D1371831

RANDOM HOUSE

WEBSTER'S
ENGLISH
LANGUAGE
DESK REFERENCE

Random House

Webster's English Language Desk Reference

RANDOM HOUSE
New York

STAFF

Sol Steinmetz, *Editorial Director*
Judy Kaplan, *Project Editor*

Editors:
Enid Pearsons, Constance A. Baboukis,
Alice Kovac Somoroff

Patricia W. Ehresmann, *Production Director*
Charlotte Staub, *Designer*

Charles Levine, *Publisher*

This work was originally published in hardcover in 1995 under the title *Random House English Language Desk Reference.*

Sections of this work have been previously published as separate works by Random House, Inc., under the following titles: *The Random House Guide to Grammar, Usage, and Punctuation, The Random House Power Vocabulary, The Random House Thesaurus, The Random House Rhyming Dictionary,* and *The Random House American Dictionary.*

Library of Congress Cataloging-in-Publication Data

Random House English language desk reference.
    Random House Webster's English language desk reference. — 1st pbk. ed.
      p. cm.
    Originally published: Random House English language desk reference. 1995.
    Includes index.
    ISBN 0-679-78000-9 (pbk.)
    1. English language—Grammar—Handbooks, manuals, etc. 2. English language—Synonyms and antonyms. 3. English language—Dictionaries. 4. Vocabulary. 5. Spellers. I. Random House (Firm) II. Title.
PE1112.R28 1997
428—dc21
                                    96-49233
                                        CIP

Random House Web address http://www.randomhouse.com/
Typeset and Printed in the United States of America
9 8 7 6 5 4 3 2 1
First Paperback Edition
New York Toronto London Sydney Auckland

CONTENTS

LIST OF TABLES AND CHARTS

PREFACE

The *Random House English Language Desk Reference* is designed to provide the reader with basic information about the English language. The six sections of the book owe their inception and creation to the collaborative efforts of professional linguists, lexicographers, and editors. The result is a language reference book that is as comprehensive as it is authoritative.

The sections on grammar and vocabulary were written by Laurie Rozakis and Eric Larsen. The Thesaurus of Synonyms and Antonyms was edited by Laurence Urdang; the Rhyming Dictionary, by Jess Stein, editor in chief of the *Random House Dictionary of the English Language, Unabridged, First Edition;* and the Desk Dictionary, by a group of lexicographers under the direction of Stuart Berg Flexner.

It is hoped that this reference guide to English will prove to be a handy resource to all individuals who seek to improve their command of the language.

PART ONE

GRAMMAR, USAGE, AND PUNCTUATION

1

GRAMMAR

PARTS OF SPEECH

Your ability to communicate ideas clearly and effectively depends on your understanding of and familiarity with English grammar. Grammatical rules and terms help define the construction of our language and show us how to use words correctly in written and spoken English.

The English language is made up of eight basic types of words, or parts of speech: nouns, pronouns, verbs, adjectives, adverbs, prepositions, conjunctions, and interjections. Our review will explain how parts of speech are arranged in structures that form the basis of speech and writing.

The part of speech is determined by the way a word is used in a sentence.

Words often serve more than one grammatical function, depending on their placement within sentences. Therefore, the same word can be a different part of speech in different sentences. For example, the word "help" can function as both a noun and a verb, according to its use in a sentence.

"Help" *as a noun:*

The offer of *help* was greatly appreciated. (Here "help" is a thing.)

"Help" *as a verb:*

They *help* the community by volunteering their time to tutor illiterate adults. (Here "help" is an action.)

Since words can work in different ways, you must first determine how the word is functioning within a sentence before you can label it as a specific part of speech. You cannot assume that any word will always be the same part of speech and fulfill the same grammatical function.

NOUNS

A noun is a word used to name a person, place, thing, or quality.

EXAMPLES:

Person	Place	Thing	Quality
Mary	library	snake	decency
Edward	yard	flowers	bravery
teacher	Ontario	justice	courage
American	coastline	mutiny	integrity
cousin	Paris	computer	sincerity
Mr. Jones	city	ballot	happiness

Some of the nouns listed above can be further classified into specific types: **Common nouns** name any of a class of people, places, or things. **Proper nouns** name specific people, places, and things.

EXAMPLES:

Common Nouns	Proper Nouns
girl	Lisa
river	Ohio River
road	Main Street

Collective nouns name groups of people or things.

EXAMPLES:

team   clan   flock   tribe   pack   committee

Mass nouns name qualities or things that cannot be counted.

EXAMPLES:

fury   gold   strength   sand   valor   flour

Compound nouns are made up of two or more words. The words may be separate, hyphenated, or combined.

EXAMPLES:

boarding pass   housework   runaway
mother-in-law   airport   schoolroom

Articles or Noun Markers

The words *a, an,* and *the,* which often precede nouns, are called **articles** or **noun markers.**

EXAMPLES:

an apple   a river   the child

PRONOUNS

A pronoun is a word used in place of a noun or a group of words functioning as a noun.

EXAMPLE:

Ellen has been working on a project for a long time. She spends eight hours a day on it. Her time is well spent, however, as she herself recognizes.

Antecedents

The meaning of a pronoun comes from the noun it represents. This noun is called the **antecedent.** In the above example, the antecedent of the pronoun *she* is *Ellen;* the antecedent of the pronoun *it* is *project.* As you can see, the antecedent usually comes before the pronoun in the sentence. Most pronouns have specific antecedents, but some do not.

Types of Pronouns

There are different types of pronouns, depending on their function within a sentence and on their form.

Personal pronouns refer to specific people. Personal pronouns that refer to the speaker are known as **first-person pronouns;** those that refer to the person spoken to are known as **second-person pronouns;** those that refer to the person, place, or thing spoken about are known as **third-person pronouns.**

first-person (singular)	*second-person*	*third-person*
I, me, my, mine	you, your, yours	he, him, his, she, her, hers, it, its

first-person (plural)	*second-person*	*third-person*
we, us, our, ours	you, yours, yours	they, them, their, theirs

Intensive pronouns add emphasis to a noun or pronoun; **reflexive pronouns** show that the subject of the sentence also receives the action of the verb and adds information to a sentence. Both intensive and reflexive pronouns end in *-self* or *-selves.*

Intensive and Reflexive Pronouns

myself   himself   itself   yourselves
yourself   herself   ourselves   themselves

EXAMPLES:

Intensive:

I **myself** have never given much thought to the matter.

Marty hung the striped wallpaper **himself.**

Reflexive:

I treated **myself** to a new pair of shoes.

Michael kept telling **himself** that it was not his fault.

Interrogative pronouns are used to introduce questions. These pronouns do not have to have a specific antecedent.

Interrogative Pronouns

which   what   who   whom   whose

EXAMPLES:

What did you call me for in the first place?

Whom have you called about this matter?

Whose dog is this?

Relative pronouns are used to tie together or relate groups of words. Relative pronouns begin subordinate clauses (see page 26).

Relative Pronouns

which   that   who   whom   whose

EXAMPLES:

Debbie enrolled in the class **that** her employer recommended.

Charles has a friend **who** lives in Toronto, Canada.

Demonstrative pronouns identify specific nouns. They can be placed before or after their antecedents.

Demonstrative Pronouns

this   that   these   those

EXAMPLES:

This is the book I told you about last week.

That is a perfect place to sit down and have lunch.

Is **that** the house with the Japanese garden in the back yard?

Indefinite pronouns take the place of a noun but they do not have to have a specific antecedent.

Common Indefinite Pronouns

much	both	little	some
several	everybody	one	none
each	anyone	all	others
many	either	any	another
most	anything	more	few
neither	anybody	nobody	everything
no one	somebody	nothing	someone
something	everybody	other	

EXAMPLES:

Specific Antecedent:

The **casserole** was so delicious that **none** was left by the end of the meal.

A **few** of the **relatives** usually lend a hand when my husband undertakes one of his home repair projects.

No Specific Antecedent:

Someone arrived at the party early, much to the embarrassment of the unprepared host and hostess.

Everyone stayed late, too.

Case

The majority of English words rely on their position within a sentence rather than their form to show their function. In most instances, the placement of a word determines whether it is a subject or object. Certain nouns and pronouns, however, change their form to indicate their use.

Case is the form a noun or pronoun assumes that shows how it is used in a sentence.

English has three cases: **nominative**, **objective**, and **possessive**. In general, pronouns take the nominative case when they function as the subject of a sentence or clause and the objective case when they function as the object of a verb or preposition. Pronouns and nouns take the possessive case to indicate ownership.

Nouns change form only in the possessive case: for example, *a dog's bark, Maria's hair*. Some pronouns, in contrast, change form in the nominative, objective, and possessive cases. The following chart shows how personal pronouns change form in the three different cases.

Personal Pronouns

Subject (Nominative case)	Object (Objective case)	Possessive (Possessive case)
I	me	my, mine
you	you	your
he	him	his
she	her	her, hers
it	it	its
we	us	our, ours
they	them	their, theirs
who	whom	whose
whoever	whomever	whoever

Nominative Case

The nominative case is sometimes called the "subjective" case because it is used when pronouns function as subjects. The following examples illustrate how personal pronouns are used in the nominative case.

EXAMPLES OF PERSONAL PRONOUNS IN THE NOMINATIVE CASE:

Subject of a Verb:

We understand that **they** will be late.

Neither **she** nor I will be attending.

Who is responsible for this situation?

Subject of a Clause:

Give a tip to the waitress **who** helped us.

Whoever wants extra hours must see me today.

She is the person **who** recommended the plan.

Appositive identifying a subject (An appositive is a word or a phrase appearing next to a noun or pronoun that explains or identifies it and is equivalent to it):

Both physicists, Marie Curie and **he**, worked on isolating radium.

Both community members, **she** and her brother, traveled to Albany this weekend to lobby for increased state aid.

Predicate Nominative:

It is **I**.

The primary supervisor is **she**.

The fastest runners are Lenore and **he**.

We Malones are fond of traveling.

The **predicate nominative** is the noun or pronoun after a linking verb that renames the subject. As a general rule, the linking verb *to be* functions as an equals sign: the words on either side must be in the same form.

Since the predicate nominative can sound overly formal in speech, many people use the colloquial: It's *me*. It's *her*. It must be *them*. In formal speech and edited writing, however, the nominative forms are used: It must be *they*. The figure at the door had been *she*, not her husband. In some instances, revising the sentence can produce a less artificial sound:

EXAMPLES:

Predicate Nominatives:

The delegates who represented the community at last evening's town board meeting were **you** and **I.**

Revision:

You and **I** represented the community at last evening's town board meeting.

Objective Case

The objective case is used when a personal pronoun is a direct object, indirect object, or object of a preposition.

EXAMPLES:

Direct Object:

Bob's jokes embarrassed **me.**

When you reach the station, call either **him** or **me.**

Indirect Object:

The glaring sun gave my friends and **us** a headache.

My aunt sent **me** a scarf from Venice.

Please give **him** some money.

Object of a Preposition:

From **whom** did you receive this card?

They fully understood why they had come with **us** rather than with **him.**

Let's keep this understanding between you and **me.**

With **than** *or* **as**

If the word following *than* or *as* begins a clause, the pronoun takes the nominative case. If the word following *than* or *as* does not introduce a clause, the pronoun takes the objective case. In some instances, the case depends on the meaning of the sentence. To help decide whether the sentence requires a pronoun in the nominative or objective case, complete the clause.

EXAMPLES:

She has been working at Smithson longer than **he** (has).

Kevin is more proficient at marketing than **I** (am).

They are going to be informed as quickly as **we** (were).

I have stayed with Julia as long as **she** (has stayed with her).

I have stayed with Julia as long as **her** [as I have stayed with her].

Uses of *Who* and *Whom*

The form of the pronoun **who** depends on its function within a clause, not within the sentence as a whole.

Subordinate Clauses and Who/Whom

In subordinate clauses, use *who* and *whoever* for all subjects, *whom* and *whomever* for all objects, regardless of whether the clause itself acts as a subject or object.

EXAMPLES:

Distribute the food to **whoever** needs it. (Since *whoever* is the subject of "needs," it is in the nominative case. Note that the entire clause *whoever needs it* is the subject of the preposition *to.*)

We did not realize **whom** the specialist called. (Since *whom* is the object of "called," it is in the objective case. Note that the entire clause *whom the specialist called* is the object of the verb "realize.")

Frederick is the lawyer **whom** most people hire for this type of work.
(Since *whom* is the object of "hire," it is in the objective case. The clause *whom most people hire for this type of work* describes the noun "lawyer.")

Questions and Who/Whom

Use *who* at the beginning of a question about a subject; use *whom* at the beginning of a question about an object.

In speech, this distinction is often not made, and *who* is used for the first word of a question, regardless of whether the question is about a subject or an object.

To determine whether to use *who* or *whom,* use a personal pronoun to construct an answer to the question. The case of the personal pronoun determines whether *who* (nominative) or *whom* (objective) is required.

EXAMPLES:

Who left the car doors open?
(Sample answer to the question: *"He* left the car doors open." Since *he* is in the nominative case, the question is about a subject and thus requires *who.)*

Whom should I see about this invoice?
(Sample answer to the question: "You should see *him."* Since *him* is in the objective case, the question is about an object and thus requires *whom.)*

Possessive Case

A pronoun takes the possessive case when it shows ownership.

With Nouns

Use the possessive case before nouns to show ownership.

EXAMPLES:

Joan left **her** coat in the movie theater.
Theirs is the store on the corner.
Our puppy cut **its** front paw on a rough brick.
Is that book really **his**?

With Gerunds

Use the possessive case before gerunds in most instances.

A gerund is the *-ing* form of the verb (examples: *swimming, snoring*) used as a noun. Possessive pronouns and nouns often precede gerunds, as in *The landlord objected to my* (not me) *having guests late at night.* In practice, however, both objective and possessive forms appear before gerunds.

EXAMPLES:

My shoveling the snow no doubt saved the postal carrier a nasty fall.
Do you mind **my** eating the rest of the cake?
She wholeheartedly supported **his** exercising.
My colleagues were really annoyed by **my** coughing.

A possessive is not used before a gerund when it would create a clumsy sentence. In these instances, rewrite the sentence to eliminate the awkward construction.

EXAMPLES:

The neighbors on the corner spread the news about **somebody's** wanting to organize a block party.
We heard the news that **somebody** wants to organize a block party.

In a Noun Position

Some possessive pronouns—*mine, his, hers, your, ours, theirs*—can be used alone in a noun position to indicate possession.

EXAMPLES:

This idea was **mine,** not yours.
Is this article really **hers**?
Do you believe that it's **theirs**?

Note: Never use an apostrophe with a possessive personal pronoun. The following personal pronouns are already possessive, so have no need for an apostrophe: *my, mine, your, yours, her, hers, its, our, ours, their,* and *theirs.* In addition, do not confuse the contraction *it's* with the possessive pronoun *its.*

Ambiguous References

Make sure that the reference is clear when two pronouns could logically refer to either of two antecedents. The following examples demonstrate how ambiguities can occur.

UNCLEAR:

The manager told Mrs. Greenberger that she will have to train her new people by June.

As the sentence is written, it is unclear whether the manager or Mrs. Greenberger will have to train the new people, and whose new people have to be trained.

CLEARER:

Since Mrs. Greenberger will have to train her new people by June, she decided to take her vacation early in the year.

If the reference to an antecedent is not specific, confusion can arise. An unclear pronoun reference can usually be clarified by rearranging the sentence or by using the noun rather than the pronoun, as the following examples show.

UNCLEAR:

When you have finished with the stamp and bound the report, please return it to the storeroom.

CLEARER:

When you have finished with the stamp and bound the report, please return the stamp to the storeroom.

Sometimes, using *it, they,* or *you* incorrectly will result in a sentence that is vague or wordy. Removing the pronoun, eliminating excess words, or revising the sentence usually produces a clearer and more vigorous style.

WORDY:

In the cookbook it says that wooden chopping boards should be disinfected with bleach.

BETTER:

The cookbook says that wooden chopping boards should be disinfected with bleach.

WORDY:

They say you should use a cold steam vaporizer instead of the traditional hot steam one.

BETTER:

The doctor says we should use a cold steam vaporizer instead of the traditional hot steam one.

VERBS

A verb is a word that expresses an action, an occurrence, or a state of being.

EXAMPLES:

Action	Occurrence	State of being
jump	become	be
swim	happen	seem
jog	drop	am
think	decide	was

Action verbs can describe mental as well as physical actions. The verb *think* from the above chart, for example, describes a mental action, one that cannot be seen. Additional examples of action verbs that describe unseen mental actions include *understand, welcome, enjoy, relish, ponder, consider,* and *deliberate.* Action verbs are divided into two groups, depending on how they function within a sentence. The division is based on whether they can stand alone or require a direct object.

Transitive verbs require a direct object. **Intransitive** verbs do not require a direct object.

EXAMPLES:

Transitive:

My son **ate** the slice of chocolate cake I was saving for my midnight snack.

My sister **baked** me another cake.

Intransitive:

My unsympathetic husband **shrugged**.

When they heard about it, my friends **laughed**.

Worst of all, even the baby **giggled**.

Many verbs can be either transitive or intransitive, depending on their function within the sentence. To check whether a verb requires an object, try to complete the sentence by asking ''what?'' or

''whom?'' The verb is transitive if your question was answered by the sentence. Consult a dictionary to check specific words.

EXAMPLES:

Transitive:

José **eats** dinner every night at 5:45.

Intransitive:

José **eats** at regular times.

Verbs that describe an occurrence or a state of being are called **linking verbs**.

Linking verbs connect parts of a sentence.

The most common linking verbs are forms of the verb *to be.* A number of other linking verbs are also commonly used.

EXAMPLES:

To be:

am	are	is
was	were	am being
are being	is being	was being
can be	could be	may be
might be	must be	shall be
have been	might have been	may have been

Other verbs:

look	grow	sound
appear	taste	smell
become	happen	remain
stay	seem	feel

EXAMPLES:

The milk **smelled** sour.

The supports **looked** fragile.

The actor **seemed** nervous when the play began.

The verb *to be,* in common with the other words on the list, does not always function as a linking verb. To determine whether the word is functioning as a linking verb or as an action verb, examine its role within the sentence.

EXAMPLE:

Linking Verb:

The child **grew** tired by the end of the evening.

Action Verb:

The child **grew** three inches last year.

The **predicate nominative** is the noun or pronoun after a linking verb that renames the subject. As a general rule, the linking verb *(to be)* functions as an equals sign: the words on both sides must be in the same form.

EXAMPLES:

We all assumed that it was he.

I am waiting for mother to call. Is that she?

There is a third kind of verb whose function is to connect individual verbs into verb phrases.

Helping verbs combine verbs to form verb phrases.

In addition to forms of *to be,* a number of other words can function as helping verbs. These include *do, does, did, has, had, have, would, will, shall, should, must, might, may, could, can.* Helping verbs are also known as **auxiliary verbs.**

EXAMPLES:

Helping Verbs:

Did you complete the project on time?

May has seen the program before.

Have you ever eaten in that restaurant?

Helping Verbs Forming Verb Phrases:

They **might have considered** my feelings in the matter.

When **will** they **be completing** their chores?

The machine operator **should** not **have been working** when he was so fatigued.

Verb Forms, Tense, Mood, and Voice

Forms

All English verbs except *to be* have four basic forms: the **infinitive,** the **past,** the **past participle,** and the **present participle.** Each is explained in the chart below.

BASIC VERB FORMS

Infinitive

Definition	*Examples*
The basic form found in the dictionary	
	(to) grin
	(to) talk
	(to) snore
	(to) walk
	(to) drop

Past Tense

Definition	*Examples*
Indicates that the verb's action occurred in the past Regular verbs add *-d* or *-ed* to the infinitive	grinned
	talked
	snored
	walked
	dropped

Past Participle

Definition	*Examples*
Used with *have, had, has* Used with form of *to be* in the passive voice Regular forms same as past tense	grinned
	talked
	snored
	walked
	dropped

Present Participle

Definition	*Examples*
Add *-ing* to infinitive Can combine with form of *to be* to show continuing action	grinning
	talking
	snoring
	walking
	dropping

Irregular Verbs

The majority of English verbs are regular and change their form by adding *-ing, -ed,* or *-d* to the infinitive. However, a substantial number of verbs do not follow this pattern. These **irregular verbs** form their past tense and past participle in a number of different ways: some change an internal vowel and add *-n* to the past participle; some retain the same form in all three forms or in the past tense and past participle; some follow no discernible pattern.

The following list includes the most common irregular verbs. For information about verbs not included below, consult a dictionary. If a verb is regular, the dictionary will list only the infinitive. If the verb is irregular, the dictionary will include the past tense and past participle along with the infinitive; if only two forms are listed, then the past tense and the past participle are identical.

COMMON IRREGULAR VERBS

Present Tense	Past Tense	Past Participle	Present Tense	Past Tense	Past Participle
arise	arose	arisen	hang (execute someone)	hanged	hanged
be	was/were	been			
bear	bore	borne, born			
beat	beat	beaten	hear	heard	heard
become	became	become	hide	hid	hidden
begin	began	begun	hold	held	held
bend	bent	bent	keep	kept	kept
bet	bet, betted	bet	kneel	knelt	knelt
bid	bid, bade	bid, bidden	know	knew	known
bind	bound	bound	lay (put down)	laid	laid
bite	bit	bitten			
blow	blew	blown	lead	led	led
break	broke	broken	lie (rest; recline)	lay	lain
bring	brought	brought			
burn	burned, burnt	burned, burnt	lose	lost	lost
			mistake	mistook	mistaken
burst	burst	burst	pay	paid	paid
buy	bought	bought	ride	rode	ridden
catch	caught	caught	ring	rang	rung
choose	chose	chosen	rise	rose	risen
cling	clung	clung	run	ran	run
come	came	come	see	saw	seen
creep	crept	crept	set	set	set
cut	cut	cut	sew	sewed	sewed, sewn
deal	dealt	dealt	shake	shook	shaken
dig	dug	dug	shrink	shrank	shrunk
dive	dived, dove	dived	sing	sang, sung	sung
do	did	done	sit	sat	sat
draw	drew	drawn	slay	slew	slain
dream	dreamed, dreamt	dreamed, dreamt	speak	spoke	spoken
			spend	spent	spent
drink	drank	drunk	spring	sprang	sprung
drive	drove	driven	stand	stood	stood
eat	ate	eaten	steal	stole	stolen
fall	fell	fallen	strike	struck	struck
fight	fought	fought	swear	swore	sworn
find	found	found	sweep	swept	swept
flee	fled	fled	swim	swam	swum
fling	flung	flung	take	took	taken
fly	flew	flown	teach	taught	taught
forbid	forbade, forbad	forbidden, forbid	tear	tore	torn
			throw	threw	thrown
forget	forgot	forgotten, forgot	wake	woke, waked	woken, waked
forgive	forgave	forgiven	wear	wore	worn
freeze	froze	frozen	weep	wept	wept
get	got	got, gotten	win	won	won
give	gave	given	wind	wound	wound
go	went	gone	wring	wrung	wrung
grow	grew	grown	write	wrote	written
hang (suspend)	hung	hung			

Tense

Tense is the verb form that indicates time of action or state of being.

Tense is different from time. The present tense, for instance, shows present time, but it can also indicate future time or a generally accepted belief.

English has three main groups of tenses: the **simple tenses** (present, past, and future), the **perfect tenses** (present perfect, past perfect, future perfect), and the **progressive tenses** (present progressive, past progressive, future progressive, present perfect progressive, past perfect progressive, and future perfect progressive).

TENSES OF REGULAR VERBS

Simple Tense (Present)	Perfect Tense	Progressive Tense
smile	have smiled	am smiling have been smiling

Simple Tense (Past)	Perfect Tense	Progressive Tense
smiled	had smiled	was smiling had been smiling

Simple Tense (Future)	Perfect Tense	Progressive Tense
will smile	will have smiled	will be smiling will have been smiling

The Simple Tenses

The simple tenses generally show that an action or state of being is taking place now, in the future, or in the past relative to the speaker or writer. The simple tenses indicate a finished, momentary, or habitual action or condition.

The Present Tense (I/We/You/They Walk, He-She Walks)

Except when the subjects are singular nouns or third-person singular pronouns, the present tense uses the infinitive form of the verb (I *walk,* you *skip,* we *jump,* they *catch*). With singular nouns or third-person singular pronouns, *-s* or *-es* is added to the infinitive (Robert *walks,* she *skips,* he *jumps,* it *catches*).

The present tense is generally used to express a number of different actions.

EXAMPLES:

To State Present Action:
Nick **prepares** the walls for painting.

To Show Present Condition:
The secretary **is** efficient.

To Show That an Action Occurs Regularly:
Louise **prepares** a report every week for her supervisor.

To Show a Condition That Occurs Regularly:
The traffic **is** usually backed up on the turnpike in the evenings.

To Indicate Future Time:
The income tax refund **arrives** tomorrow.

To State a Generally Held Belief:
Haste **makes** waste.

To State a Scientific Truth:
A body in motion **tends** to stay in motion.

To Discuss Literary Works, Films, and So On:
In *Hamlet,* Claudius **poisons** his brother, **marries** his former sister-in-law, and **seizes** the throne.

The Past Tense (I/He/She/We/You/They Walked)

With regular verbs, the past tense is formed by adding *-d* or *-ed* to the infinitive; with irregular verbs, the entire form of the verb changes. Consult the chart on page 9 for forms of irregular past-tense verbs.

EXAMPLES:

To Show Completed Actions:
Jimmy **walked** the dog last night.

To Show Completed Conditions:
Joan **was** very happy.

To Show Recurring Past Actions That Do Not Extend to the Present:
During World War II, Eric **saw** the fighting through the lens of a camera.

The Future Tense (I/He/She/We/You/They Will Walk)

The future is formed by using the helping verb *will* or *shall* with the infinitive form of the verb.

EXAMPLES:

To Show a Future Action:
Tomorrow the sun **will set** at 6:45 P.M.

To Show a Future Condition:
They **will be excited** when they see the presents.

To Indicate Intention:
The Board of Education has announced that it **will begin** repairs on the town pool as soon as possible.

To Show Probability:

The decrease in land values in the Northeast will most likely **intensify**.

The Perfect Tenses

The perfect tenses indicate that one action was or will be finished before another action. The perfect tenses are created by using a form of the helping verb **have** with the past participle.

The Present Perfect (I/We/You/They Have Walked, He-She Has Walked)

There are three main uses of the present perfect.

EXAMPLES:

To Show Completed Action:

Martin **has finished** talking to his clients.

To Show Past Action or Condition Continuing Now:

We **have been waiting** for a week.

To Show Action That Occurred at an Unspecified Past Time:

I **have reviewed** all the new procedures.

The Past Perfect (I/He/She/We/You/They Had Walked)

As with the present perfect, the past perfect has three main uses.

EXAMPLES:

To Show One Action or Condition Completed before Another:

By the time her employer returned, Linda **had completed** all her assigned tasks.

To Show an Action That Occurred Before a Specific Past Time:

By 1930, insulin **had been isolated, refined,** and **distributed**.

To Show an Unfilled Wish:

We **had hoped** to have the camper ready by summer vacation.

The Future Perfect (I/He/She/We/You/They Will Have Walked)

The future perfect has two primary uses.

EXAMPLES:

To Show a Future Action or Condition Completed before Another:

By the time you read this letter, Bill **will have left** Mexico for California.

To Show That an Action Will Be Over by a Specific Future Time:

By tomorrow, the bonds **will have lost** over fifty percent of their face value.

The Progressive Tenses

The progressive tenses show continuing action. They are created by using a form of the verb *to be* with the *-ing* form of the verb. To form questions, make negative statements, or show emphasis, a form of the helping verb *do* is used.

EXAMPLES:

Questions:

Do they **call** every Saturday?

Negative Statements:

They **do** not **call** every Saturday.

Emphasis:

They **do call** every Saturday.

The Present Progressive (I Am Walking, He/She Is Walking, We/You/They Are Walking)

There are two main uses of the present progressive.

EXAMPLES:

To Show Continuing Action or Condition:

I **am finishing** the painting while my children **are suffering** from the chicken pox.

To Show Something Is Happening, Although It May Not Be Taking Place at the Present:

Medicine **is becoming** increasingly specialized.

The Past Progressive (I Was Walking, He/She Was Walking, We/You/They Were Walking)

As with the present progressive, the past progressive has two main uses.

EXAMPLES:

To Show an Action or Condition Continuing in the Past:

She **was becoming** increasingly disenchanted with the radical diet.

To Show Two Past Actions Occurring Simultaneously:

Mike fell off his bicycle while he **was watching** a cat climb a tree.

The Future Progressive (I/He/She/We/You/They Will Be Walking)

There are two primary uses of the future progressive.

EXAMPLES:

To Show Continuing Future Action:

The grocery store clerk **will be counting** the number of manufacturers' coupons redeemed.

To Show Continuing Action at a Specific Future Time:
Carol **will be traveling** to New Orleans this summer.

The Present Perfect Progressive (I/We/You/They Have Been Walking, He/She Has Been Walking)

The present perfect progressive is used only to show that an action or condition is continuing from the past into the present and/or the future.

EXAMPLE:

The amount of pollution **has been increasing** sharply.

The Past Perfect Progressive (I/He/She/We/You/They Had Been Walking)

The past perfect progressive is used only to show that a continuing past action has been interrupted by another.

EXAMPLE:

Stephan **had been visiting** the museum that was torn down to make way for condominiums.

The Future Perfect Progressive (I/He/She/We/You/They Will Have Been Walking)

The future perfect progressive is used only to show that an action or condition will continue until a specific time in the future.

EXAMPLE:

By Monday, I **will have been working** on that project for a month.

Using Tenses
Use the appropriate sequence of verb tenses.

This refers to the relationship among the verbs within a sentence. For clarity and sense, all the verbs within a sentence must accurately reflect changes in time.

Simultaneous Actions

Sometimes all the action described by each verb in a sentence occurs at approximately the same time. In such instances, the tenses of all the verbs within a sentence will usually be the same.

EXAMPLE:

When one-year-old Jessica **blew** out the candles, her parents **rose**, **clapped**, and **cheered**.

Actions Occurring at Different Times

Many times, however, the verbs within a sentence describe actions that have occurred, are occurring, or will occur at different times. In these instances, the tenses of the verbs will be different to express the different time sequence.

In general, the tenses of verbs in independent adjacent clauses can shift as necessary to convey meaning and maintain logic.

EXAMPLE:

The hearing **was** not well controlled, but the election **will show** whether the community will continue to oppose the rezoning plans.

In many instances, however, the tenses of verbs in subordinate clauses or verbal phrases depend on the tense of the verb in the independent clause. The following guidelines are generally followed to ensure logical sentences.

If the verb in the main clause is in the past tense, verbs in subordinate clauses are usually in the past or past perfect.

Since the verb in the main clause refers to an action already finished, it is logical for the actions in the subordinate clauses to be completed as well, as the following examples show.

Main Clause
William Carlos Williams *was* a pediatrician in Paterson, New Jersey

Subordinate Clause
who *wrote* some of the most distinctive verse of the twentieth century.

Main Clause
The movie *had ended*

Subordinate Clause
by the time the pizzas *were delivered.*

Main Clause
The conference *was* over

Subordinate Clause
by the time I *arrived.*

Use infinitives logically.

The present infinitive *(to do, to tell)* expresses action occurring at the same time as or later than that of the main verb. The perfect infinitive *(to have done, to have told)* expresses action occurring before that of the main verb. The following examples indicate some possible combinations of verbs.

Main Verb (Simultaneous Actions)
I *drove*

Infinitive
to see a concert last night.

Main Verb (Present/Future)
I *want*

Infinitive

to visit Albany next summer.

Main Verb (Present/Present)

I *would like*

Infinitive

to attend the seminar.

Main Verb (Present/Past)

Julia *would like*

Infinitive

to have seen Albany last year.

Use participles logically.

The present participle expresses action occurring at the same time as that of the main verb. The past participle and the present perfect participle express action occurring before that of the main verb. The following examples indicate some possible combinations of verbs.

Participle (Present)

Chewing his pencil absently,

Main Verb

Dick *looked* into space.

Participle (Past)

Having operated the terminal for a month,

Main Verb

the assistant *knew* how to repair the malfunction.

Avoid shifting unnecessarily from one tense to another.

Illogical shifts in verb tenses confuse readers and muddle meaning. Using tenses correctly allows you to express the desired sequence of events clearly.

Mood

In grammar, mood is the verb form that shows the writer's or speaker's stance toward what he or she is saying. Different moods reveal different attitudes. In English, there are three moods: the indicative, the imperative, and the subjunctive.

The **indicative mood** is used to state a fact, ask a question, or express an opinion. Using a form of the verb *to do* with the indicative mood adds emphasis.

EXAMPLES:

Fact:

Henry James **did write** *The Turn of the Screw.*

We **do hold** soccer games only on Saturdays.

Question:

Did T. S. Eliot **have** a great impact on twentieth-century literature?

Do we hold soccer games only on Saturdays?

Opinion:

My sister **does need** my advice.

The library **does have** an excellent reference section.

The **imperative mood** is used to give directions or express commands. Frequently, the subject (usually *you*) is understood rather than stated. *Let's* or *let us* can be used before the basic form of the verb in a command.

EXAMPLES:

Command:

Get up! **Let's go** to Mario's restaurant for dinner.

Directions:

Turn left at the convenience store.

The **subjunctive mood** was traditionally used to state wishes or desires, requirements, suggestions, or conditions that are contrary to fact. It was also used in clauses beginning with *that* and with certain idioms.

Although the subjunctive mood has largely disappeared from English, it survives, somewhat inconsistently, in sentences with conditional clauses contrary to fact and in subordinate clauses after verbs like *wish:* If the school budgets *were* passed, we would have built the new wing. I wish I *were* more systematic. It is also used with some idioms and set phrases, such as Far *be* it from me . . . If *need* be, . . . *Be* that as it may. The people *be* damned. *Come* rain or *come* shine. As it *were* . . . *Come* what may.

Voice

Voice shows whether the subject of the verb acts or is acted upon. Only transitive verbs (those that take objects) can show voice.

Active Voice

When the subject of the verb does the action, the sentence is said to be in the active voice: I *hit* the ball across the field. The subject, *I,* does the action, *hit.*

Passive Voice

When the subject of the verb receives the action, the sentence is said to be in the passive voice: The ball *was hit* by me. The subject, *the ball,* receives the action, *was hit.*

To form the passive voice, add the appropriate form of *to be* (*is, was, will be, has been,* etc.) to the past participle of a verb: *is smashed, was dropped, are being removed, has been repeated, had been sent.*

To change a sentence from the active voice to the passive voice, make the direct or indirect object of the verb the subject of the verb, as shown in the following examples.

Active Voice
Storms *damaged* homes.

Passive Voice
The homes *were damaged* by storms.

Active Voice
I *will make* dinner.

Passive Voice
The dinner *will be made* by me.

Active Voice
Rover *bit* Christopher.

Passive Voice
Christopher *was bitten* by Rover.

Active Voice
Conrad *wrote Lord Jim.*

Passive Voice
Lord Jim was written by Conrad.

When to Use the Active Voice
In general, use the active voice to emphasize the performer of the verb's action. Except for a small number of specific situations, which are explained below, the active voice is usually clearer and more powerful than the passive voice.

When to Use the Passive Voice
The passive voice is more effective in certain situations.

EXAMPLES:

When You Do Not Wish to Mention the Performer of the Action:
A mistake has been made.
A check has been returned marked "insufficient funds."

When It Is Necessary to Avoid Vagueness:
Furniture is **manufactured** in Hickory, North Carolina.
(Recasting this sentence in the active voice— "They manufacture furniture in Hickory, North Carolina"—results in the vague "they.")

When the Performer of the Action Is Not Known:
Plans for fifty units of low-income housing **were unveiled** at today's county meeting.
The computer **was stolen.**

When the Result of the Action Is More Important Than the Person Performing the Action:
The driver **was arrested** for speeding.
The chief suspect **was freed** on bail pending trial.

Verbals

A verbal is a verb used as another part of speech.

Although verbals do not function within a sentence as verbs, they can be modified by adverbs and adverbial phrases. They can also take a complement. Verbals can function as nouns, adjectives, or adverbs, as the following chart explains:

Verbals and Their Grammatical Functions

Verbal	Uses
Participles	function as adjectives
Gerunds	function as nouns
Infinitives	function as adverbs, adjectives, or nouns

The **verbal phrase** is the verbal and all the words related to it.

Participial phrases function as adjectives. They can be placed before or after the word they describe: The child, *waving a bright red balloon,* stood out in the crowd.

Gerund phrases function as nouns. Gerunds always end in *-ing: Eating oat bran daily* supposedly helps people lower their cholesterol level.

Infinitive phrases can function as nouns, adjectives, or adverbs. Infinitive phrases begin with the word *to: To eat in that restaurant* is an unusual experience.

ADJECTIVES

An adjective is a word used to describe (modify) a noun or pronoun.

Adjectives add color and detail to writing by providing more precise shades of meaning. Often, adjectives give a sentence the exactness that nouns alone cannot. They describe by telling "how many," "how much," "what kind," or "which one."

EXAMPLES:

How Many?
The illness has affected **twelve** people in the apartment complex.

We could give you **additional** reasons why that would not be a wise decision, but we believe these will suffice.

How Much?

"You have had **enough** cookies for one day," the mother admonished her child.

"With a **little** more money," he remarked, "we could really spruce this place up."

What Kind?

The **gold** earrings match that sweater much better than the **silver** ones do.

The **eerie** noise seems to come from the basement.

Which One?

Those newspapers and **these** books can be recycled, but **that** plastic laundry basket cannot.

"This is the **fifth** time I've asked you to clean your room!" the father shouted at his son.

Placement of Adjectives

An adjective can come before or after the noun or pronoun it describes. More than one adjective can be used to describe the same word.

EXAMPLES:

Before the Noun:

The **red, white,** and **blue** eye shadow proclaimed her patriotism but did little for her appearance.

After the Noun:

The caretaker, **ill** with fever, was unable to carry out his duties.

Nouns and Pronouns as Adjectives

Nouns and pronouns can also function as adjectives.

EXAMPLES:

The **produce** stall is open all night.

He has always enjoyed **piano** concertos.

We look forward to our **morning** coffee break.

Common Phrases in Which Nouns Are Used as Adjectives

apple pie	flower bed	art history
truth serum	Star Wars	dance class
amusement park	flood control	horse trailer
beach towel	child care	water cooler

The **personal pronouns** *my, your, his, her, its, our, their;* the **demonstrative pronouns** *this, that, these, those;* the **interrogative pronouns** *which, what;* and the **indefinite pronouns** *some, another, both, few,* *many, most, more,* etc., can all function as adjectives as well.

EXAMPLES:

Personal Pronouns:

Did she ask for **her** superior's approval?

The team tried to give **its** support to the sidelined player.

Demonstrative Adjectives:

Are **those** socks yours or his?

This bus is rarely on time in the winter.

Interrogative Adjectives:

Which chores do you dislike the least?

What hobbies and sports do you enjoy the most?

Indefinite Adjectives:

Some people have managed to get tickets for the concert.

Anyone who wanted tickets had to be at the stadium at 4:00 A.M.

Special Adjectives

There are also three special kinds of adjectives: proper adjectives, compound adjectives, and articles.

A proper noun used as an adjective or an adjective formed from a proper noun is called a **proper adjective.** Many of these adjectives are forms of people's names, as in *Emersonian,* from the nineteenth-century writer Ralph Waldo Emerson. Others come from places, such as *Florida* oranges and *New Zealand* kiwis.

An adjective made up of two or more words is called a **compound adjective.** The words in a compound adjective may be combined or hyphenated.

The **articles** or **noun markers** *a, an,* and *the* are also considered adjectives. *The* is called the **definite article;** *a* and *an* are called **indefinite articles.** Use *a* before consonant sounds and *an* before vowel sounds, not letters. See pages 3 and 43 for further guidelines on the usage of articles.

Proper adjectives	*Compound adjectives*	*Articles*
Kafkaesque realism	nearsighted	a brick
Shavian wit (Shaw)	soft-shelled	a union
Italian food	open-and-shut	an elephant
Chinese silks	hard-working	an honest
March wind	close-by	deal
		the deal

Using Adjectives

In general, use an adjective after a linking verb.

A linking verb connects a subject with its complement, a descriptive word. The words that follow linking verbs are called **subject complements.** The words most frequently used as linking verbs include: forms of *to be (is, am, are, was, were);* verbs such as *appear, seem, believe, become, grow, turn, prove, remain;* and sensory verbs such as *sound, look, hear, smell, feel,* and *taste.*

The function of the verb within the sentence determines whether or not it is a linking verb. Use an adjective when the modifier describes the subject. When the modifier describes the verb rather than the subject, it is an adverb.

EXAMPLES:

Adjective after a Linking Verb:

The dog smelled **bad** after he fell into the garbage can.

The dog appeared **brave.**

Adverb:

The cats messed up the front yard **badly.**

Roger stood **bravely.**

Generally, after a direct object use an adverb to modify the verb; use an adjective to modify the object.

If the verb's direct object is followed by a word that describes the verb, the word must be an adverb:

verb   dir. obj.
He **mumbled** the **words** quietly.
                              describes verb

On the other hand, if the direct object is followed by a word that describes the object, the word must be an adjective:

verb   dir. obj.
Soft music **made** the **dog** quiet.
                                  modifies dir. obj.

EXAMPLES:

Adjective after a Direct Object:

verb dir. obj. adjective
His mother **called him** quiet. (His mother thought
                    modifies dir. obj.

he was quiet.)

verb
The evaluation committee **considered** the firm's

dir.obj.   adjective
work complete. (The evaluation committee be-
modifies dir. obj.

lieved that the firm had finished all its work.)

Adverb after a Direct Object:

verb dir. obj. adverb
His mother **called him** quietly. (His mother called
                    modifies verb

him in a hushed voice.)

verb
The evaluation committee **considered** the firm's

dir. obj.   adverb
work completely. (The evaluation committee eval-
              describes verb

uated the firm's work in its entirety.)

ADVERBS

An adverb is a word used to describe a verb, an adjective, or another adverb.

Like adjectives, adverbs add description and detail to writing by more closely focusing the meaning of a verb, an adjective, or another adverb. They can sometimes provide a wider range of description than adjectives alone. They describe by telling "where," "when," "how," or "to what extent."

EXAMPLES:

Where?

The pot boiled **over.**

The rain came **down.**

When?

Yesterday, I banned soda from the house; **today,** I rescinded the edict.

The children **often** speak about my instant edicts.

How?

I **quickly** changed the topic.

Life **slowly** returns to normal, but the dog moves **cautiously.**

To What Extent?

Wash your hands **completely,** please.

The child has **fully** recovered from the experience.

Placement of Adverbs

An adverb can come before or after the verb it describes. It can also come before, after, or in a verb phrase.

EXAMPLES:

Adverb before the Verb:

Today I have to get to the bank, food store, and laundry.

Adverb after the Verb:

Wendy liked to run **briskly** for twenty minutes every morning.

Adverb in a Verb Phrase:

Judging from the relatively minor damage, the firefighters must have responded **quickly** when the fire alarm sounded.

Words That Can Be Either Adjectives or Adverbs

Depending on how they are used, some words can function as both adjectives or adverbs.

EXAMPLES:

Adverb:

I was so exhausted that I went to bed **early**.

Jeannine is fortunate that she lives **close** to public transportation.

Adjective:

I had an **early** appointment this morning.

That sure was a **close** call!

Distinguishing Adverbs from Adjectives

Many adverbs end in *-ly,* but this is not a reliable way to distinguish adverbs from adjectives, because there are some adjectives that end in *-ly,* and some adverbs that have two different forms. As illustrated above, the part of speech is determined by the word's position in the sentence, not by its ending. The following chart shows some adjectives and adverbs that end in *-ly.*

EXAMPLES:

Adjectives That End in -ly	*Adverbs That End in* -ly
curly tail	paint quickly
surly child	color brightly
lovely picture	ate poorly

Further, some adverbs have two forms, one that ends in *-ly* and one that does not.

Some Common Adverbs That Have Two Forms

cheap, cheaply   high, highly   late, lately
loud, loudly   near, nearly   quick, quickly
sharp, sharply   slow, slowly   wrong, wrongly

In some instances, the choice of form depends on the idiomatic use of the word. *Nearly,* for example, is used to mean "almost," while *near* is used to mean "close in time": Summer is drawing *near* (close in time). Summer is *nearly* (almost) arrived. Today *slow* is used chiefly in spoken commands with short verbs that express motion, such as *drive* and *run* (Drive slow) and combined with present

participles to form adjectives (He was *slow-moving*). *Slowly* is commonly found in writing, and is used in both speech and writing before a verb (He *slowly* swam across the cove) as well as after (He swam *slowly* through the waves).

In general, the short forms are used more often in informal writing and speech; the long forms more often in formal discourse.

Using Adjectives and Adverbs to Make Comparisons

Many adjectives and adverbs take different forms when they are used to make comparisons. The three forms are the **positive,** the **comparative,** and the **superlative.**

Positive Degree

The positive degree is the basic form of the adjective or the adverb, the form listed in the dictionary. Since the positive degree does not indicate any comparison, the adjective or adverb does not change form.

Comparative Degree

The comparative form indicates a greater degree by comparing two things. In the comparative form, adjectives and adverbs add *-er* or *more.*

Superlative Degree

The superlative form indicates the greatest degree of difference or similarity by generally comparing three or more things. In this form, adjectives and adverbs add *-est* or *most.*

When to Use *Less/Least/More/Most* or *-er/-est*

A number of one- and two-syllable adjectives and adverbs use *-er* to form the comparative degree and *-est* to form the superlative degree. In some instances, these words use *more* and *most* when necessary to avoid awkwardness.

EXAMPLES:

Positive Form (one syllable)

blue   poor   rich

Comparative Form

bluer   poorer   richer

Superlative Form

bluest   poorest   richest

Positive Form (two syllables)

pretty   heavy   steady

Comparative Form

prettier   heavier   steadier

Superlative Form

prettiest   heaviest   steadiest

Positive Form (more/most)

childlike   youthful   golden

Comparative Form

more childlike   more youthful   more golden

Superlative Form

most childlike   most youthful   most golden

In general, most adjectives and adverbs of three or more syllables and nearly all adverbs ending in *ly* **use** *more/less* **and** *most/least* **to form the comparative and superlative degrees.**

EXAMPLES:

Positive (three or more syllables)

regular   customary   admiring

Comparative

more regular   less customary   more admiring

Superlative

most regular   least customary   most admiring

Positive (-ly endings)

slow   harsh   rude

Comparative

more slowly   less harshly   more rudely

Superlative

most slowly   least harshly   most rudely

Despite the above guidelines, there are a number of words that can add either *-er/-est* or *more/most* to form the comparative and superlative degrees. The word *steady* is a case in point. The comparative can be either *steadier* or *more steady;* the superlative can be either *steadiest* or *most steady.* Some people feel *more* and *most* place more emphasis on the comparison.

Irregular Adjectives and Adverbs

A number of adverbs and adjectives are irregular in the comparative and superlative degrees, as shown in the chart below.

Positive Adverbs	Comparative Adverbs	Superlative Adverbs
well	better	best
badly	worse	worst

Positive Adjectives	Comparative Adjectives	Superlative Adjectives
good	better	best
bad	worse	worst
little	little, less	little, least
many, some, much	more	most

Comparative Versus Superlative

In general, use the comparative form to compare two or more things; use the superlative form to compare three or more things.

EXAMPLES:

Comparative:

He was the **smarter** of the two hamsters.

Marc was the **bigger** of the two second-graders.

Louis is the **quicker** of the two runners.

Superlative:

Of the six hamsters, Twiddles is the **smartest**.

Among the six of you, Roberta is the **biggest**.

Of all the runners, Louis is the **quickest**.

Double Comparisons

Avoid using double comparatives or double superlatives: *-er* cannot be combined with *more* or *less; -est* cannot be combined with *most* or *least.*

EXAMPLES:

Amanda gets a bigger allowance because she is **older** (not "more older") than I am.

She is the **nicest** (not "most nicest") student I have this semester.

Absolutes Cannot Be Compared Further

There are a number of words whose positive degree describes their only form. Words such as *central, dead, empty, excellent, impossible, infinite, perfect, straight,* and *unique* cannot have a greater or lesser degree. Therefore, something cannot be "more unique" or "most infinite." Increasingly, however, this distinction is not followed in informal speech.

In general, avoid using comparative or superlative forms for adjectives and adverbs that cannot be compared.

Comparison of Like Objects

Balance sentences by comparing like objects.

Comparing dissimilar things can result in illogical and awkward sentences.

EXAMPLES:

Weak:

Cooking with herbs is more healthful than fat.

Better:

Cooking with herbs is more healthful than **cooking** with fat.

Weak:

His comic book collection is larger than that of his friend's.

Better:

His comic book collection is larger than that of his friend.

Other and Else

One way to avoid awkward and meaningless comparisons is to include either *other* or *else* when comparing one element of a group to the rest of the group. Without these words, you are in effect comparing the item to itself.

In general, use **other** or **else** when comparing one member of a group to the other members of the group.

EXAMPLES:

Weak:

Their landscaping is nicer than any in the neighborhood.

Better:

Their landscaping is nicer than any **other** in the neighborhood.

Weak:

That little boy hits better than anyone on the Little League team.

Better:

That little boy hits better than anyone **else** on the Little League team.

PREPOSITIONS

A preposition is a word used to connect a noun or pronoun to another word in the sentence.

Prepositions can be single or compound words.

Common Prepositions and Prepositional Phrases

about	as regards	by
above	as to	by means of
according to	aside from	by reason of
across	at	by way of
after	because of	concerning
against	before	despite
ahead of	behind	down
along	below	due to
along with	beneath	during
amid	beside	except for
among	besides	excepting
apart from	between	for
around	beyond	from
as of	but	in

in addition to	on	to
in back of	on account of	toward
in case of	onto	under
in front of	opposite	underneath
in lieu of	out	unlike
in place of	out of	until
in regard to	outside	up
in spite of	over	upon
inside	owing to	up to
instead of	past	with
into	prior to	with reference to
in view of	regarding	with regard to
like	round	with respect to
near	since	with the
next to	through	exception of
of	throughout	within
off	till	without

Prepositional Phrases

Since a preposition connects a subject to the rest of the sentence, it is often followed by either a noun or a pronoun. The group of words opening with a preposition and ending with a noun or pronoun is called a **prepositional phrase**. The **object of the preposition** is the noun or pronoun at the end of the phrase.

A prepositional phrase can be made up of any number of words, depending on the length of the sentence.

EXAMPLES:
toward the mountain
away from the ocean
by the side of the cliff
in front of the bushes
on account of his gross negligence
around the bottom

Placement of Prepositions

Since a preposition connects a subject to the rest of the sentence, it should logically be followed by either a noun or a pronoun. Traditionally, grammar guides taught that it was incorrect to end a sentence with a preposition. Nevertheless, today the practice of ending sentences with prepositions is commonly accepted.

EXAMPLES:
What did Linda do that **for**?
Josh and Carol had many things to talk **about**.

A preposition normally comes before its object, but sometimes, especially in speech, the preposition comes after its object.

Examples:

Preposition before the Object:
For a week, she couldn't get the horrible scene out of her mind.
In addition to his superb academic record, he was an outstanding athlete and humanitarian.

Preposition after the Object:
What do you want to do that for?
We know which chair you are behind!

Prepositional Phrases as Adverbs and Adjectives

Prepositional phrases can function as adverbs or adjectives. In this role, prepositional phrases add description and color to writing. In addition, prepositional phrases can function as nouns.

Examples:

Prepositional Phrase as Adverb:
He hammered rapidly underneath the overhang.
The children fly their new dragon kite in the wide-open field.

Prepositional Phrase as Adjective:
Melinda is the girl with the missing front tooth.
Living in a big city affords people the chance to take part in many cultural activities.

Prepositional Phrase as Noun:
Past the village hall is the closest supermarket.

Prepositions and Adverbs

To distinguish between prepositions and adverbs, remember that prepositions, unlike adverbs, can never function alone within a sentence. A preposition is always part of a prepositional phrase.

Examples:

Preposition:
The children went into the house.

Adverb:
They went in.

Preposition:
Crowds of people were skiing down the icy slopes.

Adverb:
After the fifth book fell down, we decided it was time to rearrange the bookshelves.

Prepositional Idioms

Many prepositional phrases are idiomatic; there is no logical reason why one expression is accepted and another not. Because idioms are not governed by rules, they are especially difficult to learn.

Following is a representative listing of some commonly used prepositional idioms. As formal and informal writing vary, so does the use of these idioms.

Common Prepositional Idioms

Abide by
I cannot *abide by* your rules.

Abide in
Kelly *abides in* Kansas.

Accede to
He will not *accede to* my demand.

Accessory of
Janice is an *accessory of* the thief.

Accessory to
Gary is an *accessory to* the deed.

Accommodate to
Marty thinks it is easy to *accommodate* oneself *to* a new location.

Accommodate with
She *accommodated* them *with* an upgraded car rental.

Accompany by
My aunt was *accompanied by* her nurse.

Accompany with
The invoice was *accompanied with* a stamped, self-addressed envelope.

Accord with
In *accord with* your wishes, they will stay at the Clarion Hotel.

According to
According to Dick, the store is opening early.

Accountable for
The parents were no longer *accountable for* any debts their children might incur.

Accountable to
The trainee was *accountable to* her superior.

Accused by
Mary was *accused by* her children of throwing out their collection of dried leaves.

Accused of
She was *accused of* lying about it, too.

Acquit with

The soldier *acquitted* himself *with* dignity.

Adapt from

Janet *adapted* the dress *from* a magazine picture.

Adapt to

Some found it hard to *adapt to* city living.

Adequate for

The land was not *adequate for* their needs.

Adequate to

Their training was *adequate to* the requirements.

Averse to

She was not *averse to* long hours.

Advise of

The patient was *advised of* the risks the surgery entailed.

Agree in

The governing board *agreed in* principle with the board's recommendations.

Agree on

They cannot *agree on* what toppings to get on the pizza.

Agree to

They finally *agreed to* sausage, mushroom, and meatball.

Agree with

I do not *agree with* Marcia.

Angry with

My dog is *angry with* me.

Capable of

The child was not *capable of* lifting the heavy box.

Charge for

I was *charged for* the coat.

Charge with

She was *charged with* manslaughter.

Commensurate with

Her raise was *commensurate with* her achievements.

Compare to

You can't *compare* a man *to* a mountain.

Compare with

How do these oranges *compare with* those?

Comply with

They had to *comply with* the directive.

Concur in

They *concurred in* urging a veto of the bill.

Concur with

His anniversary *concurred with* his birthday.

Conform to

Many people feel compelled to *conform to* community norms.

Consist in

Vincent's worth *consists in* his skill at negotiating difficult contracts.

Consist of

The handout *consists of* suggestions for community fund-raisers.

Contend for

The sprinters *contended for* the blue ribbon.

Correspond to

Your account *corresponds to* what we have already heard.

Correspond with

I have been *corresponding with* my best friend for five years.

Demand from

What did your neighbor *demand from* you in return?

Demand of

She *demanded* a full account *of* the scandal.

Differ over

They *differ over* ways to increase revenue.

Differ with

I have always *differed with* Paul over environmental issues.

Eligible for

He was *eligible for* a promotion.

Excepted from

The salary is *excepted from* further deductions.

Excluded from

The children were *excluded from* further evenings out.

Familiar to

Your face is *familiar to* me.

Familiar with

She was *familiar with* the procedure.

Find for
The judge *found for* the plaintiff.

Furnish with
I *furnished* them *with* my letters of recommendation.

Identical to
She is *identical to* her twin.

Ignorant of
They were *ignorant of* their responsibilities.

Impatient at
The mother was *impatient at* her son's behavior.

Impatient with
The mother was *impatient with* her son.

Inconsistent in
My mother is *inconsistent in* her political views.

Inconsistent with
This directive is *inconsistent with* union policy.

Independent of
The bank is now *independent of* the federal system.

Inferior to
This product is *inferior to* that one.

Influence over
The mother had a strong *influence over* her child.

Inform of
I wish people would keep me *informed of* the latest plans.

Inherent in
The capacity for change is *inherent in* all.

Liable for
Homeowners are *liable for* injuries visitors sustain on their property.

Liberal in
Linda is *liberal in* her outlook.

Liberal with
She is also very *liberal with* criticism.

Necessity for
There is no *necessity for* violence.

Necessity of
We are dealing with the *necessity of* cutting back on expenses.

Oblivious of/to
Harry was *oblivious to* his surroundings.

Part from
The mother was *parted from* her children.

Part with
Lisa *parted with* her stuffed dogs.

Precedent for
What is the *precedent for* this directive?

Prior to
Prior to the meeting, I am going to get a cup of coffee.

Reconcile to
Joel is *reconciled to* the truth.

Reconcile with
I cannot *reconcile* my attitude *with* his.

Rewarded for
She was *rewarded for* her perfect attendance.

Rewarded with
She was *rewarded with* a lovely present.

Similarity in
Is there any *similarity in* their backgrounds?

Superior to
Crestwood Manor is *superior to* Greenwood Trails.

Talk of
The lecturer *talked of* her experiences.

Talk with
I *talked with* her after the presentation.

Transfer from
Rick was *transferred from* his previous job.

Transfer to
He was *transferred to* a new office.

Unequal in
The children were *unequal in* height.

Unequal to
Beth was *unequal to* the requirements of the new position.

Use for
We have no *use for* the old drapes.

Use of
We made good *use of* them anyway.

Wait at
Kim was *waiting at* the information booth.

Wait for
She was *waiting for* me.

Wait on

The clerk *waited on* me.

CONJUNCTIONS

A conjunction is a word used to connect words, phrases, or clauses.

The three main kinds of conjunctions are **coordinating, correlative,** and **subordinating.** Adverbs can also be used to link related ideas. When adverbs are used in this way, they are called **conjunctive adverbs.**

Coordinating Conjunctions

A coordinating conjunction is a word that functions individually to connect sentence parts.

To "coordinate" implies ranking equal ideas: Medical insurance is expensive, *but* dental insurance is prohibitive.

Coordinating Conjunctions

and	but	nor	or	for	so	yet

How to Use Coordinating Conjunctions

As a general rule, use *and, but, nor,* or *or* to connect matching words, phrases, or clauses; use *for* or *so* to connect subordinate or independent clauses rather than individual words.

The conjunctions have different meanings as well: *and* shows connection; *but, nor,* and *yet* show contrast; *or* shows choice; *so* indicates result; and *for* shows causality.

EXAMPLES:

And *Shows Connection:*

The children cleaned up quickly **and** quietly.

But, Nor, *and* **Yet** *Show Contrast:*

The living room was extremely elegant **but** surprisingly comfortable.

My supervisor will never give us half days on Friday, **nor** will she agree to your other demands.

She took good care of the houseplant, **yet** it wilted and lost its leaves anyway.

Or *Shows Choice:*

You can have the spaghetti and meatballs **or** the veal and peppers.

So *Shows Result:*

We missed the dinner party, **so** we ended up eating peanut butter and jelly sandwiches.

For *Shows Causality:*

Laura stayed in the office late all week, **for** she had to finish the project by Friday.

Correlative Conjunctions

Correlative conjunctions always work in pairs to connect words, phrases, or clauses.

Correlative Conjunctions

both . . . and	neither . . . nor	whether . . . or
either . . . or	not only . . . but also	not . . . but

EXAMPLES:

Both the bank **and** the post office are closed on national holidays.

The envelopes are **neither** in the drawer **nor** in the cabinet.

Whether you agree to implement my plan or not, you have to concede that it has merit.

Either you agree to ratify our contract now, **or** we will have to once again return to the bargaining table.

Not only the children **but also** the adults were captivated by the dancing bears at the circus.

Not the renters **but** the homeowners were most deeply affected by the recent change in tax laws.

Subordinating Conjunctions

A subordinating conjunction is a word that connects two thoughts by making one subordinate to the other.

To "subordinate" suggests making one statement less important than the other: *Although* some people tried to repair the tennis courts, they were unable to gain sufficient public backing. The main idea, "they were unable to gain sufficient public backing," can stand alone because it is an **independent clause** (complete sentence); the subordinate idea, "Although some people tried to repair the tennis courts," cannot stand alone because it is a **dependent clause** (sentence fragment). Either clause may come first in the sentence.

Common Subordinating Conjunctions

after	if	though
although	if only	till
as	in order that	unless
as if	now that	until
as long as	once	when
as soon as	rather than	whenever
as though	since	where
because	so that	whereas
before	than	wherever
even if	that	while
even though		

In general, subordinating conjunctions can be used in the following instances:

To show condition	To show intent	To show identification
though	that	where
as if	in order that	that
even though	so that	when
although		who
if	*To show time*	which
since	when	
provided	while	*To show cause*
less	since	because
	until	since
	after	
	before	

EXAMPLES:

Subordinate Clause First:

Until you make up your mind, we won't be able to leave.

Although traffic was light every morning, the employee was unable to arrive at work on time.

Independent Clause First:

The little girl overheard her parents arguing in the next room **even though** they were whispering.

Please retype this letter **after** you return from lunch.

Subordinating Conjunctions Versus Prepositions

A word such as *until, before, since, till,* or *after* can function as either a preposition or a subordinating conjunction, depending on its position in a sentence. Recall that subordinating conjunctions, unlike prepositions, connect two complete ideas.

EXAMPLES:

Subordinating Conjunction:

Since you are driving in that direction anyway, please drop this movie off at the video store.

Preposition:

Since this morning, I have had a headache.

Subordinating Conjunction:

After you finish reading that book, may I borrow it?

Preposition:

After lunch, I am going shopping for a new pair of shoes.

Conjunctive Adverbs

A conjunctive adverb is a word that connects complete ideas by describing their relationship to each other.

Common Conjunctive Adverbs

accordingly	hence	nonetheless
again	however	now
also	incidentally	on the other hand
anyway	indeed	otherwise
beside	instead	similarly
certainly	likewise	still
consequently	meanwhile	then
finally	moreover	thereafter
for example	namely	therefore
further	nevertheless	thus
furthermore	next	undoubtedly

EXAMPLES:

The train is in very bad disrepair; **for example,** the air conditioning rarely works, the windows won't open, and the seats are broken.

The memo required an immediate response; **consequently,** we sent a fax.

You should not be angry at them for arriving early; **undoubtedly,** they were nervous and overestimated the time that the drive would take.

Conjunctive adverbs are also known as **transitions** because they link related ideas. You can distinguish conjunctive adverbs from coordinating and subordinating conjunctions easily by remembering that conjunctive adverbs can be moved within a sentence; conjunctions cannot.

EXAMPLES:

The taxi was late; **however,** we arrived in time to catch the entire first act.

The taxi was late; we arrived, **however,** in time to catch the entire first act.

The taxi was late; we arrived in time to catch the entire first act, **however.**

Although some versions are better, notice that the sentence makes sense regardless of the position of the conjunctive adverb. The same is not true with coordinating and subordinating conjunctions.

INTERJECTIONS

An interjection is a word used to express strong emotion. It functions independently within a sentence.

In Latin, the word *interjection* means "something thrown in." In a sense, interjections are "thrown in'' to add strong feeling. Interjections should be used sparingly in your writing. Since they are independent from the rest of the sentence, they can be set off by commas or punctuated as independent clauses.

Common Interjections

Ouch Bah Shh Oh Wow Nonsense Well
Darn Ah Bravo Hey Alas

EXAMPLES:

Darn! That cat got out again.

Oh! I didn't expect you to arrive this early.

Hey! Do you know what you're doing?

There are a number of other words that are used alone in a sentence. These include *please, thank you, yes, no, hello,* and *good-bye.* They are punctuated like interjections.

PHRASES AND CLAUSES

PHRASES

A phrase is a group of related words that does not contain a subject and a verb.

EXAMPLES:

by the river	near the pond
giving the speech	leaving this town
to win the game	their day finished

Phrases can be used as nouns, adjectives, or adverbs. They are often classified as **prepositional** (adjectival and adverbial), **appositive,** or **verbal** (participial, gerund, and infinitive).

Types of Phrases

Prepositional Phrases

A prepositional phrase is a group of words that opens with a preposition and ends with a noun or pronoun.

Prepositional phrases can function as adjectives, adverbs, or nouns.

Adjectival phrases are prepositional phrases that describe a noun or pronoun. They function as adjectives to add color and description to writing.

EXAMPLES:

The price **of the dinner** was exorbitant.

My house is the one **between the twisted oak tree and the graceful weeping willow.**

Adverbial phrases are prepositional phrases that describe a verb, adjective, or adverb. They function as adverbs within a sentence.

EXAMPLES:

The joggers ran **with determination.**

My plane is scheduled to depart **at 6 P.M.**

Appositive Phrases

An appositive phrase identifies or explains nouns and pronouns.

Nonrestrictive appositive phrases, those not necessary for the meaning of the sentence, are set off by commas. **Restrictive** appositive phrases are not set off from the sentence.

EXAMPLES:

Nonrestrictive:

The guest of honor was Dr. Brown, **a noted humanitarian.**

Michael, **a former track star,** keeps in shape by running fifty miles a week.

Restrictive:

The well-known author Maya Angelou read her poems to the large crowd.

Sally's sister Andrea is an excellent student.

Verbals

A verbal is a verb form used as another part of speech.

The verbal and all the words related to it are called a **verbal phrase.**

Participial phrases function as adjectives. They can be placed before or after the word they describe.

EXAMPLES:

Shaking with fear, the defendant stood before the jury.

She got a hamburger **drenched in mustard.**

Gerund phrases function as nouns. Gerunds always end in *-ing.*

EXAMPLES:

Swimming vigorously three times a week helps a person stay in shape.

Getting bumped from an airplane can be an expensive experience.

Infinitive phrases can function as nouns, adjectives, or adverbs. An infinitive phrase always begins with the word *to.*

EXAMPLES:

To **shop** in that store is a true nightmare.

The boss left them no choice but to **defy his** direct orders.

CLAUSES

A clause is a group of related words that contains a subject and a verb.

There are two types of clauses: **independent** (main) and **dependent** (subordinate).

An independent (main) clause can stand alone as a complete sentence. A dependent (subordinate) clause cannot stand alone as a complete sentence.

EXAMPLES:

Independent:

We swim.

He missed his train.

The little boy picked up his spaghetti carefully.

Dependent:

Swimming, **which is very good exercise**, is suitable for people of all ages.

Because he overslept, he missed his train.

Marcia, **who won the blue ribbon in the annual cooking contest**, plans to open a catering business.

Functions of Dependent Clauses

As with phrases, dependent clauses fulfill different functions within sentences. They can be classified as **adjectival** (relative), **adverbial**, **nominal** (noun), or **elliptical**.

Adjectival Clauses

An adjectival clause is a subordinate clause that describes a noun or pronoun.

An adjectival clause usually begins with one of the **relative pronouns:** *which, what, whatever, who, whose, whom, whoever, whomever,* or *that*. It may also begin with a **relative adverb:** *when, where, before, since,* or *why*. "Relative" means that the adverb "relates" a clause to the word it describes.

Adjectival clauses act as adjectives to add detail and description to writing. The relative pronouns act like subordinating conjunctions to connect one clause to another. But unlike subordinating conjunctions, relative pronouns are often subjects or objects within their clauses. A particular clause is identified by its function within a sentence.

In general, place an adjectival clause as close as possible to the word it describes to avoid confusion.

EXAMPLES:

Adjectival Clauses Beginning with a Relative Pronoun:

We hired those **who came with the strongest recommendations**.

The child **you saw in the magazine** is my youngest sister.

Adjectival Clauses Beginning with a Relative Adverb:

Did Fred tell you the reason **why he was late for work this morning**?

I remember **when my sister was a baby**.

Adverbial Clauses

An adverbial clause is a subordinate clause that describes a verb, adjective, adverb, or verbal. Since adjectival clauses function as adverbs, these clauses tell "why," "how," "where," "when," "in what manner," "to what extent," "under what condition," or "with what result."

Adverbial clauses always begin with a subordinating conjunction. Common subordinating conjunctions include: *as, as if, as soon as, as though, because, before, even if, even though, if, if only, in order that, now that, once,* and *rather than*. Refer to page 23 for a complete list of common subordinating conjunctions.

Unlike adjectival clauses, adverbial clauses can be separated from the word they describe. Adverbial clauses can be placed at the beginning, middle, or end of a sentence. If the clause is placed at the beginning or middle of a sentence, it is often set off by commas.

EXAMPLES:

Since the guests were so convivial, I soon forgot my troubles.

Did you visit the Statue of Liberty **when you were in New York**?

I decided, **after I lost an especially important file**, to make two backup copies of key documents.

Nominal (Noun) Clauses

A nominal, or noun, clause is a subordinate clause that acts as a noun.

Noun clauses can function as subjects, objects, and complements within sentences. They begin either with a relative pronoun or with a word such as *how, why, where, when, if,* or *whether*.

Noun clauses can be difficult to identify. Since so many different words can be used to begin a noun clause, the opening word itself cannot be used as a determinant. You must discover the function of the clause within the sentence to identify it as a noun clause.

EXAMPLES:

What the writer said dismayed the critics.

Whoever finishes dinner first will be allowed to pick the television show.

They talked about **whether they could take the time off from work.**

Elliptical Clauses

An elliptical clause is a subordinate clause that is grammatically incomplete but nonetheless clear because the missing element can be understood from the rest of the sentence.

The word *elliptical* comes from *ellipsis,* which means "omission." The verb from the second part of the comparison may be missing, or the relative pronouns *that, which,* and *whom* may be omitted from adjectival clauses. Often, elliptical clauses begin with *as* or *than,* although any subordinate conjunction that makes logical sense can be used. In the following examples, the omitted words are supplied in parentheses.

EXAMPLES:

Chad's younger cousin is as tall **as he** (is).

Aruba is among the islands (that) **they visited on their recent cruise.**

When (he was) **only a child,** Barry was taken on a tour around the world.

Although (they were) **common fifty years ago,** passenger pigeons are extinct today.

SENTENCES

PARTS OF A SENTENCE

A sentence is the expression of a complete thought.

There are two basic parts to every sentence: the **subject** and the **predicate.** The **simple subject** is the noun or pronoun that identifies the person, place, or thing the sentence is about. The **complete subject** is the simple subject and all the words that describe it. The **predicate** contains the verb that explains what the subject is doing. The **simple predicate** contains only the verb; the **complete predicate** contains the verb and any complements and modifiers.

EXAMPLES:

Subject
The motorcycle

Predicate
veered away from the boulder.

Subject
The new computer

Predicate
used the MS/DOS operating system.

Subject
One of Hawthorne's direct blood relatives

Predicate
was the famous "hanging judge" of the Salem witchcraft trials.

Subject
Farmingdale, in the town of Oyster Bay,

Predicate
has recently begun a massive recycling project.

Hard-to-Locate Subjects

Commands or Directions

In some instances, the subject can be difficult to locate. In commands or directions, for instance, the subject is often not stated, because it is understood to be *you.*

Subject (you)

Predicate
Please unload the dishwasher and vacuum the basement.

Subject (you)

Predicate
Just tell me what happened that evening.

Questions

In questions, too, subjects can be difficult to locate because they often follow the verb rather than come before it. Rewriting the question as a statement will make it easier to find the subject. In the rewritten statements, the subject is in italics.

Question
Are *you* planning to go to Oregon this weekend or next?

Rewritten as a Statement
You are planning to go to Oregon this weekend or next.

Question

When do you think the *report* will be ready for distribution?

Rewritten as a Statement

The *report* will be ready for distribution tomorrow, I assume.

Sentences Beginning with "There" or "Here"

Sentences that begin with "there" or "here" do not usually open with a subject. Rephrase the sentence if you cannot locate the subject. In the following examples, the subjects are in italics in the rewritten sentences.

> there *or* here
> *There* is your wallet on the table.
> *Rewritten sentence*
> Your *wallet* is there on the table.

> there *or* here
> *Here* is the sherbet from the dairy.
> *Rewritten sentence*
> The *sherbet* from the dairy is here.

Inverted Sentences

Inverted sentences place the subject after the verb for emphasis: High on the mountain overlooking the ocean was the diver. *The diver* is the subject; the rest, the predicate.

Sentence Complements

Along with a verb, complete predicates often contain a **complement.**

> A complement is a word or word group that completes the meaning of the predicate.

There are five primary kinds of sentence complements: direct objects, indirect objects, object complements, predicate nominatives, and predicate adjectives. The last two are often called **subject complements.**

Direct Objects

> A direct object is the noun, pronoun, or word acting as a noun that completes the meaning of a transitive verb.

A direct object completes the meaning of the transitive verb by receiving the action. (In transitive action verbs do not have direct objects.) To help decide if a word is a direct object, ask *What?* or *Whom?* after an action verb.

> EXAMPLES:
>
> Martha won the stuffed dog.
> (*What* did she win? The stuffed dog.)
> The hurricane damaged the trees and sidewalks.

(*What* did the hurricane damage? The trees and sidewalks.)
The waiter served Jack.
(*Whom* did the waiter serve? He served Jack.)

Indirect Objects

> An indirect object is a noun or pronoun that names the person or thing that something is done to or given to.

Indirect objects are located after the action verb and before the direct object. Obviously, they are found only in sentences that have direct objects. Indirect objects answer the questions "To whom?" "For whom?" "To what?" or "For what?"

> EXAMPLES:
>
> The assistant **gave** the **supervisor** the file folders.
>
> The receptionist **handed** the **mother** the invoice.
>
> Has the fire marshal **told** **you** about the new fire safety regulations?

Object Complements

> An object complement is a noun or adjective immediately after a direct object that either renames or describes it.

Object complements are found only in sentences that have direct objects.

> EXAMPLES:
>
> The scientists called the first duckbilled platypus a hoax.
>
> Upon closer examination, they decided that it was a reptile.

Subject Complements: Predicate Nominatives and Predicate Adjectives

The word "predicate" indicates that subject complements, as with object complements, are found in the sentence predicates.

> A subject complement is a noun, pronoun, or adjective that follows a linking verb and gives further information about the subject of a sentence.

Predicate Nominatives

> A predicate nominative is a noun or pronoun that follows a linking verb to explain the subject of a sentence.

> EXAMPLES:
>
> The new head of the division will be Henry.
>
> Which of those two movies seems the better one to see?

Predicate Adjectives

A predicate adjective is an adjective that follows a linking verb to explain the subject of a sentence.

EXAMPLES:

The vegetable soup smelled **delicious**.

My husband's collection of comic books grows **larger** and **more valuable** every day.

FORMING SENTENCES

Independent and dependent clauses can be combined in various ways to create four basic types of sentences: simple, compound, complex, and compound-complex.

Simple Sentences

A simple sentence is one independent clause, a group of words containing a subject and a predicate.

This does not mean, however, that a simple sentence must be short. Both the subject and the verb may be compounded. In addition, a simple sentence may contain describing phrases. By definition, though, a simple sentence cannot have a subordinate clause or another independent clause.

EXAMPLES:

Single Subject and Verb:
Heather shopped.
$\quad$ s $\quad\quad$ v

Compound Subject:
The **carpenter** and the **electrician** arrived
$\quad\quad$ s $\quad\quad\quad\quad$ s
simultaneously.

Compound Verb:
The shingle **flapped, folded,** and **broke** off.
$\quad\quad\quad\quad$ v $\quad\quad$ v $\quad\quad$ v

Compound Subject and Compound Verb:
Either **my mother** or **my great-aunt bought**
$\quad\quad\quad$ s $\quad\quad\quad$ s $\quad\quad$ v
and **wrapped** this lovely crystal decanter.
$\quad$ v

Phrases and Modifiers:
Freezing unexpectedly, the **water**
$\quad\quad\quad\quad\quad\quad\quad\quad\quad$ s
in the copper lines **burst** the gaskets.
$\quad\quad\quad\quad\quad\quad$ v

Compound Sentences

A compound sentence is two or more independent clauses joined together.

Since the clauses in a compound sentence are independent, each can be written as an individual sentence. A compound sentence cannot have dependent clauses. The independent clauses can be connected by a comma and a coordinating conjunction *(and, but, or, for, so, yet)* or by a semicolon. If the clauses are very short, the comma before the coordinating conjunction is often omitted.

EXAMPLES:

Mary Jones went to the store, **but** Bill Jones stayed home with the baby.

You may mail the enclosed form back to our central office, **or** you may call our customer service representative at the number listed above.

Eddie typed the report in three hours; it took him four hours to correct his errors.

Complex Sentences

A complex sentence contains one independent clause and one or more subordinate clauses.

To distinguish it from the other clauses, the independent clause in a complex sentence is called the **main clause**. In a complex sentence, each clause has its own subject and verb. The subject in the main clause is called the **subject of the sentence**; the verb in the main clause is called the **main verb**. An independent clause can stand alone as a complete sentence; a dependent clause cannot.

EXAMPLES:

As we were looking over your sign-in sheets for May and June,
$\quad\quad\quad\quad\quad$ subordinate clause
we noticed a number of minor problems.
$\quad\quad\quad\quad\quad$ main clause

While Mary went to the store,
$\quad\quad$ subordinate clause
Bill stayed with the baby.
$\quad\quad$ main clause

No one responded
$\quad\quad$ main clause
when she rang the front doorbell.
$\quad\quad\quad\quad$ subordinate clause

The owners of the small mountain inns rejoiced
main clause
as the snow fell.
subordinate clause

Compound-Complex Sentences

A compound-complex sentence has at least two independent clauses and at least one dependent clause.

The compound-complex sentence is so named because it shares the characteristics of both compound and complex sentences. Like the compound sentence, the compound-complex has at least two main clauses. Like the complex sentence, it has at least one subordinate clause. The subordinate clause can be part of an independent clause.

EXAMPLES:
Since my memo seems to outline our requirements fully,
                subordinate clause
we are circulating it to all the departments;
                main clause
please notify us if we can be of any further assistance.
                main clause

When the heat comes,
subordinate clause
the lakes dry up
 main clause
and farmers know that crops will fail.
                main clause

The length of a sentence has no bearing on its type; simple sentences can be longer than complex ones. Neither is one type "better" than any other: do not assume that a complex sentence is superior to a simple or compound sentence because it may be "harder." As a general rule, suit the sentence to the subject.

Review of Sentence Forms

The following five sentence forms are the basic templates on which all English sentences are built—no matter how complex. Note that the variations occur in the predicate section of each pattern, while the subject portion remains the same.

1. *subject + intransitive verb*
   Bond prices fell.
        s   +   v
2. *subject + transitive verb + direct object*
   Bob hummed the song.
        s   +   v   +   do

3. *subject + transitive verb + direct object + objective complement*
   The committee appointed Eve secretary.
        s   +   v   +   do   +   oc
4. *subject + linking verb + subject complement*
   The procedure was tedious.
        s   +   v + sc
5. *subject + transitive verb + indirect object + direct object*
   The clerk gave us the receipt.
        s + v + io   +   do

SENTENCE FUNCTION

In addition to the form they take, sentences can also be classified according to function. There are four main types of sentences: declarative, interrogative, imperative, and exclamatory.

Declarative Sentences

A declarative sentence makes a statement.

EXAMPLES:
On Thursday we are going to see a movie.
We have been waiting for six weeks for the movie to open.
The reviews were excellent.

Since it makes a statement, a declarative sentence always ends with a period.

Interrogative Sentences

An interrogative sentence asks a question.

EXAMPLES:
Are we going to see the movie on Tuesday?
How long have you been waiting for the movie to open?
What did the reviewers say about it?

Since it asks a question, an interrogative sentence always ends with a question mark.

Imperative Sentences

An imperative sentence makes a command.

In many instances, the subject of an imperative sentence is understood to be *you* and is thus not stated. In other instances, the sentence may be phrased as a question, but does not end with a question mark.

EXAMPLES:
Take this money in case you change your mind.
Clean up that mess!

Will you please favor us with a reply at your earliest convenience.

Would someone move those books to the other shelf, please.

Exclamatory Sentences

An exclamatory sentence conveys strong feeling.

Many exclamatory sentences are very strongly stated declarative sentences. Since the exclamatory sentence conveys strong emotion, it is not found much in formal writing. An exclamatory sentence ends with an exclamation point.

EXAMPLES:

They still have not called!

The dress is ruined!

SENTENCE ERRORS

Sentence errors fall into three main divisions: parts of sentences set off as complete (**fragments**), two or more sentences incorrectly joined (**run-ons**), and sentence parts misplaced or poorly connected to the rest of the sentence (**misplaced** or **dangling modifiers**).

Fragments

A fragment is part of a sentence presented as though it were a complete sentence.

A fragment may be missing a subject or verb or both, or it may be a subordinate clause not connected to a complete sentence. Since fragments are not complete sentences, they do not express complete thoughts.

EXAMPLES:

No Subject:

Ran to catch the bus.

Ate all the chocolate hidden in the drawer.

No Verb:

The box sitting in the trunk.

The man in the room.

No Subject or Verb:

Feeling happy.

Acting poorly.

Subordinate Clause:

When I woke him up early this morning.

If it is as pleasant as you expect today.

Correcting Fragments

Fragments are often created when phrases and subordinate clauses are punctuated as though they were complete sentences. Recall that phrases can never stand alone because they are groups of words that do not have subjects or verbs. To correct phrase fragments, add the information they need to be complete.

Subordinate clauses, on the other hand, do contain subjects and verbs. Like phrases, however, they do not convey complete thoughts. They can be completed by connecting them to main clauses. They can also be completed by dropping the subordinating conjunction. Correct each fragment in the manner that makes the most logical sense within the context of the passage and your purpose.

EXAMPLES:

Phrase fragment

a big house

Corrected

A big house at the end of the block burned down last evening.

(Fragment becomes subject; predicate is added.)

My sister recently purchased a big house.

(Fragment becomes direct object; subject and predicate added.)

She earned enough money for a big house.

(Fragment becomes object of the preposition; subject, predicate, and direct object added.)

Did you visit his newest acquisition, a big house?

(Fragment becomes appositive; subject, predicate, and direct object added.)

Subordinating Clause Fragment

When I woke him up early this morning.

Corrected

I woke him up early this morning.

(Subordinating conjunction is dropped.)

When I woke him up early this morning, he was far grouchier than I expected.

(Fragment is connected to a main clause.)

Subordinating Clause Fragment

If it is as pleasant as you expect today.

Corrected

It is as pleasant as you expect today.

(Subordinating conjunction is dropped.)

If it is as pleasant as you expect today, maybe we will have a chance to go to the beach.

(Fragment is connected to a main clause.)

Acceptable Uses of Fragments

In the majority of instances a fragment is considered a sentence error, but in a handful of cases fragments are acceptable in written speech, as explained below.

EXAMPLES:

Exclamations:
Oh dear!
What!

Commands:
Stop!
Close the door.

Questions:
What now?
Where to?

Answers:
To Smithtown.
Home.

Transitional Phrases:
One additional point.

Writers may deliberately use fragments to achieve a specific effect in their work. This technique is often used with dialogue that mimics informal speech.

Run-ons

A run-on is two complete ideas incorrectly joined.

Run-ons are generally classified as either **comma splices** or **fused sentences**.

A **comma splice** incorrectly joins two independent clauses with a comma.

A **fused sentence** runs two independent clauses together without an appropriate conjunction or mark of punctuation.

EXAMPLES:

Comma Splices:
Mary walked into the room, she found a mouse on her desk.
The vest was beautiful, it had intricate embroidery.
My sister loves *The Honeymooners,* she watches it every night at 11:00.

Fused Sentences:
Many people are afraid of computers they do not realize how easy it is to learn basic programming.

All the word processing programs come with built-in lessons you can learn to do basic word processing in an afternoon or less.

The on-line spell check and thesaurus are especially handy they do not take the place of a good dictionary.

Correcting Run-On Sentences

There are four ways to correct both comma splices and fused sentences: separate the clauses into two separate sentences, insert a comma and coordinating conjunction between clauses to create a compound sentence, insert a semicolon between clauses, or subordinate one clause to the other to create a complex sentence.

EXAMPLES:

Create Two Sentences:
Mary walked into the room. She found a mouse on her desk.
Many people are afraid of computers. They do not realize how easy it is to learn basic programming.

Insert Comma and Coordinating Conjunction:
Mary walked into the room, and she found a mouse on her desk.
Many people are afraid of computers, for they do not realize how easy it is to learn basic programming.

Insert Semicolon:
Mary walked into the room; she found a mouse on her desk.
Many people are afraid of computers; they do not realize how easy it is to learn basic programming.

Subordinate One Clause to the Other:
When Mary walked into the room, she found a mouse on her desk.
Many people are afraid of computers, since they do not realize how easy it is to learn basic programming.

Misplaced and Dangling Modifiers

A misplaced modifier occurs when the modifier appears to describe the wrong word in the sentence.

A dangling modifier occurs when a modifier does not logically or grammatically describe anything in the sentence.

As a general rule, a modifier should be placed as closely as possible to the word it modifies. When a clause, phrase, or word is placed too far from the word it modifies, the sentence may fail to convey the intended meaning and might produce ambiguity or even amusement. When this occurs, the modifier is called "misplaced."

When the noun or pronoun to which a phrase or clause refers is in the wrong place or missing, an unattached—or dangling—modifier results. As with misplaced modifiers, dangling modifiers result in confusion.

EXAMPLES:

Word Misplaced:

To get to the ski slope we **nearly** drove five hours.
(Since the modifier "nearly" describes "five," not "drove," the sentence should read: *To get to the ski slope we drove nearly five hours.*)

Phrase Misplaced:

Paul got a glimpse of the accident **in his rear-view mirror.**
(Since we can assume logically that the accident did not occur in Paul's rearview mirror, the phrase "in his rearview mirror" modifies "got a glimpse of" and should be placed closer to it. The sentence should read: *In his rearview mirror, Paul got a glimpse of the accident.*)

Clause Misplaced:

My sister purchased a dog for my brother **that they call Rover.**
(The clause "that they call Rover" describes the dog, not the brother. The sentence should read: *For my brother, my sister purchased a dog that they call Rover.*)

Dangling Modifier:

While sailing off the coast, a great white whale was seen.
(The construction is "dangling" because the lack of a subject leaves the reader wondering who saw the whale. To correct the error, revise the sentence as follows: *While sailing off the coast, we saw a great white whale.*)

Correcting Misplaced and Dangling Modifiers

Correct misplaced modifiers by placing the phrase or clause closer to the word it describes. In some instances, you can correct dangling modifiers by rewriting the sentence to add the missing word. In other cases, expand the verbal phrases into a clause.

EXAMPLES:

Misplaced Modifier

The right belongs to every person of freedom of speech.

Modifier Correctly Placed

The right of freedom of speech belongs to every person.

Misplaced Modifier

We saved the balloons for the children that had been left on the table.

Modifier Correctly Placed

We saved the balloons that had been left on the table for the children.

Dangling Modifier

While reading the book, the birds on the railing caught my eye.

Modifier Corrected

While I was reading the book, the birds on the railing caught my eye.

Dangling Modifier

To understand the process, an up-to-date text is a must.

Modifier Corrected

For you to understand the process, you must have an up-to-date text.

Dangling Modifier

Being childless for so long, the baby was a welcome addition.

Modifier Corrected

Since they were childless for so long, the baby was a welcome addition.

AGREEMENT OF SENTENCE PARTS

Agreement is what it sounds like—matching. Specifically, agreement refers to the matching of number, person, and gender within a sentence. Subjects and verbs must match in **number** (singular or plural) and **person** (first, second, or third). Pronouns and their antecedents (the words to which they refer) must also match in **gender** (masculine, feminine, or neuter). The following chart reviews number, person, and gender.

First Person:
The Speakers: I, we

Number

Singular	Plural
I am here.	*We* are here.
I was here.	*We* were here.
I begin.	*We* begin.

Second Person:
Those spoken to: you

Number
Singular	*Plural*
You are here.	*You* are here.
You were here.	*You* were here.

Third Person:
Those spoken about: he, she, it, they

Number
Singular	*Plural*
He (She) is here.	*They* are here.
It is here.	
She (He) was here.	*They* were here.
It was here.	

Gender
  Masculine
  Nouns That Name Males
  Pronouns Referring to Males: he, him

  Feminine
  Nouns That Name Females
  Pronouns Referring to Females: she, her

  Neuter
  Nouns That Name Ideas, Places, Things, Qualities
  Pronouns Referring to the Above List: it, they

Sentences that do not maintain agreement among all their elements sound clumsy; they can be ambiguous as well. Sentences in which all the parts do agree help make your point more clearly and logically. There are several situations that can cause difficulty with agreement.

A subject must agree with its verb in number.

A singular subject takes a singular verb. A plural subject takes a plural verb.

LOCATE THE SUBJECT

First, find the subject; then determine whether it is singular or plural. The subject is the noun or pronoun that is doing the action. Often, it will be located at the beginning of the sentence, as in the following example: *I* recommend that company highly. Here, the subject *I* is doing the action *recommend*.

Sometimes the subject will follow the verb, as in questions and in sentences beginning with *here* and *there*. In the following example, the verb *are* comes before the subject *roads*: There *are* two *roads* you can use. The same is true of the placement of subject and verb in the following question, as the verb *is* comes before the subject *briefcase*: Where *is* your *briefcase*?

DETERMINE IF THE SUBJECT IS SINGULAR OR PLURAL

After you have located the subject, decide whether it is singular or plural. In English, confusion arises because most present-tense **verbs** (with the notable exceptions of *be* and *have*) add *-s* or *-es* when their subject is third-person singular (He *runs* fast; She *eats* a lot), while **nouns** ending in *-s* or *-es* are plural (potatoes, computers). The following chart shows how regular English verbs are conjugated in the present tense:

Singular	*Plural*
I dream	we dream
you dream	you dream
he (she, it) dreams	they dream

There are a number of plural nouns that are regarded as singular in meaning, as well as other nouns that can be both singular and plural, depending on the context of the sentence. *Athletics, economics, news, measles, politics, physics,* and *statistics,* for example, are often treated as singular nouns. *Mathematics,* on the other hand, can idiomatically be used with either a singular or a plural verb.

EXAMPLES:

There **are** many different **views** on the subject.

A **case** of folders **is** on sale today.

Margie works long hours in her new job.

Words that intervene between a subject and a verb do not affect subject-verb agreement.

Often, a phrase or clause will intervene between a subject and a verb. These intervening words do not affect subject-verb agreement, as illustrated in the following examples.

EXAMPLES:

The **supervisor** of the department, together with his sales force, **is** taking the late-afternoon shuttle.

The **representatives** for the congressman **are** exploring alternate methods of disposing of newspapers.

A **display** of luscious foods sometimes **encourages** impulse buying.

The **profits** earned this quarter **are** much higher than we had expected.

In general, singular subjects connected by or, nor, either . . . or, or neither . . . nor take a singular verb if both subjects are singular, a plural verb if both subjects are plural.

In the following example the singular verb *has* is used since both *supervisor* and *colleague* are singular: Either your *supervisor* or your *colleague has* to take responsibility for the error. In the next example the plural verb *have* is used since both *supervisors* and *colleagues* are plural: Either *supervisors* or *colleagues have* to take responsibility for the error.

EXAMPLES:

Neither the **sled** nor the **snow shovel has** been put away.

Either the **clown** or the **magician is** scheduled to appear at the library this Sunday afternoon.

Neither **boots** nor **shoes are** included in the one-day sale.

If a subject consists of both singular and plural nouns or pronouns connected by *or* or *nor,* the verb usually agrees with the nearer noun or pronoun.

In the following sentence, the plural verb *have* agrees with the plural noun *members:* Neither the *mayor* nor the council *members* have yielded. Notice how the verb becomes singular when *mayor* and *members* switch order: Neither the council *members* nor the *mayor* has yielded. Practice in this matter varies, however, and often the presence of one plural subject, no matter what its position, results in the use of a plural verb. Sometimes writers will place the plural subject closest to the verb to avoid awkwardness.

EXAMPLES:

Neither we nor **she has** distributed the memo yet.

Neither **she** nor **we have** distributed the memo yet.

Either **Martha, Ruth,** or the **Champney girls are** planning to organize the sweet sixteen party.

Two or more subjects, phrases, or clauses connected by *and* take a plural verb.

Whether the individual subjects are singular or plural, together they form a compound subject, which is plural.

EXAMPLES:

The **president** and his **advisers were** behind schedule.

The **faculty** and **staff have** planned a joint professional retreat.

Richard and his **dog jog** before work every morning.

Sleeping late Sunday morning and **reading** the paper leisurely **help** relax me after a long week at work.

Traditionally, when the subjects joined by *and* refer to the same object or person or stand for a single idea, the entire subject is treated as a unit. Most often, the personal pronoun or article before the parts of the compound subject indicates whether the subject is indeed seen as a unit. As with other matters of agreement, this varies widely in actual use.

EXAMPLES:

Unit as Singular:

Ham and swiss is my favorite sandwich.

My **mentor and friend guides** me through difficult career decisions. (mentor and friend are the same person)

Unit as Plural:

Ham and **Swiss make** a great sandwich.

My **mentor** and my **friend guide** me through difficult career decisions. (mentor and friend are two different people)

Mixed Units:

Ham and eggs was once considered a nutritious and healthful breakfast; now, **cereal** and **fresh fruit are** considered preferable.

Nouns that refer to weight, extent, time, fractions, portions, or amount *considered as one unit* usually take a singular verb; those that indicate *separate units* usually take a plural verb.

In the first two examples below, the subjects are considered as single units and thus take a singular verb. In the last two, the subjects are considered as individual items and thus take a plural verb.

EXAMPLES:

Seventy-five cents is more than enough to buy what you want at the penny carnival.

Three fourths of the harvest **was** saved through their heroic efforts.

Half of the nails **were** rusted.

Fifty pounds of fresh chicken **are** being divided among the eager shoppers.

Collective Nouns

Collective nouns (words that are singular in form but refer to a group) may be either singular or plural, depending on the meaning of the sentence.

Collective Nouns That Are Usually Considered Singular

army	couple	number
assembly	crowd	pair
association	department	part
athletics	family	percent
audience	firm	platoon
board	group	politics
cabinet	gymnastics	press
class	half	public
commission	herd	remainder
committee	jury	series
company	legion	staff
corporation	majority	statistics
council	minority	tactics
counsel	navy	United States

Collective Nouns That Are Usually Considered Plural

assets	pliers	tidings
earnings	premises	trousers
goods	proceeds	wages
means	quarters	winnings
odds	savings	whereabouts
pincers	scissors	

Although plural in form, nouns such as *measles, blues, mumps,* and *economics* usually take a singular verb. The phrase *the number* is almost always singular, but the phrase *a number* is almost always plural. The title of a book, even when plural in form, usually takes a singular verb. The names of companies can be singular or plural.

Determine agreement for each collective noun on a sentence-by-sentence basis. If the sentence implies that the group named by the collective noun acts as a single unit, use a singular verb. If the sentence implies that the group named by the collective noun acts individually, use a plural verb.

Collective Nouns as Singular

Collective nouns are usually treated as singular when the members of the group act, or are considered, as a unit.

EXAMPLES:

The budget **committee is** evaluating expenditures this week.

The **team has** five games scheduled for September alone.

The **jury,** not the judge, **makes** the final decision.

Measles is extremely contagious.

Gotthelf & Company is hosting its annual holiday party this Friday evening.

Five hundred dollars is the amount you owe.

Agreement of collective nouns is not uniform on both sides of the Atlantic, however: standard British usage treats nouns like *legion, committee,* and *government,* for example, as plural. Keep your intended audience in mind and double-check pronoun number in the dictionary.

Pronouns

A pronoun must agree with its antecedent—the word to which the pronoun refers—in number and gender.

Traditionally, certain indefinite pronouns were always considered singular, some were always considered plural, and some could be both singular and plural. As language changes, however, many of these rules are changing. *None,* for example, was always treated as a singular pronoun, even though it has been used with both singular and plural verbs since the ninth century. When the sense is "not any persons or things," the plural is more commonly used: The rescue party searched for survivors, but *none were* found. When *none* is clearly intended to mean *not one* or *not any,* it is followed by a singular verb: Of all my court cases, *none has* been stranger than yours.

The following lists, therefore, are presented as general guidelines, not hard-and-fast rules.

In general, use singular verbs with indefinite pronouns.

As the following chart shows, most indefinite pronouns are usually considered singular in meaning.

*Indefinite Pronouns That Are
Most Often Considered Singular*

any	every	nobody
anybody	everybody	nothing
anyone	everyone	one
anything	everything	somebody
each	many a	someone
either	neither	

*Indefinite Pronouns That Are
Most Often Considered Plural*

both	many	several
few	others	

*Indefinite Pronouns That Can Be
Considered Singular or Plural*

all	none	most
any	more	some

EXAMPLES:

Each of the people observes all the safety regulations.

Few are comfortable on a job interview.

Some of the water is seeping into the wall, but some of the files remain dry.

All the food has been donated to charity.

SHIFTS

A shift is an unnecessary or illogical change of tense, voice, mood, person, number, tone or style, viewpoint, or direct and indirect quotations within a sentence, paragraph, or essay. While there are times when it is necessary to shift one of these elements to clarify meaning, unnecessary shifts confuse your reader and distort the meaning of your writing.

Avoid illogical and unnecessary shifts.

SHIFTS IN TENSE

A shift in tense occurs when the tenses of verbs within a sentence or paragraph do not logically match. Sometimes, however, it is necessary to shift tenses to indicate specific changes in meaning. In the following example, the shift in tense is necessary to underscore the parallel career choices between mother and daughter by explaining that Kathy's career will occur in the future, while her mother worked in the same field in the past: Kathy *will become* a lawyer thirty years after her mother *was admitted* to the bar. But shifts in tense not required by the meaning of the sentence are distracting to your reader, as the following examples illustrate.

EXAMPLES:

Confusing:
Michigan was a land-grant university and therefore two years of military drill will be compulsory.

Revised:
Michigan was a land grant university and therefore two years of military drill was compulsory.

Confusing:
Throughout the eighties the junk-bond market rose steadily; as a result, small investors invest heavily from 1985 to 1989.

All the children have left to go to school together.

Sometimes even when all the elements in a sentence agree, the sentence will still sound awkward. This is especially true of plural verbs with collective nouns. If this is the case, rewrite the sentence to eliminate the awkwardness.

Revised:
Throughout the eighties the junk-bond market rose steadily; as a result, small investors invested heavily from 1985 to 1989.

Confusing:
Last night I was watching my favorite television show. Suddenly the show is interrupted for a special news bulletin. I lean forward and will eagerly watch the screen for information.

Revised:
Last night I was watching my favorite television show. Suddenly the show was interrupted for a special news bulletin. I leaned forward and eagerly watched the screen for information.

SHIFTS IN VOICE

Voice shows whether the subject of the verb acts or is acted upon. When the subject of the verb does the action, the sentence is said to be in the active voice: I hit the ball across the field. When the subject of the verb receives the action, the sentence is said to be in the passive voice: The ball *was hit* by me.

As with shifts in tense, there are times when it will be necessary to shift voice within a sentence. Sometimes a shift in voice will help a reader zero in on the focus of the sentence, as in the following example: The volunteer *worked* diligently and *was rewarded* with a paid position in the organization. Shifts in voice also serve to give emphasis: Despite town board protests, planned repairs to the town swimming pool *were shelved* for the time being. Unnecessary shifts in voice, however, can confuse readers, as the following examples show.

EXAMPLES:

Confusing:
As we finished our coffee and tea, the waiters and waitresses were seen clearing the adjacent tables.

Revised:

As we **finished** our coffee and tea, **we saw** the waiters and waitresses clearing the adjacent tables.

Confusing:

The **cook mixed** the bread dough until it was blended and then **it was set** in the warm oven to rise.

Revised:

The **cook mixed** the bread dough until it was blended and then **set it** in the warm oven to rise.

OR

The **bread dough was mixed** until it was blended and then **it was set** in the warm oven to rise.

SHIFTS IN MOOD

As with tense and voice, there are occasions when writers have to shift **mood** within or between sentences to make their meaning clear. Unnecessary shifts in mood, however, can cause confusion.

Shifts in mood often occur in giving directions, when a writer moves between the **imperative mood** and the **indicative mood**. Some writers feel that directions are more effective when given in the imperative mood. The following examples illustrate annoying or confusing shifts in mood:

EXAMPLES:

Confusing:

Stroke the paint on evenly, but **you should not dab it on** corners and edges. (shift from imperative to indicative)

Revised:

Stroke the paint on evenly, but **don't dab it on** corners and edges.

OR

You should stroke the paint on evenly, but **you shouldn't dab it on** corners and edges.

Confusing:

The cleaning service asked that **they get better hours** and **they want to work fewer weekends** as well. (shift from subjunctive to indicative)

Revised:

The cleaning service asked that **they get better hours** and **that they work fewer weekends** as well.

OR

The cleaning service asked to **work better hours** and **fewer weekends**.

OR

The cleaning service wants to **work better hours** and **fewer weekends**.

SHIFTS IN PERSON

Person means the form a pronoun or verb takes to show the person or persons speaking: the first person *(I, we)*, second person *(you)*, or third person *(he, she, it, they)*. As the pronouns indicate, the **first person** is the person talking, the **second person** is the person spoken to, and the **third person** is the person, concept, or thing spoken about.

Shifts between the second- and third-person pronouns cause the most confusion. Some people feel that these shifts are the most common because English allows us to refer to people in general in both the second person *(you)* and the third person *(a person, one; people, they)*. The following examples illustrate common shifts in person and different ways to revise such shifts.

EXAMPLE:

Confusing:

When **one** shops for an automobile, **you** should research various models in consumer magazines and read all the advertisements as well as speak to salespeople. (shift from the third to the second person)

Revised:

When **you** shop for an automobile, **you** should research various models in consumer magazines and read all the advertisements as well as speak to salespeople.

OR

When **one** shops for an automobile, **one** should research various models in consumer magazines and read all the advertisements as well as speak to salespeople.

OR

When **people** shop for an automobile, **they** should research various models in consumer magazines and read all the advertisements as well as speak to salespeople.

Confusing:

When **a person** applies themselves diligently, **you** can accomplish a surprising amount.

Revised:

When **people** apply themselves diligently, **they** can accomplish a surprising amount.

OR

When **you** apply yourself diligently, **you** can accomplish a surprising amount.

OR

When **a person** applies himself or herself diligently, **he or she** can accomplish a surprising amount.

SHIFTS IN PERSPECTIVE

Shifts in **perspective** are related to shifts in person in that both change the vantage point from which a piece of writing is told. As with other shifts, there will be occasions when it is desirable to shift perspective, but unnecessary shifts confuse readers. In the following example, the perspective shifts from above the water to below without adequate transition.

EXAMPLE:

Confusing:
The frothy surface of the ocean danced with bursts of light and the fish swam lazily through the clear water and waving plants.

Revised:
The frothy surface of the ocean danced with bursts of light; **below,** the fish swam lazily through the clear water and waving plants.

SHIFTS IN NUMBER

Number indicates one (**singular**) or many (**plural**). Shifts in number occur with nouns and personal pronouns because both change form to show differences in number. Confusion with number occurs especially often between a pronoun and its antecedent and between words whose meanings relate to each other. As a general rule, shifts in number can be corrected if singular pronouns are used to refer to singular antecedents and plural pronouns are used to refer to plural antecedents. The following examples show how shifts in number can be revised for greater clarity and improved style.

EXAMPLES:

Confusing:
If **a person** does not keep up with household affairs, **they** will find that things pile up with alarming speed. (shift from singular to plural)

Revised:
If **a person** does not keep up with household affairs, **he or she** will find that things pile up with alarming speed.

OR

If **people** do not keep up with household affairs, **they** will find that things pile up with alarming speed.

Confusing:
All the repair **stations** have a good **reputation.** (*repair stations* is plural; *reputation* is singular)

Revised:
All the repair **stations** have good **reputations.**

Person and Number with Collective Nouns

Maintaining consistency of person and number is especially tricky with collective nouns, since many can be either singular or plural, depending on the context. Once you establish a collective noun as singular or plural within a sentence, maintain consistency throughout.

EXAMPLES:

Confusing:
Because my **company** bases **their** bonus on amount of income generated yearly, we must all do our share to enable **it** to give a generous bonus. (*company* can be either singular or plural)

Revised:
Because my **company** bases **its** bonus on amount of income generated yearly, we must all do our share to enable **it** to give a generous bonus.

OR

Because my **company** bases **their** bonus on amount of income generated yearly, we must all do our share to enable **them** to give a generous bonus.

Confusing:
The **jury** is divided on whether or not **they** should demand additional evidence.

Revised:
The **jury** are divided on whether or not **they** should demand additional evidence. (*jury* functioning as separate individuals)

SHIFTS IN TONE AND STYLE

Tone in writing is the writer's attitude toward his or her readers and subject. As pitch and volume convey tone in speaking, so word choice and sentence structure help convey tone in writing. Tone can be formal or informal, humorous or earnest, distant or friendly, pompous or personal, or any number of different stances. Obviously, different tones are appropriate for different audiences.

Style is a writer's way of writing. Style comprises every way a writer uses language. Elements of style include tone, word choice, figurative language, grammatical structure, rhythm, and sentence length and organization.

Generally speaking, a piece of writing is more powerful and effective if consistent tone and style are maintained throughout. Needless shifts in tone and style confuse readers and weaken the impact of a piece of writing.

EXAMPLES:

Shift:

Reporters who assert that freedom of the press can be maintained without judicial intervention are **really bananas.** (shift from elevated diction to colloquial)

Revised:

Reporters who assert that freedom of the press can be maintained without judicial intervention are **greatly mistaken.**

Shift:

Their leave-taking was marked by the same **cool** that had characterized their entire visit with us. Later, we discussed their good humor, consideration, and generosity. (shift from colloquial to standard written English)

Revised:

Their leave-taking was marked by the same **affability** that had characterized their entire visit with us. Later, we discussed their good humor, consideration, and generosity.

SHIFTS IN DIRECT AND INDIRECT QUOTATIONS

Direct quotations use quotation marks to report a speaker's exact words: "I'll be the referee for this week's game," Mr. Kinsella said. Usually, direct quotations are also marked by a phrase such as *she said* or *he remarked,* which indicates the speaker.

Indirect quotations report what was said, but not necessarily in the speaker's own words: Mr. Kinsella said that he would be the referee for this week's game. Since the remarks do not have to be reproduced exactly, indirect quotations do not use quotation marks. Often, a reported statement will be introduced by *that, who, how, if, what, why,* or *whether.*

Illogical shifts between direct and indirect quotations can become wordy, lead to illogical tense shifts, and confuse readers. As the following examples show, these errors can usually be eliminated by recording a speaker's remarks with logic and consistency regardless of whether direct or indirect quotations or a combination of the two are used.

EXAMPLES:

Wordy:

Poet and critic T. S. Eliot said that he feels that the progress of an artist was like a long process of sacrifice of self, "a continual extinction of personality."

Revised:

Poet and critic T. S. Eliot said that the progress of an artist is a long process of self-sacrifice, "a continual extinction of personality."

OR

Poet and critic T. S. Eliot said that to progress, artists must sacrifice and extinguish the self.

Confusing:

Jill asked whether we had cut down the storm-damaged tree and "Was there any further damage?"

Revised:

Jill asked whether we had cut down the storm-damaged tree and if there was any further damage.

PARALLEL STRUCTURE

Parallel structure, or **parallelism,** means that grammatical elements that share the same function will share the same form. Parallel structure ensures that ideas of equal rank are expressed in similar ways and that separate word groups appear in the same grammatical form.

Individual words, phrases, clauses, or sentences can be paralleled. For example, nouns are paired with nouns, and verbs correspond with matching verbs in tense, mood, and number. Parallel structure helps coordinate ideas and strengthen logic and symmetry.

EXAMPLES:

Words Not Parallel:

The child was **hot, cranky,** and **needed food.**

Parallel:

The child was **hot, cranky,** and **hungry.**

Phrases Not Parallel:

He has **plundered** our seas, **ravaged** our coasts, and **was burning** our towns.

Parallel:

He has **plundered** our seas, **ravaged** our coasts, **burnt** our towns . . .

Clauses Not Parallel:

The **only good** is knowledge, and evil is the **only ignorant thing.**

Parallel:

The **only good** is knowledge, and the **only evil** is ignorance.

Sentences Not Parallel:

Cursed be the social wants that sin against the strength of youth!
Cursed be the social ties that warp us from the living truth!
Cursed be the sickly forms that err from honest nature's rule!
The gold that gilds the straighten'd forehead of the fool is also **cursed.**

Parallel:

Cursed be the social wants that sin against the strength of youth!
Cursed be the social ties that warp us from the living truth!
Cursed be the sickly forms that err from honest nature's rule!
Cursed be the gold that gilds the straighten'd forehead of the fool.

PARALLEL ITEMS IN SERIES

Items in a series usually have greater impact when arranged in parallel order. The items can be words, phrases, or clauses.

EXAMPLES:

Passions, prejudices, fears, and neuroses spring from ignorance, and take the form of myth and illusions.—Sir Isaiah Berlin

When any of the four pillars of the government, religion, justice, counsel, and treasure, are mainly shaken or weakened, men have need to pray for fair weather.—Francis Bacon

PARALLEL ITEMS IN PAIRS

In the opening of *A Tale of Two Cities,* Charles Dickens arranged paired items in a series for a powerful effect:

It was the best of times, it was the worst of times,
it was the age of wisdom, it was the age of foolishness,
it was the epoch of belief, it was the epoch of incredulity,
it was the season of Light, it was the season of Darkness,
it was the spring of hope, it was the winter of despair . . .

COORDINATING AND CORRELATIVE CONJUNCTIONS

Use coordinating and correlative conjunctions to establish parallelism.

Parallel structure is especially effective with coordinating conjunctions *(and, but, or, nor, so, for, yet)* and correlative conjunctions *(both . . . and; either . . . or; neither . . . nor; not only . . . but also; whether . . . or).*

Coordinating Conjunctions

EXAMPLES:

Not Parallel:

The homemaker was **organized, efficient,** and **a hard worker.**

Parallel:

The homemaker was **organized, efficient,** and **industrious.**

Not Parallel:

Knowing how to win is important, but it is even more important **to know** how to lose.

Parallel:

Knowing how to win is important, but **knowing** how to lose is even more important.

Not Parallel:

We can **go out** to eat, or **ordering in** a pizza would do as well.

Parallel:

We can **go out** to eat, or we can **order in** a pizza.

Correlative Conjunctions

EXAMPLES:

Not Parallel:

The hosts paid attention **not only** to the refreshments, but they **also** were paying attention to the music.

Parallel:

The hosts paid attention **not only** to the refreshments but **also** to the music.

Not Parallel:

Either take down the screens **or** you clean the garage out.

Parallel:

Either take down the screens **or clean** out the garage.

Not Parallel:

Neither the **dripping cat** nor the **dog that was muddy** was welcome in my foyer.

Parallel:

Neither the **dripping cat** nor the **muddy dog** was welcome in my foyer.

CLARIFY PARALLEL CONSTRUCTION BY REPEATING WORDS

In longer sentences, repeating a preposition, an article, *to* from the infinitive, or introductory words from phrases or clauses can underscore the parallelism.

EXAMPLE:

As the winter days grow shorter and colder, and **as** cabin fever sets in, I take out my travel books and dream of exotic islands.

PARALLEL OUTLINES AND LISTS

Arranging outlined ideas and lists in parallel structure helps solidify thinking. Maintaining one format (for example, complete sentences, clauses, or phrases) throughout serves to order ideas, as the following sentence outline shows.

I. Cigarette smoke harms the health of the general public.
   A. Cigarette smoke may lead to serious diseases in nonsmokers.
      1. It leads to lung cancer.
         a. It causes emphysema.
         b. It causes mouth cancer.
      2. It leads to circulatory disease.
         a. It causes strokes.
         b. It causes heart disease.
   B. Cigarette smoke worsens less serious health conditions in nonsmokers.
      1. It aggravates allergies.
      2. It intensifies pulmonary infections.

BASIC GLOSSARY OF USAGE

Language and the way it is used change constantly. This glossary provides a concise guide to contemporary English usage. It will show you how certain words and phrases are used and why certain usage is unacceptable.

"Informal" indicates that a word or phrase is often used in everyday speech but should generally be avoided in formal discourse. "Nonstandard" means that the word or phrase is not suitable for everyday speech and writing or in formal discourse. The glossary also covers many frequently confused words and homonyms.

a/an In both spoken and written English, **an** is used before words beginning with a vowel sound (*He carried an umbrella. The Nobel is an honor*) and when the consonants *f, h, l, m, n, r, s,* and *x* are pronounced by name (*The renovations created an L-shaped room. Miles received an F in physics*). Use **a** before words beginning with a consonant sound (*What a fish! I bought a computer*) and words that start with vowels but are pronounced as consonants (*A union can be dissolved. They live in a one-room apartment*). Also use **a** with words that start with consonant letters not listed above and with the vowel *u* (*She earned a C in French. He made a U-turn*).

For words that begin with *h*, if the initial *h* is not pronounced, the word is preceded by **an** (*It will take an hour*). Adjectives such as *historic, historical, heroic,* and *habitual* are commonly preceded by **an**, especially in British English, but the use of **a** is common in both writing and speech (*She read a historical novel*). When the *h* is strongly pronounced, as in a stressed first syllable, the word is preceded by **a** (*I bought a history of Long Island*).

above Above can be used as an adjective (*The above entry is incomplete*)

or as a noun (*First, please read the above*) in referring to what has been previously mentioned in a passage. Both uses are standard in formal writing.

accept/except Accept is a verb meaning "to receive": *Please accept a gift.* Except is usually a preposition or a conjunction meaning "other than" or "but for": *He was willing to accept an apology from everyone except me.* When **except** is used as a verb, it means "to leave out": *He was excepted from the new regulations.*

accidentally/accidently The correct adverb is **accidentally**, from the root word **accidental**, not **accident** (*Russel accidentally slipped on the icy sidewalk*). **Accidently** is a misspelling.

adoptive/adopted Adoptive refers to the parent: *He resembles his adoptive father.* Adopted refers to the child: *Their adopted daughter wants to adopt a child herself.*

adverse/averse Both words are adjectives, and both mean "opposed" or "hostile." Averse, however, is used to describe a subject's opposition to something (*The minister was averse to the new trends developing in the country*), whereas adverse describes something opposed to the subject (*The adverse comments affected his self-esteem*).

advice/advise Advice, a noun, means "suggestion or suggestions": *Here's some good advice.* Advise, a verb, means "to offer ideas or suggestions": *Act as we advise you.*

affect/effect Most often, affect is a verb, meaning "to influence," and effect is a noun meaning "the result of an action": *His speech affected my mother very deeply, but had no effect on my sister at all.* Affect is also used as a noun in psychology and psychiatry to mean "emotion": *We can learn much about affect from performance.* In this usage, it is pronounced with the stress on the first syllable. Effect is also used as a verb meaning "to

bring about": *His letter effected a change in their relationship.*

aggravate/annoy In informal speech and writing, aggravate can be used as a synonym for annoy. However, in formal discourse the words mean different things and should be used in this way: *Her back condition was aggravated by lifting the child, but the child's crying annoyed her more than the pain.*

agree to/agree with Agree to means "to consent to, to accept" (usually with a plan or idea). Agree with means "to be in accord with" (usually with a person or group): *I can't believe they will agree to start a business together when they don't agree with each other on anything.*

ain't The term is nonstandard for "am not," "isn't," or "aren't." It is used in formal speech and writing only for humorous effect, usually in dialogue.

aisle/isle Aisle means "a passageway between sections of seats": *It was impossible to pass through the airplane aisle during the meal service.* Isle means "island": *I would like to be on a desert isle on such a dreary morning.*

all ready/already All ready, a pronoun and an adjective, means "entirely prepared"; already, an adverb, means "so soon" or "previously": *I was all ready to leave when I noticed that it was already dinnertime.*

all right/alright All right is always written as two words: alright is a misspelling: *Betsy said that it was all right to use her car that afternoon.*

allusion/illusion An allusion is a reference or hint: *He made an allusion to the past.* An illusion is a deceptive appearance: *The canals on Mars are an illusion.*

almost/most Almost, an adverb, means "nearly"; most, an adjective, means "the greatest part of" something. Most is not synonymous with almost, as the following example shows: *During our vacation we shop at* *that store almost every day and buy most of the available snack foods.*

In informal speech, most (as a shortened form of almost) is used as an adverb. It occurs before such pronouns as *all, anyone, anybody, everyone,* and *everybody;* the adjectives *all, any,* and *every;* and the adverbs *anywhere* and *everywhere.* For example: *Most everyone around here is related.* The use of most as an adverb is nonstandard and is uncommon in formal writing except when used to represent speech.

a lot/alot/allot A lot is always written as two words. It is used informally to mean "many": *The unrelenting heat frustrated a lot of people.* Allot is a verb meaning "to divide" or "to set aside": *We allot a portion of the yard for a garden.* Alot is not a word.

altogether/all together Altogether means "completely" or "totally"; all together means "all at one time" or "gathered together": *It is altogether proper that we recite the Pledge all together.*

allude/elude Both words are verbs. Allude means "to mention briefly or accidentally": *During our conversation, he alluded to his vacation plans.* Elude means "to avoid or escape": *The thief has successfully eluded capture for six months.*

altar/alter Altar is a noun meaning "a sacred place or platform": *The couple approached the altar for the wedding ceremony.* Alter is a verb meaning "to make different; to change": *He altered his appearance by losing fifty pounds, growing a beard, and getting a new wardrobe.*

A.M., P.M./a.m., p.m. These abbreviations for time are most frequently restricted to use with figures: *The ceremony begins at 10:00 A.M. (not ten thirty A.M.)*

among/between Among is used to indicate relationships involving more than two people or things, while between is used to show relationships involving two people or things, or to compare one thing to a group to which it belongs: *The three quarreled among themselves because she had to choose between two of them.* Between is also used to express relationships of persons or things considered individually, no matter how many: *Between holding public office, teaching, and raising a family, she has little free time.*

amount/number Amount refers to quantity that cannot be counted: *The*

amount of work accomplished before a major holiday is always negligible. Number, in contrast, refers to things that can be counted: *He has held a number of jobs in the past five months.* But some concepts, like time, can use either amount or number, depending how the elements are identified in the specific sentence: *We were surprised by the amount of time it took us to settle into our new surroundings. The number of hours it took to repair the sink pleased us.*

and etc. Since etc. means "and all the rest," and etc. is redundant; the "and" is not needed. Many prefer to use "and so forth" or "and the like" as a substitute for the abbreviation.

and/or The combination and/or is used mainly in legal and business writing. Its use should be avoided in general writing, as in *He spends his weekends watching television and/or snacking.* In such writing, either one or the other word is sufficient. If you mean either, use or; if you mean both, use and. To make a greater distinction, revise the phrasing: *He spends his weekends watching television, snacking, or both.*

and which/and who "And" is unnecessary when "which" or "who" is used to open a relative clause. Use and which or and who only to open a second clause starting with the same relative pronoun: *Elizabeth is my neighbor who goes shopping every morning and who calls me every afternoon to tell me about the sales.*

a number/the number As a subject, a number is most often plural and the number is singular: *A number of choices are available. The number of choices is limited.* As with many agreement questions, this guideline is followed more often in formal discourse than in speech and informal writing.

ante-/anti- The prefix ante- means "before" *(antecedent, antechamber, antediluvian);* the prefix anti- means against *(antigravity, antifreeze).* Anti- takes a hyphen before an *i* or a capital letter: *anti-Marxist, anti-inflationary.*

anxious/eager Traditionally, anxious means "nervous" or "worried" and consequently describes negative feelings. In addition, it is usually followed by the word "about": *I'm anxious about my exam.* Eager means "looking forward" or "anticipating enthusiastically" and consequently describes positive feelings. It is usu-

ally followed by "to": *I'm eager to get it over with.* Today, however, it is standard usage for anxious to mean "eager": *They are anxious to see their new home.*

anybody, any body/anyone, any one Anybody and anyone are pronouns; any body is a noun modified by "any" and any one is a pronoun or adjective modified by "any." They are used as follows: *Was anybody able to find any body in the debris? Will anyone help me? I have more cleaning than any one person can ever do.*

any more/anymore Any more means "no more"; anymore, an adverb, means "nowadays" or "any longer": *We don't want any more trouble. We won't go there anymore.*

anyplace Anyplace is an informal expression for "anywhere." It occurs in speech and informal writing but is best avoided in formal prose.

anyways/anyway; anywheres/anywhere Anyways is nonstandard for anyway; anywheres is nonstandard for anywhere.

apt/likely Apt is standard in all speech and writing as a synonym for "likely" in suggesting chance without inclination: *They are apt to call any moment now.* Likely, meaning "probably," is frequently preceded by a qualifying word: *The new school budget will very likely raise taxes.* However, likely without the qualifying word is standard in all varieties of English: *The new school budget will likely raise taxes.*

as Do not use as in place of *whether: We're not sure whether (not "as") you should do that.* Also avoid using as as a substitute for *because, since, while, whether, or who,* where its use may create confusion. In the following sentence, for example, as may mean "while" or "because": *As they were driving to California, they decided to see the Grand Canyon.*

as/because/since While all three words can function as subordinating conjunctions, they carry slightly different shades of meaning. As establishes a time relationship and can be used interchangeably with when or while. Because and since, in contrast, describe causes and effects: *As we brought out the food, it began to drizzle. Because (since) Nancy goes skiing infrequently, she prefers to rent skis.*

as/like When as functions as a preposition, the distinction between as and like depends on meaning: As suggests that the subject is equivalent to the description: *He was employed as a teacher.* **Like,** in contrast, suggests similarity but not equivalence: *Speakers like her excel in front of large groups.*

ascent/assent Ascent is a noun that means "a move upward or a climb": *Their ascent up Mount Ranier was especially dangerous because of the recent rock slides.* Assent can be a noun or a verb. As a verb, **assent** means "to concur, to express agreement": *The union representative assented to the agreement.* As a noun, **assent** means "an agreement": *The assent was not reached peacefully.*

assistance/assistants Assistance is a noun that means "help, support": *Please give us your assistance here for a moment.* Assistants is a plural noun that means "helpers": *Since the assistants were late, we found ourselves running behind schedule.*

assure, ensure, insure Assure is a verb that means "to promise": *The plumber assured us that the sink would not clog again.* Ensure and insure are both verbs that mean "to make certain," although some writers use insure solely for legal and financial writing and ensure for more widespread usage: *Since it is hard to insure yourself against mudslide, we did not buy the house on the hill. We left late to ensure that we would not get caught in traffic.*

at Avoid using at after "where": *Where are you seeing her (not "at")?* Whether used as an adverb or as a preposition, "where" contains the preposition "at" in its definition.

at this point in time Although the term at this point in time is widely used (especially in politics), many consider it verbose and stuffy. Instead, use "now" or "at this time": *We are not now ready to discuss the new budget.*

awful/awfully Avoid using awful or awfully to mean "very" in formal discourse: *We had an awfully busy time at the amusement park.* Although the use of awful to mean "terrible" (rather than "inspiring awe") has permeated all levels of writing and speech, consider using in its place a word that more closely matches your intended meaning: *We had an unpleasant (not "awful") time because the park was hot, noisy, and crowded.*

awhile/a while Awhile is an adverb and is always spelled as one word: *We visited awhile.* A while is a noun phrase (an article and a noun) and

is used after a preposition: *We visited for a while.*

backward/backwards In formal discourse, backward is preferred: *This stroke is easier if you use a backward motion* (adjective). *Counting backward from 100 can be an effective way to induce sleep* (adverb).

bad/badly Bad, an adjective, is used to describe a noun or pronoun. Badly, an adverb, is used to describe a verb, adjective, or another adverb. Thus: *She felt bad because her broken leg throbbed badly.*

bare/bear Bare is an adjective or a verb. As an adjective, **bare** means "naked, unadorned": *The wall looked bare without the picture.* As a verb, **bare** means "to reveal": *He bared his soul.* Bear is a noun or a verb. As a noun, **bear** refers to the animal: *The teddy bear was named after Theodore Roosevelt.* As a verb, **bear** means to carry: *He bears a heavy burden.*

because/due to the fact that/since Because or since are preferred over the wordy phrase due to the fact that: *He wrote the report longhand because (not "due to the fact") his computer was broken.*

before/prior to Prior to is used most often in a legal sense: *Prior to settling the claim, the Smiths spent a week calling the attorney general's office.* Use **before** in almost all other cases: *Before we go grocery shopping, we sort the coupons we have clipped from the newspaper.*

being as/being that Avoid both being as and being that in formal writing. Instead, use "since" or "because." For example: *Since you asked, I'll be glad to help.*

beside/besides Although both words can function as prepositions, they have different shades of meaning: beside means "next to"; besides means "in addition to" or "except": *Besides, Richard would prefer not to sit beside the dog. There is no one here besides John and me.* Besides is also an adverb meaning "in addition": *Other people besides you feel the same way about the dog.*

better/had better The verb "had" is necessary in the phrase had better and should be retained: *She had better return the lawn mower today.*

between you and I Pronouns that function as objects of prepositions are traditionally used in the objective case: *Please keep this between you and me. I would appreciate it if you could keep this between her and them.*

bi- Many words that refer to periods of time through the prefix bi- are potentially confusing. Ambiguity is avoided by using the prefix **semi-,** meaning "twice each" *(semiweekly; semimonthly; semiannual)* or by using the appropriate phrases *(twice a week; twice each month; every two months; every two years).*

bias/prejudice Generally, a distinction is made between bias and prejudice. Although both words imply "a preconceived opinion" or a "subjective point of view" in favor of something or against it, prejudice is generally used to express unfavorable feelings.

blonde/blond A blonde indicates a woman or girl with fair hair and skin. Blond, as an adjective, refers to either sex *(My three blond children. He is a cute blond boy),* but blonde, as an adjective, still applies to women: *The blonde actress and her companion made the front page of the tabloid.*

borrow/lend Borrow means "to take with the intention of returning": *The book you borrow from the library today is due back in seven days.* Lend means "to give with the intention of getting back": *I will lend you the rake, but I need it back by Saturday.* The two terms are not interchangeable.

borrow off/borrow from Borrow off, considered slang, is not used in formal speech and writing; borrow from is the preferred expression.

bottom line This overworked term is frequently used as a synonym for "outcome" or "the final result": *The bottom line is that we have to reduce inventory to maintain profits.* Careful writers and speakers eschew it for less shopworn descriptions.

brake/break The most common meaning of brake as a noun is a device for slowing a vehicle: *The car's new brakes held on the steep incline.* Brake can also mean "a thicket" or "a species of fern." Break, a verb, means "to crack or make useless": *Please be especially careful that you don't break that vase.*

breath/breathe Breath, a noun, is the air taken in during respiration: *Her breath looked like fog in the frosty morning air.* Breathe, a verb, refers to the process of inhaling and exhaling air: *"Please breathe deeply,"* the doctor said to the patient.

bring/take Bring is to carry toward the speaker: *She brings it to me.* Take is to carry away from the speaker: *She takes it away.*

bunch　Use the noun **bunch** in formal writing only to refer to clusters of things grouped together, such as grapes or bananas: *That bunch of grapes looks better than the other one.* In formal writing, use *group* or *crowd* to refer to gatherings of people; **bunch** is used to refer to groups of people or items only in speech and informal writing.

burst, bursted/bust, busted　Burst is a verb meaning "to come apart suddenly." The word **busted** is not acceptable in either speech or writing. The verb **bust** and adjective **busted** are both informal or slang terms; as such, they should not be used in formal writing.

but however/but yet　There is no reason to combine **but** with another conjunction: *She said she was leaving, yet (not "but yet") she poured another cup of coffee.*

but that/but what　As with the previous example, there is no reason to add the word **but** to either **that** or **what**: *We don't doubt that (not "but that") you will win this hand.*

buy/by　Buy, a verb, means to "acquire goods at a price": *We have to buy a new dresser.* By can be a preposition, an adverb, or an adjective. As a preposition, by means "next to": *I pass by the office building every day.* As an adverb, by means "near, at hand": *The office is close by.* As an adjective, by means "situated to one side": *They came down on a by passage.*

calculate/figure/reckon　None of these words is an acceptable substitute for *expect* or *imagine* in formal writing, although they are used in speech and informal prose.

can/may　Traditionally, may is used in formal writing to convey permission; can, ability or capacity. In speech, however, the terms are used interchangeably to mean permission: *Can (May) I borrow your hedge clippers?* Can and may are frequently but not always interchangeable when used to mean possibility: *A blizzard can (or may) occur any time during February.* In negative constructions, can't is more common than mayn't, the latter being rare: *You can't eat that taco in the den.*

cannot/can not　Cannot is occasionally spelled can not. The one-word spelling is by far the more common. The contraction can't is used mainly in speech and informal writing.

can't help but　Can't help but, as in *You can't help but like her,* is a double negative. This idiom can be replaced by the informal **can't help** or the formal **cannot but** where each is appropriate: *She can't help wishing that it was spring. I cannot but wish things had turned out differently.* While **can't help but** is common in all types of speech, avoid using it in formal writing.

canvas/canvass　Canvas, a noun, refers to a heavy cloth: *The boat's sails are made of canvas.* Canvass, a verb, means "to solicit votes": *The candidate's representatives canvass the neighborhood seeking support.*

capital/Capitol　Capital is the city or town that is the seat of government: *Paris is the capital of France.* Capitol refers to the building in Washington, D.C., in which the U.S. Congress meets: *When I was a child, we went for a visit to the Capitol building.* When used with a lowercase letter, capitol is the building of a state legislature. Capital also means "a sum of money": *After the sale of their home, they had a great deal of capital.* As an adjective, capital means "foremost" or "first-rate": *He was a capital fellow.*

cause of . . . on account of/due to　The phrases **on account of** and **due to** are unnecessary with **cause of.** Omit the phrases or revise the entire sentence: *One cause of physical and psychological problems is due to too much stress.* Change the sentence to: *Too much stress causes physical and psychological problems.*

censor/censure　Although both words are verbs, they have different meanings. To **censor** is to remove something from public view on moral or other grounds, and to **censure** is to give a formal reprimand: *The committee censored the offending passages from the book and censured the librarian for placing it on the shelves.*

center around/center on　Although both phrases are often criticized for being illogical, they have been used in writing for more than a hundred years to express the notion of collecting or gathering as if around a center point. The phrase *revolve around* is often suggested as an alternative, and the prepositions *at, in,* and *on* are considered acceptable with **center** in the following sense: *Their problems centered on their lack of expertise.*

chair/chairperson　Chairperson is used widely in academic and govern-

mental circles as an alternative to "chairman" or "chairwoman." While some reject the term **chairperson** as clumsy and unnecessary and use the term **chair** for any presiding officer, regardless of sex, **chairperson** is still standard in all types of writing and speech.

choose/chose　Choose is a verb that means "to select one thing in preference to another": *Why choose tomatoes when they are out of season?* Chose is the past tense of "to choose": *I chose tomatoes over cucumbers at the salad bar.*

cite/sight/site　To cite means to "quote a passage": *The scholar often cited passages from noted authorities to back up his opinions.* Sight is a noun that means "vision": *With her new glasses, her sight was once again perfect.* Site is a noun that means "place or location": *They picked out a beautiful site overlooking a lake for their new home.*

climatic/climactic　The word climatic comes from the word "climate" and refers to weather: *This summer's brutal heat may indicate a climatic change.* Climactic, in contrast, comes from the word "climax" and refers to a point of high drama: *In the climactic last scene the hideous creature takes over the world.*

clothes/cloths　Clothes are garments: *For his birthday, John got some handsome new clothes.* Cloths are pieces of fabric: *Use these cloths to clean the car.*

coarse/course　Coarse, an adjective, means "rough or common": *The horsehair fabric was too coarse to be made into a pillow. Although he's a little coarse around the edges, he has a heart of gold.* Course, a noun, means "a path" or "a prescribed number of classes": *They followed the bicycle course through the woods. My courses include English, math, and science.*

complement/compliment　Both words can function as either a noun or a verb. The noun **complement** means "that which completes or makes perfect": *The rich chocolate mousse was a perfect complement to the light meal.* The verb **complement** means "to complete": *The oak door complemented the new siding and windows.* The noun **compliment** means "an expression of praise or admiration": *The mayor paid the visiting officials the compliment of escorting them around town personally.* The verb **compliment** means "to pay a compliment to": *Everyone complimented her after the presentation.*

complementary/complimentary Complementary is an adjective that means "forming a complement, completing": *The complementary colors suited the mood of the room.* Complimentary is an adjective that means "expressing a compliment": *The complimentary reviews ensured the play a long run.* Complimentary also means "free": *We thanked them for the complimentary tickets.*

conformity to/conformity with Although the word conformity can be followed by either "to" or "with," conformity to is generally used when the idea of obedience is implied: *The new commissioner issued a demand for conformity to health regulation.* Conformity with is used to imply agreement or correspondence: *This is an idea in conformity with previous planning.*

consensus/consensus of The expression consensus of (*consensus of opinion*) is considered redundant, and the preferred usage is the single plural noun consensus, meaning "general agreement or concord": *Since the consensus was overwhelming, the city planners moved ahead with the proposal.* The phrase general consensus is also considered redundant. Increasingly, the word consensus is widely used attributively, as in the phrase *consensus politics.*

contact The word is both a verb and a noun. As a verb, it is frequently used imprecisely to mean "to communicate" when a more exact word (*telephone, write to, consult*) would better communicate the idea. Contact as a noun meaning "a person through whom one can obtain information" is now standard usage: *He is my contact in the state department.*

continual/continuous Use continual to mean "intermittent, repeated often" and continuous to mean "uninterrupted, without stopping": *We suffered continual losses of electricity during the hurricane. They had continuous phone service during the hurricane.* Continuous and continual are never interchangeable with regard to spatial relationships: *a continuous series of passages.*

corps/corpse Both words are nouns. A corps is a group of people acting together; the word is often used in a military context: *The officers' corps assembled before dawn for the drill.* A corpse is a dead body: *The corpse was in the morgue.*

counsel/council Counsel is a verb meaning "to give advice": *They counsel recovering gamblers.* Council is a noun meaning "a group of advisers": *The trade union council meets in Ward Hall every Thursday.*

couple/couple of Both phrases are informally used to mean "two" or "several": *I need a couple more cans of spackle. I took a couple of aspirins for my headache.* The expression a couple of is used in standard English, especially in referring to distance, money, or time: *He is a couple of feet away. I have a couple of thousand dollars in the bank. The store will open in a couple of weeks.* Couple may be treated as either a singular or plural noun.

credible/creditable/credulous These three adjectives are often confused. Credible means "believable": *The tale is unusual, but seems credible to us.* Creditable means "worthy": *Sandra sang a creditable version of the song.* Credulous means "gullible": *The credulous Marsha believed that the movie was true.*

criteria/criterion Criteria is the plural of criterion (a standard for judgment). For example: *Of all their criteria for evaluating job performance, customer satisfaction was the most important criterion.*

data/datum Data is the plural of datum (fact). Although data is often used as a singular, it should still be treated as plural in formal speech and writing: *The data pertain (not "pertains") to the first half of the experiment.* To avoid awkward constructions, most writers prefer to use a more commonplace term such as "fact" or "figure" in place of datum.

descent/dissent Descent, a noun, means "downward movement": *Much to their surprise, their descent down the mountain was harder than their ascent had been.* Dissent, a verb, means "to disagree": *The town council strongly dissented with the proposed measure.* Dissent as a noun means "difference in sentiment or opinion": *Dissent over the new proposal caused a rift between colleagues.*

desert/dessert Desert as a verb means to abandon; as a noun, an arid region: *People deserted in the desert rarely survive.* Dessert, a noun, refers to the sweet served as the final course of a meal: *My sister's favorite dessert is strawberry shortcake.*

device/devise Device is a noun meaning "invention or contrivance": *Do you think that device will really save us time?* Devise is a verb meaning "to contrive or plan": *Did he devise some device for repairing the ancient pump assembly?*

die/dye Die, as a verb, means "to cease to live": *The frog will die if released from his aquarium into the pond.* Dye as a verb means "to color or stain something": *I dye the drapes to cover the stains.*

differ from/differ with Differ from means "to be unlike"; differ with means "to disagree with": *The sisters differ from each other in appearance. We differ with you on this matter.*

different from/different than Although different from is the preferred usage (*His attitude is different from mine*), different than is widely accepted when a clause follows, especially when the word "from" would create an awkward sentence. Example: *The stream followed a different course than the map showed.*

discreet/discrete Discreet means "tactful"; discrete, "separate." For example: *Do you have a discreet way of refusing the invitation? The mosaic is made of hundreds of discrete pieces of tile.*

disinterested/uninterested Disinterested is used to mean "without prejudice, impartial" (*He is a disinterested judge*) and uninterested to mean "bored" or "lacking interest." (*They are completely uninterested in sports*).

dominant/dominate Dominant, an adjective, means "ruling, controlling": *Social scientists have long argued over the dominant motives for human behavior.* Dominate, a verb, means "to control": *Advice columnists often preach that no one can dominate you unless you allow them to.*

don't/does not Don't is the contraction for "do not," not for does not, as in *I don't care, she doesn't (not don't) care.*

done Using done as an adjective to mean "through, finished" is standard. Originally, done was used attributively (*The pact between them was a done thing*), but it has become more common as a compliment: *Are your pictures done yet? When we were done with the power saw, we removed the blade.*

double negatives Although the use of double negatives (*They never paid no dues*) was standard for many years in English, today certain uses of the double negative are universally considered unacceptable: *He didn't have nothing to do,* for example. In educated speech and writing, "anything" would be used in place of "nothing."

doubt that/doubt whether/doubt if Doubt that is used to express conviction *(I doubt that they intended to hurt your feelings);* doubt whether and doubt if are used to indicate uncertainty: *I doubt whether (or if) anyone really listened to the speaker.*

due to In formal discourse, due to is acceptable only after a form of the verb "to be": *Her aching back was due to poor posture.* Due to is not acceptable as a preposition meaning "because of" or "owing to": *Because of (not "due to") the poor weather, the bus was late.*

each When each is used as a pronoun, it takes a singular verb *(Each was born in Europe),* although plurals are increasingly used in formal speech and writing in an attempt to avoid using "he" or "his" for sentences that include females or do not specify sex: *(Each of them had their (rather than "his") own agenda.* More and more, the same pattern of pronoun agreement is being used with the singular pronouns *anyone, anybody, everyone, everybody, no one, someone,* and *somebody.* When the pronoun each is followed by an "of" phrase containing a plural noun or pronoun, usage guides suggest that the verb be singular, but the plural is used often even in formal writing: *Each of the children has (or "have") had a school physical.*

When the adjective each follows a plural subject, the verb agrees with the subject: *The rooms each have separate thermostats.*

each and every Use "each" or "every" in place of the phrase each and every, generally considered wordy: *Each of us enjoyed the concert. Every one of us stayed until the end of the performance.*

each other/one another Each other is traditionally used to indicate two members; one another for three or more: *The two children trade lunches with each other. The guests greeted one another fondly.* In standard practice, though, these distinctions are not observed in either speech or writing.

elicit/illicit Elicit, a verb, means "call forth"; illicit, an adjective, means "against the law": *The assault elicited a protest against illicit handguns.*

emigrate/immigrate Emigrate means "to leave one's own country to settle in another": *She emigrated from France.* **Immigrate** means "to enter a different country and settle there": *My father immigrated to America when he was nine years old.*

eminent/imminent Eminent means "distinguished": *Marie Curie was an eminent scientist in the final years of her life.* **Imminent** means "about to happen": *The thundershower seemed imminent.*

enthused/enthusiastic The word enthused is used informally to mean "showing enthusiasm." For formal writing and speech, use the adjective enthusiastic: *The team was enthusiastic about the quarterback's winning play.*

envelop/envelope Envelop is a verb that means "to surround": *The music envelops him in a soothing atmosphere.* **Envelope,** a noun, is a flat paper container, usually for a letter: *Be sure to put a stamp on the envelope before you mail that letter.*

especially/specially The two words are not interchangeable: especially means "particularly"; specially means "for a specific reason." For example: *I especially value my wedding ring; it was made specially for me.*

-ess/-or/-er The suffix -ess has often been used to denote feminine nouns. While many such words are still in use, English is moving increasingly toward nouns that do not denote sex differences. The most widely observed guideline today is that if the sex of the performer is not relevant to the performance of the task or function, the neutral ending -or or -er should be used in place of -ess. Thus, words such as *ambassadress, ancestress, authoress, poetess, proprietress, sculptress* are no longer used; and the airlines, for example, have replaced both *steward* and *stewardess* with *flight attendant.*

et al. Et al., the Latin abbreviation for "and other people," is fully standard for use in a citation to refer to works with more than three authors: *Harris et al.*

etc. Since etc. (et cetera) is the Latin abbreviation for "and other things," it should not be used to refer to people. In general, it should be avoided in formal writing as imprecise. In its place, provide the entire list of items or use "and so on."

-ette English nouns whose -ette ending signifies a feminine role or identity are passing out of usage. *Farmerette, suffragette, usherette,* for exam-ple, have been replaced by *farmer, suffragist,* and *usher,* respectively.

ever so often/every so often Ever so often means happening very often and every so often means happening occasionally.

everybody, every body/everyone, every one Everybody and everyone are indefinite pronouns: *Everybody likes William, and everyone enjoys his company.* **Every body** is a noun modified by "every" and every one is a pronoun modified by "every"; both refer to a person in a specific group and are usually followed by "of": *Every body of water in our area is polluted; every one of our ponds is covered in debris.*

everyday/every day Everyday is an adjective that means "used daily, typical, ordinary"; every day is made up of a noun modified by the adjective "every" and means "each day": *Every day they had to deal with the everyday business of life.*

everywheres/everywhere Everywheres is a nonstandard term for everywhere and should be avoided in speech and writing.

exam/examination Exam should be reserved for everyday speech and examination for formal writing: *The College Board examinations are scheduled for this Saturday morning at 9:00.*

except for the fact that/except that Use except that in place of the verbose phrase except for the fact that: *Except that (not "except for the fact that") the button is missing, this is a lovely skirt.*

explicit/implicit Explicit means "stated plainly"; implicit means "understood," "implied": *You know we have an implicit understanding that you are not allowed to watch any television shows that contain explicit sex.*

fair/fare Fair as an adjective means "free from bias," "ample," "unblemished," "of light hue," or "attractive." As an adverb, it means "favorably." It is used informally to mean "honest." Fare as a noun means "the price charged for transporting a person" or "food."

farther/further Traditionally, farther is used to indicate physical distance *(Is it much farther to the hotel?)* and further is used to refer to additional time, amount, or abstract ideas *(Your mother does not want to talk about this any further).*

fewer/less Traditionally, fewer, a plural noun, has most often been used to refer to individual units that can be counted: *There are fewer buttons on this shirt. No fewer than forty of the fifty voters supported the measure.* **Less**, a singular noun, is used to refer to uncountable quantities: *She eats less every day. I have less patience than I used to.*

Standard English does not usually reflect these distinctions, however. When followed by "than," **less** is used as often as **fewer** to indicate plural nouns that refer to items that can be counted: *There were no less than eight million people. No less than forty of the fifty voters supported the measure.*

figuratively/literally Figuratively, meaning "involving a figure of speech," usually implies that the statement is not true. Literally, meaning "actually, without exaggeration," implies that the statement is true: *The poet Robert Frost once figuratively described writing poetry without regular meter and rhyme as playing tennis with the net down. My sister literally passed out when she saw what had happened to her new car.*

Literally is commonly used as an intensifier meaning "in effect, virtually": *The state representative was literally buried alive in the caucus.* This usage should be avoided in formal discourse.

fix The verb **fix**, meaning "to repair," is fully accepted in all areas of speech and writing. The noun **fix**, meaning "repair" or "adjustment," is used informally.

fixing to/intend to Use **intend to** in place of the colloquial term **fixing to**: *The community intends to (not "is fixing to") raise money to help the victims of the recent fire.*

flaunt/flout Flaunt means "to show off"; **flout**, "to ignore or treat with disdain." For example: *They flouted convention when they flaunted their wealth.*

flunk/fail Use the standard term **fail** in speech and writing; **flunk** is a colloquial substitute.

former/latter Former is used to refer to the first of two items; **latter**, the second: *We enjoy both gardening and painting, the former during the summer and the latter during the winter.* When dealing with three or more items, use "first" and "last" rather than **former** and **latter**: *We enjoy gardening, painting, and skiing, but the last is very costly.*

formally/formerly Both words are adverbs. Formally means "in a formal manner": *The minister addressed the king and queen formally.* **Formerly** means "previously": *Formerly, he worked as a chauffeur; now, he is employed as a guard.*

forth/fourth Forth is an adverb meaning "going forward or away": *From that day forth, they lived happily ever after.* **Fourth** is most often used as an adjective that means "next after the third": *Mitchell was the fourth in line.*

fortuitous Fortuitous means "happening accidentally": *A fortuitous meeting with a former acquaintance led to a change in plans.* It is also used sometimes as a synonym for "lucky" or "fortunate."

from whence Although the phrase **from whence** is sometimes criticized on the grounds that "from" is redundant because it is included in the meaning of "whence," the idiom is nonetheless standard in both speech and writing: *She finally moved to Kansas, from whence she began to build a new life.*

fulsome Originally, fulsome meant "abundant," but for hundreds of years the word has been used to mean "offensive, disgusting, or excessively lavish." While the word still maintains the connotations of "excessive" or "offensive," it has also come to be used in the original sense as well: *Compare the severe furniture of the living room to the fulsome decorations in the den.*

fun Fun should not be used as an adjective in formal writing. Instead, substitute a word such as "happy," "pleasant," or "entertaining": *They had a pleasant (not "fun") afternoon at the park.*

gentleman Once used only to refer to men of high social rank, the term **gentleman** now also specifies a man of courtesy and consideration: *He behaves like a gentleman.* It is also used as a term of polite reference and address in the singular and plural: *This gentleman is waiting to be served. Are we ready to begin, gentlemen?*

get The verb **get** is used in many slang and colloquial phrases as a substitute for forms of "to be." For example: *They won't get accepted with that attitude.* In American English, an alternative past participle is **gotten**, especially in the sense of "received" and "acquired": *I have gotten (or "got") all I ever wanted.*

Both **have** *and* **has got** (meaning "must") are occasionally criticized as being redundant, but are nonetheless fully standard in all varieties of speech and writing: *You have got to carry your driver's licence at all times.*

good/well Good, an adjective, should be used to describe someone or something: *Joe is a good student.* **Well**, when used as an adverb, should describe an action: *She and Laura play well together on the swing set.* **Well**, when used as an adjective after "look," "feel" or other linking verbs, often refers to good health: *You're looking well.*

good and/very Avoid using **good and** as a substitute for **very**: *I was very (not "good and") hungry.*

graduate The passive form, once considered the only correct usage, is seldom used today: *I was graduated from the Merchant Marine Academy last May.* Although some critics condemn the use of **graduate** as a transitive verb meaning "to receive a degree or diploma from," its use is increasing in both speech and writing: *She graduated from elementary school in Cleveland.*

great The word **great** has been overused in informal writing and speech as a synonym for "enthusiastic," "good," or "clever": *She was really great at making people feel at home.*

had drank/had drunk According to some authorities, **had drank** is acceptable usage: *I had drank a gallon of milk.* **Had drunk**, though, is fully standard and the preferred usage.

has/have; has got/have got The word "got" is unnecessary; simply use **has** or **have**: *Jessica has a mild case of chicken pox.*

had ought/ought Had ought is considered wordy; the preferred usage is **ought**: *She ought (not "had ought") to heed her mother's advice.*

half/a half/a half Use either **half** or **a half**; **a half a** is considered wordy: *Please give me a half (not "a half a") piece. I'd like half that slice, please.*

hanged/hung Although both words are past-tense forms of "to hang," **hanged** is used to refer to executions (*Billy Budd was hanged*) and **hung** is used for all other meanings: *The stockings were hung by the chimney with care.*

have/of Use **have** rather than **of** after helping verbs like "could," "should," "would," "may," and "might": *They should have (not "of") let me know of their decision earlier.*

healthy/healthful Healthy means "possessing health"; **healthful**

means "bringing about health": *They believed that they were healthy people because they ate healthful food.*

he, she; he/she The pronouns **he** and **she** refer to male and female antecedents, respectively. Traditionally, when an antecedent in singular form could be either female or male, "he" was always used to refer to either sex: *A child is often apprehensive when he first begins school.* Today, however, various approaches have been developed to avoid the all-purpose "he." Many people find the construction *he/she* (or *he or she*) awkward: *A child is often apprehensive when he/she first begins school.* The blended form *s/he* has not been widely adopted, probably because of confusion over pronunciation. Most people now favor either rephrasing the sentence entirely to omit the pronoun or reconstructing the sentence in the third-person plural: *Children are often apprehensive when they first begin school.*

hopefully Hopefully means "with hope": *They waited hopefully for a look at the astronaut.* In formal writing and speech, avoid using **hopefully** to mean "it is to be hoped": *We hope (not "Hopefully") Captain Smith will come out of the hangar soon.*

how come/why How come is used informally in speech to substitute for why.

human/humane Both words are adjectives. Human means "pertaining to humanity": *The subject of the documentary is the human race.* Humane means "tender, compassionate, or sympathetic": *Many of her patients believed that her humane care speeded their recovery.*

idea/ideal Idea means "thought," while ideal means "a model of perfection" or "goal." The two words are not interchangeable. They should be used as follows: *The idea behind the blood drive is that our ideals often move us to help others.*

if/whether Use whether rather than if to begin a subordinate clause when the clause states a choice: *I don't know whether (not "if") I should stay until the end or leave right after the opening ceremony.*

impact Both the noun and verb impact are used to indicate forceful contact: *I cannot overstate the impact of the new policy on productivity.* Some speakers and writers avoid using impact as a verb to mean "to have an effect," as in *Our work here impacts on every division in the firm.*

imply/infer Imply means "to suggest without stating": *The message on Karen's postcard implies that her vacation has not turned out as she wished.* Infer means "to reach a conclusion based on understood evidence": *From her message I infer that she wishes she had stayed home.* When used in this manner, the two words describe two sides of the same process.

in Several phrases beginning with in are verbose and should be avoided in formal writing. Refer to the following chart:

Replace the phrase . . .
in this day and age

With . . .
now

Replace the phrase . . .
in spite of the fact that

With . . .
although *or* even though

Replace the phrase . . .
in the neighborhood of

With . . .
approximately *or* about

Replace the phrase . . .
in the event that

With . . .
if

The following phrases can be omitted entirely: *in a very real sense, in number, in nature, in reality, in terms of,* and *in the case of.*

in/into In is used to indicate condition or location, "positioned within": *She was in labor. The raccoon was in the woodpile.* Into, in contrast, indicates movement or a change in condition "from the outside to the inside": *The raccoon went into the shed. He went into cardiac arrest.* Into is also used as a slang expression for "involved with" or "interested in": *They are really into health foods.*

inferior than Inferior to and worse than are the generally preferred forms: *This wine is inferior to (not "inferior than") the burgundy we had last night.*

incredible/incredulous Incredible means "cannot be believed"; incredulous means "unbelieving": *The teacher was incredulous when she heard the pupil's incredible story about the fate of his term project.*

individual/person/party Individual should be used to stress uniqueness or to refer to a single human being as contrasted to a group of people: *The rights of the individual should not supersede the rights of a group.* Person is the preferred word in other contexts: *What person wouldn't want to have a chance to sail around the world?* Party is used to refer to a group: *Send the party of five this way, please.* Party is also used to refer to an individual mentioned in a legal document.

ingenious/ingenuous Ingenious means "resourceful, clever": *My sister is ingenious when it comes to turning leftovers into something delicious.* Ingenuous means "frank, artless": *The child's ingenuous manner is surprising considering her fame.*

in regards to/with regards to Both terms are considered nonstandard terms for "regarding," "in regard to," "with regard to," and "as regards." As regards (not "in regards to") your request of April 1, we have traced your shipment and it will be delivered tomorrow.

inside/outside; inside of/outside of When the words inside and outside are used as prepositions, the word of is not included: *Stay inside the house. The authorization is outside my department.* Inside of is used informally to refer to time (*I'll be there inside of an hour*), but in formal speech or writing within is the preferred usage: *The dump was cleaned up within a month.*

insignia Insignia was originally the plural of the Latin word "insigne." The plural term insignias has been standard usage since the eighteenth century.

irregardless/regardless Regardless is the standard term; avoid irregardless in both speech and writing.

is when/is where Both phrases are unacceptable and are to be avoided.

its/it's/its' Its is the possessive form if *it*: *The shrub is losing its blossoms.* It's is the contraction for *it is*: *It's a nice day.* The two are often confused because possessives are most frequently formed with -'s. Its' is nonstandard usage.

It's me/It's I The traditional rule is that personal pronouns after the verb "to be" take the nominative case (*I, she, he, we, they*). Today, however, such usage as *it's me, that's him,* *it must be them* are almost universal in informal speech. The objective forms have also replaced the nominative forms in informal speech in such constructions as *me neither, who, them?* In formal discourse, however, the nominative forms are still used: *it's I, that is he.*

-ize/-wise Use the suffix -ize to change a noun or adjective into a verb: *categorize.* Use the suffix -wise to change a noun or adjective into an adverb: *otherwise.*

kind of/sort of/type of Avoid using either kind of, sort of, or type of as synonyms for "somewhat" in formal speech and writing. Instead, use **rather**: *She was rather (not "kind of") slender.* It is acceptable to use the three terms only when the word **kind, sort,** or **type** is stressed: *This kind of cheese is hard to digest.* Do not add "a": *I don't know what kind of (not "kind of a") cheese that is.* When the word **kind, sort,** or **type** is not stressed, omit the phrase entirely: *That's an unusual (not "unusual kind of") car. She's a pleasant (not "pleasant sort of a") person.*

later/latter Later is used to refer to time; latter, the second of two items named: *It is later than you think. Of the two shirts I just purchased, I prefer the latter.* See also **former/latter.**

lay/lie Lay is a transitive verb that means "to put down" or "to place." It takes a direct object: *Please lay the soup spoon next to the teaspoon.* Lie is an intransitive verb that means "to be in a horizontal position" or "be situated." It does not take a direct object: *The puppy lies down where the old dog had always lain. The hotel lies on the outskirts of town.* The confusion arises over **lay,** which is the present tense of the verb **lay** and the past tense of the verb **lie.**

To lie (recline)

Present: *Spot lies (is lying) down.*

Future: *Spot will lie down.*

Past: *Spot lay down.*

Perfect: *Spot has (had, will have) lain down.*

To lay (put down)

Present: *He lays (is laying) his dice down.*

Future: *He will lay his dice down.*

Past: *He laid his dice down.*

Perfect: *He has (had, will have) laid his dice down.*

Although **lie** and **lay** tend to be used interchangeably in all but the most careful, formal speech, the following phrases are generally considered nonstandard and are avoided in written English: *Lay down, dears. The dog laid in the sun. Abandoned cars were laying in the junkyard. The reports have laid in the mailbox for a week.*

lead/led Lead as a verb means "to take or conduct on the way": *I plan to lead a quiet afternoon.* Led is the past tense: *He led his followers through the dangerous underbrush.* Lead, as a noun, means "a type of metal": *Pipes are made of lead.*

learn/teach Learn is to acquire knowledge: *He learned fast.* Teach is to impart knowledge: *She taught well.*

leave/let Leave and let are interchangeable only when followed by the word "alone": *Leave him alone. Let him alone.* In other instances, leave means "to depart" or "permit to remain in the same place": *If you leave, please turn off the copier. Leave the extra paper on the shelf.* Let means "to allow": *Let him work with the assistant, if he wants.*

lessen/lesson Lessen is a verb meaning "to decrease": *To lessen the pain of a burn, apply ice to the injured area.* Lesson is most often used as a noun meaning "material assigned for study": *Today, the lesson will be on electricity.*

let's Let's is often used as a word in its own right rather than as the contraction of "let us." As such, it is often used in informal speech and writing with redundant or appositional pronouns: *Let's us take in a movie. Let's you and me go for a walk.* Usage guides suggest avoiding **let's us** in formal speech and writing, although both *let's you and me* and *let's you and I* occur in the everyday speech of educated speakers. While the former conforms to the traditional rules of grammar, the latter, nevertheless, occurs more frequently.

lightening/lightning Lightening is a form of the verb that means "to brighten": *The cheerful new drapes and bunches of flowers went a long way in lightening the room's somber mood.* Lightning is most often used as a noun to mean "flashes of light generated during a storm": *The thunder and lightning frightened the child.*

like/such as Use like to compare an example to the thing mentioned and **such as** to show that the example is representative of the thing mentioned: *Judy wants to be a famous clothing designer like John Weitz, Liz Claiborne, and Yves St. Laurent. Judy has samples of many fine articles such as evening dresses, suits, and jackets.*

Many writers favor not separating **such** and **as** with an intervening word: *samples of many fine articles such as* rather than *samples of such fine articles as.*

loose/lose Loose is an adjective meaning "free and unattached": *The dog was loose again.* Loose can also be a verb meaning "let loose": *The hunters loose the dogs as soon as the ducks fall.* Lose is a verb meaning "to part with unintentionally": *He will lose his keys if he leaves them on the countertop.*

lots/lots of Both terms are used in informal speech and writing as a substitute for "a great many," "very many," or "much."

mad/angry Traditionally, **mad** has been used to mean "insane"; **angry,** "full of ire." While **mad** can be used to mean "enraged, angry," in informal usage, you should replace **mad** with **angry** in formal discourse: *The president is angry at Congress for overriding his veto.*

man The use of the term man as a synonym for "human being," both by itself and in compounds *(mankind),* is declining. Terms such as *human being(s), human race, humankind, humanity, people,* and, when necessary, *men and women* or *women and men* are widely accepted in formal usage.

-man/-person The use of the term man as the last element in compound words referring to a person of either sex who performs some function *(anchorman, chairman, spokesman)* has declined in recent years. Now such compound words are only widely used if the word refers to a male. The sex-neutral word **person** is otherwise substituted for man *(anchorperson, chairperson, spokesperson).* In other instances, a form without a suffix *(anchor, chair),* or a word that does not denote gender *(speaker),* is used.

The compound words *freshman, lowerclassmen, underclassmen* are still generally used in schools, and *freshman* is used in the U.S. Congress as well. These terms are applied to members of both sexes. As a modifier, *freshman* is used with both singular and plural nouns: *freshman athlete, freshman legislators.* See also chair/chairperson.

maybe/may be Maybe, an adverb, means "perhaps": *Maybe the newspapers can be recycled with the plastic and glass.* May be, a verb, means "could be": *It may be too difficult, however.*

me and Me and is considered nonstandard usage when part of a compound subject: *Bob and I (not "Me and Bob") decided to fly to Boston.*

media Media, the plural of medium, is used with a plural verb: *Increasingly, the radio and television media seem to be stressing sensational news.*

mighty Mighty is used informally for "very" or "extremely": *He is a mighty big fighter.*

moral/morale As a noun, moral means "ethical lesson": *Each of Aesop's fables has a clear moral.* Morale means "state of mind" or "spirit": *Her morale was lifted by her colleague's good wishes.*

more important/more importantly Both phrases are acceptable in standard English: *My donations of clothing were tax deductible; more important(ly), the clothes were given to homeless people.*

Ms. (or Ms) The title Ms. is widely used in business and professional circles as an alternative to "Mrs." and "Miss," both of which reveal a woman's marital status. Some women prefer "Mrs.," where appropriate, or the traditional "Miss," which is still fully standard for an unmarried woman or a woman whose marital status is unknown. Since Ms. is not an abbreviation, some sources spell it without a period; others use a period to parallel "Mr." It is correctly used before a woman's name but not before her husband's name: *Ms. Leslie Taubman* or *Ms. Taubman (not "Ms. Steven Taubman").*

much/many Use many rather than much to modify plural nouns: *They had many (not "much") dogs. There were too many (not "much") facts to absorb.*

Muslim/Moslem Muslim is now the preferred form for an adherent of Islam, though Moslem, the traditional form, is still in use.

mutual One current meaning of mutual is "reciprocal": *Employers and employees sometimes suffer from a mutual misunderstanding.* Mutual can also mean "held in common; shared": *Their mutual goal is clearly understood.*

myself; herself; himself; yourself The -self pronouns are intensive or reflexive, intensifying or referring to an antecedent: *Kerri herself said so. Mike and I did it ourselves.* Questions are raised when the -self forms are used instead of personal pronouns (I, me, etc.) as subjects, objects, or complements. This use of the -self forms is especially common in informal speech and writing: *Many came to welcome my wife and myself back from China.* All these forms are also used, alone or with other nouns or pronouns, after "as," "than," or "but" in all varieties of speech and writing: *Letters have arrived for everyone but the counselors and yourselves.* Although there is ample precedent in both British and American usage for the expanded uses of the -self constructions, the -self pronouns should be used in formal speech and writing only with the nouns and pronouns to which they refer: *No one except me (not "myself") saw the movie.*

nauseous/nauseated Nauseated is generally preferred in formal writing over nauseous: *The wild ride on the roller coaster made Wanda feel nauseated.*

neither . . . nor When used as a correlative, neither is almost always followed by nor: *neither Caitlyn nor her father . . .* The subjects connected by neither . . . nor take a singular verb when both subjects are singular *(Neither Caitlyn nor her father is going to watch the program)* and a plural verb when both are plural *(Neither the rabbits nor the sheep have been fed yet today).* When a singular and a plural subject are joined by these correlatives, the verb should agree with the nearer noun or pronoun: *Neither the mayor nor the council members have yielded. Neither the council members nor the mayor has yielded.*

nohow The word nohow, nonstandard usage for "in no way" or "in any way," should be avoided in speech and writing.

none None can be treated as either singular or plural depending on its meaning in a sentence. When the sense is "not any persons or things," the plural is more common: *The rescue party searched for survivors, but none were found.* When none is clearly intended to mean "not one" or "not any," it is followed by a singular verb: *Of all the ailments I have diagnosed during my career, none has been stranger than yours.*

no . . . nor/no . . . or Use no . . . or in compound phrases: *We had no milk or eggs in the house.*

nothing like, nowhere near Both phrases are used in informal speech and writing, but they should be avoided in formal discourse. Instead, use "not nearly": *The congealed pudding found in the back of the refrigerator is not nearly as old as the stale bread on the second shelf.*

nowheres/nowhere The word nowheres, nonstandard usage for nowhere, should be avoided in speech and writing.

of Avoid using of with descriptive adjectives after the adverbs "how" or "too" in formal speech and writing. This usage is largely restricted to informal discourse: *How long of a ride will it be? It's too cold of a day for swimming.*

off of/off Off of is redundant and awkward; use off: *The cat jumped off the sofa.*

OK/O.K./okay All three spellings are considered acceptable, but the phrases are generally reserved for informal speech and writing.

on account of/because of Since it is less wordy, because of is the preferred phrase: *Because of her headache, they decided to go straight home.*

on the one hand/on the other hand These two transitions should be used together: *On the one hand, we hoped for fair weather. On the other hand, we knew the rain was needed for the crops.* This usage, though, can be wordy. Effective substitutes include "in contrast," "but," "however," and "yet": *We hoped for fair weather, yet we knew the rain was needed for the crops.*

only The placement of only as a modifier is more a matter of style and clarity than of grammatical rule. In strict, formal usage, only should be placed as close as possible *before* the word it modifies. In the following sentence, for example, the placement of the word only suggests that no one but the children was examined: *The doctor examined only the children.* In the next sentence, the placement of only says that no one but the doctor did the examining: *Only the doctor examined the children.* Nonetheless, in all types of speech and writing, people often place only before the verb regardless of what it modifies. In spoken discourse, speakers may convey their intended meaning by stressing the word or construction to which only applies.

owing to the fact that "Because" is generally accepted as a less wordy substitute for owing to the fact that.

pair/pairs When modified by a number, the plural of **pair** is commonly **pairs**, especially when referring to persons: *The three pairs of costumed children led off Halloween parade.* The plural **pair** is used mainly in reference to inanimate objects or nonhumans: *There are four pair (or "pairs") of shoelaces. We have two pair (or "pairs") of rabbits.*

passed/past **Passed** is a form of the verb meaning "to go by": *Bernie passed the same buildings on his way to work each day.* **Past** can function as a noun, adjective, adverb, or preposition. As a noun, **past** means "the history of a nation, person, etc.": *The lessons of the past should not be forgotten.* As an adjective, **past** means "gone by or elapsed in time": *John is worried about his past deeds.* As an adverb, **past** means "so as to pass by": *The fire engine raced past the parked cars.* As a preposition, **past** means "beyond in time": *It's past noon already.*

patience/patients Patience, a noun, means "endurance": *Chrissy's patience makes her an ideal baby-sitter.* **Patients** are people under medical treatment: *The patients must remain in the hospital for another week.*

peace/piece Peace is "freedom from discord": *The negotiators hoped that the new treaty would bring about lasting peace.* **Piece** is "a portion of a whole" or "a short musical arrangement": *I would like just a small piece of cake, please. The piece in E flat is especially beautiful.*

people/persons In formal usage, **people** is most often included to refer to a general group, emphasizing anonymity: *We the people of the United States . . .* Use **persons** to indicate any unnamed individuals within the group: *Will the persons who left their folders on the table please pick them up at their earliest convenience?* Except when individuals are being emphasized, **people** is generally suggested for use rather than **persons**.

per; a/an Per, meaning "for each," occurs mainly in technical or statistical contexts: *This new engine averages fifty miles per hour. Americans eat fifty pounds of chicken per person per year.* It is also frequently used in sports commentary: *He scored an average of two runs per game.* A or **an** is often considered more suitable in nontechnical

use: *The silk costs ten dollars a yard. How many miles an hour can you walk?*

percent/per cent Percent comes from the English *per cent.,* an abbreviation of the Latin *per centum.* It almost always follows a number: *I made 12 percent interest by investing my money in that new account.* In formal writing, use the word rather than the symbol (%). The use of the two-word form **per cent** is diminishing.

percent/percentage Percent is used with a number, **percentage** with a modifier. **Percentage** is used most often after an adjective: *A high percentage of your earnings this year is tax deductible.*

personal/personnel Personal means "private": *The lock on her journal showed that it was clearly personal.* **Personnel** refers to employees: *Attention all personnel!* The use of **personnel** as a plural has become standard in business and government: *The personnel were dispatched to the Chicago office.*

phenomena Like words such as **criteria** and **media**, phenomena is a plural form (of "phenomenon"), meaning "an observable fact, occurrence, or circumstance": *The official explained that the disturbing phenomena we had seen for the past three evenings were nothing more than routine aircraft maneuvers.*

plain/plane Plain as an adjective means "easily understood," "undistinguished," or "unadorned": *His meaning was plain to all. The plain dress suited the gravity of the occasion.* As an adverb, **plain** means "clearly and simply": *She's just plain foolish.* As a noun, **plain** is a flat area of land: *The vast plain seemed to go on forever.* As a noun, **plane** has a number of different meanings. It most commonly refers to an airplane, but is also used in mathematics and fine arts and is a tool used to shave wood.

plenty As a noun, plenty is acceptable in standard usage: *I have plenty of money.* In informal speech and writing **plenty** is often a substitute for "very": *She was traveling plenty fast down the freeway.*

plus Plus is a preposition meaning "in addition to": *My salary plus overtime is enough to allow us a gracious life style.* Recently, **plus** has been used as a conjunctive adverb in informal speech and writing: *It's safe, plus it's economical.* This usage is still considered nonstandard.

practicable/practical Practicable means "capable of being done": *My decorating plans were too difficult to be practicable.* **Practical** means "pertaining to practice or action": *It was just not practical to paint the floor white.*

practically Use practically as a synonym for "in effect," or "virtually." It is also considered correct to use it in place of "nearly" in all varieties of speech and writing.

precede/proceed Although both words are verbs, they have different meanings. **Precede** means "to go before": *Morning precedes afternoon.* **Proceed** means "to move forward": *Proceed to the exit in an orderly fashion.*

presence/presents Presence is used chiefly to mean "attendance; close proximity": *Your presence at the ceremony will be greatly appreciated.* **Presents** are gifts: *Thank you for giving us such generous presents.*

previous to/prior to "Before" is generally preferred in place of either expression: *Before (not "previous to" or "prior to") repairing the tire, you should check to see if there are any other leaks.*

principal/principle Principal can be a noun or an adjective. As a noun, **principal** means "chief or head official" (*The principal decided to close school early on Tuesday*) or "sum of capital" (*Invest only the interest, never the principal*). As an adjective, **principal** means "first or highest": *The principal ingredient is sugar.* **Principle** is a noun only, meaning "rule" or "general truth": *Regardless of what others said, she stood by her principles.*

providing/provided Both forms can serve as subordinating conjunctions meaning "on the condition that": *Provided (Providing) that we get the contract in time, we will be able to begin work by the first of the month.* While some critics feel that **provided** is more acceptable in formal discourse, both are correct.

question of whether/question as to whether Both phrases are wordy substitutes for "whether": *Whether (not "the question of whether" or "the question as to whether") it rains or not, we are planning to go on the hike.*

quiet/quite Quiet, as an adjective, means "free from noise": *When the master of ceremonies spoke, the room became quiet.* **Quite**, an adverb, means "completely, wholly": *By the late afternoon, the children were quite exhausted.*

quotation/quote Quotation, a noun, means "a passage quoted from a speech or book": *The speaker read a quotation of twenty-five lines to the audience.* **Quote,** a verb, means "to repeat a passage from a speech, etc.": *Marci often quotes from popular novels.* Quote and quotation are often used interchangeably in speech; in formal writing, however, a distinction is still observed between the two words.

rain/reign/rein As a noun, rain means "water that falls from the atmosphere to earth." As a verb, **rain** means "to send down; to give abundantly": *The crushed piñata rained candy on the eager children.* As a noun, reign means "royal rule"; as a verb, "to have supreme control": *The monarch's reign was marked by social unrest.* As a noun, **rein** means "a leather strap used to guide an animal"; as a verb, "to control or guide": *He used the rein to control the frisky colt.*

raise/rise/raze Raise, a transitive verb, means "to elevate": *How can I raise the cost of my house?* Rise, an intransitive verb, means "to go up, to get up": *Will housing costs rise this year?* **Raze** is a transitive verb meaning "to tear down, demolish": *The wrecking crew was ready to raze the condemned building.*

rarely ever/rarely The term rarely ever is used informally in speech and writing. For formal discourse, use either rarely or hardly in place of rarely ever: *She rarely calls her mother. She hardly calls her mother.*

real/really In formal usage, real (an adjective meaning "genuine") should not be used in place of really (an adverb meaning "actually"): *The platypus hardly looked real. How did it really happen?*

reason is because/reason is since Although both expressions are commonly used in informal speech and writing, formal usage requires a clause beginning with "that" after "reason is": *The reason the pool is empty is that (not "because" or "since") the town recently imposed a water restriction.* Another alternative is to recast the sentence: *The pool is empty because the town recently imposed a water restriction.*

regarding/in regard to/with regard to/relating to/relative to/with respect to/respecting All the above expressions are wordy substitutes for "about," "concerning," or "on": *Janet spoke about (not "relative to," etc.) the PTA's plans for the September fund drive.*

relate to The phrase relate to is used informally to mean "understand" or "respond in a favorable manner": *I don't relate to chemistry.* It is rarely used in formal writing or speech.

repeat it/repeat it again Repeat it is the expression to use to indicate someone should say something for a second time: *I did not hear your name; please repeat it.* Repeat it again indicates the answer is to be said a third time. In the majority of instances, repeat it is the desired phrase; again, an unnecessary addition.

respectful/respective Respectful means "showing (or full of) respect": *If you are respectful toward others, they will treat you with consideration as well.* Respective means "in the order given": *The respective remarks were made by executive board members Joshua Whittles, Kevin McCarthy, and Warren Richmond.*

reverend/reverent As an adjective (usually capitalized), Reverend is an epithet of respect given to a clergyman: *The Reverend Mr. Jones gave the sermon.* As a noun, a reverend is "a clergyman": *In our church, the reverend opens the service with a prayer.* Reverent is an adjective meaning "showing deep respect": *The speaker began his remarks with a reverent greeting.*

right/rite/write Right as an adjective means "proper, correct" and "as opposed to left"; as a noun it means "claims or titles"; as an adverb it means "in a straight line, directly"; as a verb it means "to restore an upright position." Rite is a noun meaning "a solemn ritual": *The religious leader performed the necessary rites.* Write is a verb meaning "to form characters on a surface": *The child liked to write her name over and over.*

says/said Use said rather than says after a verb in the past tense: *At the public meeting, he stood up and said (not "says"), "The bond issue cannot pass."*

seldom ever/seldom Seldom is the preferred form in formal discourse: *They seldom (not "seldom ever") visit the beach.*

sensual/sensuous Sensual carries sexual overtones: *The massage was a sensual experience.* Sensuous means "pertaining to the senses": *The sensuous aroma of freshly baked bread wafted through the house.*

set/sit Set, a transitive verb, describes something a person does to an object: *She set the book down on the*

table. Sit, an intransitive verb, describes a person resting: *Marvin sits on the straight-backed chair.*

shall/will Today, shall is used for first-person questions requesting consent or opinion: *Shall we go for a drive? Shall I buy this dress or that?* Shall can also be used in the first person to create an elevated tone: *We shall call on you at six o'clock.* It is sometimes used with the second or third person to state a speaker's resolution: *You shall obey me.*

Traditionally, will was used for the second and third persons: *Will you attend the party? Will he and she go as well?* It is now widely used in speech and writing as the future-tense helping verb for all three persons: *I will drive, you will drive, they will drive.*

should/would Rules similar to those for choosing between "shall" and "will" have long been advanced for should and would. In current American usage, use of would far outweighs that of should. Should is chiefly used to state obligation: *I should repair the faucet. You should get the parts we need.* Would, in contrast, is used to express a hypothetical situation or a wish: *I would like to go. Would you?*

since Since is an adverb meaning "from then until now": *She was appointed in May and has been supervisor ever since.* It is also used as an adverb meaning "between a particular past time and the present, subsequently": *They had at first refused to cooperate, but have since agreed to volunteer.* As a preposition, since means "continuously from": *It has been rainy since June.* It is also used as a preposition meaning "between a past time or event and the present": *There have been many changes since the merger.* As a conjunction, since means "in the period following the time when": *He has called since he changed jobs.* Since is also used as a synonym for "because": *Since you're here early, let's begin.*

situation The word situation is often added unnecessarily to a sentence: *The situation is that we must get the painting done by the weekend.* In such instances, consider revising the sentence to pare excess words: *We must get the painting done by the weekend.*

slow/slowly Today slow is used chiefly in spoken imperative constructions with short verbs that express motion, such as "drive," "walk," "swim," and "run." For example: *Drive slow, Don't walk so slow.* Slow is also combined with present participles to form adjectives: *He was slow-moving. It was a slow-burning fire.* Slowly is found commonly in formal writing and is used in both speech and writing before a verb *(He slowly walked through the hills)* as well as after a verb *(He walked slowly through the hills).*

so Many writers object to so being used as an intensifier, noting that in such usage it is often vague: *They were so happy.* So followed by "that" and a clause usually eliminates the vagueness: *They were so happy that they had been invited to the exclusive party.*

so/so that So that, rather than so, is most often used in formal writing to avoid the possibility of ambiguity: *He visited Aunt Lucia so that he could help her clear the basement.*

some Some is often used in informal speech and writing as an adjective meaning "exceptional, unusual" and as an adverb meaning "somewhat." In more formal instances, use "somewhat" in place of some as an adverb or a more precise word such as "remarkable" in place of some as an adjective: *Those are unusual (not "some") shoes. My sister and brother-in-law are going to have to rush somewhat (not "some") to get here in time for dinner.*

somebody/some body Somebody is an indefinite pronoun: *Somebody recommended this restaurant.* Some body is a noun modified by an adjective: *I have a new spray that will give my limp hair some body.*

someone/some one Someone is an indefinite pronoun: *Someone who ate here said the pasta was delicious.* Some one is a pronoun adjective modified by "some": *Please pick some one magazine that you would like to read.*

someplace/somewhere Someplace should be used only in informal writing and speech; use somewhere for formal discourse.

sometime/sometimes/some time Traditionally, these three words have carried different meanings. Sometime means "at an unspecified time in the future": *Why not plan to visit Niagara Falls sometime?* Sometimes means "occasionally": *I visit my former college roommate sometimes.* Some time means "a span of time": *I need some time to make up my mind about what you have said.*

somewheres Somewheres is not accepted in formal writing or speech; use the standard "somewhere": *She would like to go somewhere (not "somewheres") special to celebrate New Year's Eve.*

split infinitive There is a longstanding convention that prohibits placing a word between "to" and the verb: *To understand fully another culture, you have to live among its people for many years.* This convention is based on an analogy with Latin, in which an infinitive is only one word and therefore cannot be divided. Criticism of the split infinitive was especially strong when the modeling of English on Latin was especially popular, as it was in the nineteenth century. Today many note that a split infinitive sometimes creates a less awkward sentence: *Many American companies expect to more than double their overseas investments in the next decade.*

stationary/stationery Although these two words sound alike, they have very different meanings. *Stationary* means "staying in one place": *From this distance, the satellite appeared to be stationary.* Stationery means "writing paper": *A hotel often provides stationery with its name preprinted.*

straight/strait Straight is most often used as an adjective meaning "unbending": *The path cut straight through the woods.* Strait, a noun, is "a narrow passage of water connecting two large bodies of water" or "distress, dilemma": *He was in dire financial straits.*

subsequently/consequently Subsequently means "occurring later, afterward": *We went to a new French restaurant for dinner; subsequently, we heard that everyone who had eaten the Caesar salad became ill.* Consequently means "therefore, as a result": *The temperature was above 90 degrees for a week; consequently, all the tomatoes burst on the vine.*

suppose to/supposed to; use to/used to Both suppose to and use to are incorrect. The preferred usage is supposed to or used to: *I was supposed to (not "suppose to") get up early this morning to go hiking in the mountains. I used to (not "use to") enjoy the seashore, but now I prefer the mountains.*

sure/surely When used as an adverb meaning surely, sure is considered inappropriate for formal discourse. A qualifier like "certainly" should

be used instead of sure: *My neighbors were certainly right about it.* It is widely used, however, in speech and informal writing: *They were sure right about that car.*

sure and/sure to; try and/try to Sure to and try to are the preferred forms for formal discourse: *Be sure to (not "sure and") come home early tonight. Try to (not "try and") avoid the traffic on the interstate.*

taught/taut Taught is the past tense of "to teach": *My English teachers taught especially well.* Taut is "tightly drawn": *Pull the knot taut or it will not hold.*

than/then Than, a conjunction, is used in comparisons: *Robert is taller than Michael.* Then, an adverb, is used to indicate time: *We knew then that there was little to be gained by further discussion.*

that The conjunction that is occasionally omitted, especially after verbs of thinking, saying, believing, and so forth: *She said (that) they would come by train.* The omission of the conjunction almost always occurs when the dependent clause begins with a personal pronoun or a proper name. The omission is most frequent in informal speech and writing.

that/which Traditionally, that is used to introduce a restrictive clause: *They should buy the cookies that the neighbor's child is selling.* Which, in contrast, is used to introduce nonrestrictive clauses: *The cookies, which are covered in chocolate, would make a nice evening snack.* This distinction is maintained far more often in formal writing than in everyday speech, where voice can often distinguish restrictive from nonrestrictive clauses.

that/which/who That is used to refer to animals, things, and people: *That's my dog. I like that pen. Is that your mother?* In accepted usage, who is used to refer only to people: *Who is the man over there?* Which is used to refer only to inanimate objects and animals: *Which pen do you prefer? Which dog is the one that you would like to buy?*

their/there/they're Although these three words sound alike, they have very different meanings. Their, the possessive form of "they," means "belonging to them": *Their house is new.* There can point out place *(There is the picture I was telling you about)* or function as an expletive

(There is a mouse behind you!). **They're** is a contraction for "they are": *They're not at home right now.*

them/those Them is nonstandard when used as an adjective: *I enjoyed those (not "them") apples a great deal.*

this here/these here/that there/them there Each of these phrases is nonstandard: this here for "this"; these here for "these"; that there for "that"; them there for "those."

threw/thru/through Threw, the past tense of the verb "throw," means "to hurl an object": *He threw the ball at the batter.* Through means "from one end to the other" or "by way of": *They walked through the museum all afternoon.* Through should be used in formal writing in place of thru, a colloquial spelling.

thusly/thus Thusly is a pointless synonym for thus. Speakers and writers often use thusly only for a deliberately humorous effect.

till/until/'til Till and until are used interchangeably in speech and writing; 'til, a shortened form of until, is rarely used.

time period The expression time period is redundant, since "period" is a period of time. *The local ambulance squad reported three emergency calls in a one-week period (not "time period").*

to/too/two Although the words sound alike, they are different parts of speech and have different meanings. To is a preposition indicating direction or part of an infinitive; too is an adverb meaning "also" or "in extreme"; and two is a number: *I have to go to the store to buy two items. Do you want to come too?*

too Be careful when using too as an intensifier in speech and writing: *The dog is too mean.* Adding an explanation of the excessive quality makes the sentence more logical: *The dog is too mean to trust alone with children.*

toward/towards The two words are used interchangeably in both formal and informal speech and writing.

track/tract Track, as a noun, is a path or course: *The railroad track in the Omaha station has recently been electrified.* Track as a verb, is "to follow": *Sophisticated guidance control systems are used to track the space shuttles.* Tract is "an expanse of land" or "a brief treatise": *Jonathan Swift wrote many tracts on the political problems of his day.*

try and/try to While try to is the preferred form for informal speech and writing, both phrases occur in all types of speech and writing.

type/type of In written English, type of is the preferred construction: *This is an unusual type of flower.* In informal speech and writing, it is acceptable to use type immediately before a noun: *I like this type car.*

unexceptional/unexceptionable Although both unexceptional and unexceptionable are adjectives, they have different meanings and are not interchangeable. Unexceptional means "commonplace, ordinary": *Despite the glowing reviews the new restaurant had received, we found it offered unexceptional meals and services.* Unexceptionable means "not offering any basis for exception or objection; beyond criticism": *We could not dispute his argument because it was unexceptionable.*

unique Since unique is an absolute adjective meaning "one of a kind," it cannot sensibly be used with a modifier such as "very," "most," or "extremely": *That is a unique (not "very unique" or "most unique") outfit.*

usage/use Usage is a noun that refers to the generally accepted way of doing something. The word refers especially to the conventions of language: *"Most unique" is considered incorrect usage.* Use can be either a noun or a verb. As a noun, use means "the act of employing or putting into service": *In the adult education course, I learned the correct use of tools.* Usage is often misused in place of the noun use: *Effective use (not "usage") of your time results in greater personal satisfaction.*

use/utilize/utilization Utilize means "to make use of": *They should utilize the new profit-sharing plan to decrease taxable income.* Utilization is the noun form of utilize. In most instances, however, use is preferred to either utilize or utilization as less overly formal and stilted: *They should use the new profit-sharing plan to decrease taxable income.*

used to could/used to be able to The phrase used to could is nonstandard for used to be able to: *I used to be able to (not "used to could") touch my toes.*

very The adverb very is sometimes used unnecessarily, especially in modifying an absolute adjective: *It*

was *a very unique experience.* In such instances, it clearly should be omitted. Further, very has become overworked and has lost much of its power. Use more precise modifiers such as "extremely" and "especially."

want in/want out Both phrases are informal: want in for "want to enter"; want out for "want to leave": *The dog wants to enter (not "wants in"). The cat wants to leave (not "wants out").*

way/ways Way is the preferred usage for formal speech and writing; ways is used colloquially: *They have a little way (not "ways") to go before they reach the campground.*

when/where Where and when are not interchangeable: *Weekends are occasions when (not "where") we have a chance to spend time with the family.*

where at/where to Both phrases are generally considered to be too informal to be acceptable in good writing and speech: *Where is John? (not "Where is John at?") Where is Mike going? (not "Where is Mike going to?")*

where/that Where and that are not interchangeable: *We see by the memo that (not "where") overtime has been discontinued.*

which/witch Which is a pronoun meaning "what one": *Which desk is yours?* Witch is a noun meaning "a person who practices magic": *The superstitious villagers accused her of being a witch.*

who/whoever; whom/whomever Traditionally, who/whoever is used as a subject (the nominative case) and whom/whomever as an object (the objective case). In informal speech and writing, however, since who and whom often occur at the beginning of a sentence, people usually select who, regardless of grammatical function.

without/unless Without as a conjunction is a dialectical or regional use of unless.

with regards to/with regard to/as regards/regarding Use with regard to, regarding, or as regards in place of with regards to in formal speech and writing: *As regards your inquiry, we have asked our shipping department to hold the merchandise until Monday.*

who's/whose Who's is the contraction for "who is" or "who has": *Who's the person in charge here? Who's* got the money? **Whose** is the possessive form of who: *"Whose book is this?"*

would have   Do not use the phrase would have in place of **had** in clauses that begin with "if" and express a state contrary to fact: *If the driver had (not "would have") been* wearing his seat belt, he would have escaped without injury.

would of/could of   There is no such expression as would of or could of: *He would have (not "would of") gone.* Also, of is not a substitute for " 've,": *She would've (not "would of") left earlier.*

you was   You was is nonstandard for you were: *You were (not "you was") late on Thursday.*

your/you're   Your is the possessive form of "you": *Your book is overdue at the library.* You're is the contraction of "you are": *You're just the person we need for this job.*

PUNCTUATION

Punctuation is intended to clarify the meaning of writing. It provides the key to the logic of an argument; for example, when readers see a semicolon in a work, they know the writer is linking closely related ideas. The ability to use different forms of punctuation to express ideas gives variety, coherence, and strength to writing.

END PUNCTUATION: PERIOD, QUESTION MARK, EXCLAMATION POINT

PERIOD

Use a period to end sentences that are statements, indirect questions, or mild commands. Also use a period after most abbreviations and within decimal numbers and amounts of money.

Use a Period With:

Statements

EXAMPLES:
The mayor's speech was unusually well received.
The meeting was amicable and important.

Indirect Questions
An indirect question reports what a person has asked, but not in the speaker's original words. Since the question is paraphrased, quotation marks are not used.

EXAMPLES:
He asked me when the train will leave the station.
She wanted to know whether the supplies would be back in stock by Tuesday.

Mild Commands
If you cannot decide whether to use a period or an exclamation mark after a command, use a period. Exclamation marks are used infrequently in formal writing.

EXAMPLES:
Read the next two chapters before Tuesday.
Please leave your muddy shoes on the mat outside the door.

Most Abbreviations

EXAMPLES:
H. Sammis & Sons, Inc., recently issued its annual report.
A. L. Smith just returned from a convention at the U.S. Department of Agriculture.

When a sentence ends with an abbreviation, use only one period.

EXAMPLES:
The meeting will begin promptly at 8 A.M.
I will send your files to Jeffrey Mallack, M.D.

Also note that the official two-letter postal zip code state abbreviations do not use periods. Acronyms—abbreviations formed from the first letters of the words in a name—never use periods.

EXAMPLES:

Acronyms:
UNICEF UNESCO NASA NATO
IRA AIDS OPEC NAFTA

Zip Code State Abbreviations:
NY PA CA ME MD

Within Decimal Numbers and Amounts of Money

EXAMPLES:

A sales tax of 7.5 percent is leveled on all clothing in this state.

He spent $44.50 on the shirt, $36.99 on the pants, and $22.00 on the tie.

QUESTION MARK

Use a question mark to end a sentence, clause, phrase, or single word that asks a direct question. Also use a question mark within parentheses to indicate uncertainty about the correctness of a number or date included within the sentence.

Use a Question Mark:

To Indicate a Question

EXAMPLES:

Who invited him to the party?

"Is something the matter?" she asked.

Whom shall we elect? Murray? Harris?

To Indicate Doubt about Information

EXAMPLES:

Socrates was born in 470 (?) B.C.

The codex dates back to A.D. 500 (?)

EXCLAMATION POINT

Use an exclamation point to end a sentence, clause, phrase, or single word that expresses strong emotion, such as surprise, command, and admiration.

Use an Exclamation Mark to Express:

Strong Emotion

EXAMPLES:

Go away!

What a week this has been!

PUNCTUATION WITHIN A SENTENCE: COMMA, SEMICOLON, COLON, DASH, ELLIPSIS, PARENTHESES, BRACKETS, QUOTATION MARKS, ITALICS/UNDERLINING, SOLIDUS (SLASH)

COMMA

The comma is the most often used mark of punctuation within a sentence. In general, commas separate parts of a sentence. Adding unnecessary commas or omitting necessary ones can confuse a reader and obscure the meaning of a sentence.

Use a Comma:

To Separate Independent Clauses of a Compound Sentence Linked by a Coordinating Conjunction—Such as and, but, yet, for, or, or nor—Unless the Compound Sentence Is Very Brief

EXAMPLES:

Longer Sentences:

Almost any person knows how to earn money, yet not one in a million knows how to spend it.

Bill is not in the office today, but he will be here tomorrow.

Shorter Sentences:

We must catch the train or we will miss the meeting.

Mark washed the dishes and Jim dried.

To Set Off Most Introductory Elements

An introductory element modifies (describes) a word or words in the independent clause that follows.

EXAMPLES:

Having rid themselves of their former rulers, the people now disagreed on the new leadership.

Although the details have not been fully developed, scientists are confident that people will reach the stars.

Politically, our candidate has proved to be inept.

Hurt, she left the room quickly.

Pleased with the result, he appraised his work.

The comma can be omitted after brief introductory prepositional and infinitive phrases and subordinate clauses if it is not needed for clarity.

EXAMPLES:

Comma Unnecessary:
As a child he was intractable.

Comma Is Necessary for Clarification:
In 1988, 300 people won in the lottery.

To Set Off Nonrestrictive Elements

Since it restricts, or limits the meaning of, the word or words it applies to, a **restrictive** element is essential to the meaning of the sentence and thus cannot be omitted.

EXAMPLES:

The novel that she wrote in 1989 won a literary award.

Employees who started before November 1 will be entitled to two more vacation days per year.

Since it adds information about the word or words it applies to but does not limit that meaning, a **nonrestrictive** element can be left out of a sentence without changing the meaning. Place commas before and after the nonrestrictive portion.

EXAMPLES:

Her most recent novel, written in 1989, won a literary award.

Our new car, which has whitewall tires and a leather interior, will be ready for delivery on Thursday.

To Set Off Interrupting Words or Phrases

There are several different kinds of interrupters. These include words of direct address, appositives, contrasting expressions, interjections, parenthetical expressions, and transitional words.

Words of direct address: These are words that tell to whom a comment is addressed.

EXAMPLES:

You realize, Mary, that we may never return to Paris.

Jim, where have you been?

Appositives: Appositives are words that give additional information about the preceding or following word or expression. Many appositives are nonrestrictive and are thus set off from the rest of the sentence, usually with commas. Be careful not to set off restrictive appositives, which are necessary for the meaning of the sentence.

EXAMPLES:

Nonrestrictive Appositives:
A heavy sleeper, my sister is the last to awaken.

The last to awaken is my sister, a heavy sleeper.

My sister, a heavy sleeper, is the last to awaken.

March, the month of crocuses, can still bring snow and ice.

His favorite author, Stephen King, entered the auditorium.

Mr. Case, a member of the committee, refused to comment.

Restrictive Appositives:
My friend Mary spoke at the convention.

The crowd fell silent as the author Stephen King entered the auditorium.

Contrasting expressions: Use commas to set off groups of words that show contrast.

EXAMPLES:

The boys, not the men, did most of the chores around the house.

His clever wit, not his appearance, won him many friends.

This report needs more facts, less fluff.

Interjections: Use a comma to set off any interjection. Examples of interjections include *well, my, oh, yes,* and *no.*

EXAMPLES:

Oh, here's our new neighbor.

Why, you can't mean that!

Well, can you imagine that!

Parenthetical expressions: Use commas to set off expressions that explain by providing additional information.

EXAMPLES:

You may, if you insist, demand a retraction.

If you wouldn't mind, please leave your raincoat and umbrella on the porch.

Transitional words: Transitional expressions include *however, indeed, consequently, as a result, of course, for example, in fact,* and so forth. Use a comma to distinguish these expressions from the rest of the sentence.

EXAMPLES:

Still, you must agree that he knows his business.

The use of pesticides, however, has its disadvantages.

He knew, nevertheless, that all was lost.

To Separate Items in a Series

Use a comma to separate words, phrases, and clauses that are part of a series of three or more items.

EXAMPLES:

The Danes are an industrious, friendly, generous, and hospitable people.

The chief agricultural products of Denmark are butter, eggs, potatoes, beets, wheat, barley, and oats.

It is permissible to omit the final comma before the ''and'' in a series of words as long as the absence of a comma does not interfere with clarity of meaning. In many cases, however, the inclusion or omission of the comma can significantly affect the meaning of the sentence. In the following sentence, omission of the final comma might indicate that the tanks were amphibious: *Their equipment included airplanes, helicopters, artillery, amphibious vehicles, and tanks.* As a general rule, the final comma is never wrong, and it always helps the reader see that the last two items are separate.

Do not use commas to separate two items treated as a single unit within a series, as in this example: *For breakfast he ordered orange juice, bread and butter, coffee, and bacon and eggs.*

But when the items are treated individually, each is separated by a comma, as in this sentence: *At the supermarket he bought orange juice, bread, butter, bacon, and eggs.*

Do not use commas to separate adjectives that are so closely related that they appear to form a single element with the noun they modify. Adjectives that refer to the number, age *(old, young, new)*, size, color, or location of the noun often fall within this category. To determine whether or not to use the comma in these instances, insert the word *and*. If *and* cannot replace the comma without creating an awkward sentence, it is safe to conclude that a comma is also out of place.

EXAMPLES:

twenty happy little youngsters

a dozen large blue dresses

several dingy old Western mining towns

beautiful tall white birches

But commas must be used when each adjective is considered separately, not as modifiers of other adjectives:

EXAMPLES:

the beautiful, expensive dress

the happy, smiling youngsters

He sold his business, rented his house, gave up his car, paid his creditors, and set off for Alaska.

They strolled along the city streets, browsed in the bookshops, and dined at their favorite café.

To Separate Parts of Dates, Addresses, Geographical Locations, Titles of Individuals, and Long Numbers

EXAMPLES:

The Declaration of Independence was signed on July 4, 1776.

Pearl Harbor was bombed on Sunday, December 7, 1941.

Her friend lives at 35 Fifth Avenue, New York, N.Y.

She moved from 1515 Halsted Street, Chicago, Illinois.

He lived in Lima, Peru, for fifteen years.

Dr. Martin Price, Dean of Admissions, is in the office down the hall.

This is Mr. John Winthrop, President.

The population of Grove City, Minnesota, is 34,500.

If you win this week's jackpot, the payoff is $75,000!

To Set Off Quoted Matter from the Rest of the Sentence
(See also ''Quotation Marks,'' page 65.)

EXAMPLE:

He said, ''I wish you had been at the workshop today.''

She replied, ''Unfortunately, my meeting ran late.''

''Unfortunately,'' she replied, ''my meeting ran late.''

To Set Off the Salutation of a Personal Letter and the Complimentary Close of a Personal or a Formal Letter

EXAMPLES:

Dear Midge,

Very truly yours,

To Denote an Omitted Word or Words in One or More Parallel Constructions within a Sentence

EXAMPLE:

John is studying Greek; George, Latin.

To Prevent Misreading

The comma tells the reader to stop briefly before reading on. Words may run together in confusing ways unless you use a comma to separate them. Use a comma in such sentences even though no rule requires one.

EXAMPLES:

Soon after, she quit the job for good.

The people who can, usually contribute some money to the local holiday drive.

SEMICOLON

In general, a semicolon is used to separate parts of a sentence—such as independent clauses, items in a series, and explanations or summaries—from the main clause. In choosing among the three punctuation marks that separate main clauses—the comma, the semicolon, and the colon—a writer needs to decide on the relationship between ideas. A semicolon can be used to great effect when the first clause sets up some expectation in the reader that a related idea is to follow. The semicolon then gives a brief stop before the second clause completes the thought.

In general:

The comma	links both equal and unequal sentence parts.
The semicolon	links equal and balanced sentence parts.
The colon	links unequal sentence parts.

Use a Semicolon:

To Separate Independent Clauses Not Joined by a Simple Conjunction

(See p. 66 for the use of a comma with independent clauses joined by simple conjunctions.)

EXAMPLE:

The house burned down; it was the last shattering blow.

The war must continue; we will be satisfied only with victory.

We have made several attempts to reach you by telephone; not a single call has been returned.

To Separate Independent Clauses Joined by a Conjunctive Adverb, Such as however, nevertheless, otherwise, therefore, besides, hence, indeed, instead, nonetheless, still, then, or thus

EXAMPLE:

The funds are inadequate; therefore, the project will close down.

Enrollments exceed all expectations; however, there is a teacher shortage.

He knew the tickets for the performance would be scarce; therefore, he arrived at the concert hall two hours early.

A comma is generally used after a conjunctive adverb. Commas are optional, however, with such one-syllable conjunctive adverbs as *thus* and *hence;* they are frequently omitted as well when *therefore, instead,* or any of several other conjunctive adverbs are placed at the end of clauses.

EXAMPLES:

She skipped her lunch; thus she was ravenously hungry by 4:00.

He did not take notes; he borrowed hers instead.

To Separate Long or Possibly Ambiguous Items in a Series, Especially When Those Items Already Include Commas

EXAMPLES:

The elected officers are Robert Harris, president; Charles Lawrence, vice president; Samantha Jill, treasurer; and Elisabeth Fink, secretary.

During the parade, the marchers wore red, green, and blue uniforms; carried silver banners; and sang songs.

To Precede an Abbreviation or Word That Introduces an Explanation or Summary

EXAMPLES:

On the advice of his broker, he chose to invest in major industries; i.e., steel, automobiles, and oil.

She organizes her work well; for example, by putting correspondence in folders of different colors to indicate degrees of urgency.

COLON

As a mark of introduction, the colon tells the reader that the first statement is going to be explained by the second or signals that a quotation or series will follow. In effect, the colon is a substitute for such phrases as *for example* and *namely.* A colon can often be interchanged with a dash, although a dash indicates a less formal and more abrupt shift.

Use a Colon:

To Introduce a Long Formal Statement, Summary, Explanation, Quotation, or Question

EXAMPLES:

Formal Statement:

This I believe: All men are created equal and must enjoy equally the rights that are inalienably theirs.

Summary:

They cannot pay their monthly bills because their money is tied up in their stocks and bonds: they are paper-rich and cash-poor.

Explanation:

It is a good thing to be old early: to have the fragility and sensitivity of the old, and a bit of wisdom, before the years of planning and building have run out.—Martin Gumbert

Quotation:

Richards replied: "You are right. There can be no unilateral peace just as there can be no unilateral war. No one contests that view." (Note: Use a comma, not a colon, if the quotation is a single sentence.)

Question:

This is the issue: Can an employer dismiss an employee simply because the employee laughs loudly? (Note that the first word of the sentence following the colon is capitalized. This applies to formal statements as well as to questions.)

To Introduce a Series or List of Items, Examples, or the Like

EXAMPLES:

The three committees are as follows: membership, finance, and nominations.

He named his five favorite poets: Byron, Keats, Tennyson, Hardy, and Dickinson.

It is impossible to dissociate language from science or science from language, because every natural science always involves three things: the sequence of phenomena on which the science is based, the abstract concepts which call these phenomena to mind; and the words in which the concepts are expressed.—Antoine Lavoisier

The colon should not be used after *of* or after a verb.

EXAMPLES:

The committee consisted of nine teachers, twelve parents, and six business leaders.

Possible choices include games, tapes, books, and puzzles.

To Follow the Salutation of a Formal Letter or Speech

EXAMPLES:

Dear Mr. Brodwin:

My fellow Americans:

To Whom It May Concern:

To Follow the Name of the Speaker in a Play

EXAMPLES:

Ghost: Revenge his foul and most unnatural murder.

Hamlet: Murder?

To Separate Parts of a Citation

EXAMPLES:

Genesis 3:2

Journal of Transcendentalism 15:251–255

To Separate Hours from Minutes in Indicating Time

EXAMPLES:

1:30 P.M.

12:30 A.M.

DASH

A dash is used to show sudden changes in thought or to set off certain sentence elements. Like the exclamation point, dashes are dramatic and thus should be used sparingly in formal writing. Do not confuse the dash with the hyphen (see page 000 on the hyphen).

Use a Dash To:

Mark an Abrupt Change in Thought, Shift in Tone, or Grammatical Construction in the Middle of a Sentence

EXAMPLES:

He won the game—but I'm getting ahead of the story.

She told me—does she really mean it?—that she will inform us of any changes ahead of time from now on.

Suggest Halting or Hesitant Speech

EXAMPLES:

"Well—er—it's hard to explain," he faltered. Madame de Vionnett instantly rallied.

"And you know—though it might occur to one—it isn't in the least that he's ashamed of her. She's really—in a way—extremely good looking."—Henry James

Indicate a Sudden Break or Interruption before a Sentence Is Completed

EXAMPLES:

"Harvey, don't climb up that—." It was too late.

If they discovered the truth—he did not want to think of the consequences.

Add Emphasis to Parenthetical Material or Mark an Emphatic Separation between Parenthetical Material and the Rest of the Sentence

EXAMPLES:

His influence—he was a powerful figure in the community—was a deterrent to effective opposition.

The car he was driving—a gleaming red convertible—was the most impressive thing about him.

Set Off an Appositive or an Appositive Phrase When a Comma Would Provide Less Than the Desired Emphasis on the Appositive or When the Use of Commas Might Result in Confusion Because of Commas within the Appositive Phrase

EXAMPLES:

The premier's promise of changes—land reform and higher wages—was not easily fulfilled.

The qualities Renoir valued in his painting—rich shadows, muted colors, graceful figures—flourished in the ballet dancers he used as subjects.

Replace an Offensive Word or Part of One

EXAMPLE:

Where the h— is he?

Where's that son of a —?

ELLIPSIS

The ellipsis mark consists of three spaced periods (. . .). Use it to show that part of a quotation has been left out. You can also use the ellipsis in place of a dash to indicate pauses and unfinished statements in quoted speech.

Use an Ellipsis To:

Show That Part of a Quote Has Been Omitted, to Indicate Pauses and Unfinished Statements

Original Paragraph:

He left his home in the city at age twenty. Seeking solitude, he built a log cabin in the mountains. Years later he returned to the city to find that everything had changed.

Quoted Portions:

He left his home in the city at age twenty. . . . Years later he returned to find that everything had changed. (Ellipsis indicates the omission of the second sentence. Notice that the period is retained, resulting in four spaced periods.)

He left his home. . . . Seeking solitude, he built a cabin in the mountains. (Ellipsis indicates omission at the end of the first sentence. The period from the end of the sentence follows the ellipsis marks.)

PARENTHESES

Parentheses are used to enclose nonessential material within a sentence. This can include facts, explanations, digressions, and examples that may be helpful but are not necessary for the sentence. Do not put a comma before a parenthesis.

Use Parentheses To:

Enclose Material That Is Not Part of the Main Sentence but Is Too Important to Omit

EXAMPLES:

Faulkner's novels (but not his poetry) were selected as prizes in the recent contest.

The data (see Table 14) were very impressive.

Enclose Part of a Sentence That Would Be Confusing if Enclosed by Commas

EXAMPLE:

The authors he advised (none other than Hemingway, Lewis, and Cather) would have been delighted to honor him today.

Enclose an Explanatory Item That Is Not Part of the Statement or Sentence

EXAMPLE:

He wrote to *The Paris* (Illinois) *News.*

Enclose Numbers or Letters That Designate Each Item in a Series

EXAMPLE:

The project is (1) too time-consuming, (2) too expensive, and (3) poorly staffed.

Enclose a Numerical Figure Used to Confirm a Spelled-Out Number That Comes before It

EXAMPLE:

Enclosed is a check for ten dollars ($10.00) to cover the cost of the order.

Dashes, commas, and parentheses can all be used to set off information that is not essential to the sentence. Each mark achieves a different effect:

Dashes Create the Most Emphasis

Many workers—including those in the mail room—distrust the new shipping regulations.

Commas Create Less Emphasis

Many workers, including those in the mail room, distrust the new shipping regulations.

Parentheses Create the Least Emphasis

Many workers (including those in the mail room) distrust the new shipping regulations.

BRACKETS

Brackets are used in pairs to enclose figures, phrases, or sentences, most often within a direct quotation.

Use Brackets To:

Explain, Clarify, or Correct the Contents of a Direct Quotation

EXAMPLES:

According to the Globe critic, "This [*Man and Superman*] is one of Shaw's greatest plays."

"Young as they are," he writes, "these students are afflicted with cynicism, world-weariness, and *a total disregard for tradition and authority.*" [Emphasis is mine.]

"As a result of the Gemini V mission [the flight by astronauts Cooper and Conrad in August 1965], we have proof that human beings can withstand the eight days in space required for a round trip to the moon."

"It was on August 25, 1944 [1945—Ed.] that delegates representing forty-six countries met in San Francisco."

Indicate That an Error in Fact, Spelling, Punctuation, or Language Usage Is Quoted Deliberately in an Effort to Reproduce the Original Statement with Complete Accuracy

To indicate the questionable expression, place the Latin word *"sic,"* meaning "thus," directly after it in brackets.

EXAMPLES:

"George Washington lived during the seventeenth [sic] century."

"The governor of Missisipi [sic] addressed the student body."

Enclose Stage Directions for a Play

EXAMPLE:

Juliet: [*Snatching Romeo's dagger*] . . . Oh happy dagger! This is thy sheath; [*Stabs herself*] there rest and let me die.

Enclose Comments Made in a Verbatim Transcript

EXAMPLE:

Sen. Eaton: The steady rise in taxes must be halted. [Applause]

Substitute for Parentheses with Material Already Enclosed by Parentheses

Although this use is not encountered frequently, it is sometimes used in footnotes.

EXAMPLE:

[1]See "René Descartes" (M. C. Beardsley, *The European Philosophers from Descartes to Nietzsche* [New York, 1960]).

Enclose the Publication Date, Inserted by the Editor, of an Item Appearing in an Earlier Issue of a Periodical

This is used in letters to the editor or in articles written on subjects previously reported. Parentheses may be used instead.

EXAMPLES:

Dear Sir: Your excellent article on China [April 15] brings to mind my recent experience . . .

When removing old wallpaper [*Homeowners' Monthly*, June 1990], some do-it-yourselfers neglect to . . .

QUOTATION MARKS

The main function of quotation marks is to enclose a direct quotation. Quotation marks are always used in pairs to mark the beginning and end of the quotation.

Punctuating with quotation marks is largely a matter of common sense: if a colon, semicolon, question mark, or exclamation point is part of the quotation, place it *inside* the end quotation mark; if it is not part of the quotation, place it *outside*.

Before a colon or semicolon: Place the end quotation mark *before* a colon or semicolon, as in the following example: He remembered that the boys had always called Tom "the champ"; he began to wonder if the reputation had endured.

After a question mark or exclamation point: Place the end quotation mark *after* a question mark or exclamation point only when the question or exclamation is part of the quoted passage, as in this example: "Hurry, please, before it is too late!" she cried. In all other cases, place the end quotation mark *before* the question mark or exclamation point, as shown in this example: Did Pangloss really mean it when he said, "This is the best of all possible worlds"?

Use Quotation Marks To:

Indicate a Direct Quotation

Use double quotation marks to enclose a direct quotation.

> EXAMPLE:
>
> "They've come back!" she exclaimed.
>
> "It's not in the cabinet; it's on the counter," my sister shouted out.

Use single quotation marks to enclose a quotation within a quotation.

> EXAMPLE:
>
> Reading Jill's letter, Pat said, "Listen to this! 'I've just received notice that I made the dean's list.' Isn't that great?"

As in the above examples, use a comma between the quotation and phrases such as *according to the speaker, he said, and she replied* used to introduce or conclude a quotation.

If a quotation consists of two or more consecutive paragraphs, use quotation marks at the beginning of each paragraph, but place them at the end of the last paragraph only.

Mark Words or Groups of Words That Are Quoted from the Original

> EXAMPLES:
>
> Portia's speech on "the quality of mercy" is one of the most quoted passages from Shakespeare.
>
> It was Shaw who wrote: "All great truths begin as blasphemies."

Enclose Titles of Newspaper and Magazine Articles, Essays, Short Stories, Poems, Chapters of Books, Songs, Works of Art, and Radio and Television Programs

The quotation marks are designed to distinguish the literary pieces from the books or periodicals (these are underlined or italicized) in which they appear.

> EXAMPLES:
>
> Our anthology contains such widely assorted pieces as Bacon's essay "Of Studies," Poe's "The Gold Bug," Shelley's "Ode to the West Wind," and an article on criticism from *The New Yorker*.
>
> Most people recognize Da Vinci's *Mona Lisa* and Rodin's *The Thinker*.
>
> He especially enjoyed watching reruns of *All in the Family* and *My Mother, the Car*.

Use quotation marks around the titles of plays only if they are part of a larger collection. Referred to as single volumes, they are underlined or italicized.

> EXAMPLE:
>
> "The Wild Duck" is the Ibsen play included in this edition of *Modern European Plays*.

Enclose the Names of Ships and Airplanes; Italics and Underlines May Also Be Used

> EXAMPLES:
>
> Lindbergh called the airplane in which he flew across the Atlantic the "Spirit of St. Louis."
>
> We had waited our entire lives for a chance to take a cruise on the "Queen Elizabeth."

Emphasize a Word or Phrase That Is the Subject of Discussion or to Suggest a Word or Phrase Is Being Used Ironically

> EXAMPLES:
>
> The words "imply" and "infer" are not synonymous.
>
> Such Freudian terms as "ego," "superego," "id," and "libido" have now entered popular usage and are familiar to most Americans.
>
> The radio blasting forth Kim's favorite "music" is to his parents an instrument of torture.
>
> Bob's skiing "vacation" consisted of three weeks with his leg in a cast.

ITALICS/UNDERLINING

Italics are used to emphasize or set apart specific words and phrases. In handwritten or typed papers, underlining indicates italics.

Use Italics (Underlining) To:

Distinguish Titles of Books, Newspapers, Long Poems, Magazines, Pamphlets, Published Speeches, Long Musical Compositions, Movies, Plays, Works of Art, Ships, and Aircraft

> EXAMPLES:
>
> I read *War and Peace, Beowulf,* and Lincoln's *Gettysburg Address* as part of my annual summer self-improvement kick.
>
> They enjoyed the original version of *Invasion of the Body Snatchers* far more than the remake.

Set Off Foreign Words and Phrases That Are Not in Common Use

> EXAMPLES:
>
> In his younger days he was quite a *bon vivant*.
>
> I'll be there, *deo volente*.

Refer to a Word, Letter, Number, or Expression Used As Such

Quotation marks are sometimes used instead.

EXAMPLES:

She drew a large *3* on the blackboard.

The word *fantastic* is his favorite adjective.

Do not pronounce the final *e* in *Hecate.*

Indicate Stage Directions within Brackets

EXAMPLE:

Heidi [*turning to Anita*]: Did he call me?

Anita: I didn't hear him. [*She picks up a magazine.*]

Emphasize Specific Words and Phrases

Occasionally, italics can be used to stress certain words and phrases.

EXAMPLE:

The man was *totally* bereft; he had neither friends nor relatives to lend a hand.

SOLIDUS (SLASH)

The solidus acts as a dividing line, as in dates and fractions, and in run-in passages of poetry to show verse division; it is also used between two words to indicate an option.

Use a Solidus To:

Separate Lines of Poetry within the Text

When used in this way, the solidus marks the end of a line of poetry and has equal space on either side

EXAMPLE:

William Blake's stanza on anger in "A Poison Tree" seems as appropriate today as when it was first written: "I was angry with my friend: / I told my wrath, my wrath did end. / I was angry with my foe: / I told it not, my wrath did grow."

Indicate Dates and Fractions

EXAMPLES:

winter 1990/1991

the fiscal year 1992/93

3/4 + 2/3

$x/y - y/x$

Indicate Options and Alternatives

EXAMPLE:

I have never seen the advantage of pass/fail courses.

Note: Try to avoid using he/she. Instead, make the subject plural ("they") or revise the construction completely.

PUNCTUATION WITHIN A WORD: APOSTROPHE, HYPHEN

APOSTROPHE

In contrast to other marks of punctuation, which divide words from one another, the apostrophe (') is used within a word to show the omission of one or more letters, to show possession, or (in some cases) to indicate a plural.

Use an Apostrophe To:

Denote the Omission of One or More Letters, Figures, or Numerals

Apostrophes are used to form contractions

EXAMPLES:

I am	I'm
you are	you're
he is	he's
she is	she's
they are	they're
we are	we're
it is	it's

who is	who's
cannot	can't
could not	couldn't
do not	don't
does not	doesn't
was not	wasn't
were not	weren't
would not	wouldn't
is not	isn't

Note: Will not is irregular; the contraction is "won't."

EXAMPLES:

The Spirit of '76

The class of '90

Indicate the Omission of Letters in Quoted Dialogue

EXAMPLES:

'tis a fine day

goin' fishing

Show the Possessive Case of Nouns, Indicating Ownership

To form the possessive of most singular and plural nouns and indefinite pronouns not ending in *s*, add an apostrophe and *s*.

EXAMPLES:

"The Monk's Tale" is one of Chaucer's *Canterbury Tales.*

When he would arrive at **Mary's** house was anybody's guess.

He was amazed to find that the **women's** shoes cost fifty dollars, but the **children's** shoes cost even more.

To form the possessive of *singular* nouns (both common and proper) ending in *s* or the sound of *s*, add an apostrophe and *s* unless the addition of the *s* would sound or look awkward.

EXAMPLES:

With the "s" Added:
the **horse's** mane
the **bus's** light
the **class's** average
Kansas's schools
Texas's governor
Francis's promotion

Without the "s" Added:
Socrates' concepts
for **goodness'** sake
Dickens's book

To form the possessive of *plural* nouns (both common and proper) ending in *s* or the sound of *s*, add only an apostrophe.

EXAMPLES:
farmers' problems
students' views
critics' reviews
two **weeks'** vacation
judges' opinions
the **Smiths'** travels
the **Joneses'** relatives
three **months'** delay

To form the possessive of *plural* nouns (both common and proper) not ending in *s*, add an apostrophe and *s*.

EXAMPLES:
men's clothing
children's toys

women's hats
people's observations

To form the possessive of compound words or two or more proper names, add an apostrophe and *s* to the last word of the compound.

EXAMPLES:
anyone **else's** property
brother-in-law's job
one **another's** books
editor-in-chief's pen
Japan and Germany's agreement
Lewis and Clark's expedition
the **University of South Carolina's** mascot

Note: Never use an apostrophe with a possessive personal pronoun. These personal pronouns are already possessive and therefore have no need for an apostrophe: *my, mine, your, yours, her, hers, its, our, ours, their,* and *theirs.*

Form the Plurals of Numbers, Symbols, Letters, and Words Used to Name Themselves (Add an Apostrophe and an "s")

EXAMPLES:
Dot the i's and cross the t's
33 r.p.m.'s
figure 8's
+'s and −'s
GI's
V.I.P.'s
PX's
the 1890's (or 1890s)

HYPHEN

Although a hyphen and a dash may appear to be the same at first glance, they are two very different marks of punctuation. Their form is as different as their meaning, a dash being twice as long as a hyphen. Dashes are used to separate or connect *sentence* elements; hyphens are used to separate or connect *word* elements.

Use a Hyphen:

To Spell Out a Word or Name

EXAMPLES:
r-e-a-s-o-n
G-a-e-l-i-c

To Divide a Word into Syllables

EXAMPLES:

spec-ta-to-ri-al

liv-id-ness

To Mark the Division of a Word of More Than One Sylla-
ble at the End of a Line, Indicating That the Word Is to Be
Completed on the Next Line

Do not leave a single letter at the end of a line or
fewer than three letters at the beginning of a line.
Do not divide one-syllable words.

Avoid confusing word divisions. Certain words,
when divided, will form pronounceable units that
might confuse the reader. In these instances, divide
the word at another acceptable place (*re-arrange* instead of *rear-range*).

To Separate the Parts (When Spelling Out Numerals) of a
Compound Number from Twenty-One to Ninety-Nine

EXAMPLES:

thirty-six inches to the yard

Fifty-second Street

nineteen hundred **forty-three**

To Express Decades in Words

EXAMPLES:

the **nineteen-twenties**

the **eighteen-sixties**

To Separate (When Spelling Out Numerals) the Numera-
tor from the Denominator of a Fraction, Especially a Frac-
tion That Is Used as an Adjective

EXAMPLES:

One-third cup of milk

a **three-fifths** majority

While some writers avoid hyphenating fractions
used as nouns, the practice persists.

EXAMPLES:

Three fourths (or **three-fourths**) of his con-
stituents

One fifth (**one-fifth**) of the class

Do not use a hyphen to indicate a fraction if either
the numerator or the denominator is already hyphenated.

EXAMPLES:

one **thirty-second**

twenty-one thirty-sixths

To Form Certain Compound Nouns

EXAMPLES:

secretary-treasurer

cease-fire

city-state

do-gooder

AFL-CIO

has-been

Do not hyphenate compound nouns indicating
chemical terms, military rank, or certain governmental positions.

EXAMPLES:

sodium chloride

en route

vice admiral

in vitro

attorney general

To Combine the Elements of a Compound Modifier When
Used Before the Noun It Modifies

In most cases the same modifier is not hyphenated
if it follows the noun it modifies.

EXAMPLES:

They engage in **hand-to-hand** combat.

They fought **hand to hand**.

They endured a **hand-to-mouth** existence.

They lived **hand to mouth**.

well-known expert

an expert who is **well known**.

Do not hyphenate a compound modifier that includes an adverb ending in *-ly* even when it is used
before the noun.

EXAMPLES:

his **loose-fitting** jacket

his **loosely fitting** jacket

a **well-guarded** secret

a **carefully guarded** secret

To Distinguish a Less Common Pronunciation or Mean-
ing of a Word from Its More Customary Usage

EXAMPLES:

a **recreation** hall	**re-creation** of a scene
to **recover** from an illness	**re-cover** the sofa
to **reform** a sinner	**re-form** their lines

To Prevent Possible Confusion in Pronunciation if a Prefix Results in the Doubling of a Letter, Especially a Vowel

EXAMPLES:

anti-inflationary

co-op

de-escalate

non-native

To Combine Prefixes with Proper Nouns or Adjectives

EXAMPLES:

anti-	anti-American	anti-British
mid-	mid-Victorian	mid-Atlantic
neo-	neo-Nazi	neo-Darwinism
non-	non-European	non-Asian
pan-	pan-American	Pan-Slavic
pro-	pro-French	pro-American
un-	un-American	un-British

To Combine the Following Prefixes and Suffixes with the Main Word of the Compound

EXAMPLES:

co-	co-conspirator
ex-	ex-premier
self-	self-defeating
-elect	governor-elect

To Form Most Compound Nouns and Adjectives That Begin with the Word Element Listed Below

EXAMPLES:

cross-	cross-examine	cross-stitch
double-	double-breasted	double-park
great-	great-grandfather	great-grandchild
heavy-	heavy-handed	heavy-hearted
ill-	ill-organized	ill-timed
light-	light-fingered	light-year
single-	single-minded	single-handed
well-	well-behaved	well-wisher

Concise Guide
for Writers

Punctuation

The punctuation system is presented in six charts. The first deals with sentence punctuation. The next two describe the punctuation that is used within sentences. The fourth brings together all the punctuation needed for handling quotations. The fifth is concerned with punctuation that has to do with words rather than sentences. The sixth lists some subsidiary uses of the punctuation marks. Since punctuation marks are frequently used in more than one way, some marks appear on more than one chart. Readers who are interested in the various uses of a particular mark can scan the left column of each chart to locate relevant sections.

There is a considerable amount of variation in punctuation practices. At one extreme are writers who have committed themselves to using as little punctuation as possible. At the other extreme are writers who seek to direct the reader's path through a text in painstaking detail. The principles presented here represent a middle road.

1. SENTENCE-LEVEL PUNCTUATION

Sentence punctuation depends upon how writers choose to organize the independent clauses in their texts. There are four possibilities:

Rule	Example
• (1) Ordinarily an independent clause is made into a sentence by beginning it with a capital letter and ending it with a period.	The forecast promised beautiful weather. It rained every day. Some of us still support the mayor. Others think he should retire. There's only one solution. We must reduce next year's budget.
, (2) Independent clauses may be grouped into sentences by using the words *and, but, yet, or, nor, for,* and *so.* The first clause is usually followed by a comma.	The forecast promised beautiful weather, so it rained every day. We tried to reason with him, but he had already made up his mind. Jennifer is finishing high school this year, and Joe is a junior at Yale. Take six cooking apples and put them into a flameproof dish.

Rule	Example
; (3) The writer can indicate that independent clauses are closely connected by joining them with a semicolon instead of punctuating them as separate sentences.	Some of us still support the mayor; others think he should retire. Scarcity is a basic principle of economics; we must constantly choose between guns and butter. Writer's block is a widespread affliction; even well-known and consistently productive writers experience it from time to time.
: (4) When one independent clause is followed by another that explains or exemplifies it, they can be separated by a colon. The second clause may or may not begin with a capital letter.	There's only one solution: we must reduce next year's budget. The negotiators finally agreed on a basic principle: neither side would seek to resupply its troops during the cease-fire. The conference addresses a basic question: How can we take the steps needed to protect the environment without stalling economic growth?
? Sentences that ask a question should be followed by a question mark.	Are they still planning to move their headquarters to Salt Lake City? What is the population of Norway? You can get us in free? What constitutional principle did John Marshall establish in *Marbury* v. *Madison*? in *McCullough* v. *Maryland*? in *Fletcher* v. *Peck*?
! Sentences that express strong feeling may be followed by an exclamation mark.	Watch out! That's a stupid thing to say! Wow! Connie just won the lottery!
. ! . ? End-of-sentence punctuation is sometimes used after groups of words that are not independent clauses. This is especially common in advertising and other writing that seeks to reflect the rhythms of speech.	Somerset Estates has all the features you've been looking for. Like state-of-the-art facilities. A friendly atmosphere. And a very reasonable price. Sound interesting? Phone today. No reasonable offer refused!

2. SEPARATING CLAUSES

When one of the elements in a clause is compounded, that is, when there are two or more subjects, predicates, objects, and so forth, internal punctuation is necessary.

Rule	Example
When two elements are compounded, they are usually joined together with a word like *and* or *or* without any punctuation. Occasionally more than two elements are joined in this way.	Haiti and the Dominican Republic share the island of Hispaniola. Tuition may be paid by check or charged to a major credit card. I'm taking history and English and biology this semester.

Rule	Example
, Compounds that contain more than two elements are called series. Commas are used to separate the items in a series, with a word like *and* or *or* usually occurring between the last two items. Many different kinds of clause elements can be compounded in this way.	England, Scotland, and Wales share the island of Great Britain. Cabbage is especially good with corned beef, game, or smoked meats. Environmentally conscious businesses use recycled white paper, photocopy on both sides of a sheet, and use ceramic cups. We frequently hear references to government of the people, by the people, for the people.
; When the items in a series are very long or have internal punctuation, separation by commas can be confusing, and semicolons may be used instead.	In the next year, they plan to open stores in Sewickley, Pennsylvania; Belleville, Illinois; Breckenridge, Colorado; and Martinez, California. Academically talented students were selected on the basis of grades; tests of vocabulary, memory, reading, inductive reasoning, math, and perceptual speed and accuracy; and teacher recommendations.

NOTE: Some writers omit the final comma when punctuating a series, and newspapers and magazines often follow this practice. Book publishers and educators, however, usually follow the practice recommended above.

3. SETTING OFF MODIFIERS

Another way that sentences become more complex is through the addition of free modifiers—elements that are not part of the basic sentence structure. Free modifiers can ordinarily be omitted without affecting the meaning or basic structure of the sentence. They may be added at the beginning, somewhere in the middle, or at the end.

Rule	Example
, Words that precede the subject in a sentence are potentially confusing, and they are often set off by a comma that shows the reader where the main part of the sentence begins.	Born to wealthy parents, he was able to pursue his career without financial worries. After the first few years of marriage, most couples realize that there are certain matters upon which they will never agree. Since the team was in last place, it was not surprising that only fifteen hundred fans showed up for the final game of the season.
When the introductory modifier is short, the comma is often omitted.	In this article I will demonstrate that we have chosen the wrong policy. At the present time the number of cigarette smokers is declining.
Certain kinds of introductory modifiers are followed by a comma even though they are short.	Madam Chairwoman, I suggest that the matter be put to a vote. Theoretically, she will have to get the permission of the chairman. Thoroughly chilled, he decided to set out for home. Yes, we are prepared for any motion that the prosecution may make. However, it is important to understand everyone's point of view.

Rule	Example
, , Free modifiers that occur in the middle of the sentence require two commas to set them off.	It is important, however, to understand everyone's point of view. Most new employees, after the first month, settle easily into the company's routine. Our distinguished colleague, the president of the guild, will be the keynote speaker. We can, I hope, agree on a budget for next year.
If the sentence can be read without pauses before and after the modifier, the commas may be omitted.	We can therefore conclude that the defendant is innocent of the charges. The applicant must understand before sending in the forms that the deposit fee is not refundable.
It is important to distinguish between free modifiers and other modifiers that may look very much the same but are part of the basic sentence. The latter should not be set off by commas.	This woman, who started out on the assembly line more than thirty years ago, became president of the company this week. An employee who started out on the assembly line more than thirty years ago became president of the company this week. The rock star, well known from recordings, has made a substantial contribution to the college's endowment. The rock star who recorded last year's hit has made a substantial contribution to the college's endowment.
When dates and addresses are used in sentences, each part except the first is treated as a free modifier and set off by commas. When only the month and year are given, the comma is usually omitted.	All contributions should be sent to the recording secretary at 4232 Grand Boulevard, Silver Spring, MD 70042, as soon as possible. She was born on Tuesday, December 20, 1901, in a log cabin near Casey Creek, Kentucky. We took our first trip to Alaska in August 1988.
, When free modifiers occur at the end of a sentence, they should be preceded by a comma.	It is important to understand everyone's point of view, however. She was much influenced by the Elizabethan composers, especially Byrd, Gibbons, and Dowland. Congress passed the bill in spite of the president's objections, hoping that a veto would provide an effective issue for the campaign.
There is a distinction between free modifiers at the end of a sentence and other modifiers that, if omitted, would change the meaning of the sentence. The latter should not be preceded by a comma.	We congratulate the Senate whip, who organized the filibuster. We congratulate the senator who organized the filibuster. The shortstop couldn't play, since he had a broken ankle. The shortstop hasn't played since he broke his ankle. Melanie insisted on gambling, even though she couldn't afford to lose. Don't gamble if you can't afford to lose.
When two or more free modifiers occur at the end of a sentence, each should be preceded by a comma.	Ralph sat motionless on a thin cushion, his legs folded into the lotus position, his eyes turned up so that only the whites were showing, his breathing almost imperceptible.

Rule	Example
— When a free modifier has internal punctuation or produces a very emphatic break in the sentence, commas may not seem strong enough, and dashes can be used instead.	The difficulties of marriage—sexual, financial, emotional—seem to be getting more formidable. My brother gave me a CD—a compact disc, not a certificate of deposit—for my birthday.
A dash can also be used to set off a free modifier that comes at the end of a sentence.	Only one employee in ten stays long enough to reach the senior level—a process that takes from ten to twelve years. These families had a median income of $35,000—$24,000 earned by the husband and $11,000 by the wife.
( ) Parentheses provide still another method for setting off extra elements from the rest of the sentence. They are used in a variety of ways.	There are three types of mergers: (1) horizontal (between companies); (2) vertical (between a supplier and a customer); and (3) conglomerate (between unrelated companies). The Federal Trade Commission (FTC) has issued regulations on the advertising of many products (see Appendix B for examples). The community didn't feel (and why should they?) that there was adequate police protection.

4. QUOTATIONS

Quotations are a significant feature of many texts, and a variety of ways have been developed for making clear to a reader which words are the writer's and which have been borrowed from someone else.

Rule	Example
" " When writers include the exact words of someone else, they must use quotation marks to set them off from the rest of the text.	In 1841, Ralph Waldo Emerson wrote, "I hate quotations. Tell me what you know." A quarter of a century later, he observed, "By necessity, by proclivity, and by delight, we all quote." This change of heart calls to mind another of his beliefs: "A foolish consistency is the hobgoblin of little minds."
Indirect quotations—in which writers report what someone else said without using the exact words—should not be set off by quotation marks.	Emerson said that he hated quotations and that writers should instead tell the reader what they themselves know.
When quotations are longer than two or three lines, they are often placed on separate lines. Sometimes a shorter line length and/or smaller type is also used. When this is done, quotation marks are not used.	In his essay "Notes on Punctuation," Lewis Thomas* gives the following advice to writers using quotations: If something is to be quoted, the exact words must be used. If part of it must be left out because of space limitations, it is good manners to insert three dots to indicate the omission, but it is unethical to do this if it means connecting two thoughts which the original author did not intend to have tied together.

Rule	Example
. . . **. . . .** It is sometimes convenient to omit part of a quotation. When this is done, the omission must be marked with points of ellipsis, usually with spaces between them. When the omission comes in the middle of a sentence, three points are used. When the omission includes the end of one or more sentences, four points are used.	Lewis Thomas offers the following advice: If something is to be quoted, the exact words must be used. If part of it must be left out . . . insert three dots to indicate the omission, but it is unethical to do this if it means connecting two thoughts which the original author did not intend to have tied together.
[ ] When writers insert something within a quoted passage, the insertion should be set off with brackets. Insertions are sometimes used to supply words that make a quotation easier to understand.	Lewis Thomas warns that it is "unethical to [omit words in a quotation] . . . if it means connecting two thoughts which the original author did not intend to have tied together."
Writers can make clear that a mistake in the quotation has been carried over from the original by using the word *sic*, meaning "thus."	As Senator Claghorne wrote to his constituents, "My fundamental political principals [*sic*] make it impossible for me to support the bill in its present form."
, Text that reports the source of quoted material is usually separated from it by a comma.	Marcus said, "I've decided not to apply to law school until next year." "Well," said Jennifer, "I was hoping that you would help me with my algebra tonight." "I think we should encourage young people to vote," said the mayor.
When quoted words are woven into a text so that they perform a basic grammatical function in the sentence, no punctuation is used.	According to Thoreau, most of us "lead lives of quiet desperation."
: Words that introduce a quotation formally, especially a quotation that is fairly long, are often followed by a colon.	Such demagogues should remember the words of John Stuart Mill: "We can never be sure that the opinion we are endeavoring to stifle is a false opinion; and if we were sure, stifling it would be an evil still."
' ' Quotations that are included within other quotations are set off by single quotation marks. (In British usage, single quotation marks are often used for regular quotations, and double quotation marks for included quotations.)	The witness made the same damaging statement under cross-examination: "As I entered the room, I heard him say, 'I'm determined to get even.' " *British usage:* 'As I entered the room, I heard him say, "I'm determined to get even." '
" " Final quotation marks follow other punctuation marks, except for semicolons and colons.	After dinner Ed began looking up all the unfamiliar allusions in Milton's "L'Allegro"; then, shortly after midnight, he turned to "Il Penseroso."
Question marks and exclamation marks precede final quotation marks when they refer to the quoted words. They follow when they refer to the sentence as a whole.	Once more she asked, "What do you think we should do about this?" What do you suppose Carla meant when she said, "I'm going to do something about this"? "Be off with you!" he yelled.

* *New England Journal of Medicine*, Vol. 296, pp. 1103–05 (May 12, 1977). Quoted by permission.

5. WORD-LEVEL PUNCTUATION

The punctuation covered so far is used to clarify the structure of sentences. There are also punctuation marks that are used with words.

Rule	Example
, The apostrophe is used with nouns to show possession:	The company's management resisted the union's demands. She found it impossible to decipher the students' handwriting.
(1) An apostrophe plus *s* is added to all words—singular or plural—that do not end in *-s*.	the little boy's hat the front office's ideas children's literature a week's vacation somebody else's fault the mice's tails
(2) Just an apostrophe is added at the end of plural words that end in *-s*.	the little boys' hats the farmers' demands the Joneses' yard two weeks' vacation the oil companies' profits for old times' sake
(3) There is no agreement on how to treat singular nouns that end in *-s*. Perhaps the best practice is to follow one's own pronunciation. If the possessive form has an extra syllable, then add an apostrophe and *s*; otherwise, just add an apostrophe.	Tess's bad luck Socrates' worldview for goodness' sake Williams's poems Charles Dickens' novels the class's attitude
An apostrophe is used in contractions to show where letters or numerals have been omitted.	I'm he's didn't won't let's Ma'am four o'clock readin', 'ritin', an' 'rithmetic the class of '55 the Panic of '93
An apostrophe is sometimes used when making letters or numbers plural.	This handwriting is very hard to read: the *o*'s and *a*'s look alike. The number of Ph.D.'s awarded to U.S. citizens declined in the 1980's.
. A period is used to mark shortened forms like abbreviations and initials.	Prof. M. L. Smith 14 ft. and 9 in. 4:00 p.m. John Q. Public, Jr. U.S.S.R. or USSR
- A hyphen is used at the end of a line of text when part of a word must be carried over to the next line.	. . .insta- bility
Hyphens are sometimes used to form compound words.	twenty-five mother-in-law self-confidence three-fourths president-elect ex-wife forty-one sixty-fourths double-breasted hands-on
In certain situations, hyphens are used between prefixes and root words.	catlike *but* bull-like recover *vs.* re-cover antibiotic *but* anti-intellectual coop *vs.* co-op preschool *but* pre-Columbian recreation *vs.* re-creation
Hyphens are often used to indicate that a group of words is to be understood as a unit.	hand-to-hand combat a three-hour lunch a well-dressed woman problem-solving strategies high-level talks a scholar-athlete

Rule	Example
When two modifiers containing hyphens are joined together, common elements are often not repeated.	This textbook covers both macro- and microeconomics. The study included fourth-, eighth-, and twelfth-grade students.

NOTE: It is important not to confuse the hyphen (-) with the dash (—), which is more than twice as long. The hyphen is used to group words and parts of words together, while the dash is used to clarify sentence structure. With a typewriter, a dash is formed by typing two successive hyphens (–)

6. OTHER USES OF PUNCTUATION MARKS

In addition to their main uses, punctuation marks are employed for a variety of special purposes.

Rule	Example
, Commas are used to indicate that a word or words used elsewhere in the sentence have been omitted.	Our company has found it difficult to find and keep skilled workers: the supply is limited; the demand, heavy; the turnover, high.
A comma is used after the complimentary close in a letter. In a personal letter, a comma is also used after the salutation.	Very truly yours, Dear Aunt Sally, Cordially, Dear Dad, Love, Dear Josie,
In numbers used primarily to express quantity, commas are used to divide the digits into groups of three. Commas are not ordinarily used in numbers that are used for identification.	The attendance at this year's convention was 12,347. Grain production in 1987, a drought year, was less than 90,000 tons. Norma lived at 18325 Sunset Boulevard. If you must write to us about this appliance, please mention the following serial number: AJ-3657294.
" " Quotation marks are used occasionally to indicate that a word or phrase is used in a special way. For other special uses of quotation marks, see the Italics section below.	Some anthropologists have attempted to prove "scientifically" that women are "biologically" passive and dependent. People still speak of "typing," even when they are seated in front of a computer screen.
: A colon can be used generally to call attention to what follows. It should not, however, be used between verbs or prepositions and their objects.	There were originally five Marx brothers: Groucho, Chico, Harpo, Zeppo, and Gummo. In 1988, Brooks published *Gilded Twilight: The Later Years of Melville and Twain.* The senior citizens demanded the following: better police protection, more convenient medical facilities, and a new recreational center. The senior citizens' demands included better police protection, more convenient medical facilities, and a new recreational center.
A colon is used after the salutation in a business letter.	Dear Mr. Czerny: Dear Valued Customer: Dear Ms. McFadden: Dear Frank:
— The dash can be used to indicate hesitations in speech.	"Well—uh—I'd like to try again—if you'll let me," he offered.

Rule	Example
When a list precedes a general statement about the items listed, it is followed by a dash.	Strength, endurance, flexibility—these three goals should guide each individual's quest for overall physical fitness.
■ The hyphen can be used as a substitute for *to*, with the meaning "up to and including." It should not, however, be used in conjunction with *from*.	The text of the Constitution can be found on pages 679–87. The period 1890–1914 was a particularly tranquil time in Europe. The Civil War lasted from 1861 to 1865. (*not* from 1861–1865) The San Francisco–Vancouver flight has been discontinued.

ITALICS

Rule	Example
Titles of newspapers, magazines, and books should be put in italics. Articles, essays, stories, chapters, and poems should be enclosed in quotation marks.	Her job requires her to keep up with the *New York Times,* the *Wall Street Journal,* and the *Washington Post* every day. "Song of Myself" is the first poem in Whitman's *Leaves of Grass.* Every year *Consumer Reports* runs "Best Buy Gifts" in the November issue.
Titles of plays and movies should be put in italics. Television and radio programs should be enclosed in quotation marks.	Shakespeare's *Hamlet* *The Playboy of the Western World* the movie *High Noon* Huston's *The Maltese Falcon* "Sesame Street" "60 Minutes"
Titles of works of art and long musical works should be put in italics. Shorter works such as songs should be enclosed in quotation marks. When the form of a musical work is used as its title, neither italics nor quotation marks are used.	Grant Wood's *American Gothic* Leonardo da Vinci's *Last Supper* Handel's *Messiah* *Don Giovanni* by Mozart *Porgy and Bess* "Summertime" Beethoven's Ninth Symphony Piano Sonata No. 2 in A major
The names of ships and airplanes should be put in italics.	the aircraft carrier *Intrepid* Lindbergh's *The Spirit of St. Louis*
Words and phrases from a foreign language should be put in italics. Accompanying translations are often enclosed in quotation marks. Words of foreign origin that have become familiar in an English context should not be italicized.	As a group, these artists appear to be in the avant-garde. They are not, however, to be thought of as *enfants terribles,* or "terrible children," people whose work is so outrageous as to shock or embarrass.
Words used as words, and letters used as letters, should be put in italics.	I can never remember how to spell *broccoli.* Be sure to pronounce the final *e* in *Nike.*
Italics are sometimes used to indicate that a word or words should be pronounced with extra emphasis.	The boss is *very* hard to get along with today. John loaned the tape to Robert, and *he* gave it to Sally.

NOTE: When a typewriter is used, italics are indicated by underlining. The advent of the word processor has made this substitution unnecessary. If you are preparing a manuscript for publication, however, editors and typesetters will find it easier to work with if you use underlining instead of italics.

CAPITALIZATION

Rule	Example
The important words in titles are capitalized. This includes the first and last words and all other words except articles, prepositions, and coordinating conjunctions, such as *and, but,* and *or.*	*Gone with the Wind* *The Brain: A User's Manual* *With Malice toward None* *A World to Lose* *The Universe Within* *The Great War, 1914–1918* *Sports-related Injuries* *Twentieth-Century Views*
Proper nouns—names of specific people, places, organizations, groups, events, etc.— are capitalized, as are the proper adjectives derived from them.	Martin Luther King, Jr. Jeremy Spanish Civil War United States Coast Guard Canada Canadian New Orleans Latinos Jeffersonian
When proper nouns and adjectives have taken on a specialized meaning, they are often no longer capitalized.	My brother ordered a bologna sandwich with french dressing. The shop specializes in china and plaster of paris ornaments. The address was written in india ink on a manila envelope.
Titles of people are capitalized when they precede the name, but usually not when they follow or when they are used alone.	Queen Victoria Victoria, queen of England the queen of England the queen the president's office John Dall, president of Rynex, Inc. Mr. Dall the president of the corporation
Kinship terms are capitalized when they are used before a name or alone in place of a name. They are not capitalized when they are preceded by modifiers.	I'm expecting Aunt Alice to drop by this weekend. I forgot to call Mother on her birthday I forgot to call my mother on her birthday.
Geographical features are capitalized when they are part of the official name. In the plural, they are capitalized when they precede names, but not when they follow.	The Sonoran Desert is in southern Arizona. The Arizona desert is beautiful in the spring. In recent years, Lakes Erie and Ontario have been cleaned up. The Hudson and Mohawk rivers are both in New York State.
Points of the compass are capitalized only when they are used as the name of a section of the country.	We've been driving east for over two hours. We visited the South last summer and the Southwest the year before. He was born in southwestern Nebraska.

MANUSCRIPT PREPARATION

Manuscripts should be printed or typed on standard-size paper—8½ by 11 inches. The text should be double-spaced. If the paper is being submitted for publication and will be edited and set into type, everything should be double-spaced—including block quotations, footnotes, and references—since it is difficult to edit material that has less than a full line of space between lines of text. While covers may be attractive for certain purposes, most editors and instructors find that they make manuscripts more difficult to handle efficiently. Pages must be numbered, preferably in the upper right-hand corner and far enough from the edge so that the numbers are not accidentally left off when the manuscript is photocopied. Every manuscript should be copied as a safeguard against loss of the original.

Word processing makes available several features that are not available on the conventional typewriter—italics, boldface, various typefaces, and different possibilities for spacing. If a manuscript is being prepared for its final readership, then it makes sense to use these capabilities to make it as attractive and readable as possible. On the other hand, if the manuscript will be edited and set into type, it will be easier to deal with if a single typeface is used.

FOOTNOTES

Footnotes can be used for additional material that does not fit conveniently into the text. They may be placed at the bottom of the page or at the end of the text, in which case they are often referred to as endnotes. Traditionally, footnotes have also been used to cite the sources of information, ideas, and quotations included in a text. This is no longer a recommended practice. It is now more common to include brief identifications of sources in parentheses within a text and give full information in a reference list at the end. In-text citations and reference lists are discussed in the next two sections.

IN-TEXT CITATIONS

There are two main ways of citing sources within a text: (1) the author-page system, which is widely used in the humanities; and (2) the author-date system, which has been adopted by the social sciences and some of the natural sciences. Each of these systems has several variations. The recognized standard for the author-page system is *The MLA Style Manual,* which is published by the Modern Language Association. The most widely used version of the author-date system can be found in the *Publication Manual of the American Psychological Association* (APA), 3rd ed. The brief descriptions of each system that follow are based on these two sources.

The basic technique in both systems is to include just enough information in the text to enable the reader to find the relevant item in the reference list. In the author-page system, this information includes the author of the work referred to and the relevant page number.

American novelists have always had a difficult relationship with their public (Brooks 247).

If the author is mentioned in the text, then just the page number is needed in parentheses.

As Brooks has observed, American novelists have always had a difficult relationship with their public (247).

If the reference is to a work as a whole rather than to a specific part, then no additional citation is needed.

In *Gilded Twilight,* Brooks establishes himself as the most thoughtful of poststructuralist critics.

When there is more than one item in the reference list by the same author, the title of the work referred to is included in the parentheses, usually in a shortened form.

Brooks' comments on Melville are surprisingly negative (*Gilded* 83).

When works by different authors are referred to, all the references are included in the same parentheses.

Recently critics have had surprisingly negative things to say about Melville (Brooks, *Gilded* 83; Adams and Rubens 432; Leibniz 239).

In the author-date system, the in-text citations include the author's name and the date of publication. As with the author-page system, material that already appears in the text is not repeated within the parentheses.

A recent study carried out at McGill came to the opposite conclusion (McBain, 1991).
McBain (1991) demonstrates that there is at least one alternative to the accepted view.
In a 1991 study, McBain showed that there is at least one alternative to the accepted view.

When the reference list contains more than one work published by a particular author in the same year, letters are used to distinguish among them.

Several innovative studies in the last few years have demonstrated that this matter is not as settled as was once thought (Brewer, 1989;

Fischer & Rivera, 1988; McBain, 1989a, 1989b, 1991; Silvano, Blomstedt & Meigs, 1987).

Ordinarily, page numbers are included only when there is a direct quotation.

> One respected researcher notes that little notice has been taken of "the substantial number of counterexamples that have not been either questioned or explained" (McBain, 1991, p. 238).

Notice how the two systems differ in details: for example, one uses *and,* the other *&;* one follows the author's name with a comma, while the other does not.

In some publications in the sciences, the items in the reference list are numbered and these numbers are used in citations in the text.

> One group of experiments has led researchers to believe that despite the enormous difficulties, a vaccine will eventually be produced (3,22,39). Much depends on the availability of funds and staff to carry out the work (14). Motley observes, however, that "whether the administration has the will to make the painful choices necessary is highly doubtful" (19, p. 687).

With a number system, the items in the reference list may be put in either alphabetical order or the order in which they occur in the text.

REFERENCE LISTS

The following table shows how items in the reference list would be treated in the author-page and author-date systems. It is important to realize that in following a particular style, the writer must be consistent in every detail of wording, abbreviation, spacing, and punctuation. There is space here for only a limited variety of items. Those who are preparing texts for publication will probably need to consult the relevant manual.

Sample Reference Lists

Type of Document	Author-Page System (MLA) Works Cited	Author-Date (APA) References
Journal article	Stewart, Donald C. "What Is an English Major, and What Should It Be?" *College Composition and Communication* 40 (1989): 188–202.	Roediger, H. L. (1990). Implicit memory: A commentary. *Bulletin of the Psychonomic Society, 28,* 373–380.
Journal article two authors	Brownell, Hiram H., and Heather H. Potter. "Inference Deficits in Right-Brain Damaged Patients." *Brain and Language* 27 (1986): 310–21.	Tulving, E., & Schacter, D. L. (1990). Priming and human memory systems. *Science, 247,* 301–305.
Journal article more than two authors	Mascia-Lees, Frances E., Pat Sharpe, and Colleen B. Cohen. "Double Liminality and the Black Woman Writer." *American Behavioral Scientist* 31 (1987): 101–14.	Barringer, H. R., Takeuchi, D. T., & Xenos, P. C. (1990). Education, occupational prestige and income of Asian Americans: Evidence from the 1980 Census. *Sociology of Education, 63,* 27–43.
Book	Graff, Gerald. *Professing Literature: An Institutional History.* Chicago: U of Chicago P, 1987.	Rossi, P. H. (1989). *Down and out in America: The origins of homelessness.* Chicago: University of Chicago Press.
Book revised edition	Erikson, Erik. *Childhood and Society.* 2nd ed. New York: Norton, 1963.	Kail, R. (1990). *Memory development in children* (3rd ed.). New York: Freeman.

Type of Document	Author-Page System (MLA) Works Cited	Author-Date (APA) References
Book corporate author	College Board. *College-bound Seniors: 1989 SAT Profile.* New York: College Entrance Examination Board, 1989.	American Psychiatric Association. (1987). *Diagnostic and statistical manual of mental disorders* (3rd ed., rev.). Washington, DC: Author.
Book no author	*Guidelines for the Workload of the College English Teacher.* Urbana: National Council of Teachers of English, 1987.	*Standards for educational and psychological tests.* (1985). Washington, DC: American Psychological Association.
Edited book	Kerckhove, Derrick de, and Charles J. Lumsden, eds. *The Alphabet and the Brain: The Lateralization of Writing.* Berlin: Springer-Verlag, 1988.	Campbell, J. P., Campbell, R. J., & Associates. (Eds.). (1988). *Productivity in organizations.* San Francisco, CA: Jossey-Bass.
Selection from edited book	Glover, David. "The Stuff That Dreams Are Made Of: Masculinity, Femininity, and the Thriller." *Gender, Genre and Narrative Pleasure.* Ed. Derek Longhurst. London: Unwin Hyman, 1989. 67–83.	Wilson, S. F. (1990). Community support and integration: New directions for outcome research. In S. Rose (Ed.), *Case management: An overview and assessment.* White Plains, NY: Longman.
Translated book	Lacan, Jacques. *Ecrits: A Selection.* Trans. Alan Sheridan. New York: Norton, 1977.	Michotte, A. E. (1963). The perception of causality (T. R. Miles & E. Miles, Trans.). London: Methuen. (Original work published 1946)
Republished book	Hurston, Zora Neale. *Their Eyes Were Watching God.* 1937. Urbana: U of Illinois P, 1978.	Ebbinghaus, H. (1964). *Memory: A contribution to experimental psychology.* New York: Dover. (Original work published 1885; translated 1913)
Magazine article	Miller, Mark Crispen. "Massa, Come Home." *New Republic* 16 Sept. 1981: 29–32.	Gibbs, N. (1989, April 24). How America has run out of time. *Time,* pp. 58–67.
Newspaper article	"Literacy on the Job." *USA Today* 27 Dec. 1988: 6B.	Freudenheim, M. (1987, December 29). Rehabilitation in head injuries in business and health. *New York Times,* p. D2.
Review	Kidd, John. "The Scandal of *Ulysses.*" Rev. of *Ulysses: The Corrected Text,* by Hans Walter Gabler. *New York Review of Books* 30 June 1988: 32–39.	Falk, J. S. (1990). [Review of *Narratives from the crib*]. *Language, 66,* 558–562.
Report available from ERIC	Baurer, Barbara A. *A Study of the Reliabilities and Cost Efficiencies of Three Methods of Assessment for Writing Ability.* ERIC, 1981. ED 216 357.	Hill, C., & Larsen, E. (1984). *What reading tests call for and what children do.* Washington, DC: National Institute of Education. (ERIC Document Reproduction Service No. ED 238 904)
University report	Flower, Linda. The Role of Task Representation in Reading to Write. Technical Report No. 6. Berkeley: Center for the Study of Writing at U of California, Berkeley and Carnegie Mellon U, 1987.	Elman, J., & Zipser, D. (1987). *Learning the hidden structure of speech* (Report No. 8701). Institute for Cognitive Science, University of California, San Diego.

Type of Document	Author-Page System (MLA) Works Cited	Author-Date (APA) References
Dissertation	Hubert, Henry Allan. "The Development of English Studies in Nineteenth-Century Anglo-Canadian Colleges." Diss. U of British Columbia, 1988.	Thompson, L. (1988). *Social perception in negotiation.* Unpublished doctoral dissertation, Northwestern University, Evanston, IL.
Conference paper	Moffett, James. "Censorship and Spiritual Education." The Right to Literacy Conference. Columbus, Ohio, September 1988.	Hogan, R., Raskin, R., & Fazzini, D. (1988, October). *The dark side of charisma.* Paper presented at the Conference on Psychological Measures and Leadership, San Antonio, TX.

AVOIDING SEXIST LANGUAGE

Word choices and grammatical constructions that ignore or minimize the presence and contributions of one sex in society—at home or school or the workplace, in business or professional spheres, in social or personal relationships—may be considered sexist. Many writers and speakers try to avoid such usages, and they reject as well language that calls attention to the sex of an individual when it is irrelevant to the role or situation under discussion. Here are specific suggestions for avoiding sexist language, from replacing one term with another to recasting sentences.

1. Replacing *man* or *men*, or words or expressions containing either, when they are clearly intended to refer to a person of either sex or to include members of both sexes.

Instead of	Consider using
man	human being, human, person, individual
mankind, man (collectively)	human beings, humans, humankind, humanity, people, human race, human species, society, men and women
man-made	synthetic, artificial
workingman	worker, wage earner
man in the street	average person, ordinary person

2. Using gender-neutral terms wherever possible to designate occupations, positions, roles, etc., rather than terms that specify sex. A full list of nonsexist job designations can be found in the *Dictionary of Occupational Titles* published by the U.S. Department of Labor.

   a. Avoiding terms ending in *-man* or other gender-specific forms. One approach is to use words ending in *-person*. Some of these terms, like *salesperson* and *spokesperson,* have achieved wide acceptance; others, like *councilperson* and *weatherperson,* still sound awkward to many people. When discussing an individual whose sex is known, gender-specific terms such as *anchorwoman, businessman, saleswoman,* and *salesman* can be used, although in this situation, too, many people still prefer the neutral terms.

Instead of	Consider using
anchorman	anchor
bellman, bellboy	bellhop
businessman	businessperson *or more specifically* business executive, manager, business owner, retailer, etc.
cameraman	camera operator, cinematographer
chairman	chair, chairperson
cleaning lady, cleaning woman	housecleaner, office cleaner housekeeper
clergyman	member of the clergy, cleric *or more specifically* minister, rabbi, priest, pastor, etc.
congressman	representative, member of Congress, legislator
fireman	firefighter
forefather	ancestor
housewife	homemaker
insurance man	insurance agent
layman	layperson, nonspecialist, nonprofessional
mailman, postman	mail carrier, letter carrier
policeman	police officer, law enforcement officer
salesman	salesperson, sales representative
spokesman	spokesperson, representative

Instead of	Consider using
stewardess, steward	flight attendant
weatherman	weather reporter, weathercaster, meteorologist
workman	worker

b. Avoiding "feminine" suffixes such as *-ess*, *-ette*, *-trix*, and *-enne*. Words with these suffixes are often regarded as implying triviality or inferiority on the part of the person or role involved, as well as making unnecessary reference to the person's sex.

Instead of	Consider using
authoress	author
aviatrix	aviator
poetess	poet
proprietress	proprietor
sculptress	sculptor
suffragette	suffragist
usherette	usher

A few such terms, like *actress, heiress,* and *hostess,* remain in active use, though many women prefer the terms *actor, heir,* and *host.* Several substitutions for both *waitress* and *waiter*—*waitperson, waitron,* and *server*—are gaining ground, but none has yet replaced the traditional designations. Legal terms like *executrix* and *testatrix* are still used, but with diminishing frequency.

c. Eliminating as modifiers the words *lady, female, girl, male,* and the like for terms that otherwise have no gender designation, as in *lady doctor, female lawyer, girl athlete,* or *male secretary,* unless they serve to clarify meaning. Such expressions tend to patronize the individual involved by suggesting that the norm for the role is the gender *not* specified, and that for someone of the gender specified to be found in that role is somehow remarkable or peculiar. When it is necessary to point out the female aspect of a person in a given role or occupation, using *female* or *woman* as a modifier is preferable to *lady: My grandmother was the first woman doctor to practice in this town.*

3. Referring to members of both sexes by parallel terms, names, or titles.

Instead of	Consider using
man and wife	husband and wife
men and girls	men and women, boys and girls
men and ladies	men and women, ladies and gentlemen
President Johnson and Mrs. Meir	President Johnson and Prime Minister Meir *or* Mr. Johnson and Mrs. Meir

4. Avoiding the third person singular masculine pronoun when referring to an individual who could be of either sex, as in *When a reporter covers a controversial story, he has a responsibility to present both sides of the issue.* Rephrasing the sentence in any of the following ways will circumvent this situation:

a. Structuring the sentence in the plural and using the third person plural pronouns *they/ their/theirs/them: When reporters cover controversial stories, they have a responsibility . . . .* (Some people approve the use of a plural pronoun to refer to an indefinite like *everyone* or *anyone,* as in *Everyone packed their own lunch,* but many people do not, at least in formal writing.)

b. Using either first or second person pronouns—*I/me/my/mine, we/us/our/ours, you/ your/yours*—that do not specify sex: *As a reporter covering a controversial story, I have a responsibility . . .* or *As reporters covering controversial stories, we have a responsibility . . .* or *When you are a reporter covering a controversial story, you have a responsibility . . . .*

c. Using the third person *one: As a reporter covering a controversial story, one has a responsibility . . . .* (Although common in British usage, *one* can seem stilted or excessively formal to Americans. This pronoun is most effective when used sparingly.)

d. Using both the masculine and feminine singular pronouns: *When a reporter covers a controversial story, he or she* (or *she or he*) *has a responsibility . . . .* (This approach is the one most likely to produce awkwardness. But if the pronouns are not repeated too often, it may sometimes be the most satisfactory solution.) The abbreviated forms *he/she, his/her, him/her* (and the reverse forms, with the feminine pronoun first) are also available, though they are not widely used in formal writing. The blend *s/he* is also used by some people.

e. Using the passive voice: *When controversial stories are covered, there is a responsibility to present both sides of the issue* (or *both sides of the issue should be presented*).

f. Rephrasing the sentence to avoid any pronoun: *When covering a controversial story, a reporter has a responsibility . . . .*

g. Using nouns, like *person, individual,* or a synonym appropriate to the context, instead of pronouns: *Reporters often cover controversial stories. In such cases the journalist has a responsibility . . . .*

h. Using a relative clause: *A reporter who covers a controversial story has a responsibility . . . .*

Different solutions will work better in different contexts.

5. Avoiding language that disparages, stereotypes, or patronizes either sex.

a. Avoiding reference to an adult female as a *girl;* to women collectively as *the distaff side* or *the fair sex;* to a wife as *the little woman;* to a female college student as a *coed;* to an unmarried woman as a *bachelor girl, spinster,* or *old maid.*

b. Being aware that such generalized phrases as *lawyers/doctors/farmers and their wives* or *a teacher and her students* or *a secretary and her boss* can be taken to exclude an entire sex from even the possibility of occupying a role. It is possible to choose words or forms that specify neither sex or acknowledge both sexes, as in *lawyers . . . and their spouses* (or *families* or *companions*); *a teacher and his or her students* (or *a teacher and students* or *teachers and their students*); *a secretary and his or her boss* (or *a secretary and boss*).

c. Avoiding terms like *womanly, manly, feminine,* or *masculine* in referring to traits stereotypically associated with one sex or the other. English abounds in adjectives that describe such qualities as strength or weakness, nurturing or determination or sensitivity, without intrinsic reference to maleness or femaleness.

Part Two

Vocabulary Builder

BUILDING A POWERFUL VOCABULARY

INTRODUCTION

Words are the building blocks of thought. They are the means by which we understand the ideas of others and express our own opinions. It is only logical that people who know how to use words concisely and accurately find it easier to achieve their aims.

In fact, formal education has less relationship to vocabulary achievement than you might expect; people *can* improve their word power on their own. This section will show you how to expand and improve your vocabulary in *just ten minutes a day!*

Each of the following lessons is designed to take ten minutes to complete. Do one lesson a day. Work from beginning to end because the lessons build on each other. Follow these three easy steps:

Step 1: Time

Begin by setting aside a block of ten minutes a day. Don't split your time into two five-minute segments—set aside one ten-minute period every day. Consider using ten minutes in the early morning before you begin your regular activities. Or you might want to use ten minutes on the bus, subway, or train or ten minutes during a work break. Maybe right after dinner is a convenient time for you. Whatever time you select, make it *your* time—carve it in granite! To make your work even easier, try to set aside the same time every day. You'll be surprised at how quickly your vocabulary builds.

Step 2: Place

Now, find a place where you can work undisturbed. If you know that you have difficulty tuning out the distractions of public transportation or the office lunchroom, try to study at home. Perhaps you have the ability to completely ignore extraneous chatter or music and so can concentrate in the middle of the family room or in a crowded cafeteria. Wherever you decide to study, try to settle in the same place every day. In this way, you'll set to work more quickly, concentrate better, and succeed sooner.

Step 3: Method

Ten minutes a day is all it takes to build a powerful vocabulary. To help you get into the rhythm of working in ten-minute segments, set your alarm or kitchen timer for ten minutes. When you hear the buzzer, you'll know that you've spent ten minutes on your vocabulary. Soon you'll be able to pace yourself without the timer.

TEST YOUR VOCABULARY

How Good Is Your Vocabulary?

To see how your vocabulary measures up to that of other people, take the following tests. As you go through each test, put a check mark next to any word you don't know. After you complete each test, go back and see which of your choices proved correct. Then take a minute to study the words you missed.

The first test consists of twenty-five phrases, each containing an italicized word. Circle the correct response. This test has no time limit.

1. a *lenient* supervisor
   a. short b. not strict c. inflexible d. shrewd
2. an *audacious* endeavor
   a. foolish b. serious c. expensive d. bold
3. a *latent* talent
   a. apparent b. valuable c. present but not apparent d. useless
4. a *gaudy* dress

a. expensive   b. deep green   c. flattering
d. showy
5. a *disheveled* person
a. useless   b. untidy   c. miserable   d. vicious
6. *feign* illness
a. suffer   b. pretend   c. die from   d. enjoy
7. an *agile* child
a. intelligent   b. nimble   c. neglected
d. annoying
8. a *somber* night
a. dismal   b. expensive   c. lively
d. disastrous
9. a *prosaic* event
a. extraordinary   b. irregular
c. commonplace   d. pretty
10. a *vivacious* person
a. annoying   b. dismal   c. vicious
d. spirited
11. a *baffling* situation
a. puzzling   b. obvious   c. easy   d. old
12. a *hiatus* in the schedule
a. continuation   b. uniformity   c. gap
d. beginning
13. a *lackluster* report
a. enthusiastic   b. praiseworthy   c. dull
d. wordy
14. a *prevalent* condition
a. adult   b. widespread   c. previous   d. fatal
15. a *loquacious* person
a. talkative   b. cutthroat   c. laconic
d. enthusiastic
16. an *anonymous* victim
a. willing   b. known   c. not known or named
d. foreign
17. a *vicarious* thrill
a. incomplete   b. triumphant   c. spoiled
d. indirect
18. a *languid* feeling
a. nervous   b. energetic   c. fatigued
d. robust
19. *vernacular* language
a. ordinary   b. elevated   c. formal
d. informal
20. a religious *icon*
a. gesture   b. picture   c. ritual   d. structure
21. *inclement* weather
a. fair   b. unexpected   c. foul   d. disturbing
22. a *cavalier* attitude
a. pleasant   b. dramatic   c. considerate
d. arrogant
23. a *caustic* remark
a. wise   b. biting   c. prudent
d. complimentary
24. a timely *caveat*
a. bargain   b. purchase   c. warning
d. movement

25. an *ominous* situation
a. pleasant   b. rigid   c. obvious
d. threatening

Answers: 1. b   2. d   3. c   4. d   5. b   6. b
7. b   8. a   9. c   10. d   11. a   12. c   13. c
14. b   15. a   16. c   17. d   18. c   19. a
20. b   21. c   22. d   23. b   24. c   25. d

Refer to the following chart to score your results:
 0–6   correct   Below average
 7–13 correct   Average
14–20 correct   Above average
21–25 correct   Superior

The following three tests evaluate whether you have an average, good, or excellent vocabulary. The tests have no time limit.

Test for an Average Vocabulary

If you have an average vocabulary, you should be able to match the two columns below correctly. Write your answer in the space provided. Nearly three quarters of the adults tested knew all these words.

1. IMMINENT	a. cleanse	____
2. FLUSTER	b. flashy	____
3. RIGID	c. confuse	____
4. PURGE	d. restore	____
5. REHABILITATE	e. hinder	____
6. LATENT	f. pretend	____
7. GAUDY	g. stiff	____
8. FEIGN	h. coax	____
9. CAJOLE	i. hidden	____
10. IMPEDE	j. at hand	____

Answers: 1. j   2. c   3. g   4. a   5. d   6. i
7. b   8. f   9. h   10. e

Test for a Good Vocabulary

Only half the adults tested got all of the following words correct. See how well *you* can do! Write S if the word in the second column is similar in meaning to the word in the first column or O if it is opposite.

		S or O
1. MYRIAD	few	____
2. PANACEA	cure-all	____
3. OPULENT	spare	____
4. ESCHEW	shun	____
5. NEFARIOUS	wicked	____
6. INCARCERATE	imprison	____
7. AMELIORATE	make worse	____
8. CANDOR	hypocrisy	____
9. TACITURN	talkative	____
10. VERBOSE	wordy	____

Building a Powerful Vocabulary   91

Test for an Excellent Vocabulary

Fewer than one quarter of the adults tested got all of the following words correct. In the space provided, write T if the definition is true or F if it is false.

T or F

1. *Obsequiousness* is a sign of pride.   ____
2. *Parsimonious* people are extravagant.   ____
3. Recycling is an *exigency* of the moment.   ____
4. The hawk is a *predatory* bird.   ____
5. An *aquiline* nose is straight.   ____
6. A *covert* plan is out in the open.   ____
7. It is hard to explain things to an *obtuse* person.   ____
8. Someone with *catholic* views is narrow-minded.   ____
9. A large debt *obviates* financial worries.   ____
10. *Erudite* people are well-read.   ____

PRONUNCIATION

Obviously, knowing the meaning of a word is only half the battle: you also have to know how to pronounce it. The best way to learn how to pronounce new words is by using a dictionary. It is the best source for the words you need to get you where you want to go.

LESSON 1. TEST YOUR PRONUNCIATION

How Good Is Your Pronunciation?

Let's see how you pronounce some fairly difficult words. As you work through each test, put a check mark next to any word whose pronunciation you don't know. After you finish each test, go back and see which of your choices were right. (Some words have alternate pronunciations.) Finally, take a few minutes to study the words you missed.

The following test contains twenty words. See how many you can pronounce correctly. There is no time limit.

Test 1: Pronunciation

1. badinage	11. exegesis
2. salubrious	12. dishabille
3. apocryphal	13. élan
4. putsch	14. febrile
5. effeminacy	15. gamut
6. effusive	16. obsequious
7. mandible	17. jejune
8. raison d'être	18. ribald
9. amblyopia	19. gecko
10. dacha	20. wizened

Answers: To satisfy your curiosity, here are the definitions as well as the pronunciations. To rank yourself against others, refer to the chart at the end of this section.

If you are not familiar with the pronunciation symbols, refer to the pronunciation key on page 385.

1. **badinage** (bad'n äzh', bad'n ij) light, playful banter or raillery
2. **salubrious** (sə lo͞o'brē əs) favorable to or promoting health; healthful
3. **apocryphal** (ə pok'rə fəl) of doubtful authenticity; false

4. **putsch** (po͝och) a plot to overthrow a government
5. **effeminacy** (i fem'ə nə sē) the quality of being soft or delicate to an unmanly degree in traits, tastes, habits, etc.
6. **effusive** (i fyo͞o'siv) unduly demonstrative; lacking reserve
7. **mandible** (man'də bəl) the bone of the lower jaw
8. **raison d'être** (rā'zōn de'trə) reason or justification for being or existing
9. **amblyopia** (am'blē ō'pē ə) dimness of sight, without an apparent organic cause
10. **dacha** (dä'chə) a Russian country house or villa
11. **exegesis** (ek'si jē'sis) a critical explanation or interpretation, especially of Scripture
12. **dishabille** (dis'ə bēl') the state of being carelessly or partly dressed; a state of disarray or disorder
13. **élan** (ā län') dash; impetuous ardor
14. **febrile** (fē'brəl, feb'rəl) feverish
15. **gamut** (gam'ət) the entire scale or range
16. **obsequious** (əb sē'kwē əs) servile, compliant, or deferential
17. **jejune** (ji jo͞on') insipid, dull; childish; deficient or lacking in nutritive value
18. **ribald** (rib'əld) vulgar or indecent in speech; coarsely mocking
19. **gecko** (gek'ō) a harmless nocturnal lizard
20. **wizened** (wiz'ənd) withered; shriveled

Now use this chart to score your results:
0–5 correct   Below average
6–10 correct   Average
11–15 correct   Above average
16–20 correct   Superior

Want to try again? See how many of these twenty words you can pronounce correctly. The test has no time limit.

Test 2: Pronunciation

1. vignette
2. bailiwick
3. juvenilia
4. baroque
5. flaccid
6. cupidity
7. ghee
8. sententious
9. zealous
10. ragout
11. blasé
12. cabochon
13. loath
14. quotidian
15. obdurate
16. cache
17. jocund
18. cabriolet
19. escutcheon
20. penuche

Answers: To rank yourself against others, refer to the chart at the end of this section.

1. **vignette** (vin yet′) a short, graceful literary sketch; a decorative design or small illustration used on the title page of a book or at the beginning or end of a chapter
2. **bailiwick** (bā′lə wik′) a person's area of skill, knowledge, or training; the district within which a bailiff has jurisdiction
3. **juvenilia** (jo͞o′və nil′ē ə) works, especially writings, produced in youth
4. **baroque** (bə rōk′) extravagantly ornamented; ornate; designating a style of art or music of the 17th–18th century
5. **flaccid** (flak′sid) soft and limp; flabby
6. **cupidity** (kyo͞o pid′i tē) eager or inordinate desire, especially for wealth; greed or avarice
7. **ghee** (gē) liquid butter made from the milk of cows and buffalos and clarified by boiling, used in Indian cooking
8. **sententious** (sen ten′shəs) given to excessive moralizing; self-righteous; abounding in pithy aphorisms or maxims, as a book
9. **zealous** (zel′əs) ardently active or devoted
10. **ragout** (ra go͞o′) a highly seasoned stew of meat or fish
11. **blasé** (blä zā′) indifferent to or bored with life or a particular activity
12. **cabochon** (kab′ə shon′) a precious stone of convex hemispherical or oval form, polished but not cut into facets
13. **loath** (lōth, lōth) unwilling; reluctant
14. **quotidian** (kwō tid′ē ən) daily; everyday; ordinary
15. **obdurate** (ob′do͞o rit, -dyo͞o-) unmoved by persuasion, pity, or tender feelings; unyielding
16. **cache** (kash) a hiding place
17. **jocund** (jok′ənd) cheerful; merry
18. **cabriolet** (kab′rē ə lā′) a light, two-wheeled one-horse carriage
19. **escutcheon** (i skuch′ən) a shield or shieldlike surface on which a coat of arms is depicted
20. **penuche** (pə no͞o′ chē) a candy made of brown sugar, butter, and milk, usually with nuts

Refer to the following chart to score your results:

0–6 correct   Below average
7–13 correct   Average
14–20 correct   Above average
21–25 correct   Superior

LESSON 2.

Here are several more pronunciation quizzes to provide you with additional practice.

Test 1: Pronunciation

1. dybbuk
2. hauteur
3. nacre
4. sidle
5. toque
6. viscid
7. lingua franca
8. shoji
9. guano
10. apropos
11. insouciance
12. folderol
13. cavil
14. macabre
15. elision
16. denouement
17. parvenu
18. pince-nez
19. alopecia
20. chicanery

Answers:

1. **dybbuk** (dib′ək) in Jewish folklore, a demon or the soul of a dead person that enters the body of a living person and controls him or her
2. **hauteur** (hō tûr′) a haughty manner or spirit
3. **nacre** (nā′kər) mother-of-pearl
4. **sidle** (sīd′l) to move sideways
5. **toque** (tōk) a soft, brimless, close-fitting hat for women; a chef's hat; a velvet hat with a narrow, turned-up brim, a full crown, and a plume, worn especially in the sixteenth century
6. **viscid** (vis′id) having a glutinous consistency; sticky
7. **lingua franca** (ling′gwə frang′kə) a language widely used as a means of communication among speakers of different languages
8. **shoji** (shō′jē) a light screen of translucent paper, used as a sliding door or a room divider in Japanese homes
9. **guano** (gwä′nō) a natural manure composed chiefly of the excrement of sea birds, found especially on islands near the Peruvian coast; bird lime
10. **apropos** (ap′rə pō′) appropriate; timely; to the purpose; opportunely; with reference or regard

11. **insouciance** (in sōō′sē əns) lack of care or concern; indifference
12. **folderol** (fol′də rol′) mere nonsense; foolish talk or ideas
13. **cavil** (kav′əl) to quibble; an irritating or trivial objection
14. **macabre** (mə kä′brə) gruesome; horrible; grim
15. **elision** (i lizh′ən) the omission of a vowel, consonant, or syllable in pronunciation
16. **denouement** (dā′nōō mäɴ′) the final resolution of a plot, as of a drama or novel; outcome
17. **parvenu** (pär′və nōō′, -nyōō′) a person who has suddenly acquired wealth or importance but lacks the proper social qualifications; upstart
18. **pince-nez** (pans′nā′, pins′-) a pair of eyeglasses held on the face by a spring that pinches the nose
19. **alopecia** (al′ə pē′shē ə, -sē ə) baldness
20. **chicanery** (shi kā′nə rē, chi-) trickery or deception by the use of cunning or clever tricks

Test 2: Pronunciation

1. façade	11. defalcation
2. obeisance	12. contumacious
3. gnome	13. heinous
4. diva	14. emollient
5. liaison	15. gibe
6. mauve	16. ewer
7. fiat	17. hirsute
8. kiosk	18. ogle
9. chassis	19. ennui
10. omniscient	20. canard

Answers:

1. **façade** (fə säd′) the front of a building, especially an imposing or decorative one; a superficial appearance or illusion of something
2. **obeisance** (ō bā′səns, ō bē′-) a movement of the body expressing deep respect or deferential courtesy, as before a superior; a deep bow
3. **gnome** (nōm) one of a legendary species of diminutive creatures, usually described as shriveled little old men, who inhabit the interior of the earth and act as guardians of its treasure; troll; dwarf
4. **diva** (dē′və, -vä) a distinguished female singer; prima donna
5. **liaison** (lē ā′zən, lē′ā zôɴ′, lē′ə zon′) a contact maintained between units to ensure concerted action; an illicit sexual relationship
6. **mauve** (mōv, môv) pale bluish purple
7. **fiat** (fē′ät, -at; fī′ət, -at) an authoritative decree, sanction, or order
8. **kiosk** (kē′osk, kē osk′) a kind of open pavilion or summerhouse common in Turkey and Iran; a similar structure used as a bandstand, newsstand, etc.
9. **chassis** (chas′ē, -is, shas′ē) the frame, wheels, and machinery of a motor vehicle, on which the body is supported
10. **omniscient** (om nish′ənt) having complete or infinite knowledge, awareness, or understanding; perceiving all things; all-knowing
11. **defalcation** (dē′fal kā′shən, -fôl-) the misappropriation of money held by an official, trustee, or other fiduciary
12. **contumacious** (kon′tōō mā′shəs, -tyōō-) stubbornly perverse or rebellious; obstinately disobedient
13. **heinous** (hā′nəs) hateful; odious
14. **emollient** (i mol′yənt) something that softens or soothes the skin, as a medical substance
15. **gibe** (jīb) to mock, jeer; a caustic remark
16. **ewer** (yōō′ər) a pitcher with a wide spout
17. **hirsute** (hûr′sōōt, hûr sōōt′) hairy; shaggy
18. **ogle** (ō′gəl) to look at amorously, flirtatiously, or impertinently
19. **ennui** (än wē′) weariness and discontent resulting from satiety or lack of interest; boredom
20. **canard** (kə närd′) a false story, report, or rumor, usually derogatory

WORDS OFTEN MISPRONOUNCED

abdomen	cello	clique	crosier	draught
aborigine	cerebral	colonel	crouton	drought
agile	chaise longue	compote	cuisine	duodenum
albino	chamois	conduit	dachshund	dyspepsia
apropos	chantey	consommé	debris	edifice
avoirdupois	chauffeur	corps	debut	egregious
balk	chic	corpuscle	devotee	emu
baroque	cholera	cortege	dinghy	entree
bayou	cinchona	cotillion	diphtheria	façade
brooch	clandestine	coup	diphthong	facile
buoy	clapboard	coxswain	discern	fiancé

frigate
fuchsia
fuselage
fusillade
gendarme
gentian
gestation
gibber
gladiolus
glazier
glower
gnu
gourmet
granary
guerrilla
guillotine
gunwale
habitué
harbinger
heifer
heinous
hirsute
holocaust
hosiery
iguana
imbroglio

inchoate
incognito
indigenous
interstice
inure
irascible
isosceles
isthmus
jodhpurs
joust
khaki
kohlrabi
labyrinth
lascivious
legerdemain
leisure
lemur
liaison
lien
lieu
lineage
lingerie
liturgy
llama
locale
logy

lorgnette
louver
lucid
lucre
machete
machination
mademoiselle
maestro
mannequin
marijuana
marquis
matinée
mauve
meliorate
mesa
mien
modiste
motif
murrain
myrrh
naïve
naphtha
niche
nihilism
nirvana
nom de plume

nonpareil
nougat
nuance
oblique
ocher
omniscient
onerous
onus
opiate
pachyderm
palsy
paprika
parfait
parquet
paschal
pecan
pellagra
petit
philistine
pimiento
plebeian
pneumatic
poignant
posthumous
precipice
premier

pristine
protégé
pueblo
purulent
quaff
qualm
quay
ragout
regime
renege
reveille
ricochet
rudiment
savoir-faire
short-lived
sleazy
soufflé
specious
suave
subpoena
tarpaulin
thyme
travail
usury
valance
worsted

USING PREFIXES

A prefix is a letter or group of letters placed at the beginning of a word to change its meaning. Later we will show you how knowing a handful of roots can help you figure out scores of words. Here we will begin by teaching you a few prefixes that can open the door to more powerful words. Here, for example, is a sampling of words that derive from the Latin prefix "circum-," meaning *around*.

Circum- Words

circumambulate   to walk around
circumference   the outer boundary of something

circumfluent   flowing around; encompassing
circumfuse   to surround, as with fluid
circumjacent   lying around; surrounding
circumlocution   a roundabout way of speaking
circumlunar   rotating about the moon
circumnavigate   to sail around
circumpolar   around or near one of the earth's poles
circumrotate   to rotate like a wheel
circumscribe   to encircle; mark off or delimit; restrict

LESSON 1. LATIN PREFIXES

Below are ten common Latin prefixes and their variations. Study the chart and examples. Then, to help you remember them, complete the self-tests that follow.

Prefix	Meaning	Variations	Examples
1. ad-	to, toward		adjoin, adverb
		a-	ascribe
		ac-	accede
		af-	affix
		ag-	aggregate
		at-	attempt
2. com-	with, together		commotion
		co-	cohabit, coworker
		col-	collaborate
		con-	concede, conduct
		cor-	correlate, correspond
3. de-	down		depress, deform
4. dis-	away, apart, opposite of		disagree, dishonest
		di-	divert
		dif-	diffuse

Prefix	Meaning	Variations	Examples
5. ex-	out		exchange, excavate
		e-	elongate, evaporate
		ec-	eccentric
		ef-	effluent, effuse
6. in-	in, into		inscribe, inhabit
		il-	illuminate
		im-	import, impart
		ir-	irradiate
7. in-	not		inflexible, indecent
		ig-	ignoble
		il-	illiterate, illegal
		im-	immodest, impatient
		ir-	irregular
8. pre-	before		premature
9. pro-	forward		proclaim
10. re-	again, back		recover, return

Test 1: Applying Latin Prefixes

Each of the following phrases contains an italicized word. Based on the meaning of its prefix, select the closest synonym. Circle the correct response.

1. *adjudicate* the matter
   a. sit in judgment on   b. throw out   c. argue   d. adjust
2. an *illicit* affair
   a. public   b. external   c. unlawful   d. renewed
3. an important *confederation*
   a. visit   b. return   c. church   d. alliance
4. *prolong* a speech
   a. shorten   b. dictate   c. extend   d. preserve
5. an *accredited* school
   a. second-rate   b. authorized   c. undesirable   d. separated
6. valuable *collateral*
   a. security   b. comments   c. opinions   d. animals
7. *ascribe* the phrase to
   a. write   b. scrawl   c. scribble   d. credit
8. *imbibe* too freely
   a. speak   b. drink   c. travel   d. laugh
9. *precursor* of greater things
   a. banner   b. detractor   c. forerunner   d. hope

10. *compress* metal
    a. help   b. coat   c. squeeze   d. buff

Answers: 1. a   2. c   3. d   4. c   5. b   6. a   7. d   8. b   9. c   10. c

Test 2: Defining Words

Based on the meaning of its prefix, define each of the following words.

1. accord _____
2. irradiate _____
3. predestination _____
4. reincarnation _____
5. convolution _____
6. invoke _____
7. cohabit _____
8. irrelevant _____
9. irreducible _____
10. excommunicate _____

Suggested Answers: 1. agreement   2. illuminate   3. fate; destiny   4. rebirth; resurrection   5. a rolled up or coiled condition   6. to request or call forth   7. to live together as husband and wife   8. not relevant   9. incapable of being reduced   10. to exclude from communion

LESSON 2. GREEK PREFIXES

Below are five common Greek prefixes and their variations. Study the chart and examples. Then, to help you remember the prefixes, complete the self-tests that follow.

Prefix	Meaning	Variations	Examples
1. a-	not, without		atypical, asexual
		an-	anarchy
2. apo-	off, away		apology, apostrophe
3. epi-	beside, upon		epigraph, epidermis
		ep-	epoch
4. para-	beside		paragraph, paraphrase
5. syn-	together, with		synthesis, synonym
		syl-	syllable, syllogism
		sym-	symbiosis, symphony

Test 1: Applying Greek Prefixes

Each of the following phrases contains an italicized word. Based on the meaning of its prefix, select the closest synonym. Circle your response.

Formed from:

1. a new *synagogue*
   a. combination   c. house of worship
   b. sentence   d. building
   Greek "syn-" + "-agogos," *bringer, gatherer*

2. the true *apogee*
   a. limit of endurance   c. closest point of an orbit
   b. insult   d. farthest point of an orbit
   Greek "apo-" + "ge," *earth*

3. the fifth annual *synod*
   a. church council   c. house-cleaning
   b. religious holiday   d. painting
   Greek "syn-" + "hodos," *way*

4. the sad *episode*
   a. incident   c. death
   b. anecdote   d. accident

Greek "epi-" + "hodos," *way*

5. the witty *epigram*
   a. television   c. saying
      show
   b. radio   d. song
      broadcast

Greek "epi-" + "gramma," *something written*

6. guilty of *apostasy*
   a. murder   c. an unnamed crime
   b. desertion   d. abandonment of religious faith

Greek "apo-" + "stasis," *standing*

7. *aseptic* ointment
   a. free from   c. expensive
      germs
   b. effective   d. greasy

Greek "a-" + "septos," *rotted*

8. clear and effective *syntax*
   a. treatment   c. speech
   b. word   d. magazine
      arrangement   article

Greek "syn-" + "taxis," *order*

9. injured *epidermis*
   a. leg ligament c. skin
   b. elbow   d. shinbone

Greek "epi-" + "dermis," *skin*

10. a cutting *epithet*
    a. weapon   c. knife
    b. funeral   d. descriptive
       oration   word

Greek "epi-" + "theton," *placed*

Answers: 1. c   2. d   3. a   4. a   5. c   6. d
7. a   8. b   9. c   10. d

Test 2: Matching Synonyms

Based on your knowledge of Greek prefixes, match each of the numbered words with the closest synonym. Write your answer in the space provided.

1. SYLLOGISM   a. running beside   ____
2. PARALEGAL   b. climax; highest
                        point   ____
3. ANONYMOUS   c. bottomless hole   ____
4. ANESTHETIC   d. one sent out;
                        messenger   ____
5. APOSTLE   e. logical argument   ____
6. PARALLEL   f. doubting God's
                        existence   ____
7. APOCRYPHAL   g. attorney's assistant ____
8. APOGEE   h. false; spurious   ____
9. AGNOSTIC   i. causing loss of
                        feeling   ____
10. ABYSS   j. nameless   ____

Answers: 1. e   2. g   3. j   4. i   5. d   6. a
7. h   8. b   9. f   10. c

LESSON 3. ANGLO-SAXON PREFIXES

Below are the five most common Anglo-Saxon prefixes and their variations. Study the chart and examples. Then, to help you remember the prefixes, complete the self-tests that follow.

Prefix	Meaning	Examples
a-	on, to, at, by	ablaze, afoot
be-	over, around	bespeak, besiege
mis-	wrong, badly	mistake, misspell
over-	beyond, above	overreach, overawe
un-	not	unwilling, unethical

Test 1: Applying Anglo-Saxon Prefixes

Each of the following phrases contains an italicized word. Based on the meaning of its prefix, select the closest synonym. Circle your response.

1. a *miscarriage* of justice
   a. instance   b. hero   c. failure   d. example
2. *beseech* movingly
   a. implore   b. search   c. evoke   d. refuse
3. walking two *abreast*
   a. together   b. side by side   c. back to back
   d. in tandem
4. *bestowed* on us
   a. hurled   b. smashed   c. dependent
   d. presented
5. an unfortunate *misalliance*
   a. treaty   b. conversation   c. bad deal
   d. improper marriage
6. an *overwrought* patient
   a. highly emotional   b. extremely ill   c. very
   restrained   d. overmedicated
7. an *unkempt* look
   a. funny   b. messy   c. ugly   d. pretty

8. an embarrassing *miscue*
   a. joke   b. anecdote   c. step   d. error
9. *bedaub* with clay
   a. sculpt   b. present   c. smear   d. create
10. *bemoan* his situation
    a. celebrate   b. share   c. lament   d. hide

Answers: 1. c   2. a   3. b   4. d   5. d   6. a
7. b   8. d   9. c   10. c

Test 2: Matching Synonyms

Based on your knowledge of Anglo-Saxon prefixes, match each of the numbered words with the closest synonym. Write your answer in the space provided.

1. UNFEIGNED	a. conquer	____
2. MISBEGOTTEN	b. right on the mark	____
3. BEGUILE	c. too fervent	____
4. MISCARRIAGE	d. envy; resent	____
5. BEMUSE	e. sincere; genuine	____
6. MISHAP	f. accident	____
7. OVERCOME	g. illegitimate	____
8. BEGRUDGE	h. mislead	____
9. UNERRING	i. bewilder	____
10. OVERZEALOUS	j. spontaneous abortion	____

Answers: 1. e   2. g   3. h   4. j   5. i   6. f
7. a   8. d   9. b   10. c

USING SUFFIXES

A suffix is a letter or group of letters placed at the end of a word to change its grammatical function, tense, or meaning. Suffixes can be used to create a verb from a noun or adjective or an adjective from a verb, for example. They can change a word's tense as well; "-ed" can make a present-tense verb into a past participle, for instance. They can even change a word's meaning; the suffix "-ette," for example, can make a word into its diminutive: "kitchen" into "kitchenette."

Just as recognizing a small number of prefixes can help you figure out many unfamiliar words, so knowing a few common suffixes can help you build a more powerful vocabulary.

LESSON 1. TEN POWERFUL SUFFIXES

Below are ten useful suffixes. Read through the chart and examples. To reinforce your study, complete the self-tests that follow.

Suffix	Meaning	Variations	Examples	Suffix	Meaning	Variations	Examples
1. -ate	to make		alienate, regulate	6. -er	one that does or deals with		teacher
	marked by		passionate, affectionate			-ar	scholar
						-ier	furrier
2. -en	to make		weaken, moisten			-or	bettor
3. -ism	the quality or practice of		absolutism, baptism	7. -an	one that does or deals with		comedian, historian
4. -ation	the act or condition of		allegation, affirmation	8. -al	resembling or pertaining to		natural, accidental
		-ition	recognition	9. -ous	full of		perilous
		-tion	commotion			-ious	gracious, vicious
5. -ty	the state of		modesty	10. -able	capable of being		lovable, affordable
		-ity	security worker,			-ible	reversible

Test 1: Applying Suffixes

Each of the following phrases contains an italicized word. Based on the meaning of its suffix, select the closest synonym. Circle your response.

1. *combustible* rubbish
   a. unbreakable b. able to burst c. affordable
   d. flammable

2. *pastoral* scenes
   a. clerical b. attractive c. rural d. homely

3. a *partisan* of the rebellion
   a. flag b. supporter c. sign d. result

4. a *palatial* home
   a. magnificent b. modest c. formal
   d. enjoyable

5. the *collegiate* atmosphere
   a. churchlike b. friendly c. cooperative
   d. academic

6. *assiduity* in studies
   a. alacrity b. cleverness c. diligence
   d. laziness

7. a country of *pedestrians*
   a. scholars b. walkers c. shopkeepers
   d. students

8. an *abstemious* eater
   a. aloof b. idle c. absent-minded
   d. sparing

9. *perilous* practices
   a. commonplace b. rare c. dangerous
   d. useless

10. *deleterious* effects
    a. good b. neutral c. bad d. delightful

Answers: 1. d 2. c 3. b 4. a 5. d 6. c
7. b 8. d 9. c 10. c

Test 2: Matching Synonyms

Based on your knowledge of suffixes, match each of the numbered words with the closest synonym. If in doubt, refer to the root word that follows each numbered word.

1. CULPABLE
   (Root word: Latin "culpa," *blame*)

2. PARITY
   (Root word: Latin "par," *equal*)

3. AMENABLE
   (Root word: French "amener," *to lead to*)

4. MENDACIOUS
   (Root word: Latin "mendax," *dishonest*)

5. SEMPITERNAL
   (Root word: Latin "semper," *always*)

6. NIHILISM
   (Root word: Latin "nihil," *nothing*)

7. ATAVISM
   (Root word: Latin "atavus," *remote*)

8. FEALTY
   (Root word: French "fealté," *fidelity*)

9. CASTIGATE
   (Root word: Latin "castus," *chaste*)

10. NOXIOUS
    (Root word: Latin "noxa," *harm*)

a. blameworthy

b. injurious

c. everlasting

d. reversion to type

e. equality

f. to chastise; censure

g. willing

h. total rejection of law

i. lying; false

j. faithfulness

Answers: 1. a 2. e 3. g 4. i 5. c 6. h
7. d 8. j 9. f 10. b

LESSON 2. TEN ADDITIONAL POWERFUL SUFFIXES

The following ten suffixes will help you understand countless additional words. After you read through the suffixes and their definitions, complete the two self-tests at the end of the lesson.

Suffix	Meaning	Examples	Suffix	Meaning	Examples
1. -esque	in the manner of; like	Lincolnesque	7. -less	without	guiltless; helpless
2. -aceous	resembling or having	carbonaceous	8. -ship	occupation or skill; condition of being	authorship, penmanship; friendship
3. -ic	associated with	democratic			
4. -age	act or process of; quantity or measure	marriage coverage; footage,	9. -ian	a person who is, does, or participates in	comedian
5. -itis	inflammation	tonsillitis	10. -ferous	bearing or conveying	odoriferous
6. -ish	similar to; like a	foolish; babyish			

Test 1: Matching Synonyms

Based on your knowledge of suffixes, match each of the numbered words with its closest synonym. Write your answer in the space provided.

1. WASPISH	a. inattentive, sloppy	____
2. FELLOWSHIP	b. egotistic	____
3. ANGELIC	c. distance	____
4. MILEAGE	d. huge	____
5. PICTURESQUE	e. eternal	____
6. CURVACEOUS	f. irritable	____
7. TITANIC	g. voluptuous	____
8. CARELESS	h. companionship	____
9. SELFISH	i. innocent	____
10. TIMELESS	j. colorful	____

Answers: 1. f 2. h 3. i 4. c 5. j 6. g
7. d 8. a 9. b 10. e

Test 2: Applying Suffixes

Each of the following phrases contains an italicized word. Based on the meaning of its suffix, select the closest synonym. If in doubt, refer to the root word listed in the right-hand column. Circle your response.

Root Word

1. *auriferous* mineral
   a. containing gold   b. extremely hard   c. having an odor   d. very common
   Latin "aurum," gold

2. *conical* shape
   a. humorous; amusing   b. like a cone   c. spherical   d. rigid
   Greek "konos," cone

Root Word

3. suffering from *carditis*
   a. eye infection   b. a tin ear   c. inflammation of the heart   d. stiff joints
   Greek "kardia," heart

4. graceful *Romanesque*
   a. architectural style   b. departure   c. essay   d. apology

5. *olivaceous* color
   a. oily   b. deep green   c. faded   d. attractive

6. frightful *carnage*
   a. journey   b. slaughter   c. scene   d. sensuality
   Latin "carnis," flesh

7. *satanic* nature
   a. evil   b. cheerful   c. shiny   d. generous

8. admirable *craftsmanship*
   a. display   b. individual   c. shop   d. artfulness

9. *veracious* remarks
   a. vivid   b. vicious   c. windy   d. truthful
   Latin "verus," true

10. painful *appendicitis*
    a. news   b. surgery   c. inflammation of the appendix   d. removal of the appendix

Answers: 1. a   2. b   3. c   4. a   5. b   6. b
7. a   8. d   9. d   10. c

ROOT POWER I

LATIN AND GREEK ROOTS

One of the quickest and most effective ways to improve your vocabulary is by learning to recognize the most common Latin and Greek roots, since any one of them can help you define a number of English words. Whenever you come upon an unfamiliar word, first check to see if it has a recognizable root. If you know that the Latin root "ami," for example, means *like* or *love,* you can easily figure out that "amiable" means *pleasant,*

friendly and "amorous" means *loving.* Even if you cannot define a word exactly, recognizing the root will still give you a general idea of the word's meaning. Remembering that the Greek root "geo" means *earth* would certainly help you define "geophysics" as *the physics of the earth,* but it also might help you figure out that "geocentric" has to do with the center of the earth or with the earth as a center. Begin by studying the following lists of common Latin and Greek roots and representative words.

LESSON 1. COMMON LATIN ROOTS

Root	Meaning	Example	Definition	Root	Meaning	Example	Definition
ag	act	agent	representative	port	carry	portable	movable
cad, cas	fall	cadence	rhythmic flow	rupt	break	abrupt	sudden, quick
cap, cept	take, hold	receptacle	container	scrib, script	write	inscription	engraving, writing
ced, cess	go	recessive	tending to go back	sect	cut	dissect	cut apart
cid, cis	kill, cut	incision	cut, gash	sent, sens	feel	sensitive	tender
clud, clus	shut	seclusion	separation from others	sequ, secut	follow	sequel	result
				spect	look	prospect	outlook, expectation
cred	believe	credible	believable				
cur(r), curs	run	concur	agree (i.e., run together)	sta, stat	stand	stable	fixed, firm
				tang, tact	touch	tactile	tangible
fer	bear	odoriferous	yielding an odor	termin	end	terminate	abolish, end
				tract	pull, draw	tractor	vehicle that pulls
her, hes	cling	adhere	cling, stick				
ject	throw	projection	jutting out, protrusion	ven, vent	come	convene	assemble (i.e., come together)
leg, lect	read	legible	easily readable	vert, vers	turn	invert	overturn
pel(l), puls	drive	repulse	repel (i.e., drive back)	vid, vis	see	provident	having foresight
pon, posit	put	postpone	defer	vinc, vict	conquer	invincible	unconquerable
				volv, volut	roll, turn	evolve	develop

Test 1: Applying Roots

Each of the following phrases contains an italicized word. Based on the meaning of the root, select the closest synonym. Circle your response.

1. a *captive* animal
   a. confined b. wild c. charming
   d. domestic
2. an *inverted* glass
   a. broken b. upside-down c. returned
   d. drunk from
3. an *abrupt* stop
   a. slow b. bad c. sudden d. harmful
4. a disappointing *sequel*
   a. television show b. beginning c. movie
   d. follow-up
5. *terminate* the relationship
   a. doubt b. intensify c. begin d. finish
6. an *incredible* story
   a. outlandish b. unbelievable c. foolish
   d. upsetting
7. a *recessive* trait
   a. dominant b. receding c. hurtful
   d. missing
8. *illegible* writing
   a. unreadable b. graceful c. distinct
   d. large
9. a thorough *dissection*
   a. cutting apart b. conference c. discussion
   d. putting together
10. an *unstable* relationship
    a. new b. unsteady c. one-sided
    d. unreliable
11. an *odoriferous* cheese
    a. commonplace b. brightly colored
    c. malodorous d. faded

12. an *invincible* warrior
    a. huge b. foreign c. defeated
    d. unbeatable
13. the *advent* of summer
    a. departure b. middle c. arrival
    d. complaint
14. a *provident* move
    a. prosperous b. injudicious c. prudent
    d. hurtful
15. the top-secret *projectile*
    a. missile b. project c. plan d. meeting

Answers: 1. a 2. b 3. c 4. d 5. d 6. b
7. b 8. a 9. a 10. b 11. c 12. d 13. c
14. c 15. a

Test 2: True/False

In the space provided, write T if the definition of the numbered word is true or F if it is false.

		T or F
1. ADHERE	cling	——
2. CADAVER	cavort	——
3. EVOLVE	develop	——
4. INCISION	cut	——
5. CONCURRENT	disjointed	——
6. RECLUSE	vivacious person	——
7. INSCRIPTION	story	——
8. AGENT	deputy	——
9. TACTILE	tangible	——
10. REPULSE	repel	——

Answers: 1. T 2. F 3. T 4. T 5. F 6. F
7. F 8. T 9. T 10. T

LESSON 2. COMMON GREEK ROOTS

Root	Meaning	Example	Definition
aster, astro	star	asterisk	star-shaped mark
chrom	color	chromatic	pertaining to color
chron, chrono	time	synchronize	occur simultaneously
cosmo	world	cosmopolitan	citizen of the world
dem	people	democracy	government by the people
meter	measure	thermometer	instrument that measures temperature
onym	name, word	pseudonym	a fictitious name
path	feeling	apathy	absence of feeling

Root	Meaning	Example	Definition
phob	fear	claustrophobia	fear of enclosed places
phon	sound	cacophony	harsh, discordant sound
psycho	mind	psychology	science of the mind
soph	wisdom	sophistry	subtle, tricky reasoning

Test 1: True/False

In the space provided, write T if the definition of the numbered word is true or F if it is false.

		T or F
1. EPIDEMIC	plague	___
2. HOMONYM	same-sounding name	___
3. CLAUSTROPHOBIA	fear of dogs	___
4. CACOPHONY	dissonance	___
5. APATHY	enthusiasm	___
6. ACCELEROMETER	instrument for measuring acceleration	___
7. SYNCHRONIZE	squabble	___
8. COSMOPOLITAN	international	___
9. SOPHISM	specious argument	___
10. CHROMATIC	crisp	___

Answers: 1. T   2. T   3. F   4. T   5. F   6. T
7. F   8. T   9. T   10. F

Test 2: Applying Greek Roots

Based on the meaning of its root, define each of the following words. If in doubt, check the suggested answers.

1. asteroid _____
2. chromatics _____
3. cosmos _____
4. anonymous _____
5. Anglophobia _____
6. cosmography _____
7. synchronous _____
8. pathetic _____
9. pedometer _____
10. democracy _____
11. phonograph _____
12. demographics _____
13. psychotic _____
14. sophisticated _____
15. cognition _____

Suggested Answers: 1. a small mass that orbits the sun   2. the science of colors   3. universe
4. without any name acknowledged   5. fear of things English   6. the study of the structure of the universe   7. coinciding in time   8. evoking feelings of pity   9. an instrument that measures distance covered in walking   10. government by the people   11. a sound-reproducing machine
12. the statistical data of a population   13. a person who is mentally ill   14. worldly-wise
15. act or fact of knowing

LESSON 3. "OTHER PLACES, OTHER FACES": *AL, ALL, ALTER*

An "alibi" is a defense by an accused person who claims to have been elsewhere at the time the offense was committed. The word comes from the Latin root "al," meaning *other*. Outside of law, an alibi often means an excuse, especially to avoid blame.

The Latin roots "al" and "alter," as well as the related Greek root "all" or "allo," all mean *other* or *another,* and form the basis of a number of English words. Below are ten such words. After you study the definitions and practice the pronunciations, complete the quizzes.

1. **alien** (āl′yən, ā′lē ən) a person born in and owing allegiance to a country other than the one in which he or she lives; a nonterrestrial being; foreign or strange.

   Although my neighbor is not an American citizen, he has lived in this country so long he no longer thinks of himself as an alien.

2. **allegory** (al′ə gôr′ē) a representation of an abstract meaning through concrete or material forms; figurative treatment of one subject under the guise of another.

   Nathaniel Hawthorne's short story "Young Goodman Brown" can be read as an allegory of an average person's encounter with sin and temptation.

3. **alias** (ā′lē əs) a false or assumed name, especially as used by a criminal. From the Latin word meaning *otherwise*.

   Many criminals use an alias with the same initials as their real name; Clyde Griffith, for example, took as his alias "Chester Gillett."

4. **alienate** (āl′yə nāt′, ā′lē ə-) to make indifferent or hostile. From Latin "alienare," *to make another*.

   Unkempt yards alienate prospective home buyers.

5. **altruism** (al′trōō iz′əm) unselfish concern for the welfare of others.

   Devotion to the poor, sick, and unfortunate of the world shows a person's altruism.

6. **altercation** (ôl′tər kā′shən) a heated or angry dispute; noisy argument or controversy. From Latin "altercari," *to quarrel with another*.

   The collision resulted in an altercation between the two drivers.

7. **inalienable** (in āl′yə nə bəl, -ā′lē ə-) not transferable to another; incapable of being repudiated.

   Freedom of speech is the inalienable right of every American citizen.

8. **allograft** (al′ə graft′) tissue grafted or transplanted to another member of the same species.

Allografts of vital organs have saved many lives.

9. **allogamy** (ə log′ə mē) cross-fertilization in plants. From "allo-," *other* + "-gamy," *pollination.*

   To ensure allogamy, the farmer set out many different plants close together.

10. **alter ego** (ôl′tər ē′gō) another self; an inseparable friend.

    Superman's alter ego, the mild-mannered Clark Kent, is a reporter for the *Daily Planet.*

Test 1: Matching Synonyms

Match each of the numbered words with its closest synonym. Write your answer in the space provided.

1. ALIEN	a. absolute	___
2. ALIAS	b. cross-fertilization	___
3. ALTER EGO	c. selflessness, kindness	___
4. ALLOGAMY	d. best friend	___
5. ALLEGORY	e. another name	___
6. INALIENABLE	f. transplant	___
7. ALTRUISM	g. contention, quarrel	___
8. ALIENATE	h. symbolic narrative	___
9. ALLOGRAFT	i. stranger, outcast	___
10. ALTERCATION	j. turn away, estrange	___

Answers: 1. i 2. e 3. d 4. b 5. h 6. a 7. c 8. j 9. f 10. g

Test 2: True/False

In the space provided, write T if the definition of the numbered word is true or F if it is false.

		T or F
1. ALIEN	foreign	___
2. ALIAS	excuse	___
3. ALTER EGO	egotist	___
4. ALLOGAMY	multiple marriage	___
5. ALLEGORY	moral story	___
6. INALIENABLE	without basis in fact	___
7. ALTRUISM	unselfishness	___
8. ALIENATE	estrange	___
9. ALLOGRAFT	illegal money	___
10. ALTERCATION	dispute	___

Answers: 1. T 2. F 3. F 4. F 5. T 6. F 7. T 8. T 9. F 10. T

LESSON 4. "THE BREATH OF LIFE": *ANIMA*

Ancient peoples connected the soul with the breath. They saw that when people died they stopped breathing, and they believed that the soul left the body at the same time. They also believed that when people sneezed, the soul left the body for a moment, so they muttered a hasty blessing to ensure that the soul would return quickly to its rightful place. The Latin root for air or breath, "anima," also means *soul, spirit,* or *mind,* reflecting this belief in a connection between life and breathing. Many English words come from this root.

Below are ten words linked to "anima." After you study the definitions and practice the pronunciations, complete the quizzes.

1. **animation** (an′ə mā′shən) liveliness or vivacity; the act or an instance of animating or enlivening. From Latin "animare," *to give life to.*

   In speech class we learned how to talk with animation to make our presentations more interesting.

2. **animadversion** (an′ə mad vûr′zhən, -shən) criticism; censure. From Latin "animus," *mind, spirit* + "adversio," *attention, warning.*

   The critic's animadversion on the subject of TV shows revealed his bias against popular culture.

3. **animus** (an′ə məs) hostile feeling or attitude.

   The jury's animus toward the defendant was obvious from the jurors' stony faces and stiff posture.

4. **pusillanimous** (pyo͞o′sə lan′ə məs) lacking courage or resolution; cowardly. From Latin "pusillus," *very small* + "animus," *spirit.*

   He was so pusillanimous that he wouldn't even run away from a bully.

5. **unanimity** (yo͞o′nə nim′i tē) the state or quality of being in complete agreement; undivided opinion or a consensus. From Latin "unus," *one* + "animus," *mind, spirit.*

   The school board's unanimity on the controversial issue of sex education was all the more surprising in light of their well-known individual differences.

6. **animate** (an′ə māt′) to give life or liveliness to; alive.

   Her presence animated the otherwise dull party.

7. **animalcule** (an′ə mal′kyo͞ol) a minute or microscopic organism. From Latin "animalis," *living, animal* + "-culum," *tiny thing.*

   The animalcule could not be seen with the naked eye.

8. **magnanimous** (mag nan′ə məs) generous in

forgiving an insult or injury; free from petty resentfulness. From Latin "magnus," *large, great* + "animus," *soul.*

The governor's magnanimous pardon of the offender showed his liberal nature.

9. **inanimate** (in an'ə mit) not alive or lively; lifeless.

Pinocchio was inanimate, a puppet carved from a block of wood.

10. **animism** (an'ə miz'əm) the belief that natural objects, natural phenomena, and the universe itself possess souls or consciousness.

Their belief in animism drew them to the woods, where they felt more in touch with nature's spirit.

Test 1: Matching Synonyms

Match each of the numbered words with the closest synonym. Write your answer in the space provided.

1. ANIMADVERSION	a. enliven	____
2. ANIMUS	b. harmony	____
3. PUSILLANIMOUS	c. generous	____
4. UNANIMITY	d. cowardly	____
5. ANIMATE	e. hostility	____
6. ANIMALCULE	f. spirit, zest	____
7. MAGNANIMOUS	g. a censorious remark	____
8. INANIMATE	h. a belief in spirits	____
9. ANIMATION	i. a minute organism	____
10. ANIMISM	j. inert	____

Answers: 1. g 2. e 3. d 4. b 5. a 6. i
7. c 8. j 9. f 10. h

Test 2: True/False

In the space provided, write T if the definition of the numbered word is true or F if it is false.

		T or F
1. ANIMADVERSION	praise	____
2. ANIMUS	hostility	____
3. PUSILLANIMOUS	cowardly	____
4. UNANIMITY	total agreement	____
5. ANIMATE	deaden	____
6. ANIMALCULE	small soul	____
7. MAGNANIMOUS	generous	____
8. INANIMATE	living	____
9. ANIMATION	liveliness	____
10. ANIMISM	love of animals	____

Answers: 1. F 2. T 3. T 4. T 5. F 6. F
7. T 8. F 9. T 10. F

LESSON 5. "THE YEAR OF WONDERS": *ANN, ENN*

While certain years are celebrated for great wonders, the first year that was actually designated "The Year of Wonders," *Annus Mirabilis,* was 1666. The English poet, dramatist, and critic John Dryden (1631–1700) enshrined that year as "Annus Mirabilis" in his poem of the same name, which commemorated the English victory over the Dutch and the Great Fire of London. "Annus," meaning *year,* comes from the Latin root "ann," a source of many useful English words. The same root is also written "enn" in the middle of a word.

Below are ten words drawn from this root. After you look over the definitions and practice the pronunciations, complete the quizzes that follow.

1. **per annum** (pər an'əm) by the year; yearly.

The firm promised to bill the additional interest charges per annum, the invoice to arrive every January.

2. **annual** (an' yoo əl) of, for, or pertaining to a year; yearly.

The annual enrollment in the high school has increased sharply since the new housing was built.

3. **anniversary** (an'ə vûr'sə rē) the yearly recurrence of the date of a past event, especially the date of a wedding. From Latin "ann(i)," *year* + "vers(us)," *turned* + adjectival suffix "-ary."

For their twenty-fifth wedding anniversary, the happy couple decided to have dinner at the restaurant where they first met.

4. **biennial** (bī en'ē əl) happening every two years; lasting for two years. From Latin "bi-," *two* + root "enn" + adjectival suffix "-ial."

My flowering fig tree has a biennial cycle; it blooms every two years.

5. **triennial** (trī en'ē əl) occurring every three years; lasting three years. From Latin "tri-," *three* + root "enn" + adjectival suffix "-ial."

The university has set up a triennial cycle of promotions to review candidates for advancement.

6. **decennial** (di sen'ē əl) of or for ten years; occurring every ten years. From Latin "dec-(em)," *ten* + root "enn" + adjectival suffix "-ial."

Every ten years, the PTA holds its decennial meeting in the state capital.

7. **centennial** (sen ten'ē əl) of or pertaining to a period of one hundred years; recurring once

every hundred years. From Latin "cent(um)," *hundred* + root "enn" + adjectival suffix "-ial."

To celebrate the railroad's centennial anniversary, the town's historical society restored the run-down station so it looked exactly as it did when it was built a hundred years ago.

8. **bicentennial** (bī'sen ten'ē əl) pertaining to or in honor of a two-hundredth anniversary; consisting of or lasting two hundred years.

To advertise its bicentennial festivities next year, the town has adopted the slogan "Celebrating Two Hundred Years of Progress."

9. **millennium** (mi len'ē əm) a period of one thousand years. From Latin "mille," *thousand* + root "enn" + noun suffix "-ium."

Technology advances so rapidly now that we can scarcely imagine what life will be like in the next millennium.

10. **annuity** (ə nōō' i tē, ə nyōō'-) a specified income payable each year or at stated intervals in consideration of a premium paid. From Latin "ann(uus)," *yearly* + noun suffix "-ity."

The annuity from her late husband's life-insurance policy was barely adequate for the poor widow's needs.

Test 1: Matching Synonyms

Select the best definition for each numbered word. Write your answer in the space provided.

1. BICENTENNIAL	a. every ten years	___
2. ANNIVERSARY	b. every two years	___
3. DECENNIAL	c. every two hundred years	___
4. MILLENNIUM	d. every three years	___
5. PER ANNUM	e. one thousand years	___
6. CENTENNIAL	f. fixed payment	___
7. ANNUITY	g. yearly recurrence of a date	___
8. TRIENNIAL	h. every hundred years	___
9. BIENNIAL	i. by the year	___
10. ANNUAL	j. yearly	___

Answers: 1. c 2. g 3. a 4. e 5. i 6. h
7. f 8. d 9. b 10. j

Test 2: True/False

In the space provided, write T if the definition of the numbered word is true or F if it is false.

		T or F
1. ANNUITY	every two hundred years	___
2. BICENTENNIAL	every other year	___
3. MILLENNIUM	one thousand years	___
4. ANNUAL	fixed amount of money	___
5. CENTENNIAL	every hundred years	___
6. TRIENNIAL	every three years	___
7. PER ANNUM	by order	___
8. BIENNIAL	every third year	___
9. DECENNIAL	every thousand years	___
10. ANNIVERSARY	yearly event	___

Answers: 1. F 2. F 3. T 4. F 5. T 6. T
7. F 8. F 9. F 10. T

LESSON 6. "MAN OF THE WORLD": *ANTHROPO*

In the early twentieth century, Rudolph Steiner developed an esoteric system of knowledge he called "anthroposophy." Steiner developed the word from the Greek roots "anthropo," meaning *man* or *human,* and "soph," meaning *wisdom.* He defined his philosophy as "the knowledge of the spiritual human being . . . and of everything which the spirit man can perceive in the spiritual world."

We've taken several more words from "anthropo"; below are six of them. After you look over the definitions and practice the pronunciations, complete the quizzes that follow.

1. **anthropoid** (an'thrə poid') resembling humans.
   The child was fascinated by the anthropoid ape on display in the natural history museum.
2. **anthropomorphism** (an'thrə pə môr'fizəm) the ascription of human form or attributes to a being or thing not human, such as a deity.
   To speak of the "cruel, crawling foam" is an example of anthropomorphism, for the sea is not cruel.
3. **misanthrope** (mis'ən thrōp', miz'-) a hater of humankind. From Greek "mis(o)," *hate* + "anthropos," *man.*
   In *Gulliver's Travels,* the great misanthrope Jonathan Swift depicts human beings as monstrous savages.
4. **philanthropy** (fi lan'thrə pē) good works; affection for humankind, especially as manifested in donations, as of money, to needy persons or to socially useful purposes. From Greek "phil(o)," *loving* + "anthropos," *man.*
   Thanks to the philanthropy of a wealthy patron, the new hospital wing was fully stocked with the latest equipment.
5. **anthropology** (an'thrə pol'ə jē) the science that deals with the origins, physical and cultural development, racial characteristics, and social customs and beliefs of humankind.

After the student completed the anthropology course, she visited some of the exotic cultures she had read about.

6. **anthropocentric** (an'thrə pō sen'trik) regarding humans as the central fact of the universe.

Philosophy that views and interprets the universe in terms of human experience and values is anthropocentric.

Test 1: Matching Synonyms

Select the best definition for each numbered word. Write your answer in the space provided.

1. ANTHROPOLOGY
2. PHILANTHROPY
3. ANTHROPOCENTRIC

a. believing that humans are the center of the universe ____
b. one who dislikes people ____
c. science of humankind's origins, beliefs, and customs ____

4. ANTHROPOID
5. ANTHROPOMORPHISM
6. MISANTHROPE

d. personification of inanimate things ____
e. doing good for people ____
f. humanlike ____

Answers: 1. c 2. e 3. a 4. f 5. d 6. b

Test 2: True/False

In the space provided, write T if the definition of the numbered word is true or F if it is false.

		T or F
1. MISANTHROPE	cynic	____
2. PHILANTHROPY	goodwill to humankind	____
3. ANTHROPOMORPHISM	insecurity	____
4. ANTHROPOCENTRIC	unselfish	____
5. ANTHROPOLOGY	science of flowers	____
6. ANTHROPOID	resembling humans	____

Answers: 1. F 2. T 3. F 4. F 5. F 6. T

Lesson 7. "Know Thyself": *gno*

One of the fascinating things about the study of words is the discovery of close relationships between seemingly unrelated words. Because English draws its vocabulary from many sources, it often appropriates foreign words that ultimately derive from the same source as a native English word. A good example is our word "know," which has its exact equivalent in the Latin and Greek root "gno." Here are eight words from this root. First read through the pronunciations, definitions, and examples. Then complete the quizzes that follow.

1. **cognizant** (kog'nə zənt, kon'ə-) aware. From Latin "cognoscere," *to come to know* ("co-," *together* + "gnoscere," *to know*).

He was fully cognizant of the difficulty of the mission.

2. **incognito** (in'kog nē'tō, in kog'ni tō') with one's identity concealed, as under an assumed name. From Latin "incognitus," *not known* ("in-," *not* + "cognitus," *known*).

The officer from naval intelligence always traveled incognito to avoid any problems with security.

3. **prognosticate** (prog nos'ti kāt') to forecast from present indications. From Greek "prognostikos," *knowing beforehand* ("pro-," *before* + "(gi)gno(skein)," *to know*).

The fortuneteller was able to prognosticate with the help of her tea leaves, crystal ball, and a good deal of inside information about her client.

4. **diagnostician** (di'əg no stish'ən) an expert in determining the nature of diseases. From Greek "diagnosis," *determination* (of a disease) ("dia-," *through* + "(gi)gno(skein)," *to know*).

The diagnostician was able to allay her patient's fears after the x-ray showed that he had suffered only a sprain, not a break.

5. **cognoscenti** (kon'yə shen'tē, kog'nə-) well-informed persons, especially in a particular field, as in the arts. From Italian, ultimately derived from Latin "co-," *together* + "gnoscere," *to know.*

Although the exhibit had only been open one week, the cognoscenti were already proclaiming it the show of the decade.

6. **gnostic** (nos'tik) pertaining to knowledge, especially to the esoteric knowledge taught by an early Christian mystical sect. From Greek "gnostikos," *knowing,* from the root of "(gi)gno(skein)," *to know.*

The gnostic view that everything is knowable is opposed by the agnostic view.

7. **ignoramus** (ig'nə rā'məs, -ram'əs) an extremely uninformed person. From the Latin word mean-

ing *we don't know,* derived from "ignorare," *to not know* ("i(-n-)," *not* + the root of "gno(scere)," *to come to know*).

Only an ignoramus would insist that the earth is flat.

8. **cognition** (kog nish′ən) the act or process of knowing; perception. From Latin "cognitio," derived from "cognoscere," *to come to know* ("co-," *together* + "gnoscere," *to know*).

Cognition is impaired by narcotic drugs.

Test 1: True/False

In the space provided, write T if the definition of the numbered word is true or F if it is false.

		T or F
1. GNOSTIC	knowing	_____
2. INCOGNITO	disguised	_____
3. PROGNOSTICATE	curse	_____
4. IGNORAMUS	ignorant person	_____
5. COGNOSCENTI	aromatic herb	_____
6. COGNITION	perception	_____
7. DIAGNOSTICIAN	expert mechanic	_____
8. COGNIZANT	conscious	_____

Test 2: Defining Words

Define each of the following words.

1. ignoramus _____
2. cognoscenti _____
3. cognition _____
4. incognito _____
5. gnostic _____
6. prognosticate _____
7. diagnostician _____
8. cognizant _____

LESSON 8. "RULERS AND LEADERS": *ARCH*

In Christian theology, Michael is given the title of "archangel," principal angel and primary opponent of Satan and his horde. The Greek root "arch," meaning *chief, first; rule* or *ruler,* is the basis of a number of important and useful words.

Below are ten words drawn from this root. Read the definitions and practice the pronunciations. Then study the sample sentences and see if you can use the words in sentences of your own.

1. **archenemy** (ärch′en′ə mē) a chief enemy; Satan.

    In Christian theology, Satan is the archenemy.

2. **patriarch** (pā′trē ärk′) the male head of a family or tribe. From Greek "patria," *family* + "-arches," *head, chief.*

    When we gathered for Thanksgiving dinner, our great-grandfather, the family patriarch, always sat at the head of the table.

3. **anarchy** (an′ər kē) society without rule or government; lawlessness; disorder; confusion; chaos. From Greek "an-," *not* + "arch(os)," *rule, ruler.*

    The king's assassination led to anarchy throughout the country.

4. **hierarchy** (hī′ə rär′kē, hī′rär-) any system of persons or things ranked one above another;

formerly, rule by church leaders, especially a high priest. From Greek "hieros," *sacred* + "arch(os)," *rule, ruler.*

    The new office hierarchy ranks assistant vice presidents over directors.

5. **monarchy** (mon′ər kē) rule or government by a king, queen, emperor, or empress. From Greek "mon(o)-," *one* + "arch(os)," *rule, ruler.*

    The French Revolution ended with the overthrow of the monarchy.

6. **oligarchy** (ol′i gär′kē) rule or government by a few persons. From Greek "oligos," *few* + "arch(os)," *rule, ruler.*

    After the revolution, an oligarchy of army officers ruled the newly liberated country.

7. **archbishop** (ärch′bish′əp) a bishop of the highest rank; chief bishop.

    The archbishop meets with the bishops from his area once a month to discuss their concerns.

8. **matriarch** (mā′trē ärk′) the female head of a family or tribe. From Greek "matri-," *mother* + "-arches," *head, chief.*

    The younger members of the clan usually seek out Grandma Josie, the family matriarch, for advice.

9. **archetype** (är′ki tīp′) the original pattern or model after which a thing is made; prototype.

From Greek "arch(e)-," *first, original* + "typos," *mold, type.*

Odysseus is the archetype for James Joyce's Leopold Bloom in his novel *Ulysses.*

10. **archaic** (är kā′ik) marked by the characteristics of an earlier period; antiquated. From Greek "arch(aios)," *old, early, first.*

With the advent of the pocket calculator, the slide rule has become archaic.

Test 1: Matching Synonyms

Select the best synonym for each of the italicized words. Circle your response.

1. the *archbishop* of Canterbury
   a. oldest bishop   b. youngest bishop
   c. highest-ranking bishop   d. recently appointed bishop
2. a strong *monarchy*
   a. government by a president   b. government by a consortium   c. government by the proletariat   d. government by a king or queen
3. an *archaic* device
   a. old-fashioned   b. complicated
   c. expensive   d. useful
4. a wise *patriarch*
   a. old woman   b. general   c. revolutionary
   d. male family head
5. the literary and social *archetype*
   a. concern   b. exhibition   c. prototype
   d. major problem
6. a state of *anarchy*
   a. hopefulness   b. lawlessness   c. strict order
   d. female control

7. a brutal *archenemy*
   a. less powerful enemy   b. chief enemy
   c. strict enemy   d. Gabriel
8. the iron-handed *oligarchy*
   a. government by few   b. communist state
   c. democracy   d. unstable government
9. a highly respected *matriarch*
   a. confidant   b. duke   c. male leader
   d. female family head
10. the strict governmental *hierarchy*
    a. leadership   b. promotions   c. system of ranking   d. discipline

Answers: 1. c   2. d   3. a   4. d   5. c   6. b
7. b   8. a   9. d   10. c

Test 2: True/False

In the space provided, write T if the synonym or definition of the numbered word is true or F if it is false.

			T or F
1.	PATRIARCH	male family head	____
2.	ARCHETYPE	model	____
3.	ARCHENEMY	chief enemy	____
4.	MONARCHY	royal government	____
5.	OLIGARCHY	chaos	____
6.	ARCHBISHOP	church deacon	____
7.	MATRIARCH	wife and mother	____
8.	ANARCHY	political lawlessness	____
9.	HIERARCHY	higher orders	____
10.	ARCHAIC	old-fashioned	____

Answers: 1. T   2. T   3. T   4. T   5. F   6. F
7. F   8. T   9. F   10. T

LESSON 9. "TO LIFE!": *BIO*

In 1763, the Scottish writer James Boswell was first introduced to the acclaimed English poet, playwright, and dictionary-maker Samuel Johnson, setting the stage for the birth of modern biography. From 1772 until Johnson's death in 1784, the two men were closely associated, and Boswell devoted much of his time to compiling detailed records of Johnson's activities and conversations. Seven years after Johnson's death, Boswell published his masterpiece, the *Life of Samuel Johnson.* The word "biography," *a written account of another person's life,* comes from the Greek root "bio," meaning *life,* and "graphy," meaning *writing.* Besides *life,* "bio" can also mean *living, living thing,* or *biological.*

A number of other important words come from "bio." Here's a list of eight of them. Read through the definitions and practice the pronunciations, then go on to the quizzes.

1. **biodegradable** (bī′ō di grā′də bəl) capable of being decomposed by living organisms, as paper and kitchen scraps are, as opposed to metals, glass, and plastics, which do not decay.

   After a long campaign, the local residents persuaded the supermarkets to use biodegradable paper bags rather than nondegradable plastic.
2. **biofeedback** (bī′ō fēd′bak′) a method of learning to modify one's own bodily or physiological functions with the aid of a visual or auditory display of one's brain waves, blood pressure, or muscle tension.

   Desperate to quit smoking, she made an appointment to try biofeedback.
3. **bioengineering** (bī′ō en′jə nēr′ing) the application of engineering principles and techniques to problems in medicine and biology.

   In the last few decades, bioengineering has

made important progress in the design of artificial limbs.

4. **biological clock** (bī′ə loj′i kəl klok′) an innate system in people, animals, and organisms that causes regular cycles of function or behavior.

   Recently the term "biological clock" has been used in reference to women in their late thirties and early forties who are concerned about having children before they are no longer able to reproduce.

5. **bionic** (bī on′ik) utilizing electronic devices and mechanical parts to assist humans in performing tasks, as by supplementing or duplicating parts of the body. Formed from "bio-" + "(electr)onic."

   The scientist used a bionic arm to examine the radioactive material.

6. **biopsy** (bī′op sē) the excision for diagnostic study of a piece of tissue from a living body. From "bio-" + Greek "opsis," *sight, view.*

   The doctor took a biopsy from the patient's lung to determine the nature of the infection.

7. **biota** (bī ō′tə) the plant and animal life of a region or period. From Greek "biote," *life,* from the root "bio."

   The biota from the cliffside proved more useful for conservation than the biologists had initially suspected.

8. **biohazard** (bī′ō haz′ərd) a disease-causing agent or organism, especially one produced by biological research; the health risk caused by such an agent or organism.

   Will new technology like gene splicing produce heretofore unknown biohazards to threaten the world's population?

Test 1: Definitions

Select the word that best fits the definition. Write your answer in the space provided.

____ 1. the excision for diagnostic study of a piece of tissue from a living body.
   a. biopsy b. bioengineering c. incision

____ 2. utilizing electronic devices and mechanical parts to assist humans in performing tasks.
   a. biota b. bioengineering c. bionic

____ 3. capable of decaying and being absorbed by the environment.
   a. biogenic b. biodegradable c. bionic

____ 4. a method of learning to modify one's own bodily or physiological functions.
   a. autobiography b. biofeedback
   c. biota

____ 5. the application of engineering principles and techniques to problems in medicine and biology.
   a. bioengineering b. autobiography
   c. biometry

____ 6. an innate system in people, animals, and organisms that causes regular cycles of function.
   a. biota b. bionic c. biological clock

____ 7. the plant and animal life of a region.
   a. biota b. autobiography c. biometry

____ 8. an agent or organism that causes a health risk.
   a. biopsy b. biohazard c. biota

Answers: 1. a 2. c 3. b 4. b 5. a 6. c
7. a 8. b

Test 2: True/False

In the space provided, write T if the definition of the numbered word is true or F if it is false.

		T or F
1. BIOPSY	tissue sample	____
2. BIOTA	plants and animals	____
3. BIOLOGICAL CLOCK	perpetual clock	____
4. BIOHAZARD	health risk	____
5. BIODEGRADABLE	capable of decomposing	____
6. BIONIC	superhero	____
7. BIOFEEDBACK	culinary expertise	____
8. BIOENGINEERING	railroad supervision	____

Answers: 1. T 2. T 3. F 4. T 5. T 6. F
7. F 8. F

LESSON 10. "SPEAK!": DICT, DIC

The earliest known dictionaries were found in the library of the Assyrian king at Nineveh. These clay tablets, inscribed with cuneiform writing dating from the seventh century B.C., provide important clues to our understanding of Mesopotamian culture. The first English dictionary did not appear until 1440. Compiled by the Dominican monk Gal-fridus Grammaticus, the *Storehouse for Children or Clerics,* as the title translates, consists of Latin definitions of 10,000 English words. The word "dictionary" was first used in English in 1526, in reference to a Latin dictionary by Peter Berchorius. This was followed by a Latin-English dictionary published by Sir Thomas Elyot in 1538. All these early efforts confined themselves to uncommon words and phrases not generally known or understood, because the daily language was not supposed to require explanation.

Today we understand the word "dictionary" to mean *a book containing a selection of the words of a language, usually arranged alphabetically, giving information about their meanings, pronunciations, etymologies, etc.; a lexicon.* The word comes from the Latin root "dictio," taken from "dicere," meaning *to say, state, declare, speak.* This root has given us scores of important English words. Below are eight for you to examine. After you read through their pronunciations and definitions, complete the self-tests.

1. **malediction** (mal′i dik′shən) a curse or the utterance of a curse. From Latin "male-," *evil* + "dictio," *speech, word.*

    After the witch delivered her malediction, the princess fell into a swoon.
2. **abdication** (ab′di kā′shən) the renunciation or relinquishment of something such as a throne, right, power, or claim, especially when formal.

    Following the abdication of Edward VIII for the woman he loved, his brother George VI assumed the throne of England.
3. **benediction** (ben′i dik′shən) the invocation of a blessing. From Latin "bene-," *well, good* + "dictio," *speech, word.*

    The chaplain delivered a benediction at the end of the service.
4. **edict** (ē′dikt) a decree issued by a sovereign or other authority; an authoritative proclamation or command

    Herod's edict ordered the massacre of male infants throughout his realm.
5. **predicate** (pred′i kāt′) to proclaim, declare, or affirm; base or found.

    Your acceptance into the training program is predicated upon a successful personal interview.
6. **jurisdiction** (jŏŏr′is dik′shən) the right, power, or authority to administer justice.

    The mayor's jurisdiction extends only to the

area of the village itself; outside its limits, the jurisdiction passes to the town board.
7. **dictum** (dik′təm) an authoritative pronouncement; saying or maxim.

    The firm issued a dictum stating that smoking was forbidden on the premises.
8. **predictive** (pri dik′tiv) indicating the future or future conditions; predicting.

    Although the day was clear and balmy, the brisk wind was predictive of the approaching cold snap.

Test 1: Matching Synonyms

Match each of the following numbered words with its closest synonym. Write your answer in the space provided.

1. PREDICTIVE	a. assert	____
2. EDICT	b. maxim	____
3. PREDICATE	c. indicating the future	____
4. BENEDICTION	d. authority	____
5. ABDICATION	e. decree	____
6. MALEDICTION	f. imprecation, curse	____
7. DICTUM	g. blessing	____
8. JURISDICTION	h. renunciation	____

Answers: 1. c 2. e 3. a 4. g 5. h 6. f 7. b 8. d

Test 2: True/False

In the space provided, write T if the definition of the numbered word is true or F if it is false.

		T or F
1. PREDICTIVE	indicative of the future	____
2. PREDICATE	declare	____
3. EDICT	decree	____
4. JURISDICTION	authority	____
5. DICTUM	blessing	____
6. ABDICATION	assumption	____
7. MALEDICTION	machismo	____
8. BENEDICTION	opening services	____

Answers: 1. T 2. T 3. T 4. T 5. F 6. F 7. F 8. F

LESSON 11. "LEAD ON, MACDUFF!": *DUC, DUCT*

Aqueducts, artificial channels built to transport water, were used in ancient Mesopotamia, but the ones used to supply water to ancient Rome are the most famous. Nine aqueducts were built in all; eventually they provided Rome with about thirty-eight million gallons of water daily. Parts of several are still in use, supplying water to fountains in

Rome. The word "aqueduct" comes from the Latin "aqua," meaning *water,* and "ductus," meaning *a leading* or *drawing off.*

A great number of powerful words are derived from the "duc, duct" root. Here are nine such words. Read through the definitions and practice the pronunciations. Try to use each word in a sentence of your own. Finally, work through the two self-tests at the end of the lesson to help fix the words in your memory.

1. **induce** (in d$\overline{oo}$s′, -dy$\overline{oo}$s′) to influence or persuade, as to some action.

    Try to induce her to stay at least a few hours longer.
2. **misconduct** (mis kon′dukt) improper conduct or behavior.

    Such repeated misconduct will result in a reprimand, if not an outright dismissal.
3. **abduct** (ab dukt′) to carry (a person) off or lead (a person) away illegally; kidnap.

    Jason's mother was so fearful that he might be abducted by a stranger that she refused even to let him walk to school alone.
4. **deduce** (di d$\overline{oo}$s′, -dy$\overline{oo}$s′) to derive as a conclusion from something known or assumed.

    The detective was able to deduce from the facts gathered thus far that the murder took place in the early hours of the morning.
5. **viaduct** (vī′ə dukt′) a bridge for carrying a road or railroad over a valley, gorge, or the like, consisting of a number of short spans; overpass.

    The city government commissioned a firm of civil engineers to explore the possibility of building a viaduct over the river.
6. **reductive** (ri duk′tiv) pertaining to or producing a smaller size. From Latin "reduct-, reducere," *to lead back*.

    The new electronic copier had reductive and enlargement capabilities.
7. **seduce** (si d$\overline{oo}$s′, -dy$\overline{oo}$s′) to lead astray, as from duty or rectitude.

    He was seduced by the prospect of gain.
8. **traduce** (trə d$\overline{oo}$s′, -dy$\overline{oo}$s′) to speak maliciously and falsely of; slander. From Latin "traducere," *to transfer, lead across*.

To traduce someone's character can do permanent harm to his or her reputation.
9. **ductile** (duk′til) pliable or yielding.

    The new plastic is very ductile and can be molded into many forms.

Test 1: Matching Synonyms

Match each of the numbered words with the closest synonym. Write your answer in the space provided.

1. SEDUCE	a. overpass	____
2. VIADUCT	b. shrinking	____
3. INDUCE	c. kidnap	____
4. REDUCTIVE	d. bad behavior	____
5. TRADUCE	e. infer	____
6. ABDUCT	f. entice	____
7. MISCONDUCT	g. pliable	____
8. DEDUCE	h. defame	____
9. DUCTILE	i. persuade	____

Answers: 1. f   2. a   3. i   4. b   5. h   6. c
7. d   8. e   9. g

Test 2: True/False

In the space provided, write T if the definition of the numbered word is true or F if it is false.

		T or F
1. DEDUCE	infer	____
2. DUCTILE	pliable	____
3. SEDUCE	lead astray	____
4. REDUCTIVE	magnifying	____
5. TRADUCE	malign	____
6. VIADUCT	overpass	____
7. ABDUCT	restore	____
8. MISCONDUCT	improper behavior	____
9. INDUCE	persuade	____

Answers: 1. T   2. T   3. T   4. F   5. T   6. T
7. F   8. T   9. T

LESSON 12. "JUST THE FACTS, MA'AM": FAC, FACT, FECT

We have formed a great many important and useful words from the Latin "facere," *to make* or *do*. A "facsimile," for example, derives from the Latin phrase "fac simile," meaning *to make similar,* and has come to mean *an exact copy.* Since facsimile copiers and transmitters have become very common, "facsimile" is now generally shortened and changed in spelling to "fax."

Many potent words are derived from the "fac, fact, fect" root. Eight such words follow. Learn them by completing this lesson; then try to use the root to help you figure out other "fac, fact" words you encounter.

1. **factious** (fak′shəs) given to or marked by discord; dissenting. From Latin "factio," *act of doing or of making connections; group* or *clique,* derived from "facere," *to do* or *make.*

   Factious groups threatened to break up the alliance.
2. **factotum** (fak tō′təm) a person employed to do all kinds of work, as a personal secretary or the chief servant of a household.

   Jeeves was the model of a gentleman's gentleman—the indispensable factotum of the frivolous Bertie Wooster.
3. **factitious** (fak tish′əs) made artificially; contrived.

   The report was merely a factitious account, not factual at all.
4. **facile** (fas′il) moving or acting with ease; fluent. From Latin "facilis," *easy to do,* derived from "facere," *to do.*

   With his facile mind, he often thought of startlingly original solutions to old problems.
5. **artifact** (är′tə fakt′) any object made by human skill or art. From the Latin phrase "arte factum," *(something) made with skill.*

   The archaeologists dug up many artifacts from the ancient Indian culture.
6. **facsimile** (fak sim′ə lē) an exact copy, as of a book, painting, or manuscript; a method of transmitting typed or printed material by means of radio or telegraph.

   If they could not obtain a facsimile of the document by noon, the deal would fall through.
7. **putrefaction** (pyoo′trə fak′shən) the decomposition of organic matter by bacteria and fungi. From Latin "putrere," *to rot* + "factio," *act of doing.*

   Once the putrefaction of the compost pile was complete, the gardener used the rotted material to enrich the soil.

8. **prefect** (prē′fekt) a person appointed to any of various positions of command, authority, or superintendence. From Latin "praefectus," formed from "prae," *ahead, surpassing* + "fectus," *doing* (from "facere," *to do*).

   The prefect was appointed to a term of three years.

Test 1: Definitions

Select the word that best fits the definition. Write your answer in the space provided.

____ 1. the decomposition of organic matter by bacteria and fungi
a. chemical analysis   b. hypothermia
c. putrefaction

____ 2. not natural; artificial
a. factious   b. facile   c. factitious

____ 3. an exact copy, as of a book, painting, or manuscript
a. factoid   b. facsimile   c. putrefaction

____ 4. given to dissension or strife
a. facile   b. factious   c. obsequious

____ 5. an object made by humans
a. artifact   b. factotum   c. factious

____ 6. a person employed to do all kinds of work
a. facile   b. factotum   c. faculty

____ 7. moving or acting easily
a. putrefaction   b. prefect   c. facile

____ 8. someone appointed to any of various positions of command, authority, or superintendence
a. prefect   b. facile   c. factotum

Answers: 1. c   2. c   3. b   4. b   5. a   6. b
7. c   8. a

Test 2: True/False

In the space provided, write T if the definition of the numbered word is true or F if it is false.

		T or F
1. FACTITIOUS	contrived	____
2. FACTOTUM	carrier	____
3. PUTREFACTION	rotting	____
4. ARTIFACT	machinery	____
5. FACSIMILE	instant transmission	____
6. PREFECT	administrator	____
7. FACTIOUS	dissenting	____
8. FACILE	fluent	____

Answers: 1. T   2. F   3. T   4. F   5. F   6. T
7. T   8. T

LESSON 13. "ALWAYS FAITHFUL": *FEDER, FID, FIDE*

"Semper fidelis" is Latin for *always faithful*. The phrase is the motto of the United States Marine Corps and the title of an 1888 march by John Philip Sousa. This phrase, as with a number of useful words, comes from the Latin root "fid, fide," meaning *trust, faith*.

Below are seven words derived from this root. Read through the meanings, practice the pronunciations, and complete the self-tests that follow to help fix the words in your memory.

1. **fidelity** (fi del′i tē) faithfulness; loyalty.

    Dogs are legendary for their fidelity to their masters.

2. **fiduciary** (fi dōō′shē er′ē, -dyōō′-) a person to whom property or power is entrusted for the benefit of another; trustee. From Latin "fiducia," *trust*, related to "fidere," *to trust*.

    The bank's fiduciary administers the children's trust funds.

3. **infidel** (in′fi dl, -del′) a person who does not accept a particular religious faith. From Latin "in," *not* + "fidelis," *faithful* (from "fide," *faith*).

    The ayatollah condemned Salman Rushdie as an infidel.

4. **perfidious** (pər fid′ē əs) deliberately faithless; treacherous. From Latin "perfidia" ("per-," *through* + "fide," *faith*).

    The perfidious lover missed no opportunity to be unfaithful.

5. **confide** (kən fīd′) to entrust one's secrets to another. From Latin "confidere" ("con-," *with* + "fidere," *to trust*).

    The two sisters confided in each other.

6. **bona fide** (bō′nə fīd′, bon′ə) genuine; real; in good faith.

    To their great astonishment, the offer of a free vacation was bona fide.

7. **affidavit** (af′i dā′vit) a written declaration upon oath made before an authorized official. From a Medieval Latin word meaning *(he) has declared on oath*, from Latin "affidare," *to pledge on faith*.

    In the affidavit, they swore they had not been involved in the accident.

Test 1: Matching Synonyms

Match each of the following numbered words with its closest synonym. Write your answer in the space provided.

1. CONFIDE	a. faithfulness	____
2. FIDELITY	b. heathen	____
3. BONA FIDE	c. declaration	____
4. INFIDEL	d. entrust	____
5. AFFIDAVIT	e. trustee	____
6. PERFIDIOUS	f. genuine	____
7. FIDUCIARY	g. faithless	____

Answers: 1. d 2. a 3. f 4. b 5. c 6. g 7. e

Test 2: Matching Synonyms

Select the best synonym for each numbered word. Write your answer in the space provided.

____ 1. bona fide
   a. unauthorized   b. deboned
   c. real   d. well-trained

____ 2. perfidious
   a. irreligious   b. content   c. loyal
   d. treacherous

____ 3. fidelity
   a. loyalty   b. alliance   c. great
   affection   d. random motion

____ 4. fiduciary
   a. bank teller   b. trustee
   c. insurance   d. default

____ 5. infidel
   a. warrior   b. intransigent
   c. heathen   d. outsider

____ 6. affidavit
   a. affright   b. declaration   c. loyalty
   d. betrothal

____ 7. confide
   a. combine   b. recline   c. entrust
   d. convert

Answers: 1. c 2. d 3. a 4. b 5. c 6. b 7. c

LESSON 14. "FLOW GENTLY, SWEET AFTON": *FLU*

In 1991, the upper fifth of working Americans took home more money than the other four-fifths put together—the highest proportion of wealthy people since the end of World War II. One word to describe such wealthy people is "affluent," *prosperous.* The word comes from the Latin root "fluere," meaning *to flow.* As a river would flow freely, so the money of the affluent flows easily.

Seven of the most useful and important words formed from the "flu" root follow. Study the definitions and read through the pronunciations. Then do the self-tests.

1. **flume** (flo͞om) a deep, narrow channel containing a mountain stream or torrent; an amusement-park ride through a water-filled chute or slide.

    The adults steadfastly refused to try the log flume ride, but the children enjoyed it thoroughly.

2. **confluence** (kon′flo͞o əns) a flowing together of two or more streams; their place of junction.

    The confluence of the rivers is marked by a strong current.

3. **fluent** (flo͞o′ənt) spoken or written effortlessly; easy; graceful; flowing.

    Jennifer was such a fluent speaker that she was in great demand as a lecturer.

4. **fluctuation** (fluk′cho͞o ā′shən) continual change from one course, condition, etc., to another.

    The fluctuation in temperature was astonishing, considering it was still only February.

5. **fluvial** (flo͞o′vē əl) of or pertaining to a river; produced by or found in a river.

    The contours of the riverbank were altered over the years by fluvial deposits.

6. **influx** (in′fluks′) a flowing in.

    The unexpected influx of refugees severely strained the community's resources.

7. **flux** (fluks) a flowing or flow; continuous change.

    His political views are in constant flux.

Test 1: True/False

In the space provided, write T if the definition of the numbered word is true or F if it is false.

		T or F
1. FLUCTUATION	change	____
2. FLUVIAL	deep crevasse	____
3. FLUENT	flowing	____
4. FLUX	flow	____
5. INFLUX	egress	____
6. CONFLUENCE	diversion	____
7. FLUME	feather	____

Answers: 1. T   2. F   3. T   4. T   5. F   6. F   7. F

Test 2: Matching Synonyms

Select the best definition for each numbered word. Write your answer in the space provided.

1. FLUX	a. gorge	____
2. CONFLUENCE	b. flowing easily	____
3. FLUME	c. continual shift	____
4. FLUCTUATION	d. an inflow	____
5. FLUENT	e. a flow	____
6. INFLUX	f. riverine	____
7. FLUVIAL	g. convergence	____

Answers: 1. e   2. g   3. a   4. c   5. b   6. d   7. f

LESSON 15. "IN THE BEGINNING": *GEN*

Genesis, the first book of the Old Testament, tells of the beginning of the world. The English word "genesis" is taken from the Greek word for *origin* or *source.* From the root "gen," meaning *beget, bear, kind,* or *race,* a number of powerful vocabulary builders has evolved.

Here are ten "gen" words. Study the definitions and practice the pronunciations to help you learn the words. To accustom yourself to using these new terms in your daily speech and writing, work through the two self-tests at the end of the lesson.

1. **gene** (jēn) the unit of heredity in the chromosomes that controls the development of inherited traits. From Greek "-genes," *born, begotten.*

    The gene for color blindness is linked to the Y chromosome.

2. **engender** (en jen′dər) to produce, cause, or give rise to.

    Hatred engenders violence.

3. **gentility** (jen til′i tē) good breeding or refinement.

    Her obvious gentility marked her as a member of polite society.

4. **gentry** (jen′trē) wellborn and well-bred people; in England, the class under the nobility.

   In former times, the gentry lived on large estates with grand houses, lush grounds, and many servants.

5. **genus** (jē′nəs) the major subdivision of a family or subfamily in the classification of plants and animals, usually consisting of more than one species.

   The biologist assigned the newly discovered plant to the appropriate genus.

6. **genial** (jēn′yəl, jē′nē əl) cordial; favorable for life, growth, or comfort.

   Under the genial conditions in the greenhouse, the plants grew and flourished.

7. **congenital** (kən jen′i tl) existing at or from one's birth.

   The child's congenital defect was easily corrected by surgery.

8. **eugenics** (yoo jen′iks) the science of improving the qualities of a breed or species, especially the human race, by the careful selection of parents.

   Through eugenics, scientists hope to engineer a superior race of human beings.

9. **genealogy** (jē′nē ol′ə jē) a record or account of the ancestry and descent of a person, family, group, etc.; the study of family ancestries.

   Genealogy shows that Franklin Delano Roosevelt was a cousin of Winston Churchill.

10. **congenial** (kən jēn′yəl) agreeable or pleasant; suited or adapted in disposition; compatible.

    The student enjoyed the congenial atmosphere of the library.

Test 1: Definitions

Select the word that best fits the definition. Write your answer in the space provided.

____ 1. the major subdivision of a family or subfamily in the classification of plants and animals.
   a. gene   b. genus   c. genial   d. gentry

____ 2. suited or adapted in disposition; agreeable.
   a. genial   b. congenital
   c. genealogy   d. congenial

____ 3. wellborn and well-bred people.
   a. gene   b. gentry   c. nobility
   d. gentility

____ 4. the science of improving the qualities of a breed or species.
   a. genetics   b. gentry
   c. genealogy   d. eugenics

____ 5. the unit of heredity transmitted in the chromosome.
   a. ancestry   b. DNA   c. gene   d. genus

____ 6. cordial; favorable for life, growth, or comfort.
   a. genial   b. gentry   c. eugenics
   d. hospitality

____ 7. to produce, cause, or give rise to.
   a. gentility   b. engender
   c. genealogy   d. genial

____ 8. a record or account of the ancestry of a person, family, group, etc.
   a. gene   b. genealogy   c. glibness
   d. gentry

____ 9. good breeding or refinement.
   a. reductive   b. genus   c. gentility
   d. eugenics

____ 10. existing at or from one's birth.
   a. congenital   b. genus
   c. congenial   d. gene

Answers: 1. b   2. d   3. b   4. d   5. c   6. a
7. b   8. b   9. c   10. a

Test 2: True/False

In the space provided, write T if the definition of the numbered word is true or F if it is false.

		T or F
1. GENTRY	peasants	____
2. CONGENITAL	incurable	____
3. GENIAL	debased	____
4. GENE	genetic material	____
5. EUGENICS	matricide	____
6. GENTILITY	viciousness	____
7. GENEALOGY	family history	____
8. CONGENIAL	pleasant	____
9. GENUS	subdivision	____
10. ENGENDER	cease	____

Answers: 1. F   2. F   3. F   4. T   5. F   6. F
7. T   8. T   9. T   10. F

ROOT POWER II

LESSON 1. "THIS WAY TO THE EGRESS": *GRAD, GRES, GRESS*

P. T. Barnum was a nineteenth-century American showman whose greatest undertaking was the circus he called "The Greatest Show on Earth." The circus, which included a menagerie that exhibited Jumbo the elephant and a museum of freaks, was famous all over the country. After its merger in 1881 with James Anthony Bailey's circus, the enterprise gained international renown. When Barnum's customers took too long to leave his famous exhibits, he posted a sign: "This way to the egress." Following the arrow in eager anticipation of a new oddity, the visitors were ushered through the egress—the exit.

Knowing that the root "grad, gres, gress" means *step, degree,* or *walk* might have given these suckers a few more minutes to enjoy the exhibits, and it can certainly help you figure out a number of powerful words. Here are nine words that use this Latin root. Study the definitions, practice the pronunciations, and work through the two self-tests.

1. **digress** (di gres′, dī-) to wander away from the main topic. From Latin "digressus, digredi," *to walk away* ("di-," *away, apart* + "gressus, gredi," *to walk, step*).

    The manager cautioned her salespeople that they would fare better if they did not digress from their prepared sales talks.

2. **transgress** (trans gres′, tranz-) to break or violate a law, command, moral code, etc. From Latin "transgressus, transgredi," *to step across.*

    Those who transgress the laws of their ancestors often feel guilty.

3. **retrograde** (re′ trə grād′) moving backward; having backward motion.

    Most of the townspeople regarded the new ordinance as a prime example of retrograde legislation.

4. **regression** (ri gresh′ən) the act of going or fact of having gone back to an earlier place or state.

    The child's regression could be seen in his thumbsucking.

5. **degrade** (di grād′) to reduce the dignity of (someone); deprive (someone) of office, rank, or title; lower (someone or something) in quality or character.

    He felt they were degrading him by making him wash the dishes.

6. **Congress** (kong′gris) the national legislative body of the United States, consisting of the Senate and the House of Representatives; *(lower case)* encounter; meeting.

    Congress held a special session to discuss the situation in the Middle East.

7. **gradation** (grā dā′shən) any process or change taking place through a series of stages, by degrees, or gradually. From Latin "gradatio," *series of steps,* derived from "gradus," *step, degree.*

    He decided to change his hair color by gradation rather than all at once.

8. **gradient** (grā′dē ənt) the degree of inclination, or the rate of ascent or descent, in a highway, railroad, etc.

    Although they liked the house very much, they were afraid that the driveway's steep gradient would make it hard to park a car there in the winter.

9. **progressive** (prə gres'iv) characterized by progress or reform; innovative; going forward; gradually increasing.

   The progressive legislation wiped out years of social inequity.

Test 1: Matching Synonyms

Match each of the following numbered words with its closest synonym. Write your answer in the space provided.

1. CONGRESS	a. backward moving	____
2. REGRESSION	b. depart from a subject	____
3. GRADIENT	c. disobey	____
4. PROGRESSIVE	d. meeting	____
5. DIGRESS	e. stage, degree	____
6. GRADATION	f. reversion	____
7. RETROGRADE	g. humiliate	____
8. DEGRADE	h. innovative	____
9. TRANSGRESS	i. incline	____

Answers: 1. d 2. f 3. i 4. h 5. b 6. e
7. a 8. g 9. c

Test 2: Defining Words

Define each of the following words.

1. gradient _____
2. Congress _____
3. progressive _____
4. regression _____
5. retrograde _____
6. degrade _____
7. digress _____
8. gradation _____
9. transgress _____

Suggested Answers: 1. the degree of inclination, or the rate of ascent or descent, in a highway, etc. 2. the national legislative body of the United States; a meeting or assembly 3. characterized by reform; increasing gradually 4. the act of going back to an earlier place or state 5. moving backward; having backward motion 6. to reduce (someone) to a lower rank; deprive of office, rank, or title; to lower in quality or character 7. to wander away from the main topic 8. any process or change taking place through a series of stages, by degrees, or gradually 9. to break or violate a law, command, moral code, etc.

LESSON 2. "SPLISH, SPLASH, I WAS TAKING A BATH": *HYDRO, HYDR*

According to mythology, the ancient Greeks were menaced by a monstrous nine-headed serpent with fatally poisonous breath. Killing it was no easy matter: When you lopped off one head, it grew two in its place, and the central head was immortal. Hercules, sent to destroy the serpent as the second of his twelve labors, was triumphant when he burned off the eight peripheral heads and buried the ninth under a huge rock. From its residence, the watery marsh, came the monster's name, "Hydra," from the Greek root "hydr(o)," meaning *water*.

Quite a few words are formed from the "hydro" or "hydr" root. Here are ten of them. Read through the definitions, practice the pronunciations, and then work through the two self-tests that follow.

1. **hydrostat** (hī'drə stat') an electrical device for detecting the presence of water, as from an overflow or a leak.

   The plumber used a hydrostat to locate the source of the leak in the bathroom.
2. **dehydrate** (dē hī'drāt) to deprive of water; dry out.

   Aside from being tasty and nutritious, dehy-

drated fruits and vegetables are easy to store and carry.
3. **hydrophobia** (hī'drə fō'bē ə) rabies; fear of water.

   Sufferers from hydrophobia are unable to swallow water.
4. **hydroplane** (hī'drə plān') a light, high-powered boat, especially one with hydrofoils or a stepped bottom, designed to travel at very high speeds.

   The shore police acquired a new hydroplane to help them apprehend boaters who misuse the waterways.
5. **hydroponics** (hī'drə pon'iks) the cultivation of plants by placing the roots in liquid nutrients rather than soil.

   Some scientists predict that in the future, as arable land becomes increasingly more scarce, most of our vegetables will be grown through hydroponics.
6. **hydropower** (hī'drə pou'ər) electricity generated by falling water or another hydraulic source.

   Hydropower is efficient, clean, and economical.

7. **hydrate** (hī′drāt) to combine with water.

Lime is hydrated for use in plaster, mortar, and cement.

8. **hydrangea** (hī drān′jə) a showy shrub cultivated for its large white, pink, or blue flower clusters. From Greek "hydr-," *water* + "ange-ion," *vessel.*

Hydrangeas require a great deal of water to flourish.

9. **hydrotherapy** (hī′drə ther′əpē) the treatment of disease by the scientific application of water both internally and externally.

To alleviate strained muscles, physical therapists often prescribe hydrotherapy.

10. **hydrosphere** (hī′drə sfēr′) the water on or surrounding the surface of the planet Earth, including the water of the oceans and the water in the atmosphere.

Scientists are investigating whether the greenhouse effect is influencing the hydrosphere.

Test 1: Definitions

Select the word that best fits the definition. Write your answer in the space provided.

_____ 1. electricity generated by water
   a. hydropower   b. hydrangea
   c. hydrotherapy   d. electrolysis

_____ 2. the treatment of disease by the scientific application of water both internally and externally
   a. hydrate   b. electrolysis
   c. hydrotherapy   d. hydroponics

_____ 3. a light, high-powered boat, especially one with hydrofoils or a stepped bottom
   a. hydropower   b. hydroplane
   c. hydroelectric   d. hydroship

_____ 4. rabies; fear of water
   a. hydrate   b. hydrotherapy
   c. hydroponics   d. hydrophobia

_____ 5. the water on or surrounding the surface of the globe, including the water of the oceans and the water in the atmosphere

   a. hydrosphere   b. hydrate
   c. hydrofoil   d. hydrangea

_____ 6. to deprive of water
   a. a. hydrate   b. dehydrate
   c. hydrolyze   d. hydrotherapy

_____ 7. a showy shrub with large white, pink, or blue flower clusters
   a. hydrate   b. hydrangea
   c. hydroponics   d. hydrofoil

_____ 8. the cultivation of plants by placing the roots in liquid nutrient solutions rather than soil
   a. hydrotherapy   b. hydrangea
   c. hydroponics   d. hydrolyze

_____ 9. to combine with water
   a. hydrostat   b. hydrosphere
   c. hydrangea   d. hydrate

_____ 10. an electrical device for detecting the presence of water, as from an overflow or a leak
   a. hydrosphere   b. hydrangea
   c. hydroponics   d. hydrostat

Answers: 1. a   2. c   3. b   4. d   5. a   6. b
7. b   8. c   9. d   10. d

Test 2: True/False

In the space provided, write T if the definition of the numbered word is true or F if it is false.

		T or F
1. HYDROPOWER	hydroelectric power	_____
2. HYDROPLANE	boat	_____
3. HYDROPONICS	gardening in water	_____
4. HYDROSTAT	water power	_____
5. HYDRANGEA	flowering plant	_____
6. HYDROTHERAPY	water cure	_____
7. HYDRATE	lose water	_____
8. HYDROSPHERE	bubble	_____
9. DEHYDRATE	wash thoroughly	_____
10. HYDROPHOBIA	pneumonia	_____

Answers: 1. T   2. T   3. T   4. F   5. T   6. T
7. F   8. F   9. F   10. F

LESSON 3. "AFTER ME, THE DELUGE": *LAV, LU*

The failure of Louis XV (1710–74) to provide strong leadership and badly needed reforms contributed to the crisis that brought about the French Revolution. Louis took only nominal interest in ruling his country and was frequently influenced by his mistresses. In the last years of his reign, he did cooperate with his chancellor to try to reform the government's unequal and inefficient system of taxation, but it was too late. His reported deathbed prophecy, "After me, the deluge," was fulfilled in the overthrow of the monarchy less than twenty years later. The word "deluge," meaning *flood,* comes from the Latin root "lu," *to wash.* As a flood, a deluge would indeed wash things clean.

A number of words were formed from the "lav, lu" root. Here are several examples. Study the definitions and practice the pronunciations. To help you remember the words, complete the two self-tests at the end of the lesson.

1. **dilute** (di lo͞ot′, dī-) to make thinner or weaker by adding water; to reduce the strength or effectiveness of (something). From Latin "dilutus, di-luere," *to wash away.*

    The wine was too strong and had to be diluted.

2. **lavabo** (lə vä′bō, -vä′-) the ritual washing of the celebrant's hands after the offertory in the Mass; the passage recited with the ritual. From the Latin word meaning *I shall wash,* with which the passage begins.

    The priest intoned the Latin words of the lavabo.

3. **lavage** (lə väzh′) a washing, especially the cleansing of an organ, as the stomach, by irrigation.

    Lavage is a preferred method of preventing infection.

4. **diluvial** (di lo͞o′vē əl) pertaining to or caused by a flood or deluge.

    The diluvial aftermath was a bitter harvest of smashed gardens, stained siding, and missing yard furniture.

5. **alluvium** (ə lo͞o′vē əm) a deposit of sand, mud, etc., formed by flowing water.

    Geologists study alluvium for clues to the earth's history.

6. **ablution** (ə blo͞o′shən) a cleansing with water or other liquid, especially as a religious ritual; a washing of the hands, body, etc.

    He performed his morning ablutions with vigor.

Test 1: Matching Synonyms

Select the best or closest synonym for each numbered word. Write your answer in the space provided.

_____ 1. lavage
    a. molten rock   b. sewage
    c. washing   d. religious ritual

_____ 2. alluvium
    a. great heat   b. rain   c. flood
    d. deposit of sand

_____ 3. lavabo
    a. religious cleansing   b. volcano
    c. flooding   d. lavatory

_____ 4. ablution
    a. cleansing with water   b. absence
    c. sacrifice   d. small font

_____ 5. dilute
    a. wash   b. weaken   c. cleanse
    d. liquefy

_____ 6. diluvial
    a. before the flood   b. antedate
    c. monarchy   d. of a flood

Answers: 1. c   2. d   3. a   4. a   5. b   6. d

Test 2: True/False

In the space provided, write T if the definition of the numbered word is true or F if it is false.

		T or F
1. DILUTE	reduce strength	_____
2. DILUVIAL	two-lipped	_____
3. LAVAGE	security	_____
4. ALLUVIUM	molten rock	_____
5. ABLUTION	washing	_____
6. LAVABO	religious ritual	_____

Answers: 1. T   2. F   3. F   4. F   5. T   6. T

LESSON 4. "SILVER TONGUE": *LOQUI, LOQU, LOCU*

For many years, ventriloquist Edgar Bergen amused audiences as he tried to outwit his monocled wooden dummy, Charlie McCarthy. Among the most popular entertainers of his age, Bergen astonished audiences with his mastery of ventriloquism, the art of speaking so that projected sound seems to originate elsewhere, as from a hand-manipulated dummy. This ancient skill sounds easier than it is, since it requires modifying the voice through slow exhalation, minimizing movement of the tongue and lips, and maintaining an impassive expression

to help shift viewers' attention to the illusory source of the voice.

The word "ventriloquism" comes from Latin "ventri-," *abdomen, stomach,* and the root "loqui," *to speak* (because it was believed that the ventriloquist produced sounds from his stomach). Many useful and important words were formed from the "loqui, loqu" root. Below are seven you should find especially helpful. Study the definitions and practice the pronunciations. To reinforce your learning, work through the two self-tests.

1. **obloquy** (ob'lə kwē) blame, censure, or abusive language.

    The vicious obloquy surprised even those who knew of the enmity between the political rivals.

2. **colloquial** (kə lō'kwē əl) characteristic of or appropriate to ordinary or familiar conversation rather than formal speech or writing.

    In standard American English, "He hasn't got any" is colloquial, while "He has none" is formal.

3. **soliloquy** (sə lil'ə kwē) the act of talking while or as if alone.

    A soliloquy is often used as a device in a drama to disclose a character's innermost thoughts.

4. **eloquent** (el'ə kwənt) having or exercising the power of fluent, forceful, and appropriate speech; movingly expressive.

    William Jennings Bryan was an eloquent orator famous for his "Cross of Gold" speech.

5. **interlocution** (in'tər lō kyōō'shən) conversation; dialogue.

    The interlocutions disclosed at the Watergate hearings riveted the American public to their TV sets.

6. **loquacious** (lō kwā'shəs) talking much or freely; talkative; wordy.

    After the sherry, the dinner guests became loquacious.

7. **elocution** (el'ə kyōō'shən) a person's manner of speaking or reading aloud; the study and practice of public speaking.

    After completing the course in public speaking, the pupils were skilled at elocution.

Test 1: Matching Synonyms

Match each of the numbered words with its closest synonym. Write your answer in the space provided.

1. LOQUACIOUS	a. censure	____
2. INTERLOCUTION	b. informal	____
3. ELOCUTION	c. monologue	____
4. COLLOQUIAL	d. talkative	____
5. SOLILOQUY	e. conversation	____
6. OBLOQUY	f. fluent	____
7. ELOQUENT	g. public speaking	____

Answers: 1. d 2. e 3. g 4. b 5. c 6. a 7. f

Test 2: Definitions

Select the word that best fits the definition. Write your answer in the space provided.

____ 1. a person's manner of speaking or reading aloud; the study and practice of public speaking
    a. obloquy   b. soliloquy
    c. prologue   d. elocution

____ 2. conversation; dialogue
    a. colloquial   b. interlocution
    c. monologue   d. elocution

____ 3. tending to talk; garrulous
    a. eloquent   b. colloquial
    c. loquacious   d. elocutionary

____ 4. characteristic of or appropriate to ordinary or familiar conversation rather than formal speech or writing
    a. colloquial   b. eloquent
    c. prologue   d. dialogue

____ 5. the act of talking while or as if alone
    a. circumlocution   b. dialogue
    c. soliloquy   d. obloquy

____ 6. having or exercising the power of fluent, forceful, and appropriate speech; movingly expressive
    a. interlocution   b. eloquent
    c. colloquial   d. loquacious

____ 7. censure; abusive language
    a. interlocution   b. soliloquy
    c. obloquy   d. dialogue

Answers: 1. d 2. b 3. c 4. a 5. c 6. b 7. c

LESSON 5. "STAR LIGHT, STAR BRIGHT": *LUC, LUX, LUM*

Before he was driven out of heaven because of his pride, Satan was called "Lucifer," which translates as *bringer of light*. In his epic retelling of the Bible, *Paradise Lost*, John Milton used the name "Lucifer" for the demon of sinful pride, and we call the planet Venus "Lucifer" when it appears as the morning star. "Lucifer" comes from the root "luc, lux" meaning *light*.

A number of powerful words derive from "luc" and its variations. We trust that you'll find the following seven *light* words "enlightening"! Study the definitions and practice the pronunciations. Then complete the two self-tests at the end of the lesson.

1. **pellucid** (pə lōō' sid) allowing the maximum passage of light; clear.

The pellucid waters of the Caribbean allowed us to see the tropical fish clearly.

2. **lucid** (lōō'sid) shining or bright; clearly understood.

Stephen Hawking's lucid explanation of astrophysics became a bestseller.

3. **translucent** (trans lōō' sənt, tranz-) permitting light to pass through but diffusing it so that persons, objects, etc., on the opposite side are not clearly visible.

Frosted window glass is translucent.

4. **elucidate** (i lōō'si dāt') to make light or clear; explain.

Once my math teacher elucidated the mysteries of geometry, I had no further difficulty solving the problems.

5. **lucubrate** (lōō'kyōō brāt') to work, write, or study laboriously, especially at night. From Latin "lucubrare," *to work by artificial light.*

The scholar lucubrated for many long nights in an attempt to complete his thesis.

6. **luminary** (lōō'mə ner'ē) an eminent person; an object that gives light.

Certain that the elegant woman emerging from the limousine had to be a theatrical luminary, the crowd surged forward to get a closer look.

7. **luminous** (lōō' mə nəs) radiating or emitting light; brilliant.

The luminous paint emitted an eerie glow, not at all what the designer had envisioned.

Test 1: True/False

In the space provided, write T if the definition of the numbered word is true or F if it is false.

		T or F
1. LUCID	comprehensible	___
2. ELUCIDATE	explain	___
3. LUCUBRATE	lubricate	___
4. PELLUCID	limpid, clear	___
5. LUMINOUS	reflective	___
6. LUMINARY	lightning	___
7. TRANSLUCENT	opaque	___

Answers: 1. T 2. T 3. F 4. T 5. F 6. F 7. F

Test 2: Matching Synonyms

Select the best definition for each numbered word. Write your answer in the space provided.

1. LUMINOUS	a. study hard	___
2. ELUCIDATE	b. prominent person	___
3. PELLUCID	c. brilliant	___
4. LUCUBRATE	d. permitting but diffusing light	___
5. LUCID	e. clearly understood	___
6. LUMINARY	f. allowing the passage of maximum light	___
7. TRANSLUCENT	g. clarify	___

Answers: 1. c 2. g 3. f 4. a 5. e 6. b 7. d

LESSON 6. "EVIL BE TO HIM WHO DOES EVIL": *MALE, MAL*

"Malnutrition" is defined as *a lack of the proper type and amount of nutrients required for good health.* It is estimated that more than ten million American children suffer from malnutrition; the World Health Organization reports that over 600 million people suffer from malnutrition in the emerging countries alone. Malnourished people endure a variety of side effects, including a failure to grow, increased susceptibility to infection, anemia, diarrhea, and lethargy.

The root "mal" in the word "malnourished" means *bad, evil,* and words formed around this root invariably carry negative overtones. In Latin, the root is spelled "male"; in French, it's "mal," but regardless of the spelling, the root means *evil.* Study the definitions and pronunciations of the following "mal" words until you become comfort-able with them. Then work through the two self-tests.

1. **maladjusted** (mal'ə jus'tid) badly adjusted.

Despite attempts by the psychologist to ease him into his environment, the child remained maladjusted.

2. **malefactor** (mal'ə fak'tər) a person who violates the law; a criminal.

The police issued an all-points bulletin for the apprehension of the malefactor.

3. **maladroit** (mal'ə droit') unskillful; awkward; clumsy.

With his large hands and thick fingers, the young man was maladroit at fine needlework.

4. **malevolent** (mə lev'ə lənt) wishing evil to another or others; showing ill will.

Her malevolent uncle robbed the heiress of her estate and made her a virtual prisoner.

5. **malapropism** (mal′ə prop iz′əm) a confused use of words, especially one in which one word is replaced by another of similar sound but ludicrously inappropriate meaning; an instance of such a use. The word comes from Mrs. Malaprop, a character in Sheridan's comedy *The Rivals* (1775), noted for her misapplication of words. Sheridan coined the character's name from the English word "malapropos," meaning *inappropriate,* derived from the French phrase "mal à propos," *badly (suited) to the purpose.*

"Lead the way and we'll precede" is a malapropism.

6. **malicious** (mə lish′əs) full of or characterized by evil intention.

The malicious gossip hurt the young couple's reputation.

7. **malfeasance** (mal fē′zəns) the performance by a public official of an act that is legally unjustified, harmful, or contrary to law.

Convicted of malfeasance, the mayor was sentenced to six months in jail.

8. **malignant** (mə lig′nənt) disposed to cause harm, suffering, or distress; tending to produce death, as a disease or tumor.

The patient was greatly relieved when the pathologist reported that the tumor was not malignant.

9. **malign** (mə līn′) to speak harmful untruths about; slander.

"If you malign me again," the actor threatened the tabloid reporter, "I will not hesitate to sue."

Test 1: Matching Synonyms

Match each of the numbered words with its closest synonym. Write your answer in the space provided.

1. MALADROIT	a. wishing others evil	____
2. MALICIOUS	b. harmful; fatal	____
3. MALAPROPISM	c. official misconduct	____
4. MALFEASANCE	d. bungling, tactless	____
5. MALIGN	e. badly adjusted	____
6. MALIGNANT	f. spiteful	____
7. MALEFACTOR	g. criminal	____
8. MALEVOLENT	h. revile, defame	____
9. MALADJUSTED	i. confused use of words	____

Answers: 1. d   2. f   3. i   4. c   5. h   6. b   7. g   8. a   9. e

Test 2: True/False

In the space provided, write T if the definition of the numbered word is true or F if it is false.

		T or F
1. MALEFACTOR	ranger	____
2. MALAPROPISM	faulty stage equipment	____
3. MALFEASANCE	food poisoning	____
4. MALICIOUS	spiteful	____
5. MALADJUSTED	poorly adjusted	____
6. MALIGNANT	benign	____
7. MALADROIT	clumsy	____
8. MALEVOLENT	bad winds	____
9. MALIGN	defame	____

Answers: 1. F   2. F   3. F   4. T   5. T   6. F   7. T   8. F   9. T

Lesson 7. "I do!": *mater, matr*

The word "matrimony," meaning *marriage,* derives from the Latin root "mater," *mother,* because the union of a couple was established through motherhood. Most of us accept without question the idea of matrimony based on romantic love, but this is a relatively new belief. Only recently, following the rise of the middle class and the growth of democracy, has there been a tolerance of romantic marriages based on the free choice of the partners involved. Arranged marriages, accepted almost everywhere throughout history, eventually ceased to prevail in the West, although they persist in aristocratic circles to the present. The most extreme application of the custom of arranged marriages occurred in prerevolutionary China, where the bride and groom often met for the first time only on their wedding day.

We've inherited and created a number of significant words from the "mater, matr" root. Below are eight such words to help make your vocabulary more powerful and precise. Study the definitions and pronunciations; then complete the two self-tests.

1. **maternal** (mə tûr′nl) having the qualities of a mother; related through a mother.

On his maternal side, he is related to Abigail and John Adams.

2. **matron** (mā′trən) a married woman, especially

one with children, or one who has an established social position.

The matrons got together every Thursday to play bridge or mahjong.

3. **mater** (mā′tər) informal or humorous British usage for "mother."

"Mater is off to London again," said Giles, snidely.

4. **matrix** (mā′triks) that which gives origin or form to a thing, or which serves to enclose it.

Rome was the matrix of Western civilization.

5. **alma mater** (äl′mə mä′tər, al′-) a school, college, or university where a person has studied, and, usually, from which he or she has graduated. From the Latin phrase meaning *nourishing mother*.

Ellen's alma mater was Queens College.

6. **matrilineal** (ma′trə lin′ē əl, mā′-) inheriting or determining descent through the female line.

In a matrilineal culture, the children are usually part of the mother's family.

7. **matronymic** (ma′trə nim′ik) derived from the name of the mother or another female ancestor; named after one's mother. The word is also spelled "metronymic" (mē′trə nim′ik, me′-).

Some men have matronymic middle names.

8. **matriculate** (mə trik′yə lāt′) to enroll or cause to enroll as a student, especially in a college or university.

She intends to matriculate at City College in the fall.

Test 1: Definitions

Select the word that best fits the definition. Write your answer in the space provided.

_____ 1. that which gives origin or form to a thing, or which serves to enclose it
a. matrix   b. matrimonial   c. mater
d. alma mater

_____ 2. a school, college, or university at which a person has studied, and, usually, from which he or she has graduated
a. maternal   b. alma mater
c. maternity   d. matrimony

_____ 3. inheriting or determining descent through the female line
a. femaleness   b. matrix
c. matrilineal   d. lineage

_____ 4. derived from the name of the mother or another female ancestor; named after one's mother
a. matriarch   b. matrilocal   c. alma mater   d. matronymic

_____ 5. having the qualities of a mother
a. alma mater   b. matrilineal
c. maternal   d. matrix

_____ 6. a married woman, especially one with children, or one who has an established social position
a. matrix   b. matron   c. alma mater
d. homemaker

_____ 7. to enroll or cause to enroll as a student, especially in a college or university
a. matriculate   b. graduate
c. matrix   d. alma mater

_____ 8. informal British usage for "mother"
a. mater   b. matriarch   c. matron
d. ma

Answers: 1. a   2. b   3. c   4. d   5. c   6. b
7. a   8. a

Test 2: True/False

In the space provided, write T if the definition of the numbered word is true or F if it is false.

		T or F
1. MATRIX	outer edges	____
2. ALMA MATER	stepmother	____
3. MATRILINEAL	grandmotherly	____
4. MATRICULATE	study for a degree	____
5. MATER	mother	____
6. MATERNAL	motherly	____
7. MATRONYMIC	from the mother's name	____
8. MATRON	single woman	____

Answers: 1. F   2. F   3. F   4. T   5. T   6. T
7. T   8. F

LESSON 8. "BIRTH AND REBIRTH": *NASC, NAT*

The Renaissance (also spelled Renascence) occurred between 1300 and 1600, when the feudal society of the Middle Ages became an increasingly urban, commercial economy with a central political institution. The term "Renaissance," or *rebirth*, was first applied in the mid-nineteenth century by a French historian to what has been characterized as nothing less than the birth of modern humanity and consciousness. The word goes back to Latin "renasci," *to be reborn*, from "re-," *again* + "nasci," *to be born*.

Many significant words evolved from the "nasc,

nat'' root. Here are eight such words for your consideration. First, read through the pronunciations, definitions, and sentences. Then, to reinforce your reading, complete the two self-tests.

1. **natal** (nāt′l) of or pertaining to one's birth.
   The astrologer cast a natal chart for his client.
2. **nativity** (nə tiv′i tē, nā-) birth; the birth of Christ.
   The wanderer returned to the place of his nativity.
3. **nativism** (nā′ti viz′əm) the policy of protecting the interests of native inhabitants against those of immigrants.
   The supporters of nativism staged a protest to draw attention to their demands for protection against the newcomers.
4. **innate** (i nāt′) existing from birth; inborn.
   The art lessons brought out her innate talent.
5. **nascent** (nas′ənt, nā′sənt) beginning to exist or develop.
   The nascent republic petitioned for membership in the United Nations.
6. **nationalism** (nash′ə nl iz′əm, nash′nə liz′-) national spirit or aspirations; devotion to the interests of one's own nation. From Latin "natio," *nation, race,* derived from "nasci," *to be born.*
   Many Americans feel a stirring of nationalism when they see the flag or hear the national anthem.
7. **naturalize** (nach′ər ə līz′, nach′rə-) to invest (an alien) with the rights and privileges of a citizen. From Latin "natura," *birth, nature,* derived from "nasci," *to be born.*
   To become naturalized American citizens, immigrants have to study the Constitution of their adopted country.
8. **nee** (nā) born. The word is placed after the name of a married woman to introduce her

maiden name. From French "née," going back to Latin "nata," *born,* from "nasci," *to be born.*
Madame de Staël, nee Necker, was the central figure in a brilliant salon.

Test 1: True/False

In the space provided, write T if the definition of the numbered word is true or F if it is false.

		T or F
1. NATIVISM	protectionism	___
2. NATURALIZE	admit to citizenship	___
3. NEE	foreign wife	___
4. NATAL	pertaining to birth	___
5. NATIONALISM	immigration	___
6. NATIVITY	rebirth	___
7. NASCENT	native-born	___
8. INNATE	inborn	___

Answers: 1. T 2. T 3. F 4. T 5. F 6. F 7. F 8. T

Test 2: Matching Synonyms

Select the best definition for each numbered word. Write your answer in the space provided.

1. INNATE	a. admit to citizenship	___
2. NATIONALISM	b. relating to birth	___
3. NATURALIZE	c. beginning to exist	___
4. NEE	d. birth	___
5. NATAL	e. protection of native inhabitants	___
6. NASCENT	f. inborn	___
7. NATIVISM	g. indicating maiden name	___
8. NATIVITY	h. patriotism	___

Answers: 1. f 2. h 3. a 4. g 5. b 6. c 7. e 8. d

LESSON 9. "DADDY DEAREST": *PATER, PATR*

To sociologists and anthropologists, patriarchy is a system of social organization in which descent is traced through the male line and all offspring have the father's name or belong to his people. Often, the system is connected to inheritance and social prerogatives, as in primogeniture, in which the eldest son is the sole heir. The ancient Greeks and Hebrews were a patriarchal society, as were the Europeans during the Middle Ages. While many aspects of patriarchy, such as the inheritance of the family name through the male line, persist in Western society, the exclusive male inheritance of property and other patriarchal customs are dying out.
From the "pater, patr" root, meaning *father,* we

have formed many useful words. Eight of them follow. Go through the pronunciations, definitions, and sentences to help you make the words part of your daily speech and writing. Then complete the two self-tests.

1. **patrician** (pə trish′ən) a member of the original senatorial aristocracy in ancient Rome; any person of noble or high rank.
   You could tell she was a patrician from her elegant manner.
2. **expatriate** (*v.* eks pā′trē āt′; *n.* eks pā′trē it) to banish (a person) from his or her native country; one who has left his or her native country.

Among the most famous American expatriates in the 1920s were the writers F. Scott Fitzgerald, Ernest Hemingway, and Gertrude Stein.

3. **patronage** (pā′trə nij, pa′-) the financial support or business afforded to a store, hotel, or the like, by customers, clients, or paying guests; the encouragement or support of an artist by a patron; the control of appointments to government jobs, especially on a basis other than merit alone. From Latin "patronus," *patron, protector, advocate,* derived from "pater," father.

To show its appreciation for its clients' patronage, the beauty shop offered a half-price haircut to all regular customers for the month of January.

4. **paternalism** (pə tûr′nl iz′əm) the system, principle, or practice of managing or governing individuals, businesses, nations, etc., in the manner of a father dealing benevolently and often intrusively with his children.

The employees chafed under their manager's paternalism.

5. **paternoster** (pā′tər nos′tər, pä′-, pat′ər-) the Lord's Prayer, especially in the Latin form. The term is often capitalized.

The term "paternoster" is a translation of the first two words of the prayer in the Vulgate version, "our Father."

6. **paterfamilias** (pā′tər fə mil′ē əs, pä′-, pat′ər-) the male head of a household or family.

The paterfamilias gathered his children about him.

7. **patronymic** (pa′trə nim′ik) (a name) derived from the name of a father or ancestor, especially by the addition of a suffix or prefix indicating descent; family name or surname.

Their patronymic was Williamson, meaning "son of William."

8. **patrimony** (pa′trə mō′nē) an estate inherited from one's father or ancestors; heritage.

For his share of the patrimony, John inherited the family mansion at Newport.

Test 1: Definitions

Select the word that best fits the definition. Write your answer in the space provided.

_____ 1. the Lord's Prayer
   a. patrician   b. paternoster
   c. paternalism   d. expatriate

_____ 2. derived from the name of a father or ancestor; family name or surname
   a. paterfamilias   b. patronage
   c. pater   d. patronymic

_____ 3. the male head of a household or family
   a. paterfamilias   b. patronymic
   c. patrician   d. patrimony

_____ 4. any person of noble or high rank
   a. patricide   b. patrician
   c. expatriate   d. patriot

_____ 5. the system, principle, or practice of managing or governing in the manner of a father dealing with his children
   a. paterfamilias   b. expatriate
   c. paternalism   d. patronymic

_____ 6. to banish someone from his or her native country; one who has left his or her native country
   a. repatriate   b. patronize
   c. paternalize   d. expatriate

_____ 7. an estate inherited from one's father or ancestors; heritage
   a. patrimony   b. patricide
   c. paternoster   d. patronage

_____ 8. the financial support or business afforded to a store by its clients; the support of a patron; control of appointments to government jobs
   a. patronymic   b. pater
   c. patronage   d. paterfamilias

Answers: 1. b   2. d   3. a   4. b   5. c   6. d
7. a   8. c

Test 2: Matching Synonyms

Match each of the numbered words with its closest synonym. Write your answer in the space provided.

1. PATERNOSTER	a. financial backing	_____
2. PATRONYMIC	b. exile	_____
3. PATERFAMILIAS	c. male head of a family	_____
4. PATRIMONY	d. fatherly management	_____
5. PATRONAGE	e. the Lord's Prayer	_____
6. PATERNALISM	f. aristocrat	_____
7. PATRICIAN	g. surname	_____
8. EXPATRIATE	h. inheritance	_____

Answers: 1. e   2. g   3. c   4. h   5. a   6. d
7. f   8. b

LESSON 10. "KEEP ON TRUCKIN' ": *PED, POD*

From the Latin root "ped" and the related Greek root "pod," both meaning *foot*, we have derived many words relating to movement by foot. The English word "foot" is itself a Germanic cousin of the Latin and Greek forms. One curious aberration is "peddler" (also spelled "pedlar," "pedler"), for it is *not* from the root "ped," as we would expect. The word may be derived from "pedde," a Middle English word for a lidless hamper or basket in which fish and other items were carried as they were sold in the streets, though it is generally thought to be of unknown origin.

The following eight words, however, all come from the "ped, pod" roots. Practice the pronunciations, study the definitions, and read the sentences. Then, to help set the words in your mind, complete the two self-tests that follow.

1. **quadruped** (kwod′roŏ ped′) any animal, especially a mammal, having four feet.

   Horses, dogs, and cats are all classified as quadrupeds.

2. **podiatrist** (pə dī′ə trist) a person who treats foot disorders. From Greek "pod-," *foot* + "-iatros," *physician*.

   Podiatrists were formerly known as chiropodists.

3. **chiropodist** (ki rop′ə dist, kī-) a podiatrist. From Greek "cheir," *hand* + "podos," *foot*.

   A chiropodist treats minor problems of the feet, including corns and bunions.

4. **biped** (bī′ped) a two-footed animal.

   Humans are bipeds.

5. **expedient** (ik spē′dē ənt) tending to promote some desired object; fit or suitable under the circumstances. From Latin "expedire," *to make ready*, literally *to free the feet*.

   It was expedient for them to prepare all the envelopes at the same time.

6. **pseudopod** (soō′də pod′) an organ of propulsion on a protozoan.

   Amebas use pseudopods, literally "false feet," as a means of locomotion.

7. **pedigree** (ped′i grē′) an ancestral line; lineage. From the French phrase "pied de grue," *foot of a crane* (from the claw-shaped mark used in family trees to show lineage); "pied," *foot*, going back to the Latin root "ped."

   The dog's pedigree could be traced six generations.

8. **pedometer** (pə dom′i tər) an instrument that measures distance covered in walking by recording the number of steps taken.

The race walker used a pedometer to keep track of how much distance she could cover in an hour.

Test 1: Definitions

Select the best definition for each numbered word. Write your answer in the space provided.

_____ 1. pedigree
     a. dog training b. lineage c. horse racing d. nature walking
_____ 2. biped
     a. false feet b. horses c. two-footed animal d. winged creature
_____ 3. pedometer
     a. race walking b. jogger's injury c. foot care d. measuring device
_____ 4. expedient
     a. advantageous b. extra careful c. unnecessary d. walking swiftly
_____ 5. quadruped
     a. four-footed animal b. four-wheeled vehicle c. racehorse d. four animals
_____ 6. chiropodist
     a. orthopedic surgeon
     b. chiropractor c. podiatrist
     d. physician's assistant
_____ 7. podiatrist
     a. children's doctor b. foot doctor c. chiropractor d. skin doctor
_____ 8. pseudopod
     a. false seed pod b. widow's peak c. bad seed d. organ of propulsion

Answers: 1. b   2. c   3. d   4. a   5. a   6. c
7. b   8. d

Test 2: True/False

In the space provided, write T if the definition of the numbered word is true or F if it is false.

		T or F
1. CHIROPODIST	foot doctor	_____
2. PEDIGREE	lineage	_____
3. EXPEDIENT	advantageous	_____
4. PODIATRIST	foot doctor	_____
5. QUADRUPED	four-footed animal	_____
6. PEDOMETER	scale	_____
7. PSEUDOPOD	cocoon	_____
8. BIPED	stereo	_____

Answers: 1. T   2. T   3. T   4. T   5. T   6. F
7. F   8. F

Lesson 11. "It's my pleasure": *PLAC*

"S'il vous plaît," say the French to be polite. "Plaît" derives from "plaire," *to please,* which goes back to the Latin "placere." Thus the "plac" root, meaning *please,* forms the basis of the French expression for *if you please.* Many other words, including adjectives, nouns, and verbs, also derive from this root. Below are six "pleasing" words to add to your vocabulary. Look over the pronunciations, definitions, and sentences. Then to reinforce your study, complete the two self-tests.

1. **placid** (plas'id) pleasantly peaceful or calm.
   The placid lake shimmered in the early morning sun.
2. **complacent** (kəm plā'sənt) pleased, especially with oneself or one's merits, advantages, situation, etc., often without awareness of some potential danger, defect, or the like.
   She stopped being so complacent after she lost her job.
3. **placebo** (plə sē'bō) a substance having no pharmacological effect but given to a patient or subject of an experiment who supposes it to be a medicine. From the Latin word meaning *I shall please.*
   In the pharmaceutical company's latest study, one group was given the medicine; the other, a placebo.
4. **placate** (plā'kāt) to appease or pacify.
   To placate an outraged citizenry, the Board of Education decided to schedule a special meeting.
5. **implacable** (im plak'ə bəl, -plā'kə-) incapable of being appeased or pacified; inexorable.
   Despite concessions made by the allies, the dictator was implacable.
6. **complaisant** (kəm plā'sənt, -zənt, kom'plə zant') inclined or disposed to please; obliging; gracious. From the French word for *pleasing,* derived ultimately from Latin "complacere," *to be very pleasing.*

Jill's complaisant manner belied her reputation as a martinet.

Test 1: Synonyms

Select the best synonym for each numbered word. Write your answer in the space provided.

____ 1. complaisant
   a. self-satisfied   b. fake
   c. agreeable   d. successful
____ 2. implacable
   a. obliging   b. foolish   c. calm
   d. inexorable
____ 3. placid
   a. lake   b. tranquil   c. wintery
   d. nature-loving
____ 4. complacent
   a. smug   b. wretched
   c. contemplative   d. obsessively neat
____ 5. placebo
   a. strong medicine   b. harmless
   drug   c. sugar cube   d. cure
____ 6. placate
   a. offend   b. advertise   c. cause
   d. appease

Answers: 1. c   2. d   3. b   4. a   5. b   6. d

Test 2: Matching Synonyms

Match each of the numbered words with its closest synonym. Write your answer in the space provided.

1. PLACEBO	a. self-satisfied	____
2. COMPLAISANT	b. serene	____
3. IMPLACABLE	c. harmless substance	____
4. COMPLACENT	d. incapable of being appeased	____
5. PLACATE	e. pacify	____
6. PLACID	f. obliging	____

Answers: 1. c   2. f   3. d   4. a   5. e   6. b

Lesson 12. "The City of Brotherly Love": *PHIL, PHILO*

The site of the future city of Philadelphia was settled in the mid-seventeenth century by Swedish immigrants. Later the prominent English Quaker William Penn (1644–1718) determined to establish a New World colony where religious and political freedom would be guaranteed. He first obtained from Charles II a charter for Pennsylvania (named by the king). In 1682 he surveyed the land and laid out the plan for the "City of Brotherly Love," Philadelphia. The settlement flourished from the time of its foundation, growing into a thriving center of trade and manufacturing.

The Greek root "phil, philo," meaning *love*, has given us many other words besides "Philadelphia." Here are ten of them to add to your vocabulary.

1. **philanthropy** (fi lan'thrə pē) affection for humankind, especially as manifested in donations of money, property, or work to needy persons or for socially useful purposes. From Greek "philanthropia," *love of humanity.*

   Millions of people have benefited from Andrew Carnegie's works of philanthropy.

2. **philanderer** (fi lan'dər ər) a man who makes love without serious intentions, especially one who carries on flirtations.

   When she discovered that her husband was a philanderer, she sued for divorce.

3. **bibliophile** (bib'lē ə fil', -fil) a person who loves or collects books, especially as examples of fine or unusual printing, binding, or the like. From Greek "biblion," *book* + "philos," *loving.*

   The bibliophile was excited by the prospect of acquiring a first edition of Mark Twain's *Life on the Mississippi.*

4. **philharmonic** (fil'här mon'ik) a symphony orchestra.

   The philharmonic is presenting a concert this week.

5. **philately** (fi lat'l ē) the collection and study of postage stamps. From Greek "phil-," *loving* + "ateleia," *exemption from charges* (due to a sender's prepayment shown by a postage stamp).

   To pursue his hobby of philately, the collector attended stamp exhibitions as often as possible.

6. **philhellene** (fil hel'ēn) a friend and supporter of the Greeks.

   George was a philhellene whose greatest passion was ancient Greek sculpture.

7. **philter** (fil'tər) a potion or drug that is supposed to induce a person to fall in love with someone.

   He so desperately wanted her love that he resorted to dropping a philter into her drink.

8. **Anglophile** (ang'glə fil', -fil) a person who greatly admires England or anything English.

   A devoted Anglophile, Barry visits England at least twice a year.

9. **philodendron** (fil'ə den'drən) an ornamental tropical plant.

   The word "philodendron" originally meant *fond of trees,* but now we use it to refer to a plant.

10. **philology** (fi lol'ə jē) the study of written records, their authenticity and original form, and the determination of their meaning; in earlier use, linguistics. From Greek "philo-," *loving* + "logos," *word, speech, reason.*

    The subject of philology, in its broadest sense, is culture and literature.

Test 1: Definitions

Select the word that best fits the definition. Write your answer in the space provided.

____ 1. a person who greatly admires England or anything English
   a. Anglophile   b. philhellene
   c. bibliophile   d. philanderer

____ 2. an ornamental tropical plant
   a. philanthropy   b. philodendron
   c. philately   d. Anglophile

____ 3. a love potion
   a. philhellene   b. philology
   c. philter   d. bibliophile

____ 4. the collection and study of stamps
   a. philanthropy   b. philology
   c. philharmonic   d. philately

____ 5. a symphony orchestra
   a. philodendron   b. philter
   c. philharmonic   d. philately

____ 6. a friend and supporter of the Greeks
   a. philanderer   b. philhellene
   c. Anglophile   d. bibliophile

____ 7. linguistics
   a. philter   b. philately
   c. philosophy   d. philology

____ 8. a person who loves books
   a. philanderer   b. philter
   c. Anglophile   d. bibliophile

9. concern for humanity
   a. philanthropy   b. philodendron
   c. philology   d. philter
___ 10. a man who makes love without serious intentions, especially one who carries on flirtations
   a. bibliographer   b. philanderer
   c. bibliophile   d. Anglophile

Answers: 1. a   2. b   3. c   4. d   5. c   6. b
7. d   8. d   9. a   10. b

Test 1: True/False

In the space provided, write T if the definition of the numbered word is true or F if it is false.

		T or F
1. PHILATELY	fondness for stamps	___
2. PHILHELLENE	supporter of Greek culture	___
3. BIBLIOPHILE	lover of books	___
4. PHILANDERER	womanizer	___
5. PHILODENDRON	plant	___
6. PHILOLOGY	study of geography	___
7. PHILTER	filtration	___
8. PHILANTHROPY	stinginess	___
9. PHILHARMONIC	fond of books	___
10. ANGLOPHILE	stamp collector	___

Answers: 1. T   2. T   3. T   4. T   5. T   6. F
7. F   8. F   9. F   10. F

LESSON 13. "HANG IN THERE, BABY!": *PEND*

The word "appendix" has two meanings. First, it is an organ located in the lower right side of the abdomen. A vestigial organ, it has no function in humans. Second, it refers to the supplementary material found at the back of a book. The two meanings can be surmised from their root, "pend," *to hang* or *weigh*. The appendix (vermiform appendix, strictly speaking) "hangs" in the abdomen, as the appendix "hangs" at the end of a text.

Knowing the "pend" root can help you figure out the meanings of other words as well. Below are eight such words to help you hone your language skills.

1. **append** (ə pend') to add as a supplement or accessory.
   My supervisor asked me to append this material to the report we completed yesterday.
2. **appendage** (ə pen'dij) a subordinate part attached to something; a person in a subordinate or dependent position.
   The little boy had been hanging on his mother's leg for so long that she felt he was a permanent appendage.
3. **compendium** (kəm pen'dē əm) a brief treatment or account of a subject, especially an extensive subject.
   The medical editors put together a compendium of modern medicine.
4. **stipend** (stī'pend) fixed or regular pay; any periodic payment, especially a scholarship allowance. From Latin "stips," *a coin* + "pendere," *to weigh, pay out.*
   The graduate students found their stipends inadequate to cover the cost of living in a big city.
5. **pendulous** (pen'jə ləs, pend'yə-) hanging down loosely; swinging freely.
   She had pendulous jowls.
6. **pendant** (pen' dənt) a hanging ornament.
   She wore a gold necklace with a ruby pendant.
7. **impending** (im pen'ding) about to happen; imminent.
   The impending storm filled them with dread.
8. **perpendicular** (pûr'pən dik'yə lər) vertical; upright.
   They set the posts perpendicular to the ground.

Test 1: Matching Synonyms

Match each of the numbered words with its closest synonym. Write your answer in the space provided.

1. APPENDAGE	a. upright	___
2. COMPENDIUM	b. salary	___
3. IMPENDING	c. hanging	___
4. PENDULOUS	d. adjunct	___
5. PERPENDICULAR	e. ornament	___
6. APPEND	f. summary	___
7. PENDANT	g. attach	___
8. STIPEND	h. imminently menacing	___

Answers: 1. d   2. f   3. h   4. c   5. a   6. g
7. e   8. b

Test 2: True/False

In the space provided, write T if the definition of the numbered word is true or F if it is false.

			T or F
1. PENDULOUS	swinging freely		____
2. PERPENDICULAR	curved		____
3. PENDANT	hanging ornament		____
4. STIPEND	fasten		____
5. APPEND	add		____

6. COMPENDIUM	excised section		____
7. APPENDAGE	adjunct		____
8. IMPENDING	imminent		____

Answers: 1. T 2. F 3. T 4. F 5. T 6. F
7. T 8. T

LESSON 14. "OH GOD!": *THE, THEO*

Atheism is the doctrine that denies the existence of a supreme deity. Many people have been incorrectly labeled atheists because they rejected some popular belief in divinity. The Romans, for example, felt the early Christians were atheists because they did not worship the pagan gods; Buddhists and Jains have been called atheistic because they deny a personal God. The word "atheism" comes from the Greek prefix "a-," *without,* and the root "the, theo," meaning *god.*

Many words derive from this root; the following section provides just a few useful examples.

1. **theology** (thē ol′ə jē) the field of study that deals with God or a deity.
    Modern theology is chiefly concerned with the relation between humanity and God.
2. **theism** (thē′iz′ əm) the belief in the existence of a God or deity as the creator and ruler of the universe.
    The religious seminary taught its students the philosophy of theism.
3. **monotheism** (mon′ə thē iz′əm) the doctrine or belief that there is only one God.
    Judaism and Christianity preach monotheism.
4. **theocracy** (thē ok′rə sē) a form of government in which God or a deity is recognized as the supreme ruler.
    Puritan New England was a theocracy, with ministers as governors and the Bible as the constitution.
5. **pantheism** (pan′ thē iz′əm) the doctrine that God is the transcendent reality of which the material universe and human beings are only manifestations.
    The New England philosophy of Transcendentalism that flourished in the mid-nineteenth century included elements of pantheism.
6. **apotheosis** (ə poth′ē ō′sis, ap′ə thē′ə sis) the exaltation of a person to the rank of a god; ideal example; epitome.
    This poem is the apotheosis of the Romantic spirit.

7. **theogony** (thē og′ə nē) an account of the origin of the gods.
    Hesiod wrote a theogony of the Greek gods.

Test 1: Defining Words

Define each of the following words.

1. pantheism _____
2. theology _____
3. theogony _____
4. theism _____
5. apotheosis _____
6. theocracy _____
7. monotheism _____

Suggested Answers: 1. the doctrine that God is the transcendent reality of which the material universe and human beings are only manifestations
2. the field of study that treats of the deity, its attributes, and its relation to the universe 3. an account of the origin of the gods 4. the belief in one God as the creator and ruler of the universe
5. the exaltation of a person to the rank of a god; the glorification of a person, act, principle, etc., as an ideal 6. a form of government in which God or a deity is recognized as the supreme civil ruler
7. the doctrine or belief that there is only one God

Test 2: True/False

In the space provided, write T if the definition of the numbered word is true or F if it is false.

		T or F
1. APOTHEOSIS	epitome	____
2. THEOGONY	account of the origin of the gods	____
3. THEOCRACY	religious government	____
4. THEISM	belief in rebirth	____
5. MONOTHEISM	viral illness	____
6. PANTHEISM	rejected beliefs	____
7. THEOLOGY	study of divine things	____

Answers: 1. T 2. T 3. F 4. F 5. F 6. F
7. T

LESSON 15. "CALL OUT!": VOC

The voice box (more properly called the "larynx") is the muscular and cartilaginous structure in which the vocal cords are located. The vibration of the vocal cords by air passing out of the lungs causes the formation of sounds that are then amplified by the resonating nature of the oral and nasal cavities. The root "voc," meaning *call* or *voice*, is the basis of words like "vocal," as well as a host of other powerful words. Now study the following ten "vocal" words.

1. **avocation** (av′ə kā′shən) a minor or occasional occupation; hobby. From Latin "avocatio," *distraction*, derived from "avocare," *to call away*.
   His avocation is bird-watching.

2. **vocable** (vō′ kə bəl) a word, especially one considered without regard to meaning. From Latin "vocabulum," derived from "vocare," *to call*, from "voc-, vox," *voice*.
   Lewis Carroll coined many nonsense vocables, such as *jabberwocky* and *bandersnatch*.

3. **vociferous** (vō sif′ər əs) crying out noisily; clamorous; characterized by noise or vehemence.
   She was vociferous in her support of reform legislation.

4. **advocate** (ad′və kāt′) to plead in favor of; support.
   The citizens' committee advocated a return to the previous plan.

5. **convoke** (kən vōk′) to summon to meet. From Latin "convocare" ("con-," *with, together* + "vocare," *to call*).
   They will convoke the members for a noon meeting.

6. **evoke** (i vōk′) to call up, as memories or feelings. From Latin "evocare."
   The music evoked the mood of spring.

7. **revoke** (ri vōk′) to take back or withdraw; cancel. From Latin "revocare," *to call again, recall*.
   The king revoked his earlier decree.

8. **invoke** (in vōk′) to call forth or pray for; appeal to or petition; declare to be in effect. From Latin "invocare."
   The defendant invoked the Fifth Amendment so as not to incriminate himself.

9. **equivocal** (i kwiv′ə kəl) of uncertain significance; not determined; dubious. From Latin "aequivocus" ("aequus," *equal* + "voc-, vox," *voice*).
   Despite his demands for a clear-cut decision, she would give only an equivocal response.

10. **irrevocable** (i rev′ə kə bəl) incapable of being revoked or recalled; unable to be repealed or annulled.
    Once Caesar crossed the Rubicon, his decision to begin the civil war against Pompey was irrevocable.

Test 1: Matching Synonyms

Match each of the numbered words with its closest synonym. Write your answer in the space provided.

1. CONVOKE	a. word	____
2. ADVOCATE	b. hobby	____
3. REVOKE	c. uncertain	____
4. EQUIVOCAL	d. permanent	____
5. INVOKE	e. summon	____
6. VOCABLE	f. pray for	____
7. EVOKE	g. support	____
8. VOCIFEROUS	h. loud	____
9. IRREVOCABLE	i. cancel	____
10. AVOCATION	j. call up; produce	____

Answers: 1. e 2. g 3. i 4. c 5. f 6. a 7. j 8. h 9. d 10. b

Test 2: True/False

In the space provided, write T if the definition of the numbered word is true or F if it is false.

		T or F
1. REVOKE	restore	____
2. AVOCATION	profession	____
3. VOCIFEROUS	quiet	____
4. ADVOCATE	oppose	____
5. EVOKE	stifle	____
6. EQUIVOCAL	unambiguous	____
7. INVOKE	suppress	____
8. IRREVOCABLE	changeable	____
9. CONVOKE	summon	____
10. VOCABLE	word	____

Answers: 1. F 2. F 3. F 4. F 5. F 6. F 7. F 8. F 9. T 10. T

Lesson 16. "A rose by any other name": NOMIN, NOMEN

The differences between the nominative and objective cases have baffled countless generations of English-speaking students. Is it I or me? Who or whom? The nominative case is so named because it *names* the subject, the doer of the action, whereas the objective case refers to the object, as of a verb or preposition. Here are eight words that use the root "nomin, nomen," *name*.

1. **nominee** (nom'ə nē') a person named, as to run for elective office or to fill a particular post.
   In order to qualify for consideration, the nominee was required to present a petition with three hundred verifiable signatures.
2. **misnomer** (mis nō'mər) a misapplied name or designation; an error in naming a person or thing.
   "Expert" was a misnomer; "genius" was a far more accurate description of the young chess player.
3. **nomenclature** (nō'mən klā'chər) a set or system of names or terms, as those used in a particular science or art.
   The scientific nomenclature devised by Linnaeus was a great innovation.
4. **ignominious** (ig'nə min'ē əs) disgracing one's name; humiliating; discreditable; contemptible.
   The army suffered an ignominious defeat.
5. **nominal** (nom'ə nl) being such in name only; so-called.
   The silent partner is the nominal head of the firm.
6. **nominate** (nom'ə nāt') to name (someone) for appointment or election to office.
   The delegate from Vermont was pleased to nominate a favorite son for President at the Democratic convention.

Test 1: True/False

In the space provided, write T if the definition of the numbered word is true or F if it is false.

		T or F
1. IGNOMINIOUS	foolish, ignorant	____
2. NOMINATE	name as a candidate	____
3. NOMENCLATURE	clamp	____
4. NOMINEE	candidate	____
5. NOMINAL	so-called	____
6. MISNOMER	faux pas	____

Answers: 1. F 2. T 3. F 4. T 5. T 6. F

Test 2: Synonyms

Select the best synonym for each numbered word. Write your answer in the space provided.

____ 1. ignominious
   a. ignorant b. enormous
   c. disgraceful d. successful
____ 2. nomenclature
   a. biology b. classification c. torture device d. international transport
____ 3. nominee
   a. elected official b. hereditary title
   c. candidate d. assumed name
____ 4. misnomer
   a. misapplied name b. married name c. wrong road d. misapplied remedy
____ 5. nominal
   a. a lot b. allot c. so-called
   d. summons
____ 6. nominate
   a. apply b. designate c. reject
   d. elect

Answers: 1. c 2. b 3. c 4. a 5. c 6. b

WORD HISTORIES I

LESSON 1.

Words, like people, have a past, and as with people, some words have more interesting stories than others. Knowing a word's history can help you remember it and incorporate it into your daily speech. The following ten words have especially intriguing backgrounds. Read through the histories, then complete the self-tests that follow.

1. **bootlegger** (boot′leg′ər) Originally, a "bootlegger" was a person who smuggled outlawed alcoholic liquor in the tops of his tall boots. Today the term is used to mean *someone who unlawfully makes, sells, or transports alcoholic beverages* without registration or payment of taxes.

2. **bugbear** (bug′bâr′) The word refers to *a source of fears, often groundless.* It comes from a Welsh legend about a goblin in the shape of a bear that ate up naughty children.

3. **fiasco** (fē as′kō) "Fiasco" is the Italian word for *flask* or *bottle.* How it came to mean *a complete and ignominious failure* is obscure. One theory suggests that Venetian glassblowers set aside fine glass with flaws to make into common bottles.

4. **jackanapes** (jak′ə nāps′) Today the word is used to describe *an impertinent, presumptuous young man; a whippersnapper.* Although its precise origin is uncertain, we know that the term was first used as an uncomplimentary nickname for William de la Pole, Duke of Suffolk, who was murdered in 1450. His badge was an ape's clog and chain. In a poem of the time, Suffolk was called "the Ape-clogge," and later referred to as an ape called "Jack Napes."

5. **jeroboam** (jer′ə bō′əm) We now use the term "jeroboam" to refer to *a wine bottle having a capacity of about three liters.* Historically, Jeroboam was the first king of the Biblical kingdom of Israel, described in I Kings 11:28 as "a mighty man of valor," who, three verses later, "made Israel to sin." Some authorities trace the origin of today's usage to the king, reasoning that since an oversized bottle of wine can cause sin, it too is a jeroboam.

6. **nonplus** (non plus′, non′plus) The word "nonplus" means *to make utterly perplexed, to puzzle completely.* The original Latin phrase was "non plus ultra," meaning *no more beyond,* allegedly inscribed on the Pillars of Hercules, beyond which no ship could safely sail.

7. **quisling** (kwiz′ling) This term refers to *a traitor,* a person who betrays his or her own country by aiding an enemy and often serving later in a puppet government. It is directly derived from the name of Vidkun Quisling (1887–1945), a Norwegian army officer turned fascist who collaborated with the Nazis early in World War II.

8. **bowdlerize** (bōd′lə rīz′, boud′-) In 1818, Scottish physician Dr. Thomas Bowdler published a new edition of Shakespeare's works. The value of his edition, he stated, lay in the fact that he had edited it so that all "words and expressions are omitted which cannot with propriety be read aloud to the family." Good intentions aside, he found himself being held up to ridicule. From his name is derived the word "bowdlerize," meaning *to expurgate a literary text in a prudish manner.*

9. **boycott** (boi′kot) In an attempt to break the stranglehold of Ireland's absentee landlords,

Charles Stewart Parnell advocated in 1880 that anyone who took over land from which a tenant had been evicted for nonpayment of rent should be punished "by isolating him from his kind as if he was a leper of old." The most famous application of Parnell's words occurred soon after on the estate of the Earl of Erne. Unable to pay their rents, the earl's tenants suggested a lower scale, but the manager of the estate, Captain Charles Cunningham Boycott, would not accept the reduction. In retaliation, the tenants applied the measures proposed by Parnell, not only refusing to gather crops and run the estate, but also intercepting Boycott's mail and food, humiliating him in the street, and threatening his life. Their treatment of Boycott became so famous that within a few months the newspapers were using his name to identify any such nonviolent coercive practices. Today "boycott" means *to join together in abstaining from, or preventing dealings with, as a protest.*

10. **chauvinism** (shō'və niz'əm) One of Napoleon's most dedicated soldiers, Nicolas Chauvin was wounded seventeen times fighting for his emperor. After he retired from the army, he spoke so incessantly of the majestic glory of his leader and the greatness of France that he became a laughingstock. In 1831, his name was used for a character in a play who was an almost idolatrous worshiper of Napoleon. The word "chauvin" became associated with this type of extreme hero worship and exaggerated patriotism. Today we use the term "chauvinism" to refer to *zealous and belligerent nationalism.*

Test 1: Matching Synonyms

Match each of the numbered words with its closest synonym. Write your answer in the space provided.

1. BOOTLEGGER	a. fanatical patriotism	____
2. BUGBEAR	b. total failure	____
3. FIASCO	c. expurgate	____
4. JACKANAPES	d. groundless fear	____
5. JEROBOAM	e. oversized wine bottle	____
6. NONPLUS	f. unlawful producer of alcohol	____
7. QUISLING	g. rude fellow	____
8. BOWDLERIZE	h. perplex	____
9. BOYCOTT	i. traitor	____
10. CHAUVINISM	j. strike	____

Answers: 1. f 2. d 3. b 4. g 5. e 6. h
7. i 8. c 9. j 10. a

Test 2: True/False

In the space provided, write T if the definition of the numbered word is true or F if it is false.

		T or F
1. BOWDLERIZE	expurgate	____
2. BOYCOTT	male child (Scottish)	____
3. BOOTLEGGER	petty thief	____
4. FIASCO	celebration	____
5. CHAUVINISM	fanatical patriotism	____
6. JACKANAPES	jack-of-all-trades	____
7. QUISLING	turncoat	____
8. BUGBEAR	baseless fear	____
9. JEROBOAM	ancient queen	____
10. NONPLUS	certain	____

Answers: 1. T 2. F 3. F 4. F 5. T 6. F
7. T 8. T 9. F 10. F

LESSON 2.

The origins of most of the following words can be traced to Latin. Read through the histories, then complete the self-tests.

1. **aberration** (ab'ə rā'shən) This word comes from the Latin verb "aberrare," *to wander away from.* A person with a psychological "aberration" exhibits behavior that strays from the accepted path; hence the word means *deviation from what is common, normal, or right.*

2. **abominate** (ə bom'ə nāt') "Abominate" is from the Latin "abominor," meaning *I pray that the event predicted by the omen may be averted.* The Romans murmured the word to keep away the evil spirits whenever anyone said something unlucky. Today we use it to mean *to regard with intense aversion or loathing; abhor.*

3. **abracadabra** (ab'rə kə dab'rə) This intriguing-sounding word was first used as a charm in the second century. The Romans believed that the word had the ability to cure toothaches and other illnesses. Patients seeking relief wrote the letters in the form of a triangle on a piece of parchment and wore it around their necks on a length of thread. Today "abracadabra" is used as a pretend conjuring word. It also means *meaningless talk; nonsense.*

4. **wiseacre** (wīz'ā'kər) Although the word "acre" in "wiseacre" makes it appear that the term re-

fers to a unit of measurement, "wiseacre" is actually used contemptuously to mean *a wise guy* or *a smart aleck*. The term comes from the Dutch "wijssegger," which means *soothsayer*. Since soothsayers were considered learned, it was logical to call them "wise," which is what "wijs" means. The word "acre" is a mispronunciation of the Dutch "segger," *sayer*. There is a famous story in which the word was used in its present sense. In response to the bragging of a wealthy landowner, the English playwright Ben Jonson is said to have replied, "What care we for your dirt and clods? Where you have an acre of land, I have ten acres of wit." The chastened landowner is reported to have muttered: "He's Mr. Wiseacre."

5. **ebullient** (i bul'yənt, i bŏŏl'-) This word derives from the Latin "ebullire," *to boil over*. A person who is "ebullient" is *overflowing with fervor, enthusiasm, or excitement*.

6. **enclave** (en'klāv, än'-) The word "enclave" refers to *a country or territory entirely or mostly surrounded by another country*. More generally, it means *a group enclosed or isolated within a larger one*. The word comes ultimately from Latin "inclavare," *to lock in*.

7. **expedite** (ek'spi dīt') The word "expedite" means *to speed up the progress of something*. It comes from the Latin "expedire," *to set the feet free*.

8. **expunge** (ik spunj') To indicate that a soldier had retired from service, the ancient Romans wrote a series of dots or points beneath his name on the service lists. The Latin "expungere" thus meant both *to prick through* and *to mark off on a list*. Similarly, the English word "expunge" means *to strike or blot out; to erase*.

9. **inchoate** (in kō'it, -āt) "Inchoate" comes from the Latin "inchoare," *to begin*. Thus, an "inchoate" plan is *not yet fully developed*, or *rudimentary*.

10. **prevaricate** (pri var'i kāt') Today "prevaricate" means *to speak falsely or misleadingly with deliberate intent; to lie*. It has its origin in a physical act. The Latin verb "praevaricare" means *to spread apart*. The plowman who "prevaricated," then, made crooked ridges, deviating from straight furrows in the field.

Test 1: True/False

In the space provided, write T if the definition of the numbered word is true or F if it is false.

		T or F
1. ENCLAVE	rendezvous	___
2. ABOMINATE	detest	___
3. WISEACRE	large ranch	___
4. EXPUNGE	erase	___
5. PREVARICATE	preplan	___
6. INCHOATE	illogical	___
7. ABERRATION	fidelity	___
8. EXPEDITE	slow down	___
9. ABRACADABRA	hocus-pocus	___
10. EBULLIENT	enthusiastic	___

Answers: 1. F 2. T 3. F 4. T 5. F 6. F
7. F 8. F 9. T 10. T

Test 2: Matching Synonyms

Match each of the following numbered words with its closest synonym. Write your answer in the space provided.

1. WISEACRE	a. dispatch	___
2. ENCLAVE	b. divergence	___
3. INCHOATE	c. smarty-pants	___
4. ABOMINATE	d. obliterate	___
5. ABERRATION	e. misstate	___
6. ABRACADABRA	f. enclosure	___
7. EXPUNGE	g. detest	___
8. EXPEDITE	h. mumbo-jumbo	___
9. EBULLIENT	i. incipient	___
10. PREVARICATE	j. high-spirited	___

Answers: 1. c 2. f 3. i 4. g 5. b 6. h
7. d 8. a 9. j 10. e

LESSON 3.

Powerful words may have their beginnings in historical events, myths and legends, and special terminology. Here are ten more powerful words with interesting or unusual histories. Read through the etymologies (word origins), then complete the self-tests that follow.

1. **impeccable** (im pek'ə bəl) The word comes from the Latin "impeccabilis," *without sin*. The religious meaning has been only slightly extended over the years. Today an "impeccable" reputation is *faultless, flawless, irreproachable*.

2. **ambrosia** (am brō'zhə) Originally, "ambrosia" was the food of the Olympian gods (as "nectar" was their drink). The word comes from the Greek "a-," *not*, and "brostos," *mortal*; hence, eating ambrosia conferred immortality. Today

the word means *an especially delicious food,* with the implication that the concoction is savory enough to be fit for the gods. One popular dessert by this name contains shredded coconut, sliced fruits, and cream.

3. **gerrymander** (jer′i man′dər, ger′-) In 1812, Massachusetts governor Elbridge Gerry conspired with his party to change the boundaries of voting districts to enhance their own political clout. Noticing that one such district resembled a salamander, a newspaper editor coined the term "gerrymander" to describe *the practice of dividing a state, county, etc., into election districts so as to give one political party a majority while concentrating the voting strength of the other party into as few districts as possible.*

4. **mesmerize** (mez′mə rīz′, mes′-) The Austrian doctor Friedrich Anton Mesmer first publicly demonstrated the technique of hypnotism in 1775. Today the term "mesmerize" is still used as a synonym for "hypnotize," but it has broadened to also mean *spellbind* or *fascinate.*

5. **quintessence** (kwin tes′əns) The word comes from the medieval Latin term "quinta essentia," *the fifth essence.* This fifth primary element was thought to be ether, supposedly the constituent matter of the heavenly bodies, the other four elements being air, fire, earth, and water. The medieval alchemists tried to isolate ether through distillation. These experiments gave us the contemporary meaning of the word: *the pure and concentrated essence of a substance.*

6. **desultory** (des′əl tôr′ē) Some Roman soldiers went into battle with two horses, so that when one steed wearied, the soldier could vault onto the second horse striding along parallel to the first without losing any time. The same skill was employed by circus performers, especially charioteers, who could leap between two chariots riding abreast. Such a skilled horseman was called a "desultor," *a leaper.* Perhaps because these equestrians stayed only briefly on their mounts, the word "desultory" acquired its present meaning, *lacking in consistency, constancy, or visible order.*

7. **aegis** (ē′jis) When Zeus emerged victorious from his rebellion against the Titans, he attributed his success in part to his shield, which bore at its center the head of one of the Gorgons. The shield was reputedly made of goatskin, and hence its name, "aigis," was said to derive from the Greek "aig-," the stem of "aix," *goat.* Our present use of the word to mean *protection* or *sponsorship* evolved from the notion of eighteenth-century English writers

who assumed that the "egis" of Zeus or Athena—or their Roman counterparts Jove and Minerva—protected all those who came under its influence. Today the preferred spelling of the word is "aegis."

8. **adieu** (ə dōō′, ə dyōō′) The French expression "à Dieu" literally means *to God.* It is an abbreviation of the sentence "Je vous recommande à Dieu," *I commend you to God,* used between friends at parting. Both in French and in English the word means *good-bye* or *farewell.*

9. **aloof** (ə lōōf′) The word was originally a sailor's term, "a loof," *to the luff or windward direction,* perhaps from the Dutch "te loef," *to windward.* Etymologists believe that our use of the word to mean *at a distance, especially in feeling or interest,* comes from the idea of keeping a ship's head to the wind, and thus clear of the lee shore toward which it might drift.

10. **bluestocking** (blōō′stok′ing) A "bluestocking" is *a woman with considerable scholarly, literary, or intellectual ability or interest.* The word originated in connection with intellectual gatherings held in London about 1750 in the homes of women bored by the more frivolous pastimes of their age. Lavish evening dress was not required at these affairs; in fact, to put at ease visitors who could not afford expensive clothing, the women themselves dressed simply. One of the male guests went so far as to wear his everyday blue worsted stockings rather than the black silk ones usually worn at evening social gatherings. In response to their interests and dress, the English naval officer Admiral Edward Boscawen (1711–1761) is said to have sarcastically called these gatherings "the Blue Stocking Society."

Test 1: Definitions

Select the best definition for each numbered word. Circle your answer.

1. mesmerize
   a. attack   b. burst forth   c. fascinate
2. desultory
   a. aggressive   b. fitful   c. nasty
3. aloof
   a. remote   b. sailing   c. windy
4. aegis
   a. intense interest   b. goat   c. sponsorship
5. gerrymander
   a. medieval gargoyle   b. combine for historical sense   c. redistrict for political advantage
6. impeccable
   a. guileless   b. perfect   c. impeachable

7. adieu
   a. good-bye b. hello c. about-face
8. ambrosia
   a. suppository b. flower c. delicious food
9. quintessence
   a. pith b. fruit c. oil
10. bluestocking
    a. ill-dressed woman b. intellectual woman
    c. poor man

Answers: 1. c 2. b 3. a 4. c 5. c 6. b
7. a 8. c 9. a 10. b

Test 2: Matching Synonyms

Select the best synonym for each numbered word. Write your answer in the space provided.

1. ADIEU	a. delicious food	____
2. ALOOF	b. inconsistent; random	____
3. GERRYMANDER	c. distant; remote	____
4. AMBROSIA	d. farewell	____
5. IMPECCABLE	e. sponsorship	____
6. BLUESTOCKING	f. enthrall	____
7. DESULTORY	g. without fault	____
8. AEGIS	h. concentrated essence	____
9. MESMERIZE	i. divide a political district	____
10. QUINTESSENCE	j. a well-read woman	____

Answers: 1. d 2. c 3. i 4. a 5. g 6. j
7. b 8. e 9. f 10. h

LESSON 4.

The following words are all based on Greek myths and legends. Read through their histories, then complete the self-tests.

1. **amazon** (am′ə zon′) The word comes ultimately from the Greek, but the origin of the Greek word is uncertain. "Amazon" refers to *a tall, powerful, aggressive woman*. The Amazons of legend were female warriors, allied with the Trojans against the Greeks.

2. **anemone** (ə nem′ə nē′) This spring flower is named for Anemone, daughter of the wind. It comes from Greek "anemos," *the wind*.

3. **cornucopia** (kôr′nə kō′pē ə, -nyə-) According to Greek mythology, to save the infant Zeus from being swallowed by his father, Cronus, his mother, Rhea, hid her son in a cave and tricked Cronus into swallowing a stone wrapped in a cloth. The infant was then entrusted to the care of the nymph Amaltheia, who fed him on goat's milk. One day she filled a goat's horn with fresh fruit and herbs. The horn was thereafter magically refilled, no matter how much the child ate. To the Greeks, this boundless source was the horn of Amaltheia; to the Romans, it was the "cornu copiae," from "cornu," *horn,* and "copia," *plenty.* We know a "cornucopia" as *a horn containing food or drink in endless supply* or *horn of plenty.* It is often used as a symbol of abundance.

4. **diadem** (dī′ə dem′) In his quest to create a vast, unified empire with Babylon as its capital, the Macedonian hero Alexander the Great adopted a number of Persian and Oriental customs. He began to wear a blue-edged white headband with two ends trailing to the shoul-

ders, a Persian symbol of royalty. The Greeks called this headpiece a "diadema," literally *a binding over.* The headpiece was adopted by other monarchs down through the ages and further embellished with gold and gems, eventually evolving into a rich crown. Today a "diadem" is *a crown* or *a headband worn as a symbol of royalty.*

5. **epicure** (ep′i kyŏŏr′) Epicurus was a Greek philosopher who lived from 342 to 270 B.C. He believed that pleasure, attained mainly through pure and noble thoughts, constituted the highest happiness. After his death, his disciples spread his views. Their critics argued that Epicurus's theory was little more than an excuse for debauchery. From this argument we derive the present-day meaning of "epicure," *a person with luxurious tastes or habits, especially in eating or drinking.*

6. **esoteric** (es′ə ter′ik) From the Greek "esoterikos," *inner,* the word was used to describe the secret doctrines taught by the philosopher Pythagoras to a select few of his disciples. Hence "esoteric" means *understood by or meant only for those who have special knowledge or interest; recondite.*

7. **labyrinth** (lab′ə rinth) According to the Greek myth, King Minos of Crete ordered Daedalus to build a prison for the Minotaur, a half-bull, half-human monster. Daedalus succeeded by creating a series of twisting passageways that kept the monster imprisoned. Today a "labyrinth" is *a devious arrangement of linear patterns forming a design; a maze.*

8. **lethargy** (leth′ər jē) The Greeks believed in an

afterlife. In their mythology, the dead crossed the river Lethe, which flowed through Hades, the underground realm. Anyone who drank its water forgot the past. The Greek word "lethargia" derives from "lethe," *forgetfulness.* Hence our English word "lethargy," *drowsiness* or *sluggishness.*

9. **mentor** (men′tôr, -tər) In the *Odyssey* of Homer, Mentor is Odysseus's friend and tutor to his son Telemachus. Today the word "mentor" means *trusted teacher or guide.*

10. **nemesis** (nem′ə sis) Nemesis was the Greek goddess of vengeance, whose task it was to punish the proud and the insolent. Today a "nemesis" is *an agent or act of retribution or punishment,* or *something that a person cannot conquer or achieve.*

Test 1: True/False

In the space provided, write T if the definition of the numbered word is true or F if it is false.

		T or F
1. DIADEM	crown	___
2. LABYRINTH	lazy	___
3. MENTOR	mendacious	___
4. AMAZON	female warrior	___
5. ANEMONE	mollusk	___
6. ESOTERIC	arcane	___

7. LETHARGY	lassitude	___
8. NEMESIS	downfall	___
9. CORNUCOPIA	foot ailment	___
10. EPICURE	hidden	___

Answers: 1. T 2. F 3. F 4. T 5. F 6. T
7. T 8. T 9. F 10. F

Test 2: Defining Words

Define each of the following words.

1. diadem _____
2. esoteric _____
3. mentor _____
4. nemesis _____
5. amazon _____
6. epicure _____
7. anemone _____
8. cornucopia _____
9. labyrinth _____
10. lethargy _____

Suggested Answers: 1. crown 2. meant only for the select few with special knowledge or interest 3. trusted teacher or guide 4. act of retribution, or that which a person cannot conquer or achieve 5. female warrior 6. a person with luxurious tastes or habits, especially in eating or drinking 7. flower 8. boundless source 9. maze 10. sluggishness; weariness

LESSON 5.

Now study the curious origins of these ten words and work through the two self-tests that follow.

1. **ostracize** (os′trə sīz′) The word "ostracize" comes originally from the Greek "ostrakon," *tile, potsherd, shell.* It refers to the ancient Greek practice of banishing a man by writing his name on a shell or a bit of earthen tile. Anyone considered dangerous to the state was sent into exile for ten years. The judges cast their votes by writing on the shells or pottery shards and dropping them into an urn. The word "ostracize" still retains the same sense, *to exclude, by general consent, from society.*

2. **sycophant** (sik′ə fənt, -fant′) The word "sycophant" now means *a self-seeking, servile flatterer.* Originally, it was used to refer to an informer or slanderer. Curiously, it comes from Greek "sykon," *fig,* and "-phantes," *one who shows;* thus, *a fig-shower.* One explanation for this odd coinage is that in ancient Greece a sycophant was an informer against merchants engaged in the unlawful exportation of figs.

3. **cynosure** (sī′nə sho͝or′, sin′ə-) According to the myth, Zeus chose to honor the nymph who cared for him in his infancy by placing her in the sky as a constellation. One of her stars was so brilliant and stationary that all the other stars seemed to revolve around it. To the practical-minded ancient mariners, however, the bottom three stars of the constellation looked like a dog's tail. They named the entire constellation "Cynosura," *dog's tail.* From its name we get our word "cynosure," *something that attracts attention by its brilliance or interest.* By the way, we now call the constellation "Ursa Minor," *Little Bear,* and the bright star "Polaris," *Pole Star* or *North Star.*

4. **belfry** (bel′frē) Oddly enough, this word has nothing to do with bells, except by association. Originally, a "belfry" was a movable tower rolled up close to the walls of a besieged city by soldiers in wartime. Later, a belfry was a tower to protect watchmen, or a watchtower in which alarm bells were hung, through which usage it finally became *a bell tower.* The word came into

English from Old French, which in turn may have taken it from a Germanic military term.

5. **debauch** (di bôch′) Today we define the word "debauch" as *to corrupt by sensuality, intemperance, etc.* It comes from the French word "débaucher," meaning *to entice away from work or duty.*

6. **eldorado** (el′də rä′dō, -rā′-) The word comes from Spanish legends of an incredibly wealthy city in South America, so rich that its streets were paved with gold. Many adventurers set off to find this elusive city; in 1595 Sir Walter Raleigh ventured into Guiana in a vain attempt to locate it. Among the Spaniards, the king of this fabulous land came to be called "El Dorado," *the Golden One.* Today "eldorado" is used generally to mean *any fabulously wealthy place.*

7. **esquire** (es′kwī ᵊr) In medieval times, young men who wished to become knights first had to serve other knights. Their primary duty was to act as shield bearer. Because of this duty, the young man was called an "esquire," from the French "esquier," *shield bearer,* ultimately going back to the Latin "scutum," *shield.* Later the title "esquire" came to be attached to the sons of a nobleman; eventually it referred to any man considered a gentleman. Today it is often appended to a lawyer's name; in Britain, it is applied to a member of the gentry ranking next below a knight.

8. **filibuster** (fil′ə bus′tər) In the seventeenth century, English seamen who attacked Spanish ships and brought back wealth from New Spain were called "buccaneers." In Holland, they were known as "vrijbuiters," *free robbers.* In French, the word became first "fribustier" and then "flibustier." In Spain, the term was "filibustero." Then, when the nineteenth-century American soldier of fortune William Walker tried to capture Sonora, Mexico, the Mexicans promptly dubbed him a "filibuster." Today the term refers to *the use of irregular or disruptive tactics, such as exceptionally long speeches, by a member of a legislative assembly.* The current use of the word may have arisen through a comparison of a legislator's determination to block a bill with the tactics used by William Walker to evade the law.

9. **furlong** (fûr′lông, -long) In the twelfth century, an acre of land was defined as the area a yoke of oxen could plow in one day. As such, the size varied from place to place but always greatly exceeded what we accept today as an acre. In some places, an acre was defined by the area a team of eight oxen could plow in a day—about an eighth of a Roman mile, also called a "stadium." The length of the plow's furrows were thus each about a stadium in length; this became a convenient measure of distance—a "furlang" in Old English, from "furh," *furrow,* and "lang," *long.* This measure was then standardized to an area forty rods in length by four rods in width; however, the rod was not a standard measure either. Later, when the length of a yard was standardized, "furlong" came to be used simply as a term for *a unit of distance an eighth of a mile or 220 yards in length.*

10. **galvanism** (gal′və niz′əm) In the mid-eighteenth century, Luigi Galvani, a professor of anatomy at the University of Bologna, concluded that the nerves are a source of electricity. Although Volta later proved his theory incorrect, Galvani's pioneering work inspired other scientists to produce electricity by chemical means. Today the term "galvanism," *electricity,* honors Galvani.

Test 1: Definitions

Each of the following phrases contains an italicized word. See how many you can define correctly. Write your answer in the space provided.

_____ 1. bats in the *belfry*
a. cave   b. brain   c. bell tower
d. tropical tree

_____ 2. *ostracized* from society
a. banished   b. beaten   c. walked
d. welcomed

_____ 3. a hopeless *sycophant*
a. dreamer   b. alcoholic
c. romantic   d. toady

_____ 4. travel a *furlong*
a. acre   b. year   c. week   d. less than a mile

_____ 5. seek *eldorado*
a. physical comfort   b. delicious food   c. wealthy place   d. death

_____ 6. add the title *esquire*
a. gentleman   b. married man
c. duke   d. professional

_____ 7. *debauched* by the experience
a. impoverished   b. corrupted
c. strengthened   d. enriched

_____ 8. a lengthy *filibuster*
a. entertainment   b. obstructive tactics   c. childhood   d. voyage

_____ 9. powerful *galvanism*
a. electric current   b. discoveries
c. gases   d. weapons

_____ 10. the *cynosure* of all eyes
a. defect   b. attraction   c. sky-blue color   d. cynicism

Test 2: True/False

In the space provided, write T if the definition of the numbered word is true or F if it is false.

		T or F
1. BELFRY	steeple	___
2. DEBAUCH	corrupt	___
3. ESQUIRE	attorney's title	___
4. OSTRACIZE	exclude	___
5. FILIBUSTER	obstruction	___
6. FURLONG	eighth of a mile	___
7. CYNOSURE	sarcasm	___
8. ELDORADO	Spain	___
9. GALVANISM	atomic power	___
10. SYCOPHANT	flatterer	___

Answers: 1. T 2. T 3. T 4. T 5. T 6. T
7. F 8. F 9. F 10. T

LESSON 6.

Our language is enriched by many exotic words with curious histories. Here are ten new ones to add to your growing vocabulary. Read through the etymologies and complete the two self-tests that follow.

1. **juggernaut** (jug′ər nôt′, -not′) Our modern word "juggernaut" comes from the Hindi name for a huge image of the god Vishnu, "Jagannath," at Puri, a city in Orissa, India. Each summer, the statue is moved to a new location a little less than a mile away from the old one. Early tourists to India brought back strange stories of worshipers throwing themselves under the wheels of the wagon carrying the idol. Since any shedding of blood in the presence of the god is sacrilege, what these travelers probably witnessed was a weary pilgrim being accidentally crushed to death. Thus, thanks to exaggeration and ignorance, "juggernaut" came to mean *blind and relentless self-sacrifice.* In addition, the word means *any large, overpowering, or destructive force.*

2. **iconoclast** (ī kon′ə klast′) An "iconoclast" is *a person who attacks cherished beliefs or traditional institutions.* It is from the Greek "eikon," *image,* and "klastes," *breaker.* Although the contemporary usage is figurative, the word was originally used in a literal sense to describe the great controversy within the Christian church in the eighth century over religious images. One camp held that all visual representations should be destroyed because they encouraged idol worship; the other, that such artworks simply inspired the viewers to feel more religious. By the mid-eighth century, untold numbers of relics and images had been destroyed. The issue was not settled for nearly a century, when the images were restored to the church in Constantinople.

3. **laconic** (lə kon′ik) In Sparta, the capital of the ancient Greek region of Laconia, the children were trained in endurance, cunning, modesty, and self-restraint. From the terse style of speech and writing of the Laconians we derive the English word "laconic." Today the word retains this meaning, *expressing much in few words.*

4. **gamut** (gam′ət) Guido of Arezzo, one of the greatest musicians of medieval times, is credited with being first to use the lines of the staff and the spaces between them. He used the Greek letter "gamma" for the lowest tone in the scale. This note was called "gamma ut." Contracted to "gamut," it then designated the entire scale. The word quickly took on a figurative as well as a literal sense. Today "gamut" is defined as *the entire scale or range.*

5. **guillotine** (gil′ə tēn′, gē′ə-) After the outbreak of the French Revolution, Dr. Joseph Ignace Guillotin became a member of the National Assembly. During an early debate, he proposed that future executions in France be conducted by a humane beheading machine that he had seen in operation in another country. His suggestion was received favorably; in 1791, after Dr. Guillotin had retired from public service, the machine that bears his name was designed by Antoine Louis and built by a German named Schmidt. The guillotine was first used in 1792 to behead a thief. At that time, the device was called a "Louisette" after its designer; but the public began calling it after Dr. Guillotin, the man who had first advocated its use.

6. **horde** (hôrd) Upon the death of Genghis Khan, his grandson Batu Khan led the Mongol invasion of Europe, cutting a merciless swath from Moscow to Hungary. At each post, Batu erected a sumptuous tent made of silk and leather. His followers called it the "sira ordu," *the silken camp.* In Czech and Polish the Turkic "ordu" was changed to "horda." The name came to be applied not only to Batu's tent but also to his entire Mongol army. Because of the

terror they inspired across the land, "horde" eventually referred to any Tartar tribe. Today, it means *any large crowd; swarm.*

7. **lyceum** (lī sē′əm) The Lyceum was the shrine dedicated to Apollo by the Athenians. The name came from the Greek "Lykeion," meaning *Wolf Slayer,* a nickname of Apollo. The shrine was a favorite haunt of the Athenian philosophers, especially Aristotle, who taught his disciples while walking along its paths. Thus, the word "lyceum" came to mean *an institute for popular education, providing discussions, lectures, concerts, and so forth.*

8. **macabre** (mə kä′brə, -kä′bər) In modern usage, "macabre" means *gruesome and horrible, pertaining to death.* Its history is uncertain. However, most etymologists believe that the word's use in the French phrase "Danse Macabre," *dance of Macabre,* a translation of Medieval Latin "chorea Macchabeorum," connects the word with the Maccabees, the leaders of the Jewish rebellion against Syria about 165 B.C., whose death as martyrs is vividly described in the Book of Maccabees (a part of the Apocrypha).

9. **gargantuan** (gär gan′ chо̄o ən) The sixteenth-century French writer François Rabelais created a giant he named "Gargantua" after a legendary giant of the Middle Ages. To fuel his enormous bulk—Gargantua rode on a horse as large as six elephants—he had to consume prodigious amounts of food and drink. Today we use the word "gargantuan" to mean *gigantic, enormous.*

10. **libertine** (lib′ər tēn′) In ancient Rome, "libertinus" referred to a freed slave. Since those freed from slavery were unlikely to be strict observers of the laws that had enslaved them in the first place, "libertine" came to designate *a person who is morally or sexually unrestrained.*

Test 1: Matching Synonyms

Match each of the numbered words with its closest synonym. Write your answer in the space provided.

1. LYCEUM	a. skeptic	____
2. LIBERTINE	b. academy	____
3. ICONOCLAST	c. overpowering force	____
4. HORDE	d. terse	____
5. GARGANTUAN	e. gruesome	____
6. LACONIC	f. dissolute person	____
7. GUILLOTINE	g. beheading machine	____
8. JUGGERNAUT	h. entire range	____
9. GAMUT	i. huge	____
10. MACABRE	j. crowd	____

Answers: 1. b   2. f   3. a   4. j   5. i   6. d   7. g   8. c   9. h   10. e

Test 2: Defining Words

Define each of the following words.

1. iconoclast _____
2. libertine _____
3. gamut _____
4. macabre _____
5. guillotine _____
6. laconic _____
7. gargantuan _____
8. lyceum _____
9. horde _____
10. juggernaut _____

Suggested Answers: 1. a person who attacks cherished beliefs or traditional institutions   2. a rake   3. the entire scale or range   4. horrible, gruesome   5. a machine used to behead criminals   6. terse   7. enormous, colossal 8. institute for popular education   9. large group 10. an overpowering force

LESSON 7.

The English language has adopted a prodigious number of words from unexpected sources. Read through the histories of the ten unusual words that follow and then complete the self-tests.

1. **imp** (imp) In Old English, an imp was originally a young plant or seedling. Eventually, the term came to be used figuratively to indicate a descendant of a royal house, usually a male. Probably because of the behavior of such children, the word became synonymous with a young demon. Since the sixteenth century, the original meaning of "imp" as *scion* has been completely dropped, and the word is now used exclusively to mean *a little devil or demon, an evil spirit,* or *an urchin.*

2. **kaleidoscope** (kə lī′də skо̄p′) Invented in 1816 by Scottish physicist Sir David Brewster, the "kaleidoscope" is a scientific toy constructed of a series of mirrors within a tube. When the tube is turned by hand, symmetrical, ever-changing patterns can be viewed through the eyepiece. Brewster named his toy from the Greek "kalos," *beautiful;* "eidos," *form;* and "skopos," *watcher.*

3. **knave** (nāv) In Old English, the word "knave" (then spelled "cnafa") referred to a male child, a boy. It was later applied to a boy or man employed as a servant. Many of these boys had to be wily to survive their hard lot; thus the word gradually evolved to mean *a rogue* or *rascal.*

4. **Machiavellian** (mak'ē ə vel'ē ən) The Florentine political philosopher Nicolò Machiavelli (1469–1527) was a fervent supporter of a united Italy. Unfortunately, his methods for achieving his goals placed political expediency over morality. His masterpiece, *The Prince* (1513), advocated deception and hypocrisy on the grounds that the end justifies the means. Therefore, the adjective "Machiavellian" means *unscrupulous, cunning,* and *deceptive in the pursuit of power.*

5. **indolence** (in'dl əns) Originally, "indolence" meant *indifference*. The word was used in that sense until the sixteenth century. Probably because indifference is frequently accompanied by an unwillingness to bestir oneself, the term has now come to mean *lazy* or *slothful.*

6. **incubus/succubus** (in'kyə bəs, ing'-; suk'yə bəs) In the Middle Ages, women were thought to give birth to witches after being visited in their sleep by an "incubus," or *evil male spirit.* The female version of this spirit, said to be the cause of nightmares, was a "succubus." Because the evil spirit pressed upon the sleeper's body and soul, the term "incubus" also means *something that oppresses like a nightmare.*

7. **hoyden** (hoid'n) A "hoyden" is *a boisterous, ill-bred girl; a tomboy.* The word is usually linked to the Dutch "heyden," meaning *a rustic person* or *rude peasant,* originally *a heathen* or *pagan,* and is related to the English word "heathen." At first in English the word meant *a rude, boorish man,* but beginning in the 1600s it was applied to girls in the sense of *a tomboy.* How the change came about is uncertain.

8. **guinea** (gin'ē) The guinea was a gold coin first minted in 1663 for the use of speculators trading with Africa. The coins were called "guineas" because the trade took place along the coast of Guinea. The British guinea came to be worth 21 shillings. After the establishment of the gold standard in the early nineteenth century, no more guineas were struck. In Great Britain, a pound and one shilling is still often called a "guinea."

9. **macadam** (mə kad'əm) While experimenting with methods of improving road construction, John McAdam, a Scotsman, concluded that the prevailing practice of placing a base of large stones under a layer of small stones was unnecessary. As surveyor-general for the roads of Bristol, England, in the early nineteenth century, McAdam built roads using only six to ten inches of small crushed stones, thereby eliminating the cost of constructing the base. Not only were the results impressive, the savings were so remarkable that his idea soon spread to other countries. McAdam's experiments led to our use of the term "macadam" for *a road surface* or *pavement.*

10. **mackintosh** (mak'in tosh') In 1823, Scottish chemist Charles Macintosh discovered that the newfangled substance called "rubber" could be dissolved with naphtha. This solution could be painted on cloth to produce a waterproof covering. Clothing made from Macintosh's invention came to be called "mackintoshes," or *raincoats.*

Test 1: True/False

In the space provided, write T if the definition of the numbered word is true or F if it is false.

		T or F
1. INCUBUS	evil spirit	_____
2. HOYDEN	howl	_____
3. GUINEA	rush basket	_____
4. MACADAM	raincoat	_____
5. MACKINTOSH	road surface	_____
6. IMP	male servant	_____
7. MACHIAVELLIAN	principled	_____
8. KALEIDOSCOPE	optical toy	_____
9. INDOLENCE	laziness	_____
10. KNAVE	dishonest fellow	_____

Answers: 1. T   2. F   3. F   4. F   5. F   6. F
7. F   8. T   9. T   10. T

Test 2: Matching Synonyms

Select the best definition for each numbered word. Write your answer in the space provided.

1. MACADAM	a. raincoat	_____
2. HOYDEN	b. little mischiefmaker	_____
3. GUINEA	c. laziness	_____
4. MACKINTOSH	d. optical toy	_____
5. MACHIAVELLIAN	e. pavement	_____
6. IMP	f. rogue	_____
7. KALEIDOSCOPE	g. evil spirit	_____
8. KNAVE	h. gold coin	_____
9. INDOLENCE	i. sly and crafty	_____
10. INCUBUS	j. tomboy	_____

Answers: 1. e   2. j   3. h   4. a   5. i   6. b
7. d   8. f   9. c   10. g

LESSON 8.

Now read about these ten words and complete the tests that follow.

1. **maelstrom** (māl'strəm) The word's figurative meaning, *a restless, disordered state of affairs,* is derived from its literal one. Today's meaning comes from "Maelstrom," the name of a strong tidal current off the coast of Norway. The current creates a powerful whirlpool because of its configuration. According to legend, the current was once so strong that it could sink any vessel that ventured near it.

2. **insolent** (in'sə lənt) The word comes from the Latin "insolentem," which literally meant *not according to custom.* Since those who violate custom are likely to offend, "insolent" evolved to imply that the person was also vain and conceited. From this meaning we derive our present usage, *contemptuously rude or impertinent in speech or behavior.*

3. **interloper** (in'tər lō'pər) The word "interloper" was used in the late sixteenth century to describe Spanish traders who carved out for themselves a piece of the successful trade the British had established with the Russians. The word was formed on the analogy of "landloper," meaning *one who trespasses on another's land,* from a Dutch word literally meaning *land runner.* Although the dispute over the Spanish intrusion was settled within a few years, the word remained in use to mean *one who intrudes into some region or field of trade without a proper license* or *thrusts himself or herself into the affairs of others.*

4. **halcyon** (hal'sē ən) According to classical mythology, the demigod Halcyone threw herself into the sea when she saw the drowned body of her beloved mortal husband. After her tragic death, the gods changed Halcyone and her husband into birds, which they called "halcyons," our present-day kingfishers. The Greeks believed the sea calmed as the birds built their nests and hatched their eggs upon its waves during the seven days before and after the winter solstice. This period came to be known as "halcyon days." The adjective is now used to mean *calm, peaceful, prosperous,* or *joyful.*

5. **hector** (hek'tər) Hector was a great Trojan hero, son of King Priam. As Homer recounts in the *Iliad,* Hector took advantage of his enemy Achilles's departure from the Greek camp to drive the Greeks back to their ships and slay Achilles's dearest friend, Patroclus. To the Romans, who regarded themselves as descendants of the Trojans, Hector was a symbol of courage. But in the seventeenth century, the name was applied to the gangs of bullies who terrorized the back streets of London. It is to their transgressions that we owe the present use of "hector," *to harass or persecute.*

6. **helpmeet** (help'mēt') This synonym for *helpmate, companion, wife,* or *husband* is the result of a misunderstanding. The word comes from Genesis 2:18, "And the Lord God said, It is not good that the man should be alone; I will make him an help meet for him." In this passage, "meet" means *proper* or *appropriate,* but the two words came to be read as one, resulting in the word's current spelling.

7. **hermetic** (hûr met'ik) The Greeks linked the Egyptian god Thoth with Hermes, calling him "Hermes Trismegistus," Hermes Three-Times Greatest. He was accepted as the author of the books that made up the sum of Egyptian learning, called the "Hermetic Books." Since these forty-two works largely concerned the occult sciences, "hermetic" came to mean *secret,* and in a later usage, *made airtight by fusion or sealing.*

8. **intransigent** (in tran'si jənt) When Amadeus, the son of Victor Emmanuel II of Italy, was forced to abdicate the throne of Spain in 1873, those favoring a republic attempted to establish a political party. This group was called in Spanish "los intransigentes" (from "in-," *not* + "transigente," *compromising*) because they could not come to terms with the other political parties. The term passed into English as "intransigent." Today the word retains the same meaning: *uncompromising* or *inflexible.*

9. **jitney** (jit'nē) The origin of this term has long baffled etymologists. The word first appeared in American usage in the first decade of the twentieth century as a slang term for a nickel. The word then became associated with the public motor vehicles whose fare was five cents. Some authorities have theorized that the term is a corruption of "jeton," the French word for *token.* Today a "jitney" is *a small passenger bus following a regular route at varying hours.*

10. **junket** (jung'kit) At first, the word referred to a basket of woven reeds used for carrying fish, and was ultimately derived from Latin "juncus," *reed.* Then the basket was used to prepare cheese, which in turn came to be called "junket." Since the basket also suggested the food it

could carry, "junket" later evolved to mean *a great feast*. Today we use the term in closely related meanings: *a sweet custardlike food* or *flavored milk curdled with rennet* or *a pleasure excursion*.

Test 1: Matching Synonyms

Match each numbered word with its closest synonym. Write your answer in the space provided.

1. HALCYON	a. tightly sealed	____
2. INTRANSIGENT	b. intruder	____
3. JITNEY	c. impertinent	____
4. MAELSTROM	d. peaceful	____
5. JUNKET	e. inflexible	____
6. HECTOR	f. small bus	____
7. INSOLENT	g. companion	____
8. HERMETIC	h. pleasure trip	____
9. INTERLOPER	i. harass	____
10. HELPMEET	j. disorder	____

Answers: 1. d 2. e 3. f 4. j 5. h 6. i 7. c 8. a 9. b 10. g

Test 2: True/False

In the space provided, write T if the definition of the numbered word is true or F if it is false.

		T or F
1. HALCYON	calm	____
2. JITNEY	juggler	____
3. MAELSTROM	masculine	____
4. INTRANSIGENT	uncompromising	____
5. INSOLENT	rude	____
6. INTERLOPER	welcome guest	____
7. JUNKET	refuse	____
8. HECTOR	helper	____
9. HERMETIC	airtight	____
10. HELPMEET	newcomer	____

Answers: 1. T 2. F 3. F 4. T 5. T 6. F 7. F 8. F 9. T 10. F

LESSON 9.

The interesting origins of these ten words can help you remember their current meanings. Complete the quizzes after your reading.

1. **knickers** (nik'ərz) The descendants of the Dutch settlers in New York are sometimes known as "Knickerbockers." Thus, the term for the *loosely fitting short trousers gathered at the knee* that we call "knickers" derives from the name of the people who wore them, the Knickerbockers. The pants first came to public attention in the illustrations to Washington Irving's *A History of New York from the Beginning of the World to the End of the Dutch Dynasty,* published in 1809 under the pen name Diedrich Knickerbocker. Knickers were formerly extremely popular attire for boys and young men.

2. **magenta** (mə jen'tə) On June 4, 1859, the French and Sardinian armies of Napoleon III won a decisive victory over the Austrian army in the northern fields of Italy near the small town of Magenta. At the time of the victory, scientists had just created a dye imparting a lovely reddish-purple color but had not yet named it. When the French chemists heard of the momentous triumph for their country, they named the dye "magenta" in honor of the victory. Today we call this *reddish-purple color* "magenta," but the dye itself is technically known as "fuchsin" (as in "fuchsia").

3. **garret** (gar'it) Originally, the French word "garite" referred to a watchtower from which a sentry could look out for approaching enemies. Among the things the Normans brought when they conquered England was the word "garite." In England the word came to mean a *loft* or *attic* and its spelling was altered to "garret."

4. **mandrake** (man'drāk) The original name for this narcotic herb was "mandragora," which is still its scientific name; the word comes from Greek "mandragoras," of unknown origin. In the Middle Ages, Englishmen erroneously assumed that "mandragora" came from "mandragon," a combination of "man," because of the appearance of its forked root, and "dragon," because of its noxious qualities. Since a dragon was then commonly called a "drake," the plant came to be called "mandrake."

5. **gazette** (gə zet') In the beginning of the sixteenth century, Venetians circulated a small tin coin of little value they called a "gazzetta," a diminutive of the word "gaza," magpie. Soon after, the government began to print official bulletins with news of battles, elections, and so forth. Because the cost of the newspaper was one gazzetta, the leaflet itself eventually came to be called a "gazzetta." By the end of the century, the term was used in England as well. The present spelling is the result of French influence. Today a "gazette" refers to *a newspaper* or *official government journal.*

6. **martinet** (mär'tn et', mär'tn et') Seeking to improve his army, in 1660 Louis XIV hired Col-

onel Jean Martinet, a successful infantry leader, to devise a drill for France's soldiers. Martinet drilled his soldiers to such exacting standards that his name came to be applied to any officer intent on maintaining military discipline or precision. Thus, in English, a "martinet" is *a strict disciplinarian, especially a military one.* Interestingly, in France, Martinet's name acquired no such negative connotation.

7. **gorgon** (gôr′gən) The name comes from the Greek myth of the three monstrous sisters who inhabited the region of Night. Together they were known as the "Gorgons"; their individual names were Stheno, Euryale, and Medusa. Little has been written about the first two. Medusa was the most hideous and dangerous; her appearance, with her head of writhing serpents, was so ghastly that anyone who looked directly at her was turned to stone. A secondary meaning of "gorgon" is *a mean or repulsive woman.*

8. **maudlin** (môd′lin) This word, meaning *tearfully or weakly emotional,* comes from the miracle plays of the Middle Ages. Although these plays depicted many of the Biblical miracles, the most popular theme was the life of Mary Magdalene. The English pronounced her name "maudlin," and since most of the scenes in which she appeared were tearful, this pronunciation of her name became associated with mawkish sentimentality.

9. **meander** (mē an′dər) In ancient times, the Menderes River in western Turkey was so remarkable for its twisting path that its Greek name, "Maiandros," came to mean *a winding.* In Latin this word was spelled "maeander," hence English "meander," used mainly as a verb and meaning *to proceed by a winding or indirect course.*

10. **gossamer** (gos′ə mər) In fourth-century Germany, November was a time of feasting and merrymaking. The time-honored meal was roast goose. So many geese were eaten that the month came to be called "Gänsemonat," *goose month.* The term traveled to England but in the course of migration, it became associated with the period of unseasonably warm autumn weather we now call "Indian summer." During the warm spell, large cobwebs are found draped in the grass or suspended in the air. These delicate, airy webs, which we call "gossamer," are generally believed to have taken their name from "goose summer," when their appearance was most noticeable. We now define "gossamer" as *something fine, filmy, or light;* it also means *thin and light.*

Test 1: Sentence Completion

Complete each sentence with the appropriate word from the following list.

gossamer   gorgon   maudlin
magenta   garret   meander
mandrake   knickers   gazette
martinet

1. It is pleasant to _____ slowly down picturesque country roads on crisp autumn afternoons.
2. The movie was so _____ that I was still crying when the closing credits began to roll.
3. The teacher was such a _____ that his students soon rebelled fiercely against his strict regulations.
4. In ancient days, the root of the _____ was surrounded by myths: it was believed that it could cast out demons from the sick, cause madness, or even make a person fall hopelessly in love.
5. Your entire load of white laundry will likely turn pink or even _____ if you include even a single new and previously unwashed red or purple sock.
6. Many budding artists have romantic fantasies about living in a wretched _____ and starving for the sake of their art.
7. Men rarely wear _____ any longer for playing golf, but the style was popular for many years.
8. The _____ cobwebs shredded at the slightest touch.
9. Since the daily _____ has excellent coverage of local sports, cultural events, and regional news, we tend to overlook its weak coverage of international events.
10. The gossip columnist was so mean and ugly that her victims referred to her as a _____ .

Answers: 1. meander   2. maudlin   3. martinet   4. mandrake   5. magenta   6. garret   7. knickers   8. gossamer   9. gazette   10. gorgon

Test 2: Definitions

Select the correct definition for each numbered word. Write your answer in the space provided.

_____ 1. knickers
     a. short pants   b. soccer players
     c. early settlers   d. punch line
_____ 2. meander
     a. moan   b. ramble   c. strike back
     d. starve

3. gorgon
   a. misunderstood person   b. foregone
   conclusion   c. hideous monster
   d. midget
4. magenta
   a. military victory   b. electricity
   c. machinations   d. reddish-purple
   color
5. mandrake
   a. myth   b. dragon   c. duck
   d. narcotic plant
6. garret
   a. basement   b. attic   c. garage
   d. unsuccessful artist
7. maudlin
   a. warlike   b. married   c. mawkish
   d. intense
8. martinet
   a. strict disciplinarian   b. facile
   problem   c. hawk   d. musical
   instrument
9. gazette
   a. journal   b. gazebo   c. silver coin
   d. book of maps
10. gossamer
   a. variety of goose   b. grasp   c. flimsy
   material   d. idle talk

Answers: 1. a   2. b   3. c   4. d   5. d   6. b
7. c   8. a   9. a   10. c

LESSON 10.

Knowing the backgrounds of the following ten words will give you an edge in recalling their meanings and using them in conversation to make your speech and writing more powerful. When you have studied each word, complete the two quizzes that follow.

1. **meerschaum** (mēr′shəm, -shôm) Since it is white and soft and often found along seashores, ancient people believed this white clay-like mineral was foam from the ocean turned into stone. As a result, in all languages it was called "sea foam." It was of little use until German artisans began to carve it into pipes, for as it absorbs the nicotine from the tobacco it acquires a deep honey color. Because the Germans were the first to find a use for it, the German name stuck: "meer," *sea;* "schaum," *foam.* In English "meerschaum" often means *a tobacco pipe with a bowl made of meerschaum* (the mineral).

2. **toady** (tō′dē) In the seventeenth century, people believed that toads were poisonous, and anyone who mistakenly ate a toad's leg instead of a frog's leg would die. Rather than swearing off frogs' legs, people sought a cure for the fatal food poisoning. Charlatans would sometimes hire an accomplice who would pretend to eat a toad, at which point his employer would whip out his instant remedy and "save" his helper's life. For his duties, the helper came to be called a "toad-eater." Since anyone who would consume anything as disgusting as a toad must be completely under his master's thumb, "toad-eater" or "toady" became the term for *an obsequious sycophant; a fawning flatterer.*

3. **gregarious** (gri gâr′ē əs) The Latin term for a herd of animals is "grex." Because a group of people banded together in military formation resembles a herd of animals, the word "grex" was applied to people as well as animals. The way the people grouped together was called "gregarius," *like a herd.* The word has come down to us as "gregarious," meaning *friendly* or *fond of the company of others.*

4. **miscreant** (mis′krē ənt) The word's source, the Old French "mes-," *wrongly,* and "creant," *believing,* tells us that "miscreant" was originally used to describe a heretic. The word has evolved over the centuries, however, to refer to *a base, villainous, or depraved person.*

5. **sinecure** (sī′ni kyŏŏr′, sin′i-) "Sinecure," a word meaning *an office or position requiring little or no work, especially one yielding profitable returns,* originally began as a church term, from the Latin "beneficium sine cura," *a benefice without care.* It referred to the practice of rewarding a church rector by giving him a parish for which he had no actual responsibilities. The real work was carried on by a vicar, but his absent superior received the higher recompense. Although the church practice was abolished in the mid-nineteenth century, the term is often used today in a political context.

6. **ottoman** (ot′ə mən) In the late thirteenth century, the Muslim Turks, under the leadership of Othman (also known as Osman I) established Turkey as "the Ottoman Empire." The empire was noted for its exotic silk and velvet furnishings. Travelers to the realm took some of their luxurious couches and divans back to Europe, where they became popular in France under the Bourbon kings. The French dubbed *a low, backless cushioned seat or footstool* an "otto-

mane'' after its country of origin. The English called it an ''ottoman.''

7. **namby-pamby** (nam'bē pam'bē) The term ''namby-pamby,'' used to describe anything *weakly sentimental, pretentious, or affected,* comes from Henry Carey's parody of Ambrose Philips's sentimental children's poems. Carey titled his parody ''Namby Pamby,'' taking the ''namby'' from the diminutive of ''Ambrose'' and using the first letter of his surname, ''P,'' for the alliteration. Following a bitter quarrel with Philips, Alexander Pope seized upon Carey's parody in the second edition of his *Dunciad* in 1733. Through the popularity of Pope's poem, the term ''namby-pamby'' passed into general usage.

8. **mountebank** (moun'tə bangk') During the Middle Ages, Italians conducted their banking in the streets, setting up business on convenient benches. In fact, the Italian word ''banca'' has given us our word ''bank.'' People with less honest intentions realized that it would be relatively easy to cheat the people who assembled around these benches. To attract a crowd, these con men often worked with jugglers, clowns, rope dancers, or singers. Since they always worked around a bench, they were known as ''montimbancos.'' Although the word was Anglicized to ''mountebank,'' it still refers to *a huckster or charlatan* who sells quack medicines from a platform in a public place, appealing to his audience by using tricks, storytelling, and so forth.

9. **phaeton** (fā'i tn) In Greek mythology, Helios drove the chariot of the sun across the sky each day. Helios's son Phaëton implored his father to let him drive the glittering chariot. Against his better judgment, one day Helios acceded to his son's wishes and let him drive the chariot pulled by its four powerful horses. Phaëton began well enough, but by mid-morning he wearied and could no longer control the horses. The sun fluctuated between heaven and earth, causing great destruction. To stop the devastation, Zeus hurled a thunderbolt at Phaëton, who fell lifeless to the ground. In the sixteenth century, the English drew from this legend to describe a heedless driver as a ''Phaeton.'' The word was later applied to *a light four-wheeled carriage* popular in the eighteenth century. Still later, it was applied to *a type of touring car.*

10. **mugwump** (mug'wump') This word entered the English language in a most curious fashion. In the mid-1600s, the clergyman John Eliot, known as the Apostle to the Indians, translated the Bible into the Algonquian language. When he came to the thirty-sixth chapter of Genesis, he had no word for ''duke,'' so he used ''mugquomp,'' an Algonquian term for *chief* or *great man.* Historians of the language theorize that the term might already have been in circulation at that time, but they know for certain that by 1884 it was in fairly general use. In the presidential election that year, a group of Republicans threw their support to Grover Cleveland rather than to the party's nominee, James G. Blaine. The newspapers scorned the renegade Republicans as ''mugwumps,'' those who thought themselves too good to vote for Blaine. The scorned Republicans got the last word when they adopted the same term to describe themselves, saying they were independent men proud to call themselves ''mugwumps,'' or *great men.* Today we use the term ''mugwump'' to desribe *a person who takes an independent position* or *one who is neutral on a controversial issue.*

Test 1: True/False

In the space provided, write T if the definition of the numbered word is true or F if it is false.

		T or F
1. TOADY	sycophant	____
2. MISCREANT	sociable person	____
3. MUGWUMP	political ally	____
4. NAMBY-PAMBY	cereal	____
5. GREGARIOUS	affable	____
6. PHAETON	ghost	____
7. MOUNTEBANK	impostor	____
8. MEERSCHAUM	mixup	____
9. OTTOMAN	footstool	____
10. SINECURE	sincere	____

Answers: 1. T 2. F 3. F 4. F 5. T 6. F
7. T 8. F 9. T 10. F

Test 2: Matching Synonyms

Match each of the following numbered words with its closest synonym. Write your answer in the space provided.

1. MOUNTEBANK	a. easy job	____
2. GREGARIOUS	b. knave	____
3. OTTOMAN	c. charlatan	____
4. TOADY	d. carriage	____
5. MISCREANT	e. sociable	____
6. MUGWUMP	f. independent	____
7. NAMBY-PAMBY	g. sycophant	____
8. SINECURE	h. pipe	____
9. PHAETON	i. low, backless seat	____
10. MEERSCHAUM	j. sentimental	____

Answers: 1. c 2. e 3. i 4. g 5. b 6. f
7. j 8. a 9. d 10. h

WORD HISTORIES II

LESSON 1.

Here are ten new words to enhance your word power. When you have finished reading the history of each word, complete the self-tests.

1. **oscillate** (os′ə lāt′) In ancient Rome, the grape growers hung little images with the face of Bacchus, the god of wine, on their vines. Since the Latin word for face is "os," a little face would be called an "oscillum." Because the images swung in the wind, some students of language concluded that the Latin verb "oscillare" came from a description of this motion. Most scholars have declined to make this connection, saying only that our present word "oscillate," *to swing to and fro,* is derived from Latin "oscillare," *to swing,* which in turn comes from "oscillum,"* a swing.*

2. **nabob** (nā′bob) The Mogul emperors, who ruled India from the sixteenth until the middle of the nineteenth century, delegated authority to men who acted as governors of various parts of India. To the native Indians, such a ruler was known as a "nawwab," *deputy.* The word was changed by the Europeans into "nabob." The nabobs were supposed to tithe money to the central government, but some of the nabobs withheld the money, and thereby became enormously wealthy. From their fortunes came the European custom of using the word "nabob" to refer to a person, especially a European, who had attained great wealth in India or another country of the East. The usage spread to England, and today we use the term to describe *any very wealthy or powerful person.*

3. **pander** (pan′dər) "Pander," *to act as a go-between in amorous intrigues* or *to act as a pimp or* *procurer* or *to cater basely,* comes from the medieval story of Troilus and Cressida. In his retelling, Chaucer describes how the love-stricken Troilus calls upon his friend Pandarus, kin to Cressida, to aid him in his quest for her love. Much of Chaucer's tale is devoted to the different means used by Pandarus to help Troilus win his love. Shakespeare later recycled the same legend. As the story gained in popularity the name "Pandarus" was changed in English to "pandare" and then to "pander." The noun now has the negative connotation of *pimp* or *procurer for illicit sexual intercourse.*

4. **pedagogue** (ped′ə gog′, -gôg′) Wealthy Greek families kept a special slave to supervise their sons. The slave's responsibilities included accompanying the boys as they traveled to and from school and walked in the public streets. To describe a slave's chores, the Greeks coined the term "paidagogos," *a leader of boys.* Occasionally, when the slave was an educated man captured in warfare and sold into slavery, the slave also tutored his charges. From the Greek word we derived the English word "pedagogue," *teacher* or *educator.*

5. **quack** (kwak) Noticing how the raucous shouts of the charlatans selling useless concoctions sounded like the strident quacks of ducks, the sixteenth-century Dutch called these charlatans "quacksalvers"—literally, *ducks quacking over their salves.* The term quickly spread through Europe. The English shortened it to "quack," and used it to describe *any fraudulent or ignorant pretender to medical skills,* the meaning we retain today.

6. **nepotism** (nep′ə tiz′əm) This word for *patron-*

age bestowed or favoritism shown on the basis of family relationships, as in business or politics, can be traced to the popes of the fifteenth and sixteenth centuries. To increase their power, these men surrounded themselves with people they knew would be loyal—members of their own family. Among the most popular candidates were the popes' own illegitimate sons, called "nephews," from the Latin "nepos," *a descendant,* as a mark of respect. Eventually the term "nepotism" came to mean favoritism to all family members, not just nephews.

7. **pompadour** (pom′pə dôr′, -door′) Sheltered by a wealthy family and educated as though she were their own daughter, at twenty the exquisite Jeanne Antoinette Poisson Le Normant d'Étioles married her protector's nephew and began her reign over the world of Parisian fashion. Soon after, King Louis XV took her as his mistress, established her at the court of Versailles, and gave her the estate of Pompadour. The Marquise de Pompadour created a large and high-swept hairstyle memorialized by her name. Though it has been somewhat modified, the style is still known by her name.

8. **nostrum** (nos′trəm) The word "nostrum," *a patent or quack medicine,* became very current around the time of the Great Plague in the mid-seventeenth century. Doctors were helpless to combat the disease, so charlatans and quacks scurried to fill the gap, flooding the market with their own "secret"—and useless—concoctions. To make their medicines seem more effective, they labeled them with the Latin word "nostrum." The term came to be used as a general word for any quack medicine. Ironically, "nostrum" means *our own,* as in "nostrum remedium," *our own remedy;* thus it makes no claims at all for the remedy's effectiveness.

9. **narcissism** (när′sə siz′əm) The word "narcissism," *inordinate fascination with oneself,* comes from the Greek myth of Narcissus. According to one version of the legend, an exceptionally handsome young man fell in love with his own image reflected in a pool. Because he was unable to embrace his image, he died from unrequited love. According to another version, Narcissus fell in love with his identical twin sister.

After her death, he sat and stared at his own reflection in the pool until he died from grief.

10. **nepenthe** (ni pen′thē) According to Greek legend, when Paris kidnapped Helen and took her to Troy, he wanted her to forget her previous life. In Homer's version of the tale, Paris gave Helen a drug thought to cause loss of memory. The drug was called "nepenthes." The word has come down to us with its meaning intact: *anything inducing a pleasurable sensation of forgetfulness.*

Test 1: True/False

In the space provided, write T if the definition of the numbered word is true or F if it is false.

1.	NEPENTHE	remembrance	____
2.	NEPOTISM	impartiality	____
3.	PANDER	procurer	____
4.	POMPADOUR	crewcut	____
5.	OSCILLATE	swing	____
6.	PEDAGOGUE	teacher	____
7.	NARCISSISM	self-love	____
8.	NABOB	pauper	____
9.	NOSTRUM	patent medicine	____
10.	QUACK	expert	____

Answers: 1. F 2. F 3. T 4. F 5. T 6. T 7. T 8. F 9. T 10. F

Test 2: Defining Words

Define each of the following words.

1. pompadour _____
2. nepenthe _____
3. oscillate _____
4. nostrum _____
5. quack _____
6. nabob _____
7. pander _____
8. nepotism _____
9. pedagogue _____
10. narcissism _____

Suggested Answers: 1. upswept hairstyle 2. something inducing forgetfulness 3. to swing back and forth 4. patent or useless remedy 5. medical charlatan 6. wealthy, powerful person 7. pimp or procurer 8. patronage given to family members 9. teacher 10. excessive self-love

Lesson 2.

Each of these ten words beginning with the letter "p" has a particularly captivating tale behind it. Read the stories, then complete the two tests at the end of the lesson.

1. **palaver** (pə lav′ər, -lä′vər) The word "palaver" derives ultimately from the Greek word "parabola," *comparison*, literally *a placing beside*. From this came English "parable," *a story that makes comparisons*. In Latin the word came to mean *speech, talk, word*. Later, Portuguese traders carried the term to Africa in the form "palavra" and used it to refer to the long talks with native chiefs required by local custom. English traders picked up the word in the eighteenth century, spelling it as we do today. The word retains its last meaning, *a long parley, especially one with people indigenous to a region* or *profuse, idle talk*.

2. **pannier** (pan′yər, -ē ər) The word "pannier" was first used in thirteenth-century France to mean *bread basket;* it is related to the French word "pain," *bread*. Soon it was also used to refer to a fish basket, and then a basket for toting any provisions. In later centuries, the term was applied to the baskets balanced on a donkey's back. Today we use the term to denote *a basket, especially a large one carried on a person's back*.

3. **pariah** (pə rī′ə) The term "pariah," *an outcast*, comes from the name of one of the lowest castes in India. Composed of agricultural laborers and household servants, it is not the lowest caste, but its members are still considered untouchable by the Brahmans. The British used the term "pariah" for anyone of low social standing. The term "pariah" now is used for *any outcast among his or her own people*.

4. **pecuniary** (pi kyoo′nē er′ē) The Romans measured a man's worth by the number of animals he kept on his farm. They adapted the Latin word for a farm animal, "pecu," to refer to individual wealth. But as people acquired new ways of measuring wealth, such as money and land, the Roman word evolved into "pecunia," which referred most specifically to money. From this came the adjective "pecuniary," *pertaining to or consisting of money*.

5. **phantasmagoria** (fan taz′mə gôr′ē ə) In the early years of the nineteenth century, an inventor named Philipstal created a wondrous device for producing optical illusions. By projecting colored slides onto a thin silk screen, Philipstal made his spectral images appear to move. Today, of course, we take such motion-picture illusions for granted, but in the age of the magic lantern, such visions were marvelous indeed. Philipstal named his invention "phantasmagoria," which we now apply to *a shifting series of phantasms or deceptive appearances, as in a dream*.

6. **poplin** (pop′lin) The origin of this word has nothing to do with its appearance or use. In the early fourteenth century, the papal seat was located in Avignon, France. Even after the papacy was moved to Rome, Avignon remained important for its production of a sturdy dress and upholstery fabric. The fabric came to be identified with the city in which it was made. Since Avignon remained a papal town until the late eighteenth century, the fabric came to be called "papelino," or *papal*. The English pronounced the word "poplin," giving us the present-day name for this *finely corded fabric of cotton, rayon, silk, or wool*.

7. **precipitate** (pri sip′i tāt′) The word "precipitate" is based on the Latin root "caput," meaning *head*. In fact, the word was first used to apply to those who had been executed or killed themselves by being hurled or jumping headlong from a "precipice" or high place. Later, the word came to mean *to rush headlong*. From this has come today's meaning, *to hasten the occurrence of; to bring about prematurely*.

8. **precocious** (pri kō′shəs) To the Romans, Latin "praecox," the source of English "precocious," was a culinary term meaning *precooked*. In time, however, its meaning was extended to *acting prematurely*. It is this later meaning of "precocious" that we use today, *unusually advanced in development, especially mental development*.

9. **pretext** (prē′tekst) "Pretext" comes from the Latin word "praetexta," meaning *an ornament*, such as the purple markings on a toga denoting rank. In addition to its literal sense, however, the word carried the connotation of something to cloak one's true identity. We have retained only the word's figurative meaning, *something that is put forward to conceal a true purpose or object; an ostensible reason*.

10. **procrustean** (prō krus′tē ən) According to one version of the Greek myth, Procrustes was a bandit who made his living waylaying unsuspecting travelers. He tied everyone who fell

into his grasp to an iron bed. If they were longer than the bed, he cut short their legs to make their bodies fit; if they were shorter, he stretched their bodies until they fit tightly. Hence, "procrustean" means *tending to produce conformity through violent or arbitrary means.*

Test 1: True/False

In the space provided, write T if the definition of the numbered word is true or F if it is false.

		T or F
1. PROCRUSTEAN	marine life	___
2. PECUNIARY	picayune	___
3. PRECIPITATE	play	___
4. PRETEXT	falsification	___
5. PARIAH	outcast	___
6. POPLIN	religious vestment	___
7. PALAVER	serving tray	___
8. PRECOCIOUS	advanced	___
9. PANNIER	basket	___
10. PHANTASMAGORIA	illusions	___

Answers: 1. F 2. F 3. F 4. T 5. T 6. F
7. F 8. T 9. T 10. T

Test 2: Matching Synonyms

Match each of the following numbered words with its closest synonym from the list of lettered words in the second column. Write your answer in the space provided.

1. POPLIN	a. excuse	___
2. PALAVER	b. producing conformity by violent means	___
3. PECUNIARY	c. fabric	___
4. PHANTASMAGORIA	d. fantasy	___
5. PRETEXT	e. expedite	___
6. PRECOCIOUS	f. idle chatter	___
7. PRECIPITATE	g. advanced	___
8. PARIAH	h. outcast	___
9. PROCRUSTEAN	i. basket	___
10. PANNIER	j. monetary	___

Answers: 1. c 2. f 3. j 4. d 5. a 6. g
7. e 8. h 9. b 10. i

LESSON 3.

Read through the interesting stories behind these ten words. Then work through the two self-tests to see how many of the words you can use correctly.

1. **proletariat** (prō'li târ'ē ət) "Proletariat" derives from the Latin "proletarius," *a Roman freeman who lacked property and money.* The word came from "proles," *offspring, children.* Although the freemen had the vote, many wealthy Romans despised them, saying they were useful only to have children. They called them "proletarii," *producers of children.* Karl Marx picked up the word in the mid-nineteenth century as a label for the lower-class working people of his age. "Proletariat" retains the same meaning today: *members of the working class, especially those who do not possess capital and must sell their labor to survive.*

2. **Arcadian** (är kā'dē ən) The residents of landlocked Arcadia, in ancient Greece, did not venture to other lands. As a result, they maintained traditional ways and lived what others imagined to be a simpler life. Ancient classical poets made "Arcadia" a symbol for a land of pastoral happiness. In the sixteenth century, English poet Sir Philip Sidney referred to a bucolic land he called "Arcadia." The word has retained this meaning, and today we consider residents of an "Arcadian" place to be *rustic, simple, and innocent.*

3. **rake** (rāk) "Rake," meaning *a dissolute person, especially a man,* was originally "rakehell." In the sixteenth century, this colorful term was used to describe a person so dissipated that he would "rake hell" to find his pleasures. "Rakehell" is now considered a somewhat archaic term to describe such roués; "rake" is the common word.

4. **pygmy** (pig'mē) The ancient Greeks were entranced by stories of a tribe of dwarfs in the upper Nile who were so small that they could be swallowed by cranes. To describe these tiny people, the Greeks used the word "pygmaios," which also referred to the distance on a person's arm from the elbow to the knuckles. The word became English "pygmy," *a tiny person or thing; a person or thing of small importance.*

5. **sardonic** (sär don'ik) The ancient Greeks described a plant on the island of Sardinia whose flesh, if eaten, caused the victim's face to become grotesquely convulsed, as if in scornful laughter. The Greek name for Sardinia was "Sardos"; therefore, "sardonios" came to refer to any mocking laughter. The English word eventually became "sardonic," *characterized by bitter irony or scornful derision.*

6. **tartar** (tär′tər) The fierce Genghis Khan and his successors led an army of bloodthirsty warriors, including the Ta-ta Mongols, in a series of conquests throughout Asia and into Europe. Their name, "Tartar" or "Tatar," became closely associated with brutal massacres. Today the word "tartar" refers to *a savage, ill-tempered, or intractable person.*

7. **argosy** (är′gə sē) In the Middle Ages, cities on the Mediterranean coast maintained large fleets to ship goods around the known world. Ragusa was a Sicilian city well known for its large ships, called "ragusea." In English, the initial two letters became switched, creating "argusea." From there it was a short step to "argosy," *a large merchant ship, especially one with a rich cargo.* Because of Ragusa's wealth, the word "argosy" also came to mean *an opulent supply or collection.*

8. **Balkanize** (bôl′kə nīz′) After centuries of war, in 1912 the Balkan nations united to conquer the Turks and divide the spoils among themselves. The following year, however, the Balkan nations quarreled over how to divide their booty and began to fight among themselves. From this experience comes the verb "Balkanize," *to divide a country or territory into small, quarrelsome, ineffectual states.*

9. **cravat** (krə vat′) In the late seventeenth century, the French king Louis XIV formed a special division of Croats, a Slavic people, to serve in his army. The Croats wore colorful, much-admired neckties to distinguish themselves from the other regiments. Fashionable civilians took to wearing these neckties, calling them "cravats" after a variant spelling of "Croat." The term is still used to mean *necktie,* although it is somewhat out of fashion. It also refers to a scarf worn by men.

10. **hegira** (hi jī′rə, hej′ər ə) Around the year 600, the prophet Muhammad began to preach the new faith of Islam. To escape persecution, he was forced to flee his home in Mecca. Eventually, his followers increased, and by his death in 632, he controlled Arabia. Within a century, the empire of Islam had spread throughout western Asia and northern Africa. The turning point, Muhammad's flight from Mecca, came to be called the "Hegira," after the Arabic word for *flight* or *emigration.* The "Hegira" is the starting point on the Muslim calendar, and we now apply the word to *any flight or journey to a desirable or congenial place.*

Test 1: True/False

In the space provided, write T if the definition of the numbered word is true or F if it is false.

		T or F
1. RAKE	roué	____
2. PROLETARIAT	wealthy persons	____
3. HEGIRA	flight	____
4. CRAVAT	craving	____
5. TARTAR	disciple	____
6. ARCADIAN	rustic	____
7. SARDONIC	derisive	____
8. PYGMY	monkey	____
9. ARGOSY	rich supply	____
10. BALKANIZE	vulcanize	____

Answers: 1. T 2. F 3. T 4. F 5. F 6. T
7. T 8. F 9. T 10. F

Test 2: Matching Synonyms

Select the best definition for each numbered word. Write your answer in the space provided.

1. RAKE	a. bucolic	____
2. PYGMY	b. merchant ship	____
3. CRAVAT	c. midget	____
4. ARCADIAN	d. break up into antagonistic units	____
5. ARGOSY	e. the working class	____
6. HEGIRA	f. scornful; mocking	____
7. BALKANIZE	g. necktie	____
8. PROLETARIAT	h. bad-tempered person	____
9. SARDONIC	i. journey or flight	____
10. TARTAR	j. roué	____

Answers: 1. j 2. c 3. g 4. a 5. b 6. i
7. d 8. e 9. f 10. h

LESSON 4.

Now look at the backgrounds of these ten words. Then complete the two self-tests to help you add them to your vocabulary.

1. **ballyhoo** (bal′ē hōō′) The word "ballyhoo" is of uncertain origin. Some, however, have connected it with the Irish town of Ballyhooy, known for the rowdy and often uncontrolled quarrels of its inhabitants. Today "ballyhoo" is an Americanism with a specific meaning: *a clamorous attempt to win customers or advance a cause; blatant advertising or publicity.*

2. **tawdry** (tô′drē) In the seventh century, an Englishwoman named Etheldreda fled her husband to establish an abbey. When the Venerable Bede recounted her story in the early eighth century, he claimed that her death had been caused by a tumor in her throat, which she believed was a punishment for her early vanity of wearing jewelry about her neck. Her abbey eventually became the Cathedral of Ely; her name, Audrey. In her honor, the cathedral town held an annual fair where "trifling objects" were hawked. One theory as to the development of the word "tawdry" relates to the hawkers' cry, "Saint Audrey's lace!" This became "Sin t'Audrey lace" and then "tawdry lace." By association with these cheap trinkets, the word "tawdry" has come to mean *gaudy, showy,* or *cheap.*

3. **python** (pī′thon) According to Greek myth, the sacred oracle at Delphi was at one time threatened by a terrible serpent called "Python." It was finally killed by Apollo. About 150 years ago, *a large constrictor snake often measuring more than twenty feet long* was named after this mythical monster.

4. **recalcitrant** (ri kal′si trənt) The word was formed from the Latin prefix "re-," *back,* and "calcitrare," *to kick.* Thus, a recalcitrant person is one who kicks back, resisting authority or control.

5. **copperhead** (kop′ər hed′) The term "copperhead" was coined by the New York *Tribune* in the early days of the Civil War to refer to *a Northerner who sympathized with the South.* The term came from the sneaky and poisonous copperhead snake, which strikes without warning.

6. **silhouette** (sil′ōō et′) At the urging of his mistress, Madame de Pompadour, the French king Louis XV appointed Étienne de Silhouette as his finance minister. His mission was to enact strict economy measures to rescue the government from near-bankruptcy. At the same time, there was a revival of the practice of tracing profiles created by shadows. Since they replaced more costly paintings, these outlines came to be derided as "à la Silhouette"—another of his money-saving measures. Although Silhouette lasted in office less than a year, he achieved a sort of immortality when his name became permanently associated with *a two-dimensional representation of the outline of an object, as a person's profile, generally filled in with black.*

7. **remora** (rem′ər ə) Since this odd fish impeded the progress of Roman ships by attaching itself to the vessels with its sucking disks, the Romans named it a "remora," *that which holds back; hindrance.* Today we use the term only to name the fish, though formerly it was also a synonym for *obstacle, hindrance.*

8. **caprice** (kə prēs′) "Caprice," *a sudden, unpredictable change of mind, a whim,* doesn't remind us of hedgehogs, yet these animals probably played a role in this word's past. "Caprice" comes ultimately from the Italian word "capriccio," which originally meant *fright, horror.* The word is thought to be a compound of "capo," *head,* and "riccio," *hedgehog,* because when people are very frightened, their hair stands on end, like a hedgehog's spines.

9. **treacle** (trē′kəl) Originally, "treacle" was an ointment used by the ancient Romans and Greeks against the bite of wild animals. But in the eighteenth and nineteenth centuries, competing quack medicine hawkers added sweetening to make their bitter potions more palatable. After a while, the sweetening agent itself, usually molasses, came to be called "treacle." We retain this meaning and have extended it to refer figuratively to *contrived or unrestrained sentimentality* as well.

10. **billingsgate** (bil′ingz gāt′) In the 1500s, "Belin's gate," a walled town within London, was primarily a fish market. The name was soon distorted to "billingsgate," and since many fishwives and seamen were known for their salty tongues, the word "billingsgate" came to mean *coarse or vulgar abusive language.*

Test 1: True/False

In the space provided, write T if the definition of the numbered word is true or F if it is false.

			T or F
1.	RECALCITRANT	easygoing	___
2.	CAPRICE	capable	___
3.	REMORA	renovate	___
4.	COPPERHEAD	fierce warrior	___
5.	BALLYHOO	dance	___
6.	TAWDRY	gaudy	___
7.	BILLINGSGATE	profane language	___
8.	PYTHON	snake	___
9.	TREACLE	sugar	___
10.	SILHOUETTE	outline	___

Answers: 1. F 2. F 3. F 4. F 5. F 6. T
7. T 8. T 9. F 10. T

Test 2: Matching Synonyms

Match each of the following numbered words with its closest synonym. Write your answer in the space provided.

1.	PYTHON	a.	whim	___
2.	BALLYHOO	b.	cheap	___
3.	TREACLE	c.	verbal abuse	___
4.	TAWDRY	d.	snake	___
5.	COPPERHEAD	e.	outline	___
6.	RECALCITRANT	f.	clamor	___
7.	SILHOUETTE	g.	balky	___
8.	CAPRICE	h.	mawkish sentimentality	___
9.	REMORA	i.	fish	___
10.	BILLINGSGATE	j.	Southern sympathizer	___

Answers: 1. d 2. f 3. h 4. b 5. j 6. g
7. e 8. a 9. i 10. c

LESSON 5.

The stories behind these ten words provide intriguing reading and can give your vocabulary true power. After you study the words, complete the two self-tests to see how many of the words you can use correctly.

1. **apartheid** (ə pärt′hāt, -hīt) "Apartheid," the term for *a policy of racial segregation and discrimination against nonwhites,* entered English from Afrikaans, the language of South Africa's Dutch settlers, the Boers. They created the word from the Dutch word for "apart" and the suffix "-heid," related to our suffix "-hood." Thus, the word literally means *apartness* or *separateness.* It was first used in 1947, in a South African newspaper.

2. **quixotic** (kwik sot′ik) The word "quixotic," meaning *extravagantly chivalrous or romantic,* is based on the character of Don Quixote, the chivalrous knight in Cervantes' 1605 masterpiece *Don Quixote de la Mancha.* The impractical, visionary knight was ludicrously blind to the false nature of his dreams.

3. **bromide** (brō′mīd) "Bromides" are chemicals, several of which can be used as sedatives. In 1906, the American humorist Gelett Burgess first used the word to mean *a boring person,* one who is likely to serve the same purpose as a sedative. The term was then extended to mean *a platitude,* the kind of remark one could expect from a tiresome person.

4. **profane** (prə fān′, prō-) Only fully initiated men were allowed to participate in Greek and Roman religious rites; those not admitted were called "profane," from "pro," *outside,* and "fanum," *temple.* When the word came into English, it was applied to persons or things not part of Christianity. Probably in reference to the contempt of nonbelievers, "profane" now means *characterized by irreverence for God or sacred things.*

5. **rialto** (rē al′tō) In the late sixteenth century, the Venetians erected a bridge across the Grand Canal. Since the bridge spanned deep waters, it was called the "Rialto," *deep stream.* The bridge led to the creation of a busy shopping area in the center of the city. From this shopping center we derive our present meaning of "rialto," *an exchange or mart.*

6. **thespian** (thes′pē ən) A Greek poet named Thespis, who flourished circa 534 B.C., enlarged the traditional celebrations at the festival of Dionysus by writing verses to be chanted alternately by individuals and the chorus. This opportunity to be a solo performer was a first. From the poet's name we derive the word "thespian," *an actor or actress.*

7. **salver** (sal′vər) "Salver" came into English from Spanish "salva," a kind of tray. The Spanish word derived from Latin "salvare," *to save,* from the practice of having a servant taste one's

food or drink to check for poison. Because poisoning was the method of choice for eliminating wealthy enemies in the Middle Ages, the practice of retaining a taster was commonplace among the affluent. The master's food was presented upon a separate tray, so the term "salva" came to apply to the tray as well as the tasting. Once the habit of poisoning people subsided, the English term "salver" came to mean *a tray, especially one used for serving food.*

8. **chagrin** (shə grin′) The word "chagrin," meaning *a feeling of vexation due to disappointment,* does not derive from "shagreen," *a piece of hard, abrasive leather used to polish metal,* even though both words are spelled identically in French. French scholars connect "chagrin," *vexation, grief,* with an Old French verb, "chagreiner," *to turn melancholy or gloomy,* which evolved in part from a Germanic word related to English "grim."

9. **shibboleth** (shib′ə lith, -leth′) In the twelfth chapter of Judges, Jephthah and his men were victorious over the warriors of Ephraim. After the battle, Jephthah gave his guards the password "shibboleth" to distinguish friends from foes; he picked the word because the Ephraimites could not pronounce the "sh" sound. His choice was shrewd, and many of his enemies were captured and killed. Thus, "shibboleth" has come to mean *a peculiarity of pronunciation, usage, or behavior that distinguishes a particular class or set of persons.* It also can mean *slogan; catchword.*

10. **vie** (vī) The word "vie," *to strive in competition or rivalry with another, to contend for superiority,* was originally a shortened version of "envien," a sixteenth-century gaming term meaning *to raise the stake.* The contraction, "vie," came to mean *to contend, compete.*

Test 1: True/False

In the space provided, write T if the definition of the numbered word is true or F if it is false.

T or F

1. CHAGRIN	chafe	____
2. VIE	accede	____
3. PROFANE	irreverent	____
4. SALVER	tray	____
5. QUIXOTIC	ill-tempered	____
6. RIALTO	marketplace	____
7. APARTHEID	foreigner	____
8. SHIBBOLETH	platitude	____
9. THESPIAN	actor	____
10. BROMIDE	explosive	____

Answers: 1. F 2. F 3. T 4. T 5. F 6. T
7. F 8. F 9. T 10. F

Test 2: Definitions

Select the best definition for each numbered word. Circle your answer.

____ 1. bromide
    a. cliché b. effervescence c. angst
____ 2. vie
    a. treat b. contend c. despise
____ 3. quixotic
    a. alien b. romantic c. fictional
____ 4. salver
    a. salivate b. poison c. tray
____ 5. shibboleth
    a. peculiarity b. forbidden
    c. murdered
____ 6. profane
    a. pious b. irreverent c. exploding
____ 7. thespian
    a. actress b. speech impairment
    c. playwright
____ 8. apartheid
    a. discrimination b. unity
    c. hopelessness
____ 9. rialto
    a. shipyard b. reality c. exchange
____ 10. chagrin
    a. stiff b. vexation c. smirk

Answers: 1. a 2. b 3. b 4. c 5. a 6. b
7. a 8. a 9. c 10. b

LESSON 6.

Knowing the histories of the following ten words can help you remember their meanings and use them in your speech and writing. Study the words, then work through the two tests that follow.

1. **Promethean** (prə mē′thē ən) According to Greek myth, as punishment for stealing fire from the gods and giving it to mortal humans, Prometheus was bound to the side of a mountain, where he was attacked daily by a fierce bird that feasted upon his liver. At night his wounds healed; the next day he was attacked anew. Because of his extraordinary boldness in stealing the divine fire, the word "Promethean" has come to mean *creative, boldly original.*

2. **sarcophagus** (sär kof′ə gəs) Although the majority of ancient Greeks favored burial or cremation, some obtained limestone coffins that could dissolve a body in little over a month. The coffin was called a "sarcophagus," from the Greek "sarx," *flesh,* and "phagos," *eating.* Today we use the term to refer to *a stone coffin, especially one bearing sculpture, an inscription, etc., often displayed as a monument.*

3. **quorum** (kwôr′əm) The word "quorum" was first used as part of a Latin phrase meaning *to select people for official court business.* Ultimately, it came to mean *the number of members of a group or organization required to be present to transact business; legally, usually a majority.*

4. **antimacassar** (an′ti mə kas′ər) In the 1800s, macassar oil was imported from Indonesia to England as a popular remedy for baldness. Based on its reputation, men began to apply it liberally to their pates, but the oil stained the backs of sofas and chairs where they rested their oily heads. Therefore, homemakers began to place pieces of fabric over sofa and chair backs, since these scraps could be washed more easily than stained upholstery. These fabric pieces came to be called "antimacassars"— *against macassar oil.* They survive today in the *little doilies* fastidious homemakers drape over furniture.

5. **lackey** (lak′ē) After their invasion of Spain in 711, the Moors conquered nearly the entire country and established a glittering civilization. But it was not to last. By 1100, Christians had already wrested half of Spain from the Moors. Two hundred years later, the Moors retained only a small toehold; and a hundred years after that, they were driven out of Europe entirely.

As the Moors suffered repeated defeats, their captured soldiers became servants to their Spanish conquerors. They were called "alacayo." The initial "a" was later dropped, and the word was rendered in English as "lackey," *a servile follower.*

6. **obelisk** (ob′ə lisk′) The word comes from the ancient Egyptian practice of erecting tall, thin pillars to pay homage to the sun god Ra. The Greeks called these shafts "obeliskoi." The word has come down to us as "obelisk," with its meaning intact, *a tapering four-sided shaft of stone with a pyramidal apex; a monument.*

7. **paladin** (pal′ə din) The original paladins were Charlemagne's twelve knights. According to legend, the famous paladin Roland was caught in an ambush and fought valiantly with his small band of followers to the last man. Because of his actions, "paladin" has come down to us as *any champion of noble causes.*

8. **hobnob** (hob′nob′) Those who "hobnob" with their buddies *associate on very friendly terms* or *drink together.* The word comes from the Anglo-Saxon "haebbe" and "naebbe," *to have* and *to have not.* In the 1700s, "hobnob" meant *to toast friends and host alternate rounds of drinks.* Each person thus had the pleasure of treating, creating a sense of familiarity. Today this usage survives, even if those hobnobbing are teetotalers.

9. **helot** (hel′ət, hē′lət) Around the eighth century B.C., the Spartans conquered and enslaved the people of the southern half of the Peloponnesus. They called these slaves "helots," perhaps from the Greek word meaning *to enslave.* Today "helot" still means *serf or slave; bondsman.*

10. **kowtow** (kou′tou′) The Chinese people, who were largely isolated from the West until Portuguese traders established a post outside Canton, regarded their emperor as a representation of God on earth. Those approaching the emperor had to fall to the ground and strike their heads against the floor as a sign of humility. This was called a "kowtow," from the Chinese word that meant *knock-head.* As a verb, the English word follows the original meaning, *to touch the forehead to the ground while kneeling, as an act of worship;* but from this meaning we have derived a figurative use as well: *to act in an obsequious manner; show servile deference.*

Test 1: Defining Words

Define each of the following words.

1. obelisk _____
2. Promethean _____
3. helot _____
4. sarcophagus _____
5. kowtow _____
6. lackey _____
7. antimacassar _____
8. hobnob _____
9. quorum _____
10. paladin _____

Suggested Answers: 1. shaft 2. creative, boldly original 3. serf, slave 4. coffin 5. deference 6. a servile follower 7. doily 8. associate on friendly terms; drink together 9. majority 10. champion

Test 2: True/False

In the space provided, write T if the definition of the numbered word is true or F if it is false.

		T or F
1. LACKEY	servant	_____
2. QUORUM	majority	_____
3. OBELISK	shaft	_____
4. HOBNOB	twisted logic	_____
5. PROMETHEAN	creative	_____
6. SARCOPHAGUS	cremation	_____
7. HELOT	hell-on-wheels	_____
8. ANTIMACASSAR	against travel	_____
9. KOWTOW	bow low	_____
10. PALADIN	villain	_____

Answers: 1. T 2. T 3. T 4. F 5. T 6. F 7. F 8. F 9. T 10. F

LESSON 7.

The quirky stories behind the following ten words can help you understand and remember them better. Read through the histories and complete the two self-tests to add to your mastery of language.

1. **quahog** (kwô′hôg, -hog) Despite the "hog" at the end of the word, a "quahog" has nothing to do with a pig. Rather, it is a clam; the word comes from the Algonquian (Narragansett) word "poquauhock."

2. **protean** (prō′tē ən) According to Greek legend, Proteus was a sea god who possessed the power to change his shape at will. He also had the ability to foretell the future, but those wishing to avail themselves of his power first had to steal upon him at noon when he checked his herds of sea calves, catch him, and bind him securely. Thus bound, Proteus would change shape furiously, but the petitioner who could keep him restrained until he returned to his original shape would receive the answer to his question—if he still remembered what he wanted to know. From Proteus, then, we get the word "protean," *readily assuming different forms or characters; variable.*

3. **noisome** (noi′səm) Although the words appear to have the same root, "noisome" bears no relation to "noise." "Noisome" means *offensive* or *disgusting,* as an odor, and comes from the Middle English word "noy," meaning *harm.* The root is related, however, to the word "annoy," *to molest or bother.*

4. **Ouija** (wē′jə) "Ouija" is a trademark for *a board game used to spell out messages in spiritualistic communication.* It consists of a small board, or planchette, resting on a larger board marked with words and letters. The name comes from the French and German words for *yes,* "oui" and "ja."

5. **simony** (sī′mə nē, sim′ə-) Simon the sorcerer offered to pay the Apostle Peter to teach him the wondrous cures he had seen him perform, not understanding that his feats were miracles rather than magic tricks. From Simon's name comes the term "simony," *the sin of buying or selling ecclesiastical preferments.*

6. **rigmarole** (rig′mə rōl′) In fourteenth-century England, a register of names was called a "rageman." Later it became a "ragman," then "ragman roll." As it changed, the term evolved to refer to a series of unconnected statements. By the 1700s, the word had become "rigmarole," with its present meaning, *an elaborate or complicated procedure.*

7. **bolshevik** (bōl′shə vik) At a rally of Communist leaders in 1903, Lenin garnered a majority of the votes. He cleverly dubbed his supporters "Bolsheviks," meaning *the majority.* His move was effective propaganda. Even though his supporters actually comprised only a minority, the name stuck and came to be associated with *a member of the Russian Communist party.* The word is also used in a derogatory sense to denote *an extreme political radical, a revolutionary.*

8. **misericord** (miz′ər i kôrd′, mi zer′i kôrd′) Both the *small projection on the underside of a hinged seat of a church stall that gives support, when*

the seat is lifted, to a person standing in the stall and a medieval dagger have the same name, "misericord." In a curious sense, this is because they both provide mercy, the seat giving a parishioner a resting place during a long service, the dagger delivering the coup de grâce to a wounded foe. "Misericord" comes from the Latin "misericordia," meaning *compassion*.

9. **surplice** (sûr′plis) To keep themselves warm in damp, chilly stone churches, clergymen in the Middle Ages wore fur robes. But since fur was not considered proper attire for religious men, the priests covered their furs with loose-fitting white overgarments. The word "surplice" to describe these broad-sleeved white vestments came from their function: the Latin "super," *over*, and "pellicia," *fur garment*.

10. **sylph** (silf) A German alchemist of the 1700s coined the term "Sylphis" to describe the spirits of the air. He envisioned them as looking like humans but able to move more swiftly and gracefully. Over the years, the word evolved to mean *a slender, graceful girl or woman*.

Test 1: True/False

In the space provided, write T if the definition of the numbered word is true or F if it is false.

			T or F
1. MISERICORD	wretchedness		____
2. OUIJA	board game		____
3. SIMONY	slickness		____
4. BOLSHEVIK	sheik		____
5. PROTEAN	changeable		____
6. NOISOME	clamorous		____
7. SYLPH	svelte female		____
8. QUAHOG	bivalve		____
9. RIGMAROLE	simplification		____
10. SURPLICE	clerical vestment		____

Answers: 1. F 2. T 3. F 4. F 5. T 6. F
7. T 8. T 9. F 10. T

Test 2: Matching Synonyms

Match each of the numbered words with its closest synonym from the list of lettered words in the second column. Write your answer in the space provided.

1. SYLPH	a. vestment	____
2. QUAHOG	b. medieval dagger	____
3. SURPLICE	c. ecclesiastical favors	____
4. BOLSHEVIK	d. slender girl	____
5. OUIJA	e. Communist	____
6. MISERICORD	f. involved process	____
7. NOISOME	g. variable	____
8. PROTEAN	h. clam	____
9. RIGMAROLE	i. foul	____
10. SIMONY	j. board game	____

Answers: 1. d 2. h 3. a 4. e 5. j 6. b
7. i 8. g 9. f 10. c

LESSON 8.

Now read the histories of these ten unique words. Fix them in your memory by completing the two self-tests that follow. The words can make your speech and writing more colorful, interesting, and effective.

1. **muumuu** (mōō′mōō′) This *loose dress, often brightly colored or patterned*, was first introduced into Hawaii by missionaries anxious to clothe their nude Hawaiian female converts. To accomplish their aims, the missionaries gave the Hawaiian women dresses cut in the European fashion, which the Hawaiians adapted to suit their needs and climate. The dress acquired the Hawaiian name "muumuu," which means *cut off*, because it lacked a yoke and therefore looked "cut off" at the neck.

2. **sybarite** (sib′ə rīt′) The ancient Greek colony of Sybaris in southern Italy was known for its luxurious life style. The residents were so famous for their opulent ways that the word "sybarite" came to be used for *any person devoted to luxury and pleasure*.

3. **rostrum** (ros′trəm) Today a "rostrum" is *any platform, stage, or the like for public speaking*. The word comes from the victory in 338 B.C. of the Romans over the pirates of Antium (Anzio), off the Italian coast. The victorious consul took back to Rome the prows of the six ships he had captured. These were attached to the lecterns used by Roman speakers. They came to be called "rostra," or *beaks*. We use the singular, "rostrum."

4. **lemur** (lē′mər) *An animal with a small foxlike face, woolly fur, and cute monkeylike body*, the "lemur" seems to some people to be an adorable creature. The scientist who first named this small nocturnal mammal, the eighteenth-century Swedish botanist Linnaeus, obviously had a less pleasant reaction to the animal, since the

Latin word "lemur" denotes *malevolent, frightening spirits of the dead.*

5. **spoonerism** (spoo'nə riz'əm) The English clergyman W. A. Spooner (1844–1930) was notorious for his habit of transposing the initial letters or other sounds of words, as in "a blushing crow" for "a crushing blow." Since the good reverend was not unique in his affliction, we use the word "spoonerism" to describe these *unintentional transpositions of sounds.*

6. **vermicelli** (vûr'mi chel'ē) Anyone faced with a small child determined not to eat his or her spaghetti because "it looks like worms" had better avoid explaining the origin of "vermicelli." In Italian, "vermicelli" is the plural of "vermicello," a diminutive of "verme," which does indeed mean *worm.* When dealing with recalcitrant children, it's probably better to refer to these *long, slender threads of spaghetti* simply as "pasta."

7. **pundit** (pun'dit) Today we use the word "pundit" to mean *an expert or authority;* but in the nineteenth century, the word was usually applied to a learned person in India. It comes from the Hindi word "pandit," meaning *learned man,* a Brahman with profound knowledge of Sanskrit, Hindu law, and so forth.

8. **yahoo** (yä'hoo) This word for a *coarse, uncouth person* was coined by Jonathan Swift in his 1726 novel *Gulliver's Travels.* In Swift's satire, the Yahoos were a race of humanoid brutes ruled by the Houyhnhnms, civilized horses.

9. **stoic** (stō'ik) The Stoics were philosophers of ancient Greece who believed in self-restraint. Their name comes from Greek *stoa,* "porch," where they habitually walked. Hence the word "stoic," which describes a person who is *impassive, calm, and austere.*

10. **wormwood** (wûrm'wood') "Wormwood" is the active narcotic ingredient of absinthe, a bitter green liqueur now banned in most Western countries. Originally, however, the herb was used as a folk remedy for worms in the body. Because of the herb's bitter qualities, we also use it figuratively to mean *something bitter, grievous, or extremely unpleasant.*

Test 1: True/False

In the space provided, write T if the definition of the numbered word is true or F if it is false.

		T or F
1. SPOONERISM	Midwesterner	____
2. YAHOO	oaf	____
3. WORMWOOD	bitterness	____
4. MUUMUU	murmur	____
5. PUNDIT	bad kick	____
6. LEMUR	monkeylike nocturnal mammal	____
7. SYBARITE	slender	____
8. STOIC	austere	____
9. VERMICELLI	aggravation	____
10. ROSTRUM	register	____

Answers: 1. F 2. T 3. T 4. F 5. F 6. T
7. F 8. T 9. F 10. F

Test 2: Matching Synonyms

Select the best definition for each numbered word. Write your answer in the space provided.

1. ROSTRUM	a. loose dress	____
2. YAHOO	b. something bitter	____
3. MUUMUU	c. small nocturnal mammal	____
4. SPOONERISM	d. long, thin threadlike pasta	____
5. WORMWOOD	e. impassive	____
6. SYBARITE	f. stage or platform	____
7. LEMUR	g. authority	____
8. PUNDIT	h. lover of luxury	____
9. VERMICELLI	i. transposition of sounds in words	____
10. STOIC	j. boor	____

Answers: 1. f 2. j 3. a 4. i 5. b 6. h
7. c 8. g 9. d 10. e

LESSON 9.

Here are ten more words with intriguing pasts. Read through the histories, then complete the self-tests that follow. Spend a few minutes using each of the words in a sentence to help you make them part of your everyday speech and writing.

1. **termagant** (tûr'mə gənt) The word "termagant," meaning *a violent, turbulent, or brawling woman,* comes from a mythical deity that many Europeans of the Middle Ages believed was worshiped by the Muslims. It often appeared in morality plays as a violent, overbearing personage in long robes. In modern usage, "termagant" is applied only to women.

2. **blarney** (blär'nē) According to Irish legend, anyone who kisses a magical stone set twenty

feet beneath the ground of a castle near the village of Blarney, in Ireland, will henceforth possess the gift of eloquence. One story claims the Blarney stone got its powers from the eloquence of the seventeenth-century Irish patriot Cormac McCarthy, whose soft speech won favorable terms from Elizabeth I after an Irish uprising. From this stone-kissing custom, "blarney" has come to mean *flattering or wheedling talk; cajolery.*

3. **schooner** (skōo′nər) According to legend, Captain Andrew Robinson built the first "schooner," *a sailing vessel with a foremast and a mainmast.* As it cut smoothly into the water on its maiden voyage, someone presumably was heard to exclaim, "Oh, how she scoons!" Picking up on the praise, Robinson decided to call his previously unnamed ship a "scooner." The "h" was added later. Scholars, however, doubt the veracity of this story and regard the word's source as uncertain.

4. **eunuch** (yōo′nək) A "eunuch" is *a castrated man,* especially formerly, one employed by Oriental rulers as a harem attendant. The word is based on the Greek "eunouchos," from "eune," *bed,* and "echein," *to keep,* since a eunuch is perfectly suited for guarding a woman's bed. The word is used figuratively to refer to *a weak, powerless person.*

5. **reefer** (rē′fər) The word "reefer" has several different meanings; but in the nineteenth century, the word was used to refer to sailors. The term came from a description of their duties, the taking in of the reefs. Heavy woolen coats hindered the seamen in the execution of their duties, so they wore close-fitting coats instead. These coats took their name from the sailors who wore them, and today we often refer to *any short coat or jacket of thick cloth* as a "reefer."

6. **shrew** (shrōo) In Old English, the word "shrew" described *a small, fierce rodent.* The word was later applied to *a person with a violent temper and tenacious personality* similar to the rodent's. Although "shrew" has retained this meaning, it is usually applied only to a woman.

7. **kudos** (kōo′dōz, kyōo′-) Although "kudos" has come down to us from the Greek intact in both form and meaning—*praise, glory*—in the process it has come to be regarded as a plural word, although it is singular. As a result, another new word has been formed, "kudo." Although purists still prefer "kudos is" to "kudos are," only time will tell if the transformation to kudo/kudos becomes permanent.

8. **bohemian** (bō hē′mē ən) In the early fifteenth century, a band of vagabond peasants took up residence in Paris. Knowing that they had come from somewhere in central Europe, the French dubbed the gypsies "Bohemians," in the belief that they were natives of Bohemia. Working from the stereotyped view of gypsies as free spirits, the French then applied the term "bohemian" to *a person, typically one with artistic or intellectual aspirations, who lives an unconventional life.*

9. **rhubarb** (rōo′bärb) In conventional usage, the word refers to *a long-stalked plant,* used in tart conserves and pie fillings; it is also a slang term for *quarrel* or *squabble.* The ancient Greeks gave the plant its name. Since it grew in an area outside of Greece, they called it "rha barbaron." "Rha" was the name of the plant and "barbaron" meant *foreign.*

10. **lacuna** (lə kyōo′nə) "Lacuna," *a gap or missing part; hiatus,* comes from the identical Latin word, "lacuna," meaning *a hollow.* It first entered English to refer to a missing part in a manuscript. It is also the root of "lagoon."

Test 1: True/False

In the space provided, write T if the definition of the numbered word is true or F if it is false.

		T or F
1. KUDOS	compliment	___
2. BLARNEY	cajolery	___
3. SHREW	cleverness	___
4. REEFER	woolen coat	___
5. LACUNA	hiatus	___
6. TERMAGANT	intermediate	___
7. BOHEMIAN	businesslike	___
8. SCHOONER	sailing vessel	___
9. RHUBARB	sweet	___
10. EUNUCH	castrated man	___

Answers: 1. T 2. T 3. F 4. T 5. T 6. F 7. F 8. T 9. F 10. T

Test 2: Definitions

Select the best definition for each numbered word. Write your answer in the space provided.

___ 1. kudos
   a. enclave b. martial arts
   c. acclaim d. humiliation
___ 2. eunuch
   a. hero b. warrior c. castle
   d. castrated man
___ 3. bohemian
   a. free spirit b. butcher
   c. foreigner d. master chef

_____ 4. shrew
    a. virago b. sly c. bibliophile
    d. hearty

_____ 5. lacuna
    a. hot tub b. gap c. lake d. cool
    water

_____ 6. termagant
    a. lease b. eternal c. possessive
    d. brawling woman

_____ 7. schooner
    a. release b. submarine
    c. possessive d. sailboat

_____ 8. rhubarb
    a. root b. ridicule c. squabble
    d. arrow

_____ 9. blarney
    a. mountain climbing b. sweet talk
    c. sightseeing d. luncheon meats

_____ 10. reefer
    a. coat b. renegade c. exotic fish
    d. regret

Answers: 1. c 2. d 3. a 4. a 5. b 6. d
7. d 8. c 9. b 10. a

LESSON 10.

Recalling the history of these ten words can help you remember their meanings and make them part of your stock of words. Go through the following word histories and complete the self-tests that follow. Then review the histories to help you remember the words.

1. **solecism** (sol′ə siz′əm, sō′lə-) To the ancient Greeks, the people of the colony of Soloi spoke inexcusably poor Greek. The Greeks were perhaps most offended by the Solois' errors in grammar and usage. They called such barbarous speech "soloikismos," _the language of Soloi._ Through Latin, the word became "solecism," _a substandard or ungrammatical usage; a breech of good manners or etiquette._

2. **requiem** (rek′wē əm) A "requiem" is a mass celebrated for the repose of the souls of the dead. It comes from the opening line of the Roman Catholic mass for the dead, "Requiem aeternam dona eis, Domine," meaning _Give them eternal rest, Lord._

3. **tariff** (tar′if) "Tariff," _an official schedule of duties or customs imposed by a government on imports and exports,_ comes from the Arabic term for _inventory,_ "ta'rif." Perhaps because this story is so unexciting, a false etymology claims that the word instead comes from the name of a Moorish town near the straits of Gibraltar formerly used as a base for daring pirate raids. Colorful, but not true.

4. **blitzkrieg** (blits′krēg′) The German word "Blitzkrieg," literally _a lightning war,_ describes the overwhelming Nazi attacks on Poland in 1940. In two weeks, Germany pounded Poland into submission; in six weeks, it crushed the French army. Although ultimately the Germans met defeat, their method of attack has found a place in our language, and "blitzkrieg" has come to denote _an overwhelming, all-out attack._

5. **entrepreneur** (än′trə prə nûr′, -nŏŏr′, -nyŏŏr′) "Entrepreneur" came from the French word derived from the verb "entreprendre," _to undertake._ It was initially used in English to denote a musician's manager, the person responsible for such things as organizing concerts; in the nineteenth century, the word assumed its present meaning: _a person who organizes, manages, and assumes responsibility for a business or other enterprise._

6. **spinnaker** (spin′ə kər) According to one story, in the mid-nineteenth century, a yachtsman devised a new racing sail. The name of the yacht was the "Sphinx," but the sailors had difficulty pronouncing the word. Their mispronunciation gave us the word "spinnaker," _a large, triangular sail carried by yachts as a headsail when running before the wind._

7. **reynard** (rā′närd, -nərd, ren′ərd) This _poetic name given to the fox_ comes from the medieval beast epic, stories first circulated orally throughout western Europe, then written down. Aside from countless hours of entertainment, these satirical tales have also provided us with words for other animals: "bruin" for _bear_ and "chanticleer" for _rooster._

8. **kibitzer** (kib′it sər) A "kibitzer" is _a spectator, especially at a card game, who gives unwanted advice to a player; a meddler._ This word came from Yiddish, which derived it from the German verb "kiebitzen," _to be a busybody; give unwanted advice to card players._ The verb, in turn, came from "Kiebitz," the German word for a lapwing, an inquisitive little bird given to shrill cries.

9. **lampoon** (lam pŏŏn′) "Lampoon," _a sharp, often virulent satire,_ comes from the French word "lampon," which is thought to come from "lampons," _let's drink,_ a common ending to seventeenth-century French satirical drink-

ing songs. We also use the word as a verb meaning *to mock or ridicule.*

10. **scapegoat** (skăp'gōt') The term "scapegoat," *a person made to bear the blame for others or to suffer in their place,* comes from the sixteenth chapter of Leviticus, which describes how the high priest Aaron was directed to select two goats. One goat was to be a burnt offering to the Lord; the other, an "escape goat" for atonement, was presented alive to the Lord and sent away into the wilderness to carry away the sins of the people. The word "scape" was a shortening of "escape."

Test 1: True/False

In the space provided, write T if the definition of the numbered word is true or F if it is false.

			T or F
1.	KIBITZER	busybody	——
2.	REYNARD	goat	——
3.	BLITZKRIEG	negotiations	——
4.	SOLECISM	bad grammar	——
5.	TARIFF	customs duties	——
6.	SPINNAKER	craftsperson	——

7.	REQUIEM	revival	——
8.	LAMPOON	enlighten	——
9.	SCAPEGOAT	substitute victim	——
10.	ENTREPRENEUR	organizer and manager	——

Answers: 1. T 2. F 3. F 4. T 5. T 6. F
7. F 8. F 9. T 10. T

Test 2: Matching Synonyms

Match each of the following numbered words with its closest synonym. Write your answer in the space provided.

1.	TARIFF	a. sail	——
2.	LAMPOON	b. mock	——
3.	KIBITZER	c. funeral mass	——
4.	SCAPEGOAT	d. fox	——
5.	REYNARD	e. customs duties	——
6.	REQUIEM	f. business manager	——
7.	SOLECISM	g. busybody	——
8.	BLITZKRIEG	h. grammatical error	——
9.	SPINNAKER	i. victim	——
10.	ENTREPRENEUR	j. all-out attack	——

Answers: 1. e 2. b 3. g 4. i 5. d 6. c
7. h 8. j 9. a 10. f

IMPORTED WORDS

Along with sushi, crêpes, and pizza—and their names—English has borrowed numerous words from foreign cultures. Here is a selection of "imported" words for you to add to your vocabulary.

LESSON 1. FRENCH BORROWINGS

We've borrowed so many words from French that someone once half-seriously claimed that English is little more than French badly pronounced. Some of these words have kept their original spelling, while others have become so Anglicized you may not recognize them as originally French.

1. **envoy** (en'voi, än'-) a diplomatic agent; an accredited messenger or representative.
2. **résumé** (rez'ŏŏ mā', rez'ŏŏ mā') a summing up; a brief account of personal, educational, and professional qualifications and experience, as of an applicant for a job.
3. **coup d'état** (kŏŏ'dā tä') a sudden and decisive action in politics, especially one effecting a change of government, illegally or by force.
4. **cause célèbre** (kôz'sə leb', -leb'rə) any controversy that attracts great public attention.
5. **avant-garde** (ə vänt'gärd', ə vant'-, av'än-, ä'vän-) the advance group in any field, especially in the visual, literary, or musical arts, whose works are unorthodox and experimental.
6. **laissez-faire** (les'ā fâr') the theory that government should intervene as little as possible in economic affairs.
7. **rendezvous** (rän'də vŏŏ', -dä-) an agreement between two or more people to meet at a certain time and place.
8. **cul-de-sac** (kul'də sak') a street, lane, etc., closed at one end; blind alley.
9. **esprit de corps** (e sprē' də kôr') a sense of union and of common interests and responsibilities, as developed among a group of persons associated together.
10. **idée fixe** (ē'dā fēks') a fixed idea; obsession.
11. **joie de vivre** (zhwä'də vēv', vē'vrə) a delight in being alive.
12. **milieu** (mil yŏŏ', mēl-) an environment; medium.
13. **potpourri** (pō'pŏŏ rē') a mixture of dried petals of roses or other flowers with spices, kept in a jar for their fragrance.
14. **rapport** (ra pôr', rə-) a harmonious or sympathetic relationship or connection.
15. **bon vivant** (bon'vē vänt', bôn'vē vän') a person who lives luxuriously and enjoys good food and drink.

Test 1: Matching Synonyms

Match each of the following numbered words with its closest synonym. Write your answer in the space provided.

1. RENDEZVOUS	a. togetherness	——
2. RAPPORT	b. experimental artists	——
3. CUL-DE-SAC	c. hands-off policy	——
4. BON VIVANT	d. love of life	——
5. IDÉE FIXE	e. meeting	——
6. JOIE DE VIVRE	f. environment	——
7. POTPOURRI	g. diplomatic agent	——
8. MILIEU	h. harmony	——
9. AVANT-GARDE	i. controversy	——
10. COUP D'ÉTAT	j. government overthrow	——
11. RÉSUMÉ	k. dead end	——
12. ESPRIT DE CORPS	l. list of qualifications	——
13. ENVOY	m. connoisseur	——
14. CAUSE CÉLÈBRE	n. fragrant dried flowers	——
15. LAISSEZ-FAIRE	o. obsession	——

Answers: 1. e 2. h 3. k 4. m 5. o 6. d 7. n 8. f 9. b 10. j 11. l 12. a 13. g 14. i 15. c

Test 2: True/False

In the space provided, write T if the definition of the numbered word is true or F if it is false.

		T or F
1. LAISSEZ-FAIRE	a policy of leaving alone	___
2. ESPRIT DE CORPS	harmony and union	___
3. MILIEU	setting	___
4. RENDEZVOUS	meeting	___
5. IDÉE FIXE	obsession	___
6. POTPOURRI	cooking utensils	___
7. ENVOY	letter	___
8. RAPPORT	announcement	___
9. JOIE DE VIVRE	good vintage	___
10. COUP D'ÉTAT	headache	___
11. CAUSE CÉLÈBRE	controversy	___
12. CUL-DE-SAC	dead end	___
13. BON VIVANT	good sport	___
14. RÉSUMÉ	curriculum vitae	___
15. AVANT-GARDE	front-runners	___

Answers: 1. T 2. T 3. T 4. T 5. T 6. F 7. F 8. F 9. F 10. F 11. T 12. T 13. T 14. T 15. T

LESSON 2. ADDITIONAL FRENCH BORROWINGS

Here are fifteen more words borrowed from French. Their mastery can put vigor into your vocabulary, especially in writing.

1. **tour de force** (tŏŏr'də fôrs') an exceptional achievement using the full skill, ingenuity, and resources of a person, country, or group.
2. **connoisseur** (kon'ə sûr', -sŏŏr') a person who is especially competent to pass critical judgments in art or in matters of taste.
3. **raconteur** (rak'on tûr', -tŏŏr') a person who is skilled in relating anecdotes.
4. **poseur** (pō zûr') a person who attempts to impress others by assuming or affecting a manner, degree of elegance, etc.
5. **saboteur** (sab'ə tûr') a person who deliberately destroys property, obstructs services, or undermines a cause.
6. **décolletage** (dā'kol täzh') the neckline of a dress cut low in the front or back and often across the shoulders.
7. **mêlée** (mā'lā, mā lā') a confused, general hand-to-hand fight.
8. **tout à fait** (tŏŏ' tä fā') entirely.
9. **chauffeur** (shō'fər, shō fûr') a person employed to drive another person's automobile.
10. **fiancé** (fē'än sā', fē än'sā) a man engaged to be married.
11. **protégé** (prō'tə zhā', prō'tə zhā') a person under the patronage or care of someone influential who can further his or her career.
12. **gourmet** (gŏŏr mā', gŏŏr'mā) a connoisseur in the delicacies of the table.
13. **tout de suite** (tŏŏt swēt') at once; immediately.
14. **chic** (shēk) attractive and fashionable in style; stylish.
15. **tout le monde** (tŏŏ'lə mônd') everyone; everybody.

Test 1: Defining Words

Define each of the following words.

1. tout à fait _____
2. gourmet _____
3. chauffeur _____
4. tout le monde _____
5. décolletage _____
6. tout de suite _____
7. tour de force _____
8. chic _____
9. protégé _____
10. connoisseur _____
11. raconteur _____
12. mêlée _____
13. saboteur _____
14. poseur _____
15. fiancé _____

Suggested Answers: 1. entirely 2. a connoisseur in the delicacies of the table 3. a person employed to drive another person's automobile 4. everyone; everybody 5. a low-cut neckline or backless dress 6. at once; immediately 7. an exceptional achievement using the full skill, ingenuity, and resources of a person, country, or group 8. attractive and fashionable in style 9. a person under the patronage or care of someone influential who can further his or her career 10. a person who is especially competent to pass critical judgments in art, especially one of the fine arts, or in matters of taste 11. a person who is skilled in relating anecdotes 12. a confused, general hand-to-hand fight 13. a person who destroys property, obstructs services, or subverts a cause 14. a person who attempts to impress others by assuming or affecting a manner, degree of elegance, etc. 15. a man engaged to be married

Test 2: Synonyms

Each of the following phrases contains an italicized word. Select the best synonym for each word from the choices provided. Write your answer in the space provided.

1. a daring *décolletage*
   a. low-cut dress   b. dance   c. acrobatics
   d. behavior
2. a *chic* hat
   a. French   b. imported   c. expensive
   d. stylish
3. the nervous *fiancé*
   a. engaged woman   b. engaged man
   c. executive   d. husband
4. *tout le monde* attended
   a. connoisseurs   b. specialists   c. everyone
   d. no one
5. the entertaining *raconteur*
   a. comedian   b. storyteller   c. singer
   d. poet
6. an amazing *tour de force*
   a. show of force   b. war victory
   c. humiliation   d. achievement
7. pass the butter *tout de suite*
   a. immediately   b. thank you   c. please
   d. later
8. a transparent *poseur*
   a. model   b. prank   c. fraud   d. gag
9. a captured *saboteur*
   a. spy   b. demolisher   c. turncoat
   d. revolutionary
10. my *protégé*
    a. mentor   b. tutor   c. child   d. dependent
11. a new *chauffeur*
    a. kitchen helper   b. mentor   c. chef
    d. driver
12. a violent *mêlée*
    a. free-for-all   b. storm   c. criminal   d. sea
13. a noted *connoisseur*
    a. expert   b. politician   c. hostess
    d. professor
14. completed the job *tout à fait*
    a. quickly   b. sloppily   c. entirely
    d. yesterday
15. a famous *gourmet*
    a. driver   b. waitress   c. heavy eater   d. food
    expert

Answers: 1. a   2. d   3. b   4. c   5. b   6. d
7. a   8. c   9. b   10. d   11. d   12. a   13. a
14. c   15. d

LESSON 3.

Numerous other languages have left their mark on English as well—including Italian, Spanish, and Latin. We will begin with a group of words borrowed from Italian.

ITALIAN BORROWINGS

1. alfresco (al fres′kō) out-of-doors; in the open air.
2. piazza (pē az′ə, -ä′zə) a town square.
3. dilettante (dil′i tänt′) a person who takes up an art, activity, or subject merely for amusement; dabbler.
4. fiasco (fē as′kō) a complete and ignominious failure.
5. imbroglio (im brōl′yō) a confused state of affairs; a complicated or difficult situation; bitter misunderstanding.
6. impresario (im′pri sär′ē ō′, -sâr′-) a person who organizes or manages public entertainments; a manager, director, or the like.
7. incognito (in′kog nē′tō, in kog′ni tō′) having one's identity concealed, as under an assumed name, especially to avoid notice.
8. manifesto (man′ə fes′tō) a public declaration of intentions, opinions, objectives, or motives, as one issued by a government, a sovereign, or an organization.
9. replica (rep′li kə) a copy or reproduction of a work of art.

Test 1: Matching Synonyms

Match each of the following numbered words with its closest synonym. Write your answer in the space provided.

1. FIASCO	a. manager ____
2. IMBROGLIO	b. town square ____
3. INCOGNITO	c. outdoors ____
4. IMPRESARIO	d. failure ____
5. MANIFESTO	e. public declaration ____
6. PIAZZA	f. confusion ____
7. REPLICA	g. reproduction ____
8. ALFRESCO	h. in disguise ____
9. DILETTANTE	i. dabbler ____

Answers: 1. d   2. f   3. h   4. a   5. e   6. b
7. g   8. c   9. i

Test 2: Definitions

Each of the following phrases contains an italicized word. From the three choices provided, circle the best definition.

1. an *alfresco* café
   a. open-air   b. expensive   c. famous
2. traveling *incognito*
   a. cheaply   b. under an alias   c. quickly
3. a major *fiasco*
   a. cigar   b. fault   c. failure
4. an important *manifesto*
   a. declaration   b. expansion   c. bond issue
5. a real *dilettante*
   a. expert   b. socialite   c. amateur
6. a horrible *imbroglio*
   a. confusion   b. disgrace   c. conflagration
7. a broad *piazza*
   a. forest   b. error   c. town square
8. an expensive *replica*
   a. request   b. copy   c. machine
9. a famous *impresario*
   a. singer   b. actor   c. manager

Answers: 1. a   2. b   3. c   4. a   5. c   6. a
7. c   8. b   9. c

LESSON 4. ADDITIONAL ITALIAN BORROWINGS

Italian is often said to be the most musical of the Romance languages. Make sure to practice the pronunciations of the following musical and artistic terms borrowed from Italian. The two self-tests at the end of the lesson will help you reinforce the words and their meanings.

1. **sotto voce** (sot'ō vō'chē) in a low, soft voice, so as not to be overheard.
2. **sonata** (sə nä'tə) a composition for one or two instruments, typically with three or four contrasting movements.
3. **fugue** (fyo͞og) a polyphonic composition based on one, two, or more themes that are enunciated by several voices or parts in turn, and are subject to contrapuntal treatment; in psychiatry, a period in which a patient suffers from loss of memory, often begins a new life, and upon recovery, remembers nothing from the amnesiac period. Borrowed through French from Italian "fuga," literally *a fleeing, flight.*
4. **intermezzo** (in'tər met'sō, -med'zō) a short dramatic, musical, or other entertainment of light character introduced between the acts of a drama or opera.
5. **cantata** (kən tä'tə) a choral composition, either sacred and resembling a short oratorio, or secular, as a drama set to music but not to be acted.
6. **maestro** (mī'strō) an eminent composer, teacher, or conductor of music.
7. **chiaroscuro** (kē är'ə sko͞or'ō) the distribution of light and shade in a picture.
8. **villanella** (vil'ə nel'ə) a rustic Italian part-song without accompaniment. The French word "villanelle," meaning *a short poem of fixed form,* was adapted from Italian.

Test 1: Defining Words

Define each of the following words.

1. villanella _____
2. chiaroscuro _____
3. sonata _____
4. sotto voce _____
5. maestro _____
6. cantata _____
7. intermezzo _____
8. fugue _____

Suggested Answers: 1. a part-song without accompaniment   2. the distribution of light and shade in a picture   3. a musical composition for one or two instruments, typically with three or four contrasting movements   4. in a low, soft voice   5. an eminent composer, teacher, or conductor of music   6. a choral composition   7. a short, light entertainment offered between the acts of a drama or opera   8. a polyphonic composition based on one or more themes

Test 2: True/False

In the space provided, write T if the definition of the numbered word is true or F if it is false.

		T or F
1. MAESTRO	famous musician	____
2. CHIAROSCURO	shadows	____
3. INTERMEZZO	musical interlude	____
4. CANTATA	song	____
5. SONATA	ballad	____
6. VILLANELLA	part-song	____
7. FUGUE	musical instrument	____
8. SOTTO VOCE	strident voice	____

Answers: 1. T   2. T   3. T   4. F   5. F   6. T
7. F   8. F

LESSON 5. SPANISH BORROWINGS

Our neighbors to the south have also enriched our language with a number of words that reflect the merging of Spanish culture with our own. You may find that you are already familiar with some of the following words but were unaware of their Hispanic ancestry.

1. **desperado** (des′pə rä′dō, -rā′-) a bold, reckless criminal or outlaw.
2. **fiesta** (fē es′tə) in Spain and Latin America, a festival celebrating a religious holiday; any festive celebration.
3. **siesta** (sē es′tə) a midday or afternoon rest or nap, especially as taken in Spain and Latin America.
4. **bonanza** (bə nan′zə, bō-) a rich mass of ore, as found in mining; a spectacular windfall.
5. **pronto** (pron′tō) promptly; quickly.
6. **patio** (pat′ē ō′, pä′tē ō′) a paved outdoor area adjoining a house; courtyard.
7. **bolero** (bə lâr′ō, bō-) a lively Spanish dance in triple meter; a waist-length jacket worn open in front.
8. **bravado** (brə vä′dō) swaggering display of courage.

Test 1: True/False

In the space provided, write T if the definition of the numbered word is true or F if it is false.

			T or F
1.	SIESTA	nap	____
2.	PATIO	courtyard	____
3.	BOLERO	jacket	____
4.	FIESTA	celebration	____
5.	BRAVADO	applause	____
6.	PRONTO	dappled pony	____
7.	DESPERADO	desperate lover	____
8.	BONANZA	sprawling ranch	____

Answers: 1. T   2. T   3. T   4. T   5. F   6. F   7. F   8. F

Test 2: Matching Synonyms

Select the best definition for each numbered word. Write your answer in the space provided.

1.	PRONTO	a. great, sudden wealth or luck	____
2.	BRAVADO	b. afternoon nap	____
3.	BONANZA	c. courtyard	____
4.	BOLERO	d. bold outlaw	____
5.	DESPERADO	e. festive celebration	____
6.	SIESTA	f. promptly	____
7.	PATIO	g. waist-length jacket	____
8.	FIESTA	h. swaggering show of bravery	____

Answers: 1. f   2. h   3. a   4. g   5. d   6. b   7. c   8. e

LESSON 6. ADDITIONAL SPANISH BORROWINGS

Here are some additional Spanish words to spice up your speech and writing. Study the definitions and complete the two self-tests at the end of the lesson to help you reinforce what you have learned.

1. **tango** (tang′gō) a ballroom dance of Spanish-American origin.
2. **arroyo** (ə roi′ō) a small steep-sided watercourse or gulch with a nearly flat floor, usually dry except in heavy rains.
3. **sierra** (sē er′ə) a chain of hills or mountains, the peaks of which suggest the teeth of a saw.
4. **mesa** (mā′sə) a land formation having a flat top and steep rock walls, common in arid and semi-arid parts of the United States and Mexico.
5. **chili con carne** (chil′ē kon kär′nē) a spicy Mexican-American dish of meat, beans, onion, chopped pepper, tomatoes, and seasonings.
6. **guerrilla** (gə ril′ə) a member of a small, independent band of soldiers that harass the enemy by surprise raids, sabotage, etc.
7. **mustang** (mus′tang) a small, hardy horse of the American plains.
8. **caudillo** (kou ᵗhē′lyô, -ᵗhē′yô) a head of state, especially a military dictator.

Test 1: Definitions

For each definition, select the correct vocabulary word. Write your answer in the space provided.

____ 1. a member of a band of independent soldiers who harass the enemy through surprise attacks
a. quadroon   b. arroyo   c. mustang
d. guerrilla

____ 2. a Mexican-American dish of meat, beans, tomatoes, onion, chopped pepper, and seasonings
a. sierra   b. taco   c. chili con carne
d. peccadillo

_____ 3. a small, steep-sided watercourse or gulch with a nearly flat floor
a. arroz con pollo b. tango
c. arroyo d. mesa

_____ 4. a small, hardy horse
a. arroyo b. mustang c. mesa
d. caudillo

_____ 5. a military dictator
a. caudillo b. mesa c. sierra
d. arroyo

_____ 6. a ballroom dance of Spanish-American origin
a. tango b. waltz c. quadroon
d. arroyo

_____ 7. a land formation having a flat top and steep rock walls
a. Sierra Madre b. tango c. arroyo
d. mesa

_____ 8. a chain of hills or mountains
a. quadroon b. mesa c. sierra
d. arroyo

Answers: 1. d   2. c   3. c   4. b   5. a   6. a
7. d   8. c

Test 2: Matching Synonyms

Match each of the numbered words with its closest synonym. Write your answer in the space provided.

1. MESA	a. soldier	_____
2. MUSTANG	b. saw-toothed mountains	_____
3. CAUDILLO	c. ballroom dance	_____
4. ARROYO	d. flat-topped land formation	_____
5. GUERRILLA	e. chief of state	_____
6. TANGO	f. spicy dish of meat and beans	_____
7. CHILI CON CARNE	g. dry gulch	_____
8. SIERRA	h. horse	_____

Answers: 1. d   2. h   3. e   4. g   5. a   6. c
7. f   8. b

LESSON 7. LATIN BORROWINGS

We've already encountered a great number of words with Latin roots in previous lessons, but most of them have been transformed over the centuries. Here are eight Latin words and phrases that survived intact when they were incorporated into English. All are words that can add power to your speech and writing. Study the definitions and complete the two self-tests.

1. **decorum** (di kôr′əm) dignified behavior, manners, or appearance.
2. **gratis** (grat′is, grā′tis) without charge or payment; free.
3. **in toto** (in tō′tō) in all; in the whole.
4. **odium** (ō′dē əm) intense hatred or dislike, especially toward something or someone regarded as contemptible, despicable, or repugnant.
5. **per se** (pûr sā′, sē′) by, of, for, or in itself.
6. **pro tempore** (prō′ tem′pə rē′, -rā′) temporarily; for the time being.
7. **status quo** (stā′təs kwō′, stat′əs) the existing state or condition; things as they are.
8. **terra firma** (ter′ə fûr′mə) firm or solid earth; dry land.

Test 1: Defining Words

Define each of the following words.

1. pro tempore _____
2. odium _____

3. in toto _____
4. per se _____
5. terra firma _____
6. decorum _____
7. gratis _____
8. status quo _____

Suggested Answers: 1. temporarily; for the time being   2. intense hatred or dislike   3. in all; in the whole   4. by, of, for, or in itself   5. firm or solid earth; dry land   6. dignified behavior, manners, or appearance   7. without charge or payment; free   8. the existing state or condition

Test 2: True/False

In the space provided, write T if the definition of the numbered word is true or F if it is false.

		T or F
1. STATUS QUO	existing state	_____
2. PRO TEMPORE	for the time being	_____
3. ODIUM	bad odor	_____
4. TERRA FIRMA	solid ground	_____
5. PER SE	amount	_____
6. IN TOTO	with the dog	_____
7. GRATIS	free	_____
8. DECORUM	embellishment	_____

Answers: 1. T   2. T   3. F   4. T   5. F   6. F
7. T   8. F

SPECIAL WORDS

LESSON 1. SLANG

Slang is a very informal use of vocabulary and idiom, typically formed by creative, often clever juxtapositions of images or words. It is characteristically more metaphorical, playful, elliptical, vivid, and ephemeral than ordinary language.

New slang expressions tend to come from subcultures, such as adolescents, ethnic minorities, citizen-band radio broadcasters, sports groups, criminals, and members of established institutions, such as the armed forces or labor unions. If members of the subculture have sufficient contact with the mainstream culture, the slang expression often passes into general use. For instance, "cool" *(fashionable, well-accepted)*, "nitty-gritty" *(the core or crux of some matter)*, and "The Man" *(the law)* all derive from the black culture of New York's Harlem area.

Slang develops just as other levels of language develop. In some instances, words acquire new meanings ("cat" for a *person*); in others, a meaning becomes extended ("fink," at first *a strikebreaker,* now refers to any betrayer). Words become abbreviated ("burger" for "hamburger," "perk" for "percolate"), and acronyms become widely used ("VIP"). Often words are created to deal with social and other innovations (as "tailgating," "yuppie," "hip-hop").

Slang expressions can quickly become passé ("sheik," "skiddoo," "goo-goo eyes," "the cat's pajamas," "hepcat") or standard speech ("hand-me-down" for "second-hand item"). Today, mass communication has greatly speeded up the circulation of slang expressions.

While slang invigorates a language, giving it freshness and energy, it has no place in formal speech and writing. Use it occasionally to flavor your conversation, but be careful to suit your audience and purpose. Also, make sure the words you're using are not stale and out of date.

Test: Write In

Each of the following sentences contains an italicized slang word or expression that is perfectly appropriate in the context of informal conversation. For each sentence, replace the slang word with a word or phrase that would be better suited to more formal usage and notice the effect of the change. Write your answer in the space provided.

_____ 1. He really *bugs* me when he does that.
_____ 2. Slow down! *Smokey's* up ahead behind those bushes!
_____ 3. That chore was a real *pain in the neck.*
_____ 4. Johnny was hit on the *bean* with the softball.
_____ 5. I had a lot of *moola* riding on that bet.
_____ 6. I *blew* it all at the races.
_____ 7. That franchise deal was a *ripoff.*
_____ 8. If you keep on drinking like that, you're going to get *plastered.*
_____ 9. I wish he'd quit his *bellyaching.*
_____ 10. When she's in one of those moods, she's a real *sourpuss.*
_____ 11. He *zapped* the figures marching across the screen and defeated his opponent.
_____ 12. What's your *beef?*
_____ 13. I told him to *bug off.*
_____ 14. If he doesn't start studying soon, he's going to *flunk* this course.
_____ 15. Mike is *hooked on* video games.

LESSON 2. JARGON AND ARGOT

"Get him in here stat," the doctor ordered. "Stat," a word adopted by the medical establishment from Latin "statim," is medical argot for "immediately" and is used when doctors and their assistants want to communicate quickly and efficiently. Both "jargon" and "argot" refer to the vocabulary that is peculiar to a specific group of people and that has been devised for intergroup communication or identification. Its use is also a means of restricting access by the uninitiated and creating a sense of exclusivity among group members. Though the words "jargon" and "argot" are interchangeable, "jargon" has derogatory connotations and one of its common meanings is *gibberish, nonsense*. For that reason we shall use the designation "argot" for specialized terminology.

While some argot does pass into general circulation, most of it remains incomprehensible to the layperson. Argot should be used only within the field to which it belongs; otherwise, it will probably fail to communicate your meaning. Here are some examples of argot drawn from different disciplines.

Legal Argot

on all fours   a legal precedent exactly on the mark
blacklining   marking up a legal document for changes
nit   a small point
conformed copy   a legal document with a printed rather than a signed name
counterparts   identical copies signed by different parties

Publishing Argot

dummy   a mocked-up copy to be checked, as for pagination.
proof   a trial impression of composed type taken to correct errors and make alterations
gutter   the white space formed by the inner margins of two facing pages of a book
slush pile   unsolicited manuscripts

Printing Argot

bleed   illustration or printing that extends beyond the trim size of the page
roll size   paper width
live art   the actual art being used
blanket   the rubber sheet in a printing press that transfers the image from the plate to the paper

Theater Argot

angel   a theatrical backer
spot   a spotlight
apron   the part of a stage in front of the curtain
ice   free tickets

Computer Argot

boot up   to start a computer by loading the operating system
crash   a major computer malfunction
debug   to detect and correct errors in a system
interface   connection; interaction
on-line   connected to a main computer

Aeronautics Argot

jig   a device in which an airplane part can be held while it is being worked on
BAFO   best and final offer
RFQ   request for quote
CDRL   contract data requirements list

Test: Matching Synonyms

Below are some examples of baseball argot. See how closely you can match each word or phrase with its meaning. Write your answer in the space provided.

_____ 1. fungo

_____ 2. around the horn

_____ 3. hit for the cycle

_____ 4. can of corn

_____ 5. grand slam

_____ 6. Baltimore chop

a. a high fly ball that's easy to catch

b. batter hits the ball down so it will bounce high

c. a baseball tossed in the air and struck as it comes down

d. a home run with three runners on base

e. to get a single, double, triple, and home run in one game

f. a double play started by the third baseman

Answers: 1. c   2. f   3. e   4. a   5. d   6. b

LESSON 3. DIALECT AND BRITICISMS

A dialect is a version of language spoken in a particular geographic region or by a specific group of people. Dialects frequently contain words, pronunciations, and grammatical structures that are not accepted as standard English. For example, in the British Yorkshire dialect, "something" would be rendered as "summat."

Although the Americans and the British have little difficulty communicating with each other, each country nevertheless retains a vocabulary of its own. Words used specifically by the British are known as Briticisms. Here are some of the more common ones.

Americanism	*Briticism*
bar	pub
laid off (from a job)	redundant
raincoat	mackintosh
police officer, cop	bobby
guy	bloke
candy store	sweet-shop
crazy	barmy
druggist	chemist
TV	telly
gasoline	petrol
elevator	lift
run (in a stocking)	ladder
sofa	settee
subway	underground
hood (of a car)	bonnet
naked	starkers
napkin	serviette

Americanism	*Briticism*
truck	lorry
call up (on the telephone)	ring up
French-fried potatoes	chips

Test: Matching Synonyms

Match each Briticism with its American counterpart. Write your answer in the space provided.

1. LIFT	a. napkin	——
2. UNDERGROUND	b. sofa	——
3. TELLY	c. hood (of a car)	——
4. BARMY	d. truck	——
5. CHIPS	e. guy	——
6. REDUNDANT	f. elevator	——
7. SETTEE	g. druggist	——
8. PETROL	h. TV	——
9. BLOKE	i. police officer, cop	——
10. BOBBY	j. run (in a stocking)	——
11. LORRY	k. subway	——
12. CHEMIST	l. crazy	——
13. RING UP	m. call up	——
14. MACKINTOSH	n. gasoline	——
15. SERVIETTE	o. raincoat	——
16. PUB	p. French fries	——
17. SWEET-SHOP	q. bar	——
18. LADDER	r. laid off	——
19. BONNET	s. candy store	——
20. STARKERS	t. naked	——

Answers: 1. f 2. k 3. h 4. l 5. p 6. r
7. b 8. n 9. e 10. i 11. d 12. g 13. m
14. o 15. a 16. q 17. s 18. j 19. c 20. t

PUZZLES

It's no surprise that people who love to solve word puzzles have superior vocabularies. Here are a number of different puzzles designed to add to *your* word power. There are three different types of puzzles to tease your brain and augment your vocabulary. Have fun!

LESSON 1. SUPER SIX

Most of the words in this puzzle have six letters; two of them have five. Your job is to fit each word listed below in its proper place in the puzzle. To help you get started, we've filled in one word, "mantra."

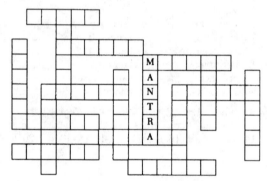

Word List

1. **cabal** (kə bal′) a small group of conspirators, especially one plotting against a government
2. **fecund** (fē′kund, fek′und) prolific, fertile, fruitful
3. **bisque** (bisk) a heavy cream soup of puréed shellfish or vegetables; ice cream made with powdered macaroons or nuts
4. **drivel** (driv′əl) nonsense
5. **bungle** (bung′gəl) to do clumsily or awkwardly; botch
6. **wimple** (wim′pəl) a woman's headcloth drawn in folds under the chin, formerly worn out of doors, and still in use by nuns
7. **morose** (mə rōs′) gloomy, depressed
8. **balsam** (bôl′səm) a fragrant resin exuded from certain trees
9. **demean** (di mēn′) to lower in dignity or standing; debase
10. **petard** (pi tärd′) an engine of war or an explosive device formerly used to blow in a door or gate, form a breach in a wall, etc.
11. **mantra** (man′trə, män′-) a word or formula to be recited or sung
12. **feisty** (fī′stē) animated, energetic, spirited, plucky
13. **welter** (wel′tər) to roll, toss, or heave, as waves; to wallow or become deeply involved
14. **supine** (soo pīn′) lying on the back
15. **beadle** (bēd′l) in British universities, an official who supervises and leads processions; mace-bearer; a parish officer who keeps order during services, waits on the clergy, etc.
16. **duress** (doo res′, dyoo-) coercion, force, constraint
17. **sinew** (sin′yoo) tendon; a source of strength

Answers:

LESSON 2. WORD FIND #1

There are seventeen words hidden in this word find puzzle. To complete the puzzle, locate and circle all the words. The words may be written forward, backward, up, or down. Good luck!

```
C A T A F A L Q U E D
R D N U C I B U R T E
U E P O I L L A C A T
C S C A R A B G D G A
I O Z O B E R M I E C
B E L B U A B I C N I
L E Z A R A S R U B T
E F O N T A N E L A S
B S A T U R N A L I A
M S I P O R P A L A M
```

Word List:

1. **malapropism** (mal′ə prop iz′əm) the act or habit of misusing words ridiculously
2. **rubicund** (roo′bi kund′) red or reddish
3. **saturnalia** (sat′ər nā′lē ə) unrestrained revelry; orgy
4. **catafalque** (kat′ə fôk′, -fôlk′, -falk′) a raised structure on which the body of a deceased person lies in state
5. **quagmire** (kwag′mī ᵊr′, kwog′-) an area of miry or boggy ground
6. **lucid** (loo′sid) crystal-clear
7. **bauble** (bô′bəl) a cheap piece of ornamentation; gewgaw
8. **masticated** (mas′ti kā′tid) chewed
9. **calliope** (kə lī′ə pē′) a musical instrument consisting of a set of harsh-sounding steam whistles that are activated by a keyboard
10. **rebozo** (ri bō′sō, -zō) a long woven scarf, worn over the head and shoulders, especially by Mexican women
11. **rubric** (roo′brik) a title, heading, direction, or the like, in a book, written or printed in red or otherwise distinguished from the rest of the text
12. **fontanel** (fon′tn el′) one of the spaces, covered by a membrane, between the bones of the fetal or young skull
13. **raze** (rāz) to wreck, demolish
14. **scarab** (skar′əb) a beetle regarded as sacred by the ancient Egyptians; a representation or image of a beetle, much used by the ancient Egyptians
15. **abnegate** (ab′ni gāt′) to surrender or renounce (rights, conveniences, etc.); deny oneself
16. **bursar** (bûr′sər, -sär) a treasurer or business officer, especially of a college or university
17. **crucible** (kroo′sə bəl) a vessel of metal or refractory material employed for heating substances to a high temperature

Answers:

LESSON 3. ACROSTIC #1

First unscramble each of the seven vocabulary words so that it matches its definition. Then use the words to fill in the appropriate spaces on the correspondingly numbered lines. When you have completed the entire puzzle, another vocabulary word will read vertically in the first spaces.

1. PONILANER having no equal
2. YOGLUE a speech or writing in praise of a person
3. MERRYPUT nonsense
4. REESIO an evening party or social gathering
5. HUNRIC a mischievous child
6. SIKKO an open pavilion
7. TEARRA errors in writing or printing

1. __ __ __ __ __ __ __ __ __
2. __ __ __ __ __ __
3. __ __ __ __ __ __ __ __
4. __ __ __ __ __ __
5. __ __ __ __ __ __

6. __ __ __ __ __
7. __ __ __ __ __ __

Word List:

soirée   errata   nonpareil
eulogy   trumpery   kiosk
urchin

Answers:

n o n p a r e i l having no equal
e u l o g y a speech or writing in praise of a person
t r u m p e r y nonsense
s o i r é e an evening party or social gathering
u r c h i n a mischievous child
k i o s k an open pavilion
e r r a t a errors in writing or printing

(netsuke (net'skē, -skā) in Japanese art, a small carved figure, originally used as a buttonlike fixture on a man's sash)

LESSON 4. WORD FIND #2

There are eighteen words hidden in this word find puzzle. To complete the puzzle, locate and circle all the words. The words may be written forward, backward, up, or down. Good luck!

```
N O N S E Q U I T U R
E B G A D F L Y B O E
T A U T O L O G Y E M
T L D U E U R O D N O
L U A R P U R L O I N
E S M N A C L O Y T S
S T S I J S U X E N T
O R O N E C N O N O R
M A N E M L O D B T A
E D S O D E N R U O T
P E J O R A T I V E E
```

Word List:

1. **nonce** (nons) the present; the immediate occasion or purpose
2. **damson** (dam'zən, -sən) the small dark-blue or purple fruit of a plum
3. **nexus** (nek'səs) a means of connecting; tie; link
4. **jape** (jāp) to jest; joke; jibe
5. **tontine** (ton'tēn, ton tēn') an annuity scheme in which subscribers share a common fund with the benefit of survivorship, the survivors' shares being increased as the subscribers die, until the whole goes to the last survivor
6. **balustrade** (bal'ə strād', bal'ə strād') a railing
7. **doxology** (dok sol'ə jē) a hymn or form of words containing an ascription of praise to God
8. **non sequitur** (non sek'wi tər, -toor') an inference or conclusion that does not follow from the premises
9. **purloin** (pər loin', pûr'loin) to take dishonestly; steal

10. **dolmen** (dōl′men, -mən, dol′-) a structure, usually regarded as a tomb, consisting of two or more large, upright stones set with a space between and capped by a horizontal stone
11. **doyen** (doi en′, doi′ən) the senior member, as in age or rank, of a group
12. **remonstrate** (ri mon′strāt) to protest
13. **nettlesome** (net′l səm) annoying; disturbing
14. **tautology** (tô tol′ə jē) needless repetition of an idea in different words, as in "widow woman"
15. **rue** (rōō) to deplore; mourn; regret
16. **gadfly** (gad′flī′) a person who repeatedly and persistently annoys or stirs up others with provocative criticism
17. **pejorative** (pə jôr′ə tiv, -jor′-) having a disparaging, derogatory, or belittling effect or force
18. **saturnine** (sat′ər nīn′) having or showing a sluggish, gloomy temperament

Answers:

```
N O N S E Q U I T U R
E B G A D F L Y B O E
T A U T O L O G Y E M
T L D U E U R O D N O
L U A R P U R L O I N
E S M N A C L O Y T S
S T S I J S U X E N T
O R O N E C N O N O R
M A N E M L O D B T A
E D S O D E N R U O T
P E J O R A T I V E E
```

LESSON 5. ACROSTIC #2

First unscramble each of the seven vocabulary words so that it matches its definition. Then use the words to fill in the appropriate spaces on the correspondingly numbered lines. When you have completed the entire puzzle, another vocabulary word will read vertically in the first spaces.

1. RACEUSA a break, usually in the middle of a verse
2. ORAMIRE a large wardrobe
3. BAMNELT moving lightly over a surface
4. SOURIOUX doting upon or submissive to one's wife
5. CANDIMENT a beggar
6. MYPONE a person, real or imaginary, from whom something, as a tribe, nation, or place, takes its name
7. FITFIN a light lunch (British usage)

1. __ __ __ __ __ __ __
2. __ __ __ __ __ __ __
3. __ __ __ __ __ __ __
4. __ __ __ __ __ __ __ __
5. __ __ __ __ __ · __ __ __

6. __ __ __ __ __ __
7. __ __ __ __ __ __

Word List:

tiffin	lambent	mendicant
eponym	caesura	armoire
uxorious		

Answers:

c a e s u r a a break, usually in the middle of a verse
a r m o i r e a large wardrobe
l a m b e n t moving lightly over a surface
u x o r i o u s doting upon or submissive to one's wife
m e n d i c a n t a beggar
e p o n y m a person, real or imaginary, from whom something, as a tribe, nation, or place, takes its name
t i f f i n a light lunch (British usage)

(**calumet** (kal′yə met′, kal′yə met′) a long, ornamented ceremonial tobacco pipe used by Native Americans)

Lesson 6. word find #3

There are fourteen words hidden in this word find puzzle. To complete the puzzle, locate and circle all the words. The words may be written forward, backward, up, or down. Good luck!

```
D  N  U  B  R  E  M  M  U  C
U  N  A  M  S  D  U  B  M  O
L  C  O  B  E  Z  A  G  A  M
C  O  A  L  E  S  C  E  H  P
I  I  M  Y  R  I  A  D  O  O
M  F  E  Y  N  E  E  R  U  T
E  T  I  O  L  O  G  Y  T  E
R  O  U  S  T  A  B  O  U  T
```

Word List:

1. **gazebo** (gə zā′bō, -zē′-) a structure, as a summerhouse or pavilion, built on a site affording a pleasant view
2. **roustabout** (roust′ə bout′) a wharf laborer or deck hand; a circus laborer
3. **compote** (kom′pōt) fruit stewed or cooked in syrup
4. **coif** (kwäf, koif) a hairstyle
5. **cummerbund** (kum′ər bund′) a wide sash worn as a waistband, especially one with horizontal pleats worn beneath a dinner jacket
6. **seer** (sēr) a prophet; mystic

7. **ombudsman** (om′bədz mən, -man′, -boodz-, ôm′-) a commissioner appointed by a legislature to hear and investigate complaints by private citizens against government officials and agencies
8. **mahout** (mə hout′) the keeper or driver of an elephant
9. **tureen** (too rēn′, tyoo-) a large, deep covered dish for serving soup or stew
10. **coalesce** (kō′ə les′) to blend; join
11. **fey** (fā) fairylike; whimsical or strange; supernatural, enchanted; in unnaturally high spirits
12. **etiology** (ē′tē ol′ə jē) the study of the causes of diseases
13. **dulcimer** (dul′sə mər) a trapezoidal zither with metal strings that are struck with light hammers
14. **myriad** (mir′ē əd) many; innumerable

Answers:

Lesson 7. the "p" patch

Each of the words in this puzzle begins with the letter "p." Your job is to fit each of the words listed below in its proper place in the puzzle. To help you get started, we've filled in one word, "pimpernel."

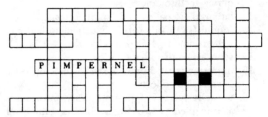

Word List:

1. **patois** (pat′wä, pä′twä, pa twä′) a rural or provincial form of speech, especially of French
2. **parse** (pärs, pärz) to describe (a word or series of words) grammatically, telling the parts of speech, inflectional forms, etc.
3. **poteen** (pə tēn′, -chēn′) illicitly distilled whiskey
4. **pimpernel** (pim′pər nel′, -nl) a plant of the primrose family, having scarlet, purplish, or white flowers that close at the approach of bad weather
5. **piebald** (pī′bôld′) having patches of black and white or of other colors
6. **paean** (pē′ən) any song of praise, joy, or thanksgiving
7. **prosody** (pros′ə dē) the science or study of poetic meters and versification

8. **pica** (pī′kə) a type size measuring twelve points
9. **pout** (pout) to sulk; look sullen
10. **pastiche** (pa stēsh′, pä-) a literary, musical, or artistic piece consisting wholly or chiefly of motifs or techniques borrowed from one or more sources
11. **pariah** (pə rī′ə) an outcast
12. **piddle** (pid′l) to waste time; dawdle
13. **placebo** (plə sē′bō) a substance having no pharmacological effect but given to a patient or subject of an experiment who supposes it to be a medicine
14. **paucity** (pô′si tē) scarcity; meagerness or scantiness
15. **peon** (pē′ən, -on) an unskilled laborer; drudge; person of low social status
16. **pupa** (pyoo′pə) an insect in the nonfeeding, usually immobile, transformation stage between the larva and the imago
17. **pinto** (pin′tō, pēn′-) piebald; mottled; spotted; a pinto horse

Answers:

	P	A	T	O	I	S		P				P			P
	A						P	I	E	B	A	L	D		A
P	A	R	S	E		P		D			A		P	O	U	T
	T					A		D			C		I		C
P	I	M	P	E	R	N	E	L		P	A	E	A	N		I
	C		E			I		E			U	■	B		T		T
	H		O			A				P	R	O	S	O	D	Y
P	O	T	E	E	N		H		P	I	C	A			

LESSON 8. WORD FIND #4

There are twenty words hidden in this word find puzzle. To complete the puzzle, locate and circle all the words. The words may be written forward, backward, up, or down. Good luck!

```
T  S  I  T  A  M  S  I  M  U  N  B
C  A  C  H  E  P  O  T  U  O  L  F
A  P  F  E  R  A  L  R  S  E  E  R
L  X  R  A  M  S  A  I  M  R  N  E
L  U  D  D  I  T  E  A  O  T  G  N
O  A  Z  Y  A  I  K  G  I  U  I  E
U  F  A  D  O  C  H  E  R  O  O  T
S  S  C  A  T  H  A  R  S  I  S  I
C  A  S  E  M  E  N  T  Y  O  L  C
```

Word List:

1. **triage** (trē äzh′) the process of sorting victims, as of a battle or disaster, to determine priority of medical treatment
2. **cachepot** (kash′pot′, -pō′) an ornamental container for holding or concealing a flowerpot
3. **frenetic** (frə net′ik) highly excited
4. **callous** (kal′əs) unfeeling
5. **miasma** (mī az′mə, mē-) noxious exhalations from putrescent matter
6. **outré** (oo trā′) beyond the bounds of what is usual or considered proper
7. **cheroot** (shə root′) a cigar having open, untapered ends
8. **feral** (fēr′əl, fer′-) wild, primitive
9. **flout** (flout) to treat with disdain, scorn, or contempt; scoff at
10. **catharsis** (kə thär′sis) purging of the emotions, especially through a work of art

11. **Luddite** (lud′īt) a member of any of various bands of English workers (1811–1816) who destroyed industrial machinery in the belief that its use diminished employment; any opponent of new technologies
12. **faux pas** (fō pä′) a social gaffe; error
13. **soigné** (swän yā′) carefully or elegantly done; well-groomed
14. **seer** (sēr) a prophet; mystic
15. **numismatist** (noo miz′mə tist, -mis′-, nyoo-) a person who collects coins
16. **pastiche** (pa stēsh′, pä-) a literary, musical, or artistic piece consisting wholly or chiefly of motifs or techniques borrowed from one or more sources
17. **heady** (hed′ē) intoxicating; exciting
18. **coda** (kō′də) a passage concluding a musical composition
19. **cloy** (kloi) to weary by excess, as of food, sweetness, or pleasure; surfeit or sate
20. **casement** (kās′mənt) a window sash opening on hinges

Answers:

```
T (S  I  T  A  M  S  I  M  U  N) B
C (A  C  H  E  P  O (T) U  O  L (F
A  P (F  E  R  A  L  R (S (E (E  R
L  X (R  A  M  S  A  I  M  R  N  E
L  U  D  D  I  T  E) A  O  T  G  N
O  A  Z (Y  A  I  K  G  I  U  I  E
U (F (A  D  O (C) H  E  R  O  O) T
S  S (C  A  T  H  A  R  S  I  S) I
C  A  S  E  M  E  N  T) Y  O  L  C)
```

LESSON 9. ACROSTIC #3

First unscramble each of the seven vocabulary words so that it matches its definition. Then use the words to fill in the appropriate spaces on the correspondingly numbered lines. When you have completed the entire puzzle, another vocabulary word will read vertically in the first spaces.

1. ZIMZUNE a crier who calls Muslims to prayer
2. NEXUPGE to erase
3. DAILYRAP the art of cutting and polishing gems; highly exact and refined in style
4. PARTIFIE a small alcoholic drink taken before dinner

5. COCARMENNY black magic; conjuration
6. TIGMEL a small tool; a cocktail
7. WESHEC to shun; avoid

1. __ __ __ __ __ __ __
2. __ __ __ __ __ __ __
3. __ __ __ __ __ __ __
4. __ __ __ __ __ __ __
5. __ __ __ __ __ __ __ __ __
6. __ __ __ __ __ __
7. __ __ __ __ __ __

Word List:

eschew	necromancy	lapidary
gimlet	muezzin	apéritif
expunge		

Answers:

<u>m u e z z i n</u> a crier who calls Muslims to prayer

<u>e x p u n g e</u> to erase

<u>l a p i d a r y</u> the art of cutting and polishing gems; highly exact and refined in style

<u>a p é r i t i f</u> a small alcoholic drink taken before dinner

<u>n e c r o m a n c y</u> black magic; conjuration

<u>g i m l e t</u> a small tool; a cocktail

<u>e s c h e w</u> to shun; avoid

(**mélange** (mā lăɴzh′, -länj′) a mixture or medley)

LESSON 10. WORD FIND #5

There are thirteen words hidden in this word find puzzle. To complete the puzzle, locate and circle all the words. The words may be written forward, backward, up, or down. Good luck!

```
S L U M G U L L I O N S M
C I T C E L C E N B O R I
A N E D E M A N A V R I N
B A H E G E M O N Y O X A
R E C A N T E D E R M I R
O A A E P I P H A N Y L E
U P C E T A U N E T X E T
S A N C T I M O N I O U S
```

Word List:

1. **slumgullion** (slum gul′yən, slum′gul′-) a stew of meat, potatoes, and vegetables
2. **oxymoron** (ok′si môr′on) a figure of speech in which a locution produces an effect by seeming self-contradictory, as in "cruel kindness" or "to make haste slowly"
3. **paean** (pē′ən) any song of praise, joy, or thanksgiving
4. **minarets** (min′ə rets′, min′ə rets′) slender towers or turrets that are attached to a mosque and from which a muezzin calls the people to prayer
5. **sanctimonious** (sangk′tə mō′nē əs) insincere, hypocritical

6. **hegemony** (hi jem′ə nē, hej′ə mō′nē) leadership or predominant influence
7. **inane** (i nān′) pointless, silly
8. **extenuate** (ik sten′yo͞o āt′) to make or try to make seem less serious, especially by offering excuses
9. **nirvana** (nir vä′nə, -van′ə, nər-) in Buddhism, freedom from the endless cycle of personal reincarnations, with their consequent suffering, as a result of the extinction of individual passion, hatred, and delusion
10. **recanted** (ri kan′tid) retracted; denied
11. **edema** (i dē′mə) abnormal accumulation of fluids in body tissues, causing swelling
12. **epiphany** (i pif′ə nē) an appearance or manifestation, especially of a deity
13. **eclectic** (i klek′tik) selecting; choosing from various sources

Answers:

```
S L U M G U L L I O N S M
C I T C E L C E N B O R I
A N E D E M A N A V R I N
B A H E G E M O N Y O X A
R E C A N T E D E R M I R
O A A E P I P H A N Y L E
U P C E T A U N E T X E T
S A N C T I M O N I O U S
```

LESSON 11. SPECTACULAR SEVEN

Each of the words in this puzzle has seven letters. Your job is to fit each of the words listed below in its proper place in the puzzle. To help you get started, we've filled in one word, "heinous," which means *reprehensible* or *evil*.

Word List:

1. **acolyte** (ak'ə līt') an altar boy
2. **pismire** (pis'mī ³r', piz'-) an ant
3. **shoguns** (shō'gənz, -gunz) the chief Japanese military commanders from the eighth to twelfth centuries, or the hereditary officials who governed Japan, with the emperor as nominal ruler, until 1868
4. **panacea** (pan'ə sē'ə) a remedy for all ills; cure-all
5. **pooh-bah** (poo'bä') a person who holds sev-

eral positions, especially ones that give him importance; a pompous person
6. **hirsute** (hûr'soot, hûr soot') hairy
7. **foibles** (foi'bəlz) minor weaknesses or failings of character
8. **debacle** (də bä'kəl, -bak'əl, dā-) a general breakup or dispersion; sudden collapse
9. **carping** (kär'ping) fault-finding; critical
10. **cuckold** (kuk'əld) the husband of an unfaithful wife
11. **distaff** (dis'taf) a staff with a cleft end for holding wool, flax, etc., from which the thread is drawn in spinning by hand; the female sex; woman's work
12. **palfrey** (pôl'frē) a riding horse, as distinguished from a war horse; a woman's horse
13. **winsome** (win'səm) cute, charming

Answers:

A		P				C	U	C	K	O	L	D
C	A	R	P	I	N	G		H				E
O		S		D	I	S	T	A	F	F		B
L	S	M	P	■	R			O				A
Y	H	E	I	N	O	U	S		I			C
T	O	R	O		U			B				L
E	G	E	H		T		P	A	L	F	R	E	Y
	U		B		E			E				
P	A	N	A	C	E	A		W	I	N	S	O	M	E
	S		H									

LESSON 12. WORD FIND #6

There are nineteen words hidden in this word find puzzle. To complete the puzzle, locate and circle all the words. The words may be written forward, backward, up, or down. Good luck!

```
P R E L A P S A R I A N
E E M E T I E R V U E O
I M B R O G L I O B H I
G O D H A R M A O G C T
N T E S P O U S E H U A
O I B T I B M A G E A R
I P A N D E M I C R G O
R E C A F F E F A K I R
R S A V O I R F A I R E
T N A C I R Y G E N A P
```

Word List:

1. **peroration** (per'ə rā'shən) the concluding part of a speech or discourse
2. **oeuvre** (ûrv, ûrv'rə) the works of a writer, painter, or the like, taken as a whole
3. **prelapsarian** (prē'lap sâr'ē ən) pertaining to conditions existing before the fall of humankind
4. **mummery** (mum'ə rē) an empty or ostentatious performance
5. **gherkin** (gûr'kin) a pickle
6. **fakir** (fə kēr', fā'kər) a Muslim or Hindu religious ascetic or mendicant monk commonly considered a wonder worker
7. **métier** (mā'tyā, mā tyā') an occupation
8. **peignoir** (pān wär', pen-, pän'wär, pen'-) a woman's dressing gown

9. **pandemic** (pan dem′ik) (of a disease) prevalent throughout an entire country or continent or the whole world

10. **savoir faire** (sav′wär fâr′) a knowledge of just what to do in any situation; tact

11. **gauche** (gōsh) uncouth; awkward

12. **imbroglio** (im brōl′yō) a confused state of affairs

13. **panegyric** (pan′i jir′ik, -jī′rik) an oration, discourse, or writing in praise of a person or thing

14. **dharma** (där′mə, dur′-) in Buddhism, the essential quality or nature, as of the cosmos or one's own character

15. **efface** (i fās′) to wipe out; cancel or obliterate; make (oneself) inconspicuous

16. **espouse** (i spouz′, i spous′) to advocate or support; marry

17. **epitome** (i pit′ə mē) a person or thing that is typical of or possesses to a high degree the features of a whole class; embodiment

18. **gambit** (gam′bit) in chess, an opening in which a player seeks by sacrificing a pawn or piece to obtain some advantage; any maneuver by which one seeks to gain an advantage

19. **cant** (kant) deceit; insincerity or hypocrisy; the private language of a group, class, or profession; singsong or whining speech

Answers:

```
P R E L A P S A R I A N
E E M E T I E R V U E O
I M B R O G L I O B H I
G O D H A R M A O G C T
N T E S P O U S E H U A
O I B T I B M A G E A R
I P A N D E M I C R G O
R E C A F F E F A K I R
R S A V O I R F A I R E
T N A C I R Y G E N A P
```

PART THREE

THESAURUS OF SYNONYMS AND ANTONYMS

IN OTHER WORDS . . .

Judicious use of this book will more than treble the average person's potential vocabulary. Over 80,000 synonyms and antonyms have been listed in categories which are numbered to correspond with the senses in which they are most commonly used, based on scientific frequency counts.

Thus, for the entry **trust,** the synonyms given for number 1. are those which are equated to the most common sense in which the word is used, "reliance on the integrity, justice, etc., of a person, or in some quality or attribute of a thing; confidence." Similarly, synonyms under following numbers correspond to meanings of decreasing frequency.

The arrangement within the entries proper varies: if the entry word is a "strong" one, synonyms will be entered in order of decreasing intensity (synonyms for **oblivious** run the gamut from *heedless* to *negligent*), and if "weak," in order of increasing "strength." Also, informal words have their synonyms given in the order of increasing formality (**coast** synonyms run from *shore* to *littoral*), while formal word synonyms go in the opposite direction.

ANTONYMS are provided only for appropriate words which have antonyms. Only a few are provided in each case, but to find more, the user need only look up the synonym entries provided for the antonyms listed.

A WORD OF CAUTION

The most important word of caution for the user of this dictionary is to remember that there is *no true synonym* for any word in English. Each word has its own set of meanings, but its use must always be appropriate to the context in which it appears. Thus no one would write "We spent the day on the littoral" instead of "We spent the day at the beach, at the shore, etc." If a selected synonym is unfamiliar, *look up the word in a good dictionary* where it will often be shown used in a sample sentence or phrase. It is only in this way that you can derive the greatest amount of use and benefit from this thesaurus.

A

abandon, *v.* 1. leave, forsake, desert, relinquish, evacuate, drop, discard, cast off, quit, vacate. 2. resign, retire, quit, abjure, forswear, withdraw, forgo. 3. abdicate, waive, give up, yield, surrender, resign, cede, renounce, repudiate.
Ant. keep, maintain; pursue.

abandoned, *adj.* 1. forsaken, left, deserted, relinquished, dropped, discarded, cast off, cast aside, cast out, rejected, demitted, sent down. 2. unrestrained. 3. wicked, depraved, unprincipled, sinful, corrupt, licentious, amoral, profligate, vicious, dissolute, shameless; shameful, immoral, incorrigible, impenitent, graceless, irreclaimable, reprobate, demoralized, vice-ridden.
Ant. virtuous, honest, good, righteous.

abase, *v.* lower, reduce, humble, degrade, downgrade, demote; disgrace, dishonor, debase, take down, humiliate.
Ant. elevate, exalt, honor.

abash, *v.* shame, embarrass, mortify, disconcert, discompose, confound, confuse; cow, humble, humiliate, discountenance, affront.

abate, *v.* 1. lessen, diminish, reduce, discount, decrease, lower, slow. 2. deduct, subtract, remit, rebate, allow, discount. 3. omit, eliminate, disallow. 4. *(law)* suppress; suspend, extinguish; annul; remove, disallow, nullify, repress. 5. diminish, lessen, decrease, lower, slow, subside, decline, sink, wane, ebb, slack off, slacken, fade, fade out, fade away.
Ant. increase, intensify.

abatement, *n.* 1. alleviation, mitigation, lessening, let-up, diminution, decrease, slackening. 2. suppression, termination, ending, end, cessation. 3. subsidence, decline, sinking, way, ebb, slack, fade-out, fading.
Ant. intensification, increase.

abbreviate, *v.* shorten, abridge, reduce, curtail, cut, contract, compress; crop, dock, pare down, prune,

truncate; condense, digest, epitomize, abstract.
Ant. lengthen, expand.

abbreviation, *n.* shortening, abridgment, compendium, reduction, curtailment, cut, contraction, compression; truncation; condensation, digest, epitome, brief, essence, heart, core, soul.
Ant. lengthening, expansion.

abdicate, *v.* renounce, disclaim, disavow, disown, repudiate; resign, retire, quit, relinquish, abandon, surrender, cede, give up, waive.
Ant. commit.

abdication, *n.* renunciation, disclaimer, disavowal, repudiation, resignation, retirement, quittance; abandonment, surrender, cession, waiver.
Ant. commitment.

abdomen, *n.* 1. stomach, belly, visceral cavity, viscera, paunch. 2. *(slang)* pot, guts, gut, potbelly, corporation, alderman, beer-barrel.

abduct, *v.* kidnap, carry off, bear off, capture, carry away, ravish, steal away, run away *or* off with, seize, rape.

abduction, *n.* kidnapping, capture, ravishment, deprehension, seizure, rape.

abductor, *n.* kidnaper, captor, ravisher, seizer, rapist.

abecedarian, *n.* 1. beginner. —*adj.* 2. alphabetical. 3. primary, basic, rudimentary.

aberrant, *adj.* 1. straying, stray, deviating, deviate, wandering, errant, erring, devious, erratic, rambling, diverging, divergent. 2. abnormal, irregular, unusual, odd, eccentric, peculiar, exceptional, weird, queer, curious, singular, strange; unconforming, nonconforming, anomalous.
Ant. direct.

aberration, *n.* 1. wandering, straying, deviation, rambling, divergence, departure. 2. strangeness, abnormality, abnormity, oddness, anomaly, ir-

regularity, eccentricity; peculiarity, curiosity, oddity. 3. unsoundness, illusion, hallucination, delusion, *lapsus mentis.*

abet, *v.* aid, assist, help, support, back, succor, sustain; countenance, sanction, uphold, second, condone, approve, favor; encourage, promote, conduce, advocate, advance, further, subsidize.
Ant. hinder.

abeyance, *n.* suspension, suspense, inactivity, hiatus, recess, deferral, intermission, interregnum, dormancy, quiescence.
Ant. operation, action.

abhor, *v.* hate, detest, loathe, abominate, despise, regard with repugnance, execrate, view with horror, shrink from, shudder at, bear malice *or* spleen.
Ant. love.

abhorrence, *n.* hate, hatred, loathing, execration, odium, abomination, aversion, repugnance, revulsion, disgust, horror, antipathy, detestation, animosity, enmity.
Ant. love.

abhorrent, *adj.* 1. hating, loathing, loathsome, execrating, execratory, antipathetic, detesting, detestable. 2. horrible, horrifying, shocking, disgusting, revolting, sickening, nauseating, repugnant, repulsive, odious; hateful, detestable, abominable, invidious. 3. remote, far, distant, removed.
Ant. amiable, lovable.

abide, *v.* 1. remain, stay, wait, wait for, tarry, sojourn. 2. dwell, reside, live, inhabit, tenant, stay. 3. remain, continue, endure, last, persist, persevere, remain steadfast *or* faithful *or* constant, go on, keep on. 4. stand by, support, second; await *or* accept the consequences of. 5. await, attend, wait for. 6. stand one's ground against, await *or* sustain defiantly. 7. put up with, stand, suffer, brook, allow, tolerate, bear, endure.

ability, *n.* 1. power, proficiency, expertness, dexterity, capacity, able-

ness, capability, knack, facility, competency, competence, enablement; puissance, prepotency. 2. faculty, talent, aptitude, skill, skillfulness, aptness, ingenuity.
Ant. inability.

abject, *adj.* 1. humiliating, disheartening, debasing, degrading. 2. contemptible, despicable, scurvy, hateful; base, mean, low, vile, groveling, corrupt; faithless, treacherous, perfidious, dishonorable, inglorious, dishonest, false, fraudulent; disgraceful, ignominious, discreditable.
Ant. supercilious; exalted.

able, *adj.* 1. qualified, fit, fitted, competent, capable, apt. 2. talented, accomplished, gifted, endowed; skilled, clever, adroit, expert, ingenious, skillful, proficient, versed.
Ant. unable, incompetent, inept.

abnormal, *adj.* nonconforming, nonconformant, irregular, erratic, anomalous, unusual, unnatural, queer, odd, peculiar, aberrant, eccentric, weird, curious, strange, singular, idiosyncratic.
Ant. normal, regular.

abnormality, *n.* abnormity, irregularity, unconformity, anomaly, peculiarity, aberrance, idiosyncrasy, singularity, curiosity; malformation, monstrosity.
Ant. regularity, normality.

abolish, *v.* suppress, put an end to, cease, void, annul, invalidate, nullify, cancel, revoke, rescind, repeal, eradicate, stamp out, annihilate, extirpate, destroy, do away with, abrogate, obliterate, erase, extinguish, put out, eliminate.
Ant. establish.

abolition, *n.* destruction, annihilation, extirpation, abrogation, obliteration, eradication, elimination, extinction; annulment, nullification, invalidation, cancellation, revocation, repeal.
Ant. establishment.

abominable, *adj.* detestable, hateful, loathsome, abhorrent, odious, contemptible, despicable, scurvy; horrible, horrifying, disgusting, nauseating, sickening, revolting, repugnant, obnoxious, foul, noxious.
Ant. likable, admirable, delightful.

abominate, *v.* abhor, regard with aversion, detest, hate, loathe, execrate, contemn, despise, regard with repugnance, view with horror, shrink from, shudder at, bear malice *or* spleen.
Ant. like, love, enjoy.

abomination, *n.* 1. hatred, loathing, abhorrence, detestation, revulsion, loathsomeness, odiousness, odium; aversion. 2. vice, sin, impurity, corruption, wickedness, evil, viciousness, depravity, immorality, amorality, profligacy, defilement, pollution, filth.

abortive, *adj.* 1. failing, unsuccessful, miscarrying, immature, premature. 2. undeveloped, underdeveloped, rudimentary, primitive. 3. *(medicine)* abortifacient. 4. *(pathology)* short, mild, without symptoms.
Ant. consummate.

abound, *v.* prevail, teem, swarm, be very prevalent, pour, stream, shower.
Ant. want, need, lack.

about, *prep.* 1. of, concerning, in regard to, respecting, with regard *or* respect *or* reference to, relating *or* relative to. 2. connected with, in connection with, relating *or* relative to. 3. near, around, round, not far from, close to. 4. near, close to, approximately, almost. 5. around, circling, encircling, inclosing, enclosing, surrounding. 6. on one's person, having, in one's possession. 7. on the point of, ready, prepared. 8. here and there, in, on, hither and yon, to and fro, back and forth, hither and thither. —*adv.* 9. near, approximately, nearly, almost, well-nigh. 10. nearby, close, not far, around. 11. on every side, in every direction, all around, everywhere, every place, all over. 12. half round, reversed, backwards, opposite direction. 13. to and fro, back and forth, hither and thither, hither and yon, here and there. 14. in succession, alternately, in rotation.

above, *adv.* 1. overhead, aloft, on high, atop, on top of. 2. higher, beyond, over, superior, surpassing. 3. before, prior, earlier, sooner, previous, first. 4. in heaven, on high, *in excelsis.* —*prep.* 5. over, in a higher place than, higher than, superior to. 6. more, greater than, more than, exceeding. 7. superior to, beyond, surpassing. —*adj.* 8. supra, said, written, mentioned previously, foregoing, preceding.

aboveboard, *adv.* 1. in open sight, without tricks, without disguise, openly, overtly, candidly, honestly, frankly, sincerely, guilelessly, unequivocally, unequivocatingly. —*adj.* 2. open, candid, overt, honest, frank, sincere, guileless, unequivocal, unequivocating.

Ant. underhand, treacherous, seditious.

abrade, *v.* wear off, wear down, scrape off; erode, wear away, rub off.

abrasion, *n.* 1. sore, scrape, cut, scratch. 2. friction, abrading, rubbing, erosion, wearing down, rubbing off.

abreast, *adv., adj.* side by side, alongside, equal, aligned, in alignment.

abridge, *v.* 1. condense, digest, scale down, reduce, epitomize, abstract. 2. curtail, reduce, lessen, diminish, contract. 3. deprive, cut off, dispossess, divest.
Ant. expand, extend.

abridgment, *n.* 1. condensation, shortening, digest, epitome, curtailment, reduction, abbreviation, contraction, retrenchment, compression; compendium, synopsis, abstract, abstraction, summary, syllabus, brief, outline, précis. 2. dispossession, limitation.
Ant. expansion, extension, enlargement.

abroad, *adv.* 1. overseas, beyond the sea, away. 2. out-of-doors, outside, out of the house. 3. astir, in circulation, bruited about. 4. broadly, widely, expansively, at large, everywhere, ubiquitously, in all directions. 5. untrue, wide of the truth.
Ant. here, domestically.

abrogate, *v.* abolish, cancel, annul, repeal, disannul, revoke, rescind, nullify, void, invalidate.
Ant. ratify, establish.

abrogation, *n.* abolition, cancellation, annulment, repeal, disannulment, revocation, rescission, nullification, invalidation.
Ant. establishment.

abrupt, *adj.* 1. sudden, unceremonious, short, precipitous, hasty, blunt, curt, brusque, uncomplaisant; rude, rough, discourteous, inconsiderate, boorish. 2. discontinuous, spasmodic, uneven. 3. steep, precipitous, acclivitous, craggy.
Ant. gradual, slow, deliberate.

abscond, *v.* depart suddenly, depart secretly, steal away, sneak off *or* out, decamp, run away, run off, escape, flee, fly, bolt.
Ant. remain.

absence, *n.* 1. want, lack, need, deficiency, defect. 2. non-appearance.
Ant. presence.

absent, *adj.* 1. away, out, not in, not present, off. 2. lacking, missing, not present, away. —*v.* 3. stay away, keep away.
Ant. present.

absent-minded, *adj.* forgetful, preoccupied, abstracted, oblivious, inattentive, wandering, withdrawn; musing, in a brown study, dreaming, daydreaming.
Ant. attentive.

absolute, *adj.* 1. complete, whole, entire, perfect, free from imperfection, ideal. 2. pure, unmixed, unadulterated, sheer, unqualified. 3. unqualified, utter, total, entire, unconditional, unrestricted, unlimited, unbound, unbounded. 4. arbitrary, despotic, autocratic, dictatorial, tyrannous, tyrannical, imperious, Nazi, Fascist, Fascistic. 5. uncompared, categorical, certain, unquestionable, unequivocal. 6. positive, affirmative, unquestionable, indubitable, certain, sure, unequivocal, unequivocating, firm, definite.
Ant. mixed; relative.

absolutely, *adv.* 1. completely, wholly, entirely, unqualifiedly, definitely, unconditionally. 2. positively, affirmatively, unquestionably, definitely, unequivocally, indubitably, really, without doubt, beyond doubt.

absolve, *v.* 1. acquit, exonerate, free from blame, exculpate, excuse, forgive, pardon, clear, release, liberate, set free, free, disentangle, discharge, loose, rid. 2. set free, loose, release, liberate, exempt. 3. pardon, excuse, forgive.
Ant. blame, censure.

absorb, *v.* 1. swallow, consume, assimilate, amalgamate, devour, engulf, ingurgitate; destroy. 2. engross, occupy.

abstinence, *n.* 1. abstemiousness, sobriety, soberness, teetotalism, moderation, temperance. 2. self-restraint, forbearance, avoidance, self-denial, nonindulgence.
Ant. indulgence.

abstract, *adj.* 1. apart, special, unrelated, separate, isolated. 2. theoretical, unpractical. 3. abstruse, difficult, deep, complex, complicated. 4. *(art)* nonrepresentational, unrealistic, unphotographic. —*n.* 5. summary, digest, epitome, abridgment, synopsis, compendium, condensation, brief; syllabus, outline, précis, gist, substance. 6. essence, distillation, condensation, substance; core, heart, idea. —*v.* 7. draw away, take away, remove, distill; separate, fractionate. 8. divert, disengage. 9. steal, purloin, rob, pilfer, shoplift, hijack. 10. separate, consider apart, isolate, dissociate; disjoin, disunite. 11. summarize, epitomize, distill, abridge, abbreviate, outline, condense, edit, digest.
Ant. concrete; interpolate.

absurd, *adj.* ridiculous, preposterous, foolish, inane, asinine, stupid, unwise, false, unreasonable, irrational, incongruous, self-contradictory.
Ant. sensible, rational.

abundance, *n.* 1. overflow, plenty, copiousness, fertility, profusion, plenteousness, prodigality, extravagance, oversupply, flood. 2. fulness, generosity, large-heartedness. 3. affluence, wealth.
Ant. lack, need, paucity.

abundant, *adj.* abounding, teeming, thick, plentiful, plenteous, flowing, copious, profuse, overflowing, rich, replete.
Ant. sparse, scarce, poor.

abuse, *v.* 1. misuse, misapply, mistreat, misemploy, misappropriate; desecrate, profane, prostitute; deceive, betray, seduce, subvert. 2. maltreat, ill-use, injure, harm, hurt. 3. revile, malign, vilify, vituperate, berate, rate, rail at, upbraid, scold, carp at, inveigh against, reproach; traduce, slander, defame, denounce, asperse, calumniate, disparage; satirize, lampoon. —*n.* 4. misuse, misapplication, mistreatment, misemployment, misappropriation; desecration, profanation, prostitution; deception, betrayal, seduction, subversion. 5. censure, adverse criticism, blame, condemnation, hostile condemnation; denunciation, vilification, malignment, vituperation, invective, slander, defamation, aspersion, calumniation, curse, disparagement; contumely, scorn, reproach, opprobrium. 6. offense, crime, corruption.
Ant. esteem; praise, acclaim.

academic, *adj.* 1. college, collegiate, university. 2. unscientific, literary, lettered, scholastic, unprofessional. 3. theoretical, unpractical, impractical. 4. conventional, formal.
Ant. illiterate.

accept, *v.* 1. receive, take. 2. admit, agree to, accede to, acquiesce in, assent to, approve, allow, concede, acknowledge. 3. resign oneself to, accommodate oneself to, yield, consent. 4. believe, acknowledge. 5. understand, construe, interpret. 6. receive, acknowledge.
Ant. reject.

accident, *n.* 1. mischance, misfortune, disaster, calamity, catastrophe, casualty, mishap, misadventure, contingency. 2. fortuity, chance.
Ant. intent, calculation.

accidental, *adj.* 1. casual, fortuitous, undesigned, unplanned, contingent. 2. nonessential, incidental, subsidiary, secondary, dispensable, expendable, adventitious.
Ant. planned, designed, essential.

accommodate, *v.* 1. oblige, serve; aid, assist, help, abet. 2. provide, supply, furnish, minister to. 3. furnish room for, board, entertain. 4. make suitable, suit, fit, adapt. 5. bring into harmony, adjust, reconcile, compose, harmonize. 6. contain, hold. 7. conform, agree, concur, assent.
Ant. inconvenience, incommode.

accompany, *v.* 1. go along, attend, join, escort, convoy, wait on. 2. coexist with, consort with. 3. associate with, consider together with, couple with.
Ant. desert, abandon, forsake.

accomplice, *n.* associate, partner, confederate, accessory.

accomplish, *v.* 1. fulfill, complete, achieve, execute, do, carry out, perform, finish, attain, consummate, culminate, dispatch, effect, effectuate, perfect, realize. 2. succeed in, be successful with *or* in, triumph over, win over. 3. equip, supply, furnish, provide.
Ant. foil.

accomplishment, *n.* 1. fulfillment, completion, effecting, execution. 2. achievement, success, consummation. 3. attainment, acquirement, acquisition, proficiency.
Ant. failure.

accord, *v.* 1. agree, assent, concur, correspond, be harmonious *or* in harmony, harmonize. 2. adapt, accommodate, reconcile, suit, fit. 3. grant, concede, yield, give up *or* in, allow, deign, vouchsafe.
Ant. conflict, disagree.

accordingly, *adv.* 1. correspondingly, conformably, agreeably. 2. in due course, consequently, hence, therefore, thus, so, wherefore.

account, *n.* 1. narrative, narration, recital, report, history, chronicle, journal, anecdote, description, story, exposé, tale. 2. explanation, elucidation. 3. explication, clearing up, exposition. 4. reason, consideration, motive, excuse, purpose. 5. consequence, importance, value, consideration, worth, distinction, repute, reputation. 6. estimation, judgment, consideration, regard. 7. profit, advantage, benefit. 8. statement, ledger, inventory, register, score, book, books. 9. record, ledger; balance. —v. 10. give an explanation for, explain, elucidate. 11. make excuse for, give reasons for, answer, reply. 12. explain, explicate. 13. cause death or capture for. 14. count, reckon, estimate, consider, regard, judge, deem, rate, assess, hold, see, view, look upon. 15. assign to, impute to, blame, credit, accuse.

accurate, *adj.* correct, exact, precise, careful, true, unerring. *Ant.* inaccurate.

accuse, *v.* 1. arraign, indict, charge, incriminate, impeach. 2. blame, inculpate, charge, involve, point to.*Ant.* exonerate.

accustomed, *adj.* 1. customary, habitual, usual, characteristic, familiar, common. 2. wont, used to, in the habit of. *Ant.* unused, unaccustomed.

ache, *v.* 1. suffer, hurt, suffer pain. —*n.* 2. pain, continued or dull pain, agony.

achieve, *v.* 1. carry through, accomplish, consummate, complete, effect, execute, do, perform, realize, reach. 2. gain, obtain, acquire, procure, secure, get, attain, realize, win. 3. effect, result. *Ant.* fail.

achievement, *n.* 1. exploit, feat, deed. 2. accomplishment, realization, attainment, consummation. *Ant.* failure.

acid, *adj.* 1. vinegary. 2. sour, tart, biting, ill-natured, ill-tempered, sarcastic, sardonic, scornful. *Ant.* sweet, mild.

acknowledge, *v.* 1. admit, confess, own, declare, grant, concede, give in, allow, agree. 2. realize, recognize. 3. accept, receive, allow. 4. appreciate, be grateful for, express gratitude for. 5. reply to, receive, indorse, admit or certify receipt of.

acquaintance, *n.* 1. associate, companion, friend. 2. personal knowledge, familiarity.

acquiesce, *v.* assent, accede, comply, agree, concur, consent, bow, submit, yield, resign or reconcile oneself, rest, be satisfied or content (with). *Ant.* protest, object.

acquire, *n.* 1. appropriate, gain, win, earn, attain; take over, take possession of, procure, secure, obtain, get. 2. accomplish, achieve. *Ant.* forfeit.

acquit, *v.* 1. absolve, exonerate, exculpate, pardon, excuse, forgive. 2.

release or discharge, liberate, set free. 3. settle, pay, fulfill. *Ant.* convict, condemn.

act, *n.* 1. feat, exploit, achievement, transaction, accomplishment, performance. 2. deed, performance. 3. decree, edict, law, statute, judgment, resolve, award. 4. record, deed, enactment, ordinance. 5. turn, routine, performance, stint. —*v.* 6. exert energy or force, operate, function, perform, do, work. 7. function, be active, substitute (for). 8. produce an effect, operate, be efficient or effective or efficacious. 9. behave, perform, conduct or deport or comport oneself. 10. pretend, sham, dissemble, feign, fake, do imitations, dissimulate, play. 11. play parts, do imitations or impersonations. 12. represent, impersonate, imitate, play the part of. 13. feign, counterfeit, fake, imitate. 14. behave as, play the part of.

action, *n.* 1. movement, work, performance, moving, working, performing, operation. 2. deed, act. 3. *(plural)* conduct, behavior. 4. energetic activity. 5. exertion, energy, effort. 6. gesture. 7. mechanism, contrivance, apparatus. 8. skirmish, brush, affair, encounter, meeting, engagement, conflict, combat, fight, battle. 9. *(law)* proceeding, process, case, suit, lawsuit. *Ant.* lethargy, inactivity.

active, *adj.* 1. acting, moving, working, operative. 2. busy, energetic, strenuous, vigorous, animated, enterprising, efficient, fervent, earnest, eager, diligent, industrious; engaged, occupied, consumed with. 3. nimble, sprightly, agile, alert, smart, quick, spirited, brisk, supple, lively. 4. practical, working, applicable, applied. 5. *(commerce)* busy, profitable; interest-bearing. 6. *(medicine)* effective, productive. *Ant.* inactive, lazy.

actual, *adj.* 1. true, genuine, real, veritable, palpable, tangible, certain, positive, absolute, sure, categorical, decided, definite, determinate, substantial. 2. now existing, present, here and now. *Ant.* unreal, untrue, fake.

acute, *adj.* 1. pointed, cuspidate, aciform, acicular, acuminate, sharp, sharpened. 2. intense, poignant, touching; severe, fierce, violent, distressing, crucial, sudden, piercing, penetrating. 3. sharp, penetrating, perceptive, keen, astute, discerning, intelligent, perspicacious, sharp-wit-

ted, shrewd, clever, knowing, wise, sage, sagacious, sapient; smart, bright, ingenious. 4. sensitive, keen. 5. alt, high, intense. *Ant.* blunt.

adapt, *v.* suit, adjust, modify, fit, reconcile, accommodate, prepare, conform, make conformable or suitable, qualify, compose.

add, *v.* 1. unite, annex, connect, affix, join; append, attach, supplement, increase, make an addition to, augment, adjoin, tack on. 2. total, tot, sum, aggregate. *Ant.* subtract, deduct.

addition, *n.* 1. uniting, adding, joining. 2. summing up. 3. increase, increment, enlargement, aggrandizement, accession; supplement, appendix, accessory, adjunct, attachment, addendum, appendage. *Ant.* deduction, subtraction.

address, *n.* 1. discourse, lecture, speech, oration. 2. location, post office. 3. residence, domicile, abode, habitation, lodging, dwelling, home quarters, house. 4. manner, bearing. 5. skillful management, skill, art, adroitness, cleverness, tact, ingenuity, technique, dexterity, ability. —*v.* 6. direct (speech or writing to), speak to; accost. 7. invoke, appeal to, apply to.

adequate, *adj.* commensurate, equal, suitable, fit for; satisfactory, competent, sufficient, enough; capable. *Ant.* inadequate, insufficient.

adhere, *v.* 1. stick fast, cleave, cling to, stick, hold, cohere. 2. be devoted, identify, be attached, be a follower, be faithful, be true. 3. hold closely or firmly to. *Ant.* separate.

adherent, *n.* 1. supporter, follower, partisan, disciple; devoté, fan, aficionado. —*adj.* 2. clinging, adhering, sticking, cleaving. *Ant.* recreant, deserter.

adjacent, *adj.* near, close, contiguous, adjoining, juxtaposed, neighboring, nearby, touching. *Ant.* distant.

adjoining, *adj.* bordering, contiguous, adjacent, near or close or next to, touching.

adjourn, *v.* 1. suspend (for a day), postpone, interrupt, put off, defer, delay, prorogue. 2. postpone, defer, transfer. *Ant.* convene; begin.

adjunct, *n.* 1. addition, appendix, supplement, attachment. 2. aide, attaché, subordinate, accessory.

adjust, *v.* 1. fit, make correspondent *or* conformable to, adapt, accommodate, suit. 2. regulate, set, repair, fix; change, alter. 3. arrange, rectify, reconcile, settle. 4. adapt oneself, make oneself suitable *or* suited for.

administer, *v.* 1. manage, conduct, control, execute; rule, govern; direct, superintend, oversee, supervise. 2. dispense, distribute, supply, job, furnish, contribute. 3. give, dispense, apply, dose, deal out, dole out. 4. tender, offer, proffer; impose. 5. provide aid, contribute assistance. 6. *(law)* act as executor; act as administrator.

admirable, *adj.* estimable, praiseworthy, fine, rare, excellent. *Ant.* abhorrent.

admiration, *n.* wonder, awe, pleasure, approbation, delight, esteem; liking, affection, regard. *Ant.* abhorrence, disgust, hatred.

admire, *v.* esteem; revere, venerate; like, delight in. *Ant.* detest, hate.

admission, *n.* 1. entrance, introduction, access, admittance, entrée, ticket, pass, Annie Oakley, key, shibboleth. 2. confession, acknowledgment, allowance, concession. *Ant.* rejection.

admit, *v.* 1. allow to enter, grant *or* afford entrance to, let in, afford access to, receive. 2. permit, allow, agree to, concede, bear. 3. acknowledge, own, avow, confess. 4. permit entrance, give access. 5. grant permission, be capable of. *Ant.* reject.

admittance, *n.* 1. entrance, admission, introduction. 2. access, reception.

admonish, *v.* 1. caution, advise, warn, counsel. 2. rebuke, censure, reprove. 3. recall to duty, remind, notify, make aware, apprise, acquaint, inform.

ado, *n.* activity, bustle, fuss, flurry, to-do, commotion, babble, stir, tumult, confusion, upset, excitement, hubbub, noise, turmoil, bother, pother. *Ant.* serenity, calm.

adolescent, *adj.* 1. immature, youthful, young. —*n.* 2. youth, teen-ager, minor. *Ant.* adult.

adore, *v.* idolize, worship, love; respect, honor, esteem, reverence, revere, venerate, idolize. *Ant.* abhor, detest, abominate, hate.

adorn, *v.* 1. embellish, add luster to. 2. decorate, enhance, beautify, deck,

bedeck, ornament, trim, bedizen, array. *Ant.* disfigure, deface.

adroit, *adj.* expert, ingenious, skillful, dexterous, clever, resourceful, ready, quick, apt, adept. *Ant.* clumsy, maladroit.

adult, *adj.* 1. mature, grown up, full-grown, ripe, of age. —*n.* 2. grown-up, man, woman. *Ant.* immature, adolescent.

advance, *v.* 1. move *or* set *or* push *or* bring forward, further, forward. 2. propose, bring to view *or* notice, adduce, propound, offer, allege. 3. improve, further, forward, promote, strengthen. 4. promote, elevate, dignify, exalt. 5. increase, raise the pride of, augment. 6. update, accelerate, quicken, hasten, speed up, bring forward. 7. furnish *or* supply on credit, lend, loan. 8. move *or* go forward, proceed, move on. 9. improve, progress, make progress, grow, increase, flourish, rise, thrive. 10. rise, increase, appreciate. —*n.* 11. moving forward, progress, procedure, way; march, procession. 12. advancement, promotion, improvement, advance, rise. 13. overture, proposal, proposition, tender, offer, proffer, offering. 14. price rise, raise, rise, increase. —*adj.* 15. going before, preceding, precedent. 16. beyond, ahead, before; prepublication. *Ant.* retreat.

advantage, *n.* 1. favorable opportunity *or* state *or* circumstance *or* means *or* situation, vantage point, superiority, superior condition. 2. benefit, avail, gain, profit, value; return, dividend; utility, usefulness, expediency, use, service. 3. superiority, ascendancy, preeminence. 4. behalf, vantage; privilege, prerogative, convenience, accommodation. —*v.* 5. be of service to, serve, avail, benefit, profit, help, aid, yield profit *or* gain to. *Ant.* disadvantage.

adversary, *n.* 1. antagonist, opponent, enemy, foe. 2. contestant, litigant, opponent. 3. Satan, the Devil, the Evil One, the Prince of Darkness, Beelzebub, the Tempter. *Ant.* ally, compatriot, friend.

adverse, *adj.* 1. antagonistic, contrary, opposite, conflicting, opposed, hostile, against, con, contra, inimical, unfriendly. 2. unfavorable, unlucky, unfortunate; calamitous, disastrous, catastrophic. 3. opposite,

confronting, opposed, facing, vis-à-vis, face-to-face. *Ant.* favorable, beneficial.

adversity, *n.* calamity, distress, catastrophe, disaster; bad luck, misfortune, misery, trouble, affliction, wretchedness. *Ant.* happiness, wealth.

advice, *n.* 1. admonition, warning, caution, counsel, opinion, recommendation, guidance, suggestion, persuasion, urging, exhortation. 2. communication, information, news, report, intelligence, tidings, word, notice, notification.

advisable, *adj.* 1. expedient, advantageous, politic, proper, fit, suitable, desirable, correct, prudent, sensible, common-sense, judicious. 2. receptive, open to suggestion *or* advice.

advise, *v.* 1. give counsel to, counsel, admonish, caution, warn, recommend to. 2. suggest, recommend. 3. inform, notify, apprise, acquaint. 4. take counsel, confer, deliberate, discuss, consult. 5. give advice, offer counsel.

advocate, *v.* 1. plead in favor of, support, urge, argue for, speak for, recommend. —*n.* 2. lawyer, attorney, counselor, counselor-at-law, counsel, barrister, solicitor; intercessor. 3. defender, vindicator, espouser, upholder, supporter, maintainer, promoter, patron, friend. *Ant.* oppose; opponent.

aesthete, *n.* dilettante, connoisseur, virtuoso, expert, discriminator, collector.

affable, *adj.* courteous, urbane, debonair, suave, civil, approachable, polite, friendly, cordial, pleasant, amiable, obliging, gracious; benign, mild, easy, casual, social. *Ant.* discourteous, boorish, reserved.

affect, *v.* 1. effect, exert influence on, accomplish, bring about, influence, sway, act on; modify, alter, transform, change. 2. move, impress, touch, stir, overcome. 3. pretend, feign, fake, assume, adopt. 4. imitate, act, mimic. 5. use, adopt, prefer, choose, select. 6. profess, pretend.

affectation, *n.* pretension, airs, mannerisms, pose, artificiality, pretense, affectedness, unnaturalness, insincerity. *Ant.* sincerity.

affected, *adj.* assumed, pretended, feigned. *Ant.* sincere, genuine.

affecting, *adj.* touching, pathetic, piteous, moving, impressive.

affection, *n.* 1. attachment, liking, friendliness, amity, fondness, devotion, friendship, tenderness, endearment, heart, love. 2. feeling, inclination, partiality, proclivity, disposition, predisposition, bent, bias. 3. *(pathology)* disease, disorder, affliction, malady, ailment, illness, complaint.
Ant. abhorrence.

affectionate, *adj.* tender, loving, fond, attentive, attached, devoted, warm, kind, sympathetic.
Ant. apathetic.

affirm, *v.* 1. state, assert, aver, maintain, declare, asseverate, depose, testify, say, pronounce. 2. establish, confirm, ratify, approve, endorse.
Ant. deny.

affliction, *n.* 1. pain, distress, grief, adversity, misfortune, trial, mishap, trouble, tribulation, calamity, catastrophe, disaster. 2. sickness, loss, calamity, persecution, suffering, misery, woe, depression, wretchedness, heartbreak; plague, scourge, epidemic.
Ant. relief.

affluent, *adj.* 1. abounding, rich, wealthy, opulent. 2. abundant, free-flowing, teeming. —*n.* 3. tributary, feeder.
Ant. poor; scarce.

affront, *n.* 1. offense, slight, disrespect, insult, impertinence, contumely, scorn, indignity, abuse, outrage, injury. 2. shame, disgrace, degradation. —*v.* 3. offend, insult, slight, abuse, outrage. 4. shame, disgrace, discountenance, confuse, confound, disconcert, abash. 5. confront, encounter, face, meet.
Ant. compliment.

afraid, *adj.* scared, fearful, alarmed, frightened, terrified, disquieted, shocked, apprehensive, timid, cowardly, pusillanimous, timorous, shy, cautious, overcautious.
Ant. bold, sanguine, confident.

age, *n.* 1. period, life, duration. 2. maturity, years of discretion. 3. old age, decline. 4. era, epoch, time, date, period. —*v.* 5. grow old, mature, ripen.
Ant. youth.

aged, *adj.* 1. old, ancient, decrepit, elderly. 2. old, of the age of.
Ant. young.

aggravate, *v.* worsen, make severe, intensify, heighten, increase, make serious *or* grave.
Ant. assuage, improve, better.

aggregate, *adj.* 1. added, combined, total, complete. —*n.* 2. sum, mass, assemblage, total, gross, body, amount. —*v.* 3. bring together, assemble, collect, amass, accumulate, gather. 4. amount to, add up to. 5. combine into a mass, form a collection.
Ant. particular.

aggressive, *adj.* 1. pugnacious, attacking, offensive, assaulting, militant, assailing. 2. energetic, vigorous, pushing, enterprising, assertive, determined, forward.
Ant. retiring, bashful, shy.

agile, *adj.* quick, light, nimble, sprightly, active, lively, brisk, ready, smart, alert, spry.
Ant. awkward.

agitate, *v.* 1. shake *or* move briskly, disturb, toss, jar. 2. move to and fro. 3. disturb, ruffle, stir *or* work up, perturb, excite, fluster. 4. discuss, debate, controvert, campaign *or* argue for, dispute. 5. plan, devise; revolve *or* turn over in the mind, cogitate, consider, deliberate. 6. arouse public interest, ferment, disturb, rouse.
Ant. tranquilize.

agitation, *n.* 1. agitating, shaking, jarring, disturbing. 2. disturbance, excitement, turmoil, tumult, storm; unrest, disquiet; struggle, conflict; perturbation, flurry, ado, to-do. 3. urging, persistence; debate, discussion, dispute, argument, campaign.
Ant. serenity, calm, tranquillity.

agony, *n.* 1. pain, distress, suffering, torment, torture, rack; throe, paroxysm, spasm, seizure, pang; ache. 2. excitement, suspense, anguish, torment, torture.
Ant. comfort.

agree, *v.* 1. assent, yield, consent, accede, concede, acquiesce, allow, comply. 2. harmonize, concur, unite, accord, combine. 3. come to an agreement *or* arrangement *or* understanding, compromise, arrive at a settlement. 4. accord, correspond, compare favorably, coincide, conform, tally, match, stand up, suit. 5. be applicable *or* appropriate *or* similar, resemble. 6. make *or* write a contract *or* bargain, contract, stipulate, bargain. 7. concede, grant, allow, let, permit.
Ant. disagree.

agreement, *n.* 1. agreeing, being in concord. 2. bargain, contract, compact, understanding, arrangement, deal. 3. unanimity, harmony, accord, concord, settlement, treaty,

pact, word, conformity, unity, uniformity.
Ant. disagreement.

aid, *v.* 1. support, help, succor, assist, serve, abet, back, second; spell, relieve. 2. promote, facilitate, ease, simplify. 3. be of help, give help *or* assistance. —*n.* 4. help, support, succor, assistance, service, furtherance; relief, charity. 5. assistant, helper, supporter, servant, aide, aide-de-camp.
Ant. hinder, obstruct; obstacle, obstruction.

ailing, *adj.* sickly, sick, ill, unwell.
Ant. healthy, well.

aim, *v.* 1. direct, point, give direction to. 2. direct, point. 3. strive, try, purpose. —*n.* 4. direction, sighting. 5. target, object, end. 6. purpose, end, object, goal; intent, intention, reason; design, scheme.

air, *n.* 1. atmosphere. 2. breeze, breath, zephyr, wind. 3. circulation, publication, publicity. 4. character, complexion, appearance, impression, aspect, look, mien; manner, demeanor, attitude, conduct, carriage, behavior, deportment, bearing. 5. affectation, haughtiness. —*v.* 6. ventilate. 7. expose, display.

alarm, *n.* 1. fear, apprehension, fright, consternation, terror, panic, dismay. 2. alarum, tocsin, distress-signal, siren. —*v.* 3. terrify, frighten, scare, startle; appall, shock; dismay, daunt.
Ant. calm, comfort.

alert, *adj.* 1. attentive, vigilant, watchful, aware, wary, observant, circumspect, heedful, cautious, on the lookout, on the qui vive. 2. nimble, brisk, lively, quick, active, agile, sprightly, spirited. —*n.* 3. vigilance, caution, wariness. 4. air-raid alarm. —*v.* 5. prepare for action, warn.
Ant. asleep, listless.

alien, *n.* 1. stranger, foreigner, immigrant. —*adj.* 2. strange, foreign. 3. adverse, hostile, opposed, unfriendly, differing, unallied, unconnected, separate.
Ant. native, friendly.

alive, *adj.* 1. existing, living, breathing, quick. 2. unextinguished, operative, functioning. 3. lively, active, alert. 4. swarming, thronged, aswarm.
Ant. dead.

allay, *v.* quiet, appease, moderate, soothe, soften, assuage, alleviate, lighten, lessen, mitigate, mollify, temper, relieve, ease.
Ant. aggravate.

allege, *v.* 1. declare, affirm, attest, state, asseverate, assert, aver. 2. plead, advance.
Ant. deny.

allegiance, *n.* duty, obligation, faithfulness, loyalty, fealty, fidelity; homage.
Ant. treason, treachery.

alleviate, *v.* ease, lessen, diminish, quell, abate, mitigate, lighten, relieve, assuage, allay, mollify.
Ant. aggravate, intensify.

alley, *n.* back street, lane, byway, street.

alliance, *n.* 1. association, coalition, combination, bloc, partnership, affiliation, connection, federation, confederacy, confederation, league, union, treaty, pact, compact. 2. marriage, intermarriage, relation, relationship. 3. affinity.

allot, *v.* 1. divide, distribute, parcel out, apportion, assign, deal out, dole out, mete out, deal, dispense, measure out. 2. appropriate, allocate, set apart, appoint.

allow, *v.* 1. let, permit, grant. 2. grant, yield, cede, relinquish, give. 3. admit, acknowledge, concede, own, confess. 4. set apart, abate, deduct, remit. 5. bear, suffer, tolerate, put up with.
Ant. forbid, prohibit; refuse.

allowance, *n.* 1. allotment, stipend. 2. deduction, discount, rebate, tret. 3. acceptance, admission, concession, acknowledgment. 4. sanction, tolerance, leave, permission, license, permit, authorization, authority, approval, approbation, imprimatur, sufferance.

ally, *v.* 1. unite, unify, join, confederate, combine, connect, league, marry, wed. 2. associate, relate. 3. join, unite. —*n.* 4. associate, partner, friend, confederate, aide, accomplice, accessory, assistant, abettor; colleague, coadjutor, auxiliary.
Ant. enemy, foe, adversary.

almost, *adv.* nearly, well-nigh, somewhat, toward, towards.

alone, *adj.* apart, lone, lonely, lonesome, single, solitary, desolate, isolated, enisled, unaccompanied, solo.
Ant. together, accompanied.

also, *adv.* in addition, too, further, likewise, besides, moreover, furthermore.

alter, *v.* 1. modify, adjust, change, permute, vary. 2. castrate, spay. 3. differ, vary, change.
Ant. preserve, keep.

alternate, *v.* 1. reciprocate. 2. act *or* follow reciprocally, interchange successively. —*adj.* 3. reciprocal, successive, in turn, one after another. —*n.* 4. substitute, stand-in.

alternative, *n.* 1. choice, option, selection, course, other. —*adj.* 2. mutually exclusive (*choice between two things*).

although, *conj.* though, even though, notwithstanding, even if, albeit.

altitude, *n.* height, elevation.

always, *adv.* 1. all the time, uninterruptedly, perpetually, everlastingly, eternally, forever, continually, ever, evermore, forevermore, unceasingly. 2. every time.
Ant. never.

amateur, *n.* dilettante, tyro, novice, nonprofessional, neophyte, greenhorn.
Ant. professional, expert.

amaze, *v.* astound, dumfound, surprise, astonish, stagger; stupefy, bewilder, confuse, perplex, daze.

ambiguous, *adj.* 1. equivocal, doubtful, dubious, unclear, uncertain, vague, indistinct, indeterminate; deceptive. 2. difficult, obscure, unclassifiable, anomalous. 3. puzzling, enigmatic, problematic.
Ant. explicit, clear.

ambition, *n.* 1. aspiration, enterprise, yearning, longing. 2. energy.
Ant. satisfaction.

ambitious, *adj.* 1. aspiring, enterprising. 2. eager, desirous, emulous. 3. showy, pretentious, ostentatious.
Ant. apathetic; humble.

ameliorate, *v.* improve, better, amend, raise, elevate, promote.
Ant. aggravate.

amiable, *adj.* 1. gracious, agreeable, kind-hearted. 2. kind, friendly, amicable.
Ant. hostile.

amid, *prep.* among, amidst, amongst, surrounded by.

among, *prep.* amid, between, surrounded by.

amorous, *adj.* 1. loving, amatory, tender. 2. enamored, in love, fond of, ardent, tender, passionate, impassioned, erotic, filled with desire, lustful, libidinous.
Ant. indifferent, cold.

ample, *adj.* 1. large, spacious, extensive, vast, great, capacious, roomy, broad, wide. 2. liberal, generous, free, abundant, copious, abounding, unrestricted, rich, lavish, inexhaustible, plenteous, plentiful, overflowing, full, bountiful, exuberant.

Ant. insufficient, meager, scanty, sparse.

amplify, *v.* 1. enlarge, extend, greaten, expand, widen, broaden, develop, augment, dilate, magnify. 2. exaggerate, overstate, blow up.
Ant. abridge, abbreviate.

amuse, *v.* entertain, divert, please, charm, cheer, enliven.
Ant. bore.

amusing, *adj.* 1. entertaining, diverting, pleasing, charming, cheering, lively. 2. comical, comic, droll, risible, laughable, delightful, mirth-provoking, funny, farcical, ludicrous, ridiculous.
Ant. boring, tedious.

ancestral, *adj.* hereditary, inherited, patrimonial.

ancestry, *n.* 1. pedigree, descent, stock, genealogy. 2. family, house, race, line, lineage.
Ant. posterity, descendants.

ancient, *adj.* 1. old, primitive. 2. old, aged, antique, antiquated, old-fashioned, out-of-date; antediluvian, prehistoric, of yore.
Ant. new, modern.

anger, *n.* 1. displeasure, resentment, exasperation, wrath, ire, fury, indignation, rage, choler, bile, spleen. —*v.* 2. displease, vex, irritate, arouse, nettle, exasperate, infuriate, enrage, incense, madden.
Ant. patience.

angry, *adj.* indignant, resentful, irate, incensed, enraged, wrathful, wroth, infuriated, furious, mad, passionate, inflamed; provoked, irritated, nettled, galled, chafed, piqued.
Ant. patient, calm.

anguish, *n.* 1. pain, pang, suffering, distress, agony, torment, torture, rack. —*v.* 2. agonize, distress, torture.
Ant. comfort.

angular, *adj.* 1. with angles *or* corners. 2. bony, gaunt, skinny, cadaverous. 3. awkward, stiff, unbending.
Ant. curved; plump; graceful.

animal, *n.* 1. creature. 2. beast, brute, monster. —*adj.* 3. living, sentient. 4. carnal, fleshly, unspiritual, physical; beastly, brutal.

animate, *v.* 1. vivify, enliven, vitalize, quicken. 2. invigorate, encourage, inspire, inspirit, hearten, energize, fortify, stimulate, arouse, waken. 3. refresh, exhilarate, buoy up, excite, fire, heat, urge, provoke, incite, kindle, prompt. —*adj.* 4. alive, lively, vigorous.
Ant. thwart; inanimate, sluggish.

animation, *n.* liveliness, vivacity, spirit, life, vigor, energy; enthusiasm, ardor, exhilaration, cheerfulness, sprightliness, buoyancy, airiness.
Ant. sluggishness.

announce, *v.* proclaim, publish, declare, report, set forth, promulgate, publicize.
Ant. suppress.

annoy, *v.* molest, harry, hector, badger, tease, irk, pester, harass, bother, worry, trouble, irritate, chafe, fret, disturb, disquiet.
Ant. comfort, soothe.

answer, *n.* 1. reply, response, retort, rejoinder. 2. solution. 3. defense, plea. —*v.* 4. reply, make reply *or* response, respond, rejoin. 5. be responsible *or* liable *or* accountable. 6. pass, serve, do, suit; suffice, be sufficient. 7. conform, correspond, be correlated. 8. reply to, respond to. 9. serve, suit, satisfy, fulfill. 10. discharge (a responsibility, debt, etc.). 11. conform *or* correspond to, be similar *or* equivalent to. 12. atone for, make amends for.
Ant. ask, question; differ.

antagonist, *n.* opponent, adversary, rival, competitor, contestant, enemy, foe.
Ant. ally, friend.

anticipate, *v.* 1. foresee, expect, foretaste, forecast. 2. expect, await, wait for. 3. preclude, obviate, prevent. 4. forestall, antedate. 5. accelerate, precipitate.
Ant. close, terminate; slow.

antipathy, *n.* 1. repugnance, dislike, aversion, disgust, abhorrence, hatred, detestation, hate, loathing, horror. 2. contrariety, opposition.
Ant. attraction, sympathy, love.

antique, *adj.* 1. ancient, old, archaic, bygone; antediluvian. 2. early, old. 3. antiquated, old-fashioned, out-of-date, obsolescent, obsolete, passé, demoded, démodé. —*n.* 4. objet d'art, bibelot, curio, rarity.
Ant. modern, new.

anxiety, *n.* 1. apprehension, fear, foreboding; worry. distress, uneasiness, disquietude, disquiet; trouble, pain. 2. solicitous desire, eagerness.
Ant. security, certainty.

anxious, *adj.* concerned, worried, apprehensive, uneasy.
Ant. secure, certain, sure, confident.

apartment, *n.* compartment, suite *or* set of rooms, flat, tenement.

apathetic, *adj.* unfeeling, passionless, emotionless, indifferent, uncon-

cerned, impassive, stoical, cool, cold, uninterested, phlegmatic, dull, lifeless, flaccid, obtuse, sluggish, torpid, callous, cold-blooded, insensible, soulless.
Ant. alert, emotional, sensitive.

ape, *v.* imitate, mimic, counterfeit, copy, affect.

apex, *n.* tip, point, vertex, summit, top, pinnacle, zenith; acme, climax.

apology, *n.* 1. excuse, plea, explanation, reparation. 2. defense, justification, vindication. 3. poor substitute, makeshift.

appall, *v.* frighten, horrify, terrify, dismay, daunt, shock, petrify.
Ant. activate, innervate.

apparel, *n.* 1. clothes, dress, garb, attire, raiment, costume, garments, habiliments, vesture, vestments, robes, rig, accouterments, trappings, outfit, equipment. 2. aspect, guise. —*v.* 3. dress, clothe, garb, attire; equip, rig, outfit, accouter; adorn, ornament, array, deck out.

apparent, *adj.* 1. plain, clear, open, evident, obvious, conspicuous, patent, unquestionable, unmistakable, manifest. 2. seeming, ostensible, unreal, specious, quasi, superficial, external. 3. visible, open, in sight, perceptible, detectable, discernible. 4. entitled.
Ant. concealed, obscure; real.

apparition, *n.* 1. specter, vision, illusion, phantom, wraith, spirit, sprite, ghost, phantasm, shade, chimera. 2. appearance, appearing, manifestation, phenomenon.

appeal, *n.* 1. entreaty, request, petition, prayer, supplication, invocation. 2. application, suit, solicitation. 3. attraction. —*v.* 4. entreat, supplicate, petition, ask, request. 5. resort.

appear, *v.* 1. become visible, come into sight *or* view, emerge, crop up, arise, turn up, see the light. 2. have an appearance, seem, look, show, have the appearance. 3. be obvious *or* manifest *or* clear.
Ant. disappear.

appearance, *n.* 1. form, being, apparition; arrival, coming, advent. 2. aspect, mien, guise, air, expression, look; manner, demeanor, presence. 3. show, seeming, semblance, face, pretense, pretext, colors.

appease, *v.* 1. pacify, quiet, soothe, calm, placate, tranquilize, mollify, alleviate, mitigate, temper, allay, assuage, ease, abate, lessen; still, hush, lull; keep down, quell, subdue. 2. satisfy, fulfill, propitiate. 3. conciliate,

propitiate, win over, make amends, accede to the demands of, make favorable.
Ant. aggravate, perturb; dissatisfy.

appendix, *n.* appendage, supplement, addendum, adjunct, appurtenance, addition, extra; enhancement, corrigendum, excursus.

appetite, *n.* 1. hunger, desire, longing, craving, thirst. 2. demand. 3. propensity, liking, relish, gusto, zest, zeal.
Ant. renunciation, anorexia.

applause, *n.* hand-clapping, shouting; approval, acclamation, approbation, acclaim, plaudit, laurel.
Ant. disapproval, condemnation.

appliance, *n.* 1. instrument, apparatus, device, tool, appurtenance; adjunct, expedient, means, way, resource. 2. application, use, practice, exercise.

applicable, *adj.* fit, suitable, suited, relevant, apt, fitting, befitting, proper, apropos, germane, pertinent, pointed.
Ant. inept.

application, *n.* 1. applying, appliance, utilization, use, practice. 2. usability, utility, relevance, aptness, aptitude, suitability, pertinence. 3. request, petition, solicitation, appeal. 4. attention, persistent effort, assiduity, industry, persistence, perseverance.
Ant. inattention, laziness.

apply, *v.* 1. lay on, place on *or* upon. 2. use, employ, put to use, effect, utilize. 3. devote, prescribe, dedicate, assign, appropriate, allot. 4. have a bearing, refer, be pertinent, hold true *or* good, be appropriate, impinge. 5. ask, petition, sue, entreat, solicit, appeal.
Ant. neglect.

appoint, *v.* 1. nominate, assign, name, elect, select, set apart, designate, point out, allot, destine. 2. constitute, ordain, establish, prescribe, direct, require, command, order, decree, impose *or* insist on. 3. fix, settle, determine, agree on *or* upon. 4. equip, rig, outfit, accouter, furnish, supply; apparel; decorate.
Ant. dismiss; strip.

appointment, *n.* 1. appointing, designating, designation, place, installation. 2. office, post, station, sinecure, position. 3. engagement, agreement, arrangement, assignation, rendezvous, tryst.

apportion, *v.* divide, allot, distribute, assign, allocate, appoint, partition, measure, mete, dole out, deal, dispense, parcel out.

appreciate, *v.* 1. esteem, prize, value, estimate *or* rate highly. 2. be aware *or* conscious of, detect. 3. raise the value of. 4. rise *or* increase in value. *Ant.* disparage; scorn.

apprehension, *n.* 1. anticipation, anxiety, misgiving, dread, fear, alarm; worry, uneasiness, suspicion, distrust, mistrust. 2. understanding, intelligence, reason. 3. view, opinion, idea, belief, sentiment. 4. arrest, seizure, capture. *Ant.* confidence, composure; release.

apprise, *v.* inform, tell, advise, give notice to, acquaint, notify, disclose to.

appropriate, *adj.* 1. fitting, suitable, suited, apt, befitting, meet, felicitous, proper, opportune, apropos, seemly, due, becoming, germane, pertinent, to the point. 2. proper, individual, unique, sui generis. —*v.* 3. set apart, direct, assign, apportion, allocate; adopt, take as one's own. *Ant.* inappropriate, inept.

approve, *v.* 1. commend, praise, recommend, appreciate, value, esteem, prize. 2. sanction, authorize, confirm, endorse, ratify, validate, uphold, support, sustain. *Ant.* disapprove.

apt, *adj.* 1. inclined, disposed, prone, liable. 2. likely. 3. clever, bright, intelligent, brilliant, ingenious; adroit, handy, dexterous, skillful, expert. 4. appropriate, suited, pertinent, relevant, fit, fitting, apt, befitting, meet, germane, applicable, apropos, felicitous. *Ant.* inapt, indisposed, malapropos.

aptitude, *n.* 1. tendency, propensity, predilection, proclivity, inclination, bent, gift, genius, talent, knack, faculty. 2. readiness, intelligence, cleverness, talent; understanding, ability, aptness. 3. fitness, suitability, applicability.

arbitrary, *adj.* 1. discretionary. 2. capricious, uncertain, unreasonable, willful, fanciful, whimsical. 3. uncontrolled, unlimited, unrestrained; absolute, despotic, dictatorial, totalitarian, tyrannical, imperious, overbearing, peremptory, domineering; Fascistic, undemocratic. *Ant.* relative.

archaic, *adj.* old, ancient, antiquated, antique, old-fashioned, out-of-date. *Ant.* modern, up-to-date.

archetype, *n.* model, form, pattern, prototype, example, type, paragon, ideal.

ardent, *adj.* 1. passionate, glowing, fervent, fervid, intense, eager, sanguine, enthusiastic, zealous; vehement, forceful, impassioned, strenuous. 2. glowing, flashing, flushed. 3. hot, burning, fiery. *Ant.* cool, apathetic.

ardor, *n.* 1. warmth, fervor, fervency, eagerness, zeal, passion, enthusiasm. 2. fire, burning, heat, warmth, glow. *Ant.* indifference.

arduous, *adj.* 1. laborious, hard, difficult, toilsome, onerous, burdensome, wearisome, exhausting, Herculean. 2. energetic, strenuous; fatiguing. 3. steep, high, acclivitous. 4. severe, unendurable. *Ant.* easy.

argue, *v.* 1. debate, discuss, reason, plead, hold. 2. contend, dispute. 3. reason upon, contest, controvert, debate, discuss, dispute. 4. maintain, support, contend. 5. persuade, drive, convince. 6. show, indicate, prove, imply, infer, betoken, evince, denote. *Ant.* agree.

argument, *n.* 1. controversy, dispute, debate, discussion. 2. reasoning, reason, proof, ground, evidence. 3. fact, statement; theme, thesis, topic, subject, matter. 4. summary, abstract, epitome, outline, précis. *Ant.* agreement.

arid, *adj.* 1. dry, moistureless, desert, parched; barren, infertile. 2. dull, lifeless, uninteresting, dry, empty, jejune. *Ant.* wet, damp.

aroma, *n.* 1. perfume, odor, scent, fragrance, bouquet, redolence. 2. subtle quality, spirit, essence, characteristic, air; suggestion, hint. *Ant.* stench.

arouse, *v.* 1. animate, stir, rouse, awaken; inspirit, inspire, excite, incite, provoke, instigate, stimulate, warm, kindle, fire. 2. awaken, get up, arise. *Ant.* alleviate, calm, mitigate.

arrange, *v.* 1. order, place, adjust, array, group, sort, dispose, classify, class, rank, distribute. 2. settle, determine, establish, adjust. 3. prepare, plan, contrive, devise, concoct, organize. 4. *(music)* adapt, adjust. 5. settle, agree, come to terms. 6. prepare, adjust, adapt, make preparations *or* plans. *Ant.* disarrange, disorder, disturb.

array, *v.* 1. arrange, order, range, marshal, rank, place, dispose, draw up. 2. clothe, apparel, dress, attire, equip, accouter, rig, outfit; deck, bedeck, ornament, trim, decorate, garnish, adorn. —*n.* 3. order, arrangement, disposition; allotment. 4. display, show, exhibit, exhibition, showing, demonstration. 5. attire, dress, clothes, raiment, apparel, garments; panoply. *Ant.* disarray.

arrest, *v.* 1. seize, apprehend, capture, catch, take, trap, take into custody, take prisoner. 2. catch, fix, secure, rivet, engage, capture, occupy, attract. 3. stop, check, bring to a standstill, stay, hinder, deter, obstruct, delay, interrupt, restrain, hold, withhold. —*n.* 4. detention, custody, imprisonment, apprehension, capture. 5. seizure, capture, rape. 6. stoppage, halt, stay, staying, check, hindrance, obstruction, deterrent, detention, restraint, delay, interruption. *Ant.* release; activate, animate; continue.

arrival, *n.* 1. advent, coming. 2. reaching, attainment. 3. arriver, comer. *Ant.* departure.

arrive, *v.* come, reach a point, attain, attain a position of success. *Ant.* depart; fail.

arrogance, *n.* haughtiness, overbearing, pride, insolence, disdain, effrontery, superciliousness, scorn, contumely, self-confidence, self-importance, conceit, egotism, hauteur. *Ant.* humility.

arrogant, *adj.* presumptuous, haughty, imperious, supercilious, assuming, proud, insolent, scornful, contumelious, overbearing, overweening, conceited, egotistic, egotistical. *Ant.* humble, self-effacing.

art, *n.* 1. trade, craft; skill, adroitness, dexterity, aptitude, ingenuity, knack, cleverness. 2. cunning, craft, guile, deceit, duplicity, wiliness, dishonesty, artfulness.

artifice, *n.* 1. ruse, device, subterfuge, wile, machination, expedient, trick, stratagem. 2. craft, trickery, guile, deception, deceit, art, cunning, artfulness, fraud, duplicity, doubledealing. 3. skillful, apt *or* artful contrivance.

artist, *n.* 1. artisan, painter, sculptor, sketcher. 2. actor, actress, thespian, singer, artiste. 3. designer, artificer, workman. 4. trickster, designer, contriver.

artless, *adj.* ingenuous, naive, unsophisticated, natural, simple, guileless, open, frank, plain, unaffected, candid, honest, sincere, true, truthful, trusting, trustful, unsuspicious, unsuspecting; unskillful, rude, crude.
Ant. cunning, sly, crafty.

ascend, *v.* 1. mount, rise, climb *or* go upward, soar, climb, arise. 2. tower. 3. climb, mount, scale, go *or* get up.
Ant. descend; fall.

ascertain, *v.* determine, establish, define, pinpoint, fix, certify, settle, verify; learn, find out, discover, uncover, get at.
Ant. guess, assume.

ascribe, *v.* attribute, impute, refer, assign, charge.

ashamed, *adj.* 1. abashed, humiliated, mortified, shamefaced, embarrassed, confused. 2. unwilling, restrained.
Ant. vain, arrogant; willing.

ask, *v.* 1. put a question to, interrogate, question, inquire of. 2. inquire, seek information. 3. request, solicit, petition, sue, appeal, seek, beseech, implore, beg, supplicate, entreat. 4. demand, expect, require, exact, call for. 5. invite, call in. 6. make inquiry, inquire, question. 7. request, petition, sue, appeal, pray, beg.
Ant. answer; refuse, decline.

aspect, *n.* 1. appearance, look, attitude, situation, condition. 2. countenance, expression, mien, visage; air. 3. view, viewpoint, point of view, attitude, outlook, prospect, direction, bearing.

aspire, *v.* desire, long, yearn.

assail, *v.* assault, set *or* fall upon, attack; abuse, impugn, maltreat, asperse, malign.

assassinate, *v.* murder, kill, blight, destroy, slay, despatch.

assault, *n.* 1. assailing, attack, onslaught, onset, combat, invasion, aggression; threat. —*v.* 2. attack, assail, storm, charge, invade; threaten.

assemble, *v.* 1. bring together, gather, congregate, collect, convene, convoke, summon, call, call together. 2. put together, manufacture, connect, set up. 3. meet, convene, congregate, gather, gather together, come together.
Ant. disperse.

assembly, *n.* 1. company, assemblage, throng, mob, gathering, convention, congress, convocation, meeting, meet. 2. congress, legislature, parlia-ment, lower house, conclave, synod, council, diet.

assent, *v.* 1. acquiesce, accede, concur, agree, fall in, consent, admit, yield, allow. —*n.* 2. agreement, concurrence, acquiescence, consent, allowance, approval, concord, accord, approbation.
Ant. refuse, deny, dissent.

assert, *v.* 1. declare, asseverate, affirm, maintain, aver, say, pronounce, allege, avow. 2. maintain, defend, uphold, support, vindicate, claim, emphasize. 3. press, make felt, emphasize.
Ant. controvert, contradict, deny.

assertion, *n.* allegation, statement, asseveration, avowal, declaration, claim, affirmation, predication, vindication, defense, maintenance, emphasis, support.
Ant. denial, contradiction.

assiduous, *adj.* constant, unremitting, continuous, applied, industrious, untiring, tireless, persistent, persisting, devoted, zealous, studious, attentive, diligent, solicitous, sedulous.
Ant. random, casual, lazy.

assign, *v.* 1. distribute, allot, apportion, allocate, measure, appropriate. 2. appoint, designate, specify; fix, determine, pinpoint. 3. ascribe, attribute, refer, adduce, allege, advance, show, offer, bring up *or* forward.

assist, *v.* help, support, aid, sustain, patronize, befriend, further, second, abet, back, speed, promote, serve, succor, relieve, spell.
Ant. impede, obstruct, hinder.

associate, *v.* 1. connect, link. 2. join, affiliate, team up with. 3. unite, combine, couple. 4. unite, combine. 5. fraternize, consort, keep company. —*n.* 6. acquaintance, consort, comrade, fellow, companion, friend, mate, peer, compeer, equal. 7. confederate, accomplice, ally, partner, colleague, fellow.
Ant. dissociate, alienate; adversary, opponent.

association, *n.* 1. organization, alliance, union, guild, society, club, fraternity, sorority, lodge; company, corporation, firm, partnership; set, coterie, clique, band. 2. companionship, intimacy, fellowship, friendship. 3. connection, combination.

assume, *v.* 1. suppose, presuppose, take for granted, infer. 2. undertake, take on, take upon oneself. 3. pretend, feign, affect, simulate, coun-terfeit, put on. 4. appropriate, arrogate, usurp.

assumption, *n.* 1. supposition, presupposition, assuming, presumption, taking for granted; hypothesis, conjecture, guess, postulate, theory. 2. arrogance, presumption, effrontery, forwardness, insolence, hauteur, haughtiness, superciliousness, lordliness, stateliness, pride, conceit.

assurance, *n.* 1. declaration, avowal, asseveration, averment, deposition. 2. pledge, warranty, surety, guaranty, oath. 3. confidence, firmness, trust, certainty. 4. courage, bravery, self-reliance, self-confidence, intrepidity, sang-froid. 5. boldness, impudence, presumption, arrogance, effrontery, rudeness, impertinence, nerve, cheek.
Ant. denial; distrust, uncertainty; cowardice, diffidence.

astonish, *v.* amaze, strike with wonder, surprise, astound, shock, startle; daze, stun, stupefy, confound, stagger, overwhelm.

astringent, *adj.* 1. (*medical*) contracting, constrictive, styptic, binding. 2. stern, severe, austere, sharp, harsh, rigorous, hard, unrelenting.

astute, *adj.* keen, shrewd, cunning, artful, crafty, sly, wily, penetrating, eagle-eyed, sharp, quick, perspicacious, ingenious, intelligent, sagacious, discerning.
Ant. ingenuous, naive, candid, unsophisticated; dull.

asylum, *n.* 1. hospital, institute, retreat, sanitarium. 2. refuge, haven, preserve, reserve, sanctuary, shelter, retreat.

atheist, *n.* agnostic, disbeliever, nonbeliever, infidel, skeptic, doubter, heathen, pagan, gentile.
Ant. theist.

atom, *n.* iota, jot, dot, whit, tittle, scintilla, mote; indivisible particle.

atrocious, *adj.* 1. wicked, cruel, heinous, flagitious, monstrous, felonious, flagrant, grievous, outrageous, diabolical, devilish, infernal, hellish. 2. bad, tasteless, execrable, detestable, abominable.
Ant. kind, benevolent; good, praiseworthy.

attach, *v.* 1. fasten to, affix, join, cement, connect, subjoin, append, add, tack on, annex. 2. go with, accompany. 3. associate, attribute, assign. 4. attract, charm, endear, enamour, captivate, engage, bind. 5. adhere, pertain, belong, obtain.
Ant. detach, separate; repel.

attachment, *n.* 1. affection, friendship, regard, admiration, fondness, liking, love, devotion; assiduity, bent, predilection. 2. tie, fastening, junction, connection. 3. device, apparatus, adjunct.
Ant. detachment, separation.

attack, *v.* 1. assail, assault, molest, threaten, interfere with, storm, charge, oppugn, engage in battle, set upon. 2. criticize, impugn, censure, blame, abuse. 3. affect. 4. begin hostilities. —*n.* 5. onslaught, assault, offense, onset, encounter, aggression.
Ant. defend; defense.

attain, *v.* 1. reach, achieve, accomplish, effect, secure, gain, procure, acquire, get, obtain, win. 2. arrive at, reach.
Ant. fail.

attempt, *v.* 1. try, undertake, seek, make an effort, essay. 2. attack, assault, assail. —*n.* 3. trial, essay, effort, endeavor, enterprise, undertaking. 4. attack, assault.
Ant. accomplish, attain.

attend, *v.* 1. be present at, frequent. 2. accompany, go with, escort. 3. minister to, serve, wait on. 4. tend, take charge of. 5. heed, listen to, pay attention to, respect. 6. be present. 7. pay attention, pay respect, give heed, listen. 8. apply oneself. 9. take care *or* charge. 10. depend, rely. 11. wait on, serve, minister.

attendant, *n.* 1. escort, companion, comrade, follower; servant, waiter, valet, footman, lackey, flunky, menial, slave. 2. attender, frequenter. 3. concomitant, accompaniment, consequence. —*adj.* 4. present, in attendance, accompanying, concomitant, consequent.

attention, *n.* 1. attending. 2. care, consideration, observation, heed, regard, mindfulness, notice, watchfulness, alertness. 3. civility, courtesy, homage, deference, respect, politeness, regard. 4. *(plural)* regard, court, courtship, suit, devotion, wooing.
Ant. inattention.

attentive, *adj.* 1. observant, regardful, mindful, heedful, thoughtful, alive, alert, awake, on the qui vive; wary, circumspect, watchful, careful. 2. polite, courteous, respectful, deferential, assiduous.
Ant. inattentive, unwary; discourteous.

attitude, *n.* 1. position, disposition, manner, bearing, mien, pose. 2. position, posture.

attract, *v.* 1. draw, cause to approach, magnetize. 2. draw, invite, allure, win, engage, captivate, endear, enamor, charm.
Ant. repel, repulse.

attribute, *v.* 1. ascribe, impute. —*n.* 2. quality, character, characteristic, property, mark; peculiarity, quirk.

audacious, *adj.* 1. bold, daring, spirited, adventurous, fearless, intrepid, brave, courageous, dauntless, venturesome, undaunted, valiant. 2. reckless, bold, impudent, presumptuous, assuming, unabashed, unashamed, shameless, flagrant, insolent, impertinent, brazen, forward.
Ant. cowardly, contumelious, feckless.

augment, *v.* 1. enlarge, extend, increase, swell, bloat. 2. increase.
Ant. reduce, abate.

austere, *adj.* 1. harsh, hard, stern, strict, forbidding, severe, formal, stiff, inflexible, rigorous, uncompromising, relentless, stringent, restrictive. 2. grave, sober, serious. 3. simple, severe, without ornament, plain. 4. rough, harsh, sour, astringent, acerb, bitter.
Ant. soothing, flexible; kind; sweet.

austerity, *n.* severity, harshness, strictness, asceticism, rigor, rigidity, rigorousness, stiffness, inflexibility.
Ant. lenience, flexibility.

authentic, *adj.* 1. reliable, trustworthy, veritable, true, accurate, authoritative. 2. genuine, real, true, unadulterated, pure, uncorrupted.
Ant. unreliable, inaccurate; sham, fraudulent, corrupt.

authoritative, *adj.* 1. official, conclusive, unquestioned, authentic. 2. impressive, positive; peremptory, dogmatic, authoritarian, dictatorial, imperious, arrogant, autocratic.
Ant. unofficial; servile.

authority, *n.* 1. control, influence, command, rule, sway, power, supremacy. 2. expert, adjudicator, arbiter, judge, sovereign. 3. statute, law, rule, ruling. 4. warrant, justification, permit, permission, sanction, liberty, authorization. 5. testimony, witness.

authorize, *v.* 1. empower, commission, allow, permit, let. 2. sanction, approve. 3. establish, entrench. 4. warrant, justify, legalize, support, back.
Ant. forbid, prohibit.

automatic, *adj.* 1. self-moving, self-acting, mechanical. 2. involuntary, uncontrollable.
Ant. manual; deliberate, intentional.

auxiliary, *adj.* 1. supporting, helping, helpful, aiding, assisting, abetting. 2. subsidiary, subordinate, secondary, ancillary, additional. —*n.* 3. helper, aide, ally, assistant, confederate.
Ant. chief, main.

available, *adj.* 1. accessible, ready, at hand, handy, usable, of use *or* service, serviceable; suitable, fit, appropriate, fitting, befitting. 2. valid, efficacious, profitable, advantageous.
Ant. unavailable; unbecoming; invalid, unprofitable.

avenge, *v.* revenge, vindicate, take vengeance, exact satisfaction for.
Ant. forgive, pardon.

average, *n.* 1. mean, mean proportion, median. 2. mediocrity. —*adj.* 3. mean, medial, normal, intermediate, middle; mediocre, middling, ordinary, passable, tolerable, satisfactory. —*v.* 4. reduce to a mean, equate; proportion. 5. show *or* produce a mean.

averse, *adj.* disinclined, reluctant, unwilling, loath, opposed.
Ant. inclined, disposed.

aversion, *n.* repugnance, disgust, antipathy, loathing, detestation, hate, hatred, abhorrence; dislike, distaste, objection, disinclination, unwillingness, reluctance.
Ant. predilection, liking; favor.

avoid, *v.* keep away from *or* clear of, shun, evade, escape, elude, fight shy of, eschew.
Ant. confront, face.

await, *v.* 1. wait for, look for, expect. 2. attend, be in store for, be ready for. 3. wait.

aware, *adj.* cognizant *or* conscious (of), informed, mindful, apprised.
Ant. unaware, oblivious.

awe, *n.* 1. reverence, respect, veneration; dread, fear, terror. —*v.* 2. solemnize; daunt, cow, frighten, intimidate.
Ant. contempt, irreverence; scorn.

awkward, *adj.* 1. clumsy, bungling, unskillful, inexpert, gauche, inept, maladroit. 2. ungraceful, ungainly, unwieldy, unmanageable, coarse, rude, crude, wooden, stiff, constrained, gawky, unrefined, unpolished, rough. 3. hazardous, dangerous. 4. trying, embarrassing.
Ant. deft, adroit, adept; graceful, refined, polished.

B

back, *n.* 1. rear, posterior, end. —*v.* 2. support, sustain, second, aid, abet, favor, assist; countenance, allow, side with, endorse, stand by. 3. reverse, move *or* push backward. 4. retire, retreat, withdraw, go backward. —*adj.* 5. hind, posterior, rear; remote, frontier, unpopulated. *Ant.* front, fore, face.

backward, *adv.* 1. rearward, back foremost, retrogressively, behind. —*adj.* 2. reversed, returning. 3. behind, late, slow, tardy, behindhand. 4. reluctant, hesitant, bashful, wavering, disinclined, timid, retired. 5. slow, retarded, undeveloped, underdeveloped, ignorant. *Ant.* forward; precocious.

bad, *adj.* 1. evil, wicked, ill, corrupt, base, depraved, unprincipled, immoral, disingenuous, rascally, mischievous, sinful, criminal, dishonest, villainous, baneful; deleterious, pernicious, harmful, hurtful, injurious, detrimental. 2. defective, worthless, poor, inferior, imperfect; incompetent, ill-qualified, inadequate. 3. incorrect, faulty. 4. invalid, unsound. 5. sick, ill. 6. regretful, sorry, contrite, wretched, upset. 7. unfavorable, unfortunate, adverse, unlucky, unhappy. 8. offensive, disagreeable, painful, mean, abominable. 9. vile, wretched, shabby, scurvy. 10. severe, serious. 11. rotten, decayed. *Ant.* good.

bag, *n.* 1. pouch, receptacle, sack, reticule, wallet. 2. handbag, purse, moneybag. —*v.* 3. catch, net, trap, entrap, kill.

balance, *n.* 1. scales. 2. equilibrium, equilibration, symmetry, equipoise, equality. 3. poise, composure, self-control, equilibrium, equipoise, self-possession. 4. counterpoise, equalizer, stabilizer. —*v.* 5. weigh, compare, equilibrate, estimate, assay. 6. counterpoise, counterbalance, offset, counteract, neutralize, countervail, compensate, allow for, make up for. 7. proportion, equalize, square, adjust.

ball, *n.* 1. sphere, globe, orb. 2. bullet, shot, missile, projectile. 3. dance, assembly, dancing-party.

ban, *v.* 1. prohibit, interdict, outlaw, forbid, proscribe, taboo. —*n.* 2. prohibition, interdiction, interdict, taboo, proscription. 3. anathema, curse, malediction, excommunication, denunciation. *Ant.* permit, allow; permission, blessing.

band, *n.* 1. company, party, troop, crew, gang, group; body; clique, coterie, set, society, association, sodality, horde, host, assembly. 2. strip, fillet, belt, tag, strap, cincture, girdle; *(heraldry)* bend. 3. cord, fetter, shackle, manacle, bond, chain. —*v.* 4. unite, confederate. 5. stripe; mark, tag, identify.

banish, *v.* 1. exile, expel, expatriate, deport, ostracize, outlaw. 2. send *or* drive *or* put away, exclude, expel, dismiss, dispel. *Ant.* admit, receive.

bank, *n.* 1. pile, heap, embankment, mount, knoll, hillock, hill, tumulus, dike. 2. slope, shore, acclivity, shoal, ridge. 3. row, ridge, tier, course. —*v.* 4. embank, border, bound, rim, edge, dike.

banter, *n.* 1. badinage, joking, jesting, pleasantry, persiflage; mockery, ridicule, derision. —*v.* 2. tease, twit, make fun of; ridicule, deride, mock, jeer, chaff.

bar, *n.* 1. rod, pole. 2. obstruction, hindrance, deterrent, stop, impediment, obstacle, barrier, barricade. 3. ridge, shoal, reef, sand-bunk, bank, sand-bar, shallow. 4. counter; saloon, café, bistro, nightclub, cocktail lounge. 5. lawyers, the legal fraternity; tribunal, judgment-seat, court. 6. stripe, band. —*v.* 7. hinder, obstruct, deter, stop, impede, barricade, prevent, prohibit, restrain. 8. exclude, shut out, eliminate, block, except. *Ant.* suffer, allow, permit.

barbarian, *n.* 1. savage, philistine, alien, brute, boor, ruffian. —*adj.* 2. rude, uncivilized, savage, primitive, barbaric, barbarous, rough, crude, coarse, untutored, ignorant, uncultivated, unlettered. 3. cruel, ferocious, wild, feral, inhuman, brutal, harsh, harsh-sounding, raucous. *Ant.* cosmopolite; refined, civilized, cultivated; kind.

bare, *adj.* 1. naked, nude, uncovered, unclothed, undressed, exposed, unprotected, unsheltered, unshielded, open. 2. unfurnished, undecorated, plain, stark, mean, poor, destitute, meager, unadorned, bald, empty, barren. 3. simple, sheer, mere, alone, sole, just. 4. unconcealed, undisguised, unreserved, conspicuous, obvious, glaring, evident, palpable. —*v.* 5. disclose, denude, lay open, expose. *Ant.* covered, dressed.

bargain, *n.* 1. compact, agreement, stipulation, arrangement, contract, convention, concord, concordat, treaty, stipulation, transaction. 2. good purchase, buy. —*v.* 3. contract, agree, stipulate, covenant, transact. 4. trade, sell, transfer.

barren, *adj.* 1. sterile, unprolific, childless, infecund, unfruitful, infertile, unproductive, poor, bare. 2. uninteresting, dull, stupid; uninstructive, unsuggestive, ineffectual, ineffective. *Ant.* fertile; interesting, effectual.

barricade, *n.* 1. barrier, obstruction, bar. —*v.* 2. obstruct, block, bar, shut in, stop up, fortify.

barrier, *n.* bar, obstruction, hindrance, barricade, stop, impediment, obstacle, restraint; fence, railing, stockade, palisade, wall; limit, boundary.

barter, *v.* trade, exchange, traffic, bargain; sell.

base, *n.* 1. bottom, stand, rest, pedestal, understructure, substructure, foot, basis, foundation, ground, groundwork; principle. 2. fundamental part, ingredient, element. 3. station, goal, starting-point, point of departure. —*adj.* 4. (morally) low, despicable, contemptible, mean-spirited, mean, degraded, degrading, selfish, cowardly. 5. servile, lowly, slavish, menial, beggarly, abject, sordid, ignoble. 6. poor, inferior, cheap, tawdry, worthless; debased, counterfeit, fake, spurious, shabby, coarse. 7. unrefined, plebeian, vulgar, lowly, humble, unknown, baseborn; impure, corrupted, corrupt, vile, venal. 8. scandalous, shameful, disreputable, disgraceful, discreditable, dishonorable, infamous, notorious. —*v.* 9. found, rest, establish, ground. *Ant.* top, peak; moral, virtuous; good, valuable; refined, pure; honorable.

bashful, *adj.* diffident, shy, abashed, timid, timorous, coy, sheepish, modest, self-effacing, embarrassed, shamefaced, ashamed. *Ant.* arrogant, immodest.

basis, *n.* bottom, base, foundation.

batter, *v.* beat, pound, belabor, smite, pelt; bruise, wound; break, shatter, shiver, smash, destroy, demolish, ruin.

battle, *n.* 1. action, skirmish, campaign, contest, conflict, engagement, military engagement *or* encounter. 2. warfare, combat, war, fight. —*v.* 3. strive, struggle, fight, combat, war, contest, conflict.

beach, *n.* 1. coast, seashore, littoral, shore, strand, sands, margin, rim. —*v.* 2. run ashore, strand, put aground.

beam, *n.* 1. girder. 2. ray, pencil, streak, gleam, suggestion, hint, glimmer. —*v.* 3. shine, gleam, glisten, glitter, radiate. 4. smile, grin.

bear, *v.* 1. support, hold up, uphold, sustain. 2. carry, transport, convey, waft; conduct, guide, take. 3. thrust, drive, force, push, press. 4. render, give, yield, afford, produce. 5. transmit, utter, spread, broadcast, advertise, exhibit, show, demonstrate. 6. sustain, endure, suffer, undergo, tolerate, brook, abide, put up with, stand, stand for, submit to; allow, admit, permit, admit of, hold up under, be capable of. 7. maintain, keep up, carry on. 8. entertain, harbor, cherish. 9. give birth to, bring forth. 10. confirm, prove. 11. hold, remain firm. 12. be patient. 13. tend, relate, be pertinent, concern, affect, refer. 14. act, operate, take effect, work, succeed.

bearing, *n.* 1. carriage, posture, manner, mein, deportment, demeanor, behavior, conduct, air. 2. relation, connection, dependency, reference, application. 3. direction, course, aim.

beat, *v.* 1. hit, pound, strike, thrash, belabor, batter, knock, thump, drub, maul, baste, pommel, thwack, whack, punch, cudgel, cane, whip, flog, lash, buffet. 2. break, forge, hammer. 3. conquer, subdue, overcome, vanquish, overpower, defeat, checkmate. 4. excel, outdo, surpass. 5. throb, pulsate. 6. win, conquer. —*n.* 7. stroke, blow. 8. pulsation, throb, tattoo, rhythm.

beautiful, *adj.* handsome, comely, seemly, attractive, lovely, pretty, fair, fine, elegant, beauteous, graceful, pulchritudinous.
Ant. ugly; inelegant, ungraceful.

beauty, *n.* 1. loveliness, pulchritude, elegance, grace, gracefulness, comeliness, seemliness, fairness, attrac-

tiveness. 2. belle. 3. grace, charm, excellence, attraction.
Ant. ugliness; witch; gracelessness.

because, *conj.* as, since, for, inasmuch as, for the reason that.

becoming, *adj.* 1. attractive, comely, neat, pretty, graceful. 2. fit, proper, apt, suitable, appropriate, meet, right, correct, decorous, congruous, fitting, seemly.
Ant. unbecoming, ugly; unfit, inappropriate, indecorous.

bedim, *v.* darken, dim, obscure, cloud, becloud.
Ant. brighten.

befitting, *adj.* fitting, proper, suitable, seemly, appropriate, becoming, fit, apt.
Ant. unbecoming, improper, unsuitable, inappropriate.

beg, *v.* ask for, entreat, pray, crave, implore, beseech, importune, petition, sue, request, supplicate, sue for, solicit.

begin, *v.* 1. commence, start, initiate, inaugurate, institute, enter upon, set about. 2. originate, create; arise.
Ant. end, conclude, die.

beginning, *n.* 1. initiation, inauguration, inception, start, commencement, outset, rise, onset, arising, emergence. 2. source, birth, origin, rise, first cause.

begrudge, *v.* envy, grudge, covet.

beguile, *v.* 1. mislead, delude, charm, cheat, deceive, befool. 2. divert, charm, amuse, entertain, cheer, solace.

behave, *v.* conduct oneself, act, deport *or* comport oneself, demean oneself, acquit oneself.
Ant. misbehave.

behavior, *n.* demeanor, conduct, manners, deportment, bearing, carriage, mien, air.
Ant. misbehavior.

belief, *n.* 1. opinion, view, tenet, doctrine, dogma, creed. 2. certainty, conviction, assurance, confidence, persuasion, believing, trust, reliance. 3. credence, credit, acceptance, assent.

belt, *n.* 1. girth, girdle, cinch, cinture, zone. 2. band, zone, strip, stripe, stretch. —*v.* 3. gird, girdle, surround, encircle.

bend, *v.* 1. curve, crook, bow, deflect, draw, flex. 2. cause to yield, subdue, persuade, influence, mold, dispose, bias, incline, direct, turn. 3. stoop, bow. 4. yield, submit, bow, stoop, kneel, give way, acquiesce, agree. 5. crook, deflect, deviate, swerve, di-

verge, incline. —*n.* 6. curve, crook, bow, rib, elbow, turn, angle, curvature, turning.

beneficial, *adj.* salutary, wholesome, serviceable, useful, favorable, helpful, profitable, advantageous.
Ant. unwholesome, unfavorable, disadvantageous.

benevolent, *adj.* kind, kindly, well-disposed, kindhearted, humane, tender, tender-hearted, unselfish, generous, liberal, obliging, benign, benignant, charitable, philanthropic, altruistic.
Ant. cruel, selfish, egotistical.

bent, *adj.* 1. curved, crooked, hooked, bowed, flexed, deflected. 2. determined, set on, resolved, fixed on. —*n.* 3. inclination, leaning, bias, tendency, propensity, proclivity, disposition, turn, penchant, predilection, partiality, liking, fondness, proneness.
Ant. straight; undecided; disinclination.

beseech, *v.* 1. implore, beg, entreat, pray, petition, obsecrate, obtest, supplicate, importune, adjure. 2. solicit, ask, entreat, beg, implore, importune, crave.

beset, *v.* 1. assail, harass, surround, encompass, encircle, enclose, besiege, beleaguer. 2. set, bestud, stud, decorate, ornament, embellish, garnish.

besides, *adv.* 1. moreover, in addition, furthermore, else, otherwise, too, also, yet, further. —*prep.* 2. over and above, in addition to, except, other than, save, distinct from.

betray, *v.* 1. deliver, expose, give up, uncover, reveal. 2. be unfaithful to, be a traitor to, deceive, be disloyal to, disappoint. 3. show, exhibit, display, manifest, indicate, imply, betoken, evince, expose, uncover, reveal.
Ant. protect, safeguard.

better, *adj.* 1. more good; more useful, more valuable; more suitable, more appropriate, more fit, more applicable. 2. larger, greater, bigger. —*v.* 3. improve, amend, ameliorate, meliorate, emend; advance, promote; reform, correct, rectify. 4. improve upon, surpass, exceed.
Ant. worse; worsen.

bewilder, *v.* confuse, perplex, puzzle, mystify; confound, nonplus, astonish, daze, stagger, befog, muddle.

bewitch, *v.* throw a spell over, charm, enchant, captivate, transport, enrapture, fascinate, hypnotize.

bias, *n.* 1. prejudice, inclination, preconception, predilection, prepossession, proclivity, propensity, proneness, partiality, predisposition, bent, leaning, tendency. —*v.* 2. prejudice, warp, predispose, bend, influence, incline, dispose. *Ant.* justness, impartiality.

bid, *v.* 1. command, order, direct, charge, require, enjoin, summon. 2. greet, wish, say. 3. offer, propose, tender, proffer. —*n.* 4. offer, proposal, proffer. *Ant.* forbid, prohibit, enjoin.

big, *adj.* 1. large, great, huge, bulky, massive, immense, tremendous, capacious, gigantic, extensive. 2. pregnant, with child, enceinte. 3. filled, teeming, overflowing, productive. 4. important, consequential, haughty, proud, arrogant, pompous, swelling, swollen, inflated, tumid, self-important, conceited, self-sufficient, bombastic, boastful. 5. generous, bighearted, kindly. *Ant.* small; trivial, nugatory.

bill, *n.* 1. account, reckoning, score, charges, invoice, statement. 2. bulletin, handbill, notice, advertisement, broadside, poster, placard, announcement, throwaway, circular. 3. beak, nib, neb, mandible.

bind, *v.* 1. band, bond, tie, make fast, fasten, secure, gird, attach. 2. encircle, border; confine, restrain, restrict. 3. engage, obligate, oblige. 4. indenture, apprentice. *Ant.* untie, unbind.

birth, *n.* 1. act of bearing, bringing forth, parturition. 2. lineage, extraction, parentage, descent, ancestry, line, blood, family, race. 3. origin, beginning, rise, nativity. *Ant.* death, end.

bit, *n.* 1. particle, speck, grain, mite, crumb, iota, jot, atom, scintilla, tittle, whit, fragment. 2. bridle, curb, control, rein, check, checkrein, restrainer.

bite, *v.* 1. gnaw, chew, champ; nip, rip, rend, tear. 2. cut, pierce; sting, burn, cause to smart. 3. corrode, erode, eat away. 4. cheat, deceive, defraud, dupe, trick, gull, make a fool of, cozen, outwit, fool, bamboozle, inveigle, mislead, beguile. —*n.* 5. nip, sting, cut. 6. food, snack; morsel, mouthful.

bitter, *adj.* 1. harsh, acrid, biting. 2. grievous, distasteful, painful, distressing, intense, sore, poignant, sorrowful, calamitous. 3. piercing, stinging, biting, nipping. 4. harsh, sarcastic, caustic, cutting, acrimonious, acerbate, severe, stern, sardonic, scornful, sneering. 5. fierce, cruel, savage, mean, merciless, ruthless, relentless, virulent, dire. *Ant.* sweet.

black, *adj.* 1. dark, dusky, sooty, inky, ebon, sable, swart, swarthy. 2. soiled, dirty, dingy, dusky, stained. 3. gloomy, sad, dismal, sullen, hopeless, dark, depressing, doleful, funereal, somber, mournful, forbidding, disastrous, calamitous. 4. amoral, evil, wicked, sinful, fiendish, inhuman, devilish, diabolic, infernal, monstrous, atrocious, horrible, outrageous, heinous, flagitious, nefarious, treacherous, traitorous, infamous, villainous. 5. ruined, desolate, empty. *Ant.* white; clean, pure, undefiled; happy; good, upright.

blackguard, *n.* churl, scoundrel, scamp, rascal, rapscallion, rogue, roué, devil, rake, wastrel, villain. *Ant.* hero, protagonist.

blame, *v.* 1. reproach, reprove, reprehend, censure, condemn, find fault, criticize, disapprove. —*n.* 2. censure, reprehension, condemnation, stricture, disapproval, disapprobation, reproach, reproof, animadversion. 3. guilt, culpability, fault, wrong, misdeed, misdoing, shortcoming, sin, defect, reproach. *Ant.* credit, honor.

blameless, *adj.* irreproachable, guiltless, unimpeachable, faultless, innocent, inculpable, not guilty, undefiled, unsullied, unspotted, spotless, unblemished. *Ant.* guilty, culpable; sullied, besmirched.

blanch, *v.* whiten, bleach, etiolate, pale, fade. *Ant.* darken, blacken.

bland, *adj.* 1. gentle, agreeable, affable, friendly, kindly, mild, amiable; suave, urbane, mild-mannered; complaisant, self-satisfied. 2. soft, mild, balmy, soothing, nonirritating. *Ant.* cruel, unfriendly; boorish, crude; irritable, irksome.

blank, *adj.* 1. unmarked, void, empty, unadorned, undistinguished. 2. amazed, astonished, nonplussed, astounded, confused, dumfounded, disconcerted. 3. complete, utter, pure, simple, unadulterated, unmixed; perfect, entire, absolute, unmitigated, unabated, unqualified, mere. —*n.* 4. space, line, area; form; void, vacancy, emptiness. *Ant.* distinguished, marked; blasé; impure; significant.

blasphemy, *n.* profanity, cursing, swearing, impiousness, sacrilege. *Ant.* reverence, piety.

blast, *n.* 1. wind, squall, gust, gale, blow, storm. 2. blare, peal, clang. 3. explosion, outburst, burst, outbreak, discharge. —*v.* 4. blow, toot, blare. 5. wither, blight, kill, shrivel. 6. ruin, destroy, annihilate. 7. explode, burst, split.

blaze, *n.* 1. fire, flame, holocaust, inferno; glow, gleam, brightness; outburst. —*v.* 2. burn, shine, flame, flare up, flicker.

bleach, *v.* 1. whiten, blanch, etiolate, pale. —*n.* 2. whitener. *Ant.* blacken, darken.

blemish, *v.* 1. stain, sully, spot, taint, injure, tarnish, mar, damage, deface, impair. —*n.* 2. stain, defect, blot, spot, speck, disfigurement, flaw, taint, fault. *Ant.* purify; purity, immaculateness.

blend, *v.* 1. mingle, combine, coalesce, mix, intermingle, commingle, amalgamate, unite, compound. —*n.* 2. mixture, combination, amalgamation. *Ant.* separate, precipitate.

blind, *adj.* 1. sightless, stone-blind, purblind. 2. ignorant, undiscerning, unenlightened, benighted. 3. irrational, uncritical, indiscriminate, headlong, rash, heedless, careless, thoughtless, unreasoning, inconsiderate. 4. hidden, concealed, obscure, remote, dim, confused, dark. 5. closed, dead-end, shut. —*n.* 6. curtain, shade, blinker, blinder, screen, cover. 7. hiding place, ambush. 8. cover, decoy, ruse, stratagem, pretense, pretext. *Ant.* discerning, enlightened; rational, discriminating; open.

blink, *v.* 1. wink, nictitate. 2. flicker, flutter, twinkle. 3. ignore, overlook, disregard, evade, avoid, condone. —*n.* 4. wink, twinkle; glance, glimpse, peep, sight.

bliss, *n.* blitheness, happiness, gladness, joy, transport, rapture, ecstasy. *Ant.* misery, unhappiness, dejection.

blithe, *adj.* joyous, merry, gay, glad, cheerful, happy, mirthful, sprightly, lighthearted, buoyant, lively, animated, elated, vivacious, joyful, blithesome. *Ant.* unhappy, miserable, cheerless.

block, *n.* 1. mass. 2. blockhead, dolt, idiot, imbecile, simpleton, fool, dunce. 3. mold. 4. blank. 5. pulley, tackle, sheave. 6. obstacle, hindrance, impediment, blocking, blockade, obstruction, stoppage, blockage, jam. —v. 7. mold, shape, form. 8. obstruct, close, hinder, deter, arrest, stop, blockade, impede, check.

Ant. genius; encourage, advance, continue.

bloody, *adj.* 1. bloodstained, sanguinary, ensanguined, gory. 2. murderous, cruel, bloodthirsty, savage, barbarous, ferocious, homicidal, inhuman, ruthless.

bloom, *n.* 1. flower, blossom, efflorescence. 2. freshness, glow, flush, vigor, prime. —v. 3. flourish, effloresce; glow.

blot, *n.* 1. spot, stain, inkstain, erasure, blotting, blotch, obliteration, blur. 2. blemish, reproach, stain, taint, dishonor, disgrace, spot. —v. 3. spot, stain, bespatter; sully, disfigure, deface. 4. darken, dim, obscure, eclipse, hide, overshadow. 5. destroy, annihilate, obliterate, efface, erase, expunge, rub out, cancel, strike out, eliminate.

blow, *n.* 1. stroke, buffet, thump, thwack, rap, slap, cuff, box, beat, knock. 2. shock, calamity, reverse, disaster, misfortune, affliction. 3. attack. 4. blast, wind, gale, gust. 5. blossom, flower, bloom. —v. 6. pant, puff, wheeze. 7. blossom, bloom, flower.

blue, *n.* 1. azure, cerulean, sky-blue, sapphire. 2. prude, censor, pedant. —adj. 3. depressed, dismal, unhappy, morose, gloomy, doleful, melancholy, dispiriting, dispirited, dejected, sad, glum, downcast, crestfallen, despondent. 4. prudish, moral, rigid, unbending, righteous, puritanical, self-righteous, severe, rigorous. 5. obscene, lewd, lascivious, licentious, indecent, risqué, ribald, irreverent, scurrilous, suggestive, immoral, amoral.

Ant. happy, mirthful.

bluff, *adj.* 1. abrupt, unconventional, blunt, direct, frank, open, honest, hearty, rough, crude. 2. steep, precipitous, abrupt. —n. 3. cliff, headland, hill, bank. 4. fraud, deceit, lie, dissembling. —v. 5. mislead, defraud, deceive, lie, dissemble, fake.

Ant. suave, diplomatic, tactful; gradual; plain.

blunt, *adj.* 1. rounded, not sharp, dull. 2. abrupt, bluff, brusque, curt, short, obtuse, difficult, gruff, uncourtly, uncivil, rough, harsh, uncourteous, discourteous, rude, impolite. 3. slow, dull, dimwitted, dullwitted, stupid, thick, stolid. —v.

4. dull, obtund. 5. numb, paralyze, deaden, stupefy, make insensible.

Ant. sharp, acute; courteous, civil, polite; quick, alert.

boast, *v.* 1. exaggerate, brag, vaunt, swagger, crow. —n. 2. bragging, rodomontade, swaggering, braggadocio.

Ant. depreciate, belittle.

body, *n.* 1. carcass, corpse, cadaver. 2. trunk, torso, substance, matter, bulk, main part; fuselage, hull. 3. collection, group; company, party, band, coterie, society, clique, set; association, corporation. 4. consistency, density, substance, thickness.

Ant. spirit, soul.

boil, *v.* 1. seethe, foam, froth, churn, stew, simmer, rage. —n. 2. ebullition. 3. furuncle, pustule.

boisterous, *adj.* rough, noisy, loud, clamorous, roaring, unrestrained, wild, tumultuous, turbulent, violent, impetuous, stormy, tempestuous, uproarious, obstreperous, roistering, vociferous.

Ant. calm, serene, pacific.

bold, *adj.* 1. fearless, courageous, brave, intrepid, daring, dauntless, valorous, valiant, heroic, manly, doughty, undaunted, hardy, spirited, mettlesome, gallant, stout-hearted, resolute. 2. forward, brazen, brassy, presumptuous, shameless, insolent, impudent, immodest, defiant, overconfident, saucy, pushing. 3. conspicuous, prominent, obvious, evident. 4. steep, abrupt, precipitous.

Ant. cowardly, timorous, timid; backward, shy; inconspicuous; gradual.

bond, *n.* 1. binder, fastener, fastening, band, cord, ligature, ligament, link, rope. 2. tie, connection, link, attraction, attachment, union. 3. bondsman, security, ward, promise; promissory note; obligation, contract, compact. 4. (*pl.*) chains, fetters, captivity, constraint, restriction, bondage; prison, imprisonment. —v. 5. mortgage. 6. cement, glue.

bondage, *n.* slavery, indenture, servitude, serfdom, thraldom, captivity, imprisonment, confinement.

Ant. freedom.

bonus, *n.* bounty, premium, reward, honorarium, gift, subsidy; dividend, perquisite.

border, *n.* 1. side, edge, margin; orphrey; periphery, circumference, lip, brim, verge, brink. 2. frontier, limit, confine, boundary. —v. 3. bound, limit, confine; adjoin.

bore, *v.* 1. perforate, drill, pierce. 2. weary, fatigue, tire, annoy. —n. 3. caliber, hole. 4. tidal wave, eagre.

Ant. amuse.

bosom, *n.* 1. breast, heart, affection. —adj. 2. intimate, close, confidential.

bother, *v.* 1. annoy, pester, worry, trouble, plague, tease, harass, vex, harry; molest, disturb. 2. bewilder, confuse.

Ant. solace, comfort.

bottom, *n.* 1. base, foot. 2. underside. 3. foundation, base, basis, groundwork. 4. seat, buttocks. —adj. 5. fundamental, basic, elementary; undermost, lowest.

Ant. top; superficial, superfluous.

bough, *n.* branch, limb, arm, shoot.

bound, *v.* 1. leap, jump, spring. 2. rebound, ricochet. —n. 3. (*usually plural*) limit, confine, boundary, verge, border. —adj. 4. constrained; destined for, tending, going.

Ant. free.

bounty, *n.* 1. generosity, munificence, charity, liberality, beneficence. 2. gift, award, present, benefaction. 3. reward, premium, bonus.

bow, *v.* 1. stoop, bend, buckle, give way. 2. yield, submit. 3. subdue, crush, depress, cast down. 4. curve, bend, inflect. —n. 5. front, forepart, prow.

brace, *n.* 1. clasp, clamp, vise. 2. stay, support, prop, strut. 3. bitstock. 4. couple, pair. —v. 5. fasten firmly, strengthen, support, back up, fortify, prop, steady. 6. tighten, tauten, make tense. 7. stimulate, strengthen, fortify.

brag, *v., n.* boast, rodomontade, bluster.

Ant. depreciate.

brains, *n.* understanding, intelligence, mind, intellect, sense, reason; capacity.

Ant. stupidity.

branch, *n.* 1. bough, limb, arm, shoot, offshoot. 2. limb, offshoot, ramification, arm. 3. section, subdivision, department; member, portion, part; article. 4. tributary, feeder. —v. 5. divide, subdivide, diverge, ramify.

bravado, *n.* boasting, swaggering, braggadocio, pretense, brag, bluster, bombast.

Ant. shame, modesty.

brave, *adj.* 1. courageous, fearless, gallant, confident, cool, chivalrous, impetuous, dashing, intrepid, daring, dauntless, doughty, bold, valiant, heroic, manly, hard, mettlesome, stout-hearted. 2. fine, showy, effective, brilliant; gay; debonair. —*n.* 3. warrior (*esp. American Indian*). —*v.* 4. face, defy, challenge, dare. *Ant.* cowardly, fearful; craven, pusillanimous.

bravery, *n.* boldness, courage, intrepidity, daring, prowess, heroism, pluck, gallantry, spirit, audacity, nerve, mettle, fearlessness, spunk, valor. *Ant.* cowardice.

brawl, *n.* 1. quarrel, squabble, argument, spat, wrangle, feud, disagreement, dispute, fracas, disturbance, disorder, row, tumult, clamor, rumpus, fray, fight, affray, altercation, melee, riot. —*v.* 2. quarrel, squabble, argue, wrangle, feud, disagree, dispute, fight, bicker.

brazen, *adj.* 1. brassy. 2. bold, forward, shameless, impudent, insolent, immodest, defiant. *Ant.* shy, diffident, modest.

breach, *n.* 1. break, rupture, fracture, crack, gap, fissure, rift, rent, opening, chasm. 2. infraction, violation, infringement. 3. alienation, disaffection, falling out, misunderstanding; split, rift, schism, severance, separation; dissension, disagreement, difference, variance, quarrel, dispute. *Ant.* observance.

break, *v.* 1. fracture, crush, shatter, splinter, shiver, smash, batter, demolish, destroy. 2. contravene, transgress, disobey, violate, infringe, infract. 3. dissolve, annul, negate, dismiss. 4. lacerate, wound, cut, injure, harm, hurt. 5. interrupt, suspend, disrupt, stop; abbreviate, curtail. 6. end, overcome. 7. exceed, outdo, surpass, beat. 8. disclose, open, unfold, divulge. 9. ruin, bankrupt, make bankrupt. 10. impair, weaken, enfeeble, enervate; dispirit. 11. tame, make obedient. 12. discharge, degrade, cashier, demote. 13. shatter, shiver; burst. 14. dissolve, separate, split. 15. escape, break loose. 16. dawn, open, appear. 17. decline, weaken. —*n.* 18. disruption, separation, rent, tear, rip, rift, schism, severance, split; breach, gap, fissure, crack, chasm, rupture, fracture. 19. suspension, stoppage, stop, caesura, hiatus, interruption, lacuna, pause, discontinuity. *Ant.* repair.

breaker, *n.* wave, comber, surge, whitecap, roller; bore, eagre.

breed, *v.* 1. beget, bear, bring forth, conceive, give birth to, produce, en-

gender, father, mother. 2. propagate, procreate, originate, create, beget, occasion, generate. 3. raise, rear, bring up, nurture; train, educate, discipline, instruct, teach, school. 4. grow, develop, flourish, arise, rise. —*n.* 5. race, lineage, strain, family, pedigree, line, extraction, stock, progeny. 6. sort, kind, species, class, denomination, order, rank, character, nature, description.

breeze, *n.* wind, air, blow, zephyr. *Ant.* calm.

brevity, *n.* 1. shortness, briefness. 2. conciseness, compactness, condensation, succinctness, pithiness; terseness, curtness. *Ant.* lengthiness.

bridle, *n.* 1. curb, restraint, check, control, governor. —*v.* 2. restrain, check, curb, control, govern. 3. bristle, ruffle. *Ant.* freedom; decontrol.

brief, *adj.* 1. short, short-lived, fleeting, transitory, ephemeral, transient, temporary. 2. concise, succinct, pithy, condensed, compact, laconic; curt, short, terse, abrupt. —*n.* 3. outline, précis, synopsis, summary, epitome, syllabus, abstract, abridgment, conspectus, compendium, breviary. —*v.* 4. abstract, summarize, outline, epitomize, abridge, abbreviate. *Ant.* long, tedious, boring.

bright, *adj.* 1. radiant, radiating, refulgent, resplendent, effulgent, lucent, lustrous, glowing, beaming, lambent, splendid, brilliant, shining, irradiant, gleaming, luminous; scintillating, sparkling, twinkling, glistening, glistering, shimmering, coruscating, glittering, flashing, flaming, blazing; shiny, sheeny, glossy, burnished; vivid, light, sunny, fulgid, fulgent. 2. clear, transparent, pellucid, translucent, lucid, limpid, unclouded, crystal, cloudless, lambent. 3. illustrious, distinguished, glorious, famous, golden, silver. 4. quick-witted, intelligent, keen, discerning, acute, ingenious, sharp, clever. 5. lively, animated, cheerful, merry, happy, sprightly, lighthearted, gay, vivacious, genial, pleasant. 6. favorable, auspicious, propitious, promising, encouraging, inspiriting, inspiring, enlivening, exhilarating. *Ant.* dull; opaque, dense; undistinguished, ignominious; slow, stupid; laconic, doleful, melancholy; unfavorable, discouraging.

brilliance, *n.* 1. brightness, splendor, luster, refulgence, effulgence,

radiance, brilliancy; sparkle, glitter, glister, gleam. 2. excellence, distinction, eminence, renown, prominence, preeminence, singularity, fame, illustriousness. *Ant.* dullness; notoriety. oblivion.

brim, *n.* rim, edge, border; orphrey; periphery, circumference, bound, brink, lip. *Ant.* center.

bring, *v.* 1. take along, conduct, convey, lead, fetch, guide, convoy, accompany, transport, carry. 2. lead, induce, prevail upon, draw. *Ant.* remove, withdraw.

brisk, *adj.* 1. active, lively, energetic, peart, quick, nimble, agile, alert, spry, on the qui vive, spirited, bright, vivacious. 2. sharp, stimulating, acute. 3. effervescent, bubbly, bubbling. *Ant.* slow, lethargic; dull; flat.

brittle, *adj.* fragile, frail, breakable, frangible. *Ant.* supple, flexible, elastic.

broad, *adj.* 1. wide. 2. large, extensive, vast, spacious, ample. 3. diffused, diffuse, open, full. 4. liberal, large, big, tolerant, open-minded, hospitable. 5. main, general, chief, important, obvious. 6. plain, clear, bold, plain-spoken, open, unconfined, free, unrestrained. 7. rough, coarse, countrified, unrefined, vulgar, indecent, indelicate, gross. *Ant.* narrow; penurious, stingy; refined, cultivated, decent.

brood, *n.* 1. offspring, litter, young, progeny, issue. 2. breed, kind, sort, line, lineage, stock, family, strain, species, class, order. —*v.* 3. incubate, sit. 4. dwell on, ponder, ruminate over, meditate on. 5. sit, hatch, set. 6. rest. 7. meditate morbidly.

brook, *n.* 1. stream, rivulet, run, runnel, runlet, streamlet, rill, burn, branch. —*v.* 2. bear, suffer, tolerate, allow, stand, endure, abide, put up with, submit to.

brother, *n.* fellow man, fellow countryman, kinsman, associate; sibling.

brownie, *n.* goblin, fairy, elf, pixie, leprechaun, nix, nixie, sprite, imp.

brush, *n.* 1. encounter, brief encounter, meeting; engagement, affair, contest, collision, action, fight, battle, skirmish, struggle, conflict. 2. bushes, scrub, thicket, copse, shrubs, bracken, brake.

brusque, *adj.* abrupt, blunt, rough, unceremonious, bluff, gruff, ungracious, uncivil, discourteous, impolite, rude, crude, curt.

Ant. courteous, courtly, polished, refined, gentle.

brutal, *adj.* 1. savage, cruel, inhuman, ruthless, pitiless, unfeeling, barbarous, barbarian, uncivilized, ferocious, brutish, barbaric, truculent. 2. crude, coarse, gross, harsh, rude, rough, uncivil, ungracious, impolite, unmannerly, ungentlemanly, brusque. 3. irrational, unreasoning, brute, unthinking. 4. bestial, beastly, animal, carnal. *Ant.* kind, sensitive; artistic; gracious, rational, sensible; human.

brute, *n.* 1. beast, quadruped. 2. barbarian. —*adj.* 3. animal, brutish, irrational, unreasoning. 4. savage, cruel, brutal. 5. sensual, carnal. *Ant.* human; kind; spiritual.

building, *n.* edifice, structure, construction, erection.

bulk, *n.* 1. size, magnitude, mass, volume, dimensions. 2. greater part, majority, most; body, mass. —*v.* 3. grow, swell, bulge, expand, enlarge, aggrandize.

bulky, *adj.* massive, ponderous, unwieldy, clumsy, cumbersome; great, big, large, huge, vast. *Ant.* small, delicate.

bunch, *n.* 1. cluster; group, lot, bundle, batch, collection. 2. knob, lump, protuberance.

bundle, *n.* 1. bunch. 2. parcel, pack, package, packet.

burden, *n.* 1. load, weight. 2. encumbrance, impediment, grievance, trial. 3. substance, core, point, essence, epitome, central idea, tenor, drift. 4. refrain, chorus. —*v.* 5. load, overload, oppress. *Ant.* disburden.

burn, *v.* 1. flame. 2. tingle, be hot, glow. 3. consume, scorch, sear, singe, char, toast, brown, tan, bronze. —*n.* 4. brook, rivulet, rill, run, runnel, streamlet, runlet.

burst, *v.* 1. explode, crack, blow up, split. 2. rend, tear, break. —*n.* 3. explosion. 4. spurt, outpouring, gust. *Ant.* implode.

bury, *v.* 1. inter, entomb, inhume, inearth. 2. sink. 3. cover, hide, conceal, secrete, shroud, enshroud. *Ant.* disinter; rise; uncover.

business, *n.* 1. occupation, trade, craft, metier, profession, calling, employment, vocation, pursuit. 2. company, concern, enterprise, corpora-

tion, firm, partnership. 3. affair, matter, concern, transaction. 4. commerce, trade, traffic. 5. function, duty, office, position.

busy, *adj.* 1. engaged, occupied, diligent, industrious, employed, working, assiduous, active, sedulous, hardworking. 2. active, brisk, bustling, spry, agile, nimble. 3. officious, meddlesome, prying. *Ant.* indolent, unoccupied, lazy.

but, *conj.* 1. however, nevertheless, yet, further, moreover, still. 2. excepting, save, except. —*prep.* 3. excepting, except, save, excluding. —*adv.* 4. only, just, no more than.

butcher, *n.* 1. meat dealer. 2. slaughterer, meat dresser. 3. murderer, slayer, killer, assassin, cutthroat, thug. —*v.* 4. kill, slaughter. 5. slaughter, massacre, murder, kill, assassinate. 6. bungle, botch, fail in.

buy, *v.* 1. purchase. 2. hire, bribe, corrupt. *Ant.* sell.

byword, *n.* 1. slogan, motto. 2. proverb, maxim, apothegm, aphorism, saw, adage, saying. 3. epithet.

C

cabin, *n.* 1. hut, shanty, shack, cot, cottage, shed, hovel. —*v.* 2. cramp, confine, enclose, restrict.

calamity, *n.* affliction, adversity, ill fortune, misery, bad luck, distress, trouble, evil, hardship, trial, reverse, mischance, mishap, blow, misfortune, disaster, catastrophe, cataclysm. *Ant.* fortune, blessing, boon.

calculate, *v.* 1. count, figure, reckon, cast, estimate, weigh, deliberate, compute, rate. 2. suit, adapt, fit, adjust. *Ant.* assume, guess.

calculation, *n.* 1. computation, figuring, reckoning, estimate, estimation. 2. estimate, forecast, expectation, prospect, anticipation. 3. forethought, planning, circumspection, caution, wariness, foresight, cautiousness, discretion, prudence, deliberation. *Ant.* guess, assumption.

call, *v.* 1. cry out. 2. announce, proclaim. 3. awaken, waken, rouse, wake up, arouse. 4. summon, invite, send

for. 5. convoke, convene, call together, assemble, muster. 6. telephone, ring up. 7. name, give a name to, label, term, designate, style, dub, christen, entitle, nominate, denominate. 8. reckon, consider, estimate, designate. 9. shout, cry, voice. 10. visit, stop. —*n.* 11. shout, cry, outcry. 12. summons, signal; invitation, bidding; appointment. 13. need, occasion; demand, claim, requisition.

callous, *adj.* 1. hard, hardened, inured, indurated. 2. unfeeling, insensible, blunt, apathetic, unimpressible, indifferent, unsusceptible, obtuse; dull, sluggish, torpid, slow. *Ant.* soft; sensitive; alert.

calm, *adj.* 1. still, quiet, smooth, motionless, tranquil, unruffled, mild, peaceful. 2. tranquil, peaceful, serene, self-possessed, cool, collected, unruffled, composed, undisturbed, sedate, aloof. —*n.* 3. stillness, serenity, calmness, quiet, smoothness, tranquillity, peacefulness, aloofness, self-possession, composure, repose,

equanimity. —*v.* 4. still, quiet, tranquilize, pacify, smooth, appease, compose; allay, assuage, mollify, soothe, soften. *Ant.* perturbed; tempestuous; excite, agitate.

can, *v.* 1. know how to, be able to, have the ability *or* power *or* right *or* qualifications *or* means to. —*n.* 2. tin, container.

cancel, *v.* 1. cross out, delete, dele, erase, expunge, obliterate, blot out, efface, rub out. 2. void, annul, countermand, revoke, rescind, counterbalance, compensate for, allow for. *Ant.* ratify.

candid, *adj.* 1. frank, open, outspoken, sincere, ingenuous, naive, artless, honest, plain, guileless, straightforward, aboveboard, free, honorable. 2. impartial, honest, just, fair, unprejudiced, unbiased. 3. white, clear, pure, unadulterated, lucid, transparent, pellucid, lucent. *Ant.* concealed, hidden, wily, deceitful; biased, prejudiced; turgid, cloudy, dull, impure.

canon, *n.* 1. rule, law, standard, formula. 2. criterion, principle, standard.

capable, *adj.* 1. able, competent, efficient, intelligent, clever, skillful, ingenious, sagacious, gifted, accomplished. 2. fitted, adapted, suited, qualified. 3. susceptible, open, admitting, allowing, permitting, permissive.
Ant. incapable.

capacious, *adj.* spacious, roomy, ample, large, broad, comprehensive, wide.
Ant. confining, narrow.

capacity, *n.* 1. cubic contents, volume, magnitude, dimensions, amplitude. 2. ability, power, aptitude, faculty, wit, genius, aptness, bent, forte, leaning, propensity, ableness, talent, discernment; caliber, cleverness, skill, skillfulness, competency, competence, readiness, capability. 3. position, relation, function, sphere, area, province; office, post, charge, responsibility.
Ant. incapacity, incompetence.

capital, *n.* 1. metropolis, seat. 2. wealth, principal, investment, worth, resources, assets, stock. —*adj.* 3. principal, first, important, chief, prime, primary, major, leading, cardinal, essential, vital. 4. excellent, first-rate, splendid, fine. 5. large-size, upper case. 6. fatal, serious.
Ant. trivial, unimportant.

capsize, *v.* overturn, upset.
Ant. right.

captivate, *v.* charm, enthrall, enchant, fascinate, hypnotize, bewitch, enamor, win, catch.
Ant. repel, repulse.

captivity, *n.* bondage, servitude, slavery, thralldom, serfdom, subjection; imprisonment, confinement, incarceration.
Ant. freedom.

capture, *v.* 1. seize, take prisoner, catch, arrest, snare, apprehend, grab, nab; imprison, incarcerate. —*n.* 2. arrest, seizure, apprehension, catch.
Ant. release.

carcass, *n.* 1. body, corpse, cadaver. 2. framework, skeleton.

care, *n.* 1. worry, anxiety, concern, solicitude, trouble. 2. heed, caution, pains, anxiety, regard, attention, vigilance, carefulness, solicitude, circumspection, alertness, watchfulness, wakefulness. 3. burden, charge, responsibility. —*v.* 4. have concern *or* regard, be solicitous *or* anxious, worry, be troubled. 5. like, be inclined *or* disposed *or* interested.

careful, *adj.* 1. cautious, circumspect, watchful, wakeful, vigilant, guarded, chary, discreet, wary, suspicious, prudent, tactful; trustworthy. 2. painstaking, meticulous, discerning, exact, thorough, concerned, scrupulous, finical, conscientious, attentive, heedful, thoughtful.
Ant. careless.

careless, *adj.* 1. inattentive, incautious, unwary, unthoughtful, forgetful, remiss, negligent, neglectful, unmindful, heedless, reckless, indiscreet, thoughtless, unconcerned. 2. negligent, inaccurate, inexact. 3. unconsidered; inconsiderate.
Ant. careful.

cargo, *n.* freight, load, burden, lading.

caricature, *n.* 1. burlesque, exaggeration, travesty, take-off, parody, farce, satire, lampoon, cartoon. —*v.* 2. burlesque, exaggerate, travesty, parody, take off, satirize, lampoon.

carnal, *adj.* 1. human, temporal, worldly, mundane, earthly, unregenerate, natural, unspiritual. 2. sensual, fleshly, bodily, animal. 3. lustful, impure, gross, lecherous, worldly, lascivious, salacious, libidinous, concupiscent, lewd, lubricious, wanton, lubricous.
Ant. spiritual, moral, intellectual.

carriage, *n.* 1. vehicle, cart, wagon, conveyance; dog-cart, brougham, hansom, victoria, calash, buckboard, carry-all, shay, sulky, surrey. 2. bearing, manner, mien, deportment, behavior, conduct, demeanor.

carry, *v.* 1. convey, bear, transport; transmit, transfer, take, bring. 2. bear, support, sustain, stand, suffer. 3. lead, impel, drive, conduct, urge. 4. effect, accomplish, gain, secure, win, capture.

case, *n.* 1. instance, example, illustration, occurrence. 2. state, circumstance, situation, condition, contingency; plight, predicament. 3. patient; action, suit, lawsuit, cause, process, trial. 4. receptacle, box, container, chest, folder, envelope, sheath. 5. frame, framework.

cast, *v.* 1. throw, fling, hurl, deposit, propel, put, toss, pitch, shy, sling, pitch. 2. throw off, shed, slough, put off, lay aside. 3. direct, turn, cause to fall, throw, shed, impart. 4. throw out, send forth, hurl, toss. 5. throw down, defeat, overwhelm. 6. part with, lose. 7. set aside, throw aside, discard, reject, dismiss, disband. 8.

emit, eject, vomit, spew forth, puke. 9. bestow, confer. 10. arrange, plan out, allot, apportion, appoint, assign. 11. mold, form, found. 12. compute, calculate, reckon; forecast, foretell. 13. ponder, consider, contrive, devise, plan. 14. throw. 15. calculate, add. 16. consider; plan, scheme. —*n.* 17. throw, fling, toss. 18. fortune, lot. 19. appearance, form, shape, mien, demeanor. 20. sort, kind, style. 21. tendency, inclination, turn, bent, trend, air. 22. turn, twist; warp. 23. tinge, tint, hue, shade, touch; dash, trace, hint, suggestion. 24. computation, calculation, addition. 25. forecast, conjecture, guess.

castle, *n.* 1. fortress, citadel, stronghold. 2. palace, chateau, mansion. 3. (*chess*) rook.

casual, *adj.* 1. unexpected, fortuitous, unforeseen, chance, accidental. 2. unpremeditated, offhand, unintentional. 3. careless, negligent, unconcerned. 4. irregular, occasional, random.
Ant. premeditated, deliberate, calculated; careful; regular, routine.

catalogue, *n.* list, roll, roster, register, record, inventory.

catastrophe, *n.* disaster, mishap, cataclysm, calamity, misfortune, mischance; end, dénouement, finale; upshot, conclusion, windup, termination.
Ant. triumph.

catch, *v.* 1. capture, apprehend, arrest. 2. ensnare, entrap, deceive, entangle. 3. surprise, detect, take unawares. 4. strike, hit. 5. lay hold of, grasp, seize, snatch, grip, entangle, clutch. 6. captivate, charm, enchant, fascinate, win, bewitch. —*n.* 7. capture, apprehension, arrest, seizure. 8. ratchet, bolt. 9. take.
Ant. release.

cause, *n.* 1. occasion, reason, ground, grounds, basis; motive, determinant, incitement, inducement. 2. purpose, object, aim, end. —*v.* 3. bring about, effect, determine, make, produce, create, originate, occasion, give rise to.

caution, *n.* 1. prudence, discretion, circumspectness, watchfulness, circumspection, heed, care, wariness, heedfulness, vigilance, forethought, providence. 2. warning, admonition, advice, injunction, counsel. —*v.* 3. warn, admonish, advise, enjoin, counsel, forewarn.
Ant. carelessness.

cautious, *adj.* prudent, careful, heedful, watchful, discreet, wary, vigilant, alert, provident, chary, circumspect, guarded. *Ant.* careless, heedless, indiscreet.

cavity, *n.* hollow, hole, void.

cease, *v.* 1. stop, desist, stay. 2. terminate, end, culminate. 3. discontinue, end. *Ant.* start, begin; continue, persist.

cede, *v.* yield, resign, surrender, relinquish, abandon, give up; make over, grant, transfer, convey. *Ant.* persist, maintain.

celebrate, *v.* 1. commemorate, honor, observe. 2. proclaim, announce. 3. praise, extol, laud, glorify, honor, applaud, commend. 4. solemnize, ritualize.

celebrated, *adj.* famous, renowned, well-known, distinguished, illustrious, eminent, famed. *Ant.* obscure, unknown.

censure, *n.* 1. condemnation, reproof, disapproval, disapprobation, blaming, criticism, blame, reproach, reprehension, rebuke, reprimand, stricture, animadversion. —*v.* 2. criticize, disapprove, condemn, find fault with. 3. reprove, rebuke, reprimand, reprehend, chide, blame, reproach. *Ant.* praise, commend.

center, *n.* 1. middle, midst. 2. pivot, hub, point, axis. *Ant.* brim, edge.

ceremony, *n.* rite, ritual, formality, observance. *Ant.* informality.

certain, *adj.* 1. confident, sure, assured, convinced, satisfied, indubitable, indisputable, unquestionable, undeniable, incontestable, irrefutable, unquestioned, incontrovertible, absolute, positive, plain, patent, obvious, clear. 2. sure, inevitable, infallible, unfailing. 3. fixed, agreed upon, settled, prescribed, determined, determinate, constant, stated, given. 4. definite, particular, special, especial. 5. unfailing, reliable, trustworthy, dependable, trusty. *Ant.* uncertain; unclear, unsure; unsettled; indefinite; fallible, unreliable.

certainty, *n.* 1. unquestionableness, inevitability, certitude, assurance, confidence, conviction. 2. fact, truth. *Ant.* doubt, uncertainty.

champion, *n.* 1. winner, victor, hero. 2. defender, protector, vindicator. 3. fighter, warrior. —*v.* 4. defend, support, maintain, fight for, advocate. *Ant.* loser; oppose.

chance, *n.* 1. fortune, fate, luck, accident, fortuity. 2. possibility, contingency, probability. 3. opportunity, opening, occasion. 4. risk, hazard, peril, danger, jeopardy. —*v.* 5. happen, occur, befall, take place. —*adj.* 6. casual, accidental, fortuitous. *Ant.* necessity, inevitability; surety.

change, *v.* 1. alter, make different, turn, transmute, transform, vary, modify. 2. exchange, substitute, convert, shift, replace; barter, trade, commute. 3. interchange. —*n.* 4. variation, alteration, modification, deviation, transformation, transmutation, mutation, conversion, transition. 5. substitution, exchange. 6. variety, novelty, innovation, vicissitude. *Ant.* remain, endure; immutability.

character, *n.* 1. individuality, personality. 2. feature, trait, characteristic. 3. nature, quality, disposition, mien, constitution, cast. 4. name, reputation, repute. 5. status, capacity. 6. symbol, mark, sign, letter, figure, emblem.

characteristic, *adj.* 1. typical, distinctive, discrete, special, peculiar, singular. —*n.* 2. feature, quality, trait, peculiarity, mark, attribute, property.

charge, *v.* 1. load, lade, burden, freight. 2. command, enjoin, exhort, order, urge, bid, require. 3. impute, ascribe. 4. blame, accuse, indict, arraign, impeach, inculpate, incriminate, involve, inform against, betray. 5. attack, assault, set on. —*n.* 6. load, burden, cargo, freight. 7. duty, responsibility, commission, office, trust, employment. 8. care, custody, superintendence, ward, management. 9. command, injunction, exhortation, order, direction, mandate, instruction, precept. 10. accusation, indictment, imputation, allegation, crimination, incrimination. 11. price, cost. 12. tax, lien, cost, expense, encumbrance, outlay, expenditure, liability, debt. 13. onset, attack, onslaught, assault, encounter.

charitable, *adj.* 1. generous, openhanded, liberal, beneficent, benign, kind, benignant, benevolent, bountiful, lavish. 2. broad-minded, liberal, lenient, considerate, mild, kindly. *Ant.* mean, stingy; narrow-minded, inconsiderate.

charm, *n.* 1. attractiveness, allurement, fascination, enchantment, bewitchment, spell, witchery, magic, sorcery. 2. trinket, bauble, jewelry; amulet. —*v.* 3. enchant, fascinate, captivate, catch, entrance, enrapture, transport, delight, please; attract, allure, enamor, bewitch; ravish. *Ant.* revulsion; disgust.

chart, *n.* map, plan.

charter, *n.* 1. privilege, immunity, guaranty, warranty. —*v.* 2. lease, hire, rent, let.

chary, *adj.* 1. careful, wary, cautious, circumspect. 2. shy, bashful, self-effacing. 3. fastidious, choosy, particular. 4. sparing, stingy, frugal. *Ant.* careless.

chaste, *adj.* virtuous, pure, moral, decent, undefiled, modest, continent; clean, elevated, unsullied; unaffected, simple, subdued, neat, straight, honest; refined, classic, elegant. *Ant.* sinful, impure, immodest; unrefined, coarse, inelegant.

chasten, *v.* discipline, punish, chastise, restrain, subdue, humble. *Ant.* indulge, humor.

cheap, *adj.* 1. inexpensive, low-priced. 2. paltry, common, mean, low, lowly, poor, inferior, base. *Ant.* dear, expensive, costly; exceptional, extraordinary, elegant.

cheat, *n.* 1. fraud, swindle, deception, trick, imposture, wile, deceit, artifice, chicanery, stratagem, hoax, imposition, snare, trap, pitfall, catch. 2. swindler, imposter, trickster, sharper, cheater, dodger, charlatan, fraud, fake, phony, mountebank, rogue, knave. —*v.* 3. deceive, defraud, trick, victimize, mislead, dupe, gudgeon, cog, gull, cozen, outwit, bamboozle, delude, hoodwink, beguile, inveigle, swindle, con; entrap, hoax, ensnare, fool, cajole; dissemble.

check, *v.* 1. stop, halt, delay, arrest. 2. curb, restrain, control, repress, chain, bridle, hinder, hobble, obstruct, curtail. 3. investigate, verify, assess, test, measure, examine, compare. 4. agree, correspond. 5. pause, stop. —*n.* 6. restraint, curb, bridle, bit, hindrance, obstacle, obstruction, impediment, control, bar, barrier, restriction, damper, interference, deterrent, repression. 7. rebuff, arrest, stoppage, cessation, repulse, halt. 8. ticket, receipt, coupon, tag, counterfoil, stub.

Ant. continue, advance, foster, support.

cheer, *n.* 1. encouragement, comfort, solace. 2. gladness, gaiety, animation, joy, mirth, glee, merriment, cheerfulness. 3. food, provisions, victuals, repast, viands. —*v.* 4. gladden, enliven, inspirit, exhilarate, animate, encourage. 5. shout, applaud, acclaim, salute. *Ant.* derision; misery; discourage, deride; boo, hiss.

cheerful, *adj.* 1. cheery, gay, blithe, happy, lively, spirited, sprightly, joyful, joyous, mirthful, buoyant, gleeful, sunny, jolly. 2. pleasant, bright, gay, winsome, gladdening, cheery, cheering, inspiring, animating. 3. hearty, robust, ungrudging, generous. *Ant.* miserable; unpleasant; stingy, mean.

cherish, *v.* 1. foster, harbor, entertain, humor, encourage, indulge. 2. nurse, nurture, nourish, support, sustain, comfort. 3. treasure, cling to, hold dear. *Ant.* abandon, scorn.

chide, *v.* 1. scold, fret, fume, chafe. 2. reprove, rebuke, censure, criticize, scold, admonish, upbraid, reprimand, blame, reprehend. *Ant.* praise, commend.

chief, *n.* 1. head, leader, ruler, chieftain, commander. —*adj.* 2. principal, most important, prime, first, supreme, leading, paramount, great, grand, cardinal, master; vital, essential. *Ant.* follower, disciple; unimportant, trivial, trifling; secondary.

chiefly, *adv.* mostly, principally, mainly, especially, particularly, eminently. *Ant.* last, lastly.

childish, *adj.* childlike, puerile, infantile, young, tender; weak, silly, simple, ingenuous, guileless, trusting, confident. *Ant.* adult, sophisticated.

chill, *n.* 1. cold, coldness, frigidity. 2. shivering, ague. 3. depression, damp. —*adj.* 4. chilly, cool, unfriendly, depressing, discouraging, bleak. —*v.* 5. cool, freeze; depress, discourage, deject, dishearten. *Ant.* warm.

choice, *n.* 1. selection, choosing, election, option, alternative, preference. —*adj.* 2. worthy, excellent, superior, fine, select, rare, uncommon, valuable, precious.

choose, *v.* select, elect, prefer, pick, cull.

chop, *v.* cut, mince.

chronic, *adj.* 1. inveterate, constant, habitual, confirmed, hardened. 2. perpetual, continuous, continuing, unending, never-ending, everlasting. *Ant.* fleeting, temporary.

chuckle, *v.*, *n.* laugh, giggle, titter. *Ant.* cry, sob.

circle, *n.* 1. ring, periphery, circumference, perimeter. 2. ring, circlet, crown. 3. compass, area, sphere, province, field, region, bounds, circuit. 4. cycle, period, series. 5. coterie, set, clique, society, club, company, class, fraternity. 6. sphere, orb, globe, ball. —*v.* 7. surround, encircle, encompass, round, bound, include. 8. orbit, circuit, revolve.

circuit, *n.* 1. course, tour, journey, revolution, orbit. 2. circumference, perimeter, periphery, boundary, compass. 3. space, area, region, compass, range, sphere, province, district, field.

civil, *adj.* polite, courteous, courtly, gracious, complaisant, respectful, deferential, obliging; affable, urbane, debonair, chivalrous, gallant, suave; refined, well-mannered, well-bred, civilized. *Ant.* uncivil, discourteous; rude; ill-mannered, unrefined.

claim, *v.* 1. demand, require, ask, call for, challenge. 2. assert, maintain, uphold. —*n.* 3. demand, request, requirement, requisition, call. 4. right, title, privilege, pretension.

clamor, *n.* 1. shouting, uproar, outcry, noise, hullabaloo. 2. vociferation. —*v.* 3. vociferate, cry out, shout. 4. importune, demand noisily. *Ant.* quiet, serenity, taciturnity.

clandestine, *adj.* secret, private, concealed, hidden, sly, underhand. *Ant.* open, candid, aboveboard.

clash, *v.* 1. clang, crash, clap, dash, clatter, clank. 2. collide. 3. conflict, struggle, disagree, interfere, content. —*n.* 4. collision. 5. conflict, opposition, disagreement, interference, struggle, contradiction. *Ant.* harmony, agreement.

clasp, *n.* 1. brooch, pin, clip, hook, fastening, catch, hasp. 2. embrace, hug, grasp. —*v.* 3. clip. 4. grasp, grip, clutch. 5. embrace, hug, clutch, grasp, fold.

clean, *adj.* 1. unsoiled, unstained, clear, unblemished, pure, flawless,

spotless, unsullied, neat, immaculate. 2. pure, purified, unmixed, unadulterated, clarified. 3. uncontaminated, not radioactive. 4. clear, readable, legible. 5. unsullied, undefiled, moral, innocent, upright, honorable, chaste. 6. neat, trim, shapely, graceful, delicate, light. 7. adroit, deft, dextrous. 8. complete, perfect, entire, whole, unabated, unimpaired. —*adv.* 9. cleanly, neatly. 10. wholly, completely, perfectly, entirely, altogether, fully, thoroughly, in all respects, out and out. —*v.* 11. scour, scrub, sweep, brush, wipe, mop, dust, wash, rinse, lave, cleanse, deterge, purify, clear; decontaminate. *Ant.* dirty, contaminated; radioactive; impure, immoral; clumsy, awkward.

cleanse, *v.* clean. *Ant.* soil.

clear, *adj.* 1. unclouded, light, bright, pellucid, limpid, diaphanous, crystalline, transparent, luminous. 2. bright, shining, lucent. 3. perceptible, understood, distinct, intelligible, orotund, comprehensible, lucid, plain, perspicuous, conspicuous, obvious. 4. distinct, evident, plain, obvious, apparent, manifest, palpable, patent, unmistakable, unequivocal, unambiguous, indisputable, undeniable, unquestionable. 5. convinced, certain, positive, definite, assured, sure. 6. innocent, pure, not guilty, unsullied, irreproachable, unblemished, clean, unspotted, unadulterated, moral, undefiled, virtuous, immaculate, spotless. 7. serene, calm, untroubled, fair, cloudless, sunny. 8. unobstructed, open, free, unimpeded, unhindered, unhampered, unencumbered, unentangled. 9. smooth, clean, even, regular, unblemished. 10. emptied, empty, free, rid. 11. limitless, unlimited, unqualified, unequivocal, boundless, free, open. 12. net. —*adv.* 13. clearly. —*v.* 14. clarify, purify, refine, clean, cleanse. 15. acquit, absolve, exonerate, vindicate, excuse, justify. 16. extricate, disentangle, disabuse, rid, disencumber, disengage. 17. liberate, free, emancipate, set free, disenthrall, loose, unchain, unfetter, let go. *Ant.* cloudy, dim, obscure; indistinct, unclear; equivocal, doubtful; guilty, culpable; troubled, disturbed, perturbed; obstructed; limited, confined.

clearly, adv. definitely, distinctly, evidently, plainly, understandably, obviously, certainly, surely, assuredly, entirely, completely, totally. Ant. confusedly, indefinitely; partly.

cleft, n. split, fissure, crack, crevice, cleaving, cleavage, rift, breach, break, fracture, cranny, gap, chasm. Ant. joint, link.

clemency, n. mildness, mercy, lenience, leniency, forbearance, compassion, tenderness, kindness, kindliness, gentleness, mercifulness. Ant. severity, austerity, cruelty, mercilessness.

clever, adj. 1. bright, quick, able, apt, smart, intelligent, expert, gifted, talented, ingenious, quick-witted. 2. skillful, adroit, dextrous, nimble, agile, handy. Ant. dull, slow, dimwitted; clumsy, awkward, maladroit.

climb, v. 1. mount, ascend, scale, surmount. 2. rise, arise. —n. 3. ascent, climbing, scaling, rise. Ant. descend; descent.

cloister, n. monastery, nunnery, convent, abbey, priory.

close, v. 1. stop, obstruct, shut, block, bar, stop up, clog, choke. 2. enclose, cover in, shut in. 3. bring together, join, unite. 4. end, terminate, finish, conclude, cease, complete. 5. terminate, conclude, cease, end. 6. come together, unite, coalesce, join. 7. grapple, fight. —adj. 8. shut, tight, closed, fast, confined. 9. enclosed, shut in. 10. heavy, unventilated, muggy, oppressive, uncomfortable, dense, thick. 11. secretive, reticent, taciturn, close-mouthed, silent, uncommunicative, incommunicative, reserved, withdrawn. 12. parsimonious, stingy, tight, closefisted, penurious, niggardly, miserly, mean. 13. scarce, rare. 14. compact, condensed, dense, thick, solid, compressed, firm. 15. near, nearby, adjoining, adjacent, neighboring, immediate. 16. intimate, confidential, attached, dear, devoted. 17. strict, searching, minute, scrupulous, exact, exacting, accurate, precise, faithful, nice. 18. intent, fixed, assiduous, intense, concentrated, earnest, constant, unremitting, relentless, unrelenting. —n. 19. end, termination, conclusion. 20. junction, union, coalescence, joining. Ant. open.

clothes, n. clothing, attire, raiment, dress, garments, vesture, habit, costume, garb, vestments, habiliments, accouterments.

cloud, n. 1. fog, haze, mist, vapor. 2. host, crowd, throng, multitude, swarm, horde, army. —v. 3. becloud, bedim, shadow, overshadow, obscure, shade. Ant. clarify.

cloudy, adj. 1. overcast, shadowy, clouded, murky, lowering, gloomy, cloudy, dismal, depressing, sullen. 2. obscure, indistinct, dim, blurred, blurry, unclear, befogged, muddled, confused, dark, turbid, muddy, opaque. Ant. clear; distinct.

club, n. 1. stick, cudgel, bludgeon, blackjack, billy; bat. 2. society, organization, association, circle, set, coterie, clique, fraternity, sorority.

clumsy, adj. 1. awkward, unskillful, ungainly, lumbering, ungraceful, lubberly. 2. unhandy, maladroit, unskillful, inexpert, bungling, ponderous, heavy, heavy-handed, inept. Ant. adroit, clever, dexterous.

coarse, adj. 1. impure, base, common, inferior, faulty, crude, rude, rough. 2. indelicate, unpolished, uncivil, impolite, gruff, bluff, boorish, churlish. 3. gross, broad, indecent, vulgar, crass, ribald, lewd, lascivious, amoral, immoral, dirty. Ant. pure, refined; civil, civilized, cultivated; decent, decorous.

coast, n. shore, seashore, strand, beach, seaside, seacoast, littoral.

coax, v. wheedle, cajole, beguile, inveigle, persuade, flatter. Ant. force, bully; deter.

coherence, n. 1. cohesion, union, connection. 2. connection, congruity, consistency, correspondence, harmony, harmoniousness, agreement, unity, rationality. Ant. incoherence.

cold, adj. 1. chilly, chill, cool, frigid, gelid, frozen, freezing. 2. dead. 3. impassionate, unemotional, unenthusiastic, passionless, apathetic, unresponsive, unsympathetic, unaffected, stoical, phlegmatic, unfeeling, unsusceptible, unimpressible, unimpressed, cool, sluggish, torpid, indifferent, cold-blooded, unconcerned, heartless, unperturbed, imperturbable. 4. polite, formal, reserved, unresponsive, unfriendly, inimical, hostile. 5. calm, deliberate, depressing, dispiriting, disheartening, uninspiring, spiritless, unaffecting, dull. 6. faint, weak. 7. bleak, raw, cutting, nipping, arctic, polar, frosty, icy, wintry, chill, chilly. —n. 8. chill, shivers, ague. Ant. warm, hot.

collect, v. gather, assemble, amass, accumulate, aggregate, scrape together. Ant. strew, broadcast, spread.

collection, n. 1. set, accumulation, mass, heap, pile, hoard, store, aggregation. 2. contribution, alms.

colloquial, adj. conversational, informal. Ant. formal.

column, n. pillar, shaft, stele, pilaster.

combat, v. 1. fight, contend, battle, oppose, struggle, contest, war, resist, withstand. —n. 2. fight, skirmish, contest, battle, struggle, conflict, war, brush, affair, encounter, engagement. Ant. support, defend.

combination, n. 1. conjunction, association, union, connection, coalescence, blending. 2. composite, compound, mixture, amalgamation, amalgam. 3. alliance, confederacy, federation, union, league, coalition, association, society, club; cartel, combine, monopoly; conspiracy, cabal.

combine, v. 1. unite, join, conjoin, associate, coalesce, blend, mix, incorporate, involve, compound, amalgamate. —n. 2. combination (def. 3.). Ant. dissociate, separate.

comfort, v. 1. soothe, console, relieve, ease, cheer, pacify, calm, solace, gladden, refresh. —n. 2. relief, consolation, solace, encouragement. Ant. agitate, discommode, incommode; discomfort, discouragement.

command, v. 1. order, direct, bid, demand, charge, instruct, enjoin, require. 2. govern, control, oversee, manage, rule, lead, preside over; dominate, overlook. 3. exact, compel, secure, demand, require, claim. —n. 4. order, direction, bidding, injunction, charge, mandate, behest, commandment, requisition, requirement, instruction, dictum. 5. control, mastery, disposal, ascendancy, rule, sway, superintendence, power, management, domination. Ant. obey.

commence, v. begin, open, start, originate, inaugurate, enter upon or into. Ant. end, finish, terminate.

commend, v. 1. recommend, laud, praise, extol, applaud, eulogize. 2. entrust. Ant. censure, blame; distrust.

commendation, n. 1. recommendation, praise, approval, approbation,

applause; medal. 2. eulogy, encomium, panegyric, praise.
Ant. censure, blame.

comment, *n.* 1. explanation, elucidation, expansion, criticism, critique, note, addendum, annotation, exposition, commentary. 2. remark, observation, criticism. —*v.* 3. remark, explain, annotate, criticize.

commerce, *n.* 1. interchange, traffic, trade, dealing, exchange, business. 2. intercourse, conversation, converse, intimacy.

commercial, *adj.* 1. mercantile, trafficking. —*n.* 2. advertisement.

common, *adj.* 1. mutual. 2. joint, united. 3. public, communal. 4. notorious. 5. widespread, general, ordinary, universal, prevalent, popular. 6. familiar, usual, customary, frequent, habitual, everyday. 7. hackneyed, trite, stale, commonplace. 8. mean, low, mediocre, inferior. 9. coarse, vulgar, ordinary, undistinguished, ill-bred.
Ant. exceptional, singular, extraordinary, separate; unfamiliar, strange.

commonplace, *adj.* 1. ordinary, uninteresting. 2. trite, hackneyed, common, banal, stereotyped. —*n.* 3. cliché, bromide.
Ant. extraordinary, original.

commotion, *n.* 1. tumult, disturbance, perturbation, agitation, disorder, pother, bustle, ado, turmoil, turbulence, riot, violence. 2. sedition, insurrection, uprising, revolution.
Ant. peace, calm, serenity.

communicate, *v.* 1. impart, transmit; give, bestow. 2. divulge, announce, declare, disclose, reveal, make known.
Ant. withhold, conceal.

community, *n.* 1. hamlet, town, village, city. 2. public, commonwealth, society. 3. agreement, identity, similarity, likeness. —*adj.* 4. common, joint, cooperative.

compact, *adj.* 1. dense, solid, firm, tightly packed, condensed. 2. concise, pithy, terse, laconic, short, sententious, succinct, brief, pointed, meaningful. —*v.* 3. condense, consolidate, compress. 4. stabilize, solidify. —*n.* 5. covenant, pact, contract, treaty, agreement, bargain, entente, arrangement, convention, concordat.
Ant. diverse, dispersed.

companion, *n.* 1. associate, comrade, partner, fellow, mate. 2. assistant; nurse, governess.

company, *n.* 1. group, band, party, troop, assemblage, body, unit. 2. companionship, fellowship, association, society. 3. assembly, gathering, concourse, crowd, circle, set, congregation. 4. firm, partnership, corporation, concern, house, syndicate, association.

compare, *v.* 1. liken, contrast. 2. vie, compete, equal, resemble.

compartment, *n.* division, section, apartment, cabin, roomette.

compassion, *n.* sorrow, pity, sympathy, feeling, ruth, mercy, commiseration, kindness, kindliness, tenderness, heart, tender-heartedness, clemency.
Ant. mercilessness, indifference.

compassionate, *adj.* pitying, sympathetic, tender, kind, merciful, tender-hearted, kindly, clement, gracious, benignant, gentle.
Ant. merciless, pitiless, harsh, cruel, mean.

compel, *v.* 1. force, drive, coerce, constrain, oblige, commit, impel, motivate, necessitate. 2. subdue, subject, bend, bow, overpower. 3. unite, drive together, herd.
Ant. coax.

compensate, *v.* 1. counterbalance, counterpoise, offset, countervail, make up for. 2. remunerate, reward, pay, recompense, reimburse. 3. atone, make amends.

compensation, *n.* 1. recompense, remuneration, payment, amends, reparation, indemnity, reward. 2. atonement, requital, satisfaction, indemnification.

compete, *v.* contend, vie, contest, rival, emulate, oppose, dispute, strive, cope, struggle.
Ant. support.

competent, *adj.* 1. fitting, suitable, sufficient, convenient, adequate, qualified, fit, apt, capable, proficient. 2. permissible, allowable.
Ant. incompetent, inapt.

competitor, *n.* opponent, contestant, rival, antagonist.
Ant. ally, friend.

complain, *v.* grumble, growl, murmur, whine, moan, bewail, lament, bemoan.

complement, *v.* 1. complete, supplement, add to, round out. —*n.* 2. supplement.

complete, *adj.* 1. whole, entire, full, intact, unbroken, unimpaired, undivided, one, perfect, developed, unabated, undiminished, fulfilled. 2. finished, ended, concluded, consummated, done, consummate, perfect, thorough; through-and-through, dyed-in-the-wool. —*v.* 3. finish, end, conclude, consummate, perfect, accomplish, do, fulfill, achieve, effect, terminate, close.
Ant. incomplete; unfinished; begin, commence, initiate.

complex, *adj.* 1. compound, composite, complicated, mixed, mingled. 2. involved, complicated, intricate, perplexing, tangled. —*n.* 3. complexus, net, network, complication, web, tangle.
Ant. simple; simplex.

compliment, *n.* 1. praise, commendation, admiration, tribute, honor, eulogy, encomium, panegyric. 2. regard, respect, civility; flattery. —*v.* 3. commend, praise, honor, flatter. 4. congratulate, felicitate.
Ant. insult, injury; decry, disparage.

comply, *v.* acquiesce, obey, yield, conform, consent, assent, agree, accede, concede.
Ant. refuse.

component, *adj.* 1. composing, constituent. —*n.* 2. element, ingredient, part.
Ant. complex.

composed, *adj.* calm, tranquil, serene, undisturbed, peaceful, cool, placid, pacific, unruffled, sedate, unperturbed, self-possessed, controlled, imperturbable, quiet.
Ant. upset, perturbed, disturbed, disquieted.

composite, *adj., n.* compound, complex.
Ant. divers.

composure, *n.* serenity, calm, calmness, tranquillity, equability, peacefulness, quiet, coolness, equanimity, self-possession.
Ant. agitation.

comprehend, *v.* 1. understand, conceive, know, grasp, see, discern, imagine, perceive. 2. include, comprise, embrace, take in, embody, contain.

comprehensive, *adj.* comprehending, inclusive, broad, wide, large, extensive, sweeping.
Ant. limited.

compress, *v.* 1. condense, squeeze, constrict, contract, press, crowd. —*n.* 2. pad, bandage.
Ant. spread, stretch.

comprise, *v.* include, comprehend, contain, embrace, embody; consist *or* be composed of.
Ant. exclude.

compulsory, *adj.* 1. compelling, coercive, constraining. 2. compelled, forced, obligatory, arbitrary, binding, necessary, unavoidable, inescapable, ineluctable.
Ant. free, unrestrained, unrestricted.

compute, *v.* reckon, calculate, estimate, count, figure.

conceal, *v.* 1. hide, secrete, cover, put away, bury, screen. 2. keep secret, hide, disguise, dissemble.
Ant. reveal.

conceit, *n.* 1. self-esteem, vanity, amour-propre, egotism, complacency. 2. fancy, imagination, whim, notion, vagary; thought, idea, belief, conception.
Ant. humility, modesty.

conceited, *adj.* vain, proud, egotistical, self-important, self-satisfied, smug, complacent, self-sufficient.
Ant. humble, modest, shy, retiring.

conceive, *v.* 1. imagine, create, ideate, think. 2. understand, apprehend, comprehend.

concentrate, *v.* 1. focus, condense. 2. intensify, purify, clarify.
Ant. dissipate, disperse.

concern, *v.* 1. affect, touch, interest, relate to, engage, involve, include. 2. disquiet, trouble, disturb. —*n.* 3. business, affair, interest, matter. 4. solicitude, anxiety, care, worry, burden, responsibility. 5. relation, bearing, appropriateness, consequence. 6. firm, company, business, establishment, corporation, partnership, house.
Ant. exclude; calm; unconcern, indifference.

conciliate, *v.* 1. placate, win over, soothe, propitiate, appease. 2. reconcile, pacify.
Ant. alienate, antagonize,

conciseness, *n.* brevity, laconicism, summary, terseness, pithiness, sententiousness.
Ant. diversity.

conclusion, *n.* 1. end, close, termination, completion, ending, finale. 2. summing up, summation. 3. result, issue, outcome. 4. settlement, arrangement, wind-up. 5. decision, judgment, determination. 6. deduction, inference.
Ant. beginning, commencement.

concur, *v.* 1. agree, consent, coincide, harmonize. 2. cooperate, combine, help, conspire, contribute.
Ant. disagree.

condemn, *v.* 1. blame, censure, disapprove. 2. doom, find guilty, sentence, damn.
Ant. liberate, release, exonerate.

condense, *v.* compress, concentrate, consolidate, contract; abridge, epitomize, digest, shorten, abbreviate, reduce, diminish, curtail.
Ant. expand.

condescend, *v.* deign, stoop, descend, degrade oneself.

condition, *n.* 1. state, case, situation, circumstance, conjuncture, circumstances. 2. requisite, prerequisite, requirement, contingency, consideration, proviso, provision, stipulation, *sine qua non.* —*v.* 3. determine, limit, restrict.

conduct, *n.* 1. behavior, demeanor, action, actions, deportment, bearing, carriage, mien, manners. 2. direction, management, execution, guidance, leadership, administration. 3. guidance, escort, leadership, convoy, guard. —*v.* 4. behave, deport, act, bear. 5. direct, manage, carry on, supervise, regulate, administrate, administer, execute, guide, lead. 6. lead, guide, escort, convoy.

confederation, *n.* alliance, confederacy, league, federation, union, coalition.

confer, *v.* 1. bestow, give, donate, grant, vouchsafe, allow, promise. 2. compare. 3. consult together, discuss, deliberate, discourse, parley, converse, advise, talk.

conference, *n.* meeting, interview, parley, colloquy, convention, consultation.

confess, *v.* acknowledge, avow, own, admit, grant, concede; declare, aver, confirm.

confidence, *n.* 1. trust, belief, faith, reliance, dependence. 2. self-reliance, assurance, boldness, intrepidity, self-confidence, courage.
Ant. distrust, mistrust; modesty.

confident, *adj.* sure, bold, believing, assured, self-assured, certain, positive, convinced; brave, intrepid.
Ant. shy, modest, diffident.

confidential, *adj.* 1. secret, restricted, private. 2. familiar, trusted, trusty, trustworthy, faithful, honorable, honest.

confine, *v.* 1. enclose, bound, circumscribe, circle, encircle, limit, bind, restrict. 2. immure, imprison, incarcerate. —*n.* 3. (*usually plural*) bounds, boundary, perimeter, periphery, limits; frontiers, borders.

confirm, *v.* 1. make certain *or* sure, assure, corroborate, verify, substanti-

ate, authenticate. 2. make valid *or* binding, ratify, sanction, approve, validate, bind. 3. make firm, strengthen, settle, establish, fix, assure.

conflict, *v.* 1. collide, clash, oppose, vary with, interfere. 2. contend, fight, combat, battle. —*n.* 3. battle, struggle, encounter, contest, collision, fight; siege, strife; contention, controversy, opposition, variance. 4. interference, discord, disunity, disharmony, inconsistency, antagonism.
Ant. harmony.

conform, *v.* 1. comply, yield, agree, assent, harmonize. 2. tally, agree, correspond, square. 3. adapt, adjust, accommodate.
Ant. disagree, dissent.

confuse, *v.* 1. jumble, disorder, disarrange, disturb, disarray. 2. confound, mix, mix up, intermingle, mingle. 3. perplex, mystify, nonplus, bewilder, astonish, surprise, disarm, shock, disconcert, embarrass, disturb. 4. disconcert, abash, mortify, shame, confound.
Ant. enlighten.

confusion, *n.* 1. perplexity, embarrassment, surprise, astonishment, shock, bewilderment, distraction. 2. disorder, disarray, disarrangement, jumble, mess, turmoil, chaos, tumult, furor, commotion, ferment, agitation, stir. 3. embarrassment, abashment, shamefacedness, shame, mortification.
Ant. enlightenment; clarity.

congenial, *adj.* sympathetic, kindred, similar, friendly, favorable, genial; agreeable, pleasing, pleasant, complaisant, suited, adapted, well-suited, suitable, apt, proper.
Ant. unsympathetic, disagreeable; unsuitable.

congress, *n.* meeting, assembly, conference, council, convention.

conjecture, *n.* 1. hypothesis, theory, guess, surmise, opinion, supposition, inference, deduction. —*v.* 2. conclude, suppose, assume, presume, suspect, surmise, hypothesize, theorize, guess.
Ant. determine, ascertain.

conjoin, *v.* associate, unite, join, combine, connect.
Ant. disjoin, dissociate.

connect, *v.* join, unite, link, conjoin, couple, associate, combine; cohere.
Ant. disconnect, disjoin.

connection, *n.* 1. junction, conjunction, union, joining, association, alli-

ance, dependence, interdependence. 2. link, yoke, connective, bond, tie, coupling. 3. association, relationship, affiliation, affinity. 4. circle, set, coterie, acquaintanceship. 5. relation, relative, kinsman; kin, kith.
Ant. disjunction, dissociation.

conquer, *v.* 1. win, gain. 2. overcome, subdue, vanquish, overpower, overthrow, subjugate, defeat, master, subject, beat, rout, crush, reduce. 3. surmount, overcome, overwhelm.
Ant. surrender, submit, give up, yield.

conquest, *n.* 1. captivation, seduction, enchantment. 2. vanquishment, victory, triumph. 3. subjugation, overthrow, defeat, mastery, subjection, rout.
Ant. surrender.

conscientious, *adj.* just, upright, honest, straightforward, incorruptible, faithful, careful, particular, painstaking, scrupulous, exacting, demanding; devoted, dedicated.
Ant. dishonest, corrupt, unscrupulous.

conscious, *adj.* 1. awake, aware, sentient, knowing, cognizant, percipient, intelligent. 2. sensible, sensitive, felt; rational, reasoning. 3. deliberate, intentional, purposeful.
Ant. unconscious.

consecrate, *v.* 1. sanctify, hallow, venerate, elevate. 2. devote, dedicate.
Ant. desecrate.

consecutive, *adj.* successive, continuous, regular, uninterrupted.
Ant. alternate, random.

consent, *v.* 1. agree, assent, permit, allow, let, concur, yield, comply, accede, acquiesce. —*n.* 2. assent, acquiescence, permission, compliance, concurrence, agreement. 3. accord, concord, agreement, consensus.
Ant. refuse, disagree; dissent.

consequence, *n.* 1. effect, result, outcome, issue, upshot, sequel, event, end. 2. importance, significance, moment, weight, concern, interest. 3. distinction, importance, singularity, weight.

consider, *v.* 1. contemplate, meditate, reflect, ruminate, ponder, deliberate, weigh, revolve, study, think about. 2. think, suppose, assume, presume. 3. regard, respect, honor.
Ant. ignore.

considerate, *adj.* thoughtful, kind, charitable, patient, concerned, well-disposed.
Ant. inconsiderate.

consideration, *n.* 1. considering, meditation, reflection, rumination, deliberation, contemplation, attention, advisement, regard. 2. regard, account. 3. recompense, payment, remuneration, fee, compensation, pay. 4. thoughtfulness, sympathy, kindness, kindliness, patience, concern. 5. importance, consequence, weight, significance, moment, interest. 6. estimation, esteem, honor.

consistent, *adj.* 1. agreeing, concordant, compatible, congruous, consonant, harmonious, suitable, apt, conformable, conforming. 2. constant, faithful, assiduous, unwavering.
Ant. inconsistent.

consolation, *n.* comfort, solace, relief, encouragement.
Ant. discomfort, discouragement.

console, *v.* comfort, solace, cheer, encourage, soothe, relieve, calm.
Ant. aggravate, agitate, disturb.

consonant, *n.* 1. sonorant, fricative, stop, continuant. —*adj.* 2. in agreement, concordant, consistent, harmonious, compatible, congruous, conformant, suitable.
Ant. vowel; discordant, inconsistent.

conspicuous, *adj.* 1. visible, manifest, noticeable, clear, marked, salient, discernible, perceptible, plain, open, apparent. 2. prominent, outstanding, obvious, striking, noteworthy, attractive, eminent, distinguished, noted, celebrated, illustrious.
Ant. unclear, imperceptible; undistinguished, trifling.

conspire, *v.* 1. complot, plot, intrigue, cabal, contrive, devise. 2. combine, concur, cooperate.

constancy, *n.* firmness, fortitude, resolution, determination, inflexibility, decision, tenacity, steadfastness, faithfulness, fidelity, fealty, devotion, loyalty; regularity, stability, immutability, uniformity, permanence, sameness.
Ant. randomness, faithlessness, irregularity, instability.

constant, *adj.* 1. invariable, uniform, stable, unchanging, fixed, immutable, invariable, unvarying, permanent. 2. perpetual, unremitting, uninterrupted, continual, recurrent, assiduous, unwavering, unfailing, persistent, persevering, determined. 3. steadfast, faithful, loyal, stanch, true, trusty, devoted, steady, resolute, firm, unshaking, unshakable, unwavering, unswerving, determined.
Ant. inconstant, variable, random,

unstable, changeable; sporadic; unsteady, wavering.

consternation, *n.* amazement, dread, dismay, bewilderment, awe, alarm, terror, fear, panic, fright, horror.
Ant. composure, equanimity.

constrain, *v.* 1. force, compel, oblige, coerce. 2. confine, check, bind, restrain, curb.
Ant. liberate, free.

constrict, *v.* compress, contract, shrink, cramp, squeeze, bind, tighten.
Ant. unbind, untie.

construct, *v.* build, frame, form, devise, erect, make, fabricate, raise.
Ant. raze.

consult, *v.* confer, deliberate.

consume, *v.* 1. destroy, expend, use up, use, exhaust, spend, waste, dissipate, squander, eat up, devour. 2. be absorbed *or* engrossed.

consummate, *v.* 1. complete, perfect, fulfill, accomplish, achieve, finish, effect, execute, do. —*adj.* 2. complete, perfect, done, finished, effected, fulfilled, excellent, supreme.
Ant. imperfect, unfinished, base.

contagious, *adj.* 1. communicable, infectious, catching. 2. noxious, pestilential, poisonous, deadly, foul.

contain, *v.* hold, accommodate, include, embody, embrace.

contaminate, *v.* defile, pollute, sully, stain, soil, tarnish, taint, corrupt, befoul, besmirch, infect, poison, vitiate.

contemplate, *v.* 1. look at, view, observe, regard, survey. 2. consider, reflect upon, meditate on, study, ponder, deliberate, think about, revolve. 3. intend, mean, purpose, design, plan.

contemplative, *adj.* reflective, meditative, thoughtful, studious, musing.
Ant. inattentive.

contemporary, *adj.* coexisting, coeval, contemporaneous.
Ant. antecedent; succeeding.

contempt, *n.* 1. scorn, disdain, derision, contumely. 2. dishonor, disgrace, shame.
Ant. respect, reverence; honor.

contemptible, *adj.* despicable, mean, low, miserable, base, vile.
Ant. splendid, admirable.

contemptuous, *adj.* disdainful, scornful, sneering, insolent, arrogant, supercilious, haughty.
Ant. humble, respectful.

contend, *v.* 1. struggle, strive, fight, battle, combat, vie, compete, rival. 2.

debate, dispute, argue, wrangle. 3. assert, maintain, claim.

content, *adj.* 1. satisfied, contented, sanguine. 2. assenting, acceding, resigned, willing, agreeable. —*v.* 3. appease, gratify, satisfy.
Ant. dissatisfy.

contention, *n.* 1. struggling, struggle, strife, discord, dissension, quarrel, disagreement, squabble, feud; rupture, break, falling out; opposition, combat, conflict, competition, rivalry, contest. 2. disagreement, dissension, debate, wrangle, altercation, dispute, argument, controversy.
Ant. agreement.

contentment, *n.* happiness, satisfaction, content, ease.
Ant. misery.

contest, *n.* 1. struggle, conflict, battle, combat, fight, encounter. 2. competition, contention, rivalry, match, tournament, tourney, game. 3. strife, dispute, controversy, debate, argument, altercation, quarrel, contention. —*v.* 4. struggle, fight, compete, contend, vie, combat, battle. 5. argue against, dispute, controvert, litigate, debate, oppose, contend against. 6. doubt, question, challenge, dispute. 7. rival, strive, compete, vie, contend for.

continual, *adj.* unceasing, incessant, ceaseless, uninterrupted, unremitting, constant, continuous, unbroken, successive, perpetual, unending, habitual, permanent, everlasting, eternal; recurrent, recurring, frequentative, repeated, repetitious, repetitive.
Ant. periodic, sporadic.

continue, *v.* 1. keep on, go onward *or* forward, persist, persevere. 2. last, endure, remain, persist. 3. remain, abide, tarry, stay, rest. 4. persist in, extend, perpetuate, prolong, carry on, maintain, retain; carry over, postpone, adjourn.
Ant. cease, interrupt.

contract, *n.* 1. agreement, compact, bargain, covenant, arrangement, pact, convention, concordat, treaty, stipulation. —*v.* 2. draw together, compress, concentrate, condense, reduce, lessen, shorten, narrow, shrivel, shrink. 3. elide, abbreviate, apocopate, abridge, epitomize.
Ant. disperse, spread.

contradict, *v.* deny, gainsay, dispute, controvert, impugn, challenge, assail.
Ant. corroborate, support.

contradictory, *adj.* contrary, opposed, opposite, opposing, antagonistic, irreconcilable, paradoxical, inconsistent, contrary.
Ant. corroborative.

contrary, *adj.* 1. opposite, opposed, contradictory, conflicting, discordant, counter, opposing. 2. untoward, unfavorable, adverse, unfriendly, hostile, oppugnant, antagonistic, disagreeable, irreconcilable. 3. perverse, self-willed, intractable, obstinate, refractory, headstrong, stubborn, pig-headed, contumacious.
Ant. obliging, compliant, tractable.

contrast, *v.* 1. oppose, compare, differentiate, discriminate, distinguish, set off. —*n.* 2. opposition, comparison, differentiation, difference, discrimination, contrariety.

contrive, *v.* plan, devise, invent, design, hatch, brew, concoct, form, make; plot, complot, conspire, scheme; manage, effect.

control, *v.* 1. dominate, command, manage, govern, rule, direct, reign over. 2. check, curb, hinder, restrain, bridle, constrain. 3. test, verify, prove. —*n.* 4. regulation, domination, command, management, direction, government, rule, reign, sovereignty, mastery, superintendence.

controversy, *n.* dispute, contention, debate, disputation, disagreement, altercation; quarrel, wrangle, argument.
Ant. concord, agreement, accord.

convene, *v.* 1. assemble, meet, congregate, collect, gather. 2. convoke, summon.
Ant. disperse, adjourn.

convenient, *adj.* 1. suited, fit, appropriate, suitable, adapted, serviceable, well-suited, favorable, easy, comfortable, agreeable, helpful, advantageous, useful. 2. at hand, accessible, handy.
Ant. inconvenient.

convention, *n.* 1. assembly, conference, convocation, meeting. 2. agreement, contract, compact, pact, treaty. 3. agreement, consent. 4. custom, precedent.

conventional, *adj.* 1. formal, conforming, conformant. 2. accepted, usual, habitual, customary, regular, common.
Ant. unconventional, unusual.

conversant, *adj.* 1. familiar, versed, learned, skilled, practiced, well-informed, proficient. 2. acquainted, associating.
Ant. unfamiliar, ignorant.

converse, *v.* 1. talk, chat, speak, discuss, confabulate. —*n.* 2. discourse, talk, conversation, discussion, colloquy. 3. opposite, reverse, transformation.

convert, *v.* 1. change, transmute, transform, proselyte, proselytize. —*n.* 2. proselyte, neophyte, disciple.
Ant. renegade, recreant.

convey, *v.* 1. carry, transport, bear, bring, transmit, lead, conduct. 2. communicate, impart.

convince, *v.* persuade, satisfy.

convoy, *v.* 1. accompany, escort, attend. —*n.* 2. escort, guard, attendance, protection.
Ant. desert.

cool, *adj.* 1. cold. 2. calm, unexcited, unmoved, deliberate, composed, collected, self-possessed, unruffled, sedate, undisturbed, placid, quiet, dispassionate, unimpassioned. 3. frigid, distant, superior, chilling, freezing, apathetic, repellent. 4. indifferent, lukewarm, unconcerned, cold-blooded. 5. audacious, impudent, shameless. —*v.* 6. allay, calm, moderate, quiet, temper, assuage, abate, dampen.
Ant. warm, tepid, lukewarm, hot.

copious, *adj.* abundant, large, ample, plentiful, overflowing, profuse, rich, full, plenteous.
Ant. scarce, scanty, meager.

copy, *n.* 1. transcript, reproduction, imitation, carbon, duplicate, facsimile. 2. original, manuscript, pattern, model, archetype. —*v.* 3. imitate, duplicate, transcribe.
Ant. original.

corporal, *adj.* corporeal, bodily, physical, material.
Ant. spiritual.

corpse, *n.* body, remains, carcass.

correct, *v.* 1. set right, rectify, amend, emend, reform, remedy, cure. 2. admonish, warn, rebuke, discipline, chasten, punish, castigate. —*adj.* 3. factual, truthful, accurate, proper, precise, exact, faultless, perfect, right, true.
Ant. ruin, spoil; incorrect, wrong.

correspond, *v.* 1. conform, agree, harmonize, accord, match, tally, concur, coincide, fit, suit. 2. communicate.
Ant. differ, diverge.

corrode, *v.* 1. eat, gnaw, consume, erode, wear away. 2. impair, deteriorate. 3. canker, rust, crumble.

corrupt, *adj.* 1. dishonest, venal, false, untrustworthy, bribable. 2. debased, depraved, base, perverted, wicked, sinful, evil, dissolute, profligate, abandoned, reprobate. 3. putrid, impure, putrescent, rotten, contaminated, adulterated, tainted, corrupted, spoiled, infected. —*v.* 4. bribe, lure, entice, demoralize, lead astray. 5. pervert, deprave, debase, vitiate. 6. infect, taint, pollute, contaminate, adulterate, spoil, defile, putrefy.

Ant. honest; honorable; pure, unspoiled, unadulterated; purify.

corruption, *n.* 1. perversion, depravity, abandon, dissolution, sinfulness, evil, immorality, wickedness, profligacy. 2. dishonesty, baseness, bribery. 3. decay, rot, putrefaction, putrescence, foulness, pollution, defilement, contamination, adulteration.

Ant. righteousness; honesty; purity.

cost, *n.* 1. price, charge, expense, expenditure, outlay. 2. sacrifice, loss, penalty, damage, detriment, suffering, pain.

costly, *adj.* valuable, dear, highpriced, sumptuous, expensive, precious, rich, splendid.

Ant. cheap.

coterie, *n.* society, association, set, circle, clique, club, brotherhood, fraternity.

cottage, *n.* cabin, lodge, hut, shack, cot, shanty.

Ant. palace, castle.

counsel, *n.* 1. advice, opinion, instruction, suggestion, recommendation, caution, warning, admonition. 2. consultation, deliberation, forethought. 3. purpose, plan, design, scheme. 4. lawyer, solicitor, barrister, advocate, counselor, adviser.

countenance, *n.* 1. aspect, appearance, look, expression, mien. 2. face, visage, physiognomy. 3. favor, encouragement, aid, assistance, support, patronage, sanction, approval, approbation. —*v.* 4. favor, encourage, support, aid, abet, patronize, sanction, approve.

Ant. condemn, prohibit.

counteract, *v.* neutralize, counterbalance, annul, countervail, offset, contravene, thwart, oppose, resist, hinder, check, frustrate, defeat.

Ant. cooperate.

counterfeit, *adj.* 1. spurious, false, fraudulent, forged. 2. sham, pretended, feigned, simulated, fraudulent, false, mock, fake, unreal, ersatz. —*n.* 3. imitation, forgery, falsification, sham. —*v.* 4. imitate, forge, copy, fake, falsify. 5. resemble. 6.

simulate, feign, sham, pretend. 7. feign, dissemble.

Ant. genuine.

countryman, *n.* 1. compatriot, fellow citizen. 2. native, inhabitant. 3. rustic, farmer, peasant, husbandman.

Ant. alien, foreigner.

couple, *n.* 1. pair, duo, duet, yoke, brace, two, span. —*v.* 2. fasten, link, join, unite, associate, pair, conjoin, connect.

Ant. separate, disjoin.

courage, *n.* fearlessness, dauntlessness, intrepidity, fortitude, pluck, spirit, heroism, daring, audacity, bravery, mettle, valor, hardihood, bravado, gallantry, chivalry.

Ant. cowardice.

course, *n.* 1. advance, direction, bearing. 2. path, route, channel, way, road, track, passage. 3. progress, passage, process. 4. process, career, race. 5. conduct, behavior, deportment. 6. method, mode, procedure. 7. sequence, succession, order, turn, regularity. 8. range, row, series, layer, order. —*v.* 9. chase, pursue, follow, hunt. 10. run, race.

courteous, *adj.* civil, polite, well-mannered, well-bred, urbane, debonair, affable, gracious, courtly, respectful, obliging.

Ant. discourteous, rude, curt, brusque.

cover, *v.* 1. overlay, overspread, envelop, enwrap, clothe, invest. 2. shelter, protect, shield, guard, defend. 3. hide, screen, cloak, disguise, secrete, veil, shroud, mask, enshroud. 4. include, comprise, provide for, take in, embrace, contain, embody, comprehend. 5. suffice, defray, offset, compensate for, counterbalance. —*n.* 6. lid, top, case, covering, tegument, integument. 7. protection, shelter, asylum, refuge, concealment, guard, defense. 8. woods, underbrush, covert, shrubbery, growth, thicket, copse. 9. veil, screen, disguise, mask, cloak.

Ant. uncover; exposure.

covet, *v.* desire, envy, long for.

Ant. relinquish, renounce.

coward, *n.* 1. poltroon, cad, dastard, milksop. —*adj.* 2. timid, cowardly.

cowardice, *n.* poltroonery, dastardliness, pusillanimity, timidity.

Ant. boldness, bravery, temerity.

cowardly, *adj.* craven, poltroon, dastardly, pusillanimous, recreant, timid, timorous, faint-hearted, white-livered, lily-livered, chicken-

hearted, yellow, fearful, afraid, scared.

Ant. brave, bold, valiant.

coxcomb, *n.* dandy, fop, dude, exquisite, beau, popinjay, jackanapes.

coy, *adj.* retiring, diffident, shy, self-effacing, bashful, modest, shrinking, timid, demure.

Ant. bold, pert, brazen, arch.

crack, *v.* 1. snap. 2. break, snap, split; crackle, craze. —*n.* 3. snap, report. 4. break, flaw, split, fissure, cleft, chink, breach, crevice, cranny, interstice.

craft, *n.* 1. skill, ingenuity, dexterity, talent, ability, aptitude, expertness. 2. skill, art, artfulness, craftiness, subtlety, artifice, cunning, deceit, guile, shrewdness, deceitfulness, deception. 3. handicraft, trade, art, vocation, metier, calling. 4. boat, vessel, ship; aircraft, airplane, plane.

craftsman, *n.* artisan, artificer, mechanic, handicraftsman, workman.

Ant. bungler, shoemaker.

crafty, *adj.* skillful, sly, cunning, deceitful, artful, wily, insidious, tricky, designing, scheming, plotting, arch, shrewd.

Ant. gullible, naive.

cram, *v.* stuff, crowd, pack, compress, squeeze, overcrowd, gorge, glut, press.

cranky, *adj.* 1. ill-tempered, cross, crotchety, cantankerous, perverse. 2. eccentric, queer, odd, strange, peculiar, curious. 3. shaky, unsteady, loose, disjointed, out of order, broken. 4. bent, twisted, crooked.

Ant. amiable, good-natured; firm; solid.

crash, *v.* 1. break, shatter, shiver, splinter, dash, smash. —*n.* 2. falling, collapse, depression, failure, ruin.

crave, *v.* 1. long for, desire, want, yearn *or* hunger for. 2. require, need. 3. beg for, beseech, entreat, implore, solicit, supplicate.

Ant. relinquish, renounce.

craven, *adj.* cowardly.

Ant. brave, bold, intrepid, fearless.

crazy, *adj.* 1. demented, insane, mad, deranged, crazed, lunatic, cracked. 2. rickety, shaky, tottering, doddering, loose. 3. weak, infirm, confused, impaired.

Ant. sane, well-balanced; firm; strong.

create, *v.* 1. produce, originate, invent, cause, occasion. 2. make, constitute.

credit, *n.* 1. belief, trust, confidence, faith, reliance, credence. 2. influence, authority, power. 3. trustworthiness, credibility. 4. repute, estimation, character; reputation, name, esteem, regard, standing, position, rank, condition; notoriety. 5. commendation, honor, merit. 6. acknowledgment, ascription. —*v.* 7. believe, trust, confide in, have faith in, rely upon. *Ant.* discredit.

creditable, *adj.* praiseworthy, meritorious, estimable, reputable, honorable, respectable. *Ant.* disreputable, dishonorable.

credulous, *adj.* believing, trusting, trustful, unsuspecting, gullible. *Ant.* incredulous, cautious, wary.

crime, *n.* offense, wrong, sin; infraction, violation, breach, misdemeanor, tort, felony: trespassing, breaking and entering, theft, robbery, assault, battery, statutory rape, rape, embezzlement, slander, libel, treason, manslaughter, murder.

criminal, *adj.* 1. felonious, unlawful, illegal, nefarious, flagitious, iniquitous, wicked, sinful, wrong. —*n.* 2. convict, malefactor, evildoer, transgressor, sinner, culprit, delinquent, offender, felon; crook, hoodlum, gangster.

cripple, *v.* disable, maim, weaken, impair, break down, ruin, destroy.

crisis, *n.* climax, juncture, exigency, strait, pinch, emergency.

criterion, *n.* standard, rule, principle, measure, parameter, touchstone, test, proof.

critic, *n.* 1. reviewer, censor, judge, connoisseur. 2. censurer, carper, faultfinder.

critical, *adj.* 1. captious, carping, censorious, faultfinding, caviling, severe. 2. discriminating, tasteful, judicial, fastidious, nice, exact, precise. 3. decisive, climacteric, crucial, determining, momentous, important. 4. dangerous, perilous, risky, suspenseful, hazardous, precarious, ticklish. *Ant.* unimportant, superficial, trivial.

criticism, *n.* 1. censure, faultfinding, stricture, animadversion, reflection. 2. review, critique, comment.

crooked, *adj.* 1. bent, curved, winding, devious, sinuous, flexuous, serpentine. 2. deformed, misshapen, disfigured, twisted, awry, askew, crippled. 3. dishonest, unscrupulous, knavish, tricky, fraudulent, dishonorable, unlawful, illegal, deceitful, insidious, crafty, treacherous. *Ant.* straight; honest, upright.

crop, *n.* 1. harvest, produce, yield. 2. craw, stomach. —*v.* 3. cut, cut short, clip, lop, mow.

cross, *n.* 1. opposing, thwarting, opposition, frustration. 2. trouble, misfortune, misery, burden. —*v.* 3. intersect, traverse. 4. oppose, thwart, frustrate, baffle, contradict, foil. 5. interbreed, mongrelize. —*adj.* 6. petulant, fractious, irascible, waspish, crabbed, cranky, curmudgeonly, churlish, sulky, cantankerous, ill-natured, peevish, sullen, ill-tempered, intemperate, impatient, complaining, snappish, irritable, fretful, moody, touchy, testy, unpleasant, unkind, mean, angry, spiteful, resentful, gloomy, glowering, morose, sour. *Ant.* supporting; aid, support; complaisant, amenable, agreeable, sweet.

crowd, *n.* 1. throng, multitude, swarm, company, host, horde, herd. 2. masses, proletariat, plebians, rabble, mob, people, populace. —*v.* 3. assemble, throng, swarm, flock together, herd. 4. push, shove, cram, pack, press, squeeze, cramp, force.

crude, *adj.* 1. unrefined, unfinished, unprepared, coarse, raw. 2. unripe, immature, undeveloped. 3. unpolished, unfinished, incomplete, coarse, boorish, uncouth, rough, rude, clumsy, awkward. 4. undisguised, blunt, bare, rough, direct. *Ant.* refined; aged, mature, ripe; complete, perfect; indirect, subtle.

cruel, *adj.* 1. barbarous, bloodthirsty, sanguinary, ferocious, fell, merciless, unmerciful, relentless, implacable, pitiless, distressing, ruthless, truculent, brutal, savage, inhuman, brutish, barbarian, unmoved, unfeeling, unrelenting. 2. severe, hard, bitter. *Ant.* kind, benevolent, beneficial.

cruelty, *n.* harshness, brutality, ruthlessness, barbarity, inhumanity, atrocity. *Ant.* kindness, benevolence.

crush, *v.* 1. squeeze, press, bruise, crumple, rumple, wrinkle, compress. 2. break, shatter, pulverize, granulate, powder, mash, smash, crumble, disintegrate. 3. put down, quell, overpower, subdue, overwhelm, overcome, quash, conquer, oppress.

cry, *v.* 1. lament, grieve, weep, bawl, sorrow, sob, shed tears, bewail, bemoan, squall, blubber, whimper, mewl, pule, wail. 2. call, shout, yell,

yowl, scream, exclaim, ejaculate, clamor, roar, bellow, vociferate. 3. yelp, bark, bellow, hoot. —*n.* 4. shout, scream, wail, shriek, screech, yell, yowl, roar, whoop, bellow. 5. exclamation, outcry, clamor, ejaculation. 6. entreaty, appeal. 7. proclamation, announcement. 8. weeping, lament, lamentation, tears. *Ant.* laugh.

crying, *adj.* 1. weeping, wailing. 2. flagrant, notorious, demanding, urgent, important, great, enormous. *Ant.* laughing; nugatory, trifling.

cunning, *n.* 1. ability, skill, adroitness, expertness. 2. craftiness, skillfulness, shrewdness, artfulness, wiliness, trickery, finesse, intrigue, artifice, guile, craft, deceit, deceitfulness, slyness, deception. —*adj.* 3. ingenious, skillful. 4. artful, wily, tricky, foxy, crafty. *Ant.* stupidity, inability; dullness; naive, gullible, dull.

curb, *n.* 1. restraint, check, control, bridle, rein, checkrein. —*v.* 2. control, restrain, check, bridle, repress. *Ant.* encourage, further, foster.

cure, *n.* 1. remedy, restorative, specific, antidote. —*v.* 2. remedy, restore, heal, make well *or* whole, mend, repair, correct.

curious, *adj.* 1. inquisitive, inquiring, prying, spying, peeping, meddlesome, interested. 2. strange, novel, unusual, singular, rare, foreign, exotic, queer, extraordianry, unique. *Ant.* blasé; common, commonplace, usual, customary.

current, *adj.* 1. present, prevailing, prevalent, general, common, circulating, widespread, popular, rife. 2. accepted, stylish, in vogue, *à la mode,* fashionable. —*n.* 3. stream, river, tide, course, progress, progression. *Ant.* outmoded, uncommon, unpopular.

curse, *n.* 1. imprecation, execration, fulmination, malediction, oath, denunciation, anathema, ban. 2. evil, misfortune, calamity, trouble, vexation, annoyance, affliction, torment, bane, thorn, plague, scourge. —*v.* 3. blaspheme, swear, imprecate, execrate, fulminate, damn, denunciate, accurse, maledict, anathematize, condemn, profane, excommunicate. 4. doom, destroy, plague, scourge, afflict, trouble, vex, annoy. *Ant.* blessing, benediction.

cursed, *adj.* 1. damned, accursed, banned, blighted. 2. execrable, dam-

nable, hateful, abominable, villainous.
Ant. blessed.

curt, *adj.* 1. short, shortened, brief,
abbreviated, concise, laconic, blunt,
terse. 2. rude, snappish, abrupt, dry.
Ant. long, drawn-out, lengthy; courteous, courtly.

curtail, *v.* lessen, diminish, decrease,
dock, shorten, abbreviate, blunt,
abridge.
Ant. extend, expand.

curtain, *n.* 1. drape, drapery, hanging, portière, lambrequin, valance,
blind, shade, shutter, shutters. 2.
cover, concealment.
Ant. window.

cushion, *n.* 1. pillow, bolster, pad;
shock-absorber. —*v.* 2. absorb,
check, slow, alleviate, meliorate.

custody, *n.* 1. keeping, guardianship,
care, custodianship, charge, safekeeping, watch, preserving, protec-

tion, preservation; possession, ownership, mastery, holding. 2.
imprisonment, confinement.

custom, *n.* 1. habit, practice, usage,
procedure, rule. 2. rule, convention,
form, observance, formality. 3. tax,
duty, impost, tribute, toll. 4. patronage, customers, patrons, clientele.

customary, *adj.* usual, habitual,
wonted, accustomed, conventional,
common, regular.
Ant. unusual, rare, uncommon, irregular.

cut, *v.* 1. gash, slash, slit, lance,
pierce, penetrate, incise, wound. 2.
wound, hurt, move, touch, slight, insult. 3. divide, sever, carve, cleave,
sunder, bisect, chop, hack, hew, fell,
saw. 4. lop off, crop. 5. reap, mow,
harvest. 6. clip, shear, pare, prune.
7. cross, intersect, transect. 8.
abridge, edit, shorten, abbreviate,
curtail. 9. lower, lessen, reduce, di-

minish. 10. dissolve, dilute, thin,
water, water down. 11. facet, make,
fashion. 12. hollow out, excavate,
dig. —*n.* 13. incision, wound, slash,
gash, slit; channel, passage, strait.
14. style, fashion, mode, kind, sort.

cutting, *n.* 1. root, shoot, leaf,
branch, limb. —*adj.* 2. sharp, keen,
incisive, trenchant, piercing. 3. mordant, mordacious, caustic, biting,
acid, wounding, sarcastic, sardonic,
bitter, severe.
Ant. dull; kind.

cynical, *adj.* distrustful, pessimistic,
sarcastic, satirical, unbelieving, dis-
believing, sneering, contemptuous,
derisive, cutting, scornful, ridicul-
ing, censorious, captious, waspish,
petulant, testy, fretful, touchy, cross,
surly, ill-tempered, ill-natured,
crusty, cantankerous.
Ant. optimistic, hopeful; good-
natured, calm, pleasant.

dainty, *adj.* 1. delicate, beautiful,
charming, exquisite, fine, elegant. 2.
toothsome, delicious, savory, palatable, tender, juicy, delectable, luscious. 3. particular, fastidious, scrupulous. 4. squeamish, finical,
overnice. —*n.* 5. delicacy, tidbit,
sweetmeat.
Ant. clumsy, inelegant; disgusting,
distasteful; sloppy.

dally, *v.* 1. sport, play, trifle, fondle,
toy, caress. 2. waste time, loiter,
delay, dawdle.
Ant. hasten, hurry.

damage, *n.* 1. injury, harm, hurt, detriment, mischief, impairment, loss.
—*v.* 2. injure, harm, hurt, impair,
mar.
Ant. improvement; improve, better.

damp, *adj.* 1. moist, humid, dank,
steamy, wet. —*n.* 2. moisture, humidity, dankness, wet, wetness,
dampness, fog, vapor, steam. 3. dejection, depression, dispiritedness,
chill, discouragement, check. —*v.* 4.
dampen, moisten, wet, humidify. 5.
check, retard, slow, inhibit, restrain,
moderate, abate, allay, slow, interfere with. 6. stifle, suffocate, extinguish.
Ant. dry, arid.

danger, *n.* hazard, risk, peril, jeopardy, liability, exposure; injury, evil.
Ant. security, safety.

dare, *v.* venture, hazard, risk, brave,
challenge, defy, endanger.

daring, *n.* 1. courage, adventurous-
ness, boldness, bravery, audacity, intrepidity, heroism. —*adj.* 2. courageous, venturesome, adventurous,
bold, brave, audacious, dauntless,
undaunted, intrepid, fearless, valiant, valorous, gallant, chivalrous,
doughty, heroic.
Ant. cowardice; timid, cowardly,
pusillanimous, fearful.

dark, *adj.* 1. dim, gloomy, murky, umbrageous, shadowy, penumbral,
dusky, unilluminated, unlit, sunless,
shady, swarthy, black, pitchy, ebon,
Cimmerian. 2. gloomy, cheerless,
dismal, sad, morose, morbid, disheartening, discouraging. 3. sullen,
frowning. 4. unenlightened, ignorant, untaught, untutored, uneducated, unlettered, benighted, in the
dark. 5. obscure, recondite, abstruse, dim, incomprehensible,
unintelligible, occult, cabalistic, mysterious, puzzling, enigmatic, enig-
matical, mystic, mystical. 6. hidden,
secret, concealed. 7. silent, reticent.
8, infernal, wicked, sinful, nefarious,
flagitious, foul, infamous, hellish,
devilish, evil, bad, satanic.
Ant. light, fair; cheerful; pleasant; intelligent, educated; clear, intelligible; open, revealed; voluble; heavenly, godly.

dart, *n.* 1. arrow, barb. —*v.* 2. spring,
start, dash, bolt, rush, fly, shoot.

dash, *v.* 1. strike, break; throw, thrust;
splash, splatter. 2. adulterate, mix,
deteriorate, mingle. 3. rush, dart,
bolt, fly. —*n.* 4. pinch, bit, suggestion, soupçon, hint, touch, tinge,
smack, sprinkle, sprinkling. 5. vigor,
spirit, élan, flourish, éclat.

daunt, *v.* 1. intimidate, overawe, subdue, dismay, frighten, appall. 2. discourage, dispirit, dishearten, thwart,
frustrate.
Ant. encourage, actuate.

dauntless, *adj.* fearless, bold, undaunted, intrepid, brave, courageous, daring, indomitable, unconquerable, valiant, valorous, heroic,
chivalrous, doughty, undismayed.
Ant. fearful, cowardly, timid, timorous.

dawn, *n.* 1. daybreak, sunrise, dawning. —*v.* 2. appear, open, begin,
break.
Ant. sunset; disappear.

dead, *adj.* 1. deceased, lifeless, extinct, inanimate, defunct, departed.
2. insensible, numb, unfeeling, indifferent, cool, cold, callous, obtuse,
frigid, unsympathetic, apathetic,
lukewarm. 3. infertile, barren, sterile. 4. still, motionless, inert, inoperative, useless, dull, inactive, unemployed. 5. extinguished, out. 6.

complete, absolute, utter, entire, total. 7. straight, direct, unerring, exact, precise, sure.
Ant. alive, live, animate; fervid, eager, warm, animated; fertile; partial; crooked, indirect, devious.

deadly, *adj.* 1. fatal, lethal, mortal. 2. implacable, sanguinary, murderous, bloodthirsty.

deal, *v.* 1. act, behave. 2. trade, do business, traffic. 3. distribute, dole, mete, dispense, apportion, allot, give, assign. —*n.* 4. bargain, arrangement, pact, contract. 5. quantity, amount, extent, degree. 6. dealing, distribution, share.
Ant. gather, collect.

dear, *adj.* 1. beloved, loved, precious, darling, esteemed. 2. expensive, high-priced, costly, high; exorbitant.
Ant. hateful; cheap.

death, *n.* 1. decease, demise, passing, departure. 2. stop, cessation, surcease, estoppage, end, finale.
Ant. life.

debar, *v.* 1. exclude, shut out. 2. prevent, prohibit, hinder, interdict, outlaw.
Ant. include, welcome; encourage, support.

debase, *v.* 1. adulterate, corrupt, vitiate, contaminate, pollute, defile, foul, befoul. 2. lower, depress, reduce, impair, deteriorate, degrade, abase, demean.
Ant. purify; elevate, raise, exalt.

debate, *n.* 1. discussion, argument, controversy, disputation, dispute, contention. 2. deliberation, consideration. —*v.* 3. discuss, dispute, argue, contend, hold. 4. deliberate, consider, discuss, argue.
Ant. agreement.

debt, *n.* liability, obligation, duty, due, debit.

decadence, *n.* decline, degeneration, retrogression, decay, fall.
Ant. flourishing, progress.

decay, *n.* 1. deteriorate, decline, retrogress, degenerate, fall, fall away, wither, perish. 2. decompose, putrefy, rot, disintegrate. —*n.* 3. decline, deterioration, degeneration, decadence, impairment, dilapidation. 4. decomposition, putrefaction, rotting, rot.
Ant. flourish, grow; progress.

deceit, *n.* 1. deceiving, concealment, fraud, deception, cheating, guile, hypocrisy, craftiness, slyness, insincerity, disingenuousness. 2. trick, stratagem, artifice, wile, trickery, chicane, chicanery, device, cozenage. 3.

falseness, duplicity, treachery, perfidy.
Ant. honesty, forthrightness.

deceitful, *adj.* 1. insincere, disingenuous, false, hollow, empty, deceiving, fraudulent, designing, tricky, wily, two-faced. 2. misleading, fraudulent, deceptive, counterfeit, illusory, fallacious.
Ant. sincere, honest, forthright; genuine.

deceive, *v.* mislead, delude, cheat, cozen, dupe, gull, fool, bamboozle, hoodwink, trick, double-cross, defraud, outwit; entrap, ensnare, betray.

decent, *adj.* 1. fitting, appropriate, suited, suitable, apt, proper, fit, becoming. 2. conformant, tasteful, modest, seemly, proper, decorous.
Ant. indecent, indecorous, improper, unfit, unsuitable.

deception, *n.* 1. deceiving, gulling. 2. artifice, sham, cheat, imposture, treachery, subterfuge, stratagem, ruse, hoax, fraud, trick, wile.

deceptive, *adj.* deceiving, misleading, delusive, fallacious, specious, false, deceitful.
Ant. genuine, authentic.

decide, *v.* determine, settle, resolve, purpose, conclude.
Ant. waver, hesitate, vacillate.

decided, *adj.* 1. unambiguous, unquestionable, definite, unmistakable, undeniable, indeniable, indisputable, indubitable, certain, sure, emphatic, pronounced, absolute, unequivocal, categorical, incontrovertible. 2. resolute, determined, resolved, unwavering, unhesitating.
Ant. undecided, ambiguous, indefinite; irresolute, hesitant.

decisive, *adj.* incontrovertible, firm, resolute, determined, conclusive, final.
Ant. indecisive, irresolute, vacillating, wavering.

deck, *v.* clothe, attire, bedeck, array, garnish, trim, dress, bedizen, adorn, embellish, decorate.
Ant. undress.

declare, *v.* 1. announce, proclaim, pronounce. 2. affirm, assert, aver, protest, make known, state, asseverate, utter. 3. manifest, reveal, disclose, publish.
Ant. deny, controvert; suppress.

decline, *v.* 1. refuse, avoid, reject, deny. 2. descend, slope, incline *or* bend downward. 3. stoop, condescend, lower oneself, abase, debase. 4. fail, weaken, deteriorate, pale, di-

minish, degenerate, decay, languish. —*n.* 5. incline, declivity, slope, hill. 6. failing, loss, enfeeblement, deterioration, degeneration, enervation, weakening, decay, diminution, lessening, retrogression.
Ant. agree; rise; improve, increase; strengthening.

decompose, *v.* 1. separate, distill, fractionate, analyze, disintegrate. 2. rot, putrefy, decay, mould.

decorous, *adj.* proper, decent, seemly, becoming, sedate, conventional, fitting, fit, suitable.
Ant. indecorous, indecent, unseemly, unbecoming, unfit.

decorum, *n.* etiquette, politeness, politesse, manners, manner, behavior, comportment, deportment, decency, propriety, dignity.
Ant. indecency, impropriety.

decrease, *v.* 1. diminish, lessen, abate, fall off, decline, contract, dwindle, shrink, wane, ebb, subside. —*n.* 2. abatement, diminution, reduction, decline, wane, subsidence, falling-off, contraction, shrinking, dwindling, lessening, ebb, ebbing.
Ant. increase.

decrepit, *adj.* weak, feeble, enfeebled, infirm, aged, superannuated, effete, broken-down.
Ant. sturdy, strong.

decry, *v.* disparage, censure, belittle, discredit, depreciate, condemn.
Ant. praise, laud, commend.

deduct, *v.* subtract, remove, detract, withdraw.
Ant. add.

deed, *n.* act, performance, exploit, achievement, action, feat.

deem, *v.* judge, regard, think, consider, hold, believe, account, count, suppose.

deep, *adj.* 1. recondite, abstruse, abstract, difficult, profound, mysterious, obscure, unfathomable. 2. grave, serious, grievous. 3. absorbing, absorbed, involved, intense, heartfelt, great, extreme. 4. penetrating, intelligent, bright, cunning, sagacious, wise, discerning, astute, shrewd, artful. —*n.* 5. ocean, sea, abyss.
Ant. shallow.

deface, *v.* mar, disfigure, deform, spoil, soil, injure, harm; blot out, efface, obliterate, erase, eliminate.
Ant. beautify.

defeat, *v.* 1. overcome, conquer, overwhelm, vanquish, subdue, overthrow, subjugate, suppress, rout, check. 2. frustrate, thwart, foil, baf-

fle, disconcert, unnerve, balk. —*n.*
3. overthrow, vanquishment, downfall, rout. 4. frustration, bafflement.
Ant. yield, surrender, submit.

defect, *n.* 1. blemish, flaw, fault, shortcoming, imperfection, mar, blotch, scar, blot, foible, weakness. 2. deficiency, want, lack, destitution. —*v.* 3. desert, abandon, revolt, rebel, betray.
Ant. sufficiency, perfection; support.

defective, *adj.* imperfect, incomplete, faulty, deficient, insufficient, inadequate.
Ant. perfect, complete, adequate.

defend, *v.* 1. guard, garrison, fortify, shield, shelter, screen, preserve, protect, keep, watch over, safeguard, secure. 2. uphold, maintain, assert, justify, plead, espouse, vindicate.
Ant. attack.

defer, *v.* delay, postpone, put off, prevent, adjourn; procrastinate.
Ant. speed, expedite.

defiant, *adj.* antagonistic, insubordinate, contumacious, refractory, recalcitrant, rebellious, insolent, resistant; daring, courageous, brave, bold.
Ant. friendly, amiable; cowardly.

definite, *adj.* 1. defined, determined, specific, particular, exact, fixed, precise, determinate. 2. certain, clear, express, sure.
Ant. indefinite, undetermined, indeterminate; uncertain, unclear.

deform, *v.* misshape, deform, disfigure, deface, efface, mar, spoil, ruin; transform.

deformed, *adj.* malformed, misshapen, crippled, disfigured.

defy, *v.* challenge, resist, dare, brave, flout, scorn, despise.
Ant. encourage, support, help.

degradation, *n.* humiliation, disgrace, debasement, dishonor, degeneration, decline, decadence, degeneracy, perversity.
Ant. exaltation.

degrade, *v.* 1. demote, depose, downgrade, lower, break, cashier. 2. debase, deprave, lower, abase, vitiate, deteriorate. 3. humiliate, dishonor, disgrace, discredit.
Ant. exalt.

dejected, *adj.* depressed, dispirited, disheartened, low-spirited, discouraged, despondent, downhearted, sad, unhappy, miserable.
Ant. happy, cheerful, lighthearted.

delay, *v.* 1. put off, defer, postpone, procrastinate. 2. impede, slow, retard, hinder, detain, stop, arrest. 3.

linger, loiter, tarry. —*n.* 4. delaying, procrastination, loitering, tarrying, dawdling, stay, stop. 5. deferment, postponement, respite, deferring.
Ant. expedite, hasten, speed.

delegate, *n.* 1. representative, deputy, envoy, ambassador, legate. —*v.* 2. depute, entrust, commission.

delete, *v.* cancel, strike or take out, dele, erase, expunge, eradicate, remove, efface, blot out.

deleterious, *adj.* injurious, hurtful, harmful, pernicious, destructive, deadly, lethal; noxious, poisonous.
Ant. salutary, beneficial, advantageous.

deliberate, *adj.* 1. weighed, considered, studied, intentional, purposive, purposeful, premeditated, voluntary, willful. 2. careful, slow, unhurried, leisurely, methodical, thoughtful, circumspect, cautious, wary. —*v.* 3. weigh, consider, ponder over, reflect, think, ruminate, meditate. 4. consult, confer.
Ant. haphazard, unintentional; careless, unwary, incautious.

delicate, *adj.* 1. fine, dainty, exquisite, nice, fragile, graceful, elegant, choice. 2. fine, slight, subtle. 3. tender, fragile, frail, dainty, slight, weak, slender, sensitive, frangible. 4. critical, precarious. 5. scrupulous, careful, painstaking, exact, exacting, precise, accurate. 6. discriminating, fastidious, careful, demanding.
Ant. rude, crude; blunt; rough, insensitive, unbreakable; careless.

delicious, *adj.* pleasing, luscious, palatable, savory, dainty, delicate.
Ant. unpleasant, bitter, acrid, unpalatable.

delight, *n.* 1. enjoyment, pleasure, transport, delectation, joy, rapture, ecstasy. —*v.* 2. please, satisfy, transport, enrapture, enchant, charm, ravish.
Ant. disgust, revulsion, displeasure; displease.

delightful, *adj.* pleasing, pleasant, pleasurable, enjoyable, charming, enchanting, agreeable, delectable, rapturous.
Ant. unpleasant, disagreeable, revolting, repellent.

deliver, *v.* 1. give up, surrender, hand over, transfer, give over, yield, resign, cede, grant, relinquish. 2. give forth, emit, cast, direct, deal, discharge. 3. utter, pronounce, announce, proclaim, declare, communicate, publish, impart, promulgate, advance. 4. set free, liberate, release,

free, emancipate. 5. redeem, rescue, save, release, extricate, disentangle.
Ant. limit, confine.

delude, *v.* mislead, deceive, beguile, cozen, cheat, dupe, gull, defraud, trick.
Ant. enlighten.

deluge, *n.* inundation, flood, downpour, overflow, cataclysm, catastrophe.

delusion, *n.* illusion, deception, trick, fancy, fallacy, error, mistake, hallucination.

demand, *v.* 1. claim, require, exact, ask for, call for, challenge. 2. ask, inquire. —*n.* 3. claim, requisition, requirement. 4. inquiry, question, asking, interrogation.
Ant. waive, relinquish.

demolish, *v.* ruin, destroy, put an end to, lay waste, raze, level.
Ant. construct, build, create.

demur, *v.* 1. object, take exception, raise or make objection; refuse. —*n.* 2. objection, hesitation, refusal.
Ant. agree, accede, consent.

demure, *adj.* 1. prudish, prim, overmodest, priggish. 2. sober, modest, serious, sedate, decorous, coy.
Ant. licentious, immodest; indecorous.

denounce, *v.* 1. condemn, assail, censure, attack, stigmatize, blame, brand, label. 2. inform against, accuse, denunciate, give away.
Ant. commend, exonerate.

deny, *v.* 1. dispute, controvert, oppose, gainsay, contradict. 2. reject, renounce, abjure, disavow. 3. refuse, repudiate, disown.
Ant. concede, agree, concur; accept; receive.

depart, *v.* 1. go away, start, set out, leave, quit, retire, withdraw, absent, go. 2. turn aside, diverge, deviate, vary. 3. die, pass on or away.
Ant. arrive; converge.

depict, *v.* 1. represent, portray, paint, limn, delineate, sketch, reproduce, draw. 2. describe.

deplore, *v.* grieve, regret, lament, bemoan, bewail, mourn.
Ant. boast.

deposit, *v.* 1. place, put, lay down, lay. 2. throw down, drop, precipitate. 3. bank, save, store, hoard; secure. —*n.* 4. sediment, deposition, precipitate; silt, mud, slime, sand, alluvium; snow, rain, sleet, hail. 5. coating; lode, vein.

depot, *n.* station, terminal; storehouse, warehouse, depository.

depraved, *adj.* corrupt, perverted, corrupted, immoral, wicked, evil, sinful, iniquitous, profligate, debased, dissolute, reprobate, degenerate, licentious, lascivious, lewd. *Ant.* upright, honest; honorable, decorous, modest.

depress, *v.* 1. dispirit, deject, oppress, dishearten, discourage, dampen, chill, sadden. 2. reduce, weaken, dull, lower. 3. devalue, cheapen. 4. humble, humiliate, abase, debase, degrade, abash. *Ant.* inspirit, encourage; elevate; gladden.

depressed, *adj.* dejected, downcast, sad, unhappy, miserable, morose, saddened, blue, despondent, melancholy, gloomy, morbid. *Ant.* happy, cheerful.

deprive, *v.* dispossess, bereave, strip, divest, disallow, deny. *Ant.* endow.

dereliction, *n.* neglect, negligence, delinquency, fault, abandonment, desertion, renunciation.

descent, *n.* 1. falling, fall, sinking, descending. 2. inclination, declination, slope, declivity, grade, decline. 3. extraction, lineage, derivation, parentage, genealogy. 4. incursion, attack, assault, raid, foray. *Ant.* ascent, rise.

describe, *v.* narrate, account, recount, tell, relate; delineate, portray, characterize, limn, represent, depict.

desert, *n.* 1. waste, wilderness. —*adj.* 2. desolate, barren, forsaken, wild, uninhabited. —*v.* 3. abandon, forsake, leave behind, give up, relinquish, leave, quit, renounce.

design, *v.* 1. plan, devise, project, contrive. 2. intend, purpose, mean, propose. 3. sketch, draw, delineate. —*n.* 4. plan, scheme, proposal, proposition, project. 5. sketch, plan, drawings, blueprint, outline, draught. 6. end, intention, purpose, intent, aim, object. 7. meaning, purport, drift. *Ant.* achieve, execute, accomplish; execution; accident, fortuity, chance.

designing, *adj.* contriving, scheming, sly, artful, cunning, tricky, wily, crafty, deceitful, treacherous, arch, Machiavellian, astute, unscrupulous. *Ant.* open, candid, frank, honest; guileless, artless, naive.

desire, *v.* 1. wish *or* long for, crave, want, wish, covet, fancy. 2. ask, request, solicit. —*n.* 3. linging, craving, yearning, wish, need, hunger, appetite, thirst. 4. request, wish, aspiration. 5. lust. *Ant.* abominate, loathe, abhor.

desolate, *adj.* 1. barren, laid waste, devastated, ravaged, scorched, destroyed. 2. deserted, uninhabited, desert, lonely, alone, lone, solitary, forsaken, lonesome. 3. miserable, wretched, unhappy, sad, woeful, woebegone, disconsolate, inconsolable, forlorn, lost, cheerless. 4. dreary, dismal, wild. —*v.* 5. lay waste, devastate, ravage, ruin, sack, destroy, despoil. 6. depopulate. 7. sadden, depress. 8. forsake, abandon, desert. *Ant.* fertile; populous, crowded; happy, delighted; cultivated; build, create; cheer.

despair, *n.* hopelessness, desperation, despondency, discouragement, gloom, disheartenment. *Ant.* encouragement, hope, optimism.

desperate, *adj.* 1. reckless, despairing, rash, headlong, frantic. 2. hopeless, serious, grave, dangerous. 3. wretched, forlorn, hopeless, desolate. 4. extreme, excessive, great, heroic, prodigious, foolhardy. *Ant.* careful; hopeful.

despicable, *adj.* despisable, contemptible, vile, base, worthless, mean, abject, low, pitiful. *Ant.* lovable, likable, worth.

despise, *v.* contemn, scorn, disdain, spurn. *Ant.* love, like, admire.

despite, *prep.* notwithstanding, in spite of.

despondency, *n.* depression, dejection, discouragement, melancholy, gloom, desperation, despair, sadness, blues. *Ant.* elation, joy, happiness.

despondent, *adj.* desponding, depressed, dejected, discouraged, disheartened, downhearted, melancholy, sad, blue, dispirited, hopeless, low-spirited. *Ant.* elated, joyful, happy.

destiny, *n.* fate, karma, kismet, lot, fortune, future, doom, destination.

destitute, *adj.* needy, poor, indigent, penniless, impoverished, poverty-stricken. *Ant.* affluent, rich, opulent.

destroy, *v.* 1. smash, dash, demolish, raze, spoil, consume, level, ruin, waste, ravage, devastate, desolate, lay waste. 2. end, extinguish, extirpate, annihilate, eradicate, slay, kill, uproot. 3. nullify, invalidate. *Ant.* create; originate, start.

destruction, *n.* 1. extinction, extermination, desolation, devastation, ruin, eradication. 2. demolition, annihilation, murder, slaughter, death, massacre, genocide. 3. plague, shipwreck, holocaust. *Ant.* birth, origin; creation.

destructive, *adj.* 1. ruinous, baleful, pernicious, mischievous, deleterious, fatal, deadly, lethal. 2. extirpative, eradicative. *Ant.* salutary; creative.

detain, *v.* 1. delay, arrest, retard, stop, slow, stay, check, keep. 2. restrain, confine, arrest. 3. keep back, withhold, retain. *Ant.* promote, encourage; advance.

detect, *v.* discover, catch, expose, descry, find, find out, ascertain, learn, hear of, hear.

deter, *v.* discourage, restrain, dissuade, hinder, prevent, stop. *Ant.* encourage, further, continue.

determine, *v.* 1. settle, decide, conclude, adjust. 2. conclude, ascertain, verify, check, certify. 3. fix, decide, establish, condition, influence, resolve. 4. impel, induce, lead, incline.

determined, *adj.* staunch, resolute, unflinching, firm, inflexible, rigid, rigorous, unfaltering, unwavering. *Ant.* irresolute, vacillating, wavering, faltering, flexible.

detest, *v.* abhor, hate, loathe, abominate, execrate, despise. *Ant.* love, like.

detestable, *adj.* abominable, hateful, execrable, loathsome, vile, odious, abhorred, abhorrent, despicable. *Ant.* lovable, likable.

detraction, *n.* detracting, disparagement, belittling, defamation, vilification, calumny, abuse, slander, aspersion, depreciation. *Ant.* praise, commendation.

detriment, *n.* loss, damage, injury, hurt, harm, impairment, disadvantage, prejudice. *Ant.* advantage, profit.

devastate, *v.* ravage, lay waste, desolate, destroy, strip, pillage, plunder, sack, spoil, despoil. *Ant.* build, erect, create.

development, *n.* 1. expansion, growth, elaboration, progress, increase. 2. opening, disclosure, developing, unfolding, maturing, maturation. 3. community, project, housing project. *Ant.* deterioration, decadence, degeneration.

deviate, *v.* 1. depart, swerve, digress, diverge, part, wander, veer, err, stray. 2. turn aside, avert.
Ant. converge.

device, *n.* 1. invention, contrivance, gadget. 2. plan, scheme, project, design, expedient. 3. wile, ruse, artifice, shift, trick, stratagem, evasion, maneuver. 4. design, figure, emblem, trademark, badge, logotype, colophon, symbol, crest, seal. 5. motto, slogan, legend. 6. (*plural*) will, desire, inclination, bent, abilities, aptitudes.

devilish, *adj.* satanic, diabolic, diabolical, demoniac, infernal, Mephistophelian, fiendish, hellish.
Ant. good, fine, upstanding, righteous, godly.

devise, *v.* order, arrange, plan, think out, contrive, invent, prepare, concoct, scheme, project, design.
Ant. disorder, disarrange.

devote, *v.* assign, apply, consign, give up, dedicate, consecrate.
Ant. resign, relinquish.

devotion, *n.* 1. dedication, consecration. 2. attachment, affection, love. 3. devotedness, zeal, ardor, eagerness, earnestness. 4. (*theology*) religion, religiousness, piety, faith, devoutness, sanctity, saintliness, godliness.

devout, *adj.* 1. pious, devoted, religious, worshipful, holy, saintly. 2. earnest, sincere, hearty, serious, honest.
Ant. atheistic, agnostic; insincere, scornful.

dexterous, *adj.* skillful, adroit, deft, handy, nimble, clever, expert, apt, ready, quick, able.
Ant. clumsy, awkward, maladroit, unapt.

dialect, *n.* 1. provincialism, idiom, localism, jargon, patois, variant. 2. branch, subfamily, subgroup. 3. language, tongue, speech.

diction, *n.* phraseology, wording, style, usage, grammar, language; distinctness, enunciation, pronunciation.

die, *v.* 1. decease, pass away *or* on, perish, expire, depart. 2. cease, end, vanish, disappear. 3. weaken, fail, subside, fade, sink, faint, decline, wither, decay. —*n.* 4. cube, block. 5. stamp.

difference, *n.* 1. discrepancy, disparity, dissimilarity, inconsistency, unlikeness, variation, diversity, imbalance, disagreement, inequality, dissimilitude, divergence, contrast,

contrariety. 2. discrimination, distinction.
Ant. similarity; agreement.

different, *adj.* 1. differing, unlike, diverse, divergent, altered, changed, contrary, contrasted, deviant, deviating, variant. 2. sundry, divers, miscellaneous, various, manifold.
Ant. similar, like; uniform, identical.

differentiate, *v.* 1. set off, distinguish, alter, change. 2. distinguish, discriminate, separate, contrast.
Ant. group together.

difficult, *adj.* 1. hard, arduous. 2. obscure, complex, intricate, perplexing. 3. austere, rigid, reserved, forbidding, unaccommodating. 4. fastidious, particular.
Ant. easy, simple; clear, plain; accommodating; careless, sloppy.

difficulty, *n.* 1. dilemma, predicament, quandary, fix, exigency, emergency. 2. trouble, problem. 3. reluctance, unwillingness, obstinacy, stubbornness. 4. demur, objection, obstacle.
Ant. ease; willingness.

diffident, *adj.* shy, self-conscious, self-effacing, bashful, abashed, embarrassed, timid, sheepish, modest.
Ant. forward, bold, unabashed.

digest, *v.* 1. understand, assimilate, study, ponder, consider, contemplate, ruminate over, reflect upon. 2. arrange, systematize, think over, classify, codify. —*n.* 3. summary, epitome, abstract, synopsis, abridgment, brief, conspectus.
Ant. expand.

digress, *v.* deviate, diverge, wander.

dilate, *v.* expand, spread out, enlarge, engross, widen, extend, swell, distend.
Ant. shrink, constrict.

dilemma, *n.* predicament, problem, question, quandary, difficulty, strait.

diligence, *n.* persistence, effort, application, industry, assiduity, perseverance, assiduousness.
Ant. carelessness, laziness.

diligent, *adj.* 1. industrious, assiduous, sedulous, occupied, busy, constant, attentive, persistent. 2. painstaking, persevering, indefatigable, untiring, tireless, unremitting, industrious.
Ant. lazy, careless; remiss.

dim, *adj.* 1. obscure, dark, shadowy, dusky, nebulous, hazy, cloud, faint, indistinct. 2. indistinct, unclear, ill-defined, blurred, vague, confused, indefinite. 3. dull, tarnished, blurred, slow, stupid, dense, foggy.

4. disparaging, adverse, uncomplimentary. —*v.* 5. darken, cloud, obscure, dull. 6. blur, dull, fade.
Ant. clear, bright, distinct; definite.

diminish, *v.* lessen, reduce, decrease, subside, ebb, dwindle, shrink, abate, contract, shrivel up.
Ant. increase.

diminutive, *adj.* little, small, tiny, dwarf, dwarflike, dwarfish, minute, microscopic, submicroscopic.
Ant. large, immense.

dip, *v.* 1. plunge, immerse, dive, duck. 2. sink, drop, incline, decline, slope downward.
Ant. rise.

diplomatic, *adj.* politic, tactful, artful.
Ant. tactless, rude, naive.

direct, *v.* 1. guide, advise, regulate, conduct, manage, control, dispose, lead, govern, rule. 2. order, command, instruct. 3. point, aim. —*adj.* 4. straight, undeviating. 5. immediate, personal, unbroken, simple, evident. 6. straightforward, downright, plain, categorical, unequivocal, unambiguous, express, open, sincere, outspoken, frank, earnest, ingenuous, obvious, naive.
Ant. divert, mislead; crooked; devious; ambiguous, sly.

dirty, *adj.* 1. soiled, foul, unclean, filthy, squalid, defiled, grimy. 2. dirtying, soiling, befouling, besmirching. 3. vile, mean, base, vulgar, low, groveling, scurvy, shabby, contemptible, despicable. 4. indecent, obscene, nasty, lascivious, lewd, lecherous, licentious, immoral, amoral. 5. contaminated, radioactive. 6. stormy, squally, rainy, foul, sloppy, disagreeable, nasty. 7. dark-colored, dingy, dull, dark, sullied, clouded.
Ant. clean; elevated, exalted; decent, moral; fair; clear.

disability, *n.* incapacity, disqualification, inability, incompetence, impotence, incapability.
Ant. ability, capacity, capability.

disable, *v.* 1. weaken, destroy, cripple, incapacitate, enfeeble, paralyze. 2. disqualify, incapacitate, eliminate.
Ant. strengthen; qualify; include.

disadvantage, *n.* 1. drawback, inconvenience, hindrance, deprivation. 2. detriment, hurt, harm, damage, injury, loss, disservice.
Ant. advantage.

disappear, *v.* vanish, fade, cease, pass away, end.
Ant. appear.

disappointment, *n.* 1. failure, defeat, frustration, unfulfillment. 2. mortifi-

cation, frustration, chagrin.
Ant. fulfillment, victory; consummation.

disaster, *n.* misfortune, calamity, mischance, mishap, accident, misadventure, blow, reverse, catastrophe, adversity, affliction.
Ant. luck, fortune.

disband, *v.* break up, disorganize, demobilize, dissolve, disperse, dismiss, scatter, separate.
Ant. organize, unite.

disburse, *v.* spend, pay, expend, lay out.
Ant. bank, save.

discern, *v.* 1. perceive, see, recognize, notice, apprehend, discover, descry, espy, come upon, behold. 2. discriminate, distinguish, differentiate, judge.

discharge, *v.* 1. unload, disburden, relieve, unburden. 2. remove, send forth, get rid of, expel, eject, emit. 3. fire, shoot, set off, detonate. 4. relieve, release, absolve, exonerate, clear, acquit, liberate, set free, free. 5. fulfill, perform, execute, observe. 6. dismiss, cashier, fire, remove, expel, send down, break. 7. pay, honor, disburse, make good on, liquidate, dissolve, settle. —*n.* 8. emission, ejection, expulsion, removal, evacuation, voiding. 9. detonation, firing, shooting. 10. fulfillment, execution, performance, observance.
Ant. load, burden.

disciple, *n.* follower, adherent, supporter; pupil, student, scholar.
Ant. leader; rebel.

discipline, *n.* 1. training, drill, exercise, instruction, practice. 2. punishment, chastisement, castigation, correction. 3. subjection, order, control, regulation, subjugation, government. 4. rules, regulations. —*v.* 5. train, exercise, drill, practice, instruct, teach, educate. 6. punish, correct, chastise, castigate.

disclose, *v.* 1. reveal, make known, divulge, show, tell, unveil, communicate. 2. uncover, lay open, expose, bring to light; muckrake.
Ant. conceal, hide; cover.

disconcert, *v.* disturb, confuse, perturb, ruffle, discompose, perplex, bewilder, frustrate, embarrass, abash; disarrange, disorder.
Ant. calm; order, arrange.

disconsolate, *adj.* inconsolable, unhappy, desolate, forlorn, heart-broken, sad, melancholy, dejected, gloomy, miserable, cheerless, sorrowful.
Ant. happy, cheerful, delighted.

discontent, *adj.* 1. discontented, dissatisfied. —*n.* 2. discontentment, dissatisfaction, uneasiness, inquietude, restlessness, displeasure.
Ant. contentment; satisfaction, pleasure, ease, restfulness.

discontinue, *v.* put an end to, interrupt, stop, cease, quit; desist.
Ant. continue, further.

discourage, *v.* 1. dishearten, dispirit, daunt, depress, deject, overawe, cow, awe, subdue, abash, embarrass, dismay, intimidate, frighten. 2. dissuade, deter, hinder, prevent, obstruct.
Ant. encourage, hearten, embolden.

discouragement. *n.* 1. depression, dejection, hopelessness, despair. 2. deterrent, damper, wet blanket, cold water, impediment, obstacle, obstruction.
Ant. encouragement.

discover, *v.* 1. learn of, ascertain, unearth, determine, ferret out, dig up; find out, detect, espy, descry, discern, see, notice. 2. originate, bring to light, invent.
Ant. conceal.

discreet, *adj.* wise, judicious, prudent, circumspect, cautious, careful, heedful, considerate, wary.
Ant. indiscreet, careless, imprudent; incautious, inconsiderate.

discrepancy, *n.* difference, inconsistency, incongruity, disagreement, discordance, contrariety, variance, variation.
Ant. similarity, congruity, consistency, concord, accord, agreement.

discriminate, *v.* 1. distinguish, set apart, differentiate. —*adj.* 2. critical, distinguishing, discriminative, discriminatory.
Ant. group, unite; indiscriminate, undistinguished.

discuss, *v.* examine, reason, deliberate, argue, debate, talk over, sift, consider.

disdain, *v.* 1. contemn, despise, scorn, spurn. —*n.* 2. contempt, scorn, contumely, contemptuousness, haughtiness, arrogance, superciliousness, hauteur.
Ant. accept, like, love; love, admiration, regard.

disdainful, *adj.* contemptuous, scornful, haughty, arrogant, supercilious, contumelious.
Ant. friendly, amiable, considerate, attentive.

disease, *n.* morbidity, illness, sickness, ailment, complaint, affection, disorder, malady, abnormality, de-

rangement, distemper, indisposition, infirmity.
Ant. health, salubriety.

disfigure, *v.* mar, deface, injure, deform, spoil, ruin, blemish.
Ant. beautify.

disgrace, *n.* 1. ignominy, shame, dishonor, infamy, disfavor, disapproval, disapprobation, disparagement, stain, taint, notoriety, baseness. 2. odium, obloquy, degradation, opprobrium, scandal. —*v.* 3. shame, dishonor, defame, disfavor, humiliate, disapprove, discredit, degrade, debase, stain, sully, taint, tarnish, reproach.

disgust, *v.* 1. sicken, nauseate, turn one's stomach. 2. offend, displease, repel, repulse, revolt, abhor, detest. —*n.* 3. distaste, nausea, loathing, hatred, abhorrence, disrelish. 4. dislike, detestation, repugnance, aversion, dissatisfaction, antipathy.
Ant. please, delight, attract; relish, liking, love; satisfaction.

disgusting, *adj.* offensive, offending, loathsome, sickening, nauseous, nauseating, repulsive, revolting, odious, hateful, repugnant, foul, abominable, abhorrent, distasteful, detestable.
Ant. delightful, delectable, attractive, beautiful.

dishonest, *adj.* unscrupulous, conniving, corrupt, knavish, thievish, deceitful, treacherous, perfidious; false, fraudulent, counterfeit.
Ant. honest.

dishonorable, *adj.* 1. ignoble, base, disgraceful, shameful, shameless, false, fraudulent. 2. infamous, notorious, unscrupulous, unprincipled, disreputable, disgraceful, scandalous, ignominious, discreditable.
Ant. honorable.

disintegrate, *v.* reduce to particles *or* fragments, break up, decay, rot, fall apart, separate.
Ant. integrate.

disinterested, *adj.* unbiased, unprejudiced, unselfish, impartial, fair, generous, liberal.
Ant. biased, prejudiced, illiberal, bigoted, selfish, partial.

dislike, *v.* 1. have an aversion *or* be averse to, be disinclined *or* reluctant. —*n.* 2. disrelish, disgust, distaste, repugnance, antipathy, loathing, aversion, antagonism.
Ant. like; relish, delight, delectation.

disloyal, *adj.* unfaithful, false, perfidious, treacherous, traitorous, trea-

sonable, subversive, disaffected, untrue, unpatriotic.
Ant. loyal, faithful, true, honest.

disloyalty, *n.* unfaithfulness, perfidy, treachery, treason, betrayal, disaffection, faithlessness, subversion.
Ant. loyalty, fealty, allegiance.

dismay, *v.* 1. discourage, dishearten, daunt, appall, terrify, horrify, frighten, scare, intimidate, disconcert, put out, alarm, paralyze. —*n.* 2. consternation, terror, horror, panic, fear, alarm.
Ant. encourage, hearten, embolden; security, confidence.

dismiss, *v.* release, let go, discharge, discard, reject, set *or* put aside; fire.
Ant. hire, employ.

disobedient, *adj.* insubordinate, contumacious, defiant, refractory, unruly, rebellious, obstinate, stubborn, unsubmissive, uncompliant.
Ant. obedient.

disobey, *v.* transgress, violate, disregard, defy, infringe.
Ant. obey.

disorder, *n.* 1. disorderliness, disarray, jumble, mess, litter, clutter, disarrangement, confusion, irregularity, disorganization, derangement. 2. disturbance, tumult, brawl, uproar, fight, unrest, quarrel, bustle, clamor, riot, turbulence. 3. ailment, malady, derangement, illness, complaint, sickness, disease, indisposition. —*v.* 4. disarrange, disarray, mess up, disorganize, unsettle, disturb, derange, discompose, upset, confuse, confound.
Ant. order.

disparity, *n.* dissimilarity, inequality, difference, distinction, dissimilitude.
Ant. similarity, equality, similitude.

dispense, *v.* deal, distribute, apportion, allot, dole.

disperse, *v.* 1. scatter, dissipate, separate. 2. spread, diffuse, disseminate, broadcast, sow, scatter. 3. dispel. 4. vanish, disappear, evanesce.
Ant. unite, combine; appear.

displace, *v.* 1. misplace, move, dislocate. 2. replace, remove, depose, oust, dismiss, cashier.

display, *v.* 1. show, exhibit, demonstrate, make visible, evince, manifest. 2. reveal, uncover, betray. 3. unfold, open out, spread out. 4. show, flourish, flaunt, parade, show off. —*n.* 5. show, exhibition, manifestation. 6. parade, ostentation, flourish, flaunting.
Ant. conceal, hide; cover.

displeasure, *n.* dissatisfaction, annoyance, disapprobation, disapproval, distaste, dislike; anger, ire, wrath, indignation, vexation; offense.
Ant. pleasure, satisfaction, approval, delight; calm, peace.

disposition, *n.* 1. temper, temperament, nature, character, humor. 2. inclination, willingness, bent, tendency, proneness, bias, predisposition, proclivity. 3. arrangement, order, grouping, location, placement. 4. settlement, outcome, finale, result, dispensation. 5. regulation, appointment, management, control, direction. 6. bestowal, endowment.
Ant. indisposition, unwillingness.

dispute, *v.* 1. argue, discuss, debate, agitate. 2. wrangle, contest, quarrel, bicker, spat, squabble, spar, brawl. 3. oppose, controvert, contradict, deny, impugn. —*n.* 4. argumentation, argument, contention, debate, controversy, disputation, altercation, quarrel, wrangle, bickering, spat, squabble, tiff.
Ant. agree, concur; agreement, concurrence.

disregard, *v.* 1. ignore, neglect, overlook, disobey, pay no attention *or* heed *or* regard to, take no notice of. 2. slight, insult. —*n.* 3. neglect, inattention, inattentiveness, oversight. 4. disrespect, slight, indifference.
Ant. regard, view, notice, note; attention; respect.

disrespectful, *adj.* discourteous, impolite, rude, crude, uncivil, impudent, impertinent, irreverent.
Ant. respectful, courteous, polite, civil, reverent.

dissatisfaction, *n.* discontent, displeasure, dislike, disappointment, disapproval, disapprobation, uneasiness.
Ant. satisfaction, approval, approbation.

dissent, *v.* 1. differ, disagree. —*n.* 2. difference, dissidence, disagreement, dissatisfaction, opposition, nonconformity, separation.
Ant. agree, concur; agreement, concurrence, satisfaction, unity.

dissipate, *v.* 1. scatter, disperse, dispel, disintegrate. 2. waste, squander. 3. scatter, disappear, vanish, disintegrate. 4. debauch.
Ant. integrate, unite; appear; join.

dissolve, *v.* 1. melt, liquefy. 2. sever, loose, loosen, free, disunite, break up; dismiss, disperse, adjourn. 3. destroy, dispel, ruin, disintegrate,

break down, terminate, end; perish, crumble, die, expire.
Ant. solidify; unite; meet; integrate; originate.

distaste, *n.* dislike, disinclination, aversion, repugnance, disgust, displeasure, dissatisfaction; disrelish.
Ant. taste, delectation, liking, love, satisfaction; relish.

distasteful, *adj.* 1. disagreeable, displeasing, offensive, repugnant, repulsive, unpleasant. 2. unpalatable, unsavory, nauseating, loathsome, disgusting, sickening.
Ant. tasteful, agreeable, pleasant, inoffensive; attractive, delightful.

distend, *v.* expand, swell, stretch, dilate, bloat, enlarge.
Ant. contract, shrink, reduce.

distinct, *adj.* 1. distinguished, distinguishable, different, individual, separate, dividual, various, varied; dissimilar. 2. definite, well-defined, clear, plain, unmistakable, unconfused.
Ant. indistinct, blurred, same; similar; indefinite, unclear, confused.

distinction, *n.* 1. difference, differentiation, discrimination. 2. honor, repute, name, fame, celebrity, renown, importance, note, account, eminence, superiority.
Ant. indifference; similarity; disrepute, dishonor.

distinguish, *v.* 1. mark, characterize. 2. discriminate, differentiate, separate, divide, classify, categorize. 3. discern, recognize, perceive, know, tell. 4. make prominent *or* conspicuous *or* eminent.

distinguished, *adj.* 1. conspicuous, marked, extraordinary. 2. noted, eminent, famed, famous, celebrated, renowned, illustrious. 3. distingué, refined.
Ant. undistinguished, common; infamous; unknown; unrefined, coarse.

distress, *n.* 1. pain, anxiety, sorrow, grief, agony, anguish, misery, adversity, hardship, trial, tribulation, suffering, trouble, affliction. 2. need, necessity, want, privation, deprivation, destitution, poverty, indigence. —*v.* 3. trouble, worry, afflict, bother, grieve, pain, make miserable *or* unhappy.
Ant. comfort; fulfillment, opulence; console, mitigate, delight.

distribute, *v.* 1. deal out, deal, allot, apportion, assign, mete, dole, dispense, give. 2. disperse, spread, scatter. 3. divide, separate, classify, categorize, dispose, sort, arrange.
Ant. collect, keep; unite.

distrust, *v.* 1. doubt, suspect, mistrust. —*n.* 2. doubt, suspicion, mistrust, misgiving.
Ant. trust, depend.

disturbance, *n.* 1. perturbation, agitation, commotion, disorder, confusion, derangement. 2. disorder, tumult, riot, uproar.
Ant. order, organization; calm, serenity.

diverge, *v.* 1. branch off, separate, fork, bifurcate, divide. 2. differ, deviate, disagree, vary.
Ant. converge, unite; agree, concur.

diverse, *adj.* 1. unlike, dissimilar, separate, different, disagreeing. 2. various, varied, multiform, manifold, variant, divergent.
Ant. similar, like.

divert, *v.* 1. turn aside, deflect. 2. draw aside *or* away, turn aside, distract. 3. distract, entertain, amuse, delight, gratify, exhilarate.
Ant. fix; weary, bore, tire.

divest, *v.* 1. strip, unclothe, denude, disrobe, undress. 2. strip, dispossess, deprive.
Ant. invest.

divide, *v.* 1. separate, sunder, cut off, sever, shear, cleave, part. 2. apportion, share, deal out, partition, distribute, portion. 3. alienate, disunite, cause to disagree, estrange. 4. distinguish, classify, sort, arrange, distribute.
Ant. unite; keep, retain; disarrange.

division, *n.* 1. partition, dividing, separation, apportionment, allotment, distribution, sharing. 2. mark, boundary, partition, demarcation. 3. section, part, compartment, partition, segment. 4. disagreement, dissension, difference, variance, rupture, disunion, discord, breach, rift, estrangement, alienation, feud.
Ant. agreement, union, accord.

divulge, *v.* disclose, reveal, make known, impart, tell, broadcast.
Ant. conceal.

do, *v.* 1. perform, act. 2. execute, finish, carry out, conclude, end, terminate, complete. 3. accomplish, finish, achieve, attain, effect, bring about, execute, carry out. 4. exert, put forth. 5. cover, traverse. 6. serve, suffice for. 7. behave, proceed, act, fare, manage.

doctrine, *n.* tenet, dogma, theory, precept, belief, principle; teachings.

dodge, *v.* equivocate, quibble, evade, be evasive, elude.

dominant, *adj.* 1. ruling, governing, controlling, most influential, pre-vailing, prevalent, common, principal, predominant, paramount, preeminent, outstanding, important, first, ascendant. 2. commanding, advantageous.
Ant. secondary, disadvantageous.

donation, *n.* gift, contribution, offering, grant, benefaction, boon, largess, present, gratuity.

doom, *n.* 1. fate, destiny, lot, fortune. 2. ruin, death. 3. judgment, decision, sentence, condemnation. —*v.* 4. destine, predestine, foreordain, decree. 5. condemn, sentence, ordain.

dormant, *adj.* 1. asleep, inactive, torpid, quiescent. 2. quiescent, inoperative, in abeyance, latent, potential, inert, suspended.
Ant. awake, active; operative; kinetic.

doubt, *v.* 1. distrust, mistrust, suspect, question. 2. hesitate, waver. —*n.* 3. undecidedness, indecision, uncertainty, faltering, irresolution, hesitation, hesitancy, vacillation, misgiving, suspense; mistrust, distrust, suspicion.
Ant. trust; decision, certainty, conviction.

doubtful, *adj.* 1. uncertain, unsure, ambiguous, equivocal, indeterminate, undecided, fifty-fifty. 2. undetermined, unsettled, indecisive, dubious, enigmatic, problematic, puzzled. 3. hesitating, hesitant, wavering, irresolute, vacillating, dubious, skeptical, incredulous.
Ant. certain, sure, unambiguous, decided; settled; unhesitating, resolute.

dowdy, *adj.* ill-dressed, frumpy, shabby, old-maidish, old-fashioned.
Ant. fashionable, chic, modish, à la mode.

downhearted, *adj.* dejected, discouraged, depressed, downcast, despondent, disheartened, sad, sorrowful, unhappy, dispirited, crestfallen.
Ant. happy.

drag, *v.* 1. draw, pull, haul, trail, tug. 2. trail, linger, loiter, slow.
Ant. drive, push; speed, expedite.

draw, *v.* 1. drag, haul, pull, tug, tow, lead. 2. attract, magnetize. 3. delineate, sketch, draught, depict, trace. 4. frame, formulate, compose, write, draw up, prepare, form. 5. suck, inhale, drain. 6. get, derive, deduce, infer, understand. 7. produce, bring in, bear. 8. draw *or* pull out, attenu-ate; extend, stretch, lengthen. 9. extract.
Ant. drive, push.

dread, *v.* 1. fear. —*n.* 2. terror, fear, apprehension. 3. awe, reverence, veneration. —*adj.* 4. frightful, dire, terrible, dreadful, horrible.
Ant. intrepidity, bravery; pleasant, delightful.

dreary, *adj.* 1. gloomy, dismal, drear, cheerless, chilling, chill, depressing, comfortless. 2. monotonous, tedious, wearisome, dull, boring, uninteresting, tiresome.
Ant. cheerful, comforting; interesting, engaging.

drench, *v.* steep, wet, soak, ret, saturate.
Ant. dry.

dress, *n.* 1. costume, frock, gown. 2. clothing, raiment, garb, attire, apparel, vesture, garments, vestments, clothes, suit, habit, habiliment. 3. regalia, array, panoply. —*v.* 4. attire, robe, garb, clothe, array, accouter, apparel, rig, deck out. 5. trim, ornament, adorn, decorate. 6. straighten, align. 7. prepare, fit.
Ant. undress.

drink, *v.* 1. imbibe, sip, quaff, swallow. 2. tipple, tope. —*n.* 3. beverage, potion, liquid refreshment, draft.

drive, *v.* 1. push, force, impel, propel, send. 2. overwork, overtask, overburden, overtax. 3. urge, constrain, impel, compel, force. 4. go, travel, ride. —*n.* 5. vigor, pressure, effort, energy.
Ant. curb, restrain.

droll, *adj.* 1. queer, odd, diverting, amusing, comical, waggish, witty, funny. —*n.* 2. wag, buffoon, jester, comedian, clown, zany, punch, merry-andrew. 3. joke, jest, clown.
Ant. common; serious.

droop, *v.* sink, bend, hang down, flag, languish, fail, weaken, decline, faint, wilt, wither, fade.
Ant. rise.

drove, *n.* herd, flock, company, crowd, host, collection.

drudgery, *n.* work, labor.

drunkard, *n.* toper, sot, tippler, drinker, inebriate, dipsomaniac, alcoholic.
Ant. teetotaler, dry.

drunken, *adj.* drunk, sotted, besotted, tipsy, inebriated, intoxicated, befuddled.
Ant. sober.

dry, *adj.* 1. arid, parched. 2. wiped *or* drained away, evaporated. 3. thirsty.

4. plain, bald, unadorned, unembellished. 5. dull, uninteresting, dreary,
tiresome, boring, tedious, jejune,
barren, vapid. 6. humorous, sarcastic, biting, sardonic, keen, sharp,
pointed, sly.
Ant. wet, drenched; interesting, fascinating; dull.

dubious, *adj.* 1. doubtful, undecided,
indeterminate, uncertain, dubitable, fluctuating, wavering. 2. questionable, equivocal, ambiguous, obscure, unclear.
Ant. definite, incisive, certain; unquestionable, unequivocal, clear.

dull, *adj.* 1. slow, obtuse, stupid,
blunted, unimaginative, sluggish,
unintelligent, stolid. 2. insensible,
unfeeling, insensate, apathetic,
unimpassioned, lifeless, callous,
dead. 3. listless, spiritless, torpid,
inactive, lifeless, inert, inanimate. 4.
boring, depressing, ennuyant, tedious, uninteresting, tiresome, drear,
dreary, vapid, wearisome, dry,
jejune. 5. blunt, dulled. —*v.* 6.
blunt, deaden, stupefy, paralyze, obtund, benumb. 7. depress, dis-

hearten, discourage, dispirit, sadden, deject.
Ant. bright, imaginative, quick; sensitive; spirited, active, animated; interesting; sharp, clever; encourage,
inspirit, hearten.

dumb, *adj.* 1. mute, speechless, silent,
voiceless. 2. stupid.
Ant. voluble, talkative, loquacious.

duplicate, *adj.* 1. double, twofold.
—*n.* 2. facsimile copy, replica, reproduction, transcript. —*v.* 3. copy, replicate, reproduce, repeat, double,
imitate.
Ant. original.

duplicity, *n.* deceitfulness, deceit,
double-dealing, deception, guile, hypocrisy, dissimulation, chicanery, artifice, fraud, dishonesty, perfidy,
treachery.
Ant. naiveté, honesty, openness, simplicity.

durable, *adj.* lasting, enduring, stable, constant, permanent.
Ant. unstable, temporary, temporal.

dusky, *adj.* 1. swarthy, dark. 2. dim,
shadowy, murky, cloudy, shady, obscure, clouded, penumbral.

Ant. fair, blond, light; clear, unclouded.

dutiful, *adj.* respectful, docile, submissive, deferential, reverential, obedient.
Ant. disrespectful, disobedient, irreverent.

duty, *n.* 1. obligation. 2. office, function, responsibility, service, business.
3. homage, respect, deference, reverence. 4. levy, tax, impost, custom,
toll, excise.

dwarf, *n.* 1. homunculus, manikin,
pygmy, midget, Lilliputian. 2. runt.
—*adj.* 3. diminutive, tiny, small, little, Lilliputian, stunted, dwarfed, undersized. —*v.* 4. stunt.
Ant. giant, colossus; huge, gigantic,
immense, colossal.

dwell, *v.* 1. abide, reside, stay, live, inhabit. 2. continue, perpetuate. 3. linger, emphasize.
Ant. leave, depart; cease, end, terminate, stop.

dwindle, *v.* diminish, lessen, decline,
decrease, wane, shrink, waste away,
degenerate, sink, decay.
Ant. increase, grow, wax.

E

earn, *v.* 1. gain, acquire, win, get, obtain, secure, procure. 2. merit, deserve.

earnest, *adj.* 1. sincere, zealous, ardent, eager, fervent, resolute, serious, fervid, determined, purposeful.
2. deep, firm, stable, intent, steady,
faithful, true.
Ant. insincere, apathetic; faithless,
unfaithful, wavering.

earth, *n.* 1. globe, world. 2. ground,
soil, turf, sod, dirt, terra firma.
Ant. heaven; sky.

earthly, *adj.* 1. terrestrial, worldly,
mundane, earthy. 2. possible, conceivable, imaginable.
Ant. spiritual; impossible, inconceivable.

ease, *n.* 1. comfort, relaxation, rest,
repose, well-being, effortlessness,
contentment, happiness. 2. tranquillity, serenity, calmness, quiet, quietude, peace. 3. informality, unaffect-
edness, naturalness, lightness,
flexibility, freedom. —*v.* 4. comfort,
relieve, disburden. 5. tranquilize,
soothe, allay, alleviate, mitigate,
abate, assuage, lighten, lessen, reduce. 6. facilitate.

Ant. discomfort, effort; disturbance,
perturbation; affectation; burden;
increase.

easy, *adj.* 1. facile, light, gentle, moderate. 2. tranquil, untroubled, comfortable, contented, satisfied, quiet,
at rest. 3. easygoing, compliant, submissive, complying, accommodating, agreeable, yelding. 4. lenient. 5.
informal, unrestrained, unconstrained, brash, unembarrassed,
smooth.
Ant. difficult, hard, immoderate;
troubled, disturbed, uncomfortable,
disagreeable, unyielding; restrained,
embarrassed.

ebb, *n.* 1. reflux, regression, regress,
retrogression. 2. decline, decay,
deterioration, degeneration, wane.
—*v.* 3. subside, abate, recede, retire.
4. decline, sink, wane, decrease,
decay, waste *or* fade away.
Ant. flow, neap; wax; increase, swell,
well; rise.

economical, *adj.* saving, provident,
sparing, thrifty, frugal; stingy, tight,
penurious.
Ant. lavish, spendthrift.

economy, *n.* 1. frugality, thriftiness,
thrift, saving. 2. management, system, method.
Ant. lavishness.

edge, *n.* 1. border, rim, lip, margin,
boundary, verge, brink. —*v.* 2. inch,
sidle.
Ant. center.

educate, *v.* teach, instruct, school,
drill, indoctrinate, train, discipline.

education, *n.* 1. instruction, schooling, tuition, training. 2. learning,
knowledge, enlightenment, culture.
Ant. illiteracy.

eerie, *adj.* fearful, awesome, weird,
uncanny, strange.
Ant. common, ordinary.

effect, *n.* 1. result, consequence, end,
outcome, issue. 2. power, efficacy,
force, validity, weight. 3. operation,
execution; accomplishment, fulfillment. 4. purport, intent, tenor, significance, signification, meaning,
import. —*v.* 5. bring about, accomplish, make happen, achieve, do,
perform, complete, consummate,
bring about, realize.
Ant. cause.

effective, *adj.* 1. capable, competent, efficient, efficacious, effectual. 2. operative, in force, active.
Ant. ineffective, incompetent, inefficient, ineffectual; inactive, inoperative.

effectual, *adj.* effective.
Ant. ineffectual.

efficacious, *adj.* effective.
Ant. ineffective.

efficient, *adj.* effective.
Ant. inefficient, ineffective.

effort, *n.* application, endeavor, exertion, nisus, attempt, struggle, striving.
Ant. ease.

egoism, *n.* self-love, egotism, selfishness, self-conceit.
Ant. altruism.

egotism, *n.* self-centeredness, egoism, boastfulness, conceit.
Ant. altruism, modesty.

elaborate, *adj.* 1. perfected, painstaking, labored, studied; detailed, ornate, intricate, complicated, complex. —*v.* 2. produce, develop, work out, refine, improve.
Ant. simple; simplify.

elect, *v.* 1. select, choose, prefer, pick out. —*adj.* 2. select, chosen, choice.
Ant. refuse, reject; spurned.

elegant, *adj.* tasteful, fine, luxurious; refined, polished, cultivated, genteel, courtly, graceful; choice, nice, superior; excellent.
Ant. inelegant, distasteful; unrefined, disgraceful; inferior.

element, *n.* 1. component, constituent, ingredient, unit, part, essential. 2. rudiments, principle, basis, basics. 3. habitat, environment, medium, milieu.
Ant. whole, nonessential; compound.

elementary, *adj.* primary, rudimentary, basic, fundamental, rudimental; uncompounded, simple, uncomplicated.
Ant. advanced, secondary; complex, complicated.

elevate, *v.* raise, lift up, exalt, heighten, increase, intensify, promote, advance, improve, enhance, dignify, refine; animate, cheer.
Ant. lower, debase, decrease; depress.

elevation, *n.* 1. eminence, height, hill; altitude. 2. loftiness, grandeur, dignity, nobility, nobleness, refinement, exaltation.
Ant. valley; depths.

eliminate, *v.* get rid of, expel, remove, exclude, reject, omit, ignore.
Ant. include, accept.

elocution, *n.* oratory, declamation, rhetoric.

elucidate, *v.* explain, explicate, clarify, make plain *or* clear.
Ant. becloud, bedim, confuse.

elude, *v.* 1. avoid, escape, evade, slip away from, shun, dodge. 2. baffle, confound, foil, thwart, confuse, frustrate, disconcert.
Ant. pursue, follow.

emanate, *v.* emerge, issue, proceed, come forth, originate, arise, spring, flow.

embarrass, *v.* 1. disconcert, abash, make uncomfortable, confuse, discomfit, discompose, chagrin. 2. complicate, make difficult, perplex, mystify. 3. impede, hamper, hinder, annoy, vex, trouble, harass, distress.
Ant. comfort, console; simplify.

embarrassment, *n.* 1. disconcertment, abashment, perplexity, confusion, discomposure, discomfort, mortification, chagrin. 2. trouble, annoyance, vexation, distress, harassment, hindrance, deterrent.
Ant. comfort, composure; encouragement.

embellish, *v.* 1. beautify, ornament, adorn, decorate, garnish, bedeck, embroider. 2. enhance, embroider, exaggerate about.
Ant. mar, disfigure, deface.

emblem, *n.* token, sign, symbol, figure, image, badge, device, mark.

embrace, *v.* 1. clasp, hug. 2. accept, adopt, espouse, welcome, seize. 3. encircle, surround, enclose, contain. 4. include, contain, comprise, comprehend, cover, embody.
Ant. exclude.

emerge, *v.* come forth, emanate, issue, spread, stream.
Ant. enter.

emergency, *n.* crisis, straits, urgency, turning-point, exigency, necessity, extremity, pinch, dilemma, quandary.

eminence, *n.* 1. repute, distinction, prominence, celebrity, renown, conspicuousness, note, fame, rank, position. 2. elevation, hill, prominence.
Ant. disrepute.

eminent, *adj.* 1. distinguished, signal, notable, noteworthy, noted, reputable, prominent, celebrated, renowned, outstanding, illustrious, conspicuous, exalted. 2. lofty, high, prominent, projecting, protruding, protuberant.
Ant. disreputable, commonplace, ordinary; low, debased; inconspicuous.

emit, *v.* 1. send *or* give forth, discharge, eject, vent, exhale, exude, expel. 2. issue, circulate, publish.
Ant. inspire, inhale, accept; hide.

emotion, *n.* feeling; sympathy, empathy.
Ant. apathy.

emphatic, *adj.* significant, marked, striking, positive, energetic, forcible, forceful, pronounced, strong, decided, unequivocal, definite.
Ant. insignificant, uncertain, unsure.

empire, *n.* 1. power, sovereignty, dominion, rule, supremacy, authority. 2. command, sway, rule, government, control.

employ, *v.* 1. use, engage, hire, retain, occupy. 2. use, apply, make use of. —*n.* 3. service, employment.

employee, *n.* worker, servant, agent, clerk, wage earner.
Ant. employer, boss.

empower, *v.* 1. authorize, warrant, commission, license, qualify, deputize. 2. enable, permit.

empty, *adj.* 1. void, vacant, blank, unoccupied, uninhabited. 2. unsatisfactory, meaningless, superficial, hollow, delusive, vain, ineffectual, ineffective, unsatisfying. 3. frivolous, foolish. —*v.* 4. unload, unburden, pour out, evacuate, drain, discharge.
Ant. full, replete, occupied, inhabited; satisfactory, effectual; serious.

emulation, *n.* competition, rivalry, contention, strife, envy.

enamor, *v.* inflame, captivate, bewitch, charm, fascinate, enchant.

enchant, *v.* fascinate, captivate, charm, enrapture, transport, bewitch, delight.
Ant. bore.

encircle, *v.* surround, encompass, environ, gird, enfold, enclose.

enclose, *v.* surround, encircle, encompass, circumscribe.
Ant. exclude.

encounter, *v.* 1. meet, confront, face. 2. contend against, engage with, attack, cope with, compete with. —*n.* 3. meeting. 4. battle, combat, conflict.

encourage, *v.* 1. inspirit, embolden, hearten, stimulate, incite; reassure, assure, console, comfort. 2. urge, abet, second, support, favor, countenance, advance, foster, promote, aid, help, foment.
Ant. discourage, dispirit.

encroach, *v.* trespass, intrude, invade, infringe.

encumber, *v.* 1. impede, hamper, retard, embarrass, obstruct, complicate, involve, entangle. 2. load, oppress, overload, burden. *Ant.* disencumber; unload, unburden.

end, *n.* 1. extremity, extreme. 2. limit, bound, boundary, termination, tip, terminus. 3. close, termination, conclusion, finish, outcome, issue, consequence, result, completion, attainment. 4. finale, conclusion, peroration. 5. purpose, aim, object, objective, intention, design, intent, drift. —*v.* 6. terminate, conclude, wind up, finish, complete, close. 7. stop, cease, discontinue, conclude. *Ant.* beginning, start; begin, commence, open; continue.

endeavor, *v.* 1. attempt, essay, try, make an effort, strive, struggle, labor; seek, aim. —*n.* 2. exertion, struggle, essay, attempt, trial.

endless, *adj.* limitless, unlimited, vast, illimitable, immeasurable, unending, boundless, infinite, interminable, incessant, unceasing, eternal, continuous, perpetual, everlasting. *Ant.* limited, finite.

endow, *v.* equip, invest, clothe, endue, enrich; confer, bestow, give. *Ant.* divest.

endowment, *n.* gift, grant, bequest, largess, bounty, present; capacity, talent, faculties, quality, power, ability, aptitude, capability, genius. *Ant.* incapacity.

endure, *v.* 1. sustain, hold out against, undergo, bear, support, suffer, experience. 2. experience, stand, tolerate, bear, brook, allow, permit, submit. 3. continue, last, persist, remain. *Ant.* fail, subside; refuse; die, perish, fail.

enemy, *n.* foe, adversary, opponent, antagonist. *Ant.* friend, ally.

energetic, *adj.* 1. forcible, vigorous, active. 2. powerful, effective, effectual, strong, efficacious, potent. *Ant.* lazy, inactive; ineffective, impotent, weak.

energy, *n.* 1. activity, exertion, power, force, operation, dynamism, vigor, potency, zeal, push, spirit, animation, life. 2. force, power, might, efficacy, strength, intensity. *Ant.* inertia, inactivity; weakness.

engender, *v.* 1. produce, cause, give rise to, beget, create, occasion, excite, stir up, incite, generate, breed. 2. procreate, beget, create, generate, breed. *Ant.* terminate; kill.

enigma, *n.* puzzle, riddle, problem, question.

enjoin, *v.* 1. charge, order, direct, prescribe, bid, command, require. 2. prohibit, proscribe, interdict, ban, preclude. *Ant.* encourage, allow.

enjoyment, *n.* delight, delectation, pleasure, gratification, happiness. *Ant.* detestation, abhorrence, displeasure.

enlarge, *v.* extend, augment, amplify, dilate, increase, aggrandize, magnify, expand, greaten. *Ant.* limit, decrease, lessen, abate.

enlighten, *v.* illumine, edify, teach, inform, instruct, educate. *Ant.* confuse.

enliven, *v.* 1. invigorate, animate, inspirit, vivify, stimulate, quicken. 2. exhilarate, gladden, cheer, brighten, inspire, delight. *Ant.* dispirit, slow; depress.

enormous, *adj.* 1. huge, immense, vast, colossal, mammoth, gigantic, prodigious, elephantine, monstrous. 2. outrageous, atrocious, flagitious, depraved, wicked, flagrant, scandalous, egregious. *Ant.* small, diminutive, tiny; honorable.

enrage, *v.* infuriate, anger, incense, inflame, provoke, madden, exasperate, aggravate. *Ant.* tranquilize, calm, assuage.

ensue, *v.* follow, succeed; issue, arise, result, flow. *Ant.* lead; precede.

entangle, *v.* 1. complicate, ensnare, enmesh, tangle, knot, mat. 2. embarrass, confuse, perplex, bewilder, involve, ensnare. *Ant.* simplify.

enterprise, *n.* 1. project, plan, undertaking, venture. 2. boldness, readiness, spirit, energy.

enterprising, *adj.* ambitious, ready, resourceful, adventurous, venturesome, dashing, bold, energetic, spirited, eager, zealous. *Ant.* smug, phlegmatic.

entertain, *v.* 1. divert, amuse, please. 2. receive, consider, admit. 3. harbor, cherish, hold. *Ant.* bore; refuse, reject; expel.

enthusiasm, *n.* eagerness, earnestness, sincerity, interest, warmth, fervor, zeal, ardor, passion, devotion. *Ant.* coolness.

enthusiast, *n.* 1. zealot, devotee, fan. 2. zealot, bigot, fanatic.

enthusiastic, *adj.* ardent, zealous, eager, fervent, passionate, vehe-

ment, fervid, burning, impassioned. *Ant.* blasé, dispassionate, cool, unenthusiastic.

entice, *v.* allure, inveigle, excite, lure, attract, decoy, tempt, seduce, coax, cajole, wheedle, persuade. *Ant.* discourage, deter, dissuade.

entire, *adj.* 1. whole, complete, unbroken, perfect, unimpaired, intact, undiminished, undivided, continuous. 2. full, complete, thorough, unqualified, unrestricted, unmitigated. —*n.* 3. entirety. *Ant.* partial, imperfect, divided; restricted, incomplete.

entitle, *v.* 1. empower, qualify. 2. name, designate, call, title, dub. *Ant.* disqualify.

entrance, *n.* 1. entry, ingress, access, entree. 2. entry, door, portal, gate, doorway, stoa, passage, inlet. 3. admission, entry, admittance. —*v.* 4. enrapture, enchant, charm, delight, transport. *Ant.* exit; disenchant.

entreat, *v.* appeal, implore, beg, beseech, obsecrate, obtest, supplicate, crave, solicit, pray, importune, petition, sue.

entreaty, *n.* supplication, appeal, suit, plea, solicitation, petition.

enumerate, *v.* count, name, recount, recapitulate, rehearse, cite.

envelop, *v.* 1. wrap, cover, enfold, hide, conceal. 2. surround, enclose, encompass, cover, enfold.

envy, *n.* 1. jealousy, enviousness, grudge, covetousness. —*v.* 2. covet, begrudge, resent. *Ant.* generosity.

ephemeral, *adj.* 1. short-lived, transitory, temporary, fleeting, momentary, brief, evanescent. —*n.* 2. will o' the wisp, St. Elmo's fire, corposant, ephemeron. *Ant.* concrete, permanent.

epicure, *n.* gastronome, gourmet, epicurean, voluptuary, sensualist, glutton, gourmand.

episode, *n.* occurrence, event, incident, happening.

epoch, *n.* age, era, period, date.

equable, *adj.* even, uniform, tranquil, steady, regular, even-tempered, temperate. *Ant.* uneven, irregular, turbulent, intemperate.

equal, *adj.* 1. proportionate, commensurate, balanced, coordinate, correspondent, equivalent, tantamount, like, alike. 2. uniform, even, regular, unvarying, invariant. 3. adequate, sufficient, competent,

suitable, fit. —*n*. 4. peer, compeer, match, mate, fellow. —*v*. 5. match, be commensurate with.
Ant. unequal, disproportionate, incommensurate, dissimilar; uneven, irregular, variable; inadequate, insufficient, unsuitable.

equip, *v*. furnish, provide, fit out, outfit, rig, array, accouter.

equipment, *n*. apparatus, paraphernalia, gear, accouterment.

equivocal, *adj*. 1. ambiguous, uncertain. 2. doubtful, uncertain, questionable, dubious, indeterminate.
Ant. unequivocal, certain; definite, unquestionable.

eradicate, *v*. remove, destroy, extirpate, abolish, obliterate, uproot, exterminate, annihilate.
Ant. insert, add; originate, create.

erase, *v*. efface, expunge, cancel, obliterate.
Ant. create.

erect, *adj*. 1. upright, standing, vertical. —*v*. 2. build, raise, construct, upraise. 3. set up, found, establish, institute.
Ant. horizontal; raze, destroy; dissolve, liquidate.

erroneous, *adj*. mistaken, incorrect, inaccurate, false, wrong, untrue.
Ant. correct, accurate, true.

error, *n*. 1. mistake, blunder, slip, oversight. 2. offense, wrongdoing, fault, sin, transgression, trespass, misdeed, iniquity.

escape, *v*. 1. flee, abscond, decamp, fly, steal away, run away. 2. shun, fly, elude, evade, avoid. —*n*. 3. flight; release.

escort, *n*. 1. convoy, guard, guide, protection, safeguard, guidance. —*v*. 2. conduct, usher, guard, guide, convoy, accompany, attend.

especially, *adv*. particularly, chiefly, principally, unusually, significantly, prominently, signally, specially, markedly.

espy, *v*. catch sight of, descry, discover, perceive, make out.
Ant. overlook.

essential, *adj*. 1. indispensable, necessary, vital, fundamental, rudimentary, elementary, basic, inherent, intrinsic, important. —*n*. 2. necessity, basic, element.
Ant. dispensable, unnecessary, unimportant.

establish, *v*. 1. set up, found, institute, form, organize, fix, settle, install. 2. verify, substantiate, prove. 3. appoint, ordain, fix, enact, decree.
Ant. liquidate, dissolve; disprove.

esteem, *v*. 1. prize, value, honor, revere, respect, appreciate, estimate, regard. —*n*. 2. respect, regard, favor, admiration, honor, reverence, veneration. 3. estimation, valuation, estimate, appreciation.
Ant. disregard; disrespect, disfavor; depreciation.

estimable, *adj*. respectable, reputable, worthy, deserving, meritorious, good, excellent.
Ant. disreputable, unworthy, bad, inferior.

estimate, *v*. 1. judge, compute, reckon, gauge, count, assess, value, evaluate, appraise. —*n*. 2. judgment, calculation, valuation, estimation, opinion, computation.

estimation, *n*. judgment, opinion, appreciation, regard, honor, veneration, esteem, respect, reverence.

eternal, *adj*. 1. endless, everlasting, infinite, unending, never-ending, interminable, unceasing, perpetual, ceaseless, permanent. 2. timeless, immortal, deathless, undying, imperishable, indestructible.
Ant. transitory, ephemeral; perishable, mortal.

etiquette, *n*. decorum, propriety, code of behavior, convention, dignity.
Ant. impropriety, indignity.

eulogize, *v*. praise, extol, laud, commend, panegyrize, applaud.
Ant. criticize, condemn.

evade, *v*. 1. escape, elude, escape from, avoid, shun, sidestep, dodge. 2. baffle, foil, elude. 3. prevaricate, equivocate, quibble, fence.
Ant. face, confront.

evaporate, *v*. 1. vaporize, dehydrate, dry. 2. disappear, fade, vanish, evanesce.
Ant. condense, sublimate.

evasion, *n*. 1. avoidance, dodging, escape. 2. prevarication, equivocation, quibbling, subterfuge, sophistry.

even, *adj*. 1. level, flat, smooth, plane. 2. parallel, level. 3. regular, equable, uniform, steady, well-balanced, in equilibrium, conforming, standard. 3. commensurate, equal; square, balanced. 4. calm, placid, tranquil, even-tempered, temperate, composed, peaceful. 5. fair, just, equitable, impartial. —*adv*. 6. still, yet; just; fully, quite, completely; indeed. —*v*. 7. level, smooth; balance, equilibrate, counterpoise.
Ant. uneven, irregular; unsteady; unequal, incommensurate; agitated, in-

temperate; unfair, unjust, prejudiced, biased.

evening, *n*. eventide, dusk, twilight, gloaming, nightfall, eve, even, sundown.
Ant. dawn, sunrise.

event, *n*. 1. occurrence, happening, affair, case, circumstance, episode, incident. 2. result, issue, consequence, outcome.

ever, *adv*. 1. continuously, eternally, perpetually, constantly, always. 2. by any chance, at all, at any time.
Ant. never.

everlasting, *adj*. eternal.
Ant. ephemeral, transitory.

evidence, *n*. 1. ground, grounds, proof, testimony. 2. indication, sign, signal. 3. information, deposition, affidavit, exhibit, testimony, proof. —*v*. 4. make clear, show, manifest, demonstrate.

evident, *adj*. plain, clear, obvious, manifest, palpable, patent, unmistakable, apparent.
Ant. concealed, hidden.

evil, *adj*. 1. wicked, bad, immoral, amoral, sinful, iniquitous, flagitious, depraved, vicious, corrupt, perverse, wrong, base, vile, nefarious, malicious, malignant, malevolent. 2. harmful, injurious, wrong, bad, pernicious, destructive, mischievous. 3. unfortunate, disastrous, miserable. —*n*. 4. wickedness, depravity, iniquity, unrighteousness, sin, corruption, baseness, badness. 5. harm, mischief, misfortune, disaster, calamity, misery, pain, woe, suffering, sorrow.
Ant. good.

exact, *adj*. 1. accurate, correct, precise, literal, faithful, close. 2. strict, rigorous, rigid, unbending, exacting, demanding, severe, scrupulous. 3. methodical, careful, punctilious, accurate, critical, nice, regular, precise, orderly. —*v*. 4. call for, demand, require, force, compel. 5. extort, wrest, wring, extract.
Ant. inexact, inaccurate, imprecise, unfaithful, free; disorderly.

exalt, *v*. 1. elevate, promote, dignify, raise, ennoble. 2. praise, extol, glorify, bless. 3. elate, make proud, please. 4. stimulate. 5. intensify.
Ant. lower, debase; damn, condemn; displease.

examination, *n*. 1. inspection, inquiry, observation, investigation, scrutiny, scanning, inquisition. 2. test, trial.

examine, *v.* 1. inspect, scrutinize, search, probe, explore, study, investigate, test. 2. catechize.

example, *n.* sample, specimen, representative, illustration, case, pattern, model.

exasperate, *v.* irritate, annoy, vex, infuriate, exacerbate, anger, incense, provoke, nettle, needle, enrage, inflame.
Ant. calm, assuage, tranquilize.

exceed, *v.* overstep, transcend, surpass, cap, top, outdo, excel, outstrip, beat.

excel, *v.* surpass, outdo, exceed, transcend, outstrip, eclipse, beat, win over, cap, top.

excellence, *n.* superiority, eminence, preeminence, transcendence, distinction; merit, virtue, purity, goodness, uprightness.
Ant. baseness; inferiority.

excellent, *adj.* good, choice, worthy, fine, first-rate, estimable, superior, better, admirable, prime.
Ant. bad, inferior, base.

except, *prep.* 1. but, save, excepting, excluding. —*v.* 2. exclude, leave out, omit, bar, reject.
Ant. including; include, admit.

exceptional, *adj.* unusual, extraordinary, irregular, peculiar, rare, strange, unnatural, anomalous, abnormal, aberrant.
Ant. customary, common, usual, normal, regular, natural.

excess, *n.* 1. superfluity, superabundance, nimiety, redundancy. 2. surplus, remainder. 3. immoderation, intemperance, over-indulgence, dissipation.
Ant. lack, need, want.

excessive, *adj.* immoderate, extravagant, extreme, exorbitant, inordinate, outrageous, unreasonable, disproportionate.
Ant. reasonable, proportionate.

exchange, *v.* 1. barter, trade, interchange, commute, swap, reciprocate. —*n.* 2. interchange, trade, traffic, business, commerce, reciprocity, barter. 3. market, bourse.
Ant. embargo.

exchangeable, *adj.* interchangeable, replaceable, returnable.

excitable, *adj.* emotional, passionate, fiery, quick-tempered, hot-tempered, hasty, irascible, irritable, choleric.
Ant. unemotional, cool, calm, serene, tranquil.

excite, *v.* 1. stir, arouse, rouse, awaken, stimulate, animate, kindle,

inflame, incite. 2. stir up, provoke, disturb, agitate, irritate, discompose.
Ant. pacify, calm, soothe.

excited, *adj.* ruffled, discomposed, stormy, perturbed, impassioned, stimulated, brisk, agitated, stirred up, agog, eager, enthusiastic.
Ant. calm, unruffled, composed, pacific.

excitement, *n.* agitation, commotion, ado, to do, perturbation, disturbance.
Ant. serenity, peace.

exclamation, *n.* outcry, ejaculation, interjection, cry, complaint, protest, vociferation, shout, clamor.

exclude, *v.* 1. bar, restrain, keep out, shut out. 2. debar, eliminate, expel, eject, reject, prohibit, withhold, except, omit, preclude; proscribe, prevent.
Ant. include; accept.

exclusive, *adj.* 1. incompatible, excluding, barring. 2. restrictive, cliquish, snobbish, fastidious. 3. single, sole, only, special. 4. select, narrow, clannish, snobbish, selfish, illiberal, narrow, narrow-minded, uncharitable. 5. fashionable, chic, aristocratic, choice.
Ant. inclusive, including; general; liberal; poor.

excursion, *n.* 1. journey, tour, trip, jaunt, junket, outing, cruise. 2. deviation, digression, episode.

excuse, *v.* 1. forgive, pardon, overlook, acquit, absolve, exonerate, exculpate. 2. apologize for, exonerate, exculpate, clear, vindicate. 3. extenuate, palliate, justify. 4. release, disoblige, free, liberate, disencumber. —*n.* 5. plea, apology, absolution, justification. 6. pretext, pretense, subterfuge, evasion, makeshift.
Ant. condemn; oblige, shackle.

execute, *v.* 1. carry out, accomplish, do, perform, achieve, effect, consummate, finish, complete. 2. kill, put to death, hang. 3. enforce, effectuate, administer; sign, seal, and deliver.

exemption, *n.* immunity, impunity, privilege, freedom, exception.
Ant. culpability.

exercise, *n.* 1. exertion, labor, toil, work, action, activity. 2. drill, practice, training, schooling, discipline. 3. practice, use, application, employment, performance, operation. 4. ceremony, ritual, procedure, observance, service. —*v.* 5. discipline, drill, train, school. 6. practice, use, apply, employ, effect, exert. 7. discharge,

perform. 8. worry, annoy, make uneasy, try, burden, trouble, pain, afflict.
Ant. laziness.

exertion, *n.* effort, action, activity, endeavor, struggle, attempt, strain, trial.

exhaust, *v.* 1. empty, drain, void. 2. use up, expend, consume, waste, squander, dissipate, spend, fritter away. 3. enervate, tire, prostrate, wear out, fatigue, weaken, cripple, debilitate. —*n.* 4. fumes, smoke, vapor, effluvium.
Ant. fill; use; innervate, invigorate, strengthen.

exhaustion, *n.* weariness, lassitude, weakness, fatigue.
Ant. energy, exhilaration, strength.

exhibit, *v.* 1. expose, present, display, show, demonstrate, offer. 2. manifest, display, show, betray, reveal, express, disclose, indicate, evince. —*n.* 3. exhibition, showing, show, display, demonstration, offering, exposition, manifestation. 4. evidence, testimony.
Ant. conceal, hide.

exhilarate, *v.* make cheerful *or* merry, cheer, gladden, enliven, inspirit, animate, inspire, elate.
Ant. depress, sadden, deject.

exonerate, *v.* 1. absolve, exculpate, clear, acquit, vindicate, justify. 2. relieve, release, discharge, except, exempt, free.
Ant. blame, condemn; imprison.

exorbitant, *adj.* exceeding, excessive, inordinate, extravagant, unreasonable, unconscionable, enormous.
Ant. reasonable, inexpensive.

expand, *v.* increase, extend, swell, enlarge, dilate, distend, inflate, bloat, aggrandize, spread *or* stretch out, unfold, develop.
Ant. contract, shrink.

expect, *v.* look forward to, anticipate, await, hope for, wait for, count on, rely on.

expectation, *n.* expectancy, anticipation, hope, trust, prospect.

expedient, *adj.* 1. advantageous, fit, suitable, profitable, advisable, proper, appropriate, desirable. —*n.* 2. device, contrivance, means, resource, shift, resort.
Ant. unsuitable, inapt, undesirable.

expedite, *v.* speed up, hasten, quicken, speed, push, accelerate, hurry, precipitate; dispatch.
Ant. slow.

expedition, *n.* 1. excursion, journey, voyage, trip, junket, safari. 2.

promptness, speed, haste, quickness, dispatch, alacrity.
Ant. sloth.

expel, *v.* drive *or* force away, drive *or* force out, discharge, eject; dismiss, oust, banish, exile, expatriate, (*British*) send down.
Ant. accept, invite.

expend, *v.* 1. use, employ, consume, spend, exhaust, use up. 2. pay, disburse, spend, lay out.
Ant. save, husband, conserve.

expense, *n.* 1. cost, charge, price, outlay, expenditure. 2. loss, injury, harm, debit, detriment.

expensive, *adj.* costly, dear, high-priced.
Ant. inexpensive, cheap, tawdry.

experience, *n.* 1. undergoing, feeling, encountering. 2. knowledge, wisdom, sagacity. —*v.* 3. meet with, undergo, feel, encounter, live through, know, observe; endure; suffer.
Ant. inexperience, naiveté.

experienced, *adj.* skilled, expert, veteran, practiced, accomplished, versed, qualified, adroit, adept.
Ant. inexperienced, inexpert, naive, artless, unqualified.

experiment, *n.* 1. test, trial, examination, proof, assay, procedure. 2. experimentation, research, investigation. —*v.* 3. try, test, examine, prove, assay.

expert, *n.* 1. specialist, authority, connoisseur, master. —*adj.* 2. trained, skilled, skillful, experienced, proficient, dexterous, adroit, clever, apt, quick.
Ant. butcher, shoemaker, dolt; untrained, inexperienced, maladroit.

explain, *v.* 1. elucidate, expound, explicate, interpret, clarify, throw light on, make plain *or* manifest. 2. account for, justify.
Ant. confuse.

explanation, *n.* 1. explaining, elucidation, explication, exposition, definition, interpretation, description. 2. meaning, interpretation, solution, key, answer, definition, account, justification.

explicit, *adj.* 1. clear, unequivocal, express, unambiguous, precise, definite, exact, categorical, determinate. 2. open, outspoken, definite, unashamed, unabashed.
Ant. unclear, equivocal, ambiguous, indefinite; clandestine, concealed.

exploit, *n.* 1. deed, feat, accomplishment, achievement. —*v.* 2. use, utilize, take advantage of.

expose, *v.* 1. lay open, subject, endanger, imperil, jeopardize. 2. bare, uncover; exhibit, display. 3. make known, betray, uncover, unveil, disclose, reveal, unmask, bring to light; muckrake.
Ant. conceal, hide.

exposition, *n.* 1. exhibit, exhibition, show, demonstration, display. 2. explanation, elucidation, commentary, treatise, critique, interpretation, exegesis, explication.

exposure, *n.* 1. exposing; disclosure, unmasking, presentation, display, divulgement, revelation, exposé. 2. aspect, orientation.
Ant. hiding, concealment.

express, *v.* 1. utter, declare, state, word, speak, assert, asseverate. 2. show, manifest, reveal, expose, indicate, exhibit, represent. 3. indicate, signify, designate, denote. 4. press *or* squeeze out. —*adj.* 5. clear, distinct, definite, explicit, plain, obvious, positive, unambiguous, categorical; unsubtle. 6. special, particular, singular, signal. 7. faithful, exact, accurate, precise, true, close. 8. swift, direct, fast, rapid, nonstop. —*n.* 9. courier, special messenger.
Ant. conceal.

expression, *n.* 1. utterance, declaration, assertion, statement. 2. phrase, term, idiom. 3. language, diction, phraseology, wording, phrasing, presentation. 4. manifestation, sign. 5. look, countenance, aspect, air, mien, intonation, tone.
Ant. silence.

expressive, *adj.* 1. meaning, significant, suggestive, meaningful, indicative. 2. lively, vivid, strong, emphatic.
Ant. expressionless, meaningless.

exquisite, *adj.* 1. dainty, beautiful, elegant, rare, delicate, appealing, charming. 2. fine, admirable, consummate, perfect, matchless, complete, valuable, precious. 3. intense, acute, keen, poignant. 4. sensitive, responsive. 5. rare, select, choice, excellent, precious, valuable, priceless; vintage. 6. refined, elegant, delicate, discriminating, polished, debonair.
Ant. ugly, hideous; imperfect, valueless, worthless; dull; vacuous, vapid; common, ordinary; poor, inferior; boorish.

extemporaneous, *adj.* extemporary, extempore, impromptu, improvised, unpremeditated, offhand, off the cuff.
Ant. prepared, premeditated.

extend, *v.* 1. stretch *or* draw out, attenuate. 2. lengthen, prolong, pro-

tract, continue. 3. expand, spread out, dilate, enlarge, widen, diffuse, fill out. 4. hold forth, offer, bestow, grant, give, impart, yield.
Ant. shorten, abbreviate; discontinue; shrink, curtail.

extension, *n.* 1. stretching, expansion, enlargement, dilation, dilatation, increase. 2. prolongation, lengthening, protraction, continuation; delay. 3. extent, limit.
Ant. shrinking, decrease; curtailment.

extensive, *adj.* 1. wide, broad, large, extended, spacious, ample, vast. 2. far-reaching, comprehensive, thorough; inclusive.

extent, *n.* space, degree, magnitude, measure, amount, scope, compass, range, expanse, stretch, reach, size; length, area, volume.

exterior, *adj.* 1. outer, outside, outward, external, outer, superficial. 2. outlying, extraneous, foreign, extrinsic. —*n.* 3. outside, face. 4. appearance, mien, aspect, face.
Ant. interior, inner; important; interior, inside.

exterminate, *v.* extirpate, annihilate, destroy, eradicate, abolish, eliminate.
Ant. create, generate, originate.

extinct, *adj.* 1. extinguished, quenched, out, put out. 2. obsolete, archaic. 3. ended, terminated, over, dead, gone, vanished.
Ant. extant; modern; begun, initiated.

extol, *v.* praise, laud, eulogize, commend, glorify, exalt, celebrate, applaud, panegyrize.
Ant. condemn, damn.

extort, *v.* extract, exact, wrest, wring, blackmail, bleed.

extract, *v.* 1. draw forth *or* out, get, pull *or* pry out. 2. deduce, divine, understand. 3. extort, exact, evoke, educe, draw out, elicit, wrest, wring, bleed. 4. derive, withdraw, distill. —*n.* 5. excerpt, quotation, citation, selection. 6. decoction, distillate, solution.

extraneous, *adj.* external, extrinsic, foreign, alien, adventitious; inappropriate, not germane, not pertinent, nonessential, superfluous.
Ant. internal, intrinsic; appropriate, pertinent, essential, vital.

extraordinary, *adj.* exceptional, special, inordinate, uncommon, singular, signal, rare, phenomenal, remarkable, unusual, egregious, unheard-of.

Ant. ordinary, common, usual, customary.

extravagant, *adj.* 1. imprudent, wasteful, lavish, spendthrift, prodigal, immoderate, excessive, inordinate, exorbitant. 2. unreasonable, fantastic, wild, foolish, absurd.
Ant. prudent, thrifty, moderate; reasonable, thoughtful, sensible.

extreme, *adj.* 1. utmost, greatest, rarest, highest; superlative. 2. outermost, endmost, ultimate, last, uttermost, remotest. 3. extravagant, immoderate, excessive, fanatical, uncompromising, radical, outré, unreasonable. 4. last, final, ultimate. —*n.* 5. farthest, furthest, remotest. 6. acme, limit, end; extremity.
Ant. reasonable.

extremity, *n.* 1. terminal, limit, end, termination, extreme, verge, border, boundary, bounds. 2. utmost, extreme.

exuberance, *n.* exuberancy, superabundance, excess, copiousness, profusion, luxuriance, lavishness, superfluity, redundancy, overflow.
Ant. paucity, lack, need, want.

F

fable, *n.* 1. legend, tale, apologue, parable, allegory, myth, story. 2. lie, untruth, falsehood, fib, fiction, invention, fabrication, forgery. —*v.* 3. lie, fib, fabricate, invent.
Ant. truth, gospel.

fabricate, *v.* 1. construct, build, frame, erect, make, manufacture. 2. assemble, put together, erect. 3. devise, invent, coin, feign; forge, fake.
Ant. destroy, raze.

fabulous, *adj.* 1. unbelievable, incredible, amazing, astonishing, astounding. 2. untrue, unreal, unrealistic, invented, fabled, fictional, fictitious, fabricated, coined, made up, imaginary.
Ant. commonplace; real, natural.

face, *n.* 1. countenance, visage, front, features, look, expression, appearance, aspect, mien; sight, presence. 2. show, pretense, pretext, exterior. 3. name, prestige, reputation. —*v.* 4. meet face to face, confront, encounter, meet, meet with. 5. oppose. 6. cover, veneer.
Ant. back; absence; interior.

facetious, *adj.* amusing, humorous, comical, funny, witty, droll, jocular.
Ant. sad.

factory, *n.* manufactory, mill, workshop, plant.

faculty, *n.* ability, capacity, aptitude, capability, knack, turn, talent.
Ant. inability, incapacity.

fade, *v.* 1. wither, droop, languish, decline, decay. 2. blanch, bleach, pale. 3. disappear, vanish, die out, pass away, evanesce.
Ant. flourish; flush; appear.

fail, *v.* 1. come short, fall short, disappoint. 2. fall off, dwindle, pass *or* die away, decline, fade, weaken, sink, wane, give out, cease, disappear. 3. desert, forsake, disappoint.
Ant. succeed.

failing, *n.* shortcoming, weakness, foible, deficiency, defect, frailty, imperfection, fault, flaw.
Ant. success, sufficiency; strength.

failure, *n.* 1. unsuccessfulness, miscarriage, abortion, failing. 2. neglect, omission, dereliction, nonperformance. 3. deficiency, insufficiency, defectiveness. 4. decline, decay, deterioration, loss. 5. bankruptcy, insolvency, failing, bust; dud.
Ant. success; adequacy, sufficiency, effectiveness.

faint, *adj.* 1. indistinct, ill-defined, dim, faded, dull. 2. feeble, halfhearted, faltering, irresolute, weak, languid, drooping. 3. feeble, languid, swooning. 4. cowardly, timorous, pusillanimous, fearful, timid, dastardly, faint-hearted. —*v.* 5. swoon, pass out, black out. —*n.* 6. swoon, unconsciousness.
Ant. strong; distinct; brave, bold.

fair, *adj.* 1. unbiased, equitable, just, honest, impartial, disinterested, unprejudiced. 2. reasonable, passable, tolerable, average, middling. 3. likely, favorable, promising, hopeful. 4. bright, sunny, cloudless; fine. 5. unobstructed, open, clear, distinct, unencumbered, plain. 6. clean, spotless, pure, untarnished, unsullied, unspotted, unblemished, unstained. 7. clear, legible, distinct. 8. light, blond, white, pale. 9. beautiful, lovely, comely, pretty, attractive, pleasing, handsome. 10. courteous, civil, polite, gracious. —*adv.* 11. straight, directly. 12. favorably, auspiciously. —*n.* 13. exhibit, exhibition, festival, kermis.
Ant. unfair.

fairy, *n.* fay, pixy, leprechaun, nix, nixie, brownie, elf, sprite.

faith, *n.* 1. confidence, trust, reliance, credit, credence, assurance. 2. belief, doctrine, tenet, creed, dogma, religion, persuasion.
Ant. discredit, distrust.

faithful, *adj.* 1. strict, thorough, true, devoted. 2. true, reliable, trustworthy, trusty. 3. stable, dependable, steadfast, stanch, loyal, constant. 4. credible, creditable, believable, trustworthy, reliable. 5. strict, rigid, accurate, precise, exact, conscientious, close. —*n.* 6. believers.
Ant. unfaithful, faithless.

faithless, *adj.* 1. disloyal, false, inconstant, fickle, perfidious, treacherous. 2. unreliable, untrustworthy, untrue. 3. untrusting; unbelieving, doubting. 4. atheistic, agnostic, heathen, infidel.
Ant. faithful.

false, *adj.* 1. erroneous, incorrect, mistaken, wrong, untrue, improper. 2. untruthful, lying, mendacious, untrue. 3. deceitful, treacherous, faithless, insincere, hypocritical, disingenuous, disloyal, unfaithful, two-faced, inconstant, recreant, perfidious, traitorous. 4. deceptive, deceiving, misleading, fallacious. 5. spurious, artificial, bogus, phony, forged, sham, counterfeit. 6. substitute, ersatz, supplementary, stand-in.
Ant. true; genuine.

falsehood, *n.* lie, fib, untruth, distortion, fabrication, fiction.
Ant. truth.

falter, *v.* 1. hesitate, vacillate, waver, tremble. 2. stammer, stutter.

fame, *n.* reputation, estimation, opinion, consensus, repute, renown, eminence, celebrity, honor, glory; notoriety.
Ant. infamy, disrepute.

familiar, *adj.* 1. common, well-known, frequent. 2. well-acquainted, conversant, well-versed. 3. easy, informal,

unceremonious, unconstrained, free. 4. intimate, close, friendly, amicable. 5. presuming, presumptive, unreserved, disrespectful. 6. tame, domesticated. —*n.* 7. friend, associate, companion.
Ant. unfamiliar, unknown.

familiarity, *n.* 1. acquaintance, knowledge, understanding. 2. intimacy, liberty, freedom, license, disrespect. 3. informality, unconstraint, freedom.
Ant. unfamiliarity.

famous, *adj.* celebrated, renowned, well-known, famed, notable, eminent, distinguished, illustrious, honored.
Ant. unknown, undistinguished.

fanatical, *adj.* zealous, enthusiastic, visionary, frenzied, rabid.
Ant. apathetic.

fancy, *n.* 1. imagination, fantasy. 2. image, conception, idea, thought, notion, impression; hallucination. 3. caprice, whim, vagary, quirk, humor, crotchet. 4. preference, liking, inclination, fondness. 5. judgment, taste, sensitivity, sensitiveness. —*adj.* 6. fine, elegant, choice. 7. ornamental, decorated, ornate. 8. fanciful, capricious, whimsical, irregular, extravagant. —*v.* 9. picture, envision, conceive, imagine. 10. like, be pleased with, take a fancy to.
Ant. plain; regular, ordinary; dislike, abhor.

fascinate, *v.* bewitch, charm, enchant, entrance, enrapture, captivate, allure, infatuate, enamor.
Ant. repel, disgust.

fashion, *n.* 1. custom, style, vogue, mode, fad, rage, craze. 2. custom, style, conventionality, conformity. 3. haut monde, beau monde, four hundred, society. 4. manner, way, mode, method, approach. 5. make, form, figure, shape, stamp, mold, pattern, model, cast. 6. kind, sort. —*v.* 7. make, shape, frame, construct, mold, form. 8. accommodate, adapt, suit, fit, adjust.

fast, *adj.* 1. quick, swift, rapid, fleet. 2. energetic, active, alert, quick. 3. dissolute, dissipated, profligate, unmoral, wild, reckless, extravagant, prodigal. 4. strong, resistant, impregnable. 5. immovable, fixed, secure, steadfast, stanch, firm. 6. inescapable, inextricable. 7. tied, knotted, fastened, fixed, tight, close. 8. permanent, lasting, enduring, eternal. 9. loyal, faithful, steadfast. 10. deep, sound, profound. 11. deceptive, insincere, inconstant, unreliable. —*adv.* 12. tightly, fixedly, firmly, securely, tenaciously. 13. quickly, swiftly, rapidly, speedily. 14. energetically, recklessly, extravagantly, wildly, prodigally.
Ant. slow, lethargic; upright, moral; weak, defenseless; feeble; temporary; disloyal, faithless; shallow; sincere, constant, reliable.

fasten, *v.* make fast, fix, secure, attach, pin, rivet, bind, tie, connect, link, hook, clasp, clinch, clamp, tether.
Ant. loosen, loose, untie.

fat, *adj.* 1. fleshy, plump, corpulent, obese, adipose, stout, portly, chubby, pudgy. 2. oily, fatty, unctuous, greasy, pinguid. 3. rich, profitable, remunerative, lucrative. 4. fertile, rich, fruitful, productive. 5. thick, broad, extended, wide. 6. plentiful, copious, abundant. 7. dull, stupid, sluggish, coarse.
Ant. thin, skinny, cadaverous; poor; scarce, scanty; barren; clever.

fatal, *adj.* 1. deadly, mortal, lethal; destructive, ruinous, pernicious, calamitous, catastrophic. 2. fateful, inevitable, doomed, predestined, foreordained, damned.
Ant. lifegiving, constructive; indeterminate.

fate, *n.* 1. fortune, luck, lot, chance, destiny, karma, kismet, doom. 2. death, destruction, ruin. —*v.* 3. predetermine, destine, predestine, foreordain, preordain.

fatherly, *adj.* paternal, protecting, protective; kind, tender, benign.

fatuous, *adj.* stupid, dense, dull, dimwitted, foolish, silly, idiotic.
Ant. clever, bright, intelligent.

fault, *n.* 1. defect, imperfection, blemish, flaw, failing, frailty, foible, weakness, shortcoming, vice. 2. error, mistake, slip. 3. misdeed, sin, transgression, trespass, misdemeanor, offense, wrong, delinquency, indiscretion, culpability.
Ant. strength.

faulty, *adj.* 1. defective, imperfect, incomplete, bad. 2. blameworthy, culpable, reprehensible, censurable.
Ant. perfect, complete, consummate; exonerated, blameless.

favor, *n.* 1. kindness, good will, benefit, good deed. 2. partiality, bias, patronage, prejudice. 3. gift, present. —*v.* 4. prefer, encourage, patronize, approve, countenance, allow. 5. facilitate, ease; propitiate, conciliate, appease. 6. aid, help, support, assist.
Ant. cruelty; disfavor; disapprove, disallow, discourage.

fear, *n.* 1. apprehension, consternation, dismay, alarm, trepidation, dread, terror, fright, horror, panic. 2. anxiety, solicitude, concern. 3. awe, reverence, veneration. —*v.* 4. be afraid of, apprehend, dread. 5. revere, venerate, reverence.
Ant. boldness, bravery, intrepidity; security, confidence.

fearless, *adj.* brave, intrepid, bold, courageous, heroic.
Ant. cowardly.

feasible, *adj.* 1. practicable, workable, possible. 2. suitable, suited, usable, practical, practicable. 3. likely, probable.
Ant. unfeasible, impractical, impossible; unsuitable, unsuited; unlikely, improbable.

feast, *n.* 1. celebration, anniversary, commemoration, ceremony, banquet, fête, entertainment, carousal. 2. repast, sumptuous repast. —*v.* 3. eat, gourmandize, glut *or* stuff *or* gorge oneself. 4. gratify, delight.

feat, *n.* achievement, accomplishment, deed, action, act, exploit.

feature, *n.* characteristic, peculiarity, trait, property, mark.

feeble, *adj.* 1. weak, feckless, ineffective, ineffectual. 2. infirm, sickly, debilitated, enervated, declining, frail. 3. faint, dim, weak.
Ant. strong, effective, effectual; healthy; clear.

feed, *v.* 1. nourish, sustain, purvey. 2. satisfy, minister to, gratify, please. 3. eat. 4. subsist. —*n.* 5. fodder, forage, provender, food.
Ant. starve.

feeling, *n.* 1. consciousness, impression; emotion, passion, sentiment, sensibility; sympathy, empathy. 2. tenderness, sensitivity, sentiment, sentimentality, susceptibility, pity. 3. sentiment, opinion, tenor. —*adj.* 4. sentient, emotional, sensitive, tender; sympathetic. 5. emotional, impassioned, passionate.
Ant. apathy, coolness; unemotional, insensitive, unsympathetic; cool.

feign, *v.* 1. invent, concoct, devise, fabricate, forge, counterfeit. 2. simulate, pretend, counterfeit, affect; emulate, imitate, mimic. 3. make believe, pretend, imagine.

female, *n.* 1. woman, girl. —*adj.* 2. feminine, womanly, maternal.
Ant. male.

ferocious, *adj.* fierce, savage, wild, cruel, violent, ravenous, rapacious. *Ant.* mild, tame, calm.

fertile, *adj.* productive, prolific, fecund, fruitful, rich, teeming. *Ant.* sterile, barren.

fervent, *adj.* fervid, ardent, earnest, warm, heated, hot, burning, glowing, fiery, inflamed, eager, zealous, vehement, impassioned, passionate, enthusiastic. *Ant.* cool, apathetic.

fervor, *n.* ardor, intensity, earnestness, eagerness, enthusiasm, passion, fire, heat, vehemence. *Ant.* coolness, apathy.

feud, *n.* hostility, quarrel, argument, difference, falling-out.

fiction, *n.* 1. novel, fantasy. 2. fabrication, figment, unreality, falsity. *Ant.* nonfiction, fact; reality.

fidelity, *n.* 1. loyalty, faithfulness, devotion, fealty. 2. accuracy, precision, faithfulness, exactness, closeness. *Ant.* disloyalty, unfaithfulness; inaccuracy.

fierce, *adj.* 1. ferocious, wild, vehement, violent, savage, cruel, fell, brutal, bloodthirsty, murderous, homicidal. 2. truculent, barbarous, untamed, furious, passionate, turbulent, impetuous. *Ant.* tame, domesticated; calm; civilized; cool, temperate.

fiery, *adj.* 1. hot, flaming, heated, fervent, fervid, burning, afire, glowing. 2. fervent, fervid, vehement, inflamed, impassioned, spirited, ardent, impetuous, passionate, fierce. *Ant.* cool, cold; dispassionate.

fight, *n.* 1. battle, war, combat, encounter, conflict, contest, scrimmage, engagement, fray, affray, action, skirmish, affair, struggle. 2. melee, struggle, scuffle, tussle, riot, row, fray. —*v.* 3. contend, strive, battle, combat, conflict, contest, engage, struggle.

figment, *n.* invention, fiction, fabrication, fable. *Ant.* fact, reality.

filthy, *adj.* 1. dirty, foul, unclean, defiled, squalid. 2. obscene, vile, dirty, pornographic, licentious, lascivious. *Ant.* clean, spotless, immaculate.

final, *adj.* 1. last, latest, ultimate. 2. conclusive, decisive. *Ant.* prime, primary.

financial, *adj.* monetary, fiscal, pecuniary.

fine, *adj.* 1. superior, high-grade, choice, excellent, admirable, elegant, exquisite, finished, consummate, perfect, refined, select, delicate. 2. powdered, pulverized, minute, small, little. 3. keen, sharp, acute. 4. skilled, accomplished, brilliant. 5. affected, ornate, ornamented, fancy. *Ant.* inferior, poor, bad, unfinished; dull; unskilled, maladroit; plain.

finish, *v.* 1. bring to an end, end, terminate, conclude, close. 2. use up, complete, consume. 3. complete, perfect, consummate, polish. 4. accomplish, achieve, execute, complete, perform, do. —*n.* 5. end, conclusion, termination, close. 6. polish, elegance, refinement. *Ant.* begin, start, commence; originate, create; beginning.

finished, *adj.* 1. ended, completed, consummated, over, done, done with; complete, consummate, perfect. 2. polished, refined, elegant, perfected; trained, experienced, practiced, qualified, accomplished, proficient, skilled, gifted, talented. *Ant.* begun; incomplete, imperfect; unrefined, inelegant; inexperienced, unqualified, unskilled, maladroit.

firm, *adj.* 1. hard, solid, stiff, rigid, inelastic, compact, condensed, compressed, dense. 2. steady, unshakable, rooted, fast, fixed, stable, secure, immovable. 3. fixed, settled, unalterable, established, confirmed. 4. steadfast, unwavering, determined, immovable, resolute, stanch, constant, steady, reliable. —*n.* 5. company, partnership, association, business, concern, house, corporation. *Ant.* flabby, flaccid, elastic, soft; unsteady, unstable; wavering, irresolute, inconstant, unreliable.

fix, *v.* 1. make, fast, fasten, pin, attach, tie, secure, stabilize, establish, set, plant, implant. 2. settle, determine, establish, define, limit. 3. assign, refer. 4. repair, mend, correct, emend. —*n.* 5. predicament, dilemma, plight, spot. *Ant.* loosen, loose, detach; unsettle; break.

flame, *n.* 1. blaze, conflagration, holocaust, inferno, fire. 2. heat, ardor, zeal, passion, fervor, warmth, enthusiasm. —*v.* 3. burn, blaze. 4. glow, burn, warm; shine, flash. 5. inflame, fire.

flash, *n.* 1. flame, outburst, flare, gleam, glare. 2. instant, split second, moment, twinkling, wink. 3. ostentation, display. —*v.* 4. glance, glint, glitter, scintillate, gleam. —*adj.* 5. showy, ostentatious, flashy, gaudy, tawdry, flaunting, pretentious, superficial. 6. counterfeit, sham, fake, false, fraudulent.

flat, *adj.* 1. horizontal, level, even, equal, plane, smooth. 2. low, supine, prone, prostrate. 3. collapsed, deflated. 4. unqualified, downright, positive, outright, peremptory, absolute. 5. uninteresting, dull, tedious, lifeless, boring, spiritless, prosaic, unanimated. 6. insipid, vapid, tasteless, stale, dead, unsavory. 7. pointless. —*adv.* 8. horizontally, levelly. 9. positively, absolutely, definitely. —*n.* 10. apartment, suite. *Ant.* vertical, upright, perpendicular; doubtful, dubious; spirited, animated; tasteful, savory; pointed.

flavor, *n.* 1. taste, savor. 2. seasoning, extract, flavoring. 3. characteristic, essence, quality, spirit, soul. 4. smell, odor, aroma, perfume, fragrance.

flaw, *n.* defect, imperfection, blot, blemish, spot, fault, crack, crevice, breach, break, cleft, fissure, rift, fracture.

flexible, *adj.* 1. pliable, pliant, flexile, limber, plastic, elastic, supple. 2. adaptable, tractable, compliant, yielding, gentle. *Ant.* inflexible, rigid, solid, firm; intractable, unyielding.

flit, *v.* fly, dart, skim along; flutter.

flock, *n.* bevy, covey, flight, gaggle; brood, hatch, litter; shoal, school; swarm; pride; drove, herd, pack; group, company, crowd.

flood, *n.* 1. deluge, inundation, overflow, flash flood, freshet. —*v.* 2. overflow, inundate, deluge, flow.

flourish, *v.* 1. thrive, prosper, be successful, grow, increase, succeed. 2. luxuriate. 3. brandish, wave. 4. parade, flaunt, display, show off, be ostentatious, boast, brag, vaunt. 5. embellish, adorn, ornament, decorate. —*n.* 6. parade, ostentation, show, display, dash. 7. decoration, ornament, adornment, embellishment. *Ant.* decline, die, fail; disfigure, mar.

flow, *v.* 1. gush, spout, stream, spurt, jet, discharge. 2. proceed, run, pour, roll on. 3. overflow, abound, teem, pour. —*n.* 4. current, flood, stream. 5. stream, river, rivulet, rill, streamlet. 6. outpouring, discharge, overflowing.

fluctuate, *v.* waver, vacillate, change, vary; wave, undulate, oscillate.

fluent, *adj.* flowing, glib, voluble, copious, smooth.
Ant. terse, curt, silent.

fluid, *n.* 1. liquid; gas, vapor. —*adj.* 2. liquid, gaseous.
Ant. solid.

fly, *v.* 1. take wing, soar, hover, flutter, flit, wing, flap. 2. elapse, pass, glide, slip.

foe, *n.* enemy, opponent, adversary, antagonist.
Ant. friend, ally, associate.

fog, *n.* 1. cloud, mist, haze; smog. 2. cloud, confusion, obfuscation, dimming, blurring, darkening. —*v.* 3. befog, becloud, obfuscate, dim, blur, darken. 4. daze, bewilder, befuddle, muddle.
Ant. clarity; clear, brighten; clarify.

foible, *n.* weakness, fault, failing, frailty, defect, imperfection, infirmity.
Ant. strength, perfection.

follow, *v.* 1. succeed, ensue. 2. conform, obey, heed, comply, observe. 3. accompany, attend. 4. pursue, chase, trail, track, trace. 5. ensue, succeed, result, come next, arise, proceed.
Ant. lead; order.

follower, *n.* 1. adherent, partisan, disciple, pupil. 2. attendant, servant; supporter, retainer, companion, associate.
Ant. leader, teacher; enemy, foe.

food, *n.* provisions, rations, nutrition, nutriment, aliment, bread, sustenance, victuals; meat, viands; diet, regimen, fare, menu.

fool, *n.* 1. simpleton, dolt, dunce, blockhead, nincompoop, ninny, numskull, ignoramus, booby, sap, dunderhead, dunderpate, idiot. 2. jester, buffoon, drool, harlequin, zany, clown, merry-andrew. 3. imbecile, moron, idiot. —*v.* 4. impose on, trick, deceive, delude, hoodwink, cozen, cheat, gull, gudgeon, hoax, dupe. 5. joke, jest, play, toy, trifle, dally, idle, dawdle, loiter, tarry.
Ant. genius.

foolish, *adj.* 1. silly, senseless, fatuous, stupid, inane, dull, vacant, vapid, slow, asinine, simple, witless. 2. ill-considered, unwise, thoughtless, irrational, imprudent, unreasonable, absurd, ridiculous, nonsensical, preposterous, foolhardy.
Ant. bright, brilliant, clever, intelligent; wise, sage, sagacious.

forbid, *v.* inhibit, prohibit, taboo, interdict, prevent, preclude, stop, obviate, deter, discourage.
Ant. allow, permit, encourage.

force, *n.* 1. strength, power, impetus, intensity, might, vigor, energy. 2. coercion, violence, compulsion, constraint, enforcement. 3. efficacy, effectiveness, effect, efficiency, validity, potency, potential. 4. effect, operation. —*v.* 5. compel, constrain, oblige, coerce, necessitate. 6. drive, propel, impel. 7. overcome, overpower, violate, ravish, rape.
Ant. weakness, frailty; ineffectiveness, inefficiency.

forecast, *v.* 1. predict, augur, foretell, foresee, anticipate. 2. prearrange, plan, contrive, project. 3. conjecture, guess, estimate. —*n.* 4. prediction, augury, conjecture, guess, estimate, foresight, prevision, anticipation, forethought, prescience.

foreigner, *n.* alien, stranger, nonnative, outsider, outlander.
Ant. native.

foresight, *n.* 1. prudence, forethought, prevision, anticipation, precaution; forecast. 2. prescience, prevision, foreknowledge, prospect.

forest, *n.* grove, wood, woods, woodland.
Ant. plain.

forgive, *v.* pardon, excuse; absolve, acquit.
Ant. blame, condemn, censure.

forlorn, *adj.* 1. abandoned, deserted, forsaken, desolate, alone, lost, solitary. 2. desolate, dreary, unhappy, miserable, wretched, pitiable, pitiful, helpless, woebegone, disconsolate, comfortless, destitute.
Ant. accompanied; happy, cheerful.

form, *n.* 1. shape, figure, outline, mold, appearance, cast, cut, configuration. 2. mold, model, pattern. 3. manner, style, arrangement, sort, kind, order, type. 4. assemblage, group. 5. ceremony, ritual, formula, formality, conformity, rule, convention. 6. document, paper, application, business form, blank. 7. method, procedure, system, mode, practice, formula, approach. —*v.* 8. construct, frame, shape, model, mold, fashion, outline, cast. 9. make, produce, create, originate. 10. compose, make up, serve for, constitute. 11. order, arrange, organize, systematize, dispose, combine. 12. instruct, teach, educate, discipline, train. 13. frame, invent, contrive, devise.

formal, *adj.* 1. academic, conventional, conformal, conforming, conformist. 2. ceremonial, ceremonious, ritual, conventional. 3. ceremonious, stiff, prim, precise, punctilious, starched. 4. perfunctory, external. 5. official, express, explicit, strict, rigid, rigorous, stodgy. 6. rigorous, methodical, regular, set, fixed, rigid, stiff.

formidable, *adj.* dread, dreadful, appalling, threatening, menacing, fearful, terrible, frightful, horrible.
Ant. pleasant, friendly, amiable.

forsake, *v.* 1. quit, leave, desert, abandon. 2. give up, renounce, forswear, relinquish, recant, drop, forgo.

fortification, *n.* 1. fortifying, strengthening, bolstering, arming. 2. fort, castle, fortress, citadel, stronghold, bulwark, fastness.

fortuitous, *adj.* accidental, chance, casual, incidental.
Ant. purposeful, intentional.

fortunate, *adj.* lucky, happy, propitious, favorable, advantageous, auspicious; successful, prosperous.
Ant. unlucky, unfortunate.

forward, *adv.* 1. onward, ahead, up ahead, in advance, frontward. 2. out, forth. —*adj.* 3. well-advanced, up front, ahead. 4. ready, prompt, eager, willing, sincere, earnest, zealous. 5. pert, bold, presumptuous, assuming, confident, impertinent, impudent, brazen, flippant. 6. radical, extreme, unconventional, progressive. 7. early, premature, future, preliminary.
Ant. backward.

foster, *v.* 1. promote, encourage, further, favor, patronize, forward, advance. 2. bring up, rear, breed, nurse, nourish, sustain, support. 3. care for, cherish.
Ant. discourage.

foul, *adj.* 1. offensive, gross, disgusting, loathsome, repulsive, repellent, noisome, fetid, putrid, stinking. 2. filthy, dirty, unclean, squalid, polluted, sullied, soiled, tarnished, stained, tainted, impure. 3. stormy, unfavorable, rainy, tempestuous. 4. abominable, wicked, vile, base, shameful, infamous, sinful, scandalous. 5. scurrilous, obscene, smutty, profane, vulgar, low, coarse. 6. unfair, dishonorable, underhanded, cheating. 7. entangled, caught, jammed, tangled. —*adv.* 8. unfairly, foully. —*v.* 9. soil, defile, sully, stain, dirty, besmirch, smut, taint, pollute, poison. 10. entangle, clog, tangle, catch. 11. defile, dishonor, disgrace, shame.
Ant. delightful, attractive, pleasant; pure; saintly, angelic; fair, honorable; clean, purify; clear; honor.

foundation, *n.* 1. base, basis, ground, footing. 2. establishment, settlement; endowment.
Ant. superstructure.

fractious, *adj.* cross, fretful, peevish, testy, captious, petulant, touchy, splenetic, pettish, waspish, snappish, irritable; unruly, refractory, stubborn.
Ant. temperate, kind, even-tempered; amenable, tractable, obedient.

fragrant, *adj.* perfumed, odorous, redolent, sweet-smelling, sweet-scented, aromatic, odoriferous.
Ant. noxious.

frail, *adj.* brittle, fragile, breakable, frangible, delicate, weak, feeble.
Ant. strong, pliant, elastic, unbreakable.

frank, *adj.* 1. open, unreserved, unrestrained, unrestricted, nonrestrictive, outspoken, candid, sincere, free, bold, truthful, uninhibited. 2. artless, ingenuous, undisguised, avowed, downright, outright, direct. —*n.* 3. signature, mark, sign, seal; franchise.
Ant. secretive, restrained, restricted; sly, artful, dissembling.

fraud, *n.* deceit, trickery, duplicity, treachery, sharp practice, breach of confidence, trick, deception, guile, artifice, ruse, stratagem, wile, hoax, humbug.
Ant. honesty.

free, *adj.* 1. unfettered, independent, at liberty, unrestrained, unrestricted. 2. unregulated, unrestricted, unimpeded, open, unobstructed. 3. clear, immune, exempt, uncontrolled, decontrolled. 4. easy, firm, swift, unimpeded, unencumbered. 5. loose, unattached, lax. 6. frank, open, unconstrained, unceremonious, familiar, informal, easy. 7. loose, licentious, ribald, lewd, immoral, libertine. 8. liberal, lavish, generous, bountiful, unstinted, munificent, charitable, open-handed. —*v.* 9. liberate, set free, release, unfetter, emancipate, manumit, deliver, disenthrall. 10. exempt, deliver. 11. rid, relieve, disengage, clear.
Ant. dependent, restrained, restricted; close, obstructed; difficult; unfamiliar; moral, upright; stingy, niggardly; confine, enthrall.

freedom, *n.* 1. liberty, independence. 2. immunity, franchise, privilege. 3. ease, facility. 4. frankness, openness, ingenuousness. 5. familiarity, license, looseness, laxity.

Ant. dependence; restriction; difficulty; secrecy; unfamiliarity, restraint.

freight, *n.* 1. cargo, shipment, load. 2. freightage, transportation, express-sage. —*v.* 3. load, lade, burden, charge.

frenzy, *n.* agitation, excitement, paroxysm, enthusiasm; rage, fury, raving, mania, insanity, delirium, derangement, aberration, lunacy, madness.
Ant. calm, coolness; sanity, judgment.

frequently, *adv.* often, many times, repeatedly.
Ant. seldom.

fresh, *adj.* 1. new, recent, novel. 2. youthful, healthy, robust, vigorous, well, hearty, hardy, strong. 3. refreshing, pure, cool, unadulterated, sweet, invigorating. 4. inexperienced, artless, untrained, raw, green, uncultivated, unskilled.
Ant. stale, old; impure, contaminated; experienced, skilled.

fret, *v.* 1. worry, fume, rage. 2. torment, worry, harass, annoy, irritate, vex, taunt, goad, tease, nettle, needle. 3. wear away, erode, gnaw, corrode, rust. —*n.* 4. annoyance, vexation, harassment, agitation, worry, irritation. 5. erosion, corrosion, eating away, gnawing. 6. fretwork, ornament.

fretful, *adj.* irritable, peevish, petulant, querulous, touchy, testy, waspish, pettish, splenetic, captious, snappish, short-tempered, ill-tempered.
Ant. calm, even-tempered, temperate, easy-going.

friend, *n.* 1. companion, crony, chum, acquaintance, intimate, confidant. 2. well-wisher, patron, supporter, backer, encourager, advocate, defender. 3. ally, associate, confrère.
Ant. enemy, foe, adversary.

friendly, *adj.* 1. kind, kindly, amicable, fraternal, amiable, cordial, genial, well-disposed, benevolent, affectionate, kind-hearted. 2. helpful, favorable, advantageous, propitious.
Ant. unfriendly, inimical; unfavorable.

fright, *n.* dismay, consternation, terror, fear, alarm, panic.
Ant. bravery, boldness.

frighten, *v.* scare, terrify, alarm, appall, shock, dismay, intimidate.

frightful, *adj.* dreadful, terrible, alarming, terrific, fearful, awful, shocking, dread, dire, horrid, horrible, hideous, ghastly, gruesome.
Ant. delightful, attractive, beautiful.

frivolous, *adj.* 1. unimportant, trifling, petty, paltry, trivial, flimsy. 2. idle, silly, foolish, childish, puerile.
Ant. important, vital; mature, adult, sensible.

froward, *adj.* perverse, contrary, refractory, obstinate, willful, disobedient, uncooperative, fractious, contumacious, wayward, unmanageable, difficult, defiant, fresh, impudent.
Ant. tractable, lenient, cooperative, easy.

frugal, *adj.* economical, thrifty, chary, provident, saving, sparing, careful, parsimonious, stingy, penurious.
Ant. lavish, wasteful.

fruitful, *adj.* prolific, fertile, fecund, productive, profitable; plentiful, abudant, rich, copious.
Ant. barren, scarce, scanty, unprofitable, fruitless.

fruitless, *adj.* 1. useless, inutile, unavailing, profitless, ineffectual, unprofitable, vain, idle, futile, abortive. 2. barren, sterile, unfruitful, unproductive, infecund, unprolific.
Ant. fruitful, useful, profitable, effectual; abundant, fertile.

frustrate, *v.* defeat, nullify, baffle, disconcert, foil, disappoint, balk, check, thwart.
Ant. encourage, foster.

fulfill, *v.* 1. carry out, consummate, execute, discharge, accomplish, achieve, complete, effect, realize, perfect. 2. perform, do, obey, observe, discharge. 3. satisfy, meet, anwer, fill, comply with. 4. complete, end, terminate, bring to an end, finish, conclude.
Ant. fail; dissatisfy; create, originate.

fume, *n.* 1. smoke, vapor, exhalation, steam. 2. rage, fury, agitation, storm. —*v.* 3. smoke, vaporize. 4. chafe, fret, rage, rave, flare up, bluster, storm.

fun, *n.* merriment, enjoyment, pleasure, amusement, divertissement, sport, diversion, joking, jesting, playfulness, gaiety, frolic.
Ant. misery, melancholy.

fundamental, *adj.* 1. basic, underlying, principal, main, central, chief, essential, primary, elementary, necessary, indispensable. 2. original, first. —*n.* 3. principle, rule, basic law, essence, essential.

Ant. superficial, superfluous, dispensable; last, common; nonessential.

funny, *adj.* amusing, diverting, comical, farcical, absurd, ridiculous, droll, witty, facetious, humorous, laughable, ludicrous, incongruous, foolish.
Ant. sad, melancholy, humorless.

furnish, *v.* 1. provide, supply; purvey, cater. 2. appoint, equip, fit up, rig, deck out, decorate, outfit, fit out.

fury, *n.* 1. passion, furor, frenzy, rage, ire, anger, wrath. 2. violence, turbulence, fierceness, impetuousness, impetuosity, vehemence. 3. shrew, virago, termagant, vixen, nag, hag, maenad, bacchante.
Ant. calm, serenity.

fuse, *v.* 1. melt, liquefy, dissolve, smelt; combine, blend, intermingle, coalesce, intermix, commingle, amalgamate, homogenize, merge. —*n.* 2. match, fusee, fuze.
Ant. solidify, separate.

fuss, *n.* 1. activity, ado, bustle, pother, to-do, stir, commotion. —*v.* 2. bother, annoy, pester.
Ant. inactivity.

futile, *adj.* 1. ineffectual, useless, unsuccessful, vain, unavailing, idle, profitless, unprofitable, bootless, worthless, valueless, fruitless, unproductive. 2. trivial, frivolous, minor, nugatory, unimportant, trifling.
Ant. effective, effectual, successful; profitable, worthy; basic, important, principal, major.

G

gaiety, *n.* 1. merriment, mirth, glee, jollity, joyousness, liveliness, sportiveness, hilarity, vivacity, life, cheerfulness, joviality, animation, spirit. 2. showiness, finery, gaudiness, brilliance, glitter, flashiness, flash.
Ant. sadness, melancholy, misery.

gain, *v.* 1. obtain, secure, procure, get, acquire, attain, earn, win. 2. reach, get to, arrive at, attain. 3. improve, better, progress, advance, forward; near, approach. —*n.* 4. profit, increase, advantage, advance; profits, winnings.
Ant. lose; worsen; retreat; losses.

gallant, *adj.* 1. brave, high-spirited, valorous, valiant, chivalrous, courageous, bold, intrepid, fearless, daring. 2. gay, showy, magnificent, splendid, fine. 3. polite, courtly, chivalrous, noble, courteous. —*n.* 4. suitor, wooer, lover, paramour.
Ant. cowardly, fearful; tawdry; impolite, discourteous.

gambol, *v., n.* frolic, spring, caper, romp, dance.

game, *n.* 1. amusement, pastime, diversion, divertissement, play, sport, contest, competition. 2. scheme, artifice, strategy, stratagem, plan, plot, undertaking, venture, adventure. 3. fun, sport, joke, diversion. 4. prey, quarry. —*adj.* 5. plucky, brave, bold, resolute, intrepid, dauntless, valorous, fearless, heroic, gallant.

gang, *n.* 1. band, group, crew, crowd, company, party, set, clique, coterie; horde. 2. squad, shift, team.

gape, *v.* 1. yawn. 2. stare, wonder, gaze. 3. split, open, dehisce, separate.

garb, *n.* 1. fashion, mode, style, cut. 2. clothes, clothing, dress, costume, attire, apparel, habiliments, habit, garments, raiment, vesture. —*v.* 3. dress, clothe, attire, array, apparel.

garish, *adj.* 1. glaring, loud, showy, tawdry, gaudy, flashy. 2. ornate, ornamented, decorated.
Ant. elegant; plain, simple.

garnish, *v.* 1. adorn, decorate, ornament, embellish, grace, enhance, beautify, trim, bedeck, bedizen, set off. —*n.* 2. decoration, ornamentation, ornament, adornment, garniture, garnishment.
Ant. strip.

garrulous, *adj.* talkative, loquacious, prating, prattling, wordy, diffuse, babbling, verbose, prolix.
Ant. taciturn, silent, reticent.

gasp, *v.* pant, puff, blow.

gather, *v.* 1. get together, collect, aggregate, assemble, muster, marshal, bring *or* draw together. 2. learn, infer, understand, deduce, assume, conclude. 3. accumulate, amass, garner, hoard. 4. pluck, garner, reap, harvest, glean, cull, crop. 5. select, cull, sort, sort out. 6. grow, increase, accrete, collect, thicken, condense. —*n.* 7. contraction, drawing together, tuck, pucker, fold, pleat, plait.
Ant. separate, disperse; decrease.

gathering, *n.* 1. assembly, meeting, assemblage, crowd, convocation, congregation, concourse, company, throng, muster. 2. swelling, boil, abscess, carbuncle, pimple, sore, pustule, tumor.

gaudy, *adj.* showy, tawdry, garish, brilliant, loud, flashy, conspicuous, obvious, vulgar, unsubtle.
Ant. elegant, refined, subtle.

gaunt, *adj.* 1. thin, emaciated, haggard, lean, spare, skinny, scrawny, lank, angular, raw-boned, meager, attenuated, slender. 2. bleak, desolate, grim, dreary.
Ant. obese, fat; populous.

gay, *adj.* 1. joyous, gleeful, jovial, glad, happy, lighthearted, lively, convivial, vivacious, animated, frolicsome, sportive, hilarious, jolly, joyful, merry, good-humored, expansive, cheerful, sprightly, blithe, airy. 2. bright, showy, fine, brilliant.
Ant. unhappy, miserable, dull.

gaze, *v., n.* stare, gape, wonder.

general, *adj.* 1. impartial, unparticular, catholic, universal. 2. common, usual, prevalent, customary, regular, ordinary, popular, nonexclusive, widespread, prevailing. 3. miscellaneous, unrestricted, unspecialized, nonspecific. 4. vague, lax, indefinite, ill-defined, inexact, imprecise.
Ant. special, partial; uncommon, unusual, extraordinary; specific; definite, exact, precise.

generally, *adv.* usually, commonly, ordinarily, often, in general.
Ant. especially, particularly, unusually.

generosity, *n.* 1. readiness, liberality, munificence, charity, bounteousness. 2. nobleness, disinterestedness, magnanimity.
Ant. stinginess, niggardliness, parsimony.

generous, *adj.* 1. munificent, bountiful, unselfish, unstinting, liberal, charitable, open-handed, beneficent. 2. noble, high-minded, magnanimous; large, big. 3. ample, plentiful, abudant, flowing, overflowing, copious.
Ant. stingy, tightfisted, selfish, nig-

gardly; small, parsimonious; scarce, scanty, barren.

genial, *adj.* 1. cheerful, sympathetic, cordial, friendly, pleasant, agreeable, kindly, well-disposed, hearty, encouraging. 2. enlivening, lively, warm, mild.
Ant. unsympathetic, unpleasant, discouraging; cool.

genius, *n.* 1. capacity, ability, talent, gift, aptitude, faculty, bent. 2. spirit, guardian angel, genie, jinn.
Ant. inability, incapacity.

gentle, *adj.* 1. soft, bland, peaceful, clement, moderate, pacific, soothing, kind, tender, humane, lenient, merciful, meek, mild, kindly, amiable, submissive, gentle-hearted, kind-hearted. 2. gradual, moderate, temperate, tempered, light, mild. 3. wellborn, noble, highborn. 4. honorable, respectable, refined, cultivated, polished, well-bred, polite, elegant, courteous, courtly. 5. manageable, tractable, tame, docile, trained, peaceable, quiet.
Ant. immoderate, turbulent, unkind, cruel, heartless; sudden, abrupt; unrefined, unpolished, impolite; intractable, wild, noisy.

get, *v.* 1. obtain, acquire, procure, secure, gain. 2. earn, win, gain. 3. learn, apprehend, grasp. 4. capture, seize upon. 5. prepare, get ready. 6. prevail on *or* upon, persuade, induce, influence, dispose. 7. beget, engender, generate, breed, procreate. 8. come to, reach, arrive. 9. become, grow.
Ant. lose.

ghastly, *adj.* 1. dreadful, horrible, frightful, hideous, grisly, dismal, terrible, shocking. 2. pale, deathly, white, wan, cadaverous.
Ant. lovely, attractive, beautiful; ruddy, robust, healthy.

ghost, *n.* 1. apparition, phantom, spirit, phantasm, wraith, revenant, shade, spook, specter, supernatural being. 2. shadow, hint, suggestion.

giddy, *adj.* 1. frivolous, light, impulsive, flighty, unstable, volatile, fickle, irresolute, mutable, changeable, inconstant, unsteady, vacillating. 2. dizzy, vertiginous, light-headed.
Ant. serious, resolute, constant; sober.

gift, *n.* 1. donation, present, contribution, offering, boon, alms, gratuity, tip, benefaction, grant, largess, subsidy, allowance, endowment, bequest, legacy, dowry, inheritance, bounty. 2. talent, endowment,

power, faculty, ability, capacity, forte, capability, genius, bent.

gigantic, *adj.* huge, enormous, tremendous, colossal, mammoth, monstrous, elephantine, immense, prodigious, herculean, titanic, cyclopean, vast, extensive, infinite.
Ant. small, tiny, infinitesimal, microscopic.

give, *v.* 1. deliver, bestow, hand over, offer, vouchsafe, impart, accord, furnish, provide, supply, donate, contribute, afford, spare, accommodate with, confer, grant, cede, relinquish, yield, turn over, assign, present. 2. enable, assign, award. 3. set forth, issue, show, present, offer. 4. assume, suppose, assign. 5. afford, yield, produce. 6. perform, make do. 7. issue, put forth, emit, publish, utter, give out (with), pronounce, render. 8. communicate, impart, divulge. 9. draw back, recede, retire, relax, cede, yield, give over, give away, sink, give up. 10. break down, fail.
Ant. receive.

glad, *adj.* 1. delighted, pleased, elated, happy, gratified, contented. 2. cheerful, joyous, joyful, happy, merry, cheery, animated, light.
Ant. miserable, unhappy, sad.

glance, *v.* 1. glitter, flash, glimpse, gleam, glisten, scintillate, shine. 2. cast, reflect. —*n.* 3. glitter, gleam; glimpse, look.

glare, *n.* 1. dazzle, flare, glitter, luster, brilliance, sparkle, flash. 2. showiness. 3. scowl, glower. —*v.* 4. shine, dazzle, gleam. 5. glower, gloat, scowl.

gleam, *n.* 1. ray, flash, beam, glimmer, glimmering. —*v.* 2. shine, glimmer, flash, glitter, sparkle, beam.

glee, *n.* joy, exultation, merriment, jollity, hilarity, mirth, joviality, gaiety, liveliness, verve, life.
Ant. misery, sadness, melancholy.

glib, *adj.* 1. fluent, voluble, talkative, ready. 2. slippery, smooth, facile, artful.
Ant. taciturn, silent, quiet; artless, guileless.

glide, *v., n.* slide, slip, flow.
Ant. stick.

glisten, *v.* glimmer, shimmer, sparkle, shine, gleam, glitter.

gloom, *n.* 1. darkness, dimness, shadow, shade, obscurity, gloominess. 2. melancholy, sadness, depression, dejection, despondency.
Ant. brightness, effulgence; joy, glee, happiness.

gloomy, *adj.* 1. dark, shaded, obscure, shadowy, dim, dusky; dismal, lowering. 2. depressed, dejected, sad, melancholy, despondent, downcast, crestfallen, downhearted, glum, dispirited, disheartened.
Ant. bright, effulgent, dazzling; happy, delighted, gleeful.

glorious, *adj.* 1. admirable, delightful. 2. famous, renowned, noted, celebrated, famed, eminent, distinguished, illustrious.
Ant. horrible; unknown; notorious.

glory, *n.* 1. praise, honor, distinction, renown, fame, eminence, celebrity. 2. resplendence, splendor, magnificence, grandeur, pomp, brilliance, effulgence. —*v.* 3. exult, rejoice, triumph.
Ant. infamy, dishonor; gloom.

gloss, *n.* 1. luster, sheen, polish, glaze, shine. 2. front, mien, appearance, pretext, pretence. 3. explanation, exegesis, critique, comment, note, interpretation, analysis, annotation, commentary. —*v.* 4. polish, shine, glaze, varnish. 5. annotate, explain, interpret, analyze.

glossy, *adj.* 1. lustrous, shiny, shining, glazed, smooth, sleek. 2. specious, plausible.

gnome, *n.* goblin, troll, sylph, gremlin.

gobble, *v.* gulp, bolt, devour, swallow.

godly, *adj.* pious, saintly, devout, religious, holy, righteous, good.
Ant. ungodly.

good, *adj.* 1. moral, righteous, religious, pious, pure, virtuous, conscientious, meritorious, worthy, exemplary, upright. 2. commendable, adroit, efficient, proficient, able, skillful, expert, ready, dexterous, clever, capable, qualified, fit, suited, suitable, convenient. 3. satisfactory, excellent, exceptional, valuable, precious, capital, admirable, commendable. 4. well-behaved, obedient, heedful. 5. kind, beneficent, friendly, kindly, benevolent, humane, favorable, well-disposed, gracious, obliging. 6. honorable, worthy, deserving, fair, unsullied, immaculate, unblemished, unimpeached. 7. reliable, safe, trustworthy, honest, competent. 8. genuine, sound, valid. 9. agreeable, pleasant, genial, cheering. 10. satisfactory, advantageous, favorable, auspicious, propitious, fortunate, profitable, useful, serviceable, beneficial. 11. ample, sufficient. 12. full, adequate, all of. 13. great, considerable, large. —*n.* 14. profit, worth, advantage, benefit, usefulness, utility, gain. 15. excellence, merit, righteousness, kindness, virtue. 16. (*plural*) property, belongings, effects, chattel, furniture. 17. (*plural*) wares, merchandise, stock, commodities. *Ant.* bad.

goodness, *n.* 1. virtue, morality, integrity, honesty, uprightness, probity, righteousness, good. 2. kindness, benevolence, generosity, kindliness, benignity, humanity. 3. excellence, worth, value, quality. 4. essence, strength. *Ant.* evil.

good will, 1. friendliness, benevolence, favor, kindness. 2. acquiescence, heartiness, ardor, zeal, earnestness.

gorge, *n.* 1. defile, pass, cleft, fissure, ravine, notch. 2. disgust, repulsion, revulsion. —*v.* 3. stuff, glut, cram, fill. 4. bolt, gulp, gobble, devour, gormandize.

gorgeous, *adj.* sumptuous, magnificent, splendid, rich, grand, resplendent, brilliant, glittering, dazzling, superb. *Ant.* poor; ugly.

gossip, *n.* 1. scandal, small talk, hearsay, palaver, idle talk, newsmongering. 2. chatterer, babbler, gabber, nosy Parker. —*v.* 3. chatter, prattle, prate, palaver, tattle.

govern, *v.* 1. rule, reign, hold sway, control, command, sway, influence, have control. 2. direct, guide, restrain, check, conduct, manage, supervise, superintend. *Ant.* obey; follow.

gown, *n.* dress, robe, frock, evening gown *or* dress.

grace, *n.* 1. attractiveness, charm, gracefulness, comeliness, ease, elegance, symmetry, beauty; polish, refinement. 2. favor, kindness, kindliness, love, good will, benignity, condescension. 3. mercy, clemency, pardon, leniency, lenity, forgiveness. 4. love, sanctity, holiness, devoutness, devotion, piety. —*v.* 5. adorn, embellish, beautify, enhance, deck, decorate, ornament; honor, dignify. *Ant.* ugliness; disfavor; condemnation; hate, abhorrence; dishonor, disgrace.

gracious, *adj.* 1. kind, kindly, benevolent, benign, courteous, polite, courtly, friendly, well-disposed, favorable. 2. compassionate, tender, merciful, lenient, clement, mild, gentle. 3. indulgent, beneficent, condescending, patronizing.

Ant. ungracious, unkind, impolite, unfavorable; dispassionate, cool, cruel, inclement.

gradual, *adj.* slow, by degrees, little by little, step by step, moderate, gentle. *Ant.* sudden, precipitous, abrupt, immoderate.

grand, *adj.* 1. imposing, stately, august, majestic, dignified, exalted, elevated, eminent, princely, regal, kingly, royal, great, illustrious. 2. lofty, magnificent, great, large, palatial, splendid, brilliant, superb, glorious, sublime, noble, fine. 3. main, principal, chief. 4. important, distinctive, pretentious. 5. complete, comprehensive, inclusive, all-inclusive. *Ant.* base, undignified; ignoble; secondary; unimportant; incomplete.

grandiloquent, *adj.* lofty, pompous, bombastic, turgid, inflated, declamatory, rhetorical, oratorical, high-flown, pretentious, haughty, highfalutin. *Ant.* base, servile, lowly.

grant, *v.* 1. bestow, confer, award, bequeath, give. 2. agree *or* accede to, admit, allow, concede, accept, cede, yield. 3. transmit, convey, transfer. —*n.* 4. cession, concession, bequest, conveyance. *Ant.* receive.

graphic, *adj.* 1. lifelike, vivid, picturesque, striking, telling. 2. diagrammatic, well-delineated, detailed.

grasp, *v.* 1. seize, hold, clasp, grip, clutch, grab, catch. 2. lay hold of, seize upon, fasten on; concentrate on, comprehend, understand. —*n.* 3. grip, hold, clutches. 4. hold, possession, mastery. 5. reach, comprehension, compass, scope. *Ant.* loose, loosen; misunderstand.

grateful, *adj.* 1. appreciative, thankful, obliged, indebted. 2. pleasing, agreeable, welcome, refreshing, pleasant, gratifying, satisfying, satisfactory. *Ant.* ungrateful; unpleasant, disagreeable, unsatisfactory.

gratify, *v.* please, indulge, humor, satisfy. *Ant.* displease, dissatisfy.

grave, *n.* 1. place of interment, tomb, sepulchre, pit, excavation. —*adj.* 2. sober, solemn, serious, dignified, sedate, earnest, staid, thoughtful. 3. weighty, momentous, important, serious, consequential, critical. *Ant.* undignified, thoughtless; unimportant, trivial, trifling.

great, *adj.* 1. immense, enormous, huge, gigantic, vast, ample, grand, large, big. 2. numerous, countless. 3. unusual, considerable, important, momentous, serious, weighty. 4. notable, remarkable, noteworthy. 5. distinguished, famous, famed, eminent, noted, prominent, celebrated, illustrious, grand, renowned. 6. consequential, important, vital, critical. 7. chief, principal, main, grand, leading. 8. noble, lofty, grand, exalted, elevated, dignified, majestic, august. 9. admirable, notable. *Ant.* small; insignificant; paltry; infamous, notorious; trivial; secondary.

greed, *n.* desire, avidity, avarice, cupidity, covetousness, greediness, voracity, ravenousness, rapacity. *Ant.* generosity.

greedy, *adj.* 1. grasping, rapacious, selfish, avaricious. 2. gluttonous, voracious, ravenous, starved, insatiable. 3. desirous, covetous, eager, anxious. *Ant.* generous, unselfish.

greet, *v.* address, welcome, hail, accost, salute.

grief, *n.* suffering, distress, sorrow, regret, anguish, heartache, woe, misery, sadness, melancholy, moroseness. *Ant.* joy, happiness, glee, delight.

grieve, *v.* 1. lament, weep, mourn, sorrow, suffer, bewail, bemoan. 2. distress, sadden, depress, agonize, break one's heart, pain. *Ant.* delight in.

grievous, *adj.* 1. distressing, sad, sorrowful, painful, lamentable, regrettable. 2. deplorable, lamentable, calamitous, heinous, outrageous, flagrant, atrocious, flagitious, dreadful, gross, shameful, iniquitous. *Ant.* delighted, happy, joyful; delightful, pleasant, favorable.

grim, *adj.* 1. stern, unrelenting, merciless, uncompromising, harsh, unyielding. 2. sinister, ghastly, repellent, frightful, horrible, dire, appalling, horrid, grisly, gruesome, hideous, dreadful. 3. severe, stern, harsh, hard, fierce, forbidding, ferocious, cruel, savage, ruthless. *Ant.* merciful, lenient, sympathetic; wonderful, delightful, pleasant; amenable, genial, congenial, amiable.

grind, *v.* 1. smooth, sharpen. 2. bray, triturate, pulverize, powder, crush, comminute, pound. 3. oppress, torment, harass, persecute, plague, afflict, trouble. 4. grate, rub, abrade.

grit, *n.* 1. sand, gravel. 2. spirit, pluck, fortitude, courage, resolution.

gross, *adj.* 1. whole, entire, total, aggregate. 2. glaring, flagrant, outrageous, shameful, heinous, grievous. 3. coarse, indelicate, indecent, low, animal, sensual, vulgar, broad, lewd. 4. large, big, bulky, massive, great. 5. thick, dense, heavy. —*n.* 6. body, bulk, mass.
Ant. partial, incomplete; delicate, decent; small, dainty.

ground, *n.* 1. land, earth, soil, mold, loam, dirt. 2. (*often plural*) foundation, basis, base, premise, motive, reason, cause, consideration, factor, account. 3. (*plural*) lees, dregs, sediment, silt, deposit. —*v.* 4. found, fix, settle, establish, base, set. 5. instruct, train.
Ant. sky, heaven; embellishment.

grow, *v.* 1. increase, swell, enlarge, dilate, greaten, expand, extend. 2. sprout, germinate; arise, originate. 3. swell, wax, extend, advance, improve. 4. raise, cultivate, produce.
Ant. decrease, shrink; wane, deteriorate.

growl, *v.* 1. snarl. 2. grumble, complain, mumble.

growth, *n.* 1. development, increase, augmentation, expansion. 2. product, outgrowth, result; produce. 3.

(*pathology*) tumor, excrescence. 4. source, production.
Ant. failure, stagnation.

grudge, *n.* 1. malice, ill will, spite, resentment, bitterness, rancor, malevolence, enmity, hatred. —*v.* 2. suffer, yield, submit to. 3. begrudge, envy.
Ant. good will, amiability.

guarantee, *n.* 1. guaranty, warrant, pledge, assurance, promise, surety, security. —*v.* 2. guaranty, secure, ensure, insure, warrant.

guard, *v.* 1. protect, keep safe, preserve, save, watch over, shield, defend, shelter. 2. hold, check, watch, be careful. —*n.* 3. protector, guardian, sentry, watchman, defender, sentinel. 4. convoy, escort. 5. defense, protection, shield, bulwark, security, aegis, safety.
Ant. attack, assault; ignore; danger.

guardian, *n.* 1. guard, protector, defender. 2. trustee, warden, keeper.
Ant. assailant.

guess, *v.* 1. conjecture, hazard, suppose, fancy, believe, imagine, think. 2. estimate, solve, answer, penetrate. —*n.* 3. notion, judgment, conclusion, conjecture, surmise, supposition.
Ant. know.

guest, *n.* visitor, company.
Ant. host.

guide, *v.* 1. lead, pilot, steer, conduct, direct, show *or* point the way, escort, instruct, induce, influence, regulate, manage, govern, rule. —*n.* 2. pilot, steersman, helmsman, director, conductor. 3. mark, sign, signal, indication, key, clue.
Ant. follow.

guile, *n.* cunning, treachery, deceit, artifice, duplicity, deception, trickery, fraud, craft, artfulness.
Ant. ingenuousness.

guileless, *adj.* artless, honest, sincere, open, candid, frank, truthful, ingenuous, naive, unsophisticated, simple-minded.
Ant. cunning, sly, deceitful, artful, treacherous.

guilt, *n.* guiltiness, culpability, criminality.
Ant. exoneration.

guiltless, *adj.* innocent, spotless, blameless, immaculate, pure, unsullied, unpolluted, untarnished.
Ant. culpable, guilty, sullied, tarnished.

guise, *n.* appearance, aspect, semblance, form, shape, fashion, mode, manner.

gush, *v.* pour, stream, spurt, flow, spout, flood.

H

habit, *n.* 1. disposition, tendency, bent, wont. 2. custom, practice, way, usage, wont, manner. 3. garb, dress, rig, habiliment. —*v.* 4. dress, clothe, garb, array, attire, deck out, rig, equip.

habitual, *adj.* confirmed, inveterate, accustomed, customary, usual, common, regular, familiar, ordinary.
Ant. rare, unaccustomed, unusual, uncommon, irregular.

habituate, *v.* accustom, familiarize, acclimate, acclimatize, train, inure, harden, make used (to).

hack, *v.* 1. cut, notch, chop, hew, mangle. 2. let, hire, lease, rent. 3. hackney. —*n.* 4. cut, notch, gash. 5. jade, nag. —*adj.* 6. hired, hackney, mercenary. 7. hackneyed, trite, clichéd, overdone, old, used, worn out, commonplace, stale, stereotyped; old hat.
Ant. novel, new.

haggard, *adj.* wild-looking, careworn, gaunt, emaciated, drawn, hollow-eyed, meager, spare, worn, wasted.
Ant. hale, hearty, robust.

haggle, *v.* 1. bargain, chaffer, higgle, palter, negotiate. 2. wrangle, dispute, cavil, argue. 3. harass, annoy, vex, tease, worry, badger, bait, fret. 4. hack, mangle, chop, cut. —*n.* 5. haggling, wrangle, dispute, argument, disagreement.

hale, *adj.* 1. robust, healthy, vigorous, sound, strong, hearty. —*v.* 2. drag, haul, pull, tug, draw.
Ant. haggard, weak, feeble.

half-hearted, *adj.* unenthusiastic, indifferent, uninterested, cold, cool, perfunctory, curt, abrupt, discouraging.
Ant. enthusiastic, eager, encouraging.

hallowed, *adj.* sacred, consecrated, holy, blessed; honored, revered.
Ant. execrative, blasphemous.

hallucination, *n.* illusion, delusion, aberration, phantasm, vision.
Ant. reality.

halt, *v.* 1. hold, stop, cease, desist. 2. waver, hesitate.
Ant. continue, persist.

hamlet, *n.* village, community, town, dorp.

hamper, *v.* 1. impede, hinder, hold back, encumber, prevent, obstruct, restrain, clog. —*n.* 2. basket; crate.
Ant. further, encourage.

handsome, *adj.* 1. comely, fine, admirable, good-looking. 2. liberal, considerable, ample, large, generous, magnanimous. 3. gracious, generous.
Ant. ugly, unattractive; stingy, penurious, parsimonious.

hang, *v.* 1. suspend, dangle. 2. execute, lynch. 3. drape, decorate, adorn, furnish. 4. depend, rely, rest; hold fast, cling, adhere. 5. be doubtful *or* undecided, waver, hesitate, demur, halt. 6. loiter, linger, hover, flot. 7. impend, be imminent.

happen, *v.* come to pass, take place, occur, chance; befall, betide.

happiness, *n.* good fortune, pleasure, contentment, gladness, bliss, content, contentedness, beatitude, blessedness, delight, joy, enjoyment, gratification, satisfaction. *Ant.* misery, dissatisfaction.

happy, *adj.* 1. joyous, joyful, glad, blithe, merry, cheerful, contented, gay, blissful, delighted, satisfied, pleased, gladdened. 2. favored, lucky, fortunate, propitious, advantageous, successful, prosperous. 3. appropriate, fitting, apt, felicitous, opportune, befitting, pertinent. *Ant.* unhappy, sad, cheerless, melancholy; unlucky, luckless, unfortunate; inappropriate, inapt.

harangue, *n.* 1. address, speech, bombast. —*v.* 2. declaim, address.

harass, *v.* trouble, harry, raid, molest, disturb, distress; plague, vex, worry, badger, pester, annoy, torment, torture.

harbor, *n.* 1. haven, port. 2. shelter, refuge, asylum, protection, cover, sanctuary, retreat. —*v.* 3. shelter, protect, lodge. 4. conceal, hide, secrete. 5. entertain, indulge, foster, cherish.

hard, *adj.* 1. solid, firm, inflexible, rigid, unyielding, resistant, resisting, adamantine, flinty, impenetrable, compact. 2. difficult, toilsome, burdensome, wearisome, exhausting, laborious, arduous, onerous, fatiguing, wearying. 3. difficult, complex, intricate, complicated, perplexing, tough, puzzling. 4. vigorous, severe, violent, stormy, tempestuous; inclement. 5. oppressive, harsh, rough, cruel, severe, unmerciful, grinding, unsparing, unrelenting. 6. severe, harsh, stern, austere, strict, exacting, callous, unfeeling, unsympathetic, impassionate, insensible, unimpressible, insensitive, indifferent, unpitying, inflexible, relentless, unyielding, cruel, obdurate, adamant, hard-hearted. 7. undeniable, irrefutable, incontrovertible. 8. unfriendly, unkind; harsh, unpleasant. 9. unsympathetic, unsentimental, shrewd, hard-headed, callous. 10. strong, spirituous, intoxicating. —*adv.* 11. energetically, vigorously, violently. 12. earnestly, intently, incessantly. 13. harshly, severely, gallingly, with difficulty. 14. solidly, firmly.

Ant. soft; easy; fair; merciful; sympathetic; kind.

harden, *v.* 1. solidify, indurate, ossify, petrify. 2. strengthen, confirm, fortify, steel, brace, nerve, toughen, inure; habituate, accustom, season, train, discipline.

hardly, *adv.* 1. barely, scarcely, nearly. 2. harshly, severely, roughly, cruelly, unkindly, rigorously.

hardship, *n.* trial, oppression, privation, need, austerity, trouble, affliction, burden, suffering, misfortune, grievance.

hardy, *adj.* 1. vigorous, hearty, sturdy, hale, robust, stout, strong, sound, healthy. 2. bold, daring, courageous, brave. *Ant.* weak, feeble, unsound, unhealthy; cowardly, pusillanimous.

harm, *n.* 1. injury, damage, hurt, mischief, detriment. 2. wrong, evil, wickedness, sinfulness. —*n.* 3. injure, hurt, damage; maltreat, molest, abuse. *Ant.* good.

harmful, *adj.* injurious, detrimental, hurtful, deleterious, pernicious, mischievous. *Ant.* beneficial.

harmonious, *adj.* 1. amicable, congenial, sympathetic. 2. consonant, congruous, concordant, consistent, correspondent, symmetrical. 3. melodious, tuneful, agreeable, concordant. *Ant.* unsympathetic; discordant, incongruous, asymmetrical; cacophonous, noisy.

harmony, *n.* 1. agreement, concord, unity, peace, amity, friendship, accord, unison. 2. congruity, consonance, conformity, correspondence, consistency, congruence, fitness, suitability. 3. melody, melodiousness, concord, euphony. *Ant.* discord, disagreement; nonconformity, unfitness; cacophony, noise.

harry, *v.* 1. harass, torment, worry, molest, plague, trouble, vex, gall, fret, disturb, harrow, chafe, annoy, pester. 2. ravage, devastate, plunder, strip, rob, pillage. *Ant.* please, delight, enrapture.

harsh, *adj.* 1. rough; ungentle, unpleasant, severe, austere, brusque, rough, hard, unfeeling, unkind, brutal, cruel, stern, acrimonious, bad-tempered, ill-natured, crabbed, morose. 2. jarring, unaesthetic, inartistic, discordant, dissonant, unharmonious. *Ant.* gentle, pleasant, kind, good-

natured; artistic, aesthetic, harmonious.

haste, *n.* 1. swiftness, celerity, alacrity, quickness, rapidity, dispatch, speed, expedition, promptitude. 2. need, hurry, flurry, bustle, ado, precipitancy, precipitation. *Ant.* sloth.

hasten, *v.* hurry, accelerate, urge, press, expedite, quicken, speed, precipitate, dispatch.

hasty, *adj.* 1. speedy, quick, hurried, swift, rapid, fast, fleet, brisk. 2. precipitate, rash, foolhardy, reckless, indiscreet, thoughtless, headlong, unthinking. 3. quick-tempered, testy, touchy, irascible, petulant, waspish, fretful, fiery, pettish, excitable, irritable, peevish. *Ant.* slow, deliberate; discreet, thoughtful; even-tempered, amiable.

hatch, *v.* 1. incubate, breed, brood. 2. contrive, devise, plan, plot, concoct, design, scheme, project. 3. shade, line. —*n.* 4. brood. 5. door, cover, deck, hatchway.

hate, *v.* 1. dislike; detest, abhor, loathe, despise, execrate, abominate. —*n.* 2. hatred. *Ant.* like, love.

hateful, *adj.* detestable, odious, abominable, execrable, loathsome, abhorrent, repugnant, invidious, obnoxious, offensive, disgusting, nauseating, revolting, vile, repulsive. *Ant.* lovable, appealing, attractive, likable.

hatred, *n.* aversion, animosity, hate, detestation, loathing, abomination, odium, horror, repugnance. *Ant.* attraction, love, favor.

haughty, *adj.* disdainful, proud, arrogant, supercilious, snobbish, lordly, contemptuous. *Ant.* humble, shy, self-effacing.

have, *v.* 1. hold, occupy, possess, own, contain. 2. get, receive, take, obtain, acquire, gain, secure, procure. 3. experience, enjoy, suffer, undergo. 4. permit, allow. 5. assert, maintain, hold, aver, state, asseverate, testify.

havoc, *n.* devastation, ruin, destruction, desolation, waste, damage.

hazard, *n.* 1. danger, peril, jeopardy, risk. 2. chance, hap, accident, luck, fortuity, fortuitousness. 3. uncertainty, doubt. —*v.* 4. venture, offer. 5. imperil, risk, endanger. *Ant.* safety, security; certainty, surety.

haze, *n.* 1. vapor, dust, mist, cloud, fog, smog. 2. obscurity, dimness,

cloud, vagueness. —*v.* 3. torment, torture, abuse, trick.
Ant. clearness, clarity.

head, *n.* 1. command, authority. 2. commander, director, chief, chieftain, leader, principal, commander in chief, master. 3. top, summit, acme. 4. culmination, crisis, conclusion. 5. cape, headland, promontory, ness. 6. source, origin, rise, beginning, headwaters. 7. froth, foam. —*adj.* 8. front, leading, topmost, chief, principal, main, cardinal, foremost, first. —*v.* 9. lead, precede, direct, command, rule, govern. 10. outdo, excel, surpass, beat.

headstrong, *adj.* willful, stubborn, obstinate, intractable, self-willed, dogged, pigheaded, froward.
Ant. amenable, tractable, genial, agreeable.

heal, *v.* 1. cure, remedy, restore. 2. amend, settle, harmonize, compose, soothe. 3. cleanse, purify, purge, disinfect.
Ant. discompose; soil, pollute, infect.

healthy, *adj.* 1. healthful, hale, sound, hearty, well, robust, vigorous, strong. 2. nutritious, nourishing, salubrious, salutary, hygienic, invigorating, bracing, wholesome.
Ant. unhealthy, ill, sick, weak; unwholesome, enervating.

heap, *n.* 1. mass, stack, pile, accumulation, collection. —*v.* 2. pile *or* heap up, amass, accumulate. 3. bestow, confer, cast.

hear, *v.* 1. listen, perceive, attend. 2. regard, heed, attend.

heat, *n.* 1. warmth, caloricity, caloric, hotness. 2. warmth, intensity, ardor, fervor, zeal. 3. ardor, flush, fever, excitement, impetuosity, vehemence, violence. —*v.* 4. stimulate, warm, stir, animate, arouse, excite, rouse.
Ant. coolness; phlegm; cool, discourage.

heathen, *n.* 1. gentile, pagan. —*adj.* 2. gentile, pagan, heathenish, irreligious, unenlightened, barbarous.
Ant. Christian.

heave, *v.* 1. raise, lift, hoist, elevate. 2. pant, exhale, breathe. 3. vomit, retch. 4. rise, swell, dilate, bulge, expand.

heavenly, *adj.* 1. blissful, beautiful, divine, seraphic, cherubic, angelic, saintly, sainted, holy, beatific, blessed, beatified, glorified. 2. celestial.
Ant. hellish, satanic, diabolical, devilish.

heavy, *adj.* 1. weighty, ponderous, massive. 2. burdensome, harsh, oppressive, depressing, onerous, distressing, severe, grievous, cumbersome. 3. broad, thick, coarse, blunt. 4. serious, intense, momentous, weighty, important, pithy, concentrated. 5. trying, difficult. 6. depressed, serious, grave, sorrowful, gloomy, mournful, melancholy, morose, morbid, dejected, sad, disconsolate, crushed, despondent, heavy-hearted, downcast, crestfallen, downhearted. 7. overcast, cloudy, lowering, oppressive, gloomy. 8. clumsy, slow. 9. ponderous, dull, tedious, tiresome, wearisome, burdensome, boring, lifeless. 10. thick, unleavened, dense, concentrated.
Ant. light.

heed, *v.* 1. pay *or* give attention to, consider, regard, notice, mark, observe, obey. —*n.* 2. attention, notice, observation, consideration, care, caution, heedfulness, watchfulness, vigilance.
Ant. disregard, ignore.

height, *n.* 1. altitude, stature, elevation, tallness. 2. hill, prominence, mountain. 3. top, peak, pinnacle, apex, eminence, acme, summit, zenith, culmination.
Ant. depth, abyss.

heinous, *adj.* hateful, odious, reprehensible, grave, wicked, infamous, flagrant, flagitious, atrocious, villainous, nefarious.
Ant. good, beneficial.

hell, *n.* Gehenna, Tartarus, inferno, Abaddon, Avernus, Hades, Erebus, pandemonium, abyss, limbo.
Ant. heaven.

help, *v.* 1. cooperate, aid, assist, encourage, befriend, support, second, uphold, back, abet, succor, save. 2. further, facilitate, promote, ease, foster. 3. relieve, ameliorate, alleviate, remedy, cure, heal, restore, improve, better. 4. refrain from, avoid, forbear. —*n.* 5. support, backing, aid, assistance, relief, succor. 6. helper, handyman, assistant.
Ant. discourage, attack.

helper, *n.* aid, assistant, supporter, auxiliary, ally, colleague, partner.

helpful, *adj.* useful, convenient, beneficial, advantageous, profitable.
Ant. useless, inconvenient, disadvantageous, uncooperative.

herd, *n.* 1. drove, flock, clutch, crowd. —*v.* 2. flock, assemble, associate, keep company.

heritage, *n.* inheritance, estate, patrimony.

heroic, *adj.* intrepid, dauntless, gallant, valorous, brave, courageous, bold, daring, fearless; epic.
Ant. cowardly, fearful.

heroism, *n.* intrepidity, valor, prowess, gallantry, bravery, courage, daring, fortitude, boldness.
Ant. cowardice.

hesitate, *v.* 1. waver, vacillate, falter. 2. demur, delay, pause, wait.
Ant. resolve, decide.

hesitation, *n.* 1. hesitancy, indecision, vacillation, irresolution, delay, uncertainty, doubt. 2. halting, stammering, faltering.
Ant. resolution, certainty.

hew, *v.* 1. cut, chop, hack. 2. make, shape, fashion, form. 3. sever, cut down, fell.

hide, *v.* 1. conceal, secrete, screen, mask, cloak, veil, shroud, cover, disguise, withhold, suppress. —*n.* 2. skin, pelt, rawhide.
Ant. open, reveal.

hideous, *adj.* horrible, frightful, ugly, grisly, grim, revolting, repellent, repulsive, detestable, odious, monstrous, dreadful, appalling, terrifying, terrible, ghastly, macabre, shocking.
Ant. beautiful, lovely, attractive.

high, *adj.* 1. lofty, tall, elevated, towering, skyscraping. 2. intensified, energetic, intense, strong. 3. expensive, costly, dear, high-priced. 4. exalted, elevated, eminent, prominent, preeminent, distinguished. 5. shrill, sharp, acute, high-pitched, strident. 6. chief, main, principal, head. 7. consequential, important, grave, serious, capital, extreme. 8. lofty, haughty, arrogant, snobbish, proud, lordly, supercilious. 9. elated, merry, hilarious, happy. 10. remote, primeval, early, antediluvian, prehistoric; northerly, arctic, southerly, polar.
Ant. low.

hill, *n.* elevation, prominence, eminence, mound, monticule, knoll, hillock, foothill.
Ant. valley, dale, glen, hollow, depth.

hinder, *v.* 1. interrupt, check, retard, impede, encumber, delay, hamper, obstruct, trammel. 2. block, thwart, prevent, obstruct.
Ant. encourage, disencumber.

hindrance, *n.* 1. impeding, stopping, stoppage, estoppage, preventing. 2. impediment, deterrent, hitch, encumbrance, obstruction, check, restraint, hobble, obstacle.
Ant. help, aid, support.

hint, *n.* 1. suggestion, implication, intimation, allusion, insinuation, innuendo, memorandum, reminder, inkling. —*v.* 2. imply, intimate, insinuate, suggest, mention.

hire, *v.* 1. engage, employ; let, lease, rent, charter. 2. bribe, reward. —*n.* 3. rent, rental; pay, stipend, salary, wages, remuneration.

history, *n.* record, chronicle, account, annals, story, relation, narrative.

hit, *v.* 1. strike. 2. reach, attain, gain, win, accomplish, achieve. 3. touch, suit, fit, befit, affect. 4. find, come upon, meet with, discover, happen upon. 5. collide, strike, clash. 6. assail. —*n.* 7. blow, stroke; success.

hitch, *v.* 1. make fast, fasten, connect, hook, tether, attach, tie, unite, harness, yoke. —*n.* 2. halt, obstruction, hindrance, catch, impediment.
Ant. loose, loosen, untie.

hoarse, *adj.* husky, throaty, guttural, gruff, harsh, grating, raucous, rough.

hoist, *v.* 1. raise, elevate, lift, heave. —*n.* 2. derrick, crane, elevator, lift.
Ant. lower.

hold, *v.* 1. have, keep, retain, possess, occupy. 2. bear, sustain, hold up, support, maintain, keep (up), continue, carry on. 3. engage in, observe, celebrate, preside over, carry on, pursue. 4. hinder, restrain, keep back, deactivate, confine, detain. 5. occupy, possess, own. 6. contain, admit. 7. think, believe, embrace, espouse, entertain, have, regard, consider, esteem, judge, deem. 8. continue, persist, last, endure, remain. 9. adhere, cling, remain, stick. —*n.* 10. grasp, grip. 11. control, influence. 12. prison, keep, tower, cell, dungeon, deep.

hole, *n.* 1. aperture, opening, cavity, excavation, pit, hollow, concavity. 2. burrow, lair, den, retreat, cave. 3. hovel, den, cot.

holy, *adj.* 1. blessed, sacred, consecrated, hallowed, dedicated. 2. saintly, godly, divine, pious, devout, spiritual, pure.
Ant. unholy, desecrated, impious, piacular, sinful, impure, corrupt.

homage, *n.* 1. respect, reverence, deference, obeisance, honor, tribute. 2. fealty, allegiance, faithfulness, fidelity, loyalty, devotion. 3. devotion, worship, adoration.
Ant. disrespect, irreverence, dishonor; faithlessness, disloyalty.

home, *n.* 1. house, apartment, residence, household, abode, dwelling, domicile, habitation. 2. refuge, retreat, institution, asylum. 3. hearth, fireside, family; rightful place.

homely, *adj.* plain, simple, unpretentious, unattractive, coarse, inelegant, uncomely, ugly.
Ant. beautiful.

honest, *adj.* 1. honorable, upright, fair, just, incorruptible, trusty, trustworthy, truthful, virtuous, moral. 2. open, sincere, candid, straightforward, frank, unreserved, ingenuous. 3. genuine, pure, unadulterated. 4. chaste, virtuous, pure, virginal, decent.
Ant. dishonest; corrupt, disingenuous, untrustworthy, secretive; false, counterfeit; impure, venal, indecent.

honesty, *n.* 1. uprightness, probity, integrity, justice, fairness, rectitude, equity, honor. 2. truthfulness, sincerity, candor, frankness, truth, veracity.
Ant. dishonesty, inequity; deceit, insincerity.

honor, *n.* 1. esteem, fame, glory, repute, reputation, credit. 2. credit, distinction, dignity. 3. respect, deference, homage, reverence, veneration, consideration, distinction. 4. privilege, favor. 5. character, principle, probity, uprightness, honesty, integrity, nobleness. 6. purity, chastity, virginity. —*v.* 7. revere, esteem, venerate, respect, reverence; adore, worship, hallow.
Ant. dishonor, disrepute, discredit; indignity; disfavor; indecency; execrate, abominate.

honorable, *adj.* 1. upright, honest, noble, highminded, just, fair, trusty, trustworthy, true, virtuous. 2. dignified, distinguished, noble, illustrious, great. 3. creditable, reputable, estimable, right, proper, equitable.
Ant. ignoble, untrustworthy, corrupt; undignified; disreputable.

hope, *n.* 1. expectation, expectancy, longing, desire. 2. confidence, trust, reliance, faith. —*v.* 3. trust, expect.
Ant. hopelessness.

hopeful, *adj.* expectant, sanguine, optimistic, confident.
Ant. hopeless.

hopeless, *adj.* 1. desperate, despairing, despondent, forlorn, disconsolate. 2. irremediable, remediless, incurable.
Ant. hopeful.

horrible, *adj.* 1. horrendous, terrible, horrid, dreadful, awful, appalling, frightful, hideous, grim, ghastly, shocking, revolting, repulsive, repellent, dire, formidable, horrifying, harrowing. 2. unpleasant, deplorable, shocking, abominable, odious.
Ant. attractive, delightful, beautiful; pleasant.

horror, *n.* 1. fear, abhorrence, terror, dread, dismay, consternation, panic, alarm. 2. aversion, repugnance, loathing, antipathy, detestation, hatred, abomination.
Ant. calm, serenity; attraction, delight, love.

hospital, *n.* retreat, sanatorium, asylum, sanitarium, clinic.

hostile, *adj.* opposed, adverse, averse, unfriendly, inimical, antagonistic, contrary, warlike, oppugnant, repugnant.
Ant. friendly, amiable, amicable.

hostility, *n.* 1. enmity, antagonism, animosity, animus, ill will, unfriendliness, opposition, hatred. 2. (*plural*) war, warfare, fighting, conflict.
Ant. friendliness, good will, love; peace, truce.

hot, *adj.* 1. heated, torrid, sultry, burning, fiery. 2. pungent, piquant, sharp, acrid, spicy, peppery, biting, blistering. 3. ardent, fervent, fervid, angry, furious, vehement, intense, excited, excitable, irascible, animated, violent, passionate, impetuous.
Ant. cold.

hotel, *n.* hostelry, hostel, inn, house, guest house, motel, tavern.

house, *n.* 1. domicile, dwelling, residence, home, household. 2. firm, company, partnership, business, establishment. —*v.* 3. lodge, harbor, shelter, reside, dwell.

hubbub, *n.* noise, tumult, uproar, clamor, din, racket, disorder, confusion, disturbance, riot.
Ant. serenity, calm.

huge, *adj.* large, extensive, mammoth, vast, gigantic, colossal, stupendous, bulky, enormous, immense, tremendous, Cyclopean.
Ant. tiny, small, infinitesimal, microscopic.

humane, *adj.* 1. merciful, kind, kindly, kindhearted, tender, human, benevolent, sympathetic, compassionate, gentle, accommodating, benignant, charitable. 2. refining, polite, cultivating, elevating, humanizing, spiritual.
Ant. inhumane, cruel, ruthless, merciless; boorish, degrading.

humble, *adj.* 1. low, lowly, unassuming, plain, common, poor, meek, modest, submissive, unpretending,

unpretentious. 2. respectful, polite, courteous, courtly. —*v.* 3. lower, abase, debase, degrade, humiliate, reduce, mortify, shame, subdue, abash, crush, break.
Ant. haughty, immodest, snobbish, conceited, pretentious; impolite, discourteous; raise, elevate.

humbug, *n.* 1. trick, hoax, fraud, imposture, deception, imposition. 2. falseness, deception, sham, pretense, hypocrisy, charlatanism. 3. cheat, impostor, swindler, charlatan, pretender, confidence man, deceiver, quack. —*v.* 4. impose upon, delude, deceive, cheat, swindle, trick, fool, dupe.

humid, *adj.* damp, dank, wet, moist.
Ant. dry.

humiliate, *v.* mortify, degrade, debase, dishonor, disgrace, abash, shame, humble.
Ant. honor, elevate, exalt.

humiliation, *n.* mortification, shame, abasement, degradation, humbling, dishonoring.
Ant. honor, elevation.

humility, *n.* lowliness, meekness, humbleness, submissiveness.
Ant. haughtiness.

humor, *n.* 1. wit, fun, facetiousness, pleasantry. 2. disposition, tendency, temperament, mood; whim, caprice, fancy, vagary. —*v.* 3. indulge, gratify.

humorous, *adj.* amusing, funny, jocose, jocular, droll, comic, comical, witty, facetious, waggish, sportive, ludicrous, laughable.
Ant. serious, sad, melancholy.

hungry, *adj.* ravenous, famishing, famished, starved, starving.
Ant. sated.

hunt, *v.* 1. chase, pursue, track. 2. search for, seek, scour. —*n.* 3. chase, pursuit, hunting; search.

hurry, *v.* 1. rush, haste, hasten, be quick, move swiftly *or* quickly. 2. hasten, urge, forward, accelerate, quicken, expedite, hustle, dispatch. —*n.* 3. bustle, haste, dispatch, celerity, speed, quickness, alacrity, promptitude, expedition. 4. bustle, ado, precipitation, flurry, flutter, confusion, perturbation.
Ant. delay, slow.

hurt, *v.* 1. injure, harm, damage, mar, impair. 2. pain, ache, grieve, afflict, wound. —*n.* 3. injury, harm, damage, detriment, disadvantage; bruise, wound.

hut, *n.* cottage, cot, cabin, shed, hovel.

hybrid, *n.* half-breed, mongrel, mutt.

hypocrite, *n.* deceiver, pretender, dissembler, pharisee.

hypocritical, *adj.* sanctimonious, pharisaical, Pecksniffian; insincere, deceiving, dissembling, pretending, false, hollow, empty, deceptive, misleading, deceitful.
Ant. honest, direct, forthright, sincere.

I

icon, *n.* picture, image, symbol, idol, representation, sign.

idea, *n.* 1. thought, conception, notion; impression, apprehension, fancy. 2. opinion, view, belief, sentiment, judgment, supposition. 3. intention, plan, object, objective, aim.

ideal, *n.* 1. example, model, conception, epitome, standard. 2. aim, object, intention, objective. —*adj.* 3. perfect, consummate, complete. 4. unreal, unpractical, impractical, imaginary, visionary, fanciful, fantastic, illusory, chimerical.

idiotic, *adj.* foolish, senseless, half-witted, stupid, fatuous, imbecilic.
Ant. intelligent, sensible.

idle, *adj.* 1. unemployed, unoccupied, inactive. 2. indolent, slothful, lazy, sluggish. 3. worthless, unimportant, trivial, trifling, insignificant, useless, fruitless, vain, ineffective, unavailing, ineffectual, abortive, baseless, groundless. 4. frivolous, vain, wasteful. —*v.* 5. waste, fritter away, idle away, loiter.
Ant. employed, occupied; active, energetic; worthy, important; thrifty.

idol, *n.* 1. image, icon, symbol, statue, false god, pagan deity. 2. favorite, fair-haired boy, darling, pet. 3. figment, delusion, illusion.

if, *conj.* 1. in case, provided, providing, granting, supposing, even though, though; whether, whether or not. —*n.* 2. condition, supposition.

ignite, *v.* kindle, fire, set fire to, set on fire.
Ant. quench.

ignoble, *adj.* 1. mean, base, ignominious, degraded, dishonorable, contemptible, vulgar, low, peasant. 2. inferior, base, mean, insignificant. 3. lowly, humble, obscure, plebeian, contemptible.
Ant. noble, honorable; superior, significant; haughty.

ignominious, *adj.* discreditable, humiliating, degrading, disgraceful, dishonorable, shameful, infamous, disreputable, opprobrious, despicable, scandalous, contemptible.
Ant. creditable, honorable, reputable.

ignominy, *n.* disgrace, dishonor, disrepute, contempt, discredit, shame, infamy, obloquy, opprobrium, scandal, odium, abasement.
Ant. credit, honor, repute, fame, distinction.

ignorant, *adj.* illiterate, unlettered, uneducated, unlearned, uninstructed, untutored, untaught, unenlightened, nescient.
Ant. literate, lettered, educated.

ignore, *v.* overlook, slight, disregard, neglect.
Ant. notice, note, regard, mark.

ill, *adj.* 1. unwell, sick, indisposed, unhealthy, ailing, diseased, afflicted. 2. evil, wicked, bad, wrong, iniquitous, naughty. 3. objectionable, unsatisfactory, poor, faulty. 4. hostile, unkindly, unkind, unfavorable, adverse. —*n.* 5. evil, wickedness, depravity, badness. 6. harm, injury, hurt, pain, affliction, misery, trouble, misfortune, calamity. 7. disease, ailment, illness, affliction. —*adv.* 8. illy, wickedly, badly. 9. poorly, unsatisfactorily. 10. unfavorably, unfortunately. 11. faultily, improperly.
Ant. well, hale, healthy; good; satisfactory; favorably, properly.

illegal, *adj.* unauthorized, unlawful, illegitimate, illicit, unlicensed.
Ant. legal, licit, authorized.

ill-mannered, *adj.* impolite, uncivil, discourteous, uncourtly, rude, coarse, uncouth, unpolished, crude, rough, ill-bred.

ill-natured, *adj.* cross, cranky, petulant, testy, snappish, unkindly, unpleasant, sulky, ill-tempered, crabbed, morose, sullen, dour, gloomy, sour, crusty, perverse, acerb, bitter.
Ant. good-natured, kindly, pleasant, amiable, friendly.

illusion, *n.* delusion, hallucination, deception, fantasy, chimera. *Ant.* fact, reality.

illustration, *n.* comparison, example, case, elucidation, explanation, explication.

image, *n.* 1. icon, idol, representation, statue. 2. reflection, likeness, effigy, figure, representation. 3. idea, conception, notion, mental picture. 4. form, appearance, semblance. 5. counterpart, facsimile, copy. —*v.* 6. imagine, conceive. *Ant.* original.

imaginary, *adj.* fanciful, unreal, visionary, baseless, chimerical, shadowy, fancied, illusory, imagined. *Ant.* real.

imagine, *v.* conceive, image, picture, conceive of, realize, think, believe, fancy, assume, suppose, guess, conjecture, hypothesize.

imbibe, *v.* drink, absorb, swallow, take in, receive.

imitate, *v.* follow, mimic, ape, mock, impersonate, copy, duplicate, reproduce, simulate, counterfeit.

immediate, *adj.* 1. instant, without delay, present, instantaneous. 2. present, next, near, close, proximate. 3. direct, unmediated. *Ant.* later.

immediately, *adv.* 1. instantly, at once, without delay, presently, directly, instanter, instantaneously, forthwith. 2. directly, closely, without intervention. *Ant.* later, anon.

immense, *adj.* huge, great, vast, extensive. *Ant.* small, tiny, submicroscopic.

immerse, *v.* 1. plunge, dip, sink, immerge, duck, douse. 2. embed, bury; involve, absorb, engage. *Ant.* withdraw; disinter.

imminent, *adj.* 1. impending, threatening, near, at hand. 2. overhanging, leaning forward. *Ant.* delayed, far off.

immoderate, *adj.* excessive, extreme, exorbitant, unreasonable, inordinate, extravagant, intemperate. *Ant.* moderate, reasonable, temperate.

immoral, *adj.* abandoned, depraved, self-indulgent, dissipated, licentious, dissolute, profligate, unprincipled, vicious, sinful, corrupt, amoral, wicked, bad, wrong, evil. *Ant.* moral, pious, good.

immunity, *n.* 1. insusceptibility. 2. exemption, franchise, privilege, license, charter, right, liberty, prerogative. *Ant.* susceptibility; proneness.

impair, *v.* injure; worsen, diminish, deteriorate, lessen. *Ant.* repair.

impart, *v.* 1. communicate, disclose, divulge, reveal, make known, tell, relate. 2. give, bestow, grant, cede, confer. *Ant.* conceal, hide.

impartial, *adj.* unbiased, just, fair, unprejudiced, disinterested, equitable. *Ant.* partial.

impatient, *adj.* 1. uneasy, restless, unquiet. 2. hasty, impetuous, vehement, precipitate, sudden, curt, brusque, abrupt. 3. irritable, testy, fretful, violent, hot. *Ant.* patient, restful, quiet; gradual, slow; calm, unperturbed.

impecunious, *adj.* penniless, poor, destitute, poverty-stricken. *Ant.* wealthy, rich.

impede, *v.* retard, slow, delay, hinder, hamper, prevent, obstruct, check, stop, block, thwart, interrupt, restrain. *Ant.* aid, encourage.

impediment, *n.* bar, hindrance, obstacle, obstruction, encumbrance, check. *Ant.* help, support, encouragement.

impel, *v.* compel, drive, urge, press on, incite, constrain, force, actuate. *Ant.* restrain.

imperfect, *adj.* 1. defective, faulty, incomplete. 2. rudimentary, undeveloped, underdeveloped, incomplete; immature. *Ant.* perfect.

imperious, *adj.* 1. domineering, overbearing, dictatorial, tyrannical, despotic, arrogant. 2. urgent, imperative, necessary. *Ant.* submissive; unnecessary.

impertinent, *adj.* 1. intrusive, presumptuous, impudent, insolent, rude, fresh, bold, arrogant, insulting, officious, saucy, pert, brazen. 2. irrelevant, inappropriate, incongruous, inapplicable. 3. trivial, silly, absurd, ridiculous, inane. *Ant.* polite, courteous; appropriate; important, serious.

impetuous, *adj.* impulsive, rash, precipitate, spontaneous, violent, hasty, furious, hot. *Ant.* planned, careful.

implacable, *adj.* unappeased, unpacified, inexorable, inflexible, unbending, relentless, unappeasable, rancorous, merciless. *Ant.* flexible, merciful.

implicate, *v.* involve, concern, entangle. *Ant.* disentangle.

implore, *v.* call upon, supplicate, beseech, entreat, crave, beg, solicit.

impolite, *adj.* uncivil, rude, discourteous, disrespectful, insolent, unpolished, unrefined, boorish, ill-mannered, rough, savage. *Ant.* polite.

importance, *n.* consequence, weight, moment, significance, import, momentousness, weightiness. *Ant.* unimportance, insignificance.

impostor, *n.* pretender, deceiver, cheat, confidence man, con man, intruder, trickster, knave, hypocrite, charlatan, mountebank.

impregnable, *adj.* unassailable, invincible, invulnerable. *Ant.* pregnable, vulnerable.

improper, *adj.* 1. inapplicable, unsuited, unfit, inappropriate, unsuitable. 2. indecent, unbecoming, unseemly, indecorous, unfitting. 3. abnormal, irregular. *Ant.* proper.

improve, *v.* 1. ameliorate, better, amend, emend, correct, right, rectify. 2. mend, gain, get better. *Ant.* worsen, impair; fail, sink.

improvident, *adj.* 1. incautious, unwary, thoughtless, careless, imprudent, heedless, without *or* lacking foresight. 2. thriftless, shiftless, neglectful, wasteful, prodigal. *Ant.* provident, cautious; thrifty.

improvised, *adj.* extemporaneous, impromptu, unpremeditated, unrehearsed, spontaneous. *Ant.* premeditated.

impudence, *n.* impertinence, effrontery, insolence, rudeness, brass, brazenness, face, lip, boldness, presumption, presumptiveness, sauciness, pertness, flippancy; (*colloquial*) nerve. *Ant.* politeness, courtesy.

impudent, *adj.* bold, brazen, brassy, presumptuous, insolent, impertinent, insulting, rude, presumptive, saucy, pert, flippant, fresh. *Ant.* polite, courteous, well-behaved.

impulsive, *adj.* emotional, impetuous, rash, quick, hasty, unpremeditated. *Ant.* cool, cold, unemotional, premeditated.

impunity, *n.* exemption, license, permission. *Ant.* responsibility, blame, culpability.

impute, *v.* attribute, charge, ascribe, refer.

inability, *n.* incapability, incapacity, disqualification, impotence, incompetence.
Ant. ability.

inaccuracy, *n.* 1. incorrectness, erroneousness, inexactness, inexactitude. 2. error, blunder, mistake, slip.
Ant. accuracy.

inaccurate, *adj.* inexact, loose, general, unspecific; incorrect, wrong, erroneous, faulty, improper.
Ant. accurate.

inactive, *adj.* inert, dormant, unmoving, immobile, inoperative; indolent, lazy, sluggish, torpid, passive, idle, slothful, dilatory.
Ant. active.

inadequate, *adj.* inapt, incompetent, insufficient, incommensurate, defective, imperfect, incomplete.
Ant. adequate.

inadvertent, *adj.* heedless, inattentive, unintentional, thoughtless, careless, negligent.
Ant. intentional, purposive, purposeful.

inanimate, *adj.* 1. lifeless, inorganic, vegetable, mineral, mechanical. 2. spiritless, lifeless, sluggish, inert, spiritless; dead, defunct.
Ant. animate, alive; spirited.

inapt, *adj.* 1. unsuited, unsuitable, inappropriate, not pertinent. 2. incapable, clumsy, awkward, slow, dull.
Ant. apt, suitable, appropriate, fit; capable, efficient.

inborn, *adj.* innate, inbred, native, natural, congenital, inherent, instinctive, inherited.
Ant. acquired, learned, conditioned, environmental.

incapable, *adj.* unable, incompetent, inefficient, impotent, unqualified; incapacious.
Ant. capable, competent, efficient, potent, qualified.

incarcerate, *v.* imprison, commit, confine, jail; constrict, enclose, restrict.
Ant. liberate, free.

incense, *n.* 1. perfume, aroma, scent, fragrance. —*v.* 2. inflame, enrage, exasperate, provoke, irritate, goad, vex, excite.

incentive, *n.* motive, inducement, incitement, enticement, stimulus, spur, impulse, goad, encouragement, prod.
Ant. discouragement.

incessant, *adj.* uninterrupted, unceasing, ceaseless, continual, contin-uous, constant, unending, never-ending, relentless, unrelenting, unremitting, perpetual, eternal, everlasting.
Ant. interrupted, spasmodic, sporadic; temporary.

incident, *n.* event, occurrence, happening, circumstance.

incidental, *adj.* fortuitous, chance, accidental, casual, contingent.
Ant. fundamental.

incisive, *adj.* 1. penetrating, trenchant, biting, acute, sarcastic, sardonic, satirical, acid, severe, cruel. 2. sharp, keen, acute.
Ant. superficial; dull.

incite, *v.* urge on, stimulate, encourage, back, prod, push, spur, goad, instigate, provoke, arouse, fire; induce.
Ant. discourage.

inclination, *n.* 1. bent, leaning, tendency, set, propensity, liking, preference, predilection, predisposition, proclivity, bias, proneness, prejudice, penchant. 2. slope, slant, leaning, inclining; verging, tending, tendency.
Ant. dislike, antipathy.

include, *v.* contain, embrace, comprise, comprehend, embody.
Ant. exclude, preclude.

income, *n.* return, returns, receipts, revenue, profits, salary, wages, pay, stipend, interest, annuity, gain, earnings.
Ant. expense, expenditure.

incommode, *v.* 1. inconvenience, discomfort, disturb, annoy, vex, trouble, discommode. 2. impede, hinder, interfere, delay.
Ant. comfort; encourage, aid, abet, support, expedite.

incompatible, *adj.* 1. inconsistent, incongruous, unsuitable, unsuited, contradictory, irreconcilable. 2. discordant, contrary, opposed, difficult, contradictory, inharmonious.
Ant. compatible, consistent, appropriate; harmonious.

incompetent, *adj.* unqualified, unable, incapable, inadequate, unfit, insufficient.
Ant. competent, efficient, able, capable. adequate, fit.

incongruous, *adj.* 1. unbecoming, inappropriate, incompatible, out of keeping, discrepant, absurd. 2. inconsonant, inharmonious, discordant. 3. inconsistent, incoherent, illogical, unfitting, contrary, contradictory.
Ant. congruous, becoming, appro-priate, proper; harmonious; logical, consistent, coherent, sensible.

inconsistent, *adj.* incompatible, inharmonious, incongruous, unsuitable, irreconcilable, incoherent, discrepant, out of keeping, inappropriate.
Ant. consistent, coherent, harmonious, suitable.

inconstant, *adj.* changeable, fickle, inconsistent, variable, moody, capricious, vacillating, wavering, mercurial, volatile, unsettled, unstable, mutable, uncertain.
Ant. constant, steady, invariant, settled, staid.

incontrovertible, *adj.* undeniable, indisputable, incontestable, unquestionable.
Ant. deniable, controvertible, disputable, questionable.

inconvenient, *adj.* awkward, inopportune, disadvantageous, troublesome, annoying, vexatious, untimely, incommodious, discommodious.
Ant. convenient, opportune, advantageous.

incorrect, *adj.* 1. wrong, not valid, untrue, false, erroneous, inexact, inaccurate. 2. improper, faulty; indecent.
Ant. correct.

increase, *v.* 1. augment, add to, enlarge, greaten; extend, prolong. 2. grow, dilate, expand, enlarge, multiply. —*n.* 3. growth, augmentation, enlargement, expansion, addition, extension.
Ant. decrease.

incredulous, *adj.* unbelieving, skeptical, doubtful, dubious.
Ant. credulous.

inculpate, *v.* charge, blame, accuse, incriminate, censure, impeach.
Ant. exonerate.

indecent, *adj.* offensive, distasteful, improper, unbecoming, unseemly, outrageous, vulgar, indelicate, coarse, rude, gross, immodest, unrefined, indecorous, obscene, filthy, lewd, licentious, lascivious, pornographic.
Ant. decent.

indefinite, *adj.* 1. unlimited, unconfined, unrestrained, undefined, undetermined, indistinct, confused. 2. vague, obscure, confusing, equivocal, dim, unspecific, doubtful, unsettled, uncertain.
Ant. definite.

independence, *n.* freedom, liberty.
Ant. dependence, reliance.

indifference, *n.* 1. unconcern, listlessness, apathy, insensibility, coolness, insensitiveness, inattention. 2. unimportance, triviality, insignificance. 3. mediocrity, inferiority.
Ant. concern, warmth, sensibility; importance, significance, superiority.

indignation, *n.* consternation, resentment, exasperation, wrath, anger, ire, fury, rage, choler.
Ant. calm, serenity, composure.

indignity, *n.* injury, slight, contempt, humiliation, affront, insult, outrage, scorn, obloquy, contumely, reproach, abuse, opprobrium, dishonor, disrespect.
Ant. dignity; honor, respect.

indiscriminate, *adj.* 1. miscellaneous, undiscriminating, undistinguishing. 2. confused, undistinguishable, mixed, promiscuous.
Ant. discriminating; distinguishing.

indispensable, *adj.* necessary, requisite, essential, needed.
Ant. dispensable, disposable, unnecessary, nonessential.

indisposed, *adj.* 1. sick, ill, unwell, ailing. 2. disinclined, unwilling, reluctant, averse, loath.
Ant. well, healthy, hardy, hale; eager, willing.

indisputable, *adj.* incontrovertible, incontestable, unquestionable, undeniable, indubitable; evident, apparent, obvious, certain, sure.
Ant. questionable, dubitable, dubious; uncertain.

indolent, *adj.* idle, lazy, slothful, slow, inactive, sluggish, torpid, listless, inert.
Ant. energetic, active, industrious.

indomitable, *adj.* invincible, unconquerable, unyielding.
Ant. yielding, weak, feeble.

induce, *v.* 1. persuade, influence, move, actuate, prompt, instigate, incite, urge, impel, spur, prevail upon. 2. bring about, produce, cause, effect, bring on.
Ant. dissuade.

inducement, *n.* incentive, motive, cause, stimulus, spur, incitement.
Ant. discouragement.

indulge, *v.* yield to, satisfy, gratify, humor, pamper, give way to, favor; suffer, foster, permit, allow.
Ant. dissatisfy; disallow, forbid.

industrious, *adj.* busy, hard-working, diligent, assiduous, operose, sedulous, persistent, persevering.
Ant. lazy, indolent.

inebriate, *v.* 1. intoxicate, make drunk; exhilarate. —*n.* 2. drunkard.

ineffectual, *adj.* 1. useless, unavailing, futile, nugatory, ineffective, fruitless, pointless, abortive, purposeless. 2. powerless, impotent, feeble, weak.
Ant. effectual, efficacious, efficient.

inefficient, *adj.* incapable, ineffective, feeble, weak.
Ant. efficient, effectual, efficacious.

inept, *adj.* 1. inapt, unfitted, unfitting, unsuitable, unsuited, inappropriate, out of place, anomalous. 2. absurd, foolish, stupid, pointless, inane, ridiculous.
Ant. fit, suitable, apt, appropriate.

inert, *adj.* inactive, immobile, unmoving, lifeless, passive, motionless.
Ant. active, kinetic.

inexorable, *adj.* unyielding, unalterable, inflexible, unbending, firm, solid, steadfast, severe; relentless, unrelenting, implacable, merciless, cruel, pitiless.
Ant. flexible, yielding; merciful, relenting.

inexpensive, *adj.* cheap, low-priced.
Ant. expensive.

inexperienced, *adj.* untrained, unskilled, raw, green, unknowledgeable, unpracticed, unschooled, untutored, uninformed, naive, uninitiated.
Ant. experienced, skilled, practiced.

infallible, *adj.* trustworthy, sure, certain, reliable, unfailing.
Ant. fallible, unreliable, uncertain.

infamous, *adj.* 1. disreputable, ill-famed, notorious. 2. disgraceful, scandalous, detestable, dishonorable, shameful, bad, nefarious, odious, wicked, outrageous, shocking, vile, base, ignominious, dark, heinous, villainous.
Ant. reputable, famed; honorable, good.

infamy, *n.* notoriety, disgrace, dishonor, discredit, shame, disrepute, obloquy, odium, opprobrium, scandal, debasement, abasement, ignominy.
Ant. honor, credit, repute.

infantile, *adj.* babyish, childish, puerile, immature, weak.
Ant. mature, adult.

infectious, *adj.* contagious, catching, communicable.

inflame, *v.* kindle, excite, rouse, arouse, incite, fire, stimulate.
Ant. discourage.

inflate, *v.* distend, swell, swell out, dilate, expand, puff up *or* out, bloat, blow up.
Ant. deflate.

inflexible, *adj.* rigid, unbending, undeviating, unyielding, rigorous, implacable, stern, relentless, unrelenting, inexorable, unremitting, immovable, resolute, steadfast, firm, stony, solid, persevering, stubborn, dogged, pigheaded, obstinate, refractory, willful, headstrong, intractable, obdurate, adamant.
Ant. flexible.

influence, *n.* 1. sway, rule, authority, power, control, predominance, direction. —*v.* 2. modify, affect, sway, impress, bias, direct, control. 3. move, impel, actuate, activate, incite, rouse, arouse, instigate, induce, persuade.

inform, *v.* 1. apprise, make known, advise, notify, tell, acquaint. 2. animate, inspire, quicken, enliven, inspirit.
Ant. conceal, hide.

informal, *adj.* 1. irregular, unusual, anomalous, unconventional, natural, easy, unceremonious. 2. colloquial, flexible.
Ant. formal, regular, customary, conventional; inflexible.

information, *n.* knowledge, news, data, facts, circumstances, situation, intelligence, advice.
Ant. secret.

infringe, *v.* 1. violate, transgress, breach, break, disobey. 2. trespass, encroach; poach.
Ant. obey.

infuriate, *v.* enrage, anger, incense.
Ant. calm, pacify.

ingenious, *adj.* clever, skillful, adroit, bright, gifted, able, resourceful, inventive.
Ant. unskillful, maladroit.

ingenuous, *adj.* unreserved, unrestrained, frank, candid, free, open, guileless, artless, innocent, naive, straightforward, sincere, openhearted.
Ant. reserved, restrained, secretive, sly, insincere.

ingredient, *n.* constituent, element, component.
Ant. whole.

inherent, *adj.* innate, inherited, native, natural, inborn, inbred, essential.
Ant. acquired.

inheritance, *n.* heritage, patrimony.

inhibit, *v.* 1. restrain, hinder, arrest, check, repress, obstruct, stop; discourage. 2. prohibit, forbid, interdict, prevent.
Ant. encourage, support, abet.

inimical, *adj.* 1. adverse, unfavorable, harmful, noxious. 2. unfriendly, hostile, antagonistic, contrary. *Ant.* friendly, favorable.

initiate, *v.* 1. begin, originate, set going, start, commence, introduce, inaugurate, open. 2. teach, instruct, indoctrinate, train. —*adj.* 3. initiated, begun, started. —*n.* 4. new member, pledge, tyro, beginner, learner, amateur, freshman. *Ant.* terminate, conclude, finish.

injure, *v.* 1. damage, impair, harm, hurt, spoil, ruin, break, mar. 2. wrong, maltreat, mistreat, abuse.

injurious, *adj.* 1. harmful, hurtful, damaging, ruinous, detrimental, pernicious, deleterious, baneful, destructive, mischievous. 2. unjust, wrongful, prejudicial, biased, inequitable, iniquitous. 3. offensive, insulting, abusive, derogatory, defamatory, slanderous, libelous, contumelious, scornful, deprecatory. *Ant.* beneficial; just; right; complimentary.

injury, *n.* 1. harm, damage, ruin, detriment, wound, impairment, mischief. 2. wrong, injustice.

inn, *n.* hotel, hostelry, hostel, tavern.

innocent, *adj.* 1. pure, untainted, sinless, virtuous, virginal, blameless, faultless, impeccable, spotless, immaculate. 2. guiltless, blameless. 3. upright, honest, forthright. 4. naive, simple, unsophisticated, artless, guileless, ingenuous. *Ant.* impure, tainted, sinful, piacular; guilty, culpable; dishonest; disingenuous, sophisticated, artful.

innumerable, *adj.* countless, numberless, many, numerous; infinite.

inquire, *v.* ask, question, query, investigate, examine. *Ant.* answer, reply.

inquiry, *n.* 1. investigation, examination, study, scrutiny, exploration, research. 2. inquiring, questioning, interrogation; query, question. *Ant.* anwer, reply.

inquisitive, *adj.* inquiring, prying, curious, scrutinizing, questioning.

insane, *adj.* deranged, demented, lunatic, crazed, crazy, maniacal, *non compos mentis,* of unsound mind, mad; paranoiac, schizophrenic, delirious; foolish, senseless, stupid, thoughtless. *Ant.* sane.

insanity, *n.* derangement, dementia, lunacy, madness, craziness, mania, aberration; dementia praecox, schizophrenia, paranoia. *Ant.* sanity, probity.

inscrutable, *adj.* impenetrable, unpenetrable, mysterious, hidden, incomprehensible, undiscoverable, inexplicable, unexplainable, unfathomable. *Ant.* penetrable, comprehensible, understandable.

insecure, *adj.* 1. unsafe, exposed, unprotected. 2. uncertain, unsure, risky. *Ant.* secure, safe; certain, sure.

insensibility, *n.* 1. unconsciousness. 2. indifference, apathy, insusceptibility. *Ant.* consciousness; concern, sensibility.

inside, *prep.* 1. within, inside of, in. —*n.* 2. interior. 3. (*plural*) innards, organs. *Ant.* outside.

insidious, *adj.* 1. corrupting, entrapping, beguiling, guileful. 2. treacherous, stealthy, deceitful, artful, cunning, sly, wily, intriguing, subtle, crafty, tricky, arch, crooked, foxy. *Ant.* upright, forthright; artless, ingenuous.

insinuate, *v.* 1. hint, suggest, intimate. 2. instill, infuse, introduce, inject, inculcate.

insolent, *adj.* bold, rude, disrespectful, impertinent, brazen, brassy, abusive, overbearing, contemptuous, insulting. *Ant.* polite, courteous, retiring; complimentary.

inspection, *n.* examination, investigation, scrutiny.

instance, *n.* case, example, illustration, exemplification.

instant, *n.* moment, minute, second, twinkling, flash, jiffy, trice.

instantly, *adv.* immediately, at once, instanter, instantaneously, forthwith, in a flash *or* trice *or* jiffy. *Ant.* later.

instruct, *v.* 1. direct, command, order, prescribe. 2. teach, train, educate, tutor, coach, drill, discipline, indoctrinate, school, inform, enlighten, apprise. *Ant.* learn, study.

instruction, *n.* 1. education, tutoring, coaching, training, drill, exercise, indoctrination, schooling, teaching. 2. order, direction, mandate, command.

instructor, *n.* teacher, tutor, pedagogue, schoolmaster, preceptor. *Ant.* student, pupil.

instrument, *n.* tool, implement, utensil.

insult, *v.* 1. affront, offend, scorn, injure, slander, abuse. —*n.* 2. affront, indignity, offense, contumely, scorn, outrage. *Ant.* compliment, dignify; dignity.

insurrection, *n.* revolt, uprising, rebellion, mutiny, insurgency.

intact, *adj.* uninjured, unaltered, sound, whole, unimpaired, complete, undiminished, unbroken, entire. *Ant.* impaired, unsound, incomplete.

integrity, *n.* 1. uprightness, honesty, honor, rectitude, right, righteousness, probity, principle, virtue, goodness. 2. wholeness, entirety, completeness. *Ant.* dishonesty, disrepute; part.

intellect, *n.* mind, understanding, reason, sense, common sense, brains. *Ant.* inanity.

intellectual, *adj.* 1. mental; intelligent; high-brow. —*n.* 2. (*colloquial*) high-brow, egghead, professor, brain, mental giant, longhair. *Ant.* sensual, low-brow; dunderpate, fool.

intelligence, *n.* 1. mind, understanding, discernment, reason, acumen, aptitude, penetration. 2. knowledge, news, information, tidings. *Ant.* stupidity.

intelligent, *adj.* 1. understanding, intellectual, quick, bright. 2. astute, clever, quick, alert, bright, apt, discerning, shrewd, smart. *Ant.* stupid, unintelligent, slow; dull.

intend, *v.* have in mind, mean, design, propose, contemplate, expect, meditate, project, aim for *or* at, purpose.

intensify, *v.* aggravate, deepen, quicken, strengthen; concentrate. *Ant.* alleviate, lessen, weaken, dilute.

intent, *n.* 1. intention, design, purpose, meaning, plan, plot, aim, end, object, mark. —*adj.* 2. fixed, steadfast, bent, resolute, set, concentrated, unshakable, eager. *Ant.* phlegmatic, undetermined, irresolute, apathetic.

intention, *n.* intent.

intentional, *adj.* deliberate, purposeful, premeditated, designed, planned, intended. *Ant.* unintentional, purposeless, unpremeditated; involuntary.

interesting, *adj.* pleasing, attractive, gratifying, engaging, absorbing, exciting, fulfilling, entertaining. *Ant.* uninteresting, dull, prosaic.

interpret, *v.* 1. explain, explicate, elucidate, shed *or* cast light on, define, translate, decipher, decode. 2. explain, construe, understand.

interrupt, *v.* 1. discontinue, suspend, intermit. 2. stop, cease, break off, disturb, hinder, interfere with. *Ant.* continue.

intimate, *adj.* 1. close, closely associated, familiar, dear, confidential. 2. private, personal, privy, secret. 3. detailed, deep, cogent, exacting, exact, precise. 4. inmost, deep within; intrinsic, inner, deeprooted, deep-seated. —*n.* 5. friend, associate, confidant, crony, familiar. —*v.* 6. hint, suggest, insinuate, allude to. *Ant.* open, public, known, blatant; enemy, foe; announce, proclaim.

intimidate, *v.* overawe, cow, subdue, dismay, frighten, alarm; discourage, dissuade. *Ant.* encourage, calm.

intolerable, *adj.* unbearable, unendurable, insufferable, insupportable. *Ant.* tolerable, bearable, endurable.

intolerant, *adj.* bigoted, illiberal, narrow, proscriptive, prejudiced, biased, dictatorial, fascistic, totalitarian, fanatical. *Ant.* tolerant, liberal, unprejudiced.

intractable, *adj.* stubborn, obstinate, unmanageable, perverse, fractious, refractory, headstrong, pigheaded, dogged, unbending, inflexible, obdurate, adamant, stony, willful, unyielding, contumacious, froward. *Ant.* tractable, amiable, amenable, easygoing, flexible.

intrinsic, *adj.* essential, native, innate, inborn, inbred, natural, true, real, genuine. *Ant.* extrinsic.

introduce, *v.* present, acquaint; lead, bring, conduct.

intrude, *v.* trespass, obtrude, encroach, violate, infringe.

inundate, *v.* flood, deluge, overflow, overspread, overwhelm, glut.

invaluable, *adj.* priceless, precious, valuable, inestimable. *Ant.* worthless.

invariable, *adj.* unalterable, unchanging, uniform, constant, invariant, changeless, unvarying; unchangeable, immutable. *Ant.* variable, changing, varying, mutable.

invective, *n.* 1. denunciation, censure, reproach, abuse, contumely, scorn. 2. accusation, vituperation, railing. —*adj.* 3. abusive, censorious, denunciatory, vituperative, captious. *Ant.* praise, honor; commendatory.

invent, *v.* 1. devise, contrive, originate, discover. 2. produce, create, imagine, fancy, conceive, fabricate, concoct.

inventory, *n.* roll, list, roster, listing, record, account, catalogue, register.

invert, *v.* reverse, turn around *or* upside down.

investigation, *n.* examination, inspection, inquiry, scrutiny, research, exploration.

invigorate, *v.* animate, innerve, enliven, strengthen, fortify, energize, quicken, vitalize. *Ant.* enervate, enfeeble, weaken, devitalize.

invincible, *adj.* unconquerable, unvanquishable, insuperable, insurmountable, impregnable, impenetrable, indomitable, persistent, unyielding, irrepressible. *Ant.* conquerable, pregnable, penetrable.

invite, *v.* 1. call, request, ask, bid, summon, solicit. 2. attract, allure, lure, tempt, entice, draw.

involuntary, *adj.* 1. unintentional, reluctant, accidental. 2. automatic, reflex, unwilled, instinctive, uncontrolled. *Ant.* voluntary, intentional.

involve, *v.* 1. include, embrace, contain, comprehend, comprise, entail, imply. 2. entangle, implicate, connect, tie, bind. *Ant.* exclude, preclude.

iota, *n.* tittle, jot, bit, whit, particle, atom, grain, mite, scrap, scintilla, trace, glimmer, shadow, spark.

irascible, *adj.* testy, short-tempered, hot-tempered, quick-tempered, touchy, temperamental, irritable, waspish, snappish, petulant, peppery, choleric. *Ant.* calm, even-tempered, temperate.

irate, *adj.* angry, enraged, furious, piqued, provoked, irritated. *Ant.* pleased, calm.

irony, *n.* sarcasm, satire, mockery, derision.

irregular, *adj.* 1. unsymmetrical, uneven. 2. unmethodical, unsystematic, disorderly, capricious, erratic, eccentric, lawless, aberrant, devious, unconforming, nonconformist, unusual, abnormal, anomalous. *Ant.* regular.

irritate, *v.* vex, annoy, chafe, fret, gall, nettle, ruffle, pique, incense, anger, ire, enrage, infuriate, exasperate, provoke. *Ant.* please, delight.

isolation, *n.* solitude, loneliness; separation, disconnection, segregation, detachment.

issue, *n.* 1. delivery, emission, sending, promulgation. 2. copy, number, edition, printing. 3. point, crux; problem, question. 4. product, effect, result, consequence, event, outcome, upshot, denouement, conclusion, end, consummation. 5. egress, outlet, vent. 6. offspring, progeny, children. —*v.* 7. put out, deliver, circulate, publish, distribute. 8. send out, discharge, emit. 9. come forth, emerge, flow out. 10. come, proceed, emanate, flow, arise, spring, originate, ensue.

itinerant, *adj.* wandering, nomadic, unsettled, roving, roaming, traveling, journeying, itinerating. *Ant.* stationary, fixed, settled.

J

jam, *v.* 1. wedge, pack, crowd, ram, force, squeeze, bruise, crush. —*n.* 2. preserve, conserve, marmalade.

jargon, *n.* 1. gibberish, babble, gabble, twaddle, nonsense, balderdash, palaver, moonshine. 2. language, cant, argot, patois, slang; lingua franca, pidgin English.

jealous, *adj.* 1. envious, resentful; suspicious. 2. solicitous, watchful, vigilant.
Ant. generous, open, trusting.

jeer, *v.* 1. deride, scoff, gibe, mock, taunt, sneer at, ridicule, flout. —*n.* 2. sneer, scoff, gibe, derision, ridicule, flout.

jeopardy, *n.* hazard, risk, danger, peril.
Ant. security.

jest, *n.* 1. witticism, joke, pleasantry, mot, quip. 2. raillery, banter; sport, fun, jape, gibe. —*v.* 3. joke, trifle (with). 4. deride, jeer, scoff, gibe.

job, *n.* position, situation, post, employment.
Ant. unemployment.

jocose, *adj.* joking, jesting, jovial, humorous, playful, facetious, waggish, witty, funny, comical, droll, sportive, jocular, merry.
Ant. serious, morose, melancholy.

jocular, *adj.* jocose.

jocund, *adj.* cheerful, merry, gay, blithe, happy, glad, joyous, joyful, frolicsome, frolicking, blithesome, jolly, playful, lively, debonair.
Ant. sad, cheerless, unhappy, miserable.

join, *v.* 1. link, couple, fasten, attach, conjoin, combine, confederate, associate, consolidate, amalgamate, connect, unite, bring together. 2. adjoin, abut, touch, be adjacent to.
Ant. separate, divide.

joke, *n.* witticism, jape, quip, jest, sally, trick, raillery, prank.

jolly, *adj.* gay, glad, happy, spirited, jovial, merry, sportive, playful, cheerful, convivial, festive, joyous, mirthful, jocund, frolicsome.
Ant. serious, morose, mirthless.

journey, *n.* 1. excursion, trip, jaunt, tour, expedition, pilgrimage, travel. —*v.* 2. travel, tour, peregrinate, roam, rove; go, proceed, fare.

jovial, *adj.* merry, jolly, convivial, gay, jocose, jocular, jocund, joyous, joyful, blithe, happy, glad, mirthful.
Ant. serious, mirthless, cheerless, unhappy.

joy, *n.* 1. satisfaction, exultation, gladness, delight, rapture. 2. happiness, felicity, bliss, pleasure, ecstasy, transport.
Ant. dissatisfaction, misery; unhappiness.

joyful, *adj.* glad, delighted, joyous, happy, blithe, buoyant, elated, jubilant, gay, merry, jocund, blithesome, jolly, jovial.
Ant. sad, unhappy, melancholy, depressed.

joyless, *adj.* sad, cheerless, unhappy, gloomy, dismal, miserable.
Ant. joyous.

judge, *n.* 1. justice, magistrate; arbiter, arbitrator, umpire, referee. —*v.* 2. try, pass sentence upon. 3. estimate, consider, regard, esteem, appreciate, reckon, deem. 4. decide, determine, conclude, form an opinion, pass judgment.

judgment, *n.* 1. verdict, decree, decision, determination, conclusion, opinion, estimate. 2. understanding, discrimination, discernment, perspicacity, sagacity, wisdom, intelli-

gence, prudence, brains, taste, penetration, discretion, common sense.

judicial, *adj.* critical, discriminating, judicious, juridical, forensic.

judicious, *adj.* 1. practical, expedient, discreet, prudent, politic. 2. wise, sensible, well-advised, rational, reasonable, sober, sound, enlightened, sagacious, considered, commonsense.
Ant. impractical, indiscreet, imprudent; silly, nonsensical, unsound, unreasonable.

jumble, *v.* 1. mix, confuse, mix up. —*n.* 2. medley, mixture, hodgepodge, hotchpotch, muddle, mess, farrago, chaos, disorder, confusion, gallimaufry, potpourri.
Ant. separate, isolate; order.

jump, *v.* 1. spring, bound, skip, hop, leap, vault. —*n.* 2. leap, bound, spring, caper, vault, hop, skip.

junction, *n.* combination, union, joining, connection, linking, coupling; juncture; seam, welt, joint.

junket, *n.* excursion.

just, *adj.* 1. upright, equitable, fair, impartial, evenhanded, right, lawful. 2. true, correct, accurate, exact, proper, regular, normal. 3. rightful, legitimate, lawful, legal; deserved, merited, appropriate, condign, suited, suitable, apt, due. 4. righteous, blameless, honest, upright, pure, conscientious, good, uncorrupt, virtuous, honorable, straightforward.
Ant. unjust.

justify, *v.* vindicate, exonerate, exculpate, absolve, acquit, defend, warrant, excuse.
Ant. inculpate, convict, indict, accuse, condemn.

K

keen, *adj.* 1. sharp, acute, honed, razor-sharp. 2. sharp, cutting, biting, severe, bitter, poignant, caustic, acrimonious. 3. piercing, penetrating, discerning, astute, sagacious, sharp-witted, quick, shrewd, clever, keen-eyed, keen-sighted, clear-sighted, clear-headed. 4. ardent, eager, zealous, earnest, fervid.
Ant. dull.

keep, *v.* 1. maintain, reserve, preserve, retain, hold, withhold, have, continue. —*n.* 2. subsistence, board and room. 3. tower, dungeon, stronghold.
Ant. lose.

keeper, *n.* guard, warden, custodian, jailer, guardian.

keeping, *n.* 1. congruity, harmony, conformity, consistency, agreement.

2. custody, protection, care, charge, guardianship, trust.
Ant. incongruity, nonconformity, inconsistency.

kill, *v.* 1. slaughter, slay, assassinate, massacre, butcher, execute; murder; hang, electrocute, behead, guillotine, strangle, garrote. 2. extinguish, destroy, do away with.
Ant. create, originate.

kind, *adj.* 1. gracious, kindhearted, kindly, good, mild, benign, bland; benevolent, benignant, beneficent, friendly, humane, generous, bounteous, accommodating; gentle, affectionate, living, tender, compassionate, sympathetic, tenderhearted, soft-hearted, good-natured. —*n.* 2. sort, nature, character, race, genus, species, breed, set, class. *Ant.* unkind.

kindhearted, *adj.* kind. *Ant.* hardhearted, cruel.

kindle, *v.* 1. set fire to, ignite, inflame, fire, light. 2. rouse, arouse, awaken, bestir, inflame, provoke, incite, stimulate, animate, foment. *Ant.* extinguish, quench.

kindly, *adj.* 1. benevolent, kind, good-natured, sympathetic, compassionate. 2. gentle, mild, benign. 3. pleasant, genial, benign. —*adv.* 4.

cordially, politely, heartily; favorably. *Ant.* unkindly, malevolent, unsympathetic; cruel, harsh; unpleasant; unfavorable.

kindness, *n.* 1. service, favor, good turn. 2. benevolence, beneficence, humanity, benignity, generosity, philanthropy, charity, sympathy, compassion, tenderness, amiability. *Ant.* unkindness, malevolence.

kingdom, *n.* monarchy, realm, sovereignty, dominion, empire, domain.

kingly, *adj.* kinglike, princely, regal, royal, imperial, sovereign, majestic, august, magnificent, grand, grandiose. *Ant.* serflike, slavish, low, lowly.

kinship, *n.* relationship, affinity, connection, bearing.

knack, *n.* 1. aptitude, aptness, facility, dexterity, skill, adroitness, dexter-

ousness, skillfulness, expertness. 2. habit, practice.

knave, *n.* rascal, rogue, scoundrel, blackguard, villain, scamp, scapegrace, swindler. *Ant.* hero.

knot, *n.* 1. group, company, cluster, clique, hand, crew, gang, squad, crowd. 2. lump, knob. 3. difficulty, perplexity, puzzle, conundrum, rebus.

know, *v.* 1. perceive, understand, apprehend, comprehend, discern. 2. recognize. 3. distinguish, discriminate.

knowledge, *n.* 1. enlightenment, erudition, wisdom, science, information, learning, scholarship, lore. 2. understanding, discernment, perception, apprehension, comprehension, judgment.

L

labor, *n.* 1. toil, work, exertion, drudgery. 2. travail, childbirth, parturition, delivery. 3. workingmen, working class; bourgeoisie. —*v.* 4. work, toil, strive, drudge. 5. be burdened *or* troubled *or* distressed, suffer. 6. overdo, elaborate. *Ant.* idleness, indolence, sloth.

labored, *adj.* overdone, overworked, overwrought, ornate, unnatural.

laborious, *adj.* 1. toilsome, arduous, onerous, burdensome, difficult, tiresome, wearisome, fatiguing. 2. diligent, hard-working, assiduous, industrious, sedulous, painstaking. *Ant.* easy, simple.

lacerate, *v.* 1. tear, mangle, maim, rend, claw. 2. hurt, injure, harm, wound, damage.

lack, *n.* 1. deficiency, need, want, dearth, scarcity, paucity, shortcoming, deficit, scantiness, insufficiency, defectiveness. —*v.* 2. want, need. *Ant.* sufficiency, copiousness, abundance.

laconic, *adj.* brief, concise, succinct, sententious, pithy, concentrated, terse, compact. *Ant.* voluble.

lag, *v.* 1. fall behind *or* back, loiter, linger. —*n.* 2. retardation, slowing, slowdown.

Ant. speed, quicken, expedite; expedition.

lament, *v.* 1. bewail, bemoan, deplore, grieve, weep, mourn *or* sorrow over *or* for. —*n.* 2. lamentation, moan, wail, wailing, moaning. 3. dirge, elegy, monody, threnody. *Ant.* rejoice.

lane, *n.* path, way, passage, track, channel, course, alley.

language, *n.* 1. speech, communication, tongue. 2. dialect, jargon, terminology, vernacular; lingo, lingua franca. 3. speech, phraseology, jargon, style, expression, diction.

languid, *adj.* 1. faint, weak, feeble, weary, exhausted, debilitated. 2. indifferent, spiritless, listless, inactive, inert, sluggish, torpid, dull. *Ant.* strong, distinct, sharp, tireless; active, energetic.

large, *adj.* 1. big, huge, enormous, immense, gigantic, colossal, massive, vast, great, extensive, broad, sizeable, grand, spacious; pompous. 2. multitudinous; abundant, copious, ample, liberal, plentiful. *Ant.* small, tiny; scanty, sparse, scarce, rare.

last, *adj.* 1. final, ultimate, latest, concluding, conclusive, utmost, extreme, terminal, hindmost. —*v.* 2. go on, continue, endure, perpetuate, remain. *Ant.* first; fail, die.

late, *adj.* 1. tardy, slow, dilatory, delayed, belated. 2. continued, lasting, protracted. 3. recent, modern, advanced. 4. former, recently deceased. *Ant.* early, fast.

latent, *adj.* hidden, concealed, veiled; potential. *Ant.* kinetic, open.

latitude, *n.* range, scope, extent, liberty, freedom, indulgence.

laud, *v.* praise, extol, applaud, celebrate, esteem, honor. *Ant.* censure, condemn, criticize.

laugh, *v.* 1. chortle, cackle, cachinnate, hawhaw, guffaw, roar; giggle, snicker, snigger, titter. —*n.* 2. chuckle, grin, smile; laughter, cachinnation. *Ant.* cry, mourn, wail.

laughable, *adj.* funny, amusing, humorous, droll, comical, ludicrous, farcical, ridiculous, risible. *Ant.* sad, melancholy.

lavish, *adj.* 1. unstinted, extravagant, excessive, prodigal, profuse, generous, openhanded; wasteful, improvident. —*v.* 2. expend, bestow, endow; waste, dissipate, squander. *Ant.* stingy, niggardly; provident; save.

lawful, *adj.* 1. legal, legitimate, valid. 2. licit, sanctioned, allowed. *Ant.* illegal, illicit, illegitimate; forbidden.

lay, *v.* 1. place, put, deposit, set, locate. 2. allay, appease, calm, still, quiet, suppress. 3. wager, bet, stake, risk. 4. impute, ascribe, attribute, charge. 5. burden, penalize, assess, impose. —*n.* 6. position, lie, site. 7. song, lyric, musical poem, poem, ode. —*adj.* 8. unclerical, laic, laical. 9. unprofessional, amateur.

lazy, *adj.* idle, indolent, slothful, slow-moving, sluggish, inert, inactive, torpid.
Ant. industrious, quick.

lead, *v.* 1. conduct, go before, precede, guide, direct, escort. 2. guide, influence, induce, persuade, convince, draw, entice, lure, allure, seduce, lead on. 3. excel, outstrip, surpass. —*n.* 4. precedence, advance, vanguard, head. 5. weight, plumb.
Ant. follow.

leading, *n.* 1. guidance, direction, lead. 2. lead, spacing, space. —*adj.* 3. chief, principal, most important, foremost, capital, ruling, governing.
Ant. deputy; secondary, following.

league, *n.* 1. covenant, compact, alliance, confederation, combination, coalition, confederacy, union. —*v.* 2. unite, combine, confederate.

lean, *v.* 1. incline, tend toward, bend, slope. 2. repose, rest, rely, depend, trust, confide. —*adj.* 3. skinny, thin, gaunt, emaciated, lank, meager. 4. sparse, barren, unfruitful, inadequate, deficient, jejune. —*n.* 5. meat, essence.
Ant. fat, obese; fertile, fruitful, adequate; superfluity, excess.

leap, *v., n.* jump, bound, spring, vault, hop.

learn, *v.* ascertain, detect, discover, memorize, acquire, hear.

learning, *n.* erudition, lore, knowledge, scholarship, store of information.

leave, *v.* 1. quit, vacate, abandon, forsake, desert, depart from, retire from, withdraw *or* escape from, relinquish, renounce. 2. desist from, stop, forbear, cease, abandon, let alone. 3. omit, forget, exclude. 4. bequeath, will, devise, transmit. —*n.* 5. permission, allowance, freedom, liberty, license.
Ant. arrive, gain.

legend, *n.* fable, myth, story, fiction.
Ant. fact, history.

legitimate, *adj.* 1. legal, lawful, licit, sanctioned. 2. normal, regular. 3. reasonable, logical, sensible, common-sense, valid, warranted, called-for, correct, proper. —*v.* 4. authorize, justify, legalize.

Ant. illegitimate; unreasonable, incorrect, improper.

leisurely, *adj.* deliberate, slow, premeditated, unhurried, easily.
Ant. unpremeditated, quick, hurried, hasty.

lengthen, *v.* extend, stretch, prolong, protract, attenuate, elongate, draw out, continue, increase.
Ant. shorten, abbreviate.

lenient, *adj.* mild, clement, merciful, easy, gentle, soothing, tender, forbearing, long-suffering.
Ant. harsh, cruel, brutal, merciless.

lessen, *v.* 1. diminish, decrease, abate, dwindle, fade, shrink. 2. diminish, decrease, depreciate, disparage, reduce, micrify, lower, degrade. 3. decrease, diminish, abate, abridge, reduce.
Ant. increase; raise; lengthen, enlarge.

let, *v.* 1. allow, permit, suffer, grant. 2. disappoint, fail. 3. lease, rent, sublet, hire.
Ant. prevent, disallow.

level, *adj.* 1. even, flat, smooth, uniform, plain, flush. 2. horizontal. 3. equal, on a par, equivalent. 4. even, equable, uniform. —*v.* 5. even, equalize, smooth, flatten. 6. raze, demolish, destroy. 7. aim, direct, point.
Ant. uneven; vertical; unequal.

liable, *adj.* 1. subject, exposed, likely, open. 2. obliged, responsible, answerable, accountable.
Ant. protected, secure.

liberal, *adj.* 1. progressive, reform. 2. tolerant, unbigoted, broad-minded, unprejudiced, magnanimous, generous, honorable. 3. generous, bountiful, beneficent, free, charitable, openhanded, munificent; abundant, ample, bounteous, unstinting, lavish, plentiful.
Ant. illiberal; intolerant, prejudiced; stingy, parsimonious, niggardly.

liberate, *v.* set free, release, emancipate, free, disengage, unfetter, disenthrall, deliver, set loose, loose, let out, discharge.
Ant. imprison, incarcerate; enthrall, enslave.

libertine, *n.* 1. rake, roué, debauchee, lecher, sensualist, profligate. —*adj.* 2. amoral, licentious, lascivious, lewd, dissolute, depraved, corrupt, perverted, immoral, sensual.
Ant. prude.

liberty, *n.* freedom, liberation, independence; franchise, permission, leave, license, privilege, immunity.

licentious, *adj.* sensual, libertine, lewd, lascivious, libidinous, lustful, lecherous, lawless, immoral, wanton, concupiscent, loose, amoral, unchaste, impure.
Ant. prudish, moral; chaste, pure.

lie, *n.* 1. falsehood, prevarication, mendacity, untruth, falsification, fib. 2. place, position, location, lay, site. —*v.* 3. falsify, prevaricate, fib. 4. recline.
Ant. truth.

life, *n.* 1. animation, vigor, vivacity, vitality, sprightliness, verve, effervescence, sparkle, spirit, activity, energy. 2. biography, memoir. 3. existence, being.

lifeless, *adj.* 1. inanimate, inorganic, mineral. 2. dead, defunct, extinct. 3. dull, inactive, inert, passive, sluggish, torpid, spiritless.
Ant. alive, animate, live, organic; alive, extant; active, animated, spirited.

lift, *v.* raise, elevate, hold up, exalt, uplift.
Ant. lower.

light, *n.* 1. illumination, radiance, daylight; dawn, sunrise, daybreak. 2. aspect, viewpoint, point of view, angle, approach. —*adj.* 3. pale, whitish, blanched. 4. buoyant, lightsome, easy. 5. shallow, humorous, slight, trivial, trifling, inconsiderable, unsubstantial, flimsy, insubstantial, gossamer, airy, flighty. 6. airy, nimble, agile, alert. 7. carefree, gay, cheery, cheerful, happy, light-hearted. 8. frivolous, lightsome, light-headed, volatile. 9. wanton. 10. dizzy, delirious, light-headed, giddy. —*v.* 11. alight, get *or* come down, descend, land, disembark. 12. kindle, set fire to, ignite, set afire, fire.
Ant. darkness, sunset; swarthy; difficult; deep, considerable, substantial; cheerless, sad; serious; board, embark, mount; quench.

lighten, *v.* 1. illuminate, brighten, shine, gleam, illume. 2. mitigate, disburden, unburden, ease. 3. cheer, gladden.
Ant. darken, adumbrate; intensify, aggravate; sadden.

light-hearted, *adj.* carefree, cheerful, lightsome, gay, cheery, joyous, joyful, blithe, glad, happy, merry, jovial, jocund.
Ant. heavy-hearted, cheerless, morose, sad, gloomy, melancholy.

likely, *adj.* apt, liable, probable, possible, suitable, appropriate.
Ant. unlikely.

liking, *n.* preference, inclination favor, disposition, bent, bias, leaning, propensity, capacity, proclivity, proneness, predilection, predisposition, tendency; partiality, fondness, affection.
Ant. dislike, disfavor, disinclination.

limb, *n.* 1. part, member, extremity; leg, arm, wing. 2. branch, bough, offshoot.

limber, *adj.* pliant, flexible, supple, pliable, lithe.
Ant. rigid, unbending, unyielding.

limit, *n.* 1. bound, extent, boundary, confine, frontier, termination. 2. restraint, restriction, constraint, check, hindrance. —*v.* 3. restrain, restrict, confine, check, hinder, bound, circumscribe, define.

limpid, *adj.* clear, transparent, pellucid, lucid, crystal-clear.
Ant. cloudy, dim, dull.

linger, *v.* remain, stay on, tarry, delay, dawdle, loiter.

link, *n.* 1. bond, tie, connection, connective, copula, vinculum. —*v.* 2. bond, join, unite, connect, league, conjoin, fasten, pin, bind, tie.
Ant. separation; separate, split, rive.

liquid, *n., adj.* fluid, liquor.
Ant. solid, gas.

lissome, *adj.* lithesome, lithe, limber, supple, agile, active, energetic.
Ant. inflexible, rigid, clumsy, awkward.

list, *n.* 1. catalogue, inventory, roll, schedule, series, register. 2. border, strip, selvage, band, edge. 3. leaning, tilt, tilting, careening. —*v.* 4. register, catalogue, enlist, enroll. 5. border, edge. 6. careen, incline, lean.

listen, *v.* hearken, hear, hark, attend, give ear, lend an ear.

listlessness, *n.* indifference, inattention, inattentiveness, heedlessness; thoughtlessness, carelessness.
Ant. concern, care, attention, attentiveness.

literature, *n.* belles-lettres, letters, humanities, writings.

litter, *n.* 1. rubbish, shreds, fragments. 2. untidiness, disorder, confusion. 3. brood. 4. stretcher. 5. straw *or* hay bedding. —*v.* 6. strew, scatter, derange, mess up, disarrange, disorder.

little, *adj.* 1. small, diminutive, minute, tiny, infinitesimal, wee. 2. short, brief. 3. weak, feeble, slight, inconsiderable, trivial, paltry, insignificant, unimportant, petty, scanty. 4. mean, narrow, illiberal, paltry,

stingy, selfish, small, niggardly. —*adv.* 5. slightly, barely, just.
Ant. large, immense, huge; important; liberal, generous.

livelihood, *n.* maintenance, living, sustenance, support, subsistence.

lively, *adj.* 1. energetic, active, vigorous, brisk, peart, vivacious, alert, spry, nimble, agile, quick. 2. animated, spirited, vivacious, sprightly, gay, blithe, blithesome, buoyant, gleeful. 3. eventful, stirring, moving. 4. strong, keen, distinct, vigorous, forceful, clear, piquant. 5. striking, telling, effective. 6. vivid, bright, brilliant, fresh, clear, glowing. 7. sparkling, fresh.
Ant. inactive, torpid; leaden; uneventful; weak, dull, unclear; ineffective; dim; stale.

living, *adj.* 1. alive, live, quick, existing; extant, surviving. 2. active, lively, strong, vigorous, quickening. —*n.* 3. livelihood, maintenance, sustenance, subsistence, support.
Ant. dead.

load, *n.* 1. burden, onus, weight, encumbrance, incubus, pressure. —*v.* 2. lade, weight, weigh down, burden, encumber, freight, oppress.
Ant. disburden, unload, lighten.

loath, *adj.* reluctant, averse, unwilling, disinclined, backward.
Ant. eager, anxious, willing.

loathe, *v.* abominate, detest, hate, abhor.
Ant. adore, love.

loathing, *n.* disgust, dislike, aversion, abhorrence, hatred, hate, antipathy; animus, animosity, hostility.
Ant. liking, love; friendship, regard.

loathsome, *adj.* disgusting, nauseating, sickening, repulsive, offensive, repellent, revolting, detestable, abhorrent, hateful, odious, abominable, execrable.
Ant. attractive, delightful, lovable.

locale, *n.* place, location, site, spot, locality.

lodge, *n.* 1. shelter, habitation, cabin, hut, cottage, cot. 2. club, association, society. —*v.* 3. shelter, harbor, house, quarter. 4. place, put, set, plant, infix, deposit, lay, settle.

lofty, *adj.* 1. high, elevated, towering, tall. 2. exalted, elevated, sublime. 3. haughty, proud, arrogant, prideful.
Ant. lowly; debased; humble.

loiter, *v.* linger, dally, dawdle, idle, loaf, delay, tarry, lag.

lone, *adj.* 1. alone, unaccompanied, solitary, lonely, secluded, apart, separate, separated; deserted, uninhab-

ited, unoccupied, unpopulated, empty. 2. isolated, solitary, sole, unique, lonely.
Ant. accompanied, together; inhabited, occupied.

lonely, *adj.* lone, solitary, lonesome, sequestered, remote, dreary.
Ant. crowded, populous.

lonesome, *adj.* lonely, alone, secluded; desolate, isolated.

long, *adj.* 1. lengthy, extensive, drawn out, attenuated, protracted, stretched, prolonged, extended. 2. overlong, long-winded, tedious, boring, wordy, prolix. —*v.* 3. crave, desire, yearn for, pine for, hanker for *or* after.
Ant. short, abbreviated; interesting; forgo.

longing, *n.* craving, desire, hankering, yearning, aspiration.
Ant. disinterest, antipathy, apathy.

look, *v.* 1. gaze, glance, watch. 2. appear, seem. 3. await, wait for, expect, anticipate. 4. face, front. 5. seek, search for. —*n.* 6. gaze, glance. 7. search, examination. 8. appearance, aspect, mien, manner, air.

loose, *adj.* 1. free, unfettered, unbound, untied, unrestrained, unrestricted, released, unattached, unfastened, unconfined. 2. uncombined. 3. lax, slack, careless, negligent, heedless. 4. wanton, libertine, unchaste, immoral, dissolute, licentious. 5. general, vague, indefinite, inexact, imprecise, ill-defined, indeterminate, indistinct. —*v.* 6. loosen, free, set free, unfasten, undo, unlock, unbind, untie, unloose, release, liberate. 7. relax, slacken, ease, loosen.
Ant. bound, fettered; combined; tight, taut; moral, chaste; definite, specific; bind, commit; tighten.

loot, *n.* 1. spoils, plunder, booty. —*v.* 2. plunder, rob, sack, rifle, despoil, ransack, pillage, rape.

loquacious, *adj.* talkative, garrulous, wordy, verbose.
Ant. taciturn, close-mouthed.

lordly, *adj.* 1. grand, magnificent, majestic, royal, regal, kingly, aristocratic, dignified, noble, lofty. 2. haughty, arrogant, lofty, imperious, domineering, insolent, overbearing, despotic, dictatorial, tyrannical.
Ant. menial, servile; humble, obedient.

lore, *n.* 1. learning, kowledge, erudition. 2. wisdom, counsel, advice, teaching, doctrine, lesson.

loss, *n.* 1. detriment, disadvantage, damage, injury, destruction. 2. privation, deprivation.
Ant. gain.

lost, *adj.* 1. forfeited, gone, missing, missed. 2. bewildered, confused, perplexed, puzzled. 3. wasted, misspent, squandered, dissipated. 4. defeated, vanquished. 5. destroyed, ruined. 6. depraved, abandoned, dissolute, corrupt, reprobate, profligate, licentious, shameless, hardened, irredeemable, irreclaimable.
Ant. found; pure, honorable, chaste.

loud, *adj.* 1. noisy, clamorous, resounding, deafening, stentorian, boisterous, tumultuous. 2. gaudy, flashy, showy, obtrusive, vulgar, obvious, blatant, coarse, rude, crude, cheap.
Ant. soft, quiet; sedate, tasteful, artistic.

love, *n.* 1. affection, predilection, liking, inclination, regard, friendliness, kindness, tenderness, fondness, devotion, warmth, attachment, passion, adoration. —*v.* 2. like, be fond of, have affection for, be enamored of, be in love with, adore, adulate, worship.
Ant. hatred, dislike; detest, abhor, abominate, hate.

lovely, *adj.* beautiful, charming, exquisite, enchanting, winning.
Ant. ugly, unattractive, homely.

low, *adj.* 1. prostrate, dead, prone, supine. 2. profound, deep. 3. feeble, weak, exhausted, sinking, dying, expiring. 4. depressed, dejected, dispirited, unhappy, sad, miserable. 5. undignified, infra dig, lowly, dishonorable, disreputable, unbecoming, disgraceful. 6. groveling, abject, sordid, mean, base, lowly, degraded, menial, servile, ignoble, vile. 7. humble, lowly, meek, lowborn, poor, plain, plebeian, vulgar, base. 8. coarse, vulgar, rude, crude. 9. soft, subdued, gentle, quiet. —*adv.* 10. cheaply, inexpensively. —*v., n.* 11. moo, bellow.
Ant. high, upright.

lowbred, *adj.* unrefined, vulgar, coarse, rude, lowborn.
Ant. refined, noble, highborn.

lower, *v.* 1. reduce, decrease, diminish, lessen. 2. soften, turn down, quiet down. 3. degrade, humble, abase, humiliate, disgrace, debase. 4. let down, drop, depress, take down, sink. 5. darken, threaten, glower; frown, scowl.
Ant. raise, increase; elevate, honor; brighten.

loyal, *adj.* faithful, true, patriotic, devoted, constant.
Ant. faithless, disloyal, treacherous.

loyalty, *n.* faithfulness, allegiance, fealty, devotion, constancy, patriotism, fidelity.
Ant. faithlessness, disloyalty.

lubricous, *adj.* 1. slippery, oily, smooth. 2. unsteady, unstable, uncertain, shifty, wavering, undependable. 3. lewd, lascivious, licentious, salacious, wanton, unchaste, incontinent, lecherous, perverse, perverted, immoral, vulgar, lustful, carnal, libidinous, dissolute, libertine, profligate, depraved, corrupt, loose, sensual, concupiscent, impure, pornographic, obscene, dirty, filthy.
Ant. dependable, sure, certain, reliable; prudish, chaste, moral.

lucid, *adj.* 1. shining, bright, lucent, radiant, brilliant, resplendent, luminous. 2. clear, transparent, pellucid, limpid, crystalline; luculent, intelligible, plain, unmistakable, obvious, distinct, evident, understandable; rational, sane, sober, sound, reasonable.
Ant. dull; unclear, dull; unreasonable.

lucky, *adj.* fortunate, fortuitous, happy, favored, blessed; auspicious, propitious, favorable, prosperous.
Ant. unfortunate, unlucky.

ludicrous, *adj.* laughable, ridiculous, amusing, comical, funny, droll, absurd, farcical.
Ant. miserable, serious, tragic.

lugubrious, *adj.* doleful, mournful, dismal, sorrowful, melancholy, gloomy, depressing.
Ant. cheerful, happy.

luminous, *adj.* 1. bright, shining, lucid, lucent, radiant, brilliant, resplendent. 2. lighted, lit, illuminated. 3. brilliant, bright, intel-

ligent, smart, clever, enlightening. 4. clear, intelligible, understandable, perspicacious, perspicuous, plain, lucid.
Ant. dull; dark; stupid; unclear, unintelligible.

lure, *n.* 1. enticement, decoy, attraction, allurement, temptation, bait; fly, minnow. —*v.* 2. allure, decoy, entice, draw, attract, tempt, seduce.

lurid, *adj.* 1. vivid, glaring, sensational; shining, fiery, red, intense, fierce, terrible, unrestrained, passionate. 2. wan, pale, pallid, ghastly, gloomy, murky, dismal, lowering.
Ant. mild, controlled; cheery.

lurk, *v.* skulk, sneak, prowl, slink, steal; lie in wait, lie in ambush, lie hidden *or* concealed.

luscious, *adj.* 1. delicious, juicy, delectable, palatable, savory. 2. sweet, cloying, saccharine, honeyed.
Ant. unpalatable, disgusting, nauseating; bitter, acrid, acid.

lush, *adj.* 1. tender, juicy, succulent, luxuriant, fresh. —*n.* 2. *(slang)* drunk, toper, tippler, dipsomaniac, alcoholic, heavy drinker.
Ant. stale, moldy.

lust, *n.* 1. desire, passion, appetite, craving, eagerness, cupidity. 2. lechery, concupiscence, carnality, lubricity, salaciousness, licentiousness, wantonness, lasciviousness, libertinism, license. —*v.* 3. crave, desire, need, want, demand, hunger for.

luster, *n.* 1. glitter, glisten, sheen, gloss. 2. brillance, brightness, radiance, luminosity, resplendence. 3. excellence, merit, distinction, glory, honor, repute, renown, eminence, celebrity, dash, élan, éclat. 4. chandelier, sconce, candelabrum.
Ant. dullness, tarnish; disrepute, dishonor.

lusty, *adj.* hearty, vigorous, strong, healthy, robust, sturdy, stout.
Ant. weak, frail, unhealthy.

luxurious, *adj.* 1. splendid, rich, sumptuous, ornate, delicate, opulent, well-appointed. 2. voluptuous, sensual, self-indulgent, epicurean.
Ant. poor, squalid.

macabre, *adj.* gruesome, horrible, grim, ghastly, morbid, weird.
Ant. beautiful, lovely, attractive, delightful.

Machiavellian, *adj.* crafty, deceitful, cunning, wily. astute, unscrupulous, clever, artful, designing, insidious, sly, shrewd, subtle, arch, crooked, tricky, intriguing, double-dealing, equivocal.
Ant. naive, ingenuous, honest.

mad, *adj.* 1. insane, lunatic, deranged, raving, distracted, crazed, maniacal, crazy. 2. furious, exasperated, angry, enraged, raging, incensed, provoked, wrathful, irate. 3. violent, furious, stormy. 4. excited, frantic, frenzied, wild, rabid. 5. senseless, foolish, imprudent, impractical, ill-advised, excessive, reckless, unsound, unsafe, harmful, dangerous, perilous. 6. infatuated, wild about, desirous.
Ant. sane; calm; serene; sensible, wise.

madden, *v.* infuriate, irritate, provoke, vex, annoy, enrage, anger, inflame, exasperate.
Ant. calm, mollify.

magic, *n.* enchantment, sorcery, necromancy, witchcraft, legerdemain, conjuring, sleight of hand.

magician, *n.* sorcerer, necromancer, witch doctor, enchanter, conjuror.

magnanimous, *adj.* 1. big, large, generous, forgiving, unselfish, liberal, disinterested. 2. noble, lofty, honorable, elevated, high-minded, exalted.
Ant. small, niggardly; base, vile.

magnificence, *n.* splendor, grandeur, impressiveness, sumptuousness, pomp, state, majesty, luxury, luxuriousness, éclat.
Ant. squalor, poverty.

magnificent, *adj.* 1. splendid, fine, superb, august, stately, majestic, imposing, sumptuous, rich, lavish, luxurious, grand, gorgeous, beautiful, princely, impressive, dazzling, brilliant, radiant, excellent, exquisite, elegant, superior, extraordinary; showy, ostentatious. 2. noble, sublime, dignified, great.
Ant. squalid, poor; base.

magnify, *v.* 1. enlarge, augment, increase, add to, amplify. 2. exaggerate, overstate.
Ant. decrease, micrify; understate.

maid, *n.* 1. girl, maiden, demoiselle, lass, lassie, virgin. 2. maidservant.

maim, *v.* mutilate, cripple, lacerate, mangle, injure, disable, wound, deface, mar, impair.

main, *adj.* 1. chief, cardinal, prime, paramount, primary, principal, leading, capital. 2. pure, sheer, utmost, direct. —*n.* 3. pipe, duct, conduit, channel. 4. force, power, strength, might, effort. 5. point, idea, crux. 6. ocean, sea, high seas.
Ant. secondary, unimportant; least; weakness.

maintain, *v.* 1. keep, continue, preserve, retain, keep up, uphold, support. 2. affirm, assert, aver, asseverate, state, hold, allege, declare. 3. contend, hold, claim, defend, vindicate, justify. 4. provide for, support, sustain, keep up.
Ant. discontinue.

maintenance, *n.* subsistence, support, livelihood, living, bread, victuals, food, provisions.
Ant. desuetude.

majestic, *adj.* regal, royal, princely, kingly, imperial, noble, lofty, stately, grand, august, dignified, imposing, pompous, splendid, magnificent, sublime.
Ant. base, squalid.

major, *adj.* greater, larger, capital.
Ant. minor.

make, *v.* 1. form, build, produce, fabricate, create, construct, manufacture, fashion, mold, shape. 2. cause, render, constitute. 3. transform, convert, change, turn, compose. 4. give rise to, prompt, occasion. 5. get, gain, acquire, obtain, secure, procure, earn, win. 6. do, effect, bring about, perform, execute, accomplish, practice, act. 7. estimate, reckon, judge, gauge. 8. cause, induce, compel, force. —*n.* 9. style, form, build, shape, brand, trade name, construction, structure, constitution. 10. disposition, character, nature. 11. quantity made, output, produce, production, product.
Ant. destroy.

maladroit, *adj.* 1. unskillful, awkward, clumsy, bungling, inept. 2. tactless, gauche.
Ant. adroit; tactful, subtle.

malady, *n.* disease, illness, sickness, affliction, disorder, complaint, ailment, indisposition.

malcontent, *adj.* dissatisfied, discontented, unsatisfied, unfulfilled.
Ant. satisfied, contented, content.

male, *adj.* masculine, manly, virile, paternal.
Ant. female.

malediction, *n.* curse, imprecation, denunciation, cursing, damning, damnation, execration; slander.
Ant. benediction, blessing.

malefactor, *n.* evildoer, culprit, criminal, felon, outlaw, offender.
Ant. benefactor.

malevolence, *n.* ill will, rancor, malignity, resentment, malice, maliciousness, spite, spitefulness, grudge, hate, hatred, venom.
Ant. benevolence, good will.

malevolent, *adj.* malicious, malignant, resentful, spiteful, begrudging, hateful, venomous, vicious, hostile, ill-natured, evil-minded, rancorous, mischievous, envious.
Ant. benevolent, friendly, amiable.

malice, *n.* ill will, spite, spitefulness, animosity, animus, enmity, malevolence, grudge, venom, hate, hatred, bitterness, rancor.
Ant. good will, benevolence.

malicious, *adj.* malevolent.
Ant. benevolent.

malign, *v.* 1. slander, libel, revile, abuse, calumniate, defame, disparage, vilify. —*adj.* 2. evil, pernicious, baleful, injurious, unfavorable, baneful. 3. malevolent.
Ant. compliment, praise; good, favorable; benevolent.

malignant, *adj.* 1. malicious, spiteful, malevolent, rancorous, bitter. 2. dangerous, perilous, harmful, hurtful, virulent, pernicious, lethal, deadly.
Ant. benevolent; benign.

malignity, *n.* malevolence.
Ant. benignity.

maltreat, *v.* mistreat, abuse, injure, ill-treat.
Ant. amuse, entertain.

mammoth, *adj.* huge, gigantic, immense, colossal.
Ant. tiny, microscopic.

manage, *v.* 1. bring about, succeed, accomplish, arrange, contrive. 2. conduct, handle, direct, govern, control, guide, regulate, engineer, rule, administer, supervise, superintend. 3. handle, wield, manipulate,

control. 4. dominate, influence; train, educate, handle.
Ant. mismanage, bungle.

management, *n.* handling, direction, control, regulation, conduct, charge, administration, superintendence, care, guidance, disposal, treatment, oversight, surveillance.
Ant. mismanagement.

manager, *n.* administrator, executive, superintendent, supervisor, boss, director, overseer, governor.
Ant. employee.

mandate, *n.* command, order, fiat, decree, ukase, injunction, edict, ruling, commission, requirement, precept, requisite, prerequisite.

maneuver, *n.* 1. procedure, move; scheme, plot, plan, design, stratagem, ruse, artifice, trick. —*v.* 2. manipulate, handle, intrigue, trick, scheme, plot, plan, design, finesse.

manful, *adj.* manly.
Ant. feminine, cowardly.

mangle, *v.* cut, lacerate, crush, slash, disfigure, maim, ruin, spoil, mar, deface, mutilate, destroy.

mania, *n.* 1. excitement, enthusiasm, craze, fad. 2. insanity, madness, aberration, derangement, dementia, frenzy, lunacy.
Ant. phobia; rationality.

manifest, *adj.* 1. evident, obvious, apparent, plain, clear, distinct, patent, open, palpable, visible, unmistakable, conspicuous. —*v.* 2. show, display, reveal, disclose, open, exhibit, evince, evidence, demonstrate, declare, express, make known.
Ant. latent, hidden, inconspicuous; conceal.

manifold, *adj.* 1. various, many, numerous, multitudinous. 2. varied, various, divers, multifarious, multifaceted.
Ant. simple, singular.

manly, *adj.* 1. manful, mannish, masculine, male, virile. 2. strong, brave, honorable, courageous, bold, valiant, intrepid, undaunted.
Ant. feminine; weak, cowardly.

manner, *n.* 1. mode, fashion, style, way, habit, custom, method, form. 2. demeanor, department, air, bearing, behavior, carriage, mien, aspect, look, appearance. 3. kind, sort. 4. nature, guise, character.

mannish, *adj.* manly.
Ant. feminine; cowardly, pusillanimous.

manufacture, *v.* assemble, fabricate, make, construct, build, compose.
Ant. destroy.

many, *adj.* numerous, multifarious, abundant, myriad, innumerable, manifold, divers, sundry, various, varied.
Ant. few.

map, *n.* chart, graph, plan, outline, diagram.

mar, *v.* damage, impair, ruin, spoil, injure, blot, deface, disfigure, deform, distort, maim.

maraud, *v.* raid, plunder, pillage, ravage, ransack.

margin, *n.* border, edge, rim, limit, confine, bound, marge, verge, brink.
Ant. center.

mariner, *n.* sailor, seaman, tar, seafarer, seafaring man.
Ant. landlubber.

mark, *n.* 1. trace, impression, line, cut, dent, stain, bruise. 2. badge, brand, sign. 3. symbol, sign, token, inscription, indication. 4. note, importance, distinction, eminence, consequence. 5. trait, characteristic, stamp, print. 6. aim, target, end, purpose, object, objective. —*v.* 7. label, tag, mark up, mark down. 8. indicate, designate, point out, brand, identify, imprint, impress, characterize. 9. destine, single out. 10. note, pay attention to, heed, notice, observe, regard, eye, spot.

marriage, *n.* 1. wedding, nuptials, wedlock, matrimony. 2. union, alliance, association, confederation.
Ant. divorce; separation.

marshal, *v.* arrange, array, order, rank, dispose; gather, convoke.
Ant. disorder; scatter.

marvelous, *adj.* 1. wonderful, wondrous, extraordinary, amazing, astonishing, astounding, miraculous. 2. improbable, incredible, unbelievable, surprising.
Ant. terrible, ordinary, commonplace; believable.

mask, *n.* 1. face-covering, veil, false face. 2. disguise, concealment, pretense, pretext, ruse, trick, subterfuge, evasion. 3. masquerade, revel, *bal masqué, ballo di maschera,* mummery. —*v.* 4. disguise, conceal, hide, veil, screen, cloak, shroud, cover.

mass, *n.* 1. aggregate, aggregation, assemblage, heap, congeries, combination. 2. collection, accumulation, conglomeration, pile, assemblage, quantity. 3. main body, bulk, majority. 4. size, bulk, massiveness, magnitude, dimension. 5. *(plural)* proletariat, working class, common people, plebeians. —*v.* 6. assemble; collect,

gather, marshal, amass, convoke; heap *or* pile up, aggregate.

massacre, *n.* 1. killing, slaughter, carnage, extermination, annihilation, butchery, murder, genocide. —*v.* 2. kill, butcher, slaughter, murder, slay.

massive, *adj.* 1. bulky, heavy, large, immense, huge, tremendous. 2. solid, substantial, great, imposing, massy, ponderous.
Ant. diminutive; flimsy.

master, *n.* 1. adept, expert. 2. employer, boss. 3. commander, chief, head, commander in chief, captain. —*adj.* 4. chief, principal, head, leading, cardinal, primary, prime, main. 5. dominating, predominant. 6. skilled, adept, expert, skillful. —*v.* 7. conquer, subdue, subject, subjugate, overcome, overpower. 8. rule, direct, govern, manage, superintend, oversee.

matchless, *adj.* peerless, unrivaled, unequaled, inimitable, unparalleled, incomparable, unmatched, consummate, exquisite.
Ant. unimportant, unimpressive.

material, *n.* 1. substance, matter, stuff. 2. element, constituent. —*adj.* 3. physical, corporeal. 4. important, essential, vital, consequent, momentous.
Ant. spiritual; immaterial.

matter, *n.* 1. substance, material, stuff. 2. thing, affair, business, question, subject, topic. 3. consequence, importance, essence, import, significance, moment. 4. trouble, difficulty. 5. ground, reason, cause. —*v.* 6. signify, be of importance, count.
Ant. insignificance; ease.

mature, *adj.* 1. ripe, aged, complete, grown, adult, full-grown, fully-developed, maturated. 2. completed, perfected, elaborated, ready, prepared. —*v.* 3. ripen, age, develop. 4. perfect, complete.
Ant. immature, childish, adolescent.

maxim, *n.* proverb, aphorism, saying, adage, apothegm.

meager, *adj.* scanty, deficient, sparse, mean, insignificant; thin, lean, emaciated, spare, gaunt, skinny, lank.
Ant. abundant.

mean, *v.* 1. intend, purpose, contemplate, destine, foreordain, predestinate, design. 2. signify, indicate, denote, imply, express. —*adj.* 3. inferior. 4. common, humble, low, undignified, ignoble, plebeian, coarse, rude, vulgar. 5. unimportant, unessential, nonessential, inconsequent, dispensable, insignificant, petty, paltry, little, poor, wretched, despicable, contemptible, low, base, vile, foul, disgusting, repulsive, repellent, depraved, immoral; small-minded. 6. unimposing, shabby, sordid, unclean, unscrupulous, squalid, poor. 7. penurious, parsimonious, illiberal, stingy, miserly, tight, niggardly, Scotch, selfish, narrow, mercenary. 8. intermediate, middle, medium, average, moderate. —n. (plural) 9. agency, instrumentality, method, approach, mode, way. 10. resources, backing, support. 11. revenue, income, substance, wherewithal, property, wealth. 12. (sing.) average, median, middle, midpoint, center.

Ant. exalted, dignified; important, essential; imposing, splendid, rich, generous; superior.

meander, v. 1. wander, stroll; wind, turn. —n. 2. labyrinth, maze, intricacy.

meaning, n. 1. tenor, gist, trend, idea, purport, significance, signification, sense, import, denotation, connotation, interpretation. 2. intent, intention, aim, object, purpose, design. —adj. 3. expressive, significant, poignant, pointed, knowing, meaningful.

Ant. insignificant, meaningless.

measureless, adj. limitless, boundless, immeasurable, immense, vast, endless, infinite, unending.

Ant. limited, finite.

mechanic, n. repairman, workman, machinist; craftsman, artificer, artisan.

meddlesome, adj. prying, curious, interfering, intrusive, officious.

mediate, v. intercede, interpose, arbitrate, reconcile, settle.

medicine, n. medication, medicament, remedy, drug, physic.

mediocre, adj. indifferent, ordinary, common, commonplace, medium, average, middling, passable, mean.

Ant. superior.

meditate, v. 1. contemplate, plan, reflect on, devise, scheme, plot, concoct, contrive, think over, dwell on. 2. reflect, ruminate, contemplate, ponder, muse, cogitate, think, study.

meditative, adj. pensive, thoughtful, reflecting, contemplative; studious.

Ant. impetuous.

medium, n. 1. mean, average, mean proportion, mean average. 2. means, agency, instrumentality, instrument. 3. environment, atmo-

sphere, ether, air, temper, conditions, influences. —adj. 4. average, mean, middling; mediocre.

meek, adj. humble, patient, submissive, spiritless, tame, yielding, forbearing, docile, unassuming, mild, peaceful, pacific, calm, soft, gentle, modest.

Ant. forward, unyielding, immodest.

meet, v. 1. join, connect, intersect, cross, converge, come together, unite. 2. encounter, come upon, confront, face. 3. encounter, oppose, conflict. 4. settle, discharge, fulfill, satisfy, gratify, answer, comply with. 5. gather, assemble, congregate, convene, collect, muster. 6. concur, agree, see eye-to-eye, unite, conjoin. —n. 7. meeting, contest, competition, match. —adj. 8. suited, suitable, apt, fitting, proper, appropriate, fit, befitting, adapted.

Ant. diverge; dissatisfy; scatter; disagree, diverge; unsuited, unapt.

melancholy, n. 1. gloom, depression, sadness, dejection, despondency, gloominess, blues, hypochondria. 2. pensiveness, thoughtfulness, sobriety, seriousness. —adj. 3. sad, depressed, dejected, gloomy, despondent, blue, dispirited, sorrowful, unhappy, disconsolate, inconsolable, miserable, dismal, doleful, lugubrious, moody, glum, down-in-the-mouth, downhearted, downcast, low-spirited. 4. sober, serious, thoughtful, pensive.

Ant. cheer, happiness; cheerful, happy.

mellow, adj. 1. ripe, full-flavored, soft, mature, well-matured. 2. softened, toned down, improved. 3. soft, rich, delicate, mellifluous, dulcet, melodious, tuneful, sweet, smooth. 4. genial, jovial, good-humored, good-natured. —v. 5. soften, ripen, develop, mature, improve, perfect.

Ant. immature.

melody, n. tune, song, air, descant, theme.

melt, v. 1. liquefy, fuse, dissolve, thaw. 2. pass, dwindle, fade, fade out, blend. 3. soften, gentle, mollify, relax.

Ant. freeze.

member, n. 1. limb, leg, arm, wing, head, branch. 2. constituent, element, part, portion.

menace, n. 1. threat, minaciousness, minacity, threatening. —v. 2. threaten, intimidate.

mend, v. 1. darn, patch, repair, renew, fix, restore, retouch. 2. correct, rectify, make better, amend,

emend, ameliorate, meliorate, improve, set right. 3. heal, recover, amend, improve, become better. —n. 4. repair, improvement, amelioration, emendation, correction, restoration, rectification, amendment, renewal.

Ant. ruin, destroy; die, languish.

mendacious, adj. lying, untrue, false, untruthful, deceitful.

Ant. truthful, honest.

menial, adj. 1. servile, mean, base, low. —n. 2. servant, domestic, attendant, footman, butler, valet, maid, maidservant, waiter; flunky, slave, underling, hireling, serf, minion, lackey.

Ant. noble, dignified; master.

mention, v. 1. refer to, allude to, name, specify, speak of, make known, impart, disclose, divulge, communicate, declare, state, tell, aver. —n. 2. reference, indirect reference, allusion.

mercenary, adj. venal, grasping, sordid, acquisitive, avaricious, covetous, penurious, parsimonious, stingy, tight, miserly, mean, niggardly, selfish.

Ant. generous, unselfish.

merciful, adj. compassionate, kind, clement, lenient, forgiving, gracious, benignant, beneficent, generous, big, large; tender, humane, kindhearted, tender-hearted, soft-hearted, sympathetic.

Ant. merciless.

merciless, adj. pitiless, cruel, hard, hard-hearted, severe, relentless, unrelenting, fell, unsympathetic, uncompassionate, unfeeling, inexorable.

Ant. merciful.

mercurial, adj. 1. sprightly, volatile, active, spirited, lively, nimble, energetic. 2. flighty, fickle, changeable, volatile, inconstant, undecided.

Ant. inactive, dispirited, phlegmatic; constant, steady.

mercy, n. 1. compassion, pity, benevolence, consideration, forgiveness, indulgence, clemency, leniency, forbearance, lenity, kindness, tenderness, mildness, gentleness. 2. disposal, discretion, disposition.

Ant. cruelty, pitilessness, harshness.

mere, adj. bare, scant, simple, pure, sheer, unmixed, entire.

Ant. considerable.

meretricious, adj. tawdry, showy, gaudy, ornate, spurious, sham, false.

Ant. genuine, sincere.

merit, *n.* 1. worth, excellence, value, desert, entitlement, due, credit. —*v.* 2. deserve, be worthy of, earn, be entitled to.

merriment, *n.* gaiety, mirth, hilarity, laughter, jollity, joviality, jocularity. *Ant.* misery, melancholy.

merry, *adj.* jolly, gay, happy, jovial, joyful, joyous, mirthful, hilarious, gleeful, blithe, blithesome, frolicsome, cheery, cheerful, glad. *Ant.* sad, unhappy.

mess, *n.* 1. dirtiness, untidiness. 2. confusion, muddle, medley, farrago, hodgepodge, hotchpotch, jumble, litter, mixture, miscellany, mélange, salmagundi. 3. unpleasantness, difficulty, predicament, plight, muddle, pickle. —*v.* 4. muddle, confuse, mix, mix up. *Ant.* tidiness; order, system; arrange.

metamorphosis, *n.* change, transformation, transmutation, mutation. *Ant.* stasis.

mete, *v.* 1. distribute, apportion, parcel out, dole, allot, deal, measure. —*n.* 2. limit, bound, boundary, term.

method, *n.* 1. mode, procedure, way, means, manner, fashion, technique, process, course. 2. order, system, arrangement, disposition, rule.

meticulous, *adj.* careful, finical, finicky, solicitous, exact, precise, demanding. *Ant.* careless, inexact, imprecise.

mettle, *n.* 1. disposition, temper, character, spirit. 2. spirit, courage, valor, pluck, vigor, ardor, fire, nerve, fiber. *Ant.* cowardice, pusillanimity.

middle, *adj.* 1. central, equidistant, halfway, medial. 2. intermediate, intervening. —*n.* 3. center, midpoint, midst. *Ant.* end, final, initial.

midst, *n.* middle, center stage, arena, center, thick, heart, core. *Ant.* rim, edge.

might, *n.* power, ability, force, main, puissance, strength, efficacy. *Ant.* weakness, inability.

mighty, *adj.* 1. powerful, strong, vigorous, robust, sturdy, puissant, potent. 2. sizable, huge, immense, enormous, vast, tremendous. *Ant.* feeble, weak, impotent; small, negligible.

migrate, *v.* immigrate, emigrate, move, resettle. *Ant.* remain, stay.

mild, *adj.* 1. amiable, gentle, temperate, kind, compassionate, indulgent,

clement, soft, pleasant. 2. placid, peaceful, tranquil, pacific, calm. 3. bland, emollient, mollifying, assuasive, soothing. *Ant.* intemperate, unkind, unpleasant; stormy, turbulent; piquant, biting, bitter.

milieu, *n.* environment, medium, background, class, sphere, surroundings, element.

mind, *n.* 1. intellect, intelligence, understanding, reason, sense. 2. brain, brains. 3. sanity, reason, mental balance. 4. disposition, temper, inclination, bent, intention, leaning, proclivity, bias. 5. opinion, sentiments, belief, contemplation, judgment, consideration. 6. purpose, intention, intent, will, wish, liking, desire, wont. 7. remembrance, recollection, recall, memory. —*v.* 8. pay attention, heed, obey, attend, attend to, mark, regard, notice, note. 9. tend, take care of, watch, look after. 10. be careful *or* cautious *or* wary. 11. care, object.

mingle, *v.* 1. mix, blend, unite, commingle, intermix, join, conjoin, combine, intermingle, concoct, compound. 2. participate, associate.

minor, *adj.* 1. lesser, smaller, inferior, secondary, subordinate, petty, inconsiderable, unimportant, small. —*n.* 2. child, adolescent. *Ant.* major.

minute, *n.* 1. moment, instant; jiffy, second. 2. *(plural)* note, memorandum, record, proceedings. —*adj.* 3. small, tiny, little, infinitesimal, minuscule, diminutive. 4. detailed, exact, precise, critical. *Ant.* tremendous, huge, large; general, inexact, rough.

miraculous, *adj.* 1. marvelous, wonderful, wondrous, extraordinary, incredible. 2. supernatural, preternatural. *Ant.* prosaic, commonplace; natural.

mirth, *n.* rejoicing, joy, joyousness, gaiety, jollity, glee, merriment, joviality, laughter, hilarity. *Ant.* sadness, misery.

misadventure, *n.* mischance, mishap, ill fortune, ill luck, misfortune; accident, disaster, calamity, catastrophe. *Ant.* luck, fortune.

miscellaneous, *adj.* indiscriminate, promiscuous, mixed, heterogeneous, divers, diversified, varied, various, mingled, confused. *Ant.* specific, special, discerning.

mischief, *n.* 1. harm, trouble, injury, damage, hurt, detriment, disadvan-

tage. 2. evil, malice, malicious mischief, vandalism; misfortune, trouble. *Ant.* good, advantage.

misconstrue, *v.* misinterpret, misread, misunderstand, misapprehend, misjudge, mistake. *Ant.* construe, understand.

misdemeanor, *n.* misbehavior, misdeed, transgression, fault, misconduct; offense, trespass.

miser, *n.* niggard, skinflint, tightwad, pinchpenny. *Ant.* Maecenas.

miserable, *adj.* 1. wretched, unhappy, uneasy, uncomfortable, distressed, disconsolate, doleful, forlorn, broken-hearted, heartbroken. 2. poverty-stricken, poor, needy, destitute, penniless. 3. contemptible, bad, wretched, mean, despicable, low, abject, worthless. 4. deplorable, pitiable, lamentable, unfortunate, unlucky, ill-starred, star-crossed, luckless; calamitous, catastrophic. *Ant.* happy; wealthy; good; fortunate, lucky.

miserly, *adj.* penurious, niggardly, cheap, stingy, parsimonious, tight-fisted, penny-pinching, close, mean. *Ant.* generous, unselfish.

misery, *n.* 1. wretchedness, distress, tribulation, woe, trial, suffering, agony, anguish, torture. 2. grief, anguish, woe, unhappiness, sorrow, torment, desolation. *Ant.* happiness, joy; delight.

misfortune, *n.* 1. ill luck, bad luck, ill fortune. 2. accident, disaster, calamity, catastrophe, reverse, affliction, mishap, mischance, adversity, distress, hardship, trouble, blow. *Ant.* luck, fortune.

misgiving, *n.* apprehension, doubt, distrust, suspicion, mistrust, hesitation. *Ant.* trust.

mislead, *v.* misguide, lead astray, misconduct, delude, deceive, misdirect. *Ant.* lead, conduct.

misplace, *v.* 1. displace, mislay, lose. 2. misapply, misbestow. *Ant.* find; apply, place.

misprint, *n.* typographical error, erratum, typo.

mist, *n.* 1. cloud, fog, fogbank, haze, smog; soup. 2. bewilderment, haze, perplexity, obscurity. —*v.* 3. fog, cloud over, drizzle, foggle. *Ant.* clarity.

mistake, *n.* 1. error, blunder, slip, inaccuracy, erratum, typo, misprint, fault, oversight. 2. misapprehension, misconception, misunderstanding. —*v.* 3. misapprehend, misconceive, misunderstand, misjudge, err. *Ant.* accuracy; understanding.

mistaken, *adj.* erroneous, wrong, incorrect, misconceived, inaccurate. *Ant.* correct, accurate.

misunderstanding, *n.* 1. mistake, misapprehension, error, misconception. 2. disagreement, dissension, discord, difference, difficulty, quarrel. *Ant.* understanding; agreement, concord.

mix, *v.* 1. blend, combine, mingle, commingle, confuse, jumble, unite, compound, amalgamate, homogenize. 2. consort, mingle, associate, join. —*n.* 3. mixture, concoction. *Ant.* separate; dissociate.

mixed, *adj.* mingled, commingled, joined; coeducational, coed. *Ant.* separated.

mixture, *n.* 1. blend, combination, compound. 2. hodgepodge, hotchpotch, gallimaufry, conglomeration, jumble, medley, melange, olio, potpourri, miscellany, farrago, salmagundi; variety, diversity. *Ant.* element, constituent.

moan, *n.* 1. groan, wail, lament, lamentation; dirge, elegy, threnody, monody. —*v.* 2. bemoan, bewail, grieve, lament, mourn, deplore.

mock, *v.* 1. ridicule, deride, taunt, flout, gibe, tantalize, tease, jeer, chaff, scoff, banter, make sport of; mimic, ape, satirize, imitate. 2. defy. 3. deceive, delude, disappoint, cheat, dupe, fool, defeat, mislead. —*n.* 4. mockery, derision, ridicule, banter, sport, sneer. —*adj.* 5. feigned, pretended, counterfeit, sham, false, spurious, fake. *Ant.* praise, honor.

mockery, *n.* 1. ridicule, derision, scorn, contumely. 2. imitation, show, mimicry. 3. travesty, pretense, pretext, sham, satire.

mode, *n.* 1. method, way, manner, style, fashion. 2. form, variety, degree, modification, graduation.

model, *n.* 1. standard, paragon, prototype, ideal, pattern, example, archetype, mold, original. 2. representation, facsimile, copy, image, imitation. —*v.* 3. form, plan, pattern, mold, shape, fashion, design.

moderate, *adj.* 1. reasonable, temperate, judicious, just, fair, deliberate, mild, cool, steady, calm, peaceful. 2. medium, average, usual. 3. mediocre, fair. 4. middle-of-the-road,

conservative, temperate. —*n.* 5. mugwump, middle-of-the-roader, conservative. —*v.* 6. allay, meliorate, pacify, calm, assuage, sober, mitigate, soften, mollify, temper, qualify, appease, abate, lessen, diminish, reduce. 7. preside, chair, arbitrate, referee, regulate, umpire. *Ant.* immoderate; unusual; radical; disturb, increase, intensify.

modern, *adj.* recent, up-to-date, late, present, new, novel, fresh, neoteric. *Ant.* old, archaic, ancient, obsolete.

modest, *adj.* 1. moderate, humble, unpretentious, decent, becoming, proper. 2. inextravagant, unostentatious, retiring, unassuming, unobtrusive. 3. decent, demure, prudish, chaste, pure, virtuous. *Ant.* immodest, immoderate, improper; extravagant.

modesty, *n.* 1. unobtrusiveness. 2. moderation, decency, propriety, simplicity, purity, chastity, prudery, prudishness. *Ant.* indecency, licentiousness.

modify, *v.* 1. change, alter, vary, qualify, temper, adjust, restrict, limit, shape, reform. 2. reduce, qualify, moderate.

moil, *v.* 1. work hard, toil, drudge, labor. —*n.* 2. toil, drudgery, labor. 3. confusion, turmoil, trouble. *Ant.* indolence, laziness.

moist, *adj.* damp, humid, dank, wet. *Ant.* dry, arid.

molest, *v.* attack, assail; harass, harry, disturb, trouble, annoy, vex, plague, tease, pester, torment, torture, irritate, fret, hector, inconvenience, discommode, worry, bother.

moment, *n.* 1. minute, instant, second, jiffy, trice, flash, twinkling. 2. importance, consequence, significance, weight, gravity, import, consideration. 3. momentum, force, power, impetus, drive. *Ant.* insignificance, inertia.

momentous, *adj.* important, consequent, vital, weighty, serious. *Ant.* unimportant, trivial, trifling.

monarchy, *n.* kingdom, realm, empire.

monetary, *adj.* pecuniary, financial; nummary, nummular.

money, *n.* 1. coin, cash, currency, specie, change; coin of the realm. 2. funds, capital, assets, property, wealth, riches. 3. (*slang*) mazuma, long green, lettuce, dough.

mongrel, *n.* 1. cross, hybrid, mutt, half-breed. —*adj.* 2. hybrid. *Ant.* purebreed, thoroughbred.

monk, *n.* friar, brother; cenobite, eremite.

monotonous, *adj.* tedious, humdrum, tiresome, uniform, boring, dull, unvaried, unvarying. *Ant.* interesting, amusing, diverting.

monster, *n.* 1. brute, griffin, gargoyle, sphinx, centaur, hippogriff. 2. mooncalf, monstrosity. 3. fiend, brute, miscreant, wretch, villain, demon, devil. —*adj.* 4. huge, enormous, monstrous.

monstrous, *adj.* 1. huge, great, large, tremendous, gigantic, monster, prodigious, enormous, immense, vast, stupendous, colossal. 2. frightful, hideous, revolting, shocking, repulsive, horrible, atrocious, terrible, dreadful, horrendous. *Ant.* small, tiny; delightful, attractive.

mood, *n.* 1. disposition, frame of mind, humor, temper, vein. 2. mode.

moody, *adj.* gloomy, sullen, ill-humored, perverse, sulky, waspish, snappish, pettish, testy, short-tempered, irritable, irascible, captious, peevish, fretful, spleeny, spenetic, spiteful, morose, intractable, stubborn. *Ant.* amiable, temperate, tractable.

moot, *adj.* 1. doubtful, debatable, disputable, disputed, unsettled. —*v.* 2. argue, debate, dispute, discuss. *Ant.* indubitable, indisputable; agree, concur.

moral, *adj.* 1. ethical, upright, honest, straightforward, righteous, open, just, good, virtuous, honorable. —*n.* 2. (*plural*) ethics, integrity, standards, morality. *Ant.* immoral, amoral.

morbid, *adj.* 1. gloomy, sensitive, extreme. 2. unwholesome, diseased, unhealthy, sick, sickly, tainted, corrupted, vitiated. *Ant.* cheerful; wholesome, salubrious.

moreover, *adv.* besides, further, furthermore, and, also, too, likewise.

morning, *n.* morn, daybreak, sunrise, dawn. *Ant.* evening.

morose, *adj.* sullen, gloomy, moody, sour, sulky, churlish, splenetic, surly, ill-humored, ill-natured, perverse. *Ant.* cheerful, happy, good-natured.

mortal, *adj.* 1. human. 2. fatal, final, lethal, deadly. —*n.* 3. human being, man. *Ant.* immortal.

mortify, *v.* 1. shame, humiliate, hum-

ble, abash, abase, subdue, restrain. 2. gangrene, necrose.
Ant. honor.

mostly, *adv.* in the main, generally, chiefly, especially, particularly, for the most part, customarily.
Ant. seldom.

motion, *n.* 1. movement, move, action. 2. gait, deportment, bearing, air. 3. gesture, movement, move. —*v.* 4. move, gesture.
Ant. stasis.

motionless, *adj.* stable, fixed, unmoving, still, transfixed, quiescent, stationary.
Ant. mobile.

motive, *n.* motivation, inducement, incentive, incitement, stimulus, spur, influence, occasion, reason, ground, cause, purpose.

mount, *v.* 1. go up, ascend, climb, scale, get up on. 2. raise, put into position, fix on. 3. prepare, produce, make ready, ready. —*n.* 4. horse, steed, charger, palfrey. 5. mountain, hill.
Ant. descend.

mountebank, *n.* quack, pitchman, charlatan, pretender, phony.

mourn, *v.* 1. grieve, lament, bewail, bemoan, sorrow for. 2. deplore.
Ant. laugh, rejoice.

move, *v.* 1. stir, advance, budge, progress, make progress, proceed, move on, remove. 2. turn, revolve, spin, gyrate, rotate, operate. 3. act, bestir oneself, take action. 4. stir, shake, agitate, excite, arouse, rouse; shift, transfer, propel. 5. prompt, actuate, induce, influence, impel, activate, incite, rouse, instigate. 6. affect,

touch. 7. propose, recommend, suggest, bring up *or* forward. —*n.* 8. motion, movement, action.

movement, *n.* 1. move, motion, change. 2. motion, progress, activity, eventfulness. 3. (*music*) part, section, division; motion, rhythm, time, tempo.
Ant. inertia, stasis.

multitude, *n.* host, crowd, throng, mass, army, swarm, collection.

mumble, *v.* murmur, mutter, muffle.
Ant. articulate, enunciate, pronounce.

mundane, *adj.* worldly, earthly, terrestrial, terraqueous, secular, temporal.
Ant. unearthly, clerical.

munificent, *adj.* liberal, generous, bountiful, beneficent, bounteous.
Ant. stingy, penurious, mean, niggardly.

murder, *n.* 1. killing, assassination, homicide, manslaughter. —*v.* 2. kill, slay, assassinate, destroy, put an end to. 3. spoil, mar, ruin, abuse.

murky, *adj.* dark, gloomy, cheerless, obscure, dim, cloudy, dusky, lowering, overcast, misty, hazy.
Ant. bright, light, clear.

murmur, *n.* 1. grumble, susurration, susurrus, mumble, complaint, plaint, whimper, mutter. —*v.* 2. mumble, mutter, whisper. 3. complain, grumble, grouse.

muse, *v.* reflect, meditate, ponder, contemplate, think of *or* about, cogitate, deliberate, ruminate, think, brood; dream.

muster, *v.* 1. assemble, gather, summon, convoke, collect, marshal, convene, congregate. —*n.* 2. gathering,

assembly, assemblage, collection, convention, congregation.
Ant. scatter, separate.

mutable, *adj.* 1. changeable, alterable, variable. 2. fickle, changing, inconstant, unstable, vacillating, unsettled, wavering, unsteady, flickering, varying, variable.
Ant. immutable, invariable; stable, settled, motionless.

mute, *adj.* silent, dumb, speechless, still.
Ant. loquacious, voluble, talkative.

mutilate, *v.* injure, disfigure, maim, damage, mar, cripple, mangle.

mutinous, *adj.* 1. seditious, insurrectionary, revolutionary, insurgent. 2. rebellious, refractory, insubordinate, unruly, contumacious, turbulent, riotous.
Ant. patriotic; obedient.

mutiny, *n.* 1. revolt, rebellion, insurrection, revolution, uprising, sedition. —*v.* 2. revolt, rebel, rise up.
Ant. obedience.

mutter, *v.* murmur.

mutual, *adj.* reciprocal, balanced, correlative, common, interchangeable.
Ant. single, singular.

mysterious, *adj.* secret, esoteric, occult, cryptic, inscrutable, mystical, obscure, puzzling, inexplicable, unexplainable, unintelligible, incomprehensible, enigmatic, impenetrable, recondite, hidden, concealed, dark, abstruse, cabalistic, unfathomable.
Ant. open.

myth, *n.* legend, story, fiction, fable, tradition, epic.

N

nag, *v.* 1. torment, pester, harass, harry, hector, importune, irritate, annoy, vex. —*n.* 2. shrew, virago, pest, termagant, maenad. 3. horse, pony.

naive, *adj.* unsophisticated, ingenuous, simple, unaffected, natural, unsuspecting, artless, guileless, candid, open, plain.
Ant. sophisticated, disingenuous, artful, sly.

naked, *adj.* 1. nude, bare, incovered, undressed, unclothed. 2. bare, stripped, destitute, desert, denuded. 3. unsheathed, exposed, bare. 4. un-

furnished, bare. 5. defenseless, unprotected, unguarded, exposed, unarmed, open. 6. simple, plain, manifest, evident, undisguised, unadorned, mere, bare, sheer. 7. plainspoken, blunt, direct, outspoken, unvarnished, uncolored, unexaggerated, plain.
Ant. covered, dressed; protected; ornate; exaggerated, embellished.

name, *n.* 1. appellation, title, label, tag, designation, epithet. 2. reputation, repute, character, credit. 3. fame, repute, note, distinction, renown, eminence, honor, praise. —*v.*

4. call, title, entitle, dub, denominate. 5. specify, mention, indicate, designate, identify, nominate.

narrate, *v.* recount, relate, tell, retail, describe, detail, recite.

narrative, *n.* story, account, recital, history, chronicle, tale, description.

narrow-minded, *adj.* prejudiced, biased, bigoted, intolerant, illiberal, partial.
Ant. liberal, broad-minded, tolerant, unprejudiced.

nasty, *adj.* 1. filthy, dirty, disgusting, unclean, foul, impure, loathsome, polluted, defiled. 2. nauseous, nauseating, disgusting, sickening, offensive, repulsive, repellent, objectionable. 3. obscene, smutty, pornographic, lewd, licentious, lascivious, indecent, ribald, gross, indelicate. 4. vicious, spiteful, ugly, bad-tempered, disagreeable. 5. unpleasant, inclement, stormy.

Ant. clean, pure, unpolluted; delightful; decent, honorable; amiable, agreeable; pleasant, fair.

nation, *n.* 1. race, stock, ethnic group, population, people, tribe. 2. state, country, commonwealth, kingdom, realm.

native, *adj.* 1. inborn, inherent, inherited, natural, innate, inbred, congenital. 2. indigenous, autochthonous, aboriginal, natural. 3. unadorned, natural, real, genuine, original. —*n.* 4. inhabitant, aborigine.

Ant. acquired; imported; decorated; foreigner, alien.

nature, *n.* 1. character, quality, attributes, qualification. 2. kind, sort, character, type, species, quality. 3. universe, world, earth. 4. reality, matter.

nauseate, *v.* 1. sicken, revolt, disgust. 2. loathe, abhor, abominate, detest, reject.

Ant. delight, enchant, attract; like, love, adore.

nauseous, *adj.* 1. sickening, revolting, nasty, repellent, disgusting, loathsome, abhorrent, detestable, despicable, nauseating, offensive. 2. ill, sick to one's stomach.

Ant. attractive, lovable; well.

near, *adj.* 1. close, nigh, at within, at hand, nearby, adjacent, contiguous, touching, adjoining, bordering, abutting. 2. imminent, impending, approaching, forthcoming, at hand. 3. related, connected, intimate, familiar, allied, attached. 4. faithful, close, accurate, literal. 5. narrow, close, niggardly, parsimonious, stingy, miserly, tight, tightfisted.

Ant. far; generous.

nearly, *adv.* 1. almost, approximately, well-nigh. 2. intimately, closely. 3. parsimoniously, penuriously.

neat, *adj.* 1. orderly, ordered, trim, tidy, spruce, smart, nice. 2. clever, effective, adroit, finished, well-planned, dexterous, apt. 3. unadulterated, undiluted, straight, unmixed, pure.

Ant. disorderly, sloppy; maladroit, ineffective; adulterated; impure.

nebulous, *adj.* 1. hazy, vague, confused, indistinct. 2. cloudy, cloud-like, nebular.

Ant. clear, fair, distinct.

necessary, *adj.* 1. essential, indispensable, required, requisite, needed, needful, vital, unavoidable. 2. involuntary. —*n.* 3. requisite, prerequisite, requirement, necessity, *sine qua non,* essential.

Ant. unnecessary, dispensable; voluntary; nonessential.

necessity, *n.* 1. needfulness, indispensability, need, indispensableness. 2. requirement, requisite, demand, necessary, *sine qua non,* essential, prerequisite. 3. compulsion, fate, destiny, kismet, karma, inevitability, inevitableness, unavoidability, unavoidableness, irresistibility. 4. poverty, neediness, indigence, necessitousness, need, want.

Ant. dispensability; wealth.

necromancy, *n.* magic, enchantment, conjuration, sorcery, divination.

need, *n.* 1. requirement, want, necessity, exigency, emergency, urgency. 2. want, necessity, lack, demand. 3. destitution, poverty, neediness, want, deprivation, necessity, indigence, penury, distress, privation. —*v.* 4. require, want, lack.

Ant. wealth, opulence.

nefarious, *adj.* 1. wicked, depraved, iniquitous, evil, abominable, detestable, atrocious, execrable, flagitious, heinous, vile, horrible, dreadful, horrendous, infamous, villainous, base.

Ant. good, honest, honorable, exalted.

neglect, *v.* 1. disregard, ignore, slight, overlook, omit, be remiss. —*n.* 2. disregard, dereliction, negligence, remissness, carelessness, failure, omission, default, inattention, heedlessness.

Ant. regard, attend; regard, attention, care.

neglectful, *adj.* disregardful, remiss, careless, negligent, inattentive, indifferent, heedless, thoughtless.

Ant. regardful, careful, thoughtful.

negligence, *n.* neglect.

Ant. regard.

negligent, *adj.* neglectful.

Ant. regardful.

negotiate, *v.* 1. arrange, arrange for, settle. 2. circulate; sell, transfer, deliver, assign.

neophyte, *n.* 1. convert, proselyte. 2. beginner, tyro, amateur, greenhorn,

novice, novitiate, pupil, student.

Ant. old hand, expert.

nerve, *n.* 1. strength, vigor, energy, power, force, might. 2. courage, firmness, steadfastness, intrepidity, fortitude, resolution, resoluteness, endurance. —*v.* 3. strengthen, fortify, innervate, invigorate, steel, brace.

Ant. weakness, frailty, cowardice; weaken, enervate.

nerveless, *adj.* feeble, weak, enervated, flaccid, spiritless, flabby, cowardly, pusillanimous.

Ant. strong, brave, bold, fearless.

nervous, *adj.* excitable, uneasy, apprehensive, fearful, timid, timorous.

Ant. confident, bold, intrepid.

new, *adj.* 1. recent, modern, up to date, late, neoteric, novel, fresh. 2. further, additional, fresh. 3. unaccustomed, unused, fresh. —*adv.* 4. recently, lately; freshly, anew, newly, afresh.

Ant. old, stale.

nice, *adj.* 1. pleasing, pleasant, agreeable, delightful, good. 2. kind, amiable, pleasant, friendly. 3. accurate, precise, skilled, delicate, fastidious, exact, exacting, critical, rigorous, strict, demanding, scrupulous. 4. tactful, careful, delicate, discriminating, discerning, particular. 5. minute, fine, subtle, refined. 6. refined, well-mannered, well-spoken. 7. suitable, proper, polite. 8. neat, trim, fastidious, finical, finicky, dainty, squeamish, fussy.

Ant. unpleasant; unkind; inaccurate; tactless, careless; unrefined; improper, impolite; sloppy.

nickname, *n.* sobriquet.

niggardly, *adj.* stingy, parsimonious, penurious, miserly, mean, tight-fisted, close-fisted, small, avaricious, mercenary; illiberal, niggard, close, tight; scanty, poor, saving, chary, sparing.

Ant. generous, liberal.

nimble, *adj.* agile, quick, lively, active, brisk, spry, ready, alert, swift, light, awake, on the qui vive.

Ant. slow, clumsy, awkward.

noble, *adj.* 1. high-born, aristocratic. 2. high-minded, magnanimous, superior, elevated, exalted, worthy, lofty, honorable, great, large, generous. 3. admirable, dignified, imposing, stately, magnificent, impressive, grand, lordly, splendid. —*n.* 4. nobleman, peer, aristocrat, lord, lady.

Ant. lowborn; base; undignified; serf, slave.

noise, *n.* 1. clamor, din, hubbub, racket, clatter, rattle, blare, uproar, outcry, tumult, ado. —*v.* 2. spread, rumor, bruit about.
Ant. quiet, peace.

noiseless, *adj.* silent, quiet, still, inaudible, soundless.
Ant. noisy, clamorous, tumultuous.

noisome, *adj.* 1. offensive, disgusting, fetid, putrid, foul, rotten. 2. harmful, injurious, poisonous, noxious, nocuous, lethal, deadly, mephitic, miasmatic, miasmal, miasmic, pestilential, hurtful, pernicious, unhealthy, detrimental, deleterious, unwholesome, baneful, destructive.
Ant. delightful; pleasant, wholesome, healthful.

noisy, *adj.* loud, stentorian, clamorous, boisterous, tumultuous, riotous, vociferous, obstreperous, blustering, blatant, uproarious.
Ant. quiet, silent, peaceful.

nominal, *adj.* titular, so-called, formal.

nonchalant, *adj.* unconcerned, indifferent, cool, apathetic, unexcited, calm, casual.
Ant. concerned, excitable.

nondescript, *adj.* odd, peculiar, strange, unclassifiable, amorphous, indescribable.
Ant. regular, natural, ordinary.

nonesuch, *n.* paragon, ideal, model, pattern, nonpareil.

nonpareil, *adj.* 1. peerless, unequaled, unparalleled. —*n.* 2. nonesuch.
Ant. average, common, ordinary.

nonplus, *v.* puzzle, confound, confuse, perplex, disconcert.

nonsense, *n.* twaddle, balderdash, senselessness, moonshine, absurdity, folly, trash.

notable, *adj.* 1. noteworthy, noted, noticeable, remarkable, signal, distinguished, unusual, uncommon, extraordinary, great, conspicuous, memorable. 2. prominent, important, eminent, distinguished, famed, famous, well-known, conspicuous,

notorious. 3. capable, thrifty, industrious, diligent, sedulous, assiduous, careful, clever, smart, alert, watchful. —*n.* 4. celebrity.
Ant. common, ordinary; unimportant, undistinguished; careless.

note, *n.* 1. memorandum, record, minute. 2. comment, remark, commentary, criticism, critique, assessment, annotation, footnote. 3. IOU. 4. eminence, distinction, repute, celebrity, fame, renown, reputation, name. 5. notice, heed, observation; consideration, regard. —*v.* 6. mark down, jot down, record, make a note of, register. 7. mention, designate, refer to, indicate, denote. 8. notice, see, perceive, spot, remark, observe, regard, look at.

noted, *adj.* famous, celebrated, distinguished, famed, notable, renowned, eminent, illustrious, well-known.
Ant. unknown, undistinguished; notorious, infamous.

notice, *n.* 1. information, intelligence, advice, news, notification, mention, announcement. 2. intimation, warning, premonition. 3. sign, placard, poster, billboard, advertisement. 4. observation, perception, attention, heed, note, cognizance. 5. comment, mention, account, criticism, critique, review. —*v.* 6. discern, perceive, see, become aware of, pay attention to, distinguish, discriminate, recognize, understand, regard, heed, note, observe, mark, remark.

notify, *v.* give notice to, inform, apprise, acquaint, make known to.

notion, *n.* 1. conception, idea, concept. 2. opinion, view, belief, sentiment, impression, judgment. 3. whim, caprice, fancy, crotchet.

notwithstanding, *prep.* 1. despite, in spite of. —*adv.* 2. nevertheless, yet, however. —*conj.* 3. although, though, however, yet, nevertheless.
Ant. on account of, because of.

nourish, *v.* 1. nurture, nurse, sustain, support, tend, attend. 2. foster, pro-

mote, promulgate, foment, succor, aid, help, encourage.
Ant. discourage; neglect.

novel, *n.* 1. romance, fiction, tale, story. —*adj.* 2. new, different.

noxious, *adj.* 1. harmful, hurtful, unhealthy, unwholesome, injurious, mephitic, miasmatic, nocuous, noisome, detrimental, baneful, deleterious, pestilential, poisonous, destructive, deadly. 2. corrupting, immoral, pernicious.
Ant. harmless, wholesome, beneficial; moral.

nucleus, *n.* center, kernel, core, heart.

nude, *adj.* uncovered, undressed, unclothed, undraped, naked, bare, exposed, denuded, stark naked, *au naturel,* in the altogether.
Ant. covered, dressed.

nugatory, *adj.* 1. trifling, worthless, futile, vain, trivial. 2. useless, ineffectual, inoperative.
Ant. important, vital; useful, effectual.

number, *n.* 1. sum, total, count, aggregate, collection. 2. numeral, digit, figure. 3. issue, copy, edition. 4. quantity, collection, company, multitude, horde, many. 5. beat, rhythm. —*v.* 6. count, enumerate, calculate, compute, reckon, numerate, tell; account; include, consist of.

numberless, *adj.* innumerable, numerous, myriad, countless, uncounted, untold, infinite.
Ant. finite.

numerous, *adj.* many, numberless.
Ant. few.

nurse, *v.* 1. tend, take care of, attend. 2. foster, cherish, succor, promote, foment, encourage, aid, abet, help. 3. nourish, nurture, feed, rear, raise. 4. suckle, feed, give suck to.
Ant. neglect.

nurture, *v.* nurse.

nutrition, *n.* food, nutriment, aliment, nourishment, sustenance, subsistence.

nymph, *n.* sylph, naiad, nereid, oceanid, oread, dryad, hamadryad.

oaf, *n.* 1. simpleton, blockhead, dunce, dolt, fool, nincompoop, ninny. 2. idiot, imbecile, moron. 3. changeling.
Ant. genius.

oath, *n.* 1. promise, vow, pledge, affirmation. 2. profanity, curse, blasphemy, malediction, imprecation.

obdurate, *adj.* 1. hard-hearted, hardened, hard, firm, obstinate, callous,

stubborn, pigheaded, unyielding, unbending, inflexible, inexorable. 2. penitent, lost, unregenerate, reprobate, irreclaimable, shameless, graceless.

Ant. soft-hearted, soft, malleable; abashed, humble.

obedient, *adj.* submissive, compliant, docile, tractable, yielding, deferential, respectful, dutiful, subservient. *Ant.* disobedient, recalcitrant, refractory.

obese, *adj.* fat, stout, plump, pudgy, corpulent, portly, gross. *Ant.* thin, skinny, slender, slim.

obfuscate, *v.* 1. confuse, stupefy, muddle, bewilder, perplex. 2. darken, obscure, adumbrate, cloud. *Ant.* clarify; brighten.

object, *n.* 1. thing, reality, fact, manifestation, phenomenon. 2. target, objective, goal, end, destination, aim. 3. purpose, reason, basis, base, target, goal, end, motive, intent, intention. —*v.* 4. protest, disapprove, be averse, refuse. *Ant.* approve.

objective, *n.* 1. end, termination, object, destination, aim, target, butt. —*adj.* 2. unprejudiced, unbiased, impartial, fair, impersonal. *Ant.* subjective, biased, personal.

obligation, *n.* 1. requirement, duty, responsibility, accountableness. 2. agreement, contract, covenant, bond, stipulation.

oblige, *v.* 1. require, constrain, compel, force, necessitate, bind, coerce. 2. obligate, bind. 3. favor, accommodate, serve, please, benefit. *Ant.* disoblige, liberate, free; unfetter.

obliterate, *v.* destroy, erase, efface, do away with, expunge, rub out, concel, dele, delete, blot out. *Ant.* construct, create, originate; restore.

oblivious, *adj.* heedless, disregardful, neglectful, careless, negligent. *Ant.* heedful, regardful, careful.

obloquy, *n.* 1. discredit, disgrace. 2. censure, blame, reproach, odium, calumny, contumely, scorn, defamation, aspersion, revilement. *Ant.* credit; exoneration, favor.

obnoxious, *adj.* 1. objectionable, offensive, odious, hateful. 2. exposed, liable, subject, answerable. *Ant.* delightful, favorable; franchised, licensed, irresponsible.

obscene, *adj.* immodest, indecent, lewd, pornographic, coarse, ribald, smutty, offensive, filthy, immoral, indelicate, impure, unchaste, gross, disgusting, lubricous. *Ant.* modest, decent, moral, pure, chaste.

obscure, *adj.* 1. unclear, uncertain, doubtful, dubious, ambiguous, mysterious. 2. inconspicuous, unnoticeable, unnoticed, unknown, undistinguished, undistinguishable, unnoted. 3. remote, retired, secluded. 4. indistinct, blurred, blurry, imperfect, dim, veiled. 5. dark, murky, dim, clouded, cloudy, gloomy, dusky, somber, shadowy, lurid, unilluminated. *Ant.* clear, certain, unambiguous, conspicuous, noted; distinct; bright.

obsequious, *adj.* 1. servile, compliant, deferential, cringing, slavish, mean, submissive. 2. deferential, fawning, sycophantic, flattering. *Ant.* haughty, overbearing, domineering.

observant, *adj.* 1. attentive, watchful, heedful, mindful, aware. 2. perceptive, quick, alert. 3. careful, obedient. *Ant.* inattentive, careless; dull; disobedient.

observation, *n.* 1. noticing, perceiving, watching, regarding, attending. 2. notice, observance, attention. 3. information, record, memorandum. 4. remark, comment, aside, utterance.

observe, *v.* 1. perceive, notice, see, discover, detect. 2. regard, witness, mark, watch, note, view. 3. remark, comment, mention; utter, say. 4. obey, comply, conform, follow, fulfill. 5. solemnize, celebrate, keep. *Ant.* ignore.

obsession, *n.* preoccupation, domination.

obsolete, *adj.* antiquated, old-fashioned, ancient, old, archaic. *Ant.* modern, new, up-to-date.

obstacle, *n.* obstruction, hindrance, impediment, interference, check, block, barrier. *Ant.* aid, support; license, franchise, permission.

obstinate, *adj.* 1. mulish, obdurate, unyielding, recusant, stubborn, perverse, unbending, contumacious, inflexible, willful, headstrong, refractory, firm, intractable, resolute, pertinacious, persistent, dogged. 2. uncontrollable, wild. *Ant.* submissive, flexible, tractable; irresolute; controlled, tame.

obstreperous, *adj.* unruly, uncontrolled, boisterous, noisy, clamorous, tumultuous, riotous, uproarious. *Ant.* obedient, calm.

obstruct, *v.* block, stop, close, occlude, oppilate, choke, clog, bar, hinder, barricade, dam up, impede, prevent; retard, slow, check, arrest, interrupt. *Ant.* encourage, help, support, further.

obstruction, *n.* 1. obstacle, hindrance, barrier, occlusion, impediment, bar. 2. stopping, estoppage. *Ant.* encouragement, furtherance; continuation.

obtain, *v.* get, acquire, procure, secure, gain, achieve, earn, win, attain. *Ant.* lose, forgo.

obviate, *v.* preclude, prevent, avert, anticipate. *Ant.* include, foster.

obvious, *adj.* plain, manifest, evident, clear, open, apparent, patent, palpable, perceptible, distinct, unmistakable. *Ant.* concealed, hidden, indistinct, imperceptible.

occasion, *n.* 1. occurrence, event, time, incident. 2. opportunity, chance, convenience, opening. 3. ground, reason, cause, motive, inducement, influence. —*v.* 4. bring about, cause, motivate, originate, create, move, give rise to, produce. *Ant.* cease, stop.

occult, *adj.* 1. mysterious, hidden, concealed, secret, undisclosed, unrevealed, unknown, mystical, recondite, cabalistic, veiled, shrouded. 2. supernatural, metaphysical. *Ant.* open, manifest, obvious; natural.

occupation, *n.* 1. calling, trade, business, profession, metier, vocation, employment, pursuit, craft. 2. possession, tenure, use, occupancy. 3. seizure, invasion, capture.

occupy, *v.* 1. take up, use, engage, employ, busy. 2. possess, capture, seize, keep, take hold of.

occur, *v.* 1. come to pass, take place, happen, befall. 2. appear, be met with, be found, arise, offer, meet the eye.

occurrence, *n.* event, incident, circumstance, affair, proceeding, transaction.

odd, *adj.* 1. different, extraordinary, unusual, strange, weird, peculiar, singular, unique, queer, quaint, eccentric, uncommon, rare, fantastic, bizarre, whimsical. 2. out-of-the-way, secluded, retired. 3. occasional, casual. —*n.* 4. (*plural*) bits, scraps, remnants, oddments.

Ant. ordinary, common, unexceptional, usual.

odious, *adj.* 1. hateful, despicable, detestable, execrable, abominable, invidious. 2. obnoxious, offensive, disgusting, loathsome, repellent, repulsive, forbidding.
Ant. attractive, lovable; inviting.

odium, *n.* 1. hatred, detestation, abhorrence, dislike, antipathy. 2. reproach, discredit, opprobrium, obloquy.
Ant. love.

odor, *n.* smell, aroma, fragrance, redolence, scent, perfume.

odoriferous, *adj.* odorous, fragrant, aromatic, perfumed, redolent.
Ant. noisome, noxious.

offend, *v.* 1. irritate, annoy, vex, chafe, provoke, nettle, mortify, gall, fret, displease, affront, insult. 2. sin, transgress, err, stumble.
Ant. please, delight, compliment.

offense, *n.* 1. transgression, wrong, sin, trespass, misdemeanor, crime, fault, felony. 2. displeasure, unpleasantness, umbrage, resentment, wrath, indignation, anger, ire. 3. attack, assault, onset, aggression. 4. besiegers, enemy, foe, attackers.
Ant. delight, pleasure; defense; allies, friends.

offensive, *adj.* 1. displeasing, irritating, annoying, vexing, vexatious, unpleasant, impertinent, rude, insolent, hateful, detestable, opprobrious, insulting, abusive. 2. disagreeable, distasteful, disgusting, repulsive, obnoxious, unpalatable, unpleasant, revolting, repellent, nauseating, nauseous, sickening, loathsome. 3. repugnant, insulting, execrable, abominable, shocking, revolting. 4. aggressive, assailant, invading, attacking.
Ant. pleasing, pleasant, polite, courteous; agreeable, tasteful, attractive; delightful; defensive.

offer, *v.* 1. present, proffer, tender. 2. propose, give, move, put forward, tender. 3. volunteer, sacrifice, immolate, present. —*n.* 4. proposal, proposition, overture; bid.
Ant. refuse; refusal, denial.

offhand, *adj.* 1. cavalier, curt, brusque, short, abrupt. 2. informal, unpremeditated, casual, extempore, impromptu, extemporaneous.
Ant. considered, premeditated, thoughtful.

office, *n.* 1. staff, organization. 2. position, post, station, berth, situation.

3. duty, function, responsibility, charge, appointment, trust. 4. service, task, work, duty.

officious, *adj.* forward, obtrusive, forceful, direct, interfering, meddlesome.
Ant. retiring, shy, backward.

often, *adv.* frequently, generally, usually, repeatedly, customarily.
Ant. seldom.

ointment, *n.* unguent, nard, salve, balm.

old, *adj.* 1. aged, elderly. 2. familiar, known. 3. former, past, ancient, primeval, olden, primitive, antediluvian, antiquated, passé, antique, old-fashioned. 4. deteriorated, dilapidated, worn, decayed. 5. experienced, practiced, skilled, adroit. 6. sedate, sensible, wise, intelligent, thoughtful.
Ant. new, modern; inexperienced, green; wild, senseless.

old-fashioned, *adj.* outmoded, obsolete, antique, passé, antiquated, old, ancient, archaic.
Ant. modern.

omen, *n.* sign, augury, foreboding, portent.

ominous, *adj.* 1. portentous, inauspicious, threatening, unpropitious. 2. significant, foreboding.
Ant. favorable, propitious; insignificant, meaningless.

omnipresent, *adj.* ubiquitous, present.
Ant. nowhere.

only, *adv.* 1. alone, solely, exclusively. 2. merely, but, just, no more than. 3. singly, uniquely. —*adj.* 4. sole, single, unique, solitary, lone. 5. distinct, exclusive, alone. —*conj.* 6. but, excepting *or* except that, however.

onus, *n.* burden, responsibility, load.
Ant. relief.

onward, *adv.* 1. forward, ahead. —*adj.* 2. forward, advanced, improved; advancing.
Ant. backward; retreating, retrograde.

ooze, *v.* 1. percolate, exude, seep, drip, drop. —*n.* 2. mire, slime, mud.
Ant. pour, flood.

opalescent, *adj.* iridescent, nacreous, polychromatic.

open, *adj.* 1. unclosed, uncovered, unenclosed. 2. accessible, available, public, unrestricted, free. 3. unfilled, unoccupied. 4. undecided, unsettled, undetermined, debatable, disputable. 5. liable, subject to, unprotected, bare, undefended, ex-

posed. 6. mild, moderate. 7. unreserved, candid, frank, ingenuous, artless, guileless, unconcealed, undisguised; sincere, honest, fair, aboveboard. 8. perforated, porous, reticulated. 9. expanded, patulous, extended, spread out, unclosed. 10. generous, liberal, free, bounteous, bountiful, munificent, magnanimous, open-handed. 11. obvious, evident, clear, apparent, plain. —*v.* 12. unclose. 13. recall, revoke. 14. uncover, lay bare, bare, expose, reveal, divulge, disclose. 15. expand, extend, spread out. 16. begin, start, commence, initiate.
Ant. closed; close.

opening, *n.* 1. gap, hole, aperture, orifice, perforation; slit, slot, breach, rift, chasm, cleft, fissure, rent. 2. beginning, start, commencement, initiation, dawn. 3. vacancy, chance, opportunity.
Ant. closing.

operate, *v.* 1. work, run, use, act. 2. manage, carry on, perform. 3. bring about, effect, produce, occasion, cause.
Ant. fail.

operation, *n.* 1. action, process, procedure, manipulation, performance, proceeding. 2. efficacy, influence, virtue, effect, force, action. 3. course, transaction, business, affair, maneuver.
Ant. failure.

operative, *n.* 1. worker, workman, artisan, hand, laborer. 2. detective, investigator, private eye, agent. —*adj.* 3. operating, exerting, influencing, influential. 4. effective, efficacious, efficient, effectual, serviceable.
Ant. inoperative; ineffectual, inefficient.

opiate, *n.* narcotic, drug, anodyne, sedative, sedation, soporific.
Ant. stimulant.

opinion, *n.* sentiment, view, conclusion, persuasion, belief, judgment, notion, conception, idea, impression, estimation.

opinionated, *adj.* obstinate, stubborn, conceited, dogmatic, prejudiced, biased, bigoted.
Ant. liberal, open-minded, unprejudiced.

opponent, *n.* adversary, antagonist, competitor, rival, contestant; enemy, foe.
Ant. ally, friend, associate.

opportune, *adj.* 1. appropriate, favorable, suitable, apt, suited, fit, fitting, fitted, fortunate, propitious. 2. convenient, timely, well-timed, lucky, felicitous, seasonable, timely. *Ant.* inopportune, inappropriate; inconvenient.

opportunity, *n.* chance, occasion, time, opportune moment.

oppose, *v.* 1. resist, combat, withstand, thwart, confront, contravene, interfere, oppugn. 2. hinder, obstruct, prevent, check. 3. offset, contrast. 4. contradict, gainsay, deny, refuse. *Ant.* support, aid, help.

opposite, *adj.* 1. facing, fronting. 2. contrary, reverse, incompatible, irreconcilable, inconsistent, unlike, differing, different. 3. opposed, adverse, refractory, hostile, antagonistic, inimical. *Ant.* compatible, consistent, like, same; friendly, amiable.

opposition, *n.* 1. opposing, resisting, combating. 2. antagonism, hostility, resistance, counteraction. 3. competition, enemy, foe, adversary, antagonist. 4. offset, antithesis, contrast. 5. contrariety, inconsistency, incompatibility, difference. *Ant.* help, support, furtherance; consistency, compatibility.

oppress, *v.* 1. depress, weigh down, burden. load. 2. maltreat, persecute, wrong. 3. overwhelm, crush, overpower, subdue, suppress. *Ant.* unburden, liberate, disencumber.

oppression, *n.* 1. cruelty, injustice, tyranny, despotism, persecution, severity. 2. hardship, misery, suffering, calamity. 3. depression, sadness, misery. *Ant.* kindness, justice; happiness, joy.

opprobrious, *adj.* 1. reproachful, infamous, abusive, scurrilous, vituperative, contemptuous, insolent, offensive, insulting, scandalous. 2. disgraceful, shameful, infamous, dishonorable, disreputable, ignominious, hateful. *Ant.* complimentary, praising, laudatory; honorable, reputable.

oppugn, *v.* criticize, argue *or* act against, dispute, doubt, question, oppose. *Ant.* favor.

option, *n.* choice, election, selection, preference.

opulent, *adj.* 1. wealthy, rich, affluent, moneyed, sumptuous, luxurious. 2. abundant, copious, plentiful. *Ant.* poor, squalid; scarce.

oracular, *adj.* 1. prophetic, portentous, auspicious. 2. authoritative, inspired, inspirational, dogmatic, sententious. 3. ambiguous, obscure, equivocal, two-faced.

oral, *adj.* verbal, spoken, mouthed, uttered, said, vocal. *Ant.* tacit, silent, taciturn.

oration, *n.* speech, address, lecture, discourse, declamation, harangue.

orb, *n.* sphere, globe, ball. *Ant.* cube.

orbit, *n.* 1. path, course. —*v.* 2. circle, circumvent.

ordain, *v.* 1. appoint, call, nominate, elect, select, destine. 2. decree, order, enact, prescribe, determine. 3. predestine, predetermine, destine, fate.

ordeal, *n.* trial, test, proof, assay.

order, *n.* 1. direction, injunction, mandate, law, ukase, command, instruction, rule, canon, prescription. 2. succession, sequence. 3. method, arrangement, harmony, regularity, symmetry. 4. disposition, array, arrangement. 5. class, kind, sort, genus, subclass; tribe, family. 6. rank, status, grade, class, degree. 7. fraternity, society, brotherhood, community. 8. peace, calm, serenity. 9. custom, usage. 10. direction, commission. —*v.* 11. direct, command, instruct, bid, require; ordain. 12. regulate, conduct, manage, run, operate, adjust, arrange, systematize.

orderly, *adj.* 1. regular, systematic, methodical. 2. well-regulated, neat, trim, organized, well-organized. 3. well-disciplined, well-trained, well-behaved. *Ant.* irregular, unsystematic; sloppy, unregulated; undisciplined.

ordinary, *adj.* 1. common, usual, customary, regular, normal, accustomed, habitual, frequent. 2. inferior, second-rate, mean, mediocre, indifferent. 3. plain, homely, common-looking, commonplace. *Ant.* uncommon, extraordinary, unusual; superior; beautiful.

organic, *adj.* 1. systematic, systematized, organized. 2. constitutional, structural, inherent, fundamental, essential, vital, radical. *Ant.* inorganic.

organize, *v.* 1. coordinate, harmonize, unite, construct, form, dispose, constitute, make, shape, frame. 2. systematize, order. 3. combine, unionize. *Ant.* destroy, ruin; disorder.

origin, *n.* 1. source, rise, fountainhead, derivation, beginning, root, cradle, foundation, birthplace. 2. parentage, birth, extraction, lineage, heritage, descent. *Ant.* end; posterity.

original, *adj.* 1. primary, primordial, primeval, primitive, aboriginal. 2. new, fresh, novel, inventive, creative. —*n.* 3. archetype, pattern, prototype, model. *Ant.* secondary; old, old-fashioned.

originate, *v.* 1. arise, spring, rise, begin, emanate, flow, proceed. 2. initiate, invent, discover, create, author. *Ant.* terminate; follow.

ornament, *n.* 1. accessory, detail, embellishment, adornment, decoration, ornamentation, design. —*v.* 2. decorate, adorn, embellish, beautify, trim, garnish, grace, bedeck. *Ant.* essential, necessity.

ornate, *adj.* elaborate, adorned, embellished, showy, splendid, sumptuous, elegant, decorated, florid; flowery. *Ant.* simple, plain.

oscillate, *v.* vibrate, vacillate, swing, fluctuate, vary.

ostensible, *adj.* apparent, professed, pretended, ostensive, specious, plausible. *Ant.* concealed, hidden, implausible.

ostentation, *n.* pretension, pretentiousness, semblance, show, showiness, pretense, pretext, display, pageantry, pomp, pompousness, flourish.

ostracize, *v.* banish, exile, expatriate, disenfranchise, excommunicate. *Ant.* accept.

outcome, *n.* end, result, consequence, issue.

outdo, *v.* surpass, excel, exceed, beat, outstrip, outdistance.

outgrowth, *n.* 1. development, product, result. 2. offshoot, excrescence.

outlaw, *n.* 1. criminal, highwayman, holdup man, robber, thief, bandit, brigand. —*v.* 2. proscribe, prohibit.

outline, *n.* 1. contour, silhouette. 2. plan, draft, drawing, rough, sketch, cartoon. —*v.* 3. delineate, draft, draw.

outlive, *v.* survive, outlast.

outrage, *n.* 1. violence, violation. 2. affront, insult, offense, abuse, indignity. —*v.* 3. shock, abuse, maltreat, injure, offend. 4. ravish, rape.

outspoken, *adj.* frank, open, unreserved, candid, free. *Ant.* reserved, taciturn.

outstanding, *adj.* 1. prominent, eminent, conspicuous, striking. 2. unsettled, unpaid, owing, due.
Ant. inconspicuous; paid, settled.

overbearing, *adj.* domineering, dictatorial, haughty, arrogant, imperious, supercilious.
Ant. humble, servile.

overcome, *v.* 1. conquer, defeat, subdue, vanquish, rout, crush. 2. surmount. 3. overpower, overwhelm, discomfit.

overlook, *v.* 1. slight, disregard, miss, neglect, ignore. 2. excuse, forgive, pardon. 3. oversee, superintend, supervise. 4. bewitch.
Ant. regard, attend.

overpower, *v.* overcome, overwhelm, vanquish, subjugate, subdue, conquer, overmaster, rout, crush, defeat, beat.

overrule, *v.* disallow, rescind, revoke, repeal, recall, repudiate, set aside, nullify, cancel, annul; prevail over, influence.
Ant. allow, permit, approve.

oversee, *v.* supervise, direct, manage, superintend, survey, watch, overlook.

oversight, *n.* 1. mistake, blunder, slip, error, erratum, omission, lapse, neglect, fault, inattention. 2. management, direction, control, superintendence, supervision, charge, surveillance, care.
Ant. attention.

overt, *adj.* open, plain, manifest, showing, apparent, public.
Ant. private, concealed, clandestine, secret.

overthrow, *v.* 1. cast down, overcome, defeat, vanquish, overwhelm, conquer, master, overpower, subju-

gate, crush. 2. upset, overturn. 3. knock down, demolish, destroy, raze, level. 4. subvert, ruin, destroy. —*n.* 5. deposition, fall, displacement. 6. defeat, destruction, ruin, rout, dispersion, demolition.
Ant. support.

overture, *n.* 1. opening, proposal, proposition, offer. 2. prelude, introduction; prologue.
Ant. finale, termination, close, end, epilogue.

overturn, *v.* 1. overthrow, destroy, vanquish, conquer, upset. 2. upset, capsize, founder.

overwhelm, *v.* 1. overpower, crush, overcome, subdue, defeat, vanquish. 2. overload, overburden, cover, bury, sink, drown, inundate.

own, *v.* 1. have, hold, possess. 2. acknowledge, admit, allow, confess, concede, avow; recognize.

P

pace, *n.* 1. step, rate; gait. 2. step, walk, trot, jog, singlefoot, amble, rack, canter, gallop, run. 3. dais, platform. —*v.* 4. step, plod, trudge, walk, move, go.

pacific, *adj.* 1. conciliatory, appeasing. 2. peaceable, peaceful, calm, tranquil, at peace, quiet, unruffled, gentle.
Ant. hostile; agitated, perturbed.

pacify, *v.* 1. quiet, calm, tranquilize, assuage, still, smooth, moderate, soften, ameliorate, mollify, meliorate, better, soothe. 2. appease, conciliate.
Ant. agitate, perturb, aggravate, worsen; estrange.

pack, *n.* 1. package, bundle, parcel, packet; knapsack. 2. set, gang, group, band, company, crew, squad. —*v.* 3. stow, compress, cram. 4. load, burden, lade.

package, *n.* 1. bundle, parcel, packet, pack, bale. 2. case, crate, carton, box.

pact, *n.* agreement, compact, contract, deal, arrangement, treaty, bond, covenant, league, union, concordat, alliance, bargain.

pagan, *n.* 1. heathen, idolater, gentile. —*adj.* 2. heathen, heathenish, gentile, irreligious, idolatrous.
Ant. Christian, believer; pious, religious.

pageant, *n.* 1. spectacle, extravaganza, show, masque. 2. display, show, procession, parade.

pain, *n.* 1. suffering, distress, torture, misery, anguish, agony, torment, throe, pang, ache, twinge, stitch. 2. (*plural*) care, efforts, labor. —*v.* 3. afflict, torture, torment, distress, hurt, harm, injure, trouble, grieve, aggrieve, disquiet, discommode, incommode, inconvenience, displease, worry, tease, irritate, vex, annoy.
Ant. joy, delight, pleasure; ease; please.

painful, *adj.* 1. distressing, torturous, agonizing, tormenting, excruciating. 2. laborious, difficult, arduous, severe.
Ant. pleasant, soothing; easy, simple.

painstaking, *adj.* careful, assiduous, diligent, sedulous, strenuous.
Ant. careless, frivolous.

pair, *n.* 1. brace, couple, span, yoke, two, team. —*v.* 2. match, mate, couple, marry, join.

palatable, *adj.* agreeable, savory, sapid, tasty, gustatory, luscious, delicious, delectable, flavorsome.
Ant. unpalatable, distasteful, tasteless, flavorless.

pale, *adj.* 1. pallid, wan, white, ashy, ashen, colorless. 2. dim, faint, feeble, obscure. —*v.* 3. blanch, etiolate, whiten. —*n.* 4. picket, stake. 5. en-

closure, fence, barrier, paling, limits, bounds, confines.
Ant. ruddy, hale, hearty; robust; blacken, soil.

palpable, *adj.* 1. obvious, evident, manifest, plain, unmistakable. 2. tangible, material, real, corporeal.
Ant. obscure, unclear; intangible, spiritual.

palpitate, *v.* pulsate, throb, flutter, beat.

paltry, *adj.* trifling, petty, minor, trashy, mean, worthless, contemptible, insignificant, unimportant, trivial, inconsiderable, slight.
Ant. important, major, significant, considerable, essential.

pamper, *v.* indulge, gratify, humor, coddle, baby, cater to, spoil.
Ant. discipline.

pandemic, *adj.* general, prevalent, universal, epidemic.
Ant. isolated, unique, singular.

panegyric, *n.* eulogy, encomium, tribute; commendation, praise.
Ant. condemnation, invective.

panic, *n.* 1. terror, fright, alarm. —*v.* 2. terrorize, frighten.
Ant. security; soothe, calm.

pant, *v.* 1. gasp, breathe heavily, puff, blow. 2. long, yearn, thirst, hunger, desire. 3. throb, pulsate, palpitate. —*n.* 4. puff, gasp, heave; throb.

paragon, *n.* model, ideal, pattern, nonesuch, masterpiece.

parallel, *adj.* 1. corresponding, similar, analogous, like, resembling, correspondent. 2. tonic, harmonic. —*n.* 3. match, counterpart. 4. correspondence, analogy, similarity, resemblance, likeness. —*v.* 5. match, resemble. 6. equal, be equivalent to.
Ant. unique, unlike, singular, unusual; dissimilarity; differ.

paralyze, *v.* stun, shock, benumb, unnerve, deaden.

paramount, *adj.* superior, preeminent, chief, principal.
Ant. base, inferior, unimportant.

paraphernalia, *n.* belongings, effects; equipment, apparatus, appointments, appurtenances, accouterments, trappings, rig, equipage.

paraphrase, *n.* 1. rendering, version, translation. —*v.* 2. restate, render, translate; explain, explicate, interpret.

parasite, *n.* yes-man, sycophant, leech, hanger-on, bloodsucker, toady, flatterer, flunky.

parcel, *n.* 1. package, bundle, pack, packet. 2. quantity, lot, group, batch, collection. 3. lot, plot, tract, acreage, portion, land. —*v.* 4. divide, distribute, mete out, apportion, deal out, allot.

pardon, *n.* 1. indulgence, allowance, excuse, forgiveness; remission, amnesty, absolution. —*v.* 2. forgive, absolve, remit, condone, excuse, overlook; acquit, clear, release.
Ant. censure, blame.

pare, *v.* 1. peel; clip, cut, shave. 2. diminish, lessen, clip, reduce.
Ant. increase.

parentage, *n.* birth, descent, lineage, ancestry, origin, extraction, pedigree, family, stock.

parity, *n.* equality; equivalence, correspondence, similarity, analogy, parallelism, likeness; sameness.
Ant. inequality, dissimilarity, difference.

parley, *n.* 1. conference, discussion, talk, conversation, discourse. —*v.* 2. confer, discuss, speak, converse, talk, discourse.

parody, *n.* travesty, burlesque, imitation, caricature.

parry, *v.* 1. ward off, avert, avoid, evade, elude; prevent, obviate, preclude. —*n.* 2. prevention; avoidance, evasion.
Ant. encourage, further.

parsimonious, *adj.* sparing, frugal, stingy, tight, tight-fisted, close, niggardly, miserly, illiberal, mean, close-fisted, grasping, avaricious, penurious, covetous.
Ant. generous, open-handed, unsparing.

parsimony, *n.* economy, frugality, niggardliness, stinginess, miserliness, sparingness, closeness, illiberality, close-fistedness, tight-fistedness, cupidity, meanness.
Ant. generosity, liberality.

part, *n.* 1. portion, division, piece, fragment, fraction, section, constituent, component, ingredient, element, member, organ. 2. allotment, share, apportionment, portion, lot, dividend, concern, participation, interest, stock. 3. (*usually plural*) region, quarter, district, section. 4. duty, function, role, office, responsibility, charge. —*v.* 5. divide, break, cleave, separate, sever, sunder, disunite, dissociate, dissever, disconnect, disjoin, detach. 6. share, allot, portion, parcel out, apportion, distribute, deal out, mete out. 7. depart, leave, go, quit; pass on *or* away, die.
Ant. all, none, nothing, everything.

partake, *v.* participate, share.

partial, *adj.* 1. incomplete, unfinished, imperfect, limited. 2. constituent, component. 3. biased, prejudiced, one-sided, unfair, unjust, influenced.
Ant. complete, perfect; unbiased, unprejudiced, liberal, just, fair.

partiality, *n.* 1. bias, favor, prejudice, one-sidedness, injustice, unfairness, favoritism. 2. fondness, liking, preference, bent, leaning, tendency, predilection, inclination.
Ant. justice, fairness; dislike, disfavor.

participate, *v.* share, partake.

particle, *n.* 1. mite, whit, jot, iota, tittle, bit, mote, grain, ace, scrap, speck. 2. molecule, atom, meson, deuteron, electron, positron, neutron, neutrino.

particular, *adj.* 1. special, specific, especial. 2. one, individual, single, separate, distinct, discrete. 3. noteworthy, marked, unusual, notable, extraordinary; peculiar, singular, strange, odd, uncommon. 4. exceptional, especial, characteristic, distinctive. 5. certain, personal, special. 6. detailed, descriptive, minute, circumstantial, critical, scrupulous, strict, careful, exact, precise. 7. critical, finical, finicky, discriminating, dainty, nice, fastidious, scrupulous. —*n.* 8. point, detail, circumstance, item, feature, particularity.
Ant. general, overall; common, ordinary; inexact, imprecise; undiscriminating, indiscriminate.

particularly, *adv.* 1. exceptionally, especially, specially. 2. specially, especially, individually, characteristically, uniquely, separately, discretely, unusually, specifically, singly. 3. in detail, minutely, exactly, precisely, strictly.
Ant. generally; commonly, usually, customarily.

partisan, *n.* 1. adherent, supporter, follower, disciple. —*adj.* 2. biased, partial.
Ant. leader; unbiased, impartial.

partition, *n.* 1. division, distribution, portion, share, allotment, apportionment. 2. separation, division. 3. part, section, division, segment, piece. 4. barrier, wall, dividing wall, screen. —*v.* 5. divide, separate, apportion, portion, parcel out, deal out, mete out, share.
Ant. unity; unite, blend.

partner, *n.* 1. sharer, partaker, associate, accessory, accomplice, participant, colleague. 2. husband, wife, spouse.

party, *n.* 1. group, gathering, assembly, assemblage, company. 2. body, faction, circle, coterie, clique, set, combination, ring, league, alliance. 3. attachment, devotion, partisanship.

parvenu, *n.* upstart, snob, Johnny-come-lately, climber.

pass, *v.* 1. go, move, proceed. 2. disregard, pass over, skim over, skim, ignore. 3. transcend, exceed, surpass, excel. 4. spend; circulate. 5. convey, transfer, transmit, send, deliver. 6. sanction, approve, okay, enact. 7. express, pronounce, utter, deliver. 8. leave, go away, depart. 9. end, terminate, expire, cease. 10. go on, happen, take place, occur. 11. vanish, fade, die, disappear. —*n.* 12. notch, defile, ravine, gorge, gulch, canyon, channel. 13. permission, license, ticket, passport, visa. 14. thrust, lunge. 15. stage, state, juncture, situation, condition.
Ant. attend, regard, note, notice; disapprove; arrive, come; initiate, begin, start; appear.

passage, *n.* 1. paragraph, verse, line, section, clause, text, passus. 2. way, route, avenue, channel, road, path, byway, lane, street, thoroughfare. 3. movement, transit, transition, passing. 4. voyage, trip, tour, excursion, journey. 5. progress, course. 6. passing, enactment. 7. exchange, altercation, dispute, encounter, combat, skirmish, conflict, affair. 8. transference, transmission. —*v.* 9. cross, pass, voyage.

passion, *n.* 1. feeling, emotion, zeal, ardor, fervor, transport, rapture, excitement, impulse; hope, fear, joy, grief, anger, love, desire. 2. love, desire, attachment, affection, fondness, warmth. 3. anger, ire, resentment, fury, wrath, rage, vehemence, indignation.

Ant. coolness, apathy.

passionate, *adj.* 1. impassioned, emotional, ardent, vehement, excited, excitable, impulsive, fervent, fervid, zealous, warm, enthusiastic, earnest, glowing, burning, fiery; animated, impetuous, violent. 2. quick-tempered, irascible, short-tempered, testy, touchy, choleric, hasty, hotheaded, fiery.

Ant. dispassionate, cool, cold; calm, collected.

passive, *adj.* 1. inactive, quiescent, inert, receptive, prone. 2. suffering, receiving, submitting, submissive, patient, unresisting.

Ant. active, energetic; hostile, resisting.

password, *n.* watchword, shibboleth, countersign.

pastime, *n.* diversion, amusement, sport, entertainment, recreation.

patch, *v.* mend, repair, restore, fix, correct, emend; settle, smooth.

Ant. break, crack, ruin, spoil.

patent, *n.* 1. invention. —*adj.* 2. patented, trademarked, copyrighted. 3. open, manifest, evident, plain, clear, apparent, obvious, palpable, unmistakable, conspicuous, unconcealed.

Ant. concealed, hidden, unclear, dim.

path, *n.* way, walk, lane, trail, footpath, pathway, route, course, track, passage, road, avenue.

pathetic, *adj.* 1. pitiable, touching, moving, affecting, tender, plaintive. 2. emotional, pathetical.

Ant. cruel, ruthless; unemotional, apathetical.

patience, *n.* 1. calmness, composure, endurance, fortitude, stoicism, stability, courage, self-possession, inner strength, submissiveness, submission, sufferance, resignation. 2. perseverance, diligence, assiduity, sedulousness, indefatigability, indefatigableness, persistence.

Ant. hostility; weakness, frailty; fatigue.

patient, *n.* 1. invalid. —*adj.* 2. persevering, diligent, persistent, sedulous,

assiduous, indefatigable, untiring. 3. long-suffering, submissive, resigned, passive, unrepining, calm. 4. quiet, calm, serene, unruffled, unexcited, self-possessed, stoical, composed. 5. susceptible.

Ant. hostile, agitated; excited, perturbed; unsusceptible, impervious.

patron, *n.* 1. customer, client. 2. protector, supporter, advocate, defender.

Ant. critic.

pattern, *n.* 1. decoration, design, figure. 2. style, type, kind, sort. 3. original, model, paragon, example, exemplar, guide, archetype, prototype. 4. sample, example, specimen; illustration. —*v.* 5. model, imitate, copy, follow.

paucity, *n.* smallness, fewness, sparseness, scarcity, poverty.

Ant. abundance.

pause, *n.* 1. rest, wait, hesitation, suspension, lacuna, hiatus, interruption, delay, intermission, break; stop, halt, cessation, stoppage. —*v.* 2. hesitate, waver, deliberate, wait, rest, interrupt, tarry, delay. 3. cease, stop, arrest, halt, desist, forbear.

Ant. continuity, continuousness.

pay, *v.* 1. settle, liquidate, discharge. 2. satisfy, compensate, reimburse, remunerate, recompense; reward; indemnify. 3. yield, be profitable to, repay, requite. 4. punish, repay, retaliate, requite, revenge. 5. make amends, suffer, be punished, make compensation. —*n.* 6. payment, wages, salary, income, stipend, remuneration, emolument, fee, allowance. 7. requital, reward, punishment, just deserts. —*adj.* 8. profitable, interest-bearing, goldbearing, precious, valuable.

Ant. dissatisfy; unprofitable.

payment, *n.* pay.

peace, *n.* 1. agreement, treaty, armistice, truce, pact, accord, entente, entente cordiale, amity, harmony, concord. 2. order, security. 3. calm, quiet, tranquillity, peacefulness, calmness.

Ant. insecurity; agitation, disturbance.

peaceable, *adj.* pacific, peaceful, amicable, friendly, amiable, mild, gentle; calm, tranquil, serene, quiet.

Ant. hostile, unfriendly; noisy.

peaceful, *adj.* tranquil, placid, serene, unruffled, calm, complacent; composed, dignified, gracious, mellow; unexcited, unagitated, pacific.

Ant. perturbed, disturbed.

peak, *n.* point, top, crest, summit, arete, acme, pinnacle.

Ant. base, bottom, abyss.

peccadillo, *n.* petty sin *or* offense, slight crime, trifling fault; shortcoming, weakness.

peculiar, *adj.* 1. strange, odd, queer, eccentric, bizarre, uncommon, unusual, extraordinary, singular, exceptional. 2. distinguished, distinctive. 3. characteristic, appropriate, proper, individual, particular, select, especial, special, specific, unique, exclusive.

Ant. usual, common, ordinary; general, unspecific.

peculiarity, *n.* 1. idiosyncrasy, characteristic, odd trait. 2. singularity, oddity, rarity, eccentricity. 3. distinction, feature, characteristic.

pecuniary, *adj.* monetary, financial, nummular.

pedestrian, *n.* 1. walker, stroller. —*adj.* 2. on foot, walking, afoot. 3. commonplace, prosaic, dull.

Ant. interesting, fascinating, engaging.

pedigree, *n.* genealogy, descent, family tree, family, heritage, ancestry, lineage, line, race, derivation; patrimony.

peek, *v.* peep, peer, pry.

peel, *v.* 1. strip, skin, decorticate, pare, flay. —*n.* 2. skin, rind, bark.

Ant. cover, plate.

peer, *n.* 1. equal, compeer, match. 2. nobleman, lord; duke, count, marquis, earl, viscount, baron.

peerless, *adj.* matchless, unequaled, unsurpassed, unique, superlative, unmatched.

peevish, *adj.* cross, querulous, fretful, vexatious, vexed, captious, discontented, petulant, testy, irritable, crusty, snappish, waspish, acrimonious, splenetic, short-tempered, illtempered, ill-natured, unpleasant, disagreeable, nasty.

Ant. good-natured, friendly, pleasant, amiable, agreeable.

pejorative, *adj.* depreciative, deprecatory, disparaging, opprobrious.

Ant. favorable, complimentary.

pellucid, *adj.* translucent; limpid, clear, crystalline, crystal-clear, transparent.

Ant. dull, opaque.

pelt, *v.* 1. strike (*with missiles*), beat, belabor, batter. —*n.* 2. blow, stroke. 3. skin, hide, peltry.

penetrate, *v.* 1. pierce, bore, probe, enter; permeate, sink in. 2. affect *or* impress deeply, touch. 3. understand, discern, comprehend, fathom.

penetrating, *adj.* 1. piercing, sharp, acute, subtle. 2. acute, discerning, critical, keen, shrewd, sharp, sharp-witted, intelligent, wise, sagacious. *Ant.* blunt; uncritical, silly, stupid, undiscriminating.

penitent, *adj.* sorry, contrite, repentant, atoning, amending, remorseful.

penniless, *adj.* poor, indigent, poverty-stricken, destitute, needy, necessitous, inpecunious. *Ant.* rich, wealthy.

pensive, *adj.* serious, sober, thoughtful, meditative, reflective, dreamy, wistful; contemplative, thinking. *Ant.* frivolous, silly, unthinking, thoughtless, vapid.

pent-up, *adj.* confined, restrained; frustrated.

penurious, *adj.* mean, parsimonious, stingy, tight, tightfisted, close-fisted, close, miserly, niggardly, mercenary. *Ant.* generous.

penury, *n.* poverty, destitution, indigence, need, want. *Ant.* wealth, opulence, abundance.

people, *n.* 1. community, tribe, race, nation, clan, family. 2. persons, human beings, humans, men, man; folks. 3. populace, commonalty, public. —*v.* 4. populate; stock.

peppery, *adj.* 1. pungent, hot, spicy. 2. sharp, stinging, biting. 3. irascible, irritable, hot-tempered, short-tempered, hot-headed, touchy, testy, petulant, snarling, snappish, waspish, churlish, choleric. *Ant.* mild, tasteless; insipid; calm, amiable, friendly, good-natured.

perceive, *v.* 1. see, discern, notice, note, discover, observe, descry, espy, distinguish. 2. apprehend, understand, see, discern, appreciate. *Ant.* ignore.

perceptible, *adj.* cognizable, appreciable, understandable, discernible, apparent, perceivable. *Ant.* undiscernible, concealed.

perception, *n.* 1. cognition, recognition, perceiving, apprehension, understanding, discernment. 2. percept. *Ant.* misapprehension, misunderstanding.

perdition, *n.* ruin, damnation, destruction, downfall, hell. *Ant.* blessedness, sanctity.

peremptory, *adj.* 1. imperative, undeniable, irrefutable; categorical, positive, absolute. 2. dictatorial, im-

perious, dogmatic, arbitrary, authoritative. *Ant.* refutable, indefinite, uncertain, unsure; obedient; lenient.

perennial, *adj.* lasting, enduring, perpetual, perdurable, everlasting, permanent, imperishable, undying, deathless, eternal, immortal; constant, incessant, continual, uninterrupted, unceasing. *Ant.* evanescent, temporary, flimsy, mortal; inconstant; sporadic.

perfect, *adj.* 1. complete, finished, completed, full, consummate. 2. faultless, spotless, unblemished, excellent, exquisite. 3. skilled, adept, adroit, expert, accomplished. 4. typical, exact; thorough, sound, unqualified, pure, unmixed, unadulterated. —*v.* 5. complete, finish, bring to perfection, consummate, accomplish. *Ant.* incomplete, unfinished; imperfect; maladroit; mixed, impure.

perfidious, *adj.* faithless, treacherous, false, disloyal, dishonest; unfaithful, traitorous, deceitful, venal, untrustworthy. *Ant.* faithful, honest, loyal, trustworthy.

perfidy, *n.* treachery, faithlessness, traitorousness, treason, disloyalty. *Ant.* allegiance, faithfulness, faith, loyalty.

perform, *v.* 1. carry out, execute, do, discharge, transact. 2. fulfill, accomplish, achieve, effect. *Ant.* fail.

perfume, *n.* 1. essence, attar, scent, toilet water; incense. 2 redolence, scent, odor, smell, aroma, fragrance. *Ant.* stench, stink, noxiousness.

perfunctory, *adj.* mechanical, indifferent, careless, superficial, negligent, slovenly, heedless, reckless, uninterested, thoughtless. *Ant.* careful, diligent, thoughtful.

peril, *n.* 1. risk, jeopardy, danger, hazard. —*v.* 2. imperil, endanger, risk. *Ant.* safety, security.

period, *n.* 1. interval, age, era, epoch, term, time. 2. course, cycle.

periphery, *n.* 1. boundary, circumference, perimeter. 2. surface, outside. *Ant.* center; meat.

perish, *v.* 1. die, pass away, pass on, expire, decease. 2. decay, wither, shrivel, rot, molder, disappear, vanish. *Ant.* appear.

perky, *adj.* jaunty, pert, brisk. *Ant.* flaccid, retiring.

permanent, *adj.* lasting, unchanging, unchanged, unaltered, stable, immutable, invariant, invariable, constant; enduring, durable, abiding, perpetual, everlasting, remaining, perdurable. *Ant.* unstable, temporary, variable, inconstant; temporal.

permeate, *v.* pass through, penetrate, pervade, diffuse through, osmose, saturate, sink in.

permission, *n.* liberty, license, enfranchisement, franchise, leave, permit, liberty, freedom, allowance, consent. *Ant.* refusal.

permit, *v.* 1. allow, let, tolerate, agree to, endure, suffer. —*n.* 2. license, franchise, permission. *Ant.* refuse, disallow.

pernicious, *adj.* 1. ruinous, harmful, hurtful, detrimental, deleterious, injurious, destructive, damaging, baneful, noxious. 2. deadly, fatal, lethal. 3. evil, wicked, malevolent, malicious, bad. *Ant.* beneficial, salubrious, healthful; good.

perpendicular, *adj.* vertical, upright, standing. *Ant.* horizontal, parallel.

perpetual, *adj.* everlasting, permanent, continuing, continuous, enduring, constant, eternal, ceaseless, unceasing, incessant, unending, endless, uninterrupted, interminable, infinite. *Ant.* temporary, finite, impermanent; discontinuous.

perplex, *v.* 1. confuse, puzzle, bewilder, mystify, confound. 2. complicate, confuse, tangle, snarl, entangle, involve, encumber. 3. hamper, discourage, vex, annoy, bother, trouble, harass, disturb. *Ant.* clarify; disencumber; encourage, calm.

persecute, *v.* 1. oppress, harass, badger, molest, vex, afflict. 2. punish, discriminate against; torture, torment. 3. importune, annoy, tease, bother, pester, harass, harry.

perseverance, *n.* persistence, tenacity, pertinacity, resolution, doggedness, determination, steadfastness, indefatigability. *Ant.* irresolution.

persevere, *v.* persist, continue, keep on, last, stick it out, hold on. *Ant.* fail, cease, desist.

persist, *v.* 1. persevere, continue, last, endure, remain. 2. insist. *Ant.* stop, discontinue.

persistent, *adj.* 1. persisting, persevering, enduring, indefatigable, pertinacious, tenacious, stubborn, pigheaded, immovable, steadfast. 2. continued, continual, continuous, repeated, constant, steady.
Ant. amenable, obedient; inconstant, sporadic.

person, *n.* 1. human being, human, man, somebody, individual, personage, one. 2. character, part, role.

personality, *n.* character; personal identity.

perspicacious, *adj.* keen, perceptive, discerning, acute, penetrating, sharp-witted, clear-sighted.
Ant. dull, stupid, dim-witted.

perspicacity, *n.* perception, discernment, penetration, shrewdness, acuity, astuteness, insight, sharpness, acumen.
Ant. dullness, stupidity.

perspicuity, *n.* clearness, clarity, lucidity, transparency, plainness, distinctness, explicitness, intelligibility.
Ant. dimness, opacity.

perspicuous, *adj.* clear, lucid, intelligible, plain, distinct, explicit, transparent, unequivocal.
Ant. opaque, unintelligible, indistinct, unclear, confused, clouded.

persuade, *v.* 1. prevail on, induce, urge, influence, actuate, move, entice, impel. 2. win over, convince, satisfy.
Ant. dissuade, discourage.

pert, *adj.* bold, forward, impertinent, saucy, presumptuous, impudent, flippant.
Ant. retiring, shy, bashful; polite, courteous.

pertinacious, *adj.* tenacious, persevering, persistent, dogged.
Ant. relenting, flexible.

pertinacity, *n.* perseverance, persistence, tenacity, tenaciousness, inflexibility, firmness, steadfastness, determination, resolution.
Ant. flexibility.

pertinent, *adj.* pertaining, relating, relevant, apt, appropriate, apposite, fit, fitting, fitted, suited, suitable, applicable, proper.
Ant. irrelevant, inappropriate, unsuited, unsuitable, improper.

perturb, *v.* 1. disturb, disquiet, agitate, stir up, trouble. 2. disturb, derange, disorder, confuse, addle, muddle.
Ant. pacify, calm, tranquilize; clarify.

pervade, *v.* permeate, diffuse, fill; penetrate, pass through.

perverse, *adj.* 1. contrary, contumacious, disobedient, wayward, cantankerous. 2. willful, persistent, obstinate, stubborn, headstrong, pigheaded, dogged, intractable, unyielding. 3. wicked, evil, bad, sinful, piacular, perverted, distorted.
Ant. amiable, obedient; amenable, tractable; good.

perverted, *adj.* wicked, misguided, misapplied, distorted.
Ant. straight, good, sensible.

pessimistic, *adj.* cynical, gloomy, dark, foreboding.
Ant. optimistic, rosy, bright.

pest, *n.* 1. nuisance, annoyance. 2. pestilence, plague, scourge, bane; epidemic, pandemic.

pester, *v.* harass, annoy, vex, torment, torture, molest, harry, hector, tease, trouble, plague, nettle, disturb, provoke, bother, worry, gall, badger, irritate, chafe.
Ant. please, delight, entertain, divert.

pet, *n.* 1. favorite, darling; lap-dog. 2. peevishness, cantankerousness, moodiness. —*v.* 3. fondle, indulge, baby, caress. 4. sulk, be peevish.

petition, *n.* 1. request, supplication, suit, prayer, entreaty, solicitation, appeal, application. —*v.* 2. entreat, supplicate, beg, pray, appeal, solicit, sue.

petty, *adj.* 1. unimportant, trifling, paltry, nugatory, trivial, lesser, little, small, insignificant, negligible, inconsiderable, slight, diminutive. 2. narrow, narrow-minded, small. 3. mean, ungenerous, stingy, miserly.
Ant. important, considerable, significant; broad-minded; generous.

petulance, *n.* petulancy, irritability, peevishness, fretfulness, pettishness, testiness, waspishness.
Ant. calm, tranquillity.

petulant, *adj.* irritable, peevish, fretful, vexatious, waspish, snappish, testy, short-tempered, hot-headed, hot-tempered, peppery, pettish, touchy, irascible, cross, snarling, captious, acrimonious.
Ant. even-tempered, temperate, pleasant.

phantasm, *n.* apparition, specter, phantom, vision, illusion, ghost.
Ant. reality.

phantom, *n.* 1. phantasm. —*adj.* 2. unreal, illusive, spectral, illusory, phantasmal; imaginary, hallucinatory.
Ant. real, flesh-and-blood, material.

phenomenon, *n.* 1. fact, occurrence, event, incident, circumstance. 2. prodigy, marvel, wonder, miracle.

philander, *v.* flirt, coquet, trifle, dally.

phlegm, *n.* 1. mucus. 2. sluggishness, stoicism, apathy, indifference. 3. coolness, calm, self-possession, coldness, impassivity, impassiveness.
Ant. concern; interest, warmth.

phobia, *n.* dread, fear; aversion, hatred.
Ant. like, attraction, love.

phraseology, *n.* diction, expression, style, language.

physical, *adj.* 1. bodily, corporeal, corporal, mortal; tangible, sensible. 2. material, real, natural.
Ant. mental, spiritual; unnatural, unreal.

pick, *v.* 1. choose, select, cull. 2. criticize, find fault with. 3. steal, rob, pilfer. 4. pierce, indent, dig into, break up, peck. 5. pluck, gather, reap, collect, get, acquire. —*n.* 6. pickax. 7. choice, selection, choicest part, best. 8. plectrum.

picture, *n.* 1. painting, drawing, photograph, representation. 2. image, representation, similitude, semblance, likeness. 3. description, account, representation. 4. motion picture, movie, screen play, photoplay, film. —*v.* 5. imagine; depict, describe, delineate, paint, draw, represent.

picturesque, *adj.* 1. striking, interesting, colorful, scenic, beautiful. 2. graphic, vivid, impressive; intense, lively.
Ant. uninteresting, dull.

piece, *n.* 1. portion, quantity, segment, section, scrap, shred, fragment, part. 2. thing, example, instance, specimen. 3. short story, story, article, essay, composition, paper, theme, novella; poem, ode, sonnet; play. —*v.* 4. mend, patch. 5. complete, enlarge, extend, augment, add to.
Ant. all, everything; none, nothing.

pierce, *v.* 1. penetrate, enter, run through *or* into, perforate, stab, puncture, bore, drill. 2. affect, touch, move, rouse, strike, thrill, excite.

piety, *n.* 1. reverence, regard, respect. 2. godliness, devoutness, devotion, sanctity, grace, holiness.
Ant. irreverence, disrespect.

pile, *n.* 1. assemblage, collection, mass, heap, accumulation. 2. pyre, burning ghat. 3. building, edifice, structure. 4. pier, post. 5. hair, down; wool, fur, pelage; nap. —*v.* 6. heap up, accumulate, assemble, amass, collect.

pilgrim, *n.* 1. palmer, crusader. 2. wayfarer, sojourner, traveler, wanderer.

pilgrimage, *n.* journey, trip, excursion, tour, expedition.

pillage, *v.* 1. rob, plunder, rape, despoil, sack, spoil. —*n.* 2. booty, plunder, spoils. 3. rapine, depredation, devastation, spoliation.

pillar, *n.* shaft, column, stele, lally-column, support, pier, prop.

pillow, *n.* cushion, pad, bolster.

pin, *n.* 1. peg, fastening, bolt. 2. brooch. —*v.* 3. fasten, fix.

pinnacle, *n.* peak, eminence, culmination, tower, summit, apex, acme, zenith. *Ant.* base.

pious, *adj.* 1. devout, reverent, godly, religious, holy. 2. sacred. *Ant.* impious, irreligious, unholy; unsacred, defiled.

piquant, *adj.* 1. pungent, sharp, flavorsome, tart, spicy. 2. stimulating, interesting, attractive, sparkling. 3. smart, racy, sharp, clever. *Ant.* insipid; uninteresting, unattractive; dull.

pique, *v.* 1. offend, nettle, sting, irritate, chafe, vex; affront, wound, displease. 2. interest, stimulate, excite, incite, stir, spur, prick, goad. *Ant.* please, delight; compliment.

pirate, *n.* plunderer, filibuster, freebooter, picaroon, buccaneer, corsair.

pit, *n.* 1. hole, cavity, burrow, hollow. 2. excavation, well, pitfall, trap. 3. hollow, depression, dent, indentation. 4. stone, pip, seed, core.

piteous, *adj.* pathetic, pitiable, deplorable, wretched, miserable; affecting, distressing, moving, pitiful, lamentable, woeful, sorrowful, sad, mournful, morose, doleful. *Ant.* good, fine, pleasant, delightful.

pitiful, *adj.* 1. pitiable, pathetic, piteous. 2. contemptible, deplorable, mean, low, base, vile, despicable. *Ant.* superior, delightful, lovable.

pitiless, *adj.* merciless, cruel, mean, unmerciful, ruthless, implacable, relentless, inexorable, hard-hearted. *Ant.* merciful, soft-hearted, kind, kindly.

pity, *n.* 1. sympathy, compassion, commiseration, condolence, mercy. —*v.* 2. commiserate, be *or* feel sorry for, sympathize with, feel for. *Ant.* apathy, cruelty, ruthlessness.

placate, *v.* appease, satisfy, conciliate. *Ant.* dissatisfy, displease.

place, *n.* 1. space, plot, spot, location, locale, locality, site. 2. position, situation, circumstances. 3. job, post, office, function, duty, charge, responsibility, employment, rank. 4. region, area, section, sector. 5. residence, dwelling, house, home, domicile, abode. 6. stead, lien. 7. opportunity, occasion, reason, ground, cause. —*v.* 8. position, range, order, dispose, arrange, situate, put, set, locate, station, deposit, lay, seat, fix, establish. 9. appoint, hire, induct. 10. identify, connect. *Ant.* misplace, displace; forget.

placid, *adj.* calm, peaceful, unruffled, tranquil, serene, quiet, undisturbed. *Ant.* turbulent, tumultuous, perturbed.

plague, *n.* 1. epidemic, pestilence, disease, Black Death, Great Plague, Oriental Plague. 2. affliction, calamity, evil, curse. 3. trouble, vexation, annoyance, nuisance, torment. —*v.* 4. trouble, torment, torture, molest, bother, incommode. discommode. 5. vex, harry, hector, harass, fret, worry, pester, badger, annoy, tease, irritate, disturb.

plain, *adj.* 1. clear, distinct, lucid, unambiguous, unequivocal, intelligible, understandable, perspicuous, evident, manifest, obvious, unmistakable, patent, apparent. 2. downright, sheer, direct, transparent. 3. unambiguous, candid, outspoken, blunt, direct, frank, guileless, artless, ingenuous, open, unreserved, honest, sincere, open-hearted. 4. homely, unpretentious, homey, simple, unadorned, frugal. 5. ugly, homely, unattractive. 6. ordinary, common, commonplace, unostentatious. 7. flat, level, plane, smooth, even. —*n.* 8. mesa, plateau, savanna, prairie, pampas. *Ant.* unclear, ambiguous, unintelligible; artful, sly, cunning, deceptive, insincere; beautiful, attractive; uncommon, extraordinary.

plaintive, *adj.* sorrowful, melancholy, mournful, sad, wistful; discontented. *Ant.* happy, pleasant.

plan, *n.* 1. scheme, plot, complot, procedure, project, formula, method, system, design, contrivance. 2. drawing, sketch, floorplan, draft, map, chart, diagram, representation. —*v.* 3. arrange, scheme, plot, design, devise, contrive, invent, concoct, hatch.

platform, *n.* 1. stage, dais, rostrum, pulpit; landing. 2. principles, beliefs, tenets.

plausible, *adj.* 1. specious, deceptive, deceiving, deceitful, hypocritical. 2. fair-spoken, glib, convincing. *Ant.* implausible.

play, *n.* 1. drama, piece, show; comedy, tragedy, melodrama, farce. 2. amusement, recreation, game, sport, diversion, pastime. 3. fun, jest, trifling, frolic. 4. action, activity, movement, exercise, operation, motion. 5. freedom, liberty, scope, elbow-room. —*v.* 6. act, perform, enact, characterize, impersonate, personate. 7. compete, contend with *or* against, engage. 8. use, employ. 9. stake, bet, wager. 10. represent, imitate, emulate, mimic. 11. do, perform, bring about, execute. 12. toy, trifle, sport, dally, caper, romp, disport, frolic, gambol, skip, revel, frisk. *Ant.* work.

plead, *v.* 1. entreat, appeal, beg, supplicate. 2. argue, persuade, reason. 3. allege, cite, make a plea, apologize, answer, make excuse.

pleasant, *adj.* 1. pleasing, agreeable, enjoyable, pleasurable, acceptable, welcome, gratifying. 2. delightful, congenial, polite, courteous, friendly, personable, amiable. 3. fair, sunny. 4. gay, sprightly, merry, cheery, cheerful, lively, sportive, vivacious. 5. jocular, facetious, playful, humorous, witty, amusing, clever, jocose. *Ant.* unpleasant, displeasing.

pleasing, *adj.* agreeable, plesant, acceptable, pleasurable, charming, delightful, interesting, engaging. *Ant.* disagreeable, unpleasant, unacceptable.

pleasure, *n.* 1. happiness, gladness, delectation, enjoyment, delight, joy, well-being, satisfaction, gratification. 2. luxury, sensuality, voluptuousness. 3. will, desire, choice, preference, purpose, wish, mind, inclination, predilection. *Ant.* displeasure, unhappiness; disinclination.

plentiful, *adj.* bountiful, ample, plenteous, copious, abundant, full, rich, fertile, fruitful, bounteous, productive, exuberant, luxuriant. *Ant.* sparse, scanty, barren, fruitless.

plenty, *n.* fullness, abundance, copiousness, plenteousness, plentifulness, profusion, luxuriance, exuberance, affluence, overflow, extravagance, prodigality; superabundance, overfullness, plethora. *Ant.* paucity, scarcity.

pliant, *adj.* pliable, supple, flexible, flexile, lithe, limber; compliant, easily influenced, yielding, adaptable, manageable, tractable, ductile, facile, docile. *Ant.* inflexible; unyielding, rigid, intractable.

plight, *n.* 1. condition, state, situation, predicament, category, case, dilemma. —*v.* 2. propose, pledge, hypothecate.

plod, *v.* 1. walk heavily, pace, trudge. 2. toil, moil, labor, drudge, sweat.

plot, *n.* 1. plan, scheme, complot, intrigue, conspiracy, cabal, stratagem, machination. 2. story, theme, thread, story line. —*v.* 3. devise, contrive, concoct, brew, hatch, frame. 4. conspire, scheme, contrive.

pluck, *v.* 1. pull, jerk, yank, snatch, tug, tear, rip. —*n.* 2. courage, resolution, spirit, bravery, boldness, determination, mettle, nerve.

plump, *adj.* 1. fleshy, fat, chubby, stout, portly, corpulent, obese, round. 2. direct, downright, blunt, unqualified, unreserved, complete, full. —*v.* 3. gain weight; fatten. 4. drop, sink, fall. —*n.* 5. fall, drop. —*adv.* 6. directly, bluntly, suddenly, abruptly. *Ant.* thin, slender, skinny; subtle.

plunder, *v.* 1. rob, despoil, fleece, pillage, ravage, rape, sack, devastate, strip, lay waste. —*n.* 2. pillage, rapine, spoliation, robbery, theft, plundering. 3. loot, booty, spoils.

plunge, *v.* 1. immerse, submerge, dip. 2. dive; rush, hasten; descend, drop, hurtle over. —*n.* 3. leap, dive, rush, dash, dip.

poetry, *n.* verse, meter, rhythm, poesy, numbers.

poignant, *adj.* 1. distressing, heartfelt, serious, intense, severe, bitter, sincere. 2. keen, strong, biting, mordant, caustic, acid, pointed. 3. pungent, piquant, sharp, biting, acrid, stinging. *Ant.* superfluous, trivial; mild.

pointed, *adj.* 1. sharp, piercing, penetrating, epigrammatic, stinging, piquant, biting, mordant, sarcastic, caustic, severe, keen. 2. directed, aimed, explicit, marked, personal. 3. marked, emphasized, accented, accentuated. *Ant.* blunt, dull, mild.

poise, *n.* 1. balance, equilibrium, equipoise, counterpoise. 2. composure, self-possession, steadiness, stability, self-control, control. 3. suspense, indecision. 4. carriage, mien, demeanor, savoir-faire, breeding, behavior. —*v.* 5. balance, equilibrate. *Ant.* instability, unsteadiness; decision.

poison, *n.* 1. toxin, venom, virus. —*v.* 2. envenom, infect. 3. corrupt, ruin, vitiate, contaminate, pollute, taint, canker.

policy, *n.* 1. course (*of action*), expediency, tactic, approach, procedure, rule, management, administration, handling. 2. prudence, widsom, sagacity, shrewdness, acumen, astuteness, discretion, skill, art, cunning, stratagem. *Ant.* ingenuousness, naiveté.

polish, *v.* 1. brighten, smooth, burnish, shine. 2. finish, refine, civilize, make elegant. —*n.* 3. smoothness, gloss, shine, sheen, luster, brightness, brilliance. 4. refinement, elegance, poise, grace. *Ant.* dull.

polished, *adj.* 1. smooth, glossy, burnished, shining, shiny, shined, lustrous, brilliant. 2. refined, cultured, finished, elegant, polite, poised. 3. flawless, excellent, perfect. *Ant.* dull, dim; unrefined, impolite; inelegant; imperfect.

polite, *adj.* well-mannered, courteous, civil, well-bred, gracious, genteel, urbane, polished, poised, courtly, cultivated, refined, finished, elegant. *Ant.* impolite, rude, discourteous, uncivil.

politic, *adj.* 1. sagacious, prudent, wise, tactful, diplomatic, discreet, judicious, provident, astute, wary, prudential. 2. shrewd, artful, sly, cunning, underhanded, tricky, foxy, clever, subtle, Machiavellian, wily, intriguing, scheming, crafty, unscrupulous, strategic. 3. expedient, judicious, political. *Ant.* imprudent, indiscreet, improvident; artless, ingenuous, direct, open, honest.

pollute, *v.* 1. befoul, dirty, defile, soil, taint, tarnish, stain, contaminate, vitiate, corrupt, debase, deprave. 2. desecrate, profane, blaspheme, violate, dishonor, defile. *Ant.* purify; honor, revere, respect.

ponder, *v.* consider, meditate, reflect, cogitate, deliberate, ruminate, muse, think, study; weigh, contemplate, examine. *Ant.* forget, ignore.

ponderous, *adj.* 1. heavy, massive, weighty, bulky. 2. important; momentous, weighty. *Ant.* light, weightless; unimportant.

poor, *adj.* 1. needy, indigent, necessitous, straitened, destitute, penniless, poverty-stricken, impecunious, impoverished, reduced, hard up, distressed. 2. deficient, insufficient, meager, lacking, incomplete. 3. faulty, inferior, unsatisfactory, substandard, shabby, jerry-built, seedy, worthless, valueless. 4. sterile, barren, unfertile, fruitless, unproductive. 5. lean, emaciated, thin, skinny, meager, hungry, underfed, lank, gaunt, shrunk. 6. cowardly, abject, mean, base. 7. scanty, paltry, meager, insufficient, inadequate. 8. humble, unpretentious. 9. unfortunate, hapless, unlucky, star-crossed, doomed, luckless, miserable, unhappy, pitiable, piteous. *Ant.* rich, wealthy; sufficient, adequate, complete; superior; fertile; well-fed; bold, brave; bold, pretentious; fortunate, lucky.

popular, *adj.* 1. favorite, approved, accepted, received, liked. 2. common, prevailing, current, general, prevalent, in vogue, faddish. *Ant.* unpopular; uncommon, rare, unusual.

port, *n.* harbor, haven, refuge, anchorage.

portent, *n.* indication, omen, augury, sign, warning, presage.

portion, *n.* 1. part, section, segment, piece, bit, scrap, morsel, fragment. 2. share, allotment, quota, dole, dividend, division, apportionment, lot. 3. serving. 4. dowry, dot. —*v.* 5. divide, distribute, allot, apportion, deal *or* parcel out. 6. endow. *Ant.* all, everything; none, nothing.

portray, *v.* picture, delineate, limn, depict, paint, represent, sketch.

pose, *v.* 1. sit, model; attitudinize. 2. state, assert, propound. —*n.* 3. attitude, posture, position; affectation.

position, *n.* 1. station, place, locality, spot, location, site, locale, situation, post. 2. situation, condition, state, circumstances. 3. status, standing, rank, place. 4. post, job, situation, place, employment. 5. placement, disposition, array, arrangement. 6. posture, attitude, pose. 7. proposition, thesis, contention, principle, dictum, predication, assertion, doctrine. —*v.* 8. put, place, situate. 9. locate, fix, position.

positive, *adj.* 1. explicit, express, sure, certain, definite, precise, clear, un-

equivocal, categorical, unmistakable, direct. 2. arbitrary, enacted, decided, determined, decisive, unconditional. 3. incontrovertible, substantial, indisputable, indubitable. 4. stated, expressed, emphatic. 5. confident, self-confident, self-assured, assured, convinced, unquestioning, over-confident, stubborn, peremptory, obstinate, dogmatic, overbearing. 6. absolute. 7. practical.
Ant. unsure, indefinite, unclear, equivocal; conditional; doubtful; tacit; tractable, self-effacing; relative; impractical, unpractical.

possess, *v.* 1. have, hold, own. 2. occupy, hold, have, control. 3. impart, inform, familiarize, acquaint, make known.
Ant. lose.

possession, *n.* 1. custody, occupation, tenure. 2. ownership.
Ant. loss.

possible, *adj.* feasible, practicable, likely, potential.
Ant. impossible, impractical, unlikely.

post, *n.* 1. column, pillar, pole, support, upright. 2. position, office, assignment, appointment. 3. station, round, beat, position. —*v.* 4. announce, advertise, publicize. 5. station, place, set.

postpone, *v.* 1. put off, defer, delay, procrastinate, adjourn. 2. subordinate.

posture, *n.* 1. position, pose, attitude. 2. position, condition, state.

potent, *adj.* 1. powerful, mighty, strong, puissant. 2. cogent, influential, efficacious.
Ant. weak, impotent, powerless, feeble, frail; ineffectual.

potential, *adj.* 1. possible. 2. capable, able, latent. —*n.* 3. possibility, potentiality.
Ant. kinetic, impossible; incapable, unable; impossibility.

pound, *v.* 1. strike, beat, thrash. 2. crush, bray, pulverize, powder, triturate, comminute. 3. impound, imprison, pen, jail, shut up, confine, coop up. —*n.* 4. pound avoirdupois, pound troy, pound sterling, pound Scots. 5. enclosure, pen, confine, trap.

poverty, *n.* 1. destitution, need, lack, want, privation, necessitousness, necessity, neediness, indigence, penury, distress. 2. deficiency, sterility, barrenness, unfruitfulness. 3. scantiness, jejuneness, sparingness, meagerness.

Ant. wealth; abundance, fertility, fruitfulness.

power, *n.* 1. ability, capability, capacity, faculty, competence, competency, might, strength, puissance. 2. strength, might, force, energy. 3. control, command, dominion, authority, sway, rule, ascendancy, influence, sovereignty, suzerainty, prerogative.
Ant. inability, incapacity, incompetence.

powerful, *adj.* 1. mighty, potent, forceful, strong. 2. cogent, influential, forcible, convincing, effective, efficacious, effectual.
Ant. weak, frail, feeble; ineffective, ineffectual.

practicable, *adj.* possible, feasible, workable, performable, doable, achievable, attainable.
Ant. impracticable, impossible, unattainable.

practical, *adj.* 1. sensible, businesslike, pragmatic, efficient. 2. judicious, discreet, sensible, discriminating, balanced, reasoned, sound, shrewd.
Ant. impractical, inefficient; indiscreet, unsound.

practice, *n.* 1. custom, habit, wont. 2. exercise, drill, experience, application, study. 3. performance, operation, action, process. 4. plotting, intriguing, trickery, chicanery; plot, intrigue, stratagem, ruse, maneuver. —*v.* 5. carry out, perform, do, drill, exercise. 6. follow, observe.
Ant. inexperience.

praise, *n.* 1. praising, commendation, acclamation, plaudit, compliment, laudation, approval, approbation, applause, kudos. 2. enconium, eulogy, panegyric. —*v.* 3. laud, approve, commend, admire, extol, celebrate, eulogize, panegyrize. 4. glorify, magnify, exalt, worship, bless, adore, honor.
Ant. condemnation, disapprobation, disapproval, criticism.

pray, *v.* importune, entreat, supplicate, beg, beseech, implore, sue, petition, invoke.

precarious, *adj.* 1. uncertain, unstable, unsure, insecure, dependent, unsteady. 2. doubtful, dubious, unreliable, undependable, risky, perilous, hazardous, dangerous. 3. groundless, unfounded, baseless.
Ant. certain, stable, sure, secure, independent, reliable, dependable; well-founded.

precaution, *n.* foresight, prudence, providence, wariness, forethought.

precious, *adj.* 1. valuable, costly, dear, invaluable, priceless. 2. dear, beloved, darling, cherished. 3. choice, fine, delicate, select, pretty. 4. arrant, gross, egregious.
Ant. inexpensive, cheap; worthless; ugly, unattractive.

precipitate, *v.* 1. hasten, accelerate, hurry, speed up, expedite, speed, rush, quicken, advance, dispatch. 2. cast down, hurl *or* fling down, plunge. —*adj.* 3. headlong, hasty, rash, reckless, indiscreet. 4. sudden, abrupt, violent.
Ant. slow, retard; considered.

precipitous, *adj.* steep, abrupt, sheer, perpendicular.
Ant. gradual, sloping.

precise, *adj.* 1. definite, exact, defined, fixed, correct, strict, explicit, accurate. 2. rigid, particular, puritanical, demanding, crucial.
Ant. indefinite, incorrect, inexact, lenient; flexible, tractable.

predatory, *adj.* predacious, plundering, ravaging, pillaging, rapacious, voracious.

predicament, *n.* dilemma, plight, quandary; situation, state, condition, position, case.

predict, *v.* foretell, prophesy, foresee, forecast, presage, augur, prognosticate, foretoken, portend, divine.

prediction, *n.* prophecy, forecast, augury, prognostication, foretoken, portent, divination, soothsaying, presage.

predilection, *n.* prepossession, favoring, partiality, predisposition, disposition, inclination, bent, preference, leaning, bias, prejudice.
Ant. disfavor, disinclination, dislike.

predominant, *adj.* ascendant, prevailing, prevalent, dominant, in sway, sovereign.
Ant. rare, retrograde.

predominate, *v.* preponderate, prevail, outweigh, overrule, surpass, dominate.

preeminent, *adj.* eminent, surpassing, dominant, superior, over, above, distinguished, excellent, peerless, unequalled, paramount, consummate, predominant, supreme.
Ant. undistinguished, inferior.

preface, *n.* introduction, foreword, preamble, prologue, proem, prelude, preliminary, prolegomena.
Ant. appendix, epilogue.

prefer, *v.* 1. like better, favor, choose, elect, select, pick out, pick, single out, fix upon, fancy. 2. put forward,

advance, present, offer, proffer, tender, promote.
Ant. exclude, dislike; retract, withdraw.

preference, *n.* choice, selection, pick, predilection.
Ant. exclusion.

prejudice, *n.* 1. preconception, bias, partiality, prejudgment, predilection, predisposition, disposition. —*v.* 2. bias, influence, warp, twist.
Ant. judgment, decision.

preliminary, *adj.* 1. preceding, introductory, preparatory, prefatory, precursive, prior. —*n.* 2. introduction, prelude, preface, prolegomena, preparation.
Ant. resulting, concluding; conclusion, end, appendix, epilogue.

premeditate, *v.* consider, plan, deliberate, precontrive, predetermine, prearrange, predesign.

premium, *n.* 1. prize, door prize, bounty. 2. bonus, gift, reward, recompense.
Ant. punishment.

preoccupied, *adj.* absorbed, engrossed, meditating, meditative, pondering, musing, concentrating, inattentive, in a brown study.
Ant. unthinking, thoughtless, frivolous.

prepare, *v.* 1. contrive, devise, plan, plan for, anticipate, get *or* make ready, provide, arrange, order. 2. manufacture, make, compound, fix, compose.
Ant. destroy, ruin.

preposterous, *adj.* absurd, senseless, foolish, inane, asinine, unreasonable, ridiculous, excessive, extravagant, irrational.
Ant. rational, reasonable, sensible.

prerogative, *n.* right, privilege, precedence, license, franchise, immunity, freedom, liberty.

presage, *n.* 1. presentiment, foreboding, foreshadowing, indication, premonition, foreknowledge. 2. portent, omen, sign, token, augury, warning, signal, prognostic. 3. forecast, prediction. —*v.* 4. portend, foreshadow, forecast, predict.

prescribe, *v.* lay down, predetermine, appoint, ordain, enjoin, direct, dictate, decree, establish, hand down, institute.

presence, *n.* 1. attendance, company. 2. nearness, vicinity, neighborhood, proximity, vicinage, closeness. 3. personality; bearing, carriage, mien, aspect, impression, appearance.
Ant. absence.

present, *adj.* 1. current, existing, extant; here, at hand, near, nearby. —*n.* 2. now. 3. gift, donation, bonus, benefaction, largess, grant, gratuity, boon, tip. —*v.* 4. give, endow, bestow, grant, confer, donate. 5. afford, furnish, yield, offer, proffer. 6. show, exhibit; introduce. 7. represent, personate, act, enact, imitate, impersonate. 8. point, level, aim, direct.
Ant. absent; then; receive.

presently, *adv.* anon, at once, immediately, directly, right away, without delay, shortly, forthwith, soon.
Ant. later.

preserve, *v.* 1. keep, conserve. 2. guard, safeguard, shelter, shield, protect, defend, save. 3. keep up, maintain, continue, uphold, sustain. 4. retain, keep.
Ant. forgo; lose.

prestige, *n.* reputation, influence, weight, importance, distinction.
Ant. disrepute, notoriety.

presume, *v.* 1. assume, presuppose, suppose, take for granted, believe. 2. venture, undertake.

presumptuous, *adj.* bold, impertinent, forward, arrogant, insolent, audacious, rude, fresh.
Ant. modest, polite.

pretend, *v.* 1. feign, affect, put on, assume, falsify, simulate, fake, sham, counterfeit. 2. allege, profess; lie. 3. make believe.

pretense, *n.* 1. pretending, feigning, shamming, make-believe; subterfuge, fabrication, pretext, excuse. 2. show, cover, cover-up, semblance, dissembling, mask, cloak, veil; pretension.

preternatural, *adj.* abnormal, unusual, peculiar, odd, strange, extraordinary, irregular, unnatural, anomalous; supernatural.
Ant. usual, common, regular, natural.

pretty, *adj.* 1. fair, attractive, comely, pleasing, beautiful. 2. fine, pleasant, excellent, splendid. —*adv.* 3. moderately, fairly, somewhat, to some extent. 4. very, quite.
Ant. ugly; unpleasant; completely.

prevail, *v.* 1. predominate, preponderate. 2. win, succeed.
Ant. lose.

prevailing, *adj.* 1. prevalent, predominant, preponderating, dominant, preponderant. 2. current, general, common. 3. superior, influential, effectual, effective, efficacious, successful.

Ant. rare, uncommon; inferior, ineffectual, ineffective, unsuccessful.

prevalent, *adj.* widespread, current, common, prevailing, extensive, predominant, predominating, accepted, used, general.
Ant. rare, unusual, uncommon.

prevaricate, *v.* equivocate, quibble, cavil, shift; fib, lie.

prevent, *v.* hinder, stop, obstruct, hamper, impede, forestall, thwart, intercept, preclude, obviate, interrupt.
Ant. encourage, aid, help, abet, support, continue.

previous, *adj.* prior, earlier, former, preceding, foregoing.
Ant. later, following.

price, *n.* charge, cost, expense, outlay, expenditure.

pride, *n.* 1. conceit, self-esteem, vanity, arrogance, vainglory, self-importance. 2. insolence, haughtiness, snobbishness, superciliousness, hauteur, presumption.
Ant. modesty; humility.

prim, *adj.* stiff, starched, formal, strait-laced, precise, proper, puritanical, rigid, blue, priggish; prunes and prisms.
Ant. flexible, informal; lewd, licentious, profligate.

primary, *adj.* 1. first, highest, chief, principal, main. 2. first, earliest, primitive, original, primeval, aboriginal. 3. elementary, beginning, opening, fundamental, basic, ordinate. 4. direct, immediate.
Ant. last, final, ultimate; secondary; indirect.

prime, *adj.* primary.
Ant. last.

primeval, *adj.* prime, primary, primordial, primitive, original, primigenial, pristine.

primitive, *adj.* 1. prehistoric, primal, primeval, prime, primary, primordial, original, aboriginal, pristine, prehistoric, first, antediluvian. 2. uncivilized, uncultured, simple, unsophisticated, quaint.
Ant. secondary; civilized, sophisticated, cultured.

principal, *adj.* 1. first, highest, prime, paramount, capital, chief, foremost, main, leading, cardinal, preeminent. —*n.* 2. chief, head, leader, chieftain. 3. headmaster, dean, master.
Ant. ancillary, secondary.

principally, *adv.* especially, chiefly, mainly, primarily, firstly, particularly.
Ant. lastly.

principle, *n.* 1. canon, rule, standard, test, parameter. 2. theorem, axiom, postulate, maxim, law, proposition. 3. doctrine, tenet, belief, opinion. 4. integrity, honesty, probity, righteousness, uprightness, rectitude, virtue, incorruptibility, goodness, trustworthiness, honor.

private, *adj.* 1. individual, personal, singular, especial, special, particular, peculiar. 2. confidential, secret, top secret, "eyes only." 3. alone, secluded, cloistered, sequestered, solitary, retired.
Ant. public, general; known; open.

privation, *n.* hardship, deprivation, loss; destitution, want, need, necessity, distress, lack.
Ant. ease, wealth.

privilege, *n.* right, immunity, leave, prerogative, advantage, license, freedom, liberty, permission, franchise.

prize, *n.* 1. reward, premium. —*v.* 2. value, esteem, appraise.

probe, *v.* examine, explore, question, investigate, scrutinize, search, sift, prove, test.
Ant. overlook, ignore.

probity, *n.* honesty, uprightness, rectitude, integrity.
Ant. dishonesty.

problem, *n.* question, doubt, uncertainty, puzzle, riddle, enigma.
Ant. certainty, certitude, surety.

procedure, *n.* 1. proceeding, conduct, management, operation, course, process. 2. act, deed, transaction, maneuver, goings-on.

proceed, *v.* 1. advance, go on, progress, move on, continue, pass on. 2. go or come forth, issue, emanate, spring, arise, result, ensue, originate.
Ant. retreat.

process, *n.* course, procedure, operation, proceeding.

proclaim, *v.* announce, declare, advertise, promulgate, publish.

proclivity, *n.* inclination, tendency, bent, leaning, propensity, predisposition, disposition, proneness, favor, bias, prejudice.
Ant. dislike, aversion.

procrastinate, *v.* delay, postpone, put off, defer, adjourn, prolong.
Ant. speed, expedite.

procure, *v.* 1. acquire, gain, get, secure, win, obtain. 2. bring about, effect, cause, contrive. 3. pander, bawd, pimp.
Ant. lose.

prod, *v.* poke, jab; goad, rouse, incite.

prodigal, *adj.* 1. reckless, profligate, extravagant, lavish, wasteful, profuse. 2. abundant, profuse, plenteous, copious, plentiful, bounteous, bountiful. —*n.* 3. spendthrift, waster, wastrel, squanderer, carouser, playboy.
Ant. cautious, provident, thrifty; scarce, scanty.

prodigious, *adj.* 1. enormous, immense, huge, gigantic, tremendous, monstrous. 2. wonderful, marvelous, amazing, stupendous, astonishing, astounding, extraordinary, miraculous, wondrous, uncommon, unusual, strange. 3. abnormal, monstrous, anomalous.
Ant. small, tiny, infinitesimal; negligible, common; normal, usual.

produce, *v.* 1. give rise to, cause, generate, occasion, originate, create, effect, make, manufacture, bring about. 2. bear, bring forth, yield, furnish, supply, afford, give. 3. exhibit, show, demonstrate, bring forward. —*n.* 4. yield, product, crops, fruits, production.
Ant. destroy, ruin; subdue, squelch; hide, conceal.

productive, *adj.* generative, creative; prolific, fertile, fruitful.
Ant. barren, sterile, unproductive.

profane, *adj.* 1. irreverent, irreligious, blasphemous, sacrilegious, piacular, wicked, impious, ungodly, godless, unredeemed, unredeemable. 2. unconsecrated, secular, temporal. 3. unholy, heathen, pagan, unhallowed, impure, polluted. 4. common, low, mean, base, vulgar. —*v.* 5. debase, misuse, defile, desecrate, violate, pollute.
Ant. sacred, repentant; spiritual; pure, hallowed, holy; elevated, exalted.

profession, *n.* 1. vocation, calling, occupation, business, employment. 2. professing, avowal, declaration, asseveration, assertion.

proffer, *v.* offer, tender, volunteer, propose, suggest, hint.
Ant. refuse.

proficient, *adj.* skilled, adept, skillful, competent, practiced, experienced, qualified, trained, conversant, accomplished, finished, able, apt.
Ant. unskilled, maladroit, awkward, clumsy, untrained, unable, inept.

profit, *n.* 1. gain, return. 2. returns, proceeds, revenue, dividend. 3. advantage, benefit, gain, good, welfare, improvement, advancement. —*v.* 4. gain, improve, advance, better.
Ant. loss; lose.

profound, *adj.* deep, intense, extreme, penetrating, sagacious; abstruse.
Ant. shallow, superficial.

profuse, *adj.* extravagant, abundant, lavish, prodigal, wasteful, profligate, improvident.
Ant. scarce, scanty, thrifty.

profusion, *n.* 1. abundance, plenty, copiousness, bounty, prodigality, profligacy, excess, waste.
Ant. scarcity, need, want; penury, niggardliness.

progress, *n.* 1. proceeding, advancement, advance, progression. 2. growth, development, improvement, increase, betterment. —*v.* 3. advance, proceed; develop, improve, grow, increase.
Ant. retrogression; recession; recede, decrease, diminish.

prohibit, *v.* 1. forbid, interdict, disallow. 2. prevent, hinder, preclude, obstruct.
Ant. allow, permit; encourage, foster, further.

prohibition, *n.* interdiction, prevention, embargo, ban, restriction.
Ant. permission.

project, *n.* 1. plan, scheme, design, proposal. 2. activity, lesson, homework. —*v.* 3. propose, contemplate, plan, contrive, scheme, plot, devise, concoct. brew, frame. 4. throw, cast, toss. 5. extend, protrude, obtrude, bulge, jut out, stick out.

prolific, *adj.* 1. fruitful, fertile, productive, teeming. 2. abundant.
Ant. fruitless, unfruitful, barren, sterile; scarce.

prolong, *v.* lengthen, extend, protract.
Ant. abbreviate, shorten, curtail.

prominent, *adj.* 1. conspicuous, noticeable, outstanding, manifest, principal, chief, important, main. 2. projecting, jutting out, protuberant, embossed. 3. important, leading, well-known, eminent, celebrated, famed, famous, distinguished.
Ant. inconspicuous, unimportant; recessed; negligible, unknown.

promiscuous, *adj.* 1. miscellaneous, hodgepodge, hotchpotch, indiscriminate, confused, mixed, intermixed, intermingled, mingled, jumbled, garbled. 2. nonselective, indiscriminate, careless.
Ant. special, discriminate, pure, unmixed; selective, careful, select.

promise, *n.* 1. word, pledge, assurance. —*v.* 2. pledge, covenant, agree, engage.

promote, *v.* 1. further, advance, encourage, forward, assist, aid, help, support. 2. elevate, raise, exalt. *Ant.* discourage, obstruct; lower, debase.

prone, *adj.* 1. inclined, disposed, liable, tending, bent. 2. prostrate, recumbent. *Ant.* averse; upright.

proof, *n.* 1. evidence, testimony, certification, confirmation, demonstration. 2. test, trial, examination, essay. 3. impression. —*adj.* 4. impenetrable, impervious, invulnerable, steadfast, firm.

propensity, *n.* inclination, bent, leaning, tendency, disposition, bias. *Ant.* disinclination, aversion, distaste.

proper, *adj.* 1. appropriate, fit, suitable, suited, adapted, convenient, fitting, befitting, correct, right, becoming, meet. 2. correct, decorous, decent, respectable, polite, well-mannered. 3. special, specific, individual, peculiar. 4. strict, accurate, precise, exact, just, formal, correct. *Ant.* improper.

property, *n.* 1. possession, possessions, goods, effects, chattels, estate, belongings. 2. land, real estate, acreage. 3. ownership, right. 4. attribute, quality, characteristic, feature.

prophesy, *v.* foretell, predict, augur, prognosticate, divine.

propitiate, *v.* appease, conciliate, pacify. *Ant.* anger, arouse.

proportion, *n.* 1. relation, arrangement; comparison, analogy. 2. size, extent, dimensions. 3. portion, part, piece, share. 4. symmetry, harmony, agreement, balance, distribution, arrangement. —*v.* 5. adjust, regulate, redistribute, arrange, balance, harmonize. *Ant.* disproportion.

proposal, *n.* plan, scheme, offer, recommendation, suggestion, design, overture, approach, proposition.

propose, *v.* 1. offer, proffer, tender, suggest, recommend, present. 2. nominate, name. 3. plan, intend, design, mean, purpose. 4. state, present, propound, pose, posit. *Ant.* refuse.

proposition, *n.* proposal.

propriety, *n.* 1. decorum, etiquette, protocol, good behavior, decency, modesty. 2. suitability, appropriateness, aptness, fitness, suitableness, seemliness. 3. rightness, justness, correctness, accuracy. *Ant.* impropriety, immodesty, indecency; unseemliness, ineptitude; inaccuracy.

prosaic, *adj.* prosy, commonplace, dull, matter-of-fact, unimaginative, vapid, humdrum, tedious, tiresome, wearisome, uninteresting. *Ant.* interesting, fascinating, beguiling.

prospect, *n.* 1. anticipation, expectation, expectance, contemplation. 2. view, scene, outlook, survey, vista, perspective. —*v.* 3. search, explore.

prosper, *v.* succeed, thrive, flourish. *Ant.* fail, die.

prosperous, *adj.* 1. fortunate, successful, flourishing, thriving. 2. wealthy, rich, well-to-do, well-off. 3. favorable, propitious, fortunate, lucky, auspicious, golden, bright. *Ant.* unfortunate, unsuccessful; poor, impoverished; unfavorable.

prostitute, *n.* 1. harlot, whore, strumpet, call girl, trollop, quean, street walker, courtesan. —*v.* 2. misapply, misuse, abuse.

protect, *v.* defend, guard, shield, cover, screen, shelter, save, harbor, house, secure. *Ant.* attack, assail.

protection, *n.* 1. preservation, guard, defense, shelter, screen, cover, security, refuge, safety. 2. shield, aegis, bulwark. 3. treaty, safe-conduct, passport, visa, pass, permit. 4. aegis, patronage, sponsorship. *Ant.* attack.

protest, *n.* 1. objection, disapproval, protestation. —*v.* 2. remonstrate, complain, object. 3. declare, affirm, assert, asseverate, avow, aver, testify, attest. *Ant.* approval; approve.

prototype, *n.* model, pattern, example, exemplar, original, archetype.

protract, *v.* draw out, lengthen, extend, prolong, continue. *Ant.* curtail, abbreviate, discontinue.

proud, *adj.* 1. contented, self-satisfied, egotistical, vain, conceited. 2. arrogant, over-weening, haughty, overbearing, self-important, over-confident, disdainful, supercilious, snooty, imperious, presumptuous. 3. honorable, creditable. 4. stately, majestic, magnificent, noble, imposing, splendid.

Ant. discontented, dissatisfied; humble, self-effacing; dishonorable; ignoble, base.

prove, *v.* 1. demonstrate, show, confirm, manifest, establish, evince, evidence, substantiate, verify, justify, ascertain, determine. 2. try, test, examine, assay. *Ant.* disprove.

proverb, *n.* maxim, saying, adage, epigram, precept, truth, saw, aphorism, by-word, apothegm.

provide, *v.* 1. furnish, supply, afford, yield, produce, contribute, give. 2. prepare, get ready, procure, provide for, make provision for. *Ant.* deprive.

provided, *conj.* on the condition *or* supposition that, if, in case, granted. *Ant.* lest.

provision, *n.* 1. stipulation, condition, if, proviso. 2. catering, purveying, supplying. 3. (*plural*) food, supplies, stores, provender, stock.

provoke, *v.* 1. anger, enrage, exasperate, irk, vex, irritate, incense, annoy, chafe, aggravate, exacerbate, infuriate, ire, nettle, affront. 2. stir up, arouse, call forth, incite, stimulate, excite, fire, rouse, inflame, animate, inspirit, instigate. 3. give rise to, induce, bring about. *Ant.* assuage, calm, propitiate.

prowl, *v.* lurk, rove, roam, wander; prey, plunder, pillage, steal.

prudence, *n.* 1. calculation, foresight, forethought, judgment, discretion, common sense, circumspection, caution, wisdom. 2. providence, care, economy, frugality, carefulness. *Ant.* carelessness, imprudence, incaution.

prudent, *adj.* 1. wise, judicious, cautious, discreet, tactful, sensible, sagacious, circumspect, careful, wary, provident. 2. provident, frugal, sparing, economical, thrifty, saving, careful. *Ant.* imprudent, indiscreet, tactless, careless; improvident, prodigal.

prudish, *adj.* modest, proper, demure, pure, coy, reserved. *Ant.* immodest, indecent.

prying, *adj.* curious, inquisitive, peeping, peering, peeking; nosy. *Ant.* blasé, unconcerned, uninterested.

pseudo, *adj.* sham, counterfeit, false, spurious, pretended, fake. *Ant.* genuine, real.

publish, *v.* 1. issue, distribute. 2. announce, proclaim, promulgate, declare, disclose, divulge, reveal, impart, advertise, publicize.
Ant. conceal, hide.

puerile, *adj.* 1. boyish, juvenile, childish, youthful. 2. childish, immature, foolish, irrational, trivial, nugatory, silly, ridiculous, idle.
Ant. manly; mature, rational.

pulsate, *v.* beat, palpitate, pulse, throb; vibrate, quiver.

punctilious, *adj.* strict, exact, precise, demanding, scrupulous, nice, careful, conscientious.
Ant. inexact, careless.

pungent, *adj.* 1. biting, acrid, hot, peppery, piquant, sharp. 2. poignant, distressing, painful. 3. caustic, biting, sarcastic, sardonic, mordant, penetrating, piercing, trenchant, cutting, severe, acrimonious, bitter, waspish. 4. stimulating, acute, keen, sharp.
Ant. mild, bland; painless; dull.

punish, *v.* 1. correct, discipline, penalize, reprove. 2. castigate, scold, berate, chastise, chasten, flog, whip, lash, scourge.
Ant. praise, laud; forgive.

pupil, *v.* disciple, scholar, student, learner, tyro, greenhorn, neophyte, novice, beginner.
Ant. teacher, expert.

purblind, *adj.* blind, sightless, dimsighted, myopic, short-sighted, near-sighted.
Ant. sighted, clear-sighted, presbyopic.

purchase, *v.* 1. buy, acquire, get, obtain, procure. 2. haul, draw, raise. —*n.* 3. buying, acquisition. 4. bargain. 5. tackle, lever, winch, capstan.
Ant. sell, lose; lower; sale.

pure, *adj.* 1. unmixed, unadulterated, uncontaminated, unalloyed, clean, unsullied, untainted, unstained, undefiled, spotless, untarnished, immaculate, unpolluted, uncorrupted. 2. unmodified, simple, homogeneous, genuine, faultless, perfect. 3. thoroughbred, purebred, pedigreed. 4. utter, sheer, unqualified, absolute. 5. innocent, chaste, undefiled, unsullied, modest, virtuous. 6. guiltless, innocent, true, guileless, honest, upright.
Ant. impure.

purge, *v.* purify, cleanse, clear, clean, clarify.
Ant. pollute.

purport, *v.* 1. profess, claim, mean, intend, signify. 2. express, imply. —*n.* 3. tenor, import, meaning, intention, claim, design, significance, signification, implication, drift, suggestion, gist, spirit.
Ant. understand, see; infer; insignificance, meaninglessness.

purpose, *n.* 1. object, intent, intention, determination, aim, end, design, view. 2. result, effect, advantage, consequence. —*v.* 3. propose, design, intend, mean, contemplate, plan.
Ant. purposelessness.

push, *v.* 1. shove, shoulder, thrust, drive, move, slide. 2. press, urge, persuade, drive, impel. —*n.* 3. attack, effort, onset.

put, *v.* 1. place, lay, set, deposit. 2. set, levy, impose, inflict. 3. render, translate. 4. express, state, utter.

puzzle, *n.* 1. riddle, enigma, problem, poser, maze, question. —*v.* 2. bewilder, perplex, confound, mystify, confuse.

pygmy, *n.* dwarf, midget, Lilliputian, runt.
Ant. giant, colossus.

Q

quaint, *adj.* 1. strange, odd, curious, unusual, extraordinary, unique, uncommon. 2. picturesque, charming, old-fashioned, antiquated, antique, archaic.
Ant. common, usual, ordinary; modern, new-fangled.

quake, *v.* 1. shake, shudder, tremble, shiver, quaver, quiver. —*n.* 2. temblor, earthquake.

qualify, *v.* 1. fit, suit, adapt, prepare, equip. 2. characterize, call, name, designate, label, signify. 3. modify, limit, mitigate, restrain, narrow, restrict. 4. moderate, mitigate, meliorate, soften, mollify, soothe, ease, assuage, temper, reduce, diminish.

quality, *n.* 1. characteristic, attribute, property, character, feature, trait. 2. nature, grade, kind, sort, description, status, rank, condition. 3. excellence, superiority, standing. 4. accomplishment, deed, feat, attainment. 5. distinction, class.
Ant. inferiority, baseness; failure.

qualm, *n.* uneasiness, compunction, scruple, twinge, remorse, misgiving.
Ant. ease, confort, security.

quandary, *n.* dilemma, predicament, strait, uncertainty, doubt.
Ant. certainty, assurance.

quarrel, *n.* 1. dispute, altercation, disagreement, argument, contention, controversy, dissension, feud, breach, break, rupture, difference, spat, tiff, fight, misunderstanding, wrangle, brawl, tumult. —*v.* 2. squabble, fall out, disagree with, differ, disagree, bicker, dispute, argue, wrangle, spar, brawl, clash, jar, fight.

queer, *adj.* strange, unconventional, odd, singular, curious, fantastic, uncommon, weird, peculiar, extraordinary, eccentric, freakish.
Ant. conventional, ordinary, common.

quell, *v.* 1. suppress, stifle, extinguish, put an end to, crush, quash, subdue, overpower, overcome. 2. vanquish, put down, defeat, conquer. 3. quiet, allay, calm, pacify, compose, lull, hush.
Ant. encourage, foster; defend, lose; agitate, disturb, perturb.

querulous, *adj.* complaining, petulant, peevish, snappish, abrupt, waspish, testy; caviling, carping, discontented, fault-finding.
Ant. calm, equable; pleased, contented.

question, *n.* 1. inquiry, query, interrogation. 2. dispute, controversy. —*v.* 3. interrogate; ask, inquire, query, examine. 4. doubt. 5. dispute, challenge.
Ant. answer, reply; agree, concur.

questionable, *adj.* doubtful, uncertain, dubitable, dubious, debatable, disputable, controvertible.
Ant. certain, sure, positive.

quibble, *n.* 1. evasion, prevarication, equivocation, sophism, shift, subterfuge, cavil. —*v.* 2. evade, prevaricate, equivocate, cavil, shuffle, trifle.

quick, *adj.* 1. prompt, immediate, rapid, fast, swift, speedy, instantaneous, fleet, hasty, hurried, expeditious. 2. impatient, hasty, abrupt, curt, short, precipitate, sharp, unceremonious; testy, waspish, snappish, irritable, peppery, irascible, petulant, touchy. 3. lively, keen, acute, sensitive, alert, sharp, shrewd, intelligent, discerning. 4. vigorous, energetic, active, nimble, animated, agile, lively, alert, brisk.
Ant. slow; patient, deliberate; calm; dull, stupid; lethargic, lazy.

quiet, *n.* 1. tranquillity, rest, repose, calm, stillness, quietude, serenity, peace, calmness, silence. 2. peace. —*adj.* 3. peaceable, peaceful, pacific, calm, tranquil, serene, silent. 4. motionless, still, unmoving, unmoved. 5. inconspicuous, subdued; repressed, unstrained, unobtrusive. —*v.* 6. still, hush, silence. 7. tranquilize, pacify, calm, compose, lull, soothe.
Ant. disturbance, perturbation; war; warlike, noisy, clamorous; conspicuous, obvious, blatant; disturb, perturb.

quit, *v.* 1. stop, cease, discontinue, desist. 2. depart from, leave, go, withdraw *or* retire from. 3. give up, let go, relinquish, release, resign, surrender. —*adj.* 4. released, free, clear, liberated, rid, absolved, acquitted, discharged.
Ant. start; initiate, originate; continue; arrive, enter; chained, confined.

quiver, *v.* 1. shake, tremble, vibrate, quake, shudder, shiver. —*n.* 2. tremble, tremor, shudder, shiver, trembling, shake. 3. arrow-case.

quixotic, *adj.* visionary, impracticable, romantic, imaginary, wild.
Ant. realistic, practicable, practical.

R

race, *n.* 1. competition, contest. 2. course, stream. 3. nation, people, clan, family, tribe, generation, stock, line, lineage, breed, kin, kindred, progeny, descendants, offspring, children. 4. man, mankind. —*v.* 5. run, speed, hurry, hasten, hie.

rack, *n.* 1. frame, framework, crib. 2. torment, anguish, torture, pain, agony. —*v.* 3. torture, distress, torment, agonize, excruciate. 4. strain, force, wrest, stretch.

racket, *n.* 1. din, uproar, noise, clamor, fuss, tumult, hubbub, outcry, disturbance. 2. excitement, gaiety, dissipation.
Ant. quiet, tranquillity, peace.

racy, *adj.* 1. vigorous, lively, animated, spirited. 2. sprightly, piquant, pungent, strong, flavorful. 3. suggestive, risqué.
Ant. dispirited, dejected; mild, bland.

radiant, *adj.* shining, bright, brilliant, beaming, effulgent, resplendent, sparkling, splendid, glittering.
Ant. dull.

radical, *adj.* 1. fundamental, basic, original, constitutional, essential, innate, ingrained. 2. thorough-going, extreme, complete, unqualified, thorough, fanatical, excessive, immoderate, extravagant, violent. —*n.* 3. extremist.
Ant. superfluous; incomplete, moderate.

radioactive, *adj.* hot, dirty.
Ant. clean.

rage, *n.* 1. anger, ire, fury, frenzy, passion, vehemence, wrath, madness, raving. 2. fury, violence, turbulence, tumultuousness, storm. 3. ardor, fervor, enthusiasm, eagerness, desire, vehemence. 4. mode, fashion, fad, craze, vogue. —*v.* 5. rave, fume, storm, chafe, fret.
Ant. calm, equanimity.

ragged, *adj.* 1. tattered, torn, shredded, rent. 2. shabby, poor, mean.
Ant. neat, whole.

raid, *n.* 1. onset, attack, seizure. 2. invasion, inroad, incursion.
Ant. defense.

raise, *v.* 1. lift, lift up, elevate, heave, hoist, loft. 2. rouse, arouse, awake, awaken, call forth, evoke, stir up, excite. 3. build, erect, construct, rear, set up. 4. cause, promote, cultivate, grow, propagate. 5. originate, engender, give rise to, bring up *or* about, produce, effect, cause. 6. invigorate, animate, inspirit, heighten, intensify. 7. advance, elevate, promote, exalt. 8. gather, collect, assemble, bring together. 9. increase, intensify, heighten, aggravate, amplify, augment, enhance, enlarge. —*n.* 10. increase, rise.
Ant. lower; pacify; destroy, raze; kill; weaken, dispirit; debase, dishonor; scatter, disperse, broadcast; decrease.

ramble, *v.* 1. stroll, amble, walk, wander, saunter, stray, roam, rove, range, straggle. —*n.* 2. walk, stroll, amble, excursion, tour.

rambling, *adj.* wandering, aimless, irregular, straggling, straying, discursive.
Ant. direct, pointed.

rampart, *n.* fortification, breastwork, bulwark, barricade, stronghold, security, guard, defense.

ramshackle, *adj.* shaky, rickety, flimsy, dilapidated.
Ant. luxurious, sumptuous.

rancor, *n.* resentment, bitterness, ill will, hatred, malice, spite, venom, malevolence, animosity, enmity.
Ant. amiability, good will, benevolence.

random, *adj.* haphazard, chance, fortuitous, casual. stray, aimless.
Ant. specific, particular.

range, *n.* 1. extent, limits, scope, sweep, latitude, reach, compass. 2. rank, class, order, kind, sort. 3. row, line, series, tier, file. 4. area, trace, region. —*v.* 5. align, rank, classify, class, order, arrange, array, dispose. 6. vary, course. 7. extend, stretch out, run, go, lie. 8. roam, rove, wander, stroll, straggle. 9. extend, be found, occupy, lie, run.

rank, *n.* 1. position, standing, station, order, class, level, division. 2. row, line, tier, series, range. 3. distinction, eminence, dignity. 4. membership, body, rank and file. 5. order, arrangement, array, alignment. —*v.* 6. arrange, line up, align, array, range. 7. classify, dispose, sort, class, arrange. —*adj.* 8. tall, vigorous, luxuriant, abundant, over-abundant, exuberant. 9. strong, gamy, pungent, offensive, noxious, fetid, rancid, putrid. 10. utter, absolute, complete, entire, sheer, gross, extravagant, excessive. 11. offensive, disgusting, repulsive, repellent, miasmatic, mephitic. 12. coarse, indecent, foul, gross.

ransom, *n.* 1. redemption, deliverance, liberation, release. —*v.* 2. redeem, release, restore, deliver, deliver up.

rapacious, *adj.* greedy, predatory, extortionate, ravenous, voracious, avaricious, grasping; predacious, raptorial, preying.
Ant. generous, yielding; parasitic.

rapid, *adj.* speedy, fast, quick, swift, fleet.
Ant. slow.

rapidity, *n.* swiftness, speed, fleetness, quickness, haste, velocity, alacrity, celerity.
Ant. sloth, lethargy.

rapture, *n.* ecstasy, joy, delight, transport, bliss, beatitude, exultation.
Ant. misery, disgust, revulsion.

rare, *adj.* 1. scarce, uncommon, exceptional, unusual, sparse, infrequent, extraordinary, singular. 2. excellent, admirable, fine, choice, exquisite, incomparable, inimitable. 3. underdone.
Ant. common, usual, frequent, ordinary; base, inferior; medium, well done.

rascal, *n.* 1. rapscallion, knave, rogue, scamp, villain, scoundrel, miscreant, scapegrace. —*adj.* 2. knavish, roguish, miscreant, dishonest, base, paltry, mean, low, rascally.

rash, *adj.* 1. hasty, impetuous, reckless, headlong, precipitate, impulsive, thoughtless, heedless, indiscreet, incautious, unwary, foolhardy, audacious. —*n.* 2. eruption, efflorescence, eczema, dermatitis, breaking out, exanthema.
Ant. thoughtful, considered, discreet, cautious.

ratify, *v.* confirm, corroborate, consent to, agree to, approve, sanction, substantiate, validate, establish.
Ant. refute, veto, disapprove.

ration, *n.* 1. allowance, portion, food. —*v.* 2. apportion, distribute, mete, dole, deal, parcel out. 3. put on rations, restrict to rations.

rational, *adj.* 1. reasonable, sensible. 2. intelligent, wise; judicious, discreet, sagacious, enlightened. 3. sane, lucid, sound, sober.
Ant. irrational, unreasonable; unintelligent, stupid, unwise, indiscreet; unsound, dim.

ravage, *n.* 1. devastation, destruction, ruin, waste, desolation, damage, havoc, despoilment, plunder, pillage. —*v.* 2. damage, mar, ruin, dev-

astate, destroy, lay waste, despoil, plunder, pillage, sack.
Ant. construction, creation; build; repair.

ravening, *adj.* ravenous.

ravenous, *adj.* ravening, voracious, greedy, starved, hungry, famished, insatiable, gluttonous, devouring; rapacious, raptorial, predacious, predatory.
Ant. sated, satisfied.

raw, *adj.* 1. unprepared, unfinished, unrefined, unmade, crude, rude, rough, makeshift. 2. uncooked. 3. ignorant, inexperienced, untrained, undisciplined, green, unskilled, untried, unpracticed. 4. frank, candid, bold, exposed. 5. damp, chilly, cold, wet, windy.
Ant. prepared, finished, refined, done, polished; cooked, done; intelligent, disciplined, skilled, secretive, dry, warm, arid.

reach, *v.* 1. get to, attain, arrive at, come to. 2. touch, seize. 3. stretch, extend. —*n.* 4. extent, distance, range, compass, area, sphere, influence, stretch, scope, grasp.
Ant. fail.

reactionary, *n., adj.* conservative.
Ant. radical.

readily, *adv.* promptly, quickly, easily; willingly, cheerfully.
Ant. slowly. lethargically; reluctantly.

ready, *adj.* 1. prepared, set, fitted, fit. 2. equipped, geared, completed, adjusted, arranged. 3. willing, agreeable, cheerful, disposed, inclined. 4. prompt, quick, alert, acute, sharp, keen, adroit, facile, clever, skillful, nimble. —*v.* 5. make ready, prepare.
Ant. unprepared, unfit; unwilling, indisposed, disinclined; slow, deliberate, unskillful.

real, *adj.* true, actual, faithful, factual, authentic, genuine; sincere, unfeigned.
Ant. false, fake, counterfeit, fraudulent; insincere.

realize, *v.* 1. grasp, understand, comprehend, conceive. 2. imagine. 3. accomplish, effect, effectuate, perform.
Ant. misunderstand; begin.

realm, *n.* 1. kingdom. 2. sovereignty, sphere, domain, province, department.

rear, *n.* 1. back, background. —*v.* 2. bring up, nurture, raise, nurse. 3. raise, elevate, lift, loft, lift up, hold up. 4. build, put up, erect, construct. 5. rise; buck.
Ant. front; face.

reason, *n.* 1. ground, cause, motive, purpose, end, design, *raison d'être*, objective, aim, object. 2. justification, explanation, excuse, rationale, ratiocination, rationalization. 3. judgment, common sense, understanding, intellect, intelligence, mind. 4. sanity. —*v.* 5. argue, ratiocinate, justify; rationalize. 6. conclude, infer. 7. bring, persuade, convince, influence.

reasonable, *adj.* 1. rational, logical, sensible, intelligent, wise, judicious, right, fair, equitable. 2. moderate, tolerable. 3. sane, rational, sober, sound.
Ant. unreasonable, illogical, irrational; immoderate, intolerable; unsound, insane.

reassure, *v.* encourage, hearten, embolden, bolster, comfort, inspirit.
Ant. disconcert, unnerve, dishearten, discourage.

rebel, *n.* 1. insurgent, insurrectionist, mutineer, traitor. —*adj.* 2. insurgent, mutinous, rebellious, insubordinate. —*v.* 3. revolt.
Ant. patriot; loyal, obedient.

rebellion, *n.* resistance, defiance, insurrection, mutiny, sedition, revolution, revolt; insubordination, disobedience, contumacy.

rebellious, *adj.* defiant, insubordinate, mutinous, rebel, seditious, insurgent, refractory, disobedient, contumacious.
Ant. subordinate, obedient, patriotic.

rebuke, *v.* 1. reprove, reprimand, censure, upbraid, chide, reproach, reprehend, admonish, scold, remonstrate with. —*n.* 2. reproof, reprimand, censure, reproach, reprehension, chiding, scolding, remonstration, expostulation.
Ant. praise.

recalcitrant, *adj.* resistant, resistive, disobedient, uncompliant, refractory, rebellious, contumacious, opposing.
Ant. obedient, compliant.

recall, *v.* 1. recollect, remember. 2. call back, revoke, rescind, retract, withdraw, recant, repeal, annul, countermand, nullify. —*n.* 3. memory, recollection. 4. revocation, retraction, repeal, withdrawal, recantation, nullification; impeachment.
Ant. forget; enforce; ratify; sanction.

recapitulate, *v.* review, summarize, repeat, reiterate.

recent, *adj.* late, modern, up-to-date, fresh, new, novel.
Ant. early, old, ancient.

reciprocal, *adj.* 1. mutual, correlative, interchangeable. —*n.* 2. equivalent, counterpart, complement. *Ant.* unequal.

recital, *n.* account, narrative, description, relation, history, story.

recite, *v.* 1. repeat, relate, narrate, recount, describe. 2. enumerate, count, number, detail, recapitulate.

reckless, *adj.* careless, rash, heedless, incautious, negligent, thoughtless, imprudent, improvident, remiss, inattentive, indifferent, regardless, unconcerned. *Ant.* careful, heedful, cautious, thoughtful, provident.

reckon, *v.* 1. count, compute, calculate, enumerate. 2. esteem, consider, regard, account, deem, estimate, judge, evaluate.

reclaim, *v.* recover, bring *or* get back, regain, restore.

recoil, *v.* 1. draw *or* shrink back, falter, flinch, quail. 2. rebound, spring *or* fly back, react, reverberate. *Ant.* advance.

recollect, *v.* recall, remember. *Ant.* forget.

recommend, *v.* 1. commend, approve, condone. 2. advise, counsel. *Ant.* condemn, disapprove.

recompense, *v.* 1. repay, remunerate, reward, requite, compensate for. —*n.* 2. compensation, payment, reward, requital, remuneration, repayment, amends, indemnification, satisfaction, retribution.

reconcile, *v.* 1. content, win over, convince, persuade. 2. pacify, conciliate, placate, propitiate, appease. 3. compose, settle, adjust, make up, harmonize, make compatible *or* consistent. *Ant.* dissuade; anger, arouse, disturb.

recondite, *adj.* 1. abstruse, profound, deep. 2. obscure, dim, mysterious, hidden, occult, dark, secret, concealed. *Ant.* clear, obvious, patent.

record, *v.* 1. set down, enter, register, enroll. —*n.* 2. account, chronicle, history, note, register, memorandum.

recount, *v.* relate, narrate, tell, recite, describe, enumerate.

recover, *v.* 1. regain, get again, reclaim, retrieve, restore. 2. heal, mend, recuperate, rally.

recreant, *adj.* 1. cowardly, craven, dastardly, base, pusillanimous, fainthearted, yellow. 2. unfaithful, disloyal, false, faithless, untrue, treach-

erous, apostate. —*n.* 3. coward, craven, dastard. 4. apostate, traitor, renegade. *Ant.* bold, brave; faithful, loyal, true; hero; patriot.

rectify, *v.* 1. set right, correct, remedy, mend, emend, amend, improve, better, ameliorate. 2. adjust, regulate, put right, straighten. *Ant.* worsen, ruin.

redeem, *v.* 1. buy *or* pay off, ransom, recover, buy back, repurchase. 2. ransom, free, liberate, rescue, save. 3. discharge, fulfill, perform.

redress, *n.* 1. reparation, restitution, amends, indemnification, compensation, satisfaction, indemnity, restoration, remedy, relief, atonement, *Wiedergutmachung.* —*v.* 2. remedy, repair, correct, amend, mend, emend, right, rectify, adjust, relieve, ease. *Ant.* blame, punishment; damage.

reduce, *v.* 1. diminish, decrease, shorten, abridge, curtail, retrench, abate, lessen, attenuate, contract. 2. subdue, suppress, subject, subjugate, conquer, vanquish, overcome, overpower, overthrow, depose. 3. debase, depress, lower, degrade. 4. control, adjust, correct. *Ant.* increase; defend; honor, exalt, elevate.

refer, *v.* 1. direct, commit, deliver, consign. 2. assign, attribute, ascribe, impute. 3. relate, apply, obtain, pertain, belong, respect. 4. advert, allude, hint at.

referee, *n.* 1. arbitrator, umpire, judge, arbiter. —*v.* 2. judge, arbitrate, umpire.

reference, *n.* 1. direction, allusion, referral, mention, citation. 2. witness. 3. testimonial, endorsement. 4. relation, regard, respect, conern.

refined, *adj.* 1. cultivated, polished, genteel, elegant, polite, courteous, courtly, civilized, well-bred. 2. purified, clarified, distilled, strained. 3. subtle. 4. minute, precise, exact, exquisite. *Ant.* unrefined, inelegant, impolite, discourteous; polluted, contaminated; obvious, direct, candid; general, inexact.

reflect, *v.* 1. mirror, cast *or* throw back, rebound. 2. reproduce, show, manifest, espouse. 3. meditate, think, ponder, ruminate, cogitate, muse, deliberate, study, comtemplate, consider.

reflection, *n.* 1. image, representation, counterpart. 2. consideration,

deliberation, cogitation, rumination, meditation, study, comtemplation, thinking, musing. 3. imputation, aspersion, reproach, censure. *Ant.* original; thoughtlessness; praise.

reflective, *adj.* pensive, meditative, contemplative, thoughtful, pondering, deliberating, reflecting, reasoning, cogitating. *Ant.* thoughtless, inconsiderate, unthinking.

reform, *n.* 1. improvement, amendment, correction, reformation, betterment, amelioration. —*v.* 2. better, rectify, correct, amend, emend, ameliorate, mend, improve, repair, restore. *Ant.* deterioration; worsen, deteriorate.

reformation, *n.* improvement, betterment, correction, reform, amendment.

refractory, *adj.* stubborn, unmanageable, obstinate, perverse, mulish, headstrong, pigheaded, contumacious, intractable, disobedient, recalcitrant, cantankerous, ungovernable, unruly. *Ant.* obedient, tractable.

refrain, *v.* 1. restrain, cease, abstain, desist, curb oneself, hold oneself back, withhold. —*n.* 2. chorus, verse, theme, burden. *Ant.* continue, persist.

refresh, *v.* 1. reinvigorate, revive, stimulate, freshen, cheer, enliven, reanimate. 2. restore, repair, renovate, renew, retouch. *Ant.* dispirit, discourage.

refuge, *n.* 1. shelter, protection, security, safety. 2. asylum, retreat, sanctuary, hiding place, haven, harbor, stronghold, cloister.

refurbish, *v.* renovate, refurnish, redecorate, brighten.

refuse, *v.* 1. decline, reject, spurn, turn down, deny, rebuff, repudiate. —*n.* 2. rubbish, trash, waste, garbage; slag, lees, dregs, scum, sediment, marc, scoria, dross. *Ant.* allow, permit, sanction, approve.

refute, *v.* disprove, rebut, confute. *Ant.* agree, concur.

regain, *v.* recover, recapture, repossess, retrieve, get back. *Ant.* lose, miss.

regal, *adj.* royal, kingly; stately, princely, splendid. *Ant.* servile.

regard, *v.* 1. look upon, think of, consider, esteem, account, judge, deem, hold, suppose, estimate. 2. respect, esteem, honor, revere, reverence, value. 3. look at, observe, notice, note, see, remark, mark. 4. relate to, concern, refer to, respect. —*n.* 5. reference, relation. 6. point, particular, detail, matter, consideration. 7. thought, concern, attention. 8. look, gaze, view. 9. respect, deference, concern, esteem, estimation, consideration, reverence. 10. liking, affection, interest, love. *Ant.* disregard; disrespect, dishonor; inattention; dislike.

regardless, *adj.* inattentive, negligent, neglectful, indifferent, heedless, disregarding, ignoring, unmindful, unconcerned. *Ant.* attentive, mindful.

region, *n.* part, area, division, district, section, portion, quarter, territory, locale, site, sphere, vicinity, vicinage, space, tract.

register, *n.* 1. record, catalogue, account book, ledger, archive. 2. roll, roster, catalogue, list, record, chronicle, schedule, annals. 3. registry, entry, registration, enrollment. —*v.* 4. enrol, list, record, catalogue, chronicle, enter. 5. demonstrate, show, evince.

regret, *v.* 1. deplore, lament, feel sorry about, grieve at, bemoan, bewail, rue, mourn for, repent. —*n.* 2. sorrow, lamentation, grief. 3. remorse, penitence, contrition, repentance, compunction. *Ant.* rejoice; joy; unregeneracy.

regular, *adj.* 1. usual, normal, customary. 2. conforming, symmetrical, uniform, even, systematic, formal, fixed, orderly, invariant, unvarying, methodical, constant. 3. recurrent, periodic, habitual, established, fixed. 4. (*colloquial*) out-and-out, thorough, complete, unregenerate, perfect. *Ant.* irregular.

regulate, *v.* control, direct, manage, rule, order, adjust, arrange, set, systematize, dispose, conduct, guide.

regulation, *n.* 1. rule, order, direction, law, precept. 2. direction, control, management, arrangement, ordering, disposition, disposal, adjustment. *Ant.* misdirection, mismanagement.

rehearse, *v.* 1. recite, act, practice, drill, train, repeat. 2. relate, enumerate, recount, delineate, describe, portray, narrate, recapitulate. *Ant.* extemporize.

reign, *n.* 1. rule, sway, dominion, sovereignty, suzerainty, power, influ-

ence. —*v.* 2. rule, govern, prevail, predominate, hold sway, influence. *Ant.* obey.

reiterate, *v.* repeat.

reject, *v.* 1. refuse, repudiate, decline, deny, rebuff, repel, renounce. 2. discard, throw away, exclude, eliminate; jettison. —*n.* 3. second. *Ant.* accept.

rejoinder, *n.* answer, reply, riposte, response, replication, surrejoinder.

relate, *v.* 1. tell, recite, narrate, recount, rehearse, report, describe, delineate, detail, repeat. 2. associate, connect, ally. *Ant.* dissociate, disconnect, separate, alienate.

relation, *n.* 1. connection, relationship, association, alliance, dependence. 2. reference, regard, respect. 3. narration, recitation, recital, description, rehearsal, relating, telling. 4. narrative, account, recital, report, story, chronicle, tale, history. *Ant.* independence.

relationship, *n.* 1. relation, connection, association. 2. kinship, affinity, family tie, consanguinity. *Ant.* dissociation.

relax, *v.* 1. loosen, slacken. 2. diminish, mitigate, weaken, lessen, reduce, remit, abate, debilitate, enfeeble, enervate. 3. ease, unbend, relent, soften. *Ant.* tighten; intensify, increase; harden.

release, *v.* 1. free, liberate, set free, loose, unloose, unfasten, set at liberty, discharge, deliver, dismiss. 2. disengage, loose, extricate. 3. proclaim, publish, announce. —*n.* 4. liberation, deliverance, emancipation, discharge, freedom. *Ant.* fasten, fetter, imprison; engage, involve; hide, conceal; incarceration, imprisonment.

relentless, *adj.* unrelenting, inflexible, rigid, stern, severe, unbending, unforgiving, unappeasable, implacable, merciless, ruthless, unmerciful, pitiless, unpitying, hard, obdurate, adamant, unyielding, remorseless, inexorable. *Ant.* relenting, flexible, soft, pliant, merciful, remorseful.

relevant, *adj.* pertinent, applicable, germane, apposite, appropriate, suitable, fitting, apt, proper, suited. *Ant.* irrelevant.

reliable, *adj.* trustworthy, trusty, dependable, infallible, unfailing. *Ant.* unreliable, untrustworthy, undependable.

relief, *n.* 1. deliverance, alleviation, ease, assuagement, mitigation, comfort. 2. help, assistance, aid, succor, redress, remedy. 3. release, replacement. *Ant.* intensity, intensification.

relieve, *v.* 1. ease, alleviate, assuage, mitigate, allay, lighten, comfort, soothe, lessen, abate, diminish. 2. unburden, disburden, ease. 3. aid, help, assist, succor, remedy, support, sustain. *Ant.* intensify, increase; burden.

religious, *adj.* 1. pious, holy, devout, faithful, reverent, godly. 2. conscientious, scrupulous, exacting, punctilious, strict, rigid, demanding. —*n.* 3. monk, friar, nun. *Ant.* irreligious, impious, unfaithful, irreverent; flexible, lenient.

relinquish, *v.* renounce, surrender, give up, resign, yield, cede, waive, forswear, forgo, abdicate, leave, forsake, desert, renounce, quit, abandon, let go, resign. *Ant.* demand, require.

relish, *n.* 1. liking, taste, enjoyment, appreciation, gusto, zest, inclination, bent, partiality, predilection, preference. 2. condiment, appetizer. 3. taste, flavor, savor. —*v.* 4. like, enjoy, appreciate, prefer. *Ant.* distaste, disfavor.

reluctant, *adj.* unwilling, disinclined, hesitant, loath, averse, indisposed. *Ant.* willing, agreeable, amenable, unhesitating.

remain, *v.* 1. continue, stay, last, abide, endure. 2. wait, tarry, delay, stay, rest. —*n.* (*plural*) 3. remnant, scrap, remainder, refuse, leavings, crumbs, orts, residue, relics. 4. corpse, dead body, cadaver. *Ant.* leave, depart.

remainder, *n.* residuum, remnant, excess, residue, rest, balance, surplus. *Ant.* insufficiency, inadequacy.

remark, *v.* 1. say, observe, note, perceive, heed, regard, notice. 2. comment, say, state. —*n.* 3. notice, regard, observation, heed, attention, consideration. 4. comment, utterance, note, observation, declaration, assertion, asseveration, statement. *Ant.* disregard, ignore; inattention.

remarkable, *adj.* notable, conspicuous, unusual, extraordinary, noteworthy, striking, wonderful, uncommon, strange, rare, distinguished, prominent, singular. *Ant.* common, usual, ordinary.

remedy, *n.* 1. cure, relief, medicine, treatment, restorative, specific, medicament, medication, ointment, nard, balm. 2. antidote, corrective, antitoxin, counteraction. —v. 3. cure, heal, put or set right, restore, recondition, repair, redress. 4. counteract, remove, correct, right. *Ant.* sicken, worsen.

remember, v. 1. recall, recollect. 2. retain, memorize, keep or bear in mind. *Ant.* forget.

remembrance, n. 1. recollection, reminiscence; memory. 2. keepsake, memento, souvenir, remembrancer, trophy, token, memorial.

remiss, adj. 1. negligent, careless, thoughtless, lax, neglectful; inattentive, heedless. 2. languid, sluggish, dilatory, slothful, slow, tardy, lax. *Ant.* careful, thoughtful, attentive; energetic, quick.

remission, n. 1. pardon, forgiveness, absolution, indulgence, exoneration, discharge. 2. abatement, diminution, lessening, relaxation, moderation, mitigation. 3. release, relinquishment. 4. decrease, subsidence, respite, stoppage, pause, interruption, relief, hiatus, suspense, suspension, abatement. *Ant.* blame, censure, conviction; increase, intensification; increase.

remissness, n. slackness, neglect, dilatoriness, languor, languidness. *Ant.* responsibility.

remit, v. 1. transmit, send, forward. 2. pardon, release, forgive, excuse, overlook, absolve. 3. slacken, abate, diminish, relax. 4. return, give back, restore, replace. 5. put off, postpone. *Ant.* retain, keep, hold; condemn; increase.

remnant, n. 1. remainder, remains, residue, residuum, rest. 2. trace, vestige.

remorse, n. regret, compunction, penitence, contrition. *Ant.* conviction, assertion, assertiveness.

remorseful, adj. regretful, penitent, contrite, repentant. *Ant.* impenitent.

remorseless, adj. relentless, pitiless, uncompassionate, unrelenting, merciless, unmerciful, ruthless, cruel, savage, implacable, inexorable. *Ant.* merciful, relenting.

remote, adj. 1. distant, far apart, far off, removed, alien, foreign, unrelated, unconnected. 2. slight, faint, inconsiderable. 3. separated, abstracted.

Ant. close, near, connected, related; considerable, substantial.

remove, v. 1. replace, displace, dislodge, transfer, transport, carry. 2. take, withdraw, separate, extract, eliminate. 3. kill, assassinate, do away with, destroy, murder.

rend, v. tear apart, split, divide, rip, rive, sunder, sever, cleave, chop, fracture, tear, dissever, crack, snap, lacerate, rupture.

render, v. 1. make, cause to be, cause to become. 2. do, perform. 3. furnish, supply, give, contribute, afford. 4. exhibit, show, demonstrate. 5. present, give, assign. 6. deliver. 7. translate, interpret. 8. give back, restore, return. 9. give up, surrender, cede, yield.

renew, v. 1. restore, replenish, restock. 2. re-create, rejuvenate, regenerate, restore, reinstate, renovate, repair, mend. 3. revive, reestablish.

renounce, v. 1. give up, put aside, forsake, forgo, relinquish, abandon, forswear, leave, quit, resign, abdicate. 2. repudiate, disown, disclaim, reject, disavow, deny, recant. *Ant.* claim, accept, desire.

renovate, v. renew.

renown, n. repute, fame, celebrity, glory, distinction, note, eminence, reputation, name, honor. *Ant.* disrepute, infamy.

rent, n. 1. rental, return, payment. 2. tear, split, fissure, slit, crack, crevice, cleft, rift, gap, opening, rip, rupture, breach, break, fracture, laceration. 3. schism, separation, disunion, breach. —v. 4. lease, let, hire.

repair, v. 1. restore, mend, remodel, renew, renovate, patch, amend, fix. 2. make good, make up for, remedy, retrieve. 3. make amends for, atone for, redress. *Ant.* break, destroy, ruin.

reparation, n. 1. (usually plural) amends, indemnification, atonement, restitution, satisfaction, compensation, Wiedergutmachung. 2. restoration, repair, renewal, renovation. *Ant.* destruction.

repay, v. payback, return, reimburse, indemnify, refund.

repeat, v. 1. reiterate, recapitulate, iterate, recite, rehearse, relate. 2. reproduce, echo, reecho, redo. —n. 3. repetition, iteration.

repel, v. 1. repulse, parry, ward off. 2. resist, withstand, rebuff, oppose, confront. 3. reject, decline, refuse, discourage. *Ant.* attract; approve, accept.

repent, v. regret, atone.

repentance, n. compunction, contrition; contriteness, penitence, remorse, sorrow, regret. *Ant.* impenitence.

replace, v. 1. supersede, supplant, substitute, succeed. 2. restore, return, make good, refund, repay; replenish.

reply, v. 1. answer, respond, echo, rejoin. —n. 2. answer, rejoinder, riposte, replication, surrejoinder, response.

represent, v. 1. designate, stand for, denote, symbolize, exemplify, image, depict, express, portray, personate, delineate, figure, present. 2. set forth, describe, state.

repress, v. 1. check, suppress, subdue, put down, quell, quash, reduce, crush. 2. check, restrain, curb, bridle, control. *Ant.* foster, support, help, aid.

reprisal, n. 1. retaliation, revenge, vengeance, redress. 2. vendetta.

reproach, v. 1. chide, abuse, reprimand, condemn, criticize, rebuke, scold, reprove, call to account, censure, blame, find fault with, shame, abash, discredit, reprehend, upbraid. —n. 2. blame, censure, upbraiding, reproof, abuse, vilification, discredit, reprehension, rebuke, criticism, remonstrance, condemnation, expostulation, disapproval, disapprobation. 3. disgrace, dishonor, shame, disrepute, odium, scandal, obloquy, opprobrium, ignominy, indignity, infamy, insult, scorn, offense. *Ant.* praise, honor.

reproduce, v. 1. copy, duplicate, repeat, imitate, represent. 2. generate, propagate, beget. *Ant.* initiate, originate.

reprove, v. rebuke, blame, censure, reproach, reprimand, upbraid, chide, lecture, reprehend, admonish, remonstrate or expostulate with. *Ant.* praise; exonerate.

repudiate, v. 1. reject, disclaim, disavow, disown, discard, renounce. 2. condemn, disapprove. *Ant.* accept; approve, commend.

repugnance, n. 1. objection, distaste, aversion, dislike, reluctance, hatred, hostility, antipathy. 2. contradictoriness, inconsistency, contrariety, unsuitableness, irreconcilableness, incompatibility. *Ant.* attractiveness, attraction, liking, sympathy; consistency, compatibility.

repugnant, *adj.* 1. distasteful, objectionable, offensive. 2. opposing, objecting, protesting, averse, unfavorable, antagonistic, inimical, adverse, contrary, hostile, opposed.
Ant. attractive, tasteful; favorable, amiable.

reputation, *n.* 1. estimation, regard, repute, standing, position, name, character. 2. credit, esteem, honor, fame, celebrity, distinction, renown.
Ant. disrepute; dishonor, infamy.

repute, *n.* 1. estimation, reputation. 2. name, distinction, credit, honor. —*v.* 3. consider, esteem, account, regard, hold, deem, reckon.
Ant. disrepute; dishonor; condemn, scorn.

request, *n.* 1. solicitation, petition, suit, entreaty, supplication, prayer. 2. demand. —*v.* 3. ask for, sue, petition, entreat, beg, supplicate, solicit, beseech, require.

require, *v.* 1. need, demand, request, order, enjoin, direct, ask. 2. obligate, necessitate, want, need, call for.
Ant. forgo.

requirement, *n.* 1. requisite, need, claim, requisition, prerequisite, demand. 2. mandate, order, command, directive, injunction, ukase, charge, claim, precept.

requisite, *adj.* 1. required, necessary, essential, indispensable, needed, needful. —*n.* 2. necessity, requirement.
Ant. dispensable, unnecessary; luxury, superfluity.

requite, *v.* 1. repay, remunerate, reimburse, recompense, pay, satisfy, compensate. 2. retaliate, avenge, revenge, punish.
Ant. dissatisfy; forgive.

rescue, *v.* 1. save, deliver, liberate, set free, release, redeem, ransom, extricate; recover, preserve. —*n.* 2. liberation, release, redemption, ransom, recovery, deliverance.
Ant. incarceration, imprisonment.

research, *n.* 1. inquiry, investigation, examination, scrutiny, study. —*v.* 2. investigate, study, inquire, examine, scrutinize.

resemblance, *n.* 1. similarity, likeness, analogy, semblance, similitude. 2. appearance, representation, semblance, image.
Ant. dissimilarity; misrepresentation.

reserve, *v.* 1. keep back, save, retain, husband, keep, hold, store up. 2. set apart, set aside, bank. —*n.* 3. reserva-

tion, qualification, exception. 4. store, stock, supply. 5. self-restraint, restraint, reticence, silence, taciturnity, constraint, coldness, coolness, retention.
Ant. splurge, squander, waste; prodigality; warmth, enthusiasm.

reside, *v.* 1. dwell, abide, live, sojourn, stay, lodge, inhabit, remain. 2. abide, lie, be present, habituate, inhere, exist.

residence, *n.* 1. dwelling, house, home, habitation, domicile, mansion, manse. 2. habitancy, stay, abode, sojourn, inhabitancy.

residue, *n.* remainder, rest, remains, residuum; surplus.

resign, *v.* 1. give up, submit, yield, cede, surrender, abdicate, relinquish, forgo, abandon, forsake, quit, leave. 2. renounce, withdraw.

resignation, *n.* 1. abdication, abandonment, surrender, relinquishment. 2. submission, meekness, patience, acquiescence, endurance, compliance, forbearance, sufferance.
Ant. application; boldness, recalcitrance.

resilient, *adj.* rebounding, elastic, recoiling; buoyant, cheerful.
Ant. rigid, inflexible, inelastic.

resist, *v.* 1. withstand, strive against, oppose, impugn, confront, assail, attack, counteract, rebuff. 2. refrain *or* abstain from.
Ant. defend; continue.

resolute, *adj.* resolved, firm, steadfast, determined, set, opinionated, purposeful, earnest, sincere, fixed, unflinching, unwavering, inflexible, hardy, unshaken, bold, undaunted, pertinacious.
Ant. weak, feeble, frail, flexible, lenient.

resolve, *v.* 1. fix *or* settle on, determine, decide, confirm, establish. 2. break up, disintegrate, separate, analyze, reduce. 3. convert, transform, reduce, change. 4. explain, explicate, solve. 5. clear, dispel, scatter, disperse. —*n.* 6. resolution, determination, decision, purpose, intention.
Ant. unite, amalgamate; consolidate; indecision.

respect, *n.* 1. particular, detail, point, regard, feature, matter. 2. relation, reference, connection, regard. 3. esteem, deference, regard, estimation, veneration, reverence, homage, honor, admiration, approbation, approval, affection, feeling. 4. discrimination, bias, partiality, prejudice,

preference, inclination. —*v.* 5. honor, revere, reverence, esteem, venerate, regard, consider, defer to, admire, adulate, adore, love. 6. regard, heed, attend, notice, consider. 7. regard, relate to, refer to.
Ant. disregard.

respectable, *adj.* 1. estimable, worthy, honorable. 2. proper, decent, honest, respected, reputable. 3. fair, fairly good, moderate, middling, passable, tolerable. 4. considerable, large, moderate.
Ant. unworthy, dishonorable; improper; poor, intolerable; small, insignificant.

respectful, *adj.* courteous, polite, well-mannered, well-bred, courtly, decorous, civil, deferential.
Ant. disrespectful, discourteous, impolite.

respite, *n.* 1. relief, delay, hiatus, cessation, postponement, interval, rest, recess. 2. stay, reprieve, suspension. —*v.* 3. relieve, delay, alleviate, postpone, put off, suspend.
Ant. intensity, perseverance.

response, *n.* answer, reply, rejoinder, replication.

responsible, *adj.* 1. accountable, answerable, liable. 2. chargeable, blamable, censurable. 3. capable, able, reliable, solvent, trustworthy, trusty, dutiful, honest.
Ant. irresponsible; innocent; incapable, unable, unreliable.

restful, *adj.* calm, tranquil, peaceful, undisturbed, serene, pacific.
Ant. perturbed, disturbed, agitated.

restitution, *n.* reparation, redress, indemnification, restoration, recompense, amends, compensation, remuneration, requital, satisfaction, repayment, *Wiedergutmachung.*

restive, *adj.* 1. uneasy, restless, nervous, impatient, ill at ease, recalcitrant, unquiet. 2. refractory, disobedient, obstinate, mulish, stubborn, pigheaded.
Ant. restful, patient, quiet, serene; obedient.

restore, *v.* 1. reestablish, replace, reinstate, renew. 2. renew, renovate, repair, mend. 3. return, give back. 4. reproduce, reconstruct, rebuild.
Ant. disestablish, destroy; break, ruin; accept, receive; raze.

restrain, *v.* 1. check, keep down, repress, curb, bridle, suppress, hold, keep, constrain. 2. restrict, circumscribe, confine, hinder, abridge, narrow.
Ant. unbridle; broaden, widen.

restrict, *v.* confine, limit, restrain, abridge, curb, circumscribe, bound. *Ant.* free, broaden, disencumber.

result, *n.* 1. outcome, consequence, effect, conclusion, issue, event, end, termination, product, fruit. —*v.* 2. spring, arise, proceed, follow, flow, come, issue, ensue, rise, originate. 3. terminate, end, resolve, eventuate. *Ant.* cause.

retain, *v.* 1. keep, hold, withhold, preserve, detain, reserve. 2. remember, recall. 3. hire, engage, employ. *Ant.* loose, lose; forget; disengage, fire.

retaliate, *v.* avenge, requite, return, repay, revenge. *Ant.* forgive, pardon.

retard, *v.* slow, delay, hinder, impede, decelerate, clog, obstruct, check. *Ant.* speed, expedite, accelerate.

reticent, *adj.* taciturn, silent, reserved, quiet, uncommunicative. *Ant.* voluble, communicative.

retire, *v.* withdraw, leave, depart, go away, retreat, retrograde, retrocede, fall back, recede; retract. *Ant.* advance, attack.

retired, *adj.* withdrawn, secluded, sequestered, cloistered, isolated, enisled, removed, apart, solitary, abstracted. *Ant.* advanced.

retort, *v.* 1. reply, respond, return, answer, retaliate, rejoin. —*n.* 2. reply, response, answer, riposte, rejoinder, surrejoinder, replication; repartee.

retreat, *n.* 1. departure, withdrawal, retirement, seclusion, privacy, solitude. 2. shelter, refuge, asylum. —*v.* 3. retire, retrocede, retrograde, withdraw, leave, depart, draw back. 4. recede, slope backward. *Ant.* advance.

retribution, *n.* requital, revenge, vengeance, retaliation, repayment, reward, recompense, compensation. *Ant.* forgiveness, pardon.

retrieve, *v.* 1. recover, regain, restore. 2. make good, repair, make amends for. 3. rescue, save.

reveal, *v.* make known, communicate, disclose, divulge, unveil, uncover, discover, publish, impart, tell, announce, proclaim. *Ant.* conceal, hide, veil, cover.

revenge, *n.* 1. vengeance, retaliation, requital, reprisal, retribution. 2. vindictiveness, revengefulness, vengefulness. —*v.* 3. avenge, retaliate, requite, vindicate. *Ant.* forgiveness, pardon.

revengeful, *adj.* vindictive, spiteful, malevolent, resentful, malicious, malignant, implacable. *Ant.* forgiving, benevolent.

reverence, *n.* 1. worship, veneration, respect, homage, awe. 2. bow, curtsy, obeisance. —*v.* 3. venerate, revere, honor, adore, adulate. *Ant.* disrespect; despise.

reverse, *adj.* 1. opposite, contrary, converse. —*n.* 2. opposite, contrary, converse, counterpart. 3. back, rear, hind. 4. check, misfortune, defeat, mishap, misadventure, affliction. —*v.* 5. transpose, invert. 6. alter, change. 7. revoke, annul, repeal, veto, rescind, overthrow, countermand. *Ant.* same.

review, *n.* 1. critique, criticism, judgment, survey. 2. rereading, study, reconsideration, reexamination. 3. inspection, examination, investigation. —*v.* 4. survey, inspect, criticize.

revive, *v.* 1. reactivate, revitalize, reanimate, resuscitate, revivify, reinvigorate, reinspirit. 2. bring back, quicken, renew, refresh, rouse. 3. recover, recall, reawake. *Ant.* kill; languish, die.

revoke, *v.* take back, withdraw, annul, cancel, reverse, rescind, repeal, retract.

revolt, *v.* 1. rebel, mutiny, rise. 2. disgust, repel, shock, nauseate, sicken. —*n.* 3. insurrection, rebellion, mutiny, revolution, uprising, overthrow, sedition. 4. aversion, disgust, loathing. *Ant.* attract, delight.

revolution, *n.* 1. overthrow, change, revolt, rebellion, mutiny. 2. cycle, rotation, circuit, turn, round.

revolve, *v.* 1. rotate, spin, circulate, turn, roll. 2. orbit, circle. 3. consider, think about, ruminate upon, ponder, reflect upon, brood over, study.

reward, *n.* 1. recompense, prize, desert, compensation, pay, remuneration, requital, merit. 2. bounty, premium, bonus. —*v.* 3. recompense, requite, compensate, pay, remunerate.

ribald, *adj.* scurrilous, offensive, coarse, mocking, abusive, wanton, irreverent, loose, indecent, low, base, mean, vile, obscene, gross, filthy, dirty, vulgar. *Ant.* pure, inoffensive, refined, polished, elegant.

rich, *adj.* 1. well-to-do, wealthy, moneyed, opulent, affluent. 2. abounding, abundant, bounteous, bountiful, fertile, plenteous, plentiful, copious, ample, luxuriant, productive, fruitful, prolific. 3. valuable, valued, precious, costly, estimable, sumptuous. 4. dear, expensive, high-priced, elegant. 5. deep, strong, vivid, bright, gay. 6. full, mellow, pear-shaped, harmonious, sweet. 7. fragrant, aromatic. *Ant.* poor, impoverished; scarce, barren, sterile; cheap; weak; dull; flat; noisome.

riddle, *n.* 1. conundrum, puzzle, enigma, poser, question, problem. 2. sieve, colander, strainer. —*v.* 3. perforate, pierce, puncture.

ridicule, *n.* 1. derision, mockery, gibes, jeers, taunts, raillery, satire, burlesque, sarcasm, sneer, banter, wit, irony. —*v.* 2. deride, banter, rally, chaff, twit, mock, taunt, make fun of, sneer at, burlesque, satirize, rail at, lampoon, jeer *or* scoff at. *Ant.* praise, honor; respect.

ridiculous, *adj.* absurd, preposterous, laughable, nonsensical, funny, ludicrous, droll, comical, farcical. *Ant.* sensible.

rife, *adj.* 1. common, prevalent, widespread, prevailing. 2. current. 3. abundant, plentiful, numerous, plenteous, abounding, multitudinous. *Ant.* rare, unusual; scarce, scanty.

right, *adj.* 1. just, good, equitable, fair, upright, honest, lawful. 2. correct, proper, suitable, fit, appropriate, convenient, becoming, *de rigueur*, befitting, seemly, *comme il faut*. 3. correct, true, accurate. 4. sound, sane, normal. 5. healthy. 6. principal, front, upper, obverse. 7. genuine, legitimate, rightful. 8. straight, true, direct. —*n.* 9. claim, title, due, ownership. 10. virtue, justice, fairness, integrity, equity, equitableness, uprightness, rectitude, goodness, lawfulness. —*adv.* 11. straight, directly. 12. quite, completely. 13. immediately. 14. precisely, exactly, just, truly, actually. 15. uprightly, righteously, rightfully, lawfully, rightly, justly, fairly, equitably. 16. properly, fittingly, appropriately, fitly, suitably. 17. advantageously, favorably, well. *Ant.* wrong.

righteous, *adj.* moral, upright, justifiable, virtuous, good, honest, fair, right, equitable. *Ant.* immoral, bad, dishonest, unfair.

rigid, *adj.* 1. stiff, unyielding, unbending, firm, hard, inflexible. 2. unmoving, immovable, static, stationary. 3. inflexible, strict, severe, stern, rigorous, austere, unbending, harsh, stringent, inelastic.

Ant. flexible, soft; compliant, elastic, lenient.

rigorous, *adj.* 1. rigid, severe, harsh, stern, austere, strict, hard, inflexible, stiff, unyielding, stringent. 2. exact, demanding, finical, accurate. 3. inclement, bitter, severe, sharp.

Ant. flexible, soft; inaccurate; fair, mild, bland.

rim, *n.* 1. edge, border, lip, margin, brim, boundary, verge, skirt, confine. —*v.* 2. edge, border, bound, margin, confine.

Ant. center, inside.

ring, *n.* 1. circlet, loop, hoop; annulus. 2. arena, rink, circle. 3. competition, contest. 4. clique, coterie, set, combination, confederacy, league; gang, mob, syndicate. —*v.* 5. surround, encircle, circle. 6. peal, resonate, vibrate, reverberate, resound, reecho; tinkle, jingle, jangle. 7. announce, proclaim, usher in *or* out, summon, call, signal.

riot, *n.* 1. outbreak, disorder, brawl, uproar, tumult, disturbance, commotion, fray, melee, altercation. 2. disorder, confusion. 3. revelry, festivity. —*v.* 4. create disorder, disturb the peace, create a disturbance, brawl, fight. 5. carouse, revel.

rip, *v.* 1. cut, tear, tear apart, slash, slit, rend. —*n.* 2. rent, tear, laceration, cut.

ripe, *adj.* 1. mature, mellow, grown, aged. 2. ruddy, full, complete, consummate, perfect, finished. 3. developed, ready, prepared, set.

Ant. immature; imperfect, unfinished; undeveloped, unprepared.

ripple, *v.* 1. wave, undulate, ruffle, purl. 2. agitate, curl, dimple. —*n.* 3. wavelet, wave, ruffling, undulation.

rise, *v.* 1. get up, arise, stand, stand up. 2. revolt, rebel, oppose, resist. 3. spring up, grow. 4. come into existence, appear, come forth. 5. occur, happen. 6. originate, issue, arise, come up, be derived, proceed. 7. move upward, ascend, mount, arise. 8. succeed, be promoted, advance. 9. swell, puff up, enlarge, increase. 10. adjourn, close. —*n.* 11. rising, ascent, mounting. 12. advance, elevation, promotion. 13. increase, augmentation, enlargement, swelling. 14. source, origin, beginning.

Ant. sink; support; die; fail; decrease, deflate; open; end.

risk, *n.* 1. hazard, chance, dangerous chance, venture, peril, jeopardy, exposure. —*v.* 2. hazard, take a chance, endanger, imperil; jeopardize. 3. venture upon, dare.

rite, *n.* ceremony, procedure, practice, observance, form, usage.

ritual, *n.* 1. ceremony, rite. —*adj.* 2. ceremonial, formal, sacramental.

Ant. unceremonious, informal.

rival, *n.* 1. competitor, contestant, emulator, antagonist, opponent. —*adj.* 2. competing, competitive, opposed, emulating, opposing. —*v.* 3. compete *or* contend with, oppose. 4. match, equal, emulate.

Ant. ally, friend; associate with.

roam, *v.* walk, go, travel, ramble, wander, peregrinate, rove, stray, stroll, range; prowl.

roar, *v.* 1. cry, bellow, bawl, shout, yell, vociferate. 2. laugh. 3. resound, boom, thunder, peal.

rob, *v.* 1. rifle, sack, steal, deprive, plunder, pillage, pilfer, pinch, shoplift. 2. defraud, cheat, deprive, rook.

robber, *n.* thief, highwayman, footpad, second-story man, kleptomaniac, shoplifter, pilferer, brigand, bandit, marauder, freebooter, pirate, picaroon, filibuster.

robust, *adj.* 1. sturdy, healthy, strong, hardy, vigorous, stalwart, hale, dusty, powerful, firm, sound, athletic, brawny, muscular, sinewy. 2. rough, rude, coarse, boisterous, rambunctious, wild.

Ant. weak, feeble, unhealthy; refined, cultivated.

rogue, *n.* rascal, scamp, rapscallion, knave, mischief-maker, villain, scoundrel, scapegrace, trickster, swindler, cheat, mountebank, quack, sharper.

roll, *v.* 1. turn, revolve, rotate, wheel, gyrate, spin, whirl, bowl. 2. wave, undulate. 3. sway, rock, swing, list, tilt. 4. wrap, enfold, envelop, cover. —*n.* 5. scroll, document. 6. register, list, inventory, catalogue, roster. 7. cylinder, roller, spindle.

roly-poly, *adj.* fat, plump, rotund, five-by-five, pudgy.

Ant. scrawny, gaunt, skinny.

romance, *n.* 1. novel, *roman,* tale, story, fiction. 2. fancy, extravagance, exaggeration; falsehood, fable, fiction, lie. 3. love affair, amour.

romantic, *adj.* 1. fanciful, unpractical, quixotic, extravagant, exaggerated, wild, imaginative, unrealistic, fantastic. 2. improbable, imaginary, fantastic, chimerical, fic-

titious, fabulous, unreal. 3. picturesque.

Ant. practical, realistic; probable.

rook, *n.* 1. crow, raven. 2. castle. 3. sharper, cardsharp, cheat, swindler. —*v.* 4. cheat, swindle, rob, fleece, defraud.

rosy, *adj.* 1. pink, reddish, roseate. 2. red, rubicund, flushed, blooming, ruddy, healthy. 3. bright, promising, cheerful, optimistic.

Ant. dark, dim, cheerless, pessimistic.

rot, *v.* 1. decompose, decay, mold, molder, putrefy, spoil, corrupt. 2. corrupt, degenerate. —*n.* 3. decay, putrefaction, decomposition, corruption, mold.

Ant. purify.

rotate, *v.* turn, spin, revolve, wheel, whirl.

rotten, *adj.* 1. decomposed, decayed, putrefied, putrescent, putrid, tainted, foul, miasmatic, noxious, ill-smelling, fetid, rank. 2. corrupt, offensive, amoral, immoral. 3. contemptible, disgusting, unwholesome, treacherous, dishonest, deceitful, corrupt. 4. soft, yielding, friable; unsound, defective.

Ant. pure; moral; wholesome, honest; hard, inflexible; sound.

roué, *n.* debauchee, rake, profligate.

rough, *adj.* 1. uneven, bumpy, irregular, rugged, jagged, scabrous, craggy. 2. shaggy, coarse, hairy, bristly, hirsute. 3. violent, disorderly, wild, boisterous, turbulent, riotous; sharp, severe, harsh. 4. disturbed, stormy, agitated, tempestuous, inclement. 5. harsh, grating, jarring, noisy, cacophonous, inharmonious, discordant, flat, raucous. 6. uncultured, indelicate, unrefined, impolite, uncivil, unpolished, rude, inconvenient, uncomfortable, crude, coarse. 7. plain, imperfect, unpolished, uncorrected, unfinished. 8. vague, inexact, incomplete. 9. crude, unwrought, undressed, unpolished, unprepared, unset, uncut.

Ant. even, regular; bald, hairless, smooth; orderly; fair; harmonious; cultured, refined; finished, polished; precise, exact; dressed, polished.

round, *adj.* 1. circular, disklike. 2. ring-shaped, hooplike, annular. 3. curved, arched. 4. cylindrical. 5. spherical, globular, rotund, orbed. 6. full, complete, entire, whole, unbroken. 7. full, sonorous. 8. vigorous, brisk, smart, quick. 9. plain, honest, straightforward, candid, outspoken, frank, open, upright, fair. 10. unmodified, positive, unqualified. —*n.* 11. circle, ring, curve. 12. cylinder, rung. 13. course, cycle, revolution, period, series, succession. *Ant.* angular, square, rectangular, polygonal.

rouse, *v.* 1. stir, excite, animate, kindle, fire, inflame, stimulate, awaken, provoke. 2. anger, provoke, incite, ire. *Ant.* calm; pacify.

rove, *v.* roam, wander, range, ramble, stroll, amble, stray.

royal, *adj.* regal, majestic, kingly, imperial, princely. *Ant.* servile.

rude, *adj.* 1. discourteous, unmannerly, ill-mannered, impolite, unrefined, uncivil, coarse, curt, brusque, saucy, pert, impertinent, impudent, fresh. 2. unlearned, untutored, uneducated, untaught, ignorant, uncultured, unrefined, untrained, uncivilized, uncouth, vulgar, boorish. 3. rough, harsh, ungentle, coarse, rugged, crude. 4. unwrought, raw, crude, rough, shapeless, amorphous. 5. inartistic, inelegant, primitive, rustic, artless, simple, unadorned, unpolished, undecorated. 6. violent, tempestuous, stormy, fierce, tumultuous, turbulent. 7. robust, sturdy, vigorous. *Ant.* courteous, mannerly; learned; gentle; artistic, elegant; calm.

rudimentary, *adj.* 1. rudimental, elementary, fundamental, primary, initial. 2. undeveloped, embryonic, elementary, imperfect. 3. vestigial, abortive. *Ant.* advanced; mature, perfect; complete.

ruffle, *v.* 1. disarrange, rearrange, disorder, rumple, wrinkle, damage, derange. 2. disturb, discompose, irritate, vex, annoy, upset, agitate, trouble, torment, plague, harry, harass, worry, molest. —*n.* 3. disturbance, perturbation, annoyance, vexation, confusion, commotion, flurry, tumult, bustle, agitation. 4. frill, trimming; ruff. 5. drumbeat. *Ant.* arrange, order; compose; composure, peace.

rugged, *adj.* 1. broken, uneven, rocky, hilly, craggy, irregular. 2. wrinkled, furrowed. 3. rough, harsh, stern, severe, hard, stormy, austere. 4. severe, hard, trying, difficult. 5. tempestuous, stormy, rough. 6. harsh, grating, inharmonious, cacophonous, scabrous. 7. rude, uncultivated, unrefined, unpolished, crude. 8. homely, plain, ugly. *Ant.* even, smooth, regular; easy, flexible; fair; harmonious; cultivated, refined; pretty, lovely, beautiful.

ruin, *n.* 1. decay, dilapidation, ruination, perdition, destruction, havoc, damage, disintegration, devastation, spoliation. 2. downfall, destruction, decay, fall, overthrow, defeat, undoing, subversion, wreck. —*v.* 3. spoil, demolish, destroy, damage, reduce to ruin. *Ant.* construction; creation; create, build.

rule, *n.* 1. principle, regulation, standard, law, canon, ruling, guide, precept, order, ukase. 2. control, government, dominion, command, domination, mastery, sway, authority, direction. —*v.* 3. administer, command, govern, manage, control, handle, lead, direct, guide, conduct. 4. decree, decide, deem, judge, settle, establish, order, demand.

ruminate, *v.* 1. chew cud. 2. ponder, muse, think, meditate, reflect.

rumor, *n.* story, talk, gossip, hearsay, bruit, news, report.

run, *v.* 1. race, hasten, hurry, hie, scud, speed, scamper. 2. flow, pour, stream; go, move, proceed. 3. melt, fuse, liquefy. 4. leak, overflow, flood, spread. 5. creep, trail, climb. 6. operate, continue. 7. extend, stretch, reach, spread. 8. contend, compete, challenge. 9. pursue, hunt, chase. 10. convey, transport, ferry, carry. 11. pierce, stab, thrust, force, drive. 12. operate, carry on, conduct, manage. 13. melt, fuse, smelt, liquefy. —*n.* 14. period, spell, interval. 15. series, set, course, passage, motion, extent, progress. 16. stream, rivulet, rill, runnel, brook, channel, burn. 17. ordinary, standard, average, regular. 18. way, track. 19. herd, school, pack, bevy, covey, brood, flock, gaggle, pride; group, company, crowd.

rupture, *n.* 1. breaking, bursting; breach, fracture, break, split, burst, disruption. 2. hernia. —*v.* 3. break, fracture, split, burst, disrupt, separate. *Ant.* seam, union; unite, organize.

rural, *adj.* rustic, unsophisticated, rugged, rough; crude, boorish. *Ant.* urban.

rush, *v.* 1. dash, hasten, run. 2. attack, overcome. —*v.* 3. busyness, haste, hurry. 4. straw, reeds, fiber. *Ant.* sloth, lethargy.

rustic, *adj.* rural. *Ant.* urban.

ruthless, *adj.* pitiless, merciless, unpitying, unmerciful, cruel, hard, harsh, severe, hard-hearted, uncompassionate, unrelenting, adamant, relentless, inexorable, fell, truculent, inhuman, ferocious, savage, barbarous. *Ant.* merciful, compassionate, humane.

S

Sabbath, *n.* Lord's day, Sunday, day of rest.

sack, *n.* 1. bag, pouch. 2. pillaging, looting, plundering, pillage, destruction, devastation, desolation, spoliation, ruin, ruination, waste, ravage, rapine. —*v.* 3. pillage, loot, rob, spoil, despoil, ruin, lay waste, plunder, devastate, demolish, destroy, ravage, rape.

sacred, *adj.* 1. consecrated, holy, sainted, venerable, hallowed, divine, worshipful. 2. dedicated, consecrated, revered. 3. secure, protected, sacrosanct, immune, inviolate, inviolable.
Ant. blasphemous.

sad, *adj.* 1. sorrowful, mournful, unhappy, despondent, disconsolate, depressed, dejected, melancholy, discouraged, gloomy, downcast, downhearted. 2. somber, dark, dull. 3. grievous, deplorable, disastrous, dire, calamitous.
Ant. happy.

safe, *adj.* 1. secure, protected, sound, guarded. 2. dependable, trustworthy, sure, reliable. 3. cautious, wary, careful. —*n.* 4. repository, strongbox, coffer, chest, safe deposit box.
Ant. unsafe.

saga, *n.* edda, epic, tale, tradition, legend, history.

sagacious, *adj.* wise, sage, shrewd, discerning, clever, intelligent, judicious, rational, acute, sharp, keen, perspicacious, sharp-witted.
Ant. unwise, irrational.

sage, *n.* 1. wise man, philosopher. —*adj.* 2. prudent, sagacious.
Ant. dolt; imprudent.

sailor, *n.* mariner, salt, tar, seaman, seafarer, seafaring man.
Ant. landlubber.

sake, *n.* 1. cause, account, interest, score, regard, consideration, respect, reason. 2. purpose, end, reason.

salacious, *adj.* lustry, lecherous, rakish, lewd, carnal, wanton, lascivious, libidinous, concupiscent; obscene, pornographic, prurient.
Ant. modest, prudish.

salient, *adj.* prominent, conspicuous, important, remarkable, striking.
Ant. inconspicuous; unimportant.

salutary, *adj.* healthy, health-giving, salubrious, wholesome.
Ant. unwholesome.

same, *adj.* 1. identical; similar, like, corresponding, interchangeable, equal. 2. agreeing; unchanging.
Ant. different; disagreeing.

sameness, *n.* identity, uniformity, monotony.
Ant. difference.

sample, *n.* specimen, example, illustration, pattern, model.

sanction, *n.* 1. authority, permission, countenance, support, ratification, solemnification, authorization. —*v.* 2. authorize, countenance, approve, confirm, ratify, support, allow, bind.
Ant. disapproval; disallow, disapprove.

sanctuary, *n.* church, temple, shrine, altar, sanctum, adytum.

sanguinary, *adj.* bloody, murderous, bloodthirsty, cruel, savage, fell, ruthless, truculent, pitiless, unmerciful, merciless.
Ant. merciful, kind.

sanguine, *adj.* cheerful, hopeful, confident, enthusiastic, buoyant, animated, lively, spirited.
Ant. morose, dispirited.

sanitary, *adj.* hygienic, unpolluted, clean, germfree; healthy, salutary.
Ant. polluted; unhealthy, unwholesome.

sapient, *adj.* wise, sage, sagacious.
Ant. stupid, dull, unwise.

sarcasm, *n.* irony, derision, bitterness, ridicule; taunt, gibe, jeer.

sarcastic, *adj.* cynical, biting, cutting, mordant, bitter, derisive, ironical, sardonic, satirical.

sardonic, *adj.* sarcastic, bitter, ironical, sneering, malignant, malicious.

satanic, *adj.* evil, wicked, diabolical, devilish, infernal, hellish, malicious, fiendish.
Ant. godly, angelic, benevolent.

satiate, *v.* cloy, glut, stuff, gorge, sate, surfeit; gall, disgust, weary.

satire, *n.* irony, sarcasm, ridicule, lampoon, pasquinade, burlesque, exposure, denunciation.

satirical, *adj.* cynical, sarcastic, sardonic, ironical, taunting, biting, keen, sharp, cutting, severe, mordant, mordacious, bitter, acid.

satisfaction, *n.* 1. gratification, enjoyment, pleasure, contentment, ease, comfort. 2. reparation, restitution, amends, expiation, atonement, compensation, indemnification, re-

muneration, recompense, requital, *Wiedergutmachung.* 3. payment, discharge, repayment.
Ant. dissatisfaction, displeasure, discomfort.

satisfy, *v.* 1. gratify, meet, appease, pacify, content, please. 2. fulfill, fill, satiate, sate, suffice, surfeit. 3. assure, convince, persuade.
Ant. dissatisfy, displease.

saturate, *v.* soak, impregnate, imbue, wet, ret, drench.
Ant. ted, dry.

saunter, *v.* stroll, walk, ramble, amble.

savage, *adj.* 1. wild, rugged, uncultivated, sylvan, rough. 2. barbarous, uncivilized, rude, unpolished, wild. 3. fierce, ferocious, wild, untamed, feral, ravenous. 4. enraged, furious, angry, irate, infuriated. 5. cruel, brutal, beastly; inhuman, fell, merciless, unmerciful, pitiless, ruthless, bloodthirsty, truculent, sanguinary.
Ant. cultivated, cultured; tame; calm; merciful.

save, *v.* 1. rescue, salvage, preserve. 2. safeguard, keep. 3. set apart, reserve, lay by, economize, hoard, store up, husband. —*prep., conj.* 4. except, but.

savor, *n.* 1. taste, flavor, relish; odor, scent, fragrance. —*v.* 2. flavor, season, spice.

say, *v.* 1. utter, pronounce, speak, remark, affirm, allege. 2. express, state, word, declare, tell, argue. 3. recite, repeat, iterate, reiterate, rehearse. 4. report, allege, maintain, hold.

scale, *n.* 1. plate, lamina, flake, peel. 2. coating, crust, incrustation. 3. pan, dish. 4. (*plural*) balance. 5. steps, degrees, series, gradation, progression. —*v.* 6. skip, play at ducks and drakes. 7. weigh, balance. 8. climb, ascend, mount. 9. progress, gradate.

scandal, *n.* 1. disgrace, damage, discredit, dishonor, offense, shame, disrepute, opprobrium, odium, ignominy. 2. defamation, gossip, slander, character assassination, aspersion, detraction, calumny, obloquy.
Ant. honor, repute; praise, kudos.

scanty, *adj.* meager, sparse, insufficient, inadequate, deficient, thin, spare, small, paltry, poor, stinted, gaunt, lean.
Ant. abundant, adequate.

scarce, *adj.* rare, insufficient, deficient; uncommon, infrequent.
Ant. abundant, sufficient.

scarcely, *adv.* hardly, barely, not quite, scantly.
Ant. definitely, full.

scare, *v.* 1. terrify, alarm, startle, frighten, shock, intimidate. —*n.* 2. fright, terror, alarm, panic.

scatter, *v.* 1. sprinkle, broadcast, strew. 2. dispel, disperse, dissipate, separate, drive away.
Ant. gather.

scene, *n.* 1. arena, stage, theater. 2. view, picture, prospect, landscape. 3. incident, episode, situation. 4. exhibition, demonstration, spectacle, show, display.

scent, *n.* 1. odor, aroma, fragrance, smell, savor, redolence, perfume. 2. track, trail, spoor. —*v.* 3. detect, perceive, smell.

schedule, *n.* 1. roll, catalogue, table, list, inventory, register. 2. timetable. —*v.* 3. enter, register, list, enroll, tabulate, classify.

scheme, *n.* 1. plan, design, program, project, system. 2. plot, intrigue, stratagem, cabal, conspiracy, contrivance, machination. 3. system, pattern, diagram, schema, arrangement. —*v.* 4. plan, plot, contrive, project, devise, design.

scholar, *n.* 1. savant, wise man, sage. 2. student, pupil, disciple, learner.
Ant. teacher.

scholarship, *n.* learning, knowledge, erudition, wisdom.
Ant. stupidity.

scoff, *n., v.* mock, scorn, jeer, gibe, sneer, taunt, ridicule.
Ant. envy, praise, exalt.

scold, *v.* 1. chide, reprove, reproach, rate, berate, censure, rail at, reprimand, blame, rebuke. —*n.* 2. nag, shrew, virago, termagant, maenad, bacchante.
Ant. praise, honor.

scope, *n.* range, extent, space, opportunity, margin, room, latitude, liberty; tract, area, length.

scorch, *v.* 1. burn, singe, char, blister, parch, shrivel. 2. criticize, excoriate, condemn.
Ant. praise, laud.

score, *n.* 1. record, account, reckoning. 2. notch, scratch, stroke, line, mark. 3. twenty. 4. account, reason, ground, consideration, motive, purpose. —*v.* 5. record, reckon, tabulate, count. 6. notch, mark, scratch, cut. 7. gain, win.

scorn, *n.* 1. contempt, disdain, contumely. 2. mockery, derision, scoff, sneer. —*v.* 3. disdain, contemn, despise, detest.
Ant. affection, pleasure.

scoundrel, *n.* villain, knave, rogue, poltroon, scamp, cad, rascal, rapscallion, miscreant, trickster, sharper, cheat, mountebank, wretch.
Ant. hero, protagonist.

scourge, *n.* 1. whip, lash, strap, thong. 2. flogging, punishment. 3. affliction, calamity, plague, band, pest, nuisance. —*v.* 4. lash, whip. 5. punish, chastise, chasten, correct, castigate, afflict, torment.

scrap, *n.* 1. fragment, piece, portion; morsel, crumb, bit, bite. —*adj.* 2. fragmentary, piecemeal; waste. —*v.* 3. break up, demolish. 4. throw away, discard.
Ant. whole.

scream, *v.* 1. shriek, screech, cry, screak. —*n.* 2. outcry, cry, shriek, screech, screak.

screen, *n.* 1. partition, shelter, cover, protection, guard, shield, defense. 2. sieve, riddle, grating. —*v.* 3. shelter, protect, veil, defend, shield, conceal, hide, cover, cloak, mask, shroud. 4. sift.

scruple, *n.* 1. hesitation, reluctance, conscience, restraint, compunction, qualm. —*v.* 2. hesitate, waver, doubt.

scrupulous, *adj.* 1. conscientious, reluctant, hesitant, cautious, wary, careful, circumspect. 2. punctilious, minute, careful, exacting, exact, precise, demanding, rigorous.
Ant. unscrupulous; careless.

scrutinize, *v.* examine, investigate, dissect, study, sift.
Ant. neglect, overlook.

scrutiny, *n.* examination, investigation, dissection, study, inquiry, inspection, inquisition, search.

scurrilous, *adj.* 1. gross, indecent, abusive, opprobrious, vituperative, reproachful, insolent, insulting, offensive, ribald. 2. coarse, jocular, derisive, vulgar, obscene.
Ant. decent, polite; proper.

scurvy, *adj.* low, mean, base, contemptible, vile, despicable, worthless.
Ant. honorable, dignified, noble.

sear, *v.* 1. burn, char, singe, scorch. 2. brand, cauterize. 3. dry up, wither. 4. harden, callus.

search, *v.* 1. look for, seek, explore, investigate, examine, scrutinize, inspect. 2. probe; pierce, penetrate.

—*n.* 3. exploration, examination, investigation, inspection, scrutiny, searching, inquiry, inquisition, pursuit, quest.

seasonable, *adj.* suitable, timely, opportune, fit, convenient, appropriate.
Ant. unseasonable, unsuitable, untimely, inopportune.

seat, *n.* 1. chair, bench, banquette, easy chair, throne, stool. 2. bottom, base, fundament. 3. site, situation, location, locality, locale.

secede, *v.* abdicate, withdraw, retire, separate, resign.
Ant. join.

secluded, *adj.* withdrawn, isolated, retired, sequestered, private.
Ant. public.

secret, *adj.* 1. clandestine, hidden, concealed, covert, private, privy, unrevealed, mysterious, unknown, cabalistic, cryptic. 2. reticent, close-mouthed, secretive. 3. retired, secluded, private. 4. occult, obscure, mysterious, latent, abstruse, recondite. —*n.* 5. mystery.
Ant. open, manifest, obvious, apparent.

secrete, *v.* hide, conceal, cover, shroud, disguise.
Ant. open, manifest.

secure, *adj.* 1. safe, protected. 2. fixed, stable, fast, fastened. 3. sure, certain, confident, assured. —*v.* 4. obtain, procure, get, acquire, gain. 5. protect, guard, safeguard. 6. make certain, ensure, assure, guarantee. 7. make firm, fasten.
Ant. insecure; unstable; unsure; lose; unloose, loosen.

sedate, *adj.* calm, quiet, composed, sober, undisturbed, unexcited, staid, cool, collected, serene, placid, tranquil, unruffled, unperturbed, imperturbable, serious, settled, demure, grave, thoughtful, contemplative.
Ant. disturbed, perturbed, excited, nervous.

sediment, *n.* lees, dregs, grounds, precipitate.

sedition, *n.* treason, mutiny, rebellion, revolt, revolution, riot, insurrection, uprising.
Ant. allegiance, patriotism.

seduce, *v.* tempt, lead astray, corrupt, entice, beguile, inveigle, decoy, allure, lure, decoy, deceive.
Ant. repel, disgust.

seductive, *adj.* tempting, captivating, alluring, enticing, attractive, beguiling; deceptive.
Ant. repulsive, repellent, abhorrent.

see, *v.* 1. perceive, look at, spy, espy, notice, discern, observe, distinguish, behold, regard. 2. view, visit, watch. 3. perceive, discern, penetrate, understand, comprehend, remark. 4. learn, ascertain, find out, determine. 5. experience, live through, know, feel, meet with, suffer, undergo. 6. receive, entertain, visit with. 7. attend, escort, accompany. 8. consider, think, deliberate. —*n.* 9. diocese, bishopric.

seedy, *adj.* shabby, worn, old.
Ant. neat, tidy, trim, modern, new.

seek, *v.* 1. search for, look for. 2. pursue, follow, solicit, go after. 3. ask for, request, inquire after.

seem, *v.* appear, look; pretend, assume.

seemly, *adj.* fitting, becoming, suited, well-suited, suitable, appropriate, proper, befitting, meet; decent, decorous, right.
Ant. unseemly.

seep, *v.* ooze, osmose.
Ant. pour.

seethe, *v.* 1. soak, steep, ret, saturate. 2. boil; surge, foam, froth.

segregate, *v.* isolate, separate, set apart, dissociate.
Ant. unite, associate, blend; desegregate.

seize, *v.* 1. grasp, grab, clutch. 2. capture, take into custody, arrest, apprehend, catch, take.
Ant. loose.

seldom, *adv.* rarely, infrequently, not often.
Ant. often, frequently.

select, *v.* 1. choose, prefer, pick, pick out. —*adj.* 2. selected, chosen, preferred, choice, special, picked, valuable, excellent. 3. careful, fastidious, exclusive, selective.

self-evident, *adj.* evident, obvious, axiomatic, self-explanatory, clear.
Ant. mysterious.

self-governed, *adj.* self-governing, autonomous, independent.
Ant. dependent.

selfish, *adj.* self-interested, self-seeking, egoistic, illiberal, parsimonious, stingy, mean.
Ant. unselfish.

self-satisfied, *adj.* self-complacent, complacent, smug, satisfied.
Ant. dissatisfied.

sell, *v.* trade, barter, vend, exchange, deal in.
Ant. buy.

semblance, *n.* 1. appearance, aspect, form, show, exterior, mien, bearing, air. 2. likeness, similarity, resemblance.
Ant. dissimilarity, difference.

send, *v.* 1. transmit, dispatch, forward, convey. 2. impel, throw, cast, hurl, toss, propel, fling, project.
Ant. receive.

sensation, *n.* 1. sense, feeling, perception. 2. excitement, stimulation, animation; agitation, commotion, perturbation.

sensational, *adj.* startling, thrilling, exciting, stimulating.
Ant. prosaic, dull.

sense, *n.* 1. feeling, perception, sensation. 2. awareness, recognition, realization, apprehension, appreciation, understanding, consciousness. 3. perception, estimation, appreciation, discernment. 4. meaning, signification, signficance, import, interpretation, denotation, connotation. 5. opinion, judgment, feeling, idea, notion, sentiment. —*v.* 6. perceive, become aware of, discern, appreciate, recognize.

senseless, *adj.* 1. insensate, unconscious, insensible, inert, knocked out, cold. 2. unperceiving, undiscerning, unappreciative, unfeeling, apathetic, uninterested. 3. stupid, foolish, silly, idiotic, inane, simple, weak-minded, witless; nonsensical, meaningless, asinine.
Ant. sensitive; intelligent.

sensibility, *n.* 1. responsiveness, alertness, awareness, susceptibility, impressibility. 2. quickness, keenness, acuteness, sensitivity, sensitiveness. 3. consciousness, appreciation, understanding, rapport. 4. delicacy, sensitiveness, perceptiveness.
Ant. insensibility; dullness; boorishness.

sensible, *adj.* 1. judicious, intelligent, sagacious, sage, wise, rational, sound, sober, reasonable. 2. cognizant, aware, conscious, understanding, observant. 3. appreciable, considerable. 4. perceptible, discernible, identifiable.
Ant. insensible, irrational, unsound; unaware; trifling.

sensitive, *adj.* 1. impressionable, susceptible, easily affected. 2. sensate. 3. delicate.
Ant. insensitive; hard, obdurate, indelicate.

sensitivity, *n.* sensibility.

sensual, *adj.* 1. voluptuous, sensuous, luxurious. 2. lewd, unchaste, gross, licentious, lascivious, dissolute.
Ant. modest, prudish.

sensuous, *adj.* sentient, feeling, sensible.
Ant. insensible.

sententious, *adj.* 1. pithy, concise, laconic, epigrammatic, terse, succinct, didactic. 2. judicial, magisterial.
Ant. prosaic, prosy, long-drawn.

sentiment, *n.* 1. attitude, disposition, opinion, feeling, judgment, thought. 2. emotion, sentimentality, sensitiveness, sensibility, tenderness.
Ant. coolness.

sentimentality, *n.* sentiment.

separate, *v.* 1. keep apart, divide, part, put apart, disjoin, disconnect, dissever, sever, disunite, sunder, disengage, dissociate, split, break up. 2. withdraw, cleave. —*adj.* 3. separated, disjoined, disunited, unattached, apart, divided, severed, detached, distinct, discrete, dissociate; apart, withdrawn, sequestered, alone, isolated. 4. independent, individual, particular.
Ant. unite, connect; together, indistinct, conglomerate; dependent, general.

sepulcher, *n.* 1. tomb, grave, burial vault, ossuary. —*v.* 2. bury, entomb, inter.
Ant. cradle, womb; unearth, disinter.

sequence, *n.* 1. following, succession, order, arrangement, series. 2. outcome, sequel, consequence, result.

seraglio, *n.* harem.

serene, *adj.* 1. calm, peaceful, tranquil, unruffled, undisturbed, imperturbable, unperturbed, placid, composed, sedate, staid, collected, cool. 2. fair, clear, unclouded, bright.
Ant. active, disturbed, upset; clouded, inclement.

serenity, *n.* calmness, composure, tranquillity, peacefulness, calm, sereneness, peace.
Ant. perturbation, disturbance.

serf, *n.* slave, esne, ryot, bondman, villein, thrall.
Ant. master.

series, *n.* sequence, succession, set, line; order, arrangement.

serious, *adj.* 1. thoughtful, grave, solemn, sober, sedate, staid, earnest. 2. weighty, important, momentous, grave, critical.
Ant. jocular; trivial.

servant, *n.* domestic, maidservant, servant-girl, employee, maid, menial, servitor, attendant, retainer, butler, footman.
Ant. master.

serve, *v.* 1. wait on, attend. 2. assist, help, aid, succor. 3. function, answer, do, suffice. 4. promote, contribute, forward, advance, assist. 5. provide, cater, satisfy, purvey.

servile, *adj.* submissive, obsequious, menial, slavish, cringing, low, fawning, abject, mean, base, sycophantic, groveling.
Ant. aggressive, overbearing, dignified.

servitude, *n.* slavery, bondage, serfdom, thralldom.

set, *v.* 1. put, place, position, pose, locate, situate, post, appoint, station, plant. 2. value, price, rate, prize, evaluate, estimate. 3. fix, appoint, ordain, settle, establish, determine. 4. prescribe, assign, predetermine. 5. adjust, arrange, order, dispose, place, regulate. 6. frame, mount. 7. calibrate, regulate. 8. decline, sink, wane, go down. 9. solidify, congeal, harden. —*n.* 10. assortment, outfit, collection, series. 11. group, clique, coterie, company, circle, class, sect. 12. direction, bent, inclination, disposition, attitude. 13. bearing, carriage, mien, posture, appearance, aspect. 14. stage, scene, secenery, decoration, setting. —*adj.* 15. fixed, prefixed, predetermined. 16. prescribed, foreordained. 17. customary, usual. 18. fixed, rigid, immovable. 19. resolved, determined, habitual, stubborn, fixed, obstinate, stiff, unyielding.

settle, *v.* 1. fix, agree upon, set, establish. 2. pay, discharge, repay, liquidate. 3. locate in, people, colonize. 4. quiet, tranquilize, calm, compose, still, pacify. 5. stabilize, establish, confirm. 6. decide, arrange, agree, adjust. 7. calm down, rest. 8. sink down, decline, subside, sink, fall.

sever, *v.* separate, divide, put *or* cut apart, part, cut, cleave, sunder, break off, disunite, disjoin, detach, disconnect.
Ant. unite.

severe, *adj.* 1. harsh, extreme, trenchant, biting, acerb, bitter, caustic, satirical, keen, stinging, mordant, mordacious, sharp, cutting. 2. serious, grave, stern, austere, rigid, rigorous, strict, strait-laced, relentless, hard, unrelenting, inexorable, abrupt, peremptory, curt, short. 3. rigid, restrained, plain, simple, unadorned, unornamented, chaste. 4. uncomfortable, distressing, unpleasant, acute, afflictive, violent, intense. 5. rigid, exact, critical, demanding, accurate, methodical, systematic, exacting.

Ant. mild; gradual; flexible; comfortable; inaccurate.

shack, *n.* cottage, cot, hut, cabin, cote.
Ant. palace.

shackle, *n.* 1. fetter, chain, anklet, handcuff, manacle, gyve, hobble. 2. impediment, obstacle, obstruction, encumbrance. —*v.* 3. confine, restrain, restrict, fetter, chain, handcuff, hobble. 4. restrict, trammel, impede, slow, stultify, dull.
Ant. liberate, free.

shade, *n.* 1. darkness, shadow, obscurity, gloom, gloominess, dusk, umbrage. 2. specter, ghost, apparition, spirit, phantom. 3. variation, amount, degree, hair, trace, hint, suggestion. 4. veil, curtain, screen. —*v.* 5. obscure, dim, darken, cloud, blur, obfuscate. 6. screen, hide, protect, conceal, cover, shelter.
Ant. light.

shake, *v.* 1. sway, vibrate, oscillate, quiver, waver, tremble, agitate, shudder, shiver, totter. 2. brandish, flourish. 3. agitate, disturb, move, intimidate, frighten, daunt. 4. unsettle, weaken, enfeeble. —*n.* 5. tremor, blow, disturbance, shock.

sham, *n.* 1. imitation, pretense. —*adj.* 2. pretended, counterfeit, false, spurious, mock. —*v.* 3. pretend; imitate, deceive, feign, defraud, impose.
Ant. genuine.

shame, *n.* 1. humiliation, mortification, abashment, chagrin. 2. disgrace, derision, ignominy, dishonor, reproach, obloquy, opprobrium, odium, infamy, contempt. 3. scandal. —*v.* 4. abash, humiliate, mortify, humble, confuse, disconcert. 5. disgrace, reproach, dishonor, scandalize, debase, tarnish, stain, taint, sully, soil.
Ant. honor.

shameful, *adj.* disgraceful, scandalous, mortifying, humiliating, dishonorable, ignominious, disreputable, outrageous, infamous, vile, base, low.
Ant. honorable.

shameless, *adj.* 1. immodest, audacious, unblushing, brazen, indecent, impudent, bold, insolent, indelicate, unabashed, unashamed. 2. corrupt, sinful, unprincipled, depraved, profligate, piacular, dissolute, reprobate, vicious, hard, hardened, stony, obdurate, adamant, incorrigible, lost.
Ant. modest, proper, principled, flexible.

shanty, *n.* cottage, shack, cot, hut, hovel, cabin, house.
Ant. castle, palace.

shape, *n.* 1. outline, silhouette, form, figure, appearance, aspect. 2. phantom, specter, manifestation. 3. guise, disguise. 4. arrangement, order, pattern. 5. condition, situation, order. 6. mold, cast, pattern, form. —*v.* 7. form, fashion, mold, model. 8. word, express, term. 9. adjust, adapt, regulate, frame.

share, *n.* 1. portion, part, allotment, contribution, quota, lot, proportion. 2. dividend, stock. —*v.* 3. divide, apportion, allot, portion, parcel out, deal out, dole, mete out. 4. partake, participate.

sharp, *adj.* 1. keen, acute, trenchant. 2. pointed, peaked. 3. abrupt, sudden. 4. distinct, marked, clear. 5. pungent, biting, acrid, spicy, burning, hot, mordacious, bitter, piquant, sour. 6. shrill, piercing, loud, high. 7. cold, piercing, freezing, nipping, biting. 8. painful, distressing, intense, severe, sore, excruciating, agonizing. 9. harsh, merciless, unmerciful, severe, acute, cutting, caustic, acid, sarcastic, sardonic, acrimonious, pointed, biting, poignant. 10. fierce, violent, intense. 11. keen, eager, hungry. 12. quick, brisk. 13. vigilant, alert, awake, on the qui vive, attentive. 14. acute, shrewd, astute, clever, penetrating, discerning, perspicacious, ingenious, discriminating, ready, smart, cunning, intelligent, bright, quick, sensitive, alert, observant, incisive, vigorous, understanding, active, reasoning. 15. dishonest, shady, unlawful, deceitful, cheating.
Ant. dull; blunt; unclear; mild; soft; warm; merciful.

shatter, *v.* break, crush, shiver, split, crack; explode.

sheer, *adj.* 1. transparent, diaphanous, thin, clear. 2. unmixed, mere, simple, pure, downright, unadulterated, unqualified, utter. 3. steep, precipitous, abrupt, perpendicular. —*adv.* 4. clear, quite, completely, totally, entirely. —*n.* 5. chiffon, voile. —*v.* 6. swerve, deviate, turn aside.
Ant. opaque; gradual.

shelter, *n.* 1. protection, refuge, retreat, asylum, cover, screen, sanctuary, shield, haven, harbor. —*v.* 2. protect, guard, cover, safeguard, shield, hide, shroud, house, harbor, defend.
Ant. open.

shimmer, *v., n.* glisten, shine, gleam, glimmer.

shine, *v.* 1. beam, glare, gleam, glisten, glimmer, shimmer, sparkle, glow, radiate. —*n.* 2. radiance, light. 3. polish, luster, gloss.

shining, *adj.* 1. radiant, gleaming, bright, brilliant, resplendent, glistening, effulgent, lustrous. 2. conspicuous, fine, outstanding, distinguished, eminent, prime, splendid, choice, excellent, select.

shipment, *n.* freight, consignment, cargo, lading.

shiver, *v., n.* tremble, quake, shudder, shake.

shock, *n.* 1. blow, impact, collision, encounter, concussion, clash. 2. disturbance, commotion, agitation. —*v.* 3. startle, stagger, surprise, stun, astound, paralyze, stupefy, bewilder, dumfound. 4. horrify, disgust, outrage, nauseate, offend, sicken, revolt. 5. collide, strike, meet.

shore, *n.* 1. beach, coast, bank, seashore, riverbank, margin, strand. 2. support, prop, brace, buttress, stay, post, beam, strut.

short, *adj.* 1. brief; low. 2. concise, brief, terse, succinct, laconic, condensed, curt, sententious. 3. abrupt, curt, sharp, petulant, short-tempered, testy, uncivil, rude. 4. scanty, poor, insufficient, deficient, inadequate, wanting, lacking. 5. substandard, inferior, unacceptable, below. 6. friable, brittle, crumbly. 7. brachycephalic. —*adv.* 8. suddenly, abruptly, without notice *or* warning. 9. briefly, curtly. *Ant.* long.

shorten, *v.* 1. curtail, abbreviate, abridge, condense, lessen, limit, restrict, reduce. 2. take in, reduce, diminish, lessen, contract. *Ant.* lengthen.

short-sighted, *adj.* 1. myopic, nearsighted. 2. indiscreet, unthinking, thoughtless, imprudent, inconsiderate, tactless. *Ant.* presbyopic, far-sighted; discreet, thoughtful, prudent.

shout, *v.* cry out, hoot, exclaim, vociferate. *Ant.* whisper.

shove, *v.* 1. push, propel. 2. jostle.

show, *v.* 1. exhibit, display, demonstrate. 2. point out, indicate. 3. guide, accompany, lead, usher, conduct. 4. interpret, make clear *or* known, clarify, elucidate, explain, discover, reveal, disclose, divulge, publish, proclaim. 5. prove, demonstrate, evidence. 6. allege, assert, asseverate; plead. 7. accord, grant, bestow, confer. 8. look, appear, seem. —*n.* 9. display, ostentation, pomp, exhibition, flourish, dash, pageantry, ceremony. 10. showing, spectacle, appearance. 11. deception, pretense, pretext, simulation, illusion. 12. trace, indication. 13. sight, spectacle, exhibition. *Ant.* hide, conceal.

showy, *adj.* ostentatious, gaudy, flashy, garish, loud. *Ant.* humble, quiet.

shrew, *n.* termagant, virago, hussy, nag, scold, bacchante, maenad.

shrewd, *adj.* astute, sharp, acute, quick, discerning, discriminating, perceptive, perspicuous, perspicacious, keen, intelligent, penetrating, ingenious, sagacious. *Ant.* dull, stupid.

shriek, *n., v.* cry, scream, screech, yell.

shrink, *v.* 1. retreat, withdraw, avoid, recoil, flinch, retire. 2. contract, wither, shrivel, lessen, diminish, decrease, dwindle, wane, peter out. *Ant.* advance; inflate, dilate, increase.

shrivel, *v.* wither, wrinkle, decrease, contract, shrink. *Ant.* blossom.

shroud, *n.* 1. winding-sheet. 2. covering, garment. —*v.* 3. cover, hide, conceal, screen, veil, obscure.

shudder, *v., n.* tremble, shiver, quiver, shake.

shun, *v.* elude, avoid, evade, eschew. *Ant.* seek.

shut, *v.* 1. close; slam. 2. confine, enclose, jail, imprison. 3. bar, exclude, prohibit, preclude. —*adj.* 4. closed, fastened. *Ant.* open.

shy, *adj.* 1. bashful, diffident, retiring, timid, coy. 2. suspicious, distrustful, wary, heedful, cautious, careful, chary, reluctant. 3. short. —*v.* 4. recoil, draw back, shrink. 5. throw, toss, hurl, pitch, cast, fling. *Ant.* forward; trusting; incautious, careless; advance.

sick, *adj.* 1. ill, unwell, ailing, infirm, indisposed. 2. (*British*) nauseous, vomiting, nauseated. 3. pale, wan, white, sickly. 4. impaired, unsound, out of order. *Ant.* well, hale, healthy.

sickly, *adj.* 1. unhealthy, ailing, sick, unwell, puny, weak, frail, feeble, infirm, weakly. 2. weak, mawkish, sentimental, faint. *Ant.* strong, healthy.

siege, *n.* blockade, besieging, attack.

sign, *n.* 1. token, indication, trace, vestige, hint, suggestion. 2. mark, symbol; abbreviation. 3. omen, presage, portent, augury, foreboding. —*v.* 4. signify, betoken, indicate, mean, signal. 5. affix a signature to.

significance, *n.* 1. importance, consequence, moment, weight. 2. import, meaning, sense, purport. 3. meaningfulness, expressiveness. *Ant.* triviality.

significant, *adj.* 1. important, consequential, momentous, weighty, critical, crucial, vital. 2. meaningful, expressive, signifying, indicative *or* suggestive of. *Ant.* insignificant.

signify, *v.* 1. signal, make known, express, indicate, communicate. 2. mean, portend, represent, denote, indicate, betoken, purport, imply.

silent, *adj.* 1. quiet, still, noiseless, soundless. 2. speechless, dumb, mute; close-mouthed, taciturn, tacit. 3. inactive, dormant, quiescent. *Ant.* noisy, clamorous; voluble, talkative; active, kinetic.

silly, *adj.* 1. foolish, stupid, dull-witted, dim-witted, witless, senseless. 2. absurd, ridiculous, inane, asinine, frivolous, nonsensical, preposterous, idiotic. *Ant.* sensible.

similar, *adj.* like, resembling. *Ant.* unlike, dissimilar, different.

similarity, *n.* likeness, resemblance, similitude, correspondence, parallelism. *Ant.* difference.

simmer, *v.* seethe, bubble, boil.

simple, *adj.* 1. clear, intelligible, understandable, unmistakable, lucid. 2. plain, unadorned, natural, unaffected, unembellished, neat. 3. unaffected, unassuming, homely, unpretentious. 4. mere, bare, elementary, simplex, uncomplicated. 5. sincere, innocent, artless, naive, guileless, ingenuous, unsophisticated. 6. humble, lowly. 7. unimportant, insignificant, trifling, trivial, nonessential, unnecessary, immaterial, inconsequential. 8. common, ordinary, usual, customary. 9. unlearned, ignorant, uneducated, untutored, stupid, dense, silly, follish, credulous, shallow. *Ant.* complicated, complex.

sin, *n.* 1. transgression, trespass, violation, crime, offense, wrong, wickedness. —*v.* 2. transgress, trespass, do wrong, offend.

since, *adv.* 1. subsequently. 2. ago, before now. —*conj.* 3. because, inasmuch as.

sincere, *adj.* candid, honest, open, earnest, guileless, artless, plain, simple; genuine, true, unaffected, real, unfeigned. *Ant.* insincere.

sincerity, *n.* honesty, candor, frankness, probity, genuineness, artlessness, ingenuousness, guilelessness. *Ant.* insincerity.

sinful, *adj.* wicked, iniquitous, depraved, evil, immoral, amoral, bad, mischievous, piacular.

singe, *v.* char, burn, scorch.

single, *adj.* 1. separate, only, individual, sole, distinct, particular. 2. alone, solitary, isolated. 3. unmarried, unwed, spinsterish, old-maid. 4. sincere, honest, whole-hearted, concentrated, unbiased. 5. simple, unmixed, pure, uncompounded, unadulterated. —*v.* 6. pick, choose, select, single out. —*n.* 7. one, individual, singleton. *Ant.* conglomerate; married, wed; insincere, biased; adulterated, mixed.

singular, *adj.* 1. extraordinary, remarkable, unusual, uncommon, rare, strange, peculiar. 2. strange, odd, bizarre, fantastic, peculiar, unusual, eccentric, queer, curious, unaccountable, exceptional, unparalleled, unprecedented. 3. unique. 4. separate, individual, single. *Ant.* plural; common.

sinister, *adj.* 1. threatening, portending, portentous, ominous, inauspicious, unlucky, unfavorable, unfortunate, disastrous. 2. bad, evil, base, wicked, sinful, piacular, depraved, corrupt, perverse, dishonest, crooked. *Ant.* benign, favorable, fortunate; good, honest.

sinuous, *adj.* 1. winding, sinuate, curved, crooked, serpentine. 2. indirect, devious, roundabout. *Ant.* straight; direct.

sip, *v.* 1. drink; absorb; extract. 2. savor, taste. —*n.* 3. drink. 4. taste, savor, sapor.

siren, *n.* seductress, temptress, Circe, vampire, vamp, mermaid.

sirocco, *n.* simoom, cyclone, windstorm, dust, storm.

sit, *v.* 1. be seated, roost, perch. 2. be situated, dwell, settle, lie, rest, remain, abide, repose, stay. 3. meet, convene. *Ant.* stand, lie.

situation, *n.* 1. location, position, site, place, locality, locale, spot. 2. condition, case, plight, state, circumstances, predicament. 3. position, post, job.

size, *n.* 1. dimensions, proportions, magnitude, extent; volume, bulk, mass. 2. amount, extent, range. 3. glue, glaze, coating. —*v.* 4. sort, catalogue; measure.

skeptic, *n.* 1. disbeliever, agnostic, atheist, doubter, cynic, infidel, heathen, nullifidian. —*adj.* 2. skeptical, cynical. *Ant.* believer, theist.

skeptical, *adj.* skeptic, doubtful, dubious, incredulous, unbelieving. *Ant.* confident.

sketch, *n.* 1. drawing, outline, draft, design, delineation. 2. skit, play, act, routine, stint. —*v.* 3. depict, draw, outline, design, rough out, delineate, portray, represent.

sketchy, *adj.* hasty, imperfect, slight, superficial. *Ant.* careful, perfect.

skilled, *adj.* skillful. *Ant.* unskilled.

skillful, *adj.* skilled, expert, ready, adroit, deft, adept, proficient, dexterous, competent, qualified, practiced, accomplished, apt, clever, ingenious, intelligent, learned, knowledgeable. *Ant.* unskillful, inexpert, maladroit, unqualified.

skin, *n.* 1. hide, pelt, fur. 2. integument, covering, peel, rind, hull, shell, husk, crust, coating, outside, film, membrane. —*v.* 3. flay, peel, pare, strip, husk, excoriate.

skip, *v.* 1. spring, jump, gambol, leap, bound, caper, hop. 2. disregard, skip over, skim over. 3. ricochet, rebound, bounce. —*n.* 4. leap, jump, spring, bound, caper, hop.

skirmish, *n.* encounter, battle, fight, conflict, combat, brush.

skulk, *v.* 1. lurk, slink, sneak, hide, lie in wait. 2. shirk, malinger.

slack, *adj.* 1. loose, relaxed. 2. indolent, negligent, lazy, remiss, weak. 3. slow, sluggish, dilatory, tardy, late, lingering. 4. dull, inactive, blunted, idle, quiet. —*n.* 5. decrease, slowing, loosening, relaxation, indolence, negligence, laziness, remissness, weakness. —*v.* 6. shirk, neglect, skulk, malinger. 7. relax, abate, reduce, slacken, moderate, mitigate. *Ant.* tight, tense, taut.

slacken, *v.* 1. deactivate, relax, slack, abate. 2. loosen, relax, relieve, abate,

mitigate, remit, lessen, diminish. 3. fail, neglect, defer. 4. restrain, check, curb, bridle, repress, subdue, control. *Ant.* tighten; increase.

slang, *n.* argot, jargon, patois, dialect, cant, colloquialism.

slant, *v.* 1. slope, lean, incline. —*n.* 2. incline, inclination, pitch, slope, obliquity, obliqueness. 3. bent, leaning, prejudice, bias, inclination.

slash, *v.* 1. cut, lash, slit, slice. 2. cut, reduce, alter, abridge, abbreviate. —*n.* 3. stroke, cut, wound, gash, slit.

slaughter, *n.* 1. killing, butchering. 2. massacre, carnage, homicide, murder, butchery, slaying, killing, bloodshed, genocide. —*v.* 3. butcher, massacre, murder, slay, kill, wipe out, devastate, decimate.

slave, *n.* bond servant, esne, thrall, ryot, villein, serf, drudge, vassal, bondman. *Ant.* master.

slavery, *n.* 1. bondage, servitude, subjection, thralldom, captivity, enthrallment. 2. toil, drudgery, moil, labor.

slavish, *adj.* 1. submissive, abject, servile, groveling, menial, drudging. 2. base, mean, ignoble, low, obsequious, fawning, sycophantic, sneaking, cringing. 3. imitative, emulative. *Ant.* independent; elevated, exalted.

slay, *v.* 1. murder, kill, slaughter, massacre, butcher, assassinate. 2. destroy, extinguish, annihilate, ruin.

sleep, *v.* 1. rest, repose, slumber, nap, drowse, doze. —*n.* 2. dormancy, inactivity, slumber, rest, repose, nap.

slender, *adj.* 1. slight, slim, thin, spare, narrow. 2. small, trivial, few, meager, trifling, insignificant, inadequate, insufficient. 3. thin, weak, fragile, feeble, fine, delicate, flimsy, frangible, breakable. *Ant.* large, fat, obese, corpulent.

slide, *v.* slip, slither, glide.

slight, *adj.* 1. small, insignificant, superficial, shallow, trivial, nugatory, paltry, unimportant. 2. slender, slim. 3. frail, flimsy, weak, feeble, delicate, fragile. 4. unsubstantial, inconsiderable. —*v.* 5. ignore, disregard, neglect, disdain, overlook, scorn. —*n.* 6. neglect, disregard, disdain, indifference, scorn, contumely, contempt, inattention. 7. affront, insult, disrespect. *Ant.* considerable; compliment.

slim, *adj.* 1. slender, thin, slight. 2. small, poor, insignificant, trifling,

trivial, nugatory, unimportant, paltry, inconsiderable, scanty, weak, unsubstantial.
Ant. fat; important.

slip, *v.* 1. slide, slither, glide. 2. be mistaken, err, blunder, mistake. —*n.* 3. mistake, error, blunder, fault, oversight; faux pas, indiscretion, backsliding. 4. scion, cutting, strip.

slope, *v., n.* slant, incline.

slothful, *adj.* idle, sluggardly, indolent, lazy, sluggish, inactive, inert, torpid, slack, supine.
Ant. industrious, active, energetic.

slovenly, *adj.* untidy, careless, loose, disorderly, slipshod.
Ant. careful, tidy, neat.

slow, *adj.* 1. deliberate, gradual, moderate, leisurely, unhurried. 2. sluggish, sluggardly, dilatory, indolent, lazy, slothful. 3. dull, dense, stupid. 4. slack. 5. dragging, late, tardy, behindhand. 6. tedious, humdrum, dull, boring. —*v.* 7. retard, hinder, impede, obstruct.
Ant. fast; advance.

sluggish, *adj.* inactive, slow, lazy, slothful, indolent, dull, inert, dronish, phlegmatic.
Ant. quick, active, energetic.

slumber, *v., n.* sleep.

slur, *v.* 1. slight, disregard, pass over, ignore, overlook. 2. calumniate, disparage, slander, depreciate, asperse. —*n.* 3. slight, innuendo, insult, affront. 4. blot, stain, stigma, brand, mark, disgrace.
Ant. compliment.

sly, *adj.* 1. cunning, wily, artful, subtle, foxy, crafty. 2. stealthy, surreptitious, furtive, insidious, secret, underhanded, clandestine. 3. mischievous, roguish, shrewd, astute, cautious.
Ant. direct, obvious.

small, *adj.* 1. little, tiny, diminutive. 2. slender, thin, slight, narrow. 3. unimportant, trivial, minor, secondary, trifling, nugatory, inconsequential, petty, paltry, insignificant. 4. humble, modest, unpretentious. 5. mean-spirited, mean, stingy, ungenerous, parsimonious, niggardly, selfish, tight, illiberal, narrow. 6. ashamed, mortified, abashed. 7. weak, feeble, faint, diluted. 8. gentle, soft, low.
Ant. large.

smart, *v.* 1. pain, hurt, sting. 2. wound, insult, affront. —*adj.* 3. sharp, keen, stinging, poignant, penetrating, painful, severe. 4. brisk, vigorous, active, energetic, effective,

lively, quick. 5. quick, prompt, nimble, agile, alert, active. 6. intelligent, bright, sharp, clever, expert, adroit. 7. shrewd, cunning, adept, quick. 8. neat, trim, dashing, spruce, pretentious, showy. 9. elegant, chic, fashionable, voguish, à la mode.
Ant. pleasure; dull, stupid.

smash, *v.* 1. break, shatter, crush, crash. 2. defeat, overthrow, destroy. 3. ruin, bankrupt. —*n.* 4. smashing, shattering, crash. 5. collision, destruction, ruin; collapse.

smirch, *v.* 1. besmirch, discolor, soil, smear, smudge, smut, smutch, dirty. 2. sully, tarnish, disgrace, taint, blot, smear. —*n.* 3. smear, mark, smudge, smut, smutch, dirt. 4. stain, blot, taint.
Ant. clean; honor.

smooth, *adj.* 1. level, even, plain, flat. 2. bald, hairless, glossy, polished, sleek. 3. flat, unruffled, calm, undisturbed. 4. regular, even, easy, fluent. 5. unruffled, undisturbed, calm, peaceful, tranquil, equable, pacific, peaceable. 6. elegant, polished, flowing, glib, voluble, soft-spoken, suave, unctuous, oily, bland. 7. pleasant, agreeable, polite, courtly, courteous. —*v.* 8. plane, stroke, scrape, level, press, flatten, iron, roll. 9. polish, refine. 10. tranquilize, calm, soothe, assuage, mollify, better. 11. gloss over, palliate, soften, soothe.
Ant. rough, uneven, irregular.

smug, *adj.* 1. complacent, self-satisfied, self-complacent, satisfied, conceited, self-sufficient, self-confident, self-important, egoistic, self-opinionated, self-reliant. 2. trim, spruce, neat, smooth, sleek.
Ant. dissatisfied.

snare, *n.* 1. trap, noose, net, seine. —*v.* 2. trap, entrap, entangle, catch.

snarl, *v.* 1. growl, grumble, complain, murmur. 2. entangle, tangle, mat, complicate, confuse, ravel, involve, knot. —*n.* 3. growl, grumble. 4. tangle, entanglement, complication, knot, confusion, involvement, intricacy, difficulty.

sneak, *v.* 1. slink, lurk, skulk, steal. —*n.* 2. sneaker, lurker.

sneer, *v.* 1. scorn, jeer, gibe, scoff, disdain, deride, ridicule, criticize, contemn. —*n.* 2. scoff, gibe, jeer, derision, disdain.

sneeze, *v.* sternutate.

snide, *adj.* derogatory, nasty, insinuating, vicious, slanderous, libelous.
Ant. complimentary, favorable.

snub, *v.* 1. disdain, contemn, mortify, humiliate, abash, humble, slight, discomfit. 2. check, rebuke, stop, reprove, reprimand. —*n.* 3. rebuke, slight, affront, insult.
Ant. accept.

soak, *v.* 1. steep, drench, wet, sop, saturate. 2. permeate, osmose, penetrate.
Ant. dry.

soar, *v.* 1. fly, glide. 2. tower, rise, ascend, mount.

sober, *adj.* 1. unintoxicated; temperate, abstinent, abstemious. 2. serious, grave, solemn, quiet, sedate, subdued, staid. 3. calm, serene, tranquil, peaceful, cool, moderate, composed, unexcited, unimpassioned, unruffled, collected, dispassionate, unconcerned, reasonable, rational, controlled, sane, sound. 4. somber, dull, neutral, dark.
Ant. drunk; wild; immoderate.

sociable, *adj.* social.
Ant. unfriendly.

social, *adj.* friendly, sociable, amiable, companionable, genial, affable, familiar.
Ant. unfriendly.

society, *n.* 1. organization, association, circle, fellowship, club, fraternity, brotherhood, company, partnership, corporation. 2. community. 3. companionship, company, fellowship, sodality.

soft, *adj.* 1. yielding, pliable, plastic, moldable, malleable, impressible. 2. smooth, agreeable, delicate. 3. gentle, low, subdued, melodious, mellifluous, dulcet, sweet, pleasing, pleasant, flowing. 4. gentle, mild, balmy, genial. 5. gentle, mild, lenient, compassionate, tender, bland, sympathetic. 6. smooth, soothing, ingratiating, mollifying. 7. impressionable, yielding, affected, compliant, flexible, irresolute, submissive, undecided, weak, delicate, sensitive. 8. sentimental, weak, feeble, poor, wishy-washy.
Ant. hard, inflexible, unyielding.

soften, *v.* 1. melt, tenderize. 2. appease, assuage, mollify, moderate, mitigate, modify, soothe, alleviate, calm, quell, still, quiet, ease, allay, abate, qualify, temper, blunt, dull.
Ant. harden.

soi-disant, *adj.* self-styled, so-called, pretended.
Ant. genuine, real.

solace, *n.* 1. comfort, alleviation, cheer, consolation, relief. —*v.* 2.

comfort, console, cheer, soothe. 3. relieve, alleviate, soothe, mitigate, assuage, allay, soften.

sole, *adj.* only, single, solitary, alone, individual, unattended, unique.

solemn, *adj.* 1. grave, sober, mirthless, unsmiling, serious. 2. impressive, awe-inspiring, august, imposing, venerable, grand, majestic, stately. 3. earnest, serious. 4. formal, dignified, serious, ceremonious, ritual, ceremonial. 5. religious, reverential, devotional, sacred, ritual. *Ant.* obstreperous; jovial; unimpressive; insincere; informal.

solicit, *v.* 1. seek, entreat, ask for, request, apply for, beseech, pray, beg, importune, urge, implore, crave, supplicate, sue, petition, appeal to. 2. influence, incite, activate, urge, impel, excite, arouse, awaken, stimulate.

solicitous, *adj.* 1. anxious, concerned, apprehensive, uneasy, troubled, disturbed, restless, restive, worried. 2. desirous, anxious to please. 3. eager. 4. careful, particular. *Ant.* unconcerned, undisturbed; careless.

solid, *adj.* 1. three-dimensional, cubic. 2. dense, compact, firm, hard. 3. unbroken, continuous, undivided, whole, entire, uniform. 4. firm, cohesive, compact. 5. dense, thick, heavy, substantial, sound, stable, stout. 6. real, genuine, complete, sound, good. 7. sober-minded, sober, sensible. 8. thorough, vigorous, strong, solid, big, great, stout. 9. united, consolidated, unanimous. 10. successful, solvent, wealthy, rich, reliable, honorable, established, well-established, sound, trustworthy, honest, safe. *Ant.* flat, two-dimensional; loose; divided; sparse; counterfeit; weak; separate; unsuccessful.

solitary, *adj.* 1. unattended, alone, lone, lonely. 2. isolated, retired, lonely, deserted, unfrequented, remote, secluded. —*n.* 3. hermit, eremite, recluse.

solitude, *n.* 1. seclusion, isolation, remoteness, loneliness, retirement, privacy. 2. desert, waste, wilderness.

somber, *adj.* 1. gloomy, dark, shadowy, dim, unlighted, dusky, murky, cloudy, dull, sunless, dismal. 2. depressing, dismal, lugubrious, mournful, doleful, funereal, melancholy. *Ant.* cheerful.

some, *adj.* 1. any, one, anyone, unspecified. 2. certain, specific, special, particular. *Ant.* none.

soothe, *v.* 1. tranquilize, calm, relieve, comfort, refresh. 2. allay, mitigate, assuage, alleviate, appease, mollify, soften, lull, balm. *Ant.* upset, disturb.

sophisticated, *adj.* 1. artificial, changed, mundane, worldly. 2. deceptive, misleading. *Ant.* unsophisticated.

sorcery, *n.* magic, witchery, enchantment, witchcraft, spell, necromancy, divination, charm.

sordid, *adj.* 1. dirty, filthy, soiled, unclean, foul, squalid. 2. mean, ignoble, amoral, degraded, depraved, low, base. 3. selfish, self-seeking, mercenary, avaricious, stingy, tight, close, close-fisted, parsimonious, penurious, miserly, niggardly. *Ant.* clean; honorable; generous.

sore, *adj.* 1. painful, sensitive, tender, irritated. 2. grieved, distressed, aggrieved, sorrowful, hurt, pained, depressed, vexed. 3. grievous, distressing, painful, depressing, severe, sharp, afflictive. —*n.* 4. infection, abscess, wound, ulcer, pustule, boil, cancer, canker. *Ant.* tough.

sorrow, *n.* 1. distress, anxiety, anguish, grief, sadness, woe, suffering, misery, wretchedness, regret. 2. affliction, adversity, trouble, misfortune. —*v.* 3. grieve, mourn, bemoan, bewail, lament. *Ant.* joy, gladness, delight.

sorrowful, *adj.* 1. grieved, sad, unhappy, melancholy, depressed, dejected, aggrieved, afflicted, mournful, plaintive, grievous, lamentable. 2. distressing, dismal, dreary, doleful, sorry, lugubrious, piteous. *Ant.* happy.

sorry, *adj.* 1. regretful, sorrowing, sympathetic, pitying. 2. pitiable, miserable, deplorable. 3. sorrowful, grieved, sad, unhappy, melancholy, depressed. 4. grievous, melancholy, dismal, mournful, painful. 5. wretched, poor, mean, pitiful, base, low, vile, abject, contemptible, bad, despicable, paltry, worthless, shabby. *Ant.* happy.

sort, *n.* 1. kind, species, phylum, genera, variety, class, group, family, description, order, race, rank, character, nature, type. 2. character, quality, nature. 3. example, pattern, sample, exemplar. 4. manner, fashion, way, method, means, style. —*v.*

5. arrange, order, classify, class, separate, divide, assort, distribute. 6. assign, join, unite.

sound, *n.* 1. noise, tone. 2. strait, channel. —*v.* 3. resound, echo. 4. utter, pronounce, express. 5. plumb, probe; dive, plunge. 6. examine, inspect, investigate, fathom, ascertain, determine. —*adj.* 7. uninjured, unharmed, unbroken, whole, entire, complete, unimpaired, healthy, hale, hearty, robust, hardy, vigorous. 8. solvent, secure, well-established. 9. reliable, trustworthy, honest, honorable. 10. true, truthful, just, fair, judicious, reasonable, rational, sane, sensible, wholesome. 11. enduring, substantial. 12. correct, orthodox, right, proper. 13. upright, honest, good, honorable, loyal, true, virtuous. 14. unbroken, deep, profound, fast, undisturbed. 15. vigorous, hearty, thorough, complete. *Ant.* unsound.

soupçon, *n.* hint, trace, suggestion, suspicion, flavor, taste, sip. *Ant.* plethora.

sour, *adj.* 1. acid, tart. 2. fermented. 3. distasteful, disagreeable, unpleasant, bitter. 4. harsh, ill-tempered, bad-tempered, austere, severe, morose, peevish, testy, short-tempered, hot-tempered, touchy, acrimonious, cross, petulant, crabbed, snappish, waspish, uncivil, rude, crude, rough. *Ant.* sweet.

sovereign, *n.* 1. monarch, king, queen, emperor, empress, prince, lord, ruler, potentate. 2. senate, government. —*adj.* 3. regal, royal, majestic, princely, imperial, monarchical, kingly. 4. supreme, chief, paramount, principal, predominant. 5. utmost, extreme, greatest. 6. potent, effective, efficacious, effectual.

spacious, *adj.* 1. ample, large, capacious, roomy, wide. 2. extensive, vast, huge, extended, tremendous, trackless. *Ant.* small, cramped, crowded.

span, *n.* 1. distance, amount, piece, length, extent; nine inches. 2. extension, reach, extent, stretch. 3. period, spell. 4. pair, team, yoke, couple, brace. —*v.* 5. measure; extend over, reach, pass over, stretch across, cross, compass.

spare, *v.* 1. forbear, omit, refrain from, withhold, keep from. 2. save, lay away *or* aside, reserve, set aside *or* apart. —*adj.* 3. reserved, extra, reserve. 4. restricted, meager, frugal, sparing, scanty, parsimonious. 5. lean, thin, slender, slight, gaunt, lank, skinny, raw-boned, emaciated. 6. economical, temperate, careful.

sparkle, *v.* 1. glisten, glitter, shine, twinkle, gleam, coruscate, scintillate. 2. effervesce, bubble. —*n.* 3. luster, spark, scintillation, glister, glitter, twinkle, twinkling, coruscation. 4. brilliance, liveliness, vivacity, spirit, glow, piquancy.

sparse, *adj.* 1. thin, scattered, here and there. 2. scanty, meager, spare, restricted. *Ant.* abundant.

speak, *v.* utter, talk, voice, converse, communicate, disclose, reveal, pronounce, say, articulate, significate.

special, *adj.* 1. distinct, distinguished, different, particular, especial, peculiar, singular, specific, plain, unambiguous, certain, individual, single, unusual, uncommon. 2. extraordinary, exceptional. *Ant.* unparticular, common; ordinary.

specific, *adj.* special. *Ant.* unspecific, nonspecific.

specimen, *n.* type, example, sample, model, pattern.

specious, *adj.* plausible, ostensible, feasible; deceptive, false, misleading. *Ant.* implausible; genuine.

specter, *n.* ghost, phantom, spirit, apparition, shade, shadow. *Ant.* reality.

speculation, *n.* 1. contemplation, consideration. 2. conclusion, supposition, conjecture, surmise, view, hypothesis, theory.

speech, *n.* 1. utterance, remark, observation, declaration, assertion, asseveration, averral, comment, mention, talk. 2. talk, oration, address, discourse, harangue. 3. language, words, lingo, tongue, dialect, patois. 4. parlance, conversation, parley, communication.

speechless, *adj.* 1. dumb, dumfounded, shocked, mute. 2. silent, dumb, mute. *Ant.* loquacious, voluble, talkative.

speed, *n.* 1. rapidity, alacrity, celerity, quickness, fleetness, velocity, swiftness, dispatch, expedition, haste, hurry. —*v.* 2. promote, advance, further, forward, expedite, favor. 3. direct, guide. 4. accelerate. *Ant.* sloth.

spend, *v.* 1. disburse, expend, pay out, dispose of, squander, throw out, waste, lavish, dissipate. 2. exhaust, use up, consume. 3. employ, use, apply, devote. *Ant.* earn.

sphere, *n.* 1. ball, orb, globe. 2. shell, ball. 3. planet, star. 4. environment, orbit, area, place, province, circle, compass, coterie, set, realm, domain, quarter. 5. stratum, walk of life, rank. *Ant.* cube.

spin, *v.* 1. draw out, twist, wind. 2. twirl, whirl, turn, rotate, gyrate. 3. produce, fabricate, evolve, develop. 4. tell, narrate, relate. 5. draw out, extend, protract, prolong, lengthen. —*n.* 6. run, ride, drive.

spineless, *adj.* limp, weak, feeble, irresolute, undetermined, thewless. *Ant.* strong.

spirit, *n.* 1. animation, vitality, soul, essence, life, mind, consciousness. 2. goblin, sprite, elf, fairy, hobgoblin; angel, genius, demon, *prāna.* 3. ghost, specter, apparition, phantom, shade, shadow. 4. God, The Holy Ghost, The Holy Spirit, The Comforter, The Spirit of God. 5. mettle, vigor, liveliness, enthusiasm, energy, zeal, zealousness, ardor, fire, vivacity, enterprise, resourcefulness. 6. temper, disposition, attitude, mood, humor, sorts, frame of mind. 7. character, nature, drift, tenor, gist, sense, complexion, quintessence, essence. 8. meaning, intent, intention, significance, purport. —*v.* 9. inspirit, vitalize, animate, instill, encourage, excite.

spirited, *adj.* excited, animated, vivacious, ardent, active, agog, energetic, lively, vigorous, courageous, mettlesome, bold. *Ant.* dispirited, inactive, indolent.

spite, *n.* 1. ill will, malevolence, maliciousness, malice, rancor, gall, malignity, venom, spleen. 2. grudge, hate, pique, hatred. —*v.* 3. annoy, thwart, injure, hurt, harm.

spiteful, *adj.* malicious, venomous, malevolent, revengeful, vindictive, mean, cruel, hateful, rancorous. *Ant.* benevolent, friendly.

splendid, *adj.* 1. gorgeous, magnificent, sumptuous, luxurious, superb, dazzling, imposing. 2. grand, beautiful, impressive. 3. glorious, renowned, famed, famous, illustrious, eminent, conspicuous, distinguished, remarkable, celebrated, brilliant, noble. 4. fine, striking, admirable. *Ant.* sordid, squalid; ignoble.

splendor, *n.* 1. magnificence, brilliance, grandeur, pomp, show, display, dash, élan, éclat. 2. distinction, glory, brilliance, fame, eminence, renown, celebrity. 3. brightness, bril-

liance, light, luster, dazzle, refulgence. *Ant.* squalor.

splenetic, *adj.* spleenish, spleeny, irritable, peevish, spiteful, vexatious, irascible, testy, fretful, touchy, edgy, petulant, snappish, waspish, cross, choleric. *Ant.* moderate, temperate.

spoil, *v.* 1. damage, impair, ruin, wreck, disfigure, destroy, demolish, mar, harm. 2. corrupt, vitiate. 3. plunder, pillage, rob, rape, despoil, ravage, waste. —*n.* 4. (*often plural*) booty, plunder, loot, pillage.

spontaneous, *adj.* unpremeditated, natural, unconstrained, voluntary, gratuitous, free, unselfish. *Ant.* premeditated.

sporadic, *adj.* scattered, occasional, isolated, unconnected, separate. *Ant.* continuous.

sport, *n.* 1. pastime, game, athletics, amusement, diversion, fun, entertainment, frolic, recreation, play. 2. derision, jesting, ridicule, mockery. 3. laughingstock. 4. toy, plaything. —*v.* 5. play, frolic, gambol, romp, caper, skip. 6. trifle, deal lightly, discount. 7. ridicule, make fun.

sportive, *adj.* 1. playful, frolicsome, jesting, jocose, merry, jocular, gay, sprightly, frisky. 2. joking, prankish, facetious. *Ant.* sober, serious.

spot, *n.* 1. mark, stain, blot, speck. 2. blemish, flaw, stain, taint, stigma. 3. place, locality, locale, site, situation. —*v.* 4. stain, mark, blot, speckle. 5. sully, blemish, stain, taint, stigmatize, soil, tarnish.

spout, *v.* 1. spurt, squirt, flow, stream, pour. —*n.* 2. pipe, tube, nozzle, nose.

sprain, *v.* strain, overstain, wrench, injure, twist.

spread, *v.* 1. unroll, unfold, open, expand, stretch out, draw out. 2. extend, stretch, expand, dilate. 3. display, set forth. 4. dispose, distribute, scatter, disperse, ted. 5. overlay, cover, coat. 6. emit, scatter, diffuse, radiate. 7. shed, scatter, diffuse, disseminate, broadcast, publish, circulate, divulge, promulgate, propagate, disperse. —*n.* 8. expansion, extension, diffusion. 9. extent, reach, compass; stretch, expanse. 10. bedspread, cloth, cover, tablecloth. 11. preserve, jam, jelly, peanut butter.

spring, *v.* 1. leap, jump, bound, hop, vault. 2. recoil, fly back, rebound. 3.

shoot, dart, fly. 4. arise, start, originate, rise, issue, emanate, flow. 5. grow, develop, increase, wax, thrive. 6. emerge, emanate, issue, flow, proceed. 7. bend, warp. 8. explode. 9. split, crack. —*n.* 10. leap, jump, hop, bound, vault. 11. elasticity, springiness, resiliency, buoyancy, vigor. 12. split, crack, fissure; bend, warp. 13. source, origin, mouth, fountainhead, head. —*adj.* 14. vernal, springtime.

sprinkle, *v.* 1. scatter, strew, spread, disperse, fling, distribute, rain. 2. diversify, intersperse.

spry, *adj.* active, nimble, agile, brisk, lively, energetic, animated, quick, smart, alert, ready, prompt. *Ant.* inactive.

spur, *n.* 1. goad, prick, rowel. 2. whip, goad, incitement, stimulus, incentive, inducement, provocation, impulse, instigation. —*v.* 3. urge, goad, prick, whip, incite, provoke, stimulate, induce, instigate. *Ant.* discourage.

spurious, *adj.* 1. counterfeit, sham, false, pretended, unauthentic, bogus, phony, mock, feigned; meretricious, deceitful, fictitious. 2. illegitimate, bastard. *Ant.* genuine.

spurn, *v.* reject, disdain, scorn, despise, refuse, contemn. *Ant.* accept.

spurt, *v.* 1. gush, spout, flow, issue, stream, jet, well, spring. —*n.* 2. outburst, jet, spout. *Ant.* drip, ooze.

squalid, *adj.* 1. foul, repulsive, unclean, dirty, filthy, nasty. 2. wretched, miserable, degraded. *Ant.* splendid.

squalor, *n.* squalidness, filth, misery, foulness. *Ant.* splendor.

squander, *v.* spend, waste, dissipate, throw away, lavish, misuse, expend. *Ant.* save.

squeamish, *adj.* 1. modest, prudish; blue. 2. moral, particular, scrupulous, fastidious, finical, finicky, dainty, delicate, hypercritical, nice. *Ant.* bold.

stab, *v.* 1. pierce, wound, gore, spear, penetrate, pin, transfix. 2. thrust, plunge. —*n.* 3. thrust, blow, wound.

stability, *n.* firmness, continuance, permanence, constancy, steadiness, steadfastness, strength, immovability, fixedness. *Ant.* instability.

stable, *n.* 1. barn, mews. —*adj.* 2. firm, steady, rigid, fixed, strong, sturdy, established, immovable, permanent, invariable, unvarying, steadfast, unchangeable, unchanging. 3. enduring, permanent, constant, perdurable, lasting, abiding, secure, fast, perpetual, eternal, everlasting. 4. unwavering, steadfast, staunch, constant, reliable, steady, solid. *Ant.* unstable.

stagger, *v.* 1. sway, reel, totter, waver, falter, vacillate. 2. hesitate, doubt. 3. shock, astound, astonish, confound, amaze, nonplus, dumfound, surprise. 4. alternate, zigzag, rearrange, reorder, overlap.

staid, *adj.* sedate, settled, sober, serious, proper, decorous, correct, quiet, composed, serene, calm, solemn, grave. *Ant.* wild, indecorous.

stain, *n.* 1. discoloration, spot, blemish, mark, imperfection, blot. 2. stigma, disgrace, dishonor, taint, blot, tarnish. 3. dye, reagent, tint. —*v.* 4. discolor, taint, spot, streak, soil, dirty, blemish, blot. 5. blemish, sully, spot, taint, soil, tarnish, disgrace, dishonor, stigmatize, corrupt, debase, defile, contaminate, pollute. 6. tint, dye, tinge, color.

stake, *n.* 1. stick, post, pale, picket, pike. 2. wager, bet. 3. (*often plural*) prize, winnings, purse. 4. risk, jeopardy, hazard. —*v.* 5. risk, hazard, jeopardize, wager, venture, bet, imperil.

stale, *adj.* 1. vapid, flat, dry, hardened, hard, tasteless, sour, insipid. 2. uninteresting, hackneyed, trite, stereotyped, old hat, old, common, commonplace. *Ant.* fresh, modern.

stalemate, *n.* impasse, deadlock, standstill.

stalwart, *adj.* 1. strong, stout, well-developed, robust, sturdy, brawny, sinewy, muscular, athletic, strapping, vigorous. 2. strong, brave, valiant, bold, valorous, intrepid, daring, fearless, firm, resolute, indomitable, gallant. 3. firm, steadfast, resolute, uncompromising, redoubtable, formidable. *Ant.* weak, feeble; fearful; infirm, unsteady.

stamina, *n.* strength, vigor, resistance, power, health, robustness. *Ant.* weakness.

stammer, *v.* stutter, pause, hesitate, falter.

stamp, *v.* 1. strike, beat, trample, crush, pound. 2. eliminate, abolish, squash, quash, eradicate. 3. impress, mark, label, brand, imprint. 4. characterize, distinguish, reveal. —*n.* 5. die, block, cut, engraving, brand, branding iron. 6. impression, design, pattern, brand, mark, print, seal. 7. character, kind, type, sort, description, cut, style, cast, mold, fashion, form, make.

stand, *v.* 1. halt, stop, pause. 2. remain, continue, persist, stay, abide, be firm *or* resolute *or* steadfast *or* steady. 3. set, erect, place, put, fix. 4. face, meet, encounter, resist, oppose. 5. endure, undergo, submit to, bear, sustain, weather, outlast. 6. tolerate, abide, stomach, endure, suffer, bear, admit, allow. —*n.* 7. halt, stop, rest, stay. 8. position, effort, determination, attitude. 9. station, post, place, position, spot. 10. platform, dais, grandstand. 11. stall, booth, table, case, counter. 12. copse, grove, forest, wood; growth, crop.

standard, *n.* 1. criterion, measure, gauge, test, model, example, exemplar, sample, basis, pattern, guide, rule. 2. grade, level. 3. emblem, flag, symbol, ensign, banner, pennant, pennon, streamer. 4. upright, support; bar, rod, timber. —*adj.* 5. basic, exemplary, guiding, sample, typical.

standing, *n.* 1. position, status, rank, credit, reputation, condition. 2. existence, continuation, duration, residence, membership, experience. 3. station, booth. —*adj.* 4. still, stationary, stagnant, unmoving, motionless. 5. continuing, continuous, unceasing, constant, permanent, unchanging, steady, lasting, durable. 6. idle, out of use, unused. 7. operative, in force, effective, in effect, established, settled.

stanza, *n.* quatrain, stave, poem, staff.

stare, *v., n.* gaze.

stark, *adj.* 1. sheer, utter, downright, arrant, simple, mere, pure, absolute, entire, unmistakable. 2. stiff, rigid. 3. harsh, grim, desolate, dreary, drear. —*adv.* 4. utterly, absolutely, completely, quite, irrevocable. *Ant.* vague.

start, *v.* 1. begin, set out *or* forth, commence, depart. 2. issue, come up, come, arise. 3. jump, jerk, twitch, spring. 4. set up, begin, establish, found, institute, initiate. —*n.* 5. beginning, outset, initiation, commencement, onset. 6. impulse, sig-

nal, go-ahead, starting gun. 7. jerk, spasm, fit, twitch, jump. 8. headstart, lead. 9. chance, opportunity.
Ant. end, terminate.

startle, *v.* 1. disturb, shock, agitate, surprise, alarm, amaze, astound, astonish, scare, frighten. —*n.* 2. shock, surprise, alarm.
Ant. calm.

state, *n.* 1. condition, case, circumstances, predicament, pass, plight, situation, status, surroundings, environment, rank, position, standing, stage. 2. constitution, structure, form, phase. 3. estate, station, rank, position, standing. 4. dignity, pomp, display, grandeur, glory, magnificence. 5. sovereign government, government, federation, commonwealth, community, territory. —*adj.* 6. public, national, government, federal. 7. ceremonial, ceremonious, pompous, stately, imposing, sumptuous, dignified. —*v.* 8. declare, aver, assert, asseverate, set forth, express, affirm, specify. 9. say. 10. fix, settle, determine, authorize.

stately, *adj.* imposing, grand, dignified, majestic, elegant, magnificent, state.
Ant. base, mean, vile.

statement, *n.* declaration, communication, report, announcement, proclamation.

station, *n.* 1. position, post, place, situation, location. 2. depot, terminal, way-station, whistle-stop. 3. standing, rank, dignity. 4. position, office, rank, calling, occupation, metier, trade, business, employment, office, appointment. —*v.* 5. assign, place, post, position, locate, establish, set, fix.

status, *n.* 1. condition, state. 2. condition, position, standing, rank.

staunch, *adj.* firm, steadfast, stable, steady, constant, resolute, true, faithful, principled, loyal, substantial, strong, sound, stout.
Ant. unsteady, disloyal.

stay, *v.* 1. remain, dwell, reside, abide, sojourn, tarry, rest, lodge. 2. continue, remain. 3. stop, halt. 4. pause, wait, delay, linger. 5. hold back, detain, restrain, obstruct, arrest, check, hinder, delay, hold, curb, prevent. 6. suspend, delay, adjourn. 7. suppress, quell. 8. appease, satisfy, curb, allay. 9. wait out. 10. support, prop, brace, buttress. 11. rest, rely *or* depend on, confide *or* trust in, lean on. 12. sustain, bolster, strengthen, uphold. —*n.* 13. stop, halt, pause, delay, standstill; inter-

ruption, break, hiatus, lacuna. 14. sojourn, rest, repose. 15. prop, brace, support; crutch. 16. rope, guy, guy wire.
Ant. leave.

steadfast, *adj.* 1. fixed, directed, fast, firm, established, stable. 2. stanch, steady, sure, dependable, reliable, resolute, constant, strong, firm, loyal, regular, purposeful, faithful, unwavering.
Ant. unsteady; weak; sporadic, unfaithful.

steady, *adj.* 1. firm, fixed, steadfast, stable, balanced, even, regular. 2. undeviating, invariable, unvarying, regular, constant, unchanging, uninterrupted, uniform, unremitting, continuous. 3. habitual, regular, constant, unchangeable. 4. firm, unwavering, steadfast. 5. settled, staid, sedate, sober. —*v.* 6. stabilize.
Ant. unsteady.

steal, *v.* 1. take, pilfer, purloin, filch, embezzle, peculate, swindle. 2. win, gain, draw, lure, allure.
Ant. provide.

stealthy, *adj.* furtive, surreptitious, secret, clandestine, sly.
Ant. obvious, open, manifest.

stem, *n.* 1. axis, stalk, trunk, petiole, peduncle, pedicel. 2. stock, family, descent, pedigree, ancestry, lineage, race. —*v.* 3. rise, arise, originate. 4. stop, check, dam up, obstruct, hinder, stay. 5. tamp, plug, tighten. 6. progress against, oppose, breast, make headway against, withstand.

stereotyped, *adj.* fixed, settled, conventional, hackneyed, overused, commonplace, trite, banal, dull, ordinary, lifeless, uninteresting, stale, boring, worn, pointless, insipid, inane.
Ant. rare, uncommon, unusual; interesting, fresh, sensible.

sterile, *adj.* 1. uncontaminated, unpolluted, uncorrupted, antiseptic. 2. barren, unproductive, fruitless, infecund.
Ant. fertile.

stern, *adj.* 1. firm, strict, adamant, unrelenting, uncomprising, severe, harsh, hard, inflexible, forbidding, unsympathetic, rough, cruel, unfeeling. 2. rigorous, austere, steadfast, rigid.
Ant. lenient, flexible.

stew, *v.* 1. simmer, boil, seethe. —*n.* 2. ragout.

stick, *n.* 1. branch, shoot, switch. 2. rod, wand, baton. 3. club, cudgel; bat. 4. thrust, stab. 5. interruption.

—*v.* 6. pierce, puncture, stab, penetrate, spear, transfix, pin, gore. 7. impale. 8. fasten, attach, glue, cement, paste. 9. adhere, cohere, cling, cleave, hold. 10. remain, stay, persist, abide. 11. hesitate, scruple, stickle, waver, doubt.

stiff, *adj.* 1. rigid, firm, solid, unflexible, unbendable, unbending, unyielding. 2. violent, strong, steady, unremitting, fresh. 3. firm, purposive, unrelenting, unyielding, resolved, obstinate, stubborn, pertinacious. 4. graceless, awkward, clumsy, inelegant, crude, harsh, abrupt. 5. formal, ceremonious, punctilious, constrained, starched, prim, priggish. 6. laborious, difficult. 7. severe, rigorous, straitlaced, austere, strict, dogmatic, uncompromising, positive, absolute, inexorable. 8. great, high. 9. taut, tight, tense. 10. dense, compact, tenacious. —*n.* 11. prude, prig.
Ant. flexible.

stifle, *v.* 1. smother, suffocate, strangle, garrote, choke. 2. keep back, repress, check, stop, suppress. 3. crush, stop, obviate, prevent, preclude, put down, destroy, suppress.
Ant. encourage, further, foster.

stigma, *n.* 1. mark, stain, reproach, taint, blot, spot, tarnish, disgrace, infamy, disrepute. 2. brand.

still, *adj.* 1. in place, at rest, motionless, stationary, unmoving, inert, quiescent. 2. soundless, quiet, hushed, noiseless, silent, mute. 3. tranquil, calm, peaceful, peaceable, pacific, placid, serene. —*conj.* 4. but, nevertheless, and yet. —*v.* 5. silence, hush, quiet, mute, stifle, muffle, smother. 6. calm, appease, allay, soothe, compose, pacify, smooth, tranquilize. —*n.* 7. stillness, quiet, hush, calm. 8. distillery.
Ant. mobile, moving; noisy, clamorous; noise.

stimulate, *v.* 1. rouse, arouse, activate, incite, animate, excite, urge, provoke, instigate, goad, spur, prod, prick, inflame, fire. 2. invigorate.
Ant. discourage.

stimulus, *n.* incentive, incitement, enticement, stimulation, motive, provocation; stimulant.
Ant. discouragement; wet blanket; soporific.

stingy, *adj.* niggardly, penurious, parsimonious, miserly, mean, close, tight, avaricious.
Ant. generous.

stint, *v.* 1. limit, restrict, confine, restrain; pinch, straiten. —*n.* 2. limit,

limitation, restriction, restraint, constraint. 3. share, rate, allotment, portion.
Ant. liberate, free.

stir, *v.* 1. move, agitate, disturb. 2. shake. 3. incite, instigate, prompt, rouse, foment, arouse, provoke, stimulate, animate, urge, goad, spur. 4. affect, excite, move. —*n.* 5. movement, bustle, ado, agitation, commotion, disorder, uproar, tumult. 6. impulse, sensation, feeling, emotion.

stock, *n.* 1. store, goods, inventory, supplies, supply, provision, reserve, hoard. 2. livestock, cattle, horses, sheep. 3. trunk, stem. 4. race, lineage, family, descent, pedigree, ancestry, line, parentage, house, tribe. 5. handle, haft. 6. pillory. —*adj.* 7. staple, standard, standing, customary, permanent. 8. common, commonplace, ordinary, usual. —*v.* 9. supply, store, fill.

stoical, *adj.* stoic, impassive, calm, austere, apathetic, imperturbable, cool, indifferent.
Ant. sympathetic, warm.

stony, *adj.* 1. rocky, pebbly, gritty. 2. unfeeling, merciless, obdurate, adamant, inflexible, stiff, hard, flinty, pitiless, unbending. 3. motionless, rigid, stock-still.

stoop, *v.* bend, lean, bow, crouch. 2. descend, condescend, deign, lower oneself. 3. stoop down, descend. —*n.* 4. descent, indignity, condescension, humiliation.

stop, *v.* 1. cease, leave off, discontinue, desist or refrain from. 2. interrupt, arrest, check, halt, restrain, intermit, terminate, end. 3. cut off, intercept, withhold, thwart, interrupt, obstruct, impede, hinder, prevent, preclude, delay, restrain, repress, suppress. 4. block, obstruct, close, seal off, blockade. 5. cease, pause, quit. —*n.* 6. halt, cessation, arrest, end, termination, check. 7. stay, sojourn, stopover. 8. station, depot, terminal. 9. block, obstruction, obstacle, hindrance, impediment; plug, stopper, cork. 10. check, control, governor.
Ant. start.

storm, *n.* 1. gale, hurricane, tempest, tornado, cyclone, sirocco, simoom, dust storm, squall, northeaster, wind, rainstorm, bise, whirlwind, hailstorm, snowstorm, blizzard, thunderstorm. 2. assault, siege, attack. 3. violence, commotion, disturbance, strife. 4. outburst, outbreak. —*v.* 5. blow; rain, snow, hail, thunder and lightning. 6. rage, rant,

fume, complain. 7. rush, attack, assault, besiege.

story, *n.* 1. narrative, tale, legend, fable, romance, anecdote, record, history, chronicle. 2. plot, theme, incident. 3. narration, recital, rehearsal, relation. 4. report, account, description, statement, allegation. 5. floor, level.

stout, *adj.* 1. bulky, thick-set, fat, corpulent, plump, portly, fleshy. 2. bold, hardy, dauntless, brave, valiant, gallant, intrepid, fearless, indomitable, courageous. 3. firm, stubborn, obstinate, contumacious, resolute. 4. strong, stalwart, sturdy, sinewy, athletic, brawny, vigorous, able-bodied. 5. thick, heavy.
Ant. slim, slender, thin; fearful; weak; light.

straight, *adj.* 1. direct, right. 2. candid, frank, open, honest, direct. 3. honorable, honest, virtuous, upright, erect, just, fair, equitable, straightforward. 4. right, correct. 5. unmodified, unaltered, unchanged.
Ant. devious, crooked.

straightforward, *adj.* 1. direct, straight, undeviating, unwavering, unswerving. 2. honest, truthful, honorable, just, fair.
Ant. devious; dishonest.

strain, *v.* 1. stretch, tighten, tauten. 2. exert. 3. sprain, impair, injure, weaken, wrench, twist, tear, overexert. 4. filter, sift, sieve, filtrate, purify, percolate, seep through. 5. clasp, hug, embrace, press. 6. filter, percolate, ooze, seep. —*n.* 7. force, pressure, effort, exertion. 8. sprain, injury, wrench. 9. family, stock, descent, race, pedigree, lineage, ancestry, extraction. 10. character, tendency, trait. 11. streak, trace, hint, suggestion.

strait, *n.* difficulty, distress, need, emergency, exigency, crisis, pinch, dilemma, predicament, plight.
Ant. ease.

strange, *adj.* 1. unusual, extraordinary, curious, bizarre, odd, queer, singular, peculiar, unfamiliar, inexplicable, unexplained, irregular, unconventional, rare, mysterious, mystifying, eccentric, abnormal, anomalous, exceptional. 2. alien, foreign, exotic, outlandish, unfamiliar. 3. unacquainted, unaccustomed, unused, unfamiliar, unknown, unexperienced. 4. distant, reserved, aloof, supercilious, superior.
Ant. usual, commonplace.

stranger, *n.* alien, foreigner, outsider.
Ant. friend, relative, ally.

strangle, *v.* garrote; choke, stifle, suffocate, smother, throttle.

stratagem, *n.* plan, scheme, trick, ruse, deception, artifice, wile, intrigue, device, maneuver, contrivance, machination.

strategy, *n.* tactics, generalship; skillful management.

stream, *n.* 1. current, rivulet, rill, streamlet, run, runnel, river. 2. flow, course, tide. 3. flow, succession, torrent, rush. —*v.* 4. pour, flow, run, issue, emit.

street, *n.* way, road, roadway, avenue, boulevard, concourse, highway; path, footpath, alley, alleyway.

strength, *n.* 1. power, force, vigor, health, might, potency, energy, capacity. 2. firmness, courage, fortitude, resolution. 3. effectiveness, efficacy, potency, cogency, soundness, validity. 4. intensity, brightness, loudness, vividness, pungency. 5. support, stay, prop, brace.
Ant. weakness.

strenuous, *adj.* vigorous, energetic, active, animated, spirited, eager, zealous, ardent, resolute, determined, forceful, earnest.
Ant. easy.

stress, *v.* 1. emphasize, accent. 2. strain. —*n.* 3. importance, significance, emphasis, weight, accent, force.
Ant. unstress, deemphasize, ease, underplay.

stretch, *v.* 1. draw out, extend, lengthen, elongate. 2. hold out, reach forth, reach, extend, stretch forth. 3. spread. 4. tighten, tauten, strain. 5. lengthen, widen, distend, dilate, enlarge, broaden. 6. strain, exaggerate. 7. recline, lie down. —*n.* 8. length, distance, tract, expanse, extent, extension, range, reach, compass.
Ant. curtail, abbreviate.

strew, *v.* scatter, sprinkle, overspread, broadcast.
Ant. gather, reap.

strict, *adj.* 1. rigid, rigorous, stringent, inflexible, stiff, severe, unbending, unyielding, exacting, demanding, stern, narrow, illiberal, uncompromising, harsh, austere, strait-laced. 2. exact, precise, accurate, scrupulous, particular. 3. close, careful, minute, critical. 4. absolute, perfect, complete.
Ant. flexible.

strife, *n.* 1. conflict, discord, variance, difference, disagreement, contra-

riety, opposition. 2. quarrel, struggle, clash, fight, conflict.
Ant. peace.

strike, *v.* 1. thrust, hit, smite, knock, beat, pound, slap, cuff, buffet. 2. catch, arrest, impress. 3. come across, meet with, meet, encounter. 4. affect, overwhelm, impress.

stringent, *adj.* 1. strict. 2. narrow, binding, restrictive. 3. urgent, compelling, constraining. 4. convincing, forceful, powerful, effective, forcible, persuasive.
Ant. flexible, mollifying, emollient; ineffective.

strip, *v.* 1. uncover, peel, decorticate, denude. 2. remove. 3. withhold, deprive, divest, dispossess, dismantle. 4. rob, plunder, despoil, pillage, sack, devastate, spoil, desolate, lay waste. —*n.* 5. band, ribbon.
Ant. cover.

strive, *v.* 1. endeavor, try, exert oneself, essay, struggle, toil. 2. contend, compete, fight, struggle.

stroke, *n.* 1. striking, blow, hitting, beating, beat, knock, rap, tap, pat, thump. 2. throb, pulsation, beat; rhythm. 3. apoplexy, paralysis, shock, attack. 4. feat, achievement, accomplishment. —*v.* 5. caress, rub gently, massage.

stroll, *v.* 1. ramble, saunter, meander. 2. wander, roam, rove, stray. —*n.* 3. ramble, saunter, promenade, walk.

strong, *adj.* 1. powerful, vigorous, hale, hearty, healthy, robust, mighty, sturdy, brawny, athletic, sinewy, hardy, muscular, stout, stalwart, Herculean. 2. powerful, able, competent, potent, capable, puissant, efficient. 3. firm, courageous, valiant, brave, valorous, bold, intrepid, fearless. 4. influential, resourceful, persuasive, cogent, impressive. 5. clear, firm, loud. 6. well-supplied, rich, substantial. 7. cogent, forceful, forcible, effective, efficacious, conclusive, potent, powerful. 8. resistive, resistant, solid, firm, secure, compact, impregnable, impenetrable. 9. firm, unfaltering, tenacious, unwavering, resolute, solid, tough, stanch, stout. 10. intoxicating, alcoholic, potent. 11. intense, brilliant, glaring, vivid, dazzling. 12. distinct, marked, sharp, stark, contrasty. 13. strenuous, energetic, forceful, vigorous, zealous, eager, earnest, ardent. 14. hearty, fervent, fervid, thoroughgoing, vehement, stubborn. 15. pungent, racy, olent, aromatic, odoriferous; sharp, piquant, spicy, hot, biting. 16. smelly, rank.
Ant. weak.

structure, *n.* 1. construction, organization, system, arrangement, form, configuration, shape. 2. building, edifice, bridge, dam, framework. 3. composition, arrangement.

struggle, *v.* 1. contend, strive, oppose, contest, fight, conflict. —*n.* 2. brush, clash, encounter, skirmish, fight, battle, conflict, strife. 3. effort, strive, endeavor, exertion, labor, pains.

strut, *v.* 1. swagger, parade. —*n.* 2. brace, support, prop, stretcher.

stubborn, *adj.* 1. obstinate, perverse, contrary, dogged, persistent, intractable, refractory, inflexible, unyielding, unbending, rigid, stiff, contumacious, headstrong, pigheaded, obdurate. 2. fixed, set, opinionated, resolute, persevering. 3. hard, tough, stiff, strong, stony.
Ant. tractable, flexible; irresolute.

student, *n.* pupil, scholar; observer.
Ant. teacher.

studied, *adj.* deliberate, premeditated, predetermined, willful, considered, elaborate.
Ant. unpremeditated.

study, *n.* 1. attention, application, investigation, inquiry, research, reading, reflection, meditation, cogitation, thought, consideration, contemplation. 2. field, area, subject. 3. zealousness, endeavor, effort, assiduity, sedulousness, assiduousness. 4. thought, reverie, abstraction. 5. library, den. —*v.* 6. read, investigate, practice. 7. think, reflect, consider, ponder, weigh, estimate, examine, contemplate, scrutinize, turn over.

stuff, *n.* 1. material, substance, matter. 2. character, qualities, capabilities. 3. rubbish, trash, waste, nonsense, twaddle, balderdash, inanity, absurdity. —*v.* 4. fill, cram, pack, crowd, press, stow. 5. stop up, choke, plug, obstruct.

stun, *v.* 1. knock out, shock, dizzy. 2. astound, stupefy, daze, astonish, amaze, overcome, bewilder, overwhelm, confound.

stupid, *adj.* 1. dull, vapid, pointless, prosaic, tedious, uninteresting, boring, insipid, flat, humdrum, tiresome, heavy. 2. foolish, inane, asinine, senseless, simple, half-witted, witless, obtuse, stolid, dumb.
Ant. bright, intelligent, clever, shrewd.

sturdy, *adj.* 1. well-built, strong, robust, stalwart, hardy, muscular, brawny, sinewy, stout, powerful. 2. firm, stout, indomitable, unbeatable, unconquerable, persevering, resolute, vigorous, determined.
Ant. weak.

style, *n.* 1. kind, sort, type, form, appearance, character. 2. mode, manner, method, approach, system. 3. fashion, elegance, smartness, chic, élan, éclat. 4. touch, characteristic, mark. 5. stylus. 6. etching, point *or* needle, graver. 7. gnomon. —*v.* 8. call, denominate, name, designate, address, entitle, title, christen, dub, characterize, term.

suave, *adj.* smooth, agreeable, polite, bland, urbane, sophisticated, worldly, mundane.
Ant. boorish.

subdue, *v.* 1. conquer, defeat, suppress, subjugate, vanquish, overcome, overpower, subject. 2. repress, reduce, overcome. 3. tame, break, discipline, domesticate. 4. tone down, soften, mollify.

subject, *n.* 1. theme, topic, conception, point, thesis, object, subject matter. 2. ground, motive, reason, rationale, cause. 3. minion, dependent, subordinate. —*adj.* 4. subordinate, subjacent, subservient, subjected, inferior. 5. obedient, submissive. 6. open, exposed, prone, liable. 7. dependent, conditional, contingent. —*v.* 8. dominate, control, influence. 9. make liable, lay open, expose.

subjective, *adj.* 1. mental, unreal, imaginary, illusory, fancied, imagined. 2. personal, individual. 3. introspective, contemplative, introversive. 4. substantial, essential, inherent.
Ant. objective.

submerge, *v.* submerse, dip, sink, plunge, immerse.

submissive, *adj.* 1. unresisting, humble, obedient, tractable, compliant, pliant, yielding, amenable, agreeable. 2. passive, resigned, patient, docile, tame, long-suffering, subdued.

submit, *v.* yield, surrender, bow, comply, obey, agree, resign.
Ant. fight.

subordinate, *adj.* 1. lower, inferior. 2. secondary, unimportant, ancillary. 3. subservient; dependent. —*n.* 4. inferior, subject. —*v.* 5. lower, subject, reduce.
Ant. superior; primary.

subside, *v.* 1. sink, lower, decline, precipitate, descend, settle. 2. quiet, abate, decrease, diminish, lessen, wane, ebb.
Ant. rise; increase.

subsidiary, *adj.* supplementary, auxiliary, tributary, subordinate, secondary, ancillary.
Ant. primary, principal.

subsidy, *n.* aid, grant, subvention, support, tribute.

substance, *n.* 1. matter, material, stuff. 2. essence, subject matter, theme, subject. 3. meaning, gist, significance, import, pith, essence.

substantial, *adj.* 1. real, actual, material, corporeal. 2. ample, considerable, sizable. 3. solid, stout, firm, strong, resolute, stable, sound. 4. wealthy, influential, responsible. 5. worthy, valuable. 6. material, essential, important.
Ant. insubstantial, immaterial: trivial; unstable, unsound; poor; unworthy; unimportant.

subtract, *v.* withdraw, take away, deduct, diminish, detract, lessen, lower.
Ant. add.

subvention, *n.* subsidy.

succeed, *v.* 1. flourish, prosper, thrive, go well, make a hit, go swimmingly, prevail. 2. follow, replace.
Ant. fail; precede.

succession, *n.* 1. order, sequence, course, series. 2. descent, transmission, lineage, race.

successive, *adj.* consecutive, following, sequential, ordered.

succor, *n.* 1. help, relief, aid, support, assistance. —*v.* 2. aid, assist, relieve, help, support.

sudden, *adj.* unexpected, abrupt, unlooked for, unforeseen, quick, unanticipated.
Ant. deliberate, premeditated, foreseen.

suffer, *v.* undergo, experience, sustain, bear, tolerate, allow, permit, stomach, stand, meet with, feel.

sufficient, *adj.* enough, adequate, ample, satisfactory, competent.
Ant. insufficient.

suggest, *v.* propose, recommend, indicate, hint, insinuate, intimate, prompt, advise.

suggestive, *adj.* expressive.

sulky, *adj.* sullen, ill-humored, resentful, aloof, moody, surly, morose, cross, splenetic, churlish.
Ant. temperate, good-natured.

sullen, *adj.* 1. silent, reserved, sulky, morose, moody. 2. ill-humored,

sour, vexatious, splenetic, bad-tempered. 3. gloomy, dismal, cheerless, clouded, overcast, somber, mournful, dark. 4. slow, sluggish, dull, stagnant.
Ant. cheerful.

sully, *v.* 1. soil, stain, tarnish, taint, blemish, disgrace, dishonor. 2. dirty, contaminate, corrupt, pollute.
Ant. honor.

summary, *n.* 1. digest, extract, abstract, brief, synopsis, compendium, epitome, essence, outline, précis, abridgment. —*adj.* 2. brief, comprehensive, concise, short, condensed, compact, succinct, pithy. 3. curt, terse, peremptory, laconic.

summit, *n.* top, peak, apex, pinnacle, acme, vertex, culmination, zenith.
Ant. base, bottom.

summon, *v.* 1. call, invite, bid; convene, convoke. 2. call forth, rouse, arouse, activate, incite.

superannuated, *adj.* old, aged, decrepit, obsolete, antiquated, antique, anile, senile, passé.
Ant. young, youthful, new, voguish.

superb, *adj.* stately, majestic, grand, magnificent, admirable, fine, excellent, exquisite, elegant, splendid, sumptuous, rich, luxurious, gorgeous.
Ant. inferior.

supercilious, *adj.* haughty, disdainful, contemptuous, arrogant, scornful, contumelious.
Ant. humble.

superficial, *adj.* shallow, external, outward, exterior, slight.
Ant. basic, profound.

superfluous, *adj.* unnecessary, extra, needless, *de trop*, redundant, excessive, superabundant.
Ant. essential.

superintend, *v.* oversee, supervise, manage, direct, control, conduct, run.

supernatural, *adj.* 1. unnatural, superhuman, miraculous, preternatural. 2. extraordinary, abnormal.

supersede, *v.* 1. replace, displace, supplant, succeed, remove. 2. void, overrule, annul, neutralize, revoke, rescind.

supplant, *v.* displace, supersede, replace, succeed, remove.

supple, *adj.* 1. flexible, pliant, pliable, lithe, limber, lissome, elastic. 2. compliant, yielding, agreeable, submissive. 3. obsequious, servile, sycophantic, groveling, slavish, cringing, fawning.
Ant. rigid, inflexible.

supplement, *n.* 1. reinforcement, extension, addition, complement, addendum, appendix, epilogue, postscript. —*v.* 2. complete, add to, complement.

supplicate, *v.* pray, entreat, petition, appeal to, beg, implore, crave, importune, sue, solicit, beseech.
Ant. order, command.

supply, *v.* 1. furnish, provide, replenish, stock, fill. 2. make up, make up for, satisfy, fulfill. 3. fill, substitute for, occupy. —*n.* 4. stock, store, inventory, hoard, reserve.

support, *v.* 1. bear, hold up, sustain, uphold. 2. undergo, endure, suffer, submit to, tolerate, bear, stand, stomach, go through, put up with. 3. sustain, keep up, maintain, provide for, nourish, nurture. 4. back, uphold, second, further, advocate, endorse, forward, defend. 5. aid, countenance, maintain, help, assist, advocate, succor, abet, relieve, patronize. 6. corroborate, confirm. —*n.* 7. maintenance, sustenance, living, livelihood, subsistence, keep. 8. help, aid, succor, assistance, relief. 9. prop, brace, stay.
Ant. fail.

suppose, *v.* 1. assume, presume, infer, presuppose, take for granted. 2. believe, think, consider, judge, deem, conclude.

sure, *adj.* 1. undoubted, indubitable, indisputable. 2. confident, certain, positive, assured, convinced. 3. reliable, certain, trusty, trustworthy, honest, infallible, unfailing. 4. firm, stable, solid, safe, secure, steady. 5. unerring, accurate, precise, certain, infallible. 6. inevitable, unavoidable, destined.
Ant. unsure, uncertain.

surfeit, *n.* 1. excess, superabundance, superfluity. 2. disgust, satiety, nausea. —*v.* 3. supply, satiate, fill, stuff, gorge, overfeed.
Ant. insufficiency.

surmise, *v.* 1. think, infer, conjecture, guess, imagine, suppose, suspect. —*n.* 2. conjecture, idea, thought, possibility, likelihood.

surpass, *v.* exceed, excel, transcend, outdo, beat, outstrip.

surplus, *n.* remainder, excess, surfeit, superabundance, residue.
Ant. insufficiency, inadequacy.

surprise, *v.* 1. astonish, amaze, astound, take unawares, startle, disconcert, bewilder, confuse. —*n.* 2. assault, attack. 3. amazement, astonishment, wonder.

surrender, *v.* 1. yield, give *or* deliver up, cede. 2. give up, abandon, relinquish, renounce, resign, waive, forgo. 3. submit, yield, capitulate, give up. —*n.* 4. resignation, capitulation, relinquishment.

surreptitious, *adj.* secret, unauthorized, stealthy, clandestine, subreptitious.
Ant. open.

surveillance, *n.* watch, care, control, management, supervision, superintendence.

survey, *v.* 1. view, scan, observe, watch, inspect, examine, scrutinize. —*n.* 2. examination, inspection. 3. poll.

survive, *v.* continue, persist, live, remain, succeed, outlive.
Ant. languish, die, fail.

susceptibility, *n.* sensibility, sensitivity, sensitiveness, susceptiveness, susceptibleness, impressibility.
Ant. insusceptibility.

suspect, *v.* 1. distrust, mistrust, doubt. 2. imagine, believe, surmise, consider, suppose, guess, conjecture. —*n.* 3. defendant. —*adj.* 4. suspected, suspicious.
Ant. trust.

suspend, *v.* 1. hang, attach. 2. defer, postpone, delay, withhold. 3. stop, cease, desist, hold up, hold off, discontinue, intermit, interrupt, arrest, debar.

suspense, *n.* 1. uncertainty, doubt, unsureness, incertitude, indetermination. 2. indecision, vacillation, hesitation, hesitancy, wavering, irresolution, scruple, misgiving. 3. suspension, intermission, pause, interruption, cessation, stop, remission, surcease, relief, respite, stay, rest, quiescence.
Ant. certainty; decision.

suspicion, *n.* 1. doubt, mistrust, misgiving, distrust. 2. imagination, notion, idea, supposition, conjecture, guess. 3. trace, hint, suggestion.
Ant. trust.

sustain, *v.* 1. hold *or* bear up, bear, carry, support, uphold. 2. undergo, support, suffer, endure, bear. 3. maintain, support, subsist, nourish, nurture. 4. purvey, supply, cater, furnish, support, aid, countenance,

help. 5. uphold, confirm, establish, approve. 6. confirm, ratify, corroborate, justify.
Ant. fail; disapprove.

swagger, *v.* 1. strut, parade. 2. boast, brag, bluster, blow. —*n.* 3. boasting, bragging, arrogance, affectation, braggadocio.

swallow, *v.* 1. eat, gorge, gulp, engorge, imbibe, drink. 2. consume, assimilate, absorb, engulf, devour. 3. accept, receive. —*n.* 4. mouthful, gulp, draught, drink.

swap, *v., n.* trade, barter, exchange.

swarm, *n.* 1. horde, bevy, crowd, multitude, throng, mass, host, flock, shoal. —*v.* 2. crowd, throng. 3. abound, teem.

swarthy, *adj.* dark, dusky, brown, dark-skinned, tawny, swart.
Ant. pale.

sway, *v.* 1. swing, wave, brandish. 2. incline, lean, bend, tend. 3. fluctuate, vacillate. 4. rule, reign, govern, prevail. 5. direct, dominate, control, influence. —*n.* 6. rule, dominion, control, power, sovereignty, government, authority, mastery, predominance, ascendency. 7. influence, power, authority, bias.

swear, *v.* 1. declare, affirm, avow, depose, state, vow, testify. 2. promise. 3. curse, imprecate, blaspheme.

sweat, *v.* 1. perspire. —*n.* 2. perspiration.

sweeping, *adj.* 1. broad, wide, extensive, comprehensive, wholesale, vast. 2. exaggerated, overstated, extravagant, unqualified, hasty.
Ant. narrow; qualified.

sweet, *adj.* 1. sugary, honeyed, syrupy, saccharine. 2. fresh, pure, clean, new. 3. musical, melodious, mellifluous, harmonious, tuneful, in tune, dulcet, tuneful, mellow. 4. fragrant, redolent, aromatic, perfumed, scented. 5. pleasing, pleasant, agreeable, pleasurable, enjoyable, delightful, charming, lovable, kind, amiable, gracious, engaging, winning, winsome, attractive, gentle. 6. dear, beloved, precious. 7. manageable, tractable, easygoing.
Ant. sour, bitter.

swell, *v.* 1. inflate, dilate, distend, grow, expand, blow up. 2. bulge, protrude. 3. grow, increase, augment, enlarge. 4. arise, grow, well up, glow, warm, thrill, heave, expand. 5. bloat, strut, swagger. —*n.* 6. bulkiness, distention, inflation, swelling. 7. bulge, protuberance, augmentation, growth. 8. wave, sea, billow. 9. (*slang*) fop, dandy, coxcomb, popinjay, blade, buck. —*adj.* (*slang*) 10. stylish, elegant, fashionable, grand. 11. grand, fine, first-rate.
Ant. decrease, diminish.

swerve, *v.* deviate, diverge, depart.

swift, *adj.* 1. speedy, quick, fleet, rapid, fast, expeditious. 2. quick, prompt, ready, eager, alert, zealous. —*n.* 3. swallow.
Ant. slow, slothful.

swindle, *v.* 1. cheat, cozen, defraud, dupe, trick, gull, victimize, deceive, con. —*n.* 2. fraud, trickery, confidence game, thimblerig, shell game, deception, knavery.

swindler, *n.* confidence man, cheat, deceiver, charlatan, mountebank, rogue, rascal, knave, sharper, trickster, impostor.

swing, *v.* 1. sway, oscillate, rock, wave, vibrate. 2. suspend, hang. —*n.* 3. sway, vibration, oscillation. 4. freedom, margin, range, scope, play, sweep. 5. jazz, ragtime.

sybarite, *n.* voluptuary, epicurean, sensualist.

sycophant, *n.* flatterer, toady, fawner, parasite, boot-licker, yes-man.

sylph, *n.* salamander, undine, nymph, gnome.

sympathetic, *adj.* 1. sympathizing, compassionate, commiserating, kind, tender, affectionate. 2. congenial, attached, affected *or* touched by.
Ant. unsympathetic.

synopsis, *n.* compendium, condensation, summary, brief, digest, epitome, abstract, abridgment, précis, outline, syllabus.

system, *n.* 1. assemblage, combination, complex, correlation. 2. plan, scheme, procedure, arrangement, classification. 3. world, universe, cosmos. 4. taxonomy, order.

T

taboo, *adj.* 1. forbidden, interdicted, prohibited, banned, sacred, unclean. —*n.* 2. prohibition, interdiction, exclusion, ostracism. *Ant.* allowed, sanctioned, approved; permission, approval.

tacit, *adj.* silent, unexpressed, unspoken, unsaid, implied, implicit, understood, inferred. *Ant.* expressed.

taciturn, *adj.* silent, reserved, uncommunicative, reticent, quiet. *Ant.* voluble, talkative.

tactful, *adj.* diplomatic, adroit, skillful, clever, perceptive, sensitive. *Ant.* tactless, maladroit.

tactics, *n.* strategy, generalship, maneuvering; maneuvers, procedure.

taint, *n.* 1. fault, defect, blemish, spot, stain, blot, flaw. 2. infection, contamination, corruption, defilement. 3. dishonor, discredit, disgrace. —*v.* 4. infect, contaminate, defile, poison, corrupt, pollute. 5. sully, tarnish, blemish, stain, blot.

take, *v.* 1. get, acquire, procure, obtain, secure. 2. seize, catch, capture, grasp. 3. grasp, grip, embrace. 4. receive, accept. 5. pick, select, choose, elect. 6. subtract, deduct. 7. carry, convey, transfer. 8. conduct, escort, lead. 9. obtain, exact, demand. 10. occupy, use up, consume. 11. attract, hold, draw. 12. captivate, charm, delight, attract, interest, engage, bewitch, fascinate, allure, enchant. 13. assume, adopt, accept. 14. ascertain, determine, fix. 15. experience, feel, perceive. 16. regard, consider, suppose, assume, presume, hold. 17. perform, discharge, assume, adopt, appropriate. 18. grasp, apprehend, comprehend, understand. 19. do, perform, execute. 20. suffer, undergo, experience, bear, stand, tolerate, submit to, endure. 21. employ, use, make use of. 22. require, need, demand. 23. deceive, cheat, trick, defraud. 24. catch, engage, fix. *Ant.* give.

tale, *n.* 1. story, narrative, fairy tale, account, fiction. 2. lie, fib, falsehood, fable.

talent, *n.* ability, aptitude, capacity, capability, gift, genius, faculty, forte. *Ant.* inability, incapability, weakness.

talk, *v.* 1. speak, converse. 2. consult, confer, discuss; gossip. 3. chatter, prattle, prate. 4. communicate. 5. utter, speak, mention. —*n.* 6. speech, talking, conversation, colloquy, discourse, dialogue, chat, communication, parley, conference, confabulation. 7. report, rumor, gossip, bruit. 8. prattle, empty words, words. 9. language, dialect, lingo.

talkative, *adj.* garrulous, loquacious, wordy, verbose, prolix, long-drawn. *Ant.* taciturn, silent.

tall, *adj.* high, elevated, towering, lofty. *Ant.* short.

tame, *adj.* 1. domesticated, mild, docile, gentle. 2. gentle, fearless. 3. tractable, docile, submissive, meek, subdued, crushed, suppressed. 4. dull, insipid, unanimated, spiritless, flat, empty, vapid, vacuous, jejune, prosaic, boring, uninteresting, tedious. 5. spiritless, cowardly, pusillanimous, dastardly. 6. cultivated. —*v.* 7. domesticate, break, subdued, make tractable. 8. soften, tone down, calm, repress, subjugate, enslave. *Ant.* wild.

tamper, *v.* 1. meddle, interfere, damage, misuse, alter. 2. bribe, suborn, seduce, lead astray, corrupt. *Ant.* neglect, ignore.

tangible, *adj.* 1. touchable, discernible, material, substantial, palpable, corporeal. 2. real, actual, genuine, certain, open, plain, positive, obvious, evident, in evidence, perceptible. 3. definite, specific, ineluctable. *Ant.* intangible; unreal, imperceptible.

tantalize, *v.* torment, tease, torture, irritate, vex, provoke.

tantamount, *adj.* equal, equivalent. *Ant.* unequal.

tar, *n.* 1. pitch, creosote, asphalt. 2. sailor, seaman, seafaring man, gob, mariner, swabby, seafarer.

tardy, *adj.* 1. late, behindhand, slack, dilatory, slow, backward. 2. slow, sluggish; reluctant. *Ant.* early, punctual.

tarnish, *v.* 1. dull, discolor. 2. sully, stain, taint, blemish, soil. —*n.* 3. stain, blot, blemish, taint. *Ant.* brighten.

tarry, *v.* 1. remain, stay, sojourn, rest, lodge, stop, abide. 2. delay, linger, loiter; wait. *Ant.* leave, depart.

task, *n.* duty, job, assignment, work, labor, drudgery, toil.

taste, *v.* 1. try, sip, savor. 2. undergo, experience, feel. 3. smack, savor. —*n.* 4. sensation, flavor, savor, scent. 5. morsel, bit, sip. 6. relish, liking, fondness, predilection, disposition, partiality, preference, predisposition. 7. discernment, perception, sense, judgment. 8. manner, style, character.

tasteless, *adj.* insipid, flat; dull, uninteresting. *Ant.* tasteful; interesting.

taunt, *v.* 1. reproach, insult, censure, upbraid, sneer at, flout, revile. 2. ridicule, mock, jeer, scoff at, make fun of, twit, provoke. —*n.* 3. gibe, jeer, sarcasm, scorn, contumely, reproach, challenge, scoff, derision, insult, reproach, censure, ridicule.

tavern, *v.* 1. bar, cafe; pub. 2. inn, hotel, public house, hostelry.

tawdry, *adj.* cheap, gaudy, showy, ostentatious, flashy, meretricious. *Ant.* expensive, elegant.

teach, *v.* instruct, educate, inform, enlighten, discipline, train, drill, tutor, school, indoctrinate. *Ant.* learn.

teacher, *n.* instructor, tutor, lecturer, professor, don. *Ant.* student, pupil.

tear, *n.* 1. (*plural*) grief, sorrow, regret, affliction, misery. 2. rip, rent, fissure. 3. rage, passion, flurry, outburst. —*v.* 4. pull apart, rend, rip, sunder, sever. 5. distress, shatter, afflict, affect. 6. rend, split, divide. 7. cut, lacerate, wound, injure, mangle.

tease, *adj.* 1. worry, irritate, bother, trouble, provoke, disturb, annoy, rail at, vex, plague, molest, harry, harass, chafe, hector. 2. separate, comb, card, shred. 3. raise a nap, teasel, dress. *Ant.* calm, assuage, mollify; unite; smooth.

tedious, *adj.* long, tiresome, irksome, wearisome, prolix, labored, wearing, exhausting, tiring, fatiguing, monotonous, dull, boring. *Ant.* interesting.

teem, *v.* 1. abound, swarm, be prolific *or* fertile. 2. empty, pour out, discharge.

tell, *v.* 1. narrate, relate, give an account of, recount, describe, report. 2. communicate, make known, apprise, acquaint, inform, teach, impart, explain. 3. announce, proclaim, publish, publicize. 4. utter, express, word, mouth, mention, speak. 5. reveal, divulge, disclose, betray, declare; acknowledge, own, confess. 6. say, make plain. 7. discern, identify, describe, distinguish, discover, make out. 8. bid, order, command, urge. 9. mention, enumerate, count, reckon, number, compute, calculate. 10. operate, have force *or* effect.

temper, *n.* 1. temperament, constitution, make-up, nature. 2. disposition, mood, humor. 3. passion, irritation, anger, resentment. 4. calmness, aloofness, moderation, coolness, equanimity, tranquillity, composure. 5. hardness, elasticity. —*v.* 6. moderate, mitigate, assuage, mollify, tone down, soften, soothe, calm, pacify, tranquilize, restrain. 7. suit, adapt, fit, accommodate, adjust. 8. moisten, mix, blend, work, knead. 9. modify, qualify.

temperament, *n.* disposition, make-up, temper, constitution, nature.

temperamental, *adj.* moody, irritable, sensitive, hypersensitive, touchy, testy, hot-tempered, bad-tempered, short-tempered.
Ant. serene, composed.

temperate, *adj.* moderate, self-restrained, continent; sober, calm, cool, detached, dispassionate.
Ant. intemperate, immoderate.

tempestuous, *adj.* turbulent, tumultuous, violent, stormy, impetuous.
Ant. peaceful, pacific, serene, calm.

temporary, *adj.* transient, transitory, impermanent, discontinuous, fleeting, passing, evanescent, short-lived, ephemeral.
Ant. permanent, infinite.

tempt, *v.* 1. induce, persuade, entice, allure, seduce, attract, lead astray, invite, inveigle, decoy, lure. 2. provoke, test, try, prove.

tempting, *adj.* enticing, inviting, seductive, attractive, alluring.
Ant. repulsive, repellent.

tenacious, *adj.* 1. retentive. 2. pertinacious, persistent, stubborn, obstinate, opinionated, sure, positive, certain. 3. adhesive, sticky, viscous, glutinous. 4. cohesive, clinging, tough.
Ant. unsure, uncertain.

tenacity, *n.* perseverance, persistency, pertinacity, obstinacy.
Ant. transitoriness.

tendency, *n.* direction, trend, disposition, predisposition, proneness, proclivity, inclination, leaning, bias, prejudice, drift, bent; movement.
Ant. failure, disinclination.

tender, *adj.* 1. soft, delicate. 2. weak, delicate, feeble. 3. young, immature, youthful. 4. gentle, delicate, soft, lenient, mild. 5. soft-hearted, sympathetic, tender-hearted, compassionate, pitiful, kind, merciful, affectionate. 6. affectionate, loving, sentimental, amatory. 7. considerate, careful, chary, reluctant. 8. acute, painful, sore, sensitive. 9. fragile, breakable, frangible, friable. 10. ticklish, delicate, sensitive. —*v.* 11. offer, proffer, present. —*n.* 12. offer, offering, proposal, proffer. 13. dinghy, skiff, rowboat, lifeboat, motorboat, boat, pinnace, gig. 14. coal car, coaler.
Ant. coarse, rough; strong; mature, adult; merciless, ruthless; apathetic; inconsiderate; tough; accept.

tenet, *n.* belief, principle, doctrine, dogma, opinion, notion, position, creed.

tense, *adj.* 1. tight, taut, stretched, rigid, strained. 2. nervous, neurotic, excited, strained.
Ant. lax; relaxed.

tentative, *adj.* experimental, trial, probationary, indefinite.
Ant. definite, confirmed.

tenuous, *adj.* 1. thin, slender, small, attenuated, minute. 2. rare, thin, rarefied. 3. unimportant, insignificant, trivial, trifling, nugatory, unsubstantial.
Ant. thick; substantial, significant.

termagant, *n.* shrew, maenad, bacchante, virago, nag, beldam, Xantippe, vixen.

terminate, *v.* 1. end, finish, conclude, close, complete. 2. bound, limit. 3. issue, result, turn out, eventuate, prove.
Ant. begin, open.

terrestrial, *adj.* earthly, mundane, worldly, terrene.
Ant. celestial.

terrible, *adj.* 1. dreadful, awful, fearful, frightful, appalling, dire, horrible, horrifying, terrifying, terrific, horrendous, horrid, gruesome, hideous, monstrous. 2. distressing, severe, extreme, excessive.
Ant. delightful, pleasant; moderate.

terror, *n.* horror, fear, panic, fright, alarm, dismay, consternation.
Ant. security, calm.

terrorize, *v.* dominate, coerce, intimidate.
Ant. ameliorate, mollify.

terse, *adj.* brief, concise, pithy, neat, compact, succinct, curt, sententious, concentrated.
Ant. attenuated.

test, *n.* 1. trial, proof, assay. 2. examination, quiz, exam. —*v.* 3. try, essay, prove, examine; refine, assay.

testimony, *n.* evidence, deposition, attestation, declaration, affirmation, corroboration.

testy, *adj.* irritable, impatient, touchy, tetchy, petulant, edgy, short-tempered, peevish, vexatious, choleric, snappish, waspish, splenetic, cross, cranky, irascible, fretful.
Ant. composed, calm.

thankful, *adj.* grateful, indebted, beholden, obliged.
Ant. thankless, ungrateful.

thaw, *v.* melt, liquefy, dissolve; warm.
Ant. freeze, solidify, sublimate, cool.

theme, *n.* 1. subject, topic, thesis, point, text. 2. composition, essay, paper. 3. motif, thread, tenor, ideas, trend.

theory, *n.* 1. assumption, hypothesis, rationale, explanation, system, conjecture, guess, plan, scheme, proposal. 2. view, contemplation, conception.

therefore, *adv.* hence, whence, wherefore, accordingly, consequently, so, then.

thersitical, *adj.* scurrilous, foulmouthed, abusive, vindictive, impudent.
Ant. honorable, polite, discreet.

thesaurus, *n.* storehouse, repository, treasury; dictionary, encyclopedia.

thick-skinned, *adj.* pachydermatous; insensitive, dull, obtuse, callous.
Ant. thin-skinned, sensitive.

thief, *n.* 1. robber; pickpocket, mugger. 2. burglar, cracksman, second-story man, housebreaker, safecracker.

thin, *adj.* 1. slim, slender, lean, skinny, poor, lank, gaunt, scrawny, emaciated. 2. sparse, scanty, meager. 3. fluid, rare, rarefied, tenuous. 4. unsubstantial, slight, flimsy. 5. transparent, weak. 6. faint, slight, poor, feeble. —*v.* 7. rarefy, dilute, reduce, diminish.
Ant. thick, fat, obese; abundant; substantial; opaque, strong; increase.

think, *v.* 1. conceive, imagine, picture. 2. mediate, ponder, consider, regard, suppose, look upon, judge, deem, esteem, count, account. 3. bear in mind, recollect, recall, remember. 4. intend, mean, design, purpose. 5. believe, suppose. 6. anticipate, expect. 7. cogitate, meditate, reflect, muse, ponder, ruminate, contemplate.

thirst, *n.* desire, craving, eagerness, hankering, yearning, hunger, appetite.
Ant. distaste, apathy.

thorough, *adj.* complete, entire, thoroughgoing, unqualified, perfect, done, finished, completed, total.
Ant. incomplete, unfinished.

thought, *n.* 1. concept, conception, opinion, judgment, belief, idea, notion, tenet, conviction, speculation, consideration, contemplation. 2. meditation, reflection, musing, cogitation, thinking. 3. intention, design, purpose, intent. 4. anticipation, expectation. 5. consideration, attention, care, regard. 6. trifle, mote.

thoughtful, *adj.* 1. contemplative, meditative, reflective, pensive, deliberative. 2. careful, heedful, mindful, regardful, considerate, attentive, discreet, prudent, wary, circumspect.
Ant. thoughtless.

thoughtless, *adj.* unthinking, careless, heedless, inattentive, inconsiderate, negligent, neglectful, remiss, unmindful, unobservant, unwatchful, reckless, flighty, scatter-brained, light-headed, giddy.
Ant. thoughtful.

thrash, *v.* beat, defeat, punish, flog, wallop, maul, drub.

threaten, *v.* menace, endanger, indicate, presage, impend, portend, augur, forebode, foreshadow, prognosticate.
Ant. protect, defend.

thrifty, *adj.* 1. frugal, provident, economical, sparing, saving. 2. thriving, prosperous, successful. 3. growing, flourishing, vigorous.
Ant. wasteful, prodigal, improvident; poor, unsuccessful; stunted.

thrive, *v.* prosper, succeed, flourish, increase, advance, luxuriate.
Ant. languish, die.

throng, *n.* 1. multitude, crowd, assemblage, swarm, horde, host. —*v.* 2. swarm, assemble, crowd, press, jostle; herd.

throw, *v.* 1. project, propel, cast, hurl, pitch, toss, fling, launch, send, let fly. —*n.* 2. cast, fling. 3. venture, chance. 4. scarf, boa, stole. 5. blanket, afghan, robe.

thrust, *v.* 1. push, force, shove, drive. 2. stab, pierce, puncture, penetrate. —*n.* 3. lunge, stab, push, drive, tilt, shove.

thwart, *v.* 1. frustrate, baffle, oppose, prevent, hinder, obstruct, defeat.

—*n.* 2. seat. —*adj.* 3. cross, transverse. 4. adverse, unfavorable.
Ant. favor, encourage, support, help.

tidy, *adj.* neat, trim, orderly.
Ant. messy, sloppy, untidy.

tie, *v.* 1. bind, fasten. 2. knot. 3. fasten, join, unite, connect, link, knit, yoke, lock. 4. confine, restrict, limit, obligate, constrain. 5. equal. —*n.* 6. cord, string, rope, band, ligature. 7. necktie, cravat. 8. knot; link, connection, bond.
Ant. loose, loosen, release.

time, *n.* 1. duration. 2. period, interval, term, spell, span, space. 3. epoch, era, period, season, age, date. 4. tempo, rhythm, measure. —*v.* 5. regulate, gauge.

timely, *adj.* seasonable, opportune, well-timed, prompt, punctual.
Ant. untimely, inappropriate, inopportune.

timid, *adj.* fearful, shy, diffident, bashful, retiring, coy, blushing, shrinking, timorous, fainthearted, tremulous, cowardly, dastardly, pusillanimous.
Ant. bold, fearless, intrepid.

tint, *n.* 1. color, hue, tinge, dye, stain, tincture; rinse; pastel. —*v.* 2. color, tinge, stain.

tirade, *n.* denunciation, outburst, harangue, declamation.

tire, *v.* 1. exhaust, weary, fatigue, jade. 2. exasperate, bore, weary, irk.

tired, *adj.* exhausted, fatigued, weary, wearied, enervated.
Ant. energetic, fiery, tireless.

tireless, *adj.* untiring, indefatigable, energetic, active.
Ant. tired, tiresome.

tiresome, *adj.* 1. wearisome, tedious, dull, fatiguing, humdrum. 2. annoying, vexatious.
Ant. interesting, enchanting.

title, *n.* 1. name, designation, epithet, appellation, denomination, cognomen. 2. championship. 3. right, claim. —*v.* 4. designate, entitle, denominate, term, call, style.

toady, *n.* sycophant, fawner, flatterer, yes-man.

toil, *n.* 1. work, labor, effort, drudgery, exertion, travail, pains. —*v.* 2. labor, work, strive, moil, exert.
Ant. indolence, sloth.

tolerance, *n.* 1. toleration, patience, sufferance, forbearance, endurance. 2. liberality, catholicity, impartiality, magnanimity, open-mindedness. 3. allowance, variation.
Ant. intolerance.

tool, *n.* instrument, implement, utensil, contrivance, device.

top, *n.* 1. apex, zenith, acme, peak, summit, pinnacle, vertex, culmination. 2. best, chief. —*adj.* 3. highest, uppermost, upper, greatest. 4. foremost, chief, principal. —*v.* 5. surpass, excel, outdo. 6. crop, prune, lop.
Ant. bottom, foot; worst; lowest; least.

topic, *n.* subject, theme, thesis, subject-matter.

torment, *v.* 1. afflict, pain, rack, torture, harass, harry, hector, vex, annoy, irritate, agonize, distress, excruciate. 2. plague, worry, annoy, pester, tease, provoke, needle, nettle, trouble, tantalize, fret. —*n.* 3. agony, torture, misery, distress, anguish.
Ant. please.

torpid, *adj.* 1. inactive, sluggish, slow, dull, apathetic, lethargic, motionless, inert, indolent. 2. dormant, hibernating, estivating.
Ant. active, energetic.

torrent, *n.* stream, flow, downpour.
Ant. drop, drip, dribble.

torrid, *adj.* 1. hot, tropical, burning, scorching, fiery, parching. 2. ardent, passionate.
Ant. arctic, frigid, cold; dispassionate, cool.

tortuous, *adj.* 1. twisted, crooked, winding, curved, twisting, bent, sinuous, serpentine, sinuate. 2. evasive, roundabout, circuitous, indirect, deceitful, ambiguous, crooked, dishonest.
Ant. straight.

torture, *n., v.* torment.

toss, *v., n.* throw.

total, *adj.* 1. whole, entire, complete, finished, final, full, absolute, utter, unqualified. —*n.* 2. sum, whole, entirety, totality, aggregate, gross. —*v.* 3. add up, amount to.

totter, *v.* 1. stagger, falter, reel. 2. sway, rock, waver. 3. shake, tremble, oscillate, quiver.

touch, *v.* 1. handle, feel. 2. tap, pat, strike, hit. 3. come up to, attain, reach, arrive at. 4. modify, improve. 5. play, perform. 6. treat, affect, impress, move, strike, stir, melt, soften. 7. deal with, treat. 8. pertain *or* relate to, concern, regard, affect. —*n.* 9. contact; contiguity. 10. stroke, pat, tap, blow. 11. hint, trace, suggestion. 12. characteristic, trait, style. 13. quality, kind.

tough, *adj.* 1. firm, strong, hard, hardy. 2. sturdy, hardy, durable. 3. hardened, incorrigible, trouble-

some, inflexible, rigid. 4. vigorous, severe, violent.
Ant. weak, feeble, sickly; flexible, soft; slight.

tour, *v.* 1. travel, visit. —*n.* 2. excursion, trip, journey, expedition.

towering, *adj.* tall, lofty, high, great, elevated.
Ant. short, low.

town, *n.* city, metropolis, borough, community, village, burgh, dorp, thorp, hamlet.
Ant. country.

toxin, *n.* poison, venom, virus.
Ant. serum, antitoxin.

trace, *n.* 1. vestige, mark, sign, track, spoor, footprint, trail, record. 2. mark, indication, evidence. 3. hint, suggestion, touch, taste, soupçon. —*v.* 4. track, follow, trail. 5. ascertain, find out, discover. 6. draw, delineate, outline, diagram. 7. copy.
Ant. abundance, plethora.

tract, *n.* 1. stretch, extent, district, territory, region. 2. space, period. 3. treatise, pamphlet, essay, sermon, homily, dissertation, disquisition.

tractable, *adj.* docile, malleable, manageable, willing, governable.
Ant. intractable.

trade, *n.* 1. commrce, traffic, business, dealing, exchange, barter. 2. purchase, sale, exchange, swap. 3. occupation, vocation, metier, livelihood, living, employment, pursuit, business, profession, craft, calling, avocation. —*v.* 4. barter, traffic *or* deal in, exchange. 5. barter, interchange, bargain, deal.

traduce, *v.* slander, calumniate, malign, defame, vilify, abuse, revile, asperse, depreciate, blemish, decry, disparage.
Ant. praise, honor.

traffic, *n., v.* trade.

tragic, *adj.* mournful, melancholy, pathetic, distressing, pitiful, calamitous, sorrowful, disastrous, fatal, dreadful.
Ant. comic.

trail, *v.* 1. drag, draw. 2. track, trace, hunt down. —*n.* 3. path, track; scent, spoor.

transact, *v.* carry on, enact, conclude, settle, perform, manage, negotiate, conduct.

transform, *v.* change, alter, metamorphose, convert, transfigure, transmute.
Ant. retain.

transgress, *v.* 1. violate, break, contravene, disobey, infringe. 2. offend, sin, err, trespass.
Ant. obey.

transient, *adj.* transitory, temporary, fleeting, passing, flitting, flying, brief, fugitive.
Ant. permanent.

transitory, *adj.* transient.
Ant. permanent.

translation, *n.* paraphrase, version, interpretation, rendering, treatment.

translucent, *adj.* semitransparent, translucid; transparent.
Ant. opaque, dense, solid.

transmit, *v.* send, forward, dispatch, convey, transport, carry, transfer, bear, remit.

transparent, *adj.* 1. transpicuous, diaphanous, clear, pellucid, lucid, limpid, crystalline; translucent. 2. open, frank, candid. 3. manifest, obvious.
Ant. opaque; clandestine, secretive; concealed.

transport, *v.* 1. carry, convey. 2. banish, exile. —*n.* 3. conveyance, transportation. 4. freighter, troopship, tanker, oiler. 5. joy, bliss, rapture, ecstasy, happiness.

trap, *n.* 1. pitfall, snare, springe. 2. ambush, pitfall, artifice, stratagem. —*v.* 3. ensnare, entrap, spring. 4. ambush.

traverse, *v.* 1. go counter to, obstruct, thwart, frustrate, contravene. 2. contradict, deny. 3. pass *or* go across, cross, cross over. —*n.* 4. obstruction, bar, obstacle. 5. crosspiece, crossbar, barrier, railing, lattice, screen. —*adj.* 6. transverse, cross.

travesty, *n., v.* burlesque, parody, lampoon, caricature, take-off.

treacherous, *adj.* 1. traitorous, unfaithful, faithless, untrustworthy, treasonable, treasonous, perfidious, disloyal. 2. deceptive, unreliable, insidious, recreant, deceitful. 3. unstable, insecure.
Ant. faithful, trustworthy, loyal; reliable; stable, secure.

treachery, *n.* betrayal, treason, disloyalty, faithlessness, perfidy.
Ant. loyalty, fealty.

treason, *n.* sedition, disloyalty, treachery, disaffection, lese majesty.
Ant. loyalty, allegiance.

treasure, *n.* 1. wealth, riches, hoard, funds; valuables, jewels. —*v.* 2. lay away, store, stock, husband, save, garner. 3. prize, cherish.

treat, *v.* 1. act *or* behave toward. 2. look upon, consider, regard, deal with. 3. discuss, deal with, handle. 4. entertain, regale, feast. 5. negotiate, settle, bargain, come to terms. —*n.*

6. feast, fête, entertainment, banquet.

tremble, *v.* 1. shake, quiver, quaver, quake, shiver, shudder. 2. vibrate, oscillate, totter. —*n.* 3. trembling, shaking, quivering.

tremendous, *adj.* 1. huge, gigantic, colossal. 2. dreadful, awful, horrid, horrendous, terrible, terrific, terrifying, horrifying, appalling.
Ant. small, tiny, microscopic.

tremor, *n.* 1. trembling, shaking, vibration, oscillation, shivering, quivering, quaking. 2. quake, earthquake, temblor.

tremulous, *adj.* 1. fearful, timorous, timid, frightened, afraid. 2. vibratory, vibrating, quivering, shaking, trembling, shivering.
Ant. fearless, intrepid; solid, firm.

trenchant, *adj.* 1. incisive, keen, sharp, cutting, bitting, sarcastic, sardonic, acute, pointed, caustic, piquant. 2. thoroughgoing, vigorous, effective.
Ant. weak, mollifying; ineffective.

trend, *n.* 1. course, drift, tendency, direction, inclination. —*v.* 2. tend, extend, stretch, run, incline.

trespass, *n.* 1. invasion, encroachment, intrusion, infringement. 2. offense, sin, wrong, transgression, crime, misdemeanor, misdeed, error, fault. —*v.* 3. encroach, infringe, intrude, invade. 4. transgress, offend, sin.

trial, *n.* 1. test, proof, experiment, examination, testing. 2. attempt, effort, endeavor, struggle, essay. 3. test, assay, criterion, proof, touchstone, standard. 4. probation. 5. affliction, suffering, tribulation, distress, sorrow, grief, trouble, misery, woe, hardship.

trick, *n.* 1. device, expedient, artifice, wile, stratagem, ruse, deception, fraud, trickery, cheating, deceit, duplicity. 2. semblance, appearance. 3. prank, joke, practical joke. 4. shift, dodge, swindle, maneuver, hoax, confidence game. 5. jugglery, sleight-of-hand, legerdemain, prestidigitation. —*v.* 6. cheat, swindle, beguile, dupe, fool, deceive, defraud, delude, cozen. 7. dress, array, deck.

trickery, *n.* artifice, trick, stratagem, fraud, deception, deceit, chicanery, knavery.
Ant. honesty.

trifling, *adj.* 1. trivial, insignificant, unimportant, petty, paltry, negligible, nugatory, slight, worthless, piddling, immaterial. 2. frivolous, shallow, light, empty.

Ant. important, significant, worthy; profound.

trim, *v.* 1. reduce, pare, clip, prune, shave, shear, cut, lop, curtail. 2. modify, adjust, prepare, arrange. 3. dress, array, deck, bedeck, ornament, decorate, adorn, embellish, garnish, trick out. —*n.* 4. condition, order, case, plight, situation, state. 5. dress, array, equipment, gear, trappings, trimmings. 6. trimming, embellishment, decoration; cutting, clipping, priming, reduction. —*adj.* 7. neat, smart, compact, tidy, well-ordered, ordered. 8. prepared, well-equipped.

Ant. augment, increase.

trip, *n.* 1. journey, voyage, excursion, pilgrimage, travel, tour, jaunt, junket. 2. stumble, misstep. 3. slip, mistake, error, blunder, erratum, lapse, oversight, miss. —*v.* 4. stumble. 5. bungle, blunder, err, slip, miss, overlook. 6. hop, skip, dance. 7. tip, tilt.

trite, *adj.* commonplace, ordinary, common, hackneyed, stereotyped, stale.

Ant. original, uncommon, unusual, extraordinary.

triumph, *n.* 1. victory, conquest, success. 2. joy, exultation, ecstasy, jubilation, celebration. —*v.* 3. win, succeed, prevail. 4. rejoice, exult, celebrate. 5. glory, be elated *or* glad, rejoice.

Ant. defeat, loss.

trivial, *adj.* trifling, petty, unimportant, insignificant, nugatory, paltry, slight, immaterial, frivolous, small.

Ant. important, significant, material.

troop, *n.* 1. assemblage, crowd, band, squad, party, body, unit, company, group, troupe. 2. herd, flock, swarm, throng. —*v.* 3. gather, flock together, swarm, throng, collect. 4. associate, consort. 5. assemble, group, convene.

trouble, *v.* 1. disturb, distress, worry, concern, agitate, upset, disorder, disarrange, confuse, derange. 2. inconvenience, put out, discommode, incommode. 3. annoy, vex, bother, irritate, irk, pester, plague, fret, torment, torture, harry, hector, harass, badger, disquiet, molest, perturb. —*n.* 4. molestation, harassment, annoyance, difficulty, embarrassment. 5. misery, distress, affliction, concern, worry, grief, agitation, care, suffering, calamity, dolor, adversity, tribulation, trial, misfortune, woe, pain, sorrow. 6. disturbance, dis-

order. 7. inconvenience, exertion, pains, effort.

Ant. calm, mollify; convenience, encourage, accommodate; happiness, fortune.

troublesome, *adj.* 1. annoying, vexatious, perplexing, galling, harassing. 2. laborious, difficult, arduous, hard, burdensome, wearisome.

Ant. simple, easy; trouble-free.

troupe, *n.* troop.

truculent, *adj.* fierce, brutal, savage, harsh, threatening, bullying, overbearing, ferocious, cruel, malevolent.

Ant. affable, amiable.

trudge, *v.* walk, pace, tramp, plod.

true, *adj.* 1. factual, actual, real, authentic, genuine, veracious, truthful, veritable. 2. sincere, honest, honorable, just, faithful, equitable, fair. 3. loyal, faithful, trusty, trustworthy, stanch, constant, steady, steadfast, unwavering, unfaltering. 4. accurate, exact, faithful, correct, precise; agreeing. 5. right, proper. 6. legitimate, rightful. 7. reliable, sure, unfailing, persevering. —*adv.* 8. truly, truthfully. 9. exactly, accurately, precisely. —*v.* 10. shape, adjust, place.

Ant. untrue.

trust, *n.* 1. reliance, confidence, assurance, security, certainty, belief, faith. 2. expectation, hope, faith. 3. credit. 4. obligation, responsibility, charge. 5. commitment, office, duty, charge. —*v.* 6. rely on, confide in, have confidence in, depend upon. 7. believe, credit. 8. expect, hope. 9. entrust, commit, consign.

Ant. mistrust, distrust.

trustworthy, *adj.* reliable, true, honest, honorable, faithful, stanch, loyal, steadfast, steady, straightforward.

truth, *n.* 1. fact, reality, verity, veracity. 2. genuineness, reality, actuality. 3. honesty, uprightness, integrity, sincerity, candor, frankness, openness, ingenuousness, probity, fidelity, virtue. 4. accuracy, precision, exactness, nicety.

Ant. lie, fiction, fabrication, untruth; fraudulence; dishonesty; inaccuracy.

try, *v.* 1. attempt, essay, endeavor, strive, put forth effort. 2. test, prove, examine, investigate. 3. melt, render; extract, refine, distill.

tryst, *n.* appointment, meeting, rendezvous, assignation.

tumid, *adj.* 1. swollen, distended, dilated, enlarged, turgid. 2. pompous, turgid, bombastic, inflated,

grandiloquent, grandiose, rhetorical, declamatory.

Ant. deflated, self-effacing.

tumult, *n.* 1. commotion, disturbance, disorder, turbulence, uproar, hubbub, fracas, agitation, affray, melee; riot, outbreak, uprising, revolt, revolution, mutiny. 2. agitation, perturbation, excitement, ferment.

Ant. peace, order; calm, serenity.

tumultuous, *adj.* 1. uproarious, turbulent, riotous, violent. 2. noisy, disorderly, irregular, boisterous, obstreperous. 3. disturbed, agitated, unquiet, restive, restless, nervous, uneasy.

Ant. calm, peaceful, pacific; regular, orderly; quiet, restful.

tuneful, *adj.* musical, melodious, harmonious, dulcet, sweet.

Ant. discordant, sour, flat.

turgid, *adj.* 1. swollen, distended, tumid. 2. pompous, bombastic.

Ant. humble.

turmoil, *n.* commotion, disturbance, tumult, agitation, disquiet, turbulence, confusion, disorder, bustle, trouble, uproar.

Ant. quiet, serenity, order, peace.

turn, *v.* 1. rotate, spin, revolve. 2. change, reverse, divert, deflect, transfer. 3. change, alter, metamorphose, transmute, transform, convert. 4. direct, aim. 5. shape, form, fashion, mold. 6. send, drive. 7. curve, bend, twist. 8. disturb, derange, infuriate, infatuate, distract. 9. sour, ferment. —*n.* 10. rotation, spin, gyration, revolution. 11. change, reversal. 12. direction, drift, trend. 13. change, deviation, twist, bend, turning, vicissitude, variation. 14. shape, form, mold, cast, fashion, manner. 15. inclination, bent, tendency, aptitude, talent, proclivity, propensity. 16. need, exigency, requirement, necessity.

tussle, *v.* 1. struggle, fight, wrestle, scuffle. —*n.* 2. struggle, fight, scuffle, conflict.

twist, *v.* 1. intertwine, braid, plait. 2. combine, associate. 3. contort, distort. 4. change, alter, pervert. 5. wind, coil, curve, bend, roll. 6. writhe, squirm, wriggle. 7. turn, spin, rotate, revolve. —*n.* 8. curve, bend, turn. 9. turning, turn, rotation, rotating, spin. 10. spiral, helix, coil. 11. turn, bent, bias, proclivity, propensity. 12. torsion, torque.

twit, *v.* 1. taunt, gibe at, banter, tease. 2. deride, reproach, upbraid.

type, *n.* 1. kind, sort, class, classification, group, family, genus, phylum, form, stamp. 2. sample, specimen, example, representative, prototype, pattern, model, exemplar, original, archetype. 3. form, character, stamp. 4. image, figure, device, sign, symbol.

tyrannical, *adj.* arbitary, despotic, dictatorial, cruel, harsh, severe, oppressive, unjust, imperious, domineering, inhuman.
Ant. judicious, unbiased, just, humane.

tyrant, *n.* despot, autocrat, dictator, oppressor.
Ant. slave, serf.

tyro, *n.* beginner, neophyte, novice, greenhorn; learner, student.
Ant. expert.

U

ubiquitous, *adj.* omnipresent, being, everywhere, present.
Ant. absent, missing.

ugly, *adj.* 1. repulsive, offensive, displeasing, ill-favored, hard-featured, unlovely, unsightly, homely. 2. revolting, terrible, base, vile, monstrous, corrupt, heinous, amoral. 3. disagreeable, unpleasant, objectionable. 4. troublesome, disadvantageous, threatening, dangerous, ominous. 5. rough, stormy, tempestuous. 6. surly, spiteful, ill-natured, quarrelsome, vicious, bad-tempered.
Ant. beautiful.

ultimate, *adj.* final, decisive, last, extreme, furthest, farthest, remotest.
Ant. prime, primary.

umbrage, *n.* offense, pique, resentment, displeasure, grudge.
Ant. pleasure.

umpire, *n.* 1. referee, arbitrator, arbiter, judge. —*v.* 2. arbitrate, referee, judge; decide, settle.

unaccountable, *adj.* 1. unanswerable, irresponsible. 2. inexplicable, inscrutable, strange, unexplainable, incomprehensible, unintelligible.
Ant. accountable.

unaccustomed, *adj.* 1. unusual, unfamiliar, new. 2. unused.
Ant. accustomed.

unaffected, *adj.* 1. sincere, genuine, honest, real, unfeigned, natural, plain, naive, simple, guileless, artless. 2. unmoved, untouched, unimpressed, unstirred.
Ant. affected.

unanimity, *n.* accord, agreement, unanimousness, harmony, unity, unison, concert.
Ant. discord, disagreement.

unapt, *adj.* 1. unfitted, unsuited, unsuitable, unfit, inappropriate, inapplicable, irrelevant. 2. unlikely, indisposed. 3. slow, inapt, unskillful, inept, incompetent, unqualified.
Ant. apt.

unassuming, *adj.* modest, unpretending, unpretentious, humble, unostentatious.
Ant. immodest, pretentious.

unbearable, *adj.* unendurable, intolerable, insufferable, insupportable.
Ant. bearable.

unbecoming, *adj.* 1. inappropriate, unsuited, unapt, unsuitable, unfitted, unfit. 2. unseemly, improper, indecent.
Ant. becoming, appropriate; seemly, proper.

unbiased, *adj.* fair, equitable, impartial, tolerant, unprejudiced, neutral, disinterested, uninterested.
Ant. biased, prejudiced.

unbounded, *adj.* 1. unlimited, boundless, limitless, immense, vast, infinite, immeasurable, endless, interminable, illimitable. 2. unrestrained, unconfined, unfettered, unchained, uncontrolled, unbridled, immoderate.
Ant. bounded, limited; restrained.

unbroken, *adj.* 1. whole, intact, complete, entire. 2. uninterrupted, continuous, deep, sound, fast, profound, undisturbed. 3. undisturbed, unimpaired.
Ant. broken, incomplete; interrupted, discontinuous; impaired.

unburden, *v.* 1. disburden, unload, relieve. 2. disclose, reveal; confess.
Ant. burden.

uncalled-for, *adj.* unnecessary, improper, unwarranted.
Ant. necessary, essential, proper.

uncanny, *adj.* strange, preternatural, supernatural, weird, odd.
Ant. common, usual, natural.

uncertain, *adj.* 1. insecure, precarious, unsure, doubtful, unpredictable, problematical, unstable, unreliable, unsafe, fallible, perilous, dangerous. 2. unassured, undecided, indeterminate, undetermined, unfixed, unsettled, indefinite, ambiguous, questionable, dubious. 3. doubtful, vague, indistinct. 4. undependable, changeable, variable, capricious, unsteady, irregular, fitful, desultory, chance.
Ant. certain.

uncivil, *adj.* 1. ill-mannered, unmannerly, rude, impolite, discourteous, disrespectful, uncouth, boorish, brusque, curt, impudent. 2. uncivilized.
Ant. civil.

unclean, *adj.* 1. dirty, soiled, filthy, nasty, foul. 2. evil, vile, base, impure, unvirtuous, unchaste, sinful, corrupt, polluted.
Ant. clean.

uncomfortable, *adj.* 1. disquieting, discomforting. 2. uneasy, ill at ease, unhappy, miserable, cheerless.
Ant. comfortable.

uncommon, *adj.* unusual, rare, scarce, infrequent, odd, singular, strange, peculiar, remarkable, queer, extraordinary, exceptional.
Ant. common.

uncommunicative, *adj.* reserved, taciturn, close-mouthed, reticent.
Ant. communicative, talkative, voluble.

uncompromising, *adj.* unyielding, inflexible, rigid, firm, steadfast, obstinate.
Ant. compromising, yielding, flexible.

unconcern, *n.* indifference, nonchalance, insouciance.
Ant. concern.

unconditional, *adj.* unrestricted, absolute, complete, unqualified, unconditioned, unreserved, categorical.
Ant. conditional, restricted, qualified.

unconscionable, *adj.* 1. unscrupulous, shady, dishonest, unlawful. 2. unreasonable, excessive, extravagant, exorbitant.
Ant. scrupulous; reasonable.

uncouth, *adj.* 1. awkward, clumsy, unmannerly, discourteous, rude, ill-mannered, uncivil. 2. unusual, strange, odd, unknown, unfamiliar.
Ant. courteous; natural, usual.

uncover, *v.* lay bare, disclose, reveal, expose, open, strip.
Ant. cover, conceal.

undaunted, *adj.* undiscouraged, fearless, brave, intrepid, undismayed.
Ant. daunted, discouraged.

undeniable, *adj.* 1. irrefutable, indisputable, indubitable, incontrovertible, incontestable, unquestionable; obvious, evident, clear, certain, sure, unimpeachable, unassailable. 2. good, unexceptionable.
Ant. doubtful, dubitable, questionable; poor.

undergo, *v.* experience, suffer, bear, tolerate, sustain, endure.
Ant. avoid.

underhand, *adj.* secret, stealthy, sly, crafty, dishonorable, clandestine, surreptitious.
Ant. open, candid.

understand, *v.* 1. perceive, grasp, realize, comprehend, interpret, conceive, know, see, apprehend, discern. 2. learn, hear. 3. accept, believe.
Ant. misunderstand.

undertow, *n.* underset, undercurrent, riptide, cross-current.

undine, *n.* sprite, water nymph, sylph.

undying, *adj.* immortal, deathless, unending, eternal, everlasting, permanent.
Ant. dying, mortal, temporary.

unearthly, *adj.* weird, ultramundane, supernatural, preternatural, ghostly, spectral, unnatural, strange.
Ant. earthly, terrestrial.

uneducated, *adj.* untutored, unschooled, unenlightened, uninstructed, uncultivated, untaught, uninformed, unlettered, illiterate, ignorant.
Ant. cultivated, cultured, literate.

unemployed, *adj.* unoccupied, idle, at liberty, jobless, between engagements.
Ant. employed, occupied.

unequaled, *adj.* unparalleled, matchless, unmatched, unrivaled, peerless, inimitable, incomparable.
Ant. parallel, rival, comparable.

unequivocal, *adj.* clear, plain, simple, direct, unambiguous, certain, obvious, evident, incontestable, absolute, explicit, unmistakable.
Ant. equivocal, ambiguous.

unerring, *adj.* unfailing, right, correct, exact, precise, sure, infallible, certain, accurate, definite.
Ant. errant, failing, fallible.

unessential, *adj.* nonessential, unimportant, dispensable, immaterial, unnecessary.
Ant. essential.

unexpected, *adj.* unforeseen, unanticipated, sudden, abrupt; surprising.

Ant. expected, foreseen, anticipated, gradual.

unfair, *adj.* biased, partial, prejudiced, unjust, inequitable.
Ant. fair.

unfaithful, *adj.* 1. false, disloyal, perfidious, faithless, treacherous, traitorous, deceitful, recreant, untrustworthy. 2. dishonest, crooked, unlawful. 3. inaccurate, inexact, imprecise. 4. fickle, untrue, inconstant; adulterous.
Ant. faithful.

unfavorable, *adj.* disadvantageous, unpropitious, adverse, inimical.
Ant. favorable.

unfeeling, *adj.* insensible, insensate, numb, callous, unsympathetic, hard, hard-hearted.
Ant. feeling, sympathetic.

unfit, *adj.* 1. unfitted, unsuited, unsuitable, inappropriate, inapt, unapt. 2. unqualified, incompetent, incapable. —*v.* 3. disqualify.
Ant. fit.

unfortunate, *adj.* unlucky, unhappy, luckless, unsuccessful, hapless, star-crossed, ill-starred.
Ant. fortunate.

unfriendly, *adj.* inimical, unkindly, hostile, unkind.
Ant. friendly.

unfruitful, *adj.* unproductive, barren, sterile, fruitless.
Ant. fruitful.

ungainly, *adj.* awkward, clumsy, ungraceful, uncouth.
Ant. graceful.

ungodly, *adj.* irreligious, impious, sinful, piacular, profane, wicked, depraved, polluted, corrupted, base, vile, evil.
Ant. godly.

unguarded, *adj.* 1. unprotected, undefended, open, naked, defenseless. 2. incautious, imprudent, thoughtless, careless.
Ant. guarded, protected; cautious, careful.

unhappy, *adj.* 1. sad, miserable, wretched, sorrowful, downcast, cheerless, disconsolate, inconsolable, distressed, afflicted. 2. unlucky, unfortunate, hapless. 3. unfavorable, inauspicious, unpropitious. 4. infelicitous, inappropriate, inapt, unapt.
Ant. happy.

unhealthful, *adj.* 1. insalubrious, unwholesome, unhealthy, noxious, poisonous, harmful. 2. ill, unhealthy, sick.
Ant. healthy, healthful, hale, hearty.

unhealthy, *adj.* 1. sickly, delicate, frail, weak, feeble, enfeebled, ill, diseased, afflicted. 2. unwholesome, unhealthful, unsanitary, unhygienic, insalubrious, deleterious, poisonous, noxious.
Ant. healthy.

uniform, *adj.* 1. invariable, unchanging, unwavering, unvarying, unvaried, unchanged, constant, regular. 2. undiversified, unvariegated, dun, solid, plain. 3. regular, even. 4. consistent, regular, constant. 5. agreeing, alike, similar. —*n.* 6. livery.
Ant. irregular, wavering; diversified; uneven; inconsistent.

unimpeachable, *adj.* irreproachable, unassailable, blameless, unexceptionable.
Ant. reproachable, censurable.

unimportant, *adj.* trivial, trifling, paltry, nugatory, secondary, insignificant, petty, slight.
Ant. important.

uninterested, *adj.* indifferent, unconcerned.
Ant. interested.

union, *n.* 1. junction, combination, unity, coalition. 2. society, association, league, confederacy, alliance. 3. marriage, matrimony, wedlock. 4. brotherhood.
Ant. separation, fissure.

unique, *adj.* 1. sole, only, single. 2. unequaled, alone, peerless. 3. rare, unusual, singular, odd, peculiar, strange, uncommon.
Ant. common, usual.

unite, *v.* 1. join, combine, incorporate, connect, conjoin, couple, link, yoke, associate. 2. combine, amalgamate, compound, blend, coalesce, fuse, weld, consolidate. 3. marry, wed.
Ant. separate, sever.

unity, *n.* 1. oneness, union, singleness, singularity, individuality. 2. concord, harmony, agreement, unison, concert, unanimity, uniformity.
Ant. disunity; disharmony.

universal, *adj.* 1. general, whole, total, entire; ecumenical. —*n.* 2. concept.
Ant. local; special.

unjust, *adj.* 1. inequitable, partial, unfair, prejudiced, biased. 2. undeserved, unjustified, unjustifiable, unmerited.
Ant. just.

unkind, *adj.* harsh, cruel, unmerciful, unfeeling, distressing.
Ant. kind.

unlawful, *adj.* illegal, illicit, illegitimate; bastard, spurious, natural.
Ant. lawful, legal.

unlike, *adj.* different, dissimilar, diverse, variant, heterogeneous.
Ant. like.

unlimited, *adj.* unrestricted, unconstrained, unrestrained, boundless, unfettered, limitless, unbounded, vast, extensive, infinite.
Ant. limited.

unlucky, *adj.* unfortunate, hapless, ill-fated, unsuccessful, ill-omened.
Ant. lucky.

unmeasured, *adj.* 1. unlimited, measureless, immense, vast, infinite. 2. unrestrained, intemperate, unconstrained; unstinting, lavish.
Ant. measured, finite; temperate, constrained.

unmerciful, *adj.* merciless, pitiless, unpitying, relentless, cruel, unsparing; unconscionable.
Ant. merciful.

unmindful, *adj.* heedless, regardless, careless, inattentive, neglectful, negligent, unobservant, forgetful.
Ant. mindful, aware.

unmistakable, *adj.* clear, plain, evident, obvious, palpable, patent.
Ant. unclear, dim.

unmitigated, *adj.* unqualified, absolute, complete, consummate.
Ant. mitigated.

unmixed, *adj.* pure, unalloyed, unmingled, unadulterated.
Ant. mixed, impure, mongrel.

unnatural, *adj.* 1. affected, forced, strained, out of character. 2. unusual, strange, abnormal, irregular, anomalous, aberrant. 3. cruel, evil, inhuman, heartless, hardhearted, brutal.
Ant. natural; humane.

unnecessary, *adj.* needless, superfluous, *de trop.*
Ant. necessary.

unnerve, *v.* discourage, disarm, shake, fluster, disconcert, upset.
Ant. steel, encourage.

unparalleled, *adj.* matchless, unmatched, unequaled, unrivaled, peerless.
Ant. equaled.

unpleasant, *adj.* unpleasing, disagreeable, unpalatable, unappetizing, offensive, obnoxious, noisome, repulsive, repellent; noxious.
Ant. pleasant.

unpractical, *adj.* impractical, visionary, speculative, theoretical.
Ant. practical.

unprejudiced, *adj.* unbiased, impartial, fair.
Ant. prejudiced, biased.

unprincipled, *adj.* unscrupulous, tricky, shrewd, dishonest, cagey, wicked, bad, evil, amoral.
Ant. principled; scrupulous.

unpretentious, *adj.* modest, unassuming, shy, abashed, bashful, self-effacing, unpretending, retiring, unobtrusive.
Ant. pretentious.

unqualified, *adj.* 1. unfit, incompetent. 2. absolute, unmitigated, out-and-out, thorough, complete, direct, unrestricted, downright.
Ant. qualified.

unquestionable, *adj.* indisputable, indubitable, incontrovertible, undeniable, irrefutable, incontestable; unexceptionable.
Ant. questionable.

unquiet, *adj.* restless, restive, turbulent, tumultuous, disturbed, agitated, upset, uneasy, nervous, perturbed, fidgety.
Ant. quiet.

unreal, *adj.* imaginary, artificial, unpractical, visionary, sham, spurious, fictitious, illusive, illusory, vague, theoretical, impractical.
Ant. real.

unreasonable, *adj.* 1. irrational, senseless, foolish, silly, preposterous, absurd, stupid, nonsensical, idiotic. 2. immoderate, exorbitant, excessive, unjust, unfair, extravagant.
Ant. reasonable.

unrefined, *adj.* 1. unpurified, coarse, harsh, crude. 2. unpolished, uncultured, ill-bred, rude, boorish, vulgar, gross.
Ant. refined.

unrelenting, *adj.* unabating, relentless, unremitting, implacable, inexorable, merciless, unmerciful, ruthless, pitiless, unpitying, uncompassionate, cruel, hard, bitter, harsh, stern, remorseless, austere.
Ant. relenting.

unreserved, *adj.* 1. full, entire, complete, unlimited. 2. frank, open, ingenuous, candid, naive, artless, guileless, undesigning, sincere.
Ant. reserved, incomplete; artful.

unruffled, *adj.* smooth, calm, unperturbed, tranquil, serene, collected, imperturbable, cool, composed, peaceful, controlled, undisturbed.
Ant. ruffled.

unruly, *adj.* ungovernable, disobedient, insubordinate, unmanageable, uncontrollable, refractory, stubborn, lawless; turbulent, tumultuous, disorderly, riotous.
Ant. obedient, subordinate.

unsatisfactory, *adj.* disappointing, inadequate, insufficient.
Ant. satisfactory.

unsavory, *adj.* tasteless, insipid; unpleasant, offensive, distasteful.
Ant. savory, tasteful.

unscrupulous, *adj.* unrestrained, unrestricted, conscienceless, unprincipled, unethical.
Ant. scrupulous, restrained.

unseasonable, *adj.* inopportune, ill-timed, untimely, inappropriate.
Ant. seasonable, opportune.

unseat, *v.* displace, depose; throw.
Ant. place.

unseemly, *adj.* unfitting, unbecoming, improper, indecorous, indecent, unbefitting, inappropriate.
Ant. seemly, fitting, becoming.

unsettled, *adj.* unstable, unsteady, shaky, undependable, unsure, unfixed, undetermined, indeterminate, changeable, wavering, vacillating, infirm, fickle, faltering, irresolute.
Ant. settled, stable, steady.

unsightly, *adj.* unpleasant, unattractive, ugly, disagreeable, hideous.
Ant. beautiful.

unskillful, *adj.* untrained, inexpert, awkward, bungling, clumsy, inapt, maladroit.
Ant. skillful.

unsophisticated, *adj.* 1. simple, artless, ingenuous, guileless, naive. 2. unadulterated, pure, genuine.
Ant. sophisticated.

unsound, *adj.* 1. diseased, defective, impaired, decayed, rotten, sickly, sick, ill, infirm, unhealthy, unwholesome. 2. fallacious, unfounded, invalid, false, erroneous, untenable, faulty. 3. fragile, breakable, frangible. 4. unreliable, unsubstantial.
Ant. sound.

unsparing, *adj.* liberal, profuse, generous, lavish, bountiful; unmerciful, merciless, ruthless, pitiless, unsympathetic, severe, unforgiving, harsh, inexorable, unrelenting, relentless, uncompromising.
Ant. illiberal, sparing, penurious.

unspeakable, *adj.* unutterable, inexpressible, ineffable, indescribable.

unstable, *adj.* 1. infirm, unsteady, precarious. 2. unsteadfast, incon-

stant, wavering, vacillating, undecided, unsettled.
Ant. stable.

unsteady, *adj.* 1. unfixed, infirm, faltering. 2. fluctuating, wavering, unsettled, vacillating, fickle, changeable, unstable. 3. irregular, unreliable.
Ant. steady.

unsuitable, *adj.* inappropriate, unfitting, unbefitting, unbecoming.
Ant. suitable.

untangle, *v.* unravel, unsnarl, disentangle.
Ant. tangle, snarl, entangle.

unthinkable, *adj.* inconceivable.
Ant. conceivable.

untidy, *adj.* slovenly, disordered; sloppy.
Ant. tidy.

untie, *v.* unfasten, loose, unknot, undo, unbind.
Ant. tie.

untimely, *adj.* unpropitious, unseasonable, inappropriate.
Ant. timely.

untruth, *n.* falsehood, fib, lie, fiction, story, tale, tall tale, fabrication, fable, forgery, invention.
Ant. truth.

unusual, *adj.* uncommon, extraordinary, exceptional, rare, strange, remarkable, singular, curious, queer, odd.
Ant. usual.

unvarnished, *adj.* plain, unembellished, unexaggerated.
Ant. embellished, exaggerated.

unwary, *adj.* incautious, unguarded, imprudent, indiscreet, hasty, careless, rash, heedless, precipitous, headlong.
Ant. wary.

unwholesome, *adj.* unhealthy, insalubrious, unhealthful, deleterious, noxious, noisome, poisonous, baneful, pernicious; corrupt.
Ant. wholesome.

unwieldy, *adj.* bulky, unmanageable, clumsy, ponderous, heavy.
Ant. manageable, light.

unwise, *adj.* foolish, imprudent, injudicious, ill-advised, indiscreet.
Ant. wise.

unwitting, *adj.* unaware, unknowing, unconscious, inadvertent, unintentional, ignorant.
Ant. intentional, aware.

unworthy, *adj.* inadequate, undeserving; worthless, base.
Ant. worthy.

unyielding, *adj.* 1. inflexible, firm, stanch, steadfast, adamant, resolute, indomitable, pertinacious, determined. 2. stubborn, obstinate, stiff, intractable, perverse, headstrong, willful.
Ant. flexible.

upbraid, *v.* reproach, chide, reprove, blame, censure, condemn.
Ant. praise, laud.

uphold, *v.* 1. support, sustain, maintain, countenance. 2. raise, elevate.
Ant. attack.

uppermost, *adj.* highest, topmost, predominant, supreme.
Ant. lowermost, lowest.

upright, *adj.* 1. erect, vertical, perpendicular, plumb. 2. honest, just, righteous, honorable, straightforward, virtuous, true, good, pure, conscientious. —*n.* 3. pole, prop, support, pile, pier, column, lally column.
Ant. horizontal, prone.

uprising, *n.* insurrection, revolt, revolution, rebellion.

uproar, *n.* disturbance, tumult, disorder, turbulence, commotion, hubbub, furor, din, clamor, noise; fracas, melee, riot.
Ant. peace.

upset, *v.* 1. overturn, capsize. 2. overthrow, defeat, depose, displace. 3. disturb, derange, unnerve, disconcert, agitate, perturb, fluster. —*n.* 4. overturn, overthrow, defeat. 5. nervousness, perturbation, disturbance. 6. disorder, mess. —*adj.* 7. overturned, capsized. 8. disordered, messy; sloppy. 9. worried, concerned, disconcerted, agitated, disturbed, perturbed, irritated.
Ant. steady, stabilize.

urbane, *adj.* courteous, polite, refined, elegant, polished, smooth, suave.
Ant. discourteous, impolite.

urge, *v.* 1. push, force, impel, drive. 2. press, push, hasten. 3. impel, con-

strain, move, activate, animate, incite, instigate, goad, stimulate, spur. 4. induce, persuade, solicit, beg, beseech, importune, entreat, implore. 5. insist upon, allege, assert, aver, declare, asseverate. 6. recommend, advocate, advise. —*n.* 7. impulse, influence, force, drive, push. 8. reflex.
Ant. deter, discourage.

urgent, *adj.* 1. pressing, compelling, forcing, driving, imperative, requiring, immediate. 2. insistent, importunate, earnest, eager.
Ant. unimportant.

use, *v.* 1. employ, utilize, make use of, apply, avail oneself of. 2. expend, consume, use up, waste, exhaust. 3. practice, put to use, exercise. 4. act *or* behave toward, treat, deal with. 5. accustom, habituate, familiarize, inure. —*n.* 6. employment, utilization, application, exercise. 7. utility, usefulness, service, advantage, profit, benefit, avail. 8. help, profit, good. 9. custom, practice, usage, habit. 10. occasion, need. 11. treatment, handling.
Ant. disuse.

useful, *adj.* 1. serviceable, advantageous, profitable, helpful, effectual, effective, efficacious, beneficial, salutary. 2. practical, practicable, workable.
Ant. useless.

useless, *adj.* 1. unavailing, futile, inutile, fruitless, vain, ineffectual, profitless, bootless, valueless, worthless, hopeless. 2. unserviceable, unusable.
Ant. useful.

usual, *adj.* habitual, accustomed, customary; common, ordinary, familiar, prevailing, prevalent, everyday, general, frequent, regular, expected, predictable, settled, constant, fixed.
Ant. unusual.

utilize, *v.* use.

utter, *v.* 1. express, speak, pronounce, say, voice. 2. publish, proclaim, announce, promulgate. 3. circulate. —*adj.* 4. complete, total, absolute, unconditional, unqualified, entire.
Ant. partial, incomplete, relative.

V

vacant, *adj.* 1. empty, void. 2. devoid *or* destitute of, lacking, wanting. 3. untenanted, unoccupied, empty. 4. free, unoccupied, unemployed, leisure, unencumbered. 5. unthinking, thoughtless. 6. vacuous, blank, inane.
Ant. full; occupied; encumbered; thoughtful.

vacillate, *v.* 1. sway, waver, reel, stagger. 2. fluctuate, waver, hesitate.

vagabond, *adj.* 1. wandering, nomadic, homeless, vagrant. 2. good-for-nothing, worthless. —*n.* 3. tramp, vagrant, hobo, gypsy, outcast, loafer. 4. scamp, rascal, knave, idler, vagrant.

vagrant, *adj., n.* vagabond.

vague, *adj.* 1. indefinite, unspecific, imprecise, obscure, dim, uncertain, unsure, indistinct, undetermined, indeterminate, unsettled. 2. unclear, unknown, unfixed, lax, loose.
Ant. definite, specific.

vain, *adj.* 1. useless, hollow, idle, worthless, unimportant, nugatory, trifling, trivial, inefficient, unavailing, unfruitful, futile, vapid. 2. conceited, egotistical, self-complacent, proud, vainglorious, arrogant, overweening, inflated.
Ant. useful; humble.

vainglory, *n.* 1. egotism, vanity, conceit. 2. pomp, show, ostentation.
Ant. humility.

valiant, *adj.* brave, bold, courageous, stout, stouthearted, intrepid.
Ant. cowardly.

valid, *adj.* just, well-founded, sound, substantial, logical, good, cogent, authoritative, effectual, efficient, efficacious, effective, binding, legal.
Ant. invalid, unjust.

valor, *n.* courage, boldness, firmness, bravery, intrepidity, spirit.
Ant. cowardice.

valuable, *adj.* 1. costly, expensive, rare, precious, dear. 2. useful, serviceable, important, estimable, worthy.
Ant. worthless.

value, *n.* 1. worth, merit, desirability, usefulness, utility, importance. 2. cost, price. 3. valuation, evaluation, estimation. 4. force, import, significance. —*v.* 5. estimate, rate, price, appraise. 6. regard, esteem, appreciate, prize.

vanish, *v.* 1. disappear, evanesce. 2. end, cease, fade.
Ant. appear; begin.

vanity, *n.* 1. pride, conceit, self-esteem, egotism, self-complacency, self-admiration. 2. hollowness, emptiness, sham, unreality, folly, triviality, futility.
Ant. humility.

vanquish, *v.* conquer, defeat, overcome, overpower, subjugate, suppress, subdue, crush, quell, rout.
Ant. lose.

vapid, *adj.* 1. lifeless, dull, flavorless, insipid, flat. 2. spiritless, unanimated, dull, uninteresting, tedious, tiresome, prosaic.
Ant. spirited, animated.

variable, *adj.* 1. changeable, alterable. 2. inconstant. fickle, vacillating, wavering, fluctuating, unsteady.
Ant. invariable; constant.

variance, *n.* 1. divergence, discrepancy, difference. 2. disagreement, dispute, quarrel, controversy, dissension, discord, strife.
Ant. invariance, similitude, sameness.

variation, *n.* 1. change, mutation, vicissitude, alteration, modification. 2. deviation, divergence, difference, discrepancy; diversity.
Ant. sameness.

variety, *n.* 1. diversity, difference, discrepancy, divergence. 2. diversity, multiplicity. 3. assortment, collection, group. 4. kind, sort, class, species.
Ant. sameness.

various, *adj.* differing, different, divers, distinct, several, many, diverse, sundry, diversified, variegated, varied.
Ant. same, similar.

vary, *v.* 1. change, alter, diversify, modify. 2. transform, metamorphose, transmute, change. 3. differ, deviate. 4. alternate.

vast, *adj.* extensive, immense, huge, enormous, gigantic, colossal, measureless, boundless, unlimited, prodigious, stupendous.
Ant. limited, small.

vault, *n.* 1. arch, ceiling, roof. 2. cellar, catacomb, crypt, tomb. 3. safe, safety deposit box. —*v.* 4. arch. 5. leap, spring, jump.

vehemence, *n.* eagerness, impetuosity, verve, fire, ardor, violence, fervor, zeal, passion, enthusiasm, fervency, fury.
Ant. coolness, apathy, antipathy.

vehement, *adj.* eager, impetuous, impassioned, passionate, violent, ardent, zealous, earnest, fervent, fervid, burning, fiery, afire, ablaze.
Ant. cool, dispassionate.

velocity, *n.* rapidity, swiftness, quickness, speed, alacrity, celerity.

venal, *adj.* corrupt, bribable, unscrupulous, mercenary, purchasable, sordid.
Ant. pure, scrupulous.

veneration, *n.* respect, reverence, awe.
Ant. disrespect, irreverence.

vengeance, *n.* avenging, revenge, retribution, requital, retaliation.
Ant. forgiveness, pardon.

venial, *adj.* excusable, forgivable, pardonable.
Ant. inexcusable, unforgivable, mortal.

venom, *n.* 1. poison, virus. 2. spite, malice, malignity, maliciousness, spitefulness, acrimony, bitterness, acerbity, malevolence, gall, spleen, hate, contempt.

venture, *n.* 1. hazard, danger, jeopardy, risk, peril. 2. speculation. —*v.* 3. endanger, imperil, risk, jeopardize, hazard. 4. dare, presume, make bold.

venturous, *adj.* 1. bold, daring, adventurous, venturesome, daring, rash, intrepid, fearless, enterprising. 2. hazardous, dangerous, risky, perilous.
Ant. fearful, cowardly; secure, safe.

verbal, *adj.* oral, nuncupative, spoken, worded.
Ant. mental, physial.

verge, *n.* 1. edge, rim, margin, brim, lip. 2. brink, limit. 3. belt, strip, border. 4. room, area, scope. 5. rod, wand, mace, staff. —*v.* 6. border, tend, lean, incline.

verse, *n.* 1. stich. 2. poetry, meter, poesy, versification, numbers. 3. stanza, strophe, stave, section.

versed, *adj.* experienced, practiced, skilled.
Ant. inexperienced, unskilled.

version, *n.* 1. translation, rendering, interpretation. 2. variant, form, rendition.

vertical, *adj.* upright, plumb, zenithal, erect, perpendicular.
Ant. horizontal.

vestige, *n.* trace, hint, suggestion, mark,, evidence, token.

vex, *v.* 1. irritate, annoy, pester, provoke, anger, irk, fret, nettle. 2. torment, plague, worry, hector, harry, harass, torture, persecute. 3. agitate, discuss, debate. *Ant.* delight.

vexatious, *adj.* disturbing, annoying, vexing, troublesome, irritating. *Ant.* delightful, pleasant.

vexed, *adj.* 1. disturbed, troubled, annoyed. 2. disputed, discussed. *Ant.* delighted.

vibrant, *adj.* 1. vibrating, shaking, oscillating; resonant. 2. pulsating, energetic, powerful, vigorous; exciting, thrilling.

vibrate, *v.* 1. oscillate; shake, tremble, quiver, shiver. 2. resound, echo.

vicarious, *adj.* substituted; delegated, deputed. *Ant.* real, actual.

vice, *n.* 1. fault, sin, depravity, iniquity, wickedness, corruption. 2. blemish, blot, imperfection, defect. *Ant.* virtue.

vicious, *adj.* 1. immoral, depraved, profligate, sinful, corrupt, bad, abandoned, iniquitous. 2. reprehensible, blameworthy, censurable, wrong, improper. 3. spiteful, malignant, malicious, malevolent. 4. faulty, defective. 5. ill-tempered, bad-tempered, refractory. *Ant.* moral; commendatory; benevolent; temperate.

victimize, *v.* dupe, swindle, cheat, deceive, trick, defraud, cozen, fool, hoodwink, beguile.

victory, *n.* conquest, triumph, success. *Ant.* defeat.

vie, *v.* compete, rival, contend, strive.

view, *n.* 1. sight, vision. 2. prospect, scene, vista. 3. aspect, appearance. 4. contemplation, examination, survey, inspection. 5. aim, intention, purpose, reason, end, design, intent, object. 6. consideration, regard. 7. account, description. 8. conception, idea, notion, opinion, theory, belief, judgment, estimation, assessment, impression, valuation. —*v.* 9. see, behold, witness, contemplate, regard, look at, survey, inspect, examine.

vigilant, *adj.* attentive, wary, alert, awake, sleepless, watchful. *Ant.* inattentive, unwary.

vigorous, *adj.* strong, active, robust, sturdy, sound, healthy, hale, energetic, forcible, powerful, effective, forceful. *Ant.* weak, inactive.

vile, *adj.* 1. wretched, bad; base, low, vicious, evil, depraved, iniquitous. 2. offensive, obnoxious, objectionable, repulsive, disgusting, despicable, revolting, repellent, nauseous, nauseating. 3. foul, vulgar, obscene. 4. poor, wretched, mean, menial, low, degraded, ignominious, contemptible. 5. valueless, paltry, trivial, trifling, niggling, nugatory. *Ant.* good, elevated.

vilify, *v.* defame, traduce, depreciate, slander, disparage, malign, calumniate, revile, abuse, blacken, asperse, slur, decry. *Ant.* commend, honor, praise.

village, *n.* town, hamlet, municipality, community.

villain, *n.* scoundrel, cad, bounder, knave, rascal, rapscallion, scamp, rogue, scapegrace, miscreant, reprobate. *Ant.* hero, protagonist.

vindicate, *v.* 1. clear, exonerate. 2. uphold, justify, maintain, defend, assert, support. *Ant.* convict, blame.

vindictive, *adj.* revengeful, vengeful, spiteful, unforgiving, rancorous, unrelenting. *Ant.* forgiving.

violation, *n.* 1. breach, infringement, transgression. 2. desecration, defilement. 3. ravishment, rape, defloration, debauchment. *Ant.* obedience.

violence, *n.* 1. injury, wrong, outrage, injustice. 2. vehemence, impetuosity, fury, intensity, severity, acuteness. 3. energy, force.

virgin, *n.* 1. maiden, maid, ingenue. —*adj.* 2. pure, unsullied, undefiled, chaste, unpolluted. 3. unmixed, unalloyed, pure, unadulterated. 4. untouched, untried, unused, fresh, new, maiden. *Ant.* defiled, polluted, impure, unchaste; adulterated.

virile, *adj.* masculine, manly, vigorous, male. *Ant.* effeminate.

virtue, *n.* 1. goodness, uprightness, morality, probity, rectitude, integrity. 2. chastity, virginity, purity. 3. justice, prudence, temperance, fortitude; faith, hope, charity. 4. excellence, merit, quality, asset. 5. effectiveness, efficacy, force, power, potency. *Ant.* vice.

virtuous, *adj.* right, upright, moral, righteous, good, chaste, pure. *Ant.* vicious.

virulent, *adj.* 1. poisonous, malignant, deadly, venomous. 2. hostile, bitter, acrimonious, acerb, spiteful, vicious. *Ant.* harmless.

virus, *n.* poison, venom, toxin.

visage, *n.* 1. face, countenance, physiognomy. 2. aspect, appearance.

viscous, *adj.* sticky, adhesive, glutinous, ropy, thick.

visible, *adj.* 1. perceptible, discernible, open. 2. understandable, discernible. 3. apparent, manifest, obvious, evident, open, clear, patent, palpable, conspicuous, observable, unmistakable. *Ant.* invisible.

vision, *n.* 1. sight. 2. perception, discernment. 3. view, image, conception, idea, anticipation. 4. apparition, specter, ghost, phantom, phantasm, illusion, chimera.

visionary, *adj.* 1. fanciful, unpractical, impractical, impracticable, fancied, unreal, ideal, imaginary, speculative, illusory, chimerical, romantic. —*n.* 2. romantic, dreamer, idealist, theorist, enthusiast. *Ant.* practical, practicable.

visitor, *n.* caller, guest, visitant. *Ant.* host, hostess.

vista, *n.* view.

vital, *adj.* indispensable, essential, necessary, important, critical. *Ant.* dispensable, secondary, unimportant.

vitriolic, *adj.* acid, bitter, caustic, scathing. *Ant.* bland, mild, sweet.

vituperate, *v.* abuse, revile, objurgate, censure, vilify, reproach, upbraid, berate, scold. *Ant.* praise, commend.

vivacious, *adj.* lively, animated, sprightly, spirited, brisk, sportive. *Ant.* inanimate, dull, inactive.

vivid, *adj.* 1. bright, brilliant, intense, clear, lucid. 2. animated, spirited, vivacious, lively, intense. 3. vigorous, energetic. 4. picturesque, lifelike, realistic. 5. perceptible, clear, discernible, apparent. 6. strong, distinct, striking. *Ant.* dull.

vocation, *n.* business, occupation, profession, calling, trade, métier, employment, pursuit.

vociferous, *adj.* clamorous, noisy, loud, obstreperous, uproarious. *Ant.* quiet, pacific, peaceful.

vogue, *n.* fashion, style, mode; currency, acceptance, favor, usage, custom, practice.

void, *adj.* 1. useless, ineffectual, vain, ineffective, nugatory. 2. empty, devoid, destitute, vacant. 3. unoccupied, vacated, unfilled. —*n.* 4. space, vacuum; gap, opening. —*v.* 5. invalidate, nullify, annul. 6. empty, discharge, evacuate, vacate, emit. *Ant.* useful; full; occupied; validate; fill.

volition, *n.* will, will-power, determination, preference, discretion, choice, option.

voluble, *adj.* fluent, glib, talkative, loquacious.
Ant. taciturn, quiet, silent.

volume, *n.* 1. book, tome; scroll, manuscript, codex, papyrus. 2. size, measure, amount, magnitude. 3. mass, quantity, amount. 4. loudness, softness.

voluntary, *adj.* 1. deliberate, considered, purposeful, willful, intentional, intended, designed, planned. 2. spontaneous, impulsive, free, unforced, natural, unconstrained.
Ant. involuntary.

voluptuous, *adj.* sensual, luxurious, epicurean.
Ant. intellectual.

voracious, *adj.* ravenous, greedy, hungry, rapacious.
Ant. apathetic.

vow, *n.*, *v.* pledge, promise.

voyage, *n.* trip, flight, cruise, sailing.

vulgar, *adj.* 1. coarse, inelegant, ribald. 2. underbred, unrefined, boorish, common, mean, ignoble, plebeian, crude, rude. 3. vernacular, colloquial.
Ant. elegant; refined; standard.

vying, *adj.* competing, competitive.

wage, *n.* 1. (*usually plural*) hire, pay, salary, stipend, earnings, emolument, compensation, remuneration, allowance. 2. recompense, return, reward. —*v.* 3. carry on, undertake, engage in.

wager, *n.* 1. stake, hazard, bet, risk, venture, pledge. —*v.* 2. stake, bet, hazard, risk, lay a wager.

waggish, *adj.* roguish, jocular, humorous, mischievous, tricky, sportive, merry, jocose, droll, comical, funny.

wagon, *n.* cart, van, truck, dray; lorry, wain; buckboard, dogcart.

wait, *v.* 1. stay, rest, expect, await, remain, be inactive *or* quiescent, linger, abide, tarry, pause, delay. —*n.* 2. delay, halt, waiting, tarrying, lingering, pause, stop. 3. ambushment, ambush.
Ant. proceed.

waive, *v.* 1. relinquish, forgo, resign, demit, surrender, renounce, give up, remit. 2. defer, put off *or* aside.
Ant. require, demand.

wake, *v.* 1. awake, rise, arise, get up. 2. rouse, waken, arouse, awaken. 3. stimulate, activate, animate, kindle, provoke, motivate. —*n.* 4. vigil, deathwatch. 5. track, path, course, trail.
Ant. sleep.

wakeful, *adj.* 1. sleepless, awake, insomnious, restless. 2. watchful, vigilant, wary, alert, observant, on the qui vive.
Ant. sleepy.

waken, *v.* wake.

walk, *v.* 1. step, stride, stroll, saunter, ambulate, perambulate, promenade, pace, march, tramp, hike, tread. —*n.* 2. stroll, promenade,

march, tramp, hike, constitutional. 3. gait, pace, step, carriage. 4. beat, sphere, area, field, course, career; conduct, behavior. 5. sidewalk, path, lane, passage, footpath, alley, avenue.

wall, *n.* 1. battlement, breastwork, bulwark, barrier, bunker, rampart, bastion. 2. barrier, obstruction. 3. embankment, dike. —*v.* 4. enclose, shut off, divide, protect; immure.

wallow, *v.* welter, flounder, roll.

wan, *adj.* pale, pallid, sickly, ashen.
Ant. ruddy, robust.

wander, *v.* 1. ramble, rove, roam, stray, range, stroll, meander, saunter. 2. move, pass, extend. 3. deviate, err, go astray, digress, swerve, veer. 4. rave, be delirious.

wane, *v.* 1. decrease, decline, diminish, fail, sink. —*n.* 2. decrease, decline, diminution; failure, decay.
Ant. wax.

want, *v.* 1. need, desire, wish, require, lack. —*n.* 2. necessity, need, requirement, desideratum. 3. lack, dearth, scarcity, scarceness, inadequacy, insufficiency, scantiness, paucity, meagerness, deficiency, defectiveness. 4. destitution, poverty, privation, penury, indigence, straits.
Ant. relinquish.

wanton, *adj.* 1. reckless, malicious, unjustifiable, careless, heedless, willful, inconsiderate, groundless. 2. deliberate, calculated, uncalled-for. 3. unruly, wild, reckless. 4. lawless, unbridled, loose, lascivious, lewd, licentious, dissolute, lustful, prurient, lecherous, salacious, incontinent, concupiscent, libidinous. 5. luxurious, magnificent, elegant, lavish. —*v.* 6. squander, waste.

Ant. justifiable, careful; lawful; prudish; inelegant; save.

warden, *n.* warder, guardian, guard, custodian, keeper, caretaker, superintendent.

warlike, *adj.* martial, military; bellicose, belligerent, hostile, inimical, unfriendly.
Ant. peaceful.

warm, *adj.* 1. lukewarm, tepid, heated. 2. hearty, enthusiastic, emotional, zealous, fervent, fervid, ardent, excited, eager. 3. cordial, hearty, glowing. 4. attached, friendly, amiable, amicable, close, inimate. 5. heated, irritated, annoyed, vexed, angry, irate, furious. 6. animated, lively, brisk, vigorous, vehement. 7. strong, fresh. —*v.* 8. warm up, heat up, heat, make warm. 9. animate, excite, waken, stir, stir up, rouse, arouse.
Ant. cool.

warn, *v.* 1. caution, admonish, forewarn. 2. notify, apprise, inform.

warning, *n.* caution, admonition, advice; omen, sign, augury, presage, portent.

warp, *v.* 1. bend, twist, turn, contort, distort, spring. 2. swerve, deviate. 3. distort, bias, pervert.
Ant. straighten.

warrant, *n.* 1. authorization, sanction, justification, commission. 2. pledge, guarantee, assurance, security, surety, warranty. 3. certificate, receipt, commission, permit, voucher, writ, order, chit. —*v.* 4. authorize, sanction, approve, justify, guarantee, vouch for. 5. assure, promise, guarantee, secure, affirm, vouch for, attest.

wary, *adj.* alert, cautious, vigilant, careful, circumspect, watchful, scrupulous, discreet.
Ant. unwary.

wash, *v.* 1. cleanse, clean, lave, launder, scrub, mob, swab, rub. 2. wet, bedew, moisten. 3. bathe. —*n.* 4. washing, ablution, cleansing, bathing. 5. fen, marsh, bog, swamp, morass, slough.

waspish, *adj.* 1. resentful, snappish. 2. irascible, petulant, testy.

waste, *v.* 1. consume, spend, throw out, expend, squander, misspend, dissipate. 2. destroy, consume, wear away, erode, eat away, reduce, wear down, emaciate, enfeeble. 3. lay waste, devastate, ruin, ravage, pillage, plunder, desolate, sack, spoil, despoil. 4. diminish, dwindle, perish, wane, decay. —*n.* 5. consumption, expenditure, dissipation, diminution, decline, emaciation, loss, destruction, decay, impairment. 6. ruin, devastation, spoliation, desolation, plunder, pillage. 7. desert, wilderness, wild. 8. refuse, rubbish, trash, garbage. —*adj.* 9. unused, useless, superfluous, extra, *de trop.* 10. uninhabited, desert, deserted, wild, desolate, barren. 11. decayed, ghost; devastated, laid waste, ruined, ravaged, sacked, destroyed. 12. rejected, refuse.
Ant. save.

watch, *v.* 1. look, see, observe. 2. contemplate, regard, mark, view, look upon. 3. wait for, await, expect. 4. guard, protect, tend. —*n.* 5. observation, inspection, attention. 6. lookout, sentinel, sentry, watchman, guard; vigil, watchfulness, alertness. 7. timepiece.

watchful, *adj.* vigilant, alert, observant, attentive, heedful, careful, circumspect, cautious, wary, wakeful, awake.
Ant. unwary, inattentive, incautious.

watchword, *n.* 1. password, countersign, shibboleth. 2. slogan, motto.

wave, *n.* 1. ridge, swell, undulation, ripple, breaker, surf, sea. —*v.* 2. undulate, fluctuate, oscillate; flutter, float, sway, rock.
Ant. hollow.

waver, *v.* 1. sway, flutter. 2. thicker, quiver. 3. shake, tremble, quiver, shiver. 4. vacillate, fluctuate, alternate, hesitate.

wax, *v.* 1. increase, extend, grow, lengthen, enlarge, dilate. 2. grow, become, come *or* get to be.
Ant. wane.

way, *n.* 1. manner, mode, fashion, method. 2. habit, custom, usage, practice, wont. 3. means, course, plan, method, scheme, device. 4. respect, particular, detail, part. 5. direction. 6. passage, progress, extent. 7. distance, space, interval. 8. path, course, passage, channel, road, route, track, avenue, highroad, highway, freeway, throughway.

wayward, *adj.* 1. contrary, headstrong, stubborn, capricious, captious, obstinate, disobedient, unruly, refractory, intractable, willful, perverse. 2. irregular, unsteady, inconstant, changeable.
Ant. agreeable, obedient, tractable; regular, constant.

weak, *adj.* 1. fragile, frail, breakable, delicate. 2. feeble, senile, anile, old, infirm, decrepit, weakly, sickly, unhealthy, unwell, debilitated, invalid. 3. impotent, ineffectual, ineffective, inefficient, inadequate, inefficacious. 4. unconvincing, inconclusive, lame, illogical, unsatisfactory, vague. 5. unintelligent, simple, foolish, stupid, senseless, silly. 6. irresolute, vacillating, unstable, unsteady, wavering, weak-kneed, fluctuating, undecided. 7. faint, slight, slender, slim, inconsiderable, flimsy, poor, trifling, trivial. 8. deficient, wanting, short, lacking, insufficient.
Ant. strong.

weaken, *v.* enfeeble, debilitate, enervate, undermine, sap, exhaust, deplete, diminish, lessen, lower, reduce, impair, minimize, invalidate.
Ant. strengthen.

weakly, *adj.* weak, feeble, sickly.
Ant. strong.

weakness, *n.* 1. feebleness, fragility. 2. flaw, defect, fault. 3. tenderness, liking, inclination.
Ant. strength.

wealth, *n.* 1. property, riches. 2. abundance, profusion. 3. assets, possessions, goods, property. 4. affluence, opulence, fortune, treasure, funds, cash, pelf.
Ant. poverty.

wealthy, *adj.* 1. rich, affluent, opulent, prosperous, well-to-do, moneyed. 2. abundant, ample, copious.
Ant. poor, poverty-stricken; scanty, scarce.

wearisome, *adj.* 1. fatiguing, tiring. 2. tiresome, boring, tedious, irksome, monotonous, humdrum, dull, prosy, prosaic, vexatious, trying.
Ant. energetic; interesting.

weary, *adj.* 1. exhausted, tired, wearied, fatigued, spent. 2. impatient,

dissatisfied. 3. tiresome, tedious, irksome, wearisome. —*v.* 4. fatigue, tire, exhaust, tire *or* wear out, jade. 5. harass, harry, irk.
Ant. energetic; patient; interesting; interest, captivate.

weave, *v.* 1. interlace, intertwine, braid, plait. 2. contrive, fabricate, construct, compose. 3. introduce, insert, intermix, intermingle.

weep, *v.* shed tears, cry, sob, lament, bewail, bemoan.
Ant. laugh, rejoice.

weigh, *v.* consider, balance, ponder, contemplate, study.

weight, *n.* influence, importance, power, moment, efficacy, import, consequence, significance.

weighty, *adj.* 1. heavy, ponderous. 2. burdensome, onerous. 3. important, momentous, significant, serious, grave, consequential.
Ant. light; unimportant, insignificant.

weird, *adj.* eerie, ghostly, unearthly, ultramundane, uncanny, mysterious, unnatural, supernatural, preternatural.
Ant. natural.

welfare, *n.* well-being, prosperity, success, happiness, weal, benefit, profit, advantage.

well, *adv.* 1. satisfactorily, favorable, advantageously, fortunately, happily. 2. commendably, meritoriously, excellently. 3. properly, correctly, skillfully, adeptly, efficiently, accurately. 4. judiciously, reasonably, suitably, properly. 5. adequately, sufficiently, satisfactorily. 6. thoroughly, soundly, abundantly, amply, fully. 7. considerably, rather, quite, fairly. 8. personally, intimately. —*adj.* 9. sound, healthy, healthful, hale, hearty. 10. satisfactory, good, fine. 11. proper, fitting, suitable, befitting, appropriate. 12. fortunate, successful, well-off, happy.
Ant. poorly, badly; ill, sick.

wet, *adj.* 1. soaked, drenched, dampened, moistened. 2. damp, moist, dank, humid. 3. humid, misty, drizzling, rainy. —*n.* 4. moisture, wetness, rain, humidity, drizzle, dampness, dankness. —*v.* 5. drench, saturate, soak, ret.
Ant. dry.

whim, *n.* fancy, notion, caprice, whimsy, humor, vagary, quirk, crotchet, chimera.
Ant. consideration.

whimsical, *adj.* capricious, notional, changeable, crotchety, freakish, fanciful, odd, peculiar, curious, singular, queer, quaint.

whine, *v.* complain, grumble; moan, cry.

whip, *v.* 1. lash, beat; flog, thrash, scourge, beat, switch, punish, flagellate, chastise; castigate. 2. pull, jerk, snatch, seize, whisk. —*n.* 3. switch, leash, scourge.

whirl, *v.* 1. gyrate, pirouette, spin, rotate, revolve, twirl, wheel. —*n.* 2. rotation, gyration, spin, revolution.

whiten, *v.* blanch, bleach, etiolate. *Ant.* blacken, darken.

whole, *adj.* 1. entire, full, total, undiminished, undivided, integral, complete, unbroken, unimpaired, perfect, uninjured, faultless, undamaged, sound, intact. —*n.* 2. totality, total, sum, entirety, aggregate, sum total. *Ant.* partial; part.

wholesome, *adj.* 1. salutary, beneficial, helpful, good. 2. healthful, salubrious, nourishing, nutritious, healthy, salutary, invigorating. *Ant.* unwholesome.

wicked, *adj.* evil, bad, immoral, amoral, unprincipled, sinful, piacular, unrighteous, ungodly, godless, impious, profane, blasphemous; profligate, corrupt, depraved, dissolute, heinous, vicious, vile, iniquitous, abandoned, flagitious, nefarious, treacherous, villainous, atrocious. *Ant.* good.

wide, *adj.* 1. broad. 2. extensive, vast, spacious, ample, comprehensive, large, expanded, distended. *Ant.* narrow.

wild, *adj.* 1. untamed, undomesticated, feral, ferine, savage, unbroken, ferocious. 2. uncultivated, uninhabited. 3. uncivilized, barbarous, barbarian. 4. violent, furious, boisterous, tempestuous, stormy, disorderly, frenzied, turbulent, impetuous. 5. frantic, mad, distracted, crazy, insane. 6. enthusiastic, eager, anxious. 7. excited. 8. undisciplined, unruly, lawless, turbulent, selfwilled, ungoverned, unrestrained, riotous, wayward, outrageous. 9. unrestrained, unbridled, uncontrolled, untrammeled. 10. reckless, rash, fantastic, extravagant, impracticable. 11. queer, grotesque, bizarre, strange, imaginary, fanciful, visionary. 12. disorderly, disheveled, unkempt. —*n.* 13. waste, wilderness, desert. *Ant.* tame, domesticated.

wilderness, *n.* wild.

wile, *n.* 1. trick, artifice, stratagem, ruse, deception, contrivance, maneuver, device. 2. deceit, cunning, trickery, chicanery, fraud, cheating, defrauding, imposture, imposition.

will, *n.* 1. determination, resolution, resoluteness, decision, forcefulness. 2. volition, choice. 3. wish, desire, pleasure, disposition, inclination. 4. purpose, determination. 5. order, direction, command, behest, bidding. —*v.* 6. decide, decree, determine, direct, command, bid. 7. bequeath, devise, leave.

willful, *adj.* 1. willed, voluntary, intentional, volitional. 2. self-willed, headstrong, perverse, obstinate, intractable, wayward, stubborn, intransigent, persistent, contrary, contumacious, refractory, disagreeable, pigheaded, cantankerous, unruly, inflexible, obdurate, adamant. *Ant.* unintentional, involuntary; tractable.

wily, *adj.* crafty, cunning, artful, sly, foxy, tricky, intriguing, arch, designing, deceitful, treacherous, crooked, seditious. *Ant.* dull, stupid.

win, *v.* 1. succeed, advance, win out. 2. obtain, gain, procure, secure, earn, acquire, achieve, attain, reach. 3. win over, persuade, convince. *Ant.* lose.

wind, *n.* 1. air, blast, breeze, gust, zephyr, draught. 2. hint, intimation, suggestion. 3. vanity, conceitedness, flatulence, emptiness. 4. winding, bend, turn, curve, twist, twisting. —*v.* 5. bend, turn, meander, curve, be devious. 6. coil, twine, twist, encircle, wreathe.

wink, *v.* 1. blink, nictitate. 2. twinkle, sparkle.

winning, *adj.* taking, engaging, charming, captivating, attractive, winsome. *Ant.* losing, repulsive.

wisdom, *n.* 1. discretion, judgment, discernment, sense, common sense, sagacity, insight, understanding, prudence. 2. knowledge, information, learning, sapience, erudition, enlightenment. *Ant.* stupidity.

wise, *adj.* 1. discerning, judicious, sage, sensible, penetrating, sagacious, intelligent, perspicacious, profound, rational, prudent, reasonable. 2. learned, erudite, schooled. —*n.* 3. manner, fashion; respect, degree. *Ant.* unwise.

wish, *v.* 1. want, crave, desire, long for; need, lack. 2. bid, direct, command, order. —*n.* 3. desire, will, want, inclination.

wit, *n.* 1. drollery, facetiousness, repartee, humor. 2. understanding, intelligence, sagacity, wisdom, intellect, mind, sense.

withdraw, *v.* 1. draw back *or* away, take back, subtract, remove; retract, recall, disavow, recant, revoke, rescind. 2. depart, retire, retreat, secede. *Ant.* advance.

wither, *v.* shrivel, fade, decay, wrinkle, shrink, dry, decline, wilt, languish, droop, waste, waste away. *Ant.* flourish, thrive.

withhold, *v.* hold back, restrain, check, keep back, suppress, repress. *Ant.* promote, advance.

withstand, *v.* resist, oppose, confront, face, face up to, hold out against. *Ant.* fail.

witness, *v.* 1. see, perceive, observe, watch, look at, mark, notice, note. 2. testify, bear witness. —*n.* 3. beholder, spectator, eyewitness. 4. testimony, evidence.

witty, *adj.* facetious, droll, humorous, funny, clever, original, sparkling, brilliant, jocose, jocular. *Ant.* silly, stupid.

wizard, *n.* enchanter, magician, sorcerer, necromancer, conjurer, charmer, diviner, seer, soothsayer.

woe, *n.* distress, affliction, trouble, sorrow, grief, misery, anguish, tribulation, trial, agony, wretchedness, disconsolateness, depression, melancholy. *Ant.* joy, happiness.

woman, *n.* female, lady. *Ant.* man.

wonder, *v.* 1. think, speculate, conjecture, mediate, ponder, question. 2. marvel, be astonished *or* astounded. —*n.* 3. surprise, astonishment, amazement, awe, bewilderment, puzzlement; admiration.

wonderful, *adj.* marvelous, extraordinary, remarkable, awesome, startling, wondrous, miraculous, prodigious, astonishing, amazing, astounding, phenomenal, unique, curious, strange, odd, peculiar. *Ant.* usual, ordinary, common.

wont, *adj.* 1. accustomed, used, habituated, wonted. —*n.* 2. custom, habit, practice, use. *Ant.* unaccustomed.

word, *n.* 1. expression, utterance; assertion, affirmation, declaration, statement, asseveration. 2. warrant, assurance, promise, pledge. 3. intelligence, tidings, news, report, account, advice, information. 4. signal, catchword, password, watchword, shibboleth, countersign. 5. order, command, bidding. —*v.* 6. express, style, phrase.

wording, *n.* diction, phrasing, expressing.

work, *n.* 1. exertion, labor, toil, drudgery, moil. 2. undertaking, task, enterprise, project, responsibility. 3. employment, industry, occupation, business, profession, trade, calling, vocation, metier. 4. deed, performance, fruit, fruition, feat, achievement. —*v.* 5. labor, toil, moil, drudge. 6. act, operate. 7. operate, use, manipulate, manage, handle. 8. bring about, perform, produce, cause, do, execute, finish, effect, originate, accomplish, achieve. 9. make, fashion, execute, finish. 10. move, persuade, influence. *Ant.* leisure, indolence, idleness, sloth.

worldly, *adj.* 1. secular, earthly, mundane, temporal, terrestrial, common. 2. mundane, urbane, cosmopolitan, suave. *Ant.* spiritual; naive.

worry, *v.* 1. fret, torment oneself, chafe, be troubled *or* vexed, fidget.

2. trouble, torment, annoy, plague, pester, bother, vex, tease, harry, hector, harass, molest, persecute, badger, irritate, disquiet, disturb. —*n.* 3. uneasiness, anxiety, apprehension, solicitude, concern, disquiet, fear, misgiving, care.

worship, *n.* 1. reverence, homage, adoration, honor. 2. regard, idolizing, idolatry, deification. —*v.* 3. revere, respect, venerate, reverence, honor, glorify, adore. 4. adore, adulate, idolize, deify, love, like. *Ant.* detest.

worth, *adj.* 1. deserving, meriting, justifying. —*n.* 2. usefulness, value, importance, merit, worthiness, credit, excellence. *Ant.* uselessness.

worthy, *adj.* commendable, meritorious, worthwhile, deserving, estimable, excellent, exemplary, righteous, upright, honest. *Ant.* unworthy.

wound, *n.* 1. injury, hurt, cut, stab, laceration, lesion, damage. 2. harm, insult, pain, grief, anguish. —*v.* 3. injure, hurt, harm, damage, cut, stab, lacerate.

wrath, *n.* anger, ire, rage, resentment, indignation, dudgeon, irritation, fury, choler, exasperation, passion. *Ant.* equanimity, pleasure, delight.

wrathful, *adj.* angry, ireful, irate, furious, enraged, raging, incensed, resentful, indignant. *Ant.* equable, pleased.

wreck, *n.* 1. ruin, destruction, devastation, desolation. 2. shipwreck. —*v.* 3. shipwreck, spoil, destroy, devastate, ruin, shatter. *Ant.* create.

wrest, *v.* extract, take. *Ant.* give, yield.

wretched, *adj.* 1. miserable, pitiable, dejected, distressed, woeful, afflicted, woebegone, forlorn, unhappy, depressed. 2. sorry, miserable, despicable, mean, base, vile, bad, contemptible, poor, pitiful, worthless. *Ant.* happy.

wrong, *adj.* 1. bad, evil, wicked, sinful, immoral, piacular, iniquitous, reprehensible, unjust, crooked, dishonest. 2. erroneous, inaccurate, incorrect, false, untrue, mistaken. 3. improper, inappropriate, unfit, unsuitable. 4. awry, amiss, out of order. —*n.* 5. evil, wickedness, misdoing, misdeed, sin, vice, immorality, iniquity. —*v.* 6. injure, harm, maltreat, abuse, oppress, cheat, defraud, dishonor. *Ant.* right.

wry, *adj.* 1. bent, twisted, crooked, distorted, awry, askew. 2. devious, misdirected, perverted. *Ant.* straight; pointed.

xanthous, *adj.* yellow.
x-ray, *v.* 1. roentgenize. —*n.* 2. roentgenogram.

xylograph, *n.* wood engraving.

xyloid, *adj.* woodlike, ligneous.

yawn, *v.* 1. gape. —*n.* 2. opening, space, chasm.
yearning, *n.* longing, craving, desire.
yield, *v.* 1. give forth, produce, furnish, supply, render, bear, impart, afford, bestow. 2. give up, cede, surrender, submit, give way, concede, relinquish, abandon, abdicate, resign, waive, forgo. 3. relax, bend,

bow. —*n.* 4. produce, harvest, fruit, crop.
young, *adj.* 1. youthful, juvenile, immature. —*n.* 2. offspring. *Ant.* old, ancient; progenitors, parents.
youngster, *n.* youth, lad, stripling, child, boy. *Ant.* oldster.

youth, *n.* 1. youngness, minority, adolescence, teens, immaturity. 2. young man, youngster, teen-ager, adolescent stripling, lad, boy, juvenile. *Ant.* maturity; man, adult.
youthful, *adj.* young. *Ant.* old.
Yule, *n.* Christmas, Christmastide.

Z

zeal, *n.* ardor, enthusiasm, diligence, eagerness, fervor, desire, endeavor, fervency, warmth, earnestness, intensity, intenseness, passion, spirit. *Ant.* apathy, coolness.

zealot, *n.* bigot, fanatic, maniac.

zealous, *adj.* ardent, enthusiastic, eager, earnest, fervid, fervent, warm, intense, passionate, spirited. *Ant.* apathetic, uninterested, dispassionate, cool.

zephyr, *n.* breeze.

zest, *n.* piquancy, interest, charm; relish, gusto, heartiness, enjoyment, spice, tang. *Ant.* dullness.

zone, *n.* 1. belt, tract, area, region, district, section, girth. 2. region, climate, clime. —*v.* 3. encircle, gird, girdle, band.

zymosis, *n.* fermentation; germination; decomposition; decay.

PART FOUR

RHYMING
DICTIONARY

This dictionary is more complete, more up to date, and easier to use than any other rhyming dictionary of its kind.

The user will find an abundant supply of rhyming words here for the final syllable in one list and for the last two syllables in the second list. These words have been selected with the modern user in mind. While many obsolete and rare words have been included, they have not been accumulated indiscriminately. Most importantly, a very large number of recent and common words—many not entered in much larger dictionaries—have been included.

Rhyming words have been placed under the most commonly used spelling for a particular sound. To facilitate the location of desired lists, cross references have been liberally entered.

Following the two lists of rhyming words is a concise glossary of terms frequently encountered in the analysis of poetry.

PRONUNCIATION KEY FOR RHYMING DICTIONARY

ă	act, bat	m	my, him	ŭ	up, love
ā	able, cape	n	now, on	ū	use, cute
â	air, dare	ng	sing, England	û	urge, burn
ä	art, calm	ŏ	box, hot	v	voice, live
b	back, rub	ō	over, no	w	west, away
ch	chief, beach	ô	order, bail	y	yes, young
d	do, bed	oi	oil, joy	z	zeal, lazy, those
ě	ebb, set	ŏŏ	book, put	zh	vision, measure
ē	equal, bee	ōō	ooze, rule	ə	occurs only in
f	fit, puff	ou	out, loud		unaccented sylla-
g	give, beg	p	page, stop		bles and indicates
h	hit, hear	r	read, cry		the sound of
ĭ	if, big	s	see, miss		a *in* alone
ī	ice, bite	sh	shoe, push		e *in* system
j	just, edge	t	ten, bit		i *in* easily
k	kept, make	th	thin, path		o *in* gallop
l	low, all	th	that, other		u *in* circus

ONE-SYLLABLE RHYMES

-a, ah, baa, bah, blah, bra, fa, ha, ja, la, ma, pa, Ra, shah, spa; à bas, éclat, faux pas, hurrah, huzza, mama, papa, pasha, pasta, Ruy Blas; baccarat, cha cha cha, panama, Panama, Shangri-la; Ali Baba, Caligula, cucaracha, tarantara; Tegucigalpa; funiculi-funicula.

-ab, bab, blab, cab, crab, dab, drab, gab, grab, jab, Mab, nab, scab, slab, stab, tab; Ahab, bedab, confab, Punjab; baobab, taxicab.

-abe, Abe, babe, wabe; outgrabe; astrolabe.

-ac. See **-ack.**

-ace, ace, base, bass, brace, case, chase, dace, face, grace, Grace, lace, mace, pace, place, plaice, race, space, Thrace, trace, vase; abase, apace, birthplace, debase, deface, disgrace, displace, efface, embrace, encase, erase, footpace, grimace, horserace, misplace, outface, outpace, replace, retrace, scapegrace, staircase, ukase, uncase, unlace; about-face, boniface, carapace, commonplace, funnyface, interlace, interspace, marketplace, steeplechase.

-aced. See **-aste.**

-ach (-ăk). See **-ack.**

-ach (-ăch). See **-atch.**

-ache (-āk). See **-ake.**

-ache (-āsh). See **-ash.**

-acht. See **-ot.**

-ack, back, black, clack, claque, crack, hack, jack, Jack, knack, lac, lack, Mac, pack, plaque, quack, rack, sac, sack, sacque, shack, slack, smack, snack, stack, tack, thwack, track, whack, wrack, yak; aback, ack-ack, alack, arrack, attack, bareback, bivouac, blackjack, bootblack, cognac, drawback, Dyak, gimcrack, haystack, hogback, horseback, humpback, hunchback, Iraq, kayak, Kodak, knickknack, macaque, Meshach, ransack, repack, rucksack, Shadrach, shellac, Slovak, ticktack, unpack, zweiback; almanac, amphibrach, applejack,

bric-a-brac, Cadillac, cardiac, cul-de-sac, Frontenac, Hackensack, hackmatack, haversack, iliac, ipecac, maniac, pickaback, piggyback, Pontiac, Sarawak, stickleback, tamarack, umiak, Univac, zodiac; ammoniac, demoniac, elegiac, symposiac; aphrodisiac, dipsomaniac, hypochondriac, kleptomaniac, pyromaniac.

-acked. See **-act.**

-acks. See **-ax.**

-act, bract, fact, pact, tact, tract; abstract, attract, compact, contact, contract, detract, diffract, distract, enact, entr'acte, exact, extract, impact, infract, intact, protract, react, redact, refract, retract, subtract, transact; abreact, cataract, counteract, interact, overact, re-enact, retroact, underact; matter-of-fact.
Also: **-ack + -ed** (as in *packed, attacked,* etc.)

-ad (-ăd), ad, add, bad, bade, brad, cad, Chad, clad, dad, fad, gad, glad, had, lad, mad, pad, plaid, sad, scad, shad, tad; Bagdad, begad, dryad, egad, footpad, forbade, gonad, monad, nomad, Pleiad, tetrad, unclad; aoudad, Dunciad, hebdomad, Iliad, ironclad, Leningrad, Petrograd, Stalingrad, Trinidad, undergrad; olympiad.

-ad (-ŏd). See **-od.**

-ade, aid, bade, blade, braid, cade, fade, glade, grade, jade, lade, laid, made, maid, neighed, paid, raid, shade, spade, staid, suède, they'd, trade, wade; abrade, afraid, alcaide, arcade, Belgrade, blockade, brigade, brocade, cascade, charade, cockade, crusade, degrade, dissuade, evade, grenade, home-made, housemaid, invade, limeade, mermaid, nightshade, parade, persuade, pervade, pomade, postpaid, prepaid, self-made, stockade, tirade, unlade, unmade, unpaid, upbraid;

accolade, Adelaide, ambuscade, balustrade, barricade, cannonade, cavalcade, centigrade, chambermaid, colonnade, custom-made, enfilade, escalade, escapade, esplanade, fusillade, gallopade, gasconade, lemonade, marinade, marmalade, masquerade, orangeade, overlade, overlaid, palisade, plantigrade, promenade, ready-made, renegade, retrograde, serenade, underpaid; harlequinade, rodomontade.
Also: **-ay + -ed** (as in *played,* etc.)
Also: **-eigh + -ed** (as in *weighed,* etc.)
Also: **-ey + -ed** (as in *preyed,* etc.)

-ade (-ăd). See **-ad.**

-ade (-ŏd). See **-od.**

-adge, badge, cadge, hadj, Madge.

-afe, chafe, safe, strafe, waif; unsafe, vouchsafe.

-aff, calf, chaff, gaff, graph, half, laugh, quaff, staff; behalf, carafe, distaff, Falstaff, flagstaff, giraffe, horselaugh, pikestaff, riffraff, seraph; autograph, cenotaph, epitaph, lithograph, monograph, paragraph, phonograph, photograph, quarterstaff, shandygaff, telegraph. See also **-off.**

-affed. See **-aft.**

-aft, aft, craft, daft, draft, draught, graft, haft, kraft, laughed, raft, shaft, Taft, waft; abaft, aircraft, ingraft, seacraft, witchcraft; handicraft, overdraft.
Also: **-aff + -ed** (as in *staffed,* etc.)
Also: **-aph + -ed** (as in *autographed,* etc.)

-ag, bag, brag, crag, drag, fag, flag, gag, hag, jag, lag, nag, quag, rag, sag, scrag, shag, slag, snag, stag, swag, tag, wag; dishrag, grabbag, ragtag, sandbag, wigwag, zigzag; Brobdingnag, bullyrag, saddlebag, scalawag.

-age (-āj), age, cage, gage, gauge, page, rage, sage, stage, swage, wage; assuage, engage, enrage, greengage, outrage, presage; disengage, overage, underage.

-age (-ĭj), bridge, midge, ridge; abridge, alnage; acreage, anchorage, appanage, arbitrage, average, beverage, brokerage, cartilage, cozenage, equipage, factorage, foliage, fuselage, hemorrhage, heritage, hermitage, lineage, mucilage, overage, parentage, parsonage, pasturage, patronage, personage, pilgrimage, privilege, reportage, sacrilege, sortilege, tutelage, vicarage.

-age (-äzh), arbitrage, badinage, barrage, collage, garage, gavage, ménage, mirage, moulage; badinage, camouflage, curettage, entourage, fuselage, persiflage, reportage.

-agm. See **-am.**

-agne. See **-ain.**

-ague, Hague, plague, Prague, vague; fainaigue.

-ah. See **-a.**

-aid (-ād). See **-ade.**

-aid (-ĕd). See **-ed.**

-aif. See **-afe.**

-aight. See **-ate.**

-aign. See **-ain.**

-ail, ail, ale, bail, bale, Braille, dale, Dale, fail, flail, frail, Gael, Gail, gale, gaol, grail, hail, hale, jail, kale, mail, male, nail, pail, pale, quail, rail, sail, sale, scale, shale, snail, stale, swale, tail, tale, they'll, trail, vale, veil, wail, wale, whale, Yale; assail, avail, bewail, bobtail, cocktail, curtail, detail, dovetail, entail, exhale, fantail, female, hobnail, impale, inhale, prevail, regale, retail, travail, unveil, wassail, wholesale; abigail, Abigail, Bloomingdale, countervail, farthingale, ginger ale, martingale, monorail, nightingale.

-ails. See **-ales.**

-aim. See **-ame.**

-ain (-ān), Aisne, bane, blain, brain, Cain, cane, chain, crane, Dane, deign, drain, fain, fane, feign, gain, grain, Jane, lain, lane, main, Maine, mane, pain, pane, plain, plane, rain, reign, rein, sane, Seine, Shane, skein, slain, Spain, sprain, stain, strain, swain, ta'en, thane, thegn, train, twain, vain, vane, vein, wain, wane, Zane; abstain, again, airplane, amain, arcane, arraign, attain, biplane, campaign, champagne, Champlain, chicane, chilblain, chow mein, cocaine, complain, constrain, contain, demesne, detain, disdain, distrain, dogbane, domain, Duquesne, Elaine, enchain, entrain, ethane, explain, germane, henbane, humane, inane, insane, Lorraine, maintain, marchpane, membrane, methane, moraine, murrain, obtain, ordain, pertain, plantain, procaine, profane, ptomaine, quatrain, refrain, regain, remain, restrain, retain, Sinn Fein, sustain, terrain, urbane; aeroplane, appertain, ascertain, cellophane, chamberlain, chatelaine, counterpane, entertain, frangipane, hurricane, hydroplane, monoplane, porcelain, scatterbrain, windowpane; legerdemain.

-ain (-ĕn). See **-en.**

-ainst, 'gainst; against.

Also: **-ence** + **-ed** (as in *fenced*, etc.)

Also: **-ense** + **-ed** (as in *condensed*, etc.)

-aint, ain't, faint, feint, mayn't, paint, plaint, quaint, saint, taint; acquaint, attaint, complaint, constraint, distraint, Geraint, restraint.

-aipse, traipse; jackanapes.

Also: **-ape** + **-s** (as in *grapes*, etc.)

-air. See **-are.**

-aire. See **-are.**

-airn, bairn, cairn.

-airs. See **-ares.**

-aise (-āz). See **-aze.**

-aise (-ĕz). See **-ez.**

-ait. See **-ate.**

-aith, eighth, faith, Faith, wraith.

-aize. See **-aze.**

-ak. See **-ack.**

-ake, ache, bake, Blake, brake, break, cake, crake, drake, fake, flake, hake, Jake, lake, make, quake, rake, sake, shake, slake, snake, spake, stake, steak, strake, take, wake; awake, backache, bespake, betake, cornflake, daybreak, earache, earthquake, forsake, heartbreak, keepsake, mandrake, mistake, namesake, opaque, outbreak, partake, retake, snowflake, sweepstake, toothache; bellyache, johnnycake, overtake, patty-cake, rattlesnake, stomach ache, undertake.

-al, Al, Hal, pal, sal, shall; banal, cabal, canal, corral, locale, morale, Natal, timbale; falderal, musicale; Guadalcanal.

-ald, bald, scald; piebald, so-called; Archibald.

Also: **-all** + **-ed** (as in *stalled*, etc.)

Also: **-aul** + **-ed** (as in *hauled*, etc.)

Also: **-awl** + **-ed** (as in *crawled*, etc.)

-ale (-āl). See **-ail.**

-ale (-ăl). See **-al.**

-ales, Wales; entrails, marseilles, Marseilles.

Also: **-ail** + **-s** (as in *fails*, etc.)

Also: **-ale** + **-s** (as in *scales*, etc.)

-alf. See **-aff.**

-alk, auk, balk, calk, chalk, gawk, hawk, squawk, stalk, talk, walk; catwalk, Mohawk; tomahawk; Manitowoc; Oconomowoc.

-all (-ăl). See **-al.**

-all (-ôl). See **-awl.**

-alled. See **-ald.**

-alm, alm, balm, calm, Guam, palm, psalm, qualm; becalm, embalm, madame, salaam.

-alp, alp, Alp, palp, scalp.

-alt (-ôlt), fault, halt, malt, salt, smalt, vault; asphalt, assault, basalt, cobalt, default, exalt; somersault.

-alt (-ălt), alt, shalt.

-alts. See **-altz.**

-altz, waltz.

Also: **-alt** + **-s** (as in *salts*, etc.)

Also: **-ault** + **-s** (as in *faults*, etc.)

-alve, calve, halve, have, salve, Slav, suave; Zouave.

-am, am, cam, Cham, clam, cram, dam, damn, drachm, dram, gram, ham, jam, jamb, lam, lamb, ma'am, Pam, pram, ram, Sam, scram, sham, slam, swam, tram, wham, yam; Assam, flimflam, madame, Siam; Abraham, aerogram, Alabam, Amsterdam, Birmingham, anagram, cablegram, cryptogram, diagram, diaphragm, dithyramb, epigram, hexagram, marjoram, monogram, Rotterdam, Surinam, telegram; ad nauseam, radiogram; parallelogram.

-amb. See **-am.**

-ame, aim, blame, came, claim, dame, fame, flame, frame, game, lame, maim, Mame, name, same, shame, tame; acclaim, aflame, became, beldame, declaim, defame, disclaim, exclaim, inflame, misname, nickname, proclaim, reclaim, surname; overcame.

-amp (-ămp), amp, camp, champ, clamp, cramp, damp, guimpe, lamp, ramp, scamp, stamp, tamp, tramp, vamp; decamp, encamp, firedamp, revamp; afterdamp.

-amp (-ŏmp). See **-omp.**

-an (-ăn), an, Ann, Anne, ban, bran, can, clan, Dan, fan, Fran, Jan, Klan, man, Nan, pan, Pan, plan, ran, scan, span, tan, than, van; afghan, Afghan, began, corban, dishpan, divan, fantan, foreran, he-man, Iran, japan, Japan, Koran, Milan, pavan, pecan, rattan, sedan, trepan,

-an

unman; Alcoran, artisan, astrakhan, Astrakhan, caravan, catalan, courtesan, Hindustan, overran, Pakistan, partisan, spick-and-span. Turkestan; Afghanistan, catamaran, orang-utan.

-an (-ŏn). See **-on.**

-ance, chance, dance, France, glance, hanse, lance, manse, pants, prance, stance, trance; advance, askance, bechance, enhance, entrance, expanse, finance, mischance, perchance, romance; circumstance.

Also: **-ant** + **-s** (as in *grants,* etc.)

-anch, blanch, Blanche, branch, ganch, ranch, stanch; carte, blanche; avalanche.

-anct, sacrosanct.

Also: **-ank** + **-ed** (as in *spanked,* etc.)

-and (-ănd), and, band, bland, brand, gland, grand, hand, land, rand, sand, stand, strand, Strand; backhand, command, demand, disband, expand, forehand, Greenland, remand, unhand, withstand; ampersand, contraband, countermand, fairyland, fatherland, four-in-hand, hinterland, Holy Land, overland, reprimand, Rio Grande, Samarkand, saraband, underhand, understand, wonderland; misunderstand, multiplicand, Witwatersrand.

Also: **-an** + **-ed** (as in *banned,* etc.)

-and (-ŏnd). See **-ond.**

-ane. See **-ain.**

-ang, bang, bhang, clang, fang, gang, gangue, hang, pang, rang, sang, slang, sprang, stang, tang, twang, whang, yang; harangue, meringue, mustang, Penang, shebang; boomerang; orangoutang.

-ange, change, grange, mange, range, strange; arrange, derange, estrange, exchange; disarrange, interchange, rearrange.

-angue. See **-ang.**

-ank, bank, blank, clank, crank, dank, drank, flank, franc, frank, Frank, hank, Hank, lank, plank, prank, rank, sank, shank, shrank, spank, stank, swank, tank, thank, yank, Yank; embank, outflank, outrank, pointblank, snowbank; mountebank.

-anked. See **-anct.**

-anned. See **-and.**

-anse. See **-ance.**

-ant (-ănt), ant, aunt, can't, cant, chant, grant, Grant, Kant, pant, plant, rant, scant, shan't, slant; aslant, decant, descant, displant,

enchant, extant, gallant, implant, Levant, recant, supplant, transplant; adamant, commandant, disenchant, gallivant; hierophant.

-ant (-ŏnt). See **-aunt.**

-ants. See **-ance.**

-ap, cap, chap, clap, flap, gap, hap, Jap, lap, map, nap, pap, rap, sap, scrap, slap, snap, strap, tap, trap, wrap, yap; claptrap, dunce cap, entrap, enwrap, foolscap, kidnap, madcap, mayhap, mishap, nightcap, unwrap; afterclap, handicap, overlap, rattletrap, thunderclap.

-ape, ape, cape, chape, crepe, drape, grape, jape, nape, rape, scrape, shape, tape; agape, escape, landscape, seascape, shipshape, undrape.

-apes. See **-aipse.**

-aph. See **-aff.**

-aphed. See **-aft.**

-apped. See **-apt.**

-aps. See **-apse.**

-apse, apse, craps, lapse, schnapps; collapse, elapse, perhaps, relapse.

Also: **-ap** + **-s** (as in *claps,* etc.)

-apt, apt, rapt, wrapt; adapt.

Also: **-ap** + **-ed** (as in *clapped,* etc.)

-aque. See **-ack.**

-ar (-är), Aar, are, bar, car, char, czar, far, jar, Loire, mar, par, parr, Saar, scar, spar, star, tar, tsar; afar, agar, ajar, armoire, bazaar, bizarre, catarrh, cigar, couloir, Dakar, debar, disbar, felspar, guitar, horsecar, hussar, lascar, Navarre, pourboire; Alcazar, au revoir, avatar, caviar, cinnabar, registrar, reservoir, samovar, seminar, Zanzibar; agar-agar.

-ar (-ôr). See **-or.**

-arb, barb, garb; rhubarb.

-arce. See **-arse.**

-arch, arch, larch, march, March, parch, starch; outmarch; countermarch.

-arch. See **-ark.**

-ard (-ärd), bard, card, chard, guard, hard, lard, nard, pard, sard, shard, yard; Bernard, bombard, canard, discard, foulard, Gerard, lifeguard, petard, placard, regard, retard; Abelard, avant-garde, bodyguard, boulevard, disregard, Hildegarde, interlard, leotard; camelopard.

Also: **-ar** + **-ed** (as in *starred,* etc.)

-ard (-ôrd). See **-ord.**

-are, air, Ayr, bare, bear, blare, care, chair, Claire, dare, e'er, ere, fair, fare, flair, flare, gare, glair, glare, hair, hare, heir, herr, lair, mare,

mayor, ne'er, pair, pare, pear, Pierre, prayer, rare, scare, share, snare, spare, square, stair, stare, swear, tare, tear, their, there, they're, ware, wear, where, yare; affair, armchair, aware, beware, coheir, compare, corsair, declare, despair, eclair, elsewhere, ensnare, fanfare, forbear, forswear, Gruyère, horsehair, howe'er, impair, mohair, Mynheer, nightmare, outstare, prepare, repair, unfair, welfare, whate'er, whene'er, where'er; anywhere, Camembert, croix de guerre, debonair, Delaware, doctrinaire, earthenware, étagère, everywhere, Frigidaire, laissez faire, maidenhair, mal de mer, millionaire, nom de guerre, outerwear, porte-cochere, solitaire, thoroughfare, unaware, underwear; vin ordinaire.

-ares, theirs; downstairs, upstairs; unawares.

Also: **-air** + **-s** (as in *stairs,* etc.)

Also: **-are** + **-s** (as in *dares,* etc.)

Also: **-ear** + **-s** (as in *swears,* etc.)

Also: **-eir** + **-s** (as in *heirs,* etc.)

-arf, corf, dwarf, wharf; endomorph, mesomorph, perimorph.

-arge, barge, charge, large, marge, Marge, sarge; discharge, enlarge, surcharge; overcharge, supercharge, undercharge.

-ark, arc, ark, bark, barque, cark, Clark, dark, hark, lark, mark, Mark, marque, park, sark, shark, snark, spark, stark; aardvark, Bismarck, debark, embark, landmark, remark, tanbark; disembark, hierarch, matriarch, oligarch, patriarch.

-arl, carl, Carl, gnarl, marl, snarl.

-arm (-ärm), arm, barm, charm, farm, harm, marm; alarm, disarm, forearm, gendarme, schoolmarm, unarm.

-arm (-ôrm). See **-orm.**

-arn (-ärn), barn, darn, Marne, tarn, yarn.

-arn (-ôrn). See **-orn.**

-arp (-ärp), carp, harp, scarp, sharp; escarp; counterscarp, pericarp.

-arp (-ôrp). See **-orp.**

-arred. See **-ard.**

-arse, farce, parse, sparse.

-arsh, harsh, marsh.

-art (-ärt), art, Bart, cart, chart, dart, hart, heart, mart, part, smart, start, tart; apart, depart, dispart, impart, sweetheart, upstart; counterpart.

-art (-ôrt). See **-ort.**

-arth. See **-orth.**

-arts. See **-artz.**

-artz, courts, shorts, quartz.
Also: **-art** + **-s** (as in *warts,* etc.)
Also: **-ort** + **-s** (as in *sorts,* etc.)
-arve, carve, starve.
-as (-ŏz), Boz, vase, was; La Paz.
-as (-ă). See **-a.**
-as (-ăs). See **-ass.**
-ase (-ās). See **-ace.**
-ase (-āz). See **-aze.**
-ased. See **-aste.**
-ash (-ăsh), ash, bash, brash, cache, cash, clash, crash, dash, flash, gash, gnash, hash, lash, mash, Nash, pash, plash, rash, sash, slash, smash, splash, thrash, trash; abash, callash, mishmash, moustache, panache, Wabash; balderdash, calabash, sabretache, succotash.
-ash (-ŏsh), bosh, gosh, gauche, josh, posh, quash, slosh, squash, swash, wash; apache, awash, galosh, goulash; mackintosh.
-ask, ask, bask, Basque, cask, casque, flask, mask, masque, Pasch, task; unmask.
-asm, chasm, plasm, spasm; orgasm, phantasm, sarcasm; cataplasm, pleonasm, protoplasm; enthusiasm, iconoclasm.
-asp, asp, clasp, gasp, grasp, hasp, rasp; enclasp, unclasp.
-ass, ass, bass, brass, class, crass, gas, glass, grass, lass, mass, pass; alas, amass, crevasse, cuirasse, harass, impasse, morass, paillasse, repass, surpass; demitasse, hippocras, looking glass, sassafras, underpass.
-assed. See **-ast.**
-ast, bast, blast, cast, caste, fast, hast, last, mast, past, vast; aghast, avast, bombast, contrast, forecast, outcast, peltast, repast, steadfast; flabbergast, overcast; ecclesiast, enthusiast, iconoclast.
Also: **-ass** + **-ed** (as in *passed,* etc.)
-aste, baste, chaste, haste, paste, taste, waist, waste; distaste, foretaste, unchaste; aftertaste.
Also: **-ace** + **-ed** (as in *placed,* etc.)
Also: **-ase** + **-ed** (as in *chased,* etc.)
-at (-ăt), at, bat, brat, cat, chat, drat, fat, flat, gat, ghat, gnat, hat, mat, Matt, Nat, pat, Pat, plat, rat, sat, slat, spat, sprat, tat, that, vat; combat, cravat, fiat, muskrat, polecat, whereat, wombat; acrobat, Ararat, autocrat, Automat, democrat, diplomat, habitat, hemostat, Kattegat, photostat, plutocrat, thermostat, tit for tat; aristocrat.
-at (-ä). See **-a.**
-at (-ŏt). See **-ot.**

-atch (-ăch), batch, catch, hatch, latch, match, patch, scratch, snatch, thatch; attach, detach, dispatch, mismatch, unlatch; bandersnatch.
-atch (-ŏch). See **-otch.**
-ate, ait, ate, bait, bate, crate, date, eight, fate, fête, frate, freight, gait, gate, grate, great, hate, Kate, late, mate, Nate, pate, plait, plate, prate, rate, sate, skate, slate, spate, state, straight, strait, trait, wait, weight; abate, aerate, agnate, alate, await, baccate, berate, bookplate, bromate, casemate, castrate, caudate, cerate, checkmate, chelate, chlorate, chromate, cirrate, citrate, classmate, cognate, collate, comate, connate, cordate, costate, create, cremate, crenate, crispate, cristate, curate, curvate, debate, deflate, delate, dentate, dictate, dilate, donate, elate, equate, estate, falcate, filtrate, flyweight, formate, frontate, frustrate, furcate, gemmate, globate, gradate, guttate, gyrate, hamate, hastate, helpmate, hydrate, inflate, ingrate, inmate, innate, instate, irate, jugate, khanate, lactate, larvate, legate, lichgate, ligate, lightweight, lobate, locate, lunate, lustrate, magnate, mandate, messmate, migrate, misdate, mismate, misstate, mutate, narrate, negate, nervate, nictate, nitrate, notate, nutate, oblate, orate, ornate, ovate, palate, palmate, palpate, peltate, pennate, phonate, phosphate, picrate, pinnate, placate, playmate, prelate, primate, private, probate, prolate, prorate, prostate, prostrate, pulsate, punctuate, quadrate, quinate, rebate, relate, restate, rotate, rugate, sedate, septate, serrate, shipmate, sigmate, spicate, stagnate, stalemate, stannate, stellate, striate, sublate, sulcate, sulfate, tannate, tartrate, template, ternate, testate, titrate, tractate, translate, truncate, vacate, vibrate, Vulgate, xanthate, zonate; abdicate, ablactate, abnegate, abrogate, accurate, acetate, actuate, addlepate, adequate, adulate, adumbrate, advocate, aggravate, aggregate, agitate, allocate, altercate, alternate, ambulate, amputate, animate, annotate, annulate, antedate, antiquate, apostate, appellate, approbate, arbitrate, arrogate, aspirate, aureate, aviate, bifurcate, Billingsgate, brachiate, bracteate, branchiate, cachinnate, calculate, calibrate, caliphate, cancellate,

candidate, captivate, carbonate, castigate, catenate, celibate, cellulate, chloridate, ciliate, circulate, clypeate, cochleate, cogitate, colligate, collimate, collocate, comminate, compensate, complicate, concentrate, confiscate, conformate, conglobate, congregate, conjugate, consecrate, constipate, consulate, consummate, contemplate, copulate, cornuate, coronate, corporate, correlate, corrugate, corticate, coruscate, crenellate, crenulate, crepitate, cucullate, culminate, cultivate, cumulate, cuneate, cuspidate, cyanate, decimate, declinate, decollate, decorate, decussate, dedicate, defalcate, defecate, dehydrate, delegate, delicate, demarcate, demonstrate, denigrate, denudate, depilate, deprecate, depredate, derogate, desecrate, desiccate, designate, desolate, desperate, detonate, devastate, deviate, digitate, diplomate, dislocate, disparate, dissipate, distillate, divagate, doctorate, dominate, duplicate, ebriate, echinate, edentate, educate, elevate, elongate, emanate, emigrate, emulate, enervate, eructate, estimate, estivate, excavate, exculpate, execrate, expiate, explanate, explicate, expurgate, extirpate, extricate, fabricate, fascinate, featherweight, fecundate, federate, fenestrate, fibrillate, fistulate, flagellate, floriate, fluctuate, fluorate, foliate, formicate, formulate, fornicate, fortunate, fructuate, fulgurate, fulminate, fumigate, geminate, generate, germinate, glaciate, gladiate, glomerate, graduate, granulate, gravitate, heavyweight, hebetate, hesitate, hibernate, hyphenate, ideate, illustrate, imbricate, imitate, immigrate, immolate, implicate, imprecate, impregnate, improvisate, incarnate, inchoate, incrassate, incubate, inculcate, inculpate, incurvate, indicate, indurate, infiltrate, innervate, innovate, inornate, insensate, insolate, inspissate, instigate, insufflate, insulate, integrate, interstate, intestate, intimate, intonate, intricate, inundate, irrigate, irritate, isolate, iterate, jubilate, khedivate, labiate, lacerate, lamellate, laminate, lancinate, lapidate, laureate, legislate, levirate, levitate, liberate, ligulate, lineate, liquidate, literate,

litigate, loricate, lubricate,
lucubrate, macerate, machinate,
maculate, magistrate, majorate,
manducate, manganate, marginate,
margravate, marquisate, masticate,
maturate, mediate, medicate,
meditate, menstruate, methylate,
micturate, militate, mitigate,
moderate, modulate, molybdate,
motivate, muriate, mutilate,
nauseate, navigate, nictitate,
niobate, nominate, nucleate,
obfuscate, objurgate, obligate,
obovate, obstinate, obviate, oculate,
oleate, omoplate, opiate,
orchestrate, ordinate, oscillate,
oscitate, osculate, overrate,
overstate, overweight, ovulate,
paginate, palliate, palpitate,
paperweight, papillate, passionate,
pastorate, patellate, pectinate,
peculate, pejorate, pendulate,
penetrate, percolate, perforate,
permeate, perorate, perpetrate,
personate, phosphorate, pileate,
pollinate, populate, postulate,
potentate, predicate, principate,
priorate, procreate, profligate,
promulgate, propagate,
propinquate, proximate, prussiate,
pullulate, pulmonate, pulverate,
pulvinate, punctuate, punctulate,
pustulate, radiate, radicate,
reclinate, recreate, rectorate,
recurvate, regulate, reinstate,
relegate, remigrate, remonstrate,
renovate, replicate, reprobate,
resonate, roseate, rostellate,
rubricate, ruminate, rusticate,
sagittate, salivate, sanitate, satiate,
saturate, scintillate, scutellate,
segmentate, segregate, selenate,
separate, septenate, sequestrate,
seriate, serrulate, shogunate,
sibilate, silicate, simulate, sinuate,
situate, spatulate, speculate,
spiculate, spiflicate, spoliate,
staminate, stearate, stellulate,
stimulate, stipulate, strangulate,
stylobate, subjugate, sublimate,
subulate, suffocate, sulfurate,
sultanate, supinate, supplicate,
suppurate, surrogate, syncopate,
syndicate, tabulate, tellurate,
temperate, tête-à-tête, titanate,
titillate, titivate, tolerate, toluate,
trabeate, tracheate, transmigrate,
tridentate, trijugate, trilobate,
triplicate, trisulcate, triturate,
tubulate, tunicate, turbinate,
ulcerate, ultimate, ululate,
umbellate, uncinate, undulate,
underrate, understate,
underweight, ungulate, urinate,
urticate, ustulate, vaccinate,

vacillate, vaginate, valerate, validate,
vanillate, variate, vegetate, venerate,
ventilate, vertebrate, vesicate,
vindicate, violate, viscerate, vitiate,
welterweight; abbreviate,
abominate, accelerate, accentuate,
accommodate, accumulate,
acidulate, acuminate, adjudicate,
adulterate, affectionate, affiliate,
agglomerate, agglutinate,
aldermanate, alienate, alleviate,
amalgamate, annihilate,
annunciate, anticipate, apiculate,
apostolate, appreciate,
appropinquate, appropriate,
approximate, areolate, articulate,
asphyxiate, assassinate, asseverate,
assimilate, associate, attenuate,
auriculate, authenticate,
calumniate, capitulate, cardinalate,
centuplicate, certificate, chalybeate,
circumvallate, coagulate,
coelenterate, collaborate, collegiate,
commemorate, commensurate,
commiserate, communicate,
compassionate, concatenate,
conciliate, confabulate,
confederate, conglomerate,
conglutinate, congratulate,
considerate, consolidate,
contaminate, conterminate,
continuate, cooperate, coordinate,
corroborate, corymbiate,
curvicaudate, curvicostate,
debilitate, decapitate, decemvirate,
degenerate, deglutinate, deliberate,
delineate, denominate, denticulate,
denunciate, depopulate,
depreciate, deracinate, desiderate,
determinate, debranchiate,
dictatorate, dilapidate, directorate,
disconsolate, discriminate,
dispassionate, disseminate,
dissimulate, dissociate, divaricate,
domesticate, duumvirate,
ebracteate, effectuate, effeminate,
ejaculate, elaborate, electorate,
electroplate, eliminate, elucidate,
emaciate, emancipate, emasculate,
enucleate, enumerate, enunciate,
episcopate, equilibrate, equivocate,
eradiate, eradicate, etiolate,
evacuate, evaginate, evaluate,
evaporate, eventuate, eviscerate,
exacerbate, exaggerate, examinate,
exasperate, excogitate, excoriate,
excruciate, exfoliate, exhilarate,
exonerate, expatiate, expatriate,
expectorate, expostulate,
expropriate, exsanguinate,
extenuate, exterminate,
extortionate, extravagate,
exuberate, facilitate, felicitate,
foraminate, gelatinate, geniculate,
gesticulate, habilitate, habituate,

hallucinate, horripilate, humiliate,
hydrogenate, hypothecate,
illiterate, illuminate, immaculate,
immediate, immoderate,
imperforate, impersonate,
importunate, impostumate,
impropriate, inaccurate,
inadequate, inanimate, inaugurate,
incarcerate, incinerate, incorporate,
incriminate, indelicate,
indoctrinate, inebriate, infatuate,
infuriate, ingeminate, ingratiate,
ingurgitate, initiate, innominate,
inoculate, inordinate, insatiate,
inseminate, inseparate, insinuate,
inspectorate, intemperate,
intercalate, interminate,
interpolate, interrogate, intimidate,
intoxicate, invaginate, invalidate,
invertebrate, investigate, inveterate,
inviduate, invigorate, inviolate,
irradiate, irradicate, itinerate,
lanceolate, legitimate, licentiate,
lineolate, lixiviate, luxuriate,
machicolate, mandibulate,
manipulate, marsupiate,
matriarchate, matriculate,
meliorate, miscalculate,
multidentate, multilobate,
multiplicate, necessitate, negotiate,
nidificate, novitiate, nudirostrate,
obliterate, officiate, operate,
operculate, orbiculate, orientate,
originate, oxygenate, pacificate,
palatinate, paniculate, participate,
particulate, patriarchate,
pediculate, penultimate,
peregrinate, permanganate,
perpetuate, petiolate, pomegranate,
pontificate, postgraduate,
precipitate, precogitate,
preconsulate, predestinate,
predominate, prejudicate,
premeditate, prenominate,
prevaricate, procrastinate,
prognosticate, proliferate,
propitiate, proportionate,
protectorate, protuberate,
quadruplicate, quintuplicate,
reanimate, recalcitrate, reciprocate,
recriminate, recuperate,
redecorate, reduplicate, refrigerate,
regenerate, regurgitate, reiterate,
rejuvenate, remunerate, repatriate,
repopulate, repudiate, resuscitate,
retaliate, reticulate, reverberate,
salicylate, somnambulate,
sophisticate, subordinate,
substantiate, syllabicate,
tergiversate, testiculate, testudinate,
trabeculate, transliterate,
triangulate, tricorporate, trifoliate,
triumvirate, variegate, vermiculate,
vesiculate, vestibulate, vicariate,
vituperate, vociferate; ameliorate,

baccalaureate, canaliculate, circumambulate, circumnavigate, circumstantiate, consubstantiate, deoxygenate, deteriorate, differentiate, discombobulate, disproportionate, domiciliate, excommunicate, imbecilitate, incapacitate, intermediate, latifoliate, misappropriate, predeterminate, proletariat, quadrifoliate, quadrigeminate, quinquefoliate, ratiocinate, recapitulate, rehabilitate, reinvigorate, secretariate, superannuate, supererogate, transubstantiate, trifoliolate, undergraduate, unifoliate.

-ath (-ăth), bath, Bath, Gath, hath, lath, math, path, rath, snath, wrath; bypath; aftermath, allopath, psychopath; homeopath, osteopath.

-ath (-ôth). See **-oth**.

-athe, bathe, lathe, scathe, swathe; unswathe.

-auce. See **-oss**.

-aud, bawd, broad, Claude, fraud, gaud, laud, Maud; abroad, applaud, belaud, defraud, maraud.
Also: **-aw** + **-ed** (as in *clawed*, etc.)

-augh. See **-aff**.

-aught. See **-ought** or **-aft**.

-aul. See **-awl**.

-auled. See **-ald**.

-ault. See **-alt**.

-aunch, craunch, haunch, launch, paunch, staunch.

-aunt, aunt, daunt, flaunt, gaunt, haunt, jaunt, taunt, vaunt, want; avaunt, romaunt.

-aunts. See **-ounce**.

-ause, cause, clause, gauze, hawse, pause, yaws; applause, because.
Also: **-aw** + **-s** (as in *claws*, etc.)

-aust. See **-ost**.

-aut. See **-ought**.

-ave (-ăv). See **-alve**.

-ave (-āv), brave, cave, crave, Dave, gave, glaive, grave, knave, lave, nave, pave, rave, save, shave, slave, stave, suave, they've, waive, wave; behave, concave, conclave, deprave, enclave, engrave, enslave, exclave, forgave, margrave, misgave, octave; architrave.

-aw, awe, caw, chaw, claw, craw, daw, draw, faugh, flaw, gnaw, haw, jaw, law, maw, paw, pshaw, raw, saw, Shaw, squaw, straw, taw, thaw, yaw; catspaw, coleslaw, cushaw, foresaw, gewgaw, guffaw, heehaw, jackdaw, jigsaw, macaw, papaw, seesaw,

southpaw, Warsaw, withdraw; Arkansas, overawe, usquebaugh.

-awd. See **-aud**.

-awed. See **-aud**.

-awk. See **-alk**.

-awl, all, awl, ball, bawl, brawl, call, crawl, drawl, fall, gall, Gaul, hall, haul, mall, maul, pall, Paul, pawl, Saul, scrawl, shawl, small, sprawl, squall, stall, tall, thrall, trawl, wall, yawl; appall, baseball, befall, Bengal, catcall, enthrall, football, footfall, forestall, install, rainfall, recall, snowfall, windfall; alcohol, basketball, caterwaul, overhaul, pentothal, waterfall, wherewithal.

-awled. See **-ald**.

-awn, awn, bawn, brawn, dawn, drawn, faun, fawn, gone, lawn, pawn, prawn, sawn, Sean, spawn, yawn; indrawn, withdrawn.

-aws. See **-ause**.

-ax, ax, flax, lax, Max, pax, sax, tax, wax; addax, Ajax, anthrax, climax, relax, syntax; battleax, Halifax, Kallikaks, parallax; Adirondacks, anticlimax.
Also: **-ack** + **-s** (as in *sacks*, etc.)

-ay, a, aye, bay, bey, brae, bray, clay, day, dray, ey, fay, Fay, fey, flay, fray, gay, gray, greige, grey, hay, jay, Kay, lay, Mae, may, May, nay, née, neigh, pay, play, pray, prey, ray, Ray, say, shay, slay, sleigh, spay, spray, stay, stray, sway, they, trait, tray, trey, way, weigh, whey; abbé, affray, agley, allay, array, assay, astray, away, belay, beret, betray, bewray, Bombay, bomb bay, bouquet, café, Calais, Cathay, causeway, chambray, convey, Coué, coupé, Courbet, croquet, curé, decay, defray, delay, dengue, dismay, display, distrait, doomsday, dragée, endplay, essay, filet, fillet, foray, Fouquet, foyer, Friday, gainsay, gangway, hearsay, heyday, horseplay, inlay, inveigh, Malay, Manet, melee, midday, mislay, moiré, Monday, Monet, moray, nosegay, obey, okay, ole!, passé, per se, pince-nez, portray, prepay, purée, purvey, relay, repay, risqué, Roget, roué, sachet, sashay, soirée, soufflé, subway, Sunday, survey, throughway, Thursday, today, tokay, touché, toupée, Tuesday, waylay, Wednesday; appliqué, cabaret, canapé, castaway, Chevrolet, consommé, deMusset, disarray, disobey, distingué, émigré, exposé, faraway, holiday, Mandalay, matinee, Milky Way, Monterey, Monterrey, negligée, Nez Percé,

popinjay, protégé(e), résumé, roundelay, runaway, Saint-Tropez, Salomé, Santa Fe, Saturday, s'il vous plait, sobriquet, stowaway, virelay, yesterday; Appian Way, cabriolet, café au lait, caloo-calay, communiqué, habitué, papier-maché, sotto voce, Tono-Bunday; Edna St. Vincent Millay.

-ayed. See **-ade**.

-ays. See **-aze**.

-aze, baize, blaze, braise, braze, chaise, craze, daze, faze, gaze, glaze, graze, haze, maize, maze, phase, phrase, praise, raise, raze; ablaze, amaze, appraise, dispraise; chrysoprase, Marseillaise, mayonnaise, nowadays, paraphrase, polonaise.
Also: **-ay** + **-s** (as in *days*, etc.)
Also: **-ey** + **-s** (as in *preys*, etc.)
Also: **-eigh** + **-s** (as in *weighs*, etc.)

-azz, as, has, jazz, razz; topaz, whereas; Alcatraz, razzmatazz.

-e. See **-ee**.

-ea. See **-ee**.

-eace. See **-ease**.

-each, beach, beech, bleach, breach, breech, each, leech, peach, preach, reach, screech, speech, teach; beseech, impeach; overreach.

-ead (-ēd). See **-eed**.

-ead (-ĕd). See **-ed**.

-eaf (-ēf). See **-ef**.

-eaf (-ēf). See **-ief**.

-eague, Grieg, klieg, league; colleague, enleague, fatigue, intrigue.

-eak (-ēk), beak, bleak, cheek, chic, clique, creak, creek, eke, freak, Greek, leak, leek, meek, peak, peek, pique, reek, seek, sheik, shriek, Sikh, sleek, sneak, speak, squeak, streak, teak, tweak, weak, week, wreak; antique, bespeak, bezique, cacique, critique, Monique, mystique, oblique, physique, relique, unique; Chesapeake, Frederique, Martinique, Mozambique, Pathétique.

-eak (-āk). See **-ake**.

-eal, ceil, creel, deal, eel, feel, heal, heel, he'll, keel, Kiel, kneel, leal, meal, Neal, Neil, peal, peel, real, reel, seal, she'll, spiel, squeal, steal, teal, veal, weal, we'll, wheel, zeal; anele, anneal, appeal, Bastille, cartwheel, Castile, chenille, conceal, congeal, Émile, genteel, ideal, Lucille, misdeal, mobile, Mobile, pastille, repeal, reveal, unreal;

cochineal, commonweal, deshabille, glockenspiel, mercantile; automobile.

-eald. See **-ield.**

-ealed. See **-ield.**

-ealm. See **-elm.**

-ealth, health, stealth, wealth; commonwealth.

-eam, beam, bream, cream, deem, dream, fleam, gleam, ream, scheme, scream, seam, seem, steam, stream, team, teem, theme; abeam, beseem, blaspheme, centime, daydream, esteem, extreme, ice cream, moonbeam, redeem, regime, supreme, trireme; academe; ancien régime.

-ean, bean, been, clean, dean, Dean, e'en, Gene, glean, green, Jean, keen, lean, lien, mean, mien, peen, preen, quean, queen, scene, screen, seen, sheen, spleen, teen, wean, ween, yean; baleen, beguine, benzine, between, caffeine, canteen, careen, chlorine, Christine, codeine, colleen, convene, cuisine, demean, demesne, eighteen, Eileen, Eugene, fifteen, foreseen, fourteen, ich dien, Kathleen, machine, marine, nineteen, obscene, Pauline, poteen, praline, protein, quinine, ravine, routine, sardine, serene, shagreen, sixteen, subvene, thirteen, tontine, tureen, unclean; Aberdeen, Abilene, Argentine, atabrine, atropine, barkentine, Benzedrine, bombazine, brigantine, contravene, crêpe de chine, damascene, evergreen, fellahin, Florentine, gabardine, gasoline, Geraldine, Ghibelline, guillotine, intervene, Josephine, kerosene, libertine, magazine, mezzanine, Nazarene, nectarine, nicotine, overseen, Paris green, quarantine, serpentine, seventeen, submarine, tambourine, tangerine, unforeseen, Vaseline, velveteen, wolverine; acetylene, aquamarine, elephantine, incarnadine, ultramarine.

-eaned. See **-iend.**

-eant. See **-ent.**

-eap. See **-eep.**

-ear. See **-eer.**

-earch. See **-urch.**

-eard (-ĭrd), beard, tiered, weird; afeard.

    Also: **-ear** + **-ed** (as in *reared,* etc.)
    Also: **-ere** + **-ed** (as in *interfered,* etc.)
    Also: **-eer** + **-ed** (as in *veered,* etc.)

-eard (-ûrd). See **-urd.**

-eared. See **-eard.**

-earl. See **-url.**

-earn. See **-urn.**

-ears. See **-ares.**

-earse. See **-erse.**

-eart. See **-art.**

-earth. See **-irth.**

-eas. See **-ease.**

-ease (-ēs), cease, crease, fleece, geese, grease, Greece, lease, Nice, niece, peace, piece; caprice, decease, decrease, increase, Maurice, obese, police, release, surcease, valise; ambergris, frontispiece, mantelpiece, masterpiece, Singalese.

-ease (-ēz), bise, breeze, cheese, ease, freeze, frieze, grease, he's, lees, pease, please, seize, she's, skis, sneeze, squeeze, tease, these, wheeze; appease, Bernice, Burmese, cerise, chemise, Chinese, disease, displease, Louise, Maltese, Thales, trapeze; ABC's, Achilles, Androcles, antifreeze, Antilles, Balinese, Cantonese, Heloise, Hercules, Japanese, Javanese, journalese, obsequies, overseas, Pekingese, Portuguese, Siamese, Viennese; anopheles, antipodes, antitheses, Hippocrates, hypotheses, parentheses, soliloquies; aborigines.
    Also: **-ea** + **-s** (as in *teas,* etc.)
    Also: **-ee** + **-s** (as in *bees, frees,* etc.)

-eased. See **-east.**

-east, beast, east, feast, least, priest, yeast; artiste.
    Also: **-ease** + **-ed** (as in *released,* etc.)

-eat (-ēt), beat, beet, bleat, cheat, Crete, eat, feat, feet, fleet, greet, heat, meat, meet, mete, neat, peat, Pete, pleat, seat, sheet, skeet, sleet, street, suite, sweet, teat, treat, wheat; accrete, aesthete, afreet, athlete, compete, complete, conceit, concrete, deadbeat, deceit, defeat, delete, deplete, discreet, discrete, effete, elite, entreat, petite, receipt, replete, retreat, secrete; bittersweet, Easy Street, incomplete, indiscreet, obsolete, overeat, parakeet.

-eat (-āt). See **-ate.**

-eat (-ĕt). See **-et.**

-eath (-ĕth), Beth, breath, death, saith, Seth; Macbeth; Elizabeth, shibboleth.

-eath (-ēth), heath, Keith, 'neath, sheath, teeth, wreath; beneath; underneath.

-eathe, breathe, seethe, sheathe, teethe, wreathe; bequeath, enwreathe.

-eau. See **-ow.**

-eave, breve, cleave, eave, eve, Eve, grieve, heave, leave, lieve, peeve, reave, reeve, sleeve, Steve, thieve, weave, we've; achieve, aggrieve, believe, bereave, conceive, deceive, khedive, naïve, perceive, qui vive, receive, relieve, reprieve, retrieve; disbelieve, interleave, make-believe.

-eb, bleb, deb, ebb, neb, reb, web; sub-deb.

-eck, beck, check, cheque, Czech, deck, fleck, heck, neck, peck, reck, speck, tech, trek, wreck; bedeck, henpeck, Quebec; Tehuantepec.

-ecked. See **-ect.**

-ecks. See **-ex.**

-ect, sect; abject, affect, bisect, collect, connect, correct, defect, deflect, deject, detect, direct, dissect, effect, eject, elect, erect, expect, infect, inject, inspect, neglect, object, pandect, perfect, prefect, project, prospect, protect, reflect, reject, respect, select, subject, suspect; architect, circumspect, dialect, disconnect, disrespect, incorrect, intellect, interject, intersect, introspect, misdirect, recollect, retrospect, vivisect.
    Also: **-eck** + **-ed** (as in *wrecked,* etc.)

-ed, bed, bled, bread, bred, dead, dread, Ed, fed, fled, Fred, head, Jed, lead, led, Ned, pled, read, red, said, shed, shred, sled, sped, spread, stead, ted, Ted, thread, tread, wed, zed; abed, ahead, behead, biped, coed, hogshead, inbred, instead, misled, outspread, unread, unsaid; aforesaid, gingerbread, loggerhead, quadruped, thoroughbred, underfed, watershed.

-ede. See **-eed.**

-edge, dredge, edge, fledge, hedge, kedge, ledge, pledge, sedge, sledge, wedge; allege, unedge.

-ee, be, Bea, bee, Cree, fee, flea, flee, free, gee, glee, he, key, knee, lea, lee, me, pea, plea, quay, sea, see, she, ski, spree, tea, thee, three, tree, we, wee, ye; acme, acne, agree, bohea, debris, decree, degree, Dundee, ennui, foresee, goatee, grandee, grantee, lessee, levee, Marie, marquee, marquis, Parsee, rupee, settee, spondee, trochee, trustee; ABC, abscissae, absentee, adobe, addressee, agony, alumnae, anomie, anomaly, amputee, apogee, assignee, Athene, baloney, botany, bourgeoisie, bumblebee, calorie, calumny, canopy, cap-a-pie, Cherokee, chickadee, chimpanzee, C.O.D., company, coterie, DDT, debauchee, destiny, devotee, disagree, ebony, felony, filagree, fleur-de-lis, fricassee, gluttony, guarantee, harmony, irony, jamboree, licensee, Lombardy, Maccabee, maître d', manatee, Niobe, nominee, Normandy, pedigree, perigee, Pharisee, Picardy, potpourri, Ptolemy, recipe, referee, refugee, repartee, reveille, Sadducee, sesame, symphony, syzygy, tyranny, vis-a-vis; abalone, anemone, apostrophe, Antigone, Ariadne, calliope, catastrophe, Euphrosyne, facsimile, Gethsemane, hyperbole, macaroni, Melpomene, Penelope, proclivity, synonymy; aborigine, Deuteronomy.

-eece. See **-ease.**

-eech. See **-each.**

-eed, bead, Bede, bleed, breed, cede, creed, deed, feed, freed, greed, heed, keyed, knead, lead, mead, Mede, meed, need, plead, read, reed, seed, screed, speed, steed, Swede, tweed, weed; concede, decreed, exceed, impede, indeed, misdeed, mislead, precede, proceed, recede, secede, stampede, succeed; aniseed, antecede, centipede, Ganymede, intercede, millipede, overfeed, supersede; velocipede; Niebelungenlied.
Also: **-ee** + **-ed** (as in *agreed*, etc.)

-eef. See **-ief.**

-eek. See **-eak.**

-eel. See **-eal.**

-eeled. See **-ield.**

-eem. See **-eam.**

-een. See **-ean.**

-eened. See **-iend.**

-eep, cheap, cheep, creep, deep, heap, jeep, keep, leap, neap, peep, reap, seep, sheep, sleep, steep, sweep, veep, weep; asleep, beweep; oversleep.

-eer, beer, bier, blear, cheer, clear, dear, deer, drear, ear, fear, fleer, gear, hear, here, jeer, Lear, leer, mere, near, peer, pier, queer, rear, sear, seer, sere, shear, sheer, smear, sneer, spear, sphere, steer, tear, tier, veer, weir, year; adhere, Aegir, amir, ampere, appear, arrear, austere, brassière, career, cashier, cashmere, cohere, compeer, emir, endear, frontier, inhere, reindeer, revere, severe, sincere, Tangier, veneer; atmosphere, auctioneer, bandoleer, bombardier, brigadier, buccaneer, cannoneer, cavalier, chandelier, chanticleer, chiffonier,

commandeer, disappear, domineer, engineer, financier, frontier, gazeteer, gondolier, grenadier, hemisphere, insincere, interfere, jardiniere, mountaineer, muleteer, musketeer, mutineer, overhear, overseer, pamphleteer, persevere, pioneer, privateer, profiteer, sonneteer, souvenir, volunteer; charioteer.

-eered. See **-eard.**

-ees. See **-ease.**

-eese. See **-ease.**

-eet. See **-eat.**

-eethe. See **-eathe.**

-eeze. See **-ease.**

-ef, chef, clef, deaf, Jeff; Khrushchev.

-eft, cleft, deft, eft, heft, left, reft, theft, weft; bereft.

-eg, beg, dreg, egg, keg, leg, Meg, peg, Peg, skeg, yegg; nutmeg, pegleg; philibeg, Winnipeg.

-ege (-ĕzh), barège, cortege, manège.

-ege (-ĭj). See **-age.**

-egm. See **-em.**

-eigh. See **-ay.**

-eighed. See **-ade.**

-eighs. See **-aze.**

-eight (-āt). See **-ate.**

-eight (-īt). See **-ite.**

-eign. See **-ain.**

-eil (-āl). See **-ail.**

-eil (-ēl). See **-eal.**

-ein (-ān). See **-ain.**

-ein (-īn). See **-ine.**

-eint. See **-aint.**

-eir. See **-are.**

-eird. See **-eard.**

-eirs. See **-ares.**

-eive. See **-eave.**

-eize. See **-ease.**

-eke. See **-eak.**

-el, bell, belle, Belle, cell, dell, dwell, ell, fell, hell, jell, knell, Nell, quell, sell, shell, smell, spell, swell, tell, well, yell; appel, befell, compel, Cornell, dispel, Estelle, excel, expel, foretell, gazelle, hotel, impel, lapel, Moselle, pastel, pell-mell, rebel, repel; asphodel, Astrophel, bagatelle, calomel, caravel, caromel, citadel, clientele, decibel, hydromel, infidel, Jezebel, muscatel, parallel, personnel, philomel, pimpernel, sentinel, undersell, villanelle; mademoiselle.

-elch, belch, squelch.

-eld, eld, geld, held, weld; beheld, unquelled, upheld, withheld.
Also: **-ell** + **-ed** (as in *spelled*, etc.)

-elf, delf, elf, Guelph, pelf, self, shelf; herself, himself, itself, myself, ourself, thyself, yourself.

-elk, elk, whelk.

-ell. See **-el.**

-elle. See **-el.**

-elled. See **-eld.**

-elm, elm, helm, realm, whelm; overwhelm.

-elp, help, kelp, whelp, yelp; self-help.

-elt, belt, Celt, dealt, dwelt, felt, Kelt, knelt, melt, pelt, smelt, spelt, svelte, veldt, welt.

-elve, delve, helve, shelve, twelve.

-em, em, femme, gem, hem, phlegm, Shem, stem, them; adquem, ad rem, ahem, begem, condemn, contemn, pro tem; apothegm, Bethlehem, diadem, requiem, strategem, theorem; ad hominem.

-eme. See **-eam.**

-emn. See **-em.**

-empt, dreamt, kempt, tempt; attempt, contempt, exempt, pre-empt, unkempt.

-en, Ben, den, fen, glen, Gwen, hen, ken, men, pen, ten, then, wen, when, wren, yen, Zen; again, amen, Cheyenne; allergen, citizen, hydrogen, nitrogen, oxygen, Saracen, specimen; comedienne, equestrienne, Parisienne, tragedienne.

-ence, cense, dense, fence, hence, pence, sense, tense, thence, whence; commence, condense, defense, dispense, expense, Hortense, immense, incense, intense, offense, pretense, suspense; abstinence, accidence, affluence, ambience, audience, confidence, consequence, continence, difference, diffidence, diligence, eloquence, eminence, evidence, excellence, frankincense, immanence, imminence, impotence, impudence, indigence, indolence, inference, influence, innocence, negligence, opulence, penitence, preference, providence, recompense, redolence, reference, residence, reticence, reverence, sapience, truculence, turbulence, vehemence, violence, virulence; beneficence, benevolence, circumference, grandiloquence, inconsequence, intelligence, intransigence, magnificence, munificence, obedience, omnipotence, pre-eminence, subservience.
Also: **-ent** + **-s** (as in *tents*, etc.)

-enced. See **-ainst**

-ench, bench, blench, clench, drench, flench, French, quench, stench, tench, trench, wench, wrench; intrench, retrench.

-end, bend, blend, end, fend, friend, lend, mend, rend, send, spend, tend, trend, vend, wend; amend, append, ascend, attend, befriend, commend, contend, defend, depend, descend, distend, emend, expend, extend, forefend, impend, intend, misspend, offend, pitchblende, portend, pretend, stipend, suspend, transcend, unbend; apprehend, comprehend, condescend, dividend, minuend, recommend, reprehend, subtrahend; overextend, superintend.
Also: **-en** + **-ed** (as in *penned*, etc.)

-ene. See **-ean.**

-enge, avenge, revenge; Stonehenge.

-ength, length, strength; full-length.

-enned. See **-end.**

-ens. See **-ense.**

-ense (-ĕns). See **-ence.**

-ense (-ĕnz), cleanse, gens, lens.
Also: **-en** + **-s** (as in *pens*, etc.)
Also: **-end** + **-s** (as in *bends*, etc.)

-ensed. See **-ainst.**

-ent, bent, blent, cent, dent, gent, Ghent, Kent, leant, lent, Lent, meant, pent, rent, scent, sent, spent, tent, Trent, vent, went; absent, accent, anent, ascent, assent, augment, cement, comment, consent, content, descent, detent, dissent, event, extent, ferment, foment, frequent, indent, intent, invent, lament, misspent, portent, present, prevent, relent, repent, resent, torment, unbent, unspent; abstinent, accident, aliment, argument, armament, banishment, battlement, betterment, blandishment, chastisement, competent, complement, compliment, condiment, confident, consequent, continent, detriment, different, diffident, diligent, dissident, document, element, eloquent, eminent, evident, excellent, exigent, filament, firmament, fraudulent, government, immanent, imminent, implement, impotent, impudent, incident, increment, indigent, innocent, insolent, instrument, languishment, liniment, malcontent, management, measurement, merriment, monument, negligent, nourishment, nutriment, occident, opulent, orient, ornament, overspent, parliament, penitent, permanent, pertinent, precedent, president, prevalent, prisonment, provident, punishment, ravishment, redolent, regiment, represent, resident, reticent, reverent, rudiment, sacrament, sentiment, settlement, subsequent, succulent, supplement, tenement, testament, underwent, vehement, violent, virulent, wonderment; accomplishment, acknowledgment, advertisement, astonishment, belligerent, benevolent, development, disarmament, embarrassment, embodiment, enlightenment, environment, establishment, experiment, impenitent, impertinent, imprisonment, improvident, intelligent, irreverent, magnificent, magniloquent, presentiment, subservient, temperament; accompaniment.

-ep, hep, nep, pep, prep, rep, repp, step, steppe, yep; Dieppe, footstep; demirep; Amenhotep.

-ept, drept, kept, sept, slept, stepped, swept, wept; accept, adept, except, inept, y-clept; intercept, overslept.

er, blur, bur, burr, cur, err, fir, fur, her, myrrh, per, purr, shirr, sir, slur, spur, stir, were, whir; astir, aver, Ben Hur, bestir, Big Sur, chasseur, chauffeur, coiffeur, concur, confer, defer, demur, deter, hauteur, incur, infer, inter, occur, prefer, recur, refer, transfer; amateur, arbiter, barrister, calendar, chronicler, chorister, colander, comforter, connoisseur, cylinder, de rigueur, disinter, dowager, gossamer, harbinger, Jennifer, Jupiter, lavender, Lucifer, mariner, massacre, messenger, minister, officer, passenger, prisoner, register, scimitar, sepulcher, traveler, voyageur; administer, astrologer, astronomer, barometer, Excalibur, idolater, thermometer.

-erb, blurb, curb, herb, kerb, Serb, verb; acerb, adverb, disturb, perturb, suburb, superb.

-erce. See **-erse.**

-erced. See **-urst.**

-erch. See **-urch.**

-erd. See **-urd.**

-ere (-âr). See **-are.**

-ere (-ēr). See **-eer.**

-ered. See **-eard.**

-erf. See **-urf.**

-erg, berg, burgh; iceberg.

-erge, dirge, merge, purge, scourge, serge, splurge, spurge, surge, urge, verge; absterge, converge, deterge, diverge, emerge, immerge, submerge; demiurge, dramaturge, thaumaturge.

-erm. See **-irm.**

-ern. See **-urn.**

-err. See **-er.**

-erred. See **-urd.**

-erse, curse, Erse, hearse, herse, nurse, purse, terse, verse, worse; accurse, adverse, amerce, asperse, averse, coerce, commerce, converse, disburse, disperse, diverse, imburse, immerse, inverse, obverse, perverse, rehearse, reverse, traverse, transverse; intersperse, reimburse, universe.

-ersed. See **-urst.**

-ert, Bert, blurt, Burt, curt, dirt, flirt, Gert, girt, hurt, Kurt, pert, shirt, skirt, spurt, squirt, wert, wort; advert, Albert, alert, assert, avert, concert, convert, covert, desert, dessert, divert, evert, exert, expert, filbert, Herbert, inert, insert, invert, overt, pervert, revert, subvert, unhurt; controvert, disconcert, extrovert, introvert, animadvert.

-erth. See **-irth.**

-erve, curve, Irv, nerve, serve, swerve, verve; conserve, deserve, incurve, innerve, observe, outcurve, preserve, reserve, unnerve.

-es. See **-ess.**

-esce. See **-ess.**

-ese. See **-ease.**

-esh, crèche, flesh, fresh, mesh, thresh; afresh, enmesh, immesh, refresh.

-esk. See **-esque.**

-esque, desk; burlesque, grotesque, Moresque; alhambresque, arabesque, humoresque, picaresque, picturesque, Romanesque, statuesque.

-ess, Bess, bless, cess, chess, cress, dress, guess, jess, Jess, less, mess, press, stress, Tess, tress, yes; abscess, access, actress, address, aggress, assess, caress, compress, confess, countess, depress, digress, distress, duress, egress, empress, excess, express, finesse, impress, ingress, largesse, Loch Ness, mattress, noblesse, obsess, oneness, oppress, possess, princess, profess, progress, recess, redress, repress, success, suppress, transgress, undress, unless; acquiesce, baroness, coalesce, comfortless, convalesce, dispossess, effervesce, Inverness, obsolesce, opalesce, overdress, poetess, politesse, prophetess, repossess, shepherdess, sorceress, votaress, wilderness; nevertheless, proprietress.

Also: many words with the suffix **-ness** (as in *smallness,* etc.) and **-less** (as in *homeless,* etc.)

-esse. See **-ess.**

-essed. See **-est.**

-est, best, blest, breast, Brest, chest, crest, geste, guest, jest, lest, nest, pest, quest, rest, test, vest, west, wrest, zest; abreast, arrest, attest, behest, bequest, Celeste, congest, contest, detest, digest, divest, incest, infest, inquest, invest, Key West, molest, protest, request, suggest, unblest, unrest; acid test, alkahest, Almagest, anapest, Budapest, Everest, manifest, disinterest.

Also: **-ess** + **-ed** (as in *pressed,* etc.)

Also: many superlative forms ending in **-est** (as in *happiest,* etc.)

-et, bet, debt, fret, get, jet, let, Lett, met, net, pet, Rhett, set, stet, sweat, threat, tret, vet, wet, whet, yet; abet, aigrette, Annette, barrette, beget, beset, brochette, brunette, cadet, Claudette, Colette, coquette, corvette, curvet, duet, egret, forget, gazette, grisette, Jeannette, octet, offset, omelet, quartet, quintet, regret, rosette, roulette, septet, sestet, sextet, soubrette, Tibet, upset, vignette; alphabet, amulet, anisette, banneret, baronet, bassinet, bayonet, cabinet, calumet, castanet, cigarette, clarinet, coronet, epaulet, epithet, etiquette, Juliet, marmoset, martinet, mignonette, minaret, minuet, parapet, pirouette, quadruplet, quintuplet, rivulet, serviette, silhouette, suffragette, tourniquet, violet, winterset; marionette.

-etch, etch, fetch, ketch, retch, sketch, stretch, vetch, wretch; outstretch.

-ete. See **-eat.**

-eth. See **-eath.**

-ette. See **-et.**

-euce. See **-use.**

-eud. See **-ude.**

-eur. See **-er.**

-euth. See **-ooth.**

-eve. See **-eave.**

-ew, blew, blue, boo, brew, chew, clue, coo, coup, crew, cue, dew, do, drew, due, ewe, few, flew, flu, flue, glue, gnu, goo, grew, hew, hue, Hugh, Jew, knew, Lew, lieu, loo,

Lou, mew, moo, mu, new, nu, pew, phew, queue, rue, screw, shoe, shrew, skew, slew, slough, sou, spew, stew, strew, sue, Sue, thew, threw, through, to, too, true, two, view, who, woo, yew, you, zoo; accrue, adieu, ado, ague, Ainu, Andrew, Anjou, anew, askew, bamboo, bedew, cachou, canoe, cashew, cuckoo, curfew, curlew, debut, emu, endue, ensue, eschew, Hindu, imbue, issue, juju, menu, mildew, Peru, pooh-pooh, pursue, purview, ragout, renew, review, shampoo, subdue, taboo, tattoo, tissue, undo, venue, voodoo, withdrew, yahoo, Zulu; avenue, barbecue, billet-doux, catechu, cockatoo, curlicue, interview, kangaroo, misconstrue, parvenu, rendezvous, residue, retinue, revenue, toodle-oo, Timbuktu; Kalamazoo, merci beaucoup.

-ewd. See **-ude.**

-ews. See **-ooze** and **-use.**

-ewt. See **-ute.**

-ex, ex, flex, hex, lex, rex, Rex, sex, specs, vex; annex, apex, codex, complex, convex, index, perplex, reflex; circumflex.

Also: **-eck** + **-s** (as in *pecks,* etc.)

-exed. See **-ext.**

-ext, next, text; pretext.

Also: **-ex** + **-ed** (as in *vexed,* etc.)

-ey (-ā). See **-ay.**

-ey (-ē). See **-ee.**

-eyed. See **-ade.**

-eys. See **-aze.**

-ez, fez, says; Juarez, malaise, Suez; Marseillaise.

-i (-ē). See **-ee.**

-i (-ī). See **-y.**

-ib, bib, crib, dib, drib, fib, glib, jib, nib, rib, sib, squib; ad-lib, Carib.

-ibe, bribe, gibe, jibe, scribe, tribe; ascribe, describe, imbibe, inscribe, prescribe, proscribe, subscribe, transcribe; circumscribe, diatribe, superscribe.

-ic. See **-ick.**

-ice, bice, Brice, dice, ice, gneiss, lice, mice, nice, price, rice, slice, spice, splice, thrice, trice, twice, vice, vise; advice, allspice, concise, device, entice, precise, suffice; edelweiss, overnice, paradise, sacrifice.

-iced. See **-ist.**

-ich. See **-itch.**

-ick, brick, chic, chick, click, crick, dick, Dick, flick, hick, kick, lick, mick, nick, Nick, pick, prick, quick,

rick, sic, sick, slick, snick, stick, thick, tick, trick, Vic, wick; beatnik, caustic, heartsick, lovesick, sputnik, toothpick, triptych, yardstick; acoustic, arsenic, artistic, bailiwick, Benedick, bishopric, Bolshevik, candlestick, candlewick, catholic, chivalric, choleric, double-quick, fiddlestick, heretic, limerick, lunatic, maverick, Menshevik, pogostick, politic, rhetoric, turmeric; archbishopric, arithmetic, cataleptic, impolitic.

-icked. See **-ict.**

-icks. See **-ix.**

-ict, Pict, strict; addict, afflict, conflict, constrict, convict, depict, evict, inflict, predict, restrict; benedict, Benedict, contradict, derelict, interdict.

Also: **-ick** + **-ed** (as in *picked,* etc.)

-id, id, bid, chid, Cid, did, grid, hid, kid, lid, mid, quid, rid, skid, slid, squid; amid, Enid, eyelid, forbid, gravid, Madrid, outbid, outdid, rabid, undid; arachnid, insipid, invalid, katydid, overbid, pyramid, underbid; caryatid.

-ide, bide, bride, chide, Clyde, glide, guide, hide, pied, pride, ride, side, slide, snide, stride, tide, wide; abide, aside, astride, backside, backslide, beside, bedside, bestride, betide, broadside, bromide, carbide, cockeyed, collide, confide, cowhide, cross-eyed, decide, deride, divide, elide, green-eyed, hillside, horsehide, inside, misguide, noontide, one-eyed, outside, oxide, pop-eyed, preside, provide, reside, seaside, subside, sulfide, wall-eyed, wayside, Yuletide, worldwide; almond-eyed, alongside, Barmecide, bonafide, Christmastide, coincide, dioxide, Eastertide, eventide, fratricide, genocide, homicide, iodide, matricide, monoxide, mountainside, open-eyed, override, parricide, peroxide, regicide, subdivide, suicide, Whitsuntide; aborticide, formaldehyde, infanticide, insecticide, tyrannicide, uxoricide.

Also: **-ie** + **-d** (as in *lied,* etc.)

Also: **-igh** + **-ed** (as in *sighed,* etc.)

Also: **-y** + **-ed** (as in *cried,* etc.)

-ides, ides; besides.

Also: **-ide** + **-s** (as in *tides, hides,* etc.)

-idge. See **-age.**

-idst, bidst, chidst, didst, hidst, midst, ridst; amidst, forbidst.

-ie (-ē). See **-ee.**

-ie (-ī). See **-y.**

-iece. See **-ease.**

-ied. See **-ide.**

-ief, beef, brief, chief, fief, feoff, grief, leaf, lief, reef, sheaf, thief; belief, fig leaf, relief; bas relief, disbelief, handkerchief, interleaf, neckerchief, Tenerife, unbelief; apéritif.

-iege, liege, siege; besiege, prestige.

-ield, field, shield, weald, wield, yield; afield; battlefield, Chesterfield.
Also: **-eal** + **-ed** (as in *healed,* etc.)
Also: **-eel** + **-ed** (as in *peeled,* etc.)

-ien. See **-ean.**

-iend (-ēnd), fiend; archfiend.
Also: **-ean** + **-ed** (as in *cleaned,* etc.)
Also: **-een** + **-ed** (as in *careened,* etc.)

-iend (-ĕnd). See **-end.**

-ier (-ĭr). See **-eer.**

-ier (-īr). See **-ire.**

-ierce, Bierce, fierce, pierce, tierce; transpierce.

-iest. See **-east.**

-ieu. See **-ew.**

-ieve. See **-eave.**

-iew. See **-ew.**

-ieze. See **-ease.**

-if, biff, cliff, glyph, griff, if, jiff, miff, riff, Riff, skiff, sniff, stiff, tiff, whiff; bindlestiff, handkerchief, hieroglyph, hippogriff, neckerchief.

-ife, fife, knife, life, rife, strife, wife; alewife, fishwife, housewife, jackknife, midwife; afterlife, Duncan Phyfe.

-iff. See **-if.**

-iffed. See **-ift.**

-ift, drift, gift, lift, rift, shift, shrift, sift, swift, thrift; adrift, snowdrift, spendthrift, spindrift, uplift.
Also: **-iff** + **-ed** (as in *whiffed,* etc.)

-ig, big, brig, dig, fig, gig, grig, jig, pig, prig, rig, sprig, swig, trig, twig, Whig, wig; brillig, renege; infra dig, periwig, thimblerig, whirligig; thingumajig.

-igh. See **-y.**

-ighed. See **-ide.**

-ighs. See **-ize.**

-ight. See **-ite.**

-ign. See **-ine.**

-igned. See **-ind.**

-igue. See **-eague.**

-ike, bike, dike, hike, Ike, like, Mike, pike, psych, shrike, spike, tyke; alike, dislike, Klondike, oblique, turnpike, unlike, Vandyke; marlinspike.

-il. See **-ill.**

-ilch, filch, milch, pilch, zilch.

-ild (-ĭld), build, gild, guild; rebuild, regild, unchilled, untilled; unfulfilled.
Also: **-ill** + **-ed** (as in *killed, skilled,* etc.)

-ild (-īld), aisled, child, mild, wild, Wilde.
Also: **-ile** + **-ed** (as in *filed,* etc.)
Also: **-yle** + **-ed** (as in *styled,* etc.)

-ile (-īl), aisle, bile, chyle, faille, file, guile, heil, I'll, isle, lisle, mile, Nile, pile, rile, smile, stile, style, tile, vile, while, wile; anile, Argyle, awhile, beguile, compile, defile, edile, erewhile, exile, gentile, meanwhile, revile, senile, servile; Anglophile, crocodile, domicile, Francophile, infantile, juvenile, mercantile, puerile, reconcile, Slavophile; aileurophile, bibliophile, Germanophile.

-ile (-ēl). See **-eal.**

-ile (-ĭl). See **-ill.**

-iled. See **-ild.**

-ilk, bilk, ilk, milk, silk.

-ill, bill, Bill, brill, chill, dill, drill, fill, frill, gill, grill, hill, ill, Jill, kill, mill, nil, Phil, pill, quill, rill, shill, shrill, sill, skill, spill, squill, squill, swill, thill, thrill, 'til, till, trill, twill, 'twill, will, Will; Brazil, distil, downhill, fulfill, instill, quadrille, Seville, uphill; chlorophyll, codicil, daffodil, domicile, imbecile, Louisville, versatile, volatile, whippoorwill.

-ille (-ēl). See **-eal.**

-ille (-ĭl). See **-ill.**

-illed. See **-ild.**

-ilt, built, gilt, guilt, hilt, jilt, kilt, lilt, milt, quilt, silt, spilt, stilt, tilt, wilt; atilt, rebuilt; Vanderbilt.

-ilth, filth, spilth, tilth.

-im, brim, dim, glim, grim, Grimm, gym, him, hymn, Jim, Kim, limb, limn, prim, rim, rim, shim, skim, slim, swim, Tim, trim, vim, whim; bedim, paynim, prelim; acronym, antonym, cherubim, eponym, homonym, interim, paradigm, pseudonym, seraphim, synonym.

-imb (-ĭm). See **-im.**

-imb (-īm). See **-ime.**

-ime, chime, chyme, climb, clime, crime, cyme, dime, grime, I'm, lime, mime, prime, rhyme, rime, slime, thyme, time; begrime, bedtime, berhyme, daytime, lifetime, meantime, sometime, springtime, sublime, upclimb; Guggenheim, maritime, overtime, pantomime, paradigm, summertime, wintertime.

-imes, betimes, ofttimes, sometimes; oftentimes.
Also: **-ime** + **-s** (as in *crimes,* etc.)
Also: **-yme** + **-s** (as in *rhymes,* etc.)

-imp, blimp, chimp, crimp, gimp, guimpe, imp, limp, pimp, primp, scrimp, shrimp, simp, skimp.

-impse, glimpse.
Also: **-imp** + **-s** (as in *skimps,* etc.)

-in, been, bin, chin, din, djinn, fin, Finn, gin, grin, in, inn, jinn, kin, pin, shin, sin, skin, spin, thin, tin, twin, whin, win; akin, bearskin, begin, Berlin, bowfin, buckskin, carbine, chagrin, Corinne, herein, sidespin, tailspin, therein; alkaline, aniline, aquiline, aspirin, crinoline, crystalline, discipline, feminine, gelatin, genuine, glycerine, harlequin, heroine, Jacobin, javelin, jessamine, mandarin, mandolin, mannequin, masculine, Mickey Finn, moccasin, paladin, peregrine, Rin-Tin-Tin, saccharin, sibylline, violin, Zeppelin; adrenalin, Alexandrine, elephantine.

-inc. See **-ink.**

-ince, blintz, chintz, mince, prince, quince, rinse, since, wince; convince, evince.
Also: **-int** + **-s** (as in *prints,* etc.)

-inch, chinch, cinch, clinch, finch, flinch, inch, lynch, pinch, winch; chaffinch, goldfinch.

-inct, tinct; distinct, extinct, instinct, precinct, succinct.
Also: **-ink** + **-ed** (as in *winked,* etc.)

-ind (-īnd), bind, blind, find, grind, hind, kind, mind, rind, wind; behind, mankind, purblind, remind, unkind, unwind; colorblind, mastermind, undersigned, womankind.
Also: **-ign** + **-ed** (as in *signed,* etc.)
Also: **-ine** + **-ed** (as in *dined,* etc.)

-ind (-ĭnd), Ind, wind; rescind; Amerind, tamarind.
Also: **-in** + **-ed** (as in *grinned,* etc.)

-ine (-īn), brine, chine, dine, fine, kine, line, mine, nine, pine, Rhine, shine, shrine, sign, sine, spine, spline, stein, swine, syne, thine, tine, trine, twine, vine, whine, wine; airline, align, assign, benign, bovine, canine, carbine, carmine, combine, condign, confine, consign, decline, define, design, divine, enshrine, entwine, feline, hircine, Holstein, incline, lifeline, malign, moonshine, opine, outshine, ovine, railline, recline, refine, repine, resign, saline, sunshine, supine, vulpine, woodbine; Adeline, alkaline, anodyne, Apennine, aquiline, Argentine, asinine, Byzantine, calcimine, calomine, Caroline, Clementine, columbine, concubine, disincline, eglantine, etamine, Florentine, interline, intertwine, iodine, leonine, Liechtenstein, palatine, porcupine, Proserpine, saturnine, serpentine, superfine, timberline, Turnverein, turpentine, underline, undermine, valentine, waterline; elephantine.

-ine (-ēn). See **-ean.**

-ine (-īn). See **-in.**

-ined. See **-ind.**

-ing, bing, bring, cling, ding, fling, king, Ming, ping, ring, sing, sling, spring, sting, string, swing, Synge, thing, wing, wring, ying; evening, hireling, mainspring, something, unsling, unstring; anything, atheling, everything, opening, underling.
Also: participles in **-ing** and gerunds (as *clamoring,* etc.)

-inge, binge, cringe, fringe, hinge, Inge, singe, springe, swinge, tinge, twinge; impinge, infringe, syringe, unhinge.

-ingue. See **-ang.**

-ink, blink, brink, chink, clink, drink, fink, ink, kink, link, mink, pink, rink, shrink, sink, skink, slink, stink, swink, think, wink, zinc; bethink, forethink, hoodwink; bobolink Humperdinck, interlink, tiddlywink.

-inked. See **-inct.**

-inks. See **-inx.**

-inned. See **-ind.**

-inse. See **-ince.**

-int, dint, flint, glint, Gynt, hint, lint, mint, print, quint, splint, sprint, squint, stint, tint; asquint, footprint, imprint, misprint, reprint, spearmint; aquatint, peppermint, septuagint.

-inth, plinth; absinthe, Corinth; hyacinth, labyrinth, terebinth.

-ints. See **-ince.**

-inx, jinx, lynx, minx, sphinx; larynx, methinks, salpinx; tiddlywinks.
Also: **-ink** + **-s** (as in *thinks,* etc.)

-ip, blip, chip, clip, dip, drip, flip, grip, grippe, gyp, hip, kip, lip, nip, pip, quip, rip, scrip, ship, sip, skip, slip, snip, strip, tip, trip, whip, yip, zip; airstrip, cowslip, equip, flagship, harelip, horsewhip, lightship, outstrip, transship, unzip; battleship, underlip, weatherstrip.

Also: words with **-ship** as suffix (as *fellowship, scholarship,* etc.)

-ipe, gripe, pipe, ripe, snipe, stipe, stripe, swipe, tripe, type, wipe; bagpipe, blowpipe, hornpipe, pitchpipe, sideswipe, tintype, unripe, windpipe; archetype, collotype, guttersnipe, Linotype, Monotype, overripe, prototype; Daguerrotype, electrotype, stereotype.

-ipse, eclipse, ellipse; apocalypse.
Also: **-ip** + **-s** (as in *chips,* etc.)

-ique. See **-eak.**

-ir. See **-er.**

-irch. See **-urch.**

-ird. See **-urd.**

-ire, briar, brier, buyer, choir, dire, fire, flyer, friar, gyre, hire, ire, liar, lyre, mire, plier, prior, pyre, quire, shire, sire, spire, squire, tire, Tyre, wire; acquire, admire, afire, aspire, attire, bemire, bonfire, conspire, desire, empire, enquire, entire, esquire, expire, grandsire, inquire, inspire, perspire, quagmire, require, respire, retire, sapphire, satire, spitfire, transpire, wildfire.
Also: **-y** + **-er** (as in *crier, modifier,* etc.)

-irge. See **-erge.**

-irk. See **-urk.**

-irl. See **-url.**

-irm, berm, firm, germ, sperm, squirm, term, worm; affirm, confirm, glowworm, grubworm, infirm; isotherm, pachyderm.

-irp. See **-urp.**

-irr. See **-er.**

-irred. See **-urd.**

-irst. See **-urst.**

-irt. See **-ert.**

-irth, berth, birth, dearth, earth, firth, girth, mirth, Perth, worth; stillbirth, unearth.

-is (-īz), biz, fizz, friz, his, is, Liz, quiz, 'tis, viz, whiz, wiz; Cadiz.

-is (-īs). See **-iss.**

-ise (-īs). See **-ice.**

-ise (-īz). See **-ize.**

-ish, dish, fish, Gish, knish, pish, squish, swish, tish, wish; anguish, bluefish, flatfish, goldfish, whitefish, whitish; angelfish, babyish, devilfish, devilish, feverish, flying fish, gibberish, kittenish, womanish; impoverish.

-isk, bisque, brisk, disc, disk, frisk, risk, whisk; asterisk, basilisk, obelisk, odalisque, tamarisk.

-ism, chrism, prism, schism; abysm, Babism, baptism, Buddhism,

Chartism, Comtism, deism, faddism, Fascism, Grecism, Jainism, Mahdism, monism, mutism, psellism, purism, Scottism, snobbism, sophism, Sufism, technism, theism, Thomism, truism, Whiggism, Yogism; absinthism, actinism, acrotism, albinism, algorism, altruism, amorphism, anarchism, aneurysm, Anglicism, animism, aphorism, archaism, asterism, atavism, atheism, atomism, Atticism, barbarism, Benthamism, Biblicism, Bolshevism, Boswellism, botulism, Brahminism, Briticism, Britishism, brutalism, Byronism, cabalism, Caesarism, Calvinism, carnalism, cataclysm, catechism, Celticism, centralism, chauvinism, classicism, cocainism, Cockneyism, Communism, cretinism, criticism, cynicism, daltonism, dandyism, Darwinism, demonism, despotism, dimorphism, ditheism, dogmatism, dowdyism, Druidism, dualism, dynamism, egoism, egotism, embolism, Englishism, erethism, ergotism, euphemism, euphonism, euphuism, exorcism, extremism, fatalism, feminism, fetishism, feudalism, fogyism, foreignism, formalism, formulism, Gallicism, galvanism, gentilism, Germanism, giantism, gigantism, gnosticism, Gothicism, grundyism, heathenism, Hebraism, hedonism, Hellenism, helotism, heroism, Hinduism, Hitlerism, humanism, humorism, hypnotism, Irishism, Islamism, Jansenism, jingoism, journalism, Judaism, Junkerism, laconism, Lamaism, Lambdacism, Latinism, legalism, Leninism, localism, Lollardism, loyalism, magnetism, mannerism, martialism, masochism, mechanism, Menshevism, mephitism, mesmerism, Methodism, microcosm, Mithraism, modernism, monadism, moralism, Mormonism, morphinism, Mosaism, Moslemism, mysticism, narcotism, nepotism, nihilism, occultism, onanism, organism, optimism, ostracism, pacifism, paganism, pantheism, paroxysm, Parseeism, pauperism, pessimism, pietism, Platonism, pluralism, pragmatism, prognathism, prosaism, pyrrhonism, Quakerism, quietism, quixotism, Rabbinism, racialism, realism, regalism, rheumatism, Romanism, rowdyism, royalism, ruralism, satanism, Saxonism, schematism, scientism, Semitism, Shakerism, shamanism,

Shintoism, sigmatism, Sinicism, skepticism, Socialism, solecism, solipsism, specialism, spiritism, spoonerism, Stalinism, stoicism, suffragism, syllogism, symbolism, synchronism, syncretism, synergism, tantalism, Taoism, terrorism, toadyism, Toryism, totemism, traumatism, tribalism, tritheism, ultraism, unionism, vandalism, verbalism, vocalism, volcanism, voodooism, vulgarism, vulpinism, witticism, Yankeeism, zealotism, Zionism; absenteeism, absolutism, achromatism, aestheticism, agnosticism, alcoholism, alienism, allotropism, amateurism, anabolism, anachronism, Anglicanism, antagonism, Arianism, asceticism, astigmatism, autochthonism, automatism, bimetallism, Byzantinism, cannibalism, capitalism, catabolism, Catholicism, charlatanism, clericalism, collectivism, commercialism, communalism, Confucianism, conservatism, democratism, determinism, diabolism, dilletantism, eclecticism, empiricism, eroticism, Evangelism, expressionism, externalism, fanaticism, favoritism, federalism, generalism, Hibernicism, Hispanicism, hooliganism, hospitalism, hyperbolism, idealism, idiotism, impressionism, invalidism, isochronism, isomerism, isomorphism, isotropism, Jacobinism, Jacobitism, Jesuitism, katabolism, laconicism, legitimism, liberalism, libertinism, literalism, Lutheranism, malapropism, mercantilism, metabolism, metachronism, militarism, moderatism, monasticism, monotheism, mutualism, narcoticism, nationalism, naturalism, negativism, neologism, nicotinism, noctambulism, nominalism, objectivism, obscurantism, obstructionism, officialism, opportunism, parallelism, parasitism, paternalism, patriotism, pedagogism, Pharisaism, Philistinism, philosophism, plagiarism, plebianism, polymerism, polymorphism, polyphonism, polytheism, positivism, probabilism, progressivism, Protestantism, provincialism, Puritanism, radicalism, rationalism, recidivism, regionalism, ritualism, romanticism, ruffianism, Sadduceeism, scholasticism, secessionism, sectionalism, secularism,

sensualism, separatism, Shavianism, somnambulism, somniloquism, subjectivism, sycophantism, syndicalism, theosophism, universalism, ventriloquism, Wesleyanism; abolitionism, agrarianism, Americanism, anthropomorphism, Bohemianism, Cartesianism, colloquialism, colonialism, conceptualism, conventionalism, cosmopolitism, equestrianism, evolutionism, existentialism, heliotropism, hermaphroditism, heteromorphism, Hibernianism, histrionicism, imperialism, incendiarism, indeterminism, indifferentism, industrialism, Manicheanism, materialism, medievalism, Mohammedanism, monometallism, Occidentalism, Orientalism, parochialism, phenomenalism, postimpressionism, professionalism, proverbialism, Republicanism, Rosicrucianism, sacerdotalism, sectarianism, sensationalism, sentimentalism, Spencerianism, spiritualism, theatricalism, Tractarianism, traditionalism, transmigrationism, Utopianism, vernacularism; antinomianism, antiquarianism, ceremonialism, Congregationalism, constitutionalism, cosmospolitanism, experimentalism, individualism, intellectualism, internationalism, presbyterianism, preternaturalism, proletarianism, supernaturalism, Unitarianism, vegetarianism; Aristotelianism, humanitarianism, utilitarianism; antidisestablishmentarianism.

-isp, crisp, lisp, wisp; will o' the wisp.

-iss, bliss, Chris, hiss, kiss, miss, Swiss, this; abyss, amiss, crevice, dismiss, jaundice, remiss, ywis; ambergris, armistice, artifice, avarice, Beatrice, benefice, chrysalis, cowardice, dentrifice, edifice, emphasis, genesis, nemesis, orifice, precipice, prejudice, synthesis, verdigris; acropolis, anabasis, analysis, antithesis, dieresis, hypothesis, metropolis, necropolis, paralysis, parenthesis, rigor mortis; metamorphosis; abiogenesis.

-ist (-īst), cist, cyst, fist, gist, grist, hist!, list, mist, schist, tryst, twist, whist, wist, wrist; artist, assist, Babist, Baptist, blacklist, Buddhist, chartist, chemist, Comtist, consist, Cubist, cueist, cyclist, deist, dentist, desist,

druggist, duellist, enlist, entwist, exist, faddist, Fascist, flautist, florist, flutist, harpist, hymnist, insist, jurist, linguist, lutist, lyrist, metrist, monist, palmist, Papist, persist, psalmist, purist, resist, sacrist, simplist, sophist, statist, stylist, subsist, theist, Thomist, tourist, Trappist, tropist, typist, Yorkist; alarmist, alchemist, algebrist, Alpinist, altruist, amethyst, amorist, analyst, anarchist, animist, annalist, aorist, aphorist, Arabist, arbalest, archaist, archivist, armorist, atheist, atomist, balloonist, banjoist, biblicist, bicyclist, bigamist, Bolshevist, botanist, canoeist, cartoonist, casuist, catalyst, catechist, centralist, chauvinist, choralist, citharist, classicist, coexist, colloquist, colonist, colorist, Communist, conformist, copyist, Calvinist, cymbalist, Darwinist, diarist, dogmatist, Donatist, dramatist, dualist, egoist, egotist, elegist, essayist, Eucharist, eulogist, euphuist, extremist, fabulist, factionist, fatalist, fetishist, feudalist, fictionist, folklorist, formalist, futurist, guitarist, Hebraist, hedonist, Hellenist, herbalist, hobbyist, homilist, humanist, humorist, hypnotist, intertwist, Jansenist, journalist, Judaist, Lamaist, lampoonist, Latinist, legalist, Leninist, librettist, liturgist, lobbyist, loyalist, machinist, martialist, mechanist, medallist, mesmerist, Methodist, Mithraist, modernist, monarchist, moralist, motorist, narcotist, nepotist, Nihilist, novelist, occultist, oculist, ophthalmist, optimist, organist, pacifist, pantheist, papalist, pessimist, pharmacist, physicist, pianist, pietist, Platonist, pluralist, portraitist, pragmatist, pre-exist, publicist, pugilist, pyrrhonist, realist, re-enlist, reformist, repealist, reservist, rhapsodist, Romanist, ruralist, Sanskritist, satirist, scientist, sciolist, Scripturist, Shamanist, Shintoist, Socialist, solecist, soloist, specialist, Stalinist, strategist, suffragist, symbolist, Talmudist, Taoist, terrorist, theorist, trombonist, Trotskyist, unionist, Vedantist, violist, vocalist, Zionist, zitherist; abortionist, absolutist, accompanist, agronomist, algebraist, alienist, Anabaptist, anatomist, antagonist, anthologist, apiarist, apologist, astrologist, automatist, autonomist, aviarist, bimetallist, biologist, capitalist, chiropodist, clarinetist, clericalist, collectivist, commercialist, communalist, concessionist, conchologist, contortionist, determinist, diplomatist, dramaturgist, economist, empiricist, enamelist, equilibrist, Esperantist, ethnologist, Evangelist, exclusionist, excursionist, expressionist, extortionist, Federalist, geologist, geometrist, horologist, hygienist, hyperbolist, idealist, illusionist, impressionist, irredentist, legitimist, liberalist, literalist, lycanthropist, manicurist, meliorist, metallurgist, militarist, misanthropist, misogamist, misogynist, monogamist, monologist, monopolist, monotheist, mosaicist, necrologist, negationist, negativist, neologist, neuropathist, noctambulist, Nominalist, nonconformist, objectivist, obscurantist, obstructionist, ocularist, opportunist, optometrist, panegyrist, parachutist, pathologist, perfectionist, philanthropist, philatelist, philogynist, phrenologist, plagiarist, polemicist, polygamist, pomologist, positivist, propagandist, protagonist, protectionist, psychiatrist, psychologist, psychopathist, rationalist, recidivist, religionist, revisionist, revivalist, ritualist, salvationist, secessionist, secularist, sensualist, separatist, soliloquist, somnambulist, somniloquist, spectroscopist, symbologist, syndicalist, synonymist, taxidermist, taxonomist, telepathist, telephonist, thaumaturgist, theologist, theosophist, therapeutist, tobacconist, traditionist, ventriloquist, violinist; abolitionist, agriculturist, anthropologist, anthropomorphist, archæologist, automobilist, caricaturist, coalitionist, conceptionalist, conceptualist, constitutionist, dermatologist, educationist, Egyptologist, elocutionist, embryologist, emigrationist, encyclopædist, entomologist, etymologist, evolutionist, federationist, floriculturist, genealogist, gynecologist, horticulturist, imperialist, insurrectionist, medievalist, melodramatist, mineralogist, miniaturist, monometallist, Occidentalist, ophthalmologist, oppositionist, Orientalist, osteopathist, pharmacologist, phenomenalist, physiologist,

postimpressionist, preferentialist, prohibitionist, revolutionist, sacerdotalist, spiritualist, traditionalist, transcendentalist, universalist, violoncellist, vivisectionist; arboriculturist, Assyriologist, bacteriologist, ceremonialist, Congregationalist, constitutionalist, controversialist, conversationalist, educationalist, experimentalist, individualist, institutionalist, intellectualist, internationalist, supernaturalist. Also: **-iss** + **-ed** (as in *missed*, etc.)

-ist (-ĭst), Christ, feist; Zeitgeist. Also: **-ice** + **-ed** (as in *sliced*, etc.)

-it, bit, bitt, chit, fit, flit, grit, hit, it, kit, knit, lit, mitt, nit, pit, Pitt, quit, sit, skit, slit, smit, spit, split, sprit, tit, twit, whit, wit, writ; acquit, admit, armpit, befit, bowsprit, commit, emit, misfit, moonlit, omit, outwit, permit, refit, remit, respite, starlit, submit, sunlit, tidbit, tomtit, transmit, unfit; apposite, benefit, counterfeit, definite, exquisite, favorite, hypocrite, infinite, Jesuit, opposite, perquisite, preterite, requisite; indefinite.

-itch, bitch, ditch, fitch, flitch, hitch, itch, niche, pitch, rich, snitch, stitch, switch, twitch, which, witch; bewitch, enrich, hemstitch, unhitch; czarevich.

-ite (-īt), bight, bite, blight, bright, cite, dight, Dwight, fight, flight, fright, height, hight, kite, knight, light, might, mite, night, plight, quite, right, rite, sight, site, sleight, slight, smite, spite, sprite, tight, trite, white, wight, wright, write; affright, alight, aright, bedight, benight, contrite, daylight, delight, despite, downright, dunnite, excite, foresight, forthright, goodnight, headlight, Hittite, hoplite, ignite, incite, indict, indite, invite, midnight, moonlight, outright, polite, recite, requite, starlight, sunlight, tonight, twilight, unite, upright, wainwright, wheelwright; acolyte, aconite, anchorite, anthracite, appetite, blatherskite, Canaanite, candlelight, copyright, disunite, dynamite, erudite, eremite, expedite, fahrenheit, Gesundheit, impolite, Leninite, Moabite, Muscovite, neophyte, overnight, oversight, parasite, plebiscite, proselyte, recondite, satellite, stalactite, stalagmite, Stalinite, troglodyte, Trotskyite, underwrite, vulcanite, watersprite, watertight, weathertight, Yemenite;

electrolyte, gemütlichkeit, hermaphrodite, Israelite, meteorite.

-ite (-ĭt). See **-it.**

-ites. See **-itz.**

-ith, frith, kith, myth, pith, smith, with; Edith, forthwith, herewith, therewith, wherewith, zenith; acrolith, Arrowsmith, monolith, otolith.

-ithe, blithe, lithe, scythe, tithe, withe, writhe.

-itz, blitz, Fritz, grits, Ritz, spitz. Also: **-it** + **-s** (as in *bits*, etc.) Also: **-ite** + **-s** (as in *favorites*, etc.)

-ive (-īv), chive, Clive, dive, drive, five, gyve, hive, I've, live, rive, shive, shrive, strive, thrive, wive; alive, archive, arrive, beehive, connive, contrive, deprive, derive, nosedive, ogive, revive, survive; overdrive.

-ive (-ĭv), give, live, sieve, spiv; active, captive, costive, cursive, dative, fictive, forgive, furtive, massive, missive, motive, native, outlive, passive, pensive, plaintive, relive, restive, sportive, suasive, votive; ablative, abortive, abrasive, absorptive, abstersive, abstractive, abusive, adaptive, additive, adductive, adhesive, adjective, adjunctive, adoptive, affective, afflictive, aggressive, allusive, amative, arrestive, aspersive, assertive, assuasive, assumptive, attentive, attractive, causative, coercive, cognitive, cohesive, collective, collusive, combative, combustive, compulsive, conative, conceptive, concessive, concussive, conclusive, concoctive, conducive, conductive, conflictive, congestive, conjunctive, connective, constrictive, constructive, consultive, consumptive, contractive, convulsive, corrective, corrosive, corruptive, creative, curative, deceptive, decisive, deductive, defective, defensive, delusive, depictive, depressive, derisive, descriptive, destructive, detective, detractive, diffusive, digestive, digressive, directive, discursive, disjunctive, disruptive, dissuasive, distinctive, distractive, divertive, divisive, divulsive, effective, effusive, elective, elusive, emissive, emotive, emulsive, evasive, excessive, exclusive, excursive, exhaustive, expansive, expensive, expletive, explosive, expressive, expulsive, extensive, extortive, extractive, extrusive, fixative, formative, fugitive, genitive, gerundive, hortative, illusive, impassive, impressive, impulsive, inactive, incentive, incisive, inclusive, incursive, inductive, infective, inflective, infusive, ingestive, inscriptive, instinctive, instructive, intensive, intrusive, invective, inventive, laudative, laxative, lenitive, locative, lucrative, narrative, negative, nutritive, objective, obstructive, obtrusive, offensive, olfactive, oppressive, optative, partitive, perceptive, percussive, perfective, permissive, perspective, persuasive, pervasive, positive, possessive, preclusive, precursive, predictive, prescriptive, presumptive, preventive, primitive, privative, productive, progressive, projective, propulsive, proscriptive, prospective, protective, protractive, protrusive, punitive, purgative, purposive, reactive, receptive, recessive, redemptive, reductive, reflective, reflexive, regressive, relative, remissive, repressive, repulsive, respective, responsive, restrictive, resumptive, retentive, retractive, revulsive, secretive, sedative, seductive, selective, sensitive, siccative, subjective, subjunctive, submissive, substantive, subtractive, subversive, successive, suggestive, suppressive, talkative, tentative, transgressive, transitive, transmissive, vibrative, vindictive, vocative; abrogative, accusative, acquisitive, admonitive, adumbrative, affirmative, alternative, appellative, attributive, augmentative, calculative, carminative, circumscriptive, circumventive, coextensive, combinative, comparative, compensative, competitive, compositive, comprehensive, connotative, consecutive, conservative, contemplative, contributive, conversative, corporative, correlative, corresponsive, counteractive, cumulative, declarative, decorative, dedicative, definitive, demonstrative, denotative, deprecative, derivative, diminutive, disputative, distributive, educative, evocative, excitative, exclamative, execrative, executive, exhibitive, exhortative, expectative, explicative, explorative, expositive, figurative, generative, germinative, hesitative, illustrative, imitative, imperative, imperceptive, inattentive, incohesive, inconclusive, indecisive, indicative, indistinctive, ineffective, inexhaustive, inexpansive,

inexpensive, inexpressive, infinitive, informative, innovative, inoffensive, inquisitive, insensitive, integrative, intransitive, introductive, introspective, intuitive, irrespective, irresponsive, irritative, iterative, judicative, legislative, locomotive, mediative medicative, meditative, nominative, operative, palliative, pejorative, perforative, preparative, prerogative, preservative, preventative, procreative, prohibitive, provocative, putrefactive, qualitative, quantitative, radiative, rarefactive, reconstructive, recreative, regulative, remonstrative, repetitive, reprehensive, reprobative, reproductive, retroactive, retrogressive, retrospective, ruminative, segregative, speculative, stupefactive, superlative, suppurative, vegetative, vindicative; accumulative, administrative, agglutinative, alleviative, alliterative, appreciative, argumentative, assimilative, associative, authoritative, coagulative, commemorative, commiserative, communicative, conciliative, confederative, cooperative, corroborative, deliberative, depreciative, discriminative, exonerative, expostulative, imaginative, initiative, inoperative, interpretative, interrogative, investigative, irradiative, manipulative, recuperative, reiterative, remunerative, representative, retaliative, significative, subordinative, vituperative; incommunicative, philoprogenitive.

-ix, fix, mix, nix, pyx, six, Styx; admix, affix, commix, infix, matrix, onyx, prefix, prolix, suffix, transfix, unfix; cicatrix, crucifix, fiddlesticks, intermix, politics; executrix; archæopteryx.
Also: **-ick** + **-s** (as in *bricks, sticks,* etc.)

-ixed. See **-ixt.**

-ixt, twixt; betwixt.
Also: **-ix** + **-ed** (as in *mixed,* etc.)

-iz. See **-is.**

-ize, guise, prize, rise, size, wise; advise, apprise, arise, assize, baptize, capsize, chastise, cognize, comprise, demise, despise, devise, disguise, incise, likewise, misprize, moonrise, revise, sunrise, surmise, surprise, unwise; advertise, aggrandize, agonize, alkalize, amortize, Anglicize, atomize, authorize,

barbarize, bastardize, bowdlerize, brutalize, canalize, canonize, carbonize, catechize, cauterize, centralize, circumcise, civilize, classicize, colonize, compromise, criticize, crystallize, deputize, dogmatize, dramatize, emphasize, energize, enterprise, equalize, eulogize, euphemize, exercise, exorcise, feminize, fertilize, feudalize, focalize, formalize, fossilize, fractionize, fraternize, Gallicize, galvanize, Germanize, glutinize, harmonize, Hellenize, humanize, hybridize, hypnotize, idolize, immunize, improvise, ionize, itemize, jeopardize, Judaize, laicize, Latinize, legalize, lionize, liquidize, localize, magnetize, martyrize, maximize, mechanize, memorize, mercerize, mesmerize, metallize, methodize, minimize, mobilize, modernize, monetize, moralize, nasalize, neutralize, normalize, organize, ostracize, otherwise, oxidize, patronize, penalize, pluralize, polarize, polemize, pulverize, realize, recognize, rhapsodize, Romanize, ruralize, Russianize, satirize, scandalize, schematize, scrutinize, sermonize, signalize, socialize, solemnize, specialize, stabilize, standardize, sterilize, stigmatize, subsidize, summarize, supervise, symbolize, sympathize, symphonize, synchronize, synthesize, systemize, tantalize, televise, temporize, terrorize, theorize, totalize, tranquilize, tyrannize, unionize, utilize, vaporize, verbalize, victimize, vitalize, vocalize, vulcanize, vulgarize, Westernize; acclimatize, actualize, allegorize, alphabetize, anæsthetize, anatomize, antagonize, anthologize, apologize, apostatize, apostrophize, capitalize, catholicize, characterize, Christianize, circularize, commercialize, decentralize, dehumanize, demobilize, democratize, demonetize, demoralize, deodorize, disorganize, economize, epitomize, extemporize, federalize, generalize, hydrogenize hypothesize, idealize, immobilize, immortalize, italicize, legitimize, liberalize, metabolize, militarize, monopolize, nationalize, naturalize, parenthesize, personalize, philosophize, plagiarize, popularize, proselytize, rationalize, regularize, reorganize, ritualize, singularize, skeletonize, soliloquize, systematize, theologize,

theosophize, visualize,
ventriloquize; Americanize,
anathematize, apotheosize,
departmentalize, etymologize,
familiarize, legitimatize, materialize,
memorialize, particularize,
professionalize, republicanize,
revolutionize, secularize,
sentimentalize, spiritualize,
universalize; constitutionalize,
individualize, institutionalize,
intellectualize, internationalize.
Also: **-y** + **-s** (as in *testifies,* etc.)
Also: **-eye** + **-s** (as in *eyes,* etc.)
Also: **-igh** + **-s** (as in *sighs,* etc.)
-o (-ō). See **-ow.**
-o (-ōō). See **-oo.**
-oach, broach, brooch, coach, loach,
poach, roach; abroach, approach,
cockroach, encroach, reproach.
-oad (-ôd). See **-aud.**
-oad (-ōd). See **-ode.**
-oaf, loaf, oaf.
-oak. See **-oke.**
-oaks. See **-oax.**
-oal. See **-ole.**
-oaled. See **-old.**
-oam. See **-ome.**
-oan. See **-one.**
-oap. See **-ope.**
-oar. See **-ore.**
-oard. See **-ord.**
-oared. See **-ord.**
-oast. See **-ost.**
-oat. See **-ote.**
-oath. See **-oth.**
-oax, coax, hoax.
Also: **-oak** + **-s** (as in *cloaks,* etc.)
Also: **-oke** + **-s** (as in *jokes,* etc.)
-ob, blob, bob, Bob, cob, Cobb, fob,
glob, gob, hob, job, knob, lob, mob,
nob, rob, slob, snob, sob, squab,
swab, throb; cabob, hobnob, nabob;
thingumbob.
-obe, globe, Job, lobe, probe, robe;
conglobe, disrobe, enrobe, unrobe;
Anglophobe, Francophobe,
Gallophobe, Russophobe,
Slavophobe.
-ock, Bach, Bloch, block, bock,
chock, clock, cock, crock, doc,
dock, flock, frock, hock, jock, Jock,
knock, loch, lock, Mach, mock,
pock, roc, rock, shock, smock, sock,
stock; ad hoc, Bankok, deadlock,
Dvořák, fetlock, Hancock, hemlock,
padlock, peacock, petcock,
Rorschach, shamrock, Sherlock,
Shylock, tick-tock, unfrock, unlock,
woodcock; alpenstock, Antioch,
hollyhock, Jabberwock, poppycock,
shuttlecock, weathercock.

-ocked. See **-oct.**
-ocks. See **-ox.**
-oct, concoct, decoct; shell-shocked.
Also: **-ock** + **-ed** (as in *flocked,* etc.)
-od, clod, cod, God, hod, nod, odd,
plod, pod, prod, quad, quod, rod,
scrod, shod, sod, squad, tod, trod,
wad; ballade, couvade, facade,
roughshod, roulade, slipshod,
unshod, untrod; decapod,
demigod, goldenrod, lycopod,
promenade.
-ode, bode, code, goad, load, lode,
mode, node, ode, road, rode,
Spode, strode, toad, woad; abode,
anode, cathode, commode,
corrode, erode, explode, implode,
forebode, railroad, reload, unload;
à la mode, discommode, episode,
overload, pigeon-toed.
Also: **-ow** + **-ed** (as in *towed,* etc.)
-odge, dodge, hodge, lodge, podge,
stodge; dislodge, hodgepodge.
-oe (-ō). See **-ow.**
-oe (-ōō). See **-ew.**
-oes (-ōz). See **-ose.**
-oes (-ŭz). See **-uzz.**
-off, cough, doff, off, scoff, soph,
trough; Khrushchev, takeoff;
philosophe. See also **-aff.**
-offed. See **-oft.**
-oft, croft, loft, oft, soft; aloft,
hayloft.
Also: **-off** + **-ed** (as in *doffed,* etc.)
Also: **-ough** + **-ed** (as in *coughed,* etc.)
-og, bog, clog, cog, dog, flog, fog,
frog, grog, hog, jog, log, nog,
Prague, slog; agog, bulldog,
eggnog, incog, unclog; analogue,
catalogue, decalogue, demagogue,
dialogue, epilogue, monologue,
pedagogue, pettifog, synagogue,
travelogue.
-ogue (-ōg), brogue, rogue, vogue;
prorogue; disembogue.
-ogue (-ŏg). See **-og.**
-oice, choice, Joyce, voice; invoice,
rejoice, Rolls Royce.
-oiced. See **-oist.**
-oid, Floyd, Freud, Lloyd, void;
avoid, devoid, Negroid, ovoid,
tabloid; alkaloid, aneroid,
anthropoid, asteroid, celluloid,
Mongoloid, trapezoid; paraboloid.
Also: **-oy** + **-ed** (as in *enjoyed,* etc.)
-oil, boil, broil, coil, foil, Hoyle,
moil, oil, roil, soil, spoil, toil;
despoil, embroil, gumboil, parboil,
recoil, tinfoil, trefoil, turmoil,
uncoil.

-oin, coign, coin, groin, join, loin,
quoin; adjoin, benzoin, Burgoyne,
conjoin, Des Moines, disjoin,
enjoin, purloin, rejoin, sirloin,
subjoin; tenderloin.
-oint, joint, point; anoint, appoint,
aroint, conjoint, disjoint, dry-point,
West Point; counterpoint,
disappoint.
-oise, noise, poise; counterpoise,
equipoise, Illinois, Iroquois;
avoirdupois.
Also: **-oy** + **-s** (as in *toys,* etc.)
-oist, foist, hoist, joist, moist.
Also: **-oice** + **-ed** (as in *voiced,* etc.)
-oit, coit, doit, quoit; adroit, Beloit,
dacoit, Detroit, exploit, introit;
maladroit.
-oke, bloke, broke, choke, cloak,
coke, Coke, croak, folk, joke, oak,
oke, poke, smoke, soak, spoke,
stoke, stroke, toque, woke, yoke,
yolk; awoke, baroque, bespoke,
convoke, evoke, invoke, provoke,
revoke; artichoke, counterstroke,
gentlefolk, masterstroke.
-okes. See **-oax.**
-ol (-ŏl), doll, loll, moll, Sol; atoll;
alcohol, capitol, folderol, parasol,
protocol, vitriol.
-ol (-ōl). See **-ole.**
-old, bold, cold, fold, gold, hold,
mold, mould, old, scold, sold, told,
wold; behold, blindfold, cuckold,
enfold, foothold, foretold, freehold,
household, retold, stronghold,
threshold, toehold, twofold, unfold,
untold, uphold, withhold; manifold,
marigold, overbold.
Also: **-oal** + **-ed** (as in *foaled,* etc.)
Also: **-ole** + **-ed** (as in *paroled,* etc.)
Also: **-oll** + **-ed** (as in *rolled,* etc.)
-ole, bole, boll, bowl, coal, dole,
droll, foal, goal, hole, Joel, knoll,
kohl, mole, pole, poll, role, roll,
scroll, shoal, skoal, sole, soul, stole,
stroll, thole, toll, troll, whole; cajole,
condole, console, control, Creole,
enroll, flagpole, loophole, Maypole,
parole, patrol, payroll, peephole,
petrol; aerosol, Anatole, barcarole,
buttonhole, camisole, girandole,
girasole, oriole, rigmarole, rock 'n'
roll, Seminole; filet of sole.
-oled. See **-old.**
-olk. See **-oke.**
-oll (-ŏl). See **-ol.**
-oll (-ōl). See **-ole.**
-olled. See **-old.**
-olt, bolt, colt, dolt, holt, jolt, molt,
poult, volt; revolt, unbolt;
thunderbolt.

-olve, solve; absolve, convolve, devolve, dissolve, evolve, involve, resolve, revolve.

-om (-ŏm), bomb, dom, from, prom, rhomb, Tom; aplomb, pogrom, pompom, therefrom, wherefrom.

-om (-ōōm). See **-oom.**

-omb (-ŏm). See **-om.**

-omb (-ōm). See **-ome.**

-omb (-ōōm). See **-oom.**

-ome (-ōm), chrome, comb, dome, foam, gnome, holm, home, loam, mome, Nome, ohm, roam, Rome, tome; aplomb, cockscomb, coulomb, Jerome; aerodrome, catacomb, currycomb, gastronome, hippodrome, honeycomb, metronome, monochrome, palindrome.

-ome (-ŭm). See **-um.**

-omp, comp, pomp, romp, swamp.

-ompt, prompt, romped, swamped.

-on (-ŏn), con, don, gone, John, on, scone, swan, wan, yon; anon, Argonne, Aswan, begone, bonbon, bygone, Ceylon, chiffon, cretonne, hereon, icon, neutron, proton, thereon, upon, Yvonne; Algernon, Amazon, antiphon, Aragon, Avalon, betatron, bevatron, colophon, decagon, deuteron, echelon, electron, epsilon, Helicon, hexagon, lexicon, Marathon, marathon, mastodon, mesotron, myrmidon, nonagon, octagon, omicron, Oregon, paragon, Parthenon, Pentagon, polygon, Rubicon, silicon, synchrotron, tarragon, upsilon; phenomenon, Saskatchewan; prolegomenon; parallelopipedon.

-on (-ŭn). See **-un.**

-once (-ŏns), Hans, nonce, sconce, wants; ensconce, response, séance; liederkranz.
Also: **-aunt** + **-s** (as in *taunts,* etc.)

-once (-ŭns). See **-unce.**

-onch. See **-onk.**

-ond, blond, blonde, bond, fond, frond, pond, wand, yond; abscond, beyond, despond, respond; correspond, demimonde, vagabond.
Also: **-on** + **-ed** (as in *donned,* etc.)

-one (-ōn), bone, blown, cone, crone, drone, flown, groan, grown, hone, Joan, known, loan, lone, moan, mohn, mown, own, phone, pone, prone, roan, Rhone, scone, shone, shown, sown, stone, throne, thrown, tone, zone; alone, atone, backbone, Bayonne, bemoan, brimstone, cologne, Cologne,

condone, curbstone, depone, dethrone, disown, enthrone, flagstone, grindstone, headstone, intone, keystone, milestone, millstone, moonstone, ozone, postpone, trombone, unknown, unsewn; baritone, chaperone, cicerone, cornerstone, dictaphone, ediphone, gramaphone, megaphone, microphone, monotone, overgrown, overthrown, saxophone, telephone, undertone, xylophone.

-one (-ŏn). See **-on.**

-one (-ŭn). See **-un.**

-ong (-ŏng), gong, long, prong, song, strong, thong, throng, tong, Tong, wrong; along, belong, dingdong, diphthong, dugong, headlong, headstrong, Hongkong, King Kong, lifelong, mahjongg, oblong, pingpong, prolong, souchong; evensong, overlong.

-ong (-ŭng). See **-ung.**

-ongue. See **-ung.**

-onk (-ŏnk), conch, conk, honk.

-onk (-ŭnk). See **-unk.**

-onned. See **-ond.**

-onse. See **-once.**

-ont (-ŏnt), font, want; Vermont; Hellespont.

-ont (-ŭnt). See **-unt.**

-oo. See **-ew.**

-ood (-ōōd), could, good, hood, should, stood, wood, would; childhood, firewood, manhood, monkshood, withstood; babyhood, brotherhood, fatherhood, hardihood, Hollywood, likelihood, livelihood, maidenhood, motherhood, neighborhood, parenthood, Robin Hood, sandalwood, sisterhood, understood, womanhood; misunderstood.

-ood (-ōōd). See **-ude.**

-oof, goof, hoof, pouf, proof, roof, spoof, woof; aloof, behoof, disproof, fireproof, rainproof, reproof, Tartuffe; waterproof, weatherproof; opera bouffe.

-ook (-ōōk), book, brook, cook, crook, hook, look, nook, rook, shook, took; betook, Chinook, forsook, mistook, nainsook, outlook, partook; overlook, pocketbook, undertook.

-ook (-ook). See **-uke.**

-ool, cool, drool, fool, ghoul, pool, rule, school, spool, stool, tool, tulle, who'll; ampoule, befool, footstool,

home rule, misrule, toadstool, whirlpool; Istanbul, Liverpool, overrule.
See also **-ule.**

-oom, bloom, boom, broom, brume, doom, flume, fume, gloom, groom, loom, plume, rheum, room, spume, tomb, whom, womb; abloom, assume, bridegroom, consume, costume, entomb, exhume, Fiume, heirloom, illume, Khartoum, legume, perfume, presume, relume, resume, simoom, subsume; anteroom, hecatomb, reassume.

-oon, boon, Boone, coon, croon, dune, goon, hewn, June, loon, moon, noon, prune, rune, soon, spoon, swoon, tune; attune, baboon, balloon, bassoon, bestrewn, buffoon, cartoon, cocoon, commune, doubloon, dragoon, eftsoon, festoon, forenoon, galloon, harpoon, high noon, immune, impugn, jejune, lagoon, lampoon, maroon, midnoon, monsoon, oppugn, platoon, poltroon, pontoon, quadroon, raccoon, Rangoon, Simoon, spittoon, tycoon, typhoon, Walloon; afternoon, brigadoon, Cameroun, honeymoon, importune, macaroon, octoroon, opportune, pantaloon, picaroon, picayune, rigadoon.

-ooned. See **-ound.**

-oop, coop, croup, droop, drupe, dupe, goop, group, hoop, jupe, Krupp, loop, poop, scoop, sloop, soup, stoop, stoup, stupe, swoop, troop, troupe, whoop; recoup; Guadeloupe, nincompoop.

-oor (-ōōr), boor, brewer, dour, moor, poor, Ruhr, sewer, spoor, sure, tour, Ur; abjure, adjure, amour, assure, brochure, contour, detour, ensure, insure, tonsure, unsure; blackamoor, cynosure, Kohinoor, paramour, petit four, reassure; affaire d'amour. See also **-ure.**

-oor (-ôr). See **-ore.**

-oors. See **-ours.**

-oose (-ōōs), Bruce, deuce, goose, juice, loose, moose, noose, puce, sluice, spruce, truce, use, Zeus; abduce, abstruse, abuse, adduce, burnoose, caboose, conduce, deduce, diffuse, disuse, excuse, induce, misuse, obtuse, papoose, produce, profuse, recluse, reduce, seduce, Toulouse, traduce, vamoose; calaboose, charlotte russe, introduce, reproduce, Syracuse; hypotenuse.

-oose (-o͞oz). See **-ooze.**

-oosed. See **-oost.**

-oost, boost, deuced, Proust, roost. Also: **-uce** + **-ed** (as in *reduced,* etc.) Also: **-oose** + **-ed** (as in *loosed,* etc.)

-oot (-o͞ot), boot, bruit, brute, chute, coot, flute, fruit, hoot, jute, loot, moot, root, route, shoot, skoot, toot; Beirut, cahoot, Canute, cheroot, galloot, recruit, uproot; Aleut, bandicoot, bumbershoot, overshoot, parachute. See also **-ute.**

-oot (-o͝ot), foot, put, soot; afoot, forefoot, hotfoot, input, output; pussyfoot, underfoot; tenderfoot.

-ooth (-o͞oth), booth, couth, ruth, Ruth, sleuth, sooth, tooth, truth, youth; Duluth, forsooth, uncouth, vermouth.

-oothe (-o͞oth), smooth, soothe.

-oove. See **-ove.**

-ooze, blues, booze, bruise, choose, cruise, lose, ooze, ruse, shoes, snooze, who's, whose; peruse; Betelgeuse. See also **-use.** Also: **-ew** + **-s** (as in *chews,* etc.) Also: **-oo** + **-s** (as in *moos,* etc.) Also: **-ue** + **-s** (as in *dues,* etc.)

-op, bop, chop, cop, crop, drop, flop, fop, hop, lop, mop, plop, pop, prop, shop, slop, sop, stop, strop, swap, top; Aesop, atop, co-op, dewdrop, eavesdrop, estop, flipflop, snowdrop, tiptop, workshop; aftercrop, lollipop, Malaprop, overstop, whistle-stop.

-ope, cope, dope, grope, hope, lope, mope, nope, ope, pope, rope, scope, slope, soap, taupe, tope, trope; elope, antelope, antipope, cantaloupe, envelope, gyroscope, horoscope, interlope, isotope, microscope, misanthrope, periscope, stethoscope, telescope; heliotrope, kaleidoscope.

-opped. See **-opt.**

-opt, copt, opt; adopt. Also: **-op** + **-ed** (as in *topped,* etc.)

-or (-ôr), for, lor, nor, or, Thor, tor, war; abhor, bailor, donor, furor, junior, lessor, senior, señor, vendor; ancestor, auditor, bachelor, chancellor, conqueror, corridor, creditor, counselor, cuspidor, dinosaur, Ecuador, editor, emperor, governor, guarantor, janitor, Labrador, matador, metaphor, meteor, minotaur, monitor, orator, picador, Salvador, senator, troubadour, visitor, warrior; ambassador, competitor, compositor, conspirator, contributor, depositor, executor,

ichthyosaur, inheritor, inquisitor, progenitor, proprietor, solicitor, toreador. See also **-ore.**

-or (-ōr). See **-ore.**

-orb, orb; absorb.

-orce. See **-orse.**

-orch, porch, scorch, torch.

-ord, board, chord, cord, fiord, ford, Ford, gourd, hoard, horde, lord, sward, sword, toward, ward; aboard, abhorred, accord, afford, award, broadsword, concord, discord, landlord, record, reward, seaboard, untoward; clavichord, harpsichord. Also: **-oar** + **-ed** (as in *roared,* etc.) Also: **-ore** + **-ed** (as in *scored,* etc.)

-ore, boar, Boer, bore, chore, core, corps, door, floor, fore, frore, four, gore, hoar, lore, more, oar, o'er, ore, pore, pour, roar, score, shore, snore, soar, sore, store, swore, tore, whore, wore, yore; adore, afore, ashore, before, claymore, deplore, encore, explore, folklore, footsore, forbore, forswore, galore, heartsore, ignore, implore, restore; albacore, battledore, Baltimore, commodore, evermore, furthermore, hellebore, heretofore, nevermore, pinafore, sagamore, semaphore, Singapore, sophomore, stevedore, sycamore, underscore. See also **-or.**

-ored. See **-ord.**

-orge, forge, George, gorge; disgorge, engorge, regorge.

-ork, cork, Cork, fork, pork, stork, torque, York; New York, pitchfork, uncork.

-orld, world. Also: **-url** + **-ed** (as in *curled,* etc.)

-orm, corm, dorm, form, norm, storm, swarm, warm; conform, deform, inform, misform, perform, reform, snowstorm, transform; chloroform, cruciform, misinform, multiform, thunderstorm, uniform, vermiform; cuneiform, iodoform.

-orn, born, borne, bourn, corn, horn, lorn, morn, mourn, scorn, shorn, sworn, thorn, torn, warn, worn; acorn, adorn, blackthorn, buckthorn, first-born, foghorn, forewarn, forlorn, forsworn, greenhorn, hawthorn, Leghorn, lovelorn, outworn, popcorn, stillborn, suborn, toilworn, unborn; alpenhorn, barleycorn, Capricorn, Matterhorn, peppercorn, unicorn, yestermorn.

-orp, dorp, thorp, warp.

-orse, coarse, corse, course, force, gorse, hoarse, horse, Morse, Norse,

source, torse; concourse, discourse, divorce, endorse, enforce, perforce, recourse, remorse, resource, seahorse, unhorse; hobbyhorse, intercourse, reinforce, watercourse.

-orst. See **-urst.**

-ort, bort, court, fort, forte, mort, ort, port, quart, short, snort, sort, sport, swart, thwart, tort, wart; abort, assort, athwart, cavort, cohort, comport, consort, contort, deport, disport, distort, escort, exhort, export, extort, import, passport, purport, rapport, report, resort, retort, seaport, transport.

-orts. See **-artz.**

-orth, forth, fourth, north, swarth; henceforth, thenceforth.

-ose (-ōs), close, dose, gross; engross, globose, glucose, jocose, morose, verbose; acerose, adipose, bellicose, cellulose, comatose, diagnose, grandiose, otiose, overdose.

-ose (-ōz), chose, close, clothes, doze, froze, gloze, hose, nose, pose, prose, rose, Rose, those; Ambrose, arose, compose, depose, disclose, dispose, enclose, expose, foreclose, impose, inclose, oppose, propose, repose, suppose, transpose, unclose, unfroze; decompose, discompose, indispose, interpose, predispose, presuppose, tuberose, twinkle-toes. Also: **-o** + **-s** (as in *punctilios,* etc.) Also: **-o** + **-es** (as in *goes,* etc.) Also: **-oe** + **-s** (as in *toes,* etc.) Also: **-ot** + **-s** (as in *depots,* etc.) Also: **-ow** + **-s** (as in *glows,* etc.)

-osk, bosk, mosque; kiosk.

-osque. See **-osk.**

-oss, boss, cos, cross, dross, floss, fosse, gloss, hoss, joss, loss, moss, os, Ross, sauce, toss; across, emboss, lacrosse, reredos; albatross, applesauce; rhinoceros.

-ost (-ôst or -ŏst), cost, frost, lost, wast; accost, exhaust; holocaust, Pentecost. Also: **-oss** + **-ed** (as in *tossed,* etc.)

-ost (-ōst), boast, coast, ghost, grossed, host, most, oast, post, roast, toast; almost, engrossed, foremost, hindmost, riposte, seacoast, signpost; aftermost, furthermost, hindermost, hitching post, innermost, lowermost, nethermost, outermost, undermost, uppermost, uttermost.

-ot, blot, clot, cot, dot, Dot, got, grot, hot, jot, knot, lot, not, plot, pot, rot, scot, Scot, shot, slot, snot, sot, spot, squat, tot, trot, watt, what, wot, yacht; allot, begot, besot, boycott, cocotte, culotte, dogtrot, ergot, forgot, foxtrot, fylfot, garotte, gavotte, grapeshot, kumquat, loquat, somewhat, unknot; Aldershot, aliquot, apricot, bergamot, Camelot, counterplot, eschalot, gallipot, Hottentot, Huguenot, Lancelot, misbegot, patriot, polyglot, tommyrot, unbegot, undershot; forget-me-not.

-otch, blotch, botch, crotch, notch, scotch, Scotch, splotch, swatch, watch; hopscotch, hotchpotch, topnotch.

-ote, bloat, boat, Choate, coat, cote, dote, float, gloat, goat, groat, moat, mote, note, oat, quote, rote, shoat, smote, stoat, throat, tote, vote, wrote; afloat, capote, connote, demote, denote, devote, emote, footnote, lifeboat, misquote, outvote, promote, remote, steamboat, topcoat, unquote; anecdote, antidote, asymptote, billygoat, creosote, nanny goat, overcoat, petticoat, redingote, table d'hôte; witenagemot.

-oth (-ôth), broth, cloth, froth, Goth, moth, swath, Thoth, troth, wroth; betroth, broadcloth, sackcloth; Ashtaroth, behemoth, Ostrogoth, Visigoth.

-oth (-ōth), both, growth, loath, oath, quoth, sloth, wroth; overgrowth, undergrowth.

-othe, clothe, loathe; betroth.

-ou (-ou). See **-ow.**

-ou (-ū). See **-ew.**

-oubt. See **-out.**

-ouch (-ouch), couch, crouch, grouch, ouch, pouch, slouch, vouch; avouch.

-ouch (-ŭch). See **-utch.**

-ouche, douche, ruche; barouche, cartouche, debouch; scaramouch.

-oud, cloud, crowd, loud, proud, shroud; aloud, becloud, enshroud, o'ercloud; overcloud, overcrowd, thundercloud.
Also: **-ow** + **-ed** (as in *bowed,* etc.)

-ough (-ôf). See **-off.**

-ough (-ou or -ō). See **-ow.**

-ough (-ŭf). See **-uff.**

-oughed. See **-oft.**

-ought, aught, bought, brought, caught, fought, fraught, naught, nought, ought, sought, taught, taut, thought, wrought; besought, Connaught, distraught, dreadnought, forethought, methought, onslaught; aeronaut,

afterthought, Argonaut, astronaut, Juggernaut, overwrought.

-oul (-oul). See **-owl.**

-oul (-ōl). See **-ole.**

-ould. See **-ood.**

-oun. See **-own.**

-ounce, bounce, flounce, frounce, ounce, pounce, trounce; announce, denounce, enounce, pronounce, renounce.
Also: **-ount** + **-s** (as in *counts,* etc.)

-ound (-ound), bound, found, ground, hound, mound, pound, round, sound, wound; abound, aground, around, astound, background, bloodhound, compound, confound, dumfound, expound, hidebound, homebound, horehound, icebound, inbound, outbound, profound, propound, rebound, redound, resound, spellbound, snowbound, surround, unbound, unfound; underground; merry-go-round.
Also: **-own** + **-ed** (as in *clowned,* etc.)

-ound (-ōōnd), wound.
Also: **-oon** + **-ed** (as in *swooned,* etc.)
Also: **-une** + **-ed** (as in *tuned,* etc.)

-ount, count, fount, mount; account, amount, discount, dismount, miscount, recount, remount, surmount; catamount, paramount, tantamount.

-ounts. See **-ounce.**

-oup. See **-oop.**

-our, bower, cower, dour, dower, flour, flower, glower, hour, lour, lower, our, power, scour, shower, sour, tower; deflower, devour, embower, empower, horsepower, manpower, sunflower, wallflower; Adenauer, cauliflower, Eisenhower, overpower.
Also: **-ow** + **-er** (as in *plower,* etc.)

-ourge. See **-erge.**

-ourn (-ôrn). See **-orn.**

-ourn (-ûrn). See **-urn.**

-ours (-ourz), ours.
Also: **-our** + **-s** (as in *devours,* etc.)
Also: **-ower** + **-s** (as in *flowers,* etc.)

-ours (-ōōrz), yours.
Also: **-oor** + **-s** (as in *boors,* etc.)
Also: **-our** + **-s** (as in *amours,* etc.)
Also: **-ure** + **-s** (as in *lures,* etc.)

-ourse. See **-orse.**

-ourt. See **-ort.**

-ourth. See **-orth.**

-ous. See **-us.**

-ouse, blouse, douse, grouse, house, louse, mouse, souse, spouse, Strauss; backhouse, birdhouse, clubhouse, delouse, doghouse,

hothouse, jailhouse, madhouse, outhouse, penthouse, poorhouse, roundhouse, storehouse, warehouse, workhouse; Fledermaus.

-oust, doused, Faust, joust, oust, soused, spoused; deloused.

-out, bout, clout, doubt, drought, flout, gout, grout, knout, kraut, lout, out, pout, rout, scout, shout, snout, spout, sprout, stout, tout, trout; ablaut, about, devout, lookout, redoubt, throughout, umlaut, without; gadabout, hereabout, knockabout, out-and-out, roundabout, roustabout, sauerkraut, thereabout, waterspout, whereabout.

-outh (-outh), drouth, mouth, south.

-outh (-ōōth). See **-ooth.**

-ove (-ŭv), dove, glove, love, of, shove; above, belove, foxglove, hereof, thereof, unglove, whereof; ladylove, turtledove.

-ove (-ōv), clove, cove, dove, drove, grove, hove, Jove, mauve, rove, shrove, stove, strove, throve, trove, wove; alcove, inwove; borogrove, interwove.

-ove (-ōōv), groove, move, prove, who've, you've; approve, behoove, disprove, improve, remove, reprove; disapprove.

-ow (-ou), bough, bow, brow, chow, cow, dhow, frau, how, now, plough, plow, prow, row, scow, slough, sow, tau, thou, vow, wow, wow; allow, avow, bow-wow, endow, enow, highbrow, hoosegow, kowtow, landau, lowbrow, Mau Mau, meow, Moldau, Moscow, powwow, snowplow, somehow, anyhow, disallow, disavow, middlebrow; Oberammergau.

-ow (-ō), beau, blow, bow, crow, do, doe, dough, eau, Flo, floe, flow, foe, fro, glow, go, grow, hoe, Joe, know, lo, low, mot, mow, no, O, oh, owe, Po, pro, rho, roe, row, sew, show, sloe, slow, snow, so, sow, stow, strow, throe, throw, toe, tow, trow, whoa, woe, Zoe; aglow, ago, although, banjo, below, bestow, Bordeaux, bravo, bubo, bureau, chapeau, château, cocoa, dado, depot, dido, Dido, duo, forego, foreknow, foreshow, Frisco, heigh-ho, hello, jabot, moonglow, oboe, outgrow, pierrot, poncho, pou sto, quarto, rainbow, rondeau, Rousseau, sabot, tableau, tiptoe, toro, trousseau, zero; abovo, afterglow, albedo, al fresco, allegro, apropos, buffalo, Buffalo, bungalow, calico, cameo, Diderot, domino, dos-à-dos, embryo, Eskimo, falsetto, folio, furbelow, gazebo, gigolo, Idaho, indigo, memento, Mexico, mistletoe, mulatto, nuncio, octavo, Ohio, oleo, overflow, overgrow, overthrow, portico, portmanteau, potato, proximo, radio, Romeo, so-and-so, sourdough, stiletto, studio, tallyho, tobacco, Tokyo, tomato, torero, torpedo, tremolo, ultimo, undergo, undertow, vertigo, vireo, volcano; Abednego, Acapulco, adagio, bravissimo, fortissimo, imbroglio, incognito, intaglio, magnifico, malapropos, mustachio, Ontario, pistachio, seraglio; ab initio, archipelago, banderillero, braggadoccio, duodecimo, impresario, oratorio, pianissimo; generalissimo.

-owd. See **-oud.**

-owed (-ōd). See **-ode.**

-owed (-oud). See **-oud.**

-ower. See **-our.**

-owl, cowl, foul, fowl, growl, howl, jowl, owl, prowl, scowl, yowl; befoul, waterfowl.

-own (-oun), brown, clown, crown, down, drown, frown, gown, noun, town; adown, downtown, embrown, nightgown, pronoun, renown, uptown; eiderdown, hand-me-down, tumble-down, upside down.

-own (-ōn). See **-one.**

-owned. See **-ound.**

-ows (-ōz). See **-ose.**

-ows (-ouz). See **-owse.**

-owse, blowse, browse, dowse, drowse, house, rouse, spouse; arouse, carouse, espouse.
Also: **-ow** + **-s** (as in *cows*, etc.)

-owth. See **-oth.**

-ox, box, cox, fox, lox, ox, phlox, pox, sox, vox; bandbox, hatbox, icebox, mailbox, postbox, smallpox; chickenpox, equinox, orthodox, paradox; heterodox.
Also: **-ock** + **-s** (as in *knocks*, etc.)

-oy, boy, buoy, cloy, coy, goy, joy, oy, ploy, poi, soy, toy, troy, Troy; ahoy, alloy, annoy, convoy, decoy, deploy, destroy, employ, enjoy, envoy, Leroy, Savoy, sepoy, viceroy; corduroy, hoi polloi, Illinois, Iroquois, misemploy, overjoy; hobbledehoy.

-oyed. See **-oid.**

-oys. See **-oise.**

-oze. See **-ose.**

-ub, bub, chub, club, cub, drub, dub, grub, hub, nub, pub, rub, scrub,

shrub, snub, stub, sub, tub; hubbub; rub-a-dub, sillabub; Beelzebub.

-ube, boob, cube, rube, Rube, tube; jujube.

-uce. See **-oose.**

-uced. See **-oost.**

-uch. See **-utch.**

-uck, buck, chuck, cluck, duck, luck, muck, pluck, puck, Puck, ruck, shuck, struck, stuck, suck, truck, tuck; amok, amuck, Canuck, potluck, roebuck, woodchuck; horror-struck, terror-struck, thunderstruck, wonderstruck.

-ucked. See **-uct.**

-ucks. See **-ux.**

-uct, duct; abduct, conduct, construct, deduct, induct, instruct, obstruct; aqueduct, misconduct, oviduct, usufruct, viaduct.
Also: **-uck** + **-ed** (as in *tucked,* etc.)

-ud, blood, bud, cud, dud, flood, mud, scud, spud, stud, sud, thud; bestud, lifeblood, rosebud.

-ude, brood, crude, dude, feud, food, Jude, lewd, mood, nude, prude, rood, rude, shrewd, snood, you'd, who'd; allude, collude, conclude, delude, denude, elude, étude, exclude, extrude, exude, include, intrude, obtrude, occlude, preclude, prelude, protrude, seclude; altitude, amplitude, aptitude, certitude, desuetude, fortitude, gratitude, habitude, interlude, lassitude, latitude, longitude, magnitude, multitude, platitude, plenitude, promptitude, pulchritude, quietude, rectitude, servitude, solitude, turpitude; beatitude, exactitude, necessitude, similitude, solicitude, vicissitude.
Also: **-ew** + **-ed** (as in *brewed,* etc.)
Also: **-oo** + **-ed** (as in *wooed,* etc.)
Also: **-ue** + **-ed** (as in *pursued,* etc.)

-udge, budge, drudge, fudge, grudge, judge, nudge, sludge, smudge, trudge; adjudge, begrudge, forejudge, misjudge, prejudge.

-ue. See **-ew.**

-ues. See **-ooze** and **-use.**

-uff, bluff, buff, chough, clough, cuff, duff, fluff, gruff, guff, huff, luff, muff, puff, rough, ruff, scruff, scuff, slough, snuff, sough, stuff, tough, tuff; breadstuff, enough, Macduff, rebuff; overstuff, powderpuff.

-ug, bug, chug, drug, dug, hug, jug, lug, mug, plug, pug, rug, shrug, slug, smug, snug, thug, tug;

humbug; bunnyhug, doodlebug, jitterbug.

-uge, huge, Scrooge, stooge; refuge; centrifuge, febrifuge, subterfuge, vermifuge.

-uice. See **-oose.**

-uise. See **-ize.**

-uke, duke, fluke, Juke, Luke, puke, snook, spook, uke; archduke, caoutchouc, peruke, rebuke; Heptateuch, Mameluke, Marmaduke, Pentateuch.

-ul (-ŭl), cull, dull, gull, hull, lull, mull, null, scull, skull, trull; annul, mogul, numskull, seagull; disannul.

-ul (-ōōl), bull, full, pull, wool; cupful, graceful, lambswool; beautiful, bountiful, dutiful, fanciful, masterful, merciful, pitiful, plentiful, powerful, Sitting Bull, sorrowful, teaspoonful, wonderful, worshipful; tablespoonful.

-ulch, gulch, mulch.

-ule, fuel, mewl, mule, pule, you'll, yule; ampule; molecule, reticule, ridicule, vestibule.
See also **-ool.**

-ulge, bulge; divulge, effulge, indulge, promulge.

-ulk, bulk, hulk, skulk, sulk.

-ull. See **-ul.**

-ulp, gulp, pulp, sculp.

-ulse, pulse; appulse, convulse, expulse, impulse, repulse.

-ult, cult; adult, consult, exult, insult, occult, result, tumult; catapult, difficult.

-um, bum, chum, come, crumb, drum, dumb, glum, grum, gum, hum, mum, numb, plum, plumb, rum, scum, slum, some, strum, stum, sum, swum, thrum, thumb; become, benumb, humdrum, spectrum, succumb; burdensome, Christendom, cranium, cumbersome, frolicsome, heathendom, humorsome, kettledrum, laudanum, martyrdom, maximum, medium, mettlesome, minimum, modicum, odium, opium, optimum, overcome, pabulum, pendulum, platinum, premium, quarrelsome, quietsome, radium, speculum, stumble bum, sugar plum, tedium, troublesome, tympanum, vacuum, venturesome, wearisome; adventuresome, aluminum, aquarium, chrysanthemum, compendium, continuum, curriculum, delirium, effluvium, emporium, encomium, exordium, fee-fi-fo-fum, geranium, gymnasium, harmonium, magnesium, millennium, opprobrium, palladium, petroleum, residuum, symposium; auditorium, crematorium, equilibrium, pandemonium, sanitarium.

-umb. See **-um.**

-ume. See **-oom.**

-ump, bump, chump, clump, dump, drump, grump, Gump, hump, jump, lump, mump, plump, pump, rump, slump, stump, thump, trump, ump; mugwump.

-un, bun, done, dun, fun, gun, Hun, none, nun, one, pun, run, shun, son, spun, stun, sun, ton, tun, won; begun, homespun, outrun, rerun, someone, undone; Albion, anyone, Chesterton, cinnamon, everyone, galleon, Galveston, garrison, halcyon, orison, overdone, overrun, simpleton, singleton, skeleton, unison, venison; accordion, comparison, oblivion, phenomenon.

-unce, dunce, once.
Also: **-unt** + **-s** (as in *bunts,* etc.)

-unch, brunch, bunch, crunch, hunch, lunch, munch, punch, scrunch.

-unct, adjunct, defunct, disjunct.
Also: **-unk** + **-ed** (as in *bunked,* etc.)

-und, bund, fund; fecund, jocund, obtund, refund, rotund; cummerbund, moribund, orotund, rubicund.
Also: **-un** + **-ed** (as in *stunned,* etc.)

-une. See **-oon.**

-uned. See **-ound.**

-ung, bung, clung, dung, flung, hung, lung, rung, slung, sprung, strung, stung, sung, swung, tongue, wrung, young; among, highstrung, Shantung, unstrung, unsung; Niebelung, overhung, underslung.

-unge, lunge, plunge, sponge; expunge; muskellunge.

-unk, bunk, chunk, drunk, dunk, flunk, funk, hunk, junk, monk, plunk, punk, shrunk, skunk, slunk, spunk, sunk, trunk; adunc, kerplunk, quidnunc, spelunk.

-unked. See **-unct.**

-unned. See **-und.**

-unt, blunt, brunt, bunt, front, grunt, hunt, punt, runt, shunt, stunt; affront, confront, forefront.

-unts. See **-unce.**

-up, cup, pup, sup, tup, up; hiccup, makeup, setup, teacup, tossup; buttercup.

-upe. See **-oop.**

-upt, abrupt, corrupt, disrupt, erupt; interrupt.
Also: **-up** + **-ed** (as in *supped,* etc.)

-ur. See **-er.**

-urb. See **-erb.**

-urch, birch, church, lurch, perch, search, smirch; besmirch, research.

-urd, bird, curd, gird, heard, herd, Kurd, surd, third, word; absurd, blackbird, lovebird, songbird, ungird, unheard; hummingbird, ladybird, mockingbird, overheard.
Also: **-er** + **-ed** (as in *conferred,* etc.)
Also: **-ir** + **-ed** (as in *stirred,* etc.)
Also: **-ur** + **-ed** (as in *occurred,* etc.)

-ure, cure, lure, pure, your, you're; allure, cocksure, coiffure, demure, endure, immure, impure, inure, manure, mature, obscure, ordure, procure, secure; amateur, aperture, armature, epicure, forfeiture, furniture, immature, insecure, ligature, overture, portraiture, premature, signature, sinecure; caricature, expenditure, investiture, literature, miniature, temperature; primogeniture. See also **-oor.**

-ures. See **-ours.**

-urf, scurf, serf, surf, turf.

-urge. See **-erge.**

-urk, burke, clerk, dirk, irk, jerk, kirk, lurk, murk, perk, quirk, shirk, smirk, Turk, work; Dunkirk, rework; handiwork, masterwork, overwork, underwork.

-url, Beryl, burl, churl, curl, earl, furl, girl, hurl, knurl, pearl, purl, swirl, twirl, whirl, whorl; uncurl, unfurl.

-urled. See **-orld.**

-urn, Berne, burn, churn, earn, erne, fern, hern, kern, learn, quern, spurn, stern, tern, turn, urn, yearn; adjourn, astern, concern, discern, eterne, intern, Lucerne, return, sojourn, unlearn; overturn, taciturn, unconcern.

-urp, burp, chirp, twerp; usurp.

-urred. See **-urd.**

-urse. See **-erse.**

-ursed. See **-urst.**

-urst, burst, curst, durst, erst, first, Hearst, thirst, verst, worst; accurst, athirst, knackwurst, outburst, sunburst; liverwurst.
Also: **-erce** + **-ed** (as in *coerced,* etc.)
Also: **-erse** + **-ed** (as in *dispersed,* etc.)
Also: **-urse** + **-ed** (as in *nursed,* etc.)

-urve. See **-erve.**

-us, bus, buss, cuss, fuss, Gus, Hus, muss, plus, pus, Russ, thus, truss, us; cirrus, discuss, nimbus, nonplus, percuss, Remus, stratus; abacus, Angelus, animus, blunderbuss, cumulus, exodus, Hesperus, impetus, incubus, nautilus, octopus, omnibus, Pegasus, platypus, radius, Romulus, Sirius, stimulus, succubus, Tantalus, terminus; esophagus, Leviticus, sarcophagus.
Also: numerous words ending in **-ous** (as *mutinous, perilous,* etc.)

-use (-ūz), blues, fuse, fuze, mews, muse, news, use; abuse, accuse, amuse, bemuse, confuse, diffuse, disuse, enthuse, excuse, infuse, misuse, refuse, suffuse, transfuse; disabuse, Syracuse. See also **-ooze.**
Also: **-ew** + **-s** (as in *stews,* etc.)
Also: **-ue** + **-s** (as in *cues,* etc.)

-use (-ōōs) or (-ūs). See **-oose.**

-use (-ōōz). See **-ooze.**

-ush (-ŭsh), blush, brush, crush, flush, gush, hush, lush, mush, plush, rush, shush, slush, thrush, tush; hairbrush; underbrush.

-ush (-ōōsh), bush, push, shush, swoosh; ambush; bramblebush, Hindu Kush.

-usk, brusque, busk, dusk, husk, musk, rusk, tusk, Usk.

-uss. See **-us.**

-ussed. See **-ust.**

-ust, bust, crust, dost, dust, gust, just, lust, must, rust, thrust, trust; adjust, adust, august, August, combust, disgust, distrust, encrust, entrust, incrust, mistrust, piecrust, robust, stardust, unjust.
Also: **-uss** + **-ed** (as in *fussed,* etc.)

-ut (-ŭt), but, butt, cut, glut, gut, hut, jut, mutt, nut, putt, rut, shut, slut, smut, strut, tut; abut, beechnut, catgut, chestnut, clearcut, crewcut, peanut, rebut, uncut, walnut; betelnut, coconut, halibut, hazelnut, occiput, scuttlebutt.

-ut (-ōōt) See **-oot.**

-utch, clutch, crutch, Dutch, hutch, much, smutch, such, touch; retouch; inasmuch, insomuch.

-ute, beaut, butte, cute, lute, mute, newt, suit, Ute; acute, astute, Canute, commute, compute, confute, depute, dilute, dispute, hirsute, impute, minute, Piute, pollute, pursuit, refute, repute, salute, transmute, volute; absolute, Aleut, attribute, constitute, destitute, disrepute, dissolute, execute, institute, persecute, prosecute, prostitute, resolute, substitute; electrocute, irresolute, reconstitute. See also **-oot.**

-uth. See **-ooth.**

-ux, crux, flux, lux, shucks, tux; conflux, efflux, influx.
Also: **-uck** + **-s** (as in *plucks,* etc.)

-uzz, buzz, coz, does, fuzz.

-y, ay, aye, buy, by, bye, cry, die, dry, dye, eye, fie, fly, fry, guy, Guy, hi, hie, high, I, lie, lye, my, nigh, phi, pi, pie, ply, pry, psi, rye, shy, sigh, sky, Skye, sly, spry, spy, sty, Thai, thigh, thy, tie, try, vie, why, wry; ally, apply, awry, belie, comply, decry, defy, deny, descry, espy, goodbye, hereby, imply, July, magpie, mudpie, outcry, outvie, popeye, rely, reply, Shanghai, shoofly, standby, supply, thereby, untie,

whereby; abaci, alibi, alkali, alumni, amplify, beautify, butterfly, by-and-by, certify, clarify, classify, codify, crucify, deify, dignify, edify, falsify, fortify, glorify, gratify, horrify, hushaby, justify, lazuli, Lorelei, lullaby, magnify, modify, mollify, mortify, multiply, mystify, notify, nullify, occupy, ossify, pacify, petrify, prophesy, purify, putrefy, qualify, ratify, rectify, sanctify, satisfy, scarify, signify, simplify, specify, stultify, stupefy, terrify, testify, typify, umblepie, unify, verify, versify, vilify; beatify, disqualify, diversify, exemplify, identify, indemnify, intensify, Lotophagi, personify, preoccupy, solidify; Aegospotami, anthropophagi.

-yle. See **-ile.**

-yled. See **-ild.**

-yme. See **-ime.**

-ymn. See **-im.**

-ymph, lymph, nymph.

-yne. See **-ine.**

-ynx. See **-inx.**

-yp. See **-ip.**

-ype. See **-ipe.**

-yph. See **-iff.**

-ypse. See **-ipse.**

-yre. See **-ire.**

-yrrh. See **-er.**

-ysm. See **-ism.**

-yst. See **-ist.**

-yte. See **-ite.**

-yth. See **-ith.**

-yve. See **-ive.**

-yx. See **-ix.**

TWO-SYLLABLE RHYMES

-abard. See **-abbard.**

-abbard, jabbered, scabbard, slabbered, tabard.

-abber (-ă-), blabber, dabber, drabber, grabber, jabber, nabber, slabber, stabber; beslabber.

-abber (-ŏ-). See **-obber.**

-abbered. See **-abbard.**

-abbet. See **-abit.**

-abbey. See **-abby.**

-abbit. See **-abit.**

-abble, babble, dabble, drabble, gabble, grabble, rabble, scabble, scrabble; bedabble, bedrabble.

-abby, abbey, cabby, crabby, flabby, grabby, scabby, shabby, tabby.

-abel. See **-able.**

-aber. See **-abor.**

-abies, babies, rabies, scabies.

-abit, abbot, babbitt, Babbitt, habit, rabbet, rabbit; cohabit, inhabit.

-able, Abel, able, babel, cable, fable, gable label, Mabel, sable, stable, table; disable, enable, unable, unstable.

-abor, caber, labor, neighbor, saber, tabor, Weber; belabor.

-abra, candelabra; abracadabra.

-aby, baby, gaby, maybe.

-accy. See **-acky.**

-acement. See **-asement.**

-acence. See **-ascence.**

-acent, jacent, naissant, nascent; adjacent, complacent, complaisant, connascent, renaissant, renascent, subjacent; circumjacent, interjacent.

-aceous. See **-acious.**

-acet. See **-asset.**

-achment. See **-atchment.**

-achne. See **-acne.**

-acial, facial, glacial, racial, spatial; abbatial, palatial, prelatial.

-acic. See **-assic.**

-acile. See **-astle.**

-acious, gracious, spacious; audacious, bulbaceous, cactaceous, capacious, cetaceous, cretaceous, crustaceous, edacious, fabaceous, fallacious, feracious, flirtatious, fugacious, fumacious, fungaceous, gemmaceous, herbaceous, Horatius, Ignatius, lappaceous, lardaceous, loquacious, marlaceous, mendacious, micaceous, minacious, misgracious, mordacious, palacious, palmaceous, pomaceous, predaceous, procacious, pugnacious, rampacious, rapacious, rutaceous, sagacious, salacious, sebaceous, sequacious, setaceous, tenacious, testaceous, tophaceous, ungracious, veracious, vexatious, vinaceous, vivacious, voracious; acanaceous, acanthaceous- alliaceous, amylaceous, arenaceous, camphoraceous, capillaceous, carbonaceous, contumacious, corallaceous, coriaceous, disputatious, efficacious, erinaceous, execratious, farinaceous, ferulaceous, foliaceous, incapacious, liliaceous, olivaceous, orchidaceous, ostentatious, perspicacious, pertinacious, resinaceous, saponaceous, violaceous; inefficacious.

-acid, acid, placid.

-acis. See **-asis.**

-acit. See **-asset.**

-acken, blacken, bracken, slacken.

-acker, backer, clacker, cracker, lacquer, packer, slacker; hijacker.

-acket, bracket, flacket, jacket, packet, placket, racket, tacket.

-ackey. See **-acky.**

-ackguard. See **-aggard.**

-ackie. See **-acky.**

-ackish, blackish, brackish, knackish, quackish.

-ackle, cackle, crackle, hackle, macle, quackle, shackle, tackle; debacle, ramshackle, unshackle; tabernacle.

-ackney. See **-acne.**

-ackpot, crackpot, jackpot.

-ackson. See **-axen.**

-acky, 'baccy, Jackie, khaki, knacky, lackey, Saki, tacky, wacky; Nagasaki.

-acle. See **-ackle.**

-acne, acne, hackney; Arachne.

-acon, bacon, Macon.

-acquer. See **-acker.**

-acre. See **-aker.**

-acter. See **-actor.**

-actic, lactic, tactic; didactic, emphractic, galactic, protactic, stalactic, syntactic; parallactic, prophylactic.

-actice, cactus, factice, practice.

-actile, dactyl, tactile, tractile; attractile, contractile, protractile, retractile; pterodactyl.

-action, action, faction, fraction, paction, taction, traction; abstraction, attraction, coaction, compaction, contaction, contraction, detraction, distraction, exaction, extraction, inaction, infraction, protraction, reaction, redaction, refraction, retraction, subaction, subtraction, transaction; arefaction, benefaction, calefaction, counteraction, interaction, labefaction, liquefaction, lubrifaction, malefaction, petrifaction, putrefaction, rarefaction, retroaction, rubefaction, satisfaction, stupefaction, tabefaction, tepefaction, tumefaction; dissatisfaction.

-active, active, tractive; abstractive, attractive, coactive, contractive, detractive, distractive, enactive, inactive, olfactive, protractive, refractive, retractive, subtractive; calefactive, counteractive, petrifactive, putrefactive, retroactive, satisfactive, stupefactive; radioactive.

-actly, abstractly, compactly, exactly; matter-of-factly.

-actor, actor, factor, tractor; abstracter, attracter, climacter, compacter, contractor, detractor, distracter, enacter, exacter, extracter, infractor, olfactor, phylacter, protractor, refractor, retractor, subtracter, transactor; benefactor, malefactor.

-actress, actress, factress; contractress, detractress; benefactress, malefactress.

-acture, facture, fracture; compacture; manufacture.

-actus. See **-actice.**

-actyl. See **-actile.**

-acy, Casey, lacy, Macy, racy, précis.

-ada, Dada; armada, cicada, Grenada, haggadah, Nevada.

-adam, Adam, madam; macadam.

-adden, gladden, madden, sadden; engladden.

-adder, adder, bladder, gadder, gladder, ladder, madder, padder, sadder; stepladder.

-addie. See **-addy.**

-adding. See **-odding.**

-addish, baddish, caddish, faddish, maddish, radish, saddish.

-addle (-ă-), addle, daddle, faddle, paddle, raddle, saddle, staddle, straddle; astraddle, skedaddle, unsaddle; fiddle-faddle.

-addle (-ŏ-). See **-oddle.**

-addock, haddock, paddock, raddock, shaddock.

-addy, caddy, daddy, faddy, haddie, laddie, paddy; finnan-haddie, sugar daddy.

-aden, Aden, Haydn, laden, maiden.

-ader, aider, grader, raider, trader; crusader, evader, invader, persuader.

-adger, badger, cadger.

-adi. See **-ady.**

-adic, nomadic, sporadic.

-adiant, gradient, radiant.

-adie. See **-ady.**

-adient. See **-adiant.**

-adish. See **-addish.**

-adle, cradle, ladle; encradle.

-adly, badly, gladly, madly, sadly.

-adness, badness, gladness, madness, sadness.

-ado (-ā dō), dado; crusado, gambado, grenado, scalado, stoccado, tornado; ambuscado, barricado, bastinado, camisado, carbonado, desperado, muscovado, renegado.

-ado (-ä dō), bravado, Mikado, passado, strappado, travado; avocado, Colorado, desperado, El Dorado, imbrocado.

-ady, braidy, cadi, glady, lady, Sadie, shady; belady, cascady, landlady.

-afer, chafer, safer, wafer; cockchafer.

-affer, chaffer, gaffer, kaffir, laugher, zaffer.

-affic. See **-aphic.**

-affick. See **-aphic.**

-affir. See **-affer.**

-affle, baffle, gaffle, haffle, raffle, scraffle, snaffle, yaffle.

-affled, baffled, raffled, scaffold, snaffled.

-affold. See **-affled.**

-affy, baffy, chaffy, daffy, draffy, taffy.

-after, after, dafter, drafter, grafter, hafter, laughter, rafter, wafter; hereafter, ingrafter, thereafter; hereinafter.

-afty, crafty, drafty, grafty.

-agar. See **-agger.**

-agate. See **-aggot.**

-agement, assuagement, encagement, engagement, enragement, presagement.

-ageous, ambagious, contagious, courageous, oragious, outrageous, rampageous, umbrageous; advantageous; disadvantageous.

-ager, cager, gauger, major, pager, sager, stager; assuager, presager.

-aggard, blackguard, haggard, laggard, staggard, staggered, swaggered.

-agger, bragger, dagger, flagger, gagger, jagger, lagger, nagger, ragger, tagger, wagger; one-bagger, three-bagger, two-bagger; agar-agar, carpet-bagger.

-aggered. See **-aggard.**

-aggie. See **-aggy.**

-aggish, haggish, naggish, waggish.

-aggle, daggle, draggle, gaggle, haggle, raggle, straggle, waggle; bedaggle, bedraggle; raggle-taggle.

-aggot, agate, faggot, maggot.

-aggy, Aggie, baggy, craggy, faggy, Maggie, naggy, scraggy, shaggy, slaggy, snaggy, waggy.

-agic, magic, tragic; ellagic, pelagic; archipelagic.

-agile, agile, fragile.

-agious. See **-ageous.**

-agnate, magnate, magnet.

-agnet. See **-agnate.**

-ago (-ā gō), dago, sago; farrago, imago, lumbago, plumbago, virago, vorago.

-ago (-ä gō), Chicago, farrago; Santiago.

-agon, dragon, flagon, wagon; pendragon, snapdragon.

-agrant, flagrant, fragrant, vagrant; infragrant.

-aic, laic; Alcaic, altaic, archaic, deltaic, Hebraic, Judaic, mosaic, Mosaic, Passaic, prosaic, sodaic, spondaic, stanzaic, trochaic, voltaic; algebraic, Alhambraic, pharisaic, Ptolemaic, tesseraic; paradisaic.

-aiden. See **-aden.**

-aider. See **-ader.**

-aidy. See **-ady.**

-aighten. See **-atan.**

-aigner. See **-ainer.**

-ailer, ailer, gaoler, jailer, paler, sailor, squalor, staler, tailor, trailer, whaler.

-ailie. See **-alely.**

-ailiff, bailiff, Caliph.

-ailing, ailing, grayling, paling.

-ailment, ailment, bailment; assailment, bewailment, curtailment, derailment, entailment, impalement, regalement.

-ailor. See **-ailer.**

-aily. See **-alely.**

-aiment. See **-ayment.**

-ainder, attainder, remainder.

-ainer, drainer, gainer, plainer, saner, stainer, strainer, trainer; abstainer, attainer, campaigner, chicaner, complainer, container, profaner, retainer.

-ainful, baneful, gainful, painful; complainful, disdainful.

-ainger. See **-anger.**

-ainly, gainly, mainly, plainly, sanely, vainly, humanely, inanely, insanely, mundanely, profanely, ungainly, urbanely.

-ainter, fainter, painter, tainter.

-aintly, faintly, quaintly, saintly; unsaintly.

-ainty, dainty, fainty, feinty.

-ainy, brainy, grainy, rainy, veiny, zany; Eugénie; Allegheny, miscellany.

-airie. See **-ary.**

-airing. See **-aring.**

-airish. See **-arish.**

-airline, airline, hairline.

-airly. See **-arely.**

-airy. See **-ary.**

-aisant. See **-acent.**

-aiser. See **-azer.**

-aissant. See **-acent.**

-aisy. See **-azy.**

-aiter. See **-ator.**

-aitress. See **-atress.**

-aiver. See **-aver.**

-ajor. See **-ager.**

-ake. See **-ocky.**

-aker, acre, baker, breaker, faker, fakir, maker, Quaker, raker, shaker, Shaker, taker, waker; bookmaker, dressmaker, grubstaker, heartbreaker, lawbreaker, matchmaker, pacemaker, peacemaker, watchmaker; circuitbreaker, undertaker.

-aki (-ă-). See **-acky.**

-aki (-ä-). See **-ocky.**

-akir. See **-aker.**

-alace. See **-allas.**

-alad, ballad, salad. See also **-alid.**

-alan. See **-allon.**

-alap. See **-allop.**

-alate. See **-allot.**

-ale. See **-olly.**

-alec. See **-alic.**

-alely, bailie, daily, gaily, grayly, halely, Haley, palely, scaly, shaly, stalely; shillay; ukelele.

-alement. See **-ailment.**

-alent, gallant, talent.

-aler. See **-ailer.**

-alet. See **-allot.**

-aley. See **-alely.**

-ali. See **-olly.**

-alic, Alec, Gallic, malic, phallic, salic; cephalic, italic, metallic, oxalic, vocalic; brachycephalic; dolichocephalic.

-alice. See **-allas.**

-alid (-ă-), pallid, valid. See also **-alad.**

-alid (-ŏ-). See **-olid.**

-alin. See **-allon.**

-aling. See **-ailing.**

-aliph. See **-ailiff.**

-allad. See **-alad.**

-allant. See **-alent.**

-allas, Alice, callous, chalice, Dallas, gallus, malice, palace, Pallas, phallus.

-allen. See **-allon.**

-aller. See **-allor.**

-allet. See **-allot.**

-allette. See **-allot.**

-alley. See **-ally.**

-allic. See **-alic.**

-allid. See **-alid.**

-allment, appallment, enthrallment, installment; disenthrallment.

-allon, Alan, Allen, gallon, Stalin, talon; ten-gallon.

-allop (-ăl-), gallop, jalap, scallop, shallop; escallop.

-allop (-ŏl-). See **ollop.**

-allor, pallor, valor; caballer.

-allot, ballot, mallet, palate, pallet, pallette, shallot, valet.

-allow (-ăl-), aloe, callow, fallow, hallow, mallow, sallow, shallow, tallow; marshmallow.

-allow (-ŏl-). See **-ollow.**

-allus. See **-allas.**

-ally, alley, bally, challis, dally, galley, pally, rally, sally, Sally, tally, valley; O'Malley; dillydally, shillyshally.

-almest. See **-almist.**

-almist, calmest, palmist, psalmist; embalmist.

-almless, balmless, palmless, psalmless, qualmless.

-almon. See **-ammon.**

-almy. See **-ami.**

-aloe. See **-allow.**

-alon. See **-allon.**

-alor. See **-allor.**

-altar. See **-alter.**

-alter, altar, alter, falter, halter, palter, psalter, salter, vaulter, Walter; assaulter, defaulter, exalter, Gibraltar, unalter.

-alty, faulty, malty, salty, vaulty, walty.

-aly. See **-alely.**

-ama, Brahma, comma, drama, lama, llama, mama, Rama, pajama; cosmorama, Dalai Lama, diorama, Fujiyama, georama, melodrama, neorama, panorama, Yokahama.

-ambeau. See **-ambo.**

-amber, amber, camber, clamber, tambour.

-ambit, ambit, gambit.

-amble, amble, bramble, Campbell, gamble, gambol, ramble, scamble, scramble, shamble; preamble.

-ambo, ambo, crambo, flambeau, Sambo, zambo.

-ambol. See **-amble.**

-ambour. See **-amber.**

-ameful, blameful, flameful, shameful.

-amel, camel, Campbell, mammal, trammel; enamel, entrammel.

-amely, gamely, lamely, namely, tamely.

-ami, balmy, palmy, swami, Tommy; pastrami, salami.

-amin. See **-amine.**

-amine, famine, gamin; examine; cross-examine, reëxamine. See also **-ammon.**

-amish, Amish, famish, rammish; affamish, enfamish.

-amlet, camlet, hamlet, Hamlet, samlet.

-ammal. See **-amel.**

-ammar. See **-ammer.**

-ammel. See **-amel.**

-ammer, clamor, crammer, dammer, gammer, glamour, grammar, hammer, rammer, shammer, slammer, stammer, yammer; enamor, sledge-hammer, windjammer; ninnyhammer, yellowhammer.

-ammish. See **-amish.**

-ammon, Ammon, gammon, mammon, salmon; backgammon. See also **-amine.**

-ammy, chamois, clammy, gammy, hammy, mammy, Sammy, shammy, tammy.

-amois. See **-ammy.**

-amon. See **-ayman.**

-amor. See **-ammer.**

-amos. See **-amous.**

-amour. See **-ammer.**

-amous, Amos, famous, hamous, squamous, shamus; biramous, mandamus; ignoramus; Nostradamus.

-ampas. See **-ampus.**

-ampbell. See **-amble** or **-amel.**

-amper, camper, cramper, damper, hamper, pamper, scamper, stamper, tamper, tramper.

-ample, ample, sample, trample; ensample, example.

-ampler, ampler, sampler, trampler; exampler.

-ampus, campus, grampus, pampas.

-amus. See **-amous.**

-ana, anna, Anna, Hannah, manna; banana, bandanna, Diana, Havana, hosanna, Montana, Nirvana, savannah, Savannah, sultana, Urbana, zenana; Indiana, Juliana, Pollyanna, Susquehanna; Americana, Louisiana.

-anate. See **-anet.**

-ancer, answer, cancer, chancer, dancer, glancer, lancer, prancer; advancer, enhancer, entrancer, merganser, romancer; chiromancer, gandy-dancer, geomancer, necromancer.

-ancet. See **-ansit.**

-anchion. See **-ansion.**

-anchor. See **-anker.**

-anchored. See **-ankered.**

-ancor. See **-anker.**

-ancy, chancy, Clancy, dancy, fancy, Nancy; mischancy, unchancy; aldermancy, austromancy, belomancy, ceromancy, chiromancy, cleromancy, consonancy, crithomancy, gastromancy, geomancy, gyromancy, hesitancy, hieromancy, hydromancy, lithomancy, mendicancy, militancy, myomancy, necromancy, occupancy, oenomancy, onomancy, pedomancy, petulancy, psychomancy, sciomancy, sibilancy, spodomancy, stichomancy, supplicancy, sycophancy, tephramancy, termagancy; aleuromancy, anthropomancy, axinomancy, bibliomancy, botanomancy, catoptromancy, coscinomancy, crystallomancy, exorbitancy, extravagancy, exuberancy, lecanomancy, ophiomancy, ornithomancy, precipitancy, sideromancy, significancy; alectoromancy, alectryomancy, meteoromancy.

-anda, Amanda, Miranda, veranda; memoranda, propaganda.

-andal. See **-andle.**

-andant, commandant, demandant.

-andem. See **-andom.**

-ander (-ăn-), candor, dander, gander, glander, grander, pander, sander, slander; backhander, bystander, commander, dittander, Leander, meander, Menander, philander, pomander; Alexander, coriander, gerrymander, oleander, salamander.

-ander (-ŏn-). See **-onder.**

-andhi. See **-andy.**

-andi. See **-andy.**

-andid. See **-andied.**

-andied, bandied, brandied, candid, candied; uncandid.

-anding, banding, branding, landing, standing; demanding, disbanding, expanding, outstanding; notwithstanding, understanding.

-andish, blandish, brandish, grandish, Standish; outlandish.

-andit, bandit, pandit.

-andle, candle, dandle, handle, sandal, scandal, vandal; manhandle, mishandle.

-andler, candler, chandler, dandler, handler.

-andom, mandom, random, tandem; avizandum, memorandum.

-andor. See **-ander.**

-andsome. See **-ansom.**

-andstand, bandstand, grandstand, handstand

-andum. See **-andom.**

-andy, Andy, bandy, brandy, candy, dandy, Gandhi, gandy, handy, Mandy, pandy, randy, sandy, Sandy; unhandy; jaborandi, jackadandy.

-aneful. See **-ainful.**

-anel. See **-annel.**

-anely. See **-ainly.**

-aneous, cutaneous, extraneous, spontaneous; instantaneous, miscellaneous, simultaneous; contemporaneous, extemporaneous.

-aner. See **-ainer.**

-anet, gannet, granite, Janet, planet; pomegranate.

-anger (-ăng ər), anger, angor, banger, clangor, ganger, hangar, hanger, languor; haranguer straphanger, paper hanger.

-anger (-ān jər), changer, danger, Grainger, granger, manger, ranger, stranger; arranger, bushranger, deranger, endanger, estranger, exchanger; disarranger, interchanger, money changer.

-angle, angle, bangle, brangle, dangle, jangle, mangle, spangle, strangle, tangle, twangle, wangle, wrangle; bemangle, bespangle, embrangle, entangle, quadrangle, triangle, untangle; disentangle, interjangle.

-angled, newfangled, star-spangled. Also: **-angle** + **-ed** (as in *tangled,* etc.)

-ango, mango, tango; contango, fandango, Pago.

-angor. See **-anger.**

-anguer. See **-anger.**

-anguish, anguish, languish.

-anguor. See **-anger.**

-angy, mangy, rangy.

-anic, panic, tannic; botanic, Brahmanic, Britannic, galvanic, Germanic, mechanic, organic, rhodanic, satanic, sultanic, tetanic, titanic, tyrannic, volcanic, vulcanic; aldermanic, charlatanic, diaphanic, lexiphanic, Messianic, oceanic, Ossianic, Puritanic, talismanic; ferricyanic, hydrocyanic, valerianic; interoceanic.

-anics, annex, panics; humanics, mechanics.

-anil. See **-annel.**

-anion, banyan, canyon; companion.

-anish, banish, clannish, mannish, planish, Spanish, vanish; evanish.

-anite. See **-anet.**

-ankard. See **-ankered.**

-anker, anchor, blanker, canker, clanker, danker, hanker, rancor, ranker, spanker, tanker.

-ankered, anchored, cankered, hankered, tankard.

-ankle, ankle, rankle.

-ankly, blankly, dankly, frankly, lankly, rankly.

-anless, manless, planless.

-anna. See **-ana.**

-annah. See **-ana.**

-annal. See **-annel.**

-annel, anil, annal, cannel, channel, flannel, panel, scrannel; empanel.

-anner, banner, canner, manner, manor, planner, scanner, spanner, tanner.

-annet. See **-anet.**

-annex. See **-anics.**

-annic. See **-anic.**

-annie. See **-anny.**

-annish. See **-anish.**

-annual. See **-anual.**

-anny, Annie, branny, canny, clanny, cranny, Danny, fanny, Fanny, granny, Mannie, nanny; uncanny; hootenanny.

-anor. See **-anner.**

-anser. See **-ancer.**

-anset. See **-ansit.**

-ansion, mansion, panchion, scansion, stanchion; expansion.

-ansit, lancet, transit; Narragansett.

-ansom, handsome, hansom, ransom, transom; unhandsome.

-answer. See **-ancer.**

-ansy, pansy, tansy; chimpanzee.

-anta, Santa; Atlanta, infanta, Vedanta; Atalanta.

-antam, bantam, phantom.

-ante. See **-anty.**

-anteau. See **-anto.**

-antel. See **-antle.**

-anter, banter, canter, cantor, chanter, grantor, panter, planter, ranter; decanter, descanter, enchanter, implanter, instanter, Levanter, recanter, transplanter, trochanter.

-anther, anther, panther.

-anti. See **-anty.**

-antic, antic, frantic, mantic; Atlantic, gigantic, pedantic, romantic; chiromantic, consonantic, corybantic, geomantic, hierophantic, hydromantic, necromantic, pyromantic, sycophantic, transatlantic.

-antine, Byzantine, Levantine; adamantine, elephantine.

-antle, cantle, mantel, mantle, scantle; immantle.

-antler, antler, mantler, pantler; dismantler.

-antling, bantling, mantling, scantling; dismantling.

-anto, canto, panto; coranto, portmanteau; Esperanto, quo warranto.

-antom. See **-antam.**

-antor. See **-anter.**

-antry, chantry, gantry, pantry.

-anty, ante, anti, auntie, chanty, Dante, scanty, shanty; Ashanti, Bacchante, andante, chianti, infante; dilettante.

-anual, annual, manual; Emmanuel.

-anuel. See **-anual.**

-any (-ā-). See **-ainy.**

-any (-ĕ-). See **-enny.**

-anyan. See **-anion.**

-anyon. See **-anion.**

-anza, stanza; bonanza; Sancho Panza; extravaganza.

-anzee. See **-ansy.**

-aoler. See **-ailer.**

-apal. See **-aple.**

-ape. See **-appy.**

-apel. See **-apple.**

-apen, capon; misshapen, unshapen.

-aper, aper, caper, draper, paper, sapor, taper, tapir, vapor; flypaper, landscaper, newspaper, sandpaper, skyscraper.

-aphic, graphic, maffick, traffic; seraphic; autographic, biographic, cacographic, calligraphic, cartographic, chirographic, clinographic, cosmographic, crytographic, diagraphic, epigraphic, epitaphic, ethnographic, geographic, hierographic, holographic, hydrographic, ichnographic, lithographic, logographic, monographic, orthographic, pantographic, paragraphic, pasigraphic, petrographic, phonographic, photographic, polygraphic, pornographic, scenographic, sciagraphic, seismographic, stenographic, stratigraphic, stylographic, telegraphic, topographic, typographic, xylographic; bibliographic, choreographic, heliographic, heterographic, ideographic, lexicographic, physiographic; autobiographic, cinematographic.

-apid, rapid, sapid, vapid.

-apir. See **-aper.**

-apist, papist, rapist; escapist, landscapist.

-aple, maple, papal, staple.

-apless, capless, hapless, napless, sapless, strapless.

-apling. See **-apling.**

-apnel, grapnel, shrapnel.

-apon. See **-apen.**

-apor. See **-aper.**

-apper, capper, clapper, dapper, flapper, mapper, napper, sapper, tapper, trapper, wrapper; entrapper, fly-sapper, kidnaper; handicapper, understrapper, whippersnapper.

-appet, lappet, tappet.

-appie. See **-appy.**

-apple, apple, chapel, dapple, grapple, scapple, scrapple, thrapple; love apple, pineapple.

-appling, dappling, grappling, sapling.

-appy, chappie, flappy, happy, knappy, nappy, sappy, scrappy, snappy, serape, slap-happy, unhappy.

-apter, apter, captor, chapter; adapter, recaptor.

-aptest. See **-aptist.**

-aption, caption; adaption, contraption, recaption.

-aptist, aptest, baptist, raptest; adaptest, inaptest; anabaptist.

-aptor. See **-apter.**

-apture, capture, rapture; enrapture, recapture.

-ara, Clara, Sarah; mascara, tiara.

-arab, arab, Arab, scarab.

-arage. See **-arriage.**

-araoh. See **-arrow.**

-arass. See **-arras.**

-arat. See **-aret.**

-arbel. See **-arble.**

-arber. See **-arbor.**

-arbered. See **-arboard.**

-arble (-är-), barbel, garbel, garble, marble; enmarble.

-arble (-ôr-), corbel, warble.

-arboard, barbered, harbored, larboard, starboard.

-arbor, arbor, barber, harbor; unharbor.

-arbored. See **-arboard.**

-arcel, parcel, sarcel, tarsal; metatarsal.

-archal. See **-arkle.**

-archer, archer, marcher, parcher, starcher; departure.

-archy, barky, darky, larky, marquee, sparky; malarkey; heterarchy, hierarchy, matriarchy, oligarchy, patriarchy.

-arden (-är-), Arden, garden, harden, pardon; beer-garden, bombardon, caseharden, enharden.

-arden (-ôr-). See **-ordon.**

-arder (-är-), ardor, carder, harder, larder; bombarder, Cunarder.

-arder (-ôr-). See **-order.**

-ardon. See **-arden.**

-ardor. See **-arder.**

-ardy, hardy, lardy, tardy; foolhardy, Lombardy, Picardy.

-arel. See **-arrel.**

-arely, barely, fairly, rarely, squarely, yarely; unfairly; debonairly.

-arent, arrant, parent; apparent, transparent.

-aret, carat, caret, carrot, claret, garret, karat, parrot.

-arfish, garfish, starfish.

-argent, argent, sergeant.

-arger, charger, larger; enlarger.

-argo, Argo, argot, cargo, largo, Margot; botargo, embargo, Wells Fargo; supercargo.

-argot. See **-argo.**

-ari (-âr-). See **-ary.**

-ari (-ăr-). See **-arry.**

-arian. See **-arion.**

-aric, baric, carrick, Garrick; agaric, barbaric, Pindaric; Balearic, cinnabaric. See also **-arrack.**

-arid. See **-arried.**

-aried. See **-arried.**

-arier. See **-arrier.**

-aring, airing, daring, fairing; seafaring, talebearing, wayfaring; overbearing.

-arion, Arian, Aryan, carrion, clarion, Marian, Marion.

-arious, Darius, various; Aquarius, bifarious, contrarious, gregarious, hilarious, nefarious, ovarious, precarious, vicarious; multifarious, Sagittarius, temerarious.

-aris, Paris, Harris, heiress; Polaris. See also **-arras.**

-arish, barish, bearish, garish, parish, rarish, sparish, squarish; debonairish.

-arius. See **-arious.**

-arken, darken, hearken.

-arkish, darkish, larkish, sparkish.

-arkle, darkle, sparkle; monarchal; patriarchal.

-arkling, darkling, sparkling.

-arkly, darkly, sparkly, starkly.

-arky. See **-archy.**

-arlak. See **-arlic.**

-arlech. See **-arlic.**

-arler, gnarler, marler, parlor, snarler.

-arlet, carlet, harlot, scarlet, starlet, varlet.

-arley. See **-arly.**

-arlic, garlic, Harlech, sarlak; pilgarlic.

-arlie. See **-arly.**

-arling, darling, marling, snarling, sparling, starling.

-arlor. See **-arler.**

-arlot. See **-arlet.**

-arly, barley, Charlie, gnarly, parley, snarly; particularly.

-armer, armor, charmer, farmer; snake charmer; baby farmer.

-arming, arming.
Also: **-arm** + **-ing** (as in *charming,* etc.)

-armless, armless, harmless.

-armor. See **-armer.**

-army, army, barmy.

-arnal. See **-arnel.**

-arnel, carnal, charnel, darnel.

-arner, garner, harner.

-arness, farness, harness.

-arning. See **-orning.**

-arnish, garnish, tarnish, varnish.

-aro. See **-arrow.**

-arol. See **-arrel.**

-aron, baron, barren, Charon, marron, Sharon; fanfaron.

-arper, harper, sharper.

-arquee. See **-archy.**

-arrack, arrack, barrack, carrack. See also **-aric.**

-arrant. See **-arent.**

-arras, arras, harass; embarrass. See also **-aris.**

-arrel (-ăr-), barrel, carol, Carol, Carroll; apparel.

-arrel (-ôr-). See **-oral.**

-arren (-ă-). See **-aron.**

-arren (-ŏ-). See **-oreign.**

-arret. See **-aret.**

-arriage, carriage, marriage; disparage, miscarriage; mismarriage; intermarriage.

-arrick. See **-aric.**

-arrie. See **-ary.**

-arried, arid, carried, harried, married, parried, tarried, varied; miscarried, remarried, unmarried, unvaried; intermarried.

-arrier, barrier, carrier, charier, farrier, harrier, marrier, parrier, tarrier.

-arrion. See **-arion.**

-arris. See **-aris.**

-arron. See **-aron.**

-arrot. See **-aret.**

-arrow, arrow, barrow, faro, farrow, harrow, Harrow, marrow, narrow, Pharaoh, sparrow, taro, yarrow; bolero, dinero, pierrot, primero, sombrero, torero; caballero; banderillero, Embarcadero.

-arry (-ăr-), barry, charry, sari, scarry, sparry, starry, tarry; aracari, carbonari, charivari, hari-kari, Mata Hari. See also **-orry.**

-arry (-är-). See **-ary.**

-arsal. See **-arcel.**

-arshal. See **-artial.**

-arsley, parsley, sparsley.

-arson, arson, Carson, parson; mene mene tekel upharsin.

-artan. See **-arten.**

-arte. See **-arty.**

-arten, barton, carton, hearten, marten, martin, Martin, smarten, Spartan, tartan; dishearten, enhearten; kindergarten.

-arter, barter, carter, charter, darter, garter, martyr, starter, tartar; bemartyr, self-starter, upstarter.

-artful, artful, cartful, heartful.

-artial, marshal, Marshall, martial, partial; immartial, impartial.

-artin. See **-arten.**

-artist, artist, Chartist, smartest.

-artle, dartle, startle.

-artlet, heartlet, martlet, partlet, tartlet.

-artly, partly, smartly, tartly.

-artner, heartener, partner, smartener; disheartener.

-arton. See **-arten.**

-artridge, cartridge, partridge.

-arture. See **-archer.**

-arty, arty, hearty, party, smarty; Astarte, ex parte.

-artyr. See **-arter.**

-arval. See **-arvel.**

-arvel, carvel, larval, marvel.

-arvest, carvest, harvest, starvest.

-arving, carving, starving.

-ary, airy, Carrie, carry, chary, dairy, eyrie, fairy, Gary, hairy, harry, Larry, marry, Mary, merry, nary, parry, prairie, scary, tarry, vary, wary; canary, contrary, miscarry, unchary, unwary, vagary; actuary, adversary, ancillary, antiquary, arbitrary, capillary, cassowary, cautionary, centenary, commentary, commissary, corollary, culinary, customary, dictionary, dietary, dignitary, dromedary, estuary, February, formulary, functionary, hari-kari, honorary, intermarry, Janissary, January, legendary, legionary, literary, luminary, mercenary, military, momentary, monetary, mortuary, necessary, ordinary, passionary, planetary, prebendary, pulmonary, reliquary, salivary, salutary, sanctuary, sanguinary, sanitary, scapulary,

secondary, secretary, sedentary, seminary, solitary, stationary, statuary, sublunary, sumptuary, temporary, tertiary, Tipperary, titulary, tributary, tumulary, tutelary, visionary, voluntary, vulnerary; ablutionary, accustomary, additionary, adminculary, apothecary, confectionary, constabulary, contemporary, contributary, depositary, epistolary, fiduciary, hereditary, imaginary, incendiary, involuntary, obituary, pecuniary, proprietary, residuary, ubiquitary, vocabulary, voluptuary; accidentiary, beneficiary, evolutionary, extraordinary, intermediary. See also **-erry.**

-aryan. See **-arion.**

-asal, basal, basil, hazel, nasal, phrasal; appraisal, witch hazel.

-ascal, paschal, rascal.

-ascar. See **-asker.**

-ascence, nascence; complacence, obeisance, renascence.

-ascent. See **-acent.**

-asement, basement, casement, placement; abasement, begracement, belacement, debasement, defacement, displacement, effacement, embracement, enlacement, erasement, misplacement, retracement, subbasement; interlacement.

-aser. See **-azer.**

-asey. See **-acy.**

-asian. See **-asion.**

-asher, Dasher, rasher; haberdasher.
Also: **-ash** + **-er** (as in *splasher,* etc.)

-ashion. See **-assion.**

-ashy (-ă-), ashy, flashy, mashie, mashy, plashy, slashy, splashy, trashy.

-ashy (-ŏ-). See **-oshy.**

-asion, Asian, suasion; abrasion, Caucasian, dissuasion, equation, Eurasian, evasion, invasion, occasion, persuasion, pervasion.

-asis, basis, crasis, glacis, phasis; oasis.

-asive, suasive; assuasive, dissuasive, evasive, invasive, persuasive, pervasive.

-asker, asker, basker, lascar, masker; Madagascar.

-asket, basket, casket, flasket, gasket.

-ason. See **-asten.**

-aspar. See **-asper.**

-asper, asper, Caspar, gasper, jasper, Jasper.
Also: **-asp** + **-er** (as in *clasper,* etc.)

-assal. See **-astle.**

-assel. See **-astle.**

-asses, molasses.
  Also: **-ass** + **-es** (as in *classes,* etc.)

-asset, asset, basset, brasset, facet, fascet, placet, tacit.

-assic, classic, boracic, Jurassic, potassic, sebacic, thoracic, Triassic.

-assie. See **-assy.**

-assing, passing.
  Also: **-ass** + **-ing** (as in *amassing,* etc.)

-assion, ashen, fashion, passion, ration; Circassian, compassion, dispassion, impassion.

-assive, massive, passive; impassive.

-assle. See **-astle.**

-assock, cassock, hassock.

-assy, brassie, brassy, chassis, classy, gassy, glassy, grassy, lassie, massy, sassy; morassy; Malagasy, Tallahassee; Haile Selassie.

-astard, bastard, castored, dastard, mastered, plastered.

-asteful, tasteful, wasteful; distasteful.

-asten, basin, caisson, chasten, hasten, mason.

-aster (-ā-), baster, chaster, haster, paster, taster, waster.

-aster (-ă-), aster, Astor, blaster, caster, castor, faster, master, pastor, piaster, plaster, vaster; bandmaster, beplaster, cadaster, disaster, schoolmaster, taskmaster; alabaster, burgomaster, criticaster, medicaster, oleaster, overmaster, poetaster, quartermaster, Zoroaster.

-astered. See **-astard.**

-astic, clastic, drastic, mastic, plastic, spastic; bombastic, dichastic, dynastic, elastic, emplastic, fantastic, gymnastic, monastic, proplastic, sarcastic, scholastic; amphiblastic, anaclastic, antiphrastic, bioplastic, ceroplastic, chiliastic, Hudibrastic, inelastic, metaphrastic, onomastic, orgiastic, paraphrastic, periphrastic, pleonastic, protoplastic, scholiastic; antonomastic, ecclesiastic, encomiastic, enthusiastic, iconoclastic.

-asting, everlasting.
  Also: **-ast** + **-ing** (as in *fasting,* etc.)

-astle, castle, facile, hassle, passel, tassel, vassal, wassail, wrastle; entassel, envassal.

-astly, ghastly, lastly, vastly.

-astor. See **-aster.**

-astored. See **-astard.**

-asty (-ās-), blasty, nasty, vasty.

-asty (-ās-), hasty, pasty, tasty.

-asy. See **-assy.**

-ata (-ātə), beta, data, eta, strata, theta, zeta; albata, dentata, errata, pro rata; postulata, ultimata, vertebrata; invertebrata.

-ata (-ätə), data, strata; cantata, errata, regatta, sonata, serenata; inamorata.

-atal, datal, fatal, natal, statal; postnatal; antenatal.

-atan, Satan, straighten, straiten.

-atant. See **-atent.**

-atcher, catcher, matcher, patcher, scratcher, snatcher, stature, thatcher; dispatcher, detacher, flycatcher.

-atchet, hatchet, latchet, ratchet.

-atchman, Scotchman, watchman.

-atchment, catchment, hatchment, ratchment; attachment, detachment, dispatchment.

-ateau, chateau, plateau; mulatto.

-ateful, fateful, grateful, hateful, plateful.

-atent, blatant, latent, natant, patent.

-ater (-ô-), daughter, slaughter, tauter, water; backwater, firewater, manslaughter, stepdaughter.

-ater (-ā-). See **-ator.**

-ather (-ăth-), blather, gather, lather, rather; foregather.

-ather (-ŏth-). See **-other.**

-athos, Athos, bathos, pathos.

-atial. See **-acial.**

-atian. See **-ation.**

-atic, attic, static; aquatic, astatic, asthmatic, chromatic, Dalmatic, dogmatic, dramatic, ecbatic, ecstatic, emphatic, erratic, fanatic, hepatic, lymphatic, phlegmatic, piratic, pneumatic, pragmatic, prismatic, quadratic, rheumatic, Socratic, stigmatic, thematic, traumatic; achromatic, acrobatic, Adriatic, aerostatic, aplanatic, aromatic, Asiatic, autocratic, automatic, bureaucratic, democratic, dichromatic, diplomatic, eleatic, emblematic, enigmatic, Hanseatic, hieratic, hydrostatic, mathematic, mobocratic, morganatic, muriatic, numismatic, operatic, pancreatic, plutocratic, problematic, symptomatic, systematic; adiabatic, anagrammatic, aristocratic, axiomatic, epigrammatic, idiocratic, idiomatic, melodramatic, physiocratic; idiosyncratic.

-atim, literatim, seriatim, verbatim.
  See also **-atum.**

-atin, matin, Latin, patin, platen, satin; Manhattan, Powhattan. See also **-atten.**

-ation, Haitian, nation, ration, station; ablation, aeration, Alsatian, carnation, castration, causation, cessation, citation, collation, creation, cremation, Dalmatian, damnation, deflation, dictation, dilation, donation, duration, elation, equation, filtration, fixation, flirtation, flotation, formation, foundation, frustration, gestation, gradation, gyration, hortation, inflation, lactation, laudation, lavation, legation, libation, location, migration, mutation, narration, natation, negation, notation, nugation, oblation, oration, ovation, phonation, plantation, predation, privation, probation, prostration, pulsation, quotation, relation, rogation, rotation, sensation, serration, stagnation, taxation, temptation, translation, vacation, venation, vexation, vibration, vocation; abdication, aberration, abjuration, ablactation, abnegation, abrogation, acceptation, acclamation, accusation, actuation, adaptation, adjuration, admiration, adoration, adulation, adumbration, aerostation, affectation, affirmation, aggravation, aggregation, agitation, allegation, allocation, alteration, altercation, alternation, angulation, amputation, animation, annexation, annotation, appellation, application, approbation, arbitration, arrogation, aspiration, assignation, association, attestation, augmentation, ausculation, aviation, avocation, bifurcation, botheration, calcination, calculation, cancellation, captivation, castigation, celebration, circulation, cogitation, collocation, coloration, combination, commendation, commutation, compensation, compilation, complication, computation, concentration, condemnation, condensation, confirmation, confiscation, conflagration, conformation, confrontation, confutation, congelation, congregation, conjugation, conjuration, connotation, consecration, conservation, consolation, constellation, consternation, consultation, consummation, contamination, contemplation, conversation, convocation, copulation, coronation, corporation, correlation, corrugation, coruscation, culmination, cultivation, cumulation, debarkation, decimation, declamation, declaration, declination, decoration, decussation, dedication, defalcation, defamation, defecation, defloration, deformation, degradation, delectation, delegation, demonstration, denotation, denudation, depilation, deportation, depravation, deprecation, depredation, deprivation, deputation, derivation, derogation, desecration, desiccation, designation, desolation, desperation, destination, detestation, detonation, devastation, deviation, dislocation, dispensation, disputation, dissertation, dissipation, distillation, divagation, divination, domination, duplication, education, elevation, elongation, emanation, emendation, emigration, emulation, enervation, equitation, eructation, estimation, estivation, evocation, exaltation, excavation, excitation, exclamation, execration, exhalation, exhortation, expectation, expiation, expiration, explanation, explication, exploitation, exploration, exportation, expurgation, extirpation, extrication, exudation, exultation, fabrication, fascination, federation, fenestration, fermentation, flagellation, fluctuation, fomentation, fornication, fulmination, fumigation, generation, germination, graduation, granulation, gravitation, habitation, hesitation, hibernation, ideation, illustration, imitation, implantation, implication, importation, imprecation, impregnation, incantation, incitation, inclination, incubation, inculcation, indentation, indication, indignation, infestation, infiltration, inflammation, information, inhalation, innovation, inspiration, installation, instigation, instillation, intimation, intonation, inundation, invitation, invocation, irrigation, irritation, isolation, jubilation, laceration, lamentation, lamination, legislation, levigation, levitation, liberation, limitation, litigation,

lubrication, lucubration, maceration, machination, malformation, mastication, maturation, mediation, medication, meditation, mensuration, ministration, mitigation, moderation, modulation, molestation, mutilation, navigation, numeration, obfuscation, objurgation, obligation, obscuration, observation, obviation, occupation, operation, ordination, orchestration, oscillation, osculation, palpitation, penetration, percolation, perforation, permeation, permutation, peroration, perpetration, perspiration, perturbation, population, postulation, predication, preparation, presentation, preservation, proclamation, procreation, procuration, profanation, profligation, prolongation, protestation, provocation, publication, punctuation, radiation, recantation, recitation, reclamation, recreation, reformation, refutation, registration, regulation, relaxation, remonstration, renovation, reparation, reputation, reservation, resignation, respiration, restoration, retardation, revelation, revocation, ruination, rumination, rustication, salutation, scintillation, segmentation, segregation, separation, sequestration, sibilation, simulation, situation, speculation, spoliation, sternutation, stimulation, sublimation, subornation, suffocation, supplication, suppuration, suspiration, syncopation, termination, titillation, toleration, transformation, transplantation, transportation, trepidation, tribulation, triplication, usurpation, vaccination, vacillation, valuation, variation, vegetation, veneration, ventilation, vindication, violation, visitation, vitiation; abbreviation, abomination, acceleration, accentuation, accommodation, accreditation, accumulation, adjudication, administration, adulteration, affiliation, agglutination, alienation, alleviation, alliteration, amalgamation, amplification, annihilation, annunciation, anticipation, appreciation, appropriation, approximation, argumentation, articulation, asphyxiation, assassination, assimilation, attenuation,

authorization, brutalization, calcification, calumniation, canonization, capitulation, carbonization, catechization, circumvallation, clarification, coagulation, codification, cohabitation, columniation, commemoration, commensuration, commiseration, communication, concatenation, conciliation, confederation, configuration, conglomeration, congratulation, consideration, consolidation, continuation, cooperation, coordination, corroboration, crystallization, debilitation, degeneration, deification, deliberation, delimitation, delineation, denomination, denunciation, depopulation, depreciation, despoliation, determination, dignification, dilapidation, disapprobation, discoloration, discrimination, disfiguration, disinclination, disintegration, dissemination, disseveration, dissimulation, dissociation, documentation, domestication, edification, effectuation, ejaculation, elaboration, elimination, elucidation, emaciation, emancipation, emasculation, embarkation, enumeration, enunciation, equalization, equilibration, equivocation, eradication, evacuation, evaporation, evisceration, exacerbation, exaggeration, examination, exasperation, excoriation, exhilaration, exoneration, expatiation, expectoration, expostulation, expropriation, extenuation, extermination, facilitation, falsification, felicitation, fertilization, fortification, fossilization, galvanization, gesticulation, glorification, gratification, habilitation, habituation, hallucination, harmonization, Hellenization, horrification, humiliation, hypothecation, idealization, illumination, imagination, immoderation, inauguration, incarceration, incineration, incorporation, incrimination, inebriation, infatuation, initiation, inoculation, insemination, insinuation, interpolation, interpretation, interrogation, intoxication, investigation, irradiation, justification, legalization, legitimation,

manifestation, manipulation,
matriculation, melioration,
misinformation, modernization,
modification, mollification,
moralization, mortification,
multiplication, mystification,
nasalization, negotiation,
notification, obliteration,
origination, organization,
ossification, pacification,
participation, perambulation,
peregrination, perpetuation,
precipitation, predestination,
predomination, premeditation,
preoccupation, prevarication,
procrastination, prognostication,
pronunciation, propitiation,
protuberation, purification,
qualification, ramification,
ratification, realization,
reciprocation, recommendation,
recrimination, rectification,
recuperation, refrigeration,
regeneration, regurgitation,
reiteration, rejuvenation,
remuneration, renunciation,
representation, repudiation,
resuscitation, retaliation,
reverberation, sanctification,
scarification, signification,
solemnization, sophistication,
specialization, specification,
subordination, symbolization,
variegation, versification,
vituperation, vivification,
vociferation; amelioration,
beatification, circumnavigation,
contraindication,
cross-examination, demonetization,
deterioration, differentiation,
discontinuation, disqualification,
diversification, electrification,
excommunication, exemplification,
experimentation, extemporization,
identification, inconsideration,
indemnification, individuation,
misrepresentation, naturalization,
personification, predetermination,
ratiocination, recapitulation,
reconciliation, spiritualization,
superannuation, supererogation,
tintinnabulation,
transubstantiation.

-atius. See **-acious.**

-ative, dative, native, sative, stative;
creative, dilative; aggregative,
cogitative, cumulative, designative,
emulative, estimative, generative,
hesitative, imitative, innovative,
legislative, meditative, operative,
predicative, procreative,
quantitative, radiative, speculative,
terminative, vegetative, violative;
appreciative, associative,

communicative, continuative,
corroborative.

-atless, Atlas, hatless.

-atling. See **-attling.**

-atly, flatly, patly, rattly.

-ato (-ā-), Cato, Plato; potato,
tomato.

-ato (-ä-), château; legato, mulatto,
tomato, staccato; obbligato,
pizzicato; inamorato. See also **-otto.**

-ator, cater, crater, freighter, gaiter,
greater, later, mater, pater, traitor,
waiter; creator, cunctator, curator,
dictator, dumbwaiter, equator,
first-rater, scrutator, spectator,
testator, third-rater; alligator, alma
mater, carburetor, commentator,
conservator, second-rater.
Also: **-ate + -er** or **-or** (as in *hater,
cultivator,* etc.)

-atress, traitress, waitress; creatress,
dictatress, spectatress; imitatress.

-atrix, matrix; cicatrix, spectatrix,
testatrix; aviatrix, generatrix,
mediatrix; administratrix.

-atron, matron, natron, patron.

-atten, baton, batten, fatten, flatten,
paten, platen, ratten. See also **-atin.**

-atter (-ă-), attar, batter, blatter,
chatter, clatter, fatter, flatter,
hatter, latter, matter, patter, ratter,
satyr, scatter, shatter, smatter,
spatter, splatter, tatter; bescatter,
bespatter, Mad Hatter.

-atter (-ŏ-). See **-otter.**

-attern, pattern, Saturn, slattern

-attle (-ă-), battle, cattle, chattel,
prattle, rattle, tattle; embattle,
Seattle; tittle-tattle.

-attle (-ŏ-). See **-ottle.**

-attler, battler, rattler, Statler, tattler.

-attling, battling, fatling, gatling,
rattling, spratling, tattling.

-atto. See **-ateau.**

-atty, batty, chatty, fatty, gnatty,
Hattie, matty, natty, patty, ratty.

-atum, datum, stratum; erratum,
pomatum, substratum; postulatum,
ultimatum; desideratum. See also
-atim.

-ature (-ā-), nature; plicature;
legislature, nomenclature.

-ature (-ă-). See **-atcher.**

-aturn. See **-attern.**

-atus (-ā-), status, stratus; afflatus,
hiatus, senatus; apparatus, literatus.

-atus (-ă-), gratis, lattice, status;
apparatus.

-aty, eighty, Haiti, Katie, matey,
platy, praty, slaty, weighty.

-atyr. See **-atter.**

-audal. See **-awdle.**

-audit, audit, plaudit.

-audy. See **-awdy.**

-auger. See **-ager.**

-augher. See **-affer.**

-aughter (-ăf-). See **-after.**

-aughter (-ô-). See **-ater.**

-aughty, haughty, naughty.

-aulic, aulic; hydraulic; interaulic.

-aulter. See **-alter.**

-aulty. See **-alty.**

-aunder, launder, maunder.

-aunter, flaunter, gaunter, haunter,
jaunter, saunter, taunter, vaunter.

-auntie. See **-anty.**

-auphin. See **-often.**

-aural. See **-oral.**

-aurel. See **-oral.**

-aurus. See **-orous.**

-auseous. See **-autious.**

-austral, austral, claustral.

-aution, caution; incaution,
precaution.

-autious, cautious, nauseous;
precautious.

-ava, brava, guava, Java, lava; cassava.

-avage, ravage, savage, scavage.

-avel, cavil, gavel, gravel, ravel,
travail, travel; unravel.

-avelin, javelin, ravelin.

-aveling, knaveling, shaveling.

-avely, bravely, gravely, knavely,
slavely, suavely.

-avement, lavement, pavement;
depravement, engravement,
enslavement.

-aven, craven, graven, haven, mavin,
raven, shaven; engraven, New
Haven.

-aver (-ă-), cadaver, palaver.

-aver (-ā-), braver, craver, favor,
flavor, graver, haver, quaver, raver,
savor, shaver, slaver, waiver, waver;
disfavor, engraver, enslaver,
papaver, lifesaver, timesaver;
demiquaver, hemiquaver,
semiquaver; hemidemisemiquaver.

-avern, cavern, tavern.

-avid, avid, gravid, pavid; impavid.

-avior, clavier, pavior, savior, wavier,
Xavier; behavior; misbehavior.

-avis, Davis, mavis; rara avis.

-avish (-ā-), bravish, knavish, slavish.

-avish (-ă-), lavish, ravish; enravish,
MacTavish.

-avo, bravo, octavo.

-avor. See **-aver.**

-avy, cavy, Davy, gravy, navy, slavey,
wavy; peccavi.

-awdle, caudal, dawdle.

-awdry, bawdry, tawdry.

-awdy, bawdy, dawdy, gaudy.

-awful, awful, lawful; unlawful.

-awning, awning, dawning, fawning, spawning, yawning.

-awny, brawny, fawny, lawny, Pawnee, scrawny, Shawnee, tawny, yawny; mulligatawny.

-awyer, foyer, lawyer, sawyer; topsawyer.

-axen, flaxen, Jackson, klaxon, Saxon, waxen; Anglo-Saxon.

-axi. See **-axy.**

-axon. See **-axen.**

-axy, flaxy, taxi, waxy; galaxy; ataraxy, Cotopaxi.

-aybe. See **-aby.**

-ayday, heyday, Mayday, payday, playday.

-ayer, layer, mayor, prayer; purveyor, soothsayer, surveyor.
Also: **-ay** + **-er** (as in *player,* etc.)

-ayey, clayey, wheyey.

-aylay, Malay, melee, waylay; ukulele.

-ayling. See **-ailing.**

-ayman, Bremen, cayman, Damon, drayman, Haman, layman, Lehman, stamen; highwayman.

-ayment, claimant, payment, raiment; defrayment, displayment, repayment.

-ayo, kayo, Mayo.

-aza, Gaza, plaza; piazza.

-azard, hazard, mazzard; haphazard.

-azel. See **-asal.**

-azen. See **-azon.**

-azer, blazer, gazer, maser, phaser, praiser, razor; appraiser; paraphraser.

-azier, brazier, glazier, grazier.

-azon, blazon, brazen, glazen, raisin, scazon; emblazon; diapason.

-azzle, basil, dazzle, frazzle, razzle; bedazzle; razzle-dazzle.

-azy, crazy, daisy, hazy, lazy, Maisie, mazy.

-ea, Leah, zea; Althea, chorea, Crimea, idea, Judea, Korea, Maria, Medea, obeah, spirea; dahabeah, diarrhea, gonorrhea, Latakia, panacea, ratafia; Cassiopeia, cavalleria, pharmacopoeia; onomatopoeia.

-eaboard, keyboard, seaboard.

-eacher, beacher, bleacher, breacher, breecher, creature, feature, leacher, peacher, preacher, reacher, screecher, teacher; beseecher, impeacher.

-eachment, preachment; impeachment.

-eachy, beachy, litchi, Nietzsche, peachy, preachy, screechy.

-eacon, beacon, deacon, weaken; archdeacon.

-eaden, deaden, leaden, redden, threaden; Armageddon.

-eading. See **-edding.**

-eadle (-ē-). See **-eedle.**

-eadle (-ĕ-). See **-eddle.**

-eadlock, deadlock, headlock, wedlock.

-eadly, deadly, medley, redly.

-eady. See **-eedy.**

-eafer. See **-ephyr.**

-eager, eager, leaguer, meager; beleaguer, intriguer; overeager.

-eah. See **-ea.**

-eaken. See **-eacon.**

-eaker. See **-aker.**

-eakly, bleakly, meekly, sleekly, treacly, weakly, weekly; biweekly, obliquely, uniquely; semiweekly.

-ealment, concealment, congealment, repealment, revealment.

-ealot. See **-ellate.**

-ealous, jealous, zealous; apellous, entellus, Marcellus, procellous, vitellus.

-ealy. See **-eely.**

-eamer, dreamer, emir, femur, lemur, reamer, schemer, steamer, streamer; blasphemer, redeemer.

-eamish, beamish, squeamish.

-eamster, deemster, seamster, teamster.

-ean, Ian, lien, paean; Aegean, Andean, astrean, Augean, Chaldean, Crimean, Judean, Korean, lethean, nymphean, pampean, plebian, plumbean, protean; amoebean, amphigean, apogean, Caribbean, empyrean, European, Galilean, gigantean, hymenean, Jacobean, Maccabean, perigean, phalangean, Tennessean; adamantean, antipodean, epicurean, terpsichorean.

-eaner, cleaner, gleaner, greener, meaner, wiener; demeanor, machiner; misdemeanor.

-eaning, gleaning, meaning.
Also: **-ean** + **-ing** (as in *cleaning,* etc.)
Also: **-een** + **-ing** (as in *preening,* etc.)
Also: **-ene** + **-ing** (as in *intervening,* etc.)
Also: **-ine** + **-ing** (as in *machining,* etc.)

-eanly, cleanly, keenly, leanly, meanly, queenly; obscenely, serenely.

-eanor. See **-eaner.**

-eany. See **-eeny.**

-eapen. See **-eepen.**

-eaper. See **-eeper.**

-earage. See **-eerage.**

-earance, clearance; appearance, arrearance, coherence, inherence; disappearance, incoherence, interference, perseverance.

-earful, cheerful, earful, fearful, sneerful.

-earing (-īr-), Bering, earring.
Also: **-ear** + **-ing** (as in *hearing,* etc.)
Also: **-eer** + **-ing** (as in *engineering,* etc.)
Also: **-ere** + **-ing** (as in *adhering,* etc.)

-earing (-âr-). See **-aring.**

-earish. See **-arish.**

-early (-īr-). See **-erely.**

-early (-ûr-). See **-urly.**

-earner, burner, earner, learner; sojourner.

-earnest, earnest, Ernest, sternest; internist.

-earning, burning, earning, learning, spurning, turning, yearning; concerning, discerning, returning.

-earsal. See **-ersal.**

-earten. See **-arten.**

-eartener. See **-artner.**

-eartlet. See **-artlet.**

-earty. See **-arty.**

-eary, aerie, beery, bleary, cheery, dearie, dreary, eerie, Erie, jeery, leery, peri, query, smeary, sneery, sphery, veery, weary; aweary; miserere.

-easant, peasant, pheasant, pleasant, present; displeasant, unpleasant; omnipresent.

-easants. See **-esence.**

-easel, Diesel, easel, measle, teasel, weasel.

-easer, beezer, Caesar, easer, freezer, friezer, geezer, greaser, leaser, pleaser, sneezer, squeezer, teaser, tweezer, wheezer; Ebenezer.

-easing, breezing, easing, freezing, pleasing, sneezing, squeezing, teasing; appeasing, displeasing, unpleasing.

-eason, reason, season, treason, wizen; unreason.

-easoned, reasoned, seasoned, treasoned, weasand, wizened; unseasoned.

-easter, Easter, feaster; northeaster, southeaster.

-easting, bee-sting, easting, feasting.

-eastly, beastly, priestly.

-easure, leisure, measure, pleasure, treasure; admeasure, displeasure, entreasure, outmeasure.

-easy (-ē sĭ), creasy, fleecy, greasy.

-easy (-ē zĭ), breezy, cheesy, easy, freezy, greasy, queasy, sleazy, sneezy, wheezy; parcheesi, speakeasy, uneasy, Zambezi.

-eaten, beaten, Cretan, cretin, eaten, Eton, heaten, sweeten, wheaten; moth-eaten, storm-beaten, unbeaten, worm-eaten; overeaten, weather-beaten.

-eater (-ē-), beater, cheater, eater, greeter, heater, liter, litre, meter, metre, neater, Peter, prætor, skeeter, sweeter, tweeter; beefeater, repeater, saltpeter, smoke-eater; centimeter, decimeter, kilometer, millimeter, overeater.

-eater (-ā-). See **-ator.**

-eather (-ē-), breather, either, neither, seether, sheather, wreather.

-eather (-ĕ-), blether, feather, heather, leather, nether, tether, weather, wether, whether; aweather, bellwether, pinfeather, together, whitleather; altogether.

-eathing, breathing, seething, sheathing, teething, wreathing; bequeathing.

-eatly. See **-etely.**

-eaty, meaty, peaty, sleety, sweetie, sweety, treaty; entreaty, Tahiti.

-eauty. See **-ooty.**

-eaven. See **-even.**

-eaver, beaver, cleaver, fever, griever, keever, lever, livre, reaver, riever, weaver, weever; achiever, believer, conceiver, deceiver, enfever, receiver; cantilever, Danny Deever, unbeliever.

-eavy. See **-evy.**

-eazy. See **-easy.**

-ebble, pebble, rebel, treble.

-ebel. See **-ebble.**

-eber. See **-abor.**

-eble. See **-ebble.**

-ebo, gazebo, placebo.

-ebtor. See **-etter.**

-ecant, piquant, precant, secant; cosecant; intersecant.

-ecca, Mecca; Rebecca.

-ecco. See **-echo.**

-ecent, decent, puissant, recent; indecent.

-echer. See **-etcher.**

-echo, echo, gecko, secco; El Greco; re-echo.

-ecian. See **-etion.**

-ecious, specious; facetious.

-ecis. See **-acy.**

-ecker, checker, chequer, wrecker; exchequer, woodpecker; double-decker, triple-decker.

-eckle, deckle, freckle, heckle, keckle, Seckel, shekel, speckle; bespeckle; Dr. Jekyll.

-eckless, feckless, fleckless, necklace, reckless, speckless.

-ecko. See **-echo.**

-eckon, beckon, reckon.

-eco. See **-echo.**

-econd, beckoned, fecund, reckoned, second.

-ectant, expectant, reflectent; disinfectant.

-ectar. See **-ector.**

-ecter. See **-ector.**

-ectful, neglectful, respectful; disrespectful.

-ectic, hectic, pectic; cachectic, eclectic; analectic, apoplectic, catalectic, dialectic.

-ectile, sectile; insectile, projectile.

-ection, flection, lection, section; affection, bisection, collection, complexion, confection, connection, convection, correction, defection, deflection, dejection, detection, direction, dissection, ejection, election, erection, infection, inflection, injection, inspection, objection, perfection, projection, protection, reflection, rejection, selection, subjection, subsection, trajection, trisection; circumspection, disaffection, disinfection, genuflexion, imperfection, indirection, insurrection, interjection, introspection, misdirection, predilection, recollection, re-election, resurrection, retrospection, venesection, vivisection.

-ective, sective; affective, collective, connective, corrective, defective, deflective, detective, directive, effective, elective, erective, infective, inflective, invective, neglective, objective, perfective, perspective, prospective, protective, reflective, rejective, respective, selective, subjective; ineffective, introspective, irrespective, retrospective.

-ectly, abjectly, correctly, directly, erectly; incorrectly, indirectly.

-ector, flector, hector, Hector, lector, nectar, rector, sector, specter, vector; collector, deflector, detector, director, ejecter, elector, injecter, inspector, objector, prospector, protector, reflector, selector.

-ecture, lecture, confecture, conjecture, prefecture, projecture; architecture.

-ecund. See **-econd.**

-edal (-ĕ-). See **-eddle.**

-edal (-ē-). See **-eedle.**

-edden. See **-eaden.**

-edding, bedding, dreading, heading, leading, redding, shedding, shredding, sledding, spreading, threading, wedding.

-eddle, heddle, medal, meddle, pedal, peddle, reddle, treadle; intermeddle.

-eddler, meddler, medlar, peddler, pedlar, treadler.

-eddy, eddy, Freddy, heady, ready, steady, Teddy; already, unready, unsteady.

-edence, credence; precedence; antecedence, intercedence.

-edent, credent, needn't, sedent; decedent, precedent; antecedent, intercedent.

-edger, dredger, edger, hedger, ledger, pledger, sledger.

-edic, Vedic; comedic; encyclopedic.

-edit, credit, edit; accredit, discredit, miscredit.

-edlar. See **-eddler.**

-edley. See **-eadly.**

-edo, credo, Lido, libido, stampedo, teredo, toledo, Toledo, torpedo, tuxedo.

-eecher. See **-eacher.**

-eecy. See **-easy.**

-eedful, deedful, heedful, needful; unheedful.

-eedle, beadle, needle, tweedle, wheedle; bipedal; centipedal, millepedal.

-eedling, needling, reedling, seedling, tweedling, wheedling.

-eedy, beady, deedy, greedy, heedy, needy, reedy, seedy, speedy, weedy; indeedy.

-eefy, beefy, leafy, reefy.

-eekly. See **-eakly.**

-eely, eely, freely, mealy, peely, really, seely, squealy, steely, wheely; genteelly.

-eeman, beeman, demon, freeman, gleeman, G-man, he-man, leman, seaman, semen.

-eemly. See **-emely.**

-eenly. See **-eanly.**

-eeny, genie, greeny, meanie, queenie, sheeny, Sweeney, teeny, weenie, weeny; Athene, Bellini, bikini, Bikini, Cellini, Houdini, martini, Puccini; Mussolini, Tetrazzini.

-eepen, cheapen, deepen, steepen.

-eeper, cheaper, creeper, deeper, keeper, leaper, peeper, reaper, sleeper, steeper, sweeper, Ypres.

-eeple. See **-eople.**

-eeply, cheaply, deeply.
Also: **-eep** + **-ly** (as in *steeply*, etc.)

-eepsie. See **-ypsy.**

-eepy, creepy, sleepy, tepee, weepy.

-eerage, clearage, peerage, pierage, steerage; arrearage.

-eerful. See **-earful.**

-eerly. See **-erely.**

-eery. See **-eary.**

-eesi. See **-easy.**

-eesy. See **-easy.**

-eeten. See **-eaten.**

-eeter. See **-eater.**

-eether. See **-eather.**

-eetle, beetle, betel, fetal; decretal.

-eetly. See **-etely.**

-eety. See **-eaty.**

-eever. See **-eaver.**

-eevish, peevish, thievish.

-eezer. See **-easer.**

-eezing. See **-easing.**

-eezy. See **-easy.**

-egal, eagle, beagle, legal, regal; illegal, vice-regal.

-eggar, beggar, egger; bootlegger.

-eggy, dreggy, eggy, leggy, Peggy.

-egian. See **-egion.**

-egion, legion, region; collegian, Glaswegian, Norwegian.

-egious. See **-igious.**

-egnant, pregnant, regnant; impregnant.

-egress, egress, Negress, regress.

-eifer. See **-ephyr.**

-eighbor. See **-abor.**

-einty. See **-ainty.**

-einy. See **-ainy.**

-eiress. See **-ris.**

-eisance. See **-ascence.**

-eist, deist, seest, theist.

-eisure. See **-easure.**

-eiter. See **-itter.**

-either (-ī-). See **-ither.**

-either (-ē-). See **-eather.**

-eiver. See **-eaver.**

-ekyll. See **-eckle.**

-elate, helot, pellet, prelate, stellate, zealot; constellate; interpellate.

-elder, elder, gelder, melder, welder.

-elding, gelding, melding, welding.

-eldom, beldam, seldom.

-ele. See **-alely.**

-elee. See **-aylay.**

-elfish, elfish, pelfish, selfish, shellfish; unselfish.

-elic, bellic, melic, relic, telic; angelic; archangelic, evangelic, philatelic.

-eline, beeline, feline.

-elion, Pelion; aphelion, chameleon, Mendelian; perihelion.

-elix, Felix, helix.

-ella, Bella, Ella, fella, Stella; capella, Louella, patella, umbrella; Cinderella, Isabella, tarantella.

-ellar. See **-eller.**

-ellen. See **-elon.**

-eller, cellar, dweller, feller, heller, seller, smeller, speller, stellar, teller; impeller, propeller, saltcellar; fortune teller, interstellar.

-ellet. See **-elate.**

-elli. See **-elly.**

-ellish, hellish, relish; embellish.

-ello, bellow, cello, felloe, fellow, hello, Jello, mellow, yellow; duello, good fellow, niello; brocatello, Donatello, Monticello, punchinello, saltarello; violoncello.

-ellous. See **-ealous.**

-ellow. See **-ello.**

-ellum, vellum; flagellum; ante-bellum, cerebellum.

-ellus. See **-ealous.**

-elly, belly, Delhi, felly, helly, jelly, Kelly, Nellie, Shelley, shelly, smelly; cancelli, rake-helly; Botticelli, Donatelli, vermicelli; Machiavelli.

-elon, Ellen, felon, Helen, melon; watermelon.

-elop, develop, envelop.

-elot. See **-ellate.**

-elter, belter, felter, kelter, melter, pelter, shelter, smelter, spelter, swelter, welter; helter-skelter.

-elving, delving, helving, shelving.

-eman. See **-eeman.**

-ember, ember, member; December, dismember, November, remember, September; disremember.

-emble, semble, tremble; assemble, dissemble; reassemble.

-embly, trembly; assembly.

-emely, seemly; extremely, supremely, unseemly.

-emer. See **-eamer.**

-emic, chemic; alchemic, endemic, pandemic, polemic, systemic, totemic; academic, epidemic, theoremic.

-emish, blemish, Flemish.

-emlin, gremlin, Kremlin.

-emma, Emma, gemma; dilemma.

-emner. See **-emor.**

-emon. See **-eeman.**

-emor, hemmer, tremor; condemner, contemner.

-emplar, templar; exemplar.

-empter, tempter; attempter, exempter, preempter.

-emption, emption; ademption, coemption, diremption, exemption, pre-emption, redemption.

-emur. See **-eamer.**

-ena. See **-ina.**

-enace. See **-ennis.**

-enal, penal, renal, venal; adrenal, machinal.

-enant, pennant, tenant; lieutenant.

-enate. See **-ennet.**

-enceforth, henceforth, thenceforth.

-encer. See **-enser.**

-encher, bencher, blencher, censure, clencher, denture, quencher, trencher, venture, wencher; adventure, debenture, indenture; misadventure, peradventure.

-enchman, Frenchman, henchman.

-encil, mensal, pencil, pensil, pensile, stencil, tensile; extensile, prehensile, utensil.

-enda, Brenda, Zenda; addenda, agenda, credenda, delenda, corrigenda, hacienda.

-endance. See **-endence.**

-endant. See **-endent.**

-endence, tendance; ascendance, attendance, dependence, impendence, resplendence, transcendence; condescendence, independence; interdependence.

-endent, pendant, pendent, splendent; appendant, ascendant, attendant, contendant, defendant, dependant, dependent, descendant, descendent, impendent, intendant, resplendent, transcendent, transplendent; independent; interdependent, superintendent.

-ender, bender, blender, fender, gender, lender, render, sender, slender, spender, splendor, tender, vendor; amender, contender, defender, emender, engender, offender, perpender, pretender, surrender, suspender, week-ender.

-ending, ending, pending.
Also: **-end** + **-ing** (as in *ascending*, etc.)

-endor. See **-ender.**

-endous, horrendous, stupendous, tremendous.

-endum, addendum, agendum, credendum; corrigendum, referendum.

-enely. See **-eanly.**

-enet. See **-ennet.**

-engthen, lengthen, strengthen.

-enial, genial, menial, venial; congenial.

-enic, phrenic, scenic, splenic; arsenic, eugenic, Hellenic, irenic; calisthenic, neurasthenic, pathogenic, photogenic, psychogenic, telegenic.

-enie. See **-ainy.**

-enim. See **-enum.**

-enin. See **-enon.**

-enish, plenish, Rhenish, wennish; replenish.

-enna, henna, senna; antenna, duenna, Gehenna, Ravenna, Siena, sienna, Vienna.

-ennant. See **-enant.**

-ennel, fennel, kennel, antennal.

-enner. See **-enor.**

-ennet, Bennett, jennet, rennet, senate, tenet.

-ennis, Dennis, menace, tenace, tennis, Venice.

-enny, any, Benny, Denny, fenny, jenny, Jenny, Kenny, Lenny, many, penny, tenney, wenny, Kilkenny.

-eno, keno, Reno, Zeno; bambino, casino, merino; Filipino, maraschino.

-enom. See **-enum.**

-enon, Lenin, pennon, tenon.

-enor, penner, tenor, tenour.

-ensely, densely, tensely; immensely, intensely.

-enser, censer, censor, denser, fencer, Spencer, Spenser, tensor; commencer, condenser, dispenser, extensor, intenser.

-ensil. See **-encil.**

-ensile. See **-encil.**

-ension. See **-ention.**

-ensive, pensive, tensive; ascensive, defensive, distensive, expensive, extensive, intensive, offensive, ostensive, protensive, suspensive, apprehensive, comprehensive, indefensive, inexpensive, influencive, inoffensive, recompensive, reprehensive; incomprehensive.

-ensor. See **-enser.**

-enta, magenta, placenta, polenta.

-ental, cental, dental, gentle, lentil, mental, rental, trental; fragmental, parental, pigmental, placental, segmental, tridental, accidental,

alimental, complemental, complimental, continental, departmental, detrimental, elemental, fundamental, governmental, incidental, instrumental, ligamental, monumental, Occidental, Oriental, ornamental, regimental, rudimental, sacramental, supplemental, testamental, transcendental; coincidental, developmental, experimental, impedimental, labiodental, temperamental, transcontinental; intercontinental.

-entance, sentence, repentance; unrepentance.

-entence. See **-entance.**

-enter, center, enter, lentor, mentor, renter, tenter; dissenter, frequenter, inventor, lamenter, off-center, precentor, re-enter, repenter, tormentor; ornamenter; experimenter.

-entful, eventful, repentful, resentful; uneventful.

-ential, agential, credential, essential, potential, prudential, sentential, sequential, tangential, torrential; confidential, consequential, deferential, differential, evidential, existential, exponential, inferential, influential, penitential, pestilential, precedential, preferential, presidential, providential, quintessential, referential, reverential, unessential; experiential, inconsequential.

-entic, authentic, identic.

-enticed. See **-entist.**

-entil. See **-ental.**

-entile, gentile; percentile.

-entin, dentin, Lenten, Trenton; San Quentin.

-enting, denting, renting, scenting, tenting, venting; absenting, accenting, assenting, augmenting, cementing, consenting, fermenting, fomenting, frequenting, lamenting, presenting, preventing, relenting, resenting, tormenting; circumventing, complimenting, ornamenting, representing, supplementing; misrepresenting.

-ention, gentian, mention, pension, tension; abstention, ascension, attention, contention, convention, declension, detention, dimension, dissension, distension, extension, intension, intention, invention, prehension, pretension, prevention, propension, recension, retention,

subvention, suspension; apprehension, circumvention, comprehension, condescension, contravention, inattention, intervention, reprehension; incomprehension, misapprehension.

-entious, contentious, dissentious, licentious, pretentious, sententious, silentious; conscientious, pestilentious.

-entist, dentist, prenticed; Adventist, apprenticed, preventist.

-entive, assentive, attentive, incentive, presentive, retentive; inattentive.

-entle. See **-ental.**

-ently, gently; intently; evidently.

-entment, contentment, presentment, relentment, resentment; discontentment, representment.

-ento, cento, lento; memento, pimento; Sacramento.

-entor, centaur, mentor, stentor; succentor.

-entor. See **-enter.**

-entous, momentous, portentous.

-entric, centric; acentric, concentric, eccentric, geocentric; anthropocentric, heliocentric.

-entry, entry, gentry, sentry.

-enture. See **-encher.**

-enty, plenty, scenty, twenty; cognoscenti; Agua Caliente, dolce far niente.

-enu, menu, venue.

-enum, denim, frenum, plenum, venom.

-eny. See **-ainy.**

-enza, cadenza; influenza.

-eo, Cleo, Leo, Rio, trio.

-eomen. See **-omen.**

-eon, aeon, Creon, Leon, neon, paean, peon; pantheon; Anacreon.

-eopard, jeopard, leopard, peppered, shepherd.

-eople, people, steeple; unpeople.

-epee. See **-eepy.**

-epherd. See **-eopard.**

-ephyr, deafer, feoffor, heifer, zephyr.

-epid, tepid, trepid; intrepid.

-epper, leper, pepper, stepper; high-stepper.

-epsy, Pepsi; apepsy, eupepsy; catalepsy, epilepsy.

-eptic, peptic, septic, skeptic; aseptic, dispeptic, eupeptic; antiseptic, cataleptic, epileptic.

-era, era, Vera; chimera; Halmahera.

-erance. See **-earance.**

-ercer. See **-urser.**

-ercion. See **-ertion.**

-erder. See **-urder.**

-erdure. See **-erger.**

-erely, cheerly, clearly, dearly, merely, nearly, queerly, sheerly, yearly; austerely, severely, sincerely; cavalierly, insincerely.

-erence. See **-earance.**

-ergeant. See **-argent.**

-ergence, convergence, divergence, emergence, resurgence, submergence.

-ergent, turgent, urgent, vergent; abstergent, assurgent, convergent, detergent, divergent, emergent, insurgent, resurgent.

-erger, merger, perjure, purger, scourger, splurger, urger, verdure, verger; converger, diverger, emerger, submerger.

-ergy. See **-urgy.**

-eri. See **-erry.**

-eric, cleric, Derek, derrick, Eric, ferric, Herrick, spheric; chimeric, enteric, generic, Homeric, hysteric, mesmeric, numeric, suberic, valeric; atmospheric, chromospheric, climacteric, esoteric, exoteric, hemispheric, isomeric, neoteric, peripheric, phylacteric.

-eries, dearies, queries, series, wearies.

-eril, beryl, Merrill, peril, sterile.

-erile. See **-eril.**

-erish, cherish, perish.

-erit, ferret, merit; demerit, inherit; disinherit.

-erjure. See **-erger.**

-erker. See **-irker.**

-erky, jerky, murky, perky, turkey.

-erkin, firkin, gherkin, jerkin, merkin, Perkin.

-erling. See **-urling.**

-erly. See **-urly.**

-ermal, dermal, thermal.

-erman, Burman, firman, German, Herman, merman, sermon. See also **-ermine.**

-erment, ferment; affirmant, averment, deferment, determent, interment, preferment, referment; disinterment.

-ermes, Burmese, fermis, Hermes.

-ermine, ermine, vermin; determine; predetermine. See also **-erman.**

-ermy, fermi, Nurmi, squirmy, wormy; diathermy, taxidermy.

-ernal, colonel, journal, kernel, sternal, urnal, vernal; cavernal,

diurnal, eternal, external, fraternal, hibernal, infernal, internal, lucernal, maternal, nocturnal, paternal, supernal; co-eternal, hodiernal, sempiternal.

-ernest. See **-earnest.**

-erning. See **-earning.**

-ernist. See **-earnest.**

-erno, Sterno; inferno.

-ero (-ē-), hero, Nero, zero.

-ero (-â-). See **-arrow.**

-errand, errand, gerund.

-errant, errant, gerent; aberrant, knight-errant, vicegerent.

-errick. See **-eric.**

-errier, burier, merrier, terrier.

-erring, derring, erring, herring.

-error, error, terror.

-errot. See **-arrow.**

-erry, berry, bury, cherry, Derry, ferry, Jerry, Kerry, merry, Perry, sherry, skerry, Terry, very, wherry; Bambury, blackberry, blueberry, cranberry, gooseberry, mulberry, raspberry, strawberry; beriberi, boysenberry, capillary, cemetery, culinary, elderberry, huckleberry, Janissary, lamasery, loganberry, millinery, monastery, Pondicherry, presbytery, stationary, stationery. See also **-ary.**

-ersal, bursal, tercel, versal; rehearsal, reversal, transversal, universal.

-ersey, furzy, jersey, Jersey, kersey.

-ersian. See **-ersion.**

-ersion, Persian, version; abstersion, aspersion, aversion, conversion, discursion, dispersion, diversion, emersion, excursion, immersion, incursion, inversion, perversion, recursion, reversion, submersion, subversion; extroversion, introversion; animadversion.

-erson, person, worsen.

-ertain, Burton, certain, curtain, Merton; uncertain.

-erter, blurter, curter, flirter, hurter, squirter; asserter, averter, converter, deserter, diverter, exerter, inserter, inverter, perverter, subverter.

-ertie. See **-irty.**

-ertile. See **-urtle.**

-ertion, tertian, version; assertion, coercion, desertion, exertion, insertion; disconcertion.

-ertive, furtive; assertive, divertive, exertive, revertive.

-ertly, curtly, pertly; alertly, expertly; inertly, invertly, overtly; inexpertly.

-erule, ferule, ferrule, perule, spherule.

-ervant, curvant, fervent, servant; conservant, observant, recurvant; unobservant.

-ervent. See **-ervant.**

-erver, fervor, nerver, server, swerver; conserver, observer, preserver, reserver, time-server.

-ervid, fervid; perfervid, scurvied.

-ervish, dervish, nervish.

-ervy. See **-urvy.**

-ery. See **-erry.**

-escence, essence; excresence, florescence, pubescence, putrescence, quiescence, quintessence, rubescence, senescence, tumescence, vitrescence; acquiescence, adolescence, coalescence, convalescence, deliquescence, effervescence, efflorescence, evanescence, fluorescence, incalescence, incandescence, iridescence, obsolescence, opalescence, phosphorescence, recrudescence.

-escent, cessant, crescent, jessant; depressant, excrescent, ignescent, incessant, liquescent, putrescent, quiescent, rubescent, senescent; adolescent, convalescent, deliquescent, effervescent, efflorescent, evanescent, fluorescent, incandescent, obsolescent, opalescent, phosphorescent, recrudescent.

-escience, nescience, prescience.

-escue, fescue, rescue; Montesquieu.

-esence, pleasance, presence; omnipresence. Also: **-easant** + **-s** (as in *peasants,* etc.)

-esent. See **-easant.**

-eshen. See **-ession.**

-esher, fresher, pressure, thresher; refresher.

-eshly, fleshly, freshly.

-eshy, fleshy, meshy.

-esian. See **-esion.**

-esion, lesion; adhesion, artesian, Cartesian, cohesion, Ephesian, Parisian, Silesian; Indonesian, Micronesian, Polynesian.

-esis, Croesus, rhesus, thesis, tmesis; mimesis; catachresis, exegesis; aposiopesis.

-essage, dressage, message, presage; expressage.

-essal. See **-estle.**

-essant. See **-escent.**

-essel. See **-estle.**

-essence. See **-escence.**

-esser. See **-essor.**

-essful, distressful, successful; unsuccessful.

-essie. See **-essy.**

-essing, blessing, dressing, guessing, pressing.
Also: **-ess** + **-ing** (as in *depressing,* etc.)
Also: **-esce** + **-ing** (as in *convalescing,* etc.)

-ession, cession, freshen, Hessian, session; accession, aggression, bull session, compression, concession, confession, depression, digression, discretion, expression, impression, ingression, obsession, oppression, possession, precession, procession, profession, progression, recession, secession, succession, suppression, transgression; indiscretion, intercession, prepossession, retrocession, retrogression, supersession.

-essive, aggressive, compressive, concessive, depressive, digressive, excessive, expressive, impressive, oppressive, possessive, progressive, recessive, regressive, repressive, successive, suppressive, transgressive; retrogressive.

-essor, dresser, guesser, lesser, lessor, presser; addresser, aggressor, assessor, compressor, confessor, depressor, oppressor, possessor, professor, successor, suppressor, transgressor; antecessor, intercessor, predecessor, second-guesser, tongue-depressor.

-essure. See **-esher.**

-essy, Bessie, dressy, Jessie, messy, Tessie, tressy.

-esta, celesta, fiesta, siesta.

-estal, festal, vestal.

-ester, Chester, ester, Esther, fester, Hester, jester, Leicester, Lester, Nestor, pester, tester, vester, wrester; Chichester, Colchester, digester, Dorchester, Eastchester, investor, Manchester, nor'wester, protester, semester, sequester, sou'wester, Sylvester, trimester, Westchester; midsemester.

-estial, bestial, celestial.

-estic, domestic, majestic; anapestic, catachrestic.

-estine, destine; clandestine, intestine, predestine.

-estive, festive, restive; attestive, congestive, digestive, suggestive, tempestive.

-estle, Cecil, nestle, pestle, trestle, vessel; Horst Wessel, redressal.

-estler, nestler, wrestler.

-esto, presto; manifesto.

-estos, cestus; asbestos.

-estral, kestrel; ancestral, fenestral, orchestral, trimestral.

-esture, gesture; divesture, investure.

-esty, chesty, cresty, resty, testy.

-esus. See **-esis.**

-etail, detail, retail.

-etal. See **-ettle.**

-etcher, etcher, fetcher, fletcher, lecher, retcher, sketcher, stretcher.

-etchy, fetchy, sketchy, stretchy, tetchy, vetchy.

-ete. See **-etty.**

-etely, fleetly, meetly, neatly, sweetly; completely, concretely, discreetly; incompletely, indiscreetly, obsoletely.

-eter. See **-eater.**

-etful, fretful; forgetful, regretful.

-ethel, Bethel, Ethel, ethyl, methyl.

-ether. See **-eather.**

-ethyl. See **-ethel.**

-etic, aesthetic, ascetic, athletic, cosmetic, emetic, frenetic, genetic, hermetic, kinetic, magnetic, mimetic, pathetic, phonetic, phrenetic, poetic, prophetic, splenetic, synthetic; abietic, alphabetic, anaesthetic, antithetic, apathetic, arithmetic, dietetic, energetic, exegetic, geodetic, homiletic, hypothetic, masoretic, parenthetic, sympathetic, theoretic; antipathetic, biogenetic, peripatetic; abiogenetic; onomatopoetic.

-etion (-ē-), Grecian; accretion, completion, concretion, deletion, depletion, excretion, repletion, secretion.

-etion (-ĕ-). See **-ession.**

-etious. See **-ecious.**

-etish. See **-ettish.**

-eto, Tito, veto; bonito, mosquito.

-etor. See **-etter.**

-etsy, Betsy, tsetse.

-etter, better, bettor, debtor, fetter, getter, letter, setter, wetter, whetter; abettor, begetter, forgetter, go-getter, typesetter, unfetter; carburetor.

-etti. See **-etty.**

-ettish, fetish, Lettish, pettish, wettish; coquettish.

-ettle, fettle, Gretel, kettle, metal, mettle, nettle, petal, settle; abettal, unsettle; Popocatapetl.

-etto, ghetto, petto; falsetto, libretto, palmetto, stiletto, terzetto, zuchetto; allegretto, lazaretto, Rigoletto.

-ettor. See **-etter.**

-etty (-ĕ-), Betty, fretty, Hetty, jetty, Lettie, netty, petit, petty, sweaty; confetti, libretti, machete, Rossetti, spaghetti; Donizetti, spermaceti.

-etty (-ī-). See **-itty.**

-etus, fetus; quietus.

-euced. See **-ucid.**

-eudal. See **-oodle.**

-eudo. See **-udo.**

-eum, lyceum, museum, Te Deum; atheneum, colosseum, mausoleum; peritoneum.

-eura. See **-ura.**

-eural. See **-ural.**

-euter. See **-ooter.**

-eutic, scorbutic; pharmaceutic, therapeutic.

-eutist. See **-utist.**

-eval. See **-evil.**

-evel, bevel, devil, level, Neville, revel; bedevil, dishevel.

-even (-ĕ-), Devon, heaven, leaven, seven; eleven, replevin.

-even (-ē-), even, Stephen, Steven; uneven.

-ever (-ĕ-), clever, ever, lever, never, sever; assever, dissever, endeavor, however, whatever, whenever, wherever, whichever, whoever, whomever; howsoever, whatsoever, whencesoever, whensoever, wheresoever, whomsoever, whosoever.

-ever (-ē-). See **-eaver.**

-evil (-ē-), evil, weevil; coeval, primeval, retrieval, upheaval; medieval.

-evil (-ē-). See **-evel.**

-evious, devious, previous.

-evy, bevy, Chevy, heavy, levee, levy; top-heavy.

-ewal. See **-uel.**

-eward, leeward, sewered, skewered, steward.

-ewdest. See **-udist.**

-ewdish. See **-udish.**

-ewdly. See **-udely.**

-ewel. See **-uel.**

-ewess, Lewis, Louis, Jewess.

-ewish, blueish, Jewish, newish, shrewish, truish.

-ewly. See **-uly.**

-ewry. See **-ury.**

-ewsy. See **-oozy.**

-ewy, bluey, buoy, chewy, cooee, dewy, fluey, gluey, gooey, hooey, Louie, Louis, pfui, screwy, thewy, viewy; chop suey.

-exas. See **-exus.**

-exer, flexor, vexer; annexer, perplexer.

-exile, exile, flexile.

-extant, extant, sextant.

-extile, sextile, textile; bissextile.

-exus, nexus, plexus, Texas; Alexis; solar plexus.

-exy, prexy, sexy; apoplexy.

-eyance, seance; abeyance, conveyance, purveyance.

-eyor. See **-ayer.**

-eyrie. See **-ary.**

-ezi. See **-easy.**

-ia. See **-ea.**

-iad, dryad, naiad, triad; jeremiad.

-ial, dial, phial, trial, vial, viol; decrial, denial, espial, retrial, sundial, supplial.

-iam, Priam, Siam; Omar Khayyam.

-ian. See **-ion.**

-iance, clients, giants, science; affiance, alliance, appliance, compliance, defiance, reliance, suppliance; misalliance.

-iant, client, giant, pliant, scient; affiant, compliant, defiant, reliant.

-iants. See **-iance.**

-iaper. See **-iper.**

-iar. See **-ier.**

-iary. See **-iry.**

-ias, bias, pious; Elias, Tobias; Ananias, nisi prius.

-iat. See **-iet.**

-ibal. See **-ible.**

-ibald. See **-ibbled.**

-ibber, bibber, cribber, dibber, fibber, gibber, glibber, jibber, nibber, squibber; ad-libber, winebibber.

-ibbet. See **-ibit.**

-ibble, cribble, dibble, dribble, fribble, kibble, nibble, quibble, scribble, sibyl, Sybil, thribble; ish-kabibble.

-ibbled, dibbled, dribbled, kibbled, nibbled, piebald, quibbled, ribald, scribbled.

-ibbling, dibbling, dribbling, nibbling, quibbling, scribbling, sibling.

-ibbly, dribbly, fribbly, glibly, nibbly, quibbly, scribbly, tribbly.

-ibbon, gibbon, ribbon.

-ibel. See **-ible.**

-iber, briber, fiber, giber, Tiber; imbiber, inscriber, prescriber, subscriber, transcriber.

-ibit, gibbet, Tibbett, zibet; cohibit, exhibit, inhibit, prohibit.

-ible, Bible, libel, tribal.

-iblet, driblet, giblet, triblet.

-ibling. See **-ibbling.**

-ibyl. See **-ibble.**

-ica, mica, Micah, pica.

-icar. See **-icker.**

-icely. See **-isely.**

-icial, comitial, initial, judicial, official; artificial, beneficial, interstitial, prejudicial, sacrificial, superficial.

-ician. See **-ition.**

-icient, deficient, efficient, omniscient, proficient, sufficient; coefficient, inefficient, insufficient.

-icious, vicious; ambitious, auspicious, capricious, delicious, factitious, fictitious, judicious, malicious, nutritious, officious, pernicious, propitious, seditious, suspicious; adventitious, avaricious, expeditious, inauspicious, injudicious, meretricious, superstitious, supposititious, surreptitious.

-icken, chicken, quicken, sicken, stricken, thicken, wicken.

-icker, bicker, dicker, flicker, kicker, knicker, licker, liquor, picker, quicker, sicker, slicker, snicker, thicker, ticker, vicar, wicker.

-icket, clicket, cricket, picket, piquet, pricket, thicket, ticket, wicket.

-ickle, chicle, fickle, mickle, nickel, pickle, prickle, sickle, stickle, strickle, tickle, trickle.

-ickly, prickly, quickly, sickly, slickly, thickly, trickly.

-ickset, quickset, thickset.

-ickshaw, kickshaw, rickshaw.

-icky, dickey, Dicky, Mickey, Nicky, quickie, rickey, sticky, thicky, tricky, Vicki; doohickey, Kon-tiki.

-icle. See **-ickle.**

-icon. See **-iken.**

-icter, lictor, stricter, victor; afflicter, conflicter, constrictor, inflicter, predicter; contradicter; boa constrictor.

-iction, diction, fiction, friction; addiction, affliction, confliction, constriction, conviction, depiction, eviction, infliction, prediction, reliction, restriction, transfixion; benediction, contradiction, dereliction, interdiction, jurisdiction, malediction, valediction.

-ictive, fictive; afflictive, conflictive, constrictive, inflictive, predictive, restrictive, vindictive; benedictive, contradictive, interdictive, jurisdictive.

-ictor. See **-icter.**

-ictualler. See **-ittler.**

-icture, picture, stricture; depicture.

-ictus, ictus; Benedictus.

-icy, icy, spicy.

-idal, bridal, bridle, idle, idol, idyl, sidle, tidal; fratricidal, homicidal, matricidal, parricidal, regicidal, suicidal; infanticidal, tyrannicidal.

-idden, bidden, chidden, hidden, midden, ridden, slidden, stridden; hag-ridden, unbidden.

-iddle, diddle, fiddle, griddle, piddle, quiddle, riddle, tiddle, twiddle.

-iddling, fiddling, kidling, middling, piddling, riddling, twiddling.

-iddy, biddy, giddy, kiddie, middy, stiddy.

-iden, guidon, Haydn, Leyden, widen; Poseidon.

-ident, bident, rident, strident, trident.

-ider, cider, eider, glider, guider, hider, rider, spider, wider; backslider, confider, divider, insider, outrider, outsider, provider.

-idget, Bridget, digit, fidget, midget.

-idgy, midgy, ridgy.

-idle. See **-idal.**

-idly, idly, widely.

-idney, kidney, Sidney.

-ido. See **-edo.**

-idol. See **-idal.**

-idy, sidy, tidy; untidy; bona fide.

-idyl. See **-idal.**

-iefly, briefly, chiefly.

-ience. See **-iance.**

-ient. See **-iant.**

-ients. See **-iance.**

-ier, briar, brier, buyer, drier, dyer, flier, friar, fryer, higher, liar, mire, nigher, plier, prior, pryer, shyer, sigher, slyer, spryer, spyer, tire, Tyre, vier.
Also: **-y** + **-er** (as in *amplifier,* etc.)
See also: **-ire.**

-iery. See **-iry.**

-iestly. See **-eastly.**

-iet, diet, fiat, quiet, riot, striate; disquiet.

-ieval. See **-evil.**

-iever. See **-eaver.**

-ifer, cipher, fifer, knifer, lifer, rifer; decipher.

-iffin, biffin, griffin, griffon, stiffen, tiffin.

-iffle, piffle, riffle, sniffle, whiffle.

-iffy, iffy, jiffy, sniffy, spiffy.

-ific, glyphic; deific, horrific, pacific, pontific, prolific, somnific, specific, terrific; beatific, calorific,

-ifle
hieroglyphic, honorific, humorific, scientific, soporific.

-ifle, Eiffel, eyeful, rifle, stifle, trifle.

-ifling, rifling, stifling, trifling.

-ifter, drifter, grifter, lifter, shifter, sifter, swifter; shoplifter, uplifter.

-iftless, driftless, shiftless, thriftless.

-ifty, clifty, drifty, fifty, nifty, rifty, shifty, thrifty.

-igate. See **-igot.**

-iggard. See **-iggered.**

-igger, bigger, chigger, digger, figger, jigger, rigger, rigor, swigger, trigger, twigger, vigor; gold digger, grave digger, outrigger.

-iggered, figgered, jiggered, niggard.

-iggle, giggle, higgle, jiggle, niggle, sniggle, squiggle, wiggle, wriggle.

-iggly, bigly, giggly, sniggly, wriggly; piggly-wiggly.

-igher. See **-ier.**

-ighland. See **-island.**

-ighly. See **-ily.**

-ighness. See **-inus.**

-ighten, brighten, Brighton, frighten, heighten, lighten, tighten, Titan, triton, whiten; enlighten.

-ightening, brightening, frightening, lightning, tightening, whitening.

-ighter, biter, blighter, brighter, fighter, kiter, lighter, miter, niter, tighter, titer, triter, writer; backbiter, first-nighter, igniter, inciter, inditer, moonlighter, prize fighter, typewriter; copywriter, dynamiter, underwriter.

-ightful, frightful, mightful, rightful, spiteful, sprightful; delightful.

-ighting. See **-iting.**

-ightly, brightly, knightly, lightly, nightly, sprightly, tightly, tritely; politely, unsightly; impolitely.

-ightning. See **-ightening.**

-ighty, blighty, flighty, mighty, mitey, nightie, whitey; almighty; Aphrodite.

-igil, sigil, strigil, vigil.

-igious, litigious, prodigious, religious; irreligious, sacrilegious.

-igit. See **-idget.**

-igly. See **-iggly.**

-igma, sigma, stigma; enigma.

-igment, figment, pigment.

-ignant, benignant, indignant, malignant.

-igner. See **-iner.**

-ignly. See **-inely.**

-ignment, alignment, assignment, confinement, consignment, designment, entwinement,

inclinement, refinement, resignment.

-igor. See **-igger.**

-igot, bigot, frigate, gigot, spigot.

-iguer. See **-eager.**

-iken, icon, lichen, liken.

-iking, biking, diking, hiking, liking, piking, spiking, striking, Viking; disliking.

-ila. See **-illa.**

-ilbert, filbert, Gilbert.

-ilding. See **-uilding.**

-ildish, childish, mildish, wildish.

-ildly, childly, mildly, wildly.

-ildor. See **-uilder.**

-ile. See **-illy.**

-ilely. See **-ily.**

-ili. See **-illy.**

-ilian. See **-illion.**

-ilient. See **-illiant.**

-ilight, highlight, skylight, twilight.

-ilious, bilious; punctilious; atrabilious, supercilious.

-ilken, milken, silken.

-ilky, milky, silky, Willkie.

-illa, Scylla, villa; cedilla, chinchilla, flotilla, gorilla, guerrilla, manila, Manila, mantilla, Priscilla, vanilla; camarilla, cascarilla, sabadilla, sequidilla, sarsaparilla.

-illful, skillful, willful; unskillful.

-illian. See **-illion.**

-illie. See **-illy.**

-illion, billion, Lillian, million, pillion, trillion; carillon, Castilian, civilian, cotillion, pavilion, postilion, quadrillion, Quintilian, quintillion, reptilian, vermilion; Maximilian.

-illage, grillage, pillage, tillage, village.

-iller, chiller, driller, filler, griller, killer, miller, pillar, Schiller, spiller, swiller, thriller, tiller; distiller, Joe Miller, maxillar; caterpillar, killer-diller, ladykiller.

-illes. See **-illies.**

-illet, billet, fillet, millet, rillet, skillet.

-illiant, brilliant; resilient.

-illiard, billiard, milliard, mill-yard.

-illie. See **-illy.**

-illies, fillies, gillies, lilies, willies; Achilles, Antilles.

-illing, billing, shilling, willing; unwilling.
Also: **-ill** + **-ing** (as in *filling*, etc.)

-illo. See **-illow.**

-illow, billow, kilo, pillow, willow; negrillo; armadillo, peccadillo.

-illy, billy, Billy, Chile, chili, chilly, filly, frilly, gillie, grilly, hilly, illy, killi, lily, Lily, Millie, Philly, shrilly, silly, stilly, Tillie, Willie; Piccadilly, piccalilli, tiger lily, water lily, willy-nilly; daffy-down-dilly.

-ilo. See **-illow.**

-ilot, eyelet, islet, pilot.

-ilter, filter, jilter, kilter, milter, philter, quilter, tilter, wilter.

-ilton, Hilton, Milton, Stilton, Wilton.

-ily (-ī-), drily, highly, Reilly, Riley, shyly, slyly, vilely, wily, wryly; O'Reilly, servilely.

-ily (-ī-). See **-illy.**

-image, image, scrimmage.

-imate, climate, primate; acclimate.

-imber, limber, timber, timbre; unlimber.

-imble, cymbal, fimble, Gimbel, nimble, symbol, thimble, tymbal, wimble.

-imbo, kimbo, limbo; akimbo.

-imely, primely, timely; sublimely, untimely.

-imen. See **-imon.**

-imer. See **-immer.**

-imey. See **-imy.**

-imic, chymic, mimic; alchymic, cherubimic, eponymic, homonymic, metonymic, metronymic, pantomimic, patronymic, synonymic.

-iming, chiming, climbing, liming, priming, rhyming, timing.

-imly, dimly, grimly, primly, trimly.

-immer, brimmer, dimmer, glimmer, grimmer, primer, shimmer, simmer, skimmer, slimmer, swimmer, trimmer.

-imming, brimming, dimming, skimming, slimming, swimming, trimming.

-immy, gimme, jimmy, Jimmy, shimmy.

-imon, Hyman, Hymen, limen, pieman, Simon.

-imper, crimper, limper, scrimper, shrimper, simper, whimper.

-imple, crimple, dimple, pimple, rimple, simple, wimple.

-imply, crimply, dimply, limply, pimply, simply.

-impy, impy, scrimpy.

-imsy, flimsy, mimsy, slimsy, whimsy.

-imy, blimey, grimy, limey, limy, rimy, slimy, stymie, thymy.

-ina (-ē-), Gina, Lena, Nina, scena, Tina; arena, catena, Christina, czarina, farina, galena, Helena, hyena, Katrina, maizena, Regina, subpoena, tsarina, verbena; Argentina, cavatina, concertina, ocarina, Pasadena, philopena, scarlatina, semolina, signorina.

-ina (-ī-), china, China, Dinah, Heine, Ina, myna; Regina; Carolina.

-inal, binal, crinal, final, spinal, trinal, vinyl; acclinal, caninal, equinal, piscinal; anticlinal, officinal, semifinal.

-inas. See **-inus.**

-inca, Inca, Katrinka.

-incher, clincher, flincher, lyncher, pincher.

-inctly, distinctly, succinctly; indistinctly.

-incture, cincture, tincture; encincture.

-inder, cinder, flinder, tinder; rescinder.

-indle, brindle, dwindle, kindle, spindle, swindle; enkindle, rekindle.

-indly, blindly, kindly; unkindly.

-indy, Hindi, Lindy, shindy, windy.

-inea. See **-inny.**

-inear. See **-innier.**

-inely, finely; benignly, caninely; divinely, supinely; saturninely.

-inement. See **-ignment.**

-iner, diner, finer, liner, miner, minor, shiner, Shriner, signer, winer; airliner, assigner, consignor, definer, designer, refiner; penny-a-liner.

-inet. See **-innet.**

-inew. See **-inue.**

-iney. See **-iny.**

-inful, sinful, skinful.

-ingent, stringent; astringent, constringent, contingent, restringent.

-inger (-ĭn-jər), cringer, fringer, ginger, hinger, injure, singer, twinger; infringer.

-inger (-ĭng-ər), bringer, flinger, ringer, singer, slinger, springer, stinger, stringer, wringer; humdinger; Meistersinger, minnesinger.

-inger (-ĭng-gər), finger, linger; malinger.

-ingle, cingle, cringle, dingle, ingle, jingle, mingle, shingle, single, swingle, tingle, tringle; commingle, Kris Kringle, surcingle; intermingle.

-ingly, jingly, mingly, shingly, singly, tingly.

-ingo, bingo, dingo, gringo, jingo, lingo, stingo; Domingo, flamingo.

-ingy (-ĭng-ē), clingy, dinghy, springy, stingy, stringy, swingy, wingy.

-ingy (-ĭn-jē), cringy, dingy, fringy, stingy, swingy, twingy.

-ini. See **-eeny.**

-inian. See **-inion.**

-inic, clinic, cynic, finic, quinic; actinic, aclinic, delphinic, fulminic, platinic, rabbinic; Jacobinic, narcotinic, nicotinic, polygynic.

-ining, dining, lining.
  Also: **-ine** + **-ing** (as in *mining,* etc.)
  Also: **-ign** + **-ing** (as in *signing,* etc.)

-inion, minion, pinion; Darwinian, dominion, opinion, Virginian; Abyssinian, Augustinian, Carolinian, Carthaginian, Palestinian.

-inish (-ĭn-), finish, Finnish, thinnish, tinnish; diminish.

-inish (-ī-), brinish, swinish.

-inist, plenist; machinist, routinist; magazinist.
  Also: **-ean** + **-est** (as in *cleanest,* etc.)
  Also: **-een** + **-est** (as in *greenest,* etc.)

-injure. See **-inger.**

-inker, blinker, clinker, drinker, inker, shrinker, sinker, slinker, stinker, thinker, tinker, winker.

-inkle, crinkle, inkle, sprinkle, tinkle, twinkle, winkle, wrinkle; besprinkle; periwinkle.

-inkling, inkling, sprinkling, tinkling, twinkling, wrinkling.

-inky, blinky, dinky, inky, kinky, pinky; Helsinki.

-inland, Finland, inland.

-inly, inly, thinly; McKinley.

-inner, dinner, finner, grinner, inner, pinner, sinner, skinner, spinner, tinner, winner; beginner, muleskinner.

-innet, ginnet, linnet, minute, spinet.

-innier, finnier, linear, skinnier.

-innish. See **-inish.**

-innow, minnow, winnow.

-inny, finny, guinea, Guinea, hinny, Minnie, ninny, pinny, Pliny, skinny, spinney, tinny, vinny, whinny, Winnie; Virginny; ignominy, pickaninny.

-ino (-ī-), lino, rhino; albino.

-ino (-ē-). See **-eno.**

-inor. See **-iner.**

-inous. See **-inus.**

-inster, minster, Münster, spinster; Leominster, Westminster.

-intel, lintel, pintle, quintal.

-inter, dinter, hinter, minter, printer, splinter, sprinter, squinter, stinter, tinter, winter.

-into, pinto, Shinto.

-intry, splintery, vintry, wintry.

-inty, Dinty, flinty, glinty, linty, minty, squinty.

-inue, sinew; continue, retinue; discontinue.

-inus, binous, dryness, highness, linous, minus, shyness, sinus, slyness, spinous, vinous; Aquinas, echinus, lupinus, salinous, Your Highness.

-inute. See **-innet.**

-iny (-ī-), briny, miny, piney, shiny, spiny, tiny, twiny, viny, whiney, winy; sunshiny.

-iny (-ī-). See **-inny.**

-inyl. See **-inal.**

-io. See **-eo.**

-ion, Bryan, ion, lion, scion, Zion; anion, cation, O'Brien, Orion; dandelion.

-iot. See **-iet.**

-ious. See **-ias.**

-ipend, ripened, stipend.

-iper, diaper, griper, piper, riper, sniper, striper, swiper, typer, viper, wiper; bagpiper; windshield wiper.

-ipher. See **-ifer.**

-iple (-ī-), disciple, ectypal.

-iple (-ī-). See **-ipple.**

-iplet, liplet, triplet.

-ipling. See **-ippling.**

-ippe. See **-ippy.**

-ipper, chipper, clipper, dipper, flipper, gypper, kipper, nipper, shipper, sipper, skipper, slipper, snipper, stripper, tipper, tripper, whipper; Yom Kippur.

-ippet, sippet, skippet, snippet, tippet, whippet.

-ippi. See **-ippy.**

-ipple, cripple, nipple, ripple, stipple, tipple, triple.

-ippling, crippling, Kipling, rippling, stippling, tippling.

-ippo, hippo, Lippo.

-ippy, chippy, drippy, grippy, lippy, nippy, slippy, snippy, zippy; Xanthippe; Mississippi.

-ipsy. See **-ypsy.**

-iptic. See **-yptic.**

-iquant. See **-ecant.**

-iquely. See **-eakly.**

-iquor. See **-icker.**

-ira, Ira, Myra; Elmira, hegira, Palmyra.

-irant, gyrant, spirant, tyrant; aspirant, conspirant, expirant.

-irate. See **-yrate.**

-irchen, birchen, urchin.

-irder. See **-urder.**

-irdie. See **-urdy.**

-irdle, curdle, girdle, hurdle; engirdle.

-irdly, birdly, curdly, thirdly; absurdly.

-ireling, hireling, squireling.

-irely, direly; entirely.

-ireme, bireme, trireme.

-iren, Byron, siren; environ.

-iric. See **-yric.**

-irgin. See **-urgeon.**

-irgy. See **-urgy.**

-irker, burker, irker, jerker, lurker, shirker, smirker, worker.

-irler. See **-urler.**

-irling. See **-urling.**

-irlish, churlish, girlish.

-irly. See **-urly.**

-irma. See **-urma.**

-irmant. See **-erment.**

-irmer, firmer, murmur, squirmer, termer; affirmer, confirmer, infirmer.

-irmish, firmish, skirmish, squirmish, wormish.

-irmy. See **-ermy.**

-iro, Cairo, giro, gyro, tyro; autogiro.

-iron. See **-iren.**

-irous. See **-irus.**

-irrup, chirrup, stirrup, syrup.

-irter. See **-erter.**

-irtle. See **-urtle.**

-irty, Bertie, cherty, dirty, flirty, Gertie, shirty, spurty, squirty, thirty.

-irus, Cyrus, virus; desirous, papyrus.

-iry, briery, diary, fiery, friary, miry, priory, spiry, squiry, wiry; enquiry.

-isal, reprisal; paradisal.

-iscal, discal, fiscal.

-iscount, discount, miscount.

-iscuit. See **-isket.**

-iscus, discus, discous, viscous; hibiscus, meniscus.

-isel. See **-izzle.**

-isely, nicely; concisely, precisely.

-iser. See **-isor.**

-isher, disher, fisher, fissure, swisher, wisher; kingfisher, well-wisher.

-ishy, fishy, swishy.

-isian. See **-ision.**

-isic. See **-ysic.**

-ision, vision; collision, concision, decision, derision, division, elision, Elysian, envision, excision, incision, misprision, Parisian, precision, prevision, provision, recision, rescission, revision; circumcision, Phonevision, stratovision, subdivision, supervision, television.

-isis, crisis, Isis, phthisis.

-isive, decisive, derisive, divisive, incisive; indecisive.

-isker, brisker, frisker, risker, whisker; bewhisker.

-isket, biscuit, brisket, tisket, trisket, wisket.

-isky, frisky, risky, whiskey.

-island, highland, island, Thailand.

-isly. See **-izzly.**

-ismal, dismal; abysmal, baptismal; cataclysmal, catechismal, paroxysmal.

-ison. See **-izen.**

-isor, geyser, Kaiser, miser, sizar, visor; adviser, divisor, incisor; supervisor.
Also: **-ise** + **-er** (as in *reviser,* etc.)
Also: **-ize** + **-er** (as in *sterilizer,* etc.)

-isper, crisper, lisper, whisper.

-ispy, crispy, lispy, wispy.

-issal. See **-istle.**

-issant. See **-ecent.**

-issile. See **-istle.**

-ission. See **-ition.**

-issor. See **-izzer.**

-issue, issue, tissue; reissue.

-issure. See **-isher.**

-ista, vista, Batista.

-istance, distance; assistance, consistence, desistance, existence, insistence, persistence, resistance, subsistence; coexistence, equidistance, nonexistence, nonresistance.

-istant, distant; assistant, consistent, existent, insistent, persistent, resistant, subsistent; coexistent, equidistant, inconsistent, nonexistent, nonresistant.

-isten, christen, glisten, listen.

-istence. See **-istance.**

-istent. See **-istant.**

-ister, bister, blister, glister, mister, sister, twister; insister, persister, resister.

-istic, cystic, fistic, mystic; ballistic, deistic, juristic, linguistic, logistic, puristic, sadistic, simplistic, sophistic, statistic, stylistic, theistic, touristic; altruistic, anarchistic, animistic, atavistic, atheistic, bolshevistic, cabalistic, casuistic, catechistic, chauvinistic, communistic, egoistic, egotistic, euphuistic, fatalistic, humanistic, journalistic, nihilistic, optimistic, pantheistic, pessimistic, pietistic, pugilistic, realistic, socialistic, solecistic, syllogistic; anachronistic, capitalistic, characteristic, idealistic, polytheistic, rationalistic, ritualistic,

sensualistic; materialistic, spiritualistic; individualistic.

-istine, Christine, pristine, Sistine; Philistine; amethystine.

-istle, bristle, fissile, gristle, istle, missal, missile, scissel, sissile, thistle, whistle; abyssal, dickcissel, dismissal, epistle.

-istmas, Christmas, isthmus.

-itain. See **-itten.**

-ital, title, vital; entitle, recital, requital, subtitle.

-itan. See **-ighten.**

-itcher, ditcher, hitcher, itcher, pitcher, richer, stitcher, switcher.

-itchy, bitchy, hitchy, itchy, pitchy, twitchy.

-ite. See **-ighty.**

-iteful. See **-ightful.**

-itely. See **-ightly.**

-itement, excitement, incitement, indictment.

-iten. See **-ighten.**

-iter. See **-ighter.**

-itey. See **-ighty.**

-ither (-ī-), blither, either, lither, neither, tither, writher.

-ither (-ĭ-), blither, dither, hither, thither, slither, whither, wither.

-ithesome, blithesome, lithesome.

-ithing, scything, tithing, writhing.

-ithy, pithy, smithy.

-iti. See **-eaty.**

-itial. See **-icial.**

-itic, critic; arthritic, dendritic, Hamitic, Levitic, mephitic, proclitic, rachitic, Semitic; biolytic, catalytic, cenobitic, eremitic, hypocritic, Jesuitic, paralytic, syphillitic.

-iting, biting, whiting; handwriting.
Also: **-ight** + **-ing** (as in *fighting,* etc.)
Also: **-ite** + **-ing** (as in *uniting,* etc.)
Also: **-ict** + **-ing** (as in *indicting,* etc.)

-ition, fission, mission; addition, admission, ambition, attrition, audition, cognition, coition, commission, condition, contrition, dentition, edition, emission, fruition, Galician, ignition, logician, magician, monition, munition, musician, nutrition, omission, optician, partition, patrician, perdition, permission, petition, physician, position, remission, rendition, sedition, submission, suspicion, tactician, tradition, transition, transmission, tuition, volition; abolition, acquisition, admonition, ammunition, apparition, apposition, coalition, competition, composition, definition, demolition, deposition, disposition, disquisition, ebullition, electrician, erudition, exhibition, expedition, exposition, extradition, imposition, inanition, inhibition, intermission, intuition, manumission, obstetrician, opposition, parturition, politician, premonition, preposition, prohibition, proposition, recognition, repetition, requisition, rhetorician, statistician, superstition, supposition, transposition; academician, arithmetician, decomposition, dialectician, geometrician, indisposition, inquisition; interposition, juxtaposition, mathematician, metaphysician, predisposition, presupposition.

-itious. See **-icious.**

-itish, British, skittish.

-itle. See **-ital.**

-itness, fitness, witness.

-iton (-ī-). See **-ighten.**

-iton (-ĭ-). See **-itten.**

-itsy. See **-itzy.**

-ittal. See **-ittle.**

-ittance, pittance, quittance; admittance, remittance.

-ittee. See **-itty.**

-itten, bitten, Britain, Briton, kitten, mitten, smitten, witan, written.

-itter, bitter, fitter, flitter, fritter, glitter, hitter, jitter, knitter, litter, pitter, quitter, sitter, spitter, splitter, titter, twitter; atwitter, committer, embitter, transmitter; baby-sitter, counterfeiter.

-itti. See **-itty.**

-ittle, brittle, knittle, little, skittle, spittle, tittle, victual, whittle; acquittal, belittle, committal, lickspittle, remittal, transmittal.

-ittler, Hitler, victualler, whittler; belittler.

-itty, city, ditty, flitty, gritty, kitty, Kitty, nitty, pity, pretty, witty; banditti, committee.

-itual, ritual; habitual.

-ity. See **-itty.**

-itzy, Fritzy, Mitzi, Ritzy; itsy bitsy.

-ival, rival; archival, arrival, revival, survival; adjectival, conjunctival; imperatival, nominatival.

-ivance, connivance, contrivance, survivance.

-ivel, civil, drivel, shrivel, snivel, swivel; uncivil.

-iven, driven, given, riven, scriven, shriven; forgiven.

-iver (-ĭv-), flivver, giver, liver, quiver, river, shiver, sliver; deliver, forgiver.

-iver (-ī-), diver, driver, fiver, hiver, Ivor, liver, shriver, skiver; conniver, contriver, deriver, reviver, survivor.

-ivet, civet, pivot, divot, privet, rivet, trivet.

-ivid, livid, vivid.

-ivil. See **-ivel.**

-ivor. See **-iver.**

-ivot. See **-ivet.**

-ivver. See **-iver.**

-ivvy. See **-ivy.**

-ivy, civvy, divvy, Livy, privy, skivvy, skivy, tivy; tantivy.

-ixer, fixer, mixer; elixir.

-ixie, Dixie, nixie, pixie, tricksy.

-ixture, fixture, mixture; admixture, commixture, immixture; intermixture.

-izard. See **-izzard.**

-izen (-ī-), dizen; bedizen, horizon.

-izen (-ĭ-), dizen, mizzen, prison, wizen; arisen, bedizen, imprison.

-izier. See **-izzier.**

-izzard, blizzard, gizzard, izzard, lizard, scissored, vizard, wizard.

-izzer, quizzer, scissor, whizzer.

-izzier, busier, dizzier, frizzier, vizier.

-izzle, chisel, drizzle, fizzle, frizzle, grizzle, mizzle, sizzle, swizzle.

-izzly, drizzly, frizzly, grisly, grizzly, sizzly.

-izzy, busy, dizzy, frizzy, Lizzie, tizzy.

-oa, boa, Goa, moa, Noah, proa; aloha, Genoa, jerboa, Samoa; protozoa.

-oader, goader, loader, odor; breechloader, corroder, exploder, foreboder, malodor; muzzleloader.

-oafy, loafy, oafy, Sophie, strophe, trophy.

-oaken. See **-oken.**

-oaker. See **-oker.**

-oaky. See **-oky.**

-oaler. See **-oller.**

-oaly. See **-oly.**

-oamer. See **-omer.**

-oaner. See **-oner.**

-oarder. See **-order.**

-oarer. See **-orer.**

-oarish, boarish, whorish.

-oarsely, coarsely, hoarsely.

-oary. See **-ory.**

-oastal, coastal, postal.

-oaster, boaster, coaster, poster, roaster, toaster; bill-poster, four-poster.

-oaten, oaten; verboten.

-oater. See **-otor.**

-oatswain. See **-osen.**

-oaty, floaty, goatee, oaty, throaty, zloty; coyote; Don Quixote.

-obate, globate, probate.

-obber, blobber, clobber, cobber, jobber, lobber, robber, slobber, sobber, swabber, throbber.

-obbin, bobbin, Dobbin, robbin, robin, Robin.

-obble, cobble, gobble, hobble, nobble, squabble, wobble.

-obbler, cobbler, gobbler, squabbler, wobbler.

-obby, bobby, Bobby, cobby, hobby, knobby, lobby, mobby, Robbie, snobby.

-obe, obi, Gobi; adobe.

-ober, prober, sober; disrober, October.

-obin. See **-obbin.**

-obo, hobo, lobo, oboe.

-obster, lobster, mobster.

-ocal, bocal, focal, local, phocal, vocal, yokel; bifocal.

-occer. See **-ocker.**

-ocean. See **-otion.**

-ocer, closer, grocer, grosser; engrosser, jocoser, moroser.

-ochee. See **-oky.**

-ocher. See **-oker.**

-ocile. See **-ostle.**

-ocker, blocker, clocker, cocker, docker, Fokker, knocker, locker, mocker, rocker, shocker, soccer, socker, stocker; knickerbocker.

-ockey. See **-ocky.**

-ocious, atrocious, ferocious, precocious.

-ocket, brocket, Crockett, docket, locket, pocket, rocket, socket, sprocket; pickpocket, vest-pocket.

-ocky, cocky, crocky, flocky, hockey, jockey, locky, rocky, sake, Saki, stocky; sukiyaki.

-oco, boko, coco, cocoa, loco; baroco, rococo; locofoco, Orinoco.

-ocoa. See **-oco.**

-ocre. See **-oker.**

-octer. See **-octor.**

-oction, concoction, decoction.

-octor, doctor, proctor; concocter, decocter.

-ocus, crocus, focus, hocus, locus; Hohokus; hocus-pocus.

-ocust, focused, locust.

-oda, coda, Rhoda, soda; Baroda, pagoda.

-odal, modal, nodal, yodel.

-odden, hodden, sodden, trodden; downtrodden, untrodden.

-odder, codder, dodder, fodder, nodder, odder, plodder, prodder, solder.

-oddess, bodice, goddess.

-odding, codding, nodding, plodding, podding, prodding, wadding.

-oddle, coddle, model, noddle, swaddle, toddle, twaddle, waddle; remodel; mollycoddle.

-oddy. See **-ody.**

-odel (-ŏ-). See **-oddle.**

-odel (-ō-). See **-odal.**

-oder. See **-oader.**

-odest, bodiced, modest, oddest; immodest.

-odger, codger, dodger, Dodger, lodger, Roger.

-odic, odic; anodic, iodic, melodic, methodic, rhapsodic, spasmodic, synodic; episodic, periodic.

-odice. See **-oddess.**

-odling, coddling, codling, godling, modeling, swaddling, toddling, twaddling, waddling.

-odly, godly, oddly; ungodly.

-odo, dodo; Quasimodo.

-odor. See **-oader.**

-odule, module, nodule.

-ody, body, cloddy, Mahdi, noddy, Roddy, shoddy, soddy, toddy, wadi; embody, nobody, somebody; anybody, busybody, everybody.

-oeia. See **-ea.**

-oem, poem, proem.

-oeman. See **-omen.**

-oer. See **-ower.**

-offal, offal, waffle.

-offee, coffee, toffee.

-offer, coffer, cougher, doffer, goffer, offer, proffer, scoffer.

-offin. See **-often.**

-offing, coughing, doffing, offing, scoffing.

-often, coffin, dauphin, often, soften.

-ofty, lofty, softy.

-oga, toga, yoga; Saratoga; Ticonderoga.

-ogan, brogan, hogan, Hogan, slogan.

-oger. See **-odger.**

-ogey. See **-ogie.**

-oggish, doggish, froggish, hoggish

-oggle, boggle, coggle, goggle, joggle, toggle; boondoggle, hornswoggle.

-oggy, boggy, cloggy, doggy, foggy, froggy, groggy, joggy, soggy.

-ogi. See **-ogie.**

-ogie, bogey, bogie, dogie, fogey, stogie, Yogi.

-ogle, bogle, ogle.

-oic, stoic; azoic, benzoic, dyspnoic, heroic; Cenozoic, Eozoic, Mesozoic, unheroic, protozoic; Paleozoic.

-oidal, colloidal, spheroidal.

-oider, voider; avoider, embroider.

-oily, coyly, doily, oily, roily.

-oiner, coiner; enjoiner, purloiner.

-ointer, jointer, pointer; anointer.

-ointment, ointment; anointment, appointment, disjointment; disappointment.

-oister, cloister, foister, hoister, moister, oyster, roister; Roister-Doister.

-oiter, goiter, loiter; exploiter, reconnoiter.

-oity, dacoity; hoity-toity.

-okay, croquet, okay, Tokay.

-okel. See **-ocal.**

-oken, broken, oaken, spoken, token; bespoken, betoken, foretoken, heartbroken, Hoboken, outspoken, unbroken, unspoken.

-oker, broker, choker, cloaker, croaker, joker, ocher, poker, soaker, smoker, stoker, stroker, yoker; convoker, evoker, invoker, provoker, revoker, stockbroker; mediocre.

-okey. See **-oky.**

-okum, hokum, locum, oakum.

-oky, choky, croaky, hokey, jokey, oaky, poky, soaky, smoky, troche, trochee; hoky-poky, okey-dokey.

-ola, cola, kola, Lola, Nola, Zola; Angola, gondola, Mazola, viola; Coca-Cola, Gorgonzola, Pensacola, Pepsi-Cola.

-olar (-ŏ-). See **-ollar.**

-olar (-ō-). See **-oller.**

-olden, golden, olden; beholden, embolden.

-older (-ōl-), bolder, boulder, colder, folder, holder, molder, moulder, older, shoulder, smolder; beholder, householder, upholder.

-older (-ŏd-). See **-odder.**

-oldly, boldly, coldly.

-oleful, bowlful, doleful, soulful.

-olely. See **-oly.**

-olemn. See **-olumn.**

-olen. See **-olon.**

-oler (-ŏ-). See **-ollar.**

-oler (-ō-). See **-oller.**

-olic, colic, frolic, rollick; bucolic, carbolic, embolic, symbolic, systolic; alcoholic, apostolic, diastolic, diabolic, epistolic, hyperbolic, melancholic, metabolic, parabolic, vitriolic.

-olid, solid, squalid, stolid.

-olish, polish; abolish, demolish.

-ollar, choler, collar, dollar, loller, scholar, squalor.

-ollard, bollard, Lollard, pollard.

-ollege. See **-owledge.**

-ollen. See **-olon.**

-oller, bowler, coaler, doler, droller, molar, polar, poller, roller, solar, stroller, toller, troller, cajoler, comptroller, consoler, controller, enroller, extoller, patroller; Holy Roller.

-ollick. See **-olic.**

-ollie. See **-olly.**

-ollins, Collins, Hollins, Rollins.

-ollo. See **-ollow.**

-ollop, dollop, lollop, scallop, trollop, wallop.

-ollow, follow, hollo, hollow, Rollo, swallow, wallow; Apollo.

-olly (-ŏ-), Bali, collie, Dollie, dolly, folly, golly, holly, jolly, Molly, polly, Polly, trolley, volley; finale, loblolly, tamale; melancholy.

-olly (-ō-). See **-oly.**

-olo, bolo, polo, solo.

-olon, colon, solon, Solon, stolen, swollen; semicolon.

-olonel. See **-ernal.**

-olor. See **-uller.**

-olster, bolster, holster; upholster.

-olter, bolter, colter, jolter, poulter; revolter.

-oltish, coltish, doltish.

-olumn, column, solemn.

-olver, solver; absolver, dissolver, evolver, resolver, revolver.

-oly (-ō-), coaly, drolly, goalie, holy, lowly, moly, shoaly, solely, slowly, wholly; Stromboli; roly-poly.

-oly (-ō-). See **-olly.**

-oma, coma, Roma, soma; aboma, aroma, diploma, Natoma, sarcoma, Tacoma; carcinoma, la paloma.

-omach, hummock, stomach.

-omain, domain, ptomaine, romaine.

-oman. See **-omen.**

-ombat, combat, wombat.

-omber. See **-omer.**

-ombie, Dombey, zombie; Abercrombie.

-omely. See **-umbly.**

-omen, bowman, foeman, gnomon, omen, Roman, showman, yeoman; abdomen, cognomen.

-oment, foment, moment; bestowment.

-omer (-ō-), comber, homer, Homer, omer, roamer; beachcomber, misnomer.

-omer (-ŭ-). See **-ummer.**

-omet, comet, grommet, vomit; Mahomet.

-omic, comic, gnomic; atomic; agronomic, anatomic, astronomic, autonomic, diatomic, economic, monatomic, taxonomic.

-omit. See **-omet.**

-omma. See **-ama.**

-ommy. See **-almy.**

-omo, chromo, Como, homo; major-domo.

-ompass, compass, rumpus; encompass.

-ompter, compter, prompter; accompter.

-onal, tonal, zonal.

-onday. See **-undy.**

-ondent, fondant, frondent; despondent, respondent; co-respondent, correspondent.

-onder, blonder, bonder, condor, fonder, ponder, squander, wander, yonder; absconder, desponder, responder; corresponder.

-one. See **-ony.**

-onely. See **-only.**

-onent, sonant; component, deponent, exponent, opponent, proponent.

-oner, boner, donor, droner, groaner, loaner, loner, moaner, owner, phoner; atoner, condoner, intoner.

-onest, honest, non est, wannest; dishonest.

-oney (-ō-). See **-ony.**

-oney (-ŭ-). See **-unny.**

-onger (-ŏ-), conger, longer, stronger, wronger; prolonger.

-onger (-ŭ-). See **-unger.**

-onging, longing, thronging, wronging; belonging, prolonging.

-ongly, strongly, wrongly.

-ongo, bongo, Congo.

-oni. See **-ony.**

-onic, chronic, conic, phonic, sonic, tonic; agonic, bubonic, Byronic, canonic, carbonic, colonic, cyclonic, demonic, draconic, euphonic, harmonic, hedonic, ionic, ironic, laconic, masonic, mnemonic, platonic, sardonic, Slavonic, symphonic, tectonic,

Teutonic; diaphonic, diatonic, embryonic, histrionic, Housatonic, hydroponic, isotonic, macaronic, monophonic, philharmonic, telephonic; architectonic.

-onion, bunion, Bunyan, onion, Runyon, trunion.

-onish, donnish, wannish; admonish, astonish, premonish.

-onkey. See **-unky.**

-only, lonely, only.

-onnet, bonnet, sonnet.

-onnie, Bonnie, bonny, Connie, Johnny, Lonny, Ronnie.

-onor (-ŏ-), goner, honor, wanner; dishonor.

-onor (-ō-). See **-oner.**

-onsil, consul, tonsil; proconsul, responsal.

-onsul. See **-onsil.**

-ontal. See **-untle.**

-onter. See **-unter.**

-ontract, contract, entr' acte.

-onus, bonus, Honus, onus.

-ony, bony, Coney, cony, crony, drony, phony, pony, stony, tony, Tony; baloney, Marconi, Shoshone, spumoni, tortoni; abalone, alimony, antimony, cicerone, lazzaroni, macaroni, matrimony, minestrone, parsimony, patrimony, sanctimony, testimony.

-ooby, booby, ruby, Ruby.

-oocher. See **-uture.**

-ooding, hooding, pudding.

-oodle, boodle, doodle, feudal, noodle, strudel; caboodle, flapdoodle, kiyoodle; Yankee Doodle.

-oody (-ŏŏ-), goody, woody.

-oody (-ōō-), broody, Judy, moody.

-oody (-ŭ-). See **-uddy.**

-ooey. See **-ewy.**

-ookie. See **-ooky.**

-ookish, bookish, rookish, spookish.

-ooky (-ŏŏ-), bookie, cooky, hookey, hooky, rookie.

-ooky (-ōō-), fluky, spooky; Kabuki.

-oolie. See **-uly.**

-oolish, coolish, foolish, mulish.

-oolly (-ŏŏ-). See **-ully.**

-oolly (-ōō-). See **-uly.**

-oomer. See **-umer.**

-oomy, bloomy, gloomy, plumy, rheumy, roomy.

-ooner. See **-uner.**

-oony, loony, moony, spoony.

-ooper, blooper, cooper, grouper, hooper, snooper, stupor, super, trooper, whooper; superduper.

-oopy, croupy, droopy, rupee, soupy, whoopee.

-oorish, boorish, Moorish.

-ooser. See **-oser.**

-oosy (-ōō zĭ). See **-oozy.**

-oosy (-ōō sĭ). See **-uicy.**

-ooter, cuter, hooter, looter, mooter, neuter, pewter, rooter, scooter, tutor; commuter, computer, disputer, freebooter, polluter, refuter.

-oothless. See **-uthless.**

-ootie. See **-ooty.**

-ooty, beauty, booty, cootie, cutie, duty, fluty, fruity, rooty, snooty, sooty; agouti.

-ooza. See **-usa.**

-oozer. See **-oser.**

-oozle, foozle, fusel, ousel; bamboozle, perusal, refusal.

-oozy, boozy, floosie, newsy, oozy, woosy.

-opal, opal, copal; Adrianople, Constantinople.

-oper (-ō-), groper, moper, roper, sloper, toper; eloper, interloper.

-oper (-ŏ-). See **-opper.**

-opey. See **-opy.**

-ophe. See **-oafy.**

-ophy. See **-oafy.**

-opic, topic, tropic; myopic; microscopic, misanthropic, philanthropic, presbyopic, spectroscopic, telescopic; heliotropic, kaleidoscopic, stereoscopic.

-ople. See **-opal.**

-opper, chopper, copper, cropper, hopper, popper, proper, shopper, stopper, topper, whopper; clodhopper, cornpopper, eavesdropper, grasshopper, improper, sharecropper, show-stopper.

-opping, chopping.
Also: **-opp** + **-ing** (as in *shopping,* etc.)

-opple, stoppel, topple; estoppel.

-oppy, choppy, copy, floppy, Hoppy, poppy, sloppy, soppy.

-opsy, copsy, dropsy, Topsy; autopsy, biopsy.

-opter, copter; adopter; helicopter.

-optic, coptic, optic; synoptic.

-option, option; adoption.

-opy (-ō-), dopey, Hopi, mopy, ropy, soapy.

-opy (-ŏ-). See **-oppy.**

-ora, aura, Cora, Dora, flora, Flora, hora, Laura, mora, Nora, Torah; Andorra, angora, Aurora, fedora, Marmora, menorah, Pandora, signora; Floradora.

-orage, borage, porridge, shorage, storage.

-oral, aural, chloral, choral, coral, floral, horal, laurel, moral, oral, quarrel, sorrel; auroral, immoral, sororal.

-orax, borax, corax, storax, thorax.

-orbel. See **-arble.**

-orchard, orchard, tortured.

-orcher, scorcher, torture.

-order, boarder, border, forder, hoarder, order, warder; disorder, recorder, rewarder.

-ordon, cordon, Gordon, Jordan, warden.

-ordship, lordship wardship

-ordy. See **-urdy.**

-ore. See **-ory.**

-orehead. See **-orrid.**

-oreign, florin, foreign, warren.

-orer, borer, corer, horror, roarer, scorer, snorer; abhorrer, adorer, explorer, ignorer, restorer.

-oresail. See **-orsel.**

-orest, florist, forest, sorest.

-orey. See **-ory.**

-organ, gorgon, Morgan, organ.

-orger, forger, gorger, ordure; disgorger.

-ori. See **-ory.**

-oric, chloric, choric, Doric, Yorick; caloric, historic, phosphoric; allegoric, metaphoric, meteoric, paregoric, prehistoric, sophomoric.

-orid. See **-orrid.**

-oris, Boris, Doris, loris, Horace, Morris, Norris.

-orker. See **-irker.**

-ormal, formal, normal; abnormal, informal, subnormal.

-orman, doorman, floorman, foreman, Mormon, Norman; longshoreman.

-ormant, dormant; conformant, informant.

-ormer, dormer, former, stormer, warmer; barnstormer, conformer, informer, performer, reformer, transformer.

-ormish. See **-irmish.**

-ormy. See **-ermy.**

-orner, corner, horner, mourner, scorner, warner; adorner, suborner.

-ornet, cornet, hornet.

-orney. See **-ourney.**

-ornful, mournful, scornful.

-orning, morning, mourning, scorning, warning; adorning, forewarning.

-orny, corny, horny, thorny.

-orough, borough, burro, burrow, furrow, thorough.

-orous, chorus, porous, Taurus, torous, torus; decorous, imporous, pylorus, sonorous; ichthyosaurus.

-orpor, torpor, warper.

-orpus, corpus, porpoise.

-orrel. See **-oral.**

-orrent, torrent, warrant; abhorrent.

-orrid, florid, forehead, horrid, torrid.

-orridge. See **-orage.**

-orris. See **-oris.**

-orror. See **-orer.**

-orrow, borrow, morrow, sorrow; tomorrow.

-orry (-ŏ-), quarry, sorry. See also **-arry** and **-ory.**

-orry (-ŭ-). See **-urry.**

-orsel, dorsal, foresail, morsel.

-orsen. See **-erson.**

-orsion. See **-ortion.**

-ortal, chortle, mortal, portal; immortal.

-orten, Horton, Morton, Norton, quartan, shorten.

-orter, mortar, porter, quarter, shorter, snorter, sorter; contorter, distorter, exporter, extorter, importer, reporter, ripsnorter, supporter.

-ortex, cortex, vortex.

-ortion, portion, torsion; abortion, apportion, consortion, contortion, distortion, extortion, proportion; disproportion.

-ortive, sportive, tortive; abortive, transportive.

-ortle. See **-ortal.**

-ortly, courtly, portly.

-ortment, assortment, comportment, deportment, disportment, transportment.

-orton. See **-orten.**

-ortune, fortune; importune, misfortune.

-orture. See **-orcher.**

-ortured. See **-orchard.**

-orty, forty, snorty, sortie, warty.

-orum, forum, quorum; decorum; ad valorem, indecorum, variorum.

-orus. See **-orous.**

-ory, dory, flory, glory, gory, hoary, lorry, storey, story, Tory; Old Glory, vainglory; allegory, a priori, category, con amore, desultory, dilatory, dormitory, gustatory, hortatory, hunky dory, inventory, laudatory, mandatory, migratory, offertory, oratory, peremptory, predatory, prefatory, promissory,

promontory, purgatory, repertory, territory; a fortiori, cacciatore, circulatory, commendatory, compensatory, conciliatory, conservatory, declaratory, defamatory, depilatory, depository, deprecatory, derogatory, exclamatory, explanatory, inflammatory, laboratory, obligatory, observatory, preparatory, reformatory, respiratory, undulatory; a posteriori, retaliatory. See also **-orry.**

-osa, osa; Formosa, mimosa; Mariposa.

-osely, closely, grossly, jocosely, morosely, verbosely.

-osen, chosen, frozen, boatswain, hosen, squozen.

-oser (-o͞o zər), boozer, bruiser, chooser, cruiser, loser. See also **-user.**

-oser (-ō sər). See **-ocer.**

-oset. See **-osit.**

-osher, josher, washer.

-oshy, boshy, sloshy, squashy, swashy, toshy, washy.

-osier, crosier, hosier, osier.

-osion, ambrosian, corrosion, erosion, explosion, implosion.

-osit, closet, posit; deposit; juxtaposit.

-osive, corrosive, erosive, explosive.

-oso. See **-uso.**

-ossal. See **-ostle.**

-osser. See **-ocer.**

-ossil. See **-ostle.**

-ossom, blossom, possum; opossum.

-ossum. See **-ossom.**

-ossy, bossy, drossy, Flossie, flossy, glossy, mossy, posse, quasi, tossy.

-ostal, costal, hostel, hostile; infracostal, intercostal, Pentecostal.

-oster (-ŏ-), coster, foster, Gloucester, roster; accoster, imposter; paternoster, Pentecoster.

-oster (-ō-). See **-oaster.**

-ostic, caustic, gnostic; acrostic, agnostic, prognostic; anacrostic, diagnostic, paracrostic, pentacostic.

-ostle, docile, dossil, fossil, jostle, throstle, wassail; apostle, colossal.

-ostler, hostler, jostler, ostler, wassailer.

-ostly, ghostly, mostly.

-ostril, costrel, nostril, rostral.

-ostrum, nostrum, rostrum.

-osure, closure; composure, disclosure, enclosure, exposure, foreclosure, reposure; discomposure.

-osy, cosy, dozy, nosy, posy, prosy, Rosie, rosy.

-ota, quota, rota; Dakota, iota; Minnesota.

-otal, dotal, notal, rotal, total; sclerotal, teetotal; anecdotal, antidotal, extradotal, sacerdotal.

-otcher, blotcher, botcher, notcher, splotcher, watcher; topnotcher.

-otchy, blotchy, botchy, splotchy; Pagliacci; Liberace.

-ote. See **-oaty.**

-otem, totem; factotum.

-oter. See **-otor.**

-other (-ŏ-), bother, father, fother, pother.

-other (-ŭ-), brother, mother, other, smother; another.

-othing, clothing, loathing.

-othy, frothy, mothy.

-otic, chaotic, demotic, despotic, erotic, exotic, hypnotic, neurotic, narcotic, osmotic, pyrotic, quixotic, zymotic; idiotic, patriotic.

-otion, Goshen, lotion, motion, notion, ocean, potion; commotion, devotion, emotion, promotion, remotion; locomotion.

-otive, motive, votive; emotive, promotive; locomotive.

-otly, hotly, motley, squatly.

-oto, otoe, photo, toto; De Soto, Kyoto.

-otor, boater, bloater, doter, floater, motor, quoter, rotor, voter; promoter, pulmotor; locomotor.

-ottage, cottage, pottage, wattage.

-ottar. See **-otter.**

-otten, cotton, gotten, Groton, rotten; begotten, forgotten; misbegotten.

-otter, blotter, clotter, cottar, cotter, dotter, hotter, jotter, knotter, ottar, otter, plotter, potter, rotter, squatter, spotter, swatter, totter, trotter; complotter.

-ottish, schottische, Scottish, sottish.

-ottle, bottle, dottle, glottal, mottle, pottle, throttle, tottle, twattle, wattle.

-otto, blotto, grotto, lotto, motto, Otto, Watteau. See also **-ato** (-ä-).

-otton. See **-otten.**

-otty, blotty, clotty, dotty, knotty, Lottie, potty, snotty, spotty.

-ouble, bubble, double, rubble, stubble, trouble.

-oubly. See **-ubbly.**

-oubter. See **-outer.**

-oucher, croucher, Goucher, sloucher, voucher.

-ouder. See **-owder.**

-oudly, loudly, proudly.

-oudy. See **-owdy.**

-oughen, roughen, toughen.

-ougher (-ŏ-). See **-offer.**

-ougher (-ŭ-). See **-uffer.**

-oughly. See **-uffly.**

-oughty. See **-outy.**

-oulder. See **-older.**

-oulful. See **-oleful.**

-ouncil, council, counsel, groundsel.

-ounder, bounder, flounder, founder, hounder, pounder, rounder, sounder; confounder, expounder, propounder.

-oundly, roundly, soundly; profoundly, unsoundly.

-ounger. See **-unger.**

-ountain, fountain, mountain.

-ounter, counter, mounter; accounter, discounter, encounter, surmounter.

-ounty, bounty, county, mounty.

-ourage, courage; demurrage, discourage, encourage.

-ouper. See **-ooper.**

-ouple, couple, supple.

-oupy. See **-oopy.**

-ouri. See **-ury.**

-ourish, currish, flourish, nourish.

-ourist. See **-urist.**

-ourly, hourly, sourly.

-ourney, Ernie, journey, tourney; attorney.

-ournful. See **-ornful.**

-ourning. See **-orning.**

-ousal, housel, ousel, spousal, tousle; arousal, carousal, espousal.

-ousel. See **-ousal.**

-ouser, Bowser, browser, dowser, houser, Mauser, mouser, rouser, schnauzer, Towser, trouser; carouser.

-ousin. See **-ozen.**

-ousle. See **-ousal.**

-ousseau. See **-uso.**

-ousy, blowsy, drowsy, frowsy, lousy, mousy.

-outer, clouter, doubter, flouter, pouter, router, scouter, shouter, stouter, touter.

-outhful. See **-uthful.**

-outy, doughty, droughty, gouty, grouty, snouty.

-ova, nova; ova, Jehovah; Casanova, Villanova; Vita nuova.

-oval, approval, disproval, removal, reproval; disapproval.

-ovel, grovel, hovel, novel.

-ovement, movement; approvement, improvement.

-oven (-ō-), cloven, woven; interwoven.

-oven (-ŭ-), coven, oven, sloven.

-over (-ō-), clover, Dover, drover, over, plover, rover, stover, trover; moreover, pushover.

-over (-ŭ-), cover, lover, plover, shover; discover, recover, uncover.

-oward, coward, cowered, flowered, Howard, powered, showered, towered.

-owboy, cowboy, ploughboy.

-owder, chowder, crowder, louder, powder, prouder.

-owdy, cloudy, dowdy, howdy, rowdy; pandowdy.

-owel, bowel, dowel, rowel, towel, trowel, vowel; avowal; disembowel.

-ower, blower, crower, goer, grower, knower, lower, mower, ower, rower, sewer, slower, sower, thrower, tower; bestower; overthrower.

-owered. See **-oward.**

-owery, bowery, cowry, dowry, flowery, houri, showery, towery.

-owing, blowing, crowing, flowing, glowing, going, growing, knowing, lowing, mowing, owing, rowing, sewing, showing, snowing, sowing, stowing, towing, throwing.
Also: **-ow** + **-ing** (as in *bestowing,* etc.)
Also: **-o** + **-ing** (as in *outgoing,* etc.)

-owledge, college, knowledge; acknowledge, foreknowledge.

-owler. See **-oller.**

-owly. See **-oly.**

-owman. See **-omen.**

-owner. See **-oner.**

-ownie. See **-owny.**

-ownsman, gownsman, townsman.

-owny, brownie, Brownie, downy, frowny, towny.

-owry. See **-owery.**

-owsy. See **-ousy.**

-owy, blowy, Bowie, Chloë, doughy, glowy, Joey, showy, snowy.

-oxen, coxswain, oxen.

-oxy, Coxey, doxy, foxy, proxy; Biloxi; orthodoxy, paradoxy; heterodoxy.

-oyal, loyal, royal; disloyal.

-oyalty, loyalty, royalty.

-oyant, buoyant, clairvoyant, flamboyant.

-oyer, annoyer, destroyer, employer, enjoyer.

-oyish, boyish, coyish.

-oyly. See **-oily.**

-oyment, deployment, employment, enjoyment; unemployment.

-oyster. See **-oister.**

-ozen (-ŭ-), cousin, cozen, dozen.

-ozen (-ō-). See **-osen.**

-ozzle, nozzle, schnozzle.

-uager. See **-ager.**

-ual. See **-uel.**

-uant, fluent, truant; pursuant.

-uba, Cuba, juba, tuba.

-ubbard. See **-upboard.**

-ubber, blubber, clubber, drubber, dubber, grubber, lubber, rubber, scrubber, snubber, stubber; landlubber; money-grubber; india rubber.

-ubberd. See **-upboard.**

-ubbish, clubbish, cubbish, grubbish, rubbish, tubbish.

-ubble. See **-ouble.**

-ubbly, bubbly, doubly, knubbly, rubbly, stubbly.

-ubby, chubby, cubby, grubby, hubby, nubby, scrubby, shrubby, stubby, tubby.

-ubic, cubic, pubic, cherubic.

-ubtle. See **-uttle.**

-ubtler. See **-utler.**

-uby. See **-ooby.**

-ucent, lucent; abducent, adducent, traducent, translucent.

-ucial, crucial; fiducial.

-ucid, deuced, lucid, mucid; pellucid.

-ucker, bucker, chukker, mucker, pucker, succor, sucker, trucker, tucker; seersucker.

-uckett, bucket, tucket; Nantucket, Pawtucket.

-uckle, buckle, chuckle, huckle, knuckle, muckle, suckle, truckle; unbuckle; honeysuckle.

-uckled. See **-uckold.**

-uckler, buckler, chuckler, knuckler; swashbuckler.

-uckling, buckling, duckling, suckling.

-uckold, cuckold.
Also: **-uckle** + **-d** (as in *buckled*, etc.)

-ucky, ducky, lucky, mucky, plucky; Kentucky, unlucky.

-ucre. See **-uker.**

-ucter. See **-uctor.**

-uction, fluxion, ruction, suction; abduction, adduction, affluxion, conduction, construction, deduction, defluxion, destruction, effluxion, induction, influxion, instruction, production, reduction, seduction, traduction; introduction, reproduction, misconstruction; overproduction, superinduction.

-uctive, adductive, conductive, constructive, deductive, destructive, inductive, instructive, obstructive, productive, reductive, seductive, traductive; introductive, reproductive, superstructive; overproductive.

-uctor, ductor; abductor, adductor, conductor, constructor, destructor, eductor, instructor, obstructer; nonconductor.

-udder, dudder, flooder, mudder, rudder, scudder, shudder, udder.

-uddhist. See **-udist.**

-uddle, cuddle, huddle, muddle, puddle, ruddle.

-uddler, cuddler, huddler, muddler.

-uddy, bloody, buddy, cruddy, muddy, ruddy, studdy, study.

-udel. See **-oodle.**

-udely, crudely, lewdly, nudely, rudely, shrewdly.

-udent, prudent, student; concludent, imprudent; jurisprudent.

-udest. See **-udist.**

-udgeon, bludgeon, dudgeon, gudgeon; curmudgeon.

-udgy, pudgy, smudgy.

-udish, crudish, dudish, lewdish, nudish, prudish, rudish, shrewdish.

-udist, Buddhist, crudest, feudist, lewdest, nudist, rudest, shrewdest.

-udo, judo, pseudo; escudo, testudo.

-udy. See **-uddy.**

-uel, crewel, cruel, dual, duel, fuel, gruel, jewel, newel; bejewel, eschewal, pursual, renewal, reviewal, subdual.

-uet, cruet, suet.

-uey. See **-ewy.**

-uffel. See **-uffle.**

-uffer, bluffer, buffer, duffer, gruffer, huffer, puffer, rougher, snuffer, stuffer, suffer, tougher.

-uffin, muffin, puffin; ragamuffin.

-uffing, bluffing, cuffing, huffing, puffing, stuffing.

-uffle, buffle, duffel, muffle, ruffle, scuffle, shuffle, snuffle, truffle.

-uffly, bluffly, gruffly, roughly, ruffly, shuffly, snuffly, toughly.

-uffy, fluffy, huffy, puffy, snuffy, stuffy.

-ufty, mufti, tufty.

-ugal. See **-ugle.**

-ugger, bugger, drugger, hugger, lugger, plugger, rugger, smugger, snugger, tugger; hugger-mugger.

-uggle, juggle, smuggle, snuggle, struggle.

-uggy, buggy, muggy, puggy, sluggy.

-ugle, bugle, frugal, fugal; MacDougall.

-ugly, smugly, snuggly, snugly, ugly.

-uicy, goosy, juicy, Lucy, sluicy; Debussy, Watusi.

-uid, druid, fluid.

-uilder, builder, gilder, guilder; bewilder, rebuilder.

-uilding, building, gilding; rebuilding.

-uin, bruin, ruin.

-uiser. See **-oser.**

-uitor. See **-ooter.**

-uker, euchre, fluker, lucre, puker; rebuker.

-uki. See **-ooky.**

-uky. See **-ooky.**

-ula, Beulah, hula; Talullah; Ashtabula, Boola Boola, hula-hula.

-ulep. See **-ulip.**

-ulgar, Bulgar, vulgar.

-ulgence, effulgence, indulgence, refulgence; self-indulgence.

-ulgent, fulgent; effulgent, indulgent, refulgent; self-indulgent.

-ulip, julep, tulip.

-ulky, bulky, hulky, sulky.

-uller, color, cruller, culler, duller, guller, luller, sculler; annuller, discolor, medullar, tricolor; Technicolor, multicolor, water color.

-ullet (-ŏŏ-), bullet, pullet.

-ullet (-ŭl-), cullet, gullet, mullet.

-ulley. See **-ully.**

-ullion, cullion, mullion, scullion.

-ully (-ŏŏ-), bully, fully, pulley, woolly.

-ully (-ŭl-), cully, dully, gully, hully, sully, Tully.

-ulsion, pulsion; compulsion, convulsion, divulsion, emulsion, expulsion, impulsion, propulsion, repulsion, revulsion.

-ulsive, compulsive, convulsive, divulsive, emulsive, expulsive, impulsive, propulsive, repulsive, revulsive.

-ultry, sultry; adultery.

-ulture, culture, vulture; agriculture, aviculture, floriculture, horticulture, pisciculture, viniculture.

-ulu, Lulu, Zulu; Honolulu.

-uly, coolie, coolly, Dooley, duly, Julie, newly, Thule, truly; unduly; Ultima Thule.

-uma, duma, puma, Yuma; mazuma; Montezuma.

-umage, fumage, plumage.

-uman. See **-umen.**

-umbent, accumbent, decumbent, incumbent, procumbent, recumbent.

-umber, cumber, Humber, lumbar, lumber, number, slumber, umber; cucumber, encumber, outnumber; disencumber.

-umber. See **-ummer.**

-umble, bumble, crumble, fumble, grumble, humble, jumble, mumble, rumble, scumble, stumble, tumble, umble.

-umbly, comely, dumbly, humbly, numbly.

-umbo, Dumbo, gumbo; mumbo-jumbo.

-umbrous, cumbrous, slumbrous; penumbrous.

-umby. See **-ummy.**

-umen, human, lumen, Truman; acumen, albumin, bitumen, illumine, inhuman, legumen; superhuman.

-umer, bloomer, boomer, fumer, humor, rumor, tumor; consumer, perfumer.

-umid, fumid, humid, tumid.

-umly. See **-umbly.**

-ummer, comer, drummer, dumber, hummer, mummer, number, plumber, scummer, summer; late-comer, midsummer, newcomer.

-ummit, plummet, summit.

-ummock. See **-omach.**

-ummy, crumby, crummy, dummy, gummy, lummy, mummy, plummy, rummy, scummy, thrummy, tummy, yummy.

-umnal, autumnal, columnal.

-umous, fumous, grumous, humous, humus, plumous, spumous, strumous.

-umper, bumper, dumper, jumper, plumper, pumper, stumper, trumper, thumper.

-umpet, crumpet, strumpet, trumpet.

-umpish, dumpish, frumpish, grumpish, lumpish, plumpish.

-umpkin, bumpkin, lumpkin, pumpkin.

-umple, crumple, rumple.

-umption, gumption; assumption, consumption, presumption, resumption.

-umptious, bumptious, scrumptious.

-umptive, assumptive, consumptive, presumptive, resumptive.

-umpus. See **-ompass.**

-umus. See **-umous.**

-una, luna, puna, Una; lacuna, vicuna.

-unar. See **-uner.**

-uncheon, bruncheon, luncheon, puncheon, truncheon.

-uncle, uncle; carbuncle.

-unction, function, junction, unction; compunction, conjunction, defunction, disjunction, expunction, injunction.

-unctive, adjunctive, conjunctive, disjunctive, subjunctive.

-uncture, juncture, puncture; conjuncture.

-undance, abundance, redundance; superabundance.

-undant, abundant, redundant; superabundant.

-unday. See **-undy.**

-under, blunder, sunder, thunder, under, wonder; asunder, jocunder, refunder, rotunder, thereunder.

-undle, bundle, rundle, trundle.

-undy, Fundy, Grundy, Monday, Sunday, undie; salmagundi.

-uner, crooner, lunar, pruner, schooner, sooner, spooner, swooner, tuner; attuner, communer, harpooner, impugner, lacunar, oppugner; importuner.

-unger (-g-), hunger, monger, younger; fishmonger, gossipmonger, newsmonger; ironmonger.

-unger (-j-), blunger, lunger, plunger, sponger; expunger.

-ungle, bungle, jungle.

-unic, Munich, punic, Punic, runic, tunic.

-union. See **-onion.**

-unkard, bunkered, drunkard, Dunkard.

-unker, bunker, drunker, dunker, flunker, funker, junker, Junker, plunker, punker.

-unky, chunky, donkey, flunkey, funky, hunky, monkey, spunky.

-unnage. See **-onnage.**

-unnel, funnel, gunwale, runnel, tunnel.

-unny, bunny, funny, gunny, honey, money, sonny, sunny, Tunney, tunny.

-unster, funster, gunster, punster.

-untal. See **-untle.**

-unter, blunter, bunter, grunter, hunter, punter; confronter.

-untle, frontal, gruntle; disgruntle; contrapuntal.

-unwale. See **-unnel.**

-uoy. See **-ewy.**

-upboard, blubbered, cupboard, Hubbard, rubbered.

-uper. See **-ooper.**

-upil. See **-uple.**

-uple, pupil; scruple, octuple, quadruple, quintuple, septuple, sextuple.

-uplet, drupelet; octuplet, quadruplet, quintuplet, septuplet, sextuplet.

-upor. See **-ooper.**

-upper, crupper, scupper, supper, upper.

-upple. See **-ouple.**

-uppy, guppy, puppy.

-ura, pleura; bravura, caesura; Angostura; coloratura; appoggiatura.

-ural, crural, jural, mural, neural, pleural, plural, rural, Ural; intermural, intramural, sinecural.

-urance, durance; assurance, endurance, insurance; reassurance.

-urban, bourbon, Durban, turban, urban; suburban; interurban.

-urchin. See **-irchen.**

-urder, girder, herder, murder, sirdar; absurder, engirder, sheepherder.

-urdle. See **-irdle.**

-urdly. See **-irdly.**

-urdy, birdie, sturdy, Verdi, wordy; hurdy-gurdy.

-urely, purely; demurely, maturely, obscurely, securely.

-urement, abjurement, allurement, immurement, obscurement, procurement.

-urer, curer, führer, furor, juror, lurer, purer; abjuror, insurer, nonjuror, procurer, securer.

-urgate, expurgate, objurgate.

-urgence. See **-ergence.**

-urgent. See **-ergent.**

-urgeon, burgeon, sturgeon, surgeon, virgin.

-urger. See **-erger.**

-urgle, burgle, gurgle.

-urgy, clergy, dirgy, surgy; liturgy; dramaturgy, metallurgy, thaumaturgy.

-uric, purpuric, sulfuric, telluric.

-urist, jurist, purist, tourist; caricaturist.

-urker. See **-irker.**

-urky. See **-erky.**

-urler, burler, curler, furler, hurler, purler, skirler, twirler, whirler.

-urlew, curlew, purlieu.

-urling, curling, furling, hurling, purling, skirling, sterling, swirling, twirling, whirling; uncurling.

-urlish. See **-irlish.**

-urloin, purloin, sirloin.

-urly, burly, churly, curly, early, girlie, knurly, pearly, Shirley, surly, twirly, whirly; hurly-burly.

-urma, Burma, derma, Irma; terra firma.

-urmese. See **-ermes.**

-urmur. See **-irmer.**

-urnal. See **-ernal.**

-urner. See **-earner.**

-urning. See **-earning.**

-urnish, burnish, furnish.

-uror. See **-urer.**

-urper, burper, chirper; usurper.

-urrage. See **-ourage.**

-urrish. See **-ourish.**

-urro. See **-orough.**

-urrow. See **-orough.**

-urry, burry, curry, flurry, furry, hurry, scurry, slurry, surrey, worry.

-ursal. See **-ersal.**

-urser, bursar, cursor, mercer, nurser, purser; disburser, precursor.

-ursor. See **-urser.**

-urtain. See **-ertain.**

-urter. See **-erter.**

-urtive. See **-ertive.**

-urtle fertile, hurtle, kirtle, myrtle, Myrtle, turtle, whirtle.

-urtly. See **-ertly.**

-urvant. See **-ervant.**

-urvy, curvy, nervy, scurvy; topsy-turvy.

-ury (-o͞o-), Curie, fury, houri, Jewry, jury; Missouri; potpourri.

-ury (-ĕ-). See **-erry.**

-usa, Sousa, Medusa; Arethusa; lallapalooza.

-usal. See **-oozle.**

-uscan, buskin, dusken, Ruskin, Tuscan; Etruscan, molluscan.

-uscle. See **-ustle.**

-usel. See **-oozle.**

-useless, useless; excuseless.

-user, user; abuser, accuser, amuser, diffuser, excuser. See also **-oser.**

-usher, blusher, brusher, crusher, flusher, gusher, husher, plusher, rusher, usher; four-flusher.

-ushy, gushy, mushy, plushy, slushy.

-usi. See **-uicy.**

-usier. See **-izzier.**

-usion, fusion; allusion, Carthusian, collusion, conclusion, confusion, contusion, delusion, diffusion, effusion, elusion, exclusion, extrusion, illusion, inclusion, infusion, intrusion, Malthusian, obtrusion, occlusion, profusion, protrusion, reclusion, seclusion, suffusion, transfusion; disillusion, interfusion.

-usive, abusive, allusive, collusive, conclusive, conducive, delusive, diffusive, effusive, exclusive, illusive, inclusive, infusive, intrusive, obtrusive, reclusive, seclusive; inconclusive.

-uskin, buskin, Ruskin.

-usky, dusky, husky, musky, tusky.

-uso, Crusoe, Rousseau, trousseau, whoso; Caruso.

-ussel. See **-ustle.**

-usset, gusset, russet.

-ussia, Prussia, Russia.

-ussian. See **-ussion.**

-ussion, Prussian, Russian; concussion, discussion, percussion; repercussion.

-ussive, concussive, discussive, percussive; repercussive.

-ussy, fussy, Gussie, hussy, mussy.

-ustard, blustered, bustard, clustered, custard, flustered, mustard, mustered.

-ustered. See **-ustard.**

-uster, bluster, buster, cluster, Custer, duster, fluster, juster, luster, muster, thruster, truster; adjuster, distruster, lackluster; co-adjuster, filibuster.

-ustic, fustic, rustic.

-ustion, fustian; combustion.

-ustle, bustle, hustle, justle, muscle, mussel, rustle, tussle.

-ustler, bustler, hustler, rustler, tussler.

-ustly, justly; augustly, robustly, unjustly.

-usty, busty, dusty, gusty, lusty, musty, rusty, trusty.

-usy. See **-izzy.**

-utal, brutal, footle, tootle; refutal.

-uter. See **-ooter.**

-utest. See **-utist.**

-uthful, ruthful, truthful, youthful; untruthful.

-uthless, ruthless, toothless, truthless.

-utie. See **-ooty.**

-utile, futile; inutile.

-ution, ablution, dilution, locution, pollution, solution, volution; absolution, attribution, comminution, constitution, contribution, convolution, destitution, devolution, diminution, dissolution, distribution, elocution, evolution, execution, institution, involution, Lilliputian, persecution, prosecution, prostitution, resolution, restitution, retribution, revolution, substitution; circumlocution, electrocution, irresolution.

-utist, cutest, flutist, lutist; pharmaceutist, therapeutist.

-utive, coadjutive, constitutive, diminutive, persecutive, resolutive.

-utor. See **-ooter.**

-uttal. See **-uttle.**

-utter, butter, clutter, cutter, flutter, gutter, mutter, putter, shutter, splutter, sputter, strutter, stutter, utter; abutter, rebutter, woodcutter.

-uttish, ruttish, sluttish.

-uttle, butle, cuttle, scuttle, shuttle, subtle; rebuttal.

-uttler. See **-utler.**

-utton, button, glutton, mutton; bachelor button.

-utty, nutty, puttee, putty, rutty, smutty.

-uture, future, moocher, suture.

-utler, butler, cutler, scuttler, subtler.

-uty. See **-ooty.**

-uxion. See **-uction.**

-uyer. See **-ier.**

-uzzle, guzzle, muzzle, nuzzle, puzzle.

-uzzler, guzzler, muzzler, nuzzler, puzzler.

-uzzy, fuzzy, hussy; fuzzy-wuzzy.

-yan. See **-ion.**

-yer. See **-ier.**

-ylla. See **-illa.**

-ylon, nylon, pylon, trylon.

-yly. See **-ily.**

-ymbal. See **-imble.**

-ymbol. See **-imble.**

-ymic. See **-imic.**

-yming. See **-iming.**

-yncher. See **-incher.**

-yness. See **-inus.**

-ynic. See **-inic.**

-ypsy, gypsy, ipse, tipsy;
Poughkeepsie.

-yptic, cryptic, diptych, glyptic,
styptic, triptych; ecliptic, elliptic;
apocalyptic.

-yra. See **-ira.**

-yrant. See **-irant.**

-yrate, gyrate, irate, lyrate;
circumgyrate, dextrogyrate.

-yric, lyric, Pyrrhic; butyric, empiric,
satiric, satyric; panegyric.

-yron. See **-iren.**

-yrtle. See **-urtle.**

-yrus. See **-irus.**

-ysian. See **-ision.**

-ysic, phthisic, physic; metaphysic.

-ysmal. See **-ismal.**

-yssal. See **-istle.**

-ystic. See **-istic.**

-ytic. See **-itic.**

A Glossary of Poetic Terms

accent, the stress or emphasis placed on certain syllables, usually indicated by a mark (´) above the stressed syllable. An unaccented syllable is usually indicated by a "short" mark (˘) above the syllable. Example:
Had we but world enough, and time

alexandrine, a line of verse consisting of six iambic feet. Example:
All clad | in Lin | coln green, | with caps | of red | and blue |

alliteration, the repetition of the same consonant sound or sound group, especially in initial stressed syllables. Example:
The soft sweet sound of Sylvia's voice

amphibrach, a foot consisting of an unaccented syllable followed by an accented and an unaccented syllable. Example (the first three feet are amphibrachs):
The clans are | impatient | and chide thy | delay |

amphimacer, a foot consisting of an accented syllable followed by an unaccented syllable and an accented syllable. Example:
Catch a star, | falling fast |

anapest, a foot consisting of two unaccented syllables followed by one accented syllable. Example:
Never hear | the sweet mu | sic of speech |

assonance, the use of identical vowel sounds in several words, often as a substitute for rhyme. Example:
Shrink his thin essence like a riveled flow'r

ballad, 1. a simple narrative poem of popular origin, composed in short stanzas, often of a romantic nature

and adapted for singing. 2. any poem written in such a style.

ballade, a poem consisting (usually) of three stanzas having an identical rhyme scheme, followed by an envoy. The final line of each stanza and the envoy is the same.

ballad stanza, a four-line stanza in which the first and third lines are in iambic tetrameter while the second and fourth lines are in iambic trimeter; the second and fourth lines rhyme. In a common variant, the alternate lines rhyme. Example:
They followed from the snowy bank
Those footsteps one by one,
Into the middle of the plank—
And further there was none.

blank verse, unrhymed verse in iambic pentameter, usually not in formal stanza units.

caesura, the main pause in a line of verse, usually near the middle. Example:
Know then thyself, | presume not God to scan

cinquain, a stanza consisting of five lines.

consonance, the use of an identical pattern of consonants in different words. Examples:
time—tome—team—tame
fall—fell—fill—full
slow—slew—slay—sly

closed couplet, a couplet whose sense is completed within its two lines. Example:
True wit is nature to advantage dress'd,
What oft was thought, but ne'er so well express'd.

couplet, two consecutive lines that rhyme. Example:
Touch her not scornfully;
Think of her mournfully.

dactyl, a foot consisting of one accented syllable followed by two unaccented syllables. Example:
Cannon to | right of them |

dimeter, a line of verse consisting of two feet.

distich, a couplet

elegy, a subjective, meditative poem, especially one that expresses grief or sorrow.

envoy, 1. a short stanza concluding a poem in certain archaic metrical forms. 2. a postscript to a poetical composition, sometimes serving as a dedication.

epic, a long narrative poem about persons of heroic stature and actions of great significance, and conforming to a rigid organization and form.

epigram, a short and pithy remark, often in verse.

feminine ending, an ending on a word in which the final syllable is unaccented. Examples:
softness, careful, another, fairest

foot, the metrical unit in poetry, consisting of one accented syllable and one or more unaccented syllables. The most commonly found feet are iamb, anapest, dactyl, and trochee. The foot is usually marked in scansion by a vertical line. Example:
I am mon | arch of all | I survey |

free verse, verse that does not adhere to a fixed pattern of meter, rhyme, or other poetic conventions.

heptameter, a line of verse consisting of seven feet.

heroic couplet, two consecutive rhyming lines in iambic pentameter. Example:

O thoughtless mortals! ever blind to
fate,
Too soon dejected, and too soon
elate.

hexameter, a line of verse consisting
of six feet.

iamb, a foot consisting of one
unaccented syllable followed by one
accented syllable. Example:
The cúr | few tólls | the knéll | of
párt | ing dáy |

internal rhyme, a rhyme that occurs
within a line. Example:
So *slight* the *light*
I could not see,
My *fair*, dear *Clair*,
That it was thee.

Italian sonnet, a sonnet written in
iambic pentameter with a rhyme
scheme usually of *abba abba cdcd*.
There are occasional variants of the
rhyme scheme in the last six lines.
The first eight lines (the *octave*)
usually present a theme or premise;
the last six lines (the *sestet*) present
the conclusion or resolution.

limerick, a five-line poem using
trimeters for the first, second, and
fifth lines and using dimeters for
the third and fourth lines. It is
usually written in a mixture of
amphibrachs and iambs.

lyric, a poem with a particularly
musical, songlike quality.

macaronic verse, verse in which two
or more languages are interlaced.

masculine ending, an ending on a
word in which the final syllable is
accented. Examples:
resound, avoid, reply, consume

meter, the basic rhythmic
description of a line in terms of its
accented and unaccented syllables.
Meter describes the sequence and
relationship of all the syllables of a
line.

monometer, a line of verse
consisting of one foot.

nonometer, a line of verse consisting
of nine feet.

octave, the first eight lines of an
Italian sonnet.

octometer, a line of verse consisting
of eight feet.

ode, a poem, usually complicated in
its metrical and stanzaic form, on a
highly serious or particularly
important theme.

onomatopoeia, the quality of a word
that imitates the sound it
designates. Examples:
honk, bang, tintinnabulation

ottava rima, a stanza written in
iambic pentameter with a rhyme
scheme of *abababcc*.

pastoral, a poem dealing with simple
rural life.

pentameter, a line of verse consisting
of five feet.

Petrarchan sonnet. See Italian
sonnet.

quatrain, a stanza consisting of four
lines.

refrain, an expression, a line, or a
group of lines that is repeated at
certain points in a poem, usually at
the end of a stanza.

rhyme, an identity of certain sounds
in different words, usually the last
words in two or more lines.

rhyme royal, a stanza written in
iambic pentameter with a rhyme
scheme of *ababbcc*.

rhyme scheme, the pattern of rhyme
used in a stanza or poem.

rondeau, a poem consisting of three
stanzas of five, three, and five lines,
using only two rhymes throughout.
A refrain appears at the end of the
second and third stanzas.

rondel, a poem consisting (usually)
of fourteen lines on two rhymes, of
which four are made up of the
initial couplet repeated in the
middle and at the end (the second
line of the couplet sometimes being
omitted at the end).

rondelet, a poem consisting of five
lines on two rhymes, the opening
word or words being used after the
second and fifth lines as an
unrhymed refrain.

run-on line, a line which does not
end at a point of sense at which
there would normally be a pause in
speech.

scansion, the process of indicating
the pattern of accented and

unaccented syllables in a line of
verse.

septet, a stanza consisting of seven
lines.

sestet, a group of six lines, especially
those at the end of a sonnet.

sestina, a poem of six six-line stanzas
and a three-line envoy, originally
without rhyme, in which each
stanza repeats the end words of the
lines of the first stanza, but in
different order. The envoy uses
these six end words again, three in
the middle of the lines and three at
the end.

Shakespearian sonnet, a sonnet
written in iambic pentameter with a
rhyme scheme of *abab cdcd efef gg*.
The theme is often presented in the
three quatrains and the poem is
concluded with the couplet.

sight rhyme, not a rhyme but two or
more words which end in identical
spelling. Examples:
though, bough, through

slant rhyme, an approximate rhyme,
usually characterized by assonance
or consonance.

song, a short and simple poem,
usually suitable for setting to
music.

sonnet, a poem consisting of
fourteen lines in iambic
pentameter. The most common
forms are the Italian sonnet (which
see) and the Shakespearian sonnet
(which see).

Spenserian stanza, a stanza
consisting of eight iambic
pentameter lines and a final iambic
hexameter line, with a rhyme
scheme of *ababbcbcc*.

spondee, a foot consisting of two
accented syllables. Example:
Spéak sóft, | stánd stíll |

stanza, a fixed pattern of lines or
rhymes, or both.

stress. See accent.

tercet, a group of three consecutive
lines that rhyme together or relate
to an adjacent tercet by rhymes.

terza rima, a poem in iambic meter
consisting of eleven-syllable lines
arranged in tercets, the middle line

of each tercet rhyming with the first and third lines of the following tercet.

tetrameter, a line of verse consisting of four feet.

trimeter, a line of verse consisting of three feet.

triolet, an eight-line stanza in which line 1 recurs as line 4 and line 7, while line 2 recurs as line 8.

triplet, a stanza consisting of three lines.

trochee, a foot consisting of one accented syllable followed by one unaccented syllable. Example:

Why so | pale and | wan, fond | lover |

vers de société, a light-spirited and witty poem, usually brief, dealing with some social fashion or foible.

verse, 1. one line of a poem. 2. a group of lines in a poem. 3. any form in which rhythm is regularized.

villanelle, a poem consisting of (usually) five tercets and a final quatrain, using only two rhymes throughout.

weak rhyme, rhyme which falls upon the unaccented (or lightly accented) syllables.

PART FIVE

DESK DICTIONARY

INTRODUCTION

ENGLISH SPELLING

The classic diatribe against the vagaries of English spelling is the one made famous by George Bernard Shaw, in which he claims that our spelling is so irregular (and so absurd!) that the common word *fish* could as well be spelled *ghoti*. The idea is as follows:

> *gh*, as in cou*gh*, equals the sound of *f*
> *o*, as in w*o*men, equals the sound of *i*
> *ti*, as in na*ti*on, equals the sound of *sh*

The trouble with this analysis, amusing though it may be, is that it does not take into account the **phonotactics** of English, what might be called "the rules of the game." Without denying that in the English language we can have more than one sound for each spelling and more than one spelling for each sound, we can point to certain regularities regarding sound-spelling correspondences, among them rules of position. Taking these into account, we can see that Shaw's suggested spelling of *ghoti* for *fish* falls apart; *gh* NEVER equals the sound of *f* at the beginning of a word, only at the end, as in *rough, cough,* or *laugh.* The use of the letter *o* to represent the "short" *i* sound is even more restricted, appearing ONLY in the word *women.* Finally, *ti* produces the *sh* sound ONLY medially, typically in suffixes like *-tion,* and *-tious.*

There are reasons for the sound-spelling irregularities in English; its history warrants them. For one thing, the number of sounds in the language is greater than the number of symbols available in our alphabet; some of these symbols must do double duty (as with "hard" and "soft" *c* and *g*) or must combine with other symbols in order to account for all the sounds. For another, English has borrowed heavily from other languages, retaining traces of their pronunciations with their spellings. In addition, spelling in general is conservative—it changes less readily than pronunciation. Modern English retains spellings that do not reflect the many changes in pronunciation that have occurred over the years, particularly during the Great Vowel Shift of the fifteenth century. Nor can any single set of spellings reflect the diversity of English dialects. English is a varied language that flourishes not only throughout North America and England, but over the entire globe. Add to this the fact that early printers were inconsistent and idiosyncratic in their spelling, and some of their misspellings have survived. All of these factors have led to the kinds of spelling irregularities that make the English language both frustrating and fascinating.

Nevertheless, for all its difficulties, English spelling is not entirely irrational. We return to "phonotactics." If certain letter combinations occur predominantly in certain portions of words, a growing familiarity with these patterns can increase your confidence in using and working with the English language. And it can help to resolve an age-old problem:

FINDING SPELLINGS WHEN YOU KNOW THE SOUNDS

The Problem

Traditionally, there has been a fundamental difficulty with making efficient use of dictionaries and similar reference books: How can you look up a word if you don't know how to spell it? Where do you look? In what part of the alphabet?

The Solution

Although no complete solution exists, a "Table of Sound-Spelling Correspondences" like the one below can help. By listing alternative spellings for each of the sounds of English, and tying these sounds and spellings together, the table allows you to relate what you already know about a word—how to SAY it—with what you are trying to find out about the word—how to SPELL it.

UNDERSTANDING THE TABLE OF SOUND-SPELLING CORRESPONDENCES

Contexts for Given Spelling Patterns

Tables showing the relationship between sounds and spellings can be found in most unabridged and desk dictionaries. The table that follows not only shows spelling patterns and the sounds they represent, but indicates which part of a word (beginning, middle, or end) is likely to contain these patterns. For example, "-ag(m)," as in "diaphragm," is shown with a preceding hyphen and with parentheses around the m, as one of the patterns representing the "short" a sound. This means that when the letters ag precede an m and the agm ends a word or syllable, ag is pronounced as a vowel, as if the g were not there. (In fact, when an agm combination is split between syllables, as in the word "syn•tag•mat•ic," so that the g ends one syllable and the m starts the next one, the g is NOT silent.)

From this example, you can see that parenthesized letters in the table indicate a CONTEXT for a given spelling pattern. Similarly, hyphens show where in a word or syllable that pattern is most likely to occur. A spelling pattern shown without any hyphens can occur in various parts of a word; some of these, like air, are also found as entire words.

Key-Word Patterns

For each sound, the table shows a large, boldface **key spelling,** followed by a familiar word (or words) in which that spelling typically occurs. This key word allows you, using your own English dialect, to fix the sound in your mind.

Following the key-word pattern is a list of other spellings for the same sound. Notice that you may pronounce some of the spellings in certain sections

differently from the sound represented. Such spellings will probably be repeated at the sounds more appropriate for your dialect. Tables of this sort usually include unusual sound-spelling associations: some that are simply rare, like the u in busy or business at the short i sound, and others that are derived from languages other than English. French spellings standing for the "long" o sound, for example, might include -eau, -eaux, and -ot. Long lists of such spelling patterns, with no indication of which ones are frequent enough to be useful, can indeed be overwhelming. To simplify our table, we have marked the common spelling patterns for each sound with an asterisk.

Note that the combination of a vowel letter plus an ellipsis (three dots) and an e stands for any spelling in which that vowel and the e are separated by a single consonant. As a general rule, this "discontinuous vowel" pattern represents the long sound of that vowel. (Long i, for example, is frequently spelled with i...e, as in ice.) But a discontinuous vowel can stand for other than long vowel sounds. In the word have, the a...e stands for a short a sound, and in the word love, o...e stands for the sound of short u.

USING THE TABLE OF SOUND-SPELLING CORRESPONDENCES

To find a word, first sound it out. Say it out loud, if necessary. Determine especially how the first syllable is pronounced. In the table, find the various spelling equivalents for that pronunciation. Finally, look for each of those spellings in this dictionary until you find the word you want.

An Instructive Example

If you say the words *persuade* and *pursue* aloud, you can hear that their initial syllables sound very much alike, something like the word *purr,* but not quite as strong. The p-sound is fairly easy to spell; initial consonants usually are. The problem is with the following sound; it is not stressed and, depending on one's dialect of English, may either have a slight r "coloring" or be followed by an audible r sound. Among the spellings listed for that sound (for which the key-word pattern is **-er** as in fath**er**), you will find ar-, ir-, and ur-. If you then look in the dictionary for p followed by each of these spellings, you will eventually find both *persuade* (under p + er) and *pursue* (under p + ur). You will have discovered that although their initial syllables sound alike, the two words you were looking for are spelled differently.

TABLE OF SOUND-SPELLING CORRESPONDENCES

VOWELS AND DIPHTHONGS

*a- as in **a**t;
-a- as in h**a**t ("short" a)

-a'a-	m*a'a*m
-ach(m)	dr*ach*m
-ag(m)	diaphr*ag*m
-ah-	d*ah*lia
-ai-	pl*ai*d
-al-	h*a*lf
-au-	l*au*gh
-ua-	g*ua*rantor
-ui-	g*ui*mpe
i(n)-, -i(n)-	*i*ngenue, l*i*ngerie
-i(m)-	t*i*mbre

*a . . . e as in **a**t**e**;
-a . . . e as in h**a**t**e** ("long" a)

-ae-	G*ae*lic
-ag(n)	champ*ag*ne
*-ai-	r*ai*n
-aigh-	str*aigh*t
-aig(n)	arr*aig*n
-ao-	g*ao*l
-au-	g*au*ge
-a(g)ue	v*ague*
*-ay	r*ay*
*é-, -é	*é*tude, expos*é*
-e . . . e	su*ede*
*-ea-	st*ea*k
-ee-	matin*ee*
eh	*eh*
*-ei-	v*ei*l
*-eig(n)	f*eig*n
*eigh-, -eigh-, -eigh	*eigh*t, w*eigh*t, w*eigh*
-eilles	Mars*eilles*
-er	dossi*er*
-es(ne)	dem*es*ne
-et	ber*et*
*-ey	ob*ey*

*air as in ch**air**

*-aire	doctrin*aire*
*-ar-	ch*ar*y
*-are	d*are*
-ayer	pr*ayer*
*-ear	w*ear*
-eer	Mynh*eer*
e'er	n*e'er*
*-eir	th*eir*
-er	mal de m*er*
*-ere	th*ere*
-ey're	th*ey're*

*ah as in hurr**ah** ("broad" a)

*-a-	f*a*ther
à	*à* la mode

-aa-	baz*aa*r
*-al(f)	h*al*f
*-al(m)	c*al*m
-as	faux p*as*
-at	éclat
-au-	l*au*gh
-e(r)-	s*er*geant
*-ea(r)-	h*ea*rth
-oi-	reserv*oi*r
-ua-	g*ua*rd
i(n)-, -i(n)-	*i*ngenue, l*i*ngerie

*e as in **e**bb ("short" e)

a-, -a-,	*a*ny, m*a*ny
ae-	*ae*sthete
-ai-	s*ai*d
-ay-	s*ay*s
*-ea-	l*ea*ther
-eg(m)	phl*eg*m
-ei-	h*ei*fer
-eo-	j*eo*pardy
-ie-	fr*ie*nd
-oe-	f*oe*tid

*ee as in k**ee**p ("long" e)

ae-, -ae-	*Ae*sop, C*ae*sar
-ay	qu*ay*
*e-, -e-	*e*qual, s*e*cret
-e	stroph*e*
*ea-, -ea-, -ea	*ea*ch, t*ea*m, t*ea*
*-ea(g)ue	l*ea*gue
e'e-	*e'e*n
*e . . . e	prec*ede*
*-ei-	rec*ei*ve
-eip(t)	rec*eip*t
-eo-	p*eo*ple
*-ey	k*ey*
-i	ran*i*
*i . . . e	mach*ine*
*-ie-	f*ie*ld
-is	debr*is*
*-i(g)ue	intr*igue*
*-i(q)ue	ant*ique*
-oe-	am*oe*ba
-uay	q*uay*
*-y	cit*y*

*i as in **i**f ("short" i)

*-a-	dam*a*ge
-ae-	an*ae*sthetic
e-	*E*ngland
-ee-	b*ee*n
*-ei-	counterf*ei*t
-ia-	carr*ia*ge
-ie-	s*ie*ve
-o-	w*o*men

(b)u(s)-	*bu*siness
-ui(l)-	b*ui*ld, g*ui*lt
*-y-	s*y*mpathetic

*i . . . e as in **ice** ("long" i)

*-ai-	f*ai*lle
ais-	*ai*sle
-ay-	k*ay*ak
aye	*aye*
*-ei-	st*ei*n
-eigh-	h*eigh*t
eye	*eye*
*-ie	p*ie*
*-igh	h*igh*
is-	*i*sland
*-uy	b*uy*
*-y-, -y	c*y*cle, sk*y*
*-ye	l*ye*

*o as in **box**

*(w)a-	w*a*nder
*-(u)a-	qu*a*drant
-ach-	y*ach*t
-au-	astron*au*t
-eau-	bur*eau*cracy
-ou-	c*ou*gh
*ho-	*ho*nor

*o as in **lo**

*-au-	m*au*ve
-aut	h*aut*boy
-aux	f*aux* pas
-eau	b*eau*
-eaux	Bord*eaux*
-eo-	y*eo*man
-ew	s*ew*
*o . . . e	r*o*te
*-oa-	r*oa*d
*-oe	t*oe*
oh	*oh*
*-ol-	y*ol*k
-oo-	br*oo*ch
-ot	dep*ot*
*-ou-	s*ou*l
*-ow	fl*ow*
*-owe	*owe*

*-aw as in **paw**

*-a-	t*a*ll
*(w)a(r)-	w*a*rrant
-ah	Ut*ah*
*-al-	w*al*k
-as	Arkans*as*
*au-, -au-	*au*thor, v*au*lt
*-augh-	c*augh*t
*-o-	alcoh*o*l
*-oa-	br*oa*d
-oo-	fl*oo*r
*-ough-	s*ough*t

*-oy as in b**oy**

-awy-	l*awy*er
-eu-	Fr*eu*d
*-oi-	*oi*l
-ois	Iroqu*ois*
-uoy	b*uoy*

*-oo- as in l**oo**k

-o-	w*o*lf
*-oul-	w*ou*ld
*-u-	p*u*ll

*oo-, *-oo-, *-oo as in **oo**ze, m**oo**d, ahch**oo**

-eu-	man*eu*ver
*-ew	gr*ew*
-iew	l*ieu*
-o-	wh*o*
o . . . e	m*o*ve
-oe	can*oe*
-oeu-	man*oeu*vre
*-ou-	tr*ou*p
*u . . . e	r*u*le
*-ue	fl*ue*
-ug(n)	imp*u*gn
*-ui-	s*ui*t

*-ow as in br**ow**

au-	*Au*f Wiedersehen
-au	land*au*
*ou-, *-ou-	*ou*t, sh*ou*t
*-ough	b*ough*

*u-, -u- as in **u**p, p**u**p

o-, *-o-	*o*ther, s*o*n
-oe-	d*oe*s
*o . . . e	l*o*ve
-oo-	bl*oo*d
-ou(ble)	tr*ou*ble

*ur-, *-ur- as in **ur**n, t**ur**n

*ear-, -ear-	*ear*n, l*ear*n
*er-, -er-	*er*mine, t*er*m
err	*err*
-eur	pos*eur*
her-	*her*b
*-ir-, -ir	th*ir*sty, f*ir*
(w)or-	w*or*k
-our-	sc*our*ge
-urr	p*urr*
-yr-	m*yr*tle

*u-, -u as in **u**tility, fu**u**ture

-eau-	b*eau*ty
-eu-	f*eu*d
*-ew	f*ew*
*hu-	*hu*man
hu . . . e	*hu*ge

-ieu	pur*lieu*
-iew	v*iew*
*u . . . e	*u*s*e*
*-ue	c*ue*
-ueue	q*ueue*
yew	*yew*
you	*you*
yu-	*Yu*kon
yu . . . e	*yu*le

*a as in **a**lone

*-e-	syst*e*m
*-i-	eas*i*ly
*-o-	gall*o*p
*-u-	circ*u*s
à	tête-*à*-tête
-ai(n)	mount*ai*n
-ei(n)	mull*ei*n
-eo(n)	dung*eo*n
-ia-	parl*ia*ment
-io-	leg*io*n
-oi-	porp*oi*se
*-ou-	curi*ou*s
-y-	mart*y*r

*-er as in fath**er**

*-ar	li*ar*
*-ir	elix*ir*
*-or	lab*or*
*-our	lab*our*
*-ur	aug*ur*
*-ure	fut*ure*
-yr	mart*yr*

CONSONANTS

(Note that consonant spelling patterns such as -*bb*-, shown with hyphens on either side, are frequently part of two adjacent syllables in a word, with part of the combination in one syllable and the rest in the next.)

*b-, *-b-, *-b as in **b**ed, am**b**er, ru**b**

*-bb-, *-bb	ho*bb*y, e*bb*
*-be	lo*be*
bh-	*bh*eesty

*ch-, -ch-, *-ch as in **ch**ief, ah**ch**oo, ri**ch**

c-	*c*ello
*-che	ni*che*
*-tch-, *-tch	ha*tch*et, ca*tch*
-te-	righ*te*ous
*-ti-	ques*ti*on
*-tu-	na*tu*ral

*d-, *-d-, *-d as in **d**o, o**d**or, re**d**

*-'d	we'*d*
*-dd-, *-dd	la*dd*er, o*dd*
*-de	fa*de*
dh-	*dh*urrie
*-ed	pull*ed*
*-ld	shou*ld*

*f-, *-f-, as in **f**eed, sa**f**er

*-fe	li*fe*
*-ff-, *-ff	mu*ff*in, o*ff*
*-ft-	so*f*ten
*-gh	tou*gh*
*-lf	ca*lf*
pf-	*pf*ennig
*ph-, -ph-, -ph	*ph*ysics, sta*ph*ylococcus, sta*ph*

*g-, *-g-, *-g as in **g**ive, a**g**ate, fo**g**

*-gg	e*gg*
*gh-	*gh*ost
*gu-	*gu*ard
*-gue	pla*gue*

*h-, *-h- as in **h**it, a**h**oy

wh-	*wh*o

*wh- as in **wh**ere (like *hw*)

*hu- as in **hu**ge (like *hyoo*)

*j- as in **j**ust

-ch	Greenwi*ch*
*-d(u)	gra*du*ate
*-dg-	ju*dg*ment
*-dge	bri*dge*
*-di-	sol*di*er
*-ge	sa*ge*
-gg-	exa*gg*erate
*g(e)-, *-g(e)-	*g*em, a*g*ent
*g(i)-, *-g(i)-	*g*in, a*g*ile
-jj-	Ha*jj*i

*k-, *-k- as in **k**eep, ma**k**ing

*c-, *-c-	*c*ar, be*c*ome
*-cc-	a*cc*ount
-cch-	ba*cch*anal
*ch-	*ch*aracter
*-ck	ba*ck*
-cq-	a*cq*uaint
-cqu-	la*cqu*er
-cque	sa*cque*
cu-	bis*cu*it
-gh	lou*gh*
*-ke	ra*ke*
-kh	Si*kh*
-lk	wa*lk*
q-	*q*adi

-q	Ira*q*
-qu-	li*qu*or
-que	pla*que*

*l-, *-l-, *-l as in *l*ive, a*l*ive, sai*l*

*-le	mi*le*
*-ll	ca*ll*
-lle	fai*lle*
-sl-	li*sl*e
-sle	ai*sle*

*m-, *-m-, *-m as in **m**ore, a**m**ount, ha**m**

-chm	dra*chm*
-gm	paradi*gm*
*-lm	ca*lm*
*-mb	li*mb*
*-me	ho*me*
mh-	*mh*o
*-mm-	ha*mm*er
-mn	hy*mn*

*n-, *-n-, *-n as in **n**ot, ce**n**ter, ca**n**

*gn-	*gn*at
*kn-	*kn*ife
mn-	*mn*emonic
*-ne	do*ne*
*-nn-	ru*nn*er
*pn(eu)-	*pn*eumatic

*-ng-, *-ng as in ri**ng**ing, ri**ng**

*-n(k)	pi*n*k
-ngg	mahjo*ngg*
-ngue	to*ngue*

*p-, *-p-, *-p as in **p**en, su**p**er, sto**p**

*-pe	ho*pe*
*-pp-	su*pp*er
-ppe	lagnia*ppe*

*r-, *-r-, *-r as in **r**ed, a**r**ise, fou**r**

*-re	pu*re*
*rh-	*rh*ythm
*-rr-	ca*rr*ot
-rrh	cata*rrh*
*wr-	*wr*ong

*s-, *-s-, *-s as in **s**ee, be**s**ide, ala**s**

*c(e)-, *-c(e)-,	*c*enter, ra*c*er
*c(i)-, *-c(i)-	*c*ity, a*c*id
*-ce	mi*ce*
*ps-	*ps*ychology
*sc-	*sc*ene
sch-	*sch*ism
*-se	mou*se*
*-ss-, *-ss	me*ss*enger, lo*ss*

*sh-, *-sh-, *-sh as in **sh**ip, a**sh**amed, wa**sh**

-ce-	o*ce*an
ch-, *-ch-	*ch*aise, ma*ch*ine
-chs-	fu*chs*ia
*-ci-	spe*ci*al
psh-	*psh*aw
s(u)-	*s*ugar
sch-	*sch*ist
*-sci-	con*sci*ence
-se-	nau*se*ous
*-si-	man*si*on
*-ss-	ti*ss*ue
*-ssi-	mi*ssi*on
*-ti-	cap*ti*on

*t-, *-t-, *-t as in **t**oe, a**t**om, ha**t**

-bt	dou*bt*
-cht	ya*cht*
ct-	*ct*enophore
*-ed	talk*ed*
*-ght	bou*ght*
phth-	*phth*isic
'-t-	'*t*was
*-te	bi*te*
th-	*th*yme
*-tt-	bo*tt*om
tw-	*tw*o

*th-, *-th-, *-th as in **th**in, e**th**er, pa**th**

chth-	*chth*onian

*th-, *-th-, -th as in **th**en, o**th**er, smoo**th**

*-the	ba*the*

*v-, *-v-, -v as in **v**isit, o**v**er, lu**v**

-f	o*f*
-ph-	Ste*ph*en
*-ve	ha*ve*
-vv-	fli*vv*er

*w-, *-w- as in **w**ell, a**w**ay

-ju-	mari*ju*ana
-o(i)-	ch*oi*r
ou(i)-	*ou*ija
(q)u-	q*u*iet
*wh-	*wh*ere

*y- as in **y**et

*-i-	un*i*on
-j-	hallelu*j*ah
-ll-	torti*ll*a

*z-, -z- as in **z**one, Bi**z**et

*-s	ha*s*
-sc-	di*sc*ern

*-se	ri*se*
x-	*x*ylem
-ze	fu*ze*
*-zz-, *-zz	bu*zz*ard, fu*zz*

-zi- as in bra**zi**er (like *zh*)

*-ge	gara*ge*
*-s(u)-	mea*s*ure
*-si	divi*si*on
*-z(u)-	a*z*ure

RULES OF SPELLING

No spelling rule should be followed blindly, for every rule has exceptions and words analogous in some forms may differ in others.

1. **Silent E Dropped.** Silent *e* at the end of a word is usually dropped before a suffix beginning with a vowel: *abide, abiding; recite, recital.*

    Exceptions: Words ending in *ce* or *ge* retain the *e* before a suffix beginning with *a* or *o* to keep the soft sound of the consonant: *notice, noticeable; courage, courageous.*

2. **Silent E Kept.** A silent *e* following a consonant (or another *e*) is usually retained before a suffix beginning with a consonant: *late, lateness; spite, spiteful.*

    Exceptions: fledgling, acknowledgment, judgment, wholly, and a few similar words.

3. **Final Consonant Doubled.** A final consonant following a single vowel in one-syllable words or in a syllable that will take the main accent when combined with a suffix is doubled before a suffix beginning with a vowel: *begin, beginning; occur, occurred.*

    Exceptions: h and *x (ks)* in final position; *transferable, gaseous,* and a few others.

4. **Final Consonant Single.** A final consonant following another consonant, a double vowel, or diphthong, or that is not in a stressed syllable, is not doubled before a suffix beginning with a vowel: *part, parting; remark, remarkable.*

    Exceptions: an unaccented syllable does not prevent doubling of the final consonant, especially in British usage: *traveller* beside *traveler,* etc.

5. **Double Consonants Remain.** Double consonants are usually retained before a suffix except when a final *l* is to be followed by *ly* or *less.* To avoid a triple *lll,* one *l* is usually dropped: *full, fully.*

    Exceptions: Usage is divided, with *skilful* beside *skillful, instalment* beside *installment,* etc.

6. **Final Y.** If the *y* follows a consonant, change *y* to *i* before all endings except *ing.* Do not change it before *ing* or if it follows a vowel: *bury, buried, burying; try, tries;* but *attorney, attorneys.*

    Exceptions: day, daily; gay, gaily; lay, laid; say, said.

7. **Final IE to Y.** Words ending in *ie* change to *y* before *ing: die, dying; lie, lying.*

8. **Double and Triple E Reduced.** Words ending in double *e* drop one *e* before an ending beginning in *e,* to avoid a triple *e.* Words ending in silent *e* usually drop the *e* before endings beginning in *e* to avoid forming a syllable. Other words ending in a vowel sound commonly retain the letters indicating the sound. *Free-ed = freed.*

9. **EI or IE.** Words having the sound of *ē* are commonly spelled *ie* following all letters but *c;* with a preceding *c,* the common spelling is *ei.* Examples: *believe, achieve, besiege;* but *conceit, ceiling, receive, conceive.* When the sound is *ā* the common spelling is *ei* regardless of the preceding letter. Examples: *eight, weight, deign.*

    Exceptions: either, neither, seize, financier; some words in which *e* and *i* are pronounced separately, such as *notoriety.*

10. **Words Ending in C.** Before an ending beginning with *e, i,* or *y,* words ending in *c* commonly add *k* to keep the *c* hard: *panic, panicky.*

11. **Compounds.** Some compounds written as a unit bring together unusual combinations of letters. They are seldom changed on this account. *Bookkeeper, roommate.*

    Exceptions: A few words are regularly clipped when compounded, such as *full* in *awful, cupful,* etc.

RULES OF WORD DIVISION

1. Do not divide a one-syllable word. This includes past tenses like *walked* and *dreamed,* which should never be split before the *-ed* ending.

2. Do not divide a word so that a single letter is left at the end of a line, as in *a•bout,* or so that a single letter starts the following line, as in *cit•y.*

3. Hyphenated compounds should preferably be divided only after the hyphen. If the first portion of the compound is a single letter, however, as in *D-day,* the word should not be divided.

4. Word segments like *-ceous, -scious, -sial, -tion, -tious* should not be divided.

5. The portion of a word left at the end of a line should not encourage a misleading pronunciation, as would be the case if *acetate,* a three-syllable word, were divided after the first *e.*

WORDS OFTEN MISSPELLED

We have listed here some of the words that have traditionally proved difficult to spell. The list includes not only "exceptions," words that defy common spelling rules, but some that pose problems even while adhering to these conventions.

aberrant	annual	believe	census	controversy
abscess	anoint	beneficial	certain	convalesce
absence	anonymous	beneficiary	challenge	convenience
absorption	answer	benefit	chandelier	coolly
abundance	antarctic	benefited	changeable	copyright
accede	antecedent	blizzard	changing	cornucopia
acceptance	anticipation	bludgeon	characteristic	corollary
accessible	antihistamine	bologna	chief	corporation
accidentally	anxiety	bookkeeping	choir	correlate
accommodate	aperitif	bouillon	choose	correspondence
according	apocryphal	boundaries	cinnamon	correspondent
accordion	apostasy	breathe	circuit	counselor
accumulate	apparent	brief	civilized	counterfeit
accustom	appearance	brilliant	clothes	courageous
achievement	appetite	broccoli	codeine	courteous
acknowledge	appreciate	bronchial	collateral	crisis
acknowledgment	appropriate	brutality	colloquial	criticism
acoustics	approximate	bulletin	colonel	criticize
acquaintance	apropos	buoy	colossal	culinary
acquiesce	arctic	buoyant	column	curiosity
acquire	arguing	bureau	coming	curriculum
acquittal	argument	bureaucracy	commemorate	cylinder
across	arouse	burglary	commission	
address	arrangement	business	commitment	debt
adequate	arthritis		committed	debtor
adherent	article	cafeteria	committee	deceive
adjourn	artificial	caffeine	comparative	decide
admittance	asked	calisthenics	comparison	decision
adolescence	assassin	camaraderie	competition	decisive
adolescent	assess	camouflage	competitive	defendant
advantageous	asthma	campaign	complaint	definite
advertisement	athlete	cancel	concede	definitely
affidavit	athletic	cancellation	conceivable	dependent
against	attorneys	candidate	conceive	de rigueur
aggravate	author	cantaloupe	condemn	descend
aggression	authoritative	capacity	condescend	descendant
aging	auxiliary	cappuccino	conferred	description
aisle		carburetor	confidential	desiccate
all right	bachelor	career	congratulate	desirable
alien	balance	careful	conscience	despair
allegiance	bankruptcy	carriage	conscientious	desperate
almost	barbiturate	carrying	conscious	destroy
although	barrette	casserole	consensus	develop
always	basically	category	consequently	development
amateur	basis	caterpillar	consistent	diabetes
analysis	beggar	cavalry	consummate	diaphragm
analytical	beginning	ceiling	continuous	different
analyze	belief	cellar	control	dilemma
anesthetic	believable	cemetery	controlled	dining

diocese
diphtheria
disappear
disappearance
disappoint
disastrous
discipline
disease
dissatisfied
dissident
dissipate
distinguish
divide
divine
doesn't
dormitory
duly
dumbbell
during

easier
easily
ecstasy
effervescent
efficacy
efficiency
efficient
eighth
eightieth
electrician
eligibility
eligible
eliminate
ellipsis
embarrass
encouraging
endurance
energetic
enforceable
enthusiasm
environment
equipped
erroneous
especially
esteemed
exacerbate
exaggerate
exceed
excel
excellent
except
exceptionally
excessive
executive
exercise

exhibition
exhilarate
existence
expense
experience
experiment
explanation
exquisite
extemporaneous
extraordinary
extremely

facilities
fallacy
familiar
fascinate
fascism
feasible
February
fictitious
fiend
fierce
fiftieth
finagle
finally
financial
foliage
forcible
forehead
foreign
forfeit
formally
forte
fortieth
fortunately
forty
fourth
friend
frieze
fundamental
furniture

galoshes
gauge
genealogy
generally
gnash
government
governor
graffiti
grammar
grateful
grievance
grievous
guarantee

guard
guidance

handkerchief
haphazard
harass
harebrained
hazard
height
hemorrhage
hemorrhoid
hereditary
heroes
hierarchy
hindrance
hoping
hors d'oeuvres
huge
humorous
hundredth
hydraulic
hygiene
hygienist
hypocrisy

icicle
identification
idiosyncrasy
imaginary
immediately
immense
impresario
inalienable
incident
incidentally
inconvenience
incredible
indelible
independent
indestructible
indictment
indigestible
indispensable
inevitable
inferred
influential
initial
initiative
innocuous
innuendo
inoculation
inscrutable
installation
instantaneous
intellectual

intelligence
intercede
interest
interfere
intermittent
intimate
inveigle
irrelevant
irresistible
island

jealous
jeopardize
journal
judgment
judicial

khaki
kindergarten
knowledge

laboratory
laid
larynx
leery
leisure
length
liable
liaison
libel
library
license
lieutenant
likelihood
liquefy
liqueur
literature
livelihood
loneliness
losing
lovable

magazine
maintenance
manageable
management
maneuver
manufacturer
maraschino
marital
marriage
marriageable
mathematics
mayonnaise
meant

medicine
medieval
memento
mileage
millennium
miniature
minuet
miscellaneous
mischievous
misspell
mistletoe
moccasin
molasses
molecule
monotonous
mortgage
murmur
muscle
mutual
mysterious

naive
naturally
necessarily
necessary
necessity
neighbor
neither
nickel
niece
ninetieth
ninety
ninth
noticeable
notoriety
nuptial

obbligato
occasion
occasionally
occurred
occurrence
offense
official
omission
omit
omitted
oneself
ophthalmology
opinion
opportunity
optimism
optimist
ordinarily
origin

original
outrageous

paean
pageant
paid
pamphlet
paradise
parakeet
parallel
paralysis
paralyze
paraphernalia
parimutuel
parliament
partial
participate
particularly
pasteurize
pastime
pavilion
peaceable
peasant
peculiar
penicillin
perceive
perform
performance
peril
permanent
permissible
perpendicular
perseverance
persistent
personnel
perspiration
persuade
persuasion
persuasive
petition
philosophy
physician
piccolo
plaited
plateau
plausible
playwright
pleasant
plebeian
pneumonia
poinsettia
politician
pomegranate
possess
possession

possibility
possible
practically
practice
precede
precedence
precisely
predecessor
preference
preferred
prejudice
preparatory
prescription
prevalent
primitive
prior
privilege
probability
probably
procedure
proceed
professor
proffer
pronounce
pronunciation
propagate
protégé(e)
psychiatry
psychology
pursuant
pursue
pursuit
putrefy

quantity
questionnaire
queue

rarefy
recede
receipt
receivable
receive
recipe
reciprocal
recognize
recommend
reference
referred
reign
relegate
relevant
relieve
religious
remembrance

reminisce
remiss
remittance
rendezvous
repetition
replaceable
representative
requisition
resistance
responsibility
restaurant
restaurateur
resuscitate
reticence
reveille
rhyme
rhythm
riddance
ridiculous
rococo
roommate

sacrifice
sacrilegious
safety
salary
sandwich
sarsaparilla
sassafras
satisfaction
scarcity
scene
scenery
schedule
scheme
scholarly
scissors
secede
secrecy
secretary
seize
seizure
separate
separately
sergeant
serviceable
seventieth
several
sheik
shepherd
sheriff
shining
shoulder
shrapnel
siege

sieve
significance
silhouette
similar
simultaneity
simultaneous
sincerely
sixtieth
skiing
socially
society
solemn
soliloquy
sophomore
sorority
sovereign
spaghetti
spatial
special
specifically
specimen
speech
sponsor
spontaneous
statistics
statute
stevedore
stiletto
stopped
stopping
strength
strictly
studying
stupefy
submitted
substantial
subtle
subtly
succeed
successful
succession
successive
sufficient
superintendent
supersede
supplement
suppress
surprise
surveillance
susceptible
suspicion
sustenance
syllable
symmetrical
sympathize

sympathy
synchronous
synonym
syphilis
systematically

tariff
temperament
temperature
temporarily
tendency
tentative
terrestrial
therefore
thirtieth
thorough
thought
thousandth
through
till
titillate
together
tonight
tournament
tourniquet
tragedy
tragically
transferred
transient
tries
truly
twelfth
twentieth
typical
tyranny

unanimous
undoubtedly
unique
unison
unmanageable
unnecessary
until
upholsterer
usable
usage
using
usually
utilize

vacancy
vacuum
vague
valuable

variety	village	whim	writing	yacht
vegetable	villain	wholly	written	yield
veil		whose	wrote	
vengeance	warrant	wield	wrought	zealous
vermilion	Wednesday	woolen		zucchini
veterinarian	weird	wretched	xylophone	
vichyssoise	wherever			

ABBREVIATIONS USED

adj.	adjective	*colloq.*	colloquial	*interj.*	interjection	*pron.*	pronoun
adv.	adverb	*conj.*	conjunction	*l.c.*	lower case	*pt.*	past tense
art.	article	*def.*	definition	*n.*	noun	*sing.*	singular
aux.	auxiliary	*esp.*	especially	*pl.*	plural	*usu.*	usually
cap.	capital	*fem.*	feminine	*prep.*	preposition	*v.*	verb

PRONUNCIATION KEY

a	act, bat	**ī**	ice, bite	**ou**	out, loud	**z**	zeal, lazy, those
ā	able, cape	**j**	just, edge	**p**	page, stop	**zh**	vision, measure
â	air, dare	**k**	kept, make	**r**	read, cry	**ə**	occurs only in un-
ä	art, calm	**l**	low, all	**s**	see, miss		accented syllables
b	back, rub	**m**	my, him	**sh**	shoe, push		and indicates the
ch	chief, beach	**n**	now, on	**t**	ten, bit		sound of
d	do, bed	**ng**	sing, England	**th**	thin, path		a *in* alone
e	ebb, set	**o**	box, hot	**th**	that, other		e *in* system
ē	equal, bee	**ō**	over, no	**u**	up, love		i *in* easily
f	fit, puff	**ô**	order, bail	**û**	urge, burn		o *in* gallop
g	give, beg	**oi**	oil, joy	**v**	voice, live		u *in* circus
h	hit, hear	**o͝o**	book, put	**w**	west, away		
i	if, big	**o͞o**	ooze, rule	**y**	yes, young		

a, *adj. or indef. art.* 1. some. 2. one. 3. any.

aard′vark′, *n.* African ant-eating mammal.

a•back′, *adv.* by surprise.

ab′a•cus, *n.* 1. calculating device using rows of movable beads. 2. slab at top of column.

a•baft′, *prep. Naut.* 1. behind. —*adv.* 2. at the stern.

a•ban′don, *v.* 1. leave completely; forsake. 2. give up. —*n.* 3. freedom from constraint. —**a•ban′doned,** *adj.* —**a•ban′don•ment,** *n.*

a•base′, *v.,* **abased, abasing.** lower; degrade. —**a•base′ment,** *n.*

a•bash′, *v.* embarrass or shame.

a•bate′, *v.,* **abated, abating.** lessen or subside. —**a•bate′ment,** *n.*

ab•at•toir′ (-twär′), *n.* slaughterhouse.

ab′bé (-ā), *n.* abbot; priest.

ab′bess, *n.* convent head.

ab′bey (-ē), *n., pl.* **-beys.** monastery or convent.

ab′bot, *n.* monastery head.

ab•bre′vi•ate′, *v.,* **-ated, -ating.** shorten. —**ab•bre′vi•a′tion,** *n.*

ABC, *n., pl.* **ABC's, ABCs.** 1. alphabet. 2. (*pl.*) fundamentals.

ab′di•cate′, *v.,* **-cated, -cating.** give up (power, office, etc.). —**ab′di•ca′-tion,** *n.*

ab′do•men (-də-), *n.* part of body between thorax and pelvis; belly. —**ab•dom′i•nal** (-dom′-), *adj.*

ab•duct′, *v.* kidnap. —**ab•duc′tion,** *n.* —**ab•duc′tor,** *n.*

a•beam′, *adv. Naut.* across a ship.

a•bed′, *adv.* in bed.

ab′er•ra′tion, *n.* 1. deviation from normal or right course. 2. mental lapse.

a•bet′, *v.,* **abetted, abetting.** encourage in wrongdoing. —**a•bet′tor, a•bet′ter,** *n.*

a•bey′ance, *n.* temporary inactivity.

ab•hor′, *v.,* **-horred, -horring.** loathe; consider repugnant. —**ab•hor′-rence,** *n.* —**ab•hor′rent,** *adj.*

a•bide′, *v.,* **abode** or **abided, abiding.** 1. remain; stay. 2. dwell. 3. wait for. 4. agree; conform. 5. *Informal.* tolerate; bear.

a•bid′ing, *adj.* steadfast; lasting.

a•bil′i•ty, *n., pl.* **-ties.** 1. power or talent. 2. competence.

ab′ject, *adj.* 1. humiliating. 2. despicable. —**ab′ject•ly,** *adv.* —**ab•jec′-tion,** *n.*

ab•jure′, *v.,* **-jured, -juring.** renounce or forswear. —**ab′ju•ra′tion,** *n.*

ab′la•tive, *adj. Gram.* denoting origin, means, etc.

a•blaze′, *adv., adj.* burning; on fire.

a′ble, *adj.,* **abler, ablest.** 1. having sufficient power or qualification. 2. competent. —**a′bly,** *adv.*

ab•lu′tion, *n.* washing, esp. as ritual.

ab′ne•gate′, *v.,* **-gated, -gating.** deny to oneself. —**ab′ne•ga′tion,** *n.*

ab•nor′mal, *adj.* not normal; not usual or typical. —**ab′nor•mal′i•ty,** *n.*

a•board′, *adv.* 1. on a ship, train, etc. —*prep.* 2. on.

a•bode′, *n.* 1. home. 2. stay.

a•bol′ish, *v.* end, annul, or make void. —**ab′o•li′tion,** *n.* —**ab′o•li′-tion•ist,** *n.*

A′-bomb′, *n.* atomic bomb.

a•bom′i•na•ble, *adj.* hateful; loathesome. —**a•bom′i•na•bly,** *adv.*

a•bom′i•nate′, *v.,* **-nated, -nating.** abhor or hate. —**a•bom′i•na′tion,** *n.*

ab′o•rig′i•nal, *adj.* 1. original; first. —*n.* 2. aborigine.

ab′o•rig•i•ne′ (-rij′ə nē′), *n.* original inhabitant of a land.

a•bort′, *v.* 1. have or cause abortion. 2. end prematurely. —**a•bor′tive,** *adj.*

a•bor′tion, *n.* expulsion of fetus before it is viable. —**a•bor′tion•ist,** *n.*

a•bound′, *v.* be or have plentifully; teem.

a•bout′, *prep.* 1. concerning. 2. near, in, on, or around. 3. ready. —*adv.* 4.

approximately. 5. *Informal.* almost. 6. on all sides. 7. oppositely. —*adj.* 8. active.

a•bove′, *adv.* 1. higher. 2. previously. 3. in or to heaven. —*prep.* 4. higher or greater than. —*adj.* 5. foregoing.

a•bove′board′, *adv., adj.* honest; fair.

a•brade′, *v.,* **abraded, abrading.** wear or scrape off. —**a•bra′sion,** *n.* —**a•bra′sive,** *n., adj.*

a•breast′, *adv., adj.* side by side.

a•bridge′, *v.,* **abridged, abridging.** shorten. —**a•bridg′ment,** *n.*

a•broad′, *adv., adj.* 1. out of one's own country. 2. in circulation.

ab′ro•gate′, *v.,* **-gated, -gating.** end, annul, or repeal. —**ab′ro•ga′tion,** *n.*

ab•rupt′, *adj.* 1. sudden; unexpected. 2. steep. —**ab•rupt′ly,** *adv.* —**ab•rupt′ness,** *n.*

ab′scess, *n.* infected, pus-filled place.

ab•scond′, *v.* depart suddenly and secretly.

ab′sent, *adj.* 1. not present. 2. lacking. —*v.* (ab sent′). 3. keep away. —**ab′sence,** *n.*

ab′sen•tee′, *n.* absent person.

ab′sent-mind′ed, *adj.* forgetful or preoccupied.

ab′sinthe, *n.* bitter, green liqueur.

ab′so•lute′, *adj.* 1. complete; perfect. 2. pure. 3. unrestricted. 4. despotic. —**ab′so•lute′ly,** *adv.*

ab•solve′ (-zolv′), *v.,* **-solved, -solving.** 1. release or free. 2. remit sins of. 3. forgive. —**ab′so•lu′tion,** *n.*

ab•sorb′, *v.* 1. take in. 2. occupy completely; fascinate. —**ab•sor′bent,** *adj., n.* —**ab•sorp′tion,** *n.* —**ab•sorp′tive,** *adj.*

ab•stain′, *v.* refrain (from). —**ab•sten′tion,** *n.*

ab•ste′mi•ous, *adj.* moderate in eating, drinking, etc.

ab′sti•nence, *n.* forebearance; self-restraint. —**ab′sti•nent,** *adj.*

ab′stract, *adj.* 1. apart from specific matter. 2. theoretical. 3. hard to understand. —*n.* 4. summary. 5. essence. —*v.* (ab strakt′) 6. remove or steal. 7. summarize. —**ab•strac′tion,** *n.*

ab•stract′ed, *adj.* preoccupied and absent-minded.

ab•struse′, *adj.* hard to understand.

ab•surd′, *adj.* ridiculous. —**ab•surd′-ly,** *adv.* —**ab•surd′i•ty, ab•surd′-ness,** *n.*

a•bun′dance, *n.* plentiful supply. —**a•bun′dant,** *adj.* —**a•bun′dant-ly,** *adv.*

a•buse′, *v.,* **abused, abusing,** *n.* —*v.* (-byoōz′) 1. use or treat wrongly. —*n.* (-byoōs′) 2. wrong use or treatment. 3. insult. —**a•bu′sive,** *adj.*

a•but′, *v.,* **abutted, abutting.** be adjacent to.

a•but′ment, *n.* structural part sustaining pressure.

a•bys′mal (-biz′-), *adj.* deep; measureless.

a•byss′, *n.* 1. very deep chasm. 2. hell. Also, **a•bysm′** (ə biz′əm).

a•ca′cia (-kā′shə), *n.* tropical tree or shrub.

ac′a•dem′ic, *adj.* Also, **ac′a•dem′i•cal.** 1. of a school, college, etc. 2. theoretical. —*n.* 2. college student or teacher.

a•cad′e•my, *n.* 1. school. 2. cultural society.

a•can′thus, *n.* Mediterranean plant.

ac•cede′, *v.,* **-ceded, -ceding.** 1. consent. 2. reach.

ac•cel′er•ate′, *v.,* **-ated, -ating.** speed up; hasten. —**ac•cel′er•a′tion,** *n.*

ac•cel′er•a′tor, *n.* pedal that controls the speed of a vehicle.

ac′cent, *n.* 1. emphasis. 2. characteristic pronunciation. 3. mark showing stress, etc. —*v.* (ak sent′) 4. emphasize.

ac•cen′tu•ate′, *v.,* **-ated, -ating.** stress or emphasize. —**ac•cen′tu•a′-tion,** *n.*

ac•cept′, *v.* 1. take or receive. 2. agree to. 3. believe. —**ac•cept′a-ble, ac•cept′ed,** *adj.* —**ac•cept′a-bil′i•ty,** *n.* —**ac•cept′a•bly,** *adv.* —**ac•cept′ance,** *n.*

ac′cess, *n.* 1. right or means of approach. 2. attack.

ac•ces′si•ble, *adj.* easy to reach or influence. —**ac•ces′si•bil′i•ty,** *n.*

ac•ces′sion, *n.* 1. attainment of an office, etc. 2. increase.

ac•ces′so•ry, *n.,* *pl.* **-ries.** 1. something added for convenience, decoration, etc. 2. one who abets a felony.

ac′ci•dence, *n.* part of grammar dealing with inflection.

ac′ci•dent, *n.* unexpected event, usually unfortunate. —**ac′ci•den′tal,** *adj.* —**ac′ci•den′tal•ly,** *adv.*

ac′ci•dent-prone′, *adj.* inclined to have accidents.

ac•claim′, *v.* 1. salute with applause, cheers, etc. —*n.* 2. applause, cheers, etc. —**ac′cla•ma′tion,** *n.*

ac•cli′mate, *v.,* **-ated, -ating.** accustom to new conditions. Also, **ac•cli′-ma•tize′.**

ac•cliv′i•ty, *n.,* *pl.* **-ties.** upward slope.

ac•com′mo•date′, *v.,* **-dated, -dating.** 1. do a favor for. 2. supply. 3. provide with room, food, etc. 4. adjust.

ac•com′mo•dat′ing, *adj.* helpful; obliging.

ac•com′mo•da′tion, *n.* 1. act of accommodating. 2. (*pl.*) space for lodging or travel.

ac•com′pa•ni•ment, *n.* 1. something added as decoration, etc. 2. subsidiary music for performer.

ac•com′pa•ny, *v.,* **-nied, -nying.** 1. go or be with. 2. provide musical accompaniment for. —**ac•com′pa•nist,** *n.*

ac•com′plice, *n.* partner in crime.

ac•com′plish, *v.* do or finish.

ac•com′plished, *adj.* 1. done; finished. 2. expert.

ac•com′plish•ment, *n.* 1. completion. 2. skill or learning.

ac•cord′, *v.* 1. agree; be in harmony. 2. cause to agree. 3. grant; allow. —*n.* 4. agreement; harmony. —**ac•cord′ance,** *n.* —**ac•cord′ant,** *adj.*

according to, 1. in keeping or proportion to. 2. on authority of.

ac•cord′ing•ly, *adv.* therefore.

ac•cor′di•on, *n.* bellowslike musical instrument.

ac•cost′, *v.* approach or confront.

ac•count′, *n.* 1. story; report. 2. explanation. 3. reason. 4. importance. 5. consideration. 6. record of transactions. —*v.* 7. explain. 8. report. 9. consider.

ac•count′a•ble, *adj.* 1. responsible. 2. explainable. —**ac•count′a•bly,** *adv.*

ac•count′ing, *n.* maintenance of transaction records. —**ac•count′-ant,** *n.* —**ac•count′an•cy,** *n.*

ac•cred′it, *v.* 1. attribute. 2. certify with credentials. —**ac•cred′i•ta′-tion,** *n.*

ac•cre′tion (-krē-), *n.* increase by growth or addition.

ac•crue′, *v.,* **-crued, -cruing.** be added (to). —**ac•cru′al,** *n.*

ac•cu′mu•late′, *v.,* **-lated, -lating.** gather; collect. —**ac•cu′mu•la′tion,** *n.* —**ac•cu′mu•la′tive,** *adj.* —**ac•cu•mu•la′tor,** *n.*

ac′cu•rate, *adj.* exact; correct. —**ac′-cu•rate•ly,** *adv.* —**ac′cu•ra•cy,** *n.*

ac•curs′ed, *adj.* 1. cursed. 2. hateful. Also, **ac•curst′.**

ac•cu′sa•tive, *adj. Gram.* denoting direct object of a verb.

ac•cuse′, *v.,* **-cused, -cusing.** blame; charge. —**ac′cu•sa′tion,** *n.* —**ac•cus′er,** *n.* —**ac•cus′a•to′ry,** *adj.*

ac•cus′tom, *v.* make used to.

ac•cus′tomed, *adj.* 1. usual; habitual. 2. habituated.

ace, *n.* 1. playing card with single spot. 2. expert, esp. military pilot.

a•cer′bi•ty (-sûr′-), *n.* 1. sourness. 2. severity.

ac′e•tate′, *n.* salt or ester of acetic acid.

a•ce′tic (-sē′-), *adj.* of or producing vinegar.

a•cet′y•lene′, *n.* gas used in welding, etc.

ache, *v.,* **ached, aching,** *n.* —*v.* 1. suffer dull pain. —*n.* 2. dull pain.

a•chieve′, *v.,* **achieved, achieving.** accomplish; bring about. —**a•chieve′ment,** *n.*

ach′ro•mat′ic (ak′-), *adj.* colorless.

ac′id, *n.* 1. chemical compound containing hydrogen replaceable by a metal to form a salt. 2. sour substance. —*adj.* 3. of acids. 4. sour or sharp. —**a•cid′i•ty,** *n.*

ac•i•do′sis, *n.* poisoning by acids.

a•cid′u•lous, (-sij′-), *adj.* sour or sharp.

ack′-ack′, *n. Slang.* anti-aircraft fire.

ac•knowl′edge, *v.,* **-edged, -edging.** 1. recognize; admit. 2. show appreciation for. —**ac•knowl′edg•ment,** *n.*

ac′me, *n.* highest point.

ac′ne, *n.* skin eruption.

ac′o•lyte′, *n.* altar attendant.

ac′o•nite′, *n.* plant yielding medicine and poison.

a′corn, *n.* fruit of the oak.

a•cous′tic, *adj.* of sound or hearing. —**a•cous′ti•cal•ly,** *adv.*

a•cous′tics, *n.* 1. science of sound. 2. sound qualities.

ac•quaint′, *v.* make known or familiar.

ac•quaint′ance, *n.* 1. someone personally known. 2. general knowledge.

ac′qui•esce′, v., **-esced**, **-escing.** agree or comply. —**ac′qui•es′cence**, n. —**ac′qui•es′cent**, adj.

ac•quire′, v., **-quired**, **-quiring.** get; obtain. —**ac•quire′ment**, n.

ac′qui•si′tion, n. 1. acquiring. 2. something acquired.

ac•quis′i•tive, adj. eager to acquire. —**ac•quis′i•tive•ness**, n.

ac•quit′, v., **-quitted**, **-quitting.** 1. free of blame or guilt. 2. behave or conduct. —**ac•quit′tal**, n.

a′cre, n. unit of land area (1/640 sq. mi. or 43,560 sq. ft.). —**a′cre•age**, n.

ac′rid, adj. sharp; biting.

ac′ri•mo•ny, n. harshness of manner or speech. —**ac′ri•mo′ni•ous**, adj.

ac′ro•bat′, n. performer on trapeze, etc. —**ac′ro•bat′ic**, adj.

ac′ro•nym, n. word formed from successive initials or groups of letters, as NATO, UNICEF.

a•cross′, prep. 1. from side to side of. 2. on the other side of. —adv. 3. from one side to another.

a•cryl′ic, n. synthetic fiber.

act, n. 1. something done. 2. law or decree. 3. part of a play, opera, etc. —v. 4. do something. 5. behave. 6. pretend. 7. perform, as on stage.

act′ing, adj. substitute.

ac′tin•ism, n. action of radiant energy in causing chemical changes. —**ac•tin′ic**, adj.

ac′tion, n. 1. process or state of being active. 2. something done. 3. behavior. 4. combat. 5. lawsuit.

ac′tion•a•ble, adj. providing grounds for a lawsuit.

ac′ti•vate′, v., **-vated**, **-vating.** make active. —**ac′ti•va′tion**, n.

ac′tive, adj. 1. in action; busy, nimble, or lively. 2. Gram. indicating that the subject performs the action of the verb. —**ac′tive•ly**, adv. —**ac•tiv′i•ty**, n.

ac′tor, n. performer in play. —**ac′tress**, n.fem..

ac′tu•al (-choo-), adj. real. —**ac′tu•al•ly**, adv. —**ac′tu•al′i•ty**, n.

ac′tu•ar′y, n., pl. **-aries.** calculator of insurance rates, etc. —**ac′tu•ar′i•al**, adj.

ac′tu•ate′, v., **-ated**, **-ating.** cause to act; effect.

a•cu′men (-kyoo′-), n. mental keenness.

ac′u•punc′ture, n. Chinese art of healing by inserting needles into the skin.

a•cute′, adj. 1. sharp; pointed. 2. severe. 3. crucial. 4. keen, clever. 5. high-pitched. —**a•cute′ly**, adv. —**a•cute′ness**, n.

ad, n. Informal. advertisement.

A.D., Anno Domini: in the year of our Lord.

ad′age, n. proverb.

a•da′gio (ə dä′ jō), adj. slow.

ad′a•mant′, n. 1. hard substance. —adj. 2. Also, **ad′a•man′tine.** unyielding.

a•dapt′, v. adjust to requirements. —**a•dapt′a•ble**, adj. —**a•dapt′a•bil′i•ty**, n. —**ad′ap•ta′tion**, n.

add, v. 1. unite or join. 2. find the sum (of). 3. increase.

ad•den′dum, n., pl. **-da.** something to be added.

ad′der, n. small, venomous snake.

ad′dict, n. 1. person habituated to a drug, etc. —v. (ə dikt′). 2. habituate (to). —**ad•dic′tion**, n. —**ad•dic′tive**, adj.

ad•di′tion, n. 1. adding. 2. anything added. 3. **in addition to**, besides. —**ad•di′tion•al**, adj. —**ad•di′tion•al•ly**, adv.

ad′di•tive, n. added ingredient.

ad′dle, v., **-dled**, **-dling.** 1. confuse. 2. spoil.

ad•dress′, n. 1. formal speech. 2. place of residence. 3. manner of speaking. 4. skill. —v. 5. speak or write (to). 6. send. 7. apply (oneself). —**ad′dress•ee′**, n.

ad•duce′, v., **-duced**, **-ducing.** present; cite.

ad′e•noid′, n. mass of tissue in upper pharynx.

a•dept′, adj. 1. skilled. —n. (ad′ept). 2. expert.

ad′e•quate, adj. sufficient; fit. —**ad′e•quate•ly**, adv. —**ad′e•qua•cy**, n.

ad•here′, v., **-hered**, **-hering.** 1. stick or cling. 2. be faithful or loyal. —**ad•her′ence**, n. —**ad•her′ent**, n., adj. —**ad•he′sion**, n. —**ad•he′sive**, n., adj.

ad hoc, for a specified purpose.

a•dieu′ (ə dyoo′, ə doo′), interj., n. French. good-by.

ad′i•os′, interj. Spanish. good-by!

ad′i•pose′, adj. fatty.

ad′ja′cent, adj. near; adjoining.

ad′jec•tive, n. word describing a noun. —**ad′jec•ti′val**, adj.

ad•join′, v. be next to.

ad•journ′, v. suspend (meeting) till another time. —**ad•journ′ment**, n.

ad•judge′, v., **-judged**, **-judging.** 1. decree or decide. 2. award.

ad•ju′di•cate′, v., **-cated**, **-cating.** decide on as a judge. —**ad•ju′di•ca′tion**, n.

ad′junct, n. something added.

ad•jure′, v., **-jured**, **-juring.** request or command, esp. under oath.

ad•just′, v. 1. fit; adapt. 2. regulate. 3. settle. —**ad•just′a•ble**, adj. —**ad•just′er, ad•jus′tor**, n. —**ad•just′ment**, n.

ad′ju•tant, n. military assistant to commandant.

ad-lib′, v., **-libbed**, **-libbing.** Informal. improvise.

ad•min′is•ter, v. 1. manage; direct. 2. dispense or give.

ad•min′is•tra′tion, n. 1. management. 2. dispensing. 3. executive officials. —**ad•min′is•tra′tive**, adj.

ad•min′is•tra′tor, n. manager.

ad′mi•ral, n. high-ranking navy officer.

ad′mi•ral•ty, n. navy department.

ad•mire′, v., **-mired**, **-miring.** regard with pleasure, approval, etc. —**ad•mir′er**, n. —**ad′mi•ra′tion**, n.

ad•mis′si•ble, adj. allowable.

ad•mis′sion, n. 1. act of admitting. 2. entrance price. 3. confession or acknowledgment.

ad•mit′, v., **-mitted**, **-mitting.** 1. allow to enter. 2. permit. 3. confess or acknowledge. —**ad•mit′tance**, n.

ad•mit′ted•ly, adv. without evasion or doubt.

ad•mix′ture, n. thing added.

ad•mon′ish, v. 1. warn. 2. reprove. —**ad′mo•ni′tion**, n. —**ad•mon′i•to′ry**, adj.

a•do′, n. activity; fuss.

a•do′be (-bē), n. sun-dried brick.

ad′o•les′cence, n. period between childhood and adulthood. —**ad′o•les′cent**, adj., n.

a•dopt′, v. take or accept as one's own. —**a•dop′tion**, n. —**a•dopt′ive**, adj.

a•dore′, v., **adored**, **adoring.** regard highly; worship. —**a•dor′a•ble**, adj. —**ad′o•ra′tion**, n.

a•dorn′, v. decorate. —**a•dorn′ment**, n.

ad•ren′al•in, n. glandular secretion that speeds heart, etc.

a•drift′, adv., adj. floating about, esp. helplessly.

a•droit′, adj. expert; deft. —**a•droit′ly**, adv. —**a•droit′ness**, n.

a·dult′, *adj.* 1. full-grown; mature. —*n.* 2. full-grown person. —**a·dult′-hood**, *n.*

a·dul′ter·ate′, *v.*, -ated, -ating. make impure. —**a·dul′ter·a′tion**, *n.* —**a·dul′ter·ant**, *n.*

a·dul′ter·y, *n.* marital infidelity. —**a·dul′ter·er**, *n.* —**a·dul′ter·ess**, *n.fem.* —**a·dul′ter·ous**, *adj.*

ad·vance′, *v.*, -vanced, -vancing. 1. move forward. 2. propose. 3. raise in rank, price, etc. 4. supply beforehand; lend. —*n.* 5. forward move. 6. promotion. 7. increase. 8. loan. 9. friendly gesture. —*adj.* 10. early. —**ad·vance′ment**, *n.*

ad·vanced′, *adj.* 1. progressive. 2. relatively learned, old, etc.

ad·van′tage, *n.* 1. more favorable condition. 2. benefit. —**ad′van·ta′-geous**, *adj.*

ad′vent, *n.* 1. arrival. 2. coming of Christ. 3. (*cap.*) month before Christmas.

ad′ven·ti′tious, *adj.* accidentally added.

ad·ven′ture, *n.*, *v.*, -tured, -turing. —*n.* 1. risky undertaking. 2. exciting event. —*v.* 3. risk or dare. —**ad·ven′tur·er**, *n.* —**ad·ven′tur·ous**, *adj.*

ad′verb, *n. Gram.* word modifying a verb, verbal noun, or other adverb. —**ad·ver′bi·al**, *adj.*

ad′ver·sar′y, *n.*, *pl.* -saries. opponent.

ad·verse′, *adj.* opposing; antagonistic. —**ad·verse′ly**, *adv.*

ad·ver′si·ty, *n.*, *pl.* -ties. misfortune.

ad·vert′, *v.* refer.

ad′ver·tise′, *v.*, -tised, -tising. bring to public notice. —**ad′ver·tis′er**, *n.* —**ad′ver·tise′ment**, *n.* —**ad′ver·tis′ing**, *n.*

ad·vice′, *n.* 1. opinion offered. 2. news.

ad·vis′a·ble, *adj.* wise; desirable. —**ad·vis′a·bil′i·ty**, *n.*

ad·vise′, *v.*, -vised, -vising. 1. offer an opinion to. 2. recommend. 3. consult (with). 4. give news. —**ad·vis′er**, **ad·vi′sor**, *n.* —**ad·vise′ment**, *n.* —**ad·vi′so·ry**, *adj.*

ad′vo·cate′, *v.*, -cated, -cating, *n.* —*v.* (-kāt′). 1. urge; recommend. —*n.* (-kit). 2. supporter of cause. 3. lawyer. —**ad′vo·ca·cy**, *n.*

adz, *n.* axlike tool.

ae′gis (ē′jis) *n.* sponsorship.

ae′on (ē′ən), *n.* long time.

aer′ate, *v.*, -ated, -ating. expose to air.

aer′i·al, *adj.* 1. of or in air. 2. lofty. —*n.* 3. radio antenna.

aer′o·dy·nam′ics, *n.* science of action of air against solids. —**aer′o·dy·nam′ic**, *adj.*

aer′o·naut′, *n.* pilot.

aer′o·nau′tics, *n.* science of flight in aircraft. —**aer′o·naut′i·cal**, *adj.*

aer′o·plane′, *n. Brit.* airplane.

aer′o·space′, *n.* 1. earth's atmosphere and the space beyond. —*adj.* 2. operating in aerospace.

aer′o·sol′, *n.* 1. liquid distributed through a gas. 2. spray of such liquid.

aes·thet′ic (es-), *adj.* 1. of beauty. 2. appreciating beauty. —**aes′thete** (-thēt), *n.*

aes·thet′ics, *n.* study of beauty.

a·far′, *adv.* at a distance.

af′fa·ble, *adj.* friendly; cordial. —**af′-fa·bil′i·ty**, *n.*

af·fair′, *n.* 1. matter of business. 2. event. 3. amorous relationship.

af·fect′, *v.* 1. act on. 2. impress (feelings). 3. pretend to possess or feel.

af·fect′ed, *adj.* 1. vain; haughty. 2. diseased; infected. —**af·fect′ed·ly**, *adv.*

af′fec·ta′tion, *n.* pretense.

af·fec′tion, *n.* 1. love. 2. disease.

af·fec′tion·ate, *adj.* loving; fond. —**af·fec′tion·ate·ly**, *adv.*

af·fi′ance (ə fī′-), *v.* -anced, -ancing. become engaged to.

af′fi·da′vit, *n.* written statement under oath.

af·fil′i·ate′, *v.*, -ated, -ating, *n.* —*v.* 1. join; connect. —*n.* (-ē it). 2. associate. —**af·fil′i·a′tion**, *n.*

af·fin′i·ty, *n.*, *pl.* -ties. 1. attraction. 2. similarity.

af·firm′, *v.* 1. state; assert. 2. ratify. —**af′fir·ma′tion**, *n.*

af·firm′a·tive, *adj.* saying yes; affirming.

af·fix′, *v.* 1. attach. —*n.* (af′iks). 2. added part.

af·flict′, *v.* distress; trouble. —**af·flic′tion**, *n.*

af′flu·ent, *adj.* rich; abundant. —**af′flu·ence**, *n.*

af·ford′, *v.* 1. have resources enough. 2. provide.

af·fray′, *n.* fight.

af·front′, *n.*, *v.* insult.

af′ghan, *n.* woolen blanket.

a·field′, *adv.* astray.

a·fire′, *adv.*, *adj.* on fire. Also, **a·flame′**.

a·float′, *adv.*, *adj.* 1. floating. 2. in circulation.

a·foot′, *adv.*, *adj.* 1. on foot. 2. in existence.

a·fore′said′, *adj.* said before. Also, **a·fore′men′tioned.**

a·fraid′, *adj.* full of fear.

a·fresh′, *adj.* again.

Af′ri·can, *n.* native of Africa. —**Af′ri·can**, *adj.*

aft, *adv. Naut.* at or toward the stern.

af′ter, *prep.* 1. behind. 2. about. 3. later than. 4. next to. 5. in imitation of. —*adv.* 6. behind. 7. later.

af′ter·ef·fect′, *n.* reaction.

af′ter·life′, *n.* life after death.

af′ter·math′, *n.* results.

af′ter·noon′, *n.* period between noon and evening.

af′ter·thought′, *n.* later thought.

af′ter·ward, *adv.* later. Also, **af′ter·wards.**

a·gain′, *adv.* 1. once more. 2. besidès.

a·gainst′, *prep.* 1. opposed to. 2. in or into contact with.

ag′ate, *n.* 1. kind of quartz. 2. child's marble.

age, *n.*, *v.*, **aged, aging.** —*n.* 1. length of time in existence. 2. stage; period. 3. legal maturity. —*v.* 4. make or become older.

ag′ed, *adj.* 1. having lived long. 2. matured. —*n.pl.* 3. elderly persons.

age′ism, *n.* discrimination against elderly persons. —**age′ist**, *n.*

age′less, *adj.* 1. apparently not aging. 2. not outdated.

a′gen·cy, *n.*, *pl.* -cies. 1. office. 2. action. 3. means.

a·gen′da, *n.pl.* matters to be dealt with.

a′gent, *n.* 1. person acting for another. 2. cause; means. 3. official.

ag·glom′er·ate′, *v.*, -ated, -ating, *adj.*, *n.* —*v.* 1. collect into a mass. —*adj.* (-ər it) 2. collected in a mass. —*n.* (-ər it). 3. such a mass. —**ag·glom′er·a′tion**, *n.*

ag′gran·dize′, *v.*, -dized, -dizing. increase in size, rank, etc. —**ag·gran′-dize·ment** (-dəz-), *n.*

ag′gra·vate′, *v.*, -vated, -vating. 1. make worse. 2. anger. —**ag′gra·va′-tion**, *n.*

ag′gre·gate, *adj.*, *n.*, *v.*, -gated, -gating. —*adj.* 1. combined. —*n.* 2. whole amount. —*v.* (-gāt′). 3. collect; gather. —**ag′gre·ga′tion**, *n.*

ag·gres′sion, *n.* hostile act; encroachment. —**ag·gres′sor**, *n.*

ag•gres′sive, *adj.* 1. boldly energetic. 2. hostile.

ag•grieve′, *v.,* **-grieved, -grieving.** wrong severely.

a•ghast′ (ə gast′), *adj.* struck with fear or horror.

ag′ile (aj′əl), *adj.* quick; nimble. **—a•gil′i•ty,** *n.*

ag′i•tate′, *v.,* **-tated, -tating.** 1. shake. 2. disturb; excite. 3. discuss. **—ag′i• ta′tion,** *n.* **—ag′i•ta′tor,** *n.*

a•glow′, *adj., adv.* glowing.

ag•nos′tic, *n.* one who believes God is beyond human knowledge. **—ag• nos′ti•cism,** *n.*

a•go′, *adj., adv.* in the past.

a•gog′, *adj.* eagerly excited.

ag′o•nize′, *v.,* **-nized, -nizing.** 1. torture. 2. suffer anxiety.

ag′o•ny, *n., pl.* **-nies.** intense pain or suffering.

a•grar′i•an, *adj.* of the land.

a•gree′, *v.,* **agreed, agreeing.** 1. consent or promise. 2. be in harmony. 3. be similar. 4. be pleasing. **—a•gree′- ment,** *n.*

a•gree′a•ble, *adj.* 1. pleasant. 2. willing. **—a•gree′a•bly,** *adv.*

ag′ri•cul′ture, *n.* science of farming. **—ag′ri•cul′tur•al,** *adj.*

a•ground′, *adv., adj. Naut.* onto the bottom.

a′gue (ā′gyoo), *n.* malarial fever.

a•head′, *adv.* 1. in front; forward. 2. winning.

a•hoy′, *interj. Naut.* Hey there!

aid, *v., n.* help.

aide-de-camp, *n., pl.* **aides-de-camp.** military assistant.

ail, *v.* trouble; distress.

ai′ler•on′, *n.* flap on airplane wing.

ail′ment, *n.* illness.

aim, *v.* 1. point or direct. 2. intend. **—***n.* 3. act of aiming. 4. target. 5. purpose. **—aim′less,** *adj.*

ain′t, *v. Illiterate or Dial.* am, is, or are not.

air, *n.* 1. mixture of gases forming atmosphere of earth. 2. appearance; manner. 3. tune. **—***v.* 4. expose to air.

air bag, bag that inflates automatically to protect passengers in a car collision.

air′borne′, *adj.* carried by air; flying.

air conditioning, control of interior air for temperature, humidity, etc. **—air-conditioned,** *adj.*

air′craft′, *n.* vehicle or vehicles for flight.

air′field′, *n.* ground area for airplanes to land on and take off from.

air′lift′, *n.* 1. major transport by air. **—***v.* 2. move by airlift.

air′line′, *n.* air transport company. Also, **airlines.**

air′man, *n.* aviator.

air′plane′, *n.* powered heavier-than-air craft with wings.

air′port′, *n.* airfield for loading, repairs, etc.

air′ship′, *n.* lighter-than-air aircraft.

air′tight′, *adj.* 1. impermeable to air. 2. perfect; free of error.

air′y, *adj.* 1. of or like air. 2. delicate. 3. unrealistic. 4. well ventilated. 5. light; gay. **—air′i•ly,** *adv.* **—air′i• ness,** *n.*

aisle, *n.* partly enclosed passageway.

a•jar′, *adj., adv.* partly opened.

a•kim′bo, *adj., adv.* with hands at hips.

a•kin′, *adj.* 1. related. 2. alike.

al′a•bas′ter, *n.* translucent gypsum.

à la carte, with each dish separately priced.

a•lac′ri•ty, *n.* quickness; readiness.

à la mode, 1. in the fashion. 2. with ice cream.

a•larm′, *n.* 1. fear of danger. 2. sudden warning. 3. call to arms. **—***v.* 4. fill with fear.

a•larm′ist, *n.* spreader of needless fear.

a•las′, *interj.* (cry of sorrow.)

al′ba•tross′, *n.* large white sea bird.

al•be′it (ôl-), *conj.* though.

al•bi′no (-bī′-), *n., pl.* **-nos.** one lacking in pigmentation.

al′bum, *n.* 1. blank book for pictures, stamps, etc. 2. container with recordings.

al•bu′men (-byoo′-), *n.* egg white.

al′che•my (-kə mē), *n.* medieval chemistry. **—al′che•mist,** *n.*

al′co•hol′, *n.* colorless intoxicating liquid formed by fermentation.

al′co•hol′ic, *adj.* 1. of alcohol. **—***n.* 2. one addicted to alcohol.

al′co•hol•ism, *n.* addiction to alcohol.

al′cove, *n.* recessed space.

al′der, *n.* small tree, usually growing in moist places.

al′der•man, *n., pl.* **-men.** representative on city council.

ale, *n.* dark, bitter beer.

a•lert′, *adj.* 1. vigilant. **—***n.* 2. air-raid alarm. **—***v.* 3. warn. **—a•lert′ly,** *adv.* **—a•lert′ness,** *n.*

al•fal′fa, *n.* forage plant.

al′ga, *n., pl.* **-gae** (-jē). water plant; seaweed.

al′ge•bra, *n.* branch of mathematics using symbols rather than specific numbers. **—al′ge•bra′ic,** *adj.*

a′li•as, *adv.* 1. otherwise known as. **—***n.* 2. assumed name.

al′i•bi′ (-bī′), *n., pl.* **-bis.** 1. defense of accused one as being elsewhere. 2. excuse.

al′ien (āl′yən), *n.* 1. foreigner. **—***adj.* 2. foreign.

al′ien•ate′, *v.,* **-ated, -ating.** lose friendship of; repel. **—al′ien•a′tion,** *n.*

al′ien•ist, *n.* psychiatrist who gives legal testimony.

a•light′, *v.* 1. dismount after travel. 2. descend to perch or sit. **—***adv., adj.* 3. lighted up.

a•lign′ (ə līn′), *v.* bring into line. **—a•lign′ment,** *n.*

a•like′, *adv.* 1. similarly. **—***adj.* 2. similar.

al′i•men′ta•ry, *adj.* of or for food.

al′i•mo′ny, *n.* money for support of a wife after separation or divorce.

a•live′, *adj.* 1. living. 2. active. 3. lively. 4. teeming; swarming.

al′ka•li′ (-lī′), *n., pl.* **-lis.** chemical that neutralizes acids to form salts. **—al′ka•line′,** *adj.*

al′ka•loid′, *n.* organic compound in plants, as morphine.

all, *adj.* 1. the whole of. 2. every. **—***n., pron.* 3. the whole; everything. **—***adv.* 4. entirely.

Al′lah, *n.* Muslim name for God.

al•lay′, *v.* quiet or lessen.

al•lege′ (ə lej′), *v.,* **-leged, -leging.** declare; state, often without proof. **—al′le•ga′tion,** *n.* **—al•leg′ed•ly,** *adv.*

al•le′giance, *n.* loyalty.

al′le•go′ry, *n., pl.* **-ries.** symbolic story. **—al′le•gor′i•cal,** *adj.*

al•le′gro, *adv. Music.* fast.

al•ler′gy, *n., pl.* **-gies.** bodily sensitiveness to certain pollens, foods, etc. **—al•ler′gic,** *adj.*

al•le′vi•ate′, *v.,* **-ated, -ating.** lessen; relieve. **—al•le′vi•a′tion,** *n.*

al′ley, *n., pl.* **-leys.** narrow street or path.

al•li′ance, *n.* 1. union; joining. 2. marriage. 3. treaty. 4. parties to treaty.

al•lied′, *adj.* 1. joined by treaty. 2. related.

al′li•ga′tor, *n.* broad-snouted type of crocodile.

all'-im•por'tant, *adj.* supremely necessary.

all'-in•clu'sive, *adj.* comprehensive.

al•lit'er•a'tion, *n.* beginning of several words with same sound.

al'lo•cate', *v.,* **-cated, -cating.** allot. **—al'lo•ca'tion,** *n.*

al•lot', *v.,* **-lotted, -lotting.** 1. divide; distribute. 2. assign. **—al•lot'ment,** *n.*

all'-out', *adj.* total; unrestricted.

al•low', *v.* 1. permit. 2. give. 3. admit. **—al•low'a•ble,** *adj.* **—al•low'ance,** *n.*

al'loy, *n.* 1. mixture of metals. **—** *v.* (ə loi'). 2. mix (metals). 3. adulterate.

all'spice', *n.* sharp, fragrant spice.

al•lude', *v.,* **-luded, -luding.** refer (to) in words. **—al•lu'sion,** *n.*

al•lure', *v.,* **-lured, -luring.** attract; tempt. **—al•lure'ment,** *n.*

al•lu'vi•um, *n.* earth deposited by rivers, etc. **—al•lu'vi•al,** *adj.*

al•ly', *v.,* **-lied, -lying,** *n., pl.* **-lies.** —*v.* 1. unite in an alliance. —*n.* (al'ī). 2. person, nation, etc., bound to another, as by treaty.

al'ma ma'ter, one's school.

al'ma•nac', *n.* calendar showing special events, etc.

al•might'y, *adj.* 1. having all power. —*n.* 2. (*cap.*) God.

al'mond (ä'mənd), *n.* edible nut of the almond tree.

al'most, *adv.* nearly.

alms (ämz), *n.* charity.

al'oe, *n.* plant yielding cathartic drug.

a•loft', *adv., adj.* high up.

a•lone', *adj., adv.* 1. apart. 2. by oneself.

a•long', *prep.* 1. through length of. —*adv.* 2. onward. 3. together; with one.

a•long'side', *adv.* 1. to one's side. —*prep.* 2. beside.

a•loof', *adv.* 1. at a distance. —*adj.* 2. reserved; indifferent. **—a•loof'ness,** *n.*

a•loud', *adv.* loudly.

al•pac'a, *n.* South American sheep with soft, silky wool.

al'pha, *n.* first letter of Greek alphabet.

al'pha•bet', *n.* letters of a language in order. **—al'pha•bet'i•cal,** *adj.* **—al'pha•bet•ize',** *v.*

al•read'y, *adv.* before this time.

al'so, *adv.* in addition.

al'tar, *n.* 1. platform for religious rites. 2. communion table.

al'ter, *v.* change. **—al'ter•a'tion,** *n.*

al'ter•ca'tion, *n.* dispute.

al'ter•nate', *v.,* **-nated, -nating,** *adj., n.* —*v.* (-nāt'). 1. occur or do in turns. —*adj.* (-nit). 2. being by turns. —*n.* (-nit). 3. substitute. **—al'ter•na'tion,** *n.*

al•ter'na•tive, *n.* 1. other choice. —*adj.* 2. offering a choice.

al•though', *conj.* even though.

al•tim'e•ter, *n.* device for measuring altitude.

al'ti•tude', *n.* height.

al'to, *n., pl.* **-tos.** lowest female voice.

al'to•geth'er, *adv.* entirely.

al'tru•ism', *n.* devotion to others. **—al'tru•ist,** *n.* **—al'tru•is'tic,** *adj.*

al'um, *n.* astringent substance, used in medicine, etc.

a•lu'mi•num, *n.* light, silvery metal. Also, *Brit.,* **al'u•min'i•um.**

a•lum'nus, *n., pl.* **-ni** (-nī). graduate. **—a•lum'na,** *n.fem., pl.* **-nae** (-nē).

al'ways, *adv.* 1. all the time. 2. every time.

am, *v.* 1st pers. sing. pres. indic. of **be.**

a.m., the period before noon. Also, **A.M.**

a•mal'gam, *n.* mixture, esp. one with mercury.

a•mal'gam•ate', *v.,* **-ated, -ating.** combine. **—a•mal'gam•a'tion,** *n.*

a•man'u•en'sis, *n., pl.* **-ses.** secretary.

am'a•ryl'lis, *n.* plant with large, lily-like flowers.

a•mass', *v.* collect.

am'a•teur' (-chŏŏr'), *n.* nonprofessional artist, athlete, etc.

am'a•to'ry, *adj.* of love.

a•maze', *v.,* **amazed, amazing.** surprise greatly. **—a•maze'ment,** *n.*

am•bas'sa•dor, *n.* diplomat of highest rank.

am'ber, *n.* 1. yellowish fossil resin. —*adj.* 2. yellowish.

am'ber•gris' (-grēs'), *n.* gray secretion of sperm whale, used in perfumes.

am'bi•dex'trous, *adj.* using both hands equally well.

am'bi•ence (-bē-), *n.* surroundings; atmosphere. Also, **am'bi•ance. —am'bi•ent,** *adj.*

am•big'u•ous, *adj.* unclear in meaning. **—am'bi•gu'i•ty,** *n.*

am•bi'tion, *n.* 1. desire for success, power, etc. 2. object so desired. **—am•bi'tious,** *adj.*

am•biv'a•lent, *adj.* with conflicting emotions. **—am•biv'a•lence,** *n.*

am'ble, *v.,* **-bled, -bling,** *n.* —*v.* 1. to go at an easy gait. —*n.* 2. easy gait.

am•bro'sia (-zhə), *n.* food of classical gods.

am'bu•lance, *n.* vehicle for sick or wounded.

am'bu•la•to'ry, *adj.* able to walk.

am'bush, *n.* 1. concealment for a surprise attack. 2. surprise attack. 3. place of such concealment. —*v.* 4. attack thus. Also, **am'bus•cade'.**

a•mel'io•rate', *v.,* **-rated, -rating.** improve. **—a•mel'io•ra'tion,** *n.*

a'men', *interj.* so be it!

a•me'na•ble, *adj.* willing; submissive.

a•mend', *v.* 1. change or correct. 2. improve. **—a•mend'ment,** *n.*

a•mends', *n.* reparation.

a•men'i•ty, *n., pl.* **-ties.** pleasant feature, etc.

A•mer'i•can, *n.* 1. citizen of the U.S. 2. native of N. or S. America. **—American,** *adj.*

A•mer'i•can•ism, *n.* 1. devotion to the U.S. 2. custom, etc., of the U.S.

am'e•thyst, *n.* violet quartz, used in jewelry.

a'mi•a•ble, *adj.* pleasantly kind or friendly. **—a'mi•a•bil'i•ty,** *n.* **—a'mi•a•bly,** *adv.*

am'i•ca•ble, *adj.* not hostile. **—am'i•ca•bly,** *adv.*

a•mid', *prep.* among. Also, **a•midst'.**

a•mi'go (-mē'-), *n., pl.* **-gos.** *Spanish.* friend.

a•miss', *adv.* 1. wrongly. —*adj.* 2. wrong.

am'i•ty, *n.* friendship.

am•mo (am'ō), *n. Slang.* ammunition.

am•mo'nia, *n.* colorless, pungent, water-soluble gas.

am'mu•ni'tion, *n.* bullets, shot, etc., for weapons.

am•ne'sia, *n.* loss of memory.

am'nes•ty, *n.* pardon for political crimes.

a•moe'ba (ə mē'bə), *n., pl.* **-bas** or **-bae** (-bē). microscopic one-celled animal.

a•mok', *adv.* amuck.

a•mong', *prep.* 1. in the midst of. 2. in the group of. Also, **a•mongst'.**

a•mor'al (ā-), *adj.* indifferent to moral standards. **—a'mo•ral'i•ty,** *n.*

am'o•rous, *adj.* inclined to, or showing, love.

a•mor'phous, *adj.* formless.

am'or•tize', *v.,* **-tized, -tizing.** pay off. **—am'or•ti•za'tion,** *n.*

a•mount', *n.* 1. sum total. 2. quantity. —*v.* 3. add up (to); equal.

a•mour', *n.* love affair.

am'pere (-pēr), *n.* unit measuring electric current.

am'per•sand', *n.* sign (&) meaning "and."

am•phet'a•mine (-mēn), *n.* drug stimulating nervous system.

am•phib'i•an, *n.* 1. animal living both in water and on land. —*adj.* 2. Also, **am•phib'i•ous.** operating on land or water.

am'phi•the'a•ter, *n.* theater with seats around a central area.

am'ple, *adj.,* **-pler, -plest.** 1. sufficient. 2. abundant. —**am'ply,** *adv.*

am'pli•fy', *v.,* **-fied, -fying.** make larger or louder. —**am'pli•fi'er,** *n.* —**am'pli•fi•ca'tion,** *n.*

am'pli•tude', *n.* 1. extent. 2. abundance.

am'pu•tate', *v.,* **-tated, -tating.** cut off (a limb). —**am'pu•ta'tion,** *n.* —**am'pu•tee',** *n.*

a•muck', *adv.* murderously insane.

am'u•let, *n.* magical charm.

a•muse', *v.,* **amused, amusing.** 1. entertain. 2. cause mirth in. —**a•muse'ment,** *n.*

an, *adj. or indef. art. before initial vowel sounds.* See **a.**

a•nach'ro•nism, *n.* chronological discrepancy. —**a•nach'ro•nis'tic,** *adj.*

an'a•con'da, *n.* large South American snake.

an'a•gram', *n.* word formed from letters of another.

a'nal, *adj.* of the anus.

an•al•ge'sic (an'əl jē'zik), *n.* drug for relieving pain.

an'a•log com•put'er, a computer that solves problems by using voltages as analogies of numerical variables.

a•nal'o•gy (-jē), *n., pl.* **-gies.** similarity in some respects. —**a•nal'o•gous** (-gəs), *adj.*

a•nal'y•sis, *n., pl.* **-ses.** 1. separation into constituent parts. 2. summary. 3. psychoanalysis. —**an'a•lyst,** *n.* —**an'a•lyt'ic,** *adj.* —**an'a•lyze',** *v.*

an'ar•chy (-kē), *n.* lawless society. —**an'ar•chism,** *n.* —**an'ar•chist,** *n.*

a•nath'e•ma, *n.* 1. solemn curse. 2. thing or person detested.

a•nat'o•my, *n.* 1. structure of an animal or plant. 2. science dealing with such structure. —**an'a•tom'i•cal,** *adj.*

an'ces•tor, *n.* person from whom one is descended. —**an'ces•try,** *n.* —**an•ces'tral,** *adj.*

an'chor, *n.* 1. heavy device for keeping boats, etc., in place. —*v.* 2. fasten by an anchor. —**an'chor•age,** *n.*

an'cho•vy (-chō vē), *n., pl.* **-vies.** small herringlike fish.

an'cient, *adj.* 1. of long ago. 2. very old. —*n.* 3. person who lived long ago.

and, *conj.* 1. with; also. 2. *Informal.* (used in place of **to** in infinitive): *Try and stop me.*

an•dan'te (-tā), *adv. Music.* at moderate speed.

and'i'rons, *n.pl.* metal supports for logs in fireplace.

an'ec•dote', *n.* short story.

a•ne'mi•a, *n.* inadequate supply of hemoglobin and red blood cells. —**a•ne'mic,** *adj.*

a•nem'o•ne', *n.* wild flower with white blossoms.

an'es•the'sia (-zhə), *n.* insensibility to pain, usually induced by a drug (**an'es•thet'ic**). —**an•es'the•tize',** *v.*

a•new', *adv.* again.

an'gel, *n.* spirit that attends God. —**an•gel'ic,** *adj.*

an'ger, *n.* 1. strong displeasure. —*v.* 2. cause anger in.

an•gi'na pec'to•ris (an jī'nə pek'tə ris), painful attack, usually caused by coronary artery disease.

an'gle, *n., v.,* **-gled, -gling.** —*n.* 1. spread between converging lines or surfaces. —*v.* 2. fish with a hook on a line. 3. try for something by artful means. 4. bend in angles. —**an'gler,** *n.*

an'gle•worm', *n.* worm used in fishing.

An'gli•can, *adj.* 1. of the Church of England. —*n.* 2. member of this church.

An'glo-Sax'on, *n.* 1. person of English descent. 2. inhabitant of England before 1066. —*adj.* 3. of Anglo-Saxons.

an'gry, *adj.,* **-grier, -griest.** 1. full of anger. 2. inflamed. —**an'gri•ly,** *adv.*

an'guish, *n.* intense pain or grief.

an'gu•lar, *adj.* having angles. —**an•gu•lar'i•ty,** *n.*

an'i•line (-lin), *n.* oily liquid used in dyes, plastics, etc.

an'i•mad•vert', *v.* criticize. —**an'i•mad•ver'sion,** *n.*

an'i•mal, *n.* 1. living thing that is not a plant. 2. beast. —*adj.* 3. of animals.

an'i•mate', *v.,* **-mated, -mating,** *adj.* —*v.* (-māt'). 1. make alive or lively. —*adj.* (-mit). 2. alive. —**an'i•ma'tion,** *n.*

an'i•mos'i•ty, *n., pl.* **-ties.** strong ill will or enmity. Also, **an'i•mus.**

an'ise (an'is), *n.* plant yielding aromatic seed (**an'i•seed'**).

an'kle, *n.* joint between foot and leg.

an'nals, *n.pl.* historical records.

an•nex', *v.* 1. add; join. —*n.* (an' eks). 2. part, etc., attached. —**an'-nex•a'tion,** *n.*

an•ni•hi•late', *v.,* **-lated, -lating.** destroy completely. —**an•ni'hi•la'tion,** *n.*

an'ni•ver'sa•ry, *n., pl.* **-ries.** annual recurrence of the date of a past event.

an'no•tate', *v.,* **-tated, -tating.** supply with notes. —**an'no•ta'tion,** *n.*

an•nounce', *v.,* **-nounced, -nouncing.** make known. —**an•nounce'-ment,** *n.* —**an•nounc'er,** *n.*

an•noy', *v.* irritate or trouble. —**an•noy'ance,** *n.*

an'nu•al, *adj.* 1. yearly. 2. living only one season. —*n.* 3. annual plant. 4. yearbook. —**an'nu•al•ly,** *adv.*

an•nu'i•ty, *n., pl.* **-ties.** annual income in return for earlier payments.

an•nul', *v.,* **-nulled, -nulling.** make void. —**an•nul'ment,** *n.*

An•nun'ci•a'tion, *n.* announcement to Virgin Mary of incarnation of Christ (March 25).

an'o•dyne' (-dīn'), *n.* medication that relieves pain.

a•noint', *v.* put oil, etc., on, as in consecration.

a•nom'a•ly, *n., pl.* **-lies.** something irregular or abnormal. —**a•nom'a•lous,** *adj.*

a•non', *adv. Archaic.* soon.

a•non'y•mous, *adj.* by someone unnamed. —**an'o•nym'i•ty,** *n.*

an•oth'er, *adj.* 1. additional. 2. different. —*n.* 3. one more. 4. different one.

an'swer, *n.* 1. reply. 2. solution. —*v.* 3. reply to. 4. suit. 5. be responsible. 6. correspond.

an'swer•a•ble, *adj.* 1. able to be answered. 2. responsible.

ant, *n.* common small insect.

ant•ac'id, *n.* medicine to counteract acids.

an•tag'o•nism', *n.* hostility. —**an•tag'o•nist,** *n.* —**an•tag'o•nis'tic,** *adj.* —**an•tag'o•nize',** *v.*

ant•arc'tic, *adj. (often cap.)* of or at the South Pole.

an•te•ced′ent (-sēd-), *adj.* 1. prior. —*n.* 2. anything that precedes.

an′te•date′, *v.*, **-dated, -dating.** 1. happen earlier than. 2. date earlier than true time.

an′te•di•lu′vi•an, *adj.* before the Flood.

an′te•lope′, *n.* deerlike animal.

an•ten′na, *n.*, *pl.* **-nae** (-nē) *for* 1. 1. feeler on the head of an insect, etc. 2. wires for transmitting radio waves, TV pictures, etc.

an•te′ri•or, *adj.* 1. earlier. 2. frontward.

an′te•room′, *n.* room before the main room.

an′them, *n.* patriotic or sacred hymn.

an′ther, *n.* pollen-bearing part of stamen.

an•thol′o•gy, *n.*, *pl.* **-gies.** collection of writings.

an′thra•cite′, *n.* hard coal.

an′thrax, *n.* malignant disease of cattle, etc.

an′thro•poid′, *adj.* resembling man.

an′thro•pol′o•gy, *n.* science of mankind. —**an′thro•pol′o•gist**, *n.*

an′ti•bi•ot′ic, *n.* substance (such as penicillin) derived from mold, etc., and used to destroy certain organisms.

an′ti•bod′y, *n.*, *pl.* **-bodies.** substance in the blood that destroys bacteria.

an′tic, *n.* 1. odd behavior. —*adj.* 2. playful.

an•tic′i•pate′, *v.*, **-pated, -pating.** 1. expect and prepare for. 2. foresee. —**an•tic′i•pa′tion**, *n.*

an′ti•cli′max, *n.* disappointing or undramatic outcome.

an′ti•dote′, *n.* medicine counteracting poison, etc.

an′ti•his′ta•mine′ (-mēn′), *n.* substance used esp. against allergic reactions.

an′ti•mat′ter, *n.* matter whose particles have charges opposite to those of common particles.

an•tip′a•thy, *n.*, *pl.* **-thies.** dislike; aversion.

an′ti•quar′i•an, *adj.* 1. of the study of antiquities. —*n.* 2. antiquary.

an′ti•quar′y (-kwer′ē), *n.*, *pl.* **-ries.** collector of antiquities.

an′ti•quat′ed, *adj.* old or obsolete.

an•tique′ (-tēk′), *adj.* 1. old or old-fashioned. —*n.* 2. valuable old object.

an•tiq′ui•ty, *n.*, *pl.* **-ties.** 1. ancient times. 2. something ancient.

an′ti•sep′tic, *adj.* 1. destroying certain germs. —*n.* 2. antiseptic substance.

an′ti•so′cial, *adj.* 1. hostile to society. 2. not sociable.

an•tith′e•sis, *n.*, *pl.* **-ses.** direct opposite.

an′ti•tox′in, *n.* substance counteracting germ-produced poisons in the body.

ant′ler, *n.* horn on deer, etc.

an′to•nym, *n.* word of opposite meaning.

a′nus, *n.* opening at lower end of alimentary canal.

an′vil, *n.* iron block on which hot metals are hammered into shape.

anx•i•e′ty (ang zī′-), *n.*, *pl.* **-ties.** 1. worried distress. 2. eagerness. —**anx′ious** (angk′shəs), *adj.* —**anx′ious•ly**, *adv.*

an′y, *adj.* 1. one; some. 2. every. —*pron.* 3. any person, etc. —**an′y•bod′y, an′y•one′**, *pron.* —**an′y•thing′**, *pron.*

an′y•how′, *adv.* in any way, case, etc. Also, **an′y•way′**.

an′y•where′, *adv.* in, at, or to any place.

a•or′ta, *n.*, *pl.* **-tas, -tae** (-tē). main blood vessel from heart.

a•pach′e, *n.* Parisian tough.

a•part′, *adv.* 1. into pieces. 2. separately.

a•part′heid (ə pärt′hīt), *n.* (in South Africa) separation of and discrimination against blacks.

a•part′ment, *n.* set of rooms in a dwelling.

ap′a•thy, *n.* lack of emotion or interest. —**ap′a•thet′ic**, *adj.*

ape, *n.*, *v.*, **aped, aping.** —*n.* 1. large, tailless, monkeylike animal. —*v.* 2. imitate stupidly.

a•pé′ri•tif (ə per′i tēf′), *n.* liquor served before meal to stimulate appetite.

ap′er•ture (-chər), *n.* opening.

a′pex, *n.* tip; summit.

a′phid, *n.* plant-sucking insect.

aph′o•rism′, *n.* brief maxim.

aph′ro•dis′i•ac′, *adj.* sexually exciting.

a′pi•ar′y, *n.*, *pl.* **-ries.** place where bees are kept.

a•piece′, *adv.* for each.

A•poc′a•lypse, *n.* revelation of the apostle John.

A•poc′ry•pha, *n.* uncanonical parts of the Bible.

a•poc′ry•phal, *adj.* not verified; dubious

ap′o•gee, *n.* remotest point of satellite orbit.

a•pol′o•gist (-jist), *n.* advocate; defender.

a•pol′o•gize′, *v.*, **-gized, -gizing.** offer apology.

a•pol′o•gy, *n.*, *pl.* **-gies.** 1. statement of regret for one's act. 2. stated defense. —**a•pol′o•get′ic**, *adj.*

ap′o•plex′y, *n.* sudden loss of bodily function due to bursting of blood vessel. —**ap′o•plec′tic**, *adj.*

a•pos′tate, *n.* deserter of one's faith, cause, etc. —**a•pos′ta•sy**, *n.*

a•pos′tle, *n.* 1. disciple sent by Jesus to preach gospel. 2. moral reformer. —**ap′os•tol′ic**, *adj.*

a•pos′tro•phe, *n.* 1. sign (') indicating an omitted letter, the possessive, or certain plurals. 2. words in passing to one person or group. —**a•pos′tro•phize′**, *v.*

a•poth′e•car′y, *n.*, *pl.* **-ries.** druggist.

ap•pall′, *v.* fill with fear and dismay. Also, **ap•pal′**. —**ap•pall′ing**, *adj.*

ap′pa•ra′tus, *n.* 1. instruments and machines for some task. 2. organization.

ap•par′el, *n.* 1. clothes. —*v.* 2. dress.

ap•par′ent, *adj.* 1. obvious. 2. seeming. —**ap•par′ent•ly**, *adv.*

ap′pa•ri′tion, *n.* specter.

ap•peal′, *n.* 1. call for aid, mercy, etc. 2. request for corroboration or review. 3. attractiveness. —*v.* 4. make an appeal.

ap•pear′, *v.* 1. come into sight. 2. seem.

ap•pear′ance, *n.* 1. act of appearing. 2. outward look.

ap•pease′, *v.*, **-peased, -peasing.** 1. placate. 2. satisfy. —**ap•pease′ment**, *n.*

ap•pel′lant, *n.* one who appeals.

ap•pel′late, *adj.* dealing with appeals.

ap•pend′, *v.* add; join.

ap•pend′age, *n.* subordinate attached part.

ap′pen•dec′to•my, *n.*, *pl.* **-mies.** surgical removal of the appendix.

ap•pen′di•ci′tis (-sī′-), *n.* inflammation of appendix.

ap•pen′dix, *n.* 1. supplement. 2. closed tube from the large intestine.

ap′per•tain′, *v.* belong or pertain.

ap′pe•tite′, *n.* desire, esp. for food. —**ap′pe•tiz′er**, *n.* —**ap′pe•tiz′•ing**, *adj.*

ap•plaud', *v.* praise by clapping, cheers, etc. —**ap•plause'**, *n.*

ap'ple, *n.* common edible fruit.

ap•pli'ance, *n.* special device or instrument.

ap'pli•ca•ble, *adj.* that can be applied.

ap'pli•cant, *n.* one who applies.

ap•ply', *v.* **-plied, -plying.** 1. put on. 2. put into practice. 3. use or devote. 4. be relevant. 5. make request. —**ap'pli•ca'tion**, *n.*

ap•point', *v.* 1. choose; name. 2. furnish. —**ap•point•ee'**, *n.* —**ap•poin'-tive**, *adj.*

ap•point'ment, *n.* 1. act of choosing or naming. 2. prearranged meeting. 3. equipment.

ap•por'tion, *v.* divide into shares. —**ap•por'tion•ment**, *n.*

ap'po•site, *adj.* suitable.

ap•praise', *v.*, **-praised, -praising.** estimate the value of. —**ap•prais'al**, *n.* —**ap•prais'er**, *n.*

ap•pre'ci•a•ble, (-shē-), *adj.* noticeable; significant.

ap•pre'ci•ate' (-shē-), *v.*, **-ated, -ating.** 1. value at true worth. 2. increase in value. —**ap•pre'ci•a'tion**, *n.* —**ap•pre'cia•tive** (-shə-), *adj.*

ap•pre•hend', *v.* 1. take into custody. 2. understand.

ap•pre•hen'sion, *n.* 1. anxiety. 2. comprehension. 3. arrest.

ap•pre•hen'sive, *adj.* worried; anxious.

ap•pren'tice, *n.*, *v.*, **-ticed, -ticing.** —*n.* 1. assistant learning a trade. —*v.* 2. bind as such an assistant. —**ap•pren'tice•ship'**, *n.*

ap•prise', *v.*, **-prised, -prising.** notify. Also, **ap•prize'**.

ap•proach', *v.* 1. come near to. 2. make a proposal to. —*n.* 3. coming near. 4. access. 5. method.

ap'pro•ba'tion, *n.* approval.

ap•pro'pri•ate', *adj.*, *v.*, **-ated, -ating.** —*adj.* (-prē it). 1. suitable; proper. —*v.* (-prē āt'). 2. designate for use. 3. take possession of. —**ap•pro'pri•ate•ly**, *adv.* —**ap•pro'pri•a'tion**, *n.*

ap•prove', *v.*, **-proved, -proving.** 1. think or speak well of. 2. confirm. —**ap•prov'al**, *n.*

ap•prox'i•mate, *adj.*, *v.*, **-mated, -mating.** —*adj.* (-mit). 1. near; similar. —*v.* (-māt'). 2. come near to. **ap•prox'i•mate'ly**, *adv.* —**ap•prox'-i•ma'tion**, *n.*

ap•pur'te•nance, *n.* accessory.

ap•pur'te•nant, *adj.* pertaining.

a'pri•cot', *n.* peachlike fruit.

A'pril, *n.* fourth month of year.

a'pron, *n.* protective garment for the front of one's clothes.

ap'ro•pos' (ap'rə pō'), *adv.* 1. opportunely. 2. with reference. —*adj.* 3. opportune.

apt, *adj.* 1. prone. 2. likely. 3. skilled; able. —**apt'ly**, *adv.* —**apt'ness**, *n.*

ap'ti•tude', *n.* skill; talent.

Aq'ua•lung', *n. Trademark.* underwater breathing device using compressed air.

aq'ua•ma•rine', *n.* 1. light greenish blue. 2. beryl of this color.

a•quar'i•um, *n.* place for exhibiting aquatic animals and plants.

a•quat'ic, *adj.* of, or living in, water.

aq'ue•duct', *n.* man-made water channel.

a'que•ous, *adj.* of or like water.

aq'ui•line', *adj.* (of a nose) curved upward.

Ar'ab, *n.* 1. member of a people living or originating in Arabia, a peninsula in SW Asia. —*adj.* 2. of the Arabs. Also, **A•ra'bi•an.**

ar'a•ble, *adj.* suitable for plowing.

ar'bit•er, *n.* judge.

ar•bit'ra•ment, *n.* judgment by an arbiter.

ar'bi•trar'y, *adj.* 1. subject to personal judgment. 2. capricious. 3. abusing powers; despotic. —**ar'bi•trar'i•ly**, *adv.*

ar'bi•trate', *v.*, **-trated, -trating.** adjudicate as, or submit to, an arbiter. —**ar'bi•tra'tion**, *n.* —**ar'bi•tra'tor**, *n.*

ar'bor, *n.* tree-shaded walk or garden.

ar•bo're•al, *adj.* of, or living in, trees.

ar•bu'tus (-byoo'-), *n.* 1. variety of evergreen shrub. 2. creeping flowering plant.

arc, *n.* 1. part of circle. 2. luminous current between two electric conductors.

ar•cade', *n.* 1. row of archways. 2. covered passage with stores.

arch, *n.* 1. upwardly curved structure. —*v.* 2. cover with an arch. —*adj.* 3. chief. 4. roguish.

ar'chae•ol'o•gy (-kē-), *n.* study of past cultures from artifacts. —**ar'-chae•o•log'i•cal**, *adj.* —**ar'chae•ol'o•gist**, *n.*

ar•cha'ic, *adj.* 1. no longer used. 2. ancient.

arch'an'gel (ärk'-), *n.* chief angel.

arch'bish'op, *n.* bishop of highest rank.

arch'duke', *n.* royal prince.

arch'er, *n.* one who shoots a bow and arrow. —**arch'er•y**, *n.*

ar'chi•pel'a•go (är'kə-), *n.*, *pl.* **-gos, -goes.** 1. body of water with many islands. 2. the islands.

ar'chi•tect', (är'kə-), *n.* designer of buildings. —**ar'chi•tec'ture**, *n.* —**ar'chi•tec'tur•al**, *adj.*

ar'chives (är'kīvz), *n.pl.* 1. documents. 2. place for documents.

arch'way', *n.* entrance covered by arch.

arc'tic, *adj.* (*often cap.*) of or at the North Pole.

ar'dent, *adj.* earnest; zealous. —**ar'-dent•ly**, *adv.*

ar'dor, *n.* zeal.

ar'du•ous (-joo-), *adj.* 1. difficult. 2. steep. 3. severe.

are, *v.* pres. indic. pl. of **be.**

ar'e•a, *n.* 1. extent of surface; region. 2. scope.

area code, three-digit number for direct long-distance telephone dialing.

a•re'na, *n.* open space for contests, etc.

aren't, contraction of **are not.**

ar'go•sy, *n.*, *pl.* **-sies.** *Poetic.* large merchant ship or fleet.

ar'gue, *v.*, **-gued, -guing.** 1. present reasons for or against something. 2. dispute. 3. persuade. —**ar'gu•ment**, *n.* —**ar'gu•men•ta'tion**, *n.*

ar'gu•men•ta'tive, *adj.* tending to dispute.

a'ri•a, *n.* operatic solo.

ar'id, *adj.* dry. —**a•rid'i•ty**, *n.*

a•right', *adv.* rightly.

a•rise', *v.*, **arose, arisen, arising.** 1. move or get up. 2. occur.

ar'is•toc'ra•cy, *n.*, *pl.* **-cies.** 1. state governed by nobility. 2. nobility. —**a•ris'to•crat**, *n.* —**a•ris'to•crat'-ic**, *adj.*

a•rith'me•tic, *n.* computation with figures.

ark, *n. Archaic.* large ship.

arm, *n.* 1. upper limb from hand to shoulder. 2. weapon. 3. combat branch. —*v.* 4. equip with weapons.

ar•ma'da (-mä'-), *n.* fleet of warships.

ar'ma•ged'don (-ged'-), *n.* crucial or final conflict.

ar'ma•ment, *n.* 1. military weapons. 2. arming for war.

arm'ful, *n.*, *pl.* **-fuls.** capacity of both arms.

ar'mi•stice, *n.* truce.

ar′mor, *n.* protective covering against weapons.

ar′mor•y, *n., pl.* **-ries.** 1. storage place for weapons. 2. military drill hall.

arm′pit′, *n.* hollow part under arm at shoulder.

ar′my, *n., pl.* **-mies.** 1. military force for land combat. 2. large group.

a•ro′ma, *n.* odor. **—ar′o•mat′ic,** *adj.*

a•round′, *adv., prep.* 1. on every side of. 2. somewhere in or near. 3. about.

a•rouse′, *v.,* **aroused, arousing.** 1. awaken. 2. stir to act.

ar•raign′ (ə rān′), *v.* 1. call to court. 2. accuse. **—ar•raign′ment,** *n.*

ar•range′, *v.,* **-ranged, -ranging.** 1. place in order. 2. plan or prepare. **—ar•range′ment,** *n.*

ar′rant, *adj.* downright.

ar•ray′, *v.* 1. arrange. 2. clothe. **—n.** 3. arrangement, as for battle. 4. clothes.

ar•rears′, *n.pl.* overdue debt.

ar•rest′, *v.* 1. seize (person) by law. 2. stop. **—n.** 3. seizure. 4. stoppage.

ar•rive′, *v.* reach a certain place. **—ar•riv′al,** *n.*

ar′ro•gant, *adj.* insolently proud. **—ar′ro•gance,** *n.* **—ar′ro•gant•ly,** *adv.*

ar′ro•gate′, *v.,* **-gated, -gating.** claim presumptuously. **—ar′ro•ga′tion,** *n.*

ar′row, *n.* pointed stick shot by a bow.

ar•roy′o (ə roi′ō), *n., pl.* **-os.** steep, dry gulch.

ar′se•nal, *n.* military storehouse or factory.

ar′se•nic, *n.* 1. metallic element. 2. poisonous powder.

ar′son, *n.* malicious burning of a building.

art, *n.* 1. production of something beautiful or extraordinary. 2. skill; ability. 3. cunning. **—v.** 4. *Archaic.* are. **—art′ful,** *adj.*

ar•te′ri•o•scle•ro′sis, *n.* hardening of arteries.

ar′ter•y, *n., pl.* **-ries.** 1. blood vessel from the heart. 2. main channel. **—ar•te′ri•al,** *adj.*

ar•te′sian (-zhən) **well,** deep well whose water rises under its own pressure.

ar•thri′tis, *n.* inflammation of a joint. **—ar•thrit′ic,** *adj.*

ar′ti•choke′, *n.* plant with an edible flower head.

ar′ti•cle, *n.* 1. literary composition. 2. thing; item. 3. the words *a, an,* or *the.*

ar•tic′u•late, *adj., v.,* **-lated, -lating.** **—adj.** (-lit). 1. clear. 2. able to speak. 3. jointed. **—v.** (-lāt′). 4. speak, esp. distinctly. 5. joint. **—ar•tic′u•la′tion,** *n.*

ar′ti•fice, *n.* trick.

ar•tif′i•cer, *n.* craftsman. Also, **ar′ti•san.**

ar′ti•fi′cial (-shəl), *adj.* 1. manufactured, esp. as an imitation. 2. affected. **—ar′ti•fi′cial•ly,** *adv.* **—ar′ti•fi′ci•al′i•ty** (-fish′ē-), *n.*

ar•til′ler•y, *n.* mounted, large guns.

art′ist, *n.* practitioner of fine art. **ar•tis′tic,** *adj.* **—art′ist•ry,** *n.*

art′less, *adj.* natural.

art′y, *adj.,* **-ier, -iest.** *Informal.* self-consciously artistic.

as, *adv.* 1. to such an extent. **—conj.** 2. in the manner, etc., that. 3. while. 4. because. **—pron.** 5. that.

as•bes′tos, *n.* fibrous material used in fireproofing.

as•cend′, *v.* climb. **—as•cent′,** *n.*

as•cend′an•cy, *n.* domination; power. **—as•cend′ant,** *adj., n.*

As•cen′sion, *n.* bodily passing of Christ to heaven.

as•cer′tain (as′ər-), *v.* find out.

as•cet′ic (ə set′ik), *n.* 1. one who lives austerely. **—adj.** 2. austere or abstemious. **—as•cet′i•cism,** *n.*

as•cor′bic ac′id, vitamin C.

as•cribe′, *v.,* **-cribed, -cribing.** attribute. **—as•crip′tion,** *n.*

a•sep′sis, *n.* absence of certain harmful bacteria. **—a•sep′tic,** *adj.*

a•sex′u•al (ā-), *adj.* without sex.

ash, *n.* 1. (*pl.* **ashes**) residue of burned matter. 2. a common tree. **—ash′y,** *adj.*

a•shamed′, *adj.* feeling shame.

ash′en, *adj.* pale gray.

a•shore′, *adv., adj.* on or to shore.

A′sian (ā′zhən), *n.* native of Asia. **—Asian,** *adj.* **—A′si•at′ic,** *adj. Offensive.* Asian.

a•side′, *adv.* 1. on or to one side. 2. separate.

as′i•nine′, *adj.* stupid.

ask, *v.* 1. put a question to. 2. request. 3. invite. 4. inquire.

a•skance′, *adv.* with doubt or disapproval.

a•skew′, *adv.* twisted.

a•sleep′, *adj., adv.* sleeping.

asp, *n.* poisonous snake.

as•par′a•gus, *n.* plant with edible shoots.

as′pect, *n.* 1. appearance. 2. phase; condition. 3. direction faced.

as′pen, *n.* variety of poplar.

as•per′i•ty, *n., pl.* **-ties.** roughness.

as•per′sion, *n.* derogatory criticism.

as′phalt, *n.* hard, black material used for pavements, etc.

as•phyx′i•ate′, *v.,* **-ated, -ating.** affect by a lack of oxygen; choke or smother. **—as•phyx′i•a′tion,** *n.*

as•pire′, *v.,* **-pired, -piring.** long, aim, or seek for. **—as•pir′ant,** *n.* **—as′pi•ra′tion,** *n.*

as′pi•rin, *n.* crystalline derivative of salicylic acid, used for relief of headaches, etc.

ass, *n.* 1. donkey. 2. fool.

as•sail′, *v.* attack. **—as•sail′ant,** *n.*

as•sas′sin, *n.* murderer, esp. of an important person. **—as•sas′si•nate′,** *v.* **—as•sas′si•na′tion,** *n.*

as•sault′, *n., v.* attack.

as•say′, *v.* analyze or evaluate. **—as•say′,** *n.*

as•sem′ble, *v.,* **-bled, -bling.** come or bring together. **—as•sem′blage, as•sem′bly,** *n.*

as•sent′, *v.* 1. agree. **—n.** 2. agreement.

as•sert′, *v.* 1. state; declare. 2. claim. 3. present (oneself) boldly. **—as•ser′tion,** *n.* **—as•ser′tive,** *adj.*

as•sess′, *v.* evaluate, as for taxes. **—as•sess′ment,** *n.* **—as•ses′sor,** *n.*

as′set, *n.* 1. item of property. 2. quality.

as•sid′u•ous (ə sij′-), *adj.* persistent; devoted. **—as•sid′u•ous•ly,** *adv.*

as•sign′ (ə sīn′), *v.* 1. give. 2. appoint. 3. transfer. **—n.** 4. one to whom something is transferred. **—as•sign′a•ble,** *adj.* **—as•sign•ee′,** *n.* **—as•sign′ment,** *n.*

as′sig•na′tion (-sig-), *n.* appointment; rendezvous.

as•sim′i•late′, *v.,* **-lated, -lating.** absorb or become absorbed; merge. **—as•sim′i•la′tion,** *n.*

as•sist′, *v., n.* help; aid. **—as•sist′ant,** *n., adj.* **—as•sist′ance,** *n.*

as•so′ci•ate′, *v.,* **-ated, -ating,** *n., adj.* **—v.** (-āt′). 1. connect or join. 2. keep company. **—n.** (-it). 3. partner; colleague. **—adj.** (-it). 4. allied. **—as•so′ci•a′tion,** *n.*

as•sort′, *v.* 1. classify. 2. vary. **—as•sort′ed,** *adj.* **—as•sort′ment,** *n.*

as•suage′ (ə swāj′), *v.,* **-suaged, -suaging.** lessen (pain, grief, etc.).

as•sume′, *v.,* **-sumed, -suming.** 1. take without proof. 2. undertake. 3. pretend. 4. take upon oneself.

as•sump′tion, *n.* 1. unverified belief. 2. undertaking. 3. (*cap.*) ascent to heaven of Virgin Mary.

as•sure', *v.*, **-sured, -suring.** 1. affirm to. 2. convince; make sure. 3. encourage. 4. insure. **—as•sur'ance**, *n.* **—as•sured'**, *adj.*

as'ter, *n.* plant with many petals around a center disk.

as'ter•isk, *n.* star (*) used in writing, etc.

a•stern', *adv.*, *adj. Naut.* toward or at the rear.

as'ter•oid', *n.* planetlike body beyond Mars.

asth'ma (az'mə), *n.* painful respiratory disorder. **—asth•mat'ic**, *adj.*, *n.*

a•stig'ma•tism, *n.* eye defect resulting in imperfect images. **—a'stig•mat'ic**, *adj.*

a•stir', *adj.*, *adv.* active.

as•ton'ish, *v.* surprise greatly; amaze. **—as•ton'ish•ment**, *n.*

as•tound', *v.* amaze greatly.

a•stray', *adj.*, *adv.* straying.

a•stride', *adv.*, *adj.*, *prep.* straddling.

as•trin'gent, *adj.* contracting; styptic.

as•trol'o•gy, *n.* study of stars to determine their influence on human affairs. **—as'tro•log'i•cal**, *adj.* **—as•trol'o•ger**, *n.*

as'tro•naut', *n.* traveler outside earth's atmosphere.

as'tro•nom'i•cal, *adj.* 1. of astronomy. 2. extremely great, high, expensive, etc.

as•tron'o•my, *n.* science of all the celestial bodies. **—as'tron'o•mer**, *n.*

as•tute', *adj.* shrewd; clever. **—as•tute'ness**, *n.*

a•sun'der, *adv.*, *adj.* apart.

a•sy'lum, *n.* home for persons needing care.

at, *prep.* (word used in indicating place, time, etc.)

ate, *v.* pt. of **eat.**

a'the•ism, *n.* belief that there is no God. **—a'the•ist**, *n.* **—a'the•is'tic**, *adj.*

a•thirst', *adj.* 1. *Archaic.* thirsty. 2. eager.

ath'lete, *n.* expert in exercises, sports, etc. **—ath•let'ic**, *adj.*

a•thwart', *adv.*, *prep.* from side to side of.

at'las, *n.* book of maps.

at'mos•phere', *n.* 1. air surrounding earth. 2. pervading mood. **—at'mos•pher'ic**, *adj.*

at'oll, *n.* ring-shaped coral island.

at'om, *n.* smallest unit making up chemical element. **—a•tom'ic**, *adj.*

atomic bomb, bomb whose force is derived from nuclear fission of certain atoms, causing the conversion of some mass to energy (**atomic energy**). Also, **atom bomb.**

at'om•iz'er, *n.* device for making a fine spray.

a•tone', *v.*, **atoned, atoning.** make amends (for). **—a•tone'ment**, *n.*

a•top', *adj.*, *adv.*, *prep.* on or at the top of.

a•tro'cious, *adj.* 1. wicked. 2. very bad. **—a•troc'i•ty**, *n.*

at'ro•phy, *n.*, *v.*, **-phied, -phying.** **—n.** 1. wasting away of the body. **—v.** 2. cause or undergo atrophy.

at•tach', *v.* 1. fasten, join, or associate. 2. take by legal authority.

at'ta•ché' (at'ə shā'), *n.* embassy official.

at•tach'ment, *n.* 1. an attaching. 2. something fastened on. 3. affectionate tie.

at•tack', *v.* 1. act against with sudden force 2. do vigorously. **—n.** 3. an attacking; onset.

at•tain', *v.* 1. reach; arrive at. 2. accomplish; fulfill. **—at•tain'a•ble**, *adj.* **—at•tain'ment**, *n.*

at'tar, *n.* perfume from flowers.

at•tempt', *v.*, *n.* try.

at•tend', *v.* 1. be present at. 2. go with. 3. take care of. 4. give heed to. **—at•tend'ance**, *n.* **—at•tend'ant**, *n.*, *adj.*

at•ten'tion, *n.* 1. act of attending. 2. careful notice. **—at•ten'tive**, *adj.* **—at•ten'tive•ly**, *adv.*

at•ten'u•ate', *v.*, **-ated, -ating.** 1. make thin. 2. lessen; abate. **—at•ten'u•a'tion**, *n.*

at•test', *v.* declare or certify as true, genuine, etc. **—at'tes•ta'tion**, *n.*

at'tic, *n.* room right under the roof.

at•tire', *v.*, **-tired, -tiring**, *n.* **—v.** 1. dress; adorn. **—n.** 2. clothes.

at'ti•tude', *n.* 1. feeling or opinion, esp. as expressed. 2. posture.

at•tor'ney, *n.*, *pl.* **-neys.** lawyer.

at•tract', *v.* 1. draw toward. 2. invite; allure. **—at•trac'tion**, *n.* **—at•trac'tive**, *adj.* **—at•trac'tive•ly**, *adv.* **—at•trac'tive•ness**, *n.*

at•trib'ute, *v.*, **-uted, -uting**, *n.* **—v.** (ə trib'yoot). 1. ascribe; credit; impute. **—n.** (at'rə byoot'). 2. special quality, aspect, etc. **—at'tri•bu'tion**, *n.*

at•tri'tion (ə trish'ən), *n.* wearing down.

at•tune', *v.*, **-tuned, -tuning.** harmonize.

au'burn, *adj.* reddish brown.

auc'tion, *n.* 1. sale of goods to highest bidders. **—v.** 2. sell by auction. **—auc'tion•eer'**, *n.*, *v.*

au•da'cious, *adj.* bold; daring. **—au•dac'i•ty** (-das'-), *n.*

au'di•ble, *adj.* that can be heard. **—au'di•bil'i•ty**, *n.* **—au'di•bly**, *adv.*

au'di•ence, *n.* 1. group of hearers or spectators. 2. formal hearing or interview.

au'di•o', *adj.* 1. of sound reception or reproduction. **—n.** 2. audible part of TV.

au'di•o•vis'u•al, *adj.* using films, TV, and recordings, as for education.

au'dit, *n.* official examination of accounts. **—au'dit**, *v.* **—au'di•tor**, *n.*

au•di'tion, *n.* 1. hearing. **—v.** 2. give a hearing to.

au'di•to'ri•um, *n.* large meeting room.

au'di•to'ry, *adj.* of hearing.

au'ger, *n.* drill.

aught, *n.* 1. anything. 2. zero (0). **—adv.** 3. at all.

aug•ment', *v.* increase. **—aug'men•ta'tion**, *n.*

au'gur (ô'gər), *v.* predict; bode. **—au'gu•ry** (-gyə-), *n.*

Au'gust, *n.* eighth month of year.

au•gust', *adj.* majestic.

auk, *n.* northern diving bird.

aunt, *n.* 1. sister of one's mother or father. 2. wife of an uncle.

au'ra, *n.* atmosphere, quality, etc.

au'ral, *adj.* of or by hearing.

au're•ole', *n.* halo.

Au•re•o•my•cin (ô'rē ō mī'sin), *n. Trademark.* antibiotic drug effective against some diseases.

au' re•voir' (ō' rə vwär'), *French.* good-bye.

au'ri•cle, *n.* 1. outer part of ear. 2. chamber in heart. **—au•ric'u•lar**, *adj.*

au•rif'er•ous, *adj.* containing gold.

aus'pice (ô'spis), *n.* (*usually pl.*) patronage.

aus•pi'cious, *adj.* favorable.

aus•tere', *adj.* 1. harsh; stern. 2. severely simple. **—aus•ter'i•ty**, *n.*

Aus•tral'ian (-trāl'-), *n.* native or citizen of Australia. **—Australian**, *adj.*

Aus'tri•an, *n.* native of Austria. **—Austrian**, *adj.*

au•then'tic, *adj.* reliable; genuine. **—au•then'ti•cal•ly**, *adv.* **—au'then•tic'i•ty**, *n.* **—au•then'ti•cate'**, *v.*

au'thor, *n.* writer or creator. **—au'thor•ship'**, *n.*

au·thor′i·tar′i·an, *adj.* favoring subjection to authority.

au·thor′i·ta′tive, *adj.* to be accepted as true.

au·thor′i·ty, *n., pl.* **-ties.** 1. right to order or decide. 2. one with such right. 3. recognized source of information, etc.

au′thor·ize′, *v.,* **-ized, -izing.** permit officially. —**auth′or·i·za′tion,** *n.*

au′to, *n.* automobile.

au′to·bi·og′ra·phy, *n., pl.* **-phies.** story of one's own life.

au·toc′ra·cy, *n., pl.* **-cies.** absolute political power. —**au′to·crat′,** *n.* —**au′to·crat′ic,** *adj.*

au′to·graph′, *n.* signature.

au′to·mat′, *n.* restaurant with coin-operated service.

au′to·mat′ic, *adj.* 1. self-acting. 2. inevitably following. —**au′to·mat′i·cal·ly,** *adv.*

au′to·ma′tion, *n.* automatically controlled machinery.

au·tom′a·ton, *n.* mechanical device or figure; robot.

au′to·mo·bile′, *n.* motor-driven passenger vehicle.

au·ton′o·my, *n.* self-government. —**au·ton′o·mous,** *adj.*

au′top·sy, *n., pl.* **-sies.** examination of body for causes of death.

au′tumn, *n.* season before winter; fall. —**au·tum′nal,** *adj.*

aux·il′ia·ry (ôg zil′yə rē) *adj., n., pl.* **-ries.** —*adj.* 1. assisting. 2. subsidiary. —*n.* 3. aid. 4. noncombat naval vessel. 5. verb preceding other verbs to express tense, etc.

a·vail′, *v.* 1. be of use, value, etc. 2. take to (oneself) advantageously. —*n.* 3. benefit; advantage.

a·vail′a·ble, *adj.* present for use. —**a·vail′a·bil′i·ty,** *n.*

av′a·lanche′, *n.* mass of snow, ice, etc., falling down mountain.

a·vant′-garde′, *adj.* progressive, esp. in art.

av′a·rice, *n.* greed. —**av′a·ri′cious,** *adj.*

a·venge′, *v.,* **avenged, avenging.** take vengeance for. —**a·veng′er,** *n.*

av′e·nue′, *n.* 1. broad street. 2. approach.

a·ver′, *v.,* **averred, averring.** affirm; declare.

av′er·age (-ij), *n., adj., v.,* **-aged, -aging.** —*n.* 1. sum of a series of numbers divided by the number of terms in the series. —*adj.* 2. of or like an average. 3. typical. —*v.* 4. find average of.

a·verse′, *adj.* unwilling. —**a·verse′ly,** *adv.* —**a·verse′ness,** *n.*

a·ver′sion, *n.* dislike.

a·vert′, *v.* 1. turn away. 2. prevent.

a′vi·ar′y (ā′-), *n., pl.* **-ries.** place in which birds are kept.

a′vi·a′tion, *n.* science of flying aircraft. —**a′vi·a′tor,** *n.* —**a′vi·a′trix,** *n.fem.*

av′id, *adj.* eager. —**a·vid′i·ty,** *n.*

av′o·ca′do (-kä′-), *n., pl.* **-dos.** tropical pear-shaped fruit.

av′o·ca′tion, *n.* hobby.

a·void′, *v.* shun; evade. —**a·void′a·ble,** *adj.* —**a·void′ance,** *n.*

av′oir·du·pois′ (av′ ər də poiz′), *n.* system of weights with 16-ounce pounds.

a·vow′, *v.* declare; confess. —**a·vow′al,** *n.*

a·wait′, *v.* wait for.

a·wake′, *v.,* **awoke** or **awaked, awaking,** *adj.* —*v.* 1. Also, **a·wak′en.**

rouse from sleep. —*adj.* 2. not asleep.

a·wak′en, *v.* awake.

a·ward′, *v.* 1. bestow; grant. —*n.* 2. thing bestowed.

a·ware′, *adj.* conscious (of). —**a·ware′ness,** *n.*

a·wash′, *adj.* overflowing with water.

a·way′, *adv.* 1. from this or that place. 2. apart. 3. aside. —*adj.* 4. absent. 5. distant.

awe, *n., v.,* **awed, awing.** —*n.* 1. respectful fear. —*v.* 2. fill with awe. —**awe′some,** *adj.*

aw′ful, *adj.* 1. fearful. 2. very bad. 3. *Informal.* very.

aw′ful·ly, *adv.* 1. very badly. 2. *Informal.* very.

a·while′, *adv.* for a short time.

awk′ward, *adj.* 1. clumsy. 2. embarrassing. 3. difficult; risky. —**awk′ward·ly,** *adv.* —**awk′ward·ness,** *n.*

awl, *n.* small drill.

awn, *n.* bristlelike part of a plant.

awn′ing, *n.* rooflike shelter, esp. of canvas.

a·wry′ (ə rī′), *adv., adj.* 1. twisted. 2. wrong.

ax, *n., pl.* **axes.** small chopping tool. Also, **axe.**

ax′i·om, *n.* accepted truth. —**ax′i·o·mat′ic,** *adj.*

ax′is, *n., pl.* **axes** (ak′sēz). line about which something turns. —**ax′i·al,** *adj.*

ax′le, *n.* bar on which a wheel turns.

ay (ā), *adv. Poetic.* always. Also, **aye.**

a′ya·tol′lah, *n.* chief Muslim leader.

aye (ī), *adv., n.* yes.

a·zal′ea, *n.* flowering evergreen shrub.

az′ure (azh′-), *adj., n.* sky-blue.

B

B, b, *n.* second letter of English alphabet.

bab′ble, *v.,* **-bled, -bling.** 1. talk indistinctly or foolishly. 2. make a murmuring sound. —**bab′ble,** *n.*

babe, *n.* 1. baby. 2. innocent person.

ba·boon′, *n.* large monkey of Africa and Arabia.

ba·bush′ka, *n.* woman's head scarf.

ba′by, *n., pl.* **-bies,** *v.,* **-bied, -bying.** —*n.* 1. infant. 2. childish person. —*v.* 3. pamper. —**ba′by·hood′,** *n.* —**ba′by·ish,** *adj.*

ba′by-sit′, *v.,* **-sat, -sitting.** tend another's baby for a few hours. —**ba′by-sit′ter,** *n.*

bac′ca·lau′re·ate (-lôr′ē it), *n.* bachelor's degree.

bach′e·lor (bach′-), *n.* 1. unmarried man. 2. person holding first degree at a college. —**bach′e·lor·hood′,** *n.* —**bach′e·lor·ship′,** *n.*

ba·cil′lus (-sil′əs), *n., pl.* **-cilli** (-sil′ī). type of bacteria.

back, *n.* 1. hinder part of human body. 2. corresponding part of ani-

mal body. 3. rear. 4. spine. —*v.* 5. sponsor. 6. move backward. 7. bet in favor of. 8. furnish or form a back. —*adj.* 9. being behind. 10. in the past. 11. overdue. —*adv.* 12. at or toward the rear. 13. toward original point or condition. 14. in return. —**back′er,** *n.* —**back′ing,** *n.*

back′bite′, *v.,* **-bit, -bitten, -biting.** discuss (someone) maliciously.

back′bone′, *n.* 1. spine. 2. strength of character. —**back′boned′,** *adj.*

back′break′ing, *adj.* fatiguing.

back′fire′, *v.* **1.** (of an engine) ignite prematurely. **2.** bring results opposite to those planned. —**back′fire′,** *n.*

back′gam′mon, *n.* board game for two persons.

back′ground′, *n.* **1.** parts in the rear. **2.** distant portions in a picture. **3.** origins; antecedents.

back′hand′ed, *adj.* **1.** with upper part of hand forward. **2.** ambiguous.

back′lash′, *n.* sudden, retaliatory reaction.

back′log′, *n.* reserve or accumulation, as of work.

back′pack′, *n.* **1.** knapsack for hiking. —*v.* **2.** hike using backpack.

back′side′, *n.* **1.** rear. **2.** rump.

back′slide′, *v.,* **-slid, -slidden** or **-slid, -sliding.** relapse into sin. —**back′-slid′er,** *n.*

back talk, impertinent talk.

back′track′, *v.* retreat slowly.

back′ward, *adv.* Also, **back′wards. 1.** toward the back or rear. **2.** back foremost. **3.** toward or in the past. —*adj.* **4.** toward the back or past. **5.** behind in time or progress. **6.** bashful. —**back′ward•ly,** *adv.* —**back′ward• ness,** *n.*

back′woods′, *n.pl.* wooded or unsettled districts. —**back′woods′man,** *n.*

ba′con, *n.* cured back and sides of a hog.

bac•ter′i•a (-tēr′ē ə), *n., pl. of* **bacterium.** simplest type of vegetable organism, involved in fermentation, production of disease, etc. —**bac• te′ri•al,** *adj.* —**bac•te′ri•al•ly,** *adv.*

bac•te′ri•ol′o•gy, *n.* science dealing with bacteria. —**bac•te′ri•o•log′i• cal,** *adj.* —**bac•te′ri•ol′o•gist,** *n.*

bad, *adj.,* **worse, worst,** *n.* —*adj.* **1.** not good. —*n.* **2.** bad thing, condition, or quality. —*v.* **3.** Also, **bade.** pt. of **bid.** —**bad′ly,** *adv.* —**bad′ness,** *n.*

badge, *n.* emblem or decoration.

badg′er, *n.* **1.** burrowing carnivorous mammal. —*v.* **2.** harass.

bad′min•ton, *n.* game similar to lawn tennis.

baf′fle, *v.,* **-fled, -fling,** *n.* —*v.* **1.** thwart; confuse. —*n.* **2.** obstacle; obstruction. —**baf′fle•ment,** *n.*

bag, *n., v.,* **bagged, bagging.** —*n.* **1.** sack or receptacle of flexible material. **2.** purse. —*v.* **3.** bulge. **4.** put into a bag. **5.** kill or catch. —**bag′gy,** *adj.* —**bag′gi•ness,** *n.*

ba′gel, *n.* hard ringlike roll.

bag′gage, *n.* trunks, suitcases, etc.

bag′pipe′, *n.* (*often pl.*) musical instrument with windbag and two or more pipes. —**bag′pip′er,** *n.*

bail, *Law* (1, 2, 4). —*n.* **1.** security for the return of a prisoner to custody. **2.** person giving bail. **3.** handle of kettle or pail. —*v.* **4.** give or obtain liberty by bail. **5.** dip water out of boat. **6. bail out,** make a parachute jump. —**bail′a•ble,** *adj.* —**bail′ee′,** *n.* —**bail′ment,** *n.* —**bail′or,** *n.* —**bail′er,** *n.*

bail′iff, *n.* public officer similar to sheriff or deputy.

bail′i•wick, *n.* **1.** district under bailiff's jurisdiction. **2.** person's area of authority, skill, etc.

bait, *n.* **1.** food used as lure in angling or trapping. —*v.* **2.** prepare with bait. **3.** set dogs upon for sport.

bake, *v.,* **baked, baking. 1.** cook by dry heat, as in an oven. **2.** harden by heat. —**bak′er,** *n.*

bak′er•y, *n., pl.* **-eries.** place for baking; baker's shop.

bal′a•lai′ka (-lī′-), *n.* musical instrument similar to guitar and mandolin.

bal′ance, *n., v.,* **-anced, -ancing.** —*n.* **1.** instrument for weighing. **2.** equilibrium. **3.** harmonious arrangement. **4.** act of balancing. **5.** remainder, as of money due. —*v.* **6.** weigh. **7.** set or hold in equilibrium. **8.** be equivalent to. **9.** reckon or adjust accounts. —**bal′anc•er,** *n.*

bal′co•ny, *n., pl.* **-nies. 1.** platform projecting from wall of building. **2.** theater gallery.

bald, *adj.* **1.** lacking hair on scalp. **2.** plain; undisguised. —**bald′ly,** *adv.* —**bald′ness,** *n.*

bale, *n., v.,* **baled, baling.** —*n.* **1.** large bundle or package. —*v.* **2.** make into bales. —**bal′er,** *n.*

bale′ful, *adj.* evil; menacing. —**bale′-ful•ly,** *adv.* —**bale′ful•ness,** *n.*

balk (bôk), *v.* **1.** stop; stop short. **2.** hinder; thwart. —*n.* **3.** obstacle; hindrance. —**balk′y,** *adj.*

ball, *n.* **1.** round or roundish body. **2.** game played with ball. **3.** social assembly for dancing. —*v.* **4.** make or form into ball.

bal′lad, *n.* **1.** narrative folk song or poem. **2.** sentimental popular song.

bal′last, *n.* **1.** heavy material carried to ensure stability. —*v.* **2.** furnish with ballast.

ball bearing, 1. bearing in which a moving part turns on steel balls. **2.** ball so used.

bal•le•ri′na (-rē′-), *n.* leading woman ballet dancer.

bal•let′ (ba lā′), *n.* theatrical entertainment by dancers.

ballistic missile, guided missile completing its trajectory in free fall.

bal•lis′tics, *n.* study of the motion of projectiles. —**bal•lis′tic,** *adj.*

bal•loon′, *n.* **1.** bag filled with a gas lighter than air, designed to float in atmosphere. —*v.* **2.** go up in balloon. —**bal•loon′ist,** *n.*

bal′lot, *n., v.,* **-loted, -loting.** —*n.* **1.** ticket or paper used in voting. **2.** vote; voting. —*v.* **3.** vote by ballot.

ball′park′, *n.* baseball grounds.

ball′point′ pen, pen laying down ink with small ball bearing.

ball′room′, *n.* room for balls or dancing.

bal′ly•hoo′, *n.* **1.** *Informal.* exaggerated publicity. —*v.* **2.** tout.

balm (bäm), *n.* **1.** fragrant, oily substance obtained from tropical trees. **2.** aromatic ointment or fragrance.

balm′y, *adj.,* **balmier, balmiest. 1.** mild; refreshing. **2.** fragrant. —**balm′i•ly,** *adv.* —**balm′i•ness,** *n.*

ba•lo′ney, *n. Informal.* **1.** bologna. **2.** false or foolish talk.

bal′sa (bôl′-), *n.* tropical American tree with very light wood.

bal′sam, *n.* **1.** fragrant substance exuded from certain trees. **2.** any of these trees. —**bal•sam′ic,** *adj.*

bal′us•ter, *n.* pillarlike support for railing.

bal′us•trade′, *n.* series of balusters supporting a railing.

bam•boo′, *n.* treelike tropical grass having a hollow woody stem.

bam•boo′zle, *v.,* **-zled, -zling.** *Informal.* confuse or trick.

ban, *v.,* **banned, banning,** *n.* —*v.* **1.** prohibit. —*n.* **2.** prohibition.

ba′nal, *adj.* trite. —**ba•nal′i•ty,** *n.*

ba•nan′a, *n.* **1.** tropical plant. **2.** fruit of this plant.

band, *n.* **1.** strip of material for binding. **2.** stripe. **3.** company of persons. **4.** group of musicians. —*v.* **5.** mark with bands. **6.** unite. —**band′mas′-ter,** *n.* —**bands′man,** *n.* —**band′-stand′,** *n.*

band′age, *n., v.,* **-aged, -aging.** —*n.* **1.** strip of cloth for binding wound. —*v.* **2.** bind with bandage. —**band′-ag•er,** *n.*

ban•dan′na, *n.* colored handkerchief with figures. Also, **ban•dan′a.**

ban′dit, *n., pl.* **-dits, ban•dit′ti.** robber; outlaw. —**ban′dit•ry,** *n.*

ban'dy, *v.*, **-died, -dying**, *adj.* —*v.* 1. strike to and fro. 2. exchange (words) back and forth. —*adj.* 3. bent outward. —**ban'dy-leg'ged**, *adj.*

bane, *n.* thing causing death or destruction.

bane'ful, *adj.* destructive. —**bane'ful·ly**, *adv.* —**bane'ful·ness**, *n.*

bang, *n.* 1. loud, sudden noise. 2. (*often pl.*) fringe of hair across forehead. —*v.* 3. make loud noise. 4. strike noisily.

ban'gle, *n.* bracelet.

ban'ish, *v.* 1. exile. 2. drive or put away. —**ban'ish·ment**, *n.*

ban'is·ter, *n.* 1. baluster. 2. (*pl.*) balustrade.

ban'jo, *n.* musical instrument similar to guitar, with circular body. —**ban'jo·ist**, *n.*

bank, *n.* 1. pile; heap. 2. slope bordering stream. 3. place or institution for receiving and lending money. —*v.* 4. border with or make into bank. 5. cover fire to make burn slowly. 6. act as bank. 7. deposit or keep money in bank. —**bank'er**, *n.* —**bank'ing**, *n.*

bank'roll', *n.* 1. money possessed. —*v.* 2. pay for; fund.

bank'rupt, *n.* 1. insolvent person. —*adj.* 2. insolvent. 3. lacking. —*v.* 4. make bankrupt. —**bank'rupt·cy**, *n.*

ban'ner, *n.* flag.

banns, *n.pl.* notice of intended marriage. Also, **bans**.

ban'quet, *n.*, *v.*, **-queted, -queting**. —*n.* 1. feast. —*v.* 2. dine or entertain at banquet. —**ban'quet·er**, *n.*

ban'tam, *n.* 1. breed of small domestic fowl. —*adj.* 2. tiny.

ban'ter, *n.* 1. teasing; raillery. —*v.* 2. address with or use banter. —**ban'ter·er**, *n.*

ban'yan, *n.* East Indian fig tree.

bap'tism, *n.* immersion in or application of water, esp. as initiatory rite in Christian church. —**bap·tis'mal**, *adj.*

Bap'tist, *n.* Christian who undergoes baptism only after profession of faith.

bap·tize', *v.*, **-tized, -tizing**. 1. administer baptism. 2. christen. —**bap·tiz'er**, *n.*

bar, *n.*, *v.*, **barred, barring**, *prep.* —*n.* 1. long, evenly shaped piece of wood or metal. 2. band; stripe. 3. long ridge in shallow waters. 4. obstruction; hindrance. 5. line marking division between two measures of music. 6. place where liquors are served. 7.

legal profession or its members. 8. railing in courtroom between public and court officers. 9. place in courtroom where prisoners are stationed. —*v.* 10. provide or fasten with a bar. 11. block; hinder. —*prep.* 12. except for. —**barred**, *adj.*

barb, *n.* 1. point projecting backward. —*v.* 2. furnish with barb. —**barbed**, *adj.*

bar·bar'i·an, *n.* 1. savage or uncivilized person. —*adj.* 2. uncivilized. —**bar·bar'i·an·ism**, *n.* —**bar·bar'ic**, *adj.* —**bar·bar'i·cal·ly**, *adv.*

bar'ba·rism, *n.* barbarian state or act.

bar·bar'i·ty, *n.*, *pl.* **-ties**. 1. cruelty. 2. crudity.

bar'ba·rous, *adj.* 1. barbarian. 2. harsh; harsh-sounding. —**bar'ba·rous·ly**, *adv.* —**bar'ba·rous·ness**, *n.*

bar'be·cue', *n.*, *v.*, **-cued, -cuing**. —*n.* 1. gathering at which animals are roasted whole. 2. animal roasted whole. —*v.* 3. broil or roast animal whole.

bar'ber, *n.* 1. one who gives haircuts, shaves, etc. —*v.* 2. shave or cut the hair.

bar·bi'tu·rate' (bär bich'ə rāt'), *n.* sedative drug.

bard, *n.* 1. ancient Celtic poet. 2. any poet. —**bard'ic**, *adj.*

bare, *adj.*, **barer, barest**, *v.*, **bared, baring**. —*adj.* 1. uncovered; unclothed. 2. unfurnished. 3. unconcealed. 4. mere. —*v.* 5. make bare. —**bare'ness**, *n.* —**bare'foot'**, *adj.*, *adv.*

bare'back', *adv.*, *adj.* without saddle.

bare'faced', *adj.* 1. undisguised. 2. impudent.

bare'ly, *adv.* 1. no more than; only. 2. nakedly.

bar'gain, *n.* 1. agreement. 2. advantageous purchase. —*v.* 3. discuss or arrive at agreement. —**bar'gain·er**, *n.*

barge, *n.*, *v.*, **barged, barging**. —*n.* 1. unpowered vessel for freight. —*v.* 2. carry by barge. 3. move clumsily. 4. *Informal.* intrude. —**barge'man**, *n.*

bar'i·tone', *n.* 1. male voice or part between tenor and bass. 2. baritone singer, instrument, etc. Also, **bar'y·tone'**.

bark, *n.* 1. cry of a dog. 2. external covering of woody plants. 3. Also, **barque**. three-masted vessel. —*v.* 4. sound a bark. 5. utter with barking sound. 6. strip off bark of. 7. rub off the skin of. —**bark'er**, *n.*

bar'ley, *n.* edible cereal plant.

bar mitz'vah (bär), Jewish religious ceremony recognizing manhood.

barn, *n.* farm building for storage and stabling. —**barn'yard'**, *n.*

bar'na·cle, *n.* type of shellfish that clings to ship bottoms, floating timber, etc. —**bar'na·cled**, *adj.*

ba·rom'e·ter, *n.* instrument for measuring atmospheric pressure. —**bar'o·met'ric**, **bar'o·met'ri·cal**, *adj.*

bar'on, *n.* member of lowest nobility. Also, *n.fem.* **bar'on·ess**. —**bar'on·age**, *n.* —**ba·ro'ni·al**, *adj.*

bar'on·et, *n.* member of hereditary British commoner order, ranking below baron. —**bar'on·et·cy**, *n.*

Ba·roque' (-rōk'), *n.* artistic style marked by grotesque effects.

bar'rack, *n.* (*usually pl.*) 1. building for lodging soldiers. —*v.* 2. lodge in barracks.

bar'ra·cu'da (-kōō'-), *n.* edible eel-like fish inhabiting warm waters.

bar·rage', *n.* barrier of concentrated artillery fire.

bar'rel, *n.*, *v.*, **-reled, -reling**. —*n.* 1. wooden cylindrical vessel with bulging sides. 2. quantity held in such vessel. —*v.* 3. put in barrel or barrels.

bar'ren, *adj.* 1. sterile; unfruitful. 2. dull. —**bar'ren·ness**, *n.*

bar'ri·cade', *n.*, *v.*, **-caded, -cading**. —*n.* 1. defensive barrier. —*v.* 2. block or defend with barricade.

bar'ri·er, *n.* obstacle; obstruction.

bar'row, *n.* flat frame for carrying load.

bar'ter, *v.* 1. trade by exchange. —*n.* 2. act of bartering.

ba·salt' (-sôlt'), *n.* dark, hard rock. —**ba·sal'tic**, *adj.*

base, *n.*, *v.*, **based, basing**, *adj.* —*n.* 1. bottom or foundation of something. 2. fundamental principle. 3. starting point. 4. *Mil.* **a.** protected place from which operations proceed. **b.** supply installation. 5. chemical compound which unites with an acid to form a salt. —*v.* 6. make foundation for. —*adj.* 7. despicable. 8. inferior. 9. counterfeit. —**base'ly**, *adv.* —**base'ness**, *n.*

base'ball', *n.* 1. game of ball played by two teams of nine players on diamond-shaped field. 2. ball used.

base'ment, *n.* story of building below the ground floor.

bash'ful, *adj.* shy; timid. —**bash'ful·ly**, *adv.* —**bash'ful·ness**, *n.*

ba'sic, *adj.* 1. rudimentary. 2. essential. —*n.* 3. (*pl.*) rudiments. —**ba'si•cal•ly,** *adv.*

bas'il (baz'-), *n.* plant of mint family.

ba•sil'i•ca, *n.* 1. ancient church. 2. Roman Catholic church.

ba'sin, *n.* 1. circular vessel for liquids. 2. area drained by river.

ba'sis, *n., pl.* **-ses.** 1. base (defs. 1, 2). 2. principal ingredient.

bask, *v.* lie in or expose to warmth.

bas'ket, *n.* receptacle woven of twigs, strips of wood, etc.

bas'ket•ball', *n.* 1. game of ball played by two teams of five players on rectangular court. 2. ball used.

bass, *adj., n., pl.* (for 3) **basses, bass.** —*adj.* 1. (bās). of the lowest musical part or range. —*n.* 2. (bās). bass part, voice, instrument, etc. 3. (bas). various edible, spiny fishes.

bas'si•net', *n.* basket with hood, used as cradle.

bas•soon', *n.* baritone woodwind instrument.

bas'tard, *n.* 1. illegitimate child. 2. *Informal.* mean person. —*adj.* 3. illegitimate in birth. 4. not pure or authentic.

baste, *v.,* **basted, basting.** 1. sew with temporary stitches. 2. moisten meat, etc., while cooking.

bat, *n., v.,* **batted, batting.** —*n.* 1. club, esp. as used in ball games. 2. nocturnal flying mammal. —*v.* 3. strike with bat. 4. take turn in batting.

batch, *n.* material, esp. bread, prepared in one operation.

bat'ed, *adj.* (of breath) held back in suspense.

bath, *n., pl.* **baths.** 1. washing of entire body. 2. water used. —**bath'room',** *n.* —**bath'tub',** *n.*

bathe, *v.,* **bathed, bathing.** 1. take a bath. 2. immerse in liquid; moisten. —**bath'er,** *n.*

bath'robe', *n.* robe worn going to and from bath.

ba•tik' (-tēk'), *n.* cloth partly waxed to resist dye.

ba•ton', *n.* staff or rod, esp. one used by orchestral conductor.

bat•tal'ion, *n.* military unit of three or more companies.

bat'ten, *n.* 1. strip of wood. —*v.* 2. fasten or furnish with battens. 3. fatten or grow fat.

bat'ter, *v.* 1. beat persistently. 2. damage by hard usage. —*n.* 3. semiliquid cooking mixture. 4. one who bats.

bat'ter•y, *n., pl.* **-teries.** 1. device for producing electricity. 2. combination of artillery pieces. 3. illegal attack by beating or wounding.

bat'tle, *n., v.,* **-tled, -tling.** —*n.* 1. hostile encounter. —*v.* 2. fight. —**bat'tle•field',** *n.* —**bat'tle•ground',** *n.* —**bat'tler,** *n.*

bat'tle•ment, *n.* indented parapet.

bat'tle•ship', *n.* heavily armed warship.

bau'ble, *n.* trinket.

baux'ite (bôk'sīt), *n.* principal ore of aluminum.

bawd'y, *adj.,* **bawdier, bawdiest.** obscene. —**bawd'i•ness,** *n.*

bawl, *v.* 1. shout out. —*n.* 2. shout.

bay, *n.* 1. inlet of sea or lake. 2. vertical section of window. 3. compartment or recess in a building. 4. deep, prolonged bark. 5. stand made by hunted animal or person. 6. reddish-brown. —*v.* 7. bark. 8. bring to bay (def. 5). —*adj.* 9. of the color bay.

bay'o•net, *n., v.,* **-neted, -neting.** —*n.* 1. daggerlike instrument attached to rifle muzzle. —*v.* 2. kill or wound with bayonet.

bay'ou (bī'oo), *n., pl.* **bayous.** arm of river, etc.

ba•zaar', *n.* market place. Also, **ba•zar'.**

ba•zoo'ka, *n.* hand-held rocket launcher used esp. against tanks.

B.C., Before Christ.

be, *v.* 1. exist. 2. occur.

beach, *n.* 1. sand or pebbles of seashore. —*v.* 2. run or pull a ship onto beach.

beach'head', *n.* part of beach landed on and seized by military force.

bea'con, *n.* 1. signal, esp. a fire. —*v.* 2. serve as beacon.

bead, *n.* 1. small ball of glass, pearl, etc., designed to be strung. 2. (*pl.*) necklace. —*v.* 3. ornament with beads. —**bead'ing,** *n.* —**bead'y,** *adj.*

bea'gle, *n.* short-legged hunting dog.

beak, *n.* 1. bill of bird. 2. beaklike object.

beak'er, *n.* large glass.

beam, *n.* 1. horizontal support secured at both ends. 2. breadth of ship. 3. ray of light or other radiation. —*v.* 4. emit beams. 5. smile radiantly. —**beam'ing,** *adj.*

bean, *n.* 1. edible seed of certain plants. 2. plant producing such seed.

bear, *v.,* **bore** (for 1–5) or **beared** (for 6), **bearing,** —*v.* 1. support. 2. carry. 3. undergo; endure. 4. move; go. 5. give birth. 6. act as bear (def. 9). —*n.* 7. large shaggy mammal. 8. clumsy or rude person. 9. speculator who counts on falling prices. —**bear'er,** *n.* —**bear'a•ble,** *adj.* —**bear'ish,** *adj.* —**bear'ish•ly,** *adv.*

beard, *n.* 1. hair on face of man. 2. similar growth or part. —*v.* 3. defy. —**beard'ed,** *adj.* —**beard'less,** *adj.*

bear'ing, *n.* 1. manner. 2. reference; relation. 3. *Mach.* part in which another part moves. 4. (*often pl.*) position; direction. 5. **bearings,** orientation.

beast, *n.* 1. animal. 2. coarse or inhuman person.

beast'ly, *adj.,* **-lier, -liest.** 1. brutish. 2. nasty. —**beast'li•ness,** *n.*

beat, *v.,* **beat, beaten** or **beat, beating,** —*v.* 1. strike repeatedly. 2. dash against. 3. mark time in music. 4. defeat. 5. throb. —*n.* 6. blow. 7. sound of a blow. 8. habitual rounds. 9. musical time. —**beat'en,** *adj.* —**beat'er,** *n.*

be•a'tif'ic, *adj.* blissful. —**be•a'tif'i•cal•ly,** *adv.*

be•at'i•tude', *n.* 1. blessedness. 2. (*often cap.*) declaration of blessedness made by Christ (Matthew 5).

beau (bō), *n., pl.* **beaus, beaux.** 1. lover. 2. fop.

beau'te•ous (byoo'-), *adj.* beautiful. —**beau'te•ous•ly,** *adv.* —**beau'te•ous•ness,** *n.*

beau'ti•ful, *adj.* having beauty. —**beau'ti•ful•ly,** *adv.*

beau'ti•fy', *v.,* **-fied, -fying.** make beautiful. —**beau'ti•fi•ca'tion,** *n.*

beau'ty, *n., pl.* **-ties.** 1. quality that excites admiring pleasure. 2. beautiful thing or person.

bea'ver, *n.* 1. amphibious rodent, valued for its fur. 2. the fur.

be•cause', *conj.* 1. for the reason that. —*adv.* 2. by reason (of).

beck, *n.* beckoning gesture.

beck'on, *v.* signal by gesture. —**beck'on•er,** *n.*

be•come', *v.,* **became, become, becoming.** 1. come to be. 2. suit. —**be•com'ing,** *adj.* —**be•com'ing•ly,** *adv.*

bed, *n., v.,* **bedded, bedding.** —*n.* 1. piece of furniture on or in which a person sleeps. 2. sleep. 3. piece of ground for planting. 4. foundation. —*v.* 5. plant in bed. —**bed'time',** *n.*

bed'bug', *n.* bloodsucking insect.

bed'ding, *n.* blankets, sheets, etc., for a bed.

bed′fast′, *adj.* unable to leave bed. Also, **bed′rid′den.**

bed′fel′low, *n.* 1. sharer of bed. 2. ally

bed′lam, *n.* 1. scene of loud confusion. 2. lunatic asylum.

Bed′ou•in (-o͞o in), *n.* 1. desert Arab. 2. nomad.

be•drag′gled, *adj.* dirty and wet.

bed′room′, *n.* sleeping room.

bed′spread′, *n.* cover for bed.

bed′stead′, *n.* frame for bed.

bee, *n.* 1. four-winged, nectar-gathering insect. 2. local gathering. —**bee′hive′**, *n.* —**bee′keep′er**, *n.*

beech, *n.* tree bearing small edible nuts (**beech′nuts′**). —**beech′en**, *adj.*

beef, *n., pl.* **beeves.** 1. bull, cow, or steer. 2. edible flesh of such an animal. 3. brawn. —**beef′y**, *adj.* —**beef′i•ness**, *n.* —**beef′steak′**, *n.*

bee′line′, *n.* direct course.

beer, *n.* beverage brewed and fermented from cereals.

beet, *n.* biennial edible plant.

bee′tle, *v.*, **-tled, -tling**, *n.* —*v.* 1. project. —*n.* 2. insect with hard, horny forewings.

be•fall′, *v.*, **-fell, -fallen, -falling.** happen; happen to.

be•fit′, *v.*, **-fitted, -fitting.** be fitting for. —**be•fit′ting**, *adj.*

be•fore′, *adv.* 1. in front. 2. earlier. —*prep.* 3. in front of. 4. previously to. 5. in future of. 6. in preference to. 7. in precedence of. 8. in presence of. —*conj.* 9. previously to time when.

be•fore′hand′, *adv.* in advance.

be•friend′, *v.* act as friend toward.

beg, *v.*, **begged, begging.** 1. ask for charity. 2. ask humbly.

be•get′, *v.*, **begot, begotten** or **begot, begetting.** procreate. —**be•get′ter**, *n.*

beg′gar, *n.* 1. one who begs alms. 2. penniless person. —*v.* 3. reduce to beggary. —**beg′gar•y**, *n.*

beg′gar•ly, *adj.* meager; penurious.

be•gin′, *v.*, **began, begun, beginning.** 1. start. 2. originate. —**be•gin′ner**, *n.* —**be•gin′ning**, *n.*

be•gone′, *interj.* depart!

be•gon′ia (bi gōn′yə), *n.* tropical flowering plant.

be•grudge′, *v.*, **-grudged, -grudging.** 1. be discontented at (another's possessions or standing). 2. give or allow reluctantly.

be•guile′ (-gīl′), *v.*, **-guiled, -guiling.** 1. delude. 2. charm; divert. —**be•guile′ment**, *n.* —**be•guil′er**, *n.*

be•half′, *n.* 1. side; part. 2. interest; favor.

be•have′, *v.*, **-haved, -having.** 1. conduct oneself. 2. act properly.

be•hav′ior, *n.* manner of behaving.

be•head′, *v.* cut off the head of.

be•hest′, *n.* urgent request.

be•hind′, *prep.* 1. at the back of. 2. later than. —*adv.* 3. at the back. 4. in arrears.

be•hold′, *v.*, **beheld, beholding.** 1. look at; see. —*interj.* 2. look! —**be•hold′er**, *n.*

be•hold′en, *adj.* obliged.

be•hoove′, *v.*, **-hooved, -hooving.** be necessary for (someone).

beige (bāzh), *n.* light brown.

be′ing, *n.* 1. existence. 2. something that exists.

be•la′bor, *v.* 1. discuss, etc., excessively. 2. beat.

be•lat′ed, *adj.* late. —**be•lat′ed•ly**, *adv.*

belch, *v.* 1. eject gas from stomach. 2. emit violently. —*n.* 3. act of belching.

bel′fry, *n., pl.* **-fries.** bell tower.

be•lie′, *v.*, **-lied, -lying.** 1. misrepresent. 2. show to be false. 3. lie about. —**be•li′er**, *n.*

be•lief′, *n.* 1. thing believed. 2. conviction. 3. faith.

be•lieve′, *v.*, **-lieved, -lieving.** 1. trust. 2. accept as true. 3. regard as likely. —**be•liev′a•ble**, *adj.* —**be•liev′er**, *n.*

be•lit′tle, *v.*, **-littled, -littling.** disparage.

bell, *n.* 1. metal instrument producing ringing sound. —*v.* 2. put bell on. 3. flare outward. —**bell′-like′**, *adj.*

belle, *n.* beautiful girl.

bel′li•cose′, *adj.* warlike.

bel•lig′er•ent (-lij′-), *adj.* 1. warlike. 2. engaged in war. —*n.* 3. nation at war. —**bel•lig′er•ence, bel•lig′er•en•cy**, *n.* —**bel•lig′er•ent•ly**, *adv.*

bel′low, *v.* 1. roar, as a bull. 2. utter in deep, loud voice. —*n.* 3. act or sound of bellowing.

bel′lows, *n.sing. and pl.* collapsing device producing strong current of air.

bel′ly, *n., pl.* **-lies**, *v.*, **-lied, -lying.** —*n.* 1. abdomen. 2. inside. 3. protuberant surface. —*v.* 4. swell out.

be•long′, *v.* 1. be a member of. 2. belong to, be the property of.

be•long′ing, *n.* possession.

be•lov′ed, *adj.* 1. greatly loved. —*n.* 2. one who is loved.

be•low′, *adv.* 1. beneath. 2. in lower rank. —*prep.* 3. lower than.

belt, *n.* 1. band for encircling waist. 2. any flexible band. —*v.* 3. gird or furnish with belt. —**belt′ing**, *n.*

be•moan′, *v.* lament.

be•mused′, *adj.* lost in thought.

bench, *n.* 1. long seat. 2. judge's seat. 3. body of judges. 4. work table.

bend, *v.*, **bent, bending**, *n.* —*v.* 1. curve. 2. become curved. 3. cause to submit. 4. turn or incline. —*n.* 5. a bending. 6. something bent.

be•neath′, *adj.* 1. in a lower place, state, etc. —*prep.* 2. under. 3. lower than. 4. unworthy of.

ben′e•dic′tion, *n.* blessing.

ben′e•fac′tion, *n.* 1. doing of good. 2. benefit conferred. —**ben′e•fac′tor**, *n.* —**ben′e•fac′tress**, *n.fem.*

be•nef′i•cent, *adj.* doing good. —**benef′i•cence**, *n.* —**be•nef′i•cent•ly**, *adv.*

ben′e•fi′cial, *adj.* helpful. —**ben′e•fi′cial•ly**, *adv.*

ben′e•fi′ci•ar•y, *n., pl.* **-aries.** one who receives benefits.

ben′e•fit, *n., v.*, **-fited, -fiting.** —*n.* 1. act of kindness. 2. entertainment for worthy cause. —*v.* 3. do good to. 4. gain advantage.

be•nev′o•lent, *adj.* desiring to do good. —**be•nev′o•lence**, *n.*

be•nign′ (bi nīn′), *adj.* 1. kind. 2. favorable. —**be•nign′ly**, *adv.*

be•nig′nant (-nig′-), *adj.* 1. kind. 2. beneficial. —**be•nig′nan•cy**, *n.* —**be•nig′nant•ly**, *adv.* —**be•nig′ni•ty**, *n.*

bent, *adj.* 1. curved. 2. determined. —*n.* 3. curve. 4. inclination.

ben′zene (-zēn), *n.* colorless inflammable liquid, used as solvent.

ben′zine (-zēn), *n.* colorless inflammable liquid, used in cleaning, dyeing, etc.

be•queath′, *v.* dispose of by will. —**be•queath′al**, *n.*

be•quest′, *n.* legacy.

be•rate′, *v.*, **-rated, -rating.** scold.

be•reave′, *v.*, **-reaved** or **-reft, -reaving.** 1. deprive of. 2. make desolate. —**be•reave′ment**, *n.*

be•ret′ (-rā′), *n.* cloth cap.

ber′i•ber′i, *n.* disease caused by vitamin deficiency.

ber′ry, *n., pl.* **-ries**, *v.*, **-ried, -rying.** —*n.* 1. small juicy fruit. —*v.* 2. produce or gather berries.

ber•serk′, *adj.* raging violently.

berth, *n.* 1. sleeping space for traveler. 2. mooring space for vessel. —*v.* 3. assign berth (def. 2) to.

ber′yl, *n.* green mineral.

be•seech′, *v.*, **-sought, -seeching.** implore; beg. —**be•seech′ing•ly**, *adv.*

be•set′, *v.*, **-set, -setting.** 1. attack on all sides. 2. surround.

be•side′, *prep.* 1. at the side of. 2. compared with. 3. in addition to. —*adv.* 4. in addition.

be•sides′, *adv.* 1. moreover. 2. otherwise. —*prep.* 3. in addition to. 4. other than.

be•siege′, *v.*, **-sieged, -sieging.** lay siege to. —**be•sieg′er**, *n.*

be•smirch′, *v.* defile.

be•speak′, *v.*, **-spoke, -spoken** or **-spoke, -speaking.** 1. ask for in advance. 2. imply.

best, *adj.* 1. of highest quality. 2. most suitable. —*adv.* 3. most excellently. 4. most fully. —*n.* 5. best thing. —*v.* 6. defeat.

bes′tial (-chǝl), *adj.* 1. beastlike. 2. brutal. —**bes•ti•al′i•ty**, *n.* —**bes′-tial•ly**, *adv.*

be•stir′, *v.*, **-stirred, -stirring.** stir up.

be•stow′, *v.* 1. present. 2. apply.

be•strew′, *v.*, **-strewed, -strewed** or **-strewn, -strewing.** 1. cover. 2. scatter.

bet, *v.*, **bet** or **betted, betting**, *n.* —*v.* 1. risk on a chance result. —*n.* 2. thing or amount bet. —**bet′ter, bet′tor**, *n.*

be•take′, *v.*, **-took, -taken, -taking.** —**betake oneself**, 1. go. 2. resort (to).

bête noire (bet nwär), most dreaded person or thing.

be•tide′, *v.*, **-tided, -tiding.** happen.

be•times′, *adv. Archaic.* 1. early. 2. soon.

be•to′ken, *v.* indicate.

be•tray′, *v.* 1. deliver or expose by treachery. 2. be unfaithful to. 3. reveal. 4. deceive. 5. seduce. —**be•tray′al**, *n.* —**be•tray′er**, *n.*

be•troth′ (bi trōth′), *v.* promise to marry. —**be•troth′al**, *n.*

bet′ter, *adj.* 1. of superior quality. 2. healthier. —*adv.* 3. in a more excellent way. 4. more. —*n.* 5. something better. 6. one's superior. —*v.* 7. improve on. —**bet′ter•ment**, *n.*

be•tween′, *prep.* 1. in the space separating. 2. intermediate to. 3. connecting. —*adv.* 4. in the intervening space or time.

bev′el, *n.*, *v.*, **-eled, -eling.** —*n.* 1. surface cutting off a corner. 2. instrument for drawing angles. —*v.* 3. cut or slant at a bevel.

bev′er•age, *n.* drink.

bev′y, *n.*, *pl.* **bevies.** 1. flock of birds. 2. group.

be•wail′, *v.* lament.

be•ware′, *v.*, **-wared, -waring.** be wary (of).

be•wil′der, *v.* confuse. —**be•wil′-dered**, *adj.* —**be•wil′der•ing**, *adj.* —**be•wil′der•ing•ly**, *adv.* —**be•wil′der•ment**, *n.*

be•witch′, *v.* enchant. —**be•witch′-ing**, *adj.* —**be•witch′ing•ly**, *adv.*

be•yond′, *prep.* 1. on the farther side of. 2. farther, more, or later on. —*adv.* 3. farther on. —*n.* 4. life after death.

bi•an′nu•al, *adj.* occurring twice a year. —**bi•an′nu•al•ly**, *adv.*

bi′as, *n.*, *v.*, **biased, biasing.** —*n.* 1. slant. 2. prejudice. —*v.* 3. prejudice.

bib, *n.* cloth to protect dress.

Bi′ble, *n.* Old and New Testaments. —**Bib′li•cal**, *adj.* —**Bib′li•cal•ly**, *adv.*

bib′li•og′ra•phy, *n.*, *pl.* **-phies.** list of associated writings.

bi•cam′er•al, *adj.* composed of two legislative bodies.

bi′cen•ten′ni•al, *n.* two-hundredth anniversary.

bi′ceps (-seps), *n.* muscle of upper arm.

bick′er, *v.* squabble.

bi′cy•cle (-si-), *n.*, *v.*, **-cled, -cling.** —*n.* 1. two-wheeled vehicle. —*v.* 2. ride a bicycle. —**bi′cy•cler, bi′cy•clist**, *n.*

bid, *v.*, **bade** or **bad** (for 1, 2) or **bid** (for 3), **bidden** or **bid, bidding**, *n.* —*v.* 1. command. 2. say. 3. offer. —*n.* 4. offer. —**bid′der**, *n.* —**bid′-ding**, *n.*

bid′da•ble, *adj.* 1. worth bidding. 2. *Archaic.* obedient.

bide, *v.*, **bided, biding.** —**bide one's time**, await opportunity.

bi•det′ (bē dā′), *n.* tub for bathing private parts.

bi•en′ni•al, *adj.* occurring every two years. —**bi•en′ni•al•ly**, *adv.*

bier, *n.* stand for a corpse or coffin.

bi•fo′cal, *adj.* 1. having two focuses. 2. (of eyeglass lens) having separate portions for near and far vision. —*n.* 3. (*pl.*) eyeglasses with bifocal lenses.

big, *adj.*, **bigger, biggest.** 1. large. 2. important. —**big′ness**, *n.*

big′a•my, *n.* crime of marrying again while legally married. —**big′a•mist**, *n.* —**big′a•mous**, *adj.*

big′horn′, *n.* wild sheep of western U.S.

bight (bīt), *n.* 1. loop of rope. 2. deep bend in seashore.

big′ot, *n.* bigoted person. —**big′ot•ry**, *n.*

big′ot•ed, *adj.* intolerant. —**big′ot•ed•ly**, *adv.*

bi•ki′ni (-kē′-), *n.* woman's brief bathing suit.

bi•lat′er•al, *adj.* on or affecting two sides.

bile, *n.* 1. digestive secretion of the liver. 2. ill nature.

bilge, *n.*, *v.*, **bilged, bilging.** —*n.* 1. outer part of ship bottom. 2. water in a bilge. 3. wide part of cask. —*v.* 4. *Naut.* cause to leak at the bilge.

bi•lin′gual, speaking or expressed in two languages. —**bi•lin′gual•ly**, *adv.*

bil′ious (-yǝs), *adj.* 1. pertaining to bile or excess bile. 2. peevish.

bill, *n.* 1. account of money owed. 2. piece of paper money. 3. draft of proposed statute. 4. written list. 5. horny part of bird's jaw. —*v.* 6. charge.

bill′board′, *n.* large outdoor advertising display panel.

bil′let, *n.*, *v.*, **-leted, -leting.** —*n.* 1. lodging for a soldier. —*v.* 2. provide with lodging.

bil′-lets-doux′ (bil′i do͞o′), *n.*, *pl.* **bil-lets-doux** (-do͞oz′), love letter.

bill′fold′, *n.* wallet.

bil′liards, *n.* game played with hard balls (**billiard balls**) on a table. —**bil′liard**, *adj.* —**bil′liard•ist**, *n.*

bil′lion, *n.* thousand million. —**bil′-lionth**, *adj.*, *n.*

bil′lion•aire′, *n.* owner of billion dollars or more.

bil′low, *n.* 1. great wave. —*v.* 2. surge. —**bil′low•y**, *adj.* —**bil′low•i•ness**, *n.*

bi•month′ly, *adv.*, *adj.* every two months.

bin, *n.*, *v.*, **binned, binning.** —*n.* 1. box for storing grain, coal, etc. —*v.* 2. store in bin.

bi′na•ry (bī′-), *adj.* involving two parts, elements, etc.

bind, *v.*, **bound, binding.** 1. tie or encircle with band. 2. unite. 3. oblige. 4. attach cover to book. —**bind′er**, *n.*

bind′ing, *n.* 1. something that binds. —*adj.* 2. obligatory.

bin′go, *n.* game of chance using cards with numbered squares.

bin′na•cle, *n.* stand for ship's compass.

bin•oc′u•lars, *n.pl.* field glasses.

bi•o•chem′is•try, *n.* chemistry of living matter. **—bi′o•chem′i•cal,** *adj.* **—bi′o′chem′i•cal•ly,** *adv.*

bi′o•de•grad′a•ble, *adj.* decaying and being absorbed into environment.

bi′o•feed′back, *n.* method for achieving physical and emotional self-control through observation of one's waves, blood pressure, etc.

bi•og′ra•phy, *n., pl.* **-phies.** written account of person's life. **—bi•og′ra•pher,** *n.* **—bi′o•graph′i•cal, bi′o•graph′ic,** *adj.* **—bi′o•graph′i•cal•ly,** *adv.*

bi•ol′o•gy, *n.* science of living matter. **—bi′o•log′i•cal,** *adj.* **—bi′o•log′i•cal•ly,** *adv.* **—bi•ol′o•gist,** *n.*

bi•on′ics, *n.* use of electronic devices to increase human strength or ability. **—bi•on′ic,** *adj.*

bi′op•sy, *n., pl.* **-sies.** examination of specimen of living tissue.

bi•par′ti•san, *adj.* representing two parties or factions.

bi′ped, *n.* 1. two-footed animal. **—***adj.* 2. having two feet.

birch, *n.* tree with smooth bark and dense wood. **—birch′en,** *adj.*

bird, *n.* vertebrate with feathers and wings.

bird′s′-eye, *adj.* seen from above.

birth, *n.* 1. fact of being born. 2. lineage. 3. origin. **—birth′day′,** *n.* **—birth′place′,** *n.*

birth control, planned contraception.

birth′mark′, *n.* mark on skin from birth.

birth′right′, *n.* hereditary right.

bis′cuit, *n.* bread in small, soft cakes. **—bis′cuit•like′,** *adj.*

bi•sect′, *v.* cut into two parts. **—bi•sec′tion,** *n.* **—bi•sec′tion•al,** *adj.* **—bi•sec′tor,** *n.*

bi•sex′u•al, *adj.* 1. being both heterosexual and homosexual. **—***n.* 2. bisexual person. **—bi•sex′u•al′i•ty,** *n.*

bish′op, *n.* 1. overseer of a diocese. 2. piece in chess.

bish′op•ric, *n.* diocese or office of bishop.

bi′son, *n., pl.* **bisons, bison.** oxlike North American mammal.

bisque (bisk), *n.* creamy soup.

bit, *n., v.,* **bitted, bitting. —***n.* 1. mouthpiece of bridle. 2. restraint. 3. small amount. 4. drill. 5. unit of computer information. **—***v.* 6. restrain with a bit.

bitch, *n.* 1. female dog. 2. *Slang.* mean or lewd woman. **—***v.* 3. *Slang.* complain.

bite, *v.,* **bit, bitten** or **bit, biting,** *n.* **—***v.* 1. cut or grip with teeth. 2. sting. 3. corrode. **—***n.* 4. act of biting. 5. wound made by biting. 6. sting. 7. piece bitten off. **—bit′er,** *n.*

bit′ing, *adj.* 1. harsh to the senses. 2. severely critical. **—bit′ing•ly,** *adv.*

bit′ter, *adj.* 1. of harsh taste. 2. hard to receive or bear. 3. intensely hostile. **—***n.* 4. something bitter. **—bit′ter•ish,** *adj.* **—bit′ter•ly,** *adv.* **—bit′ter•ness,** *n.*

bit′tern, *n.* type of heron.

bit′ters, *n.pl.* liquor with bitter vegetable ingredients.

bi•tu′men (-t$\overline{oo}$′-), *n.* asphalt or asphaltlike substance. **—bi•tu′mi•nous,** *adj.*

bi′valve′, *n.* mollusk with two shells hinged together. **—bi′valve′, bi•val′vular,** *adj.*

biv′ou•ac′ ($\overline{oo}$ ak′), *n., v.,* **-acked, -acking.** **—***n.* 1. temporary resting or assembly place for troops. **—***v.* 2. dispose or meet in bivouac.

bi•week′ly, *adv., adj.* 1. every two weeks.

bi•zarre′ (-zär′), *adj.* strange.

blab, *v.,* **blabbed, blabbing.** 1. talk idly. 2. reveal secrets.

black, *adj.* 1. without brightness or color. 2. having dark skin color. 3. without light. 4. gloomy. 5. wicked. **—***n.* 6. member of a dark-skinned people. 7. black clothing. 8. something black. **—***v.* 9. make or become black. **—black′ness,** *n.* **—black′ly,** *adv.* **—black′ish,** *adj.*

black′ball′, *n.* 1. adverse vote. **—***v.* 2. vote against. 3. ostracize.

black′ber′ry, *n., pl.* **-ries.** 1. dark-purple fruit. 2. plant bearing it.

black′bird′, *n.* black-feathered American bird.

black′board′, *n.* dark board for writing on with chalk.

black′en, *v.,* **-ened, -ening.** 1. black (def. 9). 2. defame.

black′guard (blag′ärd), *n.* 1. despicable person. **—***v.* 2. revile. **—black′guard•ly,** *adv., adj.*

black hole, area in outer space whose great density prevents radiation of light.

black′jack′, *n.* 1. short flexible club. 2. game of cards; twenty-one. **—***v.* 3. strike with a blackjack.

black′list′, *n.* list of persons in disfavor. **—black′list′,** *v.*

black′mail′, *n.* 1. extortion by intimidation. 2. payment extorted. **—***v.* 3. extort by blackmail. **—black′mail′er,** *n.*

black′out′, *n.* 1. extinction of lights. 2. loss of consciousness.

black′smith′, *n.* 1. person who shoes horses. 2. worker in iron.

black′thorn′, *n.* thorny shrub with plumlike fruit.

black′ wid′ow, poisonous spider.

blad′der, *n.* sac in body.

blade, *n.* 1. cutting part of knife, sword, etc. 2. leaf. 3. thin, flat part. 4. dashing young man. **—blad′ed,** *adj.* **—blade′like′,** *adj.*

blame, *v.,* **blamed, blaming,** *n.* **—***v.* 1. hold responsible for fault. 2. find fault with. **—***n.* 3. censure. 4. responsibility for censure. **—blam′a•ble, blame′ful, blame′wor′thy,** *adj.* **—blame′less,** *adj.*

blanch, *v.* whiten.

bland, *adj.* 1. not harsh. 2. not interesting or flavorful. **—bland′ly,** *adv.* **—bland′ness,** *n.*

blan′dish, *v.* coax. **—blan′dish•ment,** *n.*

blank, *adj.* 1. not written or printed on. 2. without interest, emotion, etc. 3. white. 4. unrhymed. **—***n.* 5. place lacking something. 6. space to be filled in. 7. paper containing such space. **—***v.* 8. make blank. **—blank′ly,** *adv.* **—blank′ness,** *n.*

blan′ket, *n.* 1. warm bed covering. **—***v.* 2. cover.

blare, *v.,* **blared, blaring,** *n.* **—***v.* 1. sound loudly. **—***n.* 2. loud, raucous noise.

blar′ney, *n., v.,* **-neyed, -neying.** **—***n.* 1. wheedling talk. **—***v.* 2. wheedle.

bla•sé′ (blä zā′), *adj.* bored; unimpressed.

blas•pheme′ (-fēm′), *v.* speak impiously or evilly. **—blas•phem′er,** *n.* **—blas′phe•mous,** *adj.* **—blas′phe•my,** *n.*

blast, *n.* 1. gust of wind. 2. loud trumpet tone. 3. stream of air. 4. explosion. 5. charge of explosive. **—***v.* 6. blow. 7. blight; destroy. 8. explode. **—blast′er,** *n.*

blast′off′, *n.* rocket launching.

bla′tant, *adj.* brazenly obvious. **—bla′tan•cy,** *n.* **—bla′tant•ly,** *adv.*

blaze, *n., v.,* **blazed, blazing. —***n.* 1. bright flame. 2. bright glow. 3. brightness. 4. mark cut on tree. 5. white spot on animal's face. **—***v.* 6. burn or shine brightly. 7. mark with blazes (def. 4).

blaz′er, *n.* sports jacket.

bla′zon (blā′zən), *v.* depict or proclaim.

bleach, *v.* 1. whiten. —*n.* 2. bleaching agent.

bleach′ers, *n.pl.* tiers of spectators' seats, usu. roofless.

bleak, *adj.* 1. bare; desolate. 2. cold. 3. dreary; depressing. —**bleak′ly,** *adv.* —**bleak′ness,** *n.*

blear, *v.* 1. dim, esp. with tears. —*n.* 2. bleared state. —**blear′y,** *adj.*

bleat, *v.* 1. cry, as sheep, goat, etc. —*n.* 2. such a cry. —**bleat′er,** *n.*

bleed, *v.,* **bled, bleeding.** lose or cause to lose blood.

blem′ish, *v.* 1. mar. —*n.* 2. defect. —**blem′ish•er,** *n.*

blend, *v.,* **blended** or **blent, blending.** 1. mix. —*n.* 2. mixture.

bless, *v.,* **blessed** or **blest, blessing.** 1. consecrate. 2. request divine favor on. 3. make happy. 4. extol as holy. —**bless′ed,** *adj.* —**bless′ing,** *n.*

blight, *n.* 1. plant disease. 2. ruin. —*v.* 3. wither; decay. 4. ruin.

blind, *adj.* 1. sightless. 2. uncomprehending; unreasonable. 3. hidden. 4. without an outlet. 5. without advance knowledge. —*v.* 6. make blind. —*n.* 7. something that blinds. 8. ruse or disguise. —**blind′ly,** *adv.* —**blind′ness,** *n.*

blind′fold′, *v.* 1. cover eyes. —*n.* 2. covering over eyes. —*adj.* 3. with covered eyes.

blink, *v.* 1. wink. 2. ignore. —*n.* 3. act of blinking. 4. gleam.

bliss, *n.* 1. gladness. 2. supreme happiness. —**bliss′ful,** *adj.*

blis′ter, *n.* 1. vesicle on the skin. —*v.* 2. raise blisters on. —**blis′ter•y,** *adj.*

blithe, *adj.* joyous; cheerful. —**blithe′ly,** *adv.*

blithe′some, *adj.* cheerful.

blitz, *n.* Also, **blitz′krieg′** (-krēg′). 1. swift, violent war, waged by surprise. —*v.* 2. attack by blitz.

bliz′zard, *n.* violent snowstorm.

bloat, *v.* swell.

bloc, *n.* political or economic confederation.

block, *n.* 1. solid mass. 2. platform. 3. obstacle. 4. single quantity. 5. unit of city street pattern. —*v.* 6. obstruct. 7. outline roughly. —**block′er,** *n.*

block•ade′, *n., v.,* **-aded, -ading.** —*n.* 1. shutting-up of place by armed force. 2. obstruction. —*v.* 3. subject to blockade.

block′head′, *n.* stupid fellow.

block′house′, *n.* fortified structure.

blond, *adj.* 1. light-colored. 2. having light-colored hair, skin, etc. —*n.* 3. blond person. —**blonde,** *adj., n.fem.*

blood, *n.* 1. red fluid in arteries and veins. 2. life. 3. bloodshed. 4. extraction. —**blood′y,** *adj.* —**blood′i•ness,** *n.* —**blood′less,** *adj.*

blood′hound′, *n.* large dog with acute sense of smell.

blood′mo•bile′, *n.* truck for receiving blood donations.

blood′shed′, *n.* slaughter.

blood′shot′, *adj.* with eye veins conspicuous.

blood′suck′er, *n.* 1. leech. 2. extortionist.

blood′thirst′y, *adj.* murderous.

bloom, *n.* 1. flower. 2. health. 3. healthy glow. —*v.* 4. blossom. 5. flourish. —**bloom′ing,** *adj.*

bloom′ers, *n.pl.* loose trousers worn by women.

blos′som, *n.* 1. flower. —*v.* 2. produce blossoms. 3. develop.

blot, *n., v.,* **blotted, blotting.** —*n.* 1. spot; stain. —*v.* 2. stain; spot. 3. dry with absorbent material. 4. destroy. —**blot′ter,** *n.*

blotch, *n.* 1. large spot or stain. —*v.* 2. blot (def. 2). —**blotch′y,** *adj.*

blouse, *n.* loosely fitting upper garment.

blow, *v.,* **blew, blown, blowing,** *n.* —*v.* 1. (of air) move. 2. drive by current of air. 3. sound a wind instrument. 4. go bad. 5. explode. 6. blossom. —*n.* 7. blast of air. 8. sudden stroke. 9. sudden shock of calamity. 10. blossoming. —**blow′er,** *n.* —**blow′y,** *adj.*

blow′out′, *n.* rupture of an automobile tire.

blow′pipe′, *n.* pipe used to concentrate stream of air or gas.

blow′torch′, *n.* device producing hot flame.

blow′up′, *n.* 1. explosion. 2. *Informal.* emotional outbreak. 3. photographic enlargement.

blub′ber, *n.* 1. fat of whales. —*v.* 2. weep.

bludg′eon (bluj′ən), *n.* 1. heavy club. —*v.* 2. strike with a bludgeon.

blue, *n., adj.,* **bluer, bluest,** *v.,* **blued, bluing** or **blueing.** —*n.* 1. color of sky. —*adj.* 2. (of skin) discolored by cold, etc. 3. melancholy. —*v.* 4. make blue. —**blue′ness,** *n.* —**blu′ish,** *adj.*

blue′ber′ry, *n., pl.* **-ries.** edible berry, usually bluish.

blue′bird′, *n.* small, blue North American bird.

blue′jay′, *n.* crested North American jay.

blue′print′, *n.* white-on-blue photocopy of line drawing. —**blue′print′,** *v.*

blues, *n.pl.* 1. melancholy. 2. melancholy jazz song.

bluff, *v.* 1. mislead by show of boldness. —*n.* 2. act of bluffing. 3. one who bluffs. 4. steep cliff or hill. —*adj.* 5. vigorously frank. 6. steep. —**bluff′ly,** *adv.* —**bluff′ness,** *n.* —**bluff′er,** *n.*

blu′ing, *n.* bleaching substance. Also, **blue′ing.**

blun′der, *n.* 1. mistake. —*v.* 2. make an error. 3. move blindly. —**blun′der•er,** *n.*

blunt, *adj.* 1. having a dull edge or point. 2. abrupt in manner. —*v.* 3. make blunt. —**blunt′ly,** *adv.* —**blunt′ness,** *n.*

blur, *v.,* **blurred, blurring,** *n.* —*v.* 1. obscure. 2. make or become indistinct. —*n.* 3. smudge. —**blur′ry,** *adj.*

blurt, *v.* utter suddenly.

blush, *v.* 1. redden. 2. feel shame. —*n.* 3. reddening. 4. reddish tinge. —**blush′ful,** *adj.* —**blush′ing•ly,** *adv.*

blus′ter, *v.* 1. be tumultuous. 2. be noisy or swaggering. —*n.* 3. tumult. 4. noisy talk. —**blus′ter•er,** *n.*

bo′a, *n., pl.* **boas.** 1. nonpoisonous snake of tropical America. 2. long scarf of silk, feathers, etc.

boar, *n.* male of swine.

board, *n.* 1. thin flat piece of timber. 2. table, esp. for food. 3. daily meals. 4. official controlling body. —*v.* 5. cover or close with boards. 6. furnish with food. 7. take meals. 8. enter a (ship, train, etc.). —**board′er,** *n.*

boast, *v.* 1. speak with pride; be proud of. 2. speak with excessive pride. —*n.* 3. thing boasted. —**boast′er,** *n.* —**boast′ful,** *adj.*

boat, *n.* 1. vessel. —*v.* 2. go or move in boat. —**boat′house′,** *n.* —**boat′man,** *n.* —**boat′ing,** *n.*

boat′swain (bō′sən), *n.* petty officer on ship.

bob, *n., v.,* **bobbed, bobbing.** —*n.* 1. short jerky motion. 2. short haircut. —*v.* 3. move jerkily. 4. cut short. —**bob′ber,** *n.*

bob′bin, *n.* reel; spool.

bob′o•link′, *n.* North American songbird.

bob′tail′, *n.* 1. short tail. —*v.* 2. cut short.

bob′white′, *n.* North American quail.

bode, *v.*, **boded, boding.** portend.

bod′ice, *n.* fitted waist.

bod′y, *n.*, *pl.* **bodies**, *v.*, **bodied, bodying.** —*n.* 1. animal's physical structure. 2. corpse. 3. main mass. 4. collective group. —*v.* 5. invest with body. —**bod′i·ly**, *adj.*, *adv.*

bod′y·guard′, *n.* guard for personal safety.

body language, conscious or unconscious communication through gestures or attitudes.

bog, *n.*, *v.*, **bogged, bogging.** —*n.* 1. swampy ground. —*v.* 2. sink or catch in a bog. —**bog′gy**, *adj.*

bog′gle, *v.*, **-gled, -gling.** 1. refuse to act. 2. overwhelm with surprise.

bo′gus, *adj.* counterfeit; fake.

bo′gy, *n.*, *pl.* **-gies.** hobgoblin. Also, **bo′gey, bo′gie.**

boil, *v.* 1. heat to bubbling point. 2. be agitated. 3. cook by boiling. —*n.* 4. act or state of boiling. 5. inflamed sore. —**boil′er**, *n.*

bois′ter·ous, *adj.* rough; noisy. —**bois′ter·ous·ly**, *adv.* —**bois′ter·ous·ness**, *n.*

bold, *adj.* 1. fearless. 2. conspicuous. —**bold′ly**, *adv.* —**bold′ness**, *n.*

boll (bōl), *n.* rounded seed vessel.

bo·lo′gna (bə lō′nē), *n.* beef and pork sausage.

Bol′she·vik, *n.*, *pl.* **-viks, -viki.** Russian communist. Also, **Bol′she·vist.** —**Bol′she·vism′**, *n.* —**Bol′she·vik, Bol′she·vis′tic**, *adj.*

bol′ster, *n.* 1. long pillow. —*v.* 2. support. —**bol′ster·er**, *n.*

bolt, *n.* 1. bar fastening a door. 2. similar part in a lock. 3. threaded metal pin. 4. sudden flight. 5. roll of cloth. 6. thunderbolt. —*v.* 7. fasten. 8. swallow hurriedly. 9. move or leave suddenly. 10. sift. —**bolt′er**, *n.*

bomb, *n.* 1. projectile with explosive charge. 2. *Slang.* total failure. —*v.* 3. attack with bombs. 4. *Slang.* fail totally. —**bomb′proof′**, *adj.*

bom·bard′, *v.* attack with artillery or bombs. —**bom·bar·dier′**, *n.* —**bombard′ment**, *n.*

bom′bast, *n.* high-sounding words. —**bom·bas′tic, bom·bas′ti·cal**, *adj.*

bomb′er, *n.* 1. airplane that drops bombs. 2. one who plants bombs.

bona fide (bō′nə fīd′, -fī′dē), *adj.* genuine.

bo·nan′za, *n.* 1. rich mass of ore. 2. good luck.

bon′bon′, *n.* piece of candy.

bond, *n.* 1. something that binds or unites. 2. bondsman. 3. written contractual obligation. 4. certificate held by creditor. —*v.* 5. put on or under bond. 6. mortgage.

bond′age, *n.* slavery.

bond′man, *n.*, *pl.* **-men.** man in bondage; male slave. Also, **bond′wom′an**, *n.fem.*

bonds′man, *n.*, *pl.* **-men.** person who gives surety for another by bond.

bone, *n.*, *v.*, **boned, boning.** —*n.* 1. piece of the skeleton. 2. hard substance composing it. —*v.* 3. remove bones of. —**bon′y**, *adj.*

bon′fire′, *n.* outdoor fire.

bon′go, *n.*, *pl.* **-gos, -goes.** small hand drum played as one of pair.

bon′net, *n.* woman's or child's head covering.

bon′sai (-sī), *n.*, *pl.* **bonsai.** dwarf tree or shrub.

bo′nus, *n.* extra payment.

boo, *interj.* (exclamation used to frighten or express contempt.)

boo′by, *n.*, *pl.* **-bies.** *Informal.* fool. Also, **boob.**

book, *n.* 1. printed or blank sheets bound together. 2. (*pl.*) accounts. 3. division of literary work. —*v.* 4. enter in book. 5. engage beforehand. —**book′bind′er**, *n.* —**book′case′**, *n.* —**book′keep′er**, *n.* —**book′let**, *n.* —**book′sell′er**, *n.* —**book′store′, book′shop′**, *n.*

book′end′, *n.* prop for books.

book′ie, *n.* bookmaker.

book′ish, *adj.* fond of reading. —**book′ish·ness**, *n.*

book′mak′er, *n.* professional bettor.

book′worm′, *n.* bookish person.

boom, *v.* 1. make a loud hollow sound. 2. flourish vigorously. —*n.* 3. loud hollow sound. 4. rapid development. 5. spar extending sail. 6. beam on derrick.

boom′er·ang′, *n.* 1. Australian throwing stick that returns in flight. —*v.* 2. make trouble for plotter rather than intended victim.

boon, *n.* 1. benefit. —*adj.* 2. convivial.

boon′dog′gle, *n.* *Informal.* useless work paid for with public money.

boor, *n.* clownish, rude person. —**boor′ish**, *adj.*

boost, *v.* 1. lift by pushing. 2. praise; advocate. 3. increase. —*n.* 4. upward push. 5. assistance. —**boost′er**, *n.*

boot, *n.* 1. covering for foot and leg. 2. kick. —*v.* 3. kick. 4. dismiss or discharge.

booth, *n.* 1. light structure for exhibiting goods, etc. 2. small compartment.

boot′leg′, *n.*, *v.*, **-legged, -legging,** *adj.* —*n.* 1. illicit liquor. —*v.* 2. deal in illicit goods. —*adj.* 3. illicit. —**boot′leg′ger**, *n.*

boo′ty, *n.*, *pl.* **-ties.** plunder.

bor′der, *n.* 1. edge; margin. 2. frontier. —*v.* 3. make a border. 4. adjoin. —**bor′der·land′**, *n.* —**bor′der·line′**, *n.*

bore, *v.*, **bored, boring**, *n.* —*v.* 1. drill into. 2. be uninteresting to. —*n.* 3. bored hole. 4. inside diameter. 5. dull person. —**bore′dom**, *n.* —**bor′er**, *n.* —**bore′some**, *adj.*

boric acid, antiseptic acid.

born, *adj.* brought from the womb.

born′-a·gain′, *adj.* having experienced Christian spiritual revival.

bor′ough, *n.* 1. small incorporated municipality. 2. division of city.

bor′row, *v.* 1. obtain on loan. 2. adopt.

bos′om, *n.* breast. —**bos′om·y**, *adj.*

boss, *n.* 1. employer; superintendent. 2. powerful politician. —*v.* 3. control; manage. 4. be domineering. —**boss′y**, *adj.*

bot′a·ny, *n.*, *pl.* **-nies.** science of plant life. —**bo·tan′i·cal, bo·tan′ic**, *adj.* —**bot′a·nist**, *n.*

botch, *v.* 1. bungle. 2. do clumsily. —*n.* 3. botched work. —**botch′y**, *adj.* —**botch′er**, *n.* —**botch′er·y**, *n.*

both, *adj.*, *pron.* 1. the two. —*conj.*, *adv.* 2. alike.

both′er, *v.* 1. annoy. 2. bewilder. —*n.* 3. annoying or disturbing thing. —**both′er·some**, *adj.*

bot′tle, *n.*, *v.*, **-tled, -tling.** —*n.* 1. sealed container for liquids. —*v.* 2. put into bottle. —**bot′tler**, *n.*

bot′tom, *n.* 1. lowest or deepest part. 2. underside. 3. lowest rank. —*v.* 4. reach or furnish with bottom.

bot′tom·less, *adj.* 1. without bottom. 2. without limit.

bottom line, basic or decisive point.

bot′u·lism′ (boch′ə-), *n.* disease caused by spoiled foods.

bough (bou), *n.* branch of tree.

boul′der, *n.* large rounded rock.

boul′e·vard′, *n.* broad avenue.

bounce, *v.*, **bounced, bouncing**, *n.* —*v.* 1. spring back. —*n.* 2. act of bouncing.

bound, *adj.* 1. in bonds. 2. made into book. 3. obligated. 4. going toward. —*v.* 5. jump. 6. limit. 7. adjoin. 8.

name boundaries of. —*n.* 9. jump. 10. (*usually pl.*) boundary.

bound′a•ry, *n., pl.* **-ries.** borderline; limit.

bound′less, *adj.* unlimited.

boun′te•ous, *adj.* 1. generous. 2. plentiful. Also, **boun′ti•ful.** —**boun′te•ous•ly,** *adv.* —**boun′te•ous•ness,** *n.*

boun′ty, *n., pl.* **-ties.** 1. generosity. 2. gift.

bou•quet′ (bō kā′, bōō-), *n.* 1. bunch of flowers. 2. aroma.

bour′bon (bûr′bən), *n.* corn whiskey.

bour•geois′ (bŏŏr zhwä′), *n., pl.* **-geois.** 1. one of the middle class. —*adj.* 2. of the middle class.

bour′geoi•sie′ (-zē′), *n.* middle class.

bout, *n.* 1. contest. 2. attack; onset.

bo′vine, *adj.* oxlike.

bow (bou, *for 1, 2, 3, 5, 9;* bō, *for 4, 6, 7, 8*), *v.* 1. bend down. 2. bend in worship, respect, etc. 3. subdue. 4. curve. —*n.* 5. inclination of head or body. 6. strip of bent wood for shooting arrow. 7. looped knot. 8. rod for playing violin. 9. front of ship. —**bow′man,** *n.*

bow′el, *n.* 1. intestine. 2. inner parts. Also, **bow′els.**

bow′er, *n.* leafy shelter.

bowl, *n.* 1. deep round dish. 2. rounded hollow part. 3. ball rolled at pins in various games. —*v.* 4. roll a ball underhand. 5. play bowling games. —**bowl′ing,** *n.*

box, *n.* 1. receptacle of wood, metal, etc. 2. compartment. 3. blow, as of the hand or fist. 4. Also, **box′wood′.** evergreen tree or shrub. —*v.* 5. put into box. 6. fight with fists. —**box′er,** *n.* —**box′ing,** *n.* —**box′like,** *adj.*

boy, *n.* male child. —**boy′hood,** *n.* —**boy′ish,** *adj.*

boy′cott, *v.* 1. abstain from dealing with or using. —*n.* 2. practice or instance of boycotting.

brace, *n., v.,* **braced, bracing.** —*n.* 1. stiffening thing or device. 2. pair. 3. character, { or }, for connecting lines. —*v.* 4. fasten with brace. 5. make steady. 6. stimulate. —**brac′er,** *n.*

brace′let, *n.* ornamental wristband.

brack′et, *n.* 1. armlike support for ledge. 2. mark, [or], for enclosing parenthetical words. —*v.* 3. furnish with or place within brackets.

brack′ish, *adj.* salty.

brad, *n.* small wire nail.

brag, *v.,* **bragged, bragging,** *n.* 1. boast. —**brag′ger,** *n.*

brag′gart, *n.* boastful person.

braid, *v.* 1. weave together. —*n.* 2. something braided.

braille, *n.* alphabet for blind.

brain, *n.* 1. soft mass of nerves in cranium. 2. intelligence. —*v.* 3. dash out the brains. —**brain′y,** *adj.* —**brain′less,** *adj.*

brain′storm′, *n.* sudden idea or impulse.

brain′wash′, *v.* indoctrinate under stress.

braise (brāz), *v.,* **braised, braising.** cook slowly in moisture.

brake, *n., v.,* **braked, braking.** —*n.* 1. device for arresting motion. 2. thicket. 3. large fern. —*v.* 4. slow or stop with a brake. —**brake′man,** *n.*

bram′ble, *n.* 1. rose plant. 2. prickly shrub. —**bram′bly,** *adj.*

bran, *n.* husk of grain.

branch, *n.* 1. division of plant's stem or trunk. 2. limb; offshoot. 3. local office, store, etc. —*v.* 4. put forth or divide into branches.

brand, *n.* 1. trademark. 2. kind; make. 3. burned mark. 4. burning piece of wood. —*v.* 5. mark with a brand.

brand′ish, *v.* shake; wave.

brand′-new′, *adj.* extremely new.

bran′dy, *n.* spirit from fermented grapes.

brass, *n.* 1. alloy of copper and zinc. 2. musical instrument such as trumpet or horn. 3. *Informal.* high-ranking officials. 4. impudence. —**brass′y,** *adj.*

bras•siere′ (-zēr′), *n.* undergarment supporting the breasts.

bra•va′do, *n., pl.* **-does, -dos.** boasting; swaggering.

brave, *adj.,* **braver, bravest,** *n., v.,* **braved, braving.** —*adj.* 1. courageous. —*n.* 2. North American Indian warrior. —*v.* 3. meet courageously. 4. defy. —**brave′ly,** *adv.* —**brave′ness,** *n.* —**brav′er•y,** *n.*

bra′vo, *interj.* well done!

brawl, *n.* 1. quarrel. —*v.* 2. quarrel noisily. —**brawl′er,** *n.*

brawn, *n.* 1. muscles. 2. muscular strength. —**brawn′y,** *adj.*

bray, *n.* 1. cry of a donkey. 2. similar sound. —*v.* 3. sound a bray. —**bray′er,** *n.*

braze, *v.,* **brazed, brazing.** work in brass. —**bra′zier** (-zhər), *n.*

bra′zen, *adj.* 1. of or like brass. 2. shameless; impudent. —*v.* 3. face boldly. —**bra′zen•ly,** *adv.* —**bra′zen•ness,** *n.*

bra′zier (-zhər), *n.* receptacle for burning charcoal.

breach, *n.* 1. a breaking. 2. gap in barrier. 3. infraction; violation. 4. break in friendship. —*v.* 5. make breach.

bread, *n.* 1. food of baked dough. 2. livelihood. 3. *Slang.* money. —*v.* 4. cover with bread crumbs. —**bread′stuff′,** *n.*

breadth, *n.* extent from side to side.

break, *v.,* **broke, broken, breaking,** *n.* —*v.* 1. separate into parts. 2. violate; dissolve. 3. fracture. 4. lacerate. 5. interrupt. 6. disclose. 7. fail; disable. 8. (*pp.* **broke**) ruin financially. 9. weaken. 10. tame. —*n.* 11. forcible disruption or separation. 12. gap. 13. attempt to escape. 14. marked change. 15. brief rest. 16. *Informal.* opportunity. —**break′a•ble,** *adj.* —**break′age,** *n.*

break′down′, *n.* 1. failure to operate. 2. nervous crisis. 3. analysis of figures.

break′er, *n.* wave breaking on land.

break′fast, *n.* 1. first meal of day. —*v.* 2. eat or supply with breakfast.

break′through′, *n.* fundamental discovery.

breast, *n.* 1. chest. 2. milk gland. 3. seat of thoughts and feelings. —*v.* 4. oppose boldly.

breath, *n.* 1. air inhaled and exhaled. 2. ability to breathe. 3. light breeze. —**breath′less,** *adj.*

breathe, *v.,* **breathed, breathing.** 1. inhale and exhale. 2. blow lightly. 3. live. 4. whisper.

breath′er (brē′thər), *n. Informal.* short rest.

breath′tak′ing (breth′-), *adj.* awesome or exciting.

breech′es, *n.pl.* trousers.

breed, *v.,* **bred, breeding,** *n.* —*v.* 1. produce. 2. raise. —*n.* 3. related animals. 4. lineage. 5. sort. —**breed′er,** *n.*

breed′ing, *n.* 1. ancestry. 2. training. 3. manners.

breeze, *n.* light current of air. —**breez′y,** *adj.*

breth′ren, *n.* a pl. of **brother.**

bre•vet′, *n.* 1. promotion without increase of pay. —*v.* 2. appoint by brevet.

bre′vi•ar′y, *n.* book of daily prayers and readings.

brev′i•ty, *n.* shortness.

brew, *v.* 1. prepare beverage such as beer or ale. 2. concoct. —*n.* 3. quantity brewed. 4. act or instance of brewing. —**brew′er,** *n.* —**brew′-er•y,** *n.*

bribe, *n.* 1. gift made for corrupt performance of duty. —*v.* 2. give or influence by bribe. —**brib′er,** *n.* —**brib′er•y,** *n.*

bric′-a-brac′, *n.* small pieces of art, curios, etc.

brick, *n.* 1. building block of baked clay. —*v.* 2. fill or build with brick. —**brick′lay′er,** *n.*

brick′bat′, *n.* 1. fragment of brick. 2. caustic criticism.

bride, *n.* woman newly married or about to be married. —**brid′al,** *adj.*

bride′groom′, *n.* man newly married or about to be married.

brides′maid′, *n.* bride's wedding attendant.

bridge, *n., v.,* **bridged, bridging.** —*n.* 1. structure spanning river, road, etc. 2. card game for four players. —*v.* 3. span.

bridge′head′, *n.* military position held on hostile river shore.

bri′dle, *n., v.,* **-dled, -dling.** —*n.* 1. harness at horse's head. 2. restraining thing. —*v.* 3. put bridle on. 4. restrain.

brief, *adj.* 1. short. 2. concise. —*n.* 3. concise statement. 4. outline of arguments and facts. —*v.* 5. instruct in advance. —**brief′ly,** *adv.* —**brief′-ness,** *n.*

brief′case′, *n.* flat carrier for business papers, etc.

bri′er, *n.* 1. prickly plant. 2. plant with woody root.

brig, *n.* 1. two-masted square-rigged ship. 2. ship's jail.

bri•gade′, *n.* 1. large military unit or body of troops. —*v.* 2. form into brigade.

brig′a•dier′, *n.* military officer between colonel and major general. Also, **brigadier general.**

brig′and, *n.* bandit.

bright, *adj.* 1. shining. 2. filled with light. 3. brilliant. 4. clever. —**bright′en,** *v.* —**bright′ly,** *adv.* —**bright′ness,** *n.*

bril′liant, *adj.* 1. sparkling. 2. illustrious. 3. highly intelligent. —*n.* 4. brilliant diamond. —**bril′liant•ly,** *adv.* —**bril′liance, bril′lian•cy, bril′-liant•ness,** *n.*

brim, *n., v.,* **brimmed, brimming.** —*n.* 1. upper edge; rim. —*v.* 2. fill or be full to brim. —**brim′ful′,** *adj.*

brin′dle, *n.* brindled coloring or animal.

brin′dled, *adj.* having dark streaks or spots.

brine, *n., v.,* **brined, brining.** —*n.* 1. salt water. 2. sea. —*v.* 3. treat with brine. —**brin′y,** *adj.*

bring, *v.,* **brought, bringing.** 1. fetch. 2. cause to come. 3. lead.

brink, *n.* edge.

brisk, *adj.* 1. lively. 2. stimulating. —**brisk′ly,** *adv.* —**brisk′ness,** *n.*

bris′ket, *n.* animal's breast.

bris′tle, *n., v.,* **-tled, -tling.** —*n.* 1. short, stiff, coarse hair. —*v.* 2. rise stiffly. 3. show indignation. —**bris′-tly,** *adv.*

Brit′ish, *adj.* of Great Britain or its inhabitants. —**Brit′ish•er,** *n.*

Brit′on, *n.* native of Great Britain.

brit′tle, *adj.* breaking readily. —**brit′-tle•ness,** *n.*

broach (brōch), *n.* 1. tool for enlarging hole. —*v.* 2. use broach. 3. pierce. 4. mention for first time.

broad, *adj.* 1. wide. 2. main. 3. liberal. —**broad′ly,** *adv.*

broad′cast′, *v.,* **-cast** or **-casted, -casting,** *n., adj.* —*v.* 1. send by radio. 2. scatter widely. —*n.* 3. something broadcasted. 4. radio program. —*adj.* 5. sent by broadcasting. —**broad′cast′er,** *n.*

broad′cloth′, *n.* fine cotton material.

broad′en, *v.* widen.

broad′-mind′ed, *adj.* tolerant.

bro•cade′, *n., v.,* **-caded, -cading.** —*n.* 1. figured woven fabric. —*v.* 2. weave with figure.

broc′co•li, *n.* green edible plant.

bro•chure′ (-shŏŏr′), *n.* pamphlet; booklet.

brogue, *n.* Irish accent.

broil, *v.* cook by direct heat. —**broil′-er,** *n.*

bro′ken, *v.* 1. pp. of **break.** —*adj.* 2. in fragments. 3. fractured. 4. incomplete. 5. weakened. 6. imperfectly spoken.

bro′ker, *n.* commercial agent. —**bro′ker•age,** *n.*

bron•chi′tis, *n.* inflammation in windpipe and chest. —**bron•chit′ic,** *adj.*

bron′co, *n., pl.* **-cos.** pony or small horse of western U.S. Also, **bron′-cho.**

bronze, *n., v.,* **bronzed, bronzing.** —*n.* 1. alloy of copper and tin. 2. brownish color. —*v.* 3. make bronzelike.

brooch (brōch), *n.* clasp or ornament.

brood, *n.* 1. group of animals born at one time. —*v.* 2. hatch. 3. think moodily. —**brood′y,** *adj.*

brook, *n.* 1. small stream. —*v.* 2. tolerate.

broom, *n.* 1. sweeping implement. 2. shrubby plant.

broom′stick, *n.* handle of a broom.

broth, *n.* thin soup.

broth′el (broth′əl), *n.* house of prostitution.

broth′er, *n., pl.* **brothers, brethren.** 1. male child of same parents. 2. member of same group. —**broth′er•hood′,** *n.* —**broth′er•ly,** *adj.*

broth′er-in-law′, *n., pl.* **brothers-in-law.** 1. husband's or wife's brother. 2. sister's husband.

brow, *n.* 1. eyebrow. 2. forehead. 3. edge of a height.

brow′beat′, *v.,* **-beat, -beaten, -beating.** bully.

brown, *n.* 1. dark reddish or yellowish color. —*adj.* 2. of this color. —*v.* 3. make or become brown.

browse, *v.,* **browsed, browsing.** 1. graze; feed. 2. examine books, etc., at leisure. —**brows′er,** *n.*

bruise, *v.,* **bruised, bruising.** 1. injure without breaking. —*n.* 2. bruised injury.

bru•net′, *adj.* dark brown, esp. of skin or hair.

bru•nette′, *n.* brunet woman or girl.

brunt, *n.* main force.

brush, *n.* 1. instrument with bristles. 2. bushy tail. 3. brief encounter. 4. dense bushes, shrubs, etc. —*v.* 5. use brush. 6. touch lightly.

brusque, *adj.* abrupt; blunt. Also, **brusk.** —**brusque′ly,** *adv.* —**brusque′ness,** *n.*

brute, *n.* 1. beast. 2. beastlike person. —*adj.* 3. not human. 4. irrational. 5. like animals. 6. savage. —**bru′tal,** *adj.* —**bru•tal′i•ty,** *n.* —**bru′tal•ly,** *adv.* —**brut′ish,** *adj.*

bub′ble, *n., v.,* **-bled, -bling.** —*n.* 1. globule of gas, esp. in liquid. 2. something infirm or unsubstantial. —*v.* 3. make or give off bubbles. —**bub′bly,** *adj.*

buc′ca•neer′, *n.* pirate.

buck, *v.* 1. leap to unseat a rider. 2. resist. —*n.* 3. male of the deer, rabbit, goat, etc.

buck′et, *n.* deep, open-topped container; pail.

buck′le, *n., v.,* **-led, -ling.** —*n.* 1. clasp for two loose ends. —*v.* 2. fasten with buckle. 3. bend. 4. set to work.

buck′ler, *n.* shield.

buck′ram, *n.* stiff cotton fabric.

buck′shot′, *n.* large lead shot.

buck′skin′, *n.* skin of buck.

buck′tooth′, *n., pl.* **-teeth.** projecting tooth.

buck′wheat′, *n.* plant with edible triangular seeds.

bu·col′ic (byōō kol′ik), *adj.* rustic; rural. —**bu·col′i·cal·ly,** *adv.*

bud, *n., v.,* **budded, budding.** —*n.* 1. small protuberance on plant. 2. small rounded part. —*v.* 3. produce buds. 4. begin to grow.

Bud′dhism (bōō′diz əm), *n.* Eastern religion. —**Bud′dhist,** *n.*

budge, *v.,* **budged, budging.** move slightly with effort.

budg′et, *v.,* **-eted, -eting.** —*n.* 1. estimate of income and expense. 2. itemized allotment of funds. —*v.* 3. plan allotment of. 4. allot. —**budg′et·ar′y,** *adv.*

buff, *n.* 1. thick light-yellow leather. 2. yellowish brown. —*adj.* 3. made or colored like buff. —*v.* 4. polish brightly.

buf′fa·lo′, *n., pl.* **-loes, -los, -lo.** large bovine mammal.

buff′er, *n.* 1. cushioning device. 2. polishing device.

buf′fet, *n., v.,* **-feted, -feting.** —*n.* 1. blow. 2. (bə fā′). cabinet for china, etc. 3. (bə fā′). food counter. —*v.* 4. strike. 5. struggle.

buf·foon′, *n.* clown.

bug, *n.* insect, esp. a beetle.

bug′gy, *n., pl.* **-gies.** light carriage.

bu′gle, *n., v.,* **-gled, -gling.** —*n.* 1. cornetlike wind instrument. —*v.* 2. sound a bugle. —**bu′gler,** *n.*

build, *v.,* **built, building,** *n.* —*v.* 1. construct. 2. form. 3. develop. —*n.* 4. manner or form of construction. —**build′er,** *n.*

build′ing, *n.* constructed shelter.

build′up′, *n. Informal.* 1. steady increase. 2. publicity campaign.

bulb, *n.* 1. fleshy-leaved, usually subterranean, bud. 2. rounded enlarged part. 3. electric lamp. —**bulb′ar, bulb′ous,** *adj.*

bulge, *n., v.,* **bulged, bulging.** —*n.* 1. rounded projection. —*v.* 2. swell out. —**bulg′y,** *adj.*

bul′gur (bōōl′gər), *n.* wheat used in parboiled, cracked, and dried form.

bulk, *n.* 1. magnitude. 2. main mass. —*v.* 3. be of or increase in magnitude.

bulk′head′, *n.* wall-like partition in a ship.

bulk′y, *adj.,* **-ier, -iest.** of great bulk.—**bulkiness,** *n.*

bull, *n.* 1. male bovine. 2. bull-like person. 3. speculator who depends on rise in prices. 4. papal document. 5. *Slang.* lying talk. —*adj.* 6. male. 7. marked by rise in prices. —**bull′ish,** *adj.*

bull′dog′, *n.* large, heavily built dog.

bull′doz′er, *n.* powerful earth-moving tractor.

bul′let, *n.* projectile for rifle or handgun.

bul′le·tin, *n.* brief account; news item.

bull′fight′, *n.* combat between man and a bull. —**bull′fight′er,** *n.*

bull′finch′, *n.* European songbird.

bull′frog′, *n.* large deep-voiced frog.

bul′lion (bōōl′yən), *n.* uncoined gold or silver.

bull′ock, *n.* castrated bull.

bull′s′-eye′, *n.* center of target.

bull terrier, dog bred from bulldog and terrier.

bul′ly, *n., pl.* **-lies,** *v.,* **-lied, -lying.** —*n.* 1. blustering, overbearing person. —*v.* 2. intimidate.

bul′rush′, *n.* large rush or rushlike plant.

bul′wark, *n.* 1. rampart. 2. protection.

bum, *n. Informal.* tramp or hobo.

bum′ble·bee′, *n.* large hairy bee.

bum′mer, *n. Slang.* frustrating or bad experience.

bump, *v.* 1. strike; collide. —*n.* 2. act or shock of bumping. 3. swelling. —**bump′y,** *adj.*

bump′er, *n.* 1. device for protection in collisions. 2. glass filled to brim. —*adj.* 3. abundant.

bun, *n.* kind of bread roll.

bunch, *n.* 1. cluster. 2. group. —*v.* 3. group; gather.

bun′dle, *n., v.,* **-dled, -dling.** —*n.* 1. group bound together. 2. package. —*v.* 3. wrap in bundle. 4. dress warmly.

bun′ga·low′, *n.* one-story cottage.

bun′gle, *v.,* **-gled, -gling,** *n.* —*v.* 1. fail to do properly. —*n.* 2. something bungled. —**bun′gler,** *n.*

bun′ion (-yən), *n.* swelling on foot.

bunk, *n.* 1. built-in bed. 2. *Slang.* deceit.

bunk′er, *n.* 1. bin. 2. underground refuge.

bun′ny, *n., pl.* **-nies.** *Informal.* rabbit.

bun′ting, *n.* 1. fabric for flags, etc. 2. flags. 3. finchlike bird.

buoy (boi), *n.* 1. float used as support or navagational marker. —*v.* 2. support by or as by buoy. 3. mark with buoy.

buoy′ant, *adj.* 1. tending to float. 2. cheerful. —**buoy′an·cy,** *n.* —**buoy′ant·ly,** *adv.*

bur, *n.* prickly seed case.

bur′den, *n.* 1. load. —*v.* 2. load heavily. —**bur′den·some,** *adj.*

bur′dock, *n.* coarse, prickly plant.

bu′reau (byōōr′ō), *n., pl.* **-eaus, -eaux.** 1. chest of drawers. 2. government department.

bu·reauc′ra·cy (byōō rok′rə sē), *n., pl.* **-cies.** 1. government by bureaus. 2. bureau officials.

bu′reau·crat′, *n.* official of a bureaucracy. —**bu′reau·crat′ic,** *adj.*

bur′glar, *n.* thief who breaks and enters. —**bur′glar·ize′,** *v.* —**bur′gla·ry,** *n.*

Bur′gun·dy, *n., pl.* **-dies.** dry red wine. Also, **bur′gun·dy.**

bur′i·al, *n.* act of burying.

bur′lap, *n.* coarse fabric of jute, etc.

bur·lesque′, *n., v.,* **-lesqued, -lesquing.** —*n.* 1. artistic travesty. 2. sexually suggestive entertainment. —*v.* 3. make a burlesque of.

bur′ly, *adj.,* **-lier, -liest.** 1. of great size. 2. brusque.

burn, *v.,* **burned** or **burnt, burning,** *n.* —*v.* 1. be on fire. 2. consume with fire; be afire. 3. heat; feel heat. 4. glow. 5. feel passion. —*n.* 6. burned place or condition. —**burn′er,** *n.*

bur′nish, *v.* 1. polish. —*n.* 2. gloss.

burp, *n.* light belch. —**burp,** *v.*

burr, *n.* 1. cutting or drilling tool. 2. rough protuberance. 3. bur.

bur′ro, *n., pl.* **burros.** donkey.

bur′row, *n.* 1. animal's hole in ground. —*v.* 2. make or lodge in burrow. —**bur′row·er,** *n.*

burst, *v.,* **burst, bursting,** *n.* —*v.* 1. break open or issue forth violently. 2. rupture. —*n.* 3. act or result of bursting. 4. sudden display.

bur′y, *v.,* **buried, burying.** 1. put into ground and cover. 2. conceal. —**bur′i·er,** *n.*

bus, *n., pl.* **buses, busses,** *v.,* **bused** or **bussed, busing** or **bussing.** —*n.* 1. large passenger motor vehicle. —*v.* 2. move by bus.

bush, *n.* 1. low, shrubby plant. 2. land covered with bushes. —**bush′y,** *adj.* —**bush′i·ness,** *n.*

bush′el, *n.* unit of 4 pecks.

busi′ness (biz′nis), *n.* 1. occupation; profession. 2. trade. 3. trading enterprise. 4. affair; matter. —**busi′ness•man′, busi′ness•wom•an,** *n.*

bus′ing, *n.* moving of pupils by bus to achieve racially balanced classes. Also, **bus′sing.**

bust, *n.* 1. sculpture of head and shoulders. 2. bosom.

bus′tle, *v.,* -**tled, -tling.** 1. move or act energetically. —*n.* 2. energetic activity.

bus′y, *adj.,* **busier, busiest,** *v.,* **busied, busying.** —*adj.* 1. actively employed. 2. full of activity. —*v.* 3. make or keep busy. —**bus′i•ly,** *adv.* —**bus′y•ness,** *n.*

bus′y•bod′y, *n., pl.* -**bodies.** meddler.

but, *conj.* 1. on the contrary. 2. except. 3. except that. —*prep.* 4. except. —*adv.* 5. only.

butch′er, *n.* 1. dealer in meat. 2. slaughterer. —*v.* 3. kill for food. 4. bungle. —**butch′er•y,** *n.*

but′ler, *n.* chief male servant.

butt, *n.* 1. thick or blunt end. 2. object of ridicule. 3. large cask. 4. cigarette end. 5. *Slang.* buttocks. —*v.* 6. push with head or horns. 7. be adjacent; join. 8. strike with head or horns.

but′ter, *n.* 1. Also, **but′ter•fat′.** solid fatty part of milk. —*v.* 2. put butter on. —**but′ter•y,** *adj.*

but′ter•cup′, *n.* plant with yellow cup-shaped flowers.

but′ter•fly′, *n., pl.* -**flies.** insect with broad colorful wings.

but′ter•milk′, *n.* milk with its butter extracted.

but′ter•nut′, *n.* nut of walnutlike tree.

but′ter•scotch′, *n.* kind of taffy.

but′tock, *n.* protuberance of rump.

but′ton, *n.* 1. disk or knob for fastening. 2. buttonlike object. —*v.* 3. fasten with button. —**but′ton•hole′,** *n.*

but′tress, *n.* 1. structure steadying wall. —*v.* 2. support.

bux′om, *adj.* (of a woman) attractively plump. —**bux′om•ness,** *n.*

buy, *v.,* **bought, buying.** 1. acquire by payment. 2. bribe. —**buy′er,** *n.*

buzz, *n.* 1. low humming sound. —*v.* 2. make or speak with buzz. —**buz′zer,** *n.*

buz′zard, *n.* carnivorous bird.

buzz′word′, *n. Informal.* fashionable cliché used to give specious weight to argument.

by, *prep.* 1. near to. 2. through. 3. not later than. 4. past. 5. using as means or method. —*adv.* 6. near. 7. past.

by′gone′, *adj.* 1. past. —*n.* 2. something past.

by′law′, *n.* standing rule.

by′-pass′, *n.* 1. detour. —*v.* 2. avoid through by-pass.

by′-prod′uct, *n.* secondary product.

by′stand′er, *n.* chance looker-on.

byte (bīt), *n.* unit of computer information, larger than bit.

by′-word′, *n.* 1. catchword. 2. proverb.

C

C, c, *n.* third letter of English alphabet.

cab, *n.* 1. taxicab. 2. (formerly) one-horse carriage. 3. part of locomotive, truck, etc., where operator sits.

ca•bal′, *n.* group of plotters.

cab′a•ret′ (-rā′), *n.* restaurant providing entertainment.

cab′bage, *n.* 1. plant with edible head of leaves. 2. *Slang.* money.

cab′in, *n.* 1. small house. 2. room in a ship or plane.

cab′i•net, *n.* 1. advisory council. 2. piece of furniture with drawers, etc. —**cab′i•net•mak′er,** *n.*

ca′ble, *n., v.,* -**bled, -bling.** —*n.* 1. thick, strong rope. 2. cablegram. —*v.* 3. send cablegram (to).

ca′ble•gram′, *n.* telegram sent by underwater wires.

cab′ri•o•let′ (kab′rē ə lā′), *n.* 1. type of one-horse carriage. 2. automobile with folding top.

ca•ca′o (kə kā′ō), *n., pl.* -**caos.** tropical tree whose seeds yield cocoa, etc.

cache (kash), *n., v.,* **cached, caching.** —*n.* 1. hiding place for treasure, etc. —*v.* 2. hide.

cack′le, *v.,* -**led, -ling,** *n.* —*v.* 1. utter shrill, broken cry. —*n.* 2. act or sound of cackling.

cac′tus, *n., pl.* -**tuses, -ti.** leafless, spiny American plant.

cad, *n.* ungentlemanly person.

ca•dav′er, *n.* corpse. —**ca•dav′er•ous,** *adj.*

cad′die, *n., v.,* -**died, -dying.** —*n.* 1. boy who carries one's golf clubs. —*v.* 2. work as caddie. Also, **cad′dy.**

ca′dence, *n.* rhythmic flow or beat.

ca•det′, *n.* military or naval student.

ca•fé′ (ka fā′), *n.* restaurant.

caf′e•te′ri•a, *n.* self-service restaurant.

caf′feine (kaf′ēn), *n.* chemical in coffee, etc., used as stimulant. Also, **caf′fein.**

cage, *n., v.,* **caged, caging.** —*n.* 1. barred box or room. —*v.* 2. put in cage.

cais′son (kā′sən), *n.* 1. ammunition wagon. 2. airtight underwater chamber.

ca•jole′, *v.,* -**joled, -joling.** coax; wheedle. —**ca•jol′er•y,** *n.*

Ca′jun (kā′jən), *n.* Louisianan of Nova Scotia-French origin.

cake, *n., v.,* **caked, caking.** —*n.* 1. sweet baked dough. 2. compact mass. —*v.* 3. form into compact mass.

cal′a•bash′, *n.* kind of gourd.

ca•lam′i•ty, *n., pl.* -**ties.** disaster. —**ca•lam′i•tous,** *adj.*

cal′ci•mine′ (kal′sə mīn′), *n., v.,* -**mined, -mining.** —*n.* 1. type of paint for ceilings, etc. —*v.* 2. cover with calcimine.

cal′ci•um, *n.* white metallic chemical element.

cal′cu•late′, *v.,* -**lated, -lating.** compute or estimate by mathematics. —**cal′cu•la′tor,** *n.* —**cal′cu•la′tion,** *n.*

cal′cu•la′ting, *adj.* shrewd; scheming.

cal′cu•lus, *n.* branch of mathematics.

cal′dron (kôl-), *n.* large kettle.

cal′en•dar, *n.* 1. list of days, weeks, and months of year. 2. list of events.

cal′en•der, *n.* 1. press for paper, cloth, etc. —*v.* 2. press in such a machine.

calf, *n., pl.* **calves.** 1. young of cow, etc. 2. fleshy part of leg below knee.

cal′i•ber, *n.* 1. diameter of bullet or gun bore. 2. quality. Also **cal′i•bre.**

cal′i•brate′, *v.,* -**brated, -brating.** mark for measuring purposes. —**cal′i•bra′tion,** *n.*

cal′i•co′, *n.* printed cotton cloth.

cal′i•per, *n.* (*usually pl.*) compass for measuring.

ca′liph, *n.* head of a Muslim state.

cal′is•then′ics, *n.pl.* physical exercises.

calk (kôk), *v.* make watertight at joints.

call, *v.* 1. cry out loudly. 2. announce. 3. summon. 4. telephone. 5. name. 6. visit briefly. —*n.* 7. cry or shout. 8. summons. 9. brief visit. 10. need; demand. —**call′er,** *n.*

call′ing, *n.* 1. trade. 2. summons.

cal′lous (kal′əs), *adj.* 1. unsympathetic. —*v.* 2. harden.

cal′low, *adj.* immature.

cal′lus, *n., pl.* **-luses.** hardened part of the skin.

calm, *adj.* 1. undisturbed. 2. not windy. —*n.* 3. calm state. —*v.* 4. make calm. —**calm′ly,** *adv.* —**calm′- ness,** *n.*

cal′o•mel′, *n.* white powder used as cathartic.

ca•lor′ic, *adj.* of heat.

cal′o•rie, *n.* measured unit of heat, esp. of fuel or energy value of food.

ca•lum′ni•ate′, *v.,* **-ated, -ating.** slander. —**ca•lum′ni•a′tor,** *n.* —**cal′- um•ny,** *n.*

ca′lyx (kā′liks), *n., pl.* **-lyxes.** small leaflets around flower petals.

cam, *n.* device for changing circular movement to straight.

cam′bric, *n.* close-woven fabric.

cam′el, *n.* Asian or African animal with one or two humps.

cam′e•o′, *n., pl.* **-os.** carved stone with layers in contrasting colors.

cam′er•a, *n.* device for making photographs.

cam′ou•flage′ (kam′ə fläzh′), *n., v.,* **-flaged, -flaging.** —*n.* 1. protective, deceptive covering or construction. —*v.* 2. hide by camouflage.

camp, *n.* 1. place of temporary lodging, esp. in tents. 2. faction. —*v.* 3. form, or live in, camp. —**camp′er,** *n.*

cam•paign′, *n.* 1. military operation. 2. competition for political office. —*v.* 3. engage in campaign. —**cam• paign′er,** *n.*

cam′phor, *n.* white crystalline substance used as moth repellent, medicine, etc.

cam′pus, *n.* school grounds.

can, *v.,* **canned** (**could** for def. 1), **canning** (for def. 2), *n.* —*v.* 1. be able or qualified to. 2. put in airtight container. —*n.* 3. cylindrical metal container. —**can′ner,** *n.*

Ca•na′di•an, *n.* citizen of Canada. —**Canadian,** *adj.*

ca•nal′, *n.* 1. artificial waterway. 2. tubular passage. —**can′al•ize′,** *v.*

can′a•pé (kan′ə pē), *n.* morsel of food served as appetizer.

ca•nard′, *n.* rumor.

ca•nar′y, *n., pl.* **-ries.** yellow cage bird.

ca•nas′ta, *n. Cards.* type of rummy whose main object is to establish sets of seven or more cards.

can′cel, *v.,* **-celed, -celing.** 1. cross out. 2. make void. —**can′cel•la′tion,** *n.*

can′cer, *n.* malignant growth. —**can′cer•ous,** *adj.*

can′de•la′brum (-lä′-), *n., pl.* **-bra.** branched candlestick.

can′did, *adj.* frank or honest. —**can′- did•ly,** *adv.* —**can′did•ness,** *n.*

can′di•date′, *n.* one seeking to be elected or chosen. —**can′di•da•cy,** *n.*

can′dle, *n.* waxy cylinder with wick for burning. —**can′dle•stick′,** *n.*

can′dor, *n.* frankness.

can′dy, *n., pl.* **-dies,** *v.,* **-died, -dying.** —*n.* 1. sweet confection. —*v.* 2. cook in, or cover with sugar.

cane, *n., v.,* **caned, caning.** —*n.* 1. stick used in walking. 2. long, woody stem. —*v.* 3. beat with a cane.

ca′nine (kā′nīn), *adj.* 1. of dogs. —*n.* 2. animal of dog family.

can′is•ter, *n.* small box.

can′ker, *n.* ulcerous sore. —**can′ker• ous,** *adj.*

canned, *adj.* 1. put into cans or sealed jars. 2. *Informal.* recorded.

can′ni•bal, *n.* person who eats human flesh. —**can′ni•bal•ism,** *n.*

can′ni•bal•ize′, *v.,* **ized, -izing.** strip of reusable parts.

can′non, *n.* large mounted gun. —**can′non•eer′,** *n.*

can′non•ade′, *n.* long burst of cannon fire.

can′not, *v.* am, are, or is unable to.

can′ny, *adj.,* **-nier, -niest.** 1. careful. 2. shrewd. —**can′ni•ness,** *n.*

ca•noe′, *n.* light boat propelled by paddles. —**canoe′,** *v.*

can′on, *n.* 1. rule or law. 2. recognized books of Bible. 3. church official. —**ca•non′i•cal,** *adj.*

can′on•ize′, *v.,* **-ized, -izing.** declare as saint. —**can′on•i•za′tion,** *n.*

can′o•py, *n., pl.* **-pies.** overhead covering.

cant, *n.* 1. insincerely virtuous talk. 2. special jargon.

can′t, *v. Informal.* cannot.

can′ta•loupe′ (-lōp′), *n.* small melon.

can•tan′ker•ous, *adj.* ill-natured.

can•ta′ta (-tä′-), *n.* dramatic choral composition.

can•teen′, *n.* 1. container for water, etc. 2. military supply store. 3. entertainment place for soldiers, etc.

can′ter, *n.* 1. easy gallop. —*v.* 2. go at easy gallop.

can′ti•cle, *n.* hymn.

can′ti•le′ver, *n.* structure secured at one end only.

can′to, *n., pl.* **-tos.** section of a long poem.

can′tor, *n.* synagogue or church singer.

can′vas, *n.* 1. cloth used for sails, tents, etc. 2. sails.

can′vass, *v.* 1. investigate. 2. solicit votes, etc.

can′yon, *n.* narrow valley. Also, **cañon.**

cap, *n., v.,* **capped, capping.** —*n.* 1. brimless hat. 2. cover. —*v.* 3. cover. 4. surpass.

ca′pa•ble, *adj.* able; qualified. —**ca′- pa•bly,** *adv.* —**ca′pa•bil′i•ty,** *n.*

ca•pa′cious, *adj.* holding much.

ca•pac′i•ty, *n., pl.* **-ties.** 1. amount that can be contained. 2. capability. 3. position; role.

cape, *n.* 1. sleeveless coat. 2. projecting point of land.

ca′per, *v.* 1. leap playfully. —*n.* 2. playful leap.

cap′il•lar′y, *adj., n., pl.* **-ries.** —*adj.* 1. of or in a thin tube. —*n.* 2. tiny blood vessel.

cap′i•tal, *n.* 1. city in which government is located. 2. large letter. 3. money and property available for business use. 4. decorative head of structural support. —*adj.* 5. important or chief. 6. excellent. 7. (of letters) large. 8. punishable by death.

cap′i•tal•ism, *n.* system of private investment in and ownership of business. —**cap′i•tal•ist,** *n.* —**cap′i•tal• is′tic,** *adj.*

cap′i•tal•ize′, *v.,* **-ized, -izing.** 1. put in large letters. 2. use as capital in business. 3. take advantage. —**cap′i• tal•i•za′tion,** *n.*

cap′i•tol, *n.* building used by legislature, esp. (*cap.*) Congress.

ca•pit′u•late′, *v.,* **-ated, -ating.** surrender. —**ca•pit′u•la′tion,** *n.*

ca′pon, *n.* castrated rooster.

ca•price′ (kə prēs′), *n.* whim. —**ca•pri′cious,** *adj.*

cap′size, *v.,* **-sized, -sizing.** overturn; upset.

cap′stan, *n.* device turned to pull cables.

cap′sule, *n.* small sealed container. —**cap′su•lar,** *adj.*

cap′tain, *n.* 1. officer below major or rear admiral. 2. ship master. —**cap′tain•cy,** *n.*

cap′tion, *n.* heading.

cap′tious, *adj.* noting trivial faults. —**cap′tious•ly,** *adv.* —**cap′tious•ness,** *n.*

cap′ti•vate′, *v.,* **-vated, -vating.** charm. —**cap′ti•va′tion,** *n.* —**cap′ti•va′tor,** *n.*

cap′tive, *n.* prisoner. —**cap•tiv′i•ty,** *n.*

cap′ture, *v.,* **-tured, -turing,** *n.* —*v.* 1. take prisoner. —*n.* 2. act or instance of capturing. —**cap′tor,** *n.*

car, *n.* vehicle, esp. automobile.

ca•rafe′ (kə raf′), *n.* broad-mouthed bottle for wine, water, etc.

car′a•mel, *n.* confection made of burnt sugar.

car′at, *n.* 1. unit of weight for gems. 2. karat.

car′a•van′, *n.* group traveling together, esp. over deserts.

car′a•way, *n.* herb bearing aromatic seeds.

car′bide, *n.* carbon compound.

car′bine (kär′bīn), *n.* short rifle.

car′bo•hy′drate, *n.* organic compound group including starches and sugars.

car•bol′ic acid, brown germicidal liquid.

car′bon, *n.* chemical element occurring as diamonds, charcoal, etc. —**car•bon•if′er•ous,** *adj.*

carbon monoxide, chemical compound of carbon and oxygen: a poisonous gas.

Car′bo•run′dum, *n. Trademark.* abrasive material.

car′bun•cle, *n.* painful inflammation under skin.

car′bu•re′tor, *n.* mechanism that mixes gasoline and air in motor.

car′cass, *n.* dead body. Also, **car′case.**

car•cin′o•gen (kär sin′ə jən), *n.* cancer-producing substance. —**car′cin•o•gen′ic,** *adj.*

card, *n.* 1. piece of stiff paper, with one's name (**calling card**), marks for game purposes (**playing card**), etc. 2.

comb for wool, flax, etc. —*v.* 3. dress (wool, etc.) with card.

car′di•ac′, *adj.* of the heart.

car′di•gan, *n.* knitted jacket or sweater with buttons down the front.

car′di•nal, *adj.* 1. main; chief. 2. (of numbers) used to express quantities or positions in series, e.g., 3, 15, 45. 3. deep red. —*n.* 4. red bird. 5. high official of Roman Catholic Church.

car′di•o•graph′, *n.* instrument for recording movements of heart. —**car′di•o•gram′,** *n.*

care, *n., v.,* **cared, caring.** —*n.* 1. worry. 2. caution. —*v.* 3. be concerned or watchful. —**care′free′,** *adj.* —**care′ful,** *adj.* —**care′less,** *adj.*

ca•reen′, *v.* tip; sway.

ca•reer′, *n.* 1. course through life. 2. life work. 3. speed. —*v.* 4. speed.

ca•ress′, *v., n.* touch in expressing affection.

car′et, *n.* mark (∧) indicating insertion.

care′worn′, *adj.* haggard from worry.

car′go, *n., pl.* **-goes, -gos.** goods carried by ship or plane.

car′i•bou′ (-bōō′), *n.* North American reindeer.

car′i•ca•ture, *n.* mocking portrait. —**car′i•ca•ture,** *v.*

car′ies (kâr′ēz), *n.* tooth decay.

car′il•lon, *n.* musical bells.

car′mine (-min), *n., adj.* crimson or purplish red.

car′nage, *n.* massacre.

car′nal, *adj.* of the body.

car•na′tion, *n.* common fragrant flower.

car′ni•val, *n.* 1. amusement fair. 2. festival before Lent.

car′ni•vore′ (-vōr′), *n.* flesh-eating mammal. —**car•niv′o•rous,** *adj.*

car′ol, *n.* 1. Christmas song. —*v.* 2. sing joyously. —**car′ol•er,** *n.*

ca•rouse′ (kə rouz′), *n., v.,* **-roused, -rousing.** —*n.* 1. noisy or drunken feast. —*v.* 2. engage in a carouse. —**ca•rous′al,** *n.*

carp, *v.* 1. find fault. —*n.* 2. large fresh-water fish.

car′pel, *n.* seed-bearing leaf.

car′pen•ter, *n.* builder in wood. —**car′pen•try,** *n.*

car′pet, *n.* 1. fabric covering for floors. —*v.* 2. cover with carpet. —**car′pet•ing,** *n.*

car′riage, *n.* 1. wheeled vehicle. 2. posture. 3. conveyance.

car′ri•on, *n.* dead flesh.

car′rot, *n.* plant with orange edible root.

car′rou•sel′, *n.* merry-go-round.

car′ry, *v.,* **-ried, -rying.** 1. convey; transport. 2. support; bear. 3. behave. 4. win. 5. extend. 6. have in stock. 7. **carry out,** accomplish. —**car′ri•er,** *n.*

cart, *n.* small wagon. —**cart′age,** *n.*

car•tel′, *n.* syndicate controlling prices and production.

car′ti•lage, *n.* flexible connective body tissue. —**car′ti•lag′i•nous,** *adj.*

car′ton, *n.* cardboard box.

car•toon′, *n.* 1. comic or satirical drawing. 2. design for large art work. —**car•toon′ist,** *n.*

car′tridge, *n.* 1. cylindrical case containing bullet and explosive. 2. container with frequently replaced machine parts or supplies.

carve, *v.,* **carved, carving.** cut into desired form. —**carv′er,** *n.*

cas•cade′, *n.* waterfall.

case, *n., v.,* **cased, casing.** —*n.* 1. instance; example. 2. situation; state. 3. event. 4. statement of arguments. 5. medical patient. 6. lawsuit. 7. category in inflection of nouns, adjectives, and pronouns. 8. **in case,** if. 9. container. —*v.* 10. put in case.

ca′sein (kā′sēn), *n.* protein derived from milk, used in making cheese.

case′ment, *n.* hinged window.

cash, *n.* 1. money. —*v.* 2. give or get cash for.

cash′ew, *n.* small curved nut.

cash•ier′, *n.* 1. person in charge of money. —*v.* 2. dismiss in disgrace.

cash′mere (-mēr), *n.* soft wool fabric.

ca•si′no, *n., pl.* **-nos.** amusement or gambling hall.

cask, *n.* barrel for liquids.

cas′ket, *n.* coffin.

cas′se•role′, *n.* covered baking dish.

cas•sette′, *n.* compact case that holds film or recording tape.

cas′sock, *n.* long ecclesiastical vestment.

cast, *v.,* **cast, casting,** *n.* —*v.* 1. throw. 2. deposit (vote). 3. pour and mold. 4. compute. —*n.* 5. act of casting. 6. thing cast. 7. actors in play. 8. form; mold. 9. rigid surgical dressing. 10. tinge. 11. twist. —**cast′ing,** *n.*

cas′ta•net′, *n.* pieces of bone shell, etc., held in the palm and struck together as musical accompaniment.

cast′a•way′, *n.* shipwrecked person.

caste (kast), *n.* distinct social level.

cast'er, *n.* small swivel-mounted wheel. Also, **cast'or.**

cas'ti•gate', *v.,* **-gated, -gating.** scold severely. **—cas'ti•ga'tion,** *n.* **—cas'ti•ga'tor,** *n.*

cas'tle, *n., v.,* **-tled, -tling.** **—n.** 1. royal or noble residence, usually fortified. 2. chess piece; rook. **—v.** 3. *Chess.* transpose rook and king.

cas'tor oil, vegetable oil used as cathartic.

cas'trate, *v.,* **-trated, -trating.** remove testicles of. **—cas•tra'tion,** *n.*

cas'u•al, *adj.* 1. accidental; not planned. 2. not caring.

cas'u•al•ty, *n., pl.* **-ties.** 1. accident injurious to person. 2. soldier missing in action, killed, wounded, or captured.

cas'u•ist•ry (kazh'ōō-), *n.* adroit, specious argument. **—cas'u•ist,** *n.*

cat, *n.* common domestic animal.

cat'a•clysm', *n.* sudden upheaval. **—cat'a•clys'mic,** *adj.*

cat'a•comb', *n.* underground cemetery.

cat'a•logue', *n., v.,* **-logued, -loguing.** **—n.** 1. organized list. **—v.** 2. enter in catalogue. Also, **cat'a•log'.**

ca•tal'pa, *n.* tree with bell-shaped white flowers.

cat'a•ma•ran', *n.* two-hulled boat.

cat'a•mount', *n.* wild cat, as the cougar.

cat'a•pult', *n.* 1. device for hurling or launching. **—v.** 2. hurl.

cat'a•ract', *n.* 1. waterfall. 2. opacity of eye lens.

ca•tarrh' (-tär'), *n.* inflammation of respiratory mucous membranes.

ca•tas'tro•phe (-fē), *n.* great disaster. **—cat'a•stroph'ic,** *adj.*

cat'call', *n.* jeer.

catch, *v.,* **caught, catching,** *n.* **—v.** 1. capture. 2. trap or detect. 3. hit. 4. seize and hold. 5. be in time for. 6. get or contract. 7. be entangled. **—n.** 8. act of catching. 9. thing that catches. 10. thing caught. 11. tricky aspect. **—catch'er,** *n.*

catch'ing, *adj.* contagious.

catch'up, *n.* type of tomato sauce.

catch'word', *n.* slogan.

catch'y, *adj.* memorable and pleasing.

cat'e•chism' (-kiz' əm), *n.* set of questions and answers on religious principles. **—cat'e•chize',** *v.*

cat'e•gor'i•cal, *adj.* unconditional. **—cat'e•gor'i•cal•ly,** *adv.*

cat'e•go'ry, *n., pl.* **-ries.** division; class. **—cat'e•go•rize',** *v.*

ca'ter, *v.* 1. provide food, amusement, etc. 2. be too accommodating. **—ca'ter•er,** *n.*

cat'er•pil'lar, *n.* 1. wormlike larva of butterfly. 2. type of tractor.

cat'fish', *n.* American fresh-water fish.

cat'gut', *n.* string made from animal intestine.

ca•thar'tic, *adj.* 1. evacuating the bowels. **—n.** 2. medicine doing this.

ca•the'dral, *n.* main church of diocese.

Cath'o•lic, *adj.* 1. of or belonging to Roman Catholic Church. 2. (*l.c.*) universal. **—n.** 3. member of Roman Catholic Church. **—Ca•thol'i•cism',** *n.*

cat'nip, *n.* plant with scented leaves.

cat's'-paw', *n.* dupe used by another.

cat'sup, *n.* catchup.

cat'tail', *n.* tall spinelike marsh plant.

cat'tle, *n.* livestock, esp. cows. **—cat'tle•man,** *n.*

cat'ty, *adj.* maliciously gossiping.

cat'walk', *n.* narrow access walk.

Cau•ca'sian, *adj.* 1. of the so-called "white race." **—n.** 2. Caucasian person. Also **Cau'ca•soid.**

cau'cus, *n.* political conference.

cau'dal, *adj.* of the tail.

cau'li•flow'er, *n.* plant with an edible head.

cause, *n., v.,* **caused, causing.** **—n.** 1. person or thing producing an effect. 2. reason. 3. aim; purpose. **—v.** 4. bring about; produce. **—caus'al,** *adj.* **—cau•sa'tion,** *n.*

cause'way', *n.* raised road.

caus'tic (kôs'-) *adj.,* 1. burning or corroding. 2. sharply critical. **—caus'ti•cal•ly,** *adv.*

cau'ter•ize', *v.,* **-ized, -izing.** burn. **—cau'ter•y, cau'ter•i•za'tion,** *n.*

cau'tion, *n.* 1. carefulness. 2. warning. **—v.** 3. warn. **—cau'tious,** *adj.*

cav'al•cade', *n.* procession, esp. on horseback.

cav'a•lier', *n.* 1. knight or horseman. 2. courtly gentleman. **—adj.** 3. haughty; indifferent. 4. offhand.

cav'al•ry, *n.* troops on horseback or in armored vehicles. **—cav'al•ry•man,** *n.*

cave, *n., v.,* **caved, caving.** **—n.** 1. hollow space in the earth. **—v.** 2. fall or sink.

cav'ern, *n.* large cave.

cav'i•ar', *n.* roe of sturgeon, etc., eaten as a delicacy.

cav'il, *v.* 1. find trivial faults. **—n.** 2. trivial objection.

cav'i•ty, *n., pl.* **-ties.** hollow space.

ca•vort', *v.* prance about.

cay•enne' (kī en'), *n.* sharp condiment.

cay•use' (kī yōōs'), *n.* Indian pony.

CB, citizens band: private two-way radio.

cease, *v.,* **ceased, ceasing,** *n.* stop; end. **—cease'less,** *adj.*

ce'dar, *n.* common coniferous tree.

cede, *v.,* **ceded, ceding.** yield or give up.

ceil'ing, *n.* 1. upper surface of room. 2. maximum altitude.

cel'e•brate', *v.,* **-brated, -brating.** 1. observe or commemorate. 2. act rejoicingly. 3. perform ritually. 4. extol. **—cel'e•bra'tion,** *n.* **—cel'e•bra'tor,** *n.*

ce•leb'ri•ty, *n., pl.* **-ties.** 1. famous person. 2. fame.

ce•ler'i•ty (sə ler'-), *n.* speed.

cel'er•y, *n.* plant with edible leaf stalks.

ce•les'tial, *adj.* of heaven or the sky.

cel'i•ba•cy (sel'ə bə sē), *n.* 1. unmarried state. 2. sexual abstinence. **—cel'i•bate,** *n., adj.*

cell, *n.* 1. a small room or compartment. 2. microscopic biological structure. 3. electric battery. 4. organizational unit. **—cel'lu•lar,** *adj.*

cel'lar, *n.* room under building.

cel'lo (chel'ō), *n., pl.* **-los.** large violinlike instrument held vertically on floor.

cel'lo•phane', *n.* flexible, transparent wrapping material.

cel'lu•loid', *n.* hard, flammable substance.

cel'lu•lose', *n.* carbohydrate of plant origin, used in making paper, etc.

Cel'si•us, *n.* temperature scale in which water freezes at 0° and boils at 100°.

ce•ment', *n.* 1. clay-lime mixture that hardens into stonelike mass. 2. binding material. **—v.** 3. treat with cement. 4. unite.

cem'e•ter'y, *n., pl.* **-teries.** burial ground.

cen'o•taph' (sen'ə taf'), *n.* monument for one buried elsewhere.

cen'ser, *n.* incense burner.

cen'sor, *n.* 1. person eliminating undesirable words, pictures, etc. 2. official responsible for reforms. **—v.** 3. deal with as a censor. **—cen'sor•ship',** *n.*

cen•so'ri•ous, *adj.* severely critical.

cen'sure (-shər), *n., v.,* **-sured, -suring.** —*n.* 1. disapproval. —*v.* 2. rebuke.

cen'sus, *n.* count of inhabitants, etc.

cent, *n.* $\frac{1}{100}$ of a dollar; penny.

cen'taur (-tôr), *n.* imaginary monster, half horse and half man.

cen·te·nar'y, *n., pl.* **-naries.** 100th anniversary.

cen·ten'ni·al, *n.* 1. 100th anniversary. —*adj.* 2. of 100 years.

cen'ter, *n.* 1. middle point, part, or person. —*v.* 2. place or gather at center. 3. concentrate. Also, **cen'tre.**

cen'ti·grade', *adj.* Celsius.

cen'ti·gram', *n.* $\frac{1}{100}$ of gram.

cen'ti·li'ter (-lē'tər), *n.* $\frac{1}{100}$ of liter.

cen'ti·me'ter, *n.* $\frac{1}{100}$ of meter.

cen'ti·pede', *n.* insect with many legs.

cen'tral, *adj.* 1. of or at center. 2. main. —**cen'tral·ly,** *adv.*

cen'tral·ize', *v.,* **-ized, -izing.** 1. gather at a center. 2. concentrate control of. —**cen'tral·i·za'tion,** *n.*

cen·trif'u·gal (sen trif'yə gəl), *adj.* moving away from center.

cen·trip'e·tal, *adj.* moving toward center.

cen'tu·ry, *n., pl.* **-ries.** period of one hundred years.

ce·ram'ic, *adj.* of clay and similar materials.

ce're·al, *n.* 1. plant yielding edible grain. 2. food from such grain.

cer·e·bel'lum (ser'ə-), *n.* rear part of brain.

cer·e·bral (ser'ə brəl), *adj.* 1. of brain. 2. intellectual.

cerebral palsy, paralysis due to brain injury.

cer'e·brum, *n.* front, upper part of brain.

cer'e·mo'ny, *n., pl.* **-nies.** formal act or ritual. —**cer'e·mo'ni·al,** *adj., n.* —**cer'e·mo'ni·ous,** *adj.*

cer'tain, *adj.* 1. without doubt; sure. 2. agreed upon. 3. definite but unspecified. —**cer'tain·ly,** *adv.* —**cer'tain·ty,** *n.*

cer·tif'i·cate, *n.* document of proof.

cer'ti·fy', *v.,* **-fied, -fying.** 1. guarantee as certain. 2. vouch for in writing. —**cer'ti·fi·ca'tion,** *n.*

cer'ti·tude', *n.* sureness.

ces·sa'tion, *n.* stop.

ces'sion, *n.* ceding.

cess'pool', *n.* receptacle for waste, etc., from house.

Cha·blis' (shä blē'), *n.* dry white wine. Also, **cha·blis'.**

chafe, *v.,* **chafed, chafing.** make sore or warm by rubbing.

chaff, *n.* 1. husks of grain, etc. 2. worthless matter. —*v.* 3. tease.

chaf'fer, *v.* bargain.

chaf'ing dish, device for cooking food at table.

cha·grin' (shə grin'), *n.* 1. shame or disappointment. —*v.* 2. cause chagrin to.

chain, *n.* 1. connected series of links. 2. any series. 3. mountain range. —*v.* 4. fasten with chain.

chain reaction, process which automatically continues and spreads.

chair, *n.* 1. seat with a back and legs. 2. place of official or professor. 3. chairman. —*v.* 4. preside over.

chair'man, *n., pl.* **-men.** presiding officer. Also, *fem.,* **chair'wom'an;** *masc. or fem.,* **chair'per'son.**

chaise (shāz), *n.* light, open carriage.

chaise longue (shāz' lông') type of couch.

cha·let' (sha lā'), *n.* mountain house.

chal'ice, *n.* cup for ritual wine.

chalk (chôk), *n.* 1. soft limestone, used in stick form to write on chalkboards. —*v.* 2. mark with chalk. —**chalk'board',** *n.*

chal'lenge, *n., v.,* **-lenged, -lenging.** —*n.* 1. call to fight, contest, etc. 2. demand for identification. 3. objection to juror. —*v.* 4. make challenge to. —**chal'leng·er,** *n.*

cham'ber, *n.* 1. room, esp. bedroom. 2. assembly hall. 3. legislative body. 4. space in gun for ammunition.

cham'ber·maid', *n.* woman who cleans bedrooms.

cha·me'le·on (kə mē'lē ən), *n.* lizard that can change its color.

cham'ois (sham'ē), *n.* 1. European antelope. 2. soft leather from its skin.

champ, *n.* 1. *Informal.* champion. —*v.* 2. bite.

cham·pagne' (sham pān'), *n.* effervescent white wine.

cham'pi·on, *n.* 1. best competitor. 2. supporter. —*v.* 3. advocate. —*adj.* 4. best. —**cham'pi·on·ship',** *n.*

chance, *n., v.,* **chanced, chancing,** *adj.* —*n.* 1. fate; luck. 2. possibility. 3. opportunity. 4. risk. —*v.* 5. occur by chance. 6. risk. —*adj.* 7. accidental.

chan'cel, *n.* space around church altar.

chan'cel·ler·y, *n., pl.* **-ries.** position, department, or offices of chancellor.

chan'cel·lor, *n.* 1. high government official. 2. university head.

chan'cer·y, *n.* 1. high law court. 2. helpless position.

chan'cre (shang'kər), *n.* syphilitic lesion.

chan·de·lier', *n.* hanging lighting fixture.

chan'dler, *n.* 1. dealer in candles. 2. grocer.

change, *v.,* **changed, changing,** *n.* —*v.* 1. alter in condition, etc. 2. substitute for. 3. put on other clothes. —*n.* 4. alteration. 5. substitution. 6. novelty. 7. coins of low value. —**chang'er,** *n.* —**change'a·ble,** *adj.* —**change'a·bil'i·ty,** *n.*

chan'nel, *n.* 1. bed of stream. 2. wide strait. 3. access; route. 4. specific frequency band, as in television. —*v.* 5. convey or direct in channel.

chant, *n.* 1. song; psalm. —*v.* 2. sing, esp. slowly. —**chant'er,** *n.*

chant'ey (shan'-), *n.* sailors' song. Also, **chant'y.**

chan'ti·cleer', *n.* rooster.

Cha'nu·kah (hä'nə kə), *n.* Hanukkah.

cha'os, *n.* utter disorder. —**cha·ot'ic,** *adj.*

chap, *v.,* **chapped, chapping,** *n.* —*v.* 1. roughen and redden. —*n.* 2. *Informal.* fellow.

chap'el, *n.* small church.

chap'er·on' (shap'ə rōn'), *n.* 1. escort of young unmarried woman for propriety. —*v.* 2. accompany thus.

chap'lain, *n.* institutional clergyman.

chap'let, *n.* garland.

chaps, *n.pl.* leather leg protectors worn by cowboys.

chap'ter, *n.* 1. division of book, etc. 2. branch of society.

char, *v.,* **charred, charring.** burn.

char'ac·ter, *n.* 1. personal nature. 2. reputation. 3. person in fiction. 4. written or printed symbol.

char'ac·ter·is'tic, *adj.* 1. typical. —*n.* 2. distinguishing feature.

char'ac·ter·ize', *v.,* **-ized, -izing.** 1. distinguish. 2. describe. —**char'ac·ter·i·za'tion,** *n.*

cha·rade' (shə rād'), *n.* riddle in pantomime.

char'coal', *n.* carbonized wood.

charge, *v.,* **charged, charging,** *n.* —*v.* 1. load or fill. 2. put electricity through or into. 3. command or instruct. 4. accuse. 5. ask payment of. 6. attack. —*n.* 7. load or contents. 8. unit of explosive. 9. care; custody. 10. command or instruction. 11. accusation. 12. expense. 13. price. 14. attack. —**charge′a•ble**, *adj.*

charg′er, *n.* battle horse.

char′i•ot, *n.* ancient two-wheeled carriage. —**char′i•ot•eer′**, *n.*

cha•ris′ma (kə-), *n.* power to charm and inspire people. —**char′is•mat′ic**, *adj.*

char′i•ty, *n., pl.* **-ties.** 1. aid to needy persons. 2. benevolent institution. —**char′i•ta•ble**, *adj.*

char′la•tan (shär′-), *n.* pretender; fraud.

charm, *n.* 1. power to attract and please. 2. magical object, verse, etc. —*v.* 3. attract; enchant. —**charm′er**, *n.*

char′nel house, place for dead bodies.

chart, *n.* 1. sheet exhibiting data. 2. map. —*v.* 3. make a chart of.

char′ter, *n.* 1. document authorizing new corporation. —*v.* 2. establish by charter. 3. hire; lease.

char•treuse′ (shär trōōz′), *adj., n.* yellowish green.

char′wom′an, *n.* woman who cleans offices, houses, etc.

char′y, *adj.* careful.

chase, *v.*, **chased, chasing**, *n.* —*v.* 1. go after with hostility. 2. drive away. 3. ornament (metal) by engraving. —*n.* 4. act or instance of chasing. —**chas′er**, *n.*

chasm (kaz′əm), *n.* deep cleft in earth.

chas′sis (shas′ē), *n.* frame, wheels, and motor of vehicle.

chaste, *adj.* 1. virtuous. 2. simple. —**chas′ti•ty**, *n.*

chas′ten (chā′sən), *v.* punish to improve.

chas•tise′, *v.*, **-tised, -tising.** punish; beat.

chat, *v.*, **chatted, chatting**, *n.* —*v.* 1. talk informally. —*n.* 2. informal talk.

cha•teau′ (sha tō′), *n., pl.* **-teaux.** stately residence, esp. in France.

chat′tel, *n.* article of property other than real estate.

chat′ter, *v.* 1. talk rapidly or foolishly. 2. click or rattle rapidly. —*n.* 3. rapid or foolish talk.

chat′ter•box′, *n.* talkative person.

chat′ty, *adj.*, **-tier, -tiest.** loquacious.

chauf′feur (shō′fər), *n.* hired driver.

chau′vin•ism′ (shō′-), *n.* blind patriotism. —**chau′vin•ist′**, *n., adj.*

cheap, *adj.* of low price or value. —**cheap′ly**, *adv.* —**cheap′ness**, *n.* —**cheap′en**, *v.*

cheat, *v.* 1. defraud; deceive. —*n.* 2. fraud. 3. one who defrauds. —**cheat′er**, *n.*

check, *v.* 1. stop or restrain. 2. investigate; verify. 3. note with a mark. 4. leave or receive for temporary custody. —*n.* 5. stop; restraint. 6. written order for bank to pay money. 7. bill. 8. identification tag. 9. square pattern. 10. *Chess.* direct attack on king.

check′er, *n.* 1. piece used in checkers. —*v.* 2. diversify.

check′er•board′, *n.* board with 64 squares on which the game of **checkers** is played.

check′mate′, *n., v.*, **-mated, -mating.** *Chess.* —*n.* 1. inescapable check. —*v.* 2. subject to inescapable check.

ched′dar, *n.* sharp cheese.

cheek, *n.* 1. soft side of face. 2. *Informal.* impudence.

cheer, *n.* 1. shout of encouragement, etc. 2. gladness. —*v.* 3. shout encouragement to. 4. gladden. —**cheer′ful**, *adj.* —**cheer′less**, *adj.* —**cheer′y**, *adj.*

cheese, *n.* solid, edible product from milk.

cheese′burg′er, *n.* hamburger with melted cheese.

cheese′cloth′, *n.* open cotton fabric.

chee′tah, *n.* wild cat resembling leopard.

chef (shef), *n.* chief cook.

chem′i•cal, *adj.* 1. of chemistry. —*n.* 2. substance in chemistry. —**chem′i•cal•ly**, *adv.*

che•mise′ (shə mēz′), *n.* woman's undershirt.

chem′is•try, *n.* science of composition of substances. —**chem′ist**, *n.*

che′mo•ther′a•py, *n.* treatment of disease, esp. cancer, with chemicals.

chem′ur•gy, *n.* chemistry of industrial use of organic substances, as soybeans.

cheque (chek), *n. Brit.* bank check.

cher′ish, *v.* treat as dear.

cher′ry, *n., pl.* **-ries.** small red fruit of certain trees.

cher′ub, *n.* 1. (*pl.* **-ubim**) celestial being. 2. (*pl.* **-ubs**) angelic child.

chess, *n.* game for two people, each using 16 pieces on checkerboard.

chest, *n.* 1. part of body between neck and abdomen. 2. large box.

chest′nut′, *n.* 1. edible nut of certain trees. 2. reddish brown. 3. *Informal.* stale joke.

chev′i•ot (shev′ē ət), *n.* sturdy worsted fabric.

chev′ron (shev′-), *n.* set of stripes indicating military rank.

chew, *v.* crush repeatedly with teeth. —**chew′er**, *n.*

Chi•an′ti (kē än′tē), *n.* dry red wine. Also, **chi•an′ti.**

chic (shēk), *adj.* cleverly attractive.

Chi•ca′no (chi kä′nō), *n., pl.* **-nos.** Mexican-American. Also, *n.fem.,* **Chi•ca′na.**

chick, *n.* 1. young chicken. 2. *Slang.* woman, esp. young one.

chick′a•dee′, *n.* small gray North American bird.

chick′en, *n.* common domestic fowl.

chick′en pox′, contagious eruptive disease.

chic′le, *n.* substance from tropical tree, used in making chewing gum.

chic′o•ry, *n., pl.* **-ries.** plant with edible leaves and with root used in coffee.

chide, *v.*, **chided, chiding.** scold. —**chid′er**, *n.*

chief, *n.* 1. head; leader. —*adj.* 2. main; principal. —**chief′ly**, *adv.*

chief′tain, *n.* leader.

chif•fon′ (shi fon′), *n.* sheer silk or rayon fabric.

chif′fo•nier′ (shif′ə nēr′), *n.* tall chest of drawers.

chig′ger, *n.* parasitic larva of certain mites.

chil′blains′, *n.pl.* inflammation caused by overexposure to cold, etc.

child, *n., pl.* **children.** 1. baby. 2. son or daughter. —**child′birth′**, *n.* —**child′hood′**, *n.* —**child′ish**, *adj.* —**child′less**, *adj.* —**child′like′**, *adj.*

child′bed′, *n.* condition of giving birth.

chill, *n.* 1. coldness. —*adj.* 2. cold. 3. shivering. 4. not cordial. —*v.* 5. make or become cool. —**chill′ly**, *adv.*

chill factor, chill to skin from low temperature of moving air.

chime, *n., v.*, **chimed, chiming.** —*n.* 1. set of musical tubes, bells, etc. —*v.* 2. sound harmoniously.

chim′ney, *n.* passage for smoke, gases, etc.

chim′pan•zee′, *n.* large, intelligent African ape.

chin, *n.* part of face below mouth.

chi′na, *n.* ceramic ware.

chin•chil′la, *n.* small rodent valued for its fur.

Chi•nese′, *n., pl.* **-nese.** native or language of China.

chink, *n.* 1. crack. 2. short ringing sound. —*v.* 3. make such a sound.

chintz, *n.* printed cotton fabric.

chip, *n., v.,* **chipped, chipping. —***n.* 1. small flat piece, slice, etc. 2. broken place. 3. small plate carrying electric circuit. —*v.* 4. cut or break off (bits). 5. dent; mark. 6. **chip in,** contribute.

chip′munk, *n.* small striped rodent resembling squirrel.

chip′per, *adj. Informal.* lively.

chi•rop′o•dy (kī-), *n.* treatment of foot ailments. —**chi•rop′o•dist,** *n.*

chi′ro•prac′tor (kī′-), *n.* one who practices therapy based upon adjusting body structures, esp. the spine. —**chi′ro•prac′tic,** *n.*

chirp, *n.* 1. short, sharp sound of birds, etc. —*v.* 2. make such sound. Also, **chir′rup.**

chis′el, *n.* 1. tool with broad cutting tip. —*v.* 2. cut with such tool. 3. *Informal.* cheat. —**chis′el•er,** *n.*

chit′chat′, *n.* light talk.

chiv′al•ry (shiv′-), *n.* 1. ideal qualities, such as courtesy and courage. 2. environment or way of life of a knight. —**chiv′al•ric, chiv′al•rous,** *adj.*

chive, *n.* onionlike plant with slender leaves.

chlo′rine, *n.* green gaseous element. —**chlo′ric,** *adj.* —**chlor′in•ate′,** *v.*

chlo′ro•form′, *n.* liquid used as anesthetic.

chlo′ro•phyll, *n.* green coloring matter of plants.

chock, *n.* wedge; block.

choc′o•late, *n.* 1. beverage, candy, etc., made from preparation of cacao seeds. 2. dark brown.

choice, *n.* 1. act or right of choosing. 2. person or thing chosen. —*adj.* 3. excellent. —**choice′ness,** *n.*

choir, *n.* group of singers, esp. in church.

choke, *v.,* **choked, choking,** *n.* —*v.* 1. stop breath of. 2. obstruct. 3. be unable to breathe. —*n.* 4. act or sound of choking.

chol′er•a (kol′ər ə), *n.* acute, often deadly disease.

cho•les′te•rol′ (kə les′tə rôl′), *n.* biochemical in many bodily fluids and tissues, sometimes blocking arteries.

choose, *v.,* **chose, chosen, choosing.** take as one thinks best. —**choos′er,** *n.*

chop, *v.,* **chopped, chopping,** *n.* —*v.* 1. cut with blows. 2. cut in pieces. —*n.* 3. act of chopping. 4. slice of meat with rib. 5. jaw. —**chop′per,** *n.*

chop′py, *adj.* forming short waves.

chop′sticks′, *n.pl.* sticks used by Chinese and Japanese in eating.

chop suey, Chinese-style vegetable stew.

cho′ral, *adj.* of or for chorus or choir.

chord (kôrd), *n.* 1. combination of harmonious tones. 2. straight line across circle.

chore, *n.* routine job.

cho′re•og′ra•phy, *n.* art of composing dances. —**cho′re•og′ra•pher,** *n.*

chor′is•ter, *n.* choir singer.

chor′tle, *v.,* **-tled, -tling,** *n.* chuckle.

cho′rus (kô′-), *n.* 1. group of singers. 2. recurring melody. —**chor′al,** *adj.*

chow, *n. Slang.* food.

chow′der, *n.* vegetable soup containing clams or fish.

chow mein, Chinese-style stew served on fried noodles.

Christ, *n.* Jesus Christ; (in Christian belief) the Messiah.

chris′ten, *v.* baptize; name.

Chris′ten•dom (-ən-), *n.* all Christians.

Chris′tian, *adj.* 1. of Jesus Christ, his teachings, etc. —*n.* 2. believer in Christianity. —**Chris′tian•ize′,** *v.*

Chris′ti•an′i•ty, *n.* religion based on teachings of Jesus Christ.

Christ′mas, *n.* festival in honor of birth of Jesus (Dec. 25).

chro•mat′ic, *adj.* 1. of color. 2. *Music.* progressing by semitones.

chro′mi•um, *n.* lustrous metallic element. Also, **chrome.**

chron′ic, *adj.* constant; habitual. Also, **chron′i•cal.**

chron′i•cle, *n.* 1. record of events in order. —*v.* 2. record in chronicle. —**chron′i•cler,** *n.*

chro•nol′o•gy, *n.* summary of events in historical order. —**chron′o•log′i•cal,** *adj.*

chro•nom′e•ter, *n.* very exact clock.

chrys′a•lis (kris′ə-), *n.* pupa of butterfly, etc.

chry•san′the•mum, *n.* large, colorful flower of aster family.

chub, *n.* thick-bodied fresh-water fish.

chub′by, *adj.* plump.

chuck, *v.* 1. pat lightly. —*n.* 2. light pat. 3. cut of beef.

chuck′le, *v.,* **-led, -ling,** *n.* —*v.* 1. laugh softly. —*n.* 2. soft laugh.

chum, *n.* close friend. —**chum′my,** *adj.*

chump, *n. Informal.* fool.

chunk, *n.* big lump.

church, *n.* 1. place of Christian worship. 2. sect.

churl, *n.* 1. peasant. 2. boor. —**churl′ish,** *adj.*

churn, *n.* 1. agitator for making butter. —*v.* 2. agitate.

chute (shoot), *n.* sloping slide.

chut′ney, *n.* East Indian relish.

ci•ca′da (si kā′də), *n.* large insect with shrill call.

ci′der, *n.* apple juice.

ci•gar′, *n.* roll of tobacco for smoking.

cig′a•rette′, *n.* roll of smoking tobacco in paper tube.

cinch, *n.* 1. firm hold. 2. *Informal.* sure or easy thing.

cin′der, *n.* burned piece; ash.

cin′e•ma (sin′-), *n.* motion picture.

cin′e•ma•tog′ra•phy, *n.* making of motion pictures. —**cin′e•ma•tog′ra•pher,** *n.*

cin′na•mon, *n.* brown spice from bark of certain Asiatic trees.

ci′pher (sī′-), *n.* 1. the symbol (0) for zero. 2. secret writing, using code. —*v.* 3. calculate.

cir′ca (sûr′kə), *prep.* approximately.

cir′cle, *n., v.,* **-cled, -cling. —***n.* 1. closed curve of uniform distance from its center. 2. range; scope. 3. group of friends or associates. —*v.* 4. enclose or go in circle.

cir′cuit, *n.* 1. set of rounds, esp. in connection with duties. 2. electrical path or arrangement.

cir•cu′i•tous (sər kyoo′ə-), *adj.* roundabout. —**cir•cu′i•tous•ly,** *adv.*

cir′cu•lar, *adj.* 1. of or in circle. —*n.* 2. advertisement distributed widely. —**cir′cu•lar•ize′,** *v.*

cir′cu•late′, *v.,* **-lated, -lating.** move or pass around. —**cir′cu•la′tion,** *n.* —**cir′cu•la•to′ry,** *adj.*

cir′cum•cise′, *v.,* **-cised, -cising.** remove foreskin of. —**cir′cum•ci′sion,** *n.*

cir′cum•flex′, *n.* diacritical mark (^).

cir′cum•lo•cu′tion, *n.* roundabout expression.

cir′cum•nav′i•gate′, *v.,* **-gated, -gating.** sail around.

cir′cum•scribe′, *v.,* **-scribed, -scribing.** 1. encircle. 2. confine.

cir′cum•spect′, *adj.* cautious; prudent. —**cir′cum•spec′tion,** *n.*

cir′cum•stance′, *n.* 1. condition accompanying or affecting event. 2. detail. 3. wealth or condition. 4. ceremony.

cir′cum•stan′tial, *adj.* 1. of or from circumstances. 2. detailed. 3. with definite implications.

cir′cum•vent′, *v.* outwit or evade. —**cir′cum•ven′tion**, *n.*

cir′cus, *n.* show with animals, acrobats, etc.

cir′rus (sir′-), *n.* high, fleecy cloud.

cis′tern (sis′-), *n.* reservoir.

cit′a•del, *n.* fortress.

cite, *v.*, **cited**, **citing**. 1. mention in proof, etc. 2. summon. 3. commend. —**ci•ta′tion**, *n.*

cit′i•zen, *n.* 1. subject of a country. 2. inhabitant. 3. civilian. —**cit′i•zen•ship′**, *n.*

citizens band, see **CB**.

cit′ron (sit′rən), *n.* lemonlike Asian fruit.

cit′rus, *adj.* of the genus including the orange, lemon, etc.

cit′y, *n.*, *pl.* **-ies**. large town.

civ′ic, *adj.* 1. of cities. 2. of citizens.

civ′il, *adj.* 1. of citizens. 2. civilized. 3. polite. —**civ′il•ly**, *adv.* —**ci•vil′i•ty**, *n.*

ci•vil′ian, *n.* 1. nonmilitary or non-police person. —*adj.* 2. of such persons.

civ′i•li•za′tion, *n.* 1. act of civilizing. 2. civilized territory or condition.

civ′i•lize, *v.*, **-lized**, **-lizing**. convert from barbaric or primitive state.

civil war, war between parts of same state.

claim, *v.* 1. demand as one's right, property, etc. 2. assert. —*n.* 3. demand. 4. assertion. 5. something claimed. —**claim′ant**, *n.*

clair•voy′ant (klâr voi′ənt), *adj.* seeing things beyond physical vision. —**clair•voy′ant**, *n.* —**clair•voy′ance**, *n.*

clam, *n.* common mollusk, usually edible.

clam′ber, *v.* climb.

clam′my, *adj.*, **-mier**, **-miest**. cold and moist. —**clam′mi•ness**, *n.*

clam′or, *n.* 1. loud outcry or noise. —*v.* 2. raise clamor. —**clam′or•ous**, *adj.*

clamp, *n.* 1. device for holding firmly. —*v.* 2. fasten with clamp.

clan, *n.* 1. related families. 2. clique. —**clan′nish**, *adj.*

clan•des′tine (-des′tin), *adj.* done in secret.

clang, *v.* 1. ring harshly. —*n.* 2. Also, **clang′or**. harsh ring.

clank, *v.* 1. ring dully. —*n.* 2. dull ringing.

clap, *v.*, **clapped**, **clapping**, *n.* —*v.* 1. strike together, as hands in ap-

plause. 2. apply suddenly. —*n.* 3. act or sound of clapping. —**clap′per**, *n.*

clap′board (klab′ərd), *n.* horizontal overlapping boards on exterior walls.

claque (klak), *n.* hired applauders.

clar′et, *n.* dry red wine.

clar′i•fy′, *v.*, **-fied**, **-fying**. make or become clear. —**clar′i•fi•ca′tion**, *n.*

clar′i•net′, *n.* musical wind instrument.

clar′i•on, *adj.* clear and loud.

clar′i•ty, *n.* clearness.

clash, *v.* 1. conflict. 2. collide. —*n.* 3. collision. 4. conflict.

clasp, *n.* 1. fastening device. 2. hug. —*v.* 3. fasten with clasp. 4. hug.

class, *n.* 1. group of similar persons or things. 2. social rank. 3. group of students ranked together. 4. division. 5. *Slang.* excellence. —*v.* 6. place in classes. —**class′mate′**, *n.* —**class′room′**, *n.*

class action, lawsuit on behalf of persons with complaint in common.

clas′sic, *adj.* Also, **clas′si•cal**. 1. of finest or fundamental type. 2. in Greek or Roman manner. —*n.* 3. author, book, etc., of acknowledged superiority. —**clas′si•cal•ly**, *adv.* —**clas′si•cism′**, *n.*

clas′si•fied, *adj.* (of information) limited to authorized persons.

clas′si•fy′, *v.*, **-fied**, **-fying**. arrange in classes. —**clas′si•fi•ca′tion**, *n.*

class•y, *adj.*, **-i•er**, **-i•est**. *Slang.* stylish; elegant. —**class′i•ness**, *n.*

clat′ter, *v.*, *n.* rattle.

clause, *n.* part of sentence with its own subject and predicate.

claus′tro•pho′bi•a, *n.* dread of closed places.

claw, *n.* 1. sharp, curved nail on animal's foot. —*v.* 2. tear or scratch roughly.

clay, *n.* soft earth, used in making bricks, pottery, etc. —**clay′ey**, *adj.*

clean, *adj.* 1. free from dirt, blemish, etc. 2. trim. 3. complete. —*adv.* 4. in clean manner. —*v.* 5. make clean. —**clean′er**, *n.*

clean′-cut′, *adj.* 1. neat. 2. clear-cut.

clean•ly (klen′lē), *adj.* keeping or kept clean. —**clean′li•ness**, *n.*

cleanse, *v.*, **cleansed**, **cleansing**. make clean. —**cleans′er**, *n.*

clear, *adj.* 1. free from darkness, or obscurity. 2. easily perceived. 3. evident. 4. unobstructed. 5. free of obligations or encumbrances. 6. blameless. —*adv.* 7. in a clear manner. —*v.* 8. make or become clear. 9. pay in

full. 10. pass beyond. —**clear′ly**, *adv.* —**clear′ness**, *n.*

clear′ance, *n.* 1. space between objects. 2. authorization.

clear′-cut′, *adj.* apparent; obvious.

clear′ing, *n.* treeless space.

cleat, *n.* metal piece to which ropes, etc., are fastened.

cleave, *v.*, **cleft** or **cleaved**, **cleaving**. split. —**cleav′er**, *n.* —**cleav′age**, *n.*

clef, *n.* musical symbol indicating pitch.

clem′a•tis, *n.* flowering vine.

clem′ent, *adj.* 1. lenient. 2. mild. —**clem′en•cy**, *n.*

clench, *v.* close tightly.

cler′gy, *n.*, *pl.* **-gies**. religious officials. —**cler′gy•man′**, *n.*

cler′i•cal, *adj.* 1. of clerks. 2. of clergy.

clerk, *n.* 1. employee who keeps records, etc. 2. retail sales person.

clev′er, *adj.* nimble of mind. —**clev′er•ly**, *adv.* —**clev′er•ness**, *n.*

clew, *n.* 1. ball of yarn, etc. 2. *Brit.* clue.

cli•ché′ (klē shā′), *n.* trite expression.

click, *n.* 1. slight, sharp noise. —*v.* 2. make a click. 3. *Slang.* succeed.

cli′ent, *n.* one who hires a professional.

cli′en•tele′ (-tel′), *n.* patrons.

cliff, *n.* steep bank.

cli′mate, *n.* weather conditions. —**cli•mat′ic**, *adj.*

cli′max, *n.* high point; culmination. —**cli•mac′tic**, *adj.*

climb, *v.* 1. ascend; rise. 2. climb down, a. descend. b. *Informal.* retreat; compromise. —*n.* 3. ascent. —**climb′er**, *n.*

clinch, *v.* 1. fasten (a nail) by bending the point. 2. hold tightly. —*n.* 3. act of clinching. —**clinch′er**, *n.*

cling, *v.*, **clung**, **clinging**. hold firmly to.

clin′ic, *n.* hospital for nonresident or charity patients. —**clin′i•cal**, *adj.*

clink, *v.* 1. make light, ringing sound. —*n.* 2. such a sound.

clink′er, *n.* fused mass of incombustible residue.

clip, *v.*, **clipped**, **clipping**, *n.* —*v.* 1. cut with short snips or blow. 2. hit sharply. —*n.* 3. act of clipping. 4. metal clasp. 5. cartridge holder. —**clip′ping**, *n.*

clip′per, *n.* 1. cutting device. 2. fast sailing vessel.

clique (klēk), *n.* small exclusive group.

cloak, *n.* 1. loose outer garment. —*v.* 2. cover with cloak. 3. hide.

clob'ber, *v. Informal.* maul.

clock, *n.* device for measuring time.

clock'wise', *adv., adj.* in direction of turning clock hands.

clod, *n.* piece of earth.

clog, *v.,* **clogged, clogging,** *n.* —*v.* 1. hamper; obstruct. —*n.* 2. obstruction, etc. 3. heavy wooden shoe.

clois'ter, *n.* 1. covered walk. 2. monastery or nunnery.

clone, *n., v.,* **cloned, cloning.** —*n.* 1. organism created by asexual reproduction. 2. *Informal.* duplicate. —*v.* 3. grow as clone.

close, *v.,* **closed, closing,** *adj., adv., n.* —*v.* (klōz) 1. shut, obstruct, or end. 2. come to terms. —*adj.* (klōs) 3. shut. 4. confined. 5. lacking fresh air. 6. secretive. 7. stingy. 8. compact. 9. near. 10. intimate. —*adv.* (klōs) 11. in a close manner. —*n.* (klōz) 12. end. —**close'ly,** *adv.* —**close'ness,** *n.*

clos'et, *n.* 1. small room or cabinet for clothes, etc. —*adj.* 2. *Slang.* clandestine.

clot, *n., v.,* **clotted, clotting.** —*n.* 1. mass, esp. of dried blood. —*v.* 2. form clot.

cloth, *n.* fabric of threads.

clothe, *v.,* **clothed** or **clad, clothing.** dress.

clothes, *n.pl.* garments; apparel. Also, **cloth'ing.**

cloud, *n.* 1. mass of water particles, etc., high in the air. —*v.* 2. grow dark or gloomy. 3. lose or deprive of transparency. —**cloud'y,** *adj.* —**cloud'i•ness,** *n.*

clout, *n.* 1. blow from hand. 2. *Informal.* political or similar influence. —*v.* 3. strike with hand.

clove, *n.* 1. tropical spice. 2. section of plant bulb.

clo'ver, *n.* three-leaved plant, esp. for forage.

cloy, *v.* weary by excess sweetness.

club, *n., v.,* **clubbed, clubbing.** —*n.* 1. heavy stick or bat. 2. organized group. 3. playing-card figure (♣). —*v.* 4. beat with club.

club'foot', *n.* deformed foot.

cluck, *n.* 1. call of hen. —*v.* 2. utter such call.

clue, *n.* hint in solving mystery, etc.

clump, *n.* cluster.

clum'sy, *adj.,* **-sier, -siest.** awkward. —**clum'si•ly,** *adv.* —**clum'si•ness,** *n.*

clus'ter, *n.* 1. group; bunch. —*v.* 2. gather into cluster.

clutch, *v.* 1. seize; snatch. 2. hold tightly. —*n.* 3. grasp. 4. (*pl.*) capture or mastery. 5. device for engaging or disengaging machinery.

clut'ter, *v., n.* heap or litter.

coach, *n.* 1. enclosed carriage, bus, etc. 2. adviser, esp. in athletics. —*v.* 3. advise.

co•ag'u•late', *v.,* **-lated, -lating.** thicken, clot, or congeal. —**co•ag'u•la'tion,** *n.*

coal, *n.* 1. black mineral burned as fuel. —*v.* 2. take or get coal.

co'a•lesce' (-les') *v.,* **-lesced, -lescing.** unite or ally. —**co'a•les'cence,** *n.*

co'a•li'tion, *n.* alliance.

coarse, *adj.,* **-ser, -sest.** 1. rough or harsh. 2. vulgar. —**coarse'ly,** *adv.* —**coarse'ness,** *n.* —**coars'en,** *v.*

coast, *n.* 1. seashore. —*v.* 2. drift easily, esp. downhill. 3. sail along coast. —**coast'al,** *adj.*

coast'er, *n.* 1. something that coasts. 2. object protecting surfaces from moisture.

coat, *n.* 1. outer garment. 2. covering, as fur or bark. —*v.* 3. cover or enclose.

coat' of arms', emblems, motto, etc., of one's family.

coax, *v.* influence by persuasion, flattery, etc. —**coax'er,** *n.*

co•ax'i•al (-ak'sē əl), *adj.* having a common axis, as **coaxial cables** for simultaneous long-distance transmission of radio or television signals.

cob, *n.* corncob.

co'balt, *n.* 1. silvery metallic element. 2. deep blue-green.

cob'ble, *v.* 1. mend (shoes). —*n.* 2. Also, **cob'ble•stone'.** round stone for paving, etc. —**cob'bler,** *n.*

co'bra, *n.* venomous Asiatic snake.

cob'web', *n.* silky web made by spiders.

co•caine', *n.* narcotic drug used as local anesthetic and drug of abuse.

cock, *n.* 1. male bird, esp. rooster. 2. valve. 3. hammer in lock of a gun. 4. pile of hay. —*v.* 5. set cock of (a gun). 6. set aslant.

cock•ade', *n.* hat ornament.

cock'a•too', *n.* colorful crested parrot.

cock'er, *n.* small spaniel.

cock'le, *n.* 1. mollusk with radially ribbed valves. 2. inmost part.

cock'ney, *n.* 1. resident of London, esp. East End. 2. pronunciation of such persons.

cock'pit', *n.* 1. space for pilot or helmsman. 2. pit where cocks fight.

cock'roach', *n.* common crawling insect.

cock'tail', *n.* 1. drink containing mixture of liquors. 2. mixed appetizer.

co'coa, *n.* 1. powdered seeds of cacao, used esp. in making a beverage. —*adj.* 2. brown.

co'co•nut', *n.* large, hard-shelled seed of the tropical **co'co palm.**

co•coon', *n.* silky covering spun by certain larvae.

cod, *n.* edible Atlantic fish. Also, **cod'fish'.**

cod'dle, *v.,* **-dled, -dling.** 1. pamper. 2. cook in almost boiling water.

code, *n., v.,* **coded, coding.** —*n.* 1. collection of laws or rules. 2. system of signals or secret words. —*v.* 3. put in code.

co'deine (-dēn), *n.* drug derived from opium.

cod'i•cil (kod'ə səl), *n.* supplement, esp. to a will.

cod'i•fy', *v.,* **-fied, -fying.** organize into legal or formal code. —**cod'i•fi•ca'tion,** *n.*

co'ed', *n.* female student, esp. in co-educational school.

co'ed•u•ca'tion, *n.* education in classes of both sexes. —**co'ed•u•ca'tion•al,** *adj.*

co'ef•fi'cient, *n.* number by which another is multiplied.

co•erce', *v.,* **-erced, -ercing.** force; compel. —**co•er'cion,** *n.*

co•e'val, *adj.* of same age or date.

cof'fee, *n.* powdered brown seeds of certain tropical trees, used in making a beverage.

cof'fer, *n.* chest.

cof'fin, *n.* box in which body is buried.

cog, *n.* tooth on wheel (**cog'wheel'**), connecting with another such wheel.

co'gent (kō'jənt), *adj.* convincing. —**co'gen•cy,** *n.* —**co'gent•ly,** *adv.*

cog'i•tate' (koj'-), *v.,* **-tated, -tating.** ponder. —**cog'i•ta'tion,** *n.* —**cog'i•ta'tor,** *n.*

co'gnac (kōn'yak), *n.* brandy.

cog'nate, *adj.* related.

cog•ni'tion, *n.* knowing.

cog'ni•zance, *n.* notice, esp. official. —**cog'ni•zant,** *adj.*

cog•no'men, *n.* surname.

co•here′, *v.,* **-hered, -hering.** stick together. **—co•he′sion,** *n.* **—co•he′-sive,** *adj.*

co•her′ent, *adj.* making sense. **—co•her′ence,** *n.*

co′hort, *n.* 1. associate; companion. 2. group, esp. of soldiers.

coif•fure′ (kwä fyŏŏr′), *n.* arrangement of hair.

coil, *v.* 1. wind spirally or in rings. **—n.** 2. ring. 3. series of spirals or rings.

coin, *n.* 1. piece of metal issued as money. **—v.** 2. make metal into money. 3. invent. **—coin′age,** *n.* **—coin′er,** *n.*

co′in•cide′, *v.,* **-cided, -ciding.** 1. occur at same time, place, etc. 2. match. **—co•in′ci•dence,** *n.* **—co•in′ci•den′tal,** *adj.* **—co•in′ci•den′tal•ly,** *adv.*

coke, *n., v.,* **coked, coking.** **—n.** 1. solid carbon produced from coal. **—v.** 2. convert into coke.

col′an•der (kul′-), *n.* large strainer.

cold, *adj.* 1. giving or feeling no warmth. 2. not cordial. **—n.** 3. absence of heat. 4. illness marked by runny nose, etc. **—cold′ly,** *adv.* **—cold′ness,** *n.*

cold′-blood′ed, *adj.* 1. callous; unemotional. 2. with blood at same temperature as environment. **—cold′-blood′ed•ly,** *adv.* **—cold′-blood′ed•ness,** *n.*

cole′slaw′, *n.* sliced raw cabbage.

col′ic, *n.* sharp pain in abdomen or bowels.

col′i•se′um, *n.* large stadium.

col•lab′o•rate′, *v.,* **-rated, -rating.** work together. **—col•lab′o•ra′tion,** *n.* **—col•lab′o•ra′tor,** *n.*

col•lapse′, *v.,* **-lapsed, -lapsing,** *n.* **—v.** 1. fall in or together. 2. fail abruptly. **—n.** 3. a falling-in. 4. sudden failure. **—col•laps′i•ble,** *adj.*

col′lar, *n.* 1. part of garment around neck. **—v.** 2. seize by collar.

col•lat′er•al, *n.* 1. security pledged on loan. **—adj.** 2. additional. 3. on side.

col′league, *n.* associate in work, etc.

col•lect′, *v.* 1. gather together. 2. take payment of. **—adj., adv.** 3. payable on delivery. **—col•lec′tion,** *n.* **—col•lec′tor,** *n.*

col•lect′i•ble, *n.* 1. object collected. **—adj.** 2. able to be collected.

col•lec′tive, *adj.* 1. joint; by a group. **—n.** 2. socialist productive group.

col•lec′tiv•ism′, *n.* principle of communal control of means of production, etc. **—col•lec′tiv•ist,** *n.*

col′lege, *n.* school of higher learning. **—col•le′giate,** *adj.*

col•lide′, *v.,* **-lided, -liding.** come together violently.

col′lie, *n.* large, long-haired dog.

col′lier (-yər), *n.* 1. ship for carrying coal. 2. coal miner.

col•li′sion, *n.* 1. crash. 2. conflict.

col•lo′qui•al, *adj.* appropriate to casual rather than formal speech or writing. **—col•lo′qui•al•ism′,** *n.* **—col•lo′qui•al•ly,** *adv.*

col′lo•quy (-kwē), *n., pl.* **-quies.** conversation.

col•lu′sion, *n.* illicit agreement.

co•logne′ (kə lōn′), *n.* perfumed toilet water.

co′lon, *n.* 1. mark of punctuation (:). 2. part of large intestine. **—co•lon′ic,** *adj.*

colo′nel (kûr′nəl), *n.* military officer below general. **—colo′nel•cy,** *n.*

col′on•nade′ (-nād′), *n.* series of columns.

col′o•ny, *n., pl.* **-nies.** 1. group of people settling in another land. 2. territory subject to outside ruling power. 3. community. **—co•lo′ni•al,** *adj.,* *n.* **—col′o•nist,** *n.* **—col′o•nize′,** *v.*

col′or, *n.* 1. quality of light perceived by human eye. 2. pigment; dye. 3. complexion. 4. vivid description. 5. *(pl.)* flag. 6. race. **—v.** 7. give or apply color to. 8. distort in telling. Also, *Brit.,* **col′our. —col′or•a′tion,** *n.*

col′o•ra•tu′ra (-tyŏŏr′ə), *n.* lyric soprano.

col′ored, *adj.* of a race other than Caucasian.

col′or•ful, *adj.* 1. full of color. 2. vivid; interesting.

col′or•less, *adj.* 1. without color. 2. uninteresting. **—col′or•less•ly,** *adv.*

co•los′sal, *adj.* huge; vast.

co•los′sus, *n.* anything colossal.

colt, *n.* young male horse.

col′um•bine′, *n.* branching plant with bright flowers.

col′umn, *n.* 1. upright shaft or support. 2. long area of print. 3. regular journalistic piece. 4. long group of troops, ships, etc. **—co•lum′nar,** *adj.* **—col′umn•ist,** *n.*

co′ma, *n.* prolonged unconscious state.

comb, *n.* 1. toothed object, for straightening hair or fiber. 2. growth on a cock's head. 3. crest. 4. honeycomb. **—v.** 5. dress with comb. 6. search.

com′bat, *v.,* **-bated, -bating,** *n.* fight; battle. **—com•bat′ant,** *n.* **—com•bat′ive,** *adj.*

com′bi•na′tion, *n.* 1. act of combining. 2. things combined. 3. alliance. 4. sets of figures dialed to operate a lock.

com•bine′, *v.,* **-bined, -bining,** *n.* **—v.** 1. unite; join. **—n.** (kom′bīn). 2. combination. 3. machine that cuts and threshes grain.

com•bus′ti•ble, *adj.* 1. inflammable. **—n.** 2. inflammable substance.

com•bus′tion, *n.* burning.

come, *v.,* **came, come, coming.** 1. approach or arrive. 2. happen. 3. emerge.

co•me′di•an, *n.* humorous actor. **—co•me′di•enne′,** *n.fem.*

com′e•dy, *n., pl.* **-dies.** 1. humorous drama. 2. drama with happy ending.

come′ly (kum′lē), *adj.* attractive. **—come′li•ness,** *n.*

com′er, *n. Informal.* one likely to have great success.

com′et, *n.* celestial body orbiting around and lighted by sun, often with misty tail.

com′fort, *v.* 1. console or cheer. **—n.** 2. consolation. 3. ease. **—com′fort•a•ble,** *adj.* **—com′fort•a•bly,** *adv.*

com′fort•er, *n.* 1. one who comforts. 2. warm quilt.

com′ic, *adj.* 1. of comedy. 2. Also, **com′i•cal.** funny. **—n.** 3. comedian. **—com′i•cal•ly,** *adv.*

com′ma, *n.* mark of punctuation (,).

com•mand′, *v.* 1. order. 2. be in control of. 3. overlook. **—n.** 4. order. 5. control. 6. troops, etc., under commander.

com′man•dant′ (-dant′, -dänt′), *n.* 1. local commanding officer. 2. director of Marine Corps.

com′man•deer′, *v.* seize for official use.

com•mand′er, *n.* 1. chief officer. 2. *Navy.* officer below captain.

com•mand′ment, *n.* 1. command. 2. precept of God.

com•man′do, *n., pl.* **-dos, -does.** soldier making brief raids against enemy.

com•mem′o•rate′, *v.,* **-rated, -rating.** honor memory of. **—com•mem′o•ra′tion,** *n.* **—com•mem′o•ra′tive,** *adj.*

com•mence′, *v.,* **-menced, -mencing.** start.

com•mence′ment, *n.* 1. beginning. 2. graduation day or ceremonies.

com•mend′, *v.* 1. praise. 2. entrust. —**com•mend′a•ble,** *adj.* —**com′men•da′tion,** *n.* —**com•mend′a•to′ry,** *adj.*

com•men′su•rate (-shə rit), *adj.* equal or corresponding. —**com•men′su•rate•ly,** *adv.*

com′ment, *n.* 1. remark or criticism. —*v.* 2. make remarks.

com′men•tar′y, *n., pl.* **-taries.** 1. comment. 2. explanatory essay.

com′men•ta′tor, *n.* one who discusses news events, etc.

com′merce, *n.* sale or barter.

com•mer′cial, *adj.* 1. of or in commerce. —*n.* 2. *Radio & TV.* advertisement.

com•mer′cial•ize′, *v.,* **-ized, -izing.** treat as matter of profit.

com•min′gle, *v.,* **-gled, -gling.** blend.

com•mis′er•ate′, *v.,* **-ated, -ating.** feel sympathetic sorrow. —**com•mis′er•a′tion,** *n.*

com′mis•sar′, *n.* Soviet government official.

com′mis•sar′y, *n., pl.* **-saries.** store selling food and equipment.

com•mis′sion, *n.* 1. act of committing. 2. document giving authority. 3. group of persons with special task. 4. usable condition. 5. fee for agent's services. —*v.* 6. give commission to. 7. authorize. 8. put into service.

com•mis′sion•er, *n.* government official.

com•mit′, *v.,* **-mitted, -mitting.** 1. give in trust or custody. 2. refer to committee. 3. do. 4. obligate. —**com•mit′ment,** *n.*

com•mit′tee, *n.* group assigned to special duties.

com•mode′, *n.* washstand or small cabinet.

com•mo′di•ous, *adj.* roomy.

com•mod′i•ty, *n., pl.* **-ties.** article of commerce.

com′mo•dore′, *n.* officer below rear admiral.

com′mon, *adj.* 1. shared by all; joint. 2. ordinary; usual. 3. vulgar. —*n.* 4. area of public land. —**com′mon•ly,** *adv.*

com′mon•er, *n.* one of common people.

com′mon•place′, *adj.* 1. ordinary; trite. —*n.* 2. commonplace remark.

com′mons, *n.* 1. (*cap.*) elective house of certain legislatures. 2. large dining room.

com′mon•weal′, *n.* public welfare.

com′mon•wealth′, *n.* 1. democratic state. 2. people of a state.

com•mo′tion, *n.* disturbance.

com•mu′nal, *adj.* of or belonging to a community.

com•mune′ (kə myoon′), *v.,* **-muned, -muning,** *n.* —*v.* 1. talk together. —*n.* (kom′yoon), 2. small community with shared property. 3. district.

com•mu′ni•cate′, *v.,* **-cated, -cating.** 1. make known. 2. transmit. 3. exchange news, etc. —**com•mu′ni•ca•ble,** *adj.* —**com•mu′ni•ca′tion,** *n.* —**com•mu′ni•ca′tive,** *adj.* —**com•mu′ni•cant,** *n.*

com•mun′ion, *n.* 1. act of sharing. 2. group with same religion. 3. sacrament commemorating Jesus' last supper; Eucharist.

com•mu′ni•qué′ (-kā′), *n.* official bulletin.

com′mu•nism, *n.* 1. social system based on collective ownership of all productive property. 2. (*cap.*) political doctrine advocating this. —**com′mu•nist,** *n., adj.* —**com′mu•nis′tic,** *adj.*

com•mu′ni•ty, *n., pl.* **-ties.** 1. people with common culture living in one locality. 2. public.

com•mute′, *v.,* **-muted, -muting.** 1. exchange. 2. reduce (punishment). 3. travel between home and work. —**com•mu•ta′tion,** *n.* —**com•mut′er,** *n.*

com•pact′, *adj.* 1. packed together. 2. pithy. —*v.* 3. pack together. —*n.* (kom′pakt). 4. small cosmetic case. 5. agreement. —**com•pact′ly,** *adv.* —**com•pact′ness,** *n.*

com•pan′ion, *n.* 1. associate. 2. mate. —**com•pan′ion•a•ble,** *adj.* —**com•pan′ion•ate,** *adj.* —**com•pan′ion•ship′,** *n.*

com′pa•ny, *n., pl.* **-nies.** 1. persons associated for business or social purposes, etc. 2. companionship. 3. guests. 4. military unit.

com•par′a•tive, *adj.* 1. of or based on comparison. —*n.* 2. *Gram.* intermediate degree of comparison. —**com•par′a•tive•ly,** *adv.*

com•pare′, *v.,* **-pared, -paring.** 1. consider for similarities. 2. *Gram.* inflect to show intensity, etc. —**com′pa•ra•ble,** *adj.* —**com•par′i•son,** *n.*

com•part′ment, *n.* separate room, space, etc.

com′pass, *n.* 1. instrument for finding direction. 2. extent. 3. tool for making circles.

com•pas′sion, *n.* pity or sympathy. —**com•pas′sion•ate,** *adj.*

com•pat′i•ble, *adj.* congenial. —**com•pat′i•bil′i•ty,** *n.*

com•pa′tri•ot, *n.* person from one's own country.

com•pel′, *v.,* **-pelled, -pelling.** force.

com•pen′di•ous, *adj.* concise.

com•pen′di•um, *n.* full list or summary.

com′pen•sate′, *v.,* **-sated, -sating.** 1. make up for. 2. pay. —**com′pen•sa′tion,** *n.* —**com•pen′sa•to′ry,** *adj.*

com•pete′, *v.,* **-peted, -peting.** contend; rival.

com′pe•tent, *adj.* 1. able enough. 2. legally qualified. 3. sufficient. —**com′pe•tence, com′pe•ten•cy,** *n.* —**com′pe•tent•ly,** *adv.*

com′pe•ti′tion, *n.* 1. contest. 2. rivalry. —**com•pet′i•tive,** *adj.* —**com•pet′i•tor,** *n.*

com•pile′, *v.,* **-piled, -piling.** put together; assemble. —**com•pil′er,** *n.* —**com•pi•la′tion,** *n.*

com•pla′cen•cy, *n., pl.* **-cies.** satisfaction, esp. with self. Also, **com•pla′cence.** —**compla′cent,** *adj.* —**com•pla′cent•ly,** *adv.*

com•plain′, *v.* 1. express pain, dissatisfaction, etc. 2. accuse. —**com•plain′er, com•plain′ant,** *n.* —**com•plaint′,** *n.*

com•plai′sant, *adj.* agreeable; obliging.

com′ple•ment, *n.* (-mənt). 1. that which completes. 2. full amount. —*v.* (-ment′). 3. complete. —**com′ple•men′ta•ry,** *adj.*

com•plete′, *adj., v.,* **-pleted, -pleting.** —*adj.* 1. entire; perfect. —*v.* 2. make complete. —**com•plete′ly,** *adv.* —**com•plete′ness,** *n.* —**com•ple′tion,** *n.*

com•plex′, *adj.* 1. having many parts; intricate. —*n.* (kom′pleks). 2. complex whole. 3. obsession. —**com•plex′i•ty,** *n.*

com•plex′ion, *n.* color of skin.

com′pli•cate′, *v.,* **-cated, -cating.** make complex or difficult. —**com′pli•ca′tion,** *n.*

com•plic′i•ty (-plis′ə-), *n.* partnership in crime.

com′pli•ment, *n.* (-mənt). 1. expression of praise. —*v.* (-ment′). 2. express praise.

com′pli•men′ta•ry, *adj.* 1. of or being a compliment. 2. free.

com•ply′, *v.,* **-plied, -plying.** act in accordance. —**com•pli′ance,** *n.* —**com•pli′ant, com•pli′a•ble,** *adj.*

com•po'nent, *adj.* 1. composing. —*n.* 2. part of whole.

com•port', *v.* 1. conduct (oneself). 2. suit. —**com•port'ment,** *n.*

com•pose', *v.,* **-posed, -posing.** 1. make by uniting parts. 2. constitute. 3. put in order; calm. 4. create and write. 5. set printing type.

com•posed', *adj.* calm.

com•pos'er, *n.* writer, esp. of music.

com•pos'ite, *adj.* made of many parts.

com'post, *n.* decaying mixture of leaves, etc.

com•po'sure, *n.* calm.

com'pote (kom'pōt), *n.* stewed fruit.

com'pound, *adj.* 1. having two or more parts, functions, etc. —*n.* 2. something made by combining parts. 3. enclosure with buildings. —*v.* (kəm pound'). 4. combine. 5. condone (crime) for a price.

com'pre•hend', *v.* 1. understand. 2. include. —**com'pre•hen'si•ble,** *adj.* —**com'pre•hen'sion,** *n.*

com'pre•hen'sive, *adj.* inclusive. —**com'pre•hen'sive•ly,** *adv.* —**com'pre•hen'sive•ness,** *n.*

com•press', *v.* 1. press together. —*n.* (kom'pres). 2. pad applied to affected part of body. —**com•pres'sion,** *n.* —**com•pres'sor,** *n.*

com•prise', *v.,* **-prised, -prising.** consist of. Also, **com•prize'.** —**com•pris'al,** *n.*

com'pro•mise', *n.,v.,* **-mised, -mising.** —*n.* 1. agreement to mutual concessions. 2. something intermediate. —*v.* 3. settle by compromise. 4. endanger.

comp•trol'ler (kən-), *n.* controller.

com•pul'sion, *n.* compelling force. *adj.* —**com•pul'so•ry,** *adj.*

com•pul'sive, *adj.* due to or acting on inner compulsion.

com•punc'tion, *n.* remorse.

com•pute', *v.,* **-puted, -puting.** calculate; figure. —**com'pu•ta'tion,** *n.*

com•put'er, *n.* electronic apparatus for storing and retrieving data, making calculations, etc.

com•pu'ter•ize', *v.,* **-ized, -izing.** do by computer.

com'rade, *n.* close companion. —**com'rade•ship',** *n.*

con, *adj., n., v.,* **conned, conning.** —*adj.* 1. opposed. —*n.* 2. argument against. —*v.* 3. study. 4. *Informal.* deceive.

con•cave', *adj.* curved inward. —**con•cave'ly,** *adv.* —**con•cav'i•ty,** *n.*

con•ceal', *v.* hide. —**con•ceal'ment,** *n.*

con•cede', *v.,* **-ceded, -ceding.** 1. admit. 2. yield.

con•ceit', *n.* 1. excess self-esteem. 2. fanciful idea. —**con•ceit'ed,** *adj.*

con•ceive', *v.,* **-ceived, -ceiving.** 1. form (plan or idea). 2. understand. 3. become pregnant. —**con•ceiv'a•ble,** *adj.* —**con•ceiv'a•bly,** *adv.*

con•cen•trate', *v.,* **-trated, -trating,** *n.* —*v.* 1. bring to one point. 2. intensify. 3. give full attention. —*n.* 4. product of concentration. —**con'cen•tra'tion,** *n.*

con•cen'tric, *adj.* having common center.

con'cept, *n.* general notion.

con•cep'tion, *n.* 1. act of conceiving. 2. idea.

con•cern', *v.* 1. relate to. 2. involve. 3. worry. —*n.* 4. matter that concerns. 5. business firm.

con•cern'ing, *prep.* about.

con'cert, *n.* 1. musical performance. 2. accord.

con•cer•ti'na (-tē'-), *n.* small accordion.

con•ces'sion, *n.* 1. act of conceding. 2. what is conceded.

conch (kongk), *n.* spiral sea shell.

con•cil'i•ate', *v.,* **-ated, -ating.** win over; reconcile. —**con•cil'i•a'tion,** *n.* —**con•cil'i•a•to'ry,** *adj.*

con•cise', *adj.* brief; succinct. —**con•cise'ly,** *adv.* —**con•cise'ness,** *n.*

con'clave, *n.* private meeting.

con•clude', *v.,* **-cluded, -cluding.** 1. finish; settle. 2. infer. —**con•clu'sion,** *n.* —**con•clu'sive,** *adj.*

con•coct', *v.* make by combining. —**con•coc'tion,** *n.*

con•com'i•tant, *adj.* 1. accompanying. —*n.* 2. anything concomitant. —**con•com'i•tant•ly,** *adv.*

con'cord, *n.* agreement.

con•cord'ance, *n.* 1. concord. 2. index of principal words of book.

con•cor'dat, *n.* agreement, esp. between Pope and a government.

con'course, *n.* 1. assemblage. 2. place for crowds in motion.

con'crete, *adj., n., v.,* **-creted, -creting.** —*adj.* 1. real; objective. 2. made of concrete. —*n.* 3. material of cement and hard matter. —*v.* 4. (kon krēt'). become solid. —**con•crete'ly,** *adv.* —**con•crete'ness,** *n.* —**con•cre'tion,** *n.*

con'cu•bine', *n.* woman living with but not married to man.

con•cu'pis•cent (-pi sənt), *adj.* lustful.

con•cur', *v.,* **-curred, -curring.** 1. agree. 2. coincide. 3. cooperate. —**con•cur'rence,** *n.* —**con•cur'rent,** *adj.* —**con•cur'rent•ly,** *adv.*

con•cus'sion, *n.* shock or jarring from blow.

con•demn', *v.* 1. denounce. 2. pronounce guilty. 3. judge unfit. 4. acquire for public purpose. —**con'dem•na'tion,** *n.*

con•dense', *v.,* **-densed, -densing.** 1. reduce to denser form. 2. make or become compact. —**con'den•sa'tion,** *n.* —**con•dens'er,** *n.*

con'de•scend', *v.* 1. pretend equality with an inferior. 2. deign. —**con'de•scen'sion,** *n.*

con'di•ment, *n.* seasoning.

con•di'tion, *n.* 1. state of being or health. 2. fit state. 3. requirement. —*v.* 4. put in condition. —**con•di'tion•al,** *adj.* —**con•di'tion•al•ly,** *adv.*

con•dole', *v.,* **-doled, -doling.** sympathize in sorrow. —**con•do'lence,** *n.*

con'do•min'i•um, *n.* apartment house in which units are individually owned. Also, *Informal,* **con'do.**

con•done', *v.,* **-doned, -doning.** excuse.

con'dor, *n.* vulture.

con•duce', *v.,* **-duced, -ducing.** contribute; lead. —**con•du'cive,** *adj.*

con'duct, *n.* 1. behavior. 2. management. —*v.* (kən dukt'). 3. behave. 4. manage. 5. lead or carry.

con•duc'tor, *n.* 1. guide. 2. director of an orchestra. 3. official on trains. 4. anything that conveys electricity, heat, etc.

con'duit (-dwit), *n.* pipe for water, etc.

cone, *n.* 1. form tapering from round base to single point. 2. fruit of fir, pine, etc.

con•fec'tion, *n.* candy or other sweet preparation. —**con•fec'tion•er,** *n.* —**con•fec'tion•er'y,** *n.*

con•fed'er•a•cy, *n., pl.* **-cies.** 1. league. 2. (*cap.*) Confederate States of America.

con•fed'er•ate, *adj., n., v.,* **-ated, -ating.** —*adj.* (-ər it). 1. in league. 2. (*cap.*) of **Confederate States of America,** separated from U.S. during Civil War. —*n.* (-ər it). 3. ally. 4. accomplice. 5. (*cap.*) citizen of Confederate States of America. —*v.* (-ə rāt'). 6. be allied.—**con•fed'er•a'tion,** *n.*

con•fer', *v.,* **-ferred, -ferring.** 1. bestow. 2. consult. —**con•fer'ment,** *n.*

con′fer•ence, *n.* 1. meeting. 2. discussion.

con•fess′, *v.* 1. admit. 2. declare one's sins, as to priest. —**con•fes′sion,** *n.*

con•fes′sor, *n.* 1. one who confesses. 2. one who hears confessions.

con•fet′ti, *n.pl.,* bits of colored paper.

con′fi•dant′, *n.* one to whom secrets are told. —**con′fi•dante′,** *n.fem.*

con•fide′, *v.,* **-fided, -fiding.** 1. trust with secret. 2. entrust.

con′fi•dence, *n.* 1. full trust. 2. assurance. —**con′fi•dent,** *adj.* —**con′fi•dent•ly,** *adv.*

con′fi•den′tial, *adj.* 1. entrusted as secret. 2. private. —**con′fi•den′tial•ly,** *adv.*

con•fig′u•ra′tion, *n.* external form.

con•fine′, *v.,* **-fined, -fining,** *n.* —*v.* 1. keep within bounds. 2. shut or lock up. —*n.* (*pl.*) (kon′finz). 3. boundary.

con•fined′, *adj.* 1. in childbed. 2. stuffy.

con•fine′ment, *n.* 1. imprisonment. 2. childbirth.

con•firm′, *v.* 1. make sure. 2. make valid. 3. strengthen. 4. admit to full church membership. —**con′fir•ma′tion,** *n.*

con′fis•cate′ (kon′fis kāt′), *v.,* **-cated, -cating.** seize by public authority. —**con′fis•ca′tion,** *n.*

con′fla•gra′tion, *n.* fierce fire.

con•flict′, *v.* 1. oppose; clash. —*n.* (kon′flikt). 2. battle. 3. antagonism.

con′flu•ence, *n.* act or place of flowing together. —**con′flu•ent,** *adj.*

con•form′, *v.* 1. accord; adapt. 2. make similar. —**con•form′a•ble,** *adj.* —**con•form′ist,** *n.* —**con•form′ity,** *n.*

con′for•ma′tion, *n.* form.

con•found′, *v.* 1. confuse. 2. perplex.

con•front′, *v.* 1. meet or set facing. 2. challenge openly. —**con′fron•ta′tion,** *n.*

con•fuse′, *v.,* **-fused, -fusing.** 1. throw into disorder. 2. associate wrongly. 3. disconcert. —**con•fu′sion,** *n.*

con•fute′, *v.,* **-futed, -futing.** prove to be wrong. —**con′fu•ta′tion,** *n.*

con•geal′, *v.* make solid or thick. —**con•geal′ment,** *n.*

con•gen′ial, *adj.* agreeable; suited. —**con•ge′ni•al′i•ty,** *n.*

con•gen′i•tal, *adj.* from birth. —**con•gen′i•tal•ly,** *adv.*

con•gest′, *v.* fill to excess. —**con•ges′tion,** *n.*

con•glom′er•ate, *n., adj., v.,* **-ated, -ating.** —*n.* (-ər it). 1. mixture. 2. rock formed of pebbles, etc. 3. company owning variety of other companies. —*adj.* (-ər it). 4. gathered into a ball. 5. mixed. —*v.* (-ə rāt′). 6. gather into round mass. —**con•glom′er•a′tion,** *n.*

con•grat′u•late′, *v.,* **-lated, -lating.** express sympathetic joy. —**con•grat′u•la′tion,** *n.* —**con•grat′u•la•to′ry,** *adj.*

con′gre•gate′, *v.,* **-gated, -gating.** assemble. —**con′gre•ga′tion,** *n.*

con′gre•ga′tion•al, *adj.* 1. of congregations. 2. (*cap.*) denoting church denomination wherein each church acts independently. —**con′gre•ga′tion•al•ism,** *n.* —**con′gre•ga′tion•al•ist,** *n.*

con′gress, *n.* 1. national legislative body, esp. (*cap.*) of the U.S. 2. formal meeting. —**con•gres′sion•al,** *adj.* —**con′gress•man,** *n.* —**con′gress•wom′an,** *n.fem.*

con•gru′ent, *adj.* agreeing or coinciding. —**con′gru•ence,** *n.*

con•gru′i•ty, *n., pl.* **-ties.** agreement. —**con•gru′ous,** *adj.*

con′ic, *adj.* of or like cone. Also, **con′i•cal.**

co′ni•fer, *n.* tree bearing cones. —**co•nif′er•ous,** *adj.*

con•jec′ture, *n., v.,* **-tured, -turing.** guess. —**con•jec′tur•al,** *adj.*

con•join′, *v.* join together.

con′ju•gal, *adj.* of marriage. —**con′ju•gal•ly,** *adv.*

con′ju•gate′, *v.,* **-gated, -gating,** *adj.* —*v.* (-gāt′). 1. *Gram.* give in order forms of (verb). —*adj.* (-git). 2. coupled. —**con′ju•ga′tion,** *n.*

con•junc′tion, *n.* 1. combination. 2. *Gram.* word that links words, phrases, clauses, or sentences. —**con•junc′tive,** *adj.*

con′jure, *v.,* **-jured, -juring.** invoke or produce by magic. —**con′jur•er,** *n.*

con•nect′, *v.* join; link. —**con•nec′tion,** *n., Brit.* **con•nex′ion,** *n.* —**con•nec′tive,** *adj., n.*

con•nive′, *v.,* **-nived, -niving.** conspire. —**con•niv′ance,** *n.* —**con•niv′er,** *n.*

con′nois•seur′ (kon′ə sûr′), *n.* skilled judge.

con•note′, *v.,* **-noted, -noting.** signify in addition; imply. —**con′no•ta′tion,** *n.*

con•nu′bi•al, *adj.* matrimonial. —**con•nu′bi•al•ly,** *adv.*

con•quer, *v.* 1. acquire by force. 2. defeat. —**con′quer•or,** *n.* —**con′quest,** *n.*

con•san•guin′e•ous, *adj.* related by birth. —**con′san•guin′i•ty,** *n.*

con′science, *n.* recognition of right or wrong in oneself. —**con′sci•en′tious,** *adj.*

con′scion•a•ble (-shən-), *adj.* approved by conscience.

con′scious, *adj.* 1. in possession of one's senses. 2. aware. 3. deliberate. —**con′scious•ly,** *adv.* —**con′scious•ness,** *n.*

con′script, *adj.* 1. drafted. —*n.* 2. one drafted. —*v.* (kən skript′). 3. draft for military service. —**con•scrip′tion,** *n.*

con′se•crate′, *v.,* **-crated, -crating.** 1. make sacred. 2. devote. —**con′se•cra′tion,** *n.*

con•sec′u•tive, *adj.* 1. successive. 2. logical. —**con•sec′u•tive•ly,** *adv.*

con•sen′sus, *n.* agreement.

con•sent′, *v.* 1. agree; comply. —*n.* 2. assent.

con′se•quence′, *n.* 1. effect. 2. importance.

con′se•quent′, *adj.* following; resulting. —**con′se•quen′tial,** *adj.*

con′ser•va′tion, *n.* preservation, esp. of natural resources.

con•serv′a•tive, *adj.* 1. favoring existing conditions. 2. cautious. —*n.* 3. conservative person. —**con•serv′a•tive•ly,** *adv.* —**con•serv′a•tism,** *n.* —**con•serv′a•tiveness,** *n.*

con•serv′a•to′ry, *n., pl.* **-ries.** 1. school of music or drama. 2. hothouse.

con•serve′, *v.,* **-served, -serving,** *n.* —*v.* 1. keep intact. —*n.* (kon′sûrv). 2. kind of jam.

con•sid′er, *v.* 1. think over. 2. deem. 3. respect. —**con•sid′er•ate,** *adj.*

con•sid′er•a•ble, *adj.* important or sizable. —**con•sid′er•a•bly,** *adv.*

con•sid′er•a′tion, *n.* 1. thought. 2. regard. 3. fee.

con•sid′er•ing, *prep.* in view of.

con•sign′, *v.* 1. deliver. 2. entrust. 3. ship. —**con•sign′ment,** *n.*

con•sist′, *v.* be composed.

con•sist′en•cy, *n., pl.* **-cies.** 1. firmness. 2. density. 3. adherence to principles, behavior, etc. —**con•sist′ent,** *adj.* —**con•sist′ent•ly,** *adv.*

con•sis′to•ry, *n., pl.* **-ries.** church council.

con•sole′, *v.,* **-soled, -soling,** *n.* —*v.* 1. cheer in sorrow. —*n.* (kon′sōl). 2. control panel of organ or electrical system. —**con′so•la′tion**, *n.* —**con•sol′a•ble**, *adj.* —**con•sol′er**, *n.*

con•sol′i•date′, *v.*, **-dated, -dating.** 1. make or become firm. 2. unite. —**con•sol′i•da′tion**, *n.*

con′som•mé′ (kon′sə mä′), *n.* clear soup.

con′so•nant, *n.* 1. letter for a sound made by obstructing breath passage. —*adj.* 2. in agreement. —**con′so•nance**, *n.*

con′sort, *n.* 1. spouse. —*v.* (kən sôrt′). 2. associate.

con•spic′u•ous, *adj.* 1. easily seen. 2. notable. —**con•spic′u•ous•ly**, *adv.* —**con•spic′u•ous•ness**, *n.*

con•spire′, *v.*, **-spired, -spiring.** plot together. —**con•spir′a•cy**, *n.* —**con•spir′a•tor**, *n.*

con′sta•ble, *n.* police officer.

con•stab′u•lar′y, *n.*, *pl.* **-laries.** police.

con′stant, *adj.* 1. uniform. 2. uninterrupted. 3. faithful. —*n.* 4. something unchanging. —**con′stan•cy**, *n.* —**con′stant•ly**, *adv.*

con′stel•la′tion, *n.* group of stars.

con′ster•na′tion, *n.* utter dismay.

con′sti•pate′, *v.*, **-pated, -pating.** cause difficult evacuation of bowels. —**con′sti•pa′tion**, *n.*

con•stit′u•ent, *adj.* 1. being part; composing. —*n.* 2. ingredient. 3. represented voter. —**con•stit′u•en•cy**, *n.*

con′sti•tute′, *v.*, **-tuted, -tuting.** 1. compose. 2. make.

con′sti•tu′tion, *n.* 1. make-up. 2. physical condition. 3. system of governmental principles. —**con′sti•tu′tion•al**, *adj.*

con•strain′, *v.* 1. force or oblige. 2. confine. —**con•straint′**, *n.*

con•strict′, *v.* draw together; shrink. —**con•stric′tion**, *n.* —**con•stric′tor**, *n.*

con•struct′, *v.* build or devise. —**con•struc′tion**, *n.*

con•struc′tive, *adj.* 1. of construction. 2. helpful. —**con•struc′tive•ly**, *adv.*

con•strue′, *v.*, **-strued, -struing.** interpret.

con′sul, *n.* local diplomatic official. —**con′su•lar**, *adj.* —**con′su•late**, *n.*

con•sult′, *v.* 1. ask advice of. 2. refer to. 3. confer. —**con•sult′ant**, *n.* —**con′sul•ta′tion**, *n.*

con•sume′, *v.*, **-sumed, -suming.** 1. use up. 2. devour. 3. engross.

con•sum′er, *n.* 1. one that consumes. 2. purchaser of goods for personal use.

con•sum′er•ism, *n.* movement to defend consumer interests.

con•sum′mate′, *v.*, **-mated, -mating.** *adj.* (kən sum′it for *adj.*). complete or perfect. —**con′sum•ma′tion**, *n.*

con•sump′tion, *n.* 1. act of consuming. 2. amount consumed. 3. wasting disease, esp. tuberculosis of lungs. —**con•sump′tive**, *adj., n.*

con′tact, *n.* 1. a touching. 2. association. 3. business acquaintance.

contact lens, lens for correcting vision, put directly on eye.

con•ta′gion, *n.* spread of disease by contact. —**con•ta′gious**, *adj.*

con•tain′, *v.* 1. have within itself. 2. have space for. —**con•tain′er**, *n.*

con•tam′i•nate′, *v.*, **-nated, -nating.** make impure. —**con•tam′i•na′tion**, *n.*

con•temn′, *v.* scorn.

con′tem•plate′, *v.*, **-plated, -plating.** 1. consider. 2. observe. 3. intend. —**con′tem•pla′tion**, *n.*

con•tem′po•rar′y, *adj., n., pl.* **-raries.** —*adj.* 1. Also, **con•tem′po•ra′ne•ous.** of same age or period. —*n.* 2. contemporary person.

con•tempt′, *n.* 1. scorn. 2. disgrace. 3. disobedience or disrespect of court or legislature. —**con•tempt′i•ble**, *adj.* —**con•temp′tu•ous**, *adj.*

con•tend′, *v.* 1. be in struggle. 2. assert. —**con•tend′er**, *n.*

con•tent′, *adj.* 1. Also, **con•tent′ed.** satisfied. 2. willing.—*v.* 3. make content. —*n.* 4. Also, **con•tent′ment.** ease of mind. 5. (kon′tent) (*often pl.*). what is contained. 6. (kon′tent) capacity. —**con•tent′ed•ly**, *adv.*

con•ten′tion, *n.* 1. controversy. 2. assertion. —**con•ten′tious**, *adj.*

con′test, *n.* 1. struggle; competition. —*v.* (kən test′). 2. fight for. 3. dispute. —**con•test′ant**, *n.*

con′text, *n.* surrounding words or circumstances.

con•tig′u•ous, *adj.* 1. touching. 2. near.

con′ti•nent, *n.* 1. major land mass. —*adj.* 2. temperate. —**con′ti•nen′tal**, *adj.* —**con′ti•nence**, *n.*

con•tin′gen•cy, *n., pl.* **-cies.** chance; event.

con•tin′gent, *adj.* 1. conditional; possible. —*n.* 2. quota or group. 3. contingency.

con•tin′ue, *v.*, **-tinued, -tinuing.** 1. go or carry on. 2. stay. 3. extend. 4. carry over. —**con•tin′u•al**, *adj.* —**con•tin′u•al•ly**, *adv.* —**con•tin′u•ance, con•tin′u•a′tion**, *n.*

con′ti•nu′i•ty, *n., pl.* **-ties.** 1. continuous whole. 2. script.

con•tin′u•ous, *adj.* unbroken. —**con•tin′u•ous•ly**, *adv.*

con•tort′, *v.* twist; distort. —**con•tor′tion**, *n.*

con′tour (-tŏŏr), *n.* outline.

con′tra•band′, *n.* goods prohibited from shipment. —**con′tra•band′**, *adj.*

con′tra•cep′tion, *n.* prevention of pregnancy. —**con′tra•cep′tive**, *adj., n.*

con′tract, *n.* 1. written agreement. —*v.* (kən trakt′). 2. draw together; shorten. 3. acquire. 4. agree. —**con•trac′tion**, *n.*

con′trac•tor, *n.* one who supplies work by contract.

con′tra•dict′, *v.* deny as being true or correct. —**con′tra•dic′tion**, *n.* —**con′tra•dic′to•ry**, *adj.*

con•tral′to, *n., pl.* **-tos.** lowest female voice.

con•trap′tion, *n.* strange machine; gadget.

con′tra•ry, *adj., n., pl.* **-ries.** —*adj.* 1. opposite. 2. (kən trâr′ē). perverse. —*n.* 3. something contrary. —**con′tra•ri•ness**, *n.* —**con′tra•ri•ly**, —**con′tra•ri•wise′**, *adv.*

con•trast′, *v.* 1. show unlikeness. 2. compare. —*n.* (kon′trast). 3. show of unlikeness. 4. something unlike.

con′tra•vene′, *v.*, **-vened, -vening.** 1. oppose. 2. violate. —**con′tra•ven′tion**, *n.*

con•trib′ute, *v.*, **-uted, -uting.** give in part; donate. —**con′tri•bu′tion**, *n.* —**con•trib′u•tor**, *n.* —**con•trib′u•to′ry**, *adj.*

con•trite′, *adj.* penitent. —**con•tri′tion**, *n.*

con•trive′, *v.*, **-trived, -triving.** 1. plan; devise. 2. plot. —**con•triv′ance**, *n.*

con•trol′, *v.*, **-trolled, -trolling.** *n.* —*v.* 1. have direction over. 2. restrain. —*n.* 3. power of controlling. 4. restraint. 5. regulating device. —**con•trol′la•ble**, *adj.* —**con•trol′ler**, *n.*

con′tro•ver′sy, *n., pl.* **-sies.** dispute or debate. —**con′tro•ver′sial**, *adj.*

con′tro•vert′, *v.* 1. dispute. 2. discuss.

con•tu•ma′cious (-tŏŏ-), *adj.* stubbornly disobedient. —**con′tu•ma•cy**, *n.*

con′tu•me•ly, *n., pl.* **-lies.** contemptuous treatment.

con•tu′sion, *n.* bruise.

co·nun′drum, *n.* riddle involving pun.

con′ur·ba′tion, *n.* continuous mass of urban settlements.

con·va·lesce′, *v.,* **-lesced, -lescing.** recover from illness. **—con′va·les′-cence,** *n.* **—con′va·les′cent,** *adj., n.*

con·vec′tion, *n.* transference of heat by movement of heated matter.

con·vene′, *v.,* **-vened, -vening.** assemble.

con·ven′ient, *adj.* handy or favorable. **—con·ven′ience,** *n.*

con′vent, *n.* community of nuns.

con·ven′tion, *n.* 1. meeting. 2. accepted usage. **—con·ven′tion·al,** *adj.*

con·verge′, *v.,* **-verged, -verging.** meet in a point. **—con·ver′gence,** *n.* **—con·ver′gent,** *adj.*

con·ver′sant, *adj.* acquainted.

con′ver·sa′tion, *n.* informal discussion. **—con′ver·sa′tion·al,** *adj.* **—con′ver·sa′tion·al·ist,** *n.*

con·verse′, *v.,* **-versed, -versing,** *adj., n.* **—v.** 1. talk informally. **—adj., n.** (*adj.* kən vûrs′; *n.* kon′vûrs). 2. opposite. **—con·verse′ly,** *adv.*

con·vert′, *v.* 1. change. 2. persuade to different beliefs. **—n.** (kon′vûrt). 3. converted person. **—con·ver′-sion,** *n.* **—con·vert′er,** *n.*

con·vert′i·ble, *adj.* 1. able to be converted. **—n.** 2. automobile with folding top.

con·vex′, *adj.* curved outward. **—con·vex′i·ty,** *n.*

con·vey′, *v.* 1. transport. 2. transmit. **—con·vey′or,** *n.*

con·vey′ance, *n.* 1. act of conveying. 2. vehicle. 3. transfer of property.

con·vict′, *v.* 1. find guilty. **—n.** (kon′vikt). 2. convicted person.

con·vic′tion, *n.* 1. a convicting. 2. firm belief.

con·vince′, *v.,* **-vinced, -vincing.** cause to believe.

con·viv′i·al, *adj.* sociable.

con·voke′, *v.,* **-voked, -voking.** call together. **—con′vo·ca′tion,** *n.*

con′vo·lu′tion, *n.* coil.

con·voy′, *v.* 1. escort for protection. **—n.** (kon′voi). 2. ship, etc., that convoys. 3. group of ships with convoy.

con·vulse′, *v.,* **-vulsed, -vulsing.** shake violently. **—con·vul′sion,** *n.* **—con·vul′sive,** *adj.*

co′ny, *n., pl.* **-nies.** rabbit fur.

coo, *v.,* **cooed, cooing.** murmur softly. **—coo,** *n.*

cook, *v.* 1. prepare by heating. **—n.** 2. person who cooks. **—cook′book′,** *n.* **—cook′er·y,** *n.*

cook′ie, *n.* small sweet cake. Also, **cook′y.**

cool, *adj.* 1. moderately cold. 2. calm. 3. not enthusiastic. **—v.** 4. make or become cool. **—cool′er,** *n.* **—cool′-ly,** *adv.* **—cool′ness,** *n.*

coo′lie, *n.* Asiatic laborer.

coop, *n.* 1. cage for fowls. **—v.** 2. keep in coop.

coop′er, *n.* person who makes barrels.

co·op′er·ate′, *v.,* **-ated, -ating.** work or act together. Also, **co-op′er·ate′.** **—co·op′er·a′tion,** *n.*

co·op′er·a·tive (-ə tiv) *adj.* 1. involving cooperation. 2. willing to act with others. **—n.** 3. Also, **co-op.** jointly owned apartment house or business.

co·or′di·nate′, *v.,* **-nated, -nating,** *adj., n.* **—v.** (-nāt′). 1. put in same or due order. 2. adjust. **—adj.** (-nit). 3. equal. **—n.** (-nit). 4. equal. Also, **co-or′di·nate.** **—co·or′di·na′tion,** *n.* **—co·or′di·na′tor,** *n.*

coot, *n.* aquatic bird.

cop, *n. Slang.* policeman.

cope, *v.* 1. struggle successfully. **—n.** 2. cloak worn by priests.

cop′i·er, *n.* machine for making copies.

cop′ing, *n.* top course of wall.

co′pi·ous, *adj.* abundant.

cop′per, *n.* soft, reddish metallic element.

cop′per·head′, *n.* venomous snake.

cop′ra, *n.* dried coconut meat.

copse (kops), *n.* thicket. Also, **cop′-pice.**

cop′u·late′, *v.,* **-lated, -lating.** have sexual intercourse. **—cop′u·la′tion,** *n.*

cop′y, *n., pl.* **copies,** *v.,* **copied, copying.** **—n.** 1. reproduction or imitation. 2. material to be reproduced. **—v.** 3. make copy of. **—cop′y·ist,** *n.*

cop′y·right′, *n.* 1. exclusive control of book, picture, etc. **—v.** 2. secure copyright on. **—adj.** 3. covered by copyright.

co·quette′ (-ket′), *n.* female flirt.

cor′al, *n.* 1. hard substance formed of skeletons of a marine animal. 2. reddish yellow.

cord, *n.* 1. small rope. 2. *Elect.* small insulated cable. 3. unit of measurement of wood.

cor′dial, *adj.* 1. hearty; friendly. **—n.** 2. liqueur. **—cor·dial′i·ty,** *n.* **—cor′dial·ly,** *adv.*

cor′don, *n.* 1. honorary cord, ribbon, etc. 2. line of sentinels.

cor′du·roy′, *n.* ribbed cotton fabric.

core, *n., v.,* **cored, coring. —n.** 1. central part. **—v.** 2. remove core of.

cork, *n.* 1. outer bark of a Mediterranean oak tree. 2. stopper of cork, rubber, etc. **—v.** 3. stop with a cork.

cork′screw′, *n.* spiral, pointed instrument for pulling corks.

cor′mo·rant, *n.* voracious water bird.

corn, *n.* 1. maize. 2. any edible grain. 3. single seed. 4. horny callus, esp. on toe. **—v.** 5. preserve, esp. in brine.

cor′ne·a, *n.* transparent part of coat of the eye.

cor′ner, *n.* 1. place where two lines or surfaces meet. 2. exclusive control. **—v.** 3. put in corner. 4. acquire exclusive control of (stock or commodity). **—cor′ner·stone′,** *n.*

cor·net′, *n.* musical wind instrument resembling trumpet.

cor′nice, *n.* horizontal projection at top of a wall.

cor′nu·co′pi·a, *n.* horn-shaped container of food, etc.; horn of plenty.

co·rol′la, *n.* petals of a flower.

cor′ol·lar′y, *n., pl.* **-laries.** proposition proved in proving another.

co·ro′na, *n., pl.* **-nas, -nae.** circle of light, esp. around sun or moon.

cor′o·nar′y, *adj.* of arteries supplying heart tissues.

cor′o·na′tion, *n.* crowning.

cor′o·ner, *n.* official who investigates deaths not clearly natural.

cor′o·net, *n.* small crown.

cor′po·ral, *adj.* 1. physical. 2. *Mil.* lowest noncommissioned officer.

cor′po·ra′tion, *n.* legally formed association for business, etc. **—cor′-po·rate,** *adj.*

cor·po′re·al, *adj.* tangible.

corps (kōr), *n.* 1. military unit. 2. any group.

corpse, *n.* dead body.

cor′pu·lent, *adj.* fat. **—cor′pu·lence,** *n.*

cor′pus·cle (-pə səl), *n.* minute body in blood.

cor·ral′, *n., v.,* **-ralled, -ralling. —n.** 1. pen for stock. **—v.** 2. keep in corral. 3. corner or capture.

cor·rect′, *v.* 1. mark or remove errors. 2. rebuke. 3. counteract. **—adj.** 4. right. **—cor·rec′tion,** *n.* **—cor·rec′tive,** *adj., n.* **—cor·rect′ly,** *adv.*

cor′re•late′, *v.*, **-lated, -lating.** bring into mutual relation. —**cor′re•la′-tion,** *n.* —**cor•rel′a•tive,** *adj., n.*

cor′res•pond′, *v.* 1. conform or be similar. 2. communicate by letters. —**cor′re•spond′ence,** *n.*

cor′re•spond′ent, *n.* 1. writer of letters. 2. reporter in distant place. —*adj.* 3. corresponding.

cor′ri•dor, *n.* passageway.

cor•rob′o•rate′, *v.*, **-rated, -rating.** confirm. —**cor•rob′o•ra′tion,** *n.* —**cor•rob′o•ra′tive,** *adj.*

cor•rode′, *v.*, **-roded, -roding.** 1. eat away gradually. 2. be eaten away. —**cor•ro′sion,** *n.* —**cor•ro′sive,** *adj., n.*

cor′ru•gate′, *v.*, **-gated, -gating.** bend into folds. —**cor′ru•ga′tion,** *n.*

cor•rupt′, *adj.* 1. dishonest; evil. 2. tainted. —*v.* 3. make or become corrupt. —**cor•rupt′i•ble,** *adj.* —**cor•rup′tion, cor•rupt′ness,** *n.*

cor•sage′ (kôr säzh′), *n.* small bouquet to be worn.

cor′sair, *n.* pirate.

cor′set, *n.* undergarment for confining figure.

cor′tege′ (kôr tezh′), *n.* procession.

cor′tex, *n.* 1. bark. 2. outer covering of brain or other organ.

cor′ti•sone′ (-sōn′, -zōn′), *n.* hormone used esp. in treating arthritis.

cor•vette′, *n.* small fast vessel.

cos•met′ic, *n.* preparation for beautifying skin. —**cos•met′ic,** *adj.*

cos′mic, *adj.* 1. of the cosmos. 2. vast.

cos′mo•pol′i•tan, *adj.* worldly.

cos′mos, *n.* ordered universe.

cost, *n.* 1. price paid. 2. loss or penalty. —*v.* 3. require as payment. —**cost′ly,** *adj.*

cos′tume, *n., v.,* **-tumed, -tuming.** —*n.* 1. historical dress, stage garb, etc. —*v.* 2. dress or supply with costume.

co′sy, *adj.* cozy.

cot, *n.* light bed.

cote, *n.* shelter for pigeons, sheep, etc.

co′te•rie, *n.* group of social acquaintances.

co•til′lion (-til′yən), *n.* 1. elaborate dance. 2. ball, esp. for debutantes.

cot′tage, *n.* small house.

cot′ter, *n.* pin fitting into machinery opening.

cot′ton, *n.* downy plant substance made into fabric.

cot′ton•seed′, *n.* oily seed of cotton plant.

cot′ton•wood′, *n.* species of poplar.

couch, *n.* 1. bed. —*v.* 2. express.

cou′gar (kōō′-), *n.* large American feline.

cough, *v.* 1. expel air from lungs suddenly and loudly. —*n.* 2. act or sound of coughing.

could, *v.* pt. of **can.**

coun′cil, *n.* deliberative or advisory body. —**coun′cil•man,** *n.* —**coun′-cil•wo′man,** *n.fem.* —**coun′ci•lor, coun′cil•lor,** *n.*

coun′sel, *n., v.,* **-seled, -seling.** —*n.* 1. advice. 2. consultation. 3. lawyer. —*v.* 4. advise. —**coun′se•lor, coun′-sel•lor,** *n.*

count, *v.* 1. find total number. 2. name numbers to. 3. esteem. 4. rely. 5. be important. —*n.* 6. a counting. 7. total number. 8. item in indictment. 9. European nobleman.

count′down′, *n.* backward counting in time units to scheduled event.

coun′te•nance, *n., v.,* **-nanced, -nancing.** —*n.* 1. appearance; face. 2. encouragement. —*v.* 3. tolerate.

count′er, *n.* 1. table, display case, etc., in store. 2. one that counts. 3. anything opposite. —*v.* 4. oppose. 5. return (blow). —*adv., adj.* 6. contrary.

coun′ter•act′, *v.* act against; neutralize. —**coun′ter•ac′tion,** *n.*

coun′ter•bal′ance, *n., v.,* **-anced, -ancing.** —*n.* 1. anything that balances another. —*v.* (koun′tər bal′əns). 2. weigh against equally.

coun′ter•clock′wise′, *adv., adj.* opposite to direction of turning clock hands.

coun′ter•cul′ture, *n.* culture of young, etc., that rejects established values.

coun′ter•feit, *adj.* 1. fraudulently imitative. —*n.* 2. fraudulent imitation. —*v.* 3. make counterfeits. 4. feign. —**coun′ter•feit′er,** *n.*

coun′ter•mand′, *v.* revoke (command).

coun′ter•part′, *n.* match or complement.

coun′ter•point′, *n.* combining of melodies.

coun′ter•pro•duc′tive, *adj.* giving results opposite to those intended.

coun′ter•sign′, *n.* 1. secret signal. —*v.* 2. sign to confirm another signature.

count′ess, *n.* woman spouse or equal of count or earl.

count′less, *adj.* innumerable.

coun′try, *n., pl.* **-tries.** 1. region. 2. nation. 3. rural districts. —**coun′-try•man,** *n.* —**coun′try•side′,** *n.*

coun′ty, *n., pl.* **-ties.** political unit within state.

coup (kōō), *n., pl.* **coups.** daring and successful stroke.

coupe (kōōp), *n.* closed automobile with large rear compartment. Also, **cou•pé′** (kōō pā′).

cou′ple, *n., v.,* **-pled, -pling.** —*n.* 1. pair. —*v.* 2. fasten or unite. —**cou′-pler,** *n.* —**cou′pling,** *n.*

cou′plet, *n.* pair of rhyming lines.

cour′age, *n.* bravery. —**cou•ra′-geous,** *adj.*

cour′i•er, *n.* messenger.

course, *n., v.,* **coursed, coursing.** —*n.* 1. continuous passage. 2. route. 3. manner. 4. series of studies. 5. one part of meal. —*v.* 6. run.

court, *n.* 1. enclosed space. 2. level area for certain games. 3. palace. 4. assembly held by sovereign. 5. homage or attention. 6. place where justice is dealt. 7. judge or judges. —*v.* 8. woo. —**court′house′,** *n.* —**court′-ship,** *n.* —**court′yard′,** *n.*

cour′te•sy, *n., pl.* **-sies.** 1. good manners. 2. indulgence. —**cour′te•ous,** *adj.*

cour′ti•er, *n.* person in attendance at court.

court′ly, *adj.* elegant.

court′-mar′tial, *n., pl.* **courts-martial,** *v.,* **-tialed, -tialing.** —*n.* 1. military court. —*v.* 2. try by court-martial.

cous′in, *n.* child of uncle or aunt.

cove, *n.* deep recess in shoreline.

cov′e•nant, *n.* solemn agreement.

cov′er, *v.* 1. be or put something over. 2. include. 3. have in range. 4. meet or offset. —*n.* 5. something that covers. 6. concealment. —**cov′-er•ing,** *n.*

cov′er•age, *n.* 1. protection by insurance. 2. awareness and reporting of news.

cov′er•let, *n.* quilt.

cov′ert (kō′vərt), *adj.* secret or covered. —**cov′ert•ly,** *adv.*

cov′et, *v.* desire greatly or wrongfully. —**cov′et•ous,** *adj.*

cov′ey, *n., pl.* **-eys.** small flock.

cow, *n.* 1. female of bovine or other large animal. —*v.* 2. intimidate.

cow′ard, *n.* person who lacks courage. —**cow′ard•ice,** *n.* —**cow′ard•ly,** *adj., adv.*

cow′boy′, *n.* Western U.S. cattle herder. Also, **cow′hand′; cow′girl′,** *n. fem.*

cow′er, *v.* crouch in fear.

cowl, *n.* 1. hooded garment. 2. hoodlike part.

cow'slip', *n.* plant with yellow flowers.

cox'comb', *n.* dandy.

cox'swain (kok'sən), *n.* steersman of rowboat.

coy, *adj.* affectedly shy. —**coy'ly**, *adv.* —**coy'ness**, *n.*

coy•o'te (kī ō'tē), *n.* animal related to wolf.

co'zy, *adj.* intimately comfortable. —**co'zi•ly**, *adv.* —**co'zi•ness**, *n.*

crab, *n.* crustacean with broad flat body.

crab'by, *adj.* grouchy. —**crab'bi•ness**, *n.*

crack, *v.* 1. make sudden, sharp sound. 2. break without separating. —*n.* 3. sudden, sharp sound. 4. break without separation.

crack'er, *n.* 1. crisp biscuit. 2. firecracker. 3. *Slang.* yokel.

crack'le, *v.*, **-led, -ling**, *n.* —*v.* 1. crack repeatedly. —*n.* 2. crackling sound.

crack'pot', *n. Informal.* person with irrational theories.

crack'up', *n. Informal.* nervous breakdown.

cra'dle, *n.*, *v.*, **-dled, -dling.** —*n.* 1. bed on rockers for baby. —*v.* 2. place in a cradle.

craft, *n.* 1. skill; skilled trade. 2. cunning. 3. vessels or aircraft. —**crafts'-man**, *n.* —**crafts'man•ship'**, *n.*

craft'y, *adj.* sly. —**craft'i•ly**, *adv.*

crag, *n.* steep rough rock. —**crag'gy**, *adj.*

cram, *v.*, **crammed, cramming.** fill tightly.

cramp, *n.* 1. involuntary muscular contraction. —*v.* 2. affect with a cramp. 3. hamper.

cran'ber'ry, *n.*, *pl.* **-ries.** red, acid, edible berry.

crane, *n.* 1. tall wading bird. 2. lifting device or machine.

cra'ni•um, *n.* skull. —**cra'ni•al**, *adj.*

crank, *n.* 1. right-angled arm for communicating motion. 2. *Informal.* grouchy or eccentric person. —*v.* 3. turn with a crank.

crank'y, *adj.* ill-tempered. —**crank'i•ness**, *n.*

cran'ny, *n.*, *pl.* **-nies.** cleft.

crap, *n. Slang.* 1. worthless material. 2. false or meaningless statements.

crap'pie, *n.* small fish.

craps, *n.* dice game.

crash, *v.* 1. strike noisily. 2. land or fall with damage. —*n.* 3. noise or act of crashing. 4. collapse. 5. act or instance of crashing. 6. rough fabric.

crass, *adj.* gross; stupid. —**crass'ly**, *adv.* —**crass'ness**, *n.*

crate, *n.*, *v.*, **crated, crating.** —*n.* 1. box or frame for packing. —*v.* 2. put in crate.

cra'ter, *n.* cup-shaped hole, esp. in volcano or on moon.

cra•vat', *n.* necktie.

crave, *v.*, **craved, craving.** yearn or beg for.

cra'ven, *adj.* 1. cowardly. —*n.* 2. coward.

craw, *n.* crop of bird.

craw'fish', *n.* fresh-water crustacean.

crawl, *v.* 1. move slowly, as on stomach. —*n.* 2. act of crawling. 3. swimming stroke. —**crawl'er**, *n.*

cray'on, *n.* stick of colored clay or chalk.

craze, *v.*, **crazed, crazing**, *n.* —*v.* 1. make insane. 2. mark with fine cracks, as glaze. —*n.* 3. mania.

cra'zy, *adj.*, **-zier, -ziest.** insane. —**cra'zi•ly**, *adv.* —**cra'zi•ness**, *n.*

creak, *v.* 1. squeak sharply. —*n.* 2. creaking sound. —**creak'y**, *adj.*

cream, *n.* 1. fatty part of milk. —*v.* 2. make with cream. 3. work to a creamy state. 4. *Informal.* defeat utterly. —**cream'er**, *n.* —**cream'y**, *adj.*

cream'er•y, *n.*, *pl.* **-eries.** place dealing in milk products.

crease, *n.*, *v.*, **creased, creasing.** —*n.* 1. mark from folding. —*v.* 2. make creases in.

cre•ate', *v.*, **-ated, -ating.** cause to exist. —**cre•a'tion**, *n.* —**cre•a'tive**, *adj.* —**cre•a'tor**, *n.*

crea'ture, *n.* 1. animate being. 2. anything created.

cre'dence, *n.* belief.

cre•den'tial, *n.* verifying document.

cred'i•ble, *adj.* believable. —**cred'i•bil'i•ty**, *n.* —**cred'i•bly**, *adv.*

cred'it, *n.* 1. belief. 2. trustworthiness. 3. honor. 4. time allowed for payment. —*v.* 5. believe. 6. ascribe to.

cred'it•a•ble, *adj.* praiseworthy. —**cred'it•a•bly**, *adv.*

credit card, *n.* card entitling holder to charge purchases.

cred'i•tor, *n.* person owed.

cred'u•lous, *adj.* overwilling to believe. —**cre•du'li•ty**, *n.*

creed, *n.* formula of belief. Also, **cre'-do** (krē'dō).

creek (krēk, krik), *n.* brook.

creep, *v.*, **crept, creeping**, *n.* —*v.* 1. move stealthily; crawl. —*n.* 2. *Slang.* disagreeable person.

creep'y, *adj.*, **-ier, -iest.** causing uneasiness or fear.

cre'mate, *v.*, **-mated, -mating.** burn (corpse) to ashes. —**cre•ma'tion**, *n.* —**cre'ma•to'ry**, *adj.*, *n.*

Cre'ole, *n.* one of French blood born in Louisiana.

cre'o•sote', *n.* oily liquid from tar.

crepe (krāp), *n.* light crinkled fabric.

cre•scen'do (krə shen'dō), *n.*, *pl.* **-dos.** *Music.* gradual increase in loudness.

cres'cent (kres'ənt), *n.* 1. moon in its first or last quarter. 2. object having this shape.

cress, *n.* plant with pungent leaves.

crest, *n.* 1. tuft or plume. 2. figure above coat of arms.

crest'fal'len, *adj.* depressed.

cre•tonne' (kri ton'), *n.* heavily printed cotton.

cre•vasse', *n.* fissure, esp. in glacier.

crev'ice, *n.* fissure.

crew, *n.* 1. group of persons working together, as on ship. —*v.* 2. form crew of.

crib, *n.*, *v.*, **cribbed, cribbing.** —*n.* 1. child's bed. 2. rack or bin. —*v.* 3. put in a crib.

crib'bage, *n.* card game using score board with pegs.

crick, *n.* muscular spasm.

crick'et, *n.* 1. leaping, noisy insect. 2. British open-air ball game with bats.

cri'er, *n.* one who cries or announces.

crime, *n.* 1. unlawful act. 2. sin. —**crim'i•nal**, *adj.*, *n.* —**crim'i•nol'o•gy**, *n.*

crimp, *v.* 1. make wavy. —*n.* 2. crimped form.

crim'son, *n.*, *adj.* deep red.

cringe, *v.*, **cringed, cringing.** shrink in fear or servility.

crin'kle, *v.*, **-kled, -kling**, *n.* wrinkle or rustle. —**crin'kly**, *adj.*

crip'ple, *n.*, *v.*, **-pled, -pling.** —*n.* 1. lame person. —*v.* 2. make lame.

cri'sis, *n.*, *pl.* **-ses.** decisive stage or point.

crisp, *adj.* 1. brittle. 2. fresh. 3. brisk. 4. curly. —*v.* 5. make or become crisp.

criss'cross', *adj.* 1. marked with crossed lines. —*n.* 2. crisscross pattern. —*v.* 3. mark with crossed lines.

cri•te'ri•on, *n.*, *pl.* **-teria.** standard for judgment.

crit'ic, *n.* 1. skilled judge. 2. person arguing against something.

crit′i•cal, *adj.* 1. severe in judgment. 2. involving criticism. 3. crucial. —**crit′i•cal•ly**, *adv.*

crit′i•cize′, *v.*, **-cized, -cizing.** 1. discuss as a critic. 2. find fault with. Also, **crit′i•cise′.** —**crit′i•cism′**, *n.*

cri•tique′ (-tēk′), *n.* critical article.

croak, *v.* utter a low, hoarse cry.

cro•chet′ (krō shā′), *v.*, **-cheted, -cheting.** form thread into designs with hooked needle.

crock, *n.* earthen jar. —**crock′er•y**, *n.*

croc′o•dile′, *n.* large aquatic legged reptile with long, powerful jaws and tail.

cro′cus, *n., pl.* **crocuses.** small bulbous plant blooming in early spring.

crone, *n.* ugly old woman.

cro′ny, *n., pl.* **-nies.** close friend.

crook, *n.* 1. tight curve. 2. bend. 3. *U.S. Informal.* dishonest person. —*v.* 4. bend. —**crook′ed**, *adj.*

croon, *v.* 1. sing softly. —*n.* 2. such singing. —**croon′er**, *n.*

crop, *n., v.*, **cropped, cropping.** —*n.* 1. produce from the soil. 2. short whip. 3. pouch in gullet of bird. —*v.* 4. remove ends. 5. reap. 6. crop up, appear. —**crop′per**, *n.*

cro•quet′ (-kā′), *n.* game with wooden balls and mallets.

cro•quette′, *n.* fried or baked piece of chopped food.

cro′sier (krō′zhər), *n.* staff of bishop.

cross, *n.* 1. structure whose basic form has an upright with transverse piece. 2. emblem of Christianity. 3. figure resembling cross. 4. trouble. 5. mixture of breeds. —*v.* 6. make sign of cross over. 7. put, lie, or pass across. 8. oppose or frustrate. 9. mark (out). 10. mix (breeds). —*adj.* 11. transverse. 12. illhumored. —**cross′ly**, *adv.* —**cross′ness**, *n.*

cross′-ex•am′ine, *v.*, **-ined, -ining.** examine closely, as opposing witness. Also, **cross′-ques′tion.**

cross′-eye′, *n.* visual disorder. —**cross′-eyed′**, *adj.*

cross′road′, *n.* 1. road that crosses another. 2. (*pl.*) **a.** intersection. **b.** decisive point.

crotch, *n.* forked part.

crotch′et (kroch′it), *n.* 1. small hook. 2. whim.

crotch′et•y, *adj.* grumpy. —**crotch′-et•i•ness**, *n.*

crouch, *v.* 1. stoop or bend low. —*n.* 2. act or instance of crouching.

croup (krōōp), *n.* inflammation of throat.

crou′ton (krōō′ton), *n.* small cube of toasted bread.

crow, *v.* 1. cry, as cock. 2. boast. —*n.* 3. cry of cock. 4. black, harsh-voiced bird.

crow′bar′, *n.* iron bar for prying.

crowd, *n.* 1. large group of people. —*v.* 2. throng. 3. press or push.

crown, *n.* 1. cover for head, esp. of a sovereign. 2. power of a sovereign. 3. top. —*v.* 4. put crown on. 5. reward or complete.

cru′cial, *adj.* 1. decisive. 2. severe. —**cru′cial•ly**, *adv.*

cru′ci•ble, *n.* vessel for melting metals, etc.

cru′ci•fix, *n.* cross with figure of Jesus crucified.

cru′ci•fy′, *v.*, **-fied, -fying.** put to death on cross. —**cru′ci•fix′ion**, *n.*

crude, *adj.*, **cruder, crudest**, *n.* —*adj.* 1. unrefined. 2. unfinished. —*n.* 3. *Informal.* unrefined petroleum. —**crude′ly**, *adv.* —**crude′ness, cru′-di•ty**, *n.*

cru′el, *adj.* 1. disposed to inflict pain. 2. causing pain. —**cru′el•ly**, *adv.* —**cru′el•ness, cru′el•ty**, *n.*

cru′et, *n.* stoppered bottle for vinegar, etc.

cruise, *v.*, **cruised, cruising**, *n.* —*v.* 1. sail or fly at moderate speed. 2. travel for pleasure. —*n.* 3. cruising trip.

cruis′er, *n.* 1. kind of warship. 2. small pleasure boat.

crul′ler, *n.* sweet doughnutlike cake.

crumb, *n.* small bit of bread, etc.

crum′ble, *v.*, **-bled, -bling.** break into fragments; decay.

crum′ple, *v.*, **-pled, -pling**, *n.* wrinkle; rumple.

crunch, *v.* 1. chew or crush noisily. —*n.* 2. *Informal.* reduction of resources, esp. economic.

cru•sade′, *n., v.*, **-saded, -sading.** —*n.* 1. expedition to recover Holy Land from the Muslims. 2. campaign for good cause. —*v.* 3. engage in crusade. —**cru•sad′er**, *n.*

crush, *v.* 1. bruise or break by pressing. 2. subdue. —*n.* 3. dense crowd.

crust, *n.* 1. hard outer part or covering. 2. *Informal.* impertinence. —*v.* 3. cover with crust.

crus•ta′cean (-shən), *n.* sea animal having hard shell. — **crus•ta′cean**, *adj.*

crutch, *n.* 1. staff fitting under the armpit for support in walking. 2. *Informal.* temporary aid or expedient.

crux, *n., pl.* **cruxes, cruces.** vital point.

cry, *v.*, **cried, crying**, *n., pl.* **cries.** —*v.* 1. make sounds of grief, etc. 2. utter characteristic sounds. 3. shout. —*n.* 4. act or sound of crying.

crypt, *n.* underground chamber.

cryp′tic, *adj.* mysterious.

crys′tal, *n.* 1. clear transparent mineral. 2. body with symmetrical plane faces. 3. fine glass. 4. cover of watch face. —**crys′tal•line**, *adj.* —**crys′tal•lize**, *v.*

cub, *n.* young fox, bear, etc.

cub′by•hole′, *n.* small enclosed space.

cube, *n., v.*, **cubed, cubing.** —*n.* 1. solid bounded by six squares. 2. *Math.* third power of a quantity. —*v.* 3. make into cubes. 4. *Math.* raise to third power. —**cu′bic, cu′bi•cal**, *adj.*

cu′bi•cle, *n.* small room.

cuck′old, *n.* husband of unfaithful wife.

cuck′oo, *n.* small bird.

cu′cum•ber, *n.* common long edible fruit.

cud, *n.* food that cow, etc., returns to mouth for further chewing.

cud′dle, *v.*, **-dled, -dling.** hold tenderly; nestle.

cudg′el, *n., v.*, **-eled, -eling.** —*n.* 1. short thick stick. —*v.* 2. beat with cudgel.

cue, *n.* 1. (esp. on stage) something that signals speech or action. 2. rod for billiards.

cuff, *n.* 1. fold or band at end of sleeve or trouser leg. 2. slap. —*v.* 3. slap.

cui•sine′ (kwi zēn′), *n.* cookery.

cu′li•nar′y (kyōō′-), *adj.* of cooking.

cull, *v.* select best parts of.

cul′mi•nate′, *v.*, **-nated, -nating.** reach highest point. —**cul′mi•na′-tion**, *n.*

cul′pa•ble, *adj.* deserving blame. —**cul′pa•bil′i•ty**, *n.*

cul′prit, *n.* person arraigned for or guilty of an offense.

cult, *n.* religious sect or system.

cul′ti•vate′, *v.*, **-vated, -vating.** 1. prepare and care for (land). 2. develop possibilities of. —**cul′ti•va′-tion**, *n.* —**cul′ti•va′tor**, *n.*

cul′ti•vat′ed, *adj.* educated and well-mannered.

cul′ture, *n.* 1. raising of plants or animals. 2. development of mind. 3. state or form of civilization.

cul′vert, *n.* channel under road, etc.

cum′ber•some, *adj.* clumsy.

cu′mu·la·tive, *adj.* increasing by accumulation.

cu′mu·lus (kyoo′myə ləs), *n., pl.* **-li.** cloud in form of rounded heaps on flat base. **—cu′mu·lous,** *adj.*

cun′ning, *n.* 1. skill. 2. guile. **—***adj.* 3. clever. 4. sly.

cup, *n.* small open drinking vessel.

cup′board (kub′ərd), *n.* closet for dishes, etc.

cu·pid′i·ty, *n.* greed.

cu′po·la (kyoo′-), *n.* rounded dome.

cu′prous, *adj.* containing copper.

cur, *n.* worthless dog.

cu′rate, *n.* clergyman assisting rector or vicar.

cu·ra′tor, *n.* person in charge of museum collection.

curb, *n.* 1. strap for restraining horse. 2. restraint. 3. edge of sidewalk. **—***v.* 4. control.

curd, *n.* 1. substance formed when milk coagulates. **—***v.* 2. change into curd.

cur′dle, *v.,* **-dled, -dling.** congeal.

cure, *n., v.,* **cured, curing. —***n.* 1. treatment of disease. 2. restoration to health. **—***v.* 3. restore to health. 4. prepare for use. **—cur′a·ble,** *adj.* **—cur′a·tive,** *adj., n.*

cure′-all′, *n.* cure for anything; panacea.

cur′few, *n.* evening signal to leave streets.

cu′ri·o′, *n., pl.* **curios.** odd valuable article.

cu′ri·os′i·ty, *n., pl.* **-ties.** 1. desire to know. 2. odd thing.

cu′ri·ous, *adj.* 1. wanting to know. 2. prying. 3. strange. **—cu′ri·ous·ly,** *adv.*

curl, *v.* 1. form in ringlets. 2. coil. **—***n.* 3. ringlet.

cur′lew, *n.* shore bird.

curl′i·cue′, *n.* fancy curl.

cur′rant, *n.* 1. small seedless raisin. 2. edible acid berry.

cur′ren·cy, *n., pl.* **-cies.** 1. money in use in a country. 2. prevalence. 3. circulation.

cur′rent, *adj.* 1. present. 2. generally known or believed. **—***n.* 3. stream; flow. 4. water, air, etc., moving in one direction. 5. movement of electricity. **—cur′rent·ly,** *adv.*

cur·ric′u·lum, *n., pl.* **-lums, -la.** course of study.

cur′ry, *n., pl.* **-ries,** *v.,* **-ried, -rying. —***n.* 1. East Indian hot sauce or powder. **—***v.* 2. prepare with curry. 3. rub and comb (horse, etc.). 4. seek (favor) with servility.

curse, *n., v.,* **cursed** or **curst, cursing. —***n.* 1. wish that evil befall another. 2. evil so invoked. 3. profane oath. 4. cause of evil. **—***v.* 5. wish evil upon. 6. swear. 7. afflict.

cur′so·ry, *adj.* superficial.

curt, *adj.* brief, esp. rudely so. **—curt′ly,** *adv.*

cur·tail′, *v.* cut short. **—cur·tail′-ment,** *n.*

cur′tain, *n.* 1. piece of fabric hung to adorn, conceal, etc. **—***v.* 2. provide or cover with curtains.

curt′sy, *n., pl.* **-sies,** *v.,* **-sied, -sying. —***n.* 1. bow by women. **—***v.* 2. make curtsy.

cur′va·ture, *n.* 1. a curving. 2. degree of curving.

curve, *n., v.,* **curved, curving. —***n.* 1. bending line. **—***v.* 2. bend or move in a curve.

cush′ion, *n.* soft bag of feathers, air, etc.

cusp, *n.* pointed end.

cus′pid, *n.* canine tooth.

cus·pi·dor′, *n.* receptacle for spit, cigar ash, etc.

cus′tard, *n.* cooked dish of eggs and milk.

cus′to·dy, *n., pl.* **-dies.** 1. keeping; care. 2. imprisonment. **—cus·to′di·an,** *n.*

cus′tom, *n.* 1. usual practice. 2. set of such practices. 3. (*pl.*) **a.** duties on imports. **b.** agency collecting these. **—***adj.* 4. made for the individual. **—cus′tom·ar′y,** *adj.* **—cus′tom·ar′-i·ly,** *adv.*

cus′tom·er, *n.* 1. purchaser or prospective purchaser. 2. *Informal.* person.

cut, *v.,* **cut, cutting,** *n.* **—***v.* 1. sever, as with knife. 2. wound feelings of. 3. reap or trim. 4. shorten by omitting part. 5. dilute. **—***n.* 6. a cutting. 7. result of cutting. 8. straight passage. 9. engraved plate for printing.

cu·ta′ne·ous, *adj.* of the skin.

cute, *adj. Informal.* pretty or pleasing.

cu′ti·cle, *n.* epidermis, esp. around nails.

cut′lass, *n.* short curved sword.

cut′ler·y, *n.* knives, etc., collectively.

cut′let, *n.* slice of meat for frying or broiling.

cut′ter, *n.* 1. one that cuts. 2. small fast vessel. 3. light sleigh.

cy′a·nide′ (sī′ə nīd′), *n.* poisonous salt of hydrocyanic acid.

cy′cla·mate′, *n.* artificial sweetening agent.

cy′cle, *n., v.,* **-cled, -cling. —***n.* 1. recurring time or process. 2. complete set. 3. bicycle, etc. **—***v.* 4. ride bicycle. **—cy′clic, cyc′li·cal,** *adj.* **—cy′clist,** *n.*

cy′clone, *n.* 1. rotary weather system. 2. tornado. **—cy·clon′ic,** *adj.*

cy′clo·pe′di·a, *n.* encyclopedia.

cy′clo·tron′, *n.* device used in splitting atoms.

cyl′in·der, *n.* 1. round elongated solid with its ends equal parallel circles. 2. machine part or opening in this form. **—cy·lin′dri·cal,** *adj.*

cym′bal, *n.* brass plate used in orchestras.

cyn′ic, *n.* person who doubts or lacks goodness of motive. **—cyn′i·cal,** *adj.* **—cyn′i·cism,** *n.*

cy′no·sure′ (sī′nə-), *n.* object that attracts by its brilliance.

cy′press, *n.* evergreen tree of pine family.

cyst (sist), *n.* sac containing morbid matter formed in live tissue.

czar (zär), *n.* former emperor of Russia.

D

D, d, *n.* fourth letter of English alphabet.

dab, *v.,* **dabbed, dabbing.** 1. strike or apply lightly. —*n.* 2. small moist lump. —**dab′ber,** *n.*

dab′ble, *v.,* **-bled, -bling.** 1. splatter. 2. play in water. 3. be active or interested superficially. —**dab′bler,** *n.*

dachs′hund′ (däks′hŏŏnd′), *n.* long, short-legged dog.

Da′•cron, *n. Trademark.* strong synthetic fabric resembling nylon.

daf′fo•dil, *n.* plant with yellow flowers.

daft, *adj.* 1. insane. 2. foolish. Also, **daf′fy.** —**daft′ly,** *adv.*

dag′ger, *n.* short knifelike weapon.

dahl′ia (dal′yə). showy cultivated flowering plant.

dai′ly, *adj.* 1. of or occurring each day. —*n.* 2. daily newspaper.

dain′ty, *adj.,* **-tier, -tiest,** *n., pl.* **-ties.** —*adj.* 1. delicate. —*n.* 2. delicacy. —**dain′ti•ly,** *adv.* —**dain′ti•ness,** *n.*

dair′y, *n., pl.* **dairies.** place for making or selling milk, butter, etc. —**dair′y•man,** *n.*

dai′sy, *n., pl.* **-sies.** yellow-and-white flower.

dale, *n.* valley.

dal′ly, *v.,* **-lied, -lying.** 1. sport; flirt. 2. delay. —**dal′li•ance,** *n.*

Dal•ma′tian, *n.* large white-and-black dog.

dam, *n., v.,* **dammed, damming.** —*n.* 1. barrier to obstruct water. 2. female quadruped parent. —*v.* 3. obstruct with dam.

dam′age, *n., v.,* **-aged, -aging.** —*n.* 1. injury. 2. (*pl.*) payment for injury. —*v.* 3. injure. —**dam′age•a•ble,** *adj.*

dam′ask, *n.* 1. woven figured fabric. —*adj.* 2. pink.

dame, *n.* 1. woman of rank. 2. *Slang.* any woman.

damn, *v.* 1. declare bad. 2. condemn to hell. —**dam′na•ble,** *adj.* —**dam•na′tion,** *n.*

damp, *adj.* 1. moist. —*n.* 2. moisture. 3. noxious vapor. —*v.* Also, **damp′-en.** 4. moisten. 5. depress. 6. deaden. —**damp′ness,** *n.*

damp′er, *n.* 1. control for air or smoke currents. 2. discouraging influence.

dam′sel, *n.* girl.

dance, *v.,* **danced, dancing,** *n.* —*v.* 1. move rhythmically. —*n.* 2. act of dancing. 3. gathering or music for dancing. —**danc′er,** *n.* —**dance′a•ble,** *adj.*

dan′de•li•on, *n.* weed with yellow flowers.

dan′druff, *n.* scales on scalp.

dan′dy, *n., pl.* **-dies,** *adj.* —*n.* 1. fashionable dresser. —*adj.* 2. fine.

dan′ger, *n.* exposure to harm. —**dan′ger•ous,** *adj.*

dan′gle, *v.,* **-gled, -gling.** hang loosely.

dank, *adj.* unpleasantly damp. —**dank′ness,** *n.*

dap′per, *adj.* neat.

dap′ple, *n., adj., v.,* **-pled, -pling.** —*n.* 1. mottled marking. —*adj.* 2. mottled. —*v.* 3. mottle.

dare, *v.,* **dared** or **durst, dared, daring,** *n.* —*v.* 1. be bold enough. 2. challenge. —*n.* 3. challenge. —**dar′ing,** *adj., n.*

dark, *adj.* 1. lacking light. 2. blackish. 3. ignorant. —*n.* 4. absence of light. —**dark′en,** *v.* —**dark′ness,** *n.*

dark′room′, *n.* place for developing and printing films.

dar′ling, *n.* loved one.

darn, *v.* mend with rows of stitches. —**darn′er,** *n.*

dart, *n.* 1. slender pointed missile. —*v.* 2. move swiftly.

dash, *v.* 1. strike or throw violently. 2. frustrate. —*n.* 3. violent blow. 4. small quantity. 5. punctuation mark (–) noting abrupt break. 6. rush.

dash′board′, *n.* instrument board on motor vehicle.

dash′ing, *adj.* 1. lively. 2. stylish. —**dash′ing•ly,** *adv.*

das′tard, *n.* coward. —**das′tard•ly,** *adj.*

da′ta, *n.pl.* (*sing.* **datum**) facts or other information.

data processing, high-speed handling of information by computer.

date, *n., v.,* **dated, dating.** —*n.* 1. particular time. 2. fleshy, edible fruit of **date palm.** 3. appointment. —*v.* 4. exist from particular time. 5. fix date for or with.

daub, *v.* 1. cover with mud, etc. 2. paint clumsily. —*n.* 3. something daubed. —**daub′er,** *n.*

daugh′ter, *n.* female child. —**daugh′-ter•ly,** *adj.*

daugh′ter-in-law′, *n.* son's wife.

daunt, *v.* 1. frighten. 2. dishearten.

daunt′less, *adj.* bold; fearless.

dav′en•port′, *n.* large sofa.

dav′it, *n.* crane for boat, etc.

daw′dle, *v.,* **-dled, -dling.** waste time. —**daw′dler,** *n.*

dawn, *n.* 1. break of day. —*v.* 2. begin to grow light. 3. become apparent.

day, *n.* 1. period between two nights. 2. period (24 hours) of earth's rotation on its axis.

day′dream′, *n.* 1. reverie; fancy. —*v.* 2. indulge in reveries. —**day′-dream′er,** *n.*

day′light′, *n.* 1. light of day. 2. openness.

day′time′, *n.* time from sunrise to sunset.

daze, *v.,* **dazed, dazing,** *n.* —*v.* 1. stun. —*n.* 2. dazed condition.

daz′zle, *v.,* **-zled, -zling.** overwhelm with light.

DDT, strong insecticide.

dea′con, *n.* 1. cleric inferior to priest. 2. lay church officer. —**dea′con•ry,** *n.*

dead, *adj.* 1. no longer alive or active. 2. infertile. —*n.* 3. dead person or persons. —**dead′en,** *v.*

dead′line′, *n.* last allowable time.

dead′lock′, *n.* standstill.

dead′ly, *adj.,* **-lier, -liest.** 1. fatal. 2. dreary. 3. extremely accurate.

deaf, *adj.* unable to hear. —**deaf′en,** *v.* —**deaf′ness,** *n.*

deal, *v.,* **dealt, dealing,** *n.* —*v.* 1. conduct oneself toward. 2. do business. 3. distribute. —*n.* 4. transaction. 5. quantity. —**deal′er,** *n.*

dean, *n.* 1. head of academic faculty. 2. head of cathedral organization.

dear, *adj.* 1. loved. 2. expensive. —*n.* 3. dear one. —**dear′ly,** *adv.*

dearth, *n.* scarcity.

death, *n.* end of life. —**death′ly,** *adj., adv.* —**death′bed′,** *n.*

death′less, *adj.* enduring.

de•ba′cle (dā bä′kəl), *n.* 1. breakup; rout. 2. utter failure.

de•bar′, *v.,* **-barred, -barring.** exclude.

de•base′, *v.,* **-based, -basing.** reduce in quality. —**de•base′ment,** *n.*

de•bate′, *n., v.,* **-bated, -bating.** —*n.* 1. controversial discussion. —*v.* 2. argue; discuss. —**de•bat′a•ble,** *adj.* —**de•bat′er,** *n.*

de•bauch' (-bôch'), *v.* 1. corrupt; pervert. —*n.* 2. period of corrupt indulgence. —**de•bauch'er•y,** *n.*

de•bil'i•tate', *v.*, **-tated, -tating.** weaken. —**de•bil'i•ta'tion,** *n.*

de•bil'i•ty, *n.* weakness.

deb'it, *n.* 1. recorded debt. 2. account of debts. —*v.* 3. charge as debt.

deb'o•nair', *adj.* relaxed and cheerful.

de•bris' (də brē', dā'brē), *n.* rubbish; ruins.

debt, *n.* 1. something owed. 2. obligation to pay. —**debt'or,** *n.*

de•but' (-byoō'), *n.* first public appearance. —**deb'u•tante',** *n. fem.*

dec'ade, *n.* ten-year period.

dec'a•dence, *n.* decline in quality of power. —**dec'a•dent,** *adj.*

dec'a•gon', *n.* polygon with 10 angles and 10 sides.

dec•a•he'dron, *n.*, *pl.* **-drons, -dra.** solid figure with 10 faces.

de•cal'co•ma'ni•a (di kal' kə mā' ni ə), *n.* 1. transfer of pictures from specially prepared paper. 2. paper used. Also, **de'cal.**

Dec'a•logue', *n.* Ten Commandments.

de•camp', *v.* depart, esp. secretly.

de•cant', *v.* pour off.

de•cant'er, *n.* bottle.

de•cap'i•tate', *v.*, **-tated, -tating.** behead. —**de•cap'i•ta'tion,** *n.*

de•cath'lon, *n.* contest of ten events.

de•cay', *v.*, decline in quality, health, etc.

de•cease', *n.*, *v.*, **-ceased, -ceasing.** —*n.* 1. death. —*v.* 2. die. —**de•ceased',** *adj.*, *n.*

de•ceit', *n.* 1. fraud. 2. trick. —**de•ceit'ful,** *adj.*

de•ceive', *v.*, **-ceived, -ceiving.** mislead.

De•cem'ber, *n.* 12th month of year.

de•cen'cy, *n.*, *pl.* **-cies.** 1. propriety. 2. respectability. —**de'cent,** *adj.* —**de'cent•ly,** *adv.*

de•cen'tral•ize', *v.*, **-ized, -izing.** end central control of. —**de•cen'tral•i•za'tion,** *n.*

de•cep'tion, *n.* 1. act of deceiving. 2. fraud. —**de•cep'tive,** *adj.*

dec'i•bel', *n.* unit of intensity of sound.

de•cide', *v.*, **-cided, -ciding.** settle; resolve.

de•cid'ed, *adj.* unambiguous; emphatic. —**de•cid'ed•ly,** *adv.*

de•cid'u•ous (di sij'oō əs), *adj.* shedding leaves annually.

dec'i•mal, *adj.* 1. of tenths. 2. proceeding by tens. —*n.* 3. fraction in tenths, hundredths, etc., indicated by dot (**decimal point**) before numerator.

de•ci'pher (-sī'-), *v.* find meaning of. —**de•ci'pher•a•ble,** *adj.*

de•ci'sion, *n.* 1. something decided. 2. firmness of mind.

de•ci'sive, *adj.* 1. determining. 2. resolute. —**de•ci'sive•ly,** *adv.*

deck, *n.* 1. level on ship. 2. pack of playing cards. —*v.* 3. array.

de•claim', *v.* speak rhetorically. —**de•claim'er,** *n.*

dec'la•ma'tion, *n.* oratorical speech. —**de•clam'a•to'ry,** *adj.*

de•clare', *v.* 1. make known; proclaim. 2. affirm. —**dec'la•ra'tion,** *n.* —**de•clar'a•tive,** **de•clar'a•to'ry,** *adj.*

de•clen'sion, *n.* grammatical inflection or set of inflections.

dec'li•na'tion, *n.* 1. slope. 2. angular height of heavenly body.

de•cline', *v.*, **-clined, -clining,** *n.* —*v.* 1. refuse. 2. slant down. 3. give grammatical inflections. 4. fail; diminish. —*n.* 5. downward slope. 6. deterioration.

de•cliv'i•ty, *n.* downward slope.

de•code', *v.*, **-coded, -coding.** decipher from code.

de'com•pose', *v.*, **-posed, -posing.** 1. separate into constituent parts. 2. rot. —**de'com•po•si'tion,** *n.*

dec'o•rate', *v.*, **-rated, -rating.** furnish with ornament. —**dec'o•ra'tion,** *n.* —**dec'o•ra'tive,** *adj.*

dec'o•rous, *adj.* proper; dignified.

de•co'rum, *n.* propriety. —**dec'o•rous,** *adj.*

de•coy', *n.*, *v.* lure.

de•crease', *v.*, **-creased, -creasing,** *n.* —*v.* 1. lessen. —*n.* (dē'krēs). 2. lessening.

de•cree', *n.*, *v.*, **-creed, -creeing.** —*n.* 1. published command. —*v.* 2. proclaim or command.

de•crep'it, *adj.* feeble with age. —**de•crep'i•tude',** *n.*

de•crim'i•nal•ize', *v.*, **-ized, -izing.** cease to treat as crime. —**de•crim'i•nal•i•za'tion,** *n.*

de•cry', *v.*, **-cried, -crying.** disparage.

ded'i•cate', *v.*, **-cated, -cating.** 1. set apart. 2. devote. 3. inscribe (book) in honor of person or thing. —**ded'i•ca'tion,** *n.*

de•duce', *v.*, **-duced, -ducing.** derive logically; infer. —**de•duc'i•ble,** *adj.*

de•duct', *v.* subtract. —**de•duct'i•ble,** *adj.*

de•duc'tion, *n.* act or result of deducting or deducing. —**de•duc'tive,** *adj.*

deed, *n.* 1. act. 2. written conveyance of property. —*v.* 3. transfer by deed.

deem, *v.* think; estimate.

deep, *adj.* 1. extending far down or in. 2. difficult to understand. 3. profound. 4. low in pitch. —*n.* 5. deep part or space. —*adv.* 6. at great depth. —**deep'en,** *v.* —**deep'ly,** *adv.*

deep'-freeze', *v.*, **-froze, -frozen, -freezing,** *n.* —*v.* 1. freeze rapidly for preservation. —*n.* 2. refrigerator that deep-freezes.

deep'-fry', *v.*, **-fried, -frying.** cook in boiling fat. —**deep'-fry'er,** *n.*

deep'-seat'ed, *adj.* firmly implanted.

deer, *n.*, *pl.* **deer.** ruminant animal, usually horned.

de•face', *v.*, **-faced, -facing.** mar. —**de•face'ment,** *n.*

de•fame', *v.*, **-famed, -faming.** attack reputation of. —**def'a•ma'tion,** *n.*

de•fault', *n.* 1. failure; neglect. —*v.* 2. fail to meet obligation.

de•feat', *v.*, *n.* overthrow.

de•feat'ism, *n.* readiness to accept defeat. —**de•feat'ist,** *n.*

de'fect, *n.* fault; imperfection. —**de•fec'tive,** *adj.*

de•fec'tion, *n.* default in duty, loyalty, etc.

de•fend', *v.* 1. protect against attack. 2. uphold. —**de•fend'er,** *n.*

de•fend'ant, *n. Law.* accused party.

de•fense', *n.* 1. resistance to attack. 2. defending argument. —**de•fense'less,** *adj.* —**de•fen'sive,** *adj.*, *n.*

de•fer', *v.*, **-ferred, -ferring.** 1. postpone. 2. yield in opinion. 3. show respect. —**de•fer'ment,** *n.*

def'er•ence, *n.* act of showing respect. —**def'er•en'tial,** *adj.*

de•fi'ance, *n.* 1. bold resistance. 2. disregard. —**de•fi'ant,** *adj.* —**de•fi'ant•ly,** *adv.*

de•fi'cien•cy, *n.*, *pl.* **-cies.** lack; insufficiency. —**de•fi'cient,** *adj.*

def'i•cit, *n.* deficiency of funds.

de•file', *v.*, **-filed, -filing,** *n.* —*v.* 1. befoul. 2. desecrate. 3. march in file. —*n.* 4. narrow pass. —**de•file'ment,** *n.*

de•fine', *v.*, **-fined, -fining.** 1. state meaning of. 2. determine or outline precisely. —**def'i•ni'tion,** *n.*

def'i•nite, *adj.* 1. exact. 2. with fixed limits. —**def'i•nite•ly,** *adv.*

de•fin'i•tive, *adj.* conclusive. —**de•fin'i•tive•ly,** *adv.*

de•flate′, *v.*, **-flated, -flating.** release gas from.

de•fla′tion, *n.* abnormal fall in prices. —**de•fla′tion•ar′y**, *adj.*

de•flect′, *v.* turn from true course. —**de•flec′tion**, *n.*

de•form′, *v.* mar form of. —**de•form′i•ty**, *n.*

de•fraud′, *v.* cheat.

de•fray′, *v.* pay (expenses).

deft, *adj.* skillful. —**deft′ly**, *adv.* —**deft′ness**, *n.*

de•funct′, *adj.*, *n.* dead.

de•fy′, *v.*, **-fied, -fying.** challenge; resist.

de•gen′er•ate′, *v.*, **-ated, -ating,** *adj.*, *n.* —*v.* (-ə rāt′). 1. decline; deteriorate. —*adj.* (-ər it). 2. having declined. 3. corrupt. —*n.* (-ər it). 4. degenerate person. —**de•gen′er•a′tion**, *n.* —**de•gen′er•a•cy**, *n.*

de•grade′, *v.*, **-graded, -grading.** reduce in status. —**deg′ra•da′tion**, *n.*

de•gree′, *n.* 1. stage or extent. 2. 360th part of a complete revolution. 3. unit of temperature. 4. title conferred by college.

de•hu′man•ize′, *v.*, **-ized, -izing.** treat as lacking human qualities or requirements.

de•hy′drate′, *v.*, **-drated, -drating.** deprive of moisture. —**de′hy•dra′tion**, *n.*

de′i•fy′, *v.*, **-fied, -fying.** make a god of. —**de′i•fi•ca′tion**, *n.*

deign (dān), *v.* condescend; haughtily consent.

de′i•ty, *n.* god or goddess.

dé′jà vu′ (dā′zhä vōō′), feeling of having lived through same moment before.

de•ject′ed, *adj.* disheartened. —**de•jec′tion**, *n.*

de•lay′, *v.* 1. postpone. 2. hinder. —**de•lay′**, *n.* —**de•lay′er**, *n.*

de•lec′ta•ble, *adj.* delightful. —**de•lec′ta•bly**, *adv.* —**de′lec•ta′tion**, *n.*

del′e•gate, *n.*, *v.*, **-gated, -gating.** —*n.* 1. deputy. 2. legislator. —*v.* (-gāt′). 3. send as deputy. 4. commit to another. —**del′e•ga′tion**, *n.*

de•lete′, *v.*, **-leted, -leting.** cancel; erase. —**de•le′tion**, *n.*

del′e•te′ri•ous, *adj.* harmful.

de•lib′er•ate, *adj.*, *v.*, **-ated, -ating.** —*adj.* (-ər it). 1. intentional. 2. unhurried. —*v.* (-ə rāt′). 3. consider. 4. confer. —**de•lib′er•a′tion**, *n.* —**de•lib′er•ate•ly**, *adv.* —**de•lib′er•ate•ness**, *n.* —**de•lib′er•a′tive**, *adj.* —**de•lib′er•a′tor**, *n.*

del′i•ca•cy, *n.*, *pl.* **-cies.** 1. fineness. 2. nicety. 3. choice food.

del′i•cate, *adj.* 1. fine. 2. dainty. 3. fragile. 4. tactful. —**del′i•cate•ly**, *adv.*

del•i•ca•tes′sen, *n.* store that sells cooked or prepared food.

de•li′cious, *adj.* pleasing, esp. to taste. —**de•li′cious•ly**, *adv.* —**de•li′cious•ness**, *n.*

de•light′, *n.* 1. joy. —*v.* 2. please highly. 3. take joy. —**de•light′ed**, *adj.* —**de•light′ful**, *adj.*

de•lin′e•ate′, *v.*, **-ated, -ating.** sketch; outline. —**de•lin′e•a′tion**, *n.*

de•lin′quent, *adj.* 1. neglectful; guilty. —*n.* 2. delinquent one. —**de•lin′quen•cy**, *n.*

de•lir′i•um, *n.* mental disorder marked by excitement, visions, etc. —**de•lir′i•ous**, *adj.*

de•liv′er, *v.* 1. give up. 2. carry and turn over. 3. utter. 4. direct. 5. save. —**de•liv′er•ance**, *n.* —**de•liv′er•y**, *n.*

del•phin′i•um, *n.* blue garden flower.

del′ta, *n.* 1. 4th letter of Greek alphabet. 2. triangular area between branches of river mouth.

de•lude′, *v.*, **-luded, -luding.** mislead.

del′uge, *n.*, *v.*, **-uged, -uging.** —*n.* 1. great flood. —*v.* 2. flood. 3. overwhelm.

de•lu′sion, *n.* false opinion or conception. —**de•lu′sive**, *adj.*

de•luxe′ (-luks′), *adj.* of finest quality.

delve, *v.*, **delved, delving.** dig. —**delv′er**, *n.*

dem′a•gogue′ (-gôg′), *n.* unscrupulous popular leader. Also, **dem′a•gog′.** —**dem′a•gogu′er•y**, *n.*

de•mand′, *v.* 1. claim. 2. require. —*n.* 3. claim. 4. requirement.

de•mean′, *v.* 1. conduct (oneself). 2. lower in dignity. —**de•mean′or**, *n.*

de•ment′ed, *adj.* crazed.

de•mer′it, *n.* 1. fault. 2. rating for misconduct.

dem′i•god′, *n.* one partly divine and partly human.

de•mil′i•ta•rize′, *v.*, **-rized, -rizing.** free from military influence. —**de•mil′i•ta•ri•za′tion**, *n.*

de•mise′ (di mīz′), *n.*, *v.*, **-mised, -mising.** —*n.* 1. death. 2. transfer of estate. —*v.* 3. transfer.

dem′i•tasse′, *n.* small coffee cup.

de•mo′bi•lize′, *v.*, **-lized, -lizing.** disband (army). —**de•mo′bi•li•za′tion**, *n.*

de•moc′ra•cy, *n.* 1. government in which the people hold supreme power. 2. social equality. —**dem′o•crat′**, *n.* —**dem′o•crat′ic**, *adj.* —**de•moc′ra•tize′**, *v.*

dem′o•graph′ic, *adj.* of statistics on population. —**dem′o•graph′i•cal•ly**, *adv.*

de•mol′ish, *v.* destroy. —**dem′o•li′tion**, *n.*

de′mon, *n.* evil spirit.

de•mon′ic, *adj.* 1. inspired. 2. like a demon. Also, **de′mo•ni′a•cal.**

dem′on•strate′, *v.* 1. prove. 2. describe and explain. 3. manifest. 4. parade in support or opposition. —**de•mon′stra•ble**, *adj.* —**dem′on•stra′tion**, *n.* —**dem′on•stra′tor**, *n.*

de•mon′stra•tive, *adj.* 1. expressive. 2. explanatory. 3. conclusive.

de•mor′al•ize′, *v.*, **-ized, -izing.** corrupt morals, courage, etc., of. —**de•mor′al•i•za′tion**, *n.*

de•mote′, *v.* reduce in rank.

de•mur′, *v.*, **-murred, -murring,** *n.* —*v.* 1. object. —*n.* 2. objection.

de•mure′, *adj.* modest. —**de•mure′ly**, *adv.*

den, *n.* 1. cave of wild beast. 2. squalid place. 3. person's private room.

de•ni′al, *n.* 1. contradiction. 2. refusal to agree or give.

den′im, *n.* 1. heavy cotton fabric. 2. (*pl.*) trousers of this.

den′i•zen, *n.* inhabitant.

de•nom′i•nate′, *v.*, **-nated, -nating.** name specifically.

de•nom′i•na′tion, *n.* 1. name or designation. 2. sect. 3. value of piece of money. —**de•nom′i•na′tion•al**, *adj.*

de•nom′i•na′tor, *n.* lower term in fraction.

de•note′, *v.*, **-noted, -noting.** 1. indicate. 2. mean. —**de′no•ta′tion**, *n.*

de•nounce′, *v.*, **-nounced, -nouncing.** 1. condemn. 2. inform against.

dense, *adj.* 1. compact. 2. stupid. —**den′si•ty**, *n.* —**dense′ly**, *adv.* —**dense′ness**, *n.*

dent, *n.* 1. hollow. —*v.* 2. make a dent.

den′tal, *adj.* of teeth.

den′ti•frice, *n.* teeth-cleaning substance.

den′tist, *n.* person who prevents and treats oral disease. —**den′tist•ry**, *n.*

den′ture, *n.* artificial tooth or teeth.

de•nude′, *v.*, **-nuded, -nuding.** make bare. —**den′u•da′tion**, *n.*

de•nun′ci•a′tion, *n.* 1. condemnation. 2. accusation.

de•ny′, *v.*, **-nied, -nying. 1.** declare not to be true. **2.** refuse to agree or give.

de•o′dor•ant, *n.* agent for destroying odors.

de•part′, *v.* **1.** go away. **2.** die. **—de•par′ture**, *n.*

de•part′ment, *n.* **1.** part; section. **2.** branch. **—de′part•men′tal**, *adj.*

de•pend′, *v.* **1.** rely. **2.** be contingent. **—de•pend′ence**, *n.* **—de•pend′ent**, *adj., n.*

de•pend′a•ble, *adj.* reliable. **—de•pend′a•bil′i•ty**, *n.* **—de•pend′a•bly**, *adv.*

de•pict′, *v.* **1.** portray. **2.** describe. **—de•pic′tion**, *n.*

de•plete′, *v.*, **-pleted, -pleting.** reduce in amount. **—de•ple′tion**, *n.*

de•plore′, *v.*, **-plored, -ploring.** lament. **—de•plor′a•ble**, *adj.*

de•pop′u•late′, *v.*, **-lated, -lating.** deprive of inhabitants. **—de•pop′u•la′tion**, *n.*

de•port′, *v.* **1.** banish. **2.** conduct (oneself). **—de′por•ta′tion**, *n.*

de•port′ment, *n.* conduct.

de•pose′, *v.*, **-posed, -posing.** **1.** remove from office. **2.** testify. **—dep′o•si′tion**, *n.*

de•pos′it, *v.* **1.** place. **2.** place for safekeeping. **—***n.* **3.** sediment. **4.** something deposited. **—de•pos′i•tor**, *n.*

de′pot (dē′pō), *n.* **1.** station. **2.** storage base.

de•prave′, *v.*, **-praved, -praving.** corrupt. **—de•prav′i•ty**, *n.*

dep′re•cate′, *v.*, **-cated, -cating.** disapprove of. **—dep′re•ca′tion**, *n.* **—dep′re•ca•to′ry**, *adj.*

de•pre′ci•ate′ (-shi āt′), *v.*, **-ated, -ating.** **1.** reduce or decline in value. **2.** belittle. **—de•pre′ci•a′tion**, *n.*

dep′re•da′tion, *n.* robbery or destruction.

de•press′, *v.* **1.** deject. **2.** weaken. **3.** press down.

de•pres′sion, *n.* **1.** act of depressing. **2.** depressed state. **3.** depressed place. **4.** decline in business. **—de•pres′sive**, *adj.*

de•prive′, *v.*, **-prived, -priving. 1.** divest. **2.** withhold from. **—dep′ri•va′tion**, *n.*

depth, *n.* **1.** distance down. **2.** profundity. **3.** lowness of pitch. **4.** deep part.

dep′u•ta′tion, *n.* delegation.

dep′u•ty, *n., pl.* **-ties.** agent; substitute. **—dep′u•tize′**, *v.*

de•rail′, *v.* cause to run off rails.

de•range′, *v.*, **-ranged, -ranging. 1.** disarrange. **2.** make insane. **—de•range′ment**, *n.*

der′by, *n., pl.* **-bies.** stiff, rounded hat.

de•reg′u•late′, *v.*, **-lated, -lating.** free of regulation. **—de•reg′u•la′tion**, *n.*

der′e•lict, *adj.* **1.** abandoned. **2.** neglectful. **—***n.* **3.** something abandoned. **4.** vagabond; vagrant.

der′e•lic′tion, *n.* neglect; abandonment.

de•ride′, *v.*, **-rided, -riding.** mock. **—de•ri′sion**, *n.* **—de•ri′sive**, *adj.*

de•rive′, *v.*, **-rived, -riving. 1.** get from source. **2.** trace. **3.** deduce. **4.** originate. **—der′i•va′tion**, *n.*

der′o•gate′, *v.*, **-gated, -gating.** detract. **—der′o•ga′tion**, *n.* **—de•rog′a•to′ry**, *adj.*

der′rick, *n.* crane with boom pivoted at one end.

de•scend′ (di send′), *v.* **1.** move down. **2.** be descendant. **—de•scent′**, *n.*

de•scend′ant, *n.* person descended from specific ancestor; offspring.

de•scribe′, *v.*, **-scribed, -scribing. 1.** set forth in words. **2.** trace. **—de•scrib′a•ble**, *adj.* **—de•scrip′tion**, *n.* **—de•scrip′tive**, *adj.*

de•scry′ (de skrī′), *v.*, **-scried, -scrying.** happen to see.

des′e•crate′, *v.*, **-crated, -crating.** divest of sacredness. **—des′e•cra′tion**, *n.*

de•seg′re•gate′, *v.*, **-gated, -gating.** eliminate racial segregation in. **—de•seg′re•ga′tion**, *n.*

des′ert, *n.* **1.** arid region. **2.** (dizûrt′). due reward or punishment. **—***adj.* **3.** desolate; barren. **—***v.* **4.** (di zûrt′). abandon. **—de•sert′er**, *n.* **—de•ser′tion**, *n.*

de•serve′, *v.*, **-served, -serving.** have due one by right.

des′ic•cate′, *v.*, **-cated, -cating.** dry up. **—des′ic•ca′tion**, *n.*

de•sign′, *v.* **1.** plan. **2.** conceive form of. **—***n.* **3.** sketch or plan. **4.** art of designing. **5.** scheme. **6.** purpose. **—de•sign′er**, *n.*

des′ig•nate′, *v.*, **-nated, -nating. 1.** indicate. **2.** name. **—des′ig•na′tion**, *n.*

de•sign′ing, *adj.* scheming.

de•sire′, *v.*, **-sired, -siring**, *n.* **—***v.* **1.** wish for. **2.** request. **—***n.* **3.** longing. **4.** request. **5.** thing desired. **6.** lust. **—de•sir′a•ble**, *adj.* **—de•sir′ous**, *adj.* **—de•sir′a•bil′i•ty**, *n.*

de•sist′, *v.* stop.

desk, *n.* table for writing.

des′o•late, *adj., v.*, **-lated, -lating.** **—***adj.* (-ə lit). **1.** barren. **2.** lonely. **3.** dismal. **—***v.* (-ə lāt′). **4.** lay waste. **5.** make hopeless. **—des′o•la′tion**, *n.*

de•spair′, *n.* **1.** hopelessness. **—***v.* **2.** lose hope.

des′per•a′do (-rä′-), *n., pl.* **-does, -dos.** desperate criminal.

des′per•ate, *adj.* **1.** reckless from despair. **2.** despairing. **—des′per•a′tion**, *n.*

des′pi•ca•ble, *adj.* contemptible. **—des′pi•ca•bly**, *adv.*

de•spise′, *v.*, **-spised, -spising.** scorn.

de•spite′, *prep.* **1.** in spite of. **—***n.* **2.** insult.

de•spoil′, *v.* plunder.

de•spond′, *v.* lose courage or hope. **—de•spond′ent**, *adj.*

des′pot, *n.* tyrant. **—des•pot′ic**, *adj.* **—des′pot•ism′**, *n.*

des•sert′, *n.* sweet course of meal.

des′ti•na′tion, *n.* goal of journey.

des′tine (-tin), *v.*, **-tined, -tining. 1.** set apart. **2.** predetermine by fate.

des′ti•ny, *n., pl.* **-nies. 1.** future, esp. as predetermined. **2.** fate.

des′ti•tute′, *adj.* **1.** without means of support. **2.** deprived. **—des′ti•tu′tion**, *n.*

de•stroy′, *v.* **1.** ruin. **2.** end. **3.** kill.

de•stroy′er, *n.* **1.** one that destroys. **2.** fast, light naval vessel.

de•struc′tion, *n.* **1.** act or means of destroying. **2.** fact of being destroyed. **—de•struct′i•ble**, *adj.* **—de•struc′tive**, *adj.*

des′ul•to′ry, *adj.* not methodical. **—des′ul•to′ri•ly**, *adv.*

de•tach′, *v.* take off or away. **—de•tach′a•ble**, *adj.*

de•tached′, *adj.* **1.** separate. **2.** uninterested.

de•tach′ment, *n.* **1.** act of detaching. **2.** unconcern. **3.** impartiality. **4.** troops for special duty.

de•tail′, *n.* **1.** individual or minute part. **2.** in detail, with all details specified. **3.** troops for special duty. **—***v.* **4.** relate in detail. **5.** assign.

de•tain′, *v.* **1.** delay. **2.** keep in custody. **—de•ten′tion**, *n.*

de•tect′, *v.*, **1.** discover, esp. in or after some act. **2.** perceive. **—de•tec′tion**, *n.* **—de•tec′tor**, *n.*

de•tec′tive, *n.* professional investigator of crimes, etc.

dé•tente (dā tänt′), *n.* relaxation of international tension.

de•ter′, *v.*, **-terred, -terring.** discourage or restrain.

de•ter′gent, *adj.* 1. cleansing. —*n.* 2. cleansing agent.

de•te′ri•o•rate′, *v.,* **-rated, -rating.** make or become worse. —**de•te′ri•o•ra′tion,** *n.*

de•ter′mi•nate, *adj.* able to be specified.

de•ter′mi•na′tion, *n.* 1. act of determining. 2. firmness of purpose.

de•ter′mine, *v.,* **-mined, -mining.** 1. settle; decide. 2. ascertain. 3. limit. —**de•ter′mi•na•ble,** *adj.*

de•ter′mined, *adj.* firmly resolved.

de•ter′rence, *n.* discouragement, as of crime or military aggression. —**de•ter′rent,** *adj., n.*

de•test′, *v.* hate or despise. —**de•test′a•ble,** *adj.* —**de•test′a•bly,** *adv.* —**de′tes•ta′tion,** *n.*

de•throne′, *v.,* **-throned, -throning.** remove from a throne.

det′o•nate′, *v.,* **-nated, -nating.** explode. —**det′o•na′tion,** *n.*

de′tour, *n.* 1. roundabout course. —*v.* 2. make detour.

de•tract′, *v.* take away quality or reputation. —**de•trac′tion,** *n.*

det′ri•ment, *n.* loss or damage. —**det′ri•men′tal,** *adj.*

de•val′u•ate′, *v.,* **-ated, -ating.** reduce in value. Also, **de•val′ue.** —**de•val′u•a′tion,** *n.*

dev′as•tate′, *v.,* **-tated, -tating.** lay waste. —**dev′as•ta′tion,** *n.*

de•vel′op, *v.* 1. mature; perfect. 2. elaborate. 3. bring into being. 4. make (images on film) visible. —**de•vel′op•ment,** *n.* —**de•vel′op•er,** *n.*

de′vi•ate′, *v.,* **-ated, -ating.** 1. digress. 2. depart from normal.—**de′vi•a′tion,** *n.* —**de′vi•ant,** *adj.*

de•vice′, *n.* 1. contrivance. 2. plan. 3. slogan or emblem.

dev′il, *n.* 1. Satan. 2. evil spirit. 3. wicked person.

de′vi•ous, *adj.* 1. circuitous. 2. with low cunning. —**de′vi•ous•ly,** *adv.*

de•vise′, *v.,* **-vised, -vising.** 1. plan; contrive. 2. bequeath. —**de•vis′er,** *n.*

de•vi′tal•ize′, *v.,* **-ized, -izing.** remove vitality of. —**de•vi′tal•i•za′tion,** *n.*

de•void′, *adj.* destitute.

de•volve′, *v.,* **-volved, -volving.** 1. transfer or delegate. 2. fall as a duty.

de•vote′, *v.,* **-voted, -voting.** appropriate to something.

de•vot′ed, *adj.* 1. zealous. 2. dedicated.

dev′o•tee′ (dev′ə tē′), *n.* devoted one.

de•vo′tion, *n.* 1. consecration. 2. attachment or dedication. 3. (*pl.*) worship. —**de•vo′tion•al,** *adj.*

de•vour′, *v.* consume ravenously.

de•vout′, *adj.* pious.

dew, *n.* atmospheric moisture condensed in droplets. —**dew′y,** *adj.*

dex•ter′i•ty, *n.* 1. physical skill. 2. cleverness. —**dex′ter•ous,** *adj.*

dex′trose, *n.* type of sugar.

di′a•be′tes, *n.* disease causing body's inability to use sugar. —**di′a•bet′ic,** *adj., n.*

di′a•bol′ic, *adj.* fiendish. Also, **di′a•bol′i•cal.**

di′a•dem′, *n.* crown.

di′ag•nose′, *v.,* **-nosed, -nosing.** determine nature of (disease). —**di′ag•no′sis,** *n.*

di•ag′o•nal, *adj.* 1. connecting two angles. 2. oblique.

di′a•gram, *n., v.,* **-gramed, -graming.** chart or plan. —**di′a•gram•mat′ic,** *adj.*

di′al, *n., v.,* **dialed, dialing.** —*n.* 1. numbered face, as on watch, telephone, or radio. —*v.* 2. select or contact with use of dial.

di′a•lect′, *n.* language of district or class. —**di′a•lec′tal,** *adj.*

di′a•logue′, *n.* conversation between two or more people. Also, **di′a•log′.**

di•am′e•ter, *n.* straight line through center of a circle.

di′a•met′ri•cal, *adj.* 1. of diameters. 2. completely in contrast.

dia′mond, *n.* 1. hard, brilliant precious stone. 2. rhombus or square. 3. card suit. 4. baseball field.

di′a•per, *n.* 1. infant's underpants. —*v.* 2. put diaper on.

di′a•phragm′ (-fram′), *n.* 1. wall in body, as between thorax and abdomen. 2. vibrating membrane. 3. contraceptive device.

di′ar•rhe′a (dī′ə rē′ə), *n.* intestinal disorder. Also, **di′ar•rhoe′a.**

di′a•ry, *n.* personal daily record. —**di′a•rist,** *n.*

di′a•ther′my, *n.* therapeutic heating of body by electric currents.

di′a•tribe′, *n.* denunciation.

dice, *n.pl., sing.* **die,** *v.,* **diced, dicing.** —*n.* 1. small cubes, used in games. —*v.* 2. cut into small cubes.

di•chot′o•my, *n., pl.* **-mies.** division into two irreconcilable groups.

dick′er, *v.* bargain.

dic′tate, *v.,* **-tated, -tating,** *n.* —*v.* 1. say something to be written down. 2. command. —*n.* 3. command. —**dic•ta′tion,** *n.*

dic′ta•tor, *n.* nonhereditary absolute ruler. —**dic′ta•to′ri•al,** *adj.* —**dic′ta•tor•ship′,** *n.*

dic′tion, *n.* style of speaking or writing.

dic′tion•ar′y, *n., pl.* **-aries.** book on meaning, pronunciation, spelling, etc., of words.

di•dac′tic, *adj.* instructive. —**di•dac′ti•cism,** *n.*

did′n′t, *v. Informal.* did not.

die, *v.,* **died, dying,** *n., pl.* (for 3) **dies.** —*v.* 1. cease to be. 2. lose force; fade. —*n.* 3. shaping device. 4. sing. of **dice.**

die′hard′, *n.* defender of lost cause.

di•er′e•sis (dī er′ə sis), *n., pl.* **-ses.** sign (¨) over a vowel indicating separate pronunciation, as in Noël.

die′sel (dē′-), *n.* engine using air compression for ignition. —**die′sel,** *adj.*

di′et, *n., v.,* **-eted, -eting.** —*n.* 1. food. 2. food specially chosen for health, slimness, etc. 3. formal assembly. —*v.* 4. adhere to diet. —**di′e•tet′ic,** *adj.*

dif′fer, *v.* 1. be unlike. 2. disagree.

dif′fer•ence, *n.* 1. unlikeness. 2. disagreement; quarrel. 3. amount separating two quantities. —**dif′fer•ent,** *adj.* —**dif′fer•ent•ly,** *adv.*

dif′fer•en′ti•ate′, *v.,* **-ated, -ating.** 1. alter. 2. distinguish between.

dif′fi•cult′, *adj.* 1. hard to do or understand. 2. unfriendly or unmanageable. —**dif′fi•cul′ty,** *n.*

dif′fi•dent, *adj.* timid; shy. —**dif′fi•dence,** *n.*

dif•frac′tion, *n.* breaking up of rays of light to produce spectrum.

dif•fuse′, *v.,* **-fused, -fusing,** *adj.* —*v.* (-fyōōz′). 1. spread or scatter. —*adj.* (-fyōōs′). 2. not to the point. 3. spread or scattered. —**dif•fu′sion,** *n.*

dig, *v.,* **dug** or **digged, digging,** *n.* —*v.* 1. thrust down. 2. lift to extract. 3. form by extraction. —*n.* 4. sarcastic remark.

di•gest′, *v.* 1. prepare (food) for assimilation. 2. assimilate mentally. —*n.* (dī′jest). 3. collection or summary, esp. of laws. —**di•ges′tion,** *n.* —**di•ges′tive,** *adj.* —**di•gest′i•ble,** *adj.* —**di•gest′i•bil′i•ty,** *n.*

dig′it, *n.* 1. finger or toe. 2. any Arabic numeral, as 0, 1, 2, etc.

dig′it•al, *adj.* of or expressing data in numerals.

dig′ni•fied, *adj.* marked by dignity; stately.

dig′ni•fy′, *v.,* **-fied, -fying.** 1. honor. 2. honor more than is deserved.

dig·ni·ta·ry, *n.*, *pl.* **-ries.** eminent or high-ranking person.

dig·ni·ty, *n.*, *pl.* **-ties.** 1. nobility. 2. worthiness. 3. high rank, office, or title.

di·gress', *v.* wander from main purpose, theme, etc. —**di·gres'sion**, *n.*

dike, *n.* 1. bank for restraining waters. 2. ditch.

di·lap'i·dat'ed, *adj.* decayed.

di·lap'i·da'tion, *n.* ruin; decay.

di·late', *v.*, **-lated, -lating.** expand. —**di·la'tion**, *n.*

dil'a·to·ry, *adj.* delaying; tardy. —**dil'a·to'ri·ness**, *n*

di·lem'ma, *n.* predicament.

dil'et·tante' (-tänt'), *n.* superficial practitioner.

dil'i·gence, *n.* earnest effort. —**dil'i·gent**, *adj.*

dill, *n.* plant with aromatic seeds and leaves.

di·lute', *v.*, **-luted, -luting.** thin, as with water; weaken. —**di·lu'tion**, *n.*

dim, *adj.*, **dimmer, dimmest,** *v.*, **dimmed, dimming.** —*adj.* 1. not bright. 2. indistinct. —*v.* 3. make or become dim. —**dim'ly**, *adv.*

dime, *n.* coin worth 10 cents.

di·men'sion, *n.* magnitude. —**di·men'sion·al**, *adj.*

di·min'ish, *v.* lessen; reduce. —**dim'·i·nu'tion**, *n.*

di·min'u·tive, *adj.* 1. small. 2. denoting smallness, etc. —*n.* 3. diminutive form, as of word.

dim'i·ty, *n.*, *pl.* **-ties.** thin cotton fabric.

dim'ple, *n.* small hollow, esp. in cheek.

din, *n.*, *v.*, **dinned, dinning.** —*n.* 1. confused noise. —*v.* 2. assail with din.

dine, *v.*, **dined, dining.** eat or provide dinner.

din'ghy (ding'gē), *n.*, *pl.* **-ghies.** small boat. Also, **din'gey, din'gy.**

din'gy (-jē), *adj.*, **-gier, -giest.** dark; dirty.

din'ner, *n.* main meal.

di'no·saur', *n.* extinct reptile.

dint, *n.* 1. force. 2. dent.

di'o·cese' (dī'ə sēs'), *n.* district under a bishop. —**di·oc'e·san**, *adj.*, *n.*

dip, *v.*, **dipped** or **dipt, dipping.** —*v.* 1. plunge temporarily in liquid. 2. bail or scoop. 3. slope down. —*n.* 4. act of dipping. 5. downward slope.

diph·the'ri·a (dif thēr'ē ə), *n.* infectious disease of air passages, esp. throat.

diph'thong (dif'-), *n.* sound containing two vowels.

di·plo'ma, *n.* document of academic qualifications.

di·plo'ma·cy, *n.*, *pl.* **-cies.** 1. conduct of international relations. 2. skill in negotiation. —**dip'lo·mat'**, *n.*

dip'lo·mat'ic, *adj.* 1. of diplomacy. 2. tactful. —**dip'lo·mat'i·cal·ly**, *adv.*

dip'per, *n.* 1. one that dips. 2. ladle.

dip'so·ma'ni·a, *n.* morbid craving for alcohol. —**dip'so·ma'ni·ac**, *n.*

dire, *adj.* dreadful.

di·rect', *v.* 1. guide. 2. command. 3. manage. 4. address. —*adj.* 5. straight. 6. straightforward. —**di·rect'ly**, *adv.* —**di·rect'ness**, *n.* —**di·rec'tor**, *n.*

di·rec'tion, *n.* 1. act of directing. 2. line along which a thing lies or moves. —**di·rec'tion·al**, *adj.*

di·rec'to·ry, *n.*, *pl.* **-ries.** guide to locations or telephone numbers.

dire'ful, *adj.* dire.

dirge, *n.* funeral song.

dir'i·gi·ble, *n.* airship that can be steered.

dirk, *n.* dagger.

dirt, *n.* 1. filthy substance. 2. earth.

dirt'y, *adj.* **dirtier, dirtiest,** *v.*, **dirtied, dirtying.** —*adj.* 1. soiled. 2. indecent. —*v.* 3. soil. —**dirt'i·ness**, *n.*

dis·a'ble, *v.*, **-bled, -bling.** damage capability of. —**dis'a·bil'i·ty**, *n.*

dis·a·buse', *v.*, **-bused, -busing.** free from deception.

dis'ad·van'tage, *n.* 1. unfavorable circumstance. 2. injury. —**dis·ad'·van·ta'geous**, *adj.*

dis'af·fect', *v.* alienate. —**dis'af·fec'tion**, *n.*

dis'a·gree', *v.*, **-greed, -greeing.** differ in opinion. —**dis'a·gree'ment**, *n.*

dis'a·gree'a·ble, *adj.* unpleasant. —**dis'a·gree'a·bly**, *adv.*

dis'ap·pear', *v.* 1. vanish. 2. cease to exist. —**dis'ap·pear'ance**, *n.*

dis'ap·point', *v.* fail to fulfill hopes or wishes of. —**dis'ap·point'ment**, *n.*

dis'ap·prove', *v.*, **-proved, -proving.** condemn; censure. —**dis'ap·prov'·al**, *n.*

dis·arm', *v.* 1. deprive of arms. 2. reduce one's own armed power. —**dis·ar'ma·ment**, *n.*

dis'ar·range', *v.*, **-ranged, -ranging.** disorder. —**dis'ar·range'ment**, *n.*

dis'ar·ray', *n.* lack of order.

dis·as'ter, *n.* extreme misfortune. —**dis·as'trous**, *adj.*

dis'a·vow', *v.* disown. —**dis'a·vow'·al**, *n.* —**dis'a·vow'er**, *n.*

dis·band', *v.* terminate as organization. —**dis·band'ment**, *n.*

dis·bar', *v.*, **-barred, -barring.** expel from law practice. —**dis·bar'ment**, *n.*

dis'be·lieve', *v.*, **-lieved, -lieving.** reject as untrue. —**dis'be·lief'**, *n.*

dis·burse', *v.*, **-bursed, -bursing.** pay out. —**dis·burse'ment**, *n.*

disc, *n.* disk.

dis·card', *v.* 1. reject. —*n.* (dis'kärd). 2. something discarded. 3. discarded state.

dis·cern' (di sûrn'), *v.* 1. see. 2. distinguish. —**dis·cern'ing**, *adj.* —**dis·cern'ment**, *n.*

dis·charge', *v.*, **-charged, -charging.** 1. rid of load. 2. send forth. 3. shoot. 4. terminate employment of. 5. fulfill. —*n.* (dis'chärj). 6. act of discharging. 7. something discharged.

dis·ci'ple (di sī'pəl), *n.* intellectual follower.

dis'ci·pline, *n.*, *v.*, **-plined, -plining.** —*n.* 1. training in rules. 2. punishment. 3. subjection to rules. —*v.* 4. train. 5. punish. —**dis'ci·pli·nar'y**, *adj.* —**dis'ci·pli·nar'i·an**, *n.*

dis·claim', *n.* disown.

dis·close', *v.*, **-closed, -closing.** reveal. —**dis·clo'sure**, *n.*

dis'co, *n.*, *pl.* **-cos.** discotheque.

dis·col'or, *v.* change in color. —**dis·col'or·a'tion**, *n.*

dis·com'fit, *v.* 1. defeat. 2. frustrate. —**dis·com'fi·ture**, *n.*

dis·com'fort, *n.* lack of comfort.

dis'con·cert', *v.* perturb.

dis'con·nect', *v.* break connection of.

dis·con'so·late, *adj.* unhappy. —**dis·con'so·late·ly**, *adv.*

dis·con·tent', *adj.* Also **dis'con·tent'ed.** 1. not contented. —*n.* 2. lack of contentment.

dis'con·tin'ue, *v.*, **-tinued, -tinuing.** end; stop. —**dis'con·tin'u·ance**, *n.*

dis'cord, *n.* 1. lack of harmony. 2. disagreement; strife. —**dis·cord'ance**, *n.* —**dis·cord'ant**, *adj.*

dis'co·theque' (dis'kō tek'), *n.* nightclub where recorded dance music is played.

dis'count, *v.* 1. deduct. 2. advance money after deduction of interest. 3. disregard. 4. allow for exaggeration in. —*n.* 5. deduction.

dis•cour′age, *v.*, **-aged, -aging.** 1. deprive of resolution. 2. hinder. —**dis•cour′age•ment**, *n.*

dis′course, *n., v.*, **-coursed, -coursing.** —*n.* 1. talk. 2. formal discussion. —*v.* (dis kōrs′). 3. talk.

dis•cour′te•sy, *n.* lack of courtesy. —**dis•cour′te•ous**, *adj.*

dis•cov′er, *v.* learn or see for first time. —**dis•cov′er•y**, *n.* —**dis•cov′er•a•ble**, *adj.* —**dis•cov′er•er**, *n.*

dis•cred′it, *v.* 1. injure reputation of. 2. give no credit to. —*n.* 3. lack of belief. 4. disrepute.

dis•creet′, *adj.* wise; prudent. —**dis•creet′ly**, *adv.*

dis•crep′an•cy, *n., pl.* **-cies.** difference; inconsistency. —**dis•crep′ant**, *adj.*

dis•crete′, *adj.* separate.

dis•cre′tion, *n.* 1. freedom of choice. 2. prudence. —**dis•cre′tion•ar′y**, *adj.*

dis•crim′i•nate′, *v.*, **-nated, -nating.** *adj.* (-ə nāt′). 1. distinguish accurately. 2. show partiality for or against. —*adj.* (-ə nit). 3. making distinctions. —**dis•crim′i•na′tion**, *n.*

dis•cur′sive, *adj.* rambling; not wholly relevant.

dis•cuss′, *v.* talk about. —**dis•cus′sion**, *n.*

dis•dain′, *v., n.* scorn. —**dis•dain′ful**, *adj.*

dis•ease′, *n., v.*, **-eased, -easing.** —*n.* 1. ailment. —*v.* 2. affect with disease.

dis′em•bark′, *v.* land. —**dis′em′bar•ka′tion**, *n.*

dis′em•bod′y, *v.*, **-bodied, -bodying.** free from the body.

dis′en•chant′, *v.* free from enchantment or illusion. —**dis′en•chant′ment**, *n.*

dis′en•gage′, *v.*, **-gaged, -gaging.** separate; disconnect. —**dis′en•gage′ment**, *n.*

dis•fa′vor, *n.* 1. displeasure. 2. disregard. —*v.* 3. regard or treat with disfavor.

dis•fig′ure, *v.*, **-ured, -uring.** mar.

dis•fran′chise, *v.*, **-chised, -chising.** deprive of franchise.

dis•gorge′, *v.*, **-gorged, -gorging.** 1. vomit forth. 2. yield up.

dis•grace′, *n., v.*, **-graced, -gracing.** —*n.* 1. state or cause of dishonor. —*v.* 2. bring shame upon. —**dis•grace′ful**, *adj.* —**dis•grace′ful•ly**, *adv.*

dis•grun′tle, *v.*, **-tled, -tling.** make discontent.

dis•guise′, *v.*, **-guised, -guising**, *n.* —*v.* 1. conceal true identity of. —*n.* 2. something that disguises.

dis•gust′, *v.* 1. cause loathing in. —*n.* 2. loathing.

dish, *n.* 1. open shallow container. 2. article of food.

dis•heart′en, *v.* discourage.

di•shev′el, *v.*, **-eled, -eling.** let hang in disorder.

dis•hon′est, *adj.* not honest. —**dis•hon′est•ly**, *adv.* —**dis•hon′es•ty**, *n.*

dis•hon′or, *n.* 1. lack of honor. 2. disgrace. —*v.* 3. disgrace. 4. fail to honor. —**dis•hon′or•a•ble**, *adj.*

dis′il•lu′sion, *v.* free from illusion. —**dis′il•lu′sion•ment**, *n.*

dis′in•cline′, *v.*, **-clined, -clining.** make or be averse. —**dis′in•cli•na′tion**, *n.*

dis′in•fect′, *v.* destroy disease germs in. —**dis′in•fect′ant**, *n., adj.*

dis′in•gen′u•ous, *adj.* lacking frankness.

dis′in•her′it, *v.* exclude from inheritance.

dis•in′te•grate′, *v.*, **-grated, -grating.** separate into parts. —**dis•in′te•gra′tion**, *n.*

dis•in′ter•est, *n.* indifference.

dis•in′ter•est′ed, *adj.* impartial. —**dis•in′ter•est′ed•ly**, *adv.*

dis•joint′ed, *adj.* 1. separated at joints. 2. incoherent.

disk, *n.* 1. flat circular plate. 2. phonograph record.

dis•like′, *v.*, **-liked, -liking**, *n.* —*v.* 1. regard with displeasure. —*n.* 2. distaste.

dis′lo•cate′, *v.*, **-cated, -cating.** 1. displace. 2. put out of order. —**dis′lo•ca′tion**, *n.*

dis•lodge′, *v.*, **-lodged, -lodging.** force from place. —**dis•lodg′ment**, *n.*

dis•loy′al, *adj.* not loyal; traitorous. —**dis•loy′al•ty**, *n.*

dis′mal, *adj.* 1. gloomy. 2. terrible. —**dis′mal•ly**, *adv.*

dis•man′tle, *v.*, **-tled, -tling.** 1. deprive of equipment. 2. take apart.

dis•may′, *v.* 1. dishearten. —*n.* 2. disheartenment.

dis•mem′ber, *v.* deprive of limbs. —**dis•mem′ber•ment**, *n.*

dis•miss′, *v.* 1. direct or allow to go. 2. discharge. 3. reject. —**dis•mis′sal**, *n.*

dis•mount′, *v.* 1. get or throw down from saddle. 2. remove from mounting.

dis′o•be′di•ent, *adj.* not obedient. —**dis′o•be′di•ence**, *n.* —**dis′o•bey′**, *v.*

dis•or′der, *n.* 1. lack of order. 2. illness or disease. —*v.* 3. create disorder in. —**dis•or′der•ly**, *adj.*

dis•or′gan•ize′, *v.*, **-ized, -izing.** throw into disorder. —**dis•or′gan•i•za′tion**, *n.*

dis•own′, *v.* repudiate.

dis•par′age, *v.*, **-aged, -aging.** speak slightly of; belittle. —**dis•par′age•ment**, *n.*

dis•pas′sion•ate, *adj.* impartial; calm. —**dis•pas′sion•ate•ly**, *adv.*

dis•patch′, *v.* 1. send off. 2. transact quickly. 3. kill. —*n.* 4. act of sending off. 5. killing. 6. speed. 7. message or report. —**dis•patch′er**, *n.*

dis•pel′, *v.*, **-pelled, -pelling.** drive off; scatter.

dis•pen′sa•ry, *n.* place for dispensing medicines.

dis′pen•sa′tion, *n.* 1. act of dispensing. 2. divine order. 3. relaxation of law.

dis•pense′, *v.*, **-pensed, -pensing.** 1. distribute. 2. administer. 3. forgo. 4. do away. —**dis•pen′sa•ble**, *adj.* —**dis•pens′er**, *n.*

dis•perse′, *v.*, **-persed, -persing.** scatter. —**dis•per′sion, dis•per′sal**, *n.*

dis•pir′i•ted, *adj.* downhearted.

dis•place′, *v.*, **-placed, -placing.** 1. put out of place. 2. replace. —**dis•place′ment**, *n.*

dis•play′, *v., n.* exhibit.

dis•please′, *v.*, **-pleased, -pleasing.** offend. —**dis•pleas′ure** (-plezh′-), *n.*

dis•pose′, *v.*, **-posed, -posing.** 1. arrange. 2. incline. 3. decide. 4. get rid. —**dis•pos′a•ble**, *adj.* —**dis•pos′al**, *n.*

dis′po•si′tion, *n.* 1. personality or mood. 2. tendency. 3. disposal.

dis′pos•sess′, *v.* deprive of possession. —**dis′pos•ses′sion**, *n.*

dis′pro•por′tion, *n.* lack of proportion. —**dis′pro•por′tion•ate**, *adj.*

dis•prove′, *v.*, **-proved, -proving.** prove false.

dis•pute′, *v.*, **-puted, -puting**, *n.* —*v.* 1. argue or quarrel. —*n.* 2. argument; quarrel. —**dis•put′a•ble**, *adj.* —**dis•pu′tant**, *adj., n.* —**dis′pu•ta′tion**, *n.*

dis•qual′i•fy′, *v.*, **-fied, -fying.** make ineligible.

dis•qui′et, *v.* 1. disturb. —*n.* 2. lack of peace.

dis′qui•si′tion, *n.* formal discourse or treatise.

dis•re•gard′, *v.* 1. ignore. —*n.* 2. neglect.

dis•re•pair′, *n.* impaired condition.

dis•re•pute′, *n.* ill repute. —**dis•rep′u•ta•ble**, *adj.*

dis•re•spect′, *n.* lack of respect. —**dis•re•spect′ful**, *adj.*

dis•robe′, *v.*, **-robed, -robing.** undress.

dis•rupt′, *v.* break up. —**dis•rup′tion**, *n.* —**dis•rup′tive**, *adj.*

dis•sat′is•fy′, *v.*, **-fied, -fying.** make discontent. —**dis′sat•is•fac′tion**, *n.*

dis•sect′, *v.* cut apart for examination. —**dis•sec′tion**, *n.*

dis•sem′ble, *v.*, **-bled, -bling.** feign. —**dis•sem′bler**, *n.*

dis•sem′i•nate′, *v.*, **-nated, -nating.** scatter. —**dis•sem′i•na′tion**, *n.*

dis•sen′sion, *n.* 1. disagreement. 2. discord.

dis•sent′, *v.* 1. disagree. —*n.* 2. difference of opinion. —**dis•sent′er**, *n.*

dis′ser•ta′tion, *n.* formal essay or treatise.

dis′si•dent, *adj.* 1. refusing to agree or conform. —*n.* 2. dissident person.

dis•sim′i•lar, *adj.* not similar. —**dis•sim′i•lar′i•ty**, *n.*

dis•sim′u•late′, *v.*, **-lated, -lating.** disguise; dissemble. —**dis•sim′u•la′tion**, *n.*

dis′si•pate′, *v.*, **-pated, -pating.** 1. scatter. 2. squander. 3. live dissolutely. —**dis′si•pa′tion**, *n.*

dis•so′ci•ate′, *v.*, **-ated, -ating.** separate.

dis′so•lute′, *adj.* immoral; licentious. —**dis′so•lute′ly**, *adv.*

dis•solve′, *v.*, **-solved, -solving.** 1. make solution of. 2. terminate. 3. destroy. —**dis′so•lu′tion**, *n.*

dis′so•nance, *n.* inharmonious or harsh sound. —**dis′so•nant**, *adj.*

dis•suade′, *v.*, **-suaded, -suading.** persuade against.

dis′tance, *n.* 1. space between. 2. remoteness. 3. aloofness.

dis′tant, *adj.* 1. remote. 2. reserved. —**dis′tant•ly**, *adv.*

dis•taste′, *n.* dislike; aversion. —**dis•taste′ful**, *adj.*

dis•tem′per, *n.* infectious disease of dogs and cats.

dis•tend′, *v.* expand abnormally. —**dis•ten′tion**, *n.*

dis•till′, *v.* 1. obtain by evaporation and condensation. 2. purify. 3. fall in drops. —**dis•till′er**, *n.* —**dis•till′er•y**, *n.*

dis•tinct′, *adj.* 1. clear. 2. separate. —**dis•tinct′ly**, *adv.*

dis•tinc′tion, *n.* 1. act or instance of distinguishing. 2. discrimination. 3. difference. 4. eminence. —**dis•tinc′tive**, *adj.*

dis•tin′guish, *v.* 1. identify as different. 2. perceive. 3. make eminent.

dis•tort′, *v.* 1. twist out of shape. 2. hide truth or true meaning of. —**dis•tor′tion**, *n.*

dis•tract′, *v.* 1. divert attention of. 2. trouble. —**dis•trac′tion**, *n.*

dis•traught′, *adj.* absent-minded or crazed with anxiety.

dis•tress′, *n.* 1. pain or sorrow. 2. state of emergency. —*v.* 3. afflict with pain or sorrow.

dis•trib′ute, *v.*, **-uted, -uting.** 1. divide in shares. 2. spread. 3. sort. —**dis′tri•bu′tion**, *n.* —**dis•trib′u•tor**, *n.*

dis′trict, *n.* 1. political division. 2. region.

dis•trust′, *v.* 1. suspect. —*n.* 2. suspicion. —**dis•trust′ful**, *adj.*

dis•turb′, *v.* 1. interrupt rest or peace of. 2. unsettle. —**dis•turb′ance**, *n.*

dis•use′, *n.* absence of use.

ditch, *n.* trench; channel.

dit′to, *n.*, *pl.* **-tos,** *adv.* —*n.* 1. the same. —*adv.* 2. as stated before.

ditto mark, mark (″) indicating repetition.

dit′ty, *n.*, *pl.* **-ties.** simple song.

di′u•ret′ic, *adj.* promoting urination. —**di′u•ret′ic**, *n.*

di•ur′nal, *adj.* daily.

di′van, *n.* sofa.

dive, *v.*, **dived** or **dove, dived, diving,** *n.* —*v.* 1. plunge into water. 2. plunge deeply. —*n.* 3. act of diving. —**div′er**, *n.*

di•verge′, *v.*, **-verged, -verging.** 1. move or lie in different directions. 2. differ. —**di•ver′gence**, *n.* —**di•ver′gent**, *adj.*

di•verse′, *adj.* of different kinds or forms. —**di•ver′si•fy′**, *v.* —**di•ver′si•ty**, *n.* —**di•ver′si•fi•ca′tion**, *n.*

di•vert′, *v.* 1. turn aside. 2. amuse. —**di•ver′sion**, *n.*

di•vest′, *v.* deprive; dispossess.

di•vide′, *v.*, **-vided, -viding,** *n.* —*v.* 1. separate into parts. 2. apportion. —*n.* 3. zone separating drainage basins. —**di•vid′er**, *n.*

div′i•dend′, *n.* 1. number to be divided. 2. share in profits.

di•vine′, *adj.*, *n.*, *v.*, **-vined, -vining.** —*adj.* 1. of or from God or a god. 2. religious. 3. godlike. —*n.* 4. theologian or clergyman. —*v.* 5. prophesy. 6. perceive. —**div′i•na′tion**, *n.*

di•vin′i•ty, *n.*, *pl.* **-ties.** 1. divine nature. 2. god.

di•vi′sion, *n.* 1. act or result of dividing. 2. thing that divides. 3. section. 4. military unit under major general. —**di•vis′i•ble**, *adj.* —**di•vi′sion•al**, *adj.* —**di•vi′sive**, *adj.*

di•vi′sor, *n.* number dividing dividend.

di•vorce′, *n.*, *v.*, **-vorced, -vorcing.** —*n.* 1. dissolution of marriage. 2. separation. —*v.* 3. separate by divorce. —**di•vor•cee′** (-sē′), *n.fem.*

di•vulge′, *v.*, **-vulged, -vulging.** disclose.

diz′zy, *adj.*, **-zier, -ziest.** 1. giddy. 2. confused. —**diz′zi•ness**, *n.*

do, *v.*, **did, done, doing,** *n.* —*v.* 1. perform; execute. 2. behave. 3. fare. 4. finish. 5. effect. 6. render. 7. suffice. —*n.* 8. *Informal.* social gathering. 9. (dō). first note of musical scale.

doc′ile (dos′əl), *adj.* 1. readily taught. 2. tractable. —**do•cil′i•ty**, *n.*

dock, *n.* 1. wharf. 2. place for ship. 3. fleshy part of tail. 4. prisoner's place in courtroom. —*v.* 5. put into dock. 6. cut off end of. 7. deduct from (pay).

dock′et, *n.* 1. list of court cases. 2. label.

doc′tor, *n.* 1. medical practitioner. 2. holder of highest academic degree. —*v.* 3. treat medicinally.

doc′tri•naire′, *adj.* traditional; orthodox.

doc′trine, *n.* 1. principle. 2. teachings. —**doc′tri•nal**, *adj.*

doc′u•ment, *n.* paper with information or evidence.

doc′u•men′ta•ry, *adj.*, *n.*, *pl.* **-ries.** —*adj.* 1. of or derived from documents. —*n.* 2. film or TV program on factual subject.

dodge, *v.*, **dodged, dodging,** *n.* —*v.* 1. elude. —*n.* 2. act of dodging. 3. trick. —**dodg′er**, *n.*

do′do, *n.*, *pl.* **-dos, -does.** extinct bird.

doe, *n.* female deer, etc. —**doe′skin′**, *n.*

does (duz), *v.* third pers. sing. pres. indic. of **do.**

does′n't (duz′-), *v. Informal.* does not.

doff, *v.* remove.

dog, *n.*, *v.*, **dogged, dogging.** —*n.* 1. domesticated carnivore. —*v.* 2. follow closely.

dog′ged, *adj.* persistent.

dog′ger•el, *n.* bad verse.

dog′ma, *n.* system of beliefs; doctrine.

dog•mat′ic, *adj.* 1. of dogma. 2. opinionated. **—dog•mat′i•cal•ly,** *adv.*

dog′ma•tism′, *n.* aggressive assertion of opinions.

dog′wood′, *n.* flowering tree.

doi′ly, *n., pl.* **-lies.** small napkin.

dol′drums (dōl′-), *n. pl.* 1. flat calms at sea. 2. listless or depressed mood.

dole, *n., v.,* **doled, doling.** **—n.** 1. portion of charitable gift. **—v.** 2. give out sparingly.

dole′ful, *adj.* sorrowful; gloomy. **—dole′ful•ly,** *adv.*

doll, *n.* toy puppet.

dol′lar, *n.* monetary unit equal to 100 cents.

dol′or•ous, *adj.* grievous.

dol′phin, *n.* whalelike animal.

dolt, *n.* blockhead.

do•main′, *n.* 1. ownership of land. 2. realm.

dome, *n.* spherical roof or ceiling.

do•mes′tic, *adj.* 1. of or devoted to the home. 2. not foreign. **—n.** 3. household servant. **—do′mes•tic′i•ty,** *n.*

do•mes′ti•cate, *v.,* **-cated, -cating.** tame. **—do•mes′ti•ca′tion,** *n.*

dom′i•cile (-səl), *n.* home.

dom′i•nate, *v.,* **-nated, -nating.** 1. rule. 2. tower above. **—dom′i•na′tion, dom′i•nance,** *n.* **—dom′i•nant,** *adj.*

dom′i•neer′, *v.* rule oppressively.

do•min′ion, *n.* 1. power of governing. 2. territory governed.

dom′i•no′, *n.* oblong dotted piece used in game of **dominoes.**

don, *v.,* **donned, donning.** put on.

do′nate, *v.,* **-nated, -nating.** give. **—do•na′tion,** *n.*

don′key, *n., pl.* **-keys.** 1. ass. 2. fool.

do′nor, *n.* giver.

doo′dle, *v.,* **-dled, -dling.** make absent-minded drawings. **—doo′dler,** *n.*

doom, *n.* 1. fate. 2. ruin. 3. judgment. **—v.** 4. destine to trouble.

dooms′day′, *n.* day the world ends; Judgment Day.

door, *n.* 1. movable barrier at entrance. 2. Also, **door′way′.** entrance. **—door′bell′,** *n.* **—door′step′,** *n.*

dope, *n. Informal.* narcotic.

dor′mant, *adj.* 1. asleep. 2. inactive. **—dor′man•cy,** *n.*

dor′mer, *n.* vertical window projecting from sloping roof.

dor′mi•to′ry, *n., pl.* **-ries.** group sleeping place.

dor′mouse′, *n., pl.* **-mice.** small rodent.

do′ry, *n., pl.* **-ries.** flat-bottomed rowboat.

dose, *n., v.,* **dosed, dosing.** **—n.** 1. quantity of medicine taken at one time. **—v.** 2. give doses to. **—dos′age,** *n.*

dos′si•er (dos′ē ā′), *n.* set of documents, as on criminal.

dot, *n., v.,* **dotted, dotting.** **—n.** 1. small spot. **—v.** 2. mark with or make dots.

do′tard (dō′tərd), *n.* senile person.

dote, *v.,* **doted, doting.** 1. be overfond. 2. be senile. **—dot′age,** *n.*

dou′ble, *adj., n., v.,* **-bled, -bling.** **—adj.** 1. twice as great, etc. 2. of two parts. 3. deceitful. **—n.** 4. double quantity. 5. duplicate. **—v.** 6. make or become double. 7. bend or fold. 8. turn back. **—doub′ly,** *adv.*

doub′le-cross′, *v. Informal.* cheat or betray.

doub′le-dig′it, *adj.* involving two-digit numbers, esp. annual inflation rate of 10% or more.

double standard, moral standard that differs for men and women.

doub′le-talk′, *n.* meaningless or evasive talk.

doubt (dout), *v.* 1. be uncertain about. **—n.** 2. uncertainty. **—doubt′less,** *adv., adj.*

doubt′ful, *adj.* 1. having doubts. 2. causing doubts or suspicion. **—doubt′ful•ly,** *adv.*

dough, *n.* mixture of flour, milk, etc., for baking.

dough′nut, *n.* ringlike cake of fried, sweet dough. **—dough′nut•like′,** *adj.*

dour (dōor, dour), *adj.* sullen.

douse, *v.,* **doused, dousing.** 1. plunge; dip. 2. extinguish.

dove, *n.* pigeon.

dove′cote′, *n.* structure for tame pigeons. Also, **dove′cot′.**

dove′tail′, *n.* 1. tenon-and-mortise joint. **—v.** 2. join by dovetail.

dow′dy, *adj.,* **-dier, -diest.** not elegant.

dow′el, *n.* wooden pin fitting into hole.

dow′er, *n.* widow's share of husband's property.

down, *adv.* 1. to, at, or in lower place or state. 2. on or to ground. 3. on paper. **—prep.** 4. in descending direction. **—n.** 5. descent. 6. soft feathers. **—v.** 7. subdue. **—down′wards, adv. —down′ward,** *adv., adj.* **—down′y,** *adj.*

down′cast′, *adj.* dejected.

down′fall′, *n.* 1. ruin. 2. fall. **—down′fall′en,** *adj.*

down′heart′ed, *adj.* dejected. **—down′heart′ed•ly,** *adv.*

down′hill′, *adv., adj.* in downward direction.

down′pour′, *n.* heavy rain.

down′right′, *adj.* 1. thorough. **—adv.** 2. completely.

down′stairs′, *adv., adj.* to or on lower floor.

down′stream′, *adv., adj.* with current of stream.

down′-to-earth′, *adj.* objective; free of whims or fancies.

down′town′, *n.* 1. central part of town. **—adj.** 2. of this part. **—adv.** 3. to or in this part.

down′trod′den, *adj.* tyrannized.

dow′ry, *n.* bride's estate.

dox•ol′o•gy, *n.* hymn praising God.

doze, *v.,* **dozed, dozing,** *n.* **—v.** 1. sleep lightly. **—n.** 2. light sleep.

doz′en, *n., pl.* **dozen, dozens.** group of twelve.

drab, *adj.,* **drabber, drabbest.** **—n.** 1. dull brownish gray. **—adj.** 2. colored drab. 3. dull; uninteresting.

draft, *n.* 1. drawing; sketch. 2. preliminary version. 3. current of air. 4. haul. 5. swallow of liquid. 6. depth in water of a ship, etc. 7. selection for military service. 8. written request for payment. **—v.** 9. plan. 10. write. 11. enlist by draft. **—draft′y,** *adj.* **—draft•ee′,** *n.*

drafts′man, *n.* person who draws plans, etc.

drag, *v.,* **dragged, dragging,** *n.* **—v.** 1. draw heavily; haul. 2. dredge. 3. trail on ground. 4. pass slowly. **—n.** 5. something used in dragging. 6. hindrance.

drag′net′, *n.* 1. net dragged along bottom of river, etc. 2. system for catching criminal.

drag′on, *n.* fabled winged reptile.

drag′on•fly′, *n.* large four-winged insect.

drain, *v.* 1. draw or flow off gradually. 2. empty; dry. 3. exhaust. **—n.** 4. channel or pipe for draining. **—drain′er,** *n.* **—drain′age,** *n.*

drake, *n.* male duck.

dram, *n.* 1. apothecaries' weight, equal to ⅛ ounce. 2. small drink of liquor.

dra′ma, *n.* story acted on stage.

dra•mat′ic, *adj.* 1. of plays or theater. 2. highly vivid. **—dra•mat′i•cal•ly,** *adv.*

dra•mat'ics, *n.* 1. theatrical art. 2. exaggerated conduct or emotion.

dram'a•tist, *n.* playwright.

dram'a•tize', *v.,* **-tized, -tizing.** put in dramatic form. **—dram'a•ti•za'-tion,** *n.*

drape, *v.,* **draped, draping,** *n.* —*v.* 1. cover with fabric. 2. arrange in folds. —*n.* 3. draped hanging. **—dra'-per•y,** *n.*

dras'tic, *adj.* extreme. **—dras'ti•cal•ly,** *adv.*

draught (draft), *n.* draft.

draw, *v.,* **drew, drawn, drawing,** *n.* —*v.* 1. pull; lead. 2. take out. 3. attract. 4. sketch. 5. take in. 6. deduce. 7. stretch. 8. make or have as draft. —*n.* 9. act of drawing. 10. part that is drawn. 11. equal score. 12. *Informal.* attraction to public.

draw'back', *n.* disadvantage.

draw'bridge', *n.* bridge that can be drawn up.

draw'er, *n.* 1. sliding compartment. 2. (*pl.*) trouserlike undergarment. 3. person who draws.

draw'ing, *n.* picture, esp. in lines.

drawl, *v.* 1. speak slowly. —*n.* 2. drawled utterance.

dray, *n.* low, strong cart. **—dray'man,** *n.*

dread, *v.* 1. fear. —*n.* 2. fear. 3. awe. —*adj.* 4. feared. 5. revered.

dread'ful, *adj.* 1. very bad. 2. inspiring dread.

dread'ful•ly, *adv. Informal.* very.

dream, *n.* 1. ideas imagined during sleep. 2. reverie. —*v.* 3. have dream (about). 4. fancy. **—dream'er,** *n.* **—dream'y,** *adj.*

drear'y, *adj.,* **drearier, dreariest.** gloomy or boring.

dredge, *n.,* *v.,* **dredged, dredging.** —*n.* 1. machine for moving earth at the bottom of river, etc. —*v.* 2. use, or move with dredge. 3. sprinkle with flour.

dregs, *n.pl.* sediment.

drench, *v.* soak.

dress, *n.* 1. woman's garment. 2. clothing. —*v.* 3. clothe. 4. ornament. 5. prepare. 6. treat (wounds). **—dress'mak'er,** *n.* **—dress'mak'ing,** *n.*

dress'er, *n.* bureau.

dress'ing, *n.* 1. sauce or stuffing. 2. application for wound.

drib'ble, *v.,* **-bled, -bling,** *n.* —*v.* 1. fall in drops. 2. bounce repeatedly. —*n.* 3. trickling stream.

dri'er, *n.* dryer.

drift, *n.* 1. deviation from set course. 2. tendency. 3. something driven, esp. into heap. —*v.* 4. carry or be carried by currents. **—drift'er,** *n.*

drill, *n.* 1. boring tool. 2. methodical training. 3. furrow for seeds. 4. sowing machine. 5. strong twilled cotton. —*v.* 6. pierce with drill. 7. train methodically. **—drill'er,** *n.*

drink, *v.,* **drank, drunk, drinking,** *n.* —*v.* 1. swallow liquid. 2. swallow alcoholic liquids. —*n.* 3. liquid for quenching thirst. 4. alcoholic beverage. **—drink'er,** *n.*

drip, *v.,* **dripped** or **dript, dripping.** 1. fall or let fall in drops. —*n.* 2. act of dripping.

drive, *v.,* **drove, driven, driving,** *n.* —*v.* 1. send by force. 2. control; guide. 3. convey or travel in vehicle. 4. impel. —*n.* 5. military offensive. 6. strong effort. 7. trip in vehicle. 8. road for driving. **—driv'er,** *n.*

drive'-in', *adj.* 1. accommodating persons in automobiles. —*n.* 2. a drive-in theater, bank, etc.

driv'el, *v.,* **-eled, -eling,** *n.* —*v.* 1. let saliva flow from mouth. 2. talk foolishly. —*n.* 3. foolish talk.

drive'way', *n.* road on private property.

driz'zle, *v.,* **-zled, -zling,** *n.* rain in fine drops.

droll (drōl), *adj.* amusingly odd. **—droll'er•y,** *n.*

drom'e•dar'y, *n.,* *pl.* **-daries.** one-humped camel.

drone, *v.,* **droned, droning,** *n.* —*v.* 1. make humming sound. 2. speak dully. —*n.* 3. monotonous tone. 4. male of honeybee.

droop, *v.* 1. sink or hang down. 2. lose spirit. —*n.* 3. act of drooping. **—droop'y,** *adj.*

drop, *n.,* *v.,* **dropped** or **dropt, dropping.** —*n.* 1. small, spherical mass of liquid. 2. small quantity. 3. fall. 4. steep slope. —*v.* 5. fall or let fall. 6. end; cease. 7. visit. **—drop'per,** *n.*

drop'out', *n.* student who quits before graduation.

drop'sy, *n.* excessive fluid in body.

dross, *n.* refuse.

drought (drout), *n.* dry weather. Also, **drouth.**

drove, *n.* 1. group of driven cattle. 2. crowd.

drown, *v.* suffocate by immersion in liquid.

drowse, *v.,* **drowsed, drowsing.** be sleepy. **—drow'sy,** *adj.*

drub, *v.,* **drubbed, drubbing.** 1. beat. 2. defeat.

drudge, *n.,* *v.,* **drudged, drudging.** —*n.* 1. person doing hard, uninteresting work. —*v.* 2. do such work. **—drudg'er•y,** *n.*

drug, *n.,* *v.,* **drugged, drugging.** —*n.* 1. therapeutic chemical. 2. narcotic. —*v.* 3. mix or affect with drug. **—drug'store',** *n.*

drug'gist, *n.* person who prepares drugs.

drum, *n.,* *v.,* **drummed, drumming.** —*n.* 1. percussion musical instrument. 2. eardrum. —*v.* 3. beat on or as on drum. **—drum'mer,** *n.* **—drum'stick',** *n.*

drunk, *adj.* intoxicated. Also, **drunk'-en.**

drunk'ard, *n.* habitually drunk person.

dry, *adj.,* **drier, driest,** *v.,* **dried, drying.** —*adj.* 1. not wet. 2. rainless. 3. not yielding liquid. 4. thirsty. 5. dull; boring. 6. not expressing emotion. 7. not sweet. —*v.* 8. make or become dry. **—dry'er,** *n.* **—dry'ly,** *adv.* **—dry'ness,** *n.*

dry'-clean', *v.* clean with solvents. **—dry'-clean'er,** *n.*

du'al, *adj.* 1. of two. 2. double.

dub, *v.,* **dubbed, dubbing.** name formally.

du'bi•ous, *adj.* doubtful.

du'cal, *adj.* of dukes.

duch'ess, *n.* 1. duke's wife. 2. woman equal in rank to duke.

duch'y (duch'ē), *n.* 1. territory of duke. 2. small state.

duck, *v.* 1. plunge under water. 2. stoop or bend quickly. 3. avoid. —*n.* 4. act or instance of ducking. 5. swimming bird. 6. heavy cotton fabric. **—duck'ling,** *n.*

duck'bill', *n.* small, egg-laying mammal.

duct, *n.* tube or canal in body.

duc'tile, *adj.* 1. readily stretched. 2. compliant. **—duc•til'i•ty,** *n.*

dud, *n. Informal.* failure.

dudg'eon, *n.* indignation.

due, *adj.* 1. payable. 2. proper. 3. attributable. 4. expected. —*n.* 5. (*sometimes pl.*). something due. —*adv.* 6. in a straight line.

du'el, *n.* 1. prearranged combat between two persons. —*v.* 2. fight in duel. **—du'el•er, du'el•ist,** *n.*

du•et', *n.* music for two performers.

duke, *n.* 1. ruler of duchy. 2. nobleman below prince.

dull, *adj.* 1. stupid. 2. not brisk. 3. tedious. 4. not sharp. 5. dim. —*v.* 6. make or become dull. —**dul′ly,** *adv.* —**dull′ness, dul′ness,** *n.*

du′ly, *adv.* 1. properly. 2. punctually.

dumb, *adj.* 1. unable to speak. 2. without speech. 3. stupid.

dumb′bell′, *n.* 1. weighted bar for exercising. 2. *Informal.* stupid person.

dum·found′, *v.* strike dumb with amazement. Also, **dumb·found′.**

dum′my, *n., pl.* **-mies,** *adj.* —*n.* 1. model or copy. 2. *Informal.* **a.** mute. **b.** stupid person. —*adj.* 3. counterfeit.

dump, *v.* 1. drop heavily. 2. empty. —*n.* 3. place for dumping.

dump′ling, *n.* 1. mass of steamed dough. 2. pudding.

dump′y, *adj.* squat. —**dump′i·ness,** *n.*

dun, *v.,* **dunned, dunning,** *n.* —*v.* 1. demand payment of. —*n.* 2. demand for payment. 3. dull brown.

dunce, *n.* stupid person.

dune, *n.* sand hill formed by wind.

dung, *n.* manure; excrement.

dun′ga·ree′, *n.* coarse cotton fabric for work clothes (**dungarees**).

dun′geon, *n.* cell, esp. underground.

dunk, *v.* dip in beverage before eating.

du′o·de′num (dōō′ ə dē′nəm), *n.* uppermost part of small intestine.

dupe, *n., v.,* **duped, duping.** —*n.* 1. deceived person. —*v.* 2. deceive.

du′pli·cate, *adj., n., v.,* **-cated, -cating.** —*adj.* (-kit). 1. exactly like. 2. double. —*n.* (-kit). 3. copy. —*v.* (-kāt′). 4. copy. 5. double. —**du′pli·ca′tion,** *n.* —**du′pli·ca′tor,** *n.*

du·plic′i·ty (-plis′-), *n., pl.* **-ties.** deceitfulness.

du′ra·ble, *adj.* enduring. —**du′ra·bil′i·ty,** *n.* —**du′ra·bly,** *adv.*

dur′ance, *n.* imprisonment.

du·ra′tion, *n.* continuance in time.

du·ress′, *n.* compulsion.

dur′ing, *prep.* in the course of.

dusk, *n.* dark twilight. —**dusk′y,** *adj.*

dust, *n.* 1. fine particles of earth, etc. 2. dead body. —*v.* 3. free from dust. 4. sprinkle. —**dust′y,** *adj.*

du′ti·ful, *adj.* doing one's duties. Also, **du′te·ous.** —**du′ti·ful·ly,** *adv.*

du′ty, *n., pl.* **-ties.** 1. moral or legal obligation. 2. function. 3. tax, esp. on imports.

dwarf, *n.* 1. abnormally small person, etc. —*v.* 2. make or make to seem small.

dwell, *v.,* **dwelt** or **dwelled, dwelling.** 1. reside. 2. linger, esp. in words. —**dwell′ing,** *n.*

dwin′dle, *v.,* **-dled, -dling.** shrink; lessen.

dye, *n., v.,* **dyed, dyeing.** —*n.* 1. coloring material. —*v.* 2. color by wetting. —**dye′ing,** *n.* —**dy′er,** *n.*

dyke, *n., v.* dike.

dy·nam′ic, *adj.* 1. of force. 2. energetic. Also, **dy·nam′i·cal.** —**dy·nam′i·cal·ly,** *adv.* —**dyn′a·mism,** *n.*

dy′na·mite′, *n., v.,* **-mited, -miting.** —*n.* 1. powerful explosive. —*v.* 2. blow up with dynamite.

dy′na·mo′, *n., pl.* **-mos.** machine for generating electricity.

dy′nas·ty (dī′-), *n., pl.* **-ties.** rulers of same family. —**dy·nas′tic,** *adj.*

dys′en·ter′y (dis′-), *n.* infectious disease of bowels.

dys·pep′sia (dis pep′shə), *n.* indigestion. —**dys·pep′tic,** *adj.*

E

E, e, *n.* fifth letter of English alphabet.

each, *adj., pron.* 1. every one. —*adv.* 2. apiece.

ea′ger, *adj.* ardent. —**ea′ger·ly,** *adv.* —**ea′ger·ness,** *n.*

ea′gle, *n.* large bird of prey.

ear, *n.* 1. organ of hearing. 2. grain-containing part of cereal plant.

ear′drum′, *n.* sensitive membrane in ear.

earl, *n.* nobleman ranking below marquis. —**earl′dom,** *n.*

ear′ly, *adv.,* **-lier, -liest,** *adj.* 1. in first part of. 2. before usual time.

ear′mark′, *n.* 1. identifying mark. —*v.* 2. intend or designate.

earn, *v.* gain by labor or merit.

ear′nest, *adj.* 1. serious. —*n.* 2. portion given to bind bargain. —**ear′nest·ly,** *adv.*

earn′ings, *n.pl.* profits.

ear′ring′, *n.* ornament worn on ear lobe.

ear′shot′, *n.* hearing range.

earth, *n.* 1. planet we inhabit. 2. dry land. 3. soil.

earth′en, *adj.* made of clay or earth. —**earth′en·ware′,** *n.*

earth′ly, *adj.,* **-lier, -liest.** of or in this world.

earth′quake′, *n.* vibration of earth's surface.

earth′worm′, *n.* burrowing worm.

earth′y, *adj.,* **-ier, -iest.** 1. practical; realistic. 2. coarse; unrefined. —**earth′i·ness,** *n.*

ease, *n., v.,* **eased, easing.** —*n.* 1. freedom from work, pain, etc. 2. facility. —*v.* 3. relieve.

ea′sel, *n.* standing support, as for picture.

east, *n.* 1. direction from which sun rises. 2. (*sometimes cap.*) region in this direction. —*adj., adv.* 3. toward, in, or from east. —**east′er·ly,** *adj., adv.* —**east′ern,** *adj.* —**east′ward,** *adv., adj.* —**East′ern·er,** *n.*

East′er, *n.* anniversary of resurrection of Christ.

eas′y, *adj.,* **easier, easiest.** 1. not difficult. 2. at or giving ease. 3. affording comfort. —**eas′i·ly,** *adv.* —**eas′i·ness,** *n.*

eas′y-go′ing, *adj.* 1. casual; relaxed. 2. lenient.

eat, *v.,* **ate, eating, eaten.** 1. take into the mouth and swallow. 2. wear away or dissolve.

eaves, *n.pl.* overhanging edge of roof.

eaves′drop′, *v.,* **-dropped, -dropping.** listen secretly. —**eaves′drop′per,** *n.*

ebb, *n.* 1. fall of tide. 2. decline. —*v.* 3. flow back. 4. decline.

eb′on·y, *n.* 1. hard black wood. —*adj.* 2. very dark.

e·bul′lient, *adj.* full of enthusiasm. —**e·bul′lience,** *n.*

ec·cen′tric (ik sen′-), *adj.* 1. odd. 2. off center. —*n.* 3. odd person. 4. eccentric wheel. —**ec′cen·tric′i·ty** (-tris′-), *n.*

ec·cle′si·as′tic, *n.* 1. clergyman. —*adj.* 2. Also, **ec·cle′si·as′ti·cal.** of church or clergy.

ech′e·lon (esh′-), *n.* level of command.

ech′o, *n., pl.* **echoes,** *v.,* **echoed, echoing.** —*n.* 1. repetition of sound, esp. by reflection. —*v.* 2. emit or repeat as echo.

é·clair′, (ā-), *n.* cream-filled cake.

ec•lec'tic, *adj.* chosen from various sources.

e•clipse', *n., v.,* **eclipsed, eclipsing.** —*n.* 1. obscuring of light of sun or moon by passage of body in front of it. 2. oblivion. —*v.* 3. obscure; darken.

e•clip'tic, *n.* apparent annual path of sun.

e'co•cide', *n.* widespread destruction of natural environment.

e•col'o•gy, *n.* science of relationship between organisms and environment. —**e•col'o•gist,** *n.* —**ec'•o•log'i•cal,** *adj.*

e'co•nom'i•cal, *adj.* thrifty. —**e'co•nom'i•cal•ly,** *adv.*

e'co•nom'ics, *n.* production, distribution, and use of wealth. —**e'co•nom'ic,** *adj.* —**e•con'o•mist,** *n.*

e•con'o•mize', *v.,* **-mized, -mizing.** save; be thrifty.

e•con'o•my, *n., pl.* **-mies.** 1. thrifty management. 2. system of producing and distributing weath.

ec'o•sys'tem (ek'-), *n.* distinct ecological system.

ec'sta•sy, *n., pl.* **-sies.** 1. overpowering emotion. 2. rapture. —**ec•stat'-ic,** *adj.*

ec•u•men'i•cal, *adj.* 1. universal. 2. of or pertaining to movement for universal Christian unity. —**e•cu'men•ism,** *n.*

ec'ze•ma, *n.* itching disease of skin.

ed'dy, *n., pl.* **-dies,** *v.,* **-died, -dying.** —*n.* 1. current at variance with main current. —*v.* 2. whirl in eddies.

E'den, *n.* garden where Adam and Eve first lived; paradise.

edge, *n., v.,* **edged, edging.** —*n.* 1. border; brink. 2. cutting side. —*v.* 3. border. 4. move sidewise. —**edge'wise',** *adv.* —**edg'ing,** *n.*

ed'i•ble, *adj.* fit to be eaten. —**ed'i•bil'i•ty,** *n.*

e'dict, *n.* official decree.

ed'i•fice (-fis), *n.* building.

ed'i•fy', *v.,* **-fied, -fying.** instruct. —**ed'i•fi•ca'tion,** *n.*

ed'it, *v.* prepare for or direct publication of. —**ed'i•tor,** *n.*

e•di'tion, *n.* one of various printings of a book.

ed'i•to'ri•al, *n.* 1. article in periodical presenting its point of view. —*adj.* 2. of or written by editor.

ed'u•cate', *v.,* **-cated, -cating.** develop by instruction. —**ed'u•ca'tion,** *n.* —**ed'u•ca'tion•al,** *adj.* —**ed'u•ca'tor,** *n.*

eel, *n.* snakelike fish.

e'er, *adv. Poetic.* ever.

ee'rie, *adj.* weird.

ef•face', *v.,* **-faced, -facing.** wipe out. —**ef•face'ment,** *n.*

ef•fect', *n.* 1. result. 2. power to produce results. 3. operation. 4. (*pl.*) personal property. —*v.* 5. bring about.

ef•fec'tive, *adj.* 1. producing intended results. 2. actually in force.

ef•fec'tive•ly, *adv.* 1. in an effective way. 2. for all practical purposes.

ef•fec'tu•al, *adj.* 1. capable; adequate. 2. valid or binding.

ef•fem'i•nate, *adj.* (of man) having feminine traits.

ef'fer•vesce', *v.,* **-vesced, -vescing.** give off bubbles of gas. —**ef'fer•ves'cence,** *n.* —**ef'fer•ves'cent,** *adj.*

ef•fete' (i fēt'), *adj.* worn out.

ef'fi•ca'cious, *adj.* effective. —**ef'fi•ca•cy,** *n.*

ef•fi'cient, *adj.* acting effectively. —**ef•fi'cien•cy,** *n.* —**ef•fi'cient•ly,** *adv.*

ef'fi•gy, *n., pl.* **-gies.** visual representation of person.

ef'fort, *n.* 1. exertion of power. 2. attempt.

ef•fron'ter•y, *n.* impudence.

ef•fu'sion, *n.* free expression of feelings. —**ef•fu'sive,** *adj.*

e•gal'i•tar'i•an, *adj.* having or wishing all persons equal in rights or status. —**e•gal'i•tar'i•an•ism,** *n.*

egg, *n.* 1. reproductive body produced by animals. —*v.* 2. encourage.

egg'head', *n. Slang.* impractical intellectual.

egg'nog', *n.* drink containing eggs, milk, etc.

egg'plant', *n.* purple, egg-shaped vegetable.

e'go, *n.* self.

e'go•ism', *n.* thinking only in terms of oneself. —**e'go•ist,** *n.* —**e'go•is'tic, e'go•is'ti•cal,** *adj.*

e'go•tism', *n.* vanity. —**e'go•tist,** *n.* —**e'go•tis'tic, e'go•tis'ti•cal,** *adj.*

e•gre'gious (i grē'jəs), *adj.* flagrant.

e'gress, *n.* exit.

e'gret, *n.* kind of heron.

ei'der duck (ī'dər), large, northern sea duck yielding **eiderdown.**

eight, *n., adj.* seven plus one. —**eighth,** *adj., n.*

eight'een', *n., adj.* ten plus eight. —**eight•eenth',** *adj., n.*

eight'y, *n., adj.* ten times eight. —**eight'i•eth,** *adj., n.*

ei'ther (ē'thər, ī'thər), *adj., pron.* 1. one or the other of two. —*conj.* 2.

(introducing an alternative.) —*adv.* 3. (after negative clauses joined by **and, or, nor.**)

e•jac'u•late', *v.,* **-lated, -lating.** 1. exclaim. 2. discharge. —**e•jac'u•la'tion,** *n.*

e•ject', *v.* force out. —**e•jec'tion,** *n.* —**e•jec'tor,** *n.*

eke, *v.,* **eked, eking. eke out,** 1. supplement. 2. make (livelihood) with difficulty.

e•lab'o•rate, *adj., v.,* **-rated, -rating.** —*adj.* (-ə rit). 1. done with care and detail. —*v.* (-ə rāt'). 2. supply details; work out. —**e•lab'o•ra'tion,** *n.*

e•lapse', *v.,* **elapsed, elapsing.** (of time) pass; slip by.

e•las'tic, *adj.* 1. springy. —*n.* 2. material containing rubber. —**e•las'tic'i•ty** (-tis'-), *n.*

e•late', *v.,* **elated, elating.** put in high spirits. —**e•la'tion,** *n.*

el'bow, *n.* 1. joint between forearm and upper arm. —*v.* 2. jostle.

eld'er, *adj.* 1. older. —*n.* 2. older person. 3. small tree bearing clusters of **el'der•ber'ries.**

el'der•ly, *adj.* rather old.

eld'est, *adj.* oldest; first-born.

e•lect', *v.* 1. select, esp. by vote. —*adj.* 2. selected. —*n.* 3. (*pl.*) persons chosen. —**e•lec'tion,** *n.* —**e•lec'tive,** *adj.*

e•lec'tion•eer', *v.* work for candidate in an election.

e•lec'tor•ate, *n.* voters.

e•lec'tri'cian, *n.* one who installs or repairs electrical systems.

e•lec'tric'i•ty (-tris'-), *n.* 1. agency producing certain phenomena, as light, heat, attraction, etc. 2. electric current. —**e•lec'tric, e•lec'tri•cal,** *adj.* —**e•lec'tri•fy',** *v.*

e•lec'tro•car'di•o•gram', *n.* graphic record of heart action.

e•lec'tro•cute', *v.,* **-cuted, -cuting.** kill by electricity. —**e•lec'tro•cu'tion,** *n.*

e•lec'trode, *n.* conductor through which current enters or leaves electric device.

e•lec'trol'y•sis, *n.* decomposition by electric current. —**e•lec'tro•lyt'ic,** *adj.*

e•lec'tro•mo'tive, *adj.* of or producing electric current.

e•lec'tron, *n.* minute particle supposed to be or contain a unit of negative electricity. —**e•lec'tron'ic,** *adj.*

e•lec'tron'ics, *n.* science dealing with movement of electrons.

—e•lec′tron′ic, *adj.* —e•lec′tron′i•cal•ly, *adv.*

el′ee•mos′y•nar′y (el′ə-), *adj.* charitable.

el′e•gant, *adj.* luxurious or refined. —el′e•gance, *n.*

el′e•gy, *n., pl.* -gies. poem of mourning.

el′e•ment, *n.* 1. part of whole. 2. rudiment. 3. suitable environment. 4. (*pl.*) atmospheric forces. 5. substance that cannot be broken down chemically. 6. (*pl.*) bread and wine of the Eucharist. —el′e•men′tal, *adj.*

el′e•men′ta•ry, *adj.* of or dealing with elements or rudiments.

el′e•phant, *n.* large mammal with long trunk and tusks.

el′e•vate′, *v.,* -vated, -vating. 1. raise higher. 2. exalt.

el′e•va′tion, *n.* 1. elevated place. 2. height. 3. measured drawing of vertical face.

el′e•va′tor, *n.* 1. platform for lifting. 2. grain storage place.

e•lev′en, *n., adj.* ten plus one. —e•lev′enth, *adj., n.*

elf, *n., pl.* elves. tiny mischievous sprite. —elf′in, *adj.*

e•lic′it (-lis′-), *v.* draw forth; evoke.

el′i•gi•ble, *adj.* fit to be chosen; qualified. —el′i•gi•bil′i•ty, *n.*

e•lim′i•nate′, *v.,* -nated, -nating. get rid of. —e•lim′i•na′tion, *n.*

e•lite′ (i lēt′), *adj.* 1. chosen or regarded as finest. —*n.* (*sing.* or *pl.*) elite group of persons.

e•lit′ism, *n.* discrimination in favor of an elite.

e•lix′ir, *n.* 1. preparation supposed to prolong life. 2. kind of medicine.

elk, *n.* large deer.

el•lipse′, *n.* closed plane curve forming regular oblong figure. —el•lip′ti•cal, *adj.*

el•lip′sis, *n.* omission of word or words.

elm, *n.* large shade tree.

el′o•cu′tion, *n.* art of speaking in public.

e•lon′gate, *v.,* -gated, -gating. lengthen. —e•lon′ga′tion, *n.*

e•lope′, *v.,* eloped, eloping. run off with lover to be married. —e•lope′-ment, *n.*

el′o•quent, *adj.* fluent and forcible. —el′o•quence, *n.*

else, *adv.* 1. instead. 2. in addition. 3. otherwise.

else′where′, *adv.* somewhere else.

e•lu′ci•date′ (-lōō′sə-), *v.,* -dated, -dating. explain.

e•lude′, *v.,* eluded, eluding. 1. avoid cleverly. 2. baffle. —e•lu′sive, *adj.*

e•ma′ci•ate′ (-mā′shē-), *v.,* -ated, -ating. make lean. —e•ma′ci•a′tion, *n.*

em′a•nate′, *v.,* -nated, -nating. come forth. —em′a•na′tion, *n.*

e•man′ci•pate′, *v.,* -pated, -pating. liberate. —e•man′ci•pa′tion, *n.* —e•man′ci•pa′tor, *n.*

e•mas′cu•late′, *v.,* -lated, -lating. castrate.

em•balm′, *v.* treat (dead body) to prevent decay.

em•bank′ment, *n.* long earthen mound.

em•bar′go, *n., pl.* -goes. government restriction of movement of ships or goods.

em•bark′, *v.* 1. put or go on board ship. 2. start. —em′bar•ka′tion, *n.*

em•bar′rass, *v.* 1. make self-conscious or ashamed. 2. complicate. —em•bar′rass•ment, *n.*

em′bas′•sy, *n., pl.* -sies. 1. ambassador and staff. 2. headquarters of ambassador.

em•bed′, *v.,* -bedded, -bedding. fix in surrounding mass.

em•bel′lish, *v.* decorate. —em•bel′-lish•ment, *n.*

em′ber, *n.* live coal.

em•bez′zle, *v.,* -zled, -zling. steal (money entrusted). —em•bez′zle•ment, *n.* —em•bez′zler, *n.*

em•bit′ter, *v.* make bitter.

em′blem, *n.* symbol. —em′blem•at′-ic, *adj.*

em•bod′y, *v.,* -bodied, -bodying. 1. put in concrete form. 2. comprise. —em•bod′i•ment, *n.*

em•boss′, *v.* ornament with raised design.

em•brace′, *v.,* -braced, -bracing, *n.* —*v.* 1. clasp in arms. 2. accept willingly. 3. include. —*n.* 4. act of embracing.

em•broi′der, *v.* decorate with needlework. —em•broi′der•y, *n.*

em•broil′, *v.* involve in strife. —em•broil′ment, *n.*

em′bry•o′, *n.* organism in first stages of development. —em′bry•on′ic, *adj.*

e•mend′, *v.* correct. —e′men•da′-tion, *n.*

em′er•ald, *n.* green gem.

e•merge′, *v.,* emerged, emerging. come forth or into notice. —e•mer′-gence, *n.*

e•mer′gen•cy, *n., pl.* -cies. urgent occasion for action.

e•mer′i•tus, *adj.* retaining title after retirement.

em′er•y, *n.* mineral used for grinding, etc.

e•met′ic, *n.* medicine that induces vomiting.

em′i•grate′, *v.,* -grated, -grating. leave one's country to settle in another. —em′i•grant, *n.* —em′i•gra′-tion, *n.*

em′i•nence, *n.* high repute. —em′i•nent, *adj.*

em′is•sar′y, *n., pl.* -saries. agent on mission.

e•mit′, *v.,* emitted, emitting. 1. send forth. 2. utter.

e•mol′u•ment (-yə-), *n.* salary.

e•mo′tion, *n.* state of feeling. —e•mo′tion•al, *adj.*

em′pa•thy, *n.* sensitive awareness of another's feelings. —em′pa•thize′, *v.*

em′per•or, *n.* ruler of empire. —em′press, *n.fem.*

em′pha•sis, *n., pl.* -ses. greater importance; stress. —em•phat′ic, *adj.* —em′pha•size′, *v.*

em′pire, *n.* nations under one ruler.

em•ploy′, *v.* 1. use or hire. —*n.* 2. employment. —em•ploy′ee, *n.* —em•ploy′er, *n.* —em•ploy′ment, *n.*

em•po′ri•um, *n.* large store.

em•pow′er, *v.* authorize to act for one.

emp′ty, *adj.,* -tier, -tiest, *v.,* -tied, -tying. —*adj.* 1. containing nothing. —*v.* 2. deprive of contents. 3. become empty. —emp′ti•ness, *n.*

e′mu (ē′myōō), *n.* large flightless Australian bird.

em′u•late′, *v.,* -lated, -lating. try to equal or excel. —em′u•la′tion, *n.*

e•mul′si•fy′, *v.,* -fied, -fying. make into emulsion.

e•mul′sion, *n.* 1. milklike mixture of liquids. 2. light-sensitive layer on film.

en•a′ble, *v.,* -bled, -bling. give power, means, etc., to.

en•act′, *v.* 1. make into law. 2. act the part of. —en•act′ment, *n.*

e•nam′el, *n., v.,* -eled, -eling. —*n.* 1. glassy coating fused to metal, etc. 2. paint giving an enamellike surface. 3. outer surface of teeth. —*v.* 4. apply enamel to.

en•am′or, *v.* cause to be in love.

en•camp′, *v.,* settle in camp. —en•camp′ment, *n.*

en•chant′, *v.* bewitch; beguile; charm. —**en•chant′ment,** *n.*

en•cir′cle, *v.,* **-cled, -cling.** surround.

en′clave, *n.* country, etc., surrounded by alien territory.

en•close′, *v.,* **-closed, -closing.** 1. close in on all sides. 2. put in envelope. —**en•clo′sure,** *n.*

en•co′mi•um (-kō′-), *n.* praise; eulogy.

en•com′pass, *v.* 1. encircle. 2. contain.

en′core, *interj.* 1. again! bravo! —*n.* 2. additional song, etc.

en•coun′ter, *v.* 1. meet, esp. unexpectedly. —*n.* 2. casual meeting. 3. combat.

en•cour′age, *v.,* **-aged, -aging.** inspire or help. —**en•cour′age•ment,** *n.*

en•croach′, *v.* trespass. —**en•croach′ment,** *n.*

en•cum′ber, *v.* impede; burden. —**en•cum′brance,** *n.*

en•cyc′li•cal (-sik′-), *n.* letter from Pope to bishops.

en•cy′clo•pe′di•a, *n.* reference book giving information on many topics. Also, **en•cy′clo•pae′di•a.** —**en•cy′clo•pe′dic,** *adj.*

end, *n.* 1. extreme or concluding part. 2. close. 3. purpose. 4. result. —*v.* 5. bring or come to an end. 6. result. —**end′less,** *adj.*

en•dan′ger, *v.* expose to danger.

en•dear′, *v.* make beloved. —**en•dear′ment,** *n.*

en•deav′or, *v., n.* attempt.

end′ing, *n.* close.

en′dive, *n.* plant for salad.

en•dorse′, *v.,* **-dorsed, -dorsing.** 1. approve or support. 2. sign on back of (a check, etc.). —**en•dorse′ment,** *n.*

en•dow′, *v.* 1. give permanent fund to. 2. equip. —**en•dow′ment,** *n.*

en•dure′, *v.,* **-dured, -during.** 1. tolerate. 2. last. —**en•dur′a•ble,** *adj.* —**en•dur′ance,** *n.*

en•e•ma, *n.* liquid injection into rectum.

en′em•y, *n., pl.* **-mies.** adversary; opponent.

en′er•gy, *n., pl.* **-gies.** capacity for activity; vigor. —**en•er•get′ic,** *adj.*

en′er•vate′, *v.,* **-vated, -vating.** weaken.

en•fee′ble, *v.,* **-bled, -bling.** weaken.

en•fold′, *v.* wrap around.

en•force′, *v.* **-forced, -forcing.** compel obedience to. —**en•force′ment,** *n.*

en•fran′chise, *v.,* **-chised, -chising.** admit to citizenship.

en•gage′, *v.,* **-gaged, -gaging.** 1. occupy. 2. hire. 3. please. 4. betroth. 5. interlock with. 6. enter into conflict with. —**en•gage′ment,** *n.*

en•gen′der (-jen′-), *v.* cause.

en′gine, *n.* 1. machine for converting energy into mechanical work. 2. locomotive.

en′gi•neer′, *n.* 1. expert in engineering. 2. engine operator. —*v.* 3. contrive.

en′gi•neer′ing, *n.* art of practical application of physics, chemistry, etc.

Eng′lish, *n.* language of the people of England, Australia, the U.S., etc. —**Eng′lish,** *adj.* —**Eng′lish•man,** *n.* —**Eng′lish•wom′an,** *n.fem.*

en•grave′, *v.,* **-graved, -graving.** cut into hard surface for printing. —**en•grav′er,** *n.* —**en•grav′ing,** *n.*

en•gross′, *v.* occupy wholly.

en•gulf′, *v.* swallow up.

en•hance′, *v.,* **-hanced, -hancing.** increase.

e•nig′ma, *n.* something puzzling. —**en′ig•mat′ic,** *adj.*

en•join′, *v.* prohibit.

en•joy′, *v.* find pleasure in or for. —**en•joy′a•ble,** *adj.* —**en•joy′ment,** *n.*

en•large′, *v.,* **-larged, -larging.** make or grow larger. —**en•large′ment,** *n.*

en•light′en, *v.* impart knowledge to. —**en•light′en•ment,** *n.*

en•list′, *v.* enroll for service. —**en•list′ment,** *n.*

en•liv′en, *v.* make active.

en′mi•ty, *n.* hatred.

en•nui′ (än′wē′), *n.* boredom.

e•nor′mi•ty, *n., pl.* **-ties.** 1. extreme wickedness. 2. grievous crime; atrocity.

e•nor′mous, *adj.* huge; gigantic.

e•nough′, *adj.* 1. adequate. —*n.* 2. adequate amount. —*adv.* 3. sufficiently.

en•quire′, *v.,* **-quired, -quiring.** inquire. —**en•quir′y,** *n.*

en•rage′, *v.,* **-raged, -raging.** make furious.

en•rich′, *v.* make rich or better. —**en•rich′ment,** *n.*

en•roll′, *v.* take into group or organization. —**en•roll′ment,** *n.*

en route (än rōōt′), on the way.

en•sem′ble (än säm′bəl), *n.* assembled whole.

en•shrine′, *v.,* **-shrined, -shrining.** cherish.

en′sign (-sīn; *Mil.* -sən), *n.* 1. flag. 2. lowest commissioned naval officer.

en•slave′, *v.,* **-slaved, -slaving.** make slave of. —**en•slave′ment,** *n.*

en•sue′, *v.,* **-sued, -suing.** follow.

en•sure′, *v.,* **-sured, -suring.** make certain; secure.

en•tail′, *v.* involve.

en•tan′gle, *v.,* **-gled, -gling.** involve; entrap. —**en•tan′gle•ment,** *n.*

en′ter, *v.* 1. come or go in. 2. begin. 3. record.

en′ter•prise′, *n.* 1. project. 2. initiative.

en′ter•pris′ing, *adj.* showing initiative.

en′ter•tain′, *v.* 1. amuse. 2. treat as guest. 3. hold in mind. —**en′ter•tain′er,** *n.* —**en•ter•tain′ment,** *n.*

en•thu′si•asm′, *n.* lively interest. —**en•thu′si•as′tic,** *adj.*

en•tice′, *v.,* **-ticed, -ticing.** lure. —**en•tice′ment,** *n.*

en•tire′, *adj.* whole. —**en•tire′ly,** *adv.* —**en•tire′ty,** *n.*

en•ti′tle, *v.,* **-tled, -tling.** permit (one) to claim something.

en′ti•ty, *n., pl.* **-ties.** real or whole thing.

en•tomb′, *v.* bury.

en′to•mol′o•gy, *n.* study of insects. —**en′to•mol′o•gist,** *n.*

en′tou•rage′ (än′tōō räzh′), *n.* group of personal attendants.

en′trails, *n.pl.* internal parts of body, esp. intestines.

en′trance, *n., v.,* **-tranced, -trancing.** —*n.* (en′trans). 1. act of entering. 2. place for entering. 3. admission. —*v.* (en trans′). 4. charm.

en•trap′, *v.,* **-trapped, -trapping.** 1. catch in a trap. 2. entice into guilty situation. —**en•trap′ment,** *n.*

en•treat′, *v.* implore.

en•treat′y, *n., pl.* **-ies.** earnest request.

en•tree (än′trā) *n.* main dish of meal.

en•trench′, *v.* fix in strong position.

en′tre•pre•neur′ (än′trə prə nûr′), *n.* independent business manager.

en•trust′, *v.* give in trust.

en′try, *n., pl.* **-tries.** 1. entrance. 2. recorded statement, etc. 3. contestant.

e•nu′mer•ate′, *v.,* **-ated, -ating.** list; count. —**e•nu′mer•a′tion,** *n.*

e•nun′ci•ate′ (-sē-), *v.,* **-ated, -ating.** say distinctly. —**e•nun′ci•a′tion,** *n.*

en•vel′op, *v.* wrap; surround. —**en•vel′op•ment,** *n.*

en′ve•lope′, *n.* 1. covering for letter. 2. covering; wrapper.

en•vi′ron•ment, *n.* surrounding things, conditions, etc.

en•vi′ron•men′tal•ist, *n.* person working to protect environment from pollution or destruction.

en•vi′rons, *n.pl.* outskirts.

en′voy, *n.* 1. diplomatic agent. 2. messenger.

en′vy, *n., pl.* **-vies,** *v.,* **-vied, -vying.** —*n.* 1. discontent at another's good fortune. 2. thing coveted. —*v.* 3. regard with envy. —**en′vi•a•ble,** *adj.* —**en′vi•ous,** *adj.*

en′zyme (-zīm), *n.* bodily substance capable of producing chemical change in other substances.

e′on, *n.* aeon.

ep′au•let′ (ep′ə-), *n.* shoulder piece worn on uniform. Also **ep′au•lette′.**

e•phem′er•al, *adj.* short-lived.

ep′ic, *adj.* 1. describing heroic deeds. —*n.* 2. epic poem.

ep′i•cure′, *n.* connoisseur of food and drink. —**ep′i•cu•re′an,** *adj., n.*

ep′i•dem′ic, *adj.* 1. affecting many persons at once. —*n.* 2. epidemic disease.

ep′i•der′mis, *n.* outer layer of skin.

ep′i•glot′tis, *n.* thin structure that covers larynx during swallowing.

ep′i•gram′, *n.* terse, witty statement. —**ep′i•gram•mat′ic,** *adj.*

ep′i•lep′sy, *n.* nervous disease often marked by convulsions. —**ep′i•lep′-tic,** *adj., n.*

ep′i•logue′, *n.* concluding part or speech.

E•piph′a•ny, *n.* festival, Jan. 6, commemorating the Wise Men's visit to Christ.

e•pis′co•pa•cy, *n., pl.* **-cies.** church government by bishops.

e•pis′co•pal, *adj.* 1. governed by bishops. 2. (*cap.*) designating Anglican Church or branch of it. —**E•pis′-co•pa′lian,** *n., adj.*

ep′i•sode′, *n.* incident. —**ep′i•sod′-ic,** *adj.*

e•pis′tle, *n.* letter.

ep′i•taph′, *n.* inscription on tomb.

ep′i•thet′, *n.* descriptive term for person or thing.

e•pit′o•me, *n.* 1. summary. 2. typical specimen. —**e•pit′o•mize′,** *v.*

e plu′ri•bus u′num, *Latin.* out of many, one (motto of the U.S.).

ep′och (ep′ək), *n.* distinctive period of time.

ep•ox′y, *n., pl.* **-ies.** tough synthetic resin, used in glues, etc.

eq′ua•ble, *adj.* even; temperate. —**eq′ua•bly,** *adv.*

e′qual, *adj., n., v.,* **equaled, equaling.** —*adj.* 1. alike in quantity, rank, size, etc. 2. uniform. 3. adequate. —*n.* 4. one that is equal to. —*v.* 5. be equal to. —**e•qual′i•ty,** *n.* —**e′qual•ize′,** *v.* —**e′qual•ly,** *adv.*

e′qua•nim′i•ty, *n.* calmness.

e•quate′, *v.,* **equated, equating.** make or consider as equal.

e•qua′tion, *n.* expression of equality of two quantities.

e•qua′tor, *n.* imaginary circle around earth midway between poles. —**e′qua•to′ri•al,** *adj.*

e•ques′tri•an, *adj.* 1. of horse riders or horsemanship. —*n.* 2. Also, *fem.,* **e•ques′tri•enne′.** horse rider.

e′qui•dis′tant, *adj.* equally distant.

e′qui•lat′er•al, *adj.* having all sides equal.

e′qui•lib′ri•um, *n.* balance.

e′quine, *adj.* of horses.

e′qui•nox′, *n.* time when night and day are of equal length. —**e′qui•noc′tial,** *adj., n.*

e•quip′, *v.,* **equipped, equipping.** furnish; provide. —**e•quip′ment,** *n.*

eq′ui•ta•ble, *adj.* just; fair. —**eq′ui•ta•bly,** *adv.*

eq′ui•ty, *n., pl.* **-ties.** 1. fairness. 2. share.

e•quiv′a•lent, *adj., n.* equal.

e•quiv′o•cal, *adj.* 1. ambiguous. 2. questionable.

e•quiv′o•cate′, *v.,* **-cated, -cating.** express oneself ambiguously or indecisively. —**e•quiv′o•ca′tion,** *n.*

e′ra, *n.* period of time.

e•rad′i•cate′, *v.,* **-cated, -cating.** remove completely. —**e•rad′i•ca′tion,** *n.*

e•rase′, *v.,* **erased, erasing.** rub out. —**e•ras′er,** *n.* —**e•ra′sure,** *n.*

ere, *prep., conj. Archaic.* before.

e•rect′, *adj.* 1. upright. —*v.* 2. build. —**e•rec′tion,** *n.*

er′mine, *n.* kind of weasel.

e•rode′, *v.,* **eroded, eroding.** wear away. —**e•ro′sion,** *n.*

e•rot′ic, *adj.* of sexual love.

e•rot′i•ca, *n.pl.* erotic literature and art.

err (ûr), *v.* 1. be mistaken. 2. sin.

er′rand, *n.* special trip.

er′rant, *adj.* roving.

er•rat′ic, *adj.* uncontrolled or irregular.

er•ro′ne•ous, *adj.* incorrect.

er′ror, *n.* 1. mistake. 2. sin.

er•satz′ (er zäts′), *n., adj.,* substitute.

erst′while, *adj.* former.

er′u•dite′, *adj.* learned. —**er′u•di′-tion,** *n.*

e•rupt′, *v.* burst forth. —**e•rup′tion,** *n.*

er′y•sip′e•las, *n.* infectious skin disease.

es′ca•late′, *v.,* **-lated, -lating.** increase in intensity or size. —**es′ca•la′tion,** *n.*

es′ca•la′tor, *n.* moving stairway.

es′ca•pade′, *n.* wild prank.

es•cape′, *v.,* **-caped, -caping,** *n.* —*v.* 1. get away. 2. elude. —*n.* 3. act or means of escaping.

es•cape′ment, *n.* part of clock that controls speed.

es•cap′ism, *n.* attempt to forget reality through fantasy. —**es•cap′ist,** *n., adj.*

es•chew′, *v.* avoid.

es′cort, *n.* (es′kôrt). 1. accompanying person or persons for guidance, courtesy, etc. —*v.* (es kôrt′). 2. accompany as escort.

es′crow, *n.* legal contract kept by third person until its provisions are fulfilled.

es•cutch′eon, *n.* coat of arms.

e•soph′a•gus, *n.* tube connecting mouth and stomach.

es′o•ter′ic, *adj.* intended for select few.

es•pe′cial, *adj.* special. —**es•pe′cial•ly,** *adv.*

es′pi•o•nage′ (-näzh′, -nij), *n.* work or use of spies.

es•pouse′, *v.,* **-poused, -pousing.** 1. advocate. 2. marry. —**es•pous′al,** *n.*

es•pres′so, *n.* coffee made with steam.

es•py′, *v.,* **-pied, -pying.** catch sight of.

Es•quire′, *n. Brit.* title of respect after man's name. *Abbr.:* Esq.

es′say, *n.* 1. short nonfiction work. 2. attempt. —*v.* (ə sā′). 3. try.

es′say•ist, *n.* writer of essays.

es′sence, *n.* 1. intrinsic nature. 2. concentrated form of substance or thought.

es•sen′tial, *adj.* 1. necessary. —*n.* 2. necessary thing.

es•sen′tial•ly, *adv.* basically; necessarily.

es•tab′lish, *v.* 1. set up permanently. 2. prove.

es•tab′lish•ment, *n.* 1. act of establishing. 2. institution or business. 3. (*often cap.*) group controlling government and social institutions.

es•tate′, *n.* 1. landed property. 2. one's possessions.

es•teem′, *v.* 1. regard. —*n.* 2. opinion.

es′thete, *n.* aesthete.

es′ti•ma•ble, *adj.* worthy of high esteem.

es′ti•mate′, *v.,* -mated, -mating, *n.* —*v.* (-māt′). 1. calculate roughly. —*n.* (es′tə mit). 2. rough calculation. 3. opinion. —**es′ti•ma′tion,** *n.*

es•trange′, *v.,* -tranged, -tranging. alienate.

es′tu•ar′y, *n., pl.* -aries. part of river affected by sea tides.

et cet′er•a (set′-), and so on. *Abbr.:* etc.

etch, *v.* cut design into (metal, etc.) with acid. —**etch′ing,** *n.*

e•ter′nal, *adj.* 1. without beginning or end. —*n.* 2. (*cap.*) God. —**e•ter′ni•ty,** *n.* —**e•ter′nal•ly,** *adv.*

e′ther, *n.* 1. colorless liquid used as an anesthetic. 2. upper part of space.

e•the′re•al, *adj.* 1. delicate. 2. heavenly.

eth′ics, *n.pl.* principles of conduct. —**eth′i•cal,** *adj.* —**eth′i•cal•ly,** *adv.*

eth′nic, *adj.* 1. sharing a common culture. —*n.* 2. member of minority group.

eth′yl, *n.* fluid containing lead, added to gasoline.

et′i•quette′, *n.* conventions of social behavior.

et′y•mol′o•gy, *n., pl.* -gies. history of word or words.

eu′ca•lyp′tus, *n., pl.* -ti. Australian tree.

Eu′cha•rist (ū′kə-), *n.* Holy Communion.

eu•gen′ics, *n.* science of improving human race.

eu′lo•gy, *n., pl.* -gies. formal praise. —**eu′lo•gize′,** *v.*

eu′nuch (-nək), *n.* castrated man.

eu′phe•mism, *n.* substitution of mild expression for blunt one. —**eu′phe•mis′tic,** *adj.*

eu′pho•ny, *n.* pleasant sound. —**eu•pho′ni•ous,** *adj.*

Eu′ro•pe′an, *n.* native of Europe. —**Eu′ro•pe′an,** *adj.*

eu′tha•na′sia, *n.* mercy killing.

e•vac′u•ate′, *v.,* -ated, -ating. 1. vacate; empty. 2. remove. 3. help to flee. —**e•vac′u•a′tion,** *n.*

e•vade′, *v.,* evaded, evading. avoid or escape from by cleverness. —**e•va′sion,** *n.* —**e•va′sive,** *adj.*

e•val′u•ate′, *v.,* -ated, -ating. appraise. —**e•val′u•a′tion,** *n.*

e′van•gel′i•cal, *adj.* of or in keeping with Gospel.

e•van′ge•list, *n.* 1. preacher. 2. writers of Gospel.

e•vap′o•rate′, *v.,* -rated, -rating. change into or pass off as vapor. —**e•vap′o•ra′tion,** *n.*

eve, *n.* evening before.

e′ven, *adj.* 1. smooth. 2. uniform. 3. equal. 4. divisible by 2. 5. calm. —*adv.* 6. hardly. 7. indeed. —*v.* 8. make even. —**e′ven•ly,** *adv.* —**e′ven•ness,** *n.*

eve′ning, *n.* early part of night; end of day.

e•vent′, *n.* anything that happens. —**e•vent′ful,** *adj.*

e•ven′tu•al, *adj.* final. —**e•ven′tu•al•ly,** *adv.*

e•ven′tu•al′i•ty, *n., pl.* -ties. possible event.

ev′er, *adv.* at all times.

ev′er•green′, *adj.* 1. having its leaves always green. —*n.* 2. evergreen plant.

ev′er•last′ing, *adj.* lasting forever or indefinitely.

eve′ry, *adj.* 1. each. 2. all possible. —**eve′ry•bod′y, eve′ry•one′,** *pron.* —**eve′ry•thing′,** *pron.* —**eve′ry•where′,** *adv.* —**eve′ry•day′,** *adj.*

e•vict′, *v.* remove from property by law. —**e•vic′tion,** *n.*

e′vi•dence, *n., v.,* -denced, -dencing. —*n.* 1. grounds for belief. —*v.* 2. prove.

ev′i•dent, *adj.* clearly so. —**ev′i•dent•ly,** *adv.*

e′vil, *adj.* 1. wicked. 2. unfortunate. —**e′vil•ly,** *adv.*

e•vince′, *v.,* evinced, evincing. 1. prove. 2. show.

e•voke′, *v.,* evoked, evoking. call forth.

e•volve′, *v.,* evolved, evolving. develop gradually. —**ev′o•lu′tion,** *n.*

ewe (yoo), *n.* female sheep.

ew′er, *n.* wide-mouthed pitcher.

ex•act′, *adj.* 1. precise; accurate. —*v.* 2. demand; compel. —**ex•act′ly,** *adv.*

ex•act′ing, *adj.* severe.

ex•ag′ger•ate′, *v.,* -ated, ating. magnify beyond truth. —**ex•ag′ger•a′tion,** *n.*

ex•alt′, *v.* 1. elevate. 2. extol. —**ex′al•ta′tion,** *n.*

ex•am′ine, *v.,* -ined, -ining. 1. investigate. 2. test. 3. interrogate. —**ex•am′i•na′tion,** *n.* —**ex•am′in•er,** *n.*

ex•am′ple, *n.* 1. typical one. 2. model. 3. illustration.

ex•as′per•ate′, *v.,* -ated, -ating. make angry. —**ex•as′per•a′tion,** *n.*

ex′ca•vate′, *v.,* -vated, -vating. 1. dig out. 2. unearth. —**ex•ca•va′tion,** *n.*

ex•ceed′, *v.* go beyond; surpass.

ex•ceed′ing•ly, *adv.* very.

ex•cel′, *v.,* -celled, -celling. be superior (to).

ex′cel•len•cy, *n.* 1. title of honor. 2. excellence.

ex′cel•lent, *adj.* remarkably good. —**ex′cel•lence,** *n.*

ex•cel′si•or, *n.* fine wood shavings.

ex•cept′, *prep.* 1. excluding. —*v.* 2. exclude. 3. object. —**ex•cep′tion,** *n.*

ex•cep′tion•a•ble, *adj.* causing objections.

ex•cep′tion•al, *adj.* unusual. —**ex•cep′tion•al•ly,** *adv.*

ex′cerpt (ek′sûrpt), *n.* passage from longer writing.

ex•cess′ (ik ses′). *n.* 1. amount over that required. —*adj.* (ek′ses). 2. more than necessary, usual, or desirable.

ex•ces′sive, *adj.* more than desirable. —**ex•ces′sive•ly,** *adv.*

ex•change′, *v.,* -changed, -changing, *n.* —*v.* 1. change for something else. —*n.* 2. act of exchanging. 3. thing exchanged. 4. trading place. —**ex•change′a•ble,** *adj.*

ex•cheq′uer, *n. Brit.* treasury.

ex′cise, *n., v.,* -cised, -cising. —*n.* (ek′sīz). 1. tax on certain goods. —*v.* (ik sīz′). 2. cut out. —**ex•ci′sion,** *n.*

ex•cite′, *v.,* -cited, -citing. 1. stir up. (emotions, etc.). 2. cause. —**ex•cit′a•ble,** *adj.* —**ex•cite′ment,** *n.*

ex•claim′, *v.* cry out. —**ex′cla•ma′tion,** *n.*

ex•clude′, *v.,* -cluded, -cluding. shut out. —**ex•clu′sion,** *n.*

ex•clu′sive, *adj.* 1. belonging or pertaining to one. 2. excluding others. 3. stylish; chic. —**ex•clu′sive•ly,** *adv.*

ex′com•mu′ni•cate′, *v.,* -cated, -cating. cut off from membership. —**ex′com•mu•ni•ca′tion,** *n.*

ex•co′ri•ate′, *v.,* -ated, -ating. denounce. —**ex•co′ri•a′tion,** *n.*

ex′cre•ment, *n.* bodily waste matter.

ex•cres′cence, *n.* abnormal growth. —**ex•cres′cent,** *adj.*

ex•crete′, *v.,* -creted, -creting. eliminate from body. —**ex•cre′tion,** *n.* —**ex′cre•to•ry,** *adj.*

ex•cru′ci•ate′ (-shē-), *v.*, **-ated, -ating.** torture.

ex′cul•pate′, *v.*, **-pated, -pating.** free of blame. **—ex′cul•pa′tion.**

ex•cur′sion, *n.* short trip.

ex•cuse′, *v.*, **-cused, -cusing,** *n.* **—***v.* (ik skyo͞oz′). 1. pardon. 2. apologize for. 3. justify. 4. seek or grant release. **—***n.* (ik skyo͞os′). 5. reason for being excused.

ex′e•crate′, *v.*, **-crated, -crating.** 1. abominate. 2. curse. **—ex′e•cra•ble,** *adj.*

ex′e•cute′, *v.*, **-cuted, -cuting.** 1. do. 2. kill legally. **—ex′e•cu′tion,** *n.* **—ex′e•cu′tion•er,** *n.*

ex•ec′u•tive, *adj.* 1. responsible for directing affairs. **—***n.* 2. administrator.

ex•ec′u•tor, *n.* person named to carry out provisions of a will. **—ex•ec′u•trix′,** *n.fem.*

ex•em′pla•ry, *adj.* 1. worthy of imitation. 2. warning.

ex•em′pli•fy′, *v.*, **-fied, -fying.** show or serve as example. **—ex•em′pli•fi•ca′tion,** *n.*

ex•empt′, *v.* free from obligation. **—ex•emp′tion,** *n.*

ex′er•cise′, *n.*, *v.*, **-cised, -cising. —***n.* 1. action to increase skill or strength. 2. performance. 3. (*pl.*) ceremony. **—***v.* 4. put through exercises. 5. use.

ex•ert′, *v.* put into action. **—ex•er′tion,** *n.*

ex•hale′, *v.*, **-haled, -haling.** breathe out. **—ex′ha•la′tion,** *n.*

ex•haust′, *v.* 1. use up. 2. fatigue greatly. **—***n.* 3. used gases from engine. **—ex•haus′tion,** *n.*

ex•haus′tive, *adj.* thorough.

ex•hib′it, *v.*, *n.* show; display. **—ex′hi•bi′tion,** *n.*

ex′hi•bi′tion•ism′, *n.* desire or tendency to display onself. **—ex′hi•bi′tion•ist,** *n.*

ex•hil′a•rate′, *v.*, **-rated, -rating.** cheer; stimulate. **—ex•hil′a•ra′tion,** *n.*

ex•hort′, *v.* advise earnestly. **—ex′hor•ta′tion,** *n.*

ex•hume′ (ig zyo͞om′), *v.*, **-humed, -huming.** dig up dead body, etc.

ex′i•gen•cy, *n.* urgent requirement. **—ex′i•gent,** *adj.*

ex′ile, *n.* 1. enforced absence from one's country or home. 2. one so absent. **—***v.* 3. send into exile.

ex•ist′, *v.* be; live. **—ex•ist′ence,** *n.* **—ex•ist′ent,** *adj.*

ex′is•ten′tial, *adj.* of human life; based on or confirming experience.

ex′it, *n.* 1. way out. 2. departure.

ex′o•dus, *n.* departure.

ex of•fi′ci•o′ (-fish′ē-o), because of the office one holds.

ex•on′er•ate′, *v.*, **-ated, -ating.** free of blame. **—ex•on′er•a′tion,** *n.*

ex•or′bi•tant (ig zôr′bi tənt), *adj.* excessive, esp. in cost. **—ex•or′bi•tance,** *n.*

ex′or•cise′, *v.*, **-cised, -cising.** expel (evil spirit). **—ex′or•cism′,** *n.*

ex•ot′ic, *adj.* foreign; alien.

ex•pand′, *v.* increase; spread out. **—ex•pan′sion,** *n.* **—ex•pan′sive,** *adj.*

ex•panse′, *n.* wide extent.

ex•pa′ti•ate′ (-pā′shē-), *v.*, **-ated, -ating.** talk or write at length.

ex•pa′tri•ate′, *v.*, **-ated, -ating,** *n.*, *adj.* **—***v.* 1. exile. 2. remove (oneself) from homeland. **—***n.* (-ət) 3. expatriated person. **—***adj.* (-ət) 4. exiled; banished.

ex•pect′, *v.* look forward to. **—ex•pect′an•cy,** *n.* **—ex•pect′ant,** *adj.* **—ex′pec•ta′tion,** *n.*

ex•pec′to•rate′, *v.*, **-rated, -rating.** spit.

ex•pe′di•ent, *adj.* 1. desirable in given circumstances. 2. conducive to advantage. **—***n.* 3. expedient means. **—ex•pe′di•en•cy,** *n.*

ex′pe•dite′, *v.*, **-dited, -diting.** speed up. **—ex′pe•dit′er,** *n.*

ex′pe•di′tion, *n.* 1. journey to explore or fight. 2. promptness. **—ex′pe•di′tion•ar′y,** *adj.*

ex•pel′, *v.*, **-pelled, -pelling.** force out.

ex•pend′, *v.* 1. use up. 2. spend. **—ex•pend′i•ture,** *n.*

ex•pend′a•ble, *adj.* 1. available for spending. 2. that can be sacrificed if necessary.

ex•pense′, *n.* 1. cost. 2. cause of spending.

ex•pen′sive, *adj.* costing much.

ex•pe′ri•ence, *n.*, *v.*, **-enced, -encing.** **—***n.* 1. something lived through. 2. knowledge from such things. **—***v.* 3. have experience of.

ex•per′i•ment, *n.* (-ə mənt). 1. test to discover or check something. **—***v.* (-ment′). 2. perform experiment. **—ex•per′i•men′tal,** *adj.*

ex′pert, *n.* (eks′pûrt). 1. skilled person. **—***adj.* (ik spûrt′). 2. skilled. **—ex•pert′ly,** *adv.* **—ex•pert′ness,** *n.*

ex′per•tise′ (-tēz′), *n.* expert skill.

ex′pi•ate′, *v.*, **-ated, -ating.** atone for. **—ex′pi•a′tion,** *n.*

ex•pire′, *v.*, **-pired, -piring.** 1. end. 2. die. 3. breathe out. **—ex′pi•ra′tion,** *n.*

ex•plain′, *v.* 1. make plain. 2. account for. **—ex′pla•na′tion,** *n.* **—ex•plan′a•to′ry,** *adj.*

ex•ple′tive, *n.* word, etc., added for emphasis.

ex•plic′it (-plis′-), *adj.* 1. clearly stated. 2. outspoken. **—ex•plic′it•ly,** *adv.*

ex•plode′, *v.*, **-ploded, -ploding.** burst violently. **—ex•plo′sion,** *n.* **—ex•plo′sive,** *n.*, *adj.*

ex′ploit, *n.* (eks′ploit). 1. notable act. **—***v.* (ik sploit′). 2. use, esp. selfishly. **—ex′ploi•ta′tion,** *n.*

ex•plore′, *v.*, **-plored, -ploring.** examine from end to end. **—ex′plo•ra′tion,** *n.* **—ex•plor′er,** *n.* **—ex•plor′a•to′ry,** *adj.*

ex•po′nent, *n.* 1. person who explains. 2. symbol; typical example.

ex•port′, *v.* (ik spôrt′). 1. send to other countries. **—***n.* (eks′pôrt). 2. what is sent. **—ex′por•ta′tion,** *n.*

ex•pose′, *v.*, **-posed, -posing.** 1. lay open to harm, etc. 2. reveal. 3. allow light to reach (film). **—ex•po′sure,** *n.*

ex′po•sé′ (-zā′), *n.* exposure of wrongdoing.

ex′po•si′tion, *n.* 1. public show. 2. explanation.

ex•pos′i•to′ry (-poz′i-) *adj.* serving to expound or explain.

ex•pos′tu•late′ (-pos′chə-), *v.*, **-lated, -lating.** argue protestingly. **—ex•pos′tu•la′tion,** *n.*

ex•pound′, *v.* state in detail.

ex•press′, *v.* 1. convey in words, art, etc. 2. press out. **—***adj.* 3. definite. **—***n.* 4. fast or direct train, etc. 5. delivery system. **—ex•pres′sion,** *n.* **—ex•pres′sive,** *adj.*

ex•press′way′, *n.* road for high-speed traffic.

ex•pro′pri•ate′, *v.*, **-ated, -ating.** take for public use. **—ex•pro′pri•a′tion,** *n.*

ex•pul′sion, *n.* act of driving out.

ex•punge′, *v.*, **-punged, -punging.** obliterate.

ex′pur•gate′, *v.*, **-gated, -gating.** remove objectionable parts from.

ex′qui•site, *adj.* delicately beautiful.

ex′tant (ek′stənt), *adj.* still existing.

ex•tem′po•ra′ne•ous, *adj.* impromptu.

ex•tend′, *v.* 1. stretch out. 2. offer. 3. reach. 4. increase. —**ex•ten′sion**, *n.*

ex•ten′sive, *adj.* far-reaching; broad. —**ex•ten′sive•ly**, *adv.*

ex•tent′, *n.* degree of extension.

ex•ten′u•ate′, *v.*, **-ated, -ating.** lessen (fault).

ex•te′ri•or, *adj.* 1. outer. —*n.* 2. outside.

ex•ter′mi•nate′, *v.*, **-nated, -nating.** destroy. —**ex•ter′mi•na′tion**, *n.* —**ex•ter′mi•na′tor**, *n.*

ex•ter′nal, *adj.* outer.

ex•tinct′, *adj.* no longer existing. —**ex•tinc′tion**, *n.*

ex•tin′guish, *v.* put out; end.

ex′tir•pate′, *v.*, **-pated, -pating.** destroy totally; tear out by roots.

ex•tol′, *v.*, **-tolled, -tolling.** praise.

ex•tort′, *v.* get by force, threat, etc. —**ex•tor′tion**, *n.* —**ex•tor′tion•ate**, *adj.*

ex′tra, *adj.* additional.

ex•tract′, *v.* (ik strakt′). 1. draw out. —*n.* (eks′trakt). 2. something extracted. —**ex•trac′tion**, *n.*

ex′tra•dite′, *v.*, **-dited, -diting.** deliver (fugitive) to another state or nation. —**ex′tra•di′tion**, *n.*

ex•tra′ne•ous, *adj.* irrelevant. —**ex•tra′ne•ous•ly**, *adv.*

ex•traor′di•nar′y, *adj.* unusual.

ex′tra•sen′so•ry, *adj.* beyond one's physical senses.

ex•trav′a•gant, *adj.* 1. spending imprudently. 2. immoderate. —**ex•trav′a•gance**, *n.*

ex•treme′, *adj.* 1. farthest from ordinary. 2. very great. 3. final or outermost. —*n.* 4. utmost degree. —**ex•treme′ly**, *adv.*

ex•trem′i•ty, *n.*, *pl.* **-ties.** 1. extreme part. 2. limb of body. 3. distress.

ex′tri•cate′, *v.*, **-cated, -cating.** disentangle.

ex′tro•vert′, *n.* person interested in things outside himself.

ex•u′ber•ant, *adj.* 1. joyful; vigorous. 2. lavish. —**ex•u′ber•ance**, *n.*

ex•ude′, *v.*, **-uded, -uding.** ooze out. —**ex′u•da′tion**, *n.*

ex•ult′, *v.* rejoice. —**ex•ult′ant**, *adj.* —**ex′ul•ta′tion**, *n.*

eye, *n.*, *v.*, **eyed, eying** or **eyeing.** —*n.* 1. organ of sight. 2. power of seeing. 3. close watch. —*v.* 4. watch closely. —**eye′ball′**, *n.* —**eye′sight′**, *n.*

eye′brow′, *n.* ridge and fringe of hair over eye.

eye′glass′, *n.* lens worn for better vision.

eye′lash′, *n.* short hair at edge of eyelid.

eye′let, *n.* small hole.

eye′lid′, *n.* movable skin covering the eye.

eye′tooth′, *n.* canine tooth.

eye′wit′ness, *n.* person who sees event.

F

F, f, *n.* sixth letter of English alphabet.

fa′ble, *n.* 1. short tale with moral. 2. untrue story.

fab′ric, *n.* cloth.

fab′ri•cate′, *v.*, **-cated, -cating.** 1. construct. 2. devise (lie). —**fab′ri•ca′tion**, *n.*

fab′u•lous, *adj.* 1. marvelous. 2. suggesting fables.

fa•çade′ (fə säd′), *n.* 1. building front. 2. pretentious appearance.

face, *n.*, *v.*, **faced, facing.** —*n.* 1. front part of head. 2. surface. 3. appearance. 4. self-respect. —*v.* 5. look toward. 6. confront. —**fa′cial**, *adj.*

fac′et, (fas′it), *n.* 1. surface of cut gem. 2. aspect.

fa•ce′tious, *adj.* joking, esp. annoyingly so.

fac′ile (fas′il), *adj.* glibly easy.

fa•cil′i•tate′, *v.*, **-tated, -tating.** make easier.

fa•cil′i•ty, *n.*, *pl.* **-ties.** 1. thing that makes task easier. 2. dexterity.

fac′ing, *n.* decorative or protective outer material.

fac•sim′i•le (fak sim′ə lē), *n.* exact copy.

fact, *n.* truth. —**fac′tu•al**, *adj.*

fac′tion, *n.* competing internal group. —**fac′tion•al**, *adj.*

fac′tious, *adj.* causing strife.

fac′tor, *n.* 1. element. 2. one of two numbers multiplied.

fac′to•ry, *n.*, *pl.* **-ries.** place where goods are made.

fac′ul•ty, *n.*, *pl.* **-ties.** 1. special ability. 2. power. 3. body of teachers.

fad, *n.* temporary fashion; craze.

fade, *v.*, **faded, fading.** 1. lose freshness, color or vitality. 2. disappear gradually.

fag, *v.*, **fagged, fagging**, *n.* —*v.* 1. exhaust. —*n.* 2. Also **fag′got.** *Offensive.* homosexual.

fag′ot, *n.* bundle of firewood.

Fahr′en•heit′ (far′ən hīt′), *adj.* measuring temperature so that water freezes at 32° and boils at 212°.

fail, *v.* 1. be unsuccessful or lacking (in). 2. become weaker. 3. cease functioning. —**fail′ure**, *n.*

fail′ing, *n.* weak point of character.

faille (fil, fāl), *n.* ribbed fabric.

fail′-safe′, *adj.* ensured against failure of a mechanical system, etc., or against consequences of its failure.

faint, *adj.* 1. lacking force or strength. —*v.* 2. lose consciousness briefly. —**faint′ly**, *adv.*

fair, *adj.* 1. behaving or thinking justly. 2. moderately good. 3. sunny. 4. light-hued. 5. attractive. —*n.* 6. exhibition. —**fair′ly**, *adv.* —**fair′ness**, *n.*

fair′y, *n.*, *pl.* **fairies.** 1. tiny supernatural being. 2. *Offensive.* homosexual. —**fair′y•land′**, *n.*

faith, *n.* 1. confidence. 2. religious belief. 3. loyalty. —**faith′less**, *adj.*

faith′ful, *adj.* 1. loyal. 2. having religious belief. 3. copying accurately. —**faith′ful•ly**, *adv.* —**faith′ful•ness**, *n.*

fake, *v.*, **faked, faking**, *n.*, *adj. Informal.* —*v.* 1. pretend or counterfeit. —*n.* 2. thing faked. —*adj.* 3. designed to deceive. —**fak′er**, *n.*

fa•kir′ (fə kēr′), *n.* Muslim or Hindu monk.

fal′con (fôl′kən), *n.* bird of prey.

fall, *v.*, **fell, fallen, falling**, *n.* —*v.* 1. descend; drop. 2. happen. —*n.* 3. descent. 4. autumn.

fal′la•cy, *n.*, *pl.* **-cies.** 1. false belief. 2. unsound argument. —**fal•la′cious**, *adj.*

fal′li•ble, *adj.* liable to error. —**fal′li•bil′i•ty**, *n.*

fall′out′, *n.* radioactive particles carried by air.

fal′low, *adj.* plowed and not seeded.

false, *adj.* 1. not true. 2. faithless. 3. deceptive. —**false′hood**, *n.* —**fal′si•ty**, *n.* —**fal′si•fy**, *v.*

fal·set′to, *n.,* *pl.* **-tos.** unnaturally high voice.

fal′ter, *v.* hesitate; waver.

fame, *n.* wide reputation.

fa·mil′iar, *adj.* 1. commonly known. 2. intimate. —**fa·mil′i·ar′i·ty,** *n.* —**fa·mil′iar·ize′,** *v.*

fam′i·ly, *n.,* *pl.* **-lies.** 1. parents and their children. 2. relatives. —**fa·mil′i·al,** *adj.*

fam′ine, *n.* scarcity of food.

fam′ish, *v.* starve.

fa′mous, *adj.* renowned; celebrated.

fan, *n., v.,* **fanned, fanning.** —*n.* 1. device for causing current of air. 2. *Informal.* devotee. —*v.* 3. blow upon with fan. 4. stir up.

fa·nat′ic, *n.* person excessively devoted to cause. —**fa·nat′i·cal,** *adj.* —**fa·nat′i·cism′,** *n.*

fan′ci·er, *n.* person interested in something, as dogs.

fan′cy, *n., pl.* **-cies,** *adj.,* **-cier, -ciest,** *v.,* **-cied, -cying.** —*n.* 1. imagination. 2. thing imagined. 3. whim. 4. taste. —*adj.* 5. ornamental. —*v.* 6. imagine. 7. crave. —**fan′ci·ful,** *adj.*

fan′fare′, *n.* 1. chorus of trumpets. 2. showy flourish.

fang, *n.* long, sharp tooth.

fan′ta·size′, *v.,* **-sized, -sizing.** have fantasies.

fan·tas′tic, *adj.* 1. wonderful and strange. 2. fanciful. Also, **fan·tas′ti·cal.** —**fan·tas′ti·cal·ly,** *adv.*

fan′ta·sy, *n., pl.* **-sies.** 1. imagination. 2. imagined thing.

far, *adv., adj.,* **farther, farthest.** at or to great distance.

farce, *n.* light comedy.

fare, *n., v.,* **fared, faring.** —*n.* 1. price of passage. 2. food. —*v.* 3. eat. 4. get along. 5. go.

Far East, countries of east and southeast Asia.

fare′well′, *interj., n., adj.* good-by.

far′-fetched′, *adj.* not reasonable or probable.

farm, *n.* 1. tract of land for agriculture. —*v.* 2. cultivate land. —**farm′er,** *n.* —**farm′house′,** *n.* —**farm′yard′,** *n.*

far′-off′, *adj.* distant.

far′-out′, *adj. Slang.* extremely unconventional.

far′-reach′ing, *adj.* of widespread influence.

far′row, *n.* 1. litter of pigs. —*v.* 2. (of swine) bear.

far′-sight′ed, *adj.* 1. seeing distant objects best. 2. planning for future.

far′ther, *compar. of* **far.** —*adv.* 1. at or to a greater distance. —*adj.* 2. more distant. 3. additional.

far′thest, *superl. of* **far.** —*adv.* 1. at or to the greatest distance. —*adj.* 2. most distant.

fas′ci·nate′, *v.,* **-nated, -nating.** attract irresistibly. —**fas′ci·na′tion,** *n.*

fas′cism (fash′iz əm), *n.* principle of strong undemocratic government. —**fas′cist,** *n., adj.* —**fa·scis′tic,** *adj.*

fash′ion, *n.* 1. prevailing style. 2. manner. —*v.* 3. make.

fash′ion·a·ble, *adj.* of the latest style. —**fash′ion·a·bly,** *adv.*

fast, *adj.* 1. quick; swift. 2. secure. —*adv.* 3. tightly. 4. swiftly. —*v.* 5. abstain from food. —*n.* 6. such abstinence.

fast′back′, *n.* rear of automobile, curved downward.

fas′ten, *v.* 1. fix securely. 2. seize. —**fas′ten·er, fas′ten·ing,** *n.*

fas·tid′i·ous, *adj.* highly critical and demanding. —**fas·tid′i·ous·ly,** *adv.*

fast′ness, *n.* fortified place.

fat, *n., adj.,* **fatter, fattest.** —*n.* 1. greasy substance. —*adj.* 2. fleshy. —**fat′ty,** *adj.*

fa′tal, *adj.* causing death or ruin. —**fa′tal·ly,** *adv.*

fa′tal·ism, *n.* belief in unchangeable destiny. —**fa′tal·is′tic,** *adj.*

fa·tal′i·ty, *n., pl.* **-ties.** 1. fatal disaster. 2. fate.

fate, *n., v.,* **fated, fating.** —*n.* 1. destiny. 2. death or ruin. —*v.* 3. destine.

fate′ful, *adj.* involving important or disastrous events.

fa′ther, *n.* 1. male parent. 2. (*cap.*) God. 3. priest.

fa′ther-in-law′, *n.* father of one's spouse.

fath′om, *n.* 1. nautical measure equal to six feet. —*v.* 2. understand.

fa·tigue′, *n., v.,* **-tigued, -tiguing.** —*n.* 1. weariness. 2. (*pl.*) military work clothes. —*v.* 3. weary.

fat′ten, *v.* make or grow fat or prosperous.

fat′u·ous (fach′-), *adj.* 1. foolish or stupid. 2. unreal. —**fa·tu′i·ty,** *n.*

fau′cet, *n.* valve for liquids.

fault, *n.* defect. —**faul′ty,** *adj.*

faun, *n.* Roman deity, part man and part goat.

faux pas′ (fō pä′), error, esp. social.

fa′vor, *n.* 1. kind act. 2. high regard. —*v.* 3. prefer. 4. oblige. 5. resemble. Also, **fa′vour.** —**fa′vor·a·ble,** *adj.* —**fa′vor·ite,** *adj., n.*

fa′vor·it·ism, *n.* preference shown toward certain persons.

fawn, *n.* 1. young deer. —*v.* 2. seek favor by servility.

faze, *v.,* **fazed, fazing.** *Informal.* daunt.

fear, *n.* 1. feeling of coming harm. 2. awe. —*v.* 3. be afraid of. 4. hold in awe. —**fear′ful,** *adj.* —**fear′less,** *adj.*

fea′si·ble, *adj.* able to be done. —**fea′si·bil′i·ty,** *n.*

feast, *n.* 1. sumptuous meal. 2. religious celebration. —*v.* 3. provide with or have feast.

feat, *n.* remarkable deed.

feath′er, *n.* one of the growths forming bird's plumage. —**feath′er·y,** *adj.*

fea′ture, *n., v.,* **-tured, -turing.** —*n.* 1. part of face. 2. special part, article, etc. —*v.* 3. give prominence to.

Feb′ru·ar′y, *n.* second month of year.

fe′ces (fē′sēz), *n.pl.* excrement.

fe′cund (fē′kund), *adj.* productive. —**fe·cun′di·ty,** *n.*

fed′er·al, *adj.* 1. of states in permanent union. 2. (*cap.*) of U.S. government.

fed′er·ate′, *v.,* **-ated, -ating.** unite in league. —**fed′er·a′tion,** *n.*

fe·do′ra, *n.* man's hat.

fee, *n.* 1. payment for services, etc. 2. ownership.

fee′ble, *adj.,* **-bler, -blest.** weak. —**fee′bly,** *adv.*

feed, *v.,* **fed, feeding,** *n.* —*v.* 1. give food to. 2. eat. —*n.* 3. food. —**feed′er,** *n.*

feed′back′, *n.* 1. return of part of output of a process to its input. 2. informative response.

feel, *v.,* **felt, feeling,** *n.* —*v.* 1. perceive or examine by touch. 2. be conscious of. 3. have emotions. —*n.* 4. touch. —**feel′ing,** *adj., n.*

feign (fān), *v.* pretend.

feint (fānt), *n.* 1. deceptive move. —*v.* 2. make feint.

fe·lic′i·tate′, *v.,* **-tated, -tating.** congratulate. —**fe·lic′i·ta′tion,** *n.*

fe·lic′i·tous, *adj.* suitable.

fe·lic′i·ty, *n.* happiness.

fe′line (fē′līn), *adj.* of or like cats.

fell, *v.* cut or strike down.

fel′low, *n.* 1. man. 2. companion. 3. equal. 4. member of learned or professional group. —**fel′low·ship′,** *n.*

fel′on, *n.* criminal.

fel′o·ny, *n., pl.* **-nies.** serious crime. —**fe·lo′ni·ous,** *adj.*

felt, *n.* 1. matted fabric. —*adj.* 2. of felt.

fe′male, *adj.* 1. belonging to sex that brings forth young. —*n.* 2. female person or animal.

fem′i•nine, *adj.* of women. —**fem′i•nin′i•ty,** *n.*

fem′in•ism, *n.* support of feminine causes. —**fem′in•ist,** *adj., n.*

fe′mur (fē′-), *n.* thigh bone.

fence, *n., v.,* **fenced, fencing.** —*n.* 1. wall-like enclosure around open area. —*v.* 2. fight with sword for sport. —**fenc′ing,** *n.*

fend, *v.* ward off.

fend′er, *n.* metal part over automobile wheel.

fer′ment, *n.* 1. substance causing fermentation. 2. agitation. —*v.* (fər ment′). 3. cause or undergo fermentation.

fer′men•ta′tion, *n.* chemical change involving effervescence or decomposition.

fern, *n.* nonflowering plant with feathery leaves.

fe•ro′cious, *adj.* savagely fierce. —**fe•roc′i•ty,** *n.*

fer′ret, *n.* 1. kind of weasel. —*v.* 2. search intensively.

fer′rous, *adj.* of or containing iron. Also, **fer′ric.**

fer′ry, *n., pl.* **-ries,** *v.,* **-ried, -rying.** —*n.* 1. Also, **fer′ry•boat′.** boat making short crossings. 2. place where ferries operate. —*v.* 3. carry or pass in ferry.

fer′tile, *adj.* 1. producing abundantly. 2. able to bear young. —**fer•til′i•ty,** *n.* —**fer′ti•lize′,** *v.* —**fer′ti•liz′er,** *n.*

fer′vent, *adj.* deeply earnest. —**fer′ven•cy, fer′vor,** *n.*

fer′vid, *adj.* vehement.

fes′tal, *adj.* of feasts.

fes′ter, *v.* 1. generate pus. 2. rankle.

fes′ti•val, *n.* celebration or feast. Also, **fes•tiv′i•ty.** —**fes′tive,** *adj.*

fes•toon′, *n.* 1. garland hung between two points. —*v.* 2. adorn with festoons.

fetch, *v.* go and bring.

fete (fāt, fet), *n., v.,* **feted, feting.** —*n.* 1. festival. 2. party. —*v.* 3. honor with a fete.

fet′id, *adj.* stinking; rank.

fe′tish, *n.* object worshiped. Also, **fe′tich.**

fet′lock, *n.* 1. part of horse's leg behind hoof. 2. tuft of hair on this part.

fet′ter, *n.* 1. shackle for feet. —*v.* 2. put fetters on. 3. restrain from action.

fet′tle, *n.* condition.

fe′tus, *n.* unborn offspring.

feud, *n.* lasting hostility.

feu′dal•ism, *n.* system by which land is held in return for service. —**feu′dal,** *adj.*

fe′ver, *n.* bodily condition marked by high temperature, rapid pulse, etc. —**fe′ver•ish,** *adj.*

few, *adj., n.* not many.

fez, *n.* felt cap.

fi′an•cé′ (fē′än sā′), *n.* betrothed man. —**fi′an•cée′,** *n.fem.*

fi•as′co (fē as′kō), *n.* failure.

fi′at (fī′ət), *n.* decree.

fib, *n., v.,* **fibbed, fibbing.** mild lie.

fi′ber, *n.* threadlike piece. Also, **fi′bre.**

fib′u•la, *n.* outer thinner bone from knee to ankle.

fick′le, *adj.* inconstant; disloyal.

fic′tion, *n.* 1. narrative on imaginary events. 2. something made up. —**fic•ti′tious,** *adj.*

fid′dle, *n., v.,* **-dled, -dling.** —*n.* 1. violin. —*v.* 2. play folk or popular tunes on violin. 3. trifle. —**fid′dler,** *n.*

fi•del′i•ty, *n.* faithfulness.

fidg′et, *v.* 1. move restlessly. —*n.* 2. (*pl.*) restlessness.

fi•du′cial (-shəl), *adj.* based on trust, as paper money not backed by precious metal.

fi•du′ci•ar′y (-shē-), *adj., n., pl.* **-aries.** —*adj.* 1. being a trustee. 2. held in trust. —*n.* 3. trustee.

field, *n.* 1. open ground. 2. area of interest.

fiend, *n.* 1. devil. 2. cruel person. 3. *Informal.* addict. —**fiend′ish,** *adj.*

fierce, *adj.* wild; violent. —**fierce′ly,** *adv.*

fier′y, *adj.* 1. of or like fire. 2. ardent.

fi•es′ta, *n.* festival.

fife, *n.* high-pitched flute.

fif′teen′, *n., adj.* ten plus five. —**fif•teenth′,** *adj., n.*

fifth, *adj.* 1. next after fourth. —*n.* 2. fifth part.

fifth column, traitorous group within a country.

fif′ty, *n., adj.* ten times five. —**fif′ti•eth,** *adj., n.*

fig, *n.* fruit of semitropical tree.

fight, *n., v.,* **fought, fighting.** battle. —**fight′er,** *n.*

fig′ment, *n.* imagined story.

fig′ur•a•tive, *adj.* not literal. —**fig′ur•a•tive•ly,** *adv.*

fig′ure, *n., v.,* **-ured, -uring.** —*n.* 1. written symbol, esp. numerical. 2. amount. 3. shape. —*v.* 4. compute. 5. be prominent.

fig′ure•head′, *n.* powerless leader.

fig′ur•ine′, *n.* miniature statue.

fil′a•ment, *n.* fine fiber.

fil′bert, *n.* kind of nut.

filch, *v.* steal.

file, *n., v.,* **filed, filing.** —*n.* 1. storage place for documents. 2. line of persons, etc. 3. metal rubbing tool. —*v.* 4. arrange or keep in file. 5. march in file. 6. rub with file.

fil′i•al, *adj.* befitting sons and daughters.

fil′i•bus′ter, *n.* obstruction of legislation by prolonged speaking.

fil′i•gree′, *n.* ornamental work of fine wires.

fill, *v.* 1. make full. 2. pervade. 3. supply. —*n.* 4. full supply. —**fill′ing,** *n.*

fil•let′ (fi lā′), *n.* narrow strip, esp. of meat or fish. Also, **fi′let.**

fil′lip, *n.* thing that rouses or excites.

fil′ly, *n., pl.* **-lies.** young female horse.

film, *n.* 1. thin coating. 2. roll or sheet with photographically sensitive coating. 3. motion picture. —*v.* 4. make motion picture of.

film′strip′, strip of still pictures for projecting on screen.

film′y, *adj.,* **-ier, -iest.** 1. partly transparent. 2. indistinct; blurred.

fil′ter, *n.* 1. device for straining substances. —*v.* 2. remove by or pass through filter.

filth, *n.* 1. dirt. 2. obscenity. —**filth′y,** *adj.*

fin, *n.* winglike organ on fishes.

fi′nal, *adj.* last. —**fi•nal′i•ty,** *n.* —**fi′nal•ly,** *adv.*

fi•na′le (fi nä′lē), *n.* last part.

fi•nance′, *n., v.,* **-nanced, -nancing.** —*n.* 1. money matters. 2. (*pl.*) funds. —*v.* 3. supply with money. —**fi•nan′cial,** *adj.*

fin•an•cier′ (-sēr′), *n.* professional money handler.

finch, *n.* small bird.

find, *v.,* **found, finding,** *n.* —*v.* 1. come upon. 2. learn. —*n.* 3. discovery.

fine, *adj.,* **finer, finest,** *n., v.,* **fined, fining.** —*adj.* 1. excellent. 2. delicate; thin. —*n.* 3. money exacted as penalty. —*v.* 4. subject to fine.

fin′er•y, *n.* showy dress.

fi•nesse′, *n.* artful delicacy.

fin′ger, *n.* one of five terminal parts of hand. —**fin′ger•print**′, *n., v.*

fin′i•cal, *adj.* too fussy. Also, **fin′-ick•y.**

fi′nis (fin′is, fī′nis), *n.* end.

fin′ish, *v.* 1. end. 2. perfect. 3. give desired surface to. —*n.* 4. completion. 5. surface coating or treatment.

fiord (fyôrd), *n.* narrow arm of sea.

fir, *n.* cone-bearing evergreen tree.

fire, *n., v.,* **fired, firing.** —*n.* 1. burning. 2. ardor. 3. discharge of firearms. —*v.* 4. set on fire. 5. discharge. 6. *Informal.* dismiss.

fire′arm′, *n.* gun.

fire′fly′, *n., pl.* **-flies.** nocturnal beetle with light-producing organ.

fire′man (fīr′mən), *n., pl.* **-men.** 1. firefighter. 2. man maintaining fires.

fire′place′, *n.* semiopen place for fire.

fire′plug′, *n.* hydrant with water for fighting fires.

fire′proof′, *adj.* safe against fire.

fire′side′, *n.* area close to fireplace; hearth.

fire′trap′, *n.* dilapidated building.

fire′works′, *n.pl.* devices ignited for display of light and noise.

firm, *adj.* 1. hard or stiff. 2. fixed. 3. resolute. —*v.* 4. make or become firm. —*n.* 5. business organization. —**firm′ly,** *adv.* —**firm′ness,** *n.*

fir′ma•ment, *n.* sky.

first, *adj., adv.* 1. before all others. —*n.* 2. first thing, etc.

first aid, immediate treatment for injuries, etc.

fis′cal (-kəl), *adj.* financial.

fish, *n., pl.* **fish, fishes,** *v.* —*n.* 1. cold-blooded aquatic vertebrate. —*v.* 2. try to catch fish. —**fish′er•man,** *n.* —**fish′er•y,** *n.*

fis′sion (fish′ən), *n.* division into parts. —**fis′sion•a•ble,** *adj.*

fis′sure (fish′ər), *n.* narrow opening.

fist, *n.* closed hand.

fit, *adj.,* **fitter, fittest,** *v.,* **fitted, fitting,** *n.* —*adj.* 1. well suited. 2. in good condition. —*v.* 3. be or make suitable. 4. equip. —*n.* 5. manner of fitting. 6. sudden attack of illness or emotion.

fit′ful, *adj.* irregular.

fit′ting, *adj.* 1. appropriate. —*n.* 2. attached part. 3. trial of new clothes, etc., for fit.

five, *n., adj.* four plus one.

fix, *v.* 1. make fast or steady. 2. repair. 3. prepare. —**fix′er,** *n.*

fix•a′tion, *n.* excessive attachment or bias.

fix′ings, *n.pl. Informal.* things accompanying main item.

fix′ture, *n.* something fixed in place.

fizz, *v., n.* hiss.

fiz′zle, *v.,* **-zled, -zling.** —*v.* 1. hiss weakly. 2. *Informal.* fail. —*n.* 3. act of fizzling.

flab′ber•gast′, *v. Informal.* astound.

flab′by, *adj.,* **-bier, -biest.** limp; not firm.

flac′cid (flak′sid), *adj.* flabby.

flag, *n., v.,* **flagged, flagging.** —*n.* 1. cloth with symbolic colors or design. 2. plant with long narrow leaves. 3. Also, **flag′stone**′. paving stone. —*v.* 4. signal with flags (def. 1).

flag′el•late′ (flaj′-), *v.,* **-lated, -lating.** whip; flog. —**flag′el•la′tion,** *n.*

flag′on, *n.* large bottle.

fla′grant, *adj.* glaring. —**fla′gran•cy,** *n.*

flag′ship′, *n.* ship of senior naval officer.

flail, *n.* 1. hand instrument for threshing. —*v.* 2. strike or strike at as with flail.

flair, *n.* aptitude; talent.

flak, *n.* antiaircraft fire.

flake, *n., v.,* **flaked, flaking.** —*n.* 1. small thin piece. —*v.* 2. separate in flakes.

flam•boy′ant, *adj.* highly vivid.

flame, *n., v.,* **flamed, flaming.** blaze.

fla•min′go, *n.* tall, red, aquatic bird.

flange, *n.* projecting rim.

flank, *n.* 1. side. —*v.* 2. be at side of. 3. pass around side of.

flan′nel, *n.* soft wool fabric.

flap, *v.,* **flapped, flapping,** *n.* —*v.* 1. swing loosely and noisily. 2. move up and down. —*n.* 3. flapping movement. 4. something hanging loosely. 5. *Informal.* emotionally agitated state.

flare, *v.,* **flared, flaring,** *n.* —*v.* 1. burn with unsteady or sudden flame. 2. spread outward. —*n.* 3. signal fire.

flash, *n.* 1. brief light. 2. instant. 3. news dispatch. —*v.* 4. gleam suddenly.

flash′bulb′, *n.* bulb giving burst of light for photography.

flash′cube′, *n.* device containing four flashbulbs.

flash′light′, *n.* portable battery-powered light.

flash′y, *adj.,* **-ier, -iest.** *Informal.* showy. —**flash′i•ness,** *n.*

flask, *n.* kind of bottle.

flat, *adj.,* **flatter, flattest,** *n.* —*adj.* 1. level. 2. horizontal. 3. not thick. 4. uncompromising. 5. dull. 6. below musical pitch. —*n.* 7. something flat. 8. apartment. —**flat′ly,** *adv.* —**flat′ness,** *n.* —**flat′ten,** *v.*

flat′car′, *n.* railroad car without sides or top.

flat′ter, *v.* praise insincerely. —**flat′ter•y,** *n.*

flaunt, *v.* display boldly.

fla′vor, *n.* 1. taste. —*v.* 2. give flavor to. —**fla′vor•ing,** *n.*

flaw, *n.* defect.

flax, *n.* linen plant.

flay, *v.* strip skin from.

flea, *n.* small, blood-sucking insect.

fleck, *n.* 1. speck. —*v.* 2. spot.

fledg′ling, *n.* young bird.

flee, *v.,* **fled, fleeing.** run away from.

fleece, *n., v.,* **fleeced, fleecing.** —*n.* 1. wool of sheep. —*v.* 2. swindle. —**fleec′y,** *adj.*

fleet, *n.* 1. organized group of ships, aircraft, or road vehicles. —*adj.* 2. swift.

fleet′ing, *adj.* temporary; not lasting.

flesh, *n.* 1. muscle and fat of animal body. 2. body. 3. soft part of fruit or vegetable. —**flesh′y,** *adj.*

flesh′ly, *adj.* carnal.

flex, *v.* bend. —**flex′i•ble,** *adj.* —**flex′i•bil′i•ty,** *n.*

flick, *n.* 1. light stroke. —*v.* 2. strike lightly.

flick′er, *v.* 1. glow unsteadily. —*n.* 2. unsteady light.

fli′er, *n.* aviator.

flight, *n.* 1. act or power of flying. 2. trip through air. 3. steps between two floors. 4. hasty departure.

flight′y, *adj.,* **-ier, -iest.** capricious. —**flight′i•ness,** *n.*

flim′sy, *adj.,* **-sier, -siest.** weak or thin. —**flim′si•ness,** *n.*

flinch, *v.* shrink.

fling, *v.,* **flung, flinging,** *n.* —*v.* 1. throw violently. —*n.* 2. act of flinging.

flint, *n.* hard stone that strikes sparks. —**flint′y,** *adj.*

flip, *v.,* **flipped, flipping,** *n.* —*v.* 1. move by snapping finger. —*n.* 2. such movement.

flip′pant, *adj.* pert; disrespectful. —**flip′pan•cy,** *n.*

flip′per, *n.* broad flat limb.

flirt, *v.* 1. trifle in love. —*n.* 2. person who flirts. —**flir•ta′tion,** *n.* —**flir•ta′tious,** *adj.*

flit, *v.,* **flitted, flitting.** move swiftly.

float, *v.* 1. rest or move on or in liquid, air, etc. —*n.* 2. something that floats. 3. decorated parade wagon.

flock, *n.* 1. group of animals. —*v.* 2. gather in flock.

floe, *n.* field of floating ice.

flog, *v.*, **flogged, flogging.** beat; whip.

flood, *n.* 1. overflowing of water. —*v.* 2. overflow or cover with water, etc.

flood′light′, *n.* artificial light for large area.

floor, *n.* 1. bottom surface of room, etc. 2. level in building. 3. right to speak. —*v.* 4. furnish with floor. 5. knock down.

floor′ing, *n.* material for floors.

flop, *v.*, **flopped, flopping,** *n. Informal.* —*v.* 1. fall flatly. 2. fail. 3. flap. —*n.* 4. act of flopping.

flop′py, *adj.*, **-pier, -piest.** limp. —**flop′pi•ness,** *n.*

flo′ral, *adj.* of flowers.

flor′id, *adj.* ruddy. —**flo•rid′i•ty,** *n.*

flo′rist, *n.* dealer in flowers.

floss, *n.* 1. silky fiber from certain plants. 2. fiber for cleaning between teeth.

flo•til′la, *n.* small fleet.

flot′sam, *n.* floating wreckage.

flounce, *v.*, **flounced, flouncing,** *n.* —*v.* 1. go with an angry fling. —*n.* 2. flouncing movement. 3. ruffle for trimming.

floun′der, *v.* 1. struggle clumsily. —*n.* 2. clumsy effort. 3. flat edible fish.

flour, *n.* finely ground meal.

flour′ish (flûr′-), *v.* 1. thrive. 2. brandish. —*n.* 3. act of brandishing. 4. decoration.

flout, *v.* mock; scorn.

flow, *v.* 1. move in stream. —*n.* 2. act or rate of flowing.

flow′er, *n.*, *v.* blossom; bloom. —**flow′er•y,** *adj.*

flu, *n.* influenza.

fluc′tu•ate′, *v.*, **-ated, -ating.** vary irregularly. —**fluc′tu•a′tion,** *n.*

flue, *n.* duct for smoke, etc.

flu′ent, *adj.* writing and speaking with ease. —**flu′en•cy,** *n.* —**flu′ent•ly,** *adv.*

fluff, *n.* downy particles. —**fluff′y,** *adj.*

flu′id, *n.* 1. substance that flows. —*adj.* 2. liquid or gaseous.

fluke, *n.* 1. lucky chance. 2. flounder (def. 3).

flume, *n.* channel; trough.

flun′ky, *n.*, *pl.* **-kies.** male servant or follower.

fluo•res′cence, *n.* emission of light upon exposure to radiation, etc. —**fluo•res′cent,** *adj.*

fluorescent lamp, tubular lamp using phosphors to produce radiation of light.

fluor′i•da′tion (floٙor′ə dā′shən), *n.* addition of fluorides to drinking water to reduce tooth decay.

fluor•ide′, *n.* chemical compound containing fluorine.

fluor′o•scope′ (floٙor′ə-), *n.* device for examining the body with x-rays.

flur′ry, *n.*, *pl.* **-ries.** 1. gust of wind, rain, etc. 2. agitated state.

flush, *n.* 1. rosy glow. —*v.* 2. redden. 3. wash out with water. —*adj.* 4. even with surrounding surface. 5. well supplied.

flus′ter, *v.* confuse.

flute, *n.*, *v.*, **fluted, fluting.** —*n.* 1. musical wind instrument. 2. groove. —*v.* 3. form flutes in.

flut′ter, *v.* 1. wave in air. —*n.* 2. agitation.

flux, *n.* 1. a flowing. 2. continuous change. 3. substance that promotes fusion of metals.

fly, *v.*, **flew, flown, flying,** *n.*, *pl.* **flies.** —*v.* 1. move or direct through air. 2. move swiftly. —*n.* 3. winged insect. —**fly′er,** *n.*

flying saucer, disk-shaped missile or plane, thought to come from outer space.

fly′leaf′, *n.*, *pl.* **-leaves.** blank page in front or back of a book.

fly′wheel′, *n.* wheel for equalizing speed of machinery.

foal, *n.* young horse.

foam, *n.* 1. mass of tiny bubbles. —*v.* 2. form foam.

fob, *n.* chain or ribbon attached to a watch.

fo′cus, *n.*, *pl.* **-cuses, -ci** (-sī) *v.*, **-cused, -cusing.** —*n.* 1. point at which refracted rays of light, etc., meet. 2. state of sharpness for image from optical device. 3. central point. —*v.* 4. bring into focus. —**fo′cal,** *adj.*

fod′der, *n.* livestock food.

foe, *n.* enemy.

fog, *n.* thick mist. —**fog′gy,** *adj.* —**fog′gi•ness,** *n.*

fo′gy, *n.*, *pl.* **-gies.** old-fashioned person.

foi′ble, *n.* weak point.

foil, *v.* 1. frustrate. —*n.* 2. thin metallic sheet. 3. thing that sets off another by contrast. 4. thin, pointed sword for fencing.

foist, *v.* impose falsely.

fold, *v.* 1. bend over upon itself. 2. wrap. 3. collapse. —*n.* 4. folded part. 5. enclosure for sheep.

fold′er, *n.* 1. folded printed sheet. 2. outer cover.

fo′li•age, *n.* leaves.

fo′li•o′, *n.* 1. sheet of paper folded once. 2. book printed on such sheets.

folk, *n.* people.

folk′lore′, *n.* customs and beliefs of people.

folk′lor•ist, *n.* expert on folklore. —**folk′lor•is′tic,** *adj.*

folk′sy, *adj.*, **-sier, -siest.** *Informal.* suggesting genial simplicity. —**folk′si•ness,** *n.*

fol′li•cle, *n.* 1. seed vessel. 2. small cavity, sac, or gland.

fol′low, *v.* 1. come or go after. 2. conform to. 3. work at. 4. move along. 5. watch or understand. 6. result.

fol′low•er, *n.* 1. person who follows. 2. disciple.

fol′low•ing, *n.* group of admirers or disciples.

fol′ly, *n.*, *pl.* **-lies.** foolishness.

fo•ment′, *v.* foster.

fond, *adj.* 1. having affection. 2. foolish. —**fond′ness,** *n.*

fon′dant, *n.* sugar paste used in candies.

fon′dle, *v.*, **-dled, -dling.** caress.

fon•due′, *n.* dip of melted cheese, liquor, and seasonings.

font (font), *n.* 1. receptacle for baptismal water. 2. printing type style.

food, *n.* what is taken in for nourishment.

fool, *n.* 1. person acting stupidly. —*v.* 2. trick. 3. act frivolously. —**fool′ish,** *adj.*

fool′har′dy, *adj.*, **-dier, -diest.** rash.

fool′proof′, *adj.* proof against accident.

foot, *n.*, *pl.* **feet,** *v.* —*n.* 1. part of leg on which body stands. 2. unit of length equal to 12 inches. 3. lowest part; base. —*v.* 4. walk. —**foot′-print′,** *n.*

foot′ball′, *n.* game played with pointed leather ball.

foot′hill′, *n.* hill at foot of mountains.

foot′hold′, *n.* 1. secure place for foot to rest. 2. firm basis for progress.

foot′ing, *n.* 1. secure position. 2. basis for relationship.

foot′man, *n.* male servant.

foot′note′, *n.* note at foot of page.

foot'-pound', *n.* work done by force of one pound moving through distance of one foot.

foot'step', *n.* sound of walking.

fop, *n.* haughty, overdressed man. —**fop'pish**, *adj.*

for, *prep.* 1. with the purpose of. 2. in the interest of. 3. in place of. 4. in favor of. 5. during. —*conj.* 6. seeing that. 7. because.

for'age, *n., v.,* **-aged, -aging.** —*n.* 1. food for stock. —*v.* 2. search for supplies.

for'ay, *n.* raid.

for•bear', *v.,* **-bore, -borne, -bearing.** 1. refrain from. 2. be patient. —**for•bear'ance**, *n.*

for•bid', *v.,* **-bade** or **-bad, -bidden** or **-bid, -bidding.** give order against.

for•bid'ding, *adj.* intimidating or discouraging.

force, *n., v.,* **forced, forcing.** —*n.* 1. strength. 2. coercion. 3. armed group. 4. influence. —*v.* 5. compel. 6. make yield. —**force'ful**, *adj.*

for'ceps, *n.* medical tool for seizing and holding.

for'ci•ble, *adj.* by means of force. —**for'ci•bly**, *adv.*

ford, *n.* 1. place for crossing water by wading. —*v.* 2. cross at ford.

fore, *adj., adv.* 1. at the front. 2. earlier. —*n.* 3. front.

fore'arm', *n.* arm between elbow and wrist.

fore'bear', *n.* ancestor.

fore•bode', *v.,* **-boded, -boding.** portend.

fore'cast', *v.,* **-cast, -casting,** *n.* —*v.* 1. predict. —*n.* 2. prediction.

fore'cas•tle (fōk'səl, fōr'kas'əl), *n.* forward part of the upper deck.

fore•close', *v.,* **-closed, -closing.** deprive of the right to redeem (mortgage, etc.). —**fore•clo'sure**, *n.*

fore'fa'ther, *n.* ancestor.

fore'front', *n.* foremost place.

fore'gone' conclusion, inevitable result.

fore'ground', *n.* nearest area.

fore'head, *n.* part of face above eyes.

fore•warn', *v.* warn in good time.

for'eign, *adj.* 1. of or from another country. 2. from outside. —**for'eign•er**, *n.*

fore'man, *n.* man in charge of work crew or jury.

fore'most', *adj.* first.

fore'noon', *n.* daylight time before noon.

fo•ren'sic, *adj.* of or for public discussion or courtroom procedure.

fore'run'ner, *n.* predecessor.

fore•see', *v.,* **-saw, -seen, -seeing.** see beforehand. —**fore'sight'**, *n.*

fore•shad•ow, *v.* indicate beforehand.

fore'skin', *n.* skin on end of penis.

for'est, *n.* land covered with trees. —**for'est•er**, *n.* —**for'est•ry**, *n.*

fore•stall', *v.* thwart by earlier action.

fore•tell', *v.,* **-told, -telling.** predict.

fore'thought', *n.* 1. prudence. 2. previous calculation.

for•ev'er, *adv.* always.

fore'word', *n.* introductory statement.

for'feit, *n.* 1. penalty. —*v.* 2. lose as forfeit. —*adj.* 3. forfeited. —**for'fei•ture**, *n.*

for•gath'er, *v.* assemble.

forge, *n., v.,* **forged, forging.** —*n.* 1. place for heating metal before shaping. —*v.* 2. form by heating and hammering. 3. imitate fraudulently. 4. move ahead persistently. —**forg'er**, *n.* —**forg'er•y**, *n.*

for•get', *v.,* **-got, -gotten, -getting.** fail to remember. —**for•get'ful**, *adj.*

for•get'-me-not', *n.* small plant with blue flowers.

for•give', *v.,* **-gave, -given, -giving.** grant pardon. —**for•giv'a•ble**, *adj.* —**for•give'ness**, *n.*

for•go', *v.,* **-went, -gone, -going.** do without.

fork, *n.* 1. pronged instrument. 2. point of division. —*v.* 3. branch.

for•lorn', *adj.* abandoned.

form, *n.* 1. shape. 2. mold. 3. custom; standard practice. 4. document to be filled in. —*v.* 5. shape. —**form'a•tive**, *adj.*

for'mal, *adj.* 1. according to custom or standard practice. 2. ceremonious. 3. precisely stated. —**for'mal•ly**, *adv.* —**for'mal•ize'**, *v.*

form•al'de•hyde', *n.* solution used as disinfectant, etc.

for•mal'i•ty, *n., pl.* **-ties.** 1. accordance with custom. 2. act done as matter of standard practice.

for'mat, *n.* general design or arrangement.

for•ma'tion, *n.* 1. act or instance of forming. 2. material that forms. 3. pattern of ships, aircraft, etc., moving together.

form'a•tive, *adj.* 1. giving or acquiring form. 2. that shape or mature one's personality, etc.

for'mer, *adj.* 1. earlier. 2. first-mentioned. —**for'mer•ly**, *adv.*

for'mi•da•ble, *adj.* awesome.

for'mu•la, *n., pl.* **-las, -lae.** 1. scientific description. 2. set form of words.

for'mu•late', *v.,* **-lated, -lating.** state systematically. —**for'mu•la'tion**, *n.*

for'ni•cate', *v.,* **-cated, -cating.** have illicit sexual relations. —**for'ni•ca'tion**, *n.* —**for'ni•ca'tor**, *n.*

for•sake', *v.,* **-sook, -saken, -saking.** desert; abandon.

for•swear', *v.,* **-swore, -sworn, -swearing.** 1. renounce. 2. perjure.

for•syth'i•a, *n.* shrub bearing yellow flowers.

fort, *n.* fortified place.

forte (fôrt), *n.* 1. one's strong point. —*adv.* (fôr'tā). 2. *Music.* loudly.

forth, *adv.* 1. onward. 2. into view. 3. abroad.

forth'com'ing, *adj.* about to appear.

forth'right', *adj.* direct in manner or speech.

forth'with', *adv.* at once.

for'ti•fi•ca'tion, *n.* defensive military construction.

for'ti•fy', *v.,* **-fied, -fying.** strengthen.

for•tis'si•mo', *adj., adv. Music.* very loud.

for'ti•tude', *n.* patient courage.

fort'night', *n.* two weeks.

for'tress, *n.* fortified place.

for•tu'i•tous (-tyoo'-), *adj.* accidental. —**for•tu'i•tous•ly**, *adv.* —**for•tu'i•ty**, *n.*

for'tu•nate, *adj.* lucky. —**for'tu•nate•ly**, *adv.*

for'tune, *n.* 1. wealth. 2. luck.

for'ty, *n., adj.* ten times four. —**for'ti•eth**, *adj., n.*

fo'rum, *n.* assembly for public discussion.

for'ward, *adv.* 1. onward. —*adj.* 2. advanced. 3. bold. —*v.* 4. send on.

fos'sil, *n.* petrified remains of animal or plant. —**fos'sil•ize'**, *v.*

fos'ter, *v.* 1. promote growth. —*adj.* 2. reared in a family but not related.

foul, *adj.* 1. filthy; dirty. 2. abominable. 3. unfair. —*n.* 4. violation of rules in game. —*v.* 5. make or become foul. 6. entangle. —**foul'ly**, *adv.*

found, *v.* establish.

foun•da'tion, *n.* 1. base for building, etc. 2. organization endowed for public benefit. 3. act of founding.

foun′der, *v.* 1. fill with water and sink. 2. go lame. —*n.* 3. person who founds.

found′ling, *n.* abandoned child.

found′ry, *n., pl.* **-ries.** place where molten metal is cast.

foun′tain, *n.* 1. spring of water. 2. source. Also, **fount.**

four, *n., adj.* three plus one. —**fourth,** *n., adj.*

four′teen′, *n., adj.* ten plus four. —**four′teenth′,** *adj., n.*

fowl, *n.* bird, esp. hen or rooster.

fox, *n.* carnivorous animal of dog family.

fox′glove′, *n.* tall plant with bell-shaped flowers.

fox′hole′, *n.* small pit used for cover in battle.

fox trot, dance for couples.

fox′y, *adj.,* **-ier, -iest.** cunning.

foy′er, *n.* lobby.

fra′cas (frā′-), *n.* tumult.

frac′tion, *n.* part of whole. —**frac′-tion•al,** *adj.*

frac′tious, *adj.* unruly.

frac′ture, *n., v.,* **-tured, -turing.** —*n.* 1. break. —*v.* 2. break or crack.

frag′ile, *adj.* easily damaged. —**fra•gil′i•ty,** *n.*

frag′ment, *n.* 1. broken part. 2. bit. —**frag′men•tar′•y,** *adj.*

fra′grance, *n.* pleasant smell. —**fra′-grant,** *adj.*

frail, *adj.* weak; fragile. —**frail′ty,** *n.*

frame, *n., v.,* **framed, framing.** —*n.* 1. enclosing border. 2. skeleton. —*v.* 3. devise. 4. put in frame. —**frame′-work′,** *n.*

franc (frangk), *n.* French coin.

fran′chise (-chīz), *n.* 1. right to vote. 2. right to do business.

frank, *adj.* 1. candid. —*v.* 2. mail without charge.

frank′furt•er, *n.* small sausage.

frank′in•cense′ (-sens′), *n.* aromatic resin.

fran′tic, *adj.* wildly excited. —**fran′ti•cal•ly,** *adv.*

fra•ter′nal, *adj.* brotherly.

fra•ter′ni•ty, *n., pl.* **-ties.** male society.

frat′er•nize′, *v.,* **-nized, -nizing.** associate fraternally or intimately. —**frat′er•ni•za′tion,** *n.*

fraud, *n.* trickery. —**fraud′u•lent,** *adj.* —**fraud′u•lent•ly,** *adv.*

fraught, *adj.* full; charged.

fray, *n.* 1. brawl. —*v.* 2. ravel.

fraz′zle, *v.,* **-zled, -zling,** *n. Informal.* —*v.* 1. fray. 2. fatigue. —*n.* 3. state of fatigue.

freak, *n.* unnaturally formed creature or object.

freck′le, *n.* small brownish spot on skin.

free, *adj.,* **freer, freest,** *adv., v.,* **freed, freeing.** —*adj.* 1. having personal rights or liberty. 2. independent. 3. open. 4. provided without charge. —*adv.* 5. without charge. —*v.* 6. make free. —**free′dom,** *n.*

free′boot′er, *n.* pirate.

free′-for-all′, *n. Informal.* brawl; melee.

free′lance′, *adj., n., v.,* **-lanced, -lancing.** *adj.* 1. hiring out one's work job by job. —*n.* 2. Also, **free′-lanc′er.** freelance worker. —*v.* 3. work as freelance.

free′think′er, *n.* person with original religious opinions.

free′way′, *n.* major highway.

freeze, *v.,* **froze, frozen, freezing,** *n.* —*v.* 1. harden into ice. 2. fix (prices, etc.) at a specific level. 3. make unnegotiable. —*n.* 4. act or instance of freezing. —**freez′er,** *n.*

freight, *n.* 1. conveyance of goods. 2. goods conveyed. 3. price paid.

freight′er, *n.* ship carrying mainly freight.

French, *n.* language or people of France. —**French,** *adj.* —**French′-man,** *n.* —**French′wom′an,** *n.fem.*

French horn, coiled brass wind instrument.

fre•net′ic, *adj.* frantic.

fren′zy, *n., pl.* **-zies.** wild excitement.

fre′quen•cy, *n., pl.* **-cies.** 1. state of being frequent. 2. rate of recurrence. 3. *Physics.* number of cycles in a unit of time.

fre′quent, *adj.* 1. occurring often. —*v.* (fri kwent′). 2. visit often.

fres′co, *n., pl.* **-coes, -cos.** painting on damp plaster.

fresh, *adj.* 1. new. 2. not salt. 3. *Informal.* impudent. —**fresh′en,** *v.* —**fresh′ly,** *adv.* —**fresh′ness,** *n.*

fresh′et, *n.* sudden flood.

fresh′man, *n., pl.* **-men.** first-year student.

fret, *n., v.,* **fretted, fretting.** —*n.* 1. vexation. 2. interlaced design. —*v.* 3. ornament with fret. 4. worry. —**fret′ful,** *adj.* —**fret′work′,** *n.*

fri′a•ble, *adj.* crumbly.

fri′ar, *n.* member of Roman Catholic monastic order.

fric′as•see′, *n.* stewed meat or fowl.

fric′tion, *n.* 1. act or effect of rubbing together. 2. conflict. —**fric′tion•al,** *adj.*

Fri′day, *n.* sixth day of week.

friend, *n.* 1. person attached to another by personal regard. 2. (*cap.*) Quaker; member of **Society of Friends,** a Christian sect. —**friend′ly,** *adj.* —**friend′ship,** *n.*

frieze (frēz), *n.* decorative band.

frig′ate (frig′it), *n.* 1. fast sailing warship. 2. destroyerlike warship.

fright, *n.* 1. sudden fear. 2. shocking thing. —**fright′en,** *v.*

fright′ful, *adj.* 1. causing fright. 2. *Informal.* ugly; tasteless.

fright′ful•ly, *adv. Informal.* very.

frig′id, *adj.* 1. very cold. 2. coldly disapproving. 3. lacking sexual appetite. —**fri•gid′i•ty, frig′id•ness,** *n.*

frill, *n.* 1. ruffle. 2. unnecessary feature. —*v.* 3. ruffle. —**frill′y,** *adj.*

fringe, *n.* border of lengths of thread, etc.

frip′per•y, *n., pl.* **-peries.** cheap finery.

frisk, *v.* leap playfully. —**frisk′y,** *adj.*

frit′ter, *v.* 1. squander little by little. —*n.* 2. fried batter cake.

friv′o•lous, *adj.* not serious or appropriate. —**fri•vol′i•ty,** *n.*

friz, *v., n.* curl.

fro, *adv.* from; back.

frock, *n.* 1. dress. 2. loose robe.

frog, *n.* 1. small, tailless, web-footed amphibian. 2. hoarseness.

frol′ic, *n., v.,* **-icked, -icking.** —*n.* 1. fun; gaiety. —*v.* 2. play merrily.

from, *prep.* 1. out of. 2. because of. 3. starting at.

frond, *n.* divided leaf.

front, *n.* 1. foremost part. 2. area of battle. 3. appearance; pretense. 4. false operation concealing illegal activity. —*adj.* 5. of or at the front. —*v.* 6. face. —**fron′tal,** *adj.*

front′age, *n.* front extent of property.

fron•tier′, *n.* 1. border of a country. 2. outer edge of civilization. —**fron•tiers′man,** *n.*

fron′tis•piece′, *n.* picture preceding title page.

frost, *n.* 1. state of freezing. 2. cover of ice particles. —*v.* 3. cover with frost or frosting. —**frost′y,** *adj.*

frost′bite′, *n.* gangrenous condition caused by extreme cold.

frost′ing, *n.* 1. sweet preparation for covering cakes. 2. lusterless finish for glass, etc.

froth, *n., v.* foam. —**froth′y,** *adj.*

fro′ward, *adj.* perverse.

frown, *v.* 1. show concentration or displeasure on face. —*n.* 2. frowning look.

frowz′y, *adj.* **-ier, -iest.** slovenly.

fruc′ti•fy′, *v.,* **-fied, -fying.** 1. bear fruit. 2. make productive. —**fruc′ti•fi•ca′tion,** *n.*

fru′gal, *adj.* thrifty. —**fru•gal′i•ty,** *n.*

fruit, *n.* 1. edible product of a plant. 2. result.

fruit′ful, *adj.* productive; successful.

fruit′less, *adj.* vain; without success.

fru•i′tion, *n.* attainment.

frus′trate′, *v.,* **-trated, -trating.** thwart. —**frus•tra′tion,** *n.*

frus′tum, *n.* segment of conical solid with parallel top and base.

fry, *v.,* **fried, frying,** *n., pl.* **fries,** (for 4) **fry.** —*v.* 1. cook in fat over direct heat. —*n.* 2. something fried. 3. feast of fried things. 4. young of fishes.

fuch′sia (fyoo′shə), *n.* plant with drooping flowers.

fudge, *n.* kind of candy.

fuel, *n., v.,* **-eled, -eling.** —*n.* 1. substance that maintains fire. —*v.* 2. supply with or take in fuel.

fu′gi•tive, *n.* 1. fleeing person. —*adj.* 2. fleeing. 3. impermanent.

ful′crum, *n.* support on which lever turns.

ful•fill′, *v.* 1. carry out. 2. satisfy. —**ful•fill′ment, ful•fil′ment,** *n.*

full, *adj.* 1. filled. 2. complete. 3. abundant. —*adv.* 4. completely. 5. very. —**ful′ly,** *adv.* —**full′ness,** *n.*

full′-fledged′, *adj.* fully developed.

ful′mi•nate′, *v.,* **-nated, -nating,** *n.* —*v.* 1. explode loudly. 2. issue denunciations. —*n.* 3. explosive chemical salt. —**ful′mi•na′tion,** *n.*

ful′some, *adj.* excessive.

fum′ble, *v.,* **-bled, -bling,** *n.* —*v.* 1. grope clumsily. 2. drop. —*n.* 3. act of fumbling.

fume, *n., v.,* **fumed, fuming.** —*n.* 1. vapor. —*v.* 2. emit or treat fumes. 3. show anger.

fu′mi•gate′, *v.,* **-gated, -gating.** disinfect with fumes. —**fu′mi•ga′tion,** *n.*

fun, *n.* play; joking.

func′tion, *n.* 1. proper activity. 2. formal social gathering. —*v.* 3. act; operate. —**func′tion•al,** *adj.*

func′tion•ar′y, *n., pl.* **-aries.** official.

fund, *n.* 1. stock of money. —*v.* 2. pay for.

fun′da•men′tal, *adj.* 1. basic. —*n.* 2. basic principle. —**fun′da•men′tal•ly,** *adv.*

fun′da•men′tal•ist, *n.* believer in literal interpretation of Bible. —**fun′da•men′tal•ism,** *n.*

fu′ner•al, *n.* burial rite. —**fu′ner•al,** *adj.*

fu•ne′re•al, *adj.* 1. mournful. 2. of funerals.

fun′gus, *n., pl.* **fungi** (-jī). plant of group including mushrooms and molds. —**fun′gous,** *adj.*

funk, *n. Informal.* fear or depression.

fun′nel, *n.* 1. cone-shaped tube. 2. smokestack of vessel.

fun′ny, *adj.,* **-nier, -niest.** 1. amusing. 2. *Informal.* strange.

fur, *n., v.,* **furred, furring.** —*n.* 1. thick hairy skin of animal. 2. garment made of fur. —*v.* 3. trim with fur. —**fur′ry,** *adj.*

fur′be•low′, *n.* showy trimming.

fur′bish, *v.* polish; renew.

fu′ri•ous, *adj.* 1. full of fury. 2. violent. —**fu′ri•ous•ly,** *adv.*

furl, *v.* roll tightly.

fur′long, *n.* one eighth of mile; 220 yards.

fur′lough, *n.* 1. leave of absence. 2. temporary layoff from work. —*v.* 3. give a furlough to.

fur′nace, *n.* structure in which to generate heat.

fur′nish, *v.* 1. provide. 2. fit out with furniture.

fur′nish•ing, *n.* 1. article of furniture, etc. 2. clothing accessory.

fur′ni•ture, *n.* tables, chairs, beds, etc.

fu′ror, *n.* general excitement.

fur′ri•er, *n.* dealer or worker in furs.

fur′row, *n.* 1. trench made by plow. 2. wrinkle. —*v.* 3. make furrows in.

fur′ther, *adv.* 1. to a greater distance or extent. 2. moreover. —*adj.* 3. more. —*v.* 4. promote. —**fur′ther•ance,** *n.*

fur′ther•more′, *adv.* in addition.

fur′thest, *adj.* 1. most distant or remote. —*adv.* 2. to greatest distance.

fur′tive, *adj.* stealthy. —**fur′tive•ly,** *adv.* —**fur′tive•ness,** *n.*

fu′ry, *n., pl.* **-ries.** 1. violent passion, esp. anger. 2. violence.

furze, *n.* low evergreen shrub.

fuse, *n., v.,* **fused, fusing.** —*n.* 1. safety device that breaks an electrical connection under excessive current. 2. Also, **fuze.** device for igniting explosive. —*v.* 3. blend, esp. by melting together. —**fu′si•ble,** *adj.* —**fu′sion,** *n.*

fu′se•lage′ (fyoo′sə läzh′), *n.* framework of an airplane.

fu′sil•lade′ (fyoo′sə lād′), *n.* simultaneous gunfire.

fuss, *n.* 1. needless concern or activity. —*v.* 2. make or put into fuss. —**fuss′y,** *adj.*

fu′tile, *adj.* useless; unsuccessful. —**fu•til′i•ty,** *n.*

fu′ture, *n.* 1. time to come. —*adj.* 2. that is to come. —**fu•tu′ri•ty,** *n.*

fuzz, *n.* fluff. —**fuzz′y,** *adj.* —**fuzz′i•ness,** *n.*

G

G, g, *n.* 1. seventh letter of English alphabet. 2. suitable for all ages: motion-picture classification.

gab, *n., v.,* **gabbed, gabbing.** *Informal.* chatter. —**gab′by,** *adj.*

gab′ar•dine′ (-dēn′), *n.* firm, woven fabric.

ga′ble, *n.* triangular wall from eaves to roof ridge.

gad, *v.,* **gadded, gadding.** wander restlessly.

gad′fly′, *n., pl.* **-flies.** annoyingly critical person.

gadg′et, *n. Informal.* any ingenious device.

gaff, *n.* 1. hook for landing fish. 2. spar on the upper edge of fore-and-aft sail.

gag, *v.,* **gagged, gagging,** *n.* —*v.* 1. stop up mouth to keep (person) silent. 2. suppress statements of. 3. retch. —*n.* 4. something that gags. 5. *Informal.* joke.

gage, *n., v.,* **gaged, gaging.** —*n.* 1. token of challenge. 2. pledge. 3. gauge. —*v.* 4. gauge.

gag′gle, *n.* flock of geese or persons.

gai′e•ty, *n.* merriment.

gai′ly, *adv.* merrily.

gain, *v.* 1. obtain. 2. earn. 3. improve. 4. move faster than another. —*n.* 5. profit. —**gain′ful,** *adj.*

gain′say′, *v.,* **-said, -saying.** contradict.

gait, *n.* manner of walking.

gai′ter, *n.* 1. covering for lower leg, worn over the shoe. 2. kind of shoe.

ga′la, *adj.* festive.

gal′ax•y, *n., pl.* **-axies.** 1. (*often cap.*) Milky Way. 2. brilliant assemblage.

gale, *n.* strong wind.

gall (gôl), *v.* 1. chafe. 2. irritate. —*n.* 3. sore due to rubbing. 4. bile. 5. *Informal.* impudence. 6. abnormal growth on plants.

gal′lant, *adj.* chivalrous. —**gal′lant•ry,** *n.*

gal′le•on, *n.* large sailing vessel.

gal′ler•y, *n., pl.* **-leries.** 1. corridor. 2. balcony. 3. place for art exhibits.

gal′ley, *n., pl.* **-leys.** 1. vessel propelled by many oars. 2. kitchen of ship.

gal′li•vant′, *v.* gad frivolously.

gal′lon, *n.* unit of capacity equal to 4 quarts.

gal′lop, *v.* 1. run at full speed. —*n.* 2. fast gait.

gal′lows, *n.* wooden frame for execution by hanging.

gall′stone′, *n.* stone formed in bile passages.

ga•lore′, *adv.* in abundance.

ga•losh′es, *n.pl.* overshoes.

gal•van′ic, *adj.* 1. producing or caused by electric current. 2. stimulating; exciting.

gal′va•nize′, *v.,* **-nized, -nizing.** 1. stimulate by or as by galvanic current. 2. coat with zinc.

gam′bit, *n.* 1. sacrificial move in chess. 2. clever tactic.

gam′ble, *v.,* **-bled, -bling,** *n.* —*v.* 1. play for stakes at game of chance. —*n.* 2. *Informal.* uncertain venture. —**gam′bler,** *n.*

gam′bol, *v.,* **-boled, -boling,** *n.* frolic.

game, *n.* 1. pastime or contest. 2. wild animals, hunted for sport. —*adj.* 3. brave and willing. 4. lame.

gam′in, *n.* street urchin. —**gam′ine** (-ēn), *n.fem.*

gam′ut, *n.* full range.

gan′der, *n.* male goose.

gang, *n.* 1. group; band. 2. work crew. 3. band of criminals.

gan′gling, *adj.* awkwardly tall and thin.

gan′gli•on (-ən), *n.* nerve center.

gang′plank′, *n.* temporary bridge to docked vessel.

gan′grene (gang′grēn), *n.* dying of tissue. —**gan′gre•nous,** *adj.*

gang′ster, *n.* member of criminal gang.

gang′way′, *n.* 1. entrance to ship. 2. narrow passage. —*interj.* 3. (gang′ wā′). make way!

gant′let, *n.* double row of men beating offender passing between them.

gaol (jāl), *n., v. Brit.* jail.

gap, *n.* 1. opening; vacant space. 2. ravine.

gape, *v.,* **gaped, gaping.** 1. open mouth as in wonder. 2. open wide.

gar, *n.* long, slim fish.

ga•rage′, *n.* place where motor vehicles are kept or repaired.

garb, *n.* 1. clothes. —*v.* 2. clothe.

gar′bage, *n.* kitchen refuse.

gar′ble, *v.,* **-bled, -bling.** misquote or mix up.

gar′den, *n.* 1. area for growing plants. —*v.* 2. make or tend garden. —**gar′den•er,** *n.*

gar•de′nia, *n.* flowering evergreen shrub.

gar′gle, *v.,* **-gled, -gling,** *n.* —*v.* 1. rinse throat. —*n.* 2. liquid for gargling.

gar′goyle, *n.* grotesque head forming rain outlet.

gar′ish, *adj.* glaring; showy.

gar′land, *n.* 1. wreath of flowers, etc. —*v.* 2. deck with garland.

gar′lic, *n.* plant with edible, pungent bulb. —**gar′lick•y,** *adj.*

gar′ment, *n.* article of dress.

gar′ner, *v.* store.

gar′net, *n.* deep-red gem.

gar′nish, *v.* 1. adorn. —*n.* 2. decoration.

gar′nish•ee′, *v.,* **-nisheed, -nisheeing.** attach (money or property of defendant).

gar′ret, *n.* attic.

gar′ri•son, *n.* 1. body of defending troops. —*v.* 2. provide with garrison.

gar•rote′ (-gə rot′), *n., v.,* **-roted, -roting.** —*n.* 1. strangulation. —*v.* 2. strangle.

gar′ru•lous, *adj.* talkative. —**gar•ru′li•ty,** *n.*

gar′ter, *n.* fastening to hold up stocking.

gas, *n., pl.* **gases,** *v.,* **gassed, gassing.** —*n.* 1. fluid substance, often burned for light or heat. 2. gasoline. —*v.* 3. overcome with gas. —**gas′e•ous,** *adj.*

gash, *n.* 1. long deep cut. —*v.* 2. make gash in.

gas′ket, *n.* ring or strip used as packing.

gas′o•hol′, *n.* mixture of gasoline and alcohol, used as auto fuel.

gas′o•line′, *n.* inflammable liquid from petroleum, used esp. as motor fuel.

gasp, *n.* 1. sudden short breath. —*v.* 2. breathe in gasps.

gas′tric, *adj.* of stomachs.

gas′tro•nom′i•cal, *adj.* of good eating.

gate, *n.* movable hinged barrier.

gate′way′, *n.* passage or entrance.

gath′er, *v.* 1. bring or come together. 2. infer. 3. harvest. —*n.* 4. pucker.

gauche (gōsh), *adj.* unsophisticated, socially clumsy.

gaud′y, *adj.,* **gaudier, gaudiest.** vulgarly showy.

gauge (gāj), *v.,* **gauged, gauging,** *n.* —*v.* 1. estimate. 2. measure. —*n.* 3. standard of measure. 4. distance between railroad rails.

gaunt, *adj.* haggard; bleak.

gaunt′let, *n.* 1. large-cuffed glove. 2. gantlet.

gauze (gôz), *n.* transparent fabric. —**gauz′y,** *adj.*

gav′el, *n.* chairman's mallet.

gawk, *v.* stare stupidly.

gawk′y, *adj.* clumsy. —**gawk′i•ness.** *n.*

gay, *adj.,* **gayer, gayest,** *n.* —*adj.* 1. joyous. 2. bright. 3. *Slang.* homosexual. —*n.* 4. *Slang.* homosexual. —**gay′ly,** *adv.*

gaze, *v.,* **gazed, gazing,** *n.* —*v.* 1. look steadily. —*n.* 2. steady look.

ga•zelle′, *n.* small, graceful antelope.

ga•zette′, *n.* newspaper.

gaz′et•teer′ (-tēr′), *n.* geographical dictionary.

gear, *n.* 1. toothed wheel that engages with another. 2. equipment. —*v.* 3. connect by gears. 4. adjust.

gee (jē), *v.,* **geed, geeing.** *interj.* turn right.

Gei′ger counter (gī′gər), instrument for measuring radioactivity.

gei′sha (gā′shə), *n.* Japanese woman entertainer.

gel′a•tin, *n.* substance from animal skins, etc., used in jellies, glue, etc. —**ge•lat′i•nous,** *adj.*

geld′ing, *n.* castrated male horse.

gel′id (jel′id), *adj.* icy.

gem, *n.* precious stone.

gen′darme (zhän′därm), *n.* French policeman.

gen′der, *n. Gram.* set of classes including all nouns, distinguished as masculine, feminine, neuter.

gene, *n.* biological unit that carries inherited traits.

ge·ne·al′o·gy, *n., pl.* **-gies.** study or account of ancestry.

gen′er·al, *adj.* 1. of or including all. 2. usual. 3. undetailed. —*n.* 4. highest-ranking army officer. —**gen′er·al·ly**, *adv.*

gen′er·al′i·ty, *n., pl.* **-ties.** general statement offered as accepted truth.

gen′er·al·ize′, *v.,* **-ized, -izing.** make generalities. —**gen′er·al·i·za′tion,** *n.*

gen′er·ate′, *v.,* **-ated, -ating.** produce. —**gen′er·a′tive,** *adj.*

gen′er·a′tion, *n.* 1. all individuals born in one period. 2. such period (about 30 years). 3. production.

gen′er·a′tor, *n.* device for producing electricity, gas, etc.

ge·ner′ic, *adj.* 1. of entire categories. 2. (of merchandise) unbranded.

gen′er·ous, *adj.* 1. giving freely. 2. abundant. —**gen′er·os′i·ty,** *n.*

gen′e·sis (jen′-), *n.* birth or origin.

ge·net′ics, *n.* science of heredity. —**ge·net′ic,** *adj.*

gen′ial (jēn′-), *adj.* openly friendly. —**ge′ni·al′i·ty,** *n.* —**gen′ial·ly,** *adv.*

ge′nie (jē′nē), *n.* spirit.

gen′i·tals, *n.pl.* sexual organs. —**gen′i·tal,** *adj.*

gen′ius (jēn′-), *n., pl.* **-iuses.** 1. exceptional natural ability. 2. person having such ability.

gen′o·cide′ (jen′ə-), *n.* planned extermination of national or racial group.

gen·teel′, *adj.* self-consciously refined. —**gen·til′i·ty,** *n.*

gen′tian (jen′shən), *n.* herb with blue flowers.

gen′tile (-tīl), *adj.* not Jewish. —**gentile,** *n.*

gen′tle, *adj.,* **-tler, -tlest.** 1. mild; kindly. 2. respectable. 3. careful in handling things. —**gen′tle·ness,** *n.* —**gen′tly,** *adv.*

gen′tle·man, *n., pl.* **-men.** man of good breeding and manners.

gen′tri·fi·ca′tion, *n.* replacement of existing population by others with more wealth or status. —**gen′tri·fy,** *v.*

gen′try, *n.* wellborn people.

gen′u·flect′ (jen′yŏŏ-), *v.* kneel partway in reverence. —**gen′u·flec′tion,** *n.*

gen′u·ine (-in), *adj.* real.

ge′nus (jē′-), *n., pl.* **genera, genuses.** biological group including several species.

ge·og′ra·phy, *n.* study of earth's surface, climate, etc. —**ge′o·graph′i·cal,** *adj.*

ge·ol′o·gy, *n.* science of earth's structure. —**ge′o·log′i·cal,** *adj.*

ge·om′e·try, *n.* branch of mathematics dealing with shapes. —**ge′o·met′ri·cal,** *adj.*

ge′o·pol′i·tics, *n.* study of politics in relation to geography. —**ge′o·po·lit′i·cal,** *adj.*

ge·ra′ni·um, *n.* small plant with showy flowers.

ger′i·at′rics (jer′-), *n.* branch of medicine dealing with aged persons. —**ger′i·at′ric,** *adj.*

germ, *n.* 1. microscopic disease-producing organism. 2. seed or origin.

Ger′man, *n.* native or language of Germany. —**German,** *adj.*

ger·mane′, *adj.* pertinent.

ger′mi·cide′, *n.* agent that kills germs. —**ger′mi·cid′al,** *adj.*

ger′mi·nate′, *v.,* **-nated, -nating.** begin to grow.

ger′und (jer′-), *n.* noun form of a verb.

ges·ta′tion (jes-), *n.* period of being carried in womb.

ges·tic′u·late′, *v.,* **-lated, -lating.** make gestures. —**ges·tic′u·la′tion,** *n.*

ges′ture, *n., v.,* **-tured, -turing.** —*n.* 1. expressive movement of body, head, etc. 2. act demonstrating attitude or emotion. —*v.* 3. make expressive movements.

get, *v.,* **got, got** or **gotten, getting.** 1. obtain. 2. cause to be or do. 3. be obliged to. 4. arrive. 5. become.

gew′gaw (gyŏō′-), *n.* gaudy ornament.

gey′ser (gī′zər), *n.* hot spring that emits jets of water.

ghast′ly, *adj.* 1. frightful. 2. deathly pale.

gher′kin (gûr′-), *n.* small cucumber.

ghet′to, *n.* 1. (formerly) Jewish part of city. 2. city area in which poor minorities are forced to live.

ghost, *n.* disembodied soul of dead person. —**ghost′ly,** *adj.*

ghoul (gŏōl), *n.* 1. spirit that preys on dead. 2. person morbidly interested in misfortunes. —**ghoul′ish,** *adj.*

G.I., *Informal.* enlisted soldier.

gi′ant, *n.* 1. man of superhuman size or strength. 2. man of extraordinary

accomplishments. —**gi′ant·ess,** *n.fem.*

gib′ber (jib′-), *v.* speak unintelligibly. —**gib′ber·ish,** *n.*

gib′bet (jib′-), *n.* gallows with projecting arm.

gib′bon (gib′-), *n.* small, long-armed ape.

gibe (jīb), *v.,* **gibed, gibing,** *n.* jeer.

gib′lets (jib′-), *n.pl.* heart, liver, and gizzard of a fowl.

gid′dy, *adj.,* **-dier, -diest.** 1. frivolous. 2. dizzy.

gift, *n.* 1. present. 2. act of giving. 3. power of giving. 4. talent.

gift′ed, *adj.* talented.

gi·gan′tic, *adj.* like or befitting giants.

gig′gle, *v.,* **-gled, -gling,** *n.* —*v.* 1. laugh lightly in silly way. —*n.* 2. silly laugh.

gig′o·lo′ (jig′-), *n.* male professional escort.

gild, *v.,* **gilded** or **gilt, gilding.** coat with gold.

gill, *n.* 1. (gil). breathing organ on fish. 2. (jil). unit of liquid measure, ¼ pint (4 fluid ounces).

gilt, *n.* gold used for gilding.

gim′crack′ (jim′-), *n.* useless trifle.

gim′let (gim′-), *n.* small tool for boring holes.

gim′mick, *n. Slang.* device or trick.

gin, *n., v.,* **ginned, ginning.** —*n.* 1. flavored alcoholic drink. 2. machine for separating cotton from its seeds. 3. trap. —*v.* 4. put (cotton) through gin.

gin′ger, *n.* plant with spicy root used in cookery.

gin′ger·ly, *adj.* 1. wary. —*adv.* 2. warily.

ging′ham, *n.* yarn-dyed cotton fabric.

gin′seng (jin′-), *n.* plant with a medicinal root.

gi·raffe′, *n.* tall, long-necked animal of Africa.

gird, *v.,* **girt** or **girded, girding.** 1. encircle with or as with belt. 2. prepare.

gird′er, *n.* horizontal structural beam.

gir′dle, *n., v.,* **-dled, -dling.** —*n.* 1. encircling band. 2. light corset. —*v.* 3. encircle.

girl, *n.* female child or young woman.

girth, *n.* 1. distance around. —*v.* 2. gird.

gist (jist), *n.* essential meaning.

give, *v.,* **gave, given, giving,** *n.* —*v.* 1. bestow. 2. emit. 3. present. 4. yield. —*n.* 5. elasticity.

give′a•way′, *n. Informal.* 1. revealing act, remark, etc. 2. TV show in which contestants compete for prizes.

giv′en, *adj.* preexisting as element of problem.

giz′zard, *n.* muscular stomach of birds.

gla′cier, *n.* mass of ice moving slowly down slope.

glad, *adj.*, **gladder, gladdest.** 1. pleased; happy. 2. causing joy. —**glad′den**, *v.* —**glad′ness**, *n.*

glade, *n.* open space in forest.

glad′i•a′tor, *n.* Roman swordsman fighting for public entertainment.

glad′i•o′lus (glad′ē ō′ləs), *n.* plant bearing spikes of flowers. Also, **glad′i•o′la.**

glad′ly, *adv.* 1. with pleasure. 2. willingly.

glam′our, *n.* alluring charm. —**glam′or•ous**, *adj.* —**glam′or•ous•ly**, *adv.*

glance, *v.*, **glanced, glancing,** *n.* —*v.* 1. look briefly. 2. strike obliquely. —*n.* 3. brief look.

gland, *n.* body organ that secretes some substance. —**glan′du•lar**, *adj.*

glan′ders, *n.* disease of horses.

glare, *n.*, *v.*, **glared, glaring.** —*n.* 1. strong light. 2. fierce look. 3. bright, smooth surface. —*v.* 4. shine with strong light. 5. stare fiercely.

glass, *n.* 1. hard, brittle, transparent substance. 2. (*pl.*) eyeglasses. 3. drinking vessel of glass. 4. anything made of glass. —*adj.* 5. of glass. —*v.* 6. cover with glass. —**glass′y**, *adj.* —**glass′ware′**, *n.*

glaze, *v.*, **glazed, glazing,** *n.* —*v.* 1. furnish with glass. 2. put glossy surface on. 3. make (eyes) expressionless. —*n.* 4. glossy coating.

gla′zier (-zhər), *n.* person who installs glass.

gleam, *n.* 1. flash of light. —*v.* 2. emit gleams.

glean, *v.* gather laboriously, as grain left by reapers. —**glean′ing**, *n.*

glee, *n.* joy; mirth. —**glee′ful**, *adj.*

glen, *n.* narrow valley.

glib, *adj.* suspiciously fluent. —**glib′ly**, *adv.* —**glib′ness**, *n.*

glide, *v.*, **glided, gliding,** *n.* —*v.* 1. move smoothly and gradually. —*n.* 2. gliding movement.

glid′er, *n.* motorless heavier-than-air aircraft.

glim′mer, *n.* 1. faint unsteady light. —*v.* 2. shine faintly.

glimpse, *n.*, *v.*, **glimpsed, glimpsing.** —*n.* 1. brief view. —*v.* 2. catch glimpse of.

glint, *n.*, *v.* gleam.

glis′ten, *v.*, *n.* sparkle. Also, **glit′ter, glis′ter.**

glitch, *n. Slang.* malfunction; hitch.

gloam′ing, *n.* dusk.

gloat, *v.* gaze or speak with unconcealed triumph.

globe, *n.* 1. earth; world. 2. sphere depicting the earth. 3. any sphere. —**glob′al**, *adj.*

glob′ule, (glob′yōol), *n.* small sphere. —**glob′u•lar**, *adj.*

gloom, *n.* 1. low spirits. 2. darkness.

gloom′y, *adj.*, **-ier, -iest.** 1. dejected; low-spirited. 2. depressing. 3. dark; dismal.

glor′i•fied, *adj.* made to seem better than is really so.

glo′ri•fy′, *v.*, **-fied, -fying.** 1. extol. 2. make glorious. —**glor′i•fi•ca′tion**, *n.*

glo′ry, *n.*, *pl.* **glories,** *v.*, **gloried, glorying.** —*n.* 1. great praise or honor. 2. magnificence. 3. heaven. —*v.* 4. exult. —**glor′i•ous**, *adj.*

gloss, *n.* 1. external show. 2. shine. 3. explanation of text. —*v.* 4. put gloss on. 5. annotate. 6. explain away. —**glos′sy**, *adj.*

glos′sa•ry, *n.*, *pl.* **-ries.** list of difficult words with definitions.

glot′tis, *n.* opening at upper part of larynx.

glove, *n.*, *v.*, **gloved, gloving.** —*n.* 1. hand covering with sheath for each finger. —*v.* 2. cover with glove.

glow, *n.* 1. light emitted by heated substance. 2. brightness or warmth. —*v.* 3. shine.

glow′er (glou′-), *v.* 1. frown sullenly. —*n.* 2. frown.

glow′worm′, *n.* kind of firefly.

glu′cose′, *n.* sugar found in fruits.

glue, *n.*, *v.*, **glued, gluing.** —*n.* 1. adhesive substance, esp. from gelatin. —*v.* 2. fasten with glue.

glum, *adj.* gloomily sullen.

glut, *v.*, **glutted, glutting,** *n.* —*v.* 1. feed or fill to excess. —*n.* 2. full supply. 3. surfeit.

glu′ten (glōō′-), *n.* substance left in flour after starch is removed.

glut′ton, *n.* 1. greedy person. 2. weasellike northern animal. —**glut′ton•ous**, *adj.* —**glut′ton•y**, *n.*

glyc′er•in, *n.* sweet, oily alcohol.

gnarl (närl), *n.* knot on a tree.

gnarled (närld), *adj.* bent and distorted.

gnash (nash), *v.* grind (the teeth) together, as in rage.

gnat (nat), *n.* small fly.

gnaw (nô), *v.* wear away by biting.

gnome (nōm), *n.* dwarf in superstition.

gnu (nōō), *n.*, *pl.* **gnus, gnu.** African antelope.

go, *v.*, **went, gone, going.** 1. move; depart. 2. act. 3. become. 4. harmonize.

goad, *n.* 1. pointed stick. 2. stimulus. —*v.* 3. drive with goad. 4. tease; taunt.

goal, *n.* 1. aim. 2. terminal in race or game.

goat, *n.* horned mammal related to sheep.

goat•ee′, *n.* pointed beard.

gob, *n.* 1. mass. 2. *Slang.* sailor.

gob′ble, *v.*, **-bled, -bling,** *n.* —*v.* 1. eat greedily. 2. make cry of male turkey. —*n.* 3. this cry.

gob′ble•de•gook′, *n.* meaningless or roundabout official speech or writing.

gob′bler, *n.* male turkey.

go′-be•tween′, *n.* intermediary.

gob′let, *n.* stemmed glass.

gob′lin, *n.* elf.

God, *n.* 1. Supreme Being. 2. (*l.c.*) deity. —**god′dess**, *n.fem.*

god′ly, *adj.*, **-lier, -liest.** 1. of God or gods. 2. conforming to religion. —**god′li•ness**, *n.*

god′par′ent, *n.* sponsor of child at baptism. —**god′child′**, *n.* —**god′-fath′er**, *n.* —**god′moth′er**, *n.*

god′send′, *n.* anything unexpected but welcome.

goes (gōz), third pers. sing. pres. indic. of **go.**

gog′gles, *n.pl.* protective eyeglasses.

goi′ter, *n.* enlargement of thyroid gland.

gold, *n.* 1. precious yellow metal. 2. bright yellow. —**gold′en**, *adj.*

gold′en•rod′, *n.* plant bearing clusters of yellow flowers.

gold′fish′, *n.* small, gold-colored fish.

golf, *n.* game played on outdoor course with special clubs and small ball.

gon′do•la (gon′də lə, gon dō′lə), *n.* 1. narrow canal boat used in Venice. 2. low-sided freight car. —**gon′do•lier′** (-lēr′), *n.*

gong, *n.* brass or bronze disk sounded with soft hammer.

gon′or•rhe′a (gon′ə rē′ə), *n.* contagious venereal disease.

good, *adj.* 1. morally excellent. 2. of high or adequate quality. 3. kind. 4. skillful. —*n.* 5. benefit. 6. excellence. 7. (*pl.*) possessions. 8. (*pl.*) cloth.

good′ly, *adj.*, **-lier, -liest.** numerous; abundant.

good′-by′, *interj.*, *n.*, *pl.* **-bys.** farewell. Also, **good′-bye′.**

good′will′, *n.* friendly feelings or intentions.

Good Friday, Friday before Easter.

goof, *Informal.* —*n.* 1. fool. 2. blunder. —*v.* 3. blunder.

goose, *n.*, *pl.* **geese.** web-footed water bird.

goose′ber′ry, *n.*, *pl.* **-ries.** tart edible acid fruit.

go′pher, *n.* burrowing rodent.

gore, *n.*, *v.*, **gored, goring.** —*n.* 1. clotted blood. 2. triangular insert of cloth. —*v.* 3. pierce with horn or tusk. 4. finish with gores (def. 2). —**gor′y,** *adj.*

gorge, *n.*, *v.*, **gorged, gorging.** —*n.* 1. narrow rocky cleft. —*v.* 2. stuff with food.

gor′geous, *adj.* splendid.

go•ril′la, *n.* large African ape.

gos′ling, *n.* young goose.

gos′pel, *n.* 1. teachings of Christ and apostles. 2. absolute truth.

gos′sa•mer, *n.* 1. filmy cobweb. —*adj.* 2. like gossamer.

gos′sip, *n.*, *v.*, **-siped, -siping.** —*n.* 1. idle talk, esp. about others. 2. person given to gossip. —*v.* 3. talk idly about others.

gouge, *n.*, *v.*, **gouged, gouging.** —*n.* 1. chisel with hollow blade. —*v.* 2. dig out with gouge. 3. extract by coercion. —**goug′er,** *n.*

gou′lash, *n.* seasoned meat stew.

gourd (gōrd), *n.* dried shell of kind of cucumber.

gour•mand′ (gŏŏr mänd′), *n.* enthusiastic or greedy eater.

gour′met (gŏŏr′mā), *n.* lover of fine food.

gout, *n.* painful disease of joints. —**gout′y,** *adj.*

gov′ern, *v.* 1. rule. 2. influence. 3. regulate.

gov′ern•ess, *n.* woman who teaches children in their home.

gov′ern•ment, *n.* 1. system of rule. 2. political governing body. —**gov′ern•men′tal,** *adj.*

gov′er•nor, *n.* 1. person who governs. 2. device that controls speed.

gown, *n.* 1. woman's dress. 2. loose robe.

grab, *v.*, **grabbed, grabbing,** *n.* —*v.* 1. seize eagerly. —*n.* 2. act of grabbing.

grace, *n.*, *v.*, **graced, gracing.** —*n.* 1. beauty of form, movement, etc. 2. good will. 3. God's love. 4. prayer said at table. —*v.* 5. lend grace to; favor. —**grace′ful,** *adj.* —**grace′less,** *adj.*

gra′cious, *adj.* kind.

gra•da′tion, *n.* change in series of stages.

grade, *n.*, *v.*, **graded, grading.** —*n.* 1. degree in a scale. 2. scholastic division. 3. Also, **gra′di•ent.** slope. —*v.* 4. arrange in grades. 5. level.

grad′u•al, *adj.* changing, moving, etc., by degrees. —**grad′u•al•ly,** *adv.*

grad′u•ate, *n.*, *adj.*, *v.*, **-ated, -ating.** —*n.* (-it). 1. recipient of diploma. —*adj.* (-it). 2. graduated. 3. of or for graduates. —*v.* (-āt′). 4. receive or confer diploma or degree. 5. mark in measuring degrees. —**grad′u•a′tion,** *n.*

graf•fi′to, *n.*, *pl.* **-ti.** casual inscription in public place.

graft, *n.* 1. twig, etc., inserted in another plant to unite with it. 2. profit through dishonest use of one's position. —*v.* 3. make graft. 4. make dishonest profits. —**graft′er,** *n.*

gra′ham, *adj.* made of unsifted whole-wheat flour.

grain, *n.* 1. seed of cereal plant. 2. particle. 3. pattern of wood fibers. —**grain′y,** *adj.*

gram, *n.* metric unit of weight.

gram′mar, *n.* features of a language as a whole. —**gram•mat′i•cal,** *adj.* —**gram•mar′i•an,** *n.*

gran′a•ry (grān′-), *n.*, *pl.* **-ries.** storehouse for grain.

grand, *adj.* 1. large; major. 2. impressive.

grand′child′, *n.* child of one's son or daughter. —**grand′son′,** *n.* —**grand′daugh′ter,** *n.fem.*

gran•dee′ (-dē′), *n.* nobleman.

gran′deur, *n.* imposing greatness.

gran′di•ose′, *adj.* grand or pompous.

grand′par′ent, *n.* parent of parent. —**grand′fa′ther,** *n.* —**grand′moth′er,** *n.fem.*

grand′stand′, *n.* sloped open-air place for spectators.

grange, *n.* farmers' organization.

gran′ite, *n.* granular rock.

gra•no′la, *n.* cereal of dried fruit, grains, nuts, etc.

grant, *v.* 1. bestow. 2. admit. —*n.* 3. thing granted.

gran′u•late′, *v.*, **-lated, -lating.** form into granules. —**gran′u•la′tion,** *n.*

gran′ule, *n.* small grain. —**gran′u•lar,** *adj.*

grape, *n.* smooth-skinned fruit of **grape′vine′.**

grape′fruit′, *n.* large yellow citrus fruit.

graph, *n.* diagram showing relations by lines, etc.

graph′ic, *adj.* 1. vivid. 2. of writing, painting, etc. —**graph′i•cal•ly,** *adv.*

graph′ite (-īt), *n.* soft, dark mineral.

grap′nel, *n.* hooked device for grasping.

grap′ple, *n.*, *v.*, **-pled, -pling.** —*n.* 1. hook for grasping. —*v.* 2. try to grasp. 3. try to cope.

grasp, *v.* 1. seize and hold. 2. understand. —*n.* 3. act of gripping. 4. mastery.

grasp′ing, *adj.* greedy.

grass, *n.* 1. ground-covering herbage. 2. cereal plant.

grass′hop′per, *n.* leaping insect.

grate, *v.*, **grated, grating,** *n.* —*v.* 1. irritate. 2. make harsh sound. 3. rub into small bits. —*n.* 4. Also, **grat′ing.** metal framework. —**grat′er,** *n.*

grate′ful, *adj.* 1. thankful. 2. welcome as news. —**grate′ful•ly,** *adv.*

grat′i•fy′, *v.*, **-fied, -fying.** please. —**grat′i•fi•ca′tion,** *n.*

gra′tis (grat′is), *adv.*, *adj.* free of charge.

grat′i•tude′, *n.* thankfulness.

gra•tu′i•tous (-tōō′-), *adj.* 1. free of charge. 2. without reasonable cause.

gra•tu′i•ty, *n.*, *pl.* **-ties.** tip.

grave, *n.* 1. place of or excavation for burial. —*adj.* 2. solemn. 3. important. —**grave′yard′,** *n.*

grav′el, *n.* small stones.

grav′i•ta′tion, *n.* force of attraction between bodies. —**grav′i•tate′,** *v.*

grav′i•ty, *n.* 1. force attracting bodies to the earth's center. 2. serious character.

gra′vy, *n.*, *pl.* **-vies.** juices from cooking meat.

gray, *n.* 1. color between black and white. —*adj.* 2. of this color. 3. ambiguous. 4. vaguely depressing.

gray matter, nerve tissue of brain and spinal cord.

graze, *v.*, **grazed, grazing.** 1. feed on grass. 2. brush in passing.

grease, *n., v.,* **greased, greasing.** —*n.* 1. animal fat. —*v.* 2. put grease on or in. —**greas′y,** *adj.*

great, *adj.* 1. very large. 2. important. —**great′ly,** *adv.*

grebe (grēb), *n.* diving bird.

greed, *n.* excessive desire. —**greed′y,** *adj.*

Greek, *n.* native or language of Greece. —**Greek,** *adj.*

green, *adj.* 1. of color of vegetation. 2. unripe. 3. inexperienced. —*n.* 4. green color. 5. grassy land.

green′er•y, *n.* plants; foliage.

green′house′, *n.* building where plants are grown.

greet, *v.* 1. address in meeting. 2. react to; receive. —**greet′ing,** *n.*

gre•gar′i•ous (gri gâr′-), *adj.* fond of company.

grem′lin, *n.* mischievous elf.

gre•nade′, *n.* explosive hurled missile.

gren′a•dier′, *n. Brit.* member of special infantry regiment.

grey, *n., adj.* gray.

grey′hound′, *n.* slender fleet-footed dog.

grid, *n.* 1. covering of crossed bars. 2. system of crossed lines.

grid′dle, *n.* shallow frying pan or plate.

grid′i′ron, *n.* 1. grill. 2. football field.

grief, *n.* keen sorrow.

griev′ance, *n.* 1. wrong. 2. complaint against wrong.

griev′ous, *adj.* causing grief, pain, etc.

grieve, *v.,* **grieved, grieving.** feel sorrow; inflict sorrow on.

grill, *n.* 1. barred utensil for broiling. —*v.* 2. broil on grill. 3. question persistently.

grille (gril), *n.* ornamental metal barrier.

grim, *adj.,* **grimmer, grimmest.** 1. stern. 2. harshly threatening. —**grim′ly,** *adv.* —**grim′ness,** *n.*

gri•mace′ (*n.* grim′əs, *v.* gri mās′), *n., v.,* **-maced, -macing.** smirk.

grime, *n.* dirt. —**grim′y,** *adj.*

grin, *v.,* **grinned, grinning.** —*v.* 1. smile openly and broadly. —*n.* 2. broad smile.

grind, *v.,* **ground, grinding,** *n.* —*v.* 1. wear, crush, or sharpen by friction. 2. turn crank. —*n.* 3. *Informal.* dreary routine. —**grind′stone,** *n.*

grip, *n., v.,* **gripped, gripping.** —*n.* 1. grasp. 2. handclasp. 3. small suitcase. 4. handle. —*v.* 5. grasp.

gripe, *v.,* **griped, griping,** *n.* —*v.* 1. grasp. 2. produce pain in bowels. 3. *Informal.* complain. —*n.* 4. *Informal.* complaint.

grippe (grip), *n.* influenza.

gris′ly, *adj.,* **-lier, -liest.** gruesome.

grist, *n.* grain to be ground. —**grist′mill′,** *n.*

gris′tle, *n.* cartilage.

grit, *n., v.,* **gritted, gritting.** —*n.* 1. fine particles. 2. courage. —**grit′ty,** *adj.*

grits, *n.pl.* ground grain.

griz′zly, *adj.* gray, as hair or fur. Also, **griz′zled.**

groan, *n.* 1. moan of pain, derision, etc. —*v.* 2. utter groans. —**groan′er,** *n.*

gro′cer, *n.* dealer in foods, etc.

gro′cer•y, *n., pl.* **-ies.** 1. store selling food. 2. (*usually pl.*) food bought at such a store.

grog′gy, *adj.* dizzy. —**grog′gi•ness,** *n.*

groin, *n.* hollow where thigh joins abdomen.

grom′met, *n.* eyelet.

groom, *n.* 1. person in charge of horses or stables. 2. bridegroom. —*v.* 3. make neat.

grooms′man, *n., pl.* **-men.** attendant of bridegroom.

groove, *n., v.,* **grooved, grooving.** —*n.* 1. furrow. —*v.* 2. form groove in.

grope, *v.,* **groped, groping.** feel blindly.

gross, *adj.* 1. before deductions. 2. flagrant. —*n.* 3. amount before deductions. 4. twelve dozen. —**gross′-ly,** *adv.* —**gross′ness,** *n.*

gro•tesque′, *adj.* fantastic.

grot′to, *n., pl.* **-tos, -toes.** cave.

grouch, *Informal.* —*v.* 1. sulk. —*n.* 2. sulky person. 3. sullen mood. —**grouch′y,** *adj.*

ground, *n.* 1. earth's solid surface. 2. tract of land. 3. motive. 4. (*pl.*) dregs. —*adj.* 5. of or on ground. —*v.* 6. instruct in elements. 7. run aground.

ground′hog′, *n.* woodchuck.

ground′work′, *n.* basic work.

group, *n.* 1. number of persons or things placed or considered together. —*v.* 2. place in or form group.

grouse, *n.* game bird of America and Britain.

grove, *n.* small wood.

grov′el, *v.,* **-eled, -eling.** humble oneself, esp. by crouching.

grow, *v.,* **grew, grown, growing.** increase in size; develop. —**grow′er,** *n.*

growl, *n.* 1. guttural, angry sound. —*v.* 2. utter growls.

grown′up′, *n.* adult.

growth, *n.* 1. act of growing. 2. something that has grown.

grub, *n., v.,* **grubbed, grubbing.** —*n.* 1. larva. 2. drudge. 3. *Informal.* food. —*v.* 4. dig.

grub′by, *adj.* 1. dirty. 2. sordid. —**grub′bi•ness,** *n.*

grudge, *n.* lasting malice.

gru′el, *n., v.,* **-eled, -eling.** —*n.* 1. thin cereal. —*v.* 2. exhaust.

grue′some, *adj.* revoltingly sinister.

gruff, *adj.* surly.

grum′ble, *v.,* **-bled, -bling.** murmur in discontent. —**grum′bler,** *n.*

grump′y, *adj.* surly.

grunt, *n.* 1. guttural sound. —*v.* 2. utter grunts.

guar′an•tee′, *n., v.,* **-teed, -teeing.** —*n.* 1. pledge given as security. —*v.* 2. pledge. 2. assure. Also, **guar′an•ty′.** —**guar′an•tor′,** *n.*

guard, *v.* 1. watch over. —*n.* 2. person who guards. 3. body of guards. 4. close watch.

guard′i•an, *n.* 1. person who guards. 2. person entrusted with care of another.

gu•ber•na•to′ri•al, *adj.* of governors.

guer•ril′la (gə ril′ə), *n.* soldier belonging to an independent band.

guess, *v.* 1. form opinion on incomplete evidence. 2. be right in such opinion. *n.* 3. act of guessing.

guess′work′, *n.* 1. act of guessing. 2. conclusions from guesses.

guest, *n.* 1. visitor. 2. customer at hotel, restaurant, etc.

guf•faw′, *n.* 1. loud laughter. —*v.* 2. laugh loudly.

guid′ance, *n.* 1. act or instance of guiding. 2. advice over period of time.

guide, *v.,* **guided, guiding,** *n.* —*v.* 1. show the way. —*n.* 2. one that guides.

guided missile, radio-controlled aerial missile.

gui′don (gī′dən), *n.* small flag.

guild, *n.* commercial organization for common interest.

guile, *n.* cunning. —**guile′less,** *adj.*

guil′lo•tine′ (gil′ə tēn′), *n.* machine for beheading.

guilt, *n.* fact or feeling of having committed a wrong. —**guilt′y,** *adj.*

guin′ea fowl (gin′ē), plump domesticated fowl. —**guinea hen.**

guinea pig, 1. South American rodent. 2. subject, esp. human, of experiment.

guise (gīz), n. outward appeareance.

gui•tar′, n. stringed musical instrument.

gulch, n. ravine.

gulf, n. 1. arm of sea. 2. abyss.

gull, n. 1. web-footed sea bird. 2. dupe.—v. 3. cheat; trick.

gul′let, n. throat.

gul′li•ble, adj. easily deceived. —**gul′li•bil′i•ty,** n.

gul′ly, n., pl. **-lies.** deep channel cut by running water.

gulp, v. 1. swallow in large mouthfuls. —n. 2. act of gulping.

gum, n., v., **gummed, gumming.** —n. 1. sticky substance from plants. 2. chewing gum. 3. tissue around teeth. —v. 4. smear with gum. —**gum′my,** adj.

gum′bo, n. okra.

gun, n., v., **gunned, gunning.** —n. 1. tubular weapon which shoots missiles with explosives. —v. 2. hunt with gun. —**gun′ner,** n. —**gun′ner•y,** n.

gun′cot′ton, n. explosive made of cotton and acids.

gun′ny, n. coarse material used for sacks.

gun′pow′der, n. explosive mixture.

gun′wale (gun′əl), n. upper edge of vessel's side.

gup′py, n., pl. **-pies.** tiny tropical fish.

gur′gle, v., **-gled, -gling,** n. —v. 1. flow noisily. —n. 2. sound of gurgling.

gu′ru, n. 1. Hindu spiritual teacher. 2. any respected leader.

gush, v. 1. flow or emit suddenly. 2. talk effusively. —n. 3. sudden flow. —**gush′y,** adj.

gush′er, n. jet of petroleum from underground.

gus′set, n. angular insertion, as in clothing.

gust, n. 1. blast of wind. 2. outburst. —**gust′y,** adj.

gus′ta•to′ry, adj. of taste.

gus′to, n. keen enjoyment.

gut, n., v., **gutted, gutting.** —n. 1. intestine. 2. (pl.) Informal. courage. —v. 3. destroy interior of.

gut′ta-per′cha, n. juice of some tropical trees.

gut′ter, n. channel for leading off rainwater.

gut′tur•al, adj. 1. of or in throat. —n. 2. guttural sound. —**gut′tur•al•ly,** adv.

guy, n. 1. rope, etc., used to guide or steady object. 2. Informal. fellow.

guz′zle, v., **-zled, -zling.** drink greedily.

gym•na′si•um (jim-), n. place for physical exercise. Informal, **gym.**

gym′nast, n. performer of gymnastics.

gym•nas′tics, n.pl. physical exercises. —**gym•nas′tic,** adj.

gy′ne•col′o•gy (gī′nə-), n. branch of medicine dealing with care of women. —**gy′ne•col′o•gist,** n.,

gyp (jip), v., **gypped, gypping.** Informal. cheat.

gyp′sum, n. soft, common mineral.

Gyp′sy, n., pl. **-sies.** member of wandering people.

gy′rate, v., **-rated, -rating.** whirl. —**gy•ra′tion,** n.

gy′ro•scope′ (jī′rə-), n. rotating wheel mounted to maintain absolute direction in space.

H

H, h, n. eighth letter of English alphabet.

hab′er•dash′er•y, n. shirts and men's furnishings. —**hab′er•dash′er,** n.

hab′it, n. 1. customary practice or act. 2. garb. —**ha•bit′u•al** (hə bich′ōō əl), adj. —**ha•bit′u•al•ly,** adv. —**ha•bit′u•ate′,** v. —**ha•bit′u•a′tion,** n.

hab′it•a•ble, adj. able to be habited. —**hab′it•a•bly,** adv.

hab′i•tant, n. resident.

hab′i•tat′, n. natural dwelling place.

hab′i•ta′tion, n. place of abode.

ha•bit′u•ate′, v., **-ated, -ating.** accustom; make used to.

ha•bit′u•é′ (hə bich′ōō ā′), n. habitual frequenter.

hack, v. 1. cut or chop roughly. 2. cough sharply. —n. 3. cut or notch. 4. artistic drudge. 5. vehicle for hire. —adj. 6. trite; routine.

hack′ney, n., pl. **-neys.** horse or carriage for hire.

hack′neyed, adj. trite; common.

hack′saw′, n. saw for cutting metal.

had′dock, n. food fish of northern Atlantic.

haft, n. handle.

hag, n. repulsive old woman.

hag′gard, adj. gaunt with fatigue.

hag′gle, v., **-gled, -gling.** argue over price.

hail, n. 1. ice balls falling from sky. 2. shout. 3. salutation. —v. 4. pour down hail. 5. greet. 6. call out to.

hair, n. 1. filament on human head, animal body, etc. 2. hairs collectively. —**hair′y,** adj. —**hair′i•ness,** n. —**hair′dres′ser,** n. —**hair′pin′,** n.

hair′breadth′, n. narrow margin of safety. Also, **hairs′breadth′.**

hair′do′, n. woman's hair arrangement.

hair′spray′, n. liquid spray for holding the hair in place.

hale, v., **haled, haling,** adj. —v. 1. summon forcibly. —adj. 2. healthy.

half, n., pl. **halves,** adj., adv. —n. 1. one of two equal parts. —adj. 2. being half. 3. incomplete. —adv. 4. partly.

half′-breed′, n. offspring of parents of two races.

half′-heart′ed, adj. unenthusiastic. —**half′-heart′ed•ly,** adv. —**half-heart′ed•ness,** n.

half′-wit′, n. stupid or foolish person. —**half′-wit′ted,** adj.

hal′i•but, n. large edible fish.

hal′i•to′sis, n. offensive breath.

hall, n. 1. corridor. 2. large public room.

hal′le•lu′jah (-lōō′yə), interj. Praise ye the Lord! Also, **hal′le•lu′iah.**

hal′low, v. consecrate.

Hal′low•een′, n. eve (Oct. 31) of All Saints' Day. Also, **Hal′low•e′en′.**

hal•lu′ci•na′tion, n. illusory perception.

hall′way′, n. corridor.

ha′lo, n. radiance surrounding a head.

halt, v. 1. falter; limp. 2. stop. —adj. 3. lame. —n. 4. stop.

hal′ter, n. 1. strap for horse. 2. noose. 3. woman's sport waist.

halve, *v.,* **halved, halving.** divide in half.

ham, *n.* meat from rear thigh of hog.

ham′burg′er, *n.* sandwich of ground beef in bun.

ham′let, *n.* small village.

ham′mer, *n.* 1. tool for pounding. —*v.* 2. pound with hammer. —**ham′mer•er,** *n.*

ham′mock, *n.* hanging bed of canvas, etc.

ham′per, *v.* 1. impede. —*n.* 2. large basket.

hand, *n.* 1. terminal part of arm. 2. worker. 3. side as viewed from certain point. 4. style of handwriting. 5. pledge of marriage. 6. cards held by player. —*v.* 7. pass by hand.

hand′bag′, *n.* woman's purse.

hand′ball′, *n.* ball game played against a wall.

hand′book′, *n.* small guide or manual.

hand′cuff′, *n.* 1. shackle for wrist. —*v.* 2. put handcuff on.

hand′ful, *n.* 1. amount hand can hold. 2. difficult problem.

hand′gun′, *n.* pistol.

hand′i•cap′, *n., v.,* **-capped, -capping.** —*n.* 1. disadvantage. —*v.* 2. subject to disadvantage.

hand′i•craft′, *n.* 1. manual skill. 2. work or products requiring such skill. Also, **hand′craft′.**

hand′i•work′, *n.* 1. work done by hand. 2. personal work or accomplishment.

hand′ker•chief (hang′kər-), *n.* small cloth for wiping face, etc.

han′dle, *n., v.,* **-dled, -dling.** —*n.* 1. part to be grasped. —*v.* 2. feel or grasp. 3. manage. 4. *Informal.* endure. 5. deal in. —**han′dler,** *n.*

hand′made′, *adj.* made individually by workman.

hand′out′, *n.* 1. alms. 2. item of publicity.

hand′some, *adj.* 1. of fine appearance. 2. generous.

hand′-to-mouth′, *adj.* providing bare existence; precarious.

hand′writ′ing, *n.* writing done by hand.

hand′y, *adj.,* **handier, handiest.** 1. convenient. 2. dexterous. 3. useful.

han′dy•man′, *n., pl.* **-men.** worker at miscellaneous physical chores.

hang, *v.,* **hung** or **hanged, hanging,** *n.* —*v.* 1. suspend. 2. suspend by neck until dead. —*n.* 3. manner of hanging. —**hang′ing,** *n.* —**hang′man,** *n.* —**hang′er,** *n.*

hang′ar, *n.* shed, esp. for aircraft.

hang glider, kitelike glider for soaring through the air from hilltops, etc.

hang′o′ver, *n.* ill feeling from too much alcohol.

hang′up′, *n. Informal.* obsessive problem.

hank, *n.* skein of yarn.

han′ker, *v.* yearn.

han′som, *n.* two-wheeled covered cab.

Ha′nuk•kah (hä′-), *n.* annual Jewish festival.

hap′haz′ard, *adj.* 1. accidental. —*adv.* 2. by chance.

hap′less, *adj.* unlucky.

hap′pen, *v.* occur. —**hap′pen•ing,** *n.*

hap′py, *adj.,* **-pier, -piest.** 1. pleased; glad. 2. pleasurable. 3. bringing good luck. —**hap′pi•ly,** *adv.* —**hap′pi•ness,** *n.*

ha•rangue′, *n., v.,* **-rangued, -ranguing.** —*n.* 1. vehement speech. —*v.* 2. address in harangue.

har′ass, *v.* annoy; disturb. —**har′ass•ment,** *n.*

har′bin•ger (-bin jər), *n., v.* herald.

har′bor, *n.* 1. sheltered water for ships. 2. shelter. —*v.* 3. give shelter.

hard, *adj.* 1. firm; not soft. 2. difficult. 3. severe. 4. indisputable. —**hard′en,** *v.* —**hard′ness,** *n.*

hard′-core′, *adj.* 1. unalterably committed. 2. graphic; explicit.

hard′hat′, *n.* 1. worker's helmet. —*adj.* 2. *Informal.* obstinately conservative or intolerant.

hard′ly, *adv.* barely.

hard′ship, *n.* severe toil, oppression, or need.

hard′tack′, *n.* hard biscuit.

hard′ware′, *n.* 1. metalware. 2. the machinery of a computer.

har′dy, *adj.,* **-dier, -diest.** 1. fitted to endure hardship. 2. daring. —**har′di•ness,** *n.*

hare, *n.* mammal resembling rabbit.

hare′brained′, *adj.* foolish.

hare′lip′, *n.* split upper lip.

har′em (hâr′əm), *n.* 1. women's section of Oriental palace. 2. the women there.

hark, *v.* listen. Also, **hark′en.**

har′lot, *n.* prostitute. —**har′lot•ry,** *n.*

harm, *n.* 1. injury. 2. evil. —*v.* 3. injure. —**harm′ful,** *adj.*

harm′less, *adj.* 1. causing no harm. 2. immune from legal action. —**harm′less•ly,** *adv.* —**harm′less•ness,** *n.*

har•mon′i•ca, *n.* musical reed instrument.

har′mo•ny, *n.* 1. agreement. 2. combination of agreeable musical sounds. —**har•mon′ic,** *adj.* —**har′mo•nize′,** *v.* —**har•mon′i•ous,** *adj.*

har′ness, *n.* 1. horse's working gear. —*v.* 2. put harness on.

harp, *n.* 1. plucked musical string instrument. —*v.* 2. dwell persistently in one's words. —**harp′ist, harp′er,** *n.*

har•poon′, *n.* 1. spear used against whales. —*v.* 2. strike with harpoon.

harp′si•chord′, *n.* keyboard instrument with plucked strings.

har′ri•er, *n.* hunting dog.

har′row, *n.* 1. implement for leveling or breaking up plowed land. —*v.* 2. draw a harrow over. 3. distress.

har′ry, *v.,* **-ried, -rying.** harass.

harsh, *adj.* 1. rough. 2. unpleasant. 3. highly severe. —**harsh′ly,** *adv.* —**harsh′ness,** *n.*

hart, *n.* male deer.

har′vest, *n.* 1. gathering of crops. 2. season for this. 3. crop. —*v.* 4. reap. —**har′vest•er,** *n.*

has (haz), *v.* third pers. sing. pres. indic. of **have.**

hash, *n.* 1. chopped meat and potatoes. 2. *Slang.* hashish. —*v.* 3. chop.

hash′ish, *n.* narcotic of Indian hemp.

hasn′t, contraction of **has not.**

hasp, *n.* clasp for door, lid, etc.

has′sock, *n.* cushion used as footstool, etc.

has′sle, *n., v. Informal.* —*n.* 1. quarrel. —*v.* 2. harass.

has′ten, *v.* hurry. —**haste, hast′i•ness,** *n.* —**hast′y,** *adj.* —**hast′i•ly,** *adv.*

hat, *n.* covering for head. —**hat′ter,** *n.*

hatch, *v.* 1. bring forth young from egg. 2. be hatched. —*n.* 3. cover for opening. —**hatch′er•y,** *n.*

hatch′et, *n.* small ax.

hatch′way′, *n.* opening in ship's deck.

hate, *v.,* **hated, hating,** *n.* —*v.* 1. feel or show enmity toward. —*n.* 2. Also, **hat′red.** strong dislike.

hate′ful, *adj.* 1. full of hate. 2. arousing hate. —**hate′ful•ly,** *adv.* —**hate′ful•ness,** *n.*

haugh′ty, *adj.,* **-tier, -tiest.** disdainfully proud. —**haugh′ti•ly,** *adv.* —**haugh′ti•ness,** *n.*

haul, *v.* 1. pull; drag. —*n.* 2. pull. 3. distance of carrying. 4. thing hauled. 5. something gained.

haunch, *n.* hip.

haunt, *v.* 1. visit often, esp. as ghost. —*n.* 2. place of frequent visits.

have, *v.,* **had, having.** 1. possess; contain. 2. get. 3. be forced or obligated. 4. be affected by. 5. give birth to.

ha′ven, *n.* 1. harbor. 2. place of shelter.

haven't, contraction of **have not.**

hav′er•sack′, *n.* bag for rations, etc.

hav′oc, *n.* devastation.

haw, *v.* 1. turn left. —*n.* 2. command to turn left.

hawk, *n.* 1. bird of prey. —*v.* 2. hunt with hawks. 3. peddle.

haw′ser, *n.* cable for mooring or towing ship.

haw′thorn′, *n.* small cultivated tree.

hay, *n.* grass cut and dried for fodder. —**hay′field′,** *n.* —**hay′stack′,** *n.*

hay fever, disorder of eyes and respiratory tract, caused by pollen.

hay′wire′, *adj. Informal.* amiss.

haz′ard, *n., v.* risk. —**haz′ard•ous,** *adj.*

haze, *v.,* **hazed, hazing,** *n.* —*v.* 1. play abusive tricks on. —*n.* 2. mistlike obscurity. —**ha′zy,** *adj.*

ha′zel, *n.* 1. tree bearing edible nut (**ha′zel•nut′**). 2. light reddish brown.

H′-bomb′, *n.* hydrogen bomb.

he, *pron.* 1. male mentioned. —*n.* 2. male.

head, *n.* 1. part of body joined to trunk by neck. 2. leader. 3. top or foremost part. —*adj.* 4. at the head. 5. leading or main. —*v.* 6. lead. 7. move in certain direction.

head′ache′, *n.* 1. pain in upper part of head. 2. worrying problem.

head′ing, *n.* caption.

head′line′, *n.* title of newspaper article.

head′long′, *adj., adv.* in impulsive manner.

head′quar′ters, *n.* center of command or operations.

head′strong′, *adj.* willful.

head′way′, *n.* progress.

head′y, *adj.,* **-ier, -iest.** 1. impetuous. 2. intoxicating.

heal, *v.* 1. restore to health. 2. get well.

health, *n.* 1. soundness of body. 2. physical condition. —**health′ful,** *adj.* —**health′y,** *adj.*

heap, *n., v.* pile.

hear, *v.,* **heard, hearing.** 1. perceive by ear. 2. listen. 3. receive report. —**hear′er,** *n.* —**hear′ing,** *n.*

heark′en, *v.* listen.

hear′say′, *n.* gossip; indirect report.

hearse, *n.* funeral vehicle.

heart, *n.* 1. muscular organ keeping blood in circulation. 2. seat of life or emotion. 3. compassion. 4. vital part. —**heart′less,** *adj.* —**heart′less•ly,** *adv.* —**heart′less•ness,** *n.*

heart′ache′, *n.* grief.

heart′en, *v.* encourage.

heart′-rend′ing, *adj.* causing sympathetic grief.

hearth, *n.* place for fires.

heart′y, *adj.,* **heartier, heartiest.** 1. cordial. 2. genuine. 3. vigorous. 4. substantial. —**heart′i•ly,** *adv.*

heat, *n.* 1. warmth. 2. form of energy raising temperature. 3. intensity of emotion. 4. sexual arousal, esp. female. —*v.* 5. make or become hot. 6. excite. —**heat′er,** *n.*

heat′ed, *adj.* 1. supplied with heat. 2. emotionally charged.

heath, *n.* 1. Also, **heath′er.** low evergreen shrub. 2. waste land bearing shrubs.

hea′then, *n., adj.* pagan.

heave, *v.* 1. raise with effort. 2. lift and throw. 3. *Slang.* vomit. 4. rise and fall. —*n.* 5. act or instance of heaving.

heav′en, *n.* 1. abode of God, angels, and spirits of righteous dead. 2. (*often pl.*) sky. 3. bliss. —**heav′en•ly,** *adj.*

heav′y, *adj.,* **heavier, heaviest.** 1. of great weight. 2. substantial. 3. clumsy; indelicate. —**heav′i•ly,** *adv.* —**heav′i•ness,** *n.*

heav′y-du′ty, *adj.* made for hard use.

heav′y-hand′ed, *adj.* tactless; clumsy.

heav′y-heart′ed, *adj.* preoccupied with sorrow or worry. —**heav′y-heart′ed•ness,** *n.*

heav′y-set′, *adj.* large in body.

He′brew, *n.* 1. member of people of ancient Palestine. 2. their language, now the national language of Israel. —**He′brew,** *adj.*

hec′tare (hek′târ), *n.* 10,000 square meters (2.47 acres).

heck′le, *v.,* **-led, -ling.** harass with questions, etc. —**heck′ler,** *n.*

hec′tic, *adj.* marked by excitement, passion, etc. —**hec′ti•cal•ly,** *adv.*

hec′tor, *v., n.* bully.

hedge, *n., v.,* **hedged, hedging.** —*n.* 1. Also, **hedge′row′.** fence of bushes or

small trees. —*v.* 2. surround with hedge. 3. offset (risk, bet, etc.).

hedge′hog′, *n.* spiny European mammal.

he′don•ist, *n.* person living for pleasure. —**he′do•nis′tic,** *adj.* —**he′don•ism,** *n.*

heed, *v.* 1. notice. 2. pay serious attention to. —**heed,** *n.* —**heed′ful,** *adj.* —**heed′less,** *adj.*

heel, *n.* 1. back of foot below ankle. 2. part of shoe, etc., covering this. —*v.* 3. furnish with heels. 4. lean to one side.

hef′ty, *adj.,* **-ier, -iest.** 1. heavy. 2. sturdy.

heif′er (hef′ər), *n.* young cow without issue.

height, *n.* 1. state of being high. 2. altitude. 3. apex. —**height′en,** *v.*

hei′nous (hā′nəs), *adj.* hateful.

heir (âr), *n.* inheritor. —**heir′ess,** *n.fem.*

heir′loom′, *n.* possession long kept in family.

hel′i•cop′ter, *n.* heavier-than-air craft lifted by horizontal propeller.

he′li•o•trope′ (hē′lē ə trōp′), *n.* shrub with fragrant flowers.

he′li•um, *n.* light, gaseous element.

hell, *n.* abode of condemned spirits. —**hell′ish,** *adj.*

hel•lo′, *interj.* (exclamation of greeting.)

helm, *n.* 1. control of rudder. 2. steering apparatus. —**helms′man,** *n.*

hel′met, *n.* protective head covering.

help, *v.* 1. aid. 2. save. 3. relieve. 4. avoid. —*n.* 5. aid; relief. 6. helping person or thing. —**help′er,** *n.* —**help′ful,** *adj.*

help′less, *adj.* unable to act for oneself.

hel′ter-skel′ter, *adv.* in a disorderly way.

hem, *v.,* **hemmed, hemming,** *n.* —*v.* 1. confine. 2. fold and sew down edge of cloth. —*n.* 3. hemmed border.

hem′i•sphere′, *n.* 1. half the earth or sky. 2. half sphere. —**hem′i•spher′i•cal,** *adj.*

hem′lock, *n.* coniferous tree.

hem′or•rhage (hem′ə rij), *n.* discharge of blood.

hem′or•rhoid′ (hem′ə roid′), *n.* (*usually pl.*) painful dilation of blood vessels in anus.

hemp, *n.* tall herb whose fiber is used for rope, etc.

hen, *n.* 1. female domestic fowl. 2. female bird. —**hen′ner•y,** *n.*

hence, *adv.* 1. therefore. 2. from now on. 3. from this place, etc. —*interj.* 4. depart!

hence′forth′, *adv.* from now on.

hench′man, *n.* associate in wrong-doing.

hen′na, *n.* red dye.

her, *pron.* 1. objective case of **she.** —*adj.* 2. of or belonging to female.

her′ald, *n.* 1. messenger or forerunner. 2. proclaimer. —*v.* 3. proclaim. 4. give promise of.

her′ald•ry, *n.* art of devising and describing coats of arms, tracing genealogies, etc. —**he•ral′dic,** *adj.*

herb (ûrb, hûrb), *n.* annual flowering plant with nonwoody stem. —**her•ba′ceous,** *adj.* —**herb′al,** *adj.*

herb′age, *n.* 1. nonwoody plants. 2. leaves and stems of herbs.

herd, *n.* 1. animals feeding or moving together. —*v.* 2. go in herd. 3. tend herd. —**herd′er, herds′man,** *n.*

here, *adv.* 1. in or to this place. 2. present.

here•af′ter, *adv.* 1. in the future. —*n.* 2. future life.

here•by′, *adv.* by this.

he•red′i•tar′y, *adj.* 1. passing from parents to offspring. 2. of heredity. 3. by inheritance. —**he•red′i•tar′i•ly,** *adv.*

he•red′i•ty, *n.* transmission of traits from parents to offspring.

here•in′, *adv.* in this place.

her′e•sy, *n., pl.* **-sies.** unorthodox opinion or doctrine. —**her′e•tic,** *n.* —**he•ret′i•cal,** *adj.*

here′to•fore′, *adv.* before now.

here′with′, *adv.* along with this.

her′it•age, *n.* 1. inheritance. 2. traditions and history.

her•met′ic, *adj.* airtight. Also, **hermet′i•cal.** —**her•met′i•cal•ly,** *adv.*

her′mit, *n.* religious recluse.

her′mit•age, *n.* hermit's abode.

her′ni•a (hûr′nē ə), *n.* rupture in abdominal wall, etc.

he′ro, *n., pl.* **heroes.** 1. man of valor, nobility, etc. 2. main male character in story. —**her′oine,** *n.fem.* —**he•ro′ic, he•ro′i•cal,** *adj.* —**her′o•ism′,** *n.*

her′o•in, *n.* morphinelike drug.

her′on, *n.* long-legged wading bird.

her′ring, *n.* north Atlantic food fish.

hers, *pron.* 1. form of possessive **her.** 2. her belongings or family.

her•self′, *pron.* emphatic or reflexive form of **her.**

hertz, *n., pl.* **hertz.** radio frequency of one cycle per second.

hes′i•tate′, *v.,* **-tated, -tating.** 1. hold back in doubt. 2. pause. 3. stammer. —**hes′i•tant,** *adj.* —**hes′i•ta′tion, hes′i•tan•cy,** *n.*

het′er•o•dox′, *adj.* unorthodox. —**het′er•o•dox′y,** *n.*

het′er•o•ge′ne•ous, *adj.* 1. unlike. 2. varied.

het′er•o•sex′u•al, *adj.* sexually attracted to opposite sex. —**het′er•o•sex′u•al,** *n.*

hew, *v.,* **hewed, hewed** or **hewn, hewing.** 1. chop or cut. 2. cut down. —**hew′er,** *n.*

hex′a•gon′, *n.* six-sided polygon. —**hex•ag′o•nal,** *adj.*

hey′day′, *n.* time of greatest vigor.

hi′ber•nate′, *v.,* **-nated, -nating.** spend winter in dormant state. —**hi′ber•na′tion,** *n.*

hic′cup, *n.* 1. sudden involuntary drawing in of breath. —*v.* 2. have hiccups. Also, **hic′cough** (hik′up).

hick′o•ry, *n.* tree bearing edible nut (**hickory nut**).

hide, *v.,* **hid, hidden** or **hid, hiding,** *n.* —*v.* 1. conceal or be concealed. —*n.* 2. animal's skin.

hid′e•ous, *adj.* 1. very ugly. 2. revolting.

hie, *v.,* **hied, hieing** or **hying.** *Archaic.* go hastily.

hi′er•ar′chy, *n.* graded system of officials.

hi′er•o•glyph′ic, *adj.* Also, **hi′er•o•glyph′i•cal.** 1. of picture writing, as among ancient Egyptians. —*n.* 2. hieroglyphic symbol.

high, *adj.* 1. tall. 2. lofty. 3. expensive. 4. shrill. 5. *Informal.* exuberant with drink or drugs. —*adv.* 6. at or to high place, rank, etc.

high′brow′, *adj. Informal.* pretentious.

high′ fi•del′i•ty, reproduction of sound without distortion. —**high′-fi•del′i•ty,** *adj.*

high′-flown′, *adj.* 1. pretentious. 2. bombastic.

high′-hand′ed, *adj.* overbearing.

high′lands (-ləndz), *n.* elevated part of country.

high′light′, *v.,* **-lighted, -lighting,** *n.* —*v.* 1. emphasize. —*n.* 2. important event, scene, etc. 3. area of strong reflected light.

high′ly, *adv.* 1. in high place, etc. 2. very; extremely

high′ness, *n.* 1. high state. 2. (*cap.*) title of royalty.

high′rise′, *n.* high building. —**high-rise,** *adj.*

high′road′, *n.* highway.

high′ school′, *n.* school for grades 9 through 12.

high′-spir′it•ed, *adj.* proud; bold.

high′-strung′, *adj.* nervous.

high′way′, *n.* main road.

high′way•man, *n., pl.* **-men.** highway robber.

hi′jack′, *v.* seize (plane, truck, etc.) by force. —**hi′jack′er,** *n.*

hike, *v.,* **hiked, hiking,** *n.* —*v.* 1. walk long distance. —*n.* 2. long walk. —**hik′er,** *n.*

hi•lar′i•ous, *adj.* 1. very gay. 2. very funny. —**hi•lar′i•ous•ly,** *adv.* —**hi•lar′i•ty,** *n.*

hill, *n.* high piece of land. —**hill′y,** *adj.*

hill′bil′ly, *n., pl.* **-lies.** *Informal.* 1. Southern mountaineer. 2. yokel; rustic.

hill′ock, *n.* little hill.

hilt, *n.* sword handle.

him, *pron.* objective case of **he.**

him•self′, *pron.* reflexive or emphatic form of **him.**

hind, *adj.* 1. rear. —*n.* 2. female deer.

hin′der, *v.* 1. retard. 2. stop. —**hin′drance,** *n.*

hind′most′, *adj.* last.

hind′sight′, *n.* keen awareness of how one should have avoided past mistakes.

Hin′du, *n.* native of India who worships many gods. —**Hindu,** *adj.* —**Hin′du•ism,** *n.*

hinge, *n., v.,* **hinged, hinging.** —*n.* 1. joint on which door, lid, etc., turns. —*v.* 2. depend. 3. furnish with hinges.

hint, *n.* 1. indirect suggestion. —*v.* 2. give hint.

hin′ter•land′, *n.* area remote from cities.

hip, *n.* projecting part of each side of body below waist.

hip′pie, *n. Slang.* person rejecting conventional cultural or moral values.

hip′po•drome′, *n.* arena, esp. for horse events.

hip′po•pot′a•mus, *n.* large African water mammal.

hire, *v.,* **hired, hiring,** *n.* —*v.* 1. purchase services or use of. —*n.* 2. payment for services or use.

hire′ling, *n.* person whose loyalty can be bought.

hir′sute (hûr′sōot), *adj.* hairy.

his, *pron.* 1. possessive form of **he.** 2. his belongings.

His•pan'ic, *n.* person of Spanish descent. —**Hispanic,** *adj.*

hiss, *v.* 1. make prolonged *s* sound. 2. express disapproval in this way. —*n.* 3. hissing sound.

his•tor'ic, *adj.* 1. Also, **his•tor'i•cal.** of history. 2. important in or surviving from the past. —**his•tor'i•cal•ly,** *adv.*

his'to•ry, *n.* 1. knowledge, study, or record of past events. 2. pattern of events determining future. —**his•to'ri•an,** *n.*

his•tri•on'ics, *n.pl.* exaggerated, esp. melodramatic, behavior. —**his'tri•on'ic,** *adj.*

hit, *v.,* **hit, hitting,** *n.* —*v.* 1. strike. 2. collide with. 3. meet. 4. guess. —*n.* 5. collision. 6. blow. 7. success. —**hit'ter,** *n.*

hitch, *v.* 1. fasten. 2. harness to cart, etc. 3. raise or move jerkily. —*n.* 4. fastening or knot. 5. obstruction. 6. jerk.

hitch'hike', *v.,* **-hiked, -hiking.** beg a ride. —**hitch'hik'er,** *n.*

hith'er, *adv.* to this place. —**hith'er•ward,** *adv.*

hith'er•to', *adv.* until now.

hive, *n.* shelter for bees.

hives, *n.pl.* eruptive skin condition.

hoa'gie, *n.* mixed sandwich in long roll. Also, **hoa'gy.**

hoar, *adj.* 1. white with age or frost. 2. old. Also, **hoar'y.**

hoard, *n.* 1. accumulation for future use. —*v.* 2. accumulate as hoard. —**hoard'er,** *n.*

hoarse, *adj.* gruff in tone.

hoax, *n.* 1. mischievous deception. —*v.* 2. deceive; trick.

hob'ble, *v.,* **-bled, -bling.** 1. limp. 2. fasten legs to prevent free movement.

hob'by, *n.,* *pl.* **-bies.** favorite avocation or pastime.

hob'by•horse', *n.* 1. rocking toy for riding. 2. favorite subject for discussion.

hob'nob', *v.,* **-nobbed, -nobbing.** associate on social terms.

ho'bo, *n.* tramp; vagrant.

hock, *n.* joint in hind leg of horse, etc.

hock'ey, *n.* game played with bent clubs (**hockey sticks**) and ball or disk.

ho'cus-po'cus, *n.* 1. sleight of hand. 2. trickery.

hod, *n.* 1. trough for carrying mortar, bricks, etc. 2. coal scuttle.

hodge'podge', *n.* mixture; jumble.

hoe, *n.,* *v.,* **hoed, hoeing.** —*n.* 1. implement for breaking ground, etc. —*v.* 2. use hoe on.

hog, *n.,* *v.,* **hogged, hogging.** —*n.* 1. omnivorous mammal used for food. 2. greedy or filthy person. —*v.* 3. *Informal.* take greedily.

hogs'head', *n.* large cask.

hoist, *v.* 1. lift, esp. by machine. —*n.* 2. hoisting apparatus. 3. act or instance of lifting.

hold, *v.,* **held, holding,** *n.* —*v.* 1. have in hand. 2. possess. 3. sustain. 4. adhere. 5. celebrate. 6. restrain or detain. 7. believe. 8. consider. —*n.* 9. grasp. 10. influence. 11. cargo space below ship's deck. —**hold'er,** *n.* —**hold'ing,** *n.*

hold'up', *n.* 1. delay. 2. robbery with threats.

hole, *n.,* *v.,* **holed, holing.** —*n.* 1. opening. 2. cavity. 3. burrow. —*v.* 4. drive into hole.

hol'i•day', *n.* 1. day or period without work. —*adj.* 2. festive.

ho'li•ness, *n.* holy state or character.

hol'lan•daise', *n.* rich egg-based sauce.

hol'low, *adj.* 1. empty within. 2. sunken. 3. dull. 4. unreal. —*n.* 5. cavity. —*v.* 6. make hollow.

hol'ly, *n.* shrub with bright-red berries.

hol'ly•hock', *n.* tall flowering plant.

hol'o•caust' (hol'ə kôst'), *n.* 1. great destruction, esp. by fire. 2. (*cap.*) Nazi killing of Jews during World War II.

ho'lo•gram', *n.* three-dimensional image made by a laser.

ho•log'ra•phy, *n.* process of making holograms.

hol'ster, *n.* case for pistol.

ho'ly, *adj.,* **-lier, -liest.** 1. sacred. 2. dedicated to God.

Ho'ly Ghost', third member of Trinity. Also, **Holy Spirit.**

hom'age, *n.* reverence or respect.

home, *n.* 1. residence. 2. native place or country. —*adv.* 3. to or at home. —**home'land',** *n.* —**home'ward,** *adv., adj.* —**home'less,** *adj.* —**home'made',** *adj.*

home'ly, *adj.,* **-lier, -liest.** plain.

home'sick', *adj.* longing for home. —**home'sick'ness,** *n.*

home'spun', *adj.* 1. spun at home. 2. unpretentious. —*n.* 3. cloth made at home.

home'stead, *n.* dwelling with its land and buildings.

hom'ey, *adj.,* **-ier, -iest.** cozy.

hom'i•cide', *n.* killing of one person by another. —**hom'i•cid'al,** *adj.*

hom'i•ly, *n.* sermon.

hom'i•ny, *n.* 1. hulled corn. 2. coarse flour from corn.

ho•mo•ge'ne•ous, *adj.* 1. unvaried in content. 2. alike. —**ho'mo•ge•ne'i•ty,** *n.*

ho•mog'e•nize', *v.,* **-nized, -nizing.** form by mixing and emulsifying.

hom'o•nym, *n.* word like another in sound, but not in meaning.

ho•mo•sex'u•al, *adj.* 1. sexually attracted to same sex. —*n.* 2. homosexual person.

hone, *n.,* *v.,* **honed, honing.** —*n.* 1. fine whetstone. —*v.* 2. sharpen to fine edge.

hon'est, *adj.* 1. trustworthy. 2. sincere. 3. virtuous. —**hon'es•ty,** *n.*

hon'ey, *n.* sweet fluid produced by bees (**hon'ey•bees'**).

hon'ey•comb', *n.* wax structure built by bees to store honey.

hon'ey•dew' melon, sweet muskmelon.

hon'eyed (-ēd), *adj.* sweet or flattering, as speech.

hon'ey•moon', *n.* holiday trip of newly married couple. —**hon'ey•moon'er,** *n.*

hon'ey•suck'le, *n.* shrub bearing tubular flowers.

honk, *n.* 1. sound of automobile horn. 2. nasal sound of goose, etc. —*v.* 3. make such sound.

hon'or, *n.* 1. public or official esteem. 2. something as token of this. 3. good reputation. 4. high ethical character. 5. chastity. —*v.* 6. revere. 7. confer honor. 8. show regard for. 9. accept as valid.

hon'or•a•ble, *adj.* 1. worthy of honor. 2. of high principles. —**hon'or•a•bly,** *adv.*

hon'or•ar'y, *adj.* conferred as honor.

hood, *n.* 1. covering for head and neck. 2. automobile-engine cover.

hood'lum, *n.* violent petty criminal.

hood'wink', *v.* deceive.

hoof, *n.,* *pl.* **hoofs, hooves.** horny covering of animal foot.

hook, *n.* 1. curved piece of metal for catching, etc. 2. fishhook. 3. sharp curve. —*v.* 4. seize, etc., with hook.

hoop, *n.* circular band.

hoot, *v.* 1. shout in derision. 2. (of owl) utter cry. —*n.* 3. owl's cry. 4. shout of derision.

hop, *v.,* **hopped, hopping,** *n.* —*v.* 1. leap, esp. on one foot. —*n.* 2. such a leap. 3. twining plant bearing cones used in brewing. 4. (*pl.*) the cones.

hope, *n., v.,* **hoped, hoping.** —*n.* 1. feeling that something desired is possible. 2. object of this. 3. confidence. —*v.* 4. look forward to with hope. —**hope′ful,** *adj.* —**hope′less,** *adj.*

hop′per, *n.* funnel-shaped trough for grain, etc.

horde, *n.* 1. multitude. 2. nomadic group.

hore′hound′, *n.* herb containing bitter juice.

ho•ri′zon, *n.* apparent boundary between earth and sky.

hor′i•zon′tal, *adj.* 1. at right angles to vertical. 2. level. —*n.* 3. horizontal line, etc.

hor′mone, *n.* endocrine-gland secretion that activates specific organ, mechanism, etc.

horn, *n.* 1. hard growth on heads of cattle, goats, etc. 2. hornlike part. 3. musical wind instrument. —**horn′y,** *adj.*

hor′net, *n.* large wasp.

horn′pipe′, *n.* 1. lively dance. 2. music for it.

hor′o•scope′, *n.* chart of heavens used in astrology.

hor′ri•ble, *adj.* dreadful. Also **hor•ren′dous,** *adj.* —**hor′ri•bly,** *adv.*

hor′rid, *adj.* abominable.

hor′ror, *n.* intense fear or repugnance. —**hor′ri•fy′,** *v.*

hors-d'oeuvre′ (ôr dûrv′), *n., pl.* **-d'oeuvres′** (-dûrv′). tidbit served before meal.

horse, *n.* 1. large domesticated quadruped. 2. cavalry. 3. frame with legs for bearing work, etc. —**horse′back′,** *n., adv.* —**horse′man,** *n.* —**horse′wo′man,** *n.fem.* —**horse′hair′,** *n.*

horse′pow′er, *n.* unit of power, equal to 550 foot-pounds per second.

horse′rad′ish, *n.* cultivated plant with pungent root.

horse′shoe′, *n.* 1. ∪-shaped iron plate nailed to horse's hoof. 2. arrangement in this form.

hor′ti•cul′ture, *n.* cultivation of gardens. —**hor′ti•cul′tur•ist,** *n.*

ho•san′na, *interj.* praise the Lord!

hose, *n.* 1. stockings. 2. flexible tube for water, etc.

ho′sier•y (-zha rē), *n.* stockings.

hos′pi•ta•ble, *adj.* showing hospitality. —**hos′pi•ta•bly,** *adv.*

hos′pi•tal, *n.* institution for treatment of sick and injured. —**hos′pi•tal•ize′,** *v.*

hos′pi•tal′i•ty, *n.* warm reception of guests, etc.

host, *n.* 1. entertainer of guests. 2. great number. 3. (*cap.*) bread consecrated in Eucharist. —**host′ess,** *n.fem.*

hos′tage, *n.* person given or held as security.

hos′tel, *n.* inexpensive transient lodging.

hos′tile (-tal), *adj.* 1. opposed; unfriendly. 2. of enemies. —**hos•til′i•ty,** *n.*

hot, *adj.,* **hotter, hottest.** 1. of high temperature. 2. feeling great heat. 3. sharp-tasting. 4. ardent.

hot′bed′, *n.* 1. covered and heated bed of earth for growing plants. 2. place where something thrives and spreads.

hot′-blood′ed, *adj.* excitable.

ho•tel′, *n.* house offering food, lodging, etc.

hot′head′, *n.* impetuous or rash person.

hot′house′, *n.* greenhouse.

hot line, system for instantaneous communications of major importance.

hot rod, *Slang.* car (usu. old) with speeded-up engine.

hound, *n.* 1. hunting dog. —*v.* 2. hunt or track.

hour, *n.* period of 60 minutes. —**hour′ly,** *adj., adv.*

hour′glass′, *n.* timepiece operating by visible fall of sand.

house, *n., pl.* **houses,** *v.,* **housed, housing.** —*n.* (hous). 1. building, esp. for residence, rest, etc. 2. family. 3. legislative or deliberative body. 4. commercial firm. —*v.* (houz). 5. provide with a house.

house′fly′, *n., pl.* **-flies.** common insect.

house′hold′, *n.* 1. people of house. —*adj.* 2. domestic.

house′keep′er, *n.* person who manages a house. —**house′keeping′,** *n.*

house′wife′, *n., pl.* **-wives.** woman in charge of household. —**house′wife′ly,** *adj.*

house′work′, *n.* work done in housekeeping.

hous′ing, *n.* 1. dwellings collectively. 2. container.

hov′el, *n.* small, mean dwelling.

hov′er, *v.* 1. stay fluttering or suspended in air. 2. linger about.

Hov′er•craft′, *n. Trademark.* vehicle that can skim over water on cushion of air.

how, *adv.* 1. in what way. 2. to, at, or in what extent, price, or condition. 3. why.

how•ev′er, *conj.* 1. nevertheless. —*adj.* 2. to whatever extent.

howl, *v.* 1. utter loud long cry. 2. wail. —*n.* 3. cry of wolf, etc. 4. wail.

hub, *n.* central part of wheel.

hub′bub, *n.* confused noise.

huck′le•ber′ry, *n.* dark-blue or black edible berry of heath shrub.

huck′ster, *n.* peddler.

hud′dle, *v.,* **-dled, -dling,** *n.* —*v.* 1. crowd together. —*n.* 2. confused heap or crowd.

hue, *n.* 1. color. 2. outcry.

huff, *n.* fit of anger.

hug, *v.,* **hugged, hugging,** *n.* —*v.* 1. clasp in arms. 2. stay close to. —*n.* 3. tight clasp.

huge, *adj.* very large in size or extent. —**huge′ly,** *adv.* —**huge′ness,** *n.*

hulk, *n.* hull remaining from old ship.

hulk′ing, *adj.* bulky; clumsy. Also, **hulk′y.**

hull, *n.* 1. outer covering of seed or fruit. 2. body of ship. —*v.* 3. remove hull of.

hul′la•ba•loo′, *n. Informal.* uproar.

hum, *v.,* **hummed, humming,** *n.* —*v.* 1. make low droning sound. 2. sing with closed lips. —*n.* 3. be busy or active. 4. indistinct murmur.

hu′man, *adj.* 1. of or like people or their species. —*n.* 2. Also, **human being.** a person.

hu•mane′, *adj.* tender; compassionate. —**hu•mane′ly,** *adv.*

hu•man′i•tar′i•an, *adj.* 1. philanthropic. —*n.* 2. philanthropist.

hu•man′i•ty, *n.* 1. humankind. 2. human state or quality. 3. kindness.

hu′man•kind′, *n.* people collectively.

hu′man•ly, *adv.* by human means.

hum′ble, *adj.,* **-bler, -blest,** *v.,* **-bled, -bling.** —*adj.* 1. low in rank, etc. 2. meek. —*v.* 3. abase. —**hum′ble•ness,** *n.* —**hum′bly,** *adv.*

hum′bug, *n.* 1. hoax. 2. falseness.

hum′drum′, *adj.* dull.

hu′mid, *adj.* (of air) moist. —**hu•mid′i•fy′,** *v.* —**hu•mid′i•ty,** *n.*

hu′mi•dor′, *n.* humid box or chamber.

hu•mil′i•ate′, *v.,* **-ated, -ating.** lower pride or self-respect of. —**hu•mil′i•a′tion,** *n.*

hu•mil′i•ty, *n.* humbleness.

hum′ming•bird′, *n.* very small American bird.

hu′mor, *n.* 1. funniness. 2. mental disposition. 3. whim. —*v.* 4. indulge mood or whim of. **—hu′mor•ist,** *n.* **—hu′mor•ous,** *adj.*

hump, *n.* 1. rounded protuberance. —*v.* 2. raise in hump.

hump′back′, *n.* 1. back with hump. 2. person with such a back. Also, **hunch′back′.**

hunch, *v.* 1. push out or up in a hump. —*n.* 2. hump. 3. guess or suspicion.

hun′dred, *n., adj.* ten times ten. **—hun′dredth,** *adj., n.*

hun′ger, *n.* 1. feeling caused by need of food. —*v.* 2. be hungry.

hun′gry, *adj.,* **-grier, -griest.** 1. craving food. 2. desirous. **—hun′gri•ly,** *adv.* **—hung′ri•ness,** *n.*

hunt, *v.* 1. chase to catch or kill. 2. search for. —*n.* 3. act of hunting. 4. search. **—hunt′er,** *n.* **—hunt′ress,** *n.fem.*

hur′dle, *n., v.,* **-dled, -dling.** —*n.* 1. barrier in race track. —*v.* 2. leap over.

hurl, *v.* drive or throw forcefully. **—hurl′er,** *n.*

hur•rah′, *interj.* (exclamation of joy, triumph, etc.) Also, **hur•ray′.**

hur′ri•cane′, *n.* violent storm.

hur′ry, *v.,* **-ried, -rying,** *n., pl.* **-ries.** —*v.* 1. drive, move, or act with haste. —*n.* 2. need for haste. 3. haste.

hurt, *v.,* **hurt, hurting,** *n.* —*v.* 1. injure or pain. 2. harm. 3. offend. —*n.* 4. injury or damage. **—hurt′ful,** *adj.*

hur′tle, *v.,* **-tled, -tling.** strike or rush violently.

hus′band, *n.* 1. man of married pair. —*v.* 2. manage prudently. **—hus′band•ry,** *n.*

hush, *interj.* 1. (command to be silent.) —*n.* 2. silence.

husk, *n.* 1. dry covering of fruits and seeds. —*v.* 2. remove husk.

husk′y, *adj.,* **-ier, -iest.** 1. big and strong. 2. hoarse.

hus′sy, *n., pl.* **-sies.** 1. ill-behaved girl. 2. lewd woman.

hus′tle, *v.,* **-tled, -tling,** *n.* —*v.* 1. work energetically. 2. force or shove violently. —*n.* 3. energetic activity. 4. discourteous shoving.

hus′tler, *n. Slang.* 1. person eager for success. 2. swindler. 3. prostitute.

hut, *n.* small humble dwelling.

hutch, *n.* pen for small animals.

hy′a•cinth, *n.* bulbous flowering plant.

hy′brid, *n.* offspring of organisms of different breeds, species, etc.

hy•dran′gea (-jə), *n.* flowering shrub.

hy′drant, *n.* water pipe with outlet.

hy•drau′lic, *adj.* 1. of or operated by liquid. 2. of hydraulics.

hy•drau′lics, *n.* science of moving liquids.

hy′dro•e•lec′tric, *adj.* of electricity generated by hydraulic energy. **—hy′dro•e•lec′tric′i•ty,** *n.*

hy′dro•foil′, *n.* powered vessel that can skim on water.

hy′dro•gen, *n.* inflammable gas, lightest of elements.

hydrogen bomb, powerful bomb utilizing thermonuclear fusion.

hy′dro•pho′bi•a, *n.* 1. rabies. 2. fear of water.

hy′dro•plane′, *n.* 1. airplane that lands on water. 2. light, high-speed motorboat.

hy•e′na, *n.* carnivorous African mammal.

hy′giene, *n.* science of preserving health. **—hy′gi•en′ic,** *adj.*

hymn, *n.* song of praise.

hym′nal, *n.* book of hymns. Also, **hymn′book′.**

hyper-, *prefix.* excessive; too much.

hy′per•ac′tive, *adj.* abnormally active. **—hy′per•ac•tiv′i•ty,** *n.*

hy•per′bo•le′ (-bə lē′), *n.* exaggeration for rhetorical effect.

hy′per•crit′i•cal, *adj.* excessively critical.

hy′per•ten′sion, *n.* abnormally high blood pressure.

hy′phen, *n.* short line (-) connecting parts or syllables of a word. **—hy′phen•ate′,** *v.* **—hy′phen•a′tion,** *n.*

hyp•no′sis, *n., pl.* **-ses.** artificially produced sleeplike state. **—hyp•not′ic,** *adj.* **—hyp′no•tism′,** *n.* **—hyp′no•tize′,** *v.*

hy′po•chon′dri•a (-kon′-), *n.* morbid fancies of ill health. **—hy′po•chon′dri•ac′,** *n., adj.*

hy•poc′ri•sy, *n., pl.* **-sies.** pretense of virtue, piety, etc.

hyp′o•crite, *n.* person given to hypocrisy. **—hyp′o•crit′i•cal,** *adj.*

hy′po•der′mic, *adj.* introduced under the skin, as needle.

hy•pot′e•nuse, *n.* side of right triangle opposite right angle.

hy•poth′e•sis, *n.* 1. proposed explanation. 2. guess. **—hy′po•thet′i•cal,** *adj.*

hys′ter•ec′to•my, *n., pl.* **-mies.** surgical removal of uterus.

hys•te′ri•a (-ster′-, -stēr′-), *n.* 1. senseless emotionalism. 2. psychological disorder. **—hys•ter′i•cal** (-ster′-), *adj.*

hys•ter′ics (-ster′-), *n.pl.* fit of hysteria.

I

I, i, *n.* 1. ninth letter of English alphabet. —*pron.* 2. subject form of first person singular pronoun.

i′bis, *n.* wading bird.

ice, *n., v.,* **iced, icing.** —*n.* 1. water frozen solid. 2. frozen dessert. —*v.* 3. cover with ice or icing. 4. cool with ice. —**i′cy,** *adj.*

ice′berg′, *n.* mass of ice floating at sea.

ice′box′, *n.* food chest cooled by ice.

ich′thy•ol′o•gy (ik′thi-), *n.* study of fishes. —**ich′thy•ol′o•gist,** *n.*

i′ci•cle, *n.* hanging tapering mass of ice.

ic′ing, *n.* preparation for covering cakes.

i′con, *n.* sacred image.

i•con′o•clast′, *n.* attacker of cherished beliefs. —**i•con′o•clas′tic,** *adj.*

i•de′a, *n.* conception in mind; thought.

i•de′al, *n.* 1. conception or standard of perfection. —*adj.* 2. being an ideal. 3. not real. —**i•de′al•ly,** *adv.* —**i•de′al•ize′,** *v.*

i•de′al•ism′, *n.* belief in or behavior according to ideals. —**i•de′al•ist,** *n.* —**i•de′al•is′tic,** *adj.*

i•den′ti•cal, *adj.* same.

i•den′ti•fy′, *v.,* **-fied, -fying.** 1. recognize as particular person or thing. 2. regard as or prove to be identical. —**i•den′ti•fi•ca′tion,** *n.*

i•den′ti•ty, *n.* 1. fact of being same. 2. self.

i′de•ol′o•gy, *n., pl.* **-gies.** beliefs of group, esp. political. —**i′de•o•log′i•cal,** *adj.*

id′i•om, *n.* 1. expression peculiar to a language. 2. dialect. —**id′i•o•mat′-ic,** *adj.*

id′i•o•syn′cra•sy, *n., pl.* **-sies.** unusual individual trait.

id′i•ot, *n.* utterly foolish person. —**id′i•ot′ic,** *adj.* —**id′i•ot′i•cal•ly,** *adv.* —**id′i•o•cy,** *n.*

i′dle, *adj., v.,* **idled, idling.** —*adj.* 1. doing nothing. 2. valueless. 3. groundless. —*v.* 4. do nothing. —**i′dler,** *n.* —**i′dly,** *adv.*

i′dol, *n.* object worshiped or adored. —**i′dol•ize′,** *v.*

i•dol′a•try, *n.* worship of idols. —**i•dol′a•ter,** *n.* —**i•dol′a•trous,** *adj.*

i′dyl, *n.* composition describing simple pastoral scene. Also, **i′dyll.** —**i•dyl′lic,** *adj.*

if, *conj.* 1. in case that. 2. whether. 3. though.

ig′loo, *n.* snow hut.

ig′ne•ous, *adj.* 1. produced by great heat. 2. of fire.

ig•nite′, *v.,* **-nited, -niting.** set on or catch fire. —**ig•ni′tion,** *n.*

ig•no′ble, *adj.* 1. dishonorable. 2. humble. —**ig•no′bly,** *adv.*

ig′no•min′i•ous, *adj.* 1. humiliating. 2. contemptible. —**ig′no•min′y,** *n.*

ig′no•ra′mus (-rā′-), *n.* ignorant person.

ig′no•rant, *adj.* 1. lacking knowledge. 2. unaware. —**ig′no•rance,** *n.*

ig•nore′, *v.,* **-nored, -noring.** disregard.

i•gua′na (i gwä′nə), *n.* large tropical lizard.

ilk, *n.* family or kind.

ill, *adj.* 1. not well; sick. 2. evil. 3. unfavorable. —*n.* 4. evil; harm. 5. ailment. —*adv.* 6. badly. 7. with difficulty.

ill′-ad•vised′, *adj.* showing bad judgment.

ill′-bred′, *adj.* rude.

ill′-fat′ed, *adj.* unlucky; doomed.

il•le′gal, *adj.* unlawful. —**il•le′gal•ly,** *adv.*

il•leg′i•ble, *adj.* hard to read. —**il•leg′i•bil′i•ty,** *n.*

il′le•git′i•mate, *adj.* 1. unlawful. 2. born out of wedlock. —**il′le•git′i•ma•cy,** *n.*

il•lib′er•al, *adj.* 1. not generous. 2. narrow in attitudes or beliefs.

il•lic′it, *adj.* unlawful; not allowed.

il•lit′er•ate, *adj.* 1. unable to read and write. —*n.* 2. illiterate person. —**il•lit′er•a•cy,** *n.*

ill′ness, *n.* bad health.

il•log′i•cal, *adj.* not logical. —**il•log′i•cal•ly,** *adv.*

ill′-treat′, *v.* abuse. —**ill′-treat′ment,** *n.*

il•lu′mi•nate′, *v.,* **-nated, -nating.** supply with light. Also, **il•lu′mine.** —**il•lu′mi•na′tion,** *n.*

il•lu′sion, *n.* false impression or appearance. —**il•lu′sive, il•lu′so•ry,** *adj.*

il′lus•trate′, *v.,* **-trated, -trating.** 1. explain with examples, etc. 2. furnish with pictures. —**il′lus•tra′tion,** *n.* —**il•lus′tra•tive,** *adj.* —**il′lus•tra′tor,** *n.*

il•lus′tri•ous, *adj.* 1. famous. 2. glorious.

im-, *prefix.* variant of **in-.**

im′age, *n.* 1. likeness. 2. idea. 3. conception of one's character. —*v.* 4. mirror.

im′age•ry, *n.* use of figures of speech.

im•ag′ine, *v.,* **-ined, -ining.** 1. form mental images. 2. think; guess. —**im•ag′i•na′tion,** *n.* —**im•ag′i•na′tive,** *adj.* —**im•ag′i•nar′y,** *adj.* —**im•ag′i•na•ble,** *adj.*

I•mam′ (i mäm′), *n.* Muslim religious leader.

im•bal′ance, *n.* lack of balance.

im′be•cile (-sil), *n.* 1. person of defective mentality. —*adj.* 2. mentally feeble. —**im′be•cil′i•ty,** *n.*

im•bibe′, *v.,* **-bibed, -bibing.** drink. —**im•bib′er,** *n.*

im•bro′glio (-brōl′yō), *n.* complicated affair.

im•bue′, *v.,* **-bued, -buing.** 1. inspire. 2. saturate.

im′i•tate′, *v.,* **-tated, -tating.** 1. copy. 2. counterfeit. —**im′i•ta′tive,** *adj.* —**im′i•ta′tor,** *n.* —**im′i•ta′tion,** *n.*

im•mac′u•late, *adj.* 1. spotlessly clean. 2. pure.

im′ma•nent, *adj.* being within. —**im′ma•nence,** *n.*

im′ma•te′ri•al, *adj.* 1. unimportant. 2. spiritual.

im′ma•ture′, *adj.* not mature. —**im′ma•tu′ri•ty,** *n.*

im•meas′ur•a•ble, *adj.* limitless. —**im•meas′ur•a•bly,** *adv.*

im•me′di•ate, *adj.* 1. without delay. 2. nearest. 3. present. —**im•me′di•a•cy,** *n.* —**im•me′di•ate•ly,** *adv.*

im′me•mo′ri•al, *adj.* beyond memory or record.

im•mense′, *adj.* 1. vast. 2. boundless. —**im•men′si•ty,** *n.* —**im•mense′ly,** *adv.*

im•merse′, *v.,* **-mersed, -mersing.** 1. plunge into liquid. 2. absorb, as in study. —**im•mer′sion,** *n.*

im′mi•grant, *n.* person who immigrates.

im′mi•grate′, *v.,* **-grated, -grating.** come to new country. —**im′mi•gra′tion,** *n.*

im′mi•nent, *adj.* about to happen. —**im′mi•nence,** *n.*

im•mo′bile, *adj.* not moving. —**im′mo•bil′i•ty,** *n.* —**im•mo′bi•lize′,** *v.*

im•mod′er•ate, *adj.* excessive. —**im• mod′er•ate•ly,** *adv.*

im•mod′est, *adj.* not modest. —**im• mod′es•ty,** *n.*

im′mo•late′, *v.,* **-lated, -lating.** sacrifice. —**im′mo•la′tion,** *n.*

im•mor′al, *adj.* not moral. —**im′mo• ral′i•ty,** *n.* —**im•mor′al•ly,** *adv.*

im•mor′tal, *adj.* 1. not subject to death or oblivion. —*n.* 2. immortal being. —**im′mor•tal′i•ty,** *n.* —**im• mor′tal•ize′,** *v.*

im•mov′a•ble, *adj.* 1. fixed. 2. unchanging.

im•mune′, *adj.* 1. protected from disease. 2. exempt. —**im•mu′ni•ty,** *n.* —**im′mu•nize′,** *v.*

im•mure′, *v.,* **-mured, -muring.** confine within walls.

im•mu′ta•ble, *adj.* unchangeable. —**im•mu′ta•bil′i•ty,** *n.*

imp, *n.* little demon. —**imp′ish,** *adj.*

im′pact, *n.* act of striking together.

im•pair′, *v.* lessen in value or effectiveness. —**im•pair′ment,** *n.*

im•pale′, *v.,* **-paled, -paling.** fix upon sharp stake, etc.

im•pal′pa•ble, *adj.* that cannot be felt or understood.

im•pan′el, *v.,* **-eled, -eling.** list for jury duty.

im•part′, *v.* 1. tell. 2. give.

im•par′tial, *adj.* unbiased. —**im′par• ti•al′i•ty,** *n.* —**im•par′tial•ly,** *adv.*

im•pas′sa•ble, *adj.* not to be passed through or along.

im′passe (-pas), *n.* deadlock.

im•pas′sioned, *adj.* full of passion.

im•pas′sive, *adj.* 1. emotionless. 2. calm. —**im•pas′sive•ly,** *adv.*

im•pa′tience, *n.* lack of patience. —**im•pa′tient,** *adj.* —**im•pa′tient• ly,** *adv.*

im•peach′, *v.* try for misconduct in office. —**im•peach′ment,** *n.*

im•pec′ca•ble, *adj.* faultless. —**im• pec′ca•bly,** *adv.*

im′pe•cu′ni•ous, *adj.* without money.

im•pede′, *v.,* **-peded, -peding.** hinder. —**im•ped′i•ment,** *n.*

im•ped′i•men′ta, *n.pl.* baggage, etc., carried with one.

im•pel′, *v.,* **-pelled, -pelling.** urge forward.

im•pend′, *v.* be imminent.

im•pen′e•tra•ble, *adj.* that cannot be penetrated. —**im•pen′e•tra•bil′i• ty,** *n.* —**im•pen′e•tra•bly,** *adv.*

im•per′a•tive, *adj.* 1. necessary. 2. denoting command.

im′per•cep′ti•ble, *adj.* 1. very slight. 2. not perceptible. —**im′per•cep′ti• bly,** *adv.*

im•per′fect, *adj.* 1. having defect. 2. not complete. 3. *Gram.* denoting action in progress. —**im′per•fec′tion,** *n.* —**im•per′fect•ly,** *adv.*

im•pe′ri•al (-pēr′-), *adj.* of an empire or emperor.

im•pe′ri•al•ism′, *n.* policy of extending rule over other peoples. —**im• pe′ri•al•ist,** *n., adj.* —**im•pe′ri•al• is′tic,** *adj.*

im•per′il, *v.,* **-iled, -iling.** endanger.

im•pe′ri•ous, *adj.* domineering. —**im•pe′ri•ous•ly,** *adv.*

im•per′ish•a•ble, *adj.* immortal; not subject to decay. —**im•per′ish•a• bly,** *adv.*

im•per′me•a•ble, *adj.* not permitting penetration. —**im•per′me•a•bil′i• ty,** *n.*

im•per′son•al, *adj.* without personal reference or bias. —**im•per′son•al• ly,** *adv.*

im•per′son•ate′, *v.,* **-ated, -ating.** act the part of. —**im•per′son•a′tion,** *n.* —**im•per′son•a′tor,** *n.*

im•per′ti•nence, *n.* 1. rude presumption. 2. irrelevance. —**im•per′ti• nent,** *adj.* —**im•per′ti•nent•ly,** *adv.*

im•per•turb′a•ble, *adj.* calm.

im•per′vi•ous, *adj.* not allowing penetration. —**im•per′vi•ous•ly,** *adv.*

im•pet′u•ous, *adj.* rash or hasty. —**im•pet′u•os′i•ty,** *n.* —**im•pet′u• ous•ly,** *adv.*

im′pe•tus, *n.* 1. stimulus. 2. force of motion.

im•pi′e•ty, *n., pl.* **-ties.** 1. lack of piety. 2. act showing this. —**im′pi• ous,** *adj.*

im•pinge′, *v.,* **-pinged, -pinging.** 1. strike; collide. 2. encroach.

imp′ish, *adj.* implike; mischievous.

im•pla′ca•ble, *adj.* not to be placated.

im•plant′, *v.* instill.

im•plaus′i•ble, *adj.* not plausible. —**im•plau′si•bil′i•ty,** *n.*

im′ple•ment, *n.* instrument or tool.

im′pli•cate′, *v.,* **-cated, -cating.** involve as guilty.

im′pli•ca′tion, *n.* 1. act of implying. 2. thing implied. 3. act of implicating.

im•plic′it (-plis′it), *adj.* 1. unquestioning; complete. 2. implied. —**im• plic′it•ly,** *adv.*

im•plore′, *v.,* **-plored, -ploring.** urge or beg.

im•ply′, *v.,* **-plied, -plying.** 1. indicate. 2. suggest.

im•po•lite′, *adj.* rude.

im•pol′i•tic, *adj.* not wise or prudent.

im•pon′der•a•ble, *adj.* that cannot be weighed.

im•port′, *v.* 1. bring in from another country. 2. matter; signify. —*n.* (im′- pōrt). 3. anything imported. 4. significance. —**im′por•ta′tion,** *n.* —**im•port′er,** *n.*

im•por′tant, *adj.* 1. of some consequence. 2. prominent. —**im•por′- tance,** *n.*

im′por•tune′ (tyo͞on′), *v.,* **-tuned, -tuning.** beg persistently. —**im•por′- tu•nate,** *adj.*

im•pose′, *v.,* **-posed, -posing.** 1. set as obligation. 2. intrude (oneself). 3. deceive. —**im′po•si′tion,** *n.*

im•pos′ing, *adj.* impressive.

im•pos′si•ble, *adj.* that cannot be done or exist. —**im•pos′si•bil′i•ty,** *n.* —**im•pos′si•bly,** *adv.*

im′post, *n.* tax or duty.

im•pos′tor, *n.* person who defrauds under false name. Also, **im•pos′ter.** —**im•pos′ture,** *n.*

im′po•tence, *n.* 1. lack of power. 2. lack of sexual powers. —**im′po•tent,** *adj.*

im•pound′, *v.* seize by law.

im•pov′er•ish, *v.* make poor.

im•prac′ti•cal, *adj.* not usable or useful.

im′pre•ca′tion, *n.* curse.

im′pre•cise′, *adj.* not precise.

im•preg′na•ble, *adj.* resistant to or proof against attack.

im•preg′nate, *v.,* **-nated, -nating.** 1. make pregnant. 2. saturate. —**im′- preg•na′tion,** *n.*

im•press′, *v.* 1. affect with respect, etc. 2. fix in mind. 3. stamp. 4. force into public service. —*n.* (im′pres). 5. act of impressing. —**im•pres′sive,** *adj.*

im•pres′sion, *n.* 1. effect on mind or feelings. 2. notion. 3. printed or stamped mark.

im•pres′sion•a•ble, *adj.* easily influenced, esp. emotionally. —**im• pres′sion•a•bly,** *adv.*

im′print, *n.* 1. mark made by pressure. 2. sign of event, etc., making impression.

im•pris′on, *v.* put in prison. —**im• pris′on•ment,** *n.*

im•prob′a•ble, *adj.* unlikely. —**im• prob′a•bil′i•ty,** *n.* —**im•prob′a•bly,** *adv.*

im•promp′tu, *adj., adv.* without preparation.

im•prop′er, *adj.* not right, suitable, or proper. —**im′pro•pri′e•ty,** *n.* —**im•prop′er•ly,** *adv.*

im•prove′, *v.,* **-proved, -proving.** 1. make or become better. 2. use wisely. —**im•prove′ment,** *n.*

im′pro•vise′, *v.,* **-vised, -vising.** prepare for or perform at short notice. —**im′pro•vi•sa′tion,** *n.*

im•pru′dent, *adj.* not prudent; unwise.

im′pu•dent, *adj.* shamelessly bold. —**im′pu•dence,** *n.* —**im′pu•dent•ly,** *adv.*

im•pugn′ (-pyōōn′), *v.* attack verbally.

im′pulse, *n.* 1. inciting influence. 2. sudden inclination. —**im•pul′sive,** *adj.*

im•pu′ni•ty, *n.* exemption from punishment.

im•pure′, *adj.* 1. not pure. 2. immoral. —**im•pu′ri•ty,** *n.*

im•pute′, *v.,* **-puted, -puting.** attribute.

in, *prep.* 1. within. 2. into. 3. while; during. 4. into some place. —*adv.* 5. inside; within.

in-, common prefix meaning ''not'' or ''lacking,'' as in the list below.

in′ad•vert′ent, *adj.* 1. heedless. 2. unintentional. —**in′ad•vert′ence,** *n.*

in•al′ien•a•ble, *adj.* not to be taken away or transferred.

in•ane′, *adj.* silly.

in′ar•tic′u•late, *adj.* not clear in expression.

in′as•much′ as, 1. seeing that. 2. to the extent that.

in•au′gu•rate′, *v.,* **-rated, -rating.** 1. induct into office. 2. begin. —**in•au′gu•ral,** *adj., n.* —**in•au′gu•ra′-tion,** *n.*

in′can•des′cence (-des′əns), *n.* glow of intense heat. —**in′can•des′cent,** *adj.*

in′can•ta′tion, *n.* 1. magic ritual. 2. spell.

in′ca•pac′i•tate′, *v.,* **-tated, -tating.** make unfit. —**in′ca•pac′i•ty,** *n.*

in•car′cer•ate′, *v.,* **-ated, -ating.** imprison. —**in•car′cer•a′tion,** *n.*

in•car′nate (-nit), *adj.* embodied in flesh. —**in′car•na′tion,** *n.*

in•cen′di•ar′y (-sen′-), *adj., n., pl.* **-aries.** —*adj.* 1. of or for setting fires. 2. arousing strife. —*n.* 3. person who maliciously sets fires.

in•cense′, *v.,* **-censed, -censing,** *n.* —*v.* (in sens′). 1. enrage. —*n.* (in′ sens). 2. substance burned to give a sweet odor.

in•cen′tive, *n.* stimulus; motivation.

in•cep′tion, *n.* beginning.

in•ces′sant, *adj.* uninterrupted. —**in•ces′sant•ly,** *adv.*

in′cest, *n.* sexual relations between close relatives. —**in•ces′tu•ous,** *adj.*

inch, *n.* unit of length, $\frac{1}{12}$ foot.

in•cho′ate (-kō′it), *adj.* just begun; incomplete.

in′ci•dence, *n.* range of occurrence or effect.

in′ci•dent, *n.* 1. happening. 2. side event. —*adj.* 3. likely. 4. naturally belonging. —**in′ci•den′tal,** *adj., n.* —**in′ci•den′tal•ly,** *adv.*

in•cin′er•ate′, *v.,* **-ated, -ating.** burn to ashes. —**in•cin′er•a′tor,** *n.*

in•cip′i•ent (-sip′), *adj.* beginning. —**in•cip′i•ence,** *n.*

in•cise′ (-sīz′), *v.,* **-cised, -cising.** cut into; engrave. —**in•ci′sion,** *n.*

in•ci′sive, *adj.* 1. sharp. 2. uncomfortably sharp, as criticism.

in•ci′sor, *n.* cutting tooth.

in•cite′, *v.,* **-cited, -citing.** urge to action.

in•cline′, *v.,* **-clined, -clining,** *n.* —*v.* 1. tend. 2. slant. 3. dispose. —*n.* (in′ klīn). 4. slanted surface or railroad. —**in′cli•na′tion,** *n.*

in•close′, *v.,* **-closed, -closing.** enclose.

in•clude′, *v.,* **-cluded, -cluding.** 1. contain. 2. have among others. —**in•clu′sion,** *n.* —**in•clu′sive,** *adj.*

in•cog′ni•to′ (in kog′nə tō′), *adj., adv.* using assumed name.

in′come, *n.* money received.

in•com′pa•ra•ble, *adj.* unequaled. —**in•com′pa•ra•bly,** *adv.*

in•con•sid′er•ate, *adj.* thoughtless.

in•con′ti•nent, *adj.* 1. unable to control bodily discharges. 2. lacking sexual self-restraint. —**in•con′ti•nence,** *n.*

in•cor′po•rate′, *v.,* **-rated, -rating.** 1. form a corporation. 2. include as part. —**in•cor′po•ra′tion,** *n.*

in•cor′ri•gi•ble, *adj.* not to be reformed.

in•crease′, *v.,* **-creased, -creasing,** *n.* —*v.* 1. make or become more or greater. —*n.* (in′krēs). 2. instance of increasing. 3. growth or addition. —**in•creas′ing•ly,** *adv.*

in•cred′i•ble, *adj.* unbelievable; amazing. —**in•cred′i•bly,** *adv.*

in•cred′u•lous, *adj.* not believing.

in′cre•ment, *n.* growth.

in•crim′i•nate′, *v.,* **-nated, -nating.** charge with or involve in crime. —**in•crim′i•na′tion,** *n.*

in•crust′, *v.* cover with crust or outer layer. —**in′crus•ta′tion,** *n.*

in′cu•bate′, *v.,* **-bated, -bating.** keep warm, as eggs for hatching. —**in′cu•ba′tion,** *n.*

in′cu•ba′tor, *n.* heated case for incubating.

in•cul′cate, *v.,* **-cated, -cating.** teach; instill.

in•cum′bent, *adj.* 1. obligatory. —*n.* 2. office holder. —**in•cum′ben•cy,** *n.*

in•cur′, *v.,* **-curred, -curring.** bring upon oneself.

in•cur′sion, *n.* raid.

in•debt′ed, *adj.* obligated by debt. —**in•debt′ed•ness,** *n.*

in′de•ci′sion, *n.* inability to decide.

in•deed′, *adv.* 1. in fact. —*interj.* 2. (used to express surprise, contempt, etc.)

in′de•fat′i•ga•ble, *adj.* tireless.

in•del′i•ble, *adj.* that cannot be erased.

in•dem′ni•fy′, *v.,* **-fied, -fying.** compensate for or insure against loss, etc. —**in•dem′ni•ty,** *n.*

in•dent′, *v.* 1. notch. 2. set back from margin. —**in′den•ta′tion, in•den′-tion,** *n.*

in′de•pend′ent, *adj.* 1. free. 2. not influenced by or dependent on others. —**in′de•pend′ence,** *n.*

in′de•struct′i•ble, *adj.* that cannot be destroyed.

in′dex, *n., pl.* **-dexes, -dices,** *v.* —*n.* 1. list of names, topics, etc., with page references. 2. indicator. —*v.* 3. provide with index.

In′dian, *n.* 1. native of India. 2. Also, **Amer′ican In′dian.** member of the

in′a•bil′i•ty	in•ad′e•qua•cy	in′ap•pro′pri•ate	in•au′di•ble	in•cau′tious
in′ac•ces′si•ble	in•ad′e•quate	in•apt′i•tude′	in′aus•pi′cious	in′ci•vil′i•ty
in•ac′cu•ra•cy	in′ad•mis′si•ble	in′ar•tis′tic	in•cal′cu•la•ble	in•clem′ent
in•ac′cu•rate	in′ad•vis′a•ble	in′at•ten′tion	in•ca′pa•ble	in′co•her′ence
in•ac′tive	in•an′i•mate	in′at•ten′tive	in′ca•pac′i•ty	in′co•her′ent

aboriginal peoples of N. and S. America. —**Indian**, *adj.*

in'di•cate', *v.*, **-cated, -cating.** 1. be a sign of. 2. point to. —**in'di•ca'tion**, *n.* —**in•dic'a•tive**, *adj.* —**in'di•ca'tor**, *n.*

in•dict' (-dīt'), *v.* accuse. —**in•dict'ment**, *n.*

in•dif'fer•ent, *adj.* 1. without interest or concern. 2. moderate. —**in•dif'fer•ence**, *n.*

in•dig'e•nous (-dij'ə nəs), *adj.* native.

in'di•gent, *adj.* needy; destitute. —**in'di•gence**, *n.*

in•di•ges'tion, *n.* difficulty in digesting food.

in'dig•na'tion, *n.* righteous anger. —**in•dig'nant**, *adj.*

in•dig'ni•ty, *n., pl.* **-ties.** 1. loss of dignity. 2. cause of this.

in'di•go', *n.* blue dye.

in'dis•crim'i•nate, *adj.* done at random; haphazard.

in•dis•pose', *v.*, **-posed, -posing.** 1. make ill. 2. make unwilling.

in•dite', *v.*, **-dited, -diting.** write.

in'di•vid'u•al, *adj.* 1. single; particular. 2. of or for one only. —*n.* 3. single person, animal, or thing. —**in'di•vid'u•al'i•ty**, *n.* —**in'di•vid'u•al•ly**, *adv.*

in'di•vid'u•al•ist, *n.* person dependent only on self.

in•doc'tri•nate', *v.*, **-nated, -nating.** train to accept doctrine. —**in•doc'tri•na'tion**, *n.*

in'do•lent, *adj.* lazy. —**in'do•lence**, *n.*

in•dom'i•ta•ble, *adj.* that cannot be conquered or dominated.

in'door', *adj.* done, used, etc., inside a building. —**in•doors'**, *adv.*

in•du'bi•ta•ble, *adj.* undoubted. —**in•du'bi•ta•bly**, *adv.*

in•duce', *v.*, **-duced, -ducing.** 1. persuade; influence. 2. cause; bring on. —**in•duce'ment**, *n.*

in•duct', *v.* bring into office, military service, etc.

in•duc'tion, *n.* 1. reasoning from particular facts. 2. act of inducting. —**in•duc'tive**, *adj.*

in•dulge', *v.*, **-dulged, -dulging.** 1. accommodate whims, appetites, etc., of. 2. accommodate one's own

whims, appetites, etc. —**in•dul'gence**, *n.* —**in•dul'gent**, *adj.*

in•dus'tri•ous, *adj.* hard-working. —**in•dus'tri•ous•ly**, *adv.*

in•dus'tri•al•ist, *n.* owner of industrial plant.

in•dus'tri•al•ize', *v.*, **-ized, -izing.** convert to modern industrial methods.

in'dus•try, *n., pl.* **-tries.** 1. trade or manufacture, esp. with machinery. 2. diligent work. —**in•dus'tri•al**, *adj.*

in•e'bri•ate', *v.*, **-ated, -ating**, *n.* —*v.* (in ē'brī āt'). 1. make drunk. —*n.* (-it). 2. drunken person.

in•ef'fa•ble, *adj.* that cannot be described.

in'ef•fec'tu•al, *adj.* futile; unsatisfactory.

in•ept', *adj.* careless; unskilled.

in•eq'ui•ty, *n., pl.* **-ties.** injustice.

in•ert', *adj.* 1. without inherent power to move, resist, or act. 2. slow-moving. —**in•er'tia**, *n.*

in•ev'i•ta•ble, *adj.* not to be avoided. —**in•ev'i•ta•bil'i•ty**, *n.* —**in•ev'i•ta•bly**, *adv.*

in•ex'o•ra•ble, *adj.* unyielding. —**in•ex'o•ra•bly**, *adv.*

in'ex•plic•a•ble, *adj.* not to be explained.

in'ex•tri•ca•ble, *adj.* that cannot be freed or disentangled. —**in•ex'tri•ca•bly**, *adv.*

in•fal'li•ble, *adj.* never failing or making mistakes. —**in•fal'li•bly**, *adv.*

in'fa•my, *n.* evil repute. —**in'fa•mous**, *adj.*

in'fant, *n.* small baby. —**in'fan•cy**, *n.* —**in'fan•tile'**, *adj.*

in'fan•try, *n.* soldiers who fight on foot. —**in'fan•try•man**, *n.*

in•fat'u•ate', *v.*, **-ated, -ating.** inspire with foolish passion.

in•fect', *v.* affect, esp. with disease germs. —**in•fec'tion**, *n.*

in•fec'tious, *adj.* spreading readily.

in•fer', *v.*, **-ferred, -ferring.** conclude or deduce. —**in'fer•ence**, *n.*

in•fe'ri•or, *adj.* 1. less good, important, etc. —*n.* 2. person inferior to others. —**in•fe'ri•or'i•ty**, *n.*

in•fer'nal, *adj.* 1. of hell. 2. *Informal.* outrageous

in•fer'no, *n.* hell.

in•fest', *v.* overrun; trouble. —**in'fes•ta'tion**, *n.*

in'fi•del, *n.* unbeliever.

in'fight'ing, *n.* conflict within group.

in•fil'trate, *v.*, **-trated, -trating.** pass in, as by filtering. —**in'fil•tra'tion**, *n.*

in'fi•nite, *adj.* 1. vast; endless. —*n.* 2. that which is infinite. —**in•fin'i•ty**, *n.*

in'fin•i•tes'i•mal, *adj.* immeasurably small.

in•fin'i•tive, *n.* simple form of verb.

in•firm', *adj.* feeble; weak. —**in•fir'mi•ty**, *n.*

in•fir'ma•ry, *n., pl.* **-ries.** hospital.

in•flame', *v.*, **-flamed, -flaming.** 1. set afire. 2. redden. 3. excite. 4. cause bodily reaction marked by redness, pain, etc. —**in•flam'ma•ble**, *adj.* —**in•flam'ma•to'ry**, *adj.* —**in'flam•ma'tion**, *n.*

in•flate', *v.*, **-flated, -flating.** swell or expand with gas.

in•fla'tion, *n.* 1. rise in prices when currency or credit expands faster than available goods or services. 2. act of inflating. —**in•fla'tion•ar'y**, *adj.*

in•flect', *v.* 1. bend. 2. modulate. 3. display forms of a word. —**in•flec'tion**, *n.* —**in•flec'tion•al**, *adj.*

in•flict', *v.* impose harmfully. —**in•flic'tion**, *n.*

in'flu•ence, *n.* 1. power to affect another. 2. something that does this. —*v.* 3. move, affect, or sway. —**in'flu•en'tial**, *adj.*

in'flu•en'za, *n.* acute contagious disease caused by virus.

in'flux', *n.* instance of flowing in.

in•form', *v.* supply with information. —**in•form'ant**, *n.* —**in•form'er**, *n.* —**in•form'a•tive**, *adj.*

in'for•ma'tion, *n.* factual knowledge. —**in'for•ma'tion•al**, *adj.*

in•frac'tion, *n.* violation.

in'fra•red', *n.* part of invisible spectrum.

in•fringe', *v.*, **-fringed, -fringing.** violate; encroach. —**in•fringe'ment**, *n.*

in•fu'ri•ate', *v.*, **-ated, -ating.** enrage.

in•fuse', *v.*, **-fused, -fusing.** 1. instill. 2. steep. —**in•fu'sion**, *n.*

in•gen'ious (-jēn'-), *adj.* inventive; clever. —**in•ge•nu'i•ty**, *n.*

---

in'com•men'su•rate	**in'com•plete'**	**in'con•se•quen'tial**	**in'con•stan•cy**	**in'con•ven'ient**
in'com•pat'i•bil'i•ty	**in'com•pre•hen'si•ble**	**in'con•sist'en•cy**	**in'con•stant**	**in'cor•rect'**
in'com•pat'i•ble	**in'con•ceiv'a•ble**	**in'con•sist'ent**	**in'con•test'a•ble**	**in'cor•rupt'i•ble**
in'com•pe'tence	**in'con•clu'sive**	**in'con•sol'a•ble**	**in'con•tro•vert'i•ble**	**in•cur'a•ble**
in'com•pe•tent	**in'con•gru•ous**	**in'con•spic'u•ous**	**in'con•ven'ience**	**in•de'cen•cy**

in•gen′u•ous (-jen′-), *adj.* artlessly sincere.

in′got (ing′gət), *n.* cast mass of metal.

in•grained′, *adj.* fixed firmly.

in′grate, *n.* ungrateful person.

in•gra′ti•ate′ (-grā′shē āt′), *v.*, **-ated, -ating.** get (oneself) into someone's good graces.

in•gre′di•ent, *n.* element or part of mixture.

in′gress, *n.* entrance.

in•hab′it, *v.* live in. —**in•hab′it•ant,** *n.*

in•hale′, *v.*, **-haled, -haling.** breathe in. —**in′ha•la′tion,** *n.*

in•here′, *v.*, **-hered, -hering.** be inseparable part or element. —**in•her′ent,** *adj.*

in•her′it, *v.* become heir to. —**in•her′it•ance,** *n.*

in•hib′it, *v.* restrain or hinder. —**in′-hi•bi′tion,** *n.*

in•hu′man, *adj.* 1. brutal. 2. not human. —**in′hu•man′i•ty,** *n.*

in•im′i•cal, *adj.* 1. adverse. 2. hostile.

in•im′i•ta•ble, *adj.* not to be imitated.

in•iq′ui•ty, *n.*, *pl.* **-ties.** 1. wicked injustice. 2. sin. —**in•iq′ui•tous,** *adj.*

in•i′tial, *adj.*, *n.*, *v.*, **-tialed, -tialing.** —*adj.* 1. of or at beginning. —*n.* 2. first letter of word. —*v.* 3. sign with initials of one's name.

in•i′ti•ate′, *v.*, **-ated, -ating.** 1. begin. 2. admit with ceremony. —**in•i′ti•a′tion,** *n.*

in•i′ti•a•tive, *n.* 1. beginning action. 2. readiness to begin action.

in•ject′, *v.* force, as into tissue. —**in•jec′tion,** *n.* —**in•jec′tor,** *n.*

in•junc′tion, *n.* order or admonition.

in′jure, *v.*, **-jured, -juring.** 1. hurt. 2. do wrong to. —**in•ju′ri•ous,** *adj.* —**in′ju•ry,** *n.*

ink, *n.* 1. writing fluid. —*v.* 2. mark with ink. —**ink′y,** *adj.*

ink′ling, *n.* hint.

in′land, *adj.* 1. of or in the interior of a region. 2. not foreign. —*adv.* 3. of or toward inland area. —*n.* 4. inland area.

in′-law′, *n.* relative by marriage.

in•lay′, *v.*, **-laid, -laying,** *n.* —*v.* (in lā′). 1. ornament with design set in surface. —*n.* (in′lā′). 2. inlaid work.

in′let, *n.* narrow bay.

in′mate′, *n.* person dwelling with others.

in′most′, *adj.* farthest within. Also, **in′ner•most′.**

inn, *n.* 1. hotel. 2. tavern.

in•nate′, *adj.* natural; born into one.

in′ner, *adj.* 1. being farther within. 2. spiritual.

in′ning, *n. Baseball.* one round of play for both teams.

in′no•cence, *n.* 1. freedom from guilt. 2. lack of worldly knowledge. —**in′no•cent,** *adj.*, *n.*

in•noc′u•ous, *adj.* harmless.

in′no•vate′, *v.*, **-vated, -vating.** bring in something new. —**in′no•va′tion,** *n.* —**in′no•va′tor,** *n.* —**in′no•va′-tive,** *adj.*

in′nu•en′do, *n.*, *pl.* **-dos, -does.** hint of wrong.

in•nu′mer•a•ble, *adj.* 1. very numerous. 2. that cannot be counted.

in•oc′u•late′, *v.*, **-lated, -lating.** immunize with disease in mild form. —**in•oc′u•la′tion,** *n.*

in•or′di•nate, *adj.* excessive. —**in•or′di•nate•ly,** *adv.*

in′put′, *n.* 1. power, etc., supplied to machine. 2. information given computer.

in′quest, *n.* legal inquiry, esp. by coroner.

in•quire′, *v.*, **-quired, -quiring.** 1. ask. 2. make investigation. —**in•quir′y,** *n.*

in′qui•si′tion, *n.* investigation. —**in•quis′i•tor,** *n.*

in•quis′i•tive, *adj.* having great curiosity.

in′road′, *n.* encroachment.

in•sane′, *adj.* mentally deranged. —**in•san′i•ty,** *n.*

in•sa′ti•a•ble, *adj.* impossible to satisfy.

in•scribe′, *v.*, **-scribed, -scribing.** 1. write or engrave. 2. dedicate. —**in•scrip′tion,** *n.*

in•scru′ta•ble, *adj.* that cannot be understood. —**in•scru′ta•bil′i•ty,** *n.*

in′sect, *n.* small six-legged animal with body in three parts.

in•sec′ti•cide′, *n.* chemical for killing insects.

in•sem′i•nate′, *v.*, **-nated, -nating.** 1. sow seed in. 2. impregnate. —**in•sem′i•na′tion,** *n.*

in•sen′sate, *adj.* without feeling.

in•sert′, *v.* 1. put or set in. —*n.* (in′sûrt). 2. something inserted. —**in•ser′tion,** *n.*

in•side′, *prep.*, *adv.* 1. within. —*n.* (in′sīd′). 2. inner part. —*adj.* (in′sīd′). 3. inner.

in•sid′i•ous, *adj.* artfully treacherous.

in′sight′, *n.* discernment.

in•sig′ni•a, *n.pl.* badges of rank, honor, etc.

in•sin′u•ate′, *v.*, **-ated, -ating.** 1. hint slyly. 2. put into mind. 3. make one's way artfully. —**in•sin′u•a′tion,** *n.*

in•sip′id, *adj.* without flavor.

in•sist′, *v.* be firm or persistent. —**in•sist′ence,** *n.* —**in•sist′ent,** *adj.*

in′so•far′, *adv.* to such extent.

in′so•lent, *adj.* boldly rude. —**in′so•lence,** *n.*

in•sol′vent, *adj.* without funds to pay one's debts. —**in•sol′ven•cy,** *n.*

in•som′ni•a, *n.* sleeplessness.

in•spect′, *v.* view critically or officially. —**in•spec′tion,** *n.*

in•spec′tor, *n.* 1. person with duty to inspect. 2. minor police official.

in•spire′, *v.*, **-spired, -spiring.** 1. arouse (emotion, etc.). 2. prompt to extraordinary actions. 3. inhale. —**in′spi•ra′tion,** *n.* —**in′spi•ra′-tion•al,** *adj.*

in•stall′, *v.* 1. put in position for use. 2. establish. —**in′stal•la′tion,** *n.*

in•stall′ment, *n.* division, as of payment or story. Also, **in•stal′ment.**

in′stance, *n.*, *v.*, **-stanced, -stancing.** —*n.* 1. case; example. 2. urging. —*v.* 3. cite.

in′stant, *n.* 1. moment. 2. this month. —*adj.* 3. immediate. —**in′stant•ly, in•stan′ter,** *adv.*

in′stan•ta′ne•ous, *adj.* occurring, etc., in an instant. —**in′stan•ta′ne-ous•ly,** *adv.*

in•stead′, *adv.* in another's place.

in′step′, *n.* upper arch of foot.

in′sti•gate′, *v.*, **-gated, -gating.** incite to action. —**in′sti•ga′tion,** *n.* —**in′-sti•ga′tor,** *n.*

in•still′, *v.* introduce slowly. Also, **in•stil′.** —**in•still′ment,** *n.*

in•de′cent	in•def′i•nite	in′di•gest′i•ble	in′dis•put′a•ble	in′ef•fec′tive
in•de•ci′sive	in•del′i•ca•cy	in′di•rect′	in′dis•tinct′	in′ef•fi′cien•cy
in•dec′o•rous	in•del′i•cate	in′dis•creet′	in′dis•tin′guish•a•ble	in′ef•fi′cient
in•de•fen′si•ble	in•de•scrib′a•ble	in′dis•cre′tion	in′di•vis′i•ble	in•el′i•gi•ble
in•de•fin′a•ble	in•de•ter′mi•nate	in′dis•pen′sa•ble	in•ed′i•ble	in′e•qual′i•ty

in′stinct, *n.* natural impulse or talent. —**in•stinc′tive,** *adj.*

in′sti•tute′, *v.,* **-tuted, -tuting,** *n.* —*v.* 1. establish. 2. put into effect. —*n.* 3. society or organization. 4. established law, custom, etc.

in′sti•tu′tion, *n.* 1. organization with public purpose. 2. established tradition, etc. 3. act of instituting. —**in′-sti•tu′tion•al,** *adj.*

in•struct′, *v.* 1. order. 2. teach. —**in•struc′tion,** *n.* —**in•struc′tive,** *adj.* —**in•struc′tor,** *n.*

in′stru•ment, *n.* 1. tool. 2. device for producing music. 3. means; agent. 4. legal document. —**in′stru•men′-tal,** *adj.* —**in′stru•men•tal′i•ty,** *n.*

in′su•lar, *adj.* 1. of islands. 2. narrow in viewpoint. —**in′su•lar′i•ty,** *n.*

in′su•late′, *v.,* **-lated, -lating.** cover with nonconducting material. —**in′-su•la′tion,** *n.* —**in′su•la′tor,** *n.*

in′su•lin, *n.* synthetic hormone used to treat diabetes.

in•sult′, *v.* 1. treat with open contempt. —*n.* (in′sult). 2. such treatment.

in•su′per•a•ble, *adj.* that cannot be overcome.

in•sure′, *v.,* **-sured, -suring.** 1. make certain. 2. guarantee payment in case of harm to or loss of. —**in•sur′-ance,** *n.* —**in•sur′er,** *n.*

in•sur′gent, *n.* 1. rebel. —*adj.* 2. rebellious.

in′sur•rec′tion, *n.* armed revolt.

in•tact′, *adj.* undamaged; whole.

in′take′, *n.* 1. point at which something is taken in. 2. what is taken in.

in′te•ger (-jər), *n.* 1. whole number. 2. entity.

in′te•gral, *adj.* 1. necessary to completeness. 2. entire.

in′te•grate′, *v.,* **-grated, -grating.** 1. bring into whole. 2. complete. 3. abolish segregation by race. —**in′te•gra′tion,** *n.*

in•teg′ri•ty, *n.* 1. soundness of character; honesty. 2. perfect condition.

in•teg′u•ment, *n.* skin, rind, etc.

in′tel•lect′, *n.* 1. understanding. 2. mental capacity.

in′tel•lec′tu•al, *adj.* 1. of intellect. 2. devising or employing concepts in dealing with problems. —**in′tel•**

lec′tu•al, *n.*—**in′tel•lec′tu•al•ly,** *adv.*

in•tel′li•gence, *n.* 1. ability to learn and understand. 2. news. 3. gathering of secret information. —**in•tel′-li•gent,** *adj.*

in•tel′li•gi•ble, *adj.* understandable. —**in•tel′li•gi•bil′i•ty,** *n.* —**in•tel′li•gi•bly,** *adv.*

in•tend′, *v.* plan; design.

in•tense′, *adj.* 1. extremely powerful. 2. emotional. —**in•ten′si•fy′,** *v.* —**in•ten′si•ty,** *n.*

in•ten′sive, *adj.* thoroughgoing.

in•tent′, *n.* 1. purpose. —*adj.* 2. firmly concentrated 3. firmly purposeful. —**in•tent′ly,** *adv.*

in•ten′tion, *n.* 1. purpose. 2. meaning. —**in•ten′tion•al,** *adj.*

in•ter′ (-tûr′), *v.,* **-terred, -terring.** bury.

in′ter•cede′, *v.,* **-ceded, -ceding.** act or plead in behalf. —**in′ter•ces′-sion,** *n.*

in′ter•cept′, *v.* stop or check passage. —**in′ter•cep′tion,** *n.* —**in′ter•cep′-tor,** *n.*

in′ter•change′, *v.,* **-changed, -changing,** *n.* —*v.* (in′tər chānj′). 1. exchange. 2. alternate. —*n.* (in′tər chānj′). 3. act or place of interchanging.

in′ter•course′, *n.* 1. dealings. 2. sexual relations.

in′ter•de•pend′ent, *adj.* mutually dependent.

in′ter•dict′, *n.* 1. decree that prohibits. —*v.* (in′tər dikt′). 2. prohibit. —**in′ter•dic′tion,** *n.*

in′ter•est, *n.* 1. feeling of attention, curiosity, etc. 2. business or ownership. 3. benefit. 4. payment for use of money. —*v.* 5. excite or hold interest of.

in′ter•face′, *n.* 1. group of practices, theories, etc., shared by different academic disciplines, vocations, etc. —*v.* 2. to share; be in harmony or agreement.

in′ter•fere′, *v.,* **-fered, -fering.** 1. hamper. 2. intervene. 3. meddle. —**in′ter•fer′ence,** *n.*

in′ter•im, *n.* 1. meantime. —*adj.* 2. temporary.

in•te′ri•or, *adj.* 1. inside. 2. inland. —*n.* 3. interior part.

in′ter•ject′, *v.* add or include abruptly.

in′ter•jec′tion, *n.* 1. act of interjecting. 2. something interjected. 3. interjected word that forms a complete utterance, as *indeed!*

in′ter•lard′, *v.* mix in.

in′ter•loc′u•tor, *n.* participant in conversation.

in′ter•loc′u•to′ry, *adj.* 1. of or in conversation. 2. *Law.* not final.

in′ter•lop′er, *n.* intruder.

in′ter•lude′, *n.* 1. intervening episode, time, etc. 2. performance in intermission.

in′ter•mar′ry, *v.,* **-ried, -rying.** (of groups) become connected by marriage. —**in′ter•mar′riage,** *n.*

in′ter•me′di•ar′y, *adj., n., pl.* **-aries.** —*adj.* 1. intermediate. —*n.* 2. person negotiating between others.

in′ter•me′di•ate, *adj.* being or acting between two others.

in•ter′ment, *n.* burial.

in•ter′mi•na•ble, *adj.* seeming to be without end; endless. —**in•ter′mi•na•bly,** *adv.*

in′ter•mis′sion, *n.* interval between acts in drama, etc.

in′ter•mit′tent, *adj.* alternately ceasing and starting again.

in•tern′, *v.* 1. hold within certain limits; confine. —*n.* (in′tûrn). 2. Also, **in′terne.** resident assistant physician on hospital staff. —**in•tern′ment,** *n.*

in•ter′nal, *adj.* 1. interior; inner. 2. not foreign; domestic. —**in•ter′nal•ly,** *adv.*

in′ter•na′tion•al, *adj.* 1. among nations. 2. of many nations.

in′ter•na′tion•al•ism′, *n.* principle of international cooperation. —**in′-ter•na′tion•al•ist,** *n.*

in′ter•na′tion•al•ize′, *v.,* **-ized, -izing.** control internationally.

in′ter•ne′cine (-nē′sīn), *adj.* mutually destructive.

in′ter•play′, *n.* reciprocal action.

in•ter′po•late′, *v.,* **-lated, -lating.** insert to alter or clarify meaning. —**in•ter′po•la′tion,** *n.*

in′ter•pose′, *v.,* **-posed, -posing.** 1. place between things. 2. intervene.

in•ter′pret, *v.* 1. explain. 2. construe. 3. translate. —**in•ter′pre•ta′tion,** *n.* —**in•ter′pret•er,** *n.*

---

in•eq′ui•ta•ble	**in′ex•haust′i•ble**	**in′fe•lic′i•tous**	**in′for•mal′i•ty**	**in′har•mon′ic**
in′es•cap′a•ble	**in′ex•pen′sive**	**in•fer′tile**	**in′fre′quen•cy**	**in′har•mo′ni•ous**
in•es′ti•ma•ble	**in′ex•pe′ri•enced**	**in′fi•del′i•ty**	**in•fre′quent**	**in•hos′pi•ta•ble**
in′ex•act′	**in′ex•pres′si•ble**	**in•flex′i•ble**	**in•glo′ri•ous**	**in′hu•mane′**
in′ex•cus′a•ble	**in•fea′si•ble**	**in•for′mal**	**in•grat′i•tude′**	**in′ju•di′cious**

in'ter•ra'cial, *adj.* of, for, or between persons of different races.

in'ter'ro•gate', *v.,* **-gated, -gating.** question. **—in'ter'ro•ga'tion,** *n.* **—in'ter•rog'a•tive,** *adj.* **—in'ter'ro•ga'tor,** *n.*

in'ter•rupt', *v.* break in; stop. **—in'ter•rup'tion,** *n.*

in'ter•sect', *v.* divide by crossing; cross. **—in'ter•sec'tion,** *n.*

in'ter•sperse' (-spûrs'), *v.,* **-spersed, -spersing.** 1. scatter at random. 2. vary with something scattered.

in'ter•state', *adj.* involving number of states.

in•ter'stice (-tûr'stis), *n.* chink or opening.

in'ter•val, *n.* 1. intervening time or space. 2. difference in musical pitch.

in'ter•vene', *v.,* **-vened, -vening.** 1. come or be between. 2. mediate. **—in'ter•ven'tion,** *n.* **—in'ter•ven'tion•ist,** *n.*

in'ter•view', *n.* 1. conversation to obtain information. 2. meeting. **—v.** 3. have interview with. **—in'ter•view'er,** *n.*

in•tes'tate, *adj.* 1. without having made a will. 2. not disposed of by will.

in•tes'tine, *n.* lower part of alimentary canal. **—in•tes'ti•nal,** *adj.*

in'ti•mate, *adj., n., v.,* **-mated, -mating.** **—adj.** 1. close; friendly. 2. private. 3. thorough. **—n.** 4. intimate friend. **—v.** (-māt'). 5. imply. **—in'ti•ma•cy,** *n.* **—in'ti•ma'tion,** *n.* **—in'ti•mate•ly,** *adv.*

in•tim'i•date', *v.,* **-dated, -dating.** make timid; frighten. **—in•tim'i•da'tion,** *n.*

in'to, *prep.* to inside of.

in•tone', *v.,* **-toned, -toning.** 1. use particular spoken tone. 2. chant. **—in'to•na'tion,** *n.*

in•tox'i•cate', *v.,* **-cated, -cating.** affect with or as with alcoholic liquor. **—in•tox'i•ca'tion,** *n.*

in•trac'ta•ble, *adj.* stubborn; unmanageable.

in'tra•mu'ral, *adj.* within one school.

in•tran'si•gent (-sə jənt), *adj.* uncompromising. **—in•tran'si•gence,** *n.*

in•tran'si•tive, *adj.* (of verb) not having a direct object.

in'tra•ve'nous, *adj.* within or into vein.

in•trep'id, *adj.* fearless. **—in'tre•pid'i•ty,** *n.*

in'tri•cate, *adj.* confusingly complicated. **—in'tri•ca•cy,** *n.*

in•trigue' (in trēg'), *v.,* **-trigued, -triguing,** *n.* **—v.** 1. interest by puzzling. 2. plot. **—n.** 3. crafty design or plot.

in•trin'sic, *adj.* inherent; basic. **—in•trin'si•cal•ly,** *adv.*

in'tro•duce', *v.,* **-duced, -ducing.** 1. bring to notice, use, etc. 2. be preliminary to. 3. make (person) known to another. **—in'tro•duc'tion,** *n.* **—in'tro•duc'to•ry,** *adj.*

in'tro•spec'tion, *n.* examination of one's own thoughts and motives. **—in'tro•spec'tive,** *adj.*

in'tro•vert', *n.* person concerned chiefly with his own thoughts. **—in'tro•ver'sion,** *n.*

in•trude', *v.,* **-truded, -truding.** come or bring in without welcome. **—in•trud'er,** *n.* **—in•tru'sion,** *n.* **—in•tru'sive,** *adj.*

in•tu•i'tion, *n.* instinctive perception. **—in•tu'i•tive,** *adj.*

in'un•date', *v.,* **-dated, -dating.** flood. **—in'un•da'tion,** *n.*

in•ure' (in yŏor'), *v.,* **-ured, -uring.** accustom; harden.

in•vade', *v.,* **-vaded, -vading.** enter as an enemy. **—in•vad'er,** *n.* **—in•va'sion,** *n.*

in'va•lid, *n.* 1. sick person. **—adj.** 2. sick. 3. for invalids. 4. (in val'id). not valid. **—in•val'i•date',** *v.*

in•val'u•a•ble, *adj.* priceless.

in•vec'tive, *n.* 1. censure. 2. harsh taunts or accusations.

in•veigh' (-vā'), *v.* attack violently in words.

in•vei'gle (-vē'gəl), *v.* **-gled, -gling.** lure into action.

in•vent', *v.* devise (something new). **—in•ven'tion,** *n.* **—in•ven'tive,** *adj.* **—in•ven'tor,** *n.*

in'ven•to'ry, *n., pl.* **-tories.** list or stock of goods.

in•verse', *adj.* 1. reversed. 2. opposite. 3. inverted.

in•vert', *v.* 1. turn upside down. 2. reverse. 3. make contrary. **—in•ver'sion,** *n.*

in•ver'te•brate (-brit), *adj.* 1. without backbone. **—n.** 2. invertebrate animal.

in•vest', *v.* 1. spend money, esp. so as to get larger amount in return. 2. clothe; cover. 3. furnish. 4. besiege. **—in•vest'ment,** *n.* **—in•ves'tor,** *n.*

in•ves'ti•gate', *v.,* **-gated, -gating.** examine in detail. **—in•ves'ti•ga'tion,** *n.* **—in•ves'ti•ga'tor,** *n.*

in•vet'er•ate, *adj.* confirmed in habit.

in•vid'i•ous, *adj.* 1. likely to arouse envy. 2. offensively unjust.

in•vig'or•ate', *v.,* **-ated, -ating.** give vigor to.

in•vin'ci•ble, *adj.* unconquerable. **—in•vin'ci•bil'i•ty,** *n.*

in•vi'o•la•ble, *adj.* that must not or cannot be violated. **—in•vi'o•la•bil'i•ty,** *n.*

in•vi'o•late, *adj.* 1. not hurt or desecrated. 2. undisturbed.

in•vite', *v.,* **-vited, -viting.** 1. ask politely. 2. act so as to make likely. 3. attract. **—in'vi•ta'tion,** *n.*

in'vo•ca'tion, *n.* prayer for aid, guidance, etc.

in'voice, *n., v.,* **-voiced, -voicing.** **—n.** 1. list with prices of goods sent to buyer. **—v.** 2. list on invoice.

in•voke', *v.,* **-voked, -voking.** 1. beg for. 2. call on in prayer. 3. cite as authoritative.

in•volve', *v.,* **-volved, -volving.** 1. include as necessary. 2. complicate. 3. implicate. 4. engross. **—in•volve'ment,** *n.*

in'ward, *adv.* 1. Also, **in'wards.** toward the interior. **—adj.** 2. toward the interior. 3. inner. **—n.** 4. inward part.

i'o•dine', *n.* nonmetallic element used in medicine.

i'on, *n.* electrically charged particle.

IOU, written acknowledgment of debt.

ip'e•cac', *n.* drug from root of South American shrub.

i•ras'ci•ble (i ras'ə bəl), *adj.* easily angered.

ire, *n.* anger. **—i'rate,** *adj.*

ir'i•des'cence (-des'əns), *n.* play of rainbowlike colors. **—ir'i•des'cent,** *adj.*

in•jus'tice	**in•sen'si•tive**	**in•sol'u•ble**	**in'sup•press'i•ble**	**in•tol'er•a•ble**
in'of•fen'sive	**in'sep'a•ra•ble**	**in'sta•bil'i•ty**	**in'sur•mount'a•ble**	**in•tol'er•ance**
in•op'er•a•tive	**in'sig•nif'i•cance**	**in'sub•or'di•nate**	**in'sus•cep'ti•ble**	**in•tol'er•ant**
in'op•por•tune'	**in'sig•nif'i•cant**	**in'sub•or'di•na'tion**	**in•tan'gi•ble**	**in•var'i•a•ble**
in'or•gan'ic	**in'sin•cere'**	**in•suf'fer•a•ble**	**in•tem'per•ance**	**in•vis'i•ble**
in'se•cure'	**in'sin•cer'i•ty**	**in'suf•fi'cient**	**in•tem'per•ate**	**in•vis'i•bly**

i′ris, *n.* 1. colored part of the eye. 2. perennial plant with showy flowers.

irk, *v.* vex; annoy. **—irk′some,** *adj.*

i′ron, *n.* 1. metallic element. 2. implement for pressing cloth. 3. (*pl.*) shackles. **—***adj.* 4. of or like iron. **—***v.* 5. press with iron (def. 2).

iron curtain, barrier between Communist and non-Communist areas.

i′ro•ny, *n., pl.* **-nies.** 1. figure of speech in which meaning is opposite to what is said. 2. outcome contrary to expectations. **—i•ron′i•cal, i•ron′ic,** *adj.* **—i•ron′i•cal•ly,** *adv.*

ir•ra′di•ate′, *v.,* **-ated, -ating.** 1. illuminate. 2. expose to radiation. 3. shine. **—ir•ra′di•a′tion,** *n.*

ir•ra′tion•al, *adj.* without reason or judgment.

ir•rec′on•cil′a•ble, *adj.* 1. that cannot be brought into agreement. 2. bitterly opposed.

ir′re•deem′a•ble, *adj.* that cannot be redeemed.

ir′re•duc′i•ble, *adj.* that cannot be reduced.

ir•ref′u•ta•ble, *adj.* not refutable.

ir•reg′u•lar, *adj.* 1. not symmetrical. 2. not fixed. 3. not conforming to rule or normality. **—ir•reg′u•lar′i•ty,** *n.*

ir•rel′e•vant, *adj.* not relevant. **—ir•rel′e•vance,** *n.*

ir′re•li′gious, *adj.* impious.

ir′rep′a•ra•ble, *adj.* that cannot be rectified. **—ir′rep′a•ra•bly,** *adv.*

ir′re•press′i•ble, *adj.* that cannot be repressed. **—ir′re•press′i•bly,** *adv.*

ir′re•proach′a•ble, *adj.* blameless.

ir′re•sist′i•ble, *adj.* not to be withstood.

ir•res′o•lute′, *adj.* undecided.

ir•re•spec′tive, *adj.* without regard to.

ir′re•spon′si•ble, *adj.* not concerned with responsibilities.

ir′re•triev′a•ble, *adj.* that cannot be recovered.

ir•rev′er•ent, *adj.* lacking respect.

ir•rev′o•ca•ble, *adj.* not to be revoked or annulled.

ir′ri•gate′, *v.,* **-gated, -gating.** supply with water. **—ir′ri•ga′tion,** *n.*

ir′ri•ta•ble, *adj.* easily angered. **—ir′ri•ta•bil′i•ty,** *n.*

ir′ri•tate′, *v.,* **-tated, -tating.** 1. anger or vex. 2. make sensitive. 3. excite to action. **—ir′ri•ta′tion,** *n.* **—ir′ri•tant,** *n.*

ir•rup′tion, *n.* 1. bursting in. 2. invasion.

is, *v.* third pers. sing. pres. indic. of **be.**

i′sin•glass′, *n.* 1. transparent substance from some fish. 2. mica.

Is•lam′, *n.* religious faith founded by Muhammad (A.D. 570–632).

is′land, *n.* body of land surrounded by water.

isle, *n.* small island.

ism, *n.* doctrine.

i′so•late′, *v.,* **-lated, -lating.** set apart. **—i′so•la′tion,** *n.*

i′so•la′tion•ist, *n.* person opposed to participation in world affairs. **—i′so•la′tion•ism,** *n.*

i′so•met′rics, *n.pl.* exercises in which one body part is tensed against another.

i•sos′ce•les′ (ī sos′ə lēz′), *adj.* (of triangle) having two sides equal.

i′so•tope′, *n.* one of two or more forms of an element that vary in atomic weight.

is′sue, *v.,* **-sued, -suing,** *n.* **—***v.* 1. send out. 2. publish. 3. distribute. 4. emit. 5. emerge. **—***n.* 6. act of issuing. 7. thing issued. 8. point in question. 9. offspring. 10. result. **—is′su•ance,** *n.*

isth′mus (is′məs), *n.* strip of land connecting two larger bodies.

it, *pron.* third pers. sing. neuter pronoun.

I•tal′ian, *n.* native or language of Italy. **—Italian,** *adj.*

i•tal′ic, *n.* printing type that slopes to right. Also, **i•tal′ics. —i•tal′i•cize′,** *v.* **—i•tal′ic,** *adj.*

itch, *v.* 1. feel irritation of skin. **—***n.* 2. itching sensation. 3. restless desire.

i′tem, *n.* separate article.

i′tem•ize′, *v.,* **-ized, -izing.** state by items; list. **—i′tem•i•za′tion,** *n.*

it′er•ate, *v.,* **-ated, -ating.** say or do repeatedly. **—it′er•a′tion,** *n.* **—it′er•a′tive,** *adj.*

i•tin′er•ant, *adj.* 1. traveling. **—***n.* 2. person who goes from place to place.

i•tin′er•ar′y, *n., pl.* **-aries.** 1. route. 2. plan of travel.

its, *adj.* possessive form of **it.**

it′s, contraction of **it is.**

itself, *pron.* reflexive form of **it.**

i′vo•ry, *n., pl.* **-ries.** 1. hard white substance in tusks of elephant, etc. 2. yellowish white.

i′vy, *n., pl.* **ivies.** climbing evergreen vine. **—i′vied,** *adj.*

J

J, j, *n.* tenth letter of English alphabet.

jab, *v.,* **jabbed, jabbing,** *n.* poke; thrust.

jab′ber, *v.* 1. talk rapidly or indistinctly. **—***n.* 2. such talk.

jack, *n.* 1. lifting device. 2. person. 3. knave in playing cards. 4. male. 5. flag; ensign. **—***v.* 6. raise with jack.

jack′al, *n.* wild dog of Asia and Africa.

jack′ass′, *n.* 1. male donkey. 2. fool.

jack′et, *n.* 1. short coat. 2. any covering.

jack′knife′, *n.* folding pocket knife.

jack rabbit, large rabbit of western America.

jade, *n., v.,* **jaded, jading. —***n.* 1. valuable green stone. 2. old horse. **—***v.* 3. weary.

jag, *n.* 1. projection; ragged edge. 2. *Slang.* drunken spree. **—jag′ged,** *adj.*

jag′uar (-wär), *n.* large South American wildcat.

jail, *n.* 1. prison. **—***v.* 2. put in prison. **—jail′er,** *n.*

ja•lop′y, *n., pl.* **-pies.** old, decrepit automobile.

jam, *v.,* **jammed, jamming,** *n.* **—***v.* 1. push or squeeze. 2. make or become unworkable. **—***n.* 3. people or objects jammed together. 4. *Informal.*

difficult situation. 5. preserve of entire fruit.

jamb, *n.* side post of door or window.

jam′bo•ree′, *n.* merry gathering.

jan′gle, *v.,* **-gled, -gling. —***v.* 1. sound harshly. **—***n.* 2. harsh sound.

jan′i•tor, *n.* caretaker of building. **—jan′i•tress,** *n.fem.*

Jan′u•ar′y, *n.* first month of year.

Jap′a•nese′, *n., pl.* **-nese.** native or language of Japan. **—Japanese,** *adj.*

jar, *n., v.,* **jarred, jarring. —***n.* 1. broad-mouthed bottle. 2. unpleasant sound. 3. sudden shock or shake. **—***v.* 4. shock or shake. 5. conflict.

jar′gon, *n.* language meaningful only to particular trade, etc.

jas′mine, *n.* fragrant shrub.

jas′per, *n.* precious quartz.

jaun′dice (jôn′-), *n.* illness causing yellowed skin, etc.

jaun′diced, *adj.,* 1. skeptical. 2. envious.

jaunt, *n.* short trip.

jaun′ty, *adj.* **-tier, -tiest.** sprightly. —**jaun′ti•ly,** *adv.* —**jaun′ti•ness,** *n.*

jave′lin, *n.* spear.

jaw, *n.* either of two bones forming mouth.

jay, *n.* noisy colorful bird.

jay′walk′, *v.* cross street improperly. —**jay′walk′er,** *n.*

jazz, *n.* popular music of black American origin.

jeal′ous, *adj.* 1. resentful of another's success, etc. 2. vigilant, esp. against rivalry. —**jeal′ous•y,** *n.*

jeans, *n.pl.* cotton trousers.

Jeep, *n.* *Trademark.* small rugged type of automobile.

jeer, *v.* 1. deride. —*n.* 2. deriding shout.

Je•ho′vah, *n.* God.

jel′ly, *n., pl.* **-lies,** *v.,* **-lied, -lying.** —*n.* 1. soft, semisolid food, as fruit juice boiled down with sugar. —*v.* 2. make into, or provide with, jelly.

jel′ly•fish′, *n.* marine animal with soft, jellylike body.

jen′ny, *n., pl.* **-nies.** 1. spinning machine. 2. female donkey, wren, etc.

jeop′ard•ize′ (jep′-), *v.,* **-ized, -izing.** risk; endanger. —**jeop′ard•y,** *n.*

jerk, *n.* 1. quick, sharp thrust, pull, etc. 2. *Slang.* stupid, naïve person. —*v.* 3. give jerk to. —**jerk′y,** *adj.*

jer′ry-built′, *adj.* flimsily made.

jer′sey, *n.* type of sweater or shirt.

jest, *n., v.* joke; banter. —**jest′er,** *n.*

Je′sus, *n.* founder of Christian religion. Also called **Jesus Christ.**

jet, *n., v.,* **jetted, jetting,** *adj.* —*n.* 1. stream under pressure. 2. Also, **jet plane.** plane operated by jet propulsion. —*v.* 3. spout. —*adj.* 4. deep black.

jet lag, fatigue after jet flight to different time zone.

jet propulsion, propulsion of plane, etc., by reactive thrust of jet. —**jet′-pro•pelled′,** *adj.*

jet′sam, *n.* goods thrown overboard to lighten distressed ship.

jet′ti•son, *v.* cast (jetsam) out.

jet′ty, *n., pl.* **-ties.** wharf; pier.

Jew, *n.* 1. follower of Judaism. 2. descendant of Biblical Hebrews. —**Jew′ish,** *adj.*

jew′el, *n.* precious stone; gem. —**jew′el•er,** *n.* —**jew′el•ry,** *n.*

jib, *n.* triangular sail on forward mast.

jibe, *v.,* **jibed, jibing.** 1. jeer; taunt. 2. *Informal.* be consistent.

jif′fy, *n., pl.* **-fies.** short time.

jig, *n., v.,* **jigged, jigging.** —*n.* 1. lively folk dance. —*v.* 2. dance a jig.

jig′gle, *v.,* **-gled, -gling.** —*v.* 1. move back and forth, etc. —*n.* 2. act of jiggling.

jilt, *v.* reject (a previously encouraged suitor).

jin′gle, *v.,* **-gled, -gling,** *n.* —*v.* 1. make repeated clinking sound. —*n.* 2. clink; tinkle. 3. very simple verse. ˉ

jin•rik′i•sha (jin rik′shô), *n.* two-wheeled Oriental cart, pulled by man.

jinx, *n.* *Informal.* cause of bad luck.

jit′ter•bug′, *n.* person who dances to popular music with unusual and exaggerated motions.

jit′ters, *n.pl.* *Informal.* nervousness. —**jit′ter•y,** *adj.*

job, *n., v.,* **jobbed, jobbing.** —*n.* 1. piece of work. 2. employment. —*v.* 3. sell wholesale. —**job′less,** *adj.*

job′ber, *n.* 1. wholesaler. 2. dealer in odd lots of merchandise.

jock′ey, *n., pl.* **-eys,** *v.,* **-eyed, -eying.** —*n.* 1. rider of race horses. —*v.* 2. maneuver.

jo•cose′, *adj.* jesting; merry. Also, **joc′und.** —**jo•cos′i•ty,** *n.*

joc′u•lar, *adj.* joking.

jodh′purs (jod′pərz), *n.pl.* riding breeches.

jog, *v.,* **jogged, jogging,** *n.* —*v.* 1. nudge; shake. 2. go at steady pace. —*n.* 3. nudge. 4. steady pace. 5. projection.

join, *v.* 1. put together. 2. become member of.

join′er, *n.* 1. assembler of woodwork. 2. *Informal.* person who likes to join clubs, etc. —**join′er•y,** *n.*

joint, *n.* 1. place or part in which things join. 2. movable section. 3. cheap, sordid place. 4. *Slang.* marijuana cigarette. —*adj.* 5. shared or sharing. —*v.* 6. join or divide at joint. —**joint′ly,** *adv.*

joist, *n.* floor beam.

joke, *n., v.,* **joked, joking.** —*n.* 1. amusing remark, story, etc. —*v.* 2. make or tell joke. 3. speak only to amuse. —**jok′er,** *n.* —**jok′ing•ly,** *adv.*

jol′ly, *adj.,* **-lier, -liest,** *v.,* **-lied, -lying,** *adv.* —*adj.* 1. gay; merry. —*v.* 2. keeping good humor. —*adv.* 3. *Brit. Informal.* very. —**jol′li•ness, jol′li•ty,** *n.*

jolt, *v., n.* jar; shake.

jon′quil, *n.* fragrant yellow or white narcissus.

josh, *v.* *Informal.* tease.

jos′tle, *v.,* **-tled, -tling,** *n.* —*v.* 1. push rudely. —*n.* 2. rude push.

jot, *n., v.,* **jotted, jotting.** —*n.* 1. bit. —*v.* 2. write.

jour′nal, *n.* 1. daily record. 2. periodical. 3. part of shaft in contact with bearing.

jour′nal•ism′, *n.* newspaper writing. —**jour′nal•ist,** *n.* —**jour′nal•is′tic,** *adj.*

jour′ney, *n.* 1. act or course of traveling. —*v.* 2. travel.

jour′ney•man, *n., pl.* **-men.** hired skilled worker.

joust (joust), *n.* fight between mounted knights.

jo′vi•al, *adj.* vigorously cheerful. —**jo′vi•al′i•ty,** *n.*

jowl, *n.* jaw or cheek.

joy, *n.* gladness; delight. —**joy′ful, joy′ous,** *adj.*

ju′bi•lant, *adj.* rejoicing. —**ju′bi•la′tion,** *n.*

ju′bi•lee′, *n.* celebration, esp. of anniversary.

Ju′da•ism′, *n.* religion of the Jewish people.

judge, *n., v.,* **judged, judging.** —*n.* 1. person making authoritative decisions. 2. discriminating person; connoisseur. —*v.* 3. decide on. —**judg′er,** *n.*

judg′ment, *n.* 1. decision, as in court of law. 2. good sense.

ju•di′cial, *adj.* 1. of justice, courts of law, or judges. 2. thoughtful; wise. —**ju•di′cial•ly,** *adv.*

ju•di′ci•ar′y, *n., pl.* **-aries,** *adj.* —*n.* 1. legal branch of government. —*adj.* 2. of judges, etc.

ju•di′cious, *adj.* wise; prudent.

jug, *n.* 1. container for liquids. 2. *Slang.* prison.

jug′gle, *v.,* **-gled, -gling.** perform tricks tossing things. —**jug′gler,** *n.*

jug′u•lar, *adj.* 1. of the neck. —*n.* 2. large vein in neck.

juice, *n.* liquid part of plant, fruit, etc. —**juic′y,** *adj.*

ju•jit′su, *n.* Japanese method of wrestling. Also, **ju′do.**

juke box, coin-operated phonograph.

Ju•ly′, *n.* seventh month of year.

jum′ble, *n., v.,* **-bled, -bling.** —*n.* 1. confused mixture. —*v.* 2. make jumble of.

jum′bo, *adj.* very large.

jump, *v.* 1. spring up; leap. 2. raise. —*n.* 3. spring; leap. 4. rise. 5. *Informal.* advantage.

jump′er, *n.* 1. one that jumps. 2. sleeveless dress worn over blouse.

jump′y, *adj.* **-ier, -iest.** nervous. —**jump′i•ly**, *adv.* —**jump′i•ness**, *n.*

junc′tion, *n.* 1. union. 2. place of joining.

junc′ture, *n.* 1. point of time. 2. crisis. 3. joint.

June, *n.* sixth month of year.

jun′gle, *n.* wildly overgrown tropical land.

jun′ior, *adj.* 1. younger. 2. lower. —*n.* 3. third-year student.

ju′ni•per, *n.* coniferous evergreen shrub or tree.

junk, *n.* 1. useless material; rubbish. 2. type of Chinese ship. —*v.* 3. discard.

jun′ket, *n.* 1. custard. 2. trip or picnic. —*v.* 3. entertain.

jun′ta (hŏōn′tə), *n.* military clique.

Ju′pi•ter, *n.* 1. chief Roman god. 2. largest of sun's planets.

ju′ris•dic′tion, *n.* authority, range of control, etc., of judge or the like. —**ju′ris•dic′tion•al**, *adj.*

ju′ris•pru′dence, *n.* science of law.

ju′rist, *n.* expert in law.

ju′ror, *n.* member of jury. Also, **ju′-ryman**, *fem.* **jur′y•wom′an.**

ju′ry, *n., pl.* **-ries.** group of persons selected to make decisions, esp. in law court.

just, *adj.* 1. fair; right. 2. legal. 3. true. —*adv.* 4. exactly. 5. barely. 6. only. —**just′ly**, *adv*

jus′tice, *n.* 1. fairness; rightness. 2. administration of law. 3. high judge.

jus′ti•fy′, *v.,* **-fied, -fying.** 1. show to be true, right, etc. 2. defend. —**jus′-ti•fi•ca′tion**, *n.* —**jus′ti•fi′a•ble**, *adj.*

jut, *v.,* **jutted, jutting**, *n.* —*v.* 1. project. —*n.* 2. projection.

jute, *n.* East Indian plant whose fibers are used for fabrics, etc.

ju′ve•nile, *adj.* 1. young. —*n.* 2. young person. 3. young male lead. 4. book for children.

jux′ta•pose′, *v.* **-posed, -posing.** place close for comparison.

K

K, k, *n.* eleventh letter of English alphabet.

kai′ser (kī′-), *n.* German emperor.

kale, *n.* type of cabbage.

ka•lei′do•scope′ (-lī′-), *n.* optical device in which colored bits change patterns continually. —**ka•lei′do•scop′ic**, *adj.*

kan′ga•roo′, *n.* Australian marsupial with long hind legs used for leaping.

ka′pok, *n.* silky down from seeds of certain tropical trees, used in pillows, etc.

ka•put′ (-pŏōt′), *adj. Informal.* 1. extinct. 2. out of order.

kar′at, *n.* 1/24 part: unit for measuring purity of gold.

ka•ra′te (kə rä′tē), *n.* Japanese technique of unarmed combat.

kar′ma, *n.* fate as the result of one's actions in successive incarnations.

ka′ty•did, *n.* large green grasshopper.

kay′ak (kī′ak), *n.* Eskimo canoe, esp. of skin.

keel, *n.* 1. central framing member of ship's bottom. —*v.* 2. fall sideways.

keen, *adj.* 1. sharp. 2. excellent. 3. intense. 4. eager. —*v.* 5. wail; lament. —**keen′ly**, *adv.* —**keen′ness**, *n.*

keep, *v.,* **kept, keeping**, *n.* —*v.* 1. continue. 2. detain. 3. support. 4. maintain. 5. withhold. 6. observe. 7. last. —*n.* 8. board and lodging. —**keep′-er**, *n.*

keep′ing, *n.* 1. conformity. 2. care.

keep′sake′, *n.* souvenir.

keg, *n.* small barrel.

ken, *n.* knowledge.

ken′nel, *n.* doghouse.

ker′chief, *n.* cloth head covering.

ker′nel, *n.* center part of nut.

ker′o•sene′, *n.* type of oil.

ketch′up, *n.* catchup.

ket′tle, *n.* pot for boiling liquids, etc.

ket′tle•drum′, *n.* large drum with round bottom.

key, *n.* 1. part for operating lock. 2. explanation. 3. operating lever. 4. musicial tonality. 5. reef. —*adj.* 6. chief. —*v.* 7. intensify; excite.

key′board′, *n.* 1. row of keys on piano, etc. —*v.* 2. insert (data) into computer.

key′note′, *n.* 1. basic note of a musical piece. 2. theme of meeting, etc.

key′stone′, *n.* stone forming summit of arch.

khak′i (kak′ē), *adj., n.* yellowish brown.

khan (kän), *n.* Asiatic ruler.

kib•butz′ (-bŏŏts′), *n., pl.* **-but′zim.** Israeli collective community.

kib′itz•er, *n. Informal.* person offering unwanted advice. —**kib′itz**, *v.*

kick, *v.* 1. strike with foot. 2. recoil. 3. *Informal.* complain. —*n.* 4. act or result of kicking. 5. *Informal.* thrill.

kid, *n., v.,* **kidded, kidding.** —*n.* 1. young goat. 2. leather from its skin.

3. *Informal.* child. —*v.* 4. *Informal.* fool; tease.

kid′nap, *v.* abduct, esp. for ransom. —**kid′nap•er**, *n.*

kid′ney, *n.* 1. gland that secretes urine. 2. kind.

kill, *v.* 1. end life of; murder. 2. destroy; cancel. —*n.* 3. animal slain. —**kill′er**, *n.*

kiln (kil, kiln), *n.* large furnace for making bricks, etc.

kil′o•cy′cle, *n.* kilohertz.

kil′o•gram′, *n.* 1000 grams. Also, **kilo.**

kil′o•hertz′, *n., pl.* **-hertz.** radio frequency of 1000 cycles per second. Also, *formerly,* **kil′o•cy′cle.**

kil′o•li′ter (-lē′-), *n.* 1000 liters.

ki•lom′e•ter, *n.* 1000 meters.

kil′o•watt′, *n.* 1000 watts.

kilt, *n.* man's skirt, worn in Scotland.

ki•mo′no (-nə), *n., pl.* **-nos.** loose dressing gown.

kin, *n.* relatives. Also, **kins′folk′.** —**kins′man**, *n.* —**kins′wom′an,** *n.fem.* —**kin′ship**, *n.*

kind, *adj.* 1. compassionate; friendly. —*n.* 2. type; group. —**kind′ness**, *n.*

kin′der•gar′ten, *n.* school for very young children.

kin′dle, *v.,* **-dled, -dling.** 1. set afire. 2. rouse.

kin′dling, *n.* material for starting fire.

kind′ly, *adj.,* **-lier, -liest,** *adv.* —*adj.* 1. kind; gentle. —*adv.* 2. in kind manner. 3. cordially; favorably. —**kind′-li•ness,** *n.*

kin′dred, *adj.* 1. related; similar. —*n.* 2. relatives.

kin′e•scope′, *n.* 1. television tube. 2. filmed recording of television show.

king, *n.* supreme male ruler. —**king′-ly,** *adj.*

king′dom, *n.* government ruled by king or queen.

king′fish′er, *n.* colorful, fish-eating bird.

king′-size′, *adj.* extra large.

kink, *n., v.* twist; curl. —**kink′y,** *adj.*

kip′per, *n.* salted, dried fish.

kis′met (kiz′met), *n.* fate.

kiss, *v.* 1. touch with lips in affection, etc. —*n.* 2. act of kissing. 3. type of candy.

kit, *n.* set of tools, supplies, etc.

kitch′en, *n.* room for cooking. —**kitch′en•ware′,** *n.*

kitch′en•ette′, *n.* small, compact kitchen.

kite, *n.* 1. light, paper-covered frame flown in wind on long string. 2. type of falcon.

kit′ten, *n.* young cat. Also, **kit′ty.**

kit′ten•ish, *adj.* playfully coy or cute.

klep′to•ma′ni•a, *n.* irresistible desire to steal. —**klep′to•ma′ni•ac′,** *n.*

knack, *n.* special skill.

knap′sack′, *n.* supply bag carried on back.

knave, *n.* dishonest rascal. —**knav′-ish,** *adj.*

knead (nēd), *v.* mix (dough).

knee, *n.* middle joint of leg.

knee′cap′, *n.* flat bone at front of knee.

kneel, *v.,* **knelt** or **kneeled, kneeling.** be on one's knees.

knell, *n.* slow, deep sound of bell.

knick′ers, *n.pl.* type of breeches.

knick′knack′, *n.* trinket.

knife, *n., pl.* **knives.** cutting blade in handle.

knight, *n.* 1. chivalrous soldier of noble birth. 2. holder of honorary rank. 3. piece in chess. —*v.* 4. name man a knight. —**knight′hood,** *n.* —**knight′ly,** *adj., adv.*

knit, *v.,* **knitted** or **knit, knitting.** form netlike fabric. —**knit′ting,** *n.*

knob, *n.* rounded handle. —**knob′by,** *adj.*

knock, *v.* 1. strike hard; pound. 2. *Informal.* criticize. —*n.* 3. hard blow, etc. 4. *Informal.* criticism. —**knock′-er,** *n.*

knoll (nōl), *n.* small hill.

knot, *n., v.,* **knotted, knotting.** —*n.* 1. intertwining of cords to bind. 2. cluster. 3. lump. 4. hard mass where branch joins tree trunk. 5. one nautical mile per hour. —*v.* 6. tie or tangle. —**knot′ty,** *adj.*

knout, *n.* whip.

know, *v.,* **knew, known, knowing,** *n.* —*v.* 1. understand, remember, or experience. —*n.* 2. *Informal.* state of knowledge, esp. of secrets. —**know′-a•ble,** *adj.*

know′-how′, *n. Informal.* skill.

knowl′edge, *n.* facts, etc., known.

know′ledge•a•ble, *adj.* well-informed.

knuck′le, *n.* joint of a finger.

Ko′dak, *n. Trademark.* small camera.

kohl′ra′bi (kōl′rä′bē), *n.* variety of cabbage.

kook (kook), *n. Slang.* eccentric. —**kook′y,** *adj.*

Ko•ran′, *n.* sacred scripture of Islam.

ko′sher, *adj.* (among Jews) permissible to eat.

kow′tow′, *v.* bow respectfully.

ku′dos (-dōs, -döz), *n.* praise; glory.

kum′quat′, *n.* small citrus fruit of Chinese shrub.

kung′ fu′, Chinese technique of unarmed combat.

L

L, l, *n.* twelfth letter of English alphabet.

la′bel, *n., v.,* **-beled, -beling.** —*n.* 1. tag bearing information. —*v.* 2. put label on.

la′bi•um, *n., pl.* **-bia.** liplike part of body. —**la′bi•al,** *adj.*

la′bor, *n.* 1. bodily toil; work. 2. childbirth. —*v.* 3. work. Also, *Brit.,* **la′-bour.** —**la′bor•er,** *n.*

la′bored, *adj.* done with difficulty.

lab′o•ra•to′ry, *n., pl.* **-ries.** place for scientific work.

la•bo′ri•ous, *adj.* involving much labor.

lab′y•rinth (lab′ə-), *n.* 1. maze. 2. internal ear.

lac, *n.* resinous secretion of Asiatic insect.

lace, *n., v.,* **laced, lacing.** —*n.* 1. fancy network of threads. 2. cord. —*v.* 3. fasten with lace. —**lac′y,** *adj.*

lac′er•ate′ (las′ə-), *v.,* **-ated, -ating.** tear; mangle. —**lac′er•a′tion,** *n.*

lach′ry•mal (lak′rə məl), *adj.* of or producing tears.

lach′ry•mose′, *adj.* tearful.

lack, *n.* 1. deficiency. —*v.* 2. be wanting.

lack′a•dai′si•cal, *adj.* listless.

lack′ey, *n., pl.* **-eys.** manservant.

lack′lus′ter, *adj.* uninteresting.

la•con′ic (lə kon′ik), *adj.* using few words. —**la•con′i•cal•ly,** *adv.*

lac′quer, *n.* 1. kind of varnish. —*v.* 2. coat with lacquer.

la•crosse′ (lə krôs′), *n.* game of ball played with long rackets.

lac′tic, *adj.* of or from milk.

la•cu′na (lə kyoo′nə), *n., pl.* **-nae** (-nē), **-nas.** 1. cavity. 2. gap.

lad, *n.* boy.

lad′der, *n.* structure of two sidepieces with steps between.

lad′en, *adj.* loaded heavily.

lad′ing, *n.* cargo; freight.

la′dle, *n., v.,* **-dled, -dling.** —*n.* 1. large deep-bowled spoon. —*v.* 2. dip with ladle.

la′dy, *n., pl.* **-dies.** 1. woman of refinement. 2. mistress of household. 3. title of noblewoman. —**la′dy•like′,** *adj.*

la′dy•bug′, *n.* small spotted beetle. Also, **la′dy•bird′.**

la′dy•fin′ger, *n.* small oblong cake.

lag, *v.,* **lagged, lagging,** *n.* —*v.* 1. move slowly or belatedly. —*n.* 2. instance of lagging.

la′ger (lä′gər), *n.* kind of beer.

lag′gard, *adj.* 1. lagging. —*n.* 2. person who lags.

la•goon′, *n.* shallow pond connected with river, lake, or sea.

lair, *n.* den of beast.

lais′sez-faire′ (les′ā fer′), *adj.* without interfering in trade, others' affairs, etc.

la′i•ty, *n.pl.* laymen.

lake, *n.* large body of water enclosed by land.

la′ma, *n.* Himalayan or Mongolian Buddhist priest.

lamb, *n.* young sheep.

lam'bent, *adj.* flickering or glowing lightly. **—lam'ben•cy,** *n.*

lame, *adj.,* **lamer, lamest,** *v.,* **lamed, laming.** **—***adj.* 1. crippled. 2. inadequate. **—***v.* 3. make lame.

la•ment', *v.* 1. mourn; regret. **—***n.* 2. Also, **lam'en•ta'tion.** expression of lament. **—lam'en•ta•ble,** *adj.*

lam'i•na, *n., pl.* **-nae** (-nē) **-nas.** thin layer.

lam'i•nate, *v.,* **-nated, -nating,** *adj.* **—***v.* 1. split into thin layers. 2. cover or form with layers. **—***adj.* 3. Also, **lam'i•nat'ed.** made of layers. **—lam'i•na'tion,** *n.*

lamp, *n.* light source. **—lamp'shade',** *n.* **—lamp'post',** *n.*

lamp'black', *n.* pigment from soot.

lam•poon', *n.* 1. vicious satire. **—***v.* 2. satirize.

lam'prey, *n.* eellike fish.

lance, *n., v.,* **lanced, lancing.** **—***n.* 1. long spear. **—***v.* 2. open with lancet.

lan'cet, *n.* sharp-pointed surgical tool.

land, *n.* 1. part of the earth's surface above water. 2. region. **—***v.* 3. bring or come to land. 4. fall to earth or floor.

lan'dau (-dô), *n.* carriage with folding top.

land'ing, *n.* 1. act of one that lands. 2. place for landing persons and goods. 3. platform between stairs.

land'lord', *n.* man who owns and leases property. **—land'la'dy,** *n.fem.*

land'lub'ber, *n.* person unused to sea.

land'mark', *n.* 1. prominent object serving as a guide. 2. anything prominent of its kind.

land'scape', *n., v.,* **-scaped, -scaping.** **—***n.* 1. broad view of rural area. **—***v.* 2. arrange trees, shrubs, etc., for effects.

land'slide', *n.* fall of earth or rock.

lane, *n.* narrow road.

lan'guage, *n.* 1. speech. 2. any means of communication.

lan'guid, *adj.* without vigor.

lan'guish, *v.* 1. be or become weak. 2. pine. **—lan'guor,** *n.* **—lan'guor•ous,** *adj.*

lank, *adj.* lean; gaunt. Also, **lank'y.**

lan'o•lin, *n.* fat from wool.

lan'tern, *n.* case for enclosing light.

lan'yard (lan'yərd), *n.* short rope.

lap, *v.,* **lapped, lapping,** *n.* **—***v.* 1. lay or lie partly over. 2. wash against. 3. take up with tongue. **—***n.* 4. overlapping part. 5. one circuit of racecourse. 6. part of body of sitting person from waist to knees.

la•pel', *n.* folded-back part on front of a garment.

lap'i•dar'y, *n., pl.* **-daries,** *adj.* **—***n.* 1. worker in gems. **—***adj.* 2. meticulous in detail.

lap'in, *n.* rabbit.

lapse, *n., v.,* **lapsed, lapsing.** **—***n.* 1. slight error; negligence. 2. slow passing. **—***v.* 3. pass slowly. 4. make error. 5. slip downward. 6. become void.

lar'ce•ny, *n., pl.* **-nies.** theft.

larch, *n.* tree of pine family.

lard, *n.* 1. rendered fat of hogs. **—***v.* 2. apply lard to.

lard'er, *n.* pantry.

large, *adj.,* **larger, largest,** *n.* **—***adj.* 1. great in size or number. **—***n.* 2. at large, a. at liberty. b. in general.

large'ly, *adv.* 1. in large way. 2. generally.

lar•gess', *n.* generous gifts. Also, **lar•gesse'.**

lar'go, *Music.* slowly.

lar'i•at, *n.* long, noosed rope.

lark, *n.* 1. small songbird. 2. frolic.

lark'spur, *n.* plant with flowers on tall stalks.

lar'va, *n., pl.* **-vae** (-vē) young of insect between egg and pupal stages. **—lar'val,** *adj.*

lar'yn•gi'tis (-jī'-), *n.* inflammation of larynx.

lar'ynx, *n., pl.* **larynges, larynxes.** cavity at upper end of windpipe. **—la•ryn'ge•al,** *adj.*

las•civ'i•ous (lə siv'-), *adj.* lewd.

la'ser, *n.* device for amplifying radiation of frequencies of visible light.

lash, *n.* 1. flexible part of whip. 2. blow with whip. 3. eyelash. **—***v.* 4. strike with or as with lash. 5. bind.

lass, *n.* girl.

las'si•tude', *n.* weakness.

las'so, *n., v.,* **-soed, -soing.** **—***n.* 1. lariat. **—***v.* 2. catch with lasso.

last, *adj.* 1. latest. 2. final. **—***adv.* 3. most recently. 4. finally. **—***n.* 5. that which is last. **—***v.* 6. endure. **—last'ly,** *adv.*

latch, *n.* 1. device for fastening door or gate. **—***v.* 2. fasten with latch.

late, *adj., adv.,* **later, latest.** 1. after proper time. 2. being or lasting well along in time. 3. recent. 4. deceased.

late'ly, *adv.* recently.

la'tent, *adj.* hidden; dormant. **—la'ten•cy,** *n.*

lat'er•al, *adj.* on or from the side.

la'tex, *n.* milky plant juice yielding rubber.

lath (lath), *n.* 1. narrow wood strip. 2. material for holding plaster. **—***v.* 3. cover with laths.

lathe (lāth), *n.* machine for turning wood, etc., against a shaping tool.

lath'er, *n.* 1. froth made with soap and water. 2. froth from sweating. **—***v.* 3. form or cover with lather.

Lat'in, *n.* 1. language of ancient Rome. 2. member of any people speaking Latin-based language. **—Latin,** *adj.*

Latin America, countries in South and Central America where Spanish or Portuguese is spoken.

lat'i•tude', *n.* 1. distance from equator. 2. freedom.

la•trine' (-trēn'), *n.* toilet, esp. in army.

lat'ter, *n.* 1. being second of two. 2. later.

lat'tice, *n.* structure of crossed strips. **—lat'tice•work',** *n.*

laud, *v.* praise. **—laud'a•ble,** *adj.* **—laud'a•to'ry,** *adj.*

lau'da•num (lô'də nəm), *n.* tincture of opium.

laugh, *v.* 1. express mirth audibly. **—***n.* 2. act or sound of laughing. **—laugh'ter,** *n.*

laugh'a•ble, *adj.* ridiculous.

launch, *v.* 1. set afloat. 2. start. 3. throw. **—***n.* 4. large, open motorboat.

launch pad, platform for launching rockets. Also, **launch'ing pad.**

laun'der, *v.* wash and iron. **—laun'dress,** *n.fem.*

laun'dry, *n., pl.* **-dries.** 1. clothes, etc., to be washed. 2. place where clothes, etc., are laundered.

lau'rel, *n.* 1. small glossy evergreen tree. 2. (*pl.*) honors.

la'va, *n.* molten rock from volcano.

lav'a•to'ry, *n., pl.* **-ries.** 1. bathroom. 2. washbowl.

lave, *v.,* **laved, laving.** bathe.

lav'en•der, *n.* 1. pale purple. 2. fragrant shrub yielding **oil of lavender.**

lav'ish, *adj.* 1. extravagant. **—***v.* 2. expend or give abundantly. **—lav'ish•ly,** *adv.*

law, *n.* 1. rules under which people live. 2. rule. 3. legal action. **—law'-a•bid'ing,** *adj.* **—law'less,** *adj.* **—law'mak'er,** *n.*

law'ful, *adj.* permitted by law. **—law'ful•ly,** *adv.*

lawn, *n.* 1. grass-covered land kept mowed. 2. thin cotton or linen fabric.

law'suit', *n.* prosecution of claim in court.

law'yer, *n.* person trained in law.

lax, *adj.* 1. careless. 2. slack. —**lax'i•ty,** *n.*

lax'a•tive, *adj.* 1. mildly purgative. —*n.* 2. laxative agent.

lay, *v.,* **laid, laying,** *n., adj.* —*v.* 1. put down. 2. produce eggs. 3. ascribe. 4. devise. 5. pt. of **lie.** —*n.* 6. position. 7. song. —*adj.* 8. not clerical or professional. —**lay'man,** *n.*

lay'er, *n.* one thickness.

lay•ette', *n.* outfit for newborn child.

lay'out', *n.* arrangement.

la'zy, *adj.,* **lazier, laziest.** 1. unwilling to work. 2. slow-moving. —**la'zi•ly,** *adv.* —**la'zi•ness,** *n.*

lea, *n.* meadow.

leach, *v.* soak through or in.

lead (lēd for 1–4; led for 5–7), *v.,* **led, leading,** *n.* —*v.* 1. guide by going before or with. 2. influence. 3. afford passage. —*n.* 4. foremost place or part. 5. heavy malleable metal. 6. plummet. 7. graphite used in pencils. —**lead'en,** *adj.* —**lead'er,** *n.* —**lead'er•ship',** *n.*

leaf, *n., pl.* **leaves,** *v.* —*n.* 1. flat green part on stem of plant. 2. thin sheet. —*v.* 3. thumb through. —**leaf'y,** *adj.*

leaf'let, *n.* 1. small leaf. 2. pamphlet.

league, *n., v.,* **leagued, leaguing.** 1. alliance; pact. 2. unit of distance, about three miles. —*v.* 3. unite in league.

leak, *n.* 1. unintended hole. —*v.* 2. pass or let pass through leak. 3. allow to be known unofficially. —**leak'age,** *n.* —**leak'y,** *adj.*

lean, *v.,* **leaned** or **leant, leaning,** *n., adj.* —*v.* 1. bend. 2. depend. —*n.* 3. inclination. 4. lean flesh. —*adj.* 5. not fat. —**lean'ness,** *n.*

leap, *v.,* **leaped** or **leapt, leaping,** *n.* —*v.* 1. spring through air; jump. —*n.* 2. jump.

leap year, year of 366 days.

learn, *v.* acquire knowledge or skill. —**learn'er,** *n.* —**learn'ing,** *n.*

learn'ed, *adj.* knowing much; scholarly.

lease, *n., v.,* **leased, leasing.** —*n.* 1. contract conveying property for certain time. —*v.* 2. get by means of lease.

leash, *n.* line for holding dog.

least, *adj.* 1. smallest. —*n.* 2. least amount, etc. —*adv.* 3. to least extent, etc.

leath'er, *n.* prepared skin of animals. —**leath'er•y,** *adj.*

leave, *v.,* **left, leaving,** *n.* —*v.* 1. depart from. 2. let remain or be. 3. have remaining. 4. bequeath. —*n.* 5. permission. 6. farewell. 7. furlough.

leav'en (lev'-), *n.* 1. Also, **leav'en•ing.** fermenting agency to raise dough. —*v.* 2. produce fermentation.

lech'er•ous (lech'ər əs), *adj.* lustful. —**lech'er•y,** *n.*

lec'tern, *n.* stand for speaker's papers.

lec'ture, *n., v.,* **-tured, -turing.** —*n.* 1. instructive speech. —*v.* 2. give lecture. —**lec'tur•er,** *n.*

ledge, *n.* narrow shelf.

ledg'er, *n.* account book.

lee, *n.* 1. shelter. 2. side away from the wind. 3. (*pl.*) dregs. —**lee,** *adj.* —**lee'ward,** *adj., adv., n.*

leech, *n.* blood-sucking worm.

leek, *n.* plant resembling onion.

leer, *n.* 1. sly or insinuating glance. —*v.* 2. look with leer.

lee'way', *n.* 1. *Naut.* drift due to wind. 2. extra time, space, etc.

left, *adj.* 1. on side toward west when facing north. —*n.* 2. left side. 3. political side favoring liberal or radical reform. —**left'-hand',** *adj.* —**left'-hand'ed,** *adj.* —**left'ist,** *n., adj.*

leg, *n.* 1. one of limbs supporting a body. 2. any leglike part.

leg'a•cy, *n., pl.* **-cies.** anything bequeathed.

le'gal, *adj.* of or according to law. —**le•gal'i•ty,** *n.* —**le'gal•ize',** *v.*

leg'a•tee', *n.* person bequeathed legacy.

le•ga'tion, *n.* 1. diplomatic minister and staff. 2. official residence of minister.

leg'end, *n.* 1. story handed down by tradition. 2. inscription. —**leg'end•ar'y,** *adj.*

leg'er•de•main', (lej'ər də mān'), *n.* sleight of hand.

leg'ging, *n.* covering for leg.

leg'i•ble, *adj.* easily read. —**leg'i•bil'i•ty,** *n.* —**leg'i•bly,** *adv.*

le'gion, *n.* 1. military unit. 2. multitude.

leg'is•late', *v.,* **-lated, -lating.** 1. make laws. 2. effect by law. —**leg'is•la'tion,** *n.* —**leg'is•la'tive,** *adj.* —**leg'is•la'tor,** *n.*

leg'is•la'ture, *n.* law-making body.

le•git'i•mate, *adj.* 1. lawful. 2. after right or established principles. 3. born to a married couple. —**le•git'i•ma•cy,** *n.*

le•git'i•mize', *v.,* **-mized, -mizing.** show to be or treat as legitimate.

leg'ume (leg'yoom), *n.* plant of group including peas and beans. —**le•gu'mi•nous,** *adj.*

lei (lā), *n., pl.* **leis.** wreath of flowers for neck.

lei'sure (lē'zhər), *n.* 1. freedom from work. —*adj.* 2. unoccupied; at rest.

lei'sure•ly, *adj.* unhurried.

lem'on, *n.* yellowish fruit of citrus tree.

lem'on•ade', *n.* beverage of lemon juice and sweetened water.

le'mur (lē'mər), *n.* small monkeylike animal.

lend, *v.,* **lent, lending.** 1. give temporary use of. 2. give; provide. —**lend'er,** *n.*

length, *n.* size or extent from end to end. —**length'en,** *v.* —**length'wise',** *adv., adj.* —**length'y,** *adj.*

le'ni•ent, *adj.* merciful; not severe. —**le'ni•ence, le'ni•en•cy,** *n.*

lens, *n., pl.* **lenses.** glass for changing convergence of light rays.

Lent, *n.* season of fasting preceding Easter. —**Lent'en,** *adj.*

len'til, *n.* pealike plant.

le'o•nine' (lē'ə nīn'), *adj.* of or like the lion.

leop'ard, *n.* large fierce spotted animal.

lep'er (lep'ər), *n.* person afflicted with leprosy.

lep're•chaun', *n.* Irish sprite.

lep'ro•sy, *n.* disease marked by skin ulcerations.

les'bi•an (lez'-), *adj., n.* female homosexual.

le'sion (lē'zhən), *n.* 1. injury. 2. morbid change in bodily part.

less, *adv.* 1. to smaller extent. —*adj.* Also, **les'ser.** 2. smaller. 3. lower in importance. —*n.* 4. Also, **lesser.** smaller amount, etc. —*prep.* 5. minus. —**less'en,** *v.*

les•see', *n.* one granted a lease.

les'ser, *adj.* 1. compar. of **little.** 2. minor.

les'son, *n.* 1. something to be studied. 2. reproof. 3. useful experience.

les'sor, *n.* one granting a lease.

lest, *conj.* for fear that.

let, *v.,* **let, letting,** *n.* —*v.* 1. permit. 2. rent out. 3. contract for work. —*n.* 4. release. 5. hindrance.

le′thal, *adj.* deadly.

leth′ar•gy, *n.*, *pl.* **-gies.** drowsy dullness. —**le•thar′gic,** *adj.*

let′ter, *n.* 1. written communication. 2. written component of word. 3. actual wording. 4. (*pl.*) literature. —*v.* 5. write with letters.

let′tered, *adj.* literate; learned.

let′ter•head′, *n.* printed information at top of letter paper.

let′tuce, *n.* plant with large leaves used in salad.

leu•ke′mi•a, *n.* cancerous disease of blood cells.

lev′ee, *n.* 1. embankment to prevent floods. 2. (Also, le vē′). reception.

lev′el, *adj.*, *n.*, *v.*, **-eled, -eling.** —*adj.* 1. even. 2. horizontal. 3. well-balanced. —*n.* 4. height; elevation. 5. level position. 6. device for determining horizontal plane. —*v.* 7. make or become level. 8. aim. —**lev′el•er,** *n.*

lev′er, *n.* bar moving on fixed support to exert force.

lev′er•age, *n.* power or action of lever.

le•vi′a•than (-vī′-), *n.* sea monster.

lev′i•ty, *n.* lack of seriousness.

lev′y, *v.*, **levied, levying,** *n.*, *pl.* **levies.** —*v.* 1. raise or collect by authority. 2. make (war). —*n.* 3. act of levying. 4. something levied.

lewd, *adj.* obscene. —**lewd′ly,** *adv.* —**lewd′ness,** *n.*

lex′i•cog′ra•phy, *n.* writing of dictionaries. —**lex′i•cog′ra•pher,** *n.*

lex′i•con, *n.* dictionary.

li′a•bil′i•ty, *n.*, *pl.* **-ties.** 1. debt. 2. disadvantage. 3. state of being liable.

li′a•ble, *adj.* 1. likely. 2. subject to obligation or penalty.

li′ai•son′ (lē′ə zon′), *n.* 1. contact to ensure cooperation. 2. intimacy; affair.

li′ar, *n.* person who tells lies.

li′bel, *n.*, *v.*, **-beled, -beling.** —*n.* 1. defamation in writing or print. —*v.* 2. publish libel against. —**li′bel•ous,** *adj.*

lib′er•al, *adj.* 1. favoring extensive individual liberty. 2. tolerant. 3. generous. —*n.* 4. liberal person. —**lib′er•al•ism,** *n.* —**lib′er•al′i•ty,** *n.* —**lib′er•al•ize,** *v.*

lib′er•ate, *v.*, **-ated, -ating.** set free. —**lib′er•a′tion,** *n.* —**lib′er•a′tor,** *n.*

lib′er•tine′ (-tēn′), *n.* dissolute man.

lib′er•ty, *n.*, *pl.* **-ties.** 1. freedom; independence. 2. right to use place. 3. impertinent freedom.

li•bi′do (-bē-), *n.* sexual desire. —**li•bid′i•nous,** *adj.*

li′brar′y, *n.*, *pl.* **-ries.** 1. place for collection of books, etc. 2. collection of books, etc. —**li•brar′i•an,** *n.*

li•bret′to (li-), *n.*, *pl.* **-tos, -ti.** words of musical drama.

li′cense, *n.*, *v.*, **-censed, -censing.** —*n.* 1. formal permission. 2. undue freedom. —*v.* 3. grant license to. Also, **li′cence.**

li•cen′tious, *adj.* lewd; lawless.

li′chen (lī′kən), *n.* crustlike plant on rocks, trees, etc.

lic′it (lis′it), *adj.* lawful.

lick, *v.* 1. pass tongue over. 2. *Informal.* beat or defeat. —*n.* 3. act of licking. 4. place where animals lick salt.

lic′o•rice, *n.* plant root used in candy, etc.

lid, *n.* 1. movable cover. 2. eyelid.

lie, *n.*, *v.*, **lied, lying.** —*n.* 1. deliberately false statement. —*v.* 2. tell lie.

lie, *v.*, **lay, lain, lying,** *n.* —*v.* 1. assume or have reclining position. 2. be or remain. —*n.* 3. manner of lying.

lief, *adv.* gladly.

liege (lēj), *n.* 1. lord. 2. vassal.

lien (lēn), *n.* right in another's property as payment on claim.

lieu (lōō), *n.* stead.

lieu•ten′ant, *n.* 1. commissioned officer in army or navy. 2. aide. —**lieu•ten′an•cy,** *n.*

life, *n.*, *pl.* **lives.** 1. distinguishing quality of animals and plants. 2. period of being alive. 3. living things. 4. mode of existence. 5. animation. —**life′long′,** *adj.* —**life′time′,** *n.* —**life′less,** *adj.*

life′-size′, *adj.* of the actual size of a person, etc.

life′ style′. person's general pattern of living.

lift, *v.* 1. move or hold upward. 2. raise or rise. —*n.* 3. act of lifting. 4. help. 5. ride. 6. exaltation. 7. *Brit.* small elevator.

lift′-off′, *n.* departure from ground by rocket, etc., under own power.

lig′a•ment, *n.* band of tissue.

light, *n.*, *adj.*, *v.*, **lighted** or **lit, lighting.** —*n.* 1. that which makes things visible or gives illumination. 2. daylight. 3. aspect. 4. enlightenment. —*adj.* 5. not dark. 6. not heavy. 7. not serious. —*v.* 8. ignite. 9. illuminate. 10. alight; land. 11. happen (upon). —**light′ly,** *adv.* —**light′ness,** *n.*

light′-heart′ed, *adj.* cheerful; without worry.

light′-head′ed, *adj.* as if about to faint.

light′en, *v.* 1. become or make less dark. 2. lessen in weight. 3. mitigate. 4. cheer.

light′er, *n.* 1. something that lights. 2. barge.

light′house′, *n.* tower displaying light to guide seamen.

light′ning, *n.* flash of light in sky.

light′-year′, *n.* distance that light travels in one year.

lig′nite (lig′nīt), *n.* kind of coal.

like, *v.*, **liked, liking,** *adj.*, *prep.*, *conj.*, *n.* —*v.* 1. find agreeable. 2. wish. —*adj.* 3. resembling; similar to. —*prep.* 4. in like manner with. —*conj.* 5. *Informal.* as; as if. —*n.* 6. like person or thing; match. 7. preference. —**lik′a•ble, like′a•ble,** *adj.*

like′ly, *adj.*, **-lier, -liest,** *adv.* —*adj.* 1. probable. 2. suitable; promising. —*adv.* 3. probably. —**like′li•hood′,** *n.*

lik′en, *v.* compare.

like′ness, *n.* 1. image; picture. 2. fact of being like.

like′wise′, *adv.* 1. also. 2. in like manner.

li′lac (lī′lək), *n.* fragrant flowering shrub.

lilt, *n.* rhythmic swing.

lil′y, *n.*, *pl.* **lilies.** bulbous plant with erect stems and showy flowers.

li′ma bean, flat, edible bean.

limb, *n.* 1. jointed part of an animal body. 2. branch.

lim′ber, *adj.* 1. flexible; supple. —*v.* 2. make or become limber.

lim′bo, *n.* 1. region on border of hell or heaven. 2. state of oblivion.

Lim′burg′er, *n.* soft strong cheese.

lime, *n.*, *v.*, **limed, liming.** —*n.* 1. oxide of calcium, used in mortar, etc. 2. small, greenish, acid fruit of tropical tree. —*v.* 3. treat with lime.

lime′light′, *n.* 1. strong light used on stage. 2. public notice; fame.

lim′er•ick (lim′-), *n.* humorous five-line verse.

lime′stone′, *n.* rock consisting chiefly of powdered calcium.

lim′it, *n.* 1. farthest extent; boundary. —*v.* 2. fix or keep within limits. —**lim′it•less,** *adj.*

lim′it•ed, *adj.* 1. restricted 2. (of trains, etc.) making few stops. —*n.* 3. limited train, etc.

lim′ou·sine′ (lim′ə zēn′), *n.* enclosed automobile for several passengers.

limp, *v.* 1. walk unevenly. —*n.* 2. lame movement. —*adj.* 3. not stiff or firm.

lim′pet, *n.* small, cone-shelled, marine animal.

lim′pid, *adj.* clear.

lin′den, *n.* tree with heart-shaped leaves.

line, *n., v.,* **lined, lining.** —*n.* 1. long thin mark. 2. row; series. 3. course of action, etc. 4. boundary. 5. string, cord, etc. 6. occupation. —*v.* 7. form line. 8. mark with line. 9. cover inner side of.

lin′e·age (lin′ē ij), *n.* ancestry.

lin′e·al, *adj.* 1. of direct descent. 2. Also, **lin′e·ar.** in or of a line.

lin′e·a·ment, *n.* feature, as of face.

lin′en, *n.* 1. fabric made from flax. 2. articles of linen or cotton.

lin′er, *n.* 1. ship or airplane on regular route. 2. lining.

line′-up′, *n.* order.

lin′ger, *v.* 1. stay on. 2. persist. 3. delay.

lin′ge·rie′ (län′zhə rā′), *n.* women's undergarments.

lin′go, *n., pl.* **-goes.** *Informal.* language.

lin′gual, *adj.* 1. of the tongue. 2. of languages.

lin·gui′ni (-gwē′nē), *n. pl.* pasta in slender flat form.

lin′guist, *n.* person skilled in languages.

lin·guis′tics, *n.* science of language. —**lin·guis′tic,** *adj.*

lin′i·ment, *n.* liquid applied to bruises, etc.

lin′ing, *n.* inner covering.

link, *n.* 1. section of chain. 2. bond. —*v.* 3. unite. —**link′age,** *n.*

links, *n.pl.* golf course.

lin′net, *n.* small songbird.

li·no′le·um, *n.* floor covering made of cork, oil, etc.

Lin′o·type, *n. Trademark.* keyboard machine for casting solid type.

lin′seed′, *n.* seed of flax.

lin′sey-wool′sey, *n., pl.* **-seys.** fabric of linen and wool.

lint, *n.* bits of thread.

lin′tel, *n.* beam above door or window.

li′on, *n.* 1. large tawny animal of Africa and Asia. 2. person of note. —**li′on·ess,** *n.fem.*

lip, *n.* 1. fleshy margin of the mouth. 2. projecting edge.

lip′stick′, *n.* coloring for lips.

liq′ue·fy′, *v.,* **-fied, -fying.** become liquid. —**liq′ue·fac′tion,** *n.*

li·queur′ (li kûr′), *n.* strong, sweet, alcoholic drink.

liq′uid, *n.* 1. fluid of molecules remaining together. —*adj.* 2. of or being a liquid. 3. in or convertible to cash.

liq′ui·date′, *v.,* **-dated, -dating.** 1. settle, as debts. 2. convert into cash. 3. eliminate. —**liq′ui·da′tion,** *n.*

liq′uor, *n.* 1. alcoholic beverage. 2. liquid.

lisle (līl), *n.* strong linen or cotton thread.

lisp, *n.* 1. pronunciation of *s* and *z* like *th.* —*v.* 2. speak with lisp.

list, *n.* 1. series of words, names, etc. 2. inclination to side. —*v.* 3. make or enter on list. 4. incline.

lis′ten, *v.* attend with ear. —**lis′ten·er,** *n.*

list′less, *adj.* spiritless.

lit′a·ny, *n., pl.* **-nies.** form of prayer.

li′ter (lē′-), *n.* metric unit of capacity, = 1.0567 U.S. quarts. Also, *Brit.,* **li′tre.**

lit′er·al, *adj.* exactly as written or stated. —**lit′er·al·ly,** *adv.*

lit′er·al-mind′ed, *adj.* interpreting without imagination.

lit′er·ar′y, *adj.* of books and writings.

lit′er·ate, *adj.* 1. able to read and write. 2. educated. —*n.* 3. literate person. —**lit′er·a·cy,** *n.*

lit′er·a·ture, *n.* writings, esp. those of notable expression and thought.

lithe (līth), *adj.* limber. Also, **lithe′-some.**

lith′o·graph′, *n.* print made from prepared stone or plate. —**li·thog′ra·pher,** *n.* —**li·thog′ra·phy,** *n.*

lit′i·gant, *n.* person engaged in lawsuit.

lit′i·gate′, *v.,* **-gated, -gating.** carry on lawsuit. —**lit′i·ga′tion,** *n.*

lit′mus, *n.* blue coloring matter turning red in acid solution.

lit′ter, *n.* 1. disordered array. 2. young from one birth. 3. stretcher. 4. bedding for animals. —*v.* 5. strew in disorder.

lit′tle, *adj.* 1. small. 2. mean. —*adv.* 3. not much. —*n.* 4. small amount.

lit′ur·gy (lit′ər jē), *n., pl.* **-gies.** form of worship. —**li·tur′gi·cal,** *adj.*

liv′a·ble, *adj.* habitable or endurable.

live (liv *for 1–5;* līv *for 6–8*), *v.,* **lived, living,** *adj.* —*v.* 1. be alive. 2. endure in reputation. 3. rely for food, etc. 4.

dwell. 5. pass (life). —*adj.* 6. alive. 7. energetic. 8. effective.

live′li·hood′, *n.* means of supporting oneself.

live′ly, *adj.,* **-lier, -liest,** *adv.* —*adj.* 1. active; spirited. —*adv.* 2. vigorously. —**live′li·ness,** *n.*

liv′er, *n.* abdominal organ that secretes bile.

liv′er·wurst′, *n.* liver sausage.

liv′er·y, *n., pl.* **-eries.** 1. uniform of male servants. 2. keeping of horses for hire.

live′stock′, *n.* domestic farm animals.

liv′id, *adj.* 1. dull-blue. 2. furious.

liv′ing, *adj.* 1. live. 2. sufficient for living. —*n.* 3. condition of life. 4. livelihood.

liz′ard, *n.* four-legged reptile.

lla′ma (lä′mə), *n.* South American animal.

lo, *interj.* behold!

load, *n.* 1. cargo; anything carried. 2. charge of firearm. —*v.* 3. put load on. 4. oppress. 5. charge (firearm). —**load′er,** *n.*

load′stone′, *n.* magnetic stone. Also, **lode′stone′.**

loaf, *n., pl.* **loaves,** *v.* —*n.* 1. shaped mass of bread, etc. —*v.* 2. idle. —**loaf′er,** *n.*

loam, *n.* loose fertile soil.

loan, *n.* 1. act of lending. 2. something lent. —*v.* 3. lend.

loath, *adj.* reluctant.

loathe, *v.,* **loathed, loathing.** feel disgust at; despise. —**loath′some,** *adj.*

lob, *v.,* **lobbed, lobbing,** *n.* —*v.* 1. strike or hurl in a high curve. —*n.* 2. tennis ball so struck.

lob′by, *n., pl.* **-bies,** *v.,* **-bied, -bying.** —*n.* 1. vestibule or entrance hall. 2. group that tries to influence legislators. —*v.* 3. try to influence legislators. —**lob′by·ist,** *n.*

lobe, *n.* roundish projection. —**lo′bar, lo′bate,** *adj.*

lob′ster, *n.* edible marine shellfish.

lo′cal, *adj.* 1. of or in particular area. —*n.* 2. local branch of trade union. 3. train that makes all stops. —**lo′cal·ly,** *adv.*

lo·cale′ (-kal′), *n.* setting; place.

lo·cal′i·ty, *n., pl.* **-ties.** place; area.

lo′cal·ize′, *v.,* **-ized, -izing.** confine to particular place. —**lo′cal·i·za′tion,** *n.*

lo′cate, *v.,* **-cated, -cating.** find or establish place of.

lo·ca′tion, *n.* 1. act or instance of locating. 2. place where something is.

lock, *n.* 1. fastener preventing unauthorized access. 2. place in canal for moving vessels from one water level to another. 3. part of firearm. 4. tress of hair. —*v.* 5. secure with lock. 6. shut in or out. 7. join firmly.

lock′er, *n.* closet with lock.

lock′et, *n.* small case worn on necklace.

lock′jaw′, *n.* disease in which jaws become tightly locked.

lock′out′, *n.* business closure to force acceptance of employer's terms of work.

lock′smith′, *n.* person who makes or repairs locks.

lo′co•mo′tion, *n.* act of moving about.

lo′co•mo′tive, *n.* engine that pulls railroad cars.

lo′cust, *n.* 1. kind of grasshopper. 2. flowering American tree.

lo•cu′tion (lō kyoo′shən), *n.* phrase; expression.

lode, *n.* veinlike mineral deposit.

lode′star′, *n.* star that shows the way.

lodge, *n.*, *v.*, **lodged, lodging.** —*n.* 1. hut or house. 2. secret society. —*v.* 3. live or house temporarily. 4. fix or put; become fixed. —**lodg′er,** *n.*

lodg′ing, *n.* 1. temporary housing. 2. (*pl.*) rooms.

lodg′ment, *n.* 1. lodging. 2. something lodged. Also, **lodge′ment.**

loft, *n.* attic or gallery.

loft′y, *adj.,* **loftier, loftiest.** 1. tall. 2. exalted or elevated. —**loft′i•ly,** *adv.*

log, *n.,* *v.,* **logged, logging.** —*n.* 1. trunk of felled tree. 2. Also, **log′-book′.** record of events. —*v.* 3. fell and cut up trees. 4. record in log. —**log′ger,** *n.*

lo′gan•ber′ry, *n.,* *pl.* **-ries.** dark-red, acid fruit.

log′a•rithm, *n.* *Math.* symbol of number of times a number must be multiplied by itself to equal a given number.

loge (lōzh), *n.* box in theater.

log′ger•head′, *n.* 1. stupid person. 2. at loggerheads, disputing.

log′ic, *n.* science of reasoning. —**log′i•cal,** *adj.* —**log′i•cal•ly,** *adv.* —**lo•gi′cian,** *n.*

lo•gis′tics, *n.* science of military supply. —**lo•gis′tic, lo•gis′ti•cal,** *adj.*

lo′gy (lō′gē), *adj.,* **-gier, -giest.** heavy; dull.

loin, *n.* part of body between ribs and hipbone.

loi′ter, *v.* linger. —**loi′ter•er,** *n.*

loll, *v.* 1. recline indolently. 2. hang loosely.

lol′li•pop′, *n.* hard candy on stick.

lone, *adj.* alone.

lone′ly, *adj.* 1. alone. 2. wishing for company. 3. isolated. —**lone′li•ness,** *n.*

lone′some, *adj.* 1. depressed by solitude. 2. lone.

long, *adj.,* **longer, longest,** *adv.,* *v.* —*adj.* 1. of great or specified length. —*adv.* 2. for long space of time. —*v.* 3. yearn. —**long′ing,** *n.*

lon•gev′i•ty (lon jev′-), *n.* long life.

long′hand′, *n.* ordinary handwriting.

lon′gi•tude′, *n.* distance east and west on earth's surface.

lon′gi•tu′di•nal, *adj.* 1. of longitude. 2. lengthwise.

long′shore′man, *n.* man who loads and unloads vessels.

long′-wind′ed, *adj.* speaking or spoken at excessive length.

look, *v.* 1. direct the eyes. 2. seem. 3. face. 4. seek. —*n.* 5. act of looking. 6. appearance.

look′ing glass, mirror.

look′out′, *n.* 1. watch. 2. person for keeping watch. 3. place for keeping watch. 4. *Informal.* personal problem.

loom, *n.* 1. device for weaving fabric. —*v.* 2. weave on loom. 3. appear as large and indistinct.

loon, *n.* diving bird.

loop, *n.* 1. circular form from length of material or line. —*v.* 2. form a loop.

loop′hole′, *n.* 1. small opening in wall, etc. 2. means of evasion.

loose, *adj.,* **looser, loosest,** *v.,* **loosed, loosing.** —*adj.* 1. free; unconfined. 2. not firm or tight. 3. not exact. 4. dissolute. —*v.* 5. free. 6. shoot. —**loos′en,** *v.* —**loose′ly,** *adv.* —**loose′ness,** *n.*

loot, *n.* 1. spoils. —*v.* 2. plunder. —**loot′er,** *n.*

lop, *v.,* **lopped, lopping.** cut off.

lop′sid′ed, *adj.* uneven.

lo•qua′cious, *adj.* talkative. —**lo•quac′i•ty** (-kwas′ə tē), *n.*

lord, *n.* 1. master. 2. British nobleman. 3. (*cap.*) God. 4. (*cap.*) Jesus Christ. —*v.* 5. domineer. —**lord′ly,** *adj.* —**lord′ship,** *n.*

lore, *n.* learning.

lor•gnette′ (lôr nyet′), *n.* eyeglasses on long handle.

lor′ry, *n.,* *pl.* **-ries.** *Brit.* truck.

lose, *v.,* **lost, losing.** 1. fail to keep. 2. misplace. 3. fail to win. 4. be unaware of surroundings. 5. bring to ruin. —**los′er,** *n.*

loss, *n.* 1. disadvantage from losing. 2. something lost. 3. waste.

lot, *n.* 1. object drawn to decide question by chance. 2. allotted share. 3. piece of land. 4. large amount or number.

lo′tion, *n.* medicinal liquid for skin.

lot′ter•y, *n.,* *pl.* **-teries.** sale of tickets on prizes to be awarded by lots.

lo′tus, *n.* water lily of Egypt and Asia.

loud, *adj.* 1. strongly audible. 2. blatant. —**loud′ly,** *adv.* —**loud′ness,** *n.*

loud′-mouth′, *n.* a braggart, gossip, etc. —**loud′-mouthed′,** *adj.*

loud′speak′er, *n.* device for reproducing sound at higher volume.

lounge, *v.,* **lounged, lounging,** *n.* —*v.* 1. pass time idly. 2. loll. —*n.* 3. kind of sofa. 4. public parlor.

louse, *n.,* *pl.* **lice.** blood-sucking insect.

lous′y, *adj.,* **-ier, -iest.** 1. *Informal.* bad; poor. 2. troubled with lice. —**lous′i•ness,** *n.*

lout, *n.* boor.

lou′ver (loo′vər), *n.* arrangement of slits for ventilation.

lov′a•ble, *adj.* attracting love. Also, **love′a•ble.** —**lov′a•bly,** *adv.*

love, *n.,* *v.,* **loved, loving.** —*n.* 1. strong affection. 2. sweetheart. —*v.* 3. have love for. —**lov′er,** *n.* —**love′-less,** *adj.* —**lov′ing•ly,** *adv.*

love′ly, *adj.,* **-lier, -liest.** charming.

love′sick′, *adj.* sick from intensity of love.

low, *adj.* 1. not high or tall. 2. prostrate. 3. weak. 4. humble or inferior. 5. not loud. —*adv.* 6. in or to low position. 7. in quiet tone. —*n.* 8. something that is low. 9. moo. —*v.* 10. moo.

low′brow′, *n.* 1. uncultured person. —*adj.* 2. typical of a lowbrow.

low′er (lō′ər *for 1, 2;* lou′ər *for 3–5*), *v.* 1. reduce or diminish. 2. make or become lower. 3. be threatening. 4. frown. —*n.* 5. lowering appearance.

low′ly, *adj.,* **-lier, -liest.** humble; meek.

loy′al, *adj.* faithful. —**loy′al•ty,** *n.*

loz′enge (loz′inj), *n.* 1. flavored candy, often medicated. 2. diamond shape.

lub′ber, *n.* clumsy person.

lu′bri•cant, *n.* lubricating substance.

lu′bri•cate′, *v.*, **-cated, -cating.** oil or grease, esp. to diminish friction. —**lu′bri•ca′tion**, *n.* —**lu′bri•ca′tor**, *n.*

lu•bri′cious (-brish′əs), *adj.* 1. lewd. 2. slippery. Also, **lu′bri•cous** (-kəs).

lu′cid (lōō′sid), *adj.* 1. bright. 2. clear in thought or expression. 3. rational. —**lu•cid′i•ty, lu′cid•ness**, *n.* —**lu′cid•ly**, *adv.*

luck, *n.* 1. chance. 2. good fortune. —**luck′less**, *adj.*

luck′y, *adj.*, **-ier, -iest.** having or due to good luck. —**luck′i•ly**, *adv.*

lu′cra•tive, *adj.* profitable.

lu′cre (lōō′kər), *n.* gain or money.

lu′di•crous, *adj.* ridiculous. —**lu′di•crous•ly**, *adv.*

luff, *v.* 1. sail into wind. —*n.* 2. act of luffing.

lug, *v.*, **lugged, lugging**, *n.* —*v.* 1. pull or carry with effort. 2. haul. —*n.* 3. projecting handle.

lug′gage, *n.* baggage.

lu•gu′bri•ous (lōō gōō′-), *adj.* excessively mournful or gloomy.

luke′warm′, *adj.* slightly warm.

lull, *v.* 1. soothe, esp. to sleep. —*n.* 2. brief stillness.

lull′a•by, *n.*, *pl.* **-bies.** song to lull baby.

lum•ba′go, *n.* muscular pain in back.

lum′bar, *adj.* of loins.

lum′ber, *n.* 1. timber made into boards, etc. —*v.* 2. cut and prepare timber. 3. encumber. 4. move heavily. —**lum′ber•man**, *n.*

lum′ber•jack′, *n.* person who fells trees.

lu′mi•nar′y, *n.*, *pl.* **-naries.** 1. celestial body. 2. person who inspires many.

lu•min•es′cent, *adj.* luminous at relatively low temperatures. —**lu′min•es′cence**, *n.*

lu′mi•nous, *adj.* giving or reflecting light. —**lu′mi•nos′i•ty**, *n.*

lump, *n.* 1. irregular mass. 2. swelling. 3. aggregation. —*adj.* 4. including many. —*v.* 5. put together. 6. endure. —**lump′y**, *adj.*

lu′na•cy, *n.* insanity.

lu′nar, *adj.* 1. of or according to moon. 2. Also, **lu′nate.** crescent-shaped.

lu′na•tic, *n.* 1. insane person. —*adj.* 2. for the insane. 3. crazy.

lunch, *n.* 1. Also, **lunch′eon.** light meal, esp. at noon. —*v.* 2. eat lunch.

lunch′eon•ette′, *n.* restaurant for quick, simple lunches.

lung, *n.* respiratory organ.

lunge, *n.*, *v.*, **lunged, lunging.** —*n.* 1. sudden forward movement. —*v.* 2. make lunge.

lurch, *n.* 1. sudden lean to one side. 2. helpless plight. —*v.* 3. make lurch.

lure, *n.*, *v.*, **lured, luring.** —*n.* 1. bait. —*v.* 2. decoy; entice.

lu′rid, *adj.* 1. glaringly lighted. 2. intended to be exciting; sensational.

lurk, *v.* 1. loiter furtively. 2. exist unperceived.

lus′cious, *adj.* delicious.

lush, *adj.* 1. tender and juicy. 2. abundant.

lust, *n.* 1. strong desire. —*v.* 2. have strong desire. —**lust′ful**, *adj.*

lus′ter, *n.* gloss; radiance. Also, **lus′tre.** —**lus′trous**, *adj.*

lust′y, *adj.*, **lustier, lustiest.** vigorous. —**lust′i•ly**, *adv.*

lute, *n.* stringed musical instrument.

Lu′ther•an, *adj.* of Protestant sect named for Martin Luther.

lux•u′ri•ant (lug zhōŏr′ē ənt), *adj.* profuse; abundant. —**lux•u′ri•ance**, *n.*

lux•u′ri•ate′ (-ē āt′), *v.*, **-ated, -ating.** revel; delight.

lux′u•ry (luk′shə rē), *n.*, *pl.* **-ries.** something enjoyable but not necessary. —**lux•u′ri•ous**, *adj.*

ly•ce′um, *n.* hall for lectures, etc.

lye, *n.* alkali solution.

ly′ing-in′, *adj.* 1. of or for childbirth. —*n.* 2. childbirth.

lymph, *n.* yellowish matter from body tissues. —**lym•phat′ic**, *adj.*

lynch, *v.* put to death without legal authority.

lynx, *n.*, *pl.* **lynxes, lynx.** kind of wild cat.

lyre, *n.* ancient harplike instrument.

lyr′ic, *adj.* Also, **lyr′i•cal.** 1. (of poetry) musical. 2. of or writing such poetry. 3. ardently expressive. —*n.* 4. lyric poem. 5. (*pl.*) words for song. —**lyr′i•cal•ly**, *adv.* —**lyr′i•cism**, *n.*

M

M, m, *n.* thirteenth letter of English alphabet.

ma, *n. Informal.* mother.

ma′am, *n. Informal.* madam.

ma•ca′bre, *adj.* gruesome.

mac•ad′am, *n.* road-making material containing broken stones. —**mac•ad′am•ize′,** *v.*

mac′a•ro′ni, *n.* 1. tube-shaped food made of wheat. 2. fop.

mac′a•roon′, *n.* small cookie, usually containing almonds.

ma•caw′, *n.* tropical American parrot.

mace, *n.* 1. spiked war club. 2. staff of office. 3. spice from part of nutmeg seed. 4. (*cap.*) *Trademark.* chemical for subduing rioters, etc.

ma•che′te (mə shet′ē), *n.* heavy knife.

Mach′i•a•vel′li•an (mak′-), *adj.* wily.

mach′i•na′tion (mak′-), *n.* cunning plan.

ma•chine′, *n.* 1. apparatus or mechanical device. 2. group controlling political organization.

ma•chin′er•y, *n.* machines or mechanisms.

ma•chin′ist, *n.* operator of powered tool, ship's engines, etc.

ma•chis′mo (-chēz′-), *n.* exaggerated masculinity as basis for code of behavior.

ma′cho (mä′-), *adj.* virile; manly.

mack′er•el, *n.* common food fish.

mack′i•naw′, *n.* short, heavy, woolen coat.

mack′in•tosh′, *n.* raincoat of rubberized cloth.

mac′ra•mé′, *n.* decorative work of knotted cords.

mac′ro•bi•ot′ic, *adj.* of or giving long life.

mac′ro•cosm, *n.* universe.

mad, *adj.*, **madder, maddest.** 1. insane. 2. *Informal.* angry. 3. violent. —**mad′man′,** *n.* —**mad′den,** *v.* —**mad′ly,** *adv.* —**mad′ness,** *n.*

Mad′a•gas′car, *n.* island republic E. of Africa. —**Mad′a•gas′can,** *n.*, *adj.*

mad′am, *n.* female term of address.

mad′ame, *n.*, *pl.* **mesdames** (mā dam′). French term of address for a married woman.

mad′e•moi•selle′ (mad′ mwə zel′), *n.*, *pl.* **mademoiselles, mes-**

demoiselles. French term of address for unmarried woman.

Ma•don′na, *n.* Virgin Mary.

mad′ras, *n.* light cotton fabric.

mad′ri•gal, *n.* song for several voices unaccompanied.

mael′strom (māl′-), *n.* 1. whirlpool. 2. confusion.

maes′tro (mīs′-), *n.* master, esp. of music.

Ma′fi•a, *n.* criminal society.

mag′a•zine′, *n.* 1. periodical publication. 2. storehouse for ammunition, etc. 3. cartridge receptacle in repeating weapon.

ma•gen′ta (-jen′-), *n.* reddish purple.

mag′got, *n.* larva of fly.

Ma′gi (mā′jī), *n.pl. Bible.* the three wise men.

mag′ic, *n.* 1. seemingly supernatural production of effects. —*adj.* Also, **mag′i•cal.** 2. of magic. 3. enchanting. —**ma•gi′cian,** *n.*

mag′is•te′ri•al, *adj.* masterlike; authoritative.

mag′is•trate, *n.* civil public official.

mag•nan′i•mous, *adj.* generous; high-minded. —**mag′na•nim′i•ty,** *n.*

mag′nate (-nāt), *n.* business leader.

mag•ne′sia, *n.* magnesium oxide, used as laxative.

mag•ne′si•um (-zē), *n.* light, silvery, metallic element.

mag′net, *n.* metal body that attracts iron or steel. —**mag•net′ic,** *adj.*

mag′net•ism′, *n.* 1. characteristic property of magnets. 2. science of magnets. 3. great personal charm. —**mag′net•ize′,** *v.*

mag•ne′to, *n.* small electric generator.

mag•nif′i•cence, *n.* 1. splendor; grandeur. 2. nobility. 3. supreme excellence. —**mag•nif′i•cent,** *adj.*

mag′ni•fy, *v.,* **-fied, -fying.** 1. increase apparent size. 2. enlarge. —**mag′ni•fi•ca′tion,** *n.* —**mag′ni•fi′er,** *n.*

mag•nil′o•quent, *adj.* grandiose or pompous in expression. —**mag•nil′o•quence,** *n.*

mag′ni•tude′, *n.* 1. size or extent. 2. brightness, as of star.

mag•no′li•a, *n.* tree with large, usually fragrant, flowers.

mag′pie′, *n.* black-and-white bird that steals.

ma′ha•ra′jah, *n.* (formerly) ruling prince in India. —**ma′ha•ra′nee,** *n.fem.*

mah′-jongg′, *n.* Chinese game.

ma•hog′a•ny, *n.* tropical American tree.

Ma•hom′et, *n.* Muhammad.

maid, *n.* 1. unmarried woman. 2. female servant.

maid′en, *n.* 1. young unmarried woman. —*adj.* 2. of maidens. 3. unmarried. 4. initial. —**maid′en•ly,** *adj.* —**maid′en•li•ness,** *n.*

mail, *n.* 1. material delivered by postal system. 2. postal system. 3. armor, usually flexible. —*adj.* 4. of mail. —*v.* 5. send by mail. —**mail′box′,** *n.* —**mail′man′,** *n.*

maim, *v.* cripple; impair.

main, *adj.* 1. chief; principal. —*n.* 2. chief pipe or duct. 3. strength. 4. ocean. —**main′ly,** *adv.*

main′land′, *n.* continental land rather than island.

main′spring′, *n.* chief spring of mechanism.

main′stay′, *n.* chief support.

main′stream′, *n.* customary trend of behavior, opinion, etc.

main•tain′, *v.* 1. support. 2. assert. 3. keep in order. —**main′te•nance,** *n.*

mai′tre d′hô•tel′ (me′tr dō tel′), headwaiter. Also, **mai′tre d′′** (mā′tər dē′).

maize (māz), *n.* corn.

maj′es•ty, *n.* 1. regal grandeur. 2. sovereign. —**ma•jes′tic,** *adj.* —**ma•jes′ti•cal•ly,** *adv.*

ma•jol′i•ca, *n.* kind of pottery.

ma′jor, *n.* 1. army officer above captain. 2. person of legal age. —*adj.* 3. larger or more important.

ma′jor-do′mo, *n.* steward.

ma′jor•ette′, *n.* girl leader of marchers.

major general, army officer above brigadier general.

ma•jor′i•ty, *n.* 1. greater number. 2. full legal age.

make, *v.,* **made, making,** *n.* —*v.* 1. bring into existence; form. 2. cause; force. 3. earn. 4. accomplish. —*n.* 5. style. 6. manufacture. —**mak′er,** *n.*

make′-be•lieve′, *n.* 1. pretending to oneself that fanciful thing is true. —*adj.* 2. fictitious.

make′shift′, *n., adj.* substitute.

make′-up′, *n.* 1. cosmetics. 2. organization; composition.

mal′ad•just′ment, *n.* 1. faulty adjustment. 2. inability to adapt to social conditions. —**mal′ad•just′ed,** *adj.*

mal′ad•min′is•ter, *v.* mismanage.

mal′a•droit′, *adj.* awkward.

mal′a•dy, *n., pl.* **-dies.** illness.

ma•laise′ (-lāz′), *n.* 1. bodily discomfort. 2. vague uneasiness.

ma•lar′i•a, *n.* mosquito-borne disease. —**ma•lar′i•al,** *adj.*

mal′con•tent′, *n.* dissatisfied person.

mal de mer′, seasickness.

male, *adj.* 1. of sex that begets young. —*n.* 2. male person, etc.

mal′e•dic′tion, *n.* curse.

mal′e•fac′tor, *n.* person who does wrong.

ma•lev′o•lent, *adj.* wishing evil. —**ma•lev′o•lence,** *n.*

mal•fea′sance (-fē′-), *n.* misconduct in office.

mal•formed′, *adj.* badly formed. —**mal′for•ma′tion,** *n.*

mal′ice, *n.* evil intent. —**ma•li′cious,** *adj.*

ma•lign′ (-līn′), *v.* 1. speak ill of. —*adj.* 2. evil.

ma•lig′nan•cy, *n., pl.* **-cies.** 1. malignant state. 2. cancerous growth.

ma•lig′nant, *adj.* 1. causing harm or suffering. 2. deadly.

ma•lin′ger, *v.* feign sickness. —**ma•lin′ger•er,** *n.*

mall, *n.* 1. shaded walk. 2. covered shopping center.

mal′lard, *n.* wild duck.

mal′le•a•ble, *adj.* 1. that may be hammered or rolled into shape. 2. readily influenced. —**mal′le•a•bil′i•ty, mal′le•a•ble•ness,** *n.*

mal′let, *n.* wooden-headed hammer.

mal′low, *n.* kind of herb.

mal′nu•tri′tion, *n.* improper nutrition.

mal•o′dor•ous, *adj.* smelling bad.

mal•prac′tice, *n.* improper professional behavior.

malt, *n.* germinated grain used in liquor-making.

mal•treat′, *v.* abuse.

ma′ma, *n. Informal.* mother.

mam′mal, *n.* vertebrate animal whose young are suckled.

mam′ma•ry, *adj.* of breasts.

mam′mon, *n.* 1. material wealth; riches. 2. greed for riches.

mam′moth, *n.* 1. large extinct kind of elephant. —*adj.* 2. huge.

mam′my, *n., pl.* **-mies.** mother.

man, *n., pl.* **men,** *v.,* **manned, manning.** —*n.* 1. male human being. 2. person. 3. human race. —*v.* 4. supply with crew. 5. serve.

man′a•cle, *n., v.,* **-cled, -cling.** handcuff.

man′age, *v.*, **-aged**, **-aging**. 1. take care of. 2. direct. **—man′age•a•ble**, *adj.* **—man′a•ger**, *n.* **—man′a•ge′ri•al**, *adj.*

man′age•ment, *n.* 1. direction; control. 2. persons in charge.

ma•ña′na (mä nyä′nä), *n. Spanish.* tomorrow.

man′da•rin, *n.* public official in Chinese Empire.

man′date, *n.* 1. authority over territory granted to nation by other nations. 2. territory under such authority. 3. command, as to take office. **—man′date**, *v.*

man′da•to•ry, *adj.* officially required.

man′do•lin′, *n.* plucked stringed musical instrument.

man′drake, *n.* narcotic herb.

man′drel, *n.* rod or axle in machinery.

man′drill, *n.* kind of baboon.

mane, *n.* long hair at neck of some animals.

ma•neu′ver (-nōō′-), *n., v.*, **-vered**, **-vering.** **—n.** 1. planned movement, esp. in war. **—v.** 2. change position by maneuver. 3. put in certain situation by intrigue. **—ma•neu′ver•a•ble**, *adj.*

man′ful, *adj.* resolute. **—man′ful•ly**, *adv.*

man′ga•nese′, *n.* hard metallic element.

mange (mänj), *n.* skin disease of animals. **—man′gy**, *adj.*

man′ger, *n.* trough for feeding stock.

man′gle, *v.*, **-gled**, **-gling**, *n.* **—v.** 1. disfigure, esp. by crushing. 2. put through mangle. **—n.** 3. device with rollers for ironing.

man′go, *n., pl.* **-goes.** fruit of tropical tree.

man′grove, *n.* kind of tropical tree.

man′han′dle, *v.*, **-dled**, **-dling.** handle roughly.

man•hat′tan, *n.* cocktail of whiskey and vermouth.

man′hole′, *n.* access hole to sewer, drain, etc.

man′hood, *n.* 1. manly qualities. 2. state of being a man.

ma′ni•a, *n.* 1. great excitement. 2. violent insanity.

ma′ni•ac′, *n.* raving lunatic. **—ma•ni′a•cal** (-nī′-), *adj.*

man′ic, *adj.* irrationally excited or lively.

man′i•cure′, *n.* skilled care of fingernails and hands. **—man′i•cure′**, *v.* **—man′i•cur′ist**, *n.*

man′i•fest′, *adj.* 1. evident. **—v.** 2. show plainly. **—n.** 3. list of cargo and passengers. **—man′i•fes•ta′tion**, *n.*

man′i•fes′to, *n., pl.* **-toes.** public declaration of philosophy or intentions.

man′i•fold′, *adj.* 1. of many kinds or parts. **—v.** 2. copy.

man′i•kin, *n.* model of human body.

ma•nip′u•late′, *v.*, **-lated**, **-lating.** handle with skill or cunning. **—ma•nip′u•la′tion**, *n.* **—ma•nip′u•la′tor**, *n.*

man′kind′, *n.* 1. human race. 2. men.

man′ly, *adj.*, **-lier**, **-liest.** strong; brave.

man′na, *n.* divine food.

man′ne•quin (-kin), *n.* model for displaying clothes.

man′ner, *n.* 1. way of doing, acting, etc. 2. (*pl.*) way of acting in society. 3. sort.

man′ner•ism, *n.* peculiarity of manner.

man′ner•ly, *adj.* polite.

man′nish, *adj.* like a man.

man′-of-war′, *n.* warship.

man′or, *n.* large estate. **—ma•no′ri•al**, *adj.*

man′pow′er, *n.* available labor force.

man′sard, *n.* roof with two slopes of different pitch on all sides.

manse, *n.* house and land of parson.

man′serv′ant, *n.* male servant, as valet.

man′sion, *n.* stately house.

man′slaugh′ter, *n.* murder without malice.

man′tel, *n.* ornamental structure around fireplace.

man•til′la, *n.* lace head scarf of Spanish women.

man′tis, *n.* kind of carnivorous insect.

man′tle, *n., v.*, **-tled**, **-tling.** **—n.** 1. loose cloak. **—v.** 2. envelop. 3. blush.

man′tra, *n.* Hindu verbal formula for recitation.

man′u•al, *adj.* 1. of or done with hands. **—n.** 2. small informational book. 3. keyboard. **—man′u•al•ly**, *adv.*

man′u•fac′ture, *n., v.*, **-tured**, **-turing.** **—n.** 1. making of things, esp. in great quantity. 2. thing made. **—v.** 3. make. **—man′u•fac′tur•er**, *n.*

ma•nure′, *n., v.*, **-ured**, **-uring.** **—n.** 1. fertilizer, esp. dung. **—v.** 2. apply manure to.

man′u•script′, *n.* handwritten or typed document.

man′y, *adj.* 1. comprising a large number; numerous. **—n.** 2. large number.

map, *n., v.*, **mapped**, **mapping.** **—n.** 1. flat representation of earth, etc. **—v.** 2. show by map. 3. plan.

ma′ple, *n.* northern tree.

mar, *v.*, **marred**, **marring.** damage.

mar′a•schi′no (-skē′-), *n.* wild-cherry flavoring.

mar′a•thon′, *n.* long contest.

ma•raud′, *v.* plunder. **—ma•raud′er**, *n.*

mar′ble, *n.* 1. crystalline limestone used in sculpture and building. 2. small glass ball used in children's game. **—adj.** 3. of marble.

march, *v.* 1. walk with measured tread. 2. advance. **—n.** 3. act of marching. 4. distance covered in march. 5. music for marching.

March, *n.* third month of year.

mare, *n.* female horse.

mar′ga•rine (-jə-), *n.* oleomargarine.

mar′gin, *n.* 1. edge. 2. amount more than necessary. 3. difference between cost and selling price. **—mar′gin•al**, *adj.*

mar′i•gold′, *n.* common, yellow-flowered plant.

ma′ri•jua′na (mä′rə wä′nə), *n.* plant whose leaves contain a narcotic.

ma•rim′ba, *n.* xylophone with chambers for resonance.

ma•ri′na (-rē′-), *n.* docking area for small boats.

mar′i•nate′, *v.* **-nated**, **-nating.** season by steeping. Also, **mar′i•nade′.**

ma•rine′, *adj.* 1. of the sea. **—n.** 2. member of U.S. Marine Corps. 3. fleet of ships.

Marine Corps, military branch of U.S. Navy.

mar′i•ner, *n.* sailor.

mar′i•o•nette′, *n.* puppet on strings.

mar′i•tal, *adj.* of marriage. **—mar′i•tal•ly**, *adv.*

mar′i•time′, *adj.* of sea or shipping.

mar′jo•ram, *n.* herb used as seasoning.

mark, *n.* 1. any visible sign. 2. object aimed at. **—v.** 3. be feature of. 4. put mark on. 5. pay attention to. **—mark′er**, *n.*

marked, *adj.* 1. conspicuous. 2. ostentatious. 3. singled out for revenge. **—mark′ed•ly**, *adv.*

mar′ket, *n.* 1. place for selling and buying. **—v.** 2. sell or buy. **—mar′ket•a•ble**, *adj.*

marks′man, *n.,* *pl.* **-men.** good shooter. **—marks′man•ship′,** *n.*

mark′up′, *n.* price increase by retailer.

mar′lin, *n.* large game fish.

mar′ma•lade′, *n.* fruit preserve.

mar′mo•set′, *n.* small, tropical American monkey.

mar′mot (-mət), *n.* bushy-tailed rodent.

ma•roon′, *n., adj.* **1.** dark brownishred. **—v. 2.** abandon ashore.

mar•quee′ (-kē′), *n.* projecting shelter over outer door.

mar′quis (-kwis), *n.* rank of nobility below duke. Also, *Brit.* **mar′quess.** **—mar•quise′** (-kēz′), *n.fem.*

mar′qui•sette′ (-ki zet′-), *n.* delicate open fabric.

mar′riage, *n.* **1.** legal union of man and woman. **2.** wedding. **—mar′-riage•a•ble,** *adj.*

mar′row, *n.* soft interior tissue of bone.

mar′ry, *v.,* **-ried, -rying.** take, give, or unite in marriage; wed.

Mars, *n.* **1.** Roman god of war. **2.** one of the planets.

marsh, *n.* low, wet land. **—marsh′y,** *adj.*

mar′shal, *n., v.,* **-shaled, -shaling.** **—n. 1.** federal officer. **—v. 2.** rally; organize.

marsh′mal′low, *n.* gelatinous confection.

mar•su′pi•al, *n.* animal carrying its young in pouch, as the kangaroo. **—mar•su′pi•al,** *adj.*

mart, *n.* market.

mar′ten, *n.* small, American, fur-bearing animal.

mar′tial, *adj.* warlike; military. **—mar′tial•ly,** *adv.*

mar′tin, *n.* bird of swallow family.

mar′ti•net′, *n.* stern disciplinarian.

mar•ti′ni (-tē′nē), *n.* cocktail of gin and vermouth.

mar′tyr, *n.* **1.** person who willingly dies or suffers for a belief. **—v. 2.** make martyr of. **—mar′tyr•dom,** *n.*

mar′vel, *n., v.,* **-veled, -veling.** **—n. 1.** wonderful thing. **—v. 2.** wonder (at). **—mar′vel•ous,** *adj.*

Marx′ism, *n.* doctrine of eventually classless society; communism. **—Marx′ist,** *n., adj.*

mas•car′a, *n.* cosmetic for eyelashes.

mas′cot, *n.* source of good luck.

mas′cu•line, *adj.* of or like men. **—mas′cu•lin′i•ty,** *n.*

mash, *n.* **1.** soft pulpy mass. **—v. 2.** crush.

mash′ie, *n.* golf club.

mask, *n.* **1.** disguise for face. **—v. 2.** disguise.

mas′och•ism (mas′ə kiz′əm), *n.* willful suffering. **—mas′och•ist,** *n.* **—mas′och•is′tic,** *adj.*

ma′son, *n.* builder with stone, brick, etc. **—ma′son•ry,** *n.*

mas′quer•ade′, *n., v.,* **-aded, -ading.** **—n. 1.** disguise. **2.** party at which guests wear disguise. **—v. 3.** wear disguise. **—mas′quer•ad′er,** *n.*

mass, *n.* **1.** body of coherent matter. **2.** quantity or size. **3.** weight. **—v. 4.** form into a mass.

Mass, *n.* celebration of Lord's Supper.

mas′sa•cre, *n., v.,* **-cred, -cring.** **—n. 1.** killing of many. **—v. 2.** slaughter.

mas•sage′, *v.,* **-saged, -saging,** *n.* **—v. 1.** treat body by rubbing or kneading. **—n. 2.** such treatment. **—mas•seur′** (mə sûr′), *n.* **—mas•seuse′** (mə sōōs′), *n.fem.*

mas′sive, *adj.* large; heavy. **—mas′-sive•ly,** *adv.*

mast, *n.* upright pole.

mas′ter, *n.* **1.** person in control. **2.** employer or owner. **3.** skilled person. **—adj. 4.** chief. **—v. 5.** conquer.

mas′ter•ful, *adj.* asserting power or authority. **—mas′ter•ful•ly,** *adv.*

mas′ter•ly, *adj.* highly skilled.

mas′ter•mind′, *n.* **1.** supreme planner. **—v. 2.** plan as mastermind.

mas′ter•piece′, *n.* work of highest skill.

master sergeant, noncommissioned officer of highest rank.

mas′ter•y, *n.* control; skill.

mas′ti•cate′, *v.,* **-cated, -cating.** chew. **—mas′ti•ca′tion,** *n.*

mas′tiff, *n.* powerful dog.

mas′to•don′, *n.* large extinct elephantlike mammal.

mas′toid, *n.* protuberance of bone behind ear.

mas′tur•bate′, *v.,* **-bated, -bating.** practice sexual self-gratification. **—mas′tur•ba′tion,** *n.*

mat, *n., v.,* **matted, matting,** *adj.* **—n. 1.** floor covering. **2.** border for picture. **3.** padding. **4.** thick mass. **—v. 5.** cover with mat. **6.** form into mat. **—adj. 7.** lusterless.

mat′a•dor′, *n.* bullfighter.

match, *n.* **1.** short stick chemically tipped to strike fire. **2.** person or thing resembling or equaling another. **3.** game. **4.** marriage. **—v. 5.**

equal. **6.** fit together. **7.** arrange marriage for.

match′less, *adj.* unequaled. **—match′less•ly,** *adv.*

match′mak′er, *n.* arranger of marriages.

mate, *n., v.,* **mated, mating.** **—n. 1.** one of pair. **2.** officer of merchant ship. **3.** assistant. **4.** female member of couple. **—v. 5.** join; pair.

ma′ter, *n. Brit. Informal.* mother.

ma•te′ri•al, *n.* **1.** substance of which thing is made. **2.** fabric. **—adj. 3.** physical. **4.** pertinent. **—ma•te′ri•al•ly,** *adv.*

ma•te′ri•al•ism′, *n.* **1.** devotion to material objects or wealth. **2.** belief that all reality is material. **—ma•te′-ri•al•ist,** *n.* **—ma•te′ri•al•is′tic,** *adj.*

ma•te′ri•al•ize′, *v.,* **-ized, -izing.** give or assume material form.

ma•te′ri•el′, *n.* supplies, esp. military.

ma•ter′ni•ty, *n.* motherhood. **—ma•ter′nal,** *adj.*

math′e•mat′ics, *n.* science of numbers, including arithmetic and algebra. **—math′e•mat′i•cal,** *adj.* **—math′e•ma•ti′cian,** *n.*

mat′i•née′ (-nā′), *n.* afternoon performance.

mat′ins, *n.* morning prayer.

ma′tri•arch′, *n.* female ruler. **—ma′-tri•ar′chy,** *n.*

ma•tric′u•late′, *v.,* **-lated, -lating.** enroll. **—ma•tric′u•la′tion,** *n.*

mat′ri•mo′ny, *n.* marriage. **—mat′ri•mo′ni•al,** *adj.*

ma′tron, *n.* **1.** married woman. **2.** female institutional officer. **—ma′-tron•ly,** *adj.*

mat′ter, *n.* **1.** material. **2.** affair or trouble. **3.** pus. **4.** importance. **—v. 5.** be of importance.

mat′ter-of-fact′, *adj.* objective; realistic.

mat′ting, *n.* mat of rushes.

mat′tock, *n.* digging implement with one broad and one pointed end.

mat′tress, *n.* thick filled case for sleeping on.

ma•ture′ (-tyŏŏr′), *adj., v.,* **-tured, -turing.** **—adj. 1.** grown or developed. **2.** adult in manner or thought. **3.** payable. **—v. 4.** become or make mature. **—ma•tu′ri•ty,** *n.* **—ma•ture′ly,** *adv.* **—mat′u•ra′tion,** *n.*

maud′lin, *adj.* weakly sentimental.

maul, *v.* handle roughly.

mau′so•le′um, *n.* tomb in form of building.

mauve (mōv), *n.* pale purple.

mav'er•ick, *n.* 1. unbranded calf. 2. nonconformist.

maw, *n.* mouth.

mawk'ish, *adj.* sickly sentimental. —**mawk'ish•ly,** *adv.* —**mawk'ish•ness,** *n.*

max'im, *n.* general truth.

max'i•mum, *n.* 1. greatest degree or quantity. —*adj.* 2. greatest possible.

may, *v., pt.* **might.** (auxiliary verb of possibility or permission.)

May, *n.* fifth month of year.

may'be, *adv.* perhaps.

may'hem, *n.* bodily injury.

may'on•naise', *n.* salad dressing made chiefly of egg yolks, oil, and vinegar.

may'or, *n.* chief officer of city. —**may'or•al•ty,** *n.*

maze, *n.* confusing arrangement of paths.

ma•zur'ka, *n.* lively Polish dance.

me, *pers. pronoun.* objective case of **I.**

mead, *n.* liquor of fermented honey.

mead'ow, *n.* level grassland.

mead'ow•lark', *n.* common American songbird.

mea'ger, *adj.* poor; scanty. Also, **mea'gre.**

meal, *n.* 1. food served or eaten. 2. coarse grain. —**meal'y,** *adj.*

meal'y-mouthed', *adj.* avoiding candid speech.

mean, *v.,* **meant, meaning,** *adj., n.* —*v.* 1. intend (to do or signify). 2. signify. —*adj.* 3. poor; shabby. 4. hostile; malicious. 5. middle. —*n.* 6. method of achieving purpose. 7. (*pl.*) money or property. 8. intermediate quantity. —**mean'ness,** *n.*

me•an'der, *v.* wander aimlessly.

mean'ing, *n.* 1. significance. —*adj.* 2. significant. —**mean'ing•ful,** *adj.* —**mean'ing•ly,** *adv.*

mean'time', *n.* 1. time between. —*adv.* Also, **mean'while'.** 2. in time between.

mea'sles, *n.* infectious disease marked by small red spots.

meas'ly, *adj. Informal.* miserably small.

meas'ure, *v.,* **-ured, -uring.** *n.* —*v.* 1. ascertain size or extent. —*n.* 2. process of measuring. 3. dimensions. 4. instrument or system of measuring. 5. action. —**meas'ur•a•ble,** *adj.* —**meas'ure•ment,** *n.*

meas'ured, *adj.* in distinct sequence.

meat, *n.* 1. flesh of animals used as food. 2. edible part of fruit, nut, etc. 3. food.

meat'y, *adj.,* **-ier, -iest.** 1. with much meat. 2. rewarding attention.

me•chan'ic, *n.* skilled worker with machinery.

me•chan'i•cal, *adj.* of or operated by machinery.—**me•chan'i•cal•ly,** *adv.*

me•chan'ics, *n.* science of motion and of action of forces on bodies.

mech'an•ism', *n.* 1. structure of machine. 2. piece of machinery. —**mech'a•nist,** *n.*

mech'a•nis'tic, *adj.* of or like machinery.

mech'a•nize', *v.,* **-nized, -nizing.** adapt to machinery. —**mech'a•ni•za'tion,** *n.*

med'al, *n.* badgelike metal object given for merit.

med'al•ist, *n.* winner of a medal.

me•dal'lion, *n.* large medal or medallike ornament.

med'dle, *v.,* **-dled, -dling.** interfere; tamper. —**med'dler,** *n.* —**med'dle•some,** *adj.*

me'di•a, *n.* pl. of **medium** (def. 5).

me'di•an, *adj., n.* middle.

me'di•ate', *v.,* **-ated, -ating.** settle (dispute) between parties. —**me'di•a'tion,** *n.* —**me'di•a'tor,** *n.*

med'ic, *n. U.S.* doctor or medical aide.

Med'i•caid', *n.* state- and federal-supported medical care for low-income persons.

med'i•cal, *adj.* 1. of medicine. 2. curative. —**med'i•cal•ly,** *adv.*

me•dic'a•ment, *n.* healing substance.

Med'i•care', *n.* government-supported medical insurance for those 65 years old or more.

med'i•cate', *v.,* **-cated, -cating.** treat with medicine. —**med'i•ca'tion,** *n.*

me•dic'i•nal (-dis'-), *adj.* curative; remedial. —**me•dic'i•nal•ly,** *adv.*

med'i•cine, *n.* 1. substance used in treating disease. 2. art of preserving or restoring physical health.

me'di•e'val, *adj.* of the Middle Ages.

me'di•e'val•ism, *n.* 1. a characteristic of the Middle Ages. 2. devotion to medieval ideals, etc.

me'di•e'val•ist, *n.* 1. expert in medieval history, etc. 2. one devoted to medieval ideals, etc.

me'di•o'cre, *adj.* undistinguished. —**me'di•oc'ri•ty,** *n.*

med'i•tate', *v.,* **-tated, -tating.** think intensely; consider. —**med'i•ta'tion,** *n.* —**med'i•ta'tive,** *adj.*

me'di•um, *n., pl.* **-diums** for 1–5, **-dia** for 1–3, 5, *adj.* —*n.* 1. something intermediate or moderate. 2. means of

doing. 3. environment. 4. person believed able to communicate with dead. 5. means of public communication. —*adj.* 6. intermediate.

med'ley, *n., pl.* **-leys.** mixture, as of tunes.

meek, *adj.* submissive.

meer'schaum (mir'shəm), *n.* claylike mineral, used for tobacco pipes.

meet, *v.,* **met, meeting,** *n., adj.* —*v.* 1. come into contact with. 2. make acquaintance of. 3. satisfy. —*n.* 4. equal. 5. meeting, esp. for sport. —*adj.* 6. proper.

meet'ing, *n.* 1. a coming together. 2. persons gathered.

meg'a-, *prefix.* one million.

meg'a•hertz', *n., pl.* **-hertz.** *Elect.* one million cycles per second.

meg'a•lo•ma'ni•a, *n.* delusion of greatness, riches, etc.

meg'a•lop'o•lis, *n.* very large urbanized area. Also, **me•gap'o•lis.**

meg'a•phone', *n.* cone-shaped device for magnifying sound.

meg'a•ton', *n.* one million tons, esp. of TNT as equivalent in explosive force.

mel'an•cho'li•a, *n.* mental disease marked by great depression.

mel'an•chol'y, *n.* 1. low spirits; depression. —*adj.* 2. sad.

mé•lange' (mā länj'), *n.* mixture.

me'lee (mā'lā), *n.* confused, general fight.

mel'io•rate' (mēl'yə rāt'), *v.,* **-rated, -rating.** improve. —**mel'io•ra'tion,** *n.* —**mel'io•ra'tive,** *adj.*

mel•lif'lu•ous, *adj.* soft and sweet in speech.

mel'low, *adj.* 1. soft and rich. 2. genial. —*v.* 3. make or become mellow.

me•lo'de•on, *n.* reed organ.

me•lo'di•ous, *adj.* tuneful.

mel'o•dra'ma, *n.* play emphasizing theatrical effects and strong emotions. —**mel'o•dra•mat'ic,** *adj.*

mel'o•dy, *n., pl.* **-dies.** arrangement of musical sounds. —**me•lod'ic,** *adj.*

mel'on, *n.* edible fruit of certain annual vines.

melt, *v.,* **melted, melted** or **molten, melting.** 1. make or become liquid, esp. by heat. 2. soften.

melt'down', *n.* melting of nuclear reactor core, causing escape of radiation.

mel'ton, *n.* smooth woolen fabric.

mem'ber, *n.* 1. part of structure or body. 2. one belonging to organization. —**mem'ber•ship',** *n.*

mem′brane, *n.* thin film of tissue in animals and plants.

me•men′to, *n., pl.* **-tos, -toes.** reminder.

mem′oir (-wär), *n.* 1. (*pl.*) personal recollection. 2. biography.

mem′o•ra•bil′i•a, *n.pl.* souvenirs.

mem′o•ra•ble, *adj.* worth remembering. **—mem′o•ra•bly,** *adv.*

mem′o•ran′dum, *n., pl.* **-dums, -da.** written statement or reminder. Also, **mem′o.**

me•mo′ri•al, *n.* 1. something honoring memory of a person or event. **—adj.** 2. serving as memorial.

mem′o•rize′, *v.,* **-rized, -rizing.** commit to memory.

mem′o•ry, *n., pl.* **-ries.** 1. faculty of remembering. 2. something that is remembered. 3. length of time of recollection. 4. reputation after death.

men′ace, *v.,* **-aced, -acing,** *n.* **—v.** 1. threaten evil to. **—n.** 2. something that threatens.

mé•nage′ (mā näzh′), *n.* household.

me•nag′er•ie, *n.* collection of animals.

mend, *v.* repair; improve. **—mend′er,** *n.*

men•da′cious, *adj.* untruthful. **—men•dac′i•ty,** *n.*

men′di•cant, *n.* beggar.

me′ni•al, *adj.* 1. humble; servile. **—n.** 2. servant.

men′in•gi′tis (-jī′-), *n.* inflammation of membranes surrounding brain and spinal cord.

men′o•pause′, *n.* cessation of menses, usually between ages of 45 and 50.

men′ses, *n.pl.* monthly discharge of blood from uterus. **—men′stru•al,** *adj.* **—men′stru•ate′,** *v.* **—men•stru•a′tion,** *n.*

men′sur•a•ble (-shər-), *adj.* measurable. **—men′su•ra′tion,** *n.*

mens′wear′, *n.* clothing for men.

men′tal, *adj.* of or in mind. **—men′tal•ly,** *adv.*

men•tal′i•ty, *n., pl.* **-ties.** 1. mental ability. 2. characteristic mental attitude.

men′thol, *n.* colorless alcohol from peppermint oil. **—men′thol•at′ed,** *adj.*

men′tion, *v.* 1. speak or write of. **—n.** 2. reference.**—men′tion•a•ble,** *adj.*

men′tor, *n.* adviser; teacher.

men′u, *n.* list of dishes that can be served.

me•ow′, *n.* 1. sound cat makes. **—v.** 2. make such sound.

mer′can•tile′ (-tēl, -tīl), *adj.* of or engaged in trade.

mer′ce•nar′y (-sə-), *adj., n., pl.* **-naries.** **—adj.** 1. acting only for profit. **—n.** 2. hired soldier.

mer′cer•ize′, *v.,* **-ized, -izing.** treat (cottons) for greater strength.

mer′chan•dise′, *n., v.,* **-dised, -dising.** **—n.** 1. goods; wares. **—v.** 2. buy and sell.

mer′chant, *n.* person who buys and sells goods for profit.

merchant marine, commercial vessels of nation.

mer•cu′ri•al, *adj.* 1. of mercury. 2. sprightly. 3. changeable in emotion.

mer′cu•ry, *n.* 1. heavy metallic element. 2. (*cap.*) one of the planets. 3. (*cap.*) Roman god of commerce.

mer′cy, *n., pl.* **-cies.** 1. pity; compassion. 2. act of compassion. **—mer′ci•ful,** *adj.* **—mer′ci•less,** *adj.*

mere, *adj.* only; simple. **—mere′ly,** *adv.*

mer′e•tri′cious, *adj.* falsely attractive.

merge, *v.,* **merged, merging.** combine. **—merg′er,** *n.*

me•rid′i•an, *n.* circle on earth's surface passing through the poles.

me•ringue′ (-rang′), *n.* egg whites and sugar beaten together.

me•ri′no, *n., pl.* **-nos.** kind of sheep.

mer′it, *n.* 1. excellence or good quality. **—v.** 2. deserve. **—mer′i•to′ri•ous,** *adj.*

mer′maid′, *n.* imaginary sea creature, half woman and half fish. **—mer′man′,** *n.masc.*

mer′ry, *adj.,* **-rier, -riest.** gay; joyous. **—mer′ri•ly,** *adv.* **—mer′ri•ment,** *n.*

mer′ry-go-round′, *n.* revolving amusement ride.

mer′ry•mak′ing, *n.* festivities; hilarity. **—mer′ry-ma′ker,** *n.*

me′sa (mā′-), *n.* high, steep-walled plateau.

mesh, *n.* 1. open space of net. 2. net itself. 3. engagement of gears. **—v.** 4. catch in mesh. 5. engage.

mes′mer•ize′, *v.,* **-ized, -izing.** hypnotize. **—mes′mer•ism′,** *n.*

mes•quite′ (-kēt′), *n.* common tree of southwest U.S.

mess, *n.* 1. dirty or disorderly condition. 2. group taking meals together regularly. 3. meals so taken. **—v.** 4. disorder; make dirty. 5. eat in company. **—mess′y,** *adj.*

mes′sage, *n.* communication.

mes′sen•ger, *n.* bearer of message.

Mes•si′ah, *n.* 1. expected deliverer. 2. (in Christian theology) Jesus Christ.

mes•ti′zo (mes tē′zō), *n., pl.* **-zos, -zoes.** person part-Spanish, part-Indian. Also, **mes•ti′za,** *fem.*

me•tab′o•lism′, *n.* biological processes of converting food into living matter and matter into energy. **—met′a•bol′ic,** *adj.*

met′al, *n.* 1. elementary substance such as gold or copper. 2. mettle. **—me•tal′lic,** *adj.* **—met′al•ware′,** *n.*

met′al•lur′gy, *n.* science of working with metals. **—met′al•lur′gist,** *n.*

met′a•mor′phose, *v.,* **-phosed, -phosing.** transform.

met′a•mor•pho•sis, *n., pl.* **-ses.** change.

met′a•phor, *n.* figure of speech using analogy. **—met′a•phor′i•cal,** *adj.*

met′a•phys′ics, *n.* branch of philosophy concerned with ultimate nature of reality. **—met′a•phys′ical,** *adj.* **—met′a•phy•si′cian,** *n.*

mete, *v.,* **meted, meting.** allot.

me′te•or, *n.* celestial body passing through earth's atmosphere. **—me′te•or′ic,** *adj.*

me′te•or•ite′, *n.* meteor reaching earth.

me′te•or•ol′o•gy, *n.* science of atmospheric phenomena, esp. weather. **—me′te•or•olog′i•cal,** *adj.* **—me′te•orol′o•gist,** *n.*

me′ter, *n.* 1. unit of length in metric system, equal to 39.37 inches. 2. rhythmic arrangement of words. 3. device for measuring flow. **—v.** 4. measure. Also, *Brit.,* **me′tre.** **—met′ric, met′ri•cal,** *adj.*

meth′od, *n.* system of doing. **—me•thod′i•cal, me•thod′ic,** *adj.* **—me•thod′i•cal•ly,** *adv.*

me•tic′u•lous, *adj.* minutely careful.

metric, *adj.* of decimal system of weights and measures, based on meter and gram. **—met′ri•cize′,** *v.* **—met′ri•ca′tion,** *n.*

met′ro•nome′, *n.* device for marking tempo.

me•trop′o•lis, *n., pl.* **-lises.** great city.

met′ro•pol′i•tan, *adj.* 1. of or in city. 2. of cities and urban areas.

met′tle, *n.* 1. spirit. 2. disposition.

Mex′i•can, *n.* native of Mexico. **—Mexican,** *adj.*

mez′za•nine′, *n.* low story between two main floors; balcony.

mi•as′ma (mī-), *n., pl.* **-mata, -mas.** vapors from decaying organic matter.

mi′ca, *n.* shiny mineral occurring in thin layers.

mi′cro-, *prefix.* extremely small.

mi′crobe, *n.* microorganism, esp. one causing disease.

mi′cro•cosm, *n.* world in miniature.

mi′cro•fiche (-fēsh′), *n.* small sheet of microfilm.

mi′cro•film′, *n.* very small photograph of book page, etc. **—mi′cro•film′,** *v.*

mi•crom′e•ter, *n.* device for measuring minute distances.

mi′cro•or•gan•ism′, *n.* microscopic organism.

mi′cro•phone′, *n.* instrument for changing sound waves into changes in electric current.

mi′cro•scope′, *n.* instrument for inspecting minute objects.

mi′cro•scop′ic, *adj.* 1. of microscopes. 2. extremely small.

mi′cro•wave′, *n.* short radio wave used in radar, cooking, etc.

mid, *adj.* 1. middle. **—prep.** 2. amid.

mid′day′, *n.* noon.

mid′dle, *adj.* 1. equally distant from given limits. 2. medium. **—n.** 3. middle part.

Middle Ages, period of European history, about A.D. 476 to 1500.

Middle East, area including Israel and Arab countries of NE Africa and SW Asia.

mid′dle•man′, *n.* merchant who buys direct from producer.

mid′dle•weight′, *n.* boxer weighing 147–160 pounds.

mid′dling, *adj.* 1. medium. **—n.** 2. (*pl.*) coarse parts of grain.

mid′dy, *n., pl.* **-dies.** blouse with square back collar.

midge, *n.* minute fly.

midg′et, *n.* very small person or thing.

mid′land, *n.* interior of country.

mid′night′, *n.* 12 o'clock at night.

mid′riff, *n.* part of body between the chest and abdomen.

mid′ship′man, *n., pl.* **-men.** rank of student at U.S. Naval or Coast Guard academy.

midst, *n.* middle.

mid′way′, *adj., adv.* 1. in or to middle. **—n.** 2. area of rides, games, shows, etc., at carnival.

mid′wife′, *n.* woman who assists at childbirth.

mien (mēn), *n.* air; bearing.

miff, *n.* 1. petty quarrel. **—v.** 2. offend.

might, *v.* 1. pt. of **may. —n.** 2. strength; power.

might′y, *adj.,* **mightier, mightiest,** *adv.* **—adj.** 1. powerful; huge. **—adv.** 2. *Informal.* very. **—might′i•ness,** *n.*

mi′graine, *n.* painful headache.

mi′grate′, *v.,* **-grated, -grating.** go from one region to another. **—mi•gra′tion,** *n.* **—mi′gra•to′ry,** *adj.* **—mi′grant,** *adj., n.*

mi•ka′do, *n.* emperor of Japan.

mike, *n. Informal.* microphone.

mil, *n.* one thousandth of inch.

mi•la′dy, *n.* my lady.

milch, *adj.* giving milk.

mild, *adj.* gentle; temperate. **—mild′ly,** *adv.* **—mild′ness,** *n.*

mil′dew, *n.* 1. discoloration caused by fungus. **—v.** 2. affect with mildew.

mile, *n.* unit of distance, equal on land to 5280 ft.

mile′age, *n.* 1. miles traveled. 2. travel allowance.

mile′stone′, *n.* 1. marker showing road distance. 2. important event.

mi•lieu′ (mē lyōō′), *n.* environment.

mil′i•tant, *adj.* warlike; aggressive.

mil′i•ta•rism, *n.* 1. military spirit. 2. domination by military. **—mil′i•ta•rist,** *n.* **—mil′i•ta•ris′tic,** *adj.*

mil′i•tar•ize′, *v.,* **-ized, -izing.** equip with military weapons.

mil′i•tar′y, *adj.* 1. of armed forces, esp. on land. **—n.** 2. armed forces or soldiers collectively.

mil′i•tate′, *v.,* **-tated, -tating.** act (for or against).

mi•li′tia (-lish′ə), *n.* organization for emergency military service. **—mi•li′tia•man,** *n.*

milk, *n.* 1. white liquid secreted by female mammals to feed their young. **—v.** 2. draw milk from. **—milk′y,** *adj.* **—milk′maid′,** *n.* **—milk′man′,** *n.*

milk′weed′, *n.* plant with milky juice.

Milk′y Way′, *Astron.* galaxy containing sun and earth.

mill, *n.* 1. place where manufacturing is done. 2. device for grinding. 3. one tenth of a cent. **—v.** 4. grind or treat with mill. 5. groove edges of (coin). 6. move about in confusion. **—mill′er,** *n.*

mil•len′ni•um, *n.* 1. future period of joy. 2. future reign of Christ on earth.

mil′let, *n.* cereal grass.

mil′li•gram′, *n.* one thousandth of gram.

mil′li•li′ter, *n.* one thousandth of liter.

mil′li•me′ter, *n.* one thousandth of meter.

mil′li•ner, *n.* person who makes or sells women's hats.

mil′li•ner′y, *n.* 1. women's hats. 2. milliner's shop.

mil′lion, *n., adj.* 1000 times 1000. **—mil′lionth,** *adj., n.*

mil′lion•aire′, *n.* person having million dollars or more.

mill′stone′, *n.* stone for grinding grain.

milt, *n.* male secretion of fish.

mime, *n.* pantomimist; clown.

mim′e•o•graph′, *n.* 1. stencil device for duplicating. **—v.** 2. copy with mimeograph.

mim′ic, *v.,* **-icked, -icking,** *n.* **—v.** 1. imitate speech or actions of. **—n.** 2. person who mimics. **—mim′ic•ry,** *n.*

mi•mo′sa, *n.* semitropical tree or shrub.

min′a•ret′, *n.* tower for calling Muslims to prayer.

mince, *v.,* **minced, mincing.** 1. chop fine. 2. speak, move, or behave with affected elegance. **—minc′ing•ly,** *adv.*

mince′meat′, *n.* cooked mixture of finely chopped meat, raisins, spices, etc., used in pies.

mind, *n.* 1. thinking or feeling part of human or animal. 2. intellect. 3. inclination. **—v.** 4. heed; obey.

mind′ful, *adj.* careful.

mind′less, *adj.* 1. heedless. 2. without intelligence.

mine, *pron., n., v.,* **mined, mining.** **—pron.** 1. possessive form of **I. —n.** 2. excavation in earth for getting out metals, coal, etc. 3. stationary explosive device used in war. **—v.** 4. dig or work in mine. 5. lay explosive mines. **—min′er,** *n.*

min′er•al, *n.* 1. inorganic substance. 2. substance obtained by mining. **—adj.** 3. of minerals.

min′er•al′o•gy, *n.* science of minerals. **—min′er•al•og′i•cal,** *adj.* **—min′er•al•o•gist,** *n.*

min′e•stro′ne (min′i strō′nē), *n.* thick vegetable soup.

min′gle, *v.,* **-gled, -gling.** associate; mix.

min′i•a•ture, *n.* 1. greatly reduced form. 2. tiny painting. **—adj.** 3. on small scale.

min′i•a•tur•ize′, v., **-ized, -izing.** make in or reduce to very small size. —**min′i•a•tur•i•za′tion,** n.

min′im, n. smallest unit of liquid measure.

min′i•mize′, v., **-mized, -mizing.** make minimum.

min′i•mum, n. 1. least possible quantity, degree, etc. —adj. 2. Also, **min′i•mal.** least; lowest.

min′ion, n. servile follower.

min′is•ter, n. 1. person authorized to conduct worship. 2. government representative abroad. 3. head of governmental department. —v. 4. give care. —**min′is•te′ri•al,** adj. —**min′is•tra′tion,** n.

min′is•try, n., pl. **-ries.** 1. religious calling. 2. clergy. 3. duty or office of a department of government. 4. body of executive officials. 5. act of ministering.

mink, n. semiaquatic fur-bearing animal.

min′now, n. tiny fish.

mi′nor, adj. 1. lesser in size, importance, etc. 2. under legal age. 3. Music. less than major by half tone or having such intervals. —n. 4. person under legal age.

mi•nor′i•ty, n., pl. **-ties.** 1. smaller number or part. 2. relatively small population group. 3. state or time of being under legal age.

min′strel, n. 1. musician or singer, esp. in Middle Ages. 2. comedian in blackface.

mint, n. 1. aromatic herb. 2. place where money is coined. —v. 3. make coins.

min′u•end′, n. number from which another is to be subtracted.

min′u•et′, n. stately dance.

mi′nus, prep. 1. less. —adj. 2. less than.

mi′nus•cule′ (min′əs-), adj. tiny.

min′ute, n. 1. sixty seconds. 2. (pl.) record of proceedings. —adj. (mī nyoo̅t′). 3. extremely small. 4. attentive to detail. —**mi•nute′ly,** adv.

mi•nu′ti•ae′ (-shē ē′), n.pl. trifling matters.

minx, n. saucy girl.

mir′a•cle, n. supernatural act or effect. —**mi•rac′u•lous,** adj.

mi•rage′, n. atmospheric illusion in which images of far-distant objects are seen.

mire, n., v., **mired, miring.** —n. 1. swamp; mud. —v. 2. stick fast in mire. 3. soil. —**mir′y,** adj.

mir′ror, n. 1. reflecting surface. —v. 2. reflect.

mirth, n. gaiety, —**mirth′ful,** adj. —**mirth′less,** adj.

mis′ad•ven′ture, n. mishap.

mis′an•thrope′, n. hater of mankind. —**mis′an•throp′ic,** adj.

mis′ap•ply′, v., **-plied, -plying.** use wrongly. —**mis′ap•pli•ca′tion,** n.

mis′ap•pre•hend′, v. misunderstand. —**mis′ap•pre•hen′sion,** n.

mis′ap•pro′pri•ate′, v., **-ated, -ating.** use wrongly as one's own. —**mis′ap•pro′pri•a′tion,** n.

mis•be•got′ten, adj. ill-conceived.

mis•be•have′, v., **-haved, -having.** behave badly. —**mis′be•hav′ior,** n.

mis•cal′cu•late′, v., **-lated, -lating.** judge badly. —**mis′cal•cu•la′tion,** n.

mis•car′riage, n. 1. premature birth resulting in death of fetus. 2. failure.

mis•car′ry, v., **-ried, -rying.** 1. go wrong. 2. have miscarriage.

mis′ce•ge•na′tion (mis′i jə-), n. sexual union between persons of different races.

mis′cel•la′ne•ous, adj. unclassified; various.

mis•chance′, n. bad luck.

mis′chief, n. 1. trouble, caused willfully. 2. tendency to tease. —**mis′chie•vous,** adj.

mis′con•ceive′, v., **-ceived, -ceiving.** misunderstand. —**mis′con•cep′tion,** n.

mis•con′duct, n. improper or illegal conduct.

mis′con•strue′, v., **-strued, -struing.** misinterpret.

mis′cre•ant, n. villain.

mis•de•mean′or, n. minor offense.

mi′ser, n. hoarder of wealth. —**mi′ser•ly,** adj.

mis′er•a•ble, adj. 1. wretched. 2. deplorable. 3. contemptible. —**mis′er•a•bly,** adv.

mis′er•y, n., pl. **-eries.** wretched condition.

mis•fire′, v., **-fired, -firing.** fail to fire.

mis•fit′, 1. poor fit. 2. Also, **mis′fit.** maladjusted person.

mis•for′tune, n. bad luck.

mis•giv′ing, n. apprehension; doubt.

mis•guide′, v., **-guided, -guiding.** guide wrongly.

mis′hap, n. unlucky accident.

mish′mash′ (mish′mäsh′), n. jumble; hodgepodge.

mis′in•form′, v. give false information to. —**mis′in•for•ma′tion,** n.

mis′in•ter′pret, v. interpret wrongly. —**mis′in•ter′pre•ta′tion,** n.

mis•judge′, v., **-judged, -judging.** judge wrongly. —**mis•judg′ment,** n.

mis•lay′, v., **-laid, -laying.** 1. put in place later forgotten. 2. misplace.

mis•lead′, v., **-led, -leading.** lead wrongly.

mis•man′age, v., **-aged, -aging.** manage badly. —**mis•man′age•ment,** n.

mis•no′mer, n. misapplied name.

mi•sog′y•ny (-soj′ə-), n. hatred of women. —**mi•sog′y•nist,** n.

mis•place′, v., **-placed, -placing.** 1. forget location of. 2. place unwisely.

mis′print′, n. error in printing.

mis′pro•nounce′, v., **-nounced, -nouncing.** pronounce wrongly. —**mis′pro•nun′ci•a′tion,** n.

mis•quote′, v., **-quoted, -quoting.** quote incorrectly. —**mis′quo•ta′tion,** n.

mis′rep•re•sent′, v. give wrong idea of. —**mis′rep•re•sen•ta′tion,** n.

mis•rule′, n. bad or unwise rule. —**mis•rule′,** v.

miss, v., n., pl. **misses.** —v. 1. fail to hit, catch, meet, do, etc. 2. note or feel absence of. —n. 3. (cap.) title of respect for unmarried woman. 4. girl. 5. failure to hit, catch, etc.

mis′sal, n. book of prayers, etc., for celebrating Mass.

mis•shap′en, adj. deformed.

mis′sile, n. object thrown or shot, as lance or bullet.

mis′sion, n. 1. group sent abroad for specific work. 2. duty. 3. air operation against enemy. 4. missionary post.

mis′sion•ar′y, n., pl. **-aries,** adj. —n. 1. person sent to propagate religious faith. —adj. 2. of religious missions.

mis′sive, n. written message.

mis•spell′, v. spell wrongly.

mis•state′, v., **-stated, -stating.** state wrongly. —**mis•state′ment,** n.

mis•step′, n. error.

mist, n. light, thin fog. —**mist′y,** adj.

mis•take′, n., v., **-took, -taken, -taking.** —n. 1. error in judgment, action, or belief. —v. 2. take or regard wrongly. 3. misunderstand. 4. be in error.

Mis′ter, n. title of respect for man. Abbr.: **Mr.**

mis′tle•toe′, n. parasitic plant.

mis•treat′, v. treat badly. —**mis•treat′ment,** n.

mis′tress, n. 1. female head of household. 2. female owner. 3. woman illicitly acting as wife.

mis•tri′al, *n.* trial ended without verdict because of legal error.

mis•trust′, *n.* lack of trust. —**mis•trust′,** *v.*

mis•un•der•stand′, *v.*, **-stood, -standing.** understand wrongly. —**mis•un•der•stand′ing,** *n.*

mis•use′, *n.*, *v.*, **-used, -using.** —*n.* (-yoos′). 1. improper use. —*v.* (-yooz′). 2. use badly or wrongly. 3. abuse.

mite, *n.* 1. tiny parasitic insect. 2. small thing or bit.

mi′ter, *v.* 1. join two pieces on diagonal. —*n.* 2. such joint. 3. tall cap worn by bishops. Also, *Brit.,* **mi′tre.**

mit′i•gate′, *v.*, **-gated, -gating.** make less severe.

mitt, *n.* thick glove.

mit′ten, *n.* fingerless glove.

mix, *v.*, **mixed** or **mixt, mixing,** *n.* —*v.* 1. put together; combine. 2. associate. 3. confuse. —*n.* 4. mixture. 5. mess. —**mix′ture,** *n.*

mne•mon′ic (nē-), *adj.* aiding memory.

moan, *n.* 1. low groan. —*v.* 2. utter moans.

moat, *n.* deep, water-filled ditch around fortification.

mob, *n.*, *v.*, **mobbed, mobbing.** —*n.* 1. crowd, esp. disorderly one. —*v.* 2. attack as a mob.

mo′bile, *adj.* moving easily. —**mo•bil′i•ty,** *n.*

mo′bi•lize′, *v.*, **-lized, -lizing.** make ready for war. —**mo′bi•li•za′tion,** *n.*

moc′ca•sin, *n.* 1. soft shoe. 2. poisonous snake.

mo′cha (-kə), *n.* kind of coffee.

mock, *v.* 1. mimic or ridicule. —*n.* 2. derision. —*adj.* 3. imitation.

mock′er•y, *n.*, *pl.* **-ies.** 1. derision. 2. dishonest imitation; travesty.

mock′ing•bird′, *n.* songbird with imitative voice.

mock′-up′, *n.* scale model.

mod, *adj. Informal.* fashionably up-to-date.

mode, *n.* prevailing style. —**mod′ish,** *adj.*

mod′el, *n.* 1. standard for imitation. 2. person who poses, as for artist or photographer. —*adj.* 3. serving as model. —*v.* 4. pattern after model. 5. wear as model. 6. form.

mod′er•ate, *adj.*, *n.*, *v.*, **-ated, -ating.** —*adj.* (-it). 1. not extreme. —*n.* (-it). 2. person having moderate views. —*v.* (-ə rāt′). 3. make or become less violent. 4. preside over. —**mod′er•a′tion,** *n.* —**mod′er•ate•ly,** *adv.*

mod′er•a′tor, *n.* director of group discussion.

mod′ern, *adj.* of recent time. —**mo•der′ni•ty,** *n.* —**mod′ern•ize′,** *v.*

mod′ern•is′tic, *adj.* following modern trends.

mod′est, *adj.* 1. humble in estimating oneself. 2. simple; moderate. 3. decent, moral. —**mod′est•ly,** *adv.* —**mod′es•ty,** *n.*

mod′i•cum, *n.* small amount.

mod′i•fy, *v.*, **-fied, -fying.** alter or moderate. —**mod′i•fi•ca′tion,** *n.* —**mod′i•fi′er,** *n.*

mo•diste′ (-dēst′), *n.fem.* maker of women's attire.

mod′u•late′, *v.*, **-lated, -lating.** 1. soften. 2. *Radio.* alter (electric current) in accordance with sound waves. 3. alter the pitch or key of. —**mod′u•la′tion,** *n.*

mod′ule, *n.* 1. unit of measure. 2. building unit. 3. self-contained element of spacecraft. —**mod′u•lar,** *adj.*

mo′hair′, *n.* fabric from fleece of the Angora goat.

Mo•ham′med•an•ism, *n.* Islam. —**Mo•ham′med•an,** *n.*, *adj.*

moi′e•ty, *n.*, *pl.* **-ties.** half; any part.

moil, *n.*, *v.* labor.

moist, *adj.* damp. —**mois′ten,** *v.*

mois′ture, *n.* dampness; small beads of water.

mo′lar, *n.* broad back tooth.

mo•las′ses, *n.* thick, dark syrup produced in refining sugar.

mold, *n.* 1. form for shaping molten or plastic material. 2. thing so formed. 3. fungus growth on animal or vegetable matter. 4. loose rich earth. —*v.* 5. shape or form. 6. become or make covered with mold (def. 3). —**mold′y,** *adj.*

mold′er, *v.* 1. decay. —*n.* 2. person who molds.

mold′ing, *n.* decorative strip with special cross section.

mole, *n.* 1. small, congenital spot on skin. 2. small, furred, underground mammal. —**mole′skin′,** *n.*

mol′e•cule′, *n.* smallest physical unit of a chemical element. —**mo•lec′u•lar,** *adj.*

mole′hill′, *n.* small mound of earth raised by moles.

mo•lest′, *v.* annoy by interfering with. —**mo′les•ta′tion,** *n.*

moll, *n. Slang.* female companion of gangster.

mol′li•fy′, *v.*, **-fied, -fying.** appease in temper.

mol′lusk, *n.* hard-shelled invertebrate animal. Also, **mol′lusc.**

mol′ly•cod′dle, *v.*, **-dled, -dling.** pamper.

molt, *v.* shed skin or feathers.

mol′ten, *adj.* melted.

mo′ment, *n.* 1. short space of time. 2. importance.

mo′men•tar′y, *adj.* very brief in time. —**mo′men•tar′i•ly,** *adv.*

mo•men′tous, *adj.* important.

mo•men′tum, *n.* force of moving body.

mon′ad, *n.* one-celled organism.

mon′arch, *n.* hereditary sovereign.

mon′ar•chy, *n.*, *pl.* **-chies.** 1. government by monarch. 2. country governed by monarch. —**mon′ar•chism,** *n.*

mon′as•ter′y, *n.*, *pl.* **-teries.** residence of monks. —**mo•nas′tic,** *adj.* —**mo•nas′ti•cism,** *n.*

Mon′day, *n.* second day of week.

mon′e•tar′y, *adj.* of money.

mon′ey, *n.*, *pl.* **moneys, monies.** 1. pieces of metal or certificates issued as medium of exchange. 2. wealth.

mon′eyed (-ēd) *adj.* wealthy.

mon′goose, *n.*, *pl.* **-gooses.** carnivorous animal of Asia.

mon′grel, *n.* 1. animal or plant resulting from crossing of different breeds. —*adj.* 2. of mixed breeds.

mon′i•tor, *n.* 1. pupil who assists teacher. —*v.* 2. check continuously.

mon′i•to′ry, *adj.* warning.

monk, *n.* member of secluded religious order.

mon′key, *n.*, *pl.* **-keys,** *v.*, **-keyed, -keying.** —*n.* 1. mammal strongly resembling man. —*v.* 2. trifle idly.

mon′o•chrome, *adj.* of one color. Also, **mon′o•chro•mat′ic.**

mon′o•cle, *n.* eyeglass for one eye.

mo•nog′a•my, *n.* marriage of one woman with one man. —**mo•nog′a•mous,** *adj.* —**mo•nog′a•mist,** *n.*

mon′o•gram′, *n.* design made of one's initials. —**mon′o•grammed,** *adj.*

mon′o•graph′, *n.* treatise on one subject.

mon′o•lith, *n.* structure of single block of stone. —**mon′o•lith′ic,** *adj.*

mon′o•logue′, *n.* talk by single speaker. Also, **mon′o•log′.** —**mon′o•log′ist,** *n.*

mon′o•plane′, *n.* airplane with one wing on each side.

mo•nop′o•ly, *n.*, *pl.* **-lies.** 1. exclusive control. 2. commodity, etc., so controlled. 3. company having such control. —**mo•nop′o•lis′tic,** *adj.* —**mo•nop′o•lize′,** *v.*

mon′o•syl′la•ble, *n.* word of one syllable. —**mon′o•syl•lab′ic,** *adj.*

mon′o•tone′, *n.* single tone of unvarying pitch.

mo•not′o•ny, *n.* wearisome uniformity. —**mo•not′o•nous,** *adj.*

mon•sieur′ (mə syŏŏ′), *n., pl.* **mes•sieurs′** (mā-). French term of address for man.

Mon•si′gnor (mon sē′nyər), *n., pl.* **Monsignors, Mon•si•gno′ri** (mon sē nyŏ′rē). title of certain dignitaries of Roman Catholic Church.

mon•soon′, *n.* seasonal wind of Indian Ocean.

mon′ster, *n.* 1. animal or plant of abnormal form. 2. wicked creature. 3. anything huge.

mon•stros′i•ty, *n., pl.* **-ties.** something grotesquely abnormal.

mon′strous, *adj.* 1. huge. 2. frightful.

mon•tage′ (-täzh′), *n.* blending of elements from several pictures into one.

month, *n.* any of twelve parts of calendar year.

month′ly, *adj., n., pl.* **-lies,** *adv.* —*adj.* 1. occurring, appearing, etc., once a month. 2. lasting for a month. —*n.* 3. periodical published once a month. —*adv.* 4. once a month. 5. by the month.

mon′u•ment, *n.* memorial structure.

mon′u•men′tal, *adj.* 1. imposing. 2. serving as monument.

moo, *n., v.,* **mooed, mooing.** —*n.* 1. sound cow makes. —*v.* 2. utter such sound.

mooch, *v. Informal.* try to get without paying. —**mooch′er,** *n.*

mood, *n.* frame of mind.

mood′y, *adj.,* **moodier, moodiest.** of uncertain mood. —**mood′i•ly,** *adv.*

moon, *n.* 1. body which revolves around earth monthly. 2. month. —*v.* 3. gaze dreamily.

moon′light′, *n., v.,* **-lighted, -lighting.** —*n.* 1. light from moon. —*v.* 2. work at second job after principal one.

moon′shine′, *n.* illegally made liquor. —**moon′shin′er,** *n.*

moon′stone′, *n.* pearly gem.

moor, *v.* 1. secure (ship), as at a dock. —*n.* 2. *Brit.* open peaty wasteland.

moor′ing, *n.* 1. (*pl.*) cables, etc., by which ship is moored. 2. place where ship is moored.

moose, *n., pl.* **moose.** large animal of deer family.

moot, *adj.* debatable.

mop, *n., v.,* **mopped, mopping.** —*n.* 1. piece of cloth, etc., fastened to stick, for washing or dusting. —*v.* 2. clean with mop. 3. *Mil.* **mop up,** destroy final resisting elements.

mope, *v.,* **moped, moping.** be in low spirits.

mo′ped′, *n.* motorized bicycle.

mop′pet, *n.* child.

mo•raine′ (-rān′), *n.* mass of stone, etc., left by glacier.

mor′al, *adj.* 1. of or concerned with right conduct. 2. virtuous. —*n.* 3. (*pl.*) principles of conduct. 4. moral lesson. —**mor′al•ist,** *n.* —**mor′al•is′tic,** *adj.*

mo•rale′, *n.* spirits; mood.

mo•ral′i•ty, *n.* 1. conformity to rules of right conduct. 2. moral quality.

mor′al•ize′, *v.,* **-ized, -izing.** think or pronounce on moral questions.

mor′al•ly, *adv.* 1. according to morals. 2. in one's honest belief.

mo•rass′, *n.* swamp.

mor′a•to′ri•um, *n.* 1. legal permission to delay payment of debts. 2. any temporary cessation.

mor′bid, *adj.* 1. unwholesome. 2. of disease. —**mor•bid′i•ty,** *n.* —**mor′bid•ly,** *adv.*

mor′dant, *adj.* sarcastic.

more, *adj.* 1. in greater amount or degree. 2. additional. —*n.* 3. additional or greater quantity or degree. —*adv.* 4. in addition.

more•o′ver, *adv.* besides.

mo′res (mōr′āz), *n.pl.* social and moral customs of group.

mor′ga•nat′ic, *adj.* designating marriage between royal person and commoner.

morgue, *n.* place where corpses are taken for identification.

mor′i•bund′, *adj.* dying.

Mor′mon•ism, *n.* religion founded in U.S. in 1830. —**Mor′mon,** *n., adj.*

morn′ing, *n.* 1. first part of day. —*adj.* 2. done, or occurring, in the morning.

morn′ing-glo′ry, *n., pl.* **-ries.** vine with funnel-shaped flowers.

mo•roc′co, *n.* fine leather.

mo′ron, *n.* stupid person. —**mo•ron′ic,** *adj.*

mo•rose′, *adj.* gloomily ill-humored. —**mo•rose′ly,** *adv.* —**mo•rose′ness,** *n.*

Mor′phe•us, *n.* god of dreams.

mor′phine (-fēn), *n.* narcotic found in opium.

Morse, *n.* telegraphic code of long and short signals.

mor′sel, *n.* small amount.

mor′tal, *adj.* 1. liable to death. 2. causing death. 3. to death. —*n.* 4. human being. —**mor′tal•ly,** *adv.*

mor•tal′i•ty, *n., pl.* **-ties.** 1. mortal nature. 2. relative death rate.

mor′tar, *n.* 1. bowl in which drugs, etc., are pulverized. 2. short cannon. 3. material used to bind masonry.

mort′gage (môr′-), *n., v.,* **-gaged, -gaging.** —*n.* 1. conditional transfer of property as security for debt. —*v.* 2. put mortgage on. —**mort′ga•gee′,** *n.* —**mort′ga•gor,** *n.*

mor•ti′cian, *n.* undertaker.

mor′ti•fy, *v.,* **-fied, -fying.** 1. humiliate. 2. subject (body) to austerity. —**mor′ti•fi•ca′tion,** *n.*

mor′tise, *n., v.,* **-tised, -tising.** —*n.* 1. slot in wood for tenon. —*v.* 2. fasten by mortise.

mor′tu•ar′y (-chŏŏ-), *n., pl.* **-aries.** place where bodies are prepared for burial.

mo•sa′ic, *n.* design made of small pieces of colored stone, glass, etc.

mo′sey, *v.,* **-seyed, -seying.** *Informal.* stroll.

Mos′lem, *n., adj.* Muslim.

mosque (mosk), *n.* Muslim place of prayer.

mos•qui′to, *n., pl.* **-toes, -tos.** common biting insect.

moss, *n.* small, leafy-stemmed plant growing on rocks, etc. —*v.* 2. cover with moss. —**moss′y,** *adj.*

most, *adj.* 1. in greatest amount. 2. majority of. —*n.* 3. greatest quantity. —*adv.* 4. to greatest extent.

most′ly, *adv.* 1. in most cases. 2. in greater part.

mote, *n.* particle.

mo•tel′, *n.* roadside hotel for automobile travelers.

moth, *n.* insect, some of whose larvae eat cloth.

moth′ball′, *n.* ball of camphor, etc., for repelling moths.

moth′er, *n.* 1. female parent. 2. head of group of nuns. 3. stringy substance forming on fermenting liquids. —*adj.* 4. of, like, or being mother. 5. native. —*v.* 6. act as or like mother to. —**moth′er•hood′,** *n.* —**moth′er•ly,** *adj.*

moth′er-in-law′, *n., pl.* **mothers-in-law.** mother of one's spouse.

moth′er-of-pearl′, *n.* inner layer of certain shells.

mo·tif′ (-tēf′), *n.* subject or theme.

mo′tion, *n.* 1. process of changing position. 2. action or power of movement. 3. formal proposal made in meeting. —*v.* 4. indicate by gesture. —**mo′tion·less,** *adj.*

motion picture, series of photographs projected so rapidly that objects seem to be moving.

mo′ti·vate′, *v.,* **-vated, -vating.** give motive to. —**mo′ti·va′tion,** *n.*

mo′tive, *n.* 1. purpose; goal. —*adj.* 2. of or causing motion.

mot′ley, *adj.* widely, often grotesquely, varied.

mo′tor, *n.* 1. small, powerful engine. —*adj.* 2. of or causing motion. 3. of or operated by motor. —*v.* 4. travel by automobile.

mo′tor·boat′, *n.* boat run by motor.

mo′tor·cade′, *n.* procession of automobiles.

mo′tor·car′, *n.* automobile.

mo′tor·cy′cle, *n.* heavy motor-driven bicycle.

mo′tor·ist, *n.* automobile driver.

mo′tor·ize′, *v.,* **-ized, -izing.** furnish with motors or motor-driven vehicles.

mot′tle, *v.,* **-tled, -tling.** mark with spots or blotches.

mot′to, *n.,* *pl.* **-toes, -tos.** phrase expressing one's guiding principle.

mould, *n.* mold.

mould′er, *v.* molder.

moult, *v., n.* molt.

mound, *n.* heap of earth; hill.

mount, *v.* 1. go up; get on; rise. 2. prepare for use or display. 3. fix in setting. —*n.* 4. act or manner of mounting. 5. horse for riding. 6. Also, **mounting.** support, setting, etc. 7. hill.

moun′tain, *n.* lofty natural elevation on earth's surface. —**moun′tain·ous,** *adj.*

moun′tain·eer′, *n.* 1. mountain climber. 2. dweller in mountains. —**moun′tain·eer′ing,** *n.*

moun′te·bank′, *n.* charlatan.

mourn, *v.* grieve; feel or express sorrow (for). —**mourn′er,** *n.* —**mourn′ful,** *adj.* —**mourn′ing,** *n.*

mouse, *n.,* *pl.* **mice,** *v.,* **moused, mousing.** —*n.* 1. small gray rodent. —*v.* (mouz). 2. hunt for mice.

mousse (mo͞os), *n.* frothy dessert.

mous·tache′, *n.* mustache.

mous′y, *adj.* drably quiet in air or appearance. —**mous′i·ness,** *n.*

mouth, *n.,* *pl.* **mouths,** *v.* —*n.* 1. opening through which animal takes in food. 2. any opening. —*v.* 3. utter pompously or dishonestly. —**mouth′ful′,** *n.*

mouth organ, harmonica.

mouth′piece′, *n.* 1. piece at or forming mouth. 2. person, newspaper, etc., speaking for others.

move, *v.,* **moved, moving,** *n.* —*v.* 1. change place or position. 2. change one's abode. 3. advance. 4. make formal proposal in meeting. 5. affect emotionally. —*n.* 6. act of moving. 7. purposeful action. —**mov′a·ble,** *adj., n.* —**mov′er,** *n.*

move′ment, *n.* 1. act or process of moving. 2. trend in thought. 3. works of mechanism. 4. principal division of piece of music.

moving picture, motion picture. Also, **mov′ie.**

mow, *v.,* **mowed, mowed** or **mown, mowing,** *n.* —*v.* (mō). 1. cut (grass, etc.). 2. kill indiscriminately. —*n.* (mou). 3. place in barn where hay, etc., are stored. —**mow′er,** *n.*

Ms. (miz), *n.* title of address for woman not to be distinguished as married or unmarried.

much, *adj.* 1. in great quantity or degree. —*n.* 2. great quantity. 3. notable thing. —*adv.* 4. greatly. 5. generally.

mu′ci·lage, *n.* gummy adhesive. —**mu′ci·lag′i·nous,** *adj.*

muck, *n.* 1. filth. 2. moist barn refuse. —**muck′y,** *adj.*

muck′rake′, *v.,* **-raked, -raking.** expose scandal. —**muck′rak′er,** *n.*

mu′cous (-kəs), *n.* 1. secreting mucus. 2. of or like mucus.

mucous membrane, membrane lining internal surface of organ.

mu′cus, *n.* sticky secretion of mucous membrane.

mud, *n.* wet soft earth. —**mud′dy,** *adj., v.*

mud′dle, *v.,* **-dled, -dling,** *n.* —*v.* 1. mix up; confuse. —*n.* 2. confusion.

muff, *n.* 1. tubular covering of fur, etc., for hands. —*v.* 2. bungle. 3. drop (ball) after catching.

muf′fin, *n.* small round bread.

muf′fle, *v.,* **-fled, -fling,** *n.* —*v.* 1. wrap in scarf, cloak, etc. 2. deaden (sound). —*n.* 3. something that muffles.

muf′fler, *n.* 1. heavy neck scarf. 2. device for deadening sound, as on engine.

muf′ti, *n.* civilian dress.

mug, *n.,* *v.,* **mugged, mugging.** —*n.* 1. drinking cup. 2. *Slang.* face. —*v.* 3. *Slang.* assault from the rear by choking with forearm. 4. *Slang.* grimace. —**mug′ger,** *n.*

mug′gy, *adj.,* **-gier, -giest.** hot and humid.

Mu·ham′mad, *n.* founder of Islam, A.D. 570–632.

mul′ber′ry, *n.,* *pl.* **-ries.** tree, the leaves of some of whose species are used as food by silkworms.

mulch, *n.* 1. loose covering of leaves, straw, etc., on plants. —*v.* 2. surround with mulch.

mulct (mulkt), *v.* 1. deprive of by trickery. 2. fine.

mule, *n.* 1. offspring of donkey and mare. 2. woman's house slipper.

mul′ish, *adj.* obstinate.

mull, *v.* 1. study or ruminate (over). 2. heat and spice.

mul′lah, *n.* Muslim religious teacher.

mul′lein (-in), *n.* tall, woolly-leaved weed.

mul′let, *n.* common food fish.

mul′li·gan, *n.* stew of meat and vegetables.

mul′ti·far′i·ous, *adj.* many and varied.

mul′ti·na′tion·al, *n.* corporation with operations in many countries.

mul′ti·ple, *adj.* 1. consisting of or involving many. —*n.* 2. number evenly divisible by stated other number.

mul′ti·pli·cand′, *n.* number to be multiplied by another.

mul′ti·plic′i·ty, *n.* great number or variety.

mul′ti·ply′, *v.,* **-plied, -plying.** 1. increase the number of. 2. add (number) to itself a stated number of times. —**mul′ti·pli′er,** *n.* —**mul′ti·pli·ca′tion,** *n.*

mul′ti·tude′, *n.* great number.

mul′ti·tu′di·nous, *adj.* 1. numerous. 2. having many parts.

mum, *adj.* silent.

mum′ble, *v.,* **-bled, -bling,** *n.* 1. speak quietly and unintelligibly. —*n.* 2. mumbling sound.

mum′bo jum′bo, strange ritual.

mum′mer, *n.* 1. person in festive disguise. 2. actor.

mum′mer·y, *n.* mere show.

mum′my, *n.,* *pl.* **-mies.** dead body treated to prevent decay.

mumps, *n.pl.* infectious disease marked by swelling of salivary glands.

munch, *v.* chew.

mun·dane′, *adj.* commonplace.

mu·nic′i·pal, *adj.* of a city.

mu·nic′i·pal′i·ty, *n., pl.* **-ties.** self-governing city.

mu·nif′i·cent, *adj.* extremely generous. **—mu·nif′i·cence,** *n.* **—mu·nif′i·cent·ly,** *adv.*

mu·ni′tions, *n.* weapons and ammunition used in war.

mu′ral, *n.* 1. picture painted on wall. **—***adj.* 2. of walls.

mur′der, *n.* 1. unlawful willful killing. **—***v.* 2. commit murder. **—mur′der·er,** *n.* **—mur′der·ess,** *n.fem.* **—mur′der·ous,** *adj.*

murk, *n.* darkness.

murk′y, *adj.,* **murkier, murkiest.** dark and gloomy.**—murk′i·ness,** *n.*

mur′mur, *n.* 1. low, continuous, indistinct sound. 2. complaint. **—***v.* 3. speak softly or indistinctly. 4. complain.

mur′rain (mûr′in), *n.* disease of cattle.

mus′ca·dine, *n.* American grape.

mus′cat, *n.* sweet grape.

mus′ca·tel′, *n.* wine made from muscat grapes.

mus′cle, *n., v.,* **-cled, -cling. —***n.* 1. bundle of fibers in animal body that contract to produce motion. 2. brawn. **—***v.* 3. *Informal.* force one's way. **—mus′cu·lar,** *adj.*

muse, *v.,* **mused, musing.** reflect in silence.

Muse, *n.* one of nine goddesses of the arts.

mu·se′um, *n.* place for permanent public exhibits.

mush, *n.* 1. meal boiled in water until thick, used as food. 2. anything soft. 3. *Informal.* maudlin sentiment. **—***v.* 4. travel on foot, esp. over snow with dog team. **—mush′y,** *adj.*

mush′room, *n.* 1. fleshy fungus, usually umbrella-shaped, sometimes edible. **—***adj.* 2. growing rapidly. **—***v.* 3. grow quickly.

mu′sic, *n.* 1. art of arranging sounds for effect by rhythm, melody, etc. 2.

score of musical composition. **—mu·si′cian,** *n.*

mus′i·cal, *adj.* 1. of music. 2. pleasant-sounding. 3. sensitive to or skilled in music. **—***n.* 4. Also, **mus′ical com′edy.** a play with music. **—mus′i·cal·ly,** *adv.*

musk, *n.* animal secretion, used in perfume. **—musk′y,** *adj.*

mus′ket, *n.* early hand gun.

mus′ket·eer′, *n.* soldier armed with musket.

musk′mel′on, *n.* sweet edible melon.

musk′rat′, *n.* large aquatic American rodent.

Mus′lim (muz′-), *n.* 1. follower of Islam. **—***adj.* 2. of or pertaining to Islam.

mus′lin, *n.* plain-weave cotton fabric.

muss, *Informal.* **—***n.* 1. disorder; mess. **—***v.* 2. rumple. **—muss′y,** *adj.*

mus′sel, *n.* bivalve mollusk, sometimes edible.

must, *aux. v.* 1. be obliged to. 2. may be assumed to. **—***adj.* 3. necessary. **—***n.* 4. anything necessary. 5. new wine not yet fermented.

mus′tache, *n.* hair growing on man's upper lip. Also, **mus·ta′chio** (-shō).

mus′tang, *n.* small wild horse of western U.S.

mus′tard, *n.* pungent yellow powder made from seeds of mustard plant.

mus′ter, *v.* 1. assemble, as troops; gather. **—***n.* 2. assembly.

mus′ty, *adj.* stale-smelling. **—mus′ti·ness,** *n.*

mu′ta·ble, *adj.* subject to change. **—mu·ta·bil′i·ty,** *n.*

mu·ta′tion, *n.* change.

mute, *adj., n., v.,* **muted, muting. —***adj.* 1. silent. 2. incapable of speech. **—***n.* 3. person unable to utter words. 4. device for muffling musical instrument. **—***v.* 5. deaden sound of.

mu′ti·late′, *v.,* **-lated, -lating.** injure by depriving of or damaging part. **—mu′ti·la′tion,** *n.*

mu′ti·ny, *n., pl.* **-nies,** *v.,* **-nied, -nying.** revolt against lawful authority. **—mu′ti·neer′,** *n.* **—mu′ti·nous,** *adj.*

mutt, *n. Slang.* mongrel dog.

mut′ter, *v.* 1. speak low and indistinctly; grumble. **—***n.* 2. act or sound of muttering.

mut′ton, *n.* flesh of sheep, used as food.

mu′tu·al (-chōō-), *adj.* 1. done, etc., by two or more in relation to each other; reciprocal. 2. common. **—mu′tu·al·ly,** *adv.*

muz′zle, *n., v.,* **-zled, -zling. —***n.* 1. mouth of firearm. 2. mouth part of animal's head. 3. cage this. **—***v.* 4. put muzzle on. 5. silence; gag.

my, *pron.* possessive form of **I** used before noun.

my′na, *n.* Asiatic bird sometimes taught to talk.

my·o′pi·a, *n.* near-sightedness. **—my·op′ic,** *adj.*

myr′i·ad, *n., adj.* 1. very great number. 2. ten thousand.

myr′i·a·pod′, *n.* many-legged worm.

myrrh (mûr), *n.* aromatic substance from certain plants.

myr′tle, *n.* 1. evergreen shrub. 2. periwinkle (def. 2).

my·self′, *pron., pl.* **ourselves.** 1. intensive form of **I** or **me.** 2. reflexive form of **me.**

mys′ter·y, *n., pl.* **-teries.** 1. anything secret, unknown, or unexplained. 2. obscurity. 3. secret rite. **—mys·te′ri·ous,** *adj.* **—mys·te′ri·ous·ly,** *adv.*

mys′tic, *adj.* Also, **mys′ti·cal.** 1. mysterious or occult. 2. spiritual. **—***n.* 3. believer in mysticism.

mys′ti·cism, *n.* belief in direct spiritual intuition of God, truth, etc.

mys′ti·fy′, *v.,* **-fied, -fying.** bewilder purposely. **—mys′ti·fi·ca′tion,** *n.*

myth, *n.* 1. legendary story, person, etc. 2. false popular belief. **—myth′i·cal, myth′ic,** *adj.* **—myth′i·cal·ly,** *adv.*

my·thol′o·gy, *n.* body of myths. **—myth′o·log′i·cal,** *adj.*

N

N, n, *n.* fourteenth letter of English alphabet.

nab, *v.,* **nabbed, nabbing.** *Informal.* seize; arrest.

na′bob, *n.* wealthy person.

na•celle′ (-sel′), *n.* enclosed shelter for aircraft engine.

na′dir (nā′dər), *n.* 1. lowest point. 2. point of celestial sphere directly below given point.

nag, *v.,* **nagged, nagging,** *n.* —*v.* 1. scold constantly. —*n.* 2. horse.

nai′ad (nā′ad), *n.* water nymph.

nail, *n.* 1. slender piece of metal for holding pieces of wood together. 2. horny plate at end of finger or toe. —*v.* 3. fasten with nails. 4. *Informal.* secure or seize.

na•ïve′ (nä ēv′), *adj.* simple; unsophisticated. Also, **na•if′, na•ive′.**

na•ïve•té′ (-tā′), *n.* artless simplicity.

na′ked, *adj.* 1. without clothing or covering. 2. (of eye) unassisted in seeing. 3. plain. —**na′ked•ness,** *n.*

name, *n., v.,* **named, naming.** —*n.* 1. word or words by which a person, place, or thing is designated. 2. reputation. 3. behalf or authority. —*v.* 4. give name to. 5. specify. 6. appoint. —**nam′a•ble, name′a•ble,** *adj.* —**nam′er,** *n.* —**name′less,** *adj.*

name′ly, *adv.* that is to say.

name′sake′, *n.* one having same name as another.

nan′ny, *n., pl.* **-nies.** female goat.

nap, *n., v.,* **napped, napping.** —*n.* 1. short sleep. 2. short, fuzzy fibers on the surface of cloth. —*v.* 3. raise fuzz on. 4. have short sleep.

nape, *n.* back of neck.

naph′tha (nap′-), *n.* petroleum derivative, used as solvent, fuel, etc.

naph′tha•lene′ (naf′-), *n.* white crystalline substance used in mothballs, etc.

nap′kin, *n.* piece of cloth used at table to protect clothes.

nar′cis•sism, *n.* abnormal admiration of oneself. —**nar′cis•sis′tic,** *adj.*

nar•cis′sus, *n.* spring-blooming plant, as daffodil or jonquil.

nar•cot′ic, *adj.* 1. sleep-inducing. —*n.* 2. substance that dulls pain, induces sleep, etc.

nar′rate, *v.,* **-rated, -rating.** tell. —**nar′ra′tion,** *n.* —**nar′ra•tor,** *n.*

nar′ra•tive, *n.* 1. story of events. —*adj.* 2. that narrates. 3. of narration.

nar′row, *adj.* 1. not broad or wide. 2. literal or strict in interpreting rules, etc. 3. minute. —*v.* 4. make or become narrow. —*n.* 5. narrow place, thing, etc. —**nar′row-mind′-ed,** *adj.*

nar′whal (-wəl), *n.* Arctic whale.

NASA (nas′ə), *n.* National Aeronautics and Space Administration.

na′sal, *adj.* 1. of noses. 2. spoken through nose. —*n.* 3. nasal sound. —**na′sal•ly,** *adv.*

na•stur′tium, *n.* garden plant with yellow, orange, and red flowers.

nas′ty, *adj.,* **-tier, -tiest.** 1. disgustingly unclean. 2. objectionable. —**nas′ti•ly,** *adv.* —**nas′ti•ness,** *n.*

na′tal, *adj.* of one's birth.

na′tion, *n.* 1. people living in one territory under same government. 2. people related by tradition or ancestry. —**na′tion•al,** *adj., n.* —**na′tion•al•ly,** *adv.*

na′tion•al•ism′, *n.* devotion to one's nation. —**na′tion•al•ist,** *n., adj.* —**na′tion•al•is′tic,** *adj.*

na′tion•al′i•ty, *n., pl.* **-ties.** 1. condition of being member of a nation. 2. nation.

na′tion•al•ize′, *v.,* **-ized, -izing.** bring under national control or ownership. —**na′tion•al•i•za′tion,** *n.*

na′tion•wide′, *adj., adv.* across entire nation.

na′tive, *adj.* 1. belonging to by birth, nationality, or nature. 2. of natives. —*n.* 3. person, animal, or plant native to region.

na•tiv′i•ty, *n., pl.* **-ties.** birth.

NATO (nā′tō), *n.* North Atlantic Treaty Organization.

nat′ty, *adj.,* **-tier, -tiest.** smart; trim.

nat′u•ral, *adj.* 1. of, existting in, or formed by nature. 2. to be expected in circumstances. 3. without affectation. 4. *Music.* neither sharp nor flat. —**nat′u•ral•ly,** *adv.* —**nat′u•ral•ness,** *n.*

nat′u•ral•ist, *n.* student of nature.

nat′u•ral•ize′, *v.,* **-ized, -izing.** 1. confer citizenship upon. 2. introduce to region. —**nat′u•ral•i•za′-tion,** *n.*

na′ture, *n.* 1. material world. 2. universe. 3. character of person or thing.

naught, *n.* zero.

naugh′ty, *adj.,* **-tier, -tiest.** 1. disobedient; bad. 2. improper. —**naugh′ti•ly,** *adv.* —**naugh′ti•ness,** *n.*

nau′sea (nô′shə), *n.* 1. feeling of impending vomiting. 2. disgust. —**nau′se•ate′,** *v.* —**nau′seous,** *adj.*

nau′ti•cal, *adj.* of ships, seamen, or navigation.

nau′ti•lus, *n.* mollusk having pearly shell.

na′val, *adj.* of ships or navy.

nave, *n.* main lengthwise part of church.

na′vel, *n.* pit in center surface of belly.

nav′i•gate′, *v.,* **-gated, -gating.** 1. traverse (water or air). 2. direct on a course. —**nav′i•ga′tion,** *n.* —**nav′i•ga′tor,** *n.* —**nav′i•ga•ble,** *adj.*

na′vy, *n., pl.* **-vies.** all of a nation's warships, with their crews.

nay, *adv., n.* no.

Na′zi (nä′tsē), *n., pl.* **-zis.** member of the National Socialist party in Germany, headed by Adolf Hitler. —**Na′zism,** *n.*

neap tide, tide having lowest high point.

near, *adv.* 1. close by. —*adj.* 2. close. 3. intimate. —*v.* 4. approach. —**near′ness,** *n.*

near′by′, *adj.* close.

near′ly, *adv.* almost; in close agreement.

near′-sight′ed, *adj.* seeing distinctly only at short distance. —**near′-sight′ed•ness,** *n.*

neat, *adj.* 1. orderly. 2. skillful. 3. undiluted. —**neat′ly,** *adv.* —**neat′ness,** *n.*

neb, *n.* bill or beak.

neb′u•la, *n., pl.* **-lae** (-lē′), **-las.** luminous mass of gas or far-distant stars. —**neb′u•lar,** *adj.*

neb′u•lous, *adj.* 1. hazy; vague. 2. cloudlike.

nec′es•sar′y, *adj., n., pl.* **-saries.** —*adj.* 1. that cannot be dispensed with. 2. required by facts or reason; unavoidable. —*n.* 3. something necessary. —**nec′es•sar′i•ly,** *adv.*

ne•ces′si•tate′, *v.,* **-tated, -tating.** make necessary.

ne•ces′si•ty, *n., pl.* **-ties.** 1. something necessary. 2. fact of being necessary. 3. poverty.

neck, *n.* 1. part connecting head and trunk. —*v.* 2. *Slang.* play amorously.

neck'er•chief, *n.* cloth worn around neck.

neck'lace, *n.* ornament of gems, etc., worn around neck.

neck'piece', *n.* fur scarf.

neck'tie', *n.* cloth strip worn under man's collar and tied in front.

ne•crol'o•gy, *n., pl.* **-gies.** list of persons who have died.

nec'ro•man'cy, *n.* magic. —**nec'ro•manc'er,** *n.*

ne•cro'sis, *n.* death of tissue or of organ.

nec'tar, *n.* 1. sweet secretion of flower. 2. drink of gods.

nec'tar•ine', *n.* downless peach.

nee (nā), *adj.* (of woman) born; having as maiden name. Also, **née.**

need, *n.* 1. requirement. 2. condition marked by necessity, as poverty. —*v.* 3. depend absolutely or strongly. 4. be obliged. —**need'ful,** *adj.* —**need'less,** *adj.*

nee'dle, *n., v.,* **-dled, -dling.** —*n.* 1. slender pointed implement for sewing, knitting, etc. 2. anything similar, as indicator or gauge. —*v.* 3. prod; tease.

needs, *adv.* necessarily.

need'y, *adj.,* **needier, neediest.** very poor. —**need'i•ness,** *n.*

ne'er'-do-well', *n.* person who habitually fails.

ne•far'i•ous, *adj.* wicked.

ne•gate', *v.,* **-gated, -gating.** deny; nullify. —**ne•ga'tion,** *n.*

neg'a•tive, *adj.* 1. expressing denial or refusal. 2. undistinguished. 3. *Math.* minus. 4. *Photog.* having light and shade reversed. —*n.* 5. negative statement, etc. 6. *Photog.* negative image. —**neg'a•tive•ly,** *adv.*

ne•glect', *v.* 1. disregard; fail to do. —*n.* 2. disregard; negligence. —**ne•glect'ful,** *adj.*

neg'li•gee' (-zhā'), *n.* woman's house robe.

neg'li•gent, *adj.* neglectful. —**neg'li•gence,** *n.*

neg'li•gi•ble, *adj.* unimportant.

ne•go'ti•a•ble (-shē-), *adj.* transferable, as securities. —**ne•go'ti•a•bil'i•ty,** *n.*

ne•go'ti•ate' (-shē āt'), *v.,* **-ated, -ating.** 1. deal with; bargain. 2. dispose of. —**ne•go'ti•a'tion,** *n.* —**ne•go'ti•a'tor,** *n.*

Ne'gro, *n., pl.* **-groes.** black. —**Ne'gro,** *adj.* —**Ne'groid,** *adj.*

neigh, *n.* 1. cry of horse; whinny. —*v.* 2. make cry of horse.

neigh'bor, *n.* 1. person or thing near another. —*v.* 2. be near. —**neigh'bor•ly,** *adj.*

neigh'bor•hood, *n.* 1. surrounding area. 2. district having separate identity.

nei'ther (nē'*th*ər, nī'*th*ər), *conj., adj.* not either.

nem'e•sis, *n., pl.* **-ses.** cause of one's downfall.

Ne'o•lith'ic, *adj.* of the later Stone Age.

ne•ol'o•gism (-jiz'əm), *n.* new word or phrase.

ne'on, *n.* gas used in electrical signs.

ne'o•phyte', *n.* beginner.

neph'ew, *n.* son of one's brother or sister.

nep'o•tism, *n.* official favoritism toward one's relatives.

nerd, *n. Slang.* stupid or foolish person.

nerve, *n., v.,* **nerved, nerving.** —*n.* 1. bundle of fiber that conveys impulses between brain and other parts of body. 2. courage. 3. *Informal.* presumption. 4. (*pl.*) anxiety; unease. —*v.* 5. give courage to.

nerv'ous, *adj.* 1. of nerves. 2. having or caused by disordered nerves. 3. anxious; uneasy. —**nerv'ous•ly,** *adv.* —**nerv'ous•ness,** *n.*

nerv'y, *adj.,* **-ier, -iest.** *Informal.* presumptuous.

nest, *n.* 1. place used by bird or other creature for rearing its young. 2. group of things fitting tightly together. —*v.* 3. settle in nest. 4. fit one within another.

nes'tle, *v.,* **-tled, -tling.** lie close and snug.

net, *adj., n., v.,* **netted, netting.** —*adj.* 1. exclusive of loss, expense, etc. —*n.* 2. net profit. 3. Also, **net'ting.** lacelike fabric of uniform mesh. 4. bag of such fabric. —*v.* 5. gain as clear profit. 6. cover with net. 7. ensnare.

neth'er, *adj.* lower. —**neth'er•most',** *adj.*

net'tle, *n., v.,* **-tled, -tling.** —*n.* 1. plant with stinging hairs. —*v.* 2. irritate; sting.

net'work', *n.* 1. netlike combination. 2. group of associated radio or television stations, etc.

neu'ral (nyŏŏr'əl), *adj.* of nerves or nervous system.

neu•ral'gia, *n.* sharp pain along nerve.

neu•ri'tis, *n.* inflammation of nerve. —**neu•rit'ic,** *adj.*

neu•rol'o•gy, *n.* study of nerves. —**neu•rol'o•gist,** *n.* —**neu'ro•log'i•cal,** *adj.*

neu•ro'sis, *n. pl.* **-ses.** psychoneurosis. —**neu•rot'ic,** *adj., n.*

neu'ter, *adj.* 1. neither male nor female. —*v.* 2. spay or castrate. —**neu'ter,** *n.*

neu'tral, *adj.* 1. taking no side in controversy. 2. not emphatic or positive. —*n.* 3. neutral person or state. —**neu•tral'i•ty,** *n.* —**neu'tral•ize',** *v.* —**neu'tral•ly,** *adv.* —**neu'tral•i•za'tion,** *n.*

neu'tron, *n.* particle in nucleus of atom.

nev'er, *adv.* not ever.

nev'er•the•less', *adv.* in spite of what has been said.

new, *adj.* 1. of recent origin or existence. 2. unfamiliar. —*adv.* 3. recently; freshly. —**new'ly,** *adv.* —**new'ness,** *n.*

new'el, *n.* post at the head or foot of stair.

New England, group of states in northeast U.S.

new'ly•wed', *n.* newly married person.

news, *n.* report of recent event, situation, etc.

news'cast', *n.* radio or television broadcast of news.

news'let'ter, *n.* small informative periodical for specialized group.

news'man', *n.* journalist. Also, **news'wom'an,** *n.fem.*

news'pa'per, *n.* periodical containing news, etc. —**news'pa'per•man',** *n.* —**news'pa'per•wom'an,** *n.fem.*

news'print', *n.* paper on which newspapers are printed.

news'reel', *n.* motion picture of news events.

news'stand', *n.* sales booth for periodicals, etc.

newt, *n.* salamander.

new year, 1. (*cap.*) first day of year. 2. year approaching.

next, *adj.* 1. nearest after. —*adv.* 2. in nearest place after. 3. at first subsequent time.

nex'us, *n., pl.* **nexus.** link or series.

ni'a•cin, *n.* nicotinic acid.

nib, *n.* 1. beak of bird. 2. pen point.

nib'ble, *v.,* **-bled, -bling,** *n.* —*v.* 1. bite off in small bits. —*n.* 2. small morsel.

nib'lick, *n.* golf club.

nice, *adj.,* **nicer, nicest. 1.** agreeable. **2.** precise. **3.** fastidious. —**nice′ly,** *adv.*

ni′ce•ty, *n., pl.* **-ties. 1.** subtle point. **2.** refinement.

niche (nich), *n.* **1.** recess in wall. **2.** proper role or vocation.

nick, *n.* **1.** notch or hollow place in surface. **2.** precise or opportune moment. —*v.* **3.** make nick in.

nick′el, *n.* **1.** hard silver-white metal. **2.** five-cent coin.

nick′el•o′de•on, *n.* **1.** early, cheap motion-picture house. **2.** coin-operated automatic piano, etc.

nick′name′, *n., v.,* **-named, -naming.** —*n.* **1.** name used informally. —*v.* **2.** give nickname to.

nic′o•tine′ (-tēn′), *n.* poison found in tobacco.

nic′o•tin′ic acid, vitamin from nicotine, used against pellagra.

niece, *n.* daughter of one's brother or sister.

nif′ty, *adj.,* **-tier, -tiest.** *Informal.* smart; fine.

nig′gard•ly, *adj.* **1.** stingy. **2.** meanly small.

nigh, *adv., adj.* near.

night, *n.* period between sunset and sunrise.

night′fall′, *n.* coming of night.

night′gown′, *n.* gown for sleeping. Also, **night′dress′.**

night′hawk′, *n.* nocturnal American bird.

night′in•gale′, *n.* small European bird noted for male's song.

night′ly, *adj., adv.* every night.

night′mare′, *n.* **1.** bad dream. **2.** harrowing event.

night′shade′, *n.* plant sometimes used in medicine.

ni′hil•ism (nī′ə liz′ əm), *n.* total disbelief in principles. —**ni′hil•ist,** *n.* —**ni′hil•is′tic,** *adj.*

nil, *n.* nothing.

nim′ble, *adj.,* **-bler, -blest.** agile; quick. —**nim′bly,** *adv.* —**nim′ble• ness,** *n.*

nim′rod, *n.* hunter.

nin′com•poop′, *n.* fool.

nine, *n., adj.* eight plus one. —**ninth,** *n., adj.*

nine′pins′, *n.pl.* bowling game played with nine wooden pins.

nine′teen′, *n., adj.* ten plus nine. —**nine′teenth′,** *n., adj.*

nine′ty, *n., adj.* ten times nine. —**nine′ti•eth,** *adj., n.*

nin′ny, *n., pl.* **-nies.** fool.

nip, *v.,* **nipped, nipping,** *n.* —*v.* **1.** pinch or bite. **2.** check growth of. **3.** affect sharply. **4.** sip. —*n.* **5.** pinch. **6.** biting quality. **7.** sip. —**nip′py,** *adj.*

nip′ple, *n.* **1.** milk-discharging protuberance on breast. **2.** nipple-shaped object.

nir•va′na (nir vä′nə), *n.* **1.** (in Buddhism) freedom from all passion. **2.** state of bliss; salvation.

nit, *n.* egg of louse.

ni′ter, *n.* white salt used in gunpowder, etc. Also, **ni′tre.**

nit′-pick′, *v. Informal.* argue or find fault pettily.

ni′trate, *n.* **1.** salt of nitric acid. **2.** fertilizer containing nitrates.

ni′tro•gen, *n.* colorless, odorless, tasteless gas, used in explosives, fertilizers, etc.

ni′tro•glyc′er•in, *n.* colorless, highly explosive oil.

ni′trous, *adj.* **1.** of niter. **2.** Also, **ni′-tric.** containing nitrogen.

nit′ty-grit′ty, *n. Slang. (often pl.)* essentials of situation. —**nitty-gritty,** *adj.*

nit′wit′, *n.* simpleton.

nix, *adv. Informal.* no.

no, *adv., n., pl.* **noes,** *adj.* —*adv.* **1.** word used to express dissent, denial, or refusal. —*n.* **2.** negative vote. —*adj.* **3.** not any.

no•bil′i•ty, *n., pl.* **-ties. 1.** noble class. **2.** noble quality.

no′ble, *adj.,* **-bler, -blest,** *n.* —*adj.* **1.** of high rank by birth. **2.** admirable or magnificent. —*n.* **3.** person of noble rank. —**no′ble•man,** *n.* —**no′ble•wom′an,** *n.fem.* —**no′bly,** *adv.*

no′bod′y, *n., pl.* **-bodies. 1.** no one. **2.** no one of importance.

noc•tur′nal, *adj.* **1.** of night. **2.** occurring or active by night.

noc′turne, *n.* dreamy or pensive musical composition.

nod, *v.,* **nodded, nodding,** *n.* —*v.* **1.** incline head briefly. **2.** become sleepy. **3.** sway gently. **4.** be absentminded. —*n.* **5.** brief inclination of head.

node, *n.* **1.** protuberance. **2.** difficulty. **3.** joint in plant stem.

nod′ule, *n.* small knob or lump. —**nod′u•lar,** *adj.*

no′-fault′, *adj.* (of auto accident insurance, divorces, etc.) effective without establishing fault.

nog′gin, *n.* small mug.

noise, *n., v.,* **noised, nois•ing.** —*n.* **1.** sound, esp. loud or harsh. —*v.* **2.** spread rumors. —**noise′less,** *adj.* —**nois′y,** *adj.* —**nois′i•ly,** *adv.* —**nois′i•ness,** *n.*

noi′some, *adj.* offensive or noxious.

no′mad, *n.* wanderer. —**no•mad′ic,** *adj.*

nom de plume (nom′ də plōōm′), name assumed by writer.

no′men•cla′ture (-klā′chər), *n.* set or system of names.

nom′i•nal, *adj.* **1.** in name only; so-called. **2.** trifling. —**nom′i•nal•ly,** *adv.*

nom′i•nate′, *v.,* **-nated, -nating. 1.** propose as candidate. **2.** appoint. —**nom′i•na′tion,** *n.* —**nom′i•na′-tor,** *n.*

nom′i•na•tive, *adj.* **1.** denoting noun or pronoun used as the subject of a sentence. —*n.* **2.** nominative case.

nom′i•nee′, *n.* one nominated.

non′a•ge•nar′i•an, *n.* person 90 to 99 years old.

nonce, *n.* present occasion.

non′cha•lant′ (non′shə länt′), *adj.* coolly unconcerned. —**non′cha• lance′,** *n.* —**non′cha•lant′ly,** *adv.*

non′com•mis′sioned, *adj. Mil.* not commissioned.

non′com•mit′tal, *adj.* not committing oneself. —**non′com•mit′tal•ly,** *adv.*

non•con•duc′tor, *n.* substance that does not readily conduct heat, electricity, etc.

non′con•form′ist, *n.* person who refuses to conform.

non′de•script′, *adj.* of no particular kind.

none, *pron. sing. and pl.* **1.** not one; not any. —*adv.* **2.** in no way.

non•en′ti•ty, *n., pl.* **-ties. 1.** unimportant person or thing. **2.** nonexistent thing.

none′the•less′, *adv.* nevertheless.

no′-no′, *n. Informal.* forbidden thing.

non′pa•reil′ (non′pə rel′), *adj.* **1.** having no equal. —*n.* **2.** person or thing without equal.

non•par′ti•san, *adj.* **1.** not taking sides. **2.** belonging to no party.

non•plus′, *v.,* **-plused, -plusing.** puzzle completely.

non′sec•tar′i•an, *adj.* of no one sect. —**nonsectarian,** *n.*

non′sense, *n.* **1.** senseless or absurd words or action. **2.** anything useless. —**non•sen′si•cal,** *adj.*

non se′qui•tur, irrelevant statement.

non'stop', *adj.*, *adv.* without intermediate stops. Also, **non-stop.**

noo'dle, *n.* thin strip of dough, cooked in soup, etc.

nook, *n.* 1. corner of room. 2. secluded spot.

noon, *n.* 12 o'clock in daytime. —**noon'time'**, **noon'tide'**, *n.*

noose, *n.*, *v.*, **noosed, noosing.** —*n.* 1. loop with running knot that pulls tight. —*v.* 2. catch by noose.

nor, *conj.* or not: used with **neither.**

Nor'dic, *n.* person marked by tall stature, blond hair, and blue eyes. —**Nor'dic**, *adj.*

norm, *n.* standard.

nor'mal, *adj.* 1. of standard type; usual. 2. at right angles. —*n.* 3. standard; average. 4. perpendicular line. —**nor'mal•cy**, **nor'mal'i•ty**, *n.* —**nor'mal•ize'**, *v.* —**nor'mal•i•za'tion**, *n.* —**nor'mal•ly**, *adv.*

normal school, school for training teachers.

north, *n.* 1. cardinal point of compass, on one's right facing the setting sun. 2. territory in or to north. —*adj.* 3. toward, in, or from north. —*adv.* 4. toward north. —**north'er•ly**, *adj.*, *adv.* —**north'ern**, *adj.* —**north'ern•er**, *n.* —**north'ward**, *adj.*, *adv.*

north'east', *n.* point or direction midway between north and east. —**north'east'**, *adj.*, *adv.* —**north'east'ern**, *adj.*

north'west', *n.* point or direction midway between north and west. —**north'west'**, *adj.*, *adv.* —**north'west'ern**, *adj.*

nose, *n.*, *v.*, **nosed, nosing.** —*n.* 1. part of head containing nostrils. 2. sense of smell. 3. projecting part. —*v.* 4. smell. 5. pry or head cautiously.

nose dive, downward plunge. —**nose'-dive'**, *v.*

nose'gay', *n.* small bouquet.

nos•tal'gia, *n.* yearning for past. —**nos•tal'gic**, *adj.*

nos'tril, *n.* external opening of nose for breathing and smelling.

nos'trum, *n.* medicine allegedly having special powers.

nos'y, *adj.*, **-ier, -iest.** *Informal.* unduly inquisitive. Also, **nos'ey.**

not, *adv.* word expressing negation, denial, or refusal.

no'ta•ble, *adj.* 1. worthy of note; important. —*n.* 2. prominent person. —**no'ta•bly**, *adv.*

no'ta•rize', *v.*, **-rized, -rizing.** authenticate by notary.

no'ta•ry, *n.*, *pl.* **-ries.** official authorized to verify documents. Also, **notary public.**

no•ta'tion, *n.* 1. note. 2. special symbol. —**no•ta'tion•al**, *adj.*

notch, *n.* 1. angular cut. —*v.* 2. make notch in.

note, *n.*, *v.*, **noted, noting.** —*n.* 1. brief record, comment, etc. 2. short letter. 3. importance. 4. notice. 5. paper promising payment. 6. musical sound or written symbols. —*v.* 7. write down. 8. notice. —**note'book'**, *n.*

not'ed, *adj.* famous.

note'wor'thy, *adj.* notable.

noth'ing, *n.* 1. not anything. 2. trivial action, thing, etc. —*adv.* 3. not at all.

no'tice, *n.*, *v.*, **-ticed, -ticing.** —*n.* 1. information; warning. 2. note, etc., that informs or warns. 3. attention; heed. —*v.* 4. pay attention to; perceive. 5. mention. —**no'tice•a•ble**, *adj.* —**no'tice•a•bly**, *adv.*

no'ti•fy', *v.*, **-fied, -fying.** give notice to. —**no'ti•fi•ca'tion**, *n.*

no'tion, *n.* 1. idea; conception. 2. opinion. 3. whim. 4. (*pl.*) small items, as pins or threads.

no•to'ri•ous, *adj.* widely known, esp. unfavorably. —**no'to•ri'e•ty**, *n.*

not'with•stand'ing, *prep.* 1. in spite of. —*adv.* 2. nevertheless. —*conj.* 3. although.

nou'gat (noo'gət), *n.* pastelike candy with nuts.

nought, *n.* naught.

noun, *n.* word denoting person, place, or thing.

nour'ish, *v.* sustain with food. —**nour'ish•ment**, *n.*

nov'el, *n.* 1. long fictitious narrative. —*adj.* 2. unfamiliar. —**nov'el•ist**, *n.*

nov'el•ty, *n.*, *pl.* **-ties.** 1. unfamiliarity. 2. unfamiliar or amusing thing.

No•vem'ber, *n.* eleventh month of year.

nov'ice, *n.* 1. beginner. 2. person just received into a religious order.

no•vi'ti•ate (-vish'ē it), *n.* probationary period.

No'vo•caine', *n.* *Trademark.* local anesthetic.

now, *adv.* 1. at present time. 2. immediately. —*conj.* 3. since. —*n.* 4. the present.

now'a•days', *adv.* in these times.

no'where', *adv.* not anywhere.

nox'ious, *adj.* harmful.

noz'zle, *n.* projecting spout.

nth (enth), *adj.* utmost.

nu'ance (nyoo'äns), *n.* shade of expression, etc.

nub, *n.* gist.

nu'bile (nyoo'bil), *adj.* marriageable.

nuclear physics, branch of physics dealing with atoms.

nu'cle•us, *n.*, *pl.* **-clei, -cleuses.** 1. central part about which other parts are grouped. 2. central body of living cell. 3. central core of atom. —**nu'cle•ar**, *adj.*

nude, *adj.* naked. —**nu'di•ty**, *n.* —**nude'ly**, *adv.*

nudge, *v.*, **nudged, nudging**, *n.* —*v.* 1. push slightly. —*n.* 2. slight push.

nud'ism, *n.* practice of going naked for health. —**nud'ist**, *n.*

nu'ga•to'ry, *adj.* 1. trifling. 2. futile.

nug'get, *n.* lump.

nui'sance, *n.* annoying thing or person.

nuke, *n.* *Slang.* nuclear weapon or power plant.

null, *adj.* of no effect.

null'i•fy', *v.*, **-fied, -fying.** 1. make null. 2. make legally void. —**nul'li•fi•ca'tion**, *n.*

numb, *adj.* 1. deprived of feeling or movement. —*v.* 2. make numb. —**numb'ness**, *n.*

num'ber, *n.* 1. sum of group of units. 2. numeral. 3. one of series or group. 4. large quantity. —*v.* 5. mark with number. 6. count. 7. amount to in numbers.

num'ber•less, *adj.* too numerous to count.

nu'mer•al, *n.* 1. word or sign expressing number. —*adj.* 2. of numbers.

nu'mer•ate', *v.*, **-ated, -ating.** number; count. —**nu'mer•a'tion**, *n.*

nu'mer•a'tor, *n.* part of fraction written above the line, showing number of parts taken.

nu•mer'i•cal, *adj.* of, denoting, or expressed by number. —**nu•mer'i•cal•ly**, *adv.*

nu'mer•ous, *adj.* very many.

nu'mis•mat'ics, *n.* science of coins and medals.

num'skull', *n.* *Informal.* dunce. Also, **numb'skull'.**

nun, *n.* woman living with religious group under strict vows.

nun'ci•o' (nun'shē ō'), *n.*, *pl.* **-cios.** diplomatic representative of a Pope.

nun′ner•y, *n., pl.* **-eries.** convent.

nup′tial, *adj.* 1. of marriage. —*n.* 2. (*pl.*) marriage ceremony.

nurse, *n., v.,* **nursed, nursing.** —*n.* 1. person who cares for sick or children. —*v.* 2. tend in sickness. 3. look after carefully. 4. suckle.

nurs′er•y, *n., pl.* **-eries.** 1. room set apart for young children. 2. place where young trees or plants are grown.

nur′ture, *v.,* **-tured, -turing,** *n.* —*v.* 1. feed and care for during growth. —*n.* 2. upbringing. 3. nourishment.

nut, *n.* 1. dry fruit consisting of edible kernel in shell. 2. the kernel. 3. perforated, threaded metal block used to screw on end of bolt, etc. —**nut′-crack′er,** *n.* —**nut′shell′,** *n.*

nut′meg, *n.* aromatic seed of East Indian tree.

nu′tri•a (nyōō′trē ə), *n.* fur resembling beaver.

nu′tri•ent, *adj.* nourishing. —**nu′tri•ent,** *n.*

nu′tri•ment, *n.* nourishment.

nu•tri′tion, *n.* 1. food. 2. process by which organism converts food into living tissue. —**nu•tri′tious, nu′-tritive,** *adj.* —**nu•tri′tion•al,** *adj.*

nuts, *adj. Informal.* crazy.

nut′ty, *adj.,* **-tier, -tiest.** 1. tasting of or like nuts. 2. *Informal.* insane; senseless. —**nut′ti•ness,** *n.*

nuz′zle, *v.,* **-zled, -zling.** 1. thrust nose (against). 2. cuddle.

ny′lon, *n.* 1. tough, elastic synthetic substance used for yarn, bristles, etc. 2. (*pl.*) stockings of nylon.

nymph, *n.* beautiful goddess living in woodlands, waters, etc.

nym′pho•ma′ni•a, *n.* uncontrollable sexual desire in women. —**nym′-pho•ma′ni•ac′,** *n.*

O, o, *n.* 1. fifteenth letter of English alphabet. —*interj.* 2. expression of surprise, gladness, pain, etc. 3. word used before name in archaic form of address.

o′, *prep.* abbreviated form of **of.**

oaf, *n.* clumsy, rude person. —**oaf′-ish,** *adj.*

oak, *n.* tree having hard wood. —**oak′en,** *adj.*

oa′kum, *n.* loose fiber used in calking seams.

oar, *n.* 1. flat-bladed shaft for rowing boat. —*v.* 2. row. —**oars′man,** *n.*

oar′lock′, *n.* support on gunwale for oar.

o•a′sis, *n., pl.* **-ses.** fertile place in desert.

oat, *n.* cereal grass having edible seed. —**oat′meal′,** *n.*

oath, *n.* 1. solemn affirmation; vow. 2. curse.

ob′du•rate, *adj.* stubborn; not sorry or penitent. —**ob′du•ra•cy,** *n.*

o•bei′sance (-bā′-), *n.* 1. bow or curtsy. 2. homage.

ob′e•lisk, *n.* tapering, four-sided monumental shaft.

o•bese′ (ō bēs′), *adj.* very fat. —**o•bes′i•ty,** *n.*

o•bey′, *v.* 1. do as ordered by. 2. respond to, as controls. —**o•be′di•ence,** *n.* —**o•be′di•ent,** *adj.* —**o•be′di•ent•ly,** *adv.*

ob•fus′cate (-fus′kāt), *v.,* **-cated, -cating.** confuse; make unclear. —**ob′fus•ca′tion,** *n.*

o•bit′u•ar′y, *n., pl.* **-aries.** notice of death.

ob′ject, *n.* 1. something solid. 2. thing or person to which attention is directed. 3. end; motive. 4. noun or pronoun that represents goal of action. —*v.* (əb jekt′). 5. make protest. —**ob•jec′tion,** *n.* —**ob•jec′tor,** *n.*

ob•jec′tion•a•ble, *adj.* causing disapproval; offensive.

ob•jec′tive, *n.* 1. something aimed at. 2. objective case. —*adj.* 3. real or factual. 4. unbiased. 5. being object of perception or thought. 6. denoting word used as object of sentence. —**ob•jec′tive•ly,** *adv.* —**ob′jec•tiv′i•ty,** *n.*

ob′jur•gate′, *v.,* **-gated, -gating.** scold. —**ob′jur•ga′tion,** *n.* —**ob•jur′ga•to′ry,** *adj.*

ob′late, *adj.* (of spheroid) flattened at poles.

ob•la′tion, *n.* offering; sacrifice.

ob′li•gate′, *v.,* **-gated, -gating.** bind morally or legally. —**ob′li•ga′tion,** *n.* —**ob•lig′a•to′ry,** *adj.*

o•blige′, *v.,* **obliged, obliging.** 1. require; bind. 2. place under debt of gratitude.

o•blig′ing, *adj.* willing to help.

o•blique′ (ə blēk′), *adj.* 1. slanting. 2. indirect. —**o•blique′ly,** *adv.* —**o•bliq′ui•ty,** *n.*

ob•lit′er•ate′, *v.,* **-ated, -ating.** remove all traces of. —**ob•lit′er•a′-tion,** *n.*

ob•liv′i•on, *n.* 1. state of being forgotten. 2. forgetfulness. —**ob•liv′i•ous,** *adj.*

ob′long, *adj.* 1. longer than broad. —*n.* 2. oblong rectangle.

ob′lo•quy, *n., pl.* **-quies.** public disgrace.

ob•nox′ious, *adj.* offensive. —**ob•nox′ious•ly,** *adv.*

o′boe, *n.* wind instrument. —**o′bo•ist,** *n.*

ob•scene′, *adj.* offensive to decency. —**ob•scene′ly,** *adv.* —**ob•scen′i•ty,** *n.*

ob•scu′rant•ism, *n.* willful obscuring of something presented to public. —**ob•scu′rant•ist,** *n., adj.*

ob•scure′, *adj., v.,* **-scured, -scuring.** —*adj.* 1. not clear. 2. not prominent. 3. dark. —*v.* 4. make obscure. —**ob′-scu•ra′tion,** *n.* —**ob•scu′ri•ty,** *n.* —**ob•scure′ly,** *adv.*

ob•se′qui•ous, *adj.* servilely deferential.

ob′se•quy, *n., pl.* **-quies.** funeral rite.

ob•serv′ance, *n.* 1. act of observing or conforming. 2. due celebration. —**ob•serv′ant,** *adj.*

ob•serv′a•to′ry, *n., pl.* **-ries.** place equipped for observing stars, etc.

ob•serve′, *v.,* **-served, -serving.** 1. see; notice; watch. 2. remark. 3. pay respect to or perform duly. —**ob′-ser•va′tion,** *n.* —**ob•serv′er,** *n.*

ob•sess′, *v.* be constantly in thoughts of. —**ob•ses′sion,** *n.* —**ob•ses′sive,** *adj.*

ob′so•les′cent (-les′ənt), *adj.* becoming obsolete. —**ob′so•les′cence,** *n.*

ob′so•lete′, *adj.* no longer in use.

ob′sta•cle, *n.* something in the way.

ob•stet′rics, *n.* branch of medicine concerned with childbirth. —**ob′-ste•tri′cian,** *n.* —**ob•stet′ric,** *adj.*

ob′sti•nate, *adj.* 1. firm; stubborn. 2. not yielding to treatment. —**ob′sti•na•cy,** *n.* —**ob′sti•nate•ly,** *adv.*

ob•strep′er•ous, *adj.* unruly.

ob•struct′, *v.* block; hinder. —**ob•struc′tion,** *n.* —**ob•struc′tive,** *adj.*

ob•struc′tion•ism, *n.* perverse desire to be obstructive. —**ob•struc′tion•ist,** *n., adj.*

ob•tain′, *v.* 1. get or acquire. 2. prevail. —**ob•tain′a•ble,** *adj.*

ob•trude′, *v.,* **-truded, -truding.** thrust forward; intrude. —**ob•tru′-sion,** *n.* —**ob•tru′sive,** *adj.*

ob•tuse′, *adj.* 1. blunt; not rounded. 2. not perceptive. 3. (of angle) between 90° and 180°.

ob′verse, *n.* 1. front. 2. side of coin having principal design. 3. counterpart. —*adj.* (ob vûrs′). 4. facing. 5. corresponding.

ob′vi•ate′, *v.,* **-ated, -ating.** take preventive measures against; avoid.

ob′vi•ous, *adj.* 1. readily perceptible. 2. not subtle. —**ob′vi•ous•ly,** *adv.* —**ob′vi•ous•ness,** *n.*

oc′a•ri′na (ok′ə rē′nə), *n.* egg-shaped wind instrument.

oc•ca′sion, *n.* 1. particular time. 2. important time. 3. opportunity. 4. reason. —*v.* 5. give cause for. —**oc•ca′sion•al,** *adj.* —**oc•ca′sion•al•ly,** *adv.*

Oc′ci•dent (ok′sə-), *n.* West, esp. Europe and Americas. —**Oc′ci•den′tal,** *adj., n.*

oc•clude′, *v.,* **-cluded, -cluding.** close; shut. —**oc•clu′sion,** *n.*

oc•cult′, *adj.* 1. outside ordinary knowledge. —*n.* 2. occult matters.

oc′cu•pa′tion, *n.* 1. trade; calling. 2. possession. 3. military seizure. —**oc′cu•pa′tion•al,** *adj.*

oc′cu•py, *v.,* **-pied, -pying.** 1. inhabit or be in. 2. require as space. 3. take possession of. 4. hold attention of. —**oc′cu•pan•cy,** *n.* —**oc′cu•pant,** *n.*

oc•cur′, *v.,* **-curred, -curring.** 1. take place. 2. appear. 3. come to mind. —**oc•cur′rence,** *n.*

o′cean, *n.* 1. large body of salt water covering much of earth. 2. any of its five main parts. —**o′ce•an′ic,** *adj.*

o′ce•a•nog′ra•phy, *n.* study of oceans. —**o′ce•a•no•graph′ic,** *adj.* —**o′ce•a•nog′ra•pher,** *n.*

o′ce•lot′ (ō′sə-), *n.* small American wildcat.

o′cher (ō′kər), *n.* yellow-to-red earth used as pigment. Also, **o′chre.**

o′clock′, *adv.* of or by the clock.

oc′ta•gon′, *n.* plane figure with eight sides and eight angles.

oc′tane, *n.* colorless liquid hydrocarbon found in petroleum.

oc′tave, *n. Music.* 1. eighth tone from given tone. 2. interval between such tones.

oc•ta′vo (-tā′-), *n.* book whose pages are printed 16 to a sheet.

oc•tet′, *n.* group of eight, esp. musicians. Also, **oc•tette′.**

Oc•to′ber, *n.* tenth month of year.

oc′to•ge•nar′i•an, *n.* person 80 to 89 years old.

oc′to•pus, *n.* large, soft-bodied, eight-armed sea mollusk.

oc′u•lar, *adj.* of eyes.

oc′u•list, *n.* doctor skilled in eye-treatment.

odd, *adj.* 1. eccentric; bizarre. 2. additional; not part of set. 3. not evenly divisible by two.

odd′i•ty, *n., pl.* **-ties.** 1. queerness. 2. odd person or thing.

odds, *n.* 1. chances; probability for or against. 2. state of disagreement. 3. odd things.

ode, *n.* poem of praise.

o′di•ous, *adj.* hateful.

o′di•um, *n.* 1. discredit; reproach. 2. hatred.

o′dor, *n.* quality that affects sense of smell; scent. —**o′dor•ous,** *adj.*

o′dor•if′er•ous, *adj.* having odor, esp. pleasant.

o′er, *prep., adv. Poetic.* over.

of, *prep.* particle indicating: 1. being from. 2. belonging to.

off, *adv.* 1. up or away. 2. deviating. 3. out of operation or effect. —*prep.* 4. up or away from. —*adj.* 5. no longer in operation or effect. 6. in error. 7. on one's way.

of′fal, *n.* refuse; garbage; carrion.

off′beat′, *adj. Informal.* unconventional.

of•fend′, *v.* displease greatly.

of•fend′er, *n.* 1. person who offends. 2. person who commits crime.

of•fense′, *n.* 1. wrong; sin. 2. displeasure. 3. attack. Also, **of•fence′.** —**of•fen′sive,** *adj., n.*

of′fer, *v.* 1. present. 2. propose; suggest. —*n.* 3. proposal; bid. —**of′fer•ing,** *n.*

of′fer•to′ry, *n., pl.* **-ries.** 1. *Rom. Cath. Ch.* offering to God of bread and wine during Mass. 2. collection at religious service.

off′hand′, *adj.* 1. Also, **off′hand′ed.** done without previous thought; informal. 2. curt; brusque. —**off′hand′,** **off′hand′ed•ly,** *adv.*

of′fice, *n.* 1. place of business. 2. position of authority or trust. 3. duty; task. 4. religious service.

of′fi•cer, *n.* person of rank or authority.

of•fi′cial, *n.* 1. person who holds office. —*adj.* 2. authorized. 3. pertaining to public office. —**of•fi′cial•ly,** *adv.*

of•fi′ci•ate, *v.,* **-ated, -ating.** perform official duties. —**of•fi′ci•a′tor,** *n.*

of•fi′cious, *adj.* too forward in offering unwanted help.

off′ing, *n.* 1. distant area. 2. foreseeable future.

off′set′, *v.,* **-set, -setting.** compensate for.

off′shoot′, *n.* branch.

off′shore′, *adj., adv.* in water and away from shore.

off′spring′, *n.* children or descendants.

oft, *adv. Poetic.* often.

of′ten, *adv.* 1. frequently. 2. in many cases.

o′gle, *v.,* **ogled, ogling,** *n.* —*v.* 1. eye with impertinent familiarity. —*n.* 2. ogling glance.

o′gre (ō′gər), *n.* hideous man-eating giant. —**o′gre•ish,** *adj.* —**o′gress,** *n.fem.*

oh, *interj.* (exclamation of surprise, etc.)

ohm (ōm), *n.* unit of electrical resistance.

oil, *n.* 1. greasy combustible liquid used for lubricating, heating, etc. —*v.* 2. supply with oil. —*adj.* 3. of oil. —**oil′er,** *n.* —**oil′y,** *adj.*

oil′cloth′, *n.* fabric made waterproof with oil.

oint′ment, *n.* salve.

O.K., *adj., adv., v.,* **O.K.'d, O.K.'ing,** *n., pl.* **O.K.'s.** —*adj., adv.* (ō′kā′). 1. all right; correct. —*v.* (ō′kā′). 2. approve. —*n.* (ō′kā′). 3. agreement or approval. Also, **OK, o′kay′.**

o′kra, *n.* tall garden plant with edible pods.

old, *adj.* 1. far advanced in years or time. 2. of age. 3. Also, **old′en.** former; ancient. 4. experienced. —*n.* 5. former time.

old′-fash′ioned, *adj.* having style, ideas, etc., of an earlier time.

old′ster, *n. Informal.* elderly person.

old′-tim′er, *n. Informal.* elderly person.

Old World, Europe, Asia, and Africa. —**old′-world′,** *adj.*

o′le•ag′i•nous (ō′lē aj′ə nəs), *adj.* oily.

o′le•an′der, *n.* poisonous evergreen flowering shrub.

o•le•o•mar′ga•rine (-jə rin, -rēn′), *n.* edible fat made of vegetable oils and skim milk. Also, **o′le•o′**, **o′le•o•mar′ga•rin.**

ol•fac′to•ry, *adj.* pertaining to sense of smell.

ol′i•garch′ (-gärk′), *n.* ruler in an oligarchy.

ol′i•gar′chy, *n., pl.* **-chies.** government by small group. —**ol′i•gar′chic**, *adj.*

ol′ive, *n.* 1. evergreen tree valued for its small, oily fruit. 2. yellowish green.

om′buds•man, *n., pl.* **-men.** official who investigates private individuals' complaints against government. Also, *fem.* **om′buds•wom′an.**

om′e•let, *n.* eggs beaten with milk and fried or baked. Also, **om′e•lette.**

o′men, *n.* sign indicative of future.

om′i•nous, *adj.* threatening evil. —**om′i•nous•ly**, *adv.*

o•mit′, *v.*, **omitted, omitting.** 1. leave out. 2. fail to do, etc. —**o•mis′sion**, *n.*

om′ni•bus′, *n., pl.* **-buses.** 1. bus. 2. anthology.

om•nip′o•tent, *adj.* almighty. —**om•nip′o•tence**, *n.*

om′ni•pres′ent, *adj.* present everywhere at once.

om•nis′cient (om nish′ənt), *adj.* knowing all things. —**om•nis′cience**, *n.*

om•niv′o•rous, *adj.* eating all kinds of foods.

on, *prep.* particle expressing: 1. position in contact with supporting surface. 2. support; reliance. 3. situation or direction. 4. basis. —*adv.* 5. onto a thing, place, or person. 6. forward. 7. into operation. —*adj.* 8. near.

once, *adv.* 1. formerly. 2. single time. 3. at any time. —*conj.* 4. if ever; whenever.

once′-o′ver, *n. Informal.* quick survey.

on′com′ing, *adj.* approaching.

one, *adj.* 1. single. 2. some. 3. common to all. —*n.* 4. first and lowest whole number. 5. single person or thing. —*pron.* 6. person or thing.

one′ness, *n.* unity.

on′er•ous (on′-), *adj.* burdensome.

one•self′, *pron.* person's self. Also, **one's self.**

one′-sid′ed, *adj.* 1. with all advantage on one side. 2. biased.

one′-time′, *adj.* being such before; former.

one′-track′, *adj. Informal.* obsessed with one subject.

on′go•ing, *adj.* in progress; continuing.

on′ion, *n.* common plant having edible bulb.

on′look′er, *n.* spectator; witness.

on′ly, *adv.* 1. alone; solely. 2. merely. —*adj.* 3. sole. —*conj.* 4. but.

on′rush′, *n.* rapid advance.

on′set′, *n.* 1. violent attack. 2. beginning.

on′slaught′, *n.* attack.

on′to, *prep.* upon; on.

o′nus (ō′nəs), *n.* burden.

on′ward, *adv.* 1. toward or at point ahead. —*adj.* 2. moving forward.

on′yx, *n.* quartz occurring in varicolored bands.

ooze, *v.*, **oozed, oozing**, *n.* —*v.* 1. leak out slowly; exude. —*n.* 2. something that oozes. 3. soft mud.

o•pac′i•ty (ō pas′-), *n.* state of being opaque.

o′pal, *n.* precious stone, often iridescent.

o′pa•les′cent, *adj.* with opallike play of color. —**o′pa•les′cence**, *n.*

o•paque′ (ō pāk′), *adj.* 1. not transmitting light. 2. not shining. 3. not clear.

OPEC (ō′pek), *n.* Organization of Petroleum Exporting Countries.

o′pen, *adj.* 1. not shut. 2. not enclosed or covered. 3. available; accessible. 4. candid. —*v.* 5. make or become open. 6. begin. 7. come apart. —*n.* 8. any open space.

o′pen-and-shut′, *adj.* easily solved or decided; obvious.

o′pen-hand′ed, *adj.* generous.

o′pen•ing, *n.* 1. unobstructed or unoccupied place. 2. gap or hole. 3. beginning. 4. opportunity.

o′pen-mind′ed, *adj.* without prejudice. —**o′pen-mind′ed•ness**, *n.*

op′er•a, *n.* sung drama. —**op′er•at′ic**, *adj.*

op′er•a•ble, *adj.* 1. able to be operated. 2. curable by surgery.

op′er•ate′, *v.*, **-ated, -ating.** 1. work or run. 2. exert force or influence. 3. use surgery. —**op′er•a′tion**, *n.* —**op′er•a′tor**, *n.*

op′er•a′tion•al, *adj.* 1. concerning operations. 2. in working order. 3. in operation.

op′er•a′tive, *n.* 1. workman. 2. detective. —*adj.* 3. effective.

op′er•et′ta, *n.* light opera.

oph•thal′mi•a (of thal′mē ə), *n.* inflammation of eye.

oph′thal•mol′o•gy, *n.* branch of medicine dealing with eye. —**oph′thal•mol′o•gist**, *n.*

o′pi•ate (ō′pē it), *n.* medicine containing opium.

o•pin′ion, *n.* unproven belief or judgment.

o•pin′ion•at′ed, *adj.* conceitedly stubborn in opinions.

o′pi•um, *n.* narcotic juice of poppy.

o•pos′sum, *n.* pouched mammal of southern U.S.

op•po′nent, *n.* 1. person on opposite side, as in contest. 2. person opposed to something.

op′por•tune′, *adj.* appropriate; timely.

op′por•tun′ism, *n.* unprincipled use of opportunities. —**op′por•tun′ist**, *n.* —**op′por•tun•is′tic**, *adj.*

op′por•tu′ni•ty, *n., pl.* **-ties.** temporary possible advantage.

op•pose′, *v.*, **-posed, -posing.** 1. resist or compete with. 2. hinder. 3. set as an obstacle. 4. cause to disfavor something. —**op′po•si′tion**, *n.*

op′po•site, *adj.* 1. in corresponding position on other side. 2. completely different. —*n.* 3. one that is opposite.

op•press′, *v.* 1. weigh down. 2. treat harshly as matter of policy. —**op•pres′sion**, *n.* —**op•pres′sive**, *adj.* —**op•pres′sor**, *n.*

op•pro′bri•um, *n.* disgrace and reproach. —**op•pro′bri•ous**, *adj.*

op′tic, *adj.* of eyes.

op′ti•cal, *adj.* 1. acting by means of sight and light. 2. made to assist sight. 3. visual. 4. of optics. —**op′ti•cal•ly**, *adv.*

op•ti′cian, *n.* maker of eyeglasses.

op′tics, *n.* branch of science dealing with light and vision.

op′ti•mal, *adj.* optimum.

op′ti•mism′, *n.* 1. disposition to hope for best. 2. belief that good will prevail over evil. —**op′ti•mist**, *n.* —**op′ti•mis′tic**, *adj.*

op′ti•mum, *adj., n.* best.

op′tion, *n.* 1. power of choosing or deciding. 2. choice made. —**op′tion•al**, *adj.*

op•tom′e•try, *n.* art of testing eyes for eyeglasses. —**op•tom′e•trist**, *n.*

op′u•lent, *adj.* wealthy. —**op′u•lence**, *n.*

o′pus, (ō′ pəs), *n., pl.* **opera.** work, esp. musical, usually numbered.

or, *conj.* (particle used to connect alternatives.)

or'a•cle, *n.* 1. answer by the gods to question. 2. medium giving the answer. —**o•rac'u•lar,** *adj.*

o'ral, *adj.* 1. spoken. 2. of mouths. —**o'ral•ly,** *adv.*

or'ange, *n.* 1. round, reddish-yellow citrus fruit. 2. reddish yellow.

or'ange•ade', *n.* drink with base of orange juice.

o•rang'-u•tan', *n.* large, long-armed ape. Also, **o•rang'-ou•tang',** **o•rang'.**

o•ra'tion, *n.* formal speech.

or'a•tor, *n.* eloquent public speaker.

or'a•to'ri•o, *n.* religious work for voices and orchestra in dramatic form.

or'a•to'ry, *n.,* *pl.* **-ries.** 1. eloquent speaking. 2. small room for prayer. —**or'a•tor'i•cal,** *adj.*

orb, *n.* 1. sphere. 2. any of heavenly bodies.

or'bit, *n.* 1. path of planet, etc., around another body. 2. cavity in skull for eyeball. —**or'bit•al,** *adj.*

or'chard, *n.* plot of fruit trees.

or'ches•tra, *n.* 1. *Music.* large company of instrumental performers. 2. space in theater for musicians. 3. main floor of theater. —**or•ches'-tral,** *adj.*

or'ches•trate', *v.,* **-trated, -trating.** arrange music for orchestra. —**or'-ches•tra'tion,** *n.*

or'chid (ôr'kid), *n.* 1. tropical plant with oddly shaped blooms. 2. light purple.

or•dain', *v.* 1. invest as clergyman. 2. appoint or direct.

or•deal', *n.* severe test.

or'der, *n.* 1. authoritative command. 2. harmonious arrangement. 3. group bound by common religious rules. 4. list of goods or services desired. —*v.* 5. give an order. 6. arrange.

or'der•ly, *adj., adv., n., pl.* **-lies.** —*adj.* 1. methodical. 2. well-behaved. —*adv.* 3. according to rule. —*n.* 4. attendant. —**or'der•li•ness,** *n.*

or'di•nal, *adj.* 1. showing position in series, as *first, second,* etc. —*n.* 2. ordinal number.

or'di•nance, *n.* law.

or'di•nar'y, *adj., n., pl.* **-naries.** —*adj.* 1. usual; normal. —*n.* 2. ordinary condition, etc. —**or'di•nar'i•ly,** *adv.*

or'di•na'tion, *n.* act or ceremony of ordaining. Also, **or•dain'ment.**

ord'nance, *n.* military weapons of all kinds.

ore, *n.* metal-bearing rock.

o•reg'a•no, *n.* plant with leaves used as seasoning.

or'gan, *n.* 1. large musical keyboard instrument sounded by air forced through pipes, etc. 2. part of animal or plant with specific function. 3. means of communication. —**or'-gan•ist,** *n.*

or'gan•dy, *n.,* *pl.* **-dies.** thin stiff cotton fabric.

or•gan'ic, *adj.* 1. of bodily organs. 2. of carbon compounds. 3. basic; essential. —**or•gan'i•cal•ly,** *adv.*

or'gan•ism, *n.* anything living or formerly alive.

or'gan•ize', *v.,* **-ized, -izing.** form into coordinated whole; systematize. —**or'gan•i•za'tion,** *n.* —**or'gan•iz'-er,** *n.* —**or'gan•i•za'tion•al,** *adj.*

or'gasm, *n.* sexual climax.

or'gy, *n.,* *pl.* **-gies.** wild revelry. —**or'-gi•as'tic,** *adj.*

o'ri•ent, *n.* (ōr'ē ənt). 1. (*cap.*) countries of Asia. —*v.* (ōr'ē ent'). 2. set facing certain way. 3. inform about one's situation. —**O'ri•en'tal,** *adj.* —**o'ri•en•ta'tion,** *n.*

o'ri•en•teer'ing, *n.* sport of finding way across unfamiliar country.

or'i•fice (ôr'ə fis), *n.* opening.

or'i•gin, *n.* 1. source. 2. beginning. 3. circumstances of birth or ancestry.

o•rig'i•nal, *adj.* 1. first. 2. novel. 3. being new work. 4. capable of creating something original. —*n.* 5. primary form. 6. thing copied or imitated. 7. beginning. —**o•rig'i•nal'i•ty,** *n.*

o•rig'i•nal•ly, *adv.* 1. at first. 2. in original manner.

o•rig'i•nate', *v.,* **-nated, -nating.** 1. come to be. 2. give origin to. —**o•rig'i•na'tor,** *n.* —**o•rig'i•na'-tion,** *n.*

o'ri•ole', *n.* bright-colored bird of Europe and America.

or'i•son (ôr'i zən), *n.* prayer.

Or'lon, *n. Trademark.* synthetic fabric resembling nylon.

or'na•ment, *n.* (ôr'nə mənt). 1. something added to beautify. —*v.* (ôr'nə ment'). 2. adorn; decorate. —**or'na•men'tal,** *adj.* —**or'na•men•ta'tion,** *n.*

or•nate', *adj.* elaborately ornamented. —**or•nate'ly,** *adv.*

or'ner•y, *adj. Informal.* ill-tempered.

or'ni•thol'o•gy, *n.* study of birds. —**or'ni•thol'o•gist,** *n.* —**or'ni•tho•log'i•cal,** *adj.*

o'ro•tund', *adj.* 1. rich and clear in voice. 2. pompous; bombastic.

or'phan, *n.* 1. child whose parents are both dead. —*adj.* 2. of or for orphans. —*v.* 3. bereave of parents.

or'phan•age, *n.* home for orphans.

or'ris, *n.* kind of iris.

or'tho•dox', *adj.* 1. sound and correct in doctrine. 2. conventional. 3. (*cap.*) of Christian churches common in eastern Europe and adjacent areas. —**or'tho•dox'y,** *n.*

or•thog'ra•phy, *n.* spelling. —**or'-tho•graph'ic,** **or'tho•graph'i•cal,** *adj.*

or'tho•pe'dics, *n.* branch of medicine dealing with bone deformities. —**or'tho•pe'dist,** *n.* —**or'tho•pe'-dic,** *adj.*

os'cil•late' (os'ə-), *v.,* **-lated, -lating.** swing to and fro. —**os'cil•la'tion,** *n.* —**os'cil•la'tor,** *n.*

os'cu•late' (os'kyə-), *v.,* **-lated, -lating.** kiss. —**os'cu•la'tion,** *n.* —**os'cu•la•to'ry,** *adj.*

o'sier (ō'zhər), *n.* tough flexible twig.

os•mo'sis, *n.* diffusion of liquid through membrane.

os'prey, *n.* large hawk.

os'se•ous, *adj.* of, like, or containing bone.

os'si•fy', *v.,* **-fied, -fying.** make or become bone. —**os'si•fi•ca'tion,** *n.*

os•ten'si•ble, *adj.* merely apparent or pretended. —**os•ten'si•bly,** *adv.*

os'ten•ta'tion, *n.* pretentious display. —**os'ten•ta'tious,** *adj.*

os'te•op'a•thy, *n.* treatment of disease by manipulating affected part. —**os'te•o•path',** *n.* —**os'te•o•path'ic,** *adj.*

os'tra•cize' (os'trə sīz'), *v.,* **-cized, -cizing.** exclude from society; banish. —**os'tra•cism,** *n.*

os'trich, *n.* large, swift-footed, flightless bird.

oth'er, *adj.* 1. additional. 2. different. 3. being remaining one. 4. former. —*pron.* 5. other person or thing.

oth'er•wise', *adv.* 1. in other ways or circumstances. —*adj.* 2. of other sort.

o'ti•ose' (ō'shē ōs'), *adj.* 1. idle. 2. futile.

ot'ter, *n.* aquatic mammal.

ot'to•man, *n.* low, cushioned seat.

ought, *aux. v.* 1. be bound by obligation, or reasoning. —*n.* 2. cipher (0).

ounce, *n.* unit of weight equal to ¹⁄₁₆ lb. avoirdupois or ¹⁄₁₂ lb. troy.

our, *pron. or adj.* possessive form of **we**, used before noun.

ours, *pron. or adj.* possessive form of **we**, used predicatively.

our•selves', *pron.* 1. reflexive substitute for **us.** 2. intensive with or substitute for **we** or **us.**

oust, *v.* eject; force out.

oust'er, *n.* ejection.

out, *adv.* 1. away from some place. 2. so as to emerge or project. 3. until conclusion. 4. to depletion. 5. so as to be extinguished, etc. —*adj.* 6. away from some place. 7. extinguished, etc. —*prep.* 8. out from. 9. away along. —*n.* 10. means of evasion.

out'-and-out', *adj.* utter; thorough.

out'board', *adj., adv.* on exterior of ship or boat.

out'bound', *adj.* headed for the open sea.

out'break', *n.* 1. sudden occurrence. 2. riot.

out'burst', *n.* bursting forth.

out'cast', *n.* exiled or rejected person.

out'come', *n.* consequence.

out'crop', *n.* emerging stratum at earth's surface.

out'cry', *n., pl.* **-cries.** expression of distress or protest.

out•dat'ed, *adj.* obsolete.

out•dis'tance, *v.,* **-tanced, -tancing.** leave behind, as in racing.

out•do', *v.,* **-did, -done, -doing.** surpass.

out'door', *adj.* done or occurring in open air. —**out'doors'**, *adv., n.*

out'er, *adj.* 1. farther out. 2. on outside.

out'field', *n.* part of baseball field beyond diamond. —**out'field'er**, *n.*

out'fit', *n., v.,* **-fitted, -fitting.** —*n.* 1. set of articles for any purpose. 2. organized group of persons. —*v.* 3. equip. —**out'fit'ter**, *n.*

out'flank', *v.* go beyond flank of.

out'go', *n.* expenditure.

out'grow', *v.,* **-grew, -grown, -growing.** grow too large or mature for.

out'growth', *n.* 1. natural result. 2. offshoot.

out'ing, *n.* pleasure trip.

out•land'ish, *adj.* strange.

out'last', *v.* endure after.

out'law', *n.* 1. habitual criminal. 2. person excluded from protection of law. —*v.* 3. prohibit by law. 4. deny

protection of law to. —**out'law'ry,** *n.*

out'lay', *n.* expenditure.

out'let', *n.* 1. opening or passage out. 2. market for goods.

out'line', *n., v.,* **-lined, -lining.** —*n.* 1. line by which object is bounded. 2. drawing showing only outer contour. 3. general description. —*v.* 4. draw or represent in outline.

out'live', *v.,* **-lived, -living.** live longer or later than.

out'look', *n.* 1. view from place. 2. mental view. 3. prospect.

out'ly'ing, *adj.* remote.

out'mod'ed, *adj.* obsolete.

out•num'ber, *v.* be more numerous than.

out'-of-date', *adj.* obsolete.

out'pa'tient, *n.* patient visiting hospital to receive treatment.

out'post', *n.* 1. sentinel station away from main army. 2. place away from main area.

out'put', *n.* 1. production. 2. quantity produced.

out'rage', *n., v.,* **-raged, -raging.** —*n.* 1. gross violation of law or decency. —*v.* 2. subject to outrage. —**out•ra'geous**, *adj.*

out'right', *adj.* 1. utter; thorough. —*adv.* (out'rīt'). 2. without concealment; completely.

out'set', *n.* beginning.

out'side', *n.* 1. outer side, aspect, etc. 2. space beyond enclosure. —*adj.* 3. being, done, etc., on the outside. —*adv.* 4. on or to the outside. —*prep.* (out'sīd'). 5. at the outside of.

out•sid'er, *n.* person not belonging.

out'skirts', *n.pl.* bordering parts.

out•smart', *v. Informal.* outwit.

out'spo'ken, *adj.* candid.

out'spread', *adj.* extended.

out'stand'ing, *adj.* 1. prominent. 2. not yet paid.

out'strip', *v.,* **-stripped, -stripping.** 1. excel. 2. outdistance.

out'ward, *adj.* 1. external. —*adv.* 2. Also, **out'wards.** toward the outside. —**out'ward•ly**, *adv.*

out'weigh', *v.* exceed in importance.

out'wit', *v.,* **-witted, -witting.** defeat by superior cleverness.

out•worn', *adj.* 1. no longer vital or appropriate. 2. useless because of wear.

o'val, *adj.* egg-shaped; elliptical. Also, **o'vate.**

o'va•ry, *n., pl.* **-ries.** female reproductive gland. —**o•var'i•an**, *adj.*

o•va'tion, *n.* enthusiastic applause.

ov'en, *n.* chamber for baking or drying.

o'ver, *prep.* 1. above in place, authority, etc. 2. on. 3. across; through. 4. in excess of. 5. concerning. 6. during. —*adv.* 7. so as to affect whole surface. 8. above. 9. again. —*adj.* 10. finished. 11. remaining. 12. upper. 13. surplus.

o'ver•age (ō'vər ij), *n.* 1. surplus. —*adj.* (ō'vər āj'). 2. beyond desirable age.

o'ver•all', *adj.* 1. including everything. —*n.* 2. (*pl.*) loose, stout trousers.

o'ver•awe', *v.,* **-awed, -awing.** dominate with impressiveness or force.

o'ver•bear'ing, *adj.* arrogant; domineering.

o'ver•board', *adv.* over side of ship into water.

o'ver•cast', *adj.* 1. cloudy. 2. gloomy.

o'ver•coat', *n.* coat worn over ordinary clothing.

o'ver•come', *v.,* **-came, -come, -coming.** defeat; overpower.

o'ver•do', *v.,* **-did, -done, -doing.** 1. do to excess. 2. exaggerate.

o'ver•dose', *n.* excessive dose.

o'ver•draw', *v.,* **-drew, -drawn, -drawing.** draw upon (account, etc.) in excess of one's balance. —**o'ver•draft'**, *n.*

o'ver•drive', *n.* arrangement of gears providing propeller speed greater than engine crankshaft speed.

o'ver•due', *adj.* due some time before.

o'ver•flow', *v.,* **-flowed, -flown, -flowing**, *n.* —*v.* 1. flow or run over; flood. —*n.* (ō'vər flō'). 2. instance of overflowing. 3. something that runs over.

o'ver•grow', *v.,* **-grew, -grown, -growing.** cover with growth.

o'ver•hand', *adv.* with hand above shoulder.

o'ver•hang', *v.,* **-hung, -hanging**, *n.* —*v.* 1. project over. 2. threaten. —*n.* (ō'vər hang'). 3. projection.

o'ver•haul', *v.* 1. investigate thoroughly, as for repair. 2. overtake. —*n.* 3. complete examination.

o'ver•head', *adv.* 1. aloft. —*n.* (ō'vər hed'). 2. general business expense.

o'ver•hear', *v.,* **-heard, -hearing.** hear without speaker's intent.

o'ver•joyed', *adj.* very happy.

o'ver•kill', *n.* 1. *mil.* ability to kill more, esp. by nuclear weapons, than is needed for victory. 2. any greatly excessive amount.

o'ver•land', *adv., adj.* across open country.

o'ver•lap', *v.*, **-lapped, -lapping**, *n.* —*v.* 1. extend over and beyond. —*n.* (ō'vər lap'). 2. overlapping part.

o'ver•lay', *v.* **-laid, -laying**, *n.* —*v.* 1. spread over. —*n.* 2. something used in overlaying.

o'ver•look', *v.* 1. fail to notice. 2. afford view over.

o'ver•ly', *adv. Informal.* excessively.

o'ver•night', *adv.* 1. during the night. 2. on previous night.

o'ver•pass', *n.* bridge crossing other traffic.

o'ver•pow'er, *v.* 1. overwhelm in feeling. 2. subdue.

o'ver•rate', *v.*, **-rated, -rating**. esteem too highly.

o'ver•reach', *v.* 1. extend beyond. 2. defeat (oneself), as by excessive eagerness.

o'ver•re•act', *v.* react too emotionally. —**o'ver•re•ac'tion**, *n.*

o'ver•ride', *v.*, **-rode, -ridden, -riding**. prevail over; supersede.

o'ver•rule', *v.*, **-ruled, -ruling**. rule against.

o'ver•run', *v.*, **-ran, -run, -running**. 1. swarm over. 2. overgrow.

o'ver•seas', *adv.* over or across the sea.

o'ver•see', *v.*, **-saw, -seen, -seeing**. supervise. —**o'ver•se'er**, *n.*

o'ver•shad'ow, *v.* be more important than.

o'ver•shoe', *n.* shoe worn over another shoe to keep out wet or cold.

o'ver•sight', *n.* 1. error of neglect. 2. supervision.

o'ver•sleep', *v.*, **-slept, -sleeping**. sleep beyond desired time.

o'ver•state', *v.*, **-stated, -stating**. exaggerate in describing. —**o'ver•state'ment**, *n.*

o'ver•step', *v.*, **-stepped, -stepping**. exceed.

o'ver•stuffed', *adj.* (of furniture) having the frame padded and covered.

o•vert', *adj.* 1. not concealed. 2. giving perceptible cause or provocation.

o'ver•take', *v.*, **-took, -taken, -taking**. catch up with.

o'ver•throw', *v.*, **-threw, -thrown, -throwing**, *n.* —*v.* 1. defeat; put end to. —*n.* (ō'vər thrō'). 2. act of overthrowing.

o'ver•time', *n.* time worked in addition to regular hours. —**o'ver•time'**, *adv., adj.*

o'ver•tone', *n.* 1. additional meaning. 2. musical tone added to basic tone.

o'ver•ture', *n.* 1. offer. 2. musical prelude to opera, etc.

o'ver•turn', *v.* 1. tip off base. 2. defeat.

o'ver•view', *n.* overall perception or description.

o'ver•ween'ing, *adj.* conceited.

o'ver•weight', *n.* 1. excess of weight. —*adj.* (ō'vər wāt'). 2. weighing more than is normal.

o'ver•whelm', *v.* 1. weigh upon overpoweringly; crush. 2. stun, as with attention.

o'ver•work', *v.*, **-worked** or **-wrought, -working**, *n.* —*v.* 1. work too hard. —*n.* (ō'vər wûrk'). 2. work beyond one's strength.

o'ver•wrought', *adj.* highly excited.

o'void, *adj.* egg-shaped.

o'vum, *n.*, *pl.* **ova**. female reproductive cell.

owe, *v.*, **owed, owing**. be obligated to pay or give to another.

owl, *n.* nocturnal bird of prey. —**owl'ish**, *adj.*

owl'et, *n.* small owl.

own, *adj.* 1. of or belonging to. —*v.* 2. possess. 3. acknowledge. —**own'er**, *n.* —**own'er•ship'**, *n.*

ox, *n.*, *pl.* **oxen**. adult castrated male bovine.

ox'ide, *n.* compound of oxygen and another element.

ox'i•dize', *v.*, **-dized, -dizing**. 1. add oxygen to. 2. rust. —**ox'i•di•za'tion, ox'i•da'tion**, *n.*

ox'y•a•cet'y•lene' (ok'sē ə set'ə lēn'), *adj.* denoting a mixture of oxygen and acetylene used for cutting and welding steel.

ox'y•gen, *n.* colorless, odorless gas necessary to life and fire.

oys'ter, *n.* edible, irregularly shaped mollusk.

o'zone, *n.* form of oxygen present in upper atmosphere.

P

P, p, *n.* sixteenth letter of English alphabet.

pace, *n., v.*, **paced, pacing**. —*n.* 1. rate of movement or progress. 2. variable lineal measure, about 30 inches. 3. step or gait. —*v.* 4. set pace for. 5. step slowly and regularly. —**pac'er**, *n.*

pace'mak'er, *n.* 1. one that sets pace. 2. electrical device for controlling heartbeat.

pach'y•derm' (pak'ə-), *n.* thick-skinned mammal, as the elephant.

pa•cif'ic, *adj.* peaceful.

pac'i•fism', *n.* principle of abstention from violence. —**pac'i•fist'**, *n.* —**pa'ci•fis'tic**, *adj.*

pac'i•fy', *v.*, **-fied, -fying**. 1. calm. 2. appease. —**pac'i•fi'er**, *n.* —**pac'i•fi•ca'tion**, *n.*

pack, *n.* 1. bundle. 2. group or complete set. —*v.* 3. make into compact mass. 4. fill with objects. 5. cram. —**pack'er**, *n.*

pack'age, *n., v.*, **-aged, -aging**. —*n.* 1. bundle; parcel. 2. container. —*v.* 3. put into package.

pack'et, *n.* 1. small package. 2. passenger boat, esp. with fixed route.

pact, *n.* agreement.

pad, *n., v.*, **padded, padding**. —*n.* 1. soft, cushionlike mass. 2. bound package of writing paper. 3. dull sound of walking. —*v.* 4. furnish with padding. 5. expand with false or useless matter. 6. walk with dull sound.

pad'ding, *n.* material with which to pad.

pad'dle, *n., v.*, **-dled, -dling**. —*n.* 1. short oar for two hands. —*v.* 2. propel with paddle. 3. play in water.

pad'dock, *n.* enclosed field for horses.

pad'dy, *n., pl.* **-dies**. rice field.

pad'lock', *n.* 1. portable lock with U-shaped shackle. —*v.* 2. lock with padlock. 3. forbid access to.

pae'an (pē'ən), *n.* song of praise.

pa'gan, *n.*, 1. worshiper of idols. —*adj.* 2. idolatrous; heathen. —**pa'gan•ism**, *n.*

page, *n., v.,* **paged, paging.** —*n.* 1. written or painted surface. 2. boy servant. —*v.* 3. number pages of. 4. seek by calling by name.

pag′eant, *n.* elaborate spectacle. —**pag′eant•ry,** *n.*

pa•go′da, *n.* Far Eastern temple tower, esp. Buddhist.

pail, *n.* cylindrical container for liquids; bucket.

pain, *n.* 1. bodily or mental suffering. 2. (*pl.*) effort. 3. penalty. —*v.* 4. hurt. —**pain′ful,** *adj.* —**pain′ful•ly,** *adv.* —**pain′less,** *adj.*

pains′tak′ing, *adj.* very careful.

paint, *n.* 1. liquid coloring matter used as coating. —*v.* 2. represent in paint. 3. apply paint to. —**paint′er,** *n.* —**paint′ing,** *n.*

pair, *n., pl.* **pairs, pair,** *v.* —*n.* 1. combination of two, esp. matching. —*v.* 2. form or arrange in pairs.

pais′ley, *n.* fabric woven in colorful, detailed pattern.

pa•jam′as, *n.pl.* two-piece nightclothes.

pal, *n. Informal.* comrade.

pal′ace, *n.* official residence of sovereign.

pal′an•quin′ (-kēn′), *n.* enclosed chair or bed carried on men's shoulders.

pal′at•a•ble, *v.* agreeable to taste.

pal′ate, *n.* roof of mouth. —**pal′a•tal,** *adj.*

pa•la′tial, *adj.* splendidly built or furnished. —**pa•la′tial•ly,** *adv.*

pa•lav′er, *n.* 1. conference. 2. flattery. 3. idle talk.

pale, *adj.,* **paler, palest,** *v.,* **paled, paling,** *n.* —*adj.* 1. without intensity of color; near-white. 2. dim. —*v.* 3. become or make pale. —*n.* 4. stake; picket. 5. bounds. 6. enclosed area.

pa′le•o•lith′ic, *adj.* denoting early Stone Age.

pal′ette (pal′it), *n.* board on which painter lays and mixes colors.

pal′frey (pôl′-), *n., pl.* **-freys.** riding horse.

pal′ing, *n.* pale fence.

pal′i•sade′, *n.* 1. fence of pales. 2. line of tall cliffs.

pall (pôl), *n.* 1. cloth spread over coffin. 2. something seen or felt as gloomy. —*v.* 3. become wearisome or distasteful.

pall′bear′er, *n.* person who attends the coffin at funeral.

pal′let, *n.* 1. straw mattress. 2. implement for shaping, used by potters. 3. projecting lip on pawl.

pal′li•ate′, *v.,* **-ated, -ating.** mitigate; excuse. —**pal′li•a′tive,** *adj.*

pal′lid, *adj.* pale.

pal′lor, *n.* paleness.

palm, *n.* 1. inner surface of hand. 2. tall, unbranched tropical tree. —*v.* 3. conceal in palm of hand.

pal•met′to, *n., pl.* **-tos, -toes.** species of palm.

palm′is•try, *n.* art of telling fortunes from patterns of lines on palms of hands.

palm′y, *adj.,* **palmier, palmiest.** thriving.

pal′o•mi′no (-mē′-), *n., pl.* **-nos.** light-tan horse.

pal′pa•ble, *adj.* obvious; tangible. —**pal′pa•bly,** *adv.*

pal′pi•tate′, *v.,* **-tated, -tating.** pulsate with unnatural rapidity. —**pal′-pi•ta′tion,** *n.*

pal′sy (pôl′zē), *n., pl.* **-sies,** *v.,* **-sied, -sying.** —*n.* 1. paralysis. 2. muscular condition with tremors. —*v.* 3. afflict with palsy.

pal′try, *adj.,* **-trier, -triest.** trifling.

pam′pas, *n.* vast South American plains.

pam′per, *v.* indulge; coddle.

pam′phlet, *n.* thin booklet, cheaply printed. 2. argumentative treatise.

pam′phlet•eer′, *n.* writer of pamphlets.

pan, *n., v.,* **panned, panning.** —*n.* 1. broad shallow metal dish for cooking. —*v.* 2. wash (gravel, etc.) in seeking gold. 3. *Informal.* criticize harshly.

Pan, *n.* Greek god of shepherds.

pan′a•ce′a (-sē′ə), *n.* cure-all.

pan′cake′, *n.* flat fried batter cake.

pan′cre•as, *n.* gland near stomach secreting a digestive fluid. —**pan′cre•at′ic,** *adj.*

pan′da, *n.* bearlike Asiatic animal.

pan′de•mo′ni•um, *n.* uproar.

pan′der, *n.* 1. person who caters to base passions of others. —*v.* 2. act as pander. —**pan′der•er,** *n.*

pane, *n.* glass section of window.

pan′e•gyr′ic (-jir′ik), *n.* eulogy.

pan′el, *n.* 1. bordered section of wall, door, etc. 2. list of persons called for jury duty. 3. public discussion group. —*v.* 4. arrange in or ornament with panels. —**pan′el•ing,** *n.* —**pan′el•ist,** *n.*

pang, *n.* sudden feeling of distress.

pan′han′dle, *v.,* **-dled, -dling.** *Informal.* beg. —**pan′han′dler,** *n.*

pan′ic, *n.* demoralizing terror. —**pan′ick•y,** *adj.* —**pan′ic-strick′en,** *adj.*

pan′i•cle, *n.* loose flower cluster.

pan′o•ply, *n., pl.* **-plies.** suit of armor.

pan′o•ram′a, *n.* 1. view over wide area. 2. continuously changing scene. —**pan′o•ram′ic,** *adj.*

pan′sy, *n., pl.* **-sies.** 1. species of violet. 2. *Brit.* (*Derog.*) homosexual.

pant, *v.* 1. breathe hard and quickly. 2. long eagerly.

pan′ta•loons′, *n.pl. Archaic.* trousers.

pan′ther, *n.* cougar, puma, or leopard.

pan′ties, *n.pl.* women's underpants. Also, **pan′ty.**

pan′to•graph′, *n.* instrument for copying traced figures on any scale.

pan′to•mime′, *n., v.,* **-mimed, -miming.** —*n.* 1. expression by mute gestures. 2. play in this form. —*v.* 3. express in pantomime.

pan′try, *n.* room for kitchen supplies. —**pan′to•mim′ist,** *n.*

pants, *n.pl. Informal.* trousers.

panty hose, one-piece stockings plus panties for women.

pan′zer, *adj.* 1. armored. —*n.* 2. tank or other armored vehicle.

pap, *n.* soft food.

pa′pa, *n. Informal.* father.

pa′pa•cy, *n.* office or dignity of the Pope.

pa′pal, *adj.* of the Pope.

pa′paw (pô′pô), *n.* small North American tree.

pa•pa′ya, *n.* melonlike tropical American fruit.

pa′per, *n.* 1. thin fibrous sheet for writing, etc. 2. document. 3. treatise. 4. newspaper. —*v.* 5. decorate with wallpaper. —*adj.* 6. of paper. —**pa′per•y,** *adj.* —**pa′per•weight′** *n.*

pa′per•back′, *n.* book cheaply bound in paper.

pa′pier-mâ•ché′ (pā′pər mə shā′), *n.* molded paper pulp.

pa•pil′la, *n., pl.* **-pillae** (pil′ē). small protuberance, as those concerned with touch, taste, and smell. —**pap′-il•lar′y,** *adj.*

pa′pist, *n., adj. Disparaging.* Roman Catholic. —**pa′pism,** *n.*

pa•poose′, *n.* North American Indian baby. Also, **pap•poose′.**

pap•ri′ka (pa prē′-), *n.* mild spice from dried ground fruit of a pepper plant.

pa•py′rus (-pī′-), *n., pl.* **-pyri.** tall aquatic plant made into paper by ancient Egyptians.

par, *n.* 1. equality in value or standing. 2. average amount, etc.

par′a•ble, *n.* allegory conveying moral.

pa•rab′o•la, *n.* a ∪-shaped curve, surface, object, etc. —**par•a•bol′ic,** *adj.*

par′a•chute′, *n., v.,* **-chuted, -chuting.** —*n.* 1. umbrellalike apparatus used to fall safely through air. —*v.* 2. drop or fall by parachute. —**par′a•chut′ist,** *n.*

pa•rade′, *n., v.,* **-raded, -rading.** —*n.* 1. public procession or assembly for display. —*v.* 2. march in display. 3. display ostentatiously. —**pa•rad′er,** *n.*

par′a•digm (-dim), *n.* example or pattern.

par′a•dise′, *n.* 1. heaven. 2. garden of Eden. 3. best place or condition.

par′a•dox′, *n.* true statement that appears self-contradictory. —**par′a•dox′i•cal,** *adj.*

par′af•fin, *n.* waxy substance from petroleum, used in candles, etc.

par′a•gon′, *n.* model of excellence.

par′a•graph′, *n.* 1. distinct portion of written or printed matter, begun on new line. —*v.* 2. divide into paragraphs.

par′a•keet′, *n.* small parrot.

par′al•lax′, *n.* apparent displacement of object viewed due to changed position of viewer.

par′al•lel′, *adj.* 1. having same direction. 2. having same characteristics. —*n.* 3. anything parallel. —*v.* 4. be parallel to.

par′al•lel′o•gram, *n.* a four-sided figure whose opposite sides are parallel.

pa•ral′y•sis, *n., pl.* **-ses.** loss of voluntary muscular control. —**par′a•lyt′ic,** *n., adj.* —**par′a•lyze′,** *v.*

par′a•med′ic, *n.* person performing paramedical services.

par′a•med′i•cal, *adj.* practicing medicine in secondary capacity.

pa•ram′e•ter, *n.* determining factor.

par′a•mount′, *adj.* greatest; utmost.

par′a•mour′, *n.* lover of married person.

par′a•noi′a, *n.* mental disorder marked by systematized delusions. —**par′a•noi′ac,** *adj., n.*

par′a•pet, *n.* wall at edge of roof or terrace.

par′a•pher•nal′ia, *n.pl.* 1. equipment. 2. belongings.

par′a•phrase′, *v.,* **-phrased, -phrasing,** *n.* —*v.* 1. restate in other words. —*n.* 2. such restatement.

par′a•ple′gi•a (-plē′-), *n.* paralysis of lower part of body. —**par′a•pleg′ic** (-plēj′-), *n., adj.*

par′a•pro•fes′sion•al, *adj.* engaged in profession in partial or secondary capacity. —**paraprofessional,** *n.*

par′a•site′, *n.* animal or plant that lives on another organism. —**par′a•sit′ic,** *adj.*

par′a•sol′, *n.* sun umbrella.

par′a•troops′, *n.* force of soldiers (**paratroopers**) who reach battle by parachuting from planes.

par′boil′, *v.* precook.

par′cel, *n.* 1. goods wrapped together; bundle. 2. part. —*v.* 3. divide.

parch, *v.* dry by heat.

par•chee′si, *n.* game resembling backgammon.

parch′ment, *n.* skin of sheep, etc., prepared for writing on.

par′don, *n.* 1. polite indulgence. 2. forgiveness. —*v.* 3. excuse; forgive. —**par′don•a•ble,** *adj.*

pare, *v.,* **pared, paring.** cut off outer part of.

par′e•gor′ic, *n.* soothing medicine.

par′ent, *n.* father or mother. —**pa•ren′tal,** *adj.* —**par′ent•hood′,** *n.*

par′ent•age, *n.* descent.

pa•ren′the•sis, *n., pl.* **-ses.** 1. upright curves ( ) used to mark off interpolation. 2. material so interpolated. —**par′en•thet′ic, par′en•thet′i•cal,** *adj.* —**par′en•thet′i•cal•ly,** *adv.*

pa•re′sis, *n.* incomplete paralysis.

par•fait′ (pär fā′), *n.* frothy frozen dessert.

pa•ri′ah (-rī′-), *n.* outcast.

par′i•mu′tu•el, *n.* form of betting on races.

par′ish, *n.* ecclesiastical district. —**pa•rish′ion•er,** *n.*

par′i•ty, *n.* 1. equality. 2. similarity. 3. guaranteed level of farm prices.

park, *n.* 1. tract of land set apart for public. —*v.* 2. place vehicle.

par′ka, *n.* hooded garment.

par′lance, *n.* way of speaking.

par′lay, *v.* reinvest original amount and its earnings.

par′ley, *n., pl.* **-leys,** *v.,* **-leyed, -leying.** —*n.* 1. conference between combatants. —*v.* 2. hold parley.

par′lia•ment, *n.* legislative body, esp. (*cap.*) of United Kingdom.

par′lia•men′ta•ry, *adj.* 1. of, by, or having a parliament. 2. in accordance with rules of debate.

par′lor, *n.* room for receiving guests.

pa•ro′chi•al, *adj.* 1. of a parish. 2. narrow; provincial. —**pa•ro′chi•al•ism,** *n.*

par′o•dy, *n., pl.* **-dies,** *v.,* **-died, -dying.** —*n.* 1. humorous imitation. —*v.* 2. imitate in ridicule.

pa•role′, *n., v.,* **-roled, -roling.** —*n.* 1. conditional release from prison. —*v.* 2. put on parole.

par′ox•ysm, *n.* sudden violent outburst. —**par′ox•ys′mal,** *adj.*

par•quet′ (-kā′), *n.* floor of inlaid design.

par′ri•cide′ (-sīd′), *n.* crime of killing one's father.

par′rot, *n.* 1. hook-billed, bright-colored bird capable of being taught to talk. —*v.* 2. repeat senselessly.

par′ry, *v.,* **-ried, -rying,** *n., pl.* **-ries.** —*v.* 1. ward off; evade. —*n.* 2. act of parrying.

parse, *v.,* **parsed, parsing.** describe (word or sentence) grammatically.

par′si•mo′ny, *n.* excessive frugality. —**par′si•mo′ni•ous,** *adj.*

pars′ley, *n.* garden herb used in seasoning.

pars′nip, *n.* plant with white edible root.

par′son, *n.* clergyman.

par′son•age, *n.* house provided for parson.

part, *n.* 1. portion of a whole. 2. share. 3. (*pl.*) personal qualities. —*v.* 4. separate.

par•take′, *v.,* **-took, -taken, -taking.** have share.

par′tial, *adj.* 1. being part; incomplete. 2. biased. 3. especially fond. —**par•tial′i•ty,** *n.* —**par′tial•ly,** *adv.*

par•tic′i•pate′, *v.,* **-pated, -pating.** take part; share (in). —**par•tic′i•pant, par•tic′i•pa′tor,** *n.* —**par•tic′i•pa′tion,** *n.*

par′ti•ci•ple, *n.* adjective derived from verb. —**par′ti•cip′i•al,** *adj.*

par′ti•cle, *n.* 1. tiny piece. 2. functional word.

par•tic′u•lar, *adj.* 1. pertaining to some one person, thing, etc. 2. noteworthy. 3. attentive to details. —*n.* 4. detail. —**par•tic′u•lar•ly,** *adv.*

part′ing, *n.* departure or separation.

par′ti•san, *n.* 1. adherent. 2. guerrilla.

par•ti′tion, *n.* 1. division into portions. 2. interior wall. —*v.* 3. divide into parts.

part′ly, *adv.* not wholly.

part′ner, *n.* 1. sharer; associate. 2. joint owner. —**part′ner•ship′,** *n.*

par′tridge, *n.* game bird.

par•tu•ri′tion, *n.* childbirth.

par′ty, *n., pl.* **-ties.** 1. group of people with common purpose. 2. social gathering. 3. person concerned.

pas′chal (pas′kəl), *adj.* of Passover or Easter.

pa•sha′, *n.* (formerly) Turkish official.

pass, *v.,* **passed, passed** or **past, passing,** *n.* —*v.* 1. go past, by, or through. 2. omit. 3. approve. 4. convey. 5. proceed. 6. go by; elapse. 7. die. 8. be accepted. 9. go unchallenged. —*n.* 10. narrow route through barrier. 11. permission or license. 12. free ticket. 13. state of affairs. —**pass′er,** *n.*

pas′sa•ble, *adj.* adequate. —**pas′sa•bly,** *adv.*

pas′sage, *n.* 1. section of writing, etc. 2. freedom to pass. 3. movement; transportation. 4. corridor. 5. lapse. 6. act of passing. —**pas′sage•way′,** *n.*

pass′book′, *n.* booklet recording depositor's bank balance, etc.

pas•sé′ (pa sā′), *adj.* out-of-date.

pas′sen•ger, *n.* traveler on vehicle or craft.

pass′er-by′, *n., pl.* **passers-by.** person who passes by.

pass′ing, *adj.* brief; transitory.

pas′sion, *n.* 1. very strong emotion. 2. sexual love. 3. (*cap.*) sufferings of Christ. —**pas′sion•ate,** *adj.* —**pas′sion•ate•ly,** *adv.* —**pas′sion•less,** *adj.*

pas′sive, *adj.* 1. not in action. 2. acted upon. 3. submitting without resistance. 4. designating voice of verbs indicating subject acted upon. —**pas′sive•ly,** *adv.* —**pas′sive•ness, pas•siv′i•ty,** *n.*

pass′key′, *n.* master key.

Pass′o′ver, *n.* annual Jewish feast.

pass′port, *n.* official document giving permission to travel abroad.

pass′word′, *n.* secret word.

past, *adj.* 1. gone by, as in time. 2. of an earlier time. 3. designating a tense or verb formation showing time gone by. —*n.* 4. time or events gone by. 5. past tense. —*adv.* 6. so as to pass by. —*prep.* 7. after. 8. beyond.

pas′ta (päs′-), *n.* Italian flour-and-egg mixture, as spaghetti or macaroni.

paste, *n., v.,* **pasted, pasting.** —*n.* 1. soft sticky mixture. 2. shiny glass used for gems. —*v.* 3. fasten with paste. —**past′y,** *adj.*

paste′board′, *n.* firm board made of layers of paper.

pas•tel′, *n.* soft color.

pas′tern, *n.* part of a horse's foot between the fetlock and the hoof.

pas′teur•ize′, *v.,* **-ized, -izing.** heat (milk, etc.) to destroy certain bacteria. —**pas′teur•i•za′tion,** *n.*

pas•tiche′ (-tēsh′), *n.* artistic work made up of borrowed details.

pas•tille′ (-tēl′), *n.* flavored or medicated lozenge.

pas′time′, *n.* diversion.

pas′tor, *n.* minister.

pas′to•ral, *adj.* 1. having rural charm. 2. of shepherds. 3. of pastors.

pas′to•rale′ (-räl′), *n.* dreamy musical composition.

pas•tra′mi (-trä′-), *n.* seasoned smoked or pickled beef.

pas′try, *n.* food made of rich paste, as pies.

pas′tur•age, *n.* grazing ground.

pas′ture, *n., v.,* **-tured, -turing.** —*n.* 1. grassy ground for grazing cattle. —*v.* 2. graze on pasture.

pat, *v.,* **patted, patting,** *n., adj., adv.* —*v.* 1. strike gently with flat object, hand, etc. —*n.* 2. light stroke. 3. small mass. —*adj.* 4. apt; to the point. —*adv.* 5. perfectly. 6. unwaveringly.

patch, *n.* 1. piece of material used to mend or protect. 2. any small piece. —*v.* 3. mend, esp. with patches. —**patch′work′,** *n.*

patch′y, *adj.,* **-ier, -iest.** irregular in surface or quality. —**patch′i•ness,** *n.*

pate, *n.* crown of head.

pa•tel′la, *n., pl.* **-tellae** (tel′ē). kneecap.

pat′ent, *n.* 1. exclusive right to make, use, and sell invention. —*adj.* 2. protected by patent. 3. (*also* pā′tənt). evident; plain. —*v.* 4. secure patent on.

pa•ter′nal, *adj.* 1. fatherly. 2. related through father. —**pa•ter′nal•ly,** *adv.*

pa•ter′nal•ism, *n.* benevolent control. —**pa•ter′nal•is′tic,** *adj.*

pa•ter′ni•ty, *n.* fatherhood.

pa′ter•nos′ter, *n.* Lord's Prayer.

path, *n.* 1. Also, **path′way′.** narrow way. 2. route. 3. course of action.

pa•thet′ic, *adj.* arousing pity. —**pa•thet′i•cal•ly,** *adv.*

path′o•log′i•cal, *adj.* sick; morbid. —**path′o•log′i•cal•ly,** *adv.*

pa•thol′o•gy, *n.* study of disease. —**pa•thol′o•gist,** *n.*

pa′thos (pā′-), *n.* quality or power of arousing pity.

pa′tient, *n.* 1. person under care of a doctor. —*adj.* 2. enduring pain, annoyance, or delay calmly. —**pa′tience,** *n.* —**pa′tient•ly,** *adv.*

pat′i•na (pə tē′nə), *n.* film on old bronze, etc.

pa′ti•o′, *n., pl.* **-tios.** inner open court.

pa′tri•arch′, *n.* 1. venerable old man. 2. male head of tribe or family. —**pa′tri•ar′chal,** *adj.*

pa′tri•ar′chy, *n., pl.* **-arch•ies.** family group ruled by a father.

pa•tri′cian, *adj.* aristocratic.

pat′ri•mo′ny, *n., pl.* **-nies.** inherited estate.

pa′tri•ot, *n.* person who loves, supports, and defends his country. —**pa′tri•ot′ic,** *adj.* —**pa′tri•ot′ism,** *n.* —**pa′tri•ot′i•cal•ly,** *adv.*

pa•trol′, *v.,* **-trolled, -trolling,** *n.* —*v.* 1. pass through in guarding. —*n.* 2. person or group assigned to patrol. —**pa•trol′man,** *n.*

pa′tron, *n.* 1. supporter. 2. regular customer.

pa′tron•age, *n.* 1. support by patron. 2. political control of appointments to office.

pa′tron•ize′, *v.,* **-ized, -izing.** 1. buy from, esp. regularly. 2. treat condescendingly.

pat′ter, *v.* 1. move or strike with slight tapping sounds. 2. speak glibly. —*n.* 3. pattering sound. 4. rapid, glib speech.

pat′tern, *n.* 1. surface design. 2. characteristic mode of development, etc. 3. model for copying. —*v.* 4. make after pattern.

pat′ty, *n., pl.* **-ties.** little pie or wafer.

pau′ci•ty (pô′sə tē), *n.* scarceness.

paunch, *n.* belly, esp. when large. —**paunch′y,** *adj.*

pau′per, *n.* poor person.

pause, *n., v.,* **paused, pausing.** —*n.* 1. temporary stop. —*v.* 2. make pause.

pave, *v.,* **paved, paving.** 1. cover with solid road surface. 2. prepare. —**pave′ment,** *n.*

pa•vil′ion, *n.* 1. light open shelter. 2. tent.

paw, *n.* 1. foot of animal with nails or claws. —*v.* 2. strike or scrape with paw.

pawl, *n.* pivoted bar engaging with teeth of ratchet wheel.

pawn, *v.* 1. deposit as security for loan. —*n.* 2. state of being pawned. 3. piece used in chess. —**pawn′shop′,** *n.*

pawn′bro′ker, *n.* person who lends money on pledged articles.

pay, *v.,* **paid, paying.** —*v.* 1. give money required to. 2. give as compensation. 3. yield profit. 4. let out (rope). —*n.* 5. wages. 6. paid employ. —**pay′a•ble,** *adj.* —**pay•ee′,** *n.* —**pay′er,** *n.* —**pay′ment,** *n.*

pay′load′, *n.* 1. revenue-producing freight, etc. 2. contents to be carried.

pay′-off′, *n.* 1. *Informal.* final consequence. 2. awaited payment.

pea, *n.* round edible seed of common legume.

peace, *n.* freedom from war, trouble, or disturbance. —**peace′mak′er,** *n.* —**peace′time′,** *n.*

peace′ful, *adj.* 1. at peace. 2. desiring peace. Also, **peace′a•ble. —peace′-ful•ly,** *adv.* —**peace′ful•ness,** *n.*

peach, *n.* sweet juicy pinkish fruit.

pea′cock′, *n.* male of peafowl, having iridescent tail feathers of green, blue, and gold.

pea′fowl′, *n.* bird of pheasant family.

pea′hen′, *n.* female peafowl.

pea jacket, short heavy coat worn by seamen.

peak, *n.* 1. pointed top. 2. highest point.

peaked, *adj.* 1. having peak. 2. (pē′kid). sickly, haggard.

peal, *n.* 1. loud prolonged sound as of bells or thunder. 2. set of bells. —*v.* 3. sound in a peal.

pea′nut′, *n.* pod or edible seed of leguminous plant that ripens underground.

pear, *n.* elongated edible fruit.

pearl, *n.* hard, smooth, near-white gem formed within shell of an oyster. —**pearl′y,** *adj.*

peas′ant, *n.* farmer or farm worker.

peat, *n.* organic soil dried for fuel. —**peat′y,** *adj.*

peb′ble, *n.* small, rounded stone. —**peb′bly,** *adj.*

pe•can′ (pi kän′), *n.* smooth-shelled nut.

pec′ca•dil′lo, *n., pl.* **-loes, -los.** trifling sin.

pec′ca•ry, *n., pl.* **-ries.** wild pig.

peck, *v.* 1. strike with beak. —*n.* 2. pecking stroke. 3. dry measure of eight quarts.

pec′tin, *n.* substance in ripe fruit that forms jelly when evaporated.

pec′to•ral, *adj.* of the chest.

pec′u•late′, *v.,* **-lated, -lating.** embezzle. —**pec′u•la′tion,** *n.*

pe•cul′iar, *adj.* 1. strange; odd. 2. uncommon. 3. exclusive. —**pe•cu′li•ar′i•ty,** *n.* —**pe•cul′iar•ly,** *adv.*

pe•cu′ni•ar′y, *adj.* of money.

ped′a•gogue′, *n.* teacher. —**ped′a•go′gy,** *n.* —**ped′a•gog′ic, ped′a•gog′i•cal,** *adj.* —**ped′a•gog′i•cal•ly,** *adv.*

ped′al, *n., v., adj.* —*n.* 1. lever worked by foot. —*v.* 2. work pedals of. —*adj.* 3. (pē′dəl). of feet.

ped′ant, *n.* person excessively concerned with details. —**pe•dan′tic,** *adj.* —**ped′ant•ry,** *n.*

ped′dle, *v.,* **-dled, -dling.** carry about for sale. —**ped′dler,** *n.*

ped′es•tal, *n.* base for column, statue, etc.

pe•des′tri•an, *n.* 1. walker. —*adj.* 2. walking. 3. prosaic.

pe′di•at′rics, *n.* study of care and diseases of children. —**pe′di•a•tri′cian,** *n.* —**pe′di•at′ric,** *adj.*

pe•dic′u•lous, *adj.* having lice.

ped′i•gree′, *n.* 1. certificate of ancestry. 2. ancestry. —**ped′i•greed′,** *adj.*

ped′i•ment, *n.* gablelike architectural feature.

peek, *v., n.* peep (defs. 1–3; 5).

peel, *v.* 1. remove or lose skin, bark, etc. —*n.* 2. skin of fruit, etc.

peen, *n.* sharp end of hammer head.

peep, *v.* 1. look through small opening. 2. look furtively. 3. show slightly. 4. utter shrill little cry. —*n.* 5. quick look. 6. weak sound. —**peep′er,** *n.*

peer, *n.* 1. equal. 2. nobleman. —*v.* 3. look closely.

peer′age, *n.* 1. rank of peer. 2. list of peers.

peer′less, *adj.* without equal. —**peer′less•ness,** *n.*

peeve, *v.* **peeved, peeving.** annoy; vex.

pee′vish, *adj.* discontented; cross.

peg, *n., v.,* **pegged, pegging.** —*n.* 1. pin of wood, metal, etc. —*v.* 2. fasten with pegs.

pe′koe, *n.* black tea.

pel′i•can, *n.* large-billed bird.

pel•la′gra (pə lā′-), *n.* chronic disease from inadequate diet.

pel′let, *n.* little ball.

pell′-mell′, *adv.* in disorderly haste.

pel•lu′cid (pə loo′sid), *adj.* 1. translucent. 2. clear.

pelt, *v.* 1. throw. 2. assail. —*n.* 3. blow with something thrown. 4. skin of beast.

pel′vis, *n.* basinlike cavity in lower part of body trunk. —**pel′vic,** *adj.*

pen, *n., v.,* **penned** or (for 4) **pent, penning.** —*n.* 1. instrument for writing with ink. 2. small enclosure. —*v.* 3. write with pen. 4. confine in pen.

pe′nal (pē′nəl), *adj.* of, given as, or subject to punishment. —**pe′nal•ize′,** *v.*

pen′al•ty, *n., pl.* **-ties.** 1. punishment. 2. disadvantage.

pen′ance, *n.* punishment as penitence for sin.

pence, *n. Brit. pl.* of **penny.**

pen′chant, *n.* liking.

pen′cil, *n.* enclosed stick of graphite, etc., for marking.

pend, *v.* remain undecided.

pend′ant, *n.* 1. hanging ornament. 2. match; counterpart.

pend′ent, *adj.* hanging.

pend′ing, *prep.* 1. until. —*adj.* 2. undecided.

pen′du•lous, *adj.* hanging.

pen′du•lum, *n.* weight hung to swing freely.

pen′e•trate′, *v.,* **-trated, -trating.** 1. pierce; permeate. 2. enter. 3. understand; have insight. —**pen′e•tra•ble,** *adj.* —**pen′e•tra′tion,** *n.*

pen′guin, *n.* flightless aquatic bird.

pen′i•cil′lin (pen′ə sil′in), *n.* antibacterial substance produced in certain molds.

pen•in′su•la, *n.* piece of land nearly surrounded by water. —**pen•in′su•lar,** *adj.*

pe′nis, *n.* male organ of copulation.

pen′i•tent, *adj.* 1. sorry for sin or fault. —*n.* 2. penitent person. —**pen′i•tence,** *n.*

pen′i•ten′tia•ry, *n., pl.* **-ries.** prison.

pen′knife′, *n.* small pocket knife.

pen′man, *n., pl.* **-men.** person skilled in writing. —**pen′man•ship′,** *n.*

pen′nant, *n.* flag, usually tapered. Also, **pen′non.**

pen′ny, *n., pl.* **-nies,** *Brit.* **pence.** small coin, equal to one cent in the U.S. and Canada, and to ¹⁄₁₀₀ pound in United Kingdom. —**pen′ni•less,** *adj.*

pen′ny•weight′, *n.* (in troy weight) 24 grains, or ¹⁄₂₀ of an ounce.

pe•nol′o•gy, *n.* science of punishment of crime and management of prisoners. —**pe•nol′o•gist,** *n.*

pen′sion, *n.* 1. fixed periodic payment for past service, etc. 2. (pän sē ōn′) (in France) boarding house or school. —*v.* 3. give pension to.

pen′sion•er, *n.* person receiving pension.

pen′sive, *adj.* gravely thoughtful. —**pen′sive•ly,** *adv.* —**pen′sive•ness,** *n.*

pent, *adj.* confined.

pen′ta•gon′, *n.* plane figure having five sides and five angles.

pen•tam′e•ter, *n.* verse or line of five feet.

Pen′ta•teuch′ (-tyook′), *n. Bible.* first five books of the Old Testament.

Pen′te•cost′, *n.* 1. Christian festival; Whitsunday. 2. Jewish religious festival.

pent′house′, *n.* rooftop apartment or dwelling.

pent′-up′, *adj.* restrained.

pe′nult, *n.* next to last syllable of word.

pe•nul′ti•mate (pi nul′tə mit), *adj.* being or occurring next to last.

pe•num′bra, *n.* partial shadow outside complete shadow of celestial body in eclipse. —**pe•num′bral,** *adj.*

pe•nu′ri•ous (pə nyŏŏr′-), *adj.* 1. meanly stingy. 2. in great poverty.

pen′u•ry, *n.* poverty.

pe′on, *n.* 1. unskilled worker. 2. worker in bondage to pay off debts.

pe′on•age, *n.* labor in bondage.

pe′o•ny, *n., pl.* **-nies.** perennial plant with large showy flowers.

peo′ple, *n.* 1. body of persons constituting nation or ethnic group. 2. persons in general. 3. person's relatives. —*v.* 4. populate.

pep, *n., v.,* **pepped, pepping.** *Informal.* —*n.* 1. vigor. —*v.* 2. give vigor to. —**pep′py,** *adj.*

pep′per, *n.* 1. pungent condiment from dried berries of certain plants. 2. hollow, edible, green-to-red fruit of certain plants. —*v.* 3. season with pepper. 4. pelt with shot or missiles. —**pep′per•y,** *adj.*

pep′per•mint′, *n.* aromatic oil of herb, used as flavoring.

pep′sin, *n.* juice secreted in stomach that digests proteins.

pep′tic, *adj.* digestive.

per, *prep.* through; for; by means of.

per′ad•ven′ture, *adv. Archaic.* maybe.

per•am′bu•late′, *v.,* **-lated, -lating.** walk about or through. —**per•am′-bu•la′tion,** *n.*

per•am′bu•la′tor, *n.* baby carriage.

per•cale′, *n.* smooth, closely woven cotton fabric.

per•ceive′, *v.,* **-ceived, -ceiving.** 1. gain knowledge of by seeing, hearing, etc. 2. understand. —**per•ceiv′-a•ble,** *adj.* —**per•cep′ti•ble,** *adj.* —**per•cep′tion,** *n.*

per•cent′, *n.* number of parts in each hundred. Also, **per cent.**

per•cent′age, *n.* 1. proportion or rate per hundred. 2. *Informal.* profit; advantage.

per′cept, *n.* result of perceiving.

per•cep′tive, *adj.* 1. keen. 2. showing perception.

perch, *n.* 1. place for roosting. 2. linear measure of 5½ yards. 3. square rod (30¼ sq. yards). 4. common food fish. —*v.* 5. set or rest on perch.

per•chance′, *adv. Poetic.* maybe; by chance.

per′co•late′, *v.,* **-lated, -lating.** filter through. —**per′co•la′tion,** *n.*

per′co•la′tor, *n.* kind of coffee pot.

per•cus′sion, *n.* 1. violent impact. —*adj.* 2. sounded by striking. —**per•cus′sion•ist,** *n.*

per•di′tion, *n.* ruin; hell.

per′e•gri•nate′, *v.,* **-nated, -nating.** travel on foot. —**per′e•gri•na′tion,** *n.*

per•emp′to•ry, *adj.* permitting no denial or refusal. —**per•emp′to•ri•ly,** *adv.* —**per•emp′to•ri•ness,** *n.*

per•en′ni•al, *adj.* 1. lasting indefinitely. 2. living more than two years. —*n.* 3. perennial plant. —**per•en′ni•al•ly,** *adv.*

per′fect, *adj.* 1. complete; faultless; correct. 2. *Gram.* denoting action already completed. —*n.* 3. *Gram.* perfect tense. —*v.* (pər fekt′). 4. finish; improve; make faultless. —**per•fec′-tion,** *n.* —**per′fect•ly,** *adv.*

per•fec′tion•ism, *n.* insistence on perfection. —**per•fec′tion•ist,** *n.*

per•fi′dy, *n., pl.* **-dies.** treachery; faithlessness. —**per•fid′i•ous,** *adj.*

per′fo•rate′, *v.,* **-rated, -rating.** make holes through. —**per′fo•ra′tion,** *n.*

per•force′, *adv.* of necessity.

per•form′, *v.* 1. carry out; do. 2. act, as on stage. —**per•for′mance,** *n.* —**per•form′er,** *n.*

per•fume′, *n., v.,* **-fumed, -fuming.** —*n.* 1. sweet-smelling liquid. 2. sweet smell. —*v.* (pər fyoom′). 3. impart fragrance to.

per•func′to•ry, *adj.* done without care or attention. —**per•func′to•ri•ly,** *adv.* —**per•func′to•ri•ness,** *n.*

per•haps′, *adv.* maybe.

per′i•gee′ (-jē′), *n.* point nearest earth in orbit of a heavenly body.

per′i•he′li•on, *n.* point nearest sun in orbit of a planet or comet.

per′il, *n.* 1. danger. —*v.* 2. endanger. —**per′il•ous,** *adj.*

per•im′e•ter, *n.* 1. outer boundary of plane figure. 2. length of boundary. —**pe•rim′e•tral, per′i•met′ric,** *adj.*

pe′ri•od, *n.* 1. portion of time. 2. mark (.) ending declarative sentence, etc.

pe′ri•od′ic, *adj.* recurring regularly or intermittently. —**pe′ri•od′i•cal•ly,** *adv.*

pe′ri•od′i•cal, *n.* 1. publication issued at regular intervals. —*adj.* 2. periodic.

pe•riph′er•al, *adj.* 1. located on periphery. 2. only partly relevant.

pe•riph′er•y, *n., pl.* **-eries.** 1. external boundary. 2. external surface.

per′i•scope′, *n.* optical instrument consisting of a tube in which mirrors or prisms reflect to give a view from below or behind an obstacle.

per′ish, *v.* 1. die, esp. violently. 2. decay. —**per′ish•a•ble,** *adj.,* *n.*

per′i•to•ni′tis (-nī′-), *n.* inflammation of the abdominal wall.

per′i•win′kle, *n.* 1. edible marine snail. 2. trailing evergreen plant.

per′jure, *v.,* **-jured, -juring.** make (oneself) guilty of perjury. —**per′-jur•er,** *n.*

per′ju•ry, *n., pl.* **-ries.** false statement made willfully under oath.

perk, *v.* 1. move or raise jauntily. 2. become lively. —**perk′y,** *adj.*

per′ma•nent, *adj.* lasting indefinitely. —**per′ma•nence, per′ma•nen•cy,** *n.* —**per′ma•nent•ly,** *adv.*

per′me•ate′, *v.,* **-ated, -ating.** penetrate; pervade. —**per′me•a′tion,** *n.* —**per′me•a•ble,** *adj.*

per•mis′sion, *n.* authority granting request. —**per•mis′si•ble,** *adj.* —**per•mis′si•bly,** *adv.*

per•mis′sive, *adj.* 1. giving permission. 2. loose or lax in discipline.

per•mit′, *v.,* **-mitted, -mitting,** *n.* —*v.* (pər mit′). 1. allow; agree to. 2. afford opportunity. —*n.* (pûr′mit). 3. written order giving permission.

per′mu•ta′tion, *n.* alteration; change in order.

per•ni′cious, *adj.* 1. highly hurtful. 2. deadly.

per′o•ra′tion, *n.* concluding part of speech.

per•ox′ide, *n.* 1. oxide containing large amount of oxygen. 2. antiseptic liquid (**hydrogen peroxide**).

per•pen•dic′u•lar, *adj.* 1. upright; vertical. 2. meeting given line at right angles. —*n.* 3. perpendicular line or position.

per′pe•trate′, *v.*, **-trated, -trating.** commit (crime, etc.). **—per′pe•tra′-tion,** *n.* **—per′pe•tra′tor,** *n.*

per•pet′u•al, *adj.* 1. lasting forever. 2. unceasing. **—per•pet′u•ate′,** *v.*

per′pe•tu′i•ty, *n.* endless duration.

per•plex′, *v.* confuse mentally, **—per•plex′i•ty,** *n.*

per′qui•site, *n.* incidental profit in addition to fixed pay.

per′se•cute′, *v.*, **-cuted, -cuting.** oppress persistently, esp. for one's beliefs. **—per′se•cu′tion,** *n.* **—per′se•cu′tor,** *n.*

per′se•vere′, *v.*, **-vered, -vering.** continue steadfastly. **—per′se•ver′ance,** *n.*

per•sim′mon, *n.* soft, astringent fruit.

per•sist′, *v.* 1. continue firmly in spite of opposition. 2. endure. **—per•sist′ence,** *n.* **—per•sist′ent,** *adj.* **—per•sist′ent•ly,** *adv.*

per′son, *n.* 1. human being. 2. individual personality. 3. body.

per′son•a•ble, *adj.* attractive in appearance and manner.

per′son•age, *n.* distinguished person.

per′son•al, *adj.* 1. of, by, or relating to a certain person. 2. *Gram.* denoting class of pronouns that refer to speaker, person addressed, or thing spoken of. **—per′son•al•ly,** *adv.*

per′son•al′i•ty, *n.*, *pl.* **-ties.** 1. distinctive personal character. 2. famous person. 3. personal remark.

per′son•al•ize′, *v.*, **-ized, -izing.** 1. make personal. 2. treat as if human.

per•son′i•fy′, *v.*, **-fied, -fying.** 1. attribute personal character to. 2. embody; typify. 3. impersonate. **—per•son′i•fi•ca′tion,** *n.*

per′son•nel′, *n.* employees.

per•spec′tive, *n.* 1. art of depicting on surface so as to show space relationships. 2. balanced mental view.

per′spi•ca′cious, *adj.* mentally keen. **—per′spi•cac′i•ty,** *n.*

per•spic′u•ous, *adj.* clear to understanding. **—per′spi•cu′i•ty,** *n.*

per•spire′, *v.*, **-spired, -spiring.** sweat. **—per′spi•ra′tion,** *n.*

per•suade′, *v.*, **-suaded, -suading.** 1. prevail on to act as suggested. 2. convince. **—per•sua′sive,** *adj.*

per•sua′sion, *n.* 1. act or power of persuading. 2. conviction or belief. 3. religious system.

pert, *adj.* bold; saucy. **—pert′ly,** *adv.* **—pert′ness,** *n.*

per•tain′, *v.* have reference; belong.

per′ti•na′cious, *adj.* holding tenaciously to purpose, opinion, etc.

per′ti•nent, *adj.* relevant. **—per′ti•nence, per′ti•nen•cy,** *n.* **—per′ti•nent•ly,** *adv.*

per•turb′, *v.* disturb greatly. **—per′-tur•ba′tion,** *n.*

pe•ruse′ (-rooz′), *v.*, **-rused, -rusing.** read, esp. with care. **—pe•ru′sal,** *n.*

per•vade′, *v.*, **-vaded, -vading.** extend or be present throughout. **—per•va′sive,** *adj.*

per•verse′, *adj.* 1. stubbornly contrary. 2. counter to what is considered normal. **—per•ver′si•ty,** *n.* **—per•verse′ly,** *adv.*

per•vert′, *v.* 1. turn from right or moral course or use. —*n.* (pûr′-vûrt). 2. perverted person. **—per•ver′sion,** *n.*

pe′so (pā′sō), *n.* monetary unit and coin of Mexico, Cuba, etc.

pes′si•mism, *n.* 1. disposition to expect worst. 2. belief that all things tend to evil. **—pes′si•mist,** *n.* **—pes′-si•mis′tic,** *adj.* **—pes′si•mis′ti•cal•ly,** *adv.*

pest, *n.* troublesome thing or person.

pes′ter, *v.* annoy; harass.

pes′ti•cide′, *n.* insect poison.

pes′ti•lence, *n.* deadly epidemic disease. **—pes′ti•lent,** *adj.*

pes′tle, *n.* instrument for pounding or crushing.

pet, *n.*, *adj.*, *v.*, **petted, petting.** —*n.* 1. tamed animal that is cared for affectionately. 2. favorite. 3. fit of peevishness. —*adj.* 4. treated as pet. —*v.* 5. indulge or fondle.

pet′al, *n.* leaf of blossom.

pe′ter, *v. Informal.* diminish gradually.

pet′it (pet′ē), *adj. Law.* petty.

pe•tite′ (-tēt′), *adj.* (of woman) tiny.

pe•ti′tion, *n.* 1. request, esp. formal one. —*v.* 2. present petition. **—pe•ti′tion•er,** *n.*

pet′rel, *n.* small oceanic bird.

pet′ri•fy′, *v.*, **-fied, -fying.** 1. turn into stone. 2. paralyze with fear.

pet′ro•dol′lars, *n.pl.* money surpluses of petroleum-exporting countries.

pet′rol, *n. Brit.* gasoline.

pe•tro′le•um, *n.* oily liquid occurring naturally: source of gasoline, kerosene, paraffin, etc.

pe•trol′o•gy, *n.* study of rocks.

pet′ti•coat′, *n.* underskirt.

pet′tish, *adj.* petulant.

pet′ty, *adj.*, **-tier, -tiest.** 1. small or trivial. 2. small-minded. **—pet′ti•ness,** *n.*

pet′u•lant (pech′-), *adj.* showing impatient irritation. **—pet′u•lance,** *n.*

pe•tu′ni•a, *n.* plant with funnel-shaped flowers.

pew, *n.* enclosed bench or seats in church.

pe′wee, *n.* any of certain small birds.

pew′ter, *n.* alloy containing much tin.

PG, parental guidance recommended: motion-picture classification.

pha′e•ton (fā′ə tən), *n.* open carriage or automobile.

pha′lanx, *n.*, *pl.* **phalanxes, phalanges** (fə lan′jēz). 1. compact body, as of troops, etc. 2. any of bones of fingers or toes.

phal′lus, *n.*, *pl.* **phalli.** 1. penis. 2. image of penis as symbol of fertility. **—phal′lic,** *adj.*

phan′tasm, *n.* apparition.

phan•tas′ma•go′ri•a, *n.* shifting series of illusions.

phan′tom, *n.* 1. dreamlike or ghostlike image; apparition. —*adj.* 2. unreal.

Phar′aoh (fâr′ō), *n.* title of ancient Egyptian kings.

Phar′i•see′, *n.* 1. member of ancient Jewish sect. 2. (*l.c.*) self-righteous person.

phar′ma•ceu′tic (-soo′-), *adj.* pertaining to pharmacy. Also, **phar′ma•ceu′ti•cal.**

phar′ma•col′o•gy, *n.* study of drugs. **—phar′ma•col′o•gist,** *n.*

phar′ma•co•poe′ia (-pē′ə), *n.* authoritative book on medicines.

phar′ma•cy, *n.*, *pl.* **-cies.** 1. art or practice of preparing medicines. 2. place for dispensing medicines. **—phar′ma•cist,** *n.*

phar′ynx, *n.*, *pl.* **pharynges** (fə rin′jēz), **pharynxes.** tube connecting mouth and nasal passages with esophagus. **—pha•ryn′ge•al,** *adj.*

phase, *n.* 1. stage of change. 2. aspect of changing thing.

phase′out′, *n.* gradual dismissal or termination.

pheas′ant, *n.* large, long-tailed, bright-colored bird.

phe′no•bar′bi•tal′, *n.* white powder used as sedative.

phe′nol, *n.* carbolic acid. **—phe•no′-lic,** *adj.*

phe•nom′e•non′, *n.*, *pl.* **-ena.** 1. something observable. 2. extraordinary thing or person. —**phe•nom'e•nal**, *adj.* —**phe•nom'e•nal•ly**, *adv.*

phi'al, *n.* vial.

phi•lan'der, *v.* (of man) make love lightly. —**phi•lan'der•er**, *n.*

phi•lan'thro•py, *n., pl.* **-pies.** 1. love of mankind. 2. benevolent act, work, or institution. —**phil'an•throp'ic, phil'an•throp'i•cal**, *adj.* —**phi•lan'thro•pist**, *n.*

phi•lat'e•ly, *n.* collection and study of postage stamps, etc. —**phil'a•tel'ic**, *adj.* —**phi•lat'e•list**, *n.*

phil'har•mon'ic, *adj.* 1. music-loving. —*n.* 2. large orchestra.

phil'is•tine' (fil'ə stēn'), *n.* person indifferent to art or culture.

phi•lol'o•gy, *n.* linguistics. —**phi•lol'o•gist**, *n.*

phi•los'o•pher, *n.* 1. person versed in philosophy. 2. person guided by reason. 3. person who remains calm under difficulties.

phi•los'o•phy, *n., pl.* **-phies.** 1. study of truths underlying being and knowledge. 2. system of philosophical belief. 3. principles of particular field of knowledge or action. 4. calmness. —**phil'o•soph'ic, phil'o•soph'i•cal**, *adj.* —**phi•los'o•phize'**, *v.*

phil'ter, *n.* magic potion.

phle•bot'o•my, *n., pl.* **-mies.** *Med.* practice of opening a vein to let blood. —**phle•bot'o•mize'**, *v.*

phlegm (flem), *n.* 1. thick mucus secreted in the respiratory passages. 2. apathy.

phleg•mat'ic, *adj.* unemotional or unenthusiastic. —**phleg•mat'i•cal•ly**, *adv.*

phlox, *n.* garden plant with showy flowers.

pho'bi•a, *n.* morbid fear.

phoe'be (fē'bē), *n.* small American bird.

Phoe'bus (fē'-), *n.* Greek sun god.

phoe'nix (fē'niks), *n.* mythical bird burning, then rising reborn from its ashes.

phone, *n., v.,* **phoned, phoning.** *Informal.* telephone.

pho•net'ics, *n.* science of speech sounds. —**pho•net'ic**, *adj.* —**pho•net'i•cal•ly**, *adv.*

pho'no•graph', *n.* sound-producing machine using records. —**pho'no•graph'ic**, *adj.*

pho'ny, *adj.,* **-nier, -niest,** *n., pl.* **-nies.** *Informal.* —*adj.* 1. false; fraudulent. —*n.* 2. something phony. —**pho'ni•ness**, *n.*

phos'gene (-jēn), *n.* poisonous gas.

phos'phate, *n.* 1. salt of phosphoric acid. 2. fertilizer containing phosphorus.

phos'phor (fos'fər), *n.* substance showing luminescence when struck by ultraviolet light, etc.

phos'pho•resce', *v.,* **-resced, -rescing.** be luminous without perceptible heat. —**phos'pho•res'cence**, *n.* —**phos'pho•res'cent**, *adj.*

phos'pho•rus, *n.* solid nonmetallic element present in all forms of life. —**phos•phor'ic, phos'pho•rous**, *adj.*

pho'to, *n., pl.* **-tos.** *Informal.* photograph.

pho'to•cop'y, *n., pl.* **-copies.** photographic copy. —**pho'to•cop'y**, *v.*

pho'to•e•lec'tric, *adj.* of or using electrical effects produced by light.

pho'to•en•grav'ing, *n.* process of obtaining a relief-printing surface by photographic reproduction. —**pho'to•en•grav'er**, *n.*

pho'to•gen'ic (-jen'-), *adj.* looking attractive in photographs.

pho'to•graph', *n.* 1. picture produced by photography. —*v.* 2. take photograph. —**pho•tog'ra•pher**, *n.*

pho•tog'ra•phy, *n.* process of obtaining images on sensitized surface by action of light. —**pho'to•graph'ic**, *adj.*

pho'to•sen'si•tive, *adj.* sensitive to light.

Pho'to•stat', *n.* 1. *Trademark.* camera for photographing documents, etc. 2. (*l.c.*) the photograph. —*v.* 3. (*l.c.*) make photostatic copy. —**pho'to•stat'ic**, *adj.*

pho'to•syn'the•sis, *n.* conversion by plants of carbon dioxide and water into carbohydrates, aided by light and chlorophyll.

phrase, *n., v.,* **phrased, phrasing.** —*n.* 1. sequence of words used as unit. 2. minor division of musical composition. —*v.* 3. express in particular way.

phra'se•ol'o•gy, *n.* 1. manner of verbal expression. 2. expressions.

phre•net'ic, *adj.* frenetic.

phre•nol'o•gy, *n.* theory that mental powers are shown by shape of skull. —**phre•nol'o•gist**, *n.*

phy'lum, *n., pl.* **-la.** primary classification of plants or animals.

phys'ic, *n.* medicine, esp. one that purges.

phys'i•cal, *adj.* 1. of the body. 2. of matter. 3. of physics. —**phys'i•cal•ly**, *adv.*

phy•si'cian, *n.* medical doctor.

phys'ics, *n.* science of matter, motion, energy, and force. —**phys'i•cist**, *n.*

phys'i•og'no•my, *n., pl.* **-mies.** face.

phys'i•og'ra•phy, *n.* study of earth's surface.

phys'i•ol'o•gy, *n.* science dealing with functions of living organisms. —**phys'i•o•log'i•cal**, *adj.* —**phys'i•ol'o•gist**, *n.* —**phys'i•o•log'i•cal•ly**, *adv.*

phys'i•o•ther'a•py, *n.* treatment of disease by massage, exercise, etc.

phy•sique' (-zēk'), *n.* physical structure.

pi (pī), *v.* the letter π as symbol for ratio of circumference to diameter.

pi•a•nis'si•mo, *adj., adv. Music.* very soft.

pi•an'o, *n., pl.* **-anos,** *adj., adv.* —*n.* 1. Also, **pi•an'o•for'te.** musical keyboard instrument in which hammers strike upon metal strings. —*adj.* (pē ä'nō). 2. *Music.* soft. —*adv.* (pē ä'nō). 3. *Music.* softly. —**pi•an'ist**, *n.*

pi•az'za, *n.* veranda.

pi'ca (pī'-), *n.* 1. size of printing type. 2. unit of measure in printing (about ⅙ inch).

pic'a•yune', *adj.* petty; insignificant.

pic'ca•lil'li, *n.* spiced vegetable relish.

pic'co•lo', *n., pl.* **-los.** small shrill flute.

pick, *v.* 1. choose. 2. gather; pluck. 3. dig or break into, esp. with pointed instrument. 4. nibble listlessly. —*n.* 5. choice. 6. right to choose. 7. Also, **pick'ax', pick'axe'.** sharp-pointed tool for breaking rock, etc. —**pick'er**, *n.*

pick'er•el, *n.* small pike.

pick'et, *n.* 1. pointed post or stake. 2. demonstrator from labor union in front of work place. 3. body of troops posted to warn of enemy attack. —*v.* 4. enclose with pickets. 5. put pickets in front of.

pick'le, *n., v.,* **-led, -ling.** —*n.* 1. cucumber, etc., preserved in spiced vinegar. —*v.* 2. preserve in vinegar or brine.

pick'pock'et, *n.* person who steals from others' pockets.

pick'up', *n.* 1. ability to accelerate rapidly. 2. small open-body truck.

pic'nic, *n., v.,* **-nicked, -nicking.** —*n.* 1. outing and meal in the open. —*v.* 2. have picnic. —**pic'nick•er**, *n.*

pic'ture, *n., v.,* **-tured, -turing.** —*n.* 1. painting, photograph, etc., on flat surface. 2. motion picture. —*v.* 3. represent in picture. 4. imagine. —**pic•to′ri•al**, *adj.*

pic′tur•esque′, *adj.* striking to see.

pid′dling, *adj.* trivial; negligible.

pidg′in English (pij′in), English trade jargon used in Orient, West Africa, etc.

pie, *n.* baked dish of fruit, meat, etc., in pastry crust.

pie′bald′, *adj.* having patches of different colors.

piece, *n.*, *v.*, **pieced, piecing.** —*n.* 1. limited or single portion. 2. one part of a whole. 3. artistic work. 4. rifle or cannon. —*v.* 5. make or enlarge by joining pieces.

piece′meal′, *adv.* 1. gradually. 2. into fragments.

pied, *adj.* many-colored.

pie′plant′, *n.* rhubarb.

pier, *n.* 1. structure at which vessels are moored. 2. masonry support.

pierce, *v.*, **pierced, piercing.** 1. make hole or way into or through. 2. make (hole) in.

pi′e•ty, *n.* quality of being pious.

pig, *n.* 1. swine, esp. young. 2. oblong bar of metal. —**pig′gish**, *adj.*

pi′geon, *n.* short-legged bird with compact body.

pi′geon•hole′, *n.*, *v.*, **-holed, -holing.** —*n.* 1. small compartment, as in desk, etc. —*v.* 2. classify. 3. put aside and ignore.

pig′head′ed, *adj.* perversely stubborn.

pig iron, crude iron from blast furnace.

pig′ment, *n.* coloring matter. —**pig′men•tar′y**, *adj.*

pig′men•ta′tion, *n.* coloration.

pig′my, *n.*, *pl.* **-mies.** pygmy.

pig′tail′, *n.* hanging braid at back of head.

pike, *n.* 1. large slender fresh-water fish. 2. metal-headed shaft. 3. highway.

pik′er, *n. Slang.* person who does things cheaply or meanly.

pi•las′ter, *n.* shallow decorative imitation of column.

pile, *n.*, *v.*, **piled, piling.** —*n.* 1. heap. 2. device for producing energy by nuclear reaction. 3. Also, **pil′ing.** upright driven into ground as foundation member or to retain earth. 4. hair; down; wool; fur. 5. nap (def. 2). 6. *pl.* hemorrhoids. —*v.* 7. lay in pile. 8. accumulate.

pil′fer, *v.* steal, esp. from storage. —**pil′fer•age**, *n.*

pil′grim, *n.* 1. traveler, esp. to sacred place. 2. (*cap.*) early Puritan settler of Massachusetts. —**pil′grim•age**, *n.*

pill, *n.* small mass of medicine to be swallowed.

pil′lage, *v.*, **-laged, -laging.** *n.* plunder.

pil′lar, *n.* upright shaft of masonry.

pill′box′, *n.* 1. small fort. 2. box for pills.

pil′lo•ry, *n.*, *pl.* **-ries,** *v.*, **-ried, -rying.** —*n.* 1. wooden framework used to confine and expose offenders. —*v.* 2. put in pillory. 3. expose to public contempt.

pil′low, *n.* bag of feathers, etc., used as support for head. —**pil′low•case′**, *n.*

pi′lot, *n.* 1. operator of aircraft or ship. 2. expert in navigation. —*v.* 3. steer; guide. —*adj.* 4. experimental.

pi•men′to, *n.* dried fruit of tropical tree; allspice.

pi•mien′to (-myen′-), *n.* variety of garden pepper.

pimp, *n.*, *v.* —*n.* 1. manager of prostitutes. —*v.* 2. act as pimp.

pim′per•nel′, *n.* variety of primrose.

pim′ple, *n.* small swelling of skin. —**pim′ply**, *adj.*

pin, *n.*, *v.*, **pinned, pinning.** —*n.* 1. slender pointed piece of metal, wood, etc., for fastening. —*v.* 2. fasten with pin. 3. hold fast; bind.

pin′a•fore′, *n.* 1. child's apron. 2. sleeveless dress.

pince′-nez′ (pans′ nā′), *n.* pair of eyeglasses supported by spring pinching the nose.

pin′cers, *n.* gripping tool with two pivoted limbs.

pinch, *v.* 1. squeeze, as between finger and thumb. 2. cramp or affect sharply. 3. economize. —*n.* 4. act of pinching; nip. 5. tiny amount. 6. distress; emergency. —**pinch′er**, *n.*

pinch′-hit′, *v.*, **-hit, -hitting.** substitute.

pine, *v.*, **pined, pining,** *n.* —*v.* 1. long painfully. 2. fail in health from grief, etc. —*n.* 3. cone-bearing evergreen tree with needle-shaped leaves. —**pin′y**, *adj.*

pine′ap′ple, *n.* edible fruit of tropical plant.

pin′feath′er, *n.* undeveloped feather.

Ping′-Pong′, *n. Trademark.* variety of tennis played on table.

pin′ion (-yən), *n.* 1. feather or wing. 2. small cogwheel. —*v.* 3. bind (the arms).

pink, *n.* 1. pale red. 2. fragrant garden flower. 3. highest degree. —**pink**, *adj.*

pin′na•cle, *n.* lofty peak or position.

pi′noch′le (pē′nuk′əl), *n.* game using 48 cards. Also, **pi′noc′le.**

pin′point′, *v.* identify precisely.

pint, *n.* liquid and dry measure equal to one-half quart.

pin′tle, *n.* pin or bolt.

pin′to, *adj.*, *n.*, *pl.* **-tos.** —*adj.* 1. piebald. —*n.* 2. piebald horse.

pin′up′, *n.* unframed picture of beautiful girl.

pin′wheel′, *n.* windmill-like toy that spins on stick.

pi′o•neer′, *n.* 1. early arrival in new territory. 2. first one in any effort. —*v.* 3. act as pioneer.

pi′ous, *adj.* 1. reverential; devout. 2. sacred. —**pi′ous•ly**, *adv.* —**pi′ous•ness**, *n.*

pip, *n.* 1. small fruit seed. 2. spot on playing card, domino, etc. 3. disease of fowls.

pipe, *n.*, *v.*, **piped, piping.** —*n.* 1. tube for conveying fluid. 2. tube with bowl at one end for smoking tobacco. 3. tube used in or as musical instrument. —*v.* 4. play on pipe. 5. convey by pipe. —**pip′er**, *n.* —**pipe′line′**, *n.*

pip′ing, *n.* 1. pipes. 2. sound of pipes. 3. kind of trimming.

pip′pin, *n.* kind of apple.

pi′quant (pē′kənt), *adj.* agreeably sharp. —**pi′quan•cy**, *n.*

pique (pēk), *v.*, **piqued, piquing,** *n.* —*v.* 1. arouse resentment in. 2. excite (curiosity, etc.). —*n.* 3. irritated feeling.

pi•qué′ (pi kā′), *n.* corded cotton fabric.

pi′ra•cy, *n.*, *pl.* **-cies.** 1. robbery at sea. 2. illegal use of patented or copyrighted material. —**pi′rate**, *n.*, *v.*

pir′ou•ette′ (pir′ōō et′), *v.*, **-etted, -etting,** *n.* —*v.* 1. whirl about on the toes. —*n.* 2. such whirling.

pis′ca•to′ri•al (pis′kə-), *adj.* of fishing.

pis•ta′chi•o′ (pis tä′shē ō′), *n.*, *pl.* **-chios.** nut with edible greenish kernel.

pis′til, *n.* seed-bearing organ of flower.

pis′tol, *n.* short hand-held gun.

pis′ton, *n.* part moving back and forth under pressure in engine cylinder.

pit, *n., v.,* **pitted, pitting.** —*n.* 1. hole in ground or other surface. 2. hollow in body. 3. part of main floor of theater. 4. stone of fruit. —*v.* 5. mark with pits. 6. set in enmity or opposition. 7. remove pit from.

pitch, *v.* 1. throw. 2. set at certain point. 3. fall forward. 4. drop and rise, as ship. —*n.* 5. height. 6. musical tone. 7. slope. 8. sticky dark substance from coal tar. 9. sap that exudes from bark of pines.

pitch'blende', *n.* mineral: principal ore of uranium and radium.

pitched, *adj.* fought with all available troops.

pitch'er, *n.* 1. container with spout for liquids. 2. person who pitches.

pitch'fork', *n.* sharp-tined fork for handling hay.

pit'e•ous, *adj.* pathetic.

pit'fall', *n.* trap; hazard.

pith, *n.* 1. spongy tissue. 2. essence. 3. strength. —**pith'y,** *adj.* —**pith'i•ness,** *n.*

pit'i•a•ble, *adj.* 1. deserving pity. 2. contemptible. —**pit'i•a•bly,** *adv.*

pit'i•ful, *adj.* 1. deserving pity. 2. exciting contempt. 3. full of pity. —**pit'i•ful•ly,** *adv.* —**pit'i•ful•ness,** *n.*

pit'tance, *n.* meager income.

pi•tu'i•tar'y (pi tyoo'ə ter'ē), *adj.* denoting gland at base of brain.

pit'y, *n., pl.* **pities,** *v.,* **pitied, pitying.** —*n.* 1. sympathetic sorrow. 2. cause for regret. —*v.* 3. feel pity for. —**pit'i•less,** *adj.* —**pit'i•less•ly,** *adv.*

piv'ot, *n.* 1. short shaft on which something turns. —*v.* 2. turn on or provide with pivot. —**piv'ot•al,** *adj.*

pix'y, *n., pl.* **pixies.** fairy. Also, **pix'ie.**

piz'za (pēt'sə), *n.* dish of cheese, tomato sauce, etc., on baked crust.

piz'zer•i•a (pēt'sə rē'ə), *n.* restaurant serving mainly pizza.

plac'a•ble, *adj.* forgiving.

plac'ard, *n.* public notice posted or carried.

pla'cate, *v.,* **-cated, -cating.** appease. —**pla•ca'tion,** *n.*

place, *n., v.,* **placed, placing.** —*n.* 1. particular portion of space. 2. function. 3. social standing. 4. stead. —*v.* 5. take place, occur. 6. put in place. 7. identify from memory. —**place'ment,** *n.*

pla•ce'bo (plə sē'bō), *n., pl.* **-bos, -boes.** pill, etc., containing no medication, given to reassure patient.

pla•cen'ta (-sen'-), *n.* organ in uterus which attaches to and nourishes fetus.

plac'er, *n.* surface gravel containing gold particles.

plac'id, *adj.* serene. —**pla•cid'i•ty,** *n.* —**plac'id•ly,** *adv.*

pla'gia•rize' (-plā'jə rīz'), *v.,* **-rized, -rizing.** copy and claim as one's own work of another. —**pla'gia•rism,** *n.* —**pla'gia•rist,** *n.*

plague, *n., v.,* **plagued, plaguing.** —*n.* 1. often fatal epidemic disease. 2. affliction or vexation. —*v.* 3. trouble; annoy.

plaid (plad), *n.* 1. fabric woven in many-colored cross bars. —*adj.* 2. having such pattern.

plain, *adj.* 1. distinct. 2. evident. 3. candid. 4. ordinary; unpretentious. 5. without pattern. 6. flat. —*adv.* 7. clearly. 8. candidly. —*n.* 9. level area. —**plain'ly,** *adv.* —**plain'ness,** *n.*

plaint, *n.* complaint.

plain'tiff, *n.* one who brings suit in court.

plain'tive, *adj.* melancholy. —**plain'tive•ly,** *adv.* —**plain'tive•ness,** *n.*

plait, *n., v.* 1. braid. 2. pleat.

plan, *n., v.,* **planned, planning.** —*n.* 1. scheme of action or arrangement. 2. drawing of projected structure. —*v.* 3. make plan. —**plan'ner,** *n.*

plane, *n., adj., v.,* **planed, planing.** —*n.* 1. flat surface. 2. level. 3. airplane. 4. sharp-bladed tool for smoothing. —*adj.* 5. flat. —*v.* 6. glide. 7. smooth with plane.

plan'et, *n.* solid heavenly body revolving about sun. —**plan'e•tar'y,** *adj.*

plan'e•tar'i•um, *n.* 1. optical device that projects a representation of heavens on a dome. 2. museum with such device.

plank, *n.* 1. long flat piece of timber. 2. point in political platform.

plant, *n.* 1. any member of vegetable group of living things. 2. equipment for business or process. —*v.* 3. set in ground for growth. 4. furnish with plants. —**plant'er,** *n.* —**plant'like',** *adj.*

plan'tain (-tin), *n.* 1. tropical banana-like plant. 2. common flat-leaved weed.

plan•ta'tion, *n.* farm, esp. with one crop.

plaque (plak), *n.* monumental tablet.

plas'ma, *n.* clear liquid part of blood or lymph.

plas'ter, *n.* 1. pasty composition of lime, sand, and water for covering walls, etc. 2. medicinal preparation spread on cloth and applied to body. —*v.* 3. cover or treat with plaster.

plas'tic, *adj.* 1. of or produced by molding. 2. moldable. 3. three-dimensional. 4. (of surgery) remedying or restoring defective, injured, or lost parts. —*n.* 5. organic material that is hardened after shaping. —**plas•tic'i•ty,** *n.*

plate, *n., v.,* **plated, plating.** —*n.* 1. shallow round dish for food. 2. gold or silver ware. 3. sheet of metal used in printing. 4. shaped holder for false teeth. —*v.* 5. coat with metal. —**plat'er,** *n.*

pla•teau', *n.* raised plain.

plat'form, *n.* 1. raised flooring or structure. 2. set of announced political principles.

plat'i•num, *n.* precious, malleable metallic element.

plat'i•tude', *n.* trite remark. —**plat'i•tud'i•nous,** *adj.*

pla•ton'ic, *adj.* without sexual involvement.

pla•toon', *n.* small military or police unit.

plat'ter, *n.* large shallow dish for serving meat, etc.

plat'y•pus (-ə pəs), *n., pl.* **-puses, -pi.** duckbill.

plau'dit (plô'dit), *n.* (usually pl.) applause.

plau'si•ble, *adj.* apparently true, reasonable, or trustworthy. —**plau'si•bil'i•ty,** *n.* —**plau'si•bly,** *adv.*

play, *n.* 1. dramatic composition. 2. action for recreation. 3. fun. 4. change. 5. freedom of movement. —*v.* 6. act in a play. 7. engage in game. 8. perform on musical instrument. 9. amuse oneself. 10. move about lightly. —**play'er,** *n.* —**play'ful,** *adj.* —**play'ful•ly,** *adv.* —**play'ful•ness,** *n.* —**play'go'er,** *n.* —**play'mate',** *n.*

play'-off', *n.* extra game played to break a tie.

play'thing', *n.* toy.

play'wright', *n.* writer of plays.

pla'za, *n.* public square, esp. in Spanish-speaking countries.

plea, *n.* 1. defense; justification. 2. entreaty.

plead, *v.,* **pleaded** or **pled, pleading.** 1. make earnest entreaty. 2. allege formally in court. 3. argue (case at law). 4. allege in justification. —**plead'er,** *n.*

pleas'ant, *adj.* agreeable; pleasing. —**pleas'ant•ly,** *adv.*

pleas'ant•ry, *n., pl.* **-ries.** good-humored remark.

please, *v.,* **pleased, pleasing.** be or act to pleasure of; seem good. —**pleas'ing•ly,** *adv.*

pleas'ure, *n.* 1. enjoyment. 2. person's will or desire.

pleat, *n.* 1. double fold of cloth. —*v.* 2. fold in pleats.

ple•be'ian (plə bē'ən), *adj.* of common people.

pleb'i•scite' (-sīt'), *n.* direct vote by citizens on public question.

plec'trum, *n.* object for picking strings of musical instrument.

pledge, *n., v.,* **pledged, pledging.** —*n.* 1. solemn promise. 2. property delivered as security on a loan. 3. toast. —*v.* 4. bind by pledge. 5. promise. 6. deliver as pledge.

ple'na•ry, *adj.* full; complete.

plen'i•po•ten'ti•ar'y (-shē er'ē), *n., pl.* **-aries,** *adj.* —*n.* 1. diplomat with full authority. —*adj.* 2. having full authority.

plen'i•tude', *n.* abundance.

plen'ty, *n.* 1. abundant supply. —*adv. Informal.* 2. very. —**plen'te•ous, plen'ti•ful,** *adj.*

pleth'o•ra, *n.* superabundance.

pleu'ri•sy, *n.* inflammation of chest membranes.

Plex'i•glas', *n. Trademark.* light, durable transparent plastic.

pli'a•ble, *adj.* easily bent or influenced. —**pli'a•bil'i•ty,** *n.* —**pli'a•bly,** *adv.*

pli'ant, *adj.* pliable. —**pli'an•cy,** *n.*

pli'ers, *n.pl.* small pincers.

plight, *n.* 1. distressing condition. —*v.* 2. promise.

plod, *v.,* **plodded, plodding.** 1. walk heavily. 2. work laboriously. —**plod'der,** *n.*

plot, *n., v.,* **plotted, plotting.** —*n.* 1. secret scheme. 2. main story of fictional work. 3. small area of ground. —*v.* 4. plan secretly. 5. mark (chart course) on. 6. divide into plots. —**plot'ter,** *n.*

plov'er (pluv'ər), *n.* shore bird.

plow, *n.* 1. implement for cutting and turning soil. 2. similar implement for removing snow. —*v.* 3. cut or turn with plow. 4. force way, as through water. Also, **plough.** —**plow'man,** *n.*

plow'share', *n.* blade of plow.

pluck, *v.* 1. pull out from fixed position. 2. sound (strings of musical instrument). —*n.* 3. pull or tug. 4. courage.

pluck'y, *adj.,* **-ier, -iest.** courageous.

plug, *n., v.,* **plugged, plugging.** —*n.* 1. object for stopping hole. 2. device on electrical cord that establishes contact in socket. 3. *Slang.* advertisement; favorable mention. —*v.* 4. stop with or insert plug. 5. *Slang.* advertise or mention favorably. 6. work steadily. —**plug'ger,** *n.*

plum, *n.* 1. oval juicy fruit. 2. deep purple. 3. *Informal.* favor widely desired. —**plum'like',** *adj.*

plumb, *n.* 1. plummet. —*adj.* 2. perpendicular. —*adv.* 3. vertically. 4. exactly. 5. *Informal.* completely. —*v.* 6. make vertical. 7. measure depth of.

plumb'ing, *n.* system of water pipes, etc. —**plumb'er,** *n.*

plume, *n., v.,* **plumed, pluming.** —*n.* 1. feather, esp. large one. 2. ornamental tuft. —*v.* 3. preen. 4. furnish with plumes. —**plum'age,** *n.*

plum'met, *n.* 1. weight on line for sounding or establishing verticals. —*v.* 2. plunge.

plump, *adj.* 1. somewhat fat or thick. —*v.* 2. make or become plump. 3. fall or drop heavily. —*n.* 4. heavy fall. —*adv.* 5. directly. 6. heavily.

plun'der, *v.* 1. rob by open violence. —*n.* 2. act of plundering. 3. loot.

plunge, *v.,* **plunged, plunging,** *n.* —*v.* 1. dip suddenly. 2. rush. 3. pitch forward. —*n.* 4. dive. —**plung'er,** *n.*

plu'ral, *adj.* 1. of, being, or containing more than one. —*n.* 2. plural form. —**plur'al•ize',** *v.*

plu•ral'i•ty, *n.* 1. excess of votes given leading candidate over next candidate. 2. majority.

plus, *prep.* 1. increased by. —*adj.* 2. involving addition. 3. positive. —*n.* 4. something additional.

plush, *n.* long-piled fabric.

plu'to•crat', *n.* 1. wealthy person. 2. member of wealthy governing class. —**plu•toc'ra•cy,** *n.*

plu•to'ni•um, *n.* radioactive element.

ply, *v.,* **plied, plying,** *n., pl.* **plies.** —*v.* 1. work with by hand. 2. carry on, as trade. 3. tempt repeatedly. 4. travel regularly. —*n.* 5. fold; thickness.

ply'wood', *n.* board of thin sheets of wood glued together.

p.m., after noon. Also, **P.M.**

pneu•mat'ic (nyoo-), *adj.* 1. of air or other gases. 2. operated by or filled with air. —**pneu•mat'i•cal•ly,** *adv.*

pneu•mo'nia, *n.* inflammation of lungs.

poach, *v.* 1. take game or fish illegally. 2. cook (egg without shell) in hot water. —**poach'er,** *n.*

pock, *n.* mark on skin from smallpox, etc.

pock'et, *n.* 1. small bag sewed into garment. 2. pouch; cavity. —*adj.* 3. small. —*v.* 4. put into one's pocket. 5. take as profit. 6. suppress.

pock'et•book', *n.* purse.

pod, *n., v.,* **podded, podding.** —*n.* 1. seed covering. —*v.* 2. produce pod.

po'di•um, *n.* small raised platform.

po'em, *n.* composition in verse. —**po'et,** *n.* —**po'et•ess,** *n.fem.*

po'et•ry, *n.* rhythmical composition of words. —**po•et'ic, po•et'i•cal,** *adj.*

po•grom' (pə grum'), *n.* organized massacre, esp. of Jews.

poign'ant, (poin'yənt), *adj.* keenly distressing. —**poign'an•cy,** *n.*

poin•set'ti•a (poin set'ē ə), *n.* tropical plant with scarlet flowers.

point, *n.* 1. sharp end. 2. projecting part. 3. dot. 4. definite position or time. 5. compass direction. 6. basic reason, assertion, etc. 7. detail. 8. unit of printing measure. —*v.* 9. indicate. 10. direct. —**point'less,** *adj.*

point'-blank', *adj.* 1. direct; plain. —*adv.* 2. directly.

point'er, *n.* 1. one that points. 2. long stick for pointing. 3. breed of hunting dog.

poise, *n., v.,* **poised, poising.** —*n.* 1. balance. 2. composure. —*v.* 3. balance. 4. be in position for action.

poi'son, *n.* 1. substance that kills or harms seriously. —*v.* 2. harm with poison. —**poi'son•er,** *n.* —**poi'son•ous,** *adj.*

poke, *v.,* **poked, poking,** *n.* thrust.

pok'er, *n.* 1. rod for poking fires. 2. card game.

pok'y, *adj.,* **pokier, pokiest.** *Informal.* slow; dull. Also, **poke'y.** —**pok'i•ness,** *n.*

po'lar, *adj.* 1. arctic or antarctic. 2. in opposition or contrast. 3. of magnetic poles. —**po•lar'i•ty,** *n.*

pole, *n., v.,* **poled, poling.** —*n.* 1. long slender piece, esp. of wood. 2. unit of length equal to 16½ ft.; rod. 3. square rod, 30¼ sq. yards. 4. each end of axis. 5. each end of magnet, etc., showing strongest opposite force. 6. (*cap.*) native or citizen of Poland. —*v.* 7. propel with a pole.

pole'cat', *n.* small bad-smelling mammal.

po•lem′ics (-lem′iks), *n.* art or practice of argument. —**po•lem′ic,** *n.,* *adj.*

po•lice′, *n., v.,* **-liced, -licing.** —*n.* 1. organized civil force for enforcing law. —*v.* 2. keep in order. —**po•lice′man,** *n.* —**po•lice′wom′an,** *n.fem.*

pol′i•cy, *n., pl.* **-cies.** 1. definite course of action. 2. insurance contract.

pol′i•o•my′e•li′tis (pōl′ē ō mī′ə lī′tis), *n.* infantile paralysis. Also, **po′-li•o′.**

pol′ish (pol′-), *v.* 1. make or become smooth and glossy. —*n.* 2. polishing substance. 3. gloss. 4. refinement.

Pol′ish (pōl′-), *n.* language or people of Poland. —**Pol′ish,** *adj.*

Po′lit•bu′ro (pol′ it byoor′ō), *n.* executive committee of Communist Party of U.S.S.R.

po•lite′, *adj.* showing good manners; refined. —**po•lite′ly,** *adv.* —**po•lite′ness,** *n.*

pol′i•tic, *adj.* 1. prudent; expedient. 2. political.

pol′i•tick′ing, *n.* political self-aggrandizement.

pol′i•tics, *n.* 1. science or conduct of government. 2. political affairs, methods, or principles. —**po•lit′i•cal,** *adj.* —**pol′i•ti′cian,** *n.* —**po•lit′-i•cal•ly,** *adv.*

pol′ka, *n.* lively dance.

polka dot, pattern of dots on fabric.

poll, *n.* 1. voting or votes at election. 2. list of individuals, as for voting. 3. (*pl.*) place of voting. 4. analysis of public opinion. 5. head. —*v.* 6. receive votes. 7. vote. 8. ask opinions of.

pol′len, *n.* powdery fertilizing element of flowers. —**pol′li•nate′,** *v.*—**pol′li•na′tion,** *n.*

pol•lute′, *v.,* **-luted, -luting.** contaminate or make foul. —**pol•lu′tion,** *n.* —**pol•lut′ant,** *n.*

po′lo, *n.* game played on horseback.

pol′o•naise′ (-nāz′), *n.* slow dance.

pol′ter•geist (pōl′tər gīst′), *n.* boisterous, often destructive ghost.

pol•troon′, *n.* coward.

pol′y•an′dry, *n.* practice of having more than one husband at a time.

pol′y•es′ter, *n.* artificial material for plastics and synthetics.

po•lyg′a•my, *n.* practice of having many spouses, esp. wives, at one time. —**po•lyg′a•mist,** *n.* —**po•lyg′-a•mous,** *adj.*

pol′y•gon′, *n.* figure having three or more straight sides. —**po•lyg′o•nal,** *adj.*

pol′y•he′dron, *n., pl.* **-drons, -dra.** solid figure having four or more sides.

pol′yp, *n.* 1. projecting growth from mucous surface. 2. simple, sedentary aquatic animal form.

pol′y•phon′ic, *adj.* having many musical parts.

pol′y•syl•lab′ic, *adj.* consisting of many syllables.

po•made′, *n.* scented hair ointment.

pome′gran′ate (pom′gran′it), *n.* red, many-seeded fruit of Asiatic tree.

pom′mel (pum′əl), *n., v.,* **-meled, -meling.** —*n.* 1. knob. —*v.* 2. strike; beat.

pomp, *n.* stately display.

pom′pa•dour′ (-dōr′), *n.* arrangement of hair brushed back.

pom′pon, *n.* ornamental tuft.

pomp′ous, *adj.* affectedly dignified or serious. —**pomp•pos′i•ty, pomp′-ous•ness,** *n.* —**pomp′ous•ly,** *adv.*

pon′cho, *n., pl.* **-chos.** blanketlike cloak.

pond, *n.* small lake.

pon′der, *v.* meditate.

pon′der•ous, *adj.* heavy; not graceful.

pone, *n.* unleavened corn bread.

pon•gee′ (-jē′), *n.* silk fabric.

pon′iard (pon′yərd), *n.* dagger.

pon′tiff, *n.* 1. pope. 2. chief priest; bishop. —**pon•tif′i•cal,** *adj.*

pon•tif′i•cate′, *v.,* **-cated, -cating.** speak with affected air of authority.

pon•toon′, *n.* floating support.

po′ny, *n., pl.* **-nies.** small horse.

poo′dle, *n.* kind of dog with thick, curly hair.

pool, *n.* 1. body of still water. 2. group of persons or things available for use. 3. game resembling billiards. —*v.* 4. put into common fund.

poop, *n.* upper deck on afterpart of a ship.

poor, *adj.* 1. having little wealth. 2. wanting. 3. inferior. 4. unfortunate. —*n.* 5. poor persons. —**poor′ly,** *adv.* —**poor′ness,** *n.*

pop, *v.,* **popped, popping,** *n., adv.* —*v.* 1. make or burst with a short, quick sound. 2. shoot. —*n.* 3. short, quick sound. 4. effervescent soft drink. —*adv.* 5. suddenly.

pop′corn′, *n.* kind of corn whose kernels burst in dry heat.

pope, *n.* (*often cap.*) head of Roman Catholic Church.

pop′lar, *n.* any of certain fast-growing trees.

pop′lin, *n.* corded fabric.

pop′o′ver, *n.* very light muffin.

pop′py, *n., pl.* **-pies.** showy-flowered herbs, one species of which yields opium.

pop′u•lace, *n.* people of a place.

pop′u•lar, *adj.* 1. generally liked and approved. 2. of the people. 3. prevalent. —**pop′u•lar′i•ty,** *n.* —**pop′u•lar•ize′,** *v.* —**pop′u•lar•ly,** *adv.*

pop′u•late′, *v.,* **-lated, -lating.** inhabit.

pop′u•la′tion, *n.* 1. total number of persons inhabiting given area. 2. body of inhabitants.

pop′u•lous, *adj.* with many inhabitants.

por′ce•lain, *n.* glassy ceramic ware; china.

porch, *n.* exterior shelter on building.

por′cine (pôr′sīn), *adj.* of or like swine.

por′cu•pine′, *n.* rodent with stout quills.

pore, *v.,* **pored, poring,** *n.* —*v.* 1. ponder or read intently. —*n.* 2. minute opening in skin.

por′gy, *n.* fleshy salt-water food fish.

pork, *n.* flesh of hogs as food.

pork barrel, government funds available for popular local improvements.

por•nog′ra•phy, *n.* obscene literature or art. —**por′no•graph′ic,** *adj.* —**por•nog′ra•pher,** *n.*

po′rous, *adj.* permeable by water, air, etc. —**po′rous•ness, po•ros′i•ty,** *n.*

por′poise, *n.* gregarious aquatic mammal.

por′ridge, *n.* boiled cereal.

por′rin•ger, *n.* round dish for soup, etc.

port, *n.* 1. place where ships load and unload. 2. harbor. 3. left side of vessel, facing forward. 4. sweet red wine. —**port,** *adj.*

port′a•ble, *adj.* readily carried. —**port′a•bil′i•ty,** *n.*

por′tage, *n.* 1. overland route between navigable streams. 2. carrying.

por′tal, *n.* door or gate, esp. a large one.

por•tend′, *v.* indicate beforehand.

por′tent, *n.* 1. omen. 2. ominous significance. —**por•ten′tous,** *adj.*

por′ter, *n.* 1. train attendant. 2. doorman. 3. laborer who carries.

por'ter•house', *n.* choice cut of beef-steak.

port•fo'li•o', *n.* 1. portable case for papers, etc. 2. cabinet post.

port'hole', *n.* opening in ship's side.

por'ti•co', *n.*, *pl.* **-coes, -cos.** roof supported by columns.

por'tion, *n.* 1. part of a whole. 2. share. —*v.* 3. divide into shares.

port'ly, *adj.* 1. fat. 2. stately. —**port'li•ness**, *n.*

por'trait, *n.* picture, sculpture, etc., showing specific person. —**por'trai•ture**, *n.*

por•tray', *v.* represent faithfully, as in picture. —**por•tray'al**, *n.*

Por'tu•guese', *n.*, *pl.* **-guese.** native or language of Portugal. —**Portuguese**, *adj.*

por'tu•lac'a (pōr'chə lak'ə), *n.* low-growing garden plant.

pose, *v.*, **posed, posing**, *n.* —*v.* 1. assume or feign attitude or character. 2. take or give specific position. 3. ask (question). —*n.* 4. position or character assumed.

po'ser, *n.* 1. person who poses, as for artist. 2. difficult question.

po•seur' (pō zûr'), *n.* affected person.

posh, *adj.* elegant; luxurious.

po•si'tion, *n.* 1. place or attitude. 2. belief or argument on question. 3. social or organizational standing. 4. job. —*v.* 5. place.

pos'i•tive, *adj.* 1. explicit; not denying or questioning. 2. emphatic. 3. confident. 4. showing lights and shades of original. 5. *Gram.* denoting first degree of comparison. 6. denoting more than zero. 7. deficient in electrons. 8. revealing presence of thing tested for. —*n.* 9. something positive. —**pos'i•tive•ly**, *adv.* —**pos'i•tive•ness**, *n.*

pos'se (pos'ē), *n.* body of men assisting sheriff.

pos•sess', *v.* 1. under ownership or domination. 2. have as quality. 3. obsess or craze. 4. (of man) succeed in having sexual relations with. —**pos•ses'sor**, *n.* —**pos•ses'sion**, *n.*

pos•ses'sive, *adj.* 1. denoting possession. 2. obsessed with dominating another.

pos'si•ble, *adj.* that may be, happen, etc. —**pos'si•bil'i•ty**, *n.* —**pos'si•bly**, *adv.*

pos'sum, *n.* opossum.

post, *n.* 1. upright support. 2. position of duty or trust. 3. station for soldiers or traders. 4. *Chiefly Brit.*

mail. —*v.* 5. put up. 6. station at post. 7. *Chiefly Brit.* mail. 8. enter in ledger. 9. hasten. 10. inform. —*adv.* 11. with speed.

post'age, *n.* charge for mailing.

post'al, *adj.* concerning mail.

post•bel'lum, *adj.* after war, esp. U.S. Civil War.

post'er, *n.* large public notice.

pos•te'ri•or, *adj.* 1. situated behind. 2. later. —*n.* 3. buttocks.

pos•ter'i•ty, *n.* descendants.

post'haste', *adv.* speedily.

post'hu•mous (pos'chə məs), *adj.* 1. published after author's death. 2. born after father's death. —**post'hu•mous•ly**, *adv.*

post'man, *n.* mail carrier.

post'mark', *n.* official mark on mail showing place and time of mailing. —**post'mark'**, *v.*

post'mas'ter, *n.* official in charge of post office.

post me•rid'i•em', afternoon.

post-mor'tem, *adj.* 1. following death. —*n.* 2. examination of dead body.

post office, government office responsible for postal service.

post'paid', *adv.*, *adj.* with postage paid in advance.

post•pone', *v.*, **-poned, -poning.** delay till later. —**post•pone'ment**, *n.*

post'script', *n.* note added to letter after signature.

pos'tu•late', *v.*, **-lated, -lating**, *n.* —*v.* (pos'chə lāt'). 1. require. 2. assume without proof. —*n.* (-lit). 3. something postulated.

pos'ture, *n.*, *v.*, **-tured, -turing.** —*n.* 1. position of the body. —*v.* 2. place in particular position. 3. behave affectedly; pose.

post'war', *adj.* after a war.

po'sy, *n.*, *pl.* **-sies.** flower or bouquet.

pot, *n.*, *v.*, **potted, potting.** —*n.* 1. round deep container for cooking, etc. 2. total stakes at cards. —*v.* 3. put into pot.

po'ta•ble, *adj.* drinkable.

pot'ash', *n.* potassium carbonate, esp. from wood ashes.

po•tas'si•um, *n.* light metallic element.

po•ta'tion, *n.* drink.

po•ta'to, *n.*, *pl.* **-toes.** edible tuber of common garden plant.

po'tent, *adj.* 1. powerful. 2. having sexual power. —**po'tence, po'ten•cy**, *n.* —**po'tent•ly**, *adv.*

po'ten•tate', *n.* sovereign.

po•ten'tial, *adj.* 1. possible. 2. latent. —*n.* 3. possibility, esp. for development. —**po•ten'ti•al'i•ty**, *n.* —**po•ten'tial•ly**, *adv.*

poth'er, *n.*, *v.* fuss.

po'tion, *n.* drink.

pot'pour•ri' (pō'pə rē'), *n.* miscellany.

pot'ter, *n.* 1. person who makes earthen pots. —*v.* 2. putter (def. 1).

pot'ter•y, *n.* ware made of clay and baked.

pouch, *n.* 1. bag or sack. 2. baglike sac.

poul'tice (pōl'tis), *n.* soft moist mass applied as medicament.

poul'try, *n.* domestic fowls.

pounce, *v.*, **pounced, pouncing**, *n.* —*v.* 1. seize suddenly. —*n.* 2. sudden capture.

pound, *n.*, *pl.* **pounds, pound**, *v.* —*n.* 1. unit of weight: in U.S., **pound avoirdupois** (16 ounces) and **pound troy** (12 ounces). 2. British monetary unit. 3. enclosure for stray animals. —*v.* 4. strike repeatedly and heavily. 5. crush by pounding.

pound cake, *n.* rich, sweet cake.

pour, *v.* 1. cause to flow; flow. —*n.* 2. abundant flow.

pout, *v.* 1. look sullen. —*n.* 2. sullen look or mood.

pov'er•ty, *n.* 1. poorness. 2. lack.

pow'der, *n.* 1. solid substance crushed to fine loose particles. —*v.* 2. reduce to powder. 3. apply powder to. —**pow'der•y**, *adj.*

pow'er, *n.* 1. ability to act; strength. 2. faculty. 3. authority; control. 4. person, nation, etc., having great influence. 5. mechanical energy. 6. product of repeated multiplications of number by itself. 7. magnifying capacity of an optical instrument. —**pow'er•ful**, *adj.* —**pow'er•ful•ly**, *adv.* —**pow'er•less**, *adj.* —**pow'er•less•ly**, *adj.*

pow'wow', *n. Informal.* conference.

pox, *n.* disease marked by skin eruptions.

prac'ti•ca•ble, *adj.* feasible.

prac'ti•cal, *adj.* 1. of or from practice. 2. useful. 3. level-headed. 4. concerned with everyday affairs. 5. virtual. —**prac'ti•cal'i•ty**, *n.* —**prac'ti•cal•ly**, *adv.*

prac'tice, *n.*, *v.*, **-ticed, -ticing.** —*n.* 1. habit; custom. 2. actual performance. 3. repeated performance in learning. 4. professional activity. —*v.* Also, **prac'tise.** 5. do habitually or as profession. 6. do repeatedly in acquiring skill. —**prac'ticed,** *adj.*

prac•ti'tion•er, *n.* person engaged in a profession.

prag•mat'ic, *adj.* concerned with practical values and results. —**prag'ma•tist,** *n.* —**prag•mat'i•cal•ly,** *adv.*

prai'rie, *n.* broad flat treeless grassland.

praise, *n., v.,* **praised, praising.** —*n.* 1. words of admiration or strong approval. 2. grateful homage. —*v.* 3. give praise to. 4. worship. —**praise'wor'thy,** *adj.* —**prais'er,** *n.*

pram, *n. Brit. Informal.* baby carriage.

prance, *v.,* **pranced, prancing,** *n.* —*v.* 1. step about gaily or proudly. —*n.* 2. act of prancing. —**pranc'er,** *n.*

prank, *n.* playful trick. —**prank'ster,** *n.*

prate, *v.,* **prated, prating.** talk foolishly.

prat'tle, *v.,* **-tled, -tling,** *n.* —*v.* 1. chatter foolishly or childishly. —*n.* 2. chatter. —**prat'tler,** *n.*

prawn, *n.* large shrimplike shellfish.

pray, *v.* make prayer.

prayer, *n.* 1. devout petition to or spiritual communication with God. 2. petition. —**prayer'ful,** *adj.*

preach, *v.* 1. advocate. 2. deliver (sermon). —**preach'er,** *n.*

pre•am'ble, *n.* introductory declaration.

pre•car'i•ous, *adj.* uncertain; dangerous. —**pre•car'i•ous•ly,** *adv.*

pre•cau'tion, *n.* prudent advance measure. —**pre•cau'tion•ar'y,** *adj.*

pre•cede', *v.,* **-ceded, -ceding.** go before. —**prec'e•dence,** *n.*

prec'e•dent, *n.* past case used as example or guide.

pre'cept, *n.* rule of conduct.

pre•cep'tor, *n.* teacher.

pre'cinct, *n.* bounded or defined area.

pre'cious, *adj.* 1. valuable. 2. beloved. 3. affectedly refined. —**pre'cious•ly,** *adv.*

prec'i•pice (pres'ə pəs), *n.* sharp cliff.

pre•cip'i•tate' *v.,* **-tated, -tating,** *adj., n.* —*v.* 1. hasten occurrence of. 2. separate (solid from solution). 3. condense (as vapor into rain). 4. fling down. —*adj.* (-tit). 5. rash or impetuous; hasty. —*n.* (-tit). 6. substance precipitated. 7. condensed moisture. —**pre•cip'i•ta'tion,** *n.*

pre•cip'i•tous, *adj.* 1. like a precipice. 2. precipitate.

pré•cis' (prā sē'), *n.* summary.

pre•cise', *adj.* 1. definite; exact. 2. distinct. 3. strict. —**pre•ci'sion, pre•cise'ness,** *n.* —**pre•cise'ly,** *adv.*

pre•clude', *v.,* **-cluded, -cluding.** prevent. —**pre•clu'sion,** *n.* —**pre•clu'sive,** *adj.*

pre•co'cious, *adj.* forward in development. —**pre•coc'i•ty,** *n.*

pre•cur'sor, *n.* 1. predecessor. 2. harbinger.

pre•da'cious, *adj.* predatory. Also, **pre•da'ceous.**

pred'a•tor, *n.* animal that preys.

pred'a•tor'y (pred'ə tōr'ē), *adj.* 1. plundering. 2. feeding on other animals.

pred'e•ces'sor, *n.* one who precedes another.

pre•des'ti•na'tion, *n.* 1. determination beforehand. 2. destiny. —**pre•des'tine,** *v.*

pre•dic'a•ment, *n.* trying or dangerous situation.

pred'i•cate, *v.,* **-cated, -cating,** *adj., n.* —*v.* (-kāt'). 1. declare. 2. find basis for. —*adj.* (-kit). 3. *Gram.* belonging to predicate. —*n.* (-kit). 4. *Gram.* part of sentence that expresses what is said of subject. —**pred'i•ca'tion,** *n.*

pre•dict', *v.* tell beforehand. —**pre•dic'tion,** *n.* —**pre•dict'a•ble,** *adj.* —**pre•dic'tor,** *n.*

pre•di•lec'tion (pred'-), *n.* preference.

pre•dom'i•nate', *v.,* **-nated, -nating.** 1. be more powerful or common. 2. control. —**pre•dom'i•nance,** *n.* —**pre•dom'i•nant,** *adj.* —**pre•dom'i•nant•ly,** *adv.*

pre•em'i•nent, *adj.* superior; outstanding. —**pre•em'i•nence,** *n.* —**pre•em'i•nent•ly,** *adv.*

pre•empt', *v.* 1. acquire or reserve before others. 2. occupy to establish prior right to buy. Also, **pre-empt'.** —**pre•emp'tion,** *n.*

preen, *v.* trim or dress (oneself) carefully.

pre•fab'ri•cate', *v.,* **-cated, -cating.** construct in parts before final assembly elsewhere. —**pre'fab•ri•ca'tion,** *n.* —**pre'fab,** *n. Informal.*

pref'ace, *n., v.,* **-aced, -acing.** —*n.* 1. preliminary statement. —*v.* 2. provide with or serve as preface. —**pref'a•to'ry,** *adj.*

pre'fect, *n.* magistrate.

pre•fer', *v.,* **-ferred, -ferring.** 1. like better. 2. present (criminal charge, etc.).

pref'er•a•ble, *adj.* more desirable. —**pref'er•a•bly,** *adv.*

pref'er•ence, *n.* 1. liking of one above others. 2. person or thing preferred. 3. granting of advantage to one especially. —**pref'er•en'tial,** *adj.*

pre•fer'ment, *n.* promotion.

pre'fix, *n.* 1. syllable or syllables put before word to qualify its meaning. —*v.* (prē fiks'). 2. put before.

preg'nant, *adj.* 1. being with child. 2. filled; fraught. 3. momentous. —**preg'nan•cy,** *n.*

pre•hen'sile (-sil), *adj.* adapted for grasping.

pre'his•tor'ic, *adj.* of time before recorded history.

prej'u•dice, *n., v.,* **-diced, -dicing.** —*n.* 1. opinion formed without specific evidence. 2. disadvantage. —*v.* 3. affect with prejudice. —**prej'u•di'cial,** *adj.* —**prej'u•di'cial•ly,** *adv.*

prel'ate, *n.* high church official.

pre•lim'i•nar'y, *adj., n., pl.* **-naries.** —*adj.* 1. introductory. —*n.* 2. preliminary stage or action.

prel'ude, *n.* 1. *Music.* **a.** preliminary to more important work. **b.** brief composition, esp. for piano. 2. preliminary to major action or event.

pre•ma•ture', *adj.* 1. born, occurring, or maturing too soon. 2. overhasty. —**pre'ma•ture'ly,** *adv.* —**pre'ma•ture'ness, pre'ma•tu'ri•ty,** *n.*

pre•med'i•tate', *v.,* **-tated, -tating.** plan in advance. —**pre'med•i•ta'tion,** *n.*

pre•mier' (pri mēr'), *n.* 1. prime minister. —*adj.* 2. chief.

pre•miere' (pri mēr'), *n.* first public performance.

prem'ise, *n.* 1. (*pl.*) building with its grounds. 2. statement from which conclusion is drawn.

pre'mi•um, *n.* 1. contest prize. 2. bonus. 3. periodic insurance payment.

pre•mo•ni'tion, *n.* foreboding. —**pre•mon'i•to'ry,** *adj.*

pre•oc'cu•py', *v.,* **-pied, -pying.** engross completely. —**pre•oc'cu•pa'tion,** *n.*

pre'or•dain', *v.* decree in advance.

pre•pare', *v.,* **-pared, -paring.** 1. make or get ready. 2. manufacture. —**prep'a•ra'tion,** *n.* —**pre•par'a•to'ry,** *adj.* —**pre•par'ed•ness,** *n.*

pre•pon'der•ant, *adj.* superior in force or numbers. —**pre•pon'der•ance,** *n.*

prep′o•si′tion, *n.* word placed before noun or adjective to indicate relationship of space, time, means, etc. —**prep′o•si′tion•al,** *adj.*

pre′pos•sess′ing, *adj.* impressing favorably.

pre•pos′ter•ous, *adj.* absurd.

pre•req′ui•site, *adj.* 1. required in advance. —*n.* 2. something prerequisite.

pre•rog′a•tive, *n.* special right or privilege.

pres′age (pres′ij), *v.,* **-aged, -aging.** 1. portend. 2. predict.

pres′by•te′ri•an, *adj.* 1. (of religious group) governed by presbytery. 2. (*cap.*) designating Protestant church so governed. —*n.* 3. (*cap.*) member of Presbyterian Church.

pres′by•ter′y, *n., pl.* **-teries.** body of church elders and (in Presbyterian churches) ministers.

pre′sci•ence (prē′shē əns), *n.* foresight. —**pre′sci•ent,** *adj.*

pre•scribe′, *v.,* **-scribed, -scribing.** 1. order for use, as medicine. 2. order. —**pre•scrip′tion,** *n.* —**pre•scrip′tive,** *adj.*

pres′ence, *n.* 1. fact of being present. 2. vicinity. 3. perceived personal quality, esp. when impressive.

pres′ent, *adj.* 1. being or occurring now. 2. being at particular place. 3. *Gram.* denoting action or state now in progress. —*n.* 4. present time. 5. present tense. 6. thing bestowed as gift. —*v.* (pri zent′). 7. give, bring, or offer. 8. exhibit. —**pres′en•ta′tion,** *n.*

pre•sent′a•ble, *adj.* suitable in looks, dress, etc. —**pre•sent′a•bly,** *adv.*

pre•sen′ti•ment, *n.* feeling of impending evil.

pres′ent•ly, *adv.* 1. at present. 2. soon.

pre•sent′ment, *n.* presentation.

pre•serve′, *v.,* **-served, -serving.** 1. keep alive. 2. keep safe. 3. maintain. 4. prepare (food) for long keeping. —*n.* 5. preserved fruit. 6. place where game is protected. —**pres′er•va′tion,** *n.* —**pre•serv′a•tive,** *n., adj.* —**pre•serv′er,** *n.*

pre•side′, *v.,* **-sided, -siding.** act as chairman.

pres′i•dent, *n.* 1. highest executive of republic. 2. chief officer. —**pres′i•den•cy,** *n.*

press, *v.* 1. act upon with weight or force. 2. oppress; harass. 3. insist upon. 4. urge to hurry or comply. —*n.* 5. newspapers, etc., collectively.

6. device for pressing or printing. 7. crowd. 8. urgency. —**press′er,** *n.*

press′ing, *adj.* urgent.

pres′sure, *n.* 1. exertion of force by one body upon another. 2. harassment. 3. urgency.

pres′ti•dig′i•ta′tion (-dij′ə-), *n.* sleight of hand. —**pres′ti•dig′i•ta′tor,** *n.*

pres•tige′ (-tēzh′), *n.* distinguished reputation.

pres′to, *adv. Music.* quickly.

pre•sume′ (-zōōm′), *v.,* **-sumed, -suming.** 1. take for granted. 2. act with unjustified boldness. —**pre•sum′a•ble,** *adj.* —**pre•sum′a•bly,** *adv.* —**pre•sump′tion** (-zump′-), *n.* —**pre•sump′tu•ous,** *adj.*

pre′sup•pose′, *v.,* **-posed, -posing.** assume. —**pre•sup′po•si′tion,** *n.*

pre•tend′, *v.* 1. make false appearance or claim. 2. make believe. 3. claim, as sovereignty. —**pre•tend′er,** *n.* —**pre•tense′,** *n.*

pre•ten′sion, *n.* 1. ostentation. 2. act of pretending. —**pre•ten′tious,** *adj.* —**pre•ten′tious•ly,** *adv.* —**pre•ten′tious•ness,** *n.*

pret′er•it, *Gram.* —*adj.* 1. denoting action in past. —*n.* 2. preterit tense.

pre′ter•nat′u•ral, *adj.* supernatural.

pre′text, *n.* ostensible reason; excuse.

pret′ty, *adj.,* **-tier, -tiest,** *adv.* —*adj.* 1. pleasingly attractive. —*adv.* 2. moderately. 3. very. —**pret′ti•fy′,** *v.* —**pret′ti•ly,** *adv.* —**pret′ti•ness,** *n.*

pret′zel, *n.* crisp, elongated or knotted biscuit.

pre•vail′, *v.* 1. be widespread. 2. exercise persuasion. 3. gain victory.

prev′a•lent, *adj.* widespread; general. —**prev′a•lence,** *n.*

pre•var′i•cate, *v.,* **-cated, -cating.** speak evasively; lie. —**pre•var′i•ca′tion,** *n.* —**pre•var′i•ca′tor,** *n.*

pre•vent′, *v.* hinder; stop. —**pre•vent′a•ble, pre•vent′i•ble,** *adj.* —**pre•ven′tion,** *n.* —**pre•ven′tive, pre•vent′a•tive,** *adj., n.*

pre′view′, *n., v.* view or show in advance.

pre′vi•ous, *adj.* occurring earlier. —**pre′vi•ous•ly,** *adv.*

prey, *n.* 1. animal hunted as food by another animal. 2. victim. —*v.* 3. seize prey. 4. victimize another. 5. be obsessive.

price, *n., v.,* **priced, pricing.** —*n.* 1. amount for which thing is sold. 2. value. —*v.* 3. set price on. 4. *Informal.* ask the price of.

price′less, *adj.* too valuable to set price on.

pric′ey, *adj.,* **-ier, -iest.** *Informal.* high-priced. —**pric′i•ness,** *n.*

prick, *n.* 1. puncture by pointed object. —*v.* 2. pierce. 3. point.

prick′le, *n.* sharp point. —**prick′ly,** *adj.*

pride, *n., v.,* **prided, priding.** —*n.* 1. high opinion of worth of oneself or that associated with one. 2. self-respect. 3. that which one is proud of. —*v.* 4. feel pride. —**pride′ful,** *adj.*

priest, *n.* person authorized to perform religious rites; clergyman. —**priest′ess,** *n.fem.* —**priest′hood,** *n.*

prig, *n.* self-righteous person. —**prig′gish,** *adj.*

prim, *adj.* stiffly proper. —**prim′ly,** *adv.* —**prim′ness,** *n.*

pri′ma don′na (prē′mə don′ə), 1. principal female opera singer. 2. temperamental person.

pri′ma•ry, *adj., n., pl.* **-ries.** —*adj.* 1. first in importance or in order. 2. earliest. —*n.* 3. preliminary election for choosing party candidates.

pri′mate (-māt), *n.* 1. high church official. 2. mammal of order including man, apes, and monkeys.

prime, *adj., n., v.,* **primed, priming.** —*adj.* 1. first in importance or quality. 2. original. —*n.* 3. best stage or part. —*v.* 4. prepare for special purpose or function.

prime minister, chief minister in some governments.

prim′er, *n.* elementary book, esp. for reading.

pri•me′val, *adj.* of earliest time.

prim′i•tive, *adj.* 1. earliest. 2. simple; unrefined. —**prim′i•tive•ly,** *adv.* —**prim′i•tive•ness,** *n.*

primp, *v.* dress fussily.

prim′rose′, *n.* early-flowering garden perennial.

prince, *n.* high-ranking male member of royalty. —**prin′cess,** *n.fem.*

prince′ly, *adj.* lavish.

prin′ci•pal, *adj.* 1. chief. —*n.* 2. chief; leader. 3. head of school. 4. person authorizing another to act for him. 5. capital sum, distinguished from interest. —**prin′ci•pal•ly,** *adv.*

prin′ci•pal′i•ty, *n., pl.* **-ties.** state ruled by prince.

prin′ci•ple, *n.* 1. rule of conduct or action. 2. fundamental truth or doctrine. 3. fundamental cause or factor.

print, *v.* 1. reproduce from inked types, plates, etc. 2. write in letters like those of print. 3. produce (photograph) from negative. —*n.* 4. state of being printed. 5. (of book) present availability for sale. 6. print lettering. 7. anything printed. —**print′er,** *n.* —**print′a•ble,** *adj.*

print′out′, *n.* printed output of computer.

pri′or, *adj.* 1. earlier. —*adv.* 2. previously. —*n.* 3. officer in religious house. —**pri′or•ess,** *n.fem.* —**pri′o•ry,** *n.*

pri•or′i•ty, *n., pl.* **-ties.** 1. state of being earlier. 2. precedence.

prism (priz′əm), *n.* transparent body for dividing light into its spectrum. —**pris•mat′ic,** *adj.*

pris′on, *n.* building for confinement of criminals. —**pris′on•er,** *n.*

pris′tine (-tēn), *adj.* original; pure.

pri′vate, *adj.* 1. belonging to particular person or group. 2. free of outside knowledge or intrusion. —*n.* 3. soldier of lowest rank. —**pri′va•cy,** *n.* —**pri′vate•ly,** *adv.*

pri′va•teer′, *n.* privately owned vessel commissioned to fight. —**pri′va•teer′ing,** *n.*

pri•va′tion, *n.* lack; need.

priv′i•lege, *n., v.,* **-leged, -leging.** —*n.* 1. special advantage. —*v.* 2. grant privilege to.

priv′y, *adj., n., pl.* **privies.** —*adj.* 1. participating in shared secret. 2. private. —*n.* 3. outdoor toilet.

prize, *n., v.,* **prized, prizing.** —*n.* 1. reward for victory, superiority, etc. 2. thing worth striving for. —*v.* 3. esteem highly.

pro, *n., pl.* **pros,** *adj.* 1. *Informal.* professional. —*adv.* 2. in favor of a plan, etc.

prob′a•ble, *adj.* 1. likely to occur, etc. 2. affording ground for belief. —**prob′a•bil′i•ty,** *n.* —**prob′a•bly,** *adv.*

pro′bate, *n., adj., v.,* **-bated, -bating.** —*n.* 1. authentication of will. —*adj.* 2. of probate. —*v.* 3. establish will's validity.

pro•ba′tion, *n.* 1. act of testing. 2. conditional release, as from prison. 3. period in which to redeem past failures or mistakes. —**pro•ba′tion•ar′y,** *adj.*

probe, *v.,* **probed, probing,** *n.* —*v.* 1. examine thoroughly. —*n.* 2. surgical instrument for exploring wounds, etc. —**prob′er,** *n.*

pro′bi•ty, *n.* honesty.

prob′lem, *n.* matter involving uncertainty or difficulty. —**prob′lem•at′-ic, prob′lem•at′i•cal,** *adj.*

pro•bos′cis (-bos′is), *n., pl.* **-boscises.** flexible snout, as elephant's trunk.

pro•ced′ure (-sē′jər), *n.* course of action. —**pro•ced′ur•al,** *adj.*

pro•ceed′, *v.* 1. go forward. 2. carry on action. 3. issue forth. —*n.* (prō′sēd). 4. (*pl.*). sum derived from sale, etc.

pro•ceed′ing, *n.* 1. action or conduct. 2. (*pl.*) **a.** records of society. **b.** legal action.

proc′ess, *n.* 1. series of actions toward given end. 2. continuous action. 3. legal summons. 4. projecting growth. —*v.* 5. treat by particular process.

pro•ces′sion, *n.* ceremonial movement; parade.

pro•ces′sion•al, *n.* 1. hymn sung during procession. 2. hymnal.

pro•claim′, *v.* announce publicly. —**proc′la•ma′tion,** *n.*

pro•cliv′i•ty, *n., pl.* **-ties.** natural tendency.

pro•cras′ti•nate′, *v.,* **-nated, -nating.** delay from temperamental causes. —**pro•cras′ti•na′tion,** *n.* —**pro•cras′ti•na′tor,** *n.*

pro•cure′, *v.* **-cured, -curing.** 1. get; obtain. 2. cause. 3. hire prostitutes. —**pro•cure′ment,** *n.*

pro•cur′er, *n.* 1. one that procures. 2. Also, **pro•cur′ess,** *fem.* person who arranges for prostitution.

prod, *v.,* **prodded, prodding,** *n.* —*v.* 1. poke. 2. incite; goad. —*n.* 3. poke. 4. goading instrument.

prod′i•gal, *adj.* 1. wastefully extravagant. 2. lavish. —*n.* 3. spendthrift.

prod′i•gal′i•ty, *n., pl.* **-ties.** extravagance; lavishness.

pro•di′gious (-dij′əs), *adj.* huge; wonderful.

prod′i•gy, *n., pl.* **-gies.** 1. very gifted person. 2. wonderful thing.

pro•duce′, *v.,* **-duced, -ducing,** *n.* —*v.* 1. bring into existence; create. 2. bear, as young, fruit. 3. exhibit. —*n.* (prō′dōos). 4. product. 5. agricultural products. —**pro•duc′er,** *n.* —**pro•duc′tion,** *n.* —**pro•duc′tive,** *adj.* —**pro′duc•tiv′i•ty,** *n.*

prod′uct, *n.* 1. thing produced; result. 2. result obtained by multiplying.

pro•fane′, *adj., v.,* **-faned, -faning.** —*adj.* 1. irreverent toward sacred things. 2. secular. —*v.* 3. defile. 4. treat (sacred thing) with contempt. —**prof′a•na′tion,** *n.*

pro•fan′i•ty, *n., pl.* **-ties.** 1. profane quality. 2. blasphemous or vulgar language.

pro•fess′, *v.* 1. declare. 2. affirm faith in. 3. claim.

pro•fes′sion, *n.* 1. learned vocation. 2. declaration; assertion.

pro•fes′sion•al, *adj.* 1. following occupation for gain. 2. of or engaged in profession. —*n.* 3. professional person. —**pro•fes′sion•al•ly,** *adv.*

pro•fes′sor, *n.* college teacher of highest rank. —**pro′fes•so′ri•al,** *adj.*

prof′fer, *v., n.* offer.

pro•fi′cient, *adj.* expert. —**pro•fi′-cien•cy,** *n.* —**pro•fi′cient•ly,** *adv.*

pro′file, *n.* side view.

prof′it, *n.* 1. pecuniary gain from business transaction. 2. net gain after costs. 3. benefit. —*v.* 4. gain advantage. 5. make profit. —**prof′it•a•ble,** *adj.* —**prof′it•a•bly,** *adv.* —**prof′it•less,** *adj.*

prof′it•eer′, *n.* 1. person who makes unfair profit. —*v.* 2. act as profiteer.

prof′li•gate (-git), *adj.* 1. immoral. 2. extravagant. —**prof′li•gate,** *n.* —**prof′li•ga•cy,** *n.*

pro•found′, *adj.* 1. thinking deeply. 2. intense. 3. deep. —**pro•found′ly,** *adv.* —**pro•fun′di•ty,** *n.*

pro•fuse′, *adj.* extravagant; abundant. —**pro•fuse′ly,** *adv.* —**pro•fu′-sion, pro•fuse′ness,** *n.*

pro•gen′i•tor, *n.* forefather.

prog′e•ny, *n.pl.* children; offspring.

prog•no′sis, *n., pl.* **-noses** (-nō′sēz). medical forecast.

prog•nos′ti•cate′, *v.,* **-cated, -cating.** predict. —**prog•nos′ti•ca′tion,** *n.*

pro′gram, *n., v.,* **-grammed, -gramming.** —*n.* 1. plan of things to do. 2. schedule of entertainments. 3. television or radio show. 4. plan for computerized problem solving. —*v.* 5. make program for or including. —**pro′gram•mer,** *n.*

prog′ress, *n.* 1. advancement. 2. permanent improvement. 3. growth. —*v.* (prə gres′). 4. make progress. —**pro•gres′sion,** *n.* —**pro•gres′sive,** *adj., n.* —**pro•gres′sive•ly,** *adv.*

pro•hib′it, *v.* forbid; prevent.

pro′hi•bi′tion, *n.* 1. act of prohibiting,. 2. (*cap.*) period, 1920–33, when manufacture and sale of alcoholic drinks was forbidden in U.S. —**pro′-hi•bi′tion•ist,** *n.*

pro•hib′i•tive, *adj.* 1. serving to prohibit. 2. too expensive.

proj′ect, *n.* 1. something planned. —*v.* (prə jekt′). 2. plan; contemplate. 3. impel forward. 4. display upon surface, as motion picture or map. 5. extend out; protrude. —**pro•jec′tion,** *n.* —**pro•jec′tor,** *n.*

pro•jec′tile, *n.* object fired with explosive force.

pro′le•tar′i•at, *n.* working or impoverished class. —**pro′le•tar′i•an,** *adj., n.*

pro•lif′er•ate′, *v.,* -ated, -ating. spread rapidly. —**pro•lif′er•a′tion,** *n.*

pro•lif′ic, *adj.* productive.

pro•logue, *n.* introductory part of novel, play, etc.

pro•long′, *v.* lengthen.

prom′e•nade′ (-nād′, -näd′), *n., v.,* -naded, -nading. —*n.* 1. leisurely walk. 2. space for such walk. —*v.* 3. take promenade.

prom′i•nent, *adj.* 1. conspicuous. 2. projecting. 3. well-known. —**prom′i•nence,** *n.* —**prom′i•nent•ly,** *adv.*

pro•mis′cu•ous, *adj.* indiscriminate. —**prom′is•cu′i•ty,** *n.* —**pro•mis′cu•ous•ly,** *adv.*

prom′ise, *n., v.,* -ised, -ising. —*n.* 1. assurance that one will act as specified. 2. indication of future excellence. —*v.* 3. assure by promise. 4. afford ground for expectation. —**prom′is•ing,** *adj.*

prom′is•so•ry, *adj.* containing promise, esp. of payment.

prom′on•to•ry, *n., pl.* -ries. high peak projecting into sea or overlooking low land.

pro•mote′, *v.,* -moted, -moting. 1. further progress of. 2. advance. 3. organize. —**pro•mot′er,** *n.* —**pro•mo′tion,** *n.*

prompt, *adj.* 1. ready to act. 2. done at once. —*v.* 3. incite to action. 4. suggest (action, etc.). —**prompt′er,** *n.* —**prompt′ly,** *adv.* —**prompt′ness,** **promp′ti•tude′,** *n.*

prom′ul•gate, *v.,* -gated, -gating. proclaim formally. —**prom′ul•ga′tion,** *n.* —**prom′ul•ga′tor,** *n.*

prone, *adj.* 1. likely; inclined. 2. lying flat, esp. face downward.

prong, *n.* point.

pro′noun′, *n.* word used as substitute for noun. —**pro•nom′i•nal,** *adj.*

pro•nounce′, *v.,* -nounced, -nouncing. 1. utter, esp. precisely. 2. declare to be. 3. announce. —**pro•nounce′ment,** *n.*

pro•nounced′, *adj.* 1. strongly marked. 2. decided.

pro•nun′ci•a′tion, *n.* production of sounds of speech.

proof, *n.* 1. evidence establishing fact. 2. standard strength, as of liquors. 3. trial printing. —*adj.* 4. resisting perfectly.

proof′read′, *v.,* -read, -reading. read (printers' proofs, etc.) to mark errors. —**proof′read′er,** *n.*

prop, *n., v.,* propped, propping. —*n.* 1. rigid support. —*v.* 2. support with prop.

prop′a•gan′da, *n.* doctrines disseminated by organization. —**prop′a•gan′dist,** *n.* —**prop′a•gan′dize,** *v.*

prop′a•gate′, *v.,* -gated, -gating. 1. reproduce; cause to reproduce. 2. transmit (doctrine, etc.). —**prop′a•ga′tion,** *n.*

pro•pel′, *v.,* -pelled, -pelling. drive forward. —**pro•pel′lant, pro•pel′lent,** *n.*

pro•pel′ler, *n.* screwlike propelling device.

pro•pen′si•ty, *n.* inclination.

prop′er, *adj.* 1. suitable; fitting. 2. correct. 3. designating particular person, place, or thing. —**prop′er•ly,** *adv.*

prop′er•ty, *n., pl.* -ties. 1. that which one owns. 2. attribute.

proph′e•sy (-sī), *v.,* -sied, -sying. foretell; predict. —**proph′e•cy** (-sē), *n.*

proph′et, *n.* 1. person who speaks for God. 2. inspired leader. 3. person who predicts. —**pro•phet′ic,** *adj.* —**pro•phet′i•cal•ly,** *adv.*

pro′phy•lax′is (prō′fə lak′sis), *n.* protection from or prevention of disease. —**pro′phy•lac′tic,** *adj., n.*

pro•pin′qui•ty, *n.* nearness.

pro•pi′ti•ate′ (prə pish′ē āt′), *v.,* -ated, -ating. appease.

pro•pi′tious, *adj.* favorable. —**pro•pi′tious•ly,** *adv.*

pro•po′nent, *n.* advocate; supporter.

pro•por′tion, *n.* 1. comparative or proper relation of dimensions or quantities. 2. symmetry. 3. (*pl.*) dimensions. —*v.* 4. adjust in proper relation. —**pro•por′tion•al,** *adj.*

pro•por′tion•ate, *adj.* being in due proportion. —**pro•por′tion•ate•ly,** *adv.*

pro•pos′al, *n.* 1. proposition. 2. offer of marriage.

pro•pose′, *v.,* -posed, -posing. 1. suggest. 2. intend. 3. offer marriage.

prop′o•si′tion, *n.* 1. proposed plan. 2. statement that affirms or denies. 3. proposal of illicit sex. —*v.* 4. make proposition to.

pro•pound′, *v.* offer for consideration.

pro•pri′e•tor, *n.* owner or manager. —**pro•pri′e•tar′y,** *adj.*

pro•pri′e•ty, *n., pl.* -ties. 1. appropriateness. 2. (*pl.*) morality; correctness.

pro•pul′sion, *n.* propelling force.

pro•rate′, *v.,* -rated, -rating. divide proportionately.

pro•sa′ic, *adj.* commonplace. —**pro•sa′i•cal•ly,** *adv.*

pro•scribe′, *v.* -scribed, -scribing. prohibit. —**pro•scrip′tion,** *n.*

prose, *n.* ordinary language; not verse.

pros′e•cute′, *v.,* -cuted, -cuting. 1. begin legal proceedings against. 2. go on with (task, etc.). —**pros′e•cu′tion,** *n.* —**pros′e•cu′tor,** *n.*

pros′e•lyte′ (pros′ə līt′), *n., v.,* -lyted, -lyting. convert. —**pros′e•lyt•ize′,** *v.*

pros′pect, *n.* 1. likelihood of success. 2. outlook; view. 3. potential customer. —*v.* 4. search. —**pro•spec′tive,** *adj.* —**pros′pec•tor,** *n.*

pro•spec′tus, *n.* description of new investment or purchase.

pros′per, *v.* be successful. —**pros•per′i•ty,** *n.* —**pros′per•ous,** *adj.* —**pros′per•ous•ly,** *adv.*

pros′tate, *n.* gland in males at base of bladder.

pros′ti•tute′, *n., v.,* -tuted, -tuting. —*n.* 1. woman who engages in sexual intercourse for money. —*v.* 2. put to base use. —**pros′ti•tu′tion,** *n.*

pros′trate, *v.,* -trated, -trating, *adj.* —*v.* 1. lay (oneself) down, esp. in humility. 2. exhaust. —*adj.* 3. lying flat. 4. helpless. 5. exhausted. —**pros•tra′tion,** *n.*

pros′y, *adj.,* prosier, prosiest. dull.

pro•tag′o•nist, *n.* main character.

pro•tect′, *v.* defend, as from attack or annoyance. —**pro•tec′tion,** *n.* —**pro•tec′tive,** *adj.* —**pro•tec′tive•ly,** *adv.* —**pro•tec′tor,** *n.*

pro•tec′tor•ate, *n.* 1. relation by which strong partly controls weaker state. 2. such weaker state.

pro′té•gé′ (prō′tə zhā′), *n., pl.* -gés. one under friendly patronage of another. —**pro′té•gée′,** *n.fem.*

pro′tein, *n.* nitrogenous compound required for life processes.

pro′test, *n.* 1. objection. —*v.* (prə test′). 2. express objection. 3. declare. —**prot′es•ta′tion,** *n.*

Prot′es•tant, *n.* Christian who is not Roman Catholic or Eastern Orthodox. —**Prot′es•tant•ism′,** *n.*

pro•to•col′, *n.* diplomatic etiquette.

pro′ton, *n.* part of atom bearing positive charge.

pro•to•plasm′, *n.* basis of living matter.

pro•to•type′, *n.* model; first or typical version. **—pro′to•typ′i•cal,** *adj.*

pro•tract′, *v.* lengthen. **—pro•trac′tion,** *n.*

pro•trac′tor, *n.* instrument for measuring angles.

pro•trude′, *v.,* **-truded, -truding.** project; extend. **—pro•tru′sion,** *n.* **—pro•tru′sive,** *adj.*

pro•tu′ber•ant, *adj.* bulging out. **—pro•tu′ber•ance,** *n.*

proud, *adj.* 1. having pride. 2. arrogant. 3. magnificent. **—proud′ly,** *adv.*

prove, *v.,* **proved, proving.** 1. establish as fact. 2. test. 3. be or become ultimately. **—prov′a•ble,** *adj.*

prov′en•der, *n.* fodder.

prov′erb, *n.* wise, long-current saying. **—pro•ver′bi•al,** *adj.*

pro•vide′, *v.,* **-vided, -viding.** 1. supply. 2. yield. 3. prepare beforehand. **—pro•vid′er,** *n.*

pro•vid′ed, *conj.* if.

prov′i•dence, *n.* 1. God's care. 2. economy.

prov′i•dent, *adj.* showing foresight; prudent.

prov′i•den′tial, *adj.* coming as godsend.

prov′ince, *n.* 1. administrative unit of country. 2. sphere.

pro•vin′cial, *adj.* 1. of province. 2. narrow-minded; unsophisticated.

pro•vi′sion, *n.* 1. something stated as necessary or binding. 2. act of providing. 3. what is provided. 4. arrangement beforehand. 5. (*pl.*) food supply. **—v.** 6. supply with provisions.

pro•vi′sion•al, *adj.* temporary.

pro•vi′so, *n., pl.* **-sos, -soes.** something required in agreement.

pro•voke′, *v.,* **-voked, -voking.** 1. exasperate. 2. arouse. **—prov′o•ca′tion,** *n.* **—pro•voc′a•tive,** *adj.* **—pro•voc′a•tive•ly,** *adv.*

pro′vost marshal (prō′vō), *Mil.* head of police.

prow, *n.* fore part of ship or aircraft.

prow′ess, *n.* 1. bravery. 2. exceptional ability.

prowl, *v.* roam or search stealthily. **—prowl′er,** *n.*

prox•im′i•ty, *n.* nearness.

prox′y, *n., pl.* **proxies.** agent.

prude, *n.* person overly concerned with proprieties. **—prud′ish,** *adj.*

pru′dence, *n.* practical wisdom; caution. **—pru′dent, pru•den′tial,** *adj.*

prune, *v.,* **pruned, pruning,** *n.* **—v.** 1. cut off (branches, etc.). **—n.** 2. kind of plum, often dried.

pru′ri•ent (prŏŏr′ē ənt), *adj.* having lewd thoughts. **—pru′ri•ence,** *n.*

pry, *v.,* **pried, prying,** *n.* **—v.** 1. look or inquire too curiously. 2. move with lever. **—n.** 3. act of prying. 4. prying person. 5. lever.

psalm, *n.* sacred song.

pseu′do (sōō′dō), *adj.* false; imitation.

pseu′do•nym, *n.* false name used by writer.

psy′che (sī′kē), *n.* human soul or mind.

psy′che•del′ic (sī′kə del′ik), *adj.* noting a mental state of extreme feelings, distorted sense perceptions, hallucinations, etc.

psy•chi′a•try, *n.* science of mental diseases. **—psy′chi•at′ric,** *adj.* **—psy•chi′a•trist,** *n.*

psy′chic, *adj.* Also, **psy′chi•cal.** 1. of the psyche. 2. supernatural.

psy•cho•a•nal′y•sis, *n.* 1. study of conscious and unconscious psychological processes. 2. treatment of psychoneuroses according to such study. **—psy′cho•an′a•lyst,** *n.* **—psy′cho•an′a•lyze′,** *v.*

psy•chol′o•gy, *n.* science of mental states and behavior. **—psy′cho•log′i•cal,** *adj.* **—psy′cho•log′i•cal•ly,** *adv.* **—psy•chol′o•gist,** *n.*

psy′cho•neu•ro′sis, *n., pl.* **-ses.** emotional disorder. **—psy′cho•neu•rot′ic,** *adj., n.*

psy•chop′a•thy (-kop′-), *n.* mental disease. **—psy′cho•path′ic,** *adj.* **—psy′cho•path′,** *n.*

psy•cho′sis, *n., pl.* **-ses.** severe mental disease. **—psy•chot′ic,** *adj., n.*

psy′cho•so•mat′ic, *adj.* (of physical disorder) caused by one's emotional state.

psy′cho•ther′a•py, *n.* science of curing mental disorders. **—psy′cho•ther′a•pist,** *n.*

ptar′mi•gan (tär′-), *n.* species of mountain grouse.

pto′maine (tō′-), *n.* substance produced during decay of plant and animal matter.

pub, *n. Brit. Informal.* tavern.

pu′ber•ty (pyōō′-), *n.* sexual maturity.

pub′lic, *adj.* 1. of or for people generally. 2. open to view or knowledge of all. **—n.** 3. people. **—pub′lic•ly,** *adv.*

pub′li•ca′tion, *n.* 1. publishing of book, etc. 2. item published.

pub•lic′i•ty, *n.* 1. public attention. 2. material promoting this.

pub′li•cize′, *v.,* **-cized, -cizing.** bring to public notice.

pub′lish, *v.* 1. issue (book, paper, etc.) for general distribution. 2. announce publicly. **—pub′lish•er,** *n.*

puck′er, *v., n.* wrinkle.

pud′ding (pŏŏd′-), *n.* soft dish, usually dessert.

pud′dle (pud′-), *n., v.,* **-dled, -dling.** **—n.** 1. small pool of water, esp. dirty water. **—v.** 2. fill with puddles.

pudg′y, *adj.,* **pudgier, pudgiest.** short and fat. **—pudg′i•ness,** *n.*

pueb′lo (pweb′lō), *n., pl.* **-los.** village of certain Southwestern Indians.

pu′er•ile (pyōō′ər il), *adj.* childish. **—pu′er•il′i•ty,** *n.*

puff, *n.* 1. short quick blast, as of wind. 2. inflated part. 3. anything soft and light. **—v.** 4. blow with puffs. 5. breathe hard and fast. 6. inflate. **—puff′y,** *adj.*

puf′fin, *n.* sea bird.

pug, *n.* kind of dog.

pu′gil•ism, *n.* boxing. **—pu′gil•ist,** *n.*

pug•na′cious, *adj.* fond of fighting. **—pug•nac′i•ty,** *n.*

puke, *v.,* **puked, puking,** *n. Slang.* vomit.

pul′chri•tude′, *n.* beauty.

pull, *v.* 1. draw; haul. 2. tear. 3. move with force. **—n.** 4. act of pulling. 5. force. 6. handle. 7. *Informal.* influence in politics, etc.

pul′let, *n.* young hen.

pul′ley, *n., pl.* **-leys.** wheel for guiding rope.

Pull′man, *n.* railroad sleeping car.

pul′mo•nar′y, *adj.* of lungs.

pulp, *n.* 1. soft fleshy part, as of fruit or tooth. 2. any soft mass. **—v.** 3. make or become pulp. **—pulp′y,** *adj.*

pul′pit, *n.* clergyman's platform in church.

pul′sar (-sär), *n.* source of pulsating radio energy among stars.

pul′sate, *v.,* **-sated, -sating.** throb. **—pul•sa′tion,** *n.*

pulse, *n., v.,* **pulsed, pulsing.** **—n.** 1. steady beat of arteries caused by heart's contractions. **—v.** 2. pulsate.

pul′ver•ize′, *v.,* **-ized, -izing.** reduce to powder. **—pul′ver•i•za′tion,** *n.*

pu′ma, *n.* cougar.

pum′ice, *n.* porous volcanic glass used as abrasive.

pum′mel, *n.* pommel.

pump, *n.* 1. apparatus for raising or driving fluids. 2. light low shoe. —*v.* 3. raise or drive with pump. 4. *Informal.* try to get information from.

pum′per•nick′el, *n.* hard, sour rye bread.

pump′kin, *n.* large orange fruit of garden vine.

pun, *n., v.,* **punned, punning. —***n.* 1. play with words alike in sound but different in meaning. —*v.* 2. make pun.

punch, *n.* 1. thrusting blow. 2. tool for piercing material. 3. sweetened beverage. —*v.* 4. hit with thrusting blow. 5. drive (cattle). 6. cut or indent with punch. **—punch′er,** *n.*

punc•til′i•ous, *adj.* exact or careful in conduct.

punc′tu•al, *adj.* on time. **—punc′tu•al′i•ty,** *n.* **—punc′tu•al•ly,** *adv.*

punc′tu•ate′, *v.,* **-ated, -ating.** 1. mark with punctuation. 2. accent periodically.

punc′tu•a′tion, *n.* use of commas, semicolons, etc.

punc′ture, *n., v.,* **-tured, -turing. —***n.* 1. perforation. —*v.* 2. perforate with pointed object.

pun′dit, *n.* learned man; sage.

pun′gent, *adj.* 1. sharp in taste. 2. biting. **—pun′gen•cy,** *n.* **—pun′gent•ly,** *adv.*

pun′ish, *v.* subject to pain, confinement, loss, etc., for offense. **—pun′ish•a•ble,** *adj.* **—pun′ish•ment,** *n.*

pu′ni•tive, *adj.* punishing.

punt, *n.* 1. kick in football. 2. shallow flat-bottomed boat. —*v.* 3. kick (dropped ball) before it touches ground. 4. propel (boat) with pole.

pu′ny, *adj.,* **-nier, -niest.** weakly.

pup, *n.* Also, **pup′py.** young dog.

pu′pa (pyoo′pə), *n., pl.* **-pae, -pas.** insect in stage between larva and winged adult. **—pu′pal,** *adj.*

pu′pil, *n.* 1. person being taught. 2. opening in iris of eye.

pup′pet, *n.* 1. doll or figure manipulated by hand or strings. —*adj.* 2. ruled or directed by foreign power.

pur′chase, *v.,* **-chased, -chasing,** *n.* —*v.* 1. buy. —*n.* 2. acquisition by payment. 3. what is purchased. 4. leverage. **—pur′chas•er,** *n.*

pure, *adj.,* **purer, purest.** 1. free from anything different or hurtful. 2. abstract. 3. absolute. 4. chaste. **—pure′ly,** *adv.* **—pure′ness,** *n.*

pu•rée′ (pyoo rā′), *n.* cooked sieved food.

pur′ga•to′ry, *n., pl.* **-ries.** *Rom. Cath. Theol.* condition or place of purification, after death, from venial sins.

purge, *v.,* **purged, purging,** *n.* —*v.* 1. cleanse; purify. 2. rid. 3. clear by causing evacuation. —*n.* 4. act or means of purging. **—pur•ga′tion,** *n.* **—pur′ga•tive,** *adj., n.*

pu′ri•fy′, *v.,* **-fied, -fying.** make or become pure. **—pu′ri•fi•ca′tion,** *n.*

Pu′rim (poor′im), *n.* Jewish commemorative festival.

Pu′ri•tan, *n.* 1. member of strict religious group originating in 16th-century England. 2. (*l.c.*) person of strict morality. **—pu′ri•tan′i•cal,** *adj.*

pu′ri•ty, *n.* condition of being pure.

purl, *v.* knit with inverted stitch.

pur•loin′, *v.* steal.

pur′ple, *n., adj.* blended red and blue.

pur•port′, *v.* 1. claim. 2. imply. —*n.* (pûr′pōrt) 3. meaning.

pur′pose, *n., v.,* **-posed, -posing. —***n.* 1. object; aim; intention. —*v.* 2. intend. **—pur′pose•ful,** *adj.* **—pur′pose•less,** *adj.*

purr, *v.* 1. utter low continuous sound, as by cat. —*n.* 2. this sound.

purse, *n., v.,* **pursed, pursing. —***n.* 1. small case for carrying money. 2. sum of money offered as prize. —*v.* 3. pucker.

purs′er, *n.* financial officer.

pur•su′ant, *adv.* according.

pur•sue′, *v.,* **-sued, -suing.** 1. follow to catch. 2. carry on (studies, etc.). **—pur•su′ance,** *n.* **—pur•su′er,** *n.*

pur•suit′, *n.* 1. act of pursuing. 2. quest. 3. occupation.

pu′ru•lent (pyoor′ə lənt), *adj.* full of pus. **—pu′ru•lence,** *n.*

pur•vey′, *v.* provide; supply. **—pur•vey′ance,** *n.* **—pur•vey′or,** *n.*

pus, *n.* liquid matter found in sores, etc.

push, *v.* 1. exert force on to send away. 2. urge. —*n.* 3. act of pushing. 4. strong effort. **—push′er,** *n.*

push′o′ver, *n. Informal.* one easily victimized or overcome.

pu•sil•lan′i•mous, *adj.* cowardly.

puss′y, *n., pl.* **pussies.** cat. Also, **puss.**

puss′y•foot′, *v.* go stealthily.

pussy willow, small American willow.

pus′tule (-chool), *n.* pimple containing pus.

put, *v.* 1. move or place. 2. set, as to task. 3. express. 4. apply. 5. impose. 6. throw. —*n.* 7. throw.

pu′ta•tive, *adj.* reputed.

pu′tre•fy′, *v.,* **-fied, -fying.** rot. **—pu′tre•fac′tion,** *n.*

pu′trid, *adj.* rotten.

putt, *v.* 1. strike (golf ball) gently and carefully. —*n.* 2. such strike.

put′ter, *v.* 1. busy oneself ineffectively. —*n.* 2. club for putting.

put′ty, *n., v.,* **-tied, -tying. —***n.* 1. cement of whiting and linseed oil. —*v.* 2. secure with putty.

puz′zle, *n., v.,* **-zled, -zling. —***n.* 1. device or question offering difficulties. —*v.* 2. perplex. **—puz′zle•ment,** *n.*

pyg′my, *n., pl.* **-mies.** dwarf.

py′lon, *n.* tall thin structure.

py′or•rhe′a, *n.* disease of gums.

pyr′a•mid, *n.* 1. solid with triangular sides meeting in point. —*v.* 2. increase gradually. **—py•ram′i•dal,** *adj.*

pyre, *n.* heap of wood, esp. for burning corpse.

py′rite, *n.* common yellow mineral of low value.

py′ro•ma′ni•a, *n.* mania for setting fires. **—py′ro•ma′ni•ac′,** *n.*

py′ro•tech′nics, *n.* fireworks. **—py′ro•tech′nic,** *adj.*

py′thon, *n.* large snake that kills by constriction.

Q

Q, q, *n.* seventeenth letter of English alphabet.

quack, *n.* pretender to medical skill. —**quack′er•y,** *n.*

quad′ran′gle, *n.* 1. plane figure with four angles and four sides. 2. Also, *Informal,* **quad.** enclosed four-sided area. —**quad•ran′gu•lar,** *adj.*

quad′rant, *n.* 1. arc of 90°. 2. instrument for measuring altitudes.

quad′ra•phon′ic, *adj.* of sound reproduced through four recording tracks.

quad′ri•lat′er•al, *adj.* 1. four-sided. —*n.* 2. four-sided plane figure.

qua•drille′ (kwə dril′), *n.* square dance for four couples.

quad′ru•ped′, *n.* four-footed animal.

quad•ru′ple, *adj., n., v.,* **-pled, -pling.** —*adj.* 1. of four parts. 2. four times as great. —*n.* 3. number, etc., four times as great as another. —*v.* 4. increase fourfold.

quad•ru′plet, *n.* one of four children born at one birth.

quad•ru′pli•cate, *n.* group of four copies.

quaff (kwaf), *v.* drink heartily.

quag′mire′, *n.* boggy ground.

qua′hog (kwô′hog), *n.* edible American clam.

quail, *n., pl.* **quails, quail,** *v.* —*n.* 1. game bird resembling domestic fowls. —*v.* 2. lose courage; show fear.

quaint, *adj.* pleasingly odd. —**quaint′ly,** *adv.* —**quaint′ness,** *n.*

quake, *v.,* **quaked, quaking,** *n.* —*v.* 1. tremble. —*n.* 2. earthquake.

Quak′er, *n.* member of Society of Friends.

qual′i•fy′, *v.,* **-fied, -fying.** 1. make proper or fit. 2. modify. 3. mitigate. 4. show oneself fit. —**qual′i•fi•ca′-tion,** *n.*

qual′i•ty, *n., pl.* **-ties.** 1. characteristic. 2. relative merit. 3. excellence. —**qual′i•ta′tive,** *adj.*

qualm (kwäm), *n.* 1. misgiving; scruple. 2. feeling of illness.

quan′da•ry, *n., pl.* **-ries.** dilemma.

quan′ti•ty, *n., pl.* **-ties.** 1. amount; measure. 2. *Math.* something having magnitude. —**quan′ti•ta′tive,** *adj.*

quar′an•tine′, *n., v.,* **-tined, -tining.** —*n.* 1. strict isolation to prevent spread of disease. —*v.* 2. put in quarantine.

quar′rel, *n.* 1. angry dispute. —*v.* 2. disagree angrily. —**quar′rel•some,** *adj.*

quar′ry, *n., pl.* **-ries,** *v.,* **-ried, -rying.** —*n.* 1. pit from which stone is taken. 2. object of pursuit. —*v.* 3. get from quarry.

quart, *n.* measure of capacity: in liquid measure, ¼ gallon, in dry measure, ⅛ peck.

quar′ter, *n.* 1. one of four equal parts. 2. coin worth 25 cents. 3. (*pl.*) place of residence. 4. mercy. —*v.* 5. divide into quarters. 6. lodge. —*adj.* 7. being a quarter.

quar′ter•back′, *n.* position in football.

quar′ter•ly, *adj., n., pl.* **-lies,** *adv.* —*adj.* 1. occurring, etc., each quarter year. —*n.* 2. quarterly publication. —*adv.* 3. once each quarter year.

quar′ter•mas′ter, *n.* 1. military officer in charge of supplies, etc. 2. naval officer in charge of signals, etc.

quar•tet′, *n.* group of four. Also, **quar•tette′.**

quar′to, *n.* book page printed from sheets folded twice.

quartz, *n.* common crystalline mineral.

qua′sar (kwā′zär), *n.* astronomical source of powerful radio energy.

quash, *v.* subdue; suppress.

qua′si (kwā′zī), *adj.* 1. resembling; to be regarded as if. —*adv.* 2. seemingly.

quat′rain, *n.* four-line stanza.

qua′ver, *v.* 1. quiver. 2. speak tremulously. —*n.* 3. quavering tone.

quay (kē), *n.* landing beside water.

quea′sy (kwē′zē), *adj.,* **-sier, -siest.** 1. nauseated. 2. uneasy.

queen, *n.* 1. wife of king. 2. female sovereign. 3. fertile female of bees, ants, etc. —*v.* 4. reign as queen.

queer, *adj.* 1. strange; odd. —*n.* 2. *Offensive.* homosexual. —*v.* 3. *Slang.* ruin; impair. —**queer′ly,** *adv.* —**queer′ness,** *n.*

quell, *v.* suppress.

quench, *v.* slake or extinguish.

quer′u•lous, *adj.* fretful.

que′ry (kwēr′ē), *n., pl.* **-ries,** *v.,* **-ried, -rying.** question.

quest, *n., v.* search.

ques′tion, *n.* 1. sentence put in a form to elicit information. 2. problem for discussion or dispute. —*v.* 3. ask a question. 4. doubt. —**ques′-tion•a•ble,** *adj.* —**ques′tion•er,** *n.*

ques′tion•naire′, *n.* list of questions.

queue (kyōō), *n., v.,* **queued, queuing.** —*n.* 1. line of persons. 2. braid of hair hanging down the back. —*v.* 3. form in a line.

quib′ble, *v.,* **-bled, -bling,** *n.* —*v.* 1. speak ambiguously in evasion. 2. make petty objections. —*n.* 3. act of quibbling. —**quib′bler,** *n.*

quiche (kēsh), *n.* pielike dish of cheese, onion, etc.

quick, *adj.* 1. prompt; done promptly. 2. swift. 3. alert. —*n.* 4. living persons. 5. sensitive flesh. —*adv.* 6. quickly. —**quick′ly,** *adv.* —**quick′-ness,** *n.*

quick′en, *v.* 1. hasten. 2. rouse. 3. become alive.

quick′lime′, *n.* untreated lime.

quick′sand′, *n.* soft sand yielding easily to weight.

quick′sil′ver, *n.* mercury.

quid, *n.* portion for chewing.

qui•es′cent (kwī es′ənt), *adj.* resting; inactive. —**qui•es′cence,** *n.*

qui′et, *adj.* 1. being at rest. 2. peaceful. 3. silent. 4. restrained. —*v.* 5. make or become quiet. 6. tranquillity. —**qui′et•ly,** *adv.* —**qui′et•ness,** **qui′e•tude′,** *n.*

qui•e′tus (kwī ē′təs), *n.* 1. final settlement. 2. release from life.

quill, *n.* large feather.

quilt, *n.* padded and lined bed covering.

quince, *n.* yellowish acid fruit.

qui′nine, *n.* bitter substance used esp. in treating malaria.

quin•tes′sence, *n.* essential substance.

quin•tet′, *n.* group of five. Also, **quin•tette′.**

quin•tu′plet, *n.* one of five children born at one birth.

quip, *n., v.,* **quipped, quipping.** —*n.* 1. witty or sarcastic remark. —*v.* 2. make quip.

quire, *n.* set of 24 uniform sheets of paper.

quirk, *n.* peculiarity.

quis′ling, *n.* traitor.

quit, *v.,* **quitted, quitting.** 1. stop. 2. leave. 3. relinquish. —**quit′ter,** *n.*

quit′claim′, *n.* 1. transfer of one's interest. —*v.* 2. give up claim to.

quite, *adv.* 1. completely. 2. really.

quits, *adj.* with no further payment or revenge due.

quit′tance, *n.* 1. requital. 2. discharge from debt.

quiv′er, *v.* 1. tremble. —*n.* 2. trembling. 3. case for arrows.

quix•ot′ic, *adj.* extravagantly idealistic; impractical.

quiz, *v.,* **quizzed, quizzing,** *n., pl.* **quizzes.** —*v.* 1. question. —*n.* 2. informal questioning.

quiz′zi•cal, *adj.* comical. —**quiz′zi•cal•ly,** *adv.*

quoit, *n.* flat ring thrown to encircle peg in game of **quoits.**

quon′dam, *adj.* former.

quo′rum, *n.* number of members needed to transact business legally.

quo′ta, *n.* proportional share due.

quote, *v.,* **quoted, quoting,** *n.* —*v.* 1. repeat verbatim. 2. cite. 3. state (price of). —*n.* 4. *Informal.* quotation. —**quota′tion,** *n.* —**quot′a•ble,** *adj.*

quoth, *v. Archaic.* said.

quo′tient, *n. Math.* number of times one quantity is contained in another.

R

R, r, *n.* 1. eighteenth letter of English alphabet. 2. those less than 17 years old must be accompanied by adult: motion-picture classification.

rab′bi, *n., pl.* **-bis.** Jewish clergyman. —**rab•bin′ic, rab•bin′i•cal,** *adj.*

rab′bit, *n.* small, long-eared mammal.

rab′ble, *n.* mob.

rab′id, *adj.* 1. irrationally intense. 2. having rabies. —**rab′id•ly,** *adv.*

ra′bies (rā′bēz), *n.* fatal disease transmitted by bite of infected animal.

rac•coon′, *n.* small nocturnal carnivorous mammal.

race, *n., v.,* **raced, racing.** —*n.* 1. contest of speed. 2. onward course or flow. 3. group of persons of common origin. 4. any class or kind. —*v.* 5. engage in race. 6. move swiftly. —**rac′er,** *n.* —**ra′cial,** *adj.*

ra•ceme′ (rā sēm′), *n.* cluster of flowers along stem.

rac′ism, *n.* hatred of or prejudice against another race.

rack, *n.* 1. framework to hold various articles. 2. toothed bar engaging with teeth of pinion. 3. instrument of torture. 4. destruction. —*v.* 5. torture. 6. strain.

rack′et, *n.* 1. noise. 2. illegal or dishonest business. 3. Also, **rac′quet.** framed network used as bat in tennis, etc.

rack′e•teer′, *n.* criminal engaged in racket.

rac′on•teur′ (rak′on tûr′), *n.* skilled storyteller.

ra•coon′, *n.* raccoon.

rac′y, *adj.,* **racier, raciest.** 1. lively. 2. risqué. —**rac′i•ness,** *n.*

ra′dar, *n.* electronic device capable of locating unseen objects by radio wave.

ra′di•al, *adj.* of rays or radii.

ra′di•ant, *adj.* 1. emitting rays of light. 2. bright; exultant. 3. emitted in rays, as heat. —**ra′di•ance,** *n.* —**ra′di•ant•ly,** *adv.*

ra′di•ate′, *v.,* **-ated, -ating.** 1. spread like rays from center. 2. emit or issue in rays. —**ra′di•a′tion,** *n.*

ra′di•a′tor, *n.* heating device.

rad′i•cal, *adj.* 1. fundamental. 2. favoring drastic reforms. —*n.* 3. person with radical ideas. 4. atom or group of atoms behaving as unit in chemical reaction. —**rad′i•cal•ism,** *n.* —**rad′i•cal•ly,** *adv.*

ra′di•o′, *n.* 1. way of transmitting sound by electromagnetic waves, without wires. 2. apparatus for sending or receiving such waves.

ra′di•o•ac′tive, *adj.* emitting radiation from the atomic nucleus, as radium, for example, does. —**ra′di•o•ac•tiv′i•ty,** *n.*

rad′ish, *n.* crisp root of garden plant, eaten raw.

ra′di•um, *n.* radioactive metallic element.

ra′di•us, *n., pl.* **-dii, -diuses.** 1. straight line from center of a circle to circumference. 2. one of the bones of the forearm.

raf′fi•a, *n.* fiber made from leafstalks of a Madagascan palm.

raf′fle, *n., v.,* **-fled, -fling.** —*n.* 1. lottery in which chances are sold. —*v.* 2. dispose of by raffle.

raft, *n.* floating platform of logs, etc.

raft′er, *n.* framing member of roof.

rag, *n.* worthless bit of cloth, esp. one torn. —**rag′ged,** *adj.*

rag′a•muf′fin, *n.* ragged child.

rage, *n., v.,* **raged, raging.** —*n.* 1. violent anger. 2. object of popular enthusiasm. —*v.* 3. be violently angry. 4. prevail violently.

rag′lan, *n.* loose garment with sleeves continuing to collar.

ra•gout′ (ra gōō′), *n.* stew.

rag′weed′, *n.* plant whose pollen causes hay fever.

raid, *n.* 1. sudden attack. —*v.* 2. attack suddenly. —**raid′er,** *n.*

rail, *n.* 1. horizontal bar, used as barrier, support, etc. 2. one of pair of railroad tracks. 3. railroad as means of transport. 4. wading bird. —*v.* 5. complain bitterly.

rail′ing, *n.* barrier of rails and posts.

rail′ler•y, *n.* banter.

rail′road′, *n.* 1. road with fixed rails on which trains run. —*v.* 2. operate railroad.

rail′way′, *n. Chiefly Brit.* railroad.

rai′ment, *n.* clothing.

rain, *n.* 1. water falling from sky in drops. 2. rainfall. —*v.* 3. fall or send down as rain. —**rain′y,** *adj.*

rain′bow′, *n.* arc of colors sometimes seen in sky opposite sun during rain. —**rain′bow•like′,** *adj.*

rain′coat′, *n.* waterproof coat.

rain′fall′, *n.* amount of rain.

raise, *v.,* **raised, raising,** *n.* —*v.* 1. lift up. 2. set upright. 3. cause to appear. 4. grow. 5. collect. 6. rear. 7. cause (dough) to expand. 8. end (siege). —*n.* 9. increase, esp. in pay.

rai′sin, *n.* dried sweet grape.

ra′jah (-jə), *n.* (formerly) Indian king or prince.

rake, *n., v.,* **raked, raking.** —*n.* 1. long-handled implement with teeth for gathering or smoothing ground. 2. dissolute person. 3. slope. —*v.* 4. gather, smooth, etc., with rake. 5. fire guns the length of (target).

rak′ish, *adj.* 1. jaunty. 2. dissolute.

ral′ly, *v.,* **-lied, -lying,** *n., pl.* **-lies.** —*v.* 1. bring into order again. 2. call or come together. 3. revive. 4. come to aid. 5. tease. —*n.* 6. renewed order. 7. renewal of strength. 8. mass meeting.

ram, *n., v.,* **rammed, ramming.** —*n.* 1. male sheep. 2. device for battering, forcing, etc. —*v.* 3. strike forcibly.

ram′ble, *v.,* **-bled, -bling,** *n.* —*v.* 1. stroll idly. 2. talk vaguely. —*n.* 3. leisurely stroll. —**ram′bler,** *n.*

ram′i•fy′, *v.,* **-fied, -fying.** divide into branches. —**ram′i•fi•ca′tion,** *n.*

ramp, *n.* sloping surface between two levels.

ram′page, *n., v.,* **-paged, -paging.** —*n.* (ram′pāj). 1. violent behavior. —*v.* (ram pāj′). 2. move furiously about.

ramp′ant, *adj.* 1. vigorous; unrestrained. 2. standing on hind legs.

ram′part, *n.* mound of earth raised as bulwark.

ram′rod′, *n.* rod for cleaning or loading gun.

ram′shack′le, *adj.* rickety.

ranch, *n.* large farm, esp. for raising stock. —**ranch′er,** *n.*

ran′cid (-sid) *adj.* stale. —**ran•cid′i•ty,** *n.*

ran′cor (rang′kər), *n.* lasting resentment. —**ran′cor•ous,** *adj.*

ran′dom, *adj.* without aim or consistency.

range, *n., v.,* **ranged, ranging.** —*n.* 1. limits; extent. 2. place for target shooting. 3. distance between gun and target. 4. row. 5. mountain chain. 6. grazing area. 7. cooking stove. —*v.* 8. arrange. 9. pass over (area). 10. vary.

rang′er, *n.* 1. warden of forest tract. 2. civil officer who patrols large area.

rank, *n.* 1. class, group, or standing. 2. high position. 3. row. 4. (*pl.*) enlisted men. —*v.* 5. arrange. 6. put or be in particular rank. 7. be senior in rank. —*adj.* 8. growing excessively. 9. offensively strong in smell. 10. utter; gross. —**rank′ly,** *adv.* —**rank′ness,** *n.*

ran′kle, *v.,* **-kled, -kling.** irritate.

ran′sack, *v.* search thoroughly.

ran′som, *n.* 1. sum demanded for prisoner. —*v.* 2. pay ransom for.

rant, *v.* 1. speak wildly. —*n.* 2. violent speech. —**rant′er,** *n.*

rap, *v.,* **rapped, rapping,** *n.* —*v.* 1. strike quickly and sharply. —*n.* 2. sharp blow.

ra•pa′cious, *adj.* plundering; greedy.

rape, *n., v.,* **raped, raping.** —*n.* 1. forcible violation of woman. 2. abduction or seizure. —*v.* 3. commit

rape on. 4. abduct or seize. —**rap′ist,** *n.*

rap′id, *adj.* 1. swift. —*n.* 2. (*pl.*) swift-moving part of river. —**ra•pid′i•ty, rap′id•ness,** *n.* —**rap′id•ly,** *adv.*

ra′pi•er (rā′pē ər), *n.* slender sword.

rap′ine (rap′in), *n.* plunder.

rap•port′ (ra pôr′), *n.* sympathetic relationship.

rapt, *adj.* engrossed.

rap′ture, *n.* ecstatic joy. —**rap′tur•ous,** *adj.*

rare, *adj.,* **rarer, rarest.** 1. unusual. 2. thin, as air. 3. (of meat) not thoroughly cooked. —**rar′i•ty,** *n.* —**rare′ly,** *adv.* —**rare′ness,** *n.*

rare′bit (râr′bit), *n.* dish of melted cheese.

rar′e•fy′, *v.,* **-fied, -fying.** make or become thin, as air.

ras′cal, *n.* dishonest person. —**ras•cal′i•ty,** *n.*

rash, *adj.* 1. thoughtlessly hasty. —*n.* 2. skin eruption. —**rash′ly,** *adv.* —**rash′ness,** *n.*

rash′er, *n.* thin slice of bacon or ham.

rasp, *v.* 1. scrape as with file. 2. irritate. 3. speak gratingly. —*n.* 4. coarse file. 5. rasping sound.

rasp′ber′ry (raz′-), *n., pl.* **-ries.** small juicy red or black fruit.

rat, *n.* rodent larger than mouse.

ratch′et, *n.* wheel or bar having teeth that catch pawl to control motion.

rate, *n., v.,* **rated, rating.** —*n.* 1. charge in proportion to something that varies. 2. degree of speed, etc. —*v.* 3. estimate or fix rate. 4. consider; judge.

rath′er, *adv.* 1. somewhat. 2. in preference. 3. on the contrary.

rat′i•fy′, *v.,* **-fied, -fying.** confirm formally.

ra′tio (-shō) *n.* relative number or extent; proportion.

ra′ti•oc′i•na′tion (rash′ē os′-), *n.* reasoning.

ra′tion, *n.* 1. fixed allowance. —*v.* 2. apportion. 3. put on ration.

ra′tion•al, *adj.* 1. sensible. 2. sane. —**ra′tion•al•ly,** *adv.* —**ra′tion•al′i•ty,** *n.*

ra′tion•ale′ (rash′ə nal′), *n.* reasonable basis for action.

ra′tion•al•ism, *n.* advocacy of precise reasoning as source of truth. —**ra′tion•al•ist,** *n.* —**ra′tion•al•is′tic,** *adj.*

ra′tion•al•ize′, *v.,* **-ized, -izing.** 1. find reason for one's behavior or attitude. 2. make rational. —**ra′tion•al•i•za′tion,** *n.*

rat•tan′, *n.* hollow stem of climbing palm.

rat′tle, *v.,* **-tled, -tling,** *n.* —*v.* 1. make series of short sharp sounds. 2. chatter. 3. *Informal.* disconcert. —*n.* 4. sound of rattling. 5. child's toy that rattles.

rat′tle•snake′, *n.* venomous American snake.

rau′cous (rô′kəs), *adj.* hoarse; harsh. —**rau′cous•ly,** *adv.*

rav′age, *n., v.,* **-aged, -aging.** ruin. —**rav′ag•er,** *n.*

rave, *v.,* **raved, raving.** talk wildly.

rav′el, *v.* 1. disengage threads. 2. tangle. 3. solve. —*n.* 4. tangle. 5. disengaged thread.

ra′ven, *n.* large shiny black bird.

rav′en•ous, *adj.* very hungry; greedy.

ra•vine′, *n.* deep, narrow valley.

rav′ish, *v.* 1. fill with joy. 2. rape. —**rav′ish•er,** *n.* —**rav′ish•ment,** *n.*

raw, *adj.* 1. in the natural state. 2. uncooked. 3. open. 4. untrained. —*n.* 5. raw or naked flesh. —**raw′ness,** *n.*

raw′hide′, *n.* untanned hide, as of cattle.

ray, *n.* 1. narrow beam of light. 2. trace. 3. line outward from center. 4. flat-bodied deep-sea fish.

ray′on, *n.* silklike synthetic fabric.

raze, *v.,* **razed, razing.** demolish.

ra′zor, *n.* sharp-edged instrument for shaving.

re, *n.* 1. (rā). *Music.* second tone of scale. —*prep.* 2. (rē). with reference to.

re-, prefix indicating: 1. repetition, as reprint, rearm. 2. withdrawal.

reach, *v.* 1. come to. 2. be able to touch. 3. extend. —*n.* 4. act of reaching. 5. extent.

re•act′, *v.* 1. act upon each other. 2. respond.

re•ac′tion, *n.* 1. extreme political conservatism. 2. responsive action. —**re•ac′tion•ar′y,** *n., adj.*

re•ac′tor, *n.* 1. one that reacts. 2. apparatus for producing useful nuclear energy.

read, *v.,* **read, reading.** 1. observe and understand (printed matter, etc.). 2. register. —**read′a•ble,** *adj.* —**read′er,** *n.* —**read′er•ship′,** *n.*

read′ing, *n.* 1. amount read at one time. 2. interpretation of written or musical work.

read′y, *adj., v.,* **readied, readying,** *n.* —*adj.* 1. fully prepared. 2. willing. 3. apt. —*v.* 4. make ready. —*n.* 5. state of being ready. —**read′i•ly,** *adv.* —**read′i•ness,** *n.*

read'y-made', *adj.* ready for use when bought.

re'al, *adj.* 1. actual. 2. genuine. 3. denoting immovable property. —**re•al'i•ty, re'al•ness,** *n.* —**re'al•ly,** *adv.*

real estate, land with buildings, etc., on it. Also, **re'al•ty.**

re'al•ist, *n.* person accepting things as they are. —**re'al•is'tic,** *adj.*

re'al•ize', *v.,* **-ized, -izing.** 1. understand clearly. 2. make real. 3. get as profit. —**re'al•i•za'tion,** *n.*

realm (relm), *n.* 1. kingdom. 2. special field.

Re'al•tor, *n.* real estate broker.

ream, *n.* 1. twenty quires of paper. —*v.* 2. enlarge (hole) with a **ream'er.**

reap, *v.* harvest. —**reap'er,** *n.*

rear, *n.* 1. back part. —*adj.* 2. of or at rear. —*v.* 3. care for to maturity. 4. raise; erect. 5. rise on hind legs.

rear admiral, naval officer above captain.

re•arm', *v.* arm again. —**re•arm'a•ment,** *n.*

rea'son, *n.* 1. cause for belief, act, etc. 2. sound judgment. 3. sanity. —*v.* 4. think or argue logically. 5. infer. —**rea'son•ing,** *n.* —**rea'son•er,** *n.*

rea'son•a•ble, *adj.* showing sound judgment. —**rea'son•a•bly,** *adv.*

re•as•sure', *v.,* **-sured, -suring.** restore confidence of. —**re•as•sur'ance,** *n.*

re'bate, *v.,* **-bated, -bating,** *n.* —*v.* 1. return (part of amount paid). —*n.* 2. amount rebated.

re•bel', *v.,* **-belled, -belling,** *n.* —*v.* (ri bel'). 1. rise in arms against one's government. 2. resist any authority. —*n.* (reb'əl). 3. one who rebels. —**re•bel'lion,** *n.* —**re•bel'lious,** *adj.*

re•bound', *v.* 1. bound back after impact. —*n.* (rē'bound'). 2. act of rebounding.

re•buff', *n.* 1. blunt check or refusal. —*v.* 2. check; repel.

re•buke', *v.,* **-buked, -buking,** *n.* reprimand.

re'bus, *n.* puzzle in which pictures and symbols combine to represent a word.

re•but', *v.,* **-butted, -butting.** refute. —**re•but'tal,** *n.*

re•cal'ci•trant (ri kal'sə trənt), *adj.* resisting control. —**re•cal'ci•trance,** *n.*

re•call', *v.* 1. remember. 2. call back. 3. withdraw. —*n.* 4. act of recalling.

re•cant', *v.* retract.

re'ca•pit'u•late (-pich'ə-), *v.,* **-lated, -lating.** review; sum up. —**re'ca•pit'u•la'tion,** *n.*

re•cede', *v.,* **-ceded, -ceding.** move or appear to move back.

re•ceipt', *n.* 1. written acknowledgment of receiving. 2. (*pl.*) amount received. 3. act of receiving.

re•ceiv'a•ble, *adj.* still to be paid.

re•ceive', *v.,* **-ceived, -ceiving.** 1. take (something offered or delivered). 2. experience. 3. welcome (guests). 4. accept.

re•ceiv'er, *n.* 1. one that receives. 2. device, as radio, that receives electrical signals and converts them to sound, etc. 3. person put in charge of property in litigation. —**re•ceiv'er•ship,** *n.*

re'cent, *adj.* happening, etc., lately. —**re'cen•cy,** *n.* —**re'cent•ly,** *adv.*

re•cep'ta•cle, *n.* container.

re•cep'tion, *n.* 1. act of receiving. 2. fact or manner of being received. 3. social function.

re•cep'tive, *adj.* quick to understand and consider ideas.

re•cess', *n.* 1. temporary cessation of work. 2. alcove. 3. (*pl.*) inner part. —*v.* 4. take or make recess.

re•ces'sion, *n.* 1. withdrawal. 2. economic decline.

re•ces'sion•al, *n.* hymn sung during recession of clergyman and choir.

rec'i•pe', *n.* formula, esp. in cookery.

re•cip'i•ent, *n.* 1. receiver. —*adj.* 2. receiving.

re•cip'ro•cal, *adj.* 1. mutual. —*n.* 2. thing in reciprocal position. —**re•cip'ro•cal•ly,** *adv.*

re•cip'ro•cate', *v.,* **-cated, -cating.** 1. give, feel, etc., in return. 2. move alternately backward and forward. —**re•cip'ro•ca'tion,** *n.*

rec'i•proc'i•ty, *n.* interchange.

re•cit'al, *n.* musical entertainment.

re•cite', *v.,* **-cited, -citing.** 1. repeat from memory. 2. narrate. —**rec'i•ta'tion,** *n.*

reck'less, *adj.* careless. —**reck'less•ly,** *adv.* —**reck'less•ness,** *n.*

reck'on, *v.* 1. calculate. 2. esteem. 3. *Informal.* suppose. 4. deal (with). —**reck'on•er,** *n.*

reck'on•ing, *n.* 1. settling of accounts. 2. navigational calculation.

re•claim', *v.* make usable, as land. —**rec'la•ma'tion,** *n.*

re•cline', *v.,* **-clined, -clining.** lean back.

rec'luse, *n.* person living in seclusion.

re•cog'ni•zance, *n.* bond pledging one to do a particular act.

rec'og•nize', *v.,* **-nized, -nizing.** 1. identify or perceive from previous knowledge. 2. acknowledge formally. 3. greet. —**rec'og•ni'tion,** *n.* —**rec'og•niz'a•ble,** *adj.*

re•coil', *v.* 1. shrink back. 2. spring back. —*n.* 3. act of recoiling.

rec'ol•lect', *v.* remember. —**rec'ol•lec'tion,** *n.*

rec'om•mend', *v.* 1. commend as worthy. 2. advise. —**rec'om•men•da'tion,** *n.*

rec'om•pense', *v.,* **-pensed, -pensing,** *n.* —*v.* 1. repay or reward for services, injury, etc. —*n.* 2. such compensation.

rec'on•cile', *v.,* **-ciled, -ciling.** 1. bring into agreement. 2. restore to friendliness. —**rec'on•cil'i•a'tion,** *n.* —**rec'on•cil'a•ble,** *adj.*

re•con'noi•ter, *v.* search area, esp. for military information. —**re•con'nais•sance** (ri kon'ə səns), *n.*

re•cord', *v.* 1. set down in writing. 2. register for mechanical reproduction. —*n.* (rek'ərd). 3. what is recorded. 4. object from which sound is mechanically reproduced. 5. best rate, etc., yet attained. —*adj.* (rek'ərd). 6. making or being a record. —**re•cord'er,** *n.*

re•count', *v.* narrate.

re-count', *v.* 1. count again. —*n.* (rē'kount'). 2. a second count.

re•coup' (ri kōōp'), *v.* recover; make up.

re'course, *n.* resort for help.

re•cov'er, *v.* 1. get back. 2. reclaim. 3. regain health. —**re•cov'er•a•ble,** *adj.* —**re•cov'er•y,** *n.*

rec're•a'tion, *n.* refreshing enjoyment. —**rec're•a'tion•al,** *adj.*

re•crim'i•nate', *v.,* **-nated, -nating.** accuse in return. —**re•crim'i•na'tion,** *n.*

re•cruit', *n.* 1. new member of military or other group. —*v.* 2. enlist (men).

rec'tan'gle, *n.* parallelogram with four right angles. —**rec•tan'gu•lar,** *adj.*

rec'ti•fy', *v.,* **-fied, -fying.** correct. —**rec'ti•fi'a•ble,** *adj.* —**rec'ti•fi'er,** *n.*

rec'ti•lin'e•ar, *adj.* 1. forming straight line. 2. formed by straight lines.

rec'ti•tude', *n.* rightness of behavior.

rec'tor, *n.* 1. clergyman in charge of parish, etc. 2. head of university, etc.

rec′to•ry, *n., pl.* **-ries.** parsonage.

rec′tum, *n.* lowest part of intestine. **—rec′tal,** *adj.*

re•cum′bent, *adj.* lying down. **—re•cum′ben•cy,** *n.*

re•cu′per•ate′ (-kōō′-), *v.,* **-ated, -ating.** regain health. **—re•cu′per•a′tion,** *n.*

re•cur′, *v.,* **-curred, -curring.** 1. occur again. 2. return in thought, etc. **—re•cur′rence,** *n.* **—re•cur′rent•ly,** *adv.*

re•cy′cle, *v.* **-cled, -cling.** treat (refuse) to extract reusable material.

red, *n., adj.,* **redder, reddest. —n.** 1. color of blood. 2. leftist radical in politics. **—adj.** 3. of or like red. 4. radically to left in politics. **—red′den,** *v.*

re•deem′, *v.* 1. pay off. 2. recover. 3. fulfill. 4. deliver from sin by sacrifice. **—re•deem′er,** *n.* **—re•deem′a•ble,** *adj.* **—re•demp′tion,** *n.*

red′-let′ter, *adj.* memorable.

red′lin•ing, *n.* refusal by banks to grant mortgages in specified urban areas.

red′o•lent, *adj.* 1. odorous. 2. suggestive. **—red′o•lence,** *n.*

re•doubt′, *n.* small isolated fort.

re•dound′, *v.* occur as result.

re•dress′, *v.* 1. set right (wrong). **—n.** (rē′dres). 2. act of redressing.

red tape, excessive attention to prescribed procedure.

re•duce′, *v.,* **-duced, -ducing.** 1. make less in size, rank, etc. 2. put into simpler form or state. 3. remove body weight. **—re•duc′i•ble,** *adj.* **—re•duc′tion,** *n.* **—re•duc′er,** *n.*

re•dun′dant, *adj.* 1. excess. 2. wordy. **—re•dun′dance, re•dun′dan•cy,** *n.* **—re•dun′dant•ly,** *adv.*

red′wood′, *n.* huge evergreen tree of California.

reed, *n.* 1. tall marsh grass. 2. musical pipe made of hollow stalk. 3. small piece of cane or metal at mouth of wind instrument. **—reed′y,** *adj.*

reef, *n.* 1. narrow ridge near the surface of water. 2. *Naut.* part of sail rolled or folded to reduce area. **—v.** 3. shorten (sail) by rolling or folding.

reef′er, *n.* 1. short heavy coat. 2. *Slang.* marijuana cigarette.

reek, *v.* 1. smell strongly and unpleasantly. **—n.** 2. such smell.

reel, *n.* 1. turning object for wound cord, film, etc. 2. lively dance. **—v.** 3. wind on reel. 4. tell easily and at length. 5. sway or stagger. 6. whirl.

reeve, *v.,* **reeved** or **rove, reeved** or **roven, reeving.** pass (rope) through hole.

re•fec′to•ry, *n.* dining hall.

re•fer′, *v.,* **-ferred, -ferring.** 1. direct attention. 2. direct or go for information. 3. apply. **—re•fer′ral,** *n.*

ref′er•ee′, *n.* 1. judge. **—v.** 2. act as referee.

ref′er•ence, *n.* 1. act or fact of referring. 2. something referred to. 3. person from whom one seeks recommendation. 4. testimonial.

ref′er•en′dum, *n.* submission to popular vote of law passed by legislature.

re•fill′, *v.* 1. fill again. **—n.** (rē′fil′). 2. second filling.

re•fine′, *v.,* **-fined, -fining.** 1. free from impurities or error. 2. teach good manners, taste, etc. **—re•fin′er,** *n.* **—re•fine′ment,** *n.*

re•fin′er•y, *n., pl.* **-eries.** establishment for refining, esp. petroleum.

re•flect′, *v.* 1. cast back. 2. show; mirror. 3. bring (credit or discredit) on one. 4. think. **—re•flec′tion,** *n.* **—re•flec′tive,** *adj.* **—re•flec′tor,** *n.*

re′flex, *adj.* 1. denoting involuntary action. 2. bent. **—n.** 3. involuntary movement.

re•flex′ive, *adj.* 1. (of verb) having same subject and object. 2. (of pronoun) showing identity with subject.

re•for′est, *v.* replant with forest trees.

re•form′, *n.* 1. correction of what is wrong. **—v.** 2. change for better. **—re•form′er,** *n.* **—ref′or•ma′tion,** *n.*

re•form′a•to•ry, *n., pl.* **-ries.** prison for young offenders.

re•frac′tion, *n.* change of direction of light or heat rays in passing to another medium. **—re•fract′,** *v.* **—re•frac′tive,** *adj.* **—re•frac′tor,** *n.*

re•frac′to•ry, *adj.* stubborn.

re•frain′, *v.* 1. keep oneself (from). **—n.** 2. recurring passage in song, etc.

re•fresh′, *v.* 1. reinvigorate, as by rest, etc. 2. stimulate. **—re•fresh′ment,** *n.* **—re•fresh′er,** *adj., n.*

re•frig′er•ate′, *v.,* **-ated, -ating.** make or keep cold. **—re•frig′er•ant,** *adj., n.* **—re•frig′er•a′tion,** *n.*

re•frig′er•a′tor, *n.* cabinet for keeping food cold.

ref′uge, *n.* shelter from danger.

ref′u•gee′, *n.* person who flees for safety.

re•fund′, *v.* 1. give back (money). **—n.** (rē′fund). 2. repayment.

re•fur′bish, *v.* renovate.

re•fuse′, *v.,* **-fused, -fusing,** *n.* **—v.** 1. decline to accept. 2. deny (request). **—n.** 3. (ref′yōos). rubbish. **—re•fus′al,** *n.*

re•fute′, *v.,* **-futed, -futing.** prove false or wrong. **—ref′u•ta•ble,** *adj.* **—ref′u•ta′tion,** *n.*

re•gain′, *v.* get again.

re′gal, *adj.* royal.

re•gale′, *v.,* **-galed, -galing.** 1. entertain grandly. 2. feast.

re•ga′li•a, *n.pl.* emblems of royalty, office, etc.

re•gard′, *v.* 1. look upon with particular feeling. 2. respect. 3. look at. 4. concern. **—n.** 5. reference. 6. attention. 7. respect and liking.

re•gard′ing, *prep.* concerning.

re•gard′less, *adv.* 1. without regard; in spite of. **—adj.** 2. heedless.

re•gat′ta, *n.* boat race.

re•gen′er•ate′, *v.,* **-ated, -ating,** *adj.* **—v.** 1. make over for the better. 2. form anew. **—adj.** (-ət). 3. regenerated. **—re•gen′er•a′tion,** *n.* **—re•gen′er•a′tive,** *adj.*

re′gent, *n.* 1. person ruling in place of sovereign. 2. university governor. **—re′gen•cy,** *n.*

re•gime′ (rā zhēm′), *n.* system of rule.

reg′i•men, *n.* 1. course of diet, etc., for health. 2. rule.

reg′i•ment (-mənt), *n.* 1. infantry unit. **—v.** (rej′ə ment′). 2. subject to strict, uniform discipline. **—reg′i•men′tal,** *adj.* **—reg′i•men•ta′tion,** *n.*

re′gion, *n.* area; district. **—re′gion•al,** *adj.* **—re′gion•al•ly,** *adv.*

reg′is•ter, *n.* 1. written list; record. 2. range of voice or instrument. 3. device for controlling passage of warm air. **—v.** 4. enter in register. 5. show. 6. enter oneself on list of voters. **—reg′is•tra′tion,** *n.*

reg′is•trar′, *n.* official recorder.

reg′is•try, *n.* 1. registration. 2. place where register is kept. 3. register.

re•gress′, *v.* return to previous, inferior state. **—re•gres′sion,** *n.* **—re•gres′sive,** *adj.*

re•gret′, *v.,* **-gretted, -gretting,** *n.* **—v.** 1. feel sorry about. **—n.** 2. feeling of loss or sorrow. **—re•gret′ta•ble,** *adj.* **—re•gret′ful,** *adj.*

reg′u•lar, *adj.* 1. usual. 2. symmetrical. 3. recurring at fixed times. 4. orderly. 5. denoting permanent army. **—n.** 6. regular soldier. **—reg′u•lar′i•ty,** *n.***—reg′u•lar•ly,** *adv.*

reg′u•late′, *v.*, **-lated, -lating.** 1. control by rule, method, etc. 2. adjust. —**reg′u•la′tion**, *n.* —**reg′u•la′tor**, *n.*

re•gur′gi•tate′, *v.*, **-tated, -tating.** cast or surge back, esp. from stomach. —**re•gur′gi•ta′tion**, *n.*

re′ha•bil′i•tate′, *v.*, **-tated, -tating.** restore to good condition. —**re′ha•bil′i•ta′tion**, *n.*

re•hearse′, *v.*, **-hearsed, -hearsing.** 1. act or direct in practice for performance. 2. recount in detail. —**re•hears′al**, *n.*

reign, *n.* 1. royal rule. —*v.* 2. have sovereign power or title.

re′im•burse′, *v.*, **-bursed, -bursing.** repay, as for expenses. —**re′im•burse′ment**, *n.*

rein, *n.* narrow strap fastened to bridle or bit for controlling animal.

re′in•car•na′tion, *n.* continuation of soul after death in new body.

rein′deer′, *n.* large arctic deer.

re′in•force′, *v.*, **-forced, -forcing.** strengthen with support, troops, etc. —**re′in•force′ment**, *n.*

re•it′er•ate′, *v.*, **-ated, -ating.** repeat. —**re•it′er•a′tion**, *n.*

re•ject′, *v.* 1. refuse or discard. —*n.* (rē′jekt). 2. something rejected. —**re•jec′tion**, *n.*

re•joice′, *v.*, **-joiced, -joicing.** be or make glad.

re•join′, *v.* answer.

re•join′der, *n.* response.

re•ju′ve•nate′, *v.*, **-nated, -nating.** make young and vigorous again. —**re•ju′ve•na′tion**, *n.*

re•lapse′, *v.*, **-lapsed, -lapsing.** 1. fall back into former state or practice. —*n.* 2. act or instance of relapsing.

re•late′, *v.*, **-lated, -lating.** 1. tell. 2. establish or have relation.

re•la′tion, *n.* 1. connection. 2. relative. 3. narrative. —**re•la′tion•ship′**, *n.*

rel′a•tive, *n.* 1. person connected with another by blood or marriage. —*adj.* 2. comparative. 3. designating word that introduces subordinate clause. —**rel′a•tive•ly**, *adv.*

rel′a•tiv′i•ty, *n.* principle that time, mass, etc. are relative, not absolute concepts.

re•lax′, *v.* 1. make or become less tense, firm, etc. 2. slacken. —**re′lax•a′tion**, *n.*

re′lay, *n.* 1. fresh supply of men, etc., to relieve others. —*v.* 2. carry forward by relays.

re•lease′, *v.*, **-leased, -leasing, n.** —*v.* 1. let go; discharge. —*n.* 2. act or instance of releasing.

rel′e•gate′, *v.*, **-gated, -gating.** 1. consign. 2. turn over. —**rel′e•ga′tion**, *n.*

re•lent′, *v.* become more mild or forgiving. —**re•lent′less**, *adj.*

rel′e•vant, *adj.* having to do with matter in question. —**rel′e•vance**, *n.*

re•li′a•ble, *adj.* trustworthy. —**re•li′a•bil′i•ty**, *n.* —**re•li′a•bly**, *adv.*

re•li′ance, *n.* 1. trust. 2. confidence. —**re•li′ant**, *adj.*

rel′ic, *n.* 1. object surviving from past. 2. personal memorial of sacred person.

re•lief′, *n.* 1. alleviation of pain, distress, etc. 2. help. 3. pleasant change. 4. projection.

re•lieve′, *v.*, **-lieved, -lieving.** 1. ease; alleviate. 2. break sameness of. 3. release or discharge from duty.

re•li′gion, *n.* 1. recognition and worship of controlling superhuman power. 2. particular system of religious belief. —**re•li′gious**, *adj.* —**re•li′gious•ly**, *adv.* —**re•li′gious•ness**, *n.*

re•lin′quish, *v.* give up; surrender.

rel′ish, *n.* 1. enjoyment. 2. chopped pickles, etc. —*v.* 3. take enjoyment in.

re•luc′tant, *adj.* unwilling. —**re•luc′tance**, *n.* —**re•luc′tant•ly**, *adv.*

re•ly′, *v.*, **-lied, -lying.** put trust in.

re•main′, *v.* 1. continue to be. 2. stay; be left. —*n.pl.* 3. that which remains. 4. corpse.

re•main′der, *n.* that which remains.

re•mand′, *v.* send back, as to jail or lower court of law.

re•mark′, *v.* 1. say casually. 2. attention. —*n.* 3. comment. 4. notice.

re•mark′a•ble, *adj.* extraordinary. —**re•mark′a•bly**, *adv.*

rem′e•dy, *v.*, **-died, -dying, n., pl. -dies.** —*v.* 1. cure or alleviate. 2. correct. —*n.* 3. something that remedies. —**re•me′di•al**, *adj.*

re•mem′ber, *v.* 1. recall to or retain in memory. 2. mention as sending greetings. —**re•mem′brance**, *n.*

re•mind′, *v.* cause to remember. —**re•mind′er**, *n.*

rem′i•nisce′, *v.*, **-nisced, -niscing.** recall past experiences. —**rem′i•nis′cence**, *n.* —**rem′i•nis′cent**, *adj.*

re•miss′, *adj.* negligent.

re•mit′, *v.*, **-mitted, -mitting.** 1. send money. 2. pardon. 3. abate. —**re•mis′sion**, *n.*

re•mit′tance, *n.* money, etc., sent.

re•mit′tent, *adj.* (of illness) less severe at times.

rem′nant, *n.* 1. small remaining part. 2. trace.

re•mod′el, *v.* renovate.

re•mon′strance, *n.* protest.

re•mon′strate, *v.*, **-strated, -strating.** protest; plead in protest. —**re′mon•stra′tion, re•mon′strance**, *n.*

re•morse′, *n.* regret for wrongdoing. —**re•morse′ful**, *adj.* —**re•morse′less**, *adj.*

re•mote′, *adj.* 1. far distant. 2. faint. —**re•mote′ly**, *adv.* —**re•mote′ness**, *n.*

re•move′, *v.*, **-moved, -moving, n.** —*v.* 1. take away or off. 2. move to another place. —*n.* 3. distance of separation. —**re•mov′al**, *n.* —**re•mov′a•ble**, *adj.*

re•mu′ner•ate′, *v.*, **-ated, -ating.** pay for work, etc. —**re•mu′ner•a′tion**, *n.* —**re•mu′ner•a′tive**, *adj.*

ren′ais•sance′ (ren′ə säns′), *n.* 1. revival. 2. (*cap.*) cultural period marked by interest in culture of antiquity.

rend, *v.* 1. tear apart. 2. disturb with noise. 3. distress.

ren′der, *v.* 1. cause to be. 2. do, show, or furnish. 3. deliver officially. 4. perform. 5. give back. 6. melt (fat). —**ren•di′tion**, *n.*

ren′dez•vous′ (rän′də vōō′), *n.* appointment or place to meet.

ren′e•gade′, *n.* deserter.

re•nege′ (ri nig′), *v.*, **-neged, -neging.** *Informal.* break promise.

re•new′, *v.* 1. begin or do again. 2. make like new; replenish. —**re•new′al**, *n.*

re•nounce′, *v.*, **-nounced, -nouncing.** give up voluntarily. —**re•nounce′ment**, *n.*

ren′o•vate′, *v.*, **-vated, -vating.** repair; refurbish. —**ren′o•va′tion**, *n.*

re•nown′, *n.* fame.

rent, *n.* 1. Also, **rent′al.** payment for use of property. 2. tear; violent break. —*v.* 3. grant or have use of in return for rent.

re•nun′ci•a′tion, *n.* act of renouncing.

re•pair′, *v.* 1. restore to good condition. 2. go. —*n.* 3. work of repairing. 4. good condition. —**rep′a•ra•ble**, *adj.*

rep′a•ra′tion, *n.* amends for injury.

rep′ar•tee′, *n.* exchange of wit; banter.

re•past′, *n.* meal.

re•pa′tri•ate′, *v.*, **-ated, -ating.** send back to one's native country. —**re•pa′tri•a′tion**, *n.*

re•pay, *v.*, **-paid, -paying.** pay back. —**re•pay′ment**, *n.*

re•peal′, *v.* 1. revoke officially. —*n.* 2. revocation.

re•peat′, *v.* 1. say, tell, or do again. —*n.* 2. act of repeating. 3. musical passage to be repeated. —**re•peat′edly**, *adv.*

re•peat′er, *n.* 1. one that repeats. 2. gun firing several shots in rapid succession.

re•pel′, *v.*, **-pelled, -pelling.** 1. drive back; thrust away. 2. excite disgust or suspicion. —**re•pel′lent**, *adj., n.*

re•pent′, *v.* feel contrition. —**re•pent′ance**, *n.* —**re•pent′ant**, *adj.* —**re•pent′ant•ly**, *adv.*

re′per•cus′sion, *n.* 1. indirect result. 2. echo.

rep′er•toire′ (rep′ər twär′), *n.* group of works that performer or company can perform. Also, **rep′er•to′ry.**

rep′e•ti′tion, *n.* repeated action, utterance, etc. —**rep′e•ti′tious**, *adj.*

re•place′, *v.*, **-placed, -placing.** 1. take place of. 2. provide substitute for. —**re•place′ment**, *n.* —**re•place′a•ble**, *adj.*

re•plen′ish, *v.* make full again. —**re•plen′ish•ment**, *n.*

re•plete′, *adj.* abundantly filled. —**re•ple′tion**, *n.*

rep′li•ca, *n.* copy.

re•ply′, *v.*, **-plied, -plying**, *n.*, *pl.* **-plies.** answer.

re•port′, *n.* 1. statement of events or findings. 2. rumor. 3. loud noise. —*v.* 4. tell of (events or findings). 5. present oneself. 6. inform against. 7. write about for newspaper. —**re•port′er**, *n.*

re•pose′, *n.*, *v.*, **-posed, -posing.** —*n.* 1. rest or sleep. 2. tranquillity. —*v.* 3. rest or sleep. 4. put, as trust. —**re•pose′ful**, *adj.*

re•pos′i•tor′y, *n.*, *pl.* **-tories.** place where things are stored.

re′pos•sess′, *v.* take back.

rep′re•hen′si•ble, *adj.* blameworthy. —**rep′re•hen′si•bly**, *adv.*

rep′re•sent′, *v.* 1. express; signify. 2. act or speak for. 3. portray. —**rep′re•sen•ta′tion**, *n.*

rep′re•sent′a•tive, *n.* 1. one that represents another or others. 2. member of legislative body. —*adj.* 3. representing. 4. typical.

re•press′, *v.* 1. inhibit. 2. suppress. —**re•pres′sive**, *adj.* —**re•pres′sion**, *n.*

re•prieve′, *v.*, **-prieved, -prieving**, *n.* respite.

rep′ri•mand′, *n.* 1. severe reproof. —*v.* 2. reprove severely.

re•pris′al, *n.* infliction of injuries in retaliation.

re•proach′, *v.* 1. blame; upbraid. —*n.* 2. blame; discredit. —**re•proach′ful**, *adj.*

rep′ro•bate′, *n.*, *adj.*, *v.*, **-bated, -bating.** —*n.* 1. hopelessly bad person. —*adj.* 2. depraved. —*v.* 3. condemn. —**rep′ro•ba′tion**, *n.*

re′pro•duce′, *v.*, **-duced, -ducing.** 1. copy or duplicate. 2. produce by propagation. —**re′pro•duc′tion**, *n.* —**re′pro•duc′tive**, *adj.*

re•proof′, *n.* censure.

re•prove′, *v.*, **-proved, -proving.** blame.

rep′tile, *n.* creeping animal, as lizard or snake.

re•pub′lic, *n.* state governed by representatives elected by citizens.

re•pub′li•can, *adj.* 1. or or favoring republic. 2. (*cap.*) of **Republican party**, one of two major political parties of U.S. —*n.* 3. (*cap.*) member of Republican party.

re•pu′di•ate′, *v.*, **-ated, -ating.** reject as worthless, not binding, or false. —**re•pu′di•a′tion**, *n.*

re•pug′nant, *adj.* distasteful. —**re•pug′nance**, *n.*

re•pulse′, *v.*, **-pulsed, -pulsing**, *n.* —*v.* 1. drive back with force. —*n.* 2. act of repulsing. 3. rejection. —**re•pul′sion**, *n.*

re•pul′sive, *adj.* disgusting.

rep′u•ta•ble, *adj.* of good reputation. —**rep′u•ta•bly**, *adv.*

rep′u•ta′tion, *n.* 1. public estimation of character. 2. good name.

re•pute′, *n.*, *v.*, **-puted, -puting.** —*n.* 1. reputation. —*v.* 2. give reputation to. —**re•put′ed•ly**, *adv.*

re•quest′, *v.* 1. ask for. —*n.* 2. act of requesting. 3. what is requested.

Req′ui•em (rek′wē əm). *n.* *Rom. Cath. Ch.* Mass for dead.

re•quire′, *v.*, **-quired, -quiring.** 1. need. 2. demand. —**re•quire′ment**, *n.*

req′ui•site, *adj.* 1. necessary. —*n.* 2. necessary thing.

req′ui•si′tion, *n.* 1. formal order or demand. —*v.* 2. take for official use.

re•quite′, *v.*, **-quited, -quiting.** make return to or for. —**re•quit′al** (-kwī′təl), *n.*

re•scind′ (-sind′), *v.* annul; revoke.

res′cue, *v.*, **-cued, -cuing.** —*v.* 1. free from danger, capture, etc. —*n.* 2. act of rescuing. —**res′cu•er**, *n.*

re•search′, *n.* diligent investigation. —**re•search′er**, *n.*

re•sem′ble, *v.*, **-bled, -bling.** be similar to. —**re•sem′blance**, *n.*

re•sent′, *v.* feel indignant or injured at. —**re•sent′ful**, *adj.* —**re•sent′ment**, *n.*

res′er•va′tion, *n.* 1. act of withholding or setting apart. 2. particular doubt or misgiving. 3. advance assurance of accommodations. 4. tract of land for use of an Indian tribe.

re•serve′, *v.*, **-served, -serving**, *n.*, *adj.* —*v.* 1. keep back; set apart. —*n.* 2. something reserved. 3. part of military force held in readiness to support active forces. 4. reticence; aloofness. —*adj.* 5. kept in reserve.

re•serv′ist, *n.* member of military reserves.

res′er•voir′ (rez′ər vôr′), *n.* 1. place where water is stored for use. 2. supply.

re•side′, *v.*, **-sided, -siding.** 1. dwell. 2. be vested, as powers.

res′i•dence, *n.* 1. dwelling place. 2. act or fact of residing. —**res′i•dent**, *n.* —**res′i•den′tial**, *adj.*

res′i•due′, *n.* remainder. —**re•sid′u•al**, *adj.*

re•sign′, *v.* 1. give up (job, office, etc.). 2. submit, as to fate or force. —**res′ig•na′tion**, *n.*

re•sil′i•ent (ri zil′yənt), *adj.* 1. springing back. 2. recovering readily from adversity. —**re•sil′i•ence**, *n.*

res′in, *n.* exudation from some plants, used in medicines, etc. —**res′in•ous**, *adj.*

re•sist′, *v.* withstand; offer opposition to. —**re•sist′ant**, *adj.* —**re•sist′ance**, *n.* —**re•sist′er**, *n.*

res′o•lute′, *adj.* determined on action or result. —**res′o•lute′ly**, *adv.* —**res′o•lute′ness**, *n.*

res′o•lu′tion, *n.* 1. formal expression of group opinion. 2. determination. 3. solution of problem.

re•solve′, *v.*, **-solved, -solving**, *n.* —*v.* 1. decide firmly. 2. state formally. 3. clear away. 4. solve. —*n.* 5. resolution.

res′o•nant, *adj.* 1. resounding. 2. rich in sound. —**res′o•nance**, *n.* —**res′o•nant•ly**, *adv.*

re•sort′, *v.* 1. apply or turn (to) for use, help, etc. 2. go often. —*n.* 3. place much frequented, esp. for recreation. 4. recourse.

re•sound′ (-zound′), *v.* echo.

re•source′, *n.* 1. source of aid or supply. 2. (*pl.*) wealth.

re•source′ful, *adj.* clever. **—re•source′ful•ly,** *adv.* **—re•source′ful•ness,** *n.*

re•spect′, *n.* 1. detail; point. 2. reference. 3. esteem. *—v.* 4. hold in esteem. **—re•spect′er,** *n.*

re•spect′a•ble, *adj.* 1. worthy of respect. 2. decent. **—re•spect′a•bil′i•ty,** *n.* **—re•spect′a•bly,** *adv.*

re•spect′ful, *adj.* showing respect. **—re•spect′ful•ly,** *adv.* **—re•spect′-ful•ness,** *n.*

re•spect′ing, *prep.* concerning.

re•spec′tive, *adj.* in order previously named. **—re•spec′tive•ly,** *adv.*

res′pi•ra′tor, *n.* apparatus to produce artificial breathing.

re•spire′, *v.,* **-spired, -spiring.** breathe. **—res′pi•ra′tion,** *n.* **—res′-pi•ra•to′ry,** *adj.*

res′pite, *n., v.,* **-pited, -piting.** *—n.* 1. temporary relief or delay. *—v.* 2. relieve or cease temporarily.

re•splend′ent, *adj.* gleaming. **—re•splend′ence,** *n.*

re•spond′, *v.* answer.

re•spond′ent, *adj.* 1. answering. *—n.* 2. *Law.* defendant.

re•sponse′, *n.* reply. **—re•spon′sive,** *adj.* **—re•spon′sive•ly,** *adv.*

re•spon′si•bil′i•ty, *n., pl.* **-ties.** 1. state of being responsible. 2. obligation. 3. initiative.

re•spon′si•ble, *adj.* 1. causing or allowing things to happen. 2. capable of rational thought. 3. reliable. **—re•spon′si•bly,** *adv.*

rest, *n.* 1. refreshing quiet. 2. cessation from motion, work, etc. 3. support. 4. *Music.* interval of silence. 5. remainder; others. *—v.* 6. be quiet or at ease. 7. cease from motion. 8. lie or lay. 9. be based. 10. rely. 11. continue to be. **—rest′ful,** *adj.* **—rest′ful•ly,** *adv.* **—rest′ful•ness,** *n.* **—rest′less,** *adj.* **—rest′less•ly,** *adv.* **—rest′less•ness,** *n.*

res′tau•rant, *n.* public eating place.

res′tau•ra•teur′, *n.* restaurant owner.

res′ti•tu′tion, *n.* 1. reparation. 2. return of rights, etc.

res′tive, *adj.* restless. **—res′tive•ly,** *adv.*

re•store′, *v.,* **-stored, -storing.** 1. bring back, as to use or good condition. 2. give back. **—res′to•ra′tion,** *n.* **—re•stor′a•tive,** *adj., n.*

re•strain′, *v.* 1. hold back. 2. confine.

re•straint′, *n.* 1. restraining influence. 2. confinement. 3. constraint.

re•strict′, *v.* confine; limit. **—re•stric′tion,** *n.* **—re•stric′tive,** *adj.*

re•sult′, *n.* 1. outcome; consequence. *—v.* 2. occur as result. 3. end. **—re•sult′ant,** *adj., n.*

re•sume′, *v.,* **-sumed, -suming.** 1. go on again. 2. take again. **—re•sump′-tion,** *n.*

ré•su•mé (rez′ oͦo mā′), *n.* summary, esp. of education and work.

re•sur′gent, *adj.* rising again. **—re•sur′gence,** *n.*

res′ur•rect′, *v.* bring to life again. **—res′ur•rec′tion,** *n.*

re•sus′ci•tate′ (-sus′ə-), *v.* revive. **—re•sus′ci•ta′tion,** *n.*

re′tail, *n.* 1. sale of goods to consumer. *—v.* 2. sell at retail. **—re′tail•er,** *n.*

re•tain′, *v.* 1. keep or hold. 2. engage. **—re•tain′a•ble,** *adj.*

re•tain′er, *n.* 1. fee paid to secure services. 2. old servant.

re•tal′i•ate′, *v.,* **-ated, -ating.** return like for like, esp. evil. **—re•tal′i•a′-tion,** *n.* **—re•tal′i•a•to′ry,** *adj.*

re•tard′, *v.* delay; hinder. **—re′tar•da′tion,** *n.*

re•tard′ed, *adj.* 1. slow or weak in mental development. *—n.pl.* 2. retarded persons.

retch, *v.* try to vomit.

re•ten′tion, *n.* 1. retaining. 2. power of retaining. 3. memory. **—re•ten′-tive,** *adj.*

ret′i•cent, *adj.* saying little. **—ret′i•cence,** *n.* **—ret′i•cent•ly,** *adv.*

ret′i•na, *n.* coating on back part of eyeball that receives images.

ret′i•nue′ (-nyōͦo′), *n.* train of attendants.

re•tire′, *v.,* **-tired, -tiring.** 1. withdraw. 2. go to bed. 3. end working life. **—re•tire′ment,** *n.*

re•tir′ing, *adj.* shy.

re•tort′, *v.* 1. reply smartly. *—n.* 2. sharp or witty reply. 3. long-necked vessel used in distilling.

re•touch′, *v.* improve (picture) by marking.

re•tract′, *v.* withdraw. **—re•trac′-tion,** *n.* **—re•tract′a•ble,** *adj.*

re•treat′, *n.* 1. forced withdrawal. 2. private place. *—v.* 3. make a retreat. 4. withdraw.

re•trench′, *v.* reduce expenses. **—re•trench′ment,** *n.*

ret′ri•bu′tion, *n.* fair or just return. **—re•trib′u•tive,** *adj.*

re•trieve′, *v.,* **-trieved, -trieving.** *—v.* 1. regain or restore. 2. make amends for. 3. recover (killed

game). *—n.* 4. recovery. **—re•triev′-er,** *n.*

ret′ro•ac′tive, *adj.* applying also to past. **—ret′ro•ac′tive•ly,** *adv.*

ret′ro•fit′, *v.,* **-fitted, -fitting.** refit with newly developed equipment.

ret′ro•grade′, *adj., v.,* **-graded, -grading.** *—adj.* 1. moving backward. *—v.* 2. move backward. 3. degenerate.

ret′ro•gress′, *v.* return to earlier or more primitive condition. **—ret′ro•gres′sion,** *n.* **—ret′ro•gres′sive,** *adj.*

ret′ro•spect′, *n.* occasion of looking back. **—ret′ro•spec′tive,** *adj.* **—ret′-ro•spec′tion,** *n.*

re•turn′, *v.* 1. go or come back to former place or condition. 2. put or bring back. 3. reply. *—n.* 4. act or fact of returning. 5. recurrence. 6. requital. 7. reply. 8. (*often pl.*) profit. 9. report. **—re•turn′a•ble,** *adj.*

re•u•nite′, *v.,* **-nited, -niting.** unite after separation. **—re•un′ion,** *n.*

rev, *n., v.,* **revved, revving.** *Informal.* *—n.* 1. revolution (in machinery). *—v.* 2. increase speed of (motor).

re•vamp′, *v.* renovate.

re•veal′, *v.* disclose.

rev•eil•le (rev′ə lē), *n. Mil.* signal for awakening.

rev′el, *v.* 1. enjoy greatly. 2. make merry. *—n.* 3. merry-making. **—rev′e•ler,** *n.* **—rev′el•ry,** *n.*

rev′e•la′tion, *n.* disclosure.

re•venge′, *n., v.,* **-venged, -venging.** *—n.* 1. harm in return for harm; retaliation. 2. vindictiveness. *—v.* 3. take revenge. **—re•venge′ful,** *adj.* **—re•veng′er,** *n.*

rev′e•nue′, *n.* income, esp. of government or business.

re•ver′ber•ate′, *v.,* **-ated, -ating.** 1. echo back. 2. reflect. **—re•ver′ber•a′tion,** *n.*

re•vere′, *v.,* **-vered, -vering.** hold in deep respect.

rev′er•ence, *n., v.,* **-enced, -encing.** *—n.* 1. deep respect and awe. *—v.* 2. regard with reverence. **—rev′er•ent, rev′eren′tial,** *adj.* **—rev′er•ent•ly,** *adv.*

rev′er•end, *adj.* (*often cap.*) title used with name of clergyman.

rev′er•ie, *n.* fanciful musing. Also, **rev′er•y.**

re•verse′, *adj., n., v.,* **-versed, -versing.** *—adj.* 1. opposite in position, action, etc. 2. of or for backward motion. *—n.* 3. reverse part, position, etc. 4. misfortune. *—v.* 5. turn in the opposite position, direction, or condition. **—re•vers′i•ble,** *adj.*

re•vert′, *v.* go back to earlier state, topic, etc. —**re•ver′sion,** *n.*

re•view′, *n.* 1. critical article. 2. repeated viewing. 3. inspection. —*v.* 4. view again. 5. inspect. 6. survey. 7. write a review of. —**re•view′er,** *n.*

re•vile′, *v.,* **-viled, -viling.** speak abusively to. —**re•vile′ment,** *n.* —**re•vil′er,** *n.*

re•vise′, *v.,* **-vised, -vising.** change or amend content of. —**re•vi′sion,** *n.* —**re•vis′er,** *n.*

re•vi′sion•ism, *n.* departure from accepted doctrine. —**re•vi′sion•ist,** *n., adj.*

re•vi′tal•ize′, *v.,* **-ized, -izing.** bring new vitality to.

re•viv′al, *n.* 1. restoration to life, use, etc. 2. religious awakening. —**re•viv′al•ist,** *n.*

re•vive′, *v.,* **-vived, -viving.** bring back to consciousness, use, notice, etc. —**re•viv′er,** *n.*

re•viv′i•fy, *v.,* **-fied, -fying.** bring back to life.

re•voke′, *v.,* **-voked, -voking.** annul or repeal. —**rev′o•ca•ble,** *adj.* —**rev′o•ca′tion,** *n.*

re•volt′, *v.* 1. rebel. 2. feel disgust. —*n.* 3. rebellion. 4. loathing.

rev′o•lu′tion, *n.* 1. overthrow of established government. 2. fundamental change. 3. rotation. —**rev′o•lu′tion•ar′y,** *adj., n.* —**rev′o•lu′tion•ist,** *n.*

rev′o•lu′tion•ize′, *v.,* **-ized, -izing.** cause fundamental change in.

re•volve′, *v.,* **-volved, -volving.** 1. turn round, as on axis. 2. consider.

re•volv′er, *n.* pistol with revolving cylinder holding cartridges.

re•vue′, *n.* light topical theatrical show.

re•vul′sion, *n.* violent change of feeling, esp. to disgust.

re•ward′, *n.* 1. recompense for merit, service, etc. —*v.* 2. give or receive reward.

rhap′so•dy, *n., pl.* **-dies.** 1. exaggerated expression of enthusiasm. 2. irregular musical composition.

rhe′o•stat′, *n.* device for regulating electric current.

rhe′sus, *n.* kind of monkey found in India.

rhet′o•ric, *n.* 1. skillful use of language. 2. exaggerated speech. —**rhe•tor′i•cal,** *adj.*

rheu′ma•tism′, *n.* disease affecting extremities or back. —**rheu•mat′ic,** *adj., n.*

rhine′stone′, *n.* artificial diamond-like gem.

rhi•noc′er•os, *n.* large thick-skinned mammal with horned snout.

rho•do•den′dron, *n.* flowering evergreen shrub.

rhom′bus, *n., pl.* **-buses, -bi.** oblique-angled parallelogram with all sides equal.

rhu′barb, *n.* garden plant with edible leaf stalks.

rhyme, *n., v.,* **rhymed, rhyming.** —*n.* 1. agreement in end sounds of lines or words. 2. verse with such correspondence. —*v.* 3. make or form rhyme.

rhythm, *n.* movement with uniformly recurring beat. —**rhyth′mic, rhyth′mi•cal,** *adj.* —**rhyth′mi•cal•ly,** *adv.*

rib, *n., v.,* **ribbed, ribbing.** —*n.* 1. one of the slender curved bones enclosing chest. 2. riblike part. —*v.* 3. furnish with ribs. 4. *Informal.* tease.

rib′ald, *adj.* bawdy in speech. —**rib′ald•ry,** *n.*

rib′bon, *n.* strip of silk, rayon, etc.

ri′bo•fla′vin (rī′bō flā′vin), *n.* important vitamin in milk, fresh meat, eggs, etc.

rice, *n.* edible starchy grain of grass grown in warm climates.

rich, *adj.* 1. having great possessions. 2. abounding; fertile. 3. costly. 4. containing butter, eggs, cream, etc. 5. strong; vivid. 6. mellow. —*n.* 7. rich people. —**rich′ly,** *adv.* —**rich′ness,** *n.*

rich′es, *n.pl.* wealth.

rick, *n.* stack of hay, etc.

rick′ets, *n.* childhood disease often marked by bone deformities.

rick′et•y, *adj.* shaky.

rick′shaw, *n.* two-wheeled passenger vehicle pulled by man.

ric′o•chet′ (rik′ə shā′), *v.,* **-cheted, -cheting,** *n.* —*v.* 1. rebound from a flat surface. —*n.* 2. such a movement.

rid, *v.,* **rid** or **ridded, ridding.** clear or free of. —**rid′dance,** *n.*

rid′dle, *n., v.,* **-dled, -dling.** —*n.* 1. puzzling question or matter. 2. coarse sieve. —*v.* 3. speak perplexingly. 4. pierce with many holes. 5. put through sieve.

ride, *v.,* **rode, ridden, riding,** *n.* —*v.* 1. be carried in traveling. 2. sit on and manage (horse, etc.). 3. rest on something. —*n.* 4. journey on a horse, etc.

rid′er, *n.* 1. person that rides. 2. clause attached to legislative bill before passage.

ridge, *n., v.,* **ridged, ridging.** —*n.* 1. long narrow elevation. —*v.* 2. form with ridge.

rid′i•cule′, *n., v.,* **-culed, -culing.** —*n.* 1. derision. —*v.* 2. deride.

ri•dic′u•lous, *adj.* absurd. —**ri•dic′u•lous•ly,** *adv.*

rife, *adj.* 1. widespread. 2. abounding.

riff′raff′, *n.* rabble.

ri′fle, *n., v.,* **-fled, -fling.** —*n.* 1. shoulder firearm with spirally grooved barrel. —*v.* 2. cut spiral grooves in (gun barrel). 3. search through to rob. 4. steal. —**ri′fle•man,** *n.*

rift, *n.* split.

rig, *v.,* **rigged, rigging,** *n.* —*v.* 1. fit with tackle and other parts. 2. put together as makeshift. 3. manipulate fraudulently or artificially. —*n.* 4. arrangement of masts, booms, tackle etc. 5. equipment; outfit. —**rig′ger,** *n.*

rig′ging, *n.* ropes and chains that support and work masts, sails, etc.

right, *adj.* 1. just or good. 2. correct. 3. in good condition. 4. on side that is toward the east when one faces north. 5. straight. —*n.* 6. that which is right. 7. right side. 8. that justly due one. 9. conservative side in politics. —*adv.* 10. directly; completely. 11. set correctly. 12. in right position. 13. correct. —**right′ly,** *adv.* —**right′ness,** *n.* —**right′ist,** *adj., n.*

right angle, 90-degree angle.

right′eous, *adj.* virtuous. —**right′eous•ly,** *adv.* —**right′eous•ness,** *n.*

right′ful, *adj.* belonging by or having just claim. —**right′ful•ly,** *adv.*

rig′id, *adj.* 1. stiff; inflexible. 2. rigorous. —**ri•gid′i•ty,** *n.* —**rig′id•ly,** *adv.*

rig′ma•role′, *n.* confused talk.

rig′or, *n.* 1. strictness. 2. hardship. —**rig′or•ous,** *adj.* —**rig′or•ous•ly,** *adv.*

ri′gor mor′tis, stiffening of body after death.

rile, *v.,* **riled, riling.** *Informal.* vex.

rill, *n.* small brook.

rim, *n., v.,* **rimmed, rimming.** —*n.* 1. outer edge. —*v.* 2. furnish with rim.

rime, *n., v.,* **rimed, riming.** —*n.* 1. rhyme. —*v.* 2. rough white frost. 3. cover with rime.

rind, *n.* firm covering, as of fruit or cheese.

ring, *n., v.,* **rang, rung** (for 11, **ringed**), **ringing.** —*n.* 1. round band for a finger. 2. any circular band. 3. enclosed area. 4. group cooperating for selfish purpose. 5. ringing sound. 6. telephone call. —v. 7. sound clearly and resonantly. 8. seem; appear. 9. be filled with sound. 10. signal by bell. 11. form ring around. —**ring'er,** n.

ring'lead'er, n. leader in mischief.

ring'let, n. curl of hair.

ring'worm', n. contagious skin disease.

rink, n. floor or sheet of ice for skating on.

rinse, v., **rinsed, rinsing,** n. —v. 1. wash lightly. —n. 2. rinsing act. 3. preparation for rinsing.

ri'ot, n. 1. disturbance by mob. 2. wild disorder. —v. 3. take part in riot. —**ri'ot•ous,** adj.

rip, v., **ripped, ripping,** n. tear. —**rip'-per,** n.

ripe, adj., **riper, ripest.** fully developed; mature. —**rip'en,** v. —**ripe'ly,** adv. —**ripe'ness,** n.

rip'-off', n. Slang. theft or exploitation.

rip'ple, v., **-pled, -pling,** n. —v. 1. form small waves. —n. 2. pattern of small waves.

rise, v., **rose, risen, rising,** n. —v. 1. get up. 2. revolt. 3. appear. 4. originate. 5. move upward. 6. increase. 7. (of dough) expand. —n. 8. upward movement. 9. origin. 10. upward slope. —**ris'er,** n.

ris'i•bil'i•ty (riz'-), n., pl. **-ties.** faculty of laughing.

risk, n. 1. dangerous chance. —v. 2. expose to risk. 3. take risk of. —**risk'y,** adj.

ris•qué' (-kā'), adj. almost immodest.

rite, n. ceremonial act.

rit'u•al, n. system of religious or other rites. —**rit'u•al•ism',** n.

ri'val, n. 1. competitor. 2. equal. —adj. 3. being a rival. —v. 4. compete with. 5. match. —**ri'val•ry,** n.

rive, v., **rived, rived** or **riven, riving.** split.

riv'er, n. large natural stream of water.

riv'et, n. 1. metal bolt hammered after insertion. —v. 2. fasten with rivets.

riv'u•let, n. small stream.

roach, n. cockroach.

road, n. 1. open way for travel. 2. Also, **road'stead'.** anchorage near shore.

road'ster, n. open single-seated automobile.

roam, v. wander; rove.

roan, adj. 1. (of horses) sorrel, chestnut, or bay with gray or white spots. —n. 2. roan horse.

roar, v. 1. make loud, deep sound. —n. 2. loud, deep sound. 3. loud laughter.

roast, v. 1. cook by dry heat. —n. 2. roasted meat.

rob, v., **robbed, robbing.** deprive of unlawfully. —**rob'ber,** n. —**rob'-ber•y,** n.

robe, n., v., **robed, robing.** —n. 1. long loose garment. 2. wrap or covering. —v. 3. clothe, esp ceremonially.

rob'in, n. red-breasted bird.

ro'bot, n. mechanical man.

ro•bust', adj. strong and healthy.

rock, n. 1. mass of stone. 2. Also, **rock-'n'-roll.** popular music with steady, insistent rhythm. —v. 3. move back and forth. —**rock'y,** adj.

rock'er, n. curved support of cradle or **rock'ing chair.**

rock'et, n. tube propelled by discharge of gases from it.

ro•co'co, n. elaborate decorative style of many curves. —**ro•co'co,** adj.

rod, n. 1. slender shaft. 2. linear measure of 5½ yards.

ro'dent, n. small gnawing or nibbling mammal.

ro'de•o', n. exhibition of cowboy skills.

roe, n., pl. **roes, roe.** 1. small old-world deer. 2. fish eggs or spawn.

rog'er, interj. (message) received.

rogue, n. rascal. —**ro'guish,** adj. —**ro'guer•y,** n.

roil, v. 1. make muddy. 2. vex. —**roil'y,** adj.

roist'er, v. 1. swagger. 2. carouse. —**roist'er•er,** n.

role, n. part of function, as of character in play. Also, **rôle.**

roll, v. 1. move by turning. 2. rock. 3. have deep, loud sound. 4. flatten with roller. 5. form into roll or ball. —n. 6. list; register. 7. anything cylindrical. 8. small cake. 9. deep long sound. —**roll'er,** n.

roller skate, skate with four wheels. —**roller-skate,** v.

rol'lick•ing, adj. jolly.

ro•maine', n. kind of lettuce.

Ro'man, 1. native or citizen of Rome or Roman Empire. 2. (l.c.) upright style of printing type. —**Ro'man,** adj.

Roman Catholic Church, Christian Church of which Pope (Bishop of Rome) is head. —**Roman Catholic.**

ro•mance', n., v., **-manced, -mancing.** —n. 1. colorful, imaginative tale. 2. colorful, fanciful quality. 3. love affair. —v. 4. act romantically. 5. tell fanciful, false story. —**ro•man'tic,** adj. —**ro•man'ti•cal•ly,** adv.

Roman numerals, system of numbers using letters as symbols: I = 1, V = 5, X = 10, L = 50, C = 100, D = 500, M = 1,000.

ro•man'ti•cism, n. romantic spirit or artistic style or movement. —**ro•man'ti•cist,** n.

romp, v., n. frolic.

romp'ers, n.pl. child's loose outer garment.

rood (rōod), n. 1. crucifix. 2. one-quarter of an acre.

roof, n., pl. **roofs.** 1. upper covering of building. —v. 2. provide with roof. —**roof'er,** n.

rook (rōok), n. 1. European crow. 2. chess piece; castle. —v. 3. cheat.

rook'ie, n. Slang. recruit.

room, n. 1. separate space within building. 2. space. —v. 3. lodge. —**room'er,** n. —**room'mate',** n. —**room'y,** adj.

roost, n. 1. perch where fowls rest at night. —v. 2. sit on roost.

roost'er, n. male chicken.

root, n. 1. part of plant growing underground. 2. embedded part. 3. origin. 4. quantity that, when multiplied by itself so many times, produces given quantity. —v. 5. establish roots. 6. implant. 7. root out, exterminate. 8. dig with snout. 9. Informal. cheer encouragingly. —**root'er,** n.

rope, n., v., **roped, roping.** —n. 1. strong twisted cord. —v. 2. fasten or catch with rope.

ro'sa•ry, n., pl. **-ries.** Rom. Cath. Ch. 1. series of prayers. 2. string of beads counted in saying rosary.

rose, n. thorny plant having showy, fragrant flowers.

ro'se•ate, adj. 1. rose-colored. 2. promising; bright.

ro•sette', n. rose-shaped ornament.

Rosh' Ha•sha'na (rōsh' hä shä'nə), Jewish New Year.

ros'in, n. solid left after distilling off turpentine from pine resin.

ros'ter, n. list of persons, groups, events, etc.

ros'trum, n. speakers' platform.

ros'y, adj., **rosier, rosiest.** 1. pinkish-red. 2. cheerful. 3. bright. —**ros'i•ly,** adv. —**ros'i•ness,** n.

rot, *v.,* **rotted, rotting,** *n.* —*v.* 1. decay. —*n.* 2. decay. 3. disease marked by decay of tissue.

ro′tate, *v.,* **-tated, -tating.** turn on or as on axis. —**ro′ta•ry,** *adj.* —**ro•ta′-tion,** *n.* —**ro•ta′tor,** *n.*

rote, *n.* 1. routine way. 2. by rote, from memory in mechanical way.

ro•tis′ser•ie, *n.* rotating machine for roasting.

ro′tor, *n.* rotating part.

rot′ten, *adj.* 1. decaying. 2. corrupt. —**rot′ten•ly,** *adv.* —**rot′ten•ness,** *n.*

ro•tund′, *adj.* round. —**ro•tun′di•ty,** *n.*

ro•tun′da, *n.* round room.

rou•é′ (rōō ā′), *n.* dissolute person.

rouge, *n., v.,* **rouged, rouging.** —*n.* 1. red cosmetic for cheeks and lips. 2. red polishing agent for metal. —*v.* 3. color with rouge.

rough, *adj.* 1. not smooth. 2. violent in action or motion. 3. harsh. 4. crude. —*n.* 5. rough thing or part. —*v.* 6. make rough. —**rough′ly,** *adv.* —**rough′ness,** *n.*

rough′age, *n.* coarse part, as of digested food.

rou•lette′ (rōō-), *n.* gambling game based on spinning disk.

round, *adj.* 1. circular, curved, or spherical. 2. complete. 3. expressed as approximate number. 4. sonorous. —*n.* 5. something round. 6. complete course, series, etc. 7. part of beef thigh between rump and leg. 8. song in which voices enter at intervals. —*adv.* 9. in or as in a circle. 10. in circumference. —*prep.* 11. around. —*v.* 12. make or become round. 13. complete. 14. bring together. —**round′ness,** *n.*

round′a•bout′, *adj.* indirect.

round′ly, *adv.* unsparingly.

round′up′, *n.* 1. bringing together. 2. summary.

rouse, *v.,* **roused, rousing.** stir up; arouse.

roust′a•bout′, *n.* heavy laborer.

rout, *n.* 1. defeat ending in disorderly flight. —*v.* 2. force to flee in disorder.

route (rōōt), *n., v.,* **routed, routing.** —*n.* 1. course of travel. —*v.* 2. send by or plan route.

rou•tine′, *n.* 1. regular order of action. —*adj.* 2. like or by routine. 3. ordinary.

rove, *v.,* **roved, roving.** wander aimlessly. —**rov′er,** *n.*

row (rō), *v.* 1. propel by oars. 2. (rou). dispute noisily. —*n.* 3. trip in rowboat. 4. persons or things in line. 5. (rou). noisy dispute. —**row′boat′,** *n.*

row′dy, *adj.,* **-dier, -diest,** *n., pl.* **-dies.** —*adj.* 1. rough and disorderly. —*n.* 2. rowdy person.

roy′al, *adj.* of kings or queens. —**roy′al•ly,** *adv.*

roy′al•ist, *n.* person favoring royalty. —**royalist,** *adj.* —**roy′al•ism,** *n.*

roy′al•ty, *n., pl.* **-ties.** 1. royal persons. 2. royal power. 3. share of proceeds, paid to an author, inventor, etc.

rub, *v.,* **rubbed, rubbing,** *n.* —*v.* 1. apply pressure or friction to in cleaning, smoothing, etc. 2. press against with friction. —*n.* 3. act of rubbing. 4. difficulty.

rub′ber, *n.* 1. elastic material from a tropical tree. 2. *pl.* overshoes. —**rub′ber•ize′,** *v.* —**rub′ber•y,** *adj.*

rub′bish, *n.* 1. waste. 2. nonsense.

rub′ble, *n.* broken stone.

ru•bi•cund′ (rōō′bə kund′), *adj.* red.

ru′by, *n., pl.* **-bies.** deep-red gem.

ruck′sack′, *n.* type of knapsack.

rud′der, *n.* turning flat piece for steering vessel or aircraft.

rud′dy, *adj.,* **-dier, -diest.** having healthy red color.

rude, *adj.,* **ruder, rudest.** 1. discourteous. 2. unrefined; crude. —**rude′ly,** *adv.* —**rude′ness,** *n.*

ru′di•ment (rōō′-), *n.* basic thing to learn. —**ru′di•men′ta•ry,** *adj.*

rue, *v.,* **rued, ruing.** regret. —**rue′ful,** *adj.*

ruff, *n.* deep full collar.

ruf′fi•an, *n.* rough or lawless person.

ruf′fle, *v.,* **-fled, -fling,** *n.* —*v.* 1. make uneven. 2. disturb. 3. gather in folds. 4. beat (drum) softly and steadily. —*n.* 5. break in evenness. 6. band of cloth, etc., gathered on one edge. 7. soft steady beat.

rug, *n.* floor covering.

rug′ged, *adj.* 1. roughly irregular. 2. severe. —**rug′ged•ly,** *adv.* —**rug′ged•ness,** *n.*

ru′in, *n.* 1. downfall; destruction. 2. (*pl.*) remains of fallen building, etc. —*v.* 3. bring or come to ruin or ruins. —**ru′in•a′tion,** *n.* —**ru′in•ous,** *adj.*

rule, *n., v.,* **ruled, ruling.** —*n.* 1. principle; regulation. 2. control. 3. ruler (def. 2). —*v.* 4. control. 5. decide in the manner of a judge. 6. mark with ruler. —**rul′ing,** *n., adj.*

rul′er, *n.* 1. person who rules. 2. straight-edged strip for measuring, drawing lines, etc.

rum, *n.* alcoholic liquor made esp. from molasses.

rum′ba, *n.* Cuban dance.

rum′ble, *v.,* **-bled, -bling,** *n.* —*v.* 1. make long, deep, heavy sound. —*n.* 2. such sound.

ru′mi•nant, *n.* 1. cud-chewing mammal, as cows. —*adj.* 2. cud-chewing.

ru′mi•nate′, *v.,* **-nated, -nating.** 1. chew cud. 2. meditate. —**ru′mi•na′-tion,** *n.*

rum′mage, *v.,* **-maged, -maging.** search.

rum′my, *n.* 1. card game. 2. *Slang.* drunkard.

ru′mor, *n.* 1. unconfirmed but widely repeated story. —*v.* 2. tell as rumor.

rump, *n.* hind part of body.

rum′ple, *v.,* **-pled, -pling,** *n.* wrinkle or ruffle.

rum′pus, *n. Informal.* noise; disturbance.

run, *v.,* **ran, run, running.** 1. advance quickly. 2. be candidate. 3. flow; melt. 4. extend. 5. operate. 6. be exposed to. 7. manage. —*n.* 8. act or period of running. 9. raveled line in knitting. 10. freedom of action. 11. scoring unit in baseball.

run′-a•round′, *n. Informal.* evasive treatment.

run′a•way′, *n.* 1. fugitive; deserter. 2. something that has broken away from control. —*adj.* 3. escaped; fugitive. 4. uncontrolled.

run′-down′, *adj.* 1. fatigued; weary. 2. fallen into disrepair. 3. (of spring-operated machine) not running because of not being wound.

rune, *n.* any of the characters of the alphabet used by ancient Germanic-speaking peoples. —**ru′nic,** *adj.*

rung, *n.* 1. ladder step. 2. bar between chair legs.

run′ner, *n.* 1. one that runs. 2. messenger. 3. blade of skate. 4. strip of fabric, carpet, etc.

run′ner-up′, *n.* competitor finishing in second place.

runt, *n.* undersized person or thing.

run′way′, *n.* strip where airplanes take off and land.

rup′ture, *n., v.,* **-tured, -turing.** —*n.* 1. break. 2. hernia. —*v.* 3. break. 4. affect with hernia.

ru′ral, *adj.* of or in the country.

ruse, *n.* trick.

rush, *v.* 1. move with speed or violence. —*n.* 2. act of rushing. 3. hostile attack. 4. grasslike herb growing in marshes. —*adj.* 5. requiring or marked by haste.

rus′set, *n.* reddish brown.

Rus′sian, *n.* native or language of Russia. —**Russian,** *adj.*

rust, *n.* 1. red-orange coating that forms on iron and steel exposed to air and moisture. 2. plant disease.

—*v.* 3. make or become rusty. —**rust′y,** *adj.*

rus′tic, *adj.* 1. rural. 2. simple. —*n.* 3. country person.

rus′ti•cate′, *v.,* **-cated, -cating.** go to or live in the country.

rus′tle, *v.,* **-tled, -tling.** —*v.* 1. make small soft sounds. 2. steal (cattle, etc.). —*n.* 3. rustling sound. —**rus′tler,** *n.*

rut, *n., v.,* **rutted, rutting.** —*n.* 1. furrow or groove worn in the ground. 2. period of sexual excitement in male deer, goats, etc. —*v.* 3. make ruts in. 4. be in rut. —**rut′ty,** *adj.*

ru•ta•ba′ga (rōō′tə bā′gə), *n.* yellow turnip.

ruth′less, *adj.* pitiless. —**ruth′less•ness,** *n.*

rye, *n.* cereal grass used for flour, feed, and whiskey.

S

S, s, *n.* nineteenth letter of English alphabet.

Sab′bath, *n.* day of religious observance and rest, observed on Saturday by Jews and on Sunday by most Christians.

sab•bat′i•cal, *n.* 1. paid leave of absence for study. —*adj.* 2. (*cap.*) of the Sabbath.

sa′ber, *n.* one-edged sword. Also, **sa′bre.**

sa′ble, *n.* small mammal with dark-brown fur.

sab′o•tage′, *n., v.,* **-taged, -taging.** —*n.* 1. willful injury to equipment, etc. —*v.* 2. attack by sabotage. —**sab′o•teur′,** *n.*

sac, *n.* baglike part.

sac′cha•rin (sak′ə rin), *n.* sweet substance used as sugar substitute.

sac′cha•rine, *adj.* 1. overly sweet. —*n.* 2. saccharin.

sac′er•do′tal (sas′ ər-), *adj.* priestly.

sa•chet′ (-shā′), *n.* small bag of perfumed powder.

sack, *n.* 1. large stout bag. 2. bag. 3. *Brit. Slang.* dismissal. 4. plundering. —*v.* 5. put into a sack. 6. *Brit. Slang.* dismiss. 7. plunder; loot. —**sack′ing,** *n.*

sack′cloth′, *n.* coarse cloth worn for penance.

sac′ra•ment, *n.* 1. solemn rite in Christian church. 2. (*cap.*) Eucharist. —**sac′ra•men′tal,** *adj.*

sa′cred, *adj.* 1. holy. 2. secured against violation. —**sa′cred•ly,** *adv.* —**sa′cred•ness,** *n.*

sac′ri•fice′, *n., v.,* **-ficed, -ficing.** —*n.* 1. offer of life, treasure, etc., to deity. 2. surrender of something for purpose. —*v.* 3. give as sacrifice —**sac′ri•fi′cial,** *adj.*

sac′ri•lege (-lij), *n.* profanation of anything sacred. —**sac′ri•le′gious,** *adj.*

sac′ris•tan (sak′ri stan), *n.* sexton.

sac′ris•ty, *n., pl.* **-ties.** room in church, etc., where sacred objects are kept.

sac′ro•il′i•ac′, *n.* joint in lower back.

sac′ro•sanct′, *adj.* sacred.

sad, *adj.,* **sadder, saddest.** sorrowful. —**sad′den,** *v.* —**sad′ly,** *adv.* —**sad′ness,** *n.*

sad′dle, *n., v.,* **-dled, -dling.** —*n.* 1. seat for rider on horse, etc. 2. anything resembling saddle. —*v.* 3. put saddle on. 4. burden.

sad′ism, *n.* morbid enjoyment in being cruel. —**sad′ist,** *n.* —**sa•dis′tic,** *adj.*

sa•fa′ri (sə fär′ē), *n.* (in E. Africa) journey; hunting expedition.

safe, *adj.,* **safer, safest,** *n.* —*adj.* 1. secure or free from danger. 2. dependable. —*n.* 3. stout box for valuables. —**safe′ty,** *n.* —**safe′ly,** *adv.* —**safe′keep′ing,** *n.*

safe′guard′, *n.* 1. something that ensures safety. —*v.* 2. protect.

saf′fron, *n.* bright yellow seasoning.

sag, *v.,* **sagged, sagging,** *n.* —*v.* 1. bend, esp. in middle, from weight or pressure. 2. hang loosely. —*n.* 3. sagging place.

sa′ga, *n.* heroic tale.

sa•ga′cious, *adj.* shrewd and practical. —**sa•gac′i•ty,** *n.*

sage, *n., adj.,* **sager, sagest.** —*n.* 1. wise man. 2. herb with gray-green leaves used in seasoning. —*adj.* 3. wise; prudent. —**sage′ly,** *adv.* —**sage′ness,** *n.*

sa′go, *n.* starchy substance from some palms.

sa′hib (sä′ib), *n.* (in India) term of respect for European.

said, *adj.* named before.

sail, *n.* 1. sheet spread to catch wind to propel vessel or windmill. 2. trip on sailing vessel. —*v.* 3. move by action of wind. 4. travel over water. —**sail′or,** *n.*

sail′fish′, *n.* large fish with upright fin.

saint, *n.* holy person. —**saint′hood,** *n.* —**saint′ly,** *adj.*

sake, *n.* 1. interest; account. 2. purpose. 3. (sä′kē). rice wine.

sal′a•ble, *adj.* subject to or fit for sale. Also, **sale′a•ble.**

sa•la′cious (-lā′shəs), *adj.* lewd.

sal′ad, *n.* dish esp. of raw vegetables or fruit.

sal′a•man′der, *n.* small amphibian.

sa•la′mi, *n.* kind of sausage.

sal′a•ry, *n., pl.* **-ries.** fixed payment for regular work. —**sal′a•ried,** *adj.*

sale, *n.* 1. act of selling. 2. opportunity to sell. 3. occasion of selling at reduced prices. —**sales′man,** *n.* —**sales′la′dy, sales′wom′an,** *n.fem.* —**sales′per′son,** —**sales′people,** *n.pl.* —**sales′room′,** *n.*

sa′li•ent (sā′-), *adj.* 1. conspicuous. 2. projecting. —*n.* 3. projecting part. —**sa′li•ence,** *n.* —**sa′li•ent•ly,** *adv.*

sa′line (sā′līn), *adj.* salty. —**sa•lin′i•ty,** *n.*

sa•li′va, *n.* fluid secreted into mouth by glands. —**sal′i•var′y,** *adj.*

sal′low, *adj.* having sickly complexion.

sal′ly, *n., pl.* **-lies,** *v.,* **-lied, -lying.** —*n.* 1. sudden attack by besieged troops. 2. outward burst or rush. 3. witty remark. —*v.* 4. make sally.

salm′on, *n.* pink-fleshed food fish of northern waters.

sa•lon′, *n.* 1. drawing room. 2. art gallery.

sa•loon′, *n.* 1. place where intoxicating liquors are sold and drunk. 2. public room.

salt, *n.* 1. sodium chloride, occurring as mineral, in sea water, etc. 2. chemical compound derived from acid and base. 3. wit. 4. *Informal.* sailor.

—*v.* 5. season or preserve with salt. —**salt'y**, *adj.*

SALT, *n.* Strategic Arms Limitation Talks.

salt'pe'ter, *n.* potassium nitrate.

sa•lu'bri•ous, *adj.* healthful. —**sa•lu'bri•ous•ly**, *adv.* —**sa•lub'ri•ty**, *n.*

sal'u•ta'ry, *adj.* healthful; beneficial.

sal'u•ta'tion, *n.* 1. salute. 2. formal opening of letter.

sa•lute', *v.*, **-luted, -luting,** *n.* —*v.* 1. express respect or good will, esp. in greeting. —*n.* 2. act of saluting.

sal'vage, *n.*, *v.*, **-vaged, -vaging.** —*n.* 1. act of saving ship or cargo at sea. 2. property saved. —*v.* 3. save from shipwreck or destruction.

sal•va'tion, *n.* 1. deliverance. 2. deliverance from sin.

salve (sav), *n.*, *v.*, **salved, salving.** —*n.* 1. ointment for sores. —*v.* 2. apply salve to.

sal'ver, *n.* tray.

sal'vi•a, *n.* plant of mint family.

sal'vo, *n.* discharge of guns, bombs, etc., in rapid series.

Sa•mar'i•tan, *n.* compassionate and helpful person.

same, *adj.* 1. identical or corresponding. 2. unchanged. 3. just mentioned. —*n.* 4. same person or thing. —**same'ness**, *n.*

sam'o•var', *n.* metal urn.

sam'pan, *v.* small Far Eastern boat.

sam'ple, *n.*, *adj.*, *v.*, **-pled, -pling.** —*n.* 1. small amount to show nature or quality. —*adj.* 2. as sample. —*v.* 3. test by sample.

sam'pler, *n.* needlework done to show skill.

san'a•to'ri•um, *n.* sanitarium.

sanc'ti•fy', *v.*, **-fied, -fying.** 1. make holy. 2. give sanction to. —**sanc'ti•fi•ca'tion**, *n.*

sanc'ti•mo'ny, *n.* hypocritical devoutness. —**sanc'ti•mo'ni•ous**, *adj.*

sanc'tion, *n.* 1. permission or support. 2. legal action by group of states against another state. —*v.* 3. authorize; approve.

sanc'ti•ty, *n.* 1. holiness. 2. sacred character.

sanc'tu•ar'y, *n.*, *pl.* **-aries.** 1. holy place. 2. area around altar. 3. place of immunity from arrest or harm.

sanc'tum, *n.* private place.

sand, *n.* 1. fine grains of rock. 2. (*pl.*) sandy region. —*v.* 3. smooth with sandpaper. —**sand'er**, *n.* —**sand'y**, *adj.*

san'dal, *n.* shoe consisting of sole and straps.

san'dal•wood', *n.* fragrant wood.

sand'pa'per, *n.* 1. paper coated with sand. —*v.* 2. smooth with sandpaper.

sand'pip'er, *n.* small shore bird.

sand'stone', *n.* rock formed chiefly of sand.

sand'wich, *n.* 1. two slices of bread with meat, etc., between. —*v.* 2. insert.

sane, *adj.*, **saner, sanest.** free from mental disorder; rational. —**sane'ly**, *adv.*

san'gui•nar'y, *adj.* 1. bloody. 2. bloodthirsty.

san'guine (-gwin), *adj.* 1. hopeful. 2. red.

san'i•tar'i•um, *n.* place for treatment of invalids and convalescents.

san'i•tar'y, *adj.* of health. —**san'i•tar'i•ly**, *adv.*

san'i•ta'tion, *n.* application of sanitary measures.

san'i•ty, *n.* 1. soundness of mind. 2. good judgment.

San'skrit, *n.* extinct language of India.

sap, *n.*, *v.*, **sapped, sapping.** —*n.* 1. trench dug to approach enemy's position. 2. juice of woody plant. —*v.* 3. *Slang.* fool. 4. weaken; undermine. —**sap'per**, *n.*

sa'pi•ent, *adj.* wise. —**sa'pi•ence**, *n.*

sap'ling, *n.* young tree.

sap'phire, *n.* deep-blue gem.

sap'suck'er, *n.* kind of woodpecker.

sar'casm, *n.* 1. harsh derision. 2. ironical gibe. —**sar•cas'tic**, *adj.* —**sar•cas'ti•cal•ly**, *adv.*

sar•coph'a•gus, *n.*, *pl.* **-gi.** stone coffin.

sar•dine', *n.* small fish, often preserved in oil.

sar•don'ic, *adj.* sarcastic. —**sar•don'i•cal•ly**, *adv.*

sa'ri (sär'ē), *n.* length of cloth used as dress in India.

sa•rong', *n.* skirtlike garment.

sar'sa•pa•ril'la (sas'pə ril'ə), *n.* tropical American plant.

sar•to'ri•al, *adj.* of tailors or tailoring.

sash, *n.* 1. band of cloth usually worn as belt. 2. framework for panes of window, etc.

sas'sa•fras', *n.* American tree with aromatic root bark.

Sa'tan, *n.* chief evil spirit; devil. —**sa•tan'ic**, *adj.*

satch'el, *n.* handbag.

sate, *v.*, **sated, sating.** satisfy or surfeit.

sa•teen', *n.* glossy cotton fabric.

sat'el•lite', *n.* 1. body that revolves around planet. 2. subservient follower.

sa'ti•ate' (-shē-), *v.*, **-ated, -ating.** surfeit. —**sa'ti•a'tion, sa•ti'e•ty**, *n.*

sat'in, *n.* glossy silk or rayon fabric. —**sat'in•y**, *adj.*

sat'ire, *n.* use of irony or ridicule in exposing vice, folly, etc. —**sa•tir'i•cal, sa•tir'ic**, *adj.* —**sa•tir'i•cal•ly**, *adv.*

sat'i•rize', *v.*, **-rized, -rizing.** subject to satire. —**sat'i•rist**, *n.*

sat'is•fy', *v.*, **-fied, -fying.** 1. fulfill desire, need, etc. 2. convince. 3. pay. —**sat'is•fac'tion**, *n.* —**sat'is•fac'to•ry**, *adj.* —**sat'is•fac'to•ri•ly**, *adv.*

sat'u•rate', *v.*, **-rated, -rating.** soak completely. —**sat'u•ra'tion**, *n.*

Sat'ur•day, *n.* seventh day of week.

Sat'urn, *n.* major planet.

sat'ur•nine' (-nīn'), *adj.* gloomy.

sa'tyr (sā'tər), *n.* 1. woodland deity, part man and part goat. 2. lecherous person.

sauce, *n.* 1. liquid or soft relish. 2. stewed fruit.

sau'cer, *n.* small shallow dish.

sau'cy, *adj.*, **-cier, -ciest.** impertinent. —**sau'ci•ly**, *adv.* —**sau'ci•ness**, *n.*

sauer'kraut', *n.* chopped fermented cabbage.

sau'na (sô'-), *n.* bath heated by steam.

saun'ter, *v.*, *n.* stroll.

sau'sage, *n.* minced seasoned meat, often in casing.

sau•té' (sō tā'), *v.*, **-téed, -téeing.** cook in a little fat.

sau•terne' (sō tûrn'), *n.* sweet white wine.

sav'age, *adj.* 1. wild; uncivilized. 2. ferocious. —*n.* 3. uncivilized person. —**sav'age•ly**, *adv.* —**sav'age•ry**, *n.*

sa•vant' (sə vänt'), *n.* learned man.

save, *v.*, **saved, saving,** *prep.*, *conj.* —*v.* 1. rescue or keep safe. 2. reserve. —*prep.*, *conj.* 3. except.

sav'ing, *adj.* 1. rescuing; redeeming. 2. economical. —*n.* 3. economy. 4. (*pl.*) money put by. —*prep.* 5. except. 6. respecting.

sav'ior, *n.* 1. one who rescues. 2. (*cap.*) Christ. Also, **sav'iour.**

sa'voir-faire' (sav'wär fâr'), *n.* competence in social matters.

sa'vor, *n.*, *v.* taste or smell.

sa'vor•y, *adj.* 1. pleasing in taste or smell. —*n.* 2. aromatic plant.

saw, *n.*, *v.*, **sawed, sawing.** —*n.* 1. toothed metal blade. —*v.* 2. cut with saw. —**saw'mill,** *n.* —**saw'yer,** *n.*

sax'o•phone', *n.* musical wind instrument.

say, *v.*, **said, saying,** *n.* —*v.* 1. speak; declare; utter. 2. declare as truth. —*n.* 3. *Informal.* right to speak or choose.

say'ing, *n.* proverb.

say'so', *n. Informal.* personal assurance; word.

scab, *n.*, *v.*, **scabbed, scabbing.** —*n.* 1. crust forming over sore. 2. worker who takes striker's place. —*v.* 3. form scab. —**scab'by,** *adj.*

scab'bard, *n.* sheath for sword blade, etc.

sca'bies, *n.* infectious skin disease.

scaf'fold, *n.* 1. Also, **scaf'fold•ing.** temporary framework used in construction. 2. platform on which criminal is executed.

scal'a•wag', *n.* rascal.

scald, *v.* 1. burn with hot liquid or steam. 2. heat just below boiling. —*n.* 3. burn caused by scalding.

scale, *n.*, *v.*, **scaled, scaling.** —*n.* 1. one of flat hard plates covering fish, etc. 2. flake. 3. device for weighing. 4. series of measuring units. 5. relative measure. 6. succession of musical tones. —*v.* 7. remove or shed scales. 8. weigh. 9. climb with effort. 10. reduce proportionately. —**scal'y,** *adj.* —**scal'i•ness,** *n.*

scal'lion, *n.* small green onion.

scal'lop (skol'əp, skal'-), *n.* 1. bivalve mollusk. 2. one of series of curves on a border. —*v.* 3. finish with scallops.

scalp, *n.* 1. skin and hair of top of head. —*v.* 2. cut scalp from. 3. buy and resell at unofficial price. —**scalp'er,** *n.*

scal'pel, *n.* small surgical knife.

scam, *n. Slang.* scheme to cheat or defraud.

scamp, *n.* rascal.

scam'per, *v.* 1. go quickly. —*n.* 2. quick run.

scan, *v.*, **scanned, scanning.** 1. examine closely. 2. glance at. 3. analyze verse meter.

scan'dal, *n.* 1. disgraceful act; disgrace. 2. malicious gossip. —**scan'dal•ous,** *adj.* —**scan'dal•mon'ger,** *n.*

scan'dal•ize', *v.*, **-ized, -izing.** offend; shock.

scant, *adj.* barely adequate. Also, **scant'y.** —**scant'i•ly,** *adv.* —**scant'i•ness,** *n.*

scape'goat', *n.* one made to bear blame for others.

scape'grace', *n.* scamp; rascal.

scap'u•la, *n.*, *pl.* **-lae, -las.** shoulder blade. —**scap'u•lar,** *n.*

scar, *n.*, *v.*, **scarred, scarring.** —*n.* 1. mark left by wound, etc. —*v.* 2. mark with scar.

scar'ab, *n.* beetle.

scarce, *adj.*, **scarcer, scarcest.** 1. insufficient. 2. rare. —**scar'ci•ty,** *n.*

scarce'ly, *adv.* 1. barely. 2. definitely not.

scare, *v.*, **scared, scaring,** *n.* —*v.* 1. frighten. —*n.* 2. sudden fright.

scare'crow', *n.* object set up to frighten birds away from planted seed.

scarf, *n.*, *pl.* **scarfs** or **scarves.** band of cloth esp. for neck.

scar'i•fy', *v.*, **-fied, -fying.** 1. scratch (skin, etc.). 2. loosen (soil).

scar'let, *n.* bright red.

scarlet fever, contagious disease marked by fever and rash.

scar'y, *adj.* **-ier, -iest.** causing fear.

scat, *v.*, **scatted, scatting.** run off.

scathe, *v.*, **scathed, scathing.** criticize harshly.

scat'ter, *v.* throw loosely about.

scav'enge, *v.*, **-enged, -enging.** 1. cleanse. 2. search for food. —**scav'en•ger,** *n.*

sce•nar'i•o', *n.* plot outline, esp. of motion picture.

scene, *n.* 1. location of action. 2. view. 3. subdivision of play. 4. display of emotion. —**sce'nic,** *adj.*

scen'er•y, *n.* 1. features of landscape. 2. stage set.

scent, *n.* 1. distinctive odor. 2. trail marked by this. 3. sense of smell. —*v.* 4. smell. 5. perfume.

scep'ter (sep'-), *n.* rod carried as emblem of royal power. Also, **scep'tre.**

scep'tic, *n.* skeptic.

sched'ule (skej'-), *n.*, *v.*, **-uled, -uling.** —*n.* 1. timetable or list. —*v.* 2. enter on schedule.

scheme, *n.*, *v.*, **schemed, scheming.** —*n.* 1. plan; design. 2. intrigue. —*v.* 3. plan or plot. —**schem'er,** *n.*

schism (siz'əm), *n.* division within church, etc.; disunion. —**schis•mat'ic,** *adj.*, *n.*

schist (shist), *n.* layered crystalline rock.

schiz'oid (skit'soid), *adj.* having personality disorder, marked by depression, withdrawal, etc.

schiz'o•phre'ni•a (skit'sə frē'nē ə), *n.* kind of mental disorder.

schlock (shlok), *n. Informal.* inferior merchandise. —**schlock, schlock'y,** *adj.*

schmaltz (shmälts), *n. Informal.* sentimental art, esp. music. —**schmaltz'y,** *adj.*

schol'ar, *n.* 1. learned person. 2. pupil. —**schol'ar•ly,** *adj.*

schol'ar•ship', *n.* 1. learning. 2. aid granted to promising student.

scho•las'tic, *adj.* of schools or scholars. —**scho•las'ti•cal•ly,** *adv.*

school, *n.* 1. place for instruction. 2. regular meetings of teacher and pupils. 3. believers in doctrine or theory. 4. group of fish, whales, etc. —*v.* 5. educate; train. —**school'book',** *n.* —**school'house',** *n.* —**school'mate',** *n.* —**school'room',** *n.* —**school'teach'er,** *n.*

schoon'er, *n.* kind of sailing vessel.

schwa (shwä), *n.* vowel sound in certain unstressed syllables, as *a* in *sofa;* usually represented by ə.

sci•at'i•ca (sī-), *n.* neuralgia in hip and thigh. —**sci•at'ic,** *adj.*

sci'ence, *n.* systematic knowledge, esp. of physical world. —**sci•en•tif'ic,** *adj.* —**sci•en•tif'i•cal•ly,** *adv.* —**sci'en•tist,** *n.*

science fiction, fiction dealing with space travel, robots, etc.

scim'i•tar (sim'-), *n.* curved sword.

scin•til'la (sin-), *n.* particle, esp. of evidence.

scin'til•late', *v.*, **-lated, -lating.** sparkle. —**scin'til•la'tion,** *n.*

sci'on (sī'ən), *n.* 1. descendant. 2. shoot cut for grafting.

scis'sors, *n.* cutting instrument with two pivoted blades.

scle•ro'sis (skli-), *n.* hardening, as of tissue. —**scle•rot'ic,** *adj.*

scoff, *v.* 1. jeer. —*n.* 2. derision. —**scoff'er,** *n.*

scold, *v.* 1. find fault; reprove. —*n.* 2. scolding woman.

sconce, *n.* wall bracket for candles, etc.

scone, *n.* small flat cake.

scoop, *n.* 1. small deep shovel. 2. bucket of steam shovel, etc. 3. act of scooping. 4. quantity taken up. 5. *Informal.* earliest news report. —*v.* 6. take up with scoop. 7. *Informal.* best (competing news media) with scoop (def. 5).

scoot, *v.* go swiftly.

scoot'er, *n.* low two-wheeled vehicle.

scope, *n.* extent.

scorch, *v.* 1. burn slightly. —*n.* 2. superficial burn.

score, *n., pl.* **scores,** (for 3) **score,** *v.,* **scored, scoring.** —*n.* 1. points made in game, etc. 2. notch. 3. group of twenty. 4. account; reason. 5. piece of music arranged in parts. —*v.* 6. earn points in game. 7. notch or cut. 8. criticize. —**scor′er,** *n.*

scorn, *n.* 1. contempt. 2. mockery. —*v.* 3. regard or refuse with scorn. —**scorn′ful,** *adj.* —**scorn′ful•ly,** *adv.*

scor′pi•on, *n.* small venomous spiderlike animal.

Scot, *n.* native or inhabitant of Scotland. —**Scot′tish,** *adj., n.pl.*

Scotch, *adj.* 1. (loosely) Scottish. —*n.* 2. (*pl.*) (loosely) Scottish people. 3. whiskey made in Scotland.

scotch, *v.* 1. make harmless. 2. put an end to.

scoun′drel, *n.* rascal.

scour, *v.* 1. clean by rubbing. 2. range in searching.

scourge (skûrj), *n., v.,* **scourged, scourging.** —*n.* 1. whip. 2. cause of affliction. —*v.* 3. whip.

scout, *n.* 1. person sent ahead to examine conditions. —*v.* 2. examine as scout. 3. reject with scorn.

scow, *n.* flat-bottomed, flat-ended boat.

scowl, *n.* 1. fierce frown. —*v.* 2. frown fiercely.

scrab′ble, *v.,* **-bled, -bling.** 1. scratch with hands, etc. 2. scrawl.

scrag, *n.* scrawny creature. —**scrag′-gy,** *adj.*

scrag′gly, *adj.,* **-glier, -gliest.** shaggy.

scram′ble, *v.,* **-bled, -bling,** *n.* —*v.* 1. move with difficulty, using feet and hands. 2. mix together. —*n.* 3. scrambling progression. 4. struggle for possession.

scrap, *n., adj., v.,* **scrapped, scrapping.** —*n.* 1. small pieces. 2. *Informal.* fight. —*adj.* 3. discarded material. 4. in scraps or as scraps. —*v.* 5. break up; discard. —**scrap′py,** *adj.*

scrap′book′, *n.* blank book for clippings, etc.

scrape, *v.,* **scraped, scraping,** *n.* —*v.* 1. rub harshly. 2. remove by scraping. 3. collect laboriously. —*n.* 4. act or sound of scraping. 5. scraped place. 6. predicament. —**scrap′er,** *n.*

scrap′ple, *n.* sausagelike food of pork, corn meal, and seasonings.

scratch, *v.* 1. mark, tear, or rub with something sharp. 2. strike out. —*n.* 3. mark from scratching. 4. standard. —**scratch′y,** *adj.*

scrawl, *v.* 1. write carelessly or awkwardly. —*n.* 2. such handwriting.

scraw′ny, *adj.,* **-nier, -niest.** thin. —**scraw′ni•ness,** *n.*

scream, *n.* 1. loud sharp cry. —*v.* 2. utter screams.

screech, *n.* 1. harsh shrill cry. —*v.* 2. utter screeches.

screen, *n.* 1. covered frame. 2. anything that shelters or conceals. 3. wire mesh. 4. surface for displaying motion pictures. —*v.* 5. shelter with screen. 6. sift through screen.

screw, *n.* 1. machine part or fastener driving or driven by twisting. 2. propeller. 3. coercion. —*v.* 4. hold with screw. 5. turn as screw.

screw′driv′er, *n.* tool for turning screws.

scrib′ble, *v.,* **-bled, -bling.** —*v.* 1. write hastily or meaninglessly. —*n.* 2. piece of such writing.

scribe, *n.* penman.

scrim′mage, *n., v.,* **-maged, -maging.** —*n.* 1. rough struggle. 2. play in football. —*v.* 3. engage in scrimmage.

scrimp, *v.* economize.

scrip, *n.* certificate, paper money, etc.

script, *n.* 1. handwriting. 2. manuscript.

Scrip′ture, *n.* Bible. —**scrip′tur•al,** *adj.*

scrof′u•la, *n.* tuberculous disease, esp. of lymphatic glands.

scroll, *n.* roll of inscribed paper.

scro′tum, *n.* pouch of skin containing testicles. —**scro′tal,** *adj.*

scrounge, *v.,* **scrounged, scrounging.** *Informal.* 1. beg or mooch. 2. search. —**scroung′er,** *n.*

scrub, *v.,* **scrubbed, scrubbing,** *n., adj.* —*v.* 1. clean by rubbing. —*n.* 2. low trees or shrubs. 3. anything small or poor. —*adj.* 4. small or poor. —**scrub′by,** *adj.*

scruff, *n.* nape.

scru′ple, *n.* restraint from conscience.

scru′pu•lous, *adj.* 1. having scruples. 2. careful. —**scru′pu•lous•ly,** *adv.*

scru′ti•nize′, *v.,* **-nized, -nizing.** examine closely. —**scru′ti•ny,** *n.*

scu′ba, *n.* self-contained breathing device for swimmers.

scud, *v.,* **scudded, scudding.** move quickly.

scuff, *v.* 1. shuffle. 2. mar by hard use.

scuf′fle, *n., v.,* **-fled, -fling.** —*n.* 1. rough, confused fight. —*v.* 2. engage in scuffle.

scull, *n.* 1. oar used over stern. 2. light racing boat. —*v.* 3. propel with scull.

scul′ler•y, *n.* workroom off kitchen.

sculp′ture, *n.* 1. three-dimensional art of wood, marble, etc. 2. piece of such work. —**sculp′tor,** *n.* —**sculp′-tress,** *n.fem.*

scum, *n.* 1. film on top of liquid. 2. worthless persons. —**scum′my,** *adj.*

scup′per, *n.* opening in ship's side to drain off water.

scur′ril•ous, *adj.* coarsely abusive or derisive. —**scur′ril•ous•ly,** *adv.* —**scur•ril′i•ty, scur′ril•ous•ness,** *n.*

scur′ry, *v.,* **-ried, -rying,** *n., pl.* **-ries.** hurry.

scur′vy, *n., adj.,* **-vier, -viest.** —*n.* 1. disease from inadequate diet. —*adj.* 2. contemptible.

scut′tle, *n., v.,* **-tled, -tling.** —*n.* 1. covered opening, esp. on flat roof. 2. coal bucket. —*v.* 3. sink intentionally. 4. scurry.

scythe (sīth), *n.* curved, handled blade for mowing by hand.

sea, *n.* 1. ocean. 2. body of salt water smaller than ocean. 3. turbulence of water. —**sea′board′, sea′shore′,** *n.* —**sea′coast′,** *n.* —**sea′port′,** *n.* —**sea′go′ing,** *adj.*

sea′far′ing, *adj.* traveling by or working at sea.

sea horse, small fish with beaked head.

seal, *n., pl.* **seals,** (also for 3) **seal,** *v.* —*n.* 1. imprinted device affixed to document. 2. means of closing. 3. marine animal with large flippers. —*v.* 4. affix seal to. 5. close by seal. —**seal′ant,** *n.*

sea lion, large seal.

seam, *n.* 1. line formed in sewing two pieces together. —*v.* 2. join with seam.

sea′man, *n., pl.* **-men.** sailor. —**sea′-man•ship′,** *n.*

seam′stress, *n.* woman who sews.

seam′y, *adj.,* **seamier, seamiest.** 1. sordid. 2. having seams. —**seam′i•ness,** *n.*

sé′ance (sā′äns), *n.* meeting to attempt communication with spirits.

sea′plane′, *n.* airplane equipped with floats.

sea′port′, *n.* port for seagoing vessels.

sear, *v.* 1. burn or char. 2. dry up.

search, *v.* 1. examine as in looking for something. 2. investigate. —*n.* 3. examination or investigation. —**search′er,** *n.*

search′light′, *n.* device for throwing strong beam of light.

sea′sick′ness, *n.* nausea from motion of ship. —**sea′sick′,** *adj.*

sea'son, *n.* 1. any of four distinct periods of year. 2. best or usual time. —*v.* 3. flavor with salt, spices, etc. —**sea'sonal,** *adj.*

sea'son•a•ble, *adj.* appropriate to time of year.

sea'son•ing, *n.* flavoring, as salt, spices, or herbs.

seat, *n.* 1. place for sitting. 2. right to sit, as in Congress. 3. site; location. 4. established center. —*v.* 5. place on seat. 6. find seats for. 7. install.

sea'weed', *n.* plant growing in sea.

sea'wor'thy, *adj.* fit for sea travel.

se•ba'ceous (-shəs), *adj.* fatty; greasy.

se•cede', *v.,* **-ceded, -ceding.** withdraw from nation, alliance, etc. —**se•ces'sion,** *n.*

se•clude', *v.,* **-cluded, -cluding.** locate in solitude. —**se•clu'sion,** *n.*

sec'ond, *adj.* 1. next after first. 2. another. —*n.* 3. one that is second. 4. person who aids another. 5. (*pl.*) imperfect goods. 6. sixtieth part of minute of time or degree. —*v.* 7. support; further. —*adv.* 8. in second place. —**sec'ond•ly,** *adv.*

sec'ond•ar'y, *adj.* 1. next after first. 2. of second rank or stage. 3. less important. —**sec'ond•ar'i•ly,** *adv.*

sec'ond-hand', *adj.* 1. not new. 2. not original.

se'cret, *adj.* 1. kept from knowledge of others. —*n.* 2. something secret or hidden. —**se'cre•cy,** *n.* —**se'cret•ly,** *adv.*

sec're•tar'i•at, *n.* group of administrative officials.

sec're•tar'y, *n.,* *pl.* **-taries.** 1. office assistant. 2. head of department of government. 3. tall writing desk. —**sec're•tar'i•al,** *adj.*

se•crete', *v.,* **-creted, -creting.** 1. separate or prepare from blood. 2. hide.

se•cre'tion, *n.* 1. glandular function of secreting, as bile or milk. 2. product secreted. —**se•cre'to•ry,** *adj.*

se•cre'tive, *adj.* 1. disposed to keep things secret. 2. secretory. —**se•cre'tive•ly,** *adv.* —**se•cre'tive•ness,** *n.*

sect, *n.* group with common religious faith. —**sec•tar'i•an,** *adj., n.*

sec'tion, *n.* 1. separate or distinct part. —*v.* 2. divide into sections. —**sec'tion•al,** *adj.*

sec'tor, *n.* 1. plane figure bounded by two radii and an arc. 2. part of combat area.

sec'u•lar, *adj.* worldly; not religious. —**sec'u•lar•ize',** *v.*

se•cure', *adj., v.,* **-cured, -curing.** —*adj.* 1. safe. 2. firmly in place. 3. certain. —*v.* 4. get. 5. make secure. —**se•cure'ly,** *adv.*

se•cu'ri•ty, *n., pl.* **-ties.** 1. safety. 2. protection. 3. pledge given on loan. 4. certificate of stock, etc.

se•dan', *n.* closed automobile for four or more.

se•date', *adj.* 1. quiet; sober. —*v.* 2. give sedative to. —**se•date'ly,** *adv.* —**se•date'ness,** *n.*

sed'a•tive, *adj.* 1. soothing. 2. relieving pain or excitement. —*n.* 3. sedative medicine.

sed'en•tar'y, *adj.* characterized by sitting.

Se'der (sā'dər), *n.* ceremonial dinner at Passover.

sedge, *n.* grasslike marsh plant.

sed'i•ment, *n.* matter settling to bottom of liquid. —**sed'i•men'ta•ry,** *adj.*

se•di'tion, *n.* incitement to rebellion. —**se•di'tious,** *adj.*

se•duce', *v.,* **-duced, -ducing.** 1. corrupt; tempt. 2. induce to surrender chastity. —**se•duc'tion,** *n.* —**se•duc'tive,** *adj.*

sed'u•lous, *adj.* diligent.

see, *v.,* **saw, seen, seeing,** *n.* —*v.* 1. perceive with the eyes. 2. find out. 3. make sure. 4. escort. —*n.* 5. office or jurisdiction of bishop.

seed, *n.* 1. propagating part of plant. 2. offspring. —*v.* 3. sow seed. 4. remove seed from. —**seed'less,** *adj.*

seed'ling, *n.* plant grown from seed.

seed'y, *adj.,* **seedier, seediest.** 1. having many seeds. 2. shabby. —**seed'i•ness,** *n.*

see'ing, *conj.* inasmuch as.

seek, *v.,* **sought, seeking.** 1. search for. 2. try. —**seek'er,** *n.*

seem, *v.* appear (to be or do).

seem'ing, *adj.* apparent. —**seem'ing•ly,** *adv.*

seem'ly, *adj.,* **-lier, -liest.** decorous. —**seem'li•ness,** *n.*

seep, *v.* ooze; pass gradually. —**seep'age,** *n.*

seer, *n.* 1. person who sees. 2. prophet. —**seer'ess,** *n.fem.*

seer'suck'er, *n.* crinkled cotton fabric.

see'saw', *n.* 1. children's sport played on balancing plank. —*v.* 2. alternate, waver, etc., as on seesaw.

seethe, *v.,* **seethed, seething.** boil; foam.

seg'ment, *n.* 1. part; section. —*v.* 2. divide into segments. —**seg'men•**

ta'tion, *n.* —**seg•men'tal, seg•men'ta•ry,** *adj.*

seg're•gate', *v.,* **-gated, -gating.** separate from others. —**seg're•ga'tion,** *n.*

seine (sān), *n., v.,* **seined, seining.** —*n.* 1. kind of fishing net. —*v.* 2. fish with seine.

seis'mic (sīz'-), *adj.* of or caused by earthquakes.

seis'mo•graph', *n.* instrument for recording earthquakes.

seize, *v.,* **seized, seizing.** 1. take by force or authority. 2. understand.

seiz'ure (sē'zhər), *n.* 1. act of seizing. 2. attack of illness.

sel'dom, *adv.* not often.

se•lect', *v.* 1. choose. —*adj.* 2. selected. 3. choice. —**se•lec'tion,** *n.* —**se•lec'tive,** *adj.*

se•lect'man, *n.* town officer in New England.

self, *n., pl.* **selves,** *adj.* —*n.* 1. person's own nature. 2. personal advantage or interests. —*adj.* 3. identical.

self'-as•sur'ance, *n.* confidence in one's ability or rightness. —**self'as•sured',** *adj.*

self'-cen'tered, *adj.* interested only in oneself.

self'-con'fi•dence, *n.* faith in one's own judgment, ability, etc. —**self'-con'fident,** *adj.*

self'-de•ter'mi•na'tion, *n.* right or ability to choose government or actions.

self'-ev'i•dent, *adj.* obvious.

self'-im'age, *n.* conception or evaluation of oneself.

self'-in'ter•est, *n.* consideration of things to one's benefit.

self'ish, *adj.* caring only for oneself. —**self'ish•ly,** *adv.* —**self'ish•ness,** *n.*

self'-made', *adj.* owing success entirely to one's own efforts.

self'-pos•sessed', *adj.* calm; poised. —**self'-pos•ses'sion,** *n.*

self'-re•spect', *n.* proper esteem for oneself. —**self'-re•spect'ing,** *adj.*

self'-right'eous (-rī'chəs), *adj.* convinced one is morally right. —**self'-right'eous•ness,** *n.*

self'same', *adj.* identical.

self'-styled', *adj.* so called only by oneself.

self'-willed', *adj.* stubborn; obstinate.

sell, *v.,* **sold, selling.** 1. part with for payment. 2. betray. 3. be for sale. —**sell'er,** *n.*

selt'zer, *n.* effervescent mineral water.

sel′vage, *n.* finished edge on fabric.

se•man′tics, *n.* study of meanings of words.

sem′a•phore′, *n.* apparatus for signaling.

sem′blance, *n.* 1. appearance. 2. copy.

se′men, *n.* male reproductive fluid.

se•mes′ter, *n.* half school year.

sem′i•an′nu•al, *adj.* occurring every half-year. **—sem′i•an′nu•al•ly,** *adv.*

sem′i•cir′cle, *n.* half circle. **—sem′i•cir′cu•lar,** *adj.*

sem′i•co′lon, *n.* mark of punctuation (;) between parts of sentence.

sem′i•nar′, *n.* class of advanced students.

sem′i•nar′y, *n., pl.* **-naries.** school, esp. for young women or for divinity students.

sem′i•pre′cious, *adj.* of moderate value.

sen′ate, *n.* legislative body, esp. (*cap.*) upper house of legislatures of United States, Canada, etc. **—sen′a•tor,** *n.* **—sen′a•to′ri•al,** *adj.*

send, *v.,* **sent, sending.** 1. cause to go. 2. have conveyed. 3. emit. **—send′er,** *n.*

se•nile′ (sē′nīl), *adj.* feeble, esp. because of old age. **—se•nil′i•ty,** *n.*

sen′ior, *adj.* 1. older. 2. of higher rank. 3. denoting last year in school. **—n.** 4. senior person. **—sen•ior′i•ty,** *n.*

senior citizen, person 65 years of age or more.

se•ñor′ (se nyôr′), *n., pl.* **-ñores.** *Spanish.* 1. gentleman. 2. Mr. or sir. **—se•ño′ra,** *n.fem.*

se•ño•ri′ta (se′nyô rē′tä), *n. Spanish.* 1. Miss. 2. young lady.

sen•sa′tion, *n.* 1. operation of senses. 2. mental condition from such operation. 3. cause of excited interest.

sen•sa′tion•al, *adj.* 1. startling; exciting. 2. of sensation. **—sen•sa′tion•al•ly,** *adv.*

sense, *n., v.,* **sensed, sensing. —n.** 1. faculty for perceiving physical things. (sight, hearing, smell, etc.). 2. feeling so produced. 3. (*pl.*) consciousness. 4. (*often pl.*) rationality; prudence. 5. meaning. **—v.** 6. perceive by senses. **—sense′less,** *adj.*

sen′si•bil′i•ty, *n., pl.* **-ties.** 1. capacity for sensation. 2. (*often pl.*) sensitive feeling.

sen′si•ble, *adj.* 1. wise or practical. 2. aware. **—sen′si•bly,** *adv.*

sen′si•tive, *adj.* 1. having sensation. 2. easily affected. **—sen′si•tiv′i•ty,** *n.*

sen′si•tize′, *v.,* **-tized, -tizing.** make sensitive.

sen′so•ry, *adj.* of sensation or senses.

sen′su•al, *adj.* 1. inclined to pleasures of the senses. 2. lewd. **—sen′su•al•ist,** *n.* **—sen′su•al•ism,** *n.* **—sen′su•al•ly,** *adv.*

sen′su•ous, *adj.* 1. of or affected by senses. 2. giving or seeking enjoyment through senses. **—sen′su•ous•ly,** *adv.* **—sen′su•ous•ness,** *n.*

sen′tence, *n., v.,* **-tenced, -tencing. —n.** 1. group of words expressing complete thought. 2. judgment; opinion. 3. assignment of punishment. **—v.** 4. pronounce sentence on.

sen•ten′tious, *adj.* 1. using maxims. 2. affectedly judicious. 3. pithy.

sen′tient (-shənt), *adj.* having feeling. **—sen′tience,** *n.*

sen′ti•ment, *n.* 1. opinion. 2. emotion. 3. expression of belief or emotion.

sen′ti•men′tal, *adj.* expressing or showing tender emotion. **—sen′ti•men′tal•ist,** *n.* **—sen′ti•men′tal•ism,** *n.* **—sen′ti•men•tal′i•ty,** *n.* **—sen′ti•men′tal•ly,** *adv.*

sen′ti•nel, *n.* guard.

sen′try, *n., pl.* **-tries.** soldier on watch.

se′pal (sē′pəl), *n.* leaflike part of flower.

sep′a•rate′, *v.,* **-rated, -rating,** *adj.* **—v.** (-rāt′). 1. keep, put, or come apart. **—adj.** (-rit). 2. not connected; being apart. **—sep′a•ra′tion,** *n.* **—sep′a•ra•ble,** *adj.* **—sep′a•rate•ly,** *adv.*

sep′a•ra′tor, *n.* apparatus for separating ingredients.

se′pi•a, *n.* 1. brown pigment. 2. dark brown.

sep′sis, *n.* infection in blood. **—sep′tic,** *adj.*

Sep•tem′ber, *n.* ninth month of year.

sep•tet′, *n.* group of seven. Also, **sep•tette′.**

septic tank, tank for decomposition of sewage.

sep′tu•a•ge•nar′i•an (sep′chŏŏ ə-), *n.* person 70 to 79 years old.

sep′ul•cher (-kər), *n.* burial place. Also, **sep′ul•chre. —se•pul′chral,** *adj.*

se′quel, *n.* 1. subsequent event; result. 2. literary work continuing earlier one.

se′quence, *n.* 1. succession; series. 2. result.

se•ques′ter, *v.* 1. seclude. 2. seize and hold. **—se′ques•tra′tion,** *n.*

se′quin, *n.* small spangle.

se•quoi′a, *n.* very large tree of northwest U.S.

se•ra′pe (sə rä′pē), *n.* blanketlike wrap used in Mexico.

ser′aph, *n., pl.* **-aphs, -aphim.** angel of highest order. **—se•raph′ic,** *adj.*

sere, *adj.* withered.

ser′e•nade′, *n., v.,* **-naded, -nading. —n.** 1. music performed as compliment outside at night. **—v.** 2. compliment with serenade.

ser′en•dip′i•ty, *n.* luck in making discoveries.

se•rene′, *adj.* 1. calm. 2. fair. **—se•ren′i•ty,** *n.* **—se•rene′ly,** *adv.*

serf, *n.* slave. **—serf′dom,** *n.*

serge, *n.* stout twilled fabric.

ser′geant, *n.* noncommissioned officer above corporal.

se′ri•al, *n.* 1. story, etc., appearing in installments. **—adj.** 2. of serial. 3. of or in series. **—se′ri•al•ly,** *adv.*

se′ries, *n.* things in succession.

se′ri•ous, *adj.* 1. solemn. 2. important.

ser′mon, *n.* religious discourse.

ser′pent, *n.* snake. **—ser′pen•tine′** (-tēn′), *adj.*

ser′rat•ed (ser′ā tid), *adj.* toothed; notched. Also, **ser′rate** (ser′it).

se′rum, *n.* 1. pale-yellow liquid in blood. 2. such liquid from animal immune to certain disease.

serv′ant, *n.* 1. person employed at domestic work.

serve, *v.,* **served, serving.** 1. act as servant. 2. help. 3. do official duty. 4. suffice. 5. undergo (imprisonment, etc.). 6. deliver.

serv′ice, *n., v.,* **-iced, -icing. —n.** 1. helpful activity. 2. domestic employment. 3. armed forces. 4. act of public worship. 5. set of dishes, etc. **—v.** 6. keep in repair.

serv′ice•a•ble, *adj.* usable.

serv′ice•man, *n., pl.* **-men.** 1. person in armed forces. 2. gasoline station attendant.

ser′vile (-vil), *adj.* slavishly obsequious. **—ser′vil′i•ty,** *n.*

ser′vi•tor, *n.* servant.

ser′vi•tude′, *n.* bondage.

ses′a•me, *n.* small edible seed of tropical plant.

ses′qui•cen•ten′ni•al, *n.* 150th anniversary. **—ses′qui•cen•ten′ni•al,** *adj.*

ses′sion, *n.* sitting, as of a court or class.

set, *v.,* **set, setting,** *n., adj.* **—v.** 1. put or place. 2. put (broken bone) in position. 3. arrange (printing type). 4. pass below horizon. 5. sit on eggs. 6. become firm. 7. start. —*n.* 8. group; complete collection. 9. radio or television receiver. 10. represented setting of action in drama. —*adj.* 11. prearranged. 12. fixed. 13. resolved.

set′back′, *n.* return to worse condition.

set•tee′, *n.* small sofa.

set′ter, *n.* kind of hunting dog.

set′ting, *n.* 1. surroundings. 2. music for certain words.

set′tle, *v.,* **-tled, -tling.** 1. agree. 2. pay. 3. take up residence. 4. colonize. 5. quiet. 6. come to rest. 7. deposit dregs. —**set′tle•ment,** *n.* —**set′tler,** *n.*

set′up′, *n. Informal.* situation in detail.

sev′en, *n., adj.* six plus one. —**sev′enth,** *adj., n.*

sev′en•teen′, *n., adj.* sixteen plus one. —**sev′en•teenth′,** *adj., n.*

sev′en•ty, *n., adj.* ten times seven. —**sev′en•ti′eth,** *adj., n.*

sev′er, *v.* separate; break off. —**sev′er•ance,** *n.*

sev′er•al, *adj.* 1. some, but not many. 2. respective. 3. various. —*n.* 4. some.

se•vere′, *adj.* 1. harsh. 2. serious. 3. plain. 4. violent or hard. —**se•ver′i•ty,** *n.* —**se•vere′ly,** *adv.*

sew (sō), *v.,* **sewed, sewed** or **sewn, sewing.** join or make with thread and needle. —**sew′er,** *n.*

sew′age (sōō′-), *n.* wastes carried by sewers.

sew′er, *n.* conduit for refuse, etc.

sex, *n.* 1. character of being male or female. 2. sexual intercourse. —**sex′u•al,** *adj.* —**sex′u•al•ly,** *adv.*

sex′ism, *n.* bias because of sex, esp. against women. —**sex′ist,** *n., adj.*

sex′tant, *n.* astronomical instrument for finding position.

sex•tet′, *n.* group of six. Also, **sex•tette′.**

sex′ton, *n.* church caretaker.

sex′tu•ple, *adj.* sixfold.

shab′by, *adj.,* **-bier, -biest.** 1. worn; wearing worn clothes. 2. mean. —**shab′bi•ly,** *adv.* —**shab′bi•ness,** *n.*

shack, *n.* rough cabin.

shack′le, *n., v.,* **-led, -ling.** —*n.* 1. iron bond for wrist, ankle, etc. 2. U-shaped bolt of padlock. —*v.* 3. put shackle on; restrain.

shad, *n.* kind of herring.

shade, *n., v.,* **shaded, shading.** —*n.* 1. slightly dark, cool place. 2. ghost. 3. degree of color. 4. slight amount. —*v.* 5. protect from light.

shad′ow, *n.* 1. dark image made by body intercepting light. 2. shade. 3. trace. —*v.* 4. shade. 5. follow secretly. —**shad′ow•y,** *adj.*

shad′y, *adj.,* **-ier, -iest.** 1. in shade. 2. arousing suspicion. —**shad′i•ness,** *n.*

shaft, *n.* 1. long slender rod. 2. beam. 3. revolving bar in engine. 4. vertical space.

shag, *n.* 1. matted wool, hair, etc. 2. napped cloth. —**shag′gy,** *adj.*

shah, *n. (formerly)* ruler of Persia (now Iran).

shake, *v.,* **shook, shaken, shaking,** *n.* —*v.* 1. move with quick irregular motions. 2. tremble. 3. agitate. —*n.* 4. act of shaking. 5. tremor. —**shak′er,** *n.*

shake′up′, *n. Informal.* organizational reform.

shak′y, *adj.,* **-ier, -iest.** 1. not firm; insecure. 2. quavering. 3. affected by fright. —**shak′i•ly,** *adv.* —**shak′i•ness,** *n.*

shale, *n.* kind of layered rock.

shall, *v.* 1. am (is, are) going to. 2. am (is, are) obliged or commanded to.

shal•lot′, *n.* small onionlike plant.

shal•low, *adj.* not deep.

sham, *n.* 1. pretense or imitation. —*adj.* 2. pretended.

sham′ble, *v.,* **-bled, -bling,** *n.* —*v.* 1. walk awkwardly. —*n.* 2. shambling gait. 3. (*pl.*) scene of confusion.

shame, *n., v.,* **shamed, shaming.** —*n.* 1. painful feeling from wrong or foolish act or circumstance. 2. disgrace. —*v.* 3. cause to feel shame. —**shame′ful,** *adj.* —**shame′less,** *adj.*

shame′faced′, *adj.* 1. bashful. 2. showing shame.

sham•poo′, *v.,* **-pooed, -pooing,** *n.* —*v.* 1. wash (hair or rug). —*n.* 2. act of shampooing. 3. soap, etc., for shampooing.

sham′rock, *n.* plant with three-part leaf.

shang′hai, *v.,* **-haied, -haiing.** (formerly) abduct for service as sailor.

shank, *n.* part of leg between knee and ankle.

shan′ty, *n., pl.* **-ties.** rough hut.

shape, *n., v.,* **shaped, shaping.** —*n.* 1. form. 2. nature. —*v.* 3. give form to; take form. 4. adapt. —**shape′less,** *adj.*

shape′ly, *adj.,* **-lier, -liest.** handsome in shape. —**shape′li•ness,** *n.*

share, *n., v.,* **shared, sharing.** —*n.* 1. due individual portion. 2. portion of corporate stock. —*v.* 3. distribute. 4. use, enjoy, etc., jointly. —**shar′er,** *n.* —**share′hold′er,** *n.*

shark, *n.* 1. marine fish, often ferocious. 2. person who victimizes.

sharp, *adj.* 1. having thin cutting edge or fine point. 2. abrupt. 3. keen. 4. shrewd. 5. raised in musical pitch. —*adv.* 6. punctually. —*n.* 7. musical tone one half step above given tone. —**sharp′en,** *v.* —**sharp′en•er,** *n.* —**sharp′ly,** *adv.* —**sharp′ness,** *n.*

sharp′er, *n.* swindler.

sharp′shoot′er, *n.* skilled shooter.

shat′ter, *v.* break in pieces.

shave, *v.,* **shaved, shaved** or **shaven, shaving,** *n.* —*v.* 1. remove hair with razor. 2. cut thin slices. —*n.* 3. act of shaving.

shav′ings, *n.pl.* thin slices of wood.

shawl, *n.* long covering for head and shoulders.

she, *pron.* female last mentioned.

sheaf, *n., pl.* **sheaves.** bundle.

shear, *v.,* **sheared, sheared** or **shorn, shearing.** clip, as wool.

shears, *n.pl.* large scissors.

sheath, *n., pl.* **sheaths.** 1. case for sword blade. 2. any similar covering.

sheathe, *v.,* **sheathed, sheathing.** put into or enclose in sheath.

shed, *v.,* **shed, shedding,** *n.* —*v.* 1. pour forth. 2. cast (light). 3. throw off. —*n.* 4. simple enclosed shelter.

sheen, *n.* brightness.

sheep, *n., pl.* **sheep.** mammal valued for fleece and flesh.

sheep′ish, *adj.* embarrassed or timid.

sheer, *adj.* 1. very thin. 2. complete. 3. steep. —*v., n.* 4. swerve.

sheet, *n.* 1. large piece of cloth used as bedding. 2. broad thin mass or piece. 3. rope or chain to control sail.

sheik, *n.* (Arab) chief.

shek′el (shek′əl), *n.* ancient Hebrew coin.

shelf, *n., pl.* **shelves.** 1. horizontal slab on wall, etc., for holding objects. 2. ledge.

shell, *n.* 1. hard outer covering. 2. shotgun. cartridge. 3. explosive missile from cannon. 4. light racing boat. —*v.* 5. remove shell from. 6. take from shell. 7. bombard with shells.

shel•lac′, *n., v.,* **-lacked, -lacking.** —*n.* 1. substance used in varnish. 2. varnish. —*v.* 3. coat with shellac.

shell′fish′, *n.* aquatic animal having shell.

shel′ter, *n.* 1. place of protection. —*v.* 2. protect.

shelve, *v.*, **shelved, shelving.** 1. put on shelf. 2. lay aside. 3. furnish with shelves. 4. slope.

she•nan′i•gans, *n.pl. Informal.* mischief.

shep′herd, *n.* 1. man who tends sheep. —*v.* 2. guide while guarding. —**shep′herd•ess**, *n.fem.*

sher′bet, *n.* frozen fruit-flavored dessert.

sher′iff, *n.* county law-enforcement officer.

sher′ry, *n., pl.* **-ries.** strong wine served as cocktail.

shield, *n.* 1. plate of armor carried on arm. —*v.* 2. protect.

shift, *v.* 1. move about. 2. interchange positions. —*n.* 3. act of shifting. 4. period of work.

shift′less, *adj.* resourceless or lazy.

shift′y, *adj.*, **shiftier, shiftiest.** tricky; devious. —**shift′i•ly**, *adv.* —**shift′i•ness**, *n.*

shil•le′lagh (shə lā′lē), *n.* rough Irish walking stick.

shil′ling, *n.* former British coin, 20th part of pound.

shil′ly-shal′ly, *v.*, **-lied, -lying.** be irresolute.

shim′mer, *v.* 1. glow faintly; flicker. —*n.* 2. faint glow. —**shim′mer•y**, *adj.*

shim′my, *n., pl.* **-mies,** *v.*, **-mied, -mying.** *Informal.* —*n.* 1. vibration. —*v.* 2. vibrate.

shin, *n.* front of leg from knee to ankle.

shine, *v.*, **shone** or (for 4) **shined, shining**, *n.* —*v.* 1. give forth light. 2. sparkle. 3. excel. 4. polish. —*n.* 5. radiance. 6. polish. —**shin′y**, *adj.*

shin′gle, *n., v.*, **-gled, -gling.** —*n.* 1. thin slab used in overlapping rows as covering. 2. close haircut. —*v.* 3. cover with shingles. 4. cut (hair) short.

shin′gles, *n.* skin disease marked by blisters.

shin′ny, *n.* form of hockey.

ship, *n., v.*, **shipped, shipping.** —*n.* 1. vessel for use on water. —*v.* 2. send as freight. 3. engage to serve on ship. —**ship′board′**, *n.* —**ship′mate′**, *n.* —**ship′ment**, *n.* —**ship′per**, *n.* —**ship′ping**, *n.*

ship′shape′, *adj., adv.* in good order.

ship′wreck′, *n.* destruction of ship.

ship′wright′, *n.* carpenter in ship repair or construction.

shire, *n. Brit.* county.

shirk, *v.* 1. evade (obligation). —*n.* 2. Also, **shirk′er.** person who shirks.

shirr, *v.* 1. gather (cloth) on parallel threads. 2. bake (eggs).

shirt, *n.* man's upper garment.

shiv′er, *v.* 1. tremble as with cold. 2. splinter. —*n.* 3. quiver. 4. splinter. —**shiv′er•y**, *adj.*

shoal, *n.* 1. shallow part of stream. 2. large number, esp. of fish.

shoat, *n.* young pig.

shock, *n.* 1. violent blow, impact, etc. 2. anything emotionally upsetting. 3. state of nervous collapse. 4. group of sheaves of grain. 5. bushy mass of hair, etc. —*v.* 6. strike with force, horror, etc.

shod′dy, *adj.* of poor quality. —**shod′di•ly**, *adv.* —**shod′di•ness**, *n.*

shoe, *n., v.*, **shod, shoeing.** —*n.* 1. external covering for foot. 2. shoelike machine part. —*v.* 3. provide with shoes. —**shoe′string′**, *n.*

shoe′horn′, *n.* shaped object to assist in slipping into shoe.

shoe′mak′er, *n.* person who makes or mends shoes.

shoot, *v.* 1. hit or kill with bullet, etc. 2. discharge (firearm, bow, etc.). 3. pass or send rapidly along. 4. emit. 5. grow; come forth. —*n.* 6. shooting contest. 7. young twig, etc. —**shoot′er**, *n.*

shop, *n., v.*, **shopped, shopping.** —*n.* 1. store. 2. workshop. —*v.* 3. inspect or purchase goods. —**shop′per**, *n.*

shop′lift′er, *n.* person who steals from shops while posing as customer.

shore, *v.*, **shored, shoring**, *n.* —*v.* 1. prop. —*n.* 2. prop. 3. land beside water. 4. land or country.

shorn, *pp.* of **shear.**

short, *adj.* 1. not long or tall. 2. rudely brief. 3. scanty. 4. inferior. 5. crumbly, as pastry. —*adv.* 6. abruptly. —*n.* 7. anything short. 8. (*pl.*) short, loose trousers. 9. short circuit. —**short′en**, *v.* —**short′ly**, *adv.* —**short′ness**, *n.*

short′age, *n.* scarcity.

short circuit, *Elect.* abnormal connection between two points in circuit.

short′com′ing, *n.* defect.

short′cut′, *n.* shorter way to goal.

short′en•ing, *n.* lard, etc., used to make pastry short.

short′hand′, *n.* system of swift handwriting.

short′-lived′ (-līvd′), *adj.* lasting but short time.

short′ly, *adv.* in short time.

short′-sight′ed, *adj.* lacking foresight.

shot, *n., pl.* **shots** or (for 3), **shot.** 1. discharge of firearm, bow, etc. 2. range of fire. 3. (*often pl.*) lead pellets. 4. act or instance of shooting. 5. person who shoots. 6. heavy metal ball.

shot′gun′, *n.* kind of smoothbore gun.

should, *v.* pt. of **shall.**

shoul′der, *n.* 1. part of body from neck to upper joint of arm or foreleg. 2. unpaved edge of road. —*v.* 3. push as with shoulder. 4. take up, as burden.

shout, *v.* 1. call or speak loudly. —*n.* 2. loud cry. —**shout′er**, *n.*

shove, *v.*, **shoved, shoving**, *n.* —*v.* 1. push hard. —*n.* 2. hard push.

shov′el, *n.* 1. implement with broad scoop and handle. —*v.* 2. dig or clear with shovel. —**shov′el•er**, *n.*

show, *v.*, **showed, shown** or **showed, showing**, *n.* —*v.* 1. display. 2. guide. 3. explain. 4. prove. 5. be visible. —*n.* 6. exhibition. 7. acted entertainment. 8. appearance.

show′down′, *n.* decisive confrontation.

show′er, *n.* 1. short fall of rain. 2. any similar fall. 3. bath in which water falls from above. —*v.* 4. rain briefly. 5. give liberally. —**show′er•y**, *adj.*

show′y, *adj.*, **showier, showiest.** conspicuous; ostentatious.

shrap′nel, *n.* shell filled with missiles.

shred, *n., v.*, **shredded** or **shred, shredding.** —*n.* 1. torn piece or strip. 2. bit. —*v.* 3. reduce to shreds.

shrew, *n.* 1. quarrelsome woman. 2. small mouselike mammal. —**shrew′ish**, *adj.*

shrewd, *adj.* astute. —**shrewd•ly**, *adv.* —**shrewd′ness**, *n.*

shriek, *n.* 1. loud shrill cry. —*v.* 2. utter shrieks.

shrike, *n.* predatory bird.

shrill, *adj.* 1. high-pitched; sharp. —*v.* 2. cry shrilly. —**shril′ly**, *adv.* —**shrill′ness**, *n.*

shrimp, *n.* small long-tailed edible shellfish.

shrine, *n.* place for sacred relics.

shrink, *v.*, **shrank** or **shrunk, shrunk** or **shrunken, shrinking.** 1. draw back. 2. become smaller.

shrink′age, *n.* 1. act of shrinking. 2. amount of shrinking.

shriv′el, *v.* wrinkle in drying.

shroud, *n.* 1. burial gown or cloth. 2. (*pl.*) set of ropes supporting masts of vessel. —*v.* 3. wrap; cover.

shrub, *n.* woody perennial plant. —**shrub′ber•y**, *n.*

shrug, *v.*, **shrugged, shrugging**, *n.* —*v.* 1. move shoulders to show ignorance, indifference, etc. —*n.* 2. this movement.

shuck, *n.* 1. husk. 2. shell. —*v.* 3. remove shucks from.

shud′der, *v.* 1. tremble, as from horror. —*n.* 2. this movement.

shuf′fle, *v.*, **-fled, -fling**, *n.* —*v.* 1. drag feet in walking. 2. mix (playing cards). 3. shift. —*n.* 4. shuffling gait. 5. act of shuffling of cards.

shuf′fle•board′, *n.* game played on marked floor surface.

shun, *v.*, **shunned, shunning**. avoid.

shunt, *v.* divert; sidetrack.

shut, *v.*, **shut, shutting**, *adj.* —*v.* 1. close. 2. confine. 3. exclude. —*adj.* 4. closed.

shut′ter, *n.* 1. cover for window. 2. device for opening and closing camera lens.

shut′tle, *n.*, *v.*, **-tled, -tling.** —*n.* 1. device for moving thread back and forth in weaving. 2. bus, plane, etc., moving between two destinations. —*v.* 3. move quickly back and forth.

shut′tle•cock′, *n.* feathered object hit back and forth in badminton.

shy, *adj.*, **shier, shiest**, *v.*, **shied, shying**, *n.*, *pl.* **shies.** —*adj.* 1. bashful. 2. wary. 3. short. —*v.* 4. start aside, as in fear. 5. throw suddenly. —*n.* 6. shying movement. 7. sudden throw. —**shy′ly**, *adv.* —**shy′ness**, *n.*

shy′ster, *n. Informal.* unscrupulous lawyer.

sib′i•lant, *adj.* 1. hissing. —*n.* 2. hissing sound. —**sib′i•lance**, *n.*

sib′ling, *n.* brother or sister.

sic, *v.*, **sicked, sicking**, *adv.* —*v.* 1. urge to attack. —*adv.* 2. *Latin.* so (it reads).

sick, *adj.* 1. ill; not well. 2. of sickness. 3. nauseated. —*n.pl.* 4. sick people. —**sick′ly**, *adv.* —**sick′ness**, *n.* —**sick′en**, *v.*

sick′le, *n.* reaping implement with curved blade.

sick′ly, *adj.*, **-lier, -liest**, *adv.* 1. ailing. 2. faint; weak. —*adv.* 3. in sick manner.

side, *n.*, *adj.*, *v.*, **sided, siding.** —*n.* 1. edge. 2. surface. 3. part other than front, back, top, or bottom. 4. aspect. 5. region. 6. faction. —*adj.* 7.

at, from, or toward side. 8. subordinate. —*v.* 9. align oneself.

side′board′, *n.* dining-room cupboard.

side′burns′, *n.pl.* short whiskers in front of ears.

side′long′, *adj.*, *adv.* to or toward the side.

si•de′re•al, *adj.* of or determined by stars.

side′sad′dle, *adv.* with both legs on one side of a saddle.

side′-step′, *v.*, **-stepped, -stepping.** avoid, as by stepping aside.

side′swipe′, *v.*, **-swiped, -swiping.** strike along side.

side′track′, *v.* divert.

side′walk′, *n.* paved walk along street.

side′ward, *adj.* toward one side. —**side′ward, side′wards**, *adv.*

side′ways′, *adj.*, *adv.* 1. with side foremost. 2. toward or from a side. Also, **side′wise′**.

sid′ing, *n.* short railroad track for halted cars.

si′dle, *v.*, **-dled, -dling.** move sideways or furtively.

siege, *n.* surrounding of place to force surrender.

si•en′na, *n.* yellowish- or reddish-brown pigment.

si•es′ta, *n.* midday nap or rest.

sieve (siv) *n.*, *v.*, **sieved, sieving.** —*n.* 1. meshed implement for separating coarse and fine loose matter. —*v.* 2. sift.

sift, *v.* separate with sieve. —**sift′er**, *n.*

sigh, *v.* 1. exhale audibly in grief, weariness, etc. 2. yearn. —*n.* 3. act or sound of sighing.

sight, *n.* 1. power of seeing. 2. glimpse; view. 3. range of vision. 4. device for guiding aim. 5. interesting place. —*v.* 6. get sight of. 7. aim by sights. —**sight′less**, *adj.*

sight′ly, *adj.*, **-lier, -liest.** pleasing to sight. —**sight′li•ness**, *n.*

sight′see′ing, *n.* visiting new places of interest. —**sight′se′er**, *n.* —**sight′-see′**, *v.*

sign, *n.* 1. indication. 2. conventional mark, figure, etc. 3. advertising board. —*v.* 4. put signature to. —**sign′er**, *n.*

sig′nal, *n.*, *adj.*, *v.*, **-naled, -naling.** —*n.* 1. symbolic communication. —*adj.* 2. serving as signal. 3. notable. —*v.* 4. communicate by symbols. —**sig′nal•er**, *n.*

sig′nal•ize′, *v.*, **-ized, -izing.** make notable.

sig′nal•ly, *adv.* notably.

sig′na•to′ry, *n.*, *pl.* **-ries.** signer.

sig′na•ture, *n.* 1. person's name in own handwriting. 2. musical sign.

sig′net, *n.* small seal.

sig•nif′i•cance, *n.* 1. importance. 2. meaning. —**sig•nif′i•cant**, *adj.*

sig′ni•fy′, *v.*, **-fied, -fying.** 1. make known. 2. mean. —**sig′ni•fi•ca′tion**, *n.*

si′lence, *n.*, *v.*, **-lenced, -lencing.** —*n.* 1. absence of sound. 2. muteness. —*v.* 3. bring to silence. —**si′lent**, *adj.* —**si′lent•ly**, *adv.*

sil′hou•ette′ (sil′ $\overline{oo}$ et′), *n.*, *v.*, **-etted, -etting.** —*n.* 1. filled-in outline. —*v.* 2. show in silhouette.

sil′i•ca, *n.* silicon dioxide, appearing as quartz, sand, flint, etc.

sil′i•con, *n.* abundant nonmetallic element.

silk, *n.* 1. fine soft fiber produced by silkworms. 2. thread or cloth made of it. —*adj.* 3. Also, **silk′en, silk′y.** of silk.

silk′worm′, *n.* caterpillar that spins silk to make its cocoon.

sill, *n.* horizontal piece beneath window, door, or wall.

sil′ly, *adj.*, **-lier, -liest.** 1. stupid. 2. absurd. —**sil′li•ness**, *n.*

si′lo, *n.*, *pl.* **-los.** airtight structure to hold green fodder.

silt, *n.* 1. earth, etc., carried and deposited by a stream. —*v.* 2. fill with silt.

sil′ver, *n.* 1. valuable white metallic element. 2. coins, utensils, etc., of silver. 3. whitish gray. —*adj.* 4. of or plated with silver. 5. eloquent. 6. indicating 25th anniversary. —**sil′ver•y**, *adj.*

sil′ver•ware′, *n.* silver table articles.

sim′i•an, *n.* 1. ape or monkey. —*adj.* 2. of apes or monkeys.

sim′i•lar, *adj.* with general likeness. —**sim′i•lar′i•ty**, *n.* —**sim′i•lar•ly**, *adv.*

sim′i•le′, *n.* phrase expressing resemblance.

si•mil′i•tude′, *n.* 1. likeness. 2. comparison.

sim′mer, *v.* remain or keep near boiling.

sim′per, *v.* 1. smile affectedly. —*n.* 2. affected smile.

sim′ple, *adj.*, **-pler, -plest.** 1. easy to grasp, use, etc. 2. plain. 3. mentally weak. —**sim•plic′i•ty**, *n.* —**sim′ply**, *adv.*

sim′ple•ton, *n.* fool.

sim′pli•fy′, *v.*, **-fied, -fying.** make simpler. —**sim′pli•fi•ca′tion**, *n.*

sim·plis'tic, *adj.* foolishly or naïvely simple. **—sim·plis'ti·cal·ly,** *adv.*

sim·u·late', *v.,* **-lated, -lating.** feign; imitate. **—sim'u·la'tion,** *n.* **—sim'u·la'tive,** *adj.*

si'mul·ta'ne·ous, *adj.* occurring at the same time. **—si'mul·ta'ne·ous·ly,** *adv.* **—si'mul·ta·ne'i·ty, —si'mul·ta'ne·ous·ness,** *n.*

sin, *n., v.,* **sinned, sinning. —n.** 1. offense, esp. against divine law. **—v.** 2. commit sin. **—sin'ful,** *adj.* **—sin'ful·ly,** *adv.* **—sin'ful·ness,** *n.*

since, *adv.* 1. from then till now. 2. subsequently. **—conj.** 3. from time when. 4. because.

sin·cere', *adj.,* **-cerer, -cerest.** honest; genuine. **—sin·cer'i·ty,** *n.* **—sin·cere'ly,** *adv.*

si'ne·cure' (sī'ni kyŏŏr'), *n.* job without real responsibilities.

sin'ew, *n.* 1. tendon. 2. strength. **—sin'ew·y,** *adj.*

sing, *v.,* **sang** or **sung, sung, singing.** 1. utter words to music. 2. acclaim. **—sing'er,** *n.*

singe, *v.,* **singed, singeing,** *n.* scorch.

sin'gle, *adj., v.,* **-gled, -gling,** *n.* **—adj.** 1. one only. 2. unmarried. **—v.** 3. select. **—n.** 4. something single. **—sin'gly,** *adv.*

sing'song', *adj.* monotonous in rhythm.

sin'gu·lar, *adj.* 1. extraordinary. 2. separate. 3. denoting one person or thing. **—n.** 4. singular number or form. **—sin'gu·lar'i·ty,** *n.* **—sin'gu·lar·ly,** *adv.*

sin'is·ter, *adj.* threatening evil.

sink, *v.,* **sank** or **sunk, sunk** or **sunken, sinking,** *n.* **—v.** 1. descend or drop. 2. deteriorate gradually. 3. submerge. 4. dig (a hole, etc.). 5. bury (pipe, etc.). **—n.** 6. basin connected with drain. **—sink'er,** *n.*

sin'ner, *n.* person who sins.

sin'u·ous, *adj.* winding.

si'nus, *n.* cavity or passage.

sip, *v.,* **sipped, sipping,** *n.* **—v.** 1. drink little at a time. **—n.** 2. act of sipping. 3. amount taken in sip.

si'phon, *n.* 1. tube for drawing liquids by gravity and suction to another container. **—v.** 2. move by siphon.

sir, *n.* 1. formal term of address to man. 2. title of knight or baronet.

sire, *n., v.,* **sired, siring. —n.** 1. male parent. **—v.** 2. beget.

si'ren, *n.* 1. mythical, alluring sea nymph. 2. noise-making device used on emergency vehicles.

sir'up, *n.* syrup.

si'sal, *n.* fiber used in ropes.

sis'ter, *n.* 1. daughter of one's parents. 2. nun. **—sis'ter·hood',** *n.* **—sis'ter·ly,** *adj.*

sis'ter-in-law', *n., pl.* **sisters-in-law.** 1. sister of one's spouse. 2. wife of one's brother.

sit, *v.,* **sat, sitting.** 1. rest on lower part of trunk of body. 2. be situated. 3. pose. 4. be in session. 5. seat. **—sit'ter,** *n.*

site, *n.* position; location.

sit'-in', *n.* passive protest by demonstrators who occupy premises or seats refused to them.

sit'u·ate', *v.,* **-ated, -ating.** settle; locate.

sit'u·a'tion, *n.* 1. location. 2. condition. 3. job.

six, *n., adj.* five plus one. **—sixth,** *adj., n.*

six'teen', *n., adj.* ten plus six. **—six·teenth',** *adj., n.*

six'ty, *n., adj.* ten times six. **—six'ti·eth,** *adj., n.*

siz'a·ble, *adj.* fairly large. Also, **size'a·ble.**

size, *n., v.,* **sized, sizing. —n.** 1. dimensions or extent. 2. great magnitude. 3. Also, **sizing.** coating for paper, cloth, etc. **—v.** 4. sort according to size. 5. treat with sizing.

siz'zle, *v.,* **-zled, -zling,** *n.* **—v.** 1. make hissing sound, as in frying. **—n.** 2. sizzling sound.

skate, *n., pl.* **skates** or (for 3) **skate,** *v.,* **skated, skating. —n.** 1. steel runner fitted to shoe for gliding on ice. 2. roller skate. 3. flat-bodied marine fish; ray. **—v.** 4. glide on skates. **—skat'er,** *n.*

skate'board', *n.* oblong board on roller-skate wheels.

skein (skān), *n.* coil of yarn or thread.

skel'e·ton, *n.* bony framework of human or animal. **—skel'e·tal,** *adj.*

skep'tic, *n.* person who doubts or questions. **—skep'ti·cal·ly,** *adv.* **—skep'ti·cal,** *adj.* **—skep'ti·cism',** *n.*

sketch, *n.* 1. simple hasty drawing. 2. rough plan. **—v.** 3. make sketch (of).

sketch'y, *adj.,* **-ier, -iest.** vague; approximate. **—sketch'i·ly,** *adv.*

skew'er, *n.* pin for holding meat, etc., while cooking.

ski, *n., pl.* **skis,** *v.,* **skied, skiing. —n.** 1. slender board fastened to shoe for traveling over snow. **—v.** 2. travel by skis. **—ski'er,** *n.*

skid, *n., v.,* **skidded, skidding. —n.** 1. surface on which to support or slide heavy object. 2. act of skidding. **—v.** 3. slide on skids. 4. slip.

skiff, *n.* small boat.

skill, *n.* expertness; dexterity. **—skilled,** *adj.* **—skill'ful,** *adj.* **—skill'ful·ly,** *adv.*

skil'let, *n.* frying pan.

skim, *v.,* **skimmed, skimming.** 1. remove from surface of liquid. 2. move lightly on surface.

skimp, *v.* scrimp.

skimp'y, *adj.,* **skimpier, skimpiest.** scant. **—skimp'i·ness,** *n.*

skin, *n., v.,* **skinned, skinning. —n.** 1. outer covering, as of body. **—v.** 2. strip of skin. **—skin'ner,** *n.*

skin'flint', *n.* stingy person.

skin'ny, *adj.* very thin.

skip, *v.,* **skipped, skipping,** *n.* **—v.** 1. spring; leap. 2. omit; disregard. **—n.** 3. light jump.

skip'per, *n.* 1. master of ship. **—v.** 2. act as skipper of.

skir'mish, *n.* 1. brief fight between small forces. **—v.** 2. engage in skirmish. **—skir'mish·er,** *n.*

skirt, *n.* 1. part of gown, etc., below waist. 2. woman's garment extending down from waist. 3. (*pl.*) outskirts. **—v.** 4. pass around edge of. 5. border.

skit, *n.* short comedy.

skit'tish, *adj.* apt to shy; restless.

skul·dug'ger·y, *n.* trickery.

skulk, *v.* sneak about; lie hidden. **—skulk'er,** *n.*

skull, *n.* bony framework around brain.

skunk, *n.* small, striped, fur-bearing mammal.

sky, *n., pl.* **skies.** region well above earth. **—sky'ward',** *adv., adj.*

sky'dive', *v.,* **-dived, -diving.** make parachute jump with longest free fall possible. **—sky'div'er,** *n.*

sky'jack', *v. Informal.* capture (aircraft) while in flight. **—sky'jack'er,** *n.*

sky'light', *n.* window in roof, ceiling, etc.

sky'line', *n.* 1. outline against sky. 2. apparent horizon.

sky'rock'et, *n.* firework that rises into air before exploding.

sky'scrap'er, *n.* building with many stories.

slab, *n.* broad flat piece of material.

slack, *adj.* 1. loose. 2. inactive. **—adv.** 3. slackly. **—n.** 4. slack part. 5. inactive period. —v. 6. slacken. —**slack′-ly**, adv. —**slack′ness**, n.

slack′en, v. 1. make or become slack. 2. weaken.

slacks, n.pl. loose trousers.

slag, n. refuse matter from smelting metal from ore.

slake, v., **slaked, slaking.** 1. allay (thirst, etc.). 2. treat (lime) with water.

slam, v., **slammed, slamming,** n. —v. 1. shut noisily. —n. 2. this sound.

slan′der, n. 1. false, defamatory spoken statement. —v. 2. utter slander against. —**slan′der•ous,** adj.

slang, n. markedly informal language. —**slang′y,** adj.

slant, v. 1. slope. —n. 2. slope. 3. opinion. —**slant′ing•ly,** adv.

slap, v., **slapped, slapping,** n. —v. 1. strike, esp. with open hand. —n. 2. such blow.

slash, v. 1. cut, esp. violently and at random. —n. 2. such cut.

slat, n., v., **slatted, slatting.** —n. 1. thin narrow strip. —v. 2. furnish with slats.

slate, n., v., **slated, slating.** —n. 1. kind of layered rock. 2. dark bluish gray. 3. list of nominees. —v. 4. put in line for appointment.

slat′tern, n. untidy woman. —**slat′tern•ly,** adj.

slaugh′ter, n. 1. killing, esp. of animals for food. —v. 2. kill for food. 3. massacre. —**slaugh′ter•house′,** n.

slave, n., v., **slaved, slaving.** —n. 1. person owned by another. —v. 2. drudge. —**slav′er•y,** n.

slav′er, v. let saliva run from mouth.

slav′ish (slāv′-), adj. 1. without originality. 2. servile. —**slav′ish•ly,** adv.

slaw, n. chopped seasoned raw cabbage.

slay, v., **slew, slain, slaying.** kill. —**slay′er,** n.

slea′zy (slē′zē), adj., **-zier, -ziest.** shoddy. —**sleaz′i•ness,** n.

sled, n., v., **sledded, sledding.** —n. 1. vehicle traveling on snow. —v. 2. ride on sled.

sledge, n., v., **sledged, sledging.** —n. 1. heavy sledlike vehicle. 2. Also, **sledge′ham′mer.** large heavy hammer. —v. 3. travel by sledge.

sleek, adj. 1. smooth; glossy. —v. 2. smooth. —**sleek′ly,** adv. —**sleek′ness,** n.

sleep, v., **slept, sleeping,** n. —v. 1. rest during natural suspension of consciousness. —n. 2. state or period of sleeping. —**sleep′less,** adj. —**sleep′y,** adj. —**sleep′i•ly,** adv.

sleep′er, n. 1. person who sleeps. 2. railroad car equipped for sleeping. 3. raillike foundation member. 4. unexpected success.

sleet, n. hard frozen rain.

sleeve, n. part of garment covering arm.

sleigh, n. light sled.

sleight of hand (slīt), skill in conjuring or juggling.

slen′der, adj. 1. small in circumference. 2. scanty or weak. —**slen′der•ize′,** v. —**slen′der•ness,** n.

sleuth, n. detective.

slew, pt. of **slay.**

slice, n., v., **sliced, slicing.** —n. 1. broad flat piece. —v. 2. cut into slices. —**slic′er,** n.

slick, adj. 1. sleek. 2. sly. 3. slippery. —n. 4. oil-covered area. —v. 5. smooth.

slick′er, n. raincoat.

slide, v., **slid, sliding,** n. —v. 1. move easily; glide. —n. 2. act of sliding. 3. area for sliding. 4. landslide. 5. glass plate used in microscope. 6. transparent picture.

slight, adj. 1. trifling; small. 2. slim. —v. 3. treat as unimportant. —n. 4. such treatment; snub. —**slight′ness,** n.

slight′ly, adv. barely; partly.

slim, adj., **slimmer, slimmest.** 1. slender. 2. poor. —v. 3. make or become slim. —**slim′ly,** adv. —**slim′ness,** n.

slime, n. 1. thin sticky mud. 2. sticky secretion of plants or animals. —**slim′y,** adj.

sling, n., v., **slung, slinging.** —n. 1. straplike device for hurling stones. 2. looped rope, bandage, etc., as support. —v. 3. hurl. 4. hang loosely.

slink, v., **slunk, slinking.** go furtively. —**slink′y,** adj.

slip, v., **slipped, slipping,** n. —v. 1. move or go easily. 2. escape. 3. make mistake. —n. 4. act of slipping. 5. mistake. 6. undergarment. 7. space between piers for vessel. 8. twig for propagating. —**slip′page,** n.

slip′per, n. light shoe.

slip′per•y, adj. 1. causing slipping. 2. tending to slip.

slip′shod′, adj. careless.

slit, v., **slit, slitting,** n. —v. 1. cut apart or in strips. —n. 2. narrow opening.

slith′er, v. slide.

sliv′er, n., v. splinter.

slob′ber, v., n. slaver.

sloe, n. small sour fruit of blackthorn.

slog, v., **slogged, slogging.** plod heavily. —**slog′ger,** n.

slo′gan, n. motto.

sloop, n. kind of sailing vessel.

slop, v., **slopped, slopping,** n. —v. 1. spill liquid. —n. 2. spilled liquid. 3. swill.

slope, v., **sloped, sloping,** n. —v. 1. incline; slant. —n. 2. amount of inclination. 3. sloping surface.

slop′py, adj. **-pier, -piest.** 1. untidy. 2. careless. —**slop′pi•ly,** adv. —**slop′pi•ness,** n.

slosh, v. splash.

slot, n. narrow opening.

sloth (slôth), n. 1. laziness. 2. tree-living South American mammal. —**sloth′ful,** adj.

slouch, v. 1. move or rest droopingly. —n. 2. drooping posture. —**slouch′y,** adj.

slough, n. 1. (slou). muddy area. 2. (slo͞o). marshy pond or inlet. 3. (sluf). cast-off skin or dead tissue. —v. (sluf). 4. be shed. 5. cast off.

slov′en (sluv′ən), n. untidy or careless person. —**slov′en•ly,** adj., adv.

slow, adj. 1. not fast. 2. not intelligent or perceptive. 3. running behind time. —adv. 4. slowly. —v. 5. make or become slow. —**slow′ly,** adv. —**slow′ness,** n.

slow′down′, n. slackening of pace or speed.

sludge, n. mud.

slue, v., **slued, sluing.** turn round.

slug, v., **slugged, slugging,** n. —v. 1. hit with fists. —n. 2. slimy, crawling mollusk having no shell. 3. billet. 4. counterfeit coin. —**slug′ger,** n.

slug′gard, n. lazy person.

slug′gish, adj. inactive; slow. —**slug′gish•ly,** adv. —**slug′gish•ness,** n.

sluice (slo͞os), n. channel with gate to control flow.

slum, n. squalid, overcrowded residence or neighborhood.

slum′ber, v., n. sleep.

slump, v. 1. drop heavily or suddenly. —n. 2. act of slumping.

slur, v. **slurred, slurring,** n. —v. 1. say indistinctly. 2. disparage. —n. 3. slurred sound. 4. disparaging remark.

slush, n. partly melted snow. —**slush′y,** adj.

slut, n. slatternly or dissolute woman.

sly, adj., **slyer, slyest** or **slier, sliest.** 1. cunning. 2. stealthy. —**sly′ly,** adv. —**sly′ness,** n.

smack, *v.* 1. separate (lips) noisily. 2. slap. 3. have taste or trace. —*n.* 4. smacking of lips. 5. loud kiss. 6. slap. 7. taste. 8. trace. 9. small fishing boat.

small, *adj.* 1. not big; little. 2. not great in importance, value, etc. 3. ungenerous. —*adv.* 4. in small pieces. —*n.* 5. small part, as of back. —**small′ness,** *n.*

small′pox′, *n.* contagious disease marked by fever and pustules.

smart, *v.* 1. cause or feel sharp superficial pain. —*adj.* 2. sharp; severe. 3. clever. 4. stylish. —*n.* 5. sharp local pain. —**smart′ly,** *adv.* —**smart′ness,** *n.*

smart′en, *v.* improve in appearance.

smash, *v.* 1. break to pieces. —*n.* 2. act of smashing; destruction.

smat′ter•ing, *n.* slight knowledge.

smear, *v.* 1. rub with dirt, grease, etc. 2. sully. —*n.* 3. smeared spot. 4. slanderous attack.

smell, *v.* 1. perceive with nose. 2. have odor. —*n.* 3. faculty of smelling. 4. odor.

smelt, *n., pl.* **smelts, smelt,** *v.* —*n.* 1. small edible fish. —*v.* 2. melt (ore or metal). —**smelt′er,** *n.*

smi′lax, *n.* delicate twining plant.

smile, *v.,* **smiled, smiling,** *n.* —*v.* 1. assume look of pleasure, etc. 2. look favorably. —*n.* 3. smiling look.

smirch, *v.* 1. soil or sully. —*n.* 2. stain.

smirk, *v.* 1. smile smugly or affectedly. —*n.* 2. such a smile.

smite, *v.,* **smote, smitten** or **smit, smiting.** 1. strike. 2. charm.

smith, *n.* worker in metal.

smith′er•eens′, *n.pl.* fragments.

smith′y, *n., pl.* **smithies.** blacksmith's shop.

smock, *n.* long, loose overgarment.

smog, *n.* smoke and fog.

smoke, *n., v.,* **smoked, smoking.** —*n.* 1. visible vapor from burning. —*v.* 2. emit smoke. 3. draw into mouth and puff out tobacco smoke. 4. treat with smoke. —**smok′er,** *n.* —**smok′y,** *adj.*

smol′der, *v.* 1. burn without flame. 2. exist suppressed. Also, **smoul′der.**

smooth, *adj.* 1. even in surface. 2. easy; tranquil. —*v.* 3. make smooth. —*n.* 4. smooth place. —**smooth′ly,** *adv.* —**smooth′ness,** *n.*

smooth′bore′, *adj.* (of gun) not rifled.

smor′gas•bord′, *n.* table of assorted foods.

smoth′er, *v.* suffocate.

smudge, *n., v.,* **smudged, smudging.** —*n.* 1. dirty smear. 2. smoky fire. —*v.* 3. soil.

smug, *adj.* 1. self-satisfied. 2. trim. —**smug′ly,** *adv.* —**smug′ness,** *n.*

smug′gle, *v.,* **-gled, -gling.** 1. import or export secretly and illegally. 2. bring or take secretly. —**smug′gler,** *n.*

smut, *n.* 1. soot. 2. smudge. 3. obscenity. 4. plant disease. —**smut′ty,** *adj.*

snack, *n.* light meal.

snaf′fle, *n.* kind of bit used on bridle.

snag, *n., v.,* **snagged, snagging.** —*n.* 1. sharp projection. 2. obstacle. —*v.* 3. catch on snag.

snail, *n.* crawling, single-shelled mollusk.

snake, *n., v.,* **snaked, snaking.** —*n.* 1. scaly limbless reptile. —*v.* 2. move like snake. 3. drag. —**snak′y,** *adj.*

snap, *v.,* **snapped, snapping,** *n., adj.* —*v.* 1. make sudden sharp sound. 2. break abruptly. 3. bite (at). 4. photograph. —*n.* 5. snapping sound. 6. kind of fastener. 7. *Informal.* easy thing. —*adj.* 8. unconsidered.

snap′drag′on, *n.* plant with spikes of flowers.

snap′pish, *adj.* cross.

snap′py, *adj.* **-pier, -piest.** 1. quick. 2. smart; stylish.

snap′shot′, *n.* unposed photograph.

snare, *n., v.,* **snared, snaring.** —*n.* 1. kind of trap. 2. strand across skin of small drum. —*v.* 3. entrap.

snarl, *v., n.* 1. growl. 2. tangle.

snatch, *v.* 1. grab. —*n.* 2. grabbing motion. 3. scrap of melody, etc. —**snatch′er,** *n.*

sneak, *v.* 1. go or act furtively. —*n.* 2. person who sneaks. —**sneak′y,** *adj.*

sneak′er, *n.* rubber-soled shoe.

sneer, *v.* 1. show contempt. —*n.* 2. contemptuous look or remark.

sneeze, *v.,* **sneezed, sneezing,** *n.* —*v.* 1. emit breath suddenly and forcibly from nose. —*n.* 2. act of sneezing.

snick′er, *n.* derisive, stifled laugh. —**snick′er,** *v.* Also, **snig′ger.**

sniff, *v.* 1. inhale quickly and audibly. —*n.* 2. such an inhalation. Also, **snif′fle.**

snip, *v.,* **snipped, snipping,** *n.* —*v.* 1. cut with small, quick strokes. —*n.* 2. small piece cut off. 3. cut. 4. *(pl.)* large scissors.

snipe, *n., v.,* **sniped, sniping.** —*n.* 1. shore bird. —*v.* 2. shoot from concealment. —**snip′er,** *n.*

sniv′el, *v.* 1. weep weakly. 2. run at nose.

snob, *n.* person overconcerned with position, wealth, etc. —**snob′bish,** *adj.* —**snob′ber•y,** *n.*

snood, *n.* band or net for hair.

snoop, *Informal.* —*v.* 1. prowl or pry. —*n.* 2. Also, **snoop′er.** person who snoops.

snooze, *v.,* **snoozed, snoozing,** *n. Informal.* nap.

snore, *v.,* **snored, snoring,** *n.* —*v.* 1. breathe audibly in sleep. —*n.* 2. sound of snoring. —**snor′er,** *n.*

snor′kel, *n.* ventilating device for submarines.

snort, *v.* 1. exhale loudly and harshly. —*n.* 2. sound of snorting.

snot, *n. Informal.* nasal mucus.

snout, *n.* projecting nose and jaw.

snow, *n.* 1. white crystalline flakes that fall to earth. —*v.* 2. fall, as snow. —**snow′drift′,** *n.* —**snow′fall′,** *n.* —**snow′flake′,** *n.* —**snow′storm′,** *n.* —**snow′y,** *adj.*

snow′ball′, *n.* 1. ball of snow. 2. flowering shrub. —*v.* 3. grow rapidly.

snow′mo•bile′, *n.* motor vehicle built to travel on snow.

snow′shoe′, *n.* racketlike shoe for walking on snow.

snub, *v.,* **snubbed, snubbing,** *n., adj.* —*v.* 1. treat with scorn. 2. check or stop. —*n.* 3. rebuke or slight. —*adj.* 4. (of nose) short and turned up.

snuff, *v.* 1. inhale. 2. smell. 3. extinguish. —*n.* 4. powdered tobacco.

snuf′fle, *v.,* **-fled, -fling,** *n.* sniff.

snug, *adj.,* **snugger, snuggest.** 1. cozy. 2. trim; neat. —**snug′ly,** *adv.*

snug′gle, *v.,* **-gled, -gling.** nestle.

so, *adv.* 1. in this or that way. 2. to such degree. 3. as stated. —*conj.* 4. consequently. 5. in order that.

soak, *v.* 1. wet thoroughly. 2. absorb. —**soak′er,** *n.*

soap, *n.* 1. substance used for washing. —*v.* 2. rub with soap. —**soap′y,** *adj.*

soar, *v.* fly upward.

sob, *v.,* **sobbed, sobbing,** *n.* —*v.* 1. weep convulsively. —*n.* 2. convulsive breath.

so′ber, *adj.* 1. not drunk. 2. quiet; grave. —*v.* 3. make or become sober. —**so•bri′e•ty, so′ber•ness,** *n.* —**so′ber•ly,** *adv.*

so′-called′, *adj.* called thus.

soc′cer, *n.* game resembling football.

so′cia•ble, *adj.* friendly. —**so′cia•bly,** *adv.* —**so′cia•bil′i•ty,** *n.*

so′cial, *adj.* 1. devoted to companionship. 2. of human society. —**so′cial•ly,** *adv.*

so′cial•ism, *n.* theory advocating community ownership of means of production, etc. —**so′cial•ist,** *n.* —**so′cial•is′tic,** *adj.*

so′cial•ize′, *v.,* **-ized, -izing.** 1. associate with others. 2. put on socialistic basis.

so•ci′e•ty, *n., pl.* **-ties.** 1. group of persons with common interests. 2. human beings generally. 3. fashionable people.

Society of Friends, sect founded 1650; Quakers.

so′ci•ol′o•gy, *n.* science of social relations and institutions. —**so′ci•o•log′i•cal,** *adj.* —**so′ci•ol′o•gist,** *n.*

sock, *n. Informal.* short stocking.

sock′et, *n.* holelike part for holding another part.

sod, *n.* grass with its roots.

so′da, *n.* 1. drink made with soda water. 2. preparation containing sodium.

so•dal′i•ty, *n., pl.* **-ties.** association.

soda water, water charged with carbon dioxide.

sod′den, *adj.* 1. soaked. 2. stupid. —**sod′den•ness,** *n.*

so′di•um, *n.* soft whitish metallic element.

sod′o•my (sod′-), *n.* unnatural sexual intercourse.

so′fa (sō′fə), *n.* couch with back and arms.

soft, *adj.* 1. yielding readily. 2. gentle; pleasant. 3. not strong. 4. (of water) free from mineral salts. 5. without alcohol. —**sof′ten,** *v.* —**soft′ly,** *adv.* —**soft′ness,** *n.*

soft′ware′, *n.* programs, charts, etc., for use with a computer.

sog′gy, *adj.* 1. soaked. 2. damp and heavy. —**sog′gi•ness,** *n.*

soil, *v.* 1. dirty; smudge. —*n.* 2. spot or stain. 3. sewage. 4. earth; ground.

soi•rée′ (swä rā′), *n.* evening party.

so′journ, *v.* 1. dwell briefly. —*n.* 2. short stay.

sol′ace (sol′is), *n., v.* comfort in grief.

so′lar, *adj.* of the sun.

so•lar′i•um (-lâr′-), *n., pl.* **-iums, -ia.** glass-enclosed room for enjoying sunlight.

sol′der (sod′ər), *n.* 1. fusible alloy for joining metal. —*v.* 2. join with solder.

sol′dier, *n.* 1. member of army. —*v.* 2. serve as soldier. —**sol′dier•ly,** *adj.* —**sol′dier•y,** *n.*

sole, *n., v.,* **soled, soling,** *adj.* —*n.* 1. bottom of foot or shoe. 2. edible flat-fish. —*v.* 3. put sole on. —*adj.* 4. only. —**sole′ly,** *adv.*

sol′emn, *adj.* 1. grave; serious. 2. sacred. —**so•lem′ni•ty,** *n.* —**sol′emn•ly,** *adv.*

sol′em•nize′, *v.,* **-nized, -nizing.** observe with ceremonies. —**sol′em•ni•za′tion,** *n.*

so•lic′it (-lis′-), *v.* entreat; request. —**so•lic′i•ta′tion,** *n.*

so•lic′i•tor, *n.* 1. person who solicits. 2. *Brit.* lawyer.

so•lic′it•ous, *adj.* anxious; concerned. —**so•lic′it•ous•ly,** *adv.* —**so•lic′i•tude′,** *n.*

sol′id, *adj.* 1. having length, breadth, and thickness. 2. not hollow. 3. dense. 4. substantial. 5. entire. —*n.* 6. solid body. —**so•lid′i•fy′,** *v.* —**so•lid′i•ty,** *n.*

sol′i•dar′i•ty, *n., pl.* **-ties.** community of interests, etc.

sol′id•ly, *adv.* 1. so as to be solid. 2. whole-heartedly; fully.

so•lil′o•quy (-kwē), *n., pl.* **-quies.** speech when alone. —**so•lil′o•quize′,** *v.*

sol′i•taire′, *n.* 1. card game for one person. 2. gem set alone.

sol′i•tar′y, *adj.* 1. alone. 2. single. 3. secluded. —**sol′i•tude′,** *n.*

so′lo, *n.* performance by one person. —**so′lo•ist,** *n.*

sol′stice, *n.* time in summer (June 21) or winter (Dec. 21) when sun is at its farthest from equator.

sol′u•ble, *adj.* able to be dissolved. —**sol′u•bil′i•ty,** *n.* —**sol′u•bly,** *adv.*

so•lu′tion, *n.* 1. explanation or answer. 2. dispersion of one substance in another. 3. resulting substance.

solve, *v.,* **solved, solving.** find explanation of. —**solv′a•ble,** *adj.* —**solv′er,** *n.*

sol′vent, *adj.* 1. able to pay one's debts. 2. causing dissolving. —*n.* 3. agent that dissolves. —**sol′ven•cy,** *n.*

som′ber, *adj.* gloomy; dark. Also, **som′bre.** —**som′ber•ly,** *adv.*

som•bre′ro (-brâr′ō), *n.* tall, broad-brimmed hat.

some, *adj.* 1. being an unspecified one or number. 2. certain. *pron.* 3. unspecified number or amount.

some′bod′y, *pron.* some person. Also, **some′one′.**

some′day′, *adv.* at some distant time.

some′how′, *adv.* in some way.

som′er•sault′, *n.* heels-over-head turn of body.

some′thing′, *n.* unspecified thing.

some′time′, *adv.* 1. at indefinite time. —*adj.* 2. former.

some′times′, *adv.* at times.

some′what′, *adv.* to some extent.

some′where′, *adv.* in, at, or to unspecified place.

som•nam′bu•lism, *n.* sleep-walking. —**som•nam′bu•list,** *n.*

som′no•lent, *adj.* sleepy. —**som′no•lence,** *n.*

son, *n.* male offspring.

so•na′ta, *n.* instrumental composition.

song, *n.* music or verse for singing. —**song′ster,** *n.* —**song′stress,** *n.fem.*

son′ic, *adj.* of sound.

son′-in-law′, *n., pl.* **sons-in-law.** husband of one's daughter.

son′net, *n.* fourteen-line poem in fixed form

so•no′rous, *adj.* 1. resonant. 2. grandiose in expression. —**so•nor′i•ty,** *n.* —**so•no′rous•ly,** *adv.*

soon, *adv.* in short time.

soot, *n.* black substance in smoke. —**soot′y,** *adj.*

soothe, *v.,* **soothed, soothing.** calm; allay.

sooth′say′er, *n.* person who predicts.

sop, *n., v.,* **sopped, sopping.** —*n.* 1. food dipped in liquid. 2. something given to pacify. —*v.* 3. soak (food). 4. absorb.

so•phis′ti•cat′ed, *adj.* worldly; not simple. —**so•phis′ti•cate** (-kit), *n.* —**so•phis′ti•ca′tion,** *n.*

soph′ist•ry, *n., pl.* **-ries.** clever but unsound reasoning. —**soph′ist,** *n.*

soph′o•more′, *n.* second-year student.

soph′o•mor′ic, *adj.* intellectually immature.

so′po•rif′ic, *adj.* 1. causing sleep. —*n.* 2. soporific agent.

so•pran′o, *n., pl.* **-pranos.** 1. highest singing voice. 2. singer with such voice.

sor′cer•er, *n.* magician. Also, *fem.* **sor′cer•ess.** —**sor′cer•y,** *n.*

sor′did, *adj.* 1. dirty. 2. ignoble.

sore, *adj.,* **sorer, sorest,** —*adj.* 1. painful or tender. 2. grieved. 3. causing misery. 4. *Informal.* annoyed. —*n.* 5. sore spot. —**sore′ly,** *adv.* —**sore′ness,** *n.*

sor′ghum (-gəm), *n.* cereal used in making syrup, etc.

so•ror′i•ty, *n., pl.* **-ties.** club of women or girls.

sor′rel, *n.* 1. reddish brown. 2. sorrel horse. 3. salad plant.

sor'row, *n.* 1. grief; regret; misfortune. —*v.* 2. feel sorrow. —**sor'row•ful,** *adj.* —**sor'row•ful•ly,** *adv.* —**sor'row•ful•ness,** *n.*

sor'ry, *adj.* 1. feeling regret or pity. 2. wretched.

sort, *n.* 1. kind or class. 2. character. 3. manner. —*v.* 4. separate; classify. —**sort'er,** *n.*

sor'tie (sôr'tē), *n.* 1. attack by defending troops. 2. combat mission.

SOS, call for help.

so'-so', *adj.* 1. neither good nor bad. —*adv.* 2. tolerably.

sot, *n.* drunkard. —**sot'tish,** *adj.*

souf•fle' (soo flā'), *n.* fluffy baked dish.

sough (sou), *v.* 1. rustle or murmur, as wind. —*n.* 2. act of soughing.

sought, pt. and pp. of **seek.**

soul, *n.* 1. thinking and feeling part of man. 2. essential quality. 3. person. —*adj.* 4. of black customs and culture. —**soul'ful,** *adj.* —**soul'less,** *adj.*

sound, *n.* 1. sensation affecting organs of hearing, produced by vibrations (**sound waves**). 2. special tone. 3. noise. 4. inlet or passage of sea. —*v.* 5. make sound. 6. say. 7. give certain impression. 8. measure depth of. 9. examine; question. —*adj.* 10. healthy; strong. 11. reliable. 12. valid. —**sound'proof',** *adj.* —**sound'ly,** *adv.* —**sound'ness,** *n.*

soup, *n.* liquid food of meat, vegetables, etc.

sour, *adj.* 1. acid in taste; tart. 2. spoiled. 3. disagreeable. —*v.* 4. turn sour. —**sour'ly,** *adv.* —**sour'ness,** *n.*

source, *n.* origin.

souse, *v.,* **soused, sousing,** *n.* —*v.* 1. immerse; drench. 2. pickle. —*n.* 3. act of sousing. 4. pickled food.

south, *n.* 1. point of compass opposite north. 2. this direction. 3. territory in this direction. —*adj., adv.* 4. toward, in, or from south. —**south'er•ly,** *adj., adv.* —**south'ern,** *adj.* —**south'ern•er,** *n.* —**south'ward,** *adj., adv.*

south'east', *n.,* point or direction midway between south and east. —**south'east',** *adj., adv.*

south'west', *n.* point or direction midway between south and west. —**south'west',** *adj., adv.*

sou've•nir' (soo'və nēr'), *n.* memento.

sov'er•eign (sov'rin), *n.* 1. monarch. 2. (formerly) British gold coin worth one pound. —*adj.* 3. of a sovereign; supreme. —**sov'er•eign•ty,** *n.*

so'vi•et', *n.* 1. (in USSR) governing body. —*adj.* 2. (*cap.*) of USSR.

sow, *v.* 1. (sō). plant seed. —*n.* 2. (sou). female hog. —**sow'er,** *n.*

soy'bean', *n.* nutritious seed of leguminous plant.

spa, *n.* resort at mineral spring.

space, *n., v.,* **spaced, spacing.** —*n.* 1. unlimited expanse. 2. particular part of this. 3. linear distance. 4. interval of time. —*v.* 5. divide into space. 6. set at intervals.

space'craft', *n., pl.* **-craft.** vehicle for traveling in outer space.

space'ship', *n.* rocket vehicle for travel between planets.

spa'cious, *adj.* large; vast. —**spa'cious•ly,** *adv.* —**spa'cious•ness,** *n.*

spade, *n., v.,* **spaded, spading.** —*n.* 1. tool with blade for digging. 2. (*pl.*) suit of playing cards. —*v.* 3. dig with spade.

spa•ghet'ti, *n.* cordlike food paste.

span, *n., v.,* **spanned, spanning.** —*n.* 1. distance between extended thumb and little finger. 2. space between two supports. 3. full extent. 4. team of animals. —*v.* 5. extend over.

span'gle, *n., v.,* **-gled, -gling.** —*n.* 1. small bright ornament. —*v.* 2. decorate with spangles.

span'iel, *n.* kind of dog.

Span'ish, *n.* language or people of Spain. —**Spanish,** *adj.*

spank, *v.* 1. strike on buttocks. —*n.* 2. such blow.

spank'ing, *adj.* brisk, vigorous.

spar, *v.,* **sparred, sparring,** *n.* —*v.* 1. box. 2. bandy words. —*n.* 3. *Naut.* mast, yard, etc. 4. bright crystalline mineral.

spare, *v.,* **spared, sparing,** *adj.,* **sparer, sparest.** —*v.* 1. deal gently with. 2. part with easily. —*adj.* 3. kept in reserve. 4. extra. 5. lean.

spare'rib', *n.* cut of pork ribs.

spark, *n.* 1. burning particle. 2. flash of electricity. 3. trace.

spar'kle, *v.,* **-kled, -kling,** *n.* —*v.* 1. emit sparks. 2. glitter. 3. produce little bubbles. —*n.* 4. little spark. 5. brightness.

spark plug, device in internal-combustion engine that ignites fuel.

spar'row, *n.* small, common, hardy bird.

sparse, *adj.,* **sparser, sparsest.** thinly distributed. —**spar'si•ty, sparse'ness,** *n.* —**sparse'ly,** *adv.*

Spar'tan, *adj.* austere.

spasm, *n.* sudden involuntary muscular contraction.

spas•mod'ic, *adj.* 1. of spasms. 2. intermittent. —**spas•mod'i•cal•ly,** *adv.*

spas'tic, *adj.* of or marked by spasms.

spat, *n.* petty quarrel.

spa'tial, *adj.* of or in space.

spat'ter, *v., n.* sprinkle in many fine drops.

spat'u•la (spach'-), *n.* broad-bladed implement.

spav'in (spav'ən), *n.* disease of hock joint in horses.

spawn, *n.* 1. eggs of fish, mollusks, etc. —*v.* 2. produce spawn.

spay, *v.* neuter or castrate (dog, cat, etc.).

speak, *v.,* **spoke, spoken, speaking.** 1. talk; say. 2. deliver speech.

speak'er, *n.* 1. person who speaks. 2. presiding officer.

spear, *n.* 1. long staff bearing sharp head. —*v.* 2. pierce with spear.

spear'head', *n.* 1. head of spear. 2. leader. —*v.* 3. lead.

spear'mint', *n.* aromatic herb.

spe'cial, *adj.* 1. particular; in nature or purpose. 2. unusual. —*n.* 3. special thing or person. —**spe'cial•ly,** *adv.*

spe'cial•ize', *v.,* **-ized, -izing.** study of work in special field. —**spe'cial•ist,** *n.* —**spe'cial•i•za'tion,** *n.*

spe'cial•ty, *n., pl.* **-ties.** field of special interest or competence.

spe'cie (spē'shē), *n.* coined money.

spe'cies, *n.* class of related individuals.

spe•cif'ic, *adj.* definite. —**spe•cif'i•cal•ly,** *adv.*

spec'i•fi•ca'tion, *n.* 1. act of specifying. 2. detailed requirement.

spec'i•fy', *v.,* **-fied, -fying.** mention or require specifically.

spec'i•men, *n.* anything typical of its kind.

spe'cious (spē'shəs), *adj.* plausible but deceptive. —**spe'cious•ly,** *adv.* —**spe'cious•ness,** *n.*

speck, *n.* 1. spot or particle. —*v.* 2. spot.

speck'le, *n., v.,* **-led, -ling.** —*n.* 1. small spot. —*v.* 2. mark with speckles.

spec'ta•cle, *n.* 1. sight. 2. public display. 3. (*pl.*) eyeglasses.

spec•tac'u•lar, *adj.* dramatic; thrilling.

spec'ta•tor, *n.* observer.

spec'ter, *n.* ghost. Also, **spec'tre.** —**spec'tral,** *adj.*

spec'tro•scope', *n.* instrument for producing and examining spectra.

spec′trum, *n., pl.* **-tra** (-trə), **-trums.** band of colors formed when light ray is dispersed.

spec′u•late′, *v.,* **-lated, -lating.** 1. think; conjecture. 2. invest at some risk. **—spec′u•la′tion,** *n.* **—spec′u•la′tive,** *adj.* **—spec′u•la′tor,** *n.*

speech, *n.* 1. power of speaking. 2. utterance. 3. talk before audience. 4. language. **—speech′less,** *adj.*

speed, *n., v.,* **sped** or **speeded, speeding.** *—n.* 1. swiftness. 2. rate of motion *—v.* 3. increase speed of. 4. move swiftly. **—speed′er,** *n.* **—speed′y,** *adj.* **—speed′i•ly,** *adv.*

speed•om′e•ter, *n.* device for indicating speed.

spell, *v.,* **spelled** or **spelt, spelling,** *n.* *—v.* 1. give letters of in order. 2. (of letters) form. 3. signify. 4. relieve at work. *—n.* 5. enchantment. 6. brief period. **—spell′er,** *n.*

spell′bound′, *adj.* fascinated.

spend, *v.,* **spent, spending.** 1. pay out. 2. pass (time). 3. use up. **—spend′er,** *n.*

spend′thrift′, *n.* extravagant spender.

sperm, *n.* male reproductive fluid or cell. **—sper•mat′ic,** *adj.*

sper′ma•cet′i (-set′ē), *n.* waxy substance from large square-headed whale (**sperm whale**).

spew, *v., n.* vomit.

sphere, *n.* 1. round ball. 2. particular field of influence or competence. **—spher′i•cal,** *adj.*

sphe′roid, *n.* body approximately spherical.

sphinc′ter, *n.* muscle closing anus or other body opening. **—sphinc′ter•al,** *adj.*

sphinx, *n.* figure of creature with man's head and lion's body.

spice, *n., v.,* **spiced, spicing.** *—n.* 1. aromatic plant substance used as seasoning. *—v.* 2. season with spice. **—spic′y,** *adj.*

spi′der, *n.* wingless, web-spinning insectlike animal. **—spi′der•y,** *adj.*

spiel, *n. Slang.* high-pressure sales talk.

spig′ot, *n.* faucet.

spike, *n., v.,* **spiked, spiking.** *—n.* 1. large strong nail. 2. stiff, pointed part. 3. ear of grain. 4. stalk of flowers. *—v.* 5. fasten or pierce with spikes. 6. frustrate or stop.

spill, *v.,* **spilled** or **spilt, spilling.** 1. run or let run over. 2. shed (blood). **—spil′lage,** *n.*

spill′way′, *n.* overflow passage.

spin, *v.,* **spun, spinning,** *n.* *—v.* 1. make yarn or thread from fiber. 2. secrete filament. 3. whirl. *—n.* 4. spinning motion. 5. short ride. **—spin′ner,** *n.*

spin′ach (-ich), *n.* plant with edible leaves.

spin′dle, *n.* 1. tapered rod. 2. any shaft or axis.

spin′dling, *adj.* tall and thin. Also, **spin′dly.**

spine, *n.* 1. Also, **spinal column.** connected series of bones down back. 2. any spinelike part. 3. stiff bristle or thorn. **—spi′nal,** *adj.* **—spin′y,** *adj.*

spine′less, *adj.* weak in character.

spin′et, *n.* small piano.

spin′ster, *n.* unmarried woman, esp. elderly.

spi′ral, *n.* 1. curve made by circling a point while approaching or receding from it. *—adj.* 2. like or of spiral. *—v.* 3. move spirally. **—spi′ral•ly,** *adv.*

spire, *n.* tall tapering structure, esp. on tower or roof.

spi•re′a (spī rē′ə), *n.* common garden shrub. Also, **spiraea.**

spir′it, *n.* 1. vital principle in man; soul. 2. supernatural being. 3. feelings. 4. vigor. 5. intent. 6. (*pl.*) alcoholic liquor. 7. (*cap.*) Holy Ghost. *—v.* 8. carry off secretly. **—spir′it•ed,** *adj.* **—spir′it•less,** *adj.*

spir′it•u•al, *adj.* 1. of or in spirit; ethereal. 2. religious. *—n.* 3. religious song. **—spir′it•u•al•ly,** *adv.* **—spir′it•u•al′i•ty,** *n.*

spir′it•u•al•ism, *n.* belief that spirits of dead communicate with living. **—spir′it•u•al•ist,** *n., adj.*

spir′it•u•ous, *adj.* 1. alcoholic. 2. distilled.

spit, *v.,* **spat** or **spit** (for 2 **spitted**), **spitting,** *n.* *—v.* 1. eject from mouth. 2. pierce. *—n.* 3. saliva. 4. *Informal.* image. 5. rod for roasting meat. 6. projecting point of land.

spite, *n., v.,* **spited, spiting.** *—n.* 1. malice; grudge. *—v.* 2. annoy out of spite. **—spite′ful,** *adj.* **—spite′ful•ly,** *adv.* **—spite′ful•ness,** *n.*

spit′tle, *n.* saliva.

spit•toon′, *n.* cuspidor.

splash, *v.* 1. dash water, mud, etc. *—n.* 2. act or sound of splashing. 3. spot. **—splash′y,** *adj.*

splat′ter, *v.* splash widely.

splay, *v., adj.* spread out.

spleen, *n.* 1. ductless organ near stomach. 2. ill humor. **—sple•net′ic,** *adj.*

splen′did, *adj.* gorgeous; superb; fine. **—splen′did•ly,** *adv.* **—splen′dor,** *n.*

splice, *v.,* **spliced, splicing,** *n.* *—v.* 1. join, as ropes or boards. *—n.* 2. spliced joint.

splint, *n.* 1. brace for broken part of body. 2. strip of wood for weaving. *—v.* 3. brace with splints.

splin′ter, *n.* 1. thin sharp fragments. *—v.* 2. break into splinters.

split, *v.,* **split, splitting,** *n., adj.* *—v.* 1. separate; divide. 2. burst. *—n.* 3. crack or breach. *—adj.* 4. cleft; divided.

splotch, *n., v.,* blot; stain. **—splotch′y,** *adj.*

splurge, *n., v.,* **splurged, splurging.** *—n.* 1. big display or expenditure. *—v.* 2. make splurge; be extravagant.

splut′ter, *v.* 1. talk vehemently and incoherently. *—n.* 2. spluttering talk.

spoil, *v.,* **spoiled** or **spoilt, spoiling,** *n.* *—v.* 1. damage; ruin. 2. become tainted. *—n.* 3. (*pl.*) booty. 4. waste material. **—spoil′age,** *n.* **—spoil′er,** *n.*

spoke, *n.* bar between hub and rim of wheel.

spokes′man, *n., pl.* **-men.** person speaking for others.

sponge, *n., v.,* **sponged, sponging.** *—n.* 1. marine animal. 2. its light framework or imitation, used to absorb liquids. *—v.* 3. clean with sponge. 4. impose or live on another. **—spong′er,** *n.* **—spon′gy,** *adj.*

spon′sor, *n.* 1. one that recommends or supports. 2. godparent. 3. advertiser on radio or television. *—v.* 4. act as sponsor for.

spon•ta′ne•ous, *adj.* 1. arising without outside cause. 2. impulsive. **—spon•ta′ne•ous•ly,** *adv.* **—spon′ta•ne′i•ty, spon•ta′ne•ous•ness,** *n.*

spook, *Informal.* *—n.* 1. ghost. *—v.* 2. frighten. **—spook′y,** *adj.*

spool, *n.* cylinder on which something is wound.

spoon, *n.* 1. utensil for stirring or taking up food. *—v.* 2. lift in spoon. **—spoon′ful,** *n.*

spoor (spŏŏr), *n.* trail of wild animal.

spo•rad′ic, *adj.* occasional; scattered. **—spo•rad′i•cal•ly,** *adv.*

spore, *n.* seed, as of ferns.

sport, *n.* 1. athletic pastime. 2. diversion. 3. abnormally formed plant or animal. *—adj.* 4. of or for sport. *—v.* 5. play. **—sports′man,** *n.* **—sports′-**

man•ly, *adj.* —**sports′man•ship′**, *n.* —**sports′wear′**, *n.*

spor′tive, *adj.* playful. —**spor′tive•ly**, *adv.* —**spor′tive•ness**, *n.*

spot, *n.*, *v.*, **spotted**, **spotting**, *adj.* —*n.* 1. blot; speck. 2. locality. —*v.* 3. stain with spots. 4. notice. —*adj.* 5. made, done, etc., at once. —**spot′less**, *adj.* —**spot′ter**, *n.* —**spot′ty**, *adj.*

spouse, *n.* husband or wife.

spout, *v.* 1. discharge (liquid, etc.) with force. 2. utter insincerely. —*n.* 3. pipe or lip on container.

sprain, *v.* 1. injure by wrenching. —*n.* 2. such injury.

sprat, *n.* herringlike fish.

sprawl, *v.* 1. stretch out ungracefully. —*n.* 2. sprawling position.

spray, *n.* 1. liquid in fine particles. 2. appliance for producing spray. 3. branch of flowers, etc. —*v.* 4. scatter, as spray. 5. apply spray to. —**spray′er**, *n.*

spread, *v.*, **spread**, **spreading**, *n.* —*v.* 1. stretch out. 2. extend. 3. scatter. —*n.* 4. extent. 5. diffusion. 6. cloth cover. 7. preparation for eating on bread. —**spread′er**, *n.*

spree, *n.* frolic.

sprig, *n.* twig or shoot.

spright′ly, *adj.*, **-lier**, **-liest.** lively. —**spright′li•ness**, *n.*

spring, *v.*, **sprang** or **sprung**, **sprung**, **springing**, *n.*, *adj.* —*v.* 1. leap. 2. grow or proceed. 3. disclose. —*n.* 4. leap; jump. 5. natural fountain. 6. season after winter. 7. elastic device. —*adj.* 8. of or for spring (def. 6). —**spring′time′**, *n.* —**spring′y**, *adj.*

sprin′kle, *v.*, **-kled**, **-kling**, *n.* —*v.* 1. scatter in drops. 2. rain slightly. —*n.* 3. instance of sprinkling. 4. something sprinkled. —**sprin′kler**, *n.*

sprint, *v.* 1. run fast. —*n.* 2. short fast run. —**sprint′er**, *n.*

sprite, *n.* elf; fairy.

sprock′et, *n.* tooth on wheel for engaging with chain.

sprout, *v.* 1. begin to grow; bud. —*n.* 2. plant shoot.

spruce, *adj.*, **sprucer**, **sprucest**, *v.*, *n.* —*adj.* 1. trim; neat. —*v.* 2. make spruce. —*n.* 3. cone-bearing evergreen tree.

spry, *adj.* nimble. —**spry′ly**, *adv.* —**spry′ness**, *n.*

spud, *n.* 1. spadelike tool. 2. *Informal.* potato.

spume, *n.* foam.

spunk, *n.* *Informal.* courage; spirit. —**spunk′y**, *adj.*

spur, *n.*, *v.*, **spurred**, **spurring.** —*n.* 1. sharp device worn on heel to goad horse. 2. spurlike part. —*v.* 3. prick with spur. 4. urge.

spu′ri•ous (spyŏŏr′-), *adj.* not genuine. —**spu′ri•ous•ly**, *adv.* —**spu′ri•ous•ness**, *n.*

spurn, *v.* scorn; reject.

spurt, *v.* 1. gush or eject in jet. 2. speed up briefly. —*n.* 3. forceful gush. 4. brief increase of effort.

sput′nik, *n.* first man-made satellite, launched by Russia in 1957.

sput′ter, *v.* 1. emit violently in drops. 2. splutter. —*n.* 3. act or sound of sputtering.

spu′tum (spyōō′-), *n.* spittle, esp. mixed with mucus.

spy, *n.*, *pl.* **spies**, *v.*, **spied**, **spying.** —*n.* 1. secret observer, esp. military. —*v.* 2. watch secretly. 3. sight.

squab, *n.* young pigeon.

squab′ble, *n.*, *v.*, **-bled**, **-bling.** —*n.* 1. petty quarrel. —*v.* 2. have squabble.

squad, *n.* small group.

squad′ron, *n.* unit in Navy, Air Force, etc.

squal′id (skwol′id), *adj.* dirty or wretched. —**squal′id•ly**, *adv.* —**squal′id•ness**, *n.*

squall (skwôl), *n.* 1. strong gust of wind, etc. 2. loud cry. —*v.* 3. cry loudly. —**squall′y**, *adj.*

squal′or (skwol′ər), *n.* squalid state.

squan′der, *v.* use or spend wastefully.

square, *n.*, *v.*, **squared**, **squaring**, *adj.*, **squarer**, **squarest**, *adv.* —*n.* 1. plane figure with four equal sides and four right angles. 2. anything square. 3. tool for checking right angles. 4. product of number multiplied by itself. —*v.* 5. make square. 6. adjust; agree. 7. multiply by itself. —*adj.* 8. being a square. 9. level. 10. honest. —*adv.* 11. directly. —**square′ly**, *adv.* —**square′ness**, *n.*

squash, *v.* 1. crush; suppress. —*n.* 2. game resembling tennis. 3. fruit of vinelike plant.

squat, *v.*, **squatted** or **squat**, **squatting**, *adj.*, *n.* —*v.* 1. sit with legs close under body. 2. settle on land illegally or to acquire title. —*adj.* 3. Also, **squat′ty.** stocky. —*n.* 4. squatting position. —**squat′ter**, *n.*

squaw, *n.* American Indian woman.

squawk, *n.* 1. loud harsh cry. —*v.* 2. utter squawks. —**squawk′er**, *n.*

squeak, *n.* 1. small shrill sound. —*v.* 2. emit squeaks. —**squeak′y**, *adj.* —**squeak′er**, *n.*

squeal, *n.* 1. long shrill cry. —*v.* 2. utter squeals. —**squeal′er**, *n.*

squeam′ish, *adj.* 1. prudish. 2. overfastidious. —**squeam′ish•ly**, *adv.* —**squeam′ish•ness**, *n.*

squee′gee, *n.* implement for cleaning glass surfaces.

squeeze, *v.*, **squeezed**, **squeezing**, *n.* —*v.* 1. press together. 2. cram. —*n.* 3. act of squeezing. 4. hug.

squelch, *v.* 1. crush. 2. silence. —*n.* 3. crushing retort. —**squelch′er**, *n.*

squib, *n.* 1. short witty item or paragraph. 2. hissing firecracker.

squid, *n.* marine mollusk.

squint, *v.* 1. look with eyes partly closed. 2. be cross-eyed. —*n.* 3. squinting look. 4. cross-eyed condition.

squire, *n.*, *v.*, **squired**, **squiring.** —*n.* 1. country gentleman. 2. escort. —*v.* 3. escort.

squirm, *v.*, *n.* wriggle.

squir′rel, *n.* bushy-tailed, tree-living rodent.

squirt, *v.* 1. gush; cause to gush. —*n.* 2. jet of liquid.

SST, supersonic transport.

stab, *v.*, **stabbed**, **stabbing**, *n.* —*v.* 1. pierce with pointed weapon. —*n.* 2. thrust with or wound from pointed weapon.

sta′bi•lize, *v.*, **-lized**, **-lizing.** make or keep stable. —**sta′bi•li•za′tion**, *n.* —**sta′bi•liz′er**, *n.*

sta′ble, *n.*, *v.*, **-bled**, **-bling**, *adj.* —*n.* 1. building for horses, etc. —*v.* 2. keep in stable. —*adj.* 3. steady; steadfast. —**stab′ly**, *adv.* —**sta•bil′i•ty**, *n.*

stac′ca′to (stə kä′tō), *adj. Music.* disconnected; detached.

stack, *n.* 1. orderly heap. 2. (*often pl.*) book storage area. 3. funnel for smoke. —*v.* 4. pile in stack. 5. arrange unfairly.

sta′di•um, *n.*, *pl.* **-diums**, **-dia** (-ə). large open structure for games.

staff, *n.*, *pl.* **staves** (stāvz) or **staffs** for 1, 3; **staffs** for 2; *v.* —*n.* 1. stick carried as support, weapon, etc. 2. body of assistants or administrators. 3. set of five lines on which music is written. —*v.* 4. provide with staff.

stag, *n.* 1. adult male deer. —*adj.* 2. for men only.

stage, *n.*, *v.*, **staged**, **staging.** —*n.* 1. single step or degree. 2. raised platform. 3. theater. —*v.* 4. exhibit on stage.

stag′ger, *v.* 1. move unsteadily. 2. cause to reel. 3. arrange at intervals. —*n.* 4. staggering movement. 5. (*pl.*) disease of horses, etc.

stag'ing, *n.* scaffolding.

stag'nant, *adj.* 1. not flowing; foul. 2. inactive. —**stag'nate**, *v.* —**stag·na'-tion**, *n.*

staid, *adj.* sedate. —**staid'ly**, *adv.* —**staid'ness**, *n.*

stain, *n.* 1. discolored patch. 2. kind of dye. —*v.* 3. mark with stains. 4. color with stain.

stain'less, *adj.* 1. unstained. 2. not liable to rusting.

stair, *n.* series of steps between levels. —**stair'case'**, **stair'way'**, *n.*

stake, *n., v.*, **staked, staking.** —*n.* 1. pointed post. 2. something wagered. 3. (*pl.*) prize. 4. hazard. —*v.* 5. mark off with stakes. 6. wager.

sta·lac'tite, *n.* icicle-shaped formation hanging from cave roof.

sta·lag'mite, *n.* cone-shaped deposit on cave floor.

stale, *adj.*, **staler, stalest,** *v.*, **staled, staling.** —*adj.* 1. not fresh. —*v.* 2. make or become stale. —**stale'ness**, *n.*

stale'mate', *n., v.*, **-mated, -mating.** —*n.* 1. deadlocked position, orig. in chess. —*v.* 2. bring to stalemate.

stalk, *v.* 1. pursue stealthily. 2. walk in haughty or menacing way. —*n.* 3. plant stem.

stall, *n.* 1. compartment for one animal. 2. sales booth. 3. (of airplane) loss of air speed necessary for control. 4. *Slang.* pretext for delay. —*v.* 5. keep in stall. 6. stop; become stopped. 7. lose necessary air speed. 8. *Slang.* delay.

stal'lion (stal'yən), *n.* male horse.

stal'wart (stôl'wərt), *adj.* 1. robust. 2. brave. 3. steadfast. —*v.* 4. stalwart person.

sta'men, *n.* pollen-bearing organ of flower.

stam'i·na, *n.* vigor; endurance.

stam'mer, *v.* 1. speak with involuntary breaks or repetitions. —*n.* 2. such speech.

stamp, *v.* 1. trample. 2. mark. 3. put paper stamp on. —*n.* 4. act of stamping. 5. marking device. 6. adhesive paper affixed to show payment of fees.

stam·pede', *n., v.*, **-peded, -peding.** —*n.* 1. panic flight. —*v.* 2. flee in stampede.

stance, *n.* position of feet.

stanch (stônch), *adj.* 1. staunch. —*v.* 2. stop flow, esp. of blood. —**stanch'ly**, *adv.* —**stanch'ness**, *n.*

stan'chion, *n.* upright post.

stand, *v.*, **stood, standing,** *n.* —*v.* 1. rise or be upright. 2. remain firm. 3. be located. 4. be candidate. 5. endure. —*n.* 6. firm attitude. 7. place of standing. 8. platform. 9. support for small articles. 10. outdoor salesplace. 11. area of trees. 12. stop.

stand'ard, *n.* 1. approved model or rule. 2. flag. 3. upright support. —*adj.* 4. being model or basis for comparison.

stand'ard·ize', *v.*, **-ized, -izing.** make standard. —**stand'ard·i·za'tion**, *n.*

stand'-by', *n., pl.* **-bys,** *adj.* —*n.* 1. chief support. —*adj.* 2. emergency.

stand'ing, *n.* 1. status. 2. duration. —*adj.* 3. upright. 4. stagnant. 5. lasting; fixed.

stand'point', *n.* point of view.

stand'still', *n.* complete halt.

stan'za, *n.* division of poem.

sta'ple, *n., v.*, **-pled, -pling,** *adj.* —*n.* 1. bent fastener. 2. chief commodity. 3. textile fiber. —*v.* 4. fasten with staple. —*adj.* 5. chief. —**sta'pler**, *n.*

star, *n., adj., v.*, **starred, starring.** —*n.* 1. heavenly body luminous at night. 2. figure with five or six points. 3. asterisk. 4. principal performer. —*adj.* 5. principal. —*v.* 6. mark with star. 7. have leading part. —**star'ry**, *adj.*

star'board', *n.* right-hand side of vessel, facing forward. —**star'board'**, *adj., adv.*

starch, *n.* 1. white tasteless substance used as food and as a stiffening agent. 2. preparation from starch. —*v.* 3. stiffen with starch. —**starch'y**, *adj.*

stare, *v.*, **stared, staring,** *n.* —*v.* 1. gaze fixedly. —*n.* 2. fixed look.

star'fish', *n.* star-shaped marine animal.

stark, *adj.* 1. utter; sheer. 2. stiff. —*adv.* 3. utterly.

star'ling, *n.* small bird.

start, *v.* 1. begin. 2. move or issue suddenly. —*n.* 3. beginning. 4. startled movement. 5. lead. —**start'er**, *n.*

star'tle, *v.*, **-tled, -tling.** disturb suddenly.

starve, *v.*, **starved, starving.** 1. die or suffer severely from hunger. 2. kill or weaken by hunger. —**star·va'tion**, *n.*

state, *n., adj., v.*, **stated, stating.** —*n.* 1. condition. 2. pomp. 3. nation. 4. commonwealth of a federal union. 5. civil government. —*adj.* 6. ceremonious. —*v.* 7. declare. —**state'hood**, *n.* —**state'house**, *n.*

state'ly, *adj.*, **-lier, -liest.** dignified. —**state'li·ness**, *n.*

state'ment, *n.* 1. declaration. 2. report on business account.

state'room', *n.* quarters on ship, etc.

states'man, *n.* leader in government. —**states'man·ship'**, *n.*

stat'ic, *adj.* 1. fixed; at rest. —*n.* 2. atmospheric electricity. 3. interference caused by it.

sta'tion, *n.* 1. place of duty. 2. depot for trains, buses, etc. 3. status. 4. place for sending or receiving radio broadcasts. —*v.* 5. assign place to.

sta'tion·ar'y, *adj.* not moving; not movable; fixed.

sta'tion·er, *n.* dealer in stationery.

sta'tion·er'y, *n.* writing materials.

sta·tis'tics, *n.* science of collecting, classifying, and using numerical facts. —**sta·tis'ti·cal**, *adj.* —**sta·tis'-ti·cal·ly**, *adv.* —**stat'is·ti'cian**, *n.*

stat'u·ar'y, *n.* statues.

stat'ue, *n.* carved, molded, or cast figure.

stat'u·esque', *adj.* like statue; of imposing figure.

stat'u·ette', *n.* little statue.

stat'ure, *n.* 1. height. 2. achievement.

sta'tus (stā'-, sta'-), *n.* 1. social standing. 2. present condition.

status quo, *Latin.* existing state.

stat'ute, *n.* law enacted by legislature. —**stat'u·to'ry**, *adj.*

staunch (stônch), *adj.* 1. firm; steadfast; strong. —*v.* 2. stanch. —**staunch'ly**, *adv.* —**staunch'ness**, *n.*

stave, *n., v.*, **staved** or (for 3) **stove, staving.** —*n.* 1. one of curved vertical strips of barrel, etc. 2. *Music.* staff. —*v.* 3. break hole in. 4. ward (off).

stay, *v.*, **stayed, staying,** *n.* —*v.* 1. remain; continue. 2. stop or restrain. 3. support. —*n.* 4. period at one place. 5. stop; pause. 6. support; prop. 7. rope supporting mast.

stead, *n.* 1. place taken by another. 2. advantage.

stead'fast', *adj.* 1. fixed. 2. firm or loyal. —**stead'fast'ly**, *adv.* —**stead'-fast'ness**, *n.*

stead'y, *adj.*, **steadier, steadiest,** *v.*, **steadied, steadying.** —*adj.* 1. firmly fixed. 2. uniform; regular. 3. steadfast. —*v.* 4. make or become steady. —**stead'i·ly**, *adv.* —**stead'i·ness**, *n.*

steak, *n.* slice of meat or fish.

steal, *v.*, **stole, stolen, stealing.** 1. take wrongfully. 2. move very quietly.

stealth, *n.* secret procedure. —**stealth'y**, *adj.* —**stealth'i·ly**, *adv.*

steam, *n.* 1. water in form of gas or vapor. —*v.* 2. pass off as or give off steam. 3. treat with steam. —*adj.* 4.

operated by steam. 5. conducting steam. —**steam′boat′**, **steam′ship′**, *n.*

steam′er, *n.* 1. vessel moved by steam. 2. device for cooking, treating, etc., with steam.

steed, *n.* horse, esp. for riding.

steel, *n.* 1. iron modified with carbon. —*adj.* 2. of or like steel. —*v.* 3. make resolute. —**steel′y,** *adj.*

steel′yard′, *n.* kind of scale.

steep, *adj.* 1. sloping sharply. —*v.* 2. soak. 3. absorb. —**steep′ly,** *adv.* —**steep′ness,** *n.*

stee′ple, *n.* 1. lofty tower on church, etc. 2. spire.

stee′ple•chase′, *n.* horse race over obstacle course.

steer, *v.* 1. guide; direct. —*n.* 2. ox.

steer′age, *n.* part of ship for passengers paying cheapest rate.

stein, *n.* mug, esp. for beer.

stel′lar, *adj.* of or like stars.

stem, *n., v.,* **stemmed, stemming.** —*n.* 1. supporting stalk of plant, or of leaf, flower, or fruit. 2. ancestry. 3. part of word not changed by inflection. 4. *Naut.* bow. —*v.* 5. remove stem of. 6. originate. 7. stop or check. 8. make headway against.

stench, *n.* bad odor.

sten′cil, *n., v.,* **-ciled, -ciling.** —*n.* 1. sheet cut to pass design through when colored over. —*v.* 2. print with stencil.

ste•nog′ra•pher, *n.* person skilled at shorthand and typing.

ste•nog′ra•phy, *n.* writing in shorthand. —**sten′o•graph′ic,** *adj.* —**sten′o•graph′i•cal•ly,** *adv.*

sten•to′ri•an, *adj.* very loud.

step, *n., v.,* **stepped, stepping.** —*n.* 1. movement of foot in walking. 2. distance of such movement. 3. gait or pace. 4. footprint. 5. stage in process. 6. level on stair or ladder. —*v.* 7. move by steps. 8. press with foot.

step-, prefix showing relation by remarriage of parent. —**step′child,** *n.* —**step′son′,** *n.* —**step′daugh′ter,** *n.* —**step′par′ent,** *n.* —**step′fath′er,** *n.* —**step′moth′er,** *n.*

step′lad′der, *n.* ladder with flat treads.

steppe, *n.* vast plain.

ster′e•o, *n., pl.* **-eos.** stereophonic sound or equipment.

ster′e•o•phon′ic, *adj.* (of recorded sound) played through two or more speakers.

ster′e•op′ti•con, *n.* projector for slides, etc.

ster′e•o•scope′, *n.* device for viewing two pictures at once to give impression of depth.

ster′e•o•type′, *n., v.,* **-typed, -typing.** —*n.* 1. process of making printing plates from mold taken from composed type. 2. idea, etc., without originality. —*v.* 3. make stereotype of. 4. give fixed, trite form to.

ster′ile, *adj.* 1. free from living germs. 2. unable to produce offspring; barren. —**ste•ril′i•ty,** *n.*

ster′i•lize′, *v.,* **-lized, -lizing.** make sterile. —**ster′i•li•za′tion,** *n.* —**ster′i•liz′er,** *n.*

ster′ling, *adj.* 1. containing 92.5% silver. 2. of British money. 3. excellent.

stern, *adj.* 1. strict; harsh; grim. —*n.* 2. hind part of vessel. —**stern′ly,** *adv.* —**stern′ness,** *n.*

ster′num, *n.* flat bone in chest connecting with clavicle and ribs.

steth′o•scope′, *n.* medical instrument for listening to sounds in body.

ste′ve•dore′, *n.* person who loads and unloads ships.

stew, *v.* 1. cook by simmering. —*n.* 2. food so cooked.

stew′ard, *n.* 1. person who manages another's affairs, property, etc. 2. person in charge of food, supplies, etc., for ship, club, etc. 3. domestic employee on ship or airplane. —**stew′ard•ess,** *n.fem.* —**stew′ard•ship′,** *n.*

stick, *v.,* **stuck, sticking,** *n.* —*v.* 1. pierce; stab. 2. thrust. 3. cause to adhere. 4. adhere; cling. 5. persist. 6. extend. —*n.* 7. small length of wood, etc.

stick′er, *n.* 1. one that sticks. 2. adhesive label. 3. thorn.

stick′le, *v.,* **-led, -ling.** 1. argue over trifles. 2. insist on correctness. —**stick′ler,** *n.*

stick′y, *adj.,* **stickier, stickiest.** 1. adhering. 2. humid. —**stick′i•ness,** *n.*

stiff, *adj.* 1. rigid. 2. not moving easily. 3. formal. —**stiff′en,** *v.* —**stiff′ly,** *adv.* —**stiff′ness,** *n.*

sti′fle, *v.,* **-fled, -fling.** 1. smother. 2. repress.

stig′ma, *n., pl.* **stigmata, stigmas.** 1. mark of disgrace. 2. pollen-receiving part of pistil. —**stig′ma•tize′,** *v.*

stile, *n.* set of steps over fence, etc.

sti•let′to, *n., pl.* **-tos, -toes.** dagger.

still, *adj.* 1. motionless. 2. silent. 3. tranquil. —*adv.* 4. as previously. 5. until now. 6. yet. —*conj.* 7. nevertheless. —*v.* 8. make or become still.

—*n.* 9. distilling apparatus. —**stil′ly,** *adv., adj.* —**still′ness,** *n.*

still′born′, *adj.* born dead.

stilt, *n.* pole for extending stride.

stilt′ed, *adj.* stiffly dignified.

stim′u•lant, *n.* food, medicine, etc., that stimulates briefly.

stim′u•late′, *v.,* **-lated, -lating.** rouse to action. —**stim′u•la′tion,** *n.* —**stim′u•la′tive,** *adj.* —**stim′u•la′tor, stim′u•la′ter,** *n.*

stim′u•lus, *n., pl.* **-li.** something that stimulates.

sting, *v.,* **stung, stinging,** *n.* —*v.* 1. wound with pointed organ, as bees do. 2. pain sharply. 3. goad. —*n.* 4. wound caused by stinging. 5. sharp-pointed organ. —**sting′er,** *n.*

stin′gy (stin′jē), *adj.* 1. miserly. 2. scanty. —**stin′gi•ness,** *n.*

stink, *v.,* **stank** or **stunk, stunk, stinking,** *n.* —*v.* 1. emit bad odor. —*n.* 2. bad odor.

stint, *v.* 1. limit. 2. limit oneself. —*n.* 3. limitation. 4. allotted task.

sti′pend (stī′pend), *n.* regular pay.

stip′ple, *v.,* **-pled, -pling.** —*v.* 1. paint or cover with tiny dots. —*n.* 2. such painting.

stip′u•late′, *v.,* **-lated, -lating.** require as condition of agreement. —**stip′u•la′tion,** *n.*

stir, *v.,* **stirred, stirring,** *n.* —*v.* 1. mix or agitate (liquid, etc.), esp. with circular motion. 2. move. 3. rouse; excite. —*n.* 4. movement; commotion.

stir′rup, *n.* looplike support for foot, suspended from saddle.

stitch, *n.* 1. complete movement of needle in sewing, knitting, etc. 2. sudden pain. —*v.* 3. sew.

stock, *n.* 1. goods on hand. 2. livestock. 3. stem or trunk. 4. line of descent. 5. meat broth. 6. part of gun supporting barrel. 7. (*pl.*) framework in which prisoners were publicly confined. 8. capital or shares of company. —*adj.* 9. standard; common. 10. of stock. —*v.* 11. supply. 12. store. —**stock′brok′er,** *n.* —**stock′hold′er,** *n.*

stock•ade′, *n., v.,* **-aded, -ading.** —*n.* 1. barrier of upright posts. —*v.* 2. protect with stockade.

stock exchange, place where securities are bought and sold. Also, **stock market.**

stock′ing, *n.* close-fitting covering for foot and leg.

stock′pile′, *n., v.,* **-piled, -piling.** —*n.* 1. stock of goods. —*v.* 2. accumulate for eventual use.

stock'y, *adj.* **-ier, -iest.** sturdily built. **—stock'i•ly,** *adv.* **—stock'i•ness,** *n.*

stock'yard', *n.* enclosure for livestock about to be slaughtered.

stodg'y, *adj.,* **stodgier, stodgiest.** pompous and uninteresting. **—stodg'i•ness,** *n.*

sto'ic, *adj.* 1. Also, **sto'i•cal.** not reacting to pain. **—***n.* 2. person who represses emotion. **—sto'i•cal•ly,** *adv.* **—sto'i•cism',** *n.*

stoke, *v.,* **stoked, stoking.** tend (fire). **—stok'er,** *n.*

stole, *n.* scarf or narrow strip worn over shoulders.

stol'id, *adj.* unemotional; not easily moved. **—sto•lid'i•ty,** *n.* **—stol'id• ly,** *adv.*

stom'ach, *n.* 1. organ of food storage and digestion. 2. appetite; desire. **—***v.* 3. take into stomach. 4. tolerate. **—sto•mach'ic,** *adj.*

stone, *n.,* *pl.* **stones** or (for 4) **stone,** *adj.,* *v.,* **stoned, stoning,** *adv.* **—***n.* 1. hard, nonmetallic mineral substance. 2. small rock. 3. gem. 4. *Brit.* unit of weight = 14 pounds. 5. stone-like seed. 6. concretion formed in body. **—***adj.* 7. of stone. **—***v.* 8. throw stones at. 9. remove stones from. **—***adv.* 10. entirely. **—ston'y,** *adj.* **—ston'i•ly,** *adv.*

Stone Age, prehistoric period before use of metals.

stooge, *n.* 1. assistant to comedian. 2. person acting in obsequious obedience.

stool, *n.* seat without arms or back.

stoop, *v.* 1. bend forward. 2. condescend. **—***n.* 3. stooping posture. 4. small doorway or porch.

stop, *v.,* **stopped, stopping,** *n.* **—***v.* 1. cease; halt. 2. prevent. 3. close up. 4. stay. **—***n.* 5. act, instance, or place of stopping. 6. hindrance. 7. device on musical instrument to control tone. **—stop'page,** *n.*

stop'gap', *n.,* *adj.* makeshift.

stop'o'ver, *n.* temporary stop on journey.

stop'per, *n.* 1. plug. **—***v.* 2. close with stopper. Also, **stop'ple.**

stor'age, *n.* 1. place for storing. 2. act of storing. 3. state of being stored. 4. fee for storing.

store, *n.,* *v.,* **stored, storing.** **—***n.* 1. place where goods are kept for sale. 2. supply. **—***v.* 3. lay up; accumulate. 4. put in secure place. **—store'- keep'er,** *n.*

store'house', *n.* building for storage. **—store'room',** *n.*

sto'ried, *adj.* famed in history or story.

stork, *n.* wading bird with long legs and bill.

storm, *n.* 1. heavy rain, snow, etc., with strong winds. 2. violent assault. **—***v.* 3. blow, rain, etc., strongly. 4. rage. 5. attack. **—storm'y,** *adj.* **—storm'i•ly,** *adv.*

sto'ry, *n.,* *pl.* **-ries.** 1. fictitious tale. 2. plot. 3. newspaper report. 4. *Informal.* lie. 5. in level building.

stoup (stoop), *n.* basin for holy water.

stout, *adj.* 1. solidly built; fat. 2. bold or strong. 3. firm. **—***n.* 4. dark, sweet brew. **—stout'ly,** *adv.* **—stout'ness,** *n.*

stove, *n.* apparatus for giving heat.

stow, *v.* 1. put away, as cargo. 2. stow away, hide on ship, etc. to get free trip. **—stow'age,** *n.* **—stow'a•way',** *n.*

stra•bis'mus, *n.* visual defect; cross-eye.

strad'dle, *v.,* **-dled, -dling.** **—***v.* 1. have one leg on either side of. **—***n.* 2. straddling stance.

strafe, *v.,* **strafed, strafing.** shoot from airplanes.

strag'gle, *v.,* **-gled, -gling.** stray from course; ramble. **—strag'gler,** *n.*

straight, *adj.* 1. direct. 2. even. 3. honest. 4. right. **—***adv.* 5. directly. 6. in straight line. 7. honestly. **—***n.* 8. *Poker.* five-card sequence. **—straight'en,** *v.* **—straight'ness,** *n.*

straight'a•way', *adv.* at once. Also, **straight'way'.**

straight'for'ward, *adj.* direct; frank.

strain, *v.* 1. exert to utmost. 2. injure by stretching. 3. sieve; filter. 4. constrain. **—***n.* 5. great effort. 6. injury from straining. 7. severe pressure. 8. melody. 9. descendants. 10. ancestry. 11. hereditary trait. **—strain'er,** *n.*

strait, *n.* 1. narrow waterway. 2. (*pl.*) distress.

strait'en, *v.* 1. put into financial troubles. 2. restrict.

strand, *v.* 1. run aground. **—***n.* 2. shore. 3. twisted component of rope. 4. tress. 5. string, as of beads.

strange, *adj.,* **stranger, strangest.** 1. unusual; odd. 2. unfamiliar. **—strange'ly,** *adv.* **—strange'ness,** *n.*

stran'ger, *n.* person not known or acquainted.

stran'gle, *v.,* **-gled, -gling.** 1. kill by choking. 2. choke. **—stran'gler,** *n.* **—stran'gu•la'tion,** *n.*

strap, *n.,* *v.,* **strapped, strapping.** **—***n.* 1. narrow strip or band. **—***v.* 2. fasten with strap.

strat'a•gem (-jəm), *n.* plan; trick.

strat'e•gy, *n.,* *pl.* **-gies.** planning and direction of military operations. **—stra•te'gic,** *adj.* **—stra•te'gi•cal• ly,** *adv.* **—strat'e•gist,** *n.*

strat'i•fy', *v.,* **-fied, -fying.** form in layers. **—strat'i•fi•ca'tion,** *n.*

strat'o•sphere', *n.* upper region of atmosphere.

stra'tum (strā'təm), *n.,* *pl.* **strata, stratums.** layer of material.

straw, *n.* 1. stalk of cereal grass. 2. mass of dried stalks.

straw'ber'ry, *n.,* *pl.* **-ries.** fleshy fruit of stemless herb.

stray, *v.* 1. ramble; go from one's course or rightful place. **—***adj.* 2. straying. **—***n.* 3. stray creature.

streak, *n.* 1. long mark or smear. 2. vein; stratum. **—***v.* 3. mark with streaks. 4. flash rapidly.

stream, *n.* 1. flowing body of water. 2. steady flow. **—***v.* 3. flow or move in stream. 4. wave.

stream'er, *n.* long narrow flag.

stream'line', *adj.,* *n.,* *v.,* **-lined, -lining.** **—***adj.* 1. having shape past which fluids move easily. **—***n.* 2. streamline shape. **—***v.* 3. shape with streamline. 4. reorganize efficiently.

street, *n.* public city road.

street'car', *n.* public conveyance running on rails.

strength, *n.* 1. power of body, mind, position, etc. 2. intensity.

strength'en, *v.* make or grow stronger.

stren'u•ous, *adj.* vigorous; active. **—stren'u•ous•ly,** *adv.*

strep'to•coc'cus, *n.,* *pl.* **-ci.** one of group of disease-producing bacteria.

stress, *v.* 1. emphasize. **—***n.* 2. emphasis. 3. physical pressure. 4. strain.

stretch, *v.* 1. extend; spread. 2. distend. 3. draw tight. **—***n.* 4. act of stretching. 5. extension; expansion. 6. continuous length.

stretch'er, *n.* 1. canvas-covered frame for carrying sick, etc. 2. device for stretching.

strew, *v.,* **strewed, strewed** or **strewn, strewing.** scatter; sprinkle.

stri'at•ed, *adj.* furrowed; streaked. **—stri•a'tion,** *n.*

strict, *adj.* 1. exacting; severe. 2. precise. 3. careful. **—strict'ly,** *adv.* **—strict'ness,** *n.*

stric'ture, *n.* 1. adverse criticism. 2. morbid contraction of body passage.

stride, *v.,* **strode, stridden, striding,** *n.* —*v.* 1. walk with long steps. 2. straddle. —*n.* 3. long step. 4. steady pace.

stri′dent, *adj.* harsh in sound. —**stri′dent•ly,** *adv.* —**stri′dence, stri′den•cy,** *n.*

strife, *n.* conflict or quarrel.

strike, *v.,* **struck, struck** or **stricken, striking,** *n.* —*v.* 1. deal a blow. 2. hit forcibly. 3. cause to ignite. 4. impress. 5. efface; mark out. 6. afflict or affect. 7. sound by percussion. 8. discover in ground. 9. encounter. 10. (of workers) stop work to compel agreement to demands. —*n.* 11. act of striking. 12. *Baseball.* failure of batter to hit pitched ball; anything ruled equivalent. 13. *Bowling.* knocking-down of all pins with first bowl. —**strik′er,** *n.*

string, *n., v.,* **strung, stringing.** —*n.* 1. cord, thread, etc. 2. series or set. 3. cord on musical instrument. 4. plant fiber. —*v.* 5. furnish with strings. 6. arrange in row. 7. mount on string. —**stringed,** *adj.* —**string′y,** *adj.*

string bean, bean with edible pod.

strin′gent (strin′jənt), *adj.* 1. very strict. 2. urgent. —**strin′gen•cy,** *n.* —**strin′gent•ly,** *adv.*

strip, *v.,* **stripped, stripping,** *n.* —*v.* 1. remove covering or clothing. 2. rob. 3. cut into strips. —*n.* 4. long narrow piece.

stripe, *n., v.,* **striped, striping.** —*n.* 1. band of different color, material, etc. 2. welt from whipping. —*v.* 3. mark with stripes.

strip′ling, *n.* youth.

strive, *v.,* **strove, striven, striving.** try hard; struggle.

stroke, *v.,* **stroked, stroking.** —*v.* 1. rub gently. —*n.* 2. act of stroking. 3. blow. 4. attack, as of disease. 5. one complete movement. 6. piece of luck, work, etc. 7. method of swimming.

stroll, *v.* 1. walk idly. 2. roam. —**stroll′er,** *n.*

strong, *adj.* 1. vigorous; powerful; able. 2. intense; distinct. —**strong′ly,** *adv.*

strong′hold′, *n.* fortress.

strop, *n., v.,* **stropped, stropping.** —*n.* 1. flexible strap. —*v.* 2. sharpen on strop.

struc′ture, *n.* 1. form of building or arrangement. 2. something built. —**struc′tur•al,** *adj.* —**struc′tur•al•ly,** *adv.*

stru′del, *n.* fruit-filled pastry.

strug′gle, *v.,* **-gled, -gling,** *n.* —*v.* 1. contend; strive. —*n.* 2. strong effort. 3. combat. —**strug′gler,** *n.*

strum, *v.,* **strummed, strumming.** play carelessly on (stringed instrument).

strum′pet, *n.* prostitute.

strut, *v.,* **strutted, strutting,** *n.* —*v.* 1. walk in vain, pompous manner. —*n.* 2. strutting walk. 3. prop; truss.

strych′nine (strik′nin), *n.* colorless poison.

stub, *n., v.,* **stubbed, stubbing.** —*n.* 1. short remaining piece. 2. stump. —*v.* 3. strike (one's toe) against something. —**stub′by,** *adj.*

stub′ble, *n.* 1. short stumps, as of grain stalks. 2. short growth of beard. —**stub′bly,** *adj.*

stub′born, *adj.* 1. unreasonably obstinate. 2. persistent. —**stub′born•ly,** *adv.* —**stub′born•ness,** *n.*

stuc′co, *n., pl.* **-coes, -cos,** *v.,* **-coed, -coing.** —*n.* 1. plaster for exteriors. —*v.* 2. cover with stucco.

stud, *n., v.,* **studded, studding.** —*n.* 1. projecting knob, pin, etc. 2. upright prop. 3. detachable button. 4. collection of horses. 5. stallion. —*v.* 6. set or scatter with studs.

stu′dent, *n.* person who studies.

stud′ied, *adj.* deliberate.

stu′di•o′, *n.* 1. artist's workroom. 2. place equipped for radio or television broadcasting.

stud′y, *n., pl.* **studies,** *v.,* **studied, studying.** —*n.* 1. effort to learn. 2. object of study. 3. deep thought. 4. room for studying, writing, etc. —*v.* 5. make study of —**stu′di•ous,** *adj.* —**stu′di•ous•ly,** *adv.* —**stu′di•ous•ness,** *n.*

stuff, *n.* 1. material. 2. worthless matter. —*v.* 3. cram full; pack.

stuff′ing, *n.* material stuffed in something.

stuff′y, *adj.,* **stuffier, stuffiest.** 1. lacking fresh air. 2. pompous; pedantic. —**stuff′i•ness,** *n.*

stul′ti•fy′, *v.,* **-fied, -fying.** 1. cause to look foolish 2. make futile.

stum′ble, *v.,* **-bled, -bling.** 1. lose balance from striking foot. 2. come unexpectedly upon.

stump, *n.* 1. lower end of tree after top is gone. 2. any short remaining part. —*v.* 3. baffle. 4. campaign politically. 5. walk heavily.

stun, *v.,* **stunned, stunning.** 1. render unconscious. 2. amaze.

stun′ning, *adj.* strikingly attractive.

stunt, *v.* 1. check growth. 2. do stunts. —*n.* 3. performance to show skill, etc.

stu′pe•fy′, *v.,* **-fied, -fying.** 1. put into stupor. 2. stun. —**stu′pe•fac′tion,** *n.*

stu•pen′dous, *adj.* 1. amazing; marvelous. 2. immense.

stu′pid, *adj.* having or showing little intelligence. —**stu•pid′i•ty,** *n.* —**stu′pid•ly,** *adv.*

stu′por, *n.* dazed or insensible state.

stur′dy, *adj.,* **-dier, -diest.** 1. strongly built. 2. firm. —**stur′di•ly,** *adv.* —**stur′di•ness,** *n.*

stur′geon, *n.* large fish of fresh and salt water.

stut′ter, *v., n.* stammer. —**stut′ter•er,** *n.*

sty, *n., pl.* **sties.** 1. pig pen. 2. inflamed swelling on eyelid.

style, *n., v.,* **styled, styling.** —*n.* 1. particular kind. 2. mode of fashion. 3. elegance. 4. distinct way of writing or speaking. 5. pointed instrument. —*v.* 6. name; give title to. —**sty•lis′tic,** *adj.*

styl′ish, *adj.* fashionable. —**styl′ish•ly,** *adv.*

sty′lus, *n.* pointed tool for writing, etc.

sty′mie, *v.,* **-mied, -mying.** hinder or obstruct, as in golf.

styp′tic, *adj.* 1. checking bleeding. —*n.* 2. styptic substance.

suave (swäv), *adj.* smoothly agreeable. —**suave′ly,** *adv.* —**suav′i•ty, suave′ness,** *n.*

sub•al′tern (-ôl′-), *n. Brit.* low-ranking officer.

sub′com•mit′tee, *n.* committee appointed out of main committee.

sub•con′scious, *adj.* 1. existing beneath consciousness. —*n.* 2. ideas, feelings, etc., of which one is unaware. —**sub•con′scious•ly,** *adv.*

sub′di•vide′, *v.,* **-vided, -viding.** divide into parts. —**sub′di•vi′sion,** *n.*

sub•due′, *v.,* **-dued, -duing.** 1. overcome. 2. soften.

sub′ject, *n.* 1. matter of thought, concern, etc. 2. person under rule of government. 3. *Gram.* noun or pronoun that performs action of predicate. 4. one undergoing action, etc. —*adj.* 5. being a subject. 6. liable; exposed. —*v.* (səb jekt′). 7. cause to experience. 8. make liable. —**sub•jec′tion,** *n.*

sub•jec′tive, *adj.* 1. personal. 2. existing in mind. —**sub′jec•tiv′i•ty,** *n.* —**sub•jec′tive•ly,** *adv.*

sub•join′, *v.* append.

sub′ju•gate′, *v.,* **-gated, -gating.** subdue; conquer. —**sub′ju•ga′tion,** *n.* —**sub′ju•ga′tor,** *n.*

sub·junc'tive, *adj.* 1. designating verb mode of condition, impression, etc. —*n.* 2. subjunctive mode.

sub'lease', *n., v.,* **-leased, -leasing.** —*n.* (sub'lēs'). 1. lease granted by tenant. —*v.* (sub lēs'). 2. rent by sublease.

sub·let', *v.,* **-let, -letting.** (of lessee) let to another person.

sub'li·mate', *v.,* **-mated, -mating,** *n.* —*v.* (-māt'). 1. deflect (biological energies) to other channels. 2. sublime. —*n.* (-mit). 3. substance obtained in subliming. —**sub'li·ma'tion,** *n.*

sub·lime', *adj., n., v.,* **-limed, -liming.** —*adj.* 1. lofty; noble. —*n.* 2. that which is sublime. —*v.* 3. heat (substance) to vapor that condenses to solid on cooling. —**sub·lim'i·ty,** *n.* —**sub·lime'ly,** *adv.*

sub·lim'i·nal, *adj.* below threshold of consciousness. —**sub·lim'i·nal·ly,** *adv.*

sub'ma·rine', *n.* 1. vessel that can navigate under water. —*adj.* (sub'mə rēn'). 2. of submarines. 3. being under sea.

sub·merge', *v.,* **-merged, -merging.** plunge under water. —**sub·mer'gence,** *n.*

sub·merse', *v.,* **-mersed, -mersing.** submerge. —**sub·mer'sion,** *n.* —**sub·mers'i·ble,** *adj.*

sub·mis'sive, *adj.* yielding or obeying readily. —**sub·mis'sive·ly,** *adj.* —**sub·mis'sive·ness,** *n.*

sub·mit', *v.,* **-mitted, -mitting.** 1. yield; surrender. 2. offer for consideration. —**sub·mis'sion,** *n.*

sub·nor'mal, *adj.* of less than normal intelligence.

sub·or'di·nate, *adj., n., v.,* **-nated, -nating.** —*adj.* (-nit). 1. of lower rank or importance. —*n.* (-nit). 2. subordinate person or thing. —*v.* (-nāt'). 3. treat as subordinate. —**sub·or'di·na'tion,** *n.*

sub·orn', *v.* bribe or incite to crime, esp. to perjury.

sub·poe'na (sə pē'nə), *n., v.,* **-naed, -naing.** —*n.* 1. summons to appear in court. —*v.* 2. serve with subpoena.

sub·scribe', *v.,* **-scribed, -scribing.** 1. promise contribution. 2. agree; sign in agreement. 3. contract to receive periodical regularly. —**sub·scrib'er,** *n.* —**sub·scrip'tion,** *n.*

sub'se·quent, *adj.* later; following. —**sub'se·quent·ly,** *adv.*

sub·serve', *v.,* **-served, -serving.** promote; assist.

sub·ser'vi·ent, *adj.* 1. servile; submissive. 2. useful. —**sub·ser'vi·ence,** *n.* —**sub·ser'vi·ent·ly,** *adv.*

sub·side', *v.,* **-sided, -siding.** 1. sink; settle. 2. abate. —**sub·sid'ence,** *n.*

sub·sid'i·ar'y, *adj., n., pl.* **-aries.** —*adj.* 1. auxiliary. 2. subordinate. —*n.* 3. anything subsidiary.

sub'si·dy, *n., pl.* **-dies.** direct pecuniary aid, esp. by government. —**sub'si·dize',** *v.*

sub·sist', *v.* 1. exist. 2. live (as on food). —**sub·sist'ence,** *n.*

sub'stance, *n.* 1. matter or material. 2. density. 3. meaning. 4. likelihood.

sub·stand'ard, *adj.* below standard; not good enough.

sub·stan'tial, *adj.* 1. actual. 2. fairly large. 3. strong. 4. of substance. 5. prosperous. —**sub·stan'tial·ly,** *adv.*

sub·stan'ti·ate', *v.,* **-ated, -ating.** support with evidence. —**sub·stan'ti·a'tion,** *n.*

sub'stan·tive, *n.* 1. noun, pronoun, or word used as noun. —*adj.* 2. of or denoting substantive. 3. independent. 4. essential.

sub'sti·tute', *v.,* **-tuted, -tuting,** *n.* —*v.* 1. put or serve in place of another. —*n.* 2. substitute person or thing. —**sub'sti·tu'tion,** *n.*

sub'ter·fuge', *n.* means used to evade or conceal.

sub'ter·ra'ne·an, *adj.* underground.

sub'tile, *adj.* subtle.

sub'tle (sut'əl), *adj.* 1. delicate; faint. 2. discerning. 3. crafty. —**sub'tle·ty,** *n.* —**sub'tly,** *adv.*

sub·tract', *v.* take from another; deduct. —**sub·trac'tion,** *n.*

sub·trop'i·cal, *adj.* bordering on tropics.

sub'urb, *n.* district just outside city. —**sub·ur'ban,** *adj.*

sub·vert', *v.* overthrow; destroy. —**sub·ver'sion,** *n.* —**sub·ver'sive,** *adj., n.*

sub'way', *n.* underground electric railway.

suc·ceed', *v.* 1. end or accomplish successfully. 2. follow and replace.

suc·cess', *n.* 1. favorable achievement. 2. good fortune. 3. successful thing or person. —**suc·cess'ful,** *adj.* —**suc·cess'ful·ly,** *adv.*

suc·ces'sion, *n.* 1. act of following in sequence. 2. sequence of persons or things. 3. right or process of succeeding another. —**suc·ces'sive,** *adj.* —**suc·ces'sive·ly,** *adv.*

suc·ces'sor, *n.* one that succeeds another.

suc·cinct' (sək singkt'), *adj.* without useless words; concise. —**suc·cinct'ly,** *adv.* —**suc·cinct'ness,** *n.*

suc'cor, *n.* 1. help; aid. —*v.* 2. help in need.

suc'co·tash', *n.* corn and beans cooked together.

suc'cu·lent, *adj.* juicy. —**suc'cu·lence,** *n.*

suc·cumb', *v.* 1. yield. 2. die.

such, *adj.* 1. of that kind, extent, etc. —*n.* 2. such person or thing.

suck, *v.* 1. draw in by using lips and tongue. 2. absorb. —*n.* 3. act of sucking. 4. nourishment, etc., gained by sucking.

suck'er, *n.* 1. one that sucks. 2. freshwater fish. 3. *Informal.* lollipop. 4. shoot from underground stem or root. 5. *Informal.* gullible person.

suck'le, *v.,* **-led, -ling.** nurse at breast.

suck'ling, *n.* 1. infant. 2. unweaned animal.

suc'tion, *n.* tendency to draw substance into vacuum.

sud'den, *adj.* abrupt; quick; unexpected. —**sud'den·ly,** *adv.* —**sud'den·ness,** *n.*

suds, *n.pl.* 1. lather. 2. soapy water. —**suds'y,** *adj.*

sue, *v.,* **sued, suing.** 1. take legal action. 2. appeal.

suede (swād), *n.* soft, napped leather.

su'et, *n.* hard fat about kidneys, etc., esp. of cattle.

suf'fer, *v.* 1. undergo (pain or unpleasantness). 2. tolerate. —**suf'fer·er,** *n.*

suf'fer·ance, *n.* 1. tolerance. 2. endurance.

suf·fice', *v.,* **-ficed, -ficing.** be enough.

suf·fi'cient, *adj.* enough. —**suf·fi'cien·cy,** *n.* —**suf·fi'cient·ly,** *adv.*

suf'fix, *n.* element added to end of word to form another word.

suf'fo·cate', *v.,* **-cated, -cating.** kill or choke by cutting off air to lungs. —**suf'fo·ca'tion,** *n.*

suf'frage, *n.* right to vote.

suf·fuse', *v.* overspread.

sug'ar, *n.* 1. sweet substance, esp. from sugar cane or sugar beet. —*v.* 2. sweeten with sugar. —**sug'ar·y,** *adj.*

sug·gest', *v.* 1. offer for consideration or action. 2. imply. —**sug·ges'tion,** *n.*

sug·gest'i·ble, *adj.* easily led or influenced. —**sug·gest'i·bil'i·ty,** *n.*

sug·ges′tive, *adj.* suggesting, esp. something improper. **—sug·ges′tive·ly,** *adv.* **—sug·ges′tive·ness,** *n.*

su′i·cide′, *n.* 1. intentional killing of oneself. 2. person who commits suicide. **—su′i·cid′al,** *adj.*

suit, *n.* 1. set of clothes. 2. legal action. 3. division of playing cards. 4. petition. 5. wooing. —*v.* 6. clothe. 7. accommodate; adapt. 8. please.

suit′a·ble, *adj.* appropriate; fitting. **—suit′a·bly,** *adv.*

suit′case′, *n.* oblong valise.

suite (swēt), *n.* 1. series or set, as of rooms. 2. retinue.

suit′or, *n.* wooer.

sul′fa drugs, group of antibacterial substances used to treat diseases, wounds, etc.

sul′fate, *n.* salt of sulfuric acid.

sul′fide, *n.* compound of sulfur.

sul′fur, *n.* yellow nonmetallic element.

sul·fur′ic, *adj.* of or containing sulfur. Also, **sul′fur·ous.**

sulk, *v.* 1. hold sullenly aloof. —*n.* 2. fit of sulking.

sulk′y, *adj.,* **sulkier, sulkiest,** *n.* —*adj.* 1. sullen; ill-humored. —*n.* 2. two-wheeled racing carriage for one person. **—sulk′i·ly,** *adv.* **—sulk′i·ness,** *n.*

sul′len, *adj.* 1. silently ill-humored. 2. gloomy. **—sul′len·ly,** *adv.* **—sul′len·ness,** *n.*

sul′ly, *v.,* **-lied, -lying.** soil; defile.

sul′phur, *n.* sulfur.

sul′tan, *n.* ruler of Muslim country.

sul′try, *adj.,* **-trier, -triest.** hot and close. **—sul′tri·ness,** *n.*

sum, *n., v.,* **summed, summing.** —*n.* 1. aggregate of two or more numbers, etc. 2. total amount. 3. gist. —*v.* 4. total. 5. summarize.

su′mac (shōō′-), *n.* small tree with long pinnate leaves.

sum′ma·rize′, *v.,* **-rized, -rizing.** make or be summary of.

sum′ma·ry, *n., pl.* **-ries,** *adj.* —*n.* 1. concise presentation of main points. —*adj.* 2. concise. 3. prompt. **—sum·mar′i·ly,** *adv.*

sum·ma′tion, *n.* 1. act of summing up. 2. total.

sum′mer, *n.* 1. season between spring and fall. —*adj.* 2. of, like, or for summer. —*v.* 3. pass summer. **—sum′mer·y,** *adj.*

sum′mit, *n.* highest point.

sum′mon, *v.* call or order to appear.

sum′mons, *n.* message that summons.

sump, *n.* pit for collecting water, etc.

sump′tu·ous, *adj.* revealing great expense; luxurious. **—sump′tu·ous·ly,** *adv.* **—sump′tu·ous·ness,** *n.*

sun, *n., v.,* **sunned, sunning.** —*n.* 1. heat- and light-giving body of solar system. 2. sunshine. —*v.* 3. expose to sunshine. **—sun′ny,** *adj.* **—sun′beam′,** *n.*

Sun Belt, *n. Informal.* southern and southwestern U.S. Also, **Sunbelt.**

sun′burn′, *n., v.,* **-burned** or **-burnt, -burning.** —*n.* 1. superficial burn from sun's rays. —*v.* 2. affect with sunburn.

sun′dae, *n.* ice cream topped with fruit, etc.

Sun′day, *n.* first day of week.

sun′der, *v.* separate.

sun′di·al, *n.* outdoor instrument for telling time by shadow.

sun′dry (-drē), *adj., n., pl.* **-dries.** —*adj.* 1. various. —*n.* 2. (*pl.*) small items of merchandise.

sun′fish′, *n.* deep-bodied fish.

sun′flow′er, *n.* tall plant with yellow flowers.

sun′light′, *n.* light from sun.

sun′ny, *adj.,* **-nier, -niest.** 1. with much sunlight. 2. cheerful; jolly. **—sun′ni·ness,** *n.*

sun′rise′, *n.* ascent of sun above horizon. Also, **sun′up′.**

sun′set′, *n.* descent of sun below horizon. Also, **sun′down′.**

sun′shine′, *n.* light of sun.

sun′stroke′, *n.* illness from exposure to sun's rays.

sup, *v.,* **supped, supping.** eat supper.

su′per·an′nu·at′ed, *adj.* 1. retired. 2. too old for work or use.

su·perb′, *adj.* very fine. **—su·perb′ly,** *adv.*

su′per·charge′, *v.,* **-charged, -charging.** 1. charge with abundant or excess energy, etc. 2. supply air to (engine) at high pressure. **—su′per·charg′er,** *n.*

su′per·cil′i·ous (-sil′-), *adj.* haughtily disdainful. **—su′per·cil′i·ous·ly,** *adv.* **—su′per·cil′i·ous·ness,** *n.*

su′per·fi′cial, *adj.* 1. of, on, or near surface. 2. shallow, obvious, or insignificant. **—su′per·fi′ci·al′i·ty,** *n.* **—su′per·fi′cial·ly,** *adv.*

su·per′flu·ous, *adj.* 1. being more than is necessary. 2. unnecessary. **—su′per·flu′i·ty,** *n.* **—su·per′flu·ous·ly,** *adv.*

su′per·hu′man, *adj.* 1. beyond what is human. 2. exceeding human strength.

su′per·im·pose′, *v.,* **-posed, -posing.** place over something else.

su′per·in·tend′, *v.* oversee and direct. **—su′per·in·tend′ence, su′per·in·tend′en·cy,** *n.* **—su′per·in·tend′ent,** *n., adj.*

su·pe′ri·or, *adj.* 1. above average; better. 2. upper. 3. arrogant. —*n.* 4. superior person. 5. head of convent, etc. **—su·pe′ri·or′i·ty,** *n.*

su·per′la·tive, *adj.* 1. of highest kind; best. 2. highest in comparison. —*n.* 3. anything superlative. **—su·per′la·tive·ly,** *adv.*

su′per·mar′ket, *n.* self-service food store with large variety.

su′per·nat′u·ral, *adj.* 1. outside the laws of nature; ghostly. —*n.* 2. realm of supernatural beings or things.

su′per·nu′mer·ar·y, *adj., n., pl.* **-aries.** —*adj.* 1. extra. —*n.* 2. extra person or thing. 3. actor with no lines.

su′per·pow′er, *n.* large, powerful nation greatly influencing world affairs.

su′per·scribe′, *v.,* **-scribed, -scribing.** write above or on. **—su′per·scrip′tion,** *n.*

su′per·sede′, *v.,* **-seded, -seding.** replace in power, use, etc.

su′per·son′ic, *adj.* faster than speed of sound.

su′per·star′, *n.* entertainer or sports figure of world renown.

su′per·sti′tion, *n.* irrational belief in supernatural. **—su′per·sti′tious,** *adj.* **—su′per·sti′tious·ly,** *adv.*

su′per·struc′ture, *n.* upper part of building or vessel.

su′per·vene′, *v.,* **-vened, -vening.** 1. come as something extra. 2. ensue.

su′per·vise′, *v.,* **-vised, -vising.** direct and inspect. **—su′per·vi′sion,** *n.* **—su′per·vi′sor,** *n.* **—su′per·vi′so·ry,** *adj.*

su·pine′ (sōō-), *adj.* 1. lying on back. 2. passive. **—su·pine′ly,** *adv.*

sup′per, *n.* evening meal.

sup·plant′, *v.* supersede.

sup′ple, *adj.,* **-pler, -plest.** flexible; limber. **—sup′ple·ly,** *adv.* **—sup′ple·ness,** *n.*

sup′ple·ment (-mənt), *n.* 1. something added to complete or improve. —*v.* (-ment′). 2. add to or complete. **—sup′ple·men′tal, sup′ple·men′ta·ry,** *adj.*

sup′pli·cate′, *v.,* **-cated, -cating.** beg humbly. **—sup′pli·ant, sup′pli·cant,** *n., adj.* **—sup′pli·ca′tion,** *n.*

sup·ply′, *v.,* **-plied, -plying,** *n.* —*v.* 1. furnish; provide. 2. fill (a lack). —*n.*

3. act of supplying. 4. that supplied. 5. stock. —**sup•pli′er,** *n.*

sup•port′, *v.* 1. hold up; bear. 2. provide living for. 3. uphold; advocate. 4. corroborate. —*n.* 5. act of supporting. 6. maintenance; livelihood. 7. thing or person that supports. —**sup•port′a•ble,** *adj.*

sup•pose′, *v.,* **-posed, -posing.** 1. assume; consider. 2. take for granted. —**sup•pos′ed•ly,** *adv.* —**sup′po•si′tion,** *n.* —**sup′po•si′tion•al,** *adj.*

sup•press′, *v.* 1. end forcibly; subdue. 2. repress. 3. withhold from circulation. —**sup•pres′sion,** *n.* —**sup•pres′si•ble,** *adj.*

sup′pu•rate′ (sup′yə-), *v.,* **-rated, -rating.** form or discharge pus. —**sup′pu•ra′tion,** *n.* —**sup′pu•ra′tive,** *adj.*

su•preme′, *adj.* chief; greatest. —**su•prem′a•cy,** *n.* —**su•preme′ly,** *adv.*

sur•cease′, *n.* end.

sur′charge′, *n., v.,* **-charged, -charging.** —*n.* 1. extra or excessive charge, load, etc. —*v.* (sûr chärj′). 2. put surcharge on. 3. overburden.

sure, *adj.,* **surer, surest.** 1. certain; positive. 2. reliable. 3. firm. —**sure′ly,** *adv.* —**sure′ness,** *n.*

sure′-fire′, *adj. Informal.* certain to succeed.

sure′ty (sho͞or′i tē), *n., pl.* **-ties.** 1. security against loss, etc. 2. person who accepts responsibility for another.

surf, *n.* waves breaking on shore or shoals.

sur′face, *n., adj., v.,* **-faced, -facing.** —*n.* 1. outer face; outside. —*adj.* 2. superficial. —*v.* 3. smooth. 4. come to surface.

sur′feit (-fit), *n.* 1. excess, esp. of food or drink. 2. disgust at excess. —*v.* 3. overeat; satiate.

surge, *n., v.,* **surged, surging.** —*n.* 1. swelling or rolling movement or body. —*v.* 2. rise and fall.

sur′geon, *n.* person skilled in surgery.

sur′ger•y, *n., pl.* **-geries.** 1. treatment of disease, etc., by cutting and other manipulations. 2. room for surgical operations. —**sur′gi•cal,** *adj.* —**sur′gi•cal•ly,** *adv.*

sur′ly, *adj.,* **-lier, -liest.** rude; churlish. —**sur′li•ness,** *n.*

sur•mise′, *v.,* **-mised, -mising,** *n.* guess.

sur•mount′, *v.* 1. get over or on top of. 2. overcome. —**sur•mount′a•ble,** *adj.*

sur′name′, *n.* family name.

sur•pass′, *v.* 1. exceed; excel. 2. transcend.

sur′plice (-plis), *n.* white, loose-fitting robe.

sur′plus, *n., adj.* amount beyond that needed; excess.

sur•prise′, *v.,* **-prised, -prising,** *n.* —*v.* 1. come upon unexpectedly; astonish. —*n.* 2. act of surprising. 3. something that surprises. 4. feeling of being surprised.

sur•re′al•ism, *n.* art attempting to express the subconscious. —**sur•re′al•ist,** *n., adj.* —**sur′re•al•is′tic,** *adj.*

sur•ren′der, *v.* 1. yield. —*n.* 2. act of yielding.

sur′rep•ti′tious, *adj.* stealthy; secret. —**sur′rep•ti′tious•ly,** *adv.*

sur′rey, *n., pl.* **-reys.** light carriage with two or more seats.

sur′ro•gate′, *n.* 1. substitute. 2. judge concerned with wills, estates, etc.

sur•round′, *v.* encircle; enclose.

sur•round′ings, *n.pl.* environment.

sur′tax′, *n.* additional tax, esp. on high incomes.

sur•veil′lance (-vā′ləns), *n.* close watch.

sur•vey′, *v., n., pl.* **-veys.** —*v.* (sər vā′). 1. view. 2. measure or determine dimensions or nature of. —*n.* (sûr′vā). 3. methodical investigation. 4. description from surveying. —**sur•vey′or,** *n.*

sur•vive′, *v.,* **-vived, -viving.** 1. remain alive. 2. outlive. —**sur•viv′al,** *n.* —**sur•vi′vor,** *n.*

sus•cep′ti•ble (sə sep′-), *adj.* apt to be affected; liable. —**sus•cep′ti•bil′i•ty,** *n.* —**sus•cep′ti•bly,** *adv.*

sus•pect′, *v.* 1. imagine to be guilty, false, etc. 2. surmise. —*n.* (sus′pekt). 3. one suspected. —*adj.* (sus′pekt). 4. liable to doubt.

sus•pend′, *v.* 1. hang. 2. keep temporarily inactive. 3. refuse work to temporarily.

sus•pend′ers, *n.pl.* straps for holding up trousers.

sus•pense′, *n.* uncertainty; anxiety. —**suspense′ful,** *adj.*

sus•pen′sion, *n.* 1. act of suspending. 2. temporary inactivity. 3. state in which undissolved particles are dispersed in fluid.

sus•pi′cion, *n.* 1. act or instance of suspecting. 2. trace.

sus•pi′cious, *adj.* 1. having suspicions. 2. causing suspicion. —**sus•pi′cious•ly,** *adv.*

sus•tain′, *v.* support; maintain. —**sus•tain′er,** *n.*

sus′te•nance, *n.* 1. food. 2. maintenance.

su′ture (so͞o′chər), *n., v.,* **-tured, -turing.** —*n.* 1. closing of wound. 2. stitch used to close wound. 3. line joining two bones, esp. of the skull. —*v.* 4. join by suture.

su′ze•rain•ty (so͞o′zə rin tē), *n., pl.* **-ties.** sovereignty of one state over another.

svelte, *adj.* slender.

swab, *n., v.,* **swabbed, swabbing.** —*n.* 1. bit of cloth, etc., esp. on stick. —*v.* 2. clean with swab.

swad′dle, *v.,* **-dled, -dling.** bind (infant) with strips of cloth.

swag′ger, *v.* 1. walk with insolent air. —*n.* 2. swaggering gait.

swain, *n.* 1. country boy. 2. lover.

swal′low, *v.* 1. take into stomach through throat. 2. assimilate. 3. suppress. —*n.* 4. act of swallowing. 5. small graceful migratory bird.

swamp, *n.* 1. marshy ground. —*v.* 2. drench with water. 3. overwhelm. —**swamp′y,** *adj.*

swan, *n.* large long-necked swimming bird.

swap, *v.,* **swapped, swapping,** *n.* trade.

sward (swôrd), *n.* turf.

swarm, *n.* 1. group of bees comprising colony. —*v.* 2. fly off to start new colony. 3. cluster; throng.

swarth′y, *adj.,* **swarthier, swarthiest.** (esp. of skin) dark. —**swarth′i•ness,** *n.*

swash′buck′ler, *n.* swaggering fellow. —**swash′buck′ling,** *adj., n.*

swas′ti•ka, *n.* 1. kind of cross used as symbol and ornament. 2. emblem of Nazi Party.

swat, *v.,* **swatted, swatting,** *n. Informal.* —*v.* 1. strike. —*n.* 2. sharp blow.

swatch, *n.* sample of material or finish.

swath (swoth), *n.* long cut made by scythe or mowing machine.

swathe (swoth), *v.,* **swathed, swathing,** *n.* —*v.* 1. wrap closely. —*n.* 2. bandage.

sway, *v.* 1. swing to and fro. 2. influence or incline. —*n.* 3. act of swaying. 4. rule.

swear, *v.,* **swore, sworn, swearing.** 1. affirm on oath; vow. 2. use profane language. 3. bind by oath.

sweat, *v.,* **sweat** or **sweated, sweating,** *n.* —*v.* 1. excrete moisture through pores. 2. gather moisture. —*n.* 3. secretion of sweat glands. 4. process of sweating. —**sweat′y,** *adj.*

sweat′er, *n.* knitted jacket.

Swed′ish, *n.* language or people of Sweden. —**Swed′ish,** *adj.*

sweep, *v.,* **swept, sweeping,** *n.* —*v.* 1. move or clear with broom, etc. 2. clear or pass over with forceful, rapid movement. —*n.* 3. act of sweeping. 4. extent; range.

sweep′stakes′, *n.* 1. race for stakes put up by competitors. 2. lottery.

sweet, *adj.* 1. having taste of sugar or honey. 2. fragrant. 3. fresh. 4. pleasant in sound. 5. amiable. —*n.* 6. anything sweet. —**sweet′en,** *v.* —**sweet′ly,** *adv.* —**sweet′ness,** *n.*

sweet′bread′, *n.* pancreas, esp. of calf or lamb.

sweet′bri′er, *n.* fragrant wild rose.

sweet′heart′, *n.* beloved.

sweet′meat′, *n.* confection.

sweet pea, annual vine with fragrant blooms.

sweet potato, plant with sweet edible root.

sweet′ wil′liam, low plant with dense flower clusters.

swell, *v.,* **swelled, swelled** or **swollen, swelling,** *n.,* *adj.* —*v.* 1. grow in degree, force, etc. —*n.* 2. act of swelling. 3. wave. —*adj.* 4. *Informal.* excellent.

swel′ter, *v.* perspire or suffer from heat.

swerve, *v.,* **swerved, swerving,** *n.* —*v.* 1. turn aside. —*n.* 2. act of swerving.

swift, *adj.* 1. moving with speed. 2. prompt or quick. —*n.* 3. small bird. —**swift′ly,** *adv.* —**swift′ness,** *n.*

swig, *n.,* *v.,* **swigged, swigging.** *Informal.* —*n.* 1. deep drink. —*v.* 2. drink heartily.

swill, *n.* 1. moist garbage fed to hogs. —*v.* 2. guzzle.

swim, *v.,* **swam, swum, swimming,** *n.* —*v.* 1. move in water by action of limbs, etc. 2. be immersed. 3. be dizzy. —*n.* 4. period of swimming. —**swim′mer,** *n.*

swin′dle, *v.,* **-dled, -dling,** *n.* —*v.* 1. cheat; defraud. —*n.* 2. act of swindling. —**swin′dler,** *n.*

swine, *n.,* *pl.* **swine.** hog.

swing, *v.,* **swung, swinging,** *n.* —*v.* 1. move to and fro around point. 2. brandish. 3. hand loosely. —*n.* 4. act, way, or extent of swinging. 5. operation. 6. scope. 7. suspended seat for swinging.

swing′er, *n.* *Slang.* 1. person with modern attitudes. 2. sexually uninhibited person.

swipe, *n.,* *v.,* **swiped, swiping.** *Informal.* —*n.* 1. sweeping blow. —*v.* 2. deal such blow. 3. steal.

swirl, *v.,* *n.* whirl; eddy.

swish, *v.* 1. rustle. —*n.* 2. swishing sound.

Swiss, *n.pl.* people of Switzerland. —**Swiss,** *adj.*

switch, *n.* 1. flexible rod. 2. device for turning electric current on or off. 3. device for moving trains from one track to another. 4. change. —*v.* 5. whip with switch. 6. shift; divert. 7. turn (electric current) on or off.

switch′board′, *n.* panel for controlling electric circuits.

swiv′el, *n.* 1. device permitting rotation of thing mounted on it. —*v.* 2. rotate.

swol′len, *pp.* of **swell.**

swoon, *v.,* *n.* faint.

swoop, *v.* 1. sweep down upon. —*n.* 2. sweeping descent.

sword (sōrd), *n.* weapon with blade fixed in hilt or handle. —**sword′play′,** *n.* —**swords′man,** *n.*

sword′fish′, *n.* marine fish with swordlike upper jaw.

syb′a•rite′, *n.* person devoted to pleasure. —**syb′a•rit′ic,** *adj.*

syc′a•more′, *n.* 1. plane tree. 2. *Brit.* maple tree.

syc′o•phant (sik′ə fənt), *n.* flatterer; parasite. —**syc′o•phan•cy,** *n.*

syl•lab′i•cate′, *v.,* **-cated, -cating.** divide into syllables. Also, **syl•lab′i•fy′.** —**syl•lab′i•ca′tion,** *n.*

syl′la•ble, *n.* single unit of speech. —**syl•lab′ic,** *adj.*

syl′la•bus, *n.,* *pl.* **-buses, -bi** (-bī′), outline of course of study.

syl′lo•gism, *n.* three-part chain of logical reasoning.

sylph, *n.* graceful woman.

syl′van, *adj.* 1. of forests. 2. wooded.

sym′bol, *n.* 1. emblem; token; sign. 2. thing that represents something else. —**sym•bol′ic, sym•bol′i•cal,** *adj.* —**sym′bol•ize′,** *v.*

sym′me•try, *n.,* *pl.* **-tries.** pleasing balance or proportion. —**sym•met′ri•cal,** *adj.* —**sym•met′ri•cal•ly,** *adv.*

sym′pa•thize′, *v.,* **-thized, -thizing.** 1. be in sympathy. 2. feel or express sympathy. —**sym′pa•thiz′er,** *n.*

sym′pa•thy, *n.,* *pl.* **-thies.** 1. agreement in feeling; accord. 2. compassion. —**sym′pa•thet′ic,** *adj.* —**sym′pa•thet′i•cal•ly,** *adv.*

sym′pho•ny, *n.,* *pl.* **-nies.** 1. elaborate composition for orchestra. 2. harmonious combination. —**sym•phon′ic,** *adj.*

sym•po′si•um, *n.,* *pl.* **-siums, -sia.** meeting to present essays on one subject.

symp′tom, *n.* sign or indication, esp. of disease. —**symp′to•mat′ic,** *adj.*

syn′a•gogue′ (-gog′), *n.* 1. assembly of Jews for worship. 2. place of such assembly.

syn′chro•nize′, *v.,* **-nized, -nizing.** 1. occur at same time. 2. show or set to show same time. —**syn′chro•ni•za′tion,** *n.* —**syn′chro•nous,** *adj.*

syn′co•pate′, *v.,* **-pated, -pating.** 1. *Music.* play by accenting notes normally unaccented. 2. *Gram.* omit middle sound in (word). —**syn′co•pa′tion,** *n.*

syn′di•cate, *n.,* *v.,* **-cated, -cating.** —*n.* (sin′də kit). 1. combination of persons or companies for large joint enterprise. 2. agency dealing in news stories, etc. —*v.* (sin′di kāt′). 3. publish as syndicate. —**syn′di•ca′tion,** *n.*

syn′drome, *n.* characteristic group of symptoms.

syn′fu′el, *n.* synthetic fuel.

syn′od (sin′əd), *n.* meeting of church delegates.

syn′o•nym, *n.* word meaning same as another. —**syn•on′y•mous,** *adj.* —**syn•on′y•mous•ly,** *adv.*

syn•op′sis, *n.* brief summary.

syn′tax, *n.* arrangement of words into sentences, phrases, etc.

syn′the•sis, *n.,* *pl.* **-ses.** 1. combination of parts into whole. 2. such whole.

syn′the•size′, *v.,* **-sized, -sizing.** make by combining parts.

syn•thet′ic, *adj.* 1. produced artificially rather than by nature. 2. of synthesis. —**syn•thet′i•cal•ly,** *adv.*

synthetic fuel, fuel manufactured esp. from coal or shale.

syph′i•lis, *n.* infectious venereal disease. —**syph•i•lit′ic,** *adj.,* *n.*

sy•rin′ga (sə ring′gə), *n.* shrub with fragrant flowers, as lilac.

syr•inge′, *n.* device for drawing in and ejecting fluids.

syr′up, *n.* sweet thick liquid. —**syr′up•y,** *adj.*

sys′tem, *n.* 1. orderly assemblage of facts, parts, etc. 2. plan. 3. organization of one's body. —**sys′tem•at′ic,** *adj.* —**sys′tem•at′i•cal•ly,** *adv.* —**sys•tem′ic,** *adj.*

sys′tem•a•tize′, *v.,* **-tized, -tizing.** arrange in or by system.

sys′to•le′ (sis′tə lē′), *n.* regular contraction of the heart. —**sys•tol′ic,** *adj.*

T

T, t, *n.* twentieth letter of English alphabet.

tab, *n., v.,* **tabbed, tabbing.** —*n.* 1. small flap. 2. tag. —*v.* 3. furnish with tab.

Ta·bas'co, *n. Trademark.* pungent condiment sauce.

tab'by, *n., pl.* **-bies,** *adj.* —*n.* 1. striped or brindled cat. 2. silk fabric. —*adj.* 4. striped.

tab'er·nac'le, *n.* 1. temporary temple, esp. Jewish. 2. church for large congregation.

ta'ble, *n., v.,* **-bled, -bling.** —*n.* 1. piece of furniture consisting of level part on legs. 2. food. 3. company at table. 4. compact arrangement of information in parallel columns. —*v.* 5. place on or enter in table. 6. postpone deliberation on. —**ta'ble·cloth',** *n.*

tab·leau' (tab lō'), *n., pl.* **-leaux.** picture.

ta'ble d'hôte' (täb'əl dōt'), meal fixed in courses and price.

ta'ble·land', *n.* elevated, level region of considerable extent.

ta'ble·spoon', *n.* 1. large spoon in table service. 2. tablespoonful.

ta'ble·spoon·ful', *n., pl.* **-fuls.** quantity tablespoon holds, about ½ fluid ounce or 3 teaspoonfuls.

tab'let, *n.* 1. pad of writing paper. 2. small slab. 3. pill.

tab'loid, *n.* newspaper about half of ordinary size.

ta·boo', *adj., n., pl.* **-boos,** *v.,* **-booed, -booing.** —*adj.* 1. forbidden. —*n.* 2. prohibition. —*v.* 3. prohibit.

ta'bor (tā'bər), *n.* small drum.

tab'u·late', *v.,* **-lated, -lating.** arrange in table. —**tab'u·lar,** *adj.* —**tab'u·la'tion,** *n.* —**tab'u·la'tor,** *n.*

ta·chom'e·ter (tə kom'ə tər), *n.* instrument for measuring velocity.

tac'it (tas'it), *adj.* 1. silent. 2. implied. 3. unspoken. —**tac'it·ly,** *adv.*

tac'i·turn, *adj.* inclined to silence. —**tac'i·tur'ni·ty,** *n.* —**tac'i·turn·ly,** *adv.*

tack, *n.* 1. short nail with flat head. 2. straight windward run of sailing ship. —*v.* 3. fasten by tack. 4. navigate by tacks.

tack'le, *n., v.,* **-led, -ling.** —*n.* 1. fishing equipment. 2. hoisting apparatus. —*v.* 3. undertake to deal with. —**tack'ler,** *n.*

tack'y, *adj.,* **tackier, tackiest.** 1. *Informal.* shabby; dowdy. 2. slightly sticky.

tact, *n.* skill in handling delicate situations. —**tact'ful,** *adj.* —**tact'less,** *adj.*

tac·ti'cian (tak tish'ən), *n.* person versed in tactics.

tac'tics, *n.* 1. maneuvering of armed forces. 2. methods for attaining success. —**tac'ti·cal,** *adj.* —**tac'ti·cal·ly,** *adv.*

tac'tile, *adj.* of sense of touch. —**tac·til'i·ty,** *n.*

tad'pole', *n.* immature form of frogs, toads, etc.

taf'fe·ta, *n.* lustrous silk or rayon fabric.

taf'fy, *n.* molasses candy.

tag, *n., v.,* **tagged, tagging.** —*n.* 1. small paper, etc., attached as mark or label. 2. game in which players chase and touch each other. —*v.* 3. furnish with tag. 4. touch in playing tag.

tail, *n.* 1. appendage at rear of animal's body. 2. something resembling this.

tail'gate', *n., v.,* **-gated, -gating.** —*n.* 1. hinged board at back of vehicle. —*v.* 2. drive too closely behind.

tail'light', *n.* light, usually red, at the rear of automobile, train, etc.

tai'lor, *n.* maker or mender of outer garments.

tail'piece', *n.* piece, design, etc., added at end; appendage.

tail' spin', *n.* descent of airplane in steep spiral course.

taint, *n.* 1. unfavorable trace, as of dishonor. —*v.* 2. contaminate.

Tai'wan·ese' (tī'wä nēz'), *n.pl.* people of Taiwan. —**Taiwanese,** *adj.*

take, *v.,* **took, taken, taking.** 1. seize, catch, or embrace. 2. receive; obtain. 3. select. 4. remove. 5. deduct. 6. conduct. 7. travel by. 8. occupy. 9. assume. 10. require.

take'-off', *n.* 1. leaving of ground in leaping or flying. 2. place at which one takes off. 3. *Informal.* piece of mimicry.

talc, *n.* soft mineral, used for lubricants, etc. Also, **tal'cum.**

tale, *n.* story or lie.

tale'bear'er, *n.* gossip.

tal'ent, *n.* natural ability. —**tal'ent·ed,** *adj.*

tal'is·man, *n.* amulet.

talk, *v.* 1. speak; converse. 2. gossip. —*n.* 3. speech; conversation. 4. conference. 5. gossip. —**talk'a·tive,** *adj.* —**talk'er,** *n.*

talk'y, *adj.,* **-ier, -iest.** 1. containing too much talk, dialogue, etc. 2. talkative. —**talk'i·ness,** *n.*

tall, *adj.* high.

tal'low, *n.* 1. suet. 2. hardened fat for soap, etc.

tal'ly, *n., pl.* **-lies,** *v.,* **-lied, -lying.** —*n.* 1. notched stock indicating amount. 2. mark on tally. 3. record of amounts. —*v.* 4. record.

tal'ly·ho', *n., pl.* **-hos,** *interj. Chiefly Brit.* —*n.* 1. mail or pleasure coach. —*interj.* (tal'ē hō'). 2. huntsman's cry on catching sight of fox.

Tal'mud (täl'mŏŏd), *n.* collection of Jewish laws. —**Tal·mud'ic,** *adj.*

tal'on, *n.* claw.

tam, *n.* tam-o'-shanter.

ta·ma'le (tə mä'lē), *n.* Mexican dish of corn meal, meat, red peppers, etc.

tam'a·rind, *n.* tropical fruit.

tam'bou·rine' (tam'bə rēn'), *n.* small drum with metal disks in frame.

tame, *adj., v.,* **tamed, taming.** —*adj.* 1. not wild; domesticated. 2. uninterestingly conventional. —*v.* 3. domesticate. —**tam'a·ble, tame'a·ble,** *adj.* —**tame'ly,** *adv.* —**tame'ness,** *n.* —**tam'er,** *n.*

tam'-o'-shan'ter, *n.* cap with flat crown.

tamp, *v.* force down or in. —**tamp'er,** *n.*

tam'per, *v.* meddle.

tan, *v.,* **tanned, tanning,** *n., adj.* —*v.* 1. convert into leather. 2. make or become brown by exposure to sun. —*n.* 3. light brown. 4. Also, **tan'bark'.** bark used in tanning hides. —*adj.* 5. light brown. —**tan'ner,** *n.* —**tan'ner·y,** *n.*

tan'a·ger, *n.* small, brightly colored bird.

tan'dem, *adv.* 1. one behind another. —*adj.* 2. having with one following behind another. —*n.* 3. team of horses so harnessed.

tang, *n.* strong flavor.

tan'gent, *adj.* 1. touching. —*n.* 2. tangent line, etc. 3. sudden change of course, thought, etc. —**tan'gen·cy,** *n.*

tan•gen′tial, *adj.* 1. being tangent; touching. 2. not relevant. **—tan•gen′tial•ly,** *adv.*

tan′ge•rine′, *n.* loose-skinned fruit similar to orange.

tan′gi•ble, *adj.* 1. discernible by touch. 2. real. 3. definite. **—tan′gi•bil′i•ty,** *n.* **—tan′gi•bly,** *adv.*

tan′gle, *v.,* **-gled, -gling,** *n.* **—***v.* 1. come or bring together in confused mass. 2. involve. 3. snare. 4. *Informal.* come into conflict. **—***n.* 5. tangled state or mass.

tan′go, *n., pl.* **-gos,** *v.,* **-goed, -going.** **—***n.* 1. Spanish-American dance. **—***v.* 2. dance the tango.

tank, *n.* 1. large receptacle. 2. armored combat vehicle on caterpillar treads.

tank′ard, *n.* large cup.

tank′er, *n.* ship for transporting liquid bulk cargo.

tan′ta•lize′, *v.,* **-lized, -lizing.** torment by prospect of something desired. **—tan′ta•liz′ing•ly,** *adv.*

tan′ta•mount′, *adj.* equivalent.

tan′trum, *n.* noisy outburst of ill-humor.

tap, *n., v.,* **tapped, tapping. —***n.* 1. plug or faucet through which liquid is drawn. 2. light blow. **—***v.* 3. draw liquid from. 4. reach or pierce to draw something off. 5. strike lightly.

tap dance, dance in which rhythm is audibly tapped out by toe or heel. **—tap′-dance′,** *v.*

tape, *n., v.,* **taped, taping. —***n.* 1. narrow strip of flexible material. **—***v.* 2. furnish or tie with tape. 3. record on tape.

tape measure, *n.* tape marked for measuring. Also, **tape′line′.**

ta′per, *v.* 1. make or become narrower toward end. **—***n.* 2. gradual decrease. 3. small candle.

tap′es•try, *n., pl.* **-tries.** woven, figured fabric for wall hanging, etc.

tape′worm′, *n.* parasitic worm in alimentary canal.

tap′i•o′ca, *n.* granular food from starch of tuberous plants.

ta′pir (tā′pər), *n.* tropical swinelike animal.

tap′root′, *n.* main, central root pointing downward and giving off small lateral roots.

tar, *n., v.,* **tarred, tarring. —***n.* 1. dark viscid product made from coal, wood, etc. 2. sailor. **—***v.* 3. cover with tar. **—tar′ry** (tär′ē), *adj.*

tar′an•tel′la (tar′ən tel′ə), *n.* rapid, whirling southern Italian dance.

ta•ran′tu•la (-chə lə), *n.* large hairy spider.

tar′dy, *adj.,* **-dier, -diest.** late. **—tar′di•ly,** *adv.* **—tar′di•ness,** *n.*

tare (târ), *n.* 1. weed. 2. weight of a wrapping or receptacle.

tar′get, *n.* something aimed at.

tar′iff, *n.* 1. list of export or import duties. 2. one such duty.

tar′nish, *v.* 1. lose luster. 2. sully. **—***n.* 3. tarnished coating or state.

tar•pau′lin (tär pô′lin), *n.* waterproof covering of canvas, etc.

tar′pon, *n.* large game fish.

tar′ra•gon′, *n.* plant with aromatic leaves used as seasoning.

tar′ry (tar′ē), *v.,* **-ried, -rying.** 1. stay. 2. linger.

tart, *adj.* 1. sour; acid. 2. caustic. **—***n.* 3. pastry shell filled with fruit, etc. **—tart′ly,** *adv.* **—tart′ness,** *n.*

tar′tan, *n.* cloth worn by Natives of N Scotland, having crisscross pattern.

tar′tar, *n.* 1. hard deposit on teeth. 2. savage, intractable person. **—tar•tar′ic, tar′tar•ous,** *adj.*

task, *n.* 1. assigned piece of work. **—***v.* 2. put strain on.

task force, temporary group of armed units for carrying out specific mission.

task′mas′ter, *n.* assigner of tasks.

tas′sel, *n.* fringed ornament hanging from roundish knot.

taste, *v.,* **tasted, tasting,** *n.* **—***v.* 1. try flavor by taking in mouth. 2. eat or drink a little of. 3. perceive flavor. 4. have particular flavor. **—***n.* 5. act of tasting. 6. sense by which flavor is perceived. 7. flavor. 8. sense of fitness or beauty. **—taste′ful,** *adj.* **—taste′less,** *adj.* **—tast′er,** *n.*

tast′y, *adj.,* **-ier, -iest.** 1. savory. 2. tasting good. **—tast′i•ness,** *n.*

tat, *v.,* **tatted, tatting.** to do, or make by, tatting.

tat′ter, *n.* 1. torn piece. 2. (*pl.*) ragged clothing.

tat′ting, *n.* 1. the making of a kind of knotted lace with a shuttle. 2. such lace.

tat′tle, *v.,* **-tled, -tling,** *n.* **—***v.* 1. tell another's secrets. **—***n.* 2. chatter; gossip. **—tat′tler, tat′tle•tale′,** *n.*

tat•too′, *n., pl.* **-toos,** *v.,* **-tooed, -tooing. —***n.* 1. indelible marking on skin by puncturing and dyeing. 2. design so made. 3. military signal on drum, bugle, etc., to go to quarters. **—***v.* 4. mark by tattoo.

taunt, *v.* 1. reproach insultingly or sarcastically. **—***n.* 2. insulting or sarcastic gibe.

taupe (tōp), *n.* dark gray usually tinged with brown, purple, yellow, or green.

taut, *adj.* tight; tense. **—taut′ly,** *adv.* **—taut′ness,** *n.*

tau•tol′o•gy, *n., pl.* **-gies.** needless repetition. **—tau′to•log′i•cal,** *adj.*

tav′ern, *n.* 1. saloon. 2. inn.

taw (tô), *n.* 1. choice playing marble with which to shoot. 2. game of marbles.

taw′dry, *adj.,* **-drier, -driest.** gaudy; cheap. **—taw′dri•ly,** *adv.* **—taw′dri•ness,** *n.*

taw′ny, *adj., n.* dark yellow or yellow brown.

tax, *n.* 1. money regularly paid to government. 2. burdensome duty, etc. **—***v.* 3. impose tax. 4. burden. 5. accuse. **—tax′a•ble,** *adj.* **—tax•a′tion,** *n.* **—tax′pay′er,** *n.*

tax′i, *n., pl.* **taxis,** *v.,* **taxied, taxiing. —***n.* 1. taxicab. **—***v.* 2. go in taxicab. 3. (of airplane) move on ground or water under its own power.

tax′i•cab′, *n.* automobile carrying paying passengers.

tax′i•der′my, *n.* art of preserving and mounting skins of animals. **—tax′i•der′•mist,** *n.*

tax•on′o•my, *n.* classification, esp. in relation to principles or laws.

tea, *n.* 1. dried aromatic leaves of Oriental shrub. 2. beverage made by infusion of leaves in hot water. 3. afternoon meal or reception. **—tea′cup′,** *n.* **—tea′ket′tle,** *n.* **—tea′pot′,** *n.*

teach, *v.,* **taught, teaching.** impart knowledge to. **—teach′er,** *n.* **—teach′a•ble,** *adj.*

teak, *n.* East Indian tree with hard wood.

teal, *n., pl.* **teals, teal.** any of certain small fresh-water ducks.

team, *n.* 1. persons, etc., associated in joint action. **—***v.* 2. join in team. **—team′mate′,** *n.* **—team′work′,** *n.*

team′ster, *n.* driver of team or truck.

tear, *v.,* **tore, torn, tearing. —***v.* 1. pull apart by force. 2. distress. 3. divide. 4. lacerate. 5. rend. **—***n.* 6. act of tearing. 7. torn place. 8. (tēr). Also, **tear′drop′.** drop of fluid secreted by eye duct. **—tear′ful,** *adj.*

tear gas (tēr), gas, used esp. in riots, that makes eyes smart and water.

tease, *v.,* **teased, teasing.** annoy by raillery. **—teas′er,** *n.*

tea′spoon′, *n.* small spoon. **—tea′-spoon•ful′,** *n.*

teat, *n.* nipple.

tech′ni•cal, *adj.* 1. pertaining to skilled activity. 2. considered in strict sense. **—tech′ni•cal′i•ty,** *n.* **—tech′-ni•cal•ly,** *adv.*

Tech′ni•col′or (tek′-), *n. Trademark.* system of making color motion pictures.

tech•nique′ (-nēk′), *n.* skilled method. Also, **tech•nic′.**

tech•nol′o•gy, *n.* practical application of science. **—tech•no•log′i•cal,** *adj.*

Te De′um (tā dā′əm), hymn of praise and thanksgiving.

te′di•ous, *adj.* long and tiresome. **—te′di•um,** *n.* **—te′di•ous•ly,** *adv.* **—te′di•ous•ness,** *n.*

tee, *n., v.,* **teed, teeing.** *Golf.* **—n.** 1. hard mound of earth at beginning of play for each hole. 2. object from which ball is driven. **—v.** 3. place (ball) on tee. 4. strike (ball) from tee.

teem, *v.* abound; swarm.

teens, *n.* years (13–19) of ages ending in *-teen.* **—teen′-ag′er,** *n.*

tee′ter, *Informal.* **—v.** 1. seesaw. 2. walk unsteadily. **—n.** 3. seesaw.

teethe, *v.,* **teethed, teething.** grow or cut teeth.

tee•to′tal•er, *n.* person who does not drink alcoholic beverages.

tel′e•cast′, *v.,* **-cast** or **-casted, -casting,** *n.* **—v.** 1. broadcast by television. **—n.** 2. television broadcast.

tel′e•graph′, *n.* 1. electrical apparatus or process for sending message (**tel′e•gram′**). **—v.** 2. send by telegraph. **—te•leg′ra•pher,** *n.* **—tel′e•graph′ic,** *adj.* **—te•leg′ra•phy,** *n.*

te•lep′a•thy, *n.* communication between minds without physical means. **—te•lep′a•thist,** *n.* **—tel′e•path′ic,** *adj.* **—tel′e•path′i•cal•ly,** *adv.*

tel′e•phone′, *n., v.,* **-phoned, -phoning.** **—n.** 1. electrical apparatus or process for transmitting sound or speech. **—v.** 2. speak to or transmit by telephone. **—tel′e•phon′er** (-fō′nər), *n.* **—tel′e•phon′ic** (-fon′-), *adj.* **—tel′e•phon′i•cal•ly,** *adv.* **—te•leph′o•ny,** *n.*

tel′e•scope′, *n., v.,* **-scoped, -scoping.** **—n.** 1. optical instrument for enlarging image of distant objects. **—v.** 2. force or slide one object into another. **—tel′e•scop′ic,** *adj.*

Tel′e•type′, *n. Trademark.* teletypewriter.

tel′e•type′writ′er, *n.* a telegraphic apparatus with typewriter terminals.

tel′e•view′, *v.* view with a television receiver. **—tel′e•view′er,** *n.*

tel′e•vise′, *v.,* **-vised, -vising.** send or receive by television.

tel′e•vi′sion, *n.* radio or electrical transmission of images.

Tel′ex, *n. Trademark.* two-way teletypewriter system.

tell, *v.,* **told, telling.** 1. relate. 2. communicate. 3. say positively. 4. distinguish. 5. inform. 6. divulge. 7. order.

tell′er, *n.* bank cashier.

tell′tale′, *n.* 1. divulger of secrets. **—adj.** 2. revealing.

te•mer′i•ty, *n.* rash boldness.

tem′per, *n.* 1. state or habit of mind. 2. heat or passion. 3. control of one's anger. 4. state of metal after tempering. **—v.** 5. moderate. 6. heat and cool metal to obtain proper hardness, etc.

tem′per•a•ment, *n.* mental disposition.

tem′per•a•men′tal, *adj.* 1. moody or sensitive. 2. of one's personality. **—tem′per•a•men′tal•ly,** *adv.*

tem′per•ance, *n.* moderation.

tem′per•ate, *adj.* moderate. **—tem′-per•ate•ly,** *adv.* **—tem′per•ate•ness,** *n.*

Temperate Zone, part of earth's surface lying between either tropic and nearest polar circle.

tem′per•a•ture, *n.* degree of warmth or coldness.

tem′pest, *n.* violent storm, commotion, or disturbance. **—tem•pes′tu•ous,** *adj.*

tem′ple, *n.* 1. place dedicated to worship. 2. flat region at side of forehead.

tem′po, *n.* rapidity.

tem′po•ral, *adj.* 1. of time. 2. secular. **—tem′po•ral•ly,** *adv.*

tem′po•rar′y, *adj.* not permanent. **—tem′po•rar′i•ly,** *adv.*

tem′po•rize′, *v.,* **-rized, -rizing.** 1. delay by evasion or indecision. 2. compromise. **—tem′po•ri•za′tion,** *n.* **—tem′po•ri′zer,** *n.*

tempt, *v.* 1. entice. 2. appeal strongly. **—temp•ta′tion,** *n.* **—tempt′er,** *n.* **—tempt′ress,** *n.fem.*

ten, *n., adj.* nine plus one.

ten′a•ble, *adj.* defensible in argument. **—ten′a•bly,** *adv.*

te•na′cious, *adj.* 1. holding fast. 2. retentive. 3. obstinate. 4. sticky. **—te•na′cious•ly,** *adv.* **—te•nac′i•ty,** te•na′cious•ness, *n.*

ten′an•cy, *n.* holding; tenure.

ten′ant, *n.* 1. one renting from landlord. 2. occupant.

Ten Commandments, precepts spoken by God to Israel (Exodus 20, Deut. 10) or delivered to Moses (Exodus 24:12, 34) on Mount Sinai.

tend, *v.* 1. incline in action or effect. 2. lead. 3. take care of.

tend′en•cy, *n., pl.* **-cies.** 1. disposition to behave or act in certain way. 2. predisposition; preference.

ten•den′tious, *adj.* having or showing bias.

ten′der, *adj.* 1. soft; delicate; weak. 2. immature. 3. soft-hearted. 4. kind. 5. loving. 6. sensitive. **—v.** 7. present formally. 8. offer. **—n.** 9. something offered. 10. person who tends. 11. auxiliary vehicle or vessel. **—ten′-der•er,** *n.* **—ten′der•ly,** *adv.* **—ten′-der•ness,** *n.*

ten′der•foot′, *n., pl.* **-foots, -feet.** *Informal.* 1. inexperienced person; novice. 2. *Western U.S.* newcomer to ranching and mining regions.

ten′der-heart′ed, *adj.* soft-hearted; sympathetic. **—ten′der-heart′ed•ness,** *n.*

ten′der•loin′, *n.* 1. tender meat on loin of beef, pork, etc. 2. brothel district of city.

ten′don, *n.* band of fibrous tissue connecting muscle to bone or part.

ten′dril, *n.* clinging threadlike organ of climbing plants.

ten′e•ment, *n.* 1. dwelling place. 2. Also, **tenement house.** cheap apartment house.

ten′et, *n.* principle, doctrine, dogma, etc.

ten′nis, *n.* game of ball played with rackets (**tennis rackets**) on rectangular court (**tennis court**).

ten′on, *n.* projection inserted into cavity (**mortise**) to form joint.

ten′or, *n.* 1. continuous course or progress. 2. perceived meaning or intention. 3. male voice between baritone and alto. 4. singer with this voice.

ten′pins′, *n.* bowling game played with ten pins.

tense, *adj.,* **tenser, tensest,** *v.,* **tensed, tensing,** *n.* **—adj.** 1. taut; rigid. 2. emotionally strained. **—v.** 3. make or become tense. **—n.** 4. verb inflection indicating time of action or state. **—tense′ly,** *adv.* **—tense′ness,** *n.*

ten′sile (-səl), *adj.* 1. of tension. 2. ductile.

ten·sion, *n.* 1. stretching or being stretched. 2. strain. 3. strained relations.

tent, *n.* portable shelter, usually canvas.

ten·ta·cle, *n.* slender, flexible organ for feeling, etc.

ten·ta·tive, *adj.* in trial; experimental. —**ten·ta·tive·ly,** *adv.*

ten·ter·hook', *n.* 1. hook to hold cloth stretched on frame. 2. **on tenterhooks,** in suspense.

tenth, *adj., n.* next after ninth.

ten·u·ous, *adj.* 1. thin. 2. rarefied. —**ten·u·ous·ly,** *adv.* —**ten·u·i·ty, ten·u·ous·ness,** *n.*

ten·ure (-yər), *n.* 1. holding of something. 2. assurance of permanent work.

te'pee, *n.* American Indian tent.

tep·id, *adj.* lukewarm. —**te·pid'i·ty, tep'id·ness,** *n.* —**tep'id·ly,** *adv.*

te·qui'la (-kē'-), *n.* Mexican liquor.

term, *n.* 1. name for something. 2. period, as of school instruction. 3. (*pl.*) conditions of agreement or bargain. —*v.* 4. name; designate.

ter'ma·gant, *n.* shrew (def. 1).

ter'mi·nal, *adj.* 1. at end; concluding. 2. leading to death. —*n.* 3. end or extremity. 4. terminating point for trains, buses, etc. 5. point of electrical connection. —**ter'mi·nal·ly,** *adv.*

ter'mi·nate, *v.,* **-nated, -nating.** 1. end or cease. 2. occur at end. —**ter'mi·na·ble,** *adj.* —**ter'mi·na·bly,** *adv.* —**ter'mi·na'tion,** *n.*

ter'mi·nol'o·gy, *n.* terms of technical subject.

ter'mi·nus, *n.* 1. terminal. 2. goal. 3. limit.

ter'mite, *n.* destructive woodeating insect.

tern, *n.* gull-like aquatic bird.

Terp·sich'o·re (-sik'ə rē'), *n.* 1. Greek muse of dance. 2. (*l.c.*) art of dancing.

ter'race, *n., v.,* **-raced, -racing.** —*n.* 1. raised level with abrupt drop at front. 2. flat roof. 3. open area connected with house. —*v.* 4. make or furnish as or with terrace.

ter'ra cot'ta, 1. hard, usually unglazed earthenware. 2. brownish red.

ter'ra fir'ma (ter'ə fûr'mə), solid land.

ter·rain', *n.* area of land of specified nature.

ter'ra·pin, *n.* edible North American turtle.

ter·rar'i·um, *n., pl.* **-ums, -a.** glass tank for raising plants or land animals.

ter·res'tri·al, *adj.* of or living on earth.

ter'ri·ble, *adj.* 1. dreadful. 2. severe. —**ter'ri·ble·ness,** *n.* —**ter'ri·bly,** *adv.*

ter'ri·er, *n.* hunting dog.

ter·rif'ic, *adj.* 1. terrifying. 2. *Informal.* excellent.

ter'ri·fy', *v.,* **-fied, -fying.** fill with terror. —**ter'ri·fy'ing·ly,** *adv.*

ter'ri·to·ry, *n., pl.* **-ries.** 1. region. 2. land and waters of state. 3. region not a state but having elected legislature and appointed officials. —**ter'ri·to'ri·al,** *adj.* —**ter'ri·to'ri·al·ly,** *adv.*

ter'ror, *n.* intense fear.

ter'ror·ize', *v.,* **-ized, -izing.** fill with terror. —**ter'ror·ism',** *n.* —**ter'ror·ist,** *n.* —**ter'ror·is'tic,** *adj.* —**ter'ror·i·za'tion,** *n.*

ter'ry, *n., pl.* **-ries.** pile fabric with loops on both sides. Also, **terry cloth.**

terse, *adj.* concise. —**terse'ly,** *adv.* —**terse'ness,** *n.*

ter'ti·ar'y (tûr'shē-), *adj.* of third rank or stage.

test, *n.* 1. trial of or substance used to try quality, content, etc. 2. examination to evaluate student or class. —*v.* 3. subject to test.

tes'ta·ment, *n.* legal will. —**tes'ta·men'ta·ry,** *adj.*

tes'ti·cle, *n.* either of two male sex glands located in scrotum. Also, **testis.**

tes'ti·fy', *v.,* **-fied, -fying.** 1. give evidence. 2. give testimony.

tes'ti·mo'ni·al, *n.* writing certifying character, etc.

tes'ti·mo'ny, *n., pl.* **-nies.** 1. statement of witness under oath. 2. proof.

test tube, *Chem.* small cylindrical glass container.

tes'ty, *adj.* irritable. —**tes'ti·ly,** *adv.* —**tes'ti·ness,** *n.*

tet'a·nus, *n.* infectious disease marked by muscular rigidity.

tête'-à-tête' (tāt'ə tāt'), *n.* private conversation.

teth'er, *n.* 1. rope, chain, etc., for fastening animal to stake. —*v.* 2. fasten with tether.

text, *n.* 1. main body of matter in book or manuscript. 2. quotation from Scripture, esp. as subject of sermon, etc. —**tex'tu·al,** *adj.* —**tex'tu·al·ly,** *adv.*

text'book', *n.* student's book of study.

tex'tile (-tīl, -til), *n.* 1. woven material. —*adj.* 2. woven. 3. of weaving.

tex'ture, *n.* characteristic surface or composition. —**tex'tur·al,** *adj.*

than, *conj.* particle introducing second member of comparison.

than'a·top'sis, *n.* view or contemplation of death.

thane, *n. Early Eng. Hist.* person ranking between earl and ordinary freeman, holding lands of king or lord by military service.

thank, *v.* 1. express gratitude for. —*n.* 2. (*usually pl.*) expression of gratitude. —**thank'ful,** *adj.* —**thank'less,** *adj.* —**thanks'giv'ing,** *n.*

Thanksgiving Day, annual festival in acknowledgment of divine favor, usually last Thursday of November.

that, *pron., pl.* **those,** *adj., adv., conj.* —*pron., adj.* 1. demonstrative word indicating **a.** person, thing, etc. **b.** one of two persons, etc., mentioned (opposed to **this**). 2. relative pronoun used as: **a.** subject or object of relative clause. **b.** object of preposition. —*adv.* 3. to that extent. —*conj.* 4. word used to introduce dependent clause or one expressing reason, result, etc.

thatch, *n.* 1. rushes, leaves, etc., for covering roofs. —*v.* 2. cover with thatch.

thaw, *v.* 1. melt. —*n.* 2. act or instance of thawing.

the, *def. article.* 1. word used, esp. before nouns, with specifying effect. —*adv.* 2. word used to modify comparative or superlative form of adjective or adverb.

the'a·ter, *n.* 1. building for dramatic presentations, etc. 2. dramatic art. 3. place of action. Also, **the'a·tre.** —**the·at'ri·cal,** *adj.* —**the·at'ri·cal·ly,** *adv.*

thee, *pron. Archaic.* you.

theft, *n.* act or instance of stealing.

their, *pron.* 1. possessive form of **they** used before noun. 2. (*pl.*) that which belongs to them.

the'ism, *n.* belief in one God. —**the'ist,** *n.*

them, *pron.* objective case of **they.**

theme, *n.* 1. subject of discourse, etc. 2. short essay. 3. melody. —**the·mat'ic,** *adj.*

them·selves', *pron.* emphatic or reflexive form of **them.**

then, *adv.* 1. at that time. 2. soon afterward. 3. at another time. 4. besides. 5. in that case. —*adj.* 6. being such.

thence, *adv.* 1. from that place or time. 2. therefore.

thence′forth′, *adj.* from that place or time on. Also, **thence′for′ward.**

the•oc′ra•cy, *n.* government in which authorities claim to carry out divine law.

the•ol′o•gy, *n.* study dealing with God and His relations to universe. —**the′o•lo′gian,** *n.* —**the′o•log′i•cal•ly,** *adv.*

the′o•rem (thē′ə rəm), *n.* 1. *Math.* statement embodying something to be proved. 2. rule or law, esp. one expressed by equation or formula.

the′o•ret′i•cal, *adj.* 1. in theory. 2. not practical. 3. speculative. —**the′o•ret′i•cal•ly,** *adv.*

the′o•ry, *n., pl.* **-ries.** 1. proposition used to explain class of phenomena. 2. proposed explanation. 3. principles. —**the′o•rist,** *n.* —**the′o•rize′,** *v.*

the•os′o•phy, *n.* any of various forms of thought in which claim is made of special insight into divine nature or to special divine revelation.

ther′a•py, *n., pl.* **-pies.** treatment of disease. —**ther′a•pist,** *n.* —**ther′a•peu′tic** (-pyōō′tik), *adj.* —**ther′a•peu′ti•cal•ly,** *adv.* —**ther′a•peu′tics,** *n.*

there, *adv.* 1. in or at that place, point, matter, respect, etc. 2. to that place. —**there′a•bout′, there′a•bouts′,** *adv.* —**there•af′ter,** *adv.* —**there•by′,** —**there•for′,** *adv.* —**there•from′,** *adv.* —**there•in′,** *adv.* —**there•in′to,** *adv.* —**there•to′,** *adv.* —**there•un′der,** *adv.*

there′fore′, *adv.* consequently.

there•of′, *adv.* of or from that.

there•on′, *adv.* 1. on that. 2. immediately after that.

there′up•on′, *adv.* 1. immediately after that. 2. because of that. 3. with reference to that.

there•with′, *adv.* with or in addition to that.

ther′mal, *adj.* of heat.

ther•mom′e•ter, *n.* instrument for measuring temperature. —**ther′mo•met′•ric,** *adj.*

ther′mo•nu′cle•ar, *adj.* of nuclear-fusion reactions at extremely high temperatures.

ther′mo•plas′tic, *adj.* 1. soft and pliable whenever heated, as some plastics, without change of inherent properties. —*n.* 2. such plastic.

Ther′mos, *n. Trademark.* container with vacuum between double walls for heat insulation.

ther′mo•stat′, *n.* device regulating temperature of heating system, etc.

the•sau′rus, *n.* book of synonyms and antonyms.

these, *pron.* pl. of **this.**

the′sis, *n., pl.* **-ses.** 1. proposition to be proved. 2. essay based on research.

thes′pi•an, *adj.* 1. of dramatic art. —*n.* 2. actor or actress.

they, *pron.* nominative plural of **he, she,** and **it.**

thi′a•mine (thī′ə min), *n.* vitamin B₁. Also, **thi′a•min.**

thick, *adj.* 1. not thin. 2. in depth. 3. compact. 4. numerous. 5. dense. 6. husky. 7. slow-witted. —*adv.* 8. so as to be thick. —*n.* 9. something thick. —**thick′en,** *v.* —**thick′ly,** *adv.* —**thick′ness,** *n.*

thick′et, *n.* thick growth of shrubs, bushes, etc.

thick′-set′, *adj.* 1. set thickly; dense. 2. with heavy or solid body.

thick′-skinned′, *adj.* 1. having thick skin. 2. not sensitive to criticism or comtempt.

thief, *n., pl.* **thieves.** person who steals. —**thieve,** *v.* —**thiev′er•y,** *n.*

thigh, *n.* part of leg between hip and knee.

thim′ble, *n.* cap to protect finger while sewing.

thin, *adj.,* **thinner, thinnest,** *v.,* **thinned, thinning.** —*adj.* 1. having little extent between opposite sides; slender. 2. lean. 3. scanty. 4. rarefied; diluted. 5. flimsy. 6. weak. —*v.* 7. make or become thinner. —**thin′ner,** *n.* —**thin′ly,** *adv.* —**thin•ness,** *n.*

thing, *n.* 1. inanimate object. 2. entity. 3. matter. 4. item.

think, *v.,* **thought, thinking.** 1. conceive in mind. 2. meditate. 3. believe. —**think′er,** *n.* —**think′a•ble,** *adj.*

thin′-skinned′, *adj.* 1. having thin skin. 2. sensitive to criticism or contempt.

third, *adj.* 1. next after second. —*n.* 2. next after the second. 3. any of three equal parts.

third degree, *Chiefly U.S.* use of brutal measures by police (or others) in extorting information or confession.

Third World, developing countries of Asia and Africa.

thirst, *n.* 1. sensation caused by need of drink. —*v.* 2. be thirsty.

—thirst′y, *adj.* —**thirst′i•ly,** *adv.* —**thirst′i•ness,** *n.*

thir′teen′, *n., adj.* ten plus three. —**thir•teenth′,** *adj., n.*

thir′ty, *n., adj.* ten times three. —**thir′ti•eth,** *adj., n.*

this, *pron., pl.* **these,** *adj., adv.* —*pron., adj.* 1. demonstrative word indicating something as specified, present, near, etc. —*adv.* 2. to the indicated extent.

this′tle, *n.* prickly plant.

thith′er, *adv.* to that place, point, etc.

tho (thō), *conj., adv. Informal.* though.

thong, *n.* strip of hide or leather.

tho′rax, *n.* part of trunk between neck and abdomen. —**tho•rac′ic,** *adj.*

thorn, *n.* sharp spine on plant. —**thorn′y,** *adj.*

tho′ron (thōr′on), *n.* radioactive isotope produced by disintegration of the element thorium.

thor′ough (thûr′-), *adj.* complete. Also, *Informal,* **thor′o.** —**thor′ough•ly,** *adv.* —**thor′ough•ness,** *n.*

thor′ough•bred′, *adj.* 1. of pure breed. 2. well-bred. —*n.* 3. thoroughbred animal or person.

thor′ough•fare′, *n.* road, street, etc., open at both ends.

thor′ough•go•ing, *adj.* doing things thoroughly.

those, *pron., adj.* pl. of **that.**

thou, *pron.* you (now little used except provincially, archaically, in poetry or elevated prose, in addressing God, and by Quakers).

though, *conj.* 1. notwithstanding that. 2. even if. 3. nevertheless. —*adv.* 4. however.

thought, *n.* 1. mental activity. 2. idea. 3. purpose. 4. regard.

thought′ful, *adj.* 1. meditative. 2. heedful. 3. considerate. —**thought′ful•ly,** *adv.* —**thought′ful•ness,** *n.*

thought′less, *adj.* 1. showing lack of thought. 2. careless; inconsiderate. —**thought′less•ly,** *adv.*

thou′sand, *n., adj.* ten times one hundred. —**thou′sandth,** *adj., n.*

thrash, *v.* 1. beat thoroughly. 2. toss wildly. —**thrash′er,** *n.*

thread, *n.* 1. fine spun cord of flax, cotton, etc. 2. filament. 3. helical ridge of screw. 4. connected sequence. —*v.* 5. pass end of thread through needle's eye. 6. fix beads, etc., on thread.

thread′bare′, *adj.* shabby.

threat, *n.* menace. —**threat′en,** *v.*

three, *adj., n.* two plus one.

thren'o•dy, *n., pl.* **-dies.** song of lamentation.

thresh, *v.* separate grain or seeds from a plant. —**thresh'er,** *n.*

thresh'old, *n.* 1. doorway sill. 2. entrance. 3. beginning; border.

thrice, *adv.* three times.

thrift, *n.* frugality. —**thrift'less,** *adj.*

thrift'y, *adj.,* **thriftier, thriftiest.** saving; frugal. —**thrift'i•ly,** *adv.* —**thrift'i•ness,** *n.*

thrill, *v.* 1. affect with sudden keen emotion. 2. vibrate. —*n.* 3. tremor resulting from sudden emotion. —**thrill'er,** *n.*

thrive, *v.,* **thrived, thriving.** flourish.

throat, *n.* passage from mouth to stomach or lungs.

throat'y, *adj.,* **throatier, throatiest.** produced or modified in throat.

throb, *v.,* **throbbed, throbbing,** *n.* —*v.* 1. beat violently or rapidly. 2. vibrate. —*n.* 3. act of throbbing.

throe, *n.* 1. spasm. 2. (*pl.*) pangs.

throm•bo'sis, *n.* clotting of blood in circulatory system.

throne, *n.* official chair of king, bishop, etc.

throng, *n., v.* crowd.

throt'tle, *n., v.,* **-tled, -tling.** —*n.* 1. device controlling flow of fuel. —*v.* 2. choke. 3. check.

through, *prep.* 1. in at one end and out at other. 2. during all of. 3. having finished. 4. by means or reason of. —*adv.* 5. in at one end and out at other. 6. all the way. 7. to the end. 8. finished. —*adj.* 9. passing through.

through•out', *prep.* 1. in all parts of. —*adv.* 2. in every part, etc.

throw, *v.,* **threw, thrown, throwing,** *n.* —*v.* 1. propel or cast. 2. fell in wrestling. —*n.* 3. act of throwing. —**throw'er,** *n.*

throw'back', *n.* 1. setback or check. 2. reversion to ancestral type.

thru, *prep., adv., adj. Informal.* through.

thrum, *v.,* **thrummed, thrumming,** *n.* —*v.* 1. to play on stringed instrument, as guitar, by plucking strings. 2. to tap with fingers. —*n.* 3. act or sound of thrumming. —**thrum'mer,** *n.*

thrush, *n.* migratory singing bird.

thrust, *v.,* **thrust, thrusting,** *n.* —*v.* 1. push; shove. 2. stab. —*n.* 3. push; lunge. 4. stab.

thud, *n., v.* **thudded, thudding.** —*n.* 1. dull striking sound. —*v.* 2. make thudding sound.

thug, *n.* violent criminal.

thumb, *n.* 1. short, thick finger next to the forefinger. —*v.* 2. manipulate with thumb.

thumb'screw', *n.* 1. instrument of torture that compresses thumbs. 2. screw turned by thumb and finger.

thumb'tack', *n.* 1. tack with large, flat head. —*v.* 2. secure with thumbtack.

thump, *n.* 1. blow from something thick and heavy. —*v.* 2. pound.

thun'der, *n.* 1. loud noise accompanying lightning. —*v.* 2. give forth thunder. 2. speak loudly. —**thun'der•ous,** *adj.* —**thun'der•storm',** *n.* —**thun'der•show'er,** *n.*

thun'der•bolt', *n.* flash of lightning with thunder.

thun'der•clap', *n.* crash of thunder.

thun'der•cloud', *n.* electrically charged cloud producing lightning and thunder.

thun'der•head', *n.* mass of cumulous clouds warning of thunderstorms.

thun'der•struck', *adj.* astonished.

Thurs'day, *n.* fifth day of week.

thus, *adv.* 1. in this way. 2. consequently. 3. to this extent.

thwack, *v.* 1. strike hard with something flat. —*n.* 2. thwacking blow.

thwart, *v.* 1. frustrate; prevent. —*n.* 2. seat across a boat.

thy, *adj. Archaic.* your.

thyme (tīm), *n.* plant of mint family.

thy'roid, *adj.* of thyroid gland.

thyroid gland, ductless gland near windpipe.

thy•self', *pron.* 1. emphatic appositive to **thou** or **thee.** 2. substitute for reflexive **thee.**

ti•ar'a (tē âr'ə), *n.* woman's ornamental coronet.

Ti•bet'an, *n.* native or language of Tibet. —**Tibetan,** *adj.*

tib'i•a, *n., pl.* **tibiae.** bone from knee to ankle. —**tib'i•al,** *adj.*

tic, *n.* sudden twitch.

tick, *n.* 1. soft, recurring click. 2. bloodsucking mitelike animal. 3. cloth case of mattress, pillow, etc. —*v.* 4. produce tick (def. 1).

tick'er, *n.* 1. one that ticks. 2. telegraphic instrument that prints stock prices and market reports, etc., on tape (**ticker tape**). 3. *Slang.* heart.

tick'et, *n.* 1. slip indicating right to admission, transportation, etc. 2. tag. —*v.* 3. attach ticket to.

tick'ing, *n.* cotton fabric for ticks (def. 3).

tick'le, *v.,* **-led, -ling,** *n.* —*v.* 1. touch lightly so as to make tingle or itch. 2.

gratify. 3. amuse. —*n.* 4. act of tickling. —**tick'lish,** *adj.* —**tick'lish•ly,** *adv.*

tidal wave, large, destructive ocean wave produced by earthquake or the like.

tid'bit', *n.* choice bit.

tide, *n., v.,* **tided, tiding.** —*n.* 1. periodic rise and fall of ocean waters. 2. stream. —*v.* 3. help over difficulty. —**tid'al,** *adj.*

tide'wa'ter, *n.* 1. water affected by tide. —*adj.* 2. of lowland near sea.

ti'dings, *n.pl.* news.

ti'dy, *adj.,* **-dier, -diest,** *v.,* **-died, -dying.** —*adj.* 1. neat; orderly. —*n.* 2. make tidy. —**ti'di•ly,** *adv.* —**ti'di•ness,** *n.*

tie, *v.,* **tied, tying,** *n.* —*v.* 1. bind with cord, etc. 2. confine. 3. equal or be equal. —*n.* 4. something used to tie or join. 5. necktie. 6. equality in scores, votes, etc. 7. contest in which this occurs. 8. bond of kinship, affection, etc.

tier (tēr), *n.* row or rank.

tie'-up', *n.* 1. undesired stoppage of business, traffic, etc. 2. connection.

tiff, *n.* petty quarrel.

ti'ger, *n.* large striped Asian feline. —**ti'gress,** *n.fem.*

tiger lily, lily with flowers of dull-orange color spotted with black.

tight, *adj.* 1. firmly in place. 2. stretched; taut. 3. fitting closely. 4. impervious to fluids. —**tight'en,** *v.* —**tight'ly,** *adv.* —**tight'ness,** *n.*

tight'-fist'ed, *adj.* stingy.

tight'rope', *n.* rope stretched tight, on which acrobats perform feats of balancing.

tights, *n.pl.* close-fitting pants, worn esp. by acrobats, etc.

tight'wad', *n. Slang.* stingy person.

til'de (til'də), *n.* diacritical mark (˜) placed over letter.

tile, *n., v.,* **tiled, tiling.** —*n.* 1. thin piece of baked clay, etc., used as covering. —*v.* 2. cover with tiles.

til'ing, *n.* 1. operation of covering with tiles. 2. tiles collectively.

till, *prep., conj.* 1. until. —*v.* 2. labor on to raise crops. 3. plow. —*n.* 4. drawer in back of counter for money. —**till'a•ble,** *adj.* —**till'age,** *n.*

till'er, *n.* 1. one that tills. 2. handle on head of rudder.

tilt, *v.* 1. lean; slant. 2. charge or engage in joust. —*n.* 3. act of tilting. 4. slant.

tim'bale (tim'bəl), *n.* 1. a preparation of minced meat, etc., cooked in mold. 2. this mold, usually of paste, and sometimes fried.

tim′ber, *n.* 1. wood of growing trees. 2. trees. 3. wood for building. 4. wooden beam, etc. —*v.* 5. furnish or support with timber. —**tim′bered,** *adj.*

tim′ber•line′, *n.* altitude or latitude at which timber ceases to grow.

timber wolf, large brindled wolf of forested Canada and northern United States.

tim′bre, *n.* characteristic quality of a sound.

time, *n., v.,* **timed, timing.** —*n.* 1. duration. 2. period of time. 3. occasion. 4. point in time. 5. appointed or proper time. 6. (*pl.*) multiplied by. 7. meter of music. 8. rate. —*v.* 9. determine or record time. —**tim′er,** *n.*

time′-hon′ored, *adj.* long valued or used; traditional.

time′keep′er, *n.* 1. person who keeps time. 2. timepiece, esp. as regards accuracy.

time′less, *adj.* 1. eternal. 2. referring to no particular time.

time′ly, *adj.,* **-lier, -liest,** *adv.* —*adj.* 1. opportune. —*adv.* 2. opportunely.

time′piece′, *n.* clock; watch.

time′ta′ble, *n.* schedule of times of departures, work completion, etc.

tim′id, *adj.* 1. easily alarmed. 2. shy. —**tim′id•ly,** *adv.* —**ti•mid′i•ty, tim′id•ness,** *n.*

tim′ing, *n.* control of speed or occasion of an action, event, etc., so that it occurs at the proper moment.

tim′or•ous, *adj.* 1. fearful. 2. timid. —**tim′or•ous•ly,** *adv.* —**tim′or•ous• ness,** *n.*

tim′o•thy, *n.* coarse fodder grass.

tim′pa•ni′ (-nē′), *n.pl.* kettledrums. —**tim′pa•nist,** *n.*

tin, *n., v.,* **tinned, tinning.** —*n.* 1. low-melting metallic element. —*v.* 2. cover with tin. —**tin′ny,** *adj.*

tinc′ture, *n.* medicinal solution in alcohol.

tin′der, *n.* inflammable substance. —**tin′der•box′,** *n.*

tine, *n.* prong of fork.

tinge, *v.,* **tinged, tingeing** or **tinging,** *n.* —*v.* 1. impart trace of color, taste, etc., to. —*n.* 2. slight trace.

tin′gle, *v.,* **-gled, -gling,** *n.* —*v.* 1. feel or cause slight stings. —*n.* 2. tingling sensation.

tink′er, *n.* 1. *Chiefly Brit.* mender of pots, kettles, pans, etc. —*v.* 2. do the

work of a tinker. 3. work or repair unskillfully or clumsily.

tin′kle, *v.,* **-kled, -kling,** *n.* —*v.* 1. make light ringing sounds. —*n.* 2. tinkling sound.

tin′sel, *n.* 1. glittering metal in strips, etc. 2. anything showy and worthless.

tint, *n.* 1. color or hue. —*v.* 2. apply tint to.

tin′tin•nab′u•la′tion, *n.* ringing or sound of bells.

ti′ny, *adj.,* **-nier, -niest.** very small.

tip, *n., v.,* **tipped, tipping.** —*n.* 1. small gift of money. 2. piece of private information. 3. useful hint. 4. tap. 5. slender or pointed end. 6. top. —*v.* 7. give tip to. 8. furnish with tip. 9. tilt. 10. overturn. 11. tap. —**tip′per,** *n.*

tip′-off′, *n. Slang.* hint or warning.

tip′pet, *n.* scarf.

tip′ple, *v.,* **-pled, -pling.** drink alcoholic liquor. —**tip′pler,** *n.*

tip′sy, *adj.,* **-sier, -siest.** intoxicated. —**tip′si•ly,** *adv.* —**tip′si•ness,** *n.*

tip′toe′, *n., v.,* **-toed, -toeing.** —*n.* 1. tip of toe. —*v.* 2. move on tiptoes.

tip′top′, *n.* 1. extreme top. —*adj.* 2. situated at very top. 3. *Informal.* of highest excellence.

ti′rade, *n.* long denunciation or speech.

tire, *v.,* **tired, tiring,** *n.* —*v.* 1. exhaust strength, interest, patience, etc. —*n.* 2. hoop of metal, rubber, etc., around wheel. —**tire′less,** *adj.* —**tire′some,** *adj.*

tired, *adj.* 1. exhausted; fatigued. 2. weary. —**tired′ly,** *adv.* —**tired′ness,** *n.*

tis′sue, *n.* 1. substance composing organism. 2. light, gauzy fabric.

tissue paper, very thin paper.

tit for tat, equivalent given in retaliation, repartee, etc.

tithe, *n.* tenth part.

ti′tian (tish′ən), *n., adj.* yellowish or golden brown.

tit′il•late′, *v.,* **-lated, -lating.** 1. tickle. 2. excite agreeably. —**tit′il•la′tion,** *n.*

tit′i•vate′, *v.,* **-vated, -vating.** *Informal.* make smart or spruce. —**tit′i• va′tion,** *n.*

ti′tle, *n., v.,* **-tled, -tling.** —*n.* 1. name of book, picture, etc. 2. caption. 3. appellation, esp. of rank. 4. championship. 5. right to something. 6. document showing this. —*v.* 7. furnish with title.

tit′mouse′, *n., pl.* **-mice.** small bird having crest and conical bill.

tit′ter, *n.* 1. low, restrained laugh. —*v.* 2. laugh in this way.

tit′u•lar, *adj.* 1. of or having a title. 2. being so in title only. —**tit′u•lar•ly,** *adv.*

tiz′zy, *n., pl.* **-zies.** *Slang.* dither.

TNT, trinitrotoluene.

to, *prep.* 1. particle specifying point reached. 2. sign of the infinitive. —*adv.* 3. toward. 4. to and fro, to and from place or thing.

toad, *n.* tailless, froglike amphibian.

toad′stool′, *n.* fungus with umbrella-like cap.

toad′y, *n., pl.* **toadies,** *v.,* **toadied, toadying.** —*n.* 1. fawning flatterer. —*v.* 2. be toady.

toast, *n.* 1. person whose health is proposed and drunk. 2. the proposal. 3. sliced bread browned by heat. —*v.* 4. propose as toast. 5. make toast. —**toast′er,** *n.*

toast′mas′ter, *n.* person who introduces the after-dinner speakers or proposes toasts.

to•bac′co, *n.* 1. plant with leaves prepared for smoking or chewing. 2. the prepared leaves.

to•bac′co•nist, *n. Chiefly Brit.* dealer in or manufacturer of tobacco.

to•bog′gan, *n.* 1. long, narrow, flat-bottomed sled. —*v.* 2. coast on toboggan.

toc•ca′ta (tə kä′tə), *n. Music.* keyboard composition in style of improvisation.

toc′sin, *n.* signal.

to•day′, *n.* 1. this day, time, or period. —*adv.* 2. on this day. 3. at this period. Also, **to-day′.**

tod′dle, *v.,* **-dled, -dling.** go with short, unsteady steps. —**tod′dler,** *n.*

tod′dy, *n., pl.* **-dies.** drink made of alcoholic liquor and hot water, sweetened and sometimes spiced.

to-do′ (tə dōō′), *n., pl.* **-dos.** *Informal.* fuss.

toe, *n.* 1. terminal digit of foot. 2. part covering toes. —**toe′nail′,** *n.*

tof′fee, *n.* taffy.

to′ga, *n.* ancient Roman outer garment.

to•geth′er, *adv.* 1. into or in proximity, association, or single mass. 2. at same time. 3. in cooperation.

togs, *n.pl. Informal.* clothes.

toil, *n.* 1. hard, exhausting work. —*v.* 2. work hard. —**toil′er,** *n.*

toi′let, *n.* 1. receptacle for excretion. 2. bathroom. 3. Also, **toi•lette′.** act or process of dressing.

toilet water, scented liquid used as light perfume.

toil′some, *adj.* laborious or fatiguing. —**toil′some•ly,** *adv.* —**toil′some•ness,** *n.*

to•kay′ (tō kā′), *n.* 1. rich, sweet, aromatic wine. 2. the variety of grape from which it is made.

to′ken, *n.* 1. thing expressing or representing something else. 2. metal disk used as ticket, etc. —*adj.* 3. being merely a token; minimal.

to′ken•ism, *n.* minimal conformity to law or social pressure.

tol′er•a•ble, *adj.* 1. endurable. 2. fairly good. —**tol′er•a•bly,** *adv.*

tol′er•ance, *n.* fairness toward different opinions, etc. —**tol′er•ant,** *adj.* —**tol′er•ant•ly,** *adv.*

tol′er•ate′, *v.,* -ated, -ating. 1. allow. 2. put up with. —**tol′er•a′tion,** *n.*

toll, *v.* 1. sound bell slowly and repeatedly. —*n.* 2. payment, as for right to travel. 3. payment for long-distance telephone call.

tom′a•hawk′, *n.* light ax used by North American Indians, esp. in war.

Tom and Jerry, hot drink of rum, milk, and beaten eggs.

to•ma′to, *n.,* *pl.* -toes. cultivated plant with pulpy, edible fruit.

tomb, *n.* burial, etc., place for dead body; grave. —**tomb′stone′,** *n.*

tom′boy′, *n.* boisterous, romping girl. —**tom′boy′ish,** *adj.*

tom′cat′, *n.* male cat.

Tom Col′lins, tall iced drink containing gin, lemon or lime juice, and carbonated water.

tome, *n.* large book.

tom′fool′er•y, *n.,* *pl.* -eries. foolish or silly behavior.

Tom′my At′kins, any private in British army. Also, **tom′my.**

Tommy gun, *Slang.* type of submachine gun.

tom′my•rot′, *n.* *Slang.* nonsense.

to•mor′row, *n.* 1. day after this day. —*adv.* 2. on day after this day. Also, **to-mor′row.**

tom′-tom′, *n.* primitive drum.

ton, *n.* 1. unit of weight, equal to 2000 pounds (**short ton**) in U.S. and 2240 pounds (**long ton**) in Great Britain. 2. *Naut.* unit of volume, equal to 100 cubic feet.

to•nal′i•ty, *n.,* *pl.* -ties. 1. relation between tones of musical scales. 2. the tones.

tone, *n.,* *v.,* **toned, toning.** —*n.* 1. sound. 2. quality of sound. 3. quality,

etc., of voice. 4. firmness. 5. expressive quality. 6 elegance; amenity. —*v.* 7. give proper tone to. —**ton′al,** *adj.* —**ton′al•ly,** *adv.*

tongs, *n.pl.* two-armed implement for grasping.

tongue (tung), *n.* 1. organ on floor of mouth, used for tasting, etc. 2. language. 3. tonguelike thing.

tongue′-tied′, *adj.* unable to speak.

ton′ic, *n.* 1. invigorating medicine. —*adj.* 2. invigorating.

to•night′, *n.* 1. this night. —*adv.* 2. on this night. Also, **to-night′.**

ton′nage, *n.* 1. carrying capacity or total volume of vessel. 2. duty on cargo or tonnage. 3. ships.

ton•neau′ (tu nō′), *n.,* *pl.* -neaus, -neaux (-nōz′). rear compartment of automobile with seats for passengers.

ton′sil, *n.* oval mass of tissue in throat.

ton′sil•lec′to•my, *n.* removal of tonsils.

ton′sil•li′tis, *n.* inflammation of tonsils.

ton•so′ri•al, *adj.* of barbers.

ton′sure, *n.* 1. shaving of head. 2. shaved part of cleric's head.

too, *adv.* 1. also. 2. excessively.

tool, *n.* 1. mechanical instrument, as hammer or saw. 2. exploited person; dupe. —*v.* 3. decorate with tool.

toot, *v.* sound horn.

tooth, *n.,* *pl.* **teeth.** 1. hard body attached to jaw, used in chewing, etc. 2. projection. 3. taste, relish, etc. —**tooth′ache′,** *n.* —**tooth′brush′,** *n.* —**tooth′pick′,** *n.*

tooth′some, *adj.* tasty.

top, *n.,* *v.,* **topped, topping.** —*n.* 1. highest point, part, rank, etc. 2. lid. 3. child's spinning toy. —*v.* 4. put top on. 5. be top of. 6. surpass.

to′paz, *n.* colored crystalline gem.

top′coat′, *n.* light overcoat.

top′er (tō′pər), *n.* drunkard.

top hat, man's tall silk hat.

top′-heav′y, *adj.* disproportionately heavy at top.

top′ic, *n.* subject of discussion or writing.

top′i•cal, *adj.* 1. of or dealing with matters of current interest. 2. of topics 3. applied to local area. —**top′i•cal•ly,** *adv.*

top kick, *Mil. Slang.* first sergeant.

top′most, *adj.* highest.

top′notch′, *adj. Informal.* first-rate.

to•pog′ra•phy, *n.* description of features of geographical area. —**to•pog′ra•pher,** *n.* —**top′o•graph′ic, top′o•graph′i•cal,** *adj.*

top′per, *n.* 1. one that tops. 2. *Slang.* top hat. 3. short coat worn by women.

top′ple, *v.,* -pled, -pling. fall; tumble.

top′sail′ (top′sāl′; *Naut.* -səl), *n.* square sail next above lowest or chief sail.

top secret, extremely secret.

top′soil′, *n.* fertile upper soil.

top′sy-tur′vy, *adv.* 1. upside down. 2. in confusion.

toque (tōk), *n.* hat with little or no brim.

tor, *n.* hill.

To′rah (tōr′ə), *n.* 1. five books of Moses; Pentateuch. 2. (*also l.c.*) whole Jewish Scripture. Also, **To′ra.**

torch, *n.* light carried in hand.

tor′e•a•dor′, *n.* bullfighter, esp. one who fights on horseback.

tor•ment′, *v.* 1. afflict with great suffering. —*n.* (tôr′ment). 2. agony. —**tor•men′tor, tor•ment′er,** *n.*

tor•na′do, *n.,* *pl.* -does, -dos. destructive storm.

tor•pe′do, *n.,* *pl.* -does, *v.,* -doed, -doing. —*n.* 1. self-propelled missile launched in water and exploding on impact. —*v.* 2. strike with torpedo.

torpedo boat, small fast warship used to launch torpedoes.

tor′pid, *adj.* 1. inactive; sluggish. 2. dull; apathetic; lethargic. —**tor•pid′i•ty,** *n.* —**tor′pid•ly,** *adv.*

tor′por, *n.* 1. suspension of physical activity. 2. apathy.

torque (tôrk), *n.* rotating force.

tor′rent, *n.* rapid, violent stream. —**tor•ren′tial,** *adj.* —**tor•ren′tial•ly,** *adv.*

tor′rid, *n.* very hot.

Torrid Zone, part of earth's surface between tropics.

tor′sion, *n.* 1. act of twisting. 2. twisting by two opposite torques. —**tor′sion•al,** *adj.*

tor′so, *n.,* *pl.* -sos, -si. trunk of body.

tort, *n. Law.* civil wrong (other than breach of contract or trust) for which law requires damages.

tor•til′la (tôr tē′yä), *n.* a flat, round, corn-meal bread of Mexico.

tor′toise, *n.* turtle.

tor′tu•ous, *adj.* 1. twisting; winding. 2. indirect. —**tor′tu•ous•ly,** *adv.* —**tor′tu•ous•ness,** *n.*

tor′ture, *n.*, *v.*, **-tured, -turing.** —*n.* 1. infliction of great pain. —*v.* 2. subject to torture. **—tor′tur•er,** *n.* **—tor′tur•ous,** *adj.*

To′ry, *n.* 1. (also *l.c.*) conservative. 2. American supporter of Great Britain during Revolutionary period. **—To′ry•ism,** *n.*

toss, *v.* 1. throw or pitch. 2. pitch about. 3. throw upward. —*n.* 4. throw or pitch.

toss′up′, *n.* 1. tossing of coin to decide something by its fall. 2. *Informal.* even chance.

tot, *n.* small child.

to′tal, *adj.* 1. entire. 2. utter; outright. —*n.* 3. total amount. —*v.* 4. add up. **—to•tal′i•ty,** *n.* **—to′tal•ly,** *adv.*

to•tal′i•tar′i•an, *adj.* of centralized government under sole control of one party. **—to•tal′i•tar′i•an•ism,** *n.*

tote, *v.*, **toted, toting,** *n. Informal.* —*v.* 1. carry or bear, as burden. —*n.* 2. act or course of toting. 3. that which is toted.

to′tem, *n.* object in nature, often an animal, assumed as emblem of clan, family, or related group. **—to•tem′ic,** *adj.*

totem pole, pole with totemic figures, erected by Indians of northwest coast of North America.

tot′ter, *v.* 1. falter. 2. sway as if about to fall.

tou′can (tōō′kan), *n.* large-beaked tropical American bird.

touch, *v.* 1. put hand, finger, etc., in contact with something. 2. come or be in contact. 3. reach. 4. affect with sympathy. 5. refer to. —*n.* 6. act or instance of touching. 7. perception of things through contact. 8. contact. **—touch′a•ble,** *adj.* **—touch′ing,** *adj.*

touch′down′, *n. Football.* act of player in touching ball down to ground behind opponent's goal line.

touched, *adj.* 1. moved; stirred. 2. slightly crazy; unbalanced.

touch′-me-not′, *n.* yellow-flowered plant whose ripe seed vessels burst open when touched.

touch′stone′, *n.* 1. stone used to test purity of gold and silver by color produced when it is rubbed with them. 2. any criterion.

touch′y, *adj.*, **touchier, touchiest.** 1. irritable. 2. requiring tact. **—touch′i•ness,** *n.*

tough, *adj.* 1. not easily broken. 2. difficult to chew. 3. sturdy. 4. pugnacious. 5. trying. **—tough′en,** *v.* **—tough′ly,** *adv.* **—tough′ness,** *n.*

tou•pee′ (tōō pā′, -pē′), *n.* wig or patch of false hair worn to cover bald spot.

tour, *v.* 1. travel or travel through, esp. for pleasure. —*n.* 2. trip. 3. period of duty. **—tour′ist,** *n.* **—tour′ism,** *n.*

tour′na•ment, *n.* 1. meeting for contests. 2. contest between mounted knights. Also, **tour′ney.**

tour′ni•quet (tûr′nə kit), *n.* bandlike device for arresting bleeding by compressing blood vessels.

tou′sle, *v.*, **-sled, -sling.** dishevel.

tout, *Informal.* *v.* 1. solicit (business, votes, etc.) importunately. 2. proclaim; advertise. 3. give tip on (race horse, etc.). —*n.* 4. person who touts. **—tout′er,** *n.*

tow, *v.* 1. drag by rope or chain. —*n.* 2. act of towing. 3. thing towed. **—tow′boat′,** *n.*

to•ward′, *prep.* Also, **to•wards′.** 1. in direction of. 2. with respect to. 3. nearly.

tow′boat′, *n.* boat for pushing barges.

tow′el, *n.* cloth or paper for wiping.

tow′el•ing, *n.* fabric of cotton or linen used for towels.

tow′er, *n.* 1. tall structure. —*v.* 2. rise high.

tow′er•ing, *adj.* 1. very high or great. 2. violent; furious.

tow′head′ (tō′hed′), *n.* 1. head of light-colored hair. 2. person with such hair.

tow′line′ (tō′līn′), *n.* cable for towing.

town, *n.* 1. small city. 2. center of city. **—towns′man,** *n.* **—towns′peo′ple, towns′folk′,** *n.pl.*

town′ship, *n.* 1. division of county. 2. (in U.S. surveys) district 6 miles square.

tox′ic, *adj.* 1. of toxin. 2. poisonous. **—tox•ic′i•ty,** *n.*

tox′i•col′o•gy, *n.* science of poisons. **—tox′i•col′o•gist,** *n.*

tox′in, *n.* poisonous product of microorganism, plant, or animal.

toy, *n.* 1. plaything. —*v.* 2. play.

trace, *n.*, *v.*, **traced, tracing.** —*n.* 1. mark or track left by something. 2. small amount. 3. pulling part of harness. —*v.* 4. follow trace of. 5. find out. 6. draw. **—trace′a•ble,** *adj.* **—trac′er,** *n.*

trac′er•y, *n.*, *pl.* **-eries.** ornamental pattern of interlacing lines, etc.

tra′che•a (trā′kē ə), *n.*, *pl.* **-cheae** (-kē ē′). air-conveying tube from larynx to bronchi.

track, *n.* 1. parallel rails for railroad. 2. wheel rut. 3. footprint or other mark left. 4. path. 5. course. —*v.* 6. follow; pursue.

tract, *n.* 1. region. 2. brief treatise.

trac′ta•ble, *adj.* easily managed. **—trac′ta•bil′i•ty,** *n.* **—trac′ta•bly,** *adv.*

trac′tion, *n.* 1. act or instance of pulling. 2. adhesive friction.

trac′tor, *n.* self-propelled vehicle for pulling farm machinery, etc.

trade, *n.*, *v.*, **traded, trading.** —*n.* 1. buying, selling, or exchange of commodities; commerce. 2. exchange. 3. occupation. —*v.* 4. buy and sell. 5. exchange. **—trad′er,** *n.* **—trades′-man,** *n.*

trade′mark′, *n.* name, symbol, etc., identifying brand or source of things for sale.

trade name, word or phrase whereby particular class of goods is designated.

trade union, labor union.

trade wind, sea wind blowing toward equator from latitudes up to 30° away.

tra•di′tion, *n.* 1. handing-down of beliefs, customs, etc., through generations. 2. something so handed down. **—tra•di′tion•al,** *adj.* **—tra•di′tion•al•ly,** *adv.* **—tra•di′tion•al•ist,** *n.*, *adj.* **—tra•di′tion•al•ism,** *n.*

tra•duce′, *v.*, **-duced, -ducing.** slander.

traf′fic, *n.*, *v.*, **-ficked, -ficking.** —*n.* 1. traveling persons and things. 2. trade. —*v.* 3. trade. **—traf′fick•er,** *n.*

tra•ge′di•an, *n.* actor or writer of tragedy. **—tra•ge′di•enne′,** *n.fem.*

trag′e•dy, *n.*, *pl.* **-dies.** 1. serious drama with unhappy ending. 2. sad event. **—trag′ic, trag′i•cal,** *adj.* **—trag′i•cal•ly,** *adv.*

trail, *v.* 1. draw or drag. 2. be drawn or dragged. 3. track. —*n.* 4. path. 5. track, scent, etc., left.

trail′er, *n.* 1. van attached to truck for hauling freight, etc. 2. vehicle attached to car or truck with accommodations for living, working, etc.

train, *n.* 1. railroad locomotive with cars. 2. moving line of person, vehicles, etc. 3. series of events, ideas, etc. 4. trailing part. 5. retinue. —*v.* 6. instruct or undergo instruction. 7.

make fit. 8. aim; direct —**train′a•ble**, *adj.* —**train•ee′**, *n.* —**train′er**, *n.*

train′man, *n.*, *pl.* **-men.** member of crew of railroad train.

traipse, *v.*, **traipsed, traipsing.** *Informal.* walk aimlessly.

trait, *n.* characteristic.

trai′tor, *n.* 1. betrayer of trust. 2. person guilty of treason. —**trai′tor•ous**, *adj.* —**trai′tress**, *n. fem.*

tra•jec′to•ry, *n*, *pl.* **-ries.** curve described by projectile in flight.

tram, *n. Brit.* streetcar or trolley car.

tram′mel, *n.* 1. impediment to action. —*v.* 2. hamper.

tramp, *v.* 1. tread or walk firmly. 2. march. —*n.* 3. firm, heavy tread. 4. hike. 5. vagabond.

tram′ple, *v.*, **-pled, -pling.** step roughly on.

tram′po•line′ (-lēn′), *n.* cloth springboard for tumblers.

trance, *n.* half-conscious or hypnotic state.

tran′quil, *adj.* peaceful; quiet. —**tran′quil•ly**, *adv.* —**tran•quil′li•ty**, *n.* —**tran′quil•ize′**, *v.*

tran′quil•iz′er, *n.* drug to reduce tension.

trans•act′, *v.* carry on business. —**trans•ac′tion**, *n.* —**trans•ac′tor**, *n.*

trans′at•lan′tic, *adj.* 1. passing across Atlantic. 2. on other side of Atlantic.

tran•scend′ (-send′), *v.* 1. go or be beyond. 2. excel.

tran•scend′ent, *adj.* 1. extraordinary. 2. superior; supreme.

tran′scen•den′tal, *adj.* beyond ordinary human experience. —**tran′-scen•den′tal•ly**, *adv.*

tran•scribe′, *v.*, **-scribed, -scribing.** 1. copy. 2. make recording of. —**tran•scrip′tion, tran′script**, *n.* —**tran•scrib′er**, *n.*

tran′sept, *n.* transverse portion of cross-shaped church.

trans•fer′, *v.*, **-ferred, -ferring**, *n.* —*v.* (trans fûr′). 1. convey, hand over, or transport. 2. be transferred. —*n.* (trans′fər). 3. means or act of transferring. —**trans•fer′a•ble**, *adj.* —**trans•fer′ence**, *n.*

trans•fig′ure, *v.*, **-ured, -uring.** 1. transform. 2. glorify. —**trans′fig•u•ra′tion**, *n.*

trans•fix′, *v.* 1. pierce. 2. paralyze with terror, etc.

trans•form′, *v.* change in form, nature, etc. —**trans′for•ma′tion**, *n.*

trans•form′er, *n.* device for converting electrical currents.

trans•fuse′, *v.*, **-fused, -fusing.** 1. transmit, as by pouring. 2. transfer blood from one person to another. —**trans•fu′sion**, *n.*

trans•gress′, *v.* 1. go beyond limit. 2. violate law, etc. —**trans•gres′sion**, *n.* —**trans•gres′sor**, *n.*

tran′sient, *adj.* 1. transitory. —*n.* 2. transient person. —**tran′sient•ly**, *adv.*

tran•sis′tor, *n.* small electronic device replacing vacuum tube.

trans′it, *n.* passage or conveyance.

tran•si′tion, *n.* passage from one condition, etc., to another. —**tran•si′tion•al**, *adj.* —**tran•si′tion•al•ly**, *adv.*

tran′si•tive, *adj.* (of verb) regularly accompanied by direct object. —**tran′si•tive•ly**, *adv.*

tran′si•to′ry, *adj.* 1. not enduring. 2. brief. —**tran′si•to′ri•ness**, *n.*

trans•late′, *v.*, **-lated, -lating.** change from one language into another. —**trans•la′tion**, *n.* —**trans•lat′a•ble**, *adj.* —**trans•lat′or**, *n.*

trans•lit′er•ate′, *v.*, **-ated, -ating.** change into corresponding characters of another alphabet or language. —**trans′lit•er•a′tion**, *n.*

trans•lu′cent (-lōō′sənt), *adj.* transmitting light diffusely. —**trans•lu′cence, trans•lu′cen•cy**, *n.*

trans′mi•gra′tion, *n.* passage of soul into another body.

trans•mit′, *v.*, **-mitted, -mitting.** 1. send over or along. 2. communicate. 3. hand down. 4. cause or permit light, heat, etc., to pass through. 5. emit radio waves. —**trans•mis′sion, trans•mit′tal**, *n.* —**trans•mit′ter**, *n.*

trans•mute′, *v.*, **-muted, -muting.** change from one nature or form to another. —**trans•mut′a•ble**, *adj.* —**trans•mu•ta′tion**, *n.*

trans′o•ce•an′ic, *adj.* across or beyond ocean.

tran′som, *n.* 1. window above door. 2. crosspiece separating door from window, etc.

tran•son′ic, *adj.* close to speed of sound; moving 700–780 miles per hour.

trans′pa•cif′ic, *adj.* 1. passing across Pacific. 2. on other side of Pacific.

trans•par′ent, *adj.* 1. allowing objects to be seen clearly through it. 2. frank. 3. obvious. —**trans•par′en•cy**, *n.*

tran•spire′, *v.*, **-pired, -piring.** 1. occur. 2. give off waste matter, etc., from surface.

trans•plant′, *v.* plant in another place. —**trans′plan•ta′tion**, *n.*

trans•port′, *v.* 1. convey from one place to another. 2. enrapture. —*n.* (trans′pōrt). 3. something that transports. —**trans′por•ta′tion**, *n.*

trans•pose′, *v.*, **-posed, -posing.** alter relative position, order, musical key, etc. —**trans′po•si′tion**, *n.*

trans•sex′u•al, *n.* 1. person with sex surgically altered. 2. person feeling identity with opposite sex.

trans•verse′, *adj.* 1. lying across. —*n.* 2. something transverse. —**trans•verse′ly**, *adv.*

trans•ves′tite, *n.* person who dresses like opposite sex.

trap, *n.*, *v.*, **trapped, trapping.** —*n.* 1. device for catching animals. 2. scheme for catching unawares. —*v.* 3. catch in or set traps. —**trap′per**, *n.*

tra•peze′, *n.* suspended bar used in gymnastics.

trap′e•zoid′, *n.* four-sided figure with two parallel sides.

trap′pings, *n.pl.* equipment or dress.

trash, *n.* rubbish. —**trash′y**, *adj.*

trau′ma (trou′-), *n.*, *pl.* **-mata, -mas.** 1. externally produced injury. 2. experience causing permanent psychological harm. —**trau•mat′ic**, *adj.*

tra•vail′ (trə vāl′), *n.* 1. toil. 2. labor pains.

trav′el, *v.* 1. journey. 2. move. —*n.* 3. journeying. —**trav′el•er**, *n.*

trav′e•logue′ (trav′ə lôg′, -log′), *n.* lecture describing travel, usually illustrated. Also, **trav′e•log′**.

trav′erse, *v.*, **-ersed, -ersing**, *n.* —*v.* 1. pass over or through. —*n.* 2. act of traversing.

trav′es•ty, *n.*, *pl.* **-ties**, *v.*, **-tied, -tying.** —*n.* 1. literary burlesque. 2. debased likeness. —*v.* 3. make travesty on.

trawl, *n.* 1. fishing net dragged on bottom of water. —*v.* 2. fish with trawl. —**trawl′er**, *n.*

tray, *n.* flat, shallow receptacle or container.

treach′er•y, *n.*, *pl.* **-ies.** betrayal; treason. —**treach′er•ous**, *adj.*

tread, *v.*, **trod, trodden** or **trod, treading**, *n.* —*v.* 1. step, walk, or trample. 2. crush. —*n.* 3. manner of walking. 4. surface meeting road or rail. 5. horizontal surface of step. —**tread′er**, *n.*

trea′dle, *n.* lever, etc., worked by foot to drive machine.

tread′mill′, *n.* apparatus worked by treading on moving steps.

trea′son, *n.* violation of allegiance to sovereign or state. —**trea′son•a•ble, trea′son•ous,** *adj.*

treas′ure, *n., v.,* **-ured, -uring.** —*n.* 1. accumulated wealth. 2. thing greatly valued. —*v.* 3. put away for future use. 4. prize.

treas′ur•y, *n., pl.* **-uries.** 1. place for keeping public or private funds. 2. the funds. 3. government department handling funds. —**treas′ur•er,** *n.*

treat, *v.* 1. behave toward. 2. deal with. 3. relieve or cure. 4. discuss. 5. entertain. —*n.* 6. entertainment. —**treat′ment,** *n.* —**treat′a•ble,** *adj.*

trea′tise, *n.* writing on particular subject.

trea′ty, *n., pl.* **-ties.** formal agreement between states.

tre′ble, *adj., n., v.,* **-bled, -bling.** —*adj.* 1. triple. 2. of highest pitch or range. 3. shrill. —*n.* 4. treble part, singer, instrument, etc. —*v.* 5. triple. —**tre′bly,** *adv.*

tree, *n., v.,* **treed, treeing.** —*n.* 1. plant with permanent, woody, usually branched trunk. —*v.* 2. drive up tree.

tre′foil, *n.* 1. herb with leaf divided in three parts. 2. ornament based on this leaf.

trek, *v.,* **trekked, trekking,** *n.* journey.

trel′lis, *n.* lattice.

trem′ble, *v.,* **-bled, -bling,** *n.* —*v.* 1. quiver. —*n.* 2. act or state of trembling.

tre•men′dous, *adj.* extraordinarily great. —**tre•men′dous•ly,** *adv.*

trem′or, *n.* 1. involuntary shaking. 2. vibration.

trem′u•lous, *adj.* 1. trembling. 2. fearful. —**trem′u•lous•ly,** *adv.*

trench, *n.* ditch or cut.

trench′ant, *adj.* 1. incisive. 2. vigorous. —**trench′ant•ly,** *adv.*

trend, *n.* 1. tendency. 2. increasingly popular fashion.

trend′y, *adj.,* **-ier, -iest.** *Informal.* following current fads. —**trend′i•ness,** *n.*

trep′i•da′tion, *n.* tremulous alarm.

tres′pass, *v.* 1. enter property illicitly. 2. sin. —*n.* 3. act of trespassing. —**tres′pass•er,** *n.*

tress, *n.* braid of hair.

tres′tle, *n.* supporting frame or framework.

trey, *n. Cards or Dice.* three.

tri′ad, *n.* group of three.

tri′al, *n.* 1. examination before judicial tribunal. 2. test. 3. attempt. 4. state of being tested. 5. source of suffering.

tri′an′gle, *n.* figure of three straight sides and three angles. —**tri•an′gu•lar,** *adj.*

tribe, *n.* 1. people united by common descent, etc. 2. class. —**trib′al,** *adj.*

tribes′man, *n., pl.* **-men.** man belonging to tribe. —**tribes′wom′an,** *n.fem.*

trib′u•la′tion, *n.* 1. trouble. 2. affliction.

tri•bu′nal, *n.* 1. court of justice. 2. place of judgment.

trib′une, *n.* rostrum.

trib′u•tar′y, *n., pl.* **-taries,** *adj.* —*n.* 1. stream flowing into larger body of water. 2. payer of tribute. —*adj.* 3. flowing as tributary.

trib′ute, *n.* 1. personal offering, etc. 2. sum paid for peace, etc.

trice, *n.* instant.

tri′ceps (trī′seps), *n.* muscle at back of upper arm.

trich′i•no′sis (trik′ə-), *n.* disease due to parasitic worm.

trick, *n.* 1. artifice or stratagem. 2. prank. 3. knack. 4. cards won in one round. —*v.* 5. deceive or cheat by tricks. —**trick′er•y,** *n.* —**trick′y,** *adj.*

trick′le, *v.,* **-led, -ling,** *n.* —*v.* 1. flow in small amounts. —*n.* 2. trickling flow.

tri′col′or, *adj.* 1. of three colors. —*n.* 2. three-colored flag, esp. of France.

tri•cus′pid, *adj.* having three cusps or points, as tooth.

tri′cy•cle, *n.* child's vehicle with large front wheel and two smaller rear wheels.

tri′dent, *n.* three-pronged spear.

tried, *adj.* tested; proved.

tri•en′ni•al (trī-), *adj.* 1. lasting three years. 2. occurring every three years. —*n.* 3. period of three years. 4. third anniversary.

tri′fle, *n., v.,* **-fled, -fling.** —*n.* 1. article of small value. 2. trivial matter or amount. —*v.* 3. deal without due respect. 4. act idly or frivolously. —**tri′fler,** *n.* —**tri′fling,** *adj.*

tri•fo′li•ate (trī-), *adj.* having three leaves or leaflike parts.

trig′ger, *n.* 1. projecting tongue pressed to fire gun. 2. device to release spring. —*v.* 3. precipitate.

tri•go•nom′e•try, *n.* mathematical study of relations between sides and angles of triangles. —**trig′o•no•met′ric,** *adj.*

trill, *v.* 1. sing or play with vibratory effect. —*n.* 2. act or sound of trilling.

tril′lion, *n., adj.* 1 followed by 12 zeroes.

tril′o•gy, *n., pl.* **-gies.** group of three plays, operas, etc., on related theme.

trim, *v.,* **trimmed, trimming,** *n., adj.,* **trimmer, trimmest.** —*v.* 1. make neat by clipping, paring, etc. 2. adjust (sails or yards). 3. dress or ornament. —*n.* 4. proper condition. 5. adjustment of sails, etc. 6. dress or equipment. 7. trimming. —*adj.* 8. neat. 9. in good condition. —**trim′ly,** *adv.* —**trim′mer,** *n.* —**trim′ness,** *n.*

trim′ming, *n.* something used to trim.

tri•ni′tro•tol′u•ene′, *n.* high explosive, known as TNT.

Trin′i•ty, *n.* unity of Father, Son, and Holy Ghost.

trin′ket, *n.* 1. bit of jewelry, etc. 2. trifle.

tri′o, *n., pl.* **-os.** group of three.

trip, *n., v.,* **tripped, tripping.** —*n.* 1. journey. 2. stumble. —*v.* 3. stumble or cause to stumble. 4. slip. 5. tread quickly and lightly. —**trip′per,** *n.*

tri•par′tite (trī-), *adj.* 1. divided into or consisting of three parts. 2. participated in by three parties.

tripe, *n.* 1. ruminant's stomach, used as food. 2. *Slang.* worthless statements or writing.

tri′ple, *adj., v.,* **-pled, -pling.** —*adj.* 1. of three parts. 2. three times as great. —*v.* 3. make or become triple. —**tri′ply,** *adv.*

tri′plet, *n.* one of three children (**triplets**) born at a single birth.

trip′li•cate (-kit), *adj.* 1. triple. —*n.* 2. set of three copies.

tri′pod, *n.* three-legged stool, support, etc.

trite, *adj.,* **triter, tritest.** commonplace; hackneyed. —**trite′ly,** *adv.* —**trite′ness,** *n.*

trit′u•rate′, *v.,* **-rated, -rating,** *n.* —*v.* 1. to reduce to fine particles or powder; pulverize. —*n.* 2. triturated substance. —**trit′u•ra′tion,** *n.*

tri′umph, *n.* 1. victory. 2. joy over victory. —*v.* 3. be victorious or successful. 4. rejoice over this. —**tri•um′phal,** *adj.* —**tri•um′phant,** *adj.*

tri•um′vir (trī um′vər), *n., pl.* **-virs, -viri** (-və rī′). *Rom. Hist.* any of three magistrates exercising same public function. —**tri•um′vi•ral,** *adj.*

tri•um′vi•rate (trī um′və rit), *n.* 1. *Rom. Hist.* the office of triumvir. 2. government of three joint magistrates. 3. association of three, as in office.

triv′et, *n.* device protecting table top from hot objects.

triv′i•al, *adj.* trifling. —**triv′i•al′i•ty,** *n.* —**triv′i•al•ly,** *adv.*

tro′che (-kē), *n.* small tablet of medicinal substance.

tro′chee (-kē) *n.* verse foot of two syllables, long followed by short. —**tro•cha′ic,** *adj.*

trog′lo•dyte′ (trog′lə dīt′), *n.* 1. cave dweller. 2. person living in seclusion. 3. person unacquainted with affairs of the world.

troll, *v.* 1. sing in rolling voice. 2. sing as round. 3. fish with moving line. —*n.* 4. *Music.* round. 5. underground monster.

trol′ley, *n.* 1. trolley car. 2. pulley on overhead track or wire.

trolley car, electric streetcar receiving current from a trolley.

trol′lop (trol′əp), *n.* 1. untidy or slovenly woman; slattern. 2. prostitute.

trom•bone′, *n.* brass wind instrument with long bent tube. —**trom•bon′ist,** *n.*

troop, *n.* 1. assemblage. 2. cavalry unit. 3. body of police, etc. —*v.* 4. gather. 5. go or come in numbers. —**troop′er,** *n.*

troop′ship′, *n.* ship for conveyance of military troops; transport.

trope, *n.* figure of speech.

tro′phy, *n., pl.* **-phies.** 1. memento taken in hunting, war, etc. 2. silver cup, etc., given as prize.

trop′ic, *n.* 1. either of two latitudes (**tropic of Cancer** and **tropic of Capricorn**) bounding torrid zone. 2. (*pl.*) region between these latitudes. —**trop′i•cal,** *adj.* —**trop′i•cal•ly,** *adv.*

tro′pism, *n.* response of plant or animal, as in growth, to influence of external stimuli. —**tro•pis′tic,** *adj.*

trot, *v.,* **trotted, trotting,** *n.* —*v.* 1. go at gait between walk and run. 2. go briskly. 3. ride at trot. —*n.* 4. trotting gait. —**trot′ter,** *n.*

troth (trôth), *n.* 1. fidelity. 2. promise.

trou′ba•dour′ (trōō′bə dōr′), *n.* medieval lyric poet of W Mediterranean area who wrote on love and gallantry.

trou′ble, *v.,* **-bled, -bling,** *n.* —*v.* 1. distress. 2. put to or cause inconvenience. 3. bother. —*n.* 4. annoyance or difficulty. 5. disturbance. 6. inconvenience. —**trou′bler,** *n.* —**trou′ble•some,** *adj.*

troub′le-shoot′er, *n.* expert in eliminating causes of trouble.

trough (trôf), *n.* 1. open boxlike container. 2. long hollow or channel.

trounce, *v.,* **trounced, trouncing.** beat severely.

troupe (trōōp), *n.* company of performers. —**troup′er,** *n.*

trou′sers, *n.pl.* male outer garment covering legs.

trous′seau (trōō′sō), *n., pl.* **-seaux, -seaus** (-sōz), bride's outfit.

trout, *n.* fresh-water game fish.

trow′el, *n.* 2. tool for spreading or smoothing. 2. small digging tool.

troy weight, system of weights for precious metals and gems.

tru′ant, *n.* 1. student absent from school without leave. —*adj.* 2. absent from school without leave. —**tru′an•cy,** *n.*

truce, *n.* suspension of military hostilities.

truck, *n.* 1. vehicle for carrying heavy loads. 2. vegetables raised for market. 3. miscellaneous articles. —*v.* 4. transport by or drive a truck. 5. trade. —**truck′er,** *n.*

truck′le, *v.,* **-led, -ling.** submit humbly.

truckle bed, trundle bed.

truc′u•lent, *adj.* fierce. —**truc′u•lence,** *n.* —**truc′u•lent•ly,** *adv.*

trudge, *v.,* **trudged, trudging.** walk, esp. wearily. —**trudg′er,** *n.*

true, *adj.,* **truer, truest.** 1. conforming to fact. 2. real. 3. sincere. 4. loyal. 5. correct. —**tru′ly,** *adv.* —**true′ness,** *n.*

true′-blue′, *adj.* staunch; true.

truf′fle, *n.* edible fungus.

tru′ism, *n.* obvious truth.

trump, *n.* 1. playing card of suit outranking other suits. 2. the suit. —*v.* 3. take with or play trump. 4. fabricate.

trum′pet, *n.* 1. brass wind instrument with powerful, penetrating tone. —*v.* 2. blow trumpet. 3. proclaim. —**trum′pet•er,** *n.*

trun′cate, *v.,* **-cated, -cating.** shorten by cutting. —**trun•ca′tion,** *n.*

trun′cheon, *n.* club.

trun′dle, *v.,* **-dled, -dling.** —*v.* 1. roll, as on wheels. —*n.* 2. small roller, wheel, etc.

trun′dle bed, low bed on casters, usually pushed under another bed when not in use. Also, **truckle bed.**

trunk, *n.* 1. main stem of tree. 2. box for clothes, etc. 3. body of man or

animals, excepting head and limbs. 4. main body of anything. 5. elephant's long flexible nasal appendage.

truss, *v.* 1. bind or fasten. 2. furnish or support with a truss. —*n.* 3. rigid supporting frame work. 4. apparatus for confining hernia. 5. bundle.

trust, *n.* 1. reliance on person's integrity, justice, etc. 2. confident hope. 3. credit. 4. responsibility. 5. care. 6. something entrusted. 7. holding of legal title for another's benefit. 8. combination of companies, often monopolistic, controlled by central board. —*v.* 9. place confidence in. 10. rely on. 11. hope. 12. believe. 13. give credit. —**trust′ful,** *adj.* —**trust′wor′thy,** *adj.*

trus•tee′, *n.* 1. administrator of company, etc. 2. holder of trust (def. 7).

trus•tee′ship, *n.* 1. office of trustee. 2. control of territory granted by United Nations. 3. the territory.

trust′y, *adj.,* **trustier, trustiest,** *n., pl.* **trusties.** —*adj.* 1. reliable. —*n.* 2. trusted one. 3. trustworthy convict given special privileges. —**trust′i•ly,** *adv.* —**trust′i•ness,** *n.*

truth, *n.* 1. true facts. 2. conformity with fact. 3. established fact, principle, etc. —**truth′ful,** *adj.*

try, *v.,* **tried, trying.** 1. attempt. 2. test. 3. examine judicially. 4. strain endurance, patience, etc., of.

try′ing, *adj.* annoying; irksome.

try′out′, *n. Informal.* trial or test to ascertain fitness for some purpose.

tryst (trist), *n.* 1. appointment to meet. 2. the meeting. 3. place of meeting. —*v.* 4. meet.

tsar (zär), *n.* czar.

tset′se fly (tset′sē), African fly transmitting disease.

T′-shirt′, *n.* short-sleeved knitted undershirt. Also, **tee′-shirt′.**

T square, T-shaped ruler used in mechanical drawing.

tub, *n.* 1. bathtub. 2. deep, open-topped container.

tu′ba, *n.* low-pitched brass wind instrument.

tube, *n.* 1. hollow pipe for fluids, etc. 2. compressible container for toothpaste, etc. 3. railroad or vehicular tunnel. —**tu′bu•lar,** *adj.* —**tub′ing,** *n.*

tu′ber, *n.* fleshy thickening of underground stem or shoot. —**tu′ber•ous,** *adj.*

tu′ber•cle, *n.* small roundish projection, nodule, or swelling.

tu•ber′cu•lo′sis, *n.* infectious disease marked by formation of tubercles. **—tu•ber′cu•lar, tu•ber′cu•lous,** *adj.*

tube′rose′, *n.* cultivated flowering plant.

tuck, *v.* 1. thrust into narrow space or retainer. 2. cover snugly. 3. draw up in folds. —*n.* 4. tucked piece or part.

tuck′er, *n.* 1. piece of cloth worn by women about neck and shoulders. —*v.* 2. *Informal.* tire; exhaust.

Tues′day, *n.* third day of week.

tuft, *n.* 1. bunch of feathers, hairs, etc., fixed at base. 2. clump of bushes, etc., —*v.* 3. arrange in or form tufts. **—tuft′ed,** *adj.*

tug, *v.,* **tugged, tugging,** *n.* —*v.* 1. drag; haul. —*n.* 2. act of tugging. 3. tugboat.

tug′boat′, *n.* powerful vessel used for towing.

tu•i′tion, *n.* charge for instruction.

tu′lip, *n.* plant bearing showy, cup-shaped flowers.

tulle (tōol), *n.* thin silk or rayon net.

tum′ble, *v.,* **-bled, -bling,** *n.* —*v.* 1. fall over or down. 2. perform gymnastic feats. 3. roll about; toss. —*n.* 4. act of tumbling.

tum′ble-down′, *adj.* dilapidated; run-down.

tum′bler, *n.* 1. drinking glass. 2. performer of tumbling feats. 3. lock part engaging bolt.

tum′ble•weed′, *n.* plant whose upper part becomes detached and is driven about by wind.

tu′mid, *adj.* 1. swollen. 2. turgid; bombastic. **—tu•mid′i•ty,** *n.* **—tu•mes′cent,** *adj.*

tu′mor, *n.* 1. swollen part. 2. abnormal swelling. **—tu′mor•ous,** *adj.*

tu′mult, *n.* disturbance, commotion, or uproar. **—tu•mul′tu•ous,** *adj.*

tun, *n.* large cask.

tu′na, *n.* 1. large oceanic fish. 2. tunny. Also, **tuna fish.**

tun′dra, *n.* vast, treeless, arctic plain.

tune, *n., v.,* **tuned, tuning.** —*n.* 1. melody. 2. state of proper pitch, frequency, or condition. 3. harmony. —*v.* 4. adjust to correct pitch. 5. adjust to receive radio signals. **—tune′ful,** *adj.* **—tun′a•ble, tune′a•ble,** *adj.* **—tune′less,** *adj.* **—tun′er,** *n.*

tung′sten, *n.* metallic element used for electric-lamp filaments, etc.

tu′nic, *n.* 1. coat of uniform. 2. ancient Greek and Roman garment. 3. woman's upper garment.

tun′ing fork, steel instrument struck to produce pure tone of constant pitch.

tun′nel, *n.* 1. manmade underground passage. —*v.* 2. make tunnel.

tun′ny, *n.* large mackerellike fish.

tur′ban, *n.* head covering made of scarf wound round head.

tur′bid, *adj.* 1. muddy. 2. dense. 3. confused. **—tur•bid′i•ty,** *n.*

tur′bine, *n.* motor producing torque by pressure of fluid.

tur′bo•jet′, *n.* jet engine that compresses air by turbine.

tur′bu•lent, *adj.* 1. disorderly. 2. tumultuous. **—tur′bu•lence,** *n.* **—tur′bu•lent•ly,** *adv.*

tu•reen′ (tŏo rēn′), *n.* large covered dish for soup, etc.

turf, *n.* covering of grass and roots. **—turf′y,** *adj.*

tur′gid (tûr′jid), *adj.* 1. swollen. 2. pompous or bombastic. **—tur•gid′i•ty, tur′gid•ness,** *n.* **—tur′gid•ly,** *adv.*

tur′key, *n., pl.* **-keys.** large, edible American bird.

tur′moil, *n.* tumult.

turn, *v.* 1. rotate. 2. reverse. 3. divert; deflect. 4. depend. 5. sour; ferment. 6. nauseate. 7. alter. 8. become. 9. use. 10. pass. 11. direct. 12. curve. —*n.* 13. rotation. 14. change or point of change. 15. one's due time or opportunity. 16. trend. 17. short walk, ride, etc. 18. inclination or aptitude. 19. service or disservice.

turn′buck′le, *n.* link used to couple or tighten two parts.

turn′coat′, *n.* renegade.

tur′nip, *n.* 1. fleshy, edible root of cabbagelike plant. 2. the plant.

turn′key′, *n., pl.* **-keys.** keeper of prison keys.

turn′out′, *n.* 1. attendance at meeting, show, etc. 2. output.

turn′o′ver, *n.* rate of replacement, investment, trade, etc.

turn′pike′, *n.* 1. barrier across road (**turnpike road**) where toll is paid. 2. turnpike road.

turn′stile′, *n.* horizontal crossed bars in gateway.

turn′ta′ble, *n.* rotating platform.

tur′pen•tine′, *n.* 1. type of resin from coniferous trees. 2. oil yielded by this.

tur′pi•tude′, *n.* depravity.

tur′quoise (-koiz), *n.* 1. greenish-blue mineral used in jewelry. 2. bluish green.

tur′ret, *n.* 1. small tower. 2. towerlike gun shelter.

tur′tle, *n.* marine reptile with shell-encased body.

tur′tle•dove′, *n.* small Old World dove.

tusk, *n.* very long tooth, as of elephant or walrus.

tus′sle, *v.,* **-sled, -sling.** fight; scuffle.

tu′te•lage, *n.* 1. guardianship. 2. instruction. **—tu′te•lar′y, tu′te•lar,** *adj.*

tu′tor, *n.* 1. private instructor. 2. college teacher (below instructor). —*v.* 3. teach. **—tu•to′ri•al,** *adj.*

tux•e′do, *n., pl.* **-dos.** semiformal coat for men.

TV, television.

twad′dle, *n.* nonsense.

twain, *adj., n. Archaic.* two.

twang, *v.* 1. sound sharply and ringingly. 2. have nasal tone. —*n.* 3. twanging sound.

tweak, *v.* 1. seize and pull or twist. —*n.* 2. sharp pull and twist.

tweed, *n.* coarse, colored wool cloth.

tweez′ers, *n.pl.* small pincers.

twelve, *n., adj.* ten plus two. **—twelfth,** *adj., n.*

twen′ty, *n., adj.* ten times two. **—twen′ti•eth,** *adj., n.*

twice, *adv.* 1. two times. 2. doubly.

twid′dle, *v.,* **-dled, -dling.** 1. turn round and round, esp. with the fingers. 2. twirl (one's fingers) about each other.

twig, *n.* slender shoot on tree.

twi′light′, *n.* light from sky when sun is down.

twilight sleep, induced state of semi-consciousness, esp. for relatively painless childbirth.

twill, *n.* 1. fabric woven in parallel diagonal lines. 2. the weave. —*v.* 3. weave in twill.

twin, *n.* either of two children born at single birth.

twine, *n., v.,* **twined, twining.** —*n.* 1. strong thread of twisted strands. 2. twist. —*v.* 3. twist or become twisted together. 4. encircle.

twinge, *n., v.,* **twinged, twinging.** —*n.* 1. sudden, sharp pain. —*v.* 2. give or have twinge.

twin′kle, *v.,* **-kled, -kling,** *n.* —*v.* 1. shine with light, quick gleams. —*n.* 2. sly, humorous look. 3. act of twinkling.

twirl, *v.* 1. spin; whirl. —*n.* 2. a twirling.

twist, *v.* 1. combine by winding together. 2. distort. 3. combine in coil, etc. 4. wind about. 5. writhe. 6. turn. —*n.* 7. curve or turn. 8. spin. 9. wrench. 10. spiral. —**twist′er,** *n.*

twit, *v.*, **twitted, twitting.** taunt; tease.

twitch, *v.* 1. jerk; move with jerk. —*n.* 2. quick jerky movement, as of muscle.

twit′ter, *v.* 1. utter small, tremulous sounds, as bird. 2. tremble with excitement. —*n.* 3. twittering sound. 4. state of tremulous excitement.

two, *n.*, *adj.* one plus one.

two′some (-səm), *n.* pair.

ty•coon′, *n. Informal.* businessman having great wealth and power.

tyke, *n,* small child.

tympanic membrane, membrane separating middle from external ear.

tym′pa•num (tim′pə nəm), *n.* 1. middle ear. 2. tympanic membrane. —**tym•pan′ic,** *adj.*

type, *n.*, *v.*, **typed, typing.** —*n.* 1. kind or class. 2. representative specimen. 3. piece bearing a letter in relief, used in printing. 4. such pieces collectively. —*v.* 5. typewrite. —**typ′i•cal,** *adj.* —**typ′i•cal•ly,** *adv.* —**typ′i•fy,** *v.* —**typ′ist,** *n.*

type′writ′er, *n.* machine for writing mechanically. —**type′write′,** *v.*

ty′phoid fever, infectious disease marked by intestinal disorder. Also, **typhoid.**

ty•phoon′, *n.* cyclone or hurricane of western Pacific.

ty′phus, *n.* infectious disease transmitted by lice and fleas.

typ′i•fy′, *v.*, **-fied, -fying.** be typical of.

ty•pog′ra•phy, *n.* 1. art or process of printing. 2. general character of printed matter. —**ty•pog′ra•pher,** *n.* —**ty′po•graph′i•cal,** *adj.*

tyr′an•ny, *n.* 1. despotic abuse of authority. 2. state ruled by tyrant. —**ty•ran′ni•cal,** *adj.* —**tyr′an•nize′,** *v.*

ty′rant, *n.* oppressive, unjust, or absolute ruler.

ty′ro, *n.* novice.

tzar, *n.* czar.

U

U, u, *n.* twenty-first letter of English alphabet.

u•biq′ui•ty, *n.* simultaneous presence everywhere. —**u•biq′ui•tous,** *adj.*

ud′der, *n.* mammary gland, esp. of cow.

ug′ly, *adj.*, **-lier, -liest.** 1. repulsive. 2. dangerous. —**ug′li•ness,** *n.*

u′ku•le′le (yōō′ kə lā′lē), *n.* small guitar.

ul′cer, *n.* open sore, as on stomach lining. —**ul′cer•ous,** *adj.* —**ul′cer•ate′,** *v.*

ul′na, *n.* larger bone of forearm. —**ul′nar,** *adj.*

ul•te′ri•or, *adj.* 1. not acknowledged; concealed. 2. later.

ul′ti•mate, *adj.* 1. final; highest. 2. basic. —**ul′ti•mate•ly,** *adv.*

ul′ti•ma′tum (-mā′təm), *n.* final demand.

ul′tra•ma•rine′, *n.* deep blue.

ul′tra•vi′o•let, *adj.* of invisible rays beyond violet in spectrum.

um′ber, *n.* reddish brown.

um•bil′i•cus, *n.* navel. —**um•bil′i•cal,** *adj.*

um′brage, *n.* resentment.

um•brel′la, *n.* cloth-covered framework carried for protection from rain, etc.

um′pire, *n.*, *v.*, **-pired, -piring.** —*n.* 1. judge or arbitrator. —*v.* 2. be umpire in.

un-, prefix indicating negative or opposite sense, as in *unfair, unwanted,* and *unfasten.* See list at bottom of this and following page.

un•af•fect′ed, *adj.* 1. without affectation. 2. not concerned or involved.

u•nan′i•mous, *adj.* completely agreed. —**u•nan′i•mous•ly,** *adv.* —**u′na•nim′i•ty,** *n.*

un′as•sum′ing, *adj.* modest; without vanity.

un′a•wares′, *adv.* not knowingly.

un•bal′anced, *adj.* 1. out of balance. 2. irrational; deranged.

un•bend′, *v.*, **-bent, -bending.** 1. straighten. 2. act in genial, relaxed manner.

un•bend′ing, *adj.* rigidly formal or unyielding.

un•bos′om, *v.* disclose (secrets, etc.).

un•brid′led, *adj.* unrestrained.

un•called′-for′, *adj.* not warranted.

un•can′ny, *adj.* unnaturally strange or good.

un′cer•e•mo′ni•ous, *adj.* 1. informal. 2. rudely abrupt.

un′cle, *n.* brother of one's father or mother.

Uncle Sam, United States government.

un′com•pro•mis′ing, *adj.* refusing to compromise; rigid.

un′con•cern′, *n.* lack of concern; indifference.

un′con•di′tion•al, *adj.* absolute; without conditions or reservations. —**un′con•di′tion•al•ly,** *adv.*

un′con•scion•a•ble (-shən-), *adj.* not reasonable or honest.

un•couth′, *adj.* rude; boorish.

unc′tion, *n.* 1. anointment with oil. 2. soothing manner of speech.

unc′tu•ous (-chōō əs), *adj.* 1. oily. 2. overly suave.

un′der, *prep.*, *adj.*, *adv.* 1. beneath; below. 2. less than. 3. lower.

un′der•brush′, *n.* low shrubs, etc., in forest.

un′der•clothes′, *n.pl.* underwear. Also, **un′der•cloth′ing.**

un′der•cov′er, *adj.* secret.

un′der•cut′, *v.*, **-cut, -cutting.** sell at lower price than.

---

un•a′ble	un•but′ton	un•con′scious	un•doubt′ed	un•fail′ing
un′ack•now′ledged	un•cer′tain	un′con•trol′la•ble	un•dress′	un•fair′
un′a•void′a•ble	un•civ′il	un•cork′	un•due′	un•faith′ful
un′a•ware′	un•clean′	un•cov′er	un•du′ly	un′fa•mil′iar
un′be•liev′a•ble	un•cloak′	un′de•cid′ed	un•e′qual	un•fas′ten
un•born′	un•clothe′	un′de•clared′	un•err′ing	un•fit′
un•bound′ed	un•com′fort•a•ble	un′de•feat′ed	un•e′ven	un•fold′
un•bur′den	un•com′mon	un′de•ni′a•ble	un′ex•pect′ed	un′for•get′ta•ble

un′der•dog′, *n.* 1. weaker contestant, etc. 2. victim of injustice.

un′der•es′ti•mate′, *v.*, **-ated, -ating.** estimate too low.

un′der•gar′ment, *n.* item of underwear.

un′der•go′, *v.*, **-went, -gone, -going.** experience; endure.

un′der•grad′u•ate, *n.* college student before receiving his first degree.

un′der•ground′, *adj.*, *adv.* 1. under the ground. 2. secret. —*n.* (un′dər ground′). 3. secret resistance army.

un′der•hand′, *adj.* sly; secret. Also, **un′der•hand′ed.**

un′der•lie′, *v.*, **-lay, -lain, -lying.** 1. lie beneath. 2. be the cause or basis of.

un′der•mine′, *v.*, **-mined, -mining.** weaken or destroy, esp. secretly.

un′der•neath′, *prep.*, *adv.* beneath.

un′der•stand′, *v.*, **-stood, -standing.** 1. know meaning of. 2. accept as part of agreement. 3. sympathize. —**un′der•stand′ing**, *n.*

un′der•stood′, *adj.* agreed or assumed.

un′der•stud′y, *n.*, *pl.* **-dies.** substitute for performer.

un′der•take′, *v.* **-took, -taken, -taking.** 1. attempt. 2. promise. 3. arrange funerals, etc.

un′der•tak′er, *n.* funeral director; mortician.

un′der•tak′ing, *n.* enterprise; task.

un′der•wear′, *n.* garments worn next to skin, under other clothing.

un′der•world′, *n.* criminal element.

un′der•write′, *v.*, **-wrote, -written, -writing.** guarantee, esp. expense.

un•do′, *v.*, **-did, -done, -doing.** 1. return to original state. 2. untie. 3. destroy.

un′du•late′, *v.*, **-lated, -lating.** have wavy motion or form. —**un′du•la′-tion**, *n.*

un•dy′ing, *adj.* eternal; unending.

un•earth′, *v.* discover.

un•eas′y, *adj.*, **-ier, -iest.** anxious. —**un•eas′i•ly**, *adv.* —**un•eas′i•ness**, *n.*

un•feel′ing, *adj.* lacking sympathy. —**un•feel′ing•ly**, *adv.*

un•found′ed, *adj.* not supported by evidence.

un•gain′ly, *adj.* clumsy.

un′guent (ung′gwənt), *n.* salve.

un•hinge′, *v.*, **-hinged, -hinging.** 1. take off hinges. 2. upset reason of; unbalance.

u′ni•corn′, *n.* mythical horselike animal with one horn.

u′ni•form′, *adj.* 1. exactly alike. 2. even. —*n.* 3. distinctive clothing of specific group. —*v.* 4. put in uniform. —**u′ni•form′i•ty**, *n.*

u′ni•fy′, *v.*, **-fied, -fying.** make into one. —**u′ni•fi•ca′tion**, *n.*

u′ni•lat′er•al, *adj.* one-sided.

un′ion, *n.* 1. uniting; combination. 2. labor group for mutual aid on wages, etc. —**un′ion•ism′**, *n.* —**un′-ion•ize′**, *v.*

Union Jack, British flag.

u•nique′, *adj.* 1. only. 2. most unusual or rare. —**u•nique′ly**, *adv.*

u′ni•sex′, *adj.* of type or style used by both sexes.

u′ni•son, *n.* agreement.

u′nit, *n.* one of number of identical or similar things.

U′ni•tar′i•an, *n.* 1. member of Christian denomination asserting unity of God. —*adj.* 2. concerning Unitarians or their beliefs.

u•nite′, *v.*, **united, uniting.** join, make, etc., into one.

United Nations, organization of nations to preserve peace and promote human welfare.

u′ni•ty, *n.* 1. state of being one. 2. agreement. 3. uniformity.

u′ni•ver′sal, *adj.* 1. of all; general. 2. of universe. 3. having many skills, much learning, etc. —**un′i•ver′sal•ly**, *adv.* —**u′ni•ver•sal′i•ty**, *n.*

u′ni•verse′, *n.* all things that exist, including heavenly bodies.

u′ni•ver′si•ty, *n.*, *pl.* **-ties.** institution composed of various specialized colleges.

un•kempt′, *adj.* untidy.

un•lead′ed (-led′id), *adj.* (of gasoline) free of pollution-causing lead.

un•less′, *conj.*, *prep.* if not; except that.

un•let′tered, *adj.* illiterate.

un•prin′ci•pled, *adj.* without principles or ethics.

un•rav′el, *v.* 1. disentangle. 2. solve.

un•rest′, *n.* 1. restless state. 2. strong, almost rebellious, dissatisfaction.

un•ru′ly, *adj.* lawless.

un•speak′a•ble, *adj.* too disgusting to speak of. —**un•speak′a•bly**, *adv.*

un•ten′a•ble, *adj.* not defensible as true.

un•think′a•ble, *adj.* not to be imagined; impossible.

un•ti′dy, *adj.* not tidy or neat. —**un-tid′i•ly**, *adv.*

un•tie′, *v.*, **-tied, -tying.** loosen or open (something tied).

un•til′, *conj.*, *prep.* 1. up to time when. 2. before.

un′to, *prep. Archaic.* to.

un•told′, *adj.* countless.

un•touch′a•ble, *adj.* 1. beyond control or criticism. 2. too vile to touch. —**un•touch′a•ble**, *n.*

un•to•ward′, *adj.* unfavorable or unfortunate.

un•well′, *adj.* ill or ailing.

un•wield′y, *adj.* awkward to handle.

un•wit′ting, *adj.* not aware. —**un-wit′ting•ly**, *adv.*

un•wont′ed, *adj.* not habitual or usual.

up, *adv.*, *prep.*, *n.*, *v.*, **upped, upping.** —*adv.* 1. to higher place, etc. 2. erectly. 3. out of bed. 4. at bat. —*prep.* 5. to higher place, etc., on or in. —*n.* 6. rise. —*v.* 7. increase.

up•braid′, *v.* chide.

up′date′, *v.*, **-dated, -dating.** modernize, esp. in details.

up•heav′al, *n.* sudden and great movement or change.

up•hill′, *adv.* up a slope or incline. —**up′hill′**, *adj.*

up•hold′, *v.*, **-held, -holding.** support. —**up•hold′er**, *n.*

up•hol′ster, *v.* provide (furniture) with coverings, etc. —**up•hol′ster•er**, *n.*

up′keep′, *n.* maintenance.

up′land (up′lənd), *n.* elevated region.

up•lift′, *v.* 1. reform. —*n.* 2. (up′lift′). improvement. 3. inspiration.

---

un′for•giv′a•ble	un′in•tel′lig•i•ble	un•load′	un•roll′	un•typ′i•cal
un•for′tu•nate	un•in′ter•est′ed	un•lock′	un•screw′	un•used′
un•friend′ly	un′in•ter•rupt′ed	un•mask′	un•set′tle	un•u′su•al
un•god′ly	un•kind′	un′mis•tak′a•ble	un•shack′le	un•veil′
un•gra′cious	un•known′	un•nat′u•ral	un•sight′ly	un•wind′
un•guard′ed	un•lace′	un•nec′es•sar′y	un•skilled′	un•wise′
un•hap′py	un•law′ful	un•pack′	un•tan′gle	un•worn′
un•heard′-of′	un•like′	un•pop′u•lar	un•true′	un•wor′thy
un•ho′ly	un•like′ly	un•rea′son•a•ble	un•truth′	un•wrap′

up•on′, *prep.* on.

up′per, *adj.* higher. **—up′per•most′**, *adj.*

up′right′, *adj.* 1. erect. 2. righteous. **—up′right′ness**, *n.*

up′ris′ing, *n.* revolt.

up′roar′, *n.* tumult; noise; din. **—up•roar′i•ous**, *adj.*

up•root′, *v.* tear up by roots.

up•set′, *v.*, **-set**, **-setting**, *n.*, *adj.* **—v.** 1. turn over. 2. distress emotionally. 3. defeat. **—n.** 4. (up′set′). 5. overturn. 5. defeat. **—adj.** 6. disorderly. 7. distressed.

up′shot′, *n.* final result.

up′stairs′, *adv.*, *adj.* on or to upper floor.

up′start′, *n.* person newly risen to wealth or importance.

up′-to-date′, *adj.* 1. until now. 2. modern; latest.

up′ward, *adv.* to higher place. Also, **up′wards. —up′ward**, *adj.*

u•ra′ni•um, *n.* white, radioactive metallic element, important in development of atomic energy.

ur′ban, *adj.* of of or like a city.

ur•bane′, *adj.* polite or suave. **—ur•ban′i•ty**, *n.*

ur′chin, *n.* ragged child.

urge, *v.*, **urged**, **urging**, *n.* **—v.** 1. force, incite, or advocate. 2. entreat. **—n.** 3. desire; impulse.

ur′gent, *adj.* vital; pressing. **—ur′gent•ly**, *adv.* **—ur′gen•cy**, *n.*

u′ri•nate′, *v.*, **-nated**, **-nating**. pass urine. **—u′ri•na′tion**, *n.*

u′rine, *n.* secretion of kidneys.

urn, *n.* vase or pot.

us, *pron.* objective case of **we.**

us′age, *n.* 1. custom. 2. treatment.

use, *v.*, **used**, **using**, *n.* **—v.** 1. do something with aid of. 2. expend. 3. make practice of. 4. treat. 5. accustom. **—n.** (yōōs). 6. act or way of using. 7. service or value. **—us′a•ble**, *adj.* **—use′ful**, *adj.* **—use′less**, *adj.* **—us′er**, *n.*

ush′er, *n.* person who escorts to seats, as in theater.

u′su•al, *adj.* 1. customary. 2. common. **—u′su•al•ly**, *adv.*

u•surp′ (yōō zûrp′), *v.* seize without right. **—u•surp′er**, *n.*

u′su•ry (yōō′zhə rē), *n.* lending money at exorbitant rates of interest. **—u′sur•er**, *n.*

u•ten′sil, *n.* device, container, etc., esp. for kitchen.

u′ter•us, *n.*, *pl.* **-i.** part of woman's body in which fertilized ovum develops.

u•til′i•tar′i•an, *adj.* of practical use.

u•til′i•ty, *n.*, *pl.* **-ties.** 1. usefulness. 2. public service.

u′ti•lize′, *v.*, **-lized**, **-lizing**. use. **—u′ti•li•za′tion**, *n.*

ut′most′, *adj.* 1. greatest. 2. furthest.

U•to′pi•an, *adj.* impossibly perfect.

ut′ter, *v.* 1. speak; say. **—adj.** 2. complete; total. **—ut′ter•ance**, *n.*

ut′ter•ly, *adv.* completely; absolutely.

u′vu•la (yōō′vyə lə), *n.* small, fleshy part on soft palate.

ux•o′ri•ous (uk sōr′ē əs), *adj.* foolishly or excessively fond of one's wife.

V, v, *n.* twenty-second letter of English alphabet.

va•can•cy, *n.*, *pl.* **-cies.** 1. state of being vacant. 2. vacant space.

va′cant, *adj.* 1. empty. 2. devoid. 3. unintelligent. **—va′cant•ly**, *adv.*

va′cate, *v.*, **-cated**, **-cating**. 1. empty. 2. quit. 3. annul.

va•ca′tion, *n.* 1. freedom from duty, business, etc. 2. holiday. **—v.** 3. take a vacation. **—va•ca′tion•ist**, *n.*

vac′ci•nate′, *v.*, **-nated**, **-nating**. inoculate against smallpox, etc. **—vac′ci•na′tion**, *n.*

vac•cine′ (vak sēn′), *n.* substance injected into bloodstream to give immunity. **—vac′ci•nal**, *adj.*

vac′il•late′ (vas′ə-), *v.*, **-lated**, **-lating**. 1. waver; fluctuate. 2. be irresolute. **—vac′il•la′tion**, *n.*

va•cu′i•ty, *n.*, *pl.* **-ties.** 1. emptiness. 2. lack of intelligence. **—vac′u•ous**, *adj.* **—vac′u•ous•ly**, *adv.*

vac′u•um, *n.* space from which all matter has been removed.

vacuum cleaner, apparatus for cleaning by suction.

vacuum tube, sealed bulb, formerly used in radio and electronics.

vag′a•bond′, *adj.* 1. wandering; homeless. **—n.** 2. vagrant.

va•gar′y (və gâr′ē), *n.*, *pl.* **-garies.** capricious act or idea.

va•gi′na (və jī′nə), *n.*, *pl.* **-nas**, **-nae.** passage from uterus to vulva. **—vag′i•nal**, *adj.*

va′grant, *n.* 1. idle wanderer. **—adj.** 2. wandering. **—va′gran•cy**, *n.*

vague, *adj.*, **vaguer**, **vaguest.** 1. not definite. 2. indistinct. **—vague′ly**, *adv.* **—vague′ness**, *n.*

vain, *adj.* 1. futile. 2. conceited. **—vain′ly**, *adv.* **—vain′ness**, *n.*

val′ance (val′əns, vā′ləns), *n.* drapery across top of window.

vale, *n.* valley.

val′e•dic′tion, *n.* farewell. **—val′e•dic′to•ry**, *n.*

va′lence (vā′ləns), *n.* combining capacity of atom or radical.

val′en•tine′, *n.* 1. affectionate card or gift sent on February 14 (**Saint Valentine's Day**). 2. sweetheart chosen on that day.

val′et (val′it, val′ā), *n.* personal manservant.

val′iant, *adj.* brave. **—val′iance**, *n.* **—val′iant•ly**, *adv.*

val′id, *adj.* 1. sound; logical. 2. legally binding. **—val′idate′**, *v.* **—va•lid′i•ty**, *n.* **—val′id•ly**, *adv.*

va•lise′ (-lēs′), *n.* traveling bag.

val′ley, *n.* long depression between uplands or mountains.

val′or, *n.* bravery, esp. in battle. **—val′o•rous**, *adj.* **—val′o•rous•ly**, *adv.*

val′u•a•ble, *adj.* 1. of much worth, importance, etc. **—n.** 2. (*usually pl.*) valuable article. **—val′u•a•bly**, *adv.*

val′u•a′tion, *n.* estimation or estimated value.

val′ue, *n.*, *v.*, **-ued**, **-uing.** **—n.** 1. worth or importance. 2. equivalent or estimated worth. 3. conception of what is good. **—v.** 4. estimate worth of. 5. esteem. **—val′ue•less**, *adj.*

valve, *n.* device controlling flow of liquids, etc. **—val′vu•lar**, *adj.*

vamp, *n.* 1. upper front part of shoe or boot. 2. *Slang.* seductive woman. **—v.** 3. improvise (as music).

vam′pire, *n.* 1. corpse supposed to be reanimated and to suck blood of sleeping persons. 2. extortionist. 3. Also, **vampire bat.** South and Central American bat.

van, *n.* 1. vanguard. 2. covered truck for moving furniture, etc. 3. small closed truck.

van′dal, *n.* person who damages or destroys wantonly. **—van′dal•ism**, *n.*

van•dyke′, *n.* short, pointed beard.

vane, *n.* 1. weathervane. 2. one of set of blades set diagonally on a rotor to move or be moved by fluid.

van′guard′, *n.* 1. foremost part. 2. leaders of a movement.

va•nil′la, *n.* 1. tropical orchid, whose fruit (**vanilla bean**) yields flavoring extract. 2. the extract.

van′ish, *v.* disappear. **—van′ish•er,** *n.*

van′i•ty, *n., pl.* **-ties.** 1. vainness. 2. make-up table. 3. compact (def. 4).

van′quish, *v.* conquer; defeat. **—van′quish•er,** *n.*

van′tage, *n.* superior position or situation.

vap′id, *adj.* 1. insipid. 2. dull. **—va•pid′i•ty,** *n.* **—vap′id•ly,** *adv.*

va′por, *n.* 1. exhalation, as fog or mist. 2. gas. **—va′por•ous,** *adj.*

va′por•ize′, *v.,* **-ized, -izing.** change into vapor. **—va′por•i•za′tion,** *n.* **—va′por•iz′er,** *n.*

var′i•a•ble, *adj.* 1. changeable. 2. inconstant. **—***n.* 3. something variable. **—var′i•a•bil′i•ty,** *n.* **—var′i•a•bly,** *adv.*

var′i•ance, *n.* 1. divergence or discrepancy. 2. disagreement.

var′i•ant, *adj.* 1. varying. 2. altered in form. **—***n.* 3. variant form, etc.

var′i•a′tion, *n.* 1. change. 2. amount of change. 3. variant. 4. transformation of melody in harmony, etc. **—var′i•a′tion•al,** *adj.*

var′i•cose′, *adj.* abnormally swollen, as veins.

var′i•e•gate′, *v.,* **-gated, -gating.** 1. mark with different colors, etc. 2. vary. **—var′i•e•gat′ed,** *adj.*

va•ri′e•ty, *n., pl.* **-ties.** 1. diversity. 2. number of different things. 3. kind; category. 4. variant. **—va•ri′e•tal,** *adj.*

va•ri′o•la, *n.* smallpox.

var′i•ous, *adj.* 1. of different sorts. 2. several. **—var′i•ous•ly,** *adv.*

var′nish, *n.* 1. resinous solution drying in hard, glossy coat. 2. gloss. **—***v.* 3. lay varnish on.

var′y, *v.,* **varied, varying.** 1. change; differ. 2. cause to be different. 3. deviate; diverge.

vase, *n.* tall container, esp. for flowers.

vas•ec′to•my, *n., pl.* **-mies.** surgery for male sterilization.

vas′sal, *n.* 1. feudal holder of land who renders service to superior. 2. subject, follower, or slave. **—vas′sal•age,** *n.*

vast, *adj.* immense; huge. **—vast′ly,** *adv.* **—vast′ness,** *n.*

vat, *n.* large container for liquids.

vaude′ville (vôd′vil), *n.* theatrical entertainment made up of separate acts.

vault, *n.* 1. arched ceiling or roof. 2. arched space, chamber, etc. **—***v.* 3. build or cover with vault. 4. leap.

vaunt, *v.* 1. boast of. **—***n.* 2. boast.

V′-Day′, *n.* official day of victory in World War II (May 8, 1945, in Europe; August 15, 1945, in the Pacific).

veal, *n.* flesh of calf.

veep, *n. Informal.* Vice-President, esp. of U.S.

veer, *v.* change direction.

veg′e•ta•ble, *n.* 1. plant used for food. 2. any plant. **—veg′e•ta•ble, veg′e•tal,** *adj.*

veg′e•tar′i•an, *n.* 1. person who eats only vegetable food on principle (**vegetarianism**). **—***adj.* 2. of or advocating vegetarianism. 3. suitable for vegetarians.

veg′e•tate′, *v.,* **-tated, -tating.** 1. grow as plants do. 2. live dull, inactive life.

veg′e•ta′tion, *n.* 1. plants collectively. 2. act or process of vegetating. **—veg′e•ta′tive,** *adj.*

ve′he•ment (vē′ə mənt), *adj.* 1. impetuous or impassioned. 2. violent. **—ve′he•mence, ve′he•men′cy,** *n.* **—ve′he•ment•ly,** *adv.*

ve′hi•cle, *n.* means of transport, etc. **—ve•hic′u•lar,** *adj.*

veil, *n.* 1. material concealing face. 2. part of nun's headdress. 3. cover; screen. 4. pretense. **—***v.* 5. cover with veil.

vein, *n.* 1. vessel conveying blood from body to heart. 2. tubular riblike thickening, as in leaf or insect wing. 3. stratum of ore, coal, etc. 4. mood. **—***v.* 5. furnish or mark with veins.

vel′lum, *n.* parchment.

ve•loc′i•ty, *n.* speed.

vel′vet, *n.* fabric with thick, soft pile. **—vel′vet•y,** *adj.*

ve′nal, *adj.* corrupt; mercenary. **—ve′nal•ly,** *adv.* **—ve•nal′i•ty,** *n.*

vend, *v.* sell. **—ven′dor,** *n.*

ven•det′ta, *n.* long, bitter feud.

ve•neer′, *v.* 1. overlay with thin sheets of fine wood, etc. **—***n.* 2. veneered layer of wood. 3. superficial appearance.

ven′er•a•ble, *adj.* worthy of reverence. **—ven′er•a•bil′i•ty,** *n.*

ven′er•ate′, *v.,* **-ated, -ating.** revere. **—ven′er•a′tion,** *n.*

ve•ne′re•al (və nēr′ē əl), *adj.* relating to or caused by venereal intercourse.

venge′ance, *n.* revenge.

venge′ful, *adj.* seeking vengeance. **—venge′ful•ly,** *adv.*

ve′ni•al, *n.* pardonable.

ven′i•son, *n.* flesh of deer.

ven′om, *n.* 1. poisonous fluid secreted by some snakes, spiders, etc. 2. spite; malice. **—ven′om•ous,** *adj.* **—ven′om•ous•ly,** *adv.*

vent, *n.* 1. outlet, as for fluid. 2. expression. **—***v.* 3. express freely.

ven′ti•late′, *v.,* **-lated, -lating.** 1. provide with fresh air. 2. submit to discussion. **—ven′ti•la′tion,** *n.* **—ven′-ti•la′tor,** *n.*

ven′tri•cle, *n.* either of two lower cavities of heart. **—ven•tric′u•lar,** *adj.*

ven•tril′o•quism′, *n.* art of speaking so that voice seems to come from another source. **—ven•tril′o•quist,** *n.*

ven′ture, *n., v.,* **-tured, -turing.** **—***n.* 1. hazardous undertaking. **—***v.* 2. risk; dare. 3. enter daringly. **—ven′-ture•some, ven′tur•ous,** *adj.*

Ve′nus, *n.* 1. goddess of love. 2. second planet from sun.

ve•ra′cious, *adj.* truthful. **—ve•rac′-i•ty** (və ras′ə tē), *n.*

ve•ran′da, *n.* open porch. Also, **ve•ran′dah.**

verb, *n.* part of speech expressing action, occurrence, existence, etc., as "saw" in the sentence "I saw Tom."

ver′bal, *adj.* 1. of or in form of words. 2. oral. 3. word for word. 4. of verbs. **—***n.* 5. word, as noun, derived from verb. **—ver′bal•ly,** *adv.*

ver′bal•ize′, *v.,* **-ized, -izing.** express in words. **—ver′bal•i•za′tion,** *n.*

ver•ba′tim, *adv.* word for word.

ver•be′na, *n.* plant with long spikes of flowers.

ver′bi•age, *n.* 1. wordiness. 2. manner of verbal expression.

ver•bose′, *adj.* wordy. **—ver•bose′-ness, ver•bos′i•ty,** *n.*

ver′dant, *adj.* 1. green. 2. inexperienced. **—ver′dan•cy,** *n.*

ver′dict, *n.* decision.

ver′di•gris′ (vûr′də grēs′), *n.* green or bluish patina.

ver′dure (vûr′jər), *n.* 1. greenness. 2. green vegetation.

verge, *n., v.,* **verged, verging.** **—***n.* 1. edge or margin. **—***v.* 2. border. 3. incline; tend.

ver′i•fy′, *v.,* **-fied, -fying.** 1. prove to be true. 2. ascertain correctness of.

—ver′i•fi′a•ble, *adj.* **—ver′i•fi•ca′- tion,** *n.* **—ver′i•fi′er,** *n.*

ver′i•ly, *adv. Archaic.* truly.

ver′i•si•mil′i•tude′, *n.* appearance of truth.

ver′i•ta•ble, *adj.* genuine. **—ver′i• ta•bly,** *adv.*

ver′i•ty, *n., pl.* **-ties.** truth.

ver′mi•cel′li (-sel′ē), *n.* pasta in long threads.

ver•mil′ion, *n.* bright red.

ver′min, *n.pl. or sing.* troublesome animals collectively. **—ver′min•ous,** *adj.*

ver•nac′u•lar, *adj.* 1. (of language) used locally or in everyday speech. **—n.** 2. native speech. 3. language of particular group.

ver′nal, *adj.* of spring. **—ver′nal•ly,** *adv.*

ver′sa•tile, *adj.* doing variety of things well. **—ver′sa•til′i•ty,** *n.*

verse, *n.* 1. line of poem. 2. type of metrical line, etc. 3. poem. 4. poetry. 5. division of Biblical chapter.

versed, *adj.* expert; skilled.

ver′si•fy′, *v.,* **-fied, -fying.** 1. treat in or turn into verse. 2. compose verses. **—ver′si•fi′er,** *n.* **—ver′si•fi• ca′tion,** *n.*

ver′sion, *n.* 1. translation. 2. account.

ver′sus, *prep.* in opposition or contrast to.

ver′te•bra, *n., pl.* **-brae, -bras.** bone or segment of spinal column. **—ver′te•bral,** *adj.*

ver′te•brate′, *adj.* 1. having vertebrae. **—n.** 2. vertebrate animal.

ver′ti•cal, *adj.* 1. perpendicular to plane of horizon. **—n.** 2. something vertical. **—ver′ti•cal•ly,** *adv.*

ver′ti•go′, *n., pl.* **-goes.** dizziness.

ver′y, *adv., adj.,* **verier, veriest.** **—adv.** 1. extremely. **—adj.** 2. identical. 3. mere. 4. actual. 5. true.

ves′i•cle, *n.* small sac in body.

ves′per, *n.* 1. *Archaic.* evening. 2. (*pl.*) evening prayer, service, etc.

ves′sel, *n.* 1. ship or boat. 2. hollow or concave container, as dish or glass. 3. tube or duct, as for blood.

vest, *n.* 1. sleeveless garment worn under man's coat. **—v.** 2. clothe or robe. 3. put in someone's possession or control. 4. endow with powers, etc.

ves′ti•bule′, *n.* small room between entrance and main room. **—ves• tib′u•lar,** *adj.*

ves′tige, *n.* trace of something extinct. **—ves•tig′i•al,** *adj.*

vest′ment, *n.* ceremonial garment.

vest′-pock′et, *adj.* conveniently small.

ves′try, *n.* 1. room in church for vestments, or for meetings, etc. 2. church committee managing temporal affairs. **—ves′try•man,** *n.*

vetch, *n.* plant used for forage and soil improvement.

vet′er•an, *n.* 1. person who has seen service, esp. in armed forces. **—adj.** 2. experienced.

vet′er•i•nar′i•an, *n.* veterinary practitioner.

vet′er•i•nar′y, *n.* 1. veterinarian. **—adj.** 2. of medical and surgical treatment of animals.

ve′to, *n., pl.* **-toes,** *v.,* **-toed, -toing.** **—n.** 1. power or right to reject or prohibit. 2. prohibition. **—v.** 3. reject by veto.

vex, *v.* 1. irritate. 2. worry. 3. discuss vigorously. **—vex•a′tion,** *n.* **—vex• a′tious,** *adj.* **—vexed,** *adj.* **—vex′ed• ly,** *adv.*

vi′a (vī′ə), *prep.* by way of.

vi′a•ble, *adj.* capable of living.

vi′a•duct′, *n.* long highway or railroad bridge.

vi′al (vī′əl), *n.* small glass container.

vi′and, *n.* article of food.

vi′brant, *adj.* 1. resonant. 2. energetic; vital. **—vi′bran•cy,** *n.*

vi′brate, *v.,* **-brated, -brating.** 1. move very rapidly to and fro; oscillate. 2. tremble. 3. resound. 4. thrill. **—vi•bra′tion,** *n.* **—vi′bra•tor,** *n.* **—vi′bra•to′ry,** *adj.* **—vi•bra′tion• al,** *adj.*

vic′ar, *n.* 1. parish priest. 2. representative of Pope or bishop. 3. (*cap.*) Also, **Vicar of Christ.** Pope. 4. substitute. **—vic′ar•ship′,** *n.* **—vi•car′i•al,** *adj.*

vic′ar•age, *n.* residence or position of vicar.

vi•car′i•ous, *adj.* 1. done or suffered in place of another. 2. substitute. **—vi•car′i•ous•ly,** *adv.*

vice, *n.* 1. evil habit or fault. 2. immoral conduct. 3. vise. **—prep.** 4. instead of.

vice′-pres′i•dent, *n.* officer next in rank to president. **—vice′-pres′i• den•cy,** *n.*

vice′roy, *n.* ruler of country or province as deputy of sovereign. **—vice-re′gal,** *adj.*

vi′ce ver′sa, in opposite way.

vi•cin′i•ty, *n., pl.* **-ties.** neighborhood; nearby area.

vi′cious, *adj.* 1. immoral; depraved. 2. evil. 3. malicious. **—vi′cious•ly,** *adv.* **—vi′cious•ness,** *n.*

vi•cis′si•tude′ (vi sis′ə tyo͞od′), *n.* change, esp. in condition.

vic′tim, *n.* 1. sufferer from action or event. 2. dupe. 3. sacrifice. **—vic′- tim•ize′,** *v.*

vic′tor, *n.* conqueror or winner. **—vic•to′ri•ous,** *adj.* **—vic•to′ri• ous•ly,** *adv.*

vic′to•ry, *n., pl.* **-ries.** success in contest.

vict′ual (vit′əl), *n.* 1. (*pl.*) food. **—v.** 2. supply with victuals. **—vict′ual•er,** *n.*

vid′e•o′, *adj.* 1. of television **—n.** 2. television.

vid′e•o′cas•sette′, *n.* cassette for video recording.

vid′e•o•disk′, *n.* disk for reproducing recorded pictures and sound on TV set.

vid′e•o•tape′, *n., v.,* **-taped, -taping.** **—n.** 1. magnetic tape for recording TV picture and sound. **—v.** 2. record on this.

vie, *v.,* **vied, vying.** contend for superiority.

view, *n.* 1. seeing or beholding. 2. range of vision. 3. landscape, etc., within one's sight. 4. aspect. 5. mental survey. 6. purpose. 7. notion, opinion, etc. **—v.** 8. see; look at. 9. regard. **—view′er,** *n.* **—view′less,** *adj.*

view′point′, *n.* 1. place from which view is seen. 2. attitude toward something.

vig′il, *n.* period of staying awake, esp. as watch.

vig′i•lant, *adj.* 1. wary. 2. alert. **—vig′i•lance,** *n.* **—vig′i•lant•ly,** *adv.*

vig′i•lan′te (-lan′tē), *n.* person who takes law into own hands.

vi•gnette′ (vin yet′), *n., v.,* **-gnetted, -gnetting.** **—n.** 1. small decorative design. 2. photograph, etc., shading off at edges. 3. literary sketch. **—v.** 4. make vignette of.

vig′or, *n.* 1. active strength. 2. energy. **—vig′or•ous,** *adj.* **—vig′or• ous•ly,** *adv.*

Vik′ing, *n.* medieval Scandinavian raider.

vile, *adj.,* **viler, vilest.** 1. very bad. 2. offensive. 3. evil. **—vile′ly,** *adv.* **—vile′ness,** *n.*

vil′i•fy′, *v.* **-fied, -fying.** defame. **—vil′i•fi•ca′tion,** *n.* **—vil′i•fi′er,** *n.*

vil′la, *n.* luxurious country residence.

vil'lage, *n.* small town. —**vil'lag•er,** *n.*

vil'lain, *n.* wicked person. —**vil'lain• ous,** *adj.* —**vil'lain•y,** *n.*

vim, *n.* vigor.

vin'di•cate', *v.,* **-cated, -cating.** 1. clear, as from suspicion. 2. uphold or justify. —**vin'di•ca'tion,** *n.* —**vin'di•ca'tor,** *n.*

vin•dic'tive, *adj.* holding grudge; vengeful. —**vin•dic'tive•ly,** *adv.* —**vin•dic'tive•ness,** *n.*

vine, *n.* creeping or climbing plant with slender stem.

vin'e•gar, *n.* sour liquid obtained by fermentation. —**vin'e•gar•y,** *adj.*

vine'yard (vin'-), *n.* plantation of grapevines.

vin'tage, *n.* 1. wine from one harvest. 2. grape harvest.

vi'nyl (vī'nəl), *n.* type of plastic.

Vi•nyl•ite (vī'nə līt', vin'ə-), *n. Trademark.* vinyl.

vi•o'la, *n. Music.* instrument resembling violin but slightly larger.

vi'o•late', *v.,* **-lated, -lating.** 1. break or transgress. 2. break through or into. 3. desecrate. 4. rape. —**vi'o•la'tion,** *n.* —**vi'o•la'tor,** *n.*

vi'o•lent, *adj.* 1. uncontrolled, strong, or rough. 2. of destructive force. 3. intense; severe. —**vi'o•lence,** *n.* —**vi'o•lent•ly,** *adv.*

vi'o•let, *n.* 1. low herb bearing flowers, usually purple or blue. 2. bluish purple.

vi'o•lin', *n. Music.* stringed instrument played with bow. —**vi'o•lin'ist,** *n.*

vi'o•lon•cel'lo (vē'ə lən chel'ō), *n.* cello. —**vi'o•lon•cel'list,** *n.*

vi'per, *n.* 1. Old World venomous snake. 2. malicious or treacherous person. —**vi'per•ous,** *adj.*

vi•ra'go (vi rā'gō), *n., pl.* **-goes, -gos.** shrew.

vi'ral, *adj.* of or caused by virus.

vir'gin, *n.* 1. person, esp. woman, who has not had sexual intercourse. —*adj.* 2. being or like virgin. 3. untried; unused. —**vir'gin•al,** *adj.* —**vir•gin'i•ty,** *n.*

vir'ile (vir'əl), *adj.* 1. manly. 2. vigorous. 3. capable of procreation. —**vi•ril'i•ty,** *n.*

vir'tu•al, *adj.* such in effect, though not actually. —**vir'tu•al•ly,** *adv.*

vir'tue, *n.* 1. moral excellence. 2. chastity. 3. merit. —**vir'tu•ous,** *adj.* —**vir'tu•ous•ly,** *adv.* —**vir'tu•ous• ness,** *n.*

vir•tu•o'so, *n., pl.* **-sos, -si.** person of special skill, esp. in music. —**vir'tu• os'i•ty,** *n.*

vir'u•lent (vir'yə-), *adj.* 1. poisonous; malignant. 2. hostile. —**vir'u•lence, vir'u•len•cy,** *n.* —**vir'u•lent•ly,** *adv.*

vi'rus, *n.* 1. infective agent. 2. corrupting influence.

vi'sa (vē'zə), *n.* passport endorsement permitting foreign entry or immigration.

vis'age, *n.* 1. face. 2. aspect.

vis'cer•a (vis'ər ə), *n.pl.* 1. soft interior organs of body. 2. intestines. —**vis'cer•al,** *adj.*

vis'cid (vis'id), *adj.* sticky; gluelike. Also, **vis'cous** (vis'kəs). —**vis•cos'i• ty,** *n.*

vis'count (vī'-), *n.* nobleman ranking below earl or count. —**vis'count• ess,** *n.fem.*

vise, *n.* device, usually with two jaws, for holding object firmly.

vis'i•ble, *adj.* 1. capable of being seen. 2. perceptible. 3. manifest. —**vis'i•bil'i•ty,** *n.* —**vis'i•bly,** *adv.*

vi'sion, *n.* 1. power or sense of sight. 2. imagination or unusually keen perception. 3. mental image of something supernatural or imaginary. —**vi'sion•al,** *adj.*

vi'sion•ar'y, *adj., n., pl.* **-aries.** —*adj.* 1. fanciful. 2. seen in vision. 3. unreal. —*n.* 4. seer of visions. 5. bold or impractical schemer.

vis'it, *v.* 1. go to for purposes of talking, staying, etc. 2. afflict. —*n.* 3. act of visiting. 4. stay as guest. —**vis'i• tor, vis'i•tant,** *n.*

vis'it•a'tion, *n.* 1. visit. 2. bringing of good or evil, as by supernatural force.

vi'sor, *n.* front piece, as of helmet or cap.

vis'ta, *n.* extended view in one direction.

vis'u•al, *adj.* 1. of or by means of sight. 2. visible. —**vis'u•al•ly,** *adv.*

vis'u•al•ize', *v.,* **-ized, -izing.** 1. make visual. 2. form mental image of. —**vis'u•al•i•za'tion,** *n.*

vi'tal, *adj.* 1. of life. 2. living; energetic; vivid. 3. giving or necessary to life. 4. essential. —**vi'tal•ly,** *adv.*

vi•tal'i•ty, *n., pl.* **-ties.** 1. vital force. 2. physical or mental vigor. 3. power of continued existence.

vi'ta•min, *n.* food element essential in small quantities to maintain life. —**vi'ta•min'ic,** *adj.*

vi'ti•ate' (vish'ē āt'), *v.,* **-ated, -ating.** 1. impair. 2. corrupt. 3. invalidate. —**vi'ti•a'tion,** *n.*

vit're•ous, *adj.* of or like glass.

vit'ri•fy', *v.,* **-fied, -fying.** change to glass.

vit'ri•ol, *n.* 1. glassy metallic compound. 2. sulfuric acid. 3. caustic criticism, etc. —**vit'ri•ol'ic,** *adj.*

vi•tu'per•ate' (vī tyōō'-), *v.,* **-ated, -ating.** 1. criticize abusively. 2. revile. —**vi•tu'per•a'tion,** *n.* —**vi•tu'per• a'tive** (-pə rā'tiv), *adj.*

vi•va'cious, *adj.* lively; animated. —**vi•va'cious•ly,** *adv.* —**vi•va'- cious•ness, vi•vac'i•ty,** *n.*

viv'id, *adj.* 1. bright, as color or light. 2. full of life. 3. intense; striking. —**viv'id•ly,** *adv.* —**viv'id•ness,** *n.*

viv'i•sec'tion, *n.* dissection of live animal. —**viv'i•sec'tion•ist,** *n.*

vix'en, *n.* 1. ill-tempered woman. 2. female fox.

vo•cab'u•lar'y, *n., pl.* **-laries.** 1. words used by people, class, or person. 2. collection of defined words, usually in alphabetical order.

vo'cal, *adj.* 1. of the voice. 2. of or for singing. 3. articulate or talkative. —**vo'cal•ize',** *v.* —**vo'cal•i•za'tion,** *n.* —**vo'cal•ly,** *adv.*

vocal cords, membranes in larynx producing sound by vibration.

vo'cal•ist, *n.* singer.

vo•ca'tion, *n.* occupation, business, or profession. —**vo•ca'tion•al,** *adj.*

vo•cif'er•ate' (-sif'ə-), *v.,* **-ated, -ating.** cry noisily; shout. —**vo•cif'- er•a'tion,** *n.* —**vo•cif'er•ous,** *adj.* —**vo•cif'er•ous•ly,** *adv.*

vod'ka, *n.* colorless distilled liquor.

vogue, *n.* 1. fashion. 2. popular favor.

voice, *n., v.,* **voiced, voicing.** —*n.* 1. sound uttered through mouth. 2. speaking or singing voice. 3. expression. 4. choice. 5. right to express opinion. 6. verb inflection indicating whether subject is acting or acted upon. —*v.* 7. express or declare. —**voice'less,** *adj.*

void, *adj.* 1. without legal force. 2. useless. 3. empty. —*n.* 4. empty space. —*v.* 5. invalidate. 6. empty out. —**void'a•ble,** *adj.* —**void'ance,** *n.*

vol'a•tile, *adj.* 1. evaporating rapidly. 2. rapidly changeable in emotion. —**vol'a•til'i•ty,** *n.*

vol•ca'no, *n., pl.* **-noes, -nos.** 1. vent in earth from which lava, steam, etc., are expelled. 2. mountain with such vent. —**vol•can′ic**, *adj.*

vo•li′tion, *n.* act or power of willing. —**vo•li′tion•al**, *adv.*

vol′ley, *n., pl.* **-leys**, *v.* **-leyed, -leying.** —*n.* 1. discharge of many missiles together. —*v.* 2. fire volley.

volt, *n.* unit of electromotive force.

vol′u•ble, *adj.* glibly fluent. —**vol′u•bil′i•ty**, *n.* —**vol′u•bly**, *adv.*

vol′ume, *n.* 1. book. 2. size in three dimensions. 3. mass or quantity. 4. loudness or fullness of sound.

vo•lu′mi•nous, *adj.* 1. filling many volumes. 2. ample. —**vo•lu′mi•nous•ly**, *adv.*

vol′un•tar′y, *adj.* 1. done, made, etc., by free choice. 2. controlled by will. —**vol′un•tar′i•ly**, *adv.*

vol′un•teer′, *n.* 1. person who offers self, as for military duty. 2. worker forgoing pay. —*v.* 3. offer for some duty or purpose.

vo•lup′tu•ous, *adj.* luxurious; sensuous. —**vo•lup′tu•ous•ly**, *adv.* —**vo•lup′tu•ous•ness**, *n.*

vom′it, *v.* 1. eject from stomach through mouth. 2. eject with force. —*n.* 3. vomited matter.

vo•ra′cious, *adj.* greedy; ravenous. —**vo•ra′cious•ly**, *adv.* —**vo•rac′i•ty**, *n.*

vor′tex, *n., pl.* **-texes, -tices.** whirling movement or mass.

vote, *n., v.*, **voted, voting.** —*n.* 1. formal expression of wish or choice, as by ballot. 2. right to this. 3. votes collectively. —*v.* 4. cast one's vote. 5. cause to go or occur by vote. —**vot′er**, *n.*

vouch, *v.* 1. answer for. 2. give assurance, as surety or sponsor.

vouch′er, *n.* 1. one that vouches. 2. document, receipt, etc., proving expenditure.

vouch•safe′, *v.*, **-safed, -safing.** grant or permit.

vow, *n.* 1. solemn promise, pledge, or personal engagement. —*v.* 2. make vow.

vow′el, *n.* 1. speech sound made with clear channel through middle of mouth. 2. letter representing vowel.

voy′age, *n, v.*, **-aged, -aging.** —*n.* 1. journey, esp. by water. —*v.* 2. make voyage. —**voy′ag•er**, *n.*

vul′can•ize′, *v.*, **-ized, -izing.** treat rubber with sulfur and heat. —**vul′can•i•za′tion**, *n.* —**vul′can•iz′er**, *n.*

vul′gar, *adj.* 1. lacking good breeding or taste; unrefined. 2. indecent; obscene. 3. plebeian. 4. vernacular. —**vul′gar•ly**, *adv.* —**vul•gar′i•ty**, *n.*

vul′ner•a•ble, *adj.* 1. liable to physical or emotional hurt. 2. open to attack. —**vul′ner•a•bly**, *adv.* —**vul′ner•a•bil′i•ty**, *n.*

vul′ture, *n.* large, carrion-eating bird.

vul′va, *n.* external female genitals.

vy′ing, *adj.* competing.

W, w, *n.* twenty-third letter of English alphabet.

wab′ble, *v.*, **-bled, -bling**, *n.* wobble.

wad, *n., v.*, **wadded, wadding.** —*n.* 1. small soft mass. —*v.* 2. form into wad. 3. stuff.

wad′dle, *v.*, **-dled, -dling**, *n.* —*v.* 1. sway in walking, as duck. —*n.* 2. waddling gait.

wade, *v.*, **waded, wading**, *n.* —*v.* 1. walk through water, sand, etc. —*n.* 2. act of wading. —**wad′er**, *n.*

wa′fer, *n.* 1. thin crisp biscuit. 2. small disk of bread used in Eucharist.

waf′fle, *n.* batter cake baked in a double griddle (**waffle iron**).

waft, *v.* 1. float through air or over water. —*n.* 2. sound, odor, etc., wafted.

wag, *v.*, **wagged, wagging**, *n.* —*v.* 1. move rapidly back and forth. —*n.* 2. act of wagging. 3. joker. —**wag′gish**, *adj.*

wage, *n., v.*, **waged, waging.** —*n.* 1. pay; salary. 2. recompense. —*v.* 3. carry on (war, etc.).

wa′ger, *v., n.* bet.

wag′gle, *v.*, **-gled, -gling**, *n.* wag.

wag′on, *n.* four-wheeled vehicle for drawing heavy loads. Also, *Brit.*, **wag′gon.**

waif, *n.* homeless child.

wail, *n.* 1. long mournful cry. —*v.* 2. utter wails. —**wail′er**, *n.*

wain′scot, *n., v.*, **-scoted, -scoting.** —*n.* 1. woodwork lining wall. —*v.* 2. line with wainscot.

waist, *n.* 1. part of body between ribs and hips. 2. garment or part of garment for upper part of body. —**waist′line′**, *n.*

waist′coat′ (wes′kət), *n. Brit.* man's vest.

wait, *v.* 1. stay in expectation. 2. be ready. 3. await. 4. wait on; serve. —*n.* 5. act of waiting. 6. delay. 7. ambush.

wait′er, *n.* man who waits on table. —**wait′ress**, *n.fem.*

waive, *v.*, **waived, waiving.** give up; forgo.

waiv′er, *n.* statement of relinquishment.

wake, *v.*, **waked** or **woke, waked, waking**, *n.* —*v.* 1. stop sleeping; rouse from sleep. —*n.* 2. vigil, esp. beside corpse. 3. track or path, esp. of vessel.

wake′ful, *adj.* awake; alert. —**wake′ful•ly**, *adv.* —**wake′ful•ness**, *n.*

wak′en, *v.* wake.

wale, *n., v.*, **waled, waling.** —*n.* 1. mark left on skin by rod or whip. —*v.* 2. mark with wales.

walk, *v.* 1. go or traverse on foot. 2. cause to walk. —*n.* 3. act, course, or

manner of walking. 4. branch of activity. 5. sidewalk or path. —**walk′er**, *n.*

walk′ie-talk′ie, *n.* portable radio transmitter and receiver.

wall, *n.* 1. upright structure that divides, encloses, etc. —*v.* 2. enclose, divide, etc., with wall.

wall′board′, *n.* artificial material used to make or cover walls, etc.

wal′let, *n.* small flat case for paper money, etc.

wall′flow′er, *n.* perennial plant with fragrant flowers.

wal′lop, *Informal.* —*v.* 1. thrash or defeat. —*n.* 2. blow.

wal′low, *v.* 1. lie or roll in mud, etc. —*n.* 2. place where animals wallow.

wall′pa′per, *n.* decorative paper for covering walls and ceilings.

wal′nut′, *n.* northern tree valued for wood and edible nut.

wal′rus, *n.* large tusked mammal of Arctic seas.

waltz, *n.* 1. dance in triple rhythm. —*v.* 2. dance a waltz. —**waltz′er**, *n.*

wam′pum, *n.* shell beads, formerly used by North American Indians for money and ornament.

wan, *adj.* pale; worn-looking. —**wan′ly**, *adv.*

wand, *n.* slender rod or shoot.

wan′der, *v.* move aimlessly; stray. **—wan′der•er,** *n.*

wan′der•lust′, *n.* desire to travel.

wane, *v.,* **waned, waning,** *n.* —*v.* 1. (of moon) decrease periodically. 2. decline or decrease. —*n.* 3. decline or decrease.

want, *v.* 1. feel need or desire for. 2. lack; be deficient in. —*n.* 3. desire or need. 4. lack. 5. poverty.

want′ing, *adj., prep.* lacking.

wan′ton, *adj.* 1. malicious; unjustifiable. 2. lewd. —*n.* 3. loose woman. —*v.* 4. act in wanton manner. **—wan′ton•ly,** *adv.* **—wan′ton•ness,** *n.*

war, *n., v.,* **warred, warring,** *adj.* —*n.* 1. armed conflict. —*v.* 2. carry on war. —*adj.* 3. of, for, or due to war.

war′ble, *v.,* **-bled, -bling,** *n.* —*v.* 1. sing with trills, etc., as birds. —*n.* 2. warbled song.

war′bler, *n.* small songbird.

ward, *n.* 1. division of city. 2. division of hospital. 3. person under legal care of guardian or court. 4. custody. —*v.* 5. **ward off,** repel or avert.

ward′en, *n.* 1. keeper. 2. administrative head of prison.

ward′er, *n.* guard.

ward′robe′, *n.* 1. stock of clothes. 2. clothes closet.

ward′room′, *n.* living quarters for ship's officers other than captain.

ware, *n.* 1. (*pl.*) goods. 2. pottery. 3. vessels for domestic use.

ware′house′, *n., v.,* **-housed, -housing.** —*n.* 1. (wâr′hous′). storehouse for goods. —*v.* (-houz′). 2. store in warehouse.

war′fare′, *n.* waging of war.

war′like′, *adj.* waging or prepared for war.

warm, *adj.* 1. having, giving, or feeling moderate heat. 2. cordial. 3. lively. 4. kind; affectionate. —*v.* 5. make or become warm. **—warm′er,** *n.* **—warm′ly,** *adv.* **—warm′ness, warmth,** *n.*

war′mong′er, *n.* person who advocates or incites war.

warn, *v.* 1. give notice of danger, evil, etc. 2. caution. **—warn′ing,** *n., adj.* **—warn′ing•ly,** *adv.*

warp, *v.* 1. bend out of shape; distort. 2. guide by ropes. —*n.* 3. bend or twist. 4. lengthwise threads in loom.

war′rant, *n.* 1. justification. 2. guarantee. 3. document certifying or authorizing something. —*v.* 4. authorize or justify. 5. guarantee. **—war′rant•a•ble,** *adj.*

warrant officer, military officer between enlisted and commissioned grades.

war′ran•ty, *n., pl.* **-ties.** guarantee.

war′ren, *n.* place where rabbits live.

war′ri•or, *n.* soldier.

war′ship′, *n.* ship for combat.

wart, *n.* small hard elevation on skin. **—wart′y,** *adj.*

war′y (wâr′ē), *adj.,* **warier, wariest.** watchful; careful. **—war′i•ly,** *adv.* **—war′i•ness,** *n.*

was, *v.* first and third pers. sing., past indicative of **be.**

wash, *v.* 1. cleanse in or with water. 2. flow over. 3. carry in flowing. 4. cover thinly. —*n.* 5. act of washing. 6. clothes, etc., to be washed. 7. liquid covering. 8. rough water or air behind moving ship or plane. **—wash′a•ble,** *adj.* **—wash′board′,** *n.* **—wash′bowl′,** *n.* **—wash′cloth′,** *n.* **—wash′stand′,** *n.* **—wash′room′,** *n.*

wash′er, *n.* 1. machine for washing. 2. flat ring of rubber, metal, etc., to give tightness.

wash′out′, *n.* 1. destruction from action of water. 2. *Slang.* failure.

wasn′t, contraction of **was not.**

wasp, *n.* 1. stinging insect. 2. *Slang.* (*cap.* or *caps.*) white Anglo-Saxon Protestant.

wasp′ish, *adj.* irritable; snappish.

was′sail (wos′əl), *n.* 1. drinking party. 2. toast (def. 2).

waste, *v.,* **wasted, wasting,** *n., adj.* —*v.* 1. squander. 2. fail to use. 3. destroy gradually. 4. become wasted. —*n.* 5. useless expenditure. 6. neglect. 7. gradual decay. 8. devastation. 9. anything left over. —*adj.* 10. not used. 11. left over or worthless. **—waste′ful,** *adj.* **—waste′bas′ket,** *n.* **—waste′pa′per,** *n.*

wast′rel (wās′trəl), *n.* 1. spendthrift. 2. idler.

watch, *v.* 1. look attentively. 2. be careful. 3. guard. —*n.* 4. close, constant observation. 5. guard. 6. period of watching. 7. *Naut.* period of duty. 8. small timepiece. **—watch′er,** *n.* **—watch′ful,** *adj.* **—watch′man,** *n.*

watch′word′, *n.* 1. password. 2. slogan.

wa′ter, *n.* 1. transparent liquid forming rivers, seas, lakes, rain, etc. 2. surface of water. 3. liquid solution. 4. liquid organic secretion. —*v.* 5. moisten or supply with water. 6. di-

lute. 7. discharge water. —*adj.* 8. of, for, or powered by water.

wa′ter•bed′, *n.* water-filled plastic bag used as bed.

water closet, room containing flush toilet.

wa′ter•col′or, *n.* pigment mixed with water.

wa′ter•fall′, *n.* steep fall of water.

water glass, 1. vessel for drinking. 2. sodium silicate.

wa′ter•ing place, resort by water or having mineral springs.

wat′er•lil′y, *n. pl.* **-ies.** aquatic plant with showy flowers.

wa′ter-logged′, *adj.* filled or soaked with water.

wa′ter•mark′, *n.* 1. mark showing height reached by river, etc. 2. manufacturer's design impressed in paper. —*v.* 3. put watermark in (paper).

wa′ter•mel′on, *n.* large sweet juicy fruit of a vine.

wa′ter•proof′, *adj.* 1. impervious to water. —*v.* 2. make waterproof.

wa′ter•shed′, *n.* 1. area drained by river, etc. 2. high land dividing such areas.

wa′ter•spout′, *n.* tornadolike storm over lake or ocean.

wa′ter•way′, *n.* body of water as route of travel.

water wheel, wheel turned by water to provide power.

wa′ter•works′, *n.pl.* apparatus for collecting and distributing water, as for city.

wa′ter•y, *adj.* of, like, or full of water. **—wa′ter•i•ness,** *n.*

watt, *n.* unit of electric power. **—watt′age,** *n.*

wat′tle, *n.* 1. flesh hanging from throat or chin. 2. interwoven rods and twigs.

wave, *n., v.,* **waved, waving.** —*n.* 1. ridge on surface of liquid. 2. surge; rush. 3. curve. 4. vibration, as in transmission of sound, etc. 5. sign with moving hand, flag, etc. —*v.* 6. move with waves. 7. curve. 8. signal by wave. **—wav′y,** *adj.*

wa′ver, *v.* 1. sway. 2. hesitate. 3. fluctuate.

wax, *n.* 1. yellowish substance secreted by bees. 2. any similar substance. —*v.* 3. rub with wax. 4. (esp. of moon) increase. 5. become. **—wax′en,** *adj.* **—wax′er,** *n.* **—wax′y,** *adj.*

wax′wing′, *n.* small crested bird.

way, *n*. 1. manner; fashion. 2. plan; means. 3. direction. 4. road or route. 5. custom. 6. (*pl.*) timbers on which ship is built.

way'bill', *n*. list of goods with shipping directions.

way'far'er, *n*. rover.

way•lay', *v*. ambush.

way'side', *n*. 1. side of road. —*adj*. 2. beside road.

way'ward, *adj*. capricious. —**way'ward•ness**, *n*.

we, *pron*. nominative plural of **I**.

weak, *adj*. 1. not strong; fragile; frail. 2. deficient. —**weak'en**, *v*. —**weak'ness**, *n*.

weak'ling, *n*. weak creature.

weak'ly, *adj.*, **-lier, -liest**, *adv*. —*adj*. 1. sickly. —*adv*. 2. in weak manner.

weal, *n*. *Archaic*. well-being.

wealth, *n*. 1. great possessions or riches. 2. profusion. —**wealth'y**, *adj*.

wean, *v*. 1. accustom to food other than mother's milk. 2. detach from obsession or vice.

weap'on, *n*. instrument for use in fighting.

weap'on•ry, *n*. weapons collectively.

wear, *v*., **wore, worn, wearing**, *n*. —*v*. 1. have on body for covering or ornament. 2. impair or diminish gradually. 3. weary. 4. undergo wear. 5. last under use. —*n*. 6. use of garment. 7. clothing. 8. gradual impairment or diminution. —**wear'a•ble**, *adj*. —**wear'er**, *n*.

wea'ri•some, *adj*. 1. tiring. 2. tedious.

wea'ry, *adj.*, **-rier, -riest**, *v.*, **-ried, -rying**. —*adj*. 1. tired. 2. tedious. —*v*. 3. tire. —**wea'ri•ly**, *adv*. —**wea'ri•ness**, *n*.

wea'sel, *n*. small carnivorous animal.

weath'er, *n*. 1. state of atmosphere as to moisture, temperature, etc. —*v*. 2. expose to weather. 3. withstand. —*adj*. 4. of or on windward side.

weath'er•beat'en, *adj*. worn or marked by weather.

weath'er•vane', *n*. device to show direction of wind.

weave, *v*., **wove, woven** or **wove, weaving**, *n*. —*v*. 1. interlace, as to form cloth. 2. take winding course. —*n*. 3. manner of weaving. —**weav'er**, *n*.

web, *n.*, *v.*, **webbed, webbing**. —*n*. 1. something woven. 2. fabric spun by spiders. 3. membrane between toes in ducks, etc. —*v*. 4. cover with web. —**webbed'**, *adj*. —**web'bing**, *n*.

web'foot', *n*. foot with webbed toes. —**web'foot'ed**, *adj*.

wed, *v.*, **wedded, wedded** or **wed, wedding**. 1. bind or join in marriage. 2. attach firmly.

wed'ding, *n*. marriage ceremony.

wedge, *n.*, *v.*, **wedged, wedging**. —*n*. 1. angled object for splitting. —*v*. 2. split with wedge. 3. thrust or force like wedge.

wed'lock, *n*. matrimony.

Wednes'day, *n*. fourth day of week.

wee, *adj*. tiny.

weed, *n*. 1. useless plant growing in cultivated ground. 2. (*pl.*) mourning garments. —*v*. 3. free from weeds. 4. remove as undesirable. —**weed'er**, *n*. —**weed'y**, *adj*.

week, *n*. 1. seven successive days. 2. working part of week.

week'day', *n*. any day but Sunday. —**week'day'**, *adj*.

week'end', *n*. 1. Saturday and Sunday. —*adj*. 2. of or for weekend.

week'ly, *adj.*, *adv.*, *n.*, *pl.* **-lies**. —*adj*. 1. happening, appearing, etc., once a week. 2. lasting a week. —*adv*. 3. once a week. 4. by the week. —*n*. 5. weekly periodical.

weep, *v.*, **wept, weeping**. 1. shed tears. 2. mourn. —**weep'er**, *n*.

wee'vil, *n*. beetle destructive to grain, fruit, etc. —**wee'vi•ly**, *adj*.

weft, *n*. threads interlacing with warp.

weigh, *v*. 1. measure heaviness of. 2. burden. 3. consider. 4. lift. 5. have heaviness. —**weigh'er**, *n*.

weight, *n*. 1. amount of heaviness. 2. system of units for expressing weight. 3. heavy mass. 4. pressure. 5. burden. 6. importance. —*v*. 7. add weight to. —**weight'y**, *adj*. —**weight'i•ly**, *adv*. —**weight'less**, *adj*.

weird, *adj*. uncannily strange. —**weird'ly**, *adv*. —**weird'ness**, *n*.

wel'come, *n.*, *v.*, **-comed, -coming**, *adj*. —*n*. 1. friendly reception. —*v*. 2. receive or greet with pleasure. —*adj*. 3. gladly received. 4. given cordial right.

weld, *v*. 1. unite, esp. by heating and pressing. —*n*. 2. welded joint. —**weld'er**, *n*.

wel'fare', *n*. 1. well-being. 2. provision of benefits to poor.

well, *adv.*, *compar.* **better**, *superl.* **best**, *adj.*, *n.*, *v*. —*adv*. 1. excellently; properly. 2. thoroughly. —*adj*. 3. in good health. 4. good; proper. —*n*. 5. hole made in earth to reach water,

oil, etc. 6. source. 7. vertical shaft. —*v*. 8. rise or gush.

well'-be'ing, *n*. good or prosperous condition.

well'born', *adj*. of good family.

well'-bred', *adj*. showing good manners.

well'-mean'ing, *adj*. intending good. —**well'-meant'**, *adj*.

well'-nigh', *adv*. nearly.

well'-off', *adj*. 1. in good or favorable condition. 2. prosperous.

well'spring', *n*. source.

well'-to-do', *adj*. prosperous.

welt, *n*. 1. wale from lash. 2. strip around edge of shoe. 3. narrow border along seam. —*v*. 4. put welt on.

wel'ter, *v*. 1. roll, as waves. 2. wallow.

wen, *n*. small cyst.

wench, *n*. girl.

wend, *v.*, **wended, wending**. *Archaic*. go.

went, *v*. pt. of **go**.

were, *v*. past plural and pres. subjunctive of **be**.

weren't, contraction of **were not**.

were'wolf' (wēr'-), *n.*, *pl.* **-wolves**. (in folklore) human turned into wolf.

west, *n*. 1. point of compass opposite east. 2. direction of this point. 3. area in this direction. —*adj*. 4. toward, from, or in west. —*adv*. 5. toward or from west. —**west'er•ly**, *adj.*, *adv*. —**west'ern**, *adj*. —**west'ern•er**, *n*.

west'ward, *adj*. 1. moving or facing west. —*adv*. 2. Also, **west'wards**. toward west. —*n*. 3. westward part. —**west'ward•ly**, *adj.*, *adv*.

wet, *adj.*, **wetter, wettest**, *n.*, *v.*, **wet** or **wetted, wetting**. —*adj*. 1. covered or soaked with water. 2. rainy. —*n*. 3. moisture. —*v*. 4. make or become wet. —**wet'ness**, *n*.

wet'land', *n*. low land with usu. wet soil.

whack, *Informal*. *v*. 1. strike sharply. —*n*. 2. smart blow.

whale, *n.*, *pl.* **whales** or **whale**, *v.*, **whaled, whaling**. —*n*. 1. large fishlike marine mammal. —*v*. 2. kill and render whales. —**whal'er**, *n*.

whale'bone', *n*. elastic horny substance in upper jaw of some whales.

wharf, *n.*, *pl.* **wharves**. structure for mooring vessels.

wharf'age, *n*. 1. use of wharf. 2. charge for such use.

what, *pron.*, *pl.* **what**, *adv*. —*pron*. 1. which one? 2. that which. 3. such. —*adv*. 4. how much. 5. partly.

what•ev′er, *pron.* 1. anything that. 2. no matter what. —*adj.* 3. no matter what.

what′not′, *n.* small open cupboard, esp. for knickknacks.

wheal, *n.* swelling, as from mosquito bite.

wheat, *n.* grain of common cereal grass, used esp. for flour.

whee′dle, *v.,* **-dled, -dling.** influence by artful persuasion.

wheel, *n.* 1. round object turning on axis. —*v.* 2. turn on axis. 3. move on wheels. 4. turn.

wheel′bar′row, *n.* one-wheeled vehicle lifted at one end.

wheel′base′, *n. Auto.* distance between centers of front and rear wheel hubs.

wheeze, *v.,* **wheezed, wheezing,** *n.* —*v.* 1. whistle in breathing. —*n.* 2. wheezing breath. 3. trite saying.

whelm, *v.* 1. engulf. 2. overwhelm.

whelp, *n.* 1. young of dog, wolf, bear, etc. —*v.* 2. bring forth whelps.

when, *adv.* 1. at what time. —*conj.* 2. at time that. 3. and then.

whence, *adv., conj.* from what place.

when•ev′er, *adv.* at whatever time.

where, *adv.* 1. in, at, or to what place? 2. in what respect? —*conj.* 3. in, at, or to what place. 4. and there.

where′a•bouts′, *adv.* 1. where. —*n.* 2. location.

where•as′, *conj.* 1. while on the contrary. 2. considering that.

where′fore′, *adv., conj.* 1. why; for what. —*n.* 2. reason.

where•of′, *adv., conj.* of what.

where′up•on′, *conj.* 1. upon which. 2. at or after which.

wher•ev′er, *conj.* at or to whatever place.

where′with•al′, *n.* means.

whet, *v.,* **whetted, whetting.** sharpen. —**whet′stone′,** *n.*

wheth′er, *conj.* (word introducing alternative.)

whey (hwā), *n.* watery part that separates out when milk curdles.

which, *pron.* 1. what one? 2. the one that. —*adj.* 3. what one of (those mentioned).

which•ev′er, *pron.* any that.

whiff, *n.* 1. slight puff or blast. —*v.* 2. blow in whiffs.

while, *n., conj., v.,* **whiled, whiling.** —*n.* 1. time. —*conj.* 2. in time that. —*v.* 3. pass (time) pleasantly.

whim, *n.* irrational or fanciful decision or idea.

whim′per, *v.* 1. cry softly and plaintively. —*n.* 2. whimpering cry. —**whim′per•er,** *n.*

whim′sy, *n., pl.* **-sies.** fanciful idea; whim. —**whim′si•cal,** *adj.* —**whim′si•cal′i•ty,** *n.* —**whim′si•cal•ly,** *adv.*

whine, *n., v.,* **whined, whining.** —*n.* 1. low complaining sound. —*v.* 2. utter whines. —**whin′er,** *n.* —**whin′ing•ly,** *adv.*

whin′ny, *v.,* **-nied, -nying,** *n., pl.* **-nies.** neigh.

whip, *v.,* **whipped** or **whipt, whipping,** *n.* —*v.* 1. strike repeatedly; flog. 2. jerk; seize. 3. cover with thread; overcast. 4. beat (cream, etc.). 5. move quickly; lash about. —*n.* 6. instrument with lash and handle for striking. 7. party manager in legislature. —**whip′per,** *n.*

whip′cord′, *n.* fabric with diagonal ribs.

whip′per•snap′per, *n.* insignificant, presumptuous person, esp. young one.

whip′pet, *n.* small swift dog.

whip′poor•will′, *n.* nocturnal American bird.

whir, *v.,* **whirred, whirring,** *n.* —*v.* 1. move with buzzing sound. —*n.* 2. such sound. Also, **whirr.**

whirl, *v.* 1. spin or turn rapidly. 2. move quickly. —*n.* 3. whirling movement. 4. round of events, etc. —**whirl′er,** *n.*

whirl′i•gig′, *n.* toy revolving in wind.

whirl′pool′, *n.* whirling current in water.

whirl′wind′, *n.* whirling mass of air.

whisk, *v.* 1. sweep up. 2. move or carry lightly. —*n.* 3. act of whisking.

whisk′er, *n.* 1. (*pl.*) hair on man's face. 2. bristle on face of cat, etc.

whis′key, *n., pl.* **-keys.** distilled alcoholic liquor made from grain or corn. Also, **whis′ky.**

whis′per, *v.* 1. speak very softly. —*n.* 2. sound of whispering. 3. something whispered. —**whis′per•er,** *n.*

whist, *n.* card game.

whis′tle, *v.,* **-tled, -tling,** *n.* —*v.* 1. make clear shrill sound with breath, air, or steam. —*n.* 2. device for making such sounds. 3. sound of whistling. —**whis′tler,** *n.*

whit, *n.* particle; bit.

white, *adj.* 1. of color of snow. 2. having light skin. 3. pale. —*n.* 4. color without hue, opposite to black. 5. Caucasian. 6. white or light part. —**whit′en,** *v.* —**white′ness,** *n.* —**whit′ish,** *adj.*

white elephant, useless, expensive possession.

white′fish′, *n.* small food fish.

white′wash′, *n.* 1. substance for whitening walls, etc. —*v.* 2. cover with whitewash.

whith′er, *adv., conj. Archaic.* where; to what (which) place.

whit′ing, *n.* 1. small Atlantic food fish. 2. ground chalk used to whiten.

whit′low, *n.* inflammation on finger or toe.

Whit′sun•day, *n.* seventh Sunday after Easter.

whit′tle, *v.,* **-tled, -tling.** 1. cut bit by bit with knife. 2. reduce. —**whit′tler,** *n.*

whiz, *v.,* **whizzed, whizzing,** *n.* —*v.* 1. move with hum or hiss. —*n.* 2. whizzing sound. Also, **whizz.**

who, *pron.* 1. what person? 2. the person that.

whoa, *interj.* stop!

who•ev′er, *pron.* anyone that.

whole, *adj.* 1. entire; undivided. 2. undamaged. 3. *Math.* not fractional. —*n.* 4. entire amount or extent. 5. complete thing. —**whol′ly,** *adv.* —**whole′ness,** *n.*

whole′-heart′ed, *adj.* sincere.

whole′sale′, *n., adj., v.,* **-saled, -saling.** —*n.* 1. sale of goods in quantity, as to retailers. —*adj.* 2. of or engaged in wholesale. —*v.* 3. sell by wholesale. —**whole′sal′er,** *n.*

whole′some, *adj.* beneficial; healthful. —**whole′some•ly,** *adv.* —**whole′some•ness,** *n.*

whom, *pron.* objective case of **who.**

whoop, *n.* 1. loud shout or cry. 2. gasping sound characteristic of whooping cough. —*v.* 3. utter whoops.

whore (hōr), *n., v.,* **whored, whoring.** —*n.* 1. prostitute. —*v.* 2. consort with whores.

whorl, *n.* 1. circular arrangement as of leaves. 2. any spiral part.

whose, *pron.* possessive case of **who.**

who′so•ev′er, *pron.* whoever.

why, *adv., n., pl.* **whys.** —*adv.* 1. for what reason. —*n.* 2. cause or reason.

wick, *n.* soft threads that absorb fuel to be burned in candle, etc.

wick′ed, *adj.* 1. evil; sinful. 2. naughty. —**wick′ed•ly,** *adv.* —**wick′ed•ness,** *n.*

wick′er, *n.* 1. slender pliant twig. —*adj.* 2. made of wicker. —**wick′er•work′,** *n.*

wick′et, *n.* 1. small gate or opening. 2. framework in cricket and croquet.

wide, *adj.,* **wider, widest,** *adv.* —*adj.* 1. broad. 2. extensive. 3. expanded. 4. far. —*adv.* 5. far. 6. to farthest extent. —**wide′ly,** *adv.* —**wid′en,** *v.* —**wide′ness,** *n.*

wide′spread′, *adj.* occurring widely.

widg′eon, *n.* fresh-water duck.

wid′ow, *n.* 1. woman whose husband has died. —*v.* 2. make widow of. —**wid′ow•er,** *n.masc.* —**wid′ow•hood,** *n.*

width, *n.* 1. breadth. 2. piece of full wideness.

wield, *v.* 1. exercise (power, etc.). 2. brandish. —**wield′er,** *n.* —**wield′y,** *adj.*

wie′ner, *n.* small sausage; frankfurter.

wife, *n.,* *pl.* **wives,** married woman. —**wife′ly,** *adj.*

wig, *n.* artificial covering of hair for head.

wig′gle, *v.,* **-gled, -gling,** *n.* —*v.* 1. twist to and fro; wriggle. —*n.* 2. wiggling movement. —**wig′gly,** *adj.* —**wig′gler,** *n.*

wig′wag′, *v.,* **-wagged, -wagging,** *n.* —*v.* 1. signal in code with flags, etc. —*n.* 2. such signaling. 3. message so sent.

wig′wam (-wom), *n.* American Indian hut.

wild, *adj.* 1. not cultivated. 2. uncivilized. 3. violent. 4. uninhabited. 5. disorderly. —*adv.* 6. wildly. —*n.* 7. uncultivated or desolate tract. —**wild′ly,** *adv.* —**wild′ness,** *n.*

wild′cat′, *n.,* *v.,* **-catted, -catting.** —*n.* 1. large North American feline. —*v.* 2. prospect independently.

wil′der•ness, *n.* wild or desolate region.

wild′life′, *n.* animals living in nature.

wile, *n.* cunning; artifice.

will, *n.,* *v.,* **willed, willing.** —*n.* 1. power of conscious action or choice. 2. wish; pleasure. 3. attitude, either hostile or friendly. 4. declaration of wishes for disposition of property after death. —*v.* 5. decide to influence by act of will. 6. consent to. 7. give by will. —*auxiliary verb.* 8. am (is, are) about to. 9. am (is, are) willing to.

will′ful, *adj.* 1. intentional. 2. headstrong. Also, **wil′ful.** —**will′ful•ly,** *adv.* —**will′ful•ness,** *n.*

will′ing, *adj.* 1. consenting. 2. cheerfully done, given, etc. —**will′ing•ly,** *adv.* —**will′ing•ness,** *n.*

will′-o′-the-wisp′, *n.* 1. flitting, elusive light. 2. something that fascinates and deludes.

wil′low, *n.* slender tree or shrub with tough, pliant branches.

wil′low•y, *adj.* tall and slender. —**wil′low•i•ness,** *n.*

wil′ly-nil′ly, *adv.* willingly or unwillingly.

wilt, *v.* 1. wither or droop. —*n.* 2. wilted state.

wil′y, *adj.,* **wilier, wiliest.** crafty; cunning. —**wil′i•ness,** *n.*

win, *v.,* **won, winning.** 1. succeed or get by effort. 2. gain (victory). 3. persuade.

wince, *v.,* **winced, wincing,** *n.* —*v.* 1. shrink, as from pain or blow. —*n.* 2. wincing movement.

winch, *n.* 1. windlass. 2. crank.

wind (wind *for* 1–7; wīnd *for* 8–11), *n.,* *v.,* **winded** (for 5–7) or **wound** (wound) (for 8–11), **winding.** —*n.* 1. air in motion. 2. gas in stomach or bowels. 3. animal odor. 4. breath. —*v.* 5. make short of breath. 6. let recover breath. 7. expose to wind. 8. change direction. 9. encircle. 10. roll into cylinder or ball. 11. turn (handle, etc.). —**wind′y,** *adj.* —**wind′er,** *n.*

wind′break′, *n.* shelter from wind.

wind′ed, *adj.* 1. having wind. 2. out of breath.

wind′fall′, *n.* 1. something blown down. 2. unexpected luck.

wind instrument, musical instrument sounded by breath or air.

wind′lass (-ləs), *n.* drum mechanism for hoisting.

wind′mill′, *n.* mill operated by wind.

win′dow, *n.* opening for air and light, usually fitted with glass in frame.

wind′pipe′, *n.* trachea.

wind′shield′, *n.* glass shield above automobile, etc., dashboard.

wind′up′ (wīnd′-), *n.* close; end.

wind′ward, *n.* 1. quarter from which wind blows. —*adj.* 2. of, in, or to windward. —*adv.* 2. against wind.

wine, *n.,* *v.,* **wined, wining.** —*n.* 1. fermented juice, esp. of grape. 2. dark purplish red. —*v.* 3. entertain with wine. —**win′y,** *adj.*

win′er•y, *n.,* *pl.* **-eries.** place for making wine.

wing, *n.* 1. organ of flight in birds, insects, and bats. 2. winglike or projecting structure. 3. flight. 4. supporting surface of airplane. —*v.* 5. travel on wings. 6. wound in wing or arm. —**wing′ed,** *adj.*

wink, *v.* 1. close and open (eye) quickly. 2. signal by winking. 3. twinkle. —*n.* 4. winking movement.

win′ner, *n.* one that wins.

win′ning, *n.* 1. (*pl.*) that which is won. —*adj.* 2. charming. —**win′ning•ly,** *adv.*

win′now, *v.* 1. free from chaff by wind. 2. separate.

win′some, *adj.* sweetly or innocently charming. —**win′some•ly,** *adv.* —**win′some•ness,** *n.*

win′ter, *n.* 1. last season of year. —*adj.* 2. of, like, or for winter. —*v.* 3. pass winter. 4. keep during winter. —**win′try, win′ter•y,** *adj.*

win′ter•green′, *n.* creeping aromatic shrub.

wipe, *v.,* **wiped, wiping,** *n.* —*v.* 1. rub lightly. 2. remove or blot. —*n.* 3. act of wiping. —**wip′er,** *n.*

wire, *n.,* *adj.,* *v.,* **wired, wiring.** —*n.* 1. slender, flexible piece of metal. 2. *Informal.* telegram or telegraph. —*adj.* 3. made of wires. —*v.* 4. bind with wire. 5. *Elect.* install system of wires in. 6. *Informal.* telegraph.

wire′less, *adj.* 1. activated by electromagnetic waves rather than wires. —*n.* 2. *Brit.* radio.

wire′tap′, *v.,* **-tapped, -tapping,** *n.* —*v.* 1. connect secretly into telephone. —*n.* 2. act of wiretapping.

wir′y, *adj.* like wire; lean and strong. —**wir′i•ness,** *n.*

wis′dom, *n.* 1. knowledge and judgment. 2. wise sayings.

wisdom tooth, last tooth to erupt.

wise, *adj.* 1. having knowledge and judgment. 2. prudent. 3. informed. —*n.* 4. way; respect. —**wise′ly,** *adv.*

wish, *v.* 1. want; desire. 2. bid. —*n.* 3. desire. 4. that desired. —**wish′ful,** *adj.* —**wish′ful•ly,** *adv.*—**wish′ful•ness,** *n.*

wish′y-wash′y, *adj.* thin or weak.

wisp, *n.* small tuft. —**wisp′y,** *adj.*

wis•te′ri•a, *n.* climbing shrub with purple flowers. Also, **wis•tar′i•a.**

wist′ful, *adj.* 1. pensive. 2. longing. —**wist′ful•ly,** *adv.* —**wist′ful•ness,** *n.*

wit, *n.* 1. power of combining perception with clever expression. 2. person having this. 3. (*pl.*) intelligence. —*v.* 4. *Archaic.* know. 5. **to wit,** namely.

witch, *n.* 1. woman thought to practice magic. 2. *Slang.* bitch: a euphemism. —**witch′craft′,** *n.*

witch′er•y, *n.,* *pl.* **-eries.** 1. magic. 2. charm.

witch hazel, preparation for bruises, etc.

witch′ing, *adj.* suitable for sorcery.

with, *prep.* 1. accompanied by. 2. using. 3. against.

with•draw′, *v.,* **-drew, -drawn, -drawing.** 1. draw back. 2. retract. **—with•draw′al,** *n.*

with′er, *v.* shrivel; fade. **—with′er•ing•ly,** *adv.*

with′ers, *n.pl.* part of animal's back just behind neck.

with•hold′, *v.,* **-held, -holding.** hold or keep back.

with•in′, *adv.* 1. inside; inwardly. **—prep.** 2. in; inside of. 3. at point not beyond.

with•out′, *prep.* 1. lacking. 2. beyond. **—adv.** 3. outside. 4. outwardly. 5. lacking.

with•stand′, *v.,* **-stood, -standing.** resist.

wit′less, *adj.* stupid. **—wit′less•ly,** *adv.* **—wit′less•ness,** *n.*

wit′ness, *v.* 1. see. 2. testify. 3. attest by signature. **—n.** 4. person who witnesses. 5. testimony.

wit′ti•cism′, *n.* witty remark.

wit′ting, *adj.* knowing; aware. **—wit′ting•ly,** *adv.*

wit′ty, *adj.* showing wit. **—wit′ti•ly,** *adv.* **—wit′ti•ness,** *n.*

wive, *v.,* **wived, wiving.** marry.

wiz′ard, *n.* magician. **—wiz′ard•ry,** *n.*

wiz′ened (wiz′-), *adj.* shriveled.

wob′ble, *v.,* **-bled, -bling.** move unsteadily from side to side. **—wob′bly,** *adj.*

woe, *n.* grief or affliction. **—woe′ful,** *adj.* **—woe′ful•ly,** *adv.* **—woe′ful•ness,** *n.*

woe′be•gone′, *adj.* showing woe.

wok, *n.* Chinese cooking pan.

wolf, *n., pl.* **wolves,** *v.* **—n.** 1. wild carnivorous animal of dog family. **—v.** 2. *Informal.* eat ravenously. **—wolf′ish,** *adj.* **—wolf′ish•ly,** *adv.*

wolf′hound′, *n.* kind of hound.

wolf's′-bane′, *n.* poisonous plant.

wol′ver•ine′, *n.* North American mammal of weasel family.

wom′an, *n., pl.* **women.** female human being. **—wom′an•hood′,** *n.* **—wom′an•ish,** *adj.* **—wom′an•ly,** *adj.* **—wom′an•li•ness,** *n.*

womb (wo͞om), *n.* uterus.

won′der, *v.* 1. be curious about. 2. marvel. **—n.** 3. something strange. 4. Also, **won′der•ment.** amazement. **—won′der•ing•ly,** *adv.*

won′der•ful, *adj.* 1. exciting wonder. 2. excellent. **—won′der•ful•ly,** *adv.*

won′drous, *adj.* 1. wonderful. **—adv.** 2. remarkably. **—won′drous•ly,** *adv.*

wont (wunt, wŏnt), *adj.* 1. accustomed. **—n.** 2. habit. **—wont′ed,** *adj.*

won′t, contraction of **will not.**

woo, *v.* seek to win, esp. in marriage. **—woo′er,** *n.*

wood, *n.* 1. hard substance under bark of trees and shrubs. 2. timber or firewood. 3. (*often pl.*) forest. **—adj.** 4. made of wood. 5. living in woods. **—v.** 6. plant with trees. **—wood′craft′,** *n.* **—woods′man,** *n.* **—wood′y,** *adj.* **—wood′ed,** *adj.*

wood′bine′, *n.* any of various vines, as the honeysuckle.

wood′chuck′, *n.* bushy-tailed burrowing rodent. Also called **ground′hog′.**

wood′cut′, *n.* print made from a carved block of wood.

wood′en, *adj.* 1. made of wood. 2. without feeling or expression. **—wood′en•ly,** *adv.* **—wood′en•ness,** *n.*

wood′peck′er, *n.* bird with hard bill for boring.

woods′y, *adj.,* **-ier, -iest.** of or resembling woods.

wood′wind′, *n.* musical instrument of group including flute, clarinet, oboe, and bassoon.

wood′work′, *n.* wooden fittings inside building. **—wood′work′er,** *n.* **—wood′work′ing,** *n., adj.*

woof, *n.* 1. yarns from side to side in loom. 2. texture or fabric.

wool, *n.* 1. soft curly hair, esp. of sheep. 2. garments, yarn, etc., of wool. 3. curly, fine-stranded substance. **—wool′en** or (esp. *Brit.*) **wool′len,** *adj., n.* **—wool′ly,** *adj.* **—wool′li•ness,** *n.*

wool′gath′er•ing, *n.* daydreaming.

word, *n.* 1. group of letters or sounds that represents concept. 2. talk or conversation. 3. promise. 4. tidings. 5. (*pl.*) angry speech. **—v.** 6. express in words. **—word′less,** *adj.*

word′ing, *n.* way of expressing.

word processing, production of letters, reports, etc., using computers.

word′y, *adj.,* **wordier, wordiest.** using too many words. **—word′i•ness,** *n.*

work, *n., adj., v.,* **worked** or **wrought, working.** **—n.** 1. exertion; labor. 2. task. 3. employment. 4. materials on which one works. 5. result of work. 6. (*pl.*) industrial plant. **—adj.** 7. of or for work. **—v.** 8. do work. 9. operate successfully. 10. move or give. 11. solve. 12. excite. 13. ferment. **—work′a•ble,** *adj.* **—work′er,** *n.*

work′a•day′, *adj.* commonplace; uneventful.

work′house′, *n.* penal institution for minor offenders.

work′man, *n., pl.* **-men.** worker; laborer. Also, **work′ing•man′,** *fem.* **work′ing•wom′an.** **—work′man•like′,** *adj.* **—work′man•ship′,** *n.*

work′shop′, *n.* place where work is done.

world, *n.* 1. earth; globe. 2. particular part of earth. 3. things common to profession, etc.; milieu. 4. mankind. 5. universe. 6. great quantity.

world′ling, *n.* worldly person.

world′ly, *adj.,* **-lier, -liest.** 1. secular or earthly. 2. devoted to affairs of this world; sophisticated; shrewd. 3. of this world. **—world′li•ness,** *n.*

worm, *n.* 1. small slender creeping animal. 2. something suggesting worm, as screw thread. 3. (*pl.*) intestinal disorder. **—v.** 4. move like worm. 5. extract (secret) craftily. 6. free from worms. **—worm′y,** *adj.*

worm′wood′, *n.* bitter aromatic herb.

worn′-out′, *adj.* 1. exhausted. 2. destroyed by wear.

wor′ry, *v.,* **-ried, -rying,** *n., pl.* **-ries.** **—v.** 1. make or feel anxious. 2. seize with teeth and shake. **—n.** 3. anxiety. 4. cause of anxiety. **—wor′ri•er,** *n.* **—wor′ri•some,** *adj.*

worse, *adj.* 1. less good; less favorable. **—n.** 2. that which is worse. **—adv.** 3. in worse way. **—wors′en,** *v.*

wor′ship, *n., v.,* **-shiped, -shiping** or **-shipped, -shipping.** **—n.** 1. homage paid to God. 2. rendering of such homage. **—v.** 3. render religious reverence to. **—wor′ship•er,** *n.* **—wor′ship•ful,** *adj.*

worst, *adj.* 1. least satisfactory; least well. **—n.** 2. that which is worst. **—adv.** 3. in the worst way. **—v.** 4. defeat.

wor′sted (wŏos′tid), *n.* 1. firmly twisted wool yarn or thread. 2. fabric made of it.

wort (wûrt), *n.* malt infusion before fermentation.

worth, *adj.* 1. good enough to justify. 2. having value of. **—n.** 3. excellence; importance. 4. quantity of specified value. **—worth′less,** *adj.* **—worth′less•ness,** *n.*

worth'while', *adj.* repaying time and effort spent.

wor'thy, *adj.*, **-thier, -thiest**, *n.*, *pl.* **-thies**. —*adj.* 1. of adequate worth. 2. deserving. —*n.* 2. person of merit. —**wor'thi•ly**, *adv.* —**wor'thi•ness**, *n.*

would, *v.* past of **will** (defs. 8, 9).

would'-be', *adj.* wishing, pretending, or intended to be.

wound (wōōnd), *n.* 1. puncture from external violence. —*v.* 2. inflict wound. 3. grieve with insult or reproach.

wrack, *n.* ruin.

wraith, *n.* ghost.

wran'gle, *v.*, **-gled, -gling**, *n.* dispute. —**wran'gler**, *n.*

wrap, *v.*, **wrapped** or **wrapt, wrapping**, *n.* —*v.* 1. enclose; envelop. 2. wind or fold about. —*n.* 3. (*often pl.*) outdoor clothes.

wrap'per, *n.* 1. one that wraps. 2. Also, **wrapping**. outer cover. 3. long loose garment.

wrath, *n.* 1. stern or fierce anger. 2. vengeance. —**wrath'ful**, *adj.* —**wrath'ful•ly**, *adv.* —**wrath'y**, *adj.*

wreak, *v.* inflict.

wreath, *n.* circular band of leaves, etc.

wreathe, *v.*, **wreathed, wreathing.** encircle with wreath.

wreck, *n.* 1. anything reduced to ruins. 2. destruction. —*v.* 3. cause or suffer wreck. —**wreck'age**, *n.* —**wreck'er**, *n.*

wren, *n.* small active bird.

wrench, *v.* 1. twist forcibly. 2. injure by wrenching. —*n.* 3. wrenching movement. 4. tool for turning bolts, etc.

wrest, *v.* 1. twist violently. 2. get by effort. —*n.* 3. twist; wrench.

wres'tle, *v.*, **-tled, -tling**, *n.* —*v.* 1. contend with by trying to force other person down. —*n.* 2. this sport. 3. struggle. —**wres'tler**, *n.*

wretch, *n.* 1. pitiable person. 2. scoundrel.

wretch'ed, *adj.* 1. pitiable. 2. despicable. 3. pitiful. —**wretch'ed•ly**, *adv.* —**wretch'ed•ness**, *n.*

wrig'gle, *v.*, *n.* wiggle; squirm. —**wrig'gler**, *n.* —**wrig'gly**, *adj.*

wright, *n.* workman who builds.

wring, *v.*, **wrung, wringing**, *n.* —*v.* 1. twist or compress. 2. expel by wring-

ing. —*n.* 3. twist or squeeze. —**wring'er**, *n.*

wrin'kle, *n.*, *v.*, **-kled, -kling.** —*n.* 1. ridge or furrow. —*v.* 2. form wrinkles in. —**wrin'kly**, *adj.*

wrist, *n.* joint between hand and arm.

writ, *n.* 1. formal legal order. 2. writing.

write, *v.*, **wrote, written, writing.** 1. form (letters, etc.) by hand. 2. express in writing. 3. produce, as author or composer. —**writ'er**, *n.*

writhe, *v.*, **writhed, writhing**, *n.* —*v.* 1. twist, as in pain. —*n.* 2. writhing movement. —**writh'er**, *n.*

wrong, *adj.* 1. not right or good. 2. deviating from truth or fact. 3. not suitable. 4. under or inner (side). —*n.* 5. evil; injury; error. —*v.* 6. do wrong to. 7. misjudge. —**wrong'do'er**, *n.* —**wrong'do'ing**, *n.* —**wrong'ful**, *adj.* —**wrong'ly**, *adv.*

wroth (rôth), *adj.* angry.

wrought, *adj.* 1. worked. 2. shaped by beating.

wrought'-up', *adj.* perturbed.

wry, *adj.*, **wrier, wriest.** 1. twisted; distorted. 2. ironic. —**wry'ly**, *adv.* —**wry'ness**, *n.*

XYZ

X, x, *n.* 1. twenty-fourth letter of English alphabet. 2. those less than 17 years old not admitted: motion-picture classification.

xan'thic (zan'thik), *adj.* yellow.

xe'bec (zē'bek), *n.* three-masted vessel of Mediterranean.

Xmas, *n.* Christmas.

x'-ray', *n.* 1. highly penetrating type of electromagnetic ray, used esp. in medicine. —*v.* 2. photograph or treat with x-rays.

xy'lem (zī'lem), *n.* woody tissue of plants.

xy'lo•phone', *n.* musical instrument of wooden bars, played with small hammers. —**xy'lo•phon'ist**, *n.*

Y, y, *n.* twenty-fifth letter of English alphabet.

yacht, *n.* pleasure ship. —**yacht'ing**, *n.* —**yachts'man**, *n.*

ya'hoo, *n.* coarse stupid person.

yak, *n.* long-haired Tibetan ox.

yam, *n.* edible potatolike root.

yam'mer, *v. Informal.* whine or chatter.

yank, *v.* 1. pull suddenly; jerk. —*n.* 2. sudden pull; jerk.

Yan'kee, *n.* native or inhabitant of the United States, northern U.S., or New England.

yap, *v.*, **yapped, yapping**, *n.* yelp.

yard, *n.* 1. linear unit (3 feet). 2. long spar. 3. enclosed outdoor area, used as a lawn, etc.

yard'age, *n.* amount in yards.

yard'stick', *n.* 1. measuring stick one yard long. 2. criterion.

yarn, *n.* 1. many-stranded thread. 2. story.

yaw, *v.* 1. deviate. —*n.* 2. deviation.

yawl, *n.* small sailboat.

yawn, *v.* 1. open mouth wide involuntarily in sleepiness —*n.* 2. act of yawning.

yawp, *v.*, *n. Informal.* bawl.

y•clept' (ē-), *adj. Archaic.* named.

ye, *pron. Archaic.* 1. you. 2. the.

yea, *adv.*, *n.* yes.

year, *n.* period of 365 or 366 days. —**year'ly**, *adv.*, *adj.*

year'ling, *n.* animal one year old.

yearn, *v.* desire strongly. —**yearn'ing**, *adj.*, *n.*

yeast, *n.* yellowish substance, used to leaven bread, ferment liquor, etc.

yell, *v.* shout loudly.

yel'low, *n.* 1. color of butter, lemons, etc. —*adj.* 2. of or like yellow. 3. *Slang.* cowardly. —**yel'low•ish**, *adj.*

yellow fever, infectious tropical disease transmitted by certain mosquitoes. Also, **yellow jack.**

yellow jacket, yellow and black wasp.

yelp, *v.* 1. give sharp, shrill cry. —*n.* 2. such cry.

yen, *n. Informal.* desire.

yeo'man, *n.* 1. petty officer in navy. 2. independent farmer.

yes, *adv.*, *n.* expression of affirmation or assent.

yes'ter•day, *adv.*, *n.* day before today.

yet, *adv.* 1. so far; up to this (or that) time. 2. moreover. 3. still. 4. nevertheless. —*conj.* 5. but.

yew, *n.* evergreen coniferous tree.

Yid'dish, *n.* German-based Jewish language.

yield, *v.* 1. produce; give. 2. surrender. —*n.* 3. that which is yielded; product. —**yield′er,** *n.*

yip, *v.,* **yipped, yipping.** *Informal.* bark sharply.

yo′del, *v.* 1. sing with quick changes to and from falsetto. —*n.* 2. song yodeled.

yo′gi (-gē), *n.* Hindu practicing asceticism (**yo′ga**).

yo′gurt (-gərt), *n.* curdled milk product. Also, **yo′ghurt.**

yoke, *n., v.,* **yoked, yoking.** —*n.* 1. piece put across necks of oxen pulling cart, etc. 2. pair. —*v.* 3. couple with, or place in, yoke.

yo′kel, *n.* rustic.

yolk (yōk), *n.* yellow part of egg.

yon′der, *adj., adv. Archaic.* over there. Also, **yon.**

yore, *adv., adj. Archaic.* long ago.

you, *pron.* person or persons addressed.

young, *adj.* 1. in early stages of life, operation, etc. 2. of youth. —**young′ish,** *adj.*

young′ster, *n.* child.

your, *pron., adj.* possessive of **you;** (without noun following) **yours.**

you′re, contraction of **you are.**

your•self′, *pron.* emphatic or reflexive form of **you.**

youth, *n.* 1. young state. 2. early life. 3. young person or persons. —**youth′ful,** *adj.* —**youth′ful•ly,** *adv.* —**youth′ful•ness,** *n.*

yowl, *v., n.,* howl.

yu•an′ (yōō än′), *n.* Taiwanese dollar.

yuc′ca, *n.* tropical American plant.

yule, *n.* Christmas.

yule′tide′, *n.* Christmas season.

Z, z, *n.* twenty-sixth letter of English alphabet.

za′ny, *n., pl.* **-nies,** *adj.* **-nier, -niest.** —*n.* 1. clown. —*adj.* 2. silly. —**za′ni•ness,** *n.*

zap, *v.,* **zapped, zapping.** *Slang.* kill or defeat.

zeal, *n.* intense ardor or eagerness. —**zeal′ous** (zel′-), *adj.* —**zeal′ous•ly,** *adv.* —**zeal′ous•ness,** *n.*

zeal′ot (zel′-), *n.* excessively zealous person. —**zeal′ot•ry,** *n.*

ze′bra, *n.* wild, striped horselike animal.

ze′nith, *n.* 1. celestial point directly overhead. 2. highest point or state.

zeph′yr, *n.* mild breeze.

Zep′pe•lin, *n.* large dirigible of early 20th century.

ze′ro, *n., pl.* **zeroes.** 1. symbol (0) indicating nonquantity. 2. nothing. 3. starting point of a scale.

zero hour, starting time.

zest, *n.* something adding flavor, interest, etc. —**zest′ful,** *adj.* —**zest′ful•ly,** *adv.* —**zest′ful•ness,** *n.* —**zest′less,** *adj.*

zig′zag′, *n., adj., adv., v.,* **-zagged, -zagging.** —*n.* 1. line going sharply from side to side. —*adj., adv.* 2. with sharp turns back and forth. —*v.* 3. go in zigzag.

zinc, *n.* bluish metallic element. —**zinc′ous,** *adj.*

zinc oxide, salve made of zinc and oxygen.

zing, *n.* 1. sharp singing sound. —*v.* 2. make such sound. —*interj.* 3. (descriptive of such sound.)

zin′ni•a, *n.* bright, full-flowered plant.

Zi′on•ism′, *n.* advocacy of Jewish settlement of Palestine. —**Zi′on•ist,** *n., adj.*

zip, *v.,* **zipped, zipping,** *n. Informal.* —*v.* 1. go very speedily. —*n.* 2. energy.

zip code, code numbers used with address to expedite mail.

zip′per, *n.* fastener with interlocking edges.

zip′py, *adj.,* **-pier, -piest.** *Colloq.* lively; smart.

zith′er, *n.* stringed musical instrument. Also, **zith′ern.**

zo′di•ac′, *n.* imaginary belt of heavens containing paths of all major planets, divided into twelve constellations. —**zo•di′a•cal** (-dī′ə kəl), *adj.*

zom′bie, *n.* reanimated corpse.

zone, *n., v.,* **zoned, zoning.** —*n.* 1. special area, strip, etc. —*v.* 2. mark or divide into zones. —**zon′al,** *adj.*

zoo, *n.* place where live animals are exhibited. Also, **zoological garden.**

zo•ol′o•gy, *n.* science of animals. —**zo′o•log′i•cal,** *adj.* —**zo•ol′o•gist,** *n.*

zoom, *v.* speed sharply.

zo′o•pho′bi•a (zō′ə-), *n.* fear of animals.

zo′o•phyte′ (-fīt′), *n.* plantlike animal, as coral.

zuc•chet′to (zōō ket′ō), *n.* Roman Catholic ecclesiastical skullcap.

zuc•chi′ni (zōō kē′nē), *n.* cucumber-shaped squash.

zwie′back′ (swē′bak′), *n.* kind of dried, twice-baked bread.

PART SIX

READY REFERENCE GUIDE

NATIONS OF THE WORLD

Nation	Population	Area (sq. mi.)	Capital
Afghanistan	15,810,000	252,000	Kabul
Albania	3,080,000	10,632	Tirana
Algeria	23,850,000	919,352	Algiers
Angola	9,390,000	481,226	Luanda
Argentina	31,060,000	1,084,120	Buenos Aires
Armenia	3,283,000	11,490	Yerevan
Australia	16,250,000	2,974,581	Canberra
Austria	7,555,000	32,381	Vienna
Azerbaijan	7,029,000	33,430	Baku
Bahamas	236,000	5,353	Nassau
Bahrain	486,000	266	Manama
Bangladesh	104,100,000	54,501	Dhaka
Barbados	254,000	166	Bridgetown
Belarus	10,200,000	80,154	Minsk
Belgium	9,813,000	11,800	Brussels
Belize	193,000	8,866	Belmopan
Benin	4,440,000	44,290	Porto Novo
Bhutan	1,400,000	19,300	Thimphu
Bolivia	7,000,000	404,388	La Paz
Bosnia and Herzegovina	4,360,000	19,741	Sarajevo
Botswana	1,210,000	275,000	Gaborone
Brazil	155,560,000	3,286,170	Brasilia
Brunei	241,400	2,226	Bandar Seri Begawa
Bulgaria	8,761,000	42,800	Sofia
Burkina Faso	8,530,000	106,111	Ouagadougou
Burundi	5,130,000	10,747	Bujumbura
Cambodia	6,230,000	69,866	Phnom Penh
Cameroon	11,000,000	179,558	Yaoundé
Canada	25,354,000	3,690,410	Ottawa
Cape Verde	360,000	1,557	Praia
Central African Republic	2,759,000	238,000	Bangui
Chad	5,400,000	501,000	N'Djamena
Chile	12,680,000	286,396	Santiago
China	1,133,683,000	3,691,502	Beijing
Colombia	27,900,000	439,828	Bogotá
Comoros	434,166	719	Moroni
Congo	2,270,000	132,000	Brazzaville
Costa Rica	2,810,000	19,238	San José
Croatia	4,660,000	21,835	Zagreb
Cuba	10,240,000	44,200	Havana
Cyprus	680,000	3,572	Nicosia
Czech Republic	10,343,000	30,449	Prague
Denmark	5,130,000	16,576	Copenhagen
Djibouti	484,000	8,960	Djibouti
Dominica	94,000	290	Roseau
Dominican Republic	6,700,000	19,129	Santo Domingo

Nation	Population	Area (sq. mi.)	Capital
Ecuador	9,640,000	109,483	Quito
Egypt	49,280,000	386,198	Cairo
El Salvador	5,480,000	13,176	San Salvador
Equatorial Guinea	400,000	10,824	Malabo
Eritrea	3,200,000	47,076	Asmara
Estonia	1,573,000	17,413	Tallinn
Ethiopia	42,800,000	424,724	Addis Ababa
Fiji	715,000	7,078	Suva
Finland	4,940,000	130,119	Helsinki
France	56,560,000	212,736	Paris
Gabon	1,220,000	102,290	Libreville
Gambia	788,000	4,003	Banjul
Georgia	5,449,000	26,872	Tbilisi
Germany	78,420,000	137,852	Berlin
Ghana	13,800,000	91,843	Accra
Greece	9,990,000	50,147	Athens
Grenada	108,000	133	St. George's
Guatemala	8,990,000	42,042	Guatemala City
Guinea	6,530,000	96,900	Conakry
Guinea-Bissau	932,000	13,948	Bissau
Guyana	812,000	82,978	Georgetown
Haiti	5,300,000	10,714	Port-au-Prince
Honduras	4,300,000	43,277	Tegucigalpa
Hungary	10,604,000	35,926	Budapest
Iceland	247,357	39,709	Reykjavik
India	844,000.000	1,246,880	New Delhi
Indonesia	172,000,000	741,100	Jakarta
Iran	53,920,000	635,000	Tehran
Iraq	17,060,000	172,000	Baghdad
Ireland	3,540,000	27,136	Dublin
Israel	4,440,000	7,984	Jerusalem
Italy	57,400,000	116,294	Rome
Ivory Coast	11,630,000	127,520	Abidjan
Jamaica	2,300,000	4,413	Kingston
Japan	122,260,000	141,529	Tokyo
Jordan	2,970,000	37,264	Amman
Kazakhstan	16,538,000	1,049,155	Alma-Ata
Kenya	22,800,000	223,478	Nairobi
Kuwait	1,960,000	8,000	Kuwait
Kyrgyzstan	4,291,000	76,460	Bishkek
Laos	3,830,000	91,500	Vientiane
Latvia	2,681,000	25,395	Riga
Lebanon	3,500,000	3,927	Beirut
Lesotho	1,670,000	11,716	Maseru
Liberia	2,440,000	43,000	Monrovia
Libya	3,960,000	679,400	Tripoli

Nation	Population	Area (sq. mi.)	Capital
Liechtenstein	27,700	65	Vaduz
Lithuania	3,690,000	25,174	Vilnius
Luxembourg	377,100	999	Luxembourg
Macedonia	2,040,000	9,928	Skopje
Madagascar	10,919,000	226,657	Antananarivo
Malawi	7,059,000	49,177	Lilongwe
Malaysia	16,968,000	127,317	Kuala Lumpur
Maldives	214,139	115	Malé
Mali	9,092,000	478,841	Bamako
Malta	354,900	122	Valletta
Marshall Islands	50,000	70	Majuro
Mauritania	1,894,000	398,000	Nouakchott
Mauritius	1,075,000	788	Port Louis
Mexico	82,700,000	756,198	Mexico City
Micronesia	108,600	271	Kolonia
Moldova	4,341,000	13,100	Kishinev
Monaco	29,900	½	Monaco
Mongolia	2,001,000	600,000	Ulan Bator
Morocco	23,000,000	172,104	Rabat
Mozambique	14,900,000	297,731	Maputo
Myanmar (Burma)	42,600,000	261,789	Yangon
Nepal	16,630,000	54,000	Katmandu
Netherlands	14,715,000	16,163	Amsterdam
New Zealand	3,307,084	103,416	Wellington
Nicaragua	3,500,000	57,143	Managua
Niger	7,190,000	458,976	Niamey
Nigeria	88,500,000	356,669	Abuja
North Korea	21,890,000	50,000	Pyongyang
Norway	4,200,000	124,555	Oslo
Oman	1,200,000	82,800	Muscat
Pakistan	102,200,000	310,403	Islamabad
Panama	2,320,000	28,575	Panama City
Papua New Guinea	3,400,000	178,260	Port Moresby
Paraguay	4,010,000	157,047	Asunción
Peru	21,300,000	496,222	Lima
Philippines	60,477,000	114,830	Manila
Poland	37,800,000	121,000	Warsaw
Portugal	10,290,000	35,414	Lisbon
Qatar	371,863	8,500	Doha
Romania	22,823,000	91,654	Bucharest
Russian Federation	147,386,000	6,593,000	Moscow
Rwanda	6,710,000	10,169	Kigali
St. Kitts-Nevis	44,400	104	Basseterre
St. Lucia	146,000	238	Castries
St. Vincent and the Grenadines	112,614	150	Kingstown
San Marino	22,750	24	San Marino

Nations of the World *(Continued)*

Nation	Population	Area (sq. mi.)	Capital
São Tomé and Principe	115,600	387	São Tomé
Saudi Arabia	12,566,000	830,000	Riyadh
Senegal	6,980,000	76,084	Dakar
Seychelles	67,000	175	Victoria
Sierra Leone	3,880,000	27,925	Freetown
Singapore	2,610,000	240	Singapore
Slovakia	5,297,000	18,932	Bratislava
Slovenia	1,930,000	7,819	Ljubljana
Solomon Islands	285,796	11,458	Honiara
Somalia	6,260,000	246,198	Mogadishu
South Africa	29,600,000	472,000	Pretoria & Cape Town
South Korea	42,082,000	38,232	Seoul
Spain	39,000,000	194,988	Madrid
Sri Lanka	16,600,000	25,332	Colombo
Sudan	25,560,000	967,500	Khartoum
Suriname	415,000	63,251	Paramaribo
Swaziland	676,000	6,704	Mbabane
Sweden	8,414,000	173,394	Stockholm
Switzerland	6,620,000	15,944	Bern
Syria	11,400,000	71,227	Damascus
Tajikistan	5,112,000	55,240	Dushanbe
Tanzania	23,200,000	363,950	Dodoma
Thailand	53,900,000	198,242	Bangkok
Togo	3,246,000	21,830	Lomé
Trinidad and Tobago	1,243,000	1,980	Port-of-Spain
Tunisia	7,320,000	48,330	Tunis
Turkey	50,664,000	300,948	Ankara
Turkmenistan	3,534,000	188,417	Ashkhabad
Uganda	15,500,000	91,343	Kampala
Ukraine	51,704,000	233,090	Kiev
United Arab Emirates	1,600,000	32,300	Abu Dhabi
United Kingdom	53,917,000	94,242	London
United States	248,710,000	3,615,122	Washington, D.C.
Uruguay	3,080,000	172,172	Montevideo
Uzbekistan	19,906,000	172,741	Tashkent
Vanuatu	149,400	5,700	Vila
Venezuela	18,770,000	352,143	Caracas
Vietnam	64,000,000	126,104	Hanoi
Western Samoa	163,000	1,133	Apia
Yemen	12,000,000	207,000	Sanaa
Yugoslavia	10,392,000	39,449	Belgrade
Zaire	32,560,000	905,063	Kinshasa
Zambia	7,384,000	290,585	Lusaka
Zimbabwe	9,174,000	150,804	Harare

CONTINENTS

Name	Area in Sq. Mi.	Population
Asia	17,000,000	2,405,000,000
Africa	11,700,000	455,000,000
North America	9,400,000	370,000,000
South America	6,900,000	238,000,000
Antarctica	5,100,000	—
Europe	4,063,000	650,600,000
Australia	2,966,000	14,289,000

GREAT OCEANS AND SEAS OF THE WORLD

Ocean or Sea	Area sq. mi.	Area sq. km	Location
Pacific Ocean	70,000,000	181,300,000	Bounded by N and S America, Asia, and Australia
Atlantic Ocean	31,530,000	81,663,000	Bounded by N and S America, Europe, and Africa
Indian Ocean	28,357,000	73,444,630	S of Asia, E of Africa, and W of Australia
Arctic Ocean	5,540,000	14,350,000	N of North America, Asia, and the Arctic Circle
Mediterranean Sea	1,145,000	2,965,550	Between Europe, Africa, and Asia
South China Sea	895,000	2,318,050	Part of N Pacific, off coast of SE Asia
Bering Sea	878,000	2,274,000	Part of N Pacific, between N America and N Asia
Caribbean Sea	750,000	1,943,000	Between Central America, West Indies, and S America
Gulf of Mexico	700,000	1,813,000	Arm of N Atlantic, off SE coast of North America
Sea of Okhotsk	582,000	1,507,380	Arm of N Pacific, off E coast of Asia
East China Sea	480,000	1,243,200	Part of N Pacific, off E coast of Asia
Yellow Sea	480,000	1,243,200	Part of N Pacific, off E coast of Asia
Sea of Japan	405,000	1,048,950	Arm of N Pacific, between Asia mainland and Japanese Isles
Hudson Bay	400,000	1,036,000	N North America
Andaman Sea	300,000	777,000	Part of Bay of Bengal (Indian Ocean), off S coast of Asia
North Sea	201,000	520,600	Arm of N Atlantic, off coast of NW Europe
Red Sea	170,000	440,300	Arm of Indian Ocean, between N Africa and Arabian Peninsula
Black Sea	164,000	424,760	SE Europe-SW Asia
Baltic Sea	160,000	414,000	N Europe
Persian Gulf	92,200	238,800	Between Iran and Arabian Peninsula
Gulf of St. Lawrence	92,000	238,280	Arm of N Atlantic, between mainland of SE Canada and Newfoundland
Gulf of California	62,600	162,100	Arm of N Pacific, between W coast of Mexico and peninsula of Lower California

NOTABLE MOUNTAIN PEAKS OF THE WORLD

Name	Country or Region	Altitude ft.	m
Mt. Everest	Nepal-Tibet	29,028	8848
K2	Kashmir	28,250	8611
Kanchenjunga	Nepal-Sikkim	28,146	8579
Makalu	Nepal-Tibet	27,790	8470
Dhaulagiri	Nepal	26,826	8180
Nanga Parbat	Kashmir	26,660	8125
Annapurna	Nepal	26,503	8078
Gasherbrum	Kashmir	26,470	8068
Gosainthan	Tibet	26,291	8013
Nanda Devi	India	25,661	7820
Tirich Mir	Pakistan	25,230	7690
Muztagh Ata	China	24,757	7546
Communism Peak	Tajikistan	24,590	7495
Pobeda Peak	Kyrgyzstan-China	24,406	7439
Lenin Peak	Kyrgyzstan-Tajikistan	23,382	7127
Aconcagua	Argentina	22,834	6960
Huascarán	Peru	22,205	6768
Illimani	Bolivia	21,188	6458
Chimborazo	Ecuador	20,702	6310
Mt. McKinley	United States (Alaska)	20,320	6194
Mt. Logan	Canada (Yukon)	19,850	6050
Cotopaxi	Ecuador	19,498	5943
Kilimanjaro	Tanzania	19,321	5889
El Misti	Peru	19,200	5880
Demavend	Iran	18,606	5671
Orizaba (Citlaltepetl)	Mexico	18,546	5653
Mt. Elbrus	Russian Federation	18,465	5628
Popocatépetl	Mexico	17,887	5450
Ixtaccíhuatl	Mexico	17,342	5286
Mt. Kenya	Kenya	17,040	5194
Ararat	Turkey	16,945	5165
Mt. Ngaliema (Mt. Stanley)	Zaire-Uganda	16,790	5119
Mont Blanc	France	15,781	4810
Mt. Wilhelm	Papua New Guinea	15,400	4694
Monte Rosa	Italy-Switzerland	15,217	4638
Mt. Kirkpatrick	Antarctica	14,855	4528
Weisshorn	Switzerland	14,804	4512
Matterhorn	Switzerland	14,780	4505
Mt. Whitney	United States (California)	14,495	4418
Mt. Elbert	United States (Colorado)	14,431	4399
Mt. Rainier	United States (Washington)	14,408	4392
Longs Peak	United States (Colorado)	14,255	4345
Mt. Shasta	United States (California)	14,161	4315
Pikes Peak	United States (Colorado)	14,108	4300
Mauna Kea	United States (Hawaii)	13,784	4201
Grand Teton	United States (Wyoming)	13,766	4196

NOTABLE MOUNTAIN PEAKS OF THE WORLD *(Continued)*

Name	Country or Region	Altitude ft.	Altitude m
Mauna Loa	United States (Hawaii)	13,680	4170
Jungfrau	Switzerland	13,668	4166
Mt. Victoria	Papua New Guinea	13,240	4036
Mt. Erebus	Antarctica	13,202	4024
Eiger	Switzerland	13,025	3970
Mt. Robson	Canada (B.C.)	12,972	3954
Mt. Fuji	Japan	12,395	3778
Mt. Cook	New Zealand	12,349	3764
Mt. Hood	United States (Oregon)	11,253	3430
Mt. Etna	Italy	10,758	3280
Lassen Peak	United States (California)	10,465	3190
Haleakala	United States (Hawaii)	10,032	3058
Mt. Olympus	Greece	9730	2966
Mt. Kosciusko	Australia	7316	2230

WORLD TIME DIFFERENCES†

Amsterdam	6:00 P.M.	Honolulu	7:00 A.M.	Prague	6:00 P.M.
Athens	7:00 P.M.	Istanbul	7:00 P.M.	Rio de Janeiro	2:00 P.M.
Bangkok	12:00 Mid.	Lima	12:00 Noon	Rome	6:00 P.M.
Berlin	6:00 P.M.	London	5:00 P.M.	Shanghai	1:00 A.M.*
Bombay	10:30 P.M.	Madrid	6:00 P.M.	Stockholm	6:00 P.M.
Brussels	6:00 P.M.	Manila	1:00 A.M.*	Sydney (N.S.W.)	3:00 A.M.*
Buenos Aires	2:00 P.M.	Mexico City	11:00 A.M.	Tokyo	2:00 A.M.*
Cape Town	7:00 P.M.	Montreal	12:00 Noon	Vienna	6:00 P.M.
Dublin	5:00 P.M.	Moscow	8:00 P.M.	Warsaw	6:00 P.M.
Havana	12:00 Noon	Paris	6:00 P.M.	Zurich	6:00 P.M.

†at 12:00 noon Eastern Standard Time   *morning of the following day

U. S. TIME DIFFERENCES†

Atlanta	12:00 Noon	El Paso	10:00 A.M.	New Orleans	11:00 A.M.
Baltimore	12:00 Noon	Houston	11:00 A.M.	Omaha	11:00 A.M.
Boston	12:00 Noon	Indianapolis	12:00 Noon	Philadelphia	12:00 Noon
Buffalo	12:00 Noon	Kansas City	11:00 A.M.	Phoenix	10:00 A.M.
Chicago	11:00 A.M.	Los Angeles	9:00 A.M.	Pittsburgh	12:00 Noon
Cincinnati	12:00 Noon	Memphis	11:00 A.M.	Salt Lake City	10:00 A.M.
Cleveland	12:00 Noon	Miami	12:00 Noon	San Diego	9:00 A.M.
Columbus	12:00 Noon	Milwaukee	11:00 A.M.	San Francisco	9:00 A.M.
Dallas	11:00 A.M.	Minneapolis	11:00 A.M.	Seattle	9:00 A.M.
Denver	10:00 A.M.	Nashville	11:00 A.M.	St. Louis	11:00 A.M.
Des Moines	11:00 A.M.	New York	12:00 Noon	Washington, D.C.	12:00 Noon
Detroit	12:00 Noon				

†at 12:00 noon Eastern Standard Time

FACTS ABOUT THE UNITED STATES

State	Population (1990)	Area (sq. mi.)	Capital
Alabama	4,040,587	51,609	Montgomery
Alaska	550,403	586,400	Juneau
Arizona	3,665,228	113,909	Phoenix
Arkansas	2,350,725	53,103	Little Rock
California	29,760,021	158,693	Sacramento
Colorado	3,294,394	104,247	Denver
Connecticut	3,287,116	5,009	Hartford
Delaware	666,168	2,057	Dover
Florida	12,937,926	58,560	Tallahassee
Georgia	6,478,216	58,876	Atlanta
Hawaii	1,108,229	6,424	Honolulu
Idaho	1,006,749	83,557	Boise
Illinois	11,430,602	56,400	Springfield
Indiana	5,544,159	36,291	Indianapolis
Iowa	2,776,755	56,290	Des Moines
Kansas	2,477,574	82,276	Topeka
Kentucky	3,685,296	40,395	Frankfort
Louisiana	4,219,973	48,522	Baton Rouge
Maine	1,227,928	33,215	Augusta
Maryland	4,781,468	10,577	Annapolis
Massachusetts	6,016,425	8,257	Boston
Michigan	9,295,297	58,216	Lansing
Minnesota	4,375,099	84,068	St. Paul
Mississippi	2,573,216	47,716	Jackson
Missouri	5,117,073	69,674	Jefferson City
Montana	799,065	147,138	Helena
Nebraska	1,578,385	77,237	Lincoln
Nevada	1,201,833	110,540	Carson City
New Hampshire	1,109,252	9,304	Concord
New Jersey	7,730,188	7,836	Trenton
New Mexico	1,515,069	121,666	Santa Fe
New York	17,990,455	49,576	Albany
North Carolina	6,628,637	52,586	Raleigh
North Dakota	638,800	70,665	Bismarck
Ohio	10,847,115	41,222	Columbus
Oklahoma	3,145,585	69,919	Oklahoma City
Oregon	2,842,321	96,981	Salem
Pennsylvania	11,881,643	45,333	Harrisburg
Rhode Island	1,003,464	1,214	Providence
South Carolina	3,486,703	31,055	Columbia
South Dakota	696,004	77,047	Pierre
Tennessee	4,877,185	42,246	Nashville
Texas	16,986,510	267,339	Austin
Utah	1,722,850	84,916	Salt Lake City
Vermont	562,758	9,609	Montpelier
Virginia	6,187,358	40,815	Richmond

FACTS ABOUT THE UNITED STATES *(Continued)*

State	Population (1990)	Area (sq. mi.)	Capital
Washington	4,866,692	68,192	Olympia
West Virginia	1,793,477	24,181	Charleston
Wisconsin	4,891,769	56,154	Madison
Wyoming	453,588	97,914	Cheyenne
Washington, D.C.	606,900	63	—
Total U.S.	248,709,873		

MAJOR CITIES OF THE UNITED STATES (1990)

Rank	City, State	Population	Rank	City, State	Population
1	New York, N.Y.	7,322,564	37	Virginia Beach, Va.	393,069
2	Los Angeles, Calif.	3,485,398	38	Albuquerque, N. Mex.	384,736
3	Chicago, Ill.	2,783,726	39	Oakland, Calif.	372,242
4	Houston, Tex.	1,630,553	40	Pittsburgh, Pa.	369,879
5	Philadelphia, Pa.	1,585,577	41	Sacramento, Calif.	369,365
6	San Diego, Calif.	1,110,549	42	Minneapolis, Minn.	368,383
7	Detroit, Mich.	1,027,974	43	Tulsa, Okla.	367,302
8	Dallas, Tex.	1,006,877	44	Honolulu, Hawaii	365,272
9	Phoenix, Ariz.	983,403	45	Cincinnati, Ohio	364,040
10	San Antonio, Tex.	935,933	46	Miami, Fla.	358,548
11	San Jose, Calif.	782,248	47	Fresno, Calif.	354,202
12	Baltimore, Md.	736,014	48	Omaha, Nebr.	335,795
13	Indianapolis, Ind.	731,327	49	Toledo, Ohio	332,943
14	San Francisco, Calif.	723,959	50	Buffalo, N.Y.	328,123
15	Jacksonville, Fla.	635,230	51	Wichita, Kans.	304,011
16	Columbus, Ohio	632,910	52	Santa Ana, Calif.	293,742
17	Milwaukee, Wis.	628,088	53	Mesa, Ariz.	288,091
18	Memphis, Tenn.	610,337	54	Colorado Springs, Colo.	281,140
19	Washington, D.C.	606,900	55	Tampa, Fla.	280,015
20	Boston, Mass.	574,283	56	Newark, N.J.	275,221
21	Seattle, Wash.	516,259	57	St. Paul, Minn.	272,235
22	El Paso, Tex.	515,342	58	Louisville, Ky.	269,063
23	Cleveland, Ohio	505,616	59	Anaheim, Calif.	266,406
24	New Orleans, La.	496,938	60	Birmingham, Ala.	265,968
25	Nashville-Davidson, Tenn.	488,374	61	Arlington, Tex.	261,721
26	Denver, Colo.	467,610	62	Norfolk, Va.	261,229
27	Austin, Tex.	465,622	63	Las Vegas, Nev.	258,295
28	Fort Worth, Tex.	447,619	64	Corpus Christi, Tex.	257,453
29	Oklahoma City, Okla.	444,719	65	St. Petersburg, Fla.	238,629
30	Portland, Oreg.	437,319	66	Rochester, N.Y.	231,636
31	Kansas City, Mo.	435,146	67	Jersey City, N.J.	228,537
32	Long Beach, Calif.	429,433	68	Riverside, Calif.	226,505
33	Tucson, Ariz.	405,390	69	Anchorage, Alaska	226,338
34	St. Louis, Mo.	396,685	70	Lexington-Fayette, Ky.	225,366
35	Charlotte, N.C.	395,934	71	Akron, Ohio	223,019
36	Atlanta, Ga.	394,017	72	Aurora, Colo.	222,103

MAJOR CITIES OF THE UNITED STATES (1990) *(Continued)*

Rank	City, State	Population
73	Baton Rouge, La.	219,531
74	Stockton, Calif.	210,943
75	Raleigh, N.C.	207,951
76	Richmond, Va.	203,056
77	Shreveport, La.	198,525
78	Jackson, Miss.	196,637
79	Mobile, Ala.	196,278
80	Des Moines, Iowa	193,187
81	Lincoln, Nebr.	191,972
82	Madison, Wis.	191,262
83	Grand Rapids, Mich.	189,126
84	Yonkers, N.Y.	188,082
85	Hialeah, Fla.	188,004
86	Montgomery, Ala.	187,106
87	Lubbock, Tex.	186,206
88	Greensboro, N.C.	183,521
89	Dayton, Ohio	182,044
90	Huntington Beach, Calif.	181,519
91	Garland, Tex.	180,650
92	Glendale, Calif.	180,038
93	Columbus, Ga.	178,681
94	Spokane, Wash.	177,196
95	Tacoma, Wash.	176,664
96	Little Rock, Ark.	175,795
97	Bakersfield, Calif.	174,820
98	Fremont, Calif.	173,339
99	Fort Wayne, Ind.	173,072
100	Newport News, Va.	170,045
101	Worcester, Mass.	169,759
102	Knoxville, Tenn.	165,121
103	Modesto, Calif.	164,730
104	Orlando, Fla.	164,693
105	San Bernardino, Calif.	164,164
106	Syracuse, N.Y.	163,860
107	Providence, R.I.	160,728
108	Salt Lake City, Utah	159,936
109	Huntsville, Ala.	159,789
110	Amarillo, Tex.	157,615
111	Springfield, Mass.	156,983
112	Irving, Tex.	155,037
113	Chattanooga, Tenn.	152,466
114	Chesapeake, Va.	151,976
115	Kansas City, Kans.	149,767
116	Fort Lauderdale, Fla.	149,377
117	Glendale, Ariz.	148,134
118	Warren, Mich.	144,864
119	Winston-Salem, N.C.	143,485
120	Garden Grove, Calif.	143,050
121	Oxnard, Calif.	142,216
122	Tempe, Ariz.	141,865
123	Bridgeport, Conn.	141,686
124	Paterson, N.J.	140,891
125	Flint, Mich.	140,761
126	Springfield, Mo.	140,494
127	Hartford, Conn.	139,739
128	Rockford, Ill.	139,426
129	Savannah, Ga.	137,560
130	Durham, N.C.	136,611
131	Chula Vista, Calif.	135,163
132	Reno, Nev.	133,850
133	Hampton, Va.	133,793
134	Ontario, Calif.	133,179
135	Torrance, Calif.	133,107
136	Pomona, Calif.	131,723
137	Pasadena, Calif.	131,591
138	New Haven, Conn.	130,474
139	Scottsdale, Ariz.	130,069
140	Plano, Tex.	128,713
141	Oceanside, Calif.	128,398
142	Lansing, Mich.	127,321
143	Lakewood, Colo.	126,481
144	Evansville, Ind.	126,272
145	Boise City, Idaho	125,738
146	Tallahassee, Fla.	124,773
147	Laredo, Tex.	122,899
148	Hollywood, Fla.	121,697
149	Topeka, Kans.	119,883
150	Pasadena, Tex.	119,363
151	Moreno Valley, Calif.	118,779
152	Sterling Heights, Mich.	117,810
153	Sunnyvale, Calif.	117,229
154	Gary, Ind.	116,646
155	Beaumont, Tex.	114,323
156	Fullerton, Calif.	114,144
157	Peoria, Ill.	113,504
158	Santa Rosa, Calif.	113,313
159	Eugene, Oreg.	112,669
160	Independence, Mo.	112,301
161	Overland Park, Kans.	111,790
162	Hayward, Calif.	111,498
163	Concord, Calif.	111,348
164	Alexandria, Va.	111,183
165	Orange, Calif.	110,658
166	Santa Clarita, Calif.	110,642

Major Cities of the United States (1990) (Continued)

Rank	City, State	Population		Rank	City, State	Population
167	Irvine, Calif.	110,330		182	South Bend, Ind.	105,511
168	Elizabeth, N.J.	110,002		183	Springfield, Ill.	105,227
169	Inglewood, Calif.	109,602		184	Allentown, Pa.	105,090
170	Ann Arbor, Mich.	109,592		185	Thousand Oaks, Calif.	104,352
171	Vallejo, Calif.	109,199		186	Portsmouth, Va.	103,907
172	Waterbury, Conn.	108,961		187	Waco, Tex.	103,590
173	Salinas, Calif.	108,777		188	Lowell, Mass.	103,439
174	Cedar Rapids, Iowa	108,751		189	Berkeley, Calif.	102,724
175	Erie, Pa.	108,718		190	Mesquite, Tex.	101,484
176	Escondido, Calif.	108,635		191	Rancho Cucamonga, Calif.	101,409
177	Stamford, Conn.	108,056		192	Albany, N.Y.	101,082
178	Salem, Oreg.	107,786		193	Livonia, Mich.	100,850
179	Abilene, Tex.	106,654		194	Sioux Falls, S. Dak.	100,814
180	Macon, Ga.	106,612		195	Simi Valley, Calif.	100,217
181	El Monte, Calif.	106,209				

Distances Between U.S. Cities

	Atlanta	Chicago	Dallas	Denver	Los Angeles	New York	St. Louis	Seattle
Atlanta	—	592	738	1421	1981	762	516	2354
Boston	946	879	1565	1786	2739	184	1118	2831
Chicago	592	—	857	909	1860	724	251	1748
Cincinnati	377	255	870	1102	1910	613	550	2003
Cleveland	587	307	1080	1216	2054	458	558	2259
Dallas	738	857	—	683	1243	1391	547	2199
Denver	1421	909	683	—	838	1633	781	1074
Detroit	619	247	1045	1156	2052	486	463	1947
El Paso	1293	1249	543	554	702	1902	1033	1373
Kansas City	745	405	452	552	1360	1117	229	1626
Los Angeles	1981	1860	1243	838	—	2624	1589	956
Miami	614	1199	1405	1911	2611	1106	1123	2947
Minneapolis	942	350	860	840	1768	1020	492	1398
New Orleans	427	860	437	1120	1680	1186	609	2608
New York	762	724	1381	1633	2624	—	888	2418
Omaha	1016	424	617	485	1323	1148	394	1533
Philadelphia	667	671	1303	1578	2467	95	841	2647
Pittsburgh	536	461	1318	1349	2157	320	568	2168
St. Louis	516	251	547	781	1589	888	—	1890
San Francisco	2308	1856	1570	956	327	2580	1916	687
Seattle	2354	1748	2199	1074	956	2418	1890	—
Washington, D.C.	547	600	1183	1519	2426	215	719	2562

CHIEF AMERICAN HOLIDAYS

New Year's Day	January 1	Labor Day	First Monday in September
Martin Luther King Day	January 15[1]	Columbus Day	October 12[4]
Inauguration Day	January 20	Veterans Day	November 11
Lincoln's Birthday	February 12	Election Day	Tuesday after first Monday in November
Washington's Birthday	February 22[2]		
Good Friday	Friday before Easter		
Memorial Day	May 30[3]	Thanksgiving Day	Fourth Thursday in November
Independence Day	July 4	Christmas Day	December 25

[1]officially observed on 3rd Monday in January
[2]officially observed on 3rd Monday in February
[3]officially observed on last Monday in May

[4]officially observed on 2nd Monday in October

PRESIDENTS OF THE UNITED STATES

Name (and party)	State of birth	Born	Term	Died
George Washington (F)	Va.	1732	1789–1797	1799
John Adams (F)	Mass.	1735	1797–1801	1826
Thomas Jefferson (D-R)	Va.	1743	1801–1809	1826
James Madison (D-R)	Va.	1751	1809–1817	1836
James Monroe (D-R)	Va.	1758	1817–1825	1831
John Quincy Adams (D-R)	Mass.	1767	1825–1829	1848
Andrew Jackson (D)	S.C.	1767	1829–1837	1845
Martin Van Buren (D)	N.Y.	1782	1837–1841	1862
William Henry Harrison (W)	Va.	1773	1841–1841	1841
John Tyler (W)	Va.	1790	1841–1845	1862
James Knox Polk (D)	N.C.	1795	1845–1849	1849
Zachary Taylor (W)	Va.	1784	1849–1850	1850
Millard Fillmore (W)	N.Y.	1800	1850–1853	1874
Franklin Pierce (D)	N.H.	1804	1853–1857	1869
James Buchanan (D)	Pa.	1791	1857–1861	1868
Abraham Lincoln (R)	Ky.	180_	1861–1865	1865
Andrew Johnson (R)	N.C.	1808	1865–1869	1875
Ulysses Simpson Grant (R)	Ohio	1822	1869–1877	1885
Rutherford Birchard Hayes (R)	Ohio	1822	1877–1881	1893
James Abram Garfield (R)	Ohio	1831	1881–1881	1881
Chester Alan Arthur (R)	Vt.	1830	1881–1885	1886
Grover Cleveland (D)	N.J.	1837	1885–1889	1908
Benjamin Harrison (R)	Ohio	1833	1889–1893	1901
Grover Cleveland (D)	N.J.	1837	1893–1897	1908
William McKinley (R)	Ohio	1843	1897–1901	1901
Theodore Roosevelt (R)	N.Y.	1858	1901–1909	1919
William Howard Taft (R)	Ohio	1857	1909–1913	1930
Woodrow Wilson (D)	Va.	1856	1913–1921	1924
Warren Gamaliel Harding (R)	Ohio	1865	1921–1923	1923
Calvin Coolidge (R)	Vt.	1872	1923–1929	1933
Herbert Clark Hoover (R)	Iowa	1874	1929–1933	1964

Name (and party)	State of birth	Born	Term	Died
Franklin Delano Roosevelt (D)	N.Y.	1882	1933–1945	1945
Harry S. Truman (D)	Mo.	1884	1945–1953	1972
Dwight D. Eisenhower (R)	Tex.	1890	1953–1961	1969
John Fitzgerald Kennedy (D)	Mass.	1917	1961–1963	1963
Lyndon Baines Johnson (D)	Tex.	1908	1963–1969	1973
Richard Milhous Nixon (R)	Cal.	1913	1969–1974	1994
Gerald R. Ford (R)	Neb.	1913	1974–1977	
James Earl Carter, Jr. (D)	Ga.	1924	1977–1981	
Ronald Wilson Reagan (R)	Ill.	1911	1981–1989	
George H. W. Bush (R)	Mass.	1924	1989–1993	
William J. Clinton (D)	Ark.	1946	1993–	

F–Federalist; D–Democrat; R–Republican; W–Whig.

FORMS OF ADDRESS

The forms of address shown below cover most of the commonly encountered problems in correspondence. Although there are many alternative forms, the ones given here are generally preferred in conventional usage.

As a complimentary close, use "Sincerely yours," but, when particular formality is preferred, use "Very truly yours."

Government (United States)

President
Address: The President
The White House
Washington, D.C. 20500
Salutation: Dear Mr. *or* Madam President:

Vice President
Address: The Vice President
United States Senate
Washington, D.C. 20510
Salutation: Dear Mr. *or* Madam Vice President:

Cabinet Member
Address: The Honorable *(full name)*
Secretary of *(name of Department)*
Washington, D.C. *(zip code)*
Salutation: Dear Mr. *or* Madam Secretary:

Attorney General
Address: The Honorable *(full name)*
Attorney General
Washington, D.C. 20530
Salutation: Dear Mr. *or* Madam Attorney General:

Senator
Address: The Honorable *(full name)*
United States Senate
Washington, D.C. 20510
Salutation: Dear Senator *(surname)*:

Representative
Address: The Honorable *(full name)*
House of Representatives
Washington, D.C. 20515
Salutation: Dear Mr. *or* Madam *(surname)*:

Chief Justice
Address: The Chief Justice of the United States
The Supreme Court of the United States
Washington, D.C. 20543
Salutation: Dear Mr. *or* Madam Chief Justice:

Associate Justice
Address: Mr. *or* Madam Justice *(surname)*
The Supreme Court of the United States
Washington, D.C. 20543
Salutation: Dear Mr. *or* Madam Justice:

Judge of a Federal Court
Address: The Honorable *(full name)*
Judge of the *(name of court; if a district court, give district)*
(Local address)
Salutation: Dear Judge *(surname)*:

FORMS OF ADDRESS *(Continued)*

American Ambassador
Address: The Honorable *(full name)*
American Ambassador
(City), (Country)
Salutation: *Formal:* Sir: *or* Madam:
Informal: Dear Mr. *or* Madam
Ambassador:

Governor
Address: The Honorable *(full name)*
Governor of *(name of state)*
(City), (State)
Salutation: Dear Governor *(surname):*

State Senator
Address: The Honorable *(full name)*
(Name of state) Senate
(City), (State)
Salutation: Dear (Mr., Ms., Miss *or* Mrs.)
(surname):

State Representative; Assemblyman; Delegate
Address: The Honorable *(full name)*
(Name of state) House of
Representatives *(or* Assembly *or*
House of Delegates)
(City), (State)
Salutation: Dear (Mr., Ms., Miss *or* Mrs.)
(surname):

Mayor
Address: The Honorable *(full name)*
Mayor of *(name of city)*
(City), (State)
Salutation: Dear Mayor *(surname):*

Government (Canada)

Governor General
Address: (His *or* Her) Excellency *(full name)*
Government House
Ottawa, Ontario K1A 0A1
Salutation: *Formal:* Sir: *or* Madam:
Informal: Dear Governor General:

Prime Minister
Address: The Right Honourable *(full name),*
P.C., M.P.
Prime Minister of Canada
Prime Minister's Office
Ottawa, Ontario K1A 0A2
Salutation: *Formal:* Dear Sir: *or* Madam:

Informal: Dear Mr. *or* Madam Prime
Minister:

Cabinet Member
Address: The Honourable *(full name)*
Minister of *(function)*
House of Commons
Parliament Buildings
Ottawa, Ontario K1A 0A2
Salutation: *Formal:* Dear Sir: *or* Madam:
Informal: Dear (Mr., Ms., Miss *or* Mrs.)
(surname):

Senator
Address: The Honourable *(full name)*
The Senate
Parliament Buildings
Ottawa, Ontario K1A 0A4
Salutation: *Formal:* Dear Sir: *or* Madam:
Informal: Dear Senator:

Member of House of Commons
Address: (Mr., Ms., Miss *or* Mrs.) *(full name),*
M.P.
House of Commons
Parliament Buildings
Ottawa, Ontario K1A 0A6
Salutation: *Formal:* Dear Sir: *or* Madam:
Informal: Dear (Mr., Ms., Miss *or* Mrs.)
(surname):

Canadian Ambassador
Address: (Mr., Ms., Miss *or* Mrs.) *(full name)*
Canadian Ambassador to *(name of
country)*
(City), (Country)
Salutation: *Formal:* Dear Sir: *or* Madam:
Informal: Dear (Mr., Ms., Miss *or* Mrs.)
(surname):

Premier of a Province
Address: The Honourable *(full name),* M.L.A.*
Premier of the Province of *(name)***
(City), (Province)
Salutation: *Formal:* Dear Sir: *or* Madam:
Informal: Dear (Mr., Ms., Miss *or* Mrs.)
(surname):

Mayor
Address: His *or* Her Worship Mayor *(full name)*
City Hall
(City), (Province)
Salutation: Dear Sir: *or* Madam:

*For Ontario, use M.P.P.; for Quebec, use M.N.A.
**For Quebec, use "Prime Minister."

FORMS OF ADDRESS *(Continued)*

Religious Leaders

Minister, Pastor or Rector
Address: The Reverend *(full name)*
         (Title), (name of church)
         (Local address)
Salutation: Dear (Mr., Ms., Miss *or* Mrs.)
         (surname):

Rabbi
Address: Rabbi *(full name)*
         (Local address)
Salutation: Dear Rabbi *(surname):*

Catholic Cardinal
Address: His Eminence *(Christian name)*
         Cardinal *(surname)*
         Archbishop of *(province)*
         (Local address)
Salutation: *Formal:* Your Eminence:
         Informal: Dear Cardinal *(surname):*

Catholic Archbishop
Address: The Most Reverend *(full name)*
         Archbishop of *(province)*
         (Local address)
Salutation: *Formal:* Your Excellency:
         Informal: Dear Archbishop *(surname):*

Catholic Bishop
Address: The Most Reverend *(full name)*
         Bishop of *(province)*
         (Local address)
Salutation: *Formal:* Your Excellency:
         Informal: Dear Bishop *(surname):*

Catholic Monsignor
Address: The Right Reverend Monsignor *(full name)*
         (Local address)
Salutation: *Formal:* Right Reverend Monsignor:
         Informal: Dear Monsignor *(surname):*

Catholic Priest
Address: The Reverend *(full name), (initials of order, if any)*
         (Local address)
Salutation: *Formal:* Reverend Sir:
         Informal: Dear Father *(surname):*

Catholic Sister
Address: Sister *(full name)*
         (Name of organization)
         (Local address)
Salutation: Dear Sister *(full name):*

Catholic Brother
Address: Brother *(full name)*
         (Name of organization)
         (Local address)
Salutation: Dear Brother *(given name):*

Protestant Episcopal Bishop
Address: The Right Reverend *(full name)*
         Bishop of *(name)*
         (Local address)
Salutation: *Formal:* Right Reverend Sir *or* Madam:
         Informal: Dear Bishop *(surname):*

Protestant Episcopal Dean
Address: The Very Reverend *(full name)*
         Dean of *(church)*
         (Local address)
Salutation: *Formal:* Very Reverend Sir *or* Madam:
         Informal: Dear Dean *(surname):*

Methodist Bishop
Address: The Reverend *(full name)*
         Methodist Bishop
         (Local address)
Salutation: *Formal:* Reverend Sir:
         Informal: Dear Bishop *(surname):*

Mormon Bishop
Address: Bishop *(full name)*
         Church of Jesus Christ of Latter-day Saints
         (Local address)
Salutation: *Formal:* Sir:
         Informal: Dear Bishop *(surname):*

Miscellaneous

President of a university or college
Address: (Dr., Mr., Ms., Miss *or* Mrs.) *(full name)*
         President, *(name of institution)*
         (Local address)
Salutation: Dear (Dr., Mr., Ms., Miss *or* Mrs.)
         (surname):

Dean of a college or school
Address: Dean *(full name)*
         School of *(name)*
         (Name of institution)
         (Local address)
Salutation: Dear Dean *(surname):*

Professor
Address: Professor *(full name)*
         Department of *(name)*
         (Name of institution)
         (Local address)
Salutation: Dear Professor *(surname):*

PLANETS OF THE SOLAR SYSTEM

	Mean Distance from Sun in Miles	Diameter in Miles	Number of Satellites
Mercury	36,000,000	3,000	0
Venus	67,000,000	7,600	0
Earth	93,000,000	7,900	1
Mars	141,000,000	4,200	2
Jupiter	489,000,000	87,000	16
Saturn	886,000,000	72,000	15
Uranus	1,782,000,000	31,000	5
Neptune	2,793,000,000	33,000	2
Pluto	3,670,000,000	1,900	1

FIRST-MAGNITUDE STARS (In Order of Brightness)

	Distance in Light-Years*		Distance in Light-Years*
Sirius	8.6	Altair	16
Canopus	700?	Betelgeuse	200
Alpha Centauri	4.3	Aldebaran	60
Vega	26	Spica	200
Capella	50	Pollux	32
Arcturus	40	Antares	400
Rigel	600?	Fomalhaut	24
Procyon	10.4	Deneb	700?
Achernar	70	Regulus	60
Beta Centauri	300	Alpha Crucis	200

*Light-year = 5,880,000,000,000 miles

WEIGHTS AND MEASURES

Troy Weight

24 grains = 1 pennyweight
20 pennyweights = 1 ounce
12 ounces = 1 pound

Avoirdupois Weight

27 11/32 grains = 1 dram
16 drams = 1 ounce
16 ounces = 1 pound
100 pounds = 1 short hundredweight
20 short hundredweight = 1 short ton

Apothecaries' Weight

20 grains = 1 scruple
3 scruples = 1 dram
8 drams = 1 ounce
12 ounces = 1 pound

Linear Measure

12 inches = 1 foot
3 feet = 1 yard
5½ yards = 1 rod
40 rods = 1 furlong
8 furlongs (5280 feet) = 1 statute mile

Mariners' Measure

6 feet = 1 fathom
1000 fathoms (approx.) = 1 nautical mile
3 nautical miles = 1 league

Apothecaries' Fluid Measure

60 minims = 1 fluid dram
8 fluid drams = 1 fluid ounce
16 fluid ounces = 1 pint
2 pints = 1 quart
4 quarts = 1 gallon

Square Measure

144 square inches = 1 square foot
9 square feet = 1 square yard
30¼ square yards = 1 square rod
160 square rods = 1 acre
640 acres = 1 square mile

Cubic Measure

1728 cubic inches = 1 cubic foot
27 cubic feet = 1 cubic yard

Surveyors' Measure

7.92 inches = 1 link
100 links = 1 chain

Liquid Measure

4 gills = 1 pint
2 pints = 1 quart
4 quarts = 1 gallon
31½ gallons = 1 barrel
2 barrels = 1 hogshead

Dry Measure

2 pints = 1 quart
8 quarts = 1 peck
4 pecks = 1 bushel

Wood Measure

16 cubic feet = 1 cord foot
8 cord feet = 1 cord

Angular and Circular Measure

60 seconds = 1 minute
60 minutes = 1 degree
90 degrees = 1 right angle
180 degrees = 1 straight angle
360 degrees = 1 circle

METRIC SYSTEM

The metric system is a decimal system of weights and measures, adopted first in France, but now widespread over the world. It is universally used in science, mandatory for use for all purposes in a large number of countries, and permitted for use in most (as in U.S. and Great Britain).

The basic units are the *meter* (39.37 inches) for length, and the *gram* (15.432 grains) for mass or weight.

Derived units are the *liter* (0.908 U.S. dry quart, or 1.0567 U.S. liquid quart) for capacity, being the volume of 1000 grams of water under specified conditions, the *are* (119.6 square yards) for area, being the area of a square 10 meters on a side, and the *stere* (35.315 cubic feet) for volume, being the volume of a cube 1 meter on a side, the term stere being, however, usually restricted to measuring fire wood.

Names for units larger and smaller than the above are formed from the above names by the use of the following prefixes:

kilo 1000 deka 10 centi 0.01
hecto 100 deci 0.1 milli 0.001

To these are often added mega = 1,000,000, myria = 10,000, and micro = 0.000 001. Not all of the possible units are in common use.

In many countries names of old units are applied to roughly similar metric units.

Metric System *(Continued)*

Linear Measure

10 millimeters	= 1 centimeter
10 centimeters	= 1 decimeter
10 decimeters	= 1 meter
10 meters	= 1 dekameter
10 dekameters	= 1 hectometer
10 hectometers	= 1 kilometer

Square Measure

100 sq. millimeters	= 1 sq. centimeter
100 sq. centimeters	= 1 sq. decimeter
100 sq. decimeters	= 1 sq. meter
100 sq. meters	= 1 sq. dekameter
100 sq. dekameters	= 1 sq. hectometer
100 sq. hectometers	= 1 sq. kilometer

Cubic Measure

1000 cu. millimeters	= 1 cu. centimeter
1000 cu. centimeters	= 1 cu. decimeter
1000 cu. decimeters	= 1 cu. meter

Liquid Measure

10 milliliters	= 1 centiliter
10 centiliters	= 1 deciliter
10 deciliters	= 1 liter
10 liters	= 1 dekaliter
10 dekaliters	= 1 hectoliter
10 hectoliters	= 1 kiloliter

Weights

10 milligrams	= 1 centigram
10 centigrams	= 1 decigram
10 decigrams	= 1 gram
10 grams	= 1 dekagram
10 dekagrams	= 1 hectogram
10 hectograms	= 1 kilogram
100 kilograms	= 1 quintal
10 quintals	= 1 ton

FOREIGN ALPHABETS

ARABIC

Letter	Name	Transliteration
	alif	' [1], a
	bā	b
	tā	t
	thā	th
	jim	j
	ḥā	ḥ [2]
	khā	kh
	dāl	d
	dhāl	dh
	rā	r
	z̄ [3]	z
	sin	s
	shin	sh
	ṣād	ṣ
	ḍād	ḍ
	ṭā	ṭ
	ẓā	ẓ
	'ain	' [3]
	ghain	gh
	fā	f
	qāf	q [4]
	kāf	k
	lām	l
	mim	m
	nūn	n
	hā	h
	wāw	w, ū
	yā	y, i

[1] Glottal stop.
[2] A voiceless pharyngeal fricative.
[3] A voiced pharyngeal fricative.
[4] A voiceless uvular stop.

GREEK

Letter		Name	Transliteration
A	α	alpha	a
B	β	beta	b
Γ	γ	gamma	g
Δ	δ	delta	d
E	ε	epsilon	e
Z	ζ	zeta	z
H	η	eta	e (or ē)
Θ	θ	theta	th
I	ι	iota	i
K	κ	kappa	k
Λ	λ	lambda	l
M	μ	mu	m
N	ν	nu	n
Ξ	ξ	xi	x
O	o	omicron	o
Π	π	pi	p
P	ρ	rho	r
Σ	σ,ς [1]	sigma	s
T	τ	tau	t
Υ	υ	upsilon	y
Φ	φ	phi	ph
X	χ	chi	ch, kh
Ψ	ψ	psi	ps
Ω	ω	omega	o (or ō)

[1] At end of word.

HEBREW

Letter	Name	Transliteration
	aleph	'
	beth	b, bh, v
	gimel	g, gh
	daleth	d, dh
	he	h
	vav	v, w
	zayin	z
	cheth	ḥ
	teth	ṭ
	yod	y, j, i
	kaph	k, kh
	lamed	l
	mem	m
	nun	n
	samekh	s
	ayin	'
	pe	p, ph, f
	sadhe	ṣ
	koph	q
	resh	r
	shin	sh, š
	sin	ś
	tav	t

[1] At end of word.

RUSSIAN

Letter	Transliteration
	a
	b
	v
	g
	d
	e, ye
	zh, ž
	z
	i
	ĭ, y, j, i
	k
	l
	m
	n
	o
	p
	r
	s
	t
	u
	f
	kh, x
	ts, c
	ch, č
	sh, š
	shch, šč
	ˮ
	y, i
	'
	ė, eh, e
	yu, ju
	ya, ja

[1] Represents the sound (y) between an unpalatalized consonant and a vowel.
[2] Indicates that the preceding consonant is palatalized, or represents (y) between a palatalized consonant and a vowel.

PROOFREADER'S MARKS

Proofreader's marks are used both in preparing a manuscript for typesetting and in proofreading and revising printed material. These marks should be placed in the margin, in line with the place in the text where the change is to be made. If more than one change is suggested for the same line of text, diagonal slashes should separate the individual marks. The text itself should also be marked to specify the exact location of each change.

LETTERS, WORDS, SPACING, AND QUERIES

Mark in margin	Indication in text	Instruction or comment
a	Peter left town in hurry.	Insert at caret (∧)
a/a	Peter left town in hurry.	Insert at carets
ℐ or γ	Joan sent me the the book.	Delete
⌒	ma ke	Close up; no space
(delete and close)	I haven't seen them in years.	Delete and close up
stet	They phoned both Betty and Jack.	Let it stand; disregard indicated deletion or change
¶	up the river. Two years	Start new paragraph
no ¶ or *run in*	many unnecessary additives. The most dangerous one	No new paragraph
tr	the book on the table. Put the book table on the Put the table on the book.	Transpose
tr up or *tr ↑*	to Betty Steinberg who was traveling abroad. Mrs. Steinberg, an actress,	Transpose to place indicated above
tr down or *tr ↓*	in the clutch. The final score was 6-5. He pitched the last three innings but didn't have it.	Transpose to place indicated below
sp	Lunch cost me 6 dollars.	Spell out; use letters
fig	There were eighteen members present.	Set in figures; use numbers
#	It was a small village.	Insert one letter space
##	too late After the dance	Insert two letter spaces
hr #	jerotoam	Insert hair space (very thin space, as between letters)
line #	Oscar Picks # This year's Academy Awards nomination.	Insert line space
eq #	Ronnie got rid of the dog.	Equalize spacing between words or between lines
=	thre e days later	Align horizontally
‖	from one hand to another without spilling it	Align vertically
run over	enhance production. 2. It will	Start new line
□	□ Rose asked the price.	Indent or insert one em (space)
□□	□□ The Use of the Comma	Indent or insert two ems
⊏	What's Ellen's last name?	Move left
⊐	April 2, 1945	Move right
⊓	Please go now.	Move up
⊔	Well, that's that!	Move down
⊐⊏	"The Birth of Atomic Energy"	Center (heading, title, etc.)
fl	2. Three (3) skirts	Flush left; no indention
fr	Total: $89.50	Flush right; no indention
sent/? [the specific word that appears to be missing]	He the copy.	Insert this word here?
(Ok?) or (?)	by Francis G. Kellsey. She wrote	Query or verify; is this correct?
(out : see copy)	the discovery of but near the hull	Something left out in typesetting
(set?)	arrived in 1922 wrong date and	Is this part of the copy, to be set (or a marginal note)?

PUNCTUATION

Mark in margin	Indication in text	Instruction or comment
⊙	Christine teaches fifth grade	Insert period (.)
⌃	We expect Eileen Tom, and Ken.	Insert comma (,)
⌃;	I came; I saw conquered.	Insert semicolon (;)
⊙:	Jenny worked until 630 P.M.	Insert colon (:)
=	Douglas got a two thirds majority.	Insert hyphen (-)
=	Douglas got a two- thirds majority.	End-of-line hyphen is part of word
1/M	Mike then left very reluctantly.	Insert one-em dash or long dash ( )
1/N	See pages 96 124.	Insert one-en dash or short dash ( )
⌄	Don't mark the authors copy. Don't mark the authors copy.	Insert apostrophe (')
!	Watch out	Insert exclamation point (!)
?	Did Seth write to you	Insert question mark (?)
∀/∀	I always liked Stopping by Woods on a Snowy Evening.	Insert quotation marks (" ")
∀/∀	She said, "Read The Raven tonight.	Insert single quotation marks (' ')
(/) or { / }	Dorothy paid 8 pesos 800 centavos for it.	Insert parentheses (())
[/] or { / }	The "portly and profane author Dickson, presumably in his cups" was noticed by nobody else.	Insert brackets ([ ])

TYPOGRAPHIC CASE, STYLE, AND ADJUSTMENT

Mark in margin	Indication in text	Instruction or comment
ital	I've read Paradise Lost twice.	Set in italic (not roman) type
bf	See the definition at peace.	Set in boldface (heavier) type
lf	She repaired the motor easily.	Set in lightface (standard) type
rom	Gregory drove to Winnipeg.	Set in roman (not italic) type
cap or *caps* or *uc* or *u/c*	the italian role in Nato	Set as CAPITAL letter(s)
sc	He lived about 350 B.C.	Set as SMALL CAPITAL letter(s)
lc or *l/c*	Arlene enjoys Reading. I do NOT.	Set in lowercase; not capitalized
uc+lc or *c+lc* or *uc+lc*	STOP! STOP!	Set in uppercase and lowercase
(subscript)	H_2O	Set as subscript; inferior figure
(superscript)	$A^2 + B^2$	Set as superscript; superior figure
X	They drove to Miami.	Broken (damaged) letter of type
wf	Turn Right	Wrong font; not the proper typeface style or size
⑨	Bert proofread the book	Turn inverted (upside-down) letter

Signs And Symbols

Astrology

Signs of the Zodiac

♈	Aries, the Ram.
♉	Taurus, the Bull.
♊	Gemini, the Twins.
♋	Cancer, the Crab.
♌	Leo, the Lion.
♍	Virgo, the Virgin.
♎	Libra, the Scales.
♏	Scorpio, the Scorpion.
♐	Sagittarius, the Archer.
♑	Capricorn, the Goat.
♒	Aquarius, the Water Bearer.
♓	Pisces, the Fishes.

Astronomy

Astronomical Bodies

☉	1. the sun. 2. Sunday.
☽ ☾ ●	1. the moon. 2. Monday.
●●	new moon.
☽ ☽ ☽ ●	the moon, first quarter.
○ ⓣ	full moon.
☾ ⓒ ☾ ●	the moon, last quarter.
☿	1. Mercury. 2. Wednesday.
♀	1. Venus. 2. Friday.
⊕ ♁ ⊖	Earth
♂	1. Mars. 2. Tuesday.
♃	1. Jupiter. 2. Thursday.
♄	1. Saturn. 2. Saturday.
♅ ⛢	Uranus.
♆	Neptune.
♇	Pluto.
★✳	star.
☄	comet.

Biology

♂	male; a male organism, organ, or cell; a staminate flower or plant.
♀	female; a female organism, organ, or cell; a pistillate flower or plant.
□	a male.
○	a female.
×	crossed with; denoting a sexual hybrid.

Business

@	at; as in: eggs @ 99¢ per dozen.
a/c	account.
B/E	bill of exchange.
B/L	bill of lading.
B/P	bills payable.
B/R	bills receivable.
B/S	bill of sale.
c&f.	cost and freight.
c/o	care of.
L/C	letter of credit.
O/S	out of stock.
P&L	profit and loss.
w/	with.
w/o	without.
#	1. (before a figure or figures) number; numbered; as in: #40 thread. 2. (after a figure or figures) pound(s); as in: 20#.

Mathematics

Arithmetic and Algebra

+	1. plus; add. 2. positive; positive value; as: +64. 3. denoting underestimated approximate accuracy, with some figures omitted at the end; as in: $\pi = 3.14159+$.
–	1. minus; subtract. 2. negative; negative value; as: –64. 3. denoting overestimated approximate accuracy, with some figures omitted at the end; as in: $\pi = 3.1416-$.
±	1. plus or minus; add or subtract; as in: $4 \pm 2 = 6$ or 2. 2. positive or negative; as in: $\sqrt{a^2} = \pm a$. 3. denoting the probable error associated with a figure derived by experiment and observation, approximate calculation, etc.
× ·	times; multiplied by; as in: $2 \times 4 = 2 \cdot 4$.
÷/–	divided by; as in: $8 \div 2 = 8/2 = \frac{8}{2} = 4$.
:/–	denoting the ratio of (in proportion).
=	equals; is equal to.
::	equals; is equal to (in proportion); as in: $6 : 3 :: 8 : 4$.
≠ ≠	is not equal to.
≡	is identical with.
≢ ≢	is not identical with.
≈	is approximately equal to.
~	1. is equivalent to. 2. is similar to.
>	is greater than.
≫	is much greater than.
<	is less than.
≪	is much less than.
≯	is not greater than.
≮	is not less than.
≧ ≥	is equal to or greater than.
≦ ≤	is equal to or less than.

∝   varies directly as; is directly proportional to; as in: ∝.

√ ̄ √ ̄   the radical sign, indicating the square root of; as in: $\sqrt{81}$ = 9.

( )   parentheses; as in: $2(a + b)$.

[ ]   brackets; as in: $4 + 3\,[a(a + b)]$.

{ }   braces; as in:
$5 + b\{(a + b)\,[2 - a(a + b)] - 3\}$.

Note: Parentheses, brackets, and braces are used with quantities consisting of more than one member or term, to group them and show they are to be considered together.

∞   infinity.

%   percent; per hundred.

′ ″ ‴   prime, double prime, triple prime, etc., used to indicate: *a.* constants, as distinguished from the variable denoted by a letter alone. *b.* a variable under different conditions, at different times, etc.

∪   union.

∩   intersection.

⊆   is a subset of.

⊇   contains as a subset.

⊄   is not a subset of.

⊅   does not contain as a subset.

∅ O   set containing no numbers; empty set.

∈   is a member of.

∉   is not a member of.

Geometry

∠   angle (*pl.* ⦛); as in: ∠ *ABC*.

⊥   1. a perpendicular (*pl.* ⊥s). 2. is perpendicular to; as in: AB ⊥ CD.

‖   1. a parallel (*pl.* ‖s). 2. is parallel to; as in: AB‖CD.

△   triangle (*pl.* ⧍); as in: △*ABC*.

▭   rectangle; as in: ▭ABCD.

□   square: as in: □ABCD.

▱   parallelogram; as in: ▱ABCD.

○   circle (*pl.* ⊙).

≅≡   is congruent to; as in: △ABD ≅ △CEF.

~   is similar to; as in: △ACE ~ △CEF.

∴   therefore; hence.

∵   since, because.

π   the Greek letter pi, representing the ratio (3.14159+) of the circumference of a circle to its diameter.

⌢   (over a group of letters) indicating an arc of a circle; as: GH, the arc between points G and H.

°   degree(s) of arc; as in: 90°.

′   minute(s) of arc; as in: 90°30′.

″   second(s) of arc; as in: 90°30′15″.

Miscellaneous

&   the ampersand, meaning and.

&c.   et cetera; and others; and so forth; and so on.

′   foot; feet; as in: 6′ = six feet.

″   inch; inches; as in: 6′2″ = six feet, two inches.

×   1. by: used in stating dimensions; as in: 2′ × 4′ × 1′; a 2″ × 4″ board. 2. a sign (the cross) made in place of a signature by a person who cannot write; as in:

his

George × Walsh

mark.

†   1. dagger. 2. died.

‡   double dagger.

©   copyright; copyrighted.

®   registered; registered trademark.

*   1. asterisk. 2. born.

/   slash; diagonal.

¶   paragraph mark.

§   section mark.

″   ditto; indicating the same as the aforesaid: used in lists, etc.

. . .   ellipsis: used to show the omission of words, letters, etc.

˜   tilde.

ˆ   circumflex.

¸   cedilla; as in: ç.

´   acute accent.

`   grave accent.

¨   1. dieresis. 2. umlaut.

¯   macron.

˘   breve.

℞   take (L *recipe*).

°   degree(s) of temperature; as in: 99°F, 36°C.

Monetary

$ 1. dollar(s), in the United States, Canada, Liberia, etc. 2. peso(s), in Colombia, Mexico, etc. 3. cruzeiro(s), in Brazil. 4. escudo(s), in Portugal.

¢   cent(s), in the United States, Canada, etc.

£   pound(s), in United Kingdom, Ireland, etc.

p   new penny (new pence), in United Kingdom, Ireland, etc.

/s.   (formerly) shilling(s), in United Kingdom, Ireland, etc.

d.   (formerly) penny (pence), in United Kingdom, Ireland, etc.

¥   yen (*pl.* yen) in Japan.

Religion

† the cross, a symbol of Christianity.

† Celtic cross: used esp. as a symbol of the Presbyterian Church.

☨ three-barred cross; Russian cross: used esp. as a symbol of the Russian Orthodox Church.

✠ Greek Cross.

✠+ 1. a cross used by the Pope and by Roman Catholic archbishops and bishops before their names. 2. an indication inserted at those points in the service at which the sign of the cross is made.

✡ star of David; a symbol of Judaism.

☽ crescent; a symbol of Islam.

℟ response: used in prayer books.

✻ an indication used in Roman Catholic service books to separate a verse of a psalm into two parts, showing where the response begins.

℣ an indication used in service books to show the point at which a versicle begins.

Index

NOTES

NOTES

NOTES